Social Security Tax–2015

Category	Rate	Dollar Limit
OASDI	6.2%	$118,500
Medicare*	1.45%	First $200,000 of wages ($250,000 for joint returns)
	2.35%	Wages greater than $200,000 ($250,000 for joint returns)

*Only the employee is required to pay the additional Medicare tax on wages above $200,000 ($250,000 for joint returns). The employer pays Medicare tax of 1.45% on all wages.

Self-Employ[illegible]

Category	Rate	D[illegible]
OASDI	12.4%	$1[illegible],500
Medicare	2.90%	First $200,000 of self-employment income ($250,000 combined self-employment income for joint returns)
	3.80%	Self-employment income greater than $200,000 ($250,000 for joint returns)

Alternative Minimum Tax–2015

If AMTI minus the exemption amount is:		The tax is:	
Over—	But Not Over—		Of the Amount Over—
$0	$185,400*	26%	$0
$185,400*		$48,204* + 28%	$185,400

*$92,700 and $24,102 for married taxpayers filing separately.

AMT exemption amounts (before phase-outs and other adjustments):

Unmarried individuals (other than surviving spouses and heads of households)	$53,600
Married individuals filing joint returns and surviving spouses	83,400
Married individuals filing separate returns	41,700

STANDARD DEDUCTION

Filing Status	
Married individuals filing joint returns and surviving spouses	$12,600
Heads of households	9,250
Unmarried individuals (other than surviving spouses and heads of households)	6,300
Married individuals filing separate returns	6,300
Additional standard deduction for the aged and the blind	
Individual who is married and surviving spouses	1,250*
Individual who is unmarried and not a surviving spouse	1,550*
Taxpayer claimed as dependent on another taxpayer's return: Greater of (1) earned income plus $350, or (2) $1,050.	

*These amounts are $2,500 and $3,100, respectively, for a taxpayer who is both aged and blind.

PERSONAL AND DEPENDENCY EXEMPTION AND PHASE-OUTS

Personal and dependency exemption $ 4,000

Phase-outs for high income taxpayers:

Personal and dependency exemptions are reduced by 2% for each $2,500 increment (or part of increment) for AGI above the threshold amount.

Itemized deductions are reduced by 3% for each dollar of AGI above the threshold amounts (taxpayers cannot lose more than 80% of their allowable itemized deductions).

For both provisions, the AGI threshold amounts are:

Married individuals filing joint returns and surviving spouses	$309,900
Heads of households	284,050
Unmarried individuals (other than surviving spouses and heads of households)	258,250
Married individuals filing separate returns	154,950

PRENTICE HALL'S FEDERAL TAXATION

2016

COMPREHENSIVE

PRENTICE HALL'S FEDERAL TAXATION 2016 COMPREHENSIVE

EDITORS

TIMOTHY J. RUPERT
Northeastern University

THOMAS R. POPE
University of Kentucky

KENNETH E. ANDERSON
University of Tennessee

CONTRIBUTING AUTHORS

D. DALE BANDY
University of Central Florida

N. ALLEN FORD
University of Kansas

ANNA C. FOWLER
University of Texas at Austin (Emeritus)

ROBERT L. GARDNER
Brigham Young University

RICHARD J. JOSEPH
Bryant University

DAVID S. HULSE
University of Kentucky

LEANN LUNA
University of Tennessee

CHARLENE HENDERSON
Mississippi State University

MICHAEL S. SCHADEWALD
University of Wisconsin—Milwaukee

PEARSON

Boston Columbus Indianapolis New York San Francisco Hoboken
Amsterdam Cape Town Dubai London Madrid Milan Munich Paris Montreal Toronto
Delhi Mexico City São Paulo Sydney Hong Kong Seoul Singapore Taipei Tokyo

Vice President, Business Publishing: Donna Battista
Senior Acquisitions Editor: Lacey Vitetta
Editorial Assistant: Christine Donovan
Vice President, Product Marketing: Maggie Moylan
Director of Marketing, Digital Services and Products: Jeanette Koskinas
Senior Product Marketing Manager: Alison Haskins
Executive Field Marketing Manager: Lori DeShazo
Senior Strategic Marketing Manager: Erin Gardner
Team Lead, Program Management: Ashley Santora
Program Manager: Mary Kate Murray
Team Lead, Project Management: Jeff Holcomb
Project Managers: Alison Kalil and Melissa Pellerano
Operations Specialist: Carol Melville
Creative Director: Blair Brown
Art Director: Jon Boylan
Vice President, Director of Digital Strategy and Assessment: Paul Gentile
Manager of Learning Applications: Paul DeLuca
Digital Editor: Sarah Peterson
Director, Digital Studio: Sacha Laustsen
Digital Studio Manager: Diane Lombardo
Product Manager: James Bateman
Digital Content Team Lead: Noel Lotz
Digital Content Project Lead: Martha LaChance
Full-Service Project Management, Composition, and Interior Design: Integra Software Services
Cover Designer: Jon Boylan
Cover Art: Cristina Ciochina/Shutterstock
Printer/Binder: Courier Kendallville
Cover Printer: Courier Kendallville

PEARSON

10 9 8 7 6 5 4 3 2 1
ISBN-10: 0-13-410437-4
ISBN-13: 978-0-13-410437-9

OVERVIEW

CONTENTS

CHAPTER 3

CHAPTER 4

CHAPTER 5

TABLES

APPENDICES

ABOUT THE EDITORS

TIMOTHY J. RUPERT

Timothy J. Rupert is a Professor and the Golemme Administrative Chair at the D'Amore-McKim School of Business at Northeastern University. He received his B.S. in Accounting and his Master of Taxation from the University of Akron. He also earned his Ph.D. from Penn State University. Professor Rupert's research has been published in such journals as *The Accounting Review, The Journal of the American Taxation Association, Behavioral Research in Accounting, Advances in Taxation, Applied Cognitive Psychology, Advances in Accounting Education,* and *Journal of Accounting Education.* He currently is the co-editor of *Advances in Accounting Education.* In 2010, he received the Outstanding Educator Award from the Massachusetts Society of CPAs. He also has received the University's Excellence in Teaching Award and the D'Amore-McKim School's Best Teacher of the Year award multiple times. He is active in the American Accounting Association and the American Taxation Association (ATA) and has served as president, vice president, and secretary of the ATA.

THOMAS R. POPE

Thomas R. Pope is the Ernst & Young Professor of Accounting at the University of Kentucky. He received a B.S. from the University of Louisville and an M.S. and D.B.A. in business administration from the University of Kentucky. He teaches international taxation, partnership and S corporation taxation, tax research and policy, and introductory taxation and has won outstanding teaching awards at the University, College, and School of Accountancy levels. He has published articles in *The Accounting Review,* the *Tax Adviser, Taxes, Tax Notes,* and a number of other journals. Professor Pope's extensive professional experience includes eight years with Big Four accounting firms. Five of those years were with Ernst & Whinney (now part of Ernst & Young), including two years with their National Tax Department in Washington, D.C. He subsequently held the position of Senior Manager in charge of the Tax Department in Lexington, Kentucky. Professor Pope also has been a leader and speaker at professional tax conferences all over the United States and is active as a tax consultant.

KENNETH E. ANDERSON

Kenneth E. Anderson is the Pugh CPAs Professor of Accounting at the University of Tennessee. He earned a B.B.A. from the University of Wisconsin–Milwaukee and subsequently attained the level of tax manager with Arthur Young (now part of Ernst & Young). He then earned a Ph.D. from Indiana University. He teaches corporate taxation, partnership taxation, and tax strategy. Professor Anderson also is the Director of the Master of Accountancy Program. He has published articles in *The Accounting Review, The Journal of the American Taxation Association, Advances in Taxation,* the *Journal of Accountancy,* the *Journal of Financial Service Professionals,* and a number of other journals.

ABOUT THE AUTHORS

D. Dale Bandy is the Professor Emeritus in the School of Accounting at the University of Central Florida. He received a B.S. from the University of Tulsa, an M.B.A. from the University of Arkansas, and a Ph.D. from the University of Texas at Austin. He helped to establish the Master of Science in Taxation programs at the University of Central Florida and California State University, Fullerton, where he previously taught. In 1985, he was selected by the California Society of Certified Public Accountants as the Accounting Educator of the year. Professor Bandy has published 8 books and more than 30 articles in accounting and taxation. His articles have appeared in the *Journal of Taxation,* the *Journal of Accountancy, Advances in Taxation,* the *Tax Adviser, The CPA Journal, Management Accounting* and a number of other journals.

N. Allen Ford is the Larry D. Homer/KPMG Peat Marwick Distinguished Teaching Professor of Professional Accounting at the University of Kansas. He received an undergraduate degree from Centenary College in Shreveport, Louisiana, and both the M.B.A. and Ph.D. in Business from the University of Arkansas. He has published over 40 articles related to taxation, financial accounting, and accounting education in journals such as *The Accounting Review, The Journal of the American Taxation Association,* and *The Journal of Taxation.* He served as president of the American Taxation Association in 1979–80. Professor Ford has received numerous teaching awards, at the college and university levels. In 1993, he received the Byron T. Shutz Award for Distinguished Teaching in Economics and Business. In 1996 he received the Ray M. Sommerfeld Outstanding Tax Educator Award, which is jointly sponsored by the American Taxation Association and Ernst & Young and in 1998 he received the Kansas Society of CPAs Outstanding Education Award.

Anna C. Fowler is the John Arch White Professor Emeritus in the Department of Accounting at the University of Texas at Austin. She received her B.S. in accounting from the University of Alabama and her M.B.A. and Ph.D. from the University of Texas at Austin. Active in the American Taxation Association throughout her academic career, she served on the editorial board of its journal and held many positions, including president. She is a former member of the American Institute of CPA's Tax Executive Committee and a former chair of the AICPA's Regulation/Tax Subcommittee for the CPA exam. She has published a number of articles, most of which have dealt with estate planning or real estate transaction issues. In 2002, she received the Ray M. Sommerfeld Outstanding Educator Award, co-sponsored by the American Taxation Association and Ernst & Young.

Robert L. Gardner is the Robert J. Smith Professor of Accounting in the School of Accountancy at Brigham Young University (BYU). He received a B.S. and M.B.A. from the University of Utah and a Ph.D. from the University of Texas at Austin. He has authored or coauthored two books and over 25 articles in journals such as *The Tax Advisor, Journal of Corporate Taxation, Journal of Real Estate Taxation, Journal of Accounting Education, Journal of Taxation of S Corporations, and the International Tax Journal.* Professor Gardner has received several teaching awards. In 2001, he received the Outstanding Faculty Award in the Marriott School of Management at BYU. He has served on the Board of Trustees of the American Taxation Association and served as President of the ATA in 1999–2000.

Richard J. Joseph is Provost-for-Term and Chief Academic Officer of Bryant University. In this role, he oversees Bryant's faculty, academic programs, Colleges of Arts and Sciences and Business, and School of Health Sciences. Before joining Bryant, he was Provost and Global Dean of Hult International Business School. Previously, he served on the administration and tax faculty of The University of Texas at Austin. Before embarking on his academic career, Dr. Joseph worked as an international banker at Citibank, Riyadh; an investment banker at Lehman Brothers, New York; a securities trader at Becker Paribas, Dallas, and Bear Stearns, New York; and a mergers and acquisitions lawyer for the Bass Group, Fort Worth. A graduate *magna cum laude* of Harvard College, Oxford University, and The University of Texas at Austin School of Law, Dr. Joseph is co-editor of the *Handbook of Mergers and Acquisitions* (Oxford University Press) and author of *The Origins of the American Income Tax* (Syracuse University Press). He has written numerous commentaries in the *Financial Times, The Christian Science Monitor, Tax Notes,* and *Tax Notes International.*

David S. Hulse is the Deloitte-Touche Professor of Accountancy at the University of Kentucky. He received an undergraduate degree from Shippensburg University, an M.S. from Louisiana State University, and a Ph.D. from the Pennsylvania State University. He teaches introductory taxation and corporate taxation courses. Professor Hulse has published a number of articles on tax issues in academic and professional journals, including *The Journal of the American Taxation Association, Advances in Taxation,* the *Journal of Financial Service Professionals,* the *Journal of Financial Planning,* and *Tax Notes.*

LeAnn Luna is an Associate Professor of Accounting at the University of Tennessee. She is a C.P.A. and holds an undergraduate degree from Southern Methodist University, a M.T. from the University of Denver College of Law, and a Ph.D. from the University of Tennessee. She has taught introductory taxation, corporate and partnership taxation, tax research, and professional standards. Professor Luna also holds a joint appointment with the Center for Business and Economic Research at the University of Tennessee, where she interacts frequently with state policymakers on a variety of policy related issues. She has published articles in the *Journal of Accounting and Economics*, the *National Tax Journal, The Journal of the American Taxation Association, Tax Adviser, State Tax Notes,* and a number of other journals.

Charlene Henderson is a member of the faculty in the Adkerson School of Accountancy at Mississippi State University. She earned her undergraduate and graduate degrees in accounting at Mississippi State University. After working in public and private accounting, she completed the doctoral program at Arizona State University. Her teaching and research interests include both tax and financial accounting. Her research has appeared in several journals, including *Journal of the American Taxation Association, Journal of Accounting Auditing and Finance,* and *Journal of Business Finance and Accounting.*

Michael S. Schadewald, Ph.D., CPA, is on the faculty of the University of Wisconsin-Milwaukee where he teaches graduate and undergraduate courses in business taxation. A graduate of the University of Minnesota, Professor Schadewald is a co-author of several books on multistate and international taxation and has published more than 40 articles in academic and professional journals, including *The Accounting Review, Journal of Accounting Research, Contemporary Accounting Research, The Journal of the American Taxation Association, CPA Journal, Journal of Taxation*, and *The Tax Adviser*. Professor Schadewald also has served on the editorial boards of *The Journal of the American Taxation Association, Journal of State Taxation, International Tax Journal, The International Journal of Accounting, Issues in Accounting Education*, and *Journal of Accounting Education*.

PREFACE

Why is the Rupert/Pope/Anderson series the best choice for you and your students?

The Rupert/Pope/Anderson 2016 Series in Federal Taxation is appropriate for use in any first course in federal taxation, and comes in a choice of three volumes:

Federal Taxation 2016: Individuals
Federal Taxation 2016: Corporations, Partnerships, Estates & Trusts (the companion book to *Individuals*)
Federal Taxation 2016: Comprehensive (14 chapters from *Individuals* and 15 chapters from *Corporations*)

** For a customized edition of any of the chapters for these texts, contact your Pearson representative and they can create a custom text for you.

- The *Individuals* volume covers *all* entities, although the treatment is often briefer than in the *Corporations* and *Comprehensive* volumes. The *Individuals* volume, therefore, is appropriate for colleges and universities that require only one semester of taxation as well as those that require more than one semester of taxation. Further, this volume adapts the suggestions of the Model Tax Curriculum as promulgated by the American Institute of Certified Public Accountants.
- The *Corporations, Partnerships, Estates & Trusts* and *Comprehensive* volumes contain three comprehensive tax return problems whose data change with each edition, thereby keeping the problems fresh. Problem C:3-66 contains the comprehensive corporate tax return, Problem C:9-58 contains the comprehensive partnership tax return, and Problem C:11-64 contains the comprehensive S corporation tax return, which is based on the same facts as Problem C:9-58 so that students can compare the returns for these two entities.
- The *Corporations, Partnerships, Estates & Trusts* and *Comprehensive* volumes contain sections called Financial Statement Implications, which discuss the implications of Accounting Standards Codification (ASC) 740. The main discussion of accounting for income taxes appears in Chapter C:3. The financial statement implications of other transactions appear in Chapters C:5, C:7, C:8, and C:16 (*Corporations* volume only).

What's New to this Edition?

INDIVIDUALS

- Complete updating of significant court cases and IRS rulings and procedures during 2014 and early 2015.
- Complete updating for the Tax Increase Prevention Act of 2014.
- Discussion of the expiration or reduction of some deductions and credits in 2015.
- All tax rate schedules have been updated to reflect the rates and inflation adjustments for 2015.
- Whenever new updates become available, they will be accessible via MyAccountingLab.

CORPORATIONS

- The comprehensive corporate tax return, Problem C:3-66, has all new numbers for the 2014 forms.
- The comprehensive partnership tax return, Problem C:9-58, has all new numbers for the 2014 forms.
- The comprehensive S corporation tax return, Problem C:11-64, has all new numbers for the 2014 forms.
- Changes affecting 2015 tax law have been incorporated into the text where appropriate.
- All tax rate schedules have been updated to reflect the rates and inflation adjustments for 2015.
- Whenever new updates become available, they will be accessible via MyAccountingLab.

MyAccountingLab

MyAccountingLab is an online homework, tutorial, and assessment program designed to work with *Prentice Hall's Federal Taxation 2016* to engage students and improve results. MyAccountingLab's homework and practice questions are correlated to the textbook, they regenerate algorithmically to give students unlimited opportunity for practice and mastery, and they offer helpful feedback when students enter incorrect answers. Combining resources that illuminate content with accessible self-assessment, MyAccountingLab with eText provides students with a complete digital learning experience–all in one place. To register, go to http://www.pearsonmylabandmastering.com.

For Instructors

MyAccountingLab provides instructors with a rich and flexible set of course materials, along with course-management tools that make it easy to deliver all or a portion of your course online.

- **Powerful Homework and Test Manager** Create, import, and manage online homework and media assignments, quizzes, and tests. Create assignments from online questions directly correlated to this and other textbooks. Homework questions include "Help Me Solve This" guided solutions to help students understand and master concepts. You can choose from a wide range of assignment options, including time limits, proctoring, and maximum number of attempts allowed. In addition, you can create your own questions—or copy and edit ours—to customize your students' learning path.
- **Comprehensive Gradebook Tracking** MyAccountingLab's online gradebook automatically tracks your students' results on tests, homework, and tutorials and gives you control over managing results and calculating grades. All MyAccountingLab grades can be exported to a spreadsheet program, such as Microsoft® Excel. The MyAccountingLab Gradebook provides a number of student data views and gives you the flexibility to weight assignments, select which attempts to include when calculating scores, and omit or delete results for individual assignments.
- **Department-Wide Solutions** Get help managing multiple sections and working with Teaching Assistants using MyAccountingLab Coordinator Courses. After your MyAccountingLab course is set up, it can be copied to create sections or "member courses." Changes to the Coordinator Course flow down to all members, so changes only need to be made once.

We will add the most current tax information to MyAccountingLab as it becomes available.

For Students

MyAccountingLab provides students with a personalized interactive learning environment, where they can learn at their own pace and measure their progress.

- **Interactive Tutorial Exercises** MyAccountingLab's homework and practice questions are correlated to the textbook, and "similar to" versions regenerate algorithmically to give students unlimited opportunity for practice and mastery. Questions offer helpful feedback when students enter incorrect answers, and they include "Help Me Solve This" guided solutions as well as other learning aids for extra help when students need it.
- **Study Plan for Self-Paced Learning** MyAccountingLab's study plan helps students monitor their own progress, letting them see at a glance exactly which topics they need to practice. MyAccountingLab generates a personalized study plan for each student based on his or her test results, and the study plan links directly to interactive, tutorial exercises for topics the student hasn't yet mastered. Students can regenerate these exercises with new values for unlimited practice, and the exercises include guided solutions and multimedia learning aids to give students the extra help they need.

Strong Pedagogical Aids

- Appropriate blend of technical content of the tax law with a high level of readability for students.
- Focused on enabling students to apply tax principles within the chapter to real-life situations.

Real-World Example

These comments relate the text material to events, cases, and statistics occurring in the tax and business environment. The statistical data presented in some of these comments are taken from the IRS's Statistics of Income at www.irs.gov.

Book-to-Tax Accounting Comparison

These comments compare the tax discussion in the text to the accounting and/or financial statement treatment of this material. Also, the last section of Chapter C:3 discusses the financial statement implications of federal income taxes.

What Would You Do in This Situation?

Unique to the Rupert/Pope/Anderson series, these boxes place students in a decision-making role. The boxes include many *controversies* that are as yet unresolved or are currently being considered by the courts. These boxes make extensive use of **Ethical Material** as they represent choices that may put the practitioner at odds with the client.

Stop & Think

These "speed bumps" encourage students to pause and apply what they have just learned. Solutions for each issue are provided in the box.

Ethical Point

These comments provide the ethical implications of material discussed in the adjoining text. Apply what they have just learned.

Tax Strategy Tip

These comments suggest tax planning ideas related to material in the adjoining text.

Additional Comment

These comments provide supplemental information pertaining to the adjacent text.

Program Components

Materials for the instructor may be accessed at the Instructor's Resource Center (IRC) online, located at **www.pearsonhighered.com/phtax** or within the Instructor Resource section of MyAccountingLab. You may contact your Pearson representative for assistance with the registration process.

- *TaxACT 2014 Software:* Available via online purchase with Individuals, Corporations, and Comprehensive Texts. This user-friendly tax preparation program includes more than 80 tax forms, schedules, and worksheets. TaxACT calculates returns and alerts the user to possible errors or entries. Consists of forms 1040, 1065, 1120, and 1120S.
- *Instructor's Resource Manual:* Contains sample syllabi, instructor outlines, and information regarding problem areas for students. It also contains solutions to the tax form/tax return preparation problems.
- *Solutions Manual:* Contains solutions to discussion questions, problems, and comprehensive and tax strategy problems. It also contains all solutions to the case study problems, research problems, and "What Would You Do in This Situation?" boxes.
- *Test Bank:* Offers a wealth of true/false, multiple-choice, and calculative problems. A computerized program is available to adopters.
- *PowerPoint Slides:* Consists of chapter outlines, featuring images, examples, and problems throughout, to aid in class lectures.
- *Image Library:* Figures, tables, and tax forms featured in the book are provided as individual files for the convenience of instructors and students.
- *Multi-State Tax Chapter:* An entire chapter, complete with problems (and solutions) dedicated to multi-state tax practices.

Acknowledgments

Our policy is to provide annual editions and to prepare timely updated supplements when major tax revisions occur. We are most appreciative of the suggestions made by outside reviewers because these extensive review procedures have been valuable to the authors and editors during the revision process.

We also are grateful to the various graduate assistants, doctoral students, and colleagues who have reviewed the text and supplementary materials and checked solutions to maintain a high level of technical accuracy. In particular, we would like to acknowledge the following colleagues who assisted in the preparation of supplemental materials for this text:

Ann Burstein Cohen	SUNY at Buffalo
Craig J. Langstraat	University of Memphis
Kate Demarest	Carroll Community College
Allison McLeod	University of North Texas
Mitchell Franklin	LeMoyne College
Anthony Masino	East Tennessee State University

In addition, we want to thank Myron S. Scholes, Mark A. Wolfson, Merle M. Erickson, M. L. Hanlon, Edward L. Maydew, and Terry J. Shevlin for allowing us to use the model discussed in their text, *Taxes and Business Strategy: A Planning Approach*, as the basis for material in Chapter I:18.

Please send any comments to Kenneth E. Anderson or Timothy J. Rupert.

PRENTICE HALL'S FEDERAL TAXATION

2016

COMPREHENSIVE

CHAPTER 1

AN INTRODUCTION TO TAXATION

LEARNING OBJECTIVES

After studying this chapter, you should be able to

1. Discuss the history of taxation in the United States
2. Describe the three types of tax rate structures
3. Describe the various types of taxes
4. Discuss the criteria for a "good" tax structure, the objectives of the federal income tax law, and recent tax reform proposals
5. Describe the tax entities in the federal income tax system
6. Identify the various tax law sources and understand their implications for tax practice
7. Describe the legislative process for the enactment of the tax law
8. Describe the administrative procedures under the tax law
9. Describe the components of a tax practice
10. Understand the importance of computer applications in taxation

CHAPTER OUTLINE

Federal income taxes have a significant effect on business, investor, and personal decisions in the United States. Because tax rates can be as high as 35% on corporations and over 40% on individuals, virtually every transaction is impacted by income taxes. The following examples illustrate the impact of the tax law on various decisions in our society:

- Because of the deductibility of home mortgage interest and real estate taxes, an individual may decide to purchase a home rather than to continue to rent an apartment.
- An investor may decide to delay selling some stock because of the significant taxes that may result from the sale.
- A corporation may get a larger tax deduction if it leases property rather than purchasing the property.

The purpose of this text is to provide an introduction to the study of federal income taxation. However, before discussing the specifics of the U.S. federal income tax law, it is helpful to have a broad conceptual understanding of the taxation process. This chapter provides an overview of the following topics:

- Historical developments of the federal tax system
- Types of taxes levied and structural considerations
- Objectives of the tax law, including a discussion of recent tax reform proposals
- Taxpaying entities in the federal income tax system
- Tax law sources and the legislative process
- Internal Revenue Service (IRS) collection, examination, and appeals processes
- The nature of tax practice, including computer applications and tax research

KEY POINT

In many situations, the use of the tax laws to influence human behavior is deliberate. As will be seen later in this chapter, tax laws are often used to achieve social and economic objectives.

HISTORY OF TAXATION IN THE UNITED STATES

OBJECTIVE 1

Discuss the history of taxation in the United States

EARLY PERIODS

The federal income tax is the dominant form of taxation in the United States. In addition, most states and some cities and counties also impose an income tax. Both corporations and individuals are subject to such taxes.

Prior to 1913 (the date of enactment of the modern-day federal income tax), the federal government relied predominantly on customs duties and excise taxes to finance its operations. The first federal income tax on individuals was enacted in 1861 to finance the Civil War but was repealed after the war. The federal income tax was reinstated in 1894, however, that tax was challenged in the courts because the U.S. Constitution required that an income tax be apportioned among the states in proportion to their populations. This type of tax system, which would be both impractical and difficult to administer, would mean that different tax rates would apply to individual taxpayers depending on their states of residence.

In 1895, the Supreme Court ruled that the tax was in violation of the U.S. Constitution.[1] Therefore, it was necessary to amend the U.S. Constitution to permit the passage of a federal income tax law. This was accomplished by the Sixteenth Amendment, which was ratified in 1913. The Sixteenth Amendment, while being an extraordinarily important amendment, consists of one sentence.

HISTORICAL NOTE

The reinstatement of the income tax in 1894 was the subject of heated political controversy. In general, the representatives in Congress from the agricultural South and West favored the income tax in lieu of customs duties. Representatives from the industrial eastern states were against the income tax and favored protective tariff legislation.

Sixteenth Amendment to the Constitution of the United States

The Congress shall have the power to lay and collect taxes on incomes, from whatever source derived, without apportionment among the several States, and without regard to any census or enumeration.

[1] *Pollock v. Farmers' Loan & Trust Co.*, 3 AFTR 2602 (USSC, 1895). Note, however, that a federal income tax on corporations that was enacted in 1909 was held to be constitutional because it was treated as an excise tax. See *Flint v. Stone Tracy Co.*, 3 AFTR 2834 (USSC, 1911).

REVENUE ACTS FROM 1913 TO THE PRESENT

HISTORICAL NOTE

The Revenue Act of 1913 contained sixteen pages.

The Revenue Act of 1913 imposed a flat 1% tax (with no exemptions) on a corporation's net income. The rate varied from 1% to 6% for individuals, depending on the individual's income level. However, very few individuals paid federal income taxes because a $3,000 personal exemption ($4,000 for married individuals) was permitted as an offset to taxable income. These amounts were greater than the incomes of most individuals in 1913.

HISTORICAL NOTE

Before 1939, the tax laws were contained in the most current revenue act, a reenactment of a prior revenue act plus amendments. In 1939, a permanent tax code was established; it was revised in 1954 and 1986.

Various amendments to the original law were passed between 1913 and 1939 as separate revenue acts. For example, a deduction for dependency exemptions was provided in 1917. In 1939, the separate revenue acts were codified into the Internal Revenue Code of 1939. A similar codification was accomplished in 1954. The 1954 codification, which was known as the Internal Revenue Code of 1954, included the elimination of many "deadwood" provisions, a rearrangement and clarification of numerous code sections, and the addition of major tax law changes. Whenever changes to the Internal Revenue Code (IRC) are made, the old language is deleted and the new language added. Thus, the statutes are organized as a single document, and a tax advisor does not have to read through the applicable parts of all previous tax bills to find the most current law. In 1986, major changes were made to the tax law, and the basic tax law was redesignated as the Internal Revenue Code of 1986.

The federal income tax became a "mass tax" on individuals during the early 1940s. This change was deemed necessary to finance the revenue needs of the federal government during World War II. In 1939, less than 6% of the U.S. population was subject to the federal income tax; by 1945, 74% of the population was taxed.[2] To accommodate the broadened tax base and to avoid significant tax collection problems, Congress enacted pay-as-you-go withholding in 1943.

A major characteristic of the federal income tax since its inception to today is the manner in which the tax law is changed or modified. The federal income tax is changed on an **incremental** basis rather than a complete revision basis. Under so-called incrementalism, when a change in the tax law is deemed necessary by Congress, the entire law is not changed, but specific provisions of the tax law are added, changed, or deleted on an incremental basis. Thus, the federal income tax has been referred to as a "quiltwork" of tax laws, referring to the patchwork nature of the law. Without question, one of the principal reasons for the complexity of the federal income tax today is the incremental nature of tax legislation.

REVENUE SOURCES

ADDITIONAL COMMENT

In 2012, 145 million individual income tax returns were filed, and collections from individuals totaled $1.19 trillion.

As mentioned earlier, the largest source of federal revenues is individual income taxes. Other major revenue sources include Social Security (FICA) taxes and corporate income taxes (see Table I:1-1). Two notable trends from Table I:1-1 are (1) the gradual increase in social insurance taxes from 1960 to 2014 and (2) the gradual decrease in corporate income taxes for the same period. Individual income taxes have remained fairly stable during the past 50 years.

TYPICAL MISCONCEPTION

It is often assumed that the tax revenue from corporation income taxes is the largest source of tax revenue. However, the revenue generated from this tax only represents approximately 11% of total federal revenues in 2014.

▼ TABLE I:1-1
Breakdown of Federal Revenues

	1960	1975	1994	2014
Individual income taxes	44%	45%	43%	46%
Social insurance taxes and contribution	16	32	37	34
Corporation income taxes	23	15	11	11
Other	17	8	9	9
Total	100%	100%	100%	100%

Source: Council of Economic Advisers, *Economic Indicators* (Washington, DC: U.S. Government Printing Office, 1967, 1977, 2014).

[2] Richard Goode, *The Individual Income Tax* (Washington, DC: The Brookings Institution, 1964), pp. 2–4.

Types of Tax Rate Structures

OBJECTIVE 2

Describe the three types of tax rate structures

THE STRUCTURE OF INDIVIDUAL INCOME TAX RATES

Virtually all tax structures are comprised of two basic parts: the tax base and the tax rate. The tax base is the amount to which the tax rate is applied to determine the tax due. For example, an individual's tax base for the federal income tax is *taxable income*, as defined and determined by the income tax law. Similarly, the tax base for the property tax is generally the fair market value of property subject to the tax. The tax rate is merely the percentage rate applied to the tax base.

ADDITIONAL COMMENT

In the 1950s, the top marginal tax rate for individual taxpayers reached 92%. This astonishingly high rate only applied to taxpayers with very high taxable incomes but still is an extremely confiscatory tax rate.

Tax rates may be progressive, proportional, or regressive. A **progressive rate** structure is one where the rate of tax increases as the tax base increases. The most notable tax that incorporates a progressive rate structure is the federal income tax. Thus, as a taxpayer's taxable income increases, a progressively higher rate of tax is applied. For 2015, the federal income tax rates for individuals begin at 10% and increase to 15%, 25%, 28%, 33%, 35%, and 39.6% as a taxpayer's taxable income increases.[3] Examples I:1-1 and I:1-2 show how the progressive rate structure of the federal income tax operates.

EXAMPLE I:1-1 ▶ Alice, who is single, has $30,000 taxable income in 2015. Her federal income taxes for the year are $4,039, computed as follows: the first $9,225 of taxable income is taxed at 10% and the remaining $20,775 at 15%. (For tax rates, see the inside front cover.)

LEGISLATIVE BACKGROUND

Beginning with tax year 2013, the top rate for high-income individual taxpayers was increased to 39.6%. The top rate for 2012 was 35%.

Allen, who also is single, has taxable income of $60,000. A 10% rate applies to the first $9,225 of taxable income, 15% on the next $28,225, and a 25% rate applies to the taxable income over $37,450. Thus, Allen's total tax is $10,794 [(0.10 × $9,225) + (0.15 × $28,225) + (0.25 × $22,550)].

If Allen's taxable income is $120,000, a 28% rate applies to $29,250 of his taxable income ($120,000 − $90,750) because the 28% rate applies to taxable income above $90,750 for a single individual and his total tax for the year is $26,671. Thus, the tax rates are progressive because the rate of tax increases as a taxpayer's taxable income increases. ◀

Notice in Example I:1-1 that taxable income has doubled in size in the three cases, but the income taxes have more than doubled (i.e., $4,039 to $10,794 to $26,671). This demonstrates how a progressive rate structure operates.

EXAMPLE I:1-2 ▶ Assume the same facts as in Example I:1-1 except that Alice has taxable income of $200,000. Of Alice's taxable income, $10,700 ($200,000 − $189,300) is subject to the 33% rate. Alternatively, if Allen has taxable income of $425,000, $11,800 ($425,000 − $413,200) is subject to the top marginal rate of 39.6%. ◀

A **proportional tax** rate, sometimes called a **flat tax**, is one where the rate of tax is the same for all taxpayers, regardless of the level of their tax base. This type of tax rate is generally used for real estate taxes, state and local sales taxes, personal property taxes, customs duties, and excise taxes. A flat tax has been the subject of considerable discussion over the past twenty years and promises to be a controversial topic as the debate on federal income tax reform continues into the future.

EXAMPLE I:1-3 ▶ Assume the same facts as in Example I:1-1, except that a 17% tax rate applies to all amounts of taxable income. Based on the assumed flat tax rate structure, Alice's federal income tax is $5,100 on $30,000 of taxable income; Allen's tax is $10,200 on $60,000 of taxable income and $20,400 on $120,000 of taxable income. The tax rate is proportional because the 17% rate applies to both taxpayers without regard to their income level. As you can see, a proportional tax rate results in substantially lower taxes for higher income taxpayers.[4] ◀

[3] See the inside front cover for the 2015 tax rates and Chapter I:2 for a discussion of the computation procedures. 2014 rate schedules and tax tables are located immediately before Appendix A.

[4] This example assumes the same tax base (taxable income) for the flat tax as with the current federal tax. Most flat tax proposals allow only a few deductions and, therefore, would generate higher taxes than in the example.

SELF-STUDY QUESTION

Assume a tax system with a tax of $1,000 on taxable income of $10,000 and a $1,500 tax on taxable income of $20,000. Is the tax rate system progressive, proportional, or regressive?

ANSWER

This tax system is regressive. Even though the amount of tax has increased, the rate of taxation has decreased from 10% on the first $10,000 of taxable income to 5% on the second $10,000 of taxable income.

A **regressive tax** rate decreases with an increase in the tax base (e.g., income). Regressive taxes, while not consistent with the fairness of the income tax,[5] are found in the United States. The Social Security (FICA) tax is regressive because a fixed rate of tax of 6.20% for OASDI for both the employer and employee is levied up to a ceiling amount of $118,500 for 2015. So, for example, assume Taxpayer A has income subject to Social Security of $80,000 and Taxpayer B income of $400,000. Taxpayer A's OASDI would be $4,960 ($80,000 × 0.062), Taxpayer B's OASDI would be $7,347 ($118,500 × 0.062). Taxpayer A's average rate of OASDI tax is 6.2% while Taxpayer B's average rate of tax is 1.84% ($7,347/$400,000). The sales tax, which is levied by many states, is also regressive when measured against the income base.

THE STRUCTURE OF CORPORATE TAX RATES

Corporations are separate entities and are subject to income tax. The federal corporate income tax reflects a stair-step pattern of progression that tends to benefit small corporations. The corporate rates, which have not changed for several years, are as follows:[6]

Taxable Income[7]	*Tax*
First $50,000	15% of taxable income
Over $50,000 but not over $75,000	$7,500 + 25% of taxable income over $50,000
Over $75,000 but not over $100,000	$13,750 + 34% of taxable income over $75,000
Over $100,000 but not over $335,000	$22,250 + 39% of taxable income over $100,000
Over $335,000	34% of taxable income
Over $10,000,000 but not over $15,000,000	$3,400,000 + 35% of taxable income over $10,000,000
Over $15,000,000 but not over $18,333,333	$5,150,000 + 38% over $15,000,000
Over $18,333,333	35% of taxable income

MARGINAL, AVERAGE, AND EFFECTIVE TAX RATES FOR TAXPAYERS

A taxpayer's **marginal tax rate** is the tax rate applied to an incremental amount of taxable income that is added to the tax base. The marginal tax rate concept is useful for planning because it measures the tax effect of a proposed transaction.

EXAMPLE I:1-4 ▶ Tania, who is single, is considering the purchase of a personal residence that will provide a $20,000 tax deduction for interest expense and real estate taxes in 2015. Tania's taxable income would be reduced from $120,000 to $100,000 if she purchases the residence. Because a 28% tax rate applies to taxable income from $100,000 to $120,000, Tania's marginal tax rate is 28%. Thus, Tania's tax savings from purchasing the personal residence would be $5,600 (0.28 × $20,000). ◀

While the marginal tax rate measures the tax rate applicable to the next $1 of income or deduction for a taxpayer, there are two other tax rates that are used primarily by tax policymakers: average tax rate and effective tax rate. The **average tax rate** is computed by dividing the total tax liability by the amount of taxable income. This represents the average rate of tax for each dollar of taxable income. For example, a single taxpayer with taxable income of $450,000 in 2015 would incur a total tax liability of $134,569. The taxpayer's marginal tax rate is 39.6%, but his average tax rate is 29.9% ($134,569/$450,000).

[5] See the discussion of equity and fairness later in this chapter.

[6] For C corporations with taxable income over $100,000, the lower rates of tax on the first $75,000 of income are gradually phased out by applying a 5-percentage-point surtax on taxable income from $100,000 to $335,000 so that benefits of the favorable rates are eliminated once a corporation's taxable income reaches $335,000. Once taxable income exceeds $335,000 the tax equals 34% of taxable income. A 35% tax rate applies to taxable income in excess of $10 million. For corporations with taxable income in excess of $15 million, a 3 percentage-point-surtax applies to taxable income from $15 million to $18,333,333 to eliminate the lower 34% rate that applies to the first $10 million of taxable income.

[7] Also see the inside back cover for the corporation income tax rates.

ADDITIONAL COMMENT

One method of calculating economic income is to start with adjusted gross income (AGI), add back items of excludible income, such as tax-exempt bond interest, proceeds of life insurance policies, etc., and then deduct certain nondeductible business expenses, such as life insurance premiums, penalties and fines, etc.

The **effective tax rate** is the total tax liability divided by total economic income. **Total economic income** includes all types of economic income that a taxpayer has for the year. Thus, economic income is much broader than taxable income and includes most types of excludible income, such as tax-exempt bond interest, and generally permits business deductions but not personal-type deductions. It should be pointed out that economic income is *not* statutorily defined and experts may disagree on a precise calculation. The basic purpose of calculating the effective tax rate is to provide a broad measure of taxpayers' ability to pay taxes. Accordingly, the effective tax rate mainly is used by tax policy-makers to determine the fairness of the income tax system.

EXAMPLE I:1-5 ▶ Amelia, who is single, has adjusted gross income of $140,000 and economic income of $175,000 in 2015. The difference is attributable to $35,000 of tax-exempt bond interest. If Amelia has deductions of $30,000, then her taxable income is $110,000, and her total tax is $23,871. Her average tax rate is 21.70% ($23,871 ÷ $110,000). Amelia's effective tax rate is 13.64% ($23,871 ÷ $175,000). Amelia's effective tax rate is considerably lower than her average tax rate because of her substantial amount of tax-exempt income. ◀

STOP & THINK

Question: Gwen, a single taxpayer, has seen her income climb to $200,000 in the current year. She wants a tax planner to help her reduce her tax liability. In planning for tax clients, tax professionals almost exclusively use the marginal tax rate in their analysis rather than the average tax rate. Why is the marginal tax rate much more important in the tax planning process than the average tax rate?

Solution: Because tax planning is done at the margin. A single taxpayer who has taxable income of $200,000 has a marginal tax rate of 33% (at 2015 rates), but an average tax rate of 24.80%, computed as follows:

Taxable income		$200,000
Tax on first $189,300 of taxable income		$46,075.25
Remaining taxable income	$10,700	
Times: Marginal tax rate	× 0.33	3,531.00
Total tax liability		$ 49,606.25

$$\text{Average tax rate} = \frac{\text{Total tax}}{\text{Taxable income}} = \frac{\$\ 49{,}606.25}{\$200{,}000} = 24.80\%$$

If a tax planner could reduce Gwen's taxable income by $10,000, Gwen's tax liability would decrease by $3,333 ($10,000 × 0.33). When the taxpayer wants to know how much she can save through tax planning, the appropriate marginal tax rate yields the answer.

Overall, estimated effective federal income tax rates for individuals have increased slightly during the period 2003–2012,[8] amounting to 12.6% in 2012 as compared with 9.1% in 2003. For the highest 20% of households, the effective individual income tax rate increased to 18.0% in 2012 from 14.4% in 2003. The effective tax rate for individuals in the United States is relatively low compared to most other industrialized countries.

ADDITIONAL COMMENT

In the determination of tax rates, one should consider the incidence of taxation that involves the issue of who really bears the burden of the tax. If a city raises the real property tax but landlords simply raise rents to pass on the higher taxes, the tax burden is shifted to their tenants. The concept has important implications in determining any kind of average or effective tax rate.

DETERMINATION OF TAXABLE INCOME AND TAX DUE

As will be discussed in later chapters, the federal income taxes imposed on all taxpayers (individuals, corporations, estates, and trusts) are based on the determination of taxable income. In general, taxable income is computed as follows:

Total income (income from whatever source derived)		$xxx
Minus:	Exclusions (specifically defined items, such as tax-exempt bond interest)	(xx)

[8] Congressional Budget Office, *Effective Federal Tax Rates Under Current Law, 2001 to 2014* (Washington, DC:U.S. Government Printing Office, August, 2004), p. 10.

Gross income		$xxx
Minus:	Deductions (business expenses and itemized deductions)	(xx)
	Exemptions (not applicable for corporations)	(xx)
Taxable income		$xxx
Times:	Applicable tax rate	× .xx
Income tax before credits		$xxx
Minus:	Tax credits	(xx)
Total tax liability		$xxx
Minus:	Prepayments	(xx)
Balance due or refund		$xxx

Each different type of taxpayer (individuals, corporations, etc.) computes taxable income in a slightly different manner, but all use the general framework above. An introductory discussion of the various types of taxpayers is provided later in this chapter. More detailed discussions of individual taxpayers (Chapter I:2) and corporation taxpayers (Chapter I:16) are examined in this *Individuals* book. Corporations, estates, and trusts are further examined in *Prentice Hall's Federal Taxation: Corporations, Partnerships, Estates, and Trusts.*

OTHER TYPES OF TAXES

OBJECTIVE 3

Describe the various types of taxes

STATE AND LOCAL INCOME AND FRANCHISE TAXES

In addition to federal income taxes, many states and local jurisdictions impose income taxes on individuals and businesses. These state and local taxes have gradually increased over the years and currently represent a significant source of revenue for state and local governments but also represent a significant tax burden on taxpayers.

State and local income taxes vary greatly in both form and rates.[9] Only seven states do not impose an individual income tax.[10] In most instances, state income tax rates are mildly progressive and are based on an individual's federal adjusted gross income (AGI), with minor adjustments.[11] For example, a typical adjustment to a state income tax return is interest income on federal government bonds, which is subject to tax on the federal return but generally is not subject to state income taxes. Some states also allow a deduction for federal income taxes in the computation of taxable income for state income tax purposes.

ADDITIONAL COMMENT

States that do not impose a state income tax depend on other taxes to support the government mission, principally sales taxes.

States imposing a state income tax generally require the withholding of state income taxes and have established mandatory estimated tax payment procedures. The due date for filing state income tax returns generally coincides with the due date for the federal income tax returns (e.g., the fifteenth day of the fourth month following the close of the tax year for individuals).

ADDITIONAL COMMENT

State income tax rates for individuals have increased significantly in the past twenty years. Twenty-three states now have marginal tax rates of 6% or higher.

Most states impose a corporate income tax, although in some instances the tax is called a franchise tax. Franchise taxes usually are based on a weighted-average formula consisting of net worth, income, and sales.

WEALTH TRANSFER TAXES

U.S. citizens are subject to taxation on certain transfers of property to another person. The tax law provides a unified transfer tax system that imposes a single tax on transfers of property taking place during an individual's lifetime (gifts) and at death (estates). (See the inside back cover of the text for the transfer tax rate schedules.) Formerly, the gift and estate tax laws were separate and distinct. The federal estate tax was initially enacted in 1916. The original gift tax law dates back to 1932. The gift tax was originally imposed to prevent widespread avoidance of the estate tax (e.g., taxpayers could make tax-free gifts of property

[9] For a thorough discussion of state and local taxes, see the chapter entitled *Multistate Income Taxation* that accompanies this textbook in electronic form on the Prentice Hall Federal Taxation 2016 Web page at www.prenhall.com/phtax.

[10] These states are Alaska, Florida, Nevada, South Dakota, Texas, Washington, and Wyoming. New Hampshire has an income tax that is levied only on dividend and interest income and Tennessee's income tax applies only to income from stocks and bonds.

[11] See Chapter I:2 for a discussion of the AGI computation.

before their death). Both the gift and estate taxes are wealth transfer taxes levied on the transfer of property and are based on the fair market value (FMV) of the transferred property on the date of the transfer. Following are brief descriptions of the gift tax and estate tax.

KEY POINT

The $14,000 annual exclusion is an important tax-planning tool for wealthy parents who want to transfer assets to their children and thereby minimize their gift and estate taxes. A husband and wife who have three children could transfer a maximum of $84,000 [($14,000 × 2) × 3] to their children each year without incurring any gift tax.

The Federal Gift Tax. The gift tax is an excise tax that is imposed on the donor (not the donee) for transfers of property that are considered to be a taxable gift. A gift, generally speaking, is a transfer made gratuitously and with donative intent. However, the gift tax law has expanded the definition to include transfers that are not supported by full and adequate consideration.[12] To arrive at the amount of taxable gifts for the current year, a $14,000 (2015) annual exclusion is allowed per donee.[13] In addition, an unlimited marital deduction is allowed for transfers between spouses.[14] The formula for computing the gift tax is as follows:

FMV of all gifts made in the current year		$x,xxx
Minus: Annual donee exclusions ($14,000 per donee)	$xx	
Marital deduction for gifts to spouse	xx	
Charitable contribution deduction	xx	(xxx)
Plus: Taxable gifts for all prior years		xxx
Cumulative taxable gifts (tax base)		$x,xxx
Times: Unified transfer tax rates		× .xx
Tentative tax on gift tax base		$ xxx
Minus: Unified transfer taxes paid in prior years		(xx)
Unified credit		(xx)
Unified transfer tax (gift tax) due in the current year		$ xx

ADDITIONAL COMMENT

The gift tax was enacted to make the estate tax more effective. Without a gift tax, estate taxes could be easily avoided by large gifts made before death.

Note that the gift tax is cumulative over the taxpayer's lifetime (i.e., the tax calculation for the current year includes the taxable gifts made in prior years). The detailed tax rules relating to the gift tax are covered in Chapter C: 12 in both *Prentice Hall's Federal Taxation: Corporations, Partnerships, Estates, and Trusts* and the *Comprehensive* volume. The following general concepts and rules for the federal gift tax are presented as background material for other chapters of this text dealing with individual taxpayers:

- Gifts between spouses are exempted from the gift tax due to the operation of an unlimited marital deduction.
- The primary liability for payment of the gift tax is imposed on the **donor**. The donee is contingently liable for payment of the gift tax in the event of nonpayment by the donor.
- A donor is permitted a $14,000 annual exclusion for gifts of a present interest to each donee.[15]
- Charitable contributions are effectively exempted from the gift tax because an unlimited deduction is allowed.
- The tax basis of the property to the donee is generally the donor's cost. It is the lesser of the donor's cost and the property's FMV on the date of the gift if the property is sold by the donee at a loss. (See Chapter I:5 for a discussion of the gift tax basis rules.)
- A unified tax credit equivalent to a $5,000,000 deduction (adjusted for inflation, the amount is $5,430,000 for 2015) is available to offset any gift tax on taxable gifts that exceed the $14,000 annual exclusion.[16]

EXAMPLE I:1-6 ▶ Antonio makes the following gifts in the year 2015:

- $25,000 cash gift to his wife
- $15,000 contribution to the United Way

[12] Sec. 2512(b).

[13] Sec. 2503(b). The annual exclusion for gift tax purposes had been $10,000 for many years. However, for 2002–2005, the inflation adjustment increased the exclusion to $11,000, for 2006–2008, the exclusion was increased to $12,000, and for 2009–2012 to $13,000. For 2013 and later years, the current exclusion has been increased to $14,000.

[14] Sec. 2523(a).

[15] A gift of a present interest is an interest that is already in existence and the donee is currently entitled to receive the income from the property. A gift of a future interest comes into being at some future date (e.g., property is transferred by gift to a trust in which the donee is not entitled to the income from the property until the donor dies) and is not eligible for the $14,000 annual exclusion.

[16] The applicable exclusion amount has been $1,000,000 since 2002. However, beginning in 2011, the exclusion was increased to $5,000,000, adjusted for inflation. For further details, see *Prentice Hall's Federal Taxation:Corporations, Partnerships, Estates and Trusts*, 2016 Edition, Chapters C:12 and C:13.

▶ Gift of a personal automobile valued at $40,000 to his adult son

▶ Gift of a personal computer valued at $4,000 to a friend

The $25,000 gift to his wife is not taxed because of a $14,000 annual exclusion and a $11,000 marital deduction. The $15,000 contribution to the United Way is also not taxed because of the unlimited deduction for charitable contributions. The $40,000 gift Antonio made to his son is reduced by the $14,000 annual exclusion to each donee, leaving a $26,000 taxable gift.[17] The $4,000 gift to the friend is not taxed because of the annual exclusion of up to $14,000 in gifts to a donee in a tax year. Thus, total taxable gifts for the current year subject to the unified transfer tax are $26,000. ◀

STOP & THINK

Question: An important but frequently overlooked aspect of gift taxes is the interaction of gift taxes and income taxes. In many cases, gifts are made *primarily* for income tax purposes. Why would a gift be made for income tax purposes?

Solution: Gifts are frequently made to shift income from one family member to another family member who is in a lower marginal tax bracket. For example, assume Fran and Jan are married, have one 25-year-old son, earn $500,000 per year from their business, and generate $100,000 per year in dividends and interest from a substantial portfolio of stocks and bonds. With such a high level of income, Fran and Jan are in the 39.6% marginal tax bracket. If they make a gift of some of the stocks and bonds to their son, the dividends and interest attributable to the gift are taxed to the son at his marginal tax rate (maybe 10% or 15%). If the son's marginal tax rate is lower than 39.6%, the family unit reduces its overall income taxes.

The Federal Estate Tax. The federal estate tax is part of the unified transfer tax system that is based on the total property transfers an individual makes both during his or her lifetime and at death. The basic structure of the estate tax is shown in Example I:1-7.

TYPICAL MISCONCEPTION

It is sometimes thought that the federal estate tax raises significant amounts of revenue, but it has not been a significant revenue producer since World War II. Only 9,400 estate tax returns were filed in 2012 generating approximately $8.5 billion in tax revenues. This amount represents about 0.75% of revenues generated by income taxes on individuals.

EXAMPLE I:1-7 ▶ Amy dies during the current year. The formula for computing the estate tax on Amy's estate is as follows:

Gross estate (FMV of all property owned by the decedent at the date of death)	$xxx,xxx
Minus: Deductions for funeral and administration expenses, debts of the decedent, charitable contributions, and the marital deduction for property transferred to a spouse	(x,xxx)
Taxable estate	$ x,xxx
Plus: Taxable gifts made after 1976	xx
Tax base	$ x,xxx
Times: Unified transfer tax rate(s)	× .xx
Tentative tax on estate tax base	$ xxx
Minus: Tax credits (e.g., the unified tax credit equivalent to a $5,430,000 deduction in 2015)	(xx)
Gift taxes paid after 1976	(xx)
Unified transfer tax (estate tax) due	$ xx ◀

The federal estate tax has been on a roller coaster ride the last several years, with many changes and uncertainties. For a complete discussion of these developments, see *Prentice Hall's Federal Taxation: Corporations, Partnerships, Estates and Trusts, 2016 Edition, Chapter C:13*. Beginning January 1, 2013, however, more certainty exists to the estate tax law due to recent changes. The computation of the taxable estate and tax base (see Example I:1-7 above) is much the same as in prior years. However, the highest tax rate for tax years after 2012 has been increased to 40% from 35%. More importantly, the unified credit exclusion amount has been made permanent at $5 million per person and is indexed annually for inflation. For 2015, the unified credit exclusion amount is $5,430,000 ($5,340,000 for 2014). In essence, estates of individuals dying in 2015 generally will not be subject to estate taxes if their tax base is equal to or less

[17] This example assumes that the automobile is a gift rather than an obligation of support under state law and also assumes that Antonio's wife does not join with Antonio in electing to treat the gift to the son as having been made by both spouses (a gift-splitting election). In such event, donee exclusions of $28,000 (2 × $14,000) would be available, resulting in a taxable gift of only $12,000.

than $5,430,000. With this large exemption amount, most estates will not be subject to estate taxes.

The estate tax rules are discussed in more detail in Chapter C:13 of *Prentice Hall's Federal Taxation: Corporations, Partnerships, Estates, and Trusts* and in the *Comprehensive* volume. The general rules discussed below are provided as background material for subsequent chapters of this text dealing with individual taxpayers:

- The decedent's property is valued at its FMV on the date of death unless the alternative valuation date (six months after the date of death) is elected. The alternative valuation date may be elected only if the aggregate value of the gross estate decreases during the six-month period following the date of death and the election results in a lower estate tax liability.
- The basis of the property received by the estate and by the decedent's heirs is the property's FMV on the date of death (or the alternate valuation date if it is elected).
- Property transferred to the decedent's spouse is exempt from the estate tax because of the estate tax marital deduction provision.
- The unified credit is $2,117,800, based on an exclusion amount of $5,430,000 and is computed as follows: [$345,800 + 0.40 (5,430,000 − 1,000,000)].

EXAMPLE I:1-8 ▶ Barry died in 2015, leaving a $8,000,000 gross estate. Of the $8,000,000 gross estate, one-half of the estate was transferred to his wife, administrative and funeral expenses are $30,000, Barry had debts of $200,000, and the remainder of the estate was transferred to his children. The estate tax due is computed as follows:

Gross estate	$8,000,000
Minus: Marital deduction	(4,000,000)
Funeral and administrative expenses	(30,000)
Decedent's debts	(200,000)
Taxable estate	$3,770,000
Plus: Taxable gifts made after 1976	0
Tax base	$3,770,000
Tentative tax on estate tax base	$1,453,800[a]
Minus: Tax credits (unified tax credit—see above or inside back cover for table)	(2,117,800)
Unified transfer tax due	$ —0— ◀

[a]$345,800 + [0.40 × ($3,770,000 − $1,000,000)]

Because of the generous credit and deduction provisions (e.g., the unified tax credit and the unlimited marital deduction), few estates are required to pay estate taxes. As can be seen above, the gross estate of the decedent was $8 million but no estate taxes were due primarily because of the large marital deduction and the unified credit. However, estate taxes rise quickly as is demonstrated below in Example I:1-9.

EXAMPLE I:1-9 ▶ Assume the same facts for Barry as in Example I:1-8 except that Barry's gross estate is $14,000,000 rather than $8,000,000. The estate tax due is computed as follows:

Gross estate	$14,000,000
Minus: Marital deduction	(7,000,000)
Funeral and administrative expenses	(30,000)
Decedent's debts	(200,000)
Taxable estate	$ 6,770,000
Plus: Taxable gifts made after 1976	0
Tax base	$ 6,770,000
Tentative tax on estate tax base	$ 2,653,800[b]
Minus: Tax credits (unified tax credit)	(2,117,800)
Unified transfer tax due	$ 536,000 ◀

[b]$345,800 + [0.40 × ($6,770,000 − $1,000,000)]

OTHER TYPES OF TAXES

Although this text focuses primarily on the federal income tax, some mention should be made of the following other types of taxes levied by federal, state, and local governments.

ADDITIONAL COMMENT

Property taxes are a type of ad valorem tax, from the Latin phrase "according to value."

- **Property taxes** are based on the value of a taxpayer's property, which may include both real estate and personal property. Real estate taxes are a major source of revenue for local governments. In addition, some state and local governments levy a personal property tax on intangibles such as securities and tangible personal property (e.g., the value of a personal automobile).
- **Federal excise taxes** and **customs duties** on imported goods have declined in relative importance over the years but remain significant sources of revenue. Federal excise taxes are imposed on alcohol, tobacco, gasoline, telephone usage, production of oil and gas, and many other types of goods. Many state and local governments impose similar excise taxes on goods and services.
- **Sales taxes** are a major source of revenue for state and local governments. Sales taxes are imposed on retail sales of tangible personal property (e.g., clothing and automobiles). Some states also impose a sales tax on personal services (e.g., accounting and legal fees). Certain items often are exempt from the sales tax levy (e.g., food items or medicines), and the rates vary widely between individual state and local governments. Sales taxes are not deductible for federal income tax purposes unless incurred in a trade or business.

ADDITIONAL COMMENT

Proposals to decrease reliance on the federal income tax have focused primarily on consumption taxes, such as a national sales tax or a value-added tax. A value-added tax basically is a sales tax levied at each stage of production on the "value added."

- Employment taxes include Social Security (FICA) and federal and state unemployment compensation taxes. If an individual is classified as an employee, the FICA tax that is imposed on the employee is comprised of two parts: the old-age survivors, and disability insurance (OASDI) and the Medicare or hospital insurance (HI). The OASDI is 6.2% and is imposed on the first $118,500 (2015) of wages. This tax is imposed on both the employer and the employee at the same rate. Similarly, the HI portion is imposed on both the employer and the employee, but it has no ceiling on wages like the OASDI portion. In fact, the HI portion is generally 1.45% of wages, but beginning in 2013, the employee is required to pay an additional 0.9% on wages above $200,000 ($250,000 for married taxpayers filing a joint return). So while the employer will pay 1.45% on all wages, an employee who is single will pay 1.45% on the first $200,000 of wages and 2.35% on any wages over $200,000.

  If an individual is self-employed, a self-employment tax comprised of the OASDI and HI taxes is imposed. The OASDI portion is 12.4% on the individual's self-employment income of up to $118,500 (in 2015). The HI portion is 2.9% on the first $200,000 of self-employment income ($250,000 combined self-employment income for married taxpayers filing a joint return) and 3.8% on any self-employment income over that amount.
- Employers are required to pay federal and state unemployment taxes to fund the payment of unemployment benefits to former employees. The federal rate is 6.0% on the first $7,000 of wages for each employee in 2015.[19] However, a credit is granted for up to 5.4% of wages for taxes paid to the state government so that the actual amount paid to the federal government may be as low as 0.6%.[20] The amount of tax paid to the state depends on the employer's prior experience with respect to the frequency and amount of unemployment claims. In California, for example, the highest rate of unemployment tax imposed is 6.2% and this rate is subsequently adjusted down if the employer has a small number of unemployment claims to a minimum of 1.5%.

ADDITIONAL COMMENT

Revenue from employment taxes are indeed significant. In 2014, $1.024 trillion in employment taxes were collected representing 34% of all Internal Revenue Service collections.

The types of taxes and structural considerations that were previously discussed are summarized in Topic Review I:1-1.

---

[18] Self-employed individuals receive an income tax deduction equal to 50% of taxes paid on their self-employment income and this deduction is also allowed to compute the amount of self-employment income (see Secs. 164(f) and 1402(a)(12) and Chapter I:14).

[19] Sec. 3301.

[20] Sec. 3302. State unemployment taxes in some states are levied on tax bases above $7,000. For example, the wage base ceiling in North Carolina is $21,700 in 2015.

TOPIC REVIEW I:1-1

Types of Taxes and Tax Structure

Type of Tax	Tax Structure	Tax Base
Individuals:		
Federal income tax	Progressive	Gross income from all sources unless specifically excluded by law reduced by deductions and exemptions
State income tax	Progressive	Generally based on AGI for federal income tax purposes with adjustments
Federal gift tax	Progressive	FMV of all taxable gifts made during the tax year
Federal estate tax	Progressive	FMV of property owned at death plus taxable gifts made after 1976
Corporations:		
Federal corporate income tax	Progressive	Gross income from all sources unless specifically excluded by law reduced by deductions
State corporate income tax	Proportional or progressive	Federal corporate taxable income with adjustments
State franchise tax	Proportional	Usually based on a weighted-average formula consisting of net worth, income, and sales
Other Types of Taxes:		
Property taxes	Proportional	FMV of personal or real property
Excise taxes	Proportional	Customs and duties on imported and domestic goods from alcohol to telephone usage
Sales taxes	Proportional	Retail sales of tangible personal property or personal services
FICA and self-employment taxes	Regressive	Based on wages or self-employment income
Unemployment taxes	Regressive	Usually first $7,000 of an employee's wages

Criteria for a Tax Structure

OBJECTIVE 4

Discuss the criteria for a "good" tax structure, the objectives of the federal income tax law, and recent tax reform proposals

Establishing criteria for a "good" tax structure was first attempted in 1776 by economist Adam Smith.[21] Smith's four "canons of taxation"—equity, certainty, convenience, and economy—are still used today when tax policy issues are discussed. Many have added a fifth canon of simplicity. Below is a discussion of these criteria and how they relate to income taxes as well as other taxes.

EQUITY

A rather obvious criteria for a good tax is that the tax be equitable or fair to taxpayers. However, equity or fairness is elusive because of the subjectivity of the concept. What one person may conclude is fair in a particular situation may be considered totally unfair by another person. In other words, fairness is relative in nature and is extremely difficult to measure. For example, the deductibility of mortgage interest on a taxpayer's home certainly seems to be a fair provision for taxpayers. However, for taxpayers who do not own a home but live in a rental apartment, the deductibility of mortgage interest may not be considered as fair because the renter cannot deduct any portion of the rent paid. In other types of situations, the federal tax law includes various measures to ensure that taxpayers are treated fairly. For example, a foreign tax credit is available to minimize the double taxation that would otherwise occur when U.S. taxpayers earn income in a foreign country that is taxed by

[21] Adam Smith, *The Wealth of Nations* (New York: Random House, Modern Library, 1937), pp. 777–779.

KEY POINT

Using retroactive dates for changes in the tax law does not help to accomplish the objective of certainty. For example, the effective date of major changes in the estate tax was recently made on a retroactive basis. These retroactive changes created considerable uncertainty for taxpayers and their advisors.

both the United States and the country in which it is earned. (See the glossary at the end of this volume for a definition of tax credits and Chapter I:14 for a discussion of the foreign tax credit.) Two aspects of equity are commonly discussed in the tax policy literature, **horizontal equity** and **vertical equity**. Horizontal equity refers to the notion that similarly situated taxpayers should be treated equally. Thus, two taxpayers who each have income of $50,000 should both pay the same amount of tax. Vertical equity, on the other hand, implies that taxpayers who are not similarly situated should be treated differently. Thus, if Taxpayer A has income of $50,000 and Taxpayer B has income of $20,000, Taxpayers A and B should not pay the same amount of income tax. Vertical equity provides that the incidence of taxation should be borne by those who have the **ability to pay** the tax, based on income or wealth. The progressive rate structure is founded on the vertical equity premise.

CERTAINTY

A certain tax (1) ensures a stable source of government operating revenues and (2) provides taxpayers with some degree of certainty concerning the amount of their annual tax liability. A tax that is simple to understand and administer provides certainty for taxpayers. For many years, our income tax laws have been criticized as being overly complex and difficult to administer. Consider the remarks of a noted tax authority at a conference on federal income tax simplification:

> Tax advisers—at least some tax advisers—are saying that the income tax system is not working. They are saying that they don't know what the law provides, that the IRS does not know what the law provides, that taxpayers are not abiding by the law they don't know.[22]

While the above statement is over 30 years old, it is certainly still viable today. This uncertainty in the tax law causes frequent disputes between taxpayers and the IRS and has resulted in extensive litigation.

ADDITIONAL COMMENT

Humorist Jim Boren has proposed a constitutional amendment that would require any retroactive tax increases to be followed by retroactive elections for president, vice president, and all members of Congress.

The federal tax system has made some attempts to provide certainty for taxpayers. For example, the IRS issues advance rulings to taxpayers, which provides some assurance concerning the tax consequences of a proposed transaction for the taxpayer who requests the ruling. The taxpayer may rely on the ruling if the transaction is completed in accordance with the terms of the ruling request. For example, if a merger of two corporations is being considered, the transaction can be structured so that the shareholders and the corporations do not recognize gain or loss. If a favorable ruling is received and the transaction is completed as planned, the IRS cannot later assert that the merger does not qualify for tax-free treatment.

CONVENIENCE

A tax law should be easily assessed, collected, and administered. Taxpayers should not be overly burdened with the maintenance of records and compliance considerations (preparation of their tax returns, payment of their taxes, and so on). One of the reasons that the sales tax is such a popular form of tax for state and local governments is that it is convenient for taxpayers to pay and for the government to collect. The consumer need not complete a tax return or keep detailed records.

ECONOMY

ADDITIONAL COMMENT

For tax year 2009, 60% of all individual tax returns were prepared by paid tax-return preparers. This compares with 48% of returns prepared by paid return preparers in 1990. For taxpayers who file Form 1040 (as opposed to form 1040A and Form 1040EZ), 91% used paid preparers.

An economical tax structure should require only minimal compliance and administrative costs. The IRS collection costs, amounting to less than 0.5% of revenues, are minimal relative to the total collections of revenues from the federal income tax. Estimates of taxpayer compliance costs are less certain. One indicator of total compliance costs for taxpayers is the demand for tax professionals. Tax practice has been and continues to be one of the fastest growing areas in public accounting firms. Most large corporations also maintain sizable tax departments that engage in tax research, compliance, and planning activities. In addition, many commercial tax return preparer services are available to assist taxpayers who have relatively uncomplicated tax returns.

[22] Sidney L. Roberts, "The Viewpoint of the Tax Adviser: An Overview of Simplification," *Tax Adviser,* January 1979, p. 32.

Complying with the tax laws is enormously expensive for both businesses and individuals in the United States. In 2005, businesses spent an estimated $148 billion to comply with the federal tax laws, while it cost individuals about $111 billion.[23] Compliance with state and local taxes costs another $80 billion. Clearly, the cost of complying with the nation's tax laws is significant, in terms of both money and time.

A more difficult question is whether the tax structure is economical in terms of taxpayer compliance. The issues of tax avoidance and tax evasion are becoming increasingly more important. The General Accounting Office (GAO) reported that sole proprietors underreported their income by 57 percent or $68 billion in 2001.[24]

SIMPLICITY

One of the important measures of any tax system is that of simplicity, or at least, not undue complexity. Taxpayers should be able to understand and comply with any tax system within reasonable boundaries. The sales tax is an example of a tax system that is relatively simple, although the sales tax as it applies to businesses can become fairly complex. The federal income tax system in the United States has become inordinately complex over the years and complexity is one of the major criticisms of the income tax. The following is a quote from the report from the President's Advisory Panel on Federal Tax Reform:[25]

> In short, our current tax code is a complicated mess. Instead of clarity, we have opacity. Instead of simplicity, we have complexity. Instead of fair principles, we have seemingly arbitrary rules. Instead of contributing to economic growth, it detracts from growth. Time and time again, witnesses told the Panel about these failings in the tax code.

While simplicity is an admirable goal of any tax system, achieving this goal in the federal income tax system is difficult and involves the trade-off of other important objectives. For example, simplicity and fairness are almost impossible to achieve together. If the income tax law is extremely simple, like a flat tax rate on all income, the possible result is that many taxpayers will not be treated fairly. Consider this case, two taxpayers, A and B both earn $100,000 per year and we have a flat rate tax of 20% so that each taxpayer will pay $20,000 in income taxes for the year. However, assume that taxpayer B has a severe illness that requires him to pay medical expenses of $60,000 per year. Should both A and B pay the same income tax for the year? There is no absolute correct answer in this case, it depends on your definition of fairness. Thus, making the income tax law simple may not be the top priority in tax reform.

OBJECTIVES OF THE FEDERAL INCOME TAX LAW

The primary objective of the federal income tax law is to raise revenues for government operations. In recent years, the federal government has broadened its use of the tax laws to accomplish various economic and social policy objectives.

ADDITIONAL COMMENT

Among the provisions in the tax law that are designed to enhance the level of health care are the deductibility of medical expenses, deductibility of charitable contributions to hospitals, and exclusion of fringe benefits provided by employers for medical insurance premiums and medical care.

Economic Objectives. The federal income tax law is used as a fiscal policy tool to stimulate private investment, reduce unemployment, and mitigate the effects of inflation on the economy. Consider the following example: Tax credits for businesses operating in distressed urban and rural areas (empowerment zones) are allowed to provide economic revitalization of such areas. This is a clear example of using the federal income tax law to stimulate private investment in specific areas.

---

23 Scott A. Hodge, J. Scott Moody, and Wendy P. Warcholik, "The Rising Cost of Complying with the Federal Income Tax," Special Report No. 138, *Tax Foundation*, January, 2006, p. 1.

24 News Report. "Limiting Sole Proprietor Loss Deductions Could Improve Compliance But Would Also Limit Some Legitimate Losses" GAO Report GAO-09-815 Oct. 13, 2009.

25 Report of the President's Advisory Panel on Federal Tax Reform, *Simple, Fair, & Pro-Growth: Proposals to Fix America's Tax System*, November 2005, p. 2. See the discussion of tax reform in this chapter.

Many items in the tax law are adjusted for inflation by using the consumer price index, including the tax brackets, personal and dependency exemptions, and standard deduction amounts. These inflation adjustments provide relief for individual taxpayers who would otherwise be subject to increased taxes due to the effects of inflation. (See Chapter I:2 for a discussion of the tax computation for individuals.)

Encouragement of Certain Activities and Industries. The federal income tax law also attempts to stimulate and encourage certain activities, specialized industries, and small businesses. One such example is the encouragement of research activities by permitting an immediate write-off of expenses and a special tax credit for increasing research and experimental costs. Special incentives are also provided to the oil and gas industry through percentage depletion allowances and an election to deduct intangible drilling costs.

Certain favorable tax provisions are provided for small businesses, including reduced corporate tax rates of 15% on the first $50,000 of taxable income and 25% for the next $25,000 of taxable income. Favorable ordinary loss (instead of capital loss) deductions are granted to individual investors who sell their small business corporation stock at a loss, provided that certain requirements are met.[26] In addition, noncorporate investors may exclude up to 50% of the gain realized from the disposition of qualified small business stock if the stock is held for more than five years.[27]

Social Objectives. The tax law attempts to encourage or discourage certain socially desirable or undersirable activities. For example:

ADDITIONAL COMMENT

Deductible contributions made by self-employed individuals to their retirement plans (Keogh plans) totaled $20.8 billion in 2012. Charitable deductions totaled over $199 billion that same year.

- Special tax-favored pension and profit-sharing plans have been created for employees and self-employed individuals to supplement the social security retirement system.
- Charitable contributions are deductible to encourage individuals to contribute to charitable organizations.
- The claiming of a deduction for illegal bribes, fines, and penalties has been prohibited to discourage activities that are contrary to public policy.

EXAMPLE I:1-10 ► Able Corporation establishes a qualified pension plan for its employees whereby it makes all of the annual contributions to the plan. Able's contributions to the pension trust are currently deductible and not includible in the employees' gross income until the pension payments are distributed during their retirement years. Earnings on the contributed funds also are nontaxable until such amounts are distributed to the employees. ◄

EXAMPLE I:1-11 ► Anita contributes $10,000 annually to her church, which is a qualified charitable organization. Anita's marginal tax rate is 25%. Her after-tax cost of contributing to the church is only $7,500 [$10,000 − (0.25 × $10,000)]. ◄

EXAMPLE I:1-12 ► Ace Trucking Company incurs $10,000 in fines imposed by local and state governments for overloading its trucks during the current tax year. The fines are not deductible because the activity is contrary to public policy. ◄

The tax law objectives previously discussed are highlighted in Topic Review I:1-2.

Income Tax Reform Proposals. Tax reform has been a much debated topic over the years but has taken center stage recently. There has been a flurry of books, articles, and newspaper editorials that range from installing a completely new tax system to a partial revision of the current income tax. Few people support keeping the income tax

[26] Sec. 1244.

[27] Sec. 1202.

TOPIC REVIEW I:1-2

Objectives of the Tax Law

Objective	Example
Stimulate investment	Provide a tax credit for the purchase of business equipment
Prevent taxpayers from paying a higher percentage of their income in personal income taxes due to inflation (bracket creep)	Index the tax rates, standard deduction, and personal and dependency exemptions for inflation
Encourage research activities that will in turn strengthen the competitiveness of U.S. companies	Allow research expenditures to be written off in the year incurred and offer a tax credit for increasing research and experimental costs
Encourage venture capital for small businesses	Reduce corporate income tax rates on the first $75,000 of taxable income. Allow businesses to immediately expense $500,000 (2014) of certain depreciable business assets acquired each year.
Encourage social objectives	Provide a tax deduction for charitable contributions; provide favorable tax treatment for contributions to qualified pension plans

system as it currently stands. Virtually all reform proposals advocate greater simplicity of the income tax law. Recently, there has been a push to increase income tax rates on high-income individuals. Some proponents of a new tax system advocate substituting a retail sales tax at the federal level for the income tax, others favor a value-added tax system (VAT tax) that is widely used in Europe. A partial revision of what we have now is also a popular option.

At present, it is unclear as to the likelihood of any tax reform proposals. While the recommendations are well thought-out, there are other pressing matters facing Congress that may postpone implementation of tax reform in a comprehensive manner. Piecemeal changes to the tax code certainly may continue and this only ensures continued complexity in the tax law.

Entities in the Federal Income Tax System

OBJECTIVE 5

Describe the tax entities in the federal income tax system

The federal income tax law levies taxes on taxpayers. However, not all entities that file income tax returns pay income taxes. For example, a partnership is required to file a tax return but does not pay any income tax because the income (or loss) of the partnership is allocated to the partners who report the income or loss on their individual tax returns. Therefore, the various entities in the federal income tax system may be classified into two general categories, *taxpaying entities* and *flow-through entities*.[28] Taxpaying entities generally are required to pay income taxes on their taxable income. Flow-through entities, on the other hand, generally do not directly pay income taxes but merely pass the income on to a taxpaying entity. The major entities in each category are as follows:

Taxpaying Entities	*Flow-through Entities*
Individuals	Sole proprietorship
C corporations (regular corporations)	Partnerships
	S corporations
	Limited Liability Company (LLC) or Limited Liability Partnership (LLP)
	Trusts

[28] Some entities have characteristics of both categories of entities, including certain types of trusts and S corporations.

Each of these entities is discussed below. The purpose of this section is to provide an overall picture of the various entities in the federal income tax system.

TAXPAYING ENTITIES

Individuals. Individual taxpayers are the principal taxpaying entities in the federal income tax system. In 2014, income taxes paid by individual taxpayers comprised nearly 46% of total federal revenues. If Social Security taxes are included, individual taxpayers paid 80% of total federal revenues (see Table I:1-1 for details). Thus, the study of taxation of individuals is a very important topic and is discussed extensively in this *Individuals* textbook.

Individuals pay income taxes on all gross income minus allowable deductions. Gross income minus allowable deductions is referred to as *taxable income*. Gross income subject to taxation may be broadly classified into three categories:

- Earned income from sources such as salaries and wages, business income, and retirement income.
- Investment income, including interest income, dividends, capital gains, and rents and royalties.
- Flow-through income from partnerships, limited liability companies (LLCs), Subchapter S corporations, estates, and trusts.

Allowable deductions include expenses attributable to the gross income above and certain personal deductions and exemptions specifically allowed under the tax law. Gross income and allowable deductions and exemptions are discussed in detail later in this textbook.

Individual taxpayers use the tax formula below to compute their taxable income:

Total income, from whatever source derived		$xxx
Minus:	Exclusions, as provided in the tax law	(xxx)
Gross income		xxx
Minus:	Deductions for adjusted gross income	(xxx)
Adjusted gross income (AGI)		xxx
Minus:	Deductions from AGI:	
	Greater of itemized deductions or standard deduction	(xxx)
	Personal and dependency exemptions	(xxx)
Taxable income		$xxx

Exclusions are items of income that the tax law specifically exempts from taxation. They include such items as gifts, inheritances, interest income from state and local bonds, loans, and life insurance proceeds. Exclusions are discussed in Chapter I:4.

Once an individual determines that an expenditure is allowed as a deduction for tax purposes, he or she must classify the deduction as *for* AGI or *from* AGI. This classification is very important and is discussed in Chapter I:6. Deductions *for* AGI basically are (1) expenses connected with a taxpayer's business or rental property, or (2) other specified deductions, such as moving expenses, contributions to an Individual Retirement Account (IRA), alimony, and a number of other specific items. Deductions *from* AGI are either itemized deductions or the standard deduction, whichever is greater, and personal and dependency exemptions. Itemized deductions primarily are personal-type deductions of the taxpayer, such as medical expenses, state and local taxes, mortgage interest, and charitable contributions. Itemized deductions are discussed in Chapter I:7. The standard deduction is a set amount that all taxpayers may deduct. For 2015, the standard deduction is $6,300 ($12,600 for married couples filing a joint return) and is indexed annually for inflation. Thus, if a single taxpayer's itemized deductions for 2015 were $5,000, the taxpayer would deduct the standard deduction of $6,300 instead. On the other hand, if the taxpayer's itemized deductions were $7,000, the taxpayer would deduct $7,000 because that amount exceeds the standard deduction.

Personal and dependency exemptions also are specific deductions allowed to individuals. The personal exemption is for the taxpayer and spouse whereas dependency exemptions are for the taxpayer's children or other dependents. The personal and dependency exemption in 2015 is $4,000. So, a husband and wife who have two dependent children would be entitled to a deduction of $16,000 ($4,000 × 4). This exemption amount is phased-out for higher income taxpayers and is indexed annually for inflation. Personal and dependency exemptions are discussed further in Chapter I:2.

Once taxable income is determined, tax rates are applied to this amount to arrive at the income tax liability for the year. Certain credits are allowed that reduce the income tax liability on a dollar-for-dollar basis. Individual income tax rates may be found inside the front cover of this textbook. Because individuals are subject to withholding and estimated tax payment rules, they may pay a balance due or receive a refund upon filing their tax return.

ADDITIONAL COMMENT

Instead of filing Form 1040, some individual taxpayers are eligible to file simplified versions, the form 1040A or Form 1040 EZ.

Individual taxpayers are required to file a tax return annually, Form 1040, which is due on or before April 15 of the year following the taxable year. As can be seen from the tax rate schedules located on the inside cover of this textbook, rates range from 10% to 39.6%.

EXAMPLE I:1-13 ▶ Jeff Payne, a single taxpayer, is employed by a large corporation and has the following information for the current year of 2015:

INCOME AND OTHER RECEIPTS	
Salary from corporation	$120,000
Interest income from savings account	13,000
Interest on New York City bond	600
Loan from bank	20,000
Share of income from a partnership in which Jeff is a partner	8,600
Gift from Jeff's grandmother	11,000
Total	$173,200
DEDUCTIONS, EXEMPTIONS, AND PAYMENTS	
Itemized deductions	17,000
Personal exemption (2015)	4,000
Federal income taxes withheld from salary	30,000

Jeff's taxable income and income tax liability for 2015 would be computed as follows:

Total income			$173,200
Minus:	Exclusions:		
	Interest on New York City bond	$ 600	
	Loan from bank	20,000	
	Gift from Jeff's grandmother	$11,000	31,600
Gross income			141,600
Minus:	Deductions for AGI		0
Adjusted gross income (AGI)			141,600
Minus:	Deductions from AGI:		
	Itemized deductions	$17,000	
	Personal exemption	4,000	(21,000)
Taxable income			$120,600

The itemized deductions of $17,000 exceed Jeff's allowable standard deduction for 2015 of $6,300 and, therefore, are used to reduce taxable income.

To compute Jeff's income tax liability for the year, the 2015 rate schedules inside the front cover of the textbook are used. Jeff's income tax liability (using single taxpayer rates) would be $26,839.25 [$18,481.25 + 0.28($120,600 − $90,750)]. Since Jeff had $30,000 of federal income taxes withheld from his salary, he would be entitled to a tax refund of $3,160.75 ($30,000.00 − $26,839.25). ◀

Some types of income are taxed at lower rates. For example, dividends from most U.S. corporations are subject to a maximum rate of 20%. This 20% maximum rate also applies to long-term capital gains, such as gains on the sale of stocks and bonds. With these lower rates, a high-income taxpayer in the 39.6% marginal tax bracket would only pay a maximum of 20% on any qualified dividends received or long-term capital gains. The remainder of the taxpayer's income would be subject to the higher rates.

C Corporations. C corporations, many times referred to as regular corporations, also are taxpaying entities. These corporations, both publicly-held corporations traded on stock exchanges and privately-owned corporations, accounted for approximately 11% of total federal revenues in 2014. The percentage of federal revenues provided by C corporations has been steadily declining over the past 40 years, a concern of tax policymakers as more and more taxes are being shifted to individual taxpayers. A major disadvantage of C corporations is they are subject to so-called double taxation. Double taxation results from the corporation paying income tax on its taxable income and shareholders paying income tax on any dividends received from the corporation or on the gain from selling their stock in the corporation. Thus, the same corporate income is subjected to taxation twice—once at the corporate level and again at the shareholder level. For many years, much tax planning has been directed at trying to so arrange the tax affairs of a C corporation to avoid double taxation. This discussion of C corporations is divided into two parts, (1) taxation of C corporations and (2) the operation of double taxation.

Taxation of C corporations. C corporations are taxed on their taxable income in a manner similar to individuals. The major difference between corporations and individuals is that corporations are not allowed personal exemptions and personal deductions. Thus, the concept of AGI does not pertain to corporations. Taxable income for corporations is computed as follows:

Total income, from whatever source derived	$xxx
Minus: Exclusions, as provided in the tax law	(xxx)
Gross income	xxx
Minus: Deductions (ordinary and necessary expenses related to the corporation's trade or business)	(xxx)
Taxable income	$xxx

This taxable income is subject to tax rates that range from 15% to 35%. (see rate schedule in the inside rear cover of the textbook). A more detailed discussion of corporation taxation is contained in Chapter I:16 of this *Individuals* textbook and Chapter C:3 of the *Corporations, Partnerships, Estates, and Trusts* volume.

EXAMPLE I:1-14 ▶ During the current taxable year, Crimson Corporation generated gross income of $1,500,000 and had ordinary and necessary deductions of $900,000, resulting in taxable income of $600,000. Based on the corporation rate schedules, Crimson would be subject to taxes of $204,000 [$113,900 + .34($600,000 − 335,000)]. ◀

C corporations are required to file tax returns annually using Form 1120, which is due on or after the 15th day of the third month after the close of the corporation's tax year (e.g., March 15 for calendar year taxpayers).

Double taxation of C corporation earnings. As mentioned previously, C corporations are subject to double taxation. The corporation pays income tax on its taxable income and then shareholders must pay income tax on any dividends paid by the corporation or on the sale of their stock. Tax legislation in 2003 substantially reduced the impact of double taxation by reducing to 15% the maximum tax rate on most corporate dividends received by individuals. Prior to this reduction in tax rates on qualified dividends, dividends were subject to tax at regular tax rates. For tax years 2013 and forward, taxpayers who are in the 10% or 15% regular tax brackets continue to have a 0% tax rate on qualified dividends. Taxpayers who are in a marginal tax bracket above 15% and below 39.6% continue to pay a marginal tax rate of 15% on qualified dividends. However, taxpayers who are in the highest tax bracket of 39.6% now pay a marginal tax rate of 20% on qualified dividends. Thus, under current tax law, a taxpayer in the 35% marginal tax bracket (see tax rate schedules inside the front cover of this textbook) pays only a 15% tax rate on any dividends received. The same reduced tax rates apply to long-term capital gains on the sale of their corporate stock.

EXAMPLE I:1-15 ▶ Using the same facts for Crimson Corporation in Example I:1-14, assume the corporation paid dividends to shareholders during 2015 of $400,000. Further assume that the marginal tax bracket of the shareholders is 39.6%. The shareholders collectively would have to pay individual income taxes of $80,000 ($400,000 × 20%) as the maximum tax rate on qualified dividends is 20%. The total tax on the corporation's taxable income of $600,000, therefore, would be $284,000 ($204,000 paid by Crimson Corporation plus $80,000 paid by the shareholders), or an effective tax rate of 47.3% ($284,000/$600,000). The 47.3% is only federal income taxes and does not include any state or local income taxes that the corporation may have to pay. ◀

While the reduced rate of tax on qualified dividends is certainly favorable to shareholders, the double taxation of C corporation earnings is still an onerous tax. A common method to avoid this double taxation by C corporations with a small number of shareholders is to payout the corporate earnings in the form of salary and bonuses, thereby making the payout deductible by the corporation and eliminating double taxation. The Internal Revenue Service (IRS), however, may attack this plan by asserting that the salary and bonuses are unreasonably large and, in fact, a disguised dividend.

EXAMPLE I:1-16 ▶ Assume in Example I:1-14 that Crimson had only one shareholder, Joe Bank, who also is the president of the corporation. The corporation paid the entire $600,000 to Mr. Bank in the form of a bonus rather than as a dividend. The corporation could deduct the $600,000, thereby reducing its taxable income to zero. Mr. Bank would have to include the $600,000 in his personal income and would pay taxes on this amount. If his average tax rate on the $600,000 was 30%, he would owe $180,000 on the $600,000. The $180,000 would represent the total taxes of both the corporation and shareholder and would save $104,000 ($284,000 − $180,000) from the previous example. The IRS may attack this plan by alleging that Mr. Bank's salary and bonus are unreasonably high and recharacterize part of the $600,000 as a dividend. Because dividends are not deductible by the corporation, the corporation would be subject to additional income taxes. At the same time, if the IRS is successful, the portion of the salary and bonus of Mr. Bank that is recharacterized as a dividend would be subject to the maximum 20% tax rate. ◀

FLOW-THROUGH ENTITIES

The simplest form of a flow-through entity is the sole proprietorship as there are no formal requirements to form such an entity. The net income earned by the proprietor is reported on Schedule C of Form 1040. Thus, the income of the sole proprietorship merely flows to the proprietor's individual tax return. The net income of the sole proprietorship is subject to income tax only once (at the individual level) but is also subject to self-employment tax (Social Security and Medicare taxes).

Flow-through entities, such as partnership, limited liability companies (LLCs), limited liability partnerships (LLPs), and S corporations have the major advantage of being subject to only one level of taxation. All of these entities file tax returns, but, in general, the entities do not pay any income taxes. The income earned by the entity is allocated to the owners based on their proportionate ownership or some other allocation arrangement. Thus, the entity income tax return is really just an information return. The income allocated to the owners is then reported on their own tax returns. The income of the entity, therefore, is subject to a single level of taxation. This single level of tax is a major advantage of the flow-through form over C corporations.

To ensure a single level of taxation for flow-through entities, the tax law employs a unique method of basis adjustments. Every owner of the entity has an *adjusted basis* (basis) in his or her ownership interest. An owner's basis in a flow-through entity is determined as follows:

- Each owner obtains an original basis in his or her ownership interest upon the formation of the entity (investment in the entity) or purchase of the interest.
- The owner's basis increases for any additional capital contributions to the entity in subsequent years.
- The owner's basis increases for the owner's share of income for tax purposes or decreases for losses.
- The owner's basis increases for the owner's share of entity liabilities. Differences exist between partnerships and S corporations as to which liabilities are added to an owner's basis. Details on this topic are covered in later chapters of this textbook.
- The owner's basis decreases for money or property distributed to the owner by the entity.

Without these basis adjustments, the owner could be subject to double taxation upon selling his or her interest or upon dissolution of the entity. Practitioners refer to this basis as "outside basis" as opposed to "inside basis," which is the entity's basis in its assets.

EXAMPLE I:1-17 ▶ Wildcat Company is a flow-through entity with two owners, Rich and Teresa. Each owner has a $10,000 original basis in the entity. In its first year of operations, Wildcat Company earns $50,000, which is allocated $25,000 to each owner. Thus, each owner reports $25,000 in his individual income tax return even though the entity does not distribute any of the earnings to the owners. At the beginning of the second year, Rich sells his interest to Steve for $35,000. If Rich did not get an increased basis adjustment for his $25,000 of earnings, he would recognize a $25,000 gain ($35,000 selling price − $10,000 basis in the entity) on the sale of his interest, which taxes him twice on the $25,000. However, both Rich and Teresa do increase their bases to $35,000 ($10,000 original basis + $25,000 share of entity earnings) at the end of the first tax year. Therefore, when Rich sells his interest for $35,000, he incurs no additional taxable gain ($35,000 selling price − $35,000 basis in the entity = $0 gain). ◀

Below is a brief description of the four basic types of flow-through business entities.

Partnerships. A partnership is the classic flow-through entity as it has been around the longest. The Internal Revenue Code (IRC) defines a partnership as "a syndicate, group, pool, joint venture, or other incorporated organization" that carries on any business, financial operation, or venture.[29] Thus, if two or more individuals, corporations, trusts, or estates decide to operate a business or financial venture, the business or venture can be classified as a partnership. Unlike a corporation, which must file incorporation documents with the state, partnerships require no legal documentation. However, tax advisors strongly advise partnerships to have written agreements as to the operation of the partnership and how income, deductions, losses, and credits will be allocated to the partners. Most states have laws that govern the rights and restrictions of partnerships and their partners.

Partnerships file an annual income tax return which is just an information return because the partnership entity is not subject to taxation. The return, Form 1065 (U.S. Partnership Return of Income), reports the results of the partnership's operations. An accompanying form, Schedule K-1, reports the separate income, deductions, losses, and credits that flow through to the partners. The partners, in turn, take the information from their Schedule K-1 and report the various items on their individual returns.

EXAMPLE I:1-18 ▶ Donald and Minnie form a real estate company and decide to operate as a partnership, the DM Partnership. Donald is a 60% partner and Minnie is a 40% partner. Donald invests $60,000 into DM and Minnie contributes real estate with a basis and fair market value of $40,000. In its first year of operation, DM Partnership earns ordinary income of $150,000. The partnership files Form 1065 and reports the $150,000 but is not subject to any income taxation. Included in the

[29] Sec. 761(a).

partnership return are two Schedule K-1s that report $90,000 to Donald ($150,000 × 60%) and $60,000 ($150,000 × 40%) to Minnie. Donald reports $90,000 on his individual income tax return, Form 1040, and Minnie reports $60,000 on her individual return. If the partnership distributed $72,000 to Donald and $48,000 to Minnie during the year, the distributions are considered a return of capital and are not taxable to either partner. Donald's adjusted basis in his partnership interest would be $78,000 ($60,000 + $90,000 − $72,000) and Minnie's adjusted basis would be $52,000 ($40,000 + $60,000 − $48,000). ◀

S Corporations. S corporations are a special form of corporation treated by the tax laws as flow-through entities. They are incorporated under state law just as any other corporation but, if they so elect, are treated as flow-through entities for tax purposes. S corporations are so named because the rules pertaining to this type of entity are located in Subchapter S of the IRC. S corporations have been referred to as "corporations taxed like a partnership." Although this statement is partially true, important differences exist, such as a limitation on the number of shareholders, strict rules on allocation of income or losses, and several other differences. Similar to partnerships, S corporations are not taxed and income, deductions, losses, and credits flow through to its shareholders. Allocations of income, deductions, losses, and credits to shareholders are based on a per share–per day basis. Importantly, S corporation shareholders enjoy limited liability, as do C corporation shareholders.

To achieve S corporation status, the corporation must file an S election and all of its shareholders must consent to that election. S corporations annually file an information return, Form 1120S (U.S. Income Tax Return for an S Corporation), which reports the results of the corporation's operations and, like partnerships, also submits Schedule K-1 to each shareholder which reports the allocable share of income, deduction, loss, and credit that flow through to each shareholder.

Similar to partnerships, S corporations impose only a single level of taxation to its shareholders and the tax law uses basis adjustments to achieve this single level of taxation. The basis adjustments for S corporation shareholders are nearly identical to those for partnerships. The major difference is how liabilities affect the basis of S corporation shareholders. S corporation shareholders obtain basis only for *direct* loans to the corporation and they treat their debt basis separately from stock basis. Partners of a partnership generally increase their basis for all partnership liabilities.

EXAMPLE I:1-19 ▶ Paul and Peter form a corporation in Ohio as equal shareholders. Upon advice from their tax advisor, they decide to elect S corporation status for federal and state tax purposes and file the necessary forms. Both Paul and Peter invest $25,000 in the corporation and each receives 100 shares of common stock of the corporation. During the first year, the corporation reports net ordinary income of $62,000 and a long-term capital gain of $10,000 of Form 1120S. Each shareholder receives a $20,000 distribution from the corporation during the year. In Year 1, the corporation pays no federal or state income taxes, but both Paul and Peter report $31,000 of ordinary income and $5,000 of long-term capital gain on their individual returns. Since the shareholders have sufficient basis, the $20,000 distribution to each shareholder is not subject to taxation. Paul and Peter would each have a basis in their S corporation stock of $41,000 ($25,000 + $31,000 + $5,000 − $20,000) at the end of Year 1. ◀

EXAMPLE I:1-20 ▶ In Year 2, the corporation earns $74,000 of ordinary income and no capital gains. Also, on July 1 of Year 2, Peter sells one-half (50 shares) of his stock to Mary. So, from July 1 to December 31, Paul owns 50% of the corporate stock and Peter and Mary each own 25%. S corporation earnings must be allocated on a per share–per day basis, so the income of $74,000 is allocated to each shareholder as follows:

Paul	$74,000 × 365/365 × 50% = $37,000
Peter	($74,000 × 181/365 × 50%) + ($74,000 × 184/365 × 25%) = $27,674
Mary	$74,000 × 184/365 × 25% = $9,326

◀

Limited Liability Companies. A limited liability company (LLC) is a legal entity under the laws of all 50 states and the District of Columbia and is a very popular organizational form. LLCs combine the best features of a partnership and a corporation by being treated as a partnership while providing the limited liability protection of a corporation. Thus, LLC owners, called members, are subject to a single level of taxation and are not liable for the liabilties of the LLC.

An LLC is formed under state law similar to a corporation. After formed, the LLC elects whether to be taxed either as a partnership or a corporation.[30] Under Treasury Regulations, an LLC with more than one member is treated as a partnership unless the LLC affirmatively elects to be classified as a corporation. In most cases, LLCs will prefer to be classified as a partnership because of the tax advantages of a single level of taxation. If an LLC elects to be treated as a partnership, it files its tax return on Form 1065 (U.S. Partnership Return of Income). The LLC, however, is not legally a partnership; it is just treated as one for federal income tax purposes. A single member LLC is disregarded for tax purposes and the LLC income, deductions, etc. are reported directly on the member's Schedule C of Form 1040 as a sole proprietor. If an LLC elects to be taxed as a corporation under the Treasury Regulations, it would file Form 1120 (U.S. Corporation Income Tax Return). Further, S corporation status can be achieved by electing to be taxed as a corporation and then make an S election. Thus, the LLC would be considered an LLC for state law purposes but an S corporation for income tax purposes.

EXAMPLE I:1-21 ▶ Karen and David start a wholesale business and decide to operate the business as an LLC. They first must legally form the organization under state law. After the LLC is legally formed, they must decide how the LLC will be treated for income tax purposes. Because they want a single level of taxation, Karen and David elect to be treated as a partnership. Since being treated as a partnership is the default classification under Treasury Regulations, no forms need to be filed with the IRS. At the end of the first year, the LLC will file a Form 1065 and check the box indicating that the entity is an LLC filing as a partnership. All partner allocations, basis adjustments, and all other tax rules for the LLC are identical with partnership rules. ◀

Limited Liability Partnerships. All 50 states and the District of Columbia have statutes that allow a business to operate as a limited liability partnership (LLP). Basically, an LLP is similar to an LLC except that a partner of an LLP *is not* liable for any liability arising from acts of negligence or misconduct or similar acts of another partner of the LLP. Thus, an LLP is much more desirable than a general partnership where partners are liable for all partnership liabilities. Professional service organizations, such as many CPA firms, have adopted the LLP form, primarily to limit legal liability.

EXAMPLE I:1-22 ▶ The accounting firm of Gartman & Kuhn, CPAs, is operating as a general partnership and has 20 partners in the firm. The firm is concerned about the unlimited liability that exists for the partnership, especially in today's litigious environment. The firm decides to convert from a partnership to an LLP. The conversion is simple and tax-free,[31] and protects the partners of the new LLP entity against liabilities of the LLP arising from acts of negligence or misconduct of other partners or employees. ◀

OTHER ENTITIES

Trusts. Trusts are somewhat of a hybrid entity in that they may either be a taxpaying entity or flow-through entity. Also, there are a number of different types of trusts, so the discussion here is very general in nature. Trusts typically are subject to income taxation on all of its net income that is *not* distributed to the beneficiaries. The portion of net income that is distributed to beneficiaries is taxed to the beneficiaries. One drawback to the use of trusts is that the income tax rates are extremely progressive, reaching the 39.6% bracket when the taxable income of the trust reaches $12,300 in 2015. Trusts use Form 1041 to file its tax information.

EXAMPLE I:1-23 ▶ Ben establishes a trust for the benefit of his daughter. The principal amount of the trust is $500,000 and is projected to earn approximately 10% per year. In the current year, the trust earned $50,000 of investment income and had $5,000 of expenses. If the trust did not make any

[30] The LLC makes the election pursuant to the "check-the-box" Regulations, Reg. Secs. 301.7701-1 through -4.

[31] Rev. Rul. 95-37, 1995-1 C.B. 130.

distributions during the year to the daughter, the entire $45,000 (less a small exemption) would be subject to income taxation to the trust. Much of the taxable income would be subject to taxation at the 39.6% rate. Alternatively, if the trust distributed the entire $45,000 to the daughter, she would report the $45,000 on her individual tax return. Assuming she does not have significant other income, she would most likely be in the 25% marginal tax bracket. The trust's taxable income would be zero and would have no income tax liability. ◀

TAX LAW SOURCES

OBJECTIVE 6

Identify the various tax law sources and understand their implications for tax practice

The solution to any tax question may only be resolved by reference to tax law sources (also referred to as tax law authority). Tax law sources are generated from all three branches of the federal government, i.e., legislative, executive, and judicial. The principal sources of tax law are as follows:

Branch	*Tax Law Source*
Legislative	Internal Revenue Code
	Congressional Committee Reports
Executive (Administrative)	Income Tax Regulations
	Revenue Rulings
	Revenue Procedures
	Letter Rulings
Judicial	Court Decisions

ADDITIONAL COMMENT

Knowledge of tax law sources could be considered the most important topic in this book. It is similar to the old Chinese proverb that states that if you give a person a fish you have fed him for one day, but if you teach a person how to fish you have fed him for the rest of his life. By analogy, if a person has a knowledge of the tax law sources, he or she should be able to locate the answers to tax questions throughout his or her career.

A thorough knowledge of the various sources above as well as the relative weights attached to each source is vital to tax professionals. Because of the vast volume of tax law sources, the ability to "find an answer" to a tax question is of fundamental importance. In addition, the evaluation of the weight (or importance) of different sources of authority is also crucial in arriving at a proper conclusion. For example, a decision of the U.S. Supreme Court on a tax matter would certainly carry more weight than a Revenue Ruling issued by the Internal Revenue Service.

Clearly, the most authoritative source of tax law is the Internal Revenue Code, which is the tax law passed by Congress. However, Congress is not capable of anticipating every type of transaction that taxpayers might engage in, so most of the statutes in the Code contain very general language. Because of the general language contained in the Code, both administrative and judicial interpretations are necessary to apply the tax law to specific situations and transactions. Thus, the regulations and rulings of the IRS and the decisions of the courts are an integral part of the federal income tax law. For a detailed discussion of tax law sources, see Chapter I:15 (Chapter C:1 of the *Comprehensive* edition). Topic Review I:1-3 provides an overview of the tax law sources.

ENACTMENT OF A TAX LAW

OBJECTIVE 7

Describe the legislative process for the enactment of the tax law

Under the U.S. Constitution, the House of Representatives is responsible for initiating new tax legislation. However, tax bills may also originate in the Senate as riders to nontax legislative proposals. Often, major tax proposals are initiated by the President and accompanied by a Treasury Department study or proposal, and then introduced into Congress by one or more representatives from the President's political party.

STEPS IN THE LEGISLATIVE PROCESS

The specific steps in the legislative process are discussed below and are summarized in Table I:1-2. These steps typically include:

1. A tax bill is introduced in the House of Representatives and is referred to the House Ways and Means Committee.
2. The proposal is considered by the House Ways and Means Committee, and public hearings are held. Testimony may be given by members of professional groups such

TOPIC REVIEW I:1-3

Tax Law Sources

Source	Key Points	Weight of Authority
LEGISLATIVE		
Internal Revenue Code	Contains provisions governing income, estate and gift, employment, alcohol, tobacco, and excise taxes.	Serves as the highest legislative authority for tax research, planning, and compliance activities.
ADMINISTRATIVE		
Treasury Regulations	Represents interpretations of the tax code by the Secretary of the Treasury. Regulations may be initially issued in proposed, temporary, and final form and may either be interpretative or legislative in nature.	Legislative regulations have a higher degree of authority than interpretative regulations. Proposed regulations do not have authoritative weight.
IRS Rulings	The IRS issues Revenue Rulings (letter rulings or published rulings), Revenue Procedures, Information Releases, and Technical Advice Memoranda.	These pronouncements reflect the IRS's interpretation of the law and do not have the same level of scope and authority as Treasury Regulations.
JUDICIAL		
Judicial doctrines	Judicial doctrines are concepts that have evolved from Supreme Court cases that are used by the courts to decide tax issues. Examples include substance over form, tax benefit rule, and constructive receipt.	Judicial doctrines that evolve from Supreme Court cases have substantial weight of authority because they have the force and effect of law.
Judicial interpretations	Tax cases are initially considered by a trial court (i.e., the Tax Court, a Federal district court, or the U.S. Court of Federal Claims). Either the taxpayer or the IRS may appeal to an appeals court. A final appeal is to the U.S. Supreme Court.	A trial court must abide by the precedents set by the court of appeals of the same jurisdiction. An appeals court is not required to follow the decisions of another court of appeals. A Supreme Court decision is the "law of the land."

ADDITIONAL COMMENT

In 2015, the chairman of the House Ways and Means Committee was Rep. Paul Ryan of Wisconsin, and the chairman of the Senate Finance Committee was Sen. Orrin Hatch of Utah.

HISTORICAL NOTE

For many years, only a few members of Congress were CPAs. This trend is changing. As of December, 2014, ten members of the House of Representatives and two members of the Senate are CPAs.

as the American Institute of CPAs and the American Bar Association and from various special-interest groups.

3. The tax bill is voted on by the House Ways and Means Committee and, if approved, is forwarded to the House of Representatives for a vote. Amendments to the bill from individual members of the House of Representatives are generally not allowed.
4. If passed by the House, the bill is forwarded to the Senate for consideration by the Senate Finance Committee, and public hearings are held.
5. The tax bill approved by the Senate Finance Committee may be substantially different from the House of Representatives' version.
6. The Senate Finance Committee reports the Senate bill to the Senate for consideration. The Senate generally permits amendments (e.g., new provisions) to be offered on the Senate floor.
7. If approved by the Senate, both the Senate and House bills are sent to a Joint Conference Committee consisting of an equal number of members from the Senate and the House of Representatives.
8. The Senate and House bills are reconciled in the Joint Conference Committee. This process of reconciliation generally involves substantial compromise if the provisions of both bills are different. A final bill is then resubmitted to the House and Senate for approval.
9. If the Joint Conference Committee bill is approved by the House and Senate, it is sent to the President for approval or veto.
10. A presidential veto may be overturned if a two-thirds majority vote is obtained in both the House and Senate.

▼ **TABLE I:1-2**
Steps in the Legislative Process

1. Treasury studies prepared on needed tax reform
2. President makes proposals to Congress
3. House Ways and Means Committee prepares House bill
4. Approval of House bill by the House of Representatives
5. Senate Finance Committee prepares Senate bill
6. Approval of Senate bill by the Senate
7. Compromise bill approved by a Joint Conference Committee
8. Approval of Joint Conference Committee bill by both the House and Senate
9. Approval or veto of legislation by the President
10. New tax law and amendments incorporated into the Code

11. Committee reports are prepared by the staffs of the House Ways and Means Committee, the Senate Finance Committee, and the Joint Conference Committee as the bill progresses through Congress. These reports help to explain the new law before the Treasury Department drafts regulations on the tax law changes as well as to explain the intent of Congress for passing the new law.

Administration of the Tax Law and Tax Practice Issues

OBJECTIVE 8

Describe the administrative procedures under the tax law

ORGANIZATION OF THE INTERNAL REVENUE SERVICE

The IRS is the branch of the Treasury Department that is responsible for administering the federal tax law. It is organized on a type-of-taxpayer basis which allows the IRS to become more specialized. The responsibilities and functions of the various administrative branches include the following:

- The Commissioner of Internal Revenue, appointed by the President, is the chief officer of the IRS. This individual is supported by the Chief Counsel's office, which is responsible for preparing the government's case for litigation of tax disputes.
- The National Office includes a deputy commissioner, a series of assistants to the commissioner, and a chief counsel. A significant responsibility of the National Office is to process ruling requests and to prepare revenue procedures that assist taxpayers with compliance matters.
- Four operating divisions, organized functionally, including (1) Wage and Investment Income, (2) Small Business and Self-Employed, (3) Large Business and International, and (4) Tax Exempt and Government Entities.
- Tax service centers, located around the country, perform tax return processing work, based on the four divisions above. They also select tax returns for audit.
- For the 2013 fiscal year, the IRS had approximately 95,000 employees and a budget of $12 billion. In 2013, the IRS collected $2.91 trillion, 91 percent of federal government receipts.

ADDITIONAL COMMENT

A survey of members of the American Institute of CPAs found that more than half of the 1,036 members who responded had an unfavorable opinion of the IRS. However, the accountants gave the IRS good marks for courtesy and a willingness to solve problems.

In 1998, Congress enacted legislation with a major objective of reforming the manner in which the IRS administers the tax system. The taxpaying public has been increasingly critical of the IRS, especially with the allegedly insensitive and strong-arm tactics used against taxpayers. Therefore, the legislation placed a greater emphasis on serving the public and meeting taxpayer needs. While substantial organizational and operational changes to the IRS were mandated, only time will tell if this legislation will be successful. Details of the Act are outside the scope of this textbook.

ENFORCEMENT PROCEDURES

All tax returns are initially checked for mathematical accuracy and items that are clearly erroneous. The Form W-2 amounts (e.g., wages, and so on), Form 1099 information return amounts (e.g., relating to dividend and interest payments, and so on) and other forms filed with the IRS by the payer are checked against the amounts reported on the tax return. If differences are noted, the IRS Center merely sends the taxpayer a bill for the corrected amount of tax and a statement of the differences. This type of examination is referred to as a correspondence audit. In some instances, the difference is due to a classification error by the IRS, and the additional assessment can be resolved by written correspondence. A refund check may be sent to the taxpayer if an overpayment of tax has been made.

EXAMPLE I:1-24 ▶ Bart is an author of books and properly reports royalties on Schedule C (Profit or Loss from Business). The IRS computer matching of the Form 1099 information returns from the publishing companies incorrectly assumes that the royalties should be reported on Schedule E (Supplemental Income and Loss). If the IRS sends the taxpayer a statement of the difference and an adjusted tax bill, this matter (including the abatement of added tax, interest, and penalties) should be resolved by correspondence with the IRS. ◀

ADDITIONAL COMMENT

Individuals may call 800-366-4484 to report misconduct of IRS employees.

SELECTION OF RETURNS FOR AUDIT

The U.S. tax system is based on self-assessment and voluntary compliance. However, enforcement by the IRS is essential to maintain the integrity of the tax system. The IRS uses both computers and experienced personnel to select returns for examination. With respect to the use of the computer, a **Discriminant Function System (DIF)** is used to classify returns to be selected for audit. The DIF system generates a "score" for a return based on the potential for the return to generate additional tax revenue. After returns are scored under the DIF system, the returns are manually screened by experienced IRS personnel who decide which returns warrant further examination. In the aggregate, less than 1% of all individual returns are selected for examination each year. Some examples of situations where individuals are more likely to be audited include the following:

- Individuals who are sole proprietors and claim expenses in connection with their trade or businesses, especially if significant tax losses are incurred.
- Itemized deductions exceeding an average amount for the person's income level
- Filing of a refund claim by a taxpayer who has been previously audited, where substantial tax deficiencies have been assessed
- Individuals who are self-employed with substantial business income or income from a profession (e.g., a medical doctor)

ADDITIONAL COMMENT

A special task force has recommended that the percentage of returns audited be increased to 2.5%. Many individuals feel that the probability of being audited is so low as to be disregarded.

ADDITIONAL COMMENT

In 2002, the IRS launched the National Research Program (NRP) to select returns for audit. The NRP will update data compiled in the old TCMP audits and develop new statistical models for identifying returns most likely to contain errors.

Audit Procedures. Audits of most individuals are handled through an office audit procedure in an office of the IRS. In most cases, an individual is asked to substantiate a particular deduction, credit, or income item (e.g., charitable contributions that appear to be excessive). The office audit procedure does not involve a complete audit of all items on the return.

ETHICAL POINT

A CPA should not recommend a position to a client that exploits the IRS audit selection process.

EXAMPLE I:1-25 ▶ Brad obtains a divorce during the current year and reports a $30,000 deduction for alimony. The IRS may conduct an office audit to ascertain whether the amount is properly deductible as alimony and does not represent a disguised property settlement to Brad's ex-wife. Brad may be asked to submit verification (e.g., a property settlement agreement between the spouses that designates the payments as alimony). ◀

A **field audit procedure** often is used for corporations and individuals engaged in a trade or business. A field audit generally is broader in scope than the office audit (e.g., several items on the tax return may be reviewed). A field audit usually is conducted at the taxpayer's place of business or the office of his or her tax advisor.

Most large corporations are subject to annual audits. The year under audit may be several years prior to the current year because the corporation often will waive the statute of limitations pending the resolution of disputed issues.

KEY POINT

A taxpayer may appear on his or her own behalf before the IRS during an audit. An attorney or CPA in good standing is authorized to practice before the IRS upon the filing of a written statement that he or she is currently so qualified and is authorized to represent the taxpayer.

STATUTE OF LIMITATIONS

Most taxpayers feel a sense of relief after they have prepared their income tax return and have mailed it to the IRS. However, the filing of the tax return is not necessarily the end of the story for that particular taxable year. It is possible, of course, that the IRS may select their tax return for audit after the return has been initially processed or a taxpayer may have filed an amended return to correct an error or omission.

REAL-WORLD EXAMPLE

Based on an IRS audit, the Mustang Ranch, Nevada's most famous legal bordello, was assessed some $13 million in taxes. When the amount owed could not be paid, the IRS sold the property to recoup the taxes.

Both the IRS and taxpayers can make corrections to a return after it has been originally filed. Fortunately, both only have a limited time period in which to make such corrections. This time period is called the **statute of limitations** and prevents either the taxpayer or the IRS from changing a filed tax return after the time period has expired. The general rule for the statute of limitations is three years from the later of the date the tax return was actually filed or its due date.[32] However, a six-year statute of limitations applies if the taxpayer omits items of gross income that in total exceed 25% of the gross income reported on the return.[33] The statute of limitations remains open indefinitely if a fraudulent return is filed or if no return is filed.[34]

EXAMPLE I:1-26 ▶ Betty, a calendar-year taxpayer, is audited by the IRS in February 2015 for the tax year 2013. During the course of the audit, the IRS proposes additional tax for 2013, because Betty failed to substantiate certain travel and entertainment expense deductions. During the course of the audit, the IRS discovers that Betty failed to file a tax return for 2008, and in 2010 an item of gross income amounting to $26,000 was not reported. Gross income reported on the 2010 return was $72,000. Assuming Betty's 2013 return was filed on or before its due date (April 15, 2014), the IRS may assess a deficiency for 2013 because the three-year statute of limitations will not expire until April 15, 2017. A deficiency also may be assessed for the 2010 return because a six-year statute of limitations applies since the omission is more than 25% of the gross income reported on the return. A deficiency also may be assessed for 2008 as there is no statute of limitations for fraud. ◀

ADDITIONAL COMMENT

More than 150 penalties can be imposed on taxpayers. In fact, applying the penalties has become so complicated that the IRS is currently considering ways to consolidate and simplify them.

INTEREST

Interest accrues on both assessments of additional tax due and on refunds that the taxpayer receives from the government.[35] No interest is paid on a tax refund if the amount is refunded by the IRS within 45 days of the day prescribed for filing the return (e.g., April 15) determined without regard to extensions.[36] If a return is filed after the filing date, no interest is paid if the refund is made within 45 days of the date the return was filed.

EXAMPLE I:1-27 ▶ Beverly, a calendar-year taxpayer, files her 2014 tax return on March 1, 2015, and requests a $500 refund. No interest accrues on the refund amount if the IRS sends the refund check to Beverly within 45 days of the April 15, 2015, due date. ◀

ADDITIONAL COMMENT

In addition to the penalties listed on this page, the government also assesses penalties for civil fraud and criminal fraud. Criminal fraud carries a maximum penalty of $100,000, a prison sentence of up to five years, or both.

PENALTIES

Various nondeductible penalties are imposed on the net tax due for failure to comply, including

- A penalty of 5% per month (or fraction thereof) subject to a maximum of 25% for failure to file a tax return[37]

---

[32] Secs. 6501(a) and (b)(1). Similar rules apply to claims for a refund filed by the taxpayer. Section 6511(a) requires that a refund claim be filed within three years of the date the return was filed or within two years of the date the tax was paid, whichever is later.

[33] Sec. 6501(e). See also *Stephen G. Colestock*, 102 T.C. 380 (1994), where the Tax Court ruled that the extended six-year limitation period applied to a married couple's entire tax liability for the tax year at issue, not just to items that constituted substantial omissions of gross income. Thus, the IRS was able to assert an increased deficiency and additional penalties attributable to a disallowed depreciation deduction.

[34] Sec. 6501(c).

[35] Sec. 6621(a). The rate is adjusted four times a year by the Treasury Department based on the current interest rate for short-term federal obligations. The interest rate individual taxpayers must pay to the IRS on underpayments of tax is the federal short-term rate plus three percentage points. The interest rate paid to taxpayers on overpayments of tax is the federal short-term rate plus two percentage points. The annual interest rate on noncorporate underpayments and overpayments for the period January 1, 2015, through March 31, 2015, was 3% (2% in the case of a corporation).

[36] Sec. 6611(e).

[37] Sec. 6651(a)(1). The penalty assessed may be very small in some instances even though the taxpayer owes a large tax bill for the year because penalties are imposed on the net tax due. The percentages are increased to 15% per month (or fraction thereof) up to a maximum of 75% if the penalty is for fraudulent failure to file under Sec. 6651(f).

- A penalty of 0.5% per month (or fraction thereof) up to a maximum of 25% for failure to pay the tax that is due[38]
- An accuracy-related penalty of 20% of the underpayment for items such as negligence or disregard of rules or regulations, any substantial understatement of income tax, or any substantial misstatement of valuation[39]
- A 75% penalty for fraud[40]
- A penalty based on the current interest rate for underpayment of estimated taxes[41]
- Significant new penalties on tax return preparers have been enacted by Congress for taxable years 2007 and forward. In general, these new penalties are applicable for any position on a tax return where there is a "realistic possibility" (one-in-three chance) that the position would not be upheld in a court of law. The penalty is not assessed if the position is disclosed in the return.

ADDITIONAL COMMENT

Pete Rose, major league baseball's all-time hit leader, was sent to prison in 1990 for income tax evasion.

ADMINISTRATIVE APPEAL PROCEDURES

If an IRS agent issues a deficiency assessment, the taxpayer may make an appeal to the IRS Appeals Division. Some disputes involve a gray area (e.g., a situation where some courts have held for the IRS whereas other courts have held for the taxpayer on facts that are similar to the disputed issue). In such a case, the taxpayer may be able to negotiate a compromise settlement (e.g., a percentage of the disputed tax amount plus interest and penalties) with the Appeals Division based on the "hazards of litigation" (i.e., the probability of winning or losing the case if it is litigated).

COMPONENTS OF A TAX PRACTICE

OBJECTIVE 9

Describe the components of a tax practice

Tax practice is a rapidly growing field that provides substantial opportunities for tax specialists in public accounting, law, and industry. The tasks performed by a tax professional may range from the preparation of a simple Form 1040 for an individual to the conduct of tax research and planning for highly complex business situations. Tax practice consists of the following activities:

- Tax compliance and procedure (i.e., tax return preparation and representation of a client in administrative proceedings before the IRS)
- Tax research
- Tax planning and consulting
- Financial planning

TYPICAL MISCONCEPTION

Many people believe that a tax practitioner should serve in the capacity of a neutral, unbiased expert. They tend to forget that tax practitioners are being paid to represent their clients' interests. A tax practitioner may sometimes recommend a position that is defensible, but where the weight of authority is on the side of the IRS.

TAX COMPLIANCE AND PROCEDURE

Preparation of tax returns is a significant component of tax practice. Tax practitioners often prepare federal, state, and local tax returns for individuals, corporations, estates, trusts, and so on. In larger corporations, the tax return preparation (i.e., compliance) function usually is performed by a company's internal tax department staff. In such a case, a CPA or other tax practitioner may assist the client with the tax research and planning aspects of their tax practice, and may even review their return before it is filed.

An important part of tax practice consists of assisting the client in negotiations with the IRS. If a client is audited, the practitioner acts as the client's representative in discussions with the IRS agent. If a tax deficiency is assessed, the practitioner assists the client if

[38] Sec. 6651(a)(2). If the failure to file penalty (5%) and the failure to pay the tax penalty (0.5%) are both applicable, the failure to file penalty is reduced by the failure to pay penalty per Sec. 6651(c)(1). Further, the penalty is increased to 1% per month after the IRS notifies the taxpayer that it will levy on the taxpayer's assets.

[39] Sec. 6662.

[40] Sec. 6663.

[41] Sec. 6654.

an administrative appeal is contemplated with the IRS's Appellate Division. In most instances, an attorney is retained if litigation is being considered.

TAX RESEARCH

Tax research is the search for the best possible defensibly correct solution to a problem involving either a completed transaction (e.g., a sale of property) or a proposed transaction (e.g., a proposed merger of two corporations). Research involves each of the following steps:

- Determine the facts.
- Identify the issue(s).
- Identify and analyze the tax law sources (i.e., code provisions, Treasury Regulations, administrative rulings, and court cases).
- Evaluate nontax (e.g., business) implications.
- Solve the problem.
- Communicate the findings to the client.

SELF-STUDY QUESTION

Do large national CPA firms generally stress the importance of tax research in connection with tax-return preparation or tax planning?

ANSWER

The large CPA firms emphasize their skills in tax planning. Sometimes a slight alteration of a proposed transaction can save the client substantial tax dollars. This is high-value-added work and can be billed at premium rates.

Tax research may be conducted in connection with tax return preparation, tax planning, or procedural activities. A more thorough discussion of tax research is presented in Chapter I:15.

TAX PLANNING AND CONSULTING

Tax planning involves the process of structuring one's affairs so as to minimize the amount of taxes *and* maximize the after-tax return. Thus, optimal tax planning is *not* to just pay the least amount of tax but to maximize after-tax cash flows. A text on tax research and planning has delineated the following tax planning principles:[42]

- Keep sufficient records.
- Forecast the effect of future events.
- Support the plan with a sound business purpose.
- Base the plan on sound legal authorities.
- Do not carry a good plan too far.
- Make the plan flexible.
- Integrate the tax plan with other factors in decision making.
- Conduct research to learn whether a similar plan has previously proved unsuccessful (e.g., a court case involving similar facts may have upheld the IRS's position).
- Consider the "maximum" risk exposure of the client (e.g., if the plan is subsequently challenged by the IRS and the tax treatment is disallowed, what is the economic impact upon the taxpayer?).
- Consider the effect of timing (e.g., whether it is more beneficial to take a deduction in one year versus another).
- Shape the plan to the client's needs and desires.

ADDITIONAL COMMENT

Several national accounting firms have divided their tax departments into two basic groups, consulting and compliance. The tax consultants work with clients in tax planning and consulting matters and do not prepare tax returns. Tax returns are prepared by the compliance staff.

CPAs and attorneys frequently are engaged by their clients to perform consulting services to optimize the client's tax situation. For example, a major corporation client is considering the acquisition of a major international corporation and wants to make sure that the tax implications of such an acquisition are properly managed. The CPA will be engaged to perform a thorough review of the transaction to ensure that the client is fully aware of the tax results of the acquisition, and possibly may request an advance ruling from the IRS.

Because of the importance of planning in tax practice, subsequent chapters in this text include a separate section on tax planning to discuss issues that are related to the topical coverage. These tax planning principles should be kept in mind when attempting to use the tax planning recommendations. Also, a systematic approach to tax planning

[42] Norton, Fred W., *Federal Taxation: Research, Planning, and Procedures 2Ed*, © 1979. Printed and Electronically reproduced by permission of Pearson Education, Inc., Upper Saddle River, New Jersey.

developed by two noted academicians, Myron Scholes and Mark Wolfson, is discussed in Chapter I:18.

FINANCIAL PLANNING

A relatively new field for tax professionals is that of financial planning for individual clients. Since taxes are an integral part of any financial plan and since a tax specialist regularly meets with his or her clients (filing returns and other tax matters), the area of financial planning has become increasingly a part of tax practice. The typical steps in performing a financial planning engagement include the following steps:

- Determine the client's financial goals and objectives.
- Review the client's insurance coverage for adequacy and appropriateness.
- Recommend an investment strategy, including risk analysis and asset allocation.
- Review tax returns to ensure that, through proper tax planning, the client is maximizing his or her after-tax cash flow.
- Review the client's retirement plans to assure compliance with the law and possible new alternatives.
- Review all documents related to estate and gift planning and work with the client's attorney to minimize all transfer taxes and fulfill the client's objectives.

COMPUTER APPLICATIONS IN TAX PRACTICE

OBJECTIVE 10

Understand the importance of computer applications in taxation

KEY POINT

The use of computers has become very important in tax practice ranging from tax return preparation to tax research. It is essential that students having an interest in taxation develop advanced computer skills.

ADDITIONAL COMMENT

The Volunteer Income Tax Assistance (VITA) program sponsored by the IRS is aimed at taxpayers who need help with their federal return but cannot afford to pay for the assistance. Many college students put their textbook knowledge to work through VITA programs.

TAX RETURN PREPARATION

To prepare tax returns, most tax practitioners purchase tax preparation software from companies such as Commerce Clearing House or Intuit. This software allows the preparation of accurate and professional-looking tax returns. A word of caution, however, is in order. As with any computer software, the preparation of tax returns using the computer requires as much knowledge and expertise from the preparer as doing the returns by hand. A recent trend in tax return preparation is the electronic filing of tax returns, i.e., a "paperless" tax return. Taxpayers send their returns electronically to the IRS for processing, thereby saving enormous amounts of paper and, perhaps, reducing human error.

TAX PLANNING APPLICATIONS

Performing tax planning for clients involves the evaluation of alternative courses of action. This evaluation process can be very time-consuming because of the tax calculations necessary to arrive at an optimal solution. The computer has become an essential tool in this process because of the speed with which the tax calculations can be made. Many tax professionals now use sophisticated software to perform tax planning for their clients. A prime example of the use of the computer in tax planning has been in deciding whether a taxpayer should invest in a Roth Individual Retirement Account (Roth IRA) or a regular IRA (see Chapter I:9 for more details on IRAs). There are many factors to consider, including current and projected tax rates, current and projected level of income, etc. With the computer, a tax professional can vary the assumptions and create a number of alternatives within a relatively short period of time. To perform this task by hand would require an enormous commitment of time. As with most aspects of life, the impact of the computer on tax planning has been highly significant and will only increase in the future.

TAX RESEARCH APPLICATIONS

Computerized information-retrieval systems are used in tax research and are rapidly replacing books as the principal source of tax-related information. Most commercial research services are offered on the internet. The principal Internet services are RIA's *Checkpoint* and CCH's *Tax Research Network*. These commercial Internet services contain a wide range of materials available to tax researchers who subscribe to the service. In addition, the IRS has a home page (www.irs.gov) that taxpayers can access for forms, publications, and other related materials. All of the major accounting firms and many other tax organizations have home pages that allow users to access a myriad of tax information.

PROBLEM MATERIALS

DISCUSSION QUESTIONS

I:1-1 The Supreme Court in 1895 ruled that the income tax was unconstitutional because the tax needed to be apportioned among the states in proportion to their populations. Why would the requirement of proportionality be so difficult to administer?

I:1-2 Why was pay-as-you-go withholding needed in 1943?

I:1-3 Congressman Patrick indicates that he is opposed to tax proposals that call for a flat tax rate because the structure would not tax those individuals who have the ability to pay the tax. Discuss the position of the congressman, giving consideration to tax rate structures (e.g., progressive, proportional, and regressive) and the concept of equity.

I:1-4 The governor of your state stated in a recent political speech that he has never supported any income tax increases as the tax rates have remained at the same level during his entire term of office. Yet, you believe that you are paying more tax this year than in previous years even though your income has not increased. How can both you and the governor be correct? In other words, is it possible for the government to raise taxes without raising tax rates?

I:1-5 Carmen has computed that her average tax rate is 16% and her marginal tax rate is 25% for the current year. She is considering whether to make a charitable contribution to her church before the end of the tax year. Which tax rate is of greater significance in measuring the tax effect for her decision? Explain.

I:1-6 Why are the gift and estate taxes called wealth transfer taxes? What is the tax base for computing each of these taxes?

I:1-7 Cathy, who is single, makes gifts of $50,000 to each of her two adult children.
a. Who is primarily liable for the gift tax on the two gifts, Cathy or the two children?
b. If Cathy has never made a taxable gift in prior years, is a gift tax due on the two gifts?

I:1-8 Carlos inherits 100 shares of Allied Corporation stock from his father. The stock cost his father $8,000 and had a $25,000 FMV on the date of his father's death in 2015. The alternate valuation date was not elected. What is Carlos's tax basis for the Allied stock when it is received from the estate?

I:1-9 Most estates are not subject to the federal estate tax.
a. Why is this the case?
b. Do you believe most estates should be subject to the federal estate tax?

I:1-10 Indicate which of the following taxes are generally progressive, proportional, or regressive:
a. State income taxes
b. Federal estate tax
c. Corporate state franchise tax
d. Property taxes
e. State and local sales taxes

I:1-11 Carolyn operates a consulting business as a sole proprietor (unincorporated). Carolyn has been approached by one of her major clients to become an employee. If she accepts the new job, she would no longer operate her consulting business. From the standpoint of paying Social Security taxes, would Carolyn's Social Security taxes increase or decrease if she becomes an employee? Why? (Assume Carolyn will earn less than $200,000.)

I:1-12 The three different levels of government (federal, state, and local) must impose taxes to carry out their functions. For each of the types of taxes below, discuss which level of government primarily uses that type of tax.
a. Property taxes
b. Excise taxes
c. Sales taxes
d. Income taxes
e. Employment taxes

I:1-13 A "good" tax structure has five characteristics.
a. Briefly discuss the five characteristics.
b. Using the five characteristics, evaluate the following tax structures:
   1. Federal income tax
   2. State sales tax
   3. Local ad valorem property tax

I:1-14 Two commonly-recognized measures of the fairness of an income tax structure are "horizontal equity" and "vertical equity."
a. Discuss what is meant by horizontal equity and vertical equity as it pertains to the income tax.

b. Why is it so difficult to design a "fair" tax structure?

I:1-15 The primary objective of the federal income tax law is to raise revenue. What are its secondary objectives?

I:1-16 If the objectives of the federal tax system are multifaceted and include raising revenues, providing investment incentives, encouraging certain industries, and meeting desired social objectives, is it possible to achieve a simplified tax system? Explain.

I:1-17 Distinguish between *taxpaying entities* and *flow-through entities* from the standpoint of the federal income tax law.

I:1-18 Sally and Tom are married, have three dependent children, and file a joint return in 2015. If they have adjusted gross income (AGI) of $90,000 and itemized deductions of $10,000, what is their taxable income for 2015?

I:1-19 The Bruin Corporation, a C corporation, is owned 100% by John Bean and had taxable income in 2015 of $500,000. John is also an employee of the corporation. In December 2015, the corporation has decided to distribute $400,000 to John and has asked you whether it would be better to distribute the money as a dividend or salary. John is in the 39.6% marginal tax bracket. How would you respond to Bruin Corporation? Consider only income taxes for this problem.

I:1-20 Discuss what is meant by the term "double taxation" of corporations. Develop an example of double taxation using a corporation and shareholder.

I:1-21 Limited liability companies (LLCs) are very popular today as a form of organization. Assume a client asks you to explain what this type of organization is all about. Prepare a brief description of the federal income tax aspects of LLCs.

I:1-22 For flow-through entities, such as partnerships, how does the tax law use partner basis adjustments to prevent double taxation of partnership income?

I:1-23 Partnerships and S corporations are flow-through entities. In connection with filing annual tax returns, these entities must include Form K-1 in the returns. What is Form K-1, what is its purpose, and who receives the form?

I:1-24 The PDQ Partnership earned ordinary income of $150,000 in 2015. The partnership has three equal partners, Pete, Donald, and Quint. Quint, who is single, uses the standard deduction, and has other income of $15,000 (not connected with the partnership) in 2015. He receives a $30,000 distribution from the partnership during the year. What is Quint's taxable income in 2015?

I:1-25 Why is a thorough knowledge of sources of tax law so important for a professional person who works in the tax area?

I:1-26 The Internal Revenue Code is the most authoritative source of income tax law. In trying to resolve an income tax question, however, a tax researcher also consults administrative rulings (Income Tax Regulations, Revenue Rulings, etc.) and court decisions. Why wouldn't the tax researcher just consult the Code since it is the highest authority? Similarly, why is there a need for administrative rulings and court decisions?

I:1-27 Congressional committee reports are an important source of information concerning the legislative enactment of tax law.

a. Name the three Congressional committee reports that are issued in connection with a new tax bill.

b. Of what importance are Congressional committee reports to tax practitioners?

I:1-28 What is the primary service function provided by the National Office of the IRS?

I:1-29 What types of taxpayers are more likely to be audited by the IRS?

I:1-30 Anya is concerned that she will be audited by the IRS.

a. Under what circumstances is it possible that the IRS will review each line item on her tax return?

b. Is it likely that all items on Anya's return will be audited?

I:1-31 a. What does the term "hazards of litigation" mean in the context of taxation?

b. Why would the IRS or a taxpayer settle or compromise a case based on the "hazards of litigation"?

I:1-32 If a taxpayer files his or her tax return and receives a tax refund from the IRS, does this mean that the IRS feels that the return is correct and will not be subject to a future audit.

I:1-33 State the statute of limitations for transactions involving:

a. Fraud (e.g., failure to file a tax return)

b. Disallowance of tax deduction items

c. The omission of rental income equal to greater than 25% of the taxpayer's reported gross income

I:1-34 In reference to tax research, what is meant by *the best possible defensibly correct solution*?

I:1-35 The profession of tax practice involves four principal areas of activity. Discuss these four areas.

I:1-36 Many tax professionals have moved into the field of financial planning for their clients.

a. How do taxes impact financial planning for a client?

b. Why do tax professionals have a perfect opportunity to perform financial planning for their clients?

I:1-37 Is the principal goal of tax planning to absolutely minimize the amount of taxes that a taxpayer must pay?

I:1-38 Explain how a computer can assist a tax practitioner in tax planning activities and making complex tax calculations.

PROBLEMS

I:1-39 *Tax Rates.* Latesha, a single taxpayer, had the following income and deductions for the tax year 2015:

INCOME:	Salary	$ 80,000
	Business Income	25,000
	Interest income from bonds	10,000
	Tax-exempt bond interest	5,000
	TOTAL INCOME	120,000
DEDUCTIONS:	Business expenses	$ 9,500
	Itemized deductions	20,000
	Personal exemption	4,000
	TOTAL DEDUCTIONS	33,500

a. Compute Latesha's taxable income and federal tax liability for 2015 (round to dollars).
b. Compute Latesha's marginal, average, and effective tax rates.
c. For tax planning purposes, which of the three rates in Part b is the most important?

I:1-40 *Tax Rates.* Based on the amounts of taxable income below, compute the federal income tax payable in 2015 on each amount assuming the taxpayers are married filing a joint return. Also, for each amount of taxable income, compute the average tax rate and the marginal tax rate.
a. Taxable income of $30,000.
b. Taxable income of $100,000.
c. Taxable income of $375,000.
d. Taxable income of $600,000.

I:1-41 *Marginal Tax Rate.* Jill and George are married and file a joint return. They expect to have $425,000 of taxable income in the next year and are considering whether to purchase a personal residence that would provide additional tax deductions of $80,000 for mortgage interest and real estate taxes.
a. What is their marginal tax rate for purposes of making this decision?
b. What is the tax savings if the residence is acquired?

I:1-42 *Gift Tax.* Betty, a married taxpayer, makes the following gifts during the current year (2015): $20,000 to her church, $50,000 to her daughter, and $40,000 to her husband. What is the amount of Betty's taxable gifts for the current year (assuming that she does not elect to split the gifts with her spouse)?

I:1-43 *Estate Tax.* Clay, who was single, died in 2015 and has a gross estate valued at $8,500,000. Six months after his death, the gross assets are valued at $9,000,000. The estate incurs funeral and administration expenses of $125,000. Clay had debts amounting to $150,000 and bequeathed all of his estate to his children. During his life, Clay made no taxable gifts.
a. What is the amount of Clay's taxable estate?
b. What is the tax base for computing Clay's estate tax?
c. What is the amount of estate tax owed if the tentative estate tax (before credits) is $3,235,800?
d. Alternatively, if, six months after his death, the gross assets in Clay's estate declined in value to $7,500,000, can the administrator of Clay's estate elect the alternate valuation date? What are the important factors that the administrator should consider as to whether the alternate valuation date should be elected?

I:1-44 *Comparison of Tax Entities.*
a. Keith Thomas and Thomas Brooks began a new consulting business on January 1, 2015. They organized the business as a C corporation, KT, Inc. During 2015, the corporation was successful and generated revenues of $1,300,000. KT had operating expenses of $800,000 before any payments to Keith or Thomas. During 2015, KT paid dividends to Keith and Thomas in the amount of $165,000 each. Assume that Keith had other ordinary taxable income of $130,000, itemized deductions of $40,000, is married (wife has no income), and has no children. Compute the total tax liability of KT and Keith for 2015. Ignore any phaseout of itemized deductions or reduction of personal exemptions.

b. Instead of organizing the consulting business as a C corporation, assume Keith and Thomas organized the business as a limited liability company, KT, LLC. KT made a distribution of $250,000 each to Keith and Thomas during 2015. Compute the total tax liability of KT and Keith for 2015. Ignore any phaseout of itemized deductions, any phase out of personal exemptions, and additional tax on net investment income.

I:1-45 ***Partnership Income.*** Howard Gartman is a 40% partner in the Horton & Gartman Partnership. During 2015, the partnership reported the total items below (100%) on its Form 1065:

Ordinary income	$180,000
Qualified dividends	10,000
Long-term capital loss	(12,000)
Long-term capital gain	28,000
Charitable contributions	4,000
Cash distributions to partners	150,000

Howard and his wife Dawn, who file a joint return, also had the following income and deductions from sources not connected with the partnership:

Income	
Dawn's salary	$40,000
Qualified dividends	3,000
Deductions	
Mortgage interest	9,000
Real estate taxes	3,800
Charitable contributions	1,000

Howard and Dawn have two dependent children. During 2015, Dawn had $6,000 in federal income taxes withheld from her salary and Howard made four estimated tax payments of $3,000 each ($12,000 total). Compute Howard and Dawn's Federal income tax liability for 2015 and whether they have a balance due or a tax refund. Ignore the child tax credits and the election to take state sales tax as an itemized deduction.

I:1-46 ***Interest and Penalties.*** In 2014, Paul, who is single, has a comfortable salary from his job as well as income from his investment portfolio. However, he is habitually late in filing his federal income tax return. He did not file his 2014 income tax return until December 2, 2015 (due date was April 15, 2015) and no extensions of time to file the return were filed. Below are amounts from his 2014 return:

Taxable income	$140,000
Total tax liability on taxable income	32,271
Total federal tax withheld from his salary	26,808

Paul sent a check with his return to the IRS for the balance due of $5,463. He is relieved that he has completed his filing requirement for 2014 *and* has met his financial obligation to the government for 2014.

Has Paul met *all* of his financial obligations to the IRS for 2014? If not, what additional amounts will Paul be liable to pay to the IRS?

I:1-47 ***IRS Audits.*** Which of the following individuals is most likely to be audited?

a. Connie has a $20,000 net loss from her unincorporated business (a cattle ranch). She also received a $200,000 salary as an executive of a corporation.

b. Craig has AGI of $20,000 from wages and uses the standard deduction.

c. Dale fails to report $120 of dividends from a stock investment. His taxable income is $40,000 and he has no other unusually large itemized deductions or business expenses. A Form 1099 is reported to the IRS.

I:1-48 ***Statute of Limitations.*** In April 2015, Dan is audited by the IRS for the year 2013. During the course of the audit, the agent discovers that Dan's deductions for business travel and entertainment are unsubstantiated and a $600 deficiency assessment is proposed for the tax year 2013. The agent also examined some prior year returns. The agent discovers that Dan failed to report $40,000 of gross business income on his 2011 return. Gross income of $60,000 was reported in 2011. The agent also discovers that Dan failed to file a tax return in 2006.

Will the statute of limitations prevent the IRS from issuing a deficiency assessment for 2013, 2011, or 2006? Explain.

TAX STRATEGY PROBLEM

I:1-49 Pedro Bourbone is the founder and owner of a highly successful small business and, over the past several years, has accumulated a significant amount of personal wealth. His portfolio of stocks and bonds is worth nearly $5,000,000, owns real estate worth $3,000,000, and generates income from dividends and interest of nearly $250,000 per year. With his salary from the business and his dividends and interest, Pedro has taxable income of approximately $700,000 per year and is clearly in the top individual marginal tax bracket. Pedro is married and has three children, ages 16, 14, and 12. Neither his wife nor his children are employed and have no income. Pedro has come to you as his CPA to discuss ways to reduce his individual tax liability as well as to discuss the potential estate tax upon his death. You mention the possibility of making gifts each year to his children. Explain how annual gifts to his children will reduce both his income during lifetime and his estate tax at death.

CASE STUDY PROBLEM

I:1-50 John Gemstone, a wealthy client, has recently been audited by the IRS. The agent has questioned the following deduction items on Mr. Gemstone's tax return for the year under review:

- A $10,000 loss deduction on the rental of his beach cottage.
- A $20,000 charitable contribution deduction for the donation of a painting to a local art museum. The agent has questioned whether the painting is overvalued.
- A $15,000 loss deduction from the operation of a cattle breeding ranch. The agent is concerned that the ranch is not a legitimate business (i.e., is a hobby).

Your supervisor has requested that you represent Mr. Gemstone in his discussions with the IRS.

a. What additional questions should you ask Mr. Gemstone in an attempt to substantiate the deductibility of the above items?

b. What tax research procedures might be applied to build the best possible case for your client?

TAX RESEARCH PROBLEM

I:1-51 Read the following two cases and explain why the Supreme Court reached different conclusions for cases involving similar facts and issues:

- *CIR v. Court Holding Co.*, 33 AFTR 593, 45-1 USTC ¶9215 (USSC, 1945)
- *U.S. v. Cumberland Public Service Co.*, 38 AFTR 978, 50-1 USTC ¶9129 (USSC, 1950)

CHAPTER

2

DETERMINATION OF TAX

LEARNING OBJECTIVES

After studying this chapter, you should be able to

1. Use the tax formula to compute an individual's taxable income
2. Determine the amount of deductions from Adjusted Gross Income
3. Calculate the income tax for individuals
4. Explain the basic income tax rules relating to business entities
5. Explain the basic concepts of capital gains and losses
6. Compute the income tax for high-income individuals
7. Describe tax planning considerations for various tax matters
8. Describe compliance and procedural matters for filing tax returns

CHAPTER OUTLINE

Each year, over 140 million individuals and married couples file tax forms on which they compute their federal income tax. The income tax is imposed "on the taxable income of every individual."[1] The amount of tax actually owed by an individual taxpayer is determined by applying a complex set of rules that together make up the income tax law. To understand the income tax, it is necessary to study the basic formula on which the income tax computation is based. Therefore, this chapter introduces the income tax formula and begins the development of its components. Because the income tax formula constitutes the basis of the income tax, most of the remainder of this book is an expansion of the formula. In addition to individual taxpayers, about 6 million corporations and 2 million partnerships file returns each year. These entities are also discussed in this chapter.

FORMULA FOR INDIVIDUAL INCOME TAX

OBJECTIVE 1

Use the tax formula to compute an individual's taxable income

BASIC FORMULA

Most individuals compute their income tax by using the formula illustrated in Table I:2-1. The formula itself appears rather simple. However, the complexity of the income tax results from the intricate rules that must be applied in order to arrive at the amounts that enter into the formula.

The tax formula is incorporated into the income tax form. The tax formula illustrated in Table I:2-1 can be compared with Form 1040, which is reproduced in Figure I:2-1 (see page I:2-8). Some differences exist between the tax formula below and the tax form itself. For example, taxpayers generally are not required to report exclusions (nontaxable income) on their tax returns. One exception does require taxpayers to disclose tax-exempt interest income. A number of separate schedules are used to report various types of income. For example, income from a sole proprietorship is reported on Schedule C, where gross income from the business is reduced by related expenses that are deductions for adjusted gross income (AGI). Only the net income from the business actually appears on Form 1040. Also, Form 1040 is used to collect other taxes such as the self-employment tax. Hence, a line is provided for that tax on Form 1040. The main reason for differences between the formula and the form is administrative convenience. That is, there is no reason to require taxpayers to disclose income if the

ADDITIONAL COMMENT

The IRS estimates that the average taxpayer will spend 3 hours and 59 minutes in preparing just a Form 1040. When the estimated time for recordkeeping, learning about the law, and sending the form is added to the preparation time, the total time estimate jumps to 9 hours and 54 minutes. Each additional form and schedule adds even more time.

ADDITIONAL COMMENT

Comedian Jay Leno's explanation as to why the IRS calls it Form 1040 was, "For every $50 you earn, you get $10 and they get $40."

TYPICAL MISCONCEPTION

As explained in Chapter I:1, the federal income tax includes a progressive tax rate structure, meaning that the tax rate increases as the tax base increases. For example, if a taxpayer is in the 25% marginal tax bracket, some taxpayers incorrectly assume that this means that all of their income is being taxed at 25%. Instead, the actual calculation will include some of the income taxed at 10%, some at 15% and only the last portion of income taxed at 25%.

▼ **TABLE I:2-1**
Tax Formula for Individuals

Income from whatever source derived	$xxx,xxx
Minus: Exclusions	(xxx)
Gross income	$ xx,xxx
Minus: Deductions for adjusted gross income	(xxx)
Adjusted gross income	$ x,xxx
Minus: Deductions from adjusted gross income:	
Greater of itemized deductions or the standard deduction	(xx)
Personal and dependency exemptions	(xx)
Taxable income	$ x,xxx
Times: Tax rate or rates (from tax table or schedule)	× .xx
Gross tax	$ xx
Minus: Credits and prepayments	(x)
Net tax payable or refund due	$ xx

[1] Sec. 1.

income is not subject to tax, it is more simple to report business income on a separate schedule, and it is convenient to collect other taxes on the same tax form.

Examination of the formula reveals terms such as *gross income, exclusions, adjusted gross income, exemptions, gross tax,* and *credits*. These terms and others that make up the formula are defined below.

DEFINITIONS

Income. The term **income** includes both taxable and nontaxable income. Although the term is not specifically defined in the tax law, it does include income from any source.[2] Its meaning is close to that of the term **revenue**. However, it does not include a "return of capital." Thus, in the case of the sale of property, only the gain, not the entire sales proceeds, is viewed as income. This view extends to the sale of inventory, where gross profit is viewed as income, as opposed to the sale price.

TYPICAL MISCONCEPTION

It is easy to confuse an exclusion with a deduction. An exclusion is a source of income that is omitted from the tax base, whereas a deduction is an expense that is subtracted in arriving at taxable income. Both have the effect of reducing taxable income.

Exclusion. Not all income is taxable. An **exclusion** is any item of income that the tax law says is not taxable. Congress, over the years, has specifically excluded certain types of income from taxation for various social, economic, and political reasons. Chapter I:4 discusses specific exclusions and the reasons for their existence. Table I:2-2 contains a sample of the major exclusions from gross income.

ADDITIONAL COMMENT

One common exclusion, interest on state and local government bonds, must be reported on the tax return in amount only. It is not added to the other income items. In 2012, this reported tax-exempt interest totaled $71.1 billion.

Gross Income. **Gross income** is income reduced by exclusions. In other words, it is income from taxable sources and is reported on the return (excluded income need not be disclosed). Section 61(a) contains a partial list of items of gross income. The items listed in Sec. 61(a) are shown in Table I:2-3. Note, however, that Sec. 61(a) states that unless otherwise provided, "gross income means all income from whatever source derived, including (but not limited to)" the listed items of income. Thus, even though an item is omitted from the list does not necessarily mean that the item is excluded. For example, illegal income, although omitted from the list, is taxable.[3]

▼ TABLE I:2-2
Major Exclusions

Gifts and inheritances
Life insurance proceeds
Welfare and certain other transfer payments
Certain scholarships and fellowships
Certain payments for injury and sickness
Personal physical injury settlements
Worker's compensation
Medical expense reimbursements
Certain employee fringe benefits
Health plan premiums
Group term life insurance premiums (limited)
Meals and lodging
Employee discounts
Dependent care
Certain foreign-earned income
Interest on state and local government bonds
Certain interest of Series EE bonds
Certain improvements by lessee to lessor's property
Child support payments
Property settlements pursuant to a divorce
Gain from the sale of a personal residence (limited)
Distributions from Roth retirement plans

[2] Sec. 61(a).

[3] *U.S. v. Manley S. Sullivan*, 6 AFTR 6753, 1 USTC ¶236 (USSC, 1927).

▼ **TABLE I:2-3**
Gross Income Items Listed in Sec. 61(a)

Compensation for services, including fees, commissions, fringe benefits, and similar items
Gross income derived from business
Gains derived from dealings in property
Interest
Rents
Royalties
Dividends
Alimony and separate maintenance payments
Annuities
Income from life insurance and endowment contracts
Pensions
Income from the discharge of indebtedness
Distributive share of partnership gross income
Income in respect of a decedent
Income from an interest in an estate or trust

Deductions for Adjusted Gross Income. In general, taxpayers may deduct expenses that are specifically allowed by the tax law. Allowable deductions include business and investment expenses generally, along with personal expenses that are specifically provided for in the IRC, such as charitable contributions. Most purely personal expenses are not deductible.

Deductions fall into two categories for individual taxpayers: deductions *for* adjusted gross income and deductions *from* adjusted gross income. In general, **deductions for adjusted gross income** are expenses connected with a trade or business. For the most part, **deductions from adjusted gross income** are personal expenses that Congress has chosen to allow. This classification scheme, however, is not always followed. For example, alimony paid, which is not a business expense, is a deduction *for* adjusted gross income. Table I:2-4 contains a partial list of deductions *for* adjusted gross income that is taken from Sec. 62. Deductions for adjusted gross income are discussed further in Chapter I: 6.

ADDITIONAL COMMENT

In 2012, there were a total of 145 million individual income tax returns filed. 93.1 million of these returns had AGI under $50,000, and 5.2 million returns filed with AGI over $200,000.

Adjusted Gross Income. **Adjusted gross income** (AGI) is a measure of income that falls between gross income and taxable income. AGI is important because it is used in numerous other tax computations, especially to impose limitations. For example, AGI is used to establish floors for the medical deduction and casualty loss deduction and to establish a ceiling for the charitable contribution deduction.

Deductions from Adjusted Gross Income. Section 62 lists deductions *for* AGI (see Table I:2-4). Thus, any allowable deduction not listed in Sec. 62 is a deduction *from* AGI. The two categories of deductions *from* adjusted gross income are (1) itemized deductions or the standard deduction and (2) personal and dependency exemptions.[4] Deductions from AGI are discussed further in Chapter I: 7 of this textbook.

ADDITIONAL COMMENT

Itemized deductions were claimed on 31.5% of all returns filed in 2012.

Itemized Deductions and The Standard Deduction. As mentioned above, taxpayers generally cannot deduct personal expenses.[5] Congress, however, allows taxpayers to deduct specified personal expenses such as charitable contributions and medical expenses. In addition, taxpayers are allowed to itemize expenses related to the

[4] Sec. 63.

[5] Sec. 262.

▼ **TABLE I:2-4**
Deductions for Adjusted Gross Income Listed in Sec. 62

Trade and business deductions
Reimbursed employee expenses and certain expenses of performing artists
Losses from the sale or exchange of property
Deductions attributable to rents and royalties
Certain deductions of life tenants and income beneficiaries of property
Contributions to retirement plans (Keoghs and IRAs)
Penalties forfeited because of premature withdrawal of funds from time savings accounts
*One-half of self-employment taxes paid
*Health insurance costs incurred by a self-employed person
Alimony
Moving expenses
Certain required repayments of supplemental unemployment compensation
Jury duty pay remitted to an individual's employer
Certain environmental expenditures (reforestation and clean fuel)
Interest on education loans
Contribution to medical savings account

*Though not actually mentioned in Sec. 62, self-employment taxes and health insurance costs of self-employed persons are defined by Secs. 164(f) and 162(l), respectively, as trade or business deductions thereby indirectly enabling taxpayers to deduct these amounts for AGI.

ADDITIONAL COMMENT

Tax rate schedules, the standard deduction, personal exemptions, and other amounts are adjusted annually for inflation. Because of "rounding conventions," not every amount changes each year.

HISTORICAL NOTE

In 1986, when parents were required merely to list the names of their children to claim them as a dependent, 77 million children were claimed. In 1987, when taxpayers were required to list children's Social Security numbers to prove that the exemptions were valid, the number of children claimed as dependents decreased to 70 million.

HISTORICAL NOTE

As recently as 1986, the highest marginal tax rate was 50%, and as recently as 1980, it was 70%.

production or collection of income, the management of property held for the production of income, and the determination, collection, or refund of any tax.[6]

Taxpayers have the choice of claiming either itemized deductions or the standard deduction. The amount of the standard deduction varies depending on the taxpayer's filing status, age, and vision. As a practical matter, for most taxpayers the standard deduction is greater than the total itemized deductions. Taxpayers with small amounts of deductible expenses do not itemize and, in fact, do not have to keep records of medical expenses and other itemized deductions. The relationship between itemized deductions and the standard deduction is discussed later in this chapter.

Personal and Dependency Exemptions. A **personal exemption** generally is allowed for each taxpayer and his or her spouse and an additional dependency exemption is permitted for each dependent. Both personal and dependency exemptions are equal to $4,000 in 2015 and $3,950 in 2014. The amount of an exemption is adjusted annually for increases in the cost of living.

Taxable Income. **Taxable income** is adjusted gross income reduced by deductions *from* AGI. It is the amount of income that is taxed.

Tax Rates and Gross Tax. Tax rates are the percentage rates, set by Congress, at which income is taxed. There are seven tax rates ranging from 10% to 39.6%.

10%, 15%, 25%, 28%, 33%, 35%, and 39.6%

Taxpayers compute their tax by applying the percentage rates found in the tax rate schedules to taxable income. However, most taxpayers simply look in a tax table to find their gross tax. These two alternatives are discussed in more detail later in this chapter. The gross tax is the amount of tax determined by this process.

[6] Sec. 212.

▼ **TABLE I:2-5**
Partial List of Tax Credits

Refundable
Withholding from wages and back-up withholding
Estimated tax payments
Overpayment of prior year's tax
Excess Social Security taxes paid
Earned income credit
Regulated investment company credit
Payments made with extension request
Child credit (in some cases)
Nonrefundable
Adoption expense credit
Credit for the elderly and disabled
Foreign tax credit
Child and dependent care credit
Business energy credit
Research and experimentation credit
Building rehabilitation credit
American opportunity and lifetime learning credits

SELF-STUDY QUESTION

If a taxpayer is in the 25% marginal tax bracket, would he or she prefer $100 of tax credits or $300 of tax deductions?

ANSWER

The taxpayer would prefer the $100 of tax credits. The $300 of deductions will result in a tax savings of $75 ($300 × 0.25), whereas the $100 of credits would result in a tax savings of $100.

Credits and Prepayments. Tax credits, which include prepayments, are amounts that can be subtracted from the gross tax to arrive at the net tax due or refund due. Credits may be classified as either refundable or nonrefundable tax credits. **Refundable tax credits** are allowed to reduce a taxpayer's tax liability to zero and, if some credit still remains, are refundable (paid) by the government to the taxpayer. Prepayments of tax, which are amounts paid to the government during the year through means such as withholding from wages, and selected other items are classified as **refundable tax credits.** **Nonrefundable tax credits** are allowances that have been created by Congress for various social, economic, and political reasons such as the child and dependent care credits. Nonrefundable tax credits can be subtracted from the tax and may reduce the tax liability to zero. However, if the nonrefundable credits exceed the tax liability, none of the excess will be paid to the taxpayer. A partial list of refundable and nonrefundable tax credits can be found in Table I:2-5 and are covered in detail in Chapter I:14.

TAX FORMULA ILLUSTRATED

The following example illustrates the tax formula and Form 1040.

EXAMPLE I:2-1 ▶ The following facts relate to Larry S. and Jane V. Lane, who are married and file a joint return in 2014. Betty is their 9-year-old dependent daughter.

Salary	$78,000
Interest Income:	
Taxable	4,000
Exempt	500
Individual Retirement Account (IRA) contribution	5,000
Itemized deductions	15,300
Personal and dependency exemptions (3 × $3,950)	11,850
Federal income taxes withheld from salary	6,000

Their tax is computed as follows:

Income:			
	Salary		$78,000
	Taxable interest		4,000
	Tax-exempt interest		500
	Total		$82,500
Minus:	Exclusion:		
	Tax-exempt interest		(500)
Gross income			$82,000
Minus:	Deductions for AGI:		
	IRA contribution		(5,000)
Adjusted gross income			$77,000
Minus:	Deductions from AGI:		
	Itemized deductions		(15,300)
	Personal and dependency exemptions		(11,850)
Taxable income			$49,850
Gross tax (2014 tax table)			$ 6,574*
Minus:	Credits and prepayments		
	Child credit	(1,000)	
	Federal income tax withheld	(6,000)	(7,000)
Tax refund			$ 426

*The tax rate schedule will yield a tax of $6,570. This small variance results from the ranges in the tax table.

This tax is also computed on Form 1040 (see Figure I:2-1). Note that certain additional information, such as the taxpayers' address and Social Security numbers, also is included on the return.

DEDUCTIONS FROM ADJUSTED GROSS INCOME

OBJECTIVE 2

Determine the amount of deductions from Adjusted Gross Income

ITEMIZED DEDUCTIONS

Itemized deductions are claimed only if the total of such expenses exceeds the standard deduction. Here, consideration is given to which expenses may be itemized and the relationship between itemized deductions and the standard deduction.

ADDITIONAL COMMENT

In 2012, the 45.6 million taxpayers who itemized claimed $1.2 trillion in deductions. Taxes paid comprised 39.0% of the total, whereas interest paid made up 28.6%.

Deductible Items. Congress allows taxpayers to itemize specified personal expenses. These specified expenses include medical expenses, taxes, investment and residential interest, charitable contributions, casualty and theft losses, and employee expenses. In addition, taxpayers are allowed to itemize expenses related to the production or collection of nonbusiness income, the management of property held for the production of income, and the determination, collection, or refund of any tax. A partial list of itemized deductions is found in Table I:2-6.

Itemized Deduction Floors. There are four adjusted gross income floors associated with itemized deductions. AGI floors represent amounts subtracted from deductions in arriving at allowable amounts. Three of the floors apply to specific categories of itemized deductions; the remaining floor applies to total itemized deductions. The floors based on AGI are as follows:

- Medical expenses: only medical expenses in excess of 10% of AGI are deductible by taxpayers under age 65. Through 2016, taxpayers aged 65 and older may continue to use the 7.5% of AGI floor applicable to all taxpayers prior to 2013.
- Casualty losses: only casualty losses in excess of 10% of AGI are deductible.
- Miscellaneous itemized deductions: only miscellaneous itemized deductions in excess of 2% of AGI are deductible.
- The overall floor, which reduces total itemized deductions, only applies to high-income taxpayers. It is discussed later in this chapter.

Form **1040** Department of the Treasury—Internal Revenue Service (99)
U.S. Individual Income Tax Return **2014** OMB No. 1545-0074 IRS Use Only—Do not write or staple in this space.

For the year Jan. 1–Dec. 31, 2014, or other tax year beginning , 2014, ending , 20 See separate instructions.

Your first name and initial	Last name	Your social security number
Larry S.	Lane	123 45 6789
If a joint return, spouse's first name and initial	Last name	Spouse's social security number
Jane V.	Lane	987 65 4321
Home address (number and street). If you have a P.O. box, see instructions. 116 E. Edwards	Apt. no.	▲ Make sure the SSN(s) above and on line 6c are correct.
City, town or post office, state, and ZIP code. If you have a foreign address, also complete spaces below (see instructions). Lubbock, Texas 40401		**Presidential Election Campaign** Check here if you, or your spouse if filing jointly, want $3 to go to this fund. Checking a box below will not change your tax or refund. ☐ You ☐ Spouse
Foreign country name	Foreign province/state/county	Foreign postal code

Filing Status

Check only one box.

1 ☐ Single
2 ☒ Married filing jointly (even if only one had income)
3 ☐ Married filing separately. Enter spouse's SSN above and full name here. ▶
4 ☐ Head of household (with qualifying person). (See instructions.) If the qualifying person is a child but not your dependent, enter this child's name here. ▶
5 ☐ Qualifying widow(er) with dependent child

Exemptions

6a ☒ **Yourself.** If someone can claim you as a dependent, **do not** check box 6a
b ☒ **Spouse**

Boxes checked on 6a and 6b: 2

c **Dependents:**

(1) First name	Last name	(2) Dependent's social security number	(3) Dependent's relationship to you	(4) ✓ if child under age 17 qualifying for child tax credit (see instructions)
Betty	Lane	111 22 3333	Daughter	☒
				☐
				☐
				☐

If more than four dependents, see instructions and check here ▶ ☐

No. of children on 6c who:
• lived with you: 1
• did not live with you due to divorce or separation (see instructions):

Dependents on 6c not entered above:

d Total number of exemptions claimed — Add numbers on lines above ▶ 3

Income

Attach Form(s) W-2 here. Also attach Forms W-2G and 1099-R if tax was withheld.

If you did not get a W-2, see instructions.

7	Wages, salaries, tips, etc. Attach Form(s) W-2		7	78,000
8a	**Taxable** interest. Attach Schedule B if required		8a	4,000
b	**Tax-exempt** interest. **Do not** include on line 8a	8b 500		
9a	Ordinary dividends. Attach Schedule B if required		9a	
b	Qualified dividends	9b		
10	Taxable refunds, credits, or offsets of state and local income taxes		10	
11	Alimony received		11	
12	Business income or (loss). Attach Schedule C or C-EZ		12	
13	Capital gain or (loss). Attach Schedule D if required. If not required, check here ▶ ☐		13	
14	Other gains or (losses). Attach Form 4797		14	
15a	IRA distributions	15a	b Taxable amount 15b	
16a	Pensions and annuities	16a	b Taxable amount 16b	
17	Rental real estate, royalties, partnerships, S corporations, trusts, etc. Attach Schedule E		17	
18	Farm income or (loss). Attach Schedule F		18	
19	Unemployment compensation		19	
20a	Social security benefits	20a	b Taxable amount 20b	
21	Other income. List type and amount		21	
22	Combine the amounts in the far right column for lines 7 through 21. This is your **total income** ▶		22	82,000

Adjusted Gross Income

23	Educator expenses	23			
24	Certain business expenses of reservists, performing artists, and fee-basis government officials. Attach Form 2106 or 2106-EZ	24			
25	Health savings account deduction. Attach Form 8889	25			
26	Moving expenses. Attach Form 3903	26			
27	Deductible part of self-employment tax. Attach Schedule SE	27			
28	Self-employed SEP, SIMPLE, and qualified plans	28			
29	Self-employed health insurance deduction	29			
30	Penalty on early withdrawal of savings	30			
31a	Alimony paid b Recipient's SSN ▶	31a			
32	IRA deduction	32	5,000		
33	Student loan interest deduction	33			
34	Tuition and fees. Attach Form 8917	34			
35	Domestic production activities deduction. Attach Form 8903	35			
36	Add lines 23 through 35			36	5,000
37	Subtract line 36 from line 22. This is your **adjusted gross income** ▶			37	77,000

For Disclosure, Privacy Act, and Paperwork Reduction Act Notice, see separate instructions. Cat. No. 11320B Form **1040** (2014)

FIGURE I:2-1 ▶ FORM 1040 (Page 1)

Tax and Credits

38	Amount from line 37 (adjusted gross income)		38	77,000
39a	Check if: ☐ **You** were born before January 2, 1950, ☐ Blind. ☐ **Spouse** was born before January 2, 1950, ☐ Blind. } **Total boxes checked ▶ 39a** ☐			
b	If your spouse itemizes on a separate return or you were a dual-status alien, check here ▶ 39b ☐			
40	**Itemized deductions** (from Schedule A) **or** your **standard deduction** (see left margin)		40	15,300
41	Subtract line 40 from line 38		41	61,700
42	**Exemptions.** If line 38 is $152,525 or less, multiply $3,950 by the number on line 6d. Otherwise, see instructions		42	11,850
43	**Taxable income.** Subtract line 42 from line 41. If line 42 is more than line 41, enter -0-		43	49,850
44	**Tax** (see instructions). Check if any from: **a** ☐ Form(s) 8814 **b** ☐ Form 4972 **c** ☐		44	6,574
45	**Alternative minimum tax** (see instructions). Attach Form 6251		45	
46	Excess advance premium tax credit repayment. Attach Form 8962		46	
47	Add lines 44, 45, and 46 ▶		47	6,574
48	Foreign tax credit. Attach Form 1116 if required	48		
49	Credit for child and dependent care expenses. Attach Form 2441	49		
50	Education credits from Form 8863, line 19	50		
51	Retirement savings contributions credit. Attach Form 8880	51		
52	Child tax credit. Attach Schedule 8812, if required	52 1,000		
53	Residential energy credits. Attach Form 5695	53		
54	Other credits from Form: **a** ☐ 3800 **b** ☐ 8801 **c** ☐	54	54	
55	Add lines 48 through 54. These are your **total credits**		55	1,000
56	Subtract line 55 from line 47. If line 55 is more than line 47, enter -0- ▶		56	5,574

Standard Deduction for—
- People who check any box on line 39a or 39b **or** who can be claimed as a dependent, see instructions.
- All others:

Single or Married filing separately, $6,200

Married filing jointly or Qualifying widow(er), $12,400

Head of household, $9,100

Other Taxes

57	Self-employment tax. Attach Schedule SE	57	
58	Unreported social security and Medicare tax from Form: **a** ☐ 4137 **b** ☐ 8919	58	
59	Additional tax on IRAs, other qualified retirement plans, etc. Attach Form 5329 if required	59	
60a	Household employment taxes from Schedule H	60a	
b	First-time homebuyer credit repayment. Attach Form 5405 if required	60b	
61	Health care: individual responsibility (see instructions) Full-year coverage ☐	61	
62	Taxes from: **a** ☐ Form 8959 **b** ☐ Form 8960 **c** ☐ Instructions; enter code(s)	62	
63	Add lines 56 through 62. This is your **total tax** ▶	63	5,574

Payments

64	Federal income tax withheld from Forms W-2 and 1099	64 6,000		
65	2014 estimated tax payments and amount applied from 2013 return	65		
66a	**Earned income credit (EIC)**	66a		
b	Nontaxable combat pay election 66b			
67	Additional child tax credit. Attach Schedule 8812	67		
68	American opportunity credit from Form 8863, line 8	68		
69	Net premium tax credit. Attach Form 8962	69		
70	Amount paid with request for extension to file	70		
71	Excess social security and tier 1 RRTA tax withheld	71		
72	Credit for federal tax on fuels. Attach Form 4136	72		
73	Credits from Form: **a** ☐ 2439 **b** ☐ Reserved **c** ☐ Reserved **d** ☐	73		
74	Add lines 64, 65, 66a, and 67 through 73. These are your **total payments** ▶		74	6,000

If you have a qualifying child, attach Schedule EIC.

Refund

75	If line 74 is more than line 63, subtract line 63 from line 74. This is the amount you **overpaid**	75	426
76a	Amount of line 75 you want **refunded to you.** If Form 8888 is attached, check here ▶ ☐	76a	426
▶ b	Routing number ▶ **c** Type: ☐ Checking ☐ Savings		
▶ d	Account number		
77	Amount of line 75 you want **applied to your 2015 estimated tax** ▶ 77		

Direct deposit? See instructions.

Amount You Owe

78	**Amount you owe.** Subtract line 74 from line 63. For details on how to pay, see instructions ▶	78	
79	Estimated tax penalty (see instructions) 79		

Third Party Designee

Do you want to allow another person to discuss this return with the IRS (see instructions)? ☐ **Yes.** Complete below. ☐ **No**

Designee's name ▶ Phone no. ▶ Personal identification number (PIN) ▶

Sign Here

Under penalties of perjury, I declare that I have examined this return and accompanying schedules and statements, and to the best of my knowledge and belief, they are true, correct, and complete. Declaration of preparer (other than taxpayer) is based on all information of which preparer has any knowledge.

Joint return? See instructions. Keep a copy for your records.

Your signature	Date	Your occupation	Daytime phone number
Larry S. Lane	4/15/15	Attorney	555-555-1212
Spouse's signature. If a joint return, **both** must sign.	Date	Spouse's occupation	If the IRS sent you an Identity Protection PIN, enter it here (see inst.)
Jane V. Lane	4/15/15	Student	

Paid Preparer Use Only

Print/Type preparer's name	Preparer's signature	Date	Check ☐ if self-employed	PTIN
Firm's name ▶			Firm's EIN ▶	
Firm's address ▶			Phone no.	

www.irs.gov/form1040 Form **1040** (2014)

FIGURE I:2-1 ▶ FORM 1040 (continued)

▼ **TABLE I:2-6**
Partial List of Itemized Deductions

Medical expenses (over 10% of adjusted gross income for most taxpayers)
Certain taxes
- State, local, and foreign income and real property taxes
- State and local personal property taxes

Residential interest and investment interest (limited)
Charitable contributions (limited)
Casualty and theft losses (over 10% of adjusted gross income)
Miscellaneous deductions (over 2% of adjusted gross income)
- Employee expenses (e.g., professional and union dues, professional publications, travel, transportation, education, job hunting, office-in-home, special clothing, and 50% of entertainment expenses)
- Expenses for producing investment income (e.g., accounting and legal fees, safe deposit rental, fees paid to an IRA custodian)
- Tax advice and tax return preparation and related costs

Other miscellaneous deductions
- Federal estate tax attributable to income in respect of a decedent
- Gambling losses to the extent of winnings
- Amortization of bond premium
- Amounts restored under claim of right

These floors are discussed in more detail in Chapter I:7.

EXAMPLE I:2-2 ▶ **John and Jane, both under age 65, file a joint tax return in 2015 and report AGI of $170,000. Their itemized deductions include $25,000 of medical expenses and home mortgage interest of $10,000. The AGI floor reduces the medical expense deduction to $8,000 [$25,000 − (0.10 × $170,000)]. Thus, the total itemized deductions allowed is $18,000.** ◀

STANDARD DEDUCTION

Itemized deductions are claimed only if the total amount of such deductions exceeds the standard deduction. The **standard deduction** is an amount set by Congress. It varies from year to year depending on the taxpayer's filing status, age, and vision.

KEY POINT

The dollar amount of the standard deduction generally increases each year because it is indexed to the rate of inflation.

Filing Status	*Standard Deduction* 2014	*Standard Deduction* 2015
Single individual other than heads of households	$ 6,200	$ 6,300
Married couples filing joint returns and surviving spouses	12,400	12,600
Married people filing separate returns	6,200	6,300
Heads of households	9,100	9,250

The differences between the 2014 and 2015 amounts represent inflation adjustments.

In 2015, a married taxpayer's standard deduction is increased by $1,250 ($1,200 in 2014) if he or she is elderly or blind ($2,500 if the taxpayer is elderly *and* blind) or has a spouse who is elderly or blind (for a maximum possible increase of $5,000 for a married couple). If an unmarried taxpayer is elderly or blind, his or her standard deduction is increased by $1,550 (also $1,550 in 2014) and $3,100 if the taxpayer is elderly *and* blind. Thus, in 2015, a single taxpayer, age 65 and not blind, is entitled to a $7,850 ($6,300 + $1,550) standard deduction. Two special rules relating to age and blindness are noted below.

ADDITIONAL COMMENT

Of all individual returns filed in 2012, 67.1% claimed the standard deduction.

- The increase in the standard deduction for elderly taxpayers is available if the taxpayer turns 65 during the tax year. For purposes of this requirement, a taxpayer is considered to be age 65 on the day before his or her sixty-fifth birthday. Thus, a taxpayer who reaches age 65 on January 1 of a year is deemed to have reached age 65 on December 31 of the preceding year. The adjustment is allowed on the final return of a deceased taxpayer only if he or she reached age 65 before death.
- The IRC defines blindness as corrected vision in the better eye of no better than 20/200 or a field of no greater than 20 degrees. Vision is determined as of the last day of the tax year or, in the case of a deceased taxpayer, as of the date of death.

The standard deduction simplifies the computation of taxable income. As previously noted, for most taxpayers the standard deduction is greater than total itemized deductions. Those taxpayers do not itemize and, in fact, do not even have to keep records of medical expenses and other itemized deductions.

Who actually itemizes and who does not? High-income taxpayers are more likely to itemize than low-income taxpayers simply because they incur more expenses that can be itemized. This is true even though the AGI floors (previously discussed) affect high-income taxpayers more than low-income taxpayers. Another characteristic of taxpayers who generally itemize their deductions are individuals who own their homes and incur home mortgage expenses and property taxes. These two expenses are deductible and alone often exceed the standard deduction.

EXAMPLE I:2-3 ▶ In 2015, Joan is single and a homeowner who incurs property taxes on her home of $2,000, makes charitable contributions of $500, and pays mortgage interest of $6,000. Joan's adjusted gross income is $32,000. Her taxable income is computed as follows:

Adjusted gross income			$32,000
Minus:	Itemized deductions:		
	Charitable contributions	$ 500	
	Property taxes	2,000	
	Mortgage interest	6,000	(8,500)
Minus:	Personal exemption		(4,000)
Taxable income			$19,500 ◀

Joan would itemize her deductions because they ($8,500) are greater than her standard deduction ($6,300).

EXAMPLE I:2-4 ▶ Assume the same facts as in Example I:2-3 except that Joan is not a homeowner. Thus, she has no property taxes or mortgage interest but does pay rent of $800 per month for an apartment. Her taxable income is computed as follows:

Adjusted gross income		$32,000
Minus:	Standard deduction	(6,300)
Minus:	Personal exemption	(4,000)
Taxable income		$21,700 ◀

Joan uses the standard deduction of $6,300 because it is greater than her itemized deductions of $500. Rent paid for a personal apartment is not deductible.

Loss of The Standard Deduction. Congress decided that some taxpayers should not be permitted to use the standard deduction as they possibly would receive an unintended tax benefit.[7] The standard deduction is unavailable to three categories of taxpayers:

- An individual filing a return for a period less than twelve months because of a change in accounting period.
- A married taxpayer filing a separate return in instances where the other spouse itemizes.
- Nonresident aliens.

To illustrate why Congress does not permit certain taxpayers to claim the standard deduction, consider what could happen if a married couple files separate returns but only one spouse itemizes. On a separate return in 2015 when the standard deduction is $6,300, one spouse could claim all itemized deductions while the other uses the standard deduction.

EXAMPLE I:2-5 ▶ Clay and Joy, a married couple, have incomes of $35,000 and $34,000, respectively. Their itemized deductions total $9,000. They would claim a $12,600 standard deduction on a joint return. If Clay filed a separate return and claimed all of the deductions, his itemized deductions of $9,000 would be greater than the $6,300 standard deduction. If Joy could claim the standard deduction on her return, their total deductions would equal $15,300 ($9,000 + $6,300). The law, however, requires that either they both itemize or they both use the standard deduction. ◀

Limitation on the Standard Deduction. A special rule applies to any individual for whom the dependency exemption is allowable to another taxpayer. The standard deduction of the dependent is limited to the greater of (1) the dependent's earned income plus $350 in 2015 (also $350 in 2014) or (2) $1,050 in 2015 ($1,000 in 2014). The purpose of this limitation is to prevent parents from shifting unearned income, such as interest and dividends, to their children and avoid paying tax on such income. Without this rule, children could use the standard deduction to offset interest and dividends.

EXAMPLE I:2-6 ▶ Webb and Beth are married, in the 39.6% marginal tax rate bracket, and have one son, Vincent, age 15. Vincent has no income and is claimed as a dependent by his parents. Webb and Beth transfer stocks and bonds that earn $3,000 in dividends and interest to Vincent. Their goal is to shift the $3,000 of income to Vincent to utilize his standard deduction. However, since Vincent is claimed as a dependent by his parents on their return, Vincent's standard deduction is limited to $1,050, i.e., the *greater* of $1,050 or his earned income plus $350 ($0 + $350). ◀

EXAMPLE I:2-7 ▶ Assume the same facts as in Example I:2-6 except Vincent has a part-time job and earns $2,000 in wages. Vincent's standard deduction would be $2,350 ($2,000 + $350). Alternatively, if Vincent's wages were $7,000, his standard deduction would be $6,300 (the maximum for a single individual). ◀

ADDITIONAL COMMENT

As explained later in the chapter, some high-income taxpayers may have to phase out the personal and dependency exemptions.

PERSONAL EXEMPTIONS

Taxpayers cannot deduct personal expenses except for certain itemized deductions that are specifically authorized under the tax law. Congress has recognized the need to protect a small amount of income from tax in order to allow the taxpayer to meet personal expenses. Thus, almost every individual taxpayer is allowed a personal exemption of $4,000 ($3,950 in 2014). Because there are two taxpayers on a joint return filed by a married couple, they are allowed two personal exemptions. In addition, if a married person files a separate return, the taxpayer can claim a personal exemption for his or her spouse if the spouse has no gross income during the year and the spouse is not the dependent of another taxpayer.[8]

Only one personal exemption is allowed for each person. Therefore, an individual who is claimed as a dependent by another person is not entitled to a personal exemption on his

[7] Sec. 63(c)(6).

[8] Sec. 151(b).

or her own return. Despite the loss of the personal exemption, most dependents owe little or no tax because they can usually offset their small income by the standard deduction.

ADDITIONAL COMMENT

One should forsake any preconceived notions as to what constitutes a dependent before examining the dependency tests.

DEPENDENCY EXEMPTIONS

Virtually all taxpayers can claim a *personal exemption* for themselves. In addition, taxpayers may also claim a *dependency exemption* for each dependent.[9] To qualify as a dependent, an individual must meet the definition of either a *qualifying child* or a *qualifying relative*. All dependents must meet several requirements. Four requirements are common to all dependents. All dependents must:

- Have a qualifying identification number.
- Meet a citizenship test.
- Meet a separate return test.
- Not themselves claim another person as a dependent.

Additional requirements also must be met depending on whether the dependent is a qualifying child or a qualifying relative.

Requirements for All Dependents. The requirements applicable to all dependents are:

Identification number. Every dependent must have a Social Security number, and that number must be reported on the return.[10]

Citizenship. Dependents must be U.S. citizens[11] or nationals,[12] or residents of the U.S., Canada, or Mexico[13] for some part of the year.

Joint return. Married dependents cannot file joint returns. However, a taxpayer is entitled to the exemption if the dependent files a joint return solely to claim a refund of tax withheld (i.e., there is no tax on the joint return and there would have been no tax on two separate returns).[14] Married dependents should weigh the taxes that would be saved by the family from an exemption against the taxes that would be saved by filing a joint return. Depending on the circumstances, either alternative may be more beneficial.

No dependent. Dependents who file tax returns may not claim personal or dependency exemptions on their returns.

Additional Requirements for Qualifying Children. To claim a dependency exemption for an individual who is considered a *qualifying child,* the following additional requirements must be met:

- A relationship test.
- An age test.
- An abode test.
- A support test.

Relationship test. Eligible children include the taxpayer's children (including natural, adopted, foster, and stepchildren) and the taxpayer's siblings (including half-siblings and step-siblings) along with descendants of any of the above. A child is adopted if the child has been legally adopted or has been legally placed in a home for adoption.

---

[9] Sec. 152.

[10] Sec. 151(e). The IRS has the authority to disallow dependency exemptions for otherwise qualified dependents without Social Security numbers and with incorrectly reported Social Security numbers. A missing or incorrectly reported Social Security number may also bar an otherwise eligible individual from claiming head-of-household filing status.

[11] U.S. citizens living in foreign countries can claim dependency exemptions for adopted children even if the children are not U.S. citizens.

[12] A U.S. national is an individual born in an outlying possession such as American Samoa.

[13] A resident is a person who is not a U.S. citizen and who is legally residing in the United States with intent to stay here permanently (see Sec. 7701(b)).

[14] Rev. Rul. 54-567, 1954-2 C.B. 108 and Rev. Rul 65-34, 1965-1 C.B. 86. The theory is that the taxpayer is filing a claim for refund and not actually filing a tax return.

Age test. A qualifying child must be under age 19, a full-time student under age 24, or a permanently and totally disabled child.[15] A child is considered to be a student if he or she is in full-time attendance at a qualified educational institution during at least five months of the year. To be full-time, a student must carry the number of hours or courses the educational institution requires a student to take to be considered full-time.

Abode test. A qualifying child must have the same principal abode as the taxpayer for more than half of the year. A noncustodial parent meets this requirement if the custodial parent agrees in writing.

Support test. A qualifying child may not provide more than one-half of his or her own support during the year. Support is defined below in connection with the discussion of other dependents. Unlike other dependents, there is no requirement that the taxpayer provide more than one-half of the qualifying child's support, only that the dependent cannot provide more than one-half of his or her own support. This can be important in situations such as divorces where one spouse provides support, but the other has custody.

EXAMPLE I:2-8 ▶ Keith and Barbara file a joint return and have one son, Jeff, age 28. Because of a temporary illness, Jeff had to quit his job in June and moved back home to live with his parents. Keith and Barbara provided 70% of Jeff's support. Jeff earned $18,000. Jeff is not a qualifying child for purposes of the dependency exemption. Although Jeff meets the relationship, abode, and support tests, he fails the age test. ◀

Requirements for Other Relatives. A dependency exemption may also be claimed for a *qualifying relative*. To be eligible, dependents must meet the common requirements above and three additional requirements:

- ▶ Relationship test.
- ▶ Gross income test.
- ▶ Support test.

Relationship test. Other relatives must either be related to the taxpayer or reside in the taxpayer's household for the entire year. Although this group is referred to as "other qualifying relatives," that term is misleading because individuals who live with the taxpayer do not actually have to be related to the taxpayer. The relationship between the taxpayer and the dependent cannot violate local law.[16] Relatives who can be claimed as dependents even if they do not live with the taxpayer include the taxpayer's parents and their ancestors and siblings, the taxpayer's stepparents, and specified in-laws (mother, father, brother, sister, son, and daughter) along with qualifying children discussed above. As a result, a qualifying child may be claimed as a dependent if the child meets the tests described here even if the child fails the requirements for qualifying children. Thus, a son who is age 24 can be claimed as a dependent if the son meets the support and gross income tests discussed below even though that son could not be claimed as a dependent under the requirements for a qualifying child.

EXAMPLE I:2-9 ▶ Jesse supports three people, all of whom have gross income of less than $4,000, Tina, an unrelated child who lives with him; his cousin Judy, who lives in another state; and his daughter Vicki, who lives in her own home. Jesse can claim two dependency exemptions: one for Tina, who lives with him (a person who lives with the taxpayer need not be related) and one for his daughter. Jesse cannot claim a dependency exemption for Judy as cousins do not meet the relationship test. ◀

On a joint return the dependent needs to be related to only one spouse.[17] Once established, a relationship is not terminated by death or divorce.

---

[15] As noted, taxpayers attain the age 65, for purposes of the additional standard deduction, on the day before the anniversaries of their births. As a result, an individual whose birthday is January 1 is considered to be age 65 in the year prior to the individual's 65th birthday. A child whose 19th birthday falls on January 1 is considered to be under the age 19 in the previous year. The rule also is followed for purposes of determining whether the child is under age 24, and is used in connection with age 17 threshold associated with the child credit. Rev. Rul. 2003-72, 2003-2 C.B. 353.

[16] Sec. 152(f)(3). The exemption has been disallowed where the relationship constituted "cohabitation" and was illegal in the state (*Cassius L. Peacock*, III, PH T.C. Memo ¶78.030, 37 TCM 177).

[17] Reg. Sec. 1.152-2(d).

EXAMPLE I:2-10 ▶ Ken and Lisa support Lisa's mother and claim her as a dependent on a joint return. Following Lisa's death, Ken continues to support Lisa's mother. Lisa's mother continues to be Ken's mother-in-law and can be claimed as a dependent. ◀

Gross income test. The dependent's gross income must be less than the exemption amount for the year ($4,000 in 2015 and $3,950 in 2014). The statutory definition of gross income is used in applying this limitation. Therefore, nontaxable scholarships, tax-exempt bond interest, and nontaxable Social Security benefits are not considered, but salary, taxable interest, and rent are considered in deciding whether the person meets this test.

EXAMPLE I:2-11 ▶ Jim, age 22, a full-time college student, lives with his cousin who provides more than one-half of Jim's support. Jim earned $8,000 from a summer job. Even though Jim's cousin provided over one-half of his support, Jim cannot be claimed as a dependent as Jim does not meet the gross income test. Alternatively, if Jim lived with and was supported by his brother, he could be claimed as a dependent because, as a brother, Jim is a qualifying child and is exempt from the gross income test. ◀

Support test. The taxpayer must normally provide more than one-half of a dependent's financial support during the year. Support includes amounts spent by the taxpayer, the dependent, and other individuals. Welfare[18] and Social Security benefits[19] spent on support count even if they are excluded from gross income. Scholarships, however, do not count as support if the amounts are tax exempt.

EXAMPLE I:2-12 ▶ Tarer provided $3,000 of support for his mother, Mary. Tarer's sister provided $1,000. Mary spent $4,500 of her savings for her own support. Because Mary provided over one-half of her own support, she cannot be claimed as a dependent. ◀

EXAMPLE I:2-13 ▶ George's father received Social Security benefits of $6,600, of which $1,800 were deposited into a savings account. He spent the remaining $4,800 on food, clothing, and lodging. George spent $5,600 to support his father. George meets the support test because the amount saved is not counted in the support test. ◀

ADDITIONAL COMMENT

A TV set bought by a parent for his 12-year-old child and set up in her bedroom was considered support. A power lawn mower, however, bought by a parent of a 13-year-old child was not considered support. The parent had assigned the child the job of mowing the lawn, and the power mower was intended to make the job more palatable. The lawn mower was considered a family item that benefits all members of the household. (Rev. Rul. 77-282, 1977-2 C.B. 52.)

Support includes amounts spent for food, clothing, shelter, medical and dental care, education, and the like.[20] Support is not limited to these items.[21] Support does not include the value of services rendered by the taxpayer to the dependent.[22] Also, the IRS and the courts have excluded various other expenses from support.[23]

Generally, the amount of support equals the cost of the item, but in the case of support provided in a noncash form, such as lodging, the amount of support equals the fair market value or fair rental value. The cost of an item such as a television or an automobile is included in support if the item actually is support.[24]

EXAMPLE I:2-14 ▶ Vicki's mother lives with her. Vicki purchased clothing for her mother costing $800 and provided her with a room that Vicki estimates she could have rented for $2,800. Vicki spent $2,500 for groceries she shared with her mother and $1,200 for utilities. In addition, Vicki purchased a television for $750 that she placed in the living room. Vicki and her mother both used the television. Vicki's support for her mother, at a minimum, includes:

Clothing	$ 800
Rental value of room	2,800
Food	1,250
Total	$4,850

[18] Rev. Rul. 71-468, 1971-2 C.B. 115.

[19] Rev. Ruls. 57-344, 1957-2 C.B. 112, and 58-419, 1958-2 C.B. 57.

[20] Reg. Sec. 1.152-1(a)(2)(i).

[21] Examples of other items that have been held to be support include church contributions (Rev. Rul. 58-67, 1958-1 C.B. 62), telephone (*William K. Price, III,* 1961 PH T.C. Memo ¶61,173, 20 TCM 886), medical insurance premiums (*James Edward Parker,* 1959 PH T.C. Memo ¶52,182, 18 TCM 800), child care (*Marvin D. Tucker,* 1957 PH T.C. Memo ¶57,118, 16 TCM 488), toys (*Loren S. Brumber,* 1952 PH T.C. Memo ¶52,087, 11 TCM 289), and vacations (*George R. Melat,* 1953 PH T.C. Memo ¶53,141, 12 TCM 443).

[22] *Frank Markarian v. CIR.,* 16 AFTR 2d 5785, 65-2 USTC ¶9699 (7th Cir., 1965).

[23] Examples of items that have been excluded are funeral expenses (Rev. Rul. 65-307, 1965-2 C.B. 40), taxes (Rev. Rul. 58-67, 1958-1 C.B. 62), a rifle, lawn mower, boat insurance (*Harriet C. Flower v. U.S.,* 52 AFTR 1383, 57-1 USTC ¶9655 (D.C. Pa., 1957)), and life insurance premiums (*John F. Miller,* 1959 PH T.C. Memo ¶59,155, 18 TCM 673).

[24] Rev. Rul. 77-282, 1977-2 C.B. 52.

Whether a portion of the utilities could be included in support would depend on whether the rental rate for the room included utilities. The fact that the mother used the television set probably would not be sufficient to cause its cost to be viewed as support. On the other hand, if the television set was a gift to the mother, was placed in her room, and was used exclusively by her, the cost probably would qualify as support. ◀

If a taxpayer contributes a lump sum for the support of two or more individuals, the amount is allocated between the individuals on a pro rata basis unless proof exists to the contrary.[25]

EXAMPLE I:2-15 ▶ Jaime pays rent of $9,000 for an apartment occupied by his aunts Alice, Beth, and Cindy. Alice spends $4,000 toward her own support, Beth spends $2,000, and Cindy spends $2,500. Jaime is assumed to have provided $3,000 of support for each aunt. Thus, assuming the other tests are met, Jaime can claim exemptions for Beth and Cindy, but not for Alice. ◀

EXAMPLE I:2-16 ▶ Paul and Mary have three children and are unclear whether they can claim their children as dependents. Information on the children is as follows:

- Peter, age 25, who served in the military immediately after high school, is a college senior. He worked part-time earning $2,200 and provided 20% of his support.
- Mark, age 22, graduated from college in May (he was a full-time student for five months of the year), and accepted a job in June. He lived with his parents for the entire year, earned $28,000, and provided 70% of his own support.
- Ruth, age 18, graduated from high school in May, and moved into an apartment immediately after graduation. She earned $5,500 from a job and provided 30% of her own support for the year.

Assume Paul and Mary provide all the support not provided by the children. The first step is to determine whether any of the children are considered qualifying children. None of the children are qualifying children. Peter is over age 23. Mark provided more than 50% of his own support. Ruth did not live with her parents for more than one-half of the year. The second step is to determine whether any of the children are considered qualifying relatives. Peter is considered as a qualifying relative as he meets the relationship, gross income, and support tests. Mark fails both the gross income and support tests, and Ruth fails the gross income test. Thus, only Peter can be claimed as a dependent. ◀

Tie-Breaker Rules for Dependency Exemptions. More than one person can meet the requirements to claim someone as a dependent. Tie-breakers decide who receives the exemption in such situations, as follows:

- First, taxpayers who meet the requirements to claim the dependent under the qualifying child rules have priority over individuals who meet the requirements for other relatives.
- The next priority provides that parents have priority over other individuals.
- Finally, if neither of the first two tie-breakers apply, the third tie-breaker specifies that the exemption is awarded to the taxpayer with the highest AGI.

Consider a niece who lives with three aunts who contribute equal amounts to her support. Assuming other requirements are met, all three aunts satisfy the requirements to claim the niece as a dependent under the qualifying child rule. Taxpayers who meet the requirements to claim a dependent under the qualifying child rules have priority over individuals who meet the requirements for other relatives. This first tie-breaker would not determine which aunt receives the exemption as each meets the qualifying child requirement.

---

[25] Rev. Rul. 64-222, 1964-2 C.B. 47 and Rev. Rul. 72-591, 1972-2 C.B. 84.

Moving to the second tie-breaker, parents have priority over other individuals. Again, the tie-breaker will not determine which aunt receives the exemption as they are not the child's parent. Thus, in this case, the aunt with the greatest AGI would receive the exemption. In cases involving two parents, the exemption is awarded to the parent with whom the child resided for the longer period of time during the year, and if the child spent equal amounts of time with each parent, the exemption is awarded to the parent with the higher AGI.

Two provisions can override the normal operation of dependency exemption rules:

- A Multiple Support Declaration (Form 2120) can enable a taxpayer to claim a dependency exemption in situations where the taxpayer does not provide over one-half of the dependent's support. This can be very important when several individuals contribute to the support of an individual who is not a qualifying child.
- A Release of Claim to Exemption for Child of Divorced or Separated Parents (Form 8332) can enable a noncustodial parent to claim an exemption.

Multiple Support Agreements. Often several people contribute to the support of a dependent. When a group provides over one-half of the support of an individual but no one member of the group provides over one-half of the support, eligible members of the group are allowed to designate one group member to claim the exemption. Each eligible member (other than the taxpayer receiving the exemption) must agree in writing. The taxpayer claiming the exemption must complete a Multiple Support Declaration (Form 2120, shown on page I:2-18). An eligible member is one who contributes more than 10% of the dependent's support and meet all requirements for claiming a dependency exemption except the support requirement.[26]

EXAMPLE I:2-17 ▶ John T. Abel lives alone. His support comes from the following sources:

Andy (son)	$ 400
Gabe (son)	2,800
Mable (daughter)	2,000
Betty (friend)	2,800
Total	$8,000

Either Gabe or Mable can claim a dependency exemption if the other agrees in writing. Andy cannot claim the exemption because he did not provide over 10% of John's support. Betty cannot claim a dependency exemption because she is not related and John does not live with her. For this reason, Andy and Betty need not agree in writing. Form 2120 is included in the return of the taxpayer claiming the exemption. A completed Form 2120 is illustrated in Figure I:2-2. ◀

The Multiple Support Declaration can supercede the tie-breaker rules discussed above except that the agreement cannot be used to pass the exemption from a person who is entitled to claim the dependent under the qualifying child rules to a person who is entitled to claim the exemption under the other dependent's rule.[27]

ADDITIONAL COMMENT

Form 8332 may be completed each year by the custodial parent to relinquish the dependency exemption for only that year, or it may be completed once, relinquishing the exemption for all future years.

Parental Release. In the case of divorced or separated parents, the dependency exemption for children generally is awarded to the custodial parent. However, the noncustodial parent may claim the dependency exemption if the custodial spouse signs a completed Form 8332. The signed form is attached to the noncustodial spouse's return for each year the exemption is claimed. In the case of divorces prior to 2008, the noncustodial spouse can substitute a copy of pages from the divorce decree that award the exemption to the noncustodial spouse. In the case of a divorce or separation, the custodial spouse probably would be reluctant to relinquish the dependency exemption for a child. A noncustodial parent, however, might be able to negotiate the exemption in exchange for increased child support payments.

[26] Sec. 152(c).

[27] Sec. 152(d)(1)(D).

Form **2120**
(Rev. October 2005)
Department of the Treasury
Internal Revenue Service

Multiple Support Declaration

▶ **Attach to Form 1040 or Form 1040A.**

OMB No. 1545-0074

Attachment Sequence No. **114**

Name(s) shown on return: Gabe I. Abel

Your social security number: 123 : 45 : 6789

During the calendar year 2014, the eligible persons listed below each paid over 10% of the support of:

John T. Abel

Name of your qualifying relative

I have a signed statement from each eligible person waiving his or her right to claim this person as a dependent for any tax year that began in the above calendar year.

Mabel B. Abel — 222 : 11 : 0001

Eligible person's name — Social security number

402 N. Lable Lane Lawrence, NJ 08649

Address (number, street, apt. no., city, state, and ZIP code)

Eligible person's name — Social security number

Address (number, street, apt. no., city, state, and ZIP code)

Eligible person's name — Social security number

Address (number, street, apt. no., city, state, and ZIP code)

Eligible person's name — Social security number

Address (number, street, apt. no., city, state, and ZIP code)

FIGURE I:2-2 ▶ FORM 2120

EXAMPLE I:2-18 ▶ Hal and Pam obtain a divorce under the terms of which Pam receives custody of their son. Hal is ordered to pay $600 per month of child support. In absence of a written agreement to the contrary, Pam will receive the dependency exemption for the child. ◀

EXAMPLE I:2-19 ▶ Assume the same facts as in Example I:2-18 except that Pam negotiates child support payments of $800 per month and agrees in writing to allow Hal to claim the dependency exemption for the child. The written agreement will enable Hal to claim the dependency exemption for the child. ◀

EXAMPLE I:2-20 ▶ Andy and Beth obtain a divorce under the terms of which they share custody of their daughter. The divorce decree does not specify who is to receive the dependency exemption. Whoever has custody for the greater part of the year receives the dependency exemption for the daughter unless they agree otherwise in writing. If they share custody equally, the parent with the higher AGI receives the exemption. ◀

SELF-STUDY QUESTION

Beth's mother, who is a U.S. citizen, has moved to France to spend her retirement years. She has retained her U.S. citizenship, but she is now a resident of France. Is it possible for Beth to claim her mother as a dependent?

ANSWER

Yes, the mother need only be a U.S. citizen.

EXAMPLE I:2-21 ▶ In 2015, Lee, a single taxpayer with one dependent, reports AGI of $120,000. Her personal and dependency exemption amount is $8,000 ($4,000 × 2). ◀

The rules for deducting personal and dependency exemptions are summarized in Topic Review I:2-1.

CHILD CREDIT

Under Sec. 24 of the IRC, individual taxpayers may claim a "child credit" of $1,000 for each qualifying child. The credit is reduced by $50 for each $1,000 (or fraction thereof) by which the taxpayer's modified adjusted gross income exceeds a threshold amount ($110,000 on joint returns, $75,000 for single taxpayers, and $55,000 for married persons filing separate returns). Neither the amount of the credit or the phase-out thresholds is indexed for inflation. Modified adjusted gross income is AGI plus any amounts excluded from gross income under Secs. 911, 931, and 933 which relate to certain foreign earned income and possession's income. To qualify for the credit, a child must be under the age of 17 and be a "qualifying child" as defined in the above discussion of dependency exemptions. See Chapter I:14 for more information regarding the child credit.

ADDITIONAL COMMENT

There are now two credits that have similar names: the child tax credit and the child and dependent care credit. They are quite different in how the credit amounts are computed and which dependents qualify.

TOPIC REVIEW I:2-1

Personal and Dependency Exemptions

EXEMPTIONS IN GENERAL

- One exemption is available for each taxpayer (except when the taxpayer is the dependent of another) and for each dependent.
- The amount of each exemption, which is adjusted annually for inflation, is $4,000 in 2015 and $3,950 in 2014.

DEPENDENCY EXEMPTIONS

- One exemption is allowed for each dependent. As explained later in the chapter, the exemptions are phased out for higher income taxpayers.
- Each dependent must meet multiple conditions. All dependents (1) must have Social Security numbers reported on the taxpayer's return, (2) must meet a citizenship test, (3) cannot normally file a joint return, and (4) cannot claim others as dependents. Qualifying children must (1) be the taxpayer's child or sibling, (2) be under 19, a full-time student under 24, or disabled, (3) live with the taxpayer, and (4) not be self-supporting. Other qualifying relatives must (1) be related to the taxpayer, (2) have gross income less than the amount of the personal exemption, and (3) receive over one-half of their support from the taxpayer.

EXAMPLE I:2-22 ▶ Jane and Bill have two eligible dependent children and a modified AGI of $120,300. They have excess AGI of $10,300 ($120,300 − $110,000) and are entitled to a credit of $1,450 [(2 × $1,000) − (11 × $50)]. ◀

Through 2017, the child credit is partially refundable. For a taxpayer with one or two qualifying children, the refund is limited to 15% of the taxpayer's earned income in excess of $3,000.

EXAMPLE I:2-23 ▶ Georgia's two dependent children entitle her to a child credit of $2,000. Her salary is $25,000 and her gross income tax is $500. The credit offsets all of Georgia's income tax. In addition, Georgia is entitled to a refund of the balance of the credit ($1,500), as the amount is less than the limitation [$3,300 = 15% × ($25,000 − $3,000)]. ◀

In the case of a taxpayer with three or more qualifying children, the refund is limited to the greater of 15% of the taxpayer's earned income in excess of $3,000 or the excess of the taxpayer's Social Security tax paid over the taxpayer's earned income credit for the year. (See Chapter I: 14 in the Individuals volume for more detail.)

DETERMINING THE AMOUNT OF TAX

OBJECTIVE 3

Calculate the income tax for individuals

After taxable income is computed, the next step is to determine the gross tax. Most individuals determine the amount of gross tax by looking in the tax table. (See page T-2 after Chapter I:8 in *Individuals* volume or after Chapter C:15 in the *Comprehensive* volume.) This method allows the taxpayer to arrive at the gross tax without the need for multiplication and, therefore, simplifies the computation and reduces the number of errors. Individuals are required to use the tax table unless taxable income exceeds the maximum income in the table (currently $100,000), or if the taxpayer files a short period return on account of a change in the annual accounting period.

Taxpayers who cannot use the tax table instead use the tax rate schedule (located after Chapter I:18 and on the inside cover of the text). Taxpayers using the tax rate schedule must actually compute the tax.

EXAMPLE I:2-24 ▶ Liz is single and has taxable income of $48,210. Liz's tax is determined by reference to the tax table for single taxpayers. (At the time of this writing, the 2014 tax table was the most recent available.) The tax from the table is $7,913. ◀

EXAMPLE I:2-25 ▶ Jack and Pam are married, file a joint tax return, and have taxable income of $105,000 in 2015. They use the tax rate schedule to compute their tax. The tax is computed as follows:

Tax on $74,900	$10,313
Tax on remaining $30,100 at 25%	7,525
Gross tax	$17,838

◀

FILING STATUS

There are seven tax brackets applicable to individual taxpayers: 10%, 15%, 25%, 28%, 33%, 35%, and 39.6%. These rates are progressive in that as a taxpayer's income increases, the taxpayer moves into higher tax brackets. The income level at which higher tax brackets begin depends on the taxpayer's filing status. There are five different filing statuses but only four rate schedules and/or tax tables because married couples filing jointly and certain surviving spouses use the same rate schedule or tax table. The five filing statuses are as follows:

- Married filing jointly
- Surviving spouse
- Head of household
- Single
- Married filing separately

Before 1948, one rate schedule was used by all taxpayers. Married couples often filed separate returns in order to have more income taxed at lower rates. This treatment was deemed to be unfair because various states allocated income between spouses differently. Some states used a community property law system while other states used a common law system. Today, only a few states continue to use the community property law system.[28]

KEY POINT

Currently the highest tax rates are those for married filing separately, and the lowest are those for married filing jointly.

In general, community property law allocates community income equally between a husband and wife, regardless of which spouse actually earns the income. In other states, income belongs to the spouse who produces the income. With a progressive tax system, placing income on one return instead of two can result in a much greater tax. For this reason, couples residing in noncommunity property states often paid more tax than their counterparts who resided in community property states. In 1948, Congress developed the joint-rate schedule to rectify this problem. Unmarried taxpayers who headed families felt they also should receive tax relief because they shared their incomes with their families. So, in 1957, Congress created a rate schedule for heads of households. Below is a discussion of who is covered by each filing status.

SELF-STUDY QUESTION

If Congress were to adopt a truly proportional tax system, would it be necessary to have the four different tax rate schedules?

ANSWER

No, in a proportional tax system, there is no need for different rate schedules because all taxable income would be taxed at the same rate.

JOINT RETURN

Married couples may elect to file joint income tax returns.[29]

- To file a **joint return**, a couple must be legally married as of the last day of the tax year. Common law marriages are recognized. An annulled marriage is viewed as never having been valid.
- The Supreme Court has recognized same-sex marriages.[30] The IRS has applied the decision to same-sex couples who live in states that do not recognize same-sex marriages as long as the couples were married in states or foreign jurisdictions that permit such marriages. The ruling does not apply to civil unions or domestic partnerships.[31]
- Except in the case of death, spouses who file joint tax returns must have the same tax year-end.
- Both spouses must be U.S. citizens or residents. An exception allows a joint return if the nonresident alien spouse agrees to report all of his or her income on the return.[32]

STOP & THINK

Question: Some higher income couples who marry find that their tax liabilities increase even if their combined incomes remain unchanged. Others find that their tax liabilities decrease. Explain why taxes increase for some couples, but decrease for others.

Solution: Couples who marry ordinarily move from two individual returns where incomes are taxed using the rate schedule for single individuals to one return where the combined incomes are taxed using the joint rate schedule. The less progressive joint rate schedule results in a lower tax when one spouse has most of the income because more of that spouse's income is taxed at lower rates. However, when a higher income husband and wife

---

[28] Several states had either adopted or had begun to adopt community property laws in order to reduce the federal taxes paid by their residents. After the joint rate schedule was created, states without a tradition of community property law returned to common law. For a more detailed discussion of community property states, see page I:3-6.

[29] Sec. 6013.

[30] *U.S. v. Edith Windsor,* 111 AFTR2d 2013-2385, 2013-2 USTC ¶50,400. The court declared unconstitutional Sec. 3 of the *Defense of Marriage Act,* which stated that same-sex marriages would not be recognized by the federal government.

[31] Rev. Rul. 2013-17, 2013-38 IRB 201.

[32] Sec. 6013(g). Ordinarily, nonresident aliens are taxed only on U.S.-source income. Permitting a couple to take advantage of the lower tax rates on a joint return while reporting only one spouse's income would result in an unintended tax benefit.

ADDITIONAL COMMENT

Since marital status for the entire year is determined on the last day of the year, some couples actually plan for their wedding to occur on December 31 or January 1. In general, if only one person has income, the wedding should take place on December 31. If both have income, a January 1 wedding is better (for tax purposes).

have approximately equal incomes, their combined incomes are taxed at higher rates on one joint return. Even though the joint rate schedule is the least progressive, the combined tax for higher income couples is greater because the 25% and higher brackets in the joint rate schedule are less than twice as wide as the same brackets for single taxpayers. For example, for the tax year 2015, two single individuals with $85,000 of taxable income each are in the 25% tax bracket, while a married couple with $170,000 of taxable income is in the 28% bracket. This is because the 28% bracket begins at $90,750 for single taxpayers, but at $151,200 for married couples. Assuming the taxable income on the joint return is $170,000, the so-called marriage penalty is $564 because $18,800 of income is taxed at 28% instead of 25%. The additional tax is even greater for taxpayers with higher incomes. Nevertheless, because the lower tax brackets were widened in 2003, the additional tax for married couples is considerably less than it has been in the past.

SURVIVING SPOUSE

A widow or widower can file a joint return for the year his or her spouse dies if the widow or widower does not remarry. For the two years after the year of death, the widow or widower can file as a surviving spouse only if he or she meets specific conditions. The **surviving spouse** (sometimes called a qualifying widow or widower) must[33]

- Have not remarried as of the year end in which surviving spouse status is claimed.
- Be a U.S. citizen or resident.
- Have qualified to file a joint return in the year of death.
- Have at least one dependent son or daughter[34] living at home during the entire year and the taxpayer must pay over half of the expenses of the home.

KEY POINT

The surviving-spouse provision entitles the taxpayer to the lower joint return tax rate schedule and to the higher joint return standard deduction.

In the year of death, a joint return can be filed. On the joint return, the income of the deceased spouse (earned before death) and the survivor are both reported. Personal exemptions are allowed for both spouses. In the two years following death, surviving spouse status can be claimed only if the conditions outlined above are met. Only the surviving spouse's income is reported and, of course, no personal exemption is available for the deceased spouse. What the two situations have in common is that in both instances, the taxpayer can use the more favorable joint rate schedule and standard deduction amount.

EXAMPLE I:2-26 ▶ Connie and Carl are married and have no dependent children. Carl dies in the current year. Connie can file a joint return with Carl even though he did not live the entire year. Alternatively, separate returns can be filed for Connie and Carl applying the rate schedule for married individuals filing separately.

In subsequent years, Connie would file as a single taxpayer. On the other hand, if Connie and Carl had dependent children, Connie could file as a surviving spouse for the two tax years following his death. ◀

STOP & THINK

Question: Most recently-widowed individuals do not qualify for surviving spouse status. Why?

Solution: Most individuals are widowed late in life after their children are grown and have left home. As having a dependent child is a requirement for surviving spouse status, these individuals do not qualify for the special lower tax rate. Such individuals may ordinarily file a joint return in the year of the spouse's death.

ADDITIONAL COMMENT

Due in part to the high divorce rate in this country, the number of head-of-household returns has increased. In 1975, only 6% of all returns had the filing status of head-of-household. In 1996, that number was 11.6%, or 12.0 million returns. By 2012, the number was 15.0% or 21.8 million returns.

HEAD OF HOUSEHOLD

A second rate schedule or tax table is available to a head of household. The head of household rates increase more rapidly than those applicable to married taxpayers filing jointly and surviving spouses, but more slowly than those applicable to other single taxpayers. To claim head-of-household status, a taxpayer must meet all of the following conditions:[35]

[33] Sec. 2(a).
[34] Includes an adopted child or a stepchild, but not a foster child.
[35] Sec. 2(b).

- Be unmarried as of the last day of the tax year. Exceptions apply to individuals married to nonresident aliens[36] and to abandoned spouses.[37] An individual cannot claim head-of-household status in the year his or her spouse died. Such individuals must file a joint return or a separate return.
- Not be a surviving spouse.
- Be a U.S. citizen or resident.
- Pay over half of the costs of maintaining as his or her home a household in which a dependent lives for more than half of the tax year. An exception permits a taxpayer who maintains a household in which a qualifying child[38] lives for more than half of the tax year to claim head-of-household status when the qualifying child is not the taxpayer's dependent. This comes into play in the case of divorced parents when the dependency exemption goes to the non-custodial parent. A second exception permits a taxpayer to claim head-of-household status if he or she maintains a separate household for a dependent parent. This enables the parent to continue living in his or her own home.

EXAMPLE I:2-27 ▶ Brad and Ellen divorce. Ellen receives custody of their child, and Brad is ordered by the court to pay child support of $6,000 per year. Ellen agrees in writing to allow Brad to claim the dependency exemption for the child. If Ellen maintains the home in which she and her child live, she can claim head-of-household status even though the child is Brad's dependent. ◀

ADDITIONAL COMMENT

In 2012, approximately 20 married couples filed joint returns for every married couple that filed separately. 53.7 million married couples filed joint returns during the year.

As noted, the taxpayer must pay over half of the costs of maintaining the household. These expenses include property taxes, mortgage interest, rent, utility charges, upkeep and repairs, property insurance, and food consumed on the premises. Such costs do not include clothing, education, medical treatment, vacations, life insurance, transportation, or the value of services provided by the taxpayer.[39]

SINGLE TAXPAYER

An unmarried individual who does not qualify as a surviving spouse or a head of household must file as a single taxpayer. The tax rates progress more rapidly than those that apply to other unmarried taxpayers.

EXAMPLE I:2-28 ▶ Becky, a single taxpayer with no dependents, files her first tax return. She will file as a single taxpayer. ◀

KEY POINT

Several disadvantages are associated with the filing of separate returns by married individuals. For example, a taxpayer may lose all or part of the benefits of the deduction for individual retirement accounts, the child care credit, and the earned income credit.

MARRIED FILING A SEPARATE RETURN

Married individuals who choose to file separate returns must use the separate rate schedule. The rates on this schedule increase more rapidly than other individual rate schedules. The implications of joint returns versus separate returns are discussed later in this chapter.

EXAMPLE I:2-29 ▶ On December 31, Rose marries Joe. Because they were married before the year ended, they may elect to file jointly. Alternatively, they may file separate returns with each using the rate schedule applicable to separate returns. ◀

The filing requirements for individuals are summarized in Topic Review I:2-2.

KEY POINT

When one thinks of a person who would qualify as an abandoned spouse, one thinks of a person in dire financial condition. If no relief were granted, this person would be required to use the married filing separately tax rate schedule, which contains the highest rates.

ABANDONED SPOUSE

The particular rate schedule a taxpayer uses can have a great impact on the amount of tax. Without any special rule, an abandoned spouse would be required to file using the rate schedules for a married person filing separately. Congress has provided relief for taxpayers in this situation if they can meet certain conditions. A married individual can claim head-of-household status if[40]

---

[36] Specifically, this refers to an individual married to a nonresident alien if he or she meets the remaining head-of-household requirements.

[37] Abandoned spouse rules are discussed under a separate heading later in this chapter.

[38] Qualifying child has the same meaning as is associated with dependency exemptions except that the child cannot be married and must be a U.S. citizen, resident or national.

[39] Reg. Sec. 1.2-2(d).

[40] Sec. 2(c).

TOPIC REVIEW I:2-2

Filing Status and Requirements

Filing Status	Must Maintain Household	Must Have Dependent	Marital Status	Must Be Citizen	Tax Rates
Joint	No requirement	No	Married	Yes	Lowest rates, but two incomes are combined
Surviving spouse	Yes	Yes, son or daughter	Widowed in prior or second prior year	Yes	Uses same schedule as married couple filing joint return
Head of household	Yes	Generally, yes	Generally, single	Yes	Intermediate tax rates
Single	No requirement	No	Single	No	Highest tax rates for unmarried taxpayers
Separate	No requirement	No	Married	No	Highest tax rates

- The taxpayer lived apart from his or her spouse for the last six months of the year.
- The taxpayer pays over half of the cost of maintaining a household in which the taxpayer and a dependent son or daughter live for over half of the year.[41]
- The taxpayer is a U.S. citizen or resident.

The requirement that the taxpayer have a dependent child is met if a taxpayer who is otherwise qualified to claim the child as a dependent signs an agreement that allows the child's noncustodial parent to claim the dependency exemption for the child.[42]

EXAMPLE I:2-30 ▶ In October, Bob and Gail decide to separate. Gail supports their children after the separation and pays the costs of maintaining their home. Gail cannot claim abandoned spouse status because Bob lived with her for over one-half of the year. If she had obtained a divorce before the end of the year, she could have filed as a head of household. In the absence of a divorce, Gail must file a separate return, unless both Bob and Gail agree to file a joint return. ◀

EXAMPLE I:2-31 ▶ Assume the same facts as in Example I:2-30 except that Gail continues to support her children and pay household expenses during the next year. She can file as a head of household even if she has not obtained a divorce. ◀

CHILDREN WITH UNEARNED INCOME

In the past, taxpayers in high tax brackets were able to reduce their tax liability by shifting income to children and other dependents. Under prior law, no tax was due if the income was less than the dependent's personal exemption and standard deduction. Even if the shifted income was greater than these amounts, there was a tax savings if the dependent was in a low tax bracket. Under current law, three rules curtail the advantages of shifting income to dependents:

- Dependents do not receive a personal exemption on their own returns.
- A dependent's standard deduction is reduced to the greater of $1,050 in 2015 ($1,000 in 2014) or the dependent's earned income (such as salary) plus $350 (in both 2014 and 2015).
- The tax on the net unearned income (such as dividends and interest) of a child under age 18 (under age 24 in certain instances described below) is figured by reference to the parents' tax rate if it is higher than the child's rate. This provision is often called the "kiddie tax".

KEY POINT

Children under the age of 18 will not have their net unearned income taxed at their parents' tax rate until the children's unearned income exceeds $2,100.

The first two rules have been discussed previously in this chapter. How the "kiddie tax" is computed depends on the child's age.

---

[41] Includes adopted child, stepchild, and foster child.

[42] Sec. 152(e).

Prior to the year a child turns 18, the kiddie tax applies if the unearned income exceeds the $2,100 threshold in 2015 ($2,000 in 2014). For the year the child turns 18 (and only that year), the kiddie tax applies if child's earned income is less than or equal to one-half of his or her support and unearned income exceeds the $2,100 threshold in 2015 ($2,000 in 2014). From the year a child turns 19 up to and including the year the child turns 23, the kiddie tax applies only if the child is a full-time student, the child's earned income is less than or equal to one-half of his or her support, and unearned income exceeds the $2,100 threshold in 2015 ($2,000 in 2014).

EXAMPLE I:2-32 ▶ In 2015, Tim is an 18-year-old who received $2,400 of interest income and $4,500 from a part-time job. His support, which he paid himself, totaled $8,000. As he is self-supporting, his parent's cannot claim him as a dependent. The kiddie tax does not apply as his earned income exceeds one-half of his support. He is entitled to the regular standard deduction and a personal exemption. He owes no tax as these deductions exceed his income. ◀

EXAMPLE I:2-33 ▶ Assume the same facts as in Example I:2-32 except that Tim's parents provided over one-half of his support. Tim saved his earnings for college. Because Tim is a dependent, he is not entitled to a personal exemption. Tim's standard deduction is limited to the greater of $1,050 or his earned income plus $350 (but not more than $6,300). Because his earned income is $4,500, the standard deduction is $4,850 ($4,500 + $350). Therefore, Tim's taxable income is $2,050 ($6,900 AGI − $4,850 standard deduction). The kiddie tax does not apply as his earned income $4,500 exceeds one-half of his support. The application of the kiddie tax is based on whether the child has earned income, not whether the child is self supporting. Tim's regular tax rate of 10% applies resulting in a tax of $205 (10% × $2,050). ◀

When the kiddie tax applies, part of the net unearned income of the child under age 24 is taxed at the child's rate, and part at the parents' marginal tax rate if that rate is higher than the child's rate. This tax can be computed following a three-step process:

1. Compute the child's taxable income in the normal fashion for dependents as discussed earlier in this chapter.
2. Compute the child's net unearned income:

Unearned income (described below)	$xxx
Less: Statutory deduction of $1,000	(xxx)
Less: Greater of a. $1,000 of standard deduction, or b. Itemized deductions directly connected with the production of the unearned income.	(xxx)
Equals: Net unearned income	$xxx

3. Compute the child's tax:

Net unearned income times parents' marginal tax rate	$xxx
Plus: Difference between taxable income and net unearned income times child's tax rate	xxx
Equals: Child's total tax	$xxx

Unearned income is the child's investment income including dividends, taxable interest, capital gains, rents, royalties and other income that is not earned income (such as salary).[43]

EXAMPLE I:2-34 ▶ Assume the same facts as in Example I:2-32 except that Tim is age 17. His standard deduction is still $4,850 and his taxable income is also $2,050. Since Tim is under age 18, a portion of his unearned income may be subject to tax at his parents' 28% rate. The computation of Tim's tax is as follows:

[43] Sec. 1(g)(4).

1. Compute Tim's taxable income:

Wages		$4,500
Interest income		2,400
Adjusted gross income		$6,900
Standard deduction ($4,500 + $350)	$4,850	
Personal exemption	0	4,850
Taxable income		$2,050

2. Compute Tim's net unearned income:

Unearned income: Interest income	$2,400
Statutory deduction	(1,050)
Portion of standard deduction	(1,050)
Net unearned income	$ 300

3. Compute Tim's tax:

Tax on net unearned income: $300 × 28%	$ 84
Tax on taxable income minus net unearned income: ($2,050 − $300) × 10%	175
Total income tax	$ 259

◀

As discussed in more detail in Chapters I:3 and I:5, dividend income and capital gains are taxed at lower rates than other income. The long-term capital gains and dividend income of individuals in the 25% through 35% brackets are taxed 15%. Individuals in the 10% and 15% tax brackets pay no tax on dividend income or long-term capital gains, while individuals in the 39.6% tax bracket are taxed at 20%. These lower rates also apply to the kiddie tax calculation. In figuring the tax where the parents file separate returns, the tax rate of the parent with the greater taxable income is used. If the parents are divorced, the parent with custody is the relevant parent.

EXAMPLE I:2-35 ▶ Celeste, age 12 and a dependent of her parents, received $2,500 of dividend income. This was her sole source of income during the year. Her parents are in the 25% income tax bracket. Her taxable income is $1,450 ($2,500 dividend − $1,050 standard deduction) and her net unearned income is $400 ($2,500 − $1,050 − $1,050). Her tax is $60 ($1,050 × 0.00 + $400 × 0.15). The first $1,050 of taxable income is taxed at Celeste's rate for dividends, which is 0%, while the balance of her income is taxed at her parents' rate for dividends of 15%. ◀

Parents of a child subject to the kiddie tax may elect to include the child's dividend and interest income on their own return.[44] This rule eliminates the need to file a tax return for the child. To be eligible for the election, the child's gross income must come solely from dividends and interest, and such income must not exceed $10,500 in 2015 ($10,000 in 2014). Furthermore, there can be no withholding or estimated payment using the child's Social Security number. Parents use Form 8814, Parents' Election to Report Child's Interest and Dividends.

STOP & THINK

Question: Jane and Bill have three dependent teen-age children. Jane operates a retail business and Bill farms. They earn over $200,000 each year. Can they use compensation paid to children as a tax saving device?

Solution: The so called "kiddie tax" does not apply to income earned by children. In many instances, parents can employ their children in family businesses and reduce the family's tax. Individual children may be able to perform a variety of services. They may be assigned chores on the farm such as feeding livestock, milking, gathering eggs, or operating equipment. In the retail business they can be assigned tasks such as filing, answering phones, stocking shelves, making deliveries, and operating cash registers.

Jane and Bill can deduct reasonable compensation paid to the children for the services they provide. The payments are deductible by the parents on their return where it would otherwise be taxed at a high rate. Assuming compensation paid to each child is less than

[44] Sec. 1(g)(7).

the amount of the standard deduction, no income tax is owed by them. Assuming the parents continue to provide over one-half of the children's support they remain entitled to dependency exemptions.

Business income and business entities

OBJECTIVE 4

Explain the basic concepts relating to business entities

KEY POINT

The tax formula for C corporations differs from the tax formula for individuals in several important respects. The corporate tax formula does not contain an adjusted gross income figure, personal and dependency exemptions, or the standard deduction.

How business income is reported depends on the type of entity. Proprietors report their business income on Schedule C of Form 1040 (Schedule F in the case of farmers). The income is taxed on the proprietor's Form 1040 along with the taxpayer's other income. Approximately 17 million taxpayers report income on Schedule C each year.

Corporations are divided into two groups: C corporations and S corporations. **C corporations**, also called **regular corporations**, are treated as separate entities for tax purposes and pay income taxes on the corporation's taxable income. Shareholders are taxed on dividends they receive from a C corporation but are not taxed on the corporation's undistributed income. Lower tax rates apply temporarily to dividends received by individual taxpayers. See Chapter I:3. Approximately 2 million corporations file the regular corporate return, Form 1120, each year.

The tax formula for C corporations is presented in Table I:2-7. The major difference between the formulas for individual and corporate taxpayers is the fact that there is only one category of deductions for corporations. Personal expenses do not come into consideration. Therefore, there are no itemized deductions, standard deductions, or personal exemptions. The tax rates applicable to C corporations are as follows:[45]

Taxable Income	*Tax*
First $50,000	15% of taxable income
Over $50,000, but not over $75,000	$7,500 + 25% of taxable income over $50,000
Over $75,000, but not over $100,000	$13,750 + 34% of taxable income over $75,000
Over $100,000, but not over $335,000	$22,250 + 39% of taxable income over $100,000
Over $335,000, but not over $10,000,000	$113,900 + 34% of taxable income over $335,000
Over $10,000,000, but not over $15,000,000	$3,400,000 + 35% of taxable income over $10,000,000
Over $15,000,000, but not over $18,333,333	$5,150,000 + 38% of taxable income over $15,000,000
Over $18,333,333	$6,416,667 + 35% of taxable income over $18,333,333

Note that the corporate tax rates reflect a stair-step pattern of progression, with the two highest rates of 39% and 38% in the middle of the progression. The benefits of the two lowest tax rates of 15% and 25% are completely eliminated by the application of the 39% tax rate to taxable income between $100,000 and $335,000. Likewise, the benefit of the 34% tax rate on taxable income between $335,000 and $10,000,000 is eliminated by the application of a 38% tax rate on taxable income between $15,000,000 and $18,333,333.

The second group of corporations, **S corporations**, generally are not treated as separate entities for tax purposes. They are referred to as flow-through entities. S corporation shareholders are required to report their respective shares of the S corporation's income on their individual tax returns even if the income is not distributed. All shareholders must agree to the S corporation election when it is made. S corporations must also meet a series of conditions, such as having no foreign shareholders. S corporations report ordinary

[45] Income of certain personal service corporations is taxed at a flat rate of 35%.

▼ **TABLE I:2-7**
Tax Formula for C Corporations

Income from whatever source derived	$xxx
Minus: Exclusions	(xxx)
Gross income	$xxx
Minus: Deductions	(xxx)
Taxable income	$xxx
Times: Tax rates	× .xx
Gross tax	$xxx
Minus: Credits and prepayments	(xxx)
Net tax payable or refund due	$xxx

income and special items separately and shareholders in turn report their respective shares of the ordinary income and of each special item. Approximately 4 million corporations file S corporation returns, Form 1120S, each year.

In one sense, there is no formula to compute an S corporation's taxable income because the corporation normally does not pay a tax. S corporations do file returns, but the returns are more informational in nature, much like the returns of a partnership. A residual income total, known as ordinary income, is computed on the return. Special items, such as capital gains and losses and charitable contributions, are kept separate from ordinary income. This is because every item that would receive special treatment on a shareholder's return is passed through to the shareholder with its status intact. Each shareholder reports his or her share of the ordinary income and his or her share of each special item. Losses pass through and generally can be deducted by shareholders up to their respective bases in the corporation's stock. Losses are also subject to other rules, such as the at-risk and passive activity loss rules, which are covered in Chapter I:8.

Partnerships, like S corporations, are flow-through entities for tax purposes. Partners report their respective shares of the partnership's income on their tax returns even if the income is not distributed. Approximately 2 million partnerships file returns, Form 1065, each year. Like S corporations, partnerships report ordinary income and special items separately and the partners report their respective shares of the ordinary income and of each special item. Losses also pass through and generally can be deducted by partners on their returns.

EXAMPLE I:2-36 ▶ Jane is starting Jane's Computer Services and is considering alternative organizational forms. She anticipates the business will earn $100,000 from operations before compensating her for her services and before charitable contributions. Jane, who is single, has $3,000 of income from other sources and other itemized deductions of $11,000. Her compensation for services will be

WHAT WOULD YOU DO IN THIS SITUATION?

CHOICE OF RATE SCHEDULES

Jane Brown married Jim four years ago. Two years ago Jim lost his job. After looking for work for several months, Jim left town to look for work, and Jane has not heard from him. Jim's brother told Jane that he had heard that Jim lived in Texas, but a friend said he heard that Jim had been killed in an automobile accident.

Jane went back to school and completed a program as a medical technician. She returned to work this year, and she earned $35,000. She has asked you to prepare her tax return this year. She has asked you whether she should file as a single taxpayer, married person filing separately, or as a married person filing jointly. Because she has had a low income until recently, she has taken no legal steps to resolve her status. What should she do?

$50,000. Charitable contributions to be made by the business are expected to be $4,000. Other distributions to her from the business are expected to be $15,000. Compare her income tax for 2015 assuming she operates the business as a proprietorship, an S corporation, and a C corporation. Ignore payroll and other taxes.

	Proprietorship	*S Corporation*	*C Corporation*
Business Income			
Operating income	$100,000	$100,000	$100,000
Compensation paid to Jane		(50,000)	(50,000)
Contributions			(4,000)
Net	$100,000	$ 50,000	$ 46,000
Corporate income tax			$ 6,900
Jane's Income			
Business income (above)	$100,000	$ 50,000	
Compensation (above)		50,000	$ 50,000
Dividends			15,000
Other income	3,000	3,000	3,000
Adjusted Gross Income	$103,000	$103,000	$ 68,000
Contributions	($ 4,000)	($ 4,000)	
Other itemized deductions	(11,000)	(11,000)	(11,000)
Personal exemption	(4,000)	(4,000)	(4,000)
Taxable income	$ 84,000	$ 84,000	$ 53,000
Individual income tax	$ 16,794	$ 16,794	$ 7,544
Total tax	$ 16,794	$ 16,794	$ 14,444

In each of the alternatives, Jane reports other income of $3,000 and other itemized deductions of $11,000 on her personal return.

No separate return is filed for the proprietorship. Jane reports the $100,000 income from her business on Schedule C of her Form 1040 and she claims the $4,000 charitable contribution as an itemized deduction on Schedule A along with the other itemized deductions. In this case, whether Jane considers part of the income from the business to be compensation for her services is irrelevant.

With an S election, two returns are filed, a Form 1120S for the corporation and a Form 1040 on Jane's behalf. Because of the S election, the corporation pays no tax. Items reported on the Form 1120S "pass through" the corporation and are reported by Jane on her own return. The $50,000 of compensation paid to Jane by the corporation is deducted by the corporation in computing its income and is taxable to Jane. Jane also reports the remaining $50,000 of the corporation's income on her return and claims the $4,000 charitable contribution as an itemized deduction.

The C corporation is taxed as a separate entity. The corporation files a Form 1120 on which it would deduct the $50,000 of compensation paid to Jane along with the $4,000 charitable contribution and pay a $6,900 (15% × $46,000) tax on the remaining income. Jane reports the $50,000 salary along with the $15,000 dividend distributed by the corporation. Note that the dividend of $15,000 paid by the corporation is not deductible by the corporation. A special provision reduces the "double tax" on the dividends Jane receives from the corporation by subjecting the dividends to a 15% tax rate instead of the 25% rate that would otherwise apply. (See Chapter I:3.) As a result, her tax on the dividends is $2,250 (15% × $15,000) and her tax on her remaining income of $38,000 ($53,000 − $15,000) is $5,294 (from the rate schedule). Her total tax is $7,544. The total tax for the corporation and Jane is $14,444.

As shown, Jane's total current income tax will be lower if she chooses to operate her business as a C corporation even though the $15,000 paid to her as a dividend is taxed twice—once inside the corporation when it is earned and again on Jane's return. The reason the total tax is lower is because the income retained by the corporation is taxed at the corporation's marginal tax rate of 15% instead of being taxed at Jane's marginal rate of 25%. The savings will be lost in the future if the corporation distributes the retained income as a dividend. Clearly, if the plans are to distribute the retained income in the near future, it is desirable to operate as a proprietorship or an S corporation so that the distribution can be made without any future tax.

Self-employment taxes and social security taxes would also be considered when an organizational form is selected for a new business. Although detailed consideration of these taxes is found in Chapter I:14, it is noted here that the self-employment tax, which generally applies to the proprietorship and partnership forms of doing business, would be greater than the social security tax which would apply only to the wages paid to Jane by the S and C corporations. Given the facts in this case, Jane might judge the proprietorship organizational form less favorably when these taxes are taken into consideration. Jane should consider these taxes along with other taxes (e.g., state and local taxes) and other nontax factors such as liability protection before making a final decision. ◀

The detailed rules of C corporations are covered in Chapter I:16 while S corporations and partnerships are covered in Chapter I:17 of the *Individuals* volume. All three are covered more extensively in the *Corporations, Partnerships, Estates, and Trusts* volume and the *Comprehensive* volume.

TREATMENT OF CAPITAL GAINS AND LOSSES

OBJECTIVE 5

Explain the basic concepts of capital gains and losses

Capital gains and losses have been accorded favored tax treatment since 1922. Favored tax treatment essentially means that capital gains are taxed at a lower rate than is ordinary income. A purpose of the special rules is to distinguish capital appreciation from gains attributable to ordinary business transactions and speculation. This goal is accomplished by defining capital assets to not include certain business property (e.g., inventory and trade receivables) and by requiring taxpayers to hold capital assets for minimum time periods in order to benefit from the lower rates that are available to capital gains.

The discussion below is intended as a brief introduction to capital gains and losses. A detailed discussion of this topic is contained in Chapter I:5.

HISTORICAL NOTE

Net capital gains reported on individual income tax returns dropped from nearly $300 billion in 1986 to about $133 billion in 1987. The latter amount was more in line with 1984 and 1985. The large amount reported in 1986 was due to the fact that a 60% long-term capital gain deduction was available to individuals in 1986 but was repealed as of December 31, 1986. Many taxpayers sold capital assets to take advantage of the lower effective rates that existed in 1986.

DEFINITION OF *CAPITAL ASSETS*

A **capital gain** or **loss** is the gain or loss from the sale or exchange of a capital asset. Unfortunately, the tax law merely states what is not a capital asset. In other words, **capital assets** are assets other than those listed in Sec. 1221. A detailed discussion is found in Chapter I:5. Here we simply note the categories of properties included on the list, which are thereby excluded from capital asset status are inventory, trade receivables, certain properties created by the efforts of the taxpayer (such as works of art), depreciable business property and business land, and certain government publications. All other assets are considered capital assets and include investment property (such as stocks and bonds) and personal-use property (such as personal residence or automobile). As noted, a purpose of the rules applicable to capital gains and losses is to distinguish capital appreciation from gains derived from ordinary business operations. The profit from the sale of inventory and trade receivables is viewed as business profit as opposed to capital appreciation. Thus, a gain realized by an artist on the sale of one of his or her own works is ordinary income from personal services. However, gain from the sale of artwork held as an investment or for personal use would be treated as a capital gain.

TAX TREATMENT OF GAINS AND LOSSES

Capital gains and losses are divided into long-term (associated with property held over one year) and short-term (associated with property held one year or less). Individuals in the 10% and 15% tax brackets pay no tax on net long-term capital gains. Individuals in the 25% through 35% brackets are taxed at 15%, and taxpayers in the 39.6% bracket are taxed at 20%. An additional 3.8% tax that applies to investment income, including capital gains and interest, received by higher-income taxpayers is discussed below. A net short-term capital gain is taxed at the same rate as other income.

On the other hand, individuals who suffer net capital losses can deduct only up to $3,000 of the losses from other income. A net capital loss in excess of $3,000 can be carried over and offset against future capital gains or, subject to the $3,000 limitation, deducted from other income.

PROVISIONS APPLICABLE TO HIGHER-INCOME TAXPAYERS

OBJECTIVE 6

Compute the income tax for high-income individuals

In 2013, new rules increased taxes for higher-income taxpayers. Personal and dependency exemptions are now phased out for higher-income taxpayers and itemized deductions are reduced by up to 80%.

Specifically, personal and dependency exemptions are phased out at a rate of 2% for each $2,500 ($1,250 for married persons filing separate returns), or fraction thereof, of AGI above:

	2015	*2014*
Joint return and surviving spouse	$309,900	$305,050
Head-of-households	284,050	279,650
Single	258,250	254,200
Separate	154,950	152,525

These thresholds are adjusted for inflation.

EXAMPLE I:2-37 ► In 2015, Lee, a single taxpayer with one dependent, reports AGI of $200,000. Lee's personal and dependency exemptions of $8,000 ($4,000 × 2) are not subject to the phase-out. ◄

EXAMPLE I:2-38 ► In 2015, Jane, a single taxpayer with one dependent, reports AGI of $306,050. Jane's personal and dependency exemptions are reduced as follows:

Gross personal and dependency exemption amount		$8,000
Excess AGI ($306,050 − $258,250)	$47,800	
Phase-out multiples (rounded up) ($47,800/$2,500)	20	
Reduction ($8,000 × 20 × 2%)		(3,200)
Net personal and dependency exemption amount		$4,800

◄

Itemized deductions are reduced by 3% of AGI in excess of the same thresholds. The reduction cannot exceed 80% of the total itemized deductions (discussed in more detail in Chapter I:7).

EXAMPLE I:2-39 ► Jane, from Example I: 2-38,has $10,000 of home mortgage interest and property taxes of $6,000. Her gross itemized deductions of $16,000 are reduced by $1,434 [3% × ($306,050 − $258,250)] to $14,566. ◄

The phase-out of itemized deductions for higher-income taxpayers is discussed in more detail in Chapter I:7.

In addition, taxes enacted in 2010 as part of the Affordable Care Act became effective in 2013. A new payroll tax of 0.9% applies to earned income over $200,000 ($250,000 for married couples). An additional 3.8% tax applies to the lesser of investment income (including interest, capital gains, and dividends) or AGI in excess of $200,000 ($250,000 for married couples). These thresholds are not adjusted for inflation.

Tax planning considerations

OBJECTIVE 7

Describe tax planning considerations for various tax matters

SHIFTING INCOME BETWEEN FAMILY MEMBERS

Because of the progressive tax system, families often can reduce their taxes by **shifting income** to family members who are in lower tax brackets.

EXAMPLE I:2-40 ▶ Mary, who is in the 39.6% tax bracket, shifted $5,000 of income to her 25-year-old son, Steve, by making a gift of a 10%, $50,000 corporate bond. Steve had no income as he suffered a business loss. In absence of the shift, 39.6% of the income would have gone for taxes. There is no tax on Steve's return because the income is offset by his loss. ◀

EXAMPLE I:2-41 ▶ Farouk, who is in the 39.6% tax bracket, shifted $2,000 of interest income to his 25-year-old daughter, Dana, who is in the 10% tax bracket. The tax savings from the shift is $592 [(0.396 × $2,000) − (0.10 × $2,000)]. ◀

ADDITIONAL COMMENT

All 50 states have enacted laws that simplify the procedures for making gifts to minors. This type of law, which in most states is called the Uniform Gifts to Minors Act, is especially important when making gifts of securities.

As noted earlier in this chapter, the net unearned income of children under the age of 24 is taxed at their parents' tax rate. Hence, a shifting of income to young children is often an ineffective method of minimizing tax.

Shifting income must be distinguished from assigning income. Earned income is taxed to the person who produces it. Income from property is taxed to the person who owns the property. Ordering income to be paid to another is an assignment of income that does not change who is taxed on the income. Normally, in the case of income from property, ownership of the property must be transferred in order to shift the income.

EXAMPLE I:2-42 ▶ John owns stock in Valley Corporation. John orders the corporation to pay this year's dividends to his daughter. John will be taxed on the income even though he has assigned it to another person. ◀

EXAMPLE I:2-43 ▶ Kay owns stock in Valley Corporation. Kay gives the stock to her 25-year-old son. Future dividends on Valley stock will be taxed to the son instead of to Kay. ◀

Individuals often are unwilling to give property away completely. As a result, personal preference may limit the amount of tax planning that is possible.

SPLITTING INCOME

Splitting income consists of creating additional taxable entities, especially corporations, in order to reduce an individual's effective tax rate.

EXAMPLE I:2-44 ▶ Tom is a taxpayer in the 39.6% tax bracket and is involved in a variety of businesses. One business has been producing $20,000 of income per year for several years. Tom incorporates the business. The first $50,000 of a corporation's income is taxed at a 15% rate. Thus, the tax on the income is reduced by $4,920 [(0.396 × $20,000) − (0.15 × $20,000)]. ◀

The creation of a new corporate entity to split income is not always desirable because the corporation's income will be taxed to the shareholder as a dividend if it is distributed.

In addition, if income is allowed to accumulate in a corporation indefinitely, it may be subject to the accumulated earnings tax.[45]

KEY POINT

The ability to maximize itemized deductions by the timing of expenditures is somewhat limited. The two most significant items that would lend themselves to such a strategy are property taxes and charitable contributions. Prepaid interest is not deductible until accrued.

MAXIMIZING ITEMIZED DEDUCTIONS

Timing expenditures properly often can increase deductions. In general, cash-basis taxpayers deduct expenses in the year paid. If itemized deductions are less than the standard deduction, the taxpayer will receive no tax benefit from the deductions. A taxpayer in that situation could defer some payments or accelerate others to maximize expenses in one year, thereby creating a sufficient amount of deductions in that year.

EXAMPLE I:2-45 ▶ Jean's property taxes are due on January 1 of each year. Jean is a single, cash-basis, calendar-year taxpayer. Itemized deductions other than property taxes total $4,000 in each year. Jean pays the 2015 property taxes of $1,600 on January 1, 2015, and the 2016 property taxes of $1,600 on December 31, 2015. In the absence of doubling up, Jean would not be able to itemize in either year. The itemized deductions of $5,600 ($4,000 + $1,600) would be less than the standard deduction of $6,300. By doubling up, Jean has itemized deductions of $7,200 ($4,000 + $1,600 + $1,600) in 2015. ◀

Medical expenses are deductible only to the extent they exceed 10% of a taxpayer's AGI. In situations where medical expenses are just under the AGI threshold, taxpayers may be able to create a deduction by doubling up.

EXAMPLE I:2-46 ▶ Troy's AGI is $20,000. So far in 2015, Troy's medical expenses have totaled $1,800. Troy has received a bill from his dentist for $500 that is due January 15, 2016. By paying the bill in 2015, Troy will have a deduction for medical expenses of $300 [$1,800 + $500 − (0.10 × $20,000)]. This assumes that Troy's other itemized deductions exceed the standard deduction.[47] ◀

FILING JOINT OR SEPARATE RETURNS

Factors to be Considered. In general, married couples may file either joint or separate returns. As noted earlier, if one spouse has significantly more than half of their combined income, filing separately will increase the couple's total income tax. Because of the potential tax saving from a joint return and because it is simpler to prepare one return than two, most married couples file jointly.

It should be noted that the joint return is not always preferred. Separate returns may result in increased deductions. Because only one spouse's income is reported on a separate return, medical expenses are more likely to exceed the 10% of adjusted gross income floor if one spouse incurs most of the medical expenses. Similarly, casualty losses involving personal-use assets, which are allowable only to the extent that they exceed 10% of AGI, may be deductible on separate returns.

One significant impact of the joint return is the joint income tax liability. Both the husband and wife may be liable for taxes owed on a joint return. This could be a major problem if a couple separates or divorces after filing a return.

EXAMPLE I:2-47 ▶ Jim and Pat file a joint return. They are both informed as to the relevant information pertaining to the return. The next year they separate, and Jim moves out of town without leaving a forwarding address. The IRS audits their joint return and disallows $400 of charitable contributions

[46] Amounts accumulated in a corporation in excess of $250,000 may be subject to this tax. However, amounts accumulated for business purposes are exempt. This subject is discussed briefly in Chapter I:16 and extensively in *Prentice Hall's Federal Taxation: Corporations, Partnerships, Estates and Trusts.*

[47] For a discussion of restrictions on the deductibility of prepaid medical expenses, see Chapter I:7.

deducted on the original return. Pat may be held responsible for the additional taxes owed. The IRS does not have to attempt to locate Jim in order to collect the tax. ◀

ETHICAL POINT

Because innocent spouse rules are strict, it may sometimes be safer to file a separate return than run the risk of being held responsible for the acts of another.

Innocent Spouse Provision. When married couples file a joint return, each spouse generally is liable for the entire tax and any penalties imposed.[48] This is the case even if all of the income was earned by one spouse. This rule could prove unfair in some instances, especially where one spouse concealed information from the other. For that reason, the Code contains an **innocent spouse** provision. An innocent spouse is relieved of the liability for tax on unreported income if:

- The amount is attributable to erroneous items of the other spouse.
- The innocent spouse did not know and had no reason to know that there was such an understatement of tax.
- Under the circumstances, it would be inequitable to hold the innocent spouse liable for the understatement.
- The innocent spouse elects relief within two years after the IRS begins collection activities.[49]

EXAMPLE I:2-48 ▶ Dan and Joy file a joint return. Dan traveled much of the time and Joy had little information as to his whereabouts or income. Joy worked and her own salary was the sole source of her support. Their return was audited by the IRS. The audit disclosed that Dan had not reported income from a job he had held for several months during the year. In this situation, Joy may be able to use the innocent spouse provision in order to avoid being held liable for the tax on the unreported income. ◀

The election is permitted when the innocent spouse was aware of the understatement, but did not know or have reason to know the extent of the understatement. Relief is limited to the portion of the understatement attributable to the "unknown" amounts.

Separate Liability Election. Couples who file joint returns and are subsequently divorced, widowed, or separated may make a separate liability election. An electing spouse is liable only for the portion of any understatement attributable to him or her.

EXAMPLE I:2-49 ▶ Al and Ann divorce after filing a joint return. An IRS examination of the return reveals $20,000 of unreported income attributable to Al and $10,000 of unallowable deductions attributable to Ann. Together, these amounts result in an understatement of their tax by $9,000. If Ann can establish that she was unaware of Al's unreported income, she can make a separate liability election. She will be liable only for $3,000 of tax as she is responsible for only one third of the understatement. The allocation would not be different because only part of the deductions were disallowed because of an AGI floor. ◀

The election must be made within two years after the IRS begins collections efforts. The election may be made by both spouses. The election is invalid if the spouse responsible for the errors transfers assets to the "innocent" spouse in an effort to avoid payment.

Electing to Change to a Joint Return. In general, a husband and wife who file separate returns for a given year may elect to change to a joint return by filing an amended joint return. This change is permitted after the due date but must occur within three years of the due date including extensions. Taxpayers may not change from a joint return to separate returns after the due date.[50]

---

[48] Sec. 6013(d)(3).
[49] Sec. 6015(b).

[50] Reg. Sec. 1.6013-1(a). However, a couple who filed a joint return whose marriage is later annulled must file amended returns as singles (Rev. Rul. 76-255, 1976-2 C.B. 40).

COMPLIANCE AND PROCEDURAL CONSIDERATIONS

OBJECTIVE 8

Describe compliance and procedural matters for filing tax returns

ADDITIONAL COMMENT

The IRS is encouraging nonfilers (i.e., individuals and businesses who should have filed previous tax returns but did not) to come forward. The IRS estimates that approximately 10 million people fail to file their income tax returns each year.

WHO MUST FILE

Whether an individual must file a tax return is based on the amount of the individual's gross income.[51] The fact that the individual owes no tax does not mean that a return need not be filed. The gross income filing levels for taxpayers under age 65 are as follows:[52]

	2014	*2015*
Single	$ 10,150	$ 10,300
Married, filing jointly	20,300	20,600
Surviving spouse	16,350	16,600
Married, filing separately	3,950	4,000
Married, living separately from spouse at year-end	3,950	4,000
Head of household	13,050	13,250

There are three situations where taxpayers must file even if the gross income is less than the amounts shown above:

- Taxpayers who receive advance payments of the earned income credit (see Chapter I:14) must file regardless of their income levels.
- Taxpayers with net self-employment income of $400 or more must file regardless of their total gross income.
- Taxpayers who can be claimed as a dependent by another must file if they have either unearned income over $1,050 or total gross income over the standard deduction.

In general, taxpayers must file if their gross income equals or exceeds the sum of the personal exemption and the standard deduction (including the additional standard deduction due to age but not blindness). The blindness allowance and dependency exemptions are not considered. If the disallowance of the standard deduction rules apply, the standard deduction is ignored in determining whether taxpayers must file.

EXAMPLE I:2-50 ▶ In 2015, Carol is a single, self-supporting taxpayer with no dependents. Carol must file if her gross income is $10,300 or greater ($6,300 + $4,000). ◀

KEY POINT

It is possible that a taxpayer may be required to file an income tax return but still have no tax liability.

DUE DATES AND EXTENSIONS

Returns for individuals and partnerships are due on the fifteenth day of the fourth month following the close of the tax year, which for calendar-year taxpayers is April 15.[53] Returns for C corporations and S corporations are due on the fifteenth day of the third month following the close of the tax year, which for calendar-year corporations is March 15.[54] A due date that falls on a Saturday, Sunday, or a holiday is automatically extended to the next day that is not a Saturday, Sunday, or holiday.[55] As noted, individuals are required to file only if their gross income exceeds prescribed thresholds. Partnerships and corporations, however, are required to file even if they have no gross income.

Individuals may obtain an automatic extension of six months by filing Form 4868 (Application for Automatic Extension of Time to File U.S. Individual Income Tax Return). C corporations and S corporations may obtain an automatic extension of six months by filing Form 7004. Partnerships may obtain a 5 month extension by filing Form 7004.

[51] *Gross income* has its usual meaning except that the gain excluded from the sale of a personal residence and excluded foreign earned income are included (Sec. 6012(c)).
[52] Sec. 6012(a)(1).
[53] Sec. 6072(a).
[54] Sec. 6072(b).
[55] Sec. 7503.

An extension to file a return is not an extension to pay any tax that is owed. Taxpayers must project their tax liability to the best of their ability and remit with the extension any amount that has not been prepaid through withholding or estimated payments. Interest and penalty may apply to amounts paid after the regular due date. See Chapter C:15 in the *Comprehensive* volume and the *Corporations, Partnerships, Estates, and Trusts* volume for more on payment requirements.

	Individuals	*Partnerships*	*Corporations*
Returns	Forms 1040, 1040A, 1040EZ	Form 1065	Forms 1120, 1120S
Return due date	15th day of 4th month	15th day of 4th month	15th day of 3rd month
Automatic extension	Form 4868 (6 months)	Form 7004 (5 months)	Form 7004 (6 months)

ADDITIONAL COMMENT

In 2013, of the 145 million returns filed, nearly 121 million returns were filed electronically, or 83.4%. This compares with 73 million electronic returns in 2006.

USE OF FORMS 1040, 1040EZ, AND 1040A

The primary individual tax return is Form 1040. Complicated returns often involve many additional forms and schedules. Two shorter forms are available to taxpayers with less-complicated tax returns. Form 1040EZ is available to single taxpayers and married individuals who file a joint return. Such taxpayers must have taxable income of less than $50,000 and claim no dependents. To use Form 1040EZ, the taxpayer's income must consist of salary and wages plus no more than $1,500 of taxable interest income. No deductions (other than the standard deduction) or credits (other than withholding from salary and wages) can be taken on the return.

Form 1040A is available to taxpayers who have somewhat more involved returns. Form 1040A can be used by taxpayers claiming any number of exemptions or any filing status. Salary, wages, dividends, interest, pension and annuity income, and unemployment compensation can be reported on Form 1040A. Taxpayers may deduct IRA contributions. Taxpayers may also claim credits for withholding, child care, and earned income.

SELF-STUDY QUESTION

It is sometimes said that the hallmark of the U.S. federal income tax system is voluntary compliance. With so much information being reported to the IRS, how voluntary is the system?

ANSWER

The system is not very voluntary with respect to income subject to reporting. But some sources of income, such as income from self-employment, are not subject to reporting by a third party. Also, the IRS would have to audit a tax return to verify most of the deductions.

SYSTEM FOR REPORTING INCOME

There is a significant and expanding relationship between computers, tax returns, the taxpayer identification system, and information returns. The IRS keeps records based on taxpayer identification numbers. Individual taxpayers report information based on Social Security numbers, whereas employer identification numbers (EIN) are used by corporations, other taxpayers, and tax-exempt entities. Individuals who employ others have both a Social Security number and an employer identification number.

Employers, banks, stockbrokers, savings and loans, and so on report payments they make to others along with the payee's identification number. Today, the IRS computers match much of the reported information with tax returns, using the taxpayer identification number as the cross-reference. The need for accurate information returns is obvious. Some major information returns are listed below:

Basic Form	*Type of Payment*	*Required if Amount Equals or Exceeds*
1099-R	Pensions and annuities including lump sum distributions	$600
W-2	Salary, wages, etc.	600
1099-DIV	Dividends	10
1099-INT	Interest	600[56]
1099-B	Sale of a security	All
1099-G	Unemployment compensation, tax refunds, etc.	10
1099-MISC	Rent, royalties, etc.	600

This information-reporting system makes it more difficult for taxpayers to avoid IRS detection if they omit income from their returns.

[56] For banks and corporations the amount is $10.

PROBLEM MATERIALS

DISCUSSION QUESTIONS

I:2-1 a. The tax law refers to gross income, yet the term gross income is not found on Form 1040. Explain.
b. Why is it important to understand the concept of gross income even though the term is not found on Form 1040?

I:2-2 Explain the distinction between income and gross income.

I:2-3 a. Explain the distinction between a deduction and a credit.
b. Which is worth more, a $10 deduction or a $10 credit?
c. Explain the difference between refundable and nonrefundable credits.

I:2-4 List the conditions that must be met in order to claim a dependency exemption for qualifying children and qualifying relatives. Briefly explain each one.

I:2-5 a. Briefly explain the concept of support.
b. If a taxpayer provides 50% or less of another person's support, is it possible for the taxpayer to claim a dependency exemption? Explain.
c. Does support include the value of an automobile? Explain.

I:2-6 Under what circumstances must a taxpayer use a rate schedule instead of a tax table?

I:2-7 a. What determines who must file a tax return?
b. Is an individual required to file a tax return if he or she owes no tax?

I:2-8 Many homeowners itemize deductions while many renters claim the standard deduction. Explain.

I:2-9 Tax rules are often very precise. For example, a taxpayer must ordinarily provide "over 50%" of another person's support in order to claim a dependency exemption. Why is the threshold "over 50%" as opposed to "50% or more?"

I:2-10 What is the normal due date for the tax return of calendar-year taxpayers? What happens to the due date if it falls on a Saturday, Sunday, or holiday?

I:2-11 Sometimes taxpayers may not be able to file their tax returns by the normal due date. Are extensions available? How long are the extensions? Do extensions enable taxpayers to delay paying the tax they owe?

I:2-12 Can tax-exempt income qualify as support? Explain.

I:2-13 Can a scholarship qualify as support?

I:2-14 Explain the purpose of the multiple support agreement.

I:2-15 Summarize the rules that explain which parent receives the dependency exemption for children in cases of divorce.

I:2-16 What conditions must be met by a married couple before they can file a joint return?

I:2-17 Explain what is meant by the phrase *maintain a household.*

I:2-18 Under what circumstances, if any, can a married person file as a head of household?

I:2-19 a. Explain the principal difference in the tax treatment of an S corporation and a C corporation.
b. Why would a C corporation be used if an S corporation is generally exempt from tax?

I:2-20 Income earned by C corporations is taxed twice, once when the income is earned and again when it is distributed. If so, how is it possible that operating a business as a C corporation can reduce taxes.

I:2-21 a. What assets are excluded from capital asset status?
b. Are capital gains given favorable tax treatment?
c. What is the significance of an asset being classified as a capital asset?
d. Are capital losses deductible?

I:2-22 Is there any tax advantage for an individual who has held an appreciated capital asset for eleven months to delay the sale of the asset? Explain.

I:2-23 a. Explain the difference between income splitting and income shifting.
b. Why are taxpayers interested in shifting income from one tax return to another within the same family or economic unit?
c. Is there a relationship between the tax on unearned income of a minor and taxpayers who attempt to shift income?

I:2-24 a. Who is liable for additional taxes on a joint return?
b. Why is this so important?

I:2-25 Can couples change from joint returns to separate returns? Separate to joint?

ISSUE IDENTIFICATION QUESTIONS

I:2-26 This year, Yung Tseng, a U.S. citizen, supported his nephew who is attending school in the United States. Yung is a U.S. citizen, but his nephew is a citizen of Hong Kong. The nephew has a student visa, but he hopes to become a permanent U. S. resident. Other family members hope to come to the U.S. What issues must be considered by Yung?

I:2-27 Carmen and Carlos, who have filed joint tax returns for several years, separated this year. Carlos works in construction and is often paid in cash. Carlos says he only worked a few weeks this year and made $11,000. In prior years he made approximately $35,000 per year, and Carmen is surprised that his income is so low this year. Carmen received a salary of $38,000 as a medical laboratory technician. They have no dependents and claim the standard deduction. What tax issues should Carmen and Carlos consider?

I:2-28 Jane and Bill have lived in a home Bill inherited from his parents. Their son Jim lives with them. Bill and Jane obtain a divorce during the current year. Under the terms of the divorce, Jane receives possession of the home for a period of five years and custody of Jim. Bill is obligated to furnish over one-half of the cost of the maintenance, taxes, and insurance on the home and pay $6,000 of child support per year. Bill lives in an apartment. What tax issues should Jane and Bill consider?

PROBLEMS

I:2-29 *Computation of Tax.* The following information relates to two married couples:

	Lanes	*Waynes*
Salary (earned by one spouse)	$32,000	$115,000
Interest income	1,000	10,000
Deductible IRA contribution	5,000	0
Itemized deductions	15,000	15,000
Exemptions	8,000	8,000
Withholding	700	18,700

Compute the 2015 tax due or refund due for each couple. Assume that the itemized deductions have been reduced by the applicable floors. Ignore credits.

I:2-30 *Computation of Taxable Income.* The following information relates to Tom, a single taxpayer, age 18:

Salary	$1,800
Interest income	1,600
Itemized deductions	600

a. Compute Tom's taxable income assuming he is self-supporting.
b. Compute Tom's taxable income assuming he is a dependent of his parents.

I:2-31 *Joint Versus Separate Returns.* Carl and Carol have salaries of $14,000 and $22,000, respectively. Their itemized deductions total $8,500. They are married and both are under age 65.
a. Compute their taxable income assuming they file jointly.
b. Compute their taxable incomes assuming they file separate returns and that Carol claims all of the itemized deductions.

I:2-32 *Joint Versus Separate Returns.* Hal attended school much of 2015, during which time he was supported by his parents. Hal married Ruth in December 2015. Hal graduated and commenced work in 2016. Ruth worked during 2015 and earned $18,000. Hal's only income was $1,100 of interest. Hal's parents are in the 28% tax bracket. Thus, claiming Hal as a dependent would save them $1,120 (0.28 × $4,000) of taxes.
a. Compute Hal and Ruth's gross tax if they file a joint return.
b. Compute Ruth's gross tax if she files a separate return in order to allow Hal's parents to claim him as a dependent.
c. Which alternative would be better for the family? In other words, will filing a joint return save Hal and Ruth more than $1,120?

I:2-33 *Dependency Exemptions.* Wes and Tina are a married couple and provide financial assistance to several persons during the current year. For the situations below, determine whether the individuals qualify as Wes and Tina's dependents. In all of the situations below, assume that any dependency tests not mentioned have been met.

a. Brian is age 24 and Wes and Tina's son. He is a full-time student and lives in an apartment near campus. Wes and Tina provide over 50% of his support. Brian works as a waiter and earned $4,200.
b. Same as Part a except that Brian is a part-time student.
c. Sherry is age 22 and Wes and Tina's daughter. She is a full-time student and lives in the college dormitory. Wes and Tina provide over 50% of her support. Sherry works part-time as a bookkeeper and earned $5,000.
d. Same as Part c except that Sherry is a part-time student.
e. Granny, age 82, is Tina's grandmother and lives with Wes and Tina. During the current year, Granny's only sources of income were her Social Security of $4,800 and interest on U.S. bonds of $4,500. Granny uses her income to pay for 40% of her total support, Wes and Tina provide the remainder of Granny's support.

I:2-34 *Dependency Exemptions.* John and Carole file a joint return and have three children: Jack, age 23; David, age 20; and Kristen, age 15. All three children live at home the entire year. Below is information about each of the children:

- Jack: graduated from college last year and will start medical school next year. This year, Jack worked sparingly as he studied for the medical school entrance exam, but did earn $5,000. John and Carole provided 80% of Jack's support during the year.
- David: a full-time student at State U., earned $6,400 from a part-time job, and provided 40% of his own support.
- Kristen: a full-time student in high school, had no gross income, and provided none of her own support.

a. Based on the above facts, which of the children can be claimed by John and Carole this year?
b. How would your answer to Part a change if Jack began medical school this year?
c. How would your answer to Part a change if Jack earned $3,000 rather than $5,000?
d. How would your answer to Part a change if David was a part-time student rather than a full-time student?
e. How would your answer to Part a change if David provided 60% of his own support rather than 40%?

I:2-35 *Dependency Exemptions and Child Credit.* Robert provides much of the support for his daughter, Jane, and her two children. Jane earned $20,000. Robert, whose AGI is $350,000, paid the rent of $11,000 on Jane's apartment and provided an additional $15,000 support. Jane is age 30, and her children are age 7 and age 4.

a. Can Robert claim a dependency exemption for Jane?
b. Can Jane claim her children as dependents?
c. Who is entitled to the child credit?

I:2-36 *Dependency Exemptions.* Juan helps support his mother Maria, his son Jose, and a niece Norma. How many dependency exemptions can Juan claim given these additional facts?

Maria lives with Juan. She receives $12,000 of Social Security benefits which she uses to pay for food, clothing, medical expenses, and other living expenses. Juan provides Maria's room which has a rental value of $5,000 and pays an additional $4,000 toward her support.

Jose, age 12, lives with his mother, Linda. Juan pays $12,000 per year child support, and Linda provides an additional $4,000 of support.

Norma, age 20, is a part-time college student who lives in an apartment. She earned $6,000 working part-time and received a scholarship of $2,000. Norma's father provided $4,000 toward her support, and Juan provided $7,000.

I:2-37 *Dependency Exemptions.* Anna, age 65, who lives with her unmarried son, Mario, received $7,000, which was used for her support during the year. The sources of support were as follows:

Social Security benefits	$1,500
Mario	2,600
Caroline, an unrelated friend	800
Doug, Anna's son	500
Elaine, Anna's sister	1,600
Total	$7,000

a. Who is eligible to claim Anna as a dependent?
b. What must be done before Mario can claim the exemption?
c. Can anyone claim head-of-household status based on Anna's dependency exemption? Explain.
d. Can Mario claim an old age allowance for his mother? Explain.

I:2-38 *Dependency Exemption and Child Credit: Divorced Parents.* Joe and Joan divorce during the current year. Joan receives custody of their three children. Joe agrees to pay $5,000 of child support for each child.
a. Assuming no written agreement, who will receive the dependency exemption and child credit for the children? Explain.
b. Would it make any difference if Joe could prove that he provided over one-half of the support for each child?

I:2-39 *Filing Status, Dependency Exemptions, and Child Credit.* For the following taxpayers, indicate which tax form should be used, the applicable filing status, and the number of personal and dependency exemptions available, and the number of children who qualify for the child credit.
a. Arnie is a single college student who earned $7,700 working part-time. He had $200 of interest income and received $1,000 of support from his parents.
b. Buddy is a single college student who earned $7,700 working part-time. He had $1,600 of interest income and received $1,000 of support from his parents.
c. Cindy is divorced and received $6,000 of alimony from her former husband and earned $12,000 working as a secretary. She also received $1,800 of child support for her son who lives with her. According to a written agreement, her former husband is entitled to receive the dependency exemption.
d. Debbie is a widow, age 68, who receives a pension of $8,000, nontaxable social security benefits of $8,000, and interest of $4,000. She has no dependents.
e. Edith is married, but her husband left her two years ago and she has not seen him since. Edith supported herself and her daughter, age 6. She paid all household expenses. Her income of $26,000 consisted of a salary of $25,200 and interest of $800.

I:2-40 *Dependency Exemptions and Child Credit.* How many dependency exemptions are the following taxpayers entitled to, assuming the people involved are U.S. citizens? Which dependents qualify for the child credit?
a. Andrew supports his cousin Mary, who does not live with him. Mary has no income and is single.
b. Bob and Ann are filing a joint return. Bob provided over one-half of his father's support. The father received Social Security benefits of $6,000 and taxable interest income of $800. The father is single and does not live with them.
c. Clay provides 60% of his single daughter's support. She earned $3,000 while attending school during the year as a full-time student. She is 22 years old.
d. Dave provided 30% of his mother's support and she provided 55% of her own support. Dave's brother provided the remainder. The brother agreed to sign a multiple support agreement.

I:2-41 *Dependency Exemptions, Child Credits, Tax Rate Schedules, and Divorce.* Juan and Maria, who have two young children, are in the process of obtaining a divorce. Juan expects to have $200,000 of income each year while Maria expects to have $60,000 of income each year. Assume the children will live with Maria after the divorce and that Juan will pay child support.
a. What advice can you provide them regarding the dependency exemptions for the children?
b. What advice can you provide them regarding the child credit?
c. What advice can you provide regarding tax rate schedules?

I:2-42 *Marriage and Taxes.* Bill and Mary plan to marry in December 2015. Bill's salary is $32,000 and he owns his residence. His itemized deductions total $12,000. Mary's salary is $39,000. Her itemized deductions total only $1,600 as she does not own her residence. For purposes of this problem, assume 2016 tax rates, exemptions, and standard deductions are the same as 2015.
a. What will their tax be if they marry before year-end and file a joint return?
b. What will their combined taxes be for the year if they delay the marriage until 2016?
c. What factors contribute to the difference in taxes?

I:2-43 *Filing Requirement.* Which of the following taxpayers must file a 2015 return?
a. Amy, age 19 and single, has $8,050 of wages, $800 of interest, and $350 of self-employment income.
b. Betty, age 67 and single, has a taxable pension of $9,100 and Social Security benefits of $6,200.

c. Chris, age 15 and single, is a dependent of his parents. Chris has earned income of $1,900 and interest of $400.
d. Dawn, age 15 and single, is a dependent of her parents. She has earned income of $400 and interest of $1,600.
e. Doug, age 25, and his wife are separated. He earned $5,000 while attending school during the year.

I:2-44 *Head of Household.* In the following situations, indicate whether the taxpayer qualifies as a head of household.
a. Allen is divorced from his wife. He maintains a household for himself and his dependent mother.
b. Beth is divorced from her husband. She maintains a home for herself and supports an elderly aunt who lives in a retirement home.
c. Cindy was widowed last year. She maintains a household for herself and her dependent daughter, who lived with her during the year.
d. Dick is not divorced, but lived apart from his wife for the entire year. He maintains a household for himself and his dependent daughter. He does not receive any financial support from his wife.

I:2-45 *Filing Status.* For the following independent situations, determine the optimum filing status for the years in question.
a. Wayne and Celia had been married for 24 years before Wayne died in an accident in 2013. Celia and her son, Wally, age 21 in 2013, continued to live at home in 2013, 2014, 2015, and 2016. Wally worked part-time (earning $5,000 in each of the four years) and attended the university on a part-time basis. Celia provided more than 50% of Wally's support for all four years. What is Celia's filing status for 2013, 2014, 2015, and 2016?
b. Juanita is a single parent who maintained a household for her unmarried son Josh, age 19. Josh worked full-time and earned $16,000. Juanita provided approximately 40% of Josh's support but provided all the expenses of maintaining the household. What is Juanita's filing status?
c. Gomer and Gertrude are married and have one dependent son. In April, Gomer left Gertrude a note informing her that he needed his freedom and he was leaving her. As of December, Gertrude had not seen nor heard a word from Gomer since April. Gertrude fully supported her son and completely maintained the household. What is Gertrude's filing status assuming she was still legally married?

I:2-46 *Computation of Taxable Income.* Jim and Pat are married and file jointly. In 2015, Jim earned a salary of $46,000. Pat is self-employed. Her gross business income was $49,000 and her business expenses totaled $24,000. Each contributed $5,000 to a deductible IRA. Their itemized deductions total $13,000. Compute Parts a, b, and c without regard to self-employment tax.
a. Compute their gross income.
b. Compute their adjusted gross income.
c. Compute their taxable income assuming they have a dependent daughter.

I:2-47 *Itemized versus Standard Deduction.* Jan, a single taxpayer, has adjusted gross income of $250,000, medical expenses of $10,000, home mortgage interest of $3,000, property taxes of $2,000. and miscellaneous itemized deductions of $3,500. Should she itemize or claim the standard deduction?

I:2-48 *Kiddie Tax.* Debbie is 23 years old, a full-time student and a dependent of her parents. She earns $4,200 working part-time and receives $2,200 interest on savings. She saves both the salary and interest. What is her taxable income? Would her taxable income or tax be different if Debbie were 16 years old?

I:2-49 *Computation of Taxable Income.* John and Georgia are a married couple with two dependent sons. Their salaries total $130,000. They have a capital loss of $8,000 and tax-exempt interest income of $1,000. They paid home mortgage interest of $10,000, state income taxes of $4,000, and medical expenses of $3,000, and they made charitable contributions of $5,000.
a. Compute their adjusted gross income.
b. Compute their total itemized deductions.
c. What is the amount of their personal exemptions?
d. Compute their taxable income.

I:2-50 *Kiddie Tax.* Mike and Linda have three dependent children who are full-time students in 2015. Mike and Linda's taxable income is $180,000 and they provided $8,000 of support for each child. Information for each child is as follows:

	Karen	*Susan*	*Amelie*
Age	21	18	16
Wages	$3,000	$4,500	$5,900
Interest income	2,800	2,400	2,200

Compute each child's tax.

I:2-51 *Computation of Tax.* Georgia, a single taxpayer, operates a business that produces $100,000 of income before any amounts are paid to her. She has no dependents and no other income. She has itemized deductions of $18,000. Compute the *total* income tax that would be paid assuming the following additional facts. Ignore payroll taxes.

a. Georgia operates the business as an S corporation receiving a salary from the corporation of $60,000. The corporation distributes all of its remaining income to the shareholders.
b. She operates the business as a C corporation receiving a salary from the corporation of $60,000. The corporation distributes its after tax income to her as a dividend.
c. How would the total tax change in each of the first two requirements if the corporation made no payments to the owner other than the salary?

I:2-52 *Child Credit.* In 2015, Lana, a single taxpayer with AGI of $85,400, claims exemptions for three dependent children, all under age 17. What is the amount of her child credit?

I:2-53 *Capital Gains and Losses.* Bob and Anna are in the 39.6% tax bracket for ordinary income and the 20% bracket for capital gains (ignore the 3.8% additional tax on investment income for higher-income taxpayers.) They have owned several blocks of stock for many years. They are considering the sale of two blocks of stock. The sale of one block would produce a gain of $10,000. The sale of the other would produce a loss of $15,000. For purposes of this problem, ignore personal exemptions, itemized deductions and other phase-outs. They have no other gains or losses this year.

a. How much tax will they save if they sell the block of stock that produces a loss?
b. How much additional tax will they pay if they sell the block of stock that produces a gain?
c. What will be the impact on their taxes if they sell both blocks of stock?

I:2-54 *Timing of Deductions.* Virginia is a cash-basis, calendar-year taxpayer. Her salary is $20,000, and she is single. She plans to purchase a residence in 2016. She anticipates her property taxes and interest will total $7,200. Each year, Virginia contributes approximately $1,000 to charity. Her other itemized deductions total approximately $800. For purposes of this problem, assume that 2016 tax rates, exemptions, and standard deductions are the same as for 2015.

a. What will her gross tax be in 2015 and 2016 if she contributes $1,000 to charity in each year?
b. What will her gross tax be in 2015 and 2016 if she contributes $2,000 to charity in 2015 but makes no contribution in 2016?
c. What will her gross tax be in 2015 and 2016 if she makes no contribution in 2015 but contributes $2,000 in 2016?
d. Alternative c results in a lower tax than either a or b. Why?

I:2-55 *Tax Forms and Filing Status.* Which tax form is used by the following individuals?

a. Anita is single, age 68, and has a salary of $22,000 and interest of $300.
b. Betty owns an apartment complex that produced rental income of $36,000. Expenses totaled $38,500.
c. Clay's wife died last year. He qualifies as a surviving spouse. His salary is $24,000.
d. Donna is a head of household. Her salary is $27,000 and she has $200 of interest income.

I:2-56 *Computation of Tax.* Maria is a single taxpayer. Her salary is $51,000. Maria realized a short-term capital loss of $5,000. Her itemized deductions total $4,000.

a. Compute Maria's adjusted gross income.
b. Compute her taxable income.
c. Compute her tax liability.

I:2-57 *Kiddie Tax.* Ralph and Tina (husband and wife) transferred taxable bonds worth $30,000 to Pam, their 12-year-old daughter. Pam received $3,500 of interest on the bonds in the current year. Ralph and Tina have a combined taxable income of $83,000.

a. Compute Ralph and Tina's gross tax. Assume they do not include Pam's income on their return.
b. Can Ralph and Tina claim a child credit for Pam?
c. Compute Pam's taxable income and gross tax.
d. What would be Pam's tax if she were age 25?

I:2-58 *Filing Status.* Assume Gail is a wealthy widow whose husband died last year. Her dependent daughter lives with her for the entire year. Gail has interest income totaling $379,900 and she pays property taxes and home mortgage interest totaling $20,000.
a. What filing status applies to Gail?
b. Compute her taxable income and gross tax.
c. Assume that Gail does not have a daughter. What is Gail's filing status?

TAX STRATEGY PROBLEMS

I:2-59 Jack is starting a business that he expects to produce $60,000 of income this year before compensating Jack for his services. He has $1,000 of other income and itemized deductions totaling $10,000. He wants to know whether he should incorporate or operate the business as a proprietorship. If a corporation is formed, he wants to know whether he should make an S election. If he incorporates, the corporation will pay Jack a salary of $40,000. He expects to distribute an additional $5,000 of corporate profits to himself each year. Jack is single.

Required: Which organizational form, proprietorship, S corporation, or C corporation, will produce the lowest total current income tax liability for Jack and his business? Ignore payroll and other taxes.

I:2-60 Andrea, who is in the 39.6% tax bracket, is interested in reducing her taxes. She is considering several alternatives. For each alternative listed below, indicate how much tax, if any, she would save? (For this problem, ignore additional taxes or phase-outs for high-income taxpayers.)
a. Give $2,000 to a charity. Assume she itemizes.
b. Give $2,000 to a charity. Assume she does not itemize.
c. Make a gift of bonds valued at $8,000 yielding $600 of interest annually to her 15-year-old daughter who has no other income.
d. Sell the bonds from part c for $8,000 and buy tax exempt bonds yielding $300.

TAX FORM/RETURN PREPARATION PROBLEMS

I:2-61 Aida Petosa (SSN 123-45-6789) is the 12-year-old daughter of Alfredo Petosa (SSN 987-65-4321). Her only income is $2,800 of interest on savings. Alfredo qualifies as a head of household, and his taxable income is $52,000. Compute her tax using Form 8615.

I:2-62 James S. (SSN 123-45-6789) and Lulu B. Watson (SSN 987-65-4321) reside at 999 E. North Street, Richmond, Virginia 23174. They have one dependent child, Waldo, age 4 (SSN 111-22-3333) and they are both under 65 years old. They do not wish to take advantage of the presidential election campaign check-off. Other relevant information includes

James's salary as a mechanic	$19,000
Lulu's salary as a teacher	23,000
Interest (First National Bank)	2,100
Withholding	2,000

Complete their Form 1040A.

I:2-63 John R. Lane (SSN 111-44-6666) lives at 1010 Ipsen Street, Yorba Linda, California 90102. John, a single taxpayer, age 66, provided 100% of his cousin's support. The cousin lives in Arizona. He wants to take advantage of the presidential election campaign check-off. John is an accountant. Other relevant information includes

Salary	$20,000
Taxable pension	31,000
Interest income	300
IRA deduction	5,000
Itemized deductions (from Schedule A)	8,000
Withholding	6,000

Assume that Schedule A, if necessary, has already been completed. Complete Form 1040.

CASE STUDY PROBLEMS

I:2-64 Bala and Ann purchased as investments three identical parcels of land over a several-year period. Two years ago they gave one parcel to their daughter, Kim, who is now age 16. They have an offer from an investor who is interested in acquiring all three parcels. The buyer is able to purchase only two of the parcels now, but wants to purchase the third parcel two or three years from now, when he expects to have available funds to acquire the property. Because they paid different prices for the parcels, the sales will result in different amounts of gains and losses. The sale of one parcel owned by Bala and Ann will result in a $20,000 gain and the sale of the other parcel will result in a $28,000 loss. The sale of the parcel owned by Kim will result in a $19,000 gain. Kim has no other income and does not expect any significant income for several years. Bala and Ann, however, are in the 39.6% tax bracket. They do not have any other capital gains this year. Which two properties would you recommend that they sell this year? Why?

I:2-65 Larry and Sue separated at the end of the year. Larry has asked Sue to sign a joint income tax return for the year because he feels that the tax will be lower on a joint return. Larry and Sue both work. Sue received a salary of $25,000 and Larry's salary was $20,000. Larry works as a waiter at a local restaurant and received tips. The restaurant asked Larry to indicate the amount of tips he received so that they could report the information to the IRS. Larry reported to the employer that the tips amounted to $3,000, but Sue believes that the amount was probably $6,000 to $10,000. They do not have enough expenses to itemize. Sue has asked you what are the advantages and risks of filing a joint return.

TAX RESEARCH PROBLEMS

I:2-66 Ed has supported his stepdaughter, her husband, and their child since his wife's death three years ago. Ed promised his late wife that he would support her daughter from a former marriage and her daughter's husband until they both finished college. They live in another state, and meet gross income filing requirements. Is Ed entitled to dependency exemptions for the three individuals?

A partial list of research sources is

- Sec. 152
- Reg. Sec. 1.152-2
- *Desio Barbetti,* 9 T.C. 1097 (1947)

I:2-67 Bob and Sue were expecting a baby in January, but Sue was rushed to the hospital in December. She delivered the baby but it died the first night. Are Bob and Sue entitled to a dependency exemption for the baby?

Research sources include Rev. Rul. 73-156, 1973-1 C.B. 58.

I:2-68 Larry has severe vision problems and, in the past, he has claimed the additional standard deduction available to blind taxpayers. This year Larry's doctor prescribed a new type of contact lens that greatly improved his vision. Naturally, Larry was elated, but unfortunately new problems developed. He suffered severe pain, infection, and ulcers from wearing the new lens. The doctor recommended that he remove the lens and after several weeks his eyes healed. The doctor told him that he could wear the contacts again, but only for brief time periods, or the problems would recur. Can Larry claim the additional standard deduction available to blind taxpayers?

Research sources include *Emanuel Hollman,* 38 T.C. 251 (1963).

CHAPTER

3

GROSS INCOME: INCLUSIONS

LEARNING OBJECTIVES

After studying this chapter, you should be able to

1. Explain the difference between the economic, accounting, and tax concepts of income
2. Explain the principles used to determine who is taxed on a particular item of income
3. Determine when a particular item of income is taxable under both the cash and accrual methods of reporting
4. Apply the rules of Sec. 61(a) to determine whether items such as compensation, dividends, alimony, and pensions are taxable
5. Describe tax planning considerations for inclusions of gross income
6. Describe compliance and procedural considerations for gross income

CHAPTER OUTLINE

Computation of an individual's income tax liability begins with the determination of income. Although the meaning of the term *income* has long been debated by economists, accountants, tax specialists, and politicians, no universally operational definition has been accepted.

The Sixteenth Amendment to the Constitution gave Congress the power to tax "income from whatever source derived." To ensure the constitutionality of the income tax, this phrase is incorporated in Sec. 61(a), where **gross income** is defined as follows: "Except as otherwise provided . . . gross income means all income from whatever source derived."

This chapter examines the concept of income for the purpose of determining what items of income are taxable. Chapter I:4 considers items of income that are excluded from gross income. As noted in Chapter I:2, many provisions in the tax law are created by a process of political compromise. Thus, there is no single explanation of why certain items are taxable and others are not. For this reason, determining whether a particular item of income is taxable often proves difficult.

ECONOMIC, ACCOUNTING, AND TAX CONCEPTS OF INCOME

OBJECTIVE 1

Explain the difference between the economic, accounting, and tax concepts of income

ECONOMIC CONCEPT

Economists define *income* as the amount an individual could consume during a period and remain as well off at the end of the period as he or she was at the beginning of the period. To the economist, therefore, income includes both the wealth that flows to the individual and changes in the value of the individual's store of wealth. Or, more simply, income equals consumption plus the change in wealth.

EXAMPLE I:3-1 ▶ Alice earned a salary of $40,000. She consumed $30,000 of food, clothing, housing, medical care, and other goods and services. Assets owned by Alice were worth $100,000 at the beginning of the year. Her assets, including $10,000 of salary that was saved, were worth $115,000 at the end of the year. Her liabilities did not change during the year. Alice's economic income is $45,000 [$30,000 + ($115,000 − $100,000)]. ◀

Under the economist's definition, unrealized gains, as well as gifts and inheritances, are income. Furthermore, the economist adjusts for inflation when measuring income. An individual has no income to the extent that an increase in the measured value of property is caused by a decrease in the value of the measuring unit. In other words, inflation does not increase wealth and, therefore, does not cause an individual to be better off.

ACCOUNTING CONCEPT

Accountants usually measure income when it is *realized* in a transaction. Values measured by transactions are relatively objective as accountants recognize (i.e., report) income, expenses, gains, and losses that have been realized as a result of a completed transaction. Accountants believe that the economic concept of income is too subjective to be used as a basis for financial reporting and, therefore, have traditionally used historical costs in measuring income instead of using unconfirmed estimates of changes in market value. In accounting, the meaning of the term *realization* is critical to the income measurement process. *Realization* generally results upon the occurrence of two events: (1) a change in the form or substance of a taxpayer's property (or phrased another way, a severance of the economic interest in the property) and (2) a transaction with a second party. Realization occurs when a taxpayer sells property. Conversely, the mere increase in value of property owned by a taxpayer will not result in the realization of income because there has been no change in the form of the property and no transaction with a second party.

EXAMPLE I:3-2 ▶ Assume the same facts as in Example I:3-1. The amount consumed by Alice, the increase in the value of the property owned by her, and inflation are all ignored by the accountant in measuring her income. Only when she sells or otherwise disposes of the assets that have increased in value will the accountant recognize the gain. Thus, Alice's accounting income is $40,000. ◀

TAX CONCEPT OF INCOME

The income tax law essentially adopts the accountant's concept of income rather than the economist's. The reasons for this relate to matters of administrative convenience and the wherewithal-to-pay concept. However, as we will see later, there are many differences between income for tax purposes and accounting income.

In general, three conditions must be met for amounts to be taxable.

- There must be economic benefit. The economic benefit is not limited to cash payments. Employees who receive a company's stock, rather than cash, are receiving an economic benefit. Taxpayers benefit even if they direct that payments be made to other persons. As a result, employees cannot avoid being taxed on their earnings by ordering that their salaries be paid directly to creditors or family members.
- The income must be realized. In general, realization occurs when the earning process is complete and a transaction with another party takes place that permits an objective measure of the income. This objective measurement increases "administrative convenience" which is discussed below. Unlike financial accounting, there are many exceptions that result in income being reported when the taxpayer receives payment even if that is at a time other than when the earning process is complete. These exceptions result in taxes being owed when the taxpayer has the "wherewithal to pay" (see below). Taxpayers who use the "cash method" of reporting, discussed later in the chapter, are normally taxed when payment is received.
- The income must be recognized. Some items of income are not taxable because of special provisions in the tax law. For example, certain real estate exchanges and corporate reorganizations are not taxable because of statutory nonrecognition rules. In such cases, the taxpayer receives a lower basis in replacement property, and that often means the income is recognized when the replacement property is sold. The tax law also contains exclusions that exempt specific types of income such as scholarships, inheritances, and municipal bond interest. Within statutory limitations, taxpayers are never taxed on such items of income.

Administrative Convenience. The economic concept of income is considered to be too subjective to be used in determining taxable income. The need for objectivity in taxation is evident. If taxpayers were required to report increases in value as income, some individuals would certainly understate values to reduce their tax liabilities. The IRS and even the most honest taxpayer often would disagree over values and, as a result, the tax system would be extremely difficult to administer. The disputes over valuation issues would be frequent and the courts would be burdened with added litigation. This problem is evidenced by the few situations where valuations are required in the determination of tax. For example, taxpayers who contribute property to charity usually can deduct the value of the property. The courts are continuously having to resolve disputes between taxpayers and the IRS over the value of such contributions. Furthermore, in the case of certain large contributions of property, taxpayers are required to attach to their returns appraisals of the contributed property. Penalties apply to taxpayers who substantially overvalue contributions.

In some instances, objectivity is achieved at the price of equity. For example, a taxpayer who owns land that has substantially declined in value generally cannot recognize the decline in value until it is realized through a disposition of the land. Similarly, an increase in value, no matter how large, is not taxed until a sale or exchange of the property has occurred. A taxpayer with a modest salary may feel that it is unfair that he or she is taxed on the salary while another person is not taxed on unrealized gains amounting to millions of dollars. As noted above, however, it would be practically impossible to fairly and consistantly administer an income tax law that was based on values.

KEY POINT

Section 446(a) states that taxable income shall be computed under the method of accounting on the basis of which the taxpayer regularly computes his or her income in keeping his or her books. This provision would seem to require that tax accounting rules would conform to financial accounting rules. However, as will be seen later in this and other chapters, there are many differences.

Wherewithal to Pay. The wherewithal-to-pay concept holds that a tax should be collected when the taxpayer is in the best position to pay the tax. A taxpayer who sells property and collects the cash is in a better position to pay the tax than a taxpayer who owns property that is merely increasing in value without a sale.

This concept is the rationale for several tax provisions. For example, the tax law allows a taxpayer who sells property on the installment basis to report the gain as the installment payments are collected, rather than at the time of the sale. Losses, on the other hand, cannot be reported on the installment basis, as the wherewithal-to-pay is not an issue. The concept is also used to justify differences between the tax law and financial accounting principles. Prepaid income is not income from an accounting standpoint until it is earned. The tax law, however, takes the position that prepaid income is subject to taxation at the time it is collected, rather than as it is earned. At the time of collection, the taxpayer clearly has the cash available to pay the tax. If the tax were deferred until the income is earned, the taxpayer may no longer have the cash.

KEY POINT

Congress has not adopted any particular concept or theory of income for tax purposes. Except as specifically limited by statute, the definition of income is broad and general.

Gross Income Defined. Section 61(a) provides the following general definition and listing of income items:

> General Definition.—Except as otherwise provided in this subtitle, gross income means all income from whatever source derived, including (but not limited to) the following items:
>
> 1. Compensation for services, including fees, commissions, fringe benefits, and similar items
> 2. Gross income derived from business
> 3. Gains derived from dealings in property
> 4. Interest
> 5. Rents
> 6. Royalties
> 7. Dividends
> 8. Alimony and separate maintenance payments
> 9. Annuities
> 10. Income from life insurance and endowment contracts
> 11. Pensions
> 12. Income from discharge of indebtedness
> 13. Distributive share of partnership gross income
> 14. Income in respect of a decedent
> 15. Income from an interest in an estate or trust

SELF-STUDY QUESTION

Why should taxpayers who are using the cash method of accounting be required to include in gross income the value of property or services received?

ANSWER

If taxpayers were not required to include the value of property or services received in gross income, many taxpayers would arrange their financial affairs so that they would receive property or services instead of cash.

This definition certainly is not all-inclusive. For example, it does not indicate whether specific items of income such as property insurance settlements, gambling winnings, or illegal income are taxable. One point is apparent: The phrase *[e]xcept as otherwise provided* means that all sources of income are presumed to be taxable unless there is a specific exclusion in the income tax law. The IRS does not have to prove that an item of income is taxable. Rather, the taxpayer must prove that the item of income is excluded. Thus, gambling winnings and illegal income are taxable simply because no specific provisions in the tax law exclude such amounts from taxation. As we shall see, life insurance proceeds and certain other insurance proceeds are specifically excluded from gross income.

Form of Receipt. Gross income is not limited to amounts received in the form of cash. According to Reg. Sec. 1.61-1(a), income may be "realized in any form, whether in money, property, or services." The important question is whether the taxpayer receives an economic benefit. This rule covers barter transactions which are direct exchanges of property and services. Each party to the transaction is taxed on the value of the property or services received in the exchange. In general, the cost basis of property given up in a barter transaction can be subtracted from the value of the property received in arriving at the taxable amount.

EXAMPLE I:3-3 ▶ King Corporation transfers 1,000 shares of its stock to its president. The stock has no restrictions and is part of the president's compensation. The president must include the value of the stock in gross income. ◀

EXAMPLE I:3-4 ▶ Ali, an attorney, performs legal services for Paul, a painter, in exchange for Paul's promise to paint Ali's residence. Each taxpayer realizes income equal to the value of services received. Thus, Ali must report income in an amount equal to the value of the painting services provided by Paul. Paul must report the value of Ali's legal services. These amounts, assuming an arm's-length transaction, should be the same. ◀

EXAMPLE I:3-5 ▶ USA Corporation distributes an automobile to Vicki, a shareholder, in lieu of a cash dividend. Vicki must report the value of the automobile as dividend income. ◀

EXAMPLE I:3-6 ▶ Len has fallen behind on loan payments due to a bank. The bank obtains a court order requiring Len's employer to pay part of Len's wages directly to the bank. Len will be taxed on the full wages even though a portion goes directly to the bank. ◀

EXAMPLE I:3-7 ▶ Wayne borrowed $3,000 from his employer. The employer awarded year-end bonuses to other employees but told Wayne that the debt was being forgiven in lieu of a bonus. Wayne must include the $3,000 in income. ◀

? STOP & THINK

Question: As noted, income is taxable even if it is paid in a form other than cash. What problems does this produce for the IRS and taxpayers?

Solution: Two major problems are created: valuation and enforcement. First, it is necessary to determine the market value of property and services when income is received in a form other than cash. Determining values can be difficult. Second, enforcement by the IRS is made much more difficult because such income is not documented by canceled checks, credit card receipts, or other records. Thus, as demonstrated in Example I:3-4 above, many of these so-called traded services are not reported as income. This evasion of income represents billions of lost tax revenues to the government.

Indirect Economic Receipt. As indicated earlier, the taxability of income often depends on whether the taxpayer receives an economic benefit. In general, if a taxpayer benefits from an item, it is taxable. Frequently, however, an employer may make an expenditure in which its employees may incidentally or indirectly benefit. For example,

- Security guards patrol an employer's plant, protecting both the employer's property and the employees. The employees receive an indirect benefit for the protection provided by the security guards.
- An employer requires employees to undergo an annual checkup, the cost of which is paid by the employer.
- An employer provides protective clothing worn by employees while on the job.
- A shipping company provides sleeping accommodations to sailors while ships are at sea.
- A company requires certain employees to wear shoes manufactured by the company and provide regular reports on the quality of the shoes.

It is now well-established that taxpayers may exclude such indirect benefits from gross income. This judicially-developed rule holds that a benefit is excludible if it is made in order to serve the business needs of the employer and the benefit to the employee is secondary and incidental.

Congress also has established rules dealing with situations where expenditures are made primarily to benefit employees. While expenditures made by employers that primarily benefit employees are generally taxable, there are instances whereby such expenditures are not taxable. These rules, which are discussed in Chapters I:4 and I:9, permit employees to exclude certain fringe benefits (such as employee discounts) from gross income.

TO WHOM IS INCOME TAXABLE?

OBJECTIVE 2

Explain the principles used to determine who is taxed on a particular item of income

Once it is established that income is taxable, it is necessary to determine to whom it is taxable. Although such determinations are usually easy, there are circumstances where income is not necessarily taxed to the person who receives it. If physical receipt of income was the only test, a family might reduce or eliminate its income tax by having income paid to children and other members who are in low tax brackets or have no tax liability.

ASSIGNMENT OF INCOME

In 1930, the Supreme Court held in a landmark case, *Lucas v. Earl,* that an individual is taxed on the earnings from his or her personal services.[1] Specifically, the Supreme Court held that a husband was taxed on the earnings from his law practice, even though he had signed a legally enforceable agreement with his wife that the earnings would be shared equally. An agreement to assign income does not permit a person to avoid being taxed on the income. The Court used the previously developed analogy that likens income to the fruit and capital to the tree.[2] Accordingly, the fruit (income) could not be attributed to a tree other than the one on which it grew.

KEY POINT

The law makes a clear distinction between an assignment of income and an assignment of income-producing property. The income is taxable to the assignor in the former case, but where there is a bona fide gift of property the income is taxable to the assignee.

In 1940, the Supreme Court, in *Helvering v. Horst,* extended the assignment of income doctrine to income from property.[3] In this case, the taxpayer detached interest coupons from bonds and gave the coupons to his son. The son collected the interest and reported it on his own return. The Supreme Court held that the taxpayer was taxed on the interest income because he owned the bonds. This holding leads to a basic rule that the income from property is taxed to the owner of the property. To transfer the income from property, the taxpayer must transfer ownership of the property itself.[4]

ADDITIONAL COMMENT

The community property states are generally located in the western or southwestern United States. Generally these states were settled by immigrants from France and Spain, and their state laws reflect this fact. The common law is derived from English common law.

Although married couples may file joint returns today, this privilege did not become available until 1948. Assignment of income is an issue today when other individuals such as parents and children are involved, and it can still be an issue when married couples file separate returns.

ALLOCATING INCOME BETWEEN MARRIED PEOPLE

ADDITIONAL COMMENT

Community property laws are sometimes difficult to generalize. Depending on the specific law within a community property state, one-half of estimated taxes paid by one spouse may or may not be used by the other spouse on a separate return.

How income is allocated between a husband and wife depends on the state of residence. Forty-one states follow a common law property system, whereas nine states[5] use a community property system. Under common law, income is generally taxed to the individual who earns the income, either through labor or capital. For example, if a spouse holds stock separately in his or her name, that spouse will be taxed on all of the dividends received from the separately owned stock. Generally, the only **joint income** in a common law state is income from jointly owned property.[6]

In community property states, income may be either separate or community. **Community income** is considered to belong equally to the spouses. In all community property states, the income from the personal efforts of either spouse is considered to belong

---

[1] *Lucas v. Earl,* 8 AFTR 10287, 2 USTC ¶496 (USSC, 1930).

[2] The analogy had been used some ten years earlier in *Eisner v. Myrtle H. Macomber,* 3 AFTR 3020, 1 USTC ¶32 (USSC, 1920). The court originally used the analogy in efforts to distinguish income from capital.

[3] *Helvering v. Horst,* 24 AFTR 1058, 40-2 USTC ¶9787 (USSC, 1940).

[4] A series of rather specific rules allocates income between the former and current owner when income-producing property is transferred. For example, in the case of bonds transferred by gift, the IRS has ruled that interest must be allocated based on the number of days the bonds were held by each owner during the interest period (Rev. Rul. 72-312, 1972-1 C.B. 22). A similar allocation must be made if bonds are sold (Rev. Rul. 72-224, 1972-1 C.B. 30).

[5] The states are Arizona, California, Idaho, Louisiana, Nevada, New Mexico, Texas, Washington, and Wisconsin. Residents of Alaska may elect to be subject to community property law.

[6] Historically, tenancy by the entirety, a form of joint ownership between spouses, allocated all income to the husband. Today, the laws of many states allocate income from property held in tenancy by the entirety equally between the spouses.

equally to the spouses. Furthermore, income from community property is considered to be community income. Thus, if a wife's salary is used to purchase stock, subsequent dividends are community income.

Couples can have separate property even in community property states. **Separate property** consists of all property owned before marriage and gifts and inheritances acquired after marriage. Whether income from separate property is community or separate depends on the state. In Idaho, Louisiana, Texas, and Wisconsin income from separate property is community income. In Arizona, California, Nevada, New Mexico, and Washington, such income is separate income.

EXAMPLE I:3-8 ▶ A husband and wife file separate returns. The husband's salary is $40,000 and the wife's salary is $48,000. The wife received $1,000 of dividends on stock she had inherited from her parents. Interest of $1,200 was received on bonds that were purchased from the husband's salary. They received $2,600 in rent from farm land that they purchased jointly. The income would be allocated, depending on the state of residence, as follows:

California (Community Property State)	*Husband*	*Wife*
Salary	$44,000	$44,000
Dividends		1,000
Interest	600	600
Rent	1,300	1,300
Total	$45,900	$46,900
Texas (Community Property State)		
Salary	$44,000	$44,000
Dividends	500	500
Interest	600	600
Rent	1,300	1,300
Total	$46,400	$46,400
Pennsylvania (Common Law State)		
Salary	$40,000	$48,000
Dividends		1,000
Interest	1,200	
Rent	1,300	1,300
Total	$42,500	$50,300 ◀

These rules are important when couples file separate returns. The community income rules can prove to be a problem if one spouse conceals income from the other. Normally, each spouse is expected to report one-half of all community income. This treatment is inequitable if one spouse is not aware that the community income was earned. Special rules excuse an innocent spouse who fails to report community income on a separate return, provided that the spouse had no knowledge or reason to know of the item and, as a result, the inclusion of the community income would be inequitable.[7] A corresponding provision permits the IRS to include the entire amount in the income of the other spouse.[8]

STOP & THINK

Question: The tax treatment of income earned in a common law state versus a community property state can be very inconsistent. As noted, the Supreme Court, in *Lucas v. Earl,* decided that a husband was taxed on all his income even though he agreed to share that income with his wife. Nevertheless, community income in a community property state is divided equally between husbands and wives even if one spouse earned all of the income. Why the tax distinction?

Solution: *Lucas v. Earl* dealt with a case in a common law state where the husband was legally entitled to the income, but decided to divide it with his wife. In community property states, couples are legally obligated to share their incomes. The federal income tax law respects the different property law systems of the states and taxes the income of

[7] Sec. 66(b).

[8] Sec. 66(c).

persons based on state law.[9] It would be unfairly burdensome to tax individuals on income to which they never had any legal right.

INCOME OF MINOR CHILDREN

As noted earlier, whether a husband or wife is taxed on income is determined by state law. However, earnings of a minor child are taxed to the child regardless of the state's property law system. Therefore, earnings of a child from either personal services (compensation) or from property (dividends, interest, rents, etc.) are taxed to the child, not the child's parents. As noted in Chapter I:2, the unearned income of a child under age 24 may be taxed at the parents' tax rate if it is higher than the child's rate. Alternatively, the parents may elect to include the child's unearned income on their return. In the case of spouses, the spouse who has a legal right to such income determines who is taxed on it. In the case of children, however, the individual who earns the income is the individual who is taxed on it.

WHEN IS INCOME TAXABLE?

OBJECTIVE 3

Determine when a particular item of income is taxable under both the cash and accrual methods of reporting

The year in which income is taxed depends on the taxpayer's accounting method. The three primary overall accounting methods are the **cash receipts and disbursements method**, the **accrual method**, and the **hybrid method.** While taxpayers have the right to choose a method of accounting, the chosen method still must clearly reflect income as determined by the IRS. The IRS has the power to change the accounting method used by a taxpayer if, in the opinion of the IRS, the method being used does not clearly reflect income. Further, the Regulations require taxpayers to use the accrual method for determining purchases and sales when a taxpayer maintains an inventory.[10] However, the IRS has ruled that taxpayers whose annual gross receipts for the three prior years do not exceed $1 million ($10 million if the taxpayer's principal business is not the sale of inventory) are exempt from the requirement and may use the cash method.[11] This exception for small taxpayers is discussed in more detail below.

KEY POINT

Neither the IRC nor the Regulations define the terms *accounting* and *accounting method.*

Section 448 requires C corporations (and partnerships with corporate partners), tax shelters, and certain trusts to use the accrual method of accounting. Qualified personal service corporations, certain types of farms, and entities with average gross receipts under $5 million are exempt from the requirement.

Once an accounting method has been adopted, it cannot be changed without permission of the IRS. See Chapter I:11.

ADDITIONAL COMMENT

Taxpayers engaged in more than one trade or business may use a different method of accounting for each separate trade or business.

CASH METHOD

The **cash receipts and disbursements method** of accounting is used by most individual taxpayers and many small businesses. (See Chapter I:11 for a more complete discussion of who is permitted to use the cash method.) Under this method, income is reported in the year the taxpayer actually or constructively receives the income rather than in the year the income is earned. The income can be received by the taxpayer or the taxpayer's agent and be in the form of cash, other property, or services.[12] In the case of property or services, the amount included in income is the value of the property or services. An accounts receivable or other unsupported promise to pay is considered to have no value under the cash method and, as a result, no income is recognized until the receivable is collected. Topic Review I:3-1 summarizes when various types of income are reported.

ADDITIONAL COMMENT

The use of the cash receipts and disbursements method of accounting gives the taxpayer some control over the timing of the recognition of income and deductions. It also has the advantage of simplicity.

The fact that prepaid income is usually taxed when received, rather than when earned, often results in a mismatching of income and expenses.

EXAMPLE I:3-9 ▶ In December of the current year, Troy, who owns an apartment building, collects the first and last months' rent from a new tenant. Troy must report two months' rent in the current year. The

[9] See *Burns Poe v. H. G. Seaborn*, 9 AFTR 576, 2 USTC ¶611 (USSC, 1930). In 2010, the IRS Chief Counsel concluded that the rule also applies to same-sex California couples who enter into domestic partnership agreements based on the fact that California community property law applies to such couples (CCA 201021050).

[10] Reg. Sec. 1.446-1(c)(2)(i).

[11] Rev. Proc. 2002-28, 2002-1 C.B. 815, modified by Rev. Proc. 2012-20, 2012-14 I.R.B. 700.

[12] An agent can be an employee, relative, or other person authorized to receive the income.

TOPIC REVIEW I:3-1

When Income Is Taxable

Item	Cash Basis	Accrual Basis
Compensation	Year actually or constructively received.	Year earned or year received if prepaid.
Interest	Year actually or constructively received.	Year accrued or year received if prepaid.
Discount on Series E or EE Bonds	Choice of reporting interest as it accrues or at maturity.	Year accrued.
Dividends	Year actually or constructively received.	Year actually or constructively received.
Rent	Year actually or constructively received (does not apply to a deposit).	Year accrued or year received if prepaid (year accrued if services are associated, e.g., in a hotel or motel) (does not apply to a deposit).
Services (maintenance contracts, dance lessons, etc.)	Year actually or constructively received.	Year accrued or year received if prepaid except that a taxpayer may report the income as it accrues if all the services are to be performed by the end of the next tax year.
Sale of goods	Year actually or constructively received.	Year of sale or year cash is received if prepaid except may elect to report in year of sale if goods are not on hand, amount received is less than cost of item, and same accounting method is used for financial accounting.
Subscriptions (newspapers, magazines, etc.)	Year actually or constructively received.	Year earned or year cash is received, if prepaid, except may elect to report income as newspaper, etc., is published.
Memberships (automobile clubs, etc.)	Year actually or constructively received.	Year earned or year received if prepaid (certain nonstock corporations may elect to report prepaid amounts over the membership period, if the period covers three years or less).
Sale of property (other than stock)	Year actually or constructively received.	Year transaction is completed (e.g., the close of escrow in case of sale of real estate).
Sale of stock	Year transaction is executed.	Year transaction is executed.

actual expenses associated with the last month's rental are not incurred until the last month. However, Troy must report two months' income this year, but may only deduct one month's expenses. ◄

ADDITIONAL COMMENT

There is no recognized doctrine of constructive payment.

Reporting prepaid income can have harsh results because it is not offset by related deductions. If the income is taxed before the expenses are incurred, the taxpayer may not have enough cash to pay the expenses when they are incurred.[13] This burden is mitigated, in part, by Treasury Regulations and Revenue Procedures discussed in this chapter (e.g., the treatment of prepaid income, page I:3-11).

REAL-WORLD EXAMPLE

Paul Hornung, a former football player with the Green Bay Packers, was awarded an automobile in 1961 for being the outstanding player in the NFL championship game, but he did not actually receive it until 1962. He attempted to invoke the constructive receipt doctrine and report the income in 1961. The court held that he could not claim constructive receipt because the car was not set aside in the year of the award. *Paul V. Hornung*, 47 T.C. 428 (1967).

Constructive Receipt. As noted, a cash-basis taxpayer must report income in the year in which it is actually or constructively received. Constructive receipt means that the income is made available to the taxpayer so that he may draw upon it at any time. However, income is not constructively received if the taxpayer's control of its receipt is subject to substantial limitations or restrictions. This rule prevents taxpayers from deferring income that is otherwise available by merely "turning their backs" on it. A taxpayer cannot defer income recognition by refusing to accept payment until a later taxable year.

[13] This mismatching of income and expenses affects both cash and accrual basis taxpayers.

Examples of constructive receipt where taxpayers are required to report taxable income even though no cash is actually received include:

- A check received after banking hours[14]
- Interest credited to a bank savings account[15]
- Bond interest coupons that have matured but have not been redeemed[16]
- Salary available to an employee who does not accept payment[17]

An amount is not considered to be constructively received if:

- It is subject to substantial limitations or restrictions.
- The payor does not have the funds necessary to make payment.
- The amount is unavailable to the taxpayer.

EXAMPLE I:3-10 ▶ Beth owns an ordinary life insurance policy with a cash surrender value. She need not report any income as the cash surrender value increases because the requirement that she cancel the policy in order to collect the cash surrender value constitutes a substantial restriction. If she cancels the policy, she reports as income the difference between the cash surrender value collected and net premiums paid. ◀

EXAMPLE I:3-11 ▶ Cathy has received a paycheck from her employer but has been told to hold the check until the employer has sufficient funds to cover the payroll. Cathy need not report the amount of the check as income until funds are deposited to the employer's account. ◀

EXAMPLE I:3-12 ▶ Dan sold land for $100,000 in December with payment due the following February. During the negotiations, the buyer offered to pay cash. Because the parties did not agree to a cash transaction, there was no constructive receipt in December. Under the terms of the sale, funds were not available at the time of sale. Thus, Dan is permitted to defer the recognition of income until the funds become available the following year. ◀

Exceptions. There are exceptions to the basic rule that cash-basis taxpayers report income when it is actually or constructively received.

- The interest on Series E and Series EE U.S. savings bonds need not be reported until the final maturity date, which varies but may be as long as forty years after the date of issue, and can be deferred even longer if the bonds are exchanged within one year of the final maturity date for Series HH U.S. savings bonds.[18] Many taxpayers purchase bonds that mature after retirement when the taxpayers expect to be in a lower tax bracket.

EXAMPLE I:3-13 ▶ Tenisha purchases a Series EE U.S. savings bond for $2,500 that will mature in 10 years. The bond pays no interest until maturity when it will be worth $5,000. Tenisha is not required to report any interest income for tax purposes until the bond matures. At maturity, when Tenisha receives the $5,000, she will report $2,500 of interest income. If she desires to defer the interest further, she could exchange her Series EE bond for a Series HH bond within one year. ◀

- Special rules also apply to farmers and ranchers. Farmers may report crop insurance proceeds in the year following receipt if the crop would have ordinarily been sold in the following year. Ranchers who sell livestock on account of a drought, flood, or other weather related condition may delay reporting income until the following year if they can establish that the livestock sale would otherwise have taken place in a later tax year.[19] These rules help taxpayers avoid a bunching of income into one year.
- Small taxpayer exception for inventories. As noted above, taxpayers who have average annual gross receipts of $1 million or less for the prior three years ($10 million or less if the taxpayer's principal business is not the sale of inventory) are exempt from maintaining inventories and may use the cash method. The ruling was widely interpreted to

[14] *Charles F. Kahler,* 18 T.C. 31 (1952).
[15] Reg. Sec. 1.451-2(b).
[16] Ibid.
[17] *James J. Cooney,* 18 T.C. 883 (1952).
[18] Series E bonds were issued prior to 1980; Series EE bonds were issued after 1979. The interest on the Series HH bonds is taxable as received.

[19] Recognizing the volatile nature of farming and ranching, Congress established a special averaging technique for farmers and ranchers. Electing farmers and ranchers compute their tax on the average income for the current and three preceding years. Sec. 1301.

mean that small taxpayers did not need to account for inventories and could deduct the amount of their purchases in the year of payment. However, the IRS subsequently issued Rev. Proc. 2001-10, whereby it was clarified that the small taxpayer exception will only allow small taxpayers to deduct purchases of inventory in the year of purchase if (1) the inventory purchases are paid for by the end of the year and (2) the inventory is actually sold in such year. The effect of this new ruling basically is to eliminate the small taxpayer exception with respect to inventories.

EXAMPLE I:3-14 ▶ The Cheryl Corporation begins a new retail business in the current year and has sales of $400,000. The corporation has year-end accounts receivable of $15,000 and purchases $240,000 of merchandise during the year. At year-end, the corporation has not paid for $30,000 of the merchandise it had purchased and has $50,000 of inventory on hand. The corporation pays operating expenses of $140,000 during the year. As the average gross receipts are less than $1 million, the corporation can use either the cash or accrual method. The corporation's income computed under both methods is as follows:

	Accrual		*Cash*	
Sales		$400,000		$385,000
Purchases	$240,000		$210,000	
Ending inventory	50,000		20,000*	
Cost of sales		190,000		190,000
Gross profit		210,000		195,000
Expenses		140,000		140,000
Net income		$ 70,000		$ 55,000

*$50,000 − $30,000 = $20,000

The difference between the accrual and cash methods is that the sales are not reported under the cash method until such sales are actually collected. Thus, the corporation does not include year-end receivables in this year's income. The year-end receivables will be reported when the receivables are collected in later taxable years.

As can be seen above, the cost of sales under both the accrual and cash methods are the same. This is because under Rev. Proc. 2001-10, taxpayers may not deduct inventory unless it is both paid for and sold. Since $30,000 was not paid for by year-end, it is not deductible and the purchases under the cash method are $30,000 less than under the accrual method. The ending inventory under the cash method is the physical inventory of $50,000 reduced by the $30,000 of inventory on hand that has not been paid for by year-end. ◀

REAL-WORLD EXAMPLE

The Ninth Circuit Court of Appeals has held that "markers" customers gave to a gambling casino to evidence their indebtedness to the casino required accrual even though the receivables were legally unenforceable under state law. The court found that there need only be a "reasonable expectancy" that payment would be made. *Flamingo Resort, Inc. v. U.S.*, 50 AFTR 2d 82-502, 82-1 USTC ¶9136 (9th Cir., 1982).

ACCRUAL METHOD

Taxpayers using the accrual method of accounting generally report income in the year it is earned. Income is considered to have been earned when all the events have occurred that fix the right to receive the income and when the amount of income can be determined with reasonable accuracy.[20] In the case of a sale of property, income normally accrues when title passes to the buyer.[21] Income from services accrues as the services are performed.

Prepaid Income. A major exception to the normal operation of the accrual method is the rules applicable to the receipt of prepaid income. Prepaid income is generally taxable in the year of receipt. For example, if a lender receives January interest in the preceding December, it is taxable in the year received, whether the lender uses the cash or accrual method. This treatment, of course, differs from financial accounting, where the interest would be reported as it accrues.

Two important exceptions to the general rule are worth noting. Accrual-basis taxpayers may defer recognizing income in the case of certain advance payments for *goods* and in the case of certain advance payments for *services* to be rendered. A taxpayer may defer advance payments for goods (inventory) if the taxpayer's method of accounting for the sale is the same for tax and financial accounting purposes.[22]

[20] Reg. Sec. 1.451-1(a).

[21] Regulation Sec. 1.446-1(c)(1)(ii), however, does permit taxpayers the right to accrue income from the sale of inventory when the goods are shipped, when the product is delivered or accepted, or when title passes, as long as the method is consistently used.

[22] Reg. Sec. 1.451-5.

Under Rev. Proc. 2004-34, taxpayers may defer payments for future services to the year following the year in which the payment is received.[23] Revenue relating to services provided in the year payment is received is reported currently. Revenue relating to future years is reported in the year following the year of receipt even if the payments relate to multiple future years. The rule can be applied to a variety of services such as Internet service, dance lessons, maintenance contracts (but not warranties included in the sales price of a product), membership fees, and rent (if services are associated with the rent, such as a hotel or motel). The procedure is available when service and products are provided together. The procedure does not apply to rent (if services are not associated with the rent), insurance premiums, interest, or warranty contracts included in the price of a product.

EXAMPLE I:3-15 ▶ Bear Corporation, a publicly held, accrual-basis taxpayer that uses the calendar year as its tax year, sells computer courses under contracts ranging from three months to two years. When income is reported depends on the length of the contract and the month in which the contract is sold. Assume that Bear sells three contracts on July 1. One is for three months costing $90, a second is for one year costing $300, and the third for two years costing $500. The $90 charged for the three month contract is reported currently as all services are provided currently. One-half of $300 charged for the one year contract is reported currently and one-half is reported next year as one-half of the services are provided currently and one-half will be provided next year. One-fourth of the $500 charged for the two year contract is reported this year and the balance is reported next year. This is because Rev. Proc. 2004-34 does not permit income to be deferred beyond the end of the year following the year in which payment is received.

REAL-WORLD EXAMPLE

A dance studio using the accrual method was required to include in taxable income all advance payments for lessons in the form of cash and negotiable notes, plus contract installments due but remaining unpaid at year end. *Mark E. Schlude v. CIR*, 11 AFTR 2d 751, 63-1 USTC ¶9284 (USSC, 1963).

	Year Includible in Gross Income	
Length of Contract	*Current Year*	*Next Year*
3 months	$ 90	
12 months	150	$150
24 months	125	375

◀

HYBRID METHOD

The **hybrid method** of accounting is a combination of the cash and accrual methods. Under the hybrid method, some items of income or expense are reported under the cash basis and others are reported under the accrual method. The method is most often encountered in small businesses that maintain inventories and are required to use the accrual method of accounting for purchases and sales of goods. Such businesses often prefer to use the cash method of reporting for other items because the cash method is simpler and may provide greater flexibility for tax planning. A taxpayer using the hybrid method of accounting would use the accrual method with respect to purchases and sales of goods but would use the cash method in computing all other items of income and expenses.

? STOP & THINK

Question: Taxpayers who are eligible to use the cash method often choose the cash method of reporting income over the accrual method. Why is the cash method generally more favorable for income tax purposes?

Solution: Taxpayers who have the option frequently choose the cash method over the accrual method because it is simpler, offers greater tax planning opportunity, and results in taxes being owed when income is actually received. The cash method is simpler because taxpayers are not required to make the complex accruals associated with the accrual method. Planning opportunities are greater because cash basis taxpayers can deduct expenses when paid, thereby allowing taxpayers to control their tax liability. Under the accrual method, prepaid expenses are not deductible when paid, but must be deducted over the periods benefitted. Finally, cash basis taxpayers do not have to pay taxes until they receive the money. Under the accrual method, income is reported when it is earned even if it has not been received. As a result, accrual basis taxpayers sometimes have to pay the tax before they actually receive the income they have earned.

[23] 2004-1 C.B. 991.

ITEMS OF GROSS INCOME: SEC. 61(A)

OBJECTIVE 4

Apply the rules of Sec. 61(a) to determine whether items such as compensation, dividends, alimony, and pensions are taxable

Section 61(a), quoted earlier in this chapter, states that gross income includes, but is not limited to, fifteen specifically listed types of income. Several of these items are discussed below.

COMPENSATION

Compensation is payment for personal services. It includes salaries, wages, fees, commissions, tips, bonuses, and specialized forms of compensation such as director's fees, jury fees, and marriage fees received by clergymen. What the compensation is called, how it is computed, the form and frequency of payment, and whether the compensation is subject to withholding is of little significance. Similarly, the fact that the services are part-time, one-time, seasonal, or temporary is immaterial.

There are exclusions, however, for a variety of employer-provided fringe benefits such as group term life insurance premiums, health and accident insurance premiums, employee discounts, contributions to retirement plans, and education benefits. In addition, there is a limited exclusion applicable to foreign-earned income. Both fringe benefits and the foreign-earned income exclusion are discussed in Chapter I:4.

ADDITIONAL COMMENT

Salaries and wages constituted 68.2% of total AGI reported in 2012.

BUSINESS INCOME

The term *gross income* usually refers to the total amount received from a particular source. In the case of businesses that provide services (e.g., accounting and law), the gross business income is the total amount received. In the case of manufacturing, merchandising, and mining, however, gross income is total sales less the cost of goods sold. Thus, gross income for tax purposes is comparable to gross profit for financial accounting purposes.

The cost of goods sold is, in effect, treated as a return of capital. Chapter I:4 discusses a well-established tax concept that a return of capital is not income and, therefore, cannot be subject to the income tax. Chapter I:11 discusses how inventories are valued.

SELF-STUDY QUESTION

A retail company had sales of $1,000,000 and the following costs: goods sold, $400,000, salaries, $200,000, and rent and other expenses, $100,000. What is the company's gross income?

ANSWER

The gross income is $600,000. The sales figure is reduced by the cost of goods sold.

GAINS FROM DEALINGS IN PROPERTY

Gains realized from property transactions are included in gross income unless a nonrecognition rule applies. As is true with business inventories, taxpayers may deduct the cost of property in order to arrive at the gain from a property transaction.[24] The tax law contains over 30 nonrecognition rules, which allow taxpayers to postpone the recognition of gains and losses from certain types of property transactions. In a few instances, these rules allow taxpayers to permanently exclude gains from gross income.[25]

Losses are not offset against gains in computing gross income. Rather, most losses are deductions *for* adjusted gross income. Furthermore, net capital losses for individuals are subject to provisions that limit the amount that can be deducted from other income to $3,000 per year. Losses from the sale or disposition of an asset held for personal use are not deductible.

INTEREST

Interest is compensation for the use of money. Taxable interest includes interest on bank deposits, corporate bonds, mortgages, life insurance policies, tax refunds, most U.S. government obligations,[26] and foreign government obligations.[27] Nontaxable interest is discussed below.

TYPICAL MISCONCEPTION

It is sometimes mistakenly assumed that interest paid on federal obligations such as Treasury bonds, notes, and bills will also qualify for tax exemption.

Tax-Exempt Interest. Since the inception of the federal income tax in 1913, interest on obligations of states, territories, and U.S. possessions and their political subdivisions has been tax exempt.[28] Bonds issued by school districts, port authorities, toll road commissions, counties, and fire districts have been held to be tax exempt. In addition, Sec. 501(c)(3) organizations may issue up to $225 million of tax-exempt bonds. Such organizations include private universities, hospitals, churches, and similar nonprofit organizations.

---

[24] Note that *business income* and *gains from dealings in property* are overlapping terms. The gross profit from the sale of inventory is actually both business income and a gain from a property transaction. Typically, however, the phrase *gains from dealings in property* may be assumed to mean gains from dealings in property other than inventory, so as to avoid confusion.

[25] For example, Sec. 121 allows taxpayers to exclude a limited amount of gain from a sale of a personal residence.

[26] The interest on many federal obligations issued before March 1, 1942 is tax exempt.

[27] Reg. Sec. 1.61-7.

[28] Sec. 103(a)(1).

ADDITIONAL COMMENT

Many tax advisers consider the exclusion of interest on municipal bonds to be one of the few remaining tax shelters. As a result, municipal bond funds have flourished in recent years.

ADDITIONAL COMMENT

The doctrine of intergovernmental immunity also results in most states exempting from taxation income received from U.S. obligations.

SELF-STUDY QUESTION

Young parents, whose annual income is currently $50,000, begin a regular program of purchasing Series EE savings bonds for their 8-year-old daughter's college education. Is there any risk that when the bonds are redeemed the interest income will not be excludable?

ANSWER

Yes, the parents' income may increase over the years to such an extent that the interest exclusion will not be available.

As noted above, this exclusion does not extend to interest paid on most U.S. government obligations or foreign government obligations, nor does the exclusion exempt from taxation gains from the sale of state or local government bonds or interest on tax refunds paid by state and municipal governments.

There has always been some uncertainty as to whether the federal government could tax interest on state and local government obligations. The basic question is whether taxing these obligations would violate the doctrine of intergovernmental immunity in that the tax would reduce the ability of state and local governments to finance their operations because taxable bonds usually pay a higher rate of interest than tax-exempt bonds. The belief that taxing state and local government interest is unconstitutional is no longer widely held. While there have been efforts to tax interest on state and local bonds, the only changes have been to limit the use of bonds for private activities,[29] federally insured loans,[30] and arbitrage.[31]

Series EE Savings Bond Exclusion. Taxpayers may purchase and eventually redeem Series EE bonds tax-free if they use the proceeds to pay certain college expenses for themselves, a spouse, or dependents.[32]

To qualify for the exclusion:

- The bonds must be purchased after 1989 by an individual who is age 24 or older at the time of the purchase.
- The bonds must be purchased by the owner and cannot be a gift to the owner.
- The receipts from the bond redemption must be used for tuition and fees, which are first reduced by tax-exempt scholarships, veterans benefits, Hope and Lifetime Learning credits, and other similar amounts.[33]
- Married couples living together must file a joint return to obtain the exclusion.

The full amount of interest is excluded only if the combined amount of principal and interest received during the year does not exceed the net qualified educational expenses (tuition and fees reduced by exempt scholarships, etc.), and the taxpayer's 2015 modified adjusted gross income is not over $77,200 ($115,750 for married individuals filing a joint return). The exclusion is fully phased-out for taxpayers whose 2015 modified AGI is more than $92,200 ($145,750 for married individuals filing a joint return).[34]

If the net qualified education expenses are less than the total principal and interest, a portion of the interest is excluded based on the ratio of the qualified educational expenses to the total principal and interest. The tentative exclusion is equal to

$$\text{Series EE interest} \times \frac{\text{Net qualified educational expenses}}{\text{Series EE interest} + \text{Principal}}$$

EXAMPLE I:3-16 ▶ In 2015, Lois redeems Series EE bonds and receives $6,000, consisting of $1,875 of interest and $4,125 of principal. Assume that the net qualifying education expenses total $4,800. Lois's educational expenses equal 80% of the total amount received ($4,800 ÷ $6,000). Thus, her exclusion is limited to $1,500 (0.80 × $1,875). ◀

[29] Interest from state and local bonds issued for private activities such as the construction of sports facilities, convention centers, and industrial park sites is taxable. A limited amount of tax-exempt bonds can be issued each year by a state for "qualified" private activities such as airport construction, redevelopment, and student loans. The limit is the greater of $225 million or $75 per resident (Sec. 146(d)). Though exempt from regular income tax, interest from these "qualified" private activity bonds is subject to the alternative minimum tax (see Chapter I:14).

[30] Sec. 149(b).

[31] Sec. 148. Interest from state or local government bonds issued for the purpose of using the proceeds to buy higher-yield investments is taxable. Such bonds are called arbitrage bonds.

[32] Sec. 135(c).

[33] The exclusion is not permitted for amounts paid for sports, games, or hobbies unless they are part of a degree program (Sec. 135(c)(2)(B)).

[34] Each of these amounts is adjusted annually for inflation. In 2014, the phase-out started at $76,000 ($113,950 on joint returns) and ended at $91,000 ($143,950 on joint returns).

ADDITIONAL COMMENT

A child born today will require about $100,000 for a four-year college education. If interest rates are around 6%, one would have to save about $245 a month until the child entered school to be able to pay this amount.

As noted, the amount of the exclusion is further reduced if modified adjusted gross income exceeds a $77,200 threshold ($115,750 for married individuals filing a joint return). Modified adjusted gross income includes the interest from education savings bonds and certain otherwise excludable foreign income.[35] The reduction is computed as follows:

$$\text{Otherwise excludable amount} \times \frac{\text{Excess modified AGI}}{\$15{,}000\ (\$30{,}000 \text{ for joint filers})}$$

EXAMPLE I:3-17 ▶ Assume the same facts as in Example I:3-16 and that Lois is single and has other adjusted gross income of $80,325, making her total AGI $82,200 ($80,325 + $1,875). Lois's otherwise available exclusion of $1,500 is reduced by $500 to $1,000. This reduction is computed by dividing the excess modified AGI of $5,000 ($80,325 + $1,875 − $77,200) by $15,000 and multiplying the result by $1,500. ◀

One difficulty with the rules is that the phase-out of the exclusion is based on income in the year the bonds are redeemed, not the year they are purchased. As a result, some taxpayers who purchase bonds anticipating an exclusion find they are ineligible for the exclusion when the bonds are redeemed.

RENTS AND ROYALTIES

Amounts received as rents or royalties are included in gross income. As noted earlier, prepaid rent is taxable when received. Security deposits, which are refundable to tenants upon the expiration of a lease, are not included in gross income. The deposit is included in gross income only if it is not refunded upon the expiration of the lease.

EXAMPLE I:3-18 ▶ In December 2015, Buddy rents an apartment to Gary. Buddy receives the first and last months' rent plus a security deposit of $500. Buddy must include in 2015 gross income both the first and last months' rent. Assume that Gary moves out of the apartment in 2017 and Buddy keeps $300 of the security deposit to cover repairs costing $200 and five days' unpaid rent, which amounts to $100. In 2017, Buddy would include the $300 in gross income and could deduct $200 for repairs. ◀

Royalties from copyrights, patents, and oil, gas, and mineral rights are all taxable as ordinary income. **Royalties** are proceeds paid to an owner by others who do business under some right belonging to the owner. Amounts received by a lessor to cancel, amend, or modify a lease also are taxable.

? STOP & THINK

Question: Financial accounting contains extensive rules distinguishing "operating leases" from "capital leases." The IRC has no such rules. While the tax law does require the capitalization of leases that are in substance a purchase of the asset, most authority relating to the distinction comes from court cases. Why doesn't the tax law include specific rules relating to leased property?

Solution: The financial accounting rules that require businesses to capitalize some leases were established because of concern that long-term lease commitments represented unrecorded liabilities. Unrecorded liabilities distort a company's balance sheet, but may not distort reported income. Since the tax law is concerned with the reporting of income rather than the balance sheet, neither Congress nor the Treasury Department has seen the need to adopt leasing rules like those in financial accounting.

Improvements by Lessees. Improvements made by a lessee that increase the value of leased property are included in the lessor's income only if the improvements are made in lieu of paying rent or if rent is reduced because of the improvements. In such situations,

[35] Specifically, modified adjusted gross income includes amounts that qualify for the foreign earned income exclusion (Sec. 911), the exclusion for possession's income (Sec. 931), and the exclusion for income from Puerto Rico (Sec. 933). The limitation is determined after taking the partial exclusion for Social Security benefits and railroad retirement (Sec. 86), claiming the allowable deduction for retirement contributions (Sec. 219), and applying the passive loss limitation (Sec. 469).

the lessor must include the fair market value (FMV) of the improvement in gross income when it is made to the property.[36]

EXAMPLE I:3-19 ▶ Rita rents an apartment to Anna. The apartment normally would rent for $1,000 per month, but Rita agrees to accept $400 per month for the first year if Anna builds a block wall around the property. Rita estimates that she would have to pay someone $6,000 to build the wall. Rita is accepting reduced rent and must report gross income of $6,000 when the wall is added to the property. The $6,000 could be added to Rita's basis in the property and should qualify as a depreciable asset. ◀

Improvements not made in lieu of rent are not income to the lessor. No adjustment is made to the lessor's basis in the property and, therefore, no depreciation is allowable. Gain or loss is recognized only when the property is disposed of.[37] Whether the improvements are in lieu of rent depends on the intent of the parties. This determination is based on the facts of the particular situation. The rental rate, the terms of the rental agreement, and whether the improvements have an estimated useful life exceeding the term of the lease may all be indications of intent.

ADDITIONAL COMMENT

Shareholders of closely held corporations generally do not want to receive dividends from their corporations. The reason? They are taxed as ordinary income and the corporation does not receive a tax deduction for the payments.

DIVIDENDS

Dividends are included in shareholder gross income. The result is a so-called double tax because corporations are taxed on income they earn, and shareholders are taxed when the income is distributed as dividends.

As noted in the previous chapter many corporations avoid the problem of "double taxation" by making S elections which result in the corporations and their shareholders being taxed much like partnerships. Two other important provisions reduce the tax burden on dividends:

- C Corporation receiving dividends from other C Corporations may claim a "dividends received deduction" that reduces, and in some cases eliminates, the second corporate tax on the income. The amount of the dividend received deduction is generally 70% of dividends received by a corporation owning less than 20% of the distributing corporation, 80% of dividends received by a corporation owning at least 20% but less than 80% of the distributing corporation, and 100% of the dividends received by a corporation owning 80% or more of the distributing corporation. This rule is discussed more in Chapter I:16 and in-depth in *Prentice Hall's Federal Taxation: Corporations, Partnerships, Estates & Trusts* text and the *Comprehensive* volume.

ADDITIONAL COMMENT

Beginning in 2013, higher-income taxpayers (AGI greater than $200,000 for single or $250,000 for married filing jointly) have to pay an additional 3.8% tax on net investment income. Net investment income generally includes interest, dividends, rents, and capital gains.

- Lower tax rates apply to qualified dividends received by individuals. There is no tax on qualified dividends received by individuals in the 10% and 15% tax brackets. Dividends received by individuals in the 25% through 35% brackets are taxed at 15%. Dividends received by individuals in the 39.6% bracket are taxed at 20%. These lower rates apply only to stock that meets a special 60-day holding period.

In general, the above provisions apply to domestic corporations because foreign corporations are not automatically subject to the U.S. income tax. Only domestic corporations may make S elections. Dividends received from foreign corporations are generally ineligible for either the dividend received deduction or the lower tax rates discussed above.

EXAMPLE I:3-20 ▶ Georgia is in the 25% tax bracket. She owns 10% of Orange Corporation, an S corporation with $20,000 of income. The corporation distributes $1,000 to Georgia. She receives a $500 dividend from Red Corporation, a U.S. corporation, and $300 from Blue Corporation, a foreign corporation. Georgia will include $2,800 in gross income. This includes her share of Orange Corporation's income or $2,000 (10% × $20,000) along with $500 she received from Red Corporation and $300 she received from Blue Corporation. As Orange Corporation made an S-election, she must include in gross income her share of the corporation's income even though only part of it is distributed. The tax rate that applies to the $2,000 depends on the nature of the income earned by Orange Corporation. For example, part or all of the income could be

[36] Reg. Sec. 1.109-1.

[37] Reg. Sec. 1.1019-1.

treated as capital gains or dividend income if Orange earned those types of income while income from operations would be taxed at Georgia's higher tax rate of 25%. The dividend from Red Corporation qualifies for the favorable 15% tax rate as Georgia is in the 25% tax bracket. The dividend from Blue Corporation will be taxed at Georgia's regular tax rate of 25% as it was paid by a foreign corporation. ◀

EXAMPLE I:3-21 ▶ Celeste is a single taxpayer in 2015 with a salary of $46,750, qualified dividend income of $3,000, and itemized deductions of $8,000. Her taxable income is:

Adjusted gross income	$49,750
Itemized deductions	(8,000)
Personal exemption	(4,000)
Taxable income	$37,750

Her taxable income excluding dividends is $34,750 ($37,750 − $3,000), and is taxed at regular rates. The 15% tax bracket for single taxpayers ends at $37,450. As a result, $2,700 ($37,450 − $34,750) of Celeste's dividends are tax free, and the balance of the dividends or $300 ($3,000 − $2,700) is taxed at 15%.

Tax on ordinary income of $34,750 using rate schedule	$ 4,751
$2,700 of dividend income is tax free	–0–
Tax on $300 of dividend income at 15%	45
Taxable income	$ 4,796

◀

Dividends Defined. Distributions to shareholders are taxable as dividends only to the extent they are made from either the corporation's current earnings and profits (a concept similar, although not identical, to current year's net income for financial accounting purposes) or accumulated earnings and profits (a concept similar, although not identical, to beginning of the year retained earnings).[38] Earnings and profits are discussed in Chapter I:16 and in greater depth in *Prentice Hall's Federal Taxation: Corporations, Partnerships, Estates, and Trusts* text and the *Comprehensive* volume. Distributions in excess of current and accumulated earnings and profits are treated as a nontaxable recovery of capital. Such distributions reduce the shareholder's basis in the stock. Distributions in excess of the basis of the stock are classified as capital gains.

EXAMPLE I:3-22 ▶ Liz is the sole shareholder in Atlantic Corporation and has owned the stock for five years. The basis of her stock is $50,000. Atlantic distributes $40,000 to Liz. Accumulated earnings and profits at the beginning of the year equal $25,000, and current earnings and profits equal $10,000. Liz will report $35,000 of taxable dividend income and a nontaxable return of capital equal to $5,000. In addition, Liz must reduce her basis in the stock by $5,000. Alternatively, if the distribution to Liz were $100,000, she would report $35,000 of taxable dividend income, $50,000 as a nontaxable return of capital, and a $15,000 long-term capital gain. ◀

Stock Dividends. A **stock dividend** is a distribution by a corporation to its shareholders of the corporation's own stock. In 1920, the Supreme Court held that simple stock dividends could not be taxed because they were not income.[39] More precisely, income had not been realized because there was no real change in the taxpayer's interest or the risks faced by the taxpayer. Over the years, however, the exclusion for stock dividends has been narrowed. If a shareholder has the option of receiving either cash or stock, the shareholder is taxed even if he or she opts to receive stock. The option to receive cash constitutes constructive receipt of the cash. Today, many other features of a stock dividend may cause it to be taxed. For example, a distribution in which preferred stock is distributed to some common shareholders and common stock is distributed to others is taxable.[40] The recipient of a taxable stock dividend includes the value of the stock received in gross income, and that amount becomes the basis of the shares received.

ADDITIONAL COMMENT

Many mutual funds do not want their shareholders to have a large tax bill on the undistributed capital gains allocated among the shareholders. Some mutual funds will sell stocks in the portfolio that can be sold at a loss to offset gains incurred earlier in the year.

A nontaxable stock dividend has no effect on a shareholder's income in the year received. The basis of the old shares is allocated between the old shares and the new

[38] Sec. 316(a). The federal income tax became effective on March 1, 1913. Thus, income accumulated before that date can still be distributed on a tax-exempt basis.

[39] *Eisner v. Myrtle H. Macomber*, 3 AFTR 3020, 1 USTC ¶32 (USSC, 1920).

[40] Reg. Sec. 1.305-4.

shares. Furthermore, the holding period for the new shares starts on the same date as the holding period of the old.

EXAMPLE I:3-23 ▶ Carol purchases 100 shares of Mesa Corporation stock for $1,100 (or $11 per share). Carol receives 10 shares of Mesa stock as a nontaxable stock dividend. After the dividend, Carol owns 110 shares of stock with a total basis of $1,100 (or $10 per share). All of the stock is assumed to have been acquired at the time of the original purchase. ◀

REAL-WORLD EXAMPLE

In the 1989 trial of Leona Helmsley, the billionaire hotel queen, it was disclosed that she had billed her companies for millions of dollars in personal items. The items ranged from a $12.99 girdle to a $1 million limestone-and-marble pool enclosure at her estate. She was sentenced to four years in prison and fined $7.1 million. The amounts paid to her by her companies represented constructive dividends.

Capital Gain Dividends. A **capital gain dividend** is a distribution by a regulated investment company (commonly called a *mutual fund*) of capital gains realized from the sale of investments in the fund. Such dividends also include any undistributed capital gains allocated to shareholders by such companies.[41] Capital gain dividends are long-term regardless of how long the shareholder has owned the stock of the regulated investment company.

Constructive Dividends. In many corporations, the same individuals are both shareholders and employees. A corporation may not deduct dividends paid to shareholders but is permitted to deduct reasonable compensation. Questions are often raised as to whether amounts reported as compensation are really disguised dividends. If an amount called compensation is unreasonably high, it will be disallowed and reclassified as a dividend.[42] Often the reasonableness of compensation is determined by comparing the compensation paid to the employee-shareholders with amounts paid to others performing similar services.

EXAMPLE I:3-24 ▶ Carmen owns 100% of the stock in Florida Corporation and receives a $400,000 salary for serving as president. The corporation reports no taxable income and pays no dividends. Presidents of similar companies received salaries ranging from $75,000 to $160,000. The IRS probably would disallow a portion of Carmen's salary as unreasonable resulting in the corporation owing tax. The disallowed portion would be treated as a dividend. ◀

ADDITIONAL COMMENT

In one case, the taxpayer, who was also the president and principal shareholder, diverted cash from vending and pinball machines at his truck stops/restaurants to his personal use. The IRS's position was that these diverted cash amounts were a constructive dividend. *Hagaman v. CIR.*, 69 AFTR 2d 92-906 (6th Cir., 1992).

Constructive dividends are not limited to shareholder-employee compensation payments but may include situations where the shareholder also is a landlord (e.g., property is rented to the corporation at an amount greater than its fair rental value). A shareholder also may receive a constructive dividend because of a creditor or vendor relationship. It is not necessary that a dividend be formally declared or that distributions be in proportion to stock holdings. **Constructive dividends** are often distributions that are intended to result in a deduction to the corporation and taxable income (such as compensation) to the shareholder.[43] Other constructive dividends are intended to produce a nonreportable benefit to the shareholder,[44] or even result in a deduction to the corporation without income to the shareholder.[45]

ALIMONY AND SEPARATE MAINTENANCE PAYMENTS

Any payment pursuant to a divorce or legal separation must be classified as one of the following for tax purposes:

(1) Alimony;

(2) Child support; or

(3) Property settlement.

The treatment of a payment depends on its classification. Alimony is deductible by the payor spouse and taxable to the payee spouse. Neither child support payments nor property settlements have any tax ramifications, that is, they are not subject to tax to the payee spouse nor deductible by the payor spouse.

Example I:3-25 demonstrates the significant difference in taxation that can occur when a payment is classified as either alimony or a property settlement.

---

41 Sec. 852(b).

42 Sec. 162(a)(1).

43 Other examples include excessive royalties (*Peterson & Pegau Baking Co.*, 2 B.T.A. 637 (1925)) and rent (*Limericks, Inc. v. CIR*, 36 AFTR 649, 48-1 USTC ¶9146 (5th Cir., 1948)).

44 Examples include bargain sales of corporate assets to shareholders (*J. E. Timberlake v. CIR*, 30 AFTR 583, 42-2 USTC ¶9822 (4th Cir., 1942)), redemptions of a shareholder's stock (Sec. 302), and loans to shareholders that are actually dividends (*George Blood Enterprises, Inc.*, 1976 PH T.C. Memo ¶76,102, 35 TCM 436).

45 Examples include paying an employee's personal expenses (*The Lang Chevrolet Co.*, 1967 PH T.C. Memo ¶67,212, 26 TCM 1054) and purchasing assets for an employee's use (*Joseph Morgenstern*, 1955 PH T.C. Memo ¶55,086, 14 TCM 282).

EXAMPLE I:3-25 ▶ Helen earns $500,000 and, as a result of her divorce, she is required to pay William $250,000. If the payment is a property settlement, Helen cannot deduct any of the $250,000 payment and William is not required to include the payment in his income. However, if the $250,000 is alimony, Helen can deduct the full amount in computing her adjusted gross income. William reports the $250,000 as alimony income. ◀

ADDITIONAL COMMENT

Child-support payments are not treated as alimony and are neither deductible by the payor spouse nor includible in income of the payee spouse.

ADDITIONAL COMMENT

If any amount specified in the divorce instrument will be reduced due to the happening of a contingency relating to a child or reduced at a time that can clearly be associated with such contingency, the amount of the reduction is treated as child support.

ETHICAL POINT

Tax consultants who advise divorcing couples may face an ethical dilemma because advice that benefits one spouse may be detrimental to the other, and because of the need to maintain confidential client relationships.

The tax law has rather specific rules that distinguish alimony, child support, and property settlements. Under current law, in order to be treated as **alimony**, payments must meet all of the following requirements:[46]

- Be made in cash (not property)
- Be made pursuant to a divorce, separation, or a written agreement between the spouses
- Terminate at the death of the payee
- Not be designated as being other than alimony (e.g., child support)
- Be made between people who are living in separate households

These rules are summarized in Topic Review I:3-2. Certain aspects of these rules will be discussed further.

A **property settlement** is a division of property pursuant to a divorce. In general, each spouse is entitled to the property brought into the marriage and a share of the property accumulated during marriage.[47] A division of property does not result in any income to either spouse, nor does either spouse receive a tax deduction. The basis of property received by either spouse as a result of the divorce or separation remains unchanged.

EXAMPLE I:3-26 ▶ As a result of a divorce, Dawn receives stock that she purchased with her former husband during their marriage for $12,000. At the time of the divorce, the stock was worth $14,000. Neither Dawn nor her former husband reports income from the transfer of the stock because the stock was acquired as a property settlement. If Dawn subsequently sold the stock for $15,000, she would report a $3,000 gain. ◀

TOPIC REVIEW I:3-2

Tax Rules for Alimony

Treatment of Recipient

The recipient of alimony must include the amounts received in gross income. Property settlements and child support payments are not taxable.

Treatment of Payor

The payor of alimony may deduct amounts paid *for* adjusted gross income. Property settlements and child support payments are not deductible.

Applicable To

Payments must be pursuant to a divorce, separation, or a written agreement between spouses.

Requirements

Spouses must be living in separate households. Payments must be in the form of cash paid to (or for the benefit of) a spouse or former spouse. Payments must terminate at the death of the payee. Payments may not be designated as being other than alimony (such as child support or a property settlement).

Recapture

If the amount of payments declines in the second or third year, a portion of the early payments may have to be recaptured as income by the payor. The payee may deduct the same recaptured amount.

---

[46] Before 1942, alimony was not deductible (*Gould v. Gould*, 3 AFTR 2958, 1 USTC ¶13 (USSC, 1917)). The original rules were revised in 1984 and again in 1986. Prior rules apply to earlier divorces unless both spouses elect to apply current rules.

[47] How the property accumulated during marriage is divided may be determined by an agreement of the parties, or if they are unable to agree, on a basis of state law.

One unusual rule found in the current law that relates to alimony is the so-called **recapture provision.** This provision was established to prevent a large property settlement that might take place after a divorce from being disguised as alimony so as to produce a deduction for the payor. In essence, the concept of recapture in connection with a divorce means that the payor of the alimony (who has taken a deduction for such amounts in prior years) must report the recapture amount in his or her income. The payee (who has reported the income in prior years) receives a deduction for the recaptured amount. This recapture occurs because the payments that originally were reported as alimony are being reclassified as property settlements.

Recapture occurs if payments decrease sharply in either the second or third year. Specifically, the amount of second-year alimony recaptured is equal to the second-year alimony reduced by the total of \$15,000 plus the third-year alimony. The amount of first-year alimony recaptured is equal to the first-year alimony reduced by the total of \$15,000 plus the average alimony paid in the second year (reduced by the recapture for that year) and the third year. The calculation of recapture for both the first and second years is shown below.

$$R_2 = A_2 - (\$15{,}000 + A_3)$$

$$R_1 = A_1 - [\$15{,}000 + (A_2 + A_3 - R_2)/2]$$

A_i = Alimony paid in first (A_1), second (A_2), and third year (A_3), respectively.

R_i = Recaptured alimony from the first (R_1) and second year (R_2), respectively.

Both first- and second-year amounts are recaptured by requiring the payor to report the excess as income (and allowing the payee to deduct the same amount) in the third year. Recapture is not required if payments cease because of the death of either spouse or remarriage of the recipient.

EXAMPLE I:3-27 ▶ As a result of their divorce, Hal is ordered to pay to Rose \$100,000 alimony in 2015 and \$20,000 per year thereafter until her death or remarriage. Hal must recapture the amount of the decrease that exceeds \$35,000, or \$65,000 (\$100,000 − \$20,000 − \$15,000). The \$65,000 of alimony in 2015 must be reported by Hal as income during 2017. Also, Rose may deduct the \$65,000 *for* AGI in 2017. ◀

EXAMPLE I:3-28 ▶ As a result of their separation, Mary agrees to pay Tom \$20,000 per year. The payments are to cease if Tom remarries. In the year after the agreement is reached, Tom remarries and Mary discontinues the payments. No recapture is required because the payments are contingent on the remarriage of the recipient and the payments have been discontinued because of the occurrence of this contingency. ◀

PENSIONS AND ANNUITIES

ADDITIONAL COMMENT

The three largest sources of nonwage income in 2012, in rank order, were capital gains, pensions and annuities, and partnership and S corporation income.

An **annuity** is a series of regular payments that will continue for a fixed period of time or until the death of the recipient. Taxpayers occasionally purchase annuities from insurance companies to provide a source of funds during retirement years. The insurance company may agree to make payments to the insured for the remainder of the insured's life. The retired individual is assured of a steady flow of funds for life. The price paid for the annuity represents its cost. The insured taxpayer is permitted to recover this cost tax-free.

Individuals receiving an annuity are permitted to exclude their cost, but are taxed on the remaining portion of the annuity. The following steps can be followed to determine the nontaxable portion of the annuity:

ADDITIONAL COMMENT

The expected return is limited to amounts receivable as an annuity. It does not include amounts that may be paid after death, nor does it include anticipated dividends.

- Determine the **expected return multiple.** This multiple is the number of years that the annuity is expected to continue and may be a stated term, say ten years, or it may be for the remainder of the taxpayer's life. In the latter situation, the expected return multiple (life expectancy) is determined by referring to a table (see Table I:3-1) developed by the IRS.
- Determine the **expected return.** This return is computed by multiplying the amount of the annual payment by the expected return multiple.

▼ **TABLE I:3-1**
Ordinary Life Annuities (One Life) Expected Return Multiple

Age	Multiple	Age	Multiple	Age	Multiple
5	76.6	42	40.6	79	10.0
6	75.6	43	39.6	80	9.5
7	74.7	44	38.7	81	8.9
8	73.7	45	37.7	82	8.4
9	72.7	46	36.8	83	7.9
10	71.7	47	35.9	84	7.4
11	70.7	48	34.9	85	6.9
12	69.7	49	34.0	86	6.5
13	68.8	50	33.1	87	6.1
14	67.8	51	32.2	88	5.7
15	66.8	52	31.3	89	5.3
16	65.8	53	30.4	90	5.0
17	64.8	54	29.5	91	4.7
18	63.9	55	28.6	92	4.4
19	62.9	56	27.7	93	4.1
20	61.9	57	26.8	94	3.9
21	60.9	58	25.9	95	3.7
22	59.9	59	25.0	96	3.4
23	59.0	60	24.2	97	3.2
24	58.0	61	23.3	98	3.0
25	57.0	62	22.5	99	2.8
26	56.0	63	21.6	100	2.7
27	55.1	64	20.8	101	2.5
28	54.1	65	20.0	102	2.3
29	53.1	66	19.2	103	2.1
30	52.2	67	18.4	104	1.9
31	51.2	68	17.6	105	1.8
32	50.2	69	16.8	106	1.6
33	49.3	70	16.0	107	1.4
34	48.3	71	15.3	108	1.3
35	47.3	72	14.6	109	1.1
36	46.4	73	13.9	110	1.0
37	45.4	74	13.2	111	.9
38	44.4	75	12.5	112	.8
39	43.5	76	11.9	113	.7
40	42.5	77	11.2	114	.6
41	41.5	78	10.6	115	.5

Source: Reg. Sec. 1.72-9, Table V.
Note: This table should be used if any or all investments were made on or after July 1, 1986. If all investments were made before July 1, 1986, use Reg. Sec. 1.72-9, Table I (not shown).

ADDITIONAL COMMENT

If payments are paid other than monthly, the number of anticipated payments is adjusted accordingly. Thus, if payments are made quarterly, the number from the table is divided by three.

- Determine the **exclusion ratio.** This ratio is computed by dividing the investment in the contract (its cost) by the expected return (from above).
- Determine the **current year's exclusion.** This exclusion is computed by multiplying the exclusion ratio (from above) times the amount received during the year.

EXAMPLE I:3-29 ► David, age 65, purchases an annuity for $30,000. Under the terms of the annuity, David is to receive $300 per month ($3,600 per year) for the rest of his life.

- The expected return multiple is 20.0. The multiple is obtained from Table I:3-1.
- The expected return is $72,000 (20.0 × $3,600).
- The exclusion ratio is 0.4167 ($30,000 ÷ $72,000).
- The exclusion is $1,500 (0.4167 × $3,600). ◄

After the entire cost of an annuity has been recovered, the full amount of all future payments is taxable. On the other hand, if an individual dies before recovering the entire cost, the remaining unrecovered cost can be deducted as an itemized deduction on that individual's final return. Insurance companies and businesses with retirement plans compute the taxable portion of annuities and report the amounts to recipients on Form 1099.

Qualified Retirement Plan Annuities. Distributions from pensions and other qualified retirement plans are commonly paid in the form of an annuity. Both the employer and the employee often contribute funds to these plans. The employee's cost is limited to after-tax amounts contributed by the employee, usually through withholding. The employee's cost does not include employer contributions or pretax contributions made by the employee to Sec. 401(k) and similar plans.

KEY POINT

The simplified method is used only for annuity distributions from qualified retirement plans. All other annuity distributions are taxed in accordance with the general rules above.

Simplified Method. A simplified method is now used to determine the taxable portion of an annuity paid from a qualified retirement plan. Under the simplified method, the nontaxable portion of each annuity payment is equal to the employee's after-tax investment in the annuity divided by the number of anticipated payments as determined from the following table:

Age of Primary Annuitant on the Start Date	*Number of Anticipated Payments*
55 and under	360
56–60	310
61–65	260
66–70	210
71 and over	160

EXAMPLE I:3-30 ▶ Jack, age 62, retires, and receives a $1,000 per month annuity from his employer's qualified pension plan. Jack contributed $65,000 to the plan prior to his retirement. Under the simplified method, Jack would exclude $250 per month as a return of capital. This is calculated by dividing $65,000 by 260 anticipated payments. ◀

ADDITIONAL COMMENT

Unlike other retirement plans, all contributions made to Roth plans are from after-tax income. When all Roth requirements are met, distributions are tax-free. See Chapter I:9.

Plan Comparison. Plans that involve a combination of pre- and after-tax contributions are taxed less favorably than plans that have only pretax or only after-tax contributions because income earned on after-tax contributions is taxed when distributed to retired employees. For that reason, many employers today have two separate plans, one with only pretax contributions and a second with only after-tax contributions (like the Roth plan). The result is that all distributions from the pretax plan are taxable, whereas no qualified distributions from the Roth plan are taxable.

KEY POINT

Under current law, a taxpayer must generally pay tax on a portion of each withdrawal made before the normal starting date of the annuity.

Advance Payments. Many pensions contain provisions that allow taxpayers to withdraw amounts before the normal starting date. Under current law, an amount withdrawn from a pension before the starting date is considered to be in part a recovery of the employee's contributions and in part a recovery of the employer's contributions.[48] After all contributions have been withdrawn, additional withdrawals are fully taxable.

EXAMPLE I:3-31 ▶ Dick, age 45 and in good health, withdrew $2,000 from a pension plan during the current year. No exception exempts Dick from the 10% penalty. Dick had made $40,000 of after-tax contributions to the plan, and his employer had contributed $60,000. Dick must include $1,200 (0.60 × $2,000) in income. Because no exception applies, Dick must also pay an additional penalty of $120 (0.10 × $1,200). The penalty is not deductible by Dick. ◀

ADDITIONAL COMMENT

In addition to being subject to the regular income tax, any amount withdrawn may also be subject to a 10% nondeductible penalty. The penalty is not applicable to taxpayers who are age 591/2 or older. Other exceptions to the early withdrawal penalty are discussed in Chapter I:9.

INCOME FROM LIFE INSURANCE AND ENDOWMENT CONTRACTS

The face amount of life insurance received because of the death of the insured is not taxable. If the proceeds are left with the insurance company and as a result earn interest, the interest payments are taxable. (See Chapter I:4 for a detailed discussion of life insurance and endowment contracts.)

[48] Sec. 72(e).

INCOME FROM DISCHARGE OF INDEBTEDNESS

In general, the forgiveness of debt is a taxable event. The person who owed the money must report the amount forgiven as income unless one of several exceptions found in the tax law applies. These exceptions are discussed in Chapter I:4.

INCOME PASSED THROUGH TO TAXPAYER

Generally, entities are subject to income tax based on the amount of taxable income. Corporations, as an example, are subject to income taxation. As noted, certain types of entities are not subject to income taxation as their income is taxed directly to their owners rather than to the entities. Such entities are referred to as "flow-through entities." Section 61 specifically lists three such instances: the distributive share of a partnership's income, income in respect of a decedent, and income from an interest in an estate or trust. Though not mentioned in Sec. 61, similar treatment is accorded S corporations, Exchange Traded Funds, Regulated Investment Companies, and Real Estate Investment Trusts. In each case, the income that is produced by the entities merely flows through to the owners or beneficiaries of such entities. The rules can be summarized as follows:

KEY POINT

The pass-through of income by a partnership can create a situation known as phantom income. In this situation, a partner is required to report income on his or her individual tax return, but the partner may not have received a cash distribution from the partnership.

- Each partner reports his or her share of a partnership's income. Each partner deducts his or her share of the partnership's expenses. The income and deductions are reported by the partners whether or not any amount is actually distributed by the partnership during the year. The partnership's income and deductions retain their tax status.
- S corporations are taxed much like partnerships. Each shareholder in the corporation is taxed on his or her proportionate share of the corporation's income whether or not the income is actually distributed.
- Exchange Traded Funds (ETFs), Regulated Investment Companies (RICs), often called mutual funds, and Real Estate Investment Trusts (REITs) are also flow through entities. ETFs and RICs invest in securities and are required to distribute their income to shareholders who are taxed on the distributions. REITs invest in real estate and real estate loans. They too must distribute their income to investors who are taxed on the income. The distributions (dividends, interest, rents, and gains) retain their tax status when reported by ETF, RIC, and REIT investors.
- Income in respect of a decedent is income earned by an individual before death that is paid to another after the death. For example, salary earned by a husband before his death in an automobile accident may be paid to his widow. The recipient, in this case the widow, is taxed on the income if it has not been taxed to the decedent before his death.
- Income earned by estates and trusts is subject to taxation.[49] However, income distributions to beneficiaries are deductible by estates and trusts and are taxable to the beneficiaries. Thus, if a trust with \$20,000 of income distributes \$15,000 to its beneficiary, the trust is taxed on \$5,000, and \$15,000 is taxed to the beneficiary. Because of this approach estates and trusts are sometimes referred to as semi-flow-through or hybrid entities. The income taxation of estates and trusts is covered more fully in *Prentice Hall's Federal Taxation: Corporations, Partnerships, Estates, and Trusts.*

OTHER ITEMS OF GROSS INCOME

The preceding discussions considered items of gross income specifically listed in Sec. 61(a). However, the fact that an item of income is listed in Sec. 61(a) does not necessarily cause it to be taxable. Rather, the condition that causes an item of income to be taxable is that it is not specifically excluded. Some items of gross income not mentioned in Sec. 61(a) are discussed below.

[49] Note the distinction between income in respect of a decedent and the income of an estate. Income in respect of a decedent is the income earned before death that was never taxed to the decedent. An example would be interest that was accrued but unpaid at death. Income of an estate is income earned after death that is paid to the estate. An example would be interest that accrues after the decedent's death.

PRIZES, AWARDS, GAMBLING WINNINGS, AND TREASURE FINDS

In general, prizes, awards, gambling winnings, and treasure finds are taxable.[50] Winnings in contests, competitions, and quiz shows are taxable.[51] The amount to be included in gross income is the fair market value of the goods or services received. Total gambling winnings must be included in gross income.[52] This includes proceeds from lotteries, raffles, sweepstakes, and the like. Gambling losses (up to the amount of the current year's winnings) are allowable as an itemized deduction.[53] The Regulations state that a treasure find constitutes gross income to the extent of its value in the year in which it is reduced to undisputed possession.[54]

EXAMPLE I:3-32 ▶ Several years ago, Colleen purchased a used piano at an auction for $15. In the current year, she finds $4,500 of currency hidden in the piano. Colleen must report the $4,500 as income in the current year.[55] ◀

REAL-WORLD EXAMPLE

An accountant collected from a client money that was to be used to pay the client's taxes. Then the accountant appropriated the money for his own use. The accountant was held to have received unreported income. *Richard A. Reeves,* 1977 PH T.C. Memo ¶ 77,114, 36 TCM 500.

ILLEGAL INCOME

Income from illegal activities is taxable.[56] Some people find this part of the tax law surprising, but this fact serves as the basis for many criminal convictions given that few criminals report their illegal income. For example, Al Capone was convicted of income tax evasion, not bootlegging or other crimes. It is not necessary to prove that an individual had illegal income, but merely that the individual had income that was not reported.

Individuals have used varied defenses against this rule. One taxpayer was successful in convincing the Supreme Court that he should not be taxed on embezzlement gains because he had an unconditional obligation to repay the amount embezzled,[57] but the Supreme Court reversed this position in a later case.[58] The court concluded that although an obligation to repay existed, the taxpayer had no "consensual recognition" (intent) to repay. In addition to embezzlement of funds, the courts have held that a kidnapper's ransom was taxable,[59] along with profits from bookmaking,[60] card playing,[61] forgery,[62] stealing,[63] bank robbery,[64] sale of narcotics,[65] illegal sale of liquor,[66] and bribes.[67] (See Chapter I:6 for a discussion of related deductions.)

ADDITIONAL COMMENT

Welfare payments are not normally required to be included in gross income. However, if the welfare payments are fraudulently received under state or federal assistance programs, they must be included in the recipient's gross income.

UNEMPLOYMENT COMPENSATION

For many years, unemployment compensation was excluded from gross income. In 1978, Congress changed the law to fully tax unemployment compensation because these benefits are a substitute for taxable wages.

SOCIAL SECURITY BENEFITS

Social Security benefits were excluded from gross income until 1984. Between 1984 and 1993, up to 50% of Social Security benefits were taxable. Beginning in 1994, up to 85% of Social Security benefits may be taxable. Under Sec. 86, the portion of Social Security benefits that are taxable depends on the taxpayer's provisional income and filing status. *Provisional income* is computed using the following formula:

---

[50] Exclusions for scholarships and fellowships and a limited exclusion for prizes awarded for scientific, charitable, or similar meritorious achievements are discussed in Chapter I:4.
[51] Sec. 74 and Reg. Sec. 1.74-1.
[52] *U.S. v. Manley S. Sullivan,* 6 AFTR 6753, 1 USTC ¶236 (USSC, 1927).
[53] Sec. 165(d).
[54] Reg. Sec. 1.61-14(a).
[55] *Ermenegildo Cesarini v. U.S.,* 26 AFTR 2d 5107, 70-2 USTC ¶9509 (6th Cir., 1970).
[56] Reg. 1.61-14(a).
[57] *CIR v. Laird Wilcox,* 34 AFTR 811, 46-1 USTC ¶9188 (USSC, 1946).
[58] *Eugene C. James v. U.S.,* 7 AFTR 2d 1361, 61-1 USTC ¶9449 (USSC, 1961).
[59] *Murray Humphreys v. CIR,* 28 AFTR 1030, 42-1 USTC ¶9237 (7th Cir., 1942).
[60] *James P. McKenna,* 1 B.T.A. 326 (1925).
[61] *L. Weiner,* 10 B.T.A. 905 (1928).
[62] *Cass Sunstein,* 1966 PH T.C. Memo ¶66,043, 25 TCM 247.
[63] *Mathias Schira v. CIR,* 50 AFTR 1404, 57-1 USTC ¶9413 (6th Cir., 1957).
[64] *Gary Ayers,* 1978 PH T.C. Memo ¶78,341, 37 TCM 1415.
[65] *Antonino Farina v. McMahon,* 2 AFTR 2d 5918, 58-2 USTC ¶9938 (D.C. N.Y., 1958).
[66] *U.S. v. Manley S. Sullivan,* 6 AFTR 6753, 1 USTC ¶236 (USSC, 1927).
[67] *U.S. v. Patrick Commerford,* 12 AFTR 364, 1933 CCH ¶9255 (2nd Cir., 1933).

Adjusted gross income (excluding Social Security benefits)		$xx,xxx
Plus:	Tax-exempt interest	x,xxx
	Excluded foreign income	x,xxx
	50% of Social Security benefits	x,xxx
Provisional income		$xx,xxx

REAL-WORLD EXAMPLE

The requirement that tax-exempt income be included in determining the taxable portion of Social Security benefits has been challenged on the basis that such provision is unconstitutional. However, the court held that this provision placed only an indirect burden on the governmental unit that issued the tax-exempt bonds, which was not protected by the intergovernmental immunity doctrine. *H.J. Goldin v. Baker*, 59 AFTR 2d 87-444, 87-1 USTC ¶9128, (2nd Cir., 1987).

Married Filing Separately. In the case of married couples who live together but file separately, taxable Social Security benefits are equal to the lesser of:

- 85% of Social Security benefits, or
- 85% of provisional income

Married Filing Jointly. For married couples filing jointly, the computation of the taxable portion of Social Security benefits is as follows:

- If provisional income is $32,000 or less, no Social Security benefits are taxable.
- If provisional income is over $32,000 (but not over $44,000), taxable Social Security benefits equal the lesser of:
  50% of the Social Security benefits, or
  50% of the excess of provisional income over $32,000
- If provisional income is over $44,000, taxable Social Security benefits are equal to the lesser of:
  85% of the Social Security benefits, or
  85% of provisional income over $44,000, plus the lesser of (1) $6,000 or (2) 50% of Social Security benefits

Single Taxpayers. For single taxpayers (and married persons living separately), the computation of the taxable portion of Social Security benefits is as follows:

- If provisional income is $25,000 or less, no Social Security benefits are taxable.
- If provisional income is over $25,000 (but not over $34,000), taxable Social Security benefits are equal to the lesser of:
  50% of the Social Security benefits, or
  50% of the excess of provisional income over $25,000
- If provisional income is over $34,000, taxable Social Security benefits are equal to the lesser of:
  85% of the Social Security benefits, or
  85% of provisional income over $34,000, plus the lesser of (1) $4,500 or (2) 50% of Social Security benefits

EXAMPLE I:3-33 ► Holly is a single taxpayer with a taxable pension of $22,000, tax-exempt interest of $10,000, and Social Security benefits of $8,000. Her provisional income is $36,000, determined as follows:

Adjusted gross income		$22,000
Plus:	Tax-exempt interest	10,000
	50% of Social Security benefits	4,000
Provisional income		$36,000

The taxable Social Security benefits are equal to $5,700, which is the lesser of $6,800 (0.85 × $8,000) or $5,700 ($1,700* + the lesser of $4,500 or $4,000**).

*($36,000 provisional income − $34,000 threshold) × 0.85.
**50% of the Social Security benefits. ◄

The result of the computation excludes from gross income the Social Security benefits received by lower-income individuals but taxes a portion (up to 85%) of the benefits received by taxpayers with higher incomes. As the thresholds are not adjusted for inflation, an increasing number of retirees are finding that a portion of their Social Security benefits is taxable.

The term **Social Security benefits** refers to basic monthly retirement and disability benefits paid under Social Security and also to tier-one railroad retirement benefits. It does not include supplementary Medicare benefits that cover the cost of doctors' services and other medical benefits.

INSURANCE PROCEEDS AND COURT AWARDS

In general, insurance proceeds and court awards are taxable. Two exceptions are accident and health insurance benefits and the face amount of life insurance. (See Chapter I:4 for a discussion of these benefits.)

Insurance proceeds or court awards received because of the destruction of property are included in gross income only to the extent that the proceeds exceed the adjusted basis of the property. Involuntary conversion provisions permit taxpayers to avoid being taxed if they reinvest the proceeds in a qualified replacement property.[68] If the proceeds are less than the property's adjusted basis, they reduce the amount of any deductible loss. Proceeds of insurance guarding against loss of profits because of a casualty are taxable.[69] Similarly, if a taxpayer had to sue a customer to collect income owed to the taxpayer, the amount collected is taxable just as it would have been had the taxpayer collected the income without going to court.

EXAMPLE I:3-34 ▶ Gulf Corporation's factory was destroyed by fire. Gulf Corporation collected insurance of $400,000, which equaled the building's basis, and $250,000 for the profits lost during the time the company was rebuilding its factory. The $400,000 is not taxable because it constitutes a recovery of the basis of the factory. The $250,000 is taxable because it represents lost income. Recall that the income would have been taxable had it been earned by the company from regular operations. ◀

Although few exclusions are designed specifically for insurance proceeds or court awards, such amounts may be covered by other, more general exclusions. For example, Sec. 104(a)(2) excludes "damages (other than punitive damages) received . . . on account of personal physical injuries or sickness." Thus, amounts collected because of physical injury suffered in an automobile accident are excluded (see Chapter I:4).

RECOVERY OF PREVIOUSLY DEDUCTED AMOUNTS

On occasion, a taxpayer may deduct an amount in one year but recover the amount in a subsequent year. In general, the amount recovered must be included in the gross income in the year it is recovered. Cash-basis taxpayers encounter this situation more often than accrual-basis taxpayers because their expenses are generally deductible in the year they are paid. If the amount was overpaid, the taxpayer can anticipate a refund.

EXAMPLE I:3-35 ▶ During 2015, Cindy's employer withheld $1,000 from her wages for state income taxes. She claimed the $1,000 as an itemized deduction on her 2015 federal income tax return. Her itemized deductions totaled $12,000. On her 2015 state income tax return, her state income tax was only $800. As a result, Cindy received a $200 refund from the state in April 2016. Because Cindy deducted the full $1,000 in 2015, she must report the $200 refund as income on her 2016 federal income tax return. ◀

Tax Benefit Rule. As noted above, a taxpayer who recovers an amount deducted in a previous year must report as gross income the amount recovered. The amount recovered need not be included in income, however, if the taxpayer received no tax benefit. A tax benefit occurs only if the deduction reduced the tax for the year.[70] Chapter I:7 provides a more detailed discussion of the tax benefit rule.

---

[68] The involuntary conversion provisions are discussed in Chapter I:12.
[69] *Oppenheim's Inc. v. Kavanagh*, 39 AFTR 468, 50-1 USTC ¶9249 (D.C.-Mich., 1950).
[70] Sec. 111.

EXAMPLE I:3-36 ▶ In 2015, Jack's employer withheld $1,200 from his wages for state income tax. Jack claimed the $1,200 as an itemized deduction on his 2015 federal income tax return. Because of a variety of losses incurred by Jack, he reported a negative taxable income of $32,000 during 2015. The state refunded the $1,200 during 2016. Jack will not have to report the $1,200 as gross income on his federal return. He would have owed no federal income tax in 2015 even without the deduction for state income taxes. Therefore, Jack received no tax benefit from the deduction. ◀

REAL-WORLD EXAMPLE

An attorney collected fees from clients of his employer. Because the attorney and his employer were engaged in a dispute over ownership of the money, he deposited the disputed amount in a trust account. The attorney was taxable on the amounts in the year received because he had control over the funds under the claim of right doctrine. *Edward J. Costello, Jr.*, 1985 PH T.C. Memo ¶85,571, 50 TCM 1463.

CLAIM OF RIGHT

Sometimes taxpayers receive disputed amounts. For example, a contractor may receive payment on a job when the quality of the work is being questioned by the customer, a salesperson may receive commissions when there is a question as to whether the sales are final, or a litigant may receive a court award even though the case is on appeal. Under the claim of right doctrine, the recipient of a disputed amount must include the amount received in gross income as long as the use of the funds is unrestricted.

EXAMPLE I:3-37 ▶ Jane wins a court case against a customer requiring the customer to pay her $10,000. The customer is unhappy with the result of the case and indicates that he plans to appeal, but pays the $10,000 to avoid interest on the amount in the event he loses the appeal. Jane must include the $10,000 in gross income even though she will have to repay the amount if she loses the appeal. ◀

EXAMPLE I:3-38 ▶ Assume the same facts as in Example I:3-37 except that the $10,000 is placed in escrow by the court awaiting the outcome of the appeal. Jane does not have to report the amount as she does not have use of the funds. ◀

Of course, taxpayers may be required to repay the disputed amount in a subsequent year. Such taxpayers may deduct the previously reported amount in the year of repayment. The taxes saved from such a deduction, however, may be considerably less than the original tax. If the repayment is over $3,000, taxpayers have the option of reducing the current tax by the tax paid in the prior year or years on the repaid amount.[71]

EXAMPLE I:3-39 ▶ Assume the same facts as in Example I:3-37, except that after reporting the disputed $10,000 Jane loses the appeal and must repay the $10,000 to her customer. If Jane was in the 25% tax bracket when she reported the disputed amount, she would have paid a $2,500 (0.25 × $10,000) tax on the disputed amount. If she were in the 15% bracket when she made the repayment, she would recover only $1,500 by deducting the $10,000. Because the amount exceeds $3,000, Jane has the option of determining her current year's tax by deducting from the tax she would otherwise pay the $2,500 tax she paid in the earlier year. This credit is allowed in lieu of receiving a $10,000 deduction. ◀

TAX PLANNING CONSIDERATIONS

OBJECTIVE 5

Describe tax planning considerations for inclusions of gross income

SHIFTING INCOME

A family can reduce its taxes by shifting income from family members who are in high tax brackets (e.g., parents) to family members who are in low tax brackets (e.g., children). Assignment of income rules prevent shifting from being done by merely redirecting the payment. Thus, a father cannot avoid a tax on his salary by ordering his employer to pay the salary to his daughter. Nevertheless, income can be shifted by transferring ownership of the property. For example, children may own stock in the family business. Dividends on the stock are taxed to the children. In the case of a child under age 24, however, the

[71] Sec. 1341.

parents' (as opposed to the child's) tax rate often applies to unearned income in excess of $2,100. Series EE bonds may prove useful to avoid the kiddie tax because the interest is deferred until the bond is redeemed or matures. The maturity date, of course, may be after the child reaches age 24. Another shifting technique is for the child to work for the family business and be paid a reasonable salary. Such income is taxed at the child's tax rate, even if the child is under 24 years old, and can be offset by the child's own standard deduction.

Shifting of income is constrained by several factors. As noted, the assignment of income doctrine limits transfers. Reasonableness limitations constrain compensation and other payments. Furthermore, outright gifts of property are subject to gift taxes. Also, individuals are reluctant to transfer wealth to children for a variety of personal reasons. However, the tax saving potential of shifting income is often so great as to prompt many well-to-do families to use available shifting techniques.

ALIMONY

Whether payments made in connection with a divorce or separation are classified as alimony is of major tax significance. Such classification results in a deduction for the payor and income to the payee. Alimony is actually one way to shift income.

EXAMPLE I:3-40 ▶ Tony, who has a 39.6% marginal tax rate, makes payments of $40,000 to his former wife. If it is deductible as alimony, Tony will save $15,840 ($0.396 \times \$40,000$) a year in federal income taxes. The amount of tax that the former wife must pay depends on how much other income she has and whether she has deductions that reduce the tax. Her tax might be as high as her former husband's or as little as zero. ◀

ADDITIONAL COMMENT

In 2012, $11.2 billion of alimony paid was reported as a deduction, while only $8.9 billion was reported as taxable income.

Two points are clear. One is that both parties should understand the implication of having amounts treated as alimony. Second, the designation of the payments as alimony may be beneficial to both parties. The payor will, of course, benefit from a tax deduction. The payee may benefit because the payor may agree to make larger alimony payments since the payments are tax deductible.

PREPAID INCOME

As explained earlier in this chapter, prepaid income is generally taxable when received. This accelerated recognition of income may be a significant disadvantage to the taxpayer if the related expenses are incurred in a later tax year. Thus, tax planning for prepaid amounts is essential.

EXAMPLE I:3-41 ▶ Phil owns an apartment complex and requires tenants to pay the first and last months' rent before they move in. Rita, on the other hand, owns an apartment complex and requires tenants to pay the first month's rent and a refundable deposit (which equals one month's rent). Although the full amount received by Phil is taxable when it is received, only one-half of the amount received by Rita is taxable when it is received. Rita is required to refund the deposit, assuming the tenant vacates leaving the property in good condition and having paid all rent. Therefore, the deposit is not taxable. ◀

Taxpayers receiving advance payments in connection with services may be able to meet the requirements of Rev. Proc. 2004-34 (discussed earlier in the chapter); taxpayers receiving advance payments associated with the sale of merchandise may be able to meet the requirements of Reg. Sec. 1.451-5 (also discussed in this chapter). Also, special rules exist for subscription income, membership fees, crop insurance proceeds, and drought sales of livestock, all of which allow taxpayers to defer recognizing income.

TAXABLE, TAX-EXEMPT, OR TAX-DEFERRED BONDS

Which should a taxpayer choose: taxable bonds, tax-exempt bonds, or tax-deferred bonds? The answer depends on the relative interest rates and the taxpayer's current and future tax brackets. **Taxable bonds** yield the highest return, but the interest is taxable. **Tax-exempt bonds** yield a lower return. **Tax-deferred bonds** generally yield a return somewhere close to that of taxable bonds. Interest on U.S. Series EE savings bonds is tax exempt if it is used for educational purposes and if other requirements of Sec. 135 are met (see the discussion earlier in this chapter). If these conditions are not met, the tax is deferred until the bonds are redeemed. The taxpayer may be in a lower bracket when the tax is eventually paid, and in the meantime, the interest that will eventually go to pay taxes is earning additional income.

The decision between taxable and exempt bonds is a rather easy one if the risk of the investments is assumed to be approximately equal. A taxpayer should invest in exempt bonds instead of taxable bonds if the interest on the exempt bonds is greater than the interest on the taxable bonds multiplied by 1 minus the taxpayer's marginal tax bracket (expressed as a decimal). Stated in a formula, this means invest in tax-exempt bonds if

$$\begin{array}{c}\text{Return on the}\\\text{tax-exempt bonds}\end{array} > \begin{array}{c}\text{Return on the}\\\text{taxable bonds}\end{array} \times (1 - \text{Marginal tax bracket})$$

EXAMPLE I:3-42 ▶ Robert's marginal tax bracket is 39.6% and he is trying to decide between tax-exempt bonds, which pay 6% interest, and taxable bonds paying 8% interest. Robert should invest in the exempt bonds because 6% is greater than 4.83% [0.08 × (1 − 0.396)]. ◀

Comparison of taxable bonds or exempt bonds to tax-deferred bonds is more complicated. As noted, the advantages of the tax-deferred bonds are twofold. First, the taxpayer may be in a lower tax bracket when the tax is paid (e.g., taxpayers who plan to redeem the bonds after retirement). Second, the amount that will eventually go to pay the tax earns income until the tax must be paid. Although the computation is not covered here, it is noted that taxpayers who anticipate that they will be in lower tax brackets and who plan to leave funds invested for several years may benefit from choosing Series EE U.S. savings bonds over taxable bonds. See Chapter I:18 in the *Individuals* text for a further discussion of taxable, tax exempt, and tax deferred investments.

REPORTING SAVINGS BOND INTEREST

It may be desirable to purchase Series EE bonds in the child's name despite the fact that such interest is subject to the kiddie tax (see Chapter I:2). This is because there is no income tax as long as the child's annual income is less than $900. However, even if a child is not otherwise required to file a return, it is necessary to report interest on Series EE bonds annually by filing a tax return.[72] Taxpayers who have not been reporting savings bond interest annually may change to annual reporting, but are required to report both current and previously accrued interest in the year of the change.[73]

Taxpayers who report savings bond interest annually are allowed to change to the deferral method without IRS approval.[74] This is particularly useful where the decision to report interest currently was made before the imposition of the kiddie tax. Taxpayers who make this election are bound by it for five years.

---

[72] *Philip Apkin*, 86 T.C. 692 (1986).
[73] Reg. Sec. 1.454-1(a)(4), Ex. (1).
[74] Rev. Proc. 97-37, 1997-2 C.B. 455.

DEFERRED COMPENSATION ARRANGEMENTS

Deferred compensation plans can be used as a means of avoiding the constructive receipt of income. Although income is normally taxable when the funds become available to the taxpayer, an advance contractual agreement can produce different results. Corporate executives, professional athletes, and others often sign agreements providing for compensation to be paid at future dates. Such agreements can produce tax savings because the recipients expect to be in a lower tax bracket. Because the arrangements are advance contractual agreements, the deferral of income does not constitute taxpayers "turning their backs" on the income.

EXAMPLE I:3-43 ▶ Alonzo, a 35-year-old professional basketball player, signs a contract specifying that he will be paid $400,000 per year for ten years even if he does not play. Because of his age, both Alonzo and the team recognize that he will probably play for one or two more years. If the agreement had specified that he was to receive a salary of $1,300,000 per year for two years, most of the income would have been taxed at the highest rates. By spreading the amount over a longer period, Alonzo pays tax at lower rates on much of the income. Alonzo is compensated for the delayed payment by receiving a larger total amount [i.e., $4 million ($400,000 × 10 years) versus $2.6 million ($1.3 million × 2 years)]. ◀

COMPLIANCE AND PROCEDURAL CONSIDERATIONS

OBJECTIVE 6

Describe compliance and procedural considerations for gross income

Form 1040 lists various types of income. Some items of income (wages, tax refunds, alimony, pensions and annuities, unemployment compensation, Social Security benefits, and other income) are listed directly on Form 1040. Most expenses related to these items of income are deducted as miscellaneous itemized deductions on Schedule A.

Most other types of income (and related deductions) are reported on special schedules.

Topic Review I:3-3 summarizes the procedures for reporting income and related deductions.

EXAMPLE I:3-44 ▶ John J. Alexander has several items of income and related deductions:

Salary		$40,000
Deductible alimony payments		6,000
Taxable interest		300
Dividends:	Ford Motor Co.	1,150
	Omaha Mutual Fund	430
	Capital Gain Distribution: Omaha Mutual Fund	50
Rent income (depreciation, interest, repairs, and other related expenses total $9,000)		11,000

The reporting of these items of income is illustrated on page 1 of Form 1040 (Figure I:3-1) and on Schedule B of Form 1040 (Figure I:3-2). Salary and interest (because the interest is less than $1,500) are entered directly on Form 1040. Rental income would be entered on Schedule E (not illustrated), and the net income after deducting related expenses is transferred to Form 1040. Alimony received and alimony payments are reported on page 1 of Form 1040. ◀

ADDITIONAL COMMENT

The dollar amount of tax-exempt interest income is recorded on Form 1040, line 8b, but is not included in the tax base. The IRS requires the reporting of this type of income probably because it may affect the taxability of Social Security benefits.

KEY POINT

The amount labeled "total income" on line 22 of Form 1040 is not gross income, adjusted gross income, or taxable income.

TOPIC REVIEW I:3-3

Reporting of Income

Type of Income	Reported On	Related Deductions Are Claimed On
Wages, salaries, tips, etc.	Form 1040	Schedule A and various other forms: moving, Form 3903; travel, transportation, etc., Form 2106
Interest	Form 1040 (if less than $1,500), otherwise Schedule B	Schedule A (miscellaneous deductions, if any, e.g., safe deposit box fees)
Dividends	Form 1040 (if less than $1,500), otherwise Schedule B	Schedule A (miscellaneous deductions, if any, e.g., safe deposit box fees)
Refund of state or local income taxes	Form 1040 (instructions contain a worksheet)	Schedule A (miscellaneous deductions, if any, e.g., fee paid for tax advice)
Alimony	Form 1040	Schedule A (miscellaneous deductions, if any, e.g., legal fee associated with alimony)
Business income	Schedule C or C-EZ (net income or loss is transferred to Form 1040)	Schedule C or C-EZ (e.g., depreciation, advertising, repairs)
Capital gains	Schedule D	Schedule D (capital losses) or Schedule A (investment expenses)
Supplemental gains	Form 4797	Form 4797 (e.g., ordinary losses)
Pensions and annuities	Form 1040 (instructions contain a worksheet)	Schedule A (miscellaneous deductions, if any, e.g., fee paid for tax advice)
Rents, royalties, partnerships, S corporations, estates, trusts, etc.	Schedule E	Schedule E
Farm income	Schedule F	Schedule F
Unemployment compensation	Form 1040	Schedule A (miscellaneous deductions, if any, e.g., fee paid for tax advice)
Social Security benefits	Form 1040 (instructions contain a worksheet)	Schedule A (miscellaneous deductions, if any, e.g., fee paid for tax advice)
Other income	Form 1040	Schedule A (miscellaneous deductions, if any)

Problem Materials

DISCUSSION QUESTIONS

I:3-1 What phrase is found in both the Sixteenth Amendment to the Constitution and Sec. 61(a)? Why does the phrase appear in both locations?

I:3-2 Contrast the accounting and economic concepts of income.

I:3-3 Why does the tax concept of income more closely resemble the accounting concept of income than the economic concept?

I:3-4 Explain the meaning of the term *wherewithal to pay* as it applies to taxation.

I:3-5 If a loan is repaid, the lender does not have to include the repayment in gross income. There is no exclusion in the tax law that permits taxpayers to omit such amounts from gross income. How can this be explained?

I:3-6 A landlord who receives prepaid rent is required to report that amount as gross income when the payment is received. Why would Congress choose to do this? What problem does this create for the taxpayer?

I:3-7 Office space is often rented without carpet, wall covering, or window covering. Furthermore, many rental agreements specify that these improvements cannot be removed by a tenant if removal causes any damage to the property. What issue does this raise?

I:3-8 Does the fact that an item of income is paid in a form other than cash mean it is nontaxable? Explain.

I:3-9 Explain the significance of *Lucas v. Earl* and *Helvering v. Horst*.

I:3-10 Under present-day tax law, community property rules are followed in allocating income between husband and wife. Is this consistent with *Lucas v. Earl*? Explain.

Form 1040 Department of the Treasury—Internal Revenue Service (99)
U.S. Individual Income Tax Return **2014** OMB No. 1545-0074 IRS Use Only—Do not write or staple in this space.

For the year Jan. 1–Dec. 31, 2014, or other tax year beginning , 2014, ending , 20 | See separate instructions.

Your first name and initial	Last name	Your social security number
John J.	Alexander	123 45 6789
If a joint return, spouse's first name and initial	Last name	Spouse's social security number
Home address (number and street). If you have a P.O. box, see instructions. 41 Oak Street	Apt. no.	▲ Make sure the SSN(s) above and on line 6c are correct.
City, town or post office, state, and ZIP code. If you have a foreign address, also complete spaces below (see instructions). Orlando, FL 32816		**Presidential Election Campaign**
Foreign country name	Foreign province/state/county / Foreign postal code	Check here if you, or your spouse if filing jointly, want $3 to go to this fund. Checking a box below will not change your tax or refund. ☐ You ☐ Spouse

Filing Status

Check only one box.

1 ☒ Single
2 ☐ Married filing jointly (even if only one had income)
3 ☐ Married filing separately. Enter spouse's SSN above and full name here. ▶
4 ☐ Head of household (with qualifying person). (See instructions.) If the qualifying person is a child but not your dependent, enter this child's name here. ▶
5 ☐ Qualifying widow(er) with dependent child

Exemptions

6a ☒ **Yourself.** If someone can claim you as a dependent, **do not** check box 6a
b ☐ **Spouse**

Boxes checked on 6a and 6b: 1

c **Dependents:**

(1) First name Last name	(2) Dependent's social security number	(3) Dependent's relationship to you	(4) ✓ if child under age 17 qualifying for child tax credit (see instructions)
			☐
			☐
			☐
			☐

If more than four dependents, see instructions and check here ▶ ☐

No. of children on 6c who:
• lived with you
• did not live with you due to divorce or separation (see instructions)
Dependents on 6c not entered above

d Total number of exemptions claimed — Add numbers on lines above ▶ 1

Income

Attach Form(s) W-2 here. Also attach Forms W-2G and 1099-R if tax was withheld.

If you did not get a W-2, see instructions.

7	Wages, salaries, tips, etc. Attach Form(s) W-2	7	40,000
8a	**Taxable** interest. Attach Schedule B if required	8a	300
b	**Tax-exempt** interest. **Do not** include on line 8a	8b	
9a	Ordinary dividends. Attach Schedule B if required	9a	1,580
b	Qualified dividends	9b	
10	Taxable refunds, credits, or offsets of state and local income taxes	10	
11	Alimony received	11	
12	Business income or (loss). Attach Schedule C or C-EZ	12	
13	Capital gain or (loss). Attach Schedule D if required. If not required, check here ▶ ☐	13	50
14	Other gains or (losses). Attach Form 4797	14	
15a	IRA distributions 15a / b Taxable amount	15b	
16a	Pensions and annuities 16a / b Taxable amount	16b	
17	Rental real estate, royalties, partnerships, S corporations, trusts, etc. Attach Schedule E	17	2,000
18	Farm income or (loss). Attach Schedule F	18	
19	Unemployment compensation	19	
20a	Social security benefits 20a / b Taxable amount	20b	
21	Other income. List type and amount	21	
22	Combine the amounts in the far right column for lines 7 through 21. This is your **total income** ▶	22	43,930

Adjusted Gross Income

23	Educator expenses	23			
24	Certain business expenses of reservists, performing artists, and fee-basis government officials. Attach Form 2106 or 2106-EZ	24			
25	Health savings account deduction. Attach Form 8889	25			
26	Moving expenses. Attach Form 3903	26			
27	Deductible part of self-employment tax. Attach Schedule SE	27			
28	Self-employed SEP, SIMPLE, and qualified plans	28			
29	Self-employed health insurance deduction	29			
30	Penalty on early withdrawal of savings	30			
31a	Alimony paid b Recipient's SSN ▶ 987 65 4321	31a	6,000		
32	IRA deduction	32			
33	Student loan interest deduction	33			
34	Tuition and fees. Attach Form 8917	34			
35	Domestic production activities deduction. Attach Form 8903	35			
36	Add lines 23 through 35			36	6,000
37	Subtract line 36 from line 22. This is your **adjusted gross income** ▶			37	37,930

For Disclosure, Privacy Act, and Paperwork Reduction Act Notice, see separate instructions. Cat. No. 11320B Form **1040** (2014)

FIGURE I:3-1 ▶ FORM 1040 (PAGE 1)

SCHEDULE B
(Form 1040A or 1040)

Department of the Treasury
Internal Revenue Service (99)

Interest and Ordinary Dividends

▶ Attach to Form 1040A or 1040.
▶ Information about Schedule B and its instructions is at *www.irs.gov/scheduleb*

OMB No. 1545-0074
2014
Attachment Sequence No. 08

Name(s) shown on return: John J. Alexander

Your social security number: 123-45-6789

Part I Interest

(See instructions on back and the instructions for Form 1040A, or Form 1040, line 8a.)

Note. If you received a Form 1099-INT, Form 1099-OID, or substitute statement from a brokerage firm, list the firm's name as the payer and enter the total interest shown on that form.

			Amount
1	List name of payer. If any interest is from a seller-financed mortgage and the buyer used the property as a personal residence, see instructions on back and list this interest first. Also, show that buyer's social security number and address ▶	1	
2	Add the amounts on line 1	2	
3	Excludable interest on series EE and I U.S. savings bonds issued after 1989. Attach Form 8815	3	
4	Subtract line 3 from line 2. Enter the result here and on Form 1040A, or Form 1040, line 8a . . . . ▶	4	

Note. If line 4 is over $1,500, you must complete Part III.

Part II Ordinary Dividends

(See instructions on back and the instructions for Form 1040A, or Form 1040, line 9a.)

Note. If you received a Form 1099-DIV or substitute statement from a brokerage firm, list the firm's name as the payer and enter the ordinary dividends shown on that form.

			Amount
5	List name of payer ▶		
	Ford Motor Company		1,150
	Omaha Mutual Fund		430
		5	
6	Add the amounts on line 5. Enter the total here and on Form 1040A, or Form 1040, line 9a . . . . ▶	6	1,580

Note. If line 6 is over $1,500, you must complete Part III.

Part III Foreign Accounts and Trusts

(See instructions on back.)

	You must complete this part if you **(a)** had over $1,500 of taxable interest or ordinary dividends; **(b)** had a foreign account; or **(c)** received a distribution from, or were a grantor of, or a transferor to, a foreign trust.	Yes	No
7a	At any time during 2014, did you have a financial interest in or signature authority over a financial account (such as a bank account, securities account, or brokerage account) located in a foreign country? See instructions		X
	If "Yes," are you required to file FinCEN Form 114, Report of Foreign Bank and Financial Accounts (FBAR), to report that financial interest or signature authority? See FinCEN Form 114 and its instructions for filing requirements and exceptions to those requirements		X
b	If you are required to file FinCEN Form 114, enter the name of the foreign country where the financial account is located ▶		
8	During 2014, did you receive a distribution from, or were you the grantor of, or transferor to, a foreign trust? If "Yes," you may have to file Form 3520. See instructions on back		X

For Paperwork Reduction Act Notice, see your tax return instructions. Cat. No. 17146N **Schedule B (Form 1040A or 1040) 2014**

FIGURE I:3-2 ▶ SCHEDULE B

I:3-11 Ricardo owns a small unincorporated business. His 15-year-old daughter Jane works in the business on a part-time basis and was paid wages of $3,000 during the current year. Who is taxed on the child's earnings: Jane or her father? Explain.

I:3-12 Define the term *constructive receipt*. Explain its importance.

I:3-13 Explain three restrictions on the concept of constructive receipt.

I:3-14 When is income considered to be earned by an accrual-basis taxpayer?

I:3-15 a. Explain the difference between the treatment of prepaid income under the tax law and under financial accounting.
b. Why are the two treatments so different?
c. What problem does this treatment create for taxpayers?

I:3-16 Under what conditions is an accrual-basis taxpayer allowed to defer reporting amounts received in the advance of the delivery of goods?

I:3-17 Under what conditions is an accrual-basis taxpayer allowed to defer reporting advance payments received for services?

I:3-18 a. Is the interest received from government obligations taxable? Explain.
b. What impact does the fact that some bond interest is tax exempt have on interest rates?
c. Is an investor always better off buying tax-exempt bonds? Explain.

I:3-19 Corporations are taxed on the income they earn, and shareholders are taxed on the dividends they receive. What provisions in the tax law reduce this "double tax" burden?

I:3-20 Explain the relationship between dividends and earnings and profits.

I:3-21 On what basis did the Supreme Court in *Eisner v. Macomber* decide that stock dividends are nontaxable?

I:3-22 What is the significance of a constructive dividend?

I:3-23 Explain the importance of the distinction between alimony and a property settlement.

I:3-24 a. Are items of income not listed in Sec. 61 taxable? Explain.
b. Because there is no specific exclusion for unrealized income, why is it not taxable?
c. Can income be realized even when a cash-method taxpayer does not receive cash?
d. Does a cash basis taxpayer realize income upon the receipt of a note?

I:3-25 a. Briefly explain the tax benefit rule.
b. Is a taxpayer required to report the reimbursement of a medical expense by insurance as income if the reimbursement is received in the year following the year of the expenditure?

I:3-26 What opportunities are available for a taxpayer to defer the recognition of certain types of prepaid income? That is, what advice could you give someone who wishes to defer the reporting of prepaid income?

I:3-27 Taxpayers who deduct an expense one year but recover it the next year are required to include the recovered amount in gross income. The tax benefit rule provides relief if the original deduction did not result in any tax savings. Does this rule provide relief to taxpayers who are in a higher tax bracket in the year they recover the previously deducted expense?

I:3-28 George, a wealthy investor, is uncertain whether he should invest in taxable or tax-exempt bonds. What tax and nontax factors should he consider?

I:3-29 Do you agree or disagree with the following statement: A taxpayer should not have to report income when debt is forgiven because the taxpayer receives nothing. Explain.

I:3-30 Jack and June are retired and receive $10,000 of social security benefits and taxable pensions totaling $25,000. They have been offered $20,000 for an automobile that they restored after they retired. They did most of the restoration work themselves and the sale will result in a gain of $12,000. What tax issues should Jack and June consider?

ISSUE IDENTIFICATION QUESTIONS

I:3-31 State Construction Company is owned equally by Andy, Bill, and Charlie. Andy works in the corporation full-time, and Bill and Charlie work elsewhere. When Andy left his previous job to work for State, he signed a contract specifying that he would receive a salary of $50,000 per year. This year, Andy felt that the company could expand if it purchased more equipment, and he offered to delay receiving $20,000 of his salary so the funds could be used to purchase the equipment. Bill and Charlie agreed, and the equipment was purchased. It is expected that State will have enough cash to pay Andy by early March of next year. What tax issues should Andy consider?

I:3-32 Lisa and her daughter Jane are equal shareholders in Lisa's Flooring, Inc. Lisa founded the corporation and was the sole owner for over twenty years. The company is very successful and Lisa has accumulated a fairly large estate. When Jane turned age twenty-five last year, Lisa gave her half of the corporation's stock. The gift was properly reported on Lisa's gift tax return. Both Lisa and Jane now work full-time for the corporation. Lisa received a salary of $55,000 per year before Jane started working for the company. After Jane started working, Lisa reduced her salary to $15,000 and started paying Jane a salary of $50,000. Lisa indicates that she still makes most major decisions in the company, but she hopes that Jane will play a more important role as she becomes more familiar with the company. What tax issues should Lisa and the corporation consider?

I:3-33 Larry's Art Gallery sells oil paintings, lithographs, and bronzes to collectors and corporations. Customers often come to Larry looking for special pieces. In order to meet customer needs, Larry often accepts orders and then travels looking for the desired item, which he purchases and delivers to the customer. The pieces are expensive, and Larry requires customers to demonstrate their sincerity by providing deposits. If it turns out that the item costs more than expected, Larry contacts the buyer and asks for additional funds. If the item costs less than expected, Larry refunds the excess amount. Also, Larry sometimes returns amounts he received in advance because he is unable to find what the customer wants. What tax issues should Larry's Art Gallery consider?

PROBLEMS

I:3-34 *Noncash Compensation.* For each of the following items, indicate whether the individual taxpayer must include any amount in gross income.

a. Employees of Eastside Bookstore are given their birthdays off with pay.
b. Westside Hardware, Inc., gave each employee 10 shares of Westside stock worth $100 per share in lieu of a cash bonus.
c. Employees of Northside Manufacturing were allowed to take home the company's old computers when the company purchased new ones.

I:3-35 *Constructive Receipt.* Which of the following constitutes constructive receipt in the current year ended December 31?

a. A salary check received at 6:00 p.m. on December 31, after all the banks have closed.
b. A rent check received on December 30 by the manager of an apartment complex. The manager normally collects the rent for the owner. The owner was out of town.
c. A paycheck received on December 29 that was not honored by the bank because the employer's account did not have sufficient funds.
d. A check received on December 30. The check was postdated January 2 of the following year.
e. A check received on January 2. The check had been mailed on December 30.

I:3-36 *Cash and Accrual Methods.* Carmen opens a retail store. Her sales during the first year are $600,000, of which $30,000 has not been collected at year-end. Her purchases are $400,000. She still owes $20,000 to her suppliers, and at year-end she has $50,000 of inventory on hand. She incurred operating expenses of $160,000. At year-end she has not paid $15,000 of the expenses.

a. Compute her net income from the business assuming she elects the accrual method.
b. Compute her net income from the business assuming she elects the cash method.
c. Would paying the $15,000 she owes for operating expenses before year-end change her net income under accrual method of reporting? under the cash method?

I:3-37 *Series EE Bond Interest.* In 2011, Harry and Mary purchased Series EE bonds, and in 2015 redeemed the bonds, receiving $500 of interest and $1,500 of principal. Their income from other sources totaled $30,000. They paid $2,200 in tuition and fees for their dependent daughter. Their daughter is a qualified student at State University.

a. How much of the Series EE bond interest is excludable?
b. Assuming that the daughter received a $1,000 scholarship, how much of the interest is excludable? Ignore any tax credits that might be available.
c. Assuming the daughter received the $1,000 scholarship and that the parents' income from other sources is $121,250, how much of the interest is excludable?

I:3-38 *Alimony.* As a result of their divorce, Fred agrees to pay alimony to Tammy of $20,000 per year. The payments are to cease in the event of Fred's or Tammy's death or in the event of Tammy's remarriage. In addition, Tammy is to receive their residence, which cost them $100,000 but is worth $140,000.

a. Does the fact that Tammy receives the residence at the time of the divorce mean that there is a reduction in alimony, which will lead to Fred having to recapture an amount in the subsequent year?
b. How will the $20,000 payments be treated by Fred and Tammy?

c. Would recapture of the payments be necessary if payment ceased because of Tammy's remarriage?
d. What is Tammy's basis in the residence?

I:3-39 *Constructive Dividend.* Brad owns a successful corporation that has substantial earnings and profits. During the year, the following payments were made by the corporation:
a. Salary of $250,000 to Brad. Officers in other corporations performing similar services receive between $50,000 and $85,000.
b. Rent of $25,000 to Brad. The rent is paid in connection with an office building owned by Brad and used by the corporation. Similar buildings rent for about the same amount.
c. Salary of $5,000 to Brad's daughter, who worked for the company full-time during the summer and part-time during the rest of the year while she attended high school.
d. Alimony of $40,000 to Brad's former wife. Although Brad was personally obligated to make the payments, he used corporation funds to make the payments.

Discuss the likelihood of these payments being treated as constructive dividends. If a payment is deemed to be a constructive dividend, indicate how such a payment will be treated.

I:3-40 *Constructive Dividend.* Which of the following would likely be a constructive dividend?
a. An unreasonable salary paid to a shareholder.
b. An unreasonable salary paid to the daughter of a shareholder.
c. A sale of a corporation's asset to a shareholder at fair market value.
d. A payment by a corporation of a shareholder's debts.
e. A payment by a corporation of a shareholder's personal expenses.

I:3-41 *Prepaid Rent.* Stan rented an office building to Clay for $3,000 per month. On December 29, 2014, Stan received a deposit of $4,000 in addition to the first and last months' rent. Occupancy began on January 2, 2015. On July 15, 2015, Clay closed his business and filed for bankruptcy. Stan had collected rent for February, March, and April on the first of each month. Stan had received May rent on May 10, but collected no payments afterwards. Stan withheld $800 from the deposit because of damage to the property and $1,500 for unpaid rent. He refunded the balance of the deposit to Clay. What amount would Stan report as gross income for 2014? for 2015?

I:3-42 *Rental Income.* Ed owns Oak Knoll Apartments. During the year, Fred, a tenant, moved to another state. Fred paid Ed $1,000 to cancel the two-year lease he had signed. Ed subsequently rented the unit to Wayne. Wayne paid the first and last months' rents of $800 each and a security deposit of $500. Ed also owns a building that is used as a health club. The club has signed a fifteen-year lease at an annual rental of $17,000. The owner of the club requested that Ed install a swimming pool on the property. Ed declined to do so. The owner of the club finally constructed the pool himself at a cost of $15,000. What amount must Ed include in gross income?

I:3-43 *Gross Income.* Susan's salary is $44,000 and she received dividends of $600. She received a statement from SJ partnership indicating that her share of the partnership's income was $4,000. The partnership distributed $1,000 to her during the year and $600 after year-end. She won $2,000 in the state lottery and spent $50 on lottery tickets. Which amounts are taxable?

I:3-44 *Interest Income.* Holly inherited $10,000 of City of Atlanta bonds in February. In March, she received interest of $500, and in April she sold the bonds at a $200 gain. Holly redeemed Series EE U.S. savings bonds that she had purchased several years ago. The accumulated interest totaled $800. Holly received $300 of interest on bonds issued by the City of Quebec, Canada. What amount, if any, of gross income must Holly report?

I:3-45 *Annuity Income.* Tim retired during the current year at age 58. He purchased an annuity from American National Life Company for $40,000. The annuity pays Tim $500 per month for life.
a. Compute Tim's annual exclusion.
b. How much income will Tim report each year after reaching age 84?

I:3-46 *Pension Income.* Beth retires when she turns 65. She begins receiving a monthly pension of $300 from her employer's qualified retirement plan. While employed, Beth contributed $13,000 to the plan.
a. Beth uses the simplified method to compute her exclusion. Why?
b. Compute her monthly exclusion.
c. How much gross income does she report in the first year if she receives 12 monthly checks?

I:3-47 *Social Security Benefits.* Dan and Diana file a joint return. Dan earned $31,000 during the year before losing his job. Diana received Social Security benefits of $5,000.
a. Determine the taxable portion of the Social Security benefits.
b. What is the taxable portion of the Social Security benefits if Dan earned $46,000?

I:3-48 *Social Security Benefits.* Lucia is a 69-year-old single individual who receives a taxable pension of $10,000 per year and Social Security benefits of $7,000. Lucia is considering the possibility of selling stock she has owned for years and using the funds to purchase a summer home. She will realize a gain of $20,000 when she sells the stock, which has been paying $1,000 of dividends each year. Lucia says her brother recommended that she sell half of the stock this year and half next year because selling all of the stock at once would affect the tax treatment of her Social Security benefits.
a. Compute her AGI under the assumption she sells all of the stock now after receiving $1,000 dividends from the stock.
b. Repeat the computation under the assumption she sells only half of the stock this year and also receives $1,000 dividends from the stock.

I:3-49 *Social Security Benefits.* Bob is a single individual and received a salary of $27,000 before he retired in October of this year. After he retired, he received Social Security benefits of $3,000 during the year.
a. What amount, if any, of the Social Security benefits are taxable for the year?
b. Would the answer be different if Bob also had $1,000 of tax exempt interest?
c. What if he had had $10,000 of tax exempt interest?

I:3-50 *Adjusted Gross Income.* Amir, who is single, retired from his job this year. He received a salary of $25,000 for the portion of the year that he worked, tax-exempt interest of $3,000, and dividends from domestic corporations of $2,700. On September 1, he began receiving monthly pension payments of $1,000 and Social Security payments of $600. Assume an exclusion ratio of 40% for the pension. Amir owns a duplex that he rents to others. He received rent of $12,000 and incurred $17,000 of expenses related to the duplex. He continued to actively manage the property after he retired from his job. Compute Amir's adjusted gross income.

I:3-51 *Court Awards and Insurance Settlements.* What amount, if any, must be included in gross income by the following taxpayers?
a. Ann received $2,000 from her insurance company when her automobile which cost $3,000 was stolen.
b. Barry received $3,000 from his brother. Barry had initiated a lawsuit against his brother in an effort to recover $3,000 he had previously loaned to him. The brother paid Barry back before the case was tried, and Barry dropped the lawsuit.
c. Carry, an accountant, sued a client in order to collect her fee for doing tax work. Would Carry's accounting method make any difference?
d. Dave has incurred $6,000 of medical expenses so far this year. He paid $400 of the expenses himself. His insurance company paid $4,000 of the expenses. The hospital is suing Dave and the insurance company for the balance, $1,600.

I:3-52 *Claim of Right.* USA Corporation hired Jesse to install a computer system for the company and paid him $8,000 for the work. USA soon realized that there were problems with the system and asked Jesse to refund the payment. At the end of the year the dispute had not been resolved. Jesse is in the 25% tax bracket in the year he did the original work. During the next year, when he is in the 15% tax bracket, Jesse refunds the $8,000 to USA.
a. Is the original payment taxable to Jesse when he receives it?
b. What options are available to Jesse when he repays the $8,000?
c. What option would have been available to Jesse if he had been asked to repay only $2,000?

I:3-53 *Tax Planning.* Bart and Kesha are in the 39.6% tax bracket. They are interested in reducing the taxes they pay each year. They are currently considering several alternatives. For each of the following alternatives, indicate how much tax, if any, they would save.

a. Make a gift of bonds valued at $5,000 that yield $400 per year interest to their 24-year-old daughter, who has no other income.
b. Sell the bonds from Part a rather than give them to their daughter, and buy tax-exempt bonds that pay 6%. Assume the bonds can be sold for an amount equal to their basis of $5,000.
c. Give $1,000 cash to a charity. Assume they itemize deductions and ignore any phase-out of itemized deductions.
d. Pay their daughter a salary of $10,000 for services rendered in their unincorporated business.

I:3-54 *Series EE Bond Interest and Kiddie Tax.* In 2015, Ken and Lynn paid $5,000 to purchase Series EE bonds in the name of their 11-year-old son. The son has no other income, and they are in the 28% tax bracket. The taxable interest during the first year will be $400 if an election is made to accrue the interest on an annual basis.

a. Will the child owe any tax on the bond interest?
b. Does the son need to file a tax return?
c. What are the tax consequences in 2015 and subsequent years if annual gifts are made to their son?

COMPREHENSIVE PROBLEMS

I:3-55 Matt and Sandy reside in a community property state. Matt left home in April 2015 because of disputes with his wife, Sandy. Subsequently, Matt earned $15,000. Before leaving home in April, Matt earned $3,000. Sandy was unaware of Matt's whereabouts or his earnings after he left home. The $3,000 earned by Matt before he left home was spent on food, housing, and other items shared by Matt and Sandy. Matt and Sandy have one child, who lived with Sandy after the husband left home.

a. Is any portion of Matt's earnings after he left home taxable to Sandy?
b. What filing status is applicable to Sandy if she filed a return?
c. How much income would Sandy be required to report if she filed?
d. Is Sandy required to file?

I:3-56 During 2015, Gary earned $57,000 as an executive. Gary, who is single, supported his half sister, who lives in a nursing home. Gary received the following interest: $400 on City of Los Angeles bonds, $200 on a money market account, and $2,100 on a loan made to his brother.

Gary spent one week serving on a jury and received $50.

Gary received a refund of federal income taxes withheld during the prior year of $1,200 and a state income tax refund of $140. Gary had itemized deductions last year of $8,000 which included $1,000 of state income taxes.

Gary received qualified dividends from Ace Corporation of $1,000 and from Tray Corporation of $1,400. Gary's itemized deductions equal $9,000, and withholding for federal income taxes is $8,000. Compute Gary's tax due or refund due for 2015.

TAX STRATEGY PROBLEMS

I:3-57 Kamal is starting a new business in 2015 which will operate as an S corporation. This means that income earned by the corporation will be reported by shareholders even if they do not receive distributions. Kamal has $130,000 of income from other sources, and itemized deductions totaling $15,000. He expects that the new business will produce $30,000 of income each year. He is considering giving his son Rashid 20% of the stock in the corporation. Rashid is age 24, and is Kamal's dependent. Rashid's only other income is $2,000 of interest. Neither Kamal nor Rashid will be employed by the corporation. Which alternative will produce a lower income tax liability—having all stock owned by Kamal or having Kamal own 80% of the stock and Rashid own 20%? Assume Kamal's filing status is head-of-household and Rashid is single. Ignore other taxes. How would the answer be different if Rashid were age 17? Ignore credits.

I:3-58 Assume that it is December 31, and that Jake is considering making a $1,000 charitable contribution. Jake currently is in the 39.6% tax bracket, but expects that his tax bracket will be 28% next year. How much more will the deduction for the contribution be worth if it is made today compared to next year? (Ignore any phase-outs of itemized deductions.)

TAX FORM/RETURN PREPARATION PROBLEM

I:3-59 Sally W. Emanual had the following dividends and interest during the current year:

Acorn Corporation bond interest		$ 700
City of Boston bonds interest		1,000
Camp Bank interest		1,250
Jet Corporation dividend (qualified)		1,300
North Mutual fund		
Capital gain distribution	100	
Ordinary dividend (qualified)	150	
Nontaxable distribution	200	450
Blue Corporation foreign dividend		250

Additional information pertaining to Sally Emanual includes

Salary	$30,000
Rent income	12,000
Expenses related to rent income	14,000
Pension benefits	7,000
Alimony paid to Sally	4,000

The taxable portion of the pension is $7,000. Sally actively participates in the rental activity. Other relevant information includes

Address: 430 Rumsey Place, West Falls, California 92699
Occupation: Credit manager
Social Security number: 123-45-6789
Marital status: Single

Complete Sally's Schedule B and page 1 of her Form 1040. Assume Schedule E has already been prepared.

CASE STUDY PROBLEMS

I:3-60 Jim and Linda are your tax clients. They were divorced two years ago, and the divorce decree stated that Jim was to make monthly payments to Linda. The court designated $300 per month as alimony and $200 per month as child support, or a total of $6,000 per year. Jim has been unemployed for much of the year and paid Linda $2,000 that he said was for child support. In addition, Jim transferred the title to a three-year-old automobile with a $4,000 FMV and basis of $7,000 in exchange for her promise not to pursue any claim she has against him for the unpaid child support and alimony. Does Linda have to report any alimony and is Jim entitled to an alimony deduction? Draft a memo for the file that discusses the tax consequences for both Jim and Linda.

I:3-61 John and Mary (your clients) have two small children and are looking for ways to help fund the children's college education. They have heard that Series EE bonds are a tax-favored way of saving and have requested your opinion on the tax consequences. They have asked your opinion regarding the relative advantages of purchasing Series EE bonds in their names versus the children's names. John and Mary have indicated that they expect to have a high level of income in the future and that their children may receive other income sources from future inheritances. Prepare a client memo making recommendations about the tax consequences of Series EE bond investments for John and Mary.

I:3-62 Lee and Jane have been your firm's clients for most of the twenty years they have been married. Recently Lee came to you and said that he and Jane are obtaining a divorce, and he wants you to help him with some of the tax and financial issues that may come up during the divorce. The next day, Jane called asking you for the same assistance. What ethical issues do you see in this case? What possible conflicts may arise if you represent both Lee and Jane?

TAX RESEARCH PROBLEM

I:3-63 William owns a building that is leased to Lester's Machine Shop. Lester requests that William rewire the building for new equipment Lester plans to purchase. The wiring would cost about $4,000, but would not increase the value of the building because its only use is in connection with the specialized equipment. Rather than lose Lester as a lessee, William agrees to forgo one month's rent of $1,000 if Lester will pay for the wiring. Because Lester does not want to move, he agrees. What amount, if any, must William include in gross income?

A partial list of research sources is

- Sec. 109
- Reg. Sec. 1.109-1
- *CIR v. Grace H. Cunningham*, 2 AFTR 2d 5511, 58-2 USTC ¶9771 (9th Cir., 1958)

CHAPTER

4

GROSS INCOME: EXCLUSIONS

LEARNING OBJECTIVES

After studying this chapter, you should be able to

1. Determine whether an item is income
2. Determine which major statutory exclusions are available to a taxpayer
3. Describe tax planning considerations for exclusions of gross income
4. Describe compliance and procedural considerations for exclusions of gross income

CHAPTER OUTLINE

Chapter I:3 discussed items that must be included in gross income. This chapter considers items that are excluded from gross income. Under Sec. 61(a), all items of income are taxable unless specifically excluded. Taxpayers who wish to avoid being taxed have two basic alternatives. One approach is to establish that the item is not income. If an item is not income (e.g., if it is a return of capital), it is not subject to the income tax. The second approach is to establish that a specific exclusion applies to the item of income.

EXAMPLE I:4-1 ▶ Matt borrowed $10,000 from the bank. Although Matt received $10,000, it is not income because he is obligated to repay the amount borrowed. No specific statutory authority states that borrowed funds are excluded from taxation. Presumably, the fact that borrowed funds are not income is considered to be both fundamental and obvious. ◀

KEY POINT

Given the sweeping definition of *income*, it is generally difficult to establish that an item is not income.

EXAMPLE I:4-2 ▶ Sheila enrolled in State University. The university awarded her a $1,000 tuition scholarship because of her high admission test scores and grades. Section 117 excludes such scholarships from gross income. As a result, Sheila need not report the scholarship as income. ◀

The major source of exclusions are those specific items contained in the IRC. These exclusions have evolved over the years and were enacted by Congress for a variety of reasons, including social and economic objectives.

Another source of exclusions are referred to as *administrative exclusions*. Exclusions exist because specific provisions in the Internal Revenue Code allow them. While the IRS has no authority to create exclusions, the IRS does have the authority to interpret the meaning of the Code. A liberal interpretation of the statute by the IRS may result in a broad definition of what constitutes an exclusion, and such a broad definition may reasonably be termed an administrative exclusion. For example, Sec. 102 excludes gifts received from gross income. The IRS has followed the practice of excluding certain welfare benefits from gross income, presumably because such benefits may be viewed as gifts.[1] The IRS could take the position that welfare benefits are not gifts. That position would no doubt be challenged in the courts.

REAL-WORLD EXAMPLE

Grants made to Native Americans by the federal government under the Indian Financing Act of 1974 to expand Native American–owned economic enterprises are excludable from gross income. Rev. Rul. 77-77, 1977-1 C.B. 11.

The term *judicial exclusions* should be considered in the same vein. Although the courts cannot create exclusions, they can interpret the statute and decide whether a particular item is covered by a statutory exclusion.

ITEMS THAT ARE NOT INCOME

OBJECTIVE 1

Determine whether an item is income

As noted above, some items are not income and, therefore, are not subject to the income tax. In addition to amounts obtained by a loan (discussed above), four other items are not considered income:

- Unrealized income
- Self-help income
- Rental value of personal-use property
- Gross selling price of property (as opposed to the profit or gain earned on the sale)

TYPICAL MISCONCEPTION

It is sometimes erroneously assumed that severance pay, embezzlement proceeds, gambling winnings, hobby income, prizes, rewards, and tips are not taxable.

UNREALIZED INCOME

Income that is not realized is not subject to income taxation. Thus, owners of appreciated property are not taxed on their unrealized gains.

This issue of the taxability of unrealized income was addressed over 90 years ago in *Eisner v. Macomber*, where the Supreme Court held that a stock dividend cannot be taxed

[1] For example, see Rev. Rul. 57-102, 1957-1 C.B. 26, which excludes from gross income public assistance payments to blind persons.

because the taxpayer had "received nothing that answers the definition of income within the meaning of the Sixteenth Amendment."[2] An ordinary stock dividend does not alter the existing proportionate ownership interest of any stockholder, nor does it increase the value of the individual's holdings. In effect, the Court concluded that realization must occur before income is recognized. Although narrowed by subsequent legislation and litigation, ordinary stock dividends continue to be excluded from gross income even today. Perhaps more important, *Eisner v. Macomber* established realization as a criterion for the recognition of income.

SELF-HELP INCOME

TYPICAL MISCONCEPTION

When a taxpayer purchases an older house and remodels the kitchen or makes other improvements, there is a tendency to assume correctly that the taxpayer has no income from this activity, but it is often incorrectly assumed that the basis of the house can be increased by the value of the taxpayer's labor.

Although self-help income is considered as income by economists, it is not recognized as income by the IRS or by the courts. Taxpayers commonly benefit from activities such as painting their own homes or repairing their own automobiles. If a taxpayer hires someone else to do the work, the taxpayer has to earn income, pay tax on the income, and use the after-tax income to pay for the work. In either case, the taxpayer receives the same economic benefit, but the economic benefit derived from self-help is not included in the taxpayer's gross income.

This situation should be contrasted with taxable exchanges of services. A mechanic might agree to repair a painter's automobile in exchange for the painter's promise to paint the mechanic's home. In this instance, when the parties exchange services, each party realizes income equal to the value of the services received.

? STOP & THINK

Question: The discussion of self-help income refers to an exchange of services between two individuals, such as a painter and a mechanic. How can a taxable barter transaction be distinguished from an act of friendship which is repaid?

Solution: When one person helps another without any promise of repayment, the act of kindness does not represent an exchange and is not taxable. Friends help one another from time to time without contractual reciprocity. As a result, such acts are not taxable. The distinction between a taxable barter exchange and acts of friendship is not always easy to make.

RENTAL VALUE OF PERSONAL-USE PROPERTY

ADDITIONAL COMMENT

The tax situation of a homeowner is quite different than that of someone who lives in an apartment. The failure to include the rental value of the home as income in addition to the deduction of mortgage interest and property taxes favors homeowners.

Taxpayers are not taxed on the rental value of personally owned property. For example, taxpayers who own their own home receive the economic benefit of occupancy without being taxed on the rental value of the property. It would be very difficult to keep records and value benefits obtained from self-help and the personal use of property. For that reason, no significant effort has ever been made to tax such benefits.[3]

SELLING PRICE OF PROPERTY

If property is sold at a gain, the gain and not the entire sales price is taxable. Because the basic principle is almost universally accepted, the Supreme Court has never had to rule directly on whether the entire sale proceeds could be taxed. The IRS and the courts seemed to accept the basic principle even before the rule became part of the statute.[4] The primary reason for this principle (often referred to as the "recovery of capital" principle) is that a portion of the selling price represents a return of capital to the seller.

---

[2] 3 AFTR 3020, 1 USTC ¶32 (USSC, 1920).

[3] In 1928, the government tried unsuccessfully to tax the value of produce grown and consumed by a farmer (*Homer P. Morris,* 9 B.T.A. 1273 (1928)). The court stated, "To include the value of such products [would be to] in effect include in income something which Congress did not intend should be so regarded." The court did not explain how or why it reached this conclusion. In 1957, the IRS successfully disallowed the deduction of expenses incurred in raising such produce (*Robert L. Nowland v. CIR,* 51 AFTR 423, 57-1 USTC ¶9684 (4th Cir., 1957)).

[4] Section 202(a) of the Revenue Act of 1924 is the predecessor of current Sec. 1001(a), which states that only the gain portion of the sale proceeds is included in gross income. S. Rept. No. 398, 68th Cong., 1st Sess., p. 10 (1924) states that Sec. 202(a) sets forth general rules to be used in the computation of gain or loss. The Senate report further states that the provision "merely embodies in the law the present construction by the Department and the courts of the existing law."

MAJOR STATUTORY EXCLUSIONS

OBJECTIVE 2

Examine the major statutory exclusions that are available to taxpayers

While Congress has created statutory exclusions for a variety of reasons, most exclusions have been enacted for reasons of social policy or reasons of incentive. The concept of social policy, that is, a concept of social generosity or benevolence, has prompted the government to exclude items such as:

- Gifts and inheritances (Sec. 102)
- Life insurance proceeds (Sec. 101)
- Public assistance payments
- Qualified adoption expenses (Sec. 137)
- Payments for personal physical sickness and injury (Sec. 104)
- Discharge of indebtedness during bankruptcy or insolvency (Sec. 108)
- Gain on sale of personal residence (Sec. 121)
- Partial exclusions for Social Security benefits (Sec. 86)

Other exclusions may be explained in terms of economic incentive, that is, the government's desire to encourage or reward a particular type of behavior.

- Awards for meritorious achievement (Sec. 74(b))
- Various employee fringe benefits (Secs. 79, 105, 106, 124, 125, 129, 132)
- Partial exclusion for scholarships (Sec. 117)
- Foreign-earned income (Sec. 911)
- Interest on state and local government obligations (Sec. 103)

ADDITIONAL COMMENT

Tax expenditure estimates measure the decreases in individual and corporate income tax liabilities that result from provisions in income tax laws and regulations that provide economic incentives or tax relief to particular kinds of taxpayers.

Other reasons may exist for some of the exclusions listed above. For example, one reason income from the discharge of indebtedness during bankruptcy is excluded from gross income is the fact that such taxpayers would be unlikely to have the resources needed to pay the tax. (See Chapter I:3 for a discussion of tax-exempt interest and Social Security benefits, and Chapter I:12 for the treatment of gain on the sale of a personal residence.)

GIFTS AND INHERITANCES

TYPICAL MISCONCEPTION

Some people still believe that gifts above the gift exclusion amount of $14,000 are taxable to the donees. They are not since the Code specifically exempts all gifts, regardless of the amount. The donor may, however, depending on the circumstances, pay a gift tax.

Congress has excluded the value of gifts and inheritances received from gross income since the inception of the income tax in 1913. Section 102 excludes the value of property received during the life of the donor (***inter vivos* gifts**) and transfers at death (**testamentary transfers**—bequests, devises, and inheritances).[5] The recipient of such property is taxed on the income produced by the property after the transfer.[6] It should be noted that a donor, under the assignment of income doctrine, cannot avoid the income tax by making a gift of income. To avoid paying tax on income, a donor must make a gift of the underlying property.

EXAMPLE I:4-3 ▶ Stan owns stock in a corporation and orders the corporation to pay dividends on the stock to his daughter. Even though his daughter receives the dividends, Stan must include the dividends in his gross income. Stan could avoid being taxed on future dividends by giving the stock to his daughter. ◀

[5] Although excluded from gross income, such transfers may be subject to the gift tax or the estate tax which are imposed on the transferor.

[6] Reg. Sec. 1.102-1(b).

It is often difficult to distinguish gifts, which are not included in the recipient's gross income, from other transfers, which are taxable. Gifts sometimes closely resemble prizes and awards.[7]

EXAMPLE I:4-4 ▶ Tina received a free automobile for being the ten millionth paying guest at an amusement park. The automobile is not considered a gift but a prize and is taxable to Tina. ◀

Also, some payments made to employees by employers may resemble gifts.

EXAMPLE I:4-5 ▶ At Christmas, Red Corporation paid $500 cash to each employee who had been with the company for more than five years. These payments are not considered gifts for tax purposes and are taxable to the employees. ◀

REAL-WORLD EXAMPLE

Amounts received by a dealer from players in the operation of a gambling casino were not excludable as gifts even though impulsive generosity or superstition may be the dominant motive. The amounts were similar to tips, which are taxable. *Louis R. Tomburello*, 86 T.C. 540 (1986).

Whether a transfer is a gift depends on the intent of the donor. Gifts are motivated by love, affection, kindness, sympathy, generosity, admiration, or similar emotions. In the two preceding examples, the transfers were made for business motives and not necessarily for donative reasons. Thus, the automobile is a taxable prize, and the amounts paid to employees represent taxable awards for services rendered, but see the discussion of Sec. 274 later in this chapter.

Transfers of money or property between family members frequently create classification problems. For example, assume a father, who owns a business, hires his 10-year-old son to work in the business. Is the payment to the son a salary (and, therefore, deductible by the business) or is it really just a gift from the father to the son? The answer depends on the fair market value of the services performed by the son. If the son actually performs services that are commensurate with the salary paid, the payment may properly be classified as a salary. On the other hand, if the son is paid an amount that exceeds the value of the services, the excess amount will be treated as a gift.

LIFE INSURANCE PROCEEDS

Life insurance proceeds paid to a beneficiary because of the insured person's death are not taxable.[8] The exclusion applies whether the proceeds are paid in a lump sum or in installments. Amounts received in excess of the face amount of the policy usually are taxable as interest.

EXAMPLE I:4-6 ▶ Buddy is the beneficiary of a $100,000 insurance policy on his mother's life. Upon her death, he elects to receive $13,000 per year for ten years instead of the lump sum. He receives $10,000 per year tax-free ($100,000 ÷ 10), but the remaining $3,000 per year is taxable as interest. ◀

EXAMPLE I:4-7 ▶ Assume the same facts as in Example I:4-6, except that Buddy elects to receive the full $100,000 face amount upon his mother's death. None of the $100,000 is taxable. ◀

The exclusion exists because life insurance benefits closely resemble inheritances, which are not taxable.

There is one exception that may result in a portion of the face amount of a life insurance policy being included in gross income.[9] The life insurance exclusion generally is not available if the insurance policy is obtained by the beneficiary in exchange for valuable consideration from a person other than the insurance company. For example, an individual may purchase an existing life insurance policy for cash from another individual. In this situation, the exclusion for death benefits is limited to the consideration paid plus the premiums or other sums subsequently paid by the buyer.

[7] Recall that under Sec. 74 (discussed in Chapter I:3) most prizes and awards are taxable.

[8] Sec. 101(a).

[9] Sec. 101(a)(2).

EXAMPLE I:4-8 ▶ Kwame is the owner and beneficiary of a $100,000 policy on the life of his father. Kwame sells the policy to his brother Anwar for $10,000. Anwar subsequently pays premiums of $12,000. Upon his father's death, Anwar must include $78,000 [$100,000 − ($10,000 + $12,000)] in gross income. However, if Kwame gave the policy to his brother, all of the proceeds would be excluded from gross income because the gift of the policy does not constitute valuable consideration. ◀

ADDITIONAL COMMENT

The proceeds of a life insurance policy payable to named beneficiaries can be excluded from the federal estate tax when the decedent does not possess any incidents of ownership. This provision and the exclusion from gross income of life insurance proceeds underscore the favored position of life insurance.

The proceeds are excludable under the general exclusion for life insurance proceeds if the beneficiary's basis is found by reference to the transferor's basis (as would be true in the case of a gift), or if the policy is transferred to the insured, the insured's partner, a partnership that includes the insured, or a corporation in which the insured is a shareholder or officer.

Surrender or Sale of Policy. The exclusion for life insurance is available for amounts payable by reason of the death of the insured. In general, if a life policy is sold or surrendered for a lump sum before the death of the insured, the amount received is taxable to the extent that the amount received exceeds the net premiums paid.[10] On the other hand, no loss is recognized if a life insurance policy is surrendered before maturity and premiums paid exceed the cash surrender value.[11]

"Accelerated death benefits" may be excluded from gross income. Accelerated death benefits include payments made to a terminally ill person and periodic payments made to a chronically ill person. A person is terminally ill if a physician certifies that he is reasonably likely to die within 24 months. A person is chronically ill if he has a disability requiring long-term care (e.g., nursing home care). In general, the exclusion for periodic payments made to a chronically ill person is limited to the greater of $330 per day (in 2014 and 2015), or the actual cost of such care. The exclusion covers amounts received from the insurance provider or from a "viatical settlement provider" (i.e., person in the business of providing accelerated death benefits).

EXAMPLE I:4-9 ▶ Harry has been diagnosed with advanced AIDS and is expected to live less than a year. Harry is covered by a life insurance policy with a $100,000 face amount. The insurance company offers terminally ill individuals the option of receiving 75% of the policy face amount. If Harry accepts the settlement, the amount he receives is excludable from gross income because he is terminally ill. ◀

EXAMPLE I:4-10 ▶ Mary suffered a severe stroke and has been admitted to a nursing home where she is expected to remain for the rest of her life. She is certified by a licensed health care practitioner as being a "chronically ill individual." Her nursing home expenses amount to $200 per day. Mary has elected to receive $225 per day from a $1,000,000 face amount life insurance policy as accelerated death benefits. Because she is a chronically ill individual, Mary may exclude the full amount she receives as it is less than the daily limitation of $330 established by law. ◀

Dividends on Life Insurance and Endowment Policies. Dividends on life insurance and endowment policies are normally not taxable because they are considered to be a partial return of premiums paid. The dividends are taxable to the extent that the total dividends received exceed the total premiums paid. Also, if dividends are left with the insurance company and earn interest, the interest is taxable.

---

[10] Sec. 72(e)(2). In some instances where distributions are made before the recipient reaches age 59½, a 10% penalty applies (see Sec. 72(q)).

[11] *London Shoe Co. v. CIR*, 16 AFTR 1398, 35-2 USTC ¶9664 (2nd Cir., 1935).

ADDITIONAL COMMENT

Notice that to exclude awards for meritorious achievement, the award must not come into the possession of the taxpayer.

AWARDS FOR MERITORIOUS ACHIEVEMENT

As noted in Chapter I:3, prizes and awards generally are taxable. An exception is applicable to awards and prizes made for religious, charitable, scientific, educational, artistic, literary, or civic achievement if the recipient:

- Was selected without action on his or her part to enter the contest or the proceeding,
- Does not have to perform substantial future services as a condition to receiving the prize or award, and
- Designates that the payor is to pay the amount of the award to either a government unit or a charitable organization.[12]

The recipient of such an award normally would owe no tax if he or she collected the proceeds and then contributed the proceeds to a charity because the gift would qualify as a deductible charitable contribution. However, the exclusion changes AGI and thereby affects other computations. Also, this rule is beneficial in situations where the taxpayer could not deduct the full amount of the award because of the limitation on the charitable contribution deduction (generally 50% of AGI; see Chapter I:7) or in the case of a small award to a taxpayer who does not itemize.

ADDITIONAL COMMENT

Athletic scholarships for fees, books, and supplies awarded by a university to students who are expected, but not required, to participate in a particular sport can be excludable.

KEY POINT

The exclusion for scholarships does not include amounts received for room, board, and laundry.

SCHOLARSHIPS AND FELLOWSHIPS

Subject to certain limitations, scholarships are excluded from gross income.[13] A scholarship is an amount paid or allowed to a student, whether an undergraduate or graduate, to aid degree-seeking individuals.

The exclusion for scholarships is limited to the amount of the scholarship used for *qualified tuition and related expenses*. Qualified tuition and related expenses typically include tuition and fees, books, supplies, and equipment required for courses of instruction at an educational organization. The value of services and accommodations supplied such as room, board, and laundry are not excluded. The exclusion for scholarships does not extend to salary paid for services even if all candidates for a particular degree are required to perform the services.[14]

EXAMPLE I:4-11 ▶ Becky is awarded a $5,000 per year scholarship by State University. Becky spends $3,000 of the scholarship for tuition, books, and supplies, and $2,000 for room and board. In addition, Becky works part-time on campus and earns $4,000, which covers the rest of her room and board and other expenses. Becky is taxed on the $2,000 of the scholarship spent for room and board and $4,000 of salary earned from her part-time job. ◀

DISTRIBUTIONS FROM QUALIFIED TUITION PROGRAMS

Congress established *qualified tuition plans*, or so-called Section 529 plans, to assist students with higher education costs. Amounts contributed to a qualified tuition plan (QTP) on behalf of a designated beneficiary grow tax-free. Amounts may be withdrawn tax-free by the beneficiary as long as the amounts are used for qualified higher education expenses

---

[12] Sec. 74.

[13] Sec. 117.

[14] Scholarships may need to be reviewed to determine whether the amount constitutes compensation. A "scholarship" awarded to the winner of a televised beauty pageant by a profit-making corporation was ruled to be compensation for performing subsequent services for the corporation (Rev. Rul. 68-20, 1968-1 C.B. 55). An employer-paid "scholarship" was held to be compensation in a situation where the employee was on leave and was required to return to work after finishing the degree (*Richard E. Johnson v. Bingler,* 23 AFTR 2d 69-1212, 69-1 USTC ¶9348 (USSC, 1969)). However, in Ltr. Rul. 9526020 (September 10, 1995) the IRS ruled that grants to law students are not taxable even if they are conditioned upon the students agreeing to practice upon graduation in public, nonprofit, or other low paying sectors.

including tuition, books, fees, supplies, equipment, and room and board.[15] Wealthy individuals may fund QTPs as there is no income limitation. Although parents and grandparents are the most frequent donors, anyone can fund a QTP.

A QTP must be maintained either by a state government or by a private university. Plans may acquire mutual funds and similar investments. State plans (but not private university plans) may provide for the purchase of credit for future tuition in lieu of investments.

Contributions to a QTP may be distributed tax-free. The portion of a distribution that is treated as a contribution is determined under annuity rules discussed in Chapter I:3. The income portion of a QTP distribution may be excluded to the extent it is used for qualified higher education expenses. The amount of the QTP exclusion is reduced by American Opportunity and lifetime learning tax credits claimed by the beneficiary.[16] Any additional distributed income is included to the beneficiary's gross income and is subject to a 10% penalty.

Donors can change the designated beneficiary to another member of the original beneficiary's family without tax consequences. Family members include relatives, as defined for dependency exemption purposes, plus first cousins.

EXAMPLE I:4-12 ▶ For each of his two young children, David contributes $10,000 to a state established Qualified Tuition Program. There is no gift tax as the amounts are less than the $14,000 annual per donee gift tax exclusion. Current and future qualified contributions grow tax-free. Future distributions of income are tax exempt as long as the amounts do not exceed the beneficiary's qualified higher education expenses. Excess distributions are taxable and subject to a 10% penalty. ◀

PAYMENTS FOR INJURY AND SICKNESS

Sec. 104(a) excludes from gross income the "amount of any damages (other than punitive damages) . . . received . . . on account of personal physical injuries or physical sickness." Thus, for example, a taxpayer may exclude an insurance settlement for physical injury that resulted from an automobile accident. Section 104(a) does not cover amounts awarded for nonphysical injuries (such as a damaged reputation or libel) except that taxpayers may exclude reimbursements for medical expenses related to nonphysical injuries.

An attempt to challenge the constitutionality of this provision in the Court of Appeals of the District of Columbia was successful initially, but the court subsequently reversed itself.[17]

EXAMPLE I:4-13 ▶ After she was denied a promotion, Jane sued her employer claiming sex discrimination. She was awarded $5,000 to cover the medical bills she incurred because of the related emotional distress, $20,000 to punish her employer for discrimination, and $10,000 to compensate her for lost wages. The $5,000 awarded to cover medical bills is excluded from gross income, but not the amounts awarded as punitive damages or lost wages. ◀

The exclusion under Sec. 104(a) applies to damages received because of emotional distress in only two situations: (1) when the payments are for medical expenses related to the emotional distress, and (2) when the payments are for emotional distress *attributable* to a physical injury (including physical injury suffered by another person).

[15] Room and board is a qualified higher education expense only if the beneficiary is at least a half-time student.

[16] Sec. 529(c)(3)(B)(v). These credits are discussed in Chapter I:14 of this textbook.

[17] *Marrita Murphy v. CIR*, 100 AFTR2d 2007-5075, 2007-2 USTC ¶50,531, (DC Cir., 2007) reversing *Marrita Murphy v. CIR*, 98 AFTR2d 2006-6088, 2006-2 USTC ¶50,476, (DC Cir., 2006).

Sometimes, victims are awarded amounts that are intended to punish the guilty party. These so-called punitive damages are taxable even when they are awarded for physical injuries.

EXAMPLE I:4-14 ▶ Mary was injured in an automobile accident caused by another driver. Mary's daughter, Sarah, was in the automobile, but she was not physically injured. The other driver's insurance company was required by a court to pay Mary $10,000 to cover medical bills relating to her injuries, $5,000 to compensate her for emotional distress caused by the injuries, and $15,000 of punitive damages. Sarah was paid $3,000 to compensate her for distress caused by her witnessing her mother's injuries. Only the $15,000 of punitive damages are taxable to Mary as the other amounts are compensatory damages related to her physical injuries. Sarah's damage award of $3,000 is also excludable. ◀

Sec. 104(a)(3) excludes from gross income amounts collected under an accident and health insurance policy purchased by the taxpayer, even if the benefits are a substitute for lost income. In addition, Sec. 101 specifies that benefits received under a qualified long-term care insurance contract may be excluded from gross income, but limits the exclusion to the greater of $330 per day (in both 2014 and 2015) or the actual cost of such care. Such policies pay for nursing home and other types of long-term care. If the benefits exceed the actual cost of such care but are less than $330 per day, no portion of the benefits is taxable.

EXAMPLE I:4-15 ▶ Chuck purchased a disability income policy from an insurance company. Chuck subsequently suffered a heart attack. Under the terms of the policy, Chuck received $2,500 per month for the five months he was unable to work. The amounts received are not taxable, even though the payments are a substitute for the wages lost due to the illness. ◀

This exclusion is not applicable if the accident and health benefits are provided by the taxpayer's employer.[18]

EXAMPLE I:4-16 ▶ Assume the same facts as in Example I:4-15 except that Chuck's employer paid the premiums on the policy. The amounts received by Chuck are taxable. ◀

EXAMPLE I:4-17 ▶ Ruth suffered a serious stroke and was admitted to a nursing home. During the year, she was in a nursing home for 140 days. Nursing home charges, physician fees, and other related expenses totaled $38,000.

Under her long-term care insurance contract, Ruth received reimbursements of $40,000. The reimbursements are not includible in Ruth's gross income because the amounts are less than the allowed exclusion amount of $46,200 (140 days × $330). This exclusion applies even though she was reimbursed more than her actual costs. Alternatively, if the reimbursements had been $50,200, she would be required to report $4,000 ($50,200 − $46,200) as gross income. ◀

If the cost of the coverage is shared by the employer and the taxpayer, a portion of the benefits is taxable. For example, if the employer paid one-half of the premiums, one-half of the benefits would be taxable. The principal reason for the different tax treatment is that employer-paid coverage represents a tax-free employee fringe benefit, whereas employee-paid premiums are from after-tax dollars.

[18] A limited credit is available to taxpayers who receive such benefits. See Chapter I:14 for a discussion of the credit for the elderly and disabled.

In the case of an award intended to reimburse the taxpayer for medical expenses, it follows that the taxpayer cannot deduct the reimbursed medical expenses.[19] If the award exceeds the actual expense, it is not taxable except in the case of employer-financed accident and health insurance and in the case of excess long-term care discussed above.[20]

State worker's compensation laws establish fixed amounts to be paid to employees suffering specific job-related injuries. Section 104(a)(1) specifically excludes worker's compensation from gross income, even though the payments are intended, in part, to reimburse injured workers for loss of future income and even if the injuries are nonphysical.

EMPLOYEE FRINGE BENEFITS

In general, employee compensation is taxable regardless of the form it takes. Nevertheless, the tax law encourages certain types of fringe benefits by allowing an employer to deduct the cost of the benefit, by permitting the employee to exclude the benefit from gross income, or by permitting both the employer deduction and an employee exclusion. Employee fringe benefits subject to special rules include employee insurance, Sec. 132 benefits, meals and lodging, dependent care, and cafeteria plans. These fringe benefits are discussed below.

ADDITIONAL COMMENT

Many companies provide health care benefits to retired employees. However, due to mounting medical insurance bills, a rising retiree population, and an FASB rule that requires firms to recognize the associated liability, a number of companies are requiring retired workers to pick up a larger portion of their medical costs.

Employer-Paid Insurance. Employers commonly provide group insurance coverage for employees. In general, employers may deduct the premiums paid for life, health, accident, and disability insurance. Normally an employee does not have to include in gross income premiums paid on his or her behalf for health, accident, and disability insurance. Special rules applicable to life insurance premiums are discussed below.

Benefits received from medical, health, and group term life insurance coverage generally are excluded from an employee's gross income. Benefits received from a disability policy are normally taxable, but may qualify for the credit for the elderly and disabled (see Chapter I:14). The tax treatments of employer-financed and taxpayer-financed insurance coverage are compared in Topic Review I:4-1.

The rules relating to accident and health insurance are more generous than those for some other types of benefits. Under Sec. 106, employers can deduct insurance premiums and employees need not include the premiums in gross income.

? STOP & THINK

Question: How does the 2010 *Affordable Care Act* impact employer provided health insurance?

Answer: The law made a number of changes in the tax rules affecting employee health insurance. Collectively, these rules penalize individuals who do not obtain medical insurance coverage and also penalize larger employers who fail to provide adequate employee health benefits. The act creates several new taxes and changes others.

The act mandates that employers report the cost of health insurance benefits provided to employees on employee W-2's. The amount of the benefit is *not* included in employee gross income, but the reporting serves as a basis for imposing a variety of penalties that are part of the law. As noted elsewhere, the law increased the threshold for itemizing medical expense from 7.5% of AGI to 10% and limits the amount that can be contributed to a flexible spending plan for health care ($2,550 in 2015). A credit will help small employers with the cost of providing employees with health insurance coverage.

Industry specific taxes apply to tanning salons, medical device manufacturers, insurance companies, and pharmaceutical companies. Other taxes apply to high income individuals, individuals who do not have health coverage, and large employers who do not provide employee coverage.[21]

These and a number of other taxes will help subsidize health insurance costs for lower and middle income individuals.

---

[19] See Chapter I:3 for a discussion of the reimbursement of an expense deducted in a preceding year.

[20] Sec. 105(a).

[21] Beginning in 2013, a payroll tax of 0.9% applies to earned income over $200,000 ($250,000 for married couples). These high income taxpayers also face a 3.8% tax on investment income, such as interest, capital gains and dividends. Beginning in 2014, individuals who do not have health insurance coverage will be subject to a tax that will grow to the greater of $695 or 2% of gross income in 2016. Employers with 50 or more employees (100 or more in 2015) who do not provide adequate health insurance coverage must pay a tax of $2,080 (in 2015) for each employee over 30.

TOPIC REVIEW I:4-1

Treatment of Insurance

	Premiums Paid by	
	Employer	*Employee*
Medical and health Premiums	Premiums not included in employee's gross income. Premiums deductible by employer.	Premiums deductible as medical expense subject to 10% of AGI limitation (threshold is 7.5% of AGI through 2016 for taxpayers age 65 and older).
Benefits	Excluded from employee's gross income except when benefits exceed actual expenses.	Excluded from gross income.
Disability Premiums	Premiums not included in employee's gross income. Premiums deductible by employer.	Not deductible.
Benefits	Included in employee's gross income. May qualify for credit for elderly and disabled.	Excluded from gross income.
Life insurance Premiums	Included in employee's gross income (except for limited exclusion applicable to group term life insurance). Premiums deductible by employer (assuming employer is not the beneficiary).	Not deductible.
Benefits	Excluded from gross income.	Excluded from gross income.

ADDITIONAL COMMENT

The tax expenditure estimate associated with the exclusion of contributions by employers for medical insurance premiums and medical care for the year 2012 is $117 billion. This is the largest tax expenditure in the U.S. budget.

KEY POINT

The nondiscrimination requirements for self-insured accident and health plans are designed to ensure that such plans do not discriminate against rank-and-file workers.

Some employers provide self-insured accident and health plans to employees. Under such plans the employer pays employee medical expenses directly. Such plans are called Health Reimbursement Arrangements and often supplement health insurance.

Both insured and self-insured plans are subject to nondiscrimination requirements. *Discrimination* is defined in terms of an eligibility test (whether a sufficient number of non-highly compensated employees are covered) and benefits (whether non-highly compensated employees receive benefits comparable to highly compensated employees). Highly compensated employees include the five highest-paid officers, greater-than-10% shareholders, and highest-paid 25% of other employees. If a plan discriminates in favor of highly compensated employees, these employees must include in gross income any medical reimbursements they receive that are not available to other employees.

In general, life insurance premiums paid by an employer on an employee's behalf are deductible by the employer and are includable in the employee's gross income.[22] A limited exception is applicable to group term life insurance coverage. In general, premiums attributable to the first $50,000 of group term life insurance coverage may be excluded from an employee's gross income.[23] To qualify group term life insurance premiums for the exclusion, broad coverage of employees is required. Though somewhat different, the rules may be compared to those associated with self-insurance coverage.[24] The amount of coverage can vary between employees as long as the coverage bears a uniform relationship to each employee's compensation.

[22] If the employer is the beneficiary of the policy, the employee receives no economic benefit and, as a result, need not include the premiums in gross income. Such premium payments are not deductible by the employer. Subsequent benefits are not included in the employer's gross income.

[23] Sec. 79(a).

[24] For example, the rules refer to "key employees" as opposed to highly compensated employees. The term *key employee* is somewhat narrower in scope.

▼ **TABLE I:4-1**
Uniform One-Month Group Term Premiums for $1,000 of Life Insurance Coverage

Employee's age	Premiums
Under 25	$0.05
25 to 29	.06
30 to 34	.08
35 to 39	.09
40 to 44	.10
45 to 49	.15
50 to 54	.23
55 to 59	.43
60 to 64	.66
65 to 69	1.27
70 and above	2.06

EXAMPLE I:4-18 ▶ Data Corporation provides group term life insurance coverage for each full-time employee. The coverage is equal to one year's compensation. The arrangement constitutes a qualified group term life insurance plan. ◀

TYPICAL MISCONCEPTION

Many individuals erroneously believe that all life insurance coverage provided by employers is exempt from income.

In the case of coverage that exceeds $50,000, employees must include in gross income the amount established by the Regulations. (See Table I:4-1.)

EXAMPLE I:4-19 ▶ USA Corporation provides Joy, age 61, with $150,000 of group term life insurance coverage. Joy must include in gross income $792, an amount determined by reference to Table I:4-1 [($100,000/$1,000 × $.66) × 12 = $792]. ◀

The amount that must otherwise be included in an employee's gross income is reduced by any premiums paid by the employee.

If group term life insurance coverage discriminates in favor of key employees, each key employee must include in gross income the greater of the premiums paid on his or her behalf or the amount determined based on Table I:4-1 without any exclusion for the first $50,000 of coverage.

? STOP & THINK

Question: Does the fact that employers can provide health insurance and group term life insurance to employees on a tax-favored basis mean that such benefits should be provided to all employees? Explain.

Solution: No. Providing such benefits to all employees may be inefficient. Some employees have other health coverage (e.g., coverage through a spouse's employer). Employees with no dependents may not want life insurance coverage. As a result, employers who provide all employees with such benefits may be spending money on coverage that some employees neither want nor need. A cafeteria plan, discussed later in this chapter, is often a more efficient option. Such plans permit employees to choose either cash or from a menu of tax-favored benefits. This does have significant social and economic implications. As the cost of health insurance increases, more employees, especially those with lower incomes, choose cash salary over health insurance coverage. This contributes to the growing number of individuals who do not have health insurance. Once the provisions of the Affordable Care Act become effective, larger employers face penalties if employees are not covered by health insurance.

TOPIC REVIEW I:4-2

Summary of Sec. 132 Fringe Benefits

Section	Benefit	May Be Made Available To	Comments
132(b)	No-additional-cost (e.g., telephone, unused hotel rooms for hotel employees, unused airline seats for airline employees)	Employees, spouses, dependents, and retirees	The services must be of the same types that are sold to customers and in the line of business in which the employee works. Discrimination is prohibited.
132(c)	Qualified employee discounts	Employees, spouses, dependents, and retirees	Discounts on services limited to 20%. Discounts on merchandise are limited to the employer's gross profit percentage. No discount is permitted on real estate, stock, or other investment type property. Discrimination is prohibited.
132(d)	Working condition (e.g., free magazines, out-placement, and memberships)	Employees	Discrimination is permitted. Special rules apply to tuition reductions for employees of educational institutions and to an auto salesperson's demonstrator.
132(e)	De minimis (e.g., free coffee, holiday turkeys, or use of company eating facilities)	Employees	Eating facilities must be made available on a nondiscriminatory basis.
132(f)	Qualified transportation fringes (e.g., transit passes, tokens, and parking)	Employees	Limited exclusion for parking and transportation fringes. Discrimination is permitted.
132(j)(4)	Recreation and athletic facilities (e.g., gyms, pools, saunas, and tennis courts)	Employees, spouses, dependents, and retirees	If discrimination is present, employer loses deduction.
132(j)(8)	Educational assistance	Employees and former employees	Discrimination is prohibited. Now only covers job-related education and training.

ADDITIONAL COMMENT

The nondiscrimination rules do not apply to working condition fringe benefits. For example, if a corporation makes bodyguards available only to key officers, the working condition fringe benefit exclusion would still apply.

Section 132 Fringe Benefits. It has become common for employers to provide employees with such diverse benefits as free parking, membership in professional organizations, and small discounts on products sold by the employer. Section 132 was added to the IRC in 1984 to clarify whether certain types of benefits are taxable. Section 132 lists six types of fringe benefits that may be excluded from an employee's gross income (see Topic Review I:4-2). Any costs incurred by an employer to provide the specified benefits are deductible under Sec. 162 if they meet the "ordinary and necessary" test of that section.[25] Benefits covered by Sec. 132 include:

- No-additional-cost benefits (e.g., a hotel employee's use of a vacant hotel room)
- Qualified employee discounts (e.g., discounts on merchandise sold by the employer)
- Working condition benefits (e.g., membership fees in professional organizations paid by an employer)
- De minimis benefits (e.g., coffee provided by the employer)
- An exclusion of $250 per month (in both 2014 and 2015) is available for employer-financed parking. An exclusion of $130 per month (in both 2014 and 2015) is available for public transportation and commuter highway vehicles.

[25] See Chapter I:6 for a discussion of Sec. 162 and its requirements. Section 274 does provide one exception to the general rule. The costs of maintaining recreational facilities (such as swimming pools) are not deductible if the facilities are made available on a discriminatory basis (e.g., only officers may use the facilities).

- Athletic facilities (e.g., employer-owned tennis courts used by employees)
- Job-related education and training. See Chapter I:9 for a discussion of what constitutes "job-related" education and training. Chapter I:9 also discusses the possible deduction by employees of unreimbursed job-related education costs.

No-additional-cost benefits are limited to services, as opposed to property. Common examples of no-additional-cost benefits include the use of vacant hotel rooms by hotel employees and standby air flights provided to airline employees. The employer may not incur substantial additional costs, including forgone revenue, in providing the services to the employee. Thus, a hotel may allow employees to stay in vacant hotel rooms even though the hotel incurs additional utility and laundry costs as a result of the stay. However, the hotel cannot allow the employees to stay in lieu of paying guests. No-additional-cost benefits are limited to services provided to employees, their spouses, dependent children, and to retired and disabled employees. The term employee includes partners who perform services for a partnership. In addition, the benefits may be extended, on a reciprocal basis, to employees of other companies in the same line of business.

Employers may permit employees to purchase goods and services at a discount from the price charged regular customers. In the case of services, the discount is limited to 20% of the price charged regular customers. In the case of property, the discount is limited to the company's gross profit percent. No discounts are permitted on real property or investment property (e.g., houses or stocks). Further, the discounts must be from the same line of business in which the employee works. The discounts may be provided to the same persons as no-additional-cost benefits except that the discounts may not be provided on a reciprocal basis to employees of companies in the same line of business.

Discrimination is prohibited with respect to certain benefits. The benefits must be made available to employees in general rather than to highly compensated employees only. (See Topic Review I:4-2 for specific rules.)

SELF-STUDY QUESTION

Western Airlines and Central Airlines have a reciprocal agreement that permits employees of the other airline to travel for free on a standby basis. Stan, an employee of Western Airlines, takes a free flight on Central Airlines that would have cost $800. What is Stan's income?

ANSWER

None, reciprocal agreements with regard to no-additional-cost ser vices are permitted.

Employee Awards. As noted earlier, it is often difficult to distinguish between gifts and awards. The de minimis rule mentioned above permits employers to make small gifts such as a holiday turkey or a watch at retirement without the employee having to include the value of the gift in gross income. The employer is entitled to a deduction for the cost of such gifts.

Section 74 provides a similar rule for **employee achievement awards** and **qualified plan awards.**[26] Such awards must be in the form of tangible personal property other than cash and must be based on safety records or length of service. Employee achievement awards are limited to $400 for any one employee during the year. Furthermore, the awards must be presented as part of a meaningful presentation and awarded under circumstances that do not create a significant likelihood of the payment being disguised compensation. Qualified plan awards must be granted under a written plan and may not discriminate in favor of highly compensated employees. The average cost of qualified plan awards is limited to $400, but individual awards can be as large as $1,600.

- An award for length of service cannot qualify under the IRC if it is received during the employee's first five years of employment or if the employee has received a length-of-service award during the year or any of the preceding four years.
- No more than 10% of an employer's eligible employees may receive an excludable safety achievement award during any year. Eligible employees are employees whose positions involve significant safety concerns.

EXAMPLE I:4-20 ▶ Each year, USA Corporation presents length-of-service awards to employees who have been with the company five, ten, fifteen, or twenty years. The presentations are made at a luncheon sponsored by the company and include gifts such as desk clocks, briefcases, and watches, none of which cost more than $400. The awards, which qualify as employee achievement awards, are deductible by USA Corporation and are not taxable as income to USA's employees. ◀

[26] Sec. 74(c). The definitions and requirements for employee achievement awards and qualified plan awards are contained in Sec. 274(j).

Gifts to employees that do not qualify as employee achievement awards or qualified plan awards can be excluded by the employee only if the awards can be excluded as de minimis amounts under Sec. 132(e).

Meals and Lodging. Section 119 provides a limited exclusion for the value of meals and lodging that are provided to employees at either no cost or a reduced cost.

REAL-WORLD EXAMPLE

Many university presidents are furnished with personal residences, the value of which they can generally exclude from gross income.

- Meals provided by an employer may be excluded from an employee's gross income if they are furnished on the employer's premises and for the convenience of the employer.
- Lodging provided by an employer may be excluded from an employee's gross income if it is furnished on the employer's premises and for the convenience of the employer, and the employee is required to accept the lodging as a condition of employment.

REAL-WORLD EXAMPLE

A brewery provided houses on the business premises to officers. The value of the houses was excludable because it was important to have the officers available for around-the-clock operations of the business. *Adolph Coors Co.,* 1968 PH T.C. Memo ¶68, 256, 27 TCM 1351.

The requirement that meals and lodging be furnished on the premises of the employer refers to the employee's place of employment.[27] In one case, the Tax Court held that the business premises requirement was met in a situation where a hotel manager lived in a residence across the street from the hotel he managed.[28]

The convenience of the employer test considers whether a substantial noncompensatory business reason exists for providing the meals or lodging. Thus, the test is met if the owner of an apartment complex furnishes a unit to the manager of the complex because it is necessary to have the manager present on the premises even when he or she is off duty.

The value of lodging cannot be excluded from gross income unless the employee is required to accept the lodging as a condition of employment. This requirement is not met if the employee has a choice of accepting the lodging or receiving a cash allowance. Furthermore, meal allowances do not qualify for the exclusion because the employer does not actually provide the meal.[29] Section 132 (discussed earlier in this chapter) provides a de minimis exception. Some employers provide supper money to employees who must work overtime. If such benefits are occasionally provided to employees, the amount is excludable from the employees' gross income.

EXAMPLE I:4-21 ▶ A hospital maintains a cafeteria that is used by employees, patients, and visitors. Employees are provided free meals while on duty in order to be available for emergency calls. Since the meals are provided on the employer's premises and for the convenience of the employer, the value of the meals is excluded from the employees' gross income. ◀

EXAMPLE I:4-22 ▶ A state highway patrol organization provides its officers with a daily meal allowance to compensate them for meals eaten while they are on duty. Officers typically eat their meals at the restaurant of their choice. Because the officers receive cash instead of meals, the amount provided must be included in the officers' gross income. ◀

EXAMPLE I:4-23 ▶ A large corporation requires five of its employees to work overtime two evenings each year when the company takes inventory. The corporation gives each of the employees a small amount to cover the cost of the dinner for the two evenings. The amounts constitute supper money and are excluded from the employees' gross income. ◀

Section 119 provides that if employees can exclude the value of meals from gross income, the employer can deduct the full cost of the meal. Further, if more than half of the employees who receive meals meet the "convenience of the employer" test, then all employees who receive meals can exclude the value from gross income.

Meals and Entertainment. One obvious question is whether employees who are reimbursed by their employers when they entertain customers must include the reimbursement in gross income. If they must include the reimbursement in gross income, can they deduct the cost of the entertainment and meals? Assuming conditions for deductibility are met, the tax law clearly allows 50% of the cost of entertaining customers to be

[27] Reg. Sec. 1.119-1(c)(1).

[28] *Jack B. Lindeman,* 60 T.C. 609 (1973).

[29] *CIR v. Robert J. Kowalski,* 40 AFTR 2d 77-6128, 77-2 USTC ¶9748 (USSC, 1977).

deducted (discussed in Chapter I:9). Can the employee deduct the meals and entertainment that he personally consumes?

EXAMPLE I:4-24 ▶ Joe is a sales representative for Zero Corporation. As a part of his regular duties, Joe buys lunch for Wayne, a Zero Corporation customer. Fifty percent of the cost of Wayne's meal is deductible either by Joe if he pays for the luncheon without being reimbursed by his employer, or by the Zero Corporation if it reimburses Joe for the cost. Can Joe deduct 50% of the cost of his own meal if he pays for it and is not reimbursed? If Zero pays for the meal, must Joe include in his gross income the cost of his own lunch? ◀

In the above question, Joe apparently can deduct the portion of the luncheon that applies to himself. While this issue is not clear-cut, the IRS has indicated in Rev. Rul. 63-144 that it will not pursue the issue except where taxpayers claim deductions for substantial amounts of personal expenses.[30] In any case, it is an accepted practice today for taxpayers to deduct 50% of the total cost of a meal (taxpayer and customer) unless the practice is considered abusive.[31]

Employee Death Benefits. Occasionally, an employer may make payments to the family or friends of an employee who dies. In some instances, the payments might be viewed as a gift made for reasons such as the financial need of the family, kindness, or charity. Alternatively, the amount might constitute a payment of compensation based on the past services of the deceased employee. Gifts are, of course, excluded from gross income, whereas compensation is taxable. The treatment of payments made to the family or other beneficiaries of the employee's estate is determined by the following rules:

- Payments for past services (such as bonuses, accrued wages, and unused vacation pay) are taxable as income to the family and are deductible by the employer. The important issue is whether the employee would have received this amount had he or she lived. If the employer was legally obligated to make the payment at the time of the employee's death, the payments are taxable to the recipient.
- Other amounts may be either taxable compensation or excludable gifts depending on the facts and circumstances. If the amount is a gift, it is not deductible by the employer. If the amount is taxable income to the deceased employee's family, it is deductible by the employer.

In determining whether the amount is taxable, the courts have considered such factors as whether the employer derived benefit from the payment, whether the employee had been fully compensated, and whether the payment was made to the family and not to the estate. The Supreme Court stated, "The most critical consideration [in determining whether a transfer is a gift] is the transferor's 'intention'."[32] Although the case did not deal with death benefits, it did establish the importance of motive in determining whether a payment is a gift. Thus, the transfer should be made for reasons such as kindness, sympathy, generosity, affection, or admiration.

It should be noted that it is more difficult to establish that a payment is a gift in situations where the payments are made to persons owning stock in the corporation making the payment. Such payments may be construed as constructive dividends, which are not deductible by the corporation but are taxable income to the recipients.[33]

ADDITIONAL COMMENT

The $5,000 limit was placed on the exclusion for dependent care assistance programs because it was thought to be inequitable to provide an unlimited dependent care exclusion but a limited child care credit for people who pay their own child care expenses.

Dependent Care. Dependent care assistance programs are employer-financed programs that provide care for an employee's children or other dependents. An employee may exclude up to $5,000 of assistance each year ($2,500 for a married individual filing a separate return). The care must be of a type that, if paid by the employee, would qualify for the dependent care credit. Furthermore, the credit is scaled down if the employee

---

[30] Rev. Rul. 63-144, 1963-2 C.B. 129.

[31] See, however, *Richard A. Sutter*, 21 T.C. 170 (1953), where the Tax Court ruled that business meals, entertainment, etc. for one's own self are inherently personal and nondeductible. *Sutter* has been cited and upheld some 50 times.

[32] *CIR v. Mose Duberstein*, 5 AFTR 2d 1626, 60-2 USTC ¶9515 (USSC, 1960).

[33] *Ernest L. Poyner v. CIR*, 9 AFTR 2d 1151, 62-1 USTC ¶9387 (4th Cir., 1962).

WHAT WOULD YOU DO IN THIS SITUATION?

FRINGE BENEFIT

National Boats manufactures pleasure boats sold to consumers. The boats range in price from $40,000 to $1,500,000. Jake is the president of National Boats. The company provides Jake with one of its more expensive boats. The company pays for fuel, insurance, and other costs and deducts these expenses along with depreciation on the boat. The company states that Jake is responsible for testing and for demonstrating the boat to possible customers. Jake has had the same boat for two years, and the company plans to provide him with a new boat next month.

You asked Jake how often he uses the boat. He indicated that he uses it once or twice each month on weekends, except during the winter. You asked him who accompanies him, and what types of testing he conducts. He seemed reluctant to answer the question, but acknowledged that his family often accompanies him on the boat, and said that he tests it during ordinary operations to determine how it performs. He added that potential customers who have also accompanied him included neighbors and friends. What tax issues do you see?

KEY POINT

The classification of an employee as highly compensated is made on the basis of the facts and circumstances of each case. Any officers and shareholders owning more than 5% of the stock are classified as highly compensated employees.

ADDITIONAL COMMENT

The Sec. 132 education exclusion discussed earlier is not subject to a dollar limitation, but covers only training related to the employee's work.

ADDITIONAL COMMENT

About half of the large employers in the United States offer flexible spending accounts.

ADDITIONAL COMMENT

While the main benefit of a cafeteria plan is to offer tax-free choices to employees, the plan must also offer at least one taxable benefit.

ADDITIONAL COMMENT

Some plans supplement wages; others are wage reduction plans. In supplemental wage plans, employer funds are used to pay fringe benefits. In the case of wage reduction plans, employees elect to receive reduced wages in exchange for the fringe benefits. In both cases, employees receive benefits without being taxed on them.

receives benefits under the employer's plan. (See Chapter I:14 for a discussion of the child and dependent care rules.) The program cannot discriminate in favor of highly compensated employees or their dependents.[34]

Adoption Expenses. Congress provides tax benefits for qualified adoption expenses in the form of a tax credit (see Chapter I:14) or an exclusion for amounts paid pursuant to the employer's written adoption assistance plan. In 2015, an employee may exclude from gross income up to $13,400 ($13,190 in 2014) of qualified expenses paid by an employer in connection with the adoption of a child under age 18.[35] The exclusion is phased out for employees with modified adjusted gross income between $201,010 and $241,010 (between $197,880 and $237,880 in 2014).

Educational Assistance. Under Sec. 127 educational assistance plans, employers pay employee education expenses. Employees may exclude from gross income annual payments of up to $5,250. The exclusion applies to payments for tuition, fees, books, supplies, and equipment for undergraduate courses or graduate courses as well as other training.

Cafeteria Plans. Cafeteria plans are plans that offer employees the option of choosing cash or statutory nontaxable fringe benefits (such as group term life insurance, medical insurance, adoption expenses, child care, etc.). If the employee chooses cash, the cash is taxable. However, if the employee chooses a statutory nontaxable fringe benefit, the value of the benefit is excluded from gross income.[36] In other words, the fact that the employee could have chosen cash does not cause the fringe benefit to be taxed. The plan cannot discriminate in favor of highly compensated employees or their dependents or spouses.[37] Employer plans may specify what benefits are offered and may limit the amount of benefits individual employees may receive.

Cafeteria plans that allow employees to use funds to pay medical expenses are called Flexible Spending Accounts. Typically, the plans supplement medical insurance, and funds are used to pay dental bills and other medical expenses not covered by regular insurance. In general, employees annually elect to set aside funds to pay medical expenses, and the employer pays the expenses using the set-aside funds. One problem with the agreements is that they are binding for one year. As a result, the employee loses the funds if the actual medical expenses are less than the amount set aside. Rules permit employees to carry over up to $500 from one year to the next. Employers, on the other hand, are obligated to pay expenses up to the agreed

[34] Sec. 129.

[35] Sec. 137.

[36] Long-term care insurance (sometimes called nursing home insurance) can be offered to employees on a tax-favored basis, but that benefit cannot be offered as part of a flexible spending account.

[37] Sec. 125.

ADDITIONAL COMMENT

One benefit that was often used in the past was interest-free loans to employees. Under present law, interest must generally be imputed on interest-free loans. (See Chapter I:11 for a detailed discussion of rules applicable to interest-free loans.)

amount even if the full amount has not yet been withheld from the employee's wages. Thus, the employer may lose money if an employee terminates employment after incurring the designated amount of medical expenses but before the full amount is withheld.

Advantage of Fringe Benefits. The major advantage of taking fringe benefits (such as those described above) in lieu of a cash payment is the fact that employees do not have to use after-tax income to obtain the product or service.

EXAMPLE I:4-25 ▶ Dan, an employee of Central Corporation, has a $40,000 life insurance policy and pays the premiums out of his salary. Since his salary is taxable, the premiums are paid on an after-tax basis. Kay, an employee for Western Corporation, is covered by a $40,000 group term life insurance policy financed by Western Corporation. Western Corporation pays the premiums on the policy. Because the premiums are excludable, Kay does not have to report the premiums as income. ◀

EXAMPLE I:4-26 ▶ John's employer establishes a cafeteria plan which allows each employee to set aside up to $5,000 for health insurance premiums and medical reimbursements. John, whose salary has been $30,000, agrees to a salary reduction of $4,000, of which $2,600 is to cover his health insurance premiums and $1,400 is available to reimburse his medical expenses. Under the arrangement, John's salary is reduced to $26,000 for tax purposes. Neither the health insurance coverage nor the medical expense reimbursement is taxable. During the year, John incurs $1,300 of medical expenses not covered by insurance. He receives a reimbursement for all of the expenses. His employer retains the remaining $100. Alternatively, if the medical expenses were $1,800, John would receive a reimbursement of $1,400 and he must pay the remaining $400 of expenses out of after-tax salary dollars. ◀

In 2015, the maximum amount that employees can elect to contribute tax-free to a flexible spending account for health care benefits is $2,550 ($2,500 in 2014). The limitation does not apply to an elective wage reduction for an employee's share of medical insurance premiums, but does apply to reimbursements for dental bills, co-pays, and other medical expenses paid directly by an employee.

STOP & THINK

Question: Employers and employees both pay FICA taxes on salaries. Fringe benefits such as health insurance are exempt from both income taxes and FICA taxes. What is the tax effect of an employee's decision to elect health insurance coverage in exchange for a reduced salary?

Solution: The employee's income and FICA taxes are both lowered. The employer is permitted an income tax deduction for either the salary payment or the payment of the health insurance premium. The employer's FICA tax is reduced because the health insurance benefit also is exempt from that tax.

Availability of Tax-Favored Fringe Benefits to Business Owners. The exclusion for many fringe benefits is only available to employees (and in some cases spouses, dependents, and retirees). Many tax-favored fringe benefits are unavailable to proprietors and partners. As a result, a partnership can provide $50,000 of group-term life insurance to employees on a tax-favored basis, but cannot provide the benefit on a tax-favored basis to its partners. Other fringe benefits that cannot be offered to proprietors or partners on a tax-favored basis include cafeteria plans, disability insurance, medical reimbursements, achievement awards, adoptions assistance, on-premises lodging, moving expense, and commuting and parking benefits (other than de minimis).[38]

Special rules apply to health insurance premiums and retirement plan contributions for proprietors and partners. The owners deduct these payments for AGI. This results in a self-employment tax on the amounts, but no income tax.

---

[38] Benefits that can be offered to proprietors and partners on a tax-favored basis include athletic facilities, de minimis benefits, no additional cost fringe benefits, dependent care assistance, educational assistance, discounts, on-premises meals, and working condition fringes.

Shareholders, as such, are ineligible for tax-favored fringe benefits. In most cases employees of C corporations are eligible for tax-favored fringe benefits based on their wages even if they own stock. This is not true, however, for S corporation employees who own more than 2% of the corporation's stock. They are treated much like partners and proprietors with respect to fringe benefits. Health insurance premiums and retirement plan contributions made for these S corporation employee-shareholders are wages for income tax purposes. Like partners and proprietors, these S corporation employees-shareholders can deduct the amounts for AGI. Unlike partners and proprietors, the amounts are not subject to FICA or self-employment taxes.

The fact that fringe benefits provided to employee-shareholders of C corporations are treated more favorably than benefits provided to the owners of other businesses is an incentive for businesses to operate as C corporations.

ADDITIONAL COMMENT

Many U.S. embassies and consulates in foreign countries provide income tax assistance.

ADDITIONAL COMMENT

Foreign-earned income does not include amounts paid to an employee of the U.S. government or any U.S. government agency or instrumentality.

FOREIGN-EARNED INCOME EXCLUSION

In general, the income of U.S. citizens is subject to the U.S. income tax even if the income is derived from sources outside the United States. The foreign income of U.S. citizens also may be taxed by thc host country possibly leading to a substantial double tax on the same income. The double tax is mitigated by a **foreign tax credit**. Subject to limitations, U.S. citizens may subtract from their U.S. income tax liability the income taxes they pay to foreign countries. (See Chapter I:14 for a discussion of foreign tax credit.)

In the case of foreign-earned income, individuals have available the alternative option of excluding the first $100,800 in 2015 ($99,200 in 2014) of foreign-earned income from gross income.[39] The *exclusion* is available in lieu of the foreign tax credit. If both a husband and wife have foreign-earned income, each may claim an exclusion. Community property rules are ignored in determining the amount of the exclusion. Thus, if only one spouse has foreign-earned income, only one exclusion is available. The principal reasons for the exclusion are to encourage U.S. businesses to operate in foreign countries and to hire U.S. citizens and resident aliens to manage the businesses. The hope is that such operations will improve the balance of payments. Taxpayers who elect the exclusion in one year may switch to the foreign tax credit in any subsequent year. Taxpayers who change from the exclusion to the credit may not reelect the exclusion before the sixth tax year after the tax year in which the change was made.[40] The IRS can waive the six-year limitation in special situations (such as an individual employee changing the location of his or her foreign employment).

TYPICAL MISCONCEPTION

A taxpayer must be present in one or more foreign countries for 330 days during a period of twelve consecutive months, rather than 330 days during a calendar year.

Foreign-earned income includes an individual's earnings from personal services rendered in a foreign country. The place where the services are performed determines whether earned income is foreign or U.S. source income. If an individual is engaged in a trade or business in which both personal services and capital are material income-producing factors, no more than 30% of the net profits from the business may be excluded.[41] Furthermore, pensions, annuities, salary paid by the U.S. government, and deferred compensation do not qualify for the exclusion.[42]

To qualify for the foreign-earned income exclusion, the taxpayer must either be a bona fide resident of one or more foreign countries for an entire taxable year, or be present in one or more foreign countries for 330 days during a period of 12 consecutive months.[43] The exclusion limitation for a year must be prorated if the taxpayer is not present in, or a resident of, a foreign country or countries for the entire year.

EXAMPLE I:4-27 ▶ Sondra is given a temporary assignment to work in foreign country T. She arrives in T on October 19, 2015, and leaves on October 1, 2016. Although Sondra does not establish a permanent residence in T, she is present in T for at least 330 days out of a twelve-month period beginning on October 20, 2015. Thus, 73 days fall in 2015 and the rest in 2016. Sondra's exclusion for 2015 is limited to $20,160 [(73 ÷ 365) × $100,800]. She may exclude $20,160 or the income she earns in foreign country T during 2015, whichever is less. Sondra also may claim the foreign earned income exclusion in 2016 for the number of qualified days during the year. ◀

[39] Sec. 911(b)(2).
[40] Sec. 911(e)(2).
[41] Sec. 911(d)(2)(B).
[42] Sec. 911(b)(1)(B).
[43] Sec. 911(d).

Deductions directly attributable to the excluded foreign-earned income are disallowed. Expenses attributable to foreign-earned income must be allocated if foreign-earned income exceeds the exclusion. The disallowed portion is determined by multiplying the total amount of such expenses by the ratio of excluded earned income over total foreign-earned income.

EXAMPLE I:4-28 ▶ Connie earned $151,200 while employed in a foreign country for the entire year. She is entitled to an exclusion of $100,800. Connie incurred $12,000 of travel, transportation, and other deductible expenses attributable to the foreign-earned income. She may deduct only $4,000 of such expenses because $8,000 [($100,800 ÷ $151,200) × $12,000] is allocated to the excluded income and, therefore, not deductible. The $4,000 is classified as a miscellaneous itemized deduction and subject to the 2% of AGI floor associated with such deductions. ◀

Housing costs in foreign countries are often higher than in the United States. In such situations, employees may be able to increase their exclusion while self-employed individuals may be able to deduct a portion of their housing costs. Specifically, the exclusion (deduction) is available for housing costs that exceed 16% of the foreign earned income exclusion limitation or $16,128 (0.16 × $100,800) in 2015 ($15,872 in 2014). Because the maximum housing cost exclusion is 30%, the amount that can be excluded for housing costs under this rule generally is limited to $14,112 (0.14 × $100,800) in 2015 ($13,888 in 2014). The IRS provides higher amounts for cities with high cost-of-living. Further, the housing exclusion must be reduced if the taxpayer does not incur cost for the entire year.

EXAMPLE I:4-29 ▶ Wayne is employed in Quebec City, Canada, and earns a salary of $120,000. His housing costs are $38,000 for the year. Wayne can exclude $114,912 ($100,800 + $14,112) from gross income. If the housing costs had been $24,000, Wayne's foreign earned income exclusion would have totaled $108,672 [$100,800 + ($24,000 − $16,128)]. ◀

Taxpayers who exclude a portion, but not all foreign earned income, are subject to a special tax computation. The result of the computation is to apply higher tax rates to the taxable portion of the foreign earned income. (See *Prentice Hall's Federal Taxation: Corporations, Partnernerships, Estates, and Trusts*, Chapter 16.) Americans employed abroad are often subject to income and payroll taxes imposed by the host country. Americans employed abroad by foreign companies are generally exempt from FICA taxes while Americans employed abroad by American companies remain subject to FICA taxes except in instances where a tax treaty between the U.S. and the host country subjects Americans to comparable host country taxes.

INCOME FROM THE DISCHARGE OF A DEBT

If debt of a taxpayer is cancelled or forgiven, the taxpayer may have to include the cancelled amount in gross income. It is important to distinguish a debt cancellation from a gift, a bequest, or a renegotiation of the purchase price.

EXAMPLE I:4-30 ▶ Farouk loaned his daughter $4,000 to help her purchase an automobile. Several months after she purchased the automobile, but before she repaid the $4,000, Farouk's daughter married. Farouk told his daughter that he was "tearing up" the $4,000 note as a wedding present. In this instance, the amount forgiven would constitute an excludable gift and would not be taxable as income to the daughter. ◀

EXAMPLE I:4-31 ▶ Clay purchased a used automobile from a dealer for $6,000. He paid $2,000 down and agreed to pay the balance of $4,000 over three years. After Clay purchased the automobile, he determined that it was defective. Clay tried to return the automobile, but the automobile dealer refused. Clay threatened to sue the dealer. To resolve the problem, the dealer offered to reduce the balance due on the purchase-money debt from $4,000 to $2,500. Clay agreed. The transaction constitutes a reduction in the purchase price of the automobile. Clay will not recognize any income, but must reduce the basis in his automobile from $6,000 to $4,500. ◀

EXAMPLE I:4-32 ▶ Blue Corporation issued bonds for $1,000 when interest rates were low. After a few years, interest rates increased and the bond value declined to $850. Blue Corporation purchased the bonds on the open market. Blue will recognize $150 of income from the discharge of indebtedness. ◀

EXAMPLE I:4-33 ▶ Indy Coal Company has seen its business decline during the past two years. The Company has a significant amount of bank debt that was incurred over the years to fund its coal operations. In order to maintain its operations, Indy entered into an agreement with the bank whereby the bank agreed to cancel 50% of Indy's debt. Assuming Indy was solvent at the time of the cancellation, Indy must report the discharge of indebtedness as gross income. ◀

STOP & THINK

Question: In Example I:4-33, the bank agreed to cancel 50% of Indy Coal Company's debt. Why would a lender agree to unilaterally cancel a borrower's debt?

Solution: A bank might cancel a portion of a borrower's debt in order to protect the remaining portion of the debt. If the debt forced the company into bankruptcy, the bank may be able to collect none or only a small percentage of the debt. If the cancellation would help stabilize Indy, the bank may be able to collect at least 50% of the debt. Further, if Indy becomes a viable company in the years ahead, the bank will have a good customer to earn profits in the future.

REAL-WORLD EXAMPLE

A taxpayer purchased and retired its own bonds. The purchase resulted in a gain because the bonds were payable in British pounds, which had been devalued. The gain was excludable. *Kentucky & Indiana Terminal Railroad Co. v. U.S.*, 13 AFTR 2d 1148, 64-1 USTC ¶9374 (6th Cir., 1964).

The enforceability of a debt under state law may also determine whether the forgiveness results in income. For example, one case held that the forgiveness of a gambling debt was not included in gross income where the debt was unenforceable under state law.[44]

Discharge in Bankruptcy and Insolvency. Section 61(a)(12) indicates that gross income includes income from the discharge of an indebtedness. Section 108, on the other hand, provides for the following exceptions where the discharge of an indebtedness is not taxable:

- The discharge occurs in bankruptcy.
- The discharge occurs when the taxpayer is insolvent.

These exceptions are intended to allow a "fresh start" for bankrupt and other financially troubled taxpayers. Since a taxpayer is not required to include the discharge in gross income, he is required to reduce certain tax attributes. For example, if the taxpayer has a net operating loss carryover, the NOL carryover must be reduced by the excluded discharge.

If a debt is reduced during bankruptcy proceedings, the taxpayer recognizes no income even if the reduction in debt exceeds the available tax attributes. In the case of an insolvent taxpayer, no income is recognized as long as the taxpayer is insolvent after the reduction in debt takes place. A taxpayer is insolvent if the debts owed by the taxpayer exceed the FMV of assets owned. Thus, an insolvent taxpayer reduces the tax attributes to the point of solvency. From that point on, any reduction in debt results in the recognition of income even if all tax attributes have not been offset.

ADDITIONAL COMMENT

Also excludable is the income from the cancellation of a student loan pursuant to a provision under which part of the debt is discharged due to working for a period of time in certain professions for a broad class of employers.

Student Loan Forgiveness. Under Sec. 108(f)(2), the discharge of certain student loans is excluded from gross income if the discharge is contingent on the individual's performing certain public services. The loans must have been made by governmental, educational, or charitable organizations, and the loan proceeds must have been used to pay the cost of attending an educational institution or used to refinance outstanding student loans. Further, the loan forgiveness must be contingent upon the individual's working for a specified time period in certain professions, and the services must normally be performed for someone other than the lender.

EXAMPLE I:4-34 ▶ Lee borrowed $60,000 from the federal government to attend medical school. Under the terms of the loan, $20,000 of debt is forgiven for each year she practices medicine in designated low-income neighborhoods. Lee does not have to include the debt forgiveness in gross income. ◀

Home Mortgage Forgiveness. Through 2014, homeowners could exclude debt forgiveness on their principal residence of up to $2 million under Sec. 108(a)(1)(E). This provision applied only to mortgages acquired in connection with the acquisition or improvement of a taxpayer's principal residence. Taxpayers were required to reduce the basis of their residence by the amount of the exclusion.

[44] *David Zarin v. CIR*, 66 AFTR 2d 90-5679, 90-2 USTC ¶50,530 (3rd Cir., 1990).

EXCLUSION FOR GAIN FROM SMALL BUSINESS STOCK

Investing in small businesses is risky. To encourage investment, Congress enacted an exclusion for gains realized by noncorporate taxpayers on the sale or exchange of small business stock held over five years.[45] The exclusion for small business stock acquired after August 10, 1993 is 50% (except the exclusion is 75% for stock acquired from February 18, 2009 through September 27, 2010 and is 100% for stock acquired from September 28, 2010 through December 31, 2014).

Any gain remaining after the 50% and 75% exclusion is taxed at a rate of tax not greater than 28%. For each issuer of qualified small business stock, there is a limit on the amount of gain a taxpayer may exclude. The amount of gain eligible for the exclusion may not exceed the greater of $10 million, reduced by amounts previously excluded for gains on the company's stock, or ten times the taxpayer's aggregate adjusted basis of the stock disposed of during the year.[46] When measuring the taxpayer's aggregate basis for the stock to determine the maximum amount of gain to exclude, the fair market value of the assets contributed to the corporation is used.

EXAMPLE I:4-35 ▶ In February 2005, Dennis contributed property with a basis of $1,000,000 and a value of $4,000,000 to a qualified small business corporation for common stock. After holding the stock over five years, Dennis sells it for $14,000,000. He can exclude 50% of the $13,000,000 ($14,000,000 − $1,000,000) realized gain, or $6,500,000, as that amount is less than the maximum gain eligible for the exclusion $40,000,000 [the greater of $10,000,000 or $40,000,000 (10 times $4,000,000)]. If the stock had been acquired in February 2010 and held for over five years, Dennis' exclusion is 75% of the gain, or $9,750,000. If the stock had been acquired in February 2011 and held it over five years, the exclusion is 100% of the gain, or $13,000,000. ◀

Moreover, taxpayers do not have to recognize any gain if they reinvest the proceeds from the sale of small business stock in other small business stock within 60 days of the sale. Gain is recognized only to the extent that the amount realized from the sale exceeds the cost of the replacement stock. The basis of the replacement stock is reduced by the amount of gain not recognized. To qualify for the replacement provision the original stock must have been held for over 6 months.

EXAMPLE I:4-36 ▶ Assume the original facts in Example I:4-35, except that Dennis purchases $13,500,000 of small business investment stock within 60 days. Dennis is taxed only on $500,000 ($14,000,000 − $13,500,000) of his $13,000,000 realized gain. Dennis' basis for the new stock, however, is $1,000,000 ($13,500,000 cost of the new stock − $12,500,000 portion of the gain that is not taxed). ◀

A corporation may issue qualified small business stock only if the corporation is a C corporation that is not an excluded corporation with an aggregate adjusted basis of not more than $50 million of gross assets, and at least 80% of the value of its assets must be used in the active conduct of one or more qualified trades or businesses.[47]

OTHER EXCLUSIONS

The tax law contains other exclusions that are either covered elsewhere in the text or are of limited application. Table I:4-2 lists several such exclusions.

---

[45] §1202(a). The exclusion is 60% in the case of empowerment zone stock (except the exclusion is 75% for empowerment zone stock acquired from February 18, 2009 through September 27, 2010 and is 100% for stock acquired from September 28, 2010 through December 31, 2014).

[46] Sec. 1202(b)(1).

[47] Secs. 1202(d) and (e). Excluded corporations are those engaged in providing professional services (e.g., law and health), financial services (e.g., banking and insurance), hospitality (e.g., hotels and restaurants), farming, and mining and oil and gas production.

▼ **TABLE I:4-2**
Other Exclusions

Section	Applies to	Comments
121	Gain from sale of personal residence	Taxpayers may exclude up to $250,000 ($500,000 in the case of a married couple filing a joint return) of gain from the sale of a personal residence. (See Chapter I:12 for a detailed discussion of this provision.)
101(h)	Annuities paid to survivors of public safety officers	Annuities paid to survivors of public safety officers, such as firefighters and police officers, killed in the line of duty are excluded.
104(a) 112 134	Military disability pay Combat pay Military housing allowance	Military personnel may exclude disability pay, combat pay (noncommissioned personnel only), and housing allowances.
107	Housing allowance for ministers	Ministers may exclude either the rental value of their homes or a rental allowance if provided in connection with their religious duties.
119	Campus housing	A limited exclusion is provided to employees of educational institutions when they are provided with on-campus housing.
131	Foster care payments	Certain allowances received by foster care providers are excluded from gross income.
162(o)	Rural letter carrier's allowance	Rural letter carriers may exclude the "equipment maintenance allowance" they receive for the use of their personal automobiles in delivering the mail. They receive no deduction for the use of their automobiles.
408A(d)	Roth IRA distributions	Qualified distributions from Roth IRAs are excluded from gross income (see Chapter I:9 for a detailed discussion of the provisions).
530(d)	Education IRA distributions	Qualified distributions from Coverdell Education Savings Account IRAs are excluded from gross income (see Chapter I:9 for a detailed discussion of this provision).
988(e)	Personal foreign currency gains	Individuals are excused from recognizing gain on the disposition of foreign currency in any personal transaction, provided that the gain does not exceed $200.

TAX PLANNING CONSIDERATIONS

OBJECTIVE 3

Describe tax planning considerations for exclusions of gross income

EMPLOYEE FRINGE BENEFITS

The tax law encourages certain forms of fringe benefits by allowing an employer to deduct the cost of the benefit while permitting the employee to exclude the benefit from gross income. This deduction does not represent an income tax advantage to the employer because compensation, whether in the form of cash or nontaxable fringe benefits, is deductible if reasonable in amount. While employees receive the greatest income tax benefit from the exclusion of fringe benefits from gross income, employers receive a small benefit from the fact that fringe benefits are not subject to Social Security and Medicare taxes.

EXAMPLE I:4-37 ▶

USA Company has decided to offer $20,000 of group term life insurance coverage for each of its employees at an average annual premium cost of $100 per employee. Tim, an employee of USA Corporation, is in the 15% tax bracket. Because USA is offering a nontaxable fringe benefit, Tim will owe no additional income tax. If Tim had received a salary increase of $100, he would have had to pay an additional income tax of $15 ($0.15 \times \$100$). The remaining $85 of after-tax income would probably not have been sufficient to obtain the same amount of life insurance coverage. ◀

ADDITIONAL COMMENT

A case can be made for the desirability of encouraging employers to provide health insurance and other fringe benefits. However, these provisions may contribute to increases in the cost of insurance and medical care.

Excluding fringe benefits from gross income favors employees who are subject to higher tax rates.

EXAMPLE I:4-38 ▶ Assume the same facts as in Example I:4-37 except that Tim is in the 39.6% tax rate. Tim would save $39.60 (0.396 × $100) of taxes by receiving the group term life insurance coverage instead of the $100 salary increase. ◀

ADDITIONAL COMMENT
Fringe benefits offered by potential employers are important consideration factors when weighing total compensation packages.

It is not always desirable for employers to offer nontaxable fringe benefits. Some employees are not interested in certain benefits. For example, in the case of married couples where both spouses are employed, it is not necessary for both employers to provide medical insurance coverage for both spouses. Alternatively, single employees may not feel the need for group term life insurance and employees with no children are uninterested in employer-provided child care.

To avoid providing fringe benefits that are unneeded or unwanted, many employers have turned to cafeteria plans. Under cafeteria plans, employees may select from a list of nontaxable fringe benefits. On the other hand, employees who so choose may receive cash in lieu of some or all of the nontaxable benefits. Thus, each employee selects what he or she wants most. One common result is that high-tax-rate employees select the nontaxable fringe benefits, whereas other employees choose to receive cash.

SELF-HELP INCOME AND USE OF PERSONALLY OWNED PROPERTY

As noted earlier in this chapter, self-help income and income derived from the use of personal property are not taxable. Thus, self-help income and personal ownership of property are favored by the tax system. Taxpayers who rent their personal residences cannot deduct rental payments, but taxpayers who own their residences do not pay rent and may deduct interest and real estate taxes as itemized deductions. Thus, the tax law encourages ownership of personal residences.

Effective tax planning necessitates weighing the tax incentives with other nontax factors. Taxpayers with little accumulated funds may find it difficult to purchase a residence despite the availability of tax incentives. Taxpayers who move frequently may find that transaction costs such as real estate commissions and other closing costs are greater than the tax benefits obtained from home ownership. Other factors such as the personal preference of the taxpayer and anticipated inflation rates must also be considered.

Self-help income must be viewed in the same way. Taxpayers who are deciding whether to paint their own residences or hire someone else to do it must consider factors such as personal preference and the amount of income that could be produced if the time were spent working at an activity that produces taxable income.

COMPLIANCE AND PROCEDURAL CONSIDERATIONS

OBJECTIVE 4

Describe compliance and procedural considerations for exclusions of gross income

Taxpayers are usually not required to disclose excluded income on their tax returns. For example, a taxpayer who receives a tax-exempt scholarship need not disclose that income on his or her tax return. An exception is provided for tax-exempt interest and Social Security benefits, which must be disclosed on the tax return. If a taxpayer's only income is from tax-exempt sources, the taxpayer need not file a tax return. Whether an individual must file a return is based on the amount of the individual's gross income for the year (see Chapter I:2).

ADDITIONAL COMMENT
Taxpayers filing Form 1040 are asked to report any tax-exempt interest income on line 8b.

This chapter considers the taxability of various fringe benefits. The rules regarding the need for an employer to withhold federal income taxes or to report a payment on an employee's Form W-2 (Statement of Income Tax Withheld on Wages) closely parallel the gross income rules. (See Chapter I:14 for a discussion of these reporting requirements.) In general, if a fringe benefit is nontaxable, employers do not withhold from the benefit, nor do they report the benefit on the employee's W-2 at year-end. On the other hand, if the benefit is taxable, it is subject to withholding and is reported on the employee's W-2 at year-end. Thus, employers do not withhold for nontaxable meals and lodging provided to employees[48] or a moving expense reimbursement if the expenses are deductible.[49] Similarly, no withholding is required for the following fringe benefits if they are non-taxable: scholarships and fellowships covered by Sec. 117, dependent care covered by Sec. 129, and miscellaneous fringes covered by Sec. 132.

Problem Materials

DISCUSSION QUESTIONS

I:4-1 What is meant by the terms *administrative exclusion* and *judicial exclusion*?

I:4-2 There is no specific statutory exclusion for welfare benefits. Nevertheless, the IRS has ruled that such benefits are not taxable. Is this within the authority of the IRS?

I:4-3 What was the issue in the tax case *Eisner v. Macomber*? Why is the case important?

I:4-4 Most exclusions exist for one of two reasons. What are those reasons? Give examples of exclusions that exist for each.

I:4-5
a. If a gift of property is made, who is taxed on income produced by the property?
b. How can interfamily gifts reduce a family's total tax liability?

I:4-6
a. What role does intent play in determining whether a transfer is a gift and therefore not subject to the income tax?
b. Are tips received by employees from customers excludable from gross income as gifts? Explain.

I:4-7 What is the tax significance of the face amount of a life insurance policy?

I:4-8 What conditions must be met for an award to qualify for an exclusion under Sec. 74?

I:4-9 Which of the requirements for the Sec. 74 awards exclusion most severely limits its use? Does the exclusion benefit taxpayers more if they itemize their deductions or use the standard deduction?

I:4-10
a. Define the term *scholarship* as it is used in Sec. 117.
b. If a scholarship covers room and board, is it excludable?
c. If an employer provides a scholarship to an employee who is on leave of absence, is that scholarship taxable?
d. Is the amount paid by a university to students for services excludable from the students' gross income?

I:4-11 What special rules are applicable to non-degree candidates who receive scholarships?

I:4-12 Is the personal injury exclusion found in Sec. 104 limited to physical injury? Explain.

I:4-13 Answer the following questions relative to employer-financed medical and health, disability, and life insurance plans.
a. May employers deduct premiums paid on employee insurance?
b. Do employees have to include such premiums in gross income?
c. Are benefits paid to the employee included in the employee's gross income?

I:4-14 Special rules are applicable in situations where group term life insurance coverage exceeds $50,000. How are key employees treated?

I:4-15
a. What are the seven major types of fringe benefits covered by Sec. 132?
b. What tax advantage is offered relative to such benefits?
c. Are such benefits available to employees only or may the benefits also be offered to spouses, dependents, and retirees?
d. Is discrimination prohibited relative to Sec. 132 benefits?
e. What is the tax impact on the employer and employees if an employer's plan is discriminatory?

I:4-16 What conditions must be met if an employee is to exclude meals and lodging furnished by an employer?

I:4-17 The president and vice president of USA Corporation receive benefits that are unavailable to other employees. These benefits include free parking, payment of monthly expenses in a local club, discounts on products sold by the corporation, and payment of premiums on a whole life insurance policy. Which of the benefits must be

[48] Reg. Sec. 31.3401(a)-1(b)(9).

[49] See Sec. 3401 for withholding requirements for numerous special situations.

included in the gross income of the president and vice president?

I:4-18 Are the same fringe benefits that are available to employees also available to self-employed individuals?

I:4-19 If an employee takes a customer to lunch and discusses business, can the employee deduct 50% of the meal for both the customer and himself? Explain.

I:4-20 Are income distributions from a qualified state tuition program taxable?

I:4-21 What types of income qualify for the foreign-earned income exclusion?

I:4-22 Are taxpayers who claim the foreign-earned income exclusion entitled to deduct expenses incurred in producing that income? Explain.

I:4-23 a. Why is it important to distinguish debt cancellation from a gift, bequest, or renegotiation of a purchase price?
b. What happens to the basis of an asset if the taxpayer renegotiates its purchase price?

I:4-24 a. Under what conditions is the discharge of indebtedness not taxable?
b. If a father forgives a daughter's debt to him, is she required to include such amount in her gross income?

I:4-25 Bankrupt and insolvent taxpayers do not recognize income if debt is discharged. They must, however, reduce specified tax attributes. What is involved?

I:4-26 Are partners and proprietors at a disadvantage with respect to fringe benefits? Explain.

I:4-27 Why are cafeteria plans helpful in the design of an employee benefit plan that provides nontaxable fringe benefits?

I:4-28 Both high-income and low-income employees are covered by cafeteria plans. Under such plans, all employees may select from a list of nontaxable fringe benefits or they may elect to receive cash in lieu of these benefits.
a. Which group of employees is more likely to choose nontaxable fringe benefits in lieu of cash? Explain.
b. Is this result desirable from a social or economic point of view? Explain.

ISSUE IDENTIFICATION QUESTIONS

I:4-29 Luke, who retired this year, lives in a four-plex owned by Julie. Luke's income decreased when he retired, and he now has difficulty paying his rent. Julie offered to reduce Luke's rent if he would agree to mow the lawn, wash windows, and provide other maintenance services. Luke accepted, and Julie reduced the monthly rental from $650 to $300. What are the tax issues that should be considered by Luke and Julie?

I:4-30 Mildred worked as a maid for 27 years in the home of Larry and Kay. When she retired, they presented her with a check for $25,000, indicating that it was a way of showing their appreciation for her years of loyal service. What tax issues should Mildred and her employer consider?

I:4-31 Troy Department Stores offers employees discounts on merchandise carried in the store. Newly hired employees receive a 10% discount. The discount rate increases 1% each year until employees have 20 years of service when the discount rate is capped at 30%. What tax issues should Troy and the employees consider?

I:4-32 Jerry works in the human resources department of Ajax Corporation. One of his responsibilities is to interview prospective employees. Two or three days each week, Jerry takes a prospective employee to lunch, and Ajax reimburses him for the cost of the meals. What tax issues should Jerry and Ajax Corporation consider?

PROBLEMS

I:4-33 *Self-Help Income.* In which of the following situations would the taxpayer realize taxable income?
a. A mechanic performs work on his own automobile. The mechanic would have charged a customer $400 for doing the same work.
b. A mechanic repairs his neighbor's personal automobile. In exchange, the neighbor, an accountant, agrees to prepare the mechanic's tax return. The services performed are each worth $200.
c. A mechanic repairs his daughter's automobile without any charge.

I:4-34 *Excludable Gifts.* Which of the following would be includable in gross income?

a. Alice appeared on a TV quiz show and received a prize of $5,000.

b. Bart received $500 from his employer because he developed an idea that reduced the employer's production costs.

c. Chuck borrowed $500 from his mother in order to finance his last year in college. Upon his graduation, Chuck's mother told him he did not have to repay the $500. She intended the $500 to be a graduation present.

I:4-35 *Life Insurance Proceeds.* Don is the beneficiary of a $50,000 insurance policy on the life of his mother, Anna. To date, Anna has paid premiums of $16,000. What amount of gross income must be reported in each of the following cases?

a. Anna elects to cancel the policy and receives $20,000, the cash surrender value of the policy.

b. Anna dies and Don receives the face amount of the policy, $50,000.

c. Anna dies and Don elects to receive $15,000 per year for four years.

I:4-36 *Transfer of Life Insurance.* Ed is the beneficiary of a $20,000 insurance policy on the life of his mother. Because Ed needs funds, he sells the policy to his sister, Amy, for $6,000. Amy subsequently pays premiums of $9,000.

a. How much income must Amy report if she collects the face value of the policy upon the death of her mother?

b. Would Amy have to report any income if her brother had given her the policy? Assume the only payment she made was $9,000 for the premiums.

I:4-37 *Settlement of Life Insurance Policy.* Sue is age 73 and has a great deal of difficulty living independently as she suffers from severe rheumatoid arthritis. She is covered by a $400,000 life insurance policy, and her children are named as her beneficiaries. Because of her health, Sue decides to live in a nursing home, but she does not have enough income to pay her nursing home bills which are expected to total $42,000 per year. The insurance company offers disabled individuals the option of either a reduced settlement on their policies or an annuity. Given Sue's age and health she has the option of receiving $3,200 per month or a lump sum payment of $225,000. To date, Sue has paid $80,000 in premiums on the policy.

a. How much income must Sue report if she chooses the lump sum settlement?

b. How much income must Sue report if she elects the annuity?

c. How much income would Sue have to report if her nursing home bills amounted to only $36,000 per year?

I:4-38 *Insurance Policy Dividends.* Hank carries a $100,000 insurance policy on his life. Premiums paid over the years total $8,000. Dividends on the policy have totaled $6,000. Hank has left the dividends on the policy with the insurance company. During the current year, the insurance company credited $600 of interest on the accumulated dividends to Hank's account.

a. How much income is Hank obligated to report in connection with the policy?

b. Would it make any difference if the accumulated dividends equaled $9,000 instead of $6,000?

I:4-39 *Prizes and Awards.* For each of the following, indicate whether the amount is taxable:

a. Peggy won $4,000 in the state lottery.

b. Jane won a $500 prize for her entry in a poetry contest.

c. Linda was awarded $2,000 when she was selected as "Teacher of the Year" by the local school district.

I:4-40 *Scholarships.* For each of the following, indicate the amount that must be included in the taxpayer's gross income:

a. Larry was given a $1,500 tuition scholarship to attend Eastern Law School. In addition, Eastern paid Larry $4,000 per year to work part-time in the campus bookstore.

b. Marty received a $10,000 football scholarship for attending Northern University. The scholarship covered tuition, room and board, laundry, and books. Four thousand dollars of the scholarship was designated for room and board and laundry. It was understood that Marty would participate in the school's intercollegiate football program, but Marty was not required to do so.

c. Western School of Nursing requires all third-year students to work twenty hours per week at an affiliated hospital. Each student is paid $10 per hour. Nancy, a third-year student, earned $10,000 during the year.

I:4-41 *Research Grant.* Otto is a biology professor at State University. The university gave Otto a sabbatical leave to study the surface of the flatworm. During the year he received a salary of $50,000, which is less than his regular salary of $56,000. Otto also received a grant to cover expenses associated with the study. The grant was $2,000, as were his related expenses. Otto also incurred memberships and other employment related expenses totaling $1,000. How much must Otto include in gross income?

I:4-42 *Payments for Personal Injury.* Determine which of the following payments for sickness and injury must be included in the taxpayer's gross income.

a. Pat was injured in an automobile accident. The other driver's insurance company paid him $2,000 to cover medical expenses and a compensatory amount of $4,000 for pain and suffering.
b. A newspaper article stated that Quincy had been convicted of tax evasion. Quincy, in fact, had never been accused of tax evasion. He sued and won a compensatory settlement of $4,000 from the newspaper.
c. Rob, who pays the cost of a commercial disability income policy, fell and injured his back. He was unable to work for six months. The insurance company paid him $1,800 per month during the time he was unable to work.
d. Steve fell and injured his knee. He was unable to work for four months. His employer-financed disability income policy paid Steve $1,600 per month during the time he was unable to work.
e. Ted suffered a stroke. He was unable to work for five months. His employer continued to pay Ted his salary of $1,700 per month during the time he was unable to work.

I:4-43 *Employee Benefits.* Ursula is employed by USA Corporation. USA Corporation provides medical and health, disability, and group term life insurance coverage for its employees. Premiums attributable to Ursula were as follows:

Medical and health	$3,600
Disability	300
Group term life (face amount is $40,000)	200

During the year, Ursula suffered a heart attack and subsequently died. Before her death, Ursula collected $14,000 as a reimbursement for medical expenses and $5,000 of disability income. Upon her death, Ursula's husband collected the $40,000 face value of the life insurance policy.

a. What amount can USA Corporation deduct for premiums attributable to Ursula?
b. How much must Ursula include in income relative to the premiums paid?
c. How much must Ursula include in income relative to the insurance benefits?
d. How much must Ursula's widower include in income?

I:4-44 *Group Term Life Insurance.* Data Corporation has four employees and provides group term life insurance coverage for all four employees. Coverage is nondiscriminatory and is as follows:

Employee	*Age*	*Key Employee*	*Coverage*	*Actual Premiums*
Andy	62	yes	$200,000	$4,000
Bob	52	yes	40,000	700
Cindy	33	no	80,000	600
Damitria	33	no	40,000	300

a. How much may Data Corporation deduct for group term life insurance premiums?
b. How much income must be reported by each employee?

I:4-45 *Life Insurance Proceeds.* Joe is the beneficiary of a life insurance policy taken out by his father several years ago. Joe's father dies, and Joe has the option of receiving the $100,000 face value of the policy in cash or receiving annual payments of $1,000 per month for the rest of his life. Joe is now 65. Joe's father paid $32,000 in premiums over the years.

a. How much must Joe include in gross income this year if he accepts the $100,000 face amount?
b. Assume Joe elects to receive the annual payments. What is his life expectancy?
c. What is his annual exclusion?
d. How much must he report as income each year?

I:4-46 *Employee Benefits.* Al flies for AAA Airlines. AAA provides its employees with several fringe benefits. Al and his family are allowed to fly on a space-available basis on AAA Airline. Tickets used by Al and his family during the year are worth $2,000. AAA paid for a subscription to two magazines published for pilots. The subscriptions totaled $80. The airline paid for Al's meals and lodging while he was away from home overnight in connection with his job. Such meals and lodging cost AAA $10,000. Although Al could not eat while flying, he was allowed to drink coffee provided by the airline. The coffee was worth about $50. AAA provided Al with free parking, which is valued at $100 per month. The airline treated Al and his family to a one-week all-expenses-paid vacation at a resort near his home. This benefit was awarded because of Al's outstanding safety record. The value of the vacation was $2,300. Which of these benefits are taxable to Al?

I:4-47 *Employee Benefits.* Jet Corporation is involved in the purchase and rental of several large apartment complexes. Questions have been raised about the treatment of several items pertaining to Jet Corporation and its employees. Jet Corporation employs a manager for each complex. The manager is required to occupy a unit in the complex in order to be available at all hours. The average rental value of the units is $12,000 per year. The corporation's president finds that it is beneficial to the corporation if he entertains bankers and others with whom Jet does business. He does such entertaining about once each month and the corporation pays the cost. Business is discussed at the meals. The cost for the year of such entertaining was $1,500, and about one-third of the cost was attributable to meals consumed by the president.

Each year as the company closes its books, the controller and certain other members of the accounting staff must work overtime. The company pays each employee supper money totaling $25 during this period.

The corporation's vice president is expected to travel on business-related matters to visit various properties owned by the corporation. Because of the distances involved, the vice president must stay away from home several nights. Total meals and lodging incurred on the trips total $3,000, most of which is attributable to the vice president himself.

Which amounts are deductible by the corporation? Which are taxable to the employee?

I:4-48 *Death Benefits.* After a brief illness, Bill died. Bill's employer paid $20,000 to his widow. The corporation sent along a letter with the check indicating that $5,000 represented payment for Bill's accrued vacation days and back wages. The balance was being awarded in recognition of Bill's many years of loyal service. The company was obligated to pay the accrued vacation days and back wages, but the balance was discretionary.

a. Is the employer entitled to deduct the $20,000 paid to Bill's widow?
b. Is Bill's widow required to include the $20,000 in her gross income?

I:4-49 *Foreign-Earned Income Exclusion.* For each of the following cases, indicate the amount of the foreign-earned income exclusion. (Disregard the effect of exemptions for certain allowances under Sec. 912.)

a. Sam, a U.S. citizen, is an assistant to the ambassador to Spain. Sam lives and works in Spain. His salary of $90,000 is paid by the U.S. government.
b. Jim, a U.S. citizen, owns an unincorporated oil drilling company that operates in Argentina, where he resides. The business is heavily dependent on equipment owned by Jim. His profit for the year totaled $100,000.
c. Ken, a U.S. citizen, works for a large Japanese corporation. Ken is employed in the United States, but must travel to Japan several times each year. During the current year he spent sixty days in Japan. This is typical of most years. His salary is $95,000.

I:4-50 *Foreign-Earned Income Exclusion.* On January 5, 2015 Rita left the United States for Germany, where she had accepted an appointment as vice president of foreign operations. Her employer, USA Corporation, told her the assignment would last about two years. Rita decided not to establish a permanent residence in Germany because her assignment was for only two years. Her salary for the year is $301,800. Rita incurred travel, transportation, and other related expenses totaling $6,000, none of which are reimbursed.

a. What is Rita's foreign-earned income exclusion?
b. How much may she deduct for travel and transportation?

I:4-51 *Discharge of Debt.* During bankruptcy, USA Corporation debt was reduced from $780,000 to $400,000. USA Corporation's assets are valued at $500,000. USA's NOL carryover was $400,000.

a. Is USA Corporation required to report any income from the discharge of its debts?
b. Which tax attributes are reduced and by how much? Assume USA does not make any special elections when reducing its attributes.

I:4-52 *Discharge of Debt.* Old Corporation has suffered losses for several years, and its debts total $500,000; Old's assets are valued at only $380,000. Old's creditors agree to reduce

Old's debts by one-half in order to permit the corporation to continue to operate. Old's NOL carryover is $150,000.

a. What impact does the reduction in debt have on Old's NOL?
b. Is Old required to report any income?

I:4-53 *Court and Insurance Awards.* Determine whether the following items represent taxable income.

a. As the result of an age discrimination suit, Pat received a cash settlement of $40,000. One-half of the settlement represented wages lost by Pat as a result of the discrimination and the balance represented an award based on personal injury.
b. Matt sued the local newspaper for a story that reported he was affiliated with organized crime. The court awarded him $50,000 of libel damages.
c. Pam was injured in an automobile accident and received $10,000 from an employer-sponsored disability policy. In addition, her employer-financed medical insurance policy reimbursed her for $15,000 of medical expenses.

I:4-54 *Cafeteria Plan.* Jangyoun is a married taxpayer with a dependent 4-year-old daughter. His employer offers a cafeteria plan under which he can choose to receive cash or, alternatively, choose from certain fringe benefits. These benefits include health insurance that costs $9,000 and child care that costs $2,600. Assume Jangyoun is in the 28% tax bracket.

a. How much income tax will Jangyoun save if he chooses to participate in the employer's health insurance plan? Assume that he does not have sufficient medical expenses to itemize his deductions.
b. Would you recommend that Jangyoun participate in the employer's health insurance plan if his wife's employer already provides comparable health insurance coverage for the family?
c. Would you recommend that Jangyoun participate in the employer-provided child care option if he has the alternative option of claiming a child care credit of $480?

I:4-55 *Exclusion of Gain from Small Business Stock.* In 1996, Jose acquired 100% of Acorn Corporation common stock by transferring property with an adjusted basis of $1,000,000 and fair market value of $4,000,000. Acorn is a qualified small business corporation. On April 1, 2015, Jose sells all of the Acorn Corporation common stock for $16,000,000.

a. What is the amount of gain that may be excluded from Jose's gross income?
b. What would your answer be if the fair market value of the Acorn stock were only $800,000 upon its issue?
c. What would your answer be if the stock were sold after two years?
d. Can Jose avoid recognizing gain by purchasing replacement stock?

COMPREHENSIVE PROBLEM

I:4-56 Pat was divorced from her husband in 2010. During the current year she received alimony of $18,000 and child support of $4,000 for her 11-year-old son, who lives with her. Her former husband had asked her to sign an agreement giving him the dependency exemption for the child but she declined to do so. After the divorce she accepted a position as a teacher in the local school district. During the current year she received a salary of $32,000. The school district paid her medical insurance premiums of $6,900 and provided her with group term life insurance coverage of $40,000. The premiums attributable to her coverage equaled $160. During her marriage, Pat's parents loaned her $8,000 to help with the down payment on her home. Her parents told her this year that they understand her financial problems and that they were cancelling the balance on the loan, which was $5,000. They did so because they wanted to help their only daughter.

Pat received dividends from National Motor Company of $4,600 and interest on State of California bonds of $2,850.

Pat had itemized deductions of $9,100. Compute her taxable income for 2015.

TAX STRATEGY PROBLEMS

I:4-57 Sally owns a small C corporation that has provided health insurance coverage for Sally and the company's three other employees. The insurance coverage for Sally and the three employees is individual coverage, not family coverage. Sally's own family coverage is through a separate private policy. She pays the premiums out of after-tax dollars. Sally's salary is $40,000 and the salary for the other three employees averages $30,000. The premiums on the health insurance policy average $2,000 per employee per year. The provider recently informed Sally that the premiums will increase to $2,500 per employee. The spouses of her two married employees have coverage through their employers. The third employee has announced that he will marry soon and would very much like to have family health insurance coverage. The insurance provider says that family coverage will approximately double the premiums. Sally is finding the cost of providing medical insurance coverage particularly burdensome for her small business. What planning suggestions can you offer?

I:4-58 Maria was planning to paint the interior of her apartment over a three-day weekend. Her employer asked her to work all three days and will pay her $600 overtime. She called a professional painter who offered to do the job for $500. He is willing to use the paint she has already purchased. Maria is in the 28% tax bracket. Will she be better off financially to work the overtime and pay the painter or to turn down the overtime and do the work herself? What other factors should she consider?

TAX FORM/RETURN PREPARATION PROBLEMS

I:4-59 A. J. Paige, Social Security number 111-22-3333, is the vice president of marketing (Australia) for International Industries, Inc. (III). III is headquartered at 123 Main Street, Los Angeles, California 92601. A. J., who is single, accepted the position and became a resident of Australia on July 8 of last year. Her business address is 242 Main, Westview, Australia. Westview is not designated as a high housing cost city. A. J.'s visa permits her to stay in Australia indefinitely. Her only trips to the United States in the current year were for vacations (August 2 to 16 and December 21 to 28). A. J.'s contract specifies that her appointment is to last indefinitely, but states that III is to pay her $4,000 per year to cover the cost of two vacation trips to the United States. Her salary is $140,000, out of which she pays rent on an apartment of $30,000 per year. A. J. has no family or residence in the United States. She paid an income tax in Australia of $23,500. Complete a Form 2555 for 2014.

I:4-60 Alice Johnson, Social Security number 222-23-3334, is a single taxpayer and is employed as a secretary by State University of Florida. She has the following items pertaining to her income tax return for the current year:

- Received a $20,000 salary from her employer, who withheld $3,000 federal income tax.
- Received a gift of 1,000 shares of Ace Corporation stock with a $100,000 FMV from her mother. She also received $4,000 of cash dividends from the Ace Corporation. The dividends are qualified dividends.
- Received $1,000 of interest income on bonds issued by the City of Tampa.
- Received a regular stock dividend (nontaxable under Sec. 305) of 50 shares of Ace Corporation stock with a $5,000 FMV.
- Alice's employer paid $2,000 of medical and health insurance premiums on her behalf.
- Received $12,000 alimony from her ex-husband.
- State University provided $60,000 of group term life insurance. Alice is 42 years old and is not a key employee. The table in the text is applicable.
- Received a $1,000 cash award from her employer for being designated the Secretary of the Year.
- Total itemized deductions are $8,000.

Complete Form 1040 and accompanying schedules for Alice Johnson's 2014 return.

CASE STUDY PROBLEMS

I:4-61 Able Corporation is a closely held company engaged in the manufacture and retail sales of automotive parts. Able maintains a qualified pension plan for its employees but has not offered nontaxable fringe benefits.

You are a tax consultant for the company who has been asked to prepare suggestions for the adoption of an employee fringe benefit plan. Your discussions with the client's chief financial officer reveal the following:

- Employees currently pay their own premiums for medical and health insurance.
- No group term life insurance is provided.

- The company owns a vacant building that could easily be converted to a parking garage.
- Many of the employees purchase automobile parts from the company's retail outlets and pay retail price.
- The president of the corporation would like to provide a dependent care assistance program under Sec. 129 for its employees.

Required: Prepare a client memo that recommends the adoption of an employee fringe benefit program. Your recommendations should discuss the pros and cons of different types of nontaxable fringe benefits.

I:4-62 Jay Corporation owns several automobile dealerships. This year, the corporation initiated a policy of giving the top salesperson at each dealership a free vacation trip to Florida. The president believes that this is an effective sales incentive. The cost of the vacations is deductible by the corporation as compensation paid to employees, and is taxable to the recipients. Nevertheless, the president objects to reporting the value of the vacations as income on the W-2s of the recipients and to withholding taxes from wages for the value of the trips. He feels that this undermines the effectiveness of the incentive. What are the implications of this behavior for the corporation and the president?

TAX RESEARCH PROBLEMS

I:4-63 Ann is a graduate economics student at State University. State University awarded her a $1,000 scholarship. In addition, Ann works as a half-time teaching assistant in the Economics Department at State University. She is paid $7,000 per year and her tuition is waived. The salary is equal to that paid other part-time instructors. Her tuition would be $8,000 were it not for the waiver. Ann paid $500 for her books and supplies and she incurred living expenses of $7,400. Determine how much gross income Ann must report.

A partial list of research sources is

- Sec. 117(d)
- Prop. Reg. 1.117-6(d)(5)

I:4-64 Kim leased an office building to USA Corporation under a ten-year lease specifying that at the end of the lease USA had to return the building to its original condition if any modifications were made. USA changed the interior of the building, and at the end of the lease USA paid Kim $30,000 instead of making the required repairs. Does Kim have to include the payment in gross income?

A partial list of research sources is

- Sec. 109
- *Boston Fish Market Corp.*, 57 T.C. 884 (1972)
- *Sirbo Holdings Inc. v. CIR*, 31 AFTR 2d 73-1005, 73-1 USTC ¶9312 (2nd Cir., 1973)

I:4-65 As a result of a fire damaging their residence, the Taylors must stay in a motel for three weeks while their home is being restored. They pay $2,000 for the room and $500 for meals. Their homeowner's policy pays $2,500 to reimburse them for the cost. They estimate that during the five-week period they would normally spend $300 for meals. Is the reimbursement taxable?

A partial list of research sources is

- Sec. 123
- Reg. Sec. 1.123-1

I:4-66 Bold Corporation paid $25 to each full-time employee at year-end in recognition of the holidays. Bold Corporation is interested in whether the amounts are taxable income to its employees, and whether the company can deduct the amounts.

A partial list of research sources is

- Secs. 74(c), 102, 132(c), and 274(b)
- Reg. Sec. 1.132-6(e)(1)
- *Hallmark Cards, Inc. v. U.S.*, 9 AFTR 2d 391, 62-1 USTC ¶9162 (DC-Mo, 1961).
- Rev. Rul. 59-58, 1959-1 CB 17.

CHAPTER

5

PROPERTY TRANSACTIONS: CAPITAL GAINS AND LOSSES

LEARNING OBJECTIVES

After studying this chapter, you should be able to

1. Determine the realized gain or loss from the sale or other disposition of property
2. Determine the basis of property
3. Distinguish between capital assets and other assets
4. Understand how capital gains are taxed for noncorporate taxpayers
5. Understand how capital gains are taxed for corporate taxpayers
6. Recognize when a sale or exchange has occurred
7. Determine the holding period for an asset when a sale or disposition occurs
8. Describe tax planning opportunities for property transactions
9. Describe compliance and procedural considerations for property transactions

CHAPTER OUTLINE

Gross income includes "gains derived from dealings in property,"[1] and certain "losses from sale or exchange of property"[2] are allowed as deductions from gross income to determine adjusted gross income. All recognized gains and losses must eventually be classified either as *capital* or *ordinary.* Except for a brief time in the mid-to-late 1980s, long-term capital gains (LTCGs) of individual taxpayers have consistently been taxed at lower rates than ordinary gains or short-term capital gains (STCGs).[3] This preferential treatment of capital gains, more precisely LTCGs, has been a much debated topic for many years. A discussion of the reasoning for imposing lower tax rates on LTCGs is provided near the end of this chapter.

The preferential treatment of capital gains has fluctuated widely over the years. For example, in the early 1980s, taxpayers were allowed to deduct 60% of the gain. In 1991, net capital gains were taxed at a maximum rate of 28%, then reduced to 20% for most taxpayers in 1997. Congress started applying different rates to different types of LTCG in 2001, i.e., a LTCG due to the sale of a collectible has a maximum rate of 28% while a LTCG due to the sale of stock has a maximum rate of 15% or 20%. Thus, depending on the political persuasion of the government, tax rates on net capital gains have yo-yoed up and down. A significant change in the rates for adjusted net capital gains occurred in 2003 when the rates were reduced from 20% to 15% for most taxpayers (5% for lower income taxpayers). For tax years beginning after 2007, the rate is zero instead of 5%.[4] With the maximum ordinary tax rate for individuals being 39.6% today, individuals can benefit by having a gain classified as a LTCG rather than as ordinary gain or STCG. Thus, much planning is performed to attempt to arrange one's affairs to take advantage of the lower capital gain rates.

HISTORICAL NOTE

A preferential tax rate on capital gains was included in the tax law from 1921 until 1987. A modest preferential rate was reintroduced in 1991, with capital gains for noncorporate taxpayers being subject to a maximum 28% tax rate and ordinary income being subject to a maximum tax rate of 31%. The rates were reduced in 1997 and reduced again in 2003.

As explained later, a LTCG may be subject to one of five different rates [0%, 15%, 20%, 25%, or 28%] depending on what type of asset is sold and the taxpayer's regular tax rate.

Capital losses must be offset against capital gains, and net capital losses are subjected to restrictions on their deductibility. Thus, most taxpayers prefer to have losses classified as ordinary instead of capital.

ADDITIONAL COMMENT

For a discussion of the justification of preferential tax rates for LTCGs (see page I:5-30).

Most property transactions have tax consequences to the taxpayer. For example, when a sale, exchange, or abandonment occurs, the taxpayer must determine the realized gain or loss, the portion of the realized gain or loss that must be recognized (if any), and the character of the gain or loss. This chapter focuses on determining the realized gain or loss and the portion of the recognized gain or loss classified as capital or ordinary. When classifying a recognized gain or loss, (i.e., the gain or loss actually reported on the taxpayer's tax return) three important questions must be considered:

ADDITIONAL COMMENT

During 2010, many taxpayers sold capital assets to recognize LTCG taxed at 15% because the rates were expected to increase to 20% or even higher.

- What type of property has been sold or exchanged?
- When has a sale or exchange occurred?
- What is the holding period for the property?

In this chapter, these three questions are considered as well as difficulties associated with determining the basis of the property sold or exchanged and the amount of realized gains or losses.

[1] Sec. 61(a)(3).

[2] Sec. 62(a)(3).

[3] See page I:5-29 and below for a discussion of the holding period for capital assets. A capital gain or loss is long-term or short-term depending on the length of time the asset has been held by the taxpayer.

[4] Sec. 1(h)(1)(B).

Determination of Gain or Loss

OBJECTIVE 1

Determine the realized gain or loss from the sale or other disposition of property

REALIZED GAIN OR LOSS

To determine the **realized gain** or **loss**, the amount realized from the sale or exchange of property is compared with the adjusted basis of that property. A gain is realized when the amount realized is greater than the basis, and a loss is realized when the amount realized is less than the basis of the property.[5]

EXAMPLE I:5-1 ► Jack sells an asset with an adjusted basis of $10,000 to Judy for $14,000. Because the amount realized is greater than the basis, Jack has a realized gain of $4,000 ($14,000 − $10,000). ◄

Despite the fact that most transfers of property involve a sale, gains and losses may also be realized on certain other types of dispositions of property, such as exchanges, condemnations, casualties, thefts, bond retirements, and corporate distributions. However, gains and losses are generally not realized when property is disposed of by gift or bequest.

EXAMPLE I:5-2 ► Alice owns land held for investment with a basis of $20,000. The land is taken by the city by right of eminent domain, and she receives a payment of $30,000 for the land. This condemnation is treated as a sale or disposition for income tax purposes, and Alice's realized gain is $10,000 ($30,000 − $20,000). ◄

EXAMPLE I:5-3 ► Two years ago, Bob purchased stock of a newly formed corporation for $10,000. During the current year, he receives a $12,000 distribution, constituting a return of capital, from the corporation. This distribution is treated as a sale. Therefore, Bob has a realized gain of $2,000 ($12,000 − $10,000). Bob's basis for the stock is now zero because his basis of $10,000 has been recovered. ◄

There must be an identifiable event for a sale or other disposition to occur. Mere changes in the value of property are not normally recognized as a disposition for purposes of determining a realized gain or loss.

STUDY AID

Students should pay close attention to the technical terms used in tax law. For example, the similar sounding terms of "realized gain" and "recognized gain" are often different dollar amounts for the sale of an asset.

Many reasons exist for not taxing unrealized gains and losses that arise due to a mere change in value. The Treasury Regulations state that "A loss is not ordinarily sustained prior to the sale or other disposition of the property, for the reason that until such sale or other disposition occurs there remains the possibility that the taxpayer may recover or recoup the adjusted basis of the property."[6] Because of administrative difficulties associated with determining fair market value (FMV), disputes with the Internal Revenue Service (IRS) would be greatly increased if unrealized gains were taxed and unrealized losses were allowed as deductions. In addition, payment of tax on income is generally required only when a taxpayer has the wherewithal to pay the tax (e.g., the taxpayer has received cash from the sale or other disposition of property and can therefore pay the tax on the gain).

Amount Realized. The **amount realized** from a sale or other disposition of property is the sum of any money received, the FMV of all other property received, and any debt assumed by the buyer.

EXAMPLE I:5-4 ► Tony sells land to Rita for $15,000 in cash and a machine having a $3,000 FMV. Tony's amount realized is $18,000 ($15,000 + $3,000). ◄

---

[5] Sec. 1001(a).

[6] Reg. Sec. 1.1001-1(c)(1).

The determination of FMV is a question of fact and often creates considerable controversy between taxpayers and the IRS. **Fair market value (FMV)** is "the price at which property would change hands between a willing buyer and a willing seller, neither being under any compulsion to buy or sell."[7] The FMV of the asset given in the exchange may be easier to determine than the FMV of the property received. In those cases, the FMV of the property given may be used to measure the amount realized. If a buyer assumes the seller's liability or takes the property subject to the debt, the courts have included the amount of the liability when determining the amount realized.[8]

EXAMPLE I:5-5 ▶ Anna exchanges land subject to a liability of $20,000 for $35,000 of stock owned by Mario. Mario takes the property subject to the liability. The amount realized by Anna is $55,000 ($35,000 + $20,000 liability assumed by Mario). If Anna's adjusted basis for the land exchanged is $42,000, her realized gain is $13,000 ($55,000 − $42,000). ◀

In the above example, Anna receives stock with a $35,000 FMV and is relieved of a $20,000 debt. Mario's taking the property subject to the debt is equivalent to providing Anna with cash of $20,000. Thus, the amount realized by Anna is $55,000.

Generally, selling expenses such as sales commissions and advertising incurred in order to sell or dispose of the property reduce the amount realized.

EXAMPLE I:5-6 ▶ Doug sells stock of Briggs Corporation, with a basis of $10,000, for $17,000. Doug pays a sales commission of $300. The amount realized by Doug is $16,700 ($17,000 − $300), and his realized gain is $6,700 ($16,700 − $10,000). ◀

TYPICAL MISCONCEPTION

The difference between the assumption of a liability and the taking of the property subject to the debt is sometimes confusing. The latter means that the lender can satisfy the debt only by repossessing the property. In the former case, where the buyer assumes the debt, the lender can satisfy the debt by repossessing the property and by going after other assets of the buyer.

Adjusted Basis. The initial basis of property depends on how the property is acquired (e.g., by purchase, gift, or inheritance). Most property is acquired by purchase and therefore its initial basis is the cost of the property. However, if property is acquired from a decedent, its basis to the estate or heir is its FMV either at the date of death or, if the alternate valuation date is elected, six months from the date of death. The rules for determining the adjusted basis are discussed in subsequent sections of this chapter. Once the initial basis is determined, it may be adjusted upward or downward. Capital additions (also called capital expenditures) are expenditures that add to the value or prolong the life of property or adapt the property to a new or different use. Capital additions increase the basis. Capital recoveries, such as the deductions for casualty losses, cost recovery, and depreciation, reduce the basis. A property's adjusted basis can be determined by the following equation:

Initial basis
\+ Capital additions (e.g., new porch for a building)
− Capital recoveries (e.g., depreciation deduction)
= Adjusted basis

ETHICAL POINT

The taxpayer may have lost records relating to the basis of the assets acquired many years earlier. In that case, the CPA can accept estimates of the missing data made by the taxpayer.

Capital expenditures are distinguished from expenditures that are deductible as ordinary and necessary business expenses. For example, the cost of repairing a roof may be a deductible expense, whereas the cost of replacing a roof is a capital addition. It is sometimes difficult to determine whether an item is a capital expenditure or a business expense. Because of the preference for an immediate tax deduction, taxpayers normally prefer to classify expenditures as expenses rather than capital expenditures.

EXAMPLE I:5-7 ▶ Ellen pays $2,500 for a major overhaul of an automobile used in her trade or business. The $2,500 is capitalized as part of the automobile's cost rather than deducted as a repair expense. ◀

Capital recoveries reduce the adjusted basis. The most common form of capital recovery is the deduction for depreciation or cost recovery. As discussed in Chapter I:10, the modi-

[7] *CIR v. Homer H. Marshman*, 5 AFTR 2d 1528, 60-2 USTC ¶9484 (6th Cir., 1960).

[8] *Beulah B. Crane v. CIR*, 35 AFTR 776, 47-1 USTC ¶9217 (USSC, 1947).

fied accelerated cost recovery system (MACRS) is mandatory for most tangible depreciable property placed in service after 1986. The accelerated cost recovery system (ACRS) applies to most property placed in service after December 31, 1980, and before 1987.

EXAMPLE I:5-8 ▶ Jeremy paid $100,000 for equipment two years ago and has claimed depreciation deductions of $37,000 for the two years. The cost of repairs during the same period was $6,000. At the end of the two-year period, the property's adjusted basis is $63,000 ($100,000 − $37,000). The amount spent for repairs does not affect the basis. ◀

ADDITIONAL COMMENT

In addition to depreciation, other capital recoveries that reduce the adjusted basis of property include depletion, amortization, corporate distributions that are a return of basis, compensation or awards for involuntary conversions, deductible casualty losses, insurance reimbursements, and cash rebates received by a purchaser.

Recovery of Basis Doctrine. The **recovery of basis doctrine** states that taxpayers are allowed to recover the basis of an asset without being taxed because such amounts are a return of capital that the taxpayer has invested in the property. If a taxpayer receives a $12,000 return of capital distribution from a corporation when the taxpayer's basis for its investment in the corporation's stock is $10,000, the first $10,000 received represents a recovery of basis and the $2,000 excess amount is treated as a gain realized on a sale or exchange of the stock investment. In many cases, basis is recovered in the form of a deduction for depreciation, cost recovery, or a casualty loss.

TYPICAL MISCONCEPTION

It is sometimes incorrectly believed that all realized gains and losses are recognized for tax purposes. Although most realized gains are recognized, some realized losses are not. For example, losses on the sale or exchange of property held for personal use are not recognized.

RECOGNIZED GAIN OR LOSS

Realized gain or loss represents the difference between the amount realized and the adjusted basis when a sale or exchange occurs. The amount of gain or loss actually reported on the tax return is the **recognized gain or loss**. In some instances, gain or loss is not recognized due to special provisions in the tax law (e.g., a gain or loss may be deferred or a loss may be disallowed).

Losses are generally deductible if they are incurred in carrying on a trade or business, incurred in an activity engaged in for profit, and casualty and theft losses. Realized losses on the sale or exchange of assets held for personal use are not recognized for tax purposes. Therefore, a taxpayer who incurs a loss on the sale or exchange of a personal-use asset does not fully recover the basis. As explained in Chapter I:8, realized losses on personal-use assets may be recognized to some extent if the property is disposed of by casualty or theft.

EXAMPLE I:5-9 ▶ Ralph purchases a personal residence for $60,000. Deductions for depreciation are not allowed because the asset is not used in a trade or business or held for the production of income. If Ralph sells the house for $55,000, the realized loss of $5,000 is a capital loss but not deductible. He recovers only $55,000 of his original $60,000 basis. ◀

BASIS CONSIDERATIONS

OBJECTIVE 2

Determine the basis of property

COST OF ACQUIRED PROPERTY

In most cases, the basis of property is its cost. **Cost** is the amount paid for the property in cash or the FMV of other property given in the exchange. Any costs of acquiring the property and preparing the property for use are included in the cost of the property.

EXAMPLE I:5-10 ▶ Penny purchases equipment for $15,000, pays delivery costs of $300, and installation costs of $250. The cost of the equipment is $15,550. ◀

Funds borrowed and used to pay for an asset are included in the cost. Obligations of the seller that are assumed by the buyer increase the asset's cost.

EXAMPLE I:5-11 ▶ Peggy purchases an asset by paying cash of $40,000 and signs a note payable to the seller for $60,000. She also assumes a $2,000 lien against the property. Her basis for the asset is $102,000 and the amount realized by the seller is $102,000. ◀

Uniform Capitalization Rules. For financial accounting purposes, businesses must capitalize certain costs in connection with inventory, such as direct materials, direct labor, and overhead. For many years, businesses had a degree of flexibility with respect to capitalizing or expensing certain costs for tax purposes. However, the tax law now mandates one set of capitalization rules applicable to all taxpayers and all types of activities. These uniform capitalization rules, which apply principally to inventory, are provided in Sec. 263A and discussed in Chapter I:11.

The uniform capitalization rules also affect property other than inventory if the property is used in a taxpayer's trade or business or in an activity engaged in for profit. Taxes paid or accrued in connection with the acquisition of property are included as part of the cost of the acquired property. Taxes paid or accrued in connection with the disposition of property reduce the amount realized on the disposition.[9]

ADDITIONAL COMMENT

The sales tax is a good example of a tax that would be paid in connection with the acquisition of property.

EXAMPLE I:5-12 ▶ The Compact Corporation owns and operates a funeral home. The corporation purchases a hearse for $30,000 and pays sales taxes of $1,500. The cost basis for the hearse is $31,500. ◀

Capitalization of Interest. Interest on debt paid or incurred during the production period to finance production expenditures incurred to construct, build, install, manufacture, develop, or improve real or tangible personal property must be capitalized.[10] The real or tangible personal property must have "a long useful life, an estimated production period exceeding two years, or an estimated production period exceeding one year and a cost exceeding $1,000,000."[11] Property has a long useful life if it is real property or property with a class life of at least 20 years. The production period starts when "production of the property begins and ends when the property is ready to be placed in service or is ready to be held for sale."[12]

EXAMPLE I:5-13 ▶ The Indiana Corporation started construction of a $3 million motel on July 1, 2014, and borrowed an amount equal to the motel's construction costs. The motel is completed and ready for service on October 1, 2015. Interest incurred for the construction loan for the period from July 1, 2014, through October 1, 2015, is included in the motel's cost. The capitalized interest cost is depreciated over the motel's thirty-nine year recovery period (see Chapter I:10). ◀

ADDITIONAL COMMENT

If a stockholder leaves his or her stock with a broker in street name, the stockholder can specifically identify the shares sold by simply informing the broker which shares he or she wishes to sell. The date basis of the shares sold should appear on the confirmation from the broker.

Identification Problems. In most cases, the adjusted basis of property sold is easily identified. However, problems arise when property is homogenous in nature such as when an investor owns several blocks of common stock of the same corporation purchased on different dates at different prices. The Regulations require the taxpayer to adequately identify the particular stock sold or exchanged.[13] Many investors allow brokers to hold their stock in street name (i.e., the brokerage firm holds title to the stock certificates) and thus do not make a physical transfer of securities. Such investors need to provide specific instructions to the broker as to which securities should be sold. If the stock sold or exchanged is not adequately identified, the first-in, first-out (FIFO) method must be used to identify the stock. With the FIFO method, the stock sold or exchanged is presumed to come from the first lot or lots acquired.

EXAMPLE I:5-14 ▶ Judy purchased 300 shares of the Gustavel Corporation stock last year:

Month Acquired	*Size of Block*	*Basis*
January	100 shares	$4,000
May	100	5,000
October	100	6,000

In March of the current year, Judy sells 120 shares of the stock for $5,160. If Judy specifically identifies the stock sold as being all of the stock purchased in October and 20 shares purchased in May, her realized loss is $1,840 [$5,160 − ($6,000 + $1,000)]. ◀

[9] Sec. 164(a).
[10] Sec. 263A(f).
[11] Sec. 263A(f)(1)(B).
[12] Sec. 263A(f)(4)(B).
[13] Reg. Sec. 1.1012-1(c)(1).

If Judy does not specifically identify the stock sold, the FIFO method is used, and her realized gain is $160 [$5,160 − ($4,000 + $1,000)].

Owners of shares of mutual funds have more choices when determining the basis of shares sold. In addition to FIFO and specific identification, they may use an average cost method.[14]

EXAMPLE I:5-15 ▶ Colin purchased 100 shares of Bluejay Mutual Fund on May 10, 2013, for $1,000, and has been reinvesting dividends. On December 20, 2015, he sells 115 shares.

ADDITIONAL COMMENT

Because of the difficulty and complexity of tracking basis of shares in a mutual fund, the average cost method is widely used by taxpayers.

	Amount	*No. of Shares*
Purchase May 10, 2013	$1,000	100
Reinvested Dividend Nov. 1, 2013	125	10
Reinvested Dividends Nov. 1, 2014	140	7
Reinvested Dividends Nov. 1, 2015	185	8
	1,450	125
		$11.60 Average Cost

His basis for the 115 shares sold is $1,225 with FIFO, $1,334 (115 × $11.60) with average cost and could be as high as $1,350 with specific identification. Note that if he sells the shares obtained with the reinvested dividends in 2015, part of the gain or loss is short-term. ◀

PROPERTY RECEIVED AS A GIFT: GIFTS AFTER 1921

The basis of property received as a gift is generally the same as the donor's basis.[15] If the FMV of the property at time of the gift is less than the donor's basis, the donee may have to use one basis if the property is subsequently disposed of at a gain and another if the property is disposed of at a loss. As discussed later in this chapter, the basis may be increased by a portion or all of the gift tax paid because of the transfer.

Current rules for determining the donee's basis for property received as a gift are a function of the relationship between the FMV of the property at the time the gift is made and the donor's basis. If the FMV is equal to or greater than the donor's basis, the donee's basis is the same as the donor's basis for all purposes. However, if the FMV is less than the donor's basis, the donee has a dual basis for the property, that is, a basis for loss and a basis for gain. If the donee later transfers the property at a loss, the donee's basis is the property's FMV at the time of the gift (basis for loss). However, if the donee transfers the property at a gain, the donee's basis is the same as the donor's basis (basis for gain).

ADDITIONAL COMMENT

Upon receipt of property from a relative, one should inquire as to its basis at that time. It might be years later that the asset is sold and the information about the donor's basis may be lost or forgotten.

EXAMPLE I:5-16 ▶ Kevin makes a gift of property with a basis of $350 to Janet when it has a $425 FMV. If Janet sells the property for $450, she has a realized gain of $100 ($450 − $350). If Janet sells the property for $330, she has a realized loss of $20 ($330 − $350). Because the FMV of the property at the time of the gift is more than the donor's basis, the donee's basis is $350 for determining both gain and loss. ◀

The following example illustrates the scenario when a taxpayer has a dual basis. The property is received as a gift when the FMV is less than the donor's basis, so the basis for determining a gain is different from the basis for determining a loss.

EXAMPLE I:5-17 ▶ Chuck makes a gift of property with a basis of $600 to Maggie when the property has a $500 FMV. Maggie's basis for the property is $600 if the property is sold at a gain (i.e., for more than $600), but the basis is $500 if the property is sold at a loss (i.e., for less than $500). If the property is sold for $500 or more but not more than $600, no gain or loss is recognized. ◀

The dual basis rules were designed to prevent tax-avoidance schemes. Taxpayers are prevented from shifting unrealized losses to another taxpayer by making gifts of such "loss" property. For example, a low-income taxpayer who owns property that has depreciated in value might transfer the property by gift to a high-income taxpayer who would receive greater tax benefit from the deduction of the loss upon the subsequent sale of the

[14] For mutual fund investors, the IRS has authorized the use of FIFO, specific identification, or two average cost basis methods if only a portion of the fund shares is redeemed or sold. (See Reg. Sec. 1.1012-1(e) and Chapter I:17.)

[15] Sec. 1015(a).

ADDITIONAL COMMENT

If Maggie in Example I:5-17 sells the land for $750, she has a $150 gain. If she sells the land for $400, she has a $100 loss, and there is no gain or loss if she sells the land for $560.

TAX STRATEGY TIP

Donors generally should not make gifts of property that have declined in value below original cost. Since the donee's basis will be the property's FMV, the loss will never be recognized.

KEY POINT

No gift tax can be added to the basis of the property if the donor's basis is greater than the FMV of the property.

property. The loss basis rules prevent the donee from recognizing a loss on the sale of the property because the basis for loss is the lesser of the donor's basis or FMV on the date of the gift.

Effect of Gift Tax on Basis. If the donor pays a gift tax on the transfer of property, the donee's basis may be increased. This increase occurs only if the FMV of the property exceeds the donor's basis on the date of the gift. For taxable gifts after 1976, the increase in the donee's basis is equal to a pro rata portion of the gift tax attributable to the unrealized appreciation in the property. The amount of the addition to the donee's basis is determined as follows:[16]

$$\text{Gift tax paid} \times \frac{\text{FMV at time of the gift} - \text{Donor's basis}}{\text{Amount of the gift}}$$

The amount of the gift is the FMV of the property less the amount of the annual exclusion which is $14,000 in 2015.[17]

EXAMPLE I:5-18 ▶ During the current year, Cindy makes one gift of property with a $24,000 basis to Jessie when the property has a $64,000 FMV. Cindy pays a gift tax of $18,500. The amount of the gift is $50,000 ($64,000 − $14,000). Thus, 80% [($64,000 − $24,000)/$50,000] of the gift tax is added to Jessie's basis. Jessie's basis for the property for determining both gain and loss is $38,800 [$24,000 + (0.80 × $18,500)]. ◀

EXAMPLE I:5-19 ▶ During the current year, Sally makes a gift of property with a basis of $50,000 to Troy when the property has a $40,000 FMV. Sally pays a gift tax of $1,000. Troy's basis for the property is not affected by the gift tax paid by Sally because the FMV is less than the donor's basis at the time of the gift. Troy's basis for the property is $50,000 to determine gain and $40,000 to determine loss. ◀

STOP & THINK

Question: Pete wants to make a gift of either ABC common stock (basis of $44,000 and FMV of $50,000) or XYZ common stock (basis of $73,000 and FMV of $50,000) to his nephew. Pete and his nephew have the same tax rate. Which stock should he give to his nephew?

Solution: Pete should give the ABC stock to his nephew because the nephew's basis for determining a gain or loss is $44,000 plus a portion of any gift tax Pete pays. The nephew's basis for XYZ common stock is $50,000 to determine a loss and $73,000 to determine a gain. If the nephew sells XYZ stock for less than $73,000, no loss is recognized and thus some of the basis is not used. Note that Pete would have a $23,000 loss if he sells the XYZ stock for $50,000. Furthermore, the nephew's basis for the XYZ stock is not increased if Pete has to pay a gift tax on the $36,000 taxable gift.

PROPERTY RECEIVED FROM A DECEDENT

The basis of property received from a decedent who died in a year other than 2010 is the FMV of the property at the date of the decedent's death or an alternate valuation date (AVD).[18] This provision can result in either a step up (increase) or step down (decrease) in basis, but it is frequently described as the stepped-up basis rule. For decedents dying in 2010, the estate tax was repealed (see the discussion of Carryover Basis Rules below).

EXAMPLE I:5-20 ▶ Patrick inherited property having an $8 million FMV on the date of his sister's death in 2015. The decedent's basis in the property is $3.6 million. The executor of the estate does not elect the AVD. Patrick's basis for the property is $8 million. ◀

EXAMPLE I:5-21 ▶ Dianna inherited property having a $6 million FMV at the date of the decedent's death in 2015. The decedent's basis in the property is $7.2 million. The AVD is not elected. Dianna's basis for the property is $6 million. ◀

---

[16] Sec. 1015(d)(6).

[17] Sec. 1015(d)(2) and Sec. 2503(b). The annual exclusion for gifts was increased to $14,000 starting in 2013. From 2009–2012, the annual exclusion was $13,000. From 2005–2008, an annual exclusion of $12,000 per year was allowed for each donee, from 2002–2004, the annual exclusion was $11,000. Prior to 2002, the annual exclusion was $10,000. See Chapter I:1 for a limited discussion of the annual exclusion and Chapter C:12 of the *Corporations, Partnerships, Estates & Trusts* and *Comprehensive* volumes for a more detailed discussion.

[18] Sec. 1014(a).

REAL-WORLD EXAMPLE

The alternate valuation date was used in valuing the estates of many individuals owning large portfolios of common stocks who died shortly before the stock market crash in October 1987.

Instead of using the FMV on the date of death to determine the estate tax, the executor of the estate may elect to use the FMV on the AVD. The AVD is generally six months after the date of death. If the AVD is elected, the basis for all of the assets in the estate is their FMV on that date unless the property is distributed by the estate to the heirs or is sold before the AVD. If the AVD is used, property distributed or sold after the date of the decedent's death and before the AVD has a basis equal to its FMV on the date of distribution or the date of disposal.[19]

If the estate is small enough that an estate tax return is not required, the value of the property on the AVD may not be used.[20] An estate tax return must be filed if an individual dies in 2015 and the gross estate plus any previous taxable gifts exceeds $5.43 million.

EXAMPLE I:5-22 ▶ Marilyn inherited all of the property owned by an individual who died in April 2015, when the property had a $100,000 FMV. The value of the property six months later was $90,000. Because of the size of the estate, no estate tax was due. The AVD may not be used, and Marilyn's basis for the property is $100,000. Note that Marilyn does not want the AVD to be used because her basis would be $90,000 instead of $100,000. ◀

As noted above, the basis of the property to the estate and the heirs can be affected if the AVD is used to value the estate's assets. The AVD may be elected only if the value of the gross estate and the amount of estate tax after credits are reduced as a result of using the AVD.[21] This means that the aggregate value of the assets determined by using the AVD may be used only if the total value of the assets decreased during the six-month period.

EXAMPLE I:5-23 ▶ Helmut inherited all of the property owned by an individual who died in March 2015 when the FMV of the property was $5.8 million. Six months after the date of death, the property had a $5.95 million FMV. The property is distributed to Helmut in December. Use of the AVD is not permitted because the value of the gross estate has increased. Therefore, his basis in the property is $5.8 million, the FMV on the date of death. ◀

An executor may elect to use the AVD to reduce the estate taxes owed by the estate. However, the income tax basis of the property included in the estate is also reduced for heirs who inherit the property.

EXAMPLE I:5-24 ▶ Michelle inherited property with a $6.2 million FMV at the date of the decedent's death in 2015. The FMV of the property on the AVD (six months after the date of the decedent's death) is $5.74 million. The executor of the estate elects to use $5.74 million to value the property for estate tax purposes, and Michelle's basis for the property is thus $5.74 million instead of $6.2 million. ◀

Carryover Basis Rules-Special Rule for 2010. In 2001, Congress eliminated the estate tax for individuals dying in 2010; however, the estate tax was scheduled to return in 2011 and be higher than the estate tax in 2009. Most tax professionals did not expect the estate tax to actually be repealed for the year 2010, but Congress did not take action to reinstate the estate tax retroactively until December of 2010. Congress reinstated the estate tax for 2010 and future years, but estates of individuals dying in 2010 may elect to use the provisions in effect for 2010 and not have the estate tax apply.

ADDITIONAL COMMENT

At least five billionaires, including George Steinbrenner of the New York Yankees, died in 2010, and their estates were probably not subject to the estate tax.

The existence of the estate tax has implications for the basis of property transferred to others when one dies. For 2010, a modified carryover basis rule applies if the estate elects to not have the estate tax apply. A taxpayer who inherits the property will take the lesser of the decedent's basis or FMV at time of death, but the basis may be increased if the asset is appreciated. The basis may not be increased to more than the FMV, and the total amount of increase is limited to $1.3 million plus any unused built-in loss or NOL carryover. A surviving spouse may receive an additional $3 million adjustment.

If Patrick's sister in Example 5-20 died in 2010, an estate tax is due unless the estate elected to have the estate tax not apply. Because the exemption equivalent in 2010 was $5 million or less, the estate would probably have elected to pay no estate tax. If so, Patrick's basis is $4.9 million ($3,600,000 + $1,300,000). Patrick's basis is $7.9 million if the decedent was his spouse ($3,600,000 + $1,300,000 + $3,000,000). If the election is not made and the estate tax applies, Patrick's basis is the $8,000,000 FMV.

---

[19] Sec. 2032(a).

[20] Rev. Rul. 56-60, 1956-1 C.B. 443. For a decedent dying in 2011 and 2012, Sec. 6018(a) requires an estate tax return to be filed if the gross estate exceeds $5 million ($3.5 million in 2009, $2 million in 2006–2008 and $1.5 million for decedents dying in 2004 or 2005).

[21] Credits available include the unified transfer tax credit and possibly credits for gift taxes, foreign death taxes, and the credit for taxes on prior transfers.

Dianna's basis in Example 5-21 is $6 million even if the death occurred in 2010. The estate would elect to have the estate tax not apply and avoid any estate tax liability, but the basis is the same under the stepped-up basis rules and the carryover basis rules because the decedent's basis in the property is greater than its FMV.

Community Property. If the decedent and the decedent's spouse own property under community property laws,[22] one-half of the property is included in the decedent's gross estate and its basis to the surviving spouse is its FMV.[23] The surviving spouse's one-half share of the community property is also adjusted to FMV.[24] In effect, the surviving spouse's share of the community property is considered to have passed from the decedent.

EXAMPLE I:5-25 ▶ Matt and Jane, a married couple, live in Texas, a community property state, and jointly own land as community property that cost $110,000. The land has an $800,000 FMV when Jane dies, leaving all of her property to Matt. His basis for the entire property is $800,000. ◀

In a common law state, one-half of the jointly owned property is included in the decedent's estate and is adjusted to its FMV. The survivor's share of the jointly held property is not adjusted.

EXAMPLE I:5-26 ▶ Barry and Maria, a married couple, live in Iowa, a common law state, and jointly own land that cost $200,000. The property has a $700,000 FMV when Barry dies, leaving all of his property to Maria. Her basis for the land is $450,000 [$100,000 + (0.50 × $700,000)]. ◀

PROPERTY CONVERTED FROM PERSONAL USE TO BUSINESS USE

ADDITIONAL COMMENT

It is important to estimate the FMV of property at the time the property is converted from personal use to business use.

Often, taxpayers who own personal-use assets convert these assets to an income-producing use or for use in a trade or business. When this conversion occurs, the property's basis must be determined. The basis for computing depreciation is the lower of FMV or the adjusted basis of the property when the asset is transferred from personal use to an income-producing use or for use in a trade or business.[25] This rule prevents taxpayers from obtaining the benefits of depreciation to the extent that the property has declined in value during the period that it is held for personal use.

EXAMPLE I:5-27 ▶ Olga owns a boat that cost $2,000 and is used for personal enjoyment. At a time when the boat has a $1,400 FMV, Olga transfers the boat to her business of operating a marina. The basis for depreciation is $1,400 because the FMV is less than Olga's adjusted basis at the time of conversion to business use. The $600 decline ($2,000 − $1,400) that occurred while Olga used the boat for personal use may not be deducted as depreciation. ◀

REAL-WORLD EXAMPLE

A taxpayer sold a personal residence to a purchaser, and the purchaser rented the property from the taxpayer until financing could be secured. The rental agreement was executed simultaneously with the sales agreement and was incidental to the sale. The taxpayer was not permitted to recognize any loss on the sale because the property was never converted to rental property. *Henry B. Dawson*, 1972 PH T.C. Memo 31 TCM 5.

If the boat's FMV in Example I:5-27 is more than $2,000, the basis for depreciation is $2,000 because the FMV is higher than its adjusted basis at the time the asset is transferred to business use.

If a personal-use asset is transferred to business use when its FMV is less than its adjusted basis, the basis for determining a loss on a subsequent sale or disposition of the property is its FMV on the date of the conversion to business use less any depreciation taken after the transfer to business use.[26]

EXAMPLE I:5-28 ▶ Susanna purchased a personal residence in 1990 for $50,000 and converted the property to rental property in 1993 when its FMV was $46,000. Assume depreciation of $20,700 has been deducted after the conversion in 1993, and the property is sold for $21,000. The basis of the property is $25,300 ($46,000 − $20,700), and her loss on the sale is $4,300 ($21,000 − $25,300). ◀

The rule for determining basis, that is, lower of adjusted basis or FMV, applies only to the sale of converted property at a loss. The basis for determining gain is its adjusted basis when converted less depreciation taken after the transfer to business use.

EXAMPLE I:5-29 ▶ Assume the same facts as in Example I:5-28, except the property is sold for $31,000 instead of $21,000. The basis of the property is $29,300 ($50,000 − $20,700) and her gain is $1,700 ($31,000 − $29,300). ◀

[22] Community property states are Arizona, California, Idaho, Louisiana, New Mexico, Nevada, Texas, and Washington. Wisconsin has a marital property law that is basically the same as community property.
[23] Sec. 1014(a).
[24] Sec. 1014(b)(6).
[25] Reg. Sec. 1.167(g)-1.
[26] Reg. Sec. 1.165-9(b)(2).

Without the rule for determining basis of personal-use property converted to business property, taxpayers would have an incentive to convert nonbusiness assets that have declined in value to business use before selling the asset to convert nondeductible losses into deductible losses.

EXAMPLE I:5-30 ▶ Craig owns a personal-use asset with a basis of $80,000 and a $50,000 FMV. If he sells the asset for its FMV, the $30,000 loss ($50,000 − $80,000) is not deductible because losses on the sale of personal-use assets are not deductible. If Craig converts the asset to business use and then immediately sells the asset for $50,000, no loss is realized because the basis of the asset for purposes of determining loss is $50,000, the FMV when property was converted. ◀

REAL-WORLD EXAMPLE

A taxpayer purchased a group of lots and allocated the total cost evenly among the lots. The court, however, held that more cost should be allocated to the waterfront lots than to the interior lots. *Biscayne Bay Islands Co.*, 23 B.T.A. 731 (1931).

ALLOCATION OF BASIS

When property is obtained in one transaction and portions of the property are subsequently disposed of at different times, the basis of the property is allocated to the different portions of the property. Gain or loss is computed at the time of disposal for each portion. If a taxpayer purchases a 20-acre tract of land and later sells the entire tract, an allocation of basis is not needed. However, if the taxpayer divides the property into smaller tracts of land for resale, the cost of the 20-acre tract must be allocated among the smaller tracts of land.

Basket Purchase. If more than one asset is acquired in a single purchase transaction (i.e., a basket purchase), the cost must be apportioned to the various assets acquired. The allocation is based on the relative FMVs of the assets.

EXAMPLE I:5-31 ▶ Kelly purchases a duplex for $80,000 to use as a rental property. The land has a $15,000 FMV, and the building has a $65,000 FMV. Kelly's bases for the land and the building are $15,000 and $65,000, respectively. ◀

SELF-STUDY QUESTION

If Kelly in Example I:5-31 paid $2,000 for the cost of a title search and other costs that must be capitalized, what is the basis of the land and building?

ANSWER

Land $15,375
Building $66,625

Because no depreciation deduction is allowed for land, taxpayers tend to favor a liberal allocation of the total purchase price to the building. Appraisals or other measures of FMV may be used to make the allocation.

Common Costs. As in the case of financial accounting, common costs incurred to obtain or prepare an asset for service must be capitalized and allocated to the basis of the individual assets.

EXAMPLE I:5-32 ▶ Priscilla acquires three machines for $60,000, which have FMVs of $30,000, $20,000, and $10,000, respectively. Costs of delivery amount to $2,000, and costs to install the three machines amount to $1,000. The total installation and delivery costs of $3,000 are allocated to the three machines based on their FMVs.

The allocation of the $3,000 of common costs occurs as follows:

$$\text{Machine No. 1: } \frac{\$30{,}000 \text{ FMV}}{\$30{,}000 + \$20{,}000 + \$10{,}000} \times \$3{,}000 = \$1{,}500$$

$$\text{Machine No. 2: } \frac{\$20{,}000 \text{ FMV}}{\$30{,}000 + \$20{,}000 + \$10{,}000} \times \$3{,}000 = \$1{,}000$$

$$\text{Machine No. 3: } \frac{\$10{,}000 \text{ FMV}}{\$30{,}000 + \$20{,}000 + \$10{,}000} \times \$3{,}000 = \$500$$

The bases for each of the three machines are $31,500, $21,000, and $10,500, respectively. ◀

Nontaxable Stock Dividends Received. If a nontaxable stock dividend is received, a portion of the basis of the stock on which the stock dividend is received is allocated to the new shares received from the stock dividend.[27] The cost basis of the previously acquired shares is reduced by the amount of basis allocated to the stock dividend shares. If the stock received as a stock dividend is the same type as the stock owned before the dividend, the total basis of the stock owned before the dividend is allocated equally to all shares now owned.

[27] Sec. 307(a).

EXAMPLE I:5-33 ▶ Wayne owns 1,000 shares of Bell Corporation common stock with a $44,000 basis. Wayne receives a nontaxable 10% common stock dividend and now owns 1,100 shares of common stock. The basis for each share of common stock is now $40 ($44,000 ÷ 1,100). ◀

If the stock received as a stock dividend is not the same type as the stock owned before the dividend, the allocation is based on relative FMVs.

EXAMPLE I:5-34 ▶ Stacey owns 500 shares of Montana Corporation common stock with a $60,000 basis. She receives a nontaxable stock dividend payable in 50 shares of preferred stock. At time of the distribution, the common stock has a $40,000 FMV ($80 × 500 shares), and the preferred stock has a $10,000 FMV ($200 × 50 shares). After the distribution, Stacey owns 50 shares of preferred stock with a basis of $12,000 [($10,000 ÷ $50,000) × $60,000]. Thus, $12,000 of the basis of the common stock is allocated to the preferred stock and the basis of the common stock is reduced from $60,000 to $48,000. ◀

KEY POINT

Corporations issue stock rights to shareholders so that the shareholders will be able to maintain their same proportional ownership in the corporation. This is called the preemptive right.

Nontaxable Stock Rights Received. Stock rights represent rights to acquire shares of a specified corporation's stock at a specific exercise price when certain conditions are met. The exercise price is usually less than the market price when the stock rights are issued. Stock rights may be distributed to employees as compensation, and they are often issued to shareholders to encourage them to purchase more stock, thereby providing more capital for the corporation.

If the FMV of nontaxable stock rights received is less than 15% of the FMV of the stock, the basis of the stock rights is zero unless the taxpayer elects to allocate the basis between the stock rights and the stock owned before distribution of the stock rights.[28]

EXAMPLE I:5-35 ▶ Tina owns 100 shares of Bear Corporation common stock with a $27,000 basis and a $50,000 FMV. She receives 100 nontaxable stock rights with a total FMV of $4,000. Because the FMV of the stock rights is less than 15% of the FMV of the stock (0.15 × $50,000 = $7,500), the basis of the stock rights is zero unless Tina elects to make an allocation. ◀

REAL-WORLD EXAMPLE

In 1993, United States Cellular Corporation issued one right for each common share held. Each whole right entitled the holder to buy one common share for $33.

If, Tina, in the example above, elects to allocate the basis of $27,000 between the stock rights and the stock, the basis of the rights is $2,000 ([$4,000 ÷ $54,000] × $27,000) and the basis of the stock is $25,000 ([$50,000 ÷ $54,000] × $27,000).

The decision to allocate the basis affects the gain or loss realized on the sale or disposition of the stock rights because the basis of the rights is zero unless an allocation is made. Furthermore, the basis of any stock acquired by exercising the rights is affected by whether or not a portion of the basis is allocated to the rights. The basis of stock acquired by exercising the stock rights is the amount paid plus the basis of the stock rights exercised.

EXAMPLE I:5-36 ▶ George receives 10 stock rights as a nontaxable distribution, and no basis is allocated to the stock rights. With each stock right, George may acquire one share of stock for $20. If he exercises all 10 stock rights, the new stock acquired has a basis of $200 ($20 × 10 shares). If George sells all 10 stock rights for $135, he has a realized gain of $135 ($135 − $0). ◀

If the FMV of a nontaxable stock right received is equal to or greater than 15% of the FMV of the stock, the basis of the stock owned before the distribution must be allocated between the stock and the stock rights.

EXAMPLE I:5-37 ▶ Helen owns 100 shares of NMO common stock with a $14,000 basis and a $30,000 FMV. She receives 100 stock rights with a total FMV of $5,000. Because the FMV of the stock rights is at least 15% of the FMV of the stock, the $14,000 basis must be allocated between the stock rights and the stock. The basis of the stock rights is $2,000 [($5,000 ÷ $35,000) × $14,000] and the basis of the stock is $12,000 [($30,000 ÷ $35,000) × $14,000]. ◀

A recipient of stock rights generally has three courses of action. The stock rights can be sold or exchanged, in which case the basis allocated to the stock rights, if any, is used to determine gain or loss. The stock rights may be exercised, and any basis allocated to the rights is added to the purchase price of the acquired stock. The stock rights may be allowed to expire, in which case no loss is recognized, and any basis allocated to the rights is reallocated back to the stock. If the stock rights received in the above example expire without being exercised, Helen does not recognize a loss and the basis of her 100 shares of common stock is $14,000.

Property basis rules are highlighted in Topic Review I:5-1.

[28] Sec. 307(b)(1).

TOPIC REVIEW I:5-1

Property Basis Rules

Method Acquired	Basis of the Acquired Property
1. Acquired by direct purchase	1. Basis includes the amount paid for the property, costs of preparing the property for use, obligations of the seller assumed by the buyer, and liabilities to which the property is subject.
2. Acquired as a gift. (a) FMV on the date of the gift is equal to or greater than the donor's basis (b) FMV on the date of the gift is less than the donor's basis	2. (a) The donee's basis is the same as the donor's basis plus a pro rata portion of the gift tax attributable to the property's unrealized appreciation at the time of the gift. (b) The donee's gain basis is the donor's basis and the loss basis is FMV. No increase for any gift tax paid.
3. Received from a decedent* (a) AVD is not elected (b) AVD is elected	3. (a) The basis is its FMV on the date of death. (b) The basis of nondistributed property is its FMV on the AVD. If the property is distributed or sold before this date, its basis is FMV on the date of sale or distribution.
4. Converted from personal to business use	4. The basis for a loss (as well as for depreciation) is the lesser of its adjusted basis or FMV at date of conversion. The basis for a gain is its adjusted basis at date of conversion.
5. Nontaxable stock dividend	5. Basis of the stock dividend shares includes a pro rata portion of the adjusted basis of the underlying shares owned.
6. Nontaxable stock right	6. If the FMV of the rights is less than 15% of the stock's FMV, the basis of the rights is zero unless an election is made to allocate basis. Basis of the underlying stock is allocated to the rights based on the respective FMVs of the stock and rights.

* Special rules apply to decedents dying in 2010.

Definition of a Capital Asset

OBJECTIVE 3

Distinguish between capital assets and other assets

Instead of defining capital assets, Sec. 1221 provides a list of properties that are **not** capital assets. Thus, a capital asset is any property owned by a taxpayer *other* than the types of property specified in Sec. 1221. Property that is not a capital asset includes the following:

1. Inventory or property held primarily for sale to customers in the ordinary course of a trade or business.
2. Property used in the trade or business and subject to the allowance for depreciation provided in Sec. 167 or real property used in a trade or business. (As explained in Chapter I:13, these properties are referred to as *Sec. 1231 assets* if held by the taxpayer more than one year.)
3. Accounts or notes receivable acquired in the ordinary course of a trade or business for services rendered or from the sale of property described in item 1.
4. Supplies of a type regularly used or consumed in the ordinary course of a trade or business.
5. Other assets including
   a. A letter, memorandum, or similar property held by a taxpayer for whom such property was prepared or produced.
   b. A copyright; a literary, musical, or artistic composition; a letter or memorandum; or similar property held by a taxpayer whose personal efforts created such property or whose basis in the property for determining a gain is determined by reference to the basis of such property in the hands of one who created the property or one for whom such property was prepared or produced.

TYPICAL MISCONCEPTION

It is common in financial accounting classes to include property used in a trade or business in the definition of a capital asset. For example, factory buildings, machinery, trucks, and office buildings would be defined as capital assets. However, such items are not capital assets for tax purposes.

c. A U.S. government publication held by a taxpayer who receives the publication by any means other than a purchase at the price the publication is offered for sale to the public.

d. A U.S. government publication held by a taxpayer whose basis in the property for determining a gain is determined by reference to the basis of such property in the hands of a taxpayer in item 5c (e.g., certain property received by gift).

EXAMPLE I:5-38 ▶ Maxine owns a building used in her business. Other business assets include equipment, inventory, and accounts receivable. None of the assets are classified as capital assets. ◀

Chapter I:13 provides an in-depth discussion of business assets such as buildings, land, and equipment. Although these items are not capital assets, Sec. 1231 provides in many cases that the gain on the sale or exchange of such an asset is eventually taxed as LTCG.

EXAMPLE I:5-39 ▶ Eric owns an automobile held for personal use and also owns a copyright for a book he has written. Because the copyright is held by the taxpayer whose personal efforts created the property, it is not a capital asset. The automobile held for personal use is a capital asset. ◀

SELF-STUDY QUESTION

Doug owns a personal residence, an automobile, 100 shares of Ford Motor Company, and a poem he wrote for his girlfriend. Which of these assets are capital assets?

ANSWER

All of the items are capital assets except the poem, which is a literary composition that Doug created. If Doug gives the poem to his girlfriend, the poem is still not a capital asset.

By analyzing Examples I:5-38 and I:5-39, one can conclude that the classification of an asset is often determined by its use. An automobile used in a trade or business is not a capital asset but is a capital asset when held for personal use. Examples of assets that qualify as capital assets include a personal residence, land held for personal use, and investments in stocks and bonds. In addition, certain types of assets are specifically given capital asset status, such as patents, franchises, etc. These and other special assets are discussed later in this chapter.

Recently, Congress made a major change for self-created musical works. Pursuant to Sec. 1221(b)(3), a taxpayer whose personal efforts created such property may now make an election to treat the sale or exchange of musical compositions or copyrights in self-created musical works as a sale or exchange of a capital asset.

INFLUENCE OF THE COURTS

In *Corn Products Refining Co.*, the Supreme Court rendered a landmark decision when it determined that the sale of futures contracts related to the purchase of raw materials resulted in ordinary rather than capital gains and losses.[29] The Corn Products Company, a manufacturer of products made from grain corn, purchased futures contracts for corn to ensure an adequate supply of raw materials. Delivery of the corn was accepted when needed for manufacturing operations, and unneeded contracts were later sold. Corn Products contended that any gains or losses on the sale of the unneeded contracts should be capital gains and losses because futures contracts are customarily viewed as security investments, which qualify as capital assets. The Supreme Court held that these transactions represented an integral part of the business for the purpose of protecting the company's manufacturing operations and the gains and losses should, therefore, be ordinary in nature.

ADDITIONAL COMMENT

If an asset such as an automobile is used in part in a trade or business and in part for personal use, then the business part of the car is not a capital asset, but the other part is a capital asset.

Although the *Corn Products* doctrine has been interpreted as creating a nonstatutory exception to the definition of a capital asset when the asset is purchased for business purposes, the Supreme Court ruled in the 1988 *Arkansas Best Corporation* case that the motivation for acquiring assets is irrelevant to the question of whether assets are capital assets. Arkansas Best, a bank holding company, sold shares of a bank's stock that had been acquired for the purpose of protecting its business reputation. Relying on the *Corn Products* doctrine, the company deducted the loss as ordinary. The Supreme Court ruled that the loss was a capital loss because the stock is within the broad definition of the term *capital asset* in Sec. 1221 and is outside the classes of property that are excluded from capital-asset status.[30] *Arkansas Best* apparently limits the application of *Corn Products* to hedging transactions that are an integral part of a taxpayer's system of acquiring inventory.

ETHICAL POINT

A CPA should not prepare or sign a tax return for a client unless the position or issue has (1) a realistic possibility of being sustained on its merits or (2) is not frivolous and is adequately disclosed in the return.

[29] *Corn Products Refining Co. v. CIR*, 47 AFTR 1789, 55-2 USTC ¶9746 (USSC, 1955).

[30] *Arkansas Best Corporation v. CIR*, 61 AFTR 2d 88-655, 88-1 USTC ¶9210 (USSC, 1988).

OTHER IRC PROVISIONS RELEVANT TO CAPITAL GAINS AND LOSSES

A number of IRC sections provide special treatment for certain types of assets and transactions. For example, loss on the sale or exchange of certain small business stock that qualifies as Sec. 1244 stock is treated as an ordinary loss rather than a capital loss to the extent of $50,000 per year ($100,000 if the taxpayer is married and files a joint return).[31]

ADDITIONAL COMMENT

For purposes of Sec. 1236, a security is defined as any share of stock in any corporation, note, bond, debenture, or evidence of indebtedness, or any evidence of an interest in or right to subscribe to or purchase any of the above.

Dealers in Securities. Normally, a security dealer's gain on the sale or exchange of securities is ordinary income. Section 1236 provides an exception for dealers in securities if the dealer clearly identifies that the property is held for investment. This act of identification must occur before the close of the day on which the security is acquired, and the security must not be held primarily for sale to customers in the ordinary course of the dealer's trade or business at any time after the close of the day of purchase.

EXAMPLE I:5-40 ▶ Allyson, a dealer in securities, purchases Cook Corporation stock on April 8, and identifies the stock as being held for investment on that date. Four months later, Allyson sells the stock. Any gain or loss recognized due to the sale is capital gain or loss. ◀

Once a dealer clearly identifies a security as being held for investment, any loss on the sale or exchange of the security is treated as a capital loss.

EXAMPLE I:5-41 ▶ Kris, a dealer in securities, purchases Boston Corporation stock and clearly identifies the stock as being held for investment on the date of purchase. Eight months later, the security is removed from the investment account and held as inventory. If the security is later sold at a gain, the gain is an ordinary gain. However, if the stock is sold at a loss, the loss is a capital loss. ◀

Securities dealers must use the mark-to-market method for their inventory of securities. This method requires that securities be valued at FMV at the end of each taxable year. Dealers in securities recognize gain or loss each year as if the security is sold on the last day of the tax year. Gains and losses are generally treated as ordinary rather than capital. Gains or losses due to adjustments in subsequent years or resulting from the sale of the security must be adjusted to reflect gains and losses already taken into account when determining taxable income.[32]

EXAMPLE I:5-42 ▶ Jim Spikes, a dealer in securities and calendar-year taxpayer, purchases a security for inventory on October 10, 2015, for $10,000 and sells the security for $18,000 on July 1, 2016. The security's FMV on December 31, 2015, is $15,000. Jim recognizes $5,000 of ordinary income in 2015 and $3,000 of ordinary income in 2016. ◀

Real Property Subdivided for Sale. A taxpayer who engages in regular sales of real estate is considered to be a dealer, and any gain or loss recognized is ordinary gain or loss rather than capital gain or loss. A special relief provision is provided in Sec. 1237 for nondealer, noncorporate taxpayers who subdivide a tract of real property into lots (two or more pieces of real property are considered to be a tract if they are contiguous). Part or all of the gain on the sale of the lots may be treated as a capital gain if the following provisions of Sec. 1237 are satisfied:

ADDITIONAL COMMENT

The conversion of an apartment building into condominiums does not qualify under Sec. 1237, even if the property has been held for five years and no substantial improvements have been made.

- During the year of sale, the noncorporate taxpayer must not hold any other real property primarily for sale in the ordinary course of business.
- Unless the property is acquired by inheritance or devise, the lots sold must be held by the taxpayer for a period of at least five years.
- No substantial improvement may be made by the taxpayer while holding the lots if the improvement substantially enhances the value of the lot.[33]

---

31 Secs. 1244(a) and (b). (See Chapter I:8 for additional discussion on small business corporation stock losses.)

32 Sec. 475. The mark-to-market rule also applies to some securities that are not inventory, but does not apply to any security that is held for investment and certain other transactions (see Sec. 475(b)).

33 Certain improvements are not treated as substantial under Sec. 1237(b)(3) if the lot is held for at least ten years.

▶ The tract or any lot may not have been previously held primarily for sale to customers in the ordinary course of the taxpayer's trade or business unless such tract at that time was covered by Sec. 1237.

The primary advantage of Sec. 1237 is that potential controversy with the IRS is avoided as to whether a taxpayer who subdivides investment property is a dealer. Section 1237 does not apply to losses. Such losses are capital losses if the property is held for investment purposes, or ordinary losses if the taxpayer is a dealer.

If the Sec. 1237 requirements are satisfied, all gain on the sale of the first five lots may be capital gain. Starting in the tax year during which the sixth lot is sold, 5% of the selling price for all lots sold in that year and succeeding years is ordinary income.

EXAMPLE I:5-43 ▶ Jean subdivides a tract of land held as an investment into seven lots, and all requirements of Sec. 1237 are satisfied. The lots have a FMV of $10,000 each and have a basis of $4,000. Jean incurs no selling expenses and sells four lots in 2014 and three lots in 2015. In 2014, all of the $24,000 [four lots × ($10,000 − $4,000)] gain is capital gain. In 2015, the year in which the sixth lot is sold, $1,500 of the gain is ordinary income [0.05 × ($10,000 × three lots)], and the remaining $16,500 {[three lots × ($10,000 − $4,000)] − $1,500} gain is capital gain. ◀

EXAMPLE I:5-44 ▶ Assume the same facts as in the above example, except that all seven lots are sold in 2015. The amount of ordinary income recognized is $3,500 [0.05 × ($10,000 × seven lots)], and the remaining $38,500 {[seven lots × ($10,000 − $4,000)] − $3,500} gain is capital gain. ◀

ADDITIONAL COMMENT

If a taxpayer sells any lots from a tract and does not sell any others for a period of five years, the remaining property is considered a new tract.

Based on Examples I:5-43 and I:5-44, the advantage of selling no more than five lots in the first year should be apparent. Expenditures incurred to sell or exchange the lots are also treated favorably because they are first applied against the portion of the gain treated as ordinary income. Because selling expenses (e.g., commissions) are often equal to or greater than 5% of the selling price, this offset against ordinary income may result in the elimination of the ordinary income portion of the gain. Selling expenses in excess of the gain taxed as ordinary income reduce the amount realized on the sale or exchange.

Nonbusiness Bad Debt. Bad debt losses from nonbusiness debts are deductible only as short-term capital losses (STCLs),[34] regardless of when the debt occurred. A nonbusiness bad debt is deductible only in the year in which the debt becomes totally worthless.

EXAMPLE I:5-45 ▶ Two years ago, Alice loaned $4,000 to a friend. During the current year, the friend declares bankruptcy and the debt is entirely worthless. Assuming that Alice has no other gains and losses from the sale or exchange of capital assets during the year, she deducts $3,000 in determining adjusted gross income (AGI) and has a STCL carry forward of $1,000. ◀

TAX TREATMENT FOR CAPITAL GAINS AND LOSSES OF NONCORPORATE TAXPAYERS

OBJECTIVE 4

Understand how capital gains are taxed for noncorporate taxpayers

To recognize capital gain or loss, it is necessary to have a sale or exchange of a capital asset. Once it is determined that a capital gain or loss has been realized and is to be recognized, it is necessary to classify the gains and losses as either short-term or long-term. If the asset is held for one year or less, the gain or loss is classified as a short-term capital gain (STCG) or a short-term capital loss (STCL). If the capital asset is held for more than one year, the gain or loss is classified as a long-term capital gain (LTCG) or long-term capital loss (LTCL).[35]

[34] Sec. 166(d)(1)(B). Also, see discussion of bad debts in Chapter I:8.

[35] While the Taxpayer Relief Act of 1997 reduced the rates for most LTCGs, it increased the required holding period to more than 18 months to be eligible for the lower rates of 10% and 20%. During the last few months of 1997, gain resulting from the sale of a capital asset might be taxed at many different rates depending on whether or not the holding period is one year or less, more than one year but not more than 18 months, or more than 18 months. These changes in the law dramatically increased the complexity associated with the taxation of capital gains. The 1998 Restructuring and Reform Act eliminated the more than 18-month holding period requirement for tax years ending after 1997 and returned to the more than one year requirement to be LTCG.

ADDITIONAL COMMENT

The rates for long-term capital gains have been lower than rates for ordinary income for many years. However, preferential rates for qualified dividends were enacted in 2003. Qualified divi dends are now taxed at a maximum 15% or 20% rate, the same as for long-term capital gains which are ANCG.

CAPITAL GAINS

The first step in determining the taxability of capital gains is to calculate *net capital gains* (NCG), which is defined as the excess of net long-term capital gain over net short-term capital loss.[36] All capital gains are not taxed at the same rate. So, depending on the type of property, NCG could be taxed at zero, 15%, 20%, 25%, or 28%. Once NCG has been determined, a portion of NCG may be classified as *adjusted net capital gain* (ANCG) which is subject to the lower rates of zero, 15%, or 20%.

To compute NCG, first determine all STCGs, STCLs, LTCGs, LTCLs, and then net gains and losses as described below.

Net Short-Term Capital Gain. If total STCGs for the tax year exceed total STCLs for that year, the excess is defined as net short-term capital gain (NSTCG). As discussed later, NSTCG may be offset by net long-term capital loss (NLTCL).

EXAMPLE I:5-46 ▶ Hal has two transactions involving the sale of capital assets during the year. As a result of those transactions, he has a STCG of $4,000 and a STCL of $3,000. Hal's NSTCG is $1,000 and his AGI increases by $1,000. His gross income increases by $4,000, and he is entitled to a $3,000 deduction for AGI. ◀

Net Long-Term Capital Gain. If the total LTCGs for the tax year exceed the total LTCLs for that year, the excess is defined as net long-term capital gain (NLTCG). As indicated earlier, a NCG exists when NLTCG exceeds net short-term capital loss (NSTCL).

EXAMPLE I:5-47 ▶ Clay has two transactions involving the sale of capital assets during the year. As a result of the transactions, he has a LTCG of $5,000 and a LTCL of $3,000. Clay has a NLTCG and a net capital gain of $2,000. His AGI increases by $2,000. ◀

EXAMPLE I:5-48 ▶ Linda has four transactions involving the sale of capital assets during the year. As a result of the transactions, she has a STCG of $5,000, a STCL of $7,000, a LTCG of $10,000, and a LTCL of $2,000. After the initial netting of short-term and long-term gains and losses, Linda has a NSTCL of $2,000 ($7,000 − $5,000) and a NLTCG of $8,000 ($10,000 − $2,000). Because the NLTCG exceeds the NSTCL by $6,000 ($8,000 − $2,000), her NCG is $6,000. ◀

Lower Rates for Adjusted Net Capital Gain (ANCG). The tax rate that applies to a taxpayer's ANCG depends on the taxpayer's tax bracket, and can be zero, 15%, or 20%. Taxpayers with a 10% or 15% marginal tax rate have a zero percent tax rate on their ANCG. Taxpayers with a marginal tax rate more than 15% and less than 39.6% have a preferential rate of 15%, and the preferential rate is 20% if one's marginal tax rate is 39.6%.[37]

EXAMPLE I:5-49 ▶ Sandy is single with taxable income of $100,000 without considering the sale of Merck stock during 2015 for $15,000. The stock was purchased four years earlier for $3,000. Sandy has $12,000 of NLTCG which is ANCG taxed at 15%. To compute her total tax for 2015, ordinary rates would be applied to the $100,000 and then the tax on ANCG (15% × $12,000) is added. ◀

EXAMPLE I:5-50 ▶ Assume the same facts as in Example I:5-49 except Sandy's taxable income without the capital gain is $11,400. The $12,000 ANCG is taxed at a rate of zero because her taxable income is less than $37,450. Taxable income up to $37,450 is subject to ordinary tax rates of no higher than 15%.

Computation of the tax becomes more complicated if the ANCG causes taxable income to exceed the $37,450 for a single taxpayer. If a single taxpayer has taxable income of $40,000 that includes $10,000 of ANCG, the taxpayer's tax is determined as follows:

Tax on $30,000 (taxable income without the ANCG)	$4,039	[$922.50 + ($20,775 × 15%)]
+ Tax on $7,450 ($37,450 − $30,000) of the ANCG at zero	0	($7,450 × 0%)
+ Tax on $2,550 ($10,000 − $7,450) at 15% because the taxable income is greater than $37,450	$ 383	($2,550 × 15%)
Total tax	$4,422	

◀

LEGISLATIVE UPDATE

The American Tax Relief Act of 2012 retained tax relief of the zero and 15% rates provided by the Bush administration but increased the preferential tax rate to 20% of ANCG for those taxpayers with the highest marginal tax rate, 39.6%.

This change was a compromise between President Obama and most Democrats in Congress who advocated for higher tax rates on taxpayers with higher incomes and most Republicans who opposed any income tax increases.

---

36 Sec. 1222(11).

37 Sec. 1(h).

EXAMPLE I:5-51 ▶ The Danecks file a joint return with taxable income of $800,000 which includes ANCG of $100,000 and no other investment income. Their tax is determined by adding the tax on $700,000 where marginal tax rate is 39.6% to $20,000 (20% × $100,000). They are also subject to the 3.8% Medicare tax of $3,800 (3.8% × $100,000) on investment income discussed later in the chapter. ◀

SELF-STUDY QUESTION

Mary sells common stock for a gain of $10,000 on December 29, 2015. The settlement date, or date that Mary will receive the proceeds from the stockbroker, is January 2, 2016. Will Mary report the gain on her 2015 or 2016 tax return?

ANSWER

Mary is required to report the gain in the year of the sale (2015). Losses are also recognized in the year of sale.

KEY POINT

Collectibles gain, as explained below, is the net of LTCG and LTCL from the sale of collectibles. Sec. 1202 stock is qualified small business stock designed to encourage investment in small businesses.

ADJUSTED NET CAPITAL GAINS (ANCG)

When computing ANCG, one has to consider that four different types of LTCGs may exist:

1. Collectibles gain
2. Part of the gain (generally 50%) resulting from the sale or exchange of qualified small business stock as defined in Sec. 1202
3. Unrecaptured Sec. 1250 gain[38]
4. All other LTCGs

It is the fourth group of LTCGs that receives the preferential rates of zero, 15%, or 20%. The other three groups receive preferential treatment but not at the zero, 15%, or 20% rate. The first two gains above are referred to as 28% rate gain because the maximum rate for those gains is 28%; the maximum rate for unrecaptured Sec. 1250 gain is 25%. Unrecaptured Sec. 1250 gain, which is taxed at a maximum 25% rate, generally occurs when a building is sold. For the second and third types of LTCG, the special provisions only apply to gains. Net losses from sale of Sec. 1202 stock are treated as normal LTCLs, and one cannot have a loss connected with an unrecaptured Sec. 1250 gain.

ANCG is defined as NCG less the first three gains listed above. However, the computation of ANCG is tricky because one has to consider the impact of net capital losses, both short-term and long-term. Taxpayers are permitted to offset capital losses against capital gains. But, as discussed above, there are four different types of LTCG. So, if a taxpayer has both LTCG and capital losses, the capital losses are first offset within the category (collectibles, Sec. 1202 stock, etc.), then any excess loss is offset against the highest rate LTCG category first and works down to the lowest rate category (i.e., 28% rate gain first, then 25%, then 20% or 15%). This topic is discussed in more detail on page I:5-19 below.

When a taxpayer has no capital losses and no qualified dividends, ANCG is NCG reduced by the first three types of LTCG listed above. Many taxpayers will not have the first three types of LTCG and therefore, NCG and ANCG will often be the same amount.

EXAMPLE I:5-52 ▶ During 2015, Charles, whose tax rate exceeds 15% and is less than 39.6%, sold two publicly-traded stocks. The first stock resulted in a LTCG of $10,000 while the second stock resulted in a LTCG of $15,000. These were his only transactions involving capital assets during the year. Charles' NCG and ANCG is $25,000 and this gain is subject to a maximum tax rate of 15%. ◀

EXAMPLE I:5-53 ▶ Assume in the example above that Charles also had a gain on the sale of a building that resulted in an unrecaptured Sec. 1250 gain of $50,000. Charles has NCG of $75,000 and ANCG of $25,000. The $50,000 gain is taxed at a maximum rate of 25% while the $25,000 of ANCG is taxed at a maximum rate of 15%. ◀

Collectibles Gain. Gains resulting from the sale of collectibles such as artwork, rugs, antiques, stamps and most coins are taxed at a maximum rate of 28%.

EXAMPLE I:5-54 ▶ Danny, whose tax rate is 33%, purchased Bowling common stock and antique chairs three years ago for investment. He sells the assets during the current year and has a gain of $8,000 on the sale of the stock and $10,000 on the sale of the antique chairs. His NLTCG is $18,000, and his NCG is $18,000. His ANCG is $8,000 since $10,000 of the NCG is a collectibles gain. His tax on the capital gains is $4,000 [(15% × $8,000) + (28% × $10,000)]. ◀

SELF-STUDY QUESTION

Eliza, who is single, has taxable income of $60,000 including a $1,200 LTCG due to the sale of her baseball card collection. Does she receive preferential tax treatment?

ANSWER

No. Her marginal tax rate is 25% which is less than the maximum 28% rate that applies to collectibles gain. If her taxable income is $200,000, she saves $60 [(33% − 28%)($1,200)].

Sec. 1202 Gain. Sec. 1202 provides that noncorporate taxpayers may exclude a portion of the gain resulting from the sale or exchange of qualified small business stock (QSBS) issued after August 10, 1993, if the stock is held for more than five years. The exclusion depends on when the stock was acquired, as follows:

Date QSBS Acquired	*Exclusion Percentage*
Prior to February 18, 2009	50%
February 18, 2009–September 27, 2010	75%
September 28, 2010–December 31, 2014	100%

[38] Sec. 1(h)(4).

HISTORICAL NOTE

The Tax Relief, Unemployment Insurance Reauthorization, and Job Creation Act of 2010 increased the exclusion to 100% for qualified small business stock acquired after September 27, 2010, and before January 1, 2012. The acquisition period has been extended to before January 1, 2015.

Since the QSBS must be held for five years, it will be a few years before the 100% exclusion will take effect. A corporation may have QSBS only if the corporation is a C corporation and at least 80% of the value of its assets must be used in the active conduct of one or more qualified trades or businesses.[39]

If the excluded gain on QSBS is either 50% or 75%, the remaining gain is generally taxed at a maximum rate of 28%. However, the amount of any gain eligible for the exclusion may not exceed the greater of $10,000,000 or ten times the aggregate basis of the qualified stock. Thus, if gain on the sale of QSBS is $11.4 million and $5 million of the gain is excluded, $5 million of the gain is taxed at 28% and the remaining $1.4 million gain is taxed at 15% or 20%.

EXAMPLE I:5-55 ▶ Raef purchased $200,000 of newly issued Monona common stock on October 1, 2008. On December 15, 2015, he sells the stock for $4 million, resulting in a $3.8 million gain. He excludes $1.9 million of the gain, and the remaining $1.9 million of gain is Sec. 1202 gain taxed at 28%. Alternatively, if Raef purchased the Monona stock on July 11, 2010 and sold it in 2016, he could exclude $2.85 million ($3.8 × 0.75) of the gain. ◀

EXAMPLE I:5-56 ▶ Matthew, whose tax rate is 33%, has the following capital gains in 2015:

STCG	$10,000
LTCG (artwork)	12,000
LTCG (stock of AT&T)	17,000
LTCG (acquired in 2006)	200,000

Matthew may exclude $100,000 of the $200,000 Sec. 1202 gain. His NCG is $129,000 ($12,000 + $17,000 + $100,000). His ANCG is $17,000. The increase in his tax is $37,210 [33%($10,000) + 28%($12,000) + 15%($17,000) + 28%($100,000)]. ◀

ADDITIONAL COMMENT

If Raef's gain in Example I:5-55 is $12 million, he excludes $5 million, $5 million of the gain is taxed at 28%, and $2 million is taxed at 20%, given that Raef's tax rate would probably be 39.6%.

CAPITAL LOSSES

To have a capital loss, one must sell or exchange the capital asset for an amount less than its adjusted basis. As in the case of capital gains, the one-year period is used to determine whether the capital loss is short-term or long-term.

Net Short-Term Capital Loss. If total STCLs exceed total STCGs for the tax year, the excess is defined as a net short-term capital loss (NSTCL). As indicated above, the NSTCL is first offset against any NLTCG to determine net capital gain. If NSTCL exceeds NLTCG, the capital loss may be offset, on a dollar-for-dollar basis, against a noncorporate taxpayer's ordinary income for amounts up to $3,000 in any one year.[40]

EXAMPLE I:5-57 ▶ Bob has gross income of $60,000 before considering capital gains and losses. If Bob has a NLTCG of $10,000 and a NSTCL of $15,000, he has $5,000 of NSTCL in excess of NLTCG and may deduct $3,000 of the losses from gross income. Assuming no other deductions for AGI, Bob's AGI is $57,000 ($60,000 − $3,000). ◀

ADDITIONAL COMMENT

A husband and wife filing a joint return may use capital losses carried forward from years when they were single. Also, a divorced couple may use capital losses carried forward from a joint return year to their single returns.

In the above example, $10,000 of Bob's NSTCL is used to offset the $10,000 of NLTCG, and $3,000 of the NSTCL is used to reduce ordinary income. However, $2,000 of the loss is not used. This net capital loss is carried forward for an indefinite number of years.[41] The loss retains its original character and will be treated as a STCL occurring in the subsequent year. If a taxpayer dies with an unused capital loss carryover, it expires.

EXAMPLE I:5-58 ▶ Last year, Milt had a NSTCL of $8,000 and a NLTCG of $2,600. The netting of short-term and long-term gains and losses resulted in a $5,400 excess of NSTCL over NLTCG, and $3,000 of this amount was offset against ordinary income. Milt's NSTCL carryforward is $2,400. During the current year he sells a capital asset and generates a STCG of $800. His NSTCL is $1,600 ($2,400 − $800), and the loss is offset against $1,600 of ordinary income. ◀

Net Long-Term Capital Loss. If total LTCLs for the tax year exceed total LTCGs for the year, the excess is defined as net long-term capital loss (NLTCL). If there is both a NSTCG and a NLTCL, the NLTCL is initially offset against the NSTCG on a dollar-for-dollar basis. If the NLTCL exceeds the NSTCG, the excess is offset against ordinary income on a dollar-for-dollar basis up to $3,000 per year.

---

[39] Sec. 1202.

[40] Sec. 1211(b). A $1,500 limitation applies to a married individual filing a separate return.

[41] Sec. 1212(b) and Reg. Sec. 1.1212-1(b).

EXAMPLE I:5-59 ▶ In the current year, Gordon has a NLTCL of $9,000 and a NSTCG of $2,000. He must use $2,000 of the NLTCL to offset the $2,000 NSTCG, and then use $3,000 of the $7,000 ($9,000 − $2,000) NLTCL to offset $3,000 of ordinary income. Gordon's carryforward of NLTCL is $4,000 [$9,000 − ($2,000 + $3,000)]. This amount is treated as a LTCL in subsequent years. ◀

If an individual has both NSTCL and NLTCL, the NSTCL is offset against ordinary income first, regardless of when the transactions occur during the year.

EXAMPLE I:5-60 ▶ In the current year, Beth has a NSTCL of $2,800 and a NLTCL of $2,000. The entire NSTCL is offset initially against $2,800 of ordinary income. Because capital losses may offset only $3,000 of ordinary income, $200 of NLTCL is used to offset $200 ($3,000 − $2,800) of ordinary income. The NLTCL carryover to the next year is $1,800 ($2,000 − $200). ◀

TAX STRATEGY TIP

Taxpayers who have realized capital gains during the tax year should consider selling securities with a loss during the same year. The losses can be offset against the gains and tax savings result.

Capital Losses Applied to Capital Gains by Groups. Taxpayers separate their LTCGs and LTCLs into three tax rate groups: (1) 28% group, (2) 25% group, and (3) the 15% or 20% group. The 28% group includes capital gains and losses when the capital asset is a collectible held more than one year and part of the gain from the sale of QSBS held for more than five years. The 25% group consists of unrecaptured Sec. 1250 gain discussed in Chapter I:13, and there are no losses for this group. The 15% or 20% group includes capital gains and losses when the holding period is more than one year and the capital asset is not a collectible or Sec. 1202 small business stock.

When a taxpayer has NSTCL and NLTCG, the NSTCL is first offset against NLTCG from the 28% group, then the 25% group, and finally the 15% or 20% group. This treatment of NSTCL is favorable for taxpayers. Note that a taxpayer could have NLTCLs in one group, except the 25% group, and NLTCGs in another group. A net loss from the 28% group is first offset against gains in the 25% group then net gains in the 15% or 20% group. A net loss from the 15% or 20% group is first offset against net gains in the 28% group and then gains in the 25% group.[42]

EXAMPLE I:5-61 ▶ Leroy, whose tax rate is 33%, has NSTCL of $20,000, a $25,000 LTCG from the sale of a rare stamp held 16 months and an $18,000 LTCG from the sale of stock held for three years. The $20,000 NSTCL is offset against $20,000 of the collectibles gain in the 28% group. Leroy's NCG is $23,000 and his ANCG is $18,000. Leroy's tax liability increases by $4,100 [($5,000 × 28%) + ($18,000 × 15%)]. ◀

EXAMPLE I:5-62 ▶ Elizabeth, whose tax rate is 33%, has a $32,000 LTCL from the sale of stock held for four years and the following capital gains:

NSTCG	$40,000
LTCG from sale of collectible	$30,000
LTCG in the 25% group (unrecaptured Sec. 1250 gain)	$10,000

The $32,000 LTCL is offset first against $30,000 of the LTCG in the 28% group (collectibles) and then $2,000 against the unrecaptured Sec. 1250 gain. Her NLTCG is $8,000 taxed at 25% while her $40,000 NSTCG is taxed at her ordinary income rate of 33%. ◀

ADDITIONAL COMMENT

If Elizabeth in Example I:5-62 also had a $9,000 LTCG from the sale of stock held for two years, she would only be able to offset $23,000 of the LTCG in the 28% group.

STOP & THINK

Question: Srinija has a salary of $100,000. If she sells a non-personal use asset during the year and has a $40,000 loss, why is it important that the asset not be a capital asset?

Solution: Only $3,000 of a $40,000 capital loss is used as a deduction to reduce her gross income each year. Her AGI is $97,000 if the asset is a capital asset, and she has a $37,000 capital loss carryforward. All of the $40,000 loss is used to reduce her gross income if the asset is not a capital asset and her AGI is $60,000. It is possible that Srinija might not care whether or not the asset is a capital asset if she has capital gains that could be reduced by capital losses. If the asset is a personal-use asset, the loss is not deductible regardless of whether or not it is a capital asset.

[42] Notice 97-59, I.R.B. 1997-45.

KEY POINT

The lower rates made taxpayers more interested in having capital gain income instead of ordinary income. Investors preferences for growth stocks as opposed to stocks with high dividends increased.

LEGISLATIVE UPDATE

The lower rates on long-term capital gains and qualified dividends were scheduled to expire after December 31, 2012 under the so-called sunset provisions. These provisions would have increased maximum rates on long-term capital gains to 20% and subject dividends to ordinary income rates. Instead, only noncorporate taxpayers with a tax rate of 39.6% experienced an increase to 20%.

Tax Treatment for Net Capital Gain and Qualified Dividends. Congress eliminated preferential tax rates on NCG in 1986 by making the maximum ordinary income rate equal to the rate on net capital gains at 28%. However, this equality was short-lived as Congress, in 1991, increased the maximum ordinary income rate to 31% but left the NCG rate at 28%.[43] This newly-created preferential treatment for NCG's only applied to taxpayers whose tax rate exceeded 28%. The change in 1997 to rates as low as 10% benefited all noncorporate taxpayers if they held the capital asset for more than one year.

Legislation in 2003 which reduced the tax rate on qualified dividends to 5% (zero after 2007) and 15% as of January 1, 2003 dramatically changed investor preferences.[44] The current rate on qualified dividends is zero for a taxpayer with a regular tax rate of 15% or less, and 15% for a taxpayer with a regular tax rate greater than 15% but less than 39.6%. The rate is 20% when the marginal tax rate is 39.6%. This significant reduction of tax rates for dividend income has resulted in an increased interest in stocks with high dividends.

Taxpayers who own mutual funds must recognize their share of capital gains even if no distributions are received. Many mutual fund shareholders reinvest their distributions instead of withdrawing assets from the mutual fund. Mutual funds must classify the gains as short-term or long-term, and long-term gains will need to be separated by rate groups. When shareholders of a mutual fund recognize their share of capital gains when no distribution is actually received, the basis for their shares is increased.

EXAMPLE I:5-63 ▶ Eunice, whose tax rate is 35%, is a shareholder of Canyon Mutual Fund. The basis for her shares is $23,000. At the end of the current year, she received a statement from Canyon indicating her share of the following: qualified dividend income, $200; STCG, $300; 28-percent rate gain, $1,000; and ANCG of $1,500. The increase in her taxes as a result of her ownership of the mutual shares is $640 [($200 × 15%) + ($300 × 35%) + ($1,000 × 28%) + ($1,500 × 15%)]. The basis for her shares of Canyon Mutual Fund is increased to $26,000. ◀

ADDITIONAL COMMENT

Prior to 2003, noncorporate taxpayers preferred to have LTCG instead of dividend income.

The 3.8% Net Investment Income Tax (NIIT). The Affordable Care Act, which requires most U.S. citizens and legal residents to have health insurance, added a new medicare tax on certain taxpayers' net investment income. Investment income includes interest, dividends, NSTCG, NLTCG, rental, and royalty income. Starting in 2013, individuals are subject to a 3.8% surtax on the lesser of net investment income (NII) or the excess of modified AGI (MAGI) over a certain threshold amount.

MAGI is the sum of AGI plus the net foreign earned income excluded, and NII is gross investment income less allocable investment expenses. The threshold amount is $200,000 for individuals (single or head of household) or $250,000 for married couples (and surviving spouse). The threshold amounts are not indexed for inflation.

EXAMPLE I:5-64 ▶ The Robinsons file a joint return in 2015 with $325,000 of MAGI which includes $100,000 of net investment income. They must pay the new 3.8% medicare tax on $75,000 (net investment income or $325,000 less $250,000 threshold). ◀

EXAMPLE I:5-65 ▶ Pablo is single and a dentist with MAGI of $600,000 and taxable income of $430,000. MAGI includes LTCG of $220,000 from sale of Google stock and qualified dividend income of $60,000. Pablo's NIIT is $10,640 (3.8% × $280,000). Because his taxable income is more than $413,200 his income tax rate on the LTCG and dividend income is 20%, however, his total tax rate is 23.8% after considering the new medicare tax. ◀

ADDITIONAL COMMENT

Estates and certain trusts may be required to pay the new 3.8% medicare tax on NII.

TAX TREATMENT OF CAPITAL GAINS AND LOSSES: CORPORATE TAXPAYERS

OBJECTIVE 5

Understand how capital gains are taxed for corporate taxpayers

Most topics covered in this chapter concerning capital gains and losses, including the classification of an asset as a capital asset, rules for determining holding periods, and the procedure for offsetting capital losses against capital gains, apply to both corporate and noncorporate taxpayers. However, a major difference is that the lower tax rates of zero, 15%,

[43] For years prior to 1990, a myriad of rules have applied. Prior to 1987, noncorporate taxpayers received a deduction from gross income equal to 60% of the taxpayer's net capital gain. For years 1987–1990, net capital gains were subject to tax at ordinary income rates.

[44] Sec. 1(h)(11).

20%, 25%, and 28% on net capital gain for noncorporate taxpayers do not apply to corporations. A second significant difference relates to the treatment of capital losses: Unlike the noncorporate taxpayer who may deduct up to $3,000 of capital losses from ordinary income, corporations may offset capital losses only against capital gains. Corporate taxpayers may carry capital losses back to each of the three preceding tax years (the earliest of the three tax years first and then to the next two years) and forward for five years to offset capital gains in such years. When a corporate taxpayer carries a loss back to a preceding year or forward to a following year, the loss is treated as a STCL.[45]

EXAMPLE I:5-66 ▶ The Peach Corporation has income from operations of $200,000, a NSTCG of $40,000, and a NLTCL of $56,000 during the current year. The $40,000 NSTCG is offset by $40,000 NLTCL. The remaining $16,000 of NSTCL may not be offset against the $200,000 of other income but may be carried back three years and then forward five years to offset capital gains arising in these years. If Peach has NLTCG and/or NSTCG in the previous three years, a refund of taxes paid during those years will be received during the current year. ◀

HISTORICAL NOTE

The House of Representatives proposed a reduction in corporate net capital gains in 1997, but the proposal was rejected.

TYPICAL MISCONCEPTION

Because the carryover for net operating losses is 20 years, it is sometimes erroneously assumed that the carryover for corporate capital losses is also 20 years instead of five years.

Maximum Rate on Net Capital Gain for Corporations. Unlike individual taxpayers, corporations do not receive any preferential rate reductions for net capital gains. Corporations apply a maximum rate of 35% to the corporation's net capital gain.[46] However, given the present tax rates for corporations, the existence of the 35% alternative rate for net capital gain has no benefit. A corporation subject to a rate of 39% because taxable income is greater than $100,000 but not more than $335,000 does not use the maximum 35% rate. In essence, therefore, corporations are taxed on capital gains at the same rates for ordinary income.

Topic Review I:5-2 summarizes the principal differences in the tax treatment of capital gains and losses for corporate and noncorporate taxpayers.

TOPIC REVIEW I:5-2

Comparison of Corporate and Noncorporate Taxpayers: Capital Gains and Losses

	Noncorporate	Corporate
A statutory maximum tax rate applicable to net capital gain	Yes, 0%, 15%, 20%, 25%, and 28%	Yes, but rate is 35%
Offset of net capital losses against ordinary income	Yes, up to $3,000	No
Carryback of capital losses	No	Yes, three years as STCLs
Carryforward of capital losses	Yes, indefinitely	Yes, five years as STCLs

Sale or Exchange

OBJECTIVE 6

Recognize when a sale or exchange has occurred

As previously indicated, capital gains and losses result from the sale or exchange of capital assets. Although Sec. 1222 does not define a sale or an exchange, a **sale** is generally considered to be a transaction where one receives cash or the equivalent of cash, including the assumption of one's debt. An **exchange** is a transaction where one receives a reciprocal transfer of property, as distinguished from a transaction where one receives only cash or a cash equivalent.[47]

EXAMPLE I:5-67 ▶ Two years ago, Bart acquired 100 shares of Alaska Corporation common stock for $12,000 to hold as an investment. Bart sells 50 shares of the stock to Sandy for $10,000 and transfers the other 50 shares to Gail in exchange for land that has a $10,000 FMV. In each transaction, Bart realizes a $4,000 ($10,000 − $6,000) LTCG due to the sale or exchange of a capital asset. The transfer to Sandy qualifies as a sale, and the transfer to Gail qualifies as an exchange. ◀

To qualify as a sale or exchange, the transaction must be bona fide. Transactions between related parties such as family members are closely scrutinized. For example, a sale of property on credit to a relative may be a disguised gift if there is no intention of collecting the debt. If this is the case, a subsequent bad debt deduction due to the debt's

[45] Sec. 1212(a).

[46] Sec. 1201.

[47] Reg. Sec. 1.1002-1(d).

worthlessness is disallowed. In some instances, the Code specifically states that a particular transaction or event either qualifies or does not qualify for sale or exchange treatment. For example, the holder of an option who fails to exercise such an option treats the lapse of the option as a sale or exchange.[48] However, abandonment of property is generally not deemed to be a sale or exchange.[49]

WORTHLESS SECURITIES

ADDITIONAL COMMENT

The worthlessness of a security is treated as a sale or exchange so that the taxpayer is not forced to arrange for someone to buy the security for a token amount.

If a security that is a capital asset becomes worthless during the year, Sec. 165(g)(1) specifies that any loss is treated as a loss from the sale or exchange of a capital asset on the last day of the tax year. The term includes stock, a stock option, and "a bond, debenture, note or certificate, or other evidence of indebtedness, issued by a corporation or by a government or political division thereof, with interest coupons or in registered form."[50] Whether a security has become worthless during the year is a question of fact, and the taxpayer has the burden of proof to show evidence of worthlessness.[51]

EXAMPLE I:5-68 ▶ Charlotte purchased $40,000 of bonds issued by the Jet Corporation in March 2014. In February 2015, Jet is declared bankrupt, and its bonds are worthless. Charlotte has a LTCL of $40,000 because the bonds have become worthless and are deemed to have been sold on the last day of 2015. The more-than-one-year holding period requirement is satisfied by the last day of 2015. ◀

REAL-WORLD EXAMPLE

A corporation owned 76% of the stock of another company. The corporation later acquired the remaining 24% of the stock, allegedly for the purpose of avoiding interference by minority shareholders. Later the corporation claimed an ordinary loss on the worthless stock because it owned at least 80% of the stock. The Court treated the loss as a capital loss because the acquisition of the remaining stock was without a business purpose. *Hunter Mfg. Co.*, 21 T.C. 424 (1953).

Securities in Affiliated Corporations. If the security that becomes worthless is a security in a domestic affiliated corporation owned by a corporate taxpayer, the worthless security is not considered a capital asset. Thus, a corporate taxpayer's loss due to owning worthless securities in an affiliated corporation is treated as an ordinary loss. Because capital losses are of only limited benefit to corporate taxpayers, the classification of the loss as ordinary is preferable.

To qualify as an affiliated corporation, the parent corporation must own at least 80% of the voting power of all classes of stock and at least 80% of each class of nonvoting stock. The subsidiary corporation must be engaged in the active conduct of an operating business as opposed to being a passive investment company (i.e., more than 90% of its aggregate gross receipts must be from sources other than passive types of income such as royalties, dividends, and interest).[52]

EXAMPLE I:5-69 ▶ Ace Corporation owns 80% of all classes of stock issued by the same Jet Corporation described in Example I:5-68. Jet Corporation is actively engaged in an operating business and has no income from passive investments before being declared bankrupt. Ace's loss from its worthless stock investment is an ordinary loss instead of a capital loss because Jet is an affiliated corporation. Ace owns at least 80% of all classes of Jet's stock and more than 90% of Jet's gross receipts are from sources other than passive types of income. ◀

RETIREMENT OF DEBT INSTRUMENTS

Generally, the collection of a debt is not a sale or an exchange. However, if a debt instrument is retired, amounts received by the holder are treated as being received in an exchange.[53] Debt instruments include bonds, debentures, notes, certificates, and other evidences of indebtedness.

EXAMPLE I:5-70 ▶ In 2010 the Rocket Corporation issued $50,000 of five-year, interest-bearing bonds that were purchased by Elaine as an investment for $49,800. Elaine receives $50,000 at maturity in 2015. Retirement of the debt instrument is an exchange, and the $200 gain is a LTCG.[54] ◀

Although Congress has provided that retirements of debt instruments are treated as exchanges, Congress is not willing to allow taxpayers to convert large amounts of potential ordinary interest income into capital gain by purchasing debt instruments at a substantial

---

48 Sec. 1234(b) and Reg. Sec. 1.1234-1(b).

49 Reg. Secs. 1.165-2 and 1.167(a)-8.

50 Sec. 165(g)(2).

51 *Minnie K. Young v. CIR*, 28 AFTR 365, 41-2 USTC ¶9744 (2nd Cir., 1941).

52 Sec. 165(g)(3).

53 Sec. 1271(a).

54 If Rocket Corporation issued the bonds with the intention of calling the bonds before maturity, Sec. 1271(a)(2) treats the gain as ordinary income.

discount. As illustrated in Example I:5-70, a small amount of bond discount is sometimes converted to capital gain. However, if the discount is large enough to be classified as original issue discount, the discount must be amortized and included in gross income for each day the debt instrument is held for both cash and accrual method taxpayers. Original issue discount (OID) is defined as "the excess (if any) of the stated redemption price at maturity over the issue price."[55]

EXAMPLE I:5-71 ▶ On January 1, 2015, Connie purchases $100,000 of the City Corporation's newly issued bonds for $85,000. The bonds mature in 20 years. In 2015 and in subsequent years Connie must annually recognize as interest income a portion of the $15,000 of OID. ◀

The OID is considered to be zero if the amount of discount "is less than ¼ of 1% of the stated redemption price at maturity, multiplied by the number of complete years to maturity."[56] In Example I:5-70, the $200 discount is not OID because it is less than $625 (0.0025 × $50,000 × 5 years). If Connie pays more than $95,000 for the bonds in Example I:5-71, the OID is zero.

ADDITIONAL COMMENT

Two different types of bonds are sold at a discount: original issue discount (OID) bonds and market discount bonds. OID bonds are issued at a discount, whereas market discount bonds have market discount resulting from a rise in interest rates after the issuance of the bonds.

Original Issue Discount. Instead of spreading the OID ratably over the life of the bond, amortization of the discount is based on an interest amortization method called the **constant interest rate method.** The total amount of interest income is determined by multiplying the interest yield to maturity by the adjusted issue price. With this method of amortizing discount, the amount of OID amortized increases for each year the bond is held. In the above example, Connie recognizes a larger amount of interest income in 2016 than in 2015 due to amortization of the OID.

The daily portion of the OID for any accrual period is "determined by allocating to each day in any accrual period its ratable portion to the increase during such accrual period in the adjusted issue price of the debt instrument."[57] The increase in the adjusted issue price for any accrual period is shown below.

$$\text{increase in the adjusted issue price} = \left[\text{Adjusted issue price at the begining of the accrual period} \times \text{Yield to maturity}\right] - \text{Interest payments during the accrual period}$$

EXAMPLE I:5-72 ▶ On June 30, 2015, Fred purchases a 10%, $10,000 corporate bond for $9,264. The bond is issued on June 30, 2015, and matures in five years. Interest is paid semiannually, and the effective yield to maturity is 12% compounded semiannually. In 2015, Fred recognizes interest income of $556, as illustrated in Table I:5-1. The adjusted issue price as of January 1, 2016, is $9,320. This is the sum of the issue price plus any amounts of OID includible in the income of any holder since the date of issue. ◀

KEY POINT

The owner of an OID bond is normally required to accrue interest income each year regardless of the owner's method of accounting.

If a debt instrument is sold or exchanged before maturity, part of the OID is included in the seller's income. The amount to be included depends on the number of days the debt instrument is owned by the seller within the accrual period.

EXAMPLE I:5-73 ▶ Assume the same facts as in the above example, except that Fred sells the corporate bond to Carolyn on February 24, 2018 (the 55th day in the accrual period). Fred must include $23 [(55 days ÷ 181 days in the accrual period) × $75] of accrued interest for the period of January 1, 2018, to February 24, 2018, in income for 2018. Fred's basis for the bond increases by $23. Thus, his basis for determining a gain or loss is $9,603 ($9,580 + $23). ◀

Market Discount Bonds Purchased After April 30, 1993. The sale or exchange of a market discount bond may result in part or all of the gain being classified as ordinary

[55] Sec. 1273(a)(1).
[56] Sec. 1273(a)(3).
[57] Sec. 1272(a)(3).

▼ **TABLE I:5-1**
Computation for Interest Income in Examples I:5-72 and I:5-73

	Interest Received (1)	Amortization of Original Issue Discount (2)	Interest Income (3) = (1) + (2)	Taxpayer's Basis for the Bond
6-30-15				$ 9,264
12-31-15	$ 500	$ 56[a]	$ 556	9,320[b]
6-30-16	500	59	559	9,379
12-31-16	500	63	563	9,442
6-30-17	500	67	567	9,509
12-31-17	500	71	571	9,580
6-30-18	500	75	575	9,655
12-31-18	500	79	579	9,734
6-30-19	500	84	584	9,818
12-31-19	500	89	589	9,907
6-30-20	500	93[c]	593	10,000
	$5,000	$736	$5,736	

[a]6% × $9,264 − $500 = $56.
[b]$9,264 + $56 = $9,320.
[c]This figure is adjusted for rounding.

income.[58] A market discount bond is a bond that is acquired in the bond market at a discount. Market discount is the excess of the stated redemption price of the bond at maturity over the taxpayer's basis for such bond immediately after it is acquired.

EXAMPLE I:5-74 ▶ On January 1, Stephano purchased $100,000 of 8%, 20-year bonds for $82,000. The bonds were issued at par by the Solar Corporation two years ago on January 1. The bonds are market discount bonds. ◀

Similar to OID, there is a de minimis rule for determining market discount. Market discount is zero if the discount is less than ¼ of 1% of the stated redemption price of the bond at maturity multiplied by the number of complete years to maturity.[59] If Stephano paid $95,500 or more for the Solar Corporation bonds in Example I:5-74, the bonds would not be market discount bonds.[60]

Gain realized on disposition of the market discount bond is ordinary income to the extent of the accrued market discount.[61] The ratable accrual method (straight line method computed on a daily basis) is used to determine the amount of the accrued market discount recognized as ordinary income.[62] The market discount is allocated on the basis of the number of days the taxpayer held the bond relative to the number of days between the acquisition date and maturity date.

EXAMPLE I:5-75 ▶ Assume the same facts as in the above example except Stephano sells the bonds to Kimberly three years later for $86,400 on January 1st. $3,000 (3⁄18 × $18,000) of the $4,400 ($86,400 − $82,000) gain is ordinary income and the remaining gain is LTCG. If Stephano sold the bond for more than $82,000 but less than $85,000, all of the gain is ordinary income. The entire $18,000 gain is ordinary income if the bond is held to maturity. ◀

[58] Ordinary income treatment for accrued market discount does not apply to owners of taxable market discount bonds issued on or before July 18, 1984, if the bonds were acquired before May 1, 1993. Owners of tax-exempt bonds are not required to accrue market discount if the bonds were acquired before May 1, 1993 (regardless of the issue date).

[59] Sec. 1278(a)(2)(C).

[60] $100,000 × .25% × 18 years = $4,500.

[61] Sec. 1276(a)(1).

[62] Sec. 1276(b)(1). A taxpayer may elect to use the constant interest rate method (see Sec. 1276(b)(2)).

OPTIONS

The owner of an option to buy property may sell the option, exercise the option, or allow the option to expire. If the option is exercised, the amount paid for the option is added to the purchase price of the property acquired.[63]

EXAMPLE I:5-76 ▶ On August 5, 2015, Len pays $600 for an option to acquire 100 shares of Hill Corporation common stock for $80 per share at any time before December 20, 2015. Len exercises the option on November 15, 2015, and pays $8,000 for the stock. Len's basis for the 100 shares of Hill is $8,600 ($8,000 + $600), and the stock's holding period begins on November 15, 2015. ◀

ADDITIONAL COMMENT

An option is a contract in which the owner of property agrees with a potential buyer that the potential buyer has the right to buy the property at a fixed price within a certain period of time.

When an option is sold or allowed to expire, a sale or exchange has occurred and gain or loss is therefore recognized.[64] The character of the underlying property determines whether the gain or loss from the sale or expiration of the option is capital or ordinary in nature. If the optioned property is a capital asset, the option is treated as a capital asset and capital gain or loss is recognized on the sale or exchange.

EXAMPLE I:5-77 ▶ On March 2, 2015, Holly pays $270 for an option to acquire 100 shares of Arkansas Corporation stock for $30 per share at any time before December 10, 2015. As a result of an increase in the market value of the Arkansas stock, the market price of the option increases and Holly sells the option for $600 on August 2, 2015. Because the Arkansas stock is a capital asset in the hands of Holly, the option is a capital asset and she must recognize a STCG of $330 ($600 − $270). ◀

EXAMPLE I:5-78 ▶ On October 12, 2014, Mary paid $400 for an option to acquire 100 shares of Portland Corporation stock for $50 per share at any time before February 19, 2015. The price never exceeds $50 before February 19, 2015, and Mary does not exercise the option. Because the option expires, Mary recognizes a STCL of $400 in 2015. ◀

SELF-STUDY QUESTION

Marc writes a call option on stock owned by him and receives $800 on November 1, Y2. The value of the stock declines and the option is allowed to expire on February 15, Y3. When does Marc recognize the $800 gain?

ANSWER

Marc recognizes the STCG in Y3 when the transaction is completed.

Transactions in which taxpayers purchase or write options to buy (calls) are quite common today. An investor who anticipates that the market value of a stock or security (e.g., common stock) will increase during the next few months may purchase a call option instead of actually buying the stock. As indicated above, the tax treatment for the option depends on whether the call is exercised, sold, or expires. Someone, however, must be willing to write a call on the stock. Typically an owner of the same stock will write a call option. The writer of the call receives a payment for granting the right to purchase the stock at a fixed price within a given period of time.

If the call is exercised, the writer of the call adds the amount received for the call to the sales price to determine the amount realized.[65] If the call is not exercised within the given time period and thus expires, the writer retains the amount received for the option and recognizes a STCG in the year the call expires. The gain is short-term even if the option is written and held for more than a year.

EXAMPLE I:5-79 ▶ Sam owns 100 shares of Madison Corporation common stock, which he purchased on May 1, 2008, for $4,000. On November 8, 2015, Sam writes a call that gives Joan, an investor, the option to purchase Sam's 100 shares of Madison stock at $60 per share any time before April 19, 2016. The current market price of Madison stock is $56 per share, and Sam receives $520 for writing the call. If the call is exercised, Sam has a LTCG of $2,520 [($6,000 + $520) − $4,000] in the year the call is exercised. If the call is not exercised and expires on April 19, 2016, Sam must recognize a STCG of $520 in 2016. ◀

EXAMPLE I:5-80 ▶ Assume the same facts as in Example I:5-79, and consider the tax treatment for Joan, the holder of the call. If Joan exercises the call, the basis of the stock is $6,520 ($6,000 + $520). If she does not exercise the call, a STCL of $520 is recognized. If Joan sells the call, the amount received is compared with her basis in the call ($520) to compute Joan's gain or loss. ◀

KEY POINT

Note that Sam in Example I:5-79 did not have to recognize gross income when he received $520 on November 8.

[63] Rev. Rul. 58-234, 1958-1 C.B. 279.
[64] Sec. 1234(a).
[65] Rev. Rul. 58-234, 1958-1 C.B. 279.

PATENTS

To encourage technological progress and to clarify whether a transfer of rights to a patent is capital gain or ordinary income, Congress created Sec. 1235, which allows the holder of a patent to treat the gain resulting from the transfer of all substantial rights in a patent as LTCG. This tax treatment is more favorable than that accorded to producers of artistic and literary works, who receive ordinary rather than capital gain from the sale of their works.

KEY POINT

A copyright held by a taxpayer whose personal efforts created it is omitted from the definition of a capital asset. However, a patent can be considered a capital asset. In effect, the tax law could be said to favor individuals whose efforts lead to scientific or technological advancement.

Requirements for Capital Gain Treatment. Section 1235 provides that the transfer of all substantial rights to a patent by the holder of the patent is treated as a sale or exchange of a capital asset that has been held long-term. Thus, LTCG is recognized on the transfer of a patent regardless of its holding period or the character of the asset. Favorable long-term capital gain treatment applies even if the transferor of the patent receives periodic payments contingent on the productivity, use, or disposition of the property transferred.[66]

EXAMPLE I:5-81 ▶ Clay invents a small utensil used to peel shrimp. He has a patent on the utensil and transfers all rights to the patent to a manufacturing company. Clay receives $100,000 plus 40 cents per utensil sold. Because Sec. 1235 applies, the total of the lump-sum payment and the royalty payments received less his cost basis for the patent is recognized as a LTCG. ◀

Substantial Rights. The principal requirement in Sec. 1235 is that the holder must transfer all substantial rights to the patent. The Regulations state that the circumstances of the whole transaction should be considered in determining whether all substantial rights to a patent have been transferred.[67] All substantial rights have not been transferred if the patent rights of the purchaser are limited geographically within the country of issuance or the rights are for a period less than a patent's remaining life.

EXAMPLE I:5-82 ▶ Bruce, an inventor, transfers one of his U.S. patents on a manufacturing process to a manufacturer located in Utah. The manufacturer's rights to use the patent are limited to the state of Utah. Because the use of the patent is limited to a geographical area, all substantial rights have not been transferred, and Sec. 1235 does not apply. Payments received for the use of the patent are royalties and taxed as ordinary income. ◀

Definition of a Holder. Long-term capital gain treatment applies only to a holder of the patent rights. For purposes of Sec. 1235, a holder is an individual whose efforts created the property or an individual who acquires the patent rights from the creator for valuable consideration before the property covered by the patent is placed in service or used. Furthermore, the acquiring individual may not be related to the creator or be the creator's employer.

Section 1235 may not be used by corporate taxpayers because corporations are not permitted to be classified as holders. Although a partnership is not permitted to be a holder, individual partners may qualify as holders to the extent of the partner's interest in the patent owned by the partnership.

EXAMPLE I:5-83 ▶ Joy purchases a patent from Martin, whose efforts created the patent. The purchase occurs before the property is placed in service or used. Joy and Martin are unrelated individuals, and Joy is not Martin's employer. For purposes of Sec. 1235, both Joy and Martin qualify as holders. ◀

ADDITIONAL COMMENT

The scope of Sec. 1253 is very broad. A franchise "includes an agreement which gives one of the parties to the agreement the right to distribute, sell, or provide goods, services, or facilities within a specified area."

FRANCHISES, TRADEMARKS, AND TRADE NAMES

Before the enactment of Sec. 1253, significant uncertainty existed as to whether the transfer of a franchise, trademark, or trade name should be treated as a sale or exchange or as a licensing agreement. If the transfer is tantamount to a sale of the property, payments received should be treated by the transferor as a return of capital and capital gain, and the transferee should be required to capitalize and amortize such payments. However, if the

---

[66] Sec. 1235(a).

[67] Reg. Sec. 1.1235-2(b).

transfer represents a licensing agreement, the transferor should recognize ordinary income and the transferee should receive an ordinary deduction for such payments.

REAL-WORLD EXAMPLE

Shaquille O'Neal, a well-known former professional basketball player, has obtained a trademark on his nickname, Shaq. The trademark covers nearly 200 products including athletic shoes, cake decorations, bathroom tissue, bathtub toys, and kites.

Section 1253, which applies to the granting of a franchise, trademark, or trade name, as well as renewals and transfers to third parties, attempts to resolve the uncertainty by stating, "A transfer of a franchise, trademark, or trade name shall not be treated as a sale or exchange of a capital asset if the transferor retains any significant power, right, or continuing interest with respect to the subject matter of the franchise, trademark, or trade name."[68]

Examples of some rights that are to be considered a "significant power, right, or continuing interest"[69] include the right to:

- Disapprove of any assignment.
- Terminate the agreement at will.
- Prescribe standards of quality for products, product services, and facilities.
- Require the exclusive selling or advertising of the transferor's products or services.
- Require the transferee to purchase substantially all of its supplies and equipment from the transferor.

If the transferor does not retain any significant power, right, or continuing interest in the property, the transferor treats the transfer as a sale of the franchise and has the benefits of capital gain treatment. However, any amounts received that are contingent on the productivity, use, or disposition of such property must be treated as ordinary income by the transferor.

EXAMPLE I:5-84 ▶ Rose, who owns a franchise with a basis of $100,000, transfers the franchise to Ruth and retains no significant power, right, or continuing interest. Rose receives a $250,000 down payment when the agreement is signed and annual payments for five years equal to 10% of all sales in excess of $2,000,000. Rose has a capital gain of $150,000 with respect to the initial payment, but all of the payments received during the next five years will be ordinary income because they are contingent payments. ◀

Under Sec. 1253, the transferee may deduct payments that are contingent on the productivity, use, or disposition of such property as business expenses. Generally, other payments are capitalized and amortized over a period of 15 years.[70] In practice, payments received for the transfer of a franchise are generally treated as ordinary income to the transferor and are deductible by the transferee because in most franchise agreements the transferor desires to maintain significant powers, rights, or continuing interests in the franchise operation. Also, in many instances the payments are, in part, predicated on the success of the franchised business and are, therefore, established as contingent payments.

REAL-WORLD EXAMPLE

A taxpayer sold a building with the purchaser paying $500,000 and the lessee of the building paying $60,000 under a separate agreement to cancel the lease. The $60,000 was treated as ordinary income because no "sale or exchange" of the property occurred with respect to the lessee's $60,000 payment. *Gary Gurvey v. U.S.*, 57 AFTR 2d 86-1062, 86-1 USTC ¶9260 (D.C. Ill., 1986).

LEASE CANCELLATION PAYMENTS

A lease arrangement may be terminated before the lease period expires, and a lease cancellation payment may be made as consideration for the other party's agreement to terminate the lease. Either a lessor or a lessee may receive such a payment because the payment is normally made by the person who wants to cancel the lease. The tax treatment may differ significantly depending on which party is the recipient.

Payments Received by Lessor. The Supreme Court has ruled that lease cancellation payments received by a lessor are treated as ordinary income on the basis that the payments represent a substitute for rent.[71] Lease cancellation payments are included in the lessor's income in the year received, even if the lessor uses an accrual method.[72]

Payments Received by Lessee. Payments received by a lessee for canceling a lease are considered amounts received in exchange for the lease.[73] If the lease is a capital asset, any gain or loss is a capital gain or loss.

---

[68] Sec. 1253(a). Section 1253(e) prevents the basic Sec. 1253 rules from applying to the transfer of a professional sports franchise.

[69] Sec. 1253(b)(2).

[70] Sec. 197(a).

[71] *Walter M. Hort v. CIR*, 25 AFTR 1207, 41-1 USTC ¶9354 (USSC, 1941).

[72] *Farrelly-Walsh, Inc.*, 13 B.T.A. 923 (1928).

[73] Sec. 1241.

EXAMPLE I:5-85 ▶ Jim has a three-year lease on a house used as his personal residence. The lessor has an opportunity to sell the house and has agreed to pay $1,000 to Jim to cancel the lease. Assuming that Jim has no basis in the lease, the gain of $1,000 is capital gain because the lease is a capital asset. ◀

HOLDING PERIOD

OBJECTIVE 7

Determine the holding period for an asset when a sale or disposition occurs

The length of time an asset is held before it is disposed of (i.e., the *holding period*) is an important factor in determining whether any gain or loss resulting from the disposition of a capital asset is treated as long-term or short-term. To be classified as a long-term capital gain or loss, the capital asset must be held more than one year.[74] To determine the holding period, the day of acquisition is excluded and the disposal date is included.[75]

If the date of disposition is the same date as the date of acquisition, but a year later, the asset is considered to have been held for only one year. If the property is held for an additional day, the holding period is more than one year.

EXAMPLE I:5-86 ▶ Arnie purchased a capital asset on April 20, 2014, and sells the asset at a gain on April 21, 2015. The gain is classified as a LTCG. If the asset is sold on or before April 20, 2015, the gain is a STCG. ◀

ADDITIONAL COMMENT

When determining the holding period for marketable securities, it is important to use the "trade" dates, not the "settlement" dates.

The fact that all months do not have the same number of days is not a factor in determining the one-year period. Acquisitions made on the last day of any month must be held until the first day of the thirteenth subsequent month in order to have been held for more than one year.

EXAMPLE I:5-87 ▶ Alford sells stock held as an investment and recognizes a gain. If the capital asset was purchased on May 31, 2014, the gain is LTCG if the asset is sold on or after June 1, 2015. If sold on or before May 31, 2015, the gain is STCG and the lower preferential rates do not apply. ◀

ADDITIONAL COMMENT

The Securities and Exchange Commission requires investors who purchase or sell securities to deliver the funds to pay for the securities or deliver the certificates to be sold within three days of when the order is placed.

PROPERTY RECEIVED AS A GIFT

If a person receives property as a gift and uses the donor's basis to determine the gain or loss from a sale or exchange, the donor's holding period is added to the donee's holding period.[76] In other words, the donee's holding period includes the donor's holding period. If, however, the donee's basis is the FMV of the property on the date of the gift, the donee's holding period starts on the day after the date of the gift. This situation occurs when the FMV is less than the donor's basis on the date of the gift and the property is subsequently sold at a loss.

EXAMPLE I:5-88 ▶ Cindy receives a capital asset as a gift from Marc on July 4, 2015, when the asset has a $4,000 FMV. Marc acquired the property on April 12, 2015, for $3,400. If Cindy sells the asset after April 12, 2016, any gain or loss is LTCG or LTCL. Cindy's basis is the donor's cost because the FMV of the property is higher than the donor's basis on the date of the gift. Because Cindy takes Marc's basis, Marc's holding period is included. ◀

EXAMPLE I:5-89 ▶ Roy receives a capital asset as a gift from Diane on September 12, 2015, when the asset has a $6,000 FMV. Diane acquired the asset on July 1, 2014, for $6,500. If the asset is sold at a gain (i.e., for more than $6,500), Roy's holding period starts on July 1, 2014, the date when Diane acquired the property, because the donor's basis of $6,500 is used by Roy to compute the gain. If the asset is sold at a loss (i.e., for less than $6,000), Roy's holding period does not start until the day after the date of the gift, September 13, 2015, because Roy's basis is the $6,000 FMV. The FMV is used to compute the loss because it is less than the donor's basis on the date of the gift. ◀

ADDITIONAL COMMENT

The provision permitting the holding period of property received from a decedent to be deemed to be long-term is a rule of convenience. It is not necessary to try to determine when the decedent actually acquired the property.

PROPERTY RECEIVED FROM A DECEDENT

The holding period of property received from a decedent is always deemed to be long-term. If the person who receives the property from the decedent sells the property within one

[74] Sec. 1222. A six-month holding period was applied to property acquired after June 27, 1984 and before January 1, 1988.

[75] *H. M. Hooper*, 26 B.T.A. 758 (1932), and Rev. Rul. 70-598, 1970-2 C.B. 168.

[76] Sec. 1223(1) and Reg. Sec. 1.1223-1(b).

year after the decedent's death, the property is considered to be held for more than one year regardless of how long the property is actually held.[77]

EXAMPLE I:5-90 ▶ The executor of Paul's estate sells certain securities for $41,000 on September 2, 2015, which were valued in the estate at their FMV of $40,000 on June 5, 2015, the date of Paul's death. The estate has a LTCG of $1,000 because the securities are considered to have been held long-term. ◀

NONTAXABLE EXCHANGES

ADDITIONAL COMMENT

The like-kind exchange rules under Sec. 1031 allow taxpayers to trade certain types of business and investment properties with no tax consequences arising from the exchange. Like-kind exchanges are discussed in Chapter I:12.

In a nontaxable exchange, the basis of the property received is determined by taking into account the basis of the property given in the exchange. If the properties are capital assets or Sec. 1231 assets, the holding period of the property received includes the holding period of the surrendered property.[78] In essence, the holding period of the property given up in a tax-free exchange is tacked on to the holding period of the property received in the exchange.

RECEIPT OF NONTAXABLE STOCK DIVIDENDS AND STOCK RIGHTS

If a shareholder receives nontaxable stock dividends or stock rights, the holding period of the stock received as a dividend or the stock rights received includes the holding period for the stock owned by the shareholder.[79] However, if the stock rights are exercised, the holding period for the stock purchased begins with the date of exercise.

EXAMPLE I:5-91 ▶ As a result of owning Circle Corporation stock acquired three years ago, Paula receives nontaxable stock rights on June 5, 2015. Any gain or loss on the sale of the rights is long-term, regardless of whether any basis is allocated to the rights, because the holding period of the rights includes the holding period of the stock. ◀

EXAMPLE I:5-92 ▶ Assume the same facts as in the example above, except that the stock rights are exercised on August 20, 2015. The holding period for the newly acquired Circle stock begins on the date of exercise. ◀

STOP & THINK

Question: Carter owns 500 shares of Okoboji, Inc. (current market price of $310) with a basis of $101,500 acquired three years ago. In May of the current year, she receives 500 stock rights and exercises those rights that entitle her to purchase 500 shares of Okoboji at $300 per share. The current market price of the stock right is $40 per right. She plans to sell the 500 shares obtained by exercising the stock rights in January when she expects the market price to be $400 per share. Why should she elect to allocate basis to the stock rights?

Solution: If she does not allocate basis, her STCG will be $50,000 ($200,000 − $150,000). If she allocates basis to the stock rights, the basis of the 500 shares obtained when she exercises the rights is $161,600 ($150,000 + $11,600), and her STCG will be $38,400 ($200,000 − $161,600). Note that Carter might benefit by waiting a few months before selling because the gain might then be LTCG. She could sell the original 500 shares and have a LTCG.

JUSTIFICATION FOR PREFERENTIAL TREATMENT OF NET CAPITAL GAINS

Preferential treatment for capital gains was first created by the Revenue Act of 1921, which became effective on January 1, 1922. Despite almost continuous controversy concerning the need for preferential treatment, some form of preferential treatment for capital gains has existed since 1922. The range of controversy concerning the need for preferential tax treatment for capital gains is wide. Some maintain that capital gains do not

[77] Sec. 1223(11).
[78] Sec. 1223(1).
[79] Sec. 1223(5) and Reg. Sec. 1.1223-1(e).

HISTORICAL NOTE

In part the preferential treatment of net capital gains was repealed in the Tax Reform Act of 1986 because Congress believed that the reduction of individual tax rates on such forms of capital income as business profits, interest, dividends, and short-term capital gains eliminated the need for a reduced rate for net capital gains.

represent income and should not be taxed, whereas others maintain that capital gains are no different from any other type of income and should be taxed accordingly.[80] A few of the most common arguments are discussed below.

MOBILITY OF CAPITAL

Without some form of preferential treatment, taxpayers who own appreciated capital assets may be unwilling to sell or exchange the asset if high tax rates exist, despite the presence of more attractive investment opportunities. In essence, the taxpayer may be "locked in" to holding an appreciated capital asset instead of shifting resources to more profitable investments.

EXAMPLE I:5-93 ▶ Carmen owns Missouri Corporation stock with a \$4,000 basis and a \$20,000 FMV. She anticipates that the future after-tax annual return will be 10% on the Missouri stock and 12% on Kansas Corporation stock that has a similar level of risk. Assume her marginal tax rate is 35% (without consideration of favorable capital gain rates). Without preferential treatment of capital gains, Carmen will have to pay a tax of \$5,600 (\$16,000 × 0.35) on the sale of the Missouri stock and will have only \$14,400 (\$20,000 − \$5,600) to invest in the Kansas stock. With a 12% return, she will receive an investment return of only \$1,728 (\$14,400 × 0.12), as compared with \$2,000 (\$20,000 × 0.10) if she maintains the investment in the Missouri stock. ◀

ADDITIONAL COMMENT

According to *The Wall Street Journal,* twelve industrialized nations impose a zero capital gains rate (10-15-07, p. A22).

While the payment of any tax due to the sale of an asset creates somewhat of a "locked-in" effect, the effect can be reduced by lowering the tax rate. The "locked-in" effect is even stronger for older taxpayers if the basis of inherited property is FMV at time of death. A lower tax rate on net capital gain should reduce the taxpayers unwillingness to sell the asset and allow for more mobility of capital. For a brief period in the 1990s, both the top ordinary income rate and the rate on net capital gain were 28%. Today, the top rate on ordinary income is 39.6% and 20% on adjusted net capital gain.

MITIGATION OF THE EFFECTS OF INFLATION AND THE PROGRESSIVE TAX SYSTEM

Because the tax laws do not generally reflect the effect of changes in purchasing power due to inflation, the sale or exchange of a capital asset may produce inequitable results. In fact, taxes may have to be paid even where a transaction results in an inflation-adjusted loss.

EXAMPLE I:5-94 ▶ Beverly purchased a capital asset nine years ago for \$100,000. If the asset is sold today for \$180,000 and the general price level has increased by 100% during the nine-year period, Beverly will have a taxable gain of \$80,000, despite suffering an inflation-adjusted loss of \$20,000 [\$180,000 sale price − (\$100,000 × 200%)]. ◀

ADDITIONAL COMMENT

The American Assembly at Columbia University, in its final report on *Reforming and Simplifying the Federal Tax System* issued in 1985, recommends that capital gains be taxed as ordinary income if they are adjusted for inflation.

With a progressive tax system, the failure to adjust for inflation creates an even greater distortion. However, it should be noted that this distortion applies to all assets, not just capital assets.

LOWERS THE COST OF CAPITAL

By reducing the tax rate on capital gains, investors are more willing to provide businesses with capital and the cost of capital is reduced. A lower cost of capital encourages capital formation to create more jobs and improve our competitive position in the global economy. Reducing the cost of capital is particularly important for the formation and growth of small business.

[80] Walter J. Blum, "A Handy Summary of the Capital Gains Argument," *Taxes—The Tax Magazine,* 35 (April 1957), pp. 247–66.

TAX PLANNING CONSIDERATIONS

OBJECTIVE 8

Describe tax planning opportunities for property transactions

SELECTION OF PROPERTY TO TRANSFER BY GIFT

Many tax reasons exist for making gifts of property, although the donor may incur a gift tax liability if the gift is a taxable gift. For example, taxpayers may give income-producing property to a taxpayer subject to a lower tax rate, or property expected to appreciate in the future may be given away to reduce estate taxes. Individuals may annually give property of $14,000[81] or less to a donee without making a taxable gift.[82]

EXAMPLE I:5-95 ▶ Maya, who is single, owns marketable securities with a $6,200 basis and $10,400 FMV. She makes gifts of the marketable securities to Phil and cash of $14,000 to Roy. Because of the $14,000 annual exclusion per donee, Maya's gifts are not taxable gifts. ◀

EXAMPLE I:5-96 ▶ Harry, who is single and has never made a taxable gift, makes a gift of land in 2015 with a $1,564,000 basis and a $6,214,000 FMV to Rita. Harry's taxable gift is $6,200,000 ($6,214,000 − $14,000), and he incurs a gift tax liability. Rita's basis is $1,564,000 + 75% of the gift tax paid by Harry [($6,214,000 − $1,564,000)/$6,200,000 = 75%]. ◀

Individuals often reduce future estate taxes by making gifts. By using the annual exclusion, an individual may reduce future estate taxes and avoid the gift tax.

EXAMPLE I:5-97 ▶ Christine owns only one asset in 2015—cash of $7.2 million—and has no liabilities. In December of 2015, she gifted $14,000 to each of her five grandchildren. Because of the $14,000 annual exclusion per donee, Christine's gifts were not taxable gifts. By making the gifts, she reduced her potential gross estate by $70,000 (5 × $14,000). ◀

ADDITIONAL COMMENT

A husband and wife can each make a $14,000 gift to their daughter in 2015, enabling her to receive a total of $28,000 annually without the parents having a taxable gift.

The selection of which property to give is important if one is attempting to reduce future estate taxes. It is generally preferable to make gifts of properties that are expected to significantly increase in value during the postgift period before the donor's death. Any increases in value after the date of the gift are not included in the donor's gross estate.

EXAMPLE I:5-98 ▶ In 1994, Hal owned Sun Corporation stock with a $100,000 FMV and Union Corporation stock with a $100,000 FMV. Hal expected the Sun stock to increase in value at a moderate rate and the Union stock to increase at a substantial rate. In 1994, Hal made a gift of the Union stock to Dana. Hal's taxable gift in 1994 was $90,000 ($100,000 − $10,000 annual exclusion in 1994). Hal dies in the current year when the FMVs of the Sun and Union stocks are $180,000 and $425,000, respectively. The postgift appreciation of $325,000 ($425,000 − $100,000) is not included in Hal's gross estate. By giving the Union stock instead of the Sun stock in 1994, Hal reduces his gross estate by $245,000. ◀

Gifts are often made for income tax purposes to shift income to other family members who are in a lower income tax bracket than the donor.

EXAMPLE I:5-99 ▶ In 2015, Anne has a marginal tax rate of 33% and owns Atlantic Corporation bonds, which have a $5,000 basis and $8,000 FMV. The bonds pay interest of $1,400 per year. If Anne gives the bonds to her dependent child, the interest income is shifted to the child. If the child has no other income, the child's taxable income is $350 ($1,400 − $1,050 standard deduction), and the child's marginal tax rate is 10%. The gift results in an annual income tax savings to the family unit of $427 [(0.33 × $1,400) − (0.10 × $350)]. The rate of tax that is imposed may be the parent's rate (see Chapter I:2) if the child is less than 18 years old (possibly less than 24 years old after 2007) and has net unearned income in excess of $2,100.

In addition to shifting the interest income, Anne has also shifted a potential gain of $3,000. The child's basis for the bonds is $5,000 because the donee takes the donor's basis when the FMV of the property at the time of the gift is greater than the donor's basis. No gain is

[81] In 2009–2012, the annual exclusion was $13,000.

[82] Sec. 2503(b).

ADDITIONAL COMMENT

In Example I:5-99, Anne may also reduce the new 3.8% Medicare tax on net investment income.

recognized by Anne when the gift is made, and a future sale of the property by the child may be taxed at a lower income tax rate. ◀

Although gifts of appreciated property may generate desirable income tax benefits, it is not usually advantageous to make a gift of property that has a basis greater than its FMV because the donee's basis for determining a loss is the FMV. The excess of the donor's basis over the FMV at the time of the gift may never generate any tax benefit for the donor or the donee. Therefore, the donor should sell the asset and make a gift of the proceeds if the loss on the sale is deductible.

EXAMPLE I:5-100 ▶ Bob owns Red Corporation stock with an $8,000 basis and $6,000 FMV, which is held as an investment. Bob wishes to make a graduation gift of the marketable securities to Angela, although he expects her to sell the stock and purchase a car. If Angela sells the stock for $6,000, no gain or loss is recognized because her loss basis for the stock is $6,000. In addition, no loss is recognized by Bob on the gift of the stock to Angela. Instead of giving the stock, Bob should sell it to recognize a $2,000 capital loss and then give the proceeds from the sale to Angela. ◀

SELF-STUDY QUESTION

Doug owns IBM Corporation shares, which have a $50,000 FMV and basis of $75,000. Doug makes a deathbed telephone call to his stockbroker and sells the IBM shares. Assuming that Doug is in the 35% bracket and had no other capital gains or losses, calculate the tax savings associated with the sale.

ANSWER

Doug saves $1,050 ($3,000 × 0.35) unless he has capital gain income that may be offset with the capital loss. It should be noted that the loss is limited to $3,000; if Doug dies, the unused capital loss of $22,000 is lost.

The effect of gift taxes paid by the donor on the donee's basis for property received is another reason why it may be more advantageous to give appreciated property rather than property with a basis greater than its FMV. A portion of the gift taxes paid as a result of giving appreciated property is added to the property's basis. However, payment of gift taxes due to the gift of property that has a basis greater than its FMV does not result in an increase in the donee's basis.

SELECTION OF PROPERTY TO TRANSFER AT TIME OF DEATH

An integral part of gift and estate planning is the selection of property to be transferred to family members and others both during the taxpayer's lifetime and upon death. Usually, taxpayers find it advantageous to retain highly appreciated property in their estates and transfer such property at death to the taxpayer's heirs because the basis of the inherited property will be increased to its FMV at the date of death (or six months from the date of death if the alternate valuation date is elected). Of course, the impact of gift and estate taxes also play a major role in this planning process.

Investment and business assets that have declined in value (i.e., the FMV is less than the basis) should normally be sold before death to obtain an income tax deduction for the loss. If the property is not sold or otherwise disposed of before death, the basis of the inherited property is reduced to its FMV.

EXAMPLE I:5-101 ▶ Paul owns two farms of similar size and quality. Each farm has a $500,000 FMV. Paul's basis for the first farm is $100,000, and his basis for the second farm is $430,000. Eventually, Paul plans for both farms to be owned by Amy. However, he would like to transfer ownership of one farm now and retain the other farm until his death. Paul should make a gift of the second farm and transfer the first farm to Amy upon his death because the second farm has appreciated less in value. When Paul dies and devises the first farm to Amy, she will have a basis for the property equal to its FMV at the date of death even though Paul's basis is only $100,000. ◀

COMPLIANCE AND PROCEDURAL CONSIDERATIONS

OBJECTIVE 9

Describe compliance and procedural considerations for property transactions

DOCUMENTATION OF BASIS

The importance of being able to determine and document the basis of assets acquired by a taxpayer cannot be overemphasized. Accurate records of asset acquisitions, dispositions, and adjustments to basis are essential. When more than one asset is acquired at the same time, the amount paid must be allocated among the assets acquired based on their relative FMVs. Subsequent adjustments to basis, such as those due to capital improvements and depreciation deductions, must be documented.

KEY POINT

Many taxpayers do not maintain adequate records that can be used to document the basis of their most important asset, their personal residence. For example, taxpayers can increase the basis of their residence if they have the driveway paved or add a new room or porch.

Because the basis of property can be determined by reference to another person's basis for that asset (e.g., gifts), taxpayers should be particularly aware of obtaining documentation for that basis at the time of the transfer. In the case of a gift, the taxpayer's basis may be affected by any gift tax paid by the donor. A copy of the donor's gift tax return is useful in documenting the upward adjustment to the donor's basis in determining the donee's basis.

Taxpayers who inherit property may use the decedent's federal Estate Tax Return (Form 706) to determine the FMV at the time of the decedent's death or FMV as of the alternate valuation date. However, the appraised value used for estate tax purposes is only presumptively correct for basis purposes. Although the FMVs used to determine the estate tax are typically used to determine basis, neither the taxpayer nor the IRS is barred from using an FMV for basis purposes that differs from the values used for the estate tax return.[83]

Brokerage firms must report an investor's cost basis in any shares purchased after January 1, 2011 to the IRS when securities are sold. Brokers have been required for many years to report the amount of sales proceeds but must now also provide the basis. The broker will apply a FIFO rule when selecting the securities sold unless the taxpayer notifies the broker that other securities are being sold. If a taxpayer owns securities purchased at different prices and on different dates, the taxpayer may specifically identify those stocks deemed to be sold and thus may affect the amount of the gain or loss and if the gain or loss in ST or LT.

REPORTING OF CAPITAL GAINS AND LOSSES ON SCHEDULE D

KEY POINT

Schedule D refers to 28% gain which is NCG taxed at a maximum rate of 28% (collectible gain and part of the Sec. 1202 gain).

Capital gains and losses are reported by individuals on Schedule D, which is then attached to Form 1040. Part I is used to report short-term capital gains and losses, and Part II is used to report long-term capital gains and losses. Part III is a summary of Parts I and II.

Capital gains due to installment sales are first reported on a separate form before being included on Schedule D. The taxpayer's share of capital gains and losses from partnerships, S corporations, and fiduciaries is reported in Parts I and II on lines 5 and 12. The carryover of capital losses is also included in Parts I and II on lines 6 and 14.

EXAMPLE I:5-102 ▶ Virgil Schmidt, a single taxpayer, uses the following information to prepare his Schedule D for 2014. Virgil received $8,000 of qualified dividends during the year. He sold 200 shares of Tennis Corporation stock for $13,000 on June 20, 2014. The shares were purchased on October 2, 2013, for $8,700. He has an STCL carryforward from 2013 of $8,200. He sold a piano for $4,000 on May 30, 2014. The piano was purchased on April 12, 2004, for $2,500 and used by his two sons. Virgil also sold 500 shares of Golf Corporation stock for $18,000 on November 30, 2014. He had purchased the stock on April 1, 2010, for $10,000.

Virgil has STCG of $4,300 that is offset by $8,200 of STCL carryforward on line 6. His NSTCL of $3,900 ($8,200 − $4,300) is shown on line 7. His $1,500 LTCG as a result of the sale of the piano (not a collectible) and his $8,000 LTCG from the sale of the Golf Corporation stock are on lines 9 and 10. Thus, Virgil has a NLTCG of $9,500. He has ANCG of $5,600 ($9,500 − $3,900).

Because Virgil has ANCG of $5,600 and no 28% rate gains or unrecaptured Sec. 1250 gains, he computes his tax on the Qualified Dividends and Capital Gain Tax Worksheet. The preferential treatment for dividends and capital gains saves Virgil $1,768 of federal income taxes in 2014.

Virgil's taxable income including the above dividends and capital gains is $120,000. ◀

REAL-WORLD EXAMPLE

Artwork inherited by a married couple was originally valued at $12 million for estate taxes based on a blockage discount. The IRS determined that the undiscounted value was $36 million and the discounted value was $14 million. The taxpayers consented to the $14 million value but later used $36 million as the basis for the artwork after the statute of limitations had expired for the estate tax. The 9th Circuit Court of Appeals agreed with the IRS that the correct basis should be $14 million. *Janis v. Commissioner* 461 F.3d 1080 (CA-9, 2006)

The following pages include the Schedule D, Form 8949, and a worksheet that taxayers use to compute their tax if they have no 28% rate gains or unrecaptured Section 1250 gains. For Virgil in the above example, both stock transactions were reported on Form 1099-B with basis reported to the IRS.

83 Rev. Rul. 54-97, 1954-1 C.B. 113 and *Achille F. Ford v. U.S.*, 5 AFTR 2d 1157, 60-1 USTC ¶9375 (Ct. Cls., 1960).

SCHEDULE D (Form 1040)

Department of the Treasury
Internal Revenue Service (99)

Capital Gains and Losses

▶ Attach to Form 1040 or Form 1040NR.
▶ Information about Schedule D and its separate instructions is at *www.irs.gov/scheduled*.
▶ Use Form 8949 to list your transactions for lines 1b, 2, 3, 8b, 9, and 10.

OMB No. 1545-0074
2014
Attachment Sequence No. 12

Name(s) shown on return: Virgil Schmidt | **Your social security number**

Part I Short-Term Capital Gains and Losses—Assets Held One Year or Less

See instructions for how to figure the amounts to enter on the lines below. This form may be easier to complete if you round off cents to whole dollars.	(d) Proceeds (sales price)	(e) Cost (or other basis)	(g) Adjustments to gain or loss from Form(s) 8949, Part I, line 2, column (g)	(h) Gain or (loss) Subtract column (e) from column (d) and combine the result with column (g)
1a Totals for all short-term transactions reported on Form 1099-B for which basis was reported to the IRS and for which you have no adjustments (see instructions). However, if you choose to report all these transactions on Form 8949, leave this line blank and go to line 1b				
1b Totals for all transactions reported on Form(s) 8949 with **Box A** checked	13,000	8,700		4,300
2 Totals for all transactions reported on Form(s) 8949 with **Box B** checked				
3 Totals for all transactions reported on Form(s) 8949 with **Box C** checked				

4 Short-term gain from Form 6252 and short-term gain or (loss) from Forms 4684, 6781, and 8824	4	
5 Net short-term gain or (loss) from partnerships, S corporations, estates, and trusts from Schedule(s) K-1	5	
6 Short-term capital loss carryover. Enter the amount, if any, from line 8 of your **Capital Loss Carryover Worksheet** in the instructions	6	(8,200)
7 **Net short-term capital gain or (loss).** Combine lines 1a through 6 in column (h). If you have any long-term capital gains or losses, go to Part II below. Otherwise, go to Part III on the back	7	(3,900)

Part II Long-Term Capital Gains and Losses—Assets Held More Than One Year

See instructions for how to figure the amounts to enter on the lines below. This form may be easier to complete if you round off cents to whole dollars.	(d) Proceeds (sales price)	(e) Cost (or other basis)	(g) Adjustments to gain or loss from Form(s) 8949, Part II, line 2, column (g)	(h) Gain or (loss) Subtract column (e) from column (d) and combine the result with column (g)
8a Totals for all long-term transactions reported on Form 1099-B for which basis was reported to the IRS and for which you have no adjustments (see instructions). However, if you choose to report all these transactions on Form 8949, leave this line blank and go to line 8b				
8b Totals for all transactions reported on Form(s) 8949 with **Box D** checked	18,000	(10,000)		8,000
9 Totals for all transactions reported on Form(s) 8949 with **Box E** checked				
10 Totals for all transactions reported on Form(s) 8949 with **Box F** checked	4,000	(2,500)		1,500

11 Gain from Form 4797, Part I; long-term gain from Forms 2439 and 6252; and long-term gain or (loss) from Forms 4684, 6781, and 8824	11	
12 Net long-term gain or (loss) from partnerships, S corporations, estates, and trusts from Schedule(s) K-1	12	
13 Capital gain distributions. See the instructions	13	
14 Long-term capital loss carryover. Enter the amount, if any, from line 13 of your **Capital Loss Carryover Worksheet** in the instructions	14	( )
15 **Net long-term capital gain or (loss).** Combine lines 8a through 14 in column (h). Then go to Part III on the back	15	9,500

For Paperwork Reduction Act Notice, see your tax return instructions. Cat. No. 11338H **Schedule D (Form 1040) 2014**

FIGURE I:5-1 ▶ PART I–II OF SCHEDULE D FOR EXAMPLE I:5-102

Schedule D (Form 1040) 2014 Page **2**

Part III **Summary**

16	Combine lines 7 and 15 and enter the result	**16**	5,600
	• If line 16 is a **gain,** enter the amount from line 16 on Form 1040, line 13, or Form 1040NR, line 14. Then go to line 17 below. • If line 16 is a **loss,** skip lines 17 through 20 below. Then go to line 21. Also be sure to complete line 22. • If line 16 is **zero,** skip lines 17 through 21 below and enter -0- on Form 1040, line 13, or Form 1040NR, line 14. Then go to line 22.		
17	Are lines 15 and 16 **both** gains? ☐ **Yes.** Go to line 18. ☐ **No.** Skip lines 18 through 21, and go to line 22.		
18	Enter the amount, if any, from line 7 of the **28% Rate Gain Worksheet** in the instructions . . ▶	**18**	
19	Enter the amount, if any, from line 18 of the **Unrecaptured Section 1250 Gain Worksheet** in the instructions . . . . ▶	**19**	
20	Are lines 18 and 19 **both** zero or blank? ☐ **Yes.** Complete the **Qualified Dividends and Capital Gain Tax Worksheet** in the instructions for Form 1040, line 44 (or in the instructions for Form 1040NR, line 42). **Do not** complete lines 21 and 22 below. ☐ **No.** Complete the **Schedule D Tax Worksheet** in the instructions. **Do not** complete lines 21 and 22 below.		
21	If line 16 is a loss, enter here and on Form 1040, line 13, or Form 1040NR, line 14, the **smaller** of: • The loss on line 16 or • ($3,000), or if married filing separately, ($1,500) } . . . . **Note.** When figuring which amount is smaller, treat both amounts as positive numbers.	**21**	( )
22	Do you have qualified dividends on Form 1040, line 9b, or Form 1040NR, line 10b? ☐ **Yes.** Complete the **Qualified Dividends and Capital Gain Tax Worksheet** in the instructions for Form 1040, line 44 (or in the instructions for Form 1040NR, line 42). ☐ **No.** Complete the rest of Form 1040 or Form 1040NR.		

Schedule D (Form 1040) 2014

FIGURE I:5-1 ▶ PART III OF SCHEDULE D FOR EXAMPLE I:5-102

Form **8949**

Department of the Treasury
Internal Revenue Service

Sales and Other Dispositions of Capital Assets

▶ Information about Form 8949 and its separate instructions is at *www.irs.gov/form8949.*

▶ File with your Schedule D to list your transactions for lines 1b, 2, 3, 8b, 9, and 10 of Schedule D.

OMB No. 1545-0074

2014

Attachment Sequence No. 12A

Name(s) shown on return	Social security number or taxpayer identification number
Virgil Schmidt	

Before you check Box A, B, or C below, see whether you received any Form(s) 1099-B or substitute statement(s) from your broker. A substitute statement will have the same information as Form 1099-B. Either may show your basis (usually your cost) even if your broker did not report it to the IRS. Brokers must report basis to the IRS for most stock you bought in 2011 or later (and for certain debt instruments you bought in 2014 or later).

Part I **Short-Term.** Transactions involving capital assets you held 1 year or less are short term. For long-term transactions, see page 2.

Note. You may aggregate all short-term transactions reported on Form(s) 1099-B showing basis was reported to the IRS and for which no adjustments or codes are required. Enter the total directly on Schedule D, line 1a; you are not required to report these transactions on Form 8949 (see instructions).

You *must* check Box A, B, *or* C below. Check only one box. If more than one box applies for your short-term transactions, complete a separate Form 8949, page 1, for each applicable box. If you have more short-term transactions than will fit on this page for one or more of the boxes, complete as many forms with the same box checked as you need.

☑ **(A)** Short-term transactions reported on Form(s) 1099-B showing basis was reported to the IRS (see **Note** above)

☐ **(B)** Short-term transactions reported on Form(s) 1099-B showing basis was **not** reported to the IRS

☐ **(C)** Short-term transactions not reported to you on Form 1099-B

1 (a) Description of property (Example: 100 sh. XYZ Co.)	(b) Date acquired (Mo., day, yr.)	(c) Date sold or disposed (Mo., day, yr.)	(d) Proceeds (sales price) (see instructions)	(e) Cost or other basis. See the **Note** below and see *Column (e)* in the separate instructions	Adjustment, if any, to gain or loss. If you enter an amount in column (g), enter a code in column (f). **See the separate instructions.** (f) Code(s) from instructions	(g) Amount of adjustment	(h) **Gain or (loss).** Subtract column (e) from column (d) and combine the result with column (g)
200 Sh Tennis Corp.	10-2-13	6-20-14	13,000	8,700			4,300
2 Totals. Add the amounts in columns (d), (e), (g), and (h) (subtract negative amounts). Enter each total here and include on your Schedule D, **line 1b** (if **Box A** above is checked), **line 2** (if **Box B** above is checked), or **line 3** (if **Box C** above is checked) ▶			13,000	8,700			4,300

Note. If you checked Box A above but the basis reported to the IRS was incorrect, enter in column (e) the basis as reported to the IRS, and enter an adjustment in column (g) to correct the basis. See *Column (g)* in the separate instructions for how to figure the amount of the adjustment.

For Paperwork Reduction Act Notice, see your tax return instructions. Cat. No. 37768Z Form **8949** (2014)

FIGURE I:5-2

Form 8949 (2014) Attachment Sequence No. **12A** Page **2**

Name(s) shown on return. Name and SSN or taxpayer identification no. not required if shown on other side	**Social security number or taxpayer identification number**

Before you check Box D, E, or F below, see whether you received any Form(s) 1099-B or substitute statement(s) from your broker. A substitute statement will have the same information as Form 1099-B. Either may show your basis (usually your cost) even if your broker did not report it to the IRS. Brokers must report basis to the IRS for most stock you bought in 2011 or later (and for certain debt instruments you bought in 2014 or later).

Part II **Long-Term.** Transactions involving capital assets you held more than 1 year are long term. For short-term transactions, see page 1.

Note. You may aggregate all long-term transactions reported on Form(s) 1099-B showing basis was reported to the IRS and for which no adjustments or codes are required. Enter the total directly on Schedule D, line 8a; you are not required to report these transactions on Form 8949 (see instructions).

You *must* check Box D, E, *or* F below. Check only one box. If more than one box applies for your long-term transactions, complete a separate Form 8949, page 2, for each applicable box. If you have more long-term transactions than will fit on this page for one or more of the boxes, complete as many forms with the same box checked as you need.

- ☑ **(D)** Long-term transactions reported on Form(s) 1099-B showing basis was reported to the IRS (see **Note** above)
- ☐ **(E)** Long-term transactions reported on Form(s) 1099-B showing basis was **not** reported to the IRS
- ☐ **(F)** Long-term transactions not reported to you on Form 1099-B

1 (a) Description of property (Example: 100 sh. XYZ Co.)	(b) Date acquired (Mo., day, yr.)	(c) Date sold or disposed (Mo., day, yr.)	(d) Proceeds (sales price) (see instructions)	(e) Cost or other basis. See the **Note** below and see *Column (e)* in the separate instructions	**Adjustment, if any, to gain or loss.** If you enter an amount in column (g), enter a code in column (f). **See the separate instructions.** (f) Code(s) from instructions	(g) Amount of adjustment	(h) **Gain or (loss).** Subtract column (e) from column (d) and combine the result with column (g)
500 Sh Golf Corp Stock	4-1-10	11-30-14	18,000	10,000			8,000
2 Totals. Add the amounts in columns (d), (e), (g), and (h) (subtract negative amounts). Enter each total here and include on your Schedule D, **line 8b** (if **Box D** above is checked), **line 9** (if **Box E** above is checked), or **line 10** (if **Box F** above is checked) ▶			18,000	10,000			8,000

Note. If you checked Box D above but the basis reported to the IRS was incorrect, enter in column (e) the basis as reported to the IRS, and enter an adjustment in column (g) to correct the basis. See *Column (g)* in the separate instructions for how to figure the amount of the adjustment.

Form **8949** (2014)

FIGURE I:5-2

Form 8949 (2014) Attachment Sequence No. **12A** Page **2**

Name(s) shown on return. Name and SSN or taxpayer identification no. not required if shown on other side	**Social security number or taxpayer identification number**

Before you check Box D, E, or F below, see whether you received any Form(s) 1099-B or substitute statement(s) from your broker. A substitute statement will have the same information as Form 1099-B. Either may show your basis (usually your cost) even if your broker did not report it to the IRS. Brokers must report basis to the IRS for most stock you bought in 2011 or later (and for certain debt instruments you bought in 2014 or later).

Part II **Long-Term.** Transactions involving capital assets you held more than 1 year are long term. For short-term transactions, see page 1.

Note. You may aggregate all long-term transactions reported on Form(s) 1099-B showing basis was reported to the IRS and for which no adjustments or codes are required. Enter the total directly on Schedule D, line 8a; you are not required to report these transactions on Form 8949 (see instructions).

You *must* check Box D, E, *or* F below. Check only one box. If more than one box applies for your long-term transactions, complete a separate Form 8949, page 2, for each applicable box. If you have more long-term transactions than will fit on this page for one or more of the boxes, complete as many forms with the same box checked as you need.

☐ **(D)** Long-term transactions reported on Form(s) 1099-B showing basis was reported to the IRS (see **Note** above)
☐ **(E)** Long-term transactions reported on Form(s) 1099-B showing basis was **not** reported to the IRS
☑ **(F)** Long-term transactions not reported to you on Form 1099-B

1 (a) Description of property (Example: 100 sh. XYZ Co.)	(b) Date acquired (Mo., day, yr.)	(c) Date sold or disposed (Mo., day, yr.)	(d) Proceeds (sales price) (see instructions)	(e) Cost or other basis. See the **Note** below and see *Column (e)* in the separate instructions	**Adjustment, if any, to gain or loss.** If you enter an amount in column (g), enter a code in column (f). **See the separate instructions.** (f) Code(s) from instructions	(g) Amount of adjustment	(h) **Gain or (loss).** Subtract column (e) from column (d) and combine the result with column (g)
Piano	4-12-04	5-3-14	4,000	2,500			1,500
2 Totals. Add the amounts in columns (d), (e), (g), and (h) (subtract negative amounts). Enter each total here and include on your Schedule D, **line 8b** (if **Box D** above is checked), **line 9** (if **Box E** above is checked), or **line 10** (if **Box F** above is checked) ▶			4,000	2,500			1,500

Note. If you checked Box D above but the basis reported to the IRS was incorrect, enter in column (e) the basis as reported to the IRS, and enter an adjustment in column (g) to correct the basis. See *Column (g)* in the separate instructions for how to figure the amount of the adjustment.

Form **8949** (2014)

FIGURE I:5-2

Taxpayers such as Virgil in Example I:5-102 use the Qualified Dividends Capital Gain Tax Worksheet below if they either have qualified dividends or ANCG *and* do not have any 28% rate gain property or unrecaptured Section 1250 gain. This worksheet applies the lower preferential tax rates of zero or 15% for qualified dividends and ANCG.

2014 Form 1040—Line 44

Qualified Dividends and Capital Gain Tax Worksheet—Line 44 *Keep for Your Records*

Before you begin:
√ See the earlier instructions for line 44 to see if you can use this worksheet to figure your tax.
√ Before completing this worksheet, complete Form 1040 through line 43.
√ If you do not have to file Schedule D and you received capital gain distributions, be sure you checked the box on line 13 of Form 1040.

Line	Description		Amount	Amount	Amount
1.	Enter the amount from Form 1040, line 43. However, if you are filing Form 2555 or 2555-EZ (relating to foreign earned income), enter the amount from line 3 of the Foreign Earned Income Tax Worksheet	1.		120,000	
2.	Enter the amount from Form 1040, line 9b*	2.	8,000		
3.	Are you filing Schedule D?* ☑ **Yes.** Enter the **smaller** of line 15 or 16 of Schedule D. If either line 15 or line 16 is blank or a loss, enter -0- ☐ **No.** Enter the amount from Form 1040, line 13	3.	5,600		
4.	Add lines 2 and 3	4.	13,600		
5.	If filing Form 4952 (used to figure investment interest expense deduction), enter any amount from line 4g of that form. Otherwise, enter -0-	5.	-0-		
6.	Subtract line 5 from line 4. If zero or less, enter -0-	6.		13,600	
7.	Subtract line 6 from line 1. If zero or less, enter -0-	7.		106,400	
8.	Enter: $36,900 if single or married filing separately, $73,800 if married filing jointly or qualifying widow(er), $49,400 if head of household.	8.		36,900	
9.	Enter the smaller of line 1 or line 8	9.		36,900	
10.	Enter the smaller of line 7 or line 9	10.		36,900	
11.	Subtract line 10 from line 9. This amount is taxed at 0%	11.		-0-	
12.	Enter the smaller of line 1 or line 6	12.		13,600	
13.	Enter the amount from line 11	13.		-0-	
14.	Subtract line 13 from line 12	14.		13,600	
15.	Enter: $406,750 if single, $228,800 if married filing separately, $457,600 if married filing jointly or qualifying widow(er), $432,200 if head of household.	15.		406,750	
16.	Enter the smaller of line 1 or line 15	16.		120,000	
17.	Add lines 7 and 11	17.		106,400	
18.	Subtract line 17 from line 16. If zero or less, enter -0-	18.		13,600	
19.	Enter the smaller of line 14 or line 18	19.		13,600	
20.	Multiply line 19 by 15% (.15)	20.			2040
21.	Add lines 11 and 19	21.		13,600	
22.	Subtract line 21 from line 12	22.		-0-	
23.	Multiply line 22 by 20% (.20)	23.			-0-
24.	Figure the tax on the amount on line 7. If the amount on line 7 is less than $100,000, use the Tax Table to figure the tax. If the amount on line 7 is $100,000 or more, use the Tax Computation Worksheet	24.			22,968
25.	Add lines 20, 23, and 24	25.			25,008
26.	Figure the tax on the amount on line 1. If the amount on line 1 is less than $100,000, use the Tax Table to figure the tax. If the amount on line 1 is $100,000 or more, use the Tax Computation Worksheet	26.			26,776
27.	**Tax on all taxable income.** Enter the **smaller** of line 25 or line 26. Also include this amount on Form 1040, line 44. If you are filing Form 2555 or 2555-EZ, do not enter this amount on Form 1040, line 44. Instead, enter it on line 4 of the Foreign Earned Income Tax Worksheet	27.			25,008

**If you are filing Form 2555 or 2555-EZ, see the footnote in the Foreign Earned Income Tax Worksheet before completing this line.*

FIGURE I:5-3 ▶ QUALIFIED DIVIDENDS AND CAPITAL GAIN TAX WORKSHEET FOR EXAMPLE I:5-102

PROBLEM MATERIALS

DISCUSSION QUESTIONS

I:5-1 What problem may exist in determining the amount realized for an investor who exchanges common stock of a publicly traded corporation for a used building? How is the problem likely to be resolved?

I:5-2 In 2001, Ellen purchased a house for $60,000 to use as her personal residence. She paid $12,000 and borrowed $48,000 from the local savings and loan company. In 2005 she paid $10,000 to add a room to the house. In 200 7 she paid $625 to have the house painted and $800 for built-in bookshelves. As of January 1 of the current year, she has reduced the $48,000 mortgage to $44,300. What is her basis for the house?

I:5-3 Vincent pays $20,000 for equipment to use in his trade or business. He pays sales tax of $800 as a result of the purchase. Must the $800 sales tax be capitalized as part of the purchase price?

I:5-4 Sergio owns 200 shares of Palm Corporation common stock, purchased during the prior year: 100 shares on July 5, for $9,000; and 100 shares on October 15, for $12,000. When Sergio sells 50 shares for $8,000 on July 18 of the current year, he does not identify the particular shares sold. Determine the amount and character of the gain.

I:5-5 On October 21 of the current year, David receives stock of Western Corporation as a gift from his grandfather, who acquired the stock on January 20, 1995. Under what conditions would David's holding period start on?

a. October 22 of the current year?
b. January 20, 1995?

I:5-6 Jim inherits stock (a capital asset) from his brother, who died in March of 2015, when the property had a $6.9 million FMV. This property is the only property included in his brother's gross estate and there is a taxable estate. The FMV of the property as of the alternate valuation date was $6.7 million.

a. Why might the executor of the brother's estate elect to use the alternate valuation date to value the property?
b. Why might Jim prefer the executor to use FMV at time of the death to value the property?
c. If the marginal estate tax rate is 40% and Jim's marginal income tax rate is 25%, which value should the executor use?

I:5-7 Martha owns 500 shares of Columbus Corporation common stock at the beginning of the year with a basis of $82,500. During the year, Columbus declares and pays a 10% nontaxable stock dividend. What is her basis for each of the 50 shares received?

I:5-8 Mario owns 2,000 shares of Nevada Corporation common stock at the beginning of the year. His basis for the stock is $38,880. During the year, Nevada declares and pays a stock dividend. After the dividend, Mario's basis for each share of stock owned is $18. What is the percentage dividend paid by Nevada?

I:5-9 A corporate taxpayer plans to build a $6 million office building during the next 18 months. How must the corporation treat the interest on debt paid or incurred during the production period?

I:5-10 Andy owns an appliance store where he has merchandise such as refrigerators for sale. Roger, a bachelor, owns a refrigerator, which he uses in his apartment for personal use. For which individual is the refrigerator a capital asset?

I:5-11 Why did the Supreme Court rule in the *Corn Products* case that a gain due to the sale of futures contracts is ordinary income instead of capital gain?

I:5-12 When is the gain on the sale or exchange of securities by a dealer in securities classified as capital gain?

I:5-13 In 2002, Florence purchased 30 acres of land. She has not used the land for business purposes or made any substantial improvements to the property. During the current year, she subdivides the land into 15 lots and advertises the lots for sale. She sells four lots at a gain.

a. What is the character of the gain on the sale of the four lots?
b. Explain how the basis of each lot would be determined.

I:5-14 Amy has LTCGs that are taxed at different tax rates, 15%, 25% and 28%. She also has NSTCLs that amount to less than her NLTCG. The procedure for offsetting the NSTCL against the LTCGs is favorable to her. Explain.

I:5-15 Four years ago, Susan loaned $7,000 to her friend Joe. During the current year, the $7,000 loan is considered worthless. Explain how Susan should treat the worthless debt for tax purposes.

I:5-16 Why did the Supreme Court rule in *Arkansas Best* that the stock of a corporation purchased by the taxpayer to protect the taxpayer's business reputation was a capital asset?

I:5-17 The effective tax rate on gain of $1 million resulting from the sale of qualified small business stock obtained in 2005 in an initial public offering and held more than five years is 14%. Do you agree or disagree? Explain.

I:5-18 Nancy and the Minor Corporation own bonds of the East Corporation. Minor Corporation owns 80% of the stock of East Corporation. East Corporation has declared bankruptcy this year, and bondholders will receive only 26% of the face value of the debt. Explain why the loss is a capital loss for Nancy but an ordinary loss for the Minor Corporation.

I:5-19 On January 1 of the current year, the Orange Corporation issues $500,000 of 11%, 20-year bonds for $480,000. Determine the amount of original issue discount, if any.

I:5-20 Today, Juanita purchases a 15-year, 7% bond of the Sunflower Corporation issued four years ago at par. She purchases the bond as an investment at a discount from the par value. If she sells the bonds two years from now, explain why some or all of the gain may be ordinary income.

I:5-21 Judy just obtained a patent on a new product she has developed. Bell Corporation wishes to market the product and will pay 12% of all future sales of the product to Judy. How can she be sure that the payments received will be treated as a long-term capital gain?

I:5-22 When is the transferor of a franchise unable to treat the transfer as a sale or an exchange of a capital asset?

I:5-23 How does a lessor treat payments received for canceling a lease?

I:5-24 What is the first day that an individual could sell a capital asset purchased on March 31, 2015 and have a holding period of more than one year?

I:5-25 Phil, a cash-basis taxpayer, sells the following marketable securities, which are capital assets during 2015. Determine whether the gains or losses are long-term or short-term. Also determine the net capital gain and adjusted net capital gain for 2015.

Capital Asset	*Basis*	*Date Acquired*	*Trade Date in 2015*	*Sales Price*
A	$40,000	Feb. 10, 2014	Aug. 12	$52,000
B	20,000	Dec. 5, 2014	May 2	17,000
C	30,000	Apr. 9, 2013	Dec. 10	37,400

I:5-26 How might the current treatment of capital losses discourage an individual investor from purchasing stock of a high-risk, start-up company?

I:5-27 An individual taxpayer has realized a $40,000 loss on the sale of an asset that had a holding period of eight months. Explain why the taxpayer may be indifferent as to whether the asset is a capital asset.

I:5-28 If Pam transfers an asset to Fred and the asset is subject to a liability that is assumed by Fred, how does Fred's assumption of the liability affect the amount realized by Pam? How does Fred's assumption of the liability affect his basis for the property?

ISSUE IDENTIFICATION QUESTIONS

I:5-29 Mr. and Mrs. Pickens purchased a used piano in Y1 for their young son who had started taking piano lessons. In Y8 while cleaning the piano, Mrs. Pickens discovered $4,800 of old currency. They exchanged the old currency for new currency.

I:5-30 Lisa and John are in the business of breeding beavers to produce fur for sale. They recently purchased a pair of breeding beavers for $30,000 from XUN, Inc., and agreed to pay interest at 10% each year for five years. After the five-year period, they could pay the debt by delivering seven beavers to XUN, Inc., provided that each beaver was at least nine months old. Identify the tax issues involved in this situation.

I:5-31 Mike, a real estate broker in California, recently inherited a farm from his deceased uncle and plans to sell the farm to the first available buyer. His uncle purchased the property 12 years ago for $600,000. The FMV of the farm on the date of the uncle's death was $500,000. Mike sells the farm for $520,000 seven months after his uncle's death. What tax issues should Mike consider?

I:5-32 Sylvia, a dentist with excellent skills as a carpenter, started the construction of a house that she planned to give to her son as a surprise when he returned from Afghanistan, where he is serving in the military. She began construction on March 23, 2014, and finished the house on July 10, 2015, at a total cost of $70,000. Her son is expected to be home on September 1, 2015.

On July 30, 2015, Roscoe offered Sylvia $245,000 for the house and Sylvia considered the offer to be so attractive that she accepted it. She decided that she could purchase a suitable home for her son for about $200,000. What tax issues should Sylvia consider?

PROBLEMS

I:5-33 *Amount Realized.* Tracy owns a nondepreciable capital asset held for investment. The asset was purchased for $250,000 six years earlier and is now subject to a $75,000 liability. During the current year, Tracy transfers the asset to Tim in exchange for $94,000 cash and a new automobile with a $50,000 FMV to be used by Tracy for personal use; Tim assumes the $75,000 liability. Determine the amount of Tracy's LTCG or LTCL.

I:5-34 *Basis of Property Received as a Gift.* Doug receives a duplex as a gift from his uncle. The uncle's basis for the duplex and land is $90,000. At the time of the gift, the land and building have FMVs of $40,000 and $80,000, respectively. No gift tax is paid by Doug's uncle at the time of the gift.

a. To determine gain, what is Doug's basis for the land?
b. To determine gain, what is Doug's basis for the building?
c. Will the basis of the land and building be the same as in Parts a and b for purposes of determining a loss?

I:5-35 *Sale of Property Received as a Gift.* During the current year, Stan sells a tract of land for $800,000. The property was received as a gift from Maxine on March 10, 1995, when the property had a $310,000 FMV. The taxable gift was $300,000 because the annual exclusion was $10,000 in 1995. Maxine purchased the property on April 12, 1980, for $110,000. At the time of the gift, Maxine paid a gift tax of $12,000. In order to sell the property, Stan paid a sales commission of $16,000.

a. What is Stan's realized gain on the sale?
b. How would your answer to Part a change, if at all, if the FMV of the gift property was $85,000 as of the date of the gift?

I:5-36 *Sale of Asset Received as a Gift.* Bud received 200 shares of Georgia Corporation stock from his uncle as a gift on July 20, 2014, when the stock had a $45,000 FMV. His uncle paid $30,000 for the stock on April 12, 2000. The taxable gift was $45,000, because his uncle made another gift to Bud for $20,000 in January and used the annual exclusion. The uncle paid a gift tax of $1,500.

Without considering the transactions below, Bud's AGI is $45,000 in 2015. No other transactions involving capital assets occur during the year. Analyze each transaction below, independent of the others, and determine Bud's AGI in each case.

a. He sells the stock on October 12, 2015, for $48,000.
b. He sells the stock on October 12, 2015, for $28,000.
c. He sells the stock on December 16, 2015, for $42,000.

I:5-37 *Basis of Property Converted from Personal Use.* Irene owns a truck costing $15,000 and used for personal activities. The truck has a $9,600 FMV when it is transferred to her business, which is operated as a sole proprietorship.

a. What is the basis of the truck for determining depreciation?
b. What is Irene's realized gain or loss if the truck is sold for $5,000 after claiming depreciation of $4,000?

I:5-38 *Sale of Assets Received as a Gift and Inherited.* Daniel receives 400 shares of A&M Corporation stock from his aunt on May 20, 2015, as a gift when the stock has a $60,000 FMV. His aunt purchased the stock in 2005 for $42,000. The taxable gift is $60,000 because she made earlier gifts to Daniel during 2015 and used the annual exclusion. She paid a gift tax of $9,300 on the gift of A&M stock to Daniel.

Daniel also inherited 300 shares of Longhorn Corporation preferred stock when his uncle died on November 12, 2014, when the stock's FMV was $30,000. His uncle purchased the stock in 1995 for $27,600. Determine the gain or loss on the sale of A&M and Longhorn stock on December 15, 2015, under each alternative situation below.

a. A&M stock was sold for $62,600, and Longhorn stock was sold for $30,750.
b. A&M stock was sold for $58,200, and Longhorn stock was sold for $28,650.
c. Assume the same as in Part a except his aunt purchased A&M stock for $71,000 and his uncle purchased Longhorn stock for $31,200.

I:5-39 *Personal-use Property Converted to Rental Property.* Tally owns a house that she has been living in for eight years. She purchased the house for $245,000 and the FMV today is $200,000. She is moving into her friend's house and has decided to convert her residence to rental property. Assume 20% of the property's value is allocated to land.

a. What is the basis of the house for depreciation?
b. If she claims depreciation of $15,000 and sells the property six years later for $260,000 (20% allocated to land), determine the gain on the sale of the building and gain on the sale of the land.
c. How much of the gain is due to depreciation?
d. If the FMV is $290,000 when she converts the house to rental property instead of $200,000, what is the basis of the house for depreciation?

I:5-40 *Stock Rights.* Kathleen owns 500 shares of Buda Corporation common stock which was purchased on March 20, 1999, for $48,000. On October 10 of the current year, she receives a distribution of 500 stock rights. Each stock right has a $20 FMVand the FMV of the Buda common stock is $100 per share. With each stock right, she may acquire one share of Buda common stock for $95.

a. How much gross income must Kathleen recognize?
b. What is the basis of each stock right received?
c. If she sells the 500 stock rights for $10,600, what is her gain?
d. If she exercises the 500 stock rights on November 10, what is the basis of the 500 shares she receives and when does the holding period for those shares start?

I:5-41 ***Stock Rights.*** Martha Lou owns 100 shares of Blain Corporation common stock. She purchased the stock on July 25, 1986, for $4,000. On May 2 of the current year, she receives a nontaxable distribution of 100 stock rights. Each stock right has a $10 FMV, and the FMV of the Blain common stock is $70 per share. With each stock right, Martha Lou may acquire one share of Blain common for $68 per share. Assuming that she elects to allocate basis to the stock rights, answer the following:

a. What is the basis allocated to the stock rights?
b. If she sells the stock rights on June 10 for $1,080, determine the amount and character of the recognized gain?
c. If she exercises the stock rights on May 14, what is the basis of the 100 shares purchased and when does the holding period start?
d. If she does not elect to allocate basis to the stock rights, determine the amount and character of the gain if she sells the stock rights on June 10 for $1,080?

I:5-42 ***Real Property Subdivided for Sale.*** Beth acquired only one tract of land seven years ago as an investment. In order to sell the land at a higher price, she decides to subdivide it into 20 lots. She pays for improvements such as clearing and leveling, but the improvements are not considered to be substantial. Each lot has a basis of $2,000, and a selling price of $6,000. Selling expenses of $480 were incurred to sell two lots last year. This year, ten lots are sold, and selling expenses amount to $1,900. How much ordinary income and capital gain must be recognized in the prior and current year?

I:5-43 ***Marginal Tax Rates.*** Mr. and Mrs. Dunbar have taxable income of $260,000 without considering the following sales. Consider the following independent cases where capital gains are recognized and determine the marginal tax rate for the capital gain in each case. Ignore the effect of increasing AGI on deductions.

CASE A: $10,000 gain from sale of Storm Lake common stock held for seven months.
CASE B: $10,000 gain from sale of antique clock held for six years.
CASE C: $10,000 gain from sale of Ames preferred stock held for three years.

I:5-44 ***Netting Gains and Losses*** Trisha, whose tax rate is 35%, sells the following capital assets in 2015 with gains and losses as shown:

Asset	*Gain or (Loss)*	*Holding Period*
A	$15,000	15 months
B	7,000	20 months
C	(3,000)	14 months

a. Determine Trisha's increase in tax liability as a result of the three sales. All assets are stock held for investment. Ignore the effect of increasing AGI on deductions and phase-out amounts.
b. Determine her increase in tax liability if the holding period for asset B is 8 months.
c. Determine her increase in tax liability if the holding periods are the same as in Part a but asset B is an antique clock.
d. Determine her increase in tax liability if her tax rate is 39.6%.

I:5-45 ***Computing the Tax.*** Donna files as a head of household in 2015 and has taxable income of $90,000, including the sale of a stock held as an investment for two years at a gain of $20,000. Only one asset was sold during the year and Donna does not have any capital loss carryovers.

a. What is the amount of Donna's tax liability?
b. What is the amount of Donna's tax liability if the stock is held for 11 months?

I:5-46 ***Computing the Tax.*** Wayne is single and has no dependents. Without considering his $11,000 adjusted net capital gain (ANCG), his taxable income, which includes no investment income, in 2015 is as follows:

AGI		$258,250
Home mortgage interest	$22,100	
State and local income taxes	8,000	
Charitable contributions	7,000	
Personal exemption	4,000	41,100

Taxable income	$217,150

a. What is Wayne's tax liability without the ANCG?
b. What is Wayne's tax liability with the ANCG?

I:5-47 ***Computing the Sales Price.*** An investor in a 28% tax bracket owns land that is a capital asset with a $50,000 basis and a holding period of three years. The investor wishes to sell the asset at a price high enough so that he will have $120,000 in cash after paying the income taxes.
a. What is the minimum price the investor could accept?
b. What is the minimum price the investor could accept if all the gain is subject to the Medicare tax on net investment income?

I:5-48 ***Capital Gains and Losses.*** Consider the four independent situations below for an unmarried individual, and analyze the effects of the capital gains and losses on the individual's AGI. For each case, determine AGI after considering the capital gains and losses.

	Situation 1	*Situation 2*	*Situation 3*	*Situation 4*
AGI (excluding property transactions)	$40,000	$50,000	$60,000	$70,000
STCG	6,000	2,000	5,000	6,000
STCL	2,000	5,000	4,000	15,000
LTCG	3,500	15,000	10,000	9,000
LTCL	2,500	4,000	12,000	4,000

I:5-49 ***Capital Losses.*** To better understand the rules for offsetting capital losses and how to treat capital losses carried forward, analyze the following data for an unmarried individual for the period 2012 through 2015. No capital loss carryforwards are included in the figures. For each year, determine AGI and the capital losses to be carried forward to a later tax year.

	2012	*2013*	*2014*	*2015*
AGI (excluding property transactions)	$40,000	$50,000	$60,000	$70,000
STCG	4,000	5,000	7,000	10,000
STCL	9,000	3,000	5,000	12,000
LTCG	6,000	10,000	2,200	6,000
LTCL	5,000	21,000	1,000	9,500
AGI (including property transactions)	______	______	______	______
STCL to be carried forward	______	______	______	______
LTCL to be carried forward	______	______	______	______

I:5-50 ***Character of Loss.*** The Michigan Corporation owns 20% of the Wolverine Corporation. The Wolverine stock was acquired eight years ago to ensure a steady supply of raw materials. Michigan also owns 30% of Spartan Corporation and 85% of Huron Corporation. Stock in both corporations was acquired more than ten years ago for investment purposes. During the current year, Wolverine, Spartan, and Huron are deemed bankrupt, and the stocks are considered worthless. Describe how Michigan should treat its losses.

I:5-51 ***Original Issue Discount.*** On December 31, 2014, Phil purchased $20,000 of newly issued bonds of Texas Corporation for $16,568. The bonds are dated December 31, 2014. The bonds are 9%, 10-year bonds paying interest semiannually on June 30 and December 31. The bonds are priced to yield 12% compounded semiannually.
a. What is the amount of the original issue discount?
b. For the first semiannual period, what is the amount of the original issue discount Phil must recognize as ordinary income?
c. What is the total amount of interest income Phil must recognize in 2015?
d. What is Phil's basis for the bonds as of December 31, 2015?

I:5-52 On January 1, 2013, Swen paid $184,000 for $200,000 of the 8%, 20-year bonds of Penn Corporation, issued on January 1, 2009, at par. The bonds are held as an investment. Determine the gain and the character of the gain if the bonds are sold on January 1, 2015, for
a. $191,000
b. $185,750
c. $183,000

I:5-53 *Capital Gains and Losses.* During 2015, Gary receives a $50,000 salary and has no deductions for AGI. In 2014, Gary had a $5,000 STCL and no other capital losses or capital gains. Consider the following sales and determine Gary's AGI for 2015.

- An automobile purchased in 2010 for $10,800 and held for personal use is sold for $7,000.
- On April 10, 2015, stock held for investment is sold for $21,000. The stock was acquired on November 20, 2014, for $9,300.

I:5-54 *Call Options.* On February 10, 2015, Gail purchases 20 calls on Red Corporation for $250 per call. Each call represents an option to buy 100 shares of Red stock at $42 per share any time before November 25, 2015. Compute the gain or loss recognized, and determine whether the gain or loss is long-term or short-term for Gail in the following situations:

a. The 20 calls are sold on May 15, 2015, for $310 per call.
b. The calls are not exercised but allowed to expire.
c. The calls are exercised on July 15, 2015, and the 2,000 shares of Red Corporation stock are sold on July 20, 2016, for $50 per share.

I:5-55 *Call Writing.* Dan owns 500 shares of Rocket Corporation common stock. The stock was acquired two years ago for $30 per share. On October 2, 2015, Dan writes five calls on the stock, which represent options to buy the 500 shares of Rocket at $75 per share. For each call, Dan receives $210. The calls expire on June 22, 2016. Consider the following transactions and describe the tax treatment for Dan:

a. The five calls are exercised on December 4, 2015.
b. The calls are not exercised and allowed to expire.

I:5-56 *Corporate Capital Gains and Losses.* Determine the taxable income for the Columbia Corporation for the following independent cases:

Case	*Income from Operations*	*STCG (NSTCL)*	*NLTCG (NLTCL)*
A	$110,000	$30,000	$44,000
B	100,000	(50,000)	65,000
C	80,000	(37,000)	30,000
D	90,000	(15,000)	(9,000)

I:5-57 *Original Issue Discount.* On January 1, 2014, Sean purchased an 8%, $100,000 corporate bond for $92,277. The bond was issued on January 1, 2014, and matures on January 1, 2019. Interest is paid semiannually, and the effective yield to maturity is 10% compounded semiannually. On July 1, 2015, Sean sells the bond for $95,949. A schedule of interest amortization for the bond is shown in Table I:5-2.

a. How much interest income must Sean recognize in 2014?
b. How much interest income must Sean recognize in 2015?
c. How much gain must Sean recognize in 2015 on the sale of the bond?

▼ TABLE I:5-2

Interest Amortization for Problem I:5-57

	Interest Received (1)	Amortization of Discount (2)	Interest Income (3) = (1) + (2)
6-30-14	$4,000	$614	$4,614
12-31-14	4,000	645	4,645
6-30-15	4,000	677	4,677
12-31-15	4,000	711	4,711
6-30-16	4,000	747	4,747
12-31-16	4,000	783	4,783
6-30-17	4,000	823	4,823
12-31-17	4,000	864	4,864
6-30-18	4,000	907	4,907
12-31-18	4,000	952	4,952

I:5-58 *Capital Gains and Losses.* Martha has $40,000 AGI without considering the following information. During the year, she incurs a LTCL of $10,000 and has a gain of $14,000 due to the sale of a capital asset held for more than a year.

a. If the $14,000 gain is not properly classified as a LTCG (i.e., is improperly treated as an ordinary gain), determine Martha's AGI.
b. If the $14,000 gain is properly classified as a LTCG, determine her AGI.
c. If Martha has a $2,500 STCL carryover from earlier years, how would the answers to Parts a and b be affected?

I:5-59 *Capital Gains and Losses.* Without considering the following capital gains and losses, Charlene, who is single, has taxable income of $460,000 and a marginal tax rate of 39.6%. During the year, she sold stock held for nine months at a gain of $10,000; stock held for three years at a gain of $15,000; and a collectible asset held for six years at a gain of $20,000. Ignore the effect of the gains on any threshold amounts and assume that her marginal tax rate of 39.6% does not change.

a. What is her taxable income and the increase in her tax liability after considering the three gains?
b. In addition to the above three sales, assume that she sells another asset and has a STCL of $14,000. What is her taxable income and the increase in her tax liability after considering the four transactions?
c. In addition to the above three sales in Part a, assume that she sells another collectible asset held seven years as an investment and has a $27,000 capital loss. What is her taxable income and the increase in her tax liability after considering the four transactions?
d. Determine her medicare tax on net investment income in (a) if all of the $460,000 of taxable income is due to salary.

I:5-60 *Corporate Capital Gains and Losses.* In 2010, the Ryan Corporation sold a capital asset and incurred a $40,000 LTCL that was carried forward to subsequent years. That sale was the only sale of a capital asset that Ryan made until 2015, when Ryan sells a capital asset and recognizes a STCG of $53,000. Without considering the STCG from the sale, Ryan's taxable income is $250,000.

a. Determine the corporation's NSTCG for 2015.
b. Determine the corporation's 2015 taxable income.
c. If the sale of the asset in 2010 had occurred in 2009, determine the corporation's 2015 taxable income.

COMPREHENSIVE PROBLEM

I:5-61 Betty incurs the following transactions during the current year. Without considering the transactions, her 2015 AGI is $40,000. Analyze the transactions and answer the following questions:

- On March 10, 2015, she sells a painting for $2,000. Betty is the artist, and she completed the painting in 2010. Her basis for the painting is $50.
- On June 18, 2015, she receives $28,500 from the sale of stock purchased by her uncle in 2000 for $10,000, which she inherited on February 20, 2015, as a result of her uncle's death. The stock's FMV on that date is $30,000.
- On July 30, 2015, she sells land for $25,000 that was received as a gift from her brother on April 8, 2015, when the land's FMV was $30,000. Her brother purchased the land for $43,000 on October 12, 2007. No gift tax was paid.

a. What is her NSTCL or NSTCG?
b. What is her NLTCL or NLTCG?
c. What is the effect of capital gains and losses on her AGI?
d. What is her capital loss carryforward to the next year?

TAX STRATEGY PROBLEMS

I:5-62 Dale purchased Blue Corporation stock four years ago for $1,000 as an investment. He intended to hold the stock until funds were needed to help pay for his daughter's college education. Today the stock has a $6,500 FMV and Dale decides to sell the stock and give the proceeds, less any taxes paid on the sale, to Tammy, his 22-year-old daughter. Dale's marginal tax rate is 33%. Tammy has no other gross income and receives more than half of her support from Dale.

a. What advice would you give to Dale?
b. What is the cash savings if Dale follows your advice?

I:5-63 Calvin, whose tax rate is 35% is considering two alternative investments on January 1, 20Y1. He can purchase $100,000 of 10% bonds due in five years or purchase $100,000 of Hobbes, Inc. common stock. The bonds are issued at par, pay interest annually on December 31, and mature at the end of five years. Interest received can be reinvested at 10%. Assume that he knows with relative certainty that the value of the stock will increase 8% each year (i.e., the value of the Hobbes stock will be $108,000 at the end of 20Y1) and the interest and principal for the bonds will be paid as scheduled. On December 31, 20Y5, he will sell the stock or receive the bond principal plus the last interest payment. Which alternative should Calvin select if he wants to have the greater amount of money as of January 1, 20Y6? Provide supporting information for your answer.

I:5-64 On December 20 of the current year, Winneld has decided to sell all of the stock that she owns and reinvest the proceeds in state of Minnesota bonds. Without considering the sales, her taxable income is expected to exceed $500,000 this year and in future years. Information about the stocks are provided below:

Corporation	*FMV*	*Basis*	*Holding Period*
Viking, Inc.	$190,000	$140,000	7 months
Twins, Inc.	200,000	255,000	4 years
Timberwolves, Inc.	382,000	300,000	3 years

She is willing to sell some of the stock this year and the remaining stock next year if it is more advantageous to spread the sales over two years. Assume that the FMV of the stock will not change during the next 30 days, and ignore the effect of a sale on threshold amounts.

Determine the increase in her income tax for each of the following alternatives (a, b, & c) and advise Winneld.

a. Sell all stock this year.
b. Sell Twins and Timberwolves this year and Viking in March of next year.
c. Sell Viking and Twins this year and Timberwolves in March of next year.
d. Determine her Medicare tax on net investment income in Part a if she has no investment income before selling all the stock.

I:5-65 Dallas, whose tax rate is 35%, has recognized a STCL of $11,000 and a LTCG of $10,200 due to the sale of stock. In late December, he is considering the sale of an antique chair held for investment that would result in a LTCG of $5,000. If he sells the chair this year, what is the increase in his tax liability as a result of the sale? Ignore the phase out rules.

TAX FORM/RETURN PREPARATION PROBLEMS

I:5-66 Given the following information for Jane Cole, complete Schedule D of Form 1040 through Part III.

- Stock options, which she purchases on February 14 of the current year for $850, expire on October 1.
- On July 1, she sells for $1,500 her personal-use automobile acquired on March 31, 1990, for $8,000.
- On August 16, she sells for $3,100 her stock of York Corporation purchased as an investment on February 16, for $1,600.
- On March 15, she sells for $5,600 an antique ring, a gift from her grandmother on January 10, 1988, when its FMV was $1,600. The ring was purchased by her grandmother on April 2, 1979, for $1,800.
- She has a STCL carryover of $250 from last year.

I:5-67 Spencer Duck (SSN 000-22-1111) is single and his eight-year-old son, Mitch, lives with him nine months of the year in a rented condominium at 321 Hickory Drive in Ames, Iowa. Mitch lives with his mother, Spencer's ex-wife, during the summer months. His mother provides more than half of Mitch's support and Spencer has agreed to allow her to claim Mitch as her dependent. Spencer has a salary of $39,000 and itemized deductions of $4,000. Taxes withheld during the year amount to $3,221. On July 14 of the current year, he sold the following assets:

- Spencer received a K-1 from a partnership indicating that his share of the partnership STCL is $200.

- Land was sold for $35,000. The land was received as a property settlement on January 10, 2001, when the land's FMV amounted to $30,000. His ex-wife's basis for the land, purchased on January 10, 1991, was $18,600.
- A personal-use computer acquired on March 2 last year for $4,000 was sold for $2,480.
- A membership card for a prestigious country club was sold for $8,500. The card was acquired on October 10, 1993, for $6,000.
- Marketable securities held as an investment were sold for $20,000. The securities were inherited from his uncle, who died on March 10 of the current year when FMV of the securities was $21,000. The uncle purchased the securities on May 10, 1990, for $10,700.

In addition to the above sales, Spencer received a $100 refund of state income taxes paid last year. Spencer used the standard deduction last year to compute his tax liability. Prepare Form 1040 and Schedule D for the current year.

CASE STUDY PROBLEMS

I:5-68 As a political consultant for an aspiring politician, you have been hired to evaluate the following statements that pertain to capital gains and losses. Evaluate the statement and provide at least a one-paragraph explanation of each statement. As you prepare your answer, consider the fact that the aspiring politician does not have much knowledge about taxation.

a. The tax on capital gains is considered a voluntary tax.

b. High-income taxpayers receive the most benefit from preferential treatment for capital gains.

I:5-69 Your client, Apex Corporation, entered into an agreement with an executive to purchase his personal residence at its current FMV in the event that his employment is terminated by the company during a five-year period. The executive's job was terminated before the end of the five-year period and Apex acquired the house for $500,000. Due to a downturn in the real estate market, a $200,000 loss was incurred by the company upon the resale of the house. The chief financial officer of Apex insists that the loss be characterized as ordinary, based on the *Corn Products* doctrine. Your research into this matter reveals that the weight of authority heavily favors capital loss treatment (i.e., case law based on facts identical to the above issue held that the loss was capital rather than ordinary). You therefore conclude that the client's position does not have a realistic possibility of being sustained administratively or judicially on its merits if challenged by the IRS. What responsibility do you have as a tax practitioner relative to preparing the client's tax return and rendering continuing tax consulting services to the client? (See the Section *Statements on Standards for Tax Services* in Chapter I:1 for a discussion of these issues.)

TAX RESEARCH PROBLEMS

I:5-70 Tom Williams is an equal partner in a partnership with the Kansas Corporation. Williams, an inventor, produced a new process while working for the partnership, which has been patented by the partnership. Before making any use of the patent, the partnership entered into a contract granting all rights to use the process for the life of the patent to the Mason Manufacturing Co.

The time between receiving the patent and entering into the contract with Mason amounted to eight months. Mason agreed to pay 0.3% of all sales revenue generated by products produced as a result of the process. If Mason fails to make payments on a timely basis, Mason's right to use the process is forfeited and the agreement between the partnership and Mason is canceled. Will any of the proceeds collected qualify as LTCG under Sec. 1235?

A partial list of research sources is

- Reg. Sec. 1.1235-2
- *George N. Soffron*, 35 T.C. 787 (1961)

I:5-71 Lynette, a famous basketball player, is considering the possibility of transferring the sole right to use her name to promote basketball shoes produced and sold by the NIK Corporation. NIK will pay $2 million to obtain the right to use Lynette's name for the next 40 years. NIK may use the name on the shoes and as a part of any of the company's advertisements for basketball shoes. If Lynette signs the contract and receives the $2 million payment, will she have to recognize capital gain or ordinary income?

A partial list of research sources is

- Sec. 1221
- Rev. Rul. 65-261, 1965-2 C.B. 281

I:5-72 Jack, a tenured university professor, has been a malcontent for many years at Rockport University. The university has recently offered to pay $200,000 to Jack if he will relinquish his tenure position and resign. Jack is of the opinion that tenure is an intangible capital asset and the $200,000 received for release of the tenure should be a long-term capital gain. Explain why you agree or disagree.

A partial list of research sources is

- *Harry M. Flower,* 61 T.C. 140 (1973)
- *Estelle Goldman,* 1975 PH T.C. Memo ¶75,138, 34 TCM 639

I:5-73 Web Baker was hired three years ago by the Berry Corporation to serve as CEO for the company. As part of his employment contract, the corporation had agreed to purchase his residence at FMV in the event the company decided to fire him. Last year, Berry, unsatisfied with Web's performance, fired him and purchased the residence for $350,000. Berry immediately listed the house with a real estate agency. Soon after the purchase, the real estate market in the area experienced a serious decline, especially in higher-priced homes. Berry sold the house this year for $270,000 and paid selling expenses of $12,000. How should the Berry Corporation treat the $92,000 loss?

A partial list of research sources is

- Sec. 1221
- Rev. Rul. 82-204, 1982-2 C.B. 192
- *Azar Nut Co. v. CIR,* 67 AFTR 2d 91-987, 91-1 USTC ¶50,257 (5th Cir., 1991)

CHAPTER

6

DEDUCTIONS AND LOSSES

LEARNING OBJECTIVES

After studying this chapter, you should be able to

1. Distinguish between deductions *for* and *from* AGI
2. Discuss the criteria for deducting business and investment expenses
3. Examine the restrictions for deducting expenses
4. List the substantiation requirements for deducting travel and entertainment expenses
5. Explain the timing of deductions under both the cash and accrual methods of accounting
6. Discuss special disallowance rules for deductions
7. Describe tax planning considerations for deductions and losses
8. Describe compliance and procedural considerations for deductions and losses

CHAPTER OUTLINE

The next five chapters deal with deductions. As you recall from Chapters I:3 and I:4, the IRC uses the "all-inclusive" approach when dealing with items of income; that is, gross income includes all items of income unless the income item is specifically excluded by statute. In contrast, unless the IRC specifically provides a deduction, a taxpayer may not deduct an expenditure or expense. For example, a taxpayer who makes a donation to a charity during the year may deduct the donation only because the IRC specifically allows the deduction of charitable contributions under Sec. 170.

Chapter I:6 discusses the general requirements for the deductibility of taxpayer expenditures and losses. Some of these requirements apply to all taxpayers while others apply only to individuals. Chapter I:7 deals with itemized deductions for individual taxpayers, such as medical expenses, taxes, charitable contributions, interest expense, and other miscellaneous deductions. Chapter I:8 covers two major areas that apply to all taxpayers: the deductibility of losses and bad debts. Chapter I:9 discusses employee compensation and expenses, and Chapter I:10 discusses tax depreciation, amortization, and depletion.

As mentioned above, a taxpayer can only deduct an expenditure if the IRC specifically allows the deduction. However, the IRC cannot possibly specify *every* deductible expense that a taxpayer might incur. Therefore, the IRC contains a framework for analyzing the nature of an expenditure. If the expenditure meets the criteria developed in the framework, the taxpayer generally can deduct the item unless specific disallowance or limitation provisions apply. This framework provides three general categories of deductions:

(1) Expenses incurred in connection with a **trade or business** (Sec. 162);
(2) Expenses incurred by an individual in connection with the **production of income** (Sec. 212);
(3) Other types of expenses that fall within specific provisions of the IRC, such as certain types of interest expense, taxes, bad debts, and other expenditures by individuals for personal items such as medical expenses, alimony, and moving costs.

The first two categories of deductions (business expenses and production of income expenses) are for expenditures the taxpayer incurs in connection with a profit-motivated activity. Here again, the IRC does not attempt to specify every conceivable type of deductible business or investment expense. Rather, the IRC establishes general guidelines that a taxpayer must meet in order to deduct an expense as either a business or investment deduction. Thus, in general, a taxpayer may deduct any expense incurred in connection with a trade or business or for the production of income if the expense (1) falls within the general guidelines and (2) the IRC does not specifically exclude or limit the expense from deductibility. For example, although the IRC does not specifically state that a taxpayer can deduct expenditures for utilities or salaries that the taxpayer incurs in a profit-motivated business, the taxpayer can deduct these business expenses under Sec. 162 as long as the expenses meet the general guidelines of Sec. 162 and they are not subject to a specifically stated limitation or exclusion from deductibility. These general guidelines are discussed later in this chapter.

Section 212, which applies only to individuals, allows an individual to deduct expenses that the individual incurs for the:

- Production or collection of income
- Management, conservation, or maintenance of property held for the production of income
- Determination, collection, or refund of any tax

As explained later in this chapter, the general guidelines that the taxpayer must meet in order to deduct expenses incurred in both of these types of activities require that the expenses must be ordinary, necessary, and reasonable in the context of the activity in which they are incurred. Furthermore, if the taxpayer incurs a loss in either of these types of activities, the amount of the deduction may be limited.

Section 262 also provides a general rule that prevents individuals from deducting personal, living, or family expenses. However, the tax law does specifically allow individuals to deduct certain personal expenditures or losses. For example, a taxpayer may deduct casualty losses (subject to certain limitations) for personal-use property. Taxpayers may also deduct personal expenditures for certain types of interest, taxes, medical expenses, alimony, and retirement savings if the expenditures meet strict requirements. Chapters I:7, I:8, and I:9 discuss deductions and losses for personal expenditures.

CLASSIFYING DEDUCTIONS AS FOR VERSUS FROM ADJUSTED GROSS INCOME (AGI)

OBJECTIVE 1

Distinguish between deductions for and from AGI

As mentioned in Chapter I:2, the tax formula for individuals divides allowable business, investment, and personal deductions into the following two categories:

- Deductions subtracted from gross income in order to calculate adjusted gross income (*for* AGI deductions); and
- Deductions subtracted from AGI to calculate taxable income (*from* AGI deductions).

The concept of AGI applies to individual taxpayers, not to other entities such as corporations or partnerships.

Section 62 specifically identifies deductions *for* AGI. All other deductions for individuals are deductions *from* AGI. The more common *for* AGI deductions include the following, subject to certain limitations:

KEY POINT

Most *for* AGI deductions are either expenses the taxpayer incurs in a trade or business or certain investment activities. Most of the deductible personal expenses are deductible *from* AGI.

- All allowable expenses incurred in an individual's trade or business, but not including an employee's unreimbursed business expenses
- Reimbursed employee business expenses
- Certain business expenses incurred by performing artists as well as employees of a state or a political subdivision thereof
- Losses from the sale or exchange of trade, business, or investment property
- Expenses attributable to the production of rent or royalty income
- Contributions to certain pension, profit-sharing, or retirement plan arrangements
- Penalties paid to a bank or other savings institution because of the early withdrawal of funds from a certificate of deposit or time savings account
- Alimony
- Moving expenses
- Cash payments made to a qualified Health Savings Account or Archer Medical Savings Account
- Up to $2,500 of interest paid on qualified educational loans (student loan interest). As part of the American Taxpayer Relief Act of 2012, Congress permanently extended this *for* AGI deduction.
- One-half of the self-employment tax imposed on self-employed individuals and 100% of health insurance costs paid by such individuals.[1]

For individuals, the distinction between deductions *for* AGI and *from* AGI is critical for two reasons. First, as explained in Chapter I:2, the tax formula allows individuals to deduct the greater of the standard deduction or the total of the *from* AGI (itemized) deductions in arriving at taxable income. Thus, a taxpayer does not benefit from these deductions if the total deductible amount for the year does not exceed the standard deduction. Deductions *for* AGI, on the other hand, reduce AGI (and consequently taxable income) even if the taxpayer uses the standard deduction in computing taxable income.

EXAMPLE I:6-1 ▶ Brad, a single individual with no dependents, incurs $6,000 of deductible expenses and earns $75,000 in gross income during 2015. If the expenses are all deductions *from* AGI, Brad will

[1] Sections 62, 162(l) and 164(f). Other deductions *for* AGI include deductions for depreciation and depletion for life tenants and income beneficiaries of property, reforestation expenses, required repayments of supplemental unemployment compensation benefits, certain expenses incurred for clean-fuel vehicles and refueling property, jury duty pay the taxpayer remits to an employer, attorney's fees the taxpayer pays out of awards in certain types of lawsuits, and certain trade or business expenses incurred by members of an Armed Forces unit when the individual is more than 100 miles away from home in connection with performing services as a member of that unit. For tax years beginning before 2015, elementary and high school teachers could also take a limited *for* AGI deduction of up to $250 for out-of-pocket expenses they incur as a teacher, and college students in higher education could deduct qualified tuition and related expenses for their higher education up to a limit of $4,000. Currently Congress is considering extending these deductions either temporarily for a few more years, or permanently.

report taxable income of $64,700 (i.e., Brad receives a $4,000 deduction for his personal exemption and a $6,300 standard deduction). Brad receives no direct tax benefit from the expenses because they do not exceed the standard deduction. However, if the $6,000 of expenses are all deductions *for* AGI, Brad reports taxable income of $58,700 (a $6,000 *for* AGI deduction in addition to the $6,300 standard deduction and the $4,000 personal exemption).

KEY POINT

Many individuals lose the benefit of a *from* AGI deduction because that particular deduction is less than its applicable limit, or the total of the itemized deductions is less than the standard deduction. Furthermore, the IRC phases out certain itemized deductions.

	Deductions from AGI	*Deductions for AGI*
Gross income	$75,000	$75,000
Minus: *For* AGI deductions	0	(6,000)
AGI	$75,000	$69,000
Minus: Standard deduction	(6,300)	(6,300)
Personal exemption	(4,000)	(4,000)
Taxable income	$64,700	$58,700 ◀

The second important reason for the proper classification of deductions is that AGI acts as a limit on the amount of *from* AGI itemized deductions that can be taken. This limitation operates in various ways:

- Taxpayers may deduct certain itemized deductions such as medical expenses, casualty losses, and miscellaneous itemized deductions only to the extent the particular expense exceeds a prescribed percentage of AGI. For example, pursuant to Sec. 67 an individual may deduct certain miscellaneous itemized deductions only to the extent the sum of these deductions for the year exceeds 2% of the individual's AGI. These expenses include unreimbursed employee business expenses,[2] expenses incurred to produce investment income,[3] and the cost of tax advice and tax return preparation (see Chapter I:7). A taxpayer may deduct medical expenses only to the extent the medical expenses exceed 10% of the individual's AGI for the year (7.5% for individuals 65 or older through 2016). Individual taxpayers must first reduce casualty losses on personal-use property by $100 per casualty event. After this reduction, an individual may deduct casualty losses only to the extent that the sum exceeds 10% of the individual's AGI.
- AGI also acts as a limit on the deductibility of certain itemized deductions by placing a limit on the total amount of the deduction. For example, in general the deduction for charitable contributions may not exceed 50% of the taxpayer's AGI.
- Under Sec. 68(a) and (b) in 2015 the amount of certain itemized deductions for high-income taxpayers (taxpayers who are married filing jointly with AGI in excess of $309,900 and single taxpayers with AGI in excess of $258,250) is reduced by three percent of the excess. Additionally, the personal exemptions of these same high-income taxpayers also begin to be phased out when their AGI exceeds these same threshold AGI amounts.

Deductions *for* AGI are generally located in two places on the tax return. First, some deductions *for* AGI appear on the front page of Form 1040. These deductions include such items as moving expenses, alimony paid, one-half of self-employment taxes, and student loan interest. Second, other deductions appear on separate schedules, including Schedule C (Profit or Loss from Business), Schedule E (Supplemental Income or Loss), or Schedule F (Profit or Loss from Farming). The net profit or loss from these schedules carries over to the front page of Form 1040 as part of gross income. Thus, the deductions on these schedules are deductions *for* AGI. Figure I:2-1 in Chapter I:2, contains the front page of Form 1040.

---

[2] These employee business expenses include unreimbursed expenditures for travel and transportation, supplies, special clothing or uniforms, union dues, and subscriptions to trade journals. Reimbursed employee expenses are deductible *for* AGI and thus, are deductible in full. (See Chapter I:9.)

[3] These expenses include rental fees for safe deposit boxes used to hold investment property, subscriptions to investment journals, bank service charges on checking accounts used in an investment or income-producing activity, and fees paid for consulting advice. Expenses incurred in an investment or income-producing activity that generates either rental or royalty income are deductions *for* AGI.

CRITERIA FOR DEDUCTING BUSINESS AND INVESTMENT EXPENSES

OBJECTIVE 2

Discuss the criteria for deducting business and investment expenses

A taxpayer may deduct business and investment expenses only if certain requirements are met. Thus, deductible business or investment expenses must be:

- Related to a profit-motivated activity of the taxpayer (i.e., a business or investment activity rather than a personal expenditure),
- Ordinary,
- Necessary,
- Reasonable in amount,
- Properly documented (discussed later in the chapter under the heading Proper Substantiation Requirement), and
- An expense of the taxpayer (not someone else's expense).

Furthermore, as discussed later in this chapter under the heading General Restrictions on the Deductibility of Expenses, even if the expense meets the requirements for deductibility above, taxpayers may not deduct expenditures meeting certain other criteria. Thus, generally, a taxpayer cannot deduct an expenditure if it is:

- A capital expenditure,
- An expense related to tax-exempt income,
- Illegal or in violation of public policy, or
- Specifically disallowed by the tax law.

Further discussion of these criteria and related matters follows.

BUSINESS OR INVESTMENT ACTIVITY

Deductible expenditures generally originate from a profit-motivated activity. Section 162 provides all taxpayers with a deduction for their business expenses. Additionally, under Sec. 212, individuals can deduct expenses they incur for the production of income or for the maintenance and conservation of income-producing property (an investment activity). Thus, the requirement of an activity being profit-motivated is really two-pronged: (1) a determination of whether an expenditure originates from an activity engaged in for profit and (2) for individuals, a distinction between a trade or business and an investment activity.

REAL-WORLD EXAMPLE

A taxpayer attempted to deduct competitive bass fishing costs as a business expense, but the court concluded that there was no profit motive. Although the taxpayer maintained adequate business records, the taxpayer had a history of promptly ending unprofitable business ventures. His unwillingness to cease tournament bass fishing despite continued losses over several years suggested the lack of a profit motive. Moreover, the taxpayer's lifelong love of fishing suggested that the taxpayer engaged in the activity for personal pleasure rather than for profit. *Thomas W. and Pamela A. Hill*, T.C. Summary Opinion 2006-120.

Activity Engaged in for Profit. This first part of the test classifies the expense as resulting from either a profit-motivated activity or a personal activity. For individuals, classifying expenses as either profit-motivated or personal can be quite difficult. For example, is the activity of coin collecting a hobby that is personal in nature, a profit-motivated business, or an investment activity? No single objective test is available. Rather, a tax advisor must examine all the facts and circumstances surrounding the activity in which the taxpayer incurs expenses in order to make this distinction. The section in this chapter entitled Hobby Losses discusses these factors in more detail, as well as other issues dealing with the determination of whether or not a particular activity is profit-motivated.

Trade or Business Versus Investment Classification. The second part of the profit-motive test involves the determination of whether a particular activity is a trade or business of the taxpayer or only an investment. This distinction generally is important only to individuals since corporations are assumed to be engaged in a business. It is important to individuals for several reasons. First, if an individual realizes a loss on the sale of an asset that the individual used in a business, the individual may be able to deduct the loss as an ordinary loss.[4] On the other hand, if the taxpayer realizes a loss on the sale of an investment

[4] Under Sec. 1231, the exact treatment depends on the total gains and losses from such property for the year. See Chapter I:13 for a discussion of Sec. 1231.

asset, the IRC classifies the loss as a capital loss which, as explained in Chapter I:5, receives different treatment. Second, this distinction may control whether an expense of the activity is a deduction *for* AGI or a deduction *from* AGI. In general, the IRC classifies expenses incurred in a trade or business as deductions *for* AGI whereas investment expenses, other than those incurred to produce rents and royalties, are classified by the IRC as deductions *from* AGI. Additionally, under Sec. 179, taxpayers may elect to currently deduct a specified amount of tangible personal property placed into service during the year if the property is used in a trade or business. For 2015, the maximum amount that a taxpayer may elect to currently deduct under Sec. 179 is $25,000. This $25,000 deductible amount begins to phase out if the taxpayer places into service more than $200,000 of qualified property during 2015. For 2014 the maximum amount that a taxpayer could elect to currently deduct under Sec. 179 was $500,000 and the phase-out began at $2 million. Currently Congress is considering increasing the Sec. 179 deduction and limitation amounts back to what they were in 2014 either temporarily for a few more years, or permanently. (See Chapter I:10 for a discussion of the Sec. 179 expense election for capital expenditures.)

EXAMPLE I:6-2 ▶ Robin is a self-employed financial consultant. She meets daily with a variety of clients to discuss their investments. Because she must keep abreast of the latest market quotes and strategies, Robin subscribes to several trade publications, newsletters, and quote services. During the year, Robin purchased a $4,000 computer to be used exclusively in her consulting business. Robin may deduct the expenses incurred for the publications and services as deductions for AGI because she incurred them in her consulting business. Furthermore, she can currently deduct the $4,000 paid for the computer under the special rules of Sec. 179 because it is a business asset, rather than an investment asset. ◀

Expenses incurred by an individual in an investment activity, other than those incurred to produce rents and royalties, are miscellaneous itemized deductions *from* AGI and are deductible only to the extent they exceed 2% of the taxpayer's AGI for the year (see Chapter I:7).

EXAMPLE I:6-3 ▶ Steve is a wealthy attorney who invests in the stock market and keeps abreast of the latest market quotes and strategies by subscribing to several trade publications and newsletters. This year he purchased a computer he will use exclusively for tracking his investments. Steve generally spends an hour or two each day studying this information and analyzing his portfolio. The subscription expenses are deductions *from* AGI because Steve incurred the expenses in an investment (rather than a business) activity and the expenses do not relate to the production of rents and royalties. Steve cannot currently deduct the entire cost of the computer but must depreciate the cost over a period of five years. Furthermore, the deductibility of all of the above items depends on whether Steve's total miscellaneous itemized deductions exceed 2% of his AGI and whether Steve itemizes his deductions instead of using the standard deduction. ◀

ADDITIONAL COMMENT

A trade or business is an activity with a profit motive and some type of economic activity. An investment activity requires a profit motive but does not require economic activity.

Despite these important differences in treatment, the distinction between an investment activity and a trade or business is not always clear. The IRC and the Treasury Regulations do not provide a precise definition of what constitutes a trade or business. Judicial law, however, does provide some guidelines. In one of the first cases dealing with the issue, the Supreme Court stated that a trade or business involves "holding one's self out to others as engaged in the selling of goods or services."[5]

Later, another Supreme Court case emphasized that one must examine all the surrounding facts and circumstances to determine the underlying nature of an activity.[6] In that case, the taxpayer owned a large portfolio of stocks, bonds, and real estate. The taxpayer's holdings were so large that he rented offices and hired employees to help him manage the properties. The Court, however, regarded these activities as investment activities despite the size of the holdings and the amount of work and effort involved because the taxpayer merely kept records and collected interest and dividends from his securities. Other cases, however, indicate that a taxpayer who invests in stocks and bonds may be considered to be in a business if he or she frequently buys and sells securities in order to make a short-term profit on the daily swings in the market.

---

[5] *Deputy v. Pierre S. DuPont*, 23 AFTR 808, 40-1 USTC ¶9161 (USSC, 1940).

[6] *Eugene Higgins v. CIR*, 25 AFTR 1160, 41-1 USTC ¶9233 (USSC, 1941). See also *Chang H. Liang*, 23 T.C. 1040 (1955), and *Ralph E. Purvis v. CIR*, 37 AFTR 2d 76-968, 76-1 USTC ¶9270 (9th Cir., 1976); and *Samuel B. Levin v. U.S.*, 43 AFTR 2d 79-612, 79-1 USTC ¶9331 (Ct. Cls., 1979).

Legal and Accounting Fees. Taxpayers may generally deduct legal and accounting fees incurred in the regular conduct of a trade or business or for the production of income. Taxpayers may also deduct fees incurred for the determination, collection, or refund of any tax. These deductions are *for* AGI if incurred in a trade or business or for the production of rents and royalties. Legal and accounting fees incurred in the determination or collection of taxes are also *for* AGI deductions if paid to prepare a taxpayer's Schedule C (Profit or Loss from Business), Part I of Schedule E (Supplemental Income and Loss, which is used to report rental and royalty income), and Schedule F (Farm Income and Expenses).[7] All other deductible legal and accounting fees incurred by the taxpayer are deductible *from* AGI as miscellaneous itemized deductions, subject to the 2% of AGI limitation. A filled-in Schedule C and copies of Schedule E and Schedule F are provided in Appendix B.

Taxpayers may not deduct legal fees they incur in connection with the purchase of property. Instead, taxpayers must capitalize these expenses by adding them to the cost of the property. Likewise, taxpayers generally may not deduct legal expenses they incur for personal purposes.

EXAMPLE I:6-4 ▶ During the current year, Lia pays legal and accounting fees for the following:

Services rendered with regard to a contract dispute in Lia's business	$ 8,000
Services rendered in resolving a federal tax deficiency relating to Lia's business	2,500
Tax return preparation fees:	
Allocable to preparation of Schedule C	1,600
Allocable to preparation of Schedules A and B and to the remainder of Form 1040	400
Legal fees incident to a divorce	1,200
Total	$13,700

Lia may deduct $12,100 ($8,000 + $2,500 + $1,600) *for* AGI because these legal expenses are associated with Lia's business. Lia may deduct the remaining $400 of tax preparation fees as a miscellaneous itemized deduction from AGI subject to the 2% of AGI limitation. The legal fees incident to the divorce are personal expenses and generally are not deductible. However, Lia could take a partial deduction *from* AGI as a miscellaneous itemized deduction to the extent these legal fees relate to giving tax advice incident to the divorce. ◀

ORDINARY EXPENSE

A business or investment expense must also be "ordinary" in order for a taxpayer to be able to deduct the expense. Although the IRC does not provide either a definition or an application of this requirement, the Treasury Regulations under Sec. 212 indicate that for an expense to be ordinary it must be reasonable in amount and it must bear a reasonable and proximate relationship to the income-producing activity or property. This means that more than a remote connection must exist between the expense and the anticipated income. It does not mean that the property must be producing income currently.

EXAMPLE I:6-5 ▶ Ahmed purchases a plot of land, on which there is an old vacant warehouse. Ahmed anticipates making a long-term profit from the investment because the value of the land is expected to appreciate eventually due to commercial development in the area. To help cover the costs of holding the property, Ahmed plans to rent storage space in the warehouse. During the current year, although he is unable to rent the warehouse, Ahmed incurs the following expenses:

ADDITIONAL COMMENT

A General Accounting Office report finds that tax cheating is widespread among self-employed taxpayers. These workers represent only 13% of all taxpayers, but account for approximately 40% of all underreported individual income. The report identified truckers as one of the least compliant groups.

Expenses	*Amount*
Property taxes	$1,000
Interest	4,000
Insurance	800
Utilities	200

All of these expenditures qualify as ordinary deductible investment expenses under Sec. 212 because they bear a reasonable and proximate relationship to the income Ahmed hopes to obtain, even though he generated no income from the property during the year. However, Ahmed might not be able to deduct them all in the current year because of the passive loss limitations explained in Chapter I:8. ◀

[7] Rev. Rul. 92-29, 1992-1 C.B. 20.

The Supreme Court has ruled that for an expense to be ordinary it must be customary or usual in the context of a particular industry or business community.[8] Thus, an expenditure may be ordinary in the context of one type of business, but not in the context of another.

EXAMPLE I:6-6 ▶ For many years, Hank has been an officer in Green Corporation, which is engaged in the grain business. Green Corporation purchases its grain from various suppliers. Last year, Green Corporation went bankrupt and was relieved from having to pay off its debts to its suppliers. In the current year, Hank enters into a contract to act as a commissioned agent to purchase grain for Green Corporation. To reestablish a relationship with suppliers whom Hank knew previously, Hank decides to pay off as many of Green Corporation's debts as he can. Hank is under no legal obligation to do so. Hank's payments are not ordinary. Rather, they are extraordinary expenditures made for goodwill to establish Hank in a new trade or business, and they must be capitalized. ◀

An expense may be ordinary with respect to a taxpayer even though that taxpayer encounters it only once.

EXAMPLE I:6-7 ▶ For several years, Health for You, Inc., has been engaged in the business of making and selling dietary supplements. Health for You, Inc., does most of the advertisements, orders, and deliveries of the supplements through the mail. During the current year, the post office judged that some of the advertisements were false. As a result, a fraud order is issued under which the post office stamps "Fraudulent" on all letters addressed to Health for You, Inc., and then returns them to the senders. In an unsuccessful suit to prevent the post office from continuing this practice, Health for You, Inc. expends $50,000 in lawyer's fees. These fees are ordinary business expenses because Health For You, Inc. incurred them in an action that a taxpayer normally or ordinarily would have taken under these circumstances. ◀

REAL-WORLD EXAMPLE

A corporation made payments to an individual who was a 50% shareholder in the corporation. The corporation made these payments to the individual to prevent him from interfering in the management of the business and damaging the corporation's reputation. The Tax Court held that these payments were necessary business expenses. *Fairmont Homes, Inc.*, 1983 PH T.C. Memo ¶83,209, 45 TCM 1340.

The Supreme Court has also indicated that the term *ordinary* in this context refers to an expenditure that is currently deductible rather than an expenditure that must be capitalized.[9]

NECESSARY EXPENSE

In addition to being ordinary, a deductible investment or business expense must also be **necessary**. The Supreme Court has indicated that an expense is considered necessary if it is "appropriate and helpful" in the taxpayer's business.[10] To meet this appropriate or helpful standard, an expenditure need not be necessary in the sense that it is indispensable. Rather, the test is whether a reasonable or prudent businessperson would incur the same expenditure under similar circumstances.

EXAMPLE I:6-8 ▶ The expenditures in Example I:6-6 (the payment of debts from a former business) and Example I:6-7 (the payment of legal fees) are both necessary because they are appropriate and helpful in each case. However, the expenditure in Example I:6-6 is not ordinary and, therefore, is not deductible. The expenditure in Example I:6-7 is deductible because it meets both tests. ◀

REASONABLE EXPENSE

Section 162 and Treasury Regulations under Sec. 212 provide that in order to be deductible the business or investment expense must be reasonable. Problems with meeting this standard can arise when a closely-held C corporation pays a salary to an individual who is both a shareholder and an employee. In this situation, a controlling shareholder of a C corporation may receive a payment, characterized as salary, that the IRS asserts is too large for the services the individual employee rendered.

EXAMPLE I:6-9 ▶ Central Corporation pays Brian, the controlling shareholder and an employee of Central Corporation, an annual salary of $650,000. Based on several factors, such as the size of Central Corporation's total operations, Brian's duties as an employee, and a comparison of salary received by officers of comparably sized corporations, the IRS contends that Brian's salary should be no higher than $300,000. If Central successfully defends the $650,000 salary, the corporation is able to deduct the full amount as salary expense. If Central Corporation's defense is not successful, the IRS will treat

[8] *Thomas H. Welch v. Helvering*, 12 AFTR 1456, 3 USTC ¶1164 (USSC, 1933) and *Deputy v. Pierre S. DuPont*, 23 AFTR 808, 40-1 USTC ¶9161 (USSC, 1940).

[9] *CIR v. S. B. Heininger*, 31 AFTR 783, 44-1 USTC ¶9109 (USSC, 1943). See also *CIR v. Walter F. Tellier*, 17 AFTR 2d 633, 66-1 USTC ¶9319 (USSC, 1966).

[10] *Thomas H. Welch v. Helvering*, 12 AFTR 1456, 3 USTC ¶1164 (USSC, 1933).

KEY POINT

The IRS also applies the reasonable standard in determining whether a salary paid to the owner of an S corporation is too low. This may occur if the owner is attempting to avoid the payment of self-employment taxes.

KEY POINT

Since the Sec. 162(m) compensation deduction limit applies only to publicly-held corporations, privately-held corporations are faced with the general reasonable standard which looks at the particular facts and circumstances.

the excess $350,000 as a dividend to the extent of Central Corporation's earnings and profits, and Central Corporation may not take a deduction for the dividend. In either event, Brian must take the full $650,000 into income. (See the Tax Planning Considerations section in this chapter for a discussion of the use of a payback agreement in these situations.) ◀

In an attempt to link executive compensation to productivity and business performance and to discourage a common practice of increasing executive compensation despite declines in business performance, Congress enacted Sec. 162(m) which disallows a deduction for compensation paid to certain "covered employees" of publicly-held companies that exceeds a yearly amount of $1 million. The definition of a covered employee is based on the Securities Exchange Act of 1934 and states that a covered employee is the publicly-held company's chief executive officer plus the four highest paid corporate officers whose compensation is required to be reported under that Act. In 2006 the Securities Exchange Act was changed to define a covered employee as (1) the corporation's chief executive officer, (2) the corporation's principal financial officer, and (3) the corporation's three highest paid executives whose compensation is required to be reported to the corporation's shareholders. Because of this change in the Securities Exchange Act and a strict technical interpretation of the language of the law, IRS Notice 2007–49 explicitly states that the Sec. 162(m) deduction limit will now be applicable to compensation paid to (1) the company's chief executive officer and (2) the company's three highest paid executives whose compensation is required to be reported to the corporation's shareholders. The company's principal financial officer is not included in this definition. Thus, the company can deduct the principal financial officer's compensation even if the principal financial officer is among the company's three highest paid executives. This limitation does not apply to compensation based on commissions or other performance goals. Special rules and limitations apply to certain employers that are participating in the Troubled Asset Relief Program (TARP). [See Sec. 162(m)(5)].

The tests for determining whether a business or investment expense is deductible are summarized in Topic Review I:6-1.

EXPENSES AND LOSSES INCURRED DIRECTLY BY THE TAXPAYER

Generally, taxpayers may not take a deduction for a loss or expense of another person. This requirement attempts to prevent taxpayers from engaging in manipulative schemes.

EXAMPLE I:6-10 ▶ Juanita owns 60% of Hot Clothes, Inc. As CEO of Hot Clothes, Juanita travels extensively. This year Hot Clothes purchases a business jet to facilitate Juanita's travel. In addition to her business travel, Juanita also uses the jet to take several family vacations. In general, Hot Clothes may not take a deduction for

TOPIC REVIEW I:6-1

Tests for Deductibility as a Business or Investment Expense

Test	Application
Ordinary	▶ Based on the facts and circumstances. ▶ Reasonable and proximate relationship to the activity. ▶ Customary or usual in context of the industry. ▶ Need not be encountered by the taxpayer more than once.
Necessary	▶ Based on the facts and circumstances. ▶ Appropriate and helpful. ▶ Need not be indispensable. ▶ Would a reasonable or prudent businessperson incur the same expense?
Reasonable	▶ Based on the facts and circumstances. ▶ Applies to all business and investment expenses. ▶ Compensation paid to an owner-employee of a small corporation is the most commonly contested area. ▶ Compensation in excess of $1 million payable by a publicly-held corporation to its key executives may not be deductible.

Juanita's personal expenses. In order for the business to deduct these amounts, Juanita and the corporation must follow one of two procedures: (1) Juanita must report as additional compensation an amount that represents the use of the jet for her vacations, or (2) Juanita must reimburse Hot Clothes for the use of the jet for her vacations. However, even if Juanita does follow one of these procedures, the amount Hot Clothes, Inc. may deduct for Juanita's private use of the jet may be limited. ◀

This general rule requiring the taxpayer to directly incur the expense applies to all types of expenditures, whether incurred in a trade or business, an investment activity, or a personal activity for which deductions are allowed. There is one exception: under Sec. 213 taxpayers may take a deduction for medical expenses paid on behalf of a dependent. Individuals may also deduct medical expenses that they pay for a person who would qualify as a dependent except for failing to meet certain other tests (see Chapter I:2). For example, under Sec. 152, the dependent's gross income must be less than the exemption amount to qualify as a qualifying relative, but for Sec. 213 this requirement is disregarded.

EXAMPLE I:6-11 ▶ During the current year, Dan incurs $5,000 in deductible medical expenses. Dan's father, Tom, pays for all of Dan's support. Dan is 23 and is not a full-time student and therefore does not qualify as a dependent under the qualifying child rules of Sec. 152(c). Dan's gross income for the year is $15,000, which exceeds the exemption amount, and therefore Dan is not a qualifying relative of Tom under Sec. 152(d). If Tom pays Dan's medical expenses, Tom may add these expenses to his own itemized medical expenses (subject to the 10% of AGI limitation) because of the modified test in Sec. 213 even though Tom may not take a dependency exemption for Dan. ◀

GENERAL RESTRICTIONS ON THE DEDUCTIBILITY OF EXPENSES

OBJECTIVE 3

Examine the restrictions for deducting expenses

As mentioned earlier on page I:6-5, certain types of expenditures are not deductible. These types of expenditures fall within various categories discussed below.

CAPITALIZATION VERSUS EXPENSE DEDUCTION

General Capitalization Requirements. Under Sec. 162 a taxpayer may currently deduct ordinary, necessary, and reasonable business expenses that the taxpayer incurs for the operation and maintenance of tangible property the taxpayer uses in a business. However, under Sec. 263, expenditures that (1) provide a permanent improvement or "betterment" that increases the value of any property, or (2) "restore" the property are considered **capital expenditures**, which generally must be capitalized and depreciated over an appropriate number of years. The Treasury recently issued new temporary regulations that became effective in 2014. These regulations are very detailed in establishing when certain expenditures may be currently expensed and when the expenditures must be capitalized. Taxpayers must also capitalize the cost of goodwill purchased in connection with the acquisition of the assets of a going concern.[11] (See Chapter I:10 for a discussion of the amortization of goodwill.)

Although taxpayers may depreciate or amortize certain business assets, such as buildings, machinery, equipment, furniture and fixtures, purchased goodwill, and customer lists, other assets, such as land, stock, and partnership interests, are neither depreciable nor amortizable and taxpayers must wait until they sell these assets to recover the cost of the assets. In some instances, it is difficult to ascertain whether an asset is eligible for depreciation or amortization. For example, the Tax Court has held that antique violin bows and an antique bass violin are depreciable property, overriding the IRS's arguments that they should not be depreciable because they were actually appreciating in value and it was impossible to determine their useful life.[12]

As mentioned above, maintenance and repair expenditures that only keep an asset in a normal operating condition are deductible if they do not provide a permanent improvement

[11] Reg. Sec. 1.263(a)-2(h). See also *Indopco, Inc., v. CIR*, 69 AFTR 2d 92-694, 92-1 USTC ¶50,113 (USSC, 1992), where expenses incurred by a corporation that was the target of a "friendly" takeover were held to be nondeductible capital expenditures because they provided long-term benefits to the corporation. In this case, the Supreme Court held that these long-term benefits do not need to be associated with a specific identifiable asset.

[12] *Richard L. Simon*, 103 T.C. 247 (1994) and *Brian P. Liddle*, 76 AFTR 2d 95-6255, 95-2 USTC ¶50,488 (3rd Cir., 1959). The IRS has stated it will not follow these decisions. See AOD 96-9, 7/15/96.

ADDITIONAL COMMENT

Some provisions permit taxpayers to depreciate or amortize capital expenditures over a relatively short period of time. For example, there is a rapid write-off available for pollution control facilities under Sec. 169 and for organization costs of corporations under Sec. 248.

BOOK-TAX COMPARISON

Although for tax purposes a taxpayer may elect to deduct these capital expenditures, for book purposes capital expenditures must still be capitalized and depreciated or amortized. This difference in treatment gives rise to a book-tax adjustment on Schedule M-1 or M-3 of a corporation's Form 1120 or a partnership's Form 1065.

or betterment that increases the value of the property or restore the property to its normal usage. Distinguishing between a currently deductible expenditure and a capital expenditure that must be capitalized and depreciated over time can be very difficult. This difficulty has caused a lot of uncertainty and controversy for taxpayers. For example, in an old Tax Court case, the court held that expenditures incurred in replacing support beams and floor joists to shore up a sagging floor were deductible, whereas the court held that the cost of placing a new floor over an old one was a capital expenditure.[13] Because of this difficulty, the Treasury Department has recently issued new Temporary Regulations that provide more clear guidance for taxpayers. These new regulations contain many examples that can help taxpayers and their advisors distinguish the proper tax treatment of these expenditures. In any event, a tax advisor must examine all of the facts and circumstances in light of the guidance contained in these new regulations in order to determine whether any particular expenditure constitutes a deductible expense or a capitalized expenditure.

Election to Deduct Currently. Taxpayers sometimes may elect a current deduction for certain capital expenditures. Taxpayers often prefer a current deduction over capitalizing and depreciating an asset because of the time value of money. Some expenditures that taxpayers may elect to deduct currently[14] include: cost of fertilizers incurred by farmers, cost of soil and water conservation incurred by farmers, intangible drilling costs incurred in drilling oil and gas wells, costs for tertiary injectants, costs for certain mining development projects, costs incurred to remove architectural and transportation barriers to the handicapped and elderly, and costs for certain qualified research and experimental expenditures.

As mentioned previously, under Sec. 179 a taxpayer may also elect to currently deduct a limited amount of capital expenditures for new tangible property the taxpayer purchases to use in a trade or business. Additionally, for years prior to 2015 a taxpayer could elect to currently take a "50% bonus depreciation deduction" for certain qualified new property the taxpayer purchases during the year instead of depreciating the full cost of the property over its depreciable life. Currently Congress is considering extending the bonus depreciation deduction either temporarily for a few more years, or permanently. See Chapter I:10 for a discussion of the limitations of these deductions and how they apply.

Capitalization of Deduction Items. The exceptions mentioned above provide a current deduction for expenditures that are normally capital in nature. Conversely, Section 266 provides for the capitalization of certain expenses that are normally deductible. Section 266 is elective and applies to the following items:

- Interest and employment taxes incurred in transporting and installing personalty (as opposed to realty) up to the time when the taxpayer first puts the property into use.
- Annual property taxes, interest on a mortgage, and other carrying charges incurred on unimproved and unproductive real estate.
- Annual property taxes, interest, employment taxes, and other necessary expenses incurred for the development, improvement, or construction of real property, prior to the time construction is completed. For these expenses to be capitalized, the real property may be either improved or unimproved, productive or unproductive. After construction is completed, these types of expenses are fully deductible when incurred.

A taxpayer may make a new election to capitalize the expenses on unimproved and unproductive real estate each year.

EXAMPLE I:6-12 ▶ During 2015 and 2016, Nancy pays property taxes of $5,000 on a plot of land. During 2015, the land is vacant and unproductive. In 2016, Nancy uses the land as a parking lot, generating $7,000 in income. Nancy can elect to capitalize the taxes in 2015 because the property is both unimproved and unproductive. In 2016, however, the land is productive, and Nancy cannot elect to capitalize the taxes. Because the expenses relate to the production of rental income, Nancy can deduct them *for* AGI. If the land remains unproductive during 2016, Nancy can elect to capitalize the taxes paid in 2016. However, the election is optional and Nancy doesn't need to make the election for 2016 merely because she made the election for 2015. ◀

[13] *Standard Fruit Product Co.*, 1949 PH T.C. Memo ¶49,207, 8 TCM 733.

[14] See Secs. 180, 175, 263(c), 193, 616, 190, and 174 respectively.

For the development or construction of real property, if the taxpayer makes the election to capitalize the other expenses incurred during the development or construction period the election remains in effect for that year and for all subsequent years until the end of the construction period. However, a taxpayer may make the election on each new project separately.

EXAMPLE I:6-13 ▶ During the current year, Development, Inc. begins construction of an office building and a hotel. Development, Inc. incurs $20,000 in property taxes during the construction of the office building and $12,000 for the hotel. The election to capitalize the taxes on the office building does not bind Development, Inc. to make the same election with respect to the taxes on the hotel. ◀

If a taxpayer elects to capitalize this type of expense under Sec. 266, the expense increases the taxpayer's basis in the property to which the election pertains. If the property is depreciable, the taxpayer may deduct the expenses as depreciation deductions over a certain period. Taxpayers would want to make this election if they have large net operating loss (NOL) carryovers, or if they expect to be in a significantly higher tax bracket in future years and thus estimate that the benefit of the deduction will be greater in the future.

Under Sec. 263A, certain taxpayers must capitalize certain costs into inventory instead of taking a current deduction. (See Chapter I:11 for a discussion of inventories.)

SELF-STUDY QUESTION

Alpha, Inc., borrows $100,000 at a 10% rate of interest and invests the $100,000 in exempt bonds yielding 8%. Alpha is in the 35% tax bracket. Calculate what Alpha's cash flow on these transactions would be on an after-tax basis if Alpha could deduct these expenses.

ANSWER

Alpha, Inc., has $8,000 of exempt income and $10,000 of interest expense. Cash flows would be equal to ($2,000) since there is no tax benefit for the interest. If the interest expense were deductible, its after-tax cost would be $6,500 ($10,000 − $3,500). Alpha's cash flow would be $1,500 ($8,000 − $6,500), allowing Alpha to make money on an unsound investment.

EXPENSES RELATED TO EXEMPT INCOME

Under Sec. 265, taxpayers may not deduct any expense allocated or related to tax-exempt income. The purpose of this disallowance is to prevent the taxpayer from receiving a double tax benefit.

The IRC specifically disallows interest expense on debt the taxpayer incurs in order to purchase or hold tax-exempt securities. Thus, the disallowance depends on the taxpayer's intended use of the loan proceeds. Intent is generally determined by an examination of all the facts and circumstances surrounding the transaction rather than a mere statement of intent. Intent to hold tax-exempt securities is shown if the tax-exempt securities are used as collateral in securing a loan.[15] If an individual who holds tax-exempt securities later incurs some debt, no disallowance will occur if the debt is incurred to finance personal items for which an interest deduction may be taken (e.g., a mortgage on a personal residence). However, if a taxpayer incurs the debt to finance an investment, a deduction for a portion of the interest is generally disallowed. Even though the debt is not incurred to hold tax-exempt securities, the deductibility of interest may still be limited. For example, if a taxpayer incurs interest on personal debt, this interest is not deductible unless the loan qualifies as home aquisition or home equity indebtedness. (See Chapter I:7 for a discussion of limitations on the deductibility of personal interest.)

EXAMPLE I:6-14 ▶ Asian, Inc. has invested $80,000 in Gold Corporation stock, $120,000 in real estate, and $50,000 in tax-exempt municipal bonds. During the current year, Asian borrows $70,000 for the purpose of investing in a limited partnership. For the year, the company pays $6,000 interest on the loan. Under these circumstances, the IRS will presume that Asian, Inc. has incurred a portion of the debt in order to hold the tax-exempt securities and will disallow a portion of the deduction. Asian may overcome that presumption if it can show that it could not have sold the tax-exempt securities. Merely showing that the sale of the bonds would result in a loss will not overcome this presumption. ◀

BOOK-TAX COMPARISON

For book purposes, tax-exempt income and related expenses are included in the calculation of net income. For tax purposes, they are excluded from gross income resulting in a permanent book-tax difference that must be reported on schedule M-1 or M-3.

EXPENDITURES CONTRARY TO PUBLIC POLICY

Taxpayers may not deduct certain expenditures, if the payment itself is illegal or if the payment is a penalty or fine resulting from an illegal act. These nondeductible expenses generally fall within one of the following categories: illegal payments to government officials or employees; other illegal payments; kickbacks, rebates, and bribes under Medicare and Medicaid; payments of fines and penalties; and payment of treble damages under the federal antitrust laws.

REAL-WORLD EXAMPLE

A subcontractor involved with the construction of a new shopping mall made kickbacks to the supervisor of the primary contractor. The kickbacks were deductible because they were not illegal, and the kickbacks were also ordinary and necessary because the subcontractor would not have been able to continue to work if the kickbacks had not been made. *Raymond Bertolini Trucking Co. v. CIR*, 54 AFTR 2d 84-5413, 1984-2 USTC ¶9591 (6th Cir., 1984).

Bribes and Kickbacks. Under Sec. 162(c)(1), any illegal bribe or kickback made to any official or employee of a government is not deductible. This applies to payments made to: federal officials and employees; state, local, and foreign government officials and employees; and officials and employees of an agency of a government.

[15] Rev. Proc. 72-18, 1972-1 C.B. 740 and Rev. Proc. 87-53, 1987-2 C.B. 669. See also *Wisconsin Cheeseman, Inc. v. U.S.*, 21 AFTR 2d 383, 68-1 USTC ¶9145 (7th Cir., 1968).

EXAMPLE I:6-15 ▶ During February of the current year, Road Corporation enters into a contract with the State of Iowa to construct a five-mile stretch of a new highway. Under the terms of the contract, Road Corporation must complete the project by October 22 of the current year. If it is not completed and accepted by Iowa on or before that date, Iowa will fine Road Corporation $5,000 per day for every day after October 22 until the project is accepted. By October 20, the project foreman realizes that the company will not make the deadline if it complies with all the requirements imposed by the state inspector assigned to the project. To avoid the fine, the foreman arranges for the inspector to "look the other way" on several of the requirements in exchange for a payment of $8,000. Because this payment constitutes an illegal bribe to a government official, the payment is not deductible. On the other hand, assume Road Corporation does not pay the bribe and that it finishes the project four days after the deadline. In this case Road Corporation must pay $20,000 in fines. These fines are not imposed because of an illegal act. Thus, Road Corporation can deduct the $20,000 as an ordinary and necessary business expense. ◀

Taxpayers may not deduct illegal payments to officials or employees of a foreign government if the payment is unlawful under the Foreign Corrupt Practices Act of 1977, unless such payments constitute a normal way of doing business in that country. In all cases, the burden rests on the government to prove the illegality of the payment.

If a taxpayer makes illegal bribes, kickbacks, and other illegal payments to people other than a government official or employee, the payments are nondeductible if they are illegal under a federal law that subjects the payor to a criminal penalty or loss of the privilege of doing business. In addition, illegal payments under a state law imposing the same penalties are nondeductible, but only if the state generally enforces its law. Here, the definition of a kickback includes a payment for referring a client, patient, or customer.

ETHICAL POINT

A CPA discovers that a client included fines and penalties in a miscellaneous expense section of a previously filed tax return. The CPA should recommend the filing of an amended return. However, the CPA is not obligated to inform the IRS, and the CPA may not do so without the client's permission, except where required by law.

The courts and the IRS have made a distinction between an illegal nondeductible kickback and a rebate on the purchase of an item. If the seller pays a rebate directly to the purchaser, it is an adjustment to the selling price and, as such, is an *exclusion* (rather than a deduction) from gross income.[16] The distinction between the two payments seems to be that the seller and purchaser negotiate the rebate as part of the selling price.

Section 162(c)(3) specifically disallows a deduction for any kickback, rebate, or bribe under Medicare and Medicaid. Disallowed amounts include payments made by physicians or by suppliers and providers of goods and services who receive payment under the Social Security Act or a federally funded state plan. Unlike payments to foreign government or nongovernment employees and officials, these payments need not be illegal under federal or state law.

STOP & THINK

Question: Queen, Inc., is engaged in the ship and boat repair business. Since competition in this industry is very tough, Queen generally kicks back approximately 10% of any repair bill to any ship captain who brings the ship to Queen for repairs. Queen's customers include individual owners of large ocean-going yachts and fishing boats, as well as government vessels owned by state, federal, and foreign governments. During the current year, Queen paid $80,000 in kickbacks to the captains of privately-owned yachts and boats, $40,000 to the owners of privately-owned vessels, and $100,000 to the captains of state, federal, and foreign government vessels. The crews of these government vessels are government employees. What is the proper tax treatment of these payments?

Solution: The $40,000 in kickbacks paid directly to the owners of the privately-owned vessels are treated as merely a rebate in the price of the services and reduces Queen's gross income, unless the payments could result in the imposition of a criminal penalty or loss of the privilege of doing business. The kickbacks paid to the captains of the state and federal vessels are not deductible because they are paid to employees of state and federal governments. The kickbacks paid to the captains of the privately-owned vessels are not deductible if they are illegal and subject the payor to a criminal penalty or loss of the privilege to do business. Likewise, the payments to the captains of the foreign vessels are not deductible if the payments are unlawful under the Foreign Corrupt Practices Act.

16 Rev. Rul. 82-149, 1982-2 C.B. 56.

Fines and Penalties. Section 162(f) of the IRC also disallows a deduction for the payment of any fine or penalty paid to a government because of the violation of a law.

Furthermore, the IRC disallows a deduction for two-thirds of any payment the taxpayer makes for damages resulting from a conviction (or a guilty or no-contest plea) in an action regarding a criminal violation of the federal antitrust laws.[17]

EXAMPLE I:6-16 ▶ During the current year, the United States files criminal and civil actions against Allen, the president of Able Corporation, and Betty, the president of Bell Corporation, for conspiring to fix and maintain prices of electrical transformers. Both Allen and Betty enter pleas of no contest, and the appropriate judgments are entered. Subsequent to this action, Circle Corporation sues both Able and Bell Corporations for treble damages of $3,000,000. In settlement, Able and Bell Corporations each pay Circle Corporation $750,000. For these damage settlements, Able and Bell Corporations may each deduct $250,000 ($750,000 ÷ 3). ◀

Expenses Relating to an Illegal Activity. Interestingly, although the payment of an illegal bribe or kickback and the payment of a fine or penalty as the result of an illegal act are both nondeductible, other expenses incurred in an illegal business activity are generally deductible if they are ordinary, necessary, and reasonable and the taxpayer reports the income from the illegal activity.[18]

EXAMPLE I:6-17 ▶ Acme, Inc., owns and operates a small financial services business involved in the sale of securities and the lending of money. Acme often sells securities to customers in other states. However, because Acme has not registered the business with the appropriate state or federal authorities, the operation of the business is illegal. During the current year, Acme incurs the following expenses:

Interest	$ 20,000
Salaries	140,000
Depreciation	7,000
Printing	5,000
Bribe to employee of state securities commission	12,000
Total	$184,000

If Acme reports the income from this activity, the deductible expenses for the year total $172,000. The illegal bribe paid of $12,000 to the government employee is not deductible. ◀

One exception to this general rule exists. Section 280E disallows a deduction for expenses incurred in an illegal business of trafficking or dealing in drugs.

OTHER EXPENDITURES SPECIFICALLY DISALLOWED

The IRC also specifically disallows deductions for certain other expenses, even though they might meet all the requirements mentioned previously. These include political contributions and lobbying expenses and, in certain situations, business start-up expenses.

Political Contributions and Lobbying Expenses. Political contributions and lobbying expenses constitute one general category of disallowed expenses. Taxpayers may not deduct expenditures made in connection with the following:

- Influencing legislation
- Participating or intervening in any political campaign of any candidate for public office
- Attempting to influence the general public with respect to elections, legislative matters, or referendums
- Communicating directly with the President, Vice President, and certain other federal employees and officials

[17] Sec. 162(g).
[18] *CIR v. Neil Sullivan, et al.*, 1 AFTR 2d 1158, 58-1 USTC ¶9368 (USSC, 1958).

Sec. 162(e) also denies a deduction for contributions to tax-exempt organizations that carry on lobbying activities if a principal purpose of the contribution is to obtain a deduction for what otherwise would have been disallowed. Furthermore, the IRC disallows payments made for advertising in a convention or any other program if any part of the proceeds of the publication will directly or indirectly benefit a specific political party or candidate.[19]

Taxpayers may deduct lobbying expenses incurred to influence legislation on a local level if the legislation is of direct interest to the taxpayer's business. Local legislation includes actions by a legislative body of any political subdivision of a state (e.g., city or county council), but does not include any state or federal action. These deductible expenditures include expenses of communicating with or dues paid to an organization of which the taxpayer is a member. For administrative convenience, the deduction disallowance does not apply to any in-house expenditure attributable to such activities as long as the total of such expenditures for the taxable year does not exceed $2,000. In-house expenditures are expenses incurred directly by the taxpayer other than amounts paid to a professional lobbyist or dues that are allocable to lobbying. Additionally, the deduction disallowance does not apply to taxpayers engaged in the business of lobbying.

EXAMPLE I:6-18 ▶ Kensey & Associates is a large New York law firm. It is not in the lobbying business. During the year, the firm spends $6,000 to send some of its employees to Washington, D.C., to testify before a Congressional subcommittee with regard to proposed changes in the Social Security taxes imposed on employers. Such changes directly affect the firm's business because they affect the amount of taxes it must pay on behalf of its employees. The firm's ordinary and necessary expenses incurred with respect to the trip are not deductible because the expenses were incurred to influence federal rather than local legislation. ◀

If the legislation cannot reasonably be expected to directly affect the taxpayer's trade or business, the expenses are not deductible.

EXAMPLE I:6-19 ▶ Realty, LLC is a residential real estate company located in Chicago. The city of Chicago has proposed legislation to increase the hotel room tax. Realty spends time researching and traveling to speak to the Chicago City Council regarding this legislation. Although Realty, LLC incurs these expenses in an effort to influence legislation on the local level, it may not deduct these expenses because they are not of direct interest to its business. ◀

Business Investigation and Preopening Expenses. At the election of the taxpayer, Section 195 of the IRC allows a current deduction in the year in which the business starts for business start-up expenditures. The current deduction amounts to the lesser of the amount of the start-up expenditures or $5,000, with a dollar for dollar phaseout for amounts incurred over $50,000. Taxpayers must capitalize and amortize the remaining portion of start-up expenditures over a period of 180 months starting with the month in which the new business begins. Start-up expenditures specifically include three types of expenditures:

- *Business investigation expenses.* These expenses are costs a taxpayer incurs in reviewing and analyzing a prospective business before deciding whether to acquire or create it. The key here is that the taxpayer incurs the expenses before making a decision. These expenses include such items as analyses and surveys of markets, traffic patterns, products, labor supplies, and distribution facilities.

ADDITIONAL COMMENT

Costs incurred in connection with the issuance of stock or securities do not qualify as start-up costs. These costs are charged to Paid-in Capital.

- *Preopening or start-up costs.* Preopening or start-up costs are expenses incurred after a taxpayer decides to acquire or create a business but before the business activity itself has started. These costs include expenditures for training employees; advertising; securing supplies, distributors, and potential customers; and professional services in setting up the business' books and records. These costs must be incurred by a taxpayer not engaged in any existing business or engaged in a business unrelated to the business the taxpayer is acquiring or creating.

---

[19] Sec. 276(a). Nondeductible political contributions also include payments for admission to a dinner or program where the proceeds will benefit a party or candidate, or admission to an inaugural ball, party, or concert if the activity is identified with a political party or candidate.

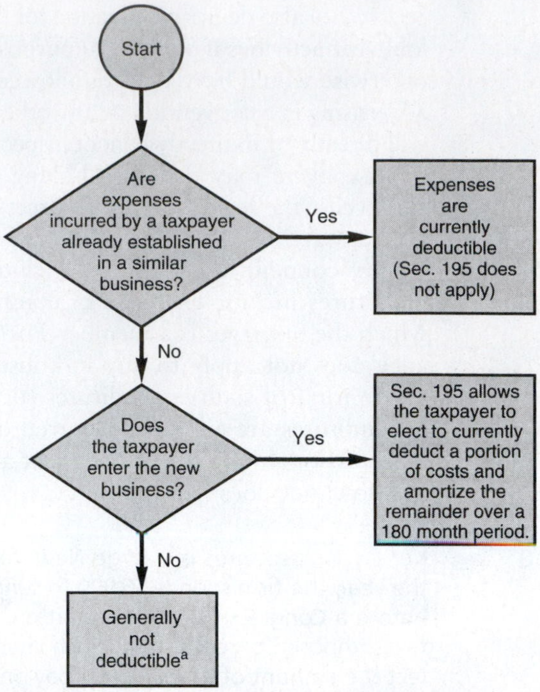

[a] Rev. Rul. 57-418, 1957-2 C.B. 143 and Rev. Rul. 77-254, 1977-2 C.B. 63; *Morton Frank*, 20 T.C. 511 (1953).

FIGURE I:6-1 ▶ DEDUCTIBILITY OF BUSINESS INVESTIGATION AND START-UP COSTS

▶ *Expenses incurred in connection with an investment activity*. These expenses are costs the taxpayer incurs in connection with an investment activity that the taxpayer anticipates will become an active trade or business.

As defined by Sec. 195, start-up expenditures do not include these same types of expenses when incurred by a taxpayer already engaged in a business similar to the new one being created or acquired. In this case, the taxpayer may deduct these expenditures currently because the expenses originate in the taxpayer's existing business. Figure I:6-1 provides a flowchart to assist in properly classifying these types of expenditures.

STOP & THINK

Question: Shauna works in an automobile manufacturing plant in Detroit, Michigan. In January of the current year, she took a two-week vacation in order to fly to Orlando, Florida. While in Orlando, she spent some time investigating the possibility of opening a store in nearby Coco Beach. In total, she spent $800 on airfare, $1,500 on hotels and food, $300 on equipment rentals, and $300 on a car rental. In addition to spending time on the beach talking to people and checking out the rental equipment, she also spent some time talking to shop owners and real estate agents. After some analysis, however, Shauna decides to keep her job in Detroit. What is the proper tax treatment for these expenditures?

Solution: In general, Sec. 162 of the IRC allows a deduction for expenses incurred in a business. Expenses incurred before the business starts are not incurred in a business and thus are not deductible under Sec. 162. However, under Sec. 195 a portion of certain expenditures such as business investigation expenses and start-up costs can be deducted currently while the remainder is capitalized and amortized over a 180-month period, beginning with the month in which the new business begins. Unfortunately Shauna did not open the new business. Thus, she may not deduct or amortize any of these expenses.

Topic Review I:6-2 summarizes the restrictions on the deductibility of these items.

TOPIC REVIEW I:6-2

Restrictions on the Deductibility of Expense Items

Item	Restrictions Imposed
1. Capital expenditures	The general rule is that the expenditure is not currently deductible if its life extends beyond the end of the year. Special elections are available to currently deduct certain capital expenditures (e.g., research and experimental costs under Sec. 174; and limited amounts per year for acquisitions of tangible personal property used in a trade or business under Sec. 179).
2. Carrying charges	An election may be made under Sec. 266 to capitalize certain expenses that are normally deductible such as property and employment taxes, interest, and carrying charges on unimproved unproductive real estate.
3. Expenses related to tax-exempt income	Expenses such as interest incurred on debt used to purchase or carry tax-exempt securities are disallowed under Sec. 265.
4. Expenditures contrary to public policy	Such expenditures are generally not deductible. Examples include bribes and kickbacks, fines and penalties, and expenses of an illegal activity involved with trafficking or dealing in drugs.
5. Legal and accounting fees	Legal and accounting fees can be either *for* AGI deductible business expenses, nondeductible personal use expenditures, or *from* AGI fees incurred in the determination of any tax (e.g., tax return preparation fees).
6. Political contributions and lobby expenses	The general rule is that such items are not deductible (e.g., costs of influencing public opinion), but there are certain exceptions (e.g., costs of appearing before local legislative bodies on topics directly related to the taxpayer's business).
7. Business investigation and preopening expenses	The following rules apply: a. Currently deductible if the taxpayer is already engaged in a similar business. b. Not deductible if the taxpayer is not currently engaged in a similar business and does not enter the new business. c. An amount equal to the lesser of the amount of the expenses or $5,000 reduced by amounts incurred over $50,000 is currently deductible with the remainder to be capitalized and amortized over a 180 month period if the taxpayer enters the new business and makes an election. d. Deductible if expenditures constitute specific items such as legal expenses incurred in drafting purchase documents in an unsuccessful attempt to acquire a specific business. However, general investigation expenditures in search of a new business are not deductible.

PROPER SUBSTANTIATION REQUIREMENT

OBJECTIVE 4

List the substantiation requirements for deducting travel and entertainment expenses

Generally, the burden of proving the existence of a deduction or loss falls on the taxpayer. Thus, a taxpayer must properly substantiate all deductible expenses. Because the IRS may audit a return and request proof, taxpayers should retain items such as receipts, cancelled checks, and paid bills. Occasionally, the courts will allow a deduction that is not properly substantiated by the taxpayer if an expenditure clearly has been made. In these cases, the court estimates the amount of the deduction based on all the facts and circumstances. This procedure is known as the *Cohan* rule and derives its name from a court case in which the judge allowed a deduction for an estimated amount of certain expenses.[20] The most prudent course of action, of course, is to retain proper documentation rather than to rely upon the *Cohan* rule.

EXAMPLE I:6-20 ▶ In April of the current year, Terry took his tax records to a CPA to have his prior year's income tax return prepared. As part of the return, the CPA attached a supplemental schedule listing all of Terry's items of income and expense. After the return was prepared and filed, Terry's records

[20] *George M. Cohan v. CIR*, 8 AFTR 10552, 2 USTC ¶489 (2nd Cir., 1930). Interestingly, the *Cohan* case dealt with travel and entertainment expenses. Because of the subsequent enactment of Sec. 274(d), the *Cohan* rule may not be used to deduct entertainment expenses. It is still effective for other types of expenses.

were stolen. Upon audit two years later, the IRS disallowed Terry's deductions because he had no records to substantiate the expenses. When the case was litigated, the court allowed deductions for an estimated amount of expenses under the *Cohan* rule because of the list that was attached to Terry's return and because the court believed that Terry had testified honestly in his own behalf.[21] ◀

HISTORICAL NOTE

Judge Learned Hand, in permitting a deduction for unsubstantiated amounts in *George M. Cohan v. CIR,* 8 AFTR 10552, 2 USTC ¶489 (2nd Cir, 1930), wrote "absolute certainty in such matters is usually impossible and it is not necessary; the Board should make as close an approximation as it can, bearing heavily if it chooses on the taxpayer whose inexactitude is of his own making."

Additionally, Sections 274 and 280F provide specific and more stringent recordkeeping requirements for travel, entertainment, business gifts, computers, and vehicles used for transportation. In these cases, the taxpayer may not take a deduction unless the taxpayer substantiates the expenditure by either an adequate record or sufficient evidence that corroborates the taxpayer's statement. This substantiation may take the form of account books, diaries, logs, receipts and paid bills, trip sheets, expense reports, and statements of witnesses. The information that requires substantiation includes the following:

- Amount of the expense
- Time and place of the travel or entertainment
- Date and description of the gift
- Business purpose of the expenditure
- Business relationship to the taxpayer of the person entertained or of the person who received the gift

The *Cohan* rule does not apply to these types of expenses. (See Chapter I:9 for a more complete discussion regarding the deductibility of these types of expenses.)

WHEN AN EXPENSE IS DEDUCTIBLE

OBJECTIVE 5

Explain the timing of deductions under both the cash and accrual methods of accounting

Because the tax law generally requires calculating taxable income annually, the question of when a particular expense is deductible is especially important. The answer to this question largely depends on the taxpayer's method of accounting.[22] The most common methods include the following:

- Cash receipts and disbursements method (cash method)
- Accrual method
- Hybrid method (a combination of the cash and accrual methods where some items are accounted for on the cash method and other items are accounted for on the accrual method)

ADDITIONAL COMMENT

Section 446(b) provides that in cases where no method of accounting has been regularly used or if the method used does not clearly reflect income, then the computation of taxable income is to be made under a method that, in the opinion of the IRS, does clearly reflect income.

Taxpayers normally use the same method for computing taxable income that they use in keeping their financial accounting records. However, except for the use of the last-in, first-out (LIFO) method of accounting for inventory, the tax law does not generally require conformity. For example, many companies use the straight-line depreciation method for financial accounting purposes and the modified accelerated cost recovery system (MACRS) for tax purposes. This difference in depreciation methods, of course, results in a book-tax M-1 or M-3 adjustment.

CASH METHOD

Under the **cash method** of accounting, expenses are generally deductible when actually paid. The cash method considers payment by check a cash payment as long as the bank subsequently honors the check. This is the case even if the payee receives the check so late on the last day of the year that the payee could not have cashed it.[23] If the taxpayer mails the check near the end of the year, the taxpayer must have evidence that the mailing took place in the year

[21] *Layard M. White,* 1980 PH T.C. Memo ¶80,582, 41 TCM 671.

[22] Methods of accounting as they relate to the reporting of income are discussed in Chapter I:3. Methods of accounting as they relate to deductibility of expenses and losses are covered in this chapter. For an overall discussion of accounting methods, see Chapter I:11.

[23] *CIR v. Estate of M. A. Bradley,* 10 AFTR 1405, 3 USTC ¶904 (6th Cir., 1932) and *Charles F. Kahler,* 18 T.C. 31 (1952).

for which the taxpayer claims a deduction. Furthermore, the cash method considers payment by credit card a cash payment at the time of the charge rather than at the time the taxpayer pays for the charge.

A mere promise to pay, or the issuance of a note payable, does not constitute a payment under the cash method. Thus, a charge on an open account with a creditor is not deductible until an actual payment of cash satisfies the charge.

EXAMPLE I:6-21 ▶ Fox, Inc., a calendar-year taxpayer, is in the plumbing repair business. The business uses the cash method of accounting. Under an arrangement with one of its suppliers, Fox and its employees can pick up supplies at any time during the month by merely signing for them. At the end of the month, the supplier sends Fox a bill for the charges. Fox always pays the bill in full during the following month. In December of the current year, Fox charges $1,500 for supplies. During the same month Fox purchases a plumbing fixture for $250 from another supplier. Fox uses its charge card at the time of purchase. Fox may deduct the $250 during the current year. However, the $1,500 charged on the open account is deductible when paid in the following year. ◀

Prepaid Expenses. In general, a capital expenditure or the prepayment of expenses by a cash method taxpayer does not result in a current deduction if the expenditure creates an asset having a useful life that extends substantially beyond the close of the tax year. This can occur when a taxpayer makes expenditures for prepaid rent, services, or interest. However, in the case of prepaid rent, a circuit court of appeals decision has held that a taxpayer may take a current deduction for the entire amount of an expenditure if the period covered by the prepayment does not exceed one year and the rent agreement obligates the taxpayer to make the prepayment.[24]

EXAMPLE I:6-22 ▶ On November 1 of the current year, Twyla Corporation enters into a lease arrangement with Rashad to rent Rashad's office space for the following 36 months. By prepaying the rent for the entire 36-month period, Twyla Inc. is able to obtain a favorable monthly lease payment of $1,800. This prepayment creates an asset (a leasehold) with a useful life that extends substantially beyond the end of the taxable year. Thus, only $3,600 ($1,800 × 2 months) of the total payment is deductible in the current year. The rest must be capitalized and amortized over the life of the lease. However, assume that under the terms of the lease, Twyla Inc. is obligated to make three annual payments of $21,600 each November 1 for the subsequent 12 months. On November 1 of the current year, Twyla Inc. pays Rashad $21,600 for the first 12-month period. Because Twyla Inc. is obligated to make the prepayment and the period covered by the prepayment does not exceed one year, the entire $21,600 is deductible in the current year using the reasoning of the previously cited circuit court decision. ◀

Prepaid Interest. The IRC requires taxpayers to deduct prepaid interest expense over the period of the loan to which the interest charge is allocated.[25] Receipt of a discounted loan does not represent prepaid interest expense. Instead, the IRC deems the interest paid when the taxpayer repays the loan.

EXAMPLE I:6-23 ▶ During the current year, Richelle borrows $1,000 from the bank for use in her business. Richelle uses the cash method of accounting in her business. Under the terms of the loan, the bank discounts the loan by $80, issuing Richelle $920. When the loan comes due in the following year, however, Richelle is to repay the full $1,000. Richelle cannot deduct the $80 of interest expense until she repays the loan in the following year. ◀

REAL-WORLD EXAMPLE

A taxpayer made an overpayment of the federal income tax in 1975. In 1979, the IRS offset the overpayment against interest the taxpayer owed to the IRS. The Tax Court held that the interest expense was deductible in 1979 rather than in 1975. *Saverio Eboli*, 93 T.C. 123 (1989).

Taxpayers often prepay interest in the form of points. A point is one percent of the loan amount. Thus, the payment of two points on a $100,000 loan amounts to $2,000. While tax law generally requires the amortization of points over the life of the loan, if a taxpayer pays points in connection with the purchase or improvement of a principal residence, the taxpayer may deduct the points when they are paid. Points that a taxpayer pays in connection with the

[24] *Martin J. Zaninovich v. CIR*, 45 AFTR 2d 80-1442, 80-1 USTC ¶9342 (9th Cir., 1980) and *Bonaire Development Co. v. CIR*, 50 AFTR 2d 82-5167, 82-2 USTC ¶9428 (9th Cir., 1982). See also *Stephen A. Keller v. CIR*, 53 AFTR 2d 84-663, 84-1 USTC ¶9194 (8th Cir., 1984).

[25] Sec. 461(g).

purchase (but not the improvement) of a principal residence are automatically deductible in the year paid if they satisfy the following four requirements:

- the closing agreement clearly designates the amount as points,
- the amount involves a computation as a percentage of the amount borrowed,
- the charging of points is an established business practice in the geographic area, and
- the points are paid in connection with the purchase of the taxpayer's principal residence which is used to secure the loan.[26]

REAL-WORLD EXAMPLE

The mortgage company will, at the end of the year, mail to the taxpayer a Form 1098 which shows the amount of interest and points paid.

Although points paid on loans incurred to *improve* the taxpayer's principal residence do not fall under this safe harbor rule, they still are currently deductible if the residence is collateral for the loan, the payment of points is an established business practice in the geographic area in which it is incurred, and the amount of the prepayment does not exceed the amount generally charged.

A taxpayer may not currently deduct points paid to refinance a mortgage on a principal residence because the points are not paid in connection with the purchase or improvement of the taxpayer's residence.[27]

EXAMPLE I:6-24 ▶ During the current year, Pam purchases a principal residence for $150,000, paying $50,000 down and financing the remainder with a 30-year mortgage secured by the property. Pam must make monthly payments on the mortgage. At the closing, Pam must pay three points as a loan origination fee. Because these points are paid in connection with the purchase of a principal residence, Pam may deduct $3,000 ($100,000 × 0.03) as interest expense during the current year. In addition, Pam may also deduct the interest portion of each monthly payment made during the year. On the other hand, assume that Pam takes out the $100,000 loan in order to refinance her home at a lower interest rate. The $3,000 prepaid interest is not currently deductible. Instead, Pam must deduct the interest ratably over the term of the loan. Thus, Pam may deduct an additional $8.33 ($3,000 ÷ 360 payments) interest expense for each payment that she makes during the year. ◀

If the taxpayer sells a home and pays off the refinanced mortgage, any unamortized portion of the points is deductible in the year of repayment. The tax law treats points paid by the seller as incurred by the purchaser and, therefore, the points are currently deductible by the purchaser if they meet the other requirements and are subtracted from the purchase price of the residence.[28]

The cash method of accounting provides some degree of flexibility to taxpayers because, under this method, taxpayers can generally deduct expenses when paid rather than when accrued. Thus, subject to the limitations mentioned above with regard to prepaid expenses, taxpayers may to some degree accelerate or defer deductions from one year to another by merely accelerating or deferring payment. However, the IRC imposes limitations on the use of the cash method. For example, taxpayers must account for inventories under the accrual method.[29] Furthermore, under Sec. 448, most C corporations (corporations that have not elected Subchapter S status), partnerships that have a C corporation as a partner, and tax shelters may not use the cash method. The IRC makes exceptions to this general rule for personal service corporations, small businesses with average annual gross receipts of $5 million or less, and businesses involved in the farming and timber businesses. (See Chapter I:11 for a complete discussion of the different accounting methods a taxpayer may use for computing taxable income.)

---

[26] Rev. Proc. 94-27, I.R.B. 94-15, 17. As explained in Chapter I:7, acquisition indebtedness incurred to acquire a personal residence is limited to $1,000,000. Hence, points that are allocated to the loan principal in excess of this limit are not deductible either.

[27] Rev. Rul. 87-22, 1987-1 C.B. 146, and Rev. Proc. 87-15, 1987-1 C.B. 624. However, the Eighth Circuit has allowed a current deduction for points paid upon the refinancing of a mortgage loan because the original loan was merely a "bridge" or temporary loan until permanent financing could be arranged. See *James R. Huntsman v. CIR*, 66 AFTR 2d 90-5020, 90-2 USTC ¶50,340 (8th Cir., 1990).

[28] Rev. Proc. 94-27, I.R.B. 94-15, 17.

[29] Reg. §1.446-1(c)(2). However, most taxpayers with less than $1,000,000 of average annual gross receipts may use the cash method. See Rev. Proc. 2001-10, 2001-1 CB 272. The cash method may also be used by select taxpayers whose annual gross receipts do not exceed $10,000,000. See Rev. Proc. 2002-28, I.R.B. 2002-18, 815.

ACCRUAL METHOD

An **accrual method** taxpayer deducts expenses in the period in which they accrue. Generally, items accrue when the transaction meets both an **all-events test** and an **economic performance test**.[30]

All-Events Test. The all-events test is met when both of the following occur:

- The existence of a liability is established.
- The amount of the liability is determined with reasonable accuracy.

EXAMPLE I:6-25 ▶ During the current year, Phil provides services for Granite, Inc. Granite uses the accrual method of accounting. Phil claims that Granite owes $10,000 for the services. Granite admits owing Phil $6,000, but contests the remaining $4,000. Because the amount of the liability can be accurately established only with respect to $6,000, Granite can deduct only that amount. If Granite pays the full $10,000, it may deduct the full amount in the year of payment, even though the contested amount ($4,000) is not resolved until a subsequent taxable year.[31] If Phil loses the lawsuit and repays Granite the $4,000, Granite will include that amount in income in the year of repayment under the tax benefit rule (see Chapter I:11). ◀

Because of the all-events test, taxpayers may not deduct additions to reserves for estimated expenses such as warranty expenses. Instead, the taxpayer deducts the expenses in the year in which such work is actually performed.

EXAMPLE I:6-26 ▶ Best Corporation uses the accrual method of accounting and is engaged in the business of painting and rustproofing automobiles. Best Corporation provides a 5-year warranty for new vehicles and a 2-year warranty for used vehicles. Best Corporation extends the warranty only to the person who owns the car at the time the car is painted. Furthermore, in order to keep the warranty in force, the customer must present the vehicle to Best Corporation for inspection each year. The warranty is void if the vehicle is involved in an accident. Even though for financial accounting purposes Best Corporation may provide a reserve for estimated warranty expenses and deduct a reasonable addition to the reserve on an annual basis, no income tax deduction is allowed until the warranty work is actually done. ◀

ADDITIONAL COMMENT

Because of this difference between the tax treatment and the financial accounting treatment, an M-1 or M-3 adjustment must be made on a corporation's Form 1120.

Economic Performance Test. To be currently deductible under the accrual method, an expense must also meet an economic performance test. Exactly when economic performance occurs depends on the type of transaction. Table I:6-1 contains a listing of various types of transactions that may arise and identifies when economic performance is deemed to have occurred under Sec. 461(h).

EXAMPLE I:6-27 ▶ On December 20 of the current year, Pit Corporation, an accrual method taxpayer, enters into a binding contract with Pat to have Pat do a deep cleaning of its offices. Under the terms of the contract, Pat is to do the work in March of the following year. The total cost of the job is $5,000. Pit pays Pat 10% down at the time the contract is signed. Because the job is not to be done until the following year, economic performance has not occurred in the current year and Pit may not deduct any portion of the expense in the current year. ◀

HISTORICAL NOTE

The economic performance test was added by Congress in the Tax Reform Act of 1984. Congress was concerned that in some situations taxpayers could deduct expenses currently, but the actual cash expenditure might not be made for several years. Taking a current deduction in such situations overstated the real cost because the time value of money was ignored.

An exception to the economic performance test provides that taxpayers may take a current deduction for recurring liabilities if all of the following occur:

- The item meets the all-events test during the year.
- Economic performance of the item occurs within the shorter of 8½ months after the close of the tax year or a reasonable period after the close of the tax year.
- The expense is recurring and the taxpayer consistently treats the item as incurred in the tax year.
- Either the item is not material or the accrual of the item in the tax year results in a more proper matching against income than accruing the item in the tax year in which economic performance occurs.

---

[30] Reg. Sec. 1.461-1(a)(2) and Sec. 461(h).

[31] Reg. Sec. 1.461-2(a)(1).

▼ **TABLE I:6-1**
When Economic Performance Is Deemed to Have Occurred

Event That Gives Rise to Liability	When Economic Performance Is Deemed to Have Occurred (i.e., when the accrual method taxpayer may take the deduction)
Another person provides the taxpayer with property or services	When the person actually provides the services[a]
Taxpayer uses property	As the taxpayer uses the property[a]
Taxpayer must provide property or services to another person	As the taxpayer provides property or services to the other person[b]
Taxpayer must make payments to another, including payments for rebates and refunds, awards or prizes, insurance or service contracts, and taxes	As the taxpayer makes payments to the other person
Taxpayer must make payments to another person because of a tort, breach of contract, violation of law, or injury claim under a worker's compensation act	As the taxpayer makes payments to the other person

[a] Economic performance may be deemed to have occurred at the earlier date of payment if the taxpayer reasonably expects the property or services to be provided within 3½ months after the payment is made. Reg. Sec. 1.461-4(d)(6)(ii).
[b] Economic performance may also occur as the taxpayer incurs costs in connection with the obligation to provide the property or services. Reg. Sec. 1.461-4(d)(4)(i).

The recurring liability exception is available for the first four types of transactions identified in Table I:6-1, but it is not available for the last type of transaction in the table.

EXAMPLE I:6-28 ▶ Beta Inc. is a calendar-year, accrual method taxpayer. Every year at the end of October, Beta enters into a contract with Sam to provide snow removal services for the parking lots at Beta corporate offices. This contract extends for five months through the end of March of the following year. Because the all-events test is met (the liability is fixed), the expense recurs every year, economic performance occurs within the requisite period of time, and the item is not material, Beta may deduct the entire expense in the year in which Beta and Sam enter into the contract. ◀

A special rule under Sec. 461(c) applies to real property taxes. Under this provision, a taxpayer may elect to accrue real property taxes ratably over the period to which the taxes relate. Once made, this election is irrevocable unless the taxpayer obtains permission from the IRS.

EXAMPLE I:6-29 ▶ Under the laws of State X, the lien date for real property taxes for the calendar year 2015 is January 1, 2015. The tax is payable in full on December 15, 2015. Alpha Corporation is an accrual-method taxpayer that has a January 31 fiscal year-end. On January 1, 2015, real property taxes of $100,000 are assessed against a building Alpha owns. Alpha pays the taxes on December 15, 2015. If Alpha does not make the election to use the ratable accrual method, Alpha cannot deduct any of the payment in its fiscal year ending January 31, 2015, because the payment date is more than 8½ months after Alpha's January 31, 2015, year end.

On the other hand, if Alpha makes the election, it may deduct $8,333 ($100,000 × 1⁄12) in its fiscal year that ends January 31, 2015, and $91,667 ($100,000 × 11⁄12) in its fiscal year that ends January 31, 2016.

If the taxes are paid on September 30, 2015, Alpha would be better off not making the ratable accrual election. In this case, the recurring item exception applies because Alpha makes the payment within 8½ months of its January 31, 2015, fiscal year end. Thus, if Alpha does not make the election, all of the $100,000 is deductible in its fiscal year ending on January 31, 2015. ◀

Topic Review I:6-3 presents the rules for determining when an expense is deductible.

TOPIC REVIEW I:6-3

When an Expense Is Deductible

CASH METHOD: DEDUCTIBLE WHEN PAID

Payment Is Made When

- Cash or other property is transferred.
- A check is delivered or mailed.
- An item is charged on a credit card.

  Note: A mere promise to pay or delivery of a note payable is not deductible under the cash method.

Prepaid Expenses

- Generally are deductible over the period covered.
- Deductible when paid if the period covered does not exceed one year.
- Prepaid interest is generally deductible ratably over the period covered by the loan.
- Points are deductible when paid if:
  - —The loan is used to purchase or improve the taxpayer's principal residence.
  - —The loan is secured by the residence.
  - —Points are established business practice in the geographical area.
  - —The points do not exceed the amount generally charged.
  - —For points paid to purchase a principal residence, the closing agreement clearly designates the amount as points and the amount must be computed as a percentage of the amount borrowed.

ACCRUAL METHOD: DEDUCTIBLE WHEN ACCRUED

In General

- Taxpayers maintaining inventories must use the accrual method of accounting (except for taxpayers with average annual gross receipts of $10 million or less).
- Accrual occurs when the item satisfies both the all-events test and economic performance.

All-Events Test

- The existence of a liability is established and
- The amount of the liability is determined.

Economic Performance

- When economic performance occurs depends on the transaction involved (see Table I:6-1).
- Occurs in the year the item meets the all-events test and all of the following tests:
  - —Actual economic performance occurs within the shorter of:
    - 8½ months after the taxable year or a reasonable period after the taxable year.
  - —The expense is recurring and receives consistent treatment from year to year.
  - —Either:
    - The item is immaterial or
    - Deducting the expense in the year it meets the all-events test results in a more proper matching of income and deductions.

SPECIAL DISALLOWANCE RULES

OBJECTIVE 6

Discuss special disallowance rules for deductions

In addition to the general rules mentioned above, certain types of transactions are subject to further limitations and disallowances. These include wash sales, transactions between related persons, gambling losses, losses associated with an activity determined to be a hobby, expenses of renting a vacation home, and expenses of an office in the taxpayer's home. Further discussion of these special disallowance rules follows.

WASH SALES

Section 1091 disallows losses incurred on wash sales of stock or securities in the year of sale. For purposes of Sec. 1091, a **wash sale** occurs when:

- A taxpayer realizes a loss on the sale of stock or securities, and

- The taxpayer acquires "substantially identical" stock or securities within a 61-day period of time that extends from 30 days before the date of sale to 30 days after the date of sale.[32]

The purpose of the wash sale rule is to prevent taxpayers from generating artificial tax losses in situations where taxpayers do not intend to reduce their holdings in the stock or securities sold.

EXAMPLE I:6-30 ▶ Leslie realizes $10,000 in short-term capital gains (STCGs) through dealings in the stock market during the current year. Realizing that STCGs are fully includible in gross income and are taxed at ordinary rates unless they are offset against realized capital losses, Leslie analyzes her portfolio to determine whether she owns any stocks that have declined in value. She finds that the FMV of her Edison Corporation common stock is only $8,000, even though she originally purchased it for $16,000. Despite this paper loss on the stock, Leslie wants to retain the stock because she feels that Edison Corporation is still a good investment. If Leslie attempts to take advantage of the paper loss on the Edison stock by selling the stock she owns and repurchasing a similar number of shares of Edison common stock within the 61-day period, Sec. 1091 disallows the loss. ◀

SELF-STUDY QUESTION

During 2012, you bought 100 shares of X stock on each of three occasions. You paid $158 a share for the first block of 100 shares, $100 a share for the second block, and $95 a share for the third block. On December 21, 2015, you sold 300 shares of X stock for $125 a share. On January 6, 2016, you bought 250 shares of identical X stock. Can you deduct the loss realized on the first block of stock?

ANSWER

You cannot deduct the loss of $33 a share on the first block because within 30 days after the date of sale you bought 250 identical shares of X stock. In addition, you cannot reduce the gain realized on the sale of the second and third blocks of stock by this loss.

At times, taxpayers may attempt to circumvent the wash sale provisions through either a sham transaction or an indirect repurchase of the securities. If this is the case, the wash sale provisions still prevent the recognition of the loss. The Supreme Court has held that losses on sales of stock by a husband were disallowed when the stockbroker was instructed to purchase the same number of shares in his wife's name.[33]

In some instances a taxpayer may attempt to circumvent the wash sale provisions by merely delaying the repurchase of the substantially identical stock. This tactic should work as long as a written agreement to repurchase the stock does not exist at the time of the sale or at any time within the 61-day period mandated by the Sec. 1091 wash sale provisions. If such an agreement exists, the courts will disallow the loss, even though the actual purchase does not occur within the 61-day period.[34]

In certain cases, taxpayers may still recognize losses on transactions that literally fall within the wash sale requirements. For example, a taxpayer may purchase stock and then sell a portion of those shares within 30 days where the intent is merely to reduce the stock holdings. Taken together, these two transactions meet the tests of Sec. 1091. However, because the purpose of the sale is to reduce the taxpayer's holdings rather than to generate an artificial tax loss, Sec. 1091 does not disallow the loss.[35] Section 1091 also does not apply to losses that a dealer in stock or securities realizes in the ordinary course of business.

If the taxpayer acquires fewer shares of stock within the 61-day period than the number of shares disposed of, Sec. 1091 disallows only a proportionate amount of the total loss.

EXAMPLE I:6-31 ▶ Several years ago, Henry purchased 100 shares of New Corporation common stock for $2,000 ($20 per share). On July 2 of the current year, Henry sells all 100 shares for $1,000. On July 30 of the current year, Henry purchases 75 shares (three-fourths of the original shares) of New Corporation common stock. As a result of the reacquisition, three-fourths of the total loss ($750) is disallowed. Henry recognizes the remaining $250 loss. ◀

Substantially Identical Stock or Securities. Only the acquisition of substantially identical stock or securities will cause a loss to be disallowed. The IRC and the Treasury Regulations do not define the term *substantially identical.* Judicial and administrative rulings have held that bonds issued by the same corporation generally are not substantially identical if they differ in terms (e.g., interest rate and term to maturity). However,

[32] Here the term *acquire* includes an acquisition of the stock either by purchase or in a taxable exchange. The term *stock or securities* includes contracts or options to acquire or sell stock or securities (see Sec. 1091(a)). The wash sale rules also apply to losses realized on the closing of a short sale of stock or securities if, within the 61-day period, substantially identical stock or securities were sold or another short sale of (or a securities futures contract to sell) substantially identical stock or securities was entered into.

[33] *John P. McWilliams v. CIR,* 35 AFTR 1184, 47-1 USTC ¶9289 (USSC, 1947).

[34] Rev. Rul. 72-225, 1972-1 C.B. 59, and *Frank Stein,* 1977 PH T.C. Memo ¶77,241, 36 TCM 992.

[35] Rev. Rul. 56-602, 1956-2 C.B. 527.

bonds of the same corporation that differ only in their maturity dates (e.g., the bonds do not come due for 16 years and mature within a few months of each other) have been held to be substantially identical. Generally, courts have not considered the preferred stock of a corporation to be substantially identical to the common stock of the same corporation.[36]

Basis of Stock. If the wash sale provisions disallow a loss, then the disallowed loss increases the basis of the recently acquired stock. This increase in basis merely causes the disallowed loss to be deferred. The taxpayer will eventually recognize the loss upon the subsequent sale or disposition of the stock that causes the loss disallowance. If there has been more than one purchase of replacement stock and the amount of stock purchased within the 61-day period exceeds the stock that is sold, the stock that is deemed to have caused the loss to be disallowed is accounted for chronologically. The holding period of the replacement stock includes the period of time the taxpayer held the stock sold.

EXAMPLE I:6-32 ▶ Ingrid enters into the following transactions with regard to Pacific Corporation common stock:

Date	*Transaction*	*Amount*
January 4, 2009	Purchases 600 shares	$30,000
October 2, 2015	Purchases 400 shares	10,000
October 12, 2015	Sells original 600 shares	12,000
October 20, 2015	Purchases 200 shares	5,000
October 25, 2015	Purchases 300 shares	8,400

Because Ingrid purchases more than 600 shares within the 61-day period before and after the date of sale (the purchases made on October 2, 20, and 25), the recognition of the entire loss of $18,000 ($30,000–$12,000) is postponed. Four hundred shares (two-thirds of the number of shares sold) are purchased on October 2 and 200 shares (one-third) are purchased on October 20. Thus, the basis of the 400 shares of stock purchased on October 2 is $22,000 [$10,000 purchase price + ($18,000 disallowed loss × 0.667)]. The basis of the 200 shares of stock purchased on October 20 is $11,000 [$5,000 + ($18,000 disallowed loss × 0.333)]. Both of these blocks of stock have a holding period that starts on January 4, 2009.[37] The basis of the 300 shares of stock purchased on October 25 is its purchase price of $8,400. Its holding period begins on October 25, 2015. ◀

STOP & THINK

Question: With regard to his investments in the stock market, the current year has been like a roller coaster ride for Doug. He now wants to do some year-end tax planning. For the year to date, he has realized a net gain of $12,000 on his stock investments. Although some of his current stock holdings have unrealized losses, he feels that they are excellent investments that will provide excellent returns in the next year or two. His stock broker has suggested that he sell enough of his holdings to realize a $12,000 loss (to offset the $12,000 capital gain) and then simply repurchase some of the stock. What advice would you give Doug as he discusses this strategy with his broker?

Solution: By realizing $12,000 in capital losses this year, Doug may be able to offset the capital gains he has already recognized. In order to recognize these losses, however, he must make sure that the wash sale provisions do not apply. Thus, he must either (1) purchase stock of different corporations or (2) delay the repurchase of the same issue of stock for at least 31 days after the date of sale. Because Doug is happy with his current investments, perhaps the second strategy is the best. Of course, other non-tax issues must also be considered. For example, does Doug think that the prices will go up quickly within the next 30 days? If so, he may lose out on some significant gains while he is waiting to repurchase the stock. Additionally, he must also consider the transaction costs (such as commissions).

36 *Marie Hanlin, Executrix v. CIR*, 39-2 USTC ¶9783 (3d Cir., 1939). However, the IRS held in Rev. Rul. 77-201, 1977-1 C.B. 250, that the convertible preferred stock of a corporation is substantially identical to its common stock if the preferred stock has the same voting rights and is subject to the same dividend restrictions as the common stock, is unrestricted as to its convertibility, and sells at relatively the same price (taking into consideration the conversion ratio).

37 An asset's holding period is important in determining whether subsequent gain or loss on the asset is long-term or short-term gain or loss. This is explained further in Chapter I:5.

TRANSACTIONS BETWEEN RELATED PARTIES

Section 267 places transactions between certain related parties under special scrutiny because of the potential for tax abuse. For example, a taxpayer could sell a piece of property at a loss to a wholly owned corporation. Without any restrictions on the deductibility of the loss, the individual could recognize the loss while still retaining effective control of the property. Under Sec. 267, related taxpayers may not take current deductions on two specific types of transactions. These transactions are:

- Losses on sales of property
- Accrued expenses that remain unpaid to the related cash method taxpayer at the end of the tax year

ADDITIONAL COMMENT

Section 267 does not define the word property, but the IRS and the courts have given it a broad meaning.

Related Parties Defined. Section 267 defines the following relationships as related parties:

- Individuals and their families. The term family includes an individual's spouse, brothers and sisters (including half-brothers and half-sisters), ancestors, and lineal descendants.
- An individual and a corporation in which the individual owns more than 50% of the value of the outstanding stock.
- Various relationships between grantors, beneficiaries, and fiduciaries of a trust or trusts, or between the fiduciary of a trust and a corporation if they meet certain ownership requirements.
- A corporation and a partnership if the same persons own more than 50% in value of the stock of the corporation and more than 50% of the partnership.
- Two corporations if the same persons own more than 50% in value of the outstanding stock of both corporations and at least one of the corporations is an S corporation.
- Other complex relationships involving trusts, corporations, and individuals.

TAX STRATEGY TIP

The related party rules many times cause the tax consequences to be different than what was expected. Be sure that your clients provide all details to you ahead of time when related parties are involved in the transaction. You might be able to help structure the transaction in a way that meets your clients' expectations.

Several of these relationships depend on an individual's ownership of a corporation. For example, if a taxpayer does not own more than 50% of a corporation's stock, the individual and the corporation are not related and a loss on the sale of business or investment property between the two is deductible. Occasionally, individuals might attempt to circumvent the related party rules by dispersing the ownership of a corporation (e.g., among close family members) while retaining economic control. To prevent these tactics, Sec. 267 contains constructive ownership rules whereby a taxpayer is deemed to own stock owned by certain other persons. These constructive ownership rules are as follows:

- Stock owned by an individual's family is treated as owned by the individual. Here the definition of *family* is the same as that of *related parties* (i.e., spouse, brothers and sisters, ancestors, and lineal descendants).
- Stock owned by a corporation, partnership, estate, or trust is treated as owned proportionately by the shareholders, partners, or beneficiaries.
- If an individual partner in a partnership owns (or is treated as owning) stock in a corporation, the individual is treated as owning any stock of that corporation owned by any other partner in the partnership. This does not occur, however, if the only stock the individual owns (or is considered to own) is through family attribution.[38]
- Stock ownership that is attributed to a shareholder or partner from an entity can be reattributed to another taxpayer under any of the constructive ownership rules. In other words, the same stock can be constructively owned by more than one person. However, stock ownership attributed to a taxpayer under the family or partner rules cannot be reattributed.

[38] Reg. Sec. 1.267(c)-1(b), Exs. (2) and (3).

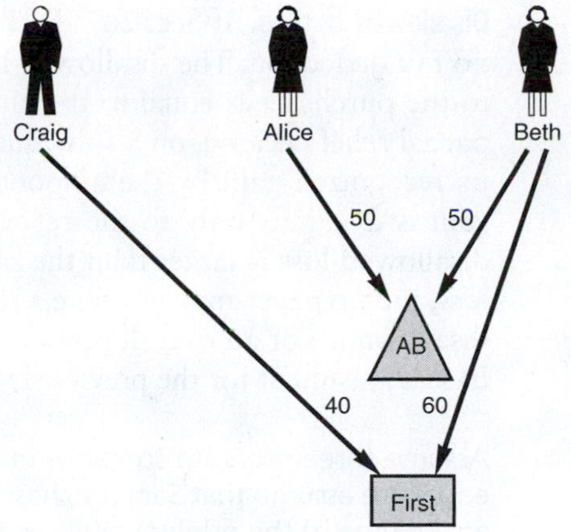

FIGURE I:6-2 ▶ ILLUSTRATION FOR EXAMPLE I:6-33

The following examples illustrate these rules.

EXAMPLE I:6-33 ▶ Alice and Beth are equal partners in the AB Partnership. Beth owns 60% of First Corporation's stock, and Craig, Alice's husband, owns the other 40%. The ownership of the partnership and the corporation is demonstrated in Figure I:6-2. Under the constructive ownership rules, Alice is considered to own Craig's 40% of the First Corporation stock. Alice is not considered to own the First Corporation stock owned by her partner, Beth, because the only First Corporation stock Alice owns (or is considered to own) is the stock owned by her husband. If Alice sells property at a loss to First Corporation, the loss is recognized because Alice does not directly or constructively own more than 50% of the First Corporation stock. ◄

EXAMPLE I:6-34 ▶ Assume the same facts as in Example I:6-33, except that the First Corporation stock is owned 50% by the AB Partnership and 25% each by Beth and Craig. The ownership of the partnership and the corporation is shown in Figure I:6-3. In addition to Craig's 25%, Alice is considered to own 50% of the stock owned by the AB Partnership because of her 50% ownership in AB. The other half of AB's stock ownership is attributed to her partner, Beth. However, Alice is also treated as owning the First Corporation stock Beth owns both actually and constructively (50%). Thus, Alice is treated as owning 100% of the First Corporation stock. In this case, Alice will not be able to recognize a loss on the sale of property to First Corporation. ◄

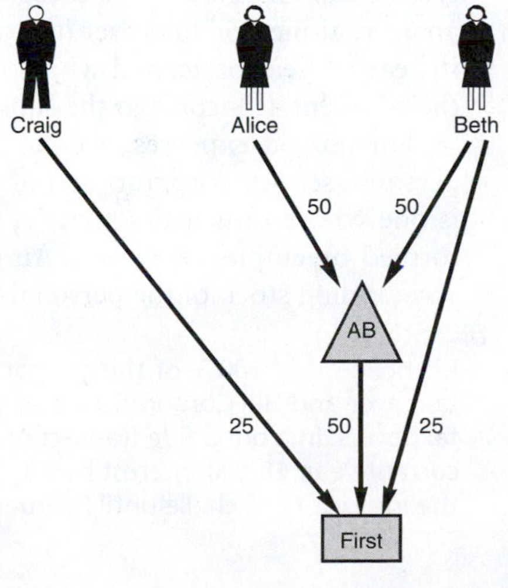

FIGURE I:6-3 ▶ ILLUSTRATION FOR EXAMPLE I:6-34

Disallowed Losses. If Sec. 267 disallows the loss, the original seller of the property receives no tax deduction. The disallowed loss has no effect on the purchaser's basis. The cost basis to the purchaser is equal to the amount paid for the property. However, Sec. 267 provides partial relief because, on a subsequent sale of the property, the related purchaser may reduce its recognized gain by the amount of the disallowed loss. This offsetting of a subsequent gain is available only to the related person who originally purchased the property. If the disallowed loss is larger than the subsequent gain, or if the purchaser sells the property at a loss, the taxpayer may not take a deduction for the unused loss. This may result in a partial disallowance of an overall economic loss for the related parties because there is no upward basis adjustment for the previously disallowed loss (as is the case for a wash sale).

EXAMPLE I:6-35 ▶ Assume three separate scenarios in which Sam sells a tract of land during the current year. In each case assume that Sam purchased the land from his father, Frank, for $10,000. Frank's basis at the time of the original sale was $15,000 in each case. Thus, Frank's $5,000 loss on each land sale was disallowed.

KEY POINT

The loss disallowance rule for related parties is more severe compared to the loss disallowance rule on wash sales. In a related party transaction, it is possible to lose the tax benefit of all or a portion of the economic loss.

	Scenario		
	1	2	3
Selling price	$17,000	$ 12,000	$ 8,000
Minus: Sam's basis	(10,000)	(10,000)	(10,000)
Sam's realized gain (loss)	$ 7,000	$ 2,000	$ (2,000)
Minus: Frank's disallowed loss (up to Sam's gain)	(5,000)	(2,000)	—0—
Sam's recognized gain (loss)	$2,000	—0—	($2,000)

In Scenario 1, Sam and Frank together have incurred an aggregate gain of $2,000 ($17,000 − $15,000). Thus, Frank's full disallowed loss reduces Sam's subsequent gain. In Scenario 2, the aggregate economic loss incurred by Sam and Frank is actually $3,000 ($12,000 − $15,000). However, the actual amount of the tax loss recognized by Sam and Frank is zero. In Scenario 3, the actual tax loss would have been $7,000 ($8,000 − $15,000) instead of $2,000 if Frank had held the land until its eventual sale. ◀

A similar rule found in Sec. 707(b)(1) disallows losses between a partner and a partnership in which the partner owns directly or indirectly over 50% of the partnership and between two partnerships in which the same people own directly or indirectly over 50% in each partnership. The constructive ownership rules of Sec. 267 apply here in determining ownership (see *Prentice Hall's Federal Taxation: Corporations, Partnerships, Estates & Trusts* text or the *Comprehensive* volume).

KEY POINT

The effect of Sec. 267 with respect to unpaid expenses is to place an accrual method taxpayer on the cash method for amounts owed to a related cash method taxpayer.

Unpaid Expenses. Under Sec. 267, a related accrual-method obligor of any accrued but unpaid expenses must defer the deduction for those expenses until the year in which the related cash-method payee recognizes the amount as income. In effect, this rule prevents an accrual-method taxpayer (the payer) from taking a deduction for an unpaid expense in the earlier year of accrual while the related cash-method taxpayer (the payee) recognizes the payment as income in the subsequent year.

For unpaid expenses, Sec. 267 expands the definition of related parties to include a personal-service corporation and any employee-owner.[39] A personal-service corporation is one whose principal activity is the performance of personal services substantially performed by employee-owners. An employee-owner is an employee who owns any of the outstanding stock of the personal-service corporation.[40]

EXAMPLE I:6-36 ▶ Michelle owns 100% of the outstanding stock of Hill Corporation. Michelle is a cash-method taxpayer and Hill Corporation is an accrual-method taxpayer. Both taxpayers are calendar-year taxpayers. In a bona fide transaction, Hill borrows some funds from Michelle. By the end of the current year, $8,000 interest had accrued on the loan. However, Hill Corporation does not pay the interest to Michelle until February of the following year. Because Michelle is a cash-method

39 Sec. 267(a)(2).

40 Secs. 269A(b) and 441(i)(2). In determining the ownership of an employee-owner, the constructive ownership rules of Sec. 318 as modified by Sec. 441(i)(2) are used. These rules differ substantially from the constructive ownership rules of Sec. 267.

taxpayer, she reports the interest income when she receives it in the following year. Although Hill is an accrual-method taxpayer, it must defer the deduction for the interest expense until it pays the interest in February of the following year. The results are the same if Hill Corporation is a personal service corporation and Michelle is an employee and owns any amount of the Hill stock. ◀

For purposes of these unpaid expenses, the definition of *related parties* also includes various relationships involving partnerships or S corporations and any person who owns (either actually or constructively) any interest in these entities.[41]

HOBBY LOSSES

Certain activities have both profit-motivated and personal attributes. In these cases, a tax advisor must examine all the relevant factors to determine the tax status of the activity since, in general, expenses incurred in a profit-motivated activity such as a business or investment are deductible, whereas most expenses associated with personal activities such as hobbies are not. Reg. Sec. 1.183-2(b) lists the factors the IRS uses to determine whether an activity is profit-motivated. These factors include the following:

- Whether the taxpayer conducts the activity in a businesslike manner.
- The expertise of the taxpayer or the taxpayer's advisors.
- The time and effort expended by the taxpayer in carrying on the activity.
- Whether the assets used in the activity are expected to appreciate in value.
- The taxpayer's success in carrying on other similar activities.
- The taxpayer's history of income or losses with respect to the activity.
- The amount of occasional profits earned, if any.
- The taxpayer's financial status.
- Any elements of personal pleasure or recreation the activity might involve.

ADDITIONAL COMMENT

Many of the court cases dealing with profit motive under Sec. 183 are ranch and farm cases. In fact, Sec. 183, now titled "Activities Not Engaged in for Profit" was originally titled "Farm Losses, etc." in the Tax Reform Act of 1969.

No one of these factors is determinative. In fact, the IRS also may consider other factors not listed. Furthermore, the IRS does not make a determination by merely counting the number of factors that are present. Instead, the decision depends on an examination of all the factors together. The IRS can, therefore, make the decision on a more subjective basis than the taxpayer might like. If the IRS asserts that an activity is a personal one (i.e., a hobby) rather than a business or investment, the burden of proof rests on the taxpayer to prove otherwise.

EXAMPLE I:6-37 ▶ Paula, a successful attorney with an annual income of $300,000, also enjoys raising and training quarter horses. She generally spends five to six hours each week training, showing, or racing the horses. Over the last four years her winnings from shows and races have amounted to $16,000. Over that same period, she has generated an additional $8,000 of income from stud fees and the sale of colts. Often Paula uses the horses to take her family or friends riding. In addition, Paula often participates in equestrian clinics and demonstrations for 4-H Clubs and other similar groups. Paula employs a high school student to feed the horses each day and clean the stalls weekly. Paula also hires a professional horse trainer for 4 hours each week to help her train the horses.

In this case, several factors such as the level of earnings, the hiring of professional help, and the amount of time spent in the activity might indicate that Paula is engaged in a business. Other factors, such as the time spent riding with family and friends, the voluntary clinics and demonstrations, and the small amount of revenue generated as compared with Paula's other income, support the position that Paula merely has a hobby of raising horses. ◀

In cases where a clear profit motive cannot be shown under the factors mentioned above, the Code provides a test whereby an activity may be presumed to be engaged in for profit. The activity meets the test if it shows a profit for any three years during a consecutive five-year period. The five-year period consists of the year in question plus the previous four years.[42] This presumption is rebuttable (i.e., if the taxpayer meets the test, the

---

[41] Sec. 267(e). A discussion of these modifications is beyond the scope of this book.

[42] Sec. 183(d). If the major part of the activity involves breeding, training, showing, or racing horses, the five-year period is extended to a seven-year period, and a profit must be shown in only two, rather than three, of the years covered by that seven-year period.

IRS has the burden of proof to show that the activity *is not* profit motivated). However, if the taxpayer fails to meet this test, the taxpayer must prove that the activity *is* profit motivated.

KEY POINT

Section 183(d) primarily serves to shift the burden of proof from the taxpayer to the IRS.

If the examination of the factors leads to the determination that the activity is a business, the taxpayer generally may deduct all qualified business expenses from the gross income, even if a net loss results.[43] However, if the factors lead to a determination that the activity is a hobby, the taxpayer can generally deduct the expenses as a miscellaneous itemized deduction but only to the extent of the gross income from the activity. A net loss may not be reported from the activity if it is a hobby.

EXAMPLE I:6-38 ▶ Lorenzo, a stockbroker, enjoys raising pedigreed poodles. Although he mainly raises them for recreation and relaxation after work, Lorenzo periodically sells some of his poodles. Lorenzo reports $850 in income and $2,900 in expenses from the activity on his 2015 tax return. Upon auditing Lorenzo's 2015 return, the IRS disallowed the expenses in excess of the income, arguing that the activity is a hobby rather than a business or investment. If Lorenzo can prove that he realized a profit from the poodle-raising operation for any three years from 2011 through 2015 inclusive, the presumption will be made that the poodles are raised for a profit and not for recreation. The IRS then has the burden of proof to show that the activity is really a hobby. If Lorenzo cannot show a profit for three years out of the five-year period, he must rely on the factors mentioned in the Treasury Regulations to convince the IRS and/or the courts that the activity is a business.

If Lorenzo's poodle-raising activity is determined to be a business, Lorenzo will report a net loss of $2,050 ($2,900 expenses − $850 income), assuming the loss is not incurred in a passive activity (see Chapter I:8). If the activity is determined to be a hobby, however, Lorenzo may deduct only $850 of the expenses (up to the amount of the gross income) as an itemized deduction. As explained later, these expenses must be deducted in a certain order. The remaining expenses are not allowed as tax deductions. ◀

Deductible Expenses. Some hobby activities generate gross income, even though profit is not a primary motive for the activity. In such situations, Sec. 183 allows the taxpayer to deduct the expenses related to the hobby, but only to the extent of the gross income from the hobby. Furthermore, a taxpayer may deduct a hobby-related expense only if it would have been deductible if incurred in a trade or business or an investment activity.

In essence, a taxpayer may deduct the hobby-related expenses as long as there is enough gross income from the activity to cover the expenses. However, a taxpayer may not generate a tax loss from a hobby and then use it to offset the taxpayer's other types of income.

Order of the Deductions. If the hobby expenses exceed the amount of gross income generated by the hobby, the expense deductions offset gross income in the following order:

- Tier 1: Expenses that are deductible even though not incurred in a trade or business (e.g., itemized deductions such as taxes, certain interest, and casualty losses)
- Tier 2: Other expenses of the hobby that could be deductible if incurred in a profit-motivated activity, but which do not reduce the tax basis of any of the assets used in the hobby (e.g., utilities and maintenance expenses)
- Tier 3: The expenses of the hobby that could be deductible if incurred in a profit-motivated activity and that reduce the basis of the hobby's assets (e.g., depreciation on fixed assets used in the hobby)[44]

ADDITIONAL COMMENT

Most hobby expenses are subject to the 2% of AGI limitation on miscellaneous itemized deductions. However, if the hobby expense is one that is deductible whether or not incurred in an income producing activity, such as real property taxes on a home, the taxpayer can include the expense in his/her itemized deductions.

To the extent that the expenses are deductible against the gross income of the activity, they are deductions *from* AGI and are deductible only if the taxpayer has itemized deductions in excess of the standard deduction. Form 1040 reports the tier 1 expenses in their respective sections on Schedule A. The tier 2 and tier 3 expenses allocated to the hobby are miscellaneous itemized deductions; therefore, these expenses are deductible only to the extent

[43] If the activity is a passive activity, however, the loss may be deferred or suspended. See Chapter I:8 for a discussion of the passive loss rules.

[44] Reg. Sec. 1.183-1(b).

they exceed 2% of AGI (see Chapter I:7). Form 1040 reports gross income from a hobby as other income. If gross income is not sufficient to cover all of the tier 1 expenses, the taxpayer may also deduct the excess tier 1 expenses as itemized deductions on Schedule A of Form 1040 because the tax law allows deductions for these expenses in any event. The tax law disallows deductions for any remaining expenses in the other two tiers, and the taxpayer may not carry them over to a subsequent year.

If depreciation expense is not deductible, the taxpayer does not need to reduce the cost basis of the asset by the amount of the disallowed depreciation expense.

EXAMPLE I:6-39 ▶ Lynn raises various plants and flowers in a small greenhouse constructed specifically for that purpose. During the current year, Lynn reports gross income from the greenhouse activities of $1,700. Lynn also incurs the following expenses:

Property taxes on the greenhouse	$1,150
Utilities	300
Depreciation (assuming the activity is considered a business)	800

If the greenhouse activity is considered to be a hobby rather than a business, the deductions Lynn may take are computed as follows:

Income from greenhouse		$1,700
Tier 1 Expenses:		
Property taxes	$1,150	
Tier 2 Expenses:		
Utilities	300	
Tier 3 Expenses:		
Depreciation[a]	250	$1,700
Total		$0

[a]Limited to greenhouse income remaining after accounting for the Tier 1 and Tier 2 expenses. ◀

REAL-WORLD EXAMPLE

Good records are very important in establishing the existence of a business rather than a hobby. A taxpayer, who owned and operated an apple orchard, asserted that he maintained sufficient business records, consisting of bank deposit slips, check stubs, and tax forms. A separate bank account was also maintained. But the taxpayer did not present any production records for the apple orchard. In fact, at trial, the taxpayer was not even certain of the exact number of trees in the orchard. Thus, the court found that due to the limited records, the taxpayer's activity was considered to be a hobby rather than a business. *Zdun*, TC Memo 1998-296 (1998).

VACATION HOME

Because owning a second home or dwelling unit may have both personal and profit-motivated attributes, Sec. 280A may disallow or limit deductions for expenses related to the rental of a vacation home that is also used as a residence by the taxpayer.

Residence Defined. For the restrictive rules of Sec. 280A to apply, the property must be a dwelling unit that qualifies as the taxpayer's residence. As used in this context, the term *dwelling unit* is quite expansive. The term dwelling unit may even include property such as boats and mobile homes. The determining factor is whether the property provides shelter and accommodations for eating and sleeping.[45] Thus, a mini-motorhome that contains the appropriate accommodations has been held to be a dwelling unit subject to the rules and limitations of Sec. 280A. The determination disregards the fact that the unit is small and cramped.

A dwelling unit qualifies as a residence if the number of days during which the taxpayer uses the property for personal use throughout the year exceeds the greater of the following:

- 14 days, or
- 10% of the number of days during the year that the property is rented at a fair rental.[46]

SELF-STUDY QUESTION

What is the maximum number of days during a year that a taxpayer may use a property for personal use and not have it considered to be used as a residence?

EXAMPLE I:6-40 ▶ Sarah owns a houseboat on Lake Powell that she personally uses for 21 days out of the year. During the year she also rents out the boat for a total of 300 days. Even though Sarah's personal use exceeds 14 days during the year, the houseboat is not considered a residence under Sec. 280A because Sarah's personal use does not exceed 30 days during the year (10% of the 300 rental days for the year). ◀

ANSWER

If a property was rented for 332 days it could be used by the taxpayer for 33 days and not be considered a residence.

[45] *Ronald L. Haberkorn*, 75 T.C. 259 (1980), and *John O. Loughlin v. U.S.*, 50 AFTR 2d 82-5827, 82-2 USTC ¶9543 (D.C. Minn., 1982).

[46] Sec. 280A(d)(1). In certain cases, this residence test might be met when a taxpayer uses a property as his or her principal residence for part of the year and rents the property for the rest of the year. This could occur, for example, when a taxpayer moves from his or her home and turns the old residence into a rental unit. In such a case, special rules prevent the home from being classified as a residence under Sec. 280A, thus preventing the application of the limitations.

For purposes of the residence test, a day of personal use includes any of the following:

- Any day the taxpayer or the taxpayer's family uses the property for personal purposes. Family is defined here as including the taxpayer's spouse, brothers and sisters, ancestors, and lineal descendants.[47]
- Any day any individual uses the property under a reciprocal-use arrangement.[48]
- Any day any individual uses the property and does not pay a fair rental for its use.[49]

Despite the family-use rule, if a taxpayer rents property at a fair rental to a family member who uses the property as a principal residence, such use does not constitute personal use by the taxpayer.

EXAMPLE I:6-41 ▶ During the current year, Peggy purchases a small house as an investment and rents the property to Stan, her married son, who uses the property as his principal residence. Stan pays his mom a fair rental for the property. Because Stan uses the property as his principal residence and pays Peggy a fair rental for the property, Peggy is not treated as personally using the house for any days during the year. Thus Peggy's personal use does not exceed the greater of 14 days or 10% of the rental days during the year, and the rules of Sec. 280A do not apply to limit the expenses that Peggy may deduct (although the passive loss rules may limit the deduction). ◀

KEY POINT

A second home is classified as either rental property, a residence, or some combination of the two. If it is classified as some combination of rental property and a residence, the expenses of the property must be allocated between the two categories.

Allocation of Expenses. When a taxpayer uses a vacation home personally as well as for rental purposes, the tax law requires the taxpayer to allocate the vacation home expenses between the taxpayer's personal use and rental use. The reason for this required allocation of the vacation home expenses is that the IRC generally allows individuals to deduct expenses attributable to the rental of property (subject to various limitations), whereas individuals generally cannot deduct expenses allocated to personal use property. The taxpayer must allocate the expenses between the two uses whether or not the property qualifies as the taxpayer's residence under the greater of (1) 14 days or (2) 10% of rental days test discussed above. If the property is considered the taxpayer's residence because the taxpayer's personal usage exceeds the greater of 14 days or 10% of the rental days during the year, the taxpayer may deduct the expenses allocated to the rental use as a *for* AGI deduction, but only to the extent of the gross income generated by the property. The property may not generate a loss which could be used to reduce other income of the taxpayer. If the allocated expenses exceed the gross income for the year, the taxpayer may carry over the excess expenses to the following year. However, the deduction in the subsequent year is also limited to the gross income of the property for the subsequent year.[50] The order for deduction of the expenses allocated to the rental use of property is the same as the order for deduction of hobby losses under the rules of Sec. 183. Example I:6-40 illustrates these rules.

Allocation Formula. Sec. 280A uses the following formula to allocate expenses between the personal use and the rental use of the property:[51]

$$\text{Rental use expenses} = \frac{\text{Number of rental days}}{\text{Total number of days used}} \times \text{Total expenses for the year}$$

The denominator of the allocation fraction is the sum of the days the property is rented plus the days the taxpayer uses it for personal purposes. The formula does not include the days that no one uses the property.

---

47 Sec. 280A(d)(2). A day during which the taxpayer spends substantially full time on repairs and maintenance does not count as a personal-use day.

48 Sec. 280A(d)(2)(B). A reciprocal-use arrangement is one whereby another person uses the taxpayer's property in exchange for the taxpayer's use of the other person's property.

49 Sec. 280A(d)(2)(C). Exactly what constitutes a fair rental must be determined by an examination of all the associated facts and circumstances.

50 Sec. 280A(c)(5)(B). The expenses that are carried over to the subsequent year are deductible to the extent of the property's gross income of that year, even though the property is not used by the taxpayer as a residence during that year.

51 Sec. 280A(e)(1).

Some courts have modified the allocation formula by using the total number of days in the year as the denominator for qualified residential interest and taxes instead of the number of days the property was used.[52] Use of this ratio allocates less interest and taxes to the rental use, allowing more of the other expenses to be deducted against the rental income. Expenses allocated to the personal use of the vacation home generally are not deductible. However, as explained in Chapter I:7, individuals may take a *from* AGI deduction for real estate taxes paid on personal use property such as a home or vacation home. In addition an individual may also include as a *from* AGI deduction certain interest expenses incurred on a "qualified residence" of the taxpayer. In order for the vacation home to qualify as a "qualified residence" the taxpayer must meet the same residence test discussed above where the taxpayer's personal usage must exceed the greater of (1) 14 days or (2) 10% of the rental days during the year.[53] Example I:6-42 and I:6-43 use the allocation formula for the interest and taxes that is sanctioned by the courts.

EXAMPLE I:6-42 ► Joan owns a cabin near the local ski resort. During the year, Joan and Joan's family use the cabin a total of 25 days. Joan also rents the cabin to out-of-state skiers for a total of 50 days during the year, generating rental income of $10,000. Joan incurs the following expenses:

Expense	*Amount*
Property taxes	$1,500
Interest on mortgage	3,000
Utilities	2,000
Insurance	1,500
Security and snow removal	2,500

SELF-STUDY QUESTION

Assume that a taxpayer rents his cabin to an individual who occupies it on a Saturday afternoon. Two weeks later the tenant leaves the cabin on a Saturday morning. Has the cabin been rented for more than 14 days?

ANSWER

No. Although the tenant was on the premises for 15 calendar days, he is treated as having rented the property for only 14 days.

Joan would have been entitled to $12,000 depreciation if the property had been entirely rental property held for investment. However, because the property is also used for personal purposes, the amount of deductions (for AGI) Joan may take with respect to the property during the year is as follows:

Item	*Calculation*	*Allocated to Rental*	*Allocated to Personal*	*Treatment of Personal Amounts*
Rental income		$10,000		
Interest	$\$\ 3{,}000 \times \frac{50}{365}$	(411)*	($2,589)	Deductible**
Taxes	$\$\ 1{,}500 \times \frac{50}{365}$	(205)*	(1,295)	Deductible***
Other expenses	$\$\ 6{,}000 \times \frac{50}{75}$	(4,000)	(2,000)	Not deductible
Depreciation	$\$12{,}000 \times \frac{50}{75}$	(5,384)****	(4,000)	Not deductible
Net Rental Income from Property		$0		

The income and expenses allocated to the rental use are reported on Schedule E. Thus, the expenses allocated to the rental use are *for* AGI deductions. The deductible interest and taxes allocated to the personal use are itemized deductions on Schedule A if Joan's total itemized deductions exceed her standard deduction.

* Under the approach favored by the IRS, $2,000 of the interest and $1,000 of the taxes would be allocated to the rental use (50/75 or 2/3 or each expense), leaving only $3,000 of the depreciation to be deducted against the gross income.

** Joan can include the interest allocated to her personal use as an itemized *from* AGI deduction because her personal usage of the cabin (25 days) exceeds 14 days (the greater of 14 days or 10% of the rental days). See Chapter I:7 and Sec. 163(h)(2) and (h)(4)(A).

*** Deductible under Sec. 164(a)(1) as an itemized **from** AGI deduction.

**** Limited to the remaining gross income. If there had been sufficient gross income, Joan could have taken $8,000 depreciation. ◄

[52] *Dorance D. Bolton v. CIR*, 51 AFTR 2d 83-305, 82-2 USTC ¶9699 (9th Cir., 1982). See also *Edith G. McKinney v. CIR*, 52 AFTR 2d 83-6281, 83-2 USTC ¶9655 (10th Cir., 1983).

[53] No deduction is allowed for interest incurred with respect to a personal residence if the debt on which the interest is paid is not secured by the property or the taxpayer has not chosen the property as a second residence for purposes of deducting the interest as qualified residential interest (see Chapter I:7). For purposes of the discussion and examples used here, the assumption is made that the interest qualifies as qualified residential interest.

EXAMPLE I:6-43 ▶ Assume all the same facts in Example I:6-42 except that during the year Joan uses the cabin for 16 days and rents the cabin out for 170 days. The allocation and deductibility of the cabin's expenses are as follows:

Item	*Calculation*	*Allocated to Rental*	*Allocated to Personal*	*Treatment of Personal Amounts*
Rental income		$10,000		
Interest	$ 3,000 × $\frac{170}{365}$	(1,397)	($1,603)	Not deductible*
Taxes	$ 1,500 × $\frac{170}{365}$	(699)	(801)	Deductible**
Other expenses	$ 6,000 × $\frac{170}{186}$	(5,484)	(516)	Not deductible
Depreciation	$12,000 × $\frac{170}{186}$	(2,420)***	(1,032)	Not deductible

* Joan cannot include the interest allocated to the personal use as an itemized deduction because her personal usage of the cabin doesn't exceed 17 days (the greater of 14 days or 10% of the rental days). See Sec. 163(h)(2) and (h)(4)(A).
**Deductible under Sec. 164(a)(1).
***Limited to the remaining gross income. ◀

Nominal Number of Rental Days. If a property qualifies as a taxpayer's residence under Sec. 280A and the taxpayer rents the property for less than 15 days during the year, the law takes the approach that the property is completely personal in nature. As such, the taxpayer does not have to report the rental income and cannot deduct any of the related expenses. However, expenses such as qualified residential interest and taxes may still be deductible as itemized deductions. (See Chapter I:7 for a discussion of the limitations on interest.)

EXAMPLE I:6-44 ▶ Assume the same facts as in Example I:6-42, except that during the year Joan rents the cabin out for only 12 days and the amount of rental income is $2,400. The cabin qualifies as Joan's residence because her personal use exceeds 14 days. Because the cabin is rented for less than 15 days during the year, Joan may only take itemized deductions of $4,500 for the qualified residential interest and taxes. She may not deduct the other expenses. In addition, she does not include the $2,400 in gross income. ◀

Nominal Number of Personal use Days. If a taxpayer does not have enough personal use days during the year to qualify the property as a residence (i.e., the personal use is not more than the greater of 14 days or 10% of the rental days), the Sec. 280A rules and limitations do not apply. In such a case the taxpayer must still allocate the expenses of the property between the personal use and the rental use days. The taxpayer may deduct the taxes allocated to the personal use as an itemized deduction. However, since the property does not qualify as the taxpayer's residence, the taxpayer may not deduct any of the interest allocated to the personal use because the interest is not "qualified residential interest" (see Chapter I:7 for a discussion of the deductibility of personal interest and qualified residential interest). The taxpayer may not deduct the tier 2 and 3 expenses allocated to the personal use. The income from the property and all of the expenses allocated to the rental use are reported on Schedule E of Form 1040. As such, the expenses are *for* AGI deductions. Any net income or loss from the property is subject to the Sec. 469 passive loss rules, which may limit the deductibility of any losses from the property (see Chapter I:8).

EXAMPLE I:6-45 ▶ Assume the same facts as in Example I:6-42 except that Joan and her family use the cabin only 10 days during the year and rent it out for 65 days of the year. Also assume that Joan chooses to use the IRS's method of allocating the interest and taxes between the personal use and the rental use of the cabin based upon the total number of days used during the year rather than on the total 365 days in the year. Since Joan does not personally use the cabin for at least 14 days, the cabin is not considered her residence and the Sec. 280A rules do not apply. Thus the interest allocated to the personal use is not deductible because it is not "qualified residential interest." Furthermore, the passive loss rules apply to the net income or loss from the property.

KEY POINT

Assume that a taxpayer owns a beachfront condo. The taxpayer personally uses the condo for only 12 days during the year and rents the property for 35 days. Section 280A does not apply because the taxpayer has not used the property for over 14 days. However, if the taxpayer cannot demonstrate a profit motive, it may still be treated as a hobby. Even if a profit motive can be shown, the loss may be limited under the passive loss limitation rules. If so, the deductibility of the expenses allocated to the rental use is limited to the gross income generated by the property. Furthermore, the interest allocated to the personal use of the property is not deductible as qualified residential interest (see Chapter I:7).

	Calculation	*Amount*
Rental income		\$10,000
Interest	$\$3{,}000 \times \frac{65}{75}$	(2,600)[a]
Taxes	$\$1{,}500 \times \frac{65}{75}$	(1,300)[a]
Other expenses	$\$6{,}000 \times \frac{65}{75}$	(5,200)
Depreciation	$\$12{,}000 \times \frac{65}{75}$	(10,400)
	Total	\$ (9,500)[b]

[a] Joan would treat the remaining \$200 in taxes (\$1,500 − \$1,300) as an itemized deduction. However, Joan may not deduct the remaining \$400 (\$3,000 − \$2,600) interest because it does not qualify as deductible residential interest.
[b] The deductibility of this \$9,500 loss may be limited by the passive loss rules (see Chapter I:8). ◄

The rule of Sec. 280A regarding the rental of residential property is summarized in Figure I:6-4.

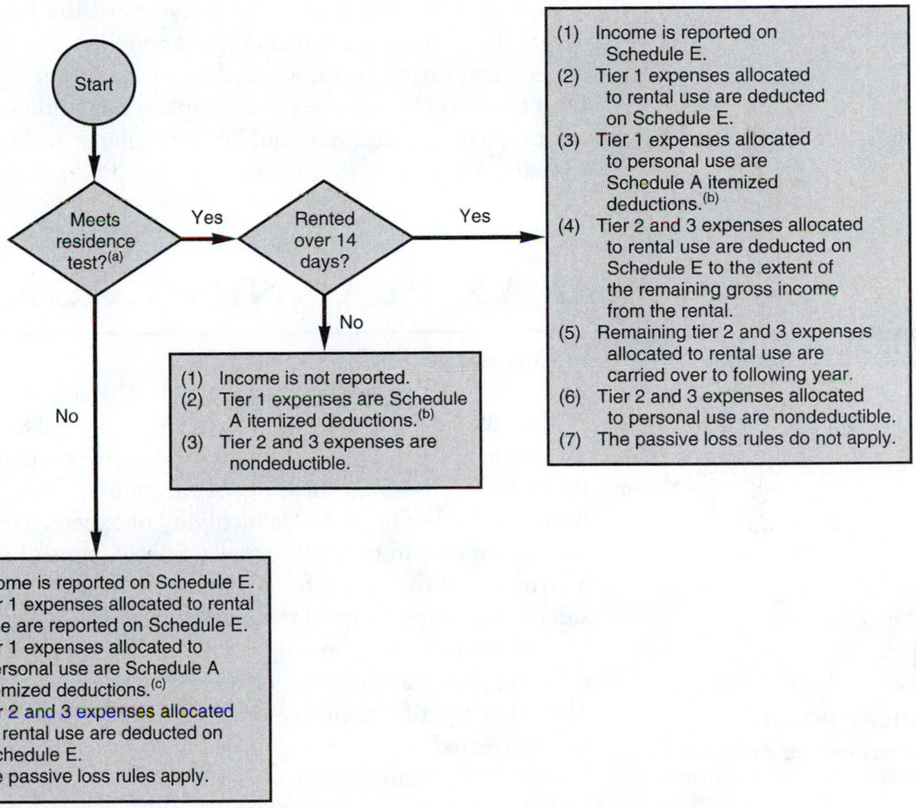

(a) Personal use is more than the larger of (1) 14 days or (2) 10% of rental days.
(b) In order for the interest to be deductible, it must be "qualified residence interest" (see Chapter 7).
(c) In order for the interest to be deductible as qualified residence interest, the property must not have been rented at all during the year. If the property has been rented out, the interest allocated to personal use is not deductible (see Chapter 7).

FIGURE I:6-4 ► SECTION 280A: LIMITATION OF DEDUCTIONS ON RENTAL OF RESIDENTIAL PROPERTY

EXPENSES OF AN OFFICE IN THE HOME

Unless the taxpayer meets certain strictly imposed requirements, Sec. 280A disallows any deduction for home office expenses. In general, for a taxpayer to deduct office-in-home expenses, the taxpayer must use the office regularly and exclusively as either of the following:

- ► The principal place of business for a trade or business of the taxpayer, or
- ► A place where the taxpayer meets or deals with clients in the normal course of business.

What would you do in this Situation?

Serious Wine or Hobby Loss?

Mr. Bouteilles Gerbeuses has been your long-time tax client. He has amassed an impressive portfolio of real estate, securities, and joint venture investments. His net worth is substantial.

Despite all his material well-being, Mr. Gerbeuses wants to take on a new challenge—that of producing fine wines. He has not had any formal wine training but he has decided to start his own winery, named *Cuvée de Prestige*. He will pattern it after the great wine houses of Europe.

He already owns several hundred acres of agriculturally zoned land in the wine producing region of the Noir Valley. It happens to adjoin his home in the Wemadeit Country Club and Retirement Resort subdivision. He anticipates a life of semi-retirement by engaging in the art of malolactic fermentation and blending of his *blanc de blancs* and *pinot noir* grapes into his own estate wine. He expects his start-up capital investment to be over $5 million and does not expect the first harvest to take place for at least seven years after the initial planting of grape vines. He expects to offset any losses by his other income.

Assuming Mr. Gerbeuses comes to you for tax advice on his new wine venture, what tax and ethical issues should be considered?

The term "principal place of business" includes a home office used by the taxpayer for administrative or management activities of the business if no other fixed location exists where the taxpayer conducts these administrative or managerial activities.

For employees to take a deduction for home office expenses, the use must also have been for the convenience of the employer. In addition, a separate structure not attached to the taxpayer's house may qualify if regularly and exclusively used in connection with the taxpayer's business. (See Chapter I:9 for a comprehensive discussion of these rules.)

TAX PLANNING CONSIDERATIONS

OBJECTIVE 7

Describe tax planning considerations for deductions and losses

HOBBY LOSSES

Deductions for expenses incurred in a hobby activity may not exceed the gross income generated by the hobby for the year. However, if the gross income exceeds the deductions from the activity in at least three out of five consecutive years (two out of seven for activities involving the breeding, training, showing, or racing of horses), tax law presumes the activity is a business, and the limits on the deductibility of expenses do not apply. Thus, if possible, taxpayers should use care in timing the realization of items of income and expense. For example, if an activity has shown a profit in only two out of the previous four years, a taxpayer may consider accelerating some of the income into the fifth year or deferring some of the expenses of the activity into the following year. Under the cash method of accounting, this can be done by delaying payment for some of the expenses or accelerating income-generating transactions. Note that meeting the three-out-of-five-year test does not automatically ensure the activity will be treated as a business. It merely compels the IRS to prove the activity is *not* a business. Under these circumstances, the IRS is less likely to challenge the deductions.

ETHICAL POINT

In some cases it is difficult to ascertain whether an activity is a trade or business or a hobby. A CPA should not prepare or sign a tax return unless he or she in good faith believes that the return takes a position that has substantial authority.

UNREASONABLE COMPENSATION

If the IRS feels that a salary payment to an officer of a corporation is excessive, it may recharacterize the excess portion as a dividend. If that happens, the corporation cannot deduct the full amount of the salary payment. To prevent a potential future disallowance, the parties may enter into a payback or hedge agreement, which provides that the employee must return to the corporation any payment held to be excessive. Under such an agreement, the employee receives a *for* AGI deduction for any amount he or she repays to the corporation. This deduction is available in the year of repayment. A payback agreement must meet the following requirements to be effective:

- The parties must enter into the agreement before actually making the payment.
- It must legally obligate the employee to repay the excess amount.[54]

[54] *Vincent E. Oswald*, 49 T.C. 645 (1968) and *J. G. Pahl*, 67 T.C. 286 (1976). See also *Ernest H. Berger*, 37 T.C. 1026 (1962).

The IRS may take the position that the existence of the payback agreement itself is evidence that the compensation is excessive. The corporation and employees can avoid this situation if they include the agreement in the general corporate bylaws rather than in a specific contract with a particular employee.[55]

TIMING OF DEDUCTIONS

Because of the time value of money, taxpayers generally prefer to deduct an expenditure as a current expense rather than capitalize it and spread the deductions over the next several years as depreciation or amortization. In addition, some capital expenditures (e.g., land) are not subject to depreciation or amortization. In some situations, however, the taxpayer may prefer to capitalize rather than expense a particular item. For example, if a taxpayer has net operating losses (NOLs) that are about to expire, a current deduction may prevent the use of these losses.[56]

In some cases it is difficult to determine whether an item should be treated as a capital expenditure or a deduction item (e.g., certain repairs may require capitalization). Because of this conflict, the Treasury has recently issued some new regulations that provide very detailed guidance on when an expenditure is to be capitalized and when it may be currently deducted. In addition, the taxpayer may elect to either capitalize or expense certain types of expenditures—such as those for research and experimentation. A tax practitioner should give consideration to the taxpayer's tax situation when making this decision. In making this decision, taxpayers and their advisors should consider NOL carryovers that might be expiring. They should also compare their current marginal tax rate with their anticipated future marginal tax rate.

COMPLIANCE AND PROCEDURAL CONSIDERATIONS

OBJECTIVE 8

Describe compliance and procedural considerations for deductions and losses

PROPER CLASSIFICATION OF DEDUCTIONS

Individuals report trade or business expenses on Schedule C (Profit or Loss from Business or Profession). It is similar to an income statement for business-related income and expenses. Income reported on Form 1040 includes the net income computed on Schedule C, because the process of arriving at the taxable income from the business involves deducting business-related expenses. Thus, these expenses are deductions *for* AGI. Similar treatment is given to expenses attributable to the production of rental and royalty income reported on Schedule E, which is an income statement. The other deductions *for* AGI have specific lines on Form 1040 itself.[57] All of these deductions appear before line 37 (where AGI appears) of Form 1040.

Deductions *from* AGI are reported on Schedule A, where they are totaled and then transferred to Line 40 of Form 1040.

A filled-in Schedule C is provided in Appendix B.

SELF-STUDY QUESTION

A professor in the Department of Accounting also teaches continuing education courses for the state CPA society as a sole proprietor. If she is a member of the state CPA society, are her dues deductible on Schedule C or as an itemized deduction?

ANSWER

Certainly, she would prefer to have the dues deductible on Schedule C so that they will not be subject to the 2% limit on miscellaneous itemized deductions. This question demonstrates the difficulty of classifying some deductions, and the answer probably depends on the primary reason for membership in the organization.

PROPER SUBSTANTIATION

The burden of proving the deductibility of any expense generally rests on the taxpayer. This has always been the case. However, in recent years Congress and the IRS have become increasingly concerned about the propriety of many deductions. In the case of travel and entertainment expenses, the Code states that taxpayers may not take a deduction for an improperly documented expense. This documentation must include the amount of the expense, the time and place of the travel or entertainment activity, the business purpose, and the business relationship of the people entertained.

BUSINESS VERSUS HOBBY

Self-employed individuals who claim a home office deduction on Schedule C must attach a Form 8829, used to allocate direct and indirect expenses to the appropriate use. Form 8829 need not be filed by employees who claim home office expenses on Form 2106.

When an activity has both profit-making and personal attributes, the burden is normally on the taxpayer to prove that the activity is a business. However, if a taxpayer can show that

[55] *Charles Schneider and Co. v. CIR*, 34 AFTR 2d 74-5422, 74-2 USTC ¶9563 (8th Cir., 1974). See also *Plastics Universal Corp.*, 1979 PH T.C. Memo ¶79,355, 39 TCM 32. Additionally, some taxpayers have been successful in defending their current level of compensation where they proved that they had been undercompensated in prior years. See *Acme Construction Co., Inc.*, 1995 RIA T.C. Memo ¶95,600, 69 TCM 1596.

[56] A NOL arises when business expenses exceed business income for a year. This excess can be carried to another year (generally back two years and forward twenty years) and is deducted against the income of that year. If the years to which the NOL is carried do not have enough income, the NOL is lost when the carryover period expires. See Chapter I:8 for a discussion of NOLs.

[57] Some of these expenses, such as employee business expenses (Form 2106) and moving expenses (Form 3903), are summarized on separate forms. These separate forms, however, are not net income statements in the same sense as Schedules C and E.

ADDITIONAL COMMENT

When a taxpayer elects to defer the determination of whether a particular activity is engaged in for profit, the statute of limitations is automatically extended for all years in the postponement period. However, the automatic extension applies only to items that might be disallowed under the hobby loss rules.

the activity has generated a profit in at least three out of five consecutive years (two out of seven for activities involving the breeding, training, showing, and racing of horses), the burden of proof shifts to the IRS. Because the statute of limitations generally runs three years after a return is filed for any particular year (i.e., for audit purposes the year closes and the IRS cannot assess any tax deficiency for that year), a potential problem exists for taxpayers who want to rely on this presumption during the first year or two of an activity's life. In these cases, the taxpayer may elect to defer the determination of whether the presumption applies until the fifth (seventh) year of operation. The election keeps the year in question open with respect to that activity until sufficient years have passed to allow for application of the presumptive test. If the taxpayer subsequently does not meet the presumptive test, the IRS can still assess a deficiency for that activity for the prior year, because the year is still open. A taxpayer makes the election by filing Form 5213 (Election to Postpone Determination as to Whether the Presumption That an Activity Is Engaged In for Profit Applies) within three years after the due date for the year in which the taxpayer first engages in the activity.

PROBLEM MATERIALS

DISCUSSION QUESTIONS

I:6-1 Why is the distinction between deductions *for* AGI and deductions *from* AGI important for individuals?

I:6-2 Sam owns a small house that he rents out to students attending the local university. Are the expenses associated with the rental unit deductions *for* or *from* AGI?

I:6-3 During the year, Sara sold a capital asset at a loss of $2,000. She had held the asset as an investment. This is the only capital asset she sold during the year. Is her deduction for this capital loss a deduction *for* or a deduction *from* AGI?

I:6-4 Joe is a single, self-employed individual who owns his own business. During 2015 Joe reported $200,000 gross income and $60,000 expenses from his business. He also paid $30,000 in alimony to his former spouse, $4,000 mortgage interest on his personal home, $6,000 for health insurance premiums, and $2,000 for medicine and doctors. Ignoring any self-employment tax on the business income, what is Joe's AGI for 2015?

I:6-5 For 2015, Mario, a single individual with no dependents, receives income of $55,000 and incurs deductible expenses of $9,000.

a. What is Mario's taxable income assuming that the expenses are deductions *for* AGI?

b. What is Mario's taxable income assuming that the expenses are miscellaneous itemized deductions *from* AGI?

I:6-6 Deductible business or investment expenses must be related to a profit-motivated activity.

a. What are the factors used in determining whether an activity is profit-motivated?

b. Why are these factors so important in making this determination?

I:6-7 If an activity does not generate a profit in three out of five consecutive years, is it automatically deemed to be a hobby? Why or why not?

I:6-8 Because expenses incurred both in a business and for the production of investment income are deductible, why is it important to determine in which category a particular activity falls?

I:6-9 In order for a business expense to be deductible it must be *ordinary, necessary,* and *reasonable*. Explain what these terms mean.

I:6-10 What are the criteria for distinguishing between a deductible expense and a capital expenditure?

I:6-11 Why are expenses related to tax-exempt income disallowed?

I:6-12 Under what circumstances may a taxpayer deduct an illegal bribe or kickback?

I:6-13 Michelle pays a CPA $400 for the preparation of her federal income tax return. Michelle's only sources of income are her salary from employment and interest and dividends from her investments.

a. Is this a deductible expense? If so, is it a deduction *for* or *from* AGI?

b. Assume the same facts as in Part a except that in addition to her salary and investment and dividend income, Michelle also owns a small business. Of the $400 fee paid to the CPA, $250 is for the preparation of her Schedule C (Profit or Loss from Business). How much, if any, of the $400 is a deductible expense? Identify it as either *for* or *from* AGI.

I:6-14 Otter Corporation sends people to the state capital to lobby the legislature to build a proposed highway that is planned to run through the area where its business is located.

a. If Otter Corp. incurs $3,200 of expenses, what part, if any, of its expenses are deductible?

b. Would it make a difference if the proposed road were a city road rather than a state highway, and Otter lobbied its local government?

c. Assume the same facts in Part a except that Otter's total in-house expenses are $1,500. Are these expenses deductible?

I:6-15 During November and December of last year, Tommy's, Inc., incurred the following expenses in investigating the feasibility of opening a new restaurant in town:

Expenses to do a market survey	$3,800
Expenses to identify potential suppliers of goods	$2,000
Expenses to identify a proper location	$1,000

Explain the proper treatment of these expenses under the following scenarios:

a. Tommy's, Inc., already owns another restaurant in town and is wanting to expand. Tommy's, Inc. opens the new restaurant in February of the current year.

b. Assume that Tommy's, Inc. is in the book selling business and feels that its bookstore business is not making a high enough return and it wants to move into the restaurant business. It opens the restaurant in February of the current year.

c. Same as Part b except Tommy's decides against opening a restaurant after getting back the results of the investigation.

I:6-16 What documentation is required in order for a travel or entertainment expense to be deductible?

I:6-17 Under what circumstances can prepaid expenses be deducted in the year of payment by a taxpayer using the cash method of accounting?

I:6-18 Under what circumstances would a taxpayer use both the cash method and the accrual method of accounting at the same time?

I:6-19 The timing of when the economic performance test is satisfied depends on the type of transaction and whether the transaction is recurring.

a. When does economic performance occur for a taxpayer who must provide property or services to another person?

b. When does economic performance occur when another person provides the taxpayer with property or services?

c. Explain the exception to the economic performance test for recurring liabilities.

I:6-20 Why did Congress enact the wash sale provisions?

I:6-21 The wash sale rules disallow a loss in the year of sale when substantially identical stock or securities are acquired by the taxpayer within a 61-day period. What types of stock or securities are considered substantially identical?

I:6-22 Under Sec. 267, current deductions may not be taken for certain transactions between related parties.

a. Who is considered a member of a taxpayer's family under the related party transaction rules of Sec. 267?

b. Identify some of the other relationships that are considered related parties for purposes of Sec. 267. Why are these other relationships included in the definition?

I:6-23 Under the related party rules of Sec. 267, why has Congress imposed the concept of constructive ownership?

I:6-24 If property is sold at a loss to a related taxpayer, under what circumstances can at least partial benefit be derived from the disallowed loss?

I:6-25 Assume that Jill is engaged in painting as a hobby. During the year, she earns $1,000 from sales of her paintings and incurs $1,300 expenses for supplies and lessons. Jill's salary from her job is $70,000. What is the tax treatment of the hobby income and expenses?

I:6-26 Under Sec. 280A, what constitutes personal use of a vacation home by the taxpayer?

I:6-27 Under Sec. 280A, how are expenses allocated to the rental use of a vacation home? In what order must the expenses be deducted against the gross income of the property?

I:6-28 Under Sec. 280A, how will a taxpayer report the income and expenses of a vacation home if it is rented out for only 12 days during the year?

ISSUE IDENTIFICATION QUESTIONS

I:6-29 David, a CPA for a large accounting firm, often works 10- to 12-hour days. As a requirement for his position, he must attend social events to recruit new clients. In addition to his job with the accounting firm, he also has private clients in his unincorporated marketing business. David purchased exercise equipment for $3,000. He works out on the equipment to maintain his stamina and good health that enable him to carry such a heavy workload. What tax issues should David consider?

I:6-30 Gus, a football player who was renegotiating his contract with the Denver Broncos, paid his ex-girlfriend $50,000 to drop a sexual assault complaint against him and keep the matter confidential. The Broncos stated that if criminal charges were filed and made public, they would terminate his employment. What tax issues should Gus consider?

I:6-31 Kathleen pays $3,000 mortgage interest on the home that she and her husband live in. Kathleen and her husband live with Molly, Kathleen's mother. The title to the home is in Kathleen's name. However, the mortgage is Molly's obligation. Kathleen claims Molly as her dependent on her current tax return. What tax issues should Kathleen consider?

I:6-32 Katie and Alan are avid boaters and water skiers. They also enjoy parasailing. This year, they started a new parasailing venture to give rides to patrons. Katie and Alan are both employed full-time in other pursuits, but they take patrons out during the summer months, on weekends and holidays. Alan has attended classes on boat operation and parasailing instruction. Katie and Alan have owned a boat for four years, but because of the heavy usage this summer, they replaced their old boat in July. They plan on replacing their boat with a new one every two years now. They use their boat in the parasailing activity and for recreational purposes. This year, Katie and Alan earned $5,400 from chartering activities and incurred $11,600 of expenses associated with their boating and parasailing. What tax issues should Katie and Alan consider?

PROBLEMS

I:6-33 *For or From AGI Deductions.* Roberta is an accountant employed by a local firm. During the year, Roberta incurs the following unreimbursed expenses:

Item	*Amount*
Travel to client locations	$750
Subscriptions to professional journals	215
Taking potential clients to lunch	400
Photocopying	60
	$1,425

a. Identify which of these expenses are deductible and the amount that is deductible by Roberta. Indicate whether they are deductible *for* or *from* AGI.

b. Would the answers to Part a change if the accounting firm reimburses Roberta for these expenses under an accountable plan?

c. Assume all of the same facts as in Part a, except that Roberta is self-employed. Identify which of the expenses are deductible, and indicate whether they are deductions *for* or *from* AGI.

I:6-34 *For vs. from AGI.* During 2015, Kent, a 40-year-old single taxpayer, reports the following items of income and expense:

Income:	
Salary	$150,000
Dividends from Alta Corporation	800
Interest income from a savings account	1,500
Rental income from a small apartment he owns	8,000
Expenses:	
Medical	6,000
Interest on a principal residence	7,000
Real property taxes on the principal residence	4,300
Charitable contributions	4,000
Casualty loss—personal	6,100
Miscellaneous itemized deductions	1,200
Loss from the sale of Delta Corporation stock (held for two years)	2,000
Expenses incurred on the rental apartment:	
Maintenance	500
Property taxes	1,000
Utilities	2,400
Depreciation	1,700
Insurance	800
Alimony payments to former wife	10,000

Assuming all of these items are deductible and that the amounts are before any limitations, what is Kent's taxable income for the year?

I:6-35 *Capitalization vs. Expense.* Sam owns a small apartment building (this is the only rental building Sam owns). During the year Sam incurs the following expenditures:

Item	*Amount*
Replace roof and roof underlying structure because of building code requirements	$30,000
Repaint the interior	3,000
Repair door handles and door locks	1,000
Replace broken windows	1,500
Replace crumbling sidewalks and stairs because of building code requirements	25,000

Discuss the proper tax treatment for these expenditures.

I:6-36 ***Political Contributions and Lobbying Expenses.*** Eljay, LLP owns several apartment complexes and office buildings. The leasing and management of these buildings constitutes Eljay's only business activity. During the current year Eljay incurred the following:

- $900 in airfare and lodging for a trip to Washington, D.C. The purpose of the trip was to protest proposed tax rate increases for individuals and corporations.
- $700 for renting space on billboards along the highway. The billboards express its concern regarding pending legislation that would significantly increase property taxes.
- $500 in airfare and hotel bills incurred on a trip to the state capital. The purpose of the trip was to meet with the legislative subcommittee on property taxation.
- $50 for a subscription to a political newsletter published by a national political party.
- $150 in making a presentation to the county council protesting a proposed increase in the property tax levy.

a. What is the total amount Eljay may deduct because of these expenditures?
b. Assume all the same facts as in Part a except that the expenses for the trip to the state capital are only $300 instead of $500. What amount may Eljay deduct because of these expenditures?

I:6-37 ***Legal and Accounting Expenses.*** Sam is a sole proprietor who owns, leases, and manages several apartment complexes and office buildings. During the current year, Sam incurs the following expenses. Which of these expenditures are deductible? Are they *for* or *from* AGI deductions?

a. $200 in attorney's fees for title searches on a new property Sam has acquired.
b. $450 in legal fees in an action brought to collect back rents.
c. $500 to his CPA for the preparation of his federal income tax return. $400 is for the preparation of Schedule C (Profit or Loss from Business).
d. $300 in attorney's fees for drafting a will.
e. $250 in attorney's fees in an unsuccessful attempt to prevent the city from rezoning the area of the city where several of his office buildings are located.

I:6-38 ***Illegal Payments.*** Damian Corporation is engaged in the business of purchasing and importing carpets from Iran. Importing these carpets from Iran is illegal. Following is a list of income and expense items for the year:

Item	*Amount*
Sales	$750,000
Cost of goods sold	270,000
Salaries	75,000
Freight	22,500
Bribes to customs officials	30,000
Lease payments on warehouses	15,000
Interest expense	12,000

a. What is the taxable income of Damian Corporation from the illegal business activity?
b. Assume the same facts as in Part a except that Damian's business consists of buying and selling marijuana and cocaine. What is Damian's taxable income from this illegal business activity?

I:6-39 ***Illegal Payments.*** Indicate whether Glenda can deduct the $5,000 payment in each of the following independent situations.

a. Glenda is a supplier of medical supplies. In order to secure a large sales contract to the regional Veterans Affairs Hospital, Glenda makes a gift of $5,000 to the hospital's purchasing agent. The payment is illegal under state law.
b. Assume the same facts as in Part a, except that the payment is made to the purchasing agent of a government-owned hospital in Brazil.
c. Assume the same facts in Part a, except that the payment is made to the purchasing agent of a privately owned hospital in Idaho.

I:6-40 ***Business Investigation Expenditures.*** During January and February of the current year, Big Bang LLC incurs $3,000 in travel, feasibility studies, and legal expenses to investigate the feasibility of opening a new entertainment gallery in one of the new suburban malls in town. Big Bang already owns two other entertainment galleries in other malls in town.

a. What is the proper tax treatment of these expenses if Big Bang decides not to open the new gallery?
b. What is the proper tax treatment of these expenses if Big Bang decides to open the new gallery?

I:6-41 *Business Investigation Expenditures.* Assume the same facts as in Problem I:6-40, except that Big Bang LLC incurs $41,000 in expenses, it does *not* already own the other entertainment galleries and it does not own anything similar.

a. What is the proper tax treatment of these expenses if Big Bang does not open the new gallery?
b. What is the proper tax treatment of these expenses if Big Bang decides to open the new gallery on May 1 of the current year and makes the appropriate election under Sec. 195?

I:6-42 *Timing of Expense Recognition.* Solutions Corporation, a computer vendor and consulting company, uses the accrual method of accounting. Its tax year is the calendar year. The following are three of the corporation's transactions during the current year:

1. Solutions Corporation hired a contractor to remodel its sales floor. The contractor completed the remodeling on November 30. On December 15, Solutions received a $5,000 bill from the contractor. Solutions immediately contacted the contractor to contest $1,000 of the total charges, arguing that it exceeded the price that was agreed upon. Solutions didn't make any payment on the bill during its current tax year.
2. Solutions offers a 2-year warranty on all of its computer systems. For sales of computers in the current year, it paid $11,500 to service warranties during the current tax year, and it expects to pay $12,000 to fulfill the remaining warranty obligations next year.
3. Every year, Solutions offers a series of six trade seminars from November 1 through April 30. It receives all registration fees from participants by October 1, before the seminars begin. As of December 31, two of the six seminars are completed, and the next seminar is scheduled for January 14–15. The expenses incurred in performing the seminars are routine each year. On the first of each month from November through April, Solutions pays the $625 monthly rent for the seminar location. On September 16, Solutions signs a contract with the seminar teacher, a computers expert and excellent public speaker. The contract requires Solutions to pay the teacher $900 after each seminar, a total of $5,400. On October 3, Solutions signs a contract with a local printing company, which will provide text materials for the seminars. Solutions pays the printer $350 after each seminar's materials are delivered the day before the seminar.

Required:

a. How should Solutions Corporation treat these transactions? What rules apply?
b. How would your answers change for each of the transactions if Solutions Corporation were a cash-method taxpayer?

I:6-43 *Prepaid Expenses.* Pamello, Inc., an engineering consulting firm, uses the cash method of accounting and is a calendar year taxpayer. Compute the amount of Pamello's current year deductions for the following transactions:

a. On November 1 of the current year, it entered into a lease to rent some office space for five years. The lease agreement states that the lease payments are $12,000 per year, payable in advance each November 1 for the following 12-month period. Under the terms of the lease, Pamello is required to pay a $5,000 deposit, refundable upon the termination of the lease.
b. On December 1 of the current year, Pamello also renewed its malpractice insurance, paying $18,000 for the three-year contract.
c. On December 31 of the current year, Pamello mailed out a check for $5,000 for drafting services performed for it during the current year by an individual who lives in another city.
d. On December 31, the firm received a shipment of $700 worth of stationery and other office supplies. Pamello has an open charge account with the office supply company, which bills the firm monthly for charges made during the year.
e. On December 31, Pamello picked up some work that a local printing company had done for it, which amounted to $1,000. The firm charged the $1,000 with its corporate credit card.

I:6-44 *Prepaid Interest.* During the current year, Richard and Alisha, a married couple who use the cash method of accounting, purchased a principal residence for $320,000. They paid $40,000 down and financed the remaining $280,000 of the purchase price with a 30-year mortgage. At the closing, they also paid $500 for an appraisal, $500 for a title search, and 1.5 points representing additional interest over the term of the loan. At the end of the year, Richard and Alisha received a statement from the mortgage company indicating that $12,000 of their total monthly payments made during the year represents interest and $1,000 is a reduction of the principal balance.

a. What is the total amount Richard and Alisha may deduct in the current year arising from the purchase and ownership of their home?
b. What is the treatment of the other items that are not deductible?

I:6-45 ***Wash Sales.*** Broward Corp. owns 1,500 shares of Silver Fox Corporation common stock. Broward Corp. purchased the 1,500 shares on April 17, 2009, for $20,000. On December 8, 2014, Broward sells 750 shares for $5,000. On January 2, 2015, Broward Corp. buys 250 shares of Silver Fox Corporation common stock for $1,750 and 50 shares of Silver Fox Corporation preferred stock for $1,000. The preferred stock is nonvoting, nonconvertible.

a. What is Broward's realized and recognized loss on the December 8 sale of stock?
b. What is Broward's basis and the holding periods of the stock?

I:6-46 ***Wash Sales.*** Cougar Corporation owns 1,000 shares of Western Corporation common stock, which it purchased on March 8, 2009, for $12,000. On October 3, 2015, Cougar purchases an additional 300 shares for $3,000. On October 12, 2015, it sells the original 1,000 shares for $8,500. On November 1, 2015, it purchases an additional 500 shares for $4,000.

a. What is Cougar's recognized gain or loss as a result of the sale on October 12, 2015?
b. What are the basis and the holding period of the stock Cougar continues to hold?
c. How would your answers to Parts a and b change if the stock Cougar purchases during 2015 is Western nonvoting, nonconvertible, preferred stock instead of Western common stock?

I:6-47 ***Constructive Ownership.*** During the current year, Troy sells land to Berry Corporation for $165,000. Troy purchased the land for investment in 2000 for $170,000. Berry Corporation is owned as follows:

Owner	*Percentage Ownership*
Tom (Troy's son)	20%
Jimmy (Troy's cousin)	15%
Jimmy's father (Troy's uncle)	30%
Angie (Troy's wife)	10%
Nicole (Angie's Sister)	25%

Troy and Jimmy are equal partners in a separate entity, TJ Partnership.

a. What is Troy's constructive ownership in Berry Corporation?
b. What is the amount of loss Troy may recognize?
c. How would your answers to Parts a and b change if TJ Partnership owned 25%, instead of Nicole?

I:6-48 ***Constructive Ownership.*** PIB Partnership is owned 20% by Sara, 40% by Steve, and 40% by Thann. Burnham, Inc. is owned 70% by PIB Partnership, 10% by Ralph, 10% by Thann, and 10% by Sara. Ralph and Thann are brothers. All other individuals are unrelated. During the current year, Ralph sold a piece of land to Burnham, Inc., for $90,000. Ralph originally purchased the land as an investment a few years ago for $100,000.

a. How much of the loss may Ralph recognize?
b. Now assume all the same facts except that the sale occurred between Thann and Burnham, Inc. How much of the loss may Thann recognize?
c. Now assume the same facts as in b except that Burnham, Inc., is owned 60% by Sara and 40% by Ralph. Thann sells the land to Burnham, Inc. How much of the loss may Thann recognize?

I:6-49 ***Related Party Transactions.*** Sally is an attorney who computes her taxable income using the cash method of accounting. Sage Corporation, owned 40% by Sally's brother, 40% by her cousin, and 20% by her grandmother, uses the accrual method of accounting. Sally is a calendar-year taxpayer, whereas Sage Corporation's fiscal year ends on January 31. During 2014, Sally does some consulting work for Sage Corporation for a fee of $10,000. The work is completed on December 15 and Sage receives Sally's invoice on that date. For each of the following assumptions, answer the following questions: During which tax year must Sally report the income? During which tax year must Sage Corporation deduct the expense?

a. The payment to Sally is made on December 27, 2014.
b. The payment to Sally is made on January 12, 2015.
c. The payment to Sally is made on February 3, 2015.

I:6-50 ***Related Party Transactions.*** During the current year, CVI Corporation sells a tract of land for $75,000. The sale is made to Sandi, CVI Corporation's sole shareholder. CVI Corporation originally purchased the land five years earlier for $98,000.

a. What is the amount of gain or loss that CVI Corporation will recognize on the sale during the current year?

b. Assume that in the following year, Sandi sells the land for $85,000. What is the amount of gain or loss Sandi will recognize? What are the tax consequences to CVI Corporation upon the subsequent sale by Sandi?
c. Assume that in the following year, Sandi sells the land for $70,000. What is the amount of gain or loss Sandi will recognize?
d. Assume that in the following year, Sandi sells the land for $105,000. What is the amount of gain or loss Sandi will recognize?

I:6-51 *Hobby Loss Presumptive Rule.* Rachel Schurtz is a high school English teacher. In her spare time, she likes to make her own body lotion, lip-gloss, and bath and shower gel. She uses the bath products herself and gives them to her friends and relatives as gifts. In 2013, Rachel started attending arts and crafts festivals three or four times a year to sell her products. She hands out her business card so her customers can buy directly from her by phone or email. In 2013, Rachel reported a net loss of $375 from the activity. In 2014, she reported a loss of $460. Rachel is audited for the year 2014, and the agent disallows the $460 loss. Rachel is confident she will make a profit on her sales in 2015, and she assumes she will continue to make a profit after 2015. Rachel is not sure that she can prove that her activity is not a hobby right now. What can she do to delay or avoid having to prove to the IRS that her loss is not a hobby loss?

I:6-52 *Hobby Loss Presumptive Rule.* Emily is an interior decorator who does consulting work for several furniture stores. Additionally, she has been designing and creating rubber stamps for the past several years. She sells the stamps to local stationary and novelty shops. Emily has reported the following net income or loss from the rubber stamp activity:

Year	*Net Income (Loss)*
2010	$ 300
2011	(900)
2012	(400)
2013	600
2014	(550)
2015	(800)

Emily is audited for the year 2015, and the agent disallows the $800 loss. Can Emily make an election for 2015 to keep the year open in anticipation of meeting the presumptive rule for the year? Why or why not?

I:6-53 *Hobby Losses.* Chuck, a dentist, raises prize rabbits for breeding and showing purposes. Assume that the activity is determined to be a hobby. During the year the activity generates the following items of income and expense:

Item	*Amount*
Sale of rabbits for breeding stock	$800
Prizes and awards	300
Property taxes on rabbit hutches	200
Feed	600
Veterinary fees	500
Depreciation on rabbit hutches	250

a. What is the total amount of deductions Chuck may take during the year with respect to the rabbit raising activities?
b. Identify which expenses may be deducted and indicate whether they are deductions *for* or *from* AGI.
c. By what amount is the cost basis of the rabbit hutches to be reduced for the year?

I:6-54 *Hobby Losses.* Assume the same facts as in Problem I:6-53, except that the income from the sale of rabbits is $1,200.
a. What is the total amount of deductions Chuck may take during the year with respect to the rabbit raising activities?
b. Identify which expenses may be deducted and indicate whether they are deductions *for* or *from* AGI.
c. By what amount is the cost basis of the rabbit hutches to be reduced for the year?

I:6-55 *Rental of Vacation Home.* During the current year, Kim incurs the following expenses with respect to her beachfront condominium in Hawaii:

Item	*Amount*
Insurance	$ 500
Repairs and maintenance	700
Interest on mortgage	3,000
Property taxes	1,000
Utilities	800

In addition to the expenses listed above, Kim could have deducted a total of $8,000 depreciation if the property had been acquired only for investment purposes. During the year, Kim uses the condominium 20 days for vacation. She also rents it out for a total of 60 days during the year, generating a total gross income of $9,000.

a. What is the total amount of deductions for and from AGI that Kim may take during the current year with respect to the condominium?

b. What is the effect on the basis of the condominium?

I:6-56 *Rental of Vacation Home.* Assume all of the same facts as in Problem I:6-55, except that during the year Kim rents the condominium a total of 14 days. How does Kim report the income and deductions from the property?

COMPREHENSIVE PROBLEMS

I:6-57 Bryce, a bank official, is married and files a joint return. During 2015 he engages in the following activities and transactions:

a. Being an avid fisherman, Bryce develops an expertise in tying flies. At times during the year, he is asked to conduct fly-tying demonstrations, for which he is paid a small fee. He also periodically sells flies that he makes. Income generated from these activities during the year is $2,500. The expenses for the year associated with Bryce's fly-tying activity include $125 personal property taxes on a small trailer that he uses exclusively for this purpose, $2,900 in supplies, $270 in repairs on the trailer, and $200 in gasoline for traveling to the demonstrations.

b. Bryce sells a small building lot to his brother for $40,000. Bryce purchased the lot four years ago for $47,000, hoping to make a profit.

c. Bryce enters into the following stock transactions: (None of the stock qualifies as small business stock.)

Date	*Transaction*
March 22	Purchases 100 shares of Silver Corporation common stock for $2,800.
April 5	Sells 200 shares of Gold Corporation common stock for $8,000. The stock was originally purchased two years ago for $5,000.
April 15	Sells 200 shares of Silver Corporation common stock for $5,400. The stock was originally purchased three years ago for $9,400.
May 20	Sells 100 shares of United Corporation common stock for $12,000. The stock was originally purchased five years ago for $10,000.

d. Bryce's salary for the year is $115,000. In addition to the items above, he also incurs $5,000 in other miscellaneous deductible itemized expenses. Assume that Bryce is not eligible for any other itemized deductions except items listed in the problem (including the election to deduct state and local sales tax instead of state and local income taxes).

Answer the following questions regarding Bryce's activities for the year.

1. Compute Bryce's taxable income for the year.

2. What is Bryce's basis in the Silver stock he continues to own?

I:6-58 Using the following facts, answer the questions below concerning Jaron's 2015 tax liability.

1. Two years ago, in November, 2013, when his wife died, Jaron left the CPA firm he was working for and started his own practice so he could have more time to spend with his four children. Jaron's children are 14, 16, 19, and 24 years old, respectively. The three youngest live at home with their father. Danny, Jaron's 19-year-old son, graduated from high school a year ago and is currently working at a local golf course. Danny earned $17,000 in the current year. Jaron's oldest daughter, Laura, is married and lives in town with her husband, Chad. Laura graduated from college two years ago and now works for a local advertising agency. What are Jaron's filing status and personal and dependency exemptions for 2015?

2. Jaron rents a small office downtown where he meets with clients and conducts business while his children are at school. He keeps all his client files and business records in this office. In the evening, he uses a converted bedroom in his home as his office. The following expenses are allocated to his home office (by square feet):

a. Depreciation	$2,150
b. Taxes	$1,500
c. Utilities	$75

Can Jaron claim a deduction for his home office?

3. Jaron owns a condominium downtown. He rented it out 270 days during the year. He also allowed Laura and her husband to stay in the home rent-free for 24 days while they were looking for a place to stay. Fortunately, the condominium wasn't rented during the time they needed it. The following items of annual income and expense relate to the condominium:

a. Rental income	$18,000
b. Interest	$3,150
c. Taxes	$1,700
d. Other expenses	$6,000
e. Depreciation	$7,090

What is the tax treatment of the condominium for Jaron in 2015?

4. On April 6, Jaron sold a parcel of land he had held for investment to a real estate development firm for $75,000. He purchased the land three years earlier from his brother for $70,000. His brother had originally purchased the land for $74,000. What is the amount and character of Jaron's gain or loss on the sale of the land?
5. On May 1, Jaron purchased 1,000 shares in Genomics Ltd. for $10 per share. In December he was forced to sell all 1,000 shares at $8 per share to avoid a conflict of interest. What is the amount and character of Jaron's gain or loss on the sale of the stock?
6. Jaron reported the following items of income and expense from his consulting practice:

a. Consulting fees received	$185,000
b. Wages expense	$47,400
c. Rent expense	$20,000
d. Depreciation	$2,100
e. Other expenses	$17,000

What is Jaron's net income from his consulting practice?

7. Calculate Jaron's 2015 income tax liability. Ignore any available credits and self employment taxes and assume the standard deduction exceeds any itemized deductions Jaron has.

TAX STRATEGY PROBLEMS

I:6-59 Danielle Anderson, your client and a cash method taxpayer, works full-time at a music store located in a mall. She assists the manager in buying decisions, serves customers on the sales floor, and plays music to draw in customers. On the weekends, she plays in various orchestras, working as an independent contractor. She does not work under a business name, maintain an office, or maintain a separate bank account for her performing activities. She always pays her bills as soon as possible, well before the bill due date. In prior years, she has taken every allowable deduction related to the performing activities. Prior year returns show the following taxable income on her Schedule C:

2011	$(5,000)
2012	2,100
2013	3,000
2014	(1,800)

Danielle has come to you on December 12, 2015. She understands that the IRS can deny losses generated by her performing business if it determines the business is actually a hobby. Because of the uncertainty of the entertainment industry, she will likely continue to generate profits in some years and losses in others. Still, she continues the activities with the intent to earn a profit.

Danielle routinely sends bills to orchestra clients at the end of the month for work she performed during the month. Most of her clients, including the Springville Orchestra, send payment within ten days of when they receive her bill.

The following is a summary of the financial position of the business for 2015 as of 12/12/2015:

Income received to date	$9,000
General expenses paid to date	9,200

Other items:	
Bill for refurbishing work on cello, due 1/2/2016	$ 300
Newspaper bill for monthly advertisement, due 1/14/2016	200
Printer bill for business cards, due 1/5/2016	500
Meals eaten while in transit to performance locations	150
Income for 12/3/2015 performance with the Springville Orchestra	1,000

What will you recommend to your client? What issues must you address? What actions will you take to ensure the most favorable tax outcome possible? What advice, if any, will you give your client for the future?

I:6-60 Peter Baumann, your client, wants to sell a printing press to Chamberlain Corporation for $50,000. Pete has used the press in his business for two years and its adjusted basis is $90,000. The Coxmann Partnership; Chloe International, Inc.; Watts, Inc., and Raleigh Corporation own Chamberlain Corporation equally. Pete and Emily Cox each own 50% of the Coxmann Partnership. Emily owns 70% of Chloe International, Inc., and Pete's sister Susan owns the other 30%. Pete's brother, Brian, owns 100% of Watts, Inc. Wade and Catherine Chamberlain, friends of Pete, own Raleigh Corporation equally. Peter wants to know what the tax consequences will be if he sells the printing press to Chamberlain Corporation. In a memo to Pete, explain any tax consequences of the proposed sale and any alternatives that would provide a better result.

TAX FORM/RETURN PREPARATION PROBLEMS

I:6-61 Dave Stevens, age 34, is a self-employed physical therapist. His wife Sarah, age 31, teaches English as a Second Language at a local language school. Dave's Social Security number is 111-11-1111. Sarah's Social Security number is 222-22-2222. Sarah and Dave have three children—Andrew, age 8; Isaac, age 6; and Mira, age 3. The children's Social Security numbers are, respectively, 333-33-3333, 444-44-4444, and 555-55-5555. They live at 12637 Pheasant Run, West Bend, Oregon 74658. They paid $8,900 in qualified residence interest and $2,400 in property taxes on their home. They had cash charitable contributions of $14,000. They also paid $180 to a CPA for preparing their federal and state income tax returns for the prior year, $100 of which was for the preparation of Dave's Schedule C. Sarah and Dave earned interest on CDs of $3,200. Sarah's salary for the year is $32,000, from which $9,600 in federal income tax and $1,400 in state income tax were withheld. Dave's office is located at Suite 402, 942 Woodview Drive, Portland, Oregon 74624, and his employer ID number is 11-1111111. Dave has been practicing for four years, and he uses the cash method of accounting. During the current year, Dave recorded the following items of income:

Revenue from patient visits	$300,000
Interest earned on the office checking balance	225

The following expenses were recorded on the office books:

Property taxes on the office	$ 4,500
Mortgage interest on the office	12,000
Depreciation on the office	4,500
Malpractice insurance	37,500
Utilities	3,750
Office staff salaries	51,000
Rent payments on equipment	15,000
Office magazine subscriptions	150
Office supplies	24,000
Medical journals	330

Dave pays $50 annually for use of a safety deposit box to store certain confidential documents related to his business. In addition to his medical practice, Dave spends 15 hours every week managing his real estate investments. To make sure he is aware of all current investment strategies and best practices, he subscribes to the following journals:

Wall Street Journal	$150
U.S. News & World Report	55
Money Magazine	45

Dave also paid $33,000 in estimated federal income taxes. Prepare Dave and Sarah's tax return (Form 1040, Schedules A, B, C, and SE) for the current year. Disregard any tax credits for which they may be eligible.

I:6-62 Lyle and Kaye James are married, have two minor children, Jessica, age 8 and Jerron, age 4, and are filing a joint tax return in the current year. They are both employed. Lyle and Kaye, ages 38 and 37, respectively, have combined salaries of $240,000, from which $48,000 of federal income tax and $10,000 of state income tax are withheld. Lyle and Kaye own two homes. Their primary residence is located at 11620 N. Mount Ave., New Haven, Connecticut 22222, and their vacation home is on the beach in Fort Lauderdale, Florida. They often rent their vacation home to supplement their income. The following items are related to the James' ownership of the two homes:

Item	*New Haven*	*Fort Lauderdale*
Rental income	$ —	$15,000
Qualified residence interest	7,200	5,000
Property taxes	1,400	1,000
Utilities	1,000	1,300
Repairs	200	300
Depreciation	0	3,500
Advertising	0	200
Insurance	1,500	1,500

The James family used their Fort Lauderdale home 20 days during the year. They rented the vacation home 60 days during the year. Lyle and Kaye jointly purchase stock in various corporations and make the following transactions in the current year. (None of the stock qualifies as small business stock.)

Date	*Transaction*	*Price Paid/Sold*
2/15	Bought 50 shares of Lake common stock (they own no other Lake stock)	$1,000
5/14	Bought 100 shares of Bass common stock (they own no other Bass stock)	3,000
5/24	Sold 25 shares of Lake common stock	250
5/27	Bought 50 shares of Lake common stock	900
	Sold 50 shares of Bass common stock	1,750
7/12	Bought 100 shares of Bass common stock	2,800

The James' have no other income or expense items. Lyle and Kaye's Social Security numbers are 111-22-3333 and 444-55-6666, respectively. Jessica and Jerron's Social Security numbers are 123-45-6789 and 888-99-1010. The James' use the IRS method of allocating all expenses between personal and rental use.

File the James' income tax return Form 1040, Schedules A, D, and E using the currently available forms and rates. Disregard the alternative minimum tax and any tax credits for which they may be eligible.

I:6-63 Scarlet Furniture Corporation, an accrual-method taxpayer, retails custom office furniture. On January 1 of the current year, Peter Marlin and John Tanner incorporated Scarlet Furniture Corporation. Peter transferred $350,000 cash for 70% of Scarlet's outstanding stock, and John transferred $150,000 cash for 30% of the outstanding stock. Scarlet generated the following financial statements at the end of its first year of operations:

Scarlet Corporation's Balance Sheet

Assets

Cash	$ 91,400
Inventory	48,000
Other Current Assets	50,000
Office Equipment	170,000
Building	250,000
Accumulated Depreciation	(20,000)
Land	550,000
Total Assets	$1,139,400

Liabilities and Owner's Equity

Accrued Expenses	$ 100,000
Long Term Debt	400,000
Common Stock	500,000
Retained Earnings	139,400
Total Liabilities and Owners' Equity	$1,139,400

Scarlet Corporation's Income Statement

Revenues	$650,000
Costs of Goods Sold	100,000
Gross Income	$550,000
Advertising Expense	40,000
Depreciation Expense	20,000*
Miscellaneous Expense	10,600**
Office Supplies	5,000
Property Tax Expense	60,000
Wages & Salaries Expense	135,000***
Warranty Expense	10,000****
Operating Income	$269,400
Interest Expense	30,000
Federal Income Tax Expense	100,000
Net Income	$139,400

*Depreciation expense for tax purposes was $120,441 because Scarlet made a Sec. 179 election to expense $105,000 of the cost of the equipment purchased this year.
**Miscellaneous expense relates to a $600 penalty fee as a result of a breached customer contract and a $10,000 fine assessed by OSHA for hazardous conditions in its storage facility.
***Wages and salary expense includes Peter's salary of $40,000 and the accrual of $15,000 of bonuses payable to Peter which Scarlet actually paid on February 10 of the following year.
****The actual expenditure paid for warranty repairs during the year is $2,000.

Scarlet does not make any sales or purchases on account. Scarlet's employer identification number is 12-34567. Its address is 789 Presidential Way, Seattle, Washington 54789. Peter Marlin's Social Security number is 555-66-8888. During the current year, the Corporation made federal estimated income tax payments of $50,000.

Prepare a Form 1120 for the initial return for Scarlet.

CASE STUDY PROBLEM

I:6-64 John and Kathy Brown have just been audited and the IRS agent disallowed the business loss they claimed in 2013. The agent asserted that the activity was a hobby, not a business.

John and Kathy live in Rochester, New York, near Lake Ontario. Kathy is a CPA, and John was formerly employed by an insurance firm. John's firm moved in 2008 and John resolved not to move to the firm's new location. Instead of seeking other employment, John felt he could supplement his income by using his fishing expertise. He had been an avid fisherman for 15 years, and he owned a large Chris-Craft fly-bridge that he chartered to paying parties.

In 2009, Kathy and John developed a business plan, established a bank account for the charter activities, developed a bookkeeping system, and acquired insurance to cover the boat and the passengers. John fulfilled all the requirements to receive a U.S. Coast Guard operating license, a New York sport trolling license, and a seller's permit. These licenses and permits were necessary to legally operate a charter boat. The first year of their activity was 2009.

John advertised in local papers and regional sport fishing magazines. He usually had three or four half-day paying parties each week. John spent at least one day per week maintaining and repairing his boat. Kathy usually accompanied John on charters three or four times each year.

John's charter activity was unprofitable the first two years. In 2011, John and Kathy restructured the activity to improve profitability. The restructuring included increasing advertising, participating in outdoor shows, and negotiating small contracts with local businesses. After the restructuring, the activity provided a small profit in 2011 and 2012.

In 2013, John started working with another insurance company in the area on a full-time basis. Even though he returned to the insurance business, John normally took two paying parties and one nonpaying, promotional party each week throughout the fishing season. John's costs unexpectedly increased and he lost $8,000 in the activity during 2013. John and Kathy deducted the entire loss on Schedule C of their 2013 tax return.

Required: Prepare a memo to the Browns recommending what position they should take and why. Show the logic used in arriving at your recommendation.

TAX RESEARCH PROBLEM

I:6-65 Richard Penn lives in Harrisburg, Pennsylvania. Richard is the president of an architectural firm. Richard has become known throughout the community for excellent work and honesty in his business dealings. Richard believes his reputation is an integral part of the success of the firm.

Oil was found recently in the area around Harrisburg and some geologists believed the reserves were large. A few well-respected businesspeople organized Oil Company to develop a few wells. Although some oil was being extracted, the oil corporation lacked capital to develop the oil fields to their expected potential. After reading the geologists' report, Richard felt that Oil Company was a good investment; therefore, he acquired 25% of the company. A short time after Richard's acquisition, the price of foreign oil decreased sharply. The drop in foreign oil prices caused Oil Company to be unprofitable due to its high production costs. Three months later Oil Company filed bankruptcy.

The bankruptcy proceedings were reported in the local newspaper. Many of Oil Company's creditors were real estate developers that engaged Richard's architectural firm to provide designs. After Oil Company declared bankruptcy the architectural firm's business noticeably decreased.

Richard felt the decline in business was related to the bankruptcy of Oil Company. Richard convinced his partner to use the accumulated earnings of the firm to repay all the creditors of Oil Company.

Richard has asked you whether his firm can deduct the expenses of repaying Oil Company's creditors. After completing your research explain to Richard why the expenses are or are not deductible.

A partial list of research sources is as follows:

- Sec. 162
- *Thomas H. Welch v. Helvering,* 12 AFTR 1456, 3 USTC ¶1164 (USSC, 1933)
- *William A. Thompson, Jr.,* 1983 PH T.C. Memo ¶83,487, 46 TCM 1109

TAX RESEARCH CASE

I:6-66 Three years ago, Paul Wilde exercised all his stock options in the start up company he helped establish and walked away with over $100 million. Since that time, he has spent all his energy, time, and effort in managing his portfolio. His investment philosophy is one of steady, careful investment in a well-balanced portfolio. Thus, although each year he engages in several sales and purchases, he generally buys and holds the securities for both the dividends and the growth potential. Consequently, most of the stock sales he makes are of securities he has held for over one year. Because his investment activities have grown so large, this year he rented a suite of offices and hired two investment advisors and five secretaries to help him. He also purchased several new computers and some new office furniture for the office.

Paul has now come to you for some tax help. Specifically, he would like to know if his activities are considered a business or an investment activity. In your explanation, please include whether the expenses incurred in the activity are deductions *for* or *from* AGI.

A partial list of research sources is as follows:

- *Higgins v. CIR,* 25 AFTR 1160, 41-1 USTC §9233 (USSC, 1941)
- *Estate of Louis Yaeger, Deceased, Judith Winters, Ralph Meisels, Abraham J. Weber and the Bank of New York,* 889 F2d 29, 89-2 USTC ¶9633 (CA-2)
- *Frederick Mayer and Jan Perry Mayer,* 67 TCM 2949 (1994)
- *Rudolph W. and Abbie A. Steffler,* 69 TCM 2940 (1995)
- Sec. 179

CHAPTER

7

ITEMIZED DEDUCTIONS

LEARNING OBJECTIVES

After studying this chapter, you should be able to

1. Identify qualified medical expenses and compute the medical expense deduction
2. Identify taxes that are deductible as itemized deductions
3. Identify different types of interest deductions
4. Compute the amount of a charitable contribution deduction and identify limitations
5. Discuss casualty and theft losses
6. Identify certain miscellaneous itemized deductions subject to the 2% of AGI limit
7. Describe tax planning considerations for itemized deductions
8. Describe compliance and procedural considerations for itemized deductions

As explained in Chapter I:6, most deductible expenses for individuals fit into three general categories:

- Expenses incurred in a trade or business
- Expenses incurred for the production of income (an investment activity) or for tax advice
- Certain specified personal expenses

If an expense is deductible based on the above categories, the expense must be classified as either *for* AGI or *from* AGI. The distinction between *for* and *from* AGI was discussed in Chapter I:6. This chapter focuses on deductions *from* AGI, also referred to as **itemized deductions**, which include medical expenses, taxes, interest, and charitable contributions. Chapter I:9 discusses other itemized deductions, such as employee business expenses, and Chapter I:8 discusses casualty losses on personal-use property.

In arriving at taxable income, individuals may subtract from AGI the larger of the standard deduction or the sum of all itemized deductions. In calculating the sum of the itemized deductions, certain deductions are subject to reductions and limitations.

MEDICAL EXPENSES

OBJECTIVE 1

Identify qualified medical expenses and compute the medical expense deduction

Medical expenses, which comprise one category of deductible personal expenditures, are deductible because Congress felt that excessive medical expenses might ultimately affect a taxpayer's ability to pay his or her federal income tax. However, under Sec. 213, taxpayers may deduct medical expenses only to the extent the expenses exceed 10% of the taxpayer's AGI. For years before 2016, the AGI limit is 7.5% for taxpayers 65 or older. To qualify as a medical expense deduction, the expenditure must be incurred for the medical care of a qualified individual. Taxpayers may not take a deduction for medical expenses to the extent the expenses are reimbursed (i.e., compensated for by insurance or otherwise).

QUALIFIED INDIVIDUALS

To deduct medical expenses, taxpayers must pay the expenses on behalf of themselves, their spouses, or their dependents.

Taxpayer's Dependent. Deductible medical expenses include those paid on behalf of a taxpayer's dependent as well as on behalf of a person for whom the taxpayer could take a dependency exemption except for the failure to meet the gross income or joint return tests.[1]

EXAMPLE I:7-1 ▶ In March of 2015, Jean's son, Steve, is involved in an automobile accident. At the time of the accident Jean is 54 years old and Steve is 25 years old. Steve has worked full-time for part of the year, earning a total of $15,000. Because Steve has no medical insurance and cannot pay the medical bills or support himself as a result of the accident, Jean pays Steve's medical expenses and supports him for the rest of the year. Because Jean provides over one-half of Steve's support for the year and Steve, except for the gross income test, otherwise qualifies as Jean's dependent, (Steve is a qualifying relative rather than a qualifying child because he is over 19 and is not a full-time student) Jean may deduct the medical expenses she pays on his behalf to the extent that these expenses, along with all of Jean's other medical expenses, exceed 10% of her AGI for the year. Jean may not claim a dependency exemption for Steve because the gross income test is not satisfied. ◀

KEY POINT

Medical expenses are deductible for a person who satisfies only the support, relationship, and citizenship dependency tests.

Children of Divorced Parents. As long as one divorced parent qualifies to claim the dependency exemption under Sec. 152(e), the parent who pays medical expenses on behalf of the children may deduct the expenses. The parent taking the medical expense deduction doesn't need to be the parent who may claim the dependency exemption.

[1] Sec. 152. See Chapter I:2 for the tests that must be met to claim a qualifying child or qualifying relative as a dependent.

QUALIFIED MEDICAL EXPENSES

The **medical expense deduction** is available only for expenditures paid for medical care. Section 213 defines *medical care* as amounts paid for

- The diagnosis, cure, mitigation, treatment, or prevention of disease
- The purpose of affecting any structure or function of the body
- Transportation primarily for and essential to the first two items listed above
- Qualified long-term care services
- Insurance covering all of the items listed above

ADDITIONAL COMMENT

In 2012 the deduction for medical expenses totaled $85.3 billion, representing 7.6% of the total dollar amount of the itemized deductions for medical expenses, taxes, interest, and charitable contributions.

Diagnosis, Cure, Mitigation, Treatment, or Prevention of Disease. Although the tax law does not precisely define the term *medical expense,* it is clear that medical expenses are deductible only if paid for procedures or treatments that are legal in the locality in which they are performed. For example, taxpayers may not deduct expenditures for controlled substances.[2] The definition of medical care includes preventive measures such as routine physical and dental examinations. However, other expenses should be "confined strictly to expenses incurred primarily for the prevention or alleviation of a physical or mental defect or illness." Thus, unless they are for routine physical or dental examinations, the expenditures must be for the purpose of curing a specific ailment rather than related to the general health of an individual. This determination is especially critical when the expenditures in question are for items such as vacations, weight loss programs, or stop smoking programs. The taxpayer may or may not incur such expenses for a specific ailment.

EXAMPLE I:7-2 ► Helmut is nervous and irritable because of pressures at work and begins to suffer angina symptoms. In order to relax and get away from it all, he takes an ocean cruise around the world. Helmut's angina symptoms ease while he is on the cruise. In a case with facts very similar to Helmut's situation, the Tax Court held that a cruise is not a proven medical necessity because the taxpayer's physician did not specifically prescribe it. Although the cruise was beneficial to Helmut's general health, it was not deductible.[3] ◄

EXAMPLE I:7-3 ► Dave enrolls in a weight reduction program on the advice of two doctors who prescribe the program as a means of relieving his obesity, hypertension, and certain hearing problems. Based on a revenue ruling issued by the IRS, these expenses qualify as deductible medical expenditures because they are incurred for a specific medical condition.[4] ◄

Although a doctor's recommendation appears to lend a great deal of weight to deductibility, it is not always sufficient. For example, a taxpayer could not deduct the cost of dancing lessons for an emotionally disturbed child, even though the lessons proved to be beneficial and were recommended by a physician. Likewise, a taxpayer suffering from arthritis could not deduct the cost of ballroom dance lessons, even though a doctor recommended the lessons. On the other hand, the IRS has ruled that the cost of a clarinet and clarinet lessons was deductible when recommended by an orthodontist to correct a malocclusion of a child's teeth.[5] In short, determining the deductibility of certain expenditures can be difficult.

ADDITIONAL COMMENT

One cannot deduct the cost of nonprescription medicine (except insulin), toothpaste, toiletries, maternity clothes, diaper service, or funeral expenses.

Range of Deductible Medical Services. According to the Treasury Regulations, typical medical expenses include payments for a wide range of medical, dental, and other diagnostic and healing services. Thus, taxpayers may deduct payments to licensed or certified medical professionals such as general practitioners, obstetricians, surgeons, ophthalmologists, opticians, dentists, and orthodontists. Furthermore, deductible medical expenditures

---

[2] Reg. Sec. 1.213-1(e)(1)(ii). See also Rev. Rul. 97-9, 1997-1 C.B. 77 and IRS Publication 502 (2014) which contains the IRS's recommended treatment for a number of medical expenses.

[3] *Daniel E. Mizl,* 1980 PH T.C. Memo ¶80,227, 40 TCM 552. Even if the taxpayer's physician had prescribed the trip, it still may not have been deductible. See Reg. Sec. 1.213-1(e)(1)(ii).

[4] Rev. Rul. 2002-19, 2002-1 C.B. 778. However, taxpayers still may not deduct the cost of diet foods or weight loss programs directed at general health or appearance. Taxpayers may deduct costs incurred for prescription medications and programs to stop-smoking, but not over-the-counter stop smoking aids. See Rev. Rul. 99-28, 1999-1 C.B. 1269.

[5] *John J. Thoene,* 33 T.C. 62 (1959), *Rose C. France v. CIR,* 50 AFTR 2d 82-5504, 1982-1 USTC ¶9225 (6th Cir., 1982), and Rev. Rul. 62-210, 1962-2 C.B. 89.

include payments for medical services rendered by individuals such as chiropractors, osteopaths, and psychotherapists who may or may not be required to be licensed or certified.[6] Taxpayers may deduct payments to Christian Science practitioners as well as for acupuncture treatment if the taxpayer receives the treatment for a specific medical purpose.[7] Qualified medical expenses also include payment for hospital services, nursing services, laboratory fees, X-rays, artificial teeth or limbs, ambulance hire, eyeglasses, and prescribed medicines and insulin. Nondeductible expenses include expenditures for nonprescription medicines, drugs, vitamins, and other types of health foods that improve the individual's general health.

To deduct costs incurred for schools and camps, the taxpayer must show that the facility has the appropriate medical equipment and regularly engages in providing medical services. For example, a court held that a taxpayer could deduct costs he incurred to send his mentally disabled son to a school with a special curriculum specifically for mentally disabled children. Similarly, another court ruled that a taxpayer could deduct the cost of sending a child with psychiatric problems to a school that specialized in learning disorders. However, taxpayers generally may not deduct the cost of sending children with special medical problems to schools or camps that do not have the proper equipment, facilities, or curriculum for such problems.

TYPICAL MISCONCEPTION

Taxpayers tend to define qualifying medical expenses too narrowly. This may be caused, in part, by comparison with expense reimbursement limitation policies of health insurance companies.

Medical Procedures Affecting any Function or Structure of The Body. Deductible medical expenditures also include payments for services affecting any function or structure of the body, even though no specific illness or disease exists. Thus, qualifying medical expenses include expenditures for such items as physical therapy, obstetrical services, eyeglasses, dental examinations and cleanings, and hearing aids. Under Sec. 213, cosmetic surgery or any other similar procedure does not qualify as a medical expense unless such surgery is necessary to correct a deformity arising from a congenital abnormality, a personal injury resulting from an accident or trauma, or a disfiguring disease. Cosmetic surgery is defined as any procedure undertaken to improve a person's appearance that does not meaningfully promote the proper function of the body or prevent or treat an illness or disease.

Transportation Essential to Medical Care. Taxpayers may deduct transportation expenses that are essential to and incurred primarily for qualified medical care. Thus, taxpayers may deduct actual out-of-pocket automobile expenditures, taxis, airfare, ambulance fees, and other forms of transportation if the travel is for medical reasons. However, the tax law disallows a deduction if the travel is undertaken for recreational purposes or for the general improvement of the taxpayer's health.

ADDITIONAL COMMENT

For 2015, the standard mileage rate for business mileage is 57.5 cents per mile. For medical and moving it is 23 cents, and for charitable purposes it is 14 cents.

In lieu of the actual cost of the use of an automobile, for 2015 the IRS allows a deduction of 23 cents for each mile that the automobile is driven for medical reasons. In addition to this standard mileage rate, taxpayers may also deduct the cost of tolls and parking.

Certain courts have held that the cost of meals and lodging while en route to a medical facility is part of deductible travel costs incurred for medical purposes. However, taxpayers may not deduct the cost of meals eaten on trips that are too short to warrant a stop for meals. Additionally, taxpayers may deduct only 50% of the cost of meals. (See Chapter I:9 for a discussion of the 50% disallowance rule for meals and entertainment.) Sec. 213(d)(2) limits the potential deduction for the cost of lodging to $50 per night. Furthermore, lodging expenses qualify as medical expenditures only if the travel is primarily for and essential to medical care, the medical care is provided in a licensed hospital (or a facility related or equivalent to a licensed hospital), and there is no significant element of personal pleasure or recreation in the travel. The tax law imposes the $50 limitation on lodging on a per-individual basis. Thus, if the patient is unable to travel alone, the taxpayer may deduct an additional $50 per night for the lodging costs of a nurse, parent, or spouse.

---

[6] Reg. Sec. 1.213-1(e)(1) and Rev. Rul. 63-91, 1963-1 C.B. 54. See also Ltr. Rul. 8919009 (February 6, 1989) where a pregnant woman was entitled to a deduction for the cost of childbirth classes to the extent that they prepared her for the childbirth. However, the cost of the classes where she received instructions on the care of the unborn child represented a flat fee that allowed a coach to attend the class with the taxpayer. Thus, one-half of the fee was deemed attributable to the coach and was not allowed as a qualified medical expense.

[7] Rev. Rul. 72-593, 1972-2 C.B. 180 and IRS Special Ruling, February 2, 1943.

Qualified Long-Term Care. Taxpayers may also deduct expenditures for qualified long-term care as medical expenses subject to the 10% of AGI limitation. Long-term care is defined as medical services required by a chronically ill individual which are provided under a prescribed plan of care. Under Sec. 7702B, such items include expenditures for diagnostic, preventive, therapeutic, curing, treating, mitigating, rehabilitative, and personal care services. A chronically ill individual generally is someone who, for a period of at least 90 days, cannot perform at least two daily living tasks such as eating, toileting (including continence), bathing, or dressing. According to Sec. 213(e)(11), if the long-term care service is provided by the individual's spouse or relative, any payment for the long-term care service is not deductible unless the spouse or relative is a licensed professional to be able to provide this care. Furthermore, services provided by a corporation or partnership in which the person owns over 50% are also not deductible.

Expenditures for long-term care insurance premiums qualify as medical deductions, subject to an annual limit based upon the age of an individual.[8]

Capital Expenditures for Medical Care. Generally, taxpayers may not currently deduct capital expenditures for federal income tax purposes. For assets used in a trade or business or held for the production of income, taxpayers must recover such costs through depreciation, cost recovery, or amortization. Capital expenditures incurred for personal medical purposes are not depreciable or amortizable. However, a current deduction is available when the capital expenditure is made to acquire an asset primarily for the medical care of the taxpayer, the taxpayer's spouse, or the taxpayer's dependents. To qualify as a deduction, the taxpayer must incur the expenditure as a medical necessity for primary use by the individual in need of medical treatment, and the expenditure must be reasonable in amount. The following are the three categories of deductible capital expenditures for medical care:[9]

- Expenditures that relate only to the sick or handicapped person, not to the permanent improvement or betterment of the taxpayer's property (e.g., eyeglasses, dogs or other animals that assist the blind or the deaf, artificial teeth and limbs, wheelchairs, crutches, and portable air conditioners purchased for the sole use of a sick or disabled person)
- Expenditures that permanently improve or better the taxpayer's residence for the purpose of providing medical care (e.g., a swimming pool installed in the home of an individual suffering from arthritis)
- Expenditures to remove structural barriers in the home of a physically disabled individual (e.g., costs of constructing entrance ramps, widening doorways and halls, lowering kitchen cabinets, and adding railings)

REAL-WORLD EXAMPLE

The cost of installing an elevator in the home upon the recommendation of a physician to help a patient with a heart condition was deductible to the extent that it did not increase the value of the home. *James E. Berry v. Wiseman*, 2 AFTR 2d 6015, 58-2 USTC ¶9870 (D.C. Okla., 1958).

Capital expenditures that relate only to the sick person (the first category) are fully deductible in the year paid. Expenditures that improve the residence (the second category) are deductible only to the extent that the amount of the expenditure exceeds the increase in the fair market value (FMV) of the residence. Expenditures to remove physical barriers in the home of a physically disabled individual (the third category) are deductible in full (i.e., the increase in the home's value is deemed to be zero). In addition, any costs of operating or maintaining the assets in all three categories are deductible as long as the medical reason for the capital expenditure continues to exist.[10] All of the above expenditures are subject to the 10% of AGI floor.

EXAMPLE I:7-4 ▶ During the current year, Rita is injured in an industrial accident. As a result, she sustains a chronic disabling leg injury, which requires her to spend much time in a wheelchair. Rita's physician recommends that a swimming pool be installed in her backyard and that she devote several hours each day to physical exercise. During the year, Rita makes the following expenditures:

Wheelchair	$ 2,500
Swimming pool	27,000
Operation and maintenance of the pool	1,800
Entrance ramp and door modification	5,000

8 For 2015, if the individual is 40 years of age or less, the annual deductible limit for the premiums is $380. For individuals over 40 but not over 50, the limit is $710. For those who are 50 but not over 60, the limit is $1,430. For those who are 60 but not over 70, the limit is $3,800. For those who are 70 or older, the limit is $4,750.

9 Reg. Sec. 1.213-1(e)(1)(iii) and H. Rept. No. 99-841, 99th Cong., 2d Sess., p. II-22 (1986).

10 Rev. Rul. 87-106, 1987-2 C.B. 67.

REAL-WORLD EXAMPLE

Taxpayers made nonrefundable advance payments required as a condition for an institution's future acceptance of their disabled child for lifetime care in the event that taxpayers could not care for the child. The amounts paid were deductible as expenses for medical care in the year paid. Rev. Rul. 75-303, 1975-2 C.B. 87. This current deduction for prepaid amounts is only available for certain lifetime care expenditures incurred in situations described in this ruling. Rev. Rul. 93-72, I.R.B. 1993-34,7.

A qualified appraiser estimates that the swimming pool increases the value of Rita's home by only $20,000. Rita's medical expenses for the year include $2,500 for the wheelchair, $7,000 for the swimming pool (the excess of the cost of the pool over the increase in the FMV of the home), $1,800 for the operation and maintenance of the pool, and $5,000 for the ramp and door modification. ◀

Costs of Living in Institutions. The entire cost of in-patient hospital care, including meals and lodging, qualifies as a medical expense. However, if an individual is in an institution other than a hospital (e.g., a nursing home or a special school for the disabled), the deductibility of the costs involved depends on the facts of the particular case. If the principal reason for the taxpayer's presence in an institution is the need for and availability of the medical care furnished by that institution, the qualified medical expenditures include the entire costs of meals, lodging, and other services necessary for furnishing the medical care. If medical care is not the principal reason for the taxpayer's presence in the institution, the institutional expenses are not deductible. Only specific medical expenses, such as doctor bills, prescription drugs, etc., are eligible for deduction.

ADDITIONAL COMMENT

A taxpayer cannot deduct the Medicare (hospital insurance benefits) tax that is withheld from wages as part of the Social Security tax.

Medical Insurance Premiums. Qualified medical expenses also include premiums paid for medical insurance, including premiums paid for supplementary medical insurance for the aged under the Social Security Act and premiums paid for qualified long-term care insurance contracts. In many cases, taxpayers pay premiums for insurance coverage that extends beyond mere medical care. For example, in addition to the standard medical care coverage, an insurance policy may provide coverage for loss of income or loss of life, limb, or sight. In such cases, the tax law allows a deduction for the medical care portion of the premium only if the cost of each type of insurance is either separately stated in the contract or furnished to the policyholder by the insurance company in a separate statement.[11]

EXAMPLE I:7-5 ▶ Each month Malazia pays $300 for an insurance policy under which she is reimbursed for any doctor or hospital charges she incurs. In addition, the policy will pay two-thirds of her regular salary each month if she becomes disabled. Finally, the policy will pay her $10,000 for the loss of any limb. At the end of the year, her insurance company issues a statement that allocates two-thirds of the premiums to the medical insurance coverage. Malazia's medical care expenditure is $2,400 ($300 × 12 × 0.667). ◀

If a taxpayer pays the premiums attributable to an individual or group medical insurance plan, the payments are deductible as medical expenses, which are itemized deductions in most cases. Self-employed individuals may deduct 100% of these amounts as deductions *for* AGI. Any amounts paid by the taxpayer's employer are excluded from the employee's gross income and are not includible in the taxpayer's medical expenses.[12]

Chapter I:9 discusses the deduction for certain medical savings accounts established for employees.

AMOUNT AND TIMING OF DEDUCTION

The amount and timing of the allowable medical expense deduction depend on when the taxpayer actually pays the medical expenses, the taxpayer's AGI, and whether the taxpayer receives any reimbursement for the medical expenses.

Timing of The Payment. In general, taxpayers may deduct medical expenses only in the year they actually pay the expenses. This rule applies regardless of the taxpayer's method of accounting or when the event that caused the expenditure occurs.[13] Thus, if taxpayers receive medical care during the year but have not paid for it as of the end of the year, taxpayers must defer the deduction for that care until the year they pay for the medical care. If the obligation is charged on a credit card, payment is deemed to have been

[11] Sec. 213(d). See also Rev. Ruls. 66-216, 1966-2 C.B. 100, and 79-175, 1979-1 C.B. 117.

[12] Sections 162 and 106.

[13] Reg. Sec. 1.213-1(a)(1). However, medical expenses paid within one year from the day following the taxpayer's death are treated as paid at the time they are incurred (see Sec. 213(c)).

made on the date of the charge, not on the later date when the taxpayer pays the credit card balance. Conversely, if medical care is prepaid, the deduction is deferred until the year the taxpayer receives the care unless there is a legal obligation to prepay or unless the prepayment is a requirement for the receipt of the medical care.[14]

Limitation on Amount Deductible. As previously noted, other than medical insurance premiums paid by self-employed individuals, the tax law allows a medical expense deduction only for the years in which the taxpayer itemizes his or her deductions and the taxpayer's expenditures for medical care exceed 10% of AGI.

EXAMPLE I:7-6 ▶ During 2015, Kelly incurs qualified medical expenditures of $6,000. Kelly is 45 and her AGI for the year is $50,000. After subtracting the floor, she has $1,000 ($6,000 − [0.1 × $50,000]) of deductible medical expenses. These medical expenses are added to Kelly's other itemized deductions to determine whether they exceed the standard deduction. ◀

SELF-STUDY QUESTION

Why does the IRS not require that the taxpayer file an amended return when a reimbursement is received in a later year?

ANSWER

The administrative burden on the IRS of processing additional returns would be too great.

Medical Insurance Reimbursements. Taxpayers may only deduct unreimbursed medical expenditures. It does not matter whether the reimbursement is from an insurance plan purchased from an insurance company, a medical reimbursement plan of an employer, or a payment resulting from litigation.

If the taxpayer receives reimbursement in the same year he or she pays for the medical expenses, the amount of the reimbursement reduces the allowed deduction. If a taxpayer receives a reimbursement in a year subsequent to the year of payment, the taxpayer must include the reimbursement in gross income in the year of receipt to the extent that the taxpayer derived a tax benefit from the deduction in the previous year. If the taxpayer did not take a deduction in the prior year, the taxpayer doesn't need to report the reimbursement as income. This may occur because the taxpayer's total itemized deductions do not exceed the standard deduction or because the taxpayer's total medical expenses do not exceed 10% of AGI. If the taxpayer took a deduction in the prior year, however, the taxpayer must report as income the lesser of the amount of the reimbursement or the amount the medical expenses reduced the taxable income in the prior year.

EXAMPLE I:7-7 ▶ During 2015, Dan, a single taxpayer under age 65, reports the following items of income and expense:

AGI	$100,000
Total qualified medical expenses	12,500
Itemized deductions other than medical	4,100

Dan's taxable income for 2015 is calculated as follows:

AGI			$100,000
Reduction: Larger of itemized deductions or standard deduction			
Medical expenses	$12,500		
Minus: 10% of AGI	(10,000)	2,500	
Other itemized deductions		4,100	
Total itemized deductions		$6,600	
Greater of itemized deductions or standard deduction ($6,300)			(6,600)
Personal exemption			(4,000)
Taxable income			$89,400

If during 2016 Dan receives a reimbursement of $1,500 for medical expenses he incurred the prior year, he must include $300 (6,600 − 6,300) in gross income for 2016, which is the amount of the tax benefit from the medical expense deduction for the prior year. This amount can be calculated by comparing Dan's actual taxable income for 2015 with what would have been his 2015 taxable income if the reimbursement had been received that year. This calculation is as follows:

[14] Rev. Rul. 78-39, 1978-1 C.B. 73 and *Robert M. Rose v. CIR*, 26 AFTR 2d 70-5653, 70-2 USTC ¶9646 (5th Cir., 1970). See also Rev. Rul. 93-72, Rev. Rul. 1993-2 C.B. 77, Rev. Rul. 75-302, 1975-2 C.B. 86, and Rev. Rul. 75-303, 1975-2 C.B. 87.

AGI			$100,000
Reduction: Larger of itemized deductions or standard deduction			
Medical expenses	$12,500		
Minus: Reimbursement	(1,500)		
Minus: 10% of AGI	(10,000)	1,000	
Other itemized deductions		4,100	
Total itemized deductions		$5,100	
Greater of itemized deductions or standard deduction ($6,300)			(6,300)
Personal exemption			(4,000)
Taxable income (assuming reimbursement was received in 2015)			$89,700
Minus: Actual 2015 taxable income			($89,400)
Tax benefit			$ 300 ◀

Topic Review I:7-1 highlights the principal requirements for the medical expense deduction previously discussed.

STOP & THINK

Question: Vince and Diane are married and file a joint tax return. For the current year they estimate their AGI at $90,000. They also estimate their itemized deductions for taxes, interest, and charitable contributions total $9,000. Up to the current date they have incurred $7,000 in deductible medical expenses. For several months they have been considering laser surgery on Diane's eyes. The total expenditure for the operations will be $5,000 and is not covered by their medical insurance. Since they already have spent so much this year on medical expenses and they do not anticipate such large expenses next year, they are considering delaying the eye operation until next year. They estimate next year's AGI to be approximately $110,000. Does this decision make sense from a tax point of view?

Solution: From a tax point of view, Vince and Diane should consider having and paying for the operation this year. If so, $5,000 is added to the prior $7,000 medical expenditures for a total of $12,000 for the year. After applying the 10% of AGI limitation, $3,000 [$12,000 − ($90,000 × 0.1)] of the medical expenses is deductible. If they wait until next year and if their estimates are correct, none of the medical expenses in either year are deductible because of the 10% of AGI limitation.

TOPIC REVIEW I:7-1

Medical Expense Deductions

Items	Deduction Rules and Limitations
Qualifying expenditures	(a) Expenditures for the diagnosis, cure, mitigation, treatment, or prevention of disease and qualified long-term care. (b) Transportation at 23¢ per mile for 2015; lodging limited to $50 per night, per person; and 50% of meals. (c) Medical and qualified long-term care insurance premiums. (d) Capital expenditures (subject to specific limitations).
Qualifying individuals	Taxpayer, spouse, dependents, children of divorced parents even if not dependent, and persons who would qualify as dependent except for the failure to meet gross income or joint return tests.
Amount and timing of the deduction	Deduct in the year paid unless prepaid, then deductible when medical treatment is received. If prepayment is required or there is a legal obligation to prepay, then deduct in year of prepayment. Medical expenses are subject to a 10% of AGI nondeductible limitation.
Treatment of insurance reimbursements	The deduction is reduced if the reimbursement is received in the year of payment. Reimbursements received in a subsequent year are included in gross income of the year received to the extent that a tax benefit was received in the earlier year.

Taxes

OBJECTIVE 2

Identify taxes that are deductible as itemized deductions

Section 164 provides taxpayers with a deduction for specifically listed taxes paid or accrued during the taxable year. Generally, cash-method taxpayers deduct the taxes when they pay for them, whereas taxpayers using the accrual method deduct taxes in the year the taxes accrue. The tax law specifically lists other taxes as nondeductible. To be deductible as a tax, the assessment in question must be a tax rather than a fee or charge imposed by a government for providing specific goods or services.

ADDITIONAL COMMENT

In 2012 the deduction for taxes totaled $483 billion, representing 43% of the total dollar amount of the itemized deductions for medical expenses, taxes, interest, and charitable contributions.

DEFINITION OF A TAX

A **tax** is a mandatory assessment levied under the authority of a political entity for the purpose of raising revenue to use for public or governmental purposes. Thus, fees, assessments, or fines imposed for specific privileges or services are not deductible as taxes under Sec. 164. These nontax items include:

- Vehicle registration and inspection fees
- Registration tags for pets
- Toll charges for highways and bridges
- Parking meter charges
- Charges for sewer, water, and other services
- Special assessments against real estate for items such as sidewalks, lighting, and streets

However, if taxpayers incur these nontax fees and charges in a business or income- producing activity, the taxpayers may either capitalize or deduct these items as ordinary and necessary business expenses or ordinary and necessary expenses incurred for the production of income.

DEDUCTIBLE TAXES

The following taxes are specifically deductible under Sec. 164:

- State, local, and foreign real property taxes
- State and local personal property taxes if based on value
- State, local, and foreign income, war profits, and excess profits taxes
- For tax years beginning before January 1, 2015, state and local sales taxes if the taxpayer makes an election to deduct these taxes instead of deducting state and local income taxes.
- The environmental tax imposed by Section 59A. Although the imposition of the Environmental Tax was imposed only for tax years beginning before January 1, 1996, §164(a)(5) still lists the tax as deductible.
- Other state, local, and foreign taxes that are paid or incurred in either a trade or business or an income-producing activity

In general, taxes imposed by the federal government are not deductible in calculating a taxpayer's income tax.[15] However, federal customs and excise taxes incurred in the taxpayer's business or income-producing activity are deductible as ordinary and necessary expenses under Secs. 162 or 212. Furthermore, an employer may deduct the *employer's* portion of Federal Social Security taxes and federal and state unemployment taxes as ordinary and necessary business expenses if the employee works in the employer's business or income-producing activity. A self-employed individual may deduct one-half of the self-employment tax imposed on the individual's self-employment income as a *for* AGI deduction.

[15] The generation-skipping transfer tax is imposed by the United States on certain distributions from a trust (see Sec. 2601) and is deductible for federal income tax purposes. Furthermore, under Sec. 691(c) a taxpayer who includes income in respect of a decedent in taxable income may deduct the estate tax attributable to that amount.

BOOK-TAX DIFFERENCE

For financial accounting purposes, all taxes are expensed in arriving at net income after taxes. However, for tax purposes, only certain taxes are deductible. This gives rise to an M-1 or M-3 adjustment.

STATE AND LOCAL INCOME TAXES

For individuals, state and local income taxes are normally an itemized (*from* AGI) deduction. Thus, a taxpayer does not receive any federal income tax benefit if these taxes, in addition to the taxpayer's other itemized deductions, do not exceed the standard deduction. Cash-method taxpayers deduct all state and local income taxes paid or withheld during the year even if the taxes are attributable to another tax year.

EXAMPLE I:7-8 ▶ During 2015, Rita had $1,500 in state income taxes withheld from her salary. On April 15, 2016, Rita pays an additional $400 when she files her 2015 state income tax return. If the sum of her itemized deductions for 2015 exceeds the 2015 standard deduction, for 2015 Rita may deduct as an itemized deduction the $1,500 in state income taxes withheld from her salary during 2015. The $400 that Rita pays on April 15, 2016, is added to her itemized deductions for 2016 even though the liability relates to her 2015 state income tax return. ◀

ADDITIONAL COMMENT

Every state except Alaska, Florida, Nevada, New Hampshire, South Dakota, Tennessee, Texas, Washington, and Wyoming impose a personal income tax. Although New Hampshire and Tennessee do not impose a personal income tax, they do tax interest and dividends at the individual level.

If a taxpayer receives a refund of state income taxes deducted in a prior year, the taxpayer must include the refund as income in the year of the refund to the extent the taxpayer received a tax benefit from the prior deduction. This calculation is similar to the calculation of the tax benefit from a medical expense reimbursement in Example I:7-7.

STATE AND LOCAL SALES TAXES

As mentioned previously, for tax years beginning before January 1, 2015, taxpayers were allowed to deduct state and local sales taxes in lieu of state and local income taxes.[16] Taxpayers electing to deduct state and local sales taxes instead of state and local income taxes had two options for determining the deductible amount. Taxpayers could deduct the actual amount of taxes paid by accumulating receipts showing the actual amount of taxes paid, or they could deduct the appropriate amount from tables provided by the Treasury Department. If a taxpayer used the amount from the tables, sales taxes paid on major purchases could be added to the table amount.

PERSONAL PROPERTY TAXES

Many state and local governments impose personal property taxes. For individuals, the key issue is whether the levy is a deductible tax under Sec. 164 or a nondeductible fee. To qualify as a deductible personal property tax, the levy must meet two basic tests:

- ▶ The tax must be an ad valorem tax on personal property. In other words, the property's value determines the amount of the tax rather than some other measure such as a vehicle's weight or model year.
- ▶ The tax must be imposed on an annual basis, even if not collected annually.[17]

If a personal property tax is based partly on value and partly on some other basis, only the ad valorem portion is deductible.

EXAMPLE I:7-9 ▶ Banner County imposes on all passenger automobiles a property tax of 1% of value plus 20 cents per pound. Clay's automobile has a value of $20,000 and weighs 1,500 pounds. Clay may deduct $200 ($20,000 × 0.01) under Sec. 164. Clay may not deduct the remaining $300 (1,500 × 0.20) under Sec. 164; however, he may deduct it as an ordinary business expense if the automobile is used in his business. ◀

ADDITIONAL COMMENT

Several states impose a tax on the value of a taxpayer's investment portfolio. This is an example of a deductible intangible personal property tax.

For individuals, personal property taxes are *from* AGI (itemized) deductions unless the individual incurs the taxes in the individual's trade or business or for the production of rental income.

REAL ESTATE TAXES

Apportionment of Taxes. When real estate is sold during the year, the federal income tax deduction for property taxes imposed on that real estate is allocated between the seller and the purchaser based on the amount of time each taxpayer owns the property during the real property tax year. The real property tax year may or may not coincide with the taxpayer's tax year. The apportionment, based on the number of days each party holds the property during the real property tax year of sale, assumes that the purchaser owns the property on the date of the sale. This apportionment is mandatory for all taxpayers even though one of

[16] In years past, Congress has extended this election. At this point in time, Congress has not extended this election beyond 2014, but may do so in the future.

[17] Reg. Sec. 1.164-3(c).

the parties (i.e., the purchaser or seller) may have actually paid the entire property tax bill. The party who actually pays the taxes (either the buyer or the seller) deducts his or her share of the taxes in the year he or she pays the taxes unless the taxpayer makes an election under Sec. 461(c) to accrue the taxes. The tax consequences do not depend on whether the agreement requires proration of the real estate taxes. Both the purchaser and the seller may deduct their apportioned share of the taxes, regardless of who actually pays the taxes. Generally the sales agreement provides for the proper apportionment of property taxes between the buyer and the seller and will state the amount of the taxes apportioned to each party separately from the selling price of the property. If the seller pays all of the taxes prior to the sale, at closing the buyer will reimburse the seller for the payment of these taxes in addition to paying the down payment. On the other hand, if the taxes are to be paid by the buyer after the purchase of the property, the amount collected from the buyer at closing is reduced by the amount of taxes allocated to the seller. This process does not impact the selling price of the property if properly allocated and accounted for at closing.[18]

ADDITIONAL COMMENT

Delinquent taxes of the seller that are paid by the buyer as part of the contract price are not deductible.

EXAMPLE I:7-10 ► The real property tax year for Bannock County is the calendar year. Property taxes for a particular real property tax year become a lien against the property as of June 30 of that year, and the owner of the property on that date becomes liable for the tax. However, the taxes are not payable until February 28 of the subsequent year. On May 30 of the current (non-leap) year, Sandy, a cash-method taxpayer, sells a building to Roger, who is also a cash-method taxpayer. The real estate taxes on the property for the current year are $1,095. Although Roger is liable for the payment of the tax, Sandy is treated as having paid $447 ($1,095 × 149/365 [the numerator of 149 is the number of days from January 1 through May 29 and the denominator is the entire real property tax year]) on the date of the sale. Thus, Sandy may deduct $447 in the year of sale. Roger may deduct his share of the taxes, equaling $648 ($1,095 × 216/365), in the subsequent year (i.e., the year during which Roger actually pays the full amount of property tax due of $1,095). On the other hand, if the taxes become a lien against the property on April 1, Sandy is the owner of the building on that date and, since she is liable for the tax, she will be the one who actually pays the tax. Under these circumstances, the result is the same (i.e., Sandy deducts $447 and Roger deducts $648) except that Roger may take the $648 deduction in the year of sale rather than in the year of payment and Sandy takes the $447 deduction in the year of payment rather than the year of sale. ◄

TYPICAL MISCONCEPTION

Taxpayers often fail to differentiate between assessments for new construction and for repairs. For example, an assessment for street repairs is deductible, but an assessment for the construction of a new street is not deductible.

Real Property Assessments for Local Benefits. Local governments often make assessments against real estate for the purpose of funding local improvements. These assessments may be for such items as street improvements, sidewalks, lighting, drainage, and sewer improvements. If the tax assessment is only against the property that benefits from the improvement, it is not deductible, even though the general public may also incidentally benefit.[19] The tax law requires capitalization of such assessments as part of the property's adjusted basis.

Real property taxes incurred on personal-use assets, such as a personal residence, are deductible *from* AGI. Real property taxes incurred on business property or property held for the production of rental income are deductions *for* AGI.

SELF-EMPLOYMENT TAX

Wages paid to an employee are subject to a payroll tax which consists of two components (Social Security, technically called OASDI, and Medicare). Both the employer and the employee pay a share of the taxes imposed. Thus, on wages paid to an employee, the employer and the employee generally each pay a tax of 6.2% for Social Security (a total of 12.4%) and 1.45% (a total of 2.9%) for Medicare. The Social Security tax is imposed on a limited amount of wages. For 2015, this wage limit is $118,500. However, the Medicare tax is imposed on both the employer and the employee without limit on the amount of the wages paid. Self-employed individuals must pay both of these taxes on their self-employment income. Because these taxes are imposed only on the self-employed individual, these taxes are imposed on the individual's self-employment income at the total 2.9% for Medicare and the total 12.4%

[18] However, if the agreement does not specifically provide and account for an apportionment of taxes, the apportionment of the taxes is still made and the seller's gain or loss on the sale (and the purchaser's basis in the property) must be adjusted either upward or downward, depending on which party actually pays the taxes.

[19] Reg. Sec. 1.164-4. However, if the assessment against the local benefits is made for maintenance, repair, or interest charges on the benefits, the assessment is deductible. The burden of proof to show how much of the assessment is deductible falls on the taxpayer (see Sec. 164(c)(1)).

(up to self-employment income of $118,500 in 2015) for Social Security. Self-employed individuals may deduct one-half of these self-employment taxes paid as a *for* AGI deduction.[20]

Starting in 2013, an additional surtax is imposed under the Patient Protection and Affordable Care Act passed by Congress in 2012. This new tax is imposed on individuals with over $200,000 in income ($250,000 for married filing jointly) and is imposed at 3.8% on investment income and 0.9% on wages and self-employment income. The reason for this 0.9% (3.8% – 2.9%) difference in these rates is that self-employment income and wages are already subject to the 2.9% Medicare tax whereas investment income is not. This new tax is imposed only on individuals, not on employers. Furthermore, unlike the Social Security tax and the Medicare tax, this new tax is not deductible by individuals.

SELF-STUDY QUESTION

Would a taxpayer normally prefer to deduct foreign taxes or take a foreign tax credit?

ANSWER

Normally the foreign tax credit is better because a credit provides a direct dollar-for-dollar reduction of the tax liability rather than a reduction of taxable income.

NONDEDUCTIBLE TAXES

The following taxes are not deductible under Sec. 164:

- Federal income taxes
- Federal estate, inheritance, legacy, succession, and gift taxes
- Federal import or tariff duties and excise taxes unless incurred in the taxpayer's business or for the production of income
- Employee's portion of Social Security and other payroll taxes
- State and local sales taxes and state inheritance, legacy, succession, and gift taxes (For years prior to 2015 individuals could elect to deduct state and local sales taxes instead of state income taxes)
- Foreign income taxes if the taxpayer elects to take the taxes as a credit against his or her federal income tax liability
- Property taxes on real estate to the extent treated as imposed on another taxpayer
- Tax imposed on wages, self-employment income, and investment income under the Patient Protection and Affordable Care Act

INTEREST

OBJECTIVE 3

Identify different types of interest deductions

In years past, taxpayers could deduct virtually all interest paid or accrued in the taxable year. Gradually, however, Congress has enacted numerous exceptions into the tax law rendering several types of interest nondeductible. For example, individuals may not deduct personal interest expense, such as interest paid on personal credit cards, automobile loans, etc. Interest incurred in connection with a trade or business is deductible. Thus, to determine the amount of interest expense deduction, individuals must properly classify their interest expense for the year. The interest expense categories include the following: active trade or business, passive activity, investment, personal, qualified residence, and student loan.

ADDITIONAL COMMENT

In 2012 the deduction for interest paid totaled $354 billion, representing 31.6% of the total dollar amount of the itemized deductions for medical expenses, taxes, interest, and charitable contributions.

DEFINITION OF INTEREST

Interest is defined as "compensation for the use or forbearance of money."[21] Thus, finance charges, carrying charges, loan discounts, premiums, loan origination fees, and points are all considered interest if they represent a cost for the use of money.

Charge for Services. In addition to interest, borrowers may incur other charges in connection with borrowing money. These service charges include fees for appraisals, title searches, bank service charges, and the annual service charge on credit cards. Unless incurred in a trade or business, these expenses are not deductible because they all represent nondeductible personal expenses. As explained in the section in this chapter entitled Personal Interest, although finance charges on credit cards represent interest rather than service costs (on page 7-16), they likewise are not deductible unless incurred in a trade or business.

Bank Service Charges and Finance Charges. Bank service charges on checking accounts are nondeductible expenses for services rendered rather than interest.

---

[20] Sec. 164(f). In calculating its taxable income subject to the income tax, an employer is able to deduct as a business expense its portion of these Social Security taxes and Medicare taxes. Thus, in order to equate the amount and deductibility of these taxes imposed on self-employed individuals, an adjustment is made to the amount of the self-employed income that is subject to these taxes. (See Chapter I:14 for a discussion of the self-employment tax.)

[21] *Deputy v. Pierre S. DuPont,* 23 AFTR 808, 40-1 USTC ¶9161 (USSC, 1940).

The annual service charge on credit cards is also a charge for services rather than interest. However, finance charges on credit cards are interest. Late payments charged by public utilities are interest expense because they do not relate to any specific service.[22] Of course, if taxpayers incur these expenses in a trade or business, they are deductible.

KEY POINT

In general, the classification of interest expense depends on the use to which the borrowed money is put, not on the nature of the property used to secure the loan.

CLASSIFICATION OF INTEREST EXPENSE

The deductibility of interest generally depends on the purpose for which the taxpayer incurs the indebtedness because interest incurred in certain activities is subject to limitation and disallowance. For example, interest expense incurred in the taxpayer's active business is deductible in full against the business income (a deduction *for* AGI, taken on Schedule C), whereas interest expense allocated to the purchase of the taxpayer's residence is subject to the limitations applicable to that type of interest and is an itemized deduction (a deduction *from* AGI). Except for certain student loan interest and certain interest on a personal residence, taxpayers may not deduct interest allocated to personal-use expenditures.

Pursuant to the Treasury Regulations, taxpayers must allocate interest expense to the different interest expense categories by identifying the use of the borrowed money. Property used as collateral in securing the debt normally has no bearing on the allocation of the interest expense.[23]

EXAMPLE I:7-11 ▶ Cathy pledges some stock and securities as collateral for a $30,000 loan. She then purchases an automobile with the proceeds of the loan. The automobile is used 100% of the time for personal use. Even though the collateral for the loan is investment property, the interest expense is allocated to a personal-use asset and is not deductible. ◀

If the taxpayer deposits borrowed funds in a bank rather than spending them immediately, the deposit is treated as an investment, and the interest on the loan is investment interest until the taxpayer withdraws or expends the funds. Then the taxpayer allocates the interest expense to a category based on the reason for making the expenditure, regardless of when the taxpayer actually pays the interest expense for the debt. This reallocation occurs as of the date the taxpayer writes the check on the account, as long as the delivery or mailing of the check occurs within a reasonable period of time.[24]

EXAMPLE I:7-12 ▶ On March 1 of the current year, José borrows $100,000 and immediately deposits the funds into an account that contains no other funds. José makes no additional deposits or payments. On May 1 of the current year, he withdraws $40,000 from the account and purchases a sailboat to be used for personal purposes. On July 1, José withdraws an additional $50,000 and purchases a passive activity. For the current year, the interest expense on the loan is categorized as follows: from March 1 through April 30, all of the expense is investment interest expense. 40% ($40,000/$100,000) of the interest expense attributable to the period May 1 through June 30 is classified as personal interest and the remainder is investment interest. The interest expense attributable to the period from July 1 to the end of the year is classified as 40% personal interest, 50% passive activity interest, and 10% investment interest. ◀

If both borrowed and personal funds are mingled in the same account, expenditures from that account are treated as coming first from the borrowed funds.[25]

EXAMPLE I:7-13 ▶ On April 1 of the current year, Diane borrows $30,000 and deposits it into a checking account that contains $10,000 of personal funds. On May 1 of the current year, Diane purchases a passive activity for $15,000, and on June 1 she purchases a personal automobile for $20,000. The $15,000 expended for the passive activity on May 1 is treated as coming from the borrowed funds. Thus, as of that date, one-half of the interest expense on the debt is reallocated from

---

22 Rev. Rul. 73-136, 1973-1 C.B. 68 and Rev. Rul. 74-187, 1974-1 C.B. 48. See also Rev. Rul. 77-417, 1977-2 CB 60, which rules that one-time charges of 2% of each new cash advance and 1% of each new check and overdraft advance on a credit card account is an interest charge if the charges are not for services performed in the maintenance of the account. Of course, interest on a credit card or interest charged by a public utility is not deductible if it is personal interest.

23 Temp. Reg. Sec. 1.163-8T. The major exception to this rule deals with home equity loans where the funds borrowed may be used for any purpose. Home equity loans are discussed later in this chapter.

24 Temp. Reg. Sec. 1.163-8T(c). If during any one month several expenditures are made from an account, the taxpayer may elect to treat all the expenditures as if made on the first day of the month. This election is made on each account separately and is available only for accounts where the borrowed funds are already in the account as of the first day of the month. If the funds are not in the account as of the first day of the month, the expenditures may be treated as made on the date that the borrowed funds are deposited in the account. See Temp. Reg. Sec. 1.163-8T(c)(4)(iv).

25 Temp. Reg. Sec. 1.163-8T(c)(4)(iii)(B). However, if an expenditure is made out of the mingled funds within 15 days of the deposit of the borrowed funds into the account, the taxpayer may designate the expenditure to which the borrowed funds are allocated.

investment interest to passive activity interest. $15,000 of the funds expended for the personal automobile on June 1 is treated as coming from the borrowed funds, and the remaining $5,000 is treated as coming from the personal funds. Thus, as of June 1, the remaining interest expense on the debt is reallocated to personal interest. ◀

When the taxpayer repays the debt, the allocation of the repayment to the expenditures made with the borrowed funds occurs in the following order: (1) personal expenditures, (2) investment expenditures and passive activity expenditures other than rental real estate, (3) passive activity expenditures in rental real estate, and (4) trade or business expenditures.

Active Trade or Business. Generally, a taxpayer may deduct without limit any interest expense incurred in the taxpayer's active trade or business. As explained in Chapter I:6, the determination of whether a particular activity constitutes a trade or business or an investment depends on an examination of all the relevant facts and circumstances. For individuals, estates, trusts, and certain corporations, however, it is not sufficient that the taxpayer incur the interest in a trade or business. In addition, the taxpayer must *materially participate* in the business. If not, the activity is considered a passive activity, and losses from the activity (including the interest expense) are subject to the passive loss limitation rules (see Chapter I:8 for a discussion of these rules). Interest incurred in an active trade or business is a deduction *for* AGI.

Passive Activity. Individuals, estates, trusts, and certain corporations that incur losses from passive activities are subject to the passive loss limitation rules explained in Chapter I:8. These rules prevent taxpayers from offsetting passive activity losses against other types of income such as salary, interest, dividends, and income from an active business. Taxpayers must include interest expense attributable to the passive activity in computing the net income or loss generated from the activity, and thus may not be able to deduct the interest under these limitation rules (see Chapter I:8 for a discussion of these rules).

Investment Interest. Individuals and other noncorporate taxpayers are limited on the deductibility of interest expense attributable to investments. Without any limitation, high-income taxpayers could realize significant tax savings by borrowing money to invest in assets that are appreciating in value but produce little or no current income. This would enable the taxpayer to offset current highly taxed income with a current interest deduction, while deferring the taxable income from the investment until it is sold at a later date. This technique also would enable taxpayers to increase their future capital gain income and reduce their current ordinary income. This procedure is favorable to individual and noncorporate taxpayers because the tax on capital gains is less than the tax on ordinary income.

Because of these concerns, Sec. 163(d) limits the current deduction for investment interest expense to the noncorporate taxpayer's net investment income for the taxable year. Any investment interest expense disallowed as a current deduction is carried over and treated as investment interest expense incurred in the following year.

EXAMPLE I:7-14 ▶ In the current year, Rita earns $27,000 in net investment income and incurs $40,000 of investment interest expense. Rita's interest expense deduction for the year is limited to $27,000, the amount of her net investment income.

The remaining investment interest expense of $13,000 ($40,000 − $27,000) may be carried over and deducted in a subsequent year. This carryover amount is treated as paid or accrued in the subsequent year and is subject to the disallowance rules that pertain to the subsequent year. ◀

Investment Interest. **Investment interest** is interest expense on indebtedness properly allocable to property held for investment. This includes property that generates portfolio types of income such as interest, dividends, annuities, and royalties. It does not include business interest, personal interest, qualified residence interest, or interest incurred in connection with any passive activity. Under Sec. 469, all rental activities are passive (see Chapter I:8 for a discussion of the passive loss limitation rules). Thus, interest incurred in owning and renting property is subject to the passive loss limitation rather than the investment interest limitation.

Investment interest also does not include interest expense incurred to purchase or hold tax-exempt securities. This interest is not deductible at all. Without this disallowance, a taxpayer could, in certain circumstances, actually borrow funds at a higher rate of interest than the rate at which they were reinvested, while still generating a positive net cash flow because the government would be subsidizing the transaction through the interest deduction on the borrowings.

Net Investment Income. For purposes of the investment interest limitation, the term **net investment income** means the excess of the taxpayer's investment income over investment expenses. Investment income is gross income from property held for investment, including items such as dividends, interest, annuities, net short-term capital gains, and royalties (if not earned in a trade or business), but excluding qualified dividends and net long-term capital gains taxed at the preferential capital gains tax rates.

Including either of these two items in the definition of investment income would increase the amount of deductible investment interest expense, which might offset other income that is taxed at higher rates. Thus, the definition of investment income generally excludes net capital gain attributable to the disposition of property held for investment and qualified dividends. However, at the election of the taxpayer, net capital gain from the disposition of investment property and qualified dividends can be included in investment income. To the extent the taxpayer elects to include gains from the disposition of investment property and qualified dividends in investment income, these items are taxed at the regular tax rates rather than at the preferential long-term capital gain rates.[26] The calculation of investment income does not include gains on business and personal-use property.

EXAMPLE I:7-15 ▶ During the current year, Michael incurs $15,000 investment interest expense, earns $7,000 of qualified dividends and $3,000 interest income. He also reports the following gains and losses from the sale of stocks and bonds during the year:

Short-term capital gains	$4,000
Short-term capital losses	(3,000)
Long-term capital gains	5,000
Long-term capital losses	(2,000)

Considering all of Michael's other income and deductions for the year, assume that he is subject to a 35% marginal tax rate. Michael's net capital gain is $3,000 (net long-term capital gain of $3,000 in excess of net short-term capital losses of $0). He also has a $1,000 ($4,000 – $3,000) net short-term capital gain. Thus, of his total capital gain of $4,000 ($9,000 of total gains – $5,000 of total losses), only $1,000 ($4,000 net gain – $3,000 net capital gain) is included in investment income. In addition, the $7,000 of qualified dividends also are not included in investment income. If Michael does not make an election, his investment income is $4,000 ($3,000 of interest plus $1,000 net short-term capital gain). He may deduct $4,000 of the investment interest expense in the current year. The excess investment interest for the current year of $11,000 ($15,000 – $4,000) is carried over to the next year. The $3,000 net capital gain and the qualified dividends are subject to the 15% tax rate on net capital gain. If Michael makes the election, his investment income is $14,000 (the $3,000 net capital gain and $7,000 of qualified dividends are included), and he may deduct $14,000 of the investment interest expense. Thus, only $1,000 ($15,000 – $14,000) of investment interest expense is not currently deductible and is carried over to the next year. However, his $3,000 net capital gain and $7,000 of qualified dividends are subject to the 35% ordinary income tax rate. ◀

ADDITIONAL COMMENT

Investment expenses are those which are deductible on the tax return, after the 2% limitation.

Investment expenses include all deductions (except interest) that are directly connected with the production of investment income. These expenses include rental fees for safe-deposit boxes, fees for investment counsel,[27] and subscriptions to investment and financial planning journals. As explained later in this chapter (see the section of this chapter titled Miscellaneous Itemized Deductions), these investment expenses are deductible only to the extent they exceed 2% of the taxpayer's AGI for the year. Only the investment

26 Secs. 1(h)(3) and 163(d)(4)(B).

27 Sec. 163(d)(4)(C). Commissions for the sale or purchase of investment property are not included here. A commission paid on the purchase of property is added to the purchase price (and the basis) of the property. A commission paid on the sale of property reduces the amount realized.

expenses remaining after application of this limitation are used in computing the net investment income. Furthermore, in computing the amount of the disallowed investment expenses, the 2% of AGI limitation applies to the noninvestment expenses first.[28] Any remaining 2% of AGI limitation then reduces the noninterest investment expenses.

EXAMPLE I:7-16 ▶ **Kevin's AGI for the current year is $200,000. Included in his AGI is $175,000 salary and $25,000 of investment income. In earning the investment income, Kevin paid investment interest expense of $33,000. He also incurred the following expenditures subject to the 2% of AGI limitation:**

Investment expenses:	
Subscriptions to investment journals	$ 700
Investment counseling	2,000
Safe-deposit box rental	300
Noninvestment expenses:	
Unreimbursed employee business expenses	1,500
Tax return preparation fees (non–business-related)	500

Kevin's investment interest expense deduction for the year is computed by first determining the deductible investment expenses (other than interest) and the net investment income.

Investment expenses:			
Subscriptions		$ 700	
Investment counseling		2,000	
Safe-deposit box rental		300	$3,000
Disallowed by the 2% limitation:			
2% of AGI ($200,000 × 0.02)	$4,000		
Unreimbursed employee expenses	(1,500)		
Tax return preparation fees	(500)		
Investment expenses (remainder of 2% limit allocated to investment expenses)			(2,000)
Deductible investment expenses			$1,000
Net investment income ($25,000 − $1,000)			$24,000

The investment interest expense deduction is limited to $24,000. The remaining investment interest of $9,000 ($33,000 – $24,000) is carried over and deducted in a subsequent year (subject to the disallowance rules that pertain to the subsequent year). ◀

Personal Interest. In general, the tax law does not allow a deduction for interest expense on debt incurred for personal purposes. Thus, taxpayers may not deduct interest on credit cards, car loans, and consumer debt. However, taxpayers generally may deduct interest on debt to acquire a personal residence. Qualified students may also deduct as a *for* AGI deduction interest incurred on certain student loans.

ADDITIONAL COMMENT

Banks and other financial institutions that receive mortgage interest from homeowners are required to report interest of $600 or more to the IRS and to the homeowners on Form 1098.

Qualified Residence Interest. Subject to certain limitations discussed below, individuals may deduct **qualified residence interest.** To be qualified residence interest, the interest payment must be either acquisition indebtedness or home equity indebtedness with respect to a qualified residence of the taxpayer. In all cases the residence must secure the debt.[29] A qualified residence (discussed below) may consist of the taxpayer's principal residence and a second residence.

Acquisition Indebtedness. Acquisition indebtedness is any debt secured by the residence and incurred in acquiring, constructing, or substantially improving the qualified residence. Debt may be treated as qualified acquisition indebtedness if the taxpayer acquires the

[28] H. Rept. No. 99-841, 99th Cong., 2d Sess., pp. II-153 and 154 (1986). The noninvestment expenses subject to the 2% of AGI limitation include unreimbursed employee business expenses, hobby expenses up to the income from the hobby, and tax return preparation fees.

[29] Sec. 163(h). If the loan is not secured by the residence, it does not qualify. In one instance the taxpayer agreed to purchase her ex-husband's interest in their residence. The terms of the sale were $10,000 down plus an unsecured $25,000 note. In a private ruling, the IRS ruled that because the note was not secured by the residence, the interest on the note was not qualified residence interest. (See Ltr. Rul. 8752010 September 18, 1987.) However, if under any state or local homestead law the security interest is ineffective or unenforceable, the interest expense still qualifies as qualified residence interest. See Sec. 163(h)(4)(C). In another letter ruling the taxpayer borrowed money to purchase a residence securing the debt by pledging stock and bonds. Here also, the IRS denied the deduction because the loan was not secured by the residence. (See Ltr. Rul. 8906031 November 10, 1988.)

residence within 90 days before or after the date that the debt is incurred. In the case of the construction or substantial improvement of a residence, debt incurred before the completion of the construction or improvement can qualify as acquisition debt to the extent of construction expenditures that are made no more than 24 months before the date the debt is incurred. Furthermore, debt incurred after construction is complete and within 90 days of the completion date may qualify as acquisition indebtedness to the extent of any construction expenditures made within the 24-month period ending on the date the debt is incurred.[30] Making payments of principal on the loan reduces the amount of acquisition debt. The only way to increase the amount of acquisition debt is to make substantial improvements to the property. The taxpayer may refinance acquisition indebtedness (and therefore treat it as acquisition indebtedness) to the extent that the principal amount of the refinancing does not exceed the principal amount of the acquisition debt immediately before the refinancing.

EXAMPLE I:7-17 ▶ Kay acquired a personal residence in 2005 for $220,000 and borrowed $140,000 on a mortgage that was secured by the property. In the current year the principal balance of the mortgage has been reduced to $100,000. Kay's acquisition indebtedness in the current year is only $100,000 and cannot be increased above $100,000 (except by indebtedness incurred to substantially improve the residence). If she refinances the existing mortgage in the current year and the refinanced debt is $110,000, only $100,000 (the principal balance of the existing acquisition indebtedness) qualifies as acquisition indebtedness. ◀

The limitation for qualified acquisition indebtedness is $1,000,000 ($500,000 for a married individual filing a separate return). Qualified acquisition indebtedness incurred before October 13, 1987 (pre-October 13, 1987 indebtedness) is not subject to any limitation. However, the aggregate amount of pre-October 13, 1987 indebtedness reduces the $1,000,000 limitation on the indebtedness incurred after October 13, 1987.

ADDITIONAL COMMENT

Many banks, in attempting to generate new loan business, have heavily advertised the tax advantages of home equity indebtedness.

Home Equity Indebtedness. Taxpayers may also deduct interest incurred on home equity indebtedness (so-called home equity loans). Subject to certain limits, home equity indebtedness is any indebtedness (other than acquisition indebtedness) secured by a qualified residence of the taxpayer. The taxpayer may use the proceeds of the loan for any purpose (including purchasing or improving a qualified residence), as long as the taxpayer's qualified residence secures the loan. However, the tax law limits home equity indebtedness to the lesser of:

- The FMV of the qualified residence in excess of the acquisition indebtedness with respect to the residence, or
- $100,000 ($50,000 for a married individual filing a separate return)

The $1,000,000 limit on acquisition indebtedness and the $100,000 limit on home equity indebtedness are two separate limits. The maximum amount of indebtedness on which a taxpayer may deduct qualified residence interest is $1,100,000 if an individual has $100,000 or more equity in the property.

EXAMPLE I:7-18 ▶ On April 23 of the current year, Kesha borrows $125,000 to purchase a new sailboat. The loan is secured by her personal residence. On that date, the outstanding balance on the original debt Kesha incurred to purchase the residence is $400,000 and the FMV of the residence is $900,000. The original debt is also secured by Kesha's residence. Kesha may deduct the interest paid on the $400,000 of acquisition indebtedness, plus the interest paid on $100,000 of the home equity loan. The interest on $25,000 ($125,000 − $100,000) is treated as personal interest and is, therefore, not deductible. The home equity loan is limited to the lesser of $100,000 or the FMV of the residence in excess of the outstanding acquisition indebtedness (the lesser of $100,000 or $500,000 ($900,000 − $400,000)). ◀

Points Paid as Qualified Residence Interest. Often taxpayers must pay **points** on real estate debt. A point is equal to 1% of the loan amount. Thus, two points paid on a $120,000 mortgage equal $2,400 (120,000 × .02). Points often represent prepaid interest because the stated

30 Notice 88-74, 1988-2 C.B. 385.

rate of interest for the loan is lower than the current rate of interest. Generally, prepaid interest paid in the form of points must be capitalized and amortized over the life of the loan. However, points paid on a loan incurred to purchase the taxpayer's principal residence (acquisition indebtedness) are automatically deductible when paid if certain requirements are met. The IRS has also indicated that points paid on Veteran Administration (VA) and Federal Home Administration (FHA) loans are also currently deductible as interest if clearly designated as points incurred in connection with the indebtedness.[31]

EXAMPLE I:7-19 ▶ During the current year, Kevin and Donna purchase a new home for $300,000, putting $100,000 down and borrowing $200,000. At the closing, they are required to pay one and one-half points as a loan discount in connection with the loan, which is secured by a mortgage against the home. The practice of charging points is an established business practice where they live.

These points represent prepaid interest on the purchase of a principal residence. Thus, in addition to the interest portion of every payment they make during the year, Kevin and Donna may also deduct $3,000 ($200,000 × 0.015) as interest paid during the year of purchase. ◀

Taxpayers must capitalize points paid on a loan to purchase property other than a principal residence or for refinancing a mortgage on a principal residence. If the property is used in a business, held as an investment, or a qualified residence (the taxpayer's principal residence and one other that the taxpayer chooses) the taxpayer may amortize the points over the life of the loan.[32]

In order for the points to be currently deductible, the purchaser of the principal residence (borrower) must have paid for them with unborrowed funds. However, amounts provided by the borrower as down payments, escrow deposits, earnest money, or other funds are treated as paid for the points. Furthermore, as long as the borrower provides sufficient funds in these other categories, he or she is treated as having paid the points even if the seller has paid for them on behalf of the borrower.[33]

In addition to interest on a qualified residence home acquisition or home equity loan, taxpayers could also deduct mortgage insurance premiums paid or accrued on a qualified residence before 2015. This deduction phased out for taxpayers with AGI in excess of $100,000. The amount of the phase-out was 10% of the amount of the qualified mortgage insurance for each $1,000 (or fraction thereof) that the taxpayer's AGI exceeded $100,000. For taxpayers married filing separately, the amount of the phase-out was 10% of the amount of the qualified mortgage insurance for each $500 (or fraction thereof) that the taxpayer's AGI exceeded $50,000. It is uncertain whether or not Congress will extend this additional deduction for years after 2014.

Qualified Residence. For any tax year, a taxpayer may have two qualified residences:

- Taxpayer's principal residence
- One other residence selected by the taxpayer, with regard to which the taxpayer meets the residence test of Sec. 280A(d)(1).

In order to meet this residence test, the taxpayer must have personally used the property more than the greater of 14 days or 10% of any rental days during the year.[34]

EXAMPLE I:7-20 ▶ Fred owns a lakeside cabin that he uses for vacations. He also rents the cabin out to others when he is not using it. During the year Fred rents the cabin out at a fair rental for 90 days. Fred personally uses the cabin for a total of 22 days. Because Fred's personal use for the year (22 days) exceeds 14 days [the greater of 14 days or 9 days (10% of the rental days)], the cabin qualifies as his residence for purposes of deducting qualified residence interest for the year. ◀

ADDITIONAL COMMENT

Whether property is a residence for tax purposes is based on all the facts and circumstances, including the good faith of the taxpayer. A residence generally includes a house, condominium, mobile home, boat, or house trailer, that contains sleeping space and toilet and cooking facilities. Treas. Reg. § 1.163-10T(p)(3)(ii).

Despite the residence test, the taxpayer may select a property that has not been rented by the taxpayer at any time during the year as the second residence on which the taxpayer may deduct qualified residence interest.

---

31 These requirements, are as follows: The points are paid upon the purchase of a principal residence; they are designated as paid in connection with the acquisition debt and are a percentage of the loan; they follow business practices and are secured by the residence. Rev. Proc. 94-27, 1994-1 C.B. 613.

32 Rev. Rul. 87-22, 1987-1 C.B. 146, and Rev. Proc. 87-15, 1987-1 C.B. 624. The 8th Circuit Court of Appeals has held in one case that points paid on refinancing a "bridge" or temporary loan are currently deductible. *James R. Huntsman v. CIR*, 66 AFTR 2d 90-5020, 90-2 USTC ¶ 50,340 (8th Cir., 1990), rev'g 91 TC 57 (1988). The IRS will not follow *Huntsman* in other circuits (IRS Action on Decision CC-1991-02, Feb. 11, 1991).

33 Reg. Sec. 1.6050H-1(f)(3). See also Rev. Proc. 94-27, 1994-1 C.B. 613.

34 Sec. 280A(d)(1). Use by the taxpayer's family as defined in Sec. 267(c)(4), other individuals under a reciprocal-use arrangement, and anyone when a fair rental is not charged counts as a day of personal use by the taxpayer.

STOP & THINK

Question: Jana is about to purchase a new sport utility vehicle for $35,000. If she pays $5,000 down, the dealer is prepared to offer her a loan for the remaining $30,000 at 6% interest. In investigating other possible sources of funds, she found out that her brokerage firm would lend her the $30,000 at 7% interest if she pledged her stock as collateral. At her local credit union, she found that she could borrow the $30,000 at 8% interest if she took out a home equity loan by using her home as security. Jana is confused about which loan she should take.

Solution: The best way to analyze this problem is to compare the after-tax interest rates of the loans. Jana may not deduct the interest paid to the car dealer because it is personal interest. Thus, its after-tax interest rate remains at 6%. Furthermore, even though Jana uses her stock holdings as collateral, the interest on the loan from the brokerage firm is non-deductible personal interest because she uses the proceeds of the loan to purchase personal property rather than investment property. Its after-tax interest rate remains at 7%. Only the interest on the home equity loan from the credit union is potentially deductible. This depends, of course, on the amount of Jana's total itemized deductions. Assuming Jana's total itemized deductions exceed the standard deduction and Jana is in the 33% marginal tax bracket, the after-tax interest rate of the home equity loan drops from 8% to 5.33% [8% × (1 − 0.33)].

Student Loan Interest. Individuals may take a *for* AGI deduction for interest paid on qualified education loans. The maximum annual interest deduction for qualified student loans is $2,500. Furthermore, the deduction is phased out if the student reports modified AGI in excess of certain amounts. For 2015 the deduction begins phasing out for a single individual with modified AGI of $65,000 (with a $15,000 phase-out range). For a student who is married filing jointly, the phase-out begins at $130,000 (with a $30,000 phase-out range).[35]

EXAMPLE I:7-21 ▶ During 2015, Ryan pays a total of $2,800 in interest on a loan incurred for qualified education expenses. Ryan is single and reports modified AGI of $74,000 for the year. Because his modified AGI of $74,000 is $9,000 more than $65,000, the maximum deduction of $2,500 is reduced by 60% ($9,000/$15,000). Ryan may take a *for* AGI deduction of $1,000 [2,500 − (60% × 2,500)]. If Ryan pays only $1,800 of interest (rather than $2,800), the potential deduction of $1,800 would be reduced by 60% to $720 [$1,800 − (60% × $1,800)]. ◀

To qualify for this deduction, the interest must be payable on a loan incurred solely to pay for qualified higher education expenses. If a taxpayer takes out a loan to pay for higher education expenses and for other purposes, none of the interest on the loan qualifies. Higher education expenses include tuition, fees, books and equipment, and room and board incurred during a time the taxpayer, the taxpayer's spouse, or the taxpayer's dependent is a student at a qualified higher education institution on at least a half-time basis. However, these qualified expenditures do not include amounts excluded from income under an employer educational assistance program or from United States savings bonds, as well as any scholarship or allowance that is excluded from income. Furthermore, to prevent a double deduction, the tax law allows no deduction to an individual for whom a dependency exemption may be taken on another person's tax return or for any amount that is deductible under any other provision of the Code.

TIMING OF THE INTEREST DEDUCTION

Under Sec. 163, deductible interest becomes deductible in the year the interest is paid or accrued. This generally means that cash method taxpayers deduct interest in the year paid, whereas accrual method taxpayers deduct interest as it accrues. However, the IRC makes exceptions to this general rule.

[35] Modified AGI includes certain excluded income from Guam, American Samoa, or Puerto Rico, as well as any income excluded under the foreign earned income provisions. Furthermore, the deduction for qualified tuition and related expenses is not allowed.

ADDITIONAL COMMENT

Points paid on the refinancing of an existing mortgage must be written off over the life of the new mortgage.

Prepaid Interest. If a cash method taxpayer prepays interest and the prepayment relates to a loan that extends beyond the end of the tax year, generally the taxpayer must capitalize the prepayment and amortize it over the periods to which the interest relates (i.e., the accrual method applies to cash method taxpayers in regards to prepaid interest). As previously discussed, the law makes one exception to this rule involving interest paid in the form of points charged in connection with the purchase or improvement of the taxpayer's principal residence. If these points represent prepaid interest, the taxpayer may deduct them in the year paid.[36]

Interest Paid with Loan Proceeds. Assuming the interest is otherwise deductible, if an individual borrows money from a third party rather than from the original lending institution and uses the funds to make a payment on a previously outstanding loan, the individual generally may deduct the interest portion of the payment. However, if the taxpayer borrows the funds used to pay the interest on the first loan from the same lender to whom the interest is due, and either (1) the purpose of the second loan is to pay the interest on the first or (2) the borrower does not have unrestricted control of the funds, then the borrower may not deduct the interest.[37]

Discounted Notes. Lending institutions often discount notes. In effect, the borrower pays the interest by repaying more money than is received when the note is signed. A cash method taxpayer can deduct this interest at the time of repayment, whereas an accrual method taxpayer must deduct the interest as it accrues over the term of the loan.

EXAMPLE I:7-22 ▶ On December 1, 2015, Stan borrows $1,000 from his credit union to use in his business. Under the terms of the contract, Stan actually receives $970 but is required to repay $1,000 on February 28, 2016 (three months later). Because Stan is a cash-method taxpayer, he may deduct the full $30 interest in 2016 when the note is repaid. If he were an accrual-method taxpayer, he could deduct $10 ($30 × 1/3) in 2015, and $20 ($30 × 2/3) in 2016. ◀

TYPICAL MISCONCEPTION

Taxpayers sometimes mistakenly assume that any business interest paid on loans between related taxpayers is not deductible. However, if the taxpayers are not governed by the Sec. 267 limitation and the interest is paid on a bona fide business loan, it is deductible.

Interest Owed to a Related Party by an Accrual Method Taxpayer. One of the purposes of Sec. 267 is to require related cash method lenders and accrual method borrowers to report the results of their joint transaction in the same year. Thus, an accrual method taxpayer who is related to a cash method creditor must defer the deduction for any accrued expense (including interest) until the year in which the taxpayer actually pays the expense and the creditor reports the income. Section 267 also disallows losses on the sale of property between related parties. Disallowance of losses between related parties is discussed in Chapter I:6.

The relationships covered by this rule are quite extensive. Some of the more common relationships include the following:

- Members of a family (defined as an individual's brothers, sisters, spouse, ancestors, and lineal descendants)
- An individual and a C corporation in which the individual owns directly or indirectly more than 50% of the outstanding stock
- A corporation and a partnership which are both over 50% owned directly or indirectly by the same people
- A partnership and any partner of the partnership
- An S Corporation and any shareholder of the S Corporation[38]

---

[36] Sec. 461(g). In order for the exception to apply, the home must be used to secure the loan, and the charging of points must be an established business practice in the area where the loan is granted. (See the discussion of the deductibility of points in this chapter under the heading Definition of *Interest* as well as the discussion in Chapter I:6.)

[37] *H. C. Franklin v. CIR*, 50 AFTR 2d 82-5551, 82-2 USTC ¶9532 (5th Cir., 1982) and *Newton A. Burgess*, 8 T.C. 47 (1947). See also *Norman W. Menz*, 80 T.C. 1174 (1983). The IRS has also announced that it will disallow a deduction for interest paid with funds obtained through a second loan from the same lender (see IRS News Release 83-93, July 6, 1983).

[38] Secs. 267(b) and (e). The list of relationships is much more extensive than those mentioned. An S corporation is one that meets certain requirements and has made an election to have its income taxed directly to its shareholders. A C corporation is one that has not made an S election. (See Chapter C:11 of *Prentice Hall's Federal Taxation: Corporations, Partnerships, Estates, and Trusts* text or Chapter C:11 of *Prentice Hall's Federal Taxation: Comprehensive* text.)

EXAMPLE I:7-23 ▶ During the current year, Lisa, a cash method taxpayer, loans some money to her 100%-owned calendar year C corporation, which uses the accrual method of accounting. As of December 31 of the current year, the corporation owes Lisa $3,000 in interest. However, because of a shortage of funds, the corporation does not actually pay the interest until February 15 of the following year. Despite the fact that the corporation uses the accrual method of accounting, the corporation cannot deduct the $3,000 until the corporation actually pays the interest to Lisa in the subsequent year. The result would be the same if the corporation were an S Corporation even if Lisa owned 50% or less of the outstanding stock. ◀

Imputed Interest. Under certain circumstances, if a taxpayer charges less than an adequate rate of interest, the IRS is authorized to impute an interest charge. This may cause the lender to have additional interest income and the borrower to have additional interest expense. The deductibility of this imputed interest expense depends on the classification of the expense (i.e. personal, investment, etc.). (See Chapter I:11 for a discussion of imputed interest.)

Topic Review I:7-2 summarizes the rules for deducting various types of interest.

TOPIC REVIEW I:7-2

Deductibility of Interest Expense

Type of Interest	Rules
Business	Deductible in full as a *for* AGI deduction.
Passive	Subject to the passive loss limits (see Chapter I:8).
Investment	Deductible as an itemized deduction to the extent of the taxpayer's net investment income for the year. Any amount not deductible is carried over to subsequent years.
Personal	Not deductible.
Qualified residence	(a) Must be attributable to debt secured by the taxpayer's principal residence and one other qualified residence selected by the taxpayer. (b) Interest on up to $1,000,000 of home acquisition indebtedness is deductible as an itemized deduction. (c) Interest on home equity debt is deductible as an itemized deduction. Home equity debt is limited to the lesser of $100,000 or the excess of the FMV of the residence over the home acquisition indebtedness.
Student Loan Interest	(a) Payable on loan incurred to pay qualified higher education expenses. (b) Taken as a *for* AGI deduction. (c) Maximum deductible amount is $2,500. The deduction is phased out ratably for modified AGI between $65,000 and $80,000 ($130,000 and $160,000 for married filing jointly).

CHARITABLE CONTRIBUTIONS

OBJECTIVE 4

Compute the amount of a charitable contribution deduction and identify limitations

Under Sec. 170, individuals who itemize their deductions and corporations can deduct **charitable contributions** to qualified organizations. With the exception of certain contributions made by corporations (explained later in this chapter), a taxpayer takes the deduction in the year the contribution is made, regardless of the taxpayer's method of accounting. The amount of the deduction depends on the type of charity receiving the contribution, the type of property contributed, and the applicable limitations.

QUALIFYING ORGANIZATION

To deduct a contribution for federal income tax purposes, a taxpayer must make the contribution to or for the use of a qualified organization.[39] Contributions made directly to

[39] The Supreme Court has ruled that in order for a contribution to be for the use of a qualifying organization, the gift must be held either in a legally enforceable trust or in a similar legal arrangement. (See *U.S. v. Harold Davis*, 65 AFTR 2d 90-1051, 90-1 USTC ¶50,270 (USSC, 1990).)

ADDITIONAL COMMENT

In 2012 the deductions for charitable contributions totaled $199 billion, representing 17.8% of the total dollar amount of the itemized deductions for medical expenses, taxes, interest, and charitable contributions.

individuals, even though the individuals may be needy, are generally not deductible.[40] Under Sec. 170, qualified organizations include the following:

- The United States, the District of Columbia, a state or possession of the United States, or a political subdivision of a state or possession
- A corporation, trust, community chest, fund or foundation created or organized under the laws of the United States, a state, possession, or the District of Columbia[41]
- A post or organization of war veterans
- A domestic fraternal society, order, or association[42]
- Certain cemetery companies

Because of the restrictions and limitations examined later in this chapter, these qualifying non-governmental are further classified into public charities and private nonoperating foundations. Different restrictions and limitations apply to each type of organization.

Public charities include:

REAL-WORLD EXAMPLE

The American Red Cross, Boy Scouts of America, United Way, Goodwill, and Indiana University are examples of public charities.

- Churches or a convention or association of churches
- Educational institutions that normally maintain a regular faculty, curriculum, and regularly enrolled students
- Organizations such as hospitals and medical schools whose principal function is medical care or medical education and research
- Government-supported organizations that exist to receive, hold, invest, and administer property for the benefit of a college or university
- Any qualified governmental unit
- Organizations that normally receive a substantial part of their support from either a governmental unit or the general public
- Certain private operating foundations[43]

TYPE OF PROPERTY CONTRIBUTED

If a taxpayer makes a contribution in cash, the amount of the contribution is easily determinable. However, in order to assure that the contribution has been properly made to a qualified charity, the taxpayer is required to maintain a record of the contribution such as a bank record or a written communication from the donee.[44] If noncash property is donated, the amount of the contribution is not as easy to identify. In the case of noncash property, the amount of the donation depends on two factors: (1) the type of property donated and (2) the type of qualifying organization (public charity or private nonoperating foundation) to whom the property is given. Furthermore, a gift of property that consists of less than the donor's entire interest in the property is not usually considered a contribution of property. Thus, for example, no charitable contribution is allowed when an individual donates the use of a vacation home for a charitable fund-raising auction.[45]

SELF-STUDY QUESTION

Doug purchases an item having a FMV of $75 for $100 in a charity auction. How much can he deduct?

ANSWER

Doug can deduct only $25 because the cash paid must be reduced by the value of the property received.

Contribution of Long-Term Capital Gain Property. In general, the amount of a donation of long-term capital gain property is its FMV. Regulation Sec. 1.170A-1(c)(2) defines a property's FMV as the price at which the property would change

40 Under certain circumstances, a taxpayer may take a deduction (limited to $50 per month) for maintaining a student as a member of his or her household. The student may not be a dependent or relative of the taxpayer and must be placed in the taxpayer's home under an arrangement with a qualifying organization (see Sec. 170(g)).

41 These organizations must be organized and operated exclusively for religious, charitable, scientific, literary, or educational purposes; to foster national or international amateur sports competition; or for the prevention of cruelty to children or animals.

42 Furthermore, gifts to these organizations must be made by individuals and must be used exclusively for religious, charitable, scientific, literary, or educational purposes, or for the prevention of cruelty to children or animals.

43 Sec. 170(b)(1)(F). The distinction between a private operating foundation and a private nonoperating foundation generally depends on the way the foundation spends or distributes its income and contributions. The details of this distinction are beyond the scope of this text.

44 Sec. 170(f)(17) and Notice 2008-16. This record must show (1)the name of the donee organization, (2) the date of the contribution, and (3) the amount of the contribution.

45 Sec. 170(f)(3), Reg. Sec. 1.170A-7(a)(1) and Rev. Rul. 89-51, 1989-1 C.B. 89. Note, however, that certain transfers of partial interests in property do qualify (e.g., the contribution of certain remainder interests to a trust, the transfer of a remainder interest in a personal residence or a farm, or a contribution of an undivided interest in property). These exceptions are beyond the scope of this text.

ADDITIONAL COMMENT

In 2004, new rules were added relating to the contribution of used vehicles and intellectual property. For a used vehicle donated to a charity, in most cases the deduction will be limited to the charity's gross proceeds on the subsequent sale of the vehicle. A taxpayer's deduction for the contribution of a patent or similar intellectual property is the taxpayer's basis in the property.

hands between a willing buyer and a willing seller, neither being under any compulsion to buy or sell and both having reasonable knowledge of relevant facts. For purposes of charitable contributions, **capital gain property** is property held over one year, on which the taxpayer would recognize a long-term capital gain if the taxpayer sold it at its FMV on the date of the contribution. If a capital loss or a short-term capital gain would be recognized on the sale of the capital asset, the property is considered to be ordinary income property for purposes of calculating the amount of the charitable contribution deduction.

Contribution to a Private Nonoperating Foundation. The tax law provides an exception to this general rule for contributions of capital gain property to private nonoperating foundations. In general, a private nonoperating foundation is an organization that does not receive funding from the general public (e.g., the Carnegie Foundation). Private nonoperating foundations distribute funds to various charitable organizations that actually perform the charitable services. The amount of the contribution of long-term capital gain property to a private nonoperating foundation is the property's FMV, reduced by the capital gain that would be recognized if the property were sold at its FMV on the date of the contribution. This means that generally the deductible amount of the contribution is the lesser of the property's adjusted basis or its FMV.[46]

EXAMPLE I:7-24 ▶ Betty purchased some land in 1991 for $10,000. In the current year, she contributes the land to the United Way. At the time of the contribution, the FMV of the property is $25,000. Because the land is long-term capital gain property donated to a public charity, the amount of the contribution is $25,000 (its FMV).

On the other hand, if Betty donates the land to Cherry Foundation, a private nonoperating foundation, the amount of the contribution is $10,000 ($25,000 − $15,000 capital gain that would be recognized if the land were sold). ◀

TYPICAL MISCONCEPTION

Many people do not understand that the unrelated use restriction applies only to tangible personal property. A gift of shares of stock (intangible property) would not be a gift of unrelated use property where the stock is sold by the donee.

Unrelated Use Property. A second exception applies to capital gain property (that is also tangible personal property) contributed to a public charity and used by the organization for purposes unrelated to the charity's function. In such cases, the amount of the contribution deduction is equal to the property's FMV minus the capital gain that would be recognized if the property were sold at its FMV. This amount generally is the property's adjusted basis. Tangible property is all property that is not intangible property (e.g., property other than stock, securities, copyrights, patents, and so on). Personal property is all property other than real estate. The taxpayer is responsible for proving that the property was not put to unrelated use. However, a taxpayer meets this burden of proof if, at the time of the contribution, the taxpayer reasonably anticipates that the property will not be put to unrelated use. The immediate sale of the property by the charitable organization is a use unrelated to its tax-exempt purpose.

EXAMPLE I:7-25 ▶ Laura purchases a painting for $3,000. Several years later she contributes the painting to a local college. The FMV of the painting is $5,000 at the time the property is contributed. The painting is both tangible personal property and capital gain property. The college places the painting in the library for display and study by art students. Because the college uses the painting for purposes related to its function as an educational institution, the amount of Laura's contribution is equal to the painting's FMV ($5,000). On the other hand, if the college had sold the painting immediately after receiving it, the presumption is that the property's use was unrelated to the college's tax-exempt purpose. In this case, Laura's contribution is only $3,000. ◀

Certain Intangibles. Under Sec. 170(e)(1)(B)(iii), a third exception applies to the contribution of certain intangibles to a charitable organization. In this case, the amount of the charitable contribution is the FMV of the property, reduced by the amount of long-term capital gain that would have been recognized if the taxpayer had sold the property. These intangibles include patents, trademarks, a trade name or secret, know-how, a purchased copyright, and certain software.

---

[46] The amount of a contribution of appreciated stock held over one year made to a private nonoperating foundation remains at its FMV.

Contribution of Ordinary Income Property

General Rule. If a taxpayer contributes ordinary income property to a charitable organization, the deduction is equal to the property's FMV minus the amount of gain that would be recognized if the taxpayer had sold the property at its FMV on the date of the contribution. In most cases, this deduction is equal to the property's adjusted basis. This rule applies regardless of the type of charitable organization to which the property is donated.

REAL-WORLD EXAMPLE

A retired congressman was not entitled to a charitable contribution of his memos and papers because the papers were ordinary income property and had no basis. *James H. Morrison*, 71 T.C. 683 (1979).

For this purpose, **ordinary income property** includes any property that would result in the recognition of income taxed at ordinary income rates if the taxpayer sold the property. Thus, ordinary income property includes inventory, works of art or manuscripts created by the taxpayer, capital assets that have been held for one year or less, and Sec. 1231 property to the extent a sale would result in the recognition of ordinary income due to depreciation recapture.[47]

EXAMPLE I:7-26 ▶ During the current year, Beta, Inc. purchases land as an investment for $10,000. Five months later, it contributes the land to the United Way. At the time of the contribution the property's FMV is $15,000. The amount of Beta's contribution is $10,000 ($15,000 − [$15,000 − $10,000]) because it held the land for less than one year. ◀

EXAMPLE I:7-27 ▶ Pork, Inc. purchased a machine a few years ago for $20,000 and used the machine in its business. During the current year, Pork, Inc. donates the machine to a local community college. At the time of the contribution, the machine's adjusted basis is $5,000 and its FMV is $8,000. Because Pork, Inc. would have recognized a $3,000 gain (all ordinary income under Sec. 1245) if the machine were sold at its FMV, the amount of the contribution is $5,000 ($8,000 − $3,000), which is equal to the machine's adjusted basis. ◀

Donation of Inventory by a Corporation. Under certain circumstances, the donation of inventory by a C corporation (not an S corporation) to certain public charities provides a larger charitable contribution deduction than the adjusted basis of the property. One of these enhanced charitable contributions involves the donation of inventory to the charity if the charity uses the inventory solely for the care of the ill, needy, or infants.[48] C corporations may also take an enhanced charitable contribution deduction for donating scientific equipment constructed by the taxpayer and donated to a college, university, or qualified research organization for use in research, experimentation, or research training in the physical or biological sciences.[49] The amount of the enhanced charitable contribution is the property's FMV, reduced by 50% (not 100%) of the ordinary income that the corporation would have recognized if it had sold the property at its FMV. However, the amount of the contribution cannot exceed twice the basis of the property.

EXAMPLE I:7-28 ▶ During 2015, Able Corporation, a manufacturer of medical supplies, donated some of its inventory to the American Red Cross. The Red Cross used the inventory for the care of the needy and ill. At the time of the contribution, the FMV of the inventory was $10,000. Able's basis in the inventory was $3,000. Because this transaction qualifies under the exception, the amount of Able's contribution (before any limitations are applied) is $6,500 [$10,000 − (0.50 × $7,000)] but the actual amount of the contribution is limited to $6,000 (2 × the $3,000 basis in the property). ◀

Contribution of Services. When a taxpayer renders services to a qualified charitable organization, the taxpayer may only deduct the unreimbursed expenses incurred incident to rendering the services. These items include out-of-pocket expenses, transportation expenses, the cost of lodging and 50% of the cost of meals while away from home, and the cost of a uniform that is required to be worn in performing the donated services but is not suitable for general wear. The out-of-pocket expenses are deductible only if the taxpayer who actually renders the services to the charity is the person who incurs these out-of-pocket expenses. Taxpayers cannot take a deduction for expenses while away from home unless they experience no

[47] Reg. Secs. 1.170A-4(b)(1) and 1.170A-4(d). Sec. 1231 property includes property used in a trade or business that is subject to depreciation. If it is sold at a gain, part or all of the gain is treated as ordinary income. Any remaining gain is subject to the Sec. 1231 rules. (See Chapter I:13 for an explanation of the depreciation recapture and Sec. 1231 rules.)

[48] Sec. 170(e)(3). These charitable organizations are known as Sec. 501(c)(3) charities. For tax years through 2014, taxpayers other than C corporations (i.e., individuals) could also take the enhanced charitable deduction if the charitable contribution was food donated for the care of the ill, needy, or infants. [see Sec. 170(e)(3)(c)(iv).]

[49] Sec. 170(e)(4). For tax years before 2012, additional enhanced charitable contribution deductions also included the donation of computer technology and equipment to public libraries and elementary and secondary schools, and the donation of books to a public library.

significant element of personal pleasure, recreation, or vacation in such travel. Instead of the actual costs of operating an automobile while performing the donated services, the law permits a deduction of 14 cents per mile.[50]

EXAMPLE I:7-29 ▶ During the current year, Tony spends a total of 100 hours developing an accounting system for the local council of the Boy Scouts of America. As an accountant, Tony earns $200 per hour. During the year, Tony also drives his car a total of 500 miles in performing the services for the Boy Scouts of America. If he uses the automatic mileage method to compute the amount of the charitable contribution, he can deduct $70 (0.14 × 500). No deduction is available for the value of 100 hours of Tony's contributed services. ◀

REAL-WORLD EXAMPLE

The cost of newspaper advertising, paper, pencils, and other supplies purchased by volunteers in connection with their involvement in the Volunteer Income Tax Assistance Program (VITA) is deductible. Rev. Rul. 80-45, 1980-1 C.B. 54.

DEDUCTION LIMITATIONS

Overall 50% Limitation. The charitable contribution deduction available for any tax year is subject to certain limitations. For individuals, the general overall limitation applicable to public charities is 50% of the taxpayer's AGI for the year. Any contributions in excess of the overall limitation may be carried forward and deducted in the subsequent five tax years. In addition, the tax law imposes further limitations on contributions of capital gain property to either a public charity or a private nonoperating foundation and all types of property contributions to private nonoperating foundations.

KEY POINT

The generosity of Congress in permitting individuals to use FMV is tempered by the 30% of AGI limitation.

30% Limitation. Under certain circumstances, a special 30% of AGI limitation applies. Contributions of capital gain property (capital assets held over one year on which a gain would be realized if sold) to public charities are generally valued at the property's FMV, but the deduction may not exceed an overall limit of 30% of AGI instead of a 50% limit. This special 30% limit does not apply, however, in the following situations:

- Capital gain property (which is tangible personal property) donated to a public charity that does not put the property to its related use. In such cases, the amount of the contribution is reduced by the capital gain that would be recognized if the property were sold.
- The taxpayer elects to reduce the amount of the charitable contribution deduction by the capital gain that the taxpayer would recognize if he or she sold the property.

EXAMPLE I:7-30 ▶ Joy donates a painting to the local university during a year in which she has AGI of $50,000. The painting, which cost $10,000 several years before, is valued at $30,000 at the time of the contribution. The university exhibits the painting in its art gallery. Because the painting is put to a use related to the university's purpose, the amount of Joy's contribution is $30,000. If Joy does not make the election, her current year charitable contribution deduction is limited to $15,000 (0.30 × $50,000 AGI). The remaining $15,000 is carried over to the subsequent five years. If she elects to reduce the amount of the contribution by the long-term capital gain, Joy's current year charitable contribution deduction is her basis of $10,000 in the property. She has no charitable contribution carryover. In this case, making the election doesn't make sense. ◀

The overall deduction limitation of 30% of AGI also applies to the contribution of all types of property other than capital gain property (e.g., cash and ordinary income property) to a private nonoperating foundation. However, further restrictions may apply to the deductibility of certain contributions to this type of charity.

20% Limitation on Capital Gain Property Contributed to Private Nonoperating Foundations. Contributions of capital gain property to private nonoperating foundations may not exceed the lesser of (1) 20% of the taxpayer's AGI or (2) 30% of the taxpayer's AGI, reduced by any contributions of capital gain property donated to a public charity.

Contributions for Athletic Events. If a taxpayer makes a contribution to a college or university and in return receives the right to purchase tickets to athletic events, the taxpayer may deduct only 80% of the payment.

Applying the Deduction Limitations. Contributions subject only to the 50% of AGI limitation are accounted for before the contributions subject to the 30% of AGI limitation.

---

[50] Sec. 170(i).

EXAMPLE I:7-31 ▶ During a year when Ted's AGI is $70,000, he donates $22,000 to his church and $18,000 to a private nonoperating charity. The church contribution is initially subject to the 50% limitation and is fully deductible because the $22,000 contribution is less than the limitation amount of $35,000 (0.50 × $70,000). Ted's deduction for the contribution to the private nonoperating charity (a 30% charity) is limited to $13,000 (the lesser of the following three amounts):

The actual contribution	$18,000
The remaining 50% limitation after the contribution to Ted's church [(0.50 × $70,000) − $22,000]	$13,000
30% of AGI (0.30 × $70,000)	$21,000 ◀

APPLICATION OF CARRYOVERS

As noted earlier, any contributions that exceed the 50% limitation may be carried over and deducted in the subsequent five years. These carryovers are subject to the limitations that apply in subsequent years. Thus, taxpayers may deduct carryovers only to the extent that the limitation of the subsequent year exceeds the contributions made during that year.

TAX PLANNING

If a taxpayer has contribution carryovers that are about to expire, the taxpayer should consider reducing the current year's contribution so that the carryovers can be deducted.

These general rules also apply with regard to the special limitations. For example, if the taxpayer donates property subject to the 30% limitation during the current year and the amount of the contribution exceeds the limitation, the excess may carry over to the five subsequent years subject to the 30% limitation in the carryover years. In the carryover year, a deduction may be taken for the excess contribution to the extent that the 30% limitation of the subsequent year exceeds the amount of the property donated during the subsequent year subject to the 30% limitation. Excess contributions of property subject to the 20% limitation may also carry over to the subsequent five years. This carryover is also subject to the special restrictions noted above for the 30% limitation. The carryovers are used in chronological order.

EXAMPLE I:7-32 ▶ Assume that for the years 2013 through 2015, Joan reports AGI and makes charitable contributions in the following amounts:

	2013	*2014*	*2015*
AGI	$40,000	$40,000	$60,000
Cash contributions subject to the 50% of AGI limitation	25,000	23,000	24,000
50% of AGI limitation	20,000	20,000	30,000

The amount of the charitable contribution deduction for each year and the order in which the deduction and carryovers are used are as follows:

	2013	*2014*	*2015*
Amount of deduction	$20,000	$20,000	$30,000
Amount of carryover			
From 2013	5,000	5,000	0
From 2014		3,000	2,000 ◀

SPECIAL RULES FOR CHARITABLE CONTRIBUTIONS MADE BY CORPORATIONS

The rules governing charitable contributions made by corporations are generally the same as those pertaining to contributions made by individuals. However, certain differences do exist.

ETHICAL POINT

A tax practitioner should not be a party to the backdating of a Board of Director's authorization of a charitable contribution pledge so that the corporation may improperly deduct the contribution in the earlier year.

Pledges Made by an Accrual Method Corporation. Generally, taxpayers may only deduct actual contributions (not pledges) made during the tax year. This rule applies to both cash and accrual method taxpayers. A major exception to this general rule exists for accrual method corporations. These accrual method corporations may elect to claim a charitable deduction for the year in which the corporation makes a pledge as long as the actual contribution is made by the fifteenth day of the third month following the close of the year in which the pledge is made.

Limitation Applicable to Corporations. Corporate charitable deductions may not exceed 10% of the corporation's taxable income for the year. This amount is computed without regard to the dividends-received deduction, net operating loss or capital loss carrybacks, or any deduction for the charitable contribution itself. Excess contributions may be carried forward for five years and are deductible only if the current-year contributions are less than the current year's 10% limitation. The corporation also uses the carryovers in chronological order.

SUMMARY OF DEDUCTION LIMITATIONS

Topic Review I:7-3 summarizes the rules governing the deduction for charitable contributions.

TOPIC REVIEW I:7-3

Deduction Rules for Charitable Contributions

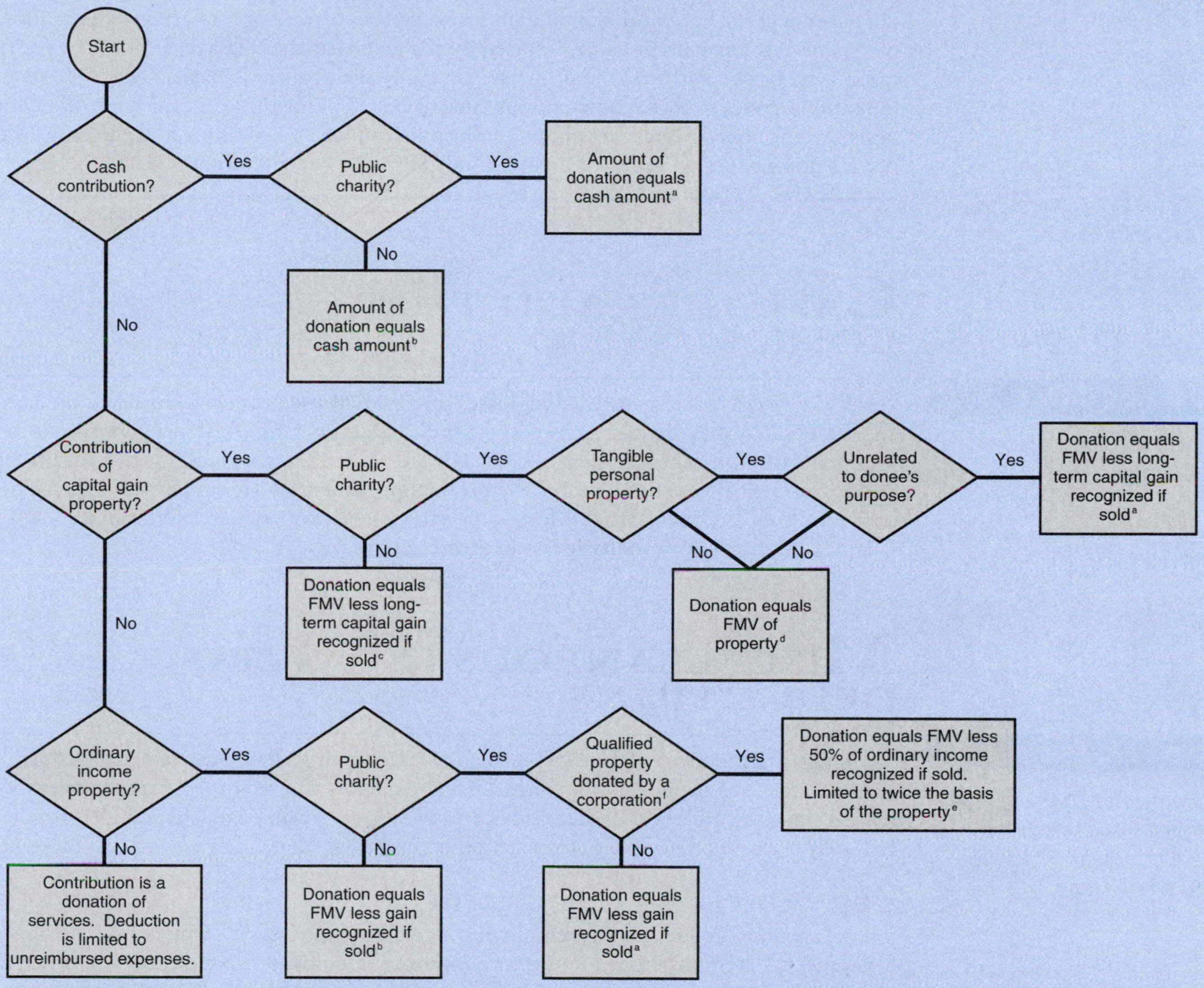

[a] Limited to 50% of AGI.
[b] Limited to lesser of (1) 30% of AGI or (2) remaining 50% of AGI after accounting for donations to public charities.
[c] Limited to lesser of (1) 20% of AGI or (2) 30% of AGI less capital gain contributions to public charities.
[d] Taxpayer may elect to scale down the amount of donation by long-term capital gain. If the election is made, limited to 50% of AGI. If no election is made, limited to 30% of AGI.
[e] Limited to 10% of the corporation's taxable income without regard to any deduction for charitable contributions, dividends received, a net operating loss carryback or a capital loss carryback.
[f] Qualified property consists of either (1) inventory or property used in a trade or business which will be used by a Sec. 501(c)(3) charity for the care of the ill, needy, or infants and (2) inventory constructed by the corporation which will be used by a qualified research institution in the physical or biological sciences.

STOP & THINK

Question: During the current year, Kim pledges to contribute $10,000 to both the Boy Scouts of America (BSA) and to a private nonoperating foundation. She wants to satisfy those pledges before the end of the year in order to take a deduction this year. She has enough cash to satisfy one of the pledges, but must either sell or donate some land in order to satisfy the other. The land she has in mind has a fair market value of $10,000 and a cost basis of $2,000. She purchased the land four years ago. Kim estimates that she will have AGI of $170,000 and will be in the 28% marginal tax bracket. Assuming that both charities would gladly accept either contribution, how should Kim satisfy these pledges?

Solution: The amount of contribution of capital gain property to a public charity is the property's fair market value. The 30% of AGI limitation applies to such contributions. However, a contribution of capital gain property to a private non-operating foundation is the property's fair market value, reduced by the gain that the taxpayer would have recognized if he or she had sold the property (generally the property's basis). The 50% of AGI limitation applies to these contributions. Since Kim's AGI for the year is so high, the limitations do not apply. Thus, Kim should contribute the land to the BSA and the cash to the private non-operating foundation, for a total charitable contribution of $20,000.

CASUALTY AND THEFT LOSSES

OBJECTIVE 5

Discuss casualty and theft losses

Generally, taxpayers may not deduct losses on personal-use property. However, under Sec. 165 individuals may deduct a casualty or theft loss on personal-use property as an itemized deduction on Schedule A of Form 1040. For individuals, casualty losses on business and investment properties held for the production of rents or royalties are deductions in computing AGI. Other casualty losses on investment property are itemized deductions. Chapter I:8 discusses casualty losses in greater depth.

MISCELLANEOUS ITEMIZED DEDUCTIONS

OBJECTIVE 6

Identify certain miscellaneous itemized deductions subject to the 2% of AGI limit

Taxpayers may deduct various types of expenses as miscellaneous itemized deductions. These deductions include employment-related expenses of employees, certain investment-related expenses, and the cost of tax advice. However, as explained in Chapter I:9, these items generally are deductible only to the extent that, in the aggregate, they exceed 2% of AGI.

CERTAIN EMPLOYEE EXPENSES

Taxpayers may deduct certain employment-related expenses as itemized deductions on Schedule A. These expenses include *unreimbursed* employee expenditures for travel and transportation, dues to professional organizations, costs of job hunting, items of protective clothing or uniforms not suitable for everyday wear, union dues, subscriptions to trade journals, and so on. Chapter I:9 provides a more detailed discussion of this topic.

EXPENSES TO PRODUCE INVESTMENT INCOME

Under Sec. 212, individuals may deduct expenses incurred to produce income. If these expenses arise in an activity that produces either rental or royalty income, they are deductions *for* AGI (see the explanation in Chapter I:6). However, if a taxpayer incurs the expenses in generating other types of investment income, such as interest, dividends, etc., the individual taxpayer may deduct such expenses on Schedule A as itemized deductions. These investment-related expenditures include items such as rental fees for safe-deposit boxes used to hold investment property, subscriptions to investment and trade journals, bank service charges on checking accounts used in an investment activity, and fees paid for consulting advice. These expenses are all subject to the 2% of AGI reduction. Flow-through entities (e.g., partnerships and S corporations) must report these types of investment expenses to their owners as separately stated items so that the 2% of AGI reduction may be applied.

ETHICAL POINT

If a client furnishes a handwritten list of his or her miscellaneous itemized deductions to a CPA, the CPA may in good faith rely on the information without verification. However, the CPA should not ignore the implications of information that is provided and should make reasonable inquiries if the information furnished appears to be incorrect, incomplete, or inconsistent.

COST OF TAX ADVICE

Section 212 provides individuals with a deduction for expenses incurred in connection with the determination, collection, or refund of any tax, including federal, state, local, and foreign income taxes as well as estate, gift, and inheritance taxes. These items include (1) tax return preparation fees, (2) appraisal fees incurred in determining the amount of a casualty loss, certain capital improvements eligible for a medical deduction, or the FMV of property donated to a qualified charity, (3) fees paid to an accountant for representation in a tax audit, (4) long-distance telephone calls responding to IRS questions, (5) costs of tax return preparation materials and books, and (6) legal fees incurred in planning the tax consequences dealing with estate planning. If an individual incurs these items in connection with the taxpayer's (1) trade or business (reported on Schedule C), (2) farm income (reported on Schedule F), or (3) an activity which produces rents or royalties (reported on Part I of Schedule E), they are *for* AGI deductions.[51] All other expenses incurred for tax advice are miscellaneous itemized deductions subject to the 2% of AGI limitation.

REAL-WORLD EXAMPLE

A taxpayer claimed that it was necessary to take a leave of absence from his job in order to appear before the Tax Court, to type various legal papers, and to take notes during the trial. He was not allowed to deduct the so-called lost wages representing the amount of vacation time spent in defending the suit. *James P. Stuart*, 1987 PH T.C. Memo ¶87,386, 54 TCM 70.

Fees not directly connected with the determination, collection, or refund of a tax or with the taxpayer's trade or business are personal expenses and are not deductible. Thus, legal fees incurred for drafting wills generally are not deductible. However, legal expenses incurred in tax fraud cases in connection with the filing of a fraudulent return generally are deductible.[52] Legal fees relating to a divorce generally are not deductible, unless they deal with tax-related items such as determining who will receive the exemption for dependent children. Chapter I:3 discusses these fees in greater detail.

REDUCTION OF CERTAIN ITEMIZED DEDUCTIONS

ADDITIONAL COMMENT

The reduction in itemized deductions obscures the true marginal tax rate applicable to high-income taxpayers and can be thought of as a hidden tax rate.

Because of concerns with the budget deficit, Congress enacted Sec. 68 several years ago which provides for a reduction in the total amount of certain itemized deductions for high-income taxpayers.[53] This reduction applies only to individuals with AGI in excess of a certain threshold amount. For 2015 this threshold amount is AGI of $309,900 for individuals filing married filing jointly and surviving spouses, $258,250 for single taxpayers, $284,050 for heads of households, and $154,950 for individuals filing married filing separately. This overall reduction applies to all itemized deductions other than medical expenses, investment interest, casualty losses, and wagering losses. The amount of the reduction is the lesser of (1) 3% of the amount the individual's AGI for the year exceeds the threshold level, or (2) 80% of the amount of the taxpayer's itemized deductions other than medical expenses, investment interest, casualty losses, and wagering losses. Furthermore, the reduction is applied after taking into account the other limitations on itemized deductions (e.g., the 2% of AGI limitation on miscellaneous itemized deductions).

[51] Rev. Rul. 92-29, 1992-1 C.B. 20.
[52] Rev. Rul. 68-662, 1968-2 C.B. 69.
[53] In 2001, Congress authorized the elimination of this reduction of itemized deductions for high-income taxpayers. This elimination began in 2006 and by 2010 the reduction was completely eliminated for 2010, 2011, and 2012 but was reinstated for years after 2012.

TAX PLANNING CONSIDERATIONS

OBJECTIVE 7

Describe tax planning considerations for itemized deductions

MEDICAL EXPENSE DEDUCTION

Working With The 10% of Agi Floor. As explained previously, a deduction for medical expenses is available to individuals only to the extent that the taxpayer's medical expenditures exceed 10% of the taxpayer's AGI for the year (7.5% of AGI for taxpayers 65 or older for tax years before 2016). Thus, many individuals find that no deduction is available, even though their medical expenses are relatively high. In these cases, taxpayers may obtain some benefit if they can bunch the medical expenses into one year. Orthodontic work, certain orthopedic treatment, noncosmetic elective surgery, and new eyeglasses are all examples of medical expenditures that may be either accelerated or delayed into a year in which other medical expenses are high or AGI is lower.

Generally, a taxpayer may take a deduction for medical expenses only in the year in which the expense is actually paid. The mere prepayment of future expenses usually does not accelerate the deduction. However, taxpayers may take a deduction in the earlier year of payment if there is a legal obligation to pay or if the prepayment is a requirement for the receipt of the medical care.[54] If the taxpayer has already received the medical treatment, but the taxpayer does not have sufficient cash to pay the bill, the taxpayer may preserve a deduction for the current year by either borrowing the cash to satisfy the bill or by using a credit card.

EXAMPLE I:7-33 ▶ During the current year, Marty is 40 and he estimates his AGI to be $70,000. Marty has already incurred $5,000 in medical expenses for himself and his family during the year. Because of the 10% of AGI limitation, Marty will not be able to deduct any of the medical expenses. Marty estimates that he will incur $4,000 in medical expenses for orthodontic work for his son next year. He doesn't think he will incur any other major medical expenses next year. Marty also estimates his AGI next year to remain the same as this year. If these estimates are correct, Marty won't be able to deduct any medical expenses in either year because the expenses for each year are less than ($7,000) 10% of his AGI in each of the years. However, if the orthodontic work is started in the current year and Marty pays for the work in the current year, he will incur a total of $9,000 in medical expenses in the current year. Thus, in the current year Marty may deduct $2,000 ($9,000 − $7,000) of the total medical expenses. This, of course, assumes that the total of Marty's itemized deductions exceeds the standard deduction for the year.

Mere prepayment in this case is not sufficient. Marty must have a portion of the orthodontic services performed in the earlier year. If he does not have sufficient cash to pay the bill in the current year, he could borrow the money or use a bank credit card. ◀

KEY POINT

Even if the medical expenses exceed 10% of AGI the taxpayer may not benefit from the deduction if the medical expenses in addition to the other itemized deductions do not exceed the standard deduction.

Multiple Support Agreements. An individual may deduct medical expenses incurred for himself or herself, his or her spouse, dependents, children of divorced parents even if not a dependent, and persons who would qualify as a dependent except for the failure to meet the gross income or joint return test. In cases where a multiple support agreement has been filed, the tax law treats the individual who is the subject of the agreement as the dependent of the taxpayer entitled to the dependency exemption. Thus, to preserve the medical expense deduction, the taxpayer entitled to the dependency exemption should pay all medical expenditures for the dependent individual.

EXAMPLE I:7-34 ▶ Amy, Bart, Clay, and Donna each provide 25% of the support of their father, Eric. Under the terms of a multiple support agreement, Bart, Clay, and Donna all agree to allow Amy to claim the dependency exemption with respect to Eric. During the year, $3,000 in medical expenses are incurred on Eric's behalf. If Amy pays these expenses, she may deduct them (subject to limitations). However, if Bart, Clay, or Donna pays these expenses, no one may claim the medical expenses as a deduction. ◀

INTEREST EXPENSE DEDUCTION

A taxpayer may deduct qualified residence interest incurred on a principal residence and one other qualified residence that the taxpayer selects. The taxpayer makes this choice annually. The taxpayer may choose any residence that is not a rental property.

[54] *Robert M. Rose v. CIR*, 26 AFTR 2d 70-5653, 70-2 USTC ¶9646 (5th Cir., 1970). See also Rev. Ruls. 75-302, 1975-2 C.B. 86, and 75-303, 1975-2 C.B. 87, both clarified by Rev. Rul. 93-72, 1993-2 C.B. 77.

In order for the second residence to qualify, the taxpayer must use it personally for more than the greater of 14 days or 10% of the rental days during the year. If this personal use test is met, however, the Sec. 280A limitations on the rental of vacation homes also apply. As explained in Chapter I:6, under these rules, taxpayers must allocate expenses between the rental use and the personal use of the property. Taxpayers may deduct the expenses allocated to the rental use only to the extent of the rental income. Of the expenses allocated to the personal use, only the taxes and interest (if the residence is selected and if the loan is secured by the residence) are deductible as itemized deductions.

If the personal use by the taxpayer does not meet the test mentioned above, the interest allocated to the personal use cannot qualify as residence interest and it becomes non deductible personal interest. Furthermore, the passive loss rules apply to the rental income and expenses allocated to the rental use of the property (see Chapter I:8). Under these rules, individuals generally can deduct losses generated from a passive activity only to the extent of the individual's passive income. Certain individuals, however, may deduct up to $25,000 of losses from the rental of real estate. Thus, the two alternatives and their consequences are as follows:

- Meet the personal use test. No loss from the rental portion of the property is deductible. However, the interest allocated to the personal use portion may be fully deductible as qualified residence interest.
- Do not meet the personal use test. The interest allocated to the personal use portion is nondeductible personal interest. However, all of the passive loss from the rental portion is deductible against passive income. Furthermore, certain individuals may deduct up to $25,000 additional passive loss.

The alternative a taxpayer chooses depends on several factors, including the amount of the taxpayer's passive income, the total amount of itemized deductions, and whether the loan is secured by the vacation home.

DEDUCTION FOR CHARITABLE CONTRIBUTIONS

SELF-STUDY QUESTION

What type of property lends itself to the "election to reduce"?

ANSWER

Property on which there is very little appreciation.

Election to Reduce the Amount of a Charitable Contribution. The election to reduce the contribution of capital gain property to public charities by the long-term capital gain that the taxpayer would recognize if he or she sold the property is an annual election that applies to all capital gain property donated to public charities during the year. Because the election increases the ceiling limitation from 30% to 50%, under certain circumstances a taxpayer may actually receive a larger deduction for the year than would normally be available if the taxpayer did not make the election.

EXAMPLE I:7-35 ▶ During the current year, Jane has AGI of $50,000. She donates a painting to the local university during the same year. The painting, valued at $30,000 at the time of contribution, cost her $25,000 several years before. The university displays the painting in its art museum. If Jane does not make the election, the amount of the contribution is equal to its FMV ($30,000). However, Jane's charitable contribution deduction for the year is limited to $15,000 ($50,000 × 0.30). If Jane makes the election to reduce the contribution amount, the deduction is reduced to $25,000 ($30,000 − $5,000 LTCG). The deduction limitation, however, increases to $25,000 for the year because the limitation is now based on 50% of AGI instead of 30%. In this case, Jane will receive a larger deduction for the year by making the election. However, the cost associated with this election is the loss of $5,000 of deduction because the total deduction is reduced from $30,000 to $25,000 if she makes the election. ◀

Many tax practitioners make this election only when preparing the taxpayer's final tax return. The taxpayer makes the election at this time because charitable contribution carryovers to the decedent's estate are not permitted.

ADDITIONAL COMMENT

To help determine the FMV of contributed property, taxpayers can refer to IRS Pub. No. 561, Determining the Value of Donated Property. (2007)

Donation of Appreciated Capital Gain Property. Instead of selling substantially appreciated capital gain property and donating the cash proceeds, the taxpayer should consider donating the property directly to a charity. If property is donated in this way, the donor receives a deduction equal to the FMV of the property and does not recognize any taxable gain on the disposition.

EXAMPLE I:7-36 ▶ Colleen wishes to satisfy a pledge of $100,000 made to a local university. She owns $100,000 worth of marketable securities purchased ten years ago for $30,000. Because the securities are marketable, the university is indifferent as to whether Colleen donates cash or the securities. Although her marginal tax rate is 35%, Colleen would be subject to a tax rate of 15% on the sale of the securities. She has enough AGI to be able to deduct the full contribution in the current year. The following chart summarizes the cash flows to Colleen under two different alternatives:

	Donate Securities	*Sell Securities and Donate Cash*
Proceeds of sale	0	$100,000
Tax on gain	0	(10,500)[a]
Cash payment to charity		(100,000)
Tax savings from the contribution deduction	$35,000[b]	35,000
Net cash flow	$35,000	$ 24,500

[a]($100,000 − $30,000) × 0.15 = $10,500.
[b]$100,000 × 0.35 = $35,000. ◀

In order to take a tax loss on business or investment property, a taxpayer should not donate property that has decreased in value. Rather, the taxpayer should sell the property, recognize the loss, and donate the cash proceeds.

COMPLIANCE AND PROCEDURAL CONSIDERATIONS

OBJECTIVE 8

Describe compliance and procedural considerations for itemized deductions

MEDICAL EXPENSES

In certain cases, expenditures qualify as both a medical care expense and a dependent care expense (i.e., expenses for household and dependent care services that the taxpayer must pay to be gainfully employed). A taxpayer who incurs an expense that qualifies under both provisions may choose to take either a medical expense deduction or a tax credit under Sec. 21.[55] However, if a taxpayer takes a credit for these expenses, they are not deductible as medical expenses.

EXAMPLE I:7-37 ▶ Joel's daughter, Debbie, has a physical disability. As a result, Joel hires a nurse who provides daily care while he is at work. During the year, Joel pays the nurse a total of $3,000. This amount qualifies for both the dependent care credit and the medical expense deduction. If Joel takes the dependent care credit, he may not deduct the $3,000 as a medical expense. Because of the limitations imposed on each, the determination of which treatment is more advantageous depends on items such as the taxpayer's AGI, other medical expenses, and total itemized deductions. ◀

ADDITIONAL COMMENT

On Form 8283, the charitable organization is required to acknowledge receipt of the gift and to file an information return if the property is sold or disposed of within two years.

CHARITABLE CONTRIBUTIONS

Over the past several years, the IRS has significantly tightened the requirements needed to properly substantiate a charitable contribution in an attempt to prevent abuses in claiming inflated charitable contributions. In order for a taxpayer to take a deduction for a cash contribution of any amount, the taxpayer must be able to substantiate the contribution with either a bank record or a written receipt from the charity. Self-created documents are not sufficient. Previously, this requirement was imposed only on cash contributions of $250 or more. In addition, when a taxpayer donates property other than cash to a qualifying charity, proper determination of the property's FMV is a critical issue. Because of actual and perceived abuses in this area, the IRS often scrutinizes and, if necessary, challenges the valuation of contributed property. This is especially true for contributions of

[55] A credit of up to 35% of expenses for child and dependent care services is allowed if the dependent is under age 13 or a spouse or dependent who is mentally or physically incapable of caring for himself or herself. The credit is reduced 1% for every $2,000 (or portion thereof) of AGI over $15,000. However, the credit may not be reduced below 20%. (See the discussion on Personal Tax Credits in Chapter I:14 for a more detailed explanation of the child and dependent care credit.)

REAL-LIFE EXAMPLE

In one case the taxpayer, a CPA, failed to support a contribution with a qualified appraisal. As a result, his charitable deduction for art and printing supplies donated to a high school was denied. To substantiate the claimed $40,000 charitable deduction, the taxpayer submitted with Form 8283 an appraisal of the donated items made by the high school's principal. The principal, however, wasn't a "qualified appraiser." *D'Arcangelo,* TC Memo 1994-572 (1994).

ADDITIONAL COMMENT

If the taxpayer's total deduction for art is $20,000 or more, he or she must include an 8 × 10 inch color photograph or a color transparency no smaller than 4 × 5 inches.

property for which no published market quotes exist. Thus, the taxpayer must (1) properly substantiate the fact that the contribution has actually been made, and (2) in the case of the contribution of property, the taxpayer may be required to acquire and retain or provide to the IRS information documenting the property's FMV. As noted below, special detailed substantiation and documentation requirements apply to the contribution of used motor vehicles, boats, and airplanes.

Proper Substantiation. As mentioned above, if the contribution is made in cash, the taxpayer must retain evidence of the donation by keeping a cancelled check or other bank record or a receipt from the charitable organization. If the contribution is in the form of noncash property, the taxpayer must maintain records containing the following:

- Name and address of the charity to which the contribution was made
- Date and location of the contribution
- Description of the property
- FMV of the property
- Method of determining the property's FMV
- Signed copy of the appraisal report if an appraiser was used[56]

For charitable contributions of $250 or more, no deduction is allowed unless the contribution is substantiated by a contemporaneous, written acknowledgment (receipt) by the donee organization.This acknowledgment must contain the following information:

- The amount of cash and a description of any property contributed
- Whether or not the organization provided any goods or services in consideration for the cash or property received, including a description and good faith estimate of the value of any goods or services provided by the organization

The acknowledgment is contemporaneous if obtained by the earlier of the date the taxpayer files a return for the year in question or the extended due date for filing such a return. This substantiation requirement is waived if the donee organization files a return that contains the required information.[57] Additionally, no deduction is allowed for a contribution of clothing or household items unless the items are in "good" condition. Unfortunately, the law does not provide guidance as to what constitutes "good" condition.

Documentation of Property's FMV. In addition to the substantiation requirement, in certain cases the taxpayer must also properly document the property's FMV. The specific documentation requirements depend upon the amount of the claimed deduction for the contributed property. If a claimed deduction for a contribution of property exceeds $500, noncorporate taxpayers (and closely held C corporations and personal service corporations) must include with their tax return a description of the property and any other information the IRS requires, including the type, location, holding period, basis, and FMV of the property. This information is reported on Form 8283 (see Appendix B). If the claimed deduction exceeds $5,000, in addition to the above requirements, all taxpayers must obtain a qualified appraisal of the property and must include with their tax return any additional information that the IRS requires. Finally, if the claimed deduction exceeds $500,000, all taxpayers are additionally required to obtain a qualified appraisal and actually attach the appraisal to their tax return. Because these documentation requirements are based on the amount of a claimed contribution, the donation of similar items of property donated to all charities will be treated as the donation of one property. This requirement prevents taxpayers from avoiding these documentation requirements by spreading out their contributions. If a partnership or an S corporation donates property, these documentation requirements are applied at the entity level. However, if the documentation requirements are not met, the deduction is denied at the partner or shareholder level. In general, these documentation rules do not apply to contributions of cash, certain intangibles, inventory, or publicly traded securities.

---

[56] Reg. Sec. 1.170A-13.

[57] Sec. 170(f)(8) and Reg. Sec. 1.170A-13(f).

Contribution of Used Motor Vehicles, Boats, and Airplanes. Special documentation rules apply to contributions of motor vehicles, boats, and airplanes if the claimed value of the property exceeds $500. However, these rules do not apply if the contributed vehicle, boat, or airplane is inventory in the hands of the donor. If these special rules apply, the substantiation rules for a donation of property exceeding $250 are no longer applicable. Instead, the charity must give the taxpayer and the IRS a contemporaneous written acknowledgment of the contribution. This acknowledgment must be included with the taxpayer's tax return. The information included in the acknowledgment and the date by which the charity must give the acknowledgment to the taxpayer depend upon whether or not the charity sells the vehicle without any significant use or any material improvement of the vehicle. In either case, the acknowledgment must include the name and taxpayer identification number of the taxpayer who donated the vehicle, as well as the vehicle identification number. If the vehicle is sold by the charity before any significant use or material improvement, the acknowledgment must also include (1) a certification that the vehicle was sold in an arm's length transaction to an unrelated party, (2) the gross proceeds from the sale, and (3) a statement that the deductible amount may not exceed the amount of the gross proceeds. This acknowledgment must be given to the taxpayer within 30 days of the contribution of the vehicle to the charity, and, as mentioned earlier, the amount of the deduction for the vehicle is limited to the gross proceeds received from the sale. On the other hand, if the charity uses or improves the vehicle, the acknowledgment must also state: (1) the intended use or improvement and the intended duration of the use and (2) a certification that the vehicle will not be transferred or sold before completion of the intended use or improvement. This acknowledgment must be given to the taxpayer within 30 days of the donation of the vehicle.[58]

EXAMPLE I:7-38 ▶ During the current year, Peter Smith (SSN. 123-45-6789) reports AGI of $250,000. Smith also makes the following charitable contributions during the year:

- Smith performs voluntary dental work three days each month in rural areas of the state. Smith drives a total of 4,000 miles on these trips during the year.
- Smith makes the following contributions by cash or check: $750 to the city library, $2,000 to the United Way, $500 to a local community college, and $4,000 to his church.
- Smith contributes a tract of land to a small rural town. The town plans to erect a public library on the site. Smith purchased the land in 1997 for $5,000. Its appraised value at the time of the contribution is $8,000.

Smith's contributions are reported on the partially completed Schedule A shown in Figure I:7-1. The out-of-pocket expenses of $560 (4,000 miles × $0.14) and the contributions by cash or check of $7,250 (library, United Way, church, and community college) are totaled and reported on line 16. The property contribution of $8,000 is separately stated on line 17. Because Smith contributes property with a value exceeding $500, Form 8283, an appraisal summary, and signed statements by the qualified appraiser and an authorized official of the organization that received the property must be attached to the return. In addition, for the donations that separately exceed $250, Peter must obtain and retain written acknowledgments from the donee organizations in order for the contributions to be deductible. ◀

TAXES

Individuals generally report their deduction for property taxes on Schedule A of Form 1040. However, if the taxpayer incurs the taxes in his or her business, they are reported on Schedule C. Taxes incurred for the production of rents and royalties are reported on Schedule E. Taxes incurred in the taxpayer's farming business are reported on Schedule F. State and local income taxes imposed on individuals are always reported on Schedule A, even if the individual is self-employed.

Real estate brokers must report any real estate tax allocable to the purchaser of a residence. (See the discussion in this chapter regarding the allocation of real estate taxes between the seller and buyer of a residence.)[59] The broker reports this information on Form 1099-S (Proceeds from Real Estate Transactions).

[58] Sec. 170(f)(11) and (f)(12).

[59] Sec. 6045(e)(4) and Notice 93-4, 1993-1 C.B. 295.

SCHEDULE A (Form 1040)

Department of the Treasury
Internal Revenue Service (99)

Itemized Deductions

▶ Information about Schedule A and its separate instructions is at *www.irs.gov/schedulea.*

▶ Attach to Form 1040.

OMB No. 1545-0074

2014

Attachment Sequence No. 07

Name(s) shown on Form 1040: Peter Smith

Your social security number: 123 45 6789

Medical and Dental Expenses		**Caution.** Do not include expenses reimbursed or paid by others.				
	1	Medical and dental expenses (see instructions)	1			
	2	Enter amount from Form 1040, line 38 [2]				
	3	Multiply line 2 by 10% (.10). But if either you or your spouse was born before January 2, 1950, multiply line 2 by 7.5% (.075) instead	3			
	4	Subtract line 3 from line 1. If line 3 is more than line 1, enter -0-			4	
Taxes You Paid	5	State and local **(check only one box):** a ☐ Income taxes, **or** b ☐ General sales taxes	5			
	6	Real estate taxes (see instructions)	6			
	7	Personal property taxes	7			
	8	Other taxes. List type and amount ▶	8			
	9	Add lines 5 through 8			9	
Interest You Paid	10	Home mortgage interest and points reported to you on Form 1098	10			
Note. Your mortgage interest deduction may be limited (see instructions).	11	Home mortgage interest not reported to you on Form 1098. If paid to the person from whom you bought the home, see instructions and show that person's name, identifying no., and address ▶	11			
	12	Points not reported to you on Form 1098. See instructions for special rules	12			
	13	Mortgage insurance premiums (see instructions)	13			
	14	Investment interest. Attach Form 4952 if required. (See instructions.)	14			
	15	Add lines 10 through 14			15	
Gifts to Charity	16	Gifts by cash or check. If you made any gift of $250 or more, see instructions	16	7,810		
If you made a gift and got a benefit for it, see instructions.	17	Other than by cash or check. If any gift of $250 or more, see instructions. You **must** attach Form 8283 if over $500	17	8,000		
	18	Carryover from prior year	18			
	19	Add lines 16 through 18			19	15,810
Casualty and Theft Losses	20	Casualty or theft loss(es). Attach Form 4684. (See instructions.)			20	
Job Expenses and Certain Miscellaneous Deductions	21	Unreimbursed employee expenses—job travel, union dues, job education, etc. Attach Form 2106 or 2106-EZ if required. (See instructions.) ▶	21			
	22	Tax preparation fees	22			
	23	Other expenses—investment, safe deposit box, etc. List type and amount ▶	23			
	24	Add lines 21 through 23	24			
	25	Enter amount from Form 1040, line 38 [25]				
	26	Multiply line 25 by 2% (.02)	26			
	27	Subtract line 26 from line 24. If line 26 is more than line 24, enter -0-			27	
Other Miscellaneous Deductions	28	Other—from list in instructions. List type and amount ▶			28	
Total Itemized Deductions	29	Is Form 1040, line 38, over $152,525? ☐ **No.** Your deduction is not limited. Add the amounts in the far right column for lines 4 through 28. Also, enter this amount on Form 1040, line 40. ☐ **Yes.** Your deduction may be limited. See the Itemized Deductions Worksheet in the instructions to figure the amount to enter.			29	
	30	If you elect to itemize deductions even though they are less than your standard deduction, check here ▶ ☐				

For Paperwork Reduction Act Notice, see Form 1040 instructions. Cat. No. 17145C **Schedule A (Form 1040) 2014**

FIGURE I:7-1 ▶ PARTIALLY COMPLETED SCHEDULE A

What would you do in this situation?

GIVING TO BOTH: GOODWILL AND THE IRS

Much has been written about abusive practices concerning the valuation of noncash property donated to qualified charities. Under Sec. 170, both corporations and individuals may deduct the FMV of property contributed to charitable organizations. Of course, a number of valuation and percentage limitations and carryover rules are applicable to both individual and corporate taxpayers.

Assume your clients, Mr. and Mrs. Nicholas Nice, come into your office on December 27 for some year-end tax planning. Your review of their tax situation indicates that they have made substantial donations of clothing and household goods to Goodwill Industries. They have obtained proper documentation for donations made during the year but do not know how to qualify for taking a charitable deduction vis-à-vis valuation, forms, and the like. They do know that their original cost basis in the donated goods was $15,000 and that the goods were in good condition at the time of the donation. What tax and ethical issues should be considered?

EXAMPLE I:7-39 ▶ During the year, Andrea incurs $1,500 in property taxes on a two-family duplex. Andrea lives in one unit and rents out the other. She also pays $100 in registration fees and $600 in personal property taxes on her automobile, based on its value. Andrea uses the automobile 80% of the time in an unincorporated business. During the current year, she also pays $2,000 in state income taxes, all of which is attributable to her income of the prior year from the unincorporated business.

Because one-half of the real estate taxes are attributable to property used to produce rental income, $750 (0.50 × $1,500) is reported on Schedule E, and the remaining personal-use portion ($750) is reported on Schedule A. Because 80% of the use of the automobile is in Andrea's business, $80 (0.80 × $100) of the registration fee is deductible as a business expense on Schedule C. The remaining $20 is not deductible because the registration fee is not a tax. However, $480 (0.80 × $600) of the personal property tax on the automobile is deductible as a business expense on Schedule C. The remaining $120 is deductible as a tax on Schedule A. Finally, even though the state income tax is related to Andrea's business income, all $2,000 of the state income tax is reported on Schedule A. Because Andrea pays the state income tax in the current year, it is deductible in the current year. ◀

PROBLEM MATERIALS

DISCUSSION QUESTIONS

I:7-1 a. For which persons may a taxpayer deduct medical expenses?
b. In the case of children of divorced parents, must the parent who is entitled to the dependency exemption pay the medical expenses of the child to ensure that the expenses are deductible? Explain.
c. Who should pay the medical expenses of an individual who is the subject of a multiple support agreement?

I:7-2 What is the definition of medical care for purposes of the medical care deduction?

I:7-3 a. What is the definition of cosmetic surgery under the Internal Revenue Code?
b. Is the cost of cosmetic surgery deductible as a medical expense? Explain.

I:7-4 a. If a taxpayer must travel away from his or her home in order to obtain medical care, which en route costs, if any, are deductible as medical expenses?
b. Are there any limits imposed on the deductibility of these expenses?

I:7-5 What are the rules dealing with the deductibility of the cost of meals and lodging incurred while away from home in order to receive medical treatment as an outpatient?

I:7-6 a. Which types of capital expenditures incurred specifically for medical purposes are deductible?
b. What limitations, if any, are imposed on the deductibility of these expenditures?

I:7-7 Bill, a plant manager, is suffering from a serious ulcer. Bill's doctor recommends that he spend three weeks fishing and hunting in the Colorado Rockies. Can Bill deduct the costs of the trip as a medical expense?

I:7-8 In what cases are medical insurance premiums paid by an individual not deductible as qualified medical expenses?

I:7-9 What is the limit placed on medical expense deductions? When can a deduction be taken for medical care? What if the medical care is prepaid?

I:7-10 a. Which taxes are specifically deductible for federal income tax purposes under Sec. 164?
b. If a tax is not specifically listed in Sec. 164, under what circumstances may it still be deductible?

I:7-11 If Susan overpays her state income tax due to excess withholdings, can she deduct the entire amount in the year withheld? When Susan receives a refund from the state how must she treat that refund for tax purposes?

I:7-12 What is an ad valorem tax? If a tax that is levied on personal property is not an ad valorem tax, under what circumstances may it still be deductible?

I:7-13 When real estate is sold during a year, why is it necessary that the real estate taxes on the property be apportioned between the buyer and seller?

I:7-14 a. Identify the different categories of interest expense an individual may incur. How is the classification of the interest determined?
b. Are these different categories of interest deductible? If so, how?

I:7-15 At times, the term *points* is used to refer to different types of charges. Define the term and describe when points are deductible.

I:7-16 In which year or years are points (representing prepaid interest on a loan) deductible?

I:7-17 Why does Sec. 267 impose a restriction on the deductibility of expenses accrued and payable by an accrual method taxpayer to a related cash method taxpayer?

I:7-18 a. What is the amount of the annual limitation placed on the deductibility of investment interest expense?
b. Explain how net investment income is calculated.
c. Is any disallowed interest expense for the year allowable as a deduction in another year? If so, when?

I:7-19 Explain what acquisition indebtedness and home equity indebtedness are with respect to a qualified residence of a taxpayer. Identify any limitations on the deductibility of interest expense on this indebtedness.

I:7-20 Explain what a qualified residence is for purposes of qualified residence interest.

I:7-21 Why is interest expense disallowed if it is incurred to purchase or hold tax-exempt obligations?

I:7-22 When is interest generally deductible for cash-method taxpayers? Explain if the general rule applies to prepaid interest, interest paid with loan proceeds, discounted notes, and personal interest. If the general rule does not apply, explain when these interest expenses are deductible.

I:7-23 a. For purposes of the charitable contribution deduction, what is capital gain property? Ordinary income property?
b. What is the significance of classifying property as either capital gain property or ordinary income property?

I:7-24 How is the *amount* of a charitable contribution of capital gain property determined if it is donated to a private nonoperating foundation? How does this determination differ if capital gain property is donated to a public charity?

I:7-25 May an individual who is married and files a joint return deduct any charitable contributions if the itemized deductions total $7,000 (of which $3,000 are qualified charitable contributions)?

I:7-26 For individuals, what is the overall deduction limitation on charitable contributions? What is the limitation for corporations?

I:7-27 If a taxpayer's charitable contributions for any tax year exceed the deduction limitations, may the excess contributions be deducted in another year? If so, in which years may they be deducted?

I:7-28 How are charitable contribution deductions reported on the tax return for individuals? What reporting requirements must be met for the contribution of property?

I:7-29 List some of the more common miscellaneous itemized deductions and identify any limitations that are imposed on the deductibility of these items.

I:7-30 Other than the 10% limitation placed on medical expenses, the 10% reduction for casualty losses on personal property, the 2% reduction applied to certain miscellaneous itemized deductions, and the fact that itemized deductions are only deductible if they exceed the standard deduction, are there any other limitations or reductions applied to itemized deductions for individuals?

ISSUE IDENTIFICATION QUESTIONS

I:7-31 Wayne and Maria file a joint tax return on which they itemize their deductions and report AGI of $50,000. During the year they incurred $1,500 of medical expenses when Maria broke her leg. Furthermore, their dentist informed them that their daughter, Alicia, needs $3,000 of orthodontic work to correct her overbite. Wayne also needs a new pair of eyeglasses that will cost $300. What tax issues should Wayne and Maria consider?

I:7-32 This year, Chuck took out a loan to purchase some raw land for investment. He paid $40,000 for the land, and he expects that within 5 years the land will be worth at least $75,000. Chuck is married, and his AGI for the year is $230,000. Chuck paid $4,300 in interest on the loan this year. Chuck has $2,600 in interest income and $1,300 in dividend income for the year. He plans to itemize his deductions so he can use the interest expense to offset his investment income. What tax issues should Chuck consider?

I:7-33 During the current year, George made contributions totaling $40,000 to an organization called the National Endowment for the Preservation of Liberty (NEPL). Later during the year, the NEPL started giving money to a political candidate to help with his campaign expenses. What tax issues should George consider?

I:7-34 During the current year, Bob has AGI of $100,000. He also donated some stock to his church. He purchased the stock two years ago for $55,000. The FMV of the stock at the time of the contribution is $60,000. Bob has $5,000 of unused excess contributions from a prior year. What tax issues should Bob consider?

PROBLEMS

I:7-35 *Medical Expense Deduction.* During 2015, Angela sustains serious injuries from a snow-skiing accident. She incurs the following expenses:

Item	*Amount*
Doctor bills	$11,700
Hospital bills	9,400
Legal fees in suit against ski resort	3,000

Angela is single and has no dependents. For the year, her salary is $58,000. She pays $600 in medical and dental insurance premiums, which is withheld from her paycheck on an after-tax basis, $2,750 in mortgage interest on her home, and $1,200 in interest on her car loan. Her health insurance provider reimburses her for $10,000 of the medical expenses. What is her 2015 taxable income?

I:7-36 ***Reimbursement of Previously Deducted Medical Expenses.*** Assume the same facts as in Problem I:7-35. In addition, assume that in 2016, Angela receives an additional $7,000 in a settlement of a lawsuit arising because of the snow-skiing accident. $4,000 of the settlement is to pay Angela's medical bills, and $3,000 is to reimburse her legal expenses. What is the proper tax treatment of this $7,000 settlement?

I:7-37 *Medical Expense Deduction.* Dan lives in Duncan, a small town in Arizona. Because of a rare blood disease, Dan is required to take special medical treatments once a month. The closest place these treatments are available to Dan is in Phoenix, 200 miles away. The treatments are provided on an outpatient basis but require him to stay overnight in Phoenix. During the year, Dan makes 12 trips to Phoenix by automobile to receive the treatments. The motel he always stays in charges $85 per night. For the year, Dan also spends a total of $250 for meals on these trips. $100 of this $250 is spent while en route to Phoenix. What is the amount of Dan's qualified medical expenses for 2015?

I:7-38 *Medical Expense Deduction.* Chad is divorced and has custody of Brett, his 14-year-old son. Chad's ex-wife has custody of their daughter, Sara. During the year, Chad incurs $3,000 for orthodontic work for Sara to correct a severe overbite and $2,000 in unreimbursed medical expenses associated with Brett's broken leg. Chad also pays $900 in health insurance premiums, which is withheld from his paycheck on a pre-tax basis. Both Brett and Sara are covered under Chad's medical insurance plan. In addition, Chad incurs $400 for prescription drugs and $1,000 in doctor bills for himself. Chad's AGI is $40,000. What is Chad's medical expense deduction for the year assuming that his other itemized deductions exceed the standard deduction?

I:7-39 *Medical Expense Deduction.* In 2015, Charla, a single taxpayer with no dependents, was severely hurt in a farm accident. Charla is 38 years old. The accident left Charla's legs 85% paralyzed. After incurring $14,000 of medical expenses at the hospital, the doctor recommended that Charla install a pool at her home for therapy. The pool cost $25,000 to install and increased the value of her home by $22,000. She spent $930 maintaining the pool in 2015 and $1,060 in 2016. Charla also purchased a wheelchair on December 28, 2015, for $2,300, which she charged to her credit card. She paid her credit card bill on January 6, 2016. She also purchased a hospital bed for $3,800 but did not pay for the bed until 2016. Charla paid her physical therapist $4,000 for services performed in 2016. Charla paid $1,200 in medical insurance premiums on an after-tax basis in both 2015 and

2016. In 2016, the insurance company reimbursed Charla $9,000 for her hospital stay in 2015. Her AGI for 2015 and 2016 is $38,000 and $43,000, respectively, not considering any of the above items. Charla has no other itemized deductions in either year.

a. What is Charla's taxable income for 2015?

b. What is Charla's medical expense deduction for 2016? How does she treat the reimbursement?

I:7-40 *Deduction of Taxes.* Joyce is a single, cash-method taxpayer. On April 11, 2014, Joyce paid $120 in state income taxes with her 2013 state income tax return. During 2014, Joyce had $1,600 in state income taxes withheld. On April 13, 2015, Joyce paid $200 with her 2014 state tax return. During 2015, she had $2,100 in state income taxes withheld from her paycheck. Upon filing her 2015 tax return on April 15, 2016, she received a refund of $450 for excess state income taxes withheld. Joyce had total AGI in 2015 and 2016 of $51,000 and $53,500, respectively. In 2015, Joyce also paid $5,500 in qualified residence interest.

a. What is the amount of state income taxes Joyce may include as an itemized deduction for 2014?

b. What is Joyce's allowed itemized deduction for state income taxes for 2015?

c. What is Joyce's taxable income for 2015?

d. What is her AGI for 2016?

I:7-41 Assume the same facts as Problem I:7-40, but change the amount of Joyce's mortgage interest to $3,000.

a. What is her taxable income for 2015?

b. What is her AGI for 2016?

I:7-42 *Deduction of Taxes.* Dawn, a single, cash-method taxpayer, paid the following taxes in 2015: Dawn's employer withheld $5,400 for federal income taxes, $2,000 for state income taxes, and $3,800 for FICA from her 2015 paychecks. Dawn purchased a new car and paid $600 in sales tax and $70 for the license. The car's FMV was $20,000 and it weighed 3,000 pounds. The county also assessed a property tax on the car. The tax was 2% of the car's value and $10 per hundredweight. Dawn uses the car 100% of the time for personal purposes. Dawn sold her house on April 15, 2015. The county's property tax on the home for 2015 is $1,850, payable on February 1, 2015. The county's real property tax year is the calendar year. Dawn's AGI for 2015 is $50,000 and her other itemized deductions exclusive of taxes are $4,000 (disregard any leap year).

a. What is Dawn's deduction for taxes in 2015?

b. Where on Dawn's tax return should she report her deduction for taxes?

I:7-43 *Apportionment of Real Estate Taxes.* On May 1 of the current year, Tara sells a building to Janet for $500,000. Tara's basis in the building is $300,000. The county in which the building is located has a real property tax year that ends on June 30. The taxes are payable by September 1 of that year. On September 1, Janet pays the annual property taxes of $6,000. Both Tara and Janet are calendar-year, cash method taxpayers. The closing agreement does not separately account for the property taxes. Disregard any leap year.

a. What amount of real property taxes may Janet deduct in the current year?

b. What amount of real property taxes may Tara deduct in the current year?

c. If no apportionment on the real property taxes is made in the sales agreement, what is Tara's total selling price of the building? Janet's basis for the building?

I:7-44 *Classification of Interest Expense.* On January 1 of the current year, Scott borrows $80,000, pledging the assets of his business as collateral. He immediately deposits the money in an interest-bearing checking account. Scott already had $20,000 in this account. On April 1, Scott invests $75,000 in a limited real estate partnership. On July 1, he buys a new ski boat for $12,000. On August 1, he makes a $10,000 capital contribution to his unincorporated business. Scott repays $50,000 of the loan on November 30 of the current year. Classify Scott's interest expense for the year.

I:7-45 *Investment Income and Deductions.* During 2015, Travis takes out a $40,000 loan, using stock he owns as collateral. He uses $10,000 to purchase a car, which he uses 100% for personal use. He uses the remaining funds to purchase stocks and bonds. He pays $3,200 interest on the loan. Travis also reports the following for the year:

AGI without any investment income	$130,000
State income taxes paid	8,400
Dividend income	10,000
Interest income	2,100

Investment expenses (exclusive of interest)	8,000
Net short term capital gains	7,300
Net long term capital gain	8,600

Travis is married and files a joint tax return. What is his net taxable income?

I:7-46 ***Qualified Residence Interest.*** During the current year, Tina purchases a beachfront condominium for $600,000, paying $150,000 down and taking out a $450,000 mortgage, secured by the property. At the time of the purchase, the outstanding mortgage on her principal residence is $700,000. This debt is secured by the residence. The FMV of the principal residence is $1,400,000. She purchased the principal residence in 1997. What is the amount of qualified indebtedness on which Tina may deduct the interest payments?

I:7-47 ***Qualified Residence Interest.*** Several years ago, Magdelena purchased a new residence for $300,000. Currently, the outstanding mortgage on the residence is $260,000. The current fair market value of the home is $330,000. Magdelena wants to borrow a sizable sum of money to pay for the college education costs of her two children and believes the interest would be deductible if she takes out a home equity loan. For each of the independent situations below, determine the amount of the home equity loan on which Magdelena may deduct the interest as qualified residence interest.

a. Magdelena borrows $50,000 as a home equity loan.

b. Magdelena borrows $80,000 as a home equity loan.

c. Alternatively, assume the current fair market value of her residence is $410,000 and she borrows $110,000 as a home equity loan.

d. Alternatively, assume the current outstanding balance of the mortgage Magdelena incurred to purchase the home is $1,200,000, the home's fair market value is $1,400,000, and she borrows $80,000 as a home equity loan.

I:7-48 ***Interest Between Related Parties.*** Crown Corporation is an accrual method taxpayer owned 55% by Brett and 45% by Susie. Brett and Susie are good friends and have been business associates for several years. BJ Partnership is a cash method taxpayer, owned 40% by Brett and 60% by Jeremy, Brett's uncle. Both Crown Corporation and BJ Partnership are calendar year entities. On January 5 of the current year, Crown borrows $50,000 from BJ Partnership and pays 8% interest on the loan. Crown must pay the interest on January first of next year.

a. What amount of interest expense can Crown Corporation deduct in the current year?

b. How would your answer change if Jeremy were Brett's brother, instead of his uncle?

I:7-49 ***Timing of Interest Deduction.*** On April 1 of the current year, Henry borrows $12,000 from the bank for a year. Because the note is discounted for the interest charge and Henry receives proceeds of $10,200, he is required to repay the face amount of the loan ($12,000) in four equal quarterly payments beginning on July 1 of the current year. Henry is a cash method individual.

a. What is the amount of Henry's interest expense deduction in the current year with respect to this loan?

b. Assume the same facts except that the initial starting date when the repayments begin is April 1 of the following year. What is the amount of Henry's interest expense deduction in the current year?

c. Assume the same facts as in Part b, except that Henry is an accrual method taxpayer and the loan will be outstanding for one year. What is the amount of his interest expense deduction in the current year?

I:7-50 ***Itemized Deductions.*** During 2015, Doug incurs the following deductible expenses: $2,300 in state income taxes, $3,000 in local property taxes, $800 in medical expenses, and $2,000 in charitable contributions. Doug is 33, single, has no dependents, and has $35,000 AGI for the year. What is the amount of Doug's taxable income?

I:7-51 ***Computation of Taxable Income.*** During 2015, James, a single, cash method taxpayer incurred the following expenditures:

Qualified medical expenses	$ 8,000
Investment interest expense	16,000
Other investment activity expenses	15,000
Qualified residence interest	12,000
Interest on loan on personal auto	2,000
Charitable contributions	3,000

State income tax paid	7,000
State sales tax paid	4,500
Property taxes	4,000
Tax return preparation and consulting fees	5,000

James' income consisted of the following items:

Salary	$70,000
Interest income	20,000
Long-term capital gains	23,000
Long-term capital losses	(15,000)

a. Compute James' taxable income for the year (assuming that he makes an election to have the net capital gain taxed at the regular tax rates). Also assume that James is 67 years old. Thus, his medical expense deduction is subject to the 7.5% rather than the 10% limit.

b. What is James' investment interest carryover (if any)?

I:7-52 ***Computation of Taxable Income.*** Assume all the same facts as in Problem I:7-51 except that James' salary income is $130,000 instead of $70,000 and that he does not make the election. Compute James' taxable income for the year.

I:7-53 ***Charitable Contributions: Services.*** Donna is an attorney who renders volunteer legal services to a Legal Aid Society, which provides legal advice to low-income individuals. The Legal Aid Society is a qualified charitable organization. During the current year she spends a total of 200 hours in this volunteer work. Her regular billing rate is $350 per hour. In addition, she spends a total of $800 in out-of-pocket costs in providing these services. She receives no compensation and is not reimbursed for her out-of-pocket costs. What is Donna's charitable contribution for the year because of these activities?

I:7-54 ***Charitable Contribution Limitations.*** In each of the following independent cases, determine the amount of the charitable contribution and the limitation that would apply. In each case, assume that the donee is a qualified public charity.

a. Sharon donates a tract of land to a charitable organization. She has held the land for seven years. Her basis in the land is $10,000 and its FMV is $40,000.

b. Assume the same facts in Part a, except that Sharon has held the land for only 11 months and that its FMV is $23,000.

c. Jack purchases a historical document for $50,000. He donates the historical document to a charitable organization two years later. The organization plans to use it for research and study. Its FMV at the time of the donation is $100,000.

d. Assume the same facts in Part c, except that the organization plans to sell the document and put the money into an endowment fund.

e. Valerie donates some inventory to a charitable organization. The inventory is not food or clothing. The inventory is purchased for $500 and its FMV is $1,200 at the time of the donation. She held the inventory for seven months.

I:7-55 ***Charitable Contributions to Private Nonoperating Foundations.*** Assume the same facts as Problem I:7-54, except that the qualified organization is a private nonoperating foundation. Determine the amount of the charitable contribution for Parts a through e.

I:7-56 ***Charitable Contribution Limitations.*** During the current year, Helen donates stock worth $50,000 to her local community college. Two years ago the stock cost Helen $40,000. Her AGI for the current year is $100,000. Beginning next year, the bulk of her income will be from tax-exempt municipal securities. Thus, she is not interested in any carryover of excess charitable contribution. What is the maximum charitable contribution deduction Helen may take this year?

I:7-57 ***Charitable Contribution Limitations.*** During the current year, Melissa reports AGI of $200,000. As part of some estate planning, she donates $30,000 to her alma mater, Middle State University, and $65,000 to a private nonoperating foundation.

a. What is the amount of Melissa's charitable deduction for the current year?

b. Assume the same facts in Part a except that she donates $45,000 to Middle State University.

I:7-58 ***Corporate Charitable Contributions.*** Circle Corporation, an accrual method taxpayer, manufactures and sells mainframe computers. In January of the current year, Circle Corporation donates a mainframe that was part of its inventory to City College. City College will use the computer for physical science research. Circle's basis in the mainframe is $300,000. The computer's FMV is $650,000. On December 15 of the current year, Circle also pledged stock to the Red Cross and promised delivery of the stock by

March 1 of the following year. The stock's FMV is $100,000 and Circle's adjusted basis in the stock is $50,000. Circle has held the stock for over one year. Circle's taxable income (before deducting any charitable contributions) for the current year is $4,000,000.

a. What is the amount of Circle's charitable contribution for the current year?

b. How much of the contribution can Circle deduct in the current year and how much may be carried over, if any?

I:7-59 *Charitable Contribution Carryovers.* Bonnie's charitable contributions and AGI for the past four years were as follows:

	2012	*2013*	*2014*	*2015*
AGI	$50,000	$55,000	$58,000	$60,000
Contributions subject to the 50% limitation	40,000	29,000	25,000	10,000

What is the amount of the charitable deduction for each year and the order in which the deduction and carryovers are used?

COMPREHENSIVE PROBLEM

I:7-60 Tim and Monica Nelson are married, file a joint return, and are your newest tax clients. They provide you with the following information relating to their 2015 tax return:

1. Tim works as a pediatrician for the county hospital. The W-2 form he received from the hospital shows wages of $150,000 and state income tax withheld of $8,500.
2. Monica spends much of her time volunteering, but also works as a substitute teacher for the local schools. During the year, she spent 900 hours volunteering. When she doesn't volunteer, she earns $8.00 per hour working as a substitute. The W-2 form she received from the school district shows total wages of $3,888 and state income tax withheld of $85.
3. On April 13, the couple paid $250 in state taxes with their 2014 state income tax return. The Nelson's state and local sales taxes in 2015 were $5,500.
4. On December 18, the Nelsons donated a small building to the Boy Scouts of America. They purchased the building three years ago for $80,000. A professional appraiser determined the fair market value of the home was $96,000 on December 12.
5. Tim and Monica both received corrective eye surgery, at a total cost of $3,000. They also paid $1,900 in health insurance premiums.
6. On June 1, the couple bought a car for $30,000, paying $18,000 down and borrowing $12,000. They paid $750 total interest on the loan in 2015.
7. On June 10, the Nelsons took out a home equity loan of $20,000 to expand their home. They paid a total of $850 interest with their monthly payments on the loan.
8. The Nelsons paid a total of $2,300 interest on their original home loan.
9. They sold stock in Cabinets, Inc. for $5,200, which they purchased for $7,900 in March of the current year. They also sold stock in The Outdoor Corporation for $12,500, which they purchased several years ago for $8,600.
10. Tim incurred the following expenses related to his profession, none of which were reimbursed by his employer:

Item	*Amount*
Subscriptions to medical journals	$400
American Medical Association (AMA) annual membership fee	250

11. During the year, the couple paid their former tax advisor $700 to prepare their prior year tax return.
12. The Nelsons do not have children, and they do not provide significant financial support to any family members.

Required: Compute the Nelson's taxable income for 2015.

TAX STRATEGY PROBLEMS

I:7-61 Dean makes a pledge of $30,000 to a local college. The college is willing to accept either cash or marketable securities in fulfillment of the pledge. Dean owns stock in Ajax Corporation worth $30,000. The stock was purchased five years ago for $10,000. Dean's marginal tax rate is 35% and he is subject to the long-term capital gains rate of 15%. Should Dean sell the stock and then donate the cash, or should he donate the stock directly? Compute the net tax benefit from each alternative and explain the difference. (Ignore the 3.8% tax on the net investment income of high-income taxpayers for this comparison.)

I:7-62 On December 1, 2015, Rebecca Ward, a single taxpayer, comes to you for tax advice. At the end of every year, she donates $5,000 to charity. She has no other itemized deductions. This year, she plans to make her charitable donation with stock. She presents you with the following information relating to her stock investments:

Corporation	*FMV on Dec. 1*	*Adjusted Basis*	*Date Purchased*
Sycamore	9,600	7,800	5/22/10
Oak	2,900	3,800	9/10/11
Redwood	5,400	4,900	6/15/15

Which stock should Rebecca donate to charity? What other tax advice would you give her?

TAX FORM/RETURN PREPARATION PROBLEMS

I:7-63 Following is a list of information for Peter and Amy Jones for the current tax year. Peter and Amy are married and have three children, Aubrynne, Bryson, and Caden. They live at 100 Main Street, Anytown, USA 00000. Peter is a lawyer working for a Native American law firm. Amy works part-time in a genetic research lab. The Jones' Social Security numbers and ages are as follows:

Name	*S.S. No.*	*Age*
Peter	111-11-1111	32
Amy	222-22-2222	28
Aubrynne	333-33-3333	5
Bryson	444-44-4444	3
Caden	555-55-5555	1

Receipts	
Peter's salary	$70,000
Amy's salary	32,000
Interest income on municipal bonds	2,400
Interest income on certificate of deposit (Universal Savings)	3,100
Dividends on GM stock	1,600

Disbursements	
Eyeglasses and exam for Aubrynne	$ 600
Orthodontic work for Bryson to correct a congenital defect	2,500
Medical insurance premiums, after-tax basis	1,800
Withholding for state income taxes	7,200
Withholding for federal income taxes	16,000
State income taxes paid with last year's tax return (paid when the return was filed in the current year)	500
Property taxes on home	1,100
Property taxes on automobile	300
Interest on home	9,700
Interest on credit cards	200
Cash contribution to church	3,900

In addition to the above, on September 17, Peter and Amy donate some Beta Trader, Inc. stock to Lakeville Community College. Beta Trader, Inc. is publicly traded. The FMV of the stock on the date of the contribution is $700. Peter and Amy had purchased the stock on November 7, 2003 for $300.

Compute Peter and Amy's income tax liability for the current year using Form 1040, Schedules A and B, and Form 8283, if necessary.

I:7-64 Kelly and Chanelle Chambers, ages 47 and 45, are married and live at 584 Thoreau Drive, Boston, MA 59483. Kelly's Social Security number is 111-11-1111 and Chanelle's is 222-22-2222. The Chambers have two children: Emma, age 23, and Chet, age 19. Their Social Security numbers are 333-33-3333 and 444-44-4444, respectively. Emma is a single college student and earned $8,000 during the summer. Kelly and Chanelle help Emma through school by paying for her room, board, and tuition. Emma lives at home during the summer. Chet has a physical handicap and lives at home. He attends a local university and earned $4,000 working for a marketing firm. In sum, Kelly and Chanelle provide more than 50% of both Emma's and Chet's total support for the year.

Kelly is a commercial pilot for a small airline. His salary is $95,000, from which $19,000 of federal income tax and $8,000 of state income tax were withheld. Kelly also pays premiums for health, disability, and life insurance. $2,000 of the premium was for health insurance, $250 for disability, and $400 for life insurance.

Chanelle owns Alliance Networks, a proprietorship that does network consulting. During the year, Chanelle's gross revenues were $23,000. She incurred the following expenses in her business:

Liability insurance	$ 700
Software rental	5,400
Journals and magazines	150
Training seminars	1,200
Supplies	1,300
Donations to a political campaign fund	800

Kelly enjoys playing guitar and plays in a band. Kelly's band has developed a local following. This year, his gross revenues were $1,200 for playing shows and $700 on CD sales. He incurred the following expenses:

Studio rent expense	$1,300
Sound system repairs	200
CD production	500
New guitar and amplifier	800

Kelly's father passed away during the year. Kelly and Chanelle received $100,000 from the life insurance policy. Neither Kelly nor Chanelle paid any of the premiums.

Chanelle purchased 100 shares of Thurston Co. stock on May 1, 1991, for $1,000. Thurston Co. was declared bankrupt during the current year.

Chet's physician recommended that he see a physical therapist to help with his disability. Kelly paid the therapist $7,000 during the year because his insurance would not cover the bills.

Kelly and Chanelle went to Las Vegas and won $5,000 at the blackjack table. The next night, they lost $6,000.

Kelly and Chanelle gave $900 to their church and, during the year, they had the following other income and expenses:

Real estate taxes	$1,400
Property taxes on car (determined by value)	500
Home mortgage interest	9,000
Credit card finance charges	2,600
Tax return preparation fees ($600 is allocable to Chanelle's business)	1,000
Sales tax on purchases during the year	6,200
Interest from a savings account	800
Interest from City of Boston Bonds	700
Dividend from 3M stock	400

Prepare Kelly and Chanelle's tax return Form 1040 and Schedules A, B, C, D, and SE for the current year.

CASE STUDY PROBLEMS

I:7-65 Brian Brown, an executive at a manufacturing enterprise, comes to you on December 1 of the current year for tax advice. He has agreed to donate a small tract of land to the Rosepark Community College. The value of the land has been appraised at $58,000. Mr. Brown purchased the land 14 months ago for $50,000. Mr. Brown's estimated AGI for the current year is $100,000. He plans to retire next year and anticipates that his AGI will fall to $35,000 for all subsequent years. He does not anticipate making any additional large charitable contributions. He understands that there are special rules dealing with charitable contributions and wants your advice in order to get the maximum overall tax benefit from his contribution. Because the college plans to use the property, selling the land is not an alternative. You are to prepare a letter to Mr. Brown explaining the tax consequences of the different alternatives. His address is 100 East Rosebrook, Mesa, Arizona 85203. For purposes of your analysis, assume that Mr. Brown is married and files a joint return. Also assume that Mr. Brown feels that an appropriate discount rate is 10%. In your analysis, use the tax rate schedules for the current year.

I:7-66 For several years, you have prepared the tax return for Alpha Corporation, a closely held corporation engaged in manufacturing garden tools. On February 20 of the current year, Bill Johnson, the president of Alpha Corporation, delivered to your office the files and information necessary for you to prepare Alpha's tax return for the immediately preceding tax year. Included in this information were the minutes of all meetings held by Alpha's Board of Directors during the year in question.

Then on February 27, Bill stops by your office and hands you an "addendum" to the minutes of the director's meeting held December 15 of the tax year for which you are preparing the tax return. The addendum is dated the same day as the director's meeting, and authorizes a charitable contribution pledge of $20,000 to the local community college. With a wink and a big smile, Bill explains that the addendum had been misplaced. In reviewing the original minutes, you find no mention of a charitable contribution pledge.

What should you do? [See Appendix E and the *Statements on Standards for Tax Services* section in Chapter I:15 (or C:1 of the *Comprehensive* volume) for a discussion of these issues.]

TAX RESEARCH PROBLEMS

I:7-67 Mark Hancock is a self-employed attorney who operates his law practice as an unincorporated sole proprietorship. In 2014, the IRS disallowed several business deductions he took in 2012 and 2013. In addition to paying the deficiency and assessed penalties, he also pays $18,000 in interest on the tax owed. Can he deduct that interest in the current year?

- Sec. 162, Sec. 163
- Reg. Sec. 1.163-9T
- *Kikalos v. Comm.*, 84 AFTR 2d 99-5933

I:7-68 Last year, Mr. Smith was involved in an automobile accident, severely injuring his legs. As part of a long-term rehabilitation process, his physician prescribes a daily routine of swimming. Because there is no readily available public facility nearby, Smith investigates the possibility of either building a pool in his own back yard or purchasing another home with a pool. In the current year he finds a new home with a pool and purchases it for $175,000. He then obtains some estimates and finds that it would cost approximately $20,000 to replace the pool in the home he has just purchased. He also obtains some real estate appraisals, which indicate that the existing pool increases the value of the home by only $8,000. During the current year, Smith also expends $500 in maintaining the pool and $1,800 in other medical expenses. What is the total amount of medical expenses he may claim in the current year? Smith's AGI for the year is $60,000.

- Sec. 213
- Reg. Sec. 1.213-1(e)(1)(iii)
- *Richard A. Polacsek,* 1981 PH T.C. Memo ¶81,569, 42 TCM 1289
- *Paul A. Lerew,* 1982 PH T.C. Memo ¶82,483, 44 TCM 918
- *Jacob H. Robbins,* 1982 PH T.C. Memo ¶82,565, 44 TCM 1254

CHAPTER

8

LOSSES AND BAD DEBTS

LEARNING OBJECTIVES

After studying this chapter, you should be able to

1. Identify transactions that may result in losses
2. Determine the proper classification for losses
3. Examine the tax treatment of passive losses
4. Identify and calculate the deduction for a casualty or theft loss
5. Compute the deduction for a bad debt
6. Compute a net operating loss deduction
7. Identify tax planning considerations for losses and bad debts
8. Identify compliance and procedural considerations for losses and bad debts

CHAPTER OUTLINE

Taxpayers often sustain losses on property they sell, exchange, or dispose of. If the taxpayer uses the property in a trade or business or holds the property for investment, the tax law generally provides a deduction for these losses. Noncorporate taxpayers may also take a limited deduction for losses on personal-use property that is either stolen or damaged in a casualty. However, in general, taxpayers may not deduct other types of losses on personal-use property (e.g., a loss they realize on the sale of a personal residence or an automobile that they use exclusively for personal purposes). Special rules allow taxpayers to take a deduction for losses they incur because of uncollectible business or nonbusiness debts. This chapter discusses the rules concerning the deductibility of these types of losses.

TRANSACTIONS THAT MAY RESULT IN LOSSES

OBJECTIVE 1

Identify transactions that may result in losses

For taxpayers to deduct a loss on property, the loss must be both *realized* and *recognized* for tax purposes. Generally, *realization* occurs in a completed (closed) transaction evidenced by an identifiable event such as a sale or exchange. This is referred to as the closed transaction doctrine. As a general rule, taxpayers who have realized losses on business or investment property may recognize such losses for tax purposes unless a specific provision holds otherwise (see pages I:8-6 and I:8-7).

EXAMPLE I:8-1 ▶ Capital Corporation purchased 500 shares of Data Corporation stock for $10,000 on February 22 of the current year. By October 31 of the same year, the price of the stock declines to $8,000. Even though Capital has suffered an economic loss on the stock, no realization event has occurred, and the corporation may not deduct the $2,000 loss. However, if Capital sells the stock for $8,000 on October 31, it realizes the loss for tax purposes in the current year. ◀

ADDITIONAL COMMENT

If property is used partly for business and partly for personal use, the loss attributable to the business portion is deductible but the loss on the personal-use portion is not unless the loss was sustained in a casualty.

KEY POINT

Anticipated losses, including those for which reserves have been established, are not deductible.

Losses on property may arise in a variety of transactions, including:

- Sale or exchange of the property
- Expropriation, seizure, confiscation, or condemnation of the property by a government
- Abandonment of the property
- Worthlessness of stock or securities
- Planned demolition of the property in order to construct other property in its place
- Destruction of the property by fire, storm, or other casualty
- Theft
- Deductible business expenses exceeding business income, giving rise to a net operating loss (NOL)

SALE OR EXCHANGE OF PROPERTY

The amount of the loss a taxpayer incurs in a sale or exchange of property equals the excess of the property's adjusted basis over the amount realized for the property.[1] The amount realized for the property equals the sum of the money received plus the fair market value (FMV) of any other property the taxpayer receives in the transaction. If the property sold or exchanged is subject to a mortgage or other liability, the amount realized by the taxpayer also includes the amount of the liability transferred to the buyer.[2] The treatment of any selling costs depends on the type of property sold or exchanged. If the property is inventory (i.e., property normally held for sale in the taxpayer's business), the selling costs are generally deductible expenses in the year in which the taxpayer incurs the expenses. However, if the sale involves property not normally held for sale by the taxpayer, the selling costs reduce the amount realized from the sale or exchange.

[1] Sec. 1001.

[2] *Beulah B. Crane v. CIR*, 35 AFTR 776, 47-1 USTC ¶9217 (USSC, 1947); and Reg. Sec. 1.1001-2.

EXAMPLE I:8-2 ▶ Four years ago, Boyer Corporation purchased a plot of land as an investment for $50,000. Unfortunately, local economic conditions worsened after Boyer, Inc. purchased the land and the land's value declined to $35,000. Boyer sells the property in the current year. At the time of the sale, the land is subject to a $10,000 mortgage. The terms of the sale are $25,000 paid in cash with the purchaser assuming the mortgage. Boyer also incurs $2,000 in sales commissions. The amount realized is $33,000 ($25,000 cash + $10,000 mortgage assumed by the buyer − $2,000 commissions). The loss on the sale is $17,000 ($50,000 basis − $33,000 amount realized). ◀

In general, taxpayers can only deduct losses they incur in the sale or exchange of property used in a trade or business or held for investment. Taxpayers cannot deduct losses they incur in the sale or exchange of personal-use property. Furthermore, the type of deduction a taxpayer may take for a loss realized on the sale or exchange of business or investment property depends on the type of property sold. For example, if inventory is sold, the loss is an ordinary loss. If the asset is a capital asset, the loss is a capital loss (see Chapter I:5). If the sale is of property used in a trade or business (a Sec. 1231 asset), the type of loss depends on the total net gain or loss realized on all the taxpayer's Sec. 1231 transactions during the year (see Chapter I:13).

EXPROPRIATED, SEIZED, CONFISCATED, OR CONDEMNED PROPERTY

A taxpayer may own property that the government expropriates, seizes, confiscates, or condemns. In these cases, the taxpayer incurs a deductible loss if the taxpayer used the property in a trade or business or held it for investment. The Tax Court has held that the confiscation, seizure, condemnation, or expropriation of property does not constitute a theft or a casualty. Rather, it is treated as a sale or exchange. Thus, no deductible loss arises if the seized property is personal-use property.[3] If the seized or condemned property is business or investment property, the classification of the loss depends on the type of property. (See the section in this chapter titled Classifying the Loss on the Taxpayer's Return.) A taxpayer may take the deduction only in the year in which the property is actually seized. Whether formal expropriation or nationalization occurs in a later year is irrelevant.[4] A taxpayer realizes gain if he or she receives compensation for the property in excess of its basis. Under certain circumstances, the taxpayer may defer this gain. (See Chapter I:12 for a discussion of the nonrecognition of gain in an involuntary conversion.)

ABANDONED PROPERTY

If a taxpayer's property becomes worthless or is not worth repairing in order to return the property to a serviceable condition, the taxpayer may simply abandon the property. If the property still has basis, the taxpayer realizes a loss. The taxpayer may not deduct such losses if the property is personal-use property. However, the taxpayer may deduct losses on business or investment property. Furthermore, because the abandonment of property is not a sale or exchange, the loss is an ordinary loss. The amount of the loss is the property's adjusted basis on the date of abandonment. The taxpayer bears the burden of proof to verify that the property was actually abandoned. If the property is depreciable (e.g., machinery and buildings), the taxpayer must actually physically abandon it to take the full amount of the loss.[5]

WORTHLESS SECURITIES

A taxpayer may take a deduction for securities that become completely worthless during the tax year.[6] Because the deduction is only available in the year the security actually becomes worthless, both the taxpayer and the IRS may have problems determining the year in which the security becomes worthless. A mere decline in value is not sufficient to create a deductible loss if the stock has any recognizable value. Furthermore, the sale of the stock for a nominal amount such as $1 does not necessarily establish that the stock became

[3] *William J. Powers*, 36 T.C. 1191 (1961) (See also *Gouhari v. U.S.*, 83 AFTR 2d 99-2726 (4th Cir., 1999).).

[4] Rev. Rul. 62-197, 1962-2 C.B. 66 as modified by Rev. Rul. 69-498, 1969-2 C.B. 31. (See also *Estate of Frank Fuchs v. CIR*, 24 AFTR 2d 69-5077, 69-2 USTC ¶9505 (2nd Cir., 1969)).

[5] Reg. Sec. 1.167(a)-8(a)(4).

[6] For this purpose, a *security* is defined in Sec. 165(g)(2) as stock in a corporation, the right to subscribe for or receive a share of stock in a corporation, or a bond, debenture, note, or certificate of indebtedness issued by a corporation or a government either in registered form or with interest coupons. Promissory notes issued by a corporation are generally not securities.

worthless in the year of the sale. The taxpayer must show that the security is completely worthless and that the security became worthless during the year.

Under Sec. 165, once the taxpayer determines the year of worthlessness, the taxpayer treats the loss as a loss from the sale of a capital asset on the last day of the tax year. Although this provision does not help in determining the year of worthlessness, it does establish a definite date for purposes of measuring whether the loss is short- or long-term. In some cases, this provision causes the loss to be long-term because it extends the date of worthlessness to the end of the year.

EXAMPLE I:8-3 ▶ On February 20 of the current year, Control Corporation enters into bankruptcy with no possibility for the shareholders to receive anything of value. Because the amount of Control Corporation's outstanding liabilities exceeds the FMV of its assets on that date, the stock of the corporation becomes worthless. Janet, a calendar-year taxpayer, owns 500 shares of Control's common stock, which she had purchased for $10,000 through her broker on June 17 of the prior year. Under Sec. 165(g), she treats the loss as having arisen from the sale of a capital asset on the last day of the current year. Thus, Janet incurs a $10,000 long-term capital loss because the holding period for the stock is more than one year. On the other hand, if Janet had received the stock directly from Control Corporation in exchange for either money or other property, and if certain other requirements are met, the stock may qualify as Sec. 1244 stock. Individuals who sustain losses on Sec. 1244 stock receive a limited amount of ordinary loss treatment rather than capital loss treatment. (See the discussion in this chapter under the heading "Losses on Sec. 1244 Stock.") ◀

Under certain circumstances, if a domestic corporation owns worthless securities of an affiliated corporation, the domestic corporation treats the loss as having arisen from the sale of a noncapital asset. This allows the corporation to treat the loss as an ordinary loss rather than as a capital loss.[7] For this exception to apply, the corporation must meet the following requirements:

- The domestic corporation that is deducting the loss must own at least 80% of the voting power of all classes of the affiliated corporation's stock and 80% of the total value of the affiliated corporation stock.
- More than 90% of the affiliated corporation's gross receipts for all its taxable years must be from nonpassive income.[8]

DEMOLITION OF PROPERTY

At times, taxpayers, intent on building their own facilities, purchase land with an existing structure that must first be removed. Taxpayers may also demolish a structure they currently use to construct new facilities. In both cases, taxpayers may not deduct any demolition costs or any loss sustained on account of the demolition. Instead, under Sec. 280B, taxpayers must add these amounts to the basis of the land on which the demolished structure previously stood.

CLASSIFYING THE LOSS ON THE TAXPAYER'S TAX RETURN

OBJECTIVE 2

Determine the proper classification for losses

If a loss is deductible, the taxpayer must determine whether the loss is an ordinary loss or a capital loss. In addition, individual taxpayers must also identify the deductible amount as either a deduction *for* or *from* AGI.

[7] As explained in Chapter I:5, the deductibility of capital losses is limited. For corporate taxpayers, capital losses must initially be offset against capital gains of the current year, and any excess loss is not deductible but may be carried back three years and forward for five years. Individuals may offset capital losses against capital gains and any excess loss is deductible up to $3,000 per year as an offset to ordinary income. Capital losses in excess of this amount for an individual are carried forward for an indefinite period. Thus, taxpayers generally prefer ordinary losses rather than capital losses.

[8] Sec. 165(g)(3). *Nonpassive income* includes all income other than royalties, rents, dividends, interest, annuities, and gains from the sale or exchange of stocks and securities.

ORDINARY VERSUS CAPITAL LOSS

Whether a deductible loss is ordinary or capital depends on the type of property involved and the transaction in which the taxpayer sustains the loss. To incur a capital loss, a sale or exchange of a capital asset must occur. If both elements (i.e., a sale or exchange and a capital asset) are not present, the deduction generally is an ordinary loss. In general, all assets *except* inventory, notes and accounts receivable, and depreciable property and land used in a trade or business (i.e., property, plant, and machinery) are classified as **capital assets.**[9]

Because a casualty is not a sale or exchange, the destruction of a capital asset in a casualty creates an ordinary rather than a capital loss. Likewise, a deductible loss realized on the abandonment of property is an ordinary loss because an abandonment is not a sale or exchange.

EXAMPLE I:8-4 ▶ On July 24 of the current year, Jermaine & Associates, LLP sells some investment property for $75,000. The property's adjusted basis is $85,000. The investment property is a capital asset. Jermaine realizes a $10,000 ($75,000 − $85,000) capital loss. If, instead, the property had been destroyed by fire and the partnership had received $75,000 in insurance proceeds, the $10,000 loss would have been an ordinary loss because a casualty is not a sale or exchange. ◀

BOOK-TAX DIFFERENCE

For book purposes, it makes no difference if a gain or loss is ordinary or capital. The full amount of the loss is deductible. However, because corporations may not deduct a capital loss in excess of its capital gains for the year, a book-tax timing (temporary) difference may arise, making an M-1 or M-3 adjustment necessary.

Certain transactions, though not actually constituting a sale or exchange, receive sale or exchange treatment. For example, as mentioned previously, if a security owned by an individual investor becomes worthless during the year, the individual treats the loss as a loss from the sale of a capital asset on the last day of the tax year, even though no sale actually occurs. Thus, the loss is a capital loss. Likewise, the taxpayer will treat a seizure or condemnation of property as a sale or exchange.

Section 1231 Property. Whether a loss on a particular transaction is treated as a capital loss may also depend on the gains and losses the taxpayer reports from other property transactions for the tax year. For instance, under Sec. 1231, taxpayers must net certain gains and losses together. If the Sec. 1231 gains exceed the Sec. 1231 losses for the year, the taxpayer treats the net gain as a long-term capital gain. However, if the losses equal or exceed the gains, both the gains and the losses are treated as ordinary. **Section 1231 property** includes real or depreciable property used in a trade or business and held for more than one year. (See Chapter I:13 for a discussion of the netting procedure under Sec. 1231.)

Losses on Sec. 1244 Stock. Taxpayers generally recognize capital gain or loss on the sale of stock or securities. For individuals, the tax law provides an exception for losses from the sale or worthlessness of small business corporation (Sec. 1244) stock. Individuals may deduct these losses as ordinary losses up to a maximum of $50,000 per tax year ($100,000 for married taxpayers filing a joint return). Any remaining loss for the year is a capital loss.

To qualify the loss as ordinary under Sec. 1244, the following requirements must be met:

- The stock must be owned by an individual or a partnership.
- The stock must have been originally issued by the corporation to the individual or to a partnership in which an individual is a partner.[10]
- The stock must be stock in a domestic (U.S.) corporation.
- The taxpayer must have received the stock in exchange for cash or property (other than stock or securities) that the taxpayer contributed to the corporation. Stock issued to the taxpayer for services rendered is not eligible for Sec. 1244 treatment.

---

[9] Sec. 1221. Certain other exceptions also exist. The definition of a capital asset is more fully examined in Chapter I:5.

[10] Stock received in certain reorganizations of corporations in exchange for Sec. 1244 stock is also considered Sec. 1244 stock. Section 1244 does not apply to stock that the individual has received through other means such as purchase in a secondary market, exchange, gift, or inheritance.

- The corporation must not have derived over 50% of its gross receipts from passive income sources during the five tax years immediately preceding the year of sale or worthlessness.[11]
- The amount of money and property contributed to both capital and paid-in surplus may not exceed $1 million at the time the corporation issues the stock.

Note that the last test listed above occurs when the corporation *actually issues the stock*. As long as the corporation's capital and paid-in surplus does not exceed $1 million at the time the stock was issued, the individual taxpayer may still report an ordinary loss on the stock even if the corporation has capital and paid-in surplus in excess of the $1 million limit at the time the loss is realized.

STOP & THINK

Question: Tony, a single taxpayer, incorporated Waffle, Inc. three years ago by contributing $70,000 in exchange for the stock. Waffle owns and operates a small restaurant. Unfortunately, Waffle's business never really became profitable. Tony has been trying to sell the Waffle stock since July of last year, but because the corporation had become insolvent, he couldn't find any buyers. In February of the current year, Waffle was judged to be bankrupt. Tony didn't receive anything for his stock. What issues should Tony's tax advisor address with regard to the Waffle, Inc. stock?

Solution: Tony's tax advisor must determine (1) the amount of any realized loss, (2) the year in which the loss is recognized, and (3) the character of the realized loss. The Waffle, Inc. stock is considered a security under Sec. 165. Whenever a security becomes completely worthless and it is determined that the owner will receive nothing for it, the owner realizes a loss to the extent of the security's basis ($70,000). The loss is deemed to be realized in the year in which the security becomes worthless. While the bankruptcy court ruled the stock to be worthless in February of the current year, the fact that Tony could not find any buyers last year because the corporation was insolvent may indicate that the stock really became worthless last year. This determination is important because Tony must recognize the loss in the year in which the stock becomes worthless. Furthermore, the stock is deemed to become worthless on the last day of that year. Since Tony received the stock directly from the corporation in exchange for contributed cash, Waffle, Inc.'s gross receipts are from business operations, and the capitalization at the time the stock was issued is less than $1 million, the stock qualifies as Sec. 1244 stock. Thus, $50,000 of the loss is characterized as ordinary loss. The remaining $20,000 is a long-term capital loss.

DISALLOWANCE POSSIBILITIES

The tax law may disallow or defer losses incurred in certain transactions and activities. Some of these transactions include:

- Transfers of property to a controlled corporation in exchange for stock of the corporation (see the discussion in Chapter C:2 of *Prentice Hall's Federal Taxation: Corporations, Partnerships, Estates & Trusts* text and Chapter C:2 of the *Comprehensive* volume)
- Exchanges of property for other property considered to be like-kind to the property given up (see the discussion in Chapter I:12)
- Property sold to certain related parties (see the discussion in Chapter I:6)
- Wash sale transactions (see the discussion in Chapter I:6)
- Losses limited because the losses exceed the amount for which the taxpayer is at risk (see the discussion in Chapter C:9 of *Prentice Hall's Federal Taxation: Corporations, Partnerships, Estates & Trusts* text and Chapter C:9 of the *Comprehensive* volume)

In addition, the passive loss rules discussed below may limit the amount of losses that individuals and certain corporations may deduct.

Topic Review I:8-1 contains a summary of loss transactions.

---

[11] For this purpose, passive income sources include royalties, rents, dividends, interest, annuities, and sales or exchanges of stocks and securities. If the corporation has not been in existence for a full five years, the gross receipts test is applied to the shorter period. If the corporation has not been in existence for an entire taxable year, the test is applied to the time period up to the date of the loss (see Sec. 1244(c)(2)).

TOPIC REVIEW I:8-1

Transactions That May Result in Losses

Type of Transaction	Result
Sale or exchange	Taxpayers may not deduct a loss on personal-use property. The tax treatment of a loss on business or investment property depends on the type of property. Losses on capital assets result in capital losses. Losses on Sec. 1231 assets are subject to the Sec. 1231 netting rules discussed in Chapter I:13.
Seizure, expropriation, confiscation, or condemnation	Treated as a sale or exchange.
Abandonment	Not treated as a sale or exchange. No deduction is allowed for a loss on personal-use property. Business or investment property is given ordinary loss treatment.
Worthless securities	Treated as a loss from the sale of the securities on the last day of the year in which the securities become worthless. This generally will result in a capital loss. However, if the requirements of Sec. 1244 are met, an individual taxpayer may treat at least part of the loss as an ordinary loss. (See Sec. 1244 stock below.) A loss realized by a corporation on worthless securities of an affiliated corporation results in an ordinary loss.
Demolition	No deductible loss is allowed. Instead, losses and costs of demolition are added to the basis of the land where the demolished structure was located.
Sec. 1244 stock	Individual taxpayers may take an ordinary loss of up to $50,000 per year ($100,000 for married filing jointly) for losses realized on qualified Sec. 1244 stock. The remaining loss is capital. The stock must have been originally issued to the individual for property or cash, and the corporation must meet the requirements to be a small business corporation.

Passive losses

OBJECTIVE 3

Examine the tax treatment of passive losses

Before 1987, taxpayers were able to reduce their income tax liability on their salary or on income from business or investment activities with deductions, losses, and credits arising in other activities. Thus, taxpayers often invested in activities, called **tax shelters**, that would spin off tax deductions and credits. Many of these tax shelters were simply *passive investments* because they did not require the taxpayer's involvement or participation. In some situations, tax shelters had real economic substance, i.e., a taxpayer's economic return in this type of shelter was not based solely on the tax benefits that the activity generated. In many cases, however, tax shelters had no real economic substance other than the creation of deductions and credits that enabled taxpayers to reduce, and sometimes eliminate, the income tax liability from their other business activities. To prevent these perceived and real abuses, Congress enacted Sec. 469, which restricts the current use of losses and credits that arise in rental activities and in other activities in which the taxpayer does not materially participate. These activities constitute passive activities. (See the "Definition of a Passive Activity" section in this chapter for an extended discussion of what constitutes a passive activity.)

HISTORICAL NOTE

Before the passive activity loss limits became effective in 1987, most tax shelters were concentrated in the areas of real estate, oil and gas, equipment leasing, farming, motion pictures, timber, and research and development. Many tax shelters took advantage of liberal depreciation rules during the early 1980s such as the rapid depreciation of real estate over a 15-year period.

COMPUTATION OF PASSIVE LOSSES AND CREDITS

In enacting the passive loss rules, Congress did not want to prevent taxpayers from currently deducting or using losses and credits generated in active business endeavors of the taxpayer. At the same time, Congress realized that certain investments (such as investments that generate interest or dividend income) normally give rise to taxable income, which could itself be sheltered by losses and credits that arise in other passive activities. Thus, Sec. 469 requires certain taxpayers to classify their income into three categories: *active income* (such as wages, salaries, and active business income), *portfolio (or investment) income,* and *passive income.* **Portfolio income** includes dividends, interest, annuities, and royalties (and allocable expenses and interest expense) not derived in the ordinary

ADDITIONAL COMMENT

Even though portfolio income and passive income from passive activities are calculated separately for purposes of the regular income tax, in general they are added together in calculating net investment income, which is subject to the 3.8% Net Investment Income Tax imposed as part of the Affordable Care Act.

course of a trade or business. Portfolio income also includes gains and losses on property that produces these types of income if the disposition of the property does not occur in the ordinary course of business.[12] Portfolio income becomes part of net investment income, which is used in computing the deduction limit for investment interest expense. (See Chapter I:7 for a discussion of the investment interest expense limitation.)

Passive Income and Losses. Taxpayers compute income and loss in the passive category separately for each passive activity in which they have invested. In general, for any tax year, a taxpayer may use losses generated in one passive activity to offset income from other passive activities, but may not use them to offset either active or portfolio income.

EXAMPLE I:8-5 ▶ During the year, Kasi, a CPA, reports $100,000 of active business income from his CPA practice. He also owns two passive activities. From activity A, he earns $10,000 of income, and from activity B, he incurs a $15,000 loss. Kasi may use $10,000 of the loss from activity B to offset the $10,000 of income from activity A. However, Kasi may not deduct the $5,000 excess loss from activity B in the current year, even though he has $100,000 of active business income. ◀

CARRYOVERS

KEY POINT

Excess passive activity losses are not "lost" because they can be carried over to future years.

A taxpayer carries over disallowed passive activity losses indefinitely and treats them as losses allocable to that specific passive activity in the following tax years. The taxpayer may use these losses, known as **suspended losses,** to offset passive activity income of the subsequent year, but generally may not offset other types of income. If a taxpayer has invested in several passive activities, and for the year some of the activities generate income while others generate losses, the loss carried over for each loss activity is a pro rata portion of the total passive loss for the year.

EXAMPLE I:8-6 ▶ Tammy reports the following income and loss for the year:

Salary	$200,000
Loss from activity X	(40,000)
Loss from activity Y	(10,000)
Income from activity Z	30,000

X, Y, and Z are all passive activities. The losses generated in activities X and Y offset the income from activity Z, but none of the salary income is offset. Thus, Tammy has a net passive loss for the year of $20,000 ($40,000 + $10,000 – $30,000), which must be carried over to subsequent years. The amount of the carryover attributable to each activity is as follows:

Activity X: $\$20{,}000 \times \frac{\$40{,}000}{\$50{,}000} = \$16{,}000$

Activity Y: $\$20{,}000 \times \frac{\$10{,}000}{\$50{,}000} = \$\ 4{,}000$ ◀

Taxable Disposition of Interest in a Passive Activity. When a taxpayer disposes of a passive activity in a taxable transaction, the taxpayer can compute the economic gain or loss generated by the activity and can deduct the suspended losses of the activity against other income. However, the amount of the total net economic loss from the asset disposed of must first offset any passive income for the year from other passive activities.[13]

EXAMPLE I:8-7 ▶ During the current year, Pam realizes $6,000 of taxable income from activity A, $1,000 of loss from activity B, and $8,000 of taxable income from activity C. All three activities are passive activities with regard to Pam. In addition, $30,000 of passive losses from activity C are carried over from prior years. During the current year, Pam sells activity C for a $15,000 taxable gain. Pam reports salary income of $90,000 for the year. Because Pam sells activity C in a fully taxable transaction, Pam may deduct $2,000 of loss against the salary income:

[12] Sec. 469(e)(1). Gain or loss on property dispositions occurring in the ordinary course of business is either passive or active business income, depending on the taxpayer's level of involvement (i.e., material participation) in the activity.

[13] Sec. 469(g). Income from the activity for prior years may also be taken into account in arriving at the net income from all passive activities for the year if it is necessary to prevent avoidance of the passive loss rules.

Income for the year from C	$ 8,000	
Gain from the sale of C	15,000	
Suspended losses from C	(30,000)	
Total loss from C		($7,000)
Income for the year from A	$ 6,000	
Loss for the year from B	(1,000)	5,000
Pam's deduction against salary income		($2,000) ◀

BOOK-TAX DIFFERENCE

Since passive losses are not limited under financial accounting rules, the limitation and carryover of passive losses for tax purposes will create a timing (temporary) difference between book and tax. However, many taxpayers subject to the passive loss rules are individuals who do not use financial accounting rules.

If the taxpayer sells the passive activity to a related party, he or she may not deduct the suspended loss until the related party sells the activity to a nonrelated person. The definition of *related persons* includes spouse, brothers and sisters, ancestors, lineal descendants, and corporations or partnerships in which the individual has a greater than 50% ownership.[14]

Although the death of a taxpayer is not a taxable disposition of the asset, some of the suspended losses may be deductible when a taxpayer dies. The amount of the deduction allowed is the amount by which the suspended losses exceed the increase in basis of the property. The decedent's final income tax return generally includes the deduction for these losses. Any suspended losses up to the amount of the increase in basis will never be deductible.[15]

EXAMPLE I:8-8 ▶ At the time that John died, he owned passive activity property with an adjusted basis of $20,000 and a FMV of $35,000. Suspended losses attributable to the property totaled $25,000. Because the increase in the basis of the property is $15,000 ($35,000 − $20,000), $15,000 of the suspended losses are lost. However, $10,000 ($25,000 suspended losses − $15,000 increase in basis) of the suspended losses are deductible on John's final income tax return. ◀

In general, the suspended losses of a passive activity become deductible only when the taxpayer completely disposes of his or her interest in the activity. However, in Treasury Reg. 1.469-4(g) the government has stated that taxpayers may treat the disposition of a substantial part of an activity as the disposition of a separate activity. This treatment is only available, however, if the taxpayer can establish with reasonable certainty the amount of income, deductions, credits, and suspended losses and credits that are allocable to that part of the activity.

Carryovers from a Former Passive Activity. The determination of whether an activity is passive with respect to a taxpayer must be made annually. Thus, an activity that was previously passive may not be passive with respect to the taxpayer for the current year. This is called a **former passive activity**. A taxpayer may deduct any loss carryover from a former passive activity against the current year's income of that activity even though the activity is not a passive activity in the current year. However, any suspended loss in excess of the activity's income for the year is still subject to the carryover limitations. Because the activity is no longer passive for the year, the current year's loss is deductible against active business income.

EXAMPLE I:8-9 ▶ Kris owns activity A, which, for the immediately preceding tax year, was considered a passive activity with regard to Kris. $10,000 in losses from activity A were disallowed and carried over to the current year. Because of Kris' increased involvement in activity A in the current year, it is not considered passive with regard to Kris for the current year. During the current year, activity A generates a $5,000 loss. During the current year, Kris also has an investment in activity B, a passive activity. Her share of activity B's income is $7,000. Kris reports $60,000 in salary. Because for the current year activity A is not a passive activity, the $5,000 current year loss is fully deductible against her salary. However, the $10,000 loss carryover from the prior year is deductible only against the $7,000 of income from passive activity B. The $3,000 ($10,000 − $7,000) excess is carried over to the subsequent year. ◀

[14] Other relationships described in Secs. 267(b) and 707(b) are also considered related parties for this purpose.

[15] Sec. 469(g)(2). For 2011 and later the basis of inherited property is its FMV on the date of death (see Chapter I:5).

Credits. A taxpayer may only use tax credits generated in a passive activity against the portion of the taxpayer's tax liability that is attributable to passive income. The taxpayer determines this amount by comparing the tax liability on all income for the year with the tax liability on all income excluding the passive income.

EXAMPLE I:8-10 ▶ Dale invests in a passive activity. For the year, he must report $10,000 of taxable income from the passive activity. Dale's share of tax credits generated by the passive activity is $5,000. Assume Dale's precredit tax liability on all income (including the $10,000 from the passive activity) is $25,000, and his precredit tax liability on all income excluding the passive activity income is $22,000. He may use only $3,000 ($25,000 − $22,000) of the tax credits generated by the passive activity. Dale must carry forward the remaining $2,000 of tax credits and can use them in a subsequent year against the portion of his tax liability attributable to his passive activity income in that year. However, these credits may never offset any portion of the tax liability attributable to nonpassive activities. (See Chapter I:14 for a discussion of credits and their carryovers.) ◀

DEFINITION OF A PASSIVE ACTIVITY

The term *passive activity* includes any trade or business in which the taxpayer does not materially participate as well as any rental activity. An important exception applies to a rental activity that is considered to be a *real property trade or business*. This exception is discussed below on page 8–14.[16] The definition of a passive activity is based on two critical elements: an identification of exactly what constitutes an activity and a determination of whether the taxpayer has materially participated in that activity.

Identification of an Activity. Identification of the activity becomes critical for several reasons. (1) The determination of whether a taxpayer materially participates in an activity is determined separately for each activity. (2) A taxpayer may deduct suspended losses of a passive activity when the taxpayer completely terminates his or her ownership of the activity. (3) As explained in a subsequent section of this chapter, taxpayers may deduct currently up to $25,000 of passive losses from rental real estate activities. Thus, taxpayers must not combine losses from passive business and rental real estate activities into one activity.

The way taxpayers combine or separate operations into activities can significantly impact the deductibility of losses generated by the activities. Taxpayers may treat one or more activities as a single activity only if they constitute an "appropriate economic unit."[17] Although the taxpayer makes this determination by examining all the relevant facts and circumstances, the following factors receive the greatest weight:

- Similarities and differences in the types of business,
- The extent of common control,
- The extent of common ownership,
- The geographical location, and
- Any interdependencies between the operations (i.e., the extent to which the operations purchase or sell goods between each other, have the same customers, are accounted for with a single set of books, etc.).

A taxpayer may treat more than one operation as a single activity, even if all of these factors do not apply. Furthermore, a taxpayer may use any reasonable method of applying the relevant facts and circumstances in grouping the activities.

EXAMPLE I:8-11 ▶ Carla owns a bakery and a movie theater in each of two different shopping malls, one located in Baltimore and the other in Philadelphia. Depending on other relevant facts and circumstances, a reasonable grouping of the operations may result in any of the following:

[16] Secs. 469(c)(1) and (c)(2). Sec. 469(c)(6) also includes investment (production of income) activities under Sec. 212 as a passive activity. Section 469(j)(8) defines the term *rental activity* as any activity where payments are principally for the use of tangible property. Pursuant to the Regulations, there are six exceptions to this general rule. These exceptions include (1) providing the use of tangible property where the average period of customer use is seven days or less, (2) the average period of customer use is 30 days or less and significant personal services are provided by the owner in conjunction with the use of the property, (3) extraordinary personal services are provided by the owner in conjunction with the use of the property, (4) the rental of the property is incidental to a nonrental activity of the taxpayer, (5) the property is customarily made available during defined business hours for nonexclusive use by various customers, or (6) the property is provided for use in a nonrental activity conducted by a partnership, S corporation, or joint venture in which the taxpayer owns an interest. The details of these exceptions are beyond the scope of this text. (See Reg. Sec. 1.469-1(e)(3)(iii).)

[17] Reg. Sec. 1.469-4.

- One activity involving all four operations
- Two activities: a bakery activity and a theater activity
- Two activities: a Baltimore activity and a Philadelphia activity
- Four activities ◄

Under the Treasury Regulations, taxpayers apparently have some degree of flexibility in determining the grouping into activities of different business operations. However, once taxpayers establish the activities, they must be consistent in grouping these activities in subsequent years unless material changes in the facts and circumstances clearly make the groupings inappropriate.

In identifying separate activities, taxpayers generally may not group rental operations with trade or business operations. However, a combination is allowed if either the rental operation is insubstantial in relation to the business operation or vice versa. Unfortunately, the Treasury Regulations do not give any guidance with regard to what is insubstantial. Furthermore, because of the special rules dealing with real estate rental activities (explained later in this chapter), the taxpayer may not combine rental activities involving real estate with rental activities involving personal property.

EXAMPLE I:8-12 ► Sandy owns a building in which she (1) operates a restaurant and (2) leases out apartments to tenants. Generally the tenants sign apartment leases of one year or longer. Of the total gross income derived from the building, 15% comes from the apartment rentals and 85% comes from the restaurant operation. If the apartment rental operation is insubstantial in relation to the restaurant operation, the taxpayer may combine the two into one activity. If it is not insubstantial, the two operations are considered two separate activities: a business activity and a rental real estate activity. ◄

Partnerships and S corporations (pass-through entities) must identify their business and rental activities by applying these rules at the partnership or S corporation level and then must report the results of their operations by activity to the partners or shareholders. Each partner or shareholder must then take the results from these activities and, using these same rules, combine them where appropriate with operations conducted either directly or through other pass-through entities. In fact, in practice taxpayers often hold real estate passive activities as either partnerships or S corporations.

Material Participation. Once each activity is identified, taxpayers must determine whether the activity is passive or active. If the taxpayer does not **materially participate** in the activity, it is deemed to be a passive activity with respect to that taxpayer. Pursuant to the Treasury Regulations,[18] taxpayers materially participate in an activity if they meet at least one of the following tests:

- The individual participates in the activity for more than 500 hours during the year.
- The individual's participation in the activity for the year constitutes substantially all of the participation in the activity by all individuals, including individuals who do not own any interest in the activity.
- The individual participates in the activity for more than 100 hours during the year, and that participation is more than any other individual's participation for the year (including participation by individuals who do not own any interest in the activity).
- The individual participates in "significant participation activities" for an aggregate of more than 500 hours during the year.[19] Thus, an individual who spends over 100 hours each in several separate significant participation activities may aggregate the time spent in these activities in order to meet the 500-hour test.
- The individual materially participated in the activity in any five years during the immediately preceding ten taxable years. These five years need not be consecutive.

[18] Temp. Reg. Sec. 1.469-5T(a).

[19] A significant participation activity is a trade or business in which the individual participates for more than 100 hours during the year but for which the individual does not meet the material participation test alone (i.e., with respect to that activity, the individual does not meet one of the other material participation tests). (See Temp. Reg. Sec. 1.469-5T(c).)

- The individual materially participated in the activity for any three years preceding the year in question, and the activity is a personal service activity.[20]
- The individual participates in the activity on a regular, continuous, and substantial basis during the year, taking into account all the relevant facts and circumstances.

ADDITIONAL COMMENT

A taxpayer may be a material participant in an activity one year and a passive investor the next year. A taxpayer must satisfy one of the material participation tests each year to be treated as a material participant for that year.

Note that the first four tests are based on the number of hours the taxpayer spent in the activity during the current year. The fifth and sixth tests are based on the material participation of the taxpayer in prior years and are designed to prevent taxpayers from asserting that retirement income is passive and offsetting it with passive losses from tax shelters. To determine whether a taxpayer materially participates in an activity, the participation of the taxpayer's spouse is also taken into account.

Limited Partnerships. A limited partner has limited liability for his or her investment in the partnership and normally is not actively involved in the business of the partnership. As a consequence, a limited partner generally does not meet the material participation test and the limited partner's investment is treated as passive. Thus, most income and deductions passed through to a limited partner from a limited partnership are passive. However, a limited partner can meet the material participation test if the individual meets either the 500 hour test or the fifth or sixth tests above (prior year tests).

Working Interest in an Oil and Gas Property. A working interest is an interest that is responsible for the cost of development or operation of the oil and gas property. This type of interest in an oil and gas property is not a passive activity as long as the taxpayer's liability in the interest is not a limited interest. Thus, even though a taxpayer may not materially participate in the activity, the passive loss rules do not apply. This is so even if the taxpayer holds the interest through an entity such as a partnership.

TAXPAYERS SUBJECT TO PASSIVE LOSS RULES

The passive loss limitation rules apply to:

- Individuals, estates, trusts
- Any closely held C corporation
- Any personal service corporation
- Certain publicly traded partnerships

Because the income and losses of partnerships and S corporations are taxed directly to the partners and shareholders, the passive loss rules do not apply to these entities.[21] Rather, the passive loss limitations apply directly at the partner or shareholder level. Thus, the situation may arise where one partner or shareholder is subject to the passive loss rules with regard to an activity conducted by the partnership or S corporation while other partners or shareholders are not.

Generally, regular corporations (i.e., C corporations) are not subject to the passive loss limitation rules. However, to prevent certain individuals from avoiding the passive loss rules through the use of a regular corporation, the passive loss rules do apply to closely held C corporations and personal service corporations.

ADDITIONAL COMMENT

Because a closely held C corporation's passive losses may offset its income from active business operations, some tax professionals advise their clients to transfer their investments in passive activities that generate passive losses to their profitable corporations.

Closely Held C Corporations. The passive loss rules apply to closely held C corporations but only on a limited basis. A **closely held C corporation** is a C corporation where more than 50% of the stock is owned by five or fewer individuals at any time during the last half of the corporation's taxable year.[22] Without this special rule involving

---

[20] A personal service activity involves rendering personal services in the fields of health, law, engineering, architecture, accounting, actuarial science, performing arts, or consulting. It also includes any other trade or business in which capital is not a material income-producing factor. (See Temp. Reg. Sec. 1.469-5T(d).)

[21] An S corporation is a corporation that has elected for federal income tax purposes to be treated as a flow-through entity. Thus, the income or losses and separately stated items of an S corporation flow through to the shareholders and are reported on their individual tax returns.

[22] Secs. 469(j)(1), 465(a)(1)(B), and 542(a)(2).

closely held C corporations, taxpayers would be motivated to transfer their investments (both portfolio investments and passive activities) to a C corporation where the portfolio income could be offset by the corporation's passive losses. Thus, as applied to a closely held C corporation, the passive loss rules prevent passive activity losses from offsetting portfolio income. However, a closely held C corporation's passive losses may offset its income from active business operations.

EXAMPLE I:8-13 ▶ All of the outstanding stock of Delta Corporation is owned equally by individuals Allen and Beth. During the current year, Delta generates $15,000 taxable income from its active business operations. It also earns $10,000 of interest and dividends from investments and reports a $30,000 loss from a passive activity. Because Delta is a closely held C corporation, the $15,000 of taxable income from the active business is offset by $15,000 of the passive loss. However, the $10,000 of portfolio income may not be offset. Thus, for the current year, Delta reports $10,000 of taxable income from its portfolio income and has a $15,000 passive loss carryover. ◀

Personal Service Corporation. A **personal service corporation** (PSC) is a regular C corporation whose principal activity is the performance of personal services that are substantially performed by owner-employees.[23] However, a corporation is not a PSC unless owner-employees own more than 10% of the value of the stock. In contrast with a closely held C corporation, the passive loss limitation rules apply in their entirety to a PSC. If a corporation is both a PSC and a closely held C corporation, the more restrictive rules for PSCs apply. Thus, a PSC cannot offset its active business income or portfolio income with losses from its passive activities.

Material participation by PSCs and closely held C corporations. Special rules apply for determining whether closely held C corporations or PSCs materially participate in an activity. These corporations materially participate in an activity only if one or more shareholders who own more than 50% in value of the outstanding stock materially participate in the activity. In addition, a closely held C corporation (other than a PSC) materially participates in an activity if it meets *all* of the following tests with regard to an activity:

1. A substantial portion of the services of at least one full-time employee is in the active management of the activity.
2. A substantial portion of the services of at least three full-time nonowner employees is directly related to the activity.
3. The Sec. 162 business deductions of the activity exceed 15% of the activity's gross income for the period.[24]

Publicly Traded Partnerships. In many cases, the tax law provisions for corporations apply to publicly traded partnerships (PTP). For purposes of the passive loss rules, a PTP is defined as any partnership if interests in the partnership are either traded on an established securities market or readily tradable on a secondary market.[25] If the corporate tax provisions apply to a PTP, the passive loss rules generally do not apply. However, if a PTP meets certain gross income requirements, the partnership tax provisions may still apply, causing its items of income, loss, and credit to flow through to the partners.[26] If this is the case, the passive loss rules apply at the partner level separately to the flow through items from each PTP. Thus, partners treat losses from a PTP as separate from any other type of income (passive, active business, or portfolio) and separate from any income from

---

[23] Secs. 469(j)(2) and 269A(b)(1). For this purpose any employee who owns any stock of the corporation is an owner-employee. This stock ownership is determined by using the Sec. 318 constructive ownership rules as modified by Sec. 469(j)(2).

[24] Secs. 469(h)(4) and 465(c)(7). Tests 1 and 2 must be met for the 12-month period ending on the last day of the tax year. Test 3 must be met for the tax year. Furthermore, the Sec. 404 deductions are also included in the 15% of gross income test.

[25] Sec. 469(k)(2). (See Chapter C:10 of *Prentice Hall's Federal Taxation: Corporations, Partnerships, Estates & Trusts* and Chapter C:10 of the *Comprehensive* volume for a definition and discussion of publicly traded partnerships.)

[26] Sec. 7704(c). For the taxable year and all preceding years beginning after Dec. 31, 1987, at least 90% of the PTP's gross income consists of dividends, interest, real property rents, income from certain gas, oil, mineral or timber activities, and gains from the sale of real estate or certain capital assets. Furthermore, certain other PTPs may also elect to continue to be treated as a partnership rather than as a corporation.

other PTPs. Partners can only carry these losses forward and offset them against income generated by that particular PTP in a subsequent year. Furthermore, a PTP loss may not offset any portfolio income that the PTP might generate. Any net income from PTPs is portfolio income.

EXAMPLE I:8-14 ▶ Mark owns interests in partnerships A and B, both of which are PTPs that are treated as partnerships. During the current year, Mark's share of the income from A is $2,000. Mark's share of B's loss is $1,200. B also generates some portfolio income. Mark's share of B's portfolio income is $800. The $1,200 loss from B may not offset any of B's $800 portfolio income. Furthermore, it may not offset any of the $2,000 income from A. The $2,000 income from A is treated as portfolio income. Thus, Mark reports $2,800 portfolio income and has a $1,200 suspended loss from B. In a subsequent year, Mark's share of any income from B can be offset by the $1,200 of suspended loss that is carried forward. ◀

A partner may deduct suspended losses from a PTP in the year the partner disposes of his or her interest in the PTP. Partners do not recognize a loss in the year that the PTP itself sells a passive activity.

REAL ESTATE BUSINESSES

In general, rental activities are considered passive activities. However, the passive activity loss rules do not apply to certain taxpayers who are involved in real property trades or businesses. Instead, these activities are treated as active businesses. A *real property trade or business* involves the development, redevelopment, construction, reconstruction, acquisition, conversion, rental, operation, management, leasing, or brokering of real property.

This exception only applies to a taxpayer if he or she meets both of the following requirements:

- ▶ More than one-half of the personal services the taxpayer performs in all trades or businesses during the year are in real property trades or businesses in which the taxpayer materially participates.
- ▶ The taxpayer performs more than 750 hours of work during the taxable year in real property trades or businesses in which the taxpayer materially participates.

In meeting these tests, personal services a taxpayer renders in his or her capacity as an employee are not treated as performed in real property trades or businesses unless the employee owns at least 5% of the employer. Furthermore, for married taxpayers filing a joint return, the exception applies only if one of the spouses separately meets both requirements. The time spent in the activity by both spouses counts toward the determination of whether or not the taxpayer meets the material participation test.

EXAMPLE I:8-15 ▶ Anwar and Anya are married and file a joint return. They own four large apartment complexes which they manage themselves. Neither is employed elsewhere. During the current year, Anya spent 500 hours keeping records and corresponding with tenants. Anwar spent 700 hours during the year maintaining and repairing the apartments. Even though all of Anya and Anwar's personal services are connected with a real property trade or business in which they materially participate, this rental activity is considered passive because neither Anwar nor Anya alone spends more than 750 hours doing services related to the rental activity. ◀

For a closely held C corporation to meet this rental real estate business exception, the corporation must derive more than one-half of its gross receipts from real property businesses in which it materially participates.

Any deduction allowed under the previously discussed exception for taxpayers involved in real property trades or businesses is not considered in determining the taxpayer's AGI for purposes of the phase-out of the $25,000 deduction available for taxpayers who actively participate in a rental real estate activity. (See the following section in this chapter for a discussion of the $25,000 active participation exception.)

KEY POINT

Up to $25,000 of passive losses attributable to rental real estate can be deducted each year against income from nonpassive sources such as salary, interest, and dividends.

OTHER RENTAL REAL ESTATE ACTIVITIES

Many rental real estate activities are not considered rental real estate businesses and are, therefore, subject to the passive loss rules. However, if an individual taxpayer meets certain requirements, the taxpayer still may deduct against other income up to $25,000 of annual losses from these passive rental real estate activities. To meet this exception, an individual must do both of the following:

- *Actively* participate in the activity
- Own at least 10% of the value of the activity for the entire tax year

Additionally, in order to take a deduction in the current year for a loss sustained in a prior year, Section 469(i) requires the taxpayer to actively participate in the activity during both years.

KEY POINT

Active participation is different from *material participation,* and is a lesser standard of involvement.

Active Participation. A taxpayer can achieve *active participation*, as opposed to material participation, without regular, continuous, and material involvement in the activity and without meeting any of the material participation tests. However, the taxpayer still must participate in making management decisions or arranging for others to provide services in a significant and bona fide sense. This includes approving new tenants, deciding on rental terms, approving expenditures, and other similar decisions. Taxpayers may achieve active participation even if they hire a rental agent and others to provide the services. However, a lessor under a net lease arrangement generally does not achieve active participation. Additionally, a limited partner generally cannot actively participate in any activity of a limited partnership.

Limitation on Deduction of Rental Real Estate Loss. Taxpayers must first apply rental real estate losses against other net passive income for the year. Taxpayers may then reduce their portfolio or active business income by up to $25,000. However, the tax law requires reduction of the $25,000 amount by 50% of the taxpayer's AGI in excess of $100,000.[27] For this purpose, AGI does not include any passive activity loss or any loss allowable to taxpayers who materially participate in real property trades or businesses (e.g., a real estate developer). Thus, if a taxpayer has AGI of $150,000 or more, the rental real estate losses are not eligible for the $25,000 deduction and are aggregated with the taxpayer's other passive losses.

ADDITIONAL COMMENT

In calculating AGI to determine the amount of the $25,000 that is phased out, married taxpayers filing joint returns must include the income of both spouses. This provision results in a marriage penalty where both spouses have income.

EXAMPLE I:8-16 ► During the current year, Penny, a married individual who files a joint return, reports the following items of income and loss:

Salary income	$120,000
Activity A (passive)	15,000
Activity B (nonbusiness rental real estate)	(50,000)

Penny owns over 10% and actively participates in activity B. Her AGI for the year is as follows:

Salary		$120,000
Passive income from activity A	$15,000	
Minus: Passive loss from activity B ($50,000, but limited to $15,000)	(15,000)	–0–
Minus: Maximum rental real estate loss (from activity B)	$25,000	
Reduced by phase-out: [($120,000 − $100,000) × 0.50]	(10,000)	
Deductible amount (but not to exceed actual loss)		(15,000)
AGI		$105,000

Penny may deduct $30,000 of the loss from activity B during the year ($15,000 as an offset to the passive income from activity A + $15,000 deductible against portfolio or active business income). Penny has $20,000 ($50,000 – $30,000) of suspended passive losses from activity B that are carried over to the following year. ◄

[27] This provision which allowed taxpayers to either (1) take a current deduction equal to 50% of certain qualified commercial revitalization expenditures on certain buildings, or (2) amortize the qualified expenditures over a 10 year period only applied to property placed into service before January 1, 2010. Even though this provision has been repealed, if a taxpayer elected to amortize the qualified expenditures over a 10 year period, the amount amortized and deducted in years after 2009 is not subject to the $25,000 passive loss limit. Further analysis of this provision is beyond the scope of this discussion. Additionally, AGI is modified by certain items that are beyond this discussion.

The $25,000 limit applies to the sum of both deductions and credits. Thus, in order to properly apply the limit, taxpayers must convert the credits into deduction equivalents. A *deduction equivalent* is an amount that, if taken as a deduction, would reduce the tax liability by an amount equal to the credits. The amount of deduction equivalents can be computed by dividing the amount of the credit by the taxpayer's marginal tax rate. If the sum of the deductions and the deduction equivalents exceeds the $25,000 limit, the taxpayer must first use the deductions.

EXAMPLE I:8-17 ▶ Hal owns over 10% of activity A, in which he actively participates. Activity A is a passive real estate rental activity. Hal's marginal tax rate is 25% and he has AGI of less than $100,000. For the year, activity A generates a $20,000 net loss and $10,000 in tax credits, which amounts to $40,000 in deduction equivalent {$10,000/25%}. After deducting the $20,000 net loss against his active business and portfolio income, Hal has a remaining real estate deduction under the limit of $5,000 ($25,000 − $20,000). Thus, Hal may use $1,250 ($5,000 × 0.25) of the credits. The remaining $8,750 ($10,000 − $1,250) of tax credits must be carried over to subsequent years. ◀

If deductions and credits exceeding the $25,000 limit arise from more than one passive activity, the taxpayer must allocate the deductions and credits between the activities.[28]

EXAMPLE I:8-18 ▶ Mary has AGI of less than $100,000 and a 25% marginal tax rate. During the year she reports a $30,000 loss from activity A and a $10,000 loss from activity B. Additionally, activity A generates $5,000 of tax credits. Both activities A and B are passive real estate rental activities in which Mary actively participates and owns over 10% of each activity. The $25,000 deduction is first allocated to the losses. Because the sum of the losses ($40,000) exceeds the limit, the deductible loss must be allocated ratably between the activities as follows:

Activity A:	$25,000 × $30,000 ÷ $40,000 = $18,750
Activity B:	$25,000 × $10,000 ÷ $40,000 = $6,250

Activity A has an $11,250 ($30,000 − $18,750) suspended loss, and activity B has a $3,750 ($10,000 − $6,250) suspended loss. In addition, activity A has $5,000 of suspended tax credits. ◀

Topic Review I:8-2 summarizes the passive activity loss rules.

? STOP & THINK

Question: Jana is a businesswoman who has successfully invested in various stock and bond funds. Now she is considering diversifying her holdings by investing in real estate. One of the alternatives she is considering is purchasing an interest in a limited partnership that invests in real estate. A friend is also urging Jana to go into a partnership with him in order to purchase a small office building they would rent out. Assume that the size of Jana's investment in the two alternatives would be exactly the same and that Jana estimates the economic results to be equivalent (e.g., she expects both to spin off equivalent losses for the first few years and then begin turning a profit). What tax issues should Jana consider when making her investment decision?

Solution: In comparing alternatives such as these, of course, the most important considerations should be the non-tax factors such as cash flow from the investment, the capital appreciation of the assets, the marketability of the investment, and the risk. For example, as a limited partner, Jana will not personally be liable for debts of the partnership or lawsuits filed against the partnership. Purchase of the office building as a general partner with her friend will cause her to be personally liable unless it is done through an LLC or LLP. Additionally, in comparing these two alternatives, certain tax issues may come into play. Both alternatives are investments in rental real estate. However, Jana is not eligible to deduct up to $25,000 of the passive losses from the limited partnership because she will

---

[28] A taxpayer may earn different types of credits, based upon the different types of investments. Furthermore, the phase-out of the $25,000 limit is treated differently for different types of credits. For example, the phase-out for the rehabilitation credit only begins when the taxpayer's AGI exceeds $200,000. Additionally, there is no phase-out applied to the credit for low income housing. (See Sec. 469(e)(3) and Chapter I:14 for a discussion of these credits.) Thus, taxpayers are required to allocate the deductions and credits among the activities and account for them in a specific order. A complete analysis of these rules is beyond the scope of this discussion. Example I:8-18 assumes both activities earn the same type of credit and are subject to the $25,000 limit.

TOPIC REVIEW I:8-2

Passive Losses

Topic	Summary
Taxpayers covered	Individuals, estates, trusts, closely held C corporations, personal service corporations, certain publicly traded partnerships.
Passive activity	Any trade or business activity in which the taxpayer does not materially participate. Includes all rental activities except for certain rental real estate activities and exceptions contained in regulations. Does not include working interests in oil and gas property.
Limitation	Passive losses are deductible against passive income, but not against active or portfolio income. Disallowed losses are carried over to subsequent years (suspended losses). Losses must be accounted for separately by activity. Activities are identified by examining the taxpayer's undertakings.
Suspended losses	Must be allocated and attributed among the passive activities that generated the losses.
Disposition of interest	Suspended losses may be deducted in the year of a taxable disposition. For inherited property, suspended losses in excess of the increase in basis may be deducted on the final return of a decedent. Losses up to the amount of the basis increase are lost.
Material participation	Must be regular, continuous, and substantial. The regulations contain seven separate tests; four based on current-year participation; two based on participation in prior years; and one based on facts and circumstances.
Real property trades or businesses	Passive activity loss rules do not apply to taxpayers who materially participate in real property trade or business activities for more than 750 hours during the year. Additionally, more than one-half of the taxpayer's personal services must be performed in real property trades or businesses in which the taxpayer materially participates.
Rental of real estate	Individuals may deduct losses up to $25,000 against active and portfolio income if they actively participate in the activity and own at least 10% of the value of the activity. Additionally, they may take certain credits generated in passive rental activities in which they actively participate. Active participation is a lesser standard than material participation, but the taxpayer must still participate in management decisions or arranging for others to provide services. The deduction and credits phase out at a 50% rate for AGI in excess of $100,000.

not actively participate in the partnership. On the other hand, if she is involved in management decisions regarding the office building held by the partnership, she will be actively participating and will be eligible for the $25,000 passive loss deduction exception. Of course, the benefit of this exception begins phasing out if her AGI exceeds $100,000.

Casualty and Theft Losses

OBJECTIVE 4

Identify and calculate the deduction for a casualty or theft loss

Taxpayers may deduct losses incurred in connection with business or investment property, but individuals generally are not allowed a deduction for losses on personal-use property. However, under Sec. 165, individuals may take a limited deduction if the loss on personal-use property arises from a fire, storm, shipwreck, other casualty, or theft. In other words, losses on personal-use property are deductible only if the loss results from a casualty. In order for an event to qualify as a casualty, the event must meet certain requirements.

Casualty Defined

According to the IRS, a deductible **casualty loss** is one that occurs in an identifiable event that is sudden, unexpected, or unusual.[29]

[29] Rev. Rul. 79-174, 1979-1 C.B. 99. See also IRS *Publication No. 547*, Casualties, Disasters, and Thefts, 2014, p.2.

Identifiable Event. Because the event that causes the loss must be *identifiable,* the act of losing or misplacing property is generally not considered a casualty.

However, in some cases, taxpayers have proven that the loss of property was the result of an identifiable event.

EXAMPLE I:8-19 ▶ One evening Troy and his wife, Lynn, go to the theater. Troy accidentally slams the car door on Lynn's hand. The impact breaks the flanges holding the diamond in her ring. As a result, the diamond falls from the ring and is lost. In this case, a deductible casualty loss has occurred.[30] ◀

KEY POINT

The taxpayer has the burden of proof to establish that a loss was caused by a casualty. The taxpayer should gather as much evidence as possible. Newspaper clippings, police reports, photographs, and insurance reports can be helpful in establishing the cause of the loss.

Sudden, Unexpected, or Unusual Events. According to the IRS, a *sudden event* is one that is swift, not gradual or progressive. An *unexpected event* is one that is ordinarily unanticipated and not intended. An *unusual event* is one that is not a day-to-day occurrence and that is not typical of the activity.

Thus, the IRS has ruled that a deductible casualty loss occurred when a taxpayer went ice fishing and his automobile fell through the ice.[31] A taxpayer whose automobile was damaged as the result of an accident also sustained a deductible casualty loss. However, a taxpayer may not deduct losses incurred in an accident caused by the taxpayer's willful negligence or willful act.[32] Damage sustained as the result of an accident in an automobile race was held to be nondeductible because accidents occur often and are not unusual events in automobile races.[33]

ADDITIONAL COMMENT

Sudden, unexpected, or unusual events must also be accompanied by an external force. For example, a blown engine in an automobile is a sudden event but because no external force caused the event, the loss is not a casualty loss.

The following are a few examples of events that the courts have held to constitute a deductible casualty loss:

- ▶ Rust and water damage to furniture and carpets caused by the bursting of a water heater
- ▶ Damage to the exterior paint of a residence caused by a severe, sudden, and unexpected concentration of chemical fumes in the air
- ▶ Loss caused by fire (unless the taxpayer sets the fire, in which case no deduction is available)
- ▶ Damage to a building caused by an unusually large blast at a nearby quarry or a jet sonic boom[34]
- ▶ Death of trees just a few days after a sudden infestation of pine beetles[35]

The following are examples of events that the courts have held *not* to be a casualty:

- ▶ Water damage to the walls and ceiling of a taxpayer's personal residence as the result of the gradual deterioration of the roof[36]
- ▶ Trees dying because of gradual suffocation of the root systems
- ▶ The loss of trees and shrubs because of disease[37]
- ▶ Damage to carpet and clothing caused by moths and carpet beetles[38]
- ▶ Damage to a road due to freezing, thawing, and gradual deterioration[39]
- ▶ Damage to a residence caused by the gradual sinking of the land underneath the home[40]
- ▶ Damage caused by drought because it occurs through progressive deterioration
- ▶ The steady weakening of a building caused by normal wind and weather conditions
- ▶ The rusting and deterioration of a water heater[41]

ETHICAL POINT

A client loses his diamond ring while fishing and wants to deduct the loss as a casualty. The CPA should not sign the tax return unless he or she believes that the client's position has a realistic possibility of being sustained on its merits if challenged, which is doubtful in this situation.

---

[30] *John P. White,* 48 T.C. 430 (1967), *acq.* 1969-2 C.B. xxv. In another case, the taxpayer convinced the Tax Court to allow a deduction for a lost diamond, even though the taxpayer could not remember a specific blow to the ring. In this instance, the taxpayer obtained an expert witness to testify that the flanges of the ring were strong enough and in good enough repair that the loss of the diamond had to have been caused by a sudden, unexpected blow rather than by progressive deterioration.

[31] Rev. Rul. 69-88, 1969-1 C.B. 58.

[32] *Willie C. Robinson,* 1984 PH T.C. Memo ¶84,188, 47 TCM 1510 and Reg. Sec. 1.165-7(a)(3).

[33] Ltr. Rul. 8227010 (March 30, 1982) contains the above examples.

[34] *Ray Durden,* 3 T.C. 1 (1944), *acq.* 1944 C.B. 8 and Rev. Rul. 60-329, 1960-2 C.B. 67.

[35] Rev. Rul. 79-174, 1979-1 C.B. 99. See also *Charles A. Smithgall v. U.S.,* 47 AFTR 2d 81-695, 81-1 USTC ¶9121 (D.C.-Ga., 1980). However, the IRS has ruled in Ltr. Rul. 8544001 (July 12, 1985) that no casualty loss results when the time interval between the infestation and the death of the trees was too long.

[36] *Lauren Whiting,* 1975 PH T.C. Memo ¶75,038, 34 TCM 241.

[37] *William R. Miller,* 1970 PH T.C. Memo ¶70,167, 29 TCM 741 and Rev. Rul. 57-599, 1957-2 C.B. 142. Modified by Rev. Rul. 79–174, 1979-1 C.B. 99. (See also *Howard F. Burns v. U.S.,* 6 AFTR 2d 6036, 61-1 USTC ¶9127 (6th Cir., 1960).)

[38] Rev. Rul. 55-327, 1955-1 C.B. 25. (See also *J. P. Meersman v. U.S.,* 18 AFTR 2d 6152, 67-1 USTC ¶9125 (6th Cir., 1966).)

[39] *Howard Stacy,* 1970 PH T.C. Memo ¶70,127, 29 TCM 542. However, the breaking up of a road over a 4-month period because of extreme weather conditions was held to be a casualty. See *Emmett J. O'Connell v. U.S.,* 29 AFTR 2d 72-596, 72-1 USTC ¶9312, (D.C. Cal., 1972). (See also *Stephen L. Shaffer,* 1983 PH T.C. Memo ¶83,677, 47 TCM 285.)

[40] *Henry W. Berry,* 1969 PH T.C. Memo ¶69,162, 28 TCM 802. (See also *David McDaniel,* 1980 PH T.C. Memo ¶80,557, 41 TCM 563.)

[41] Rev. Rul. 70-91, 1970-1 C.B. 37 and IRS *Publication No. 547* (Casualties, Disasters, and Thefts), 2014 contain the above examples.

At times it is very difficult to determine under the particular facts whether the necessary requirements of suddenness, unexpectedness, or unusualness exist. For example, as mentioned above, damage caused by the sudden infestation of pine beetles in some instances has been held to be a casualty, but in other instances it has not.[42]

THEFT DEFINED

Under Sec. 165, a taxpayer may also deduct a loss sustained as the result of a theft. This includes theft of business, investment, or personal-use property. The Treasury Regulations state that "the term theft shall be deemed to include, but shall not necessarily be limited to, larceny, embezzlement, and robbery."[43] A determination whether other actions also constitute theft often depends on whether the action involves criminal intent and is illegal under the state law where the action has occurred. Thus, the IRS has stated that blackmail, extortion, and kidnapping for ransom may also constitute theft.[44]

DEDUCTIBLE AMOUNT OF CASUALTY LOSS

The amount of a casualty loss deduction depends on the amount of the loss sustained, any insurance or other reimbursement the taxpayer received, and, in the case of personal-use property, the limitations imposed under the tax law.

Measuring the Loss. As explained below, one measurement of the amount of the loss sustained in a casualty is the amount by which the casualty reduces the property's FMV. This is measured by comparing the property's FMV immediately before and immediately after the casualty.[45] The amount of the loss may not include any reduction in the FMV of the taxpayer's surrounding but undamaged property.

EXAMPLE I:8-20 ▶ Gail purchased a vacation home for $310,000. Shortly after she purchased the property, a mudslide completely destroyed several neighboring cabins. Gail's cabin sustained no damage. After the slide, an appraisal reveals that the FMV of the cabin has declined to $250,000 because of fears that other mudslides might occur. The $60,000 reduction in the FMV of the cabin does not constitute a deductible casualty loss. ◀

ADDITIONAL COMMENT

Taxpayers cannot deduct a loss unless they own the damaged property. Therefore, a taxpayer cannot deduct amounts he or she paid to another individual for damage he or she caused to the other individual's property.

The taxpayer must use actual market value, not sentimental value, to compute the reduction in the FMV. Additionally, the cost of protecting property to prevent damage from a casualty is not a deductible loss.

If the property involved in the casualty is only partially destroyed, the amount of the loss is the lesser of the reduction in the property's FMV or the taxpayer's adjusted basis in the property.

EXAMPLE I:8-21 ▶ Troy purchased a home for $225,000 several years ago. Through the years, the value of the home appreciated until it was appraised at $325,000 in the current year. Shortly after the appraisal, a flood swept through the area and severely damaged Troy's home. After the flood, the value of the home declined to $90,000. Troy does not have any flood insurance. His loss is limited to the $225,000 basis in the home even though the economic loss is $235,000 ($325,000 − $90,000). ◀

TYPICAL MISCONCEPTION

Taxpayers sometimes think their loss should be based on the total economic loss rather than just the property's basis. Taxpayers should remember that they have not paid a tax on the appreciation in value and, therefore, should not be entitled to a deduction for a loss on the unrealized gain.

If business or investment property is totally destroyed in a casualty, the amount of the loss is the taxpayer's adjusted basis in the property, even if it is greater than the property's FMV. However, if personal-use property is totally destroyed, the amount of the loss is limited to the lesser of the reduction in the property's FMV or the property's adjusted basis.

---

[42] Rev. Rul. 79-174, 1979-1 C.B. 99 and *George K. Notter,* 1985 PH T.C. Memo ¶85,391, 50 TCM 614. A graphic illustration of the controversy that may arise when determining whether an event is a casualty can be made by comparing the following two cases. In one case the taxpayer was washing dishes. Seeing a glass of water on the windowsill, he quickly dumped the contents down the drain and turned on the garbage disposal, not realizing that his wife's rings were in the glass. Damage to the rings in this case was deemed to be a casualty (*William H. Carpenter,* 1966 PH T.C. Memo ¶66,228, 25 TCM 1186). In the second case, the taxpayer gathered up some tissues from the night stand and flushed them down the toilet, not knowing that his wife's rings were wrapped in one of them. This event was held not to be a casualty (*W.J. Keenan, Jr. v. Bowers,* 39 AFTR 849, 50-2 USTC ¶9444 (D.C.-S.C., 1950)).

[43] Reg. Sec. 1.165-8(d).

[44] Rev. Rul. 72-112, 1972-1 C.B. 60 and IRS *Publication No. 547* (Casualties, Disasters, and Thefts), 2014.

[45] Reg. Sec. 1.165-7(a)(2).

EXAMPLE I:8-22 ▶ A machine Beth uses in her business is completely destroyed by fire. At the time of the fire, the adjusted basis of the machine is $5,000 and its FMV is $3,000. Because the machine is business property, Beth's loss is $5,000. If the machine were a personal-use asset, the amount of the loss would be $3,000, the amount of the reduction in the property's FMV rather than Beth's basis of $5,000. ◀

Generally, taxpayers must establish the reduction in the FMV of the property by an appraisal. If an appraisal is difficult or impossible to obtain, the taxpayer may use the cost of the repairs instead. The repairs must meet all of the following requirements before the taxpayer may use this alternative:

KEY POINT

The reason for this difference is that taxpayers may not deduct a loss on the sale of personal-use property. Thus, taxpayers should not be able to deduct the decline in the personal property's value that occurs before the casualty.

- The repairs will bring the property back to its condition immediately before the casualty.
- The cost of the repairs is not excessive.
- The repairs do no more than repair the damage incurred in the casualty.
- The repairs do not increase the value of the property over its value immediately before the casualty.

If the same casualty destroys more than one property, the taxpayer calculates the loss on each property separately.[46] Thus, the taxpayer compares each property's basis with the reduction in the FMV of that property, rather than aggregating the basis and FMV amounts for all the properties destroyed in the casualty.

If the taxpayer receives insurance or any other type of recovery, the taxpayer must reduce the amount of the loss by these amounts. In some cases these payments may actually exceed the taxpayer's basis in the property, causing the realization of a gain. If certain requirements are met, taxpayers may defer or exclude the recognition of these gains. (See the detailed discussion of involuntary conversions in Chapter I:12.)

LIMITATIONS ON PERSONAL-USE PROPERTY

The amount an individual may deduct for a casualty loss on personal-use property is subject to two limitations: (1) losses sustained in each separate casualty must be reduced by $100, and (2) the total amount of all net casualty losses for personal-use property is reduced by 10% of the taxpayer's AGI for the year. For property destroyed in the same casualty, only $100 is deducted from all the properties (i.e., the taxpayer does not reduce the loss from each separate property by $100).

EXAMPLE I:8-23 ▶ During the year a windstorm blows over a large tree in front of Cathy's house, damaging the house and totally destroying her automobile. After the insurance reimbursement, the loss on the house amounts to $3,000, and the loss on the automobile is $2,500. Because the losses occur in the same casualty, the total amount of the loss is reduced to $5,400 ($3,000 + $2,500 − $100). If the damage to the car was sustained in a separate event such as an automobile accident, the total amount of the casualty losses incurred by Cathy during the year would have been $5,300 [($3,000 − $100) + ($2,500 − $100)]. This $5,300 or $5,400 loss is then further reduced by 10% of Cathy's AGI for the year. ◀

EXAMPLE I:8-24 ▶ As the result of a storm, Liz incurs a $4,100 casualty loss on personal-use property during the year. She also sustains a $600 theft loss. Liz's AGI for the year is $50,000. She receives no tax deduction for the casualty and theft losses because they do not exceed the following limitations:

KEY POINT

Many taxpayers cannot deduct their casualty losses because of the $100 floor and 10% of AGI limitation.

	Storm	*Theft*	*Total*
Loss before limitations	$4,100	$600	$4,700
Minus: $100 floor	(100)	(100)	(200)
	$4,000	$500	$4,500
Minus: 10% of AGI (0.10 × $50,000)			(5,000)
Deductible loss			0 ◀

[46] Reg. Sec. 1.165-7(b)(2). For personal-use property, losses on real property and improvements to the property are computed in the aggregate. Thus, no separate basis need be apportioned to the improvements. (See Reg. Secs. 1.165-7(b)(2)(ii) and 1.165-7(b)(3) Example (3).)

ADDITIONAL COMMENT

Individuals sometimes fail to file insurance claims for damage to their personal automobile for fear that their insurance rates will increase, and hope instead to deduct the loss. In this situation, the taxpayer cannot deduct the loss.

Because of these limitations, many taxpayers who sustain casualty and theft losses on personal-use property do not receive a tax deduction. Furthermore, if the taxpayer's insurance covers the property, the taxpayer cannot take a casualty loss deduction unless he or she timely files an insurance claim for the loss. This disallowance relates only to the portion of the loss covered by the insurance.

Below is a summary of the rules concerning deductibility of casualty losses:

Result of Casualty		*Business*	*Investment*	*Personal Use*
Total Destruction	Amount of Casualty[a]	Basis	Basis	Lesser of: basis or decline in FMV, reduced by $100 and 10% of AGI
	Type	For AGI	From AGI (For AGI if Rental)	From AGI
Partial Destruction	Amount of Casualty[a]	Lesser of: basis or decline in FMV	Lesser of: basis or decline in FMV	Lesser of: basis or decline in FMV, reduced by $100 and 10% of AGI
	Type	For AGI	From AGI (For AGI if Rental)	From AGI

[a] All amounts are first reduced by any insurance reimbursement.

NETTING CASUALTY GAINS AND LOSSES ON PERSONAL-USE PROPERTY

TYPICAL MISCONCEPTION

The concept of a gain on a casualty can be confusing. Nevertheless, if the insurance proceeds exceed the property's basis, a gain results.

Taxpayers must net casualty gains and losses incurred during the year on personal-use assets. These gains and losses are not combined with casualty gains and losses on business and investment property. For purposes of the netting process, the losses should be reduced by any insurance reimbursements and the $100 limitation, but not the 10% of AGI floor. If the gains exceed the losses for the year, all the gains and losses are treated as capital gains and losses.

EXAMPLE I:8-25 ▶ During the year, Pat incurs the following casualty gains and losses on personal-use assets. Assets W and X are destroyed in one casualty, and asset Y is destroyed in another. Pat acquired assets X and Y in the current year, whereas she acquired asset W several years ago.

Asset	*Reduction in FMV*	*Adjusted Basis*	*Insurance*	*Holding Period*
W	$10,000	$3,000	$10,000	More than 12 months
X	3,600	5,000	2,000	Less than one year
Y	1,600	3,000	0	Less than one year

Pat realizes a $7,000 ($10,000 – $3,000) gain on asset W because the insurance proceeds received for the asset exceed its basis. She realizes a $1,600 ($3,600 reduction in FMV – $2,000 insurance) loss on asset X. This loss is reduced to $1,500 because of the $100 reduction for personal casualty losses. She realizes a $1,600 loss on asset Y. Because this loss is realized as a result of the second casualty, the $100 limitation is deducted, resulting in a $1,500 loss from that casualty. Pat realizes a $4,000 [$7,000 – ($1,500 + $1,500)] net casualty gain for the year. Thus, the gain or loss on each asset is treated as a capital gain or loss. Pat must report a $7,000 long-term capital gain on asset W, a $1,500 short-term capital loss on asset X, and a $1,500 short-term capital loss on asset Y. ◀

If the casualty losses on personal-use property exceed the casualty gains for the year, the taxpayer must further reduce the net loss by 10% of AGI. The taxpayer performs all of these calculations (the netting process and reductions) on Form 4684. If any loss remains after the netting and reductions, the taxpayer reports the loss as an itemized deduction on Schedule A of Form 1040.

CASUALTY GAINS AND LOSSES ATTRIBUTABLE TO BUSINESS AND INVESTMENT PROPERTY

Taxpayers must net casualty gains and losses on business and investment property held over one year. (See Chapter I:13 for a discussion of the netting procedure under Sec. 1231.) If the losses exceed the gains, the business losses and losses on investment property that generate rents or royalties are *for* AGI deductions. Losses on other investment property (e.g., the theft of a security) are itemized deductions but are not subject to the 2% of AGI floor or the overall reduction of itemized deductions.[47] The $100 or 10% of AGI limitations do not apply to losses on business and investment property. Casualty gains and losses on business and investment property held one year or less are all treated as ordinary.

TIMING OF CASUALTY LOSS DEDUCTION

In general, taxpayers must deduct casualty losses in the tax year in which the taxpayer sustains the loss. In the following instances, however, taxpayers may deduct the loss in another year:

- Theft losses
- Insurance or other reimbursements that the taxpayer can reasonably expect to receive in a subsequent year
- Certain disaster losses

Theft. Taxpayers must deduct a theft loss in the tax year in which the taxpayer discovers the theft. This rule is equitable and practical because a taxpayer may not discover a theft until a subsequent year.

EXAMPLE I:8-26 ▶ Dale owns a hunting lodge in upstate New York. Sometime after his last trip to the lodge in November 2014, someone breaks into the lodge and steals several guns and paintings. Dale discovers the theft when he returns to the lodge on May 19, 2015. Dale's insurance does not cover the entire cost of the items. The loss is deductible in 2015, even though the theft may have occurred in 2014. ◀

REAL-WORLD EXAMPLE

A taxpayer had property confiscated by the Cuban government in 1960. The taxpayer left the country and could have filed for indemnity but did not because she expected to return. Later, the government took away the right of indemnity in 1961. Since she did not file for indemnity from the Cuban government when she had the chance, she was not allowed a casualty or theft loss. *Vila v. U.S.*, 23 AFTR 2d 69-1311 (1969).

Insurance and Other Reimbursements. Taxpayers must subtract any reimbursement received as compensation for a loss in arriving at the amount of the loss. This is necessary even when the taxpayer has not yet received the reimbursement, as long as there is a reasonable prospect that the taxpayer will receive it in the future. Thus, the taxpayer may not take a deduction in the year of loss if in that year a reasonable expectation of full recovery exists.[48] If no anticipation of full recovery exists, the taxpayer may deduct a loss in the year the casualty occurs for the estimated unrecovered amount. As previously mentioned, the taxpayer may not take a deduction to the extent the taxpayer has insured the personal-use property and the taxpayer does not file a timely insurance claim.

EXAMPLE I:8-27 ▶ In December of the current year, Andrea suffers a $10,000 casualty loss when her personal automobile is struck by a city bus. Although she does not receive any reimbursement from the insurance company by December 31, she reasonably expects to recover the full amount. Andrea may not deduct a casualty loss in the current year. ◀

EXAMPLE I:8-28 ▶ Assume the same facts as in Example I:8-27, except that Andrea reasonably anticipates her reimbursement from the insurance company will be only $7,000. In this case, her casualty loss in the current year is $3,000 (before reduction by the limitations). ◀

If the taxpayer does not receive the full amount of the anticipated recovery in the subsequent year, he or she may deduct the unrecovered portion. However, rather than filing an amended return for the year of loss, the taxpayer deducts the loss in the subsequent year. Thus in some cases, the taxpayer may spread the income tax consequences for a single casualty loss over two years.

---

[47] As explained in Chapter I:6, this overall reduction of itemized deductions applies to taxpayers with AGI in excess of certain threshold amounts. For surviving spouses or taxpayers filing as married filing jointly the threshold is $309,900 for 2015. For heads of households the 2015 threshold is $284,050, and for single taxpayers the 2015 threshold is $258,250. For married taxpayers filing separately the 2015 threshold is $154,950. See Sec. 68(a) and (b).

[48] Reg. Sec. 1.165-1(d)(2)(i).

EXAMPLE I:8-29 ▶ During the current year, Javier's home is damaged by an exceptionally severe blast at a nearby stone quarry owned by Acme Corporation. Although the amount of the damage is properly appraised at $20,000, Javier can reasonably anticipate a recovery of only $15,000 from Acme Corporation at the end of the current year. He does not receive any recovery from Acme during the current year. Unfortunately, in the subsequent year Acme Corporation is declared bankrupt, and Javier does not receive any reimbursement. Javier's AGI is $40,000 in the current year and $45,000 in the subsequent year. During the current year, Javier may deduct $900 {$5,000 loss reasonably anticipated in the current year − [$100 limitation + (0.10 × $40,000)]}. In the subsequent year, Javier may deduct an additional casualty loss of $10,500 [$15,000 additional loss − (0.10 × $45,000)]. ◀

If a taxpayer receives a subsequent recovery for a previously deducted loss, the taxpayer includes the reimbursement in income in the year of recovery. The taxpayer does not file an amended return. However, the amount that the taxpayer must include in income is limited to the amount of tax benefit the taxpayer received for the previous deduction.

EXAMPLE I:8-30 ▶ During the current year, Becky's automobile sustains $5,000 in damages when it is struck by another automobile. The driver of the other automobile is at fault and is uninsured, and Becky does not reasonably expect to recover any of the loss. Becky's AGI for the current year is $35,000. Becky deducts $1,400 ($5,000 loss − [$100 + $3,500]). During the subsequent year, the other driver reimburses Becky for the full amount of the damage. Because Becky received a tax benefit of only $1,400 for the loss in the year of the accident, she must only include $1,400 in gross income in the subsequent year, even though she receives a $5,000 reimbursement. Becky does not file an amended return for the year of the accident. ◀

Disaster Losses. Under certain circumstances, a taxpayer may elect to deduct a casualty loss in the year preceding the year in which the loss actually occurs. This election is available to taxpayers who suffer losses attributable to a disaster that occurs in an area subsequently declared by the President of the United States as a disaster area.[49] Thus, an individual can elect to deduct a disaster loss occurring in 2016 on his or her 2015 tax return or report it in the regular way on his or her 2016 return. The taxpayer must file an amended return (Form 1040X) unless he or she has not filed the prior year's return when the disaster is declared. This election allows taxpayers the possibility of receiving financial help sooner from potential tax refunds by filing an amendment to the prior year's return.

Topic Review I:8-3 summarizes the casualty loss deduction rules.

? STOP & THINK

Question: Due to a series of hurricanes that hit Florida during the current year, many homes, roads, and other property are destroyed. Because of the tremendous destruction, the President of the United States declares the area a disaster area. One of the properties totally destroyed is Jack's vacation home in Miami. Jack uses the home exclusively for vacationing. The value of the home is $390,000. Unfortunately, Jack had not insured the home against a hurricane. What issues must Jack consider in determining the year in which to take the casualty loss?

Solution: Since the property was destroyed in a disaster and is located in an area which the President subsequently declared as a disaster area, Jack may take the casualty deduction either in the year of the casualty or in the previous year. The year which is most beneficial is based on several factors. The destroyed property was personal use property, so the deduction is an itemized deduction that would normally be subject to the 10% of AGI limitation. Thus, Jack should compare his estimated AGI for the current year with his AGI in the last year. He also should consider his other itemized deductions, including any other casualty losses that might be subject to the $100 or 10% of AGI limitation. In addition, he should compare his marginal tax rates in the two years. Jack should also consider the time value of money, since by taking the deduction on his prior year return, he will receive the tax benefit earlier than if he takes the deduction on the current year return.

---

[49] Sec. 165(i). Additionally, the same treatment may apply under Sec. 165 to taxpayers who live in a disaster area and who are ordered by a state or local government to move from or relocate their residence because the disaster caused the residence to be unsafe. In order to qualify for this treatment, the order to move must come from the state or local government within 120 days of the date that the President determines the area to be a disaster area. If the property destroyed in a presidentially declared disaster area is the taxpayer's principal residence and the casualty results in a gain, the taxpayer may exclude a portion of the gain if certain conditions are met (see Chapter I:12).

TOPIC REVIEW I:8-3

Casualty Losses

Type of Property	Limitation and Treatment
Personal use	The amount of the loss is the lesser of the property's adjusted basis or the reduction of the asset's FMV. This amount is reduced by any insurance reimbursement. If the insurance reimbursement exceeds the property's basis, a gain is realized. To the extent the property is insured, the taxpayer must file a claim or the loss is disallowed.
	The amount of loss incurred in each separate casualty event during the year is reduced by $100.
	All casualty gains and losses for the year are netted. If the gains exceed the losses, all gains and losses are treated as capital gains and losses. If the losses exceed the gains, the net loss is reduced by 10% of AGI. Any remaining loss is an itemized deduction.
Business or investment	If the property is totally destroyed, the amount of the loss is the adjusted basis of the property. If only partially destroyed, the amount of the loss is the lesser of the property's adjusted basis or the reduction of the asset's FMV. This amount is reduced by any insurance reimbursement. A gain is realized if the insurance reimbursement exceeds the property's basis.
	For property held one year or less, the losses and gains are ordinary losses and gains. For property held over one year, the casualty gains and losses for the year are netted. The treatment depends on the total of the taxpayer's other Sec. 1231 transactions (see Chapter I:13). Business casualty losses and losses on investment property that generate rents or royalties are not subject to the $100 or 10% of AGI limitations.

Bad debts

OBJECTIVE 5

Compute the deduction for a bad debt

In addition to losses on property, taxpayers may also sustain losses generated by uncollectible debts. In dealing with a deduction for **bad debts**, taxpayers must address the following requirements and issues:

- A bona fide debtor-creditor relationship must exist between the taxpayer and some other person or entity.
- The taxpayer must have basis in the debt.
- The debt must actually have become worthless during the year.
- The type and timing of a bad debt deduction depend on whether the debt is a business or nonbusiness bad debt.

ADDITIONAL COMMENT

The tax provisions that deal with deductions for losses and the tax provisions that deal with the deductions for bad debts are mutually exclusive, and an amount properly deductible as a loss cannot be deducted as a bad debt or vice versa.

Generally, taxpayers may use only the specific write-off method of accounting when deducting the bad debt. A partial or complete recovery of a debt that was previously deducted may occur. In many cases a recovery of this type causes income recognition in the year of the recovery.

BONA FIDE DEBTOR-CREDITOR RELATIONSHIP

Only items constituting bona fide debt are eligible to be deducted as a bad debt. A **bona fide debt** is one that arises from a valid and enforceable obligation to pay a fixed or determinable sum of money and results in a debtor-creditor relationship.[50]

KEY POINT

The fact that the debtor is a related party does not preclude deduction of a bad debt, but the taxpayer must be able to document the debt as being bona fide.

Related-Party Transactions. Determining whether a bona fide loan transaction has actually taken place is especially critical when the transaction is between the taxpayer and a family member or other related party (e.g., a controlled corporation). The tax advisor must carefully examine all the facts and circumstances surrounding the transaction because a gift does not constitute a debt. The taxpayer's intent is critical. For example, if the taxpayer's intent is to provide property, cash, or services to someone else without receiving

[50] Reg. Sec. 1.166-1(c).

any consideration in return, a gift—not a loan—has been made. Some tests used to determine the taxpayer's intent include the following:

- Does a note or other written instrument exist which evidences an obligation to repay?[51]
- Have the parties established a definite schedule of repayment?
- Have the parties documented a stated reasonable rate of interest?
- Would a person unrelated to the debtor make the loan?[52]

EXAMPLE I:8-31 ▶ During the current year Maria loaned $20,000 to her son Sam, who used the money in his business. Although they signed no written note or contract, Sam orally promised to repay Maria as soon as his business became profitable. No rate of interest was stated. Unfortunately, the business failed and Sam went out of business in the subsequent year. He never repaid the loan principal or interest.

In this case, no valid debt exists because the taxpayer did not establish an interest rate or a repayment schedule. An unrelated person would not have made a loan to Sam under these conditions. In addition, Maria does not receive any consideration in return for the "loan." Since the facts indicate that the transaction is actually a gift, Maria may not claim a bad debt deduction because of Sam's failure to repay. ◀

REAL-WORLD EXAMPLE

A taxpayer advanced $8,500 to his son-in-law who operated a livestock auction barn. The taxpayer was entitled to a bad debt deduction upon default because notations on the checks indicated that they were loans and undisputed testimony indicated that repayment was to be made within 90 days. *Giffin A. Andrew*, 54 T.C. 239 (1970).

Tax advisors should also closely examine other related party transactions. For example, a loan from a shareholder to a controlled corporation may actually be an additional contribution to capital disguised as a loan. Thus, a transfer of cash by a shareholder who owns a controlling (i.e., more than 50%) interest in the stock of a corporation may indicate a capital contribution rather than a loan. Likewise, a "loan" from a corporation to a controlling shareholder may actually be a disguised dividend or a salary payment.

Third Party Debt. In some cases a taxpayer will guarantee or endorse someone else's obligation. If under the terms of the guarantee, the guarantor is required to pay the debtor's remaining outstanding principal as well as any accrued interest on the debt, the relationship between the debtor and the guarantor as well as the terms of the guarantee must be carefully analyzed. The guarantor's intent determines whether the guarantee and subsequent payment of the outstanding principal and accrued interest constitutes a gift to the debtor. If the guarantor's intent was a gift, the guarantor may not deduct the payment of the outstanding principal and accrued interest. On the other hand, if it can be proved that the guarantee was not a gift, the guarantor may deduct the principal and accrued interest as a bad debt issued to the debtor at the time of the payment.

EXAMPLE I:8-32 ▶ Ron is the sole shareholder and a full-time employee of Zip Corporation. For Zip Corporation to obtain a bank loan, Ron personally signs a guarantee that the loan will be repaid. Unfortunately, Zip Corporation defaults on the loan and Ron must repay the loan. Assume proof exists that Ron signed the guarantee to preserve his job and enhance his investment in Zip Corporation. Although Ron receives no direct consideration for having signed the note, he does receive indirect consideration in the form of continued job security and protection of his investment. Because a business or investment purpose motivated Ron to sign the loan guarantee, Ron may deduct the bad debt. On the other hand, without proof, this guarantee and subsequent payment of Zip Corporation's debt by Ron may be seen as merely an additional capital contribution by Ron to Zip Corporation. ◀

TAXPAYER'S BASIS IN THE DEBT

For a bad debt to be deductible, the creditor must have basis in the debt. The taxpayer may acquire this basis in different ways. If a taxpayer loans money, the taxpayer's basis in the debt is the amount loaned. If the debt arises because the taxpayer provides property or

---

[51] A written note or other instrument is an evidence of a bona fide debtor-creditor relationship. However, if the note or other instrument is registered or has interest coupons and is issued by a corporation or a government, the bad debt provisions of Sec. 166 do not apply. Instead, the worthless security provisions of Sec. 165 (previously discussed) apply.

[52] *Jean C. Tyler v. Tomlinson*, 24 AFTR 2d 69-5426, 69-2 USTC ¶9559 (5th Cir., 1969). (See also, *C. L. Hunt*, 1989 PH T.C. Memo ¶89,335, 57 TCM 919), where certain loans that the taxpayer made to his children were treated as bona fide loans, whereas others were treated as gifts. In that case, the children had been trading in silver futures and were required to make margin calls. Because they could not make the calls, the children's positions were involuntarily liquidated. Up to the date of the liquidation, the taxpayer had made loans to the children that were payable on demand and were subject to the prime rate of interest. These loans were evidenced by promissory notes. After the liquidation, the taxpayer continued to make loans to the children. However, these loans were not evidenced by notes. The loans up to the time of the liquidation were treated as bona fide loans and the subsequent loans were treated as gifts.

TYPICAL MISCONCEPTION

Taxpayers sometimes mistakenly assume that a cash method taxpayer can take a bad debt deduction on a debt that arose from services rendered by the taxpayer.

services for the other party, basis is established only if the taxpayer has previously included the FMV of the property or services in income. This often depends on the taxpayer's method of accounting. An accrual method taxpayer generally reports income in the year the services are performed or the property is provided. (See the discussion in Chapter I:11.) Thus, an accrual method taxpayer has a basis in either a note receivable or an open account receivable equal to the amount included in gross income (i.e., the FMV of the services). A cash method taxpayer, however, reports income only in the year in which the taxpayer receives payment in the form of cash or property. Because a note constitutes the receipt of property, a cash method taxpayer reports income (and establishes basis) in the year the note is received. However, if the cash method taxpayer does not receive a note and the receivable is an open account item, the taxpayer reports no income until the receivable is collected. Thus, the taxpayer has no basis in the receivable and does not receive a bad debt deduction if the receivable is not collected.

EXAMPLE I:8-33 ▶ In October of the current year, Jim performs some legal services for Joy. Jim bills Joy for $10,000. Joy does not sign a note for the debt. As a cash method taxpayer, Jim does not include the $10,000 in his current year's income. After repeated efforts to collect the fee, Jim discovers in June of the subsequent year that Joy has left the city and cannot be found. Jim may not deduct a bad debt for the uncollected amount in the subsequent year because he has not taken the amount into income and he has no basis in the debt. If Joy had signed a note for the debt, Jim would have reported income in the current year in an amount equal to the note's FMV. Thus, Jim can deduct the loss when the note becomes uncollectible in the subsequent year. ◀

ADDITIONAL COMMENT

Because in many cases it is difficult to pinpoint the exact time of worthlessness, the statute of limitations is extended to seven years for bad debts.

DEBT MUST BE WORTHLESS

To deduct a bad debt, the taxpayer must show that the debt is worthless. This determination is made by reference to all the pertinent evidence, including the general financial condition of the debtor and whether the debt is secured by collateral.

In proving the worthlessness of a debt, a taxpayer does not need to take legal action if the surrounding circumstances indicate that legal action probably would not result in the collection of the debt. By simply showing that legal action is not warranted, the taxpayer provides sufficient proof that the debt is worthless.[53] Indications that an unsecured debt is worthless include bankruptcy of the debtor, disappearance or death of a debtor, and repeated unsuccessful attempts at collection. Furthermore, if the surrounding circumstances warrant it, a taxpayer may deduct a worthless debt even before the debt comes due. As will be explained later in this chapter, a nonbusiness debt must be totally worthless before a deduction is allowed. However, a current deduction is allowed for a partially worthless business bad debt.

KEY POINT

Taxpayers must distinguish between business and nonbusiness bad debts because the tax treatment varies according to the type of debt.

NONBUSINESS BAD DEBTS

The distinction between a business bad debt and a nonbusiness bad debt is important because the classification of the debt determines its tax treatment. A business bad debt gives rise to an ordinary deduction, whereas a taxpayer must treat a nonbusiness bad debt as a short-term capital loss. All loans made by a corporation are assumed to be associated with the corporation's business; therefore, the provisions for nonbusiness bad debts do not apply to corporations.

TYPICAL MISCONCEPTION

Assume that a taxpayer lends money to a friend to be used in the friend's business. If the friend does not repay the loan, the debt is a nonbusiness bad debt unless the taxpayer is in the business of lending money. This type of debt is occasionally improperly classified as a business debt.

Definition of a Nonbusiness Bad Debt. A *nonbusiness debt* is defined as any debt other than (1) a debt created or acquired in connection with a trade or business of the taxpayer or (2) a debt the loss from the worthlessness of which is incurred in the taxpayer's trade or business. This determination depends on an examination of the facts and circumstances surrounding the debt in question.

A debt incurred in a taxpayer's business continues to be a business debt for that taxpayer even if, at the time the debt goes bad, the taxpayer has ceased conducting that particular business (situation (1) above). If another taxpayer acquires a business, any outstanding debt at the time the business is acquired continues to be business debt as long as the purchaser

[53] Reg. Sec. 1.166-2.

continues the business (situation (2) above). The debt is a nonbusiness debt if the person who owns the debt when it becomes worthless is not engaged in the business in which the debt is incurred either at the time the debt arose or when it becomes worthless.

EXAMPLE I:8-34 ► Matt, an individual who uses the accrual method of accounting, is engaged in the grocery business. During 2015, he extends credit to Jeff on an open account. In 2016, Matt sells his business to Joan, but retains Jeff's account. Jeff's account becomes worthless in 2016. Even though Matt is no longer engaged in the grocery business at the time the debt becomes worthless, he may deduct the loss as a business bad debt in 2016. If Joan purchases Jeff's account upon acquiring the grocery business, Joan is entitled to a business bad debt deduction in 2016 because the debt was incurred in the trade or business in which Joan is currently engaged. ◄

In addition, classification as a business debt requires a proximate relationship between the loan and the taxpayer's business.[54] According to the Supreme Court, this relationship exists if a business motive is the taxpayer's dominant motivation in making the loan. This determination must be made on a case-by-case basis. For example, when an individual stockholder who is also an employee of the corporation loans money to the corporation, is the loan a business or nonbusiness debt? Because an employee is considered to be engaged in the business of working for a corporation, a loan made to the corporation in an attempt to protect the employment relationship may be held to be a business debt. However, if the individual's dominant motive is to protect his or her stock investment, the loan is a nonbusiness debt.[55]

EXAMPLE I:8-35 ► Lisa is an individual engaged in the advertising business. If clients occasionally need additional funds to meet their cash-flow obligations, Lisa sometimes lends them money. Lisa's dominant motive for making the loans is to retain the clients. She has no ownership interests in these clients. Under these facts, if any of these loans becomes worthless, it would likely be considered a business bad debt.[56] ◄

Tax Treatment. Individuals deduct nonbusiness debts that become wholly worthless during the year as short-term capital losses. The length of time the debt is outstanding has no bearing on this treatment.

Individuals generally prefer an ordinary deduction rather than a short-term capital loss because capital losses are first used to offset capital gains. If the capital losses exceed the capital gains, the individual taxpayer is limited to an additional $3,000 tax deduction each year. Any loss in excess of this limit is carried over to subsequent years to be included in the capital gain and loss netting process in those years (see Chapter I:5).

EXAMPLE I:8-36 ► During 2015, Kim loaned her friend $10,000. The friend used the funds to invest in commodity futures. The transaction had all the characteristics of a bona fide debt rather than a mere gift to a friend. Unfortunately, the commodities market prices declined, and Kim's friend incurred substantial losses. In 2016, Kim's friend declared personal bankruptcy and Kim was unable to collect any of the loan. Kim did not recognize any other capital gains or losses during 2016. The $10,000 bad debt loss recognized in 2016 is treated as a short-term capital loss. Thus, Kim may deduct only $3,000 in 2016. The remaining $7,000 is carried forward indefinitely to 2017 and subsequent years. ◄

TYPICAL MISCONCEPTION

Partial worthlessness means that a debt is still partially recoverable. The term is sometimes erroneously applied to debt where there has been a partial recovery even though there is no prospect for further recovery.

Partial Worthlessness. As previously noted, taxpayers may not deduct a partially worthless nonbusiness debt. Thus, a taxpayer cannot deduct a loss for a nonbusiness debt that is still partially recoverable during the year.

EXAMPLE I:8-37 ► Gordon, an individual, made a $5,000, five-year interest-bearing loan to a small company in 2013. Gordon was not in the trade or business of making commercial loans. In 2015, Gordon received word from the attorney who was appointed trustee of the company that bankruptcy proceedings had been filed. The trustee indicated that, although final disposition of the case will not occur until 2016, Gordon can reasonably expect to receive only 20 cents for every $1

---

54 Reg. Sec. 1.166-5(b)(2).

55 *John M. Trent v. CIR*, 7 AFTR 2d 1599, 61-2 USTC ¶9506 (2nd Cir., 1961). See also *Charles L. Hutchinson*, 1982 PH T.C. Memo ¶82,045, 43 TCM 440 and *U.S. v. Edna Generes*, 29 AFTR 2d 72-609, 72-1 USTC ¶9259 (USSC, 1972).

56 *Stuart Bart*, 21 T.C. 880 (1954), *acq.* 1954-1 C.B. 3.

invested. Because this is a nonbusiness bad debt that is still partly recoverable in 2015, Gordon may not deduct the partial loss as a short-term capital loss in 2015 and must wait until 2016 when the case is finally settled to deduct the nonbusiness bad debt. ◀

BUSINESS BAD DEBTS

The tax treatment of losses from business bad debts differs substantially from the treatment of nonbusiness bad debts. As previously discussed, a business bad debt provides an ordinary loss deduction. Furthermore, taxpayers may also deduct a business debt that has become only partially worthless during the year.

EXAMPLE I:8-38 ▶ Assume the same facts as in Example I:8-37 except that Gordon's loan is made for business reasons (e.g., to provide assistance to a customer in financial difficulty). Because 80% of the loan is reasonably expected to be unrecoverable during 2015, Gordon may deduct $4,000 (0.80 × $5,000) as an ordinary loss in 2015. If Gordon receives only $600 in 2016 as a settlement, he may deduct an additional $400 of ordinary loss for the year. ◀

BOOK-TAX DIFFERENCES

In general, for tax purposes, taxpayers can use only the specific write-off method of accounting for bad debts. However, a corporation or other taxpayer would probably be required to use the reserve method for financial reporting purposes. This book-tax difference is one of the most common M-1 or M-3 adjustments in filing a Form 1120 for corporate taxpayers.

Accounting for the Business Bad Debt. In general, two basic methods are available to account for business bad debts: the specific write-off method and the reserve method. Except for certain specialized industries, however, taxpayers can use only the specific write-off method for tax purposes. Under the **specific write-off method**, the taxpayer deducts each bad debt individually as it becomes worthless and the taxpayer writes it off as an expense. Taxpayers use this method for (1) business bad debts that are either totally or partially worthless and (2) nonbusiness bad debts that are totally worthless. However, as previously noted, taxpayers take no deduction for partially worthless nonbusiness bad debts.

In the case of a partially worthless business bad debt, taxpayers may only deduct the worthless part of the debt. The taxpayer must prove to the satisfaction of the IRS the amount of the debt that has become worthless.

Recovery of Bad Debts. A taxpayer may collect a debt that was previously written off for tax purposes. Since the taxpayer previously deducted the uncollectible debt, the taxpayer must report the recovery as income in the year it is collected. The amount of the income that must be reported depends on the tax benefit rule discussed in Chapter I:4.

DEPOSITS IN INSOLVENT FINANCIAL INSTITUTIONS

At their election, qualified individuals may treat a loss on deposits in qualified bankrupt or insolvent financial institutions as a personal casualty loss in the year in which the individual can reasonably estimate the loss. The recognized loss is the difference between the taxpayer's basis in the deposit and a reasonable estimate of the amount that the taxpayer will receive. This treatment allows the individual an ordinary loss deduction, but subjects the loss to the personal casualty loss limitations. In lieu of this election, qualified individuals may elect to treat these losses as if they were incurred in a transaction entered into for profit (but not connected with a trade or business). This election is available only with respect to deposits that are not insured under federal law, and is limited to $20,000 ($10,000 if married and filing separately) per institution per year. This limitation is reduced by any insurance proceeds expected to be received under state law. This election also allows the individual an ordinary loss deduction but subjects the loss to the $20,000 limitation as well as the 2% of AGI floor on miscellaneous itemized deductions. If the taxpayer makes neither of these elections, the taxpayer may claim the loss as a nonbusiness bad debt (a short-term capital loss) in the year of worthlessness or partial recovery, whichever comes last.

KEY POINT

If a taxpayer incurs a casualty loss on personal use property, the amount of the deductible loss is first reduced by $100 per casualty, and then the total net casualty losses for the year are further reduced by 10% of the taxpayer's AGI for the year.

A qualified individual is any individual *except* one who:

- Owns at least 1% of the outstanding stock of the financial institution
- Is an officer of the financial institution
- Is a relative of an officer or a 1% owner of the financial institution[57]

[57] Sec. 165(l). A *relative* is defined as a sibling, spouse, aunt, uncle, nephew, niece, ancestor, or lineal descendant.

Qualified financial institutions include banks, federal or state chartered savings and loans and thrift institutions, and federal or state insured credit unions.

This election applies to all losses sustained by the individual in the same institution and cannot be revoked unless the taxpayer receives IRS permission.[58]

The treatment of business and nonbusiness bad debts for non-corporate taxpayers is summarized in Topic Review I:8-4.

TOPIC REVIEW I:8-4

Bad Debts

TYPE OF DEBT	RESULTS
Nonbusiness	Deductible as a short-term capital loss. Deductible only when the debt is totally worthless. The taxpayer must have basis in the debt.
Business	Deductible as an ordinary loss. Except for certain specialized exceptions, the specific write-off method must be used. The reserve method is not available. May deduct partial worthlessness. Must have basis in the debt.

NET OPERATING LOSSES

OBJECTIVE 6

Compute a net operating loss deduction

A **net operating loss (NOL)** under Sec. 172 generally involves only business income and expenses. An NOL occurs when taxable income for any year is negative because business expenses exceed business income. A deduction for the NOL arises when a taxpayer carries the NOL to a year in which the taxpayer has taxable income. Thus, an NOL for one year becomes a deduction against taxable income of another year. This is accomplished in one of two ways:

KEY POINT

If taxpayers were not entitled to a deduction for net operating losses, taxpayers would actually pay a tax on an amount that exceeded their economic income over a period of time. The NOL deduction permits taxpayers to offset taxable income with losses incurred in other years.

- The year's NOL is carried back and deducted from the income of a previous year. This procedure provides for a refund of some of the taxes previously paid for the prior year.
- The year's NOL is carried forward and deducted from the income of a subsequent year. This procedure provides a reduction in the taxable income of the subsequent year, thus reducing the tax liability associated with that year.

The NOL deduction is intended to mitigate the inequity caused by the interaction of the progressive rate structure and the requirement to report income on an annual basis. This inequity arises between taxpayers whose business income fluctuates widely from year to year and those whose business income remains relatively constant.

EXAMPLE I:8-39 ►

John and Julie Jones and Ken and Karen Smith are both married couples and file joint returns. Over a two-year period they both report a total of $140,000 in taxable income. However, John and Julie report $70,000 of taxable income each year; Ken and Karen report $200,000 of taxable income in the first year and a $60,000 loss in the second year. Without the NOL provisions and using the 2015 tax rates for both years, John and Julie will report a $19,156 ($9,578 + $9,578) total tax liability for the two years, whereas Ken and Karen will report a total tax liability of $43,052 on their taxable income of $200,000 in the first year.[59] Under the NOL rules, Ken and Karen can carry back the $60,000 loss in the second year to offset their taxable income in the first year. This allows them to recover a portion of the taxes paid in the first year. Based on 2015 tax rates, they would recover $16,464 of the $43,052 paid, resulting in a net tax liability for both years of $26,588 ($43,052 − $16,464). Although the total tax liability over the two years for the two couples is still unequal ($19,156 for the Joneses, and $26,588 for the Smiths), the ability to carry over NOLs substantially reduces the difference and helps provide some degree of fairness. ◄

[58] The rules dealing with this special election are found in Notice 89-28, (1989-1 C.B. 667).

[59] Using the 2015 tax rate schedules for both years.

COMPUTING THE NET OPERATING LOSS FOR INDIVIDUALS

ADDITIONAL COMMENT

In computing the NOL for corporations, only minor adjustments are necessary.

The starting point in calculating an individual's NOL is generally taxable income. As mentioned earlier in this chapter, individuals may deduct three basic types of expenses to arrive at the amount of taxable income: business-related expenses, investment-related expenses, and certain personal expenses. The NOL, however, generally attempts to measure only the economic loss that occurs when business expenses exceed business income. Thus, individual taxpayers must make several adjustments to taxable income to arrive at the amount of the NOL for any particular year. These include adjustments for an NOL deduction, a capital loss deduction, the deduction for personal exemptions, and the excess of nonbusiness deductions over nonbusiness income.

ADDITIONAL COMMENT

If taxpayers were permitted to calculate the NOL for the current year by including NOL carryovers from earlier years, they could possibly extend the carryover period beyond the statutorily established 20-year carryforward period.

Add Back any Nol Deduction. Under certain circumstances, a taxpayer might have taken a deduction for an NOL arising from another tax year in computing the taxable loss for the current loss year. Allowing this deduction to create or increase the NOL of the current loss year would provide an unwarranted benefit. Thus, taxable income for the current loss year must be increased for this deduction.

Add Back any Capital Loss Deduction. To compute taxable income, individuals may deduct up to a maximum of $3,000 capital losses in excess of capital gains in any year. Any capital loss in excess of this limit can be carried over and deducted in a subsequent tax year, subject to the same limitation. Because capital losses have their separate carryover provisions, taxpayers must add back any deduction associated with these losses to taxable income to arrive at the NOL for the current loss year. To make this adjustment, the taxpayer must follow several steps:

Step 1. A taxpayer must separate nonbusiness capital gains and losses from business capital gains and losses. The nonbusiness gains and losses are then netted, while the business gains and losses are netted separately.

Step 2. If the nonbusiness capital gains exceed the nonbusiness capital losses, the excess, along with other types of nonbusiness income, is first used to offset any nonbusiness ordinary deductions. Any nonbusiness capital gain remaining is then used to offset any business capital loss in excess of the business capital gain for the year.[60]

Step 3. If both groups of transactions result in net losses, the capital loss deduction provided by these transactions must be added back. For purposes of the NOL, no deduction is allowed for either business or nonbusiness net capital losses.

Step 4. If the taxpayer's nonbusiness capital losses exceed the nonbusiness capital gains, the losses may not be offset against the taxpayer's excess business capital gains. Allowing this offset would provide an indirect deduction for a nonbusiness economic loss.[61]

EXAMPLE I:8-40 ▶ During the current year, Nils recognizes a short-term capital loss of $10,000 on the sale of an investment capital asset. He also recognizes a $5,000 long-term capital gain on the sale of a business capital asset. For taxable income purposes, the loss is netted against the gain, leaving a $5,000 net short-term capital loss. This loss provides a $3,000 deduction from taxable income, with the remaining $2,000 being carried forward to the following year. To compute the NOL, however, none of the $10,000 nonbusiness capital loss is deductible. Thus, the $3,000 deduction as well as the $5,000 loss that offset the business capital gain must be added back because in computing taxable income the taxpayer, in essence, has received a total $8,000 reduction from the nonbusiness capital loss. ◀

Add Back the Deduction for Personal Exemptions. Because the deduction for personal and dependency exemptions is strictly a personal deduction, it must be added back to arrive at the year's NOL.

---

[60] Reg. Sec. 1.172-3. If the nonbusiness deductions exceed the nonbusiness income, the excess is added back. This adjustment is discussed later in the chapter.

[61] Sec. 172(d)(2). Note that all deductible nonbusiness capital losses involve investment property because capital losses on personal-use assets are not deductible in arriving at taxable income. To make the adjustment for any capital loss, the exclusion under Sec. 1202 for gains from small business stock is not allowed (see Chapter I:5).

ADDITIONAL COMMENT

An excess of nonbusiness deductions over nonbusiness income cannot increase the NOL. However, an excess of nonbusiness income over nonbusiness expenses can reduce the NOL.

Add Back Excess of Nonbusiness Deductions over Nonbusiness Income. Because nonbusiness deductions do not reflect an economic loss from business, they are not deductible in arriving at the NOL. However, these deductions do offset any nonbusiness income reported during the year. Nonbusiness income includes sources of income such as dividends and interest, as well as nonbusiness capital gains in excess of nonbusiness capital losses. Wages and salary, even if they are earned in part-time employment, are considered business income. Nonbusiness deductions include itemized deductions such as charitable contributions, medical expenses, and nonbusiness interest and taxes. Casualty losses on personal-use assets, however, are treated as business losses and are excluded from this adjustment.[62] If a taxpayer does not have itemized deductions in excess of the standard deduction, the standard deduction is used as the amount of the nonbusiness deductions.

Following are several independent examples demonstrating these required adjustments. In each case, assume that Nancy is a single taxpayer.

EXAMPLE I:8-41 ▶ During 2015, Nancy, who is single, reports the following taxable income:

Gross income from business		$123,000	
Minus: Business expenses		(147,000)	($24,000)
Plus: Interest income			700
Dividend income			400
AGI			($22,900)
Minus: Greater of itemized deductions or standard deduction:			
Interest expense		$ 6,000	
Taxes		4,000	
Casualty loss (reduced by the $100 floor)		1,000	
Total itemized deductions		$ 11,000	
		or	
Standard deduction		6,300	(11,000)
Minus: Personal exemption			(4,000)
Taxable income			($37,900)

Nancy's NOL for the year is computed as follows:

Taxable income			($37,900)
Nonbusiness deductions:			
Itemized deductions	$11,000		
Minus: Casualty loss	(1,000)	$ 10,000	
Minus: Nonbusiness income:			
Interest	$700		
Dividends	400	(1,100)	
Plus: Excess of nonbusiness deductions over nonbusiness income			8,900
Plus: Personal exemption			4,000
Net operating loss			($25,000)[a] ◀

[a]Note that the NOL equals the total of the $24,000 net business loss and the $1,000 casualty loss.

EXAMPLE I:8-42 ▶ During 2015, Betsy, who is single, reports the following taxable income:

Gross income from business	$123,000	
Minus: Business expenses	(147,000)	($24,000)
Plus: Interest income		700
Dividend income		400
AGI		($22,900)
Minus Greater of itemized deductions or standard deduction:		
Interest expense	$ 2,000	
	or	
Standard deduction	6,300	(6,300)
Minus: Personal exemption		(4,000)
Taxable income		($33,200)

[62] Sec. 172(d)(4)(C).

Betsy's NOL for the year is computed as follows:

Taxable income				($33,200)
Nonbusiness deductions:				
Standard deduction			$ 6,300	
Minus:	Nonbusiness income:			
	Interest	$700		
	Dividends	400	(1,100)	
Plus	Excess of nonbusiness deductions over nonbusiness income			5,200
Plus:	Personal exemption			4,000
Net operating loss				($24,000)[a] ◀

[a]Note that the NOL equals the net business loss for the year.

EXAMPLE I:8-43 ▶ **During 2015, Rachael, who is single, reports the following taxable income:**

Gross income from business		$123,000	
Minus	Business expenses	(147,000)	($24,000)
Plus:	Interest income		700
	Dividend income		400
	Salary		6,000
	Nonbusiness LTCG		10,000
AGI			($6,900)
Minus:	Greater of itemized deductions or standard deduction:		
	Interest expense	$ 6,000	
	Taxes	4,000	
Casualty (reduced by the $100 floor)		1,000	
Total itemized deductions		$ 11,000	
		or	
Standard deduction		6,300	(11,000)
Minus:	Personal exemption		(4,000)
Taxable income			($21,900)

Rachael's NOL for the year is computed as follows:

Taxable income				($21,900)
Plus:	Nonbusiness deductions:			
	Itemized deductions	$11,000		
Minus: Casualty loss		(1,000)	$ 10,000	
Minus:	Nonbusiness income:			
	Interest	$700		
	Dividends	400		
	LTCG	10,000	(11,100)	
Excess of nonbusiness deductions over nonbusiness income				0
Plus:	Personal exemption			4,000
Net operating loss				($17,900)[a] ◀

[a]Note that the NOL can also be calculated as follows:

Loss from business	($24,000)
Salary	6,000
Casualty loss	(1,000)
Excess of nonbusiness income ($11,100) over nonbusiness deductions ($10,000)	1,100
NOL	($17,900)

CARRYBACK AND CARRYOVER PERIODS

Under Sec. 172, an NOL is initially carried back for two years and is deductible as an offset to the taxable income of the carryback years. Except as noted below, taxpayers must carry the loss back first. If any loss remains, taxpayers may then carry it forward for a period of 20 years.[63] Furthermore, in both the carryback and carryforward periods, the loss must be deducted from the years in chronological order. Thus, if an NOL is sustained

[63] For NOLs arising in a farming business, in a qualified small business attributable to a Presidentially declared disaster, or in a casualty or theft sustained by an individual, the carryback period is extended to three years. These NOLs are taken after the regular NOL. Certain "specified liability losses" are entitled to a 10-year carryback. Sec. 172(b)(1)(C) and (f). Likewise, for certain losses occurring in tax years that either begin or end in 2009 or 2010, taxpayers could make a special election to carry the NOLs back for five years.

in 2015, it first must be carried back to 2013, then to 2014, followed by 2016, 2017, and so on until the loss is completely used. Any NOL that is not used during the carryover period expires and is of no further tax benefit.

If the NOL is carried back to a prior year, the taxpayer must file for a refund of taxes previously paid. If the NOL deduction is carried forward, it reduces the taxable income and the tax liability for the carryover year.

Election to Forgo Carryback Period. A taxpayer may elect not to carry back the NOL, but to carry the loss forward. This election, which is made with respect to the entire carryback period, does not extend the carryforward period beyond 20 years. This allows a taxpayer some degree of flexibility in using the NOL deduction to the greatest advantage. (See the Tax Planning Considerations section in this chapter for a discussion of this topic.)

Loss Carryovers from Two or more Years. At times, a taxpayer might have NOL carryovers that are incurred in two or more taxable years. Often these losses are carried to the same years in the carryover period. If such is the case, the loss of the earliest year is always completely used first before deducting any of the loss incurred in a subsequent year. Because of the limited carryover period, this rule is beneficial to the taxpayer.

ADDITIONAL COMMENT

An election to forgo the carryback period for the NOL of any year is irrevocable.

RECOMPUTATION OF TAXABLE INCOME IN THE CARRYOVER YEAR

When the taxpayer carries back the NOL deduction to a prior year, the taxpayer must recompute that year's taxable income. Because the NOL is attributable to a taxpayer's trade or business, it is deductible *for* AGI. As a result, the recomputation of taxable income for the carryback year may affect the deductible amount of certain itemized deductions because some of the deductions (e.g., the deductions for medical expenses, charitable contributions, and casualty losses) are limited or measured by reference to the taxpayer's AGI. All of these deductions except the deduction for charitable contributions must be recomputed using the reduced AGI amount.[64]

Once the taxpayer determines the tax refund for the carryback year, the taxpayer must calculate the amount of the NOL available to be deducted in subsequent carryover years. This is done by adjusting the recomputed income of the prior carryover year. Although certain differences exist, these adjustments are similar to those mentioned above.

The rules for computing and deducting NOLs are presented in Topic Review I:8-5.

TOPIC REVIEW I:8-5

Net Operating Losses

ITEM	RULES
Computation of NOL (adjustments to taxable income)	Add back any NOL deduction carried to the current year.
	Add back any capital loss deduction. Add back the deduction for personal and dependency exemptions. Add back the excess of nonbusiness deductions over nonbusiness income. For this purpose, casualty losses on personal-use property are treated as business losses.
Carryover period	May be carried back two years and forward twenty years (certain exceptions apply). Must be carried to the carryover years in chronological order: first carried back to the second prior year, then to the first prior year, then to the first succeeding year, etc. An election may be made to forgo the carryback. This does not extend the carryforward period. If losses from two or more years are carried to the same year, the losses from the earliest year are completely used first.

64 Reg. Sec. 1.172-5(a)(2)(ii).

Tax planning considerations

OBJECTIVE 7

Identify tax planning considerations for losses and bad debts

BAD DEBTS

To deduct a bad debt, a taxpayer must show that the debt is worthless. At times the IRS might assert that the debt being written off is either not yet worthless or that it became worthless in a previous year. If the taxpayer is unable to overcome the IRS's assertion concerning the year of worthlessness, the taxpayer might be barred from filing an amended return for the prior year because of the statute of limitations.[65] Thus, taxpayers should carefully document all efforts at collection and other facts that show the debt is worthless.

KEY POINT

If uncertainty exists as to the year in which a debt became worthless, the issue may not be settled within the normal three-year statute of limitations. For this reason, a taxpayer may claim a deduction for a worthless debt at any time within seven years.

As previously mentioned, a third-party guarantor of a loan who is required to repay the debt may, under certain circumstances, be entitled to a bad debt deduction. The guarantor must demonstrate that he or she received reasonable consideration in the form of cash or property in exchange for guaranteeing the debt. If the taxpayer does not receive proper consideration, the guarantee and subsequent payment of the loan by the guarantor is considered to be a gift rather than a loan. Reasonable consideration is also deemed to be received if the taxpayer enters into the agreement for a good faith business purpose or in accordance with normal business practice. However, if the taxpayer guarantees the debt of a spouse or a relative, the taxpayer must receive the consideration in the form of cash or property.

In the case of an outright loan between related taxpayers, the lender should always make sure to retain proper documentation to substantiate the fact that the transaction is a loan. If the taxpayer does not keep such documentation, the IRS may assert that the transaction is a gift.

CASUALTIES

A deduction is allowed for stolen property, but no deduction is allowed for lost property. Thus, taxpayers should always carefully document losses of property through theft (e.g., the filing of police reports or claims with the taxpayer's insurance company). In addition, pictures and written appraisals may be helpful to prove the amount of the loss.

NET OPERATING LOSSES

ADDITIONAL COMMENT

Normally, a taxpayer would want to carry back the NOL because of the possibility of receiving a refund in a short time period by filing the amended return. The carryover of the NOL involves waiting for a year or more to receive a tax benefit.

If a taxpayer incurs a net operating loss, the taxpayer should carefully analyze whether to elect to forgo the carryback period. Situations under which a taxpayer might elect to only carry the loss deduction forward include the following:

- A taxpayer might anticipate being in a higher marginal tax rate in future years than in the carryback years. If such is the case, the value of the deduction is higher in the carryforward years than in the carryback years. Taxpayers should consider, however, cash flows and the time value of money (e.g., the tax benefits from a refund of taxes are realized sooner if the NOL is carried back).
- General business and other tax credits that are nonrefundable (i.e., the credits are limited to the tax liability or some percentage thereof) may be reduced or eliminated for the carryback years because these credits must be recomputed based on the adjusted tax liability after applying the NOL carryback. (See Chapter I:14 for a discussion of tax credits.)

Compliance and procedural considerations

OBJECTIVE 8

Identify compliance and procedural considerations for losses and bad debts

CASUALTY LOSSES

If a taxpayer sustains a casualty loss in a location that the President of the United States declares a disaster area, he or she may make an election to deduct the loss in the year preceding the year in which the loss occurred. A taxpayer makes this election by either filing

[65] However, the statute of limitations for claims for a refund or credit because of a bad debt is extended from three years to seven years under Sec. 6511(d)(1), thus giving the taxpayer additional time if this is the case.

ADDITIONAL COMMENT

Instant access for downloading federal income tax forms, instructions, publications, etc. is available on the Internet (http://www.irs.gov).

the return for the previous year and including the loss in that year (if the return has not already been filed) or filing an amended return or claim for refund for that year.[66] The return should clearly include all the following information:

- That the election is being made
- The date of the disaster giving rise to the loss
- The city, county, and state in which the damaged property is located

The taxpayer must make the election before the due date of the return for the year in which the disaster actually occurs. Although the Regulations state that the election may not be revoked more than 90 days after it is made, the Tax Court has held that this part of the Regulation is invalid.[67]

NET OPERATING LOSSES

When an individual taxpayer carries an NOL deduction back to a prior year, the taxpayer claims a refund of taxes by either filing an amended return on Form 1040X or filing for a quick refund on Form 1045. Corporations use Form 1139. If the taxpayer uses Form 1045, the IRS must act on the application for refund within 90 days of the later of the date of the application or the last day of the month in which the return of the loss year must be filed.[68] A taxpayer must file Form 1045 within one year after the end of the year in which the NOL arose. The taxpayer must attach additional information such as pages 1 and 2 of Form 1040 for the year of loss, a copy of the application for an extension of time to file the return for the year of loss, and copies of forms or schedules for items refigured in the carryback years.

WORTHLESS SECURITIES

As explained earlier in this chapter, securities that become worthless during the taxable year are deemed to have become worthless on the last day of the year. In many cases, this treatment causes the loss to be treated as a long-term capital loss. If the loss from the worthless security is long term, the taxpayer reports it in Part II of Schedule D (Form 1040) along with the other long-term gains and losses for the year. The taxpayer reports short-term capital losses in Part I of Schedule D.

WHAT WOULD YOU DO IN THIS SITUATION?

A client comes to you with an idea to treat a loan that he made to one of his children two years ago as a bad debt. The loan is evidenced by a properly executed note with stated interest and payment dates. However, the client has not collected any loan payments or interest during the two-year period. The child is insolvent and has declared bankruptcy. Before leaving your office, the client also mentions in passing that the child is in London on vacation with other members of the family and will stay in Europe for six weeks. What would you do about classifying this loan as a bad debt?

PROBLEM MATERIALS

DISCUSSION QUESTIONS

I:8-1 What is the closed transaction doctrine, and why does it exist for purposes of recognizing a loss realized on holding property?

I:8-2 When property is disposed of, what factors influence the amount of the deductible loss?

I:8-3 Describe the usual tax consequences that apply to a worthless security.

I:8-4 Under what circumstances will a loss that is realized on a worthless security not be treated as a capital loss?

---

[66] Reg. Sec. 1.165-11(e).

[67] *Chester Matheson*, 74 T.C. 836 (1980), *acq.* 1981-2 C.B. 2.

[68] IRS, 2013 *Instructions for Filing Form 1045.*

I:8-5 What two general requirements must be met for a transaction to result in a capital loss?

I:8-6 What requirements must be met for stock to be considered Sec. 1244 stock?

I:8-7 What tax treatment applies to gains and losses on Sec. 1244 stock?

I:8-8 Describe a situation where a loss on the sale of business or investment property is not currently deductible, and explain why.

I:8-9 a. What is a passive activity?
b. Who is subject to the passive loss limitation rules?

I:8-10 a. For purposes of the passive loss rules, what is a closely held C corporation?
b. In what way do the passive loss rules differ from the regular passive loss rules when applied to closely held C corporations?

I:8-11 Why is it important to identify exactly what constitutes an activity for purposes of the passive activity rules?

I:8-12 a. If a taxpayer is involved in several different business operations during the year, how is the determination made as to how many activities these operations constitute for purposes of the passive activity loss rules?
b. Can a business operation and a rental operation ever be combined into one activity? Explain.

I:8-13 Which of the following activities are considered passive for the year? Explain. Consider each situation independently.
a. Laura owns a rental unit that she rents out to students. The rental unit is Laura's only business and she spends approximately 875 hours per year managing, collecting the rent, advertising, and performing minor repairs. At times she must hire professionals such as plumbers to do the maintenance. Is the rental unit a passive activity with respect to Laura?
b. Kami is a medical doctor who works four days a week in a medical practice that she and five other doctors formed. Last year she and her partners formed another partnership that owns and operates a medical lab. The lab employs ten technicians, one of whom also acts as manager. During the year Kami spent 120 hours in meetings, reviewing records, etc., for the lab. Is the lab a passive activity with respect to Kami?
c. Assume the same facts in part b. In addition, assume that the same group of doctors have formed two other partnerships. One is a medical supply partnership. Kami spent 150 hours working for this partnership. The medical supply partnership has five full-time employees. Kami also spent 250 hours during the year working for the other partnership. This partnership specializes in providing medical services to individuals from out of town who are staying at local hotels and motels. This partnership hires two full-time and six part-time nurses. Are the lab and the two other partnerships passive activities with respect to Kami?

I:8-14 Explain the difference between materially participating and actively participating in an activity. When is the active participation test used?

I:8-15 a. What requirements must be met in order for a taxpayer to deduct up to $25,000 of passive losses from rental real estate activities against active and portfolio income?
b. What requirements must be met in order for a real estate rental activity to be considered a real estate business that is not subject to the passive loss rules?

I:8-16 Are the losses suspended under the passive loss rules lost forever? Explain.

I:8-17 What tests must be met to qualify a loss as deductible under the casualty loss provisions? Discuss the application of each of these tests.

I:8-18 Explain how a taxable gain on property can be realized because of a casualty event such as a fire or theft. How are these gains treated?

I:8-19 During the current year, Rulon's toilet overflowed because of a mechanical problem. Rulon was outside playing croquet, and by the time he returned, the water had flooded the basement, causing damage to the carpet, walls, and ceiling. The cost of repairing the damage was $9,000. Rulon has homeowners insurance that will cover half of the damage. However, because he has already had claims this year, Rulon does not want to report the incident to his insurance company for fear of a large increase in insurance rates. Instead, Rulon wants to deduct the loss as a casualty loss on his tax return. His AGI for this year is $50,000, and he has other itemized deductions of $6,000. Rulon is single. What amount of the casualty loss may he deduct?

I:8-20 Compare and contrast the computational rules for deducting casualty losses on personal-use property with casualty losses incurred on business or investment property.

I:8-21 Under what circumstances may a loss arising from a casualty or theft be deducted in a year other than the year in which the loss occurs?

I:8-22 For individuals, how are casualty losses on personal-use property reported on the tax return? How are casualty losses on business property reported?

I:8-23 Is the $100 floor on personal-use casualty losses imposed on each individual loss item if more than one item of property is destroyed in a single casualty? Is the floor imposed before or after the casualty gains are netted against the casualty losses?

I:8-24 Sarah loans $50,000 to her best friend, John. John uses the money to open a pizza parlor next to the local high school. Three years later, when John still owed Sarah $15,000, John closed the pizza parlor and declared bankruptcy. Discuss the appropriate tax treatment for Sarah.

I:8-25 Dana is an attorney who specializes in family law. She uses the cash method of accounting and is a calendar-year taxpayer. Last year, she represented a client in a lawsuit and billed the client $5,000 for her services. Although she made repeated attempts, Dana was unable to collect the outstanding receivable. Finally, in November of the current year, she finds out that the individual has moved without leaving any forwarding address. Dana's attempts to locate the individual are futile. What is the amount of deduction that Dana may take with respect to this bad debt?

I:8-26 Under what circumstances may a taxpayer deduct a bad debt even though another party to the transaction is the creditor?

I:8-27 What is the definition of a nonbusiness debt? What is the character of the deduction for a nonbusiness bad debt?

I:8-28
a. What alternatives do individuals have in deducting a loss on a deposit in a qualified financial institution?
b. Explain when it might be better to elect one over the other.

I:8-29 A taxpayer collects a debt that was previously written off as a bad debt. What tax consequences arise if the recovery is received in a subsequent tax year?

I:8-30 What is an NOL deduction, and why is it allowed?

I:8-31 List the adjustments to an individual taxpayer's negative taxable income amount that must be made in computing an NOL for the year. What is the underlying rationale for requiring these adjustments for individuals?

I:8-32
a. What is the NOL carryback and carryover period?
b. Does a taxpayer have any choice in deciding the years to which the NOL should be carried?
c. Explain the circumstances under which a taxpayer might elect not to use the regular carryback or carryover period.

I:8-33 Can a casualty loss on a personal-use asset create or increase an NOL? Explain.

I:8-34 If an NOL is carried back to a prior year, what adjustments must be made to the prior year's taxable income? What are the possible results of the adjustments?

ISSUE IDENTIFICATION QUESTIONS

I:8-35 On January 12 of the current year, Barney Corporation, a publicly-held corporation, files for bankruptcy. During the bankruptcy proceedings it is determined that creditors will only receive 10% of what they are owed and that the shareholders will receive nothing. Sheryl, a calendar-year taxpayer, purchased 1,000 shares of Barney Corporation common stock for $7,000 on February 22 of the prior year. What tax issues should Sheryl consider?

I:8-36 Five years ago, Cora incorporated Gold, Inc., by contributing $80,000 and receiving 100% of the Gold common stock. Gold, Inc. is engaged in a retail business. Cora is single. Gold experienced financial difficulties. On December 22 of the current year, Cora sold all of her Gold stock for $5,000. What tax issues should Cora consider?

I:8-37 In a rage because of personal difficulties, Evan drove recklessly and crashed his automobile, doing $8,000 worth of damage. Fortunately, no one was injured. Since Evan received two speeding tickets during the past year, he is concerned about losing his insurance if he files an insurance claim. What tax issues should Evan consider?

I:8-38 Dan, a full-time employee of Beta, Inc., also owns 10% of its outstanding stock. The other 90% is owned by his three brothers. During the year, the president of Beta came to Dan, expressing grave concern about whether the company had the financial resources to remain in business. He mentioned specifically that a bank was threatening to force Beta to file bankruptcy if it didn't repay its $100,000 loan in full. After some negotiation, Dan agreed to loan Beta the $100,000 for one year until permanent financing could be obtained. A reasonable interest rate was set and a payment schedule was documented. Unfortunately, business did not improve, and Beta discontinued its business and did not repay the loan. What tax issues should Dan consider?

PROBLEMS

I:8-39 *Section 1244 Losses.* During the current year, Karen sells her entire interest in Central Corporation common stock for $22,000. She is the sole shareholder, and originally organized the corporation several years ago by contributing $89,000 in exchange for her stock, which qualifies as Sec. 1244 stock. Since its incorporation, Central has been involved in the manufacture of items that protect personal computers from static electricity. Unfortunately, this market is extremely competitive, and Central Corporation incurs substantial losses throughout its existence.
a. Assuming Karen is single, what are the amount and the character of the loss recognized on the sale of the Central Corporation stock?

b. Assuming Karen is married and files a joint return, what are the amount and the character of the loss recognized on the sale of the Central Corporation stock?
c. How would your answer to Part a change if Karen had originally purchased the stock from another shareholder rather than organizing the corporation?
d. How might Karen have structured the transaction in Part a to receive a greater tax advantage?

I:8-40 ***Amount and Character of Loss Transactions.*** On September 30 of the current year, Fox Corporation files for bankruptcy. At the time, it estimates that the total FMV of its assets is $725,000, whereas the total amount of its outstanding debt amounts to $950,000. Fox Corporation has been engaged in the resale of tax preparation and tax research-related books and software for several years.
a. At the time of the bankruptcy, Fox is owned by Randall, who purchased the stock from an investor for $250,000 several years ago. Randall is single. What are the amount and character of the loss sustained by Randall upon Fox's bankruptcy?
b. How would your answer to part a change if Randall originally organized Fox Corporation, capitalizing it with $250,000 of cash and assuming Fox qualifies as a small business corporation?
c. How would your answer to Part a change if Randall were a corporation instead of an individual?
d. How would your answer to Part b change if Randall were a corporation instead of an individual?

I:8-41 ***Amount and Character of Loss Transactions.*** Five years ago, Brian and his brother Boyd formed Stewart Corp., a golf apparel manufacturing corporation. At that time, Brian contributed $300,000 to the corporation in exchange for 50% of its stock. During the current year, Brian needed some cash to purchase a golf course so he sold a third of his interest in Stewart Corp. for $85,000. He also sold stock in the following companies for the amounts indicated:

Corporation	*Sales Proceeds*	*Adjusted Basis*	*When Acquired*
IBM	$15,000	$10,000	52 months ago
Microsoft	25,000	45,000	18 months ago
Tidal Radio	32,000	12,000	7 months ago
Wavetable	20,000	26,000	4 months ago

During the year Brian hired a collection agency to collect a $14,000 loan he made to an old friend, which was due in full on January 1 of the current year. The agency found no trace of his friend. Also during the year, BTR Corporation, in which he owns stock, went bankrupt. His investment was worth $94,000 on January 1, he purchased it six years ago for $100,000, and he expects to receive only $8,000 in redemption of his stock. Finally, Brian's salary for the year was $114,000 for his work as an associate professor.
a. What are the net gains and losses from the above items and their character?
b. What is Brian's AGI for the year assuming he has no other items of income or deduction?

I:8-42 ***Passive Losses.*** In the current year Alice reports $150,000 of salary income, $20,000 of income from activity X, and $35,000 and $15,000 losses from activities Y and Z, respectively. All three activities are passive with respect to Alice and are purchased during the current year. What is the amount of loss that may be deducted with respect to each of these activities? Also compute the amount of loss that must be carried over for each activity.

I:8-43 ***Passive Losses.*** In the current year Clay reports income and losses from the following activities:

Activity X	$ 28,000
Activity Y	(10,000)
Activity Z	(20,000)
Salary	100,000

Activities X, Y, and Z are all passive with respect to Clay. Activity Z has $40,000 in passive losses which are carried over from the prior year. In the current year Clay sells activity Z for a taxable gain of $30,000.
a. What is the amount of loss that Clay may deduct and what is the amount that must be carried over in the current year?
b. Based solely on the amounts above, compute Clay's AGI for the current year.

I:8-44 ***Passive Losses: Rental Real Estate.*** During the current year, Irene, a married individual who files a joint return, reports the following items of income and loss:

Salary	$130,000
Activity X (passive)	10,000
Activity Y (rental real estate, nontrade or business)	(30,000)
Activity Z (rental real estate, nontrade or business)	(20,000)

Irene actively participates in activities Y and Z and owns 100% of both Y and Z.

a. What is Irene's AGI for the year?

b. What is the amount of suspended losses (if any) that may be carried over with respect to each activity?

I:8-45 ***Passive Losses.*** In 2014, Mark purchased two separate activities. Information regarding these activities for 2014 and 2015 is as follows:

Activity	*2014 Status*	*Income (Loss)*	*Activity*	*2015 Status*	*Income (Loss)*
A	Passive	($24,000)	A	Active	$10,000
B	Passive	(8,000)	B	Passive	20,000

The 2014 losses were suspended losses for that year. During 2015, Mark also reports salary income of $120,000 and interest and dividend income of $20,000. Compute the amount (if any) of losses attributable to Activities A and B that are deductible in 2015 and any suspended losses carried to 2016.

I:8-46 ***Passive Losses.*** During the current year, Juan, a single individual, has AGI of $124,000 before taking into account any passive activity losses. He also actively participates and owns 100% of activity A, which is a real estate rental activity. For the year, activity A generates a net loss of $6,000 and $3,000 in tax credits. Juan is in the 28% tax bracket. What is the amount of suspended loss and credit from activity A that must be carried to subsequent years?

I:8-47 ***Passive Losses.*** In 2015, Julie, a single individual, reported the following items of income and deduction:

Salary	$166,000
Interest income	14,000
Long-term capital gain from sales of stock	22,000
Short-term capital losses from sales of stock	(17,000)
Loss from a passive rental real estate activity	(20,000)
Interest expense on loan to purchase stock	(21,000)
Qualified residence interest on residence	(12,000)
Charitable contributions	(8,000)
Property taxes on residence	(5,000)
Tax return preparation fees	(2,500)
Unreimbursed employee business expenses	(2,000)

Julie owns 100% and is an active participant in the rental real estate activity. What is her taxable income for 2015?

I:8-48 ***Casualty Losses.*** Tony is a carpenter who owns his own furniture manufacturing business. During the current year, vandals broke into the workshop, damaged several pieces of equipment, stole his delivery truck, and also stole his personal automobile, which he often kept in the workshop garage. The asset descriptions and related values are as follows:

Asset	*FMV Before Casualty*	*FMV After Casualty*	*Cost to Repair/Replace*	*Adjusted Basis*	*Insurance Proceeds*
Equipment A	$12,300	$4,000	$ 8,700	$ 9,000	$ 3,700
Equipment B	8,100	0	9,000	3,000	7,800
Equipment C	Not Available	Not Available	13,800	15,300	11,400
Delivery Truck	18,000	0	32,000	17,500	16,000
Automobile	15,000	0	12,000	28,000	12,000

Although he could not obtain its fair market value after the casualties, Troy decided to repair rather than replace Equipment C.

Before considering any deductions because of these casualties, Troy's AGI is $80,000. What deductions may Tony take relating to the vandalism?

I:8-49 *Theft Losses.* On December 17 of the current year, Kelly's business office safe is burglarized. The theft is discovered a few days after the burglary. $3,000 cash from the cash registers is stolen. A diamond necklace and a ring that Kelly frequently wore are also stolen. The necklace cost Kelly $2,300 many years ago and is insured for its $6,000 FMV. Kelly purchased the ring for $3,000 just two weeks before the burglary. Unfortunately, the ring and the cash are not insured. Kelly's AGI for the year, not including the items noted above, is $70,000.

a. What is Kelly's deductible theft loss in the current year?
b. What is Kelly's deductible theft loss in the current year if the theft is not discovered until January of the following year?

I:8-50 *Casualty Losses: Year of Deduction.* Jerry sprayed all of the landscaping around his house with a pesticide in June 2015. Shortly thereafter, all of the trees and shrubs unaccountably died. The FMV and the adjusted basis of the plants were $15,000. Later that year, the pesticide manufacturer announced a recall of the particular batch of pesticide that Jerry used. It also announced a program whereby consumers would be repaid for any damage caused by the improper mixture. Jerry is single and reports $38,000 AGI in 2015 and $42,000 in 2016.

a. Assume that in 2015 Jerry files a claim for his losses and receives notification that payment of $15,000 will be received in 2016. Jerry receives full payment for the damage in 2016. How should the loss and the reimbursement be reported?
b. How will your answer to Part a change if in 2016 the manufacturer files for bankruptcy and Jerry receives $1,500 in total and final payment for his claim?
c. How will your answer to Part a change if the announcement and the reimbursement do not occur until late in 2016, after Jerry has already filed his tax return for 2015?

I:8-51 *Personal-Use Casualty Losses.* In the current year Ned completely destroys his personal automobile (purchased two years earlier for $28,000) in a traffic accident. Fortunately none of the occupants are injured. The FMV of the car before the accident is $18,000; after the accident it is worthless. Ned receives a $14,000 settlement from the insurance company. Later in the same year his house is burglarized and several antiques are stolen. The antiques were purchased a number of years earlier for $8,000. Their value at the time of the theft is estimated at $12,000. They are not insured. Ned's AGI for the current year is $60,000. What is the amount of Ned's deductible casualty loss in the current year, assuming the thefts are discovered in the same year?

I:8-52 *Casualty Losses.* During 2015, Pam incurred the following casualty losses:

Asset	*FMV Before*	*FMV After*	*Basis*	*Insurance*
Business 1	$18,000	$ 0	$15,000	$ 4,000
Business 2	25,000	10,000	8,000	3,000
Business 3	20,000	0	18,000	19,000
Personal 1	12,000	0	20,000	2,000
Personal 2	8,000	5,000	10,000	0
Personal 3	9,000	0	6,000	8,000

All of the items were destroyed in the same casualty. Before considering the casualty items, Pam reports business income of $80,000, qualified residential interest of $6,000 property taxes on her personal residence of $2,000, and charitable contributions of $4,000. Compute Pam's taxable income for 2015. Pam is single.

I:8-53 *Business Bad Debt.* Elaine is a physician who uses the cash method of accounting for tax purposes. During the current year, Elaine bills Ralph $1,200 for office visits and outpatient surgery. Unfortunately, unknown to Elaine, Ralph moves away leaving no payment and no forwarding address. What is the amount of Elaine's bad debt deduction with respect to Ralph's debt?

I:8-54 *Nonbusiness Bad Debt.* During 2014, Becky loans her brother Ken $5,000, which he intends to use to establish a small business. Because Ken has no other assets and needs cash to establish the business, the agreement provides that Ken will repay the debt if (and when) sufficient funds are generated from the business. Becky and Ken do not establish an interest rate. The business is unsuccessful, and Ken is forced to file for bankruptcy in 2015. By the end of 2015, it is estimated that the creditors will receive only 20% of the amount owed. In 2016 the bankruptcy proceedings are closed, and the creditors receive 10% of the amount due on the debt. What is Becky's bad debt deduction for 2015? For 2016?

I:8-55 *Bad Debt Deduction.* Assume the same facts as in Problem I:8-54, except that Becky and Ken are not related and that under the terms of the loan Ken agrees to repay Becky the $5,000 plus interest (at a reasonable stated rate) over a five-year period. What is Becky's bad debt deduction for 2015? For 2016?

I:8-56 *Net Operating Loss Deduction.* Michelle and Mark are married and file a joint return. Michelle owns an unincorporated dental practice. Mark works part-time as a high school math teacher, and spends the remainder of his time caring for their daughter. During 2015, they report the following items:

Mark's salary	$18,000
Interest earned on savings account	1,200
Interest paid on personal residence	7,100
Itemized deductions for state and local taxes	3,400
Items relating to Michelle's dental practice	
Revenues	65,000
Payroll and salary expense	49,000
Supplies	17,000
Rent	16,400
Advertising	4,600
Depreciation	8,100

a. What is Michelle and Mark's taxable income or loss for the year?
b. What is Michelle and Mark's NOL for the year?

I:8-57 *Net Operating Loss Deduction.* Assume the same facts as in Problem I:8-56, except in addition to the other itemized deductions Michelle and Mark suffer a $4,500 deductible personal casualty loss (after limitations).
a. What is Michelle and Mark's taxable income or loss for the year?
b. What is Michelle and Mark's NOL for the year?

I:8-58 *Net Operating Loss Deduction.* Assume the same facts as in Problem I:8-56, except instead of a $3,400 itemized deduction for state and local taxes, Michelle and Mark have a $3,400 deductible casualty loss (after limitations).
a. What is Michelle and Mark's taxable income or loss for the year?
b. What is Michelle and Mark's NOL for the year?

I:8-59 *Net Operating Loss.* During 2015, Karen, a single taxpayer, reports the following income and expense items relating to her interior design business:

Revenues	$52,000
Cost of goods sold	41,000
Advertising	3,300
Office supplies	1,700
Rent	13,800
Contract labor	28,000

Karen also worked part-time during the year, earning $13,500. She reports a long-term capital gain of $4,200, and a short-term capital loss of $3,800. Her itemized deductions total $5,200.
a. What is Karen's taxable income or loss for the year?
b. What is Karen's NOL for the year?

TAX STRATEGY PROBLEMS

I:8-60 In 2012, Annie Cook and several family members formed Treehouse Rentals, Inc., in Denver, Colorado. Treehouse is a closely held C corporation engaged in the rental real estate business. Treehouse properly classifies its activities as passive. In 2012, 2013, and 2014, the corporation generated net passive losses of ($380,000), ($145,000), and ($194,000), respectively, all of which were properly suspended.

Effective January 2015, Treehouse elected to be taxed as an S corporation. Also during 2015, Treehouse sold two pieces of rental real estate property. The suspended losses related to these properties were ($63,000) and ($112,000).

Write a memo to Treehouse Rentals explaining the tax treatment of the disposition of the rental properties in 2015.

- Sec. 469, Sec. 1371
- TAM 9628002
- *St. Charles Investment Co. v. Comm.,* 86 AFTR 2d 2000-6882 (CA 10, 11/14/2000)

I:8-61 Jace Seaton is a single taxpayer living in Eugene, Oregon. From 2011 to 2014, he worked as the CEO of Wengren & Jeffers, a local architectural firm. In 2015, he left the firm to start his own company as well as spend more time golfing and travelling. On October 25, 2015, he formed Seaton & Associates, a Limited Liability Company (LLC) under Oregon law.

Upon forming the LLC, Jace received an 80% interest in the company. Two other architects, Maria Juarez and Jaman Turhoon, each received a 10% interest in the company. Jace provided all necessary capital, whereas Maria and Jamal provided experience and a commitment to work for the company. Seaton & Associates chose to be taxed as a partnership for federal income tax purposes.

During 2015, Jace worked approximately 300 hours for Seaton & Associates, and received a guaranteed payment of $100,000. Maria and Jamal each worked approximately 600 hours, and each received a guaranteed payment of $150,000. In 2015 the company generated a net loss of $530,000.

Write a memo to Jace explaining how the LLC members, particularly Jace, should treat the loss generated in 2015.

- Reg. 1.469-5T
- *Gregg v. U.S.*, 87 AFTR 2d 2001-337

I:8-62 On November 15, Alex and Deanna Kent come to you for tax advice. The Kents, a married couple that files a joint tax return, own a rental home in Southern California. From January to November 1 of the current year, they rented out the home for 210 days. Since they live in Minnesota, they are considering staying in their rental home from December 10 to 31. If they do not stay in the home during that period, it will sit vacant. They ask you if this decision would have any tax consequences. They also provide you with the following information for the year:

Rental home income and expenses:	
Rental income	$16,000
Mortgage interest	12,400
Property taxes	4,300
Homeowners Assoc. Fees	3,500
Depreciation	18,000
Other income and expenses:	
Deanna's salary	75,000
Alex's salary	65,000
Passive income (from an investment in a limited partnership)	1,000
Mortgage interest on their Minnesota home	7,800
Charitable contributions	14,200
Medical expenses	8,100
Property taxes on their Minnesota home	2,900
State income taxes	9,700

What do you recommend to the Kents?

I:8-63 Jim had $100,000 in deposits in a savings account at a bank in Page, Arizona. The bank collapsed and Jim did not receive anything for his deposits. The bank was chartered by the state of Arizona and was not insured by federal law. Jim is not sure what his options are in deducting this loss on his tax return. What can Jim do to take advantage of this loss on his tax return? He has an AGI of $110,000 and no capital gains for the current year.

TAX FORM/RETURN PREPARATION PROBLEMS

I:8-64 Heather and Nikolay Laubert are married and file a joint income tax return. Their address is 3847 Jackdaw Path, Madison, WI 58493. Nikolay's Social Security number is 000-00-1111, and Heather's is 000-00-2222. Nikolay is a mechanical engineer, and Heather is a highly renowned speech therapist. She is self-employed. They report all their income and expenses on the cash method. For 2014, they report the following items of income and expense:

Gross receipts from Heather's business	$110,000
Rent on Heather's office	12,000
Receivables written off during the year (received in Heather's business)	1,300
Subscriptions to linguistic journals for Heather	250
Salary for Heather's secretary-receptionist	22,000
Nikolay's salary	78,000
Qualified medical expenses	12,000

Property taxes on their personal residence	4,200
State income tax refund received this year (the tax benefit was received in the prior year from the state income tax deduction)	400
State income taxes withheld on Nikolay's salary	4,600
Federal income taxes withheld on Nikolay's salary	12,000
Heather's estimated tax payments	20,000
Interest paid on residence	11,000
Income tax preparation fee for the prior year's return paid this year ($500 is allocated to preparation of Schedule C)	$940

Heather and Nikolay sold the following assets:

Asset	*Acquired*	*Sold*	*Sales Price*	*Cost*
KNA stock	2/12/13	3/13/14	$14,000	$ 8,000
AEN stock	3/2/14	7/7/14	20,000	22,000
KLN stock	6/8/09	4/10/14	13,000	17,000
Motorcycle	5/3/06	9/12/14	2,500	6,000

Heather owned the KLN stock and sold it to her brother, Jacob. Heather and Nikolay used the motorcycle for personal recreation.

In addition to the items above, they donate Miner Corporation stock to their community church. The FMV of the stock on the date it is donated (8/18/14) is $6,200. It cost $2,700 when purchased on 3/12/96. Heather and Nikolay's home is burglarized during the year. The burglar stole an entertainment system (FMV $3,500; cost $5,000), an antique diamond ring and pendant (FMV $12,000; cost $10,000), and a painting (FMV $1,500; cost $1,300). The insurance company pays $1,500 for the entertainment system, $4,000 for the jewelry, and $500 for the painting. Complete Heather and Nikolay's Form 1040, Schedules A, C, D, and SE, Form 4684, and Form 8283. For purposes of this problem, disregard the alternative minimum tax and any credits.

I:8-65 Kara and Brandon Arnold are married and file a joint return. Their Social Security numbers are 000-00-1111 and 000-00-2222, respectively. Kara and Brandon have one son, Henry, age 3. His Social Security number is 000-00-3333. They live at 356 Welcome Lane, Woodbury, WA 84653. They report their income on the cash method. During 2014, they report the following items:

Salary	$103,000
Interest income from money market accounts	600
Dividend income from Davis Corp. stock	700
Cash contributions to church	6,000
Rental of a condominium in Lutsen:	
Rental income (30 days)	12,000
Interest expense	7,000
Property taxes	3,200
Maintenance	1,700
Depreciation (entire year)	7,500
Insurance	2,000
Days of personal use	16

The address of the Condo is 1127 Skyline Drive, Lutsen, WA 84666.

During the year the following events also occur:

a. In 2012, Brandon had loaned a friend $3,000 to help pay medical bills. During 2014, he discovers that his "friend" has skipped town.

b. On June 20, 2014, Brandon sells Kim Corporation stock for $16,000. He purchased the stock on December 12, 2009 for $22,000.

c. On September 19, 2014, Kara discovers that the penny stock of Roberts, Inc. she purchased on January 2 of the prior year is completely worthless. She paid $5,000 for the stock.

d. Instead of accepting $60 the utility store offers for their old dishwasher, they donate it to Goodwill on November 21, 2014. They purchased the dishwasher for $750 on March 30, 2006. The new dishwasher cost $900.

e. Kara and Brandon purchased a new residence for $250,000. As part of the closing costs, they pay two points, or $3,800, on the mortgage, which is interest rather than loan processing fees. This payment enables them to obtain a more favorable interest rate for the term of the loan. They also paid $8,400 in interest on their mortgage on their personal residence.

f. They pay $4,100 in property taxes on their residence and $7,500 in state income taxes.

g. On July 20, 2014, Kara and Brandon donate 1,000 shares of Anton, Inc. stock to the local community college. The value of the stock on that date is $10,200. Anton, Inc. is a listed stock. They had purchased the stock on November 10, 2008 for $1,000.
h. $7,000 in federal income tax was withheld during the year.

Complete Kara and Brandon's Form 1040, Schedules A, B, D, and E, Form 8283 and Form 8949. For purposes of this problem, disregard the alternative minimum tax and any credits.

CASE STUDY PROBLEMS

I:8-66 Dr. John Brown is a physician who expects to make $150,000 this year from his medical practice. In addition, Dr. Brown expects to receive $10,000 dividends and interest income.

Last year, on the advice of a friend, Dr. Brown invested $100,000 in Limited, a limited partnership. He spends no time working for Limited. Limited's operations did not turn out exactly as planned, and Dr. Brown's share of Limited's losses last year amounted to $15,000. Dr. Brown has already been informed that his share of Limited's losses this year will be $10,000.

In January of the current year, Dr. Brown set up his own laboratory. Originally he intended to have the lab only do the work for his own practice, but other physicians in the area were impressed with the quick turnaround and convenience that the lab provided and began sending their work. This year, Dr. Brown estimates that the lab will generate $30,000 of taxable income. The work in the lab is done by two full-time qualified laboratory technicians. A part-time bookkeeper is hired to keep the books. Dr. Brown has spent 320 hours to date establishing and managing the lab. He plans to hire another technician who will also manage the lab so that it can operate on its own.

In November, Dr. Brown calls you requesting some tax advice. Specifically, he would like to know what actions he should take before the end of the year in order to reduce his tax liability for the current year.

Write a memo to Dr. Brown, detailing your suggestions. His address is: Dr. John Brown, 444 Physicians Drive, Suite 100, Anytown, USA 88888.

I:8-67 In preparing the tax return for one of your clients, Jack Johnson, you notice that he has listed a deduction for a large business bad debt. Jack explains that the loan was made to his corporate employer when the corporation was experiencing extreme cash flow difficulties. In fact, Jack was very concerned at the time he made the loan that the corporation would go bankrupt. This would have been extremely bad, because not only would he have lost his job, but he also would have lost the $80,000 he had invested in the common stock of the corporation.

You know that if the loan is a business loan Jack will receive an ordinary deduction. However, if the loan is a nonbusiness debt, it becomes a short-term capital loss (and Jack can only currently deduct $3,000).

After thoroughly reviewing all of the facts, you do a complete search of the relevant judicial and administrative authority. There you find that the courts are split as to whether under these circumstances the loan should be treated as a business or nonbusiness bad debt.

What position should you take on Jack's federal income tax return? (See the *Statements on Standards for Tax Services* section in Chapter I:15 and Appendix E for a discussion of this issue.)

TAX RESEARCH PROBLEM

I:8-68 Early in 2015, Keith meets Dan through a business associate. Dan tells Keith that he is directing a business venture that purchases poorly managed restaurants in order to turn them around and make them profitable. Dan mentions that he is currently involved in acquiring a real "gold mine" but needs to raise additional cash in order to purchase it. On the strength of Dan's representations, Keith loans Dan $30,000 for the venture. An agreement is written up between Keith and Dan, wherein Dan agrees to repay Keith the entire amount over a 5-year period plus 14% interest per annum on the unpaid balance. Later in the year, however, Keith discovers that Dan had never intended to purchase the restaurant and, in fact, had used most of the money for his own benefit. Upon making this discovery, Keith sues Dan for recovery of the money, alleging that Dan falsely, fraudulently, and deceitfully represented that the money would be invested and repaid, in order to cheat and defraud Keith out of his money. Unfortunately for Keith, he is never able to recover any amount of the loan. Discuss the tax treatment that Keith may claim with regard to the loss.

A partial list of research sources is:

- *Robert S. Gerstell*, 46 T.C. 161 (1966)
- *Michele Monteleone*, 34 T.C. 688 (1960)

CHAPTER

9

EMPLOYEE EXPENSES AND DEFERRED COMPENSATION

LEARNING OBJECTIVES

After studying this chapter, you should be able to

1. Determine the classification and limitations of employee expenses
2. Determine the proper deductible amount for travel expenses
3. Understand the deductibility of transportation expenses
4. Determine the proper deductible amount for entertainment expenses under the 50% disallowance rule
5. Discuss the tax methods concerning reimbursed employee business expenses
6. Identify deductible moving expenses and determine the amount and year of deductibility
7. Describe the requirements for deducting education expenses
8. Determine whether the expenses of an office in home meet the requirements for deductibility and apply the gross income limitations
9. Discuss the tax treatment and requirements for various deferred compensation arrangements
10. Describe tax planning considerations for employee expenses
11. Describe compliance and procedural considerations for employee expenses

CHAPTER OUTLINE

This chapter discusses the tax consequences from two types of employee expenses:

- Expenditures incurred by an employee in connection with his or her job
- Deferred compensation payments made to employees

Employees routinely incur expenses in connection with their jobs, such as travel, entertainment, professional journals, etc. The tax law considers **employee expenses** to be incurred in connection with a trade or business and, therefore are deductible under Sec. 162. However, employee expenses are subject to a myriad of special rules and limitations. Because of the large number of taxpayers who are employees and the importance of the topic, this chapter discusses the rules as well as tax planning opportunities.

Deferred compensation refers to methods of compensating employees that are based on their current service, but the actual payments are deferred until future periods. Deferred compensation arrangements are very popular and widely used in business. The two principal types of deferred compensation arrangements are qualified plans and nonqualified plans. Qualified plans, such as pension and profit-sharing plans, have very favorable tax benefits but also impose strict eligibility and coverage requirements. Nonqualified plans, while not as tax advantageous as qualified plans, are very useful for highly compensated employees. Both of these types of deferred compensation arrangements are discussed later in this chapter.

CLASSIFICATION AND LIMITATIONS OF EMPLOYEE EXPENSES

OBJECTIVE 1

Determine the classification and limitations of employee expenses

Employee expenses, for purposes of the tax law, are divided into two classifications: *reimbursed* employee expenses and *unreimbursed* employee expenses. Reimbursed employee expenses are expenses incurred by the employee that are reimbursed by the employer. IRC Section 62(a)(2) provides that an employee may deduct reimbursed employee expenses *for* AGI. This presumes, of course, that the employee has included the reimbursement in his gross income. Unreimbursed employee expenses are generally deductible by employees, but are deductible *from* AGI. A more detailed discussion of the proper treatment of employee expenses under accountable and nonaccountable plans is presented later in this chapter.

ADDITIONAL COMMENT

"The income tax has made more liars out of the American people than golf has. Even when you make a tax form on the level, you don't know when its through if you are a crook or a martyr." —Will Rogers

Some of the more frequently encountered employee expenses discussed in this chapter include:

- Travel
- Transportation
- Moving
- Entertainment
- Education
- Office in home

Each of these types of employee expenses are discussed in this chapter.

NATURE OF THE EMPLOYMENT RELATIONSHIP

KEY POINT

The business expenses of a self-employed individual and the reimbursed business expenses of an employee are deductible *for* AGI. The unreimbursed business expenses of an employee are deductible *from* AGI.

An individual who provides services for another person or entity may be classified either as an employee or as a self-employed individual (also referred to as an independent contractor). If the individual is classified as self-employed, expenses are deductible *for* AGI under Sec. 162, and are reported on Schedule C of Form 1040. Conversely, expenses of employees are deductible either *for* or *from* AGI depending on whether such expenses are reimbursed or unreimbursed. In addition to the deductibility of expenses, the proper classification is also important due to employment taxes, such as Social Security and Medicare taxes. As is discussed below, self-employed taxpayers must pay both the employee and employer shares of Social Security and Medicare taxes.

Employer-Employee Relationship Defined. The Treasury Regulations provide that an employer-employee relationship generally exists where the employer has the right to control and direct the individual who provides services with regard to the end result and the means by which the result is accomplished.[1]

EXAMPLE I:9-1 ▶ Carmen is a nurse who assists a group of doctors in a clinic. Carmen is under the direct supervision of the doctors and is told what procedures to perform and when to perform them. Therefore, Carmen is classified as an employee. ◀

EXAMPLE I:9-2 ▶ Carol is a registered nurse who provides in-home services to several elderly patients. She receives instructions from the patients' doctors regarding such items as medications and diet, but Carol is directly responsible for the delivery of nursing care and is in control of the end result. Thus, Carol is self-employed. ◀

ADDITIONAL COMMENT

Anyone in a trade or business making payments of $600 or more to an independent contractor during a year must file Form 1099-MISC.

Importance of Proper Classification. As mentioned above, proper classification is important both to employers and employees. If an individual is classified as an employee, the employer must match the Social Security and Medicare taxes that are paid by the employee. In addition, employers are generally liable for unemployment taxes for their employees. Thus, an employer must pay these employment taxes to the federal and/or state governments in addition to the wages, which means that the cost of an employee generally is higher than for a non-employee. If an individual is *not* considered to be an employee, the individual is classified as self-employed (also called an independent contractor). Amounts paid to a self-employed individual are not considered to be wages and the payor is not responsible for any employment taxes. However, the self-employed individual must pay both the employee and employer portions of Social Security and Medicare taxes. This tax is referred to as the *self-employment tax*. As can be seen from the above discussion, employment taxes are shifted from the employer to the self-employed individual if the individual is not considered to be an employee.

Individuals may prefer to be classified as employees because the employee portion of the Social Security and Medicare taxes (7.65%) is only one-half of the self-employment tax rate (15.3%). Of the 7.65%, 6.2% (12.4% for self-employed individuals) is for the old age, survivors and disability insurance (OASDI) portion of the FICA tax and is assessed on a maximum income amount of $118,500 for 2015 ($117,000 in 2014). The remaining 1.45% (2.9% for self-employed individuals) portion of the FICA tax is for hospital insurance and has no ceiling limitation.[2]

NEW LEGISLATION

As discussed in Chapter I:7, total itemized deductions are subject to a 3% reduction for upper-income taxpayers beginning in 2013.

Litigation Issues and Administrative Enforcement. The determination as to whether an individual who performs services is either an employee or an independent contractor has been a major ongoing area of contention between the IRS and taxpayers. In determining whether a worker is an employee or independent contractor, the facts of the situation must be analyzed and divided into three main categories: behavioral control, financial control, and relationship of the parties. No one factor is necessarily determinative, the totality of the situation must be considered. The first category, behavioral control, entails whether the payor has the right to control how the individual does the work. *Behavioral control* is characterized by the amount of instruction as to how the work is to be done as well as the level of training that is provided to the individual. As to *financial control*, an independent contractor has a significant investment in his or her work, is not reimbursed for expenses, and has the opportunity for profit or loss. An employee generally would not have these characteristics in their role as an employee. The third category is that the *relationship of the parties* and looks at employee benefits and explicit written contracts that show the type of relationship intended. These three categories of tests are an outgrowth of the so-called "20 factor test" that was used for many years to determine whether an individual was considered an employee or independent contractor. Under either system, the determination is still a very difficult and uncertain process.

Substantial litigation has occurred in the interpretation of these factors. For example, truck drivers who were owner-operators and were engaged under contract by an interstate trucking company were considered independent contractors because they selected their

[1] Reg. Sec. 31.3401(c)-1(b).

[2] Congress granted taxpayers a 2% reduction in Social Security taxes for employees for 2011 and 2012. Thus, the total rate for Social Security (OASDI) for the two years was 5.65% (4.2% for OASDI and 1.45% for Medicare). No reduction was allowed for the employer share. This 2% payroll reduction in social security was not extended for 2013 or later years. For a more detailed discussion of the self-employment tax, see Chapter I:14.

own routes and were paid a percentage of the company's receipts for shipment.[3] However, drivers for a moving van company were considered employees because the company exercised control over their assignments.[4] The Tax Court held that cosmetologists, nail technicians, and massage therapists who performed services at a spa were not employees but rather independent contractors.[5] The individuals paid weekly rent, set their own hours and fees, and generally provided their own supplies.

LIMITATIONS ON UNREIMBURSED EMPLOYEE EXPENSES

2% Nondeductible Floor. Section 67 imposes a nondeductible floor of 2% of AGI to the following types of itemized deductions:

KEY POINT

Even if the employee expenses exceed 2% of AGI, the employee may not derive a tax benefit if the deductible employee expenses, when added to the other itemized deductions, do not exceed the standard deduction.

1) Unreimbursed employee business expenses,
2) Investment expenses,
3) Fees paid for tax advice and/or tax return preparation, and
4) Expenses allowed in connection with a hobby activity (see Chapter I:6 for details on hobby loss activities).

All of these types of expenses are referred to as **miscellaneous itemized deductions** in Sec. 67.[6] Unreimbursed employee expenses that are classified as miscellaneous itemized deductions include:

ADDITIONAL COMMENT

Unreimbursed employee business expenses first are reported by the taxpayer on Form 2106, then carried to Schedule A as a miscellaneous itemized deduction.

- Professional journals, professional dues, union dues, small tools and supplies
- Job-hunting expenses for seeking employment in the same trade or business (e.g., employment agency fees)
- The cost and maintenance of special clothing (e.g., uniforms for an airline pilot)

Investment expenses include expenses connected with the earning of investment income, such as publications and safe deposit box rentals. Other miscellaneous itemized deductions include items such as fees for tax return preparation and appraisal fees for charitable contributions.

EXAMPLE I:9-3 ▶ In 2015, Charles incurs and pays $3,000 of unreimbursed employee expenses, $1,000 of investment counseling fees, and $500 for the preparation of his 2014 income tax return. Charles's AGI is $100,000. The total miscellaneous itemized deductions are $4,500 ($3,000 + $1,000 + $500). Charles is limited to a $2,500 deduction ($4,500 − $2,000) because of the application of the 2% nondeductible floor (0.02 × $100,000 AGI = $2,000). ◀

TAX STRATEGY TIP

For taxpayers who typically do not have enough miscellaneous itemized deductions to get over the 2% floor, "bunching" of expenses in a particular tax year may allow some of the expenses to be deducted.

Exceptions to the 2% Floor. The 2% floor applies to most miscellaneous itemized deductions. However, some miscellaneous itemized deductions, such as gambling losses (see footnote 6 below), are not subject to the 2% floor. Further, itemized deductions, such as charitable contributions, mortgage interest and real estate taxes on a principal residence, are not considered miscellaneous itemized deductions and therefore not subject to the 2% nondeductible floor.

EXAMPLE I:9-4 ▶ In the current year Carmelia, who is single, incurs $1,500 of unreimbursed employee expenses, $3,000 of charitable contributions, and $7,000 of mortgage interest and real estate taxes on her principal residence. She has no other miscellaneous itemized deductions or investment expenses, and her AGI is $100,000. The $1,500 of employee expenses are not deductible because the 2% nondeductible floor ($2,000 in this case) is higher than the $1,500 of expenses. The $3,000 of charitable contributions and $7,000 of mortgage interest and real estate taxes are fully deductible as itemized deductions because Carmelia's total itemized deductions of $10,000 exceed the standard deduction amount ($6,300 for a single taxpayer in 2015). The charitable contributions, mortgage interest, and real estate taxes are not subject to the 2% nondeductible floor. ◀

---

[3] Rev. Rul. 76-226, 1976-1 CB 332

[4] *Richard N. Smith v. U.S.*, 78-1 USTC ¶9263 (CA-5, 1978).

[5] *Cheryl A. Mayfield Therapy Center*, TC Memo 2010–239.

[6] The 2% floor does not apply to certain other miscellaneous itemized deductions, including impairment-related work expenses for handicapped employees, amortizable bond premiums, certain short sale expenses, terminated annuity payments, and gambling losses to the extent of winnings.

TRAVEL EXPENSES

OBJECTIVE 2

Determine the proper deductible amount for travel expenses

DEDUCTIBILITY OF TRAVEL EXPENSES

The deductibility of travel expenses depends on the nature of the expenditure and whether the employee receives a reimbursement from the employer. The following rules apply to the deductibility of travel expenses.

- If the taxpayer is engaged in a trade or business as a self-employed individual or is engaged in an activity for the production of rental and royalty income, the travel-related expenditures are deductible *for* AGI and the 2% nondeductible floor is not applicable.
- If the taxpayer is an employee and incurs travel expenses in connection with his job, the expenses are deductible either *for* AGI or *from* AGI depending on whether the expenses are reimbursed by the employer.
- Personal travel expenses are not deductible.

HISTORICAL NOTE

The partial disallowance of business meals and entertainment of 50% was enacted because Congress believed that prior law had not focused sufficiently on the personal consumption element of deductible business meal and entertainment expenses. Congress felt that taxpayers who could arrange business settings for personal consumption were unfairly receiving a federal tax subsidy for such consumption.

Reimbursed Expenses. If business travel expenses are reimbursed and the reimbursement is included in the employee's gross income, the expenses are deductible *for* AGI.

Unreimbursed Expenses. Generally, if business travel expenses are not reimbursed by the taxpayer's employer, the expenses are a deduction *from* AGI subject to the 2% floor.

The tax rules for reporting reimbursed and unreimbursed employee business expenses are discussed in more detail later in this chapter. Table I:9-1 illustrates how travel expenses are reported.

DEFINITION OF TRAVEL EXPENSES

Travel expenses include transportation, meals, lodging, and other reasonable and necessary expenses incurred by a taxpayer while "away from home" in the pursuit of a trade or business or an employment-related activity. The term *travel expense* is more broadly defined in the IRC than is the term **transportation expense.** If an individual is not away from home, expenses related to local transportation are classified as transportation expenses rather than travel expenses. Transportation expenses for employees are deductible under certain conditions and are discussed later in this chapter.

▼ TABLE I:9-1
Classification of Travel Expenses

Situation Facts	TAX TREATMENT: Deductible *for* AGI	Deductible *from* AGI	Not Deductible
1. Cindy is a self-employed attorney who incurs travel expenses related to her business.	X[a]		
2. Jose, who lives in Dallas, is the owner of several apartment buildings in Denver. Periodically he travels to Denver to inspect and manage the properties.	X[a]		
3. Clay is an employee who is required to travel to company facilities throughout the U.S. in the conduct of his management responsibilities. Clay is not reimbursed by his employer.		X[b]	
4. Same as Situation 3, except that Clay is fully reimbursed by his employer and includes the reimbursement in his gross income.	X[a]		
5. Colleen works in New York City and travels to her parents' home in Dallas during the holidays.			X

[a] The 2% nondeductible floor is not applicable.
[b] The 2% nondeductible floor is applicable and the expenses are only deductible if in excess of the floor.

EXAMPLE I:9-5 ▶ Ahmed is away from home overnight on a job-related business trip and incurs airfare, hotel, and taxi fares amounting to $800. Because Ahmed is away from home, the $800 is treated as travel expenses. ◀

EXAMPLE I:9-6 ▶ Charlotte uses her personal automobile to make deliveries of company products to customers in the same local area of her employer's place of business. Charlotte's automobile expenses are classified as transportation expenses (rather than travel expenses) because she was not away from home when they were incurred. As is discussed later in this chapter, transportation expenses are deductible but are subject to strict recordkeeping rules. If Charlotte stopped to eat lunch alone during her delivery activities, the meals are not deductible as they are neither travel nor transportation expenses. ◀

GENERAL QUALIFICATION REQUIREMENTS

To qualify as a travel expense deduction, the following requirements must be met:

- The purpose of the trip must be connected with a trade or business or be employment-related (e.g., personal vacation trips or commuting to and from a job location are nondeductible personal expenses).[7]
- The taxpayer must be away from his tax home overnight or for a sufficient duration to require sleep or rest before returning home.

Away-from-Tax-Home Requirement. Travel expenses are deductible if the taxpayer is temporarily away from his tax home overnight. While this seems simple enough, there has been considerable controversy as to what the words actually mean. There are three important aspects of this requirement: (1) where is the taxpayer's home, (2) how is *temporarily* distinguished from *indefinite* or *permanent,* and (3) how is the term *overnight* interpreted.

TYPICAL MISCONCEPTION

There is a tendency to erroneously assume that a taxpayer's tax home is the location of his or her primary personal residence.

Taxpayer's home: The IRS's position is that a person's tax home is the location of his principal place of employment regardless of where the family residence is maintained. Thus, a taxpayer who works permanently or for an indefinite period of time away from his or her family residence is *not* considered to be away from home and, therefore, travel expenses are not deductible. In this situation, the taxpayer's *tax home* is considered to be his work location.

Temporary vs. Indefinite: To meet the away from home requirement, a taxpayer must be away from home on a temporary basis. Thus, an employee who travels out of town on a three-day business trip clearly meets this requirement. However, an employee whose primary residence is in one location but works on a permanent basis during the week at another location, and possibly has an apartment at the work location, is not considered away from home at the *work location*. In this case, the work location is considered his tax home for income tax purposes, and he is not considered to be away from home.

REAL-WORLD EXAMPLE

A taxpayer was employed by a traveling circus with headquarters in Chicago. The Tax Court held that the taxpayer's home was wherever he happened to be with the circus. Therefore, the cost of his meals and lodging was not deductible. *Nat Lewis,* 1954 PH T.C. Memo ¶54,233, 13 TCM 1167.

The determination of whether a taxpayer is away from home temporarily or indefinitely is based upon the length of time the taxpayer is at such location. Work assignments of more than one year are treated as indefinite.[8] Work assignments for one year or less are classified as either temporary or indefinite depending on the facts and circumstances of each case. If an employee is reassigned only for a temporary period, then his tax home does not change and the travel expenses are deductible. However, if the assignment is for an indefinite period, the individual's tax home shifts to the new location. The following bulleted items and examples are taken from Rev. Rul. 93-86[9] and are used to illustrate the IRS's position concerning whether a taxpayer is away from home temporarily for purposes of deducting travel expenses:

- A taxpayer accepts away from home employment where it is realistically expected that the work will be completed in six months. The actual employment period lasts ten months. Because the employment period is realistically expected to last (and does in fact last) for one year or less, the IRS's position is that the employment is temporary and the taxpayer's travel expenses are deductible.

[7] Travel expenses incurred in the production or collection of income are also deductible from AGI under Sec. 212(1), even though the travel is not connected with employment or with the conduct of a trade or business. See Rev. Rul. 84-113, 1984-2 C.B. 60.

[8] Sec. 162(a). See also Rev. Rul. 99-7, 1999-1 C.B. 361.

[9] Rev. Rul. 93-86, 1993-2 C.B. 71.

- A taxpayer accepts away from home employment where it is realistically expected that the work will be completed in 18 months but the work is actually completed in ten months. In such case the IRS's position is that the employment is treated as indefinite, regardless of whether it actually exceeds one year or not.
- A taxpayer accepts away from home employment where it is realistically expected that the work will be completed in nine months. After eight months the taxpayer is asked to remain for seven more months or a total period of more than one year. Based on these facts, the IRS's position is that the employment is temporary for eight months and the travel expenses are deductible for the eight-month period. The job is considered indefinite for the remaining seven months and no travel expense deduction is allowed for the travel expenses during this period.

Overnight test: To satisfy the overnight test, a taxpayer must show that it was reasonable for him to need to obtain sleep or rest during release time on such trips in order to meet the demands of his job.[10] Generally, costs of meals on one-day business trips are not deductible since the taxpayer was not away from home overnight. The Supreme Court held that a taxpayer who took short rest stops on long one-day business trips was not allowed to deduct his meals.[11] However, whether it is reasonable to need sleep or rest depends on the specific circumstances. A railroad conductor was allowed to deduct lodging, meals, and tips incurred during a six-hour layover on a total trip of 16 hours.[12]

EXAMPLE I:9-7 ► Roberto lives and works in Baltimore. He occasionally travels to New York City on business and stays overnight for two or three days at a time. Roberto clearly meets the away from home test and all of his travel expenses, including airfare, lodging, tips, taxi, and food (subject to the 50% disallowance) are deductible as travel expenses. ◄

EXAMPLE I:9-8 ► Tom lives with his family in Baltimore. In 2015, Tom loses his job in Baltimore and accepts a new full-time position in New York City. However, he decides not to move his family to New York but to rent an apartment and stay there during the week and return home on weekends. Tom's work assignment would be considered indefinite and the cost of his apartment, food, and other incidental expenses would not be deductible travel expenses because his tax home is New York and he is not considered to be away from home. ◄

EXAMPLE I:9-9 ► Gunther lives and works in Baltimore. Gunther's employer asks him to accept a temporary assignment in New York City for approximately seven months to work on a special project. Gunther rents an apartment in New York for the seven months, then returns to his regular office in Baltimore. Gunther's work assignment in New York is considered temporary because it is less than one year, and therefore, all of his apartment rent, food, laundry, and other incidental costs are deductible as travel expenses. Because apartments and food are expensive in New York, his travel expense deduction will be substantial. Good records to substantiate the work assignment and the expenses are very important in this case. ◄

SELF-STUDY QUESTION

A student accepts employment in another state during his summer vacation. Would the cost of his meals and lodging at the job location be deductible?

ANSWER

No, the student did not travel to the job because of the employer's business needs. *Peter F. Janss v. CIR*, 2 AFTR 2d 5927, 58-2 USTC ¶9873 (8th Cir., 1958).

BUSINESS VERSUS PLEASURE

Travel expenses are deductible only if they are incurred in the pursuit of a trade or business activity or are related to the taxpayer's employment. Thus, if a taxpayer takes a trip that is primarily personal in nature but some business is transacted, the only deductions allowed are those that are directly related to the business activity.[13] In such event, all of the traveling expenses to and from the destination are treated as nondeductible personal expenditures. However, if the trip is *primarily related* to business or employment, all of the traveling expenses to and from the destination are deductible, and meals and lodging, local transportation, and incidental expenses are allocated to the business and personal activities, respectively. In effect, an all-or-nothing approach is applied to the deductibility of traveling expenses to and from the destination depending upon the primary purpose for making the trip.

---

10 Rev. Rul. 75-168, 1975-1 C.B. 58.

11 *Correll v. U.S.*, 389 U.S. 299 (1968).

12 *Williams v. Patterson*, 286 F2d 333 (5th Cir. 1961) and Rev. Rul. 75-170, 1975-1 C.B. 60. See also *Marc G. Bissonnette*, 127 T.C. 124 (October 23, 2006), where a six-hour layover on 15-17 hour days for a ferry boat captain was held to be "away from home."

13 Reg. Sec. 1.162-2(b)(1).

In determining the primary purpose for a trip, the amount of time spent on personal activities compared to the time spent on business activities is an important factor. However, the fact that a taxpayer may spend slightly more time on personal activities than business activities will not automatically prohibit the deductibility of the transportation expenses to and from the destination. The taxpayer must clearly show that the purpose of the trip was *primarily business*.

EXAMPLE I:9-10 ▶ Dana travels to New York on a business trip for her employer and spends $500 for a roundtrip airline ticket and $200 per day for hotel, meals, and incidental expenses. She is not reimbursed for the travel expenses. Dana spends three days in business meetings and vacations for two days. Because the trip is primarily business, the traveling expenses to and from the destination (e.g., airfare) of $500 are fully deductible by Dana. Dana's meals, lodging, and incidental expenses amount to $1,000 (5 days × $200), but only $600 ($200 × 3 business days) of such travel expenses is deductible. The deductible business meal expenses are reduced by 50%, and the total amount of deductible travel expenses are subject to the nondeductible 2% floor on miscellaneous itemized deductions. A proration of the meals, lodging, and incidental expenses based on the number of days may not be appropriate if the expenses are uneven or are directly related to either business or personal activities. ◀

EXAMPLE I:9-11 ▶ Assume that the facts in Example I:9-10 are reversed (i.e., that two days are employment-related and three days are personal). Because more time was spent on personal activities, the general rule would hold that the trip is primarily personal and the traveling expenses to and from the destination of $500 are not deductible. Thus, only $400 ($200 × two business days) of travel expenses related to meals, lodging, and incidental expenses are deductible (subject to the limitations previously discussed). ◀

EXAMPLE I:9-12 ▶ Carroll, who lives and works in St. Louis, is required by his employer to attend a sales meeting in San Francisco. The meeting lasts two days. Carroll decides to take three days of vacation and sightsee in the San Francisco area. Even though Carroll spent more days on personal activities than business activities, Carroll's airfare would be deductible if he can clearly show that the primary purpose of the trip was business. ◀

REAL-WORLD EXAMPLE

It is very difficult to deduct expenses of a spouse who accompanies his or her spouse to a business meeting or convention. The accompanying spouse not only must be an employee of the corporation but the reason for accompanying his or her spouse must be for bona fide business purpose.

The IRS has ruled that the incremental expenses of an additional night's lodging and an additional day's meals that are incurred to obtain "excursion" airfare rates with respect to employees whose business travel extends over Saturday night are deductible business expenses.[14] The reimbursement for these expenses is deductible by the employer (subject to the 50% disallowance for meals). The employer is not required to report the reimbursement on the employee's Form W-2 as gross income or withhold employment taxes.

Stringent rules are applied if the taxpayer is accompanied by family members because of the likelihood that the trip is primarily for personal reasons. No deduction is permitted for travel expenses of a spouse or dependent (or other person accompanying the taxpayer) unless the person is an employee, the travel is for a bona fide business purpose, and the expenses would be otherwise deductible.[15]

FOREIGN TRAVEL

Due to the potential for abuse, special rules apply to foreign travel and foreign convention expenses.[16] Travel expenses related to foreign conventions, seminars, or similar types of meetings are disallowed unless it can be shown that the meeting is directly related to the taxpayer's trade or business (including employment) activity and that it is reasonable for the meeting to be held outside North America. In addition, complex expense allocation rules are applied to business trips made outside the United States.[17]

---

[14] PLR 9237014 (June 10, 1992).
[15] Sec. 274(m)(3).
[16] Secs. 274(c) and (h).
[17] Reg. Sec. 1.274-4. No allocation of total expenses is made to the personal-use (nondeductible) element if an individual is away from home for seven days or less or if less than 25% of the time is devoted to personal purposes. In all other cases, all of the foreign travel expenses (including transportation costs) must be apportioned between business and personal activities based on the relative percentage of time devoted to each activity.

SELF-STUDY QUESTION

Would the cost of going on a safari in Africa be deductible if the taxpayer were in the business of selling guns?

ANSWER

In an actual case, the Court held that the safari expenses were not sufficiently connected to the taxpayer's gun-selling business. Therefore, the safari costs were not deductible. *Vincent W. Eckel*, T.C. Memo 1974-33.

ADDITIONAL LIMITATIONS ON TRAVEL EXPENSES

IRC Section 274 also provides several limitations on the deductibility of certain types of travel expenses, including the following:

- Travel deductions are disallowed if the expenses are deductible only as a form of education. For example, a French language professor cannot deduct travel expenses to France if the purpose of the trip is to maintain a general familiarity with the French language and customs.
- Deductions allowed for luxury water travel (i.e., ocean liners, cruise ships, or other forms of water transportation) are limited to twice the highest per diem amount allowable for a day of domestic travel by employees in the executive branch of the federal government.
- Travel deductions to attend a convention, seminar, or meeting are not allowed if they are related to income-producing activities coming under Sec. 212. Expenses to attend a convention, seminar, or meeting are deductible if directly connected with a taxpayer's trade or business. However, expenses to attend such meetings on a U.S. cruise ship are deductible but only to a maximum amount of $2,000.

EXAMPLE I:9-13 ▶ Dawn travels from Miami on a cruise ship to attend a business meeting in Bermuda. The round-trip cost of the cruise is $6,000, and the travel is for a period of four days. If the highest daily per diem amount is $400 for a government employee, the travel expenses related to the cruise ship are limited to $3,200 ($800 per day × 4 days travel). ◀

EXAMPLE I:9-14 ▶ Assume that Dawn in Example 9-13 went on the cruise to attend a business seminar held on the cruise ship. In this case, Dawn's deductible expenses are limited to a maximum of $2,000. ◀

EXAMPLE I:9-15 ▶ Danielle is an investor in the stock market who attends investment counseling seminars. During the current year, she incurs $4,000 in travel expenses and $1,000 in registration fees to attend the seminars. None of the travel expenses are deductible because the expenses are related to income-producing activities coming under Sec. 212. The registration fees are deductible as an investment expense. If Danielle was employed as a stockbroker (rather than an investor) and attended investment seminars, her travel expenses would be deductible as well as the registration fee. ◀

TRANSPORTATION EXPENSES

OBJECTIVE 3

Understand the deductibility of transportation expenses

The deductibility and classification of transportation expenses also depends on the nature of the expenditure, as follows:

- Trade or business-related transportation expenses are deductible *for* AGI and are not subject to specific limitations.
- Transportation expenses related to the production of rental and royalty income (e.g., an owner-investor in rental properties) are deductible *for* AGI and are not subject to specific limitations.
- Reimbursed employee transportation expenses are deductible *for* AGI (assuming that an adequate accounting is made to the employer; see discussion of reimbursed employee business expenses on page I:9-17).
- Unreimbursed employee transportation expenses are deductible *from* AGI as itemized deductions subject to the 2% nondeductible floor for miscellaneous itemized deductions.
- Commuting expenses are nondeductible personal expenses.

KEY POINT

The primary difference between travel expenses and transportation expenses for tax purposes is that travel expenses are broad in nature and include transportation, lodging, meals, and other necessary expenses, whereas transportation expenses include only the cost of transportation.

DEFINITION AND CLASSIFICATION

Transportation expenses include such items as taxi fares, automobile expenses, airfares, tolls, and parking fees incurred in a trade or business or employment-related activity. Generally speaking, transportation expenses are those incurred for "local transportation" and are not treated as travel expenses because the away from home requirements have not been met. The cost of commuting to and from an employee's job location are nondeductible personal expenditures regardless of the length of the trip. Both unreimbursed employment-related travel and transportation expenses for employees are subject to the 2% floor on miscellaneous itemized deductions. If a reimbursement is received, such expenses would be deductible *for* AGI.

EXAMPLE I:9-16 ▶ Eurie's employer requires her to call on several customers at different locations in the metropolitan area during the course of the workday. Her transportation expenses (e.g., auto expenses, tolls, and parking) are deductible as transportation expenses because they are related to providing services as an employee. If Eurie is required to travel away from home overnight, the transportation costs are included with meals and lodging and deducted as a travel expense. In either situation, the unreimbursed employment-related expenses are treated as miscellaneous itemized deductions and are subject to the 2% nondeductible floor limitation. If the expenses were reimbursed by Eurie's employer and an adequate accounting is made to the employer, the expenses would be deductible *for* AGI. ◀

EXAMPLE I:9-17 ▶ David accepts a permanent job with a company located 80 miles from his principal residence. He decides not to move to the new location and drives the 160-mile roundtrip each day. None of David's transportation expenses are deductible because they are personal commuting expenses. (Note: Because the job is a permanent assignment, it is for an indefinite period rather than a temporary period and the transportation expenses are not deductible as travel expenses.) ◀

ADDITIONAL COMMENT

The IRS takes the position that the hauling of equipment, tools, etc., in an automobile for business purposes does not make the commuting expenses deductible. This position is based on the Supreme Court's decision in *Donald W. Fausner v. CIR*, 32 AFTR 2d 73-5202, 73-2 USTC ¶9515 (USSC, 1973). The Court held that it was not possible to allocate the automobile expenses between nondeductible commuting expenses and deductible business expenses. However, if the taxpayer incurs additional costs, such as in renting a trailer, these additional costs are deductible.

The following exceptions or unusual circumstances should be noted:

- Transportation expenses incurred to go from one job to another are deductible if an employee has more than one job. If the employee goes home between jobs, the deduction is only the amount it would have cost him to go directly from the first location to the second.[18]
- Certain transportation expenses related to income-producing activities are deductible under Sec. 212. Expenses are deductible *for* AGI if they are related to the production of rental or royalty income whereas expenses connected with other investment-related activities are deductible as miscellaneous itemized deductions subject to the 2% floor.
- Transportation expenses related to medical treatment may be deductible from AGI as a medical expense (subject to the limitations on the deductibility of medical expenses discussed in Chapter I:7).
- Transportation expenses related to charitable activities may be deductible as a charitable contribution (subject to the limitations on the deductibility of charitable contributions discussed in Chapter I:7).
- Transportation expenses incurred in going between the taxpayer's residence and a temporary work location outside the metropolitan area are deductible.[19] Further, assuming a taxpayer has at least one regular work location (such as his primary office location), transportation expenses are deductible in going between the taxpayer's residence and a temporary work location, regardless of the distance.[20] Thus, a CPA who is employed by a CPA firm and who maintains a regular work location (e.g., an office is provided at the CPA firm's work location) may deduct transportation expenses for trips from home to clients in the metropolitan area. Unreimbursed transportation costs for an employee are deductible *from* AGI as unreimbursed employee expenses that are subject to the 2% nondeductible floor. Transportation expenses for a self-employed individual are deductible *for* AGI.

EXAMPLE I:9-18 ▶ As shown in Figure I:9-1, Dick has two jobs that are 10 miles apart. Dick lives 5 miles from the first job site and 8 miles from the second job site. If Dick drives directly from Job 1 to Job 2, he may deduct the automobile costs associated with the 10-mile trip. If he goes home from the first job before driving to the second job, the deduction is still limited to 10 miles, even though he actually travels 13 miles. ◀

EXAMPLE I:9-19 ▶ Diana owns a duplex, which she rents to tenants. She periodically drives from her place of business to this income-producing property to collect the rents and to inspect the property. The

---

[18] IRS, *Publication No. 463* (Travel, Entertainment, Gift, and Car Expenses), 2014.

[19] Rev. Rul. 99-7, 1999-1 C.B. 361.

[20] Ibid.

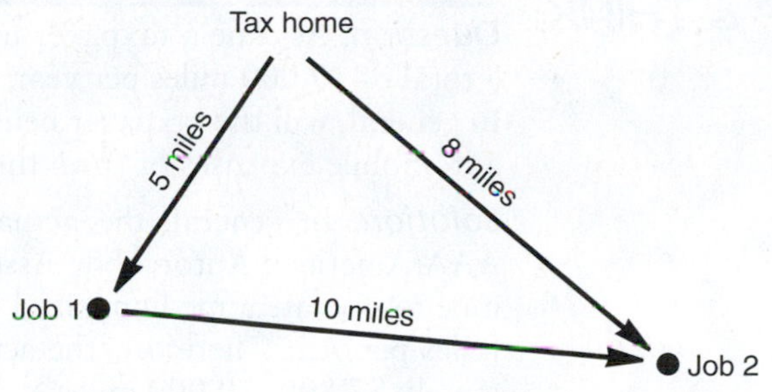

FIGURE I:9-1 ▶ ILLUSTRATION FOR EXAMPLE I:9-17

transportation expenses are deductible *for* AGI as an expense related to the production of rental income under Sec. 212. ◀

EXAMPLE I:9-20 ▶ Donna, an accountant who is employed by a CPA firm, travels from her home to an audit client located in the local metropolitan area. The firm maintains an office for Donna at their business location. She is not reimbursed for her transportation costs. The transportation costs are deductible *from* AGI as unreimbursed employee expenses that are subject to the 2% nondeductible floor. If Donna were instead a self-employed CPA operating a business from her home, her transportation expenses would be deductible *for* AGI. ◀

TREATMENT OF AUTOMOBILE EXPENSES

An employee or self-employed person may use either of two methods to deduct allowable automobile expenses. First, actual automobile expenses, including gas, oil, repairs, depreciation, interest, property taxes, license fees, and insurance are deductible based on the percentage of business miles to total miles. Detailed records to support the expenses are necessary in order to properly claim the deduction. To help reduce the burden of detailed recordkeeping, a second method, the standard mileage rate method, is available to taxpayers.

The standard mileage rate method permits a deduction based on a mileage rate of 57.5 cents per mile for the year 2015.[21] Parking and tolls for business purposes are allowed as an addition to this deduction as well as interest expense on an automobile loan and personal property taxes on the automobile. The following restrictions apply when the standard mileage rate is used:

- The standard mileage rate method cannot be used for automobiles used for hire, such as taxicabs, or for five or more automobiles used simultaneously by a taxpayer.
- If a taxpayer changes from the standard mileage rate method in one year to the actual expense method in a later year, the basis of the used automobile must be reduced by 24 cents for 2015, 22 cents for 2014, and 23 cents per mile for 2012 and 2013.[22] The modified accelerated cost-recovery system (MACRS) rules (discussed in Chapter I:10) cannot be used for computing depreciation in the year of the change and for the remaining useful life of the automobile. In such case, only the straight-line method under the alternative depreciation system (ADS) may be used (see Chapter I:10).
- A change to the standard mileage rate method is not allowed for an automobile that was previously depreciated under the MACRS rules or where an election was made under Sec. 179 to expense part or all of the automobile's cost in the year of acquisition. (See Chapter I:10 for a discussion of the Sec. 179 election.)
- The actual expense method is based on the ratio of business or employment-related miles to total miles. (See Chapter I:10 for a discussion of specific restrictions on the computation of depreciation where mixed business- and personal-use automobiles are acquired.)

ADDITIONAL COMMENT

It should be remembered that in many cases the taxpayer can choose between the automatic mileage method and calculating the actual costs of operating the car. Although the automatic mileage method has the advantage of convenience, a calculation of the actual costs might produce a larger deduction.

[21] Notice 2014-79, 2014-52 IRB, 12/10/2014. For the taxable year 2014, the standard mileage rate was 56 cents per mile.

[22] The depreciation component of the mileage rate for earlier years was 22 cents per mile for 2011, 23 cents per mile for 2010, 21 cents per mile for 2009 and 2008, 19 cents per mile for 2007, 17 cents per mile for 2006 and 2005, and 16 cents per mile for 2004 and 2003.

STOP & THINK

Question: Assume a taxpayer uses his car (original cost, $20,000) in his business, drives a total of 10,000 miles per year, and can substantiate 80% of the mileage as business use. In general, will the taxpayer benefit more from the standard mileage method of deducting automobile expenses or from the actual expenses method?

Solution: In general, the actual expenses method will yield a higher deduction. The AAA(American Automobile Association) estimates that it costs approximately $0.78 per mile to operate a medium-sized car in the United States in 2014 based on driving 10,000 miles per year. Therefore, the actual cost of operating the automobile would be approximately $7,800 (10,000 miles × $0.78). The deductible amount for tax purposes would be 80% of $7,800, or $6,240 for the actual expense method. Compare this amount with the standard mileage amount of $4,600 (10,000 miles × 80% business usage × .575/mile) and the actual expenses method yields a higher deduction. Of course, each individual situation is different and the actual results can vary based on circumstances, such as the amount of repairs, depreciation, and so on.

EXAMPLE I:9-21 ▶ Danny owns and operates a taxicab in New York City and drives 90,000 miles per year. In deducting his automobile expenses, Danny must use the actual cost method. He is not permitted to use the standard mileage method as the taxicab is an automobile for hire. ◀

EXAMPLE I:9-22 ▶ Doug acquired an automobile for use in his unincorporated business in 2012 and used the standard mileage rate method in 2012–2014. If Doug switches to the actual expense method for 2015 and later years, the automobile's adjusted basis (for depreciation purposes) must be reduced by 23 cents for 2012 and 2013 and 22 cents for 2014. Thus, if the automobile originally cost $20,000 in 2012 and was used 10,000 miles for business purposes during the initial year and 15,000 miles each in 2013 and 2014, the adjusted basis for computing depreciation in 2015 is reduced to $10,950 {$20,000 − [(0.23 × 10,000) + (0.23 × 15,000) + (0.22 × 15,000)]}. The remaining $10,950 basis must be depreciated using straight-line depreciation over the automobile's estimated useful life if the actual expense method is used. ◀

EXAMPLE I:9-23 ▶ Edith uses her automobile 50% of the time for business and employment-related use and 50% for personal use. These percentages are substantiated by records that document the total usage for the automobile. During 2015, Edith drives 3,000 miles per month or a total of 36,000 miles for the year. If the standard mileage rate method is used, she can deduct $10,350 [(0.575 × 36,000 miles) × 50%] for the business and employment-related use. Additionally, Edith may deduct any business-related parking fees and tolls. ◀

HISTORICAL NOTE

Congress enacted a "contemporaneous" records test for substantiating expenses for automobiles and certain other activities. Public outcry caused Congress to repeal this requirement. Currently, the business use of an automobile can be substantiated either by keeping adequate records or by sufficient corroborating evidence, oral or written.

REIMBURSEMENT OF AUTOMOBILE EXPENSES

An employee is entitled to deduct actual automobile expenses (or amounts derived under the standard mileage rate method if applicable) in excess of reimbursed amounts received from the employer. The computation is made on Form 2106 (Employee Business Expenses) and is reported on Schedule A of Form 1040.

EXAMPLE I:9-24 ▶ Elizabeth, who makes an adequate accounting to her employer, receives a $8,000 (20,000 miles at 40 cents per mile) reimbursement in 2015 for employment-related business miles. She also drives her car an additional 12,000 miles for personal use, or a total of 32,000 miles. She incurs the following expenses related to both business and personal use:

Gas and oil	$ 6,200
Repairs and maintenance	2,700
Depreciation	3,000
Insurance	1,900
Total	$13,800

Elizabeth also spent $100 on parking fees and tolls that were all related to business. Thus, she uses her car 62.5% (20,000 miles ÷ 32,000 miles) for business use. After subtracting the employer's $8,000 reimbursement and adding the parking fees and tolls, Elizabeth may deduct $725 [($13,800 × 0.625) + $100 − $8,000] as a miscellaneous itemized deduction (subject to the 2% nondeductible floor) in 2015. Alternatively, if 2015 is the first year she used the car in her business, she could have claimed a deduction using the standard mileage rate method. Under

ADDITIONAL COMMENT

The kind of written record that could corroborate the business use of an automobile would include account books, diaries, logs, trip sheets, expense reports, or written statements from witnesses.

the standard mileage rate method her deduction would be $3,600 [(32,000 miles × 62.5% × $0.575) + $100 business-related fees and tolls − $8,000 reimbursement]. ◀

ENTERTAINMENT EXPENSES

OBJECTIVE 4

Determine the proper deductible amount for entertainment expenses under the 50% disallowance rule

Entertainment of business customers and clients is a routine and, in many cases, an essential practice in business. Because entertainment expenses are considered ordinary and necessary practices of a business, they are deductible under either Sec. 162 or Sec. 212. However, the nature of entertainment expenses lend themselves to abuse by taxpayers. There certainly is an element of personal pleasure in taking a client or customer to a hockey game or a Philharmonic orchestra performance and allowing taxpayers to deduct such expenses creates serious enforcement problems for the IRS.

For the reasons above, Congress enacted Sec. 274, which is strictly a disallowance section and contains classification rules, restrictive tests, and specific recordkeeping requirements. To deduct entertainment expenses, taxpayers must first show that the expenditure qualifies for a deduction under Sec. 162 (trade or business expense) or Sec. 212 (investment-type expense). Then the various requirements of Sec. 274 must be adhered to in order for an entertainment expense to be deductible. Over the years, Congress has continued to tighten the rules for the deductibility of entertainment expenses.

50% DISALLOWANCE FOR MEAL AND ENTERTAINMENT EXPENSES

Section 274(n) provides that any expense incurred for either business meals or entertainment must be reduced by 50%. Business meals may be deductible either as travel expenses or as entertainment, depending on the nature of the expenditure. In either case, the 50% limit applies to the cost of food and beverages including tips and taxes but is not applicable to transportation expenses incurred going to and from a business meal. Further, any portion of a business meal that is considered lavish or extravagant is disallowed.[23] In such a situation, the 50% reduction rule is applied to the allowable portion of the business meal.

EXAMPLE I:9-25 ▶ Krishna, a self-employed individual, pays $300 for a business meal plus $18 sales tax and a $60 tip. The total cost of the meal is $378. If $150 of the meal is considered lavish or extravagant, Krishna could deduct $114 [($378 − $150) × 50%]. ◀

If an employee incurs entertainment or business meal expenses that are fully reimbursed by the employer, it is the employer rather than the employee who is limited to a deduction for 50% of the expenses. Assuming the reimbursement is made pursuant to an accountable plan (see discussion later in this chapter), the employee would not include the reimbursement in income and would not be allowed a deduction.

EXAMPLE I:9-26 ▶ Gordon incurs employment-related entertainment expenses of $1,000 and is fully reimbursed by his employer pursuant to an accountable plan. The employer may deduct $500 [$1,000 − ($1,000 × 0.50)] of entertainment expenses. Gordon would not include the $1,000 reimbursement in gross income and would not be allowed to deduct the $1,000 as a deduction. Thus, there is no overall tax effect to Gordon. ◀

Certain meals are not subject to the 50% disallowance, including meals that are treated as compensation to employees, employee picnics or other social gatherings primarily for the benefit of employees, or infrequent meals that would qualify as a de minimus fringe benefit.

CLASSIFICATION OF EXPENSES

If an individual is engaged in a trade or business (but not as an employee), allowable entertainment expenses are deductible *for* AGI. Employees, however, may deduct entertainment expenses only as a miscellaneous itemized deduction (subject to the 2% nondeductible

[23] Sec. 274(k).

floor) unless the expenses are reimbursed. The tax rules for reimbursements of employee business expenses are discussed more fully later in this chapter.

EXAMPLE I:9-27 ▶ Helen is a self-employed attorney who entertains clients and prospective clients. To the extent that these expenditures meet the Sec. 274 requirements, they are deductible by Helen as a *for* AGI expense on Schedule C of Form 1040 because Helen is engaged in a trade or business activity. The entertainment expenses are subject to the 50% limit but are not subject to the 2% nondeductible floor because the entertainment is deductible when determining AGI as a trade or business expense. ◀

ADDITIONAL COMMENT

Entertainment expenses are not considered "directly related" if there are substantial distractions. Therefore, if a meeting takes place at a sporting event, theater, or night club, the entertainment cannot be "directly related." This type of entertainment could qualify as an "associated with" expense. An example of a "directly related" expense would be the costs related to a hospitality room at a convention.

Criteria for Deduction. To be deductible as an entertainment expense, an expenditure must be either **directly related** to the active conduct of a trade or business or **associated with** the active conduct of a trade or business. Different restrictions apply to each of these categories. The Regulations under Sec. 274 provide the substantive rules for the two types of entertainment expenses.

"Directly Related" Expenses. To meet the requirements for a "directly related" **entertainment expense**, some business benefit must be expected from the business conducted other than goodwill and the expense must be incurred in a clear business setting (i.e., where there are no substantial distractions). In other words, business in anticipation of a business benefit must actually be conducted during the entertainment period.

ADDITIONAL COMMENT

With respect to the "associated with" type of expense, there is *no* requirement that the business discussion last for any specified period, or that more time be devoted to business than to entertainment.

"Associated With" Expenses. To qualify an expense as an "associated with" entertainment expenditure, the taxpayer must show a clear business purpose, such as obtaining new business or encouraging the continuation of an existing business relationship. An added restriction is placed on "associated with" entertainment in that the entertainment must directly precede or follow a bona fide business discussion. This means that the entertainment generally must occur on the same day that business is discussed.

EXAMPLE I:9-28 ▶ Holly is a lawyer who hosts a birthday party in her home. Most of the guests are law partners or clients. No formal business discussions are conducted either before or immediately following the party. The expenditures for the birthday party are not deductible because they do not meet either the "directly related" or "associated with" tests. ◀

REAL-WORLD EXAMPLE

One common way business people document a business meal is to write on the back of the credit card receipt the other person(s) at the meal and the topic discussed. Then all of the necessary substantiation requirements are present on the one piece of paper: date, time, place, amount, people present, and business discussed.

Substantiation Requirements. In addition to both the directly related and associated with requirements, Sec. 274 imposes stringent substantiation requirements for entertainment expenses. In order to deduct entertainment expenses, taxpayers are required to substantiate each expenditure for which a deduction is claimed. Lack of documentation alone will cause the disallowance of a deduction.

BUSINESS MEALS

Business meals related to travel or entertainment activities are subject to the same business-connection requirements as other types of entertainment expenses. Thus, an entertainment deduction is allowed only if the meal meets the "directly related" or "associated with" tests previously discussed. In addition, the expense must not be lavish or extravagant under the circumstances, and the taxpayer (or an employee of the taxpayer) must generally be present when the food or beverages are furnished. These requirements do not apply to a business meal associated with travel where the taxpayer claims a deduction only for his or her own expenses.

EXAMPLE I:9-29 ▶ Hank is a salesman for a manufacturing supply company. Hank meets Harold, a purchasing agent who is an important customer, for lunch during a normal business day. Business is actually conducted during the lunch, and the lunch expenses are not lavish or extravagant under the circumstances. Hank is fully reimbursed by his employer for the $30 lunch expenses after an adequate accounting of the expenses is submitted. The business meal qualifies as "directly related" entertainment because the entertainment involved the actual conduct of business where some business benefit is reasonably expected and a business discussion was conducted during the meal. Hank's employer may deduct $15 ($30 × 0.50) of entertainment expenses. ◀

WHAT WOULD YOU DO IN THIS SITUATION?

You have recently acquired a new individual tax client, Joe Windsack, who is a manufacturer's representative for a local tool and die company. You have been engaged by Windsack to prepare his individual income tax return for the current year. Before the current tax year is over, you are at a party where Windsack is also a guest. You overhear Windsack bragging to a group of people that he substantially reduces his income tax liability by overstating meal and entertainment expenses. He indicated that he overstates the deductions in several ways: (1) when he goes out to lunch or dinner that is personal in nature, such as with his family, he always uses a credit card and fictitiously writes the name of a client or prospective client on the charge card receipt, (2) when he goes out to lunch with several colleagues from his office (not business related), he charges the entire amount on his credit card (for everyone at the table), collects the cash from his colleagues for the cost of their meals, and then writes the entire amount off as a business-related meal, and (3) whenever he goes to any entertainment event, such as a ballgame, he always says that he took a client to the game with him and deducts the cost of the ticket as a business expense. When Windsack brings his tax information to you a couple of months later and you see a substantial amount of meal and entertainment expenses, what should you do?

EXAMPLE I:9-30 ▶ Assume the same facts as in Example I:9-29, except that the purchasing agent is a prospective customer and no business is actually discussed either during, directly preceding, or immediately following the meal. Thus, no deduction is allowed because no business is discussed either before, during, or after the meal. ◀

The Regulations provide that the surroundings in which food or beverages are furnished must be in an atmosphere where there are no substantial distractions to the discussion (e.g., a floor show).[24]

EXAMPLE I:9-31 ▶ Harry is a salesman who takes a customer to a local nightclub to watch a floor show and to have a few drinks. No business is discussed either before, during, or after the entertainment. The expenses for the beverages and floor show are not deductible because neither of the business meal requirements are met (i.e., the floor show produced substantial distractions, and no business was discussed). Even if business was actually discussed, no deduction would be allowed because there were substantial distractions. ◀

ENTERTAINMENT FACILITIES AND CLUB DUES

KEY POINT

Subject to very few exceptions, no deduction is permitted for costs related to yachts, swimming pools, fishing camps, tennis courts, bowling alleys, vacation resorts, etc. This highly visible type of entertainment contributed to the public perception that the tax system was unfair.

No deduction is permitted for costs (e.g., depreciation, maintenance, repairs, and so on) related to the maintenance of facilities that are used for entertainment, amusement, or recreation. Facilities include yachts, hunting lodges, beach cottages, and so on.

No deduction is permitted for any type of club dues (including business, social, athletic, luncheon, and sporting clubs, as well as airline and hotel clubs).[25] Professional, civic and public service organizations (e.g., business leagues, trade associations, chambers of commerce, boards of trade, and real estate boards) are generally not subject to the dues disallowance rules. Initiation fees that are paid only upon joining a club are treated as nondeductible capital expenditures. While club dues are not deductible, other business expenses (e.g., business meals) are deductible if the general requirements for entertainment deductions are met.

EXAMPLE I:9-32 ▶ Heidi is a self-employed CPA who entertains clients at her country club. Her club expenses include the following:

Annual dues	$ 4,000
Meal and entertainment charges related to business use	3,000
Personal-use meal charges	2,500
Initiation fee	10,000
Total expenses	$19,500

[24] Reg. Sec. 1.274-2(f)(2)(i)(b).

[25] Sec. 274(a)(3).

The only expense that is deductible is 50% of the specific business charges relating to the meals and entertainment. Thus, Heidi may deduct $1,500 ($3,000 × 0.50) *for* AGI as a business expense because she is a self-employed CPA. ◀

BUSINESS GIFTS

Business gifts are deductible but are subject to an annual ceiling amount of $25 per donee.[26] Amounts in excess of the $25 limit per donee are disallowed. The following rules and exceptions apply to determine the business gift deduction:

- Multiple gifts to each donee are aggregated for purposes of applying the $25 per donee annual limitation. Husbands and wives and other family members are treated as a single donee.
- Employee achievement awards made for length of service or safety that are under $400 per individual are excluded.[27]
- A gift from an employee to his or her supervisor does not qualify as a business gift because such gifts are personal rather than business related and are, therefore, not deductible.
- Business gifts are not subject to the 50% reduction for meals and entertainment.

EXAMPLE I:9-33 ▶ Jack, an employee, makes the following gifts during the year, none of which are reimbursed by his employer:

Jack's immediate supervisor	$20
Jack's secretary	15
Jeff (a customer of Jack's)	24
Jeff's wife (a noncustomer)	26
Total	$85

Jack's total deduction for business gifts is $40 ($15 + $25) and is classified as a miscellaneous itemized deduction subject to the 2% nondeductible floor as an employee business expense. The $20 gift to Jack's immediate supervisor is not deductible. The gifts of $24 and $26 to Jeff and Jeff's wife must be aggregated and are limited to $25. ◀

REAL-WORLD EXAMPLE

A taxpayer who had deducted the full cost of two wedding gifts, both of which were in excess of $25 apiece, was able to deduct only $25 for each gift. *Jack R. Howard,* 1981 PH T.C. Memo ¶81,250, 41 TCM 1554.

LIMITATIONS ON ENTERTAINMENT TICKETS

In addition to the general 50% meals and entertainment limitation, the cost of a ticket for any entertainment activity or facility is limited to the ticket's face value. Thus, the 50% limit applies to the face value of the ticket. Further restrictions are placed on the rental of skyboxes that are leased for more than one event.[28]

EXAMPLE I:9-34 ▶ Able Corporation acquires four tickets to a football game for $2,000 that are used for entertaining customers. The face amount of the four tickets is only $200 in total. Able's deduction for entertainment is initially limited to the $200 face value of the tickets. The deductible amount is $100 ($200 × 0.50) after applying the 50% limit on entertainment expenses. ◀

---

[26] Sec. 274(b)(1).

[27] Sec. 274(j). The total limit including both qualified and nonqualified plan awards is $1,600 per individual (see Chapter I:4).

[28] Sec. 274(l)(2). The cost of a skybox is disallowed to the extent that it exceeds the cost of the highest-priced nonluxury box seat tickets multiplied by the number of seats in the skybox (e.g., if a skybox contains 30 seats and the cost of the highest-priced nonluxury box seat for a particular event is $200, the deduction for the skybox is limited to $6,000 ($200 × 30) reduced by the 50% limitation applicable to entertainment expenses, or a total of $3,000.

REIMBURSED EMPLOYEE BUSINESS EXPENSES

OBJECTIVE 5

Discuss the tax methods concerning reimbursed employee business expenses

The tax treatment of reimbursements received by an employee from his employer for employment-related expenses depends upon whether the reimbursement is made pursuant to an **accountable** or **nonaccountable** plan. An accountable plan is a reimbursement arrangement that meets both of the following two tests.[29]

1. Substantiation—the employee must make an adequate accounting of expenses to his employer, which means that each business expense must be substantiated (an expense report, for example); and
2. Return of excess reimbursement—within a reasonable period of time, the employee is required to return to the employer any portion of the reimbursement in excess of the substantiated expenses.

ADDITIONAL COMMENT

While reimbursed business expenses under an accountable plan are technically deductions for AGI, they do not actually appear on the employee's tax return as a deduction. This is because the reimbursement itself is not included on the Form W-2.

If both of these tests are not met, amounts paid to an employee generally are treated as paid under a nonaccountable plan. However, a special rule in Reg. Sec. 1.62-2(c) provides that if an employee does not return the excess reimbursement within a reasonable time period, only the portion of the reimbursement in excess of substantiated expenses is considered as being paid under a nonaccountable plan. The portion of the reimbursement for substantiated expenses is considered as being paid under an accountable plan.

Accountable Plan. Under an accountable plan, reimbursements are included in gross income and expenses are deductible *for* AGI. Therefore, a taxpayer's AGI will not increase if employee business expenses are reimbursed under an accountable plan. Because reimbursements and expenses offset each other, when expenses are reimbursed under an accountable plan, taxpayers do not report the reimbursement or the expenses on their tax return. However, if an excess reimbursement is not returned to the employer, the excess reimbursement is included in the employee's gross income.[30]

EXAMPLE I:9-35 ▶ Anthony is an employee of the Bluechip Corporation, which maintains an accountable plan for purposes of reimbursing employee expenses. During the current year, Anthony went on a business trip and incurred $1,500 of expenses as follows: airfare, $800; lodging, $450; meals, $200; and tips, $50. Bluechip reimbursed him $1,500. Technically speaking, Anthony has gross income of $1,500 and a deduction for AGI of $1,500. But, because the reimbursement is pursuant to an accountable plan, Anthony will not report the $1,500 reimbursement in his gross income and will not deduct any of the business expenses on his tax return. ◀

EXAMPLE I:9-36 ▶ Assume the same facts as in Example I:9-35 except that Bluechip advanced Anthony $1,800, rather than $1,500, for his business trip and his expenses were the same as above. If Anthony returned the excess $300 to Bluechip within a reasonable period of time, the result would be the same as in Example I:9-35. However, if Anthony did not return the excess reimbursement (even though he is required to under the terms of the plan), Anthony must include the $300 in his gross income. The portion of the $1,800 reimbursement that pertains to the substantiated expenses, $1,500, is treated as being paid under an accountable plan. Thus, $1,500 of the reimbursement and the $1,500 of substantiated expenses are netted together and not reported. However, the excess $300 reimbursement is treated as being paid under a non accountable plan and, therefore, includible in Anthony's gross income. ◀

If an employee receives a reimbursement that is not as much as his expenses, a proration is required.

[29] Reg. Sec. 1.62-2(c).

[30] In Rev. Rul. 2006-56, 2006-2 C.B. 874, the IRS warned taxpayers that reimbursements from accountable plans must be properly substantiated and excess amounts must be returned to the employer. An accountable plan that reaches the level of a "pattern of abuse" will be reclassified as a nonaccountable plan.

EXAMPLE I:9-37 ▶ Fred, an employee, incurs employment-related expenses of $4,500 consisting of $1,200 business meals, $1,800 local transportation, and $1,500 entertainment of customers. He is only reimbursed $3,000 from his employer. Since the reimbursement is less than the amount of expenses, Fred must prorate the expenses as follows:

Expense	*Total Amount*	*Reimbursed Expense*[a]	*Unreimbursed Expense*
Business meals	$1,200	$ 800	$ 400
Local transportation	1,800	1,200	600
Entertainment	1,500	1,000	500
Total	$4,500	$3,000	$1,500

The reimbursed expenses of $3,000 are not reported by Fred and the $3,000 reimbursement is not reportable as income. The $1,500 of unreimbursed expenses are deductible *from* AGI (subject to 2% of AGI) as follows:

Business meals ($400 × 50%)	$ 200
Local transportation	600
Entertainment ($500 × 50%)	250
	$1,050

[a]Reimbursements are allocated to each expense category on a prorata basis. For example, the $800 for business meals is computed, $\frac{\$1,200}{\$4,500} \times \$3,000$. ◀

KEY POINT

Why does the government require reimbursements from nonaccountable plans to be included in the employee's gross income? Because these types of plans are often referred to as "expense accounts paid to employees as additional compensation."

Nonaccountable Plan. Under a nonaccountable plan, reimbursements are included in the employee's gross income and the expenses are deductible by the employee as miscellaneous itemized deductions, subject to the 2% of AGI floor and the 50% disallowance for meals and entertainment expenses.

EXAMPLE I:9-38 ▶ Use the same facts as in Example I:9-35 except that Bluechip does not require its employees to submit an accounting of expenses incurred. Bluechip's plan is a nonaccountable plan. Antoine must include the $1,500 in his gross income and may deduct the expenses as miscellaneous itemized deductions, subject to the 2% of AGI floor, in the amount of $1,400 [$800 + 450 + (200 × 50%) + 50]. ◀

Per Diem Allowances for Meals and Lodging. The IRS permits employers and employees to use optional "per diem allowances" for meals and lodging expenses in lieu of actual expenses. The use of per diem allowances is intended to simplify the burden of keeping detailed records for taxpayers who incur significant travel expenses. Special tables have been issued by the IRS that provide fixed per diem amounts for lodging as well as meals and incidental expenses (M&IE). The per diem allowances vary in amount depending on the city in which the travel took place. The tables list many cities in the United States as well as many cities in foreign countries. Thus, a taxpayer must only substantiate the time, place, and business purpose of the trip and then is permitted to use the per diem allowances. The per diem system is permitted only for payments under an accountable plan, the expenses must be reasonably expected to be incurred, and the amount of expenses should be in reasonable proximity to the expected actual expense amount.[31] A full discussion of this topic is outside the scope of this textbook.

EXAMPLE I:9-39 ▶ Peyton Boying is an employee of UT, Inc. UT maintains an accountable plan for reimbursing employees for their business expenses. Peyton travels extensively in the United States for business purposes. Instead of requiring Peyton to keep actual records of his travel expenses, UT reimburses Peyton the per diem amounts as allowed by the IRS. Assuming Peyton traveled exclusively in low-cost localities (see footnote below) and was away from home for 100 days, UT could reimburse Peyton in the amount of $17,200 (100 days × $172) without the necessity

[31] The IRS tables for per diem allowances paid on or after October 1, 2014, may be found in Notice 2014-57, 2014-41 IRB, or IRS Publication 1542, which is periodically updated. The rate for travel on or after October 1, 2014 for high-cost localities (specifically identified by the IRS) is $259 per day (including $65 for M&IE); low-cost localities are $172 per day (including $52 for M&IE). Further, self-employed individuals who are not reimbursed for their travel expenses may use the M&IE rate, but must substantiate lodging with actual receipts.

of Peyton keeping detailed records of his actual travel expenses. The amount that Peyton actually spent is irrelevant as the IRS will accept the per diem amounts. ◀

Table I:9-2 summarizes the concepts relating to employee business expenses and reimbursements.

▼ **TABLE I:9-2**
Treatment of Employee Reimbursements

TYPE OF PLAN	TAX EFFECT
ACCOUNTABLE PLAN	
Reimbursement = Expense	No effect, amounts are netted and not reported on employee's return.
Reimbursement > Expense	Not permissible under plan, but should it occur, excess reimbursement is included in employee's gross income.
Reimbursement < Expense	Expenses are prorated to amount of reimbursement. Reimbursed expenses—no effect; unreimbursed expenses are deductible as miscellaneous itemized deductions subject to 2% of AGI "floor" or nondeductible amount.
NONACCOUNTABLE PLAN	
Reimbursements	Always included in employee's gross income.
Expenses	Deductible as miscellaneous itemized deductions subject to 2% of AGI "floor" or nondeductible amount.

MOVING EXPENSES

OBJECTIVE 6

Identify deductible moving expenses and determine the amount and year of deductibility

Moving expenses are generally nondeductible personal expenditures. However, Sec. 217 allows a limited deduction for moving expenses for employees and self-employed people. The underlying rationale for this deduction is that such moves are similar to business expenditures because they are either employment-related or connected with a trade or business.

EXAMPLE I:9-40 ▶ Ken retires from his job and moves from Tennessee to Arizona. His moving expenses are nondeductible personal expenditures because the move is not employment-related and he is not moving to look for a new job. ◀

ADDITIONAL COMMENT

In 2012, 1.1 million taxpayers deducted moving expenses totaling $3.1 billion.

Two conditions must be met for a moving expense to be deductible:[32]

- *Distance requirement.* The new job location must be at least 50 miles farther from the taxpayer's old residence than the old residence was from the former place of employment. If an individual has no former place of employment, the new job must be at least 50 miles from the old residence.
- *Time requirement.* A new or transferred employee must be employed on a full-time basis at the new location for at least 39 weeks during the 12-month period immediately following the move. More stringent requirements must be met by self-employed people who either work as an employee at the new location or continue to be self-employed. Such individuals are subject to a 78-week minimum work period during the first two years following the move. At least 39 of the 78 weeks must be in the first 12-month period. A waiver of the time requirements is permitted for both employees and self-employed individuals if the taxpayer becomes disabled, dies, or is

ADDITIONAL COMMENT

The time requirement test ensures that taxpayers cannot use temporary jobs as a pretext for deducting the cost of moving for personal reasons.

[32] The requirements for deducting moving expenses are contained in Sec. 217 and the Treasury Regulations thereunder.

involuntarily terminated (other than for willful misconduct). Unemployed or retired individuals are generally not able to deduct moving expenses because they do not meet the 39- or 78-week test.

EXAMPLE I:9-41 ▶ Ellen is employed by the Able Company in Dallas, Texas. She lives 30 miles from her place of employment in Dallas. If Ellen accepts a new job in Houston, the new job location is 270 miles from her former residence in Dallas. The 50-mile distance requirement is satisfied because the distance from her old residence to her new job in Houston exceeds the distance from her old residence to her old job by 240 miles (270 − 30). In addition, to meet the time requirement, Ellen must be employed on a full-time basis in Houston for at least 39 weeks during the 12-month period immediately following the move. ◀

EXAMPLE I:9-42 ▶ Assume the same facts as in Example I:9-41, except that Ellen accepts a new job and moves to a new residence in a small town outside of Dallas. Her new job location is 55 miles from her former residence. The 50-mile distance requirement is not met because the distance from her old residence to her new job is 55 miles and the distance from her old residence to her old job is 30 miles; thus, the excess distance is only 25 miles. ◀

ADDITIONAL COMMENT

The individual need not be employed at the location that he or she is leaving. For example, a graduating college student who has not been employed for the most recent four years could deduct moving costs if the distance requirement is satisfied and if he or she has been employed at the *new* location for the minimum time period.

EXPENSE CLASSIFICATION

Moving expenses of an employee or a self-employed individual are deductible *for* AGI.[33] Thus, a taxpayer may receive a tax benefit from the deduction of moving expenses even if the standard deduction is used in lieu of itemizing deductions.

DEFINITION OF MOVING EXPENSES

Direct Moving Expenses. Only direct moving expenses are deductible. These expenses are deductible without limit as long as they are reasonable in amount and include:

- The cost of moving household goods and personal effects from the former residence to the new residence (e.g., moving van).
- The cost of traveling (including lodging but excluding meals) from the former residence to the new residence. If the trip is by personal automobile, a deduction of 23 cents per mile (or actual expenses) is allowed for each automobile that is driven in 2015.

KEY POINT

The standard mileage rate for purposes of the moving expense deduction is only 23 cents per mile, compared to the 2015 standard business mileage rate of 57.5 cents per mile.

The expenses of moving household goods and personal effects do not include storage charges in excess of 30 days, penalties for breaking leases, mortgage penalties, expenses of refitting drapes, or losses on deposits and club memberships.[34]

EXAMPLE I:9-43 ▶ Gail, a resident of California and a college student in that state, graduates from college and accepts a new position with an accounting firm in Atlanta. Thus, Gail is an employee of the Atlanta firm. Because the move meets the distance requirement (i.e., more than 50 miles), Gail qualifies for the deduction if she also meets the 39-week time requirement. Gail incurs the following expenses pursuant to the move: moving van, $1,200; lodging en route, $400; automobile expenses, $598 (2,600 miles × $0.23 cents per mile); and tolls and parking, $25. Assuming these expenses are reasonable, they qualify as direct moving expenses and are deductible without limitation. The cost of any meals incurred by Gail en route is not deductible. ◀

Otherwise allowable expenses of any individual other than the taxpayer are taken into account only if the individual has both the former residence and the new residence as his principal place of abode and is a member of the taxpayer's household.

EXAMPLE I:9-44 ▶ Assume the same facts as in Example I:9-43 except that Gail's son Paul is a member of her household. Additional automobile expenses (including tolls and parking) of $275 are incurred during the move because Paul owns an automobile which is driven to the new location. The $275 of additional automobile expenses are deductible as moving expenses because Paul is a member of Gail's household and his principal place of abode includes both the former and the new residences. ◀

[33] Sec. 62(a)(15). For years before 1994 moving expenses were deductible *from* AGI as an itemized deduction (not subject to the 2% nondeductible floor).

[34] Reg. Sec. 1.217-2(b)(3). In-transit storage charges for up to 30 consecutive days are allowable moving expenses.

Nondeductible Indirect Moving Expenses. In addition to the disallowed moving expenses previously discussed (e.g., meals en route, storage charges, etc.), the following indirect or moving-related expense items are not deductible:

- Househunting trips including meals, lodging, and transportation
- Temporary living expenses at the new job location
- Qualified expenses related to a sale, purchase, or lease of a residence (e.g., attorney's fees, points, or payments to a lessor to cancel a lease)

TREATMENT OF EMPLOYER REIMBURSEMENTS

Moving expense reimbursements made by an employer, either paid directly or through reimbursement, are excluded from the employee's gross income as a qualified fringe benefit under Sec. 132 to the extent that the expenses meet the requirements for deductibility (i.e., the reimbursement is for moving expenses that are otherwise deductible under Sec. 217). Moving expense reimbursements must be included in gross income if the employee actually deducted the expenses in a prior tax year or if the expenses are otherwise not deductible under Sec. 217.[35]

EXAMPLE I:9-45 ► In 2015, Ralph incurs $2,400 of moving expenses related to moving household effects and traveling to his new residence. He also incurs $2,600 of nondeductible moving-related expenses (e.g., househunting trips and temporary living expenses). Ralph receives a $5,000 reimbursement from his employer. Of the total reimbursement, $2,400 is excluded from gross income as a Sec. 132 fringe benefit. However, the $2,600 reimbursement for nondeductible moving-related expenses is included in Ralph's gross income under Sec. 82. None of the $2,400 of moving expenses may be deducted by Ralph because they were reimbursed by his employer and were not included in Ralph's gross income. ◄

EDUCATION EXPENSES

OBJECTIVE 7

Describe the requirements for deducting education expenses

Generally, education expenses are considered personal expenses and, therefore, are not deductible despite the obvious benefits that accrue to society from the pursuit of such activities. However, education expenses that are necessary in the pursuit of an employment-related or trade or business activity are deductible. It would be inequitable if such educational expenditures were not deductible because they are incurred to produce income from employment or business activities. The education expenses discussed in this chapter pertain to expenses that are related to an individual's trade or business, such as a job in the case of an employee or the business of a self-employed individual. However, there are a number of other provisions in the tax law that provide favorable tax advantages for education expenses. Most of these rules are covered elsewhere in this textbook; however, the major tax provisions dealing with education are summarized below.

- Tax credits—two important provisions benefiting education are the American Opportunity Tax Credit and the Lifetime Learning Credit. Both of these items are credits and are available for the taxpayer and his dependents and are discussed in Chapter I:14.
- Exclusion for scholarships—scholarships received by students are generally excludable from gross income under Sec. 117. See the discussion of scholarships in Chapter I:4.
- Educational assistance for employees—if an employer maintains an educational assistance plan, amounts received by the employee for tuition and other expenses are excludable from the employee's gross income under Sec. 127. This exclusion is also discussed in Chapter I:4.
- Student loan interest—a *for* AGI deduction is permitted for certain student loan interest under Sec. 221. (See Chapter I:6 for a further discussion of this topic.)

ADDITIONAL COMMENT

Attendance at a convention or professional meeting is one of the most common deductible education expenses. Almost every profession or occupation has its own society or association. Often these organizations sponsor local, regional, or national meetings. Training sessions or other types of educational activities are normally included on the program.

[35] Sec. 82 and Sec. 132(g).

- Deduction for higher education expenses—taxpayers may deduct up to $4,000 *for* AGI for tuition and related expenses under Sec. 222.[36] This deduction, as is the case for the tax credits and the student loan interest, is subject to a phase-out based on AGI. If a taxpayer's AGI does not exceed $65,000 ($130,000 on a joint return), the taxpayer may deduct up to $4,000. However, taxpayer's with AGI exceeding $65,000 but not exceeding $80,000 may deduct up to $2,000 in qualified expenses. No deduction is permitted for taxpayers with AGI in excess of $80,000 ($160,000 on a joint return). Further, taxpayers are not permitted to claim this deduction and also claim one of the tax credits above using the same expenses.
- Qualified state tuition programs—a very popular program for higher income taxpayers is the use of so-called Section 529 plans. These plans allow taxpayers to invest funds to be used for education and the income earned on such funds is not subject to tax. When amounts are withdrawn from the plan, the amounts are also not taxable if used for qualified education expenses. These plans are discussed in Chapter I:4.
- Coverdell Education IRA—these special IRAs are discussed later in this chapter and enable a taxpayer to invest up to $2,000 per year in a tax-deferred IRA.

CLASSIFICATION OF EDUCATION EXPENSES

Depending on the nature of the education-related activity, educational expenses may be either personal and nondeductible, deductible *for* AGI, deductible *from* AGI (as a miscellaneous itemized deduction), or reimbursed by an employer and excluded from gross income. Table I:9-3 illustrates the tax consequences that are accorded to various types of education expenses depending on the facts and circumstances and the type of expenditure for each case.

The discussion below focuses on the deductibility of education expenses that are related to a taxpayer's trade or business.

▼ TABLE I:9-3
Classification and Tax Treatment of Educational Expenses

Situation Facts	Classification and Tax Treatment
▶ Jeremy is a college student who is not classified as an employee and is pursuing a general course of study.	▶ The expenses are nondeductible personal expenditures regardless of whether Jeremy or his parents pay them.
▶ Irene is an employee who incurs certain employment-related educational expenses including travel, transportation, tuition, and books. Her expenses are not reimbursed by her employer.	▶ If the expenses meet the two general deduction requirements, the education expenses are deductible *from* AGI as a miscellaneous itemized deduction (subject to the 2% nondeductible floor).
▶ Jesse is an employee who receives educational assistance payments from his employer to reimburse him for certain educational expenses incurred in attending college at the undergraduate level.	▶ Educational assistance payments up to $5,250 per excluded from Jesse's gross income and are deductible by the employer as trade or business expenses if the requirements of Sec. 127 are met.[37]
▶ Jackie is a self-employed CPA who incurs education expenses including travel, transportation, books, registration fees, and so on to attend a continuing education conference.	▶ All of the education expenses are deductible *for* AGI as trade or business expenses.
▶ Jim is an employee who incurs education expenses for a continuing education course related to his employment, and the expenses are reimbursed by the employer.	▶ The reimbursement is deductible by the employer as a trade or business expense. There is no tax effect to the employee because the education expenses are offset by the reimbursement.

[36] This deduction was scheduled to expire after December 31, 2013 but has been extended for one year through 2014.

[37] The Sec. 127 exclusion is applicable for expenses paid by an employer for courses taken by employees. Qualified expenses include tuition, fees, and related expenses. Both undergraduate and graduate-level courses qualify for the exclusion.

GENERAL REQUIREMENTS FOR A DEDUCTION

TYPICAL MISCONCEPTION

Education costs include the cost of books, tuition, registration fees, and supplies. Transportation costs and travel costs are also included.

An employee generally may deduct education expenses if either of the following two requirements are met:[38]

- The expenditure is incurred to maintain or improve skills required by the individual in his or her employment, trade, or business; or
- The expenditure is incurred to meet requirements imposed by law or by the employer for retention of employment, rank, or compensation rate.

Even if one of the two requirements above are met, education expenses are not deductible if:

- The education is required to meet minimum educational requirements for qualification in the taxpayer's employment; or
- The education qualifies the taxpayer for a new trade or business (or employment activity).

ETHICAL POINT

A client asks advice from his CPA as to whether certain educational expenses are deductible. The CPA should inform the client that the advice reflects professional judgment based on an existing situation. The CPA should use cautionary language to the effect that the advice is based on facts as stated and authorities that are subject to change.

The deductibility of education expenses has been a frequent source of controversy and litigation because of the uncertainty in interpreting the above Regulations. The principal area of disagreement has been the interpretation of the term "qualifies the taxpayer for a new trade or business." If a taxpayer undertakes education and that education will *qualify* her for a new trade or business, then her expenses will not be deductible. For example, several courts have disallowed deductions to IRS agents and accountants for educational expenses incurred in obtaining a law degree, even though such training would be helpful in the taxpayer's employment.[39] The courts reasoned that the taxpayers were qualifying for a new profession (i.e., the practice of law). However, the IRS has ruled that a practicing dentist may deduct educational expenses in becoming an orthodontist under the theory that a dentist becoming an orthodontist is not entering a new trade or business.[40]

? STOP & THINK

Question: The Regulations clearly provide that if the education "qualifies" a taxpayer for a new trade or business, the cost of such education is not deductible. If taken to the extreme, could the IRS argue that *any* course would qualify an individual for a new trade or business? For example, if a person took a basket weaving course, could not the IRS argue that the person is now qualified for the new trade or business of basket weaving? How can a taxpayer support his position that the education does not qualify him for a new trade or business in order to meet the deductibility requirements?

Solution: This is a difficult question and many commentators have written that the Regulations are unfairly harsh toward taxpayers. The courts have required that the IRS be "reasonable" in its interpretations of qualification of a new trade or business. The best way for a taxpayer to support his position is to find a case where the facts are approximately the same as the taxpayer's and where the court has upheld the taxpayer's position in that case.

ADDITIONAL COMMENT

The same course could be deductible as a qualified educational expense or not depending on the particular situation of the student. For example, a CPA enrolled in a taxation course to update his or her tax knowledge could deduct the expense. On the other hand, a non-CPA taking the course as part of a series of courses meeting the requirements to sit for the CPA exam could not deduct the expense. The CPA has already met the minimum education requirements for the profession and the non-CPA has not.

Generally, a taxpayer must be employed or self-employed to be eligible for an education expense deduction. However, some courts have permitted individuals to qualify if they are unemployed for a temporary period.[41] School teachers have generally qualified for an education expense deduction in situations where the public school system requires advanced education courses as a condition for retention of employment or renewal of a teaching certificate or where state law imposes similar requirements. However, college instructors who are working on a doctorate in a college where the Ph.D. is the minimum degree for holding a permanent position generally have not been permitted to deduct the expenditures made to obtain the degree.[42] The Tax Court allowed a taxpayer to deduct the cost of earning an MBA because the education merely enhanced and maintained the skills he already had and did not qualify him for a new trade or business.[43]

---

[38] Reg. Sec. 1.162-5.

[39] *Jeffry L. Weiler*, 54 T.C. 398 (1970).

[40] Rev. Rul. 74-78, 1974-1 C.B. 44.

[41] *Robert J. Picknally*, 1977 PH T.C. Memo ¶77,321, 36 TCM 1292. The IRS has conceded that a deduction may be warranted in periods where the cessation of business activity was for periods of a year or less (Rev. Rul. 68-591, 1968-2 C.B. 73).

[42] *Kenneth C. Davis*, 65 T.C. 1014 (1976).

[43] *Daniel R. Allemeier, Jr.*, TC Memo 2005-207.

EXAMPLE I:9-46 ▶ Jane is a self-employed dentist who incurs education expenses attending a continuing education conference on new techniques in her field. Such expenditures are incurred to maintain or improve her skills as a practicing dentist (a trade or business activity). All of her educational expenses are deductible *for* AGI because Jane is currently engaged in a trade or business activity. ◀

EXAMPLE I:9-47 ▶ Juan is a business executive who incurs education expenses in the pursuit of an MBA degree in management. None of the expenses are reimbursed by Juan's employer. The expenses are deductible because they are incurred to maintain or improve Juan's skills as a manager and do not qualify Juan for a new trade or business. All of Juan's education expenses (e.g., travel, transportation, tuition, books, and word processing) are deductible *from* AGI as a miscellaneous itemized deduction (subject to the 2% nondeductible floor). ◀

EXAMPLE I:9-48 ▶ Janet is a high school teacher who is required by state law to complete a specified number of additional graduate courses to renew her provisional teaching certificate. None of the expenses are reimbursed by Janet's employer. The educational expenses are deductible *from* AGI as a miscellaneous itemized deduction (subject to the 2% nondeductible floor) because the expenditures are incurred to meet the requirements imposed by law to retain her job and do not qualify her for a new trade or business. ◀

EXAMPLE I:9-49 ▶ Jean is an accountant with a public accounting firm who incurs expenses in connection with taking the CPA examination (e.g., CPA review course fees, travel, and transportation). None of the expenses are reimbursed by Jean's employer. Even though the expenditures may improve her employment-related skills, they are not deductible because they are incurred to meet the minimum educational standards for qualification in Jean's accounting position.[44] ◀

EXAMPLE I:9-50 ▶ Joy is a tax accountant who incurs expenses to obtain a law degree. Despite the fact that the law school courses may be helpful to Joy to maintain or improve her skills as a tax practitioner, such expenses are not deductible because the taxpayer is qualifying for a new trade or business. If Joy were not a degree candidate at the law school and merely took a few tax law courses for continuing education, the educational expenses would be deductible because they are incurred to maintain or improve Joy's skills as a tax specialist and do not qualify her for a new trade or business. In such a case, the expenses are deductible *for* AGI if Joy is self-employed and *from* AGI as a miscellaneous itemized deduction (subject to the 2% nondeductible floor) if Joy is an employee. ◀

KEY POINT

The deduction for travel expenses is not permitted if the travel itself is the educational activity. Therefore, a high school teacher who teaches Spanish cannot deduct expenses incurred in living in Madrid during the summer.

OFFICE IN HOME EXPENSES

OBJECTIVE 8

Determine whether the expenses of an office in home meet the requirements for deductibility and apply the gross income limitations

Employees or self-employed individuals who use a portion of their home for trade or business or employment-related activities should be entitled to a deduction because the property is used for trade or business or employment-related activities. However, it is often difficult to determine whether a taxpayer is using a portion of the home for business or personal use.

For many years, there has been an ongoing controversy in the tax law as to the deductibility of office in home expenses. Because of the possibility of abuse by taxpayers, the IRC, Treasury Regulations, and the courts[45] have been extremely strict as to who qualifies to deduct office in home expenses. In order to promote fairness and consistency in the tax law, the definition of an office in home that qualifies for a tax deduction was expanded in 1998.

ADDITIONAL COMMENT

Approximately 28 million individuals, or 19% of the work force, work at least part-time at home.

GENERAL REQUIREMENTS FOR A DEDUCTION

Employees and self-employed individuals are permitted to deduct office in home expenses only if the office is exclusively used on a regular basis under any of the following conditions:

- The office is used as the principal place of business for *any* trade or business of the taxpayer;

[44] Rev. Rul. 69-292, 1969-1 C.B. 84.

[45] See, for example, *CIR v. Nader E. Soliman,* 71 AFTR 2d 93-463, 93-1 USTC 50,014 (USSC, 1993).

REAL-WORLD EXAMPLE

Most teachers have been denied a home office deduction because the home office is not the principal place of business. Also, most teachers cannot demonstrate that their office in the home is for the convenience of the employer because the employer typically provides an office at the school.

- The office is used as a place for meeting or dealing with patients, clients, or customers in the normal course of business; or
- If the office in home is located in a separate structure which is not attached to the dwelling unit, the office is used exclusively and regularly in connection with the taxpayer's trade or business.[46]

In addition to meeting any of these tests, an employee further must prove that the exclusive use is for the convenience of the *employer*. It is not enough that it is merely appropriate or helpful to the employee.

The first condition above has caused the major controversy in this area. Taxpayers are required to prove that the office is used exclusively as the "principal place of business." Under prior law, the principal place of business was interpreted to mean the "most important or significant place for the business," or more precisely, where the primary services were performed.

EXAMPLE I:9-51 ▶ In the *Soliman* case, Dr. Soliman was a self-employed anesthesiologist who performed medical services at three hospitals, none of which provided him with an office. He spent approximately two hours per day in his office in home where he maintained patient records and correspondence and he performed billing procedures. The office was not used as a place for meeting with or dealing with patients, clients, or customers in the normal course of his business. The U.S. Supreme Court denied a deduction for Dr. Soliman's office in home because it concluded that the essence of professional service rendered by the doctor was the actual medical treatment in the hospitals. A second factor considered by the court was the amount of time spent at the office relative to the total work effort. The effect of this case was to deny a deduction for an office in home for any type of taxpayer in a trade or business where the primary services were performed outside of the office (such as plumbers, electricians). This case was highly criticized. ◀

To combat the perceived unfairness of the *Soliman* case, Congress expanded the definition of "principal place of business" for tax years beginning after December 31, 1998. An office in home now qualifies as a taxpayer's principal place of business if:

1. the office is used by the taxpayer for *administrative or management* activities of the taxpayer's trade or business, and
2. there is no other fixed location of the trade or business where the taxpayer conducts substantial administrative or management activities of the trade or business.[47]

KEY POINT

The office-in-home deduction is available only where the office is being used for trade or business purposes. No deduction is permitted if the office is used to carry on investment activities.

Thus, the law essentially allows a deduction for an office in home even though the taxpayer provides his primary service away from the office. The above tests are clearly intended for self-employed taxpayers. However, they also apply to employees except that the additional "convenience of the employer" test will still apply.

EXAMPLE I:9-52 ▶ David is a self-employed electrician who performs his electrical services at the location of his customers. He also maintains an office where he does his administrative and management duties. David is permitted a deduction for an office in home even though his primary duties of providing electrical services are performed away from his office. ◀

EXAMPLE I:9-53 ▶ Barbara is an employee of DRK, Inc., and is provided with an office on DRK's premises. However, Barbara's job requires significant administrative work after normal working hours and she prefers to perform these duties in her office at home. Barbara may not deduct the costs of her office in home because she uses her office at home for *her* convenience, not her employer's convenience. ◀

As can be seen from the discussion above, the deduction for an office in home is generally restricted to self-employed taxpayers and employees who are not provided with an office by their employer. If a self-employed taxpayer maintains an office in home, the expenses are deductible *for* AGI. Employees must deduct the office in home expenses as miscellaneous itemized deductions, subject to the 2% nondeductible floor.

DEDUCTIONS AND LIMITATIONS

The deduction for home office expenses is computed using the following two categories of expenses: (1) Expenses directly related to the office, and (2) Expenses indirectly related to the office.

---

[46] Sec. 280A(c)(1).

[47] Ibid. For years before 1999, this new definition of principal place of business does not apply. Thus, the restrictive rules promulgated by *Soliman* apply to these years.

Direct expenses include expenses that relate solely to the office, such as painting and decorating just the office. Indirect expenses are the pro rata share of expenses that benefit the entire house or apartment, such as mortgage interest (or rent), real estate taxes, insurance, utilities, and maintenance. The office in the home expense is the sum of the direct expenses plus the pro rata share (generally based on square footage) of indirect expenses.

To compute the office in home deduction, taxpayers first subtract all expenses not connected with the office from the income generated by the business. Then, 100% of the direct expenses of the office and the percentage of indirect expenses based on the pro rata share of the house are deducted. The total of the office in home expenses cannot create a loss.

TAX STRATEGY TIP

When a taxpayer depreciates his office in the home, the office becomes business property. Upon the sale of the residence, the portion of the sale price attributable to the office will not be eligible for the sale of principal residence exclusion. Therefore, taxpayers might consider only deducting direct expenses of an in-home office to preserve the exclusion.

EXAMPLE I:9-54 ▶ Julie works as a full-time employee for a local company. She also operates a mail order business out of her home and maintains an office in her home that is used exclusively for business. The size of her home in total is 2,400 square feet and her office is 300 square feet. During the current year, she generated gross income of $18,000 and had $6,000 of business expenses, supplies, and shipping charges. She also had the following expenses in connection with the office in her home:

Painting of office	$ 600
Decorations in office	900
Mortgage interest (total)	3,200
Real estate taxes (total)	1,800
Insurance (total)	600
Utilities (total)	2,400
Depreciation (total)	800

Julie's home office expense for the current year would be computed as follows:

Direct expenses:		
Painting	$ 600	
Decorations	900	$1,500
Indirect expenses:		
Mortgage interest	3,200	
Real estate taxes	1,800	
Insurance	600	
Utilities	2,400	
Depreciation	800	
	8,800	
Business percentage (300/2,400)	×12.5%	1,100
Total expense for office in home		$2,600

Julie would be allowed to deduct the $2,600 of office in home expenses as they do not exceed the $12,000 ($18,000 − $6,000) of income from the business. If Julie only had $8,000 of gross income and $6,000 of business expenses, her office in home expenses of $2,600 would be limited to $2,000. ◀

As mentioned above, the total allowable office in home expenses may not exceed the taxpayer's net income from the business (or rental) activity.[48] This ceiling limitation on office in home deductions is intended to prevent taxpayers from recognizing tax losses if the business (or rental) activity does not produce sufficient amounts of gross income. Expenses disallowed because of the gross income limitation can be carried forward but are subject to the gross income limitation in the later year and are subject to specific ordering rules.[49]

TYPICAL MISCONCEPTION

Where a taxpayer is not entitled to an office-in-home deduction, the taxpayer can still deduct directly related business expenses (e.g., the cost of office supplies, and a MACRS deduction on filing cabinets and other equipment).

In early 2013, the IRS issued Rev. Proc. 2013-13, 2013-6 IRB (01/15/2013), which provides for an optional safe harbor that individuals can use to determine the amount of their deductible home office expenses. This safe harbor is effective for tax years beginning on or after January 1, 2013, and the same strict rules as to eligibility for a home office deduction, as discussed previously, will continue to apply. The safe harbor allows taxpayers the option of claiming as their home office deduction $5 times the square feet of qualified use (300 square feet maximum), for a maximum total deduction of $1,500.

[48] Sec. 280A(c)(5). Technically, the limitation is gross income less deductions not connected with the home office.

[49] See Prop. Reg. Sec. 1.280A-2 for the ordering rules. These rules are similar, but not identical to the ordering rules for hobby losses under Sec. 183, as follows: (1) mortgage interest and real estate taxes; (2) other deductions related to the office, such as insurance and utilities; and (3) depreciation.

Taxpayers can alternate the use of the actual expenses or the safe harbor amount each year. So, taxpayers will need to analyze each year which method to use and claim the greater amount.

Employee expense classifications and deduction limitations are summarized in Topic Review I:9-1.

TOPIC REVIEW I:9-1

Classification and Deductibility of Employee Expenses

Type of Expenditure	50% Disallowance	For or From AGI	Other Limitations
Miscellaneous itemized deductions	Applies to unreimbursed meals and entertainment	*From* AGI	Subject to 2% of AGI nondeductible floor.
Reimbursed travel expenses (adequate accounting is made)	Applies to the employer for meals portion of the travel only	*For* AGI	2% of AGI nondeductible floor applies only to employee expenses that exceed the reimbursement.
Unreimbursed travel expenses	Applies to meals portion of travel only	*From* AGI	Subject to the 2% of AGI nondeductible floor. Employee must be away from his or her tax home overnight.
Automobile expenses	Not applicable	*From* AGI	Subject to the 2% of AGI nondeductible floor. Actual costs or the standard mileage rate method may be used.
Moving expenses	Not applicable because meals are not deductible	*For* AGI	Indirect moving-related expenses are not deductible.
Entertainment expenses	Applies to all entertainment expenses	*From* AGI	Subject to the 2% of AGI non-deductible floor. Club dues and initiation fees are not deductible.
Education expenses deductible per Reg. Sec. 1.162-5	Applies to meal portion of education expenses	*From* AGI	Qualifying expenses are subject to the 2% of AGI nondeductible floor.
Office-in-home	Not applicable	*From* AGI; If trade- or business-related, the expenses are for AGI	Employment-related expenses (other than real estate taxes and interest) are subject to the 2% of AGI nondeductible floor. Gross income limitations apply to allowable expenses.

Deferred Compensation

OBJECTIVE 9

Discuss the tax treatment and requirements for various deferred compensation arrangements

Various types of benefit plans providing favorable tax treatment are available to employees and self-employed individuals. These tax benefits are provided to stimulate savings accumulations necessary for retirement. Private retirement plans should be the primary source of retirement with the Social Security system as a supplement, although in recent years, more and more retirees rely increasingly on Social Security. Favorable tax consequences generally include the following benefits:

- Deferral of taxes on amounts contributed to retirement plans until the individual retires or receives a distribution from the plan
- An immediate deduction for contributions to qualified retirement plans for the employer or self-employed individual
- Deferral of taxation on income earned on retirement plan assets
- Tax-free distributions from certain types of plans (Roth-type plans)

This section discusses *deferred compensation arrangements* including qualified pension and profit sharing plans, nonqualified deferred compensation arrangements, and self-employed retirement plans and individual retirement accounts (IRAs).

QUALIFIED PENSION AND PROFIT-SHARING PLANS

ADDITIONAL COMMENT

The Staff of the Joint Committee on Taxation estimates the revenue loss resulting from the deferral of taxes on contributions and earnings for qualified employer plans, individual retirement plans, and Keogh plans for 2012 will approximate $138 billion. This provision represents one of the largest tax expenditures of the federal government and is designed to encourage employers to establish retirement plans for their employees.

The federal tax law provides favorable tax benefits for *qualified* pension and profit-sharing plans. A **qualified plan** is one that must meet strict requirements, such as not discriminating in favor of highly compensated individuals, be formed and operated for the exclusive benefit of employees, and meet specified vesting and funding requirements. In a qualified plan, both the employer and employee receive significant tax benefits, as follows:

Employer: receives an immediate tax deduction for pension and profit-sharing contributions made on behalf of employees.

Employee: is not taxed on either employer or employee contributions or earnings of the plan assets until funds are withdrawn from the plan at retirement.[50] Thus, funds invested in a qualified plan grow tax-free during an employee's working years. Alternatively, in recent years, Roth-type plans do not allow a deduction for the employee, but all distributions at retirement age can be withdrawn completely tax free.

Types of Plans. Qualified plans[51] include:

- Pension plans
- Profit-sharing plans (including Sec. 401(k) plans)
- Stock bonus plans, including employee stock ownership plans (ESOPs)

Pension Plans. The features that distinguish a *qualified pension plan* include the following:

- Systematic and definite payments are made to a pension trust (without regard to profits) based on formulas or actuarial methods.
- A pension plan may provide for incidental benefits such as disability, death, or medical insurance benefits.

A pension plan may be either contributory or noncontributory. Under a **noncontributory pension plan**, the contributions are made solely by the employer. Under a **contributory pension plan**, the employee makes voluntary contributions into the plan that supplement any contributions made by the employer.

Pension plans also may be either defined contribution plans or defined benefit plans. In a **defined contribution pension plan**, a separate account is established for each participant and certain amounts are contributed based on a specific formula (e.g., a specified percentage of compensation). The benefits payable to the participant at retirement are based on the value of the participant's account (including the amount of earnings that accrue to the account) at the time of retirement.

EXAMPLE I:9-55 ▶ Alabama Corporation establishes a qualified pension plan for its employees that provides for employer contributions equal to 8% of each participant's salary. Retirement payments to each participant are based on the amount of accumulated benefits in the employee's account at the retirement date. The pension plan is a defined contribution plan, because the contribution rate is based on a specific and fixed percentage of compensation. ◀

KEY POINT

The trend for most companies in the U.S. is away from defined benefit plans and toward defined contribution plans. Defined contribution plans usually are less costly and the employer liability is fixed at the date of contribution rather than at some future date.

Defined benefit plans establish a contribution formula based on actuarial techniques that are sufficient to fund a fixed benefit amount to be paid upon retirement. For example, a defined benefit plan might provide fixed retirement benefits equal to 40% of an employee's average salary for the five years before retirement.

A distinguishing feature of a defined benefit plan is that forfeitures of unvested amounts (e.g., due to employee resignations) must be used to reduce the employer contributions that would otherwise be made under the plan. In a defined contribution plan, however, the forfeitures related to unvested amounts may either be reallocated to the other participants in a nondiscriminatory manner or used to reduce future employer contributions.

---

[50] An employee may not be liable for federal income taxes but may be subject to Social Security taxes and possibly local or city income taxes.

[51] Qualified plans are generally covered in Secs. 401-417 of the IRC.

Profit-Sharing Plans. A qualified **profit-sharing plan** also may be established by an employer in addition to, or in lieu of, a qualified pension plan arrangement. Profit-sharing plans include the following distinguishing features:

- A definite, predetermined formula must be used to allocate employer contributions to individual employees and to establish benefit payments.
- Annual employer contributions are not required, but substantial and recurring contributions must be made to satisfy the requirement that the plan be permanent.
- Employees may be given the option to receive cash that is fully taxable as current compensation or to defer taxation on employer contributions by having such amounts contributed to the profit-sharing trust. Plans of this type are called Sec. 401(k) plans.[52]
- Forfeitures arising under the plan may be reallocated to the remaining participants to increase their profit-sharing benefits, provided that certain nondiscrimination requirements are met.
- Lump-sum payments made to an employee before retirement may be provided following a prescribed period for the vesting of such amounts.
- Incidental benefits such as disability, death, or medical insurance may also be provided in a profit-sharing arrangement.

Roth-type Plans. Roth-type plans are a special type of back-loaded plan. Under such a plan, a taxpayer does not receive a current deduction for any current contribution to the plan, but does not include any qualified distribution from the plan in gross income. The best known of this type of plan is a Roth IRA which was first enacted in 1998 and very popular today. A discussion of Roth IRAs is presented later in this chapter. More recently, in 2006, Congress extended the Roth concept to Sec. 401(k) plans where employees can contribute funds to a Roth 401(k) plan.[53] Similar to Roth IRAs, the employee receives no current tax deduction, but all contributions plus all earnings in the plan grow tax-free. Thus, any qualified distributions (generally, distributions after age 59½) are received tax-free by taxpayer. Participants in 401(k), 403(b), or 457 plans are permitted to roll over amounts in the plan to a "qualified Roth contribution program" for tax years after December 31, 2012.

Stock Bonus Plan. A **stock bonus plan** is a special type of defined contribution plan whereby the investments of the plan are in the employer-company's own stock. The employer makes its contribution to the trust either in cash or in stock. If in cash, the amounts are invested in the company's stock. The stock is allocated and subsequently distributed to the participants. Stock bonus plan requirements are similar to profit-sharing plans. An **employee stock ownership plan (ESOP)** is a type of qualified stock bonus plan.[54] An ESOP, funded by a combination of employer and employee contributions and plan loans, invest primarily in employer stock. The stock is held for the benefit of the employees. ESOPs are attractive because the employer is allowed to reduce taxable income by deducting any dividends that are paid to the participants (or their beneficiaries) in the year such amounts are paid and are taxable to the participant. For employer securities acquired by the ESOP, the dividends-paid deduction is limited to dividends paid on employer stock acquired with an ESOP loan.

ADDITIONAL COMMENT

The tax law with respect to qualified pension and profit-sharing plans is extremely complex. A detailed study of these provisions is beyond the scope of this text.

QUALIFICATION REQUIREMENTS FOR A QUALIFIED PLAN

Qualified pension, profit-sharing, and stock bonus plans must meet complex qualification rules and requirements to achieve and maintain their favored qualifying status. A summary of the important requirements are discussed below.

- Section 401(a) requires that the plan must be for the employee's exclusive benefit. For example, the trust must follow prudent investment rules to ensure that the pension benefits will accrue for the employees' benefit.
- The plan may not discriminate in favor of highly compensated employees. Highly compensated employees are employees who meet either of two tests: (1) own more

[52] Sec. 401(k).
[53] Sec. 402A. For 2015, the maximum contribution limit to Roth 401(k) plans is $18,000 ($24,000 for taxpayers 50 years and older).
[54] Secs. 409(a) and 4975(e)(7).

than 5% of the corporation's stock in either the current or prior year or (2) receive compensation of greater than $120,000 in the prior year.[55]

- Contributions and plan benefits must bear a uniform relationship to the compensation payments made to covered employees. For example, if contributions for the benefit of the participants are based on a fixed percentage of the employee's compensation (e.g., 4%), the plan should not be disqualified despite the fact that the contributions for highly-compensated employees are greater on an actual dollar basis than those for lower paid individuals.
- Certain coverage requirements that are expressed in terms of a portion of the employees covered by the plan must be met.
- An employee's right to receive benefits from the employer's contributions must vest (i.e., become nonforfeitable) after a certain period or number of years of employment. The vesting requirement is intended to ensure that a significant percentage of employees will eventually receive retirement benefits. Employer-provided benefits must be 100% vested after 5 years of service.[56] In all cases, any employee contributions to the plan must vest immediately.

EXAMPLE I:9-56 ▶ Ken is a participant in a noncontributory qualified pension plan that provides for no vesting until an employee completes three years of service. Ken terminates his employment with the company after two years of service. Because Ken has not met the minimum vesting requirements, he is not entitled to receive any of the employer contributions that are made on his behalf. ◀

ADDITIONAL COMMENT
Most employees choose to contribute amounts to their qualified retirement plans on a pre-tax basis because of the time value of money. A current deduction (and the related tax savings) is more valuable than a deduction at retirement.

TAX TREATMENT TO EMPLOYEES AND EMPLOYERS

Employer contributions to a qualified plan are immediately deductible (subject to specific limitations on contribution amounts), and earnings on pension fund investments are tax-exempt to the plan. Amounts paid into a plan by or for an employee are not taxable until the pension payments are received, normally at retirement. At the election of the employee, amounts may be treated as having been made from either pre-tax or after-tax earnings. If amounts contributed to a qualified plan by an employee are made on a pre-tax basis, the taxable portion of the employee's earnings is reduced by the contribution amount. This has the effect of permitting a deduction for the contribution amount. When amounts are withdrawn at retirement, the entire distribution is subject to taxation.

EXAMPLE I:9-57 ▶ Larry is an employee of Cisco Corporation, which maintains a Sec. 401(k) plan. Larry contributes 5% of his gross salary into the plan on a pre-tax basis. During the current year, Larry's gross salary is $80,000 so his Sec. 401(k) contribution is $4,000. Since Larry's contribution is made on a pre-tax basis, his taxable salary for the current year will be $76,000. In effect, Larry is able to deduct the $4,000 from his salary in the current year. When Larry retires and begins withdrawing amounts from the plan, the entire amount withdrawn will be subject to income taxation. ◀

Conversely, an employee may elect to contribute to a qualified plan on an after-tax basis. If, in Example I:9-57, Larry contributed to the Sec. 401(k) plan on an after-tax basis, his taxable salary would have been $80,000. The $4,000 contributed to the plan is treated as an investment in the plan and is considered a tax-free return of capital when this amount is withdrawn at retirement.[57]

Employee Retirement Payments. An employee's retirement benefits, other than from Roth-type plans, are generally taxed under the Sec. 72 annuity rules (see Chapter I:3). If the plan is noncontributory (i.e., no employee contributions are made to the plan), all of the pension benefits when received by the employee are fully taxable. If the plan is contributory, the taxability depends on whether the employee's contributions were made on a

---

[55] Sec. 414(q). The $120,000 applicable in 2015 is subject to annual indexing for inflation. The amount for 2013 and 2014 was $115,000. Alternatively, an employer may elect to define a highly- compensated group as employees earning more than $120,000 *and* the top 20% group of employees based on compensation.

[56] Sec. 411(a)(2)(A). An alternative vesting schedule may also be used that provides for 20% vesting each year beginning in the third year of service, Sec. 411(a)(2)(B). Thus, after a total of seven years of service, an employee would be 100% vested. In addition, a faster vesting schedule is provided in Sec. 411(a)(2)(B) whereby the vesting begins after two years of service and increases at a rate of 20% per year to 100% after six years.

[57] Amounts contributed to a qualified plan on an after-tax basis are treated as an investment in the contract under the annuity rules of Sec. 72. Amounts withdrawn during retirement are taxed under the general rules of Sec. 72. (See Chapter I:3 for a discussion of taxation of annuities.)

pre-tax or after-tax basis. If the contributions were made on a pre-tax basis, *all* retirement payments received by the employee are taxable. Alternatively, if the contributions were made on an after-tax basis, each payment is treated, in part, as a tax-free return of the employee's contributions and the remainder is taxable. The excluded portion is based on the ratio of the employee's investment in the contract to the expected return under the contract. However, the total amount that may be excluded is limited to the amount of the employee's contributions to the plan. If the employee dies before the entire investment in the contract is recovered, the unrecovered amount is allowed as an itemized deduction in the year of death.

As mentioned earlier, qualified distributions from a Roth-type plan, such as a Roth 401(k), are not subject to taxation. Qualified distributions are those that have been invested in the plan for at least five years and the employee is at least age 59½.

EXAMPLE I:9-58 ► Kevin retires in 2015 at age 64 and will receive monthly annuity payments of $2,000 for life from his employer's qualified pension plan beginning in January, 2016. Kevin's investment in the contract (represented by his contributions made on an after-tax basis) is $100,000. Kevin's life expectancy per Sec. 72 is 260 months from the annuity starting date. So, for the next 260 months, Kevin can exclude $384.62 ($100,000/260 months). In 2016, Kevin would exclude $4,615.44 ($384.62 × 12 months) and $19,384.56 ($24,000.00 − $4,615.44) would be taxable. After Kevin receives payments for 260 months and his $100,000 investment in the contract is recovered, all subsequent payments are fully taxable. (See Chapter I:3 for a discussion of the annuity formula and related rules.) ◄

EXAMPLE I:9-59 ► Assume the same facts as in Example I:9-58 except that Kevin made all of his contributions to the plan on a pre-tax basis. In other words, the amount that he contributed to the plan was subtracted from his salary each year. When Kevin starts receiving payments from the plan, all amounts received will be taxable. Therefore, in 2016, Kevin will include $24,000 in his gross income. Most employees elect to "tax defer" their contributions into retirement plans in order to reduce their current year taxable income and take advantage of the time value of money principle. ◄

EXAMPLE I:9-60 ► Keith, age 61 and still employed, has maintained a Roth 401(k) plan for 10 years. All of his contributions into the plan, therefore, have been made on a post-tax basis. Keith may contribute $24,000 into his Roth 401(k) for 2015. The maximum contribution is generally $18,000, but Keith is allowed an additional $6,000 catch-up contribution as he is 50 years old or older. ◄

KEY POINT

For purposes of the limitation on employer contributions, all defined contribution plans maintained by one employer are treated as a single defined contribution plan. Furthermore, under some circumstances a group of employers can be treated as a single employer.

ADDITIONAL COMMENT

Many individuals have the option of taking their retirement savings from traditional pensions, profit-sharing plans, and 401(k)s as a lump sum or an annuity. Those who want to take a lump-sum distribution can delay taxes by transferring the money directly into a tax-deferred IRA.

Limitation on Employer Contributions. The Code places limitations on (1) amounts an employer may contribute to qualified pension, profit-sharing, and stock bonus plans and (2) amounts that the employer may deduct:

- Defined contribution plan contributions in 2015 are limited to the lesser of $53,000 or 100% of the employee's compensation.[58]
- Defined benefit plans are restricted to an annual benefit to an employee equal to the lesser of $210,000 for 2015 or 100% of the participant's average compensation for the highest three years.[59]
- An overall maximum annual employer deduction of 25% of compensation paid or accrued to plan participants is placed on defined contribution, profit-sharing, and stock bonus plans.[60] If an employer has more than one type of qualified plan (e.g., a defined benefit pension plan and a profit-sharing plan), a maximum deduction of 25% of compensation is allowed.

The distinguishing features and major requirements for qualified pension and profit-sharing plans are summarized in Topic Review I:9-2.

---

[58] Sec. 415(c). The deduction limit for 2014 was $52,000. In addition, individuals over 50 years of age are now eligible to contribute extra amounts into their plans. The amount of the so-called catch-up contributions depend on the type of plan.

[59] Sec. 415(b)(1). The benefit amount for 2014 was also $210,000. These amounts are subject to indexing each year. For participants who separated from service before January 1, 2015, the 100% average is computed by multiplying the participant's compensation limitation by 1.0178.

[60] Sec. 404(a)(3)(A).

TOPIC REVIEW I:9-2

Qualified Pension and Profit-Sharing Plans

Distinguishing Features and Major Requirements

- Employer contributions and earnings on contributed amounts are not taxed to employees until distributed or made available. The contributions are immediately deductible by the employer.
- Pension plans can be established as either defined contribution or defined benefit plans in which systematic and definite payments are made to a pension trust. Incidental benefits (e.g., death and disability payments) can be provided under the plan.
- Profit-sharing plans require the use of a predetermined allocation formula and substantial and recurring contributions must be made although annual employer contributions are not required and the contributions need not be based on profits. Section 401(k) plans can be established where employees have the option to receive cash or to have such amounts contributed to the profit-sharing trust. The employer may also establish an ESOP where the plan is funded by a contribution of the employer's stock.
- Qualified plans must be created for the employees' exclusive benefit.
- The plans may not discriminate in favor of highly compensated employees.
- Contributions and plan benefits must bear a uniform relationship to the compensation of covered employees.
- Minimum vesting requirements must be met (e.g., 100% vesting after five years).
- Employee benefits are taxed under the Sec. 72 annuity rules.
- Total employer contributions to the plan are subject to specific ceiling limitations.

KEY POINT

Because nonqualified plans are not subject to the same restrictions as imposed upon qualified plans, they do not receive the same tax benefits that are available under qualified plans. For example, the employer may not be able to deduct amounts that are set aside for employees.

NONQUALIFIED PLANS

Nonqualified deferred compensation plans are often used by employers to provide incentives or supplementary retirement benefits for executives. Common forms of nonqualified plans include the following:

- An unfunded, nonforfeitable promise to pay fixed amounts of compensation in future periods.[61]
- Restricted property plans involving property transfers (usually in the form of the employer-company stock), where the property transferred is subject to a substantial risk of forfeiture and is nontransferable.[62]

Distinguishing Characteristics of Nonqualified Plans. Nonqualified plans are not subject to the same restrictions imposed on qualified plans (such as the nondiscrimination and vesting rules), although nonqualified plans may have some vesting rules. Thus, such plans are particularly suitable for use in executive compensation planning. In general, nonqualified plans impose certain restrictions on the outright transfer of the plan's benefits to the employee. This avoids immediate taxation under the constructive receipt doctrine, which does not apply if the benefits are not yet credited, set apart, or made available so that the employee may draw on them. The amount is taxed to the employee upon the lapse of such restrictions, and the employer receives a corresponding deduction in the same year.

Unfunded Deferred Compensation Plans. Unfunded deferred compensation plans are often used to compensate highly compensated employees who desire to defer the recognition of income until future periods (e.g., a professional athlete or a business executive who receives a signing bonus may prefer to defer the recognition of income from the bonus). In general, if the promise to make the compensation payment in a future period is nonforfeitable, the agreement must not be funded (e.g., the transfer of assets to a trust for the employee's benefit) or evidenced by a negotiable note. The employer, however, may establish an *escrow account* on behalf of the employee. Such an account is used to accumulate and invest the deferred compensation amounts. If the requirements for deferral are met, the employee is taxed when the amounts are actually paid or made available, and the employer receives a corresponding deduction in the same year.[63]

---

[61] Rev. Rul. 60-31, 1960-1 C.B. 174, modified by Rev. Rul. 64-279, 1964-2 C.B. 121 and Rev. Rul. 70-435, 1970-2 C.B. 100.

[62] Sec. 83.

[63] Reg. Sec. 1.451-2(a).

EXAMPLE I:9-61 ▶ In 2015, Kelly signs an employment contract to play professional football for the Chicago Skyhawks. The contract includes a $2,000,000 signing bonus that is payable in five annual installments beginning in 2019. The bonus agreement is nonforfeitable and is unfunded. The Skyhawks have agreed to place sufficient amounts of money into an escrow account to fund the future payments to Kelly. None of the $2,000,000 bonus is deductible by the employer or taxable to Kelly when the agreement is signed in 2015. The Skyhawks do not receive a deduction for any amounts that are deposited into the escrow account during the 2015–2018 period. In 2019, Kelly receives $400,000 taxable compensation (plus interest, if any, that accrued and was paid to Kelly is also taxable) upon receipt of the initial payment, and the Skyhawks receive a corresponding tax deduction. ◀

Requirements were enacted several years ago for nonqualified deferred compensation plans.[64] While a detailed examination of these new rules is outside the scope of this textbook, some major features of the law are as follows:

- The rules apply to any plan by which executive employees are permitted to defer the receipt and taxability of compensation from the current year to a future year. In prior years, the tax laws in this area were a wide range of cases and rulings.
- If deferred amounts under a plan fail to satisfy the requirements at any time during the tax year, the recipient must pay the tax on the deferred compensation plus interest and an additional 20% excise tax.
- Distributions from the plan to recipients are subject to strict rules. Deferrals may be distributed to participants no earlier than the time of separation of service, pursuant to a fixed schedule in the plan, death, disability, an unforeseeable emergency, or upon a change in control of the company. Thus, early distributions are not generally permitted. In addition, acceleration of payment amounts are severely curtailed.
- Funding rules essentially have remained the same except that employers generally may no longer use offshore trusts.

Because of the complexity of the rules in this area, taxpayers are strongly urged to look closely at their nonqualified deferred compensation plans to ensure that they comply with the rules.

Restricted Property Plans. **Restricted property plans** are used to attract and retain key executives. Under such arrangements, the executive generally obtains an ownership interest (i.e., stock) in the corporation. Restricted property plans are governed by the income recognition rules contained in Sec. 83. Under these rules, the receipt of restricted property in exchange for services rendered is not taxable if the property is nontransferable and subject to a substantial risk of forfeiture.

The employee is treated as receiving taxable compensation based on the amount of the property's fair market value (FMV) (less any amount paid for the property) at the earlier of the time the property is no longer subject to a substantial risk of forfeiture or is transferable. The employer receives a corresponding compensation deduction at the same time the income is taxed to the employee.

EXAMPLE I:9-62 ▶ In 2015, Allied Corporation transfers 1,000 shares of its common stock to employee Karen as compensation pursuant to a restricted property plan. The FMV of the Allied stock is $10 per share on the transfer date. The restricted property agreement provides that the stock is nontransferable by Karen until the year 2017 (i.e., Karen cannot sell the stock to outsiders until year 2017). The stock is also subject to the restriction that if Karen voluntarily leaves the company before the year 2017, she must transfer the shares back to the company and will receive no benefit from the stock other than from the receipt of dividends. The FMV of the stock is $100 per share in year 2017 when the forfeiture and nontransferability restrictions lapse. Because the stock is both nontransferable and subject to a substantial risk of forfeiture from the issue date to year 2017, the tax consequences from the stock transfer are deferred for both Karen and Allied Corporation until the lapse of the nontransferability or forfeiture restrictions in year 2017. Thus, no tax consequences result in 2015 or 2016. In year 2017, Karen must report ordinary (compensation) income of $100,000 ($100 × 1,000 shares), and Allied Corporation is entitled to a corresponding compensation deduction of the same amount. Karen is taxed currently on the dividends she receives because they are not subject to any restrictions. ◀

---

[64] Sec. 409A.

KEY POINT

If an employee makes the election to be taxed immediately, he or she should be aware of the adverse consequences of leaving the company before the forfeiture restrictions lapse. The employee will not receive the property, and no deduction is allowed on the forfeiture.

Election to Be Taxed Immediately. An exception which permits an employee to elect (within 30 days after the receipt of restricted property) to recognize income immediately upon receipt of the restricted property is provided in Sec. 83(b). If the election is made, the employer is entitled to a corresponding deduction at the time the income is taxed to the employee. This election is frequently made when the fair market value of the restricted property is expected to increase significantly in the future and the future gain would be taxed as long-term capital gain.

EXAMPLE I:9-63 ▶ Assume the same facts as Example I:9-62, except that Karen elects to recognize income in 2015 (i.e., the transfer date). Karen must include $10,000 ($10 × 1,000 shares) in gross income as compensation in the current year and Allied Corporation is entitled to a corresponding deduction in the same year. Karen will report no income in 2017 when the restrictions lapse and her basis in the Allied Corporation stock remains at $10,000. If Karen sells the stock for $100,000 in the year 2017, or a later year after the restrictions lapse, Karen reports a $90,000 ($100,000 − $10,000) long-term capital gain on the sale.[65] If Karen voluntarily leaves the company before the forfeiture restrictions lapse, no deduction is allowed when the forfeiture occurs, despite the fact that Karen is previously taxed on the stock's value on the transfer date (i.e., $10,000 of income is recognized by Karen in the current year). In such event, Allied Corporation must include $10,000 in gross income in the year of the forfeiture (i.e., the amount of the deduction that is taken in the year of the transfer to the extent of any previous tax benefit). ◀

Nonqualified plan features and requirements are summarized in Topic Review I:9-3.

EMPLOYEE STOCK OPTIONS

Stock option plans are used by corporate employers to attract and retain key management employees. Both stock option and restricted property arrangements using the employer's stock permit the executive to receive a proprietary interest in the corporation. Thus, an executive may identify more closely with shareholder interests and the firm's long-run profit-maximization goals. The tax law currently includes two types of stock-option arrangements: the incentive stock option and the nonqualified stock option.[66] Each type is treated differently for tax purposes.

REAL-WORLD EXAMPLE

The use of employee stock options has come under criticism recently in the financial press. The pressure to increase earnings has been a major issue in recent corporate scandals. Further, the Financial Accounting Standards Board has issued a statement requiring the current expensing of stock options in certain circumstances.

As will be seen in the discussions below, both types of plans have their respective advantages and disadvantages. Incentive stock option arrangements generally are preferred when long-term capital gain rates are low as compared to ordinary income rates. Thus, because long-term capital gain rates are 15% or 20% and marginal tax rates for ordinary income are rather high (39.6%), interest should continue in incentive stock option arrangements. However, an employer is more favorably treated under the nonqualified stock-option rules (i.e., the employer receives a tax deduction for the compensation related to a nonqualified stock option but does not receive a corresponding deduction if an incentive stock-option plan is adopted) and may therefore still prefer to continue to use nonqualified stock options.

TOPIC REVIEW I:9-3

Nonqualified Plans

DISTINGUISHING FEATURES AND MAJOR REQUIREMENTS

1. The employee is taxed upon the lapse of restrictions imposed on the availability or withdrawal of funds and the employer receives a corresponding deduction in the same year.
2. Nonqualified plans may discriminate in favor of highly compensated employees and no minimum vesting rules are required.
3. Restricted property (usually employer stock) may be offered to executives where the incidents of taxation are deferred if the property is nontransferable and subject to a substantial risk of forfeiture. An election may be made under Sec. 83(b) to recognize income immediately upon the receipt of the restricted property.
4. Restrictions must be imposed to avoid immediate taxation to the employee under the constructive receipt doctrine.
5. To avoid immediate taxation, restricted property plans must be both nonforfeitable and subject to a substantial risk of forfeiture.

---

[65] Sec. 1223. The holding period originates on the day following the transfer date because Karen made the election to be taxed immediately under Sec. 83(b).

[66] The incentive stock option rules are provided in Sec. 422, whereas the rules governing nonqualified stock options are contained in Reg. Sec. 1.83-7.

KEY POINT

Incentive stock options have the disadvantage of not providing a compensation deduction for the employer.

KEY POINT

Incentive stock options can be a valuable tax planning tool because the earliest that they are generally taxed is when they are exercised. Also, when an employee realizes profits from stock options, those profits in certain cases may qualify as capital gains.

Incentive Stock Option Plans.

Employer Requirements. An **incentive stock option (ISO)** must meet the following plan or employer requirements:[67]

- The option price must be equal to or greater than the stock's FMV on the option's grant date.
- The option must be granted within ten years of the date the plan is adopted, and the employee must exercise the option within ten years of the grant date.
- The option must be both exercisable only by the employee and nontransferable except in the event of death.
- The employee cannot own more than 10% of the voting power of the employer corporation's stock immediately before the option's grant date.
- The total FMV of the stock options that become exercisable to an employee in any given year may not exceed $100,000 (e.g., an employee can be granted ISOs to acquire $200,000 of stock in one year, provided that no more than $100,000 is exercisable in any given year).
- Other procedural requirements must be met (e.g., shareholder approval of the plan).

Employee Requirements. In addition to the above plan requirements, the employee must meet the following requirements:

- The employee must not dispose of the stock within two years of the option's grant date nor within one year after the option's exercise date.
- The employee must be employed by the issuing company on the grant date and continue such employment until within three months before the exercise date.

If an employee meets the requirements listed above, no tax consequences occur on the grant date or the exercise date. However, the excess of the FMV over the option price on the exercise date is an adjustment for purposes of the alternative minimum tax (see Chapter I:14). When the employee sells the optioned stock, a long-term capital gain or loss is recognized. If the employee meets the two requirements, the employer does not receive a corresponding compensation deduction. If the requirements are not met, the option is treated as a nonqualified stock option.

EXAMPLE I:9-64 ▶ American Corporation grants an incentive stock option to Kay, an employee, on January 1, 2015. The option price is $100, and the FMV of the American stock is also $100 on the grant date. The option permits Kay to purchase 100 shares of American stock. Kay exercises the option on June 30, 2017, when the stock's FMV is $400. Kay sells the 100 shares of American stock on January 1, 2019, for $500 per share. Because Kay holds the stock for the required period (at least two years from the grant date and one year from the exercise date) and because Kay is employed by American Corporation on the grant date and within three months before the exercise date, all of the requirements for an ISO have been met. No income is recognized on the grant date or the exercise date, although $30,000 [($400 − $100) × 100 shares] is a tax preference item for the alternative minimum tax in 2017. Kay recognizes a $40,000 [($500 − $100) × 100 shares] long-term capital gain on the sale date in 2019. American Corporation is not entitled to a compensation deduction in any year. ◀

EXAMPLE I:9-65 ▶ Assume the same facts as Example I:9-64, except that Kay disposes of the stock on August 1, 2017, thus violating the one-year minimum holding period requirement after the exercise date. Kay must recognize ordinary income on the sale date equal to the spread between the option price and the exercise price, or $30,000 [($400 − $100) × 100 shares]. The $30,000 spread between the FMV and the option price is no longer a tax preference item because the option ceases to qualify as an ISO. American Corporation can claim a $30,000 compensation deduction in 2017. Kay also recognizes a $10,000 [($500 − $400 adjusted basis) × 100 shares] short-term capital gain on the sale date, which represents the appreciation of the stock from the exercise date to the sale date. The gain is short-term because the holding period from the exercise date to the sale date does not exceed one year. ◀

KEY POINT

With ISOs, the employee does not recognize income when the option is exercised; income is recognized only when the stock is sold. With nonqualified stock options, income is recognized when the option is exercised or on the grant date and when the stock is sold at a gain.

---

[67] Sec. 422.

Nonqualified Stock Option Plans. Stock options that do not meet the plan requirements for incentive stock options are referred to as **nonqualified stock options.** The tax treatment of nonqualified stock options depends on whether the option has a **readily ascertainable fair market value** (e.g., whether the option is traded on an established options exchange).

Readily Ascertainable Fair Market Value. If a nonqualified stock option has a readily ascertainable FMV (e.g., the option is traded on an established options exchange), the employee recognizes ordinary income on the grant date equal to the difference between the stock's FMV and the option's exercise price. The employer receives a compensation deduction on the grant date equal to the same amount of income that is recognized by the employee. In such case, no tax consequences occur on the date the option is exercised, and the employee recognizes capital gain or loss upon the sale or disposition of the stock.

No Readily Ascertainable Fair Market Value. If a nonqualified stock option has no readily ascertainable FMV, no tax consequences occur on the grant date. On the exercise date the employee recognizes ordinary income equal to the spread between the FMV of the stock and the option price, and the employer receives a corresponding compensation deduction. When the stock option is exercised, the employee's basis in the stock is equal to the option price plus the amount reported as ordinary income on the exercise date. Capital gain or loss is recognized upon the subsequent sale of the stock by the employee.

The alternative minimum tax does not apply to nonqualified stock options regardless of whether the option has a readily ascertainable FMV. Table I:9-4 illustrates the tax consequences to employees and employers for such options.

As illustrated in Table I:9-4, Kim reports a total gain of $11,000 from the nonqualified stock option transaction under both circumstances. However, the character of her profit (i.e., ordinary income or capital gain) and the timing of the profit recognition (i.e., grant date or exercise date) depends on whether the option's FMV is readily ascertainable.

The distinguishing features and major requirements for employee stock options are summarized in Topic Review I:9-4.

▼ TABLE I:9-4
Taxation of Nonqualified Stock Options

Situation Facts	Readily Ascertainable FMV	No Readily Ascertainable FMV
Grant date: On January 1, 2013, Kim is granted a nonqualified stock option to purchase 100 shares of stock from Apple Corporation (Kim's employer) at $90 per share. The stock's FMV is $100 on the grant date.	Ordinary income of $1,000 is recognized [($100 − $90) × 100 shares] by Kim in 2013. Apple Corporation receives a corresponding $1,000 compensation deduction in 2013.	No tax consequences to Kim or Apple Corporation.
Exercise date: On January 31, 2015, Kim exercises the option and acquires the 100 shares of Apple Corporation stock for the $90 option price when the FMV is $190.	No tax consequences to Kim or Apple Corporation.	Kim recognizes ordinary income in 2015 of $10,000 [($190 − $90) × 100 shares], and Apple Corporation receives a $10,000 compensation deduction.
Sale date: On February 1, 2016, Kim sells the stock for $200 per share and realizes $20,000 ($200 × 100 shares).	Kim recognizes a $10,000 ($20,000 − $10,000 basis) long-term capital gain.[a]	Kim recognizes a $1,000 ($20,000 − $19,000 basis) long-term capital gain on the sale.[b]

[a] Kim's basis includes the amount paid for the optioned stock of $9,000 plus ordinary income of $1,000 recognized on the grant date. Kim's holding period commences on the January 1, 2013, grant date for determining whether the gain is long-term.

[b] Kim's basis includes the $9,000 paid for the option stock plus the $10,000 ordinary income recognized on the exercise date. Kim's holding period commences on the January 31, 2015, exercise date for determining whether the gain is long-term.

TOPIC REVIEW I:9-4

Employee Stock Options

DISTINGUISHING FEATURES AND MAJOR REQUIREMENTS

- For an incentive stock option (ISO) plan no tax consequences occur on the grant or the exercise date (except for the recognition of a tax preference item under the AMT provisions on the exercise date). Capital gain or loss is recognized by the employee upon the sale or exchange of the stock. No deduction is allowed to the employer.
- ISOs and nonqualified stock options may be issued to highly-compensated employees without regard to nondiscrimination rules.
- If a nonqualified stock option has a readily ascertainable FMV, the employee recognizes ordinary income equal to the spread between the FMV of the stock and the option price on the grant date and the employer receives a corresponding deduction. If the option has no readily ascertainable FMV, income is recognized on the exercise date equal to the spread between the FMV of the stock and the option price and a corresponding deduction is available to the employer.
- For an ISO, the option price must be equal to or greater than the FMV of the stock on the grant date, employees cannot own more than 10% of the voting power of the employer's stock, and restrictions are placed on the total FMV of stock options that may be issued.
- To qualify under the ISO rules, a two-year holding period from the grant date is required (and at least one year after the exercise date) and the employee must continue to be employed by the company until within three months of the exercise date.

ADDITIONAL COMMENT

If you are self-employed and establish a Keogh plan, you must include any full-time employees in the plan.

PLANS FOR SELF-EMPLOYED INDIVIDUALS

Self-employed individuals, such as sole proprietors or partners who practice as a trade or business, are not considered as employees and are not eligible for the retirement plans offered to employees. However, in recent years, self-employed individuals have their own special types of retirement plans. Retirement plans of self-employed people are generally subject to the same contribution and benefit limitations as other qualified corporate plans. An individual who is an employee and also has a self-employed business generally is able to be covered under an employer-sponsored plan and a self-employed plan. There are overall limitations that apply in these circumstances.

The principal types of retirement plans for self-employed individuals include the following:

- H.R. 10 plan—this plan, also referred to as a Keogh plan, was the original self-employed plan and, although still a viable and important type of plan, is not used as much now because of the annual paperwork requirements.
- SEP IRA—this plan, a Simplified Employee Pension plan, is similar to an H.R. 10 plan but is easier to set up and administer. SEP IRAs are discussed in more detail below.
- SIMPLE plan—SIMPLE plans are relatively easy to use and administer but the contribution limits are lower than those for H.R. 10 or SEP IRA plans. SIMPLE plans are discussed in more detail below.
- Solo 401(k) plan—this plan is for solo business owners with no other employees. Solo 401(k) plans provide for a $18,000 deferral for the business owner plus a 25% of salary match by the company. The total contribution limit (including both the deferral plus the company match) in 2015 is $53,000.

KEY POINT

Keogh plans can be either defined benefit or defined contribution plans. Many individuals avoid the defined benefit type of Keogh plan due to the extra paperwork and administrative costs.

For a **defined contribution H.R. 10 plan or SEP IRA**, a self-employed individual in 2015 may contribute the smaller of $53,000 or 25% of earned income from the self-employment activity.[68] *Earned income* refers to net earnings from self-employment. However, for purposes of computing the maximum amount that may be contributed to a Keogh or SEP IRA plan by a self-employed individual, earned income must be reduced by two amounts: (1) the 50% deduction for self-employment taxes and (2) the contribution itself. Since the contribution is based on earned income *after* the contribution, the 25% contribution percentage must be reduced to 20%.[69] To compute the limitations for 2015, a maximum of $265,000 of earned income may be taken into account for any one individual.[70]

---

[68] Sec. 415(c)(1). The limitations are indexed annually for inflation.

[69] This reduction in contribution percentage is computed as follows: 0.25/1.00 + 0.25 = 0.20. If the Keogh or SEP IRA contribution rate is 15% rather than 25%, the deductible percentage would be 13.0435%, computed as above, 0.15/1.00 + 0.15 = 0.130435. Other percentages can be calculated accordingly.

[70] Secs. 401(a)(17) and 404(l). The ceiling in 2014 was $260,000.

EXAMPLE I:9-66 ▶ Larry is a self-employed CPA whose 2015 net earnings from his trade or business (before the H.R. 10 or SEP IRA plan contribution but after the deduction for one-half of the self-employment taxes paid under Sec. 164(f) [see Chapter I:14]) is $100,000. Larry may contribute $20,000 to the plan for 2015. Larry must also provide coverage for all of his eligible full-time employees under the general rules provided in the law for qualified plans (e.g., nondiscrimination, vesting, and so on).[71] ◀

EXAMPLE I:9-67 ▶ Assume the same facts as in Example I:9-66 except that Larry's earnings from his trade or business (before the plan contribution but after the deduction for one-half of the self-employment taxes) is $300,000. The maximum contribution that Larry can make on his behalf in 2015 is $53,000 ($265,000 × 0.20). Even though his earnings were $300,000, the maximum compensation that can be used to calculate the H.R. 10 or SEP IRA plan contribution in 2015 is $265,000. ◀

KEY POINT

A Keogh plan must be created no later than the last day of your tax year. However, an SEP IRA may be created by the due date of the return.

An H.R. 10 plan must be established before the end of the tax year, but contributions may be made up to the due date for the tax return (including extensions). SEP IRA plans can be setup and funded by the due date of the return, including extensions. Thus, for the tax year 2015, a taxpayer is permitted to establish a SEP IRA by April 15, 2016 (or October 15, 2016, if the return is extended). All pension contributions made by a self-employed individual for *employees* are deductible for AGI on Schedule C. The H.R. 10 or SEP IRA contribution for the self-employed individual is deductible *for* AGI on page 1 of Form 1040.

SIMPLIFIED EMPLOYEE PENSIONS (SEP IRAS)

Due to the administrative complexity associated with qualified pension and profit-sharing plans, small businesses often establish simplified employee pension (SEP IRA) plans for their employees. In an SEP, the employer makes contributions to the IRAs of its employees.[72] The following is a summary of the tax rules that apply to a SEP IRAs:

ADDITIONAL COMMENT

A self-employed person (i.e., a partner or sole proprietor) may establish an SEP rather than using an H.R. 10 plan arrangement because of reduced administrative complexity associated with a SEP.

- The employer receives an immediate tax deduction for contributions made under the plan. The annual deductible contributions for each participant are limited to the lesser of 25% of the participant's compensation (up to a ceiling of $265,000 for 2015) and the dollar limitations for defined contribution plans.[73] The maximum amount for 2015 is $53,000.
- Contributions are treated as being made on the last day of the tax year if they are made by the due date of the tax return (including extensions).
- Employer contributions must be nondiscriminatory.
- Distributions from an SEP are subject to taxation based on the IRA rules (previously discussed) including the penalty tax for premature distributions.

SIMPLE RETIREMENT PLANS

Another more recent type of retirement savings plan for small businesses is called the savings incentive match plan for employees (SIMPLE).[74] This type of plan can be adopted by employers who have 100 or fewer employees who received at least $5,000 in compensation from the employer in either of the two preceding years. A SIMPLE plan may be set up either as an IRA for each employee or part of a qualified cash or deferred arrangement (401(k) plan). Essentially, employees are allowed to make elective contributions in 2015 of up to $12,500 per year and employers are required to make matching contributions.

HISTORICAL NOTE

The IRA savings provisions were originally enacted in 1974 to provide a tax-favored retirement savings arrangement to individuals who were not covered under a qualified plan. Beginning in 1982, Congress extended IRA availability to all taxpayers. It was hoped that the extended availability would increase the level of savings and provide a discretionary retirement savings plan that was uniformly available. However, Congress in the Tax Reform Act of 1986 restricted the availability of IRAs because there was no discernible impact on aggregate personal savings.

The unique features of the SIMPLE plans are (1) that elective contributions by employees must be matched by the employer or the employer has the option of making nonelective contributions, (2) that all contributions to an employee's SIMPLE account must be fully vested, and (3) the SIMPLE plans are not subject to the special nondiscrimination rules generally applicable to qualified plans. This last feature is important in that there is no requirement that a set number of employees *participate* in the plan, the only requirement is that all employees who had $5,000 in compensation in the previous year and are reasonably expected to have $5,000 in compensation in the current year must be eligible to participate.

INDIVIDUAL RETIREMENT ACCOUNTS (IRAS)

Under current law, there are three types of IRAs that are available to taxpayers: traditional IRA, Roth IRA, and Coverdell Education Savings Account IRA.[75] Each of these three types of IRAs is discussed below.

71 Sec. 401(d).

72 Sec. 408(k).

73 Sec. 404(h)(1).

74 Sec. 408(p).

75 The Coverdell Education Savings Account was named after the late Senator Paul Coverdell of Georgia.

TRADITIONAL IRA

Traditional IRAs have been in the law for almost 40 years and taxpayers may make either deductible or nondeductible contributions to the IRA. A contribution to a traditional IRA that is deductible has two principal benefits: (1) the amount contributed to the IRA (maximum $5,500 per year for 2015) is deductible on the taxpayer's return[76] and (2) the income earned on the investments in the IRA is not subject to current taxation. However, when amounts are withdrawn from the IRA at retirement, such amounts are fully subject to taxation. Nondeductible contributions to a traditional IRA may not be deducted on the taxpayer's return, but such contributions are not subject to taxation when withdrawn from the IRA. While contributions are not subject to taxation, any earnings are subject to taxation when withdrawn.

Individuals may make deductible contributions equal to the lesser of $5,500 or 100% of compensation only if either of the following conditions exists:

- The individual is *not* an active participant in an employer-sponsored retirement plan, including tax-sheltered annuities, government plans, simplified employee pension plans, and H.R. 10 plans; or
- Individuals who are active participants in an employer-sponsored retirement plan must have an AGI equal to or below the following applicable dollar limits for 2015:[77] $61,000 ($60,000 for 2014) for an unmarried taxpayer; $98,000 ($96,000 in 2014) for a married couple filing a joint return; zero for a married individual filing separately. If an individual has AGI above these amounts, the deductible IRA contribution amounts are phased out on a pro rata basis as AGI increases from $61,000 to $71,000 for unmarried taxpayers and from $98,000 to $118,000 for married taxpayers filing a joint return.

EXAMPLE I:9-68 ► Laura is an unmarried taxpayer who is not an active participant in an employer-sponsored retirement plan or other qualified plan. In 2015, Laura's AGI is $90,000, consisting of earned income from wages. Laura is not subject to the dollar limitation because she is not an active participant in a qualified plan and may, therefore, contribute and deduct up to $5,500 to a traditional IRA. Laura's AGI is reduced to $84,500 ($90,000 − $5,500) because the amount is deductible *for* AGI. ◄

EXAMPLE I:9-69 ► Judy is an unmarried taxpayer and an active participant in her employer's qualified retirement plan. In 2015, Judy's AGI is $65,000, consisting of earned income from wages of $62,000 and interest and dividends of $3,000. Since she is an active participant in a qualified plan and her AGI is over $61,000, her deductible contribution to a traditional IRA is subject to the phaseout. Since the ceiling amount is exceeded by $4,000 ($65,000 − $61,000), the maximum IRA contribution is reduced by 40% ($4,000/$10,000), or $2,200. Thus, the maximum that Judy can contribute *and* deduct to her IRA in 2015 is $3,300 ($5,500 − $2,200). ◄

ADDITIONAL COMMENT

Banks, savings and loan associations, insurance companies, and stock brokerage firms make IRAs available to taxpayers. Usually, the amounts are invested in long-term investment accounts. However, self-directed plans are offered by some stock brokerage firms. In this type of IRA, the taxpayer can specify how the contributions will be invested.

If a taxpayer's AGI exceeds the above limits, the taxpayer may make a nondeductible contribution of up to $5,500 to a traditional IRA. The benefit of making a nondeductible contribution to an IRA is that the earnings of the IRA investments grow tax-free. Thus, even though the *earnings* of the nondeductible IRA will be taxed when distributed, the ability to allow investments to compound before-tax is a major advantage for taxpayers. However, as will be seen in the discussion of Roth IRAs below, if a taxpayer can qualify for a Roth IRA rather than a traditional nondeductible IRA, the choice clearly favors a Roth IRA. The maximum amount of a nondeductible contribution that may be made to a traditional IRA is $5,500 minus the amount that is allowed as a deduction. Also, a taxpayer may elect for all of his contributions to be nondeductible even though the contributions are otherwise eligible to be deducted.

EXAMPLE I:9-70 ► Using the same facts as in Example I:9-69, Judy is permitted to make a nondeductible contribution to her IRA of $2,200 ($5,500 − $3,300). She also could elect to designate all $5,500 as a nondeductible contribution even though she is eligible to deduct the $3,300. ◄

[76] The deductible amount to an IRA was increased from $2,000 prior to 2002 to $3,000 for 2002–2004, $4,000 for 2005–2007, $5,000 for 2008–2012, and 5,500 for 2013 and 2014. See Sec. 219 (b)(5). The deductible amount is indexed for inflation. Prior to 2002, the deductible amount was $2,000. In addition, individuals over 50 years of age are now eligible to contribute an extra $500 into their IRA in years 2002–2005 (increasing to $1,000 in 2006 and future years). These extra amounts are referred to as "catch-up contributions."

[77] Sec. 219(g).

Two special rules apply to married couples relative to traditional IRAs. First, if only one spouse is employed and this working spouse is otherwise eligible to make IRA contributions, the nonworking spouse may contribute up to $5,500 per year to an IRA (a so-called spousal IRA). Thus, a total of $11,000 may be deductible by a married couple ($5,500 to each spouse's IRA) even though only one spouse has earned income. It should be noted that even though only the working spouse must have earned income, such working spouse must have at least $11,000 of earned income in order to contribute $11,000 to the two IRAs. Second, if one spouse is covered under a qualified retirement plan but the other spouse is not covered, the non-covered spouse may contribute to a traditional deductible IRA. However, for 2015, the contribution to a traditional deductible IRA is phased out at adjusted gross incomes between $183,000 and $193,000.

EXAMPLE I:9-71 ▶ Gary and Babs are a married couple. Gary is covered under a qualified retirement plan at his job and earned $174,000 in 2015. Babs is employed as a secretary and earned $24,000 but is not covered under a qualified retirement plan. They file a joint return, have interest and dividend income of $16,000, and their AGI, therefore, is $214,000. Neither Gary nor Babs is entitled to deduct contributions to a traditional IRA. Gary cannot contribute and deduct any amount to an IRA because he is covered under another qualified plan and their AGI exceeds $118,000. Babs is also not eligible because their AGI exceeds $193,000. However, both Gary and Babs are allowed to make nondeductible contributions of $5,500 each to the IRA. ◀

EXAMPLE I:9-72 ▶ Assume the same facts as in Example I:9-71 but that Gary's income is $100,000 and their AGI is $130,000. Babs may contribute and deduct $5,500 to a traditional IRA because their AGI is less than $183,000. However, Gary may not make a deductible contribution because he is covered under a qualified plan and their AGI exceeds $118,000. Gary is permitted to make a $5,500 contribution to a nondeductible IRA. ◀

ADDITIONAL COMMENT

A contribution to an IRA for the year 2015 can be made as late as the due date for filing the 2015 return, or April 15, 2016.

The following significant tax rules apply to traditional IRAs:

- An IRA plan may be established between the end of the tax year and the due date for the tax return (not including any extensions that are permitted). Any deductible contributions made during this time are treated as a deduction for the prior year. Contributions are deductible if made by the due date for the tax return (i.e., contributions for 2015 must be made no later than April 15, 2016). Contributions to nondeductible IRAs also must be made by April 15 of the following year.
- Taxpayers who are 50 years of age or older by the end of the taxable year may contribute an additional $1,000 per year (or a total of $6,500 in 2015).
- Distributions from a traditional IRA are taxed under the annuity rules in Sec. 72. Normally distributions from an IRA are fully subject to taxation. However, if nondeductible contributions are made to an IRA, these amounts would represent the investment in the contract in calculating the exclusion ratio.
- Withdrawals by a participant before age 59½ are both includible in income and subject to a nondeductible 10% penalty tax.[78]
- Withdrawals must begin no later than April 1 of the year following the end of the tax year in which the individual reaches age 70½. IRA contributions that were deducted over the years on the taxpayer's returns are fully taxable as ordinary income when the amounts are distributed.
- A nondeductible 6% penalty is levied on excess contributions to an IRA.[79]

ADDITIONAL COMMENT

Some financial advisors recommend the following approach when someone can only afford to have limited amounts set aside for retirement. Have pre-tax dollars withheld from salary up to the employer-matching amount in 401(k) plans, then place $5,500 in a Roth IRA. This maximizes employer contributions and places the maximum amount allowable into the much favored Roth IRA.

ROTH IRA

The Roth IRA[80] is a relatively new type of IRA that is a so-called "backloaded IRA" because the tax benefits come at the end, not at the beginning, of the IRA. Contributions to a Roth IRA are nondeductible but all distributions from the IRA, including earnings, are nontaxable.

[78] Sec. 72(t). The amount subject to the 10% penalty is the portion of the amount that must be included in gross income. Exceptions to the 10% penalty are provided in the event of death, disability, and certain non-lump-sum distributions. Two additional exceptions also apply: (1) withdrawals used to pay qualified higher education costs for taxpayer, spouse, children or grandchildren and (2) up to $10,000 to buy or build the principal residence for a "first time homebuyer."

[79] Sec. 4973(b).

[80] Sec. 408A.

ADDITIONAL COMMENT

Employers may now offer their employees a Roth 401(k) option. Under a Roth 401(k), employees can contribute up to $18,000 in 2015. The Roth 401(k) plan operates in the same basic way as a regular Roth IRA.

The maximum amount that may be contributed to a Roth IRA is $5,500. However, taxpayers who are eligible for both a Roth IRA and a traditional IRA may only contribute a total of $5,500 to both types of IRAs. As with traditional IRAs, Roth IRAs are also subject to AGI phaseout limitations, although the limitation amounts are higher than with traditional IRAs.

All taxpayers may contribute up to the lesser of (1) $5,500 or (2) 100% of the taxpayer's compensation, to a Roth IRA; however, for 2015, this amount is phased-out for single taxpayers if their AGI is between $116,000 ($114,000 in 2014) and $131,000 ($183,000 and $193,000 for married couples filing a joint return and $0 for married individuals filing separate returns). The principal advantage of the Roth IRA is the nontaxability of qualified distributions. One requirement of a qualified distribution is that the distribution must meet a five-year holding period. More specifically, the distribution may not be made before the end of the five-tax-year period beginning with the first tax year for which a contribution was made to the Roth IRA. The first tax year begins on the first day of the tax year (i.e., January 1 in most cases) in which a contribution was made even though such contribution may have been made later in such tax year. In addition to satisfying the five-year test, a qualifying distribution must also meet one of the following:

- made on or after the date on which the individual attains age 59½,
- made to a beneficiary (or the individual's estate) on or after the individual's death,
- attributable to the individual being disabled, or
- a distribution for first-time homebuyer expenses (maximum of $10,000).

An important aspect of distributions from a Roth IRA is a special ordering rule for determining the taxability of nonqualifying withdrawals. Under this rule, distributions are treated as being made from contributions first and, thus, are nontaxable. After all contributions have been withdrawn, any remaining amounts are considered taxable and subject to the 10% penalty.

EXAMPLE I:9-73 ► Ray and Sandy are married and Ray is covered under his employer's qualified retirement plan. Their AGI on a joint return is $130,000. Ray can contribute $5,500 to a Roth IRA. Alternatively, however, if their AGI was $189,000, Ray would be limited to a maximum contribution of $2,200. Since their AGI exceeds the threshold of $183,000 by $6,000, the $5,500 contribution is reduced by 60% ($6,000/$10,000), or $3,300. ◄

EXAMPLE I:9-74 ► Bob, age 60 in 2015, contributes $5,500 each year to a Roth IRA in 2015, 2016, and 2017. On November 30, 2020, the value of the Roth IRA is $20,000. Bob has experienced some financial setbacks and needs to withdraw the money from the Roth IRA. If Bob withdraws $16,500 in 2020 and waits until January 2021 to withdraw the remaining $3,500, none of the distributions are taxable. This result occurs because the first $16,500 is treated as coming from contributions. The remaining $3,500 is nontaxable because Bob has met the five-year test and is over age 59½. Conversely, if Bob withdraws the entire $20,000 in 2020, $3,500 must be included in his income because the five-year test was not met. No penalty will be imposed because he is over age 59½. ◄

TAX STRATEGY TIP

Because of the tax-deferral of income within a Roth IRA and the ability to withdraw amounts at retirement tax-free, the Roth IRA generally is superior to a traditional IRA for younger taxpayers. Once a taxpayer reaches 50 years of age, the two types of IRAs become more equal.

A final aspect of Roth IRAs is the ability to "rollover" funds from an existing traditional IRA into a Roth IRA. Since the taxpayer received a deduction for the contribution into the traditional IRA, any rollover amount must be included in gross income in the year the rollover occurred, but is not subject to the 10% penalty for early withdrawals. For years prior to 2010, only taxpayers with AGI of $100,000 or less were eligible to rollover amounts from a traditional IRA to a Roth IRA. However, for tax years after 2009, the $100,000 income limit has been repealed and permits all taxpayers to convert traditional IRAs to Roth IRAs. In addition, as mentioned earlier, this rollover option has been extended to existing 401(k), 403(b), or 457 plans for years beginning in 2013. There is considerable interest in this option for taxpayers. The essential question is whether a taxpayer should convert his or her traditional IRA to a Roth IRA and pay the tax currently or keep the traditional IRA and pay the tax on a current basis as the amounts are withdrawn? The key variable in this analysis is the taxpayer's age. Younger taxpayers would definitely benefit with a Roth IRA as the amounts in the Roth IRA have years to accumulate and compound and such amounts will never be subject to taxation. Other important variables include the taxpayer's assessment of his or her future marginal tax rate and the ability to pay the tax on the rollover out of private funds.

EXAMPLE I:9-75 ▶ John has a traditional IRA that has a balance of $250,000 on June 30, 2014. He is single and has AGI of $180,000. John would like to rollover the $250,000 to a Roth IRA. John is permitted to rollover the $250,000 from his traditional IRA to a Roth IRA in 2014. He must include the $250,000 in his gross income in 2014 but no penalty is imposed. This treatment is now also available for 401(k), 403(b), or 457 plans in addition to traditional IRAs. ◀

Below is a discussion of some of the important tax rules for Roth IRAs:

- ▶ Like traditional IRAs, Roth IRAs must be established by the due date of the tax return (not including extensions). Similarly, contributions to a Roth IRA also must be made by the due date of the return (i.e., April 15, 2016, for 2015 contributions).
- ▶ Contributions to a Roth IRA are never deductible.
- ▶ Contributions to a Roth IRA are subject to special modified AGI limitations.
- ▶ Contributions to a Roth IRA can be made after the owner has reached age 70½. Similarly, no distributions are required at any age from a Roth IRA. (Remember: owners of traditional IRAs must begin taking distributions in the year after the taxpayer has reached age 70½).
- ▶ Taxpayers who are 50 years or older by the end of the taxable year may contribute an additional $1,000 per year (or a total of $6,500 in 2015).
- ▶ Withdrawals from a Roth IRA are not taxable if such withdrawals are "qualified distributions." If a withdrawal is not a qualified distribution, the amount is taxed under special ordering rules and subject to the 10% penalty.

STOP & THINK

Question: Both nondeductible contributions to a traditional IRA and contributions to a Roth IRA are similar in the sense that neither provides a tax deduction at the date of contribution. Which of the two types would be most advantageous to taxpayers?

Solution: Clearly, if a taxpayer qualifies for a Roth IRA, that type of IRA is superior to a nondeductible contribution to a traditional IRA. The reason is that distributions from a Roth IRA are totally excluded from gross income while only the principal portion of nondeductible contributions to a traditional IRA are excludable. In other words, the earnings generated in a Roth IRA are excluded from gross income whereas earnings associated with nondeductible contributions to a traditional IRA are subject to taxation. Generally, a nondeductible contribution to a traditional IRA will not be advantageous unless the taxpayer's AGI exceeds $193,000.

For a discussion of the decision whether to invest in a traditional deductible IRA or a Roth IRA, see the Tax Planning Considerations later in this chapter. Also, for a more detailed analysis including computations, see Chapter I:18 of the *Individuals* textbook.

Topic Review I:9-5 contains a table which summarizes the eligibility rules for traditional and Roth IRAs.

TOPIC REVIEW I:9-5

Traditional and Roth IRAs—Eligibility

If 2015 AGI Is	Eligible for IRA (Joint Returns) Traditional IRA (Deductible) A	B	C	Roth IRA	Traditional IRA (Nondeductible)*
Up to $98,000	Yes	Yes	Yes	Yes	Yes
$98,000–$118,000	Yes	Partially	Yes	Yes	Yes
$118,000–$183,000	Yes	No	Yes	Yes	Yes
$183,000–$193,000	Yes	No	Partially	Partially	Yes
Over $193,000	Yes	No	No	No	Yes

A If neither spouse is an active participant in an employer-sponsored plan
B For the IRA of a spouse who is an active participant in an employer-sponsored plan
C For the IRA of a spouse who is not an active participant in an employer-sponsored plan

* If AGI is not above $193,000, a nondeductible IRA will not be advantageous.

COVERDELL EDUCATION SAVINGS ACCOUNT

A special type of IRA, referred to as an Education IRA, was established to specifically assist low- and middle-income taxpayers with higher education expenses. The Education IRA was renamed the Coverdell Education Savings Account (CESA) in 2001. CESAs have a number of attractive features:

ADDITIONAL COMMENT

Any number of people may contribute funds to a Coverdell Education Savings Account for one child, but all of the contributions may not total more than $2,000 for that child.

- The maximum annual contribution into such plan is $2,000.[81]
- CESAs may be used for elementary and secondary education expenses as well as for higher education expenses, and
- Taxpayers can claim either the HOPE scholarship credit or Lifetime Learning Credit as well as excluding distributions from a CESA in the same year.

A contributor can make a *nondeductible* contribution of up to $2,000 per year into a CESA for a designated beneficiary until the beneficiary reaches age 18.[82] The contributor need not be related to the beneficiary and there is no limit on the number of CESAs that can be set up by a contributor. Distributions to the beneficiary are excluded from gross income provided the distribution does not exceed the *qualified education expenses* of the designated beneficiary during the taxable year. Qualified education expenses include tuition, fees, books, supplies, equipment, and room and board. In the case of elementary and secondary education expenses, qualified education expenses include academic tutoring and Internet access fees. Distributions in any tax year in excess of qualified education expenses are includible in the gross income of the beneficiary and subject to a 10% penalty.

Similar to other IRA-type accounts, there are phaseout limits based on the contributor's AGI. The $2,000 annual contribution is phased out for married taxpayers filing joint returns with AGI from $190,000 to $220,000 ($95,000 to $110,000 for other taxpayers). In addition, if the taxpayer claims either the HOPE scholarship credit or the Lifetime Learning Credit, the education expenses used for these credits must reduce the qualified expenses for exclusion from a CESA.

EXAMPLE I:9-76 ► Lee and Patsy are married and have two young grandchildren. To assist the grandchildren with their future education expenses, they set up a CESA for each child in 2015 and plan to deposit $2,000 in both accounts. Their AGI for 2015 is $202,000. Because their AGI exceeds $190,000, they are limited to putting $1,200 [$2,000 − $2,000(($202,000 − $190,000)/$30,000)] into the accounts in 2015. In the future, the children can withdraw amounts tax-free from their CESA to pay for qualified education expenses for elementary, secondary, or higher education. ◄

EXAMPLE I:9-77 ► Craig Shaw is about to enter State University as a freshman and plans to withdraw amounts from his CESA to help pay his expenses. His expenses for the Fall Semester 2015 are as follows:

Tuition and fees	$2,200
Books	500
Supplies	300
Room and board	2,400
Total	$5,400

Craig's parents plan on paying Craig's tuition and fees, and Craig will pay the remaining $3,200 from his CESA. Craig qualifies as a dependent of his parents for the tax year. Craig's parents plan on claiming the American Opportunity Tax Credit. Craig is not required to include the $3,200 in his gross income in 2015 as his qualified education expenses are at least $3,200. Craig's parents will use $2,200 to claim the AOTC credit. ◄

[81] Pursuant to the American Taxpayer Relief Act of 2012 (ATRA 2012), the contribution limit of $2,000 and other enhancements that were enacted in 2001 are made permanent for 2013 and future years. Without ATRA 2012, the maximum limit would have been reduced to the original limit of $500.

[82] Sec. 530. Contributions are allowed to continue past age 18 for a special-needs beneficiary.

HEALTH SAVINGS ACCOUNTS

Health Savings Accounts (HSAs) were established by Congress in 2003 to enable individuals to accumulate funds on a tax-free basis to pay qualified medical expenses currently or in the future.[83] In summary, HSAs operate as follows:

- The individual must be covered by a high-deductible health plan and not covered under any other health plan that is not a high-deductible health plan.
- Taxpayer contributes money into an HSA with a qualified trustee or custodian (much like an IRA). The taxpayer must be an eligible individual and the contributions are subject to limitations. These detailed issues are discussed below.
- The taxpayer is allowed a *for* AGI deduction in the year the contributions are made.
- Distributions from the HSA that are used exclusively to pay for qualified medical expenses (medical expenses as defined in Sec. 213(d), but not health insurance premiums) are excludable from gross income. However, any amount of the distribution that is not used to pay for qualified medical expenses is includable in the gross income of the taxpayer and subject to an additional 10% penalty. The 10% penalty is waived if the beneficiary/taxpayer is age 65 or older.

HSAs are only available to eligible individuals. An eligible individual is any individual who (1) is covered under a high-deductible health plan (HDHP), (2) is not also covered by any other health plan that is not an HDHP, (3) is not entitled to benefits under Medicare (i.e., generally, has not reached age 65), and (4) may not be claimed as a dependent on another person's tax return. An HDHP is a plan for an individual with an annual deductible in 2015 of at least $1,300 and annual out-of-pocket expenses (other than premiums) required to be paid not exceeding $6,450. For family coverage, these amounts are $2,600 and $12,900, respectively.

Annual contributions to an HSA are determined separately for each month the plan is in effect and is 1⁄12 of the *lesser* of (1) 100% of the annual deductible under the HDHP (minimum of $1,300) or (2) $3,350. For individuals with family coverage under an HDHP, the amounts are (1) 100% of the annual deductible under the HDHP (minimum of $2,600) or (2) $6,650. Catch-up contributions are permitted for individuals age 55 to 64.

EXAMPLE I:9-78 ▶ Roy, age 45, established an HDHP for his family with a $3,600 annual deductible on May 1, 2015. Roy is eligible to put $2,400 (8 months × $300) into an HSA for the calendar year 2015. The purpose of the fund is to pay for medical expenses for himself and his family. In 2015, Roy is allowed to deduct the $2,400 as a deduction for AGI. Any earnings of the fund investments are not subject to tax if the distribution is used to pay qualified medical expenses. ◀

EXAMPLE I:9-79 ▶ In 2018, Roy takes a $5,000 distribution from the HSA to make a down payment on a new automobile. Since the distribution was not used to pay qualified medical expenses, Roy must include the $5,000 in his income and pay a $500 ($5,000 × 10%) penalty in 2018. ◀

TAX PLANNING CONSIDERATIONS

OBJECTIVE 10

Describe tax planning considerations for employee expenses

MOVING EXPENSES

To be eligible for the moving expense deduction, the moving expenses must be paid in connection with the commencement of work by the taxpayer as a full-time employee or self-employed individual. Therefore, it is important to secure full-time employment or to carry on a trade or business as a self-employed individual at the new location. Taxpayers who are approaching retirement are eligible for a moving expense deduction only if they continue to work in the new location before their actual retirement (e.g., 39 weeks in the 12-month period following the move).

EXAMPLE I:9-80 ▶ Louis decides to quit his job and return to school as a full-time graduate student. Louis incurs substantial long-distance moving expenses that would otherwise be deductible to relocate to the university where the education is to be taken. No deduction is allowed unless Louis is employed on a full-time basis or is engaged in a self-employment activity at the new location. ◀

Reimbursed Amounts. Moving expense reimbursements are often greater than the amounts allowable as a deduction. This is caused by the common practice of reimbursing

[83] Sec. 223. Archer Medical Savings Accounts are similar to HSAs but cannot be established after 12/31/05. MSAs have a more restrictive definition of HDHP so there is little incentive to use them.

nondeductible items (e.g., an employer may reimburse an employee for the cost of certain indirect moving expenses such as househunting trips, which do not qualify as deductible moving expenses). This results in an increase in the employee's gross income to the extent of the excess reimbursement. From a tax planning standpoint, the employer may provide an additional payment to compensate the employee for the additional tax cost associated with the move (commonly referred to as a "gross-up").

EXAMPLE I:9-81 ▶ Austin Corporation has a policy of reimbursing transferred employees for 30% of their moving reimbursement that exceeds their deductible expenses to cover the federal and state tax costs associated with the excess reimbursement. Kathy, an employee, is transferred by the company to a new job location and incurs $6,000 of deductible moving expenses and receives an $8,000 reimbursement. Austin also will make an additional payment to Kathy of $600 (0.30 × $2,000) to cover the additional federal and state income tax costs. Kathy must include $2,600 ($2,000 + $600) of the reimbursement in gross income. ◀

PROVIDING NONTAXABLE COMPENSATION TO EMPLOYEES

Employers should consider the tax consequences to employees when changes in fringe benefit and deferred compensation arrangements are evaluated. For example, it is preferable for an employer to pay for fringe benefit items such as group term life insurance (up to $50,000 in coverage), health and accident insurance, employee parking, and so on rather than to give cash raises of a comparable amount. Such payments are nontaxable to the employee up to certain limits, whereas a comparable salary increase is fully taxable. Both types of payments are deductible by the employer.

REAL-WORLD EXAMPLE

Banks and other financial institutions in their ads sometimes compare the accumulated wealth in an IRA to the accumulated wealth in a fully taxable investment. Although the IRA is generally advantageous, the ads sometimes overstate the advantages because they fail to deduct the tax that will be paid when amounts are withdrawn from the IRA.

Consideration should also be given to increased deferred compensation benefit programs for employees, particularly highly-compensated individuals. The use of nonqualified deferred compensation plans, restricted property, and stock options result in tax deferrals and may result in the eventual recognition of capital gains that may be used to offset capital losses or that are taxed at preferential tax rates.

All eligible employees should consider establishing an individual retirement account (IRA) because of the available tax deferral benefits. Even if a premature withdrawal (i.e., before age 59½ occurs), the time value of the deferred benefits for the plan contributions and the earnings may be greater than the penalty tax imposed.

ROLLOVERS TO ROTH IRA

Taxpayers have the ability to rollover amounts from traditional IRAs as well as 401(k), 403(b), or 457 plan to a Roth IRA.[84] However, if such a rollover is made, the taxpayer must include the rollover amount in gross income in the year of the rollover. The principal benefit of the rollover is that once the amounts are in the Roth IRA, no further taxes are due on these amounts upon distribution (assuming the five-year test is met). The essential question, therefore, is whether it is advantageous to rollover amounts to a Roth IRA and pay the tax now or keep the original plan intact and pay the tax when regular distributions are made.

The decision rests on several factors, including (1) the marginal tax rate at retirement, (2) age of taxpayer, and (3) payment of tax from rollover from post-tax funds. First, if a taxpayer's marginal tax rate at retirement is expected to be lower than the current tax rate, a rollover may not be advantageous. Second, younger taxpayers are more likely to benefit from a rollover because they have more years to accumulate earnings tax-free and may be in a lower tax bracket today than at retirement. Finally, if the taxes that accrue from the rollover must be paid from the rollover funds, a rollover will probably not be in the taxpayer's favor. In other words, taxpayers should have sufficient funds from other sources to pay the tax, then the entire amount of rollover into the Roth IRA will have maximum ability to grow on a tax-free basis.

Each case must be analyzed based on the unique factors of that particular situation. However, for most taxpayers, it is generally advantageous to rollover funds from a traditional type of plan to a Roth IRA. With the higher tax rates in 2013 and the possibility of even higher tax rates in future years, the desirability of Roth conversions is increased.

[84] 401(k), 403(b), and 457 plans must have a separate "designated Roth account" for each participant in the plan.

COMPLIANCE AND PROCEDURAL CONSIDERATIONS

OBJECTIVE 11

Describe compliance and procedural considerations for employee expenses

SUBSTANTIATING TRAVEL AND ENTERTAINMENT EXPENSES

Travel and entertainment expenses are disallowed if the taxpayer does not maintain adequate records or documentary proof of the expenditures.[85] Normally, documentation includes expense statements (diary or account book) and proof of the amount, time, place, and business purpose. Strict substantiation rules are enacted in the law to curb widespread abuses in the so-called expense account living practices engaged in by some taxpayers.

KEY POINT

It is extremely important to be able to substantiate travel and entertainment expenses. The *Cohan* Rule that permits a reasonable deduction when substantiation is lacking does not apply to travel and entertainment expenses (see Chapter I:6).

To make compliance easier, the IRS formulated the following administrative procedural rules:

- If an employee makes an adequate accounting of the expenditures to the employer, it is not necessary to submit a detailed statement on the employee's tax return unless the expenses exceed the reimbursements.
- The standard mileage rate may be used to compute automobile expenses in lieu of actual expenses and is reported on Form 2106 (Employee Business Expenses).
- Taxpayers may elect an optional method for computing deductions for business travel and meal expenses in lieu of using actual costs. If a per diem allowance is paid by an employer in lieu of reimbursing actual expenses, the reimbursement is deemed to be substantiated if it does not exceed a federal per diem rate for the travel locality. In lieu of using actual expenses an employee or self-employed individual may use the applicable federal per diem rate. The taxpayer must still provide documentation of time, place, and business purpose for the expenditures.

ETHICAL POINT

The CPA has a responsibility to make sure that proper documentation has been furnished by the taxpayer to substantiate travel and entertainment expenses according to the provisions in Sec. 274(d). The CPA cannot rely on the use of estimates for these expenses despite the fact that the *AICPA's Statements on Standards for Tax Services No. 4* (see Appendix E) permits the use of estimates if it is impractical to obtain exact data and the estimated amounts appear to be reasonable.

REPORTING EMPLOYEE BUSINESS EXPENSES

Form 2106 (Employee Business Expenses) is used to report employee business expenses (see Appendix B). Part I of Form 2106 is a recap of travel and transportation expenses. Part II includes a computation of automobile expenses using either actual expenses or the standard rate mileage method. Employer reimbursements must be included in the employee's wages on Form W-2 if an adequate accounting of the expenses is not made. Employer withholding of federal income tax is also required for nonaccountable plan reimbursements. Form 2106-EZ may be used by employees who do not receive an employer reimbursement, and where the standard mileage rate is used for the current year and for the year the taxpayer's automobile was first placed in service.

Moving expenses are reported on Form 3903 (Moving Expenses) instead of Form 2106 because they are treated differently from other employee expenses (e.g., unreimbursed moving expenses are deductible *for* AGI). Expenses such as entertainment, union dues, business gifts, and education expenses are reported on Schedule A of Form 1040 as itemized deductions (see Appendix B).

A filled-in copy of Form 2106 is shown in Figure I:9-2. It includes the computations relating to the information in Example I:9-84.

EXAMPLE I:9-82 ▶ Eric Graber, SSN 000-00-0000, is single and employed as a salesman by the Houston Corporation in 2014. Eric is required to use his personal automobile for employment-related business and placed the current automobile in service on July 1, 2010. He uses only one automobile for business purposes and has elected to use the mileage method for deducting expenses. During 2014, Eric drives his automobile 80% of the time for business use and incurs the following total actual expenses:

Gas and oil	$ 7,400
Repairs	600
Depreciation	1,775
Insurance	1,400
Parking and tolls (all business related)	250
Total	$11,425

ADDITIONAL COMMENT

Many of the provisions related to employee business expenses are very complex. It has been said of the general complexity of the tax law that "If Patrick Henry thought taxation without representation was bad, he should have seen taxation with representation."

[85] Sec. 274(d).

Form **2106**

Department of the Treasury
Internal Revenue Service (99)

Employee Business Expenses

▶ Attach to Form 1040 or Form 1040NR.

▶ Information about Form 2106 and its separate instructions is available at *www.irs.gov/form2106.*

OMB No. 1545-0074

2014

Attachment Sequence No. 129

Your name	Occupation in which you incurred expenses	Social security number
Eric Graber	Sales	000 ⁞ 00 ⁞ 0000

Part I Employee Business Expenses and Reimbursements

Step 1 Enter Your Expenses		**Column A** Other Than Meals and Entertainment	**Column B** Meals and Entertainment
1 Vehicle expense from line 22 or line 29. (Rural mail carriers: See instructions.)	1	13,440	
2 Parking fees, tolls, and transportation, including train, bus, etc., that **did not** involve overnight travel or commuting to and from work .	2	250	
3 Travel expense while away from home overnight, including lodging, airplane, car rental, etc. **Do not** include meals and entertainment .	3	4,050	
4 Business expenses not included on lines 1 through 3. **Do not** include meals and entertainment	4		
5 Meals and entertainment expenses (see instructions)	5		1,350
6 **Total expenses.** In Column A, add lines 1 through 4 and enter the result. In Column B, enter the amount from line 5	6	17,740	1,350

Note: *If you were not reimbursed for any expenses in Step 1, skip line 7 and enter the amount from line 6 on line 8.*

Step 2 Enter Reimbursements Received From Your Employer for Expenses Listed in Step 1

7 Enter reimbursements received from your employer that were **not** reported to you in box 1 of Form W-2. Include any reimbursements reported under code "L" in box 12 of your Form W-2 (see instructions).	7	9,600	0

Step 3 Figure Expenses To Deduct on Schedule A (Form 1040 or Form 1040NR)

8 Subtract line 7 from line 6. If zero or less, enter -0-. However, if line 7 is greater than line 6 in Column A, report the excess as income on Form 1040, line 7 (or on Form 1040NR, line 8)	8	8,140	1,350
Note: *If **both columns** of line 8 are zero, you cannot deduct employee business expenses. Stop here and attach Form 2106 to your return.*			
9 In Column A, enter the amount from line 8. In Column B, multiply line 8 by 50% (.50). (Employees subject to Department of Transportation (DOT) hours of service limits: Multiply meal expenses incurred while away from home on business by 80% (.80) instead of 50%. For details, see instructions.)	9	8,140	675
10 Add the amounts on line 9 of both columns and enter the total here. **Also, enter the total on Schedule A (Form 1040), line 21** (or on **Schedule A (Form 1040NR), line 7**). (Armed Forces reservists, qualified performing artists, fee-basis state or local government officials, and individuals with disabilities: See the instructions for special rules on where to enter the total.) . . . . . . ▶	10		8,815

For Paperwork Reduction Act Notice, see your tax return instructions. Cat. No. 11700N Form **2106** (2014)

FIGURE I:9-2 ▶ PAGE 1 OF FORM 2106 FOR EXAMPLE I:9-82

Form 2106 (2014) Page 2

Part II Vehicle Expenses

Section A—General Information (You must complete this section if you are claiming vehicle expenses.)		(a) Vehicle 1	(b) Vehicle 2
11 Enter the date the vehicle was placed in service	11	07 / 01 / 10	/ /
12 Total miles the vehicle was driven during 2014	12	30,000 miles	miles
13 Business miles included on line 12	13	24,000 miles	miles
14 Percent of business use. Divide line 13 by line 12	14	80.00 %	%
15 Average daily roundtrip commuting distance	15	8 miles	miles
16 Commuting miles included on line 12	16	2,000 miles	miles
17 Other miles. Add lines 13 and 16 and subtract the total from line 12	17	4,000 miles	miles

	Yes	No
18 Was your vehicle available for personal use during off-duty hours?	☑ Yes	☐ No
19 Do you (or your spouse) have another vehicle available for personal use?	☑ Yes	☐ No
20 Do you have evidence to support your deduction?	☑ Yes	☐ No
21 If "Yes," is the evidence written?	☑ Yes	☐ No

Section B—Standard Mileage Rate (See the instructions for Part II to find out whether to complete this section or Section C.)

22 Multiply line 13 by 56¢ (.56). Enter the result here and on line 1	22	13,440

Section C—Actual Expenses		(a) Vehicle 1		(b) Vehicle 2	
23 Gasoline, oil, repairs, vehicle insurance, etc.	23		9,400		
24a Vehicle rentals	24a				
b Inclusion amount (see instructions)	24b				
c Subtract line 24b from line 24a	24c				
25 Value of employer-provided vehicle (applies only if 100% of annual lease value was included on Form W-2—see instructions)	25				
26 Add lines 23, 24c, and 25	26		9,400		
27 Multiply line 26 by the percentage on line 14	27		7,520		
28 Depreciation (see instructions)	28		1,420		
29 Add lines 27 and 28. Enter total here and on line 1	29		8,940		

Section D—Depreciation of Vehicles (Use this section only if you owned the vehicle and are completing Section C for the vehicle.)

		(a) Vehicle 1		(b) Vehicle 2	
30 Enter cost or other basis (see instructions)	30				
31 Enter section 179 deduction (see instructions)	31				
32 Multiply line 30 by line 14 (see instructions if you claimed the section 179 deduction)	32				
33 Enter depreciation method and percentage (see instructions)	33				
34 Multiply line 32 by the percentage on line 33 (see instructions)	34				
35 Add lines 31 and 34	35				
36 Enter the applicable limit explained in the line 36 instructions	36	1,775			
37 Multiply line 36 by the percentage on line 14	37		1,420		
38 Enter the **smaller** of line 35 or line 37. If you skipped lines 36 and 37, enter the amount from line 35. Also enter this amount on line 28 above	38		1,420		

Form **2106** (2014)

FIGURE I:9-2 ▶ PAGE 2 OF FORM 2106 FOR EXAMPLE I:9-82

During the year, Eric drives a total of 30,000 miles, of which 24,000 are business miles. Of the 6,000 personal miles, 2,000 miles are commuting to and from work (8 miles roundtrip each day). Eric receives a reimbursement of 40 cents per business mile from his employer. Eric also incurred $5,400 of unreimbursed employment-related travel and entertainment expenses. These expenses include the following:

Airfare	$ 2,500
Car rental	250
Business meals at which business was discussed	550
Laundry while traveling	100
Lodging	1,200
Entertainment of customers	800
Total	$ 5,400

Step 1, line 1: Vehicle expense (24,000 × .56)	$13,440
Step 2, line 7: (24,000 miles × $0.40)	$9,600
Section C, line 23: Actual expenses:	
Gas and oil	$7,400
Repairs	600
Insurance	1,400
Total	$ 9,400
Section C, line 28: Depreciation ($1,775 × .80)	$ 1,420

As can be seen from the completed Form 2106, Eric receives a larger deduction from the mileage method. This method has been elected by Eric. Sections C and D of Part II of Form 2106 are not necessary in this case because Eric has elected the mileage method. They are shown for illustrative purposes. ◀

REPORTING MOVING EXPENSES

Employer reimbursements for qualifying moving expenses reduce the otherwise deductible amount for the employee. Reimbursements for nondeductible moving expenses are included in gross income and should be included in total wages on the employee's Form W-2 and reported on page 1 (line 7) of Form 1040. Employers should complete Form 4782 (Employee Moving Expense Information) which summarizes the moving expense payments made to the employee and to third parties. The form is provided to an employee to properly report his moving expenses and reimbursements. Form 3903 (Moving Expenses) is used to compute the allowable moving expenses and is attached to the employee's tax return. Moving expenses are deductible *for* AGI on line 26 of page 1 of the 2014 Form 1040. Moving expenses are not subject to federal income tax withholding if it is reasonable to believe that an employee will be entitled to a deduction for such amounts. Reimbursements in excess of the deductible amounts, however, are subject to the withholding of income and social security taxes.

KEY POINT

If a taxpayer who is an employee moves in early December, the earliest that the 39-week test could be met would be early September of the following year. This is well after the April 15 due date for the individual return. The taxpayer may nevertheless deduct the moving expenses in the earlier year.

A taxpayer may deduct moving expenses, even though the tests for qualification have not been met (e.g., the 39-week test). If the individual subsequently fails to satisfy the requirements, gross income for the subsequent year must be increased by the previous tax benefit.[86] Another alternative is to wait until the tests have been met and then file an amended return (Form 1040X) for the prior year.

REPORTING OFFICE IN HOME EXPENSES

Form 8829 (Expenses for Business Use of Your Home) must be used to figure the allowable expenses for business use that are reported on Schedule C (Profit or Loss from Business) and the carryover of any nondeductible amounts from prior years. Form 4562 (Depreciation and Amortization) must also be used to compute depreciation on the office portion of the residence.

[86] Secs. 217(d)(2) and (3).

QUALIFICATION OF PENSION AND PROFIT-SHARING PLANS

The reporting requirements to establish and maintain a qualified pension or profit-sharing plan are too complex for this text. However, it should be noted that it is generally advisable for a taxpayer to obtain advance approval of the plan from the district director of the IRS by requesting a determination letter that all requirements for qualification have been met. A new determination letter should generally be requested when any material (e.g., substantial) modification is made to a plan. Material changes are frequently required when major tax legislation is enacted. In addition, several reports must be filed with the IRS and the U.S. Department of Labor.

PROBLEM MATERIALS

DISCUSSION QUESTIONS

I:9-1 Why is it important to distinguish whether an individual is an employee or an independent contractor (self-employed)?

I:9-2 Determine whether the following expenses are either deductible *for* AGI or *from* AGI or nondeductible on an employee's return. Indicate whether the expenses are subject to the 2% nondeductible floor for miscellaneous itemized deductions.

a. Automobile expenses associated with commuting to and from work
b. Legal expenses incurred to prepare the taxpayer's income tax return
c. Unreimbursed travel and transportation expenses
d. Qualified moving expenses of an employee

I:9-3 Which of the following deduction items are subject to the 2% nondeductible floor applicable to miscellaneous itemized deductions?

a. Investment counseling fees
b. Fees for tax return preparation
c. Unreimbursed professional dues for an employee
d. Gambling losses
e. Interest on a personal residence
f. Unreimbursed employee travel expenses
g. Reimbursed employee travel expenses (an adequate accounting is made to the employer and any excess reimbursement must be repaid)
h. Safe deposit box rental expenses for an investor

I:9-4 In each of the following cases involving travel expenses, indicate how each item is reported on the taxpayer's tax return. Include any limitations that might affect its deductibility.

a. Marilyn lives in Houston and owns several rental properties in Denver. To supervise the management of these properties, Marilyn incurs travel expenses including airfare, lodging, and meals while traveling to and from the location of the rental properties.
b. Marc is an employee who incurs travel expenses as a salesperson. The expenses are fully reimbursed by his employer after an adequate accounting has been made.
c. Assume the same facts as in Part b, except that the expenses are not reimbursed.
d. Kay is a self-employed attorney who incurs travel expenses (including meals) to prepare a court case in a nearby city where she spends the night.

I:9-5 Kelly is an employee who incurs $2,000 of business meal expenses in connection with business entertainment and travel, none of which are reimbursed by her employer. $500 of the business meal costs are considered to be lavish or extravagant. How much can Kelly deduct before applying the 2% nondeductible floor on miscellaneous itemized deductions?

I:9-6 Latoya, a college professor, takes a nine-month leave of absence from her employment at a college in Ohio and accepts a visiting professorship (temporary assignment) at a college in Texas. Latoya leaves her husband and children in Ohio and incurs the following expenses in connection with the temporary assignment:

Airfare to and from the temporary assignment	$ 1,000
Living expenses in the new location (including meals of $1,000)	8,000
Personal clothing	1,500
Total	$10,500

a. Which (if any) of these items can Latoya deduct?
b. Would your answer to Part a change if Latoya, after completing the nine month assignment, resigned her position in Ohio and accepted a full-time assignment with the college in Texas?

I:9-7 Louie is a full-time employee for a large corporation and also an investor in the stock market in his spare time. In the current year, Louie incurs $2,500 of travel expenses and $1,000 in registration fees related to attending investment seminars. He deducts the expenses on his income tax return as a miscellaneous itemized deduction as an investment expense. Are the travel expenses and registration fees deductible? Should they be classified as *for* AGI or *from* AGI?

I:9-8 If an employee receives a specific monthly amount from his or her employer as a reimbursement for employment-related entertainment, travel, and transportation expenses, why is it necessary to allocate a portion of the total reimbursement to each expense category?

I:9-9 If an employee receives a reimbursement of 40 cents a mile from her employer for employment-related transportation expenses, is the employee permitted to deduct the difference between the standard mileage rate and the reimbursement rate as an unreimbursed employee expense? What other alternative is available for claiming the transportation deduction?

I:9-10 If an employee (or self-employed individual) uses the standard mileage rate method for the year in which an automobile is acquired, may the actual expense method be used in a subsequent year? If so, what restrictions are imposed (if any) on depreciation methods? What adjustments to basis are required?

I:9-11 If an employee or self-employed individual uses the actual method of deducting automobile expenses and claims depreciation for the first two years of business use, can the individual switch to the standard mileage rate method for the third year and beyond?

I:9-12 Discuss the reporting procedures that should be followed by an employee to report employment-related expenses on his or her tax return under the following conditions:

a. Expenses are less than reimbursements, and no accounting is made to the employer.
b. Expenses equal reimbursements, and an adequate accounting is made to the employer.
c. Expenses exceed reimbursements, and an adequate accounting is made to the employer.
d. Expenses are less than reimbursements. An adequate accounting is made to the employer and the employee is required to repay any excess amount.

I:9-13 What are the two basic requirements that must be met to permit a deduction for moving expenses?

I:9-14 Does it matter whether a moving expense is incurred by an employee, a self-employed individual, or an unemployed person?

I:9-15 Len incurs $5,000 of deductible moving expenses in the current year and is fully reimbursed by his employer in the same year.

a. How are the expense deduction and the reimbursement reported on Len's tax return if he uses the standard deduction?
b. What tax consequences occur if the reimbursement is $5,000 but only $3,000 of the $5,000 of moving expenses are tax deductible?

I:9-16 Why are strict recordkeeping requirements required for the deduction of entertainment expenses?

I:9-17 Louis incurs "directly related" entertainment expenses of $4,000, but he is reimbursed by his employer for only $3,000 after an adequate accounting is made.

a. How are these amounts reported on Louis's tax return?
b. What are the tax consequences if Louis is unable to provide adequate documentation of the expenditures during the course of an IRS audit of his tax return?

I:9-18 Latasha is a self-employed attorney who entertains clients and potential clients in her home.

a. What requirements must be met to qualify the outlays as deductible entertainment expenses?
b. What is the difference between "directly related" and "associated with" entertainment?

I:9-19 Liz is an employee who regularly entertains customers in connection with her job. In the current year, Liz incurs $6,000 in business meal expenses that are connected with entertainment. Liz's expenses are not lavish or extravagant. She itemizes her deductions in the current year.

a. If none of these expenses are reimbursed by Liz's employer, what amounts are deductible and how are they classified?
b. How are these amounts reported by Liz and her employer if all of her expenses are reimbursed and an adequate accounting is made by Liz?

I:9-20 Atlantic Corporation provides a cafeteria for its employees. The meal charges are set at a sufficiently high level that the employees are not taxed on the subsidized eating facilities. Are Atlantic's cafeteria-related costs subject to the 50% disallowance for business meals?

I:9-21 Lynn is a salesperson who entertains clients at business luncheons. A business relationship exists for the entertainment, and there is a reasonable expectation of business benefit. However, no business discussions are generally conducted before, during, or immediately following the meals. Do the business meal expenditures qualify as entertainment expenses?

I:9-22 If an individual belongs to a country club and uses the facility primarily for business entertainment of customers, what portion of the club dues is deductible?

I:9-23 Bass Corporation purchases 10 tickets to the Super Bowl in February 2015 for entertaining its customers. Due to unusually high demand, the tickets have to be purchased from scalpers for $15,000 (10 × $1,500). The face value of the tickets is only $2,000 (10 × $200). What amount is deductible by Bass in 2015?

I:9-24 a. Discuss the two requirements for an employee expense reimbursement plan to be treated as an accountable plan.
b. How are expenses and reimbursements treated under an accountable plan?
c. How are expenses and reimbursements treated under a nonaccountable plan?

I:9-25 Martin is a tax accountant employed by a public accounting firm. He incurs the following expenses:

CPA review course	$ 400
Law school tuition and books	4,000
Accounting continuing education course (travel, fees, and transportation (including meals of $200)	600
Total	$5,000

Martin is also a degree candidate at the law school. Which (if any) of these expenditures qualify as deductible education expenses? How are they reported?

I:9-26 Discuss whether any of the following individuals are entitled to an office-in-home deduction:
a. Maggie is a self-employed management consultant who maintains an office in her home exclusively used for client meetings and other business-related activities. Maggie has no other place of business and her office is the most significant place for her business. She has substantial income from the consulting practice.
b. Marty is a college professor who writes research papers for academic journals in his office at home which is used exclusively for this purpose. Although Marty has an office at his place of employment, he finds it very convenient to maintain an office at home to avoid distractions from students and colleagues. Marty receives no income from the publication of the research articles for the year in question.
c. Bobby operates his own sole proprietorship as an electrician. He maintains an office at home where he keeps his books, takes phone calls from customers, and does the payroll for his five employees. All of his electrical work is done at the location of his customers.

I:9-27 Compare and contrast the tax advantages accruing to employers and employees from the establishment of a qualified pension or profit-sharing plan versus a nonqualified deferred compensation arrangement (e.g., a restricted property plan).

I:9-28 What is the difference between a defined benefit pension plan and a defined contribution pension plan?

I:9-29 Austin Corporation is proposing the establishment of a pension plan that will cover only employees with salaries in excess of $150,000. No other employees are covered under comparable qualified plans. What problems (if any) do you envision regarding the plan's qualification with the IRS?

I:9-30 Babson Corporation is proposing the creation of a qualified profit-sharing plan for its employees. The proposed plan provides for vesting of employer contributions after 20 years because the company wants to discourage employee turnover and does not feel that short-term employees should qualify for benefits. Will this plan qualify? Why or why not?

I:9-31 Explain how distributions from a qualified pension plan, which are made in the form of annuity payments, are reported by an employee under the following circumstances:
a. No employee contributions are made to the plan.
b. The pension plan provides for matching employee contributions.

I:9-32 Discuss the limitations and restrictions that the Internal Revenue Code places on employer contributions to qualified pension and profit-sharing plans.

I:9-33 Why are nonqualified deferred compensation plans particularly well-suited for use in executive compensation arrangements?

I:9-34 A recently-formed corporation is considering going public and anticipates substantial future appreciation in its stock. Would it be advisable for an executive/employee receiving stock (restricted property) to elect to recognize income immediately under Sec. 83(b)? Contrast the tax consequences of a restricted property arrangement for both the employer and employee when this election is made versus when it is not made. Consider the effect of the subsequent lapsing of the restrictions and the employee's sale of the stock.

I:9-35 List and discuss the qualification requirements for an incentive stock option plan (ISO). Describe the advantages and disadvantages of ISOs compared to nonqualified stock option plans.

I:9-36 What difference does it make if a nonqualified stock option has a readily ascertainable FMV on the grant date?

I:9-37 Is a self-employed individual, who is also em ployed and covered by an employer's qualified pension plan, eligible to establish an H.R. 10 or an SEP plan on his or her self-employment income?

I:9-38 What limitations are placed on self-employed individuals for contributions made to defined contribution H.R. 10 plans? Must self-employed individuals cover their full-time employees if an H.R. 10 plan is established?

I:9-39 Discuss the essential differences between a traditional IRA and a Roth IRA.

I:9-40 Would you be more favorably inclined to advise a 30-year-old individual to establish a traditional deductible IRA or a Roth IRA? Explain. Consider any tax problems involved if the IRA funds are needed before age 59½. Would your answer change for a 55-year-old individual?

I:9-41 Your client, Charley Long, age 40, has requested your advice with respect to his IRA. He has a traditional IRA with a balance of $250,000 and his current AGI is $250,000. He expects his income to increase slightly when he retires at age 65. Charley has been reading about Roth IRAs and wants your advice as to whether he should rollover the $250,000 from his traditional IRA into a Roth IRA. He has sufficient outside money to pay any taxes due on the rollover. What advice would you give Charley?

I:9-42 Sally, who is single and age 40, made deductible IRA contributions in several early years, but has not been eligible to make deductible IRA contributions for the last 5 years because she is covered under her employer's plan. Her AGI is $100,000. She is interested in making IRA contributions in the current year. What advice would you give her?

I:9-43 Discuss the major features of a Coverdell Education Savings Account (CESA).

I:9-44 The owner of an unincorporated small business is considering whether to establish a simplified employee pension (SEP) plan for its employees.

a. What nontax factors might make an SEP attractive as an alternative to establishing a qualified pension or profit-sharing plan?

b. Is the owner of the small business eligible to make contributions on his or her behalf to the SEP?

ISSUE IDENTIFICATION QUESTIONS

I:9-45 Georgia is an executive who recently completed an assignment with her employer at an away-from-home location. It was realistically expected that the assignment would be completed in 15 months but the actual time period was only 11 months. Georgia incurred $15,000 of away-from-home expenses during the 11-month period, none of which were reimbursed by her employer. What tax issues should Georgia consider?

I:9-46 Jeremy is an executive for Columbia Corporation, which is going through a restructuring of its corporate headquarters operations. Columbia has offered to relocate Jeremy from its New York headquarters to its divisional operation in South Carolina and will reimburse him for both direct and indirect moving expenses. What tax issues should Jeremy consider?

I:9-47 Juan, a self-employed medical doctor, maintains an office in his home where he maintains patient records and performs billing procedures. Most of his time is spent visiting patients and performing surgical procedures in the operating room at several local hospitals. Juan intends to deduct his expenses of his office in his home. What tax issues should Juan consider?

I:9-48 David is on the audit staff of a national accounting firm. He has been with the firm for three years and is a CPA. David has applied and been accepted into a prestigious MBA program. The program is two years in duration. David has decided to resign from the accounting firm even though the firm has indicated that it would very much like David to return to work for the firm after he receives his MBA degree. David is somewhat interested in returning to public accounting but will certainly look at all of his options when he completes the program. David wants to deduct his education expenses. What are the relevant tax issues in this case?

PROBLEMS

I:9-49 *Employment-Related Expenses.* Mike incurs the following employment-related expenses in the current year:

Actual automobile expenses	$ 2,500
Moving expenses (deductible under Sec. 217)	4,000
Entertainment expenses	1,500
Travel expenses (including $500 of business meals)	2,500
Professional dues and subscriptions	500
Total	$11,000

Mike's AGI is $120,000 before any of the above expenses are deducted. None of the expenses listed above are reimbursed by Mike's employer. He has no other miscellaneous itemized deductions and does not use the standard deduction.

a. What is the amount of Mike's deduction for employment-related expenses?
b. How are these items reported in Mike's tax return?

I:9-50 ***Travel and Entertainment.*** Monique is a self-employed manufacturer's representative (i.e., an independent contractor) who solicits business for numerous clients and receives a commission based on sales. She incurs the following expenditures during the current year:

Airfare and lodging while away from home overnight	$ 4,000
Business meals while traveling at which business is discussed	1,000
Local transportation costs for automobile, parking, tolls, etc. (business-related)	2,000
Commuting expenses	1,000
Local entertainment of customers	2,000
Total	$10,000

a. Which of the expenditures listed above (if any) are deductible by Monique?
b. Are each of these items classified as *for* AGI or *from* AGI deductions?
c. How would your answers to Parts a and b change if Monique were an employee rather than self-employed and none of the expenses were reimbursed by her employer?

I:9-51 ***Unreimbursed Employee Expenses.*** Mary is an employee of ABC corporation and incurs $3,600 of unreimbursed employment-related travel and entertainment expenses during the current year. These business expenses include the following:

Airfare	$1,500
Taxi fare	100
Meals eaten alone while away from home on business	300
Laundry	50
Lodging	650
Business meals with customers at which business is discussed	500
Entertainment of customers	500
Total	$3,600

Mary also pays $1,000 of investment counseling fees and $500 of tax return preparation fees in the current year. Mary's AGI is $70,000.

a. What is the total amount of Mary's deductible expenses?
b. Are the deductible expenses classified as *for* AGI or *from* AGI?

I:9-52 ***Travel Expenses.*** Marilyn, a business executive who lives and works in Cleveland, accepts a temporary out-of-town assignment in Atlanta for a period of ten months. Marilyn leaves her husband and children in Cleveland and rents an apartment in Atlanta during the ten-month period. Marilyn incurs the following expenses, none of which are reimbursed by her employer:

Airfare to and from Atlanta	$ 800
Airfare for weekend trips to visit her family	8,000
Apartment rent	10,000
Meals in Atlanta	8,500
Entertainment of customers	2,000
Total	$29,300

a. Which of the expenditures listed above (if any) are deductible by Marilyn (before any limitations are applied)?
b. Are each of these expenditures classified as *for* AGI or *from* AGI deductions?
c. If Marilyn's AGI is $120,000, what is the amount of the deduction for the expenditures?
d. Do the tax consequences change if Marilyn's assignment is for a period of more than one year?

e. Do the tax consequences in Parts a through c change if it was realistically expected that the work would be completed in ten months but after the ten-month period Marilyn is asked to continue for seven more months and if an additional $10,000 of travel expenses are incurred during the extended period?

I:9-53 ***Business/Personal Travel Expenses.*** In the current year, Mike's AGI is $50,000. Mike has no miscellaneous itemized deductions other than the employment-related expenses listed below. Mike attends a professional trade association convention in Los Angeles. He spends three days at the meeting and two days vacationing before the meeting. Mike's total expenses include the following:

Airfare	$ 450
Meals ($50 per day)	250
Hotel ($100 per day)	500
Entertainment of customers (business is discussed)	500
Total	$1,700

Mike's employer reimburses him for the business-related expenses and, accordingly, Mike receives a reimbursement of $1,400 ($450 + 150 + 300 + 500).

a. How much can Mike deduct for employment-related expenses?
b. How is the reimbursement reported on Mike's tax return?
c. How much of the reimbursement may Mike's employer deduct?
d. How would your answers change if Mike spent two days at the meeting and three days vacationing? Assume Mike received no reimbursement from his employer.

I:9-54 ***Employment-Related Expenses and Reimbursements.*** Maxine incurs the following employment-related business expenses in the current year:

Professional dues and subscriptions	$1,000
Airfare and lodging	2,000
Local transportation for employment-related business activities	1,000
Customer entertainment (business lunches where business is discussed)	1,000
Total	$5,000

After making an adequate accounting of the expenses, Maxine receives a reimbursement of $3,000 from her employer. Assume that Maxine's AGI is $60,000, she has other miscellaneous itemized deductions of $1,000 and she does not use the standard deduction.

a. What amount of the expenses are deductible by Maxine?
b. Are each of these expenditures classified as *for* AGI or *from* AGI deductions?
c. How would your answers to Parts a and b change if Maxine instead received a $6,000 reimbursement?

I:9-55 ***Miscellaneous Itemized Deductions.*** In the current year, Melissa, a single employee whose AGI is $100,000 before any of the items below, incurs the following expenses:

Safe deposit box rental for investments	$ 100
Tax return preparation fees	500
Moving expenses (deductible under Sec. 217)	2,000
Mortgage interest on Melissa's principal residence	12,000
Real estate taxes on Melissa's principal residence	1,800
Unreimbursed employment-related expenses (other than business meals and entertainment)	6,000
Unreimbursed employment-related expenses for business meals and entertainment (business is discussed)	1,200
Total	$23,600

a. What is the amount of Melissa's total miscellaneous itemized deductions (after deducting the 2% floor)?
b. What is the amount of Melissa's total itemized deductions?
c. What is the amount of Melissa's total itemized deductions if her AGI, after all adjustments above, is $190,000?

I:9-56 *Transportation Expenses.* Cassady, an employee of a law firm, maintains an office at the principal business location of her firm. She frequently travels directly from her home to client locations within and outside the metropolitan area. Cassady is not reimbursed for her transportation expenses and has incurred the following:

Transportation expenses associated with trips to clients within the metropolitan area	$2,000
Transportation expenses associated with trips to clients located outside the metropolitan area	3,000
Total	$5,000

a. What is the amount of Cassady's deduction for transportation expenses?
b. How is the deduction reported on Cassady's tax return?
c. What is the amount of Cassady's deduction for transportation expenses and its classification if she is self-employed and operates her office from her home? Assume that the requirements of Sec. 280A are satisfied.

I:9-57 *Auto Expenses.* Michelle is an employee who must use her personal automobile for employment-related business trips. During 2015, Michelle drives her car 60% for business use and incurs the following total expenses (100% use of car):

Gas and oil	$10,000
Repairs	1,400
Depreciation	4,700
Insurance and license fees	2,800
Parking and tolls (business related)	400
Total	$19,300

Michelle drives her car a total of 40,000 miles (24,000 business miles) during 2015 and receives a reimbursement of 40 cents per business mile from her employer. Assume that an adequate accounting is made to Michelle's employer.
a. What amount is deductible (before the 2% nondeductible floor) if Michelle uses the standard mileage method?
b. What amount is deductible (before the 2% nondeductible floor) if Michelle uses the actual cost method?
c. Can taxpayers switch back and forth between the mileage and actual methods each year?

I:9-58 *Auto Expenses.* Amelie is an employee who uses her personal automobile in connection with her job. During 2015, Amelie drove her car a total of 28,000 miles. Her business log shows that she drove 22,400 miles for business purposes. She is reimbursed $0.30 per mile from her employer for her business miles and she makes an adequate accounting to her employer. During 2015, Amelie incurred the following actual expenses based on 100% business use, that is, 28,000 miles:

Gas and oil	$ 7,800
Repairs and maintenance	2,300
Depreciation	5,800
Insurance	1,440
Licenses and fees	300
	$17,640

a. Compute Amelie's deduction before the 2% of AGI floor if she uses the actual cost method.
b. Compute Amelie's deduction before the 2% of AGI floor if she uses the standard mileage method.
c. Assume Amelie used the standard mileage method in 2015 and received the 30 cents per mile reimbursement. In addition to the automobile expenses, she made several business trips and incurred the following travel expenses:

Airfare	$ 4,600
Hotel	1,860
Meals and entertainment	720
Taxi fees and tips	280
	$7,460

None of the above expenses were personal in nature and she received total reimbursements (including the mileage reimbursement) from her employer of $11,220. If Amelie's AGI was $120,000, what is her deduction in 2015 after all limitations?

I:9-59 ***Entertainment Expenses.*** Milt, a self-employed attorney, incurs the following expenses in the current year:

Dues paid to the local chamber of commerce	$ 1,000
Business lunches for clients and prospective clients (Milt does not believe in conducting business discussions during lunch)	4,000
Entertainment of professional associates in his home (immediately following business meetings)	2,000
Country club dues (the club is used exclusively for business)	2,500
Entertainment of clients and prospective clients at the country club (meals and drinks)	1,500
Total	$11,000

a. Which of the expenditures listed above (if any) are deductible by Milt?
b. Are each of these items classified as *for* AGI or *from* AGI deductions?
c. How would your answers change if Milt was an employee rather than self-employed?

I:9-60 ***Entertainment Expenses.*** Beach Corporation purchases tickets to sporting events and uses them to entertain customers. In the current year Beach Corporation purchases the following tickets:

100 tickets to football games (face value of the tickets is $7,000)	$10,000
A skybox rented for six NFL football games (seating capacity of the skybox is 20, and the highest price of a nonluxury box seat is $100)	30,000

What amount of the entertainment expenses is deductible in the current year?

I:9-61 ***Reimbursed Employee Expenses.*** Latrisha is an employee of the Cooper Company and incurs significant employment-related expenses. During the current year, she incurred the following expenses in connection with her job:

Travel: Airfare	$ 5,850
Lodging	1,800
Meals	1,200
Entertainment of customers	2,400
Total	$11,250

a. Determine the amount of deductible expenses for both Latrisha and the Cooper Company and, for Latrisha, whether they are deductible *for* AGI or *from* AGI assuming Cooper Company maintains an accountable plan for employee expense reimbursements, if the reimbursements are alternatively:

1. $11,250
2. $9,000
3. $14,000

b. What would be the result in Part a for each of the three situations if the plan was a nonaccountable plan?

I:9-62 ***Moving Expenses.*** Michael graduates from New York University and on February 1, 2015, accepts a position with a public accounting firm in Chicago. Michael is a resident of New York. In March, Michael travels to Chicago to locate a house and starts to work in June. He incurs the following expenses, none of which are reimbursed by the public accounting firm:

Automobile expense enroute (1,000 miles at 23 cents per mile—standard mileage rate)	$ 230
Cost of meals en route	100
Househunting trip travel expenses	1,400
Moving van expenses	3,970
Commission on the sale of Michael's New York condominium	3,500
Points paid to acquire a mortgage on Michael's new residence in Chicago	1,000
Temporary living expenses for one week in Chicago (hotel and $100 in meals)	400
Expenses incurred in decorating the new residence	500
Total expenses	$11,100

a. What is Michael's moving expense deduction?
b. How are the deductible expenses classified on Michael's tax return?
c. How would your answer to Part a change if all of Michael's expenses were reimbursed by his employer and he received a check for $11,100?

I:9-63 *Education Expenses.* For each of the following independent situations, determine whether any of the expenditures qualify as deductible education expenses in connection with a trade or business (Reg. Sec. 1.162-5). Are the expenditures classified as *for* AGI or *from* AGI deductions?
a. Law school tuition and books for an IRS agent who is pursuing a law degree: $2,000.
b. Continuing professional accounting education expenses of $1,900 for a self-employed CPA: travel, $1,000 (including $200 meals); registration fees, $800; books, $100.
c. MBA education expenses totaling $5,000 for a business executive of a major corporation: tuition, $4,000; transportation, $800; and books, $200.
d. Tuition and books acquired for graduate education courses required under state law for a schoolteacher in order to renew a provisional certificate: $1,000.
e. Bar review courses for a recent law school graduate: $1,000.

I:9-64 *Education Expenses.* Anne works for a CPA firm as a secretary/receptionist and earns approximately $27,000 per year. About five years earlier, she had completed 70 credit hours at State U. To increase her career potential, she decided to enroll at the local university to continue her college education and get an undergraduate degree in accounting with the ultimate goal of obtaining her CPA certificate. During 2015, she incurred the following education expenses:

Tuition and fees	$3,500
Books and supplies	800

What are Anne's options as to the deductibility of the above expenses?

I:9-65 *Office in Home.* Nancy is a self-employed artist who uses 10% of her residence as a studio. The studio portion is used exclusively for business and is frequented by customers on a regular basis. Nancy also uses her den as an office (10% of the total floor space of her home) to prepare bills and keep records. However, the den is also used by her children as a TV room. Nancy's net income from the sale of the artwork (other than her home office expenses) amounts to $40,000 in the current year. She also incurs $1,400 of expenses directly related to the office (e.g., painting of the office, window blinds). Nancy incurs the following expenses in the current year related to her residence:

Real estate taxes	$ 2,000
Mortgage interest	5,000
Insurance	500
Depreciation	3,500
Repairs and utilities	1,000
Total	$12,000

a. Which of the expenditures above (if any) are deductible? Are they *for* AGI or *from* AGI deductions?
b. Would your answer to Part a change if Nancy's net income from painting were only $2,500 for the year? What is the amount of the office-in-home deduction and the amount of the carryover (if any) of the unused deductions? (Assume that Nancy is not subject to the hobby loss restrictions.)

I:9-66 *Office in Home.* Darrell is a self-employed consultant who uses 15% of his home exclusively as an office. Darrell operates completely out of his home office and makes all of his appointments from the office as well as keeping his books and records in the office. Darrell's gross income from his consulting business is $60,000 in 2015. He incurs $6,000 of expenses that are related to his business, such as computer and office supplies. Below are expenses that relate to Darrell's residence for 2015:

Real estate taxes	$ 4,000
Mortgage interest	8,000
Insurance	1,000
Depreciation	4,000
Repairs and utilities	1,000
Total	$18,000

a. Which of the above expenditures (if any) are deductible? Are they *for* AGI or *from* AGI deductions?
b. How would your answer change if Darrell was an employee of a consulting company and maintained an office at home in order to take work home with him so he did not have to spend so many hours at his consulting company office?

I:9-67 *Deferred Compensation Plan Requirements.* Identify whether each of the following plan features is associated with a qualified pension plan, a qualified profit-sharing plan, an employee stock ownership plan, a nonqualifed plan, or none of these plans.
a. Annual employer contributions are not required, but substantial and recurring contributions must be made based on a predetermined formula.
b. Annual, systematic, and definite employer contributions are required without regard to profits but based on actuarial methods.
c. Forfeitures must be used to reduce contributions that would otherwise be made under the plan.
d. The plan may discriminate in favor of highly compensated individuals.
e. The trust is funded with the contribution of employer stock, which is subsequently distributed to employees.

I:9-68 *Taxability of Pension Payments.* Pat is a participant in a qualified pension plan. She retires on January 1, 2015, at age 63, and receives pension payments beginning in January 2015. Her pension payments, which will be received monthly for life, amount to $1,000 per month. Pat contributed $30,000 to the pension plan on a pre-tax (or tax-deferred) basis, and the number of anticipated payments based on Pat's age of 63 years is 260 months (see IRS table in Chapter I:3) from the date she starts receiving payments.
a. What gross income will Pat recognize in 2015 and each year thereafter?
b. How would your answer to Part a change if Pat made contributions to the plan on an after-tax basis?
c. If, in Part b, Pat dies in December 2016 after receiving pension payments for two full years, what tax consequences occur in the year of death?

I:9-69 *Restricted Property.* In 2015, Bear Corporation transfers 100 shares of its stock to its employee Patrick. The stock is valued at $10 per share on the issue date. The stock is subject to the following restrictions:

- Patrick cannot transfer the stock by sale or other disposition (except in the event of death) for a five-year period.
- The stock must be forfeited to Bear Corporation if Patrick voluntarily terminates his employment with the company within a five-year period.

In the year 2020, the Bear stock is worth $100 per share when the restrictions expire.
a. Assuming that no Sec. 83(b) election is made, what are the tax consequences to Patrick and Bear Corporation in 2015?
b. What are the tax consequences to Patrick and Bear Corporation if Patrick makes a valid Sec. 83(b) election in 2015?
c. What are the tax consequences to Patrick and Bear Corporation if Patrick forfeits the stock back to the company in 2016 when the stock is worth $20 per share if an election was made under Sec. 83(b)? What would happen if no Sec. 83(b) election were made?
d. What are the tax consequences to Patrick and Bear Corporation upon the lapse of the restrictions in the year 2020 if an election has been made under Sec. 83(b)? What would the results be if no Sec. 83(b) election were made?
e. What are the tax consequences to Patrick and Bear Corporation if Patrick sells the Bear stock in the year 2021 for $120 per share if a Sec. 83(b) election is made? if no Sec. 83(b) election is made?

I:9-70 *IRAs.* On February 15, 2016, Jamal, who is single and age 30, establishes a traditional IRA and contributes $5,500 to the account. Jamal's adjusted gross income is $67,000 in 2015 and $57,000 in 2016. Jamal is an active participant in an employer-sponsored retirement plan.
a. What amount of the contribution is deductible? In what year is it deductible?
b. How is the deduction (if any) reported (i.e., *for* AGI or *from* AGI)?
c. How would your answer to Part a change, if at all, if Jamal were not an active participant in an employer-sponsored retirement plan?
d. How would your answer to Part a change if Jamal were married and files a joint return with his spouse, who has no earned income? (Assume their combined AGI is $85,000.)

I:9-71 *IRAs.* Phil, age 30, is married and files a joint return with his spouse. On February 15, 2016, Phil establishes a traditional IRA for himself and a spousal IRA for his spouse with a $11,000 contribution, $5,500 for himself and $5,500 for his wife. Phil's spouse earned $1,000 in 2015 from a part-time job, and their combined AGI is $75,000. Neither Phil nor his spouse is an active participant in an employer-sponsored retirement plan.

a. What amount of the contribution is deductible?
b. To what year does the contribution apply? (Assume that an election is made to treat Phil's spouse as having no compensation.)
c. Is the deduction reported as *for* AGI or *from* AGI?
d. How would your answer to Part a change, if at all, if Phil and his spouse were active participants in an employer-sponsored retirement plan?
e. If a portion of the contribution is nondeductible in Part d, is it possible for Phil to make a deductible and a nondeductible contribution in the same year? Explain.
f. How would your answer to Part a change if Phil and his spouse's combined AGI were $125,000 in 2015 and Phil was an active participant in an employer-sponsored retirement plan?

I:9-72 *Roth IRA.* Chatham Mae is single, age 35, and wants to make a contribution to an IRA for the year ended December 31, 2015. She is an active participant in a qualified retirement plan sponsored by her employer. Her AGI for 2015 is $122,000 before considering any IRA contribution.

a. What type of IRA, if any, is Chatham Mae eligible to make a contribution to for 2015? If she is eligible to contribute to an IRA, what is the maximum amount that she can contribute to the IRA?
b. Assume Chatham Mae contributes a total of $12,000 over six years to a Roth IRA. In 2021, she withdraws $15,000 to pay off her car loan. Her financial advisor suggested she withdraw the money from the IRA for two major reasons: (1) to eliminate her debt and (2) no tax would be due on distributions from a Roth IRA after five years. Chatham Mae wants to verify the accuracy of her advisor's advice. What would be the tax consequences of this withdrawal? Alternatively, what if Chatham Mae withdrew the $15,000 to purchase a house (she is a first-time homebuyer)?
c. Alternatively to Part b above, assume Chatham Mae has a traditional deductible IRA that has a balance of $50,000. She has been able to deduct all of her contributions to the IRA in prior years. Her financial advisor has recommended that she rollover the funds from her traditional IRA to a Roth IRA in 2015. What are the tax consequences of this rollover in 2015?

I:9-73 *Coverdell Education Savings Accounts.* Jack and Katie have five grandchildren, ages 19, 16, 15, 12, and 10. They have established Coverdell Education Savings Accounts (CESA) for each of the grandchildren and would like to contribute the maximum amount allowable to each CESA for the 2015 taxable year. Jack and Katie's AGI for 2015 is $196,000.

a. How much can Jack and Katie contribute to each grandchild's CESA in 2015?
b. Assume that the 19-year-old granddaughter is a freshman in college and makes a withdrawal of $7,000 from her CESA during the year 2015. Her college expenses for 2015 were as follows:

Tuition	$1,500
Room and board	2,500
Books and supplies	500

The extra amount withdrawn was used as a down payment on a car that the granddaughter purchased during the year. She needed the car in order to drive to school rather than having to either ride the bus or ride with a friend. What are the tax consequences of the $7,000 distribution to the granddaughter?

I:9-74 *H.R. 10 Plans.* Paula is a self-employed doctor and is considering whether to establish a defined contribution H.R. 10 plan. Paula's only employee is a full-time nurse who has been employed by Paula for seven years. Paula's net earnings from self-employment (before the H.R. 10 plan contribution but after the deduction for one-half of self-employment taxes paid) is expected to be $100,000 during the current year and in future years.

a. If the H.R. 10 plan is established, what is the maximum amount Paula can contribute for the nurse's benefit?
b. What is the maximum amount Paula can contribute for herself? Is the amount reported as a *for* AGI or *from* AGI deduction?

c. Is Paula's nurse required to be included in the plan?
d. What are the tax consequences if Paula makes a premature withdrawal from the plan before reaching age 59½?

I:9-75 *Stock Options.* Bell Corporation grants an incentive stock option to Peggy, an employee, on January 1, 2015, when the option price and FMV of the Bell stock is $80. The option entitles Peggy to buy 10 shares of Bell stock. Peggy exercises the option and acquires the stock on April 1, 2017, when the stock's FMV is $100. Peggy, while still employed by the Bell Corporation, sells the stock on May 1, 2019, for $120 per share.
a. What are the tax consequences to Peggy and Bell Corporation on the following dates: January 1, 2015; April 1, 2017; and May 1, 2019? (Assume all incentive stock option qualification requirements are met.)
b. How would your answer to Part a change if Peggy instead sold the Bell stock for $130 per share on May 1, 2017?

I:9-76 *Stock Options.* Bender Corporation grants a nonqualified stock option to Penny, an employee, on January 1, 2015, that entitled Penny to acquire 1,000 shares of Bender stock at $80 per share. On this date, the stock has a $100 FMV and the option has a readily ascertainable FMV. Penny exercises the option on January 1, 2016 (when the FMV of the stock is $150), and acquires 1,000 shares of the stock for $80 per share. Penny later sells the Bender stock on January 1, 2018, for $200 per share.
a. What are the tax consequences to Penny and Bender Corporation on the following dates: January 1, 2015; January 1, 2016; and January 1, 2018?
b. How would your answer to Part a change if the Bender stock were instead closely-held and the option had no readily ascertainable FMV?

COMPREHENSIVE PROBLEM

I:9-77 Dan and Cheryl are married, file a joint return, and have no children. Dan, age 45, is a pharmaceutical salesman and Cheryl, age 42, is a nurse at a local hospital. Dan's SSN is 400-20-1000 and Cheryl's SSN is 200-40-8000 and they reside at 2033 Palmetto Drive, Nashville, TN 28034. Dan is paid according to commissions from sales; however, his compensation is subject to withholding of income and payroll taxes. He also maintains an office in his home as the pharmaceutical company does not have an office in Nashville and when he is not traveling, Dan operates his business from his home office. During 2015, Dan earned total compensation from his job of $125,000, on which $20,000 of federal income taxes were withheld, $7,347 of OASDI, and $1,813 of Medicare taxes. State income taxes of $4,000 were withheld. Cheryl earned a salary during 2015 of $45,400, on which federal taxes withheld were $5,000, OASDI of $2,815, and Medicare taxes of $658.

During 2015, Dan and Cheryl had interest income from corporate bonds and bank accounts of $1,450 and qualified dividends from stocks of $5,950. Dan also actively trades stocks and had the following results for 2015:

LTCG	$4,900
LTCL	(3,200)
STCG	0
STCL	(7,800)

He had no capital loss carryovers from previous years.

Dan does a considerable amount of travel in connection with his job. He uses his own car and is reimbursed $0.30 per business mile. During 2015, Dan drove his car a total of 38,000 miles, of which 32,000 were business related. He also had business-related parking fees and tolls during the year of $280. Dan uses the mileage method for deducting auto expenses. Dan also had the following travel expenses while away from home during the year:

Hotel	$4,200
Meals	820
Entertainment of customers	1,080
Tips	100
Laundry and cleaning	150
Total	$6,350

Dan was reimbursed for the travel expenses by his employer, pursuant to an accountable plan, in the amount of $5,080.

Dan's expenses in connection with his office in the home were as follows:

Office supplies	$ 290
Telephone (separate line)	1,100
Utilities (entire house)	3,400
Homeowners insurance	600
Interest and property taxes (see below for totals)	
Repairs and maintenance (entire house)	800

Dan's office is 300 square feet and the total square footage of the house is 3,000 square feet. Dan and Cheryl purchased the house on June 12, 2000, for $280,000, of which $40,000 is attributable to the land.

Cheryl incurred several expenses in connection with her nursing job. She paid $450 in professional dues, $200 in professional journals, and $350 for uniforms.

Dan and Cheryl had the following other expenditures during the year:

Health insurance premiums (after-tax)	$ 4,400
Doctor bills	470
Real estate taxes on home	2,200
Personal property taxes	400
Mortgage interest	15,600
Charitable contributions—cash	9,000
Charitable contributions—GE stock owned for 5 years:	
FMV	$8,000
Adjusted basis	2,000
Tax preparation fees	750

Compute Dan and Cheryl's income tax liability for 2015. Disregard the alternative minimum tax.

TAX STRATEGY PROBLEM

I:9-78 Paul Price is the president and majority stockholder of Lightmore Communications, Inc. Lightmore is a C corporation and has been extremely successful over the past 20 years. Paul travels extensively in connection with the business to meet with existing and prospective clients. Paul's wife, Laura, would be helpful to Paul in his business entertaining if she could accompany him on many of his business trips and, furthermore, she was unable to go on these trips in the past because of their children at home. Their youngest child is now in college, and Laura's duties at home have diminished. During the current year, Laura has made a number of trips with Paul, but after conferring with the company's tax advisor, had been informed that Laura's expenses would not be deductible for tax purposes. The tax advisor suggested the possibility of putting Laura on the Lightmore payroll as an employee.

a. Would Laura's travel expenses be deductible if she was an employee of the corporation?

b. What other benefits would be available to Laura if she was an employee of the corporation?

c. Are there any detriments to putting Laura on the payroll?

TAX FORM/RETURN PREPARATION PROBLEMS

I:9-79 In 2014, Micah Johnson (SSN 000-22-1111) is employed as a manager and incurs the following unreimbursed employee business expenses:

Airplane and taxi fares	$ 4,000
Lodging away from home	5,000
Meals while away from home	1,000
Automobile expenses (related to 100% of the use of his personal automobile):	
Gasoline and oil	8,500
Repairs	1,000
Insurance	900
Depreciation	1,775
Parking and tolls (includes only business use)	100
Total	$22,275

Johnson receives a $7,800 reimbursement for the travel expenses. He did not receive any reimbursement for the auto expenses. He uses his personal automobile 80% for business use and placed his current automobile in service on October 1, 2010. Total business miles driven during the year (evenly throughout the year) amount to 26,400, his commuting miles in 2014 amount to 2,000 (average daily roundtrip of 7 miles), and other personal miles amount to 4,600 miles. Johnson's AGI is $60,000, and he has no other miscellaneous itemized deductions.

a. Calculate Johnson's expense deduction using the 2014 Form 2106 (Employee Business Expenses) based on actual automobile expenses and other employee business expenses.

b. Calculate Johnson's expense deduction for 2014 using the standard mileage rate method and other employee business expenses. (Assume that none of the restrictions on the use of the standard mileage rate method are applicable.)

I:9-80 George Large (SSN 000-11-1111) and his wife Marge Large (SSN 000-22-2222) live at 2000 Lakeview Drive, Cleveland, OH 49001 and want you to prepare their 2014 income tax return based on the information below:

George Large worked as a salesman for Toyboat, Inc. He received a salary of $80,000 ($8,500 of federal income taxes withheld and $1,800 of state income taxes withheld) plus an expense reimbursement from Toyboat of $5,000 to cover his employee business expenses. George must make an adequate accounting to his employer and return any excess reimbursement, none of the reimbursement was related to the meals and entertainment. Additionally, Toyboat provides George with medical insurance worth $7,200 per year. George drove his car a total of 24,000 miles during the year, and he placed the car in service on June 1, 2012. His log indicates that 18,000 miles were for sales calls to customers at the customers' offices and the remainder was personal mileage. George uses the standard mileage rate method. Assume his business miles were driven evenly during the year. George is a college basketball fan. He purchased two season tickets for a total of $4,000. He takes a customer to every game, and they discuss some business before, during, and after the games. George also takes clients to business lunches. His log indicates that he spent $1,500 on these business meals. George also took a five-day trip to the Toyboat headquarters in Musty, Ohio. He was so well-prepared that he finished his business in three days, so he spent the other two days sightseeing. He had the following expenses during each of the five days of his trip:

Airfare	$200
Lodging	$85/day
Meals	$50/day
Taxicabs	$20/day

Marge Large is self-employed. She repairs rubber toy boats in the basement of their home, which is 25% of the house's square footage. The business code is 811490. She had the following income and expenses:

Income from rubber toy boat repairs	$15,000
Cost of supplies	5,000
Contract labor	3,500
Telephone (business)	500

The Large's home cost a total of $150,000, of which the cost of the land was $20,000. The FMV of the house is $225,000. The house is depreciable over a 39-year recovery period. The Larges incurred the following total other expenses:

Utility bills for the house	$2,000
Real estate taxes	2,500
Mortgage interest	4,500
Cash charitable contributions	3,500

Prepare Form 1040, Schedules A, C, and SE for Form 1040, and Forms 2106 and 8829 for the 2014 year. (Assume no depreciation for this problem and that no estimated taxes were paid by the Larges.)

CASE STUDY PROBLEMS

I:9-81 Ajax Corporation is a young high-growth company engaged in the manufacture and distribution of automotive parts. Its common stock has doubled in value since the company was listed on the NASDAQ exchange about two years ago. Ajax currently has a high debt/equity ratio due to the issuance of debt to finance its capital expansion needs. Despite rapid growth in assets and profitability, Ajax has severe cash flow problems and a poor working capital ratio. The company urgently needs to attract new executives to the organization and to provide financial incentives to existing top management because of recent turnover and high growth. Approximately 55% of the common stock is owned by Andrew Ajax, who is the CEO, and his immediate family. None of the other officers own stock in the company.

You are a tax consultant for the company who has been asked to prepare suggestions after reviewing the compensation system. Your discussions with several top management individuals reveal the following aspects of corporate strategy and philosophy:

- The company needs to expand the equity capital base because of its concern for the high risk caused by large amounts of debt.
- Improvement in cash flow and liquidity would enhance its stock price and enable the company to continue its high growth rate.
- Top management feels that employee loyalty and productivity would be improved if all employees owned some stock in the company. The company currently offers a qualified pension plan to its employees and executives that provides only minimal pension benefits. No other deferred compensation or bonus arrangements are currently being offered.
- Andrew Ajax feels that the top management group should own a substantial amount of Ajax stock to ensure that the interests of management correspond with the shareholder interests (i.e., the maximization of shareholder wealth).

The following four types of executive compensation arrangements have been discussed:

- Sec. 401(k) and ESOP plans for employees.
- Encourage all employees and executives to independently fund their retirement needs beyond any Social Security benefits by establishing IRA plans.
- Provide restricted property arrangements (using Ajax stock) to attract new top level executives and to retain existing executives.
- Offer nonqualified or incentive stock options to existing and new executives.

Required: Prepare a client memo that recommends revisions to Ajax Corporation's existing compensation system for both its employee and executive groups. Your recommendations should discuss the pros and cons of different deferred compensation arrangements and should consider both tax and nontax factors.

I:9-82 Steve is part owner and manager of a small manufacturing company that makes keypads for alarm systems. The keypads are sold to several different alarm companies throughout the country. Steve must travel to several cities each year to meet with current customers and to attract new business. When you meet with Steve to obtain information to prepare his current year tax return, he tells you that he has spent about $5,000 during the current year on airfare and taking his customers out to dinner to discuss business. Because he took most of his trips in the summer and fall, and it is now April of the following year, Steve cannot remember the exact time and places of the business dinners and did not retain any receipts for the cash used to pay the bills. However, he remembers the names of the customers he went to see, the business topics that were discussed, and the restaurants where he had his meals. As Steve's tax consultant, what is your responsibility regarding the treatment of the travel and entertainment expenses under the mandates of the AICPA's *Statements on Standards for Tax Services*? Prepare a client letter explaining to Steve the requirements under Sec. 274(d) for sufficient substantiation of travel and entertainment expenses. (See the *Statements on Standards for Tax Services* section in Chapter I:15 for a discussion of these issues and Appendix E.)

TAX RESEARCH PROBLEM

I:9-83 Charley Long is a truck driver, the 18-wheeler variety. He works for Fishy Co., a seafood company in Mobile, Alabama, and drives a company truck. Charley's job entails leaving Mobile at 4:00 PM each day (five days per week) and delivering fresh fish to restaurants and wholesale fish distributors in Mississippi and Louisiana. His last stop, in Lafayette, Louisiana, is generally around 12:00 midnight. It normally takes Charley about five hours to get back to Mobile.

Charley's routine is varied. Sometimes, he drives straight back to Mobile from Lafayette. On other occasions, he will pull off at a truck stop and sleep in his cab before returning to Mobile. His cab is equipped with sleeping facilities, although small and sparse. Finally, on other occasions, Charley will spend the night in a motel along the road. The Fishy Co. has no preference as to what Charley does and has given him permission to either drive back or stay overnight. However, the company does not reimburse him for his food and lodging expenses.

When Charley drives straight back to Mobile, Charley will eat one meal. When he sleeps overnight (either in his cab or in a motel), he will eat two meals, a late dinner and breakfast. He spends an average of $10.00 for dinner and $6.00 for breakfast. The cost of his motel averages $70.00 per night. When Charley sleeps in the cab, he generally sleeps about 4–5 hours and then drives on to Mobile.

During the current year, Charley incurred the following expenses:

Meals incurred on nonstop trips	$1,000
Meals incurred when: slept in cab	800
slept in motel	600
Lodging	2,800
Total	$5,200

The IRS has disallowed all of the above expenses on the grounds that they are not bona fide travel expenses but personal expenses. Would you advise Charley to contest this issue?

A partial list of research sources is:

- Sec. 162(a)(2) and Reg. Sec. 1.162-2(a)
- *U.S. v. Correll*, 389 U.S. 299 (1967)
- *Williams v. Patterson*, 286 F.2d 333 (5th Cir. 1961)
- Rev. Rul. 75-168, 1975-1 C.B. 58 and Rev. Rul. 75-432, 1975-2 C.B. 60

CHAPTER 10

DEPRECIATION, COST RECOVERY, AMORTIZATION, AND DEPLETION

LEARNING OBJECTIVES

After studying this chapter, you should be able to

1. Explain the general concepts of tax depreciation and cost recovery
2. Calculate amortization for intangible assets and distinguish between amortizable and non-amortizable assets
3. Apply cost and percentage depletion methods and summarize the treatment for intangible drilling costs
4. Identify tax planning considerations for depreciation
5. Identify compliance and procedural considerations for depreciation

CHAPTER OUTLINE

The income tax law allows taxpayers to deduct a reasonable allowance for the exhaustion, wear and tear, and obsolescence of property used in a trade or business or held for the production of income.[1] Such deductions enable taxpayers to recover the cost of an asset under the "return of capital" doctrine. Depreciation, therefore, is the systematic allocation of the cost of an asset over its estimated economic life. The term *depreciation* relates to deductions for most tangible property; *amortization* relates to deductions for intangible property; and *depletion* relates to deductions for natural resources (oil and gas, coal, etc.) While the concepts of depreciation, amortization, and depletion are similar to those in financial accounting, the income tax rules are unique. This chapter discusses the income tax rules relating to depreciation, amortization, and depletion.

DEPRECIATION AND COST RECOVERY

OBJECTIVE 1

Explain the general concepts of tax depreciation and cost recovery

GENERAL CONSIDERATIONS

Taxpayers must use specific depreciation methods depending on *when* an asset is placed in service. Three separate depreciation and cost recovery systems are currently in place. These three distinct systems are the result of tax law changes in 1981 and 1986. The systems that taxpayers must use are as follows:

- Property placed in service after December 31, 1986. Taxpayers must use the Modified Accelerated Cost Recovery System (MACRS) as provided in Sec. 168.
- Property placed in service after December 31, 1980 and before January 1, 1987. Taxpayers must use the Accelerated Cost Recovery System (ACRS) as provided in Sec. 168.
- Property placed in service prior to 1981. Taxpayers must use the rules contained in Sec. 167. These rules basically follow financial accounting principles.

TYPICAL MISCONCEPTION

It is easy to forget that the depreciation or cost-recovery system that applies to any one asset is the system that was in effect when the property was placed in service. Property acquired in 1986 is not affected by the MACRS rules that became effective in 1987.

In this chapter, we emphasize the MACRS rules because most assets placed in service before 1987 are now fully depreciated.

The terms *depreciation* and *cost recovery* are used interchangeably in this text. The rules in Sec. 167 (or pre-ACRS) and the MACRS rules under Sec. 168 both refer to depreciation. However, the deduction under ACRS is referred to as cost recovery. In 1981, Congress initiated the original ACRS system to achieve a number of objectives, including a stimulus for private investment, improving business productivity, simplifying taxpayer compliance, and facilitating IRS administration of the tax law. Therefore, less importance was placed on the financial accounting concept of matching costs and revenues, which is the primary theory that governed the Sec. 167 depreciation rules. Congress' primary objective in 1981 was to allow businesses and investors to recover the cost of capitalized expenditures over a period of time that is substantially shorter than the property's economic useful life. Thus, the term *cost recovery* rather than *depreciation* was used under the ACRS system. The post-1986 MACRS rules more closely follow the concept of economic useful life and, therefore, the MACRS rules refer to depreciation rather than cost recovery.

HISTORICAL NOTE

Before 1954, except for the limited use of a declining-balance method, taxpayers were required to use the straight-line method.

Common Rules of All Systems. Regardless of the particular system of depreciation required (i.e., MACRS, ACRS, etc.), certain rules are common to all systems of depreciation. These common rules are discussed below.

- Depreciation may be claimed only on property used in a trade or business or for the production of income. Thus, personal-use assets, such as a personal-use automobile or the taxpayer's personal residence, are not depreciable.
- No depreciation is permitted for land or other assets that have an indefinite life. Assets such as works of art are generally not depreciable.

ADDITIONAL COMMENT

Property is considered to be "placed in service" when it is in a condition or state of readiness and is available for a specifically assigned function. This can be important in attempting to determine the first year that a depreciation deduction is available.

[1] Sec. 167(a).

ADDITIONAL COMMENT

A case held that a professional musician could depreciate a nineteenth-century violin bow. The IRS had argued the bow had an indeterminate life, but because the taxpayer played the violin, there was "wear and tear" on the bow and depreciation was allowed. *Simon v. Comm.*, 95-2 USTC ¶50,552 (CA-2, 1995).

- First-year depreciation is permitted only in the year the asset is placed in service. For example, a taxpayer may purchase a depreciable asset in December 2014 but not place it in service until January 2015. In this case, depreciation is not allowed until 2015.
- Regardless of the depreciation system, consistency is required. Taxpayers must consistently use the method selected in the year the asset was placed in service unless a change of accounting method is requested from the IRS.
- The basis of property being depreciated must be reduced by the amount of depreciation that is allowable for each taxable year. An important aspect of depreciation is determining the amount of depreciation that is *allowed* and *allowable*. The depreciation allowed is the actual depreciation claimed by the taxpayer for a particular taxable year. Allowable depreciation is the amount of depreciation to be claimed under the tax law by using the slowest possible method (i.e., straight-line using the longest permissible recovery period). If a taxpayer does not take any depreciation during a particular year, the basis of property must be reduced by the amount of depreciation that should have been taken during the year (i.e., the allowable depreciation).

EXAMPLE I:10-1 ► Maria acquires and places in service a machine (7-year property) for $50,000 to be used in her business. She elects straight-line depreciation under MACRS. Maria properly takes depreciation in the first two years in the amount of $10,714 ($3,571 in Year 1 and $7,143 in Year 2, assuming the half-year convention). However, because of a net operating loss in Year 3, Maria did not take any depreciation on the tax return. The allowable depreciation in Year 3 was $7,143. Even though Maria did not claim the $7,143 in Year 3, the basis of the machine must still be reduced by that amount. Thus, at the end of Year 3, the basis of the machine would be $32,143 ($50,000 minus the allowable accumulated depreciation of $17,857). Obviously, Maria should amend her tax return for Year 3 and deduct the allowable depreciation. This would increase her net operating loss for Year 3, which either can be carried back two years or forward 20 years. ◄

REAL-WORLD EXAMPLE

Harrah's Club in Reno, Nevada, restores antique autos and displays them. The restoration costs cannot be depreciated because the autos have an indefinite life as museum pieces. *Harrah's Club v. U.S.*, 43 AFTR 2d 79-745, 81-2 USTC ¶9677 (Ct. Cls., 1981).

Types of Property. For both property law and income tax purposes, there are two basic types of property, tangible and intangible. **Tangible property** refers to property that has physical substance, such as land, buildings, natural resources, equipment, etc. **Intangible property** refers to property that does not have physical substance, such as goodwill, patents, and stocks and bonds. The cost of tangible property (other than land, of course) is systematically written off through depreciation or depletion. Natural resources, such as oil and gas reserves, are recovered through depletion. Intangible property is written off through amortization.

Tangible property is further classified as either real property or personal property. **Real property** (often referred to as real estate or realty) is defined as land or any structure permanently attached to the land, such as buildings. **Personal property** is any tangible property that is not real property, and includes items such as equipment, vehicles, furniture, etc. It is important to distinguish between personal property and personal-use property. **Personal-use property** is any property, tangible or intangible, real or personal, that is used by the taxpayer for his own personal use rather than in a trade or business or for the production of income.

ADDITIONAL COMMENT

The IRS issued a private letter ruling that required an airline to capitalize engine overhauls rather than expensing such amounts in the current year. The IRS position requires capitalization because the overhauls involve replacement or reconditioning of a large portion of the engine's parts. This ruling has been severely criticized by the airlines industry, saying that the decision could negatively impact passenger safety.

Capitalization Versus Expense. A frequent dilemma for taxpayers is whether an expenditure should be capitalized and expensed through depreciation, or expensed entirely in the current year. As discussed in Chapter I:6, if an expenditure either improves the efficiency of an asset or extends the life of an asset beyond the end of the year, the expenditure should generally be capitalized. However, most taxpayers have established materiality limits to justify the expensing of small expenditures that technically should be considered capital expenditures. Since capitalization-expense decisions are frequently subjective in nature, disputes between the IRS and taxpayers are common.

Conversion of Personal-Use Property. If personal-use property is either converted to business-use or held for the production of income (e.g., a principal residence converted to a rental house), the property's basis for depreciation purposes is the lesser of its adjusted basis or its fair market value (FMV) determined as of the conversion date.[2]

[2] Reg. Sec. 1.168(i)-4(b)(1).

This lower of cost or market rule prevents taxpayers from depreciating the portion of the cost that represents a nondeductible loss on a personal-use asset. Chapter I:5 discusses the disposition of personal-use property.

EXAMPLE I:10-2 ▶ Marty acquired a principal residence for $115,000 in 2006. In 2015, he converts the property to rental use because he is unable to sell the house due to a depressed local real estate market. The property's FMV is only $100,000 when it is converted to rental status in 2015. The $15,000 ($115,000 − $100,000) decline in value represents a nondeductible personal loss and is not depreciable. The depreciable basis of the rental property is $100,000 (minus the portion of the property's FMV that represents land, which is not depreciable). ◀

DEPRECIATION METHODS

As mentioned previously, the depreciation method required for income tax purposes depends on the date the asset was placed in service. Assets placed in service prior to 1987 must use the old depreciation methods that were in effect during those years.[3] Under current law, for assets placed in service after 1986, the MACRS system of depreciation is required for most assets. MACRS is different from depreciation methods used for financial accounting purposes in several ways, including the following:

- MACRS does not consider salvage value in the computation of the depreciation amount.
- MACRS uses specific asset classes. Both tangible personal property and real property must be placed into specific asset classes, based on the type of property. Asset classes refer to the number of years over which the asset must be depreciated, such as 5-year property, 7-year property, etc.
- MACRS uses fewer depreciation methods, and the methods are built into the MACRS tables. Both accelerated and straight-line methods are used in MACRS, but accelerated methods are not permissible for real property. The MACRS tables are summarized in Appendix C.
- MACRS uses assumptions about when assets are either placed in service or disposed of rather than using actual dates. The applicable assumption is called a *convention*. The **half-year convention** is generally required for all tangible personal property. It assumes that all asset acquisitions or dispositions are made at the midpoint of the tax year. A special convention that may apply to tangible personal property is the **mid-quarter convention**, discussed later in this chapter. For real estate, the **mid-month convention** is used. It assumes that all asset acquisitions or dispositions are made at the midpoint of the month in which the transaction occurs.

EXAMPLE I:10-3 ▶ Golden Corporation, a calendar year taxpayer, purchases a business-use machine on March 10, 2015. For depreciation purposes, under the half-year convention, the machine is treated as if it were placed in service on July 1, 2015, and one-half year's depreciation is allowable in 2015. The half-year convention assumes all asset acquisitions and dispositions occur at the midpoint of the tax year. ◀

EXAMPLE I:10-4 ▶ Assume that Golden Corporation, in Example I:10-3 above, uses the machine for several years and decides to sell the machine on October 30, 2017. To compute the depreciation deduction for the year 2017, under the half-year convention, Golden is permitted one-half year's depreciation. This one-half year's depreciation is required even though the actual sale occurred on October 30. ◀

EXAMPLE I:10-5 ▶ Silver, Inc., a calendar year taxpayer, purchases a business-use building on March 5, 2015. For depreciation purposes, under the mid-month convention, the building is treated as if it were placed in service on March 15, 2015, and 9½ months of depreciation is allowable in 2015 (one-half of a month for March plus nine full months). ◀

[3] For assets placed into service between 1981 and 1986, taxpayers were required to use the ACRS method; for assets placed into service before 1981, a pre-ACRS method was required. Pre-ACRS methods more closely resemble depreciation methods used for financial statement purposes.

CALCULATION OF DEPRECIATION

The annual depreciation deduction involves a number of variables. Below is a discussion of these variables in connection with the two principal types of depreciable property: tangible personal property and real property.

Tangible Personal Property: Classification and Recovery Rates. Tangible personal property, such as equipment, furniture, computers, etc., is depreciable under MACRS if used in a trade or business or held for the production of income. Each piece of tangible personal property acquired must be classified into one of six asset classes.[4] Depreciation is computed using the percentages contained in Table 1 in Appendix C.

The MACRS recovery periods that apply to tangible personal property placed in service after December 31, 1986 are as follows:[5]

ADDITIONAL COMMENT

Most depreciable personal property is classified as 7-year property under MACRS.

- 3-Year — Property with a class life of 4 years or less. This category includes property such as tractor units, race horses over 12 years old, and special tools.
- 5-Year — Property with a class life of more than 4 years but less than 10 years. This category includes property such as automobiles, light and heavy-duty general purpose trucks, computers, and research and experimental (R&E) equipment.
- 7-Year — Property with a class life of 10 years or more but less than 16 years. This category includes property such as office furniture and equipment, horses, single-purpose agricultural or horticultural structures, and property with no class life and not classified elsewhere. Most types of machinery are included in this class.
- 10-Year — Property with a class life of more than 16 years, but less than 20 years. This category includes property such as barges, vessels, and petroleum and food processing equipment.
- 15-Year — Property with a class life of more than 20 years, but less than 25 years. This category includes property such as billboards, service station buildings, and land improvements.
- 20-Year — Property with a class life of 25 or more years, including property such as utilities and sewers.

KEY POINT

Notice that the recovery period for tax purposes is not necessarily dependent upon the asset's actual economic life. A property's class life and its actual economic life may be different.

KEY POINT

Remember that salvage value is not taken into consideration under the MACRS system.

Depreciation rates for the 3-year, 5-year, and 7-year recovery classes are provided in Table I:10-1. (See Table 1 in Appendix C for depreciation rates for all classes of property.) The rates are based on the 200% DB method switching to straight-line when it yields a larger amount. A half-year convention is used in the year of acquisition and zero salvage value is assumed. To properly apply the half-year convention when property is disposed of in a year before the final table year, the amount calculated from the table must be multiplied by one-half.

EXAMPLE I:10-6 ▶ In March 2015, Mary acquires and places in service a business machine which costs $20,000 and has a 7-year recovery period under MACRS rules. Assuming no Sec. 179 expensing or bonus depreciation (discussed later), the depreciation deduction for 2015 is $2,858 ($20,000 × 0.1429). MACRS depreciation deduction for the year placed in service also can be computed by applying the accelerated depreciation rate (using the half-year convention) to the basis of the assets. Thus the depreciation deduction for 2015 is $2,857 ($20,000 ÷ 7 years × 200% DB × 0.50 year). Minor differences between the two calculations are due to rounding. ◀

Certain types of property are *excluded* from MACRS depreciation, including:[6]

- Property depreciated under a method not expressed in terms of years, such as the units of production method, where the taxpayer elects to not depreciate the property under MACRS;
- Intangible assets, such as goodwill or copyrights;
- Films, videotapes, or sound recordings.

[4] To determine the class life of assets, see Rev. Proc. 87-56, modified by Rev. Proc. 88-22, which sets forth the class life of property for depreciation purposes.

[5] Sec. 168(e)(1).

[6] Sec. 168(f).

SELF-STUDY QUESTION

In Table I:10-1, how has the 20% first-year cost recovery rate for five-year property been calculated?

ANSWER

The 20% rate is calculated by multiplying the double declining-balance rate of 40% by the half-year convention of depreciation.

▼ TABLE I:10-1 (a Portion of Table 1 in Appendix C)
MACRS Percentage Rates for Tangible Personal Property (Using Half-Year Convention)

Recovery Year	Recovery Period 3-Year	5-Year	7-Year
1	33.33	20.00	14.29
2	44.45	32.00	24.49
3	14.81	19.20	17.49
4	7.41	11.52	12.49
5	—	11.52	8.93
6	—	5.76	8.92
7	—	—	8.93
8	—	—	4.46

Source: Table 1 of Rev. Proc. 87-57, 1987-2 C.B. 674.

LEGISLATIVE UPDATE

The Small Business Jobs Act of 2010 increased the election to $500,000 for 2010 and 2011. The American Taxpayer Relief Act of 2012 extended the election of $500,000 to 2013 and retroactively to 2012 (the original limit for 2012 was $139,000). The Tax Increase Prevention Act of 2014 extended the election of $500,000 to 2014. Unless Congress acts to extend the higher election amounts of recent years, the maximum amount returns to $25,000 in 2015.

Section 179 Expensing Election. In lieu of depreciating the cost of new or used tangible personal business property under the regular MACRS methods discussed above, taxpayers may elect to expense up to $25,000 (in 2015) of the acquisition cost as an ordinary deduction in the year the property is placed in service.[7] The immediate expensing election is not generally applicable to real estate.[8] The election is made on an annual basis, and the taxpayer must select the assets to which the deduction applies. MACRS rules apply to any amount of an asset's cost not expensed under Sec. 179 or claimed as bonus depreciation (for years bonus is in effect).

The maximum Sec. 179 expense amount (ceiling) has been increasing over the past several years, as shown in Table I:10-2. However, unless Congress acts to extend these higher amounts, the Sec. 179 expense amount is $25,000 for 2015.

EXAMPLE I:10-7 ▶ In July 2015, Tanya acquires and places in service equipment costing $67,000 with a 7-year MACRS recovery period for 100% business use in her sole proprietorship. Tanya elects to

▼ TABLE I:10-2
Section 179 Expense Amounts

Tax Year Beginning In	Maximum Sec. 179 Expense (Ceiling)
2015	$ 25,000
2010–2014	500,000
2008–2009	250,000
2007	125,000
2006	108,000
2005	105,000

ADDITIONAL COMMENT

In the case of a partnership, the partnership and each partner are individually subject to the annual Sec. 179 limitation.

7 Sec. 179. The Tax Increase Prevention and Reconciliation Act of 2005 extended the $100,000 base amount to 2008 and 2009 (inflation adjusted), and the Small Business and Work Opportunity Tax Act of 2007 extended it through 2010. The Economic Stimulus Act of 2008 increased the normal inflation-adjusted amount to $250,000 for 2008, the American Recovery and Reinvestment Act of 2009 extended the $250,000 into 2009. The Small Business Jobs Act of 2010 increased the amount to $500,000 for 2010 and 2011. The American Taxpayer Relief Act of 2012 extended the $500,000 amount to 2012 and 2013. The Tax Increase Prevention Act of 2014 extended the $500,000 amount to 2014.

8 The Small Business Jobs Act of 2010 allowed up to $250,000 of qualified real property to be immediately expensed in 2010 or 2011. For this provision, the qualified real property included: (1) qualified leasehold improvement property, (2) qualified restaurant property, and (3) qualified retail improvement property. The American Taxpayer Relief Act of 2012 extended this treatment to 2012 and 2013, and the Tax Increase Prevention Act of 2014 extended the treatment to 2014.

expense $25,000 of the cost under Sec. 179. Tanya's basis for MACRS depreciation is $42,000 ($67,000 − $25,000). Using the half-year convention (Table 1 of Appendix C), MACRS depreciation is $6,002 ($42,000 × 0.1429). Tanya's total 2015 depreciation is $31,002 ($25,000 + $6,002). ◀

LEGISLATIVE UPDATE

As noted, qualified property for Sec. 179 is generally tangible personal property. From 2002 to 2014, off-the-shelf computer software could be expensed under Sec. 179. This was software that was readily available for purchase by the general public, was subject to a nonexclusive license, and had not been substantially modified. Unless Congress acts to extend this treatment, this computer software will no longer be eligible to be expensed under Sec. 179 after 2014.

ADDITIONAL COMMENT

Married taxpayers who file separate tax returns are each entitled to a maximum of half the regular limitation under Sec. 179.

SELF-STUDY QUESTION

Are corporations entitled to the election to expense up to $25,000 under Sec. 179?

ANSWER

Yes, but larger corporations will not receive the benefit from it because the Sec. 179 deduction is reduced when the cost of qualified property exceeds $200,000.

The following limitations and special rules apply to the Sec. 179 election:

- The property must be purchased for use in an active trade or business (more than 50% business-use) as distinguished from property that is acquired for the production of income (e.g., personal property used in a rental activity held by an investor does not qualify).
- Qualified property is generally tangible personal property.
- The property cannot be acquired from a related party under Sec. 267 or by gift or inheritance.
- The Sec. 179 tax benefits are recaptured if the property is no longer predominantly used in a trade or business (e.g., the property is converted to personal use) at any time.[9] In the year of recapture, the taxpayer must include in gross income the amount previously expensed reduced by the amount of depreciation that would have been allowed for the period the property was held for business use.[10]
- If the total cost of qualified property placed into service during the year is more than $200,000 (in 2015), the $25,000 ceiling is reduced on a dollar-for-dollar basis by the excess amount. Thus, no deduction is permitted for the 2015 tax year if $225,000 or more of Sec. 179 property is placed in service. No carryovers of Sec. 179 depreciation under this provision are permitted. However, the portion of cost not expensed remains in the property's basis subject to MACRS depreciation.
- A second limitation on the total Sec. 179 deduction is that it cannot exceed the taxpayer's taxable income (before deducting the Sec. 179 expense) from the trade or business.[11] Any acquisition cost that cannot be deducted because of the limitation based on taxable income is carried forward for an unlimited number of years and is added to the other amounts eligible for the Sec. 179 deduction in the future year. Such carryover amount will be subject to the taxable income limitation in the carryover year.

EXAMPLE I:10-8 ▶ Pam owns an unincorporated manufacturing business. In 2015, she purchases and places in service $205,000 of qualifying equipment for use in her business. Pam's taxable income from the business (before deducting any Sec. 179 expense) is $17,000. The maximum Sec. 179 deduction of $25,000 is initially reduced by $5,000 ($205,000 − $200,000) because the total cost of qualified property placed in service during the year exceeds $200,000. Pam is allowed no carryover of the $5,000 reduced by this limitation. However, the $5,000 remains part of the equipment's basis subject to MACRS depreciation.

The remaining $20,000 ($25,000 − $5,000) Sec. 179 expense is further limited to business taxable income, so Pam's Sec. 179 deduction in 2015 will be $17,000. She may carry over $3,000 ($20,000 − $17,000) to 2016 as Sec. 179 depreciation in that year. Even though only $17,000 is deductible under Sec. 179, Pam must reduce the cost basis of the equipment by $20,000 to prevent double deduction of the Sec. 179 expense caused by the carryover. Thus, she will depreciate $185,000 ($205,000 − $20,000) using MACRS. ◀

Bonus Depreciation. In response to the terrorist attacks on September 11, 2001, Congress enacted special bonus depreciation for new qualified property placed in service after September 10, 2001 and before January 1, 2005. These special depreciation provisions were

[9] Sec. 179(d)(10).

[10] Reg. Sec. 1.179-1(e).

[11] Sec. 179(b)(3). Under Reg. Sec. 1.179-2(c)(6)(iv), employees are considered to be engaged in the active conduct of the trade or business from their employment. Thus, a small business person who is also an employee may include wages and salary derived from employment in determining taxable income for purposes of this limitation. Such amounts are considered derived from the conduct of a trade or business. For an individual, taxable income is also computed without regard to the deduction for one-half of self-employment taxes paid under Sec. 164(f) (see Chapter I:14).

effective in encouraging taxpayers to continue to invest in tangible personal property during that trying period of time. The original bonus depreciation provisions expired after December 31, 2004. However, the Economic Stimulus Act of 2008, the American Recovery and Reinvestment Act of 2009, and the Small Business Jobs Act of 2010 all reinstated 50% bonus depreciation placed in service in 2008, 2009, and 2010. Further, the Tax Relief Act of 2010 provided 100% bonus depreciation for qualified property placed in service after September 8, 2010 and before January 1, 2012. The act also extended the 50% bonus depreciation for 2012. The American Taxpayer Relief Act of 2012 provided 50% bonus depreciation for 2013. The Tax Increase Prevention Act of 2014 provided 50% bonus depreciation for 2014. Unless Congress once again acts to extend the provision, bonus depreciation will not be available after 2014.

LEGISLATIVE UPDATE

The American Taxpayer Relief Act of 2012 extended the 50% bonus depreciation that was available in 2012 to 2013. The Tax Increase Prevention Act of 2014 extended 50% bonus depreciation to 2014. Congress has not yet extended bonus depreciation for most property to 2015. However, some limited types of property (e.g., certain aircrafts) are still eligible for bonus depreciation in 2015.

While the percentage of bonus depreciation has varied across years, the specific rules discussed below are the same for the bonus depreciation property. Bonus depreciation is automatically deductible for both the regular income tax and the alternative minimum tax (AMT). Taxpayers must elect *out* of bonus depreciation if they do not wish to claim the deduction.

Qualified property (generally non-real estate) includes: (1) MACRS property with a recovery period of 20 years or less; (2) computer software (other than computer software that must be amortized under Sec. 197); or (3) qualified leasehold improvement property (see discussion of qualified leasehold improvement property later in this chapter in connection with real property). To qualify, the property must be new property and original use of the property must begin with the taxpayer. Used property does not qualify for bonus depreciation.

When the bonus depreciation rate is less than 100%, the remaining basis of qualified property is depreciated under the usual rules for depreciating such property. If the taxpayer elects to expense property under Sec. 179, the Sec. 179 expense is deducted first, then the additional first-year bonus depreciation and, third, regular MACRS depreciation.[12] In years after the first year, regular MACRS depreciation is allowable under normal rules.

EXAMPLE I:10-9 ▶ On February 10, 2014, Polar Corporation, a calendar year taxpayer, purchased and placed in service equipment costing $625,000. The equipment was 7-year MACRS property and the half-year convention applies. Polar was eligible to expense $500,000 of the cost of the equipment under Sec. 179. Polar also claimed bonus depreciation of $62,500 [($625,000 − $500,000) × 0.50]. MACRS depreciation for 2014 was $8,931 [($625,000 − $500,000 − $62,500) × 0.1429]. Thus, Polar's total 2014 depreciation on the equipment was $571,431. Polar's 2015 depreciation is $15,306 ($62,500 × 0.2449). ◀

KEY POINT

Remember, the mid-quarter convention does *not* apply to real property.

Use of the Mid-Quarter Convention. As mentioned previously, the MACRS system generally uses the half-year convention. However, the MACRS system requires the use of the **mid-quarter convention** if the aggregate basis of all *personal property* placed in service during the last three months of the year exceeds 40% of the cost of all personal property placed in service during the tax year.[13] The 40% test is applied after reducing the property's basis by Sec. 179 expensing, if elected, but not by bonus depreciation, if claimed. If the test is met, the mid-quarter convention must be used instead of the half-year convention, and special mid-quarter tables must be used to compute depreciation under this convention. (See Tables 2 through 5 in Appendix C.) Property placed in service and disposed of during the same tax year is not taken into account for purposes of the mid-quarter test,[14] nor is property expensed under Sec. 179.[15]

---

[12] Temp. Reg. 1.168(k)-1T(d)(3) Example 2.
[13] Sec. 168(d)(3).
[14] Sec. 168(d)(3)(B) and Reg. Sec. 1.168(d)-1(b)(3).
[15] PLR 9126014 (March 29, 1991).

The 40% rule prevents taxpayers from using the half-year convention and thereby obtaining one-half year's depreciation in the year of acquisition when a substantial portion of the assets are placed in service during the last quarter of the tax year.

EXAMPLE I:10-10 ▶ Michael, a calendar year taxpayer, acquires 5-year tangible personal property in 2015, does not elect Sec. 179, and places the properties in service as follows:

Date Placed in Service	*Acquisition Cost*
January 20	$45,000
April 18	50,000
November 5	77,000
Total	$172,000

Because more than 40% of the property acquired during the year is placed in service in the last three months ($77,000 ÷ $172,000 = 44.8%), the mid-quarter convention applies for all property placed in service during the year. Depreciation for 2015 is computed as follows:

Property Placed in Service	*Year 1 MACRS Depreciation*	*Appendix C Table*
January 20	$45,000 × 0.35 = $15,750	Table 2
April 18	50,000 × 0.25 = 12,500	Table 3
November 5	77,000 × 0.05 = 3,850	Table 5
Total	$32,100	

◀

EXAMPLE I:10-11 ▶ Assume the same facts as in Example I:10-10 except Michael elects to expense $25,000 under Sec. 179 and selects the property placed in service on November 5. In this case, the mid-quarter convention would not apply because not more than 40% of property (after the Sec. 179 deduction) was placed in service in the last quarter of the year [($77,000 − $25,000) ÷ ($172,000 − $25,000) = 35.4%]. Therefore, Michael uses the half-year convention, and his depreciation for 2014 is computed using Table 1 in Appendix C as follows:

Date Placed in Service	*Year 1 MACRS Depreciation*	*Sec. 179 Depreciation*	*Total 2015 Depreciation*
January 20	$45,000 × 0.20 = $ 9,000	–0–	$ 9,000
April 18	50,000 × 0.20 = 10,000	–0–	10,000
November 5	52,000* × 0.20 = 10,400	$25,000	35,400
Total			$54,400

* After Sec. 179 depreciation ($77,000 − $25,000)

In this case, the half-year convention yields larger depreciation in the first year. In some cases, the mid-quarter convention can yield a larger depreciation deduction. This situation occurs only when a large amount of property is placed in service in the first quarter of the year, yet enough property is placed in service in the fourth quarter to require the mid-quarter convention. ◀

ADDITIONAL POINT

To reflect the applicable convention, the taxpayer must manually adjust the depreciation factor found in the MACRS table for assets disposed of during the year.

Year of Disposition. The MACRS system requires that depreciation be taken in the year of disposition using the same convention that applied on acquisition (e.g., half-year, mid-month, or mid-quarter convention). Therefore, if property is disposed of during any year in which the half-year convention is applicable, the depreciation for the year of disposition will be one-half of the amount computed by using the table percentages.

EXAMPLE I:10-12 ▶ Michelle acquired machinery in March 2011 that qualified as 7-year MACRS property and had a $100,000 basis for depreciation. The half-year convention applied in the year of acquisition, and Michelle claimed no Sec. 179 depreciation on the machinery. In December 2015, Michelle sells the machinery. Michelle's depreciation deduction in 2015 is $4,465 ($100,000 × 0.0893 × 0.50). See Table 1 in Appendix C. ◀

If property is subject to the mid-quarter convention, it is treated as being disposed of at the midpoint of the quarter.

EXAMPLE I:10-13 ▶ In addition to other property acquired in the last quarter of 2011, Jason acquired $200,000 of 5-year property in May 2011 (second quarter). He depreciated all property acquired in 2011 using the mid-quarter convention. He claimed no Sec. 179 expense. If Jason sells the 5-year property on July 14, 2015 (third quarter), the property will be treated as if it were sold on August 15, 2015, which is the midpoint of the third quarter. Thus, using Table 3 in Appendix C, Jason claims $14,213 of depreciation in 2015 [($200,000 × 0.1137) × (2.5 ÷ 4)]. ◀

KEY POINT

Depreciable real property placed in service after 1986 must be depreciated using the straight-line method.

ADDITIONAL COMMENT

For purposes of determining whether at least 80% of the gross rental income is rental income from dwelling units, a taxpayer living in any part of the building includes the fair rental value of his unit in the gross rental income.

Real property falls into two categories: residential rental property and nonresidential real property. **Residential rental property** is defined as property from which at least 80% of the gross rental income is rental income from dwelling units.[16] Dwelling units include houses, apartments, and manufactured homes that are used for residential purposes but not hotels, motels, or other establishments for transient use. **Nonresidential real property** is any real property other than residential rental property.

Real Property: Classification and Recovery Rates. The MACRS recovery periods that apply to real property placed in service in years after 1986 are:

- Residential rental property: 27.5 years (Table 7 in Appendix C)
- Nonresidential real property: 39 years[17] (Tables 8 and 9 in Appendix C)

Straight-line depreciation must be used and is reflected in the tables. A mid-month convention is used in the year of acquisition and in the year of disposition.

EXAMPLE I:10-14 ▶ On October 4, 2015, Husker, Inc., acquired an office building to relocate its rapidly-growing staff. The property was purchased for $1,500,000, of which $200,000 was allocated to the underlying land. Because the property is nonresidential real property, it is classified as 39-year property. Depreciation is computed using Table 9 in Appendix C (mid-month convention), totaling $6,955 ($1,300,000 × 0.00535). In 2016, depreciation on the building will be $33,332 ($1,300,000 × 0.02564). ◀

HISTORICAL NOTE

The recovery period for nonresidential real property was extended from 31.5 years to 39 years in 1993 to offset the revenue loss from liberalizing the passive activity loss rules affecting real estate.

Taxpayers owning buildings must depreciate subsequent capital improvements. Capital improvements are depreciated over the full MACRS recovery period of the improvement, not over the remaining life or recovery period of the building. Thus, the cost of a new roof on an office building must be depreciated over 39 years, even though the building may have been placed in service several years ago.

LEGISLATIVE UPDATE

In previous years, Congress provided special treatment for qualified leasehold improvement property by allowing it to be eligible for bonus depreciation in some years and classifying it in the 15-year property class. However, without action from Congress, this treatment ends in 2015.

Qualified Leasehold Improvement Property. Qualified leasehold improvement property (QLIP) is defined as any improvement to an interior portion of nonresidential real property made by either a lessee or a lessor pursuant to a lease. The QLIP must have been placed in service more than three years after the date the building was first placed in service. Expenditures that enlarge a building or expenditures such as an elevator, an escalator, or a structural component that benefits either a common area or the internal structural framework of a building are not considered QLIP.

As discussed previously, bonus depreciation (50% or 30%) was allowed for QLIP placed in service after September 10, 2001 and before January 1, 2005 as well as for QLIP placed in service in 2008 through 2013 (50% or 100%). In recent tax legislation, Congress gave special treatment to QLIP by allowing a 15-year recovery period instead of the 39-year recovery period allowed for nonresidential real property. The shorter recovery period is effective for QLIP placed in service after December 31, 2005 and before January 1, 2015, and requires straight-line depreciation with the half-year or midquarter convention, whichever was applicable.[18]

EXAMPLE I:10-15 ▶ Shaheen Corporation leased office space to operate its business in a 20-year-old building. In early 2014, the corporation made some major leasehold improvements, such as changing the size of offices by rearranging the walls, new ductwork, and other similar capital improvements to the office. The overall size of the office did not change. The leasehold improvements were

---

[16] Secs. 168(e)(2)(A).

[17] Sec. 168(c). A 31.5-year recovery period applied to nonresidential real property placed in service on or after January 1, 1987, and before May 13, 1993.

[18] The shorter recovery period was instituted by the 2004 Jobs Act and extended by the Tax Relief and Health Care Act of 2006 and the Tax Extenders Act of 2008 to QLIP placed in service before January 1, 2010. The Tax Relief Act of 2010 extended the provision to QLIP placed in service before January 1, 2012. The American Taxpayer Relief Act of 2012 further extended the treatment of QLIP placed in service before January 1, 2014, and 2014 Tax Increase Prevention Act extended the treatment of QLIP placed in service before January 1, 2015.

completed and placed in service on July 15, 2014, at a total cost of $120,000 and were considered qualified leasehold improvement property. Normally, leasehold improvements must be depreciated over 39 years. For 2014, however, Shaheen Corporation was permitted to take both 50% bonus depreciation and 15-year straight line MACRS depreciation on the leasehold improvements. Thus, in 2014, the depreciation deduction was:

Cost of qualified leasehold improvements	$120,000
Minus: Bonus depreciation	(60,000)
Depreciable basis	60,000
Times: Depreciation rate (1/15 × 1/2)	0.03333
Depreciation on balance	$ 2,000
Total depreciation for 2014	$ 62,000

◀

Straight-Line (Method) Election Under MACRS. Instead of using the accelerated methods previously described under the MACRS rules, taxpayers may elect to use the straight-line method for tangible personal property. If the straight-line election is made, the taxpayer must use either the same depreciation period or an extended period based on the alternative depreciation system, as discussed below.[19]

EXAMPLE I:10-16 ▶ In early 2015, Delta Corporation places in service equipment costing $100,000. Delta does not elect Sec. 179 expensing and elects the straight line method under MACRS. Using a 7-year recovery period and half-year convention, Delta's depreciation for 2015 is $7,143 [($100,000 ÷ 7 years) × 0.50]. ◀

Alternative Depreciation System. The MACRS system provides an alternative depreciation system (ADS) that is required for certain property and is also available for all other depreciable assets if the taxpayer so elects.[20] The election is made on a year-by-year basis. Once the election is made for specified property, it is irrevocable. For personal property, the ADS election applies to all property within a class (all 5-year property, for example); for real property, the ADS election may be made on an individual property basis. The principal type of property for which the ADS is *required* is tangible property used predominantly outside the United States. ADS recovery periods are generally longer than recovery periods under MACRS, and ADS requires the use of the straight-line method with a half-year, mid-quarter, or mid-month convention, whichever is applicable. Thus, the ADS election is generally made by taxpayers who want to use the straight-line method over a longer recovery period. These taxpayers frequently have net operating losses or are subject to the alternative minimum tax (see Chapter I:14 for a discussion of the alternative minimum tax).

EXAMPLE I:10-17 ▶ In May 2015, Bob Roaster purchases an office building for $300,000 ($50,000 allocated to the land) as rental property. Because he has substantial net operating losses from other business ventures, Roaster elects to depreciate the building using ADS. Depreciation expense for 2015, using the mid-month convention and a 40-year life is $3,908 [$250,000 × .01563 (Table 12, Appendix C)]. If Roaster had not elected ADS, his depreciation would have been $4,013 [$250,000 × .01605 (Table 9, Appendix C)]. The difference is small because the recovery period is 39 years under regular MACRS and 40 years under ADS. ◀

If the taxpayer *elected* ADS, he or she also could use the bonus depreciation allowed in 2001-2004, and 2008–2014. For property *required* to be depreciated under ADS, however, bonus depreciation was not permitted.

The alternate depreciation system also is used to compute earnings and profits (E & P) for a corporation (see Chapter C:4), and a variation of the ADS applies to compute depreciation for property placed into service after 1986 but before 1999 for alternative minimum tax purposes for both individuals and corporations (see Chapter I:14).

Topic Review I:10-1 presents a comparison of the MACRS and ADS rules.

[19] Sec. 168(g)(7).

[20] Sec. 168(g). (See Tables 10–12 in Appendix C.)

TOPIC REVIEW I:10-1

Comparison of MACRS and ADS

	MACRS	ADS
Recovery Periods:		
Automobiles	5 years	5 years
Computers	5 years	5 years
Office machinery	5 years	6 years
Office furniture and equipment	7 years	10 years
Residential rental property	27.5 years	40 years
Nonresidential real property	39 years[b]	40 years
Personal property with no specified class life	7 years	12 years
Conventions:		
Personal property	Half-year or mid-quarter[a]	Half-year or mid-quarter[a]
Real property	Mid-month	Mid-month
Depreciation in year of sale:		
Personal property	Yes	Yes
Real property	Yes	Yes

[a] If more than 40% of the cost of personal property (after Sec. 179 expensing) is placed in service during the last quarter of year.
[b] For property placed in service prior to May 13, 1993, the recovery period is 31.5 years.

MACRS RESTRICTIONS

ETHICAL POINT

The personal use of a corporate automobile by a shareholder-employee may be a constructive dividend. Personal use by a non-shareholder-employee results in additional taxable compensation to the employee.

Personal-Use Assets. The personal-use portion of an asset's cost is not depreciable. For example, if a taxpayer owns a duplex and uses one unit as a personal residence, only the unit that is rented to tenants qualifies for depreciation.

Listed Property Rules. Because Congress was concerned about taxpayers claiming large depreciation deductions (using accelerated methods) on certain types of assets that are conducive to mixed business/personal use, it placed restrictions on assets that are classified as *listed property.* Listed property includes automobiles, computers and peripheral equipment, and property generally used for purposes of entertainment, recreation, or amusement (for example, a video recorder).[21] If a listed property's business use is greater than 50% of its total use, the taxpayer may elect Sec. 179 expensing for the business portion and may use regular MACRS tables for the remaining business portion of the asset's cost, including bonus depreciation where applicable. However, if the business use is 50% or less, the taxpayer may not elect Sec. 179 expensing, must use ADS (e.g., 5-year straight-line cost recovery for automobiles and computers), and may not use bonus depreciation (because ADS is required).

EXAMPLE I:10-18 ▶

In June 2015, Patrick acquires an automobile at a cost of $10,000. He uses it 60% for business. Assuming no Sec. 179 election, the depreciation deduction on the business-use portion of the automobile's cost is based on the MACRS system and 5-year recovery class because the automobile is predominantly used in business (i.e., more than 50%). The MACRS depreciation allowance in 2015 is $1,200 [($10,000 × 0.20) × 60% business use percentage]. (Table 1 in Appendix C.) ◀

EXAMPLE I:10-19 ▶

In June 2015, Paula acquires an automobile at a cost of $10,000. She uses it only 40% for business. Paula must use ADS to depreciate the business portion of the automobile, and Sec. 179 expensing is not allowed. The business portion is $4,000 ($10,000 × 0.40). Paula's depreciation allowance in 2015 using the straight-line method and the half-year convention is $400 [($4,000 ÷ 5 years) × 0.50]. ◀

ADDITIONAL COMMENT

Congress enacted the restrictions on automobiles in 1984 because of a concern that the tax system was underwriting the acquisition of automobiles whose cost and luxury far exceeded what was required for business needs.

Additional restrictions apply to employees who acquire listed property (e.g., an automobile, personal computer, etc.) for use in employment-related activities. In addition

[21] Before January 1, 2010, cellular telephones were listed property. However, as of January 1, 2010, cellular telephones are no longer listed property. Taxpayers are now permitted to use common-sense usage percentages. See IRS Notice 2009-46.

to the "more than 50% test," such use must be for the convenience of the *employer* and be required as a condition of employment.[22] This rule is strictly interpreted by the IRS. Further, deductions connected with listed property are also subject to substantial record-keeping requirements, similar to the requirements for entertainment expenses.[23]

EXAMPLE I:10-20 ▶ Raul, a college professor, acquired a personal computer for use at home. He used the computer 60% of the time on teaching- and research-related activities associated with his job. The remaining usage was for personal activities. Raul's employer finds that it is helpful for employees to own a personal computer but does not require them to purchase a computer as a condition of employment. Raul meets the first requirement (i.e., the 60% business usage is greater than the 50% threshold). However, the second requirement for employees (that the use must be for the convenience of the employer and required as a condition of employment) is not met. Thus, no depreciation may be taken because the employment-related use is not deemed to be business use. ◀

Recapture of Excess Cost Recovery Deductions. Taxpayers are subject to depreciation recapture on listed property if MACRS rules were used originally and the property's business-use percentage decreases to 50% or less in a subsequent year. Depreciation deductions for all years are recomputed using ADS. The excess depreciation deducted, including any Sec. 179 expense and bonus depreciation, is recaptured as ordinary income by including it in the taxpayer's gross income in the year the business-use percentage first falls to 50% or below.[24] Once the business use falls to 50% or below, ADS must be used for the current year and for all subsequent years, even if the business-use percentage increases to more than 50% in a subsequent year.

EXAMPLE I:10-21 ▶ Paul, a self-employed attorney, acquired an automobile in June 2013 for $12,000. In both 2013 and 2014, Paul's business-use percentage was 60%. Depreciation under MACRS in 2013 and 2014 were as follows:

2013: Regular MACRS depreciation assuming 100% business use ($12,000 × 0.20)	2,400
Times: Business-use percentage	0.60
Depreciation for 60% business use	$1,440
2014: Regular MACRS depreciation assuming 100% business use ($12,000 × 0.32)	$3,840
Times: Business-use percentage	0.60
Depreciation for 60% business use	$2,304

In 2015, Paul's business-use percentage declines to 40%. Therefore, he must use ADS for 2015 and also recapture the excess depreciation taken in 2013 and 2014. The recapture is computed as follows:

MACRS depreciation taken in 2013 and 2014 ($1,440 + $2,304)		$3,744
2013: Recomputed ADS depreciation ($12,000 × 0.60 × 0.10)	$ 720	
2014: Recomputed ADS depreciation ($12,000 × 0.60 × 0.20)	1,440	(2,160)
Recapture of excess depreciation in 2015 (ordinary income)		$1,584

Paul must use ADS to compute depreciation in 2015 and all subsequent years. His 2015 deduction will be $960 ($12,000 × 0.40 × 0.20). ◀

Limitations on Luxury Automobiles. Because Congress believed that the normal MACRS depreciation deduction for automobiles used for business was too generous, it placed ceilings on deductions related to luxury passenger automobiles. A passenger auto mobile is defined as a 4-wheeled vehicle which is manufactured primarily for use on public streets, roads, and highways and which is rated at 6,000 pounds or less unloaded gross vehicle weight rating (GVWR).[25] In essence, taxpayers are still allowed to fully depreciate luxury cars, but must depreciate them over longer than the normal five-year recovery period.

22 Sec. 280F(d)(3). Any other property used for transportation (e.g., a pickup truck) qualifies as listed property if the nature of the property lends itself to personal use. (See Sec. 280F(b)(4).)

23 Sec. 274(d)(4).

24 Sec. 280F(b).

25 Sec. 280F(d)(5)(A).

EXAMPLE I:10-22 ▶ In 2014, Joe purchases a $60,000 automobile that he uses 100% for business purposes. Under normal MACRS rules and without considering Sec. 179, Joe could deduct depreciation of $12,000 in the first year ($60,000 × 0.20) and $19,200 ($60,000 × 0.32) in the second year. Thus, Joe could deduct 52% ($31,200 ÷ $60,000) of the cost of his automobile in the first two years, creating considerable tax savings.

To prevent such perceived abuse, Congress has implemented ceiling limitations for MACRS depreciation on passenger automobiles placed in service (based on 100% business-use). For 2015, the ceiling limits are:

Year 1 (2015)	$3,160
Year 2 (2016)	5,100
Year 3 (2017)	3,050
Year 4 (2018 and subsequent years)	1,875

(For automobiles placed in service in prior years, see Table 6 in Appendix C.) ◀

ADDITIONAL COMMENT

The limitations on luxury automobiles mean that the depreciation deductions are limited during the normal 5-year recovery period on business automobiles costing more than $15,800 for 2015 ($3,160 ÷ 0.20).

To compute the maximum MACRS depreciation deduction for a passenger automobile for any year, taxpayers must first compute depreciation under normal MACRS rules, including Sec. 179, and then compare this amount to the ceiling limitation for that year.[26] The maximum depreciation deduction allowed for any year cannot exceed the ceiling limitation amount. Due to the ceiling limitation, taxpayers usually do not elect Sec. 179 expensing on passenger automobiles.

EXAMPLE I:10-23 ▶ Amy purchases a $60,000 automobile in 2015 that she uses 100% for business purposes. She is limited to $3,160 of depreciation, as this ceiling amount is less than regular MACRS depreciation ($60,000 × 0.20 = $12,000).

After the first year, the procedure is the same as above. The regular MACRS deduction is computed and compared with the appropriate year of the ceiling limitation and the deduction allowed cannot exceed the ceiling amount. As Table I:10-3 shows, after the regular recovery period ends for passenger automobiles placed in service in 2015, the taxpayer would be entitled to a deduction of $1,875 per year until the automobile is fully depreciated. ◀

Depreciating Mixed-Use Automobiles. Taxpayers who use passenger automobiles less than 100% for business must compute the regular MACRS depreciation amount, identify the ceiling amount, and then reduce each one by the percentage of personal use. The actual depreciation deduction for the year will be the lesser of the two reduced amounts. Complicating the matter, the taxpayer's basis in the automobile will decrease by the lesser of the *unreduced* amounts, even though that was not the amount allowed as a deduction.[27] Example 10-25 and Table 10-3 demonstrate this rule.

EXAMPLE I:10-24 ▶ Phil acquires an automobile for $60,000 in April 2015. He uses the automobile 80% for business and 20% for personal activities during 2015 and all succeeding years. Table I:10-3 lists the depreciation amounts, assuming that the 80% business use continues for the life of the automobile, but no amount is expensed under Sec. 179. At the end of the regular MACRS recovery period, the unrecovered cost of the business-use portion of the automobile may be recovered at an annual rate not to exceed $1,500 ($1,875 × 0.80). ◀

TYPICAL MISCONCEPTION

It is sometimes mistakenly believed that the Sec. 179 expensing allowance can be used to boost the first-year depreciation of luxury automobiles.

Trucks, Vans, and SUVs. As mentioned previously, limitations are placed on "passenger automobiles" that have a gross vehicle weight rating (GVWR) of 6,000 pounds or less. SUVs rated at a GVWR exceeding 6,000 pounds were not subject to the ceiling limitations, so taxpayers could expense up to $100,000 (adjusted for inflation) under Sec. 179, thus creating a major tax planning opportunity. Beginning in 2004, this controversial provision has been curtailed. For SUVs placed into service after October 22, 2004, the maximum Sec. 179

[26] Bonus depreciation also applied to property placed in service from September 11, 2001 through December 31, 2004, in 2008, in 2009, in 2010, and 2011, and was reflected in the limitations for those years.

[27] Sec. 280F(d)(8).

▼ **TABLE I:10-3**

Depreciation Amounts for Example I:10-25 (80% Business-Use Automobile)

	(A) MACRS Deduction: 100% Bus. Use (Table 1)	(B) Ceiling Limit: 100% Bus. Use (Table 6)	Deduction Allowed: 80% × Lesser of MACRS or Ceiling	Unrecovered Basis
2015				
Regular MACRS calculation ($60,000 × 0.20)	$12,000	$ 3,160	$ 2,528	$56,840[a]
2016				
Regular MACRS calculation ($60,000 × 0.32)	$19,200	$ 5,100	$ 4,080	$51,740
2017				
Regular MACRS calculation ($60,000 × 0.192)	$11,520	$ 3,050	$ 2,440	$48,690
2018				
Regular MACRS calculation ($60,000 × 0.1152)	$ 6,912	$ 1,875	$ 1,500	$46,815
2019				
Regular MACRS calculation ($60,000 × 0.1152)	$ 6,912	$ 1,875	$ 1,500	$44,940
2020				
Regular MACRS calculation ($60,000 × 0.0576)	$ 3,456	$ 1,875	$ 1,500	$43,440
Total through 2020	$60,000	$16,935	$13,548	
2021 and subsequent years until fully depreciated				
Ceiling limit		$ 1,875	$ 1,500	

[a] **Unrecovered basis** equals original basis minus the lesser of A or B [($60,000 − $3,160) in 2015] even though the annual deduction is limited to business usage.

Note: Based on the unrecovered basis of $43,440 at December 31, 2020, it would take Phil 24 more years to fully depreciate the automobile ($34,752/$1,500 = 23.2 years) based on 80% business use. The personal-use portion of the automobile's cost, $12,000 ($60,000 × 0.20), never will be depreciated and will be recovered only upon disposition.

expense amount is $25,000,[28] rather than the typically higher Sec. 179 election amounts. However, SUVs with a GVWR of greater than 6,000 pounds will continue to have significant depreciation advantages over other vehicles because the ceiling limitations do not apply.

To qualify for the truck and van depreciation deduction, a vehicle must be a passenger vehicle built on a truck chassis with an unloaded gross weight of over 6,000 pounds. A vehicle built on an automobile chassis is classified as an automobile regardless of weight, even if its manufacturer calls it an SUV.

EXAMPLE I:10-25 ▶ Two taxpayers purchase vehicles used 100% for business in July 2015, at a cost of $60,000 each. Taxpayer A purchases a BMW sedan that is considered a passenger automobile for tax purposes. Taxpayer B purchases a Ford Expedition which is rated at over 6,000 GVWR and, therefore, is not considered a passenger automobile and not subject to the ceiling limitations. Taxpayer B elects Sec. 179 expensing. The first-year depreciation for each vehicle for 2015 is computed below.

BMW:	Regular MACRS depreciation from Table 1 ($60,000 × 0.20)	$12,000
	Ceiling limitation	3,160

In this case, the maximum depreciation deduction on the vehicle for 2015 is $3,160

Ford Expedition:	Section 179 depreciation (maximum)	$25,000

ADDITIONAL COMMENT

Many SUVs have a rated GVWR of greater than 6,000 pounds, such as the Chevrolet Suburban, Dodge Durango, Hummer H1 and H2, and Toyota Sequoia. For a more complete list, go to www.carsdirect.com/home.

[28] Sec. 179(b)(5). Vehicles with a GVWR of more than 14,000 pounds are not considered SUVs and are not subject to the $25,000 limitation.

Regular MACRS depreciation from Table 1 [($60,000 − $25,000) × .020]	7,000
Total depreciation for 2015	$32,000

The Table 6 ceiling limitations do not apply because the vehicle has a GVWR of more than 6,000 pounds. ◀

This example shows the significant tax savings from buying a passenger vehicle on a truck chassis that has a GVWR of more than 6,000 pounds. It should be noted that any vehicle that avoids the ceiling limitations must be used more than 50% for business, under the general listed property rules.

Although some taxpayers avoid the ceiling limitations by purchasing heavy vehicles, other taxpayers who use light trucks and vans (6,000 GVWR or less) in their businesses are hurt by the ceiling limitations. In response to small business concerns, two recent exceptions to the ceiling limitations have been issued: (1) exemption from the ceiling limitations for vehicles that clearly are not for personal use and (2) higher ceiling limitation amounts for other light trucks and vans.

- Exemption from ceiling limitations: Certain "nonpersonal use" vehicles are completely exempt from the ceiling limitations.[29] These vehicles must be specifically modified so that they are not likely to be used more than a de minimis amount for personal purposes. This somewhat vague definition is explained further in the regulations as a van that only has a front bench for seating, has permanent shelving that fills most of the cargo area, or has been painted with advertising or the company's logo.
- Higher ceiling limitations: Even if a light truck or van does not meet the nonpersonal use criteria above, higher ceiling limitations have been issued for vehicles on a truck chassis.[30] For trucks and vans on a truck chassis that have a GVWR of 6,000 pounds or less, the ceiling amounts for 2015 (Table 6) are as follows:

	Annual Ceiling Limitations
Year 1 (2015)	$3,460
Year 2 (2016)	5,600
Year 3 (2017)	3,350
Year 4 (2018 and subsequent years)	1,975

ADDITIONAL COMMENT

The amount that can be deducted for leased automobiles is also limited.

Additional Computations for Leased Vehicles. If a taxpayer leases an automobile or light truck or van for business purposes, the deduction for rental payments is reduced to reflect the luxury auto depreciation limits imposed on purchased vehicles. If these restrictions were not applied to leased automobiles, the ceiling limitations could be avoided by leasing instead of purchasing an automobile. The leasing restriction is accomplished by requiring taxpayers to reduce their deduction by an "inclusion amount" obtained from an IRS table.[31] This amount is based on the automobile's FMV and the tax year in which the lease commences, and is prorated for the percentage of business use and number of days used during the year. Partial lease inclusion tables are provided in Tables 13 and 14 in Appendix C.

EXAMPLE I:10-26 ▶ On January 1, 2015, Jim leased and placed in service an automobile with a $39,500 FMV and annual lease payments of $7,200. Jim uses the automobile 80% for business purposes. Jim can deduct 80% of the lease payments ($7,200 × 0.80 = $5,760) but must reduce his deduction by 80% of the inclusion amount from Table 13 to reflect the luxury auto depreciation limitation. For 2015, this reduction was $27 ($34 × 0.80). Thus, Jim's auto lease deduction for 2015 was $5,733 ($5,760 − $27). For 2016, the second year, Jim's auto lease deduction is $5,700 [$5,760 − ($75 × 0.80)]. ◀

Topic Review I:10-2 summarizes the special depreciation elections and restrictions.

[29] Temp. Reg. Sec. 1.274-5T(k), T.D. 9064 (6-30-2003) amending T.D. 8061.

[30] Rev. Proc. 2003-75, 2003-2 C.B. 1018.

[31] The latest lease inclusion table is contained in Rev. Proc. 2015-19, 2015-8 I.R.B, 2/6/2015.

TOPIC REVIEW I:10-2

Special Depreciation Elections and Restrictions

SECTION 179 EXPENSING ELECTION

Maximum deduction: $25,000 (in 2015) of the total cost of qualified property placed in service during the year.

Qualified property: New or used tangible personal business-use property.

Limitations on deduction:

1. Cost limitation: The maximum Sec. 179 expense is reduced dollar-for-dollar by the excess of total qualified property cost over $200,000 (in 2015). Taxpayers may not carry forward amounts reduced by this limitation. However, the cost not expensed because of this limitation remains as basis subject to MACRS depreciation,
2. Taxable income limitation: The Sec. 179 expense after cost limitation is further limited to taxable income before the deduction. Taxpayers may carry forward amounts lost because of this limitation.

Basis reduction: The basis of qualified property for MACRS depreciation is reduced by the Sec. 179 expense (after the cost limitation reduction).

BONUS DEPRECIATION

Maximum allowed: 50% in 2014 of the cost of qualified property placed in service during the year. At the time of printing, Congress had not yet extended bonus depreciation to 2015.

Qualified Property: New (not used) property that is (1) MACRS property with a recovery period of 20 years or less, (2) computer software, or (3) qualified leasehold improvement property.

BUSINESS USE RESTRICTION

Listed property: If business use of listed property exceeds 50% of total use, taxpayers may elect Sec. 179 expensing for the business portion and may depreciate the remaining business-use portion using MACRS rules. If business use is 50% or less of total use, taxpayers may not elect Sec. 179 expensing and must depreciate listed property using ADS rules.

AUTOMOBILES, TRUCKS, AND VANS

Table 6 in Appendix C provides annual ceiling amounts for depreciation on 100% business-use automobiles and on 100% business-use trucks and vans with a GVWR of 6,000 pounds or less. The taxpayer computes regular depreciation under MACRS, including Sec. 179 expensing, and then compares that figure to the Table 6 ceiling figure. The deduction is the lesser of these two. If business-use is less than 100%, both figures must be reduced by the personal-use percentage. Basis nevertheless is adjusted by the unreduced figure. Business-use trucks and vans with a GVWR of more than 6,000 pounds are not subject to these limitations.

LEASED VEHICLES

Taxpayers who lease vehicles must subtract from their otherwise deductible lease payments as "inclusion amount" (see Tables 13 and 14 in Appendix C) to adjust the lease expense deduction for the luxury auto depreciation limitations imposed on purchased vehicles. This rule prevents individuals from avoiding the luxury auto deprecitation limits by leasing vehicles.

AMORTIZATION

OBJECTIVE 2

Calculate amortization for intangible assets and distinguish between amortizable and non-amortizable assets

HISTORICAL NOTE

Prior to the tax change in 1993, no amortization for goodwill was allowed. So, in business acquisitions, the purchaser typically tried to allocate as little of the purchase price as possible to goodwill. These allocations frequently caused disputes with the IRS. Under current law, these disputes have lessened for purchased goodwill.

Amortization deductions are allowed for a variety of intangible assets. Although amortization periods vary greatly depending on the type of asset, all intangible assets are amortized on a *straight-line basis*. The major intangible assets that may be amortized are as follows:

- Goodwill and Other Purchased Intangibles, Sec. 197
- Research and Experimental Expenditures, Sec. 174
- Computer software
- Start-up Expenditures, Sec. 195
- Organizational Expenditures, Sec. 248
- Pollution Control Facilities, Sec. 169

Several of the above intangibles are discussed below.

SEC. 197 INTANGIBLES

Sec. 197 allows a deduction for the amortization of certain acquired intangible assets. The amortization is deducted on a ratable basis (straight-line) over a 15-year period beginning with the month of acquisition.[32] In general, Sec. 197 applies only to intangible assets that are acquired in connection with the conduct of a trade or business or an activity engaged in for the production of income. Sec. 197 does not apply to an intangible asset that is internally created by the taxpayer, such as a patent resulting from the taxpayer's research and development lab. Internally-created patents and copyrights have definite and limited lives and are therefore amortizable over the defined period.[33] Internally created patents are generally amortized over 17 years; internally created copyrights over 28 years.

EXAMPLE I:10-27 ▶ On January 1, 2015, Central Corporation receives patent approval on an internally created process improvement. Legal costs associated with the patent are $100,000 and the patent has a legal life of 17 years. The patent does not qualify as a Sec. 197 intangible. The patent has a definite and limited life and is amortizable ratably over its legal life of 17 years beginning with the month of its creation. ◀

BOOK-TO-TAX ACCOUNTING COMPARISON

For financial statement reporting, a firm reduces goodwill by an impairment amount rather than by amortization.

Definition of a Sec. 197 Intangible Asset. Sec. 197 intangibles (i.e., intangible assets that are subject to 15-year ratable amortization) include the following:

- Goodwill and going concern value. Conceptually, goodwill is an intangible asset that is neither separately identified or valued but possesses characteristics that allow a business to earn greater returns than would be possible without such characteristics. These characteristics include valued employees, superior management team, loyal customer base, strategic location, etc. For income tax purposes, however, goodwill is determined in a much more practical manner. **Goodwill** is defined as the value of a trade or business that is attributable to the expectation of continued customer patronage, whether due to the name or reputation of the trade or business or to any other factor.[34] Going concern value is the added value that attaches to acquired property because it is an integral part of a going concern.
- Intangible assets relating to the workforce, such as an information base (e.g., a customer list), know-how, customers, suppliers, or similar items (e.g., the portion of the purchase price of an acquired business that is attributable to an existing employment contract for a key employee.) Know-how related intangibles include patents, copyrights, formulas, and processes.
- Licenses, permits, or other rights granted by a governmental unit or agency (e.g., the capitalized cost of acquiring a radio broadcasting license).
- Covenants not to compete. A covenant not to compete represents an agreement between a buyer and seller of a business that the seller (i.e., the selling corporation and/or its shareholders) will not compete with the buyer for a limited period. The covenant may also be limited to a geographic area. A covenant not to compete must be amortized over 15 years even though the agreement was only for five years.[35]
- Franchises, trademarks, and trade names. A franchise includes any agreement that gives one of the parties the right to distribute, sell, or provide goods, services, or facilities, within a specified area.

EXAMPLE I:10-28 ▶ In January of the current year, Chicago Corporation acquires all the net assets of Coastal Corporation for $1 million. The following intangible assets are included in the purchase agreement:

Assets	*Acquisition Cost*
Goodwill and going concern value	$100,000
Licenses	55,000
Patents	45,000
Covenant not to compete for five years	90,000

All the intangible assets above qualify as Sec. 197 intangible assets and are amortizable on a ratable basis (straight-line) over 15 years beginning with the month of acquisition. This 15-year amortization period applies to the convenant not to compete even though the convenant is only for five years. ◀

[32] Sec. 197(a).
[33] Reg. Sec. 1.167(a)-3.
[34] Reg. Sec. 1.197-2(b)(1).
[35] Frontier Chevrolet Co., 2003-1 USTC ¶50,490 (9th Cir., 2003) aff'g 116 T.C. 289 (2001).

STOP & THINK

Question: When one company purchases the assets of another company, the purchasing company may acquire goodwill. Because purchased goodwill is a Sec. 197 intangible asset and may be amortized over 15 years, determining the cost of goodwill is important. How is the "cost" of goodwill determined in an acquisition?

Solution: The IRS requires that taxpayers use the "residual method" as prescribed in Sec. 1060. Under this method, all of the assets except for goodwill are valued. The total value of these assets is then subtracted from the total purchase price, and the residual is the amount of the purchase price allocated to goodwill.

ADDITIONAL COMMENT

Sec. 1231 generally allows gains to be treated as long-term capital gains and losses to be deducted as ordinary losses. Sec. 1245 requires that gains be classified as ordinary income to the extent depreciation, amortization or depletion was claimed as an ordinary deduction in prior periods (see Chapter I:13).

Classification and Disposition of Intangible Assets. A Sec. 197 intangible asset is treated as depreciable property. Thus, a disposition is given Sec. 1231 treatment if the intangible asset is held for more than one year.[36] Gain on disposition of a Sec. 197 intangible is subject to depreciation recapture under Sec. 1245 (see Chapter I:13).[37] Loss on disposition of a Sec. 197 intangible asset, however, is not deductible if other intangibles acquired in the same acquisition of a trade or business are retained. In such case, the bases of the retained Sec. 197 intangibles are increased by the disallowed loss.[38]

EXAMPLE I:10-29 ▶ Assume the same facts as in Example I:10-28. After five years, the covenant not to compete expires. Its adjusted basis is $60,000 [$90,000 − (5/15 × $90,000)]. The $60,000 loss is not deductible, and the disallowed loss is allocated to the retained Sec. 197 assets based on their respective FMVs. ◀

EXAMPLE I:10-30 ▶ Assume the same facts as in Example I:10-28. After one year the *patent* is sold for $50,000. In the initial year, $3,000 ($45,000 ÷ 15) of amortization was deducted. The recognized gain on the sale is $8,000 ($50,000 − $42,000). Of the gain, $3,000 is recaptured as ordinary income under Sec. 1245, and $5,000 is classified as Sec. 1231 gain. ◀

RESEARCH AND EXPERIMENTAL EXPENDITURES

TYPICAL MISCONCEPTION

It is sometimes mistakenly believed that if a company constructs a new building to be used entirely as a research facility, the entire cost of the building can be expensed. However, the expensing election applies only to the depreciation allowances on the building.

In general, research and experimental (R&E) expenditures include experimental and laboratory costs incidental to the development of a product.[39] Section 174 was enacted to clarify the income tax treatment of R&E expenditures. Treasury Regulations define items that do and do not qualify as R&E expenditures. These items are summarized in Table I:10-4. For income tax purposes, the following alternatives are available for qualified R&E expenditures:

- Expense in the year paid or incurred.
- Defer (capitalize as deferred expenses) and amortize the costs as a ratable deduction over a period of 60 months or more beginning with the month in which benefits are first realized.
- Capitalize and write off the costs only when the research project is abandoned or is worthless.[40]

A taxpayer must make an election to either expense or defer and amortize the costs in the initial year the R&E expenditures are incurred. If no election is made, the costs must be capitalized. The taxpayer must continue to use the same accounting method for the R&E expenditures unless IRS approval to change methods is obtained.

Below are some important points regarding R&E expenditures:

- Most taxpayers elect to expense the R&E expenditures because they prefer the immediate tax benefit.
- The deferral and amortization method is desirable if the taxpayer is currently in a low tax rate situation or expects initial NOLs during a start-up period.
- If the deferral and amortization method is used, the amortization period of 60 or more months commences with the month in which the benefits from the expenditures are first realized.

[36] Sec. 197(f)(7).
[37] Sec. 1245(a)(2)(C).
[38] Sec. 197(f)(1).
[39] Reg. Sec. 1.174-2(a)(2). The Regulations define the term *product* to include any pilot model, formula, invention, technique, patent, or similar product.
[40] Sec. 174.

▼ **TABLE I:10-4**
Research and Experimental Expenditures

Items That Qualify	Items That Do Not Qualify[a]
▶ Costs incident to the development of an experimental or pilot model, a plant process, a product, a formula, an invention ▶ Costs associated with product improvements ▶ Costs of obtaining a patent, such as attorney fees ▶ Research contracted to others ▶ Depreciation or cost-recovery amounts attributable to capitalized R&E items (e.g., research laboratory and equipment)	▶ Expenditures for ordinary testing or inspection of materials or products for quality control purposes ▶ Efficiency surveys and management studies ▶ Marketing research, advertising, etc. ▶ Cost of acquiring another person's patent, model, production, or process ▶ Research incurred in connection with literary, historical, or similar projects

[a] Certain of these expenses may be deductible as trade or business expenses under Sec. 162, subject to amortization under Sec. 197, or treated as start-up expenditures under Sec. 195.

- R&E expenses include depreciation allowances related to capitalized expenditures. Thus, if the deferral and amortization method is used, depreciation allowances are deferred as part of the R&E expenditures that are amortized over a period of at least 60 months. Capital expenditures made in connection with R&E activities cannot be expensed when they are incurred merely because an election to expense R&E costs are made.
- A tax credit may apply to certain research expenditures. (See Chapter I:14 for a discussion of the research activities credit.) Taxpayers must reduce any R&E expense deduction by the amount of the credit claimed.

EXAMPLE I:10-31 ▶ In 2015, Control Corporation leases a research laboratory to develop new products and to improve existing products. Control Corporation, a calendar year taxpayer that uses the accrual method of accounting, incurs the following expenditures during 2015:

Laboratory supplies and materials	$ 40,000
Laboratory equipment	60,000[a]
Utilities and rent	50,000
Salaries	50,000
Total expenditures	$200,000

[a] The MACRS recovery period is 5 years at a 20% rate for the initial year.

Assume the benefits from the R&E expenditures are first realized in January 2016. If Control Corporation elects to expense the R&E expenditures, the deduction in 2015 is $152,000 ($40,000 laboratory supplies and materials + $12,000 depreciation on the equipment + $50,000 utilities and rent + $50,000 salaries). If the deferral and amortization method is elected, none of the expenditures above are deductible in 2015 because the benefits of the R&E activities are not first realized until January 2016. If the 60-month minimum amortization period is elected, the monthly amortization commencing in January 2016 is $2,533 ($152,000 ÷ 60 months). The $48,000 ($60,000 – $12,000) of laboratory equipment cost is depreciated over the remaining MACRS recovery period beginning in 2016. ◀

REAL-WORLD EXAMPLE

An airline company made payments to an aircraft manufacturer to help defray the cost of designing, developing, producing, and testing a supersonic transport prototype aircraft. These payments were considered R&E expenditures. Rev. Rul. 69-484, 1969-2 C.B. 38.

COMPUTER SOFTWARE

The amortization or depreciation of computer software depends on the nature of the software and how it is acquired. Basically, computer software is either developed by the taxpayer or acquired (purchased or leased) from an outside party.

Developed Computer Software. The cost of developing computer software that is considered R&E may either be expensed in the year the costs are incurred or, if the taxpayer so elects, capitalized and amortized over 60 months beginning with the month in which the taxpayer first realizes benefits from such expenditures, per Sec. 174. If the costs incurred to develop the software are not considered R&E costs (e.g., the software is not in the experimental stage), such costs should be depreciated on a straight line basis over 36 months beginning with the date the software is placed in service.[41]

Purchased Computer Software. Purchased computer software generally may be depreciated in two alternative ways: (1) if the software is included in the cost of the computer hardware, the software does not have to be separately stated as long as the taxpayer consistently follows this treatment. Therefore, the computer and software would be depreciated together under MACRS over five years; or (2) if the software is purchased separately, the software must be depreciated on a straight-line basis over 36 months. An exception to these rules occurs if computer software is purchased in connection with the acquisition of a number of assets of an existing trade or business. In this case, the computer software is considered to be a Sec. 197 intangible and must be amortized over a period of 15 years.[42]

EXAMPLE I:10-32 ▶ Morris Corporation purchased all the assets of an existing business on April 1, 2015 for $1,000,000. Included in the assets was some computer software that the corporation intends to use in its business. The software is specialized for use by Morris Corporation. Based on relative fair market values, the computer software is allocated a cost of $63,000. The software is considered a Sec. 197 intangible and would be amortized over 15 years beginning in the month of acquisition. For the eight-month period in calendar year 2015, Morris Corporation's amortization deduction would be $2,800 [($63,000 ÷ 15 years) × 8/12]. ◀

EXAMPLE I:10-33 ▶ Using the same facts as in Example I:10-32, if Morris Corporation had purchased computer software on April 1, 2015 (not in connection with an asset acquisition) for $63,000, the software would not be considered a Sec. 197 intangible and would be depreciable under Sec. 167(f) on a straight-line basis over a period of 36 months. Therefore, in 2015, Morris Corporation's depreciation deduction would be $14,000 [($63,000 ÷ 36) × 8 months]. ◀

Leased or Licensed Computer Software. Computer software that is leased or licensed for use in the taxpayer's trade or business generally is deductible in full in the year paid.[43]

Depletion, Intangible Drilling and Development Costs

OBJECTIVE 3

Apply cost and percentage depletion methods and summarize the treatment for intangible drilling costs

The taxation of natural resources, such as oil and gas, coal, iron ore, etc. has many of its own specific rules. This section of the text discusses some of the concepts that apply to the oil and gas industry. Other natural resources have slightly different rules, but the oil and gas industry demonstrates the normal taxation of natural resources.

The exploration, development, and operation of oil and gas properties require an outlay of various types of expenditures. Below are the four major types of oil and gas property expenditures and their income tax treatment.

- Payments for the mineral interest. These costs are capitalized and recovered through depletion.
- Intangible drilling and development costs (e.g., labor and other operating costs to clear land, erect a derrick, and drill the well). Taxpayers elect to either capitalize or immediately expense these expenditures.

[41] Sec. 167(f)(1) and Rev. Proc. 2007-16, 2007-4 I.R.B. 358.

[42] Sec. 197(e)(3)(A). If the computer software acquired in an asset acquisition is software that is readily available for purchase by the general public, such software would not be considered a Sec. 197 intangible. (See Sec. 197(e)(3)(A)(i).)

[43] Reg. Sec. 1.162-11 and Rev. Proc. 2007-4, 2007-14 I.R.B. 358.

- Tangible asset costs (e.g., machinery, pipe). These expenditures must be capitalized and depreciated under the MACRS rules.
- Operating costs after the well is producing. These expenditures are deductible under Sec. 162 as ordinary and necessary business expenses.

DEPLETION METHODS

KEY POINT

A depletion deduction is available in the case of mines, oil and gas wells, other natural resources, and timber. However, the percentage depletion method is not available in the case of timber.

Depletion, similar to depreciation, is the using up of natural resources by the process of mining (coal, for example) or drilling (oil and gas). It is calculated under the **cost depletion method** or the **percentage depletion method** for each period. The method used in any year is the one that results in the largest deduction. Thus, percentage depletion may be used in one year and cost depletion may be used in the following year.

Depletion is allowed to the taxpayer who has an **economic interest** in the property. The person who typically has an economic interest in the property is the owner of the natural resource (i.e., the oil, gas, coal, etc.). Thus, depletion may be claimed by the persons who either own the natural resource property or retain a royalty interest. A mining company that only mines coal from a property and does not own (or lease) the underlying coal is not considered to hold an economic interest and, therefore, is not allowed a depletion deduction. The landowner who owns the coal would be entitled to the depletion deduction.

ADDITIONAL COMMENT

Note that a taxpayer will deduct the greater of cost depletion or percentage depletion. If percentage depletion is used, the adjusted basis of the property is reduced by the percentage depletion amount.

Cost Depletion Method. The cost depletion method is similar to the units-of-production method of depreciation. The adjusted basis of the asset is divided by the estimated recoverable units to arrive at a per-unit depletion cost. This per-unit cost is then multiplied by the number of units sold to determine the cost depletion deduction.[44] If the original estimate of recoverable units is subsequently determined to be incorrect, the per-unit cost depletion rate must be revised and used on a prospective basis to determine cost depletion in future years.[45] It is not proper to file an amended return for the years in which the incorrect estimated unit cost was used.

EXAMPLE I:10-34 ▶ Ralph acquires an oil and gas property interest for $100,000 in 2015. The estimate of recoverable units is 10,000 barrels of oil. The per-unit cost depletion amount is $10 ($100,000 ÷ 10,000). If 3,000 units are produced and 2,000 units are sold in 2015, the cost depletion amount is $20,000 (2,000 units × $10 per unit). If cost depletion is used because it exceeds the percentage depletion amount, the cost basis of the property is reduced to $80,000 ($100,000 − $20,000) at the beginning of 2016. If the estimate of remaining recoverable units is revised downward from 8,000 units in 2016 (10,000 − 2,000 units sold in 2015) to 5,000 units (including the 1,000 barrels produced but not sold in 2015), the property's $80,000 adjusted basis is divided by 5,000 units to arrive at a new per-unit cost depletion amount of $16 for 2016. This process is continued each year until the cost of the oil and gas property interest is fully depleted. ◀

REAL-WORLD EXAMPLE

Taxpayers are entitled to a depletion deduction if they have an economic interest in the property. This economic interest may be in the form of a royalty interest where a landowner receives a certain amount per unit extracted from her land, such as $10 for each barrel of oil. The landowner would be entitled to a depletion deduction based on the royalty income received.

Percentage Depletion Method. Percentage depletion generally offers substantial tax benefits for taxpayers in the natural resources industry. The purpose of allowing percentage depletion is to encourage persons to invest and/or operate in an industry that is both capital intensive and high risk but is also vital to our national interests. Percentage depletion may be used by taxpayers for a wide variety of natural resources, such as oil and gas, coal, gold, etc. The percentage depletion method has not been available to *large* oil and gas producers since 1974; but it is still available to *small* oil and gas producers and royalty owners under a specific exemption in the law.[46] Percentage depletion is computed by multiplying the percentage depletion rate times the gross income from the property. However, the depletion amount may not exceed 50% of the taxable income from the property before depletion is deducted (100% for oil and gas properties).[47] Percentage depletion may not be calculated on any lease bonus, advance royalty, or other amount payable without regard to production from the property.

---

[44] Sec. 612.
[45] Sec. 611(a).
[46] Sec. 613A(c). To be classified as a small oil and gas producer or royalty owner, the maximum depletable quantity is based on average daily production of not more than 1,000 barrels of oil or 6 million cubic feet of natural gas.
[47] Sec. 613(a).

Whether the taxpayer uses cost depletion or percentage depletion, the amount of the depletion deduction reduces the basis of the natural resource property. Once the basis of depletable property has been reduced to zero, a taxpayer may no longer claim depletion using the cost depletion method. However, the taxpayer may continue to claim percentage depletion. Subsequent percentage depletion will not reduce the basis of the property below zero. It should be apparent that percentage depletion is a very advantageous method because the total depletion allowed over the life of the property may exceed the property's cost.[48]

Percentage depletion rates vary by the type of mineral. Depletion rates for selected minerals are as follows:

Mineral	*Depletion Rate*
Oil and gas	15%[49]
Coal, asbestos	10%
Gold, silver, copper, iron ore	15%
Sulphur and uranium	22%
Gravel, stone	5%
All other minerals	14%

EXAMPLE I:10-35 ▶ In the current year, Carmen acquires for $400,000 an oil and gas property interest with 200,000 barrels of estimated recoverable oil. During the year, 10,000 barrels of oil are sold for $250,000. Intangible drilling and development costs (IDCs) amount to $100,000 and are expensed in the current year. Other expenses are $50,000. Cost depletion is $20,000 [10,000 barrels sold × ($400,000/200,000 barrels)] in the current year. The computation of percentage depletion is as follows:

(1) Percentage depletion before taxable income limitation ($250,000 × 0.15)	$ 37,500
(2) Taxable income ceiling:	
Gross income	$250,000
Minus: Intangible drilling costs (IDCs) expensed	(100,000)
Other expenses	(50,000)
Taxable income before depletion	$100,000
(3) Percentage depletion (lesser of (1) or (2))	$ 37,500

Carmen's depletion deduction is $37,500 because the percentage depletion amount is greater than the $20,000 of cost depletion. The adjusted basis of the property is reduced by $37,500, the amount of depletion actually claimed. ◀

HISTORICAL NOTE

An Arab oil embargo to the United States in 1973 created a situation where oil prices increased significantly. Consequently, most domestic U.S. oil producers reported huge profits. This situation contributed to the repeal of the percentage depletion allowance for large oil and gas producers.

KEY POINT

The use of the percentage depletion method permits recovery of more than the cost of the property.

TREATMENT OF INTANGIBLE DRILLING AND DEVELOPMENT COSTS

Intangible drilling and development costs (**IDCs**) may either be deducted as an expense or capitalized.[50] IDCs apply only to oil, gas, and geothermal wells and basically include all expenditures, other than the acquisition costs of the underlying property, that are incurred for the drilling and preparation of wells. If the IDCs are capitalized, the amounts are added to the property's basis for determining cost depletion, and the costs are expensed through cost depletion. For a well that is nonproductive (i.e., a dry hole), an ordinary loss is allowed for any IDC costs that have been capitalized and not recovered through depletion. The amount of depletion claimed in a tax year equals the greater of the percentage depletion and cost depletion amounts. If IDCs are capitalized and cost depletion is thereby increased, little or no tax benefit may result because the percentage depletion may still produce a greater deduction than cost depletion. Therefore, it is generally preferable to expense the IDCs if the percentage depletion is expected to be more than the cost depletion and is used to compute the depletion allowance.

[48] Depletion in excess of the adjusted basis of the property is a tax preference item under Sec. 57(a)(1).

[49] For small producers and royalty owners of oil and gas properties, there is a further limitation: the percentage depletion deduction may not exceed 65% of taxable income from all sources before the depletion deduction. Sec. 613A(d)(1).

[50] Sec. 263(c).

EXAMPLE I:10-36 ▶ In the current year, Penny acquires certain rights to oil and gas property for $1,000,000, incurring $300,000 of IDCs. If the IDCs are capitalized, the basis for cost depletion purposes is $1,300,000. Assume that the cost depletion amounts are $100,000 in the current year if the IDCs are expensed and $130,000 if IDCs are capitalized. If the percentage depletion amount is $150,000, percentage depletion will be used because it is greater than either of the cost depletion amounts. Thus, expensing the IDCs permits Penny to deduct the entire $300,000 of IDCs in the current year plus $150,000 of percentage depletion. ◀

TAX PLANNING CONSIDERATIONS

OBJECTIVE 4

Identify tax planning considerations for depreciation

ALTERNATIVE DEPRECIATION SYSTEM UNDER MACRS

In some instances, it may be preferable to elect to use the alternative depreciation system (ADS) rather than the regular MACRS rules. For example, a taxpayer who anticipates losses during the next few years or who currently has NOL carryovers may elect to use ADS, which employs the straight-line method of depreciation over a longer recovery period.

EXAMPLE I:10-37 ▶ Delta Corporation has substantial NOL carryovers that will expire if not used during the next few years. Delta anticipates it will not have taxable income for each of the next seven years if the regular MACRS rules are used to depreciate its fixed asset additions. In the current year, Delta acquires new machinery and equipment at a cost of $100,000. Assuming no Sec. 179 election and no bonus depreciation, depreciation deductions using the MACRS rules and a 7-year recovery period are $14,290 (0.1429 × $100,000). Depreciation deductions under the straight-line method using ADS with a 12-year recovery period and the half-year convention are only $4,167 [($100,000 ÷ 12 years) × 0.50 year]. The ADS election increases taxable income in the current year by $10,123 and allows Delta to offset additional loss carryovers (which might otherwise expire) against this income amount. ◀

ADDITIONAL COMMENT

A taxpayer who is attempting to report a profit in three out of five years in an attempt to avoid the hobby loss rules might want to use the alternative depreciation system.

USE OF UNITS OF PRODUCTION DEPRECIATION

Many times, the MACRS depreciation system requires taxpayers to use a recovery period that is much longer than the actual useful life of the asset. For example, assume a taxpayer uses a machine in his or her business that is classified as 7-year property under MACRS. However, the machine is operated 24 hours a day, seven days a week and will completely wear out in two years. The use of the 7-year recovery period substantially understates depreciation for the machine in the two years of actual use. Under Sec. 168(f), taxpayers may exclude property from the MACRS system if the property is depreciated under the unit-of-production method or any other method not expressed in terms of years. Therefore, if the taxpayer can express the useful life of the machine in terms of some base other than years (such as machine hours, units produced, etc.), it may be possible to depreciate the machine over a much shorter period than the seven years required under MACRS.

STRUCTURING A BUSINESS COMBINATION

When a company purchases the assets of another business, the agreement must specify the amounts paid for the tangible depreciable, nondepreciable, and intangible assets. Also, the company must comply with the reporting requirements of Sec. 1060, which states that both the transferor and the transferee are bound by their written agreement as to the allocation of the purchase price to individual assets unless the IRS determines that such allocation is not appropriate. Amounts paid for tangible assets should be documented by appraisals and evidence of negotiations between the buyer and seller. Within reason, the purchaser should attempt to allocate as much of the total price to tangible depreciable assets, such as machinery and equipment. The purchaser also should consider allocating part of the purchase price to amortizable Sec. 197 intangible assets such as goodwill, covenants not to compete, patents, copyrights, licenses, and customer lists because such asset costs are recovered over a 15-year period. This is preferable to allocating the purchase price to depreciable real estate because such property must be depreciated over 39 years.

REAL-WORLD EXAMPLE

A taxpayer purchased a business that owned retail franchises. The IRS determined that amounts paid in excess of the value of the net assets represented a nondepreciable "indivisible asset." However, the taxpayer was able to show that retail franchises have limited useful lives, and was able to amortize the excess costs. *Super Food Services, Inc. v. U.S.*, 24 AFTR 2d 69-5309, 69-2 USTC ¶9558 (7th Cir., 1969).

What Would You Do in This Situation?

Your CPA firm has a long-standing tax client named Widgets R Us, Incorporated (WRU). WRU has been a worldwide leader in widget technology for years and continues to expand its global market share through a substantial program of basic research and development of widget crystallization processes. You have advised WRU as to which of these expenditures qualify as research and experimental (R&E) expenditures. In addition, you have given timely advice as to when to expense rather than capitalize these expenditures.

You are having your monthly tax conference with Ms. Ima Worthmore, president of WRU, and Mr. Stan Cunning, tax counsel of WMU. Ms. Worthmore relates to you a conversation she had with the local manager of a competitor CPA firm, Ms. Ruth Less. Ms. Less told Ms. Worthmore that she had discovered that WRU was one of the top spenders on research and development in the area and that her firm was "certified" to practice before the IRS and had experienced great success in gaining R&E write-offs for comparable firms. Ms. Less went on to say that, "For you, for this one year only, we offer to prepare your tax returns on a contingent basis. We promise to save you at least $1 million from what you are now paying the IRS through our better use of R&E write-offs, and our fee will only be 30% of the tax savings!"

Ms. Worthmore was excited that WRU might be able to pay considerably lower taxes and is somewhat perturbed because you had not brought this tax opportunity to her attention. She wants your firm to provide her with a counteroffer. How do you ethically respond to your client's request to match or better Ms. Ruth Less' proposal?

Compliance and Procedural Considerations

OBJECTIVE 5

Identify compliance and procedural considerations for depreciation

Reporting Cost Recovery, Depreciation, Depletion, and Amortization Deductions

Form 4562 is the primary reporting device for depreciation (cost recovery), depletion, and amortization. Individual taxpayers engaged in trade or business complete Form 4562 and carry the total to Schedule C of their Form 1040, using a separate 4562 for each enterprise. Corporate and other non-corporate taxpayers also use Form 4562, carrying the total to their specific returns. Individuals with rental property complete a 4562 and carry the total to Schedule E of their Form 1040.

Two exceptions to the use of Form 4562: (1) Depreciation on property used by an employee for business purposes is computed along with other employee business expenses on Form 2106, with the total carried to Schedule A of the Form 1040; (2) If a taxpayer computes depreciation only on property placed in service before the current year, Form 4562 is not required. Depreciation totals are entered directly on the applicable primary form. Taxpayers must still maintain detailed depreciation records to support the deduction.

EXAMPLE I:10-38 ► Form 4562 for 2014: George Jones, SSN 000-00-1111, is a building contractor who owns the following 100% business-use properties:

- Specialized utility repair truck (5-year property that is not listed property), costing $40,000, placed in service on February 15, 2014.
- Machinery and equipment (7-year property), costing $535,000, placed in service on June 10, 2014.
- Patent, costing $17,000, that was developed and placed in service on June 1, 2014, when it had a remaining legal life of 17 years.
- MACRS deduction for assets placed in service before 2014 is $66,000.

Jones had 2014 taxable income of $960,000 (before the Sec. 179 deduction and the deduction for one-half of self-employment taxes). George elected Sec. 179 expensing on the machinery and equipment, but elected out of claiming bonus depreciation on all qualifying property. Depreciation and amortization amounts are reported on Form 4562 and are shown in Figures I:10-1 and I:10-2. ◄

Form **4562** Department of the Treasury Internal Revenue Service (99)

Depreciation and Amortization (Including Information on Listed Property)

▶ Attach to your tax return.
▶ Information about Form 4562 and its separate instructions is at *www.irs.gov/form4562.*

OMB No. 1545-0172 | 2014 | Attachment Sequence No. 179

Name(s) shown on return	Business or activity to which this form relates	Identifying number
George Jones	Building Contractor	000-00-1111

Part I Election To Expense Certain Property Under Section 179
Note: *If you have any listed property, complete Part V before you complete Part I.*

1	Maximum amount (see instructions)	1	$500,000
2	Total cost of section 179 property placed in service (see instructions)	2	$575,000
3	Threshold cost of section 179 property before reduction in limitation (see instructions)	3	$2,000,000
4	Reduction in limitation. Subtract line 3 from line 2. If zero or less, enter -0-	4	-0-
5	Dollar limitation for tax year. Subtract line 4 from line 1. If zero or less, enter -0-. If married filing separately, see instructions	5	$500,000

6 (a) Description of property	(b) Cost (business use only)	(c) Elected cost
Truck	40,000	-0-
Machinery and Equipment	535,000	500,000
7 Listed property. Enter the amount from line 29	7	-0-

8	Total elected cost of section 179 property. Add amounts in column (c), lines 6 and 7			8	500,000
9	Tentative deduction. Enter the **smaller** of line 5 or line 8			9	500,000
10	Carryover of disallowed deduction from line 13 of your 2013 Form 4562			10	
11	Business income limitation. Enter the smaller of business income (not less than zero) or line 5 (see instructions)			11	500,000
12	Section 179 expense deduction. Add lines 9 and 10, but do not enter more than line 11			12	500,000
13	Carryover of disallowed deduction to 2015. Add lines 9 and 10, less line 12 ▶	13	-0-		

Note: *Do not use Part II or Part III below for listed property. Instead, use Part V.*

Part II Special Depreciation Allowance and Other Depreciation (Do not include listed property.**)** (See instructions.)

14	Special depreciation allowance for qualified property (other than listed property) placed in service during the tax year (see instructions)	14	
15	Property subject to section 168(f)(1) election	15	
16	Other depreciation (including ACRS)	16	

Part III MACRS Depreciation (Do not include listed property.**)** (See instructions.)

Section A

17	MACRS deductions for assets placed in service in tax years beginning before 2014	17	66,000
18	If you are electing to group any assets placed in service during the tax year into one or more general asset accounts, check here ▶ ☐		

Section B—Assets Placed in Service During 2014 Tax Year Using the General Depreciation System

(a) Classification of property	(b) Month and year placed in service	(c) Basis for depreciation (business/investment use only—see instructions)	(d) Recovery period	(e) Convention	(f) Method	(g) Depreciation deduction
19a 3-year property						
b 5-year property		40,000	5 yrs	HY	MACRS	8,000
c 7-year property		*35,000	7 yrs	HY	MACRS	5,002
d 10-year property						
e 15-year property						
f 20-year property						
g 25-year property			25 yrs.		S/L	
h Residential rental property			27.5 yrs.	MM	S/L	
			27.5 yrs.	MM	S/L	
i Nonresidential real property			39 yrs.	MM	S/L	
				MM	S/L	

Section C—Assets Placed in Service During 2014 Tax Year Using the Alternative Depreciation System

20a Class life					S/L	
b 12-year			12 yrs.		S/L	
c 40-year			40 yrs.	MM	S/L	

Part IV Summary (See instructions.)

21	Listed property. Enter amount from line 28			21	-0-
22	**Total.** Add amounts from line 12, lines 14 through 17, lines 19 and 20 in column (g), and line 21. Enter here and on the appropriate lines of your return. Partnerships and S corporations—see instructions			22	579,002
23	For assets shown above and placed in service during the current year, enter the portion of the basis attributable to section 263A costs	23			

For Paperwork Reduction Act Notice, see separate instructions. Cat. No. 12906N Form **4562** (2014)

*Line 19c: 535,000 – 500,000

FIGURE I:10-1 ▶ FORM 4562

Form 4562 (2014) Page 2

Part V **Listed Property** (Include automobiles, certain other vehicles, certain computers, and property used for entertainment, recreation, or amusement.)

Note: *For any vehicle for which you are using the standard mileage rate or deducting lease expense, complete* ***only*** *24a, 24b, columns (a) through (c) of Section A, all of Section B, and Section C if applicable.*

Section A—Depreciation and Other Information (Caution: *See the instructions for limits for passenger automobiles.)*

24a Do you have evidence to support the business/investment use claimed? ☐ **Yes** ☐ **No** **24b** If "Yes," is the evidence written? ☐ **Yes** ☐ **No**

(a) Type of property (list vehicles first)	(b) Date placed in service	(c) Business/ investment use percentage	(d) Cost or other basis	(e) Basis for depreciation (business/investment use only)	(f) Recovery period	(g) Method/ Convention	(h) Depreciation deduction	(i) Elected section 179 cost
25 Special depreciation allowance for qualified listed property placed in service during the tax year and used more than 50% in a qualified business use (see instructions) .						**25**		
26 Property used more than 50% in a qualified business use:								
		%						
		%						
		%						
27 Property used 50% or less in a qualified business use:								
		%				S/L –		
		%				S/L –		
		%				S/L –		
28 Add amounts in column (h), lines 25 through 27. Enter here and on line 21, page 1 .						**28**		
29 Add amounts in column (i), line 26. Enter here and on line 7, page 1							**29**	

Section B—Information on Use of Vehicles

Complete this section for vehicles used by a sole proprietor, partner, or other "more than 5% owner," or related person. If you provided vehicles to your employees, first answer the questions in Section C to see if you meet an exception to completing this section for those vehicles.

	(a) Vehicle 1		(b) Vehicle 2		(c) Vehicle 3		(d) Vehicle 4		(e) Vehicle 5		(f) Vehicle 6	
30 Total business/investment miles driven during the year (**do not** include commuting miles) .												
31 Total commuting miles driven during the year												
32 Total other personal (noncommuting) miles driven												
33 Total miles driven during the year. Add lines 30 through 32												
	Yes	**No**	**Yes**	**No**	**Yes**	**No**	**Yes**	**No**	**Yes**	**No**	**Yes**	**No**
34 Was the vehicle available for personal use during off-duty hours?												
35 Was the vehicle used primarily by a more than 5% owner or related person? . .												
36 Is another vehicle available for personal use?												

Section C—Questions for Employers Who Provide Vehicles for Use by Their Employees

Answer these questions to determine if you meet an exception to completing Section B for vehicles used by employees who **are not** more than 5% owners or related persons (see instructions).

	Yes	**No**
37 Do you maintain a written policy statement that prohibits all personal use of vehicles, including commuting, by your employees?		
38 Do you maintain a written policy statement that prohibits personal use of vehicles, except commuting, by your employees? See the instructions for vehicles used by corporate officers, directors, or 1% or more owners . .		
39 Do you treat all use of vehicles by employees as personal use?		
40 Do you provide more than five vehicles to your employees, obtain information from your employees about the use of the vehicles, and retain the information received?		
41 Do you meet the requirements concerning qualified automobile demonstration use? (See instructions.) . . .		

Note: *If your answer to 37, 38, 39, 40, or 41 is "Yes," do not complete Section B for the covered vehicles.*

Part VI **Amortization**

(a) Description of costs	(b) Date amortization begins	(c) Amortizable amount	(d) Code section	(e) Amortization period or percentage	(f) Amortization for this year
42 Amortization of costs that begins during your 2014 tax year (see instructions):					
Patent	6-01-14	17,000	167	17 yrs.	*583
43 Amortization of costs that began before your 2014 tax year				**43**	
44 **Total.** Add amounts in column (f). See the instructions for where to report				**44**	583

*($17,000 ÷ 17 yrs.) = $1,000 x 7/12 = $583

Form **4562** (2014)

FIGURE I:10-2 ► FORM 4562 (CONTINUED)

Problem materials

DISCUSSION QUESTIONS

I:10-1 Which of the following assets are subject to either amortization, depreciation, or cost recovery? Explain.
a. An automobile held for personal use.
b. Excess amounts paid in a business combination that are attributable to goodwill.
c. Excess amounts paid in a business combination that are attributable to customer lists that have a limited useful life.
d. A patent created internally which has a legal life of 17 years.
e. Land held for investment purposes.
f. A covenant not to compete which is entered into by the buyer and seller of a business.

I:10-2 Rick is a sole proprietor who has a small business currently operating at a loss. He would like to discontinue depreciating the fixed assets of the business for the next few years and to carry the deductions over to a future period. What tax consequences would result if Rick implements the plan to discontinue depreciation and then sells some of the depreciable assets several years later?

I:10-3 Rita acquired a personal residence two years ago for $120,000. In the current year, she purchases another residence and attempts to sell her former residence. Due to depressed housing conditions in the town where she used to live, Rita is unable to sell the house. Her former residence is now being offered for sale at $100,000 (its current FMV according to real estate appraisal experts). Rita has decided to rent the house rather than "give it away." She believes that renting the house on a permanent basis will permit her to write off the original $120,000 investment over its useful life and thus recoup her investment. What restrictions in the tax law may prevent her from accomplishing this objective? Explain.

I:10-4 Daytona Corporation, a manufacturing corporation, acquires the following business assets in the current year:

- Furniture
- Plumbing fixtures
- Land
- Goodwill and a trademark acquired in the acquisition of a business
- Automobile
- Heavy truck
- Machinery
- Building used in manufacturing activities

a. Which of the assets above are eligible for depreciation under the MACRS rules or amortization under Sec. 197?
b. What recovery period should be used for each of the assets listed above that come under the MACRS rules or under Sec. 197?

I:10-5 Robert is a sole proprietor who uses the calendar year as his tax year. On July 20, 2015 he acquired and placed in service a business machine, a 7-year asset, for $50,000. No other property was acquired in 2015.
a. What is the amount of depreciation allowed in 2015 and 2016 if Sec. 179 depreciation (first-year expense election) was not elected?
b. What is the amount of depreciation allowed in 2015 and 2016 if Sec. 179 was elected?

I:10-6 Roberta, a sole proprietor who uses the calendar year as her tax year, acquires and places in service two business machines during 2015. Machine C, a 7-year asset, was acquired on January 20, 2015, for $95,000 and Machine D, a 5-year asset, was acquired on August 1, 2015, for $50,000. No other property was acquired in 2015.
a. What is the amount of depreciation allowed in 2015 if Sec. 179 is not elected?
b. What is the amount of depreciation allowed in 2015 if Sec. 179 is elected?

I:10-7 Is a deduction allowed under the MACRS rules for depreciable real estate (used in a business or held for investment) in the year the property is sold? If so, explain how it is calculated.

I:10-8 Jose is considering acquiring a new luxury automobile costing $45,000 that will be used 100% in his business. The salesperson at the automobile dealership states that Jose will be entitled to substantial tax benefits in the initial year (2015) including:

If Sec. 179 is elected:

- A deduction of $25,000 of the acquisition cost under Sec. 179, and a $4,000 ($20,000 × 0.2) depreciation deduction, for total deductions of $29,000.

If Sec. 179 is not elected:

- A $9,000 ($45,000 × 0.2) depreciation deduction.

a. Are the salesperson's assertions relative to the tax benefits accurate? Explain.
b. Would your answer to Part a differ if the automobile were used only 60% for business purposes?
c. Would your answer to Part a differ if Jose instead were to lease the automobile?

d. Would your answers to Part a differ if the vehicle were a large SUV (gross vehicle weight rating (GVWR) greater than 6,000 pounds) rather than an automobile?

I:10-9 Would the straight-line MACRS method (using the ADS) be preferable to the regular MACRS method in the following cases? Explain.
a. Ray incurs NOLs in his business for a number of years and has NOL carryovers he would like to use.
b. Rhonda's marginal tax rate is 15% but is expected to increase to 39.6% in three years.

I:10-10 Rudy is considering whether to make the election under Sec. 179 to expense the maximum amount of the acquisition cost related to certain fixed asset additions. What advantages are associated with the Sec. 179 election?

I:10-11 Luby Corporation has maintained an office in a leased building for several years. The corporation has decided to make some significant leasehold improvements to enhance the property. How should Luby Corporation depreciate the leasehold improvements?

I:10-12 Your client is a self-employed attorney who is considering the purchase of a $32,000 automobile that will be used 80% of the time for business and a $4,000 personal computer that will be used 100% of the time for business, but is located in his home.
a. What depreciation methods and recovery periods may be used under MACRS for the automobile and the personal computer?
b. How would your answer to Part a change if your client were an employee and the computer and automobile were not required as a condition of employment?
c. What tax consequences occur in Part a if the business use of the personal computer or the automobile decreases to 50% or less in a succeeding year? Explain.

I:10-13 In recent years (through 2014), Congress enacted provisions in the tax law that permitted bonus depreciation for certain assets.
a. What types of assets typically qualified for bonus depreciation?
b. How does bonus depreciation interface with Sec. 179 first-year expensing?

I:10-14 On March 1, 2015, Sarah entered into a three-year lease of an automobile used exclusively in her business. The automobile's FMV was $58,500 at the inception of the lease. Sarah made ten monthly lease payments of $600 each during 2015. Is Sarah able to avoid the luxury automobile restrictions on depreciation by leasing instead of purchasing the automobile? Explain. (The 2015 inclusion amount for Sarah's automobile is found in Table 13 of Appendix C.)

I:10-15 What difference does it make for income tax purposes whether an intangible asset is (1) acquired in connection with a business acquisition, (2) acquired by the purchase of an individual asset (e.g., a patent), or (3) created internally? Explain.

I:10-16 In January of the current year, Park Corporation incurs $34,000 of legal costs associated with a patent that was developed internally and has a legal life of 17 years. Park also acquired for cash the net assets of Central Corporation for $1,000,000. The following assets are specified in the purchase agreement:

Land	$ 200,000
Goodwill and going concern value	100,000
Covenant not to compete	50,000
Licenses	125,000
Customer lists	25,000
Inventory	100,000
Equipment and other tangible depreciable business assets	400,000
Total	$1,000,000

a. What tax treatment should be accorded the intangible assets?
b. Assuming that you were advising Park Corporation during the negotiations before drafting the purchase agreement, what suggestions would you make regarding the allocation of the total purchase price to the individual assets? How could the purchase price of individual assets be substantiated?

I:10-17 Why do most taxpayers prefer to currently expense research and experimental expenditures?

I:10-18 In a business combination, why does the buyer generally prefer to allocate as much of the purchase price to short-lived depreciable assets, ordinary assets such as inventory, and Sec. 197 intangible assets?

I:10-19 Explain the difference between cost depletion and percentage depletion. Which of these two methods generally provides the largest deduction?

I:10-20 Simon acquires an interest in an oil property for $50,000. Intangible drilling costs (IDCs) in the initial year are $10,000. Cost depletion is $5,000 if the IDCs are expensed and $6,000 if the costs are capitalized. Percentage depletion is $15,000 if the IDCs are expensed and $20,000 if the costs are capitalized. The difference in the percentage depletion amounts is due to the 100% taxable income limitation.
a. What method (i.e., expensing or capitalization and amortization) should be elected for the treatment of the IDCs in the initial year if Simon wants to maximize his deductions?
b. Why are intangible drilling costs expensed by most taxpayers?

ISSUE IDENTIFICATION QUESTIONS

I:10-21 Georgia Corporation acquires a business automobile for $30,000 on December 31 of the current year but does not actually place the automobile into service until January 1 of the following year. What tax issues should Georgia Corporation consider?

I:10-22 Paula is planning to either purchase or lease a $50,000 automobile. She anticipates that business use of the auto will be 60% for the first two years but will decline to 40% in years three through five. Currently, Paula's marginal tax rate is 15% but she anticipates that her marginal tax rate will be 39.6% after a few years. What tax issues should Paula consider relative to the decision to purchase or lease the automobile?

I:10-23 In the current year, Coastal Corporation acquires all of the net assets of Acorn Corporation for $2,000,000. The purchase agreement allocated the following amounts to the individual assets and liabilities:

Land and building	$1,400,000
Accounts receivable	200,000
Inventory	300,000
Goodwill	400,000
Patents (remaining legal life of ten years)	100,000
Covenant not to compete	200,000
Liabilities	(600,000)
Total	$2,000,000

What tax issues should Coastal Corporation consider relative to the asset acquisitions?

I:10-24 Weiskopf, a sole proprietor and a calendar-year taxpayer, purchased $60,000 of equipment during 2015, as follows:

	Cost	*Recovery Period*
March 1	$20,000	7 years
September 18	$25,000	7 years
October 2	$15,000	5 years

Weiskopf's CPA, to maximize the depreciation deduction, elects $25,000 of Sec. 179 depreciation as follows: $20,000 on the March 1 property and $5,000 on the September 18 property. What tax issue should be considered with respect to the total depreciation deduction for the current year?

PROBLEMS

I:10-25 *Allowed Versus Allowable Depreciation.* Sandy acquired business machinery (which qualified as 7-year MACRS property) on July 15, 2012, for $10,000. In 2012, Sandy claimed a $1,429 regular MACRS depreciation deduction and she elected not to claim Sec. 179 depreciation or bonus depreciation. Because of net operating losses in 2013–2015, Sandy did not claim any depreciation deduction on her tax returns in those years. She sells the machine on July 1, 2015, for $6,000.

a. What is the adjusted basis of the machine on the sale date?

b. How much gain or loss is recognized on the sale of the machine?

I:10-26 *Conversion of Personal Asset to Business Use.* Sid purchased an automobile for personal use on January 18, 2011 for $10,000. On January 1, 2015, Sid starts a small business and begins to use the automobile exclusively in the business. The automobile's FMV on this date is $6,000. MACRS depreciation deductions are based on a 5-year recovery period.

a. What is the automobile's basis for depreciation when converted to business use in 2015?

b. Assuming Sid does not elect Sec. 179 expensing, what is Sid's depreciation deduction in 2015?

I:10-27 *MACRS 40% Test and Bonus Depreciation.* Small Corporation purchased and placed in service the following 100% business-use assets (all of the assets were purchased new). Assume that Small purchased these assets in Year 1, when 50% bonus depreciation was available on eligible property (as "eligible property" has been typically defined for years when bonus depreciation was available). Small claimed bonus depreciation but no Sec. 179 election on all eligible property in Year 1.

- Truck (light-duty, modified non-personal use) costing $20,000: Placed in service on February 15, Year 1 with a 5-year MACRS recovery period.
- Machinery costing $50,000: Placed in service on May 1, Year 1 with a 7-year MACRS recovery period.
- Land costing $60,000: Placed in service on July 1, Year 1.
- Building costing $100,000: Placed in service on December 1, Year 1 with a 39-year MACRS recovery period.
- Equipment costing $40,000:Acquired on December 24, Year 1 and placed in service on January 5, Year 2 with a 5-year MACRS recovery period.

What are Small's total depreciation deductions in Year 1 and Year 2?

I:10-28 ***MACRS 40% Test and Partial Year Depreciation.*** Large Corporation acquired and placed in service the following 100% business-use assets. Large did not elect Sec. 179 expensing on any of these properties.

- Truck (light-duty, modified non-personal use) costing $36,000: Placed in service on March 3, 2015 with a 5-year MACRS recovery period.
- Machinery costing $85,000: Placed in service on November 15, 2015 with a 7-year MACRS recovery period.
- Land costing $90,000: Placed in service on October 12, 2015.
- Building costing $280,000: Placed in service on December 4, 2015 with a 39-year MACRS recovery period.

a. What is Large's total depreciation deduction in 2015?
b. Large Corporation sells the machinery on February 2, 2017 and sells the building on September 18, 2017. What are the adjusted bases of these two assets on the dates of sale (compute accumulated depreciation to date of sale)?

I:10-29 ***Sec. 179 Expensing and MACRS Depreciation.*** Ted is in the rental real estate business. During 2015, Ted purchased and placed in service the following assets:

- Apartment building costing $300,000 (exclusive of $80,000 land): Placed in service on May 12 with a 27.5-year MACRS recovery period.
- Office furniture costing $23,000: Placed in service on April 10 with a 7-year MACRS recovery period.
- Office equipment costing $15,000: Placed in service on November 1 with a 5-year MACRS recovery period.

a. What are Ted's total depreciation deductions in 2015 assuming he does not elect Sec. 179 expensing?
b. What are Ted's total depreciation deductions in 2015 assuming he elects Sec. 179 expensing in 2015 for $23,000 on the furniture and $2,000 on the equipment? Assume Ted elects out of bonus depreciation on all qualifying properties.
c. What are Ted's total depreciation deductions in 2015 assuming he elects Sec. 179 expensing in 2015 for $10,000 on the furniture and $15,000 on the equipment?

I:10-30 ***Sec. 179 Limitations and Carryovers.*** In July 2015, Tish acquires and places in service a business machine costing $40,000 with a 7-year MACRS recovery period. Tish elects the maximum allowable Sec. 179 expense on the machine. In August 2015, she also places in service business equipment costing $165,000, with a 5-year MACRS recovery period. Tish's taxable income (before the Sec. 179 expense and the 50% of SE tax deduction) is $16,000.

a. What is Tish's allowable 2015 Sec. 179 expense on the machine? What amount can she carry over to 2016?
b. What is Tish's total 2015 depreciation deduction?
c. What are the limitations on Tish's ability to use the Sec. 179 carryover in 2016?
d. How would your answer to Part a change if Tish's business taxable income (before the Sec. 179 expense and the 50% of SE tax deduction) were $37,000 in 2015 instead of $16,000?

I:10-31 ***MACRS Dispositions.*** Tampa Corporation sold the following assets in 2015:

	Date Acquired	*Date Sold*	*Original Cost Basis*	*Depreciation/ Cost-Recovery Method*	*Recovery Period (Years)*	*Sales Price*
Automobile	1/1/12	12/1/15[a]	$ 9,000	MACRS	5	$ 1,200
Equipment	1/6/12	9/1/15[a]	20,000	MACRS	7	9,500
Building (nonresidental)	4/1/05	12/10/15	100,000	MACRS	39	240,000

[a] The half-year convention was used in the year of acquisition. Tampa did not elect Sec. 179 expense or bonus depreciation during the acquistion years.

a. What is the depreciation deduction for each asset in 2015?
b. Compute the gain or loss on each asset sold.

I:10-32 ***Sec. 179 Expensing Election and MACRS Depreciation.*** Thad acquires a machine at a cost of $27,000 for use in his business and places it in service on April 1, 2015. The machine is depreciated under MACRS, with a 7-year recovery period. This machine was his only asset acquisition of the year. Thad elects to expense $25,000 of the acquisition cost under Sec. 179.

a. What is Thad's total depreciation deduction for the machine in 2015?
b. Thad then sells the machine on October 5, 2017 for $10,000. Compute Thad's depreciation deductions for 2015 through 2017, the adjusted basis of the machine on October 5, 2017, and the gain or loss on the sale.

I:10-33 ***Sec. 179 Expensing and Mid-Quarter Convention.*** During 2015, Rita acquired and placed in service two assets for use in her business, as follows:

- Asset A: Placed in service in February at a cost of $65,000 with a 7-year MACRS recovery period.
- Asset B: Placed in service in November at a cost of $30,000 with a 7-year MACRS recovery period.

Rita elects to expense $25,000 under Sec. 179. Compute Rita's total depreciation deduction for 2015 under each of the following assumptions:

a. Rita allocates the entire $25,000 Sec. 179 expense to Asset A.
b. Rita allocates the entire $25,000 Sec. 179 expense to Asset B.

I:10-34 ***Straight-Line Depreciation.*** Long Corporation has been unprofitable for several years and has substantial NOL carryovers. Therefore, the company has elected to use straight-line MACRS for property acquisitions. Long acquires, holds, or sells the following assets in 2015:

	Date Acquired	*Date Sold*	*Original Cost Basis*	*Selling Price*	*Depreciation Method*	*Recovery Period (Years)*
Equipment	6/1/15	—	$40,000	—	SL ADS	7
Light duty truck (Nonpersonal-use)	5/1/11	12/1/15	30,000	$ 8,000	SL ADS	5
Furniture	3/1/11	—	10,000	—	SL ADS	7
Automobile	7/1/12	12/1/15	12,000	10,000	SL ADS	5

Long did not make the Sec. 179 election in any year, and elects out of bonus depreciation.

a. What is the depreciation deduction for each asset in 2015?
b. What amount of gain or loss does Long recognize on the properties sold in 2015?

I:10-35 ***Mixed Personal/Business Use.*** In 2015, Trish, a self-employed CPA and calendar year taxpayer, acquires and places in service an automobile and a personal computer. Pertinent data include the following:

Asset	*Date Acquired*	*Total Original Cost Basis*	*Portion of Business Usage*	*Sec. 179 Election*
Automobile	1/2/15	$21,000	60%	No
Personal computer	7/1/15	4,000	40%	No

For each asset, calculate the MACRS current year depreciation deduction assuming Trish does not elect Sec. 179 expensing.

I:10-36 *Employee Listed Property.* Assume the same facts as in Problem I:10-35, except Trish is an employee who uses the automobile and personal computer for employment-related activities. While both assets are helpful to Trish in performing her job duties, her employer does not require employees to purchase a car or a personal computer as a condition of employment. What is the amount of depreciation for each asset?

I:10-37 *Recapture of Depreciation Deductions Due to Personal Use.* Tammy acquired an automobile for $20,000 on July 1, 2012. She used the automobile partially for business purposes during the 2012–2015 period. The percentage of business use is as follows: 2012, 70%, 2013, 70%; 2014, 40%; 2015, 35%. The automobile is 5-year recovery property, and Tammy did not elect Sec. 179 expensing or bonus depreciation.

a. Compute the MACRS depreciation deductions for 2012–2015.

b. What amount of previously claimed depreciation deductions (if any) must Tammy recapture in 2015?

I:10-38 *Luxury Auto Limitations.* Lutz Corporation acquired a 100% business-use automobile (MACRS 5-year recovery) on July 1, 2015 for $32,000. The company did not elect Sec. 179 expensing. What is depreciation for 2015–2017, and any subsequent years?

I:10-39 *Luxury Auto Limitations.* Luby Corporation acquires a 100% business-use automobile (MACRS 5-year recovery) on July 1, 2015 for $36,000. Luby does not elect Sec. 179. What are depreciation deductions for 2015–2017?

I:10-40 *Luxury Auto Limitations.* Tracy acquires an automobile (MACRS 5-year recovery) on March 1, 2015. He uses the automobile 70% of the time in his business and 30% of the time for personal use. The automobile cost $36,000, and no amount is expensed under Sec. 179.

a. What is depreciation for 2015–2020 and any subsequent years?

b. How would your answer to Part a change if the vehicle were a SUV with a gross vehicle weight rated (GVWR) of over 6,000 pounds and Tracy elected to expense the SUV under Sec. 179?

I:10-41 *Luxury Auto Limitations—Leasing.* Troy entered into a three-year lease of a luxury automobile on January 1, 2015, for use 80% in business and 20% for personal use. The FMV of the automobile at the inception of the lease was $40,500, and Troy made 12 monthly lease payments of $600 in 2015 and 2016.

a. Before considering the effects of any lease inclusions amounts, what amount of lease payments are deductible in 2015 and 2016?

b. What portion, if any, of the "inclusion amount" must reduce Troy's lease deduction in 2015 and 2016?

c. How would your answers to Parts a and b change if the FMV of the auto was $15,000 and the monthly lease payments are $200?

I:10-42 *Amortization of Intangibles.* On January 1 of the current year, Palm Corporation purchases the net assets of Vicki's unincorporated business for $600,000. The tangible net assets have a $300,000 book value and a $400,000 FMV. The purchase agreement states that Vicki will not compete with Palm Corporation by starting a new business in the same area for a period of five years. The stated consideration received by Vicki for the covenant not to compete is $50,000. Other intangible assets included in the purchase agreement are as follows:

- Goodwill: $70,000
- Patents (12-year remaining legal life): $30,000
- Customer list: $50,000

a. How would Vicki's assets be recorded for tax purposes by Palm Corporation?

b. What is the amortization amount for each intangible asset in the current year?

I:10-43 *R&E Expenditures.* Park Corporation incurs the following costs in the initial year of doing business:

Materials and supplies for research laboratory	$ 80,000
Utilities and depreciation on research laboratory and equipment	40,000
Costs of acquiring another entity's patent for a new product	20,000
Market research salaries for surveys relative to proposed new products	60,000
Labor and supplies for quality control tests	50,000
Research costs subcontracted to a local university	35,000
Total	$285,000

Park's controller states that all of these costs are qualifying R&E expenditures and that the company policy is to expense such amounts for tax purposes in the year they are incurred. Which of these expenditures are deductible as R&E costs under Sec. 174?

I:10-44 *R&E Expenditures.* In 2015, Phoenix Corporation acquires a new research facility and hires several scientists to develop new products. No new products are developed until 2016, although the following expenditures were incurred:

Laboratory materials	$ 40,000
Research salaries	80,000
Overhead attributable to the research facility	30,000
R&E equipment placed into service (5-year MACRS recovery period)	100,000
Total	$250,000

a. What are Phoenix Corporation's deductions for R&E expenditures in 2015 and 2016 if the expensing method is elected?
b. How would your answer to Part a change if the deferral and amortization method were elected and the amortization period were 60 months?

I:10-45 *Computer Software.* Phillips Corporation, a construction company that specializes in home construction, uses special computer software to schedule jobs and keep track of job costs. It uses generic software for bookkeeping and spreadsheet analysis. During 2015, Phillips Corporation had the following transactions relating to computer software:

- The corporation purchased a new computer system on May 12, 2015, for $15,000. The system included computer hardware and built-in computer software valued at $3,000. The corporation has never separated computer software from the hardware in prior years when a computer system was purchased.
- The corporation separately purchased new bookkeeping software on September 1, 2015, for $5,760.
- On June 1, 2015, Phillips Corporation acquired another home building company to strengthen its position in higher-priced homes. The total purchase price was $700,000 allocated to specific assets as follows:

Equipment	$500,000
Goodwill	150,000
Computer software	50,000

What amount can Phillips Corporation deduct in 2015 with respect to computer software?

I:10-46 *Cost Depletion.* Tina acquires an oil and gas property interest for $200,000 in the current year. The following information about current year operations is supplied for purposes of computing the amount of Tina's depletion and intangible drilling and development cost (IDC) deductions:

Estimated recoverable units	20,000
Units produced	6,000
Units sold	4,000
IDCs	$20,000
Percentage depletion (after limitations)	$25,000

a. What is the cost depletion amount if the IDCs are expensed?
b. What is the cost depletion amount if the IDCs are capitalized?
c. How much depletion is deducted on the tax return?
d. Should the IDCs be capitalized or expensed? Explain.

I:10-47 *Percentage Depletion.* Tony has owned an oil and gas property for a number of years. The following information is provided about the property's operations in the current year:

Gross income	$500,000
Minus: Expenses (including IDCs of $100,000)	(300,000)
Taxable income (before depletion)	$200,000
Cost depletion (if IDCs are expensed)	$ 20,000
Cost depletion (if IDCs are capitalized)	$ 30,000

a. What is the percentage depletion amount if the IDCs are expensed?
b. What is the percentage depletion amount if the IDCs are capitalized?
c. What is the depletion deduction amount assuming that the IDCs are expensed?
d. Based on the information above, which method should be used for the IDCs? Explain.

COMPREHENSIVE PROBLEM

I:10-48 John and Ellen Brite (SSN 000-00-1111 and 000-00-2222, respectively) are married and file a joint return. They have no dependents. John owns an unincorporated specialty electrical lighting retail store, Brite-On. Brite-On had the following assets on January 1, 2014:

Assets	*Cost*
Old store building purchased April 1, 1999	$100,000
Equipment (7-year recovery) purchased January 10, 2009	30,000
Inventory valued using FIFO method: 4,000 light bulbs	$5/bulb

Brite-On purchased a competitor's store on March 1, 2014, for $107,000. The purchase price included the following:

New store building	$60,000 (FMV)
Land	18,000 (FMV)
Equipment (5-year recovery)	11,000 (FMV)
Inventory: 3,000 light bulbs	$ 6/bulb (cost)

On June 30, 2014, Brite-On sold the 7-year recovery period equipment for $12,000. Brite-On leased a $30,500 car for $500/month beginning on January 1, 2014. The car is used 100% for business and was driven 14,000 miles during the year.

Brite-On sold 8,000 light bulbs at a price of $15/bulb during the year. Also, Brite-On made additional purchases of 4,000 light bulbs in August 2014 at a cost of $7/bulb. Brite-On had the following revenues (in addition to the sales of light bulbs) and additional expenses:

Service revenues	$64,000
Interest expense on business loans	4,000
Auto expenses (gas, oil, etc.)	3,800
Taxes and licenses	3,300
Utilities	2,800
Salaries	24,000

John and Ellen also had some personal expenses:

Medical bills	$4,500
Real property taxes	3,800
State income taxes	4,000
Home mortgage interest	5,000
Charitable contributions (cash)	600

The Brites received interest income on a bank savings account of $275. John and Ellen made four $5,000 quarterly estimated tax payments. For self-employment tax purposes, assume John spent 100% of his time at the store while Ellen spends no time at the store.

Additional Facts:

- Equipment acquired in 2009: The Brites elected out of bonus depreciation and did not elect Sec. 179.

- Equipment acquired in 2014: The Brites elected Sec. 179 to expense the cost of the 5-year equipment but elected out of bonus depreciation.
- Assume that the lease inclusion rules require that Brite-On reduce its deductible lease expense by $8.

Compute the Brite's taxable income and balance due or refund for 2014.

TAX STRATEGY PROBLEM

I:10-49 Stan Bushart works as a customer representative for a large corporation. Stan's job entails traveling to meet with customers, and he uses his personal car 100% for business use. In 2015, Stan must decide whether to buy or lease a new car. After bargaining with several car dealers, Stan has agreed to a price of $30,000. If he buys the car, he will borrow the entire $30,000 at an annual interest rate of 8%, and his payments will be $608.29 per month over 60 months. Annual principal and interest payments are:

	Total	*Principal*	*Interest*
2015	$ 7,299	$ 5,083	$2,216
2016	7,299	5,505	1,794
2017	7,299	5,962	1,337
2018	7,299	6,457	843
2019	7,299	6,993	305
Totals:	$36,495	$30,000	$6,495

If he leases the car, his lease payment will be $450 per month for 60 months. At the end of the lease, he has the option of purchasing the car for $10,000. For simplicity, assume an average lease inclusion amount of $230 per year rather than actual amounts. Stan's marginal tax rate is 28% in each of the five years. Using present value analysis with an 8% discount rate, is Stan better off leasing or buying the car?

If Stan purchases the car, he will not elect Sec. 179 expensing or bonus depreciation. He will sell the car for $10,000 at the end of five years. If he leases the car, assume he merely turns the car in at the end of the lease.

TAX FORM/RETURN PREPARATION PROBLEMS

I:10-50 Thom Jones (SSN 000-00-1111) is an unincorporated manufacturer of widgets. He uses the LCM method to value his inventory and reports the following for 2014:

Sales (less returns and allowances)	$1,250,000
Cost of goods sold	500,000
Office expenses	10,000
Depreciation*	?
Legal services	4,000
Salary expenses	36,000
Travel expenses	30,000
Repair expenses	20,000

* Information related to Mr. Jones's depreciation:

Cost of office furniture acquired and placed in service on April 15, 2014 (7-year recovery).	$480,000
Cost of other property acquired and placed in service on August 1, 2014:	
5-year recovery property (computers-not listed property)	6,000
7-year recovery property (equipment)	54,000
Depreciation on assets purchased prior to 2014:	28,000

Complete Thom's 2014 Form 4562 and Schedule C of Form 1040, assuming Thom elects to expense the maximum amount possible under Sec. 179 but elects out of bonus depreciation.

I:10-51 Using the facts in Problem I:10-48 for John and Ellen Brite, complete their 2014 Form 1040, Schedules A, C, and SE, and Forms 4562 and 4797.

CASE STUDY PROBLEMS

I:10-52 Able Corporation is a manufacturer of electrical lighting fixtures. Able is currently negotiating with Ralph Johnson, the owner of an unincorporated business, to acquire his retail electrical lighting sales business. Johnson's assets include the following:

Assets	*Adjusted Basis*	*FMV*
Inventory of electrical fixtures	$ 30,000	$ 50,000
Store buildings	80,000	100,000
Land	40,000	100,000
Equipment: 7-year recovery period	30,000	50,000
Equipment: 5-year recovery period	60,000	100,000
Total	$240,000	$400,000

Mr. Johnson thinks that a total purchase price of $1 million in cash is warranted for the business because of its high profitability and strategic locations, and Able has agreed. Despite the fact that both parties agree that the $600,000 excess payment is goodwill, Able would prefer that it be designated as a 5-year covenant not to compete so that he can amortize it over a 5-year period.

You are a tax consultant for Able who has been asked to make recommendations as to the structuring of the purchase agreement and the amounts to be assigned to individual assets. Prepare a client memo to reflect your recommendations.

I:10-53 In 2013, the Margate Corporation acquired an automobile with a cost of $30,000 for use in its business. Shortly thereafter, Margate Corporation experienced a decline in sales. Several employees were laid off, and the automobile was not immediately needed for any of the sales personnel. Instead of letting the new automobile sit in the corporate lot, the president decided to permit a corporate officer to use the automobile for personal use. The officer used the automobile in 2013 and 2014 only. In 2015, Margate Corporation hired you as their new CPA (tax consultant). You learn that the officer's personal use of the corporate automobile took place for the two prior years without proper accounting to the IRS. As Margate Corporation's tax consultant, what actions (if any) should you take regarding the proper treatment of the automobile? What are your responsibilities as a CPA regarding this matter under the rules of the AICPA's *SSTS* No. 6? (See the *Statements on Standards for Tax Services (SSTS)* in Appendix E).

TAX RESEARCH PROBLEM

I:10-54 The Morriss Corporation is a very successful and profitable manufacturing corporation. The corporation just completed construction of new corporate offices, primarily for its top executives. The president and founder of the corporation, Mr. Timothy Couch, is an avid collector of artwork and has instructed that the lobby and selected offices be decorated with rare collections of art. These expensive works of art were purchased by the corporation in accordance with Couch's directives. Couch justified the purchase of these artworks on the premise that (1) they are excellent investments and should increase in value in the future, (2) they provide an appropriate and impressive office atmosphere when current and prospective customers visit the corporation's offices, and (3) the artwork is depreciable property and the corporation will be able to take sizable writeoffs against income. The Financial Vice-President of the corporation has requested your advice as to whether the works of art are, in fact, depreciable property. Prepare a research memorandum for the Financial Vice-President on this issue.

A partial list of research sources is provided below.

- *Rev. Rul. 68-232,* 1968-1 C.B. 70
- *Shauna C. Clinger,* 60 T.C.M. 598 (1990).
- *Simon v. Comr.,* 103 T.C. 247 (1994), *aff'd,* 95-2 USTC ¶50,552 (2d Cir. 1995) *nonacq.* 1996-2 C.B.I.
- *Liddle v. Comr.,* 103 T.C. 285 (1994), *aff'd,* 95-2 USTC ¶50,488 (3rd Cir. 1995)

CHAPTER

11

ACCOUNTING PERIODS AND METHODS

LEARNING OBJECTIVES

After studying this chapter, you should be able to

1. Explain the rules for adopting and changing an accounting period
2. Explain the differences between cash, accrual, and hybrid accounting
3. Determine what costs must be included in inventory
4. Identify the amount of income to be reported from special accounting methods
5. Compute the amount of imputed interest in certain transactions
6. Determine the tax treatment that results from changes in accounting methods
7. Describe tax planning considerations for accounting periods and methods
8. Describe compliance and procedural considerations for accounting periods and methods

CHAPTER OUTLINE

An **accounting method** is a system of rules and procedures used to determine the year in which income and expenses are reported for tax purposes. The accounting methods used to compute taxable income generally must be the same as those used in keeping the taxpayer's books and records and determine *when* income and expenses are reported, not whether they are reported. Although the accounting methods used by a taxpayer do not necessarily affect the amount of income reported over the life of a business, they do affect the tax burden in two ways. First, selecting the appropriate accounting method can accelerate deductions or defer income recognition in order to postpone tax payments, and second, because of the progressive tax rate structure, taxpayers can save taxes by spreading income over several accounting periods rather than having income bunched into one period.

EXAMPLE I:11-1 ▶ Jane, a taxpayer using the cash method of accounting, has a 28% marginal tax rate for 2015 and expects to have a 15% marginal tax rate in 2016. Jane plans to make a charitable contribution of \$1,000 in January 2016. A contribution in 2016 will reduce Jane's tax by \$150 (0.15 × \$1,000), whereas a contribution in 2015 will reduce Jane's tax by \$280 (0.28 × \$1,000). Obviously Jane may wish to accelerate the contribution in order to reduce her tax liability. ◀

ACCOUNTING PERIODS

OBJECTIVE 1

Explain the rules for adopting and changing an accounting period

Taxable income is computed on the basis of the taxpayer's annual **accounting period**, which is ordinarily 12 months (either a calendar year or a fiscal year). A **fiscal year** is a 12-month period that ends on the last day of any month other than December. The tax year must coincide with the year used to keep the taxpayer's books and records. Taxpayers who do not have books (e.g., an individual with wage income) must use the calendar year.[1] A taxpayer with a seasonal business may find a fiscal year to be advantageous. During the slow season, inventories may be lower and employees are available to take inventory and perform other accounting duties associated with the year-end. The tax year is elected on the first tax return that is filed by a taxpayer and cannot be changed without consent from the IRS.[2]

A partnership generally must use the same tax year as the partners who own the majority (greater than 50%) of partnership income and capital. If a majority of partners do not have the same year, the partnership must use the tax year of its principal partners (those with more than a 5% interest in the partnership). If the principal partners do not have the same tax year, the partnership must use the taxable year that results in the least aggregate deferral of income to the partners.[3] An exception is made for partnerships that can establish to the satisfaction of the IRS a business purpose for having a different year.

The purpose of the strict rules for selecting accounting periods is to prevent partners from deferring partnership income by choosing a different tax year for the partnership. For example, calendar-year partners might select a partnership year that ends on January 31. Because partnership income is considered to be earned by the partners on the last day of the partnership's tax year, reporting the profits would thus be deferred 11 months because the partnership year ends after the partner's year. (See the section entitled Required Payments and Fiscal Years in this chapter for further discussion of the calendar-year requirement.)

A similar rule generally requires S corporations and personal service corporations to adopt a calendar year unless the corporation has a business purpose for electing a fiscal year.[4] Taxpayers willing to make required payments or distributions may choose a fiscal year. (See the Required Payments and Fiscal Years section in this chapter.)

? STOP & THINK

Question: The tax rules related to accounting periods require most partnerships, S corporations, and personal service corporations to report on the calendar year basis.

[1] Sec. 441(g).
[2] Reg. Sec. 1.441-1(b)(4).
[3] Reg. Sec. 1.706-1(a)(3).
[4] Sec. 1378(a).

Of course, almost all individual taxpayers also report on the calendar year basis. What impact does this have on accountants?

Solution: The principal impact is a compression of tax compliance work into the "accounting busy season." A substantial portion of auditing and other accounting work also takes place at year-end. As a result, these services are also compressed into the accounting busy season. The accounting profession has sought to have these rules changed, but has, at least so far, been unsuccessful.

An improper election to use a fiscal year automatically places the taxpayer on the calendar year.[5] Thus, if the first return is filed late because of oversight, the option to choose a fiscal year is lost.

EXAMPLE I:11-2 ▶ City Corporation receives its charter but does not begin operations for three years. Tax returns are required for all years. Timely returns are not filed because City's officers are unaware that returns must be filed for inactive corporations. Thus, City Corporation must use the calendar year. City Corporation may petition the IRS for approval to use a fiscal year. ◀

ADDITIONAL COMMENT

The use of a 52–53-week year aids in budgetary matters and statistical comparisons because a four-week period, unlike a calendar month, is a uniform, fixed period.

While most tax years end on the last day of a month, the tax law allows taxpayers to use a tax year that always ends on the same day of the week, such as the last Friday in October. This means that the tax years will vary in length between 52 and 53 weeks. Taxpayers who regularly keep their books over a period that varies from 52 to 53 weeks may elect the same period for tax purposes. A 52–53-week taxable year must end either the last time a particular day occurs during a calendar month (e.g., the last Friday in October) or the occurrence of the particular day that is closest to the end of a calendar month (e.g., the Saturday closest to the end of November).[6] Under the first alternative, the year may end as many as six days before the end of the month, but must end within the month. Under the second alternative, the year may end as many as three days before or after the end of the month.

TYPICAL MISCONCEPTION

It is sometimes mistakenly believed that a tax year can end on a day in the middle of the month.

The 52–53-week year is especially useful to businesses with inventories. For example, a manufacturer might choose a 52–53-week year that ends on the last Friday in December to permit inventory to be taken over the weekend without interfering with the company's manufacturing activity. Similarly, wage accruals would be eliminated for a company with a weekly payroll if the payroll period always ends on Friday.

Although the 52–53-week year may actually end on a day other than the last day of the month, it is treated as ending on the last day of the calendar month for "effective date" changes in the tax law that would otherwise coincide with the year-end.

EXAMPLE I:11-3 ▶ Eagle Corporation has adopted a 52–53-week year. Eagle's tax year begins on December 29, 2015. Assume that a new tax rate schedule applies to tax years beginning after December 31, 2015. The new tax rate schedule is applicable to Eagle because, in the absence of the 52–53-week year, its tax period would have started on January 1, 2016. ◀

REQUIRED PAYMENTS AND FISCAL YEARS

Virtually all C corporations (other than personal service corporations) have flexibility in choosing an accounting period. Other taxpayers, such as partnerships and S corporations, may use a fiscal year if they have an acceptable business purpose. However, most of these businesses are unable to meet the rather rigid business purpose requirements outlined by the IRS. As a result, these businesses report using the calendar year concentrating most tax work during the early months of the year. Concern over this problem led Congress to enact Sec. 444 which allows partnerships, S corporations, and personal service corporations (such as incorporated medical practices) to elect a taxable year that results in a tax deferral of three months or less (e.g., a partnership with calendar-year partners may elect a September 30 year-end). This is called the **Sec. 444 election**. Furthermore, partnerships,

---

[5] *Q.A. Calhoun v. U.S.*, 33 AFTR 2d 74-305, 74-1 USTC ¶9104 (D.C. Va., 1973).

[6] Sec. 441(f).

S corporations, and personal service corporations may continue using the fiscal year they were using when the current law was passed in 1986 even if that fiscal year results in a deferral beyond three months.

ADDITIONAL COMMENT

The American Institute of Certified Public Accountants and accounting firms lobbied extensively for the provision that permits partnerships, S corporations, and personal service corporations to continue to use a fiscal year if annual required payments are made.

Partnerships and S corporations making the Sec. 444 election, however, must make annual required payments by April 15 of the following year. The purpose of the required payment is to offset the tax deferral advantage obtained when fiscal years are used.

The amount of the required payment is determined by multiplying the maximum tax rate for individuals plus 1% (40.6%) times the previous year's taxable income times a deferral ratio.[7] The deferral ratio is equal to the number of months in the deferral period divided by the number of months in the taxable year. An adjustment is made for deductible amounts distributed to the owners during the year. If the amount due is $500 or less, no payment is required.

EXAMPLE I:11-4 ▶ ABC Partnership begins operations on October 1, 2015, and elects a September 30 year-end under Sec. 444. The partnership's net income for the fiscal year ended September 30, 2016, is $100,000. ABC must make a required payment of $10,150 ($100,000 × 40.6% × 3/12) on or before April 15, 2017. ◀

The owners of businesses making such payments do not claim a credit for the amount paid. Instead, the partnership or S Corporation subtracts the previous year's required payment from the current year's required payment. If the result is negative, then the entity is entitled to a refund.

EXAMPLE I:11-5 ▶ Assume the same facts as in Example I:11-4 except that ABC Partnership's required payment for the year ended September 30, 2017 is $6,000. ABC is entitled to a refund of the difference of $4,150 ($10,150 − $6,000). ◀

Personal service corporations also may elect a fiscal year. However, deductions to shareholder/employees may be limited if distributions to such shareholder/employees during the deferral period do not exceed a minimum amount.[8] Personal service corporations are incorporated medical practices and other businesses owned by individuals who provide their services through the corporation. In general, the rules prevent a distribution pattern that creates a tax deferral. This is achieved by requiring that the deductible payments made to owners during the deferral period be at a rate no lower than during the previous fiscal year.

EXAMPLE I:11-6 ▶ Austin, Inc., is a personal service corporation of attorneys with a fiscal year ending September 30. For the year ended September 30, 2015 the company earned a profit of $480,000 before any salary payments to the owners. The entire profit, however, was paid out as wages to the owners, resulting in a taxable income of zero. To avoid any deduction limitation, Austin must pay salaries to its owners of no less than $120,000 ($480,000 × 3/12) during the period October 1, 2015, to December 31, 2015. If less than $120,000 is paid during this deferral period, deductions are limited for the year ended September 30, 2016. ◀

An option allows personal service corporations to compute the amount of the minimum distribution by using a three-year average of income and distributions.

CHANGES IN THE ACCOUNTING PERIOD

KEY POINT

The use of a natural business year helps in the matching of revenue and expense because the business is normally in a maximum state of liquidity and the problems associated with making estimates involving uncompleted transactions are reduced to a minimum.

Once adopted, an accounting period cannot normally be changed without IRS approval.[9] The IRS will usually approve a change only if the taxpayer can establish a substantial business purpose for the change (e.g., changing to a natural business year).[10] A natural business year ends at or soon after the peak income earning period (e.g., the natural business year for a department store that has a seasonal holiday business may be on January 31). A business without a peak income period may not be able to establish a natural business year and may, therefore, be precluded from changing its tax year. In general, at least

---

[7] Sec. 7519(b). The high rate discourages elections by businesses with middle and lower income owners. Businesses do not have to make similar required payments for self-employment and other taxes. As a result, there can be some advantage for businesses with higher income owners.

[8] Sec. 280H(a).

[9] Sec. 442.

[10] Rev. Proc. 2002-39, 2002-1 C.B. 1046.

25% of revenues must occur during the last two months of the year in order to qualify as a natural business year.

EXAMPLE I:11-7 ▶ USA Department Store's sales peak during the holiday season in December. During January the department store further reduces its inventory through storewide clearance sales. USA elects a "natural" business year-end of January 31 because its inventory levels are lowest at the end of January. Also, USA meets the prescribed test because at least 25% of its revenues for the year occur in December and January. ◀

In a few instances IRS approval is not required to change to another accounting period.

REAL-WORLD EXAMPLE

J.C. Penney, Kmart, and Walmart all use an accounting period ending January 31.

- A newly married person may change tax years to conform to that of his or her spouse so that a joint return may be filed. The election must be made in either the first or second year after the marriage date.[11]
- A change to a 52–53-week year that ends with reference to the same calendar month in which the former tax year ended.[12]
- A taxpayer who erroneously files tax returns using an accounting period other than that on which his or her books are kept is not required to obtain permission to file returns for later years based on the way the books are kept.[13]
- A corporation meeting the following specified conditions may change without IRS approval: (1) There has been no change in its accounting period within the past ten calendar years, (2) the resulting year does not have a net operating loss (NOL), (3) the taxable income for the resulting short tax year when annualized is at least 90% of the taxable income for the preceding full tax year, and (4) there is no change in status of the corporation (such as an S corporation election).[14]
- An existing partnership can change its tax year without prior approval if the partners with a majority interest have the same tax year to which the partnership changes or if all principal partners who do not have such a tax year concurrently change to such a tax year.[15]

There is one instance, however, when a change in tax years is required: A subsidiary corporation filing a consolidated return with its parent corporation must change its accounting period to conform with its parent's tax year.

Application for permission to change accounting periods is made on Form 1128, Application for Change in Accounting Period, on or before the due date of the return including extensions. The application must be sent to the Commissioner of the IRS, Washington, D.C.

The IRS may establish certain conditions for the taxpayer to meet before it approves the change to a new tax year. For example, the IRS has ruled that if the short period that results from a change involves a NOL greater than $50,000, the taxpayer may have to forgo a carryback of the loss.[16]

RETURNS FOR PERIODS OF LESS THAN 12 MONTHS

Most income tax returns cover an accounting period of 12 months. On two occasions, however, a taxpayer's accounting period may be less than 12 months: when the taxpayer's first or final return is filed and when the taxpayer changes accounting periods.

Taxpayers filing an initial tax return and executors filing a taxpayer's final return or corporations filing their last return are not required to annualize the year's income, nor are personal exemptions or tax credits prorated. These returns are prepared and filed, and taxes are paid as though they are returns for a 12-month period ending on the last day of

[11] Reg. Sec. 1.442-1(e). A statement should be attached to the resulting short period return indicating that the change is being made.

[12] Reg. Sec. 1.441-2(c)(2). A statement should be attached to the first return filed under the election indicating that the change is being made.

[13] Rev. Rul. 58-256, 1959-1 C.B. 215.

[14] Reg. Sec. 1.442-1(c). A statement should be attached to the return indicating that each condition is met.

[15] Reg. Sec. 1.442-1(b)(2).

[16] Rev. Proc. 2002-37, 2002-1 C.B. 1030.

the short period. An exception permits the final return of a decedent to be filed as though the decedent lived throughout the entire tax year.[17]

EXAMPLE I:11-8 ▶ ABC Partnership, which has filed its returns on a calendar-year basis, terminates on June 30. ABC's final return is due on October 15. ◀

EXAMPLE I:11-9 ▶ Joy, a single individual who has filed her returns on a calendar-year basis, dies on June 30. Joy's final return is due the following April 15. ◀

Taxpayers who change from one accounting period to another must annualize their income for the resulting short period. This prevents income earned during the resulting short period from being taxed at lower rates. Income is annualized as follows:

1. Determine modified taxable income. Individuals must compute their taxable income for the short period by itemizing their deductions (i.e., the standard deduction is not allowed) and personal and dependency exemptions must be prorated.[18]
2. Multiply modified taxable income by the following fraction:

$$\frac{12}{\text{Number of months in short period}}$$

3. Compute the tax on the resulting taxable income using the appropriate tax rate schedule.
4. Multiply the resulting tax by the following fraction:

$$\frac{\text{Number of months in short period}}{12}$$

EXAMPLE I:11-10 ▶ Pat, a single taxpayer, obtains permission to change from a calendar year to a fiscal year ending on June 30, 2015. During the six months ending June 30, 2015, Pat earns $25,000 and has $5,000 in itemized deductions.[19]

Gross Income	$25,000
Minus: Itemized deductions	(5,000)
Personal exemption [(6 ÷ 12) × $4,000]	(2,000)
Modified taxable income	$18,000
Annualized income [(12 ÷ 6) × $18,000]	$36,000
Tax on annualized income	$ 4,939
Gross tax [(6 ÷ 12) × $4,939]	$ 2,470 ◀

Topic Review I:11-1 summarizes the available accounting periods and the rules for changing accounting periods.

? STOP & THINK

Question: Why are taxpayers required to annualize when they change tax years? What provision of the tax law creates this need?

Solution: A change of tax years results in a shortened filing period during the period the change takes place. For example, a taxpayer who changes from a calendar year to a June 30 year-end reports income for only a 6-month period on the first return following the change. Less income is reported, and that income would be taxed at lower rates without annualization. Annualization is necessary because of the progressive tax rate structure.

[17] Reg. Sec. 1.443-1(a)(2).
[18] The exemptions are prorated as follows: exemptions × (number of months in the short period ÷ 12).
[19] An alternative method to compute the tax is provided in Sec. 443(b)(2) and Reg. Sec. 1.443-1(b)(2) whereby the taxpayer can elect to compute the tax for a 12-month period beginning on the first day of the short period and then convert the tax to a short-period tax.

TOPIC REVIEW I:11-1

Accounting Periods and Changes

Available Years

- Available tax years include the calendar year, a fiscal year (a year that ends on the last day of any month other than December), and a 52–53-week year (a year that always ends on the same day of the week).
- A partnership must use the tax year of its partners unless the partnership can establish a satisfactory business purpose for having a different year or if the partnership makes required payments.
- Similar rules generally require S corporations and personal service corporations to adopt a calendar year unless the corporation has a business purpose for electing a fiscal year. Taxpayers willing to make required payments or distributions may choose a fiscal year ending on September 30, October 31, or November 30.

Change in Accounting Periods

- Once adopted, an accounting period normally cannot be changed without approval by the IRS. The IRS is more likely to approve a change to a natural business year. In general, at least 25% of revenues must occur during the last two months of the year in order to qualify as a natural business year.
- Taxpayers who change from one accounting period to another must annualize their income for the resulting short period. This prevents income earned during the resulting short period from being taxed at lower rates.

Overall Accounting Methods

OBJECTIVE 2

Explain the differences between cash, accrual, and hybrid accounting

A taxpayer's method of accounting determines the year in which income is reported and expenses are deducted. Taxable income must be computed using the method of accounting regularly used by the taxpayer in keeping his or her books if that method clearly reflects income.[20] Permissible overall accounting methods are:

- Cash receipts and disbursements method (often called the cash method of accounting)
- Accrual method
- A combination of the first two methods, often called the hybrid method

KEY POINT

The Code provides the IRS with broad powers in ascertaining whether the taxpayer's accounting method clearly reflects income. It entitles the IRS to more than the usual presumption of correctness.

New taxpayers may generally choose any of the accounting methods listed above. However, the accrual method must be used for sales and cost of goods sold if inventories are an income-producing factor to the business. Exceptions permit businesses with inventories to use the cash method if their average annual gross receipts for the three preceding years do not exceed $1 million ($10 million if the taxpayer's principal business is not the sale of inventory).[21] The fact that an overall accounting method is used in one trade or business does not mean that the same method must be used in a second trade or business or for nonbusiness income and deductions.

EXAMPLE I:11-11 ► Troy, a practicing CPA, also owns an appliance store. The fact that Troy uses the accrual method of reporting income from the appliance store, where inventories are an income-producing factor, does not preclude Troy from using the cash method to report income from his service-based accounting practice. Troy could also use the cash method for reporting nonbusiness income (such as dividends) and nonbusiness expenses (such as itemized deductions). ◄

REAL-WORLD EXAMPLE

It has been held that the cash method of accounting can be used where inventories are inconsequential. *Michael Drazen,* 34 T.C. 1070 (1960).

The term *method of accounting* is used to include not only overall methods of accounting listed above but also the accounting treatment of any item.[22]

Cash Receipts and Disbursements Method

Most individuals and service businesses use the cash receipts and disbursements method of accounting. Taxpayers cannot use the cash method in a business for sales and cost of goods

[20] Sec. 446.

[21] Rev. Proc. 2002-28, 2002-1 C.B. 815, modified by Rev. Proc. 2012-20, 2012-14 IRB 700.

[22] Reg. Sec. 1.446-1(a)(1). Examples of accounting methods for specific items include Sec. 174, relating to research and experimentation expenses; Sec. 451, relating to reporting income from long-term contracts; and Sec. 453, relating to reporting income from installment sales.

sold if inventories are an income-producing factor.[23] However, as noted above, businesses with inventories are permitted to use the cash method if their average annual gross receipts for the three preceding tax years do not exceed $1 million ($10 million if the taxpayer's principal business is not the sale of inventory). However, C corporations and partnerships with a corporate partner may use the cash method only if their average annual gross receipts for the three preceding tax years do not exceed $5 million or if the business meets the requirements associated with providing personal services (i.e., if it is owned by professionals who are using the business to provide professional services).[24] Thus, a law or accounting firm can use the cash method even if its average receipts exceed $5 million. However, other C corporations with greater than $5 million average gross receipts must use the accrual method even if they have no inventory.

Under the cash receipts and disbursements method of accounting, a taxpayer is required to report income for the tax year in which payments are actually or constructively received. While it might seem that receipts under the cash method of accounting should only be recognized if the taxpayer receives cash, this is not the case. The Regulations clearly provide that gross income under the cash method includes cash, property, or services.[25] Thus, if a CPA accepts a set of golf clubs as payment from a client for services rendered, the CPA must include the fair market value of the golf clubs in his gross income. However, an accounts receivable or other unsupported promise to pay is considered to have no value and, as a result, no income is recognized until the receivable is collected. Expenses are deducted in the year paid. Because the recognition of expense is measured by the flow of cash, a taxpayer can control the year in which an expense is deductible by choosing when to make the payment. Individual taxpayers do not have the same opportunity to determine the year in which income is recognized, because the constructive receipt rule requires taxpayers to recognize income if a payment is available, even if actual payment has not been received. (See Chapter I:3 for a discussion of constructive receipt.)

KEY POINT

A taxpayer using the cash method is entitled to certain deductions that do not involve current year cash disbursements, such as depreciation, depletion, and losses.

Capitalization Requirements for Cash-Method Taxpayers. Taxpayers who use the cash receipts and disbursements method are required to capitalize fixed assets and to recover the cost through depreciation or amortization. The Regulations state that prepaid expenses must be capitalized and deducted over the life of the asset if the life of the asset extends substantially beyond the end of the tax year.[26] Typically, capitalization is required only if the life of the asset extends beyond the close of the tax year following the year of payment.[27]

EXAMPLE I:11-12 ▶ On July 1, 2015, Acme Corporation, a cash basis, calendar-year taxpayer, pays an insurance premium of $3,000 for a policy that is effective July 1, 2015, to June 30, 2016. The full $3,000 is deductible in 2015. ◀

EXAMPLE I:11-13 ▶ Assume the same facts as in Example I:11-12, except that the premium covers a three-year period beginning July 1, 2015, and ending June 30, 2018. Acme Corporation may deduct $500 in 2015, $1,000 in 2016 and 2017, and $500 in 2018. ◀

One notable exception to the one-year rule denies a deduction for prepaid interest. Cash-method taxpayers must capitalize such amounts and allocate interest over the prepayment period. A special rule allows homeowners to deduct points paid on a mortgage used to buy or improve a personal residence. The payment must be an established business practice in the area and not exceed amounts generally charged for such home loans. (See Chapter I:7 for a discussion of the deductibility of points.)

To be deductible, a payment must be more than just a refundable deposit. A taxpayer who has an option of cancelling delivery and receiving a refund of amounts prepaid is not normally entitled to deduct the amount of the deposit.

---

23 Reg. Sec. 1.471-1. However, Sec. 448(b) permits farmers to use the cash method even though they have inventories. Sec. 448(a) denies tax shelters the right to use the cash method even if they do not have inventories.

24 Secs. 448(b) and (c).

25 Reg. Sec. 1.446-1(c)(1)(i).

26 Reg. Sec. 1.461-1(a)(1).

27 *Bonaire Development Co.*, 76 T.C. 789 (1981), and *Martin J. Zaninovich v. CIR*, 45 AFTR 2d 80-1442, 80-1 USTC ¶9342 (9th Cir., 1980).

Payments can be made either by a check that is honored in due course or by the use of a credit card.[28] Payment by credit card is considered to be the equivalent of borrowing funds to pay the expense. However, a taxpayer's note is not the equivalent of cash, so if a cash method taxpayer gives a note in payment, he or she cannot take the deduction until the note is paid, even if the note is secured by collateral.[29]

ACCRUAL METHOD

For an accrual basis taxpayer, there are two tests used to determine when an item of income must be reported or an expense deducted: the **all-events test** and the **economic performance test.**

ADDITIONAL COMMENT

The phrase *reasonable accuracy* means that approximate amounts are ascertainable. Although the word *accuracy* means exactness or precision, when it is used with the word *reasonable* it implies something less than an exact amount.

All-Events Test. An accrual-method taxpayer reports an item of income when "all events" have occurred that fix the taxpayer's right to receive the item of income and the amount can be determined with reasonable accuracy.[30] Similarly, an expense is deductible when all events have occurred that establish the fact of the liability and the amount of the expense can be determined with reasonable accuracy. For deductions, the all-events test is not satisfied until economic performance has taken place.

Economic Performance Test. Economic performance (of services or property to be provided to a taxpayer) occurs when the property or services are actually provided by the other party.

EXAMPLE I:11-14 ▶ The owner of a professional football team provides medical benefits for injured players through insurance coverage. Economic performance occurs over the term of the policy rather than when the team enters into a binding contract with the insurance company or during the season when the player earns the right to medical benefits. Thus, a one-year premium is deductible over the year of the insurance coverage rather than over the term of the player's contract under which the benefit is earned. But see below for a possible waiver. ◀

Similarly, if a taxpayer is obligated to provide property or services, economic performance occurs in the year the taxpayer provides the property or service.

EXAMPLE I:11-15 ▶ Assume the same facts as in Example I:11-14 except that medical benefits are required under the terms of a player's contract. Also, the team decides to pay medical costs directly. Economic performance occurs as the team actually provides the benefits. Thus, the deduction is permitted only as medical care is provided. ◀

REAL-WORLD EXAMPLE

Before the economic performance test was added to the tax law, a company engaged in strip mining coal was able to deduct the future land reclamation costs as the coal was mined because the liability was certain and the cost could be estimated. *Ohio River Collieries,* 77 T.C. 1369 (1981).

The requirement that economic performance take place before a deduction is allowed is waived if all of the following five conditions are met:

- The all-events test, without regard to economic performance, is satisfied.
- Economic performance occurs within a reasonable period (but in no event more than 8 ½ months) after the close of the tax year.
- The item is recurring in nature, and the taxpayer consistently treats items of the same type as incurred in the tax year in which the all-events test is met.
- The taxpayer is not a tax shelter.
- Either the amount is not material or the earlier accrual of the item results in a better matching of income and expense.[31]

EXAMPLE I:11-16 ▶ Bass Corporation, a calendar year taxpayer, pays its annual insurance premium each year on April 30, the anniversary of the policy. The premium paid this year is $6,000 while last year's premium was $5,400. Accrual accounting indicates that Bass deduct $4,000 (8⁄12 × $6,000) of the premium paid this year along with $1,800 (4⁄12 × $5,400) of the premium paid last year, or a total of $5,800. As all of the conditions for the exception to the economic performance requirements are met, Bass Corporation can deduct $6,000 this year. This assumes that Bass has been consistently following the practice and deducted $5,400 last year. ◀

---

[28] Rev. Rul. 78-39, 1978-1 C.B. 73.

[29] *Frank D. Quinn Exec. v. CIR,* 24 AFTR 927, 40-1 USTC ¶9403 (5th Cir., 1940).

[30] Reg. Sec. 1.451-1(a). (See Chapter I:3 for a discussion of the all-events test as it applies to gross income.)

[31] Sec. 461(h).

TYPICAL MISCONCEPTION

It is sometimes mistakenly believed that taxpayers can deduct warranty expenses and bad debts using the allowance method instead of the direct write-off method.

Reserves for items such as product warranty expense and uncollectible accounts are commonly encountered in financial accounting. The all-events and economic performance tests prevent the use of such reserves for tax purposes. This is because the amount of such expense is not usually determinable with sufficient accuracy.

HYBRID METHOD

Taxpayers may use a combination of accounting methods as long as income is clearly reflected. Taxpayers with inventories are required to use the accrual method to report sales and purchases if their average gross receipts for the three preceding years exceeds $1 million ($10 million if the taxpayer's principal business is not the sale of inventory). These taxpayers may use the cash method to report other items of income and expense. To ensure that income is clearly reflected, certain restrictions have been placed on combining accounting methods.

KEY POINT

A taxpayer who uses the cash method in computing gross income from his or her business must use the cash method in computing expenses of such business.

Taxpayers who use the cash method of accounting in determining gross income from a trade or business must use the cash method for determining expenses of the same trade or business. Similarly, taxpayers who use the accrual method of accounting for expenses must use the accrual method in computing gross income from the trade or business.

The basic rules relating to accounting methods, the all-events test, and economic performance are summarized in Topic Review I:11-2.

? STOP & THINK

Question: If an accountant does tax work for an automobile dealer, in exchange for free use of an automobile, does the accountant have to report any income? Does it make a difference whether the accountant uses the automobile in her business? When is any taxable income reported?

Solution: The rental value of the automobile must be included in gross income. If the automobile is used in the accountant's business, a portion of the rental value is deductible as a business expense. Although it is not entirely clear, it seems that an accrual basis accountant would report income as tax services are provided to the dealer. A cash basis taxpayer would report income over the time the automobile is used.

TOPIC REVIEW I:11-2

Accounting Methods

AVAILABLE METHODS

- Permissible overall accounting methods are the cash receipts and disbursements method, the accrual method, and the hybrid method.
- The cash method is available to taxpayers without inventories and to taxpayers with inventories whose average gross receipts during the three preceding years was $1 million or less ($10 million if the taxpayer's principal business is not the sale of inventory). C corporations whose average gross receipts fall between $1 and $5 million thresholds may use the cash method if they do not have inventories. C corporations (other than personal service corporations) may not use the cash method if their average gross receipts in the three preceding tax years exceed $5 million.

ALL-EVENTS TEST AND ECONOMIC PERFORMANCE TEST

- An accrual-method taxpayer reports an item of income when all events have occurred that fix the taxpayer's right to receive the item of income and when the amount of the item can be determined with reasonable accuracy.
- An expense is deductible when all events have occurred that establish that there is a liability and when the amount of the expense can be determined with reasonable accuracy. The all-events test is not satisfied until economic performance has taken place.
- Economic performance takes place when property or services are actually provided.

INVENTORIES

OBJECTIVE 3

Determine what costs must be included in inventory

In general, manufacturing and merchandising companies are required to use the accrual method of accounting for purchases and sales of merchandise. The inventory method used by a taxpayer must conform to the best accounting practice in the trade or business, and it must clearly reflect income. However, best accounting practices (synonymous with generally accepted accounting principles) and clear reflection of income (which is determined by the IRS) occasionally conflict. The Supreme Court has held that the standard of clear reflection of income prevails in a case where the two standards conflict. In the *Thor Power Tool Co.* case, the company wrote off the cost of obsolete parts for both tax and financial accounting purposes even though the parts were kept on hand and their selling price was not reduced.[32] Regulation Sec. 1.471-4(b) states that obsolete or other slow-moving inventory cannot be written down unless the selling price is also reduced.

KEY POINT

Taxpayers cannot always use inventory methods for tax purposes that conform with generally accepted accounting principles.

Although the company's practice conformed with generally accepted accounting principles, it did not, according to the Supreme Court, clearly reflect income. Hence, generally accepted accounting principles are used only when the Regulations do not specify the treatment of an item or, alternatively, when the Regulations provide more than one alternative accounting method.

Taxpayers who value inventory at cost may write down goods that are not salable at their normal price (e.g., damaged, obsolete, or shopworn goods) only after the selling price has been reduced. Items may be valued at a bona fide selling price reduced by the direct cost of disposal.[33] The option to write down this type of merchandise is available even if the taxpayers use the LIFO inventory method.

EXAMPLE I:11-17 ▶

Stone Corporation publishes books for small academic audiences in Sanskrit and other ancient languages. There is typically one printing of a few hundred or perhaps a thousand copies of each book. Stone may sell a few copies a year of each book. Only after several years can the Corporation determine whether they will ever sell all copies of a given work. Based upon the *Thor Power Tool Co.* case, Stone Corporation cannot write off unsold copies unless they are destroyed or otherwise disposed of, and they cannot write down unsold copies unless the selling price is reduced below cost. ◀

KEY POINT

The uniform capitalization rules, included in the Tax Reform Act of 1986, require the capitalization of significant overhead costs that previously were expensed.

DETERMINATION OF INVENTORY COST

Inventories may be valued at either cost or at the lower of cost or market value. Taxpayers who use the LIFO inventory valuation method (discussed later in this chapter) may not use the lower of cost or market method. In the case of merchandise purchased, cost is the invoice price less trade discounts, plus freight and other handling charges.

Unlike financial accounting, purchasing costs (e.g., salaries of purchasing agents), warehousing costs, packaging, and administrative costs related to these functions must be allocated between cost of goods sold and inventory. The costs that must be included in inventory are found in Sec. 263A and are referred to as the Uniform Capitalization rules (UNICAP). This requirement is applicable only to taxpayers whose average gross receipts for the three preceding years exceed $10 million.[34]

ETHICAL POINT

The UNICAP rules must be followed by taxpayers. To bring a business into compliance with these rules, the taxpayer may need to make certain estimates. SRTP No. 4 provides that a CPA may use a client's estimates if such use is generally acceptable or if it is impractical to obtain exact data. If a change in the overhead application rate is contemplated, it may be desirable to request IRS approval.

In the case of goods manufactured by the taxpayer, cost is determined by using the UNICAP rules, which may be thought of as an expanded version of the full absorption costing method. Thus, direct costing and prime costing are not acceptable inventory methods. Direct labor and materials along with manufacturing overhead must be included in inventory. Under UNICAP, the following overhead items are included in inventory:

- Factory repairs and maintenance, utilities, rent, insurance, small tools, and depreciation (including the excess of tax depreciation over accounting depreciation)
- Factory administration and officers' salaries related to production
- Taxes (other than the income tax)

---

[32] *Thor Power Tool Co. v. CIR*, 43 AFTR 2d 79-362, 79-1 USTC ¶9139 (USSC, 1979).

[33] Reg. Sec. 1.471-2(c).

[34] Sec. 263A(b)(2)(B).

- Quality control and inspection
- Rework, scrap, and spoilage
- Current and past service costs of pension and profit-sharing plans
- Service support such as purchasing, payroll, and warehousing costs

Nonmanufacturing costs (e.g., advertising, selling, and research and experimentation costs) are not required to be included in inventory. Interest must be inventoried if the property is real property, long-lived property, or property requiring more than two years (one year in the case of property costing more than $1 million) to produce.

KEY POINT

Identifying the appropriate additional overhead costs to capitalize can be confusing and extremely time consuming.

The main difference between full absorption costing traditionally used for financial reporting purposes and UNICAP costing required for tax purposes is that UNICAP expands the list of overhead costs to include certain indirect costs that have not always been included in overhead for financial reporting purposes. For example, for financial reporting purposes, the costs of operating payroll and personnel departments have sometimes been considered sufficiently indirect or remote to justify omitting them from manufacturing overhead. This is true even though much of the effort of the payroll and personnel departments may be directed toward manufacturing operations. For simplicity and other reasons, overhead costs included in inventory for financial purposes are often limited to those incurred in the factory. UNICAP requires that costs associated with these departments be allocated between manufacturing and nonmanufacturing functions (e.g., sales, advertising, research and experimentation).

EXAMPLE I:11-18 ▶

Best Corporation manufactures traditional style rocking chairs in a small factory with 34 employees. The office staff consists of four employees who handle payroll, receivables, hiring, and other office responsibilities. The sales staff includes three employees who travel the region selling to furniture and craft stores. The remaining 27 employees all work in the factory. Under UNICAP, factory costs including the wages of the 27 factory workers are generally all manufacturing costs. The costs associated with the sales staff are not manufacturing costs. This would include their compensation along with related costs such as travel. Office expenses including the wages paid to the four office workers can be allocated between manufacturing overhead and sales. Reasonable allocation methods are acceptable. One possibility might be to allocate office overhead between sales and manufacturing on a basis as simple as the number of employees in sales (3) and the number in manufacturing (27). Thus, 90% of the cost of the office operation could be treated as manufacturing-related and 10% sales-related. In such case, 90% of the office expenses would be allocated to manufacturing and 10% deducted as a period cost (i.e., selling expenses). The office expenses allocated to manufacturing would in turn be allocated between cost of sales and ending inventory. This allocation could be done on a basis as simple as multiplying the allocated office expenses by the number of chairs in ending inventory and dividing by the number of chairs in the ending inventory plus the total number of chairs made during the year. ◀

A manufacturer may use standard costs to value inventory if any significant variance is reallocated pro rata to ending inventory and cost of goods sold.[35] Taxpayers may determine inventory costs by the following methods: specific identification method; first-in, first-out method (FIFO); last-in, first-out method (LIFO); or average cost method. A few taxpayers, such as an automobile or large appliance dealer, may find it practical to determine the specific cost of items in inventory. Most taxpayers, however, must rely on a flow of goods assumption (e.g., FIFO or LIFO). A discussion of the LIFO method is presented below.

LIFO Method. Many taxpayers use the LIFO cost flow assumption because, during inflationary periods, LIFO normally results in the lowest inventory value and hence the lowest taxable income. Once LIFO has been elected for tax purposes, the taxpayer's financial reports must also be prepared using LIFO.[36] This requirement to conform financial reporting often discourages companies from electing LIFO because lower earnings must be reported to shareholders. However, taxpayers may make footnote disclosure of the amount

[35] Reg. Sec. 1.471-11(d)(3).

[36] Sec. 472(c).

of net income that would have been reported under FIFO or other inventory methods.[37] Taxpayers may adopt LIFO by attaching a completed Form 970 (or by a statement acceptable to the IRS) to the return for the tax year in which the method is first used.

STOP & THINK

Question: As noted, many publicly held companies do not use LIFO inventory valuation. This is, in part, attributed to the fact that LIFO ordinarily results in lower reported income for accounting purposes than FIFO, and management prefers to report higher profits. Many small, closely-held companies also use FIFO even though their earnings are not reported to the public. Why wouldn't closely-held companies use LIFO?

Solution: There are a variety of reasons. Some businesses are very interested in how their financial statements look to banks and other lenders and to potential investors. In some industries, such as electronics, FIFO may actually provide lower inventory values. Also, LIFO cannot be used with lower of cost or market. As a result, some businesses may elect FIFO to be eligible to use lower of cost or market.

Perhaps, however, the main reason is that LIFO is more complex, and small businesses prefer to simplify their accounting. The advent of computers, accounting software, and bar codes may be having some impact on inventory valuation choices. Nevertheless, many accounting packages only track units on hand and sales revenue. They do not track inventory value (cost). Thus, the company must assign a value to inventory at year-end, and the complexity of LIFO remains a deterrent.

REAL-WORLD EXAMPLE

An automobile dealer, using the dollar-value LIFO method in maintaining its inventory, was required to use one pool for new automobiles and a separate pool for new trucks. *Fox Chevrolet, Inc.*, 76 T.C. 708 (1981).

Recordkeeping under LIFO can be cumbersome. For this reason, taxpayers are permitted to determine inventories using "dollar-value" pools and government price indexes rather than by maintaining a record of actual costs.[38] Retailers use appropriate categories in the Consumer Price Index; other taxpayers use categories in the Producer Price Index. Taxpayers using the index method must divide their inventories into one or more pools (groups of similar items). Thus, a department store might create separate pools for tools, appliances, clothing, furniture, and other products. Dividing inventory into pools can be critical because of the different inflation rates associated with various goods and because, if a particular pool is depleted, the taxpayer loses the right to use the lower prices associated with past layers. An important exception permits taxpayers with average annual gross receipts of $5 million or less for the current and two preceding tax years to use the **simplified LIFO method.**[39] The simplified LIFO method uses a single LIFO pool, thereby avoiding problems with multiple pools.

EXAMPLE I:11-19 ▶ In 2015, King Department Store changes its inventory method from FIFO to LIFO. Because King's gross receipts have never exceeded $5 million, the simplified LIFO method is available. King's year-end inventories under FIFO are as follows:

2014	$100,000
2015	$130,000

Assume the 2014 price index is 120% and the 2015 index is 125%. King must convert its 2015 inventory to 2014 prices.

$$\frac{120\%}{125\%} \times \$130{,}000 = \$124{,}800$$

A base period inventory of $100,000 is established. The increase in inventory (the 2015 layer) is valued at 2015 prices.

Base inventory (2014)	$100,000
Plus: 2015 layer [(125% ÷ 120%) × ($124,800 − $100,000)]	25,833
2015 ending inventory	$125,833

Assume the 2016 inventory valued under FIFO is $136,000 and the 2016 price index is 130%. The 2016 inventory is converted to 2014 prices.

[37] Reg. Sec. 1.472-2(e).
[38] Sec. 472(f).
[39] Sec. 474(c).

$$\frac{120\%}{130\%} \times \$136{,}000 = \$125{,}538$$

The 2016 increase in inventory (the 2016 layer) is valued at 2016 prices.

Base inventory (2014)	$100,000
2015 layer	25,833
2016 layer	800[a]
2016 ending inventory	$126,633

[a] [(130% ÷ 120%) × ($125,538 − $124,800)].

ADDITIONAL COMMENT

For tax purposes the lower of cost or market method must ordinarily be applied to each separate inventory item, but for financial accounting purposes it can be applied using an aggregate approach.

Lower of Cost or Market Method. Inventory may be valued at the **lower of cost or market**. This option is available to all taxpayers other than those who determine cost using the LIFO method.[40] The term *market* refers to replacement cost. On the date an inventory is valued, the replacement cost of each item in the inventory is compared with its cost. The lower figure is used as the inventory value. The lower of cost or market method must ordinarily be applied to each separate item in the inventory.

Recall the *Thor Power Tool* case (discussed earlier in this chapter) in which the Supreme Court distinguished market value from expected selling price. **Market value** is the price at which the taxpayer can replace the goods in question. Replacement cost is used in the lower of cost or market determination. Obsolete or other slow-moving inventory can be written down below replacement cost only if the selling price has been reduced.

Cycle Inventory Valuation. Computer technology, including bar codes and software, enables businesses to maintain real-time perpetual inventory records. Many businesses, especially those with multiple locations, do not attempt to count all inventory items on the last day of the taxable period. Instead they count inventory following a scheduled cycle. At year-end, businesses adjust quantities shown in perpetual records for shrinkage since the most recent physical count utilizing estimates based on past experiences. The IRS challenged this practice unsuccessfully arguing that the adjustments failed the "all events" test which requires that amounts must be determined with reasonable accuracy.[41] In midst of the litigation, Congress specifically permitted the method in instances where "the taxpayer makes proper adjustment to such inventories and its estimation method [for] actual shrinkage."[42]

WHAT WOULD YOU DO IN THIS SITUATION?

INVENTORY VALUATION

Jack is a new tax client. He says he and his previous accountant did not get along very well. Jack owns an automobile dealership with sales of $12 million. He has provided you with most of the information you need to prepare his tax return, but he has not yet given you the year-end inventory value. You have completed much of the work on his return, but cannot complete it without the inventory figure. You have called Jack three times about the inventory. Each time he has interrupted, and asked you what his tax liability will be at alternative inventory levels. What problem do you see?

---

40 Reg. Secs. 1.471-2(b) and (c).

41 *Wal-Mart Stores Inc. v. CIR*, 82 AFTR 2d 5601, 98-2 USTC ¶50,645 (8th Cir., 1998), *Dayton Hudson Corp. v. CIR*, 82 AFTR 2d 5610, 98-2 USTC ¶50,644 (8th Cir., 1998), and *Kroger Co.*, 1997 RIA T.C. Memo ¶97,002, 73 TCM 1637.

42 Sec. 471(b).

SPECIAL ACCOUNTING METHODS

OBJECTIVE 4

Identify the amount of income to be reported from special accounting methods

The term *method of accounting* is used to include not only overall methods of accounting (i.e., cash, accrual, and hybrid) but also the accounting treatment of specific items. Special rules have been established for two types of transactions that cover long periods of time. One rule applies to installment sales (a sale in which final payment is not received until a subsequent tax year) and a separate set of rules applies to long-term contracts (construction and similar contracts that are not completed in the same year they are started). These special rules permit taxpayers to report income from this type of transaction when they have the wherewithal to pay the tax (i.e., the year in which payment is received).

LONG-TERM CONTRACTS

Long-term contracts include building, installation, construction, or manufacturing contracts that are not completed in the same tax year in which they began.[43] A manufacturing contract is long-term only if the contract involves the manufacture of either a unique item not normally carried in finished goods inventory or items that normally require more than 12 calendar months to complete. Contracts for services (architectural, accounting, legal, and so on) do not qualify for long-term contract treatment.[44]

EXAMPLE I:11-20 ▶ Diamond Corporation manufactures two types of airplanes: small, general aviation planes that require approximately six months to complete and large jet aircrafts sold to airlines that require two years to complete. Diamond maintains an inventory of the small planes but manufactures the large planes to contract specification. Diamond can use long-term contract accounting only for the large planes. Assume Diamond also offers aircraft design assistance to the government and others who seek such services. The long-term contract method of accounting is not available for such services. ◀

HISTORICAL NOTE

The use of the completed contract method was severely restricted in the Tax Reform Act of 1986 because Congress found that several large corporations, particularly those with large defense contracts, had significant deferred taxes attributable to this method. Many of these companies had extremely low or negative tax rates for several years.

ADDITIONAL COMMENT

In general, a construction contract must involve what has historically been thought of as construction which includes erecting buildings, building dams, roads, and power plants.

The accounting method selected by a taxpayer must be used for all long-term contracts in the same trade or business.[45] In general, the income and expenses associated with long-term contracts may be accounted for by using either the **percentage of completion method** or the **modified percentage of completion method**. In limited instances (explained below), taxpayers may use the **completed contract method**. Under the percentage of completion method, income from a project is reported in installments as the work progresses. Under the completed contract method, income from a project is recognized upon completion of the contract. The modified percentage of completion method is a hybrid that combines two methods (discussed below). Alternatively, taxpayers may use any other accounting method (e.g., the accrual method) that clearly reflects income.

Costs Subject to Long-Term Contract Rules. Direct contract costs are subject to the long-term contract rules. Labor, materials, and overhead costs must be allocated to the contract and accounted for accordingly. Thus, under the completed contract method, such costs are capitalized and deducted from revenue in the year the contract is completed. Selling, marketing and advertising expenses, expenses for unsuccessful bids and proposals, and research and development costs not associated with a specific contract may be deducted currently.

In general, administrative overhead must be allocated to long-term contracts. (See the earlier list of overhead items that must be included in inventory.) This is not required of taxpayers (other than homebuilders) using the completed contract method, but as noted below, the use of the completed contract method is limited.

As previously mentioned, interest must be capitalized if the property being produced is real property, long-lived property, or property requiring more than two years (one year in

43 Reg. Sec. 1.451-3(b).

44 Rev. Proc. 2011-18, 2011-5 I.R.B. 443 and Rev. Proc. 2004-34, 2004-1 C.B. 991, modifying and superseding Rev. Proc. 71-21, 1971-2 C.B. 549, does establish rules for service contracts that extend into the year following the receipt of payment. These rules are discussed in Chapter I:3.

45 Reg. Sec. 1.451-3(a)(1).

the case of property costing more than $1 million) to produce. Interest costs directly attributable to a contract and those that could have been avoided if contract costs had not been incurred must be allocated to long-term contracts.

Completed Contract Method. Under the completed contract method of accounting, income from a contract is reported in the taxable year in which the contract is completed. This is true without regard to whether the contract price is collected in advance, upon completion of the contract, or in installments. Costs associated with the contract are accumulated in a work-in-progress account and deducted upon completion. Several courts are in conflict with regard to determining when a contract is completed. Some courts have required total completion and acceptance of the contract.[46] Other courts have held the contract to have been completed when the only work remaining consists of correcting minor defects or furnishing incidental parts.[47]

The use of the completed contract method may only be used in two limited circumstances. The method can be used by smaller companies (those whose average gross receipts for the three preceding tax years is $10 million or less) for construction contracts that are expected to take two years or less to complete and for home construction contracts.[48] It cannot be used by larger companies for manufacturing, or for other long-term contracts other than construction or for construction contracts expected to last longer than two years.

KEY POINT

In general, taxpayers with long-term contracts must compute income under the percentage of completion method for contracts entered into after July 10, 1989.

Percentage of Completion Method. Under the percentage of completion method of reporting income, the taxpayer reports a percentage of the gross income from a long-term contract based on the portion of work that has been completed. The portion of the total contract price reported in a given year is determined by multiplying the total contract price by the percentage of work completed in the year. The percentage is determined by dividing current year costs by the expected total costs.

KEY POINT

After a taxpayer has adopted an accounting method for long-term contracts, he or she must continue to use that method unless permission to change methods is granted.

Modified Percentage of Completion Method. At the beginning of a contract, it is difficult to estimate total costs. For this reason, taxpayers may elect to defer reporting any income from a contract until they have incurred at least 10% of the estimated total cost.[49] This is called the modified percentage of completion method. Under this method, if a contract has just been started as of the end of the year, the taxpayer does not have to estimate the profit on the contract during that year. The next year the taxpayer will report profit on all work that has been completed, including work done during the first year. Of course, this assumes that at least 10% of the work has been completed as of the end of the taxable year. If more than 10% of the costs are incurred during the first year, the modified percentage of completion method is identical to the regular percentage of completion method.

The completed contract method, the percentage of completion method, and the modified percentage of completion method are compared in Example I:11-21.

EXAMPLE I:11-21 ▶ In 2015, a contractor enters into a contract to construct a bridge for $1,400,000. At the outset, the contractor estimates that it will cost $1,200,000 to build the bridge. Actual costs in 2015 are $540,000 (45% of the $1,200,000 total estimated costs). Actual costs in 2016 are less than expected and amount to $600,000. The profits reported in both years of the contract are illustrated below.

	2015	2016
Completed contract		
Revenue	0	$1,400,000
Costs incurred	0	(1,140,000)
Gross profit	0	$ 260,000

46 *E. E. Black Limited v. Alsup*, 45 AFTR 1345, 54-1 USTC ¶9340 (9th Cir., 1954), and *Thompson-King-Tate, Inc. v. U.S.*, 8 AFTR 2d 5920, 62-1 USTC ¶9116 (6th Cir., 1961).

47 *Ehret-Day Co.*, 2 T.C. 25 (1943), and *Nathan Wohlfeld*, 1958 PH T.C. Memo ¶58,128, 17 TCM 677.

48 Sec. 460(e).

49 Sec. 460(a).

Percentage of completion		
Revenue	$630,000[a]	$770,000[b]
Costs incurred	(540,000)	(600,000)
Gross profit	$ 90,000	$170,000

[a] 540,000/1,200,000 × $1,400,000 = $630,000.
[b] $1,400,000 − $630,000 = $770,000.

In Example I:11-21, the modified percentage of completion method results in the same income being reported each year as the percentage of completion method because more than 10% of the estimated costs were incurred during the first year. Note that the completed contract method defers reporting income until the contract is completed, causing all income from the project to be reported in a single year. Thus, the tax is deferred but the taxpayer may end up being taxed at higher rates. As noted, the completed contract is available only for home construction contracts and to certain smaller contractors for projects of two years or less.

Look-Back Interest. Certain contracts (or portions of a contract) accounted for under either the regular or modified percentage of completion method are subject to a **look-back interest** adjustment. When a contract is completed, a computation is made to determine whether the tax paid each year during the contract is more or less than the tax that would have been paid if the actual total cost of the contract had been used rather than the estimated cost.[50] Interest is paid on any additional tax that would have been paid. The taxpayer receives interest on any additional tax that was paid.

Look-back interest is applicable only to contracts completed more than two years after the commencement date. Furthermore, look-back interest is applicable only if the contract price equals or exceeds either 1% of the taxpayer's average gross receipts for the three taxable years preceding the taxable year the contract was entered into or $1 million.[51]

Taxpayers may elect a "de minimis" exception to the "look-back" interest computation. If elected, the exception is applicable to all contracts completed within a year, and the election to use the exception can be revoked only with IRS approval. Under the exception, if income reported each year on a contract is within 10% of the recomputed "look-back income," no interest computation is made for the contract. Whether reported income is within 10% of recomputed income is determined separately for each completed contract.

EXAMPLE I:11-22 ▶ The contractor in Example I:11-21 is exempt from the look-back rule because the contract is completed within two years after the commencement date. On the other hand, if the contract took more than two years to complete, interest would be owed on the underpaid taxes for the first and subsequent contract years. The underreported income for the first year would be $33,158 [($260,000 profit × $540,000 first year's costs ÷ $1,140,000 total costs) − $90,000 first year reported income]. Assuming a 35% tax bracket, the underpaid tax for the first year is $11,605. Upon completion of the contract, interest would be paid on this amount and underpaid taxes for other years. Even if elected, the "de-minimis" exception would be inapplicable as the reported income in the first year of the contract ($90,000) is not within 10% of the income that would have been reported if actual costs had been used in the computation ($123,158 = $33,158 + $90,000). ◀

INSTALLMENT SALES METHOD

In general, the gain or loss from the sale of property is reported in the year the property is sold. If the sales proceeds are collected in years after the sale, the taxpayer may find it difficult to pay the tax on the entire amount of the gain in the year of sale. To reduce the burden, the tax law permits taxpayers to spread the gain from installment sales over the collection period. The installment method is applicable only to gains and is used to report income from an installment transaction unless the taxpayer elects not to use the

50 Sec. 460(b)(3).

51 Sec. 460(b)(3).

installment method. An **installment sale** is any disposition of property where at least one payment is received after the close of the taxable year in which the disposition occurs. The installment method is *not* applicable to sales of:

- inventory, or
- marketable securities[52]

KEY POINT

The installment sales method allows either a cash or an accrual method taxpayer to spread the gain from the sale of property over the period during which payments are received.

Computations Under Sec. 453. Income under the installment sales method is computed as follows:

SELF-STUDY QUESTION

A taxpayer sells 100 shares of Ford Motor Company stock for a gain of $800 on December 30, 2015. The taxpayer received the proceeds from the sale from the stockbroker on January 5, 2016. Can the taxpayer use the installment sales method?

ANSWER

No, the method is not applicable to sales of publicly traded property.

TYPICAL MISCONCEPTION

The selling price is sometimes confused with the contract price.

STEP 1: Compute the gross profit from the sale.

Selling price	$xx,xxx
Minus: Adjusted basis	(x,xxx)
Selling expenses	(x,xxx)
Depreciation recapture[53]	(x,xxx)
Gross profit	$ x,xxx

STEP 2: Determine the contract price.

Contract price (greater of the gross profit from above or the selling price reduced by any existing mortgage assumed or acquired by the purchaser)	$xx,xxx

STEP 3: Compute the gross profit percentage.

$$\text{Gross profit percentage} = \frac{\text{Gross profit}}{\text{Contract price}} = \text{xx\%}$$

STEP 4: Compute the gain to be reported in the year of sale.

Collections of principal received during year (exclusive of interest)	$xx,xxx
Plus: Excess mortgage (if any)[a]	x,xxx
Total	$xx,xxx
Times: Gross profit percentage	× xx%
Net gain recognized in year of sale	$ x,xxx
Plus: Depreciation recapture	x,xxx
Gain reported in year of sale	$ x,xxx

ADDITIONAL COMMENT

On the sale of a capital asset a taxpayer might elect not to use the installment sales method and report the entire gain in the year of sale if he or she has capital losses that could be used to offset the gain.

STEP 5: Compute the gain to be reported in subsequent years.

Collections of principal received	$ x,xxx
Times: Gross profit percent	× xx%
Gain reported in each of the subsequent years	$ x,xxx

[a] Mortgage − Basis − Selling expense − Depreciation recapture = Excess mortgage

Note that depreciation recapture (see Chapter I:13) must be reported in the year of the sale even if no payment is received.

EXAMPLE I:11-23 ▶ Gina, a cash basis taxpayer, sells equipment for $200,000. The equipment originally cost $70,000, and $10,000 of MACRS depreciation has been deducted before the sale. The $10,000 of depreciation must be recaptured as ordinary income under Sec. 1245. The buyer assumes the existing mortgage of $50,000, pays $10,000 down, and agrees to pay $10,000 per year for 14 years plus interest at a rate acceptable to the IRS. Selling expenses are $13,000. The selling price is $200,000 [($50,000 + $10,000) + (14 × $10,000)]. The gain to be reported is $127,000 [$200,000 − $13,000 − ($70,000 − $10,000)]. Using the steps listed above, calculations are made as follows:

[52] Sec. 453(b)(2) and (k).

[53] For a discussion of depreciation recapture, (see Chapter I:13.)

STEP 1: Compute the gross profit from the sale.

Selling price	$200,000
Minus: Adjusted basis	(60,000)
Selling expenses	(13,000)
Depreciation recapture	(10,000)
Gross profit	$117,000

STEP 2: Determine the contract price.

Greater of gross profit of $117,000 or selling price minus mortgage assumed by purchaser ($150,000 = $200,000 − $50,000)	$150,000

STEP 3: Compute the gross profit percentage.

$$\frac{\text{Gross profit}}{\text{percentage}} = \frac{\text{Gross profit (\$117,000)}}{\text{Contract price (\$150, 000)}} = 78\%$$

STEP 4: Compute the gain to be reported in the year of sale.

Principal received during year	$ 10,000
Plus: Excess mortgage	0
Total amount realized	$ 10,000
Times: Gross profit percentage	× 0.78
Gross profit	$ 7,800
Plus: Depreciation recapture	10,000
Gain reported in year of sale	$ 17,800

STEP 5: Compute the gain to be reported in subsequent years.

Principal received	$ 10,000
Times: Gross profit percentage	× 78%
Gain reported in each subsequent year	$ 7,800

Thus, the total gain reported is $127,000 [$17,800 + ($7,800 × 14)]. This is equal to the gross profit of $117,000 (which is the amount of Sec. 1231 gain reported on the sale) plus the $10,000 of depreciation recapture. As a cash basis taxpayer Gina will report the interest income as it is collected. (Figure I:11-1 at the end of this chapter illustrates this computation on Form 6252, Installment Sale Income.) ◄

REAL-WORLD EXAMPLE

When an installment obligation is assigned as collateral for a loan, the transaction is treated as a disposition of the obligation. Rev. Rul. 65-185, 1965-2 C.B. 153.

Disposition of Installment Obligations. A taxpayer who sells property on the installment basis may decide not to hold the obligation until maturity. For example, the holder may sell the obligation to a financial institution for the purpose of raising cash. Alternatively, the holder may not be able to collect the full amount of the installments because of the inability of the buyer to make payments. Thus, the holder must determine the adjusted basis of the obligation in order to compute the gain or loss realized on the disposition. The adjusted basis of an installment obligation is equal to the face amount of the obligation reduced by the gross profit that would be realized if the holder collects the face amount of the obligation. In general, this means the adjusted basis of an obligation is equal to

$$\text{Face amount} \times (100\% - \text{Gross profit percentage})$$

EXAMPLE I:11-24 ► Assume the same facts as in Example I:11-23 except that Gina immediately sells a single $10,000 installment to a bank for $9,700. Gina reports a gain of $7,500 computed as follows:

Selling price	$9,700
Minus: Adjusted basis of installment	(2,200)[a]
Recognized gain	$7,500

[a] $10,000 face amount × (100% − 78% gross profit percentage) = $2,200

Gina would have reported a gain of $7,800 had she decided not to sell the installment but to collect the face amount. Because the obligation is discounted by $300 ($10,000 − $9,700), the reported gain is reduced by $300. If the installment had not been sold immediately, the bank would probably also pay to Gina an amount for the accrued interest. In such a situation Gina would report the gain from the sale and the accrued interest as income. ◀

EXAMPLE I:11-25 ▶ Assume that Gina in Example I:11-24 is unable to collect the final $10,000 installment because the individual who purchases the property declares bankruptcy. Gina would be entitled to a bad debt deduction of $2,200, the basis of the installment. Gina does not receive a bad debt deduction for the accrued interest because the interest has not been included in her gross income. ◀

KEY POINT

A donor of property does not normally recognize gain, but a gift of certain installment obligations causes the recognition of gain.

Certain dispositions of installment obligations, such as gifts, are taxable events.[54] The main objective of this rule is to prevent income from being shifted from one taxpayer to another. Thus, if a corporation distributes an installment obligation as a dividend or if a father gives his daughter an installment obligation, gain or loss is recognized. In general, the gain or loss recognized is equal to the difference between the FMV of the obligation and its adjusted basis. In the case of a gift, the gain recognized is equal to the difference between the face of the obligation and its adjusted basis. However, certain exceptions to this rule exist. Transfers to controlled corporations under Sec. 351, certain corporate reorganizations and liquidations, transfers on the taxpayer's death, transfers incident to divorce, distributions by partnerships, and contributions of capital to a partnership are exceptions to this rule. In these cases, the recipients of the obligations report income when the installments are collected.

Repossessions of Property Sold on the Installment Basis. In general, the repossession of property sold on the installment basis is a taxable event. The gain or loss recognized is generally equal to the difference between the value of the repossessed property (reduced by any costs incurred as a result of the repossession) and the adjusted basis of any remaining installment obligations.

EXAMPLE I:11-26 ▶ Yuji sells stock of a non–publicly traded corporation with a $7,000 adjusted basis for $10,000. Yuji receives a $1,000 down payment, and the balance of $9,000 is due the following year. In the year of the sale Yuji reports a capital gain of $300 (0.30 × $1,000) under the installment method of accounting. Yuji is unable to collect the $9,000 note, and after incurring legal fees of $500, he repossesses the stock. When Yuji repossesses the stock it is worth $8,700. The adjusted basis of the note is $6,300 (0.70 × $9,000). Yuji must report a capital gain of $1,900 ($8,700 − $500 − $6,300). The basis of the stock to Yuji is its FMV at the time it is repossessed ($8,700). ◀

The amount of gain recognized from the repossession of real property is limited to the lesser of (1) the gross profit in the remaining installments reduced by the costs incurred as a result of the repossession or (2) the cash and FMV of other property received from the buyer in excess of the gain previously recognized.[55] In the case of the repossession of either real or personal property, the gain or loss retains the same character as the gain or loss on the original sale.

EXAMPLE I:11-27 ▶ Assume the same facts as in Example I:11-26, except that the property sold is land. Yuji reports a capital gain of $700, which is the lesser of $2,200 [(0.30 × $9,000) − $500] or $700 ($1,000 − $300). The basis of the land is $7,500 [$9,000 − (0.30 × $9,000) unrealized profit + $700 gain previously recognized + $500 legal fees]. ◀

Installment Sales for More Than $150,000. Special rules apply to nondealers who sell property for more than $150,000. The special rules do not apply to sales of personal use property, to sales of property used or produced in the trade or business of farming, or to sales of timeshares or residential lots.

First, if the taxpayer borrows funds using the installment obligations as security, the amount borrowed is treated as a payment received on the installment obligation.[56] This

---

54 Sec. 453B(a).
55 Sec. 1038.
56 Sec. 453A(d).

prevents the taxpayer from using the installment method to defer tax and yet obtain cash by borrowing against the installment obligation. Second, if the installment method is used, interest must be paid to the government on the deferred tax.[57] This rule, however, applies only to deferred principal payments over $5 million.[58]

KEY POINT

Installment sales between related parties cannot be used to defer the recognition of gain by the original owner when the related purchaser receives cash as result of a resale of the property.

Installment Sales Between Related Persons. Installment sales between related persons are subject to the same rules as other installment sales except when the property is resold by the related purchaser. The primary purpose of the resale rule is to prevent the original owner from deferring gain recognition by selling the property to a related person who, in turn, resells the property.

Sec. 453(e) requires the first seller to treat amounts received by the related person (second seller) as having been personally received. Thus, the first seller would be required to report the gain in the year (or years) in which proceeds are received by the second seller. This acceleration provision is applicable only if the resale takes place within two years of the initial sale. For purposes of Sec. 453(e), the term *related person* includes a spouse, children, grandchildren, and parents. Controlled corporations, partnerships, estates, and trusts are also covered.

DEFERRED PAYMENT SALES

The installment sale rules are not applicable to all sales involving future payments. The installment method cannot be used when the sale of property produces a loss. Also, a taxpayer can elect out of the installment method when a sale results in a gain. The manner in which these transactions are reported depends on the taxpayer's accounting method. For accrual method taxpayers, the total *amount receivable* from the buyer (exclusive of interest) is treated as part of the amount realized. Thus, the entire gain or loss is reported in the year of sale. For cash method taxpayers, the FMV of the installment obligation is treated as part of the amount realized in the year of sale. The amount realized, however, cannot be considered to be less than the FMV of the property sold minus any other consideration received (e.g., cash).[59]

EXAMPLE I:11-28 ▶ USA Corporation, an accrual method taxpayer, sells land for $100,000. USA receives $50,000 down and a $50,000 note payable in 12 months plus 14% interest. Assume the basis of the land is $80,000 and that it is a capital asset. Because of the buyer's poor credit, the value of the note is only $45,000. USA affirmatively elects not to report the installment sale on the installment method. USA reports a capital gain of $20,000 ($100,000 − $80,000). If USA collects the face of the note at maturity, no additional gain or loss is recognized. If USA sells the note for $45,000, a $5,000 capital loss is recognized. ◀

EXAMPLE I:11-29 ▶ Assume the same facts as in Example I:11-28, except that USA is a cash method taxpayer. If the FMV of the land is $100,000 (the stated selling price), the treatment of the transaction is exactly the same as it is using the accrual method. If the FMV of the land is assumed to be $95,000 (cash received plus FMV of the note received), USA recognizes a $15,000 ($95,000 − $80,000) capital gain in the year of the sale. If USA collects the face of the note at maturity, $5,000 of ordinary income is recognized. If USA sells the note for $45,000, no gain or loss is recognized. ◀

ADDITIONAL COMMENT

A contingent payment sale is a sale or other disposition of property in which the aggregate selling price cannot be determined by the close of the tax year in which the sale took place.

Indeterminate Market Value. In certain transactions, the value of obligations received cannot be determined (e.g., a mineral interest is sold for an amount equal to 10% of the value of future production). Under the Regulations, the value of obligations with an **indeterminate market value** is assumed to be no lower than the value of the property sold less the value of other property received.[60] Hence, if the value of property sold is determinable, the recognized gain equals the excess of the value of the property sold over its basis. On occasion, however, neither the value of the obligation received nor the value of property sold can be determined.

Temporary regulations specify how these types of transactions are to be treated.[61] The basic rules relating to special accounting methods are summarized in Topic Review I:11-3.

---

[57] The interest computation is described in Sec. 453A(c).

[58] Sec. 453A(b)(2)(B).

[59] Temp. Reg. Sec. 15A.453-1(d)(2)(ii)(A).

[60] Reg. Sec. 1.453-1(d)(3)(iii).

[61] Temp. Reg. Sec. 15A.453-1(c).

TOPIC REVIEW I:11-3

Special Accounting Methods

Long-Term Contracts

- Long-term contracts include building, installation, construction, and manufacturing contracts that are not completed in the same tax year in which they are entered into. A manufacturing contract is long-term only if the contract involves the manufacture of either a unique item not normally carried in inventory or an item that normally requires more than 12 calendar months to complete.
- Long-term contracts may be reported under the regular or the modified percentage of completion method. Under both methods income is reported as work is completed, except that under the modified percentage of completion method no income is reported until at least 10% of the work is completed.
- The completed contract method is available only for home construction contracts, for construction contracts expected to take two years or less to complete, and for use by smaller companies (those whose average gross receipts for the three preceding tax years are $10 million or less).

Installment Method

- Under the installment method gain is reported as the sales proceeds are collected. The installment method is generally not available for sales of inventory or publicly traded property. Furthermore, the method is available only for gains.
- Gain is reported as sales proceeds are collected. However, both depreciation recapture and any mortgage in excess of basis must be reported in the year of sale. Gain recognition is also accelerated in certain situations if the seller borrows against the installment obligation or if a related buyer resells the property within two years.

Imputed Interest

OBJECTIVE 5

Compute the amount of imputed interest in certain transactions

KEY POINT

Imputed interest is important because it alters the amount of gain on the sale and causes an interest expense deduction for the buyer and interest income for the seller.

TYPICAL MISCONCEPTION

Some people mistakenly assumed that the imputed interest rules do not apply if the property is sold for a loss.

Before the enactment of Sec. 1274 and the amendment of Sec. 483, property could be sold on an installment basis in a contract providing for little or no interest. Instead of charging interest, the seller charged a higher price for the property. If the property sold was a capital asset, the result of the arrangement was to reduce the interest income reported by the seller and to increase the amount of favorably taxed capital gain. Sections 483 and 1274 now *impute* interest in a deferred payment contract where no interest or a low rate of interest is provided. Another impact of the **imputed interest rules** on sellers is to reallocate payments received between interest (which is fully taxable) and principal (only the gain portion of which is taxable). The result is often an increase in the income reported in early years and a decrease in later years. The rules are generally applicable to both buyers and sellers. In certain instances, the buyer may want interest to be imputed in order to increase his interest deduction in early years.

The following transactions are exempt from the imputed interest rules:

- Debt subject to original issue discount provisions (basically bonds issued for less than face where amortization of the discount is required under Sec. 1274; see Chapter I:5)
- Sales of property for $3,000 or less
- Any sales where all of the payments are due within six months
- Sales of patents to the extent the payment is contingent on the use or disposition of the patent
- Certain carrying charges for personal property or educational services covered by Sec. 163(b) when the interest charge cannot be ascertained
- Charges for the purchase of personal-use property (purchaser only)[62]

[62] Sec. 483(d). The rule lowers the basis of a personal-use asset in order to increase any gain on the future sale of the property.

EXAMPLE I:11-30 ► Joan is involved in several transactions during the current year. No interest is stated on any of the transactions. The terms of the transactions and the applicability of the imputed interest rules are summarized below:

Transaction	*Imputation of Interest*
Purchases furniture costing $8,000 for her residence. Full price is payable within four months.	Not applicable because property is for personal use. Also, all payments are due within six months.
Sells a boat for $2,000. Payment is due in a year.	Not applicable because sales price is not more than $3,000.
Sells land for $100,000. Payment is due in five years.	Interest must be imputed because no exception is applicable.
Purchases a newly issued bond for $650 (face of $1,000).	Not applicable because transaction is subject to the original issue discount rules in Sec. 1274. Also, the price is not more than $3,000. ◄

IMPUTED INTEREST COMPUTATION

In order to avoid the imputation of interest, the stated interest rate must be at least equal to 100% of the applicable federal rate (110% of the applicable federal rate in the case of sale–lease back arrangements). Lower rates are specified for two types of transactions: (1) If the stated principal amount for qualified debt obligations that are issued in exchange for property under Sec. 1274A does not exceed $2.8 million, the interest rate is limited to 9% compounded semiannually; and (2) the interest rate is limited to 6% compounded semiannually in the case of sales of land between related individuals (unless the sales price exceeds $500,000).

The **applicable federal rate** is determined monthly and is based on the rate paid by the federal government on borrowed funds. The rate varies with the terms of the loan. Loans are divided into short-term (not over three years), mid-term (over three years but not over nine years), and long-term (over nine years).

EXAMPLE I:11-31 ► Kasi sells land for $100,000 to Bill, an unrelated person. The sales price is to be paid to Kasi at the end of five years in a single installment with no stated interest. Kasi paid $60,000 for the land. Assume the current federal rate is 10%. Because the amount of the stated principal is less than $2,800,000, interest is imputed at a rate not to exceed 9% compounded semiannually. As a result, the effective rate is 9.2025% (9% compounded semiannually), and the present value factor is .64393 ($1 \div 1.092025^5$). Thus, the present value of the final payment is $64,393 (0.64393 × $100,000). Kasi reports a $4,393 ($64,393 − $60,000) gain on the sale of the land and $35,607 ($100,000 − $64,393) interest income instead of a $40,000 gain and no interest income. The buyer is treated as incurring $35,607 in interest and has a $64,393 basis in the land. Whether the interest is deductible depends on a variety of other factors (see Chapter I:7). ◄

ACCRUAL OF INTEREST

Is imputed interest reported under the cash or the accrual method? In other words, is imputed interest reported when it accrues or when it is paid? In general, imputed interest is reported as it accrues. However, there are some major exceptions, as follows:

ADDITIONAL COMMENT

The $2 million and $2.8 million limitations are subject to inflation adjustments.

- Sales of personal residences
- Most sales of farms for $1 million or less
- Sales involving aggregate payments of $250,000 or less
- Sales of land between related persons unless the sales price exceeds $500,000[63]

In addition, if the borrower and lender jointly elect, and if the stated principal does not exceed $2 million, accrual of interest is not required. This election is not available if the lender is an accrual method taxpayer or a dealer with respect to the property sold or exchanged.[64]

[63] Sec. 1274(c)(4).

[64] Sec. 1274A(c).

EXAMPLE I:11-32 ▶ Assume the same facts as in Example I:11-31. Because the aggregate payments do not exceed $250,000, the transaction is exempt from the requirement that interest be accrued. As a result, Kasi reports interest income and Bill reports interest expense in the fifth year when the final payment is made on the transaction. Under the installment method, $4,393 gain on the sale is recognized in the fifth year. ◀

GIFT, SHAREHOLDER, AND OTHER LOANS

Imputed interest rules are not limited to installment transactions. Sec. 7872 applies to transactions involving related parties whose taxes are lowered as a result of low interest or interest-free loans. These situations include

- *Gift loans.* For example, parents in higher tax brackets loan money to their adult children without charging interest. If the children invest the borrowed money and are taxed on the income at a lower rate, the family has reduced its total tax liability in the absence of imputed interest rules.
- *Corporation shareholder loans.* In the absence of imputed interest rules, taxes may be saved by a corporation that makes an interest-free loan to a shareholder. If the corporation had invested the money and paid out the resulting income as a dividend, it would have first been taxed on the profit. By making the interest-free loan, the corporation could, in the absence of imputed interest rules, reduce its taxes by avoiding the otherwise taxable income.
- *Compensation-related loans.* Employers may loan money to employees without charging interest. Without the requirement to impute interest, this could produce tax savings if the employer was unable to deduct additional compensation because of the reasonable compensation limitation or if the employee was unable to deduct the interest, say, because the borrowed funds were used to purchase personal use property.
- *Other tax avoidance loans.* Any other low-interest or interest-free loan that produces tax savings may be subject to the imputed interest rules. For example, a club may offer its members a choice of either paying dues or making a large refundable deposit. The club can invest the money and earn interest perhaps equal to the dues. In the absence of imputed interest rules, the member avoids taxes by not having to report the income that would have been earned if the member personally invested the funds. The club is indifferent between the alternatives because both the dues and the interest income are taxable.

In general, interest is imputed on the above loans by applying the applicable federal rates discussed earlier. The resulting interest income is taxable to the lender. Whether the interest expense is deductible by the borrower is determined by applying the usual interest deduction rules (see Chapter I:7).

The imputation process involves a second step. The lender is treated as returning the imputed interest to the borrower. This is necessary because the interest was not actually paid. For example, in the case of a gift loan, the lender is treated as giving the imputed interest back to the borrower. This would not normally have income tax implications, but if the imputed interest were large enough, it could result in a gift tax. In the case of the corporation-shareholder loan, the corporation is treated as paying the imputed interest back to the shareholder as a dividend. Typically, this does not increase the corporation's tax, but it results in the recognition of dividend income to the shareholder. For compensation-related loans, the second step is to impute compensation paid by the employer and received by the employee. The compensation is taxable to the employee and, if reasonable in amount, is deductible by the employer.

There are several important exceptions intended to limit the application of imputed interest in situations where tax avoidance may be immaterial:

- Interest is not imputed on gift loans between two individuals totaling $10,000 or less, except when the borrowed funds are used to purchase income-producing property.
- If the gift loans between two individuals total $100,000 or less, the imputed interest is limited to the borrower's "net investment income" as defined by Sec. 163(d)(4). (See Chapter I:7 for a discussion of net investment income.) If the net investment income is $1,000 or less, it is not necessary to impute interest.

- Interest is not imputed on compensation-related and corporate shareholder loans totaling $10,000 or less.

These exceptions do not apply when tax avoidance is one of the principal purposes of the loans.

EXAMPLE I:11-33 ▶ Linda made interest-free gift loans to each of her four children: Andy, Bob, Cathy, and Donna. Andy borrowed $9,000 to purchase an automobile. Bob borrowed $25,000 to buy stock. Bob's net investment income is $800. Cathy also borrowed $25,000 to buy stock, but her net investment income is $1,100. Donna borrowed $120,000 to purchase a residence, and her net investment income is $500. Tax avoidance is not a motive for any of the loans. Imputation of interest is not required for the loans to Andy or Bob. The loan to Andy is exempt because the amount is less than $10,000, and the loan to Bob is exempt because his net investment income is under $1,000. Imputation of interest is required for the loans to Cathy and Donna. In the case of Cathy, the amount of imputed interest is limited to her net investment income of $1,100. The imputed interest for Donna, however, is not limited to her net investment income because the amount of the loan is over $100,000. ◀

The imputed interest rules are summarized in Topic Review I:11-4.

CHANGE IN ACCOUNTING METHODS

OBJECTIVE 6

Determine the tax treatment that results from changes in accounting methods

In general, a new taxpayer elects an accounting method by simply applying the selected method when computing income for the initial tax return.[65] If a particular item does not occur in the first year, the accounting method is elected the first year in which the item occurs.

EXAMPLE I:11-34 ▶ Gordon opened a beauty shop several years ago. Because he had no inventory, no inventory method was selected. In the current year, Gordon expanded his business to offer beauty supplies to his customers. Gordon can delay electing an inventory method until the year in which he first has an inventory. ◀

TOPIC REVIEW I:11-4

Imputed Interest

PURPOSE

The imputed interest rules are intended to prevent taxpayers from reducing their taxes by charging little or no interest on installment payment transactions and loans.

APPLIES TO

In most cases applies to both parties, the debtor and the creditor. The result is to impute interest income to the lender and interest expense to the borrower. Several exceptions exempt small transactions from imputed interest. For example, sales involving payments of $3,000 or less are generally exempt as are loans of less than $10,000.

RATE

Interest is imputed at the applicable federal rate if the stated interest rate is lower. The applicable federal rate is the rate the federal government pays on borrowed funds and is determined monthly. In general, the current rate at the time of the transaction is used throughout the term of the loan. The rate varies with the term of the loan. Loans are divided into short-term (not over three years), mid-term (over three years but not over nine years), and long-term (over nine years).

[65] Reg. Sec. 1.446-1(e)(1).

In general, once an accounting method is chosen, it cannot be changed without IRS approval. There are a few exceptions. For example, taxpayers may adopt the LIFO inventory method without prior IRS approval.[66] Once such methods are adopted, however, they cannot be changed without IRS approval.

As previously noted, the term *accounting method* indicates not only the overall accounting method used by the taxpayer, but also the treatment of any item of income or deduction.[67] A change of accounting methods should not be confused with the correction of an error. Errors include mathematical mistakes, posting errors, deductions of the wrong amount for an expense, omission of an item of taxable income, or incorrect computation of a credit. An error is normally corrected by filing an amended return for the tax year or years in which the error occurs. In general, there is a three-year statute of limitations on the correction of errors. After three years, the tax year is closed and changes cannot be made.[68]

REAL-WORLD EXAMPLE

The write-down of soil aggregate to its market value by a paving company was a change in accounting method rather than the mere correction of an accounting error. The soil aggregate was included in its election to adopt the LIFO inventory method, and the use of this method required that the soil aggregate be included at cost regardless of market value. *First National Bank of Gainesville, Trustee*, 88 T.C. 1069 (1987).

REAL-WORLD EXAMPLE

An extension of time to file the application for change of accounting method was granted because of the death of the accountant in charge of filing the application. Rev. Rul. 79-417, 1979-2 C.B. 202.

Taxpayers wishing to change accounting methods must file Form 3115 with the IRS, on or before the due date of the tax return including extensions. A duplicate copy of Form 3115 must be filed with the tax return for the year. A taxpayer who amends the original income tax return within six months of its due date may request a change of accounting methods with the amended return.[69]

In general, taxpayers initiate a change in accounting methods from an incorrect to a correct method are exempt from penalty and from retroactive application of the new reporting method. Although changes in accounting methods require IRS approval, the IRS states that approval will automatically be granted for a wide variety of changes if the taxpayer meets specific requirements that include proper filing of both Form 3115 and the current year's tax return, agreeing to take into account the Sec. 481(a) adjustment (as described below), not being under examination, and not having changed the same method of accounting within the last four years.[70] Although the IRS retains the right to again change any method of accounting adopted under these procedures it states that such changes will not be retroactive except in rare or unusual circumstances. Examples of situations where retroactive application may occur include misstatement or omission of material facts, change in material facts, and changes in applicable authority.

AMOUNT OF CHANGE

A change in accounting methods usually results in duplications or omissions of items of income or expense.

EXAMPLE I:11-35 ▶ Bonnie, a practicing CPA, has been reporting income using the cash method. In the current year, Bonnie obtains permission to change to the accrual method. At the beginning of the current year, Bonnie has $80,000 of receivables that have not been reported in prior years. The receivables were not reported in prior years because they were not collected. Although the receivables are collected in the current year, they are not taxable because, under the accrual method, Bonnie now reports income as it is earned and the income is not earned in the current year. In this case, the income was earned in prior years.

Also, assume Bonnie has accounts payable of $15,000 at the beginning of the current year. The accounts payable were not deducted in prior years because the expenses had not been paid. Furthermore, the accounts payable are not deductible in the current year even if they are paid. This is because the expenses were incurred in prior years. Obviously, the IRS expects to collect the tax on the $80,000 of receivables, and Bonnie is entitled to deduct the $15,000 of payables. In the absence of any special provision, both amounts would be omitted from the computation of taxable income. On the other hand, if the change were from the accrual

---

66 A taxpayer may adopt LIFO by merely determining year-end inventory by that method and attaching Form 970 to the tax return for the year (Reg. Sec. 1.472-3(a)).

67 Reg. Sec. 1.446-1(e)(2)(ii)(b).

68 Exceptions are applicable when the taxpayer omits from the return an amount of income that is over 25% of the gross income stated on the return (6 years) or where fraud occurs (no limitation).

69 The extension will be granted if the taxpayer follows procedures outlined in Rev. Proc. 2002-9, 2002-1 C.B. 327.

70 Rev. Proc. 97-37, 1997-2 C.B. 455.

method to the cash method, both amounts would be reported twice (in the year prior to the change because they had accrued and in the year of the change because they are collected or paid). Thus, a special provision is also needed for duplications. ◄

REPORTING THE AMOUNT OF THE CHANGE

The net amount of the change must be taken into account.[71] A positive adjustment is added to income, whereas a negative adjustment is subtracted from income. This adjustment can, of course, be made in the year of the change. If the amount is small, recognizing the full amount of the net adjustment in the year of the change is both simple and equitable. This is the only option available when the amount of the change is $3,000 or less. On the other hand, reporting a large positive adjustment in one year could push the taxpayer into a higher marginal tax bracket and result in a significant tax increase. Because the extra income is due to changing accounting methods, not increasing cash flows, the taxpayer may not have the wherewithal to pay the additional tax.

As a result, there are alternative methods that may be used to report the amount of the change. The methods that are available depend on whether the change is voluntary (a change that is initiated by the taxpayer) or involuntary (a change from an unacceptable to an acceptable method that is required by the IRS).

In the case of an involuntary change, several alternative methods are available to the IRS.[72]

In the case of voluntary changes, taxpayers must agree to report the adjustment over a period not to exceed four years. When the amount of the adjustment is $25,000 or less, taxpayers may elect to include the full amount in the current year.[73] In the case of a change spread over four years, equal portions of the change are reported in each of the four years beginning with the year of the change.

EXAMPLE I:11-36 ► Diana obtains permission to change from the accrual to the cash method of reporting income. The change results in a $30,000 negative adjustment to income. The IRS requires Diana to spread the adjustment over four years. As a result, she may deduct $7,500 per year for four years. Note that because the amount of the adjustment is spread over the current and future years, the tax savings associated with the deduction are deferred. ◄

In general, the amount of the adjustment cannot be spread over a period longer than the method being changed has been used.

REAL-WORLD EXAMPLE

A pipeline company was required to capitalize reconditioning costs on its natural gas pipelines instead of expensing these costs. *Mountain Fuel Supply Co. v. U.S.*, 28 AFTR 2d 71-5833, 71-2 USTC ¶9681 (10th Cir., 1971).

OBTAINING IRS CONSENT

Most changes in accounting method require IRS approval. Sec. 446(e) states that a taxpayer changing the method of accounting "on the basis of which he regularly computes his income in keeping his books" must obtain consent before computing taxable income under the new method. This implies that a taxpayer who has been computing taxable income on a method other than that used in computing book income does not need approval to conform the computation of taxable income to the method regularly used on the taxpayer's books. This conclusion is supported by Sec. 441(a), which requires that the same method of accounting be used in computing taxable income as is used in keeping the books. The alternative might be to require the taxpayer to conform his or her book accounting method with the tax accounting method. The answer may well be in how one defines "books." The IRS has ruled that a reconciliation of taxable income with accounting income was a part of the taxpayer's auxiliary records.[74] Hence, the taxpayer was using the same accounting method for book and tax reporting. As a result, a taxpayer who changes the method of accounting used for financial reporting may not be required to change the method of accounting used for tax reporting as long as financial income and book income are reconciled.

---

71 Sec. 481.

72 Secs. 481(a), (b)(1), (b)(2), and (c).

73 Rev. Procs. 2012-20, 2012-14 IRB 700.

74 Rev. Rul. 58-601, 1958-2 C.B. 81.

TAX PLANNING CONSIDERATIONS

OBJECTIVE 7

Describe tax planning considerations for accounting periods and methods

ACCOUNTING PERIODS

New corporations often routinely adopt a calendar year. Consideration should be given, however, to adopting a tax year for the initial reporting period that ends before the amount of taxable income exceeds the amount that is taxed at the lowest tax rates (e.g., when taxable income is $50,000 or less). This is less critical for a corporation suffering losses because the NOLs may be carried forward for a 20-year period.

In the past, taxpayers were able to defer income by selecting different tax years for partners and partnerships or S corporations and shareholders. Current law limits this opportunity. Nevertheless, partnerships and S corporations may adopt a tax year that differs from that of their owners if that year qualifies as a natural business year (i.e., at least 25% of revenues occur during the last two months of the year). Furthermore, deferral is possible in the case of estates, because they are not subject to similar restrictions on the choice of tax years.

KEY POINT

C corporations and estates have more flexibility than S corporations and partnerships in the selection of a tax year.

ACCOUNTING METHODS

New businesses should consider the tax implications of electing an accounting method. For example, taxpayers may benefit from the LIFO inventory method because LIFO typically reduces gross profit and defers the payment of taxes during inflationary periods. Similarly, service companies usually choose the cash method of reporting income because it permits receivables to be reported when collected rather than when the income is earned. Choosing an accounting method requires an understanding not only of the available accounting methods, but also the nature of the taxpayer's business. Will a specific election be to the tax advantage of the taxpayer? LIFO inventory is often recommended because, during inflationary periods, it tends to reduce inventory values and increase the cost of goods sold. In certain industries, such as the computer industry, however, costs are declining, and LIFO actually may result in a higher inventory value.

KEY POINT

The election to use an accounting method is made by filing the first tax return on the basis of that method.

In other industries, inventories may fluctuate widely from one year to the next because of changing demand, shortages of materials, strikes, or other causes. LIFO layers may have to be depleted simply to continue business operations. This can cause one of two things to happen: (1) incurring extra recordkeeping costs of LIFO for little or no benefit because the inventories are depleted before they produce significant tax deferrals or (2) depleting low-cost layers from years past, resulting in a substantial increase in taxable income in the year of occurrence.

INSTALLMENT SALES

Taxpayers normally choose the installment method of reporting income from casual sales of property. By spreading the gain from a sale over more than one tax year, the taxpayer normally remains in lower tax brackets and defers the tax. A taxpayer with low current taxable income may elect not to use the installment sale method in order to take advantage of the lower current tax rates.

COMPLIANCE AND PROCEDURAL CONSIDERATIONS

OBJECTIVE 8

Describe compliance and procedural considerations for accounting periods and methods

REPORTING INSTALLMENT SALES ON FORM 6252

Form 6252 (Installment Sale Income) is used to report income under the installment method from sales of real property and casual sales of personal property other than inventory. Figure I:11-1 illustrates how an installment sale transaction is reported. The illustration is based on Example I:11-23. A separate Form 6252 is normally used for each installment sale. Form 6252 is used in the year of the sale and any year in which the taxpayer receives a payment from the sale. Taxpayers who do not wish to use the installment method may report the transaction on either Schedule D or on Form 4797.

Form **6252**

Department of the Treasury
Internal Revenue Service

Installment Sale Income

▶ Attach to your tax return.
▶ Use a separate form for each sale or other disposition of property on the installment method.
▶ Information about Form 6252 and its instructions is at *www.irs.gov/form6252.*

OMB No. 1545-0228
2014
Attachment Sequence No. **79**

Name(s) shown on return: Gina Green | **Identifying number:** 123-45-6789

1	Description of property ▶ Equipment				
2a	Date acquired (mm/dd/yyyy) ▶ 7-01-2011 **b** Date sold (mm/dd/yyyy) ▶ 8-31-2014				
3	Was the property sold to a related party (see instructions) after May 14, 1980? If "No," skip line 4 . . . . ☐ Yes ☒ No				
4	Was the property you sold to a related party a marketable security? If "Yes," complete Part III. If "No," complete Part III for the year of sale and the 2 years after the year of sale . . . ☐ Yes ☒ No				

Part I Gross Profit and Contract Price. Complete this part for the year of sale only.

5	Selling price including mortgages and other debts. **Do not** include interest, whether stated or unstated			5	200,000
6	Mortgages, debts, and other liabilities the buyer assumed or took the property subject to (see instructions)	6	50,000		
7	Subtract line 6 from line 5	7	150,000		
8	Cost or other basis of property sold	8	70,000		
9	Depreciation allowed or allowable	9	10,000		
10	Adjusted basis. Subtract line 9 from line 8	10	60,000		
11	Commissions and other expenses of sale	11	13,000		
12	Income recapture from Form 4797, Part III (see instructions)	12	10,000		
13	Add lines 10, 11, and 12			13	83,000
14	Subtract line 13 from line 5. If zero or less, **do not** complete the rest of this form (see instructions)			14	117,000
15	If the property described on line 1 above was your main home, enter the amount of your excluded gain (see instructions). Otherwise, enter -0-			15	
16	**Gross profit.** Subtract line 15 from line 14			16	117,000
17	Subtract line 13 from line 6. If zero or less, enter -0-			17	
18	**Contract price.** Add line 7 and line 17			18	150,000

Part II Installment Sale Income. Complete this part for the year of sale **and** any year you receive a payment or have certain debts you must treat as a payment on installment obligations.

19	Gross profit percentage (expressed as a decimal amount). Divide line 16 by line 18. For years after the year of sale, see instructions			19	78%
20	If this is the year of sale, enter the amount from line 17. Otherwise, enter -0-			20	
21	Payments received during year (see instructions). **Do not** include interest, whether stated or unstated			21	10,000
22	Add lines 20 and 21			22	10,000
23	Payments received in prior years (see instructions). **Do not** include interest, whether stated or unstated	23			
24	**Installment sale income.** Multiply line 22 by line 19			24	7,800
25	Enter the part of line 24 that is ordinary income under the recapture rules (see instructions)			25	
26	Subtract line 25 from line 24. Enter here and on Schedule D or Form 4797 (see instructions)			26	7,800

Part III Related Party Installment Sale Income. Do not complete if you received the final payment this tax year.

27 Name, address, and taxpayer identifying number of related party

28 Did the related party resell or dispose of the property ("second disposition") during this tax year? . . . ☐ Yes ☐ No

29 **If the answer to question 28 is "Yes," complete lines 30 through 37 below unless one of the following conditions is met. Check the box that applies.**

- a ☐ The second disposition was more than 2 years after the first disposition (other than dispositions of marketable securities). If this box is checked, enter the date of disposition (mm/dd/yyyy) . . . ▶
- b ☐ The first disposition was a sale or exchange of stock to the issuing corporation.
- c ☐ The second disposition was an involuntary conversion and the threat of conversion occurred after the first disposition.
- d ☐ The second disposition occurred after the death of the original seller or buyer.
- e ☐ It can be established to the satisfaction of the IRS that tax avoidance was not a principal purpose for either of the dispositions. If this box is checked, attach an explanation (see instructions).

30	Selling price of property sold by related party (see instructions)	30	
31	Enter contract price from line 18 for year of first sale	31	
32	Enter the **smaller** of line 30 or line 31	32	
33	Total payments received by the end of your 2014 tax year (see instructions)	33	
34	Subtract line 33 from line 32. If zero or less, enter -0-	34	
35	Multiply line 34 by the gross profit percentage on line 19 for year of first sale	35	
36	Enter the part of line 35 that is ordinary income under the recapture rules (see instructions)	36	
37	Subtract line 36 from line 35. Enter here and on Schedule D or Form 4797 (see instructions)	37	

For Paperwork Reduction Act Notice, see page 4. Cat. No. 13601R Form **6252** (2014)

FIGURE I:11-1 ▶ REPORTING INSTALLMENT SALE INCOME ON FORM 6252 (BASED ON EXAMPLE I:11-23)

PROCEDURES FOR CHANGING TO LIFO

The LIFO method may be adopted in the initial year that inventories are maintained by merely using the method in that year. In addition, advance approval (e.g., within 180 days following the start of the year) from the IRS is not required for an adoption of the LIFO method in the initial year that inventories are maintained on the LIFO method. However, Form 970 should be filed along with the taxpayer's tax return for the year of the change.[75] The application must include an analysis of the beginning and ending inventories. Further, if a taxpayer is changing to the LIFO method from another method (e.g., FIFO), advance approval from the IRS is also not required. Form 970 must be filed with the return and the beginning inventory for LIFO purposes is the same as under the former inventory method.[76]

If the former inventory is valued based on the lower of cost or market (LCM) method, an adjustment is required to restate the beginning inventory to cost because the LCM method cannot be used under LIFO. Generally, the beginning LIFO inventory is the same as the closing inventory for the prior year, except for the required restatement of previous writedowns to market. This adjustment to the beginning inventory can be spread ratably over the year of the change and the next two years.[77]

EXAMPLE I:11-37 ▶ Delaware Corporation elects to change to the LIFO inventory method. Delaware's inventories are valued using the LCM method based on the FIFO cost-flow assumption. The FIFO cost for the ending inventory is $50,000, and its LCM amount is $35,000. The initial inventory under LIFO must be restated to its cost, or $50,000. The $15,000 ($50,000 cost − $35,000 LCM value) difference can be included in taxable income over the current year and the next two years. $5,000 is added to taxable income in each year. ◀

PROBLEM MATERIALS

DISCUSSION QUESTIONS

I:11-1 Do accounting rules determine the amount of income to be reported by a taxpayer?

I:11-2 How does a taxpayer's tax accounting method affect the amount of tax paid?

I:11-3 Most individuals use the calendar year as their tax year. What requirement, if any, in the tax law causes this?

I:11-4 Why is it desirable for a new taxpayer to select an appropriate tax year?

I:11-5 What restrictions apply to partnerships selecting a tax year?

I:11-6 Does a similar restriction apply to S corporations? Explain.

I:11-7 How could the 52–53-week year prove to be beneficial to taxpayers? Explain.

I:11-8 Under what circumstances can an individual taxpayer change tax years without IRS approval?

I:11-9 Is there any instance in which a change in tax years is required? Explain.

I:11-10 a. In what situations will a tax year cover a period of less than 12 months?
b. Under what conditions is a taxpayer required to annualize income?
c. Does annualizing income increase or decrease the taxpayer's tax liability? Explain.

I:11-11 When is a final tax return due for an individual who uses a calendar year and who dies during the year?

I:11-12 a. Is it correct to say that businesses with inventories must use the accrual method?
b. What other restrictions apply to taxpayers who are choosing an overall tax accounting method?
c. Why is the cash method usually preferred to the accrual method?

I:11-13 a. Does the term *method of accounting* refer only to overall methods of accounting? Explain.

---

75 An acceptable election is considered to have been made even if Form 970 is not filed as long as all of the information required by Reg. Sec. 1.472-3(a) is provided by the taxpayer.

76 Reg. Sec. 1.472-2(c).

77 Sec. 472(d).

b. Does a taxpayer's accounting method affect the total amount of income reported over an extended time period?
c. How can the use of an accounting method affect the total amount of tax paid over time?

I:11-14 a. When are expenses deductible by a cash method taxpayer?
b. Are the rules that determine when interest is deductible by a cash method taxpayer the same as for other expenses?
c. Is a cash method taxpayer subject to the same rules for depreciable assets as accrual method taxpayers?

I:11-15 Who may use the completed contract method of reporting income from long-term contracts?

I:11-16 When is a cash method taxpayer allowed to deduct deposits?

I:11-17 What constitutes a payment in determining when a cash-basis taxpayer is entitled to deduct an expense?

I:11-18 What is meant by economic performance?

I:11-19 What conditions must be met if the economic performance test is to be waived for an accrual-method taxpayer?

I:11-20 Is an accrual method taxpayer permitted to deduct estimated expenses? What about prepaid expenses? Explain.

I:11-21 What is the significance of the *Thor Power Tool Co.* decision?

I:11-22 a. How are overhead costs treated in determining a manufacturing company's inventory?
b. Do retailers have a similar rule?
c. Are these rules the same as for financial accounting? If not, explain.

I:11-23 What transactions are subject to the long-term contract method of reporting?

I:11-24 a. What conditions must be met in order to use the installment method?
b. Why would a taxpayer elect not to use the installment method?

I:11-25 What is the impact of having the entire gain on an installment sale consist of ordinary income from depreciation recapture?

I:11-26 What impact does the gifting of an installment obligation have on the donor?

I:11-27 What treatment is given to an installment sale involving related people?

I:11-28 What is the primary impact of the imputed interest rules on installment sales?

I:11-29 What changes in accounting method can be made without IRS approval?

I:11-30 Can the IRS require a taxpayer to change accounting methods?

I:11-31 Explain the purpose of the four-year method used in computing the tax resulting from a net adjustment due to a change in accounting methods.

I:11-32 If a taxpayer changes the method of accounting used for financial reporting purposes, must the taxpayer also change his or her method of accounting for tax purposes?

ISSUE IDENTIFICATION QUESTIONS

I:11-33 Judy's Cars, Inc., sells collectible automobiles to consumers. She employs the specific identification inventory valuation method. Prices are negotiated by Judy and individual customers. Judy accepts trade-ins when she sells an automobile. Judy negotiates the allowance for trade with the customer. Occasionally, Judy finds that it can take two or three years to sell a given automobile. Judy now has four automobiles that she has held for over two years. She expects to eventually sell those automobiles, but expects that they will sell for less than their original cost. What tax issues should Judy consider?

I:11-34 Lana operates a real estate appraisal service business in a small town serving local lenders. After noting that lenders must pay to bring in a surveyor from out of town, she completes a course and obtains a surveyor's license that enables her to provide this service also. She now provides both services as a proprietor. What tax issues should Lana consider?

I:11-35 John owns a small farm on a lake. A local developer offers John $400,000 cash for his farm. The developer believes John's farm will be very attractive to home buyers because it is on a lake. After John turns down the initial offer, the developer offers to pay John $250,000 plus an amount equal to 10% of the selling price for the homes that are developed and sold. Identify the tax issues John should consider if he accepts the offer.

I:11-36 Lee is starting a small lawn service. On the advice of his accountant, Lee has formed a corporation and made an S corporation election. The accountant has asked Lee to consider electing a fiscal year ending on the last day in February. The accountant pointed out that Lee's business is likely to slow down in the winter. Also, the accountant indicated that the February year end would permit the accountant to do Lee's accounting work after the busy season in accounting is over. What tax issues should Lee consider?

PROBLEMS

I:11-37 *Allowable Taxable Year.* For each of the following cases, indicate whether the taxpayer has selected an allowable tax year in an initial year. If the year selected is not acceptable, indicate what an acceptable year would be.

a. A corporation selects a January 15 year-end.
b. A corporation selects a March 31 year-end.
c. A corporation selects a year that ends on the last Friday in March.
d. A partnership selects a year that ends on December 31 and has three equal partners whose years end on March 31, April 30, and June 30.
e. An S corporation selects a December 31 year-end.

I:11-38 *Change in Accounting Period.* In which of the following instances is a taxpayer permitted to change accounting periods without IRS approval?

a. A calendar-year taxpayer who wishes to change to a year that ends on the last Friday in December.
b. ABC Partnership has filed its tax return using a fiscal-year ending on March 31 for over 40 years. The partnership wishes to change to a calendar year-end that coincides with its partners' year-end.
c. Iowa Corporation, a newly acquired subsidiary, wishes to change its year-end to coincide with its parent.

I:11-39 *Annualization.* Each of the following cases involves a taxable year of less than 12 months. In which situations is annualization required?

a. A new corporation formed in September elects a calendar year.
b. A calendar-year individual dies on June 15.
c. Jean, who has been using a calendar year, marries Hank, a fiscal-year taxpayer. Soon after the marriage, Jean changes her tax year to coincide with her husband's tax year.
d. A calendar-year corporation liquidates on April 20.

I:11-40 *Short Period Return.* Lavanya, a single taxpayer, is a practicing accountant. She obtains permission to change her tax year from the calendar year to a year ending July 31. Her practice income for the seven months ending July 31 is $40,000. In addition, Lavanya has $3,000 of interest income and $6,500 of itemized deductions. She is entitled to one exemption. What is her tax for the short period?

I:11-41 *Cash Basis Expenses.* How much of the following expenses are currently deductible by a cash basis taxpayer?

a. Medical prescriptions costing $20 paid by credit card (medical expenses already exceed the 10% of AGI floor).
b. Prepaid interest (not related to points) of $200 on a residential loan.
c. Taxpayer borrows $300 from the bank to make a charitable contribution. The $300 is paid to the charitable organization before the end of the tax year.
d. Taxpayer gives a note to his church indicating an intent to contribute $300.
e. A calendar-year individual mails a check for $200 to his church on December 31. The check is postmarked December 31 and clears the bank on January 4.

I:11-42 *Economic Performance.* In light of the economic performance requirement, how much is deductible by the following accrual-basis corporate taxpayers this year?

a. Camp Corporation sells products with a one-year warranty. Camp estimates that the warranty costs on products sold during this year will amount to $80,000. Camp performs $38,000 of warranty work on products sold last year and $36,000 of warranty work on products sold this year.
b. Data Corporation agrees to pay $10,000 this year and $10,000 next year to a software developer. The developer completes all work on the software and delivers the product to Data this year.
c. Palm Corporation pays $5,000 to a supplier to guarantee delivery of raw materials. The $5,000 is refundable if Palm decides not to acquire the materials.
d. This year North Corporation pays a $1,000 security deposit on space it rents for a new office. In addition, North pays current year rent of $18,000. The security deposit is refundable if the property is returned in good condition.

I:11-43 *Manufacturing Inventory.* Which of the following costs must be included in inventory by a manufacturing company?

a. Raw materials
b. Advertising
c. Payroll taxes for factory employees
d. Research and experimental costs
e. Factory insurance
f. Repairs to factory equipment
g. Factory utility costs
h. Factory rent

I:11-44 *Single-Pool LIFO.* Prime Corporation begins operations in late 2015. Prime decides to use the single-pool LIFO method. Year-end inventories under FIFO are as follows:

2015	$110,000
2016	134,000
2017	125,000

The price index for 2015 is 130%; for 2016, 134%; and 2017, 140%. What are 2016 and 2017 inventories?

I:11-45 *Installment Sale.* Ace Construction Company sells a used crane to Go Construction for $80,000. The crane, which originally cost $900,000, is fully depreciated. Under Sec. 1245 depreciation recapture rules, the entire gain is taxable as ordinary income. Ace receives a down payment of $20,000 and is to receive $20,000 per year for three additional years plus interest of 8%, which is greater than the applicable federal rate.
a. Compute the gain from the sale.
b. How much gain is taxable in the year of the sale?
c. What income does Ace report in each of the next three years?

I:11-46 *Inventory Method.* Zap Company manufactures computer hard drives. The cost of hard drives has been declining for years. Sales totaled $4,000,000 last year. Zap's ending inventory was valued at $300,000 under FIFO. The company's new president is trying to cut taxes and asks you whether the company should switch to LIFO. What do you recommend?

I:11-47 *Installment Sales.* First Company sold the following assets during the year. Indicate whether First Company can use the installment method to report each transaction. If not, how is the transaction reported? Assume First Company is an accrual basis taxpayer.
a. First Company sold stock in a publicly held company costing $35,000. First Company received a $20,000 down payment and is to receive $20,000 per year for two years plus interest.
b. First Company sold land costing $150,000. First Company received a $20,000 down payment and is to receive $20,000 per year for five years plus interest.
c. First Company initiated credit sales of merchandise. The company previously sold merchandise only to cash customers. Cash sales this year totaled $4,000,000. Credit sales totaled $500,000. At year end, First Company has receivables of $100,000. The company expects to collect only $85,000 of the current receivables.

I:11-48 *Installment Sale.* In December, Dan sells unlisted stock with a cost of $14,000 for $20,000. Dan collects $5,000 down and is scheduled to receive $5,000 per year for three years plus interest at a rate acceptable to the IRS.
a. How much gain must Dan recognize in the year of the sale? Assume Dan uses the installment method to report the gain.
b. The following January, Dan sells the three remaining installments for a total of $13,800. How much gain or loss must Dan recognize from the sale of the remaining installments?

I:11-49 *Repossession.* Lina, an attorney, sold an antique rug for $45,000 that had been in her home. The rug cost Lina $12,000 several years ago. Lina collected $15,000 down and received a one-year interest bearing note for the balance. She is unable to collect the balance, and after incurring court costs of $500, she repossesses the rug. The rug is damaged when she recovers it and is now worth only $30,000.
a. How much gain must Lina report in the year of the sale?
b. How much gain, if any, must Lina report in the year she repossesses the rug?
c. What is the basis of the rug after the repossession?

I:11-50 *Deferred Payment Sale.* Joe sells land with a $60,000 adjusted basis for $42,000. He incurs selling expenses of $2,000. The land is subject to a $10,000 mortgage. The buyer, who assumes the mortgage, pays $8,000 down and agrees to pay Joe $8,000 per year for three years plus interest. The installment obligations are worth $24,000.

a. How much gain or loss does Joe report in the year of the sale?
b. When does Joe report the interest income from the sale?
c. Does Joe report gain or loss when he collects the installment payments?

I:11-51 *Imputed Interest.* On January 30, 2015, Amy sells land to Bob for a stated price of $200,000. The full $200,000 is payable on January 30, 2017. No interest is stated. Amy, a cash-method taxpayer, purchased the land in 2010 for $130,000.
a. How much interest income must be reported by Amy on the sale? Assume a 9% rate compounded semiannually. The present value factor is 0.83856.
b. In what year is the interest reported?
c. How much gain is reported by Amy on the sale?
d. In what year is the gain reported?
e. What is Bob's basis in the land?

I:11-52 *Change of Accounting Method.* Dana manages real estate and is a cash method taxpayer. She changes to the accrual method in 2016. Dana's business income for 2016 is $30,000 computed on the accrual method. Her books show the following:

	December 31, 2015	*December 31, 2016*
Accounts receivable	$16,000	$25,300
Accounts payable	15,200	11,800

a. What adjustment is necessary to Dana's income?
b. How should Dana report the adjustment?

I:11-53 *Required Payment.* BCD Partnership has, for many years, had a March 31 year-end. The partnership's net income for the fiscal year ended March 31, 2016 is $400,000. Because of its fiscal year, BCD has $100,000 on deposit with the IRS from 2015.
a. How much must BCD add to the deposit?
b. When must BCD make the addition?
c. Will the partners receive any credit for the deposit? That is, are they permitted to treat the amount as estimated payments?

I:11-54 *Change to LIFO.* Lance Corporation's management has asked whether they may change their inventory valuation method to LIFO. They now report their inventory using FIFO. If they can change, how would they go about it? How is the related adjustment handled?

I:11-55 *Imputed Interest.* Jane loans $80,000 to John, her son, to permit him to purchase a principal residence. The loan principal is secured by John's residence, but the agreement does not specify any interest. The applicable federal rate for the year is 8%. John's net investment income is $800.
a. How much interest is imputed on the loan each year?
b. Assume that the amount of the loan is $125,000. How much interest is imputed on the loan?
c. Is John allowed to deduct the imputed interest?
d. What other tax implications are there for the loan?

I:11-56 *Long-Term Contract.* King Construction Company is engaged in a road construction contract to build a highway over a three-year period. King will receive $11,200,000 for building five miles of highway. King estimates that it will incur $10,000,000 of costs before the contract is completed. As of the end of the first year King incurred $3,000,000 of costs allocated to the contract.
a. How much income from the contract must King report during the first year?
b. Assume King incurs an additional $5,000,000 of costs during the second year. How much income is reported during that year?
c. Assume that King incurs an additional $2,500,000 of costs in the third and final year of the contract. How much does King report during the third year?
d. Will King receive or pay look-back interest? Explain.

COMPREHENSIVE PROBLEM

I:11-57 Dan turned age 65 and retired this year. He owned and operated a tugboat in the local harbor before his retirement. The boat cost $100,000 when he purchased it two years ago. A tugboat is 10-year property. Dan deducted $10,000 of depreciation on the boat the year he purchased it and he deducted $18,000 of depreciation last year. He did not elect Section 179 expensing or bonus depreciation. He sold the tugboat in November of this year for $90,000 collecting an $18,000 down payment. The buyer agreed to pay 8% interest annually on the unpaid balance and to pay $18,000 annually for four years toward the principal. The four $18,000 principal payments and related interest payments begin next year. Dan received $72,000 of business income and incurred other business expenses of $30,000 this year before he retired. He received Social Security benefits of $2,000 and withdrew $10,000 from a regular IRA account. He contributed $4,000 to his church, paid real property taxes of $2,000, and home mortgage interest of $6,500. Dan paid $200 of state income taxes when he filed last year's return earlier this year and he made estimated state income tax payments of $800 during this year and $220 after year end. In addition, Dan made federal estimated payments of $8,000. Dan is a single, cash basis taxpayer. Ignore self-employment taxes and the election to use state sales tax as an itemized deduction.

a. Compute the depreciation for the current year on the tugboat.
b. Compute the amount of gain to be reported currently on the sale of the tugboat. Assume that Dan wants to use the installment method if it can be used. The accumulated depreciation on the tugboat is subject to Sec. 1245 depreciation recapture and must be reported currently.
c. How much interest, if any, must Dan report this year?
d. What is the income from the business, excluding the gain on the sale of the tugboat?
e. What is Dan's AGI?
f. What is the amount of Dan's itemized deductions?
g. What is Dan's taxable income?

TAX STRATEGY PROBLEMS

I:11-58 Leon has a substantial portfolio of stocks and bonds as well as cash from some bonds that have recently matured. He has been looking at investing $200,000 in corporate bonds that pay 7% interest. The $14,000 of annual interest would be used to pay his 24-year-old son's tuition at State University. A friend suggested that Leon loan the money "interest free" to his son, a student who has no other income. The son would then invest the $200,000 in the corporate bonds and use the $14,000 interest to pay his tuition. Leon is in the 28% tax bracket. Would such a strategy reduce his family's tax? Assume the applicable federal rate is 6.5%.

I:11-59 Linda is selling land she has owned for many years. The land cost $80,000 and will sell for $200,000. The buyer has offered to pay $100,000 down and pay the balance next year plus interest at 8%. Assume that Linda's after tax rate of return on investments is 10%. Would she be better off receiving the installment payments or receiving cash? Assume her ordinary income is taxed at 28% and that long-term capital gains are taxed at 15%.

TAX FORM/RETURN PREPARATION PROBLEM

I:11-60 Barbara B. Kuhn (SSN 987-65-4321) purchases a fourplex on January 8, 2011, for $175,000. She allocates $25,000 of the cost to the land, and she deducts MACRS depreciation totaling $16,364. Barbara sells the fourplex on January 6, 2014, for $225,000. The buyer assumes the existing mortgage of $180,000, pays $15,000 down, and agrees to pay $15,000 per year for two years plus 12% interest. Barbara incurs selling expenses of $18,000. Complete Form 6252.

CASE STUDY PROBLEMS

I:11-61 Lavonne just completed medical school and residency. She plans to open her medical practice soon. She is not familiar with the intricacies of accounting methods and periods. On advice of her attorney, she plans to form a professional corporation (a form of organization permitted under the laws of most states that does not have the usual limited liability found with business corporations, but is taxed as a corporation). She has asked you whether she should elect a fiscal year and whether she should use the cash or accrual method of reporting income. Discuss whether the options are available to her and the implications of available choices.

I:11-62 Don owns equipment that he purchased several years ago for $400,000. Over the years he properly deducted $110,000 of depreciation. The depreciation will have to be recaptured as ordinary income on the sale. There is a $90,000 mortgage on the property. Don has an offer for the equipment from an individual who says he will pay $100,000 down and $100,000 per year for five years. There is no mention of interest. As the mortgage is nonassumable, Don will pay off the mortgage using most of the down payment. Don is age 61, and proceeds from the sale along with a pension from his employer will provide for his retirement. Don plans to retire next year. He currently has a 25% marginal tax rate. Discuss the tax implications of the sale. Is there anything Don can do to improve his situation?

I:11-63 Troy Tools manufactures over one hundred different hand tools used by mechanics, carpenters, and plumbers. Troy's cost accounting system has always been very simple. The costs allocated to inventory have included only materials, direct labor, and factory overhead. Other overhead costs such as costs of the personnel department, purchasing, payroll, and computer services have never been treated as manufacturing overhead even though many of the activities of the departments relate to the manufacturing operations. You are preparing Troy's tax return for the first time and determine that the company is not following the uniform capitalization rules prescribed in the tax law. You have explained to the company's president that there is a problem, and she is reluctant to change accounting methods. She says allocating these costs to the many products the company makes will be a time-consuming and expensive process. She feels that the cost of determining the additional amounts to include in inventory under the uniform capitalization rules will probably be more than the additional tax that the company will pay. What is the appropriate way to handle this situation? (See the *Statements on Standards for Tax Services* section in Chapter I:15 for a discussion of these issues.)

TAX RESEARCH PROBLEMS

I:11-64 Eagle and Hill Corporations discuss the terms of a land sale, and they agree to a price of $230,000. Eagle wants to use the installment sale method, but is not sure Hill is a reliable borrower. As a result, Eagle requires Hill to place the entire purchase price in escrow to be released in five yearly installments by the escrow agent. Is the installment method available to Eagle?

A partial list of research sources is:

- Rev. Rul. 77-294, 1977-2 C.B. 173
- Rev. Rul. 79-91, 1979-1 C.B. 179
- *H. O. Williams v. U.S.*, 46 AFTR 1725, 55-1 USTC ¶9220 (5th Cir., 1955)

I:11-65 Texas Corporation disassembles old automobiles for the purpose of reselling their components (i.e., different types of metals, plastics, rubber, and other materials). Texas sells some of the items for scrap, but must pay to dispose of environmentally hazardous plastics and rubber. At year-end, Texas Corporation has a difficult time determining the cost of the individual parts that are stacked in piles. In fact, it would be very expensive to even weigh some of the materials on hand. Texas has followed the practice of having two experienced employees estimate the weight of different stacks and then price them based on quotes found in trade journals. If Texas must pay to dispose of an item, it is assigned a value of zero. In other words, Texas does not value its inventory using standard FIFO or LIFO methods. Is such a practice acceptable?

A partial list of research sources is:

- Reg. Secs. 1.471-2(a) and 1.471-3(d)
- *Morrie Chaitlen,* 1978 PH T.C. Memo ¶78,006, 37 TCM 17
- *Justus & Parker Co.,* 13 BTA 127 (1928)

I:11-66 Apple Corporation has never been audited before the current year. An audit is now needed from a CPA because the company is expanding rapidly and plans to issue stock to the public in a secondary offering. A CPA firm has been doing preliminary evaluations of the Apple Corporation's accounts and records. One major problem involves the valuation of inventory under GAAP. Apple Corporation has been valuing its inventory under the cost method and no write-downs have been made for obsolescence. A review of the inventory indicates that obsolescence and excess spare parts in the inventory are two major problems. The CPA states that for GAAP the company will be required to write down its inventory by 25% of its stated amount, or $100,000, and charge this amount against net income from operations for the current period. Otherwise, a "clean opinion" will not be rendered. The company controller asks your advice regarding the tax consequences from the obsolescence and spare parts inventory write-downs for the current year and the procedures for changing to the LCM method for tax purposes. Apple Corporation is on a calendar year, and the date of your contact with the company is December 1 of the current year.

A partial list of research sources is:

- Secs. 446 and 471
- Reg. Secs. 1.446-1(e)(3), 1.471-2 and 1.471-4
- *American Liberty Pipe Line Co. v. CIR,* 32 AFTR 1099, 44-2 USTC ¶9408 (5th Cir., 1944)
- *Thor Power Tool Co. v. CIR,* 43 AFTR 2d 79-362,79-1 USTC ¶9139 (USSC, 1979)

CHAPTER

12

PROPERTY TRANSACTIONS: NONTAXABLE EXCHANGES

LEARNING OBJECTIVES

After studying this chapter, you should be able to

1. Examine the tax consequences arising from a like-kind exchange
2. Determine whether gain from an involuntary conversion may be deferred
3. Determine when a gain resulting from the sale of a principal residence is excluded
4. Describe tax planning considerations for nontaxable exchanges
5. Describe compliance and procedural considerations for nontaxable exchanges

CHAPTER OUTLINE

Taxpayers who sell or exchange property for an amount greater or less than their basis in that property have a realized gain or loss on the sale or exchange. Almost any transfer of property is treated as a sale or other disposition (see Chapter I:5). The realized gain or loss must be recognized unless a specific Code section provides for nonrecognition treatment. If the realized gain or loss is not recognized at the time of the transaction, the nonrecognized gain or loss may be deferred in some cases and excluded in others.

The general rules related to the computation of realized and recognized gains or losses are covered in Chapter I:5. This chapter discusses three of the most common transactions that may result in *nonrecognition* of a realized gain or loss:

- Like-kind exchanges under Sec. 1031 (deferred gain or loss)
- Involuntary conversions under Sec. 1033 (deferred gain)
- Sales of a personal residence under Sec. 121 (excluded gain)

KEY POINT

The transactions examined in this chapter override the normal rule that provides for the recognition of realized gains and realized losses on property used in a business or held for investment.

Nonrecognition of gain treatment for like-kind exchanges, involuntary conversions, and the sale of a residence may be partially justified by the fact that taxpayers may lack the wherewithal to pay the tax despite the existence of a realized gain. For example, a taxpayer who realizes a gain due to an involuntary conversion of property (damage from fire, storm, etc.) may have to use the amount received to replace the converted property.

A typical requirement in a nontaxable exchange is that the taxpayer is required to maintain a continuing investment in comparable property (e.g., a building is exchanged for another building). In essence, a change in form rather than a change in substance occurs.

A transaction generally considered to be nontaxable may be taxable in part. In a like-kind exchange, for example, the taxpayer may also receive money or property that is not like-kind property. If non–like-kind property or money is received, the realized gain is taxable to the extent of the sum of the money and the fair market value (FMV) of the non–like-kind property received.[1]

LIKE-KIND EXCHANGES

OBJECTIVE 1

Examine the tax consequences arising from a like-kind exchange

Section 1031(a) provides that "No gain or loss shall be recognized on the exchange of property held for productive use in a trade or business or for investment if such property is exchanged solely for property of like-kind which is to be held either for productive use in a trade or business or for investment."[2]

In a **like-kind exchange**, both the property transferred and the property received must be held either for productive use in the trade or business or for investment.

EXAMPLE I:12-1 ▶ Tom owns land used in his trade or business. He exchanges the land for other land, which is to be held for investment. No gain or loss is recognized by Tom because he has exchanged property used in a trade or business for like-kind property to be held for investment. ◀

EXAMPLE I:12-2 ▶ Dawn's automobile is held for personal use. She exchanges the automobile, with a $10,000 basis, for stock of AT&T with a $12,000 FMV. The stock is held for investment. A $2,000 gain is recognized because the automobile is not used in Dawn's trade or business or held for investment. The exchange is not a like-kind exchange because neither personal-use assets nor stock qualify as like-kind property. ◀

REAL-WORLD EXAMPLE

An exchange or trade of professional football player contracts qualifies as a like-kind exchange. Rev. Rul. 71-137, 1971-1 C.B. 104.

Section 1031 is not an elective provision. If the exchange qualifies as a like-kind exchange, nonrecognition of gain or loss is mandatory. To qualify for like-kind exchange treatment, a direct exchange must occur and the property exchanged must be like-kind. A taxpayer who prefers to recognize a loss on an exchange must structure the transaction to avoid having the exchange qualify as a like-kind exchange.

ADDITIONAL COMMENT

The mandatory nonrecognition of loss under Sec. 1031 can be avoided by selling the old property in one transaction and buying the new property in a separate, unrelated transaction.

LIKE-KIND PROPERTY DEFINED

Character of the Property. To be a nontaxable exchange under Sec. 1031, the property exchanged must be like-kind. The Treasury Regulations specify that "the words

[1] Sec. 1031(b).

[2] Sec. 1031(a).

'like-kind' have reference to the nature or character of the property and not to its grade or quality."[3] Thus, exchanges of real property qualify even if the properties are dissimiliar.

EXAMPLE I:12-3 ▶ Eric owns an apartment building held for investment. Eric exchanges the building for farmland to be used in his trade or business. The exchange is a like-kind exchange because both the building and the farmland are classified as real property and both properties are used either in business or held for investment. ◀

EXAMPLE I:12-4 ▶ Trail Corporation exchanges improved real estate for unimproved real estate, both of which are held for investment. The exchange is a like-kind exchange.[4] ◀

ADDITIONAL COMMENT

Real property is often referred to as real estate.

Location of the Property. Transfers of real property located in the U.S. and real property located outside the U.S. after July 9, 1989, are not like-kind exchanges. Exchanges of personal property predominantly used in the United States and personal property used outside of the United States that occur after June 8, 1997, are not like-kind exchanges. To determine where the property is predominantly used, the two-year period ending on the date the property is exchanged is analyzed. For property received, the location of predominant use is determined by analyzing the use during the two-year period after the property is received.

Property Must be the Same Class. An exchange is not a like-kind exchange when property of one class is exchanged for property of a different kind or class.[5] For example, if real property is exchanged for personal property (or vice versa), no like-kind exchange occurs.[6]

EXAMPLE I:12-5 ▶ Gail exchanges an office building with a $400,000 adjusted basis for an airplane with a $580,000 FMV to be used in business. This is not a like-kind exchange because the office building is real property and the airplane is personal property. Gail must recognize a $180,000 ($580,000 − $400,000) gain. ◀

EXAMPLE I:12-6 ▶ Gary exchanges a business truck for another truck to use in his business. This is an exchange of like-kind property. ◀

ADDITIONAL COMMENT

The rules in the Regulations dealing with exchanges of personal property are not interpreted as liberally as the rules relating to real property.

Property of a Like Class. The Treasury Regulations provide that personal property of a **like class** meets the definition of *like-kind*.[7] Like class property is defined as depreciable tangible personal properties within the same General Asset Class or within the same Product Class.[8] Property within a General Asset Class consists of depreciable tangible personal property described in one of the asset classes provided in Rev. Proc. 87-56 for depreciation.[9] Some of the General Asset Classes are as follows:

- Office furniture, fixtures, and equipment (Asset Class 00.11)
- Information systems such as computers and peripheral equipment (Asset Class 00.12)
- Automobiles and taxis (Asset Class 00.22)
- Buses (Asset Class 00.23)
- Light general purpose trucks (Asset Class 00.241)
- Heavy general purpose trucks (Asset Class 00.242)
- Vessels, barges, tugs, and similar water-transportation equipment except those used in marine construction (Asset Class 00.28)

For purposes of the like-kind exchange provisions, a single property may not be classified in more than one General Asset Class or more than one Product Class. Furthermore, property in any General Asset Class may not be classified in a Product Class. A property's General Asset Class or Product Class is determined as of the exchange date.

---

[3] Reg. Sec. 1.1031(a)-1(b).
[4] *Ibid.*
[5] *Ibid.*
[6] Real property includes land and property attached to land in a relatively permanent manner. Personal property that is affixed to real property in a relatively permanent manner is a fixture and is considered part of the real property. Personal property is all property that is not real property or a fixture.
[7] Reg. Sec. 1.1031(a)-2.
[8] Reg. Sec. 1.1031(a)-2(b).
[9] 1987-2 C.B. 674.

EXAMPLE I:12-7 ▶ Wint transfers a personal computer used in his trade or business for a printer to be used in his trade or business. The exchange is a like-kind exchange because both properties are in the same General Asset Class (00.12). ◀

EXAMPLE I:12-8 ▶ Renee transfers an airplane (Asset Class 00.21) used in her trade or business for a heavy general purpose truck to use in her trade or business. The properties are not of a like class because they are in different General Asset Classes. The heavy general purpose truck is in Asset Class 00.242. ◀

Example I:12-8 is taken from the Treasury Regulations, which further state: "Because each of the properties is within a General Asset Class, the properties may not be classified within a Product Class. The airplane and heavy general purpose truck are also not of a like kind. Therefore, the exchange does not qualify for nonrecognition of gain or loss under Sec. 1031."[10]

If two properties are not within a General Asset Class, it still may be possible to be considered like-kind if the properties are within the same Product Class. Property in a Product Class consists of depreciable tangible personal property listed in the North American Classification System prepared by the Office of Management and Budget.[11] The Regulations state that an exchange of a grader for a scraper is an exchange of properties of like class because neither property is in a General Asset Class and both properties are listed in the same Product Class.[12]

There are no like classes for intangible personal property, nondepreciable personal property, or personal property held for investment. To have a like-kind exchange of property held for investment, the property must be exchanged for like-kind property. To determine whether an exchange of intangible personal property is a like-kind exchange, one must consider the type of right involved as well as the underlying property to which the intangible property relates. An exchange of a copyright for a novel for a copyright on a different novel is a like-kind exchange, but the exchange of a copyright on a novel for a copyright on a song is not a like-kind exchange.[13]

ADDITIONAL COMMENT

An exchange can be a like-kind exchange for one party to the transaction but not qualify as a like-kind exchange for the other party.

Non–Like-Kind Property Exchanges. An exchange of inventory or securities does not qualify as a like-kind exchange.[14]

EXAMPLE I:12-9 ▶ Antonio, a dealer in farm equipment, exchanges a new combine for other property in the same General Asset Class to be used in Antonio's trade or business. Because Antonio is a dealer, the new combine is inventory and the exchange does not qualify as a like-kind exchange. ◀

EXAMPLE I:12-10 ▶ Nancy owns Able Corporation stock as an investment. Nancy exchanges the stock for antiques to be held as investments. This exchange is taxable because stock does not qualify as like-kind property. ◀

In most cases, to qualify as a like-kind exchange of personal property, the property must be nearly identical. For example, livestock of different sexes are not like-kind property.[15] An exchange of gold bullion held for investment for silver bullion held for investment is not a like-kind exchange. Silver and gold are intrinsically different metals and primarily are used in different ways.[16] Currency exchanges are not like-kind exchanges,[17] and the exchange of a partnership interest for an interest in another partnership is not a like-kind exchange.[18]

---

[10] Reg. Sec. 1.1031(a)-2(b)(7) Ex. 2.
[11] Reg. Sec. 1.1031(a)-2(b)(3).
[12] Reg. Sec. 1.1031(a)-2(b)(7) Ex. 3.
[13] Reg. Sec. 1.1031(a)-2(c)(1).
[14] Sec. 1031(a)(2). An exchange of stock is not a like-kind exchange. However, an exchange of stock is a nontaxable exchange if the exchange is related to a tax-free reorganization.
[15] Sec. 1031(e).
[16] Rev. Rul. 82-166, 1982-2 C.B. 190.
[17] Rev. Rul. 74-7, 1974-1 C.B. 198.
[18] Sec. 1031(a)(2).

Exchange of Securities. The like-kind exchange rules do not apply to stocks, bonds, or notes.[19] However, Sec. 1036 provides that no gain or loss is recognized on the exchange of common stock for common stock or preferred stock for preferred stock in the same corporation. Sec. 1036 applies even if voting common stock is exchanged for nonvoting common stock of the same corporation. The nontaxable exchange of stock of the same corporation may be between two stockholders or a stockholder and the corporation.[20]

Section 1036 does not apply to exchanges of common stock for preferred stock; stock for bonds of same corporation, or any kind of stock in different corporations.

EXAMPLE I:12-11 ▶ Kelly owns common stock of Best Corporation. Best issues class B common stock to Kelly in exchange for her common stock. No gain or loss is recognized because this is an exchange of common stock for common stock in the same corporation. If Best issues its preferred stock for Kelly's common stock, Kelly will have a recognized gain or loss unless the exchange is part of a tax-free reorganization. ◀

EXAMPLE I:12-12 ▶ Shirley owns 100 shares of Top Corporation common stock. The stock has a $40,000 adjusted basis and a $50,000 FMV. Bob owns 100 shares of Star Corporation common stock with a $50,000 FMV. If Shirley and Bob exchange their stock, the exchange is taxable, and Shirley has a $10,000 ($50,000 − $40,000) recognized gain. The exchange is neither a like-kind exchange nor an exchange of stock for stock of the same corporation. ◀

A DIRECT EXCHANGE MUST OCCUR

To qualify as a like-kind exchange, a direct exchange of property must occur.[21] Thus, the sale of property and the subsequent purchase of like-kind property does not qualify as a like-kind exchange unless the two transactions are interdependent.

EXAMPLE I:12-13 ▶ Karen sells a lathe used in her business to Rashad for an amount greater than the lathe's adjusted basis. After the sale, Karen purchases another lathe from David. The gain is recognized because these two transactions do not qualify as an exchange of like-kind property. ◀

A sale and a subsequent purchase may be treated as an exchange if the two transactions are interdependent. The IRS indicates that a nontaxable exchange may exist when the taxpayer sells property to a dealer and then purchases like-kind property from the same dealer.[22]

THREE-PARTY EXCHANGES

The typical two-party exchange is not always practical. If both parties do not own like-kind property that meets each other's needs, a three-party exchange might be necessary. A three-party exchange is also useful when the taxpayer is willing to exchange property for like-kind property but is not willing to sell the property to a prospective buyer. The taxpayer's unwillingness to sell the property may be motivated by the desire to avoid an immediate tax on a gain resulting from the sale of the property. Therefore, the taxpayer may arrange to have the prospective buyer purchase property from a third party that fulfills the taxpayer's needs. The three-party exchange can be an effective way of allowing the taxpayer to consummate a like-kind exchange.

EXAMPLE I:12-14 ▶ Kathy owns a farm in Nebraska, which Dick offers to purchase. Kathy is not willing to sell the farm but is willing to exchange the farm for an apartment complex in Arizona. The complex is available for sale. Dick purchases the apartment complex in Arizona from Allyson and transfers it to Kathy in exchange for Kathy's farm. The farm and the apartment complex each have a $900,000 FMV. For Kathy, the transaction qualifies as a like-kind exchange because it is a direct exchange of business real property (the farm) for investment real estate (the apartment complex). For Dick, the exchange is not a like-kind exchange. ◀

KEY POINT
Transfers of property in a three-party exchange must be part of a single, integrated plan. It is important that the taxpayers can show their intent to enter into a like-kind exchange even though contractual interdependence is not necessary to the finding of an exchange.

In the example above, the exchange is convenient for all the parties. However, it is not always this convenient to execute a three-party exchange. For example, Kathy may want

19 Reg. Sec. 1.1031(a)-1(a)(1)(ii).
20 Reg. Sec. 1.1036-1(a).
21 Sec. 1031(a).
22 Rev. Rul. 61-119, 1961-1 C.B. 395.

to own an apartment complex in Arizona, but the property she prefers may not be currently available. In this case, a nonsimultaneous exchange may occur.

TAX STRATEGY TIP
Deferred like-kind exchanges are typically used for real estate transactions. A taxpayer who has highly appreciated real estate can use a deferred, three-party, like-kind exchange to exchange the highly appreciated real estate for other real estate that is more desirable to him.

Nonsimultaneous Exchange. A nonsimultaneous exchange is treated as a like-kind exchange if the exchange is completed within a specified time period. The property to be received in the exchange must be identified within 45 days after the date of the transfer of the property relinquished in the exchange. The replacement property must be received within the earlier of 180 days after the date the taxpayer transfers the property relinquished in the exchange or the due date for filing a return (including extensions) for the year in which the transfer of the relinquished property occurs.[23]

EXAMPLE I:12-15 ▶ On May 5, 2015, Joal transfers property to Lauren, who transfers cash to an escrow agent. The escrow agent is to purchase suitable like-kind property for Joal. Joal does not have actual or constructive receipt of the cash during the delayed period. To be a like-kind exchange for Joal, the suitable like-kind property must be identified by June 19, 2015 (45 days after the transfer), and Joal must receive the property by November 1, 2015 (180 days after the transfer). ◀

EXAMPLE I:12-16 ▶ Assume the same facts as in the above example except that the transfer by Joal occurs on November 10, 2015. To be a like-kind exchange for Joal, the suitable like-kind property must be identified by December 25, 2015, and Joal must receive the property by April 15, 2016, unless Joal files an automatic four-month extension for the filing of his return (i.e., the due date is extended until August 15, 2016). In such a case, the property must be received no later than 180 days following the transfer of the property relinquished in the exchange, or by May 9, 2016 (i.e., 180 days after November 10, 2015). ◀

RECEIPT OF BOOT

TYPICAL MISCONCEPTION
In calculating the amount of gain to be recognized when boot is received, a proportionate approach is used sometimes for financial accounting purposes.

Taxpayers who want to exchange property do not always own property of equal value. To complete the exchange, non–like-kind property or money may be given or received. Cash and non–like-kind property constitute **boot.**

Gain is recognized to the extent of the boot received. However, the amount of recognized gain is limited to the amount of the taxpayer's realized gain.[24] In effect, the realized gain serves as a ceiling for the amount of the recognized gain. The receipt of boot as part of a nontaxable exchange does not cause a realized loss to be recognized.[25]

EXAMPLE I:12-17 ▶ Mario exchanges business equipment with a $50,000 adjusted basis for $10,000 cash and business equipment with a $65,000 FMV. The realized gain is $25,000 ($75,000 − $50,000). The recognized gain is $10,000 because the $10,000 of boot received is less than the $25,000 realized gain. ◀

EXAMPLE I:12-18 ▶ Mary exchanges business equipment with a $70,000 adjusted basis for $20,000 cash and business equipment with a $65,000 FMV. Her realized gain is $15,000 ($85,000 − $70,000). The $20,000 of boot received is more than the $15,000 realized gain, so $15,000 of gain is recognized. ◀

TYPICAL MISCONCEPTION
It is possible to erroneously assume that the receipt of boot causes the recognition of loss.

Taxing part or all of the gain when cash is received in like-kind exchanges is consistent with the wherewithal-to-pay concept. However, boot may not always be in the form of a liquid asset. If non–like-kind property other than cash is received as boot, the amount of the boot is the property's FMV.

EXAMPLE I:12-19 ▶ Jane exchanges land held as an investment with a $70,000 basis for other land with a $100,000 FMV and a motorcycle with a $2,000 FMV. The acquired land is to be held for investment, and the motorcycle is for personal use. Personal-use property is non–like-kind property and constitutes boot. The realized gain is $32,000 [($100,000 + $2,000) − $70,000]. The amount of boot received is equal to the FMV of the motorcycle. The recognized gain is $2,000, the lesser of the amount of boot received ($2,000) or the realized gain ($32,000). ◀

---

[23] Secs. 1031(a)(3)(A) and (B).
[24] Sec. 1031(b).
[25] Sec. 1031(c).

EXAMPLE I:12-20 ▶ Assume the same facts in Example I:12-19 except that Jane uses the motorcycle in a business. The motorcycle is boot, and a $2,000 gain is still recognized because the exchange of real property for personal property is not a like-kind exchange. ◀

SELF-STUDY QUESTION

Why is the relief of a liability treated as if one has received cash?

ANSWER

If it were not treated as such, a taxpayer could receive cash shortly before the exchange by borrowing from a bank, using the property as collateral. Then, if the taxpayer is relieved of the debt in the like-kind exchange, he or she would still have cash without having paid a tax on the gain.

Property Transfers Involving Liabilities. If a liability is assumed (or the property is taken subject to a liability), the amount of the liability is considered money received by the taxpayer on the exchange.[26] One who assumes the debt or takes the property subject to a liability is treated as having paid cash, while the party that is relieved of the debt is treated as having received cash. If each party assumes a liability of the other party, only the net liability given or received is treated as boot.[27]

EXAMPLE I:12-21 ▶ Mary exchanges land with a $550,000 FMV that is used in her business for Doug's building, which has a $450,000 FMV. Mary's basis in the land is $400,000, and the land is subject to a liability of $100,000, which Doug assumes. Mary's realized gain is $150,000 [($450,000 + $100,000) − $400,000]. Because assumption of the $100,000 liability is treated as boot, Mary recognizes a $100,000 gain. ◀

EXAMPLE I:12-22 ▶ Matt owns an office building with a $700,000 basis, which is subject to a liability of $200,000. Susan owns an apartment complex with a $900,000 FMV, which is subject to a $150,000 liability. Matt and Susan exchange buildings and assume the related liabilities. Matt's realized gain is $250,000 [($900,000 + $200,000) − ($700,000 + $150,000)]. Matt receives boot of $50,000 ($200,000 − $150,000) and recognizes a $50,000 gain. ◀

BASIS OF PROPERTY RECEIVED

Like-Kind Property Received. The basis of property received in a nontaxable exchange is equal to the adjusted basis of the property exchanged increased by gain recognized and reduced by any boot received or loss recognized on the exchange.[28]

Basis of property received in a nontaxable exchange	=	Basis of property exchanged	−	Boot received	+	Gain recognized	−	Loss recognized[29]

EXAMPLE I:12-23 ▶ Chuck, who is in the business of racing horses, exchanges a racehorse with a $30,000 basis for $10,000 cash and a trotter with an $80,000 FMV. Chuck's realized gain is $60,000 [($80,000 + $10,000) − $30,000], and $10,000 of the gain is recognized because the boot received is less than the realized gain. Chuck's basis for the replacement property (i.e., the trotter) is $30,000 ($30,000 basis of property exchanged − $10,000 of boot received + $10,000 of gain recognized). ◀

ADDITIONAL COMMENT

In effect the formula used to calculate the basis of the new property involves nothing more than journalizing the transaction and adjusting the basis of the new property by an amount needed to make the entry balance.

The basis of the like-kind property received can also be computed by subtracting the unrecognized gain from its FMV or by adding the unrecognized loss to its FMV. Chuck's $30,000 basis for the trotter in Example I:12-23 may be computed by subtracting the $50,000 of unrecognized gain from the $80,000 FMV.

EXAMPLE I:12-24 ▶ Pam, who operates a circus, exchanges an elephant with a $15,000 basis for $3,000 cash and a tiger with a $10,000 FMV. The $2,000 realized loss [($10,000 + $3,000) − $15,000] is not recognized. The receipt of boot does not cause a realized loss to be recognized. Pam's basis for the replacement property (i.e., the tiger) is $12,000 ($15,000 basis of property exchanged − $3,000 boot received). ◀

KEY POINT

The basis adjustment is the mechanism that ensures that gain or loss is temporarily postponed rather than permanently excluded.

As indicated earlier, realized gains and losses resulting from nontaxable exchanges are deferred. This deferral is reflected in the basis of property received and is illustrated in the

[26] Sec. 1031(d). If a liability is assumed, the taxpayer agrees to pay the debt. If property is taken subject to the liability, the taxpayer is responsible for the debt only to the extent that the property could be used to pay the debt.

[27] Reg. Sec. 1.1031(b)-1(c).

[28] Sec. 1031(d).

[29] A loss is recognized only when the taxpayer transfers boot with a basis greater than its FMV. Transfers of non–like-kind property (i.e., boot) are discussed in a separate section of this chapter.

two preceding examples. In Example I:12-23, the $50,000 ($60,000 − $10,000) unrecognized gain may be recognized when the trotter is sold or exchanged in a taxable transaction, because the basis of the replacement property is less than its FMV by the amount of the deferred gain. For example, if the trotter is sold in a taxable transaction for its $80,000 FMV, the $50,000 ($80,000 − $30,000 basis) of previously unrecognized gain would be recognized. In Example I:12-24, the $2,000 unrecognized loss is reflected in the basis of the tiger. If Pam sells the tiger for its $10,000 FMV, a $2,000 loss ($10,000 − $12,000 basis) is recognized.

If more than one item of like-kind property is received, the basis is allocated among the properties in proportion to their relative FMVs on the date of the exchange.

EXAMPLE I:12-25 ▶ Saul, who operates a zoo, exchanges a boa constrictor with a $300 basis for a python with a $400 FMV and an anaconda with a $600 FMV. The $700 realized gain [($400 + $600) − $300] is not recognized. The total bases of the properties received is $300. This amount is allocated to the properties (i.e., the python and the anaconda) based on their relative FMVs. Saul's basis for the python is $120 [($400 ÷ $1,000) × $300], and the basis for the anaconda is $180 [($600 ÷ $1,000) × $300]. ◀

Non–Like-Kind Property Received. The basis of non–like-kind property received is "an amount equivalent to its FMV at the date of the exchange."[30]

EXAMPLE I:12-26 ▶ Steve exchanges a punch press with a $20,000 adjusted basis for a press brake with a $50,000 FMV and $5,000 of marketable securities. Steve's realized gain is $35,000 [($50,000 + $5,000) − $20,000], and $5,000 of the realized gain is recognized due to the receipt of boot. Steve's basis for the marketable securities is $5,000, and the basis for the press brake is $20,000 ($20,000 basis of property exchanged − $5,000 boot received + $5,000 gain recognized). ◀

KEY POINT

Steve had basis of $20,000 before the exchange. Since he recognized gain of $5,000, the total basis of the two assets should be $25,000.

STOP & THINK

Question: Chris Reedy owns 40 houses that he uses as rental property. All houses have a FMV greater than their adjusted basis. Chris wishes to diversify his investments and is considering selling ten of his houses and using the proceeds to purchase other types of investment assets such as stocks, bonds, commercial parking lots and land near town that he expects to increase in value. He asks you for advice.

Solution: If he sells the ten houses, he will have a gain and must pay taxes on the gain. He could defer the gain by exchanging the houses for like-kind property. Stocks and bonds are not like-kind property, but the commercial parking lots and the land should qualify as like-kind property, therefore the tax law encourages him to exchange the houses for the commercial parking lot and/or the land.

EXCHANGES BETWEEN RELATED PARTIES

Prior to 1990, related taxpayers could often use the like-kind exchange provisions to lower taxes because the tax basis for the property received is determined by the basis of the property exchanged. Related taxpayers could take advantage of the shift in tax basis to transfer a gain on a subsequent sale to a related party.[31] However, exchanges of property between related parties are not like-kind exchanges under current law if either party disposes of the property within two years of the exchange. Any gain resulting from the original exchange is recognized in the year of the subsequent disposition.[32] Dispositions due to death or involuntary conversion, or for non–tax avoidance purposes are disregarded.[33]

ADDITIONAL COMMENT

The running of the two-year holding period is suspended during any period in which the property holder's risk of loss is substantially diminished.

EXAMPLE I:12-27 ▶ Melon Corporation, which is 100% owned by Linda, owned land with a basis of $200,000 that was held for investment. Rick wanted to purchase the land for $900,000. Linda owned an office building with a basis of $750,000 and a FMV of $900,000. Instead of selling the land to Rick, Melon Corporation exchanged the land for Linda's office building in December 2014.

---

[30] Reg. Sec. 1.1031(d)-1(c).

[31] The definition of *related parties* is the same as those for Sec. 267(a) which is discussed in Chapter I:6, and includes brothers, sisters, parents, children, and corporations where the taxpayer owns at least 50% in value. (See Sec. 1031(f)(3).)

[32] Sec. 1031(f)(1)(C).

[33] Sec. 1031(f)(2).

ADDITIONAL COMMENT

If Linda in Example I:12-27 sells the land to Rick for $910,000, she has a $150,000 recognized gain on the exchange and a $10,000 recognized gain on the sale.

Two months later, Linda sells the land to Rick for $900,000. The exchange of the land for the office building is not a like-kind exchange because one of the related parties disposes of the property within two years of the exchange. In 2015, Melon's recognized gain on the exchange of the land is $700,000 ($900,000 − $200,000) and Linda's recognized gain on the exchange of the office building is $150,000 ($900,000 − $750,000). Because Linda's basis for the land is now $900,000, no gain is recognized on the sale of the land to Rick. ◀

If the parties in Example I:12-27 were not related, a like-kind exchange occurred in 2014 and Linda's gain on the sale of the land to Rick is $150,000 ($900,000 − $750,000). Importantly, the exchange is not a like-kind exchange if Linda does not hold the land for investment or for use in her trade or business after receiving it from Melon.

TRANSFER OF NON–LIKE-KIND PROPERTY

In all of the preceding examples that include a transfer of boot, the transferor (i.e., the taxpayer) received boot. If the taxpayer transfers non–like-kind property, gain or loss equal to the difference between the FMV and the adjusted basis of the non–like-kind property surrendered must be recognized. However, if the non–like-kind property is a personal use asset, the loss is not recognized.

EXAMPLE I:12-28 ▶ Shirley exchanges land with a $30,000 basis ($46,000 FMV) and marketable securities with a $10,000 basis ($14,000 FMV) to David for land with a $60,000 FMV in a transaction that otherwise qualifies as a like-kind exchange. Because the non–like-kind property that Shirley transfers has a FMV greater than its basis, she recognizes $4,000 ($14,000 − $10,000) of gain. Shirley's basis for the land received is $44,000 ($30,000 + $10,000 + $4,000), which is the basis of both assets exchanged plus the gain recognized on the exchange. ◀

EXAMPLE I:12-29 ▶ Paul exchanges timberland held as an investment for undeveloped land with a $200,000 FMV to use in his business. Paul's basis for the timberland is $125,000. His tractor with a $6,000 basis and a $4,000 FMV is also transferred. Because the non–like-kind property (i.e., the tractor) that Paul transfers has a FMV less than its basis, he recognizes a $2,000 ($4,000 − $6,000) loss. Paul's basis for the undeveloped land is $129,000 ($125,000 + $6,000 − $2,000). ◀

In Example I:12-29, Paul recognizes a loss on the non–like-kind property he surrenders, despite receiving property in the aggregate with a FMV greater than the total adjusted basis of the transferred assets. Paul is actually making two exchanges. His exchange of timberland with a basis of $125,000 for undeveloped land with a $196,000 FMV is a like-kind exchange, but his exchange of the tractor with a basis of $6,000 for undeveloped land with a $4,000 FMV is a taxable exchange. In Example I:12-30 below, Ed also makes two exchanges. He has a realized and recognized gain as well as a realized but unrecognized loss.

EXAMPLE I:12-30 ▶ Ed owns equipment used in business with a $20,000 adjusted basis and a $15,000 FMV and marketable securities with a $10,000 basis and an $18,000 FMV. Ed exchanges the marketable securities and the equipment for business equipment in the same General Asset Class with a $33,000 FMV. Although the net realized gain is $3,000 [$33,000 − ($20,000 + $10,000)], Ed recognizes an $8,000 gain because he has transferred non–like-kind property with a $10,000 basis and an $18,000 FMV. The $5,000 realized loss on the transfer of equipment is not recognized due to the nonrecognition of gain or loss rules of Sec. 1031. Ed's basis for the equipment received is $38,000 ($20,000 + $10,000 + $8,000). ◀

KEY POINT

A taxpayer who exchanges like-kind property and non–like-kind property is actually making two exchanges.

HOLDING PERIOD FOR PROPERTY RECEIVED

ADDITIONAL COMMENT

The holding period is relevant only when the asset is a capital asset or a Sec. 1231 asset.

Like-Kind Property. The holding period of like-kind property received in a nontaxable exchange includes the holding period of the property exchanged if the like-kind property surrendered is a capital asset or an asset that is Sec. 1231 property. In essence, the holding period of the property exchanged carries over to the holding period of the like-kind property received.[34] The rule regarding the holding period carryover is consistent with the notion of a continuing investment in the underlying property that has been transferred.

[34] Sec. 1223(1) and Reg. Sec. 1.1223-1(a).

Boot. The holding period for the boot property received begins the day after the date of the exchange.[35]

EXAMPLE I:12-31 ▶ Mario owns a Van Gogh painting acquired on May 1, 1997, as an investment. He exchanges the painting on April 10, 2015, for a Picasso sculpture and marketable securities to be held as investments. The holding period for the sculpture begins on May 1, 1997, and the holding period for the marketable securities starts on April 11, 2015. ◀

The like-kind exchange provisions are summarized in Topic Review I:12-1.

TOPIC REVIEW I:12-1

Section 1031—Like-Kind Exchanges

- Gains and losses are not recognized for like-kind exchanges.
- Nonrecognition of gains and losses is mandatory if the exchange is a like-kind exchange.
- Section 1031 applies to exchanges of property used in a trade or business or held for investment.
- Property exchanged and received must be like-kind.
- Subject to certain time constraints, a nonsimultaneous exchange may qualify as a like-kind exchange.
- Some gain may be recognized if the taxpayer receives or gives non–like-kind property (boot) in an otherwise like-kind exchange.
- A loss may be recognized if the taxpayer transfers non–like-kind property (boot) in an otherwise like-kind exchange.
- The basis of property received in an exchange is the basis of the property exchanged less the boot received plus the gain recognized and less any loss recognized.
- The nonrecognized gain or loss is deferred.
- The holding period of like-kind property received includes the holding period of the property exchanged.
- Like-kind exchange treatment does not apply between related parties if property is disposed of within two years of exchange.

Involuntary Conversions

OBJECTIVE 2

Determine whether gain from an involuntary conversion may be deferred

Taxpayers who realize a gain due to the involuntary conversion of property may elect to defer recognition of the entire gain if qualifying replacement property is acquired within a specified time period at a cost equal to or greater than the amount realized from the involuntary conversion. No gain is recognized if the property is converted "into property similar or related in service or use to the property so converted."[36]

The opportunity provided in Sec. 1033 to defer recognition of the gain reflects the fact that the taxpayer maintains a continuing investment and may lack the wherewithal to pay tax on the gain that would otherwise be recognized. Furthermore, the involuntary conversion is beyond the taxpayer's control.

KEY POINT

Unlike the like-kind exchange provisions which are mandatory, the involuntary conversion provisions are elective. Further, the involuntary conversion rules apply only to gains, not losses.

Note that the gain is deferred, not excluded. The basis of the replacement property is the property's cost reduced by the amount of gain deferred. The tax treatment for an involuntary conversion is similar to the tax treatment of a like-kind exchange.

EXAMPLE I:12-32 ▶ Lenea's warehouse with a $500,000 basis is destroyed by a hurricane. She collects $650,000 from the insurance company and purchases a new warehouse for $720,000. Lenea may elect to defer recognition of the $150,000 gain ($650,000 − $500,000). If the election is made, the basis of the new warehouse is $570,000 ($720,000 − $150,000). The $150,000 gain is merely deferred rather than excluded, because an immediate sale of the replacement property at its $720,000 FMV results in a recognized gain equal to the deferred gain on the involuntarily converted property. For example, if the new warehouse is sold for $720,000, the recognized gain is $150,000 ($720,000 − $570,000). ◀

ADDITIONAL COMMENT

Property involved in an involuntary conversion need not be used in a trade or business or held for investment to qualify for the deferral of gain.

[35] Sec. 1223 and Reg. Sec. 1.1223-1(a).

[36] Sec. 1033(a)(1).

TYPICAL MISCONCEPTION

Occasionally, taxpayers fail to realize that Sec. 1033 applies only to gains, not losses.

Section 1033 does not apply to losses realized from an involuntary conversion. A taxpayer may not elect to defer recognition of a loss resulting from an involuntary conversion.

EXAMPLE I:12-33 ▶ Barry's offshore drilling rig with an $800,000 adjusted basis is destroyed by a tsunami. He collects $700,000 from the insurance company and purchases a new drilling rig for $760,000. The $100,000 loss ($700,000 − $800,000) is recognized as a casualty loss, and the basis of the new drilling rig is its $760,000 purchase price. ◀

INVOLUNTARY CONVERSION DEFINED

ADDITIONAL COMMENT

Typically, an involuntary conversion consists of either a casualty or a condemnation.

For Sec. 1033 to apply, property must be compulsorily or involuntarily converted into money or other property. An **involuntary conversion** may be due to theft, seizure, requisition, condemnation, or destruction of the property. Destruction of the property may be complete or partial.[37] For purposes of Sec. 1033, destruction of property does not have to meet the "suddenness" test if the cause of destruction otherwise falls within the general concept of a casualty.[38]

An involuntary conversion occurs when a governmental unit exercises its power of eminent domain to acquire the taxpayer's property without the taxpayer's consent. Furthermore, the threat or imminence of requisition or condemnation of property may permit a taxpayer to defer recognition of gain from the sale or exchange of property under the involuntary conversion rules. Taxpayers who transfer property due to such a threat must be careful to confirm that a decision to acquire their property for public use has been made.[39] Written confirmation of potential condemnation is particularly helpful.[40]

EXAMPLE I:12-34 ▶ Bruce owns an automobile dealership near a state university campus. On a number of occasions, the president of the university expressed an interest in acquiring Bruce's property for additional parking space. The president is not certain about the availability of funds for the purchase, and the university is reluctant to have the property condemned for its use. Based on the university's interest in the property, Bruce sells the property to the Jet Corporation. The threat or imminence of conversion does not exist merely because the property is being considered for acquisition. The sale does not constitute an involuntary conversion.[41] ◀

Threat of Condemnation. If a threat of condemnation exists and the taxpayer has reasonable grounds to believe that the property will be condemned, Sec. 1033 applies even if the taxpayer sells the property to an entity other than the governmental unit that is threatening to condemn the property.[42]

EXAMPLE I:12-35 ▶ At its regular meeting on Tuesday night, the city commission authorized the city attorney to start the process of condemning two lots owned by Beth for use as a public park. On Wednesday afternoon, Beth sells the two lots to Marty at a gain. The sale of property to Marty is an involuntary conversion, and Beth may elect to defer recognition of the gain if she satisfies the Sec. 1033 requirements. ◀

ADDITIONAL COMMENT

If the property in Example I:12-35 is later condemned, Marty may be able to defer part or all of the gain.

Conversion Must be Involuntary. The conversion must be involuntary. For example, an involuntary conversion does not occur when a taxpayer pays someone to set fire to his or her building.[43] An involuntary conversion also does not occur when a taxpayer who is developing a subdivision reserves certain property for a school site and later sells the property to the school district under condemnation proceedings. In this situation, the taxpayer was required to reserve property for a school site in order to receive zoning approval for development of the subdivision.[44]

---

37 Reg. Sec. 1.1033(a)-1.
38 Rev. Rul. 59-102, 1959-1 C.B. 200.
39 Rev. Rul. 63-221, 1963-2 C.B. 332, and *Joseph P. Balistrieri*, 1979 PH T.C. Memo ¶79,115, 38 TCM 526.
40 Rev. Rul. 63-221, 1963-2 C.B. 332.
41 *Forest City Chevrolet*, 1977 PH T.C. Memo ¶77,187, 36 TCM 768.
42 Rev. Rul. 81-180, 1981-2 C.B. 161, and *Creative Solutions, Inc. v. U.S.*, 12 AFTR 2d 5229, 1963-2 USTC ¶9615 (5th Cir., 1963).
43 Rev. Rul. 82-74, 1982-1 C.B. 110.
44 Rev. Rul. 69-654, 1969-2 C.B. 162.

REAL-WORLD EXAMPLE

Because of mounting losses and declining property values, a taxpayer decided to burn down his building to collect the fire insurance proceeds. Although the building was converted into money (insurance proceeds) as a result of its destruction, this conversion was not involuntary within the meaning of Sec. 1033. Rev. Rul. 82-74, 1982-1 C.B. 110.

Although the typical involuntary conversion generally results from a casualty or condemnation, Sec. 1033 provides that certain transactions involving livestock are to be treated as involuntary conversions.[45] For example, the destruction or sale of livestock because of disease is an involuntary conversion.

TAX TREATMENT OF GAIN DUE TO INVOLUNTARY CONVERSION INTO BOOT

Gain may be deferred if the property is involuntarily converted into money or property that is not similar or related in service or use to the converted property.[46] The taxpayer must make a proper replacement of the converted property within a specific time period and elect to defer the gain.

Realized Gain. The taxpayer's realized gain is the excess of the amount received due to the involuntary conversion over the adjusted basis of the property converted. The total award or proceeds received are reduced by expenses incurred to determine the amount realized (e.g., attorney's fees incurred in connection with determining the settlement to be received from a condemnation). If the payment of the award or proceeds is delayed, any amounts paid as interest are not included in determining the amount realized.[47] Amounts received as interest on an award for property condemned are taxed as ordinary income even if the interest is paid by a state or political subdivision.[48]

EXAMPLE I:12-36 ▶ Richard's property with a $100,000 basis is condemned by the city of Phoenix. Richard receives a $190,000 award and pays $1,000 in legal expenses for representation at the condemnation proceedings and $800 for an appraisal of the property. The amount realized is $188,200 [$190,000 − ($1,000 + $800)], and the realized gain is $88,200 ($188,200 − $100,000). Richard may elect to defer part or all of the realized gain if the requirements of Sec. 1033 are satisfied. ◀

ADDITIONAL COMMENT

Some or all of the realized gain is recognized if the cost of the replacement property is less than the amount realized.

Gain Recognized. To defer the entire gain, one must purchase replacement property with a cost equal to or greater than the amount realized from the involuntary conversion. If the replacement property is purchased for an amount less than the amount realized, that portion of the realized gain equal to the excess of the amount realized from the conversion over the cost of the replacement property must be recognized.[49] Stated differently, the recognized gain is the lesser of the realized gain or the excess of the amount realized over the cost of the replacement property.

EXAMPLE I:12-37 ▶ Bob owns a restaurant with a $200,000 basis. The restaurant is destroyed by fire, and he receives insurance proceeds of $300,000. Bob's realized gain is $100,000 ($300,000 − $200,000). He purchases another restaurant for $275,000. Bob may elect to defer $75,000 of the gain under Sec. 1033, and $25,000 ($300,000 − $275,000) of Bob's gain must be recognized because he failed to reinvest all of the $300,000 insurance proceeds in a suitable replacement property. ◀

EXAMPLE I:12-38 ▶ Stacey owns a racehorse with a $450,000 basis used for breeding purposes. The racehorse is killed by lightning, and she collects $800,000 from the insurance company. Stacey's realized gain is $350,000 ($800,000 − $450,000). She purchases another racehorse for $430,000. The entire $350,000 of gain is recognized, because the amount realized from the involuntary conversion exceeds the cost of the replacement property by $370,000 ($800,000 − $430,000) which is more than the realized gain. ◀

Basis of Replacement Property. If replacement property is purchased, the basis of the replacement property is its cost less any deferred gain. If the taxpayer elects to defer the gain, the holding period of the replacement property includes the holding period of the converted property.[50]

---

45 Secs. 1033(d) and (e). If a taxpayer sells or exchanges more livestock than normal because of a drought, the sale or exchange of the excess amount is treated as an involuntary conversion. The livestock must be other than poultry and be held by the taxpayer for draft, breeding, or dairy purposes.

46 Sec. 1033(a)(2).

47 *Flushingside Realty & Construction Co.*, 1943 PH T.C. Memo ¶43,286, 2 TCM 259.

48 *Spencer D. Stewart v. CIR*, 52 AFTR 2d 83-5885, 83-2 USTC ¶9573 (9th Cir., 1983).

49 Sec. 1033(a)(2)(A).

50 Sec. 1223(1)(A).

EXAMPLE I:12-39 ▶ Tracy owns a yacht that is held for personal use and has a $20,000 basis. The yacht is destroyed by a storm, and Tracy collects $24,000 from the insurance company. She purchases a new $35,000 yacht for personal use and elects to defer the $4,000 ($24,000 − $20,000) gain. The basis of the new yacht is $31,000 ($35,000 − $4,000). The holding period for the new yacht includes the holding period of the destroyed yacht. ◀

Severance Damages. If a portion of the taxpayer's property is condemned, the taxpayer may receive **severance damages** as compensation for a decline in the value of the retained property. For example, if access to the retained property becomes difficult or if the property is exposed to greater damage from flooding or erosion, its value may decline.

The IRS considers severance damages to be "analogous to the proceeds of property insurance; they represent compensation for damages to the property."[51] Amounts received as severance damages reduce the basis of the retained property, and any amount received in excess of the property's basis is treated as gain.[52]

EXAMPLE I:12-40 ▶ Cindy owns a 500-acre farm with a $200 basis per acre ($100,000 basis). The state condemns ten acres across the northwest corner of her farm to build a major highway. Cindy receives a condemnation award of $500 per acre for the ten acres. The highway separates the farm into a 25-acre tract and a 465-acre tract. Because her ability to efficiently use the 25-acre tract for farming is reduced, the state pays additional severance damages of $90 per acre for the 25 acres. Cindy's gain realized from condemnation of the ten acres is $3,000 [$5,000 − ($200 × 10 acres)]. The $2,250 ($90 × 25 acres) of severance damages reduce the basis of the 25-acre tract from $5,000 to $2,750 [($200 × 25 acres) − $2,250]. The reduction in basis is applied solely to the 25 acres because of its decline in value as farmland. ◀

REAL-WORLD EXAMPLE

Seven of the 18 holes of a golf course were condemned. Although 11 holes remained, it was anticipated that the course would have to be reduced to 9 holes. Therefore, $21,000 of the condemnation award was allocated to severance damages to reflect the decline in value of the two lost holes. *Marco S. Marinello Associates, Inc.*, 1975 PH T.C. Memo ¶75,078, 34 TCM 392.

The Sec. 1033 provisions concerning nonrecognition of gain may apply to severance damages. For instance, if severance damages are used to restore the retained property, only that portion of severance damages not spent for restoration reduces the basis of the retained property. A taxpayer who uses severance damages to purchase adjacent farmland to replace the portion of the farm condemned may use Sec. 1033 to defer a gain due to the receipt of the severance damages.[53]

REPLACEMENT PROPERTY

To qualify for nonrecognition of gain due to an involuntary conversion, the taxpayer must acquire qualified replacement property. With some exceptions, the **replacement property** must be "similar or related in service or use to the property so converted."[54] Taxpayers who own and use the property must use the functional-use test although replacement may be made with like-kind property in certain cases. A taxpayer who owns and leases the property that is involuntarily converted may use the taxpayer-use test.

REAL-WORLD EXAMPLE

The replacement of bowling alleys destroyed in a fire with a recreational billiards center did not pass the functional-use test. Rev. Rul. 76-319, 1976-2 C.B. 242.

Functional-Use Test. The **functional-use test** is more restrictive than the like-kind test. To be considered similar or related in service or use, the replacement property must be functionally the same as the converted property. For example, the exchange of a business building for land used in business qualifies as a like-kind exchange. Replacing a building with land does not qualify as replacement property under the involuntary conversion rules. The building must be replaced with a building that is functionally the same as the converted building.

EXAMPLE I:12-41 ▶ Julie's movie theater is destroyed by fire, and she uses the insurance proceeds to purchase a skating rink. The converted property has not been replaced with property that is similar or related in service or use under the functional-use test. The election to defer gain under Sec. 1033 is not available. ◀

---

51 Rev. Rul. 53-271, 1953-2 C.B. 36.

52 Rev. Rul. 68-37, 1968-1 C.B. 359.

53 Rev. Ruls. 69-240, 1969-1 C.B. 199, 73-35, 1973-1 C.B. 367, and 83-49, 1983-1 C.B. 191.

54 Secs. 1033(a)(2)(A) and 1033(f). The replacement of property requirement is modified when proceeds from the involuntary conversion of livestock may not be reinvested in property similar or related in use to the converted livestock because of soil contamination or other environmental contamination. Sec. 1033(f) permits the livestock to be replaced with other property, including real property, used for farming purposes.

Replacement with Like-Kind Property. If real property held for productive use in a trade or business or for investment is **condemned**, a proper replacement may be made by acquiring like-kind property.[55] This exception to the functional-use test applies only to real property used in a trade or business or held for investment.

EXAMPLE I:12-42 ▶ Ken owns a building used in his business that is condemned by the state to widen a highway. He uses the proceeds to purchase land to be held for investment. The land is a qualified replacement property because the condemned building is real property used in a trade or business, and the like-kind exchange rule may be applied to the condemnation. ◀

EXAMPLE I:12-43 ▶ Assume the same facts as in Example I:12-42 except that the building is destroyed by a violent windstorm. Ken's purchase of the investment land is not qualified replacement property because the more flexible like-kind exchange rules apply only to condemnations. He must purchase property with the same functional use as the business building. ◀

REAL-WORLD EXAMPLE

A nursery with its trees and shrubs was condemned, and the taxpayer replaced the condemned property with land and greenhouses. The replacement was considered to have been made with like-kind property. *Evert Asjes, Jr.*, 74 T.C. 1005 (1980).

If business or investment property is involuntarily converted as a result of a Presidentially declared disaster after 1994, the taxpayer may replace the property with any tangible property that is held for productive use in a trade or business.

Taxpayer-Use Test. The **taxpayer-use test** applies to the involuntary conversion of rental property owned by an investor. This test permits greater flexibility than the functional-use test. The principal requirement is that the owner-investor must lease out the replacement property that is acquired. However, the lessee is not required to use the leased property for the same functional use.[56]

EXAMPLE I:12-44 ▶ Sally owns an apartment complex that is rented to college students. The apartment complex is destroyed by fire. She uses the insurance proceeds to purchase a medical building that is leased to physicians. Sally has acquired a qualified replacement property under the taxpayer-use test, and the gain, if any, may be deferred if an election is made under Sec. 1033. ◀

? STOP & THINK

Question: Greg Stacey's motel is destroyed by fire on March 10 of the current year. The basis of the property is $400,000 and he receives $2,000,000 from the insurance company. Greg is concerned about the possibility of having to pay income tax on the $1,600,000 gain and is aware of the tax rules relating to involuntary conversions. Greg is considering replacing the destroyed motel by building either a new motel or an ice skating rink on the vacant lot. The cost of a new motel or an ice skating rink is expected to be $2,500,000, and he expects to borrow 60% of the cost. What tax advice would you give him?

Solution: Greg may defer the $1,600,000 gain if the involuntary conversion requirements are met and he makes a proper election. The principal issue is whether the replacement property is considered to be "similar in service or use" to the converted property. Because the functional-use test is applicable in this case, an ice skating rink is not similar property and the gain of $1,600,000 must be recognized. Conversely, the new motel is similar property and, since Greg is reinvesting an amount greater than $2,000,000, none of the gain is recognized. His basis in the new motel is $900,000 ($2,500,000 − deferred gain of $1,600,000). The fact that he borrows money and does not spend the $2,000,000 insurance proceeds does not prevent him from electing to defer the gain. The tax requirement is only that he must reinvest an amount equal to or greater than the $2,000,000 insurance proceeds. In this case, the tax law clearly encourages the taxpayer to build a new motel rather than an ice skating rink.

REAL-WORLD EXAMPLE

Taxpayer owned land and a warehouse held for rental purposes. Upon condemnation of this property, taxpayer invested the proceeds in a gas station on land already owned by the taxpayer which was also held for rental purposes. The taxpayer-use test applied, and taxpayer was able to defer the gain. Rev. Rul. 71-41, 1971-1 C.B. 223.

OBTAINING REPLACEMENT PROPERTY

The general rule is that the taxpayer must purchase the replacement property.[57] Taxpayers may purchase replacement property indirectly by purchasing control (i.e., 80% or more of the stock) of a corporation that owns the replacement property.[58] However,

[55] Sec. 1033(g)(1).
[56] Rev. Rul. 64-237, 1964-2 C.B. 319.
[57] To qualify as a purchase of property or stock under Sec. 1033(a)(2)(A)(ii), the unadjusted basis of the property or stock must be its cost within the meaning of Sec. 1012 without considering the basis adjustment for the deferred gain. Property acquired by inheritance, gift, or a nontaxable exchange does not qualify as replacement property (see Reg. Sec. 1.1033(a)-2(c)(4)).
[58] Sec. 1033(a)(2)(A) and Reg. Sec. 1.1033(a)-2(c).

this exception is not applicable to the purchase of like-kind property to replace condemned real property used in a trade or business or held for investment.[59]

EXAMPLE I:12-45 ▶ Hank's airplane, used in business, is hijacked and taken to a foreign country. He uses the insurance proceeds to purchase 80% of Fast Corporation stock. Fast Corporation owns an airplane which is qualified replacement property. The involuntary conversion requirements are satisfied if Hank elects to defer any gain realized. ◀

EXAMPLE I:12-46 ▶ Lynn's farm is condemned by the state for public use. She uses the proceeds to purchase 80% of Vermont Corporation stock. Vermont Corporation owns eight parking lots. A qualified replacement property has not been obtained through the stock purchase because the parking lots are not functionally the same as the farm. A qualified replacement does occur if she buys the parking lots from the Vermont Corporation. ◀

TYPICAL MISCONCEPTION

The first taxable year in which any part of the gain on the conversion is realized is the year in which the insurance proceeds are received, not the year in which the involuntary conversion took place.

TIME REQUIREMENTS FOR REPLACEMENT

To qualify for nonrecognition of gain treatment, the converted property must be replaced within a specified time period. The general rule is that the period begins with the date of disposition of the converted property and ends "two years after the close of the first taxable year in which any part of the gain upon the conversion is realized."[60] If the involuntary conversion is due to condemnation or requisition, or the threat of such, the replacement period begins on the date of the threat or imminence of the requisition or condemnation. The replacement period may be extended by obtaining permission from the IRS.[61]

EXAMPLE I:12-47 ▶ On December 8, 2015, Craig's business property was destroyed by fire. Craig receives insurance proceeds in 2016 and elects to defer recognition of the gain. He must replace the property between December 8, 2015, and December 31, 2018. The two-year time period includes 2018 because the gain is realized when the insurance proceeds are received in 2016. ◀

KEY POINT

The replacement period is three years instead of two years on the condemnation of real property used in a business or held for investment.

The replacement period is longer if the involuntary conversion is due to the condemnation of real property (excluding inventory) held for productive use in a trade or business or for investment. The replacement period ends three years after the close of the first tax year in which any part of the gain is realized.[62] This provision for a longer replacement period applies to the same type of real property that may be replaced with like-kind property.

EXAMPLE I:12-48 ▶ Beth owns a building used in her dry cleaning business. In 2015, the state condemns the building and awards Beth an amount greater than the adjusted basis of the building. Beth may replace the property with like-kind property, and the replacement period ends on December 31, 2018. ◀

The involuntary conversion rules are summarized in Topic Review I:12-2.

TOPIC REVIEW I:12-2

Section 1033: Involuntary Conversions

1. Section 1033 applies only to gains, not losses.
2. Nonrecognition of gain under Section 1033 is elective. (Nonrecognition of gain is mandatory in a direct conversion, but direct conversions seldom occur.)
3. Section 1033 applies to involuntary conversions of all types of properties.
4. Some gain may be recognized if the taxpayer replaces the involuntarily converted property with property that costs less than the amount realized in the involuntary conversion.
5. The nonrecognized gain is deferred.
6. The basis of property acquired to replace the involuntarily converted property is the cost of the property less the deferred gain.
7. Property acquired to replace the involuntarily converted property generally must be functionally related property.
8. The required replacement period generally begins with the date of disposition of the converted property and ends two years after the close of the first taxable year in which any part of the gain on the conversion is realized. (A three-year period applies to condemnations of real property used in a trade or business or held for the production of income.)

---

[59] Sec. 1033(g)(2).
[60] Sec. 1033(a)(2)(B).
[61] Sec. 1033(a)(2)(B)(ii).
[62] Sec. 1033(g)(4).

Sale of Principal Residence

OBJECTIVE 3

Determine when a gain resulting from the sale of a principal residence is excluded

Congress uses the tax law to encourage home ownership in many ways: (1) Real estate taxes and interest on a mortgage used to acquire a principal or second residence are deductible (see Chapter I:7), (2) part or all of the interest on home equity debt may be deductible, and (3) taxpayers may elect to exclude up to $250,000 ($500,000 on a joint return) of gain from the sale of a principal residence.

Individuals who sell or exchange their personal residence after May 6, 1997, may exclude up to $250,000 of gain if it was owned and occupied as a principal residence for at least two years of the five-year period before the sale or exchange. A married couple may exclude up to $500,000 when filing jointly if both meet the use test, at least one meets the ownership test and neither spouse is ineligible for the exclusion because he or she sold or exchanged a residence within the last two years.[63]

The Sec. 121 exclusion is available regardless of age, and taxpayers do not have to purchase a replacement residence. Any gain not excluded is capital gain because a personal residence is a capital asset. If long term, these gains are eligible for preferential tax rates. However, any recognized gain on the sale of a personal residence is considered to be investment income, so the gain may be subject to the 3.8% tax on net investment income due to the so-called Medicare tax on higher-income taxpayers (see Chapter I:5 for further discussion of the preferential rates and the additional tax on net investment income). A loss on the sale or exchange of a personal residence is not deductible because the residence is personal-use property.[64]

EXAMPLE I:12-49 ▶ Maki, who is single and 35 years old, sells her principal residence that she purchased four years ago and realizes a $230,000 gain. Maki may exclude the entire gain regardless of her age or whether she purchases a new principal residence. ◀

EXAMPLE I:12-50 ▶ Assume the same facts as in the above example except the realized gain is $320,000. Maki may exclude $250,000 and recognize a $70,000 LTCG. ◀

EXAMPLE I:12-51 ▶ Assume the same facts as in Example I:12-50 except Maki is married to Yixin, and they have owned and occupied the residence for the last four years. They may exclude the entire $320,000 gain. ◀

ADDITIONAL COMMENT

The elimination of taxes on up to $500,000 of gain from the sale of a personal residence has been a great benefit for many taxpayers who had large built-in gains.

Prior to the Taxpayer Relief Act of 1997, taxpayers could defer gain resulting from sale of a personal residence if they purchased another principal residence within two years at a cost greater than the adjusted sales price. Taxpayers who were at least 55 years old could exclude up to $125,000 of gain resulting from the sale of a personal residence. The deferral provision of Sec. 1034 has been repealed; the exclusion has been increased to $250,000 or $500,000; and taxpayers may exclude gain regardless of age and use the exclusion more than once.

Today, the rules for excluding gain resulting from the sale of a personal residence are more favorable for most taxpayers than the old rules because Congress wanted to eliminate the need for homeowners to maintain records for long periods of time. However, taxpayers who expect to sell their homes and have a realized gain of more than $250,000 ($500,000 if a joint return is filed) still need to maintain records. Also, taxpayers who convert their personal residence to business property or rental property will need to know the property's correct adjusted basis to compute depreciation.

Determining the Realized Gain. Gain realized is the excess of the amount realized over the property's adjusted basis.[65] The amount realized on the sale of the property is equal to the selling price less selling expenses.[66] Selling expenses include commissions, advertising, deed preparation costs, and legal expenses incurred in connection with the sale.[67]

EXAMPLE I:12-52 ▶ Kirby sells his personal residence, which has a $100,000 basis, to Maxine. To make the sale, Kirby pays a $7,000 sales commission and incurs $800 of legal costs. Maxine pays $30,000 cash and assumes Kirby's $90,000 mortgage. The amount realized is $112,200 [($30,000 + $90,000) − ($7,000 + $800)]. The realized gain is $12,200 ($112,200 − $100,000). ◀

[63] Sec. 121(a) and (b).
[64] Reg. Secs. 1.165-9(a) and 1.262-1b)(4).
[65] Reg. Sec. 1.1034-1(b)(5).
[66] Reg. Sec. 1.1034-1(b)(4).
[67] Reg. Sec. 1.1034-1(b)(4)(i).

Adjusted Basis of Residence. The original basis of a principal residence is a function of how the residence is obtained. It could be purchased, received as a gift, or inherited. The cost of a residence includes all amounts attributable to the acquisition including commissions and other purchasing expenses paid to acquire the residence.[68] Capital improvements, but not repairs, increase the adjusted basis of the residence. The costs of adding a room, installing an air conditioning system, finishing a basement, and landscaping are capital improvements. Expenses incurred to protect the taxpayer's title in the residence are also capitalized. Under Sec. 1034, which was repealed in 1997, a taxpayer who deferred gain on the sale of a principal residence was required to reduce the basis of the replacement residence by the amount of the deferred gain.[69]

EXAMPLE I:12-53 ► In 1996, Susan paid $200,000 to purchase a new residence. She paid a realtor $4,000 to help locate the house and paid legal fees of $1,200 to make certain that the seller had legal title to the property. As a result of the purchase, she deferred a gain of $50,000 from the sale a former residence in 1995. In 1997, she added a new porch to the house at a cost of $6,000 and installed central air conditioning at a cost of $5,200. Since purchasing the house, she has paid $1,500 for repairs. The adjusted basis of her house is $166,400 [$200,000 + $4,000 + $1,200 − $50,000 + $6,000 + $5,200]. ◄

Multiple Use of the Exclusion. Previously under Sec. 121, a taxpayer was limited to the exclusion once in their lifetime, and a married taxpayer whose spouse had taken the exclusion could not use the exclusion even if the taxpayer filed as married filing separately. The exclusion is now determined on an individual basis. An individual may claim the exclusion even if the individual's spouse used the exclusion within the past two years. Also, for a married couple filing a joint return when each spouse maintains a separate principal residence, the $250,000 exclusion is available for the sale or exchange of each spouse's principal residence.

EXAMPLE I:12-54 ► Krista, who has owned and used a house as her principal residence for the last seven years, marries Josh in January 2015. Josh sold his residence in October 2014 and excluded a $145,000 gain. Krista sells her residence in December 2015 and realizes a gain of $378,000. She may exclude $250,000 of the gain.

Assuming that Krista and Josh use her residence in the above example for a two-year period starting in January 2015, they could exclude up to $500,000 if she waits to sell the house until January 2017. ◄

PRINCIPAL RESIDENCE DEFINED

For Sec. 121 to apply, taxpayers must sell property that qualifies as their principal residence. Whether property is used as the taxpayer's principal residence depends upon all the facts and circumstances. If a taxpayer uses more than one property as a residence during the year, the property used a majority of the time will normally be the principal residence.[70]

EXAMPLE I:12-55 ► Lanny, a 40-year-old college professor, owns and occupies a house in Oklahoma. During the summer, he lives in a cabin in Idaho. After owning the cabin for eight years, Lanny sells it for $50,000 and realizes a gain. Gain on the sale of the cabin in Idaho must be recognized because Lanny's principal residence is in Oklahoma. ◄

KEY POINT

A taxpayer may own two or more residences, but only one of them qualifies as the principal residence.

Factors other than use of the property that are relevant when determining a taxpayer's principal residence include place of employment, mailing address for bills and correspondence, address for tax returns and voter registration, and location of religious organizations and recreational clubs with which the taxpayer is affiliated. The principal place of abode for the taxpayer's family members is also relevant.[71]

The property does not have to be one's principal residence at time of the sale to qualify for the exclusion. The exclusion applies if the property has been used as a principal residence for at least two of the five years before the sale or exchange and the exclusion has not been used within the past two years.

---

[68] Reg. Sec. 1.1034-1(c)(4).
[69] Sec. 1034(e).
[70] Reg. Sec. 1.121-1(b)(2).
[71] Reg. Sec. 1.121-1(b)(2).

EXAMPLE I:12-56 ▶ Canan owned and used a house in Buffalo as her principal residence from March 10, 2011, until November 21, 2013, when she purchased a new house in Kansas on December 1, 2013. Her brother lives in the house in Buffalo until Canan sells it on July 10, 2015, and realizes a gain of $288,000. She may exclude $250,000 and recognize a $38,000 LTCG. ◀

Condominium apartments, houseboats, and housetrailers may qualify as principal residences.[72] Stock held by a tenant-stockholder in a cooperative housing corporation is a principal residence if the dwelling that the taxpayer is entitled to occupy as a stockholder is used as his or her principal residence.[73]

ADDITIONAL COMMENT

The taxpayer does not have to be occupying the old residence at the date of sale. The taxpayer may have already moved to a new residence and be renting the old residence temporarily before its sale.

SALE OF MORE THAN ONE PRINCIPAL RESIDENCE WITHIN A TWO-YEAR PERIOD

The new exclusion provided by Sec. 121 applies to only one sale or exchange every two years. However, a portion of the gain may be excluded in certain circumstances even if the two-year requirement is not satisfied.

If a principal residence is sold within two years of a previous sale or exchange of a residence, part of the gain may be excluded if the sale or exchange is due to a change in employment, health or unforseen circumstances. The portion of the gain excluded is based on a ratio with a numerator in days or months and a denominator of 730 days or 24 months.[74] The numerator is the shorter of:

(1) the period during which the ownership and use tests were met during the five-year period ending on the date of sale, or

(2) the period of time after the date of the most recent prior sale or exchange for which the exclusion applied until the date of the current sale or exchange.[75]

The amount excluded is $250,000 or $500,000 times the above ratio.

EXAMPLE I:12-57 ▶ Winnie, who is single, sold her principal residence in Detroit on November 1, 2015, and excluded the $127,000 gain because she owned and used the residence for two of the last five years. Winnie had purchased another residence in Cleveland on October 1, 2015. She occupies the residence in Cleveland until June 12, 2016, when she moves to Dallas to accept a new job. She sells the residence in Cleveland on November 15, 2016, and realizes a gain of $40,000. Winnie may exclude all of the gain because the sale of her Cleveland residence was due to a change in employment and 254/730 of $250,000 is more than the $40,000 realized gain. She owns and uses the residence in Cleveland for 254 days, and the period between the sale of the residence in Detroit and the sale in Cleveland is 378 days. ◀

ADDITIONAL COMMENT

If Winnie's gain in Example I:12-57 is $100,000, she may exclude $86,986 (254/730 × $250,000).

Ownership and Use Tests. If a principal residence is sold before satisfying the ownership and use tests, part of the gain may be excluded if the sale is due to a change in employment, health, or unforseen circumstances. The portion of the gain excluded is determined by multiplying the amount of the exclusion (i.e., $250,000 or $500,000) by a fraction whose numerator is the number of days the use and ownership tests were met and whose denominator is 730 days (or 24 months).

EXAMPLE I:12-58 ▶ Tim, a single taxpayer who purchased his home on January 1, 2015, for $500,000, recently became ill and sells his home in order to move closer to a relative who can care for him. Tim sells his principal residence on June 14, 2015, for $620,000, realizing a gain of $120,000. Because he owned and occupied the residence for 164 days and the sale was due to a change in his health, he may exclude $56,164 ($250,000 × 164/730). ◀

For purposes of the two-year ownership rule, a taxpayer's period of ownership includes the period during which the taxpayer's deceased spouse owned the residence. When a taxpayer receives a residence from a spouse or an ex-spouse incident to a divorce, the taxpayer's period of owning the property includes the time the residence was owned by the spouse or ex-spouse.[76] When attempting to determine if the taxpayer has occupied the residence for two years, short temporary absences such as for vacation or other seasonal absence are counted as use by the taxpayer.[77]

---

[72] Rev. Rul. 64-31, 1964-1 C.B. 300.
[73] Reg. Sec. 1.1034-1(c)(3).
[74] Reg. Sec. 1.121-3(g).
[75] Sec. 121(c).
[76] Sec. 121(d)(2) and (3).
[77] Reg. Sec. 1.121-1(c)(2)(i).

EXAMPLE I:12-59 ▶ Sachie receives an $800,000 residence owned for six years by Richard, her former spouse, as part of a divorce settlement. Richard's basis for the residence is $430,000. They lived in the house for five years prior to the divorce. Three months after transfer of the residence to Sachie, she sells it for $825,000, and $250,000 of her $395,000 realized gain is excluded. Sachie must recognize a $145,000 LTCG. Sachie's period of ownership includes the six years Richard owned the residence. ◀

ADDITIONAL COMMENT

The five-year period does not include any period up to ten years during which the taxpayer or the taxpayer's spouse is on qualified official extended duty as a member of the uniformed services.

Change Due to Employment, Health, or Unforeseen Circumstances. The Treasury has issued Regulations to provide guidance as to how a homeowner may qualify for partial exclusion if the sale was before the two-year use and ownership test is satisfied or if the sale occurs within two years of a previous sale where the exclusion was used. The exceptions may apply even if a person other than the taxpayer has a change in employment or health.

A taxpayer is viewed as being eligible for partial exclusion if she sells her residence because a qualified individual has a change in employment that satisfies the test under Sec. 217 for the moving expense deduction. A qualified individual includes the taxpayer, the taxpayer's spouse, co-owner of the residence, or a person who uses the residence as a principal place of abode. Taxpayers may qualify for the exclusion and the moving expense deduction if moving to take a new job, continue with present employer or accept a job if the 50-mile distance test is satisfied. The change in employment must occur when the taxpayer is satisfying the ownership and use test for the residence except for the two-year requirement.[78]

EXAMPLE I:12-60 ▶ Mark has lived in his first house for one year in Omaha when he marries Karen. Six months later, Karen receives a job offer and they move to Florida. Mark may exclude a realized gain equal to 18/24 of $250,000, because the move is due to a change in employment of a qualified individual. ◀

When determining if the sale or exchange of the residence is due to a change in health, the definition of a "qualified individual" is expanded to include relatives who satisfy the relationship test used to determine if one is a dependent of the taxpayer. The relative must satisfy the relationship test but does not have to be a dependent to be a qualified individual. A sale or exchange is because of health if the primary reason is "to obtain, provide, or facilitate the diagnosis, cure, mitigation, or treatment of a disease, illness, or injury of a qualified individual."[79]

EXAMPLE I:12-61 ▶ Daniel has lived in his first house in Virginia for eight months when he sells the house and moves to Texas to take care of his 60-year-old father who recently suffered a stroke. Daniel may exclude a realized gain equal to 8/24 of $250,000 because the primary reason for the sale is due to the health of a qualified individual. ◀

REAL-WORLD EXAMPLE

In LTR 200601009, taxpayers who sold their home within two years of the purchase because they became aware of various criminal activities occurring in their neighborhood were allowed to utilize Sec. 121. In addition to their son being assaulted and threatened, one of the taxpayers was assaulted by the neighbors.

A sale or exchange is due to unforeseen circumstances if the primary reason for the sale or exchange is an event that the taxpayer could not reasonably have anticipated before purchasing and occupying the residence. For the unforeseen circumstances exception, a qualified individual is the same as a qualified individual for the change in employment test.

The following are specific events considered to qualify as unforeseen circumstances:

1. Involuntary conversion of residence;
2. Natural or man-made disasters or acts of war or terrorism resulting in a casualty to the residence;
3. Death of a qualified individual;
4. Loss of employment by a qualified individual if the individual is eligible for unemployment compensation;
5. Change of employment that results in the taxpayer's inability to pay housing costs and reasonable basic living expenses;
6. Divorce or legal separation;
7. Multiple births from the same pregnancy.[80]

Note that marriage and adoption are not included in the above safe-harbor list of unforeseen circumstances. One who sells her residence before meeting the two-year test because she has adopted a child will not be assured of qualifying for possible exclusion

78 Reg. Sec. 1.121-3(c).
79 Reg. Sec. 1.121-3(d).
80 Reg. Sec. 1.121-3T(e).

under the unforeseen circumstances exception. She will have to argue that the facts and circumstances justify her use of the partial exclusion.

The IRS has issued a number of letter rulings that suggest that it is willing to consider many different reasons for selling due to unforseen circumstances. In LTR 200601022, a taxpayer purchased a house, but then married someone with a child who attended a school in a different school district. They decided to temporarily use their house as rental property and rent another house for their use located in the child's school district. While living in the rented house, they had a child and decided to sell the first house because it was too small for their expanding family. Despite the fact that the taxpayer did not use the house as a principal residence, they were allowed to utilize Sec. 121.

EXAMPLE I:12-62 ▶ Benjamin purchases a house near the airport and sells it four months later because of noise caused by planes. He may not exclude any of the gain, because the airport noise is not an unforeseen circumstance. ◀

STOP & THINK

Question: Rebecca's uncle told her that she could purchase his house for $150,000 in five years provided that she could pay at least $30,000 of the purchase price in cash. Rebecca has $15,000 and is considering two alternative methods to obtain the remaining $15,000 in five years. The first alternative is to purchase $15,000 of non-dividend paying stock that she expects to increase in value to $30,000 within five years. The second alternative is to purchase an $80,000 residence by paying $15,000 and borrowing $65,000. Payments on the mortgage will be interest only for five years and amount to $450 per month. Insurance, property taxes, and other home ownership expenses average $90 per month. She expects the house to be worth $95,000 at the end of five years. She will rent an apartment for $540 per month, including utilities, if she buys the stock. Ignoring transaction costs and assuming that she does not itemize deductions, should Rebecca purchase the stock or the house?

Solution: The $15,000 gain resulting from sale of the stock is LTCG and probably taxed at 15%. If the rate is 15%, she must pay taxes of $2,250 and has only $27,750 available to purchase her uncle's house. She will have a gain of $15,000 if she sells the house but the gain is excluded. She has $30,000 of cash and is able to buy her uncle's house. The tax law encourages Rebecca to buy a principal residence.

REAL-WORLD EXAMPLE

Unlike Example I:12-62, a taxpayer in LTR 200702032 was able to utilize Sec. 121 when he sold his principal residence located near an airport because he was mislead about the amount of noise, despite his considerable efforts to determine if noise would be a problem. He sold the house at a loss, but he sued the real estate agents and the seller for their failure to disclose the excessive noise during peak periods in the early morning and evening. The defendants settled and the settlement proceeds were treated as additional proceeds from the sale of the residence resulting in a gain which the taxpayer was able to exclude.

NONQUALIFIED USE AFTER 2008

A taxpayer who owns a principal residence and a second home (rental property, vacation home, etc.) that has appreciated in value has an incentive to convert the second home to a principal residence if planning to sell the second home. The Housing Assistance Tax Act of 2008 reduced the advantage of converting residences that have not been the principal residence to one's principal residence.

Gain from the sale of a principal residence that is allocable to periods of nonqualified use after 2008 is not excluded from income. Gain allocated to periods of nonqualified use after 2008 is based on the ratio which the aggregate periods of nonqualified use after 2008 bears to the total time the property was owned. A period of nonqualified use is any period that the property is not used as a principal residence after 2008. As under prior law, any depreciation attributable to periods of business use is subject to taxation.

Any portion of the five-year period ending on the date of sale that is after the property ceases to be used as a principal residence is not considered nonqualified use, thus the taxpayer may vacate the residence before selling it without recognizing that time after moving out as nonqualified use. Absences due to change in employment, health condition, or other unforeseen circumstances are not considered nonqualified use. Also, nonqualified use does not include any period in which the taxpayer or taxpayer's spouse is serving on qualified official extended duty.

EXAMPLE I:12-63 ▶ The Eberts have owned and lived in a house on Mill Street as their personal residence for 20 years. They also own a house on Elm Street that has been used as rental property for 18 years. On May 1, 2008, they moved into the Elm Street house and used it as their principal residence until the current year when they sell the Elm Street property and realize a $700,000 gain. Any of the gain due to depreciation must be recognized, but they are eligible to exclude up to $500,000 of the remaining gain. The use of the property as rental property is not nonqualified use because it occurred before 2009. ◀

EXAMPLE I:12-64 ▶ Assume the same facts as in Example I:12-63 except the Eberts did not move into the Elm Street property until May 1, 2013, and sell the property on December 22, 2015. In this case, the period from January 1, 2009 through April 30, 2013 is nonqualified use and a prorata share of the gain after considering the gain due to depreciation is not eligible for the $500,000 exclusion. ◀

EXAMPLE I:12-65 ▶ Dale owned a house and used it as rental property for seven years until January 1, 2013, when he moved into the house and used it as a principal residence. Depreciation for the seven years that it was used as rental property is $30,000. If he sells the house on January 1, 2016, and realizes a gain of $210,000, the first $30,000 of gain is recognized because of depreciation. He may exclude 6/10* of the remaining gain of $180,000, and must recognize another $72,000 (4/10* of $180,000) due to the nonqualified use in 2009, 2010, 2011 and 2012. He used the property as a principal residence for three years, and the three years before 2009 are not considered to be nonqualified use. So, six years* of the ten-year period are eligible for the Sec. 121 exclusion. He must recognize $102,000 of the $210,000 gain and may exclude $108,000.

* To further clarify the calculations in this example, below is an explanation of the relavant time periods:

10 years = total ownership period, 1/1/06 – 1/1/16.
4 years = nonqualified use period, 1/1/09 – 12/31/12.
6 years = qualified use years, 1/1/06 – 12/31/08 and 1/1/13 – 1/1/16. ◀

INVOLUNTARY CONVERSION OF A PRINCIPAL RESIDENCE

Ordinarily, the involuntary conversion of a principal residence is governed by Sec. 1033, discussed earlier in this chapter. A gain due to an involuntary conversion of a personal residence may be deferred if the requirements of Sec. 1033 are satisfied. The functional-use test must be satisfied regardless of the type of involuntary conversion.

For purposes of Sec. 121, the destruction, theft, seizure, requisition, or condemnation of property is treated as a sale.[81] Thus, taxpayers may exclude a gain of up to $250,000 or $500,000 due to the involuntary conversion of a principal residence if the use and ownership tests are satisfied. Taxpayers normally prefer to exclude gain if the use and ownership tests are satisfied rather than defer gain under the involuntary conversion provisions.

If taxpayers make a proper and timely replacement of the residence subject to the involuntary conversion, gain may be excluded up to $250,000, or $500,000, and the remaining gain may be deferred. For purposes of applying the involuntary conversion provisions, the amount realized due to the involuntary conversion is reduced by any gain excluded under Sec. 121.[82]

EXAMPLE I:12-66 ▶ The Kochs' principal residence, with an adjusted basis of $200,000, has been used and owned by them for nine years. The house is destroyed by a hurricane, and the Kochs receive insurance proceeds of $820,000. Four months later, they purchase another residence for $900,000. The Kochs have a realized gain of $620,000 and may exclude $500,000 under Sec. 121. The remaining $120,000 gain may be deferred and the basis of their replacement residence is $780,000 ($900,000 − $120,000). ◀

Because the amount realized is reduced by the gain excluded, the Kochs could have deferred the $120,000 gain in the above example by investing only $320,000 in a replacement residence.

If gain due to the involuntary conversion of a principal residence is deferred under Sec. 1033, the holding period of the replacement residence includes the holding period of the converted property for purposes of satisfying the use and ownership tests of Sec. 121.[83] The Kochs satisfy the use and ownership requirements for Sec. 121 with respect to their new residence in Example I:12-66 because gain is deferred under Sec. 1033.

A loss due to a condemnation of a personal residence is not recognized. If the loss is due to a casualty, the loss is deductible and is treated like other casualty losses of nonbusiness property (see Chapter I:8).

TAX PLANNING CONSIDERATIONS

OBJECTIVE 4

Describe tax planning considerations for nontaxable exchanges

AVOIDING THE LIKE-KIND EXCHANGE PROVISIONS

In some cases, a taxpayer may prefer a taxable exchange to a nontaxable like-kind exchange. For instance, if the gain is taxed as a capital gain and the taxpayer has capital

[81] Sec. 121(d)(5)(A).
[82] Sec. 121(d)(5)(B).
[83] Sec. 121(d)(8).

losses to offset the gain, the taxpayer may prefer to recognize the gain during the current year. If gain on the exchange is recognized instead of deferred, the basis of the property received in the exchange is higher.

EXAMPLE I:12-67 ▶ Connie owns land with a $20,000 basis. The land is held as an investment. Connie exchanges the land for a duplex with a $100,000 FMV. Because the exchange qualifies as a like-kind exchange, no gain is recognized and Connie's basis for the duplex is $20,000. If the exchange does not qualify as a like-kind exchange (e.g., the land is a personal-use asset), Connie recognizes an $80,000 capital gain. Connie's basis for the duplex is $100,000. The basis of the duplex, except for the portion allocable to land, is eligible for depreciation. ◀

If an exchange qualifies as a like-kind exchange, no loss on the exchange is recognized. A taxpayer who prefers to recognize a loss should avoid making a like-kind exchange. It may be advantageous to sell the property to recognize the loss and then purchase the replacement asset in two independent transactions. If the sale and purchase transactions are with the same party, the IRS may maintain that the like-kind exchange rules apply because the two transactions are in substance a like-kind exchange (i.e., the judicial doctrine of substance over form might be applied).

SALE OF A PRINCIPAL RESIDENCE

Election Provision. When the requirements of Sec. 121 are satisfied, gain is excluded unless the taxpayer elects not to have Sec. 121 apply.[84]

EXAMPLE I:12-68 ▶ Paula has owned a house in Wyoming for eight years and occupied it until 18 months ago when she moved to Idaho and purchased a new house. She sells the house in Wyoming on May 23, 2015, and the realized gain is $25,000. Paula anticipates that she will move next year and have to sell the house in Idaho which has appreciated more than $100,000 since purchased. Paula may want to elect not to have Sec. 121 apply and recognize the $25,000 gain and then use the exclusion when she sells the house in Idaho next year. ◀

Property Used as Residence and for Business. If a house is used for both residential use and business use, the tax treatment depends on whether or not the business portion of the house is conducted in a separate structure. If the business portion of the house is conducted in a separate structure, the sale should be treated as a sale of two assets, the residence and the portion of the property used as a business. The Sec. 121 exclusion only applies to the residence portion of the property.

EXAMPLE I:12-69 ▶ Mormor owns a one-acre lot with a house she uses as her residence and a barn that she uses to display and sell antiques. She purchased the property in 1990 for $100,000 and $10,000 of the purchase price was allocated to the barn. Depreciation of $4,000 has been allowed for the barn. She sells the property during the current year for $300,000 and estimates that 10% of the price received is for the barn. She may exclude the $180,000 ($270,000 − $90,000) gain on the sale of the residence. Her $24,000 ($30,000 − $6,000) gain on the sale of the barn is recognized. ◀

ADDITIONAL COMMENT

As explained in Chapter I:13, Mormor's $24,000 gain in Example 69 is a Sec. 1231 gain and $4,000 is taxed at a maximum rate of 25% because it is unrecaptured Sec. 1250 gain.

If the business activity is conducted within the house and not in a separate structure, the sale does not have to be treated as a sale of two different assets. However, gain attributable to depreciation after May 6, 1997, is not eligible for the exclusion. The remaining gain is eligible for the exclusion.

EXAMPLE I:12-70 ▶ Kate purchased a house in 2005 for $200,000 and uses 15% of the house as an office. The office is used on a regular and exclusive basis and is her principal place of business. Depreciation of $3,400 has been deducted when she sells the house for $430,000. Her gain is $233,400 ($430,000 − $196,600), and she may exclude $230,000 but must recognize $3,400 of the gain. ◀

The government's decision to allow Kate to treat the property in the above example as one property instead of two is beneficial for her. If the property was viewed as two properties or if the office was in a separate structure, only $195,500 ($365,500 − $170,000) of the gain would qualify for the exclusion.

---

[84] Sec. 121(f).

EXAMPLE I:12-71 ▶ Bobbi purchased a house on March 1, 2004 and used it as her principal residence until March 1, 2006, when she rented the house to the Allens while she lived with her mother. On November 1, 2013, the Allens' lease expired and Bobbi moved back into the house. She sells the house on July 12, 2015, and realizes a gain of $210,000. She may not exclude any of the gain because she has not used the property as her principal residence for two of the last five years. ◀

If Bobbi in the above example did satisfy the two-out-of-five-year requirement, gain equal to depreciation would first be recognized. A portion of the remaining gain could not be excluded because of the nonqualified use after 2008.

EXAMPLE I:12-72 ▶ Assume the same facts as in the above example except that Bobbi sells the house on December 1, 2015. Because she has used the property as her principal residence for two of the last five years, she may exclude part of the excess of the $210,000 gain over depreciation allowed after May 6, 1997. 58 months of the use is nonqualified use because of its use as rental property for 58 months after 2008. Because she owned the property for 141 months and nonqualified use amounted to 58 months, 58/141 of the gain remaining after gain recognized due to depreciation is recognized. ◀

Compliance and Procedural Considerations

OBJECTIVE 5

Describe compliance and procedural considerations for nontaxable exchanges

REPORTING OF INVOLUNTARY CONVERSIONS

The election to defer recognition of the gain from an involuntary conversion is made by not reporting the gain as income for the first year in which gain is realized. All details pertaining to the involuntary conversion (including those relating to the replacement of the converted property) should be reported for the taxable year or years in which any of the gain is realized.[85]

ADDITIONAL COMMENT

The failure to include gain from an involuntary conversion in gross income is deemed to be an election even though the details are not reported.

A taxpayer who elects to defer recognition of the gain but does not make a proper replacement of the property within the required period of time must file an amended return for the year or years for which the election was made. An amended return may be needed if the cost of the replacement property is less than expected at the time of the election. All details pertaining to the replacement of converted property must be reported in the year in which replacement occurs.[86]

EXAMPLE I:12-73 ▶ Bob's property, with a $40,000 adjusted basis, was destroyed by a storm in 2014. Bob received $45,000 insurance proceeds in 2014 and planned to purchase property similar to the converted property in 2015 at a cost of $47,000. Bob elected to defer recognition of the gain in 2014. In 2015 the replacement property is purchased for $44,500. Bob must file an amended return for 2014 and recognize a $500 ($45,000 − $44,500) gain. ◀

ADDITIONAL COMMENT

The replacement period may be extended if special permission is obtained from the IRS.

A taxpayer who either is ineligible or does not want to defer the gain must report the gain in the usual manner. If a taxpayer does not elect to defer the gain in the year the gain is realized and the replacement period has not expired, a subsequent election may be made. In such an event, a refund claim should be filed for the tax year in which the gain was realized and previously recognized.[87]

Taxpayers who do not initially elect to defer the gain from an involuntary conversion may later make the election, but the election may not subsequently be revoked. The Tax Court has ruled that the Treasury Regulations allow the filing of an amended return for a year in which the election is made only if proper replacement is not made within the specified time period or the replacement is made at a cost lower than anticipated at the time of the election.[88] The IRS takes the position that taxpayers who designate qualifying property as replacement property may not later designate other qualifying property as the replacement property.[89]

EXAMPLE I:12-74 ▶ In 2013 Troy collected $200,000 from an insurance company as the result of the destruction of rental property with a $140,000 basis. He made the election to defer the gain realized in 2013 and attached a supporting schedule of details regarding the involuntary conversion including

[85] Reg. Sec. 1.1033(a)-2(c)(2).
[86] *Ibid.*
[87] *Ibid.*
[88] *John McShain*, 65 T.C. 686 (1976).
[89] Rev. Rul. 83-39, 1983-1 C.B. 190.

a designation of replacement property to be acquired in 2014. In 2014 Troy purchased the designated replacement rental property for $225,000. In 2015 Troy purchases other rental property for $400,000 and now wants to designate that property as the replacement property for the property destroyed in 2013. Troy may not designate the property acquired in 2015 as the replacement property because the rental property purchased in 2014 was already designated as such. ◀

REPORTING OF SALE OR EXCHANGE OF A PRINCIPAL RESIDENCE

Taxpayers only have to report the sale if any of the gain is not excluded. If the taxpayer does not qualify to exclude all of the gain or elects not to exclude the gain, the entire gain realized is reported on Schedule D either on line 1, if residence is held for one year or less, or on line 8. On the line below where the entire gain is shown, the taxpayer should indicate on the following line the amount of the gain that is being excluded as a loss (i.e., show in parentheses).

Publication 523, Selling Your Home, provides the following worksheet that may be used to determine if any gain is recognized. If the taxpayer has to utilize the exceptions to the two-year ownership and use tests, a different worksheet is provided.

Worksheet 2. **Taxable Gain on Sale of Home**

Part 1. Gain or (Loss) on Sale

1.	Selling price of home	1. ______
2.	Selling expenses (including commissions, advertising and legal fees, and seller-paid loan charges)	2. ______
3.	Subtract line 2 from line 1. This is the amount realized	3. ______
4.	Adjusted basis of home sold (from Worksheet 1, line 13)	4. ______
5.	**Gain or (loss)** on the sale. Subtract line 4 from line 3. If this is a loss, stop here	5. ______

Part 2. Exclusion and Taxable Gain

6.	Enter any depreciation allowed or allowable on the property for periods after May 6, 1997. If none, enter -0-	6. ______
7.	Subtract line 6 from line 5. If the result is less than zero, enter -0-	7. ______
8.	Aggregate number of days of nonqualified use after 2008. If none, enter -0-. If line 8 is equal to zero, skip to line 12 and enter the amount from line 7 on line 12	8. ______
9.	Number of days taxpayer owned the property	9. ______
10.	Divide the amount on line 8 by the amount on line 9. Enter the result as a decimal (rounded to at least 3 places). But do not enter an amount greater than 1.00	10. ______
11.	Gain allocated to nonqualified use. (Line 7 multiplied by line 10)	11. ______
12.	Gain eligible for exclusion. Subtract line 11 from line 7.	12. ______
13.	If you qualify to exclude gain on the sale, enter your maximum exclusion (see *Maximum Exclusion*). If you qualify for a reduced maximum exclusion, enter the amount from Worksheet 3, line 7. If you do not qualify to exclude gain, enter -0-	13. ______
14.	**Exclusion**. Enter the smaller of line 12 or line 13	14. ______
15.	**Taxable gain**. Subtract line 14 from line 5. Report your taxable gain as described under *Reporting the Sale*. **If the amount on line 6 is more than zero, complete line 16**	15. ______
16.	Enter the **smaller** of line 6 or line 15. Enter this amount on line 12 of the Unrecaptured Section 1250 Gain Worksheet in the instructions for Schedule D (Form 1040)	16. ______

PROBLEM MATERIALS

DISCUSSION QUESTIONS

I:12-1 Evaluate the following statement: The underlying rationale for the nonrecognition of a gain or loss resulting from a like-kind exchange is that the exchange constitutes a liquidation of the taxpayer's investment.

I:12-2 Why might a taxpayer want to avoid having an exchange qualify as a like-kind exchange?

I:12-3 Debbie owns office equipment with a basis of $300,000 and a holding period starting on May 10, 2004. Debbie exchanges the equipment for other office equipment owned by Doug on July 23, 2015. Doug's equipment has an FMV of $500,000. Both Debbie and Doug use the equipment in their businesses.

a. What is Debbie's basis for the office equipment received in the exchange and when does the holding period start for that equipment?
b. If Debbie and Doug are related taxpayers, explain what action could occur that would cause the exchange not to qualify as a like-kind exchange.

I:12-4 Kay owns equipment used in her business and exchanges the equipment for other like-kind equipment and marketable securities.

a. Will Kay's recognized gain ever exceed the realized gain?
b. Will Kay's recognized gain ever exceed the FMV of the marketable securities?
c. What is the basis of the marketable securities received?
d. When does the holding period of the marketable securities begin?

I:12-5 Demetrius sells word processing equipment used in his business to Edith. He then purchases new word processing equipment from Zip Corporation.

a. Do the sale and purchase qualify as a like-kind exchange?
b. When may a sale and a subsequent purchase be treated as a like-kind exchange?

I:12-6 When determining whether property qualifies as like-kind property, is the quality or grade of the property considered?

I:12-7 What is personal property of a like class that meets the definition of like-kind?

I:12-8 When does a nonsimultaneous exchange qualify as a like-kind exchange?

I:12-9 Burke is anxious to purchase land owned by Kim for use in his trade or business. Kim's basis for the land is $150,000, and Burke has offered to pay $800,000 if she will sell within the next 10 days. Kim is interested in selling but wants to avoid recognizing gain. What advice would you give?

I:12-10 Lanny wants to purchase a farm owned by Jane, but Jane does not want to recognize a gain on the transfer of the appreciated property. Explain how a three-party exchange might be used to allow Lanny to obtain the farm without Jane having to recognize a gain.

I:12-11 Does the receipt of boot in a transaction that otherwise qualifies as a like-kind exchange always cause the exchange to be at least partially taxable?

I:12-12 When must a taxpayer who gives boot recognize a gain or loss?

I:12-13 What is the justification for Sec. 1033, which allows a taxpayer to elect to defer a gain resulting from an involuntary conversion? May a taxpayer elect under Sec. 1033 to defer recognition of a loss resulting from an involuntary conversion?

I:12-14 Must property be actually condemned for the conversion of property to be classified as an involuntary conversion? Explain.

I:12-15 What are severance damages? What is the tax treatment for severance damages received if the taxpayer does not use the severance damages to restore the retained property?

I:12-16 The functional use test is often used to determine whether the replacement property is similar or related in service or use to the property converted. Explain the functional use test.

I:12-17 In what situations may a gain due to an involuntary conversion of real property be deferred if like-kind property is purchased to replace the converted property?

I:12-18 Prior to the Taxpayer Relief Act of 1997, taxpayers could defer a gain on the sale of a principal residence sold before May 7, 1997, if they purchased and occupied a new principal residence within two years before or after the sale and the cost of the new residence was at least equal to the adjusted sales price of the old residence. Some taxpayers who were at least 55 years old had a once-in-a-lifetime exclusion up to $125,000 if they owned and used the property as a principal residence for at least three years of the five-year-period ending on the date of sale. Discuss why current law with respect to the sale of a personal residence is more favorable than the law prior to the Taxpayer Relief Act of 1997.

I:12-19 One reason Congress expanded the exclusion of gain on the sale of a principal residence and eliminated the deferral provision was to eliminate the need for many taxpayers to keep records of capital improvements that increase the basis of their residence. Why might taxpayers still need to maintain such records to substantiate the adjusted basis of their principal residence?

I:12-20 Steve maintains that the cost of wallpapering his three-bedroom house is a capital expenditure while Martha maintains that the cost of wallpapering her three-bedroom house is an expense. Steve uses his house as his personal residence while Martha's house is rental property. Explain why Steve and Martha view the cost of wallpapering differently.

I:12-21 The Nelsons purchased a new residence in 1992 for $300,000 from David who owned and used the residence as rental property. When the Nelsons wanted to purchase the property, it was being rented to tenants who had four months remaining on their lease. The Nelsons paid the tenants $1,000 to relinquish the lease and vacate the property. In 1996, they added a family room to the house at a cost of $79,200. In 1998, they suffered hail damage to the roof and received $7,000 from the insurance company. They did not repair the damaged roof, and no casualty loss deduction was allowed. What is their adjusted basis for the house today?

I:12-22 What requirements must be satisfied by an unmarried taxpayer under Sec. 121 to be eligible for the election to exclude a gain up to $250,000 on the sale or exchange of a principal residence?

ISSUE IDENTIFICATION QUESTIONS

I:12-23 John owns 25% of the ABC Partnership and Jane owns 25% of the XYZ Partnership. The ABC Partnership owns a farm and produces corn and the XYZ Partnership owns a farm and produces soybeans. John and Jane agree to exchange their partnership interests. What tax issues should John and Jane consider?

I:12-24 Chauvin Oil Corporation operates primarily in the United States and owns an offshore drilling rig with an adjusted basis of $400,000 that it uses near Louisiana. Chauvin exchanges the rig for a new rig with a FMV of $1,000,000, and Chauvin also pays $250,000. Chauvin plans to expand its drilling operations to offshore sites near Finland. What tax issues should the Chauvin Oil Corporation consider?

I:12-25 Jaharta, Inc., owns land used for truck farming and cattle raising. The California Division of Highways condemned 36 acres of Jaharta's land to build a new highway. Jaharta owned a 50% interest in property being used for apricot, prune, and walnut orchards. Jaharta used the proceeds received as a result of the condemnation to purchase the remaining interest in the property being used for orchards. What tax issues should Jaharta consider?

PROBLEMS

I:12-26 *Like-Kind Property.* Which of the following exchanges qualify as like-kind exchanges under Sec. 1031?

a. Acme Corporation stock held for investment purposes for Mesa Corporation stock also held for investment purposes
b. A motel used in a trade or business for an apartment complex held for investment
c. A pecan orchard in Texas used in a trade or business for an orange grove in Florida used in a trade or business
d. A one-third interest in a general partnership for a one-fourth interest in a limited partnership
e. Inventory for equipment used in a trade or business
f. Unimproved land held as an investment for a warehouse used in a trade or business
g. An automobile used as a personal-use asset for marketable securities held for investment

I:12-27 *Like-Kind Property.* Which of the following exchanges qualify as like-kind exchanges under Sec. 1031?

a. A motel in Texas for a motel in Italy
b. An office building held for investment for an airplane to be used in the taxpayer's business
c. Land held for investment for marketable securities held for investment
d. Land held for investment for a farm to be used in the taxpayer's business

I:12-28 *Like-Kind Exchange: Boot.* Determine the realized gain or loss, the recognized gain or loss, and the basis of the equipment received for the following like-kind exchanges:

Basis of Equipment Exchanged	*FMV of Boot Received*	*FMV of Equipment Received*
$20,000	$ –0–	$85,000
45,000	14,000	70,000
60,000	25,000	65,000
70,000	38,000	60,000
90,000	22,000	55,000

I:12-29 ***Like-Kind Exchange: Personal Property.*** Beach Corporation owns a computer with a $34,000 adjusted basis. The computer is used in the company's trade or business. What is the realized and recognized gain or loss for each of the following independent transactions where the computer is exchanged for?

a. A used computer with a $70,000 FMV plus $16,000 cash.
b. A used computer with a $18,000 FMV plus $7,000 cash.
c. Marketable securities with a $61,000 FMV.

I:12-30 ***Like-Kind Exchange: Personal Property.*** Boise Corporation exchanges a machine with a $14,000 basis for a new machine with an $18,000 FMV and $3,000 cash. The machines are used in Boise's business and are in the same General Asset Class.

a. Determine Boise Corporation's recognized gain and the basis for the new machine.
b. How would your answer to Part a change if the corporation's machine is also subject to a $6,000 liability, and the liability is assumed by the other party?

I:12-31 ***Exchange of Personal Property.*** Lithuania Corporation operates a ferry service and owns four barges. Lithuania exchanges one of the barges with an adjusted basis of $350,000 for a used smaller barge with a FMV of $444,000 and a $26,000 computer. Without considering the exchange, Lithuania Corporation's taxable income is $700,000. Determine Lithuania's

a. realized gain on the exchange.
b. recognized gain.
c. basis of the new barge.
d. basis of the computer.
e. Assume that the recognized gain is $26,000 and the gain is not capital gain. What is the increase in Lithuania's tax liability as a result of the exchange?

I:12-32 ***Like-Kind Exchange: Liabilities.*** Paul owns a building used in his business with an adjusted basis of $340,000 and a $750,000 FMV. He exchanges the building for a building owned by David. David's building has a $950,000 FMV but is subject to a $200,000 liability. Paul assumes David's liability and uses the building in his business. What is Paul's

a. realized gain?
b. recognized gain?
c. basis for the building received?

I:12-33 ***Like-Kind Exchange: Liabilities.*** Helmut exchanges his apartment complex for Heidi's farm, and the exchange qualifies as a like-kind exchange. Helmut's adjusted basis for the apartment complex is $600,000 and the complex is subject to a $180,000 liability. The FMV of Heidi's farm is $770,000 and the farm is subject to a $100,000 liability. Each asset is transferred subject to the liability. What is Helmut's recognized gain and the basis of the new farm?

I:12-34 ***Like-Kind Exchange: Liabilities.*** Carol owns land used in her business with a basis of $70,000 and a fair market value of $90,000. She is planning to exchange the land for a warehouse owned by Jeff and used in his business. Jeff's warehouse has a basis of $50,000 and a fair market value of $110,000. The warehouse is also subject to a liability of $20,000. Carol has agreed to assume the liability for Jeff. What is Jeff's recognized gain and his basis in the new land?

I:12-35 ***Like-Kind Exchange: Transfer of Boot.*** Wayne exchanges unimproved land with a $50,000 basis and marketable securities with a $10,000 basis for an eight-unit apartment building having a $150,000 FMV. The land and marketable securities are held by Wayne as investments, and the apartment building is held as an investment. The marketable securities have a $25,000 FMV. What is his realized gain, recognized gain, and the basis for the apartment building?

I:12-36 ***Like-Kind Exchange: Related Parties.*** Bob owns a duplex used as rental property. The duplex has a basis of $86,000 and $300,000 FMV. He transfers the duplex to Cindy, his sister, in exchange for a triplex that she owns. The triplex has a basis of $279,000 and a

$300,000 FMV. Two months after the exchange, Cindy sells the duplex to a business associate for $312,000. Determine:
a. Bob's realized and recognized gain on the exchange.
b. Cindy's realized and recognized gain on the exchange.

I:12-37 *Like-Kind Exchange: Related Parties.* Assume the same facts as in I:12-36 except Cindy sells the duplex to a nonrelated individual more than two years after the exchange with Bob. Ignore any changes in adjusted basis due to depreciation that would have occurred after the exchange. Determine:
a. Bob's realized and recognized gain on the exchange.
b. Cindy's realized and recognized gain on the exchange.
c. Cindy's realized and recognized gain on the sale.

I:12-38 *Involuntary Conversion.* Duke Corporation owns an office building with a $400,000 adjusted basis. The building is destroyed by a tornado. The insurance company paid $750,000 as compensation for the loss. Eight months after the loss, Duke uses the insurance proceeds and other funds to acquire a new office building for $682,000 and machinery for one of the company's plants at a $90,000 cost. Assuming that Duke elects to defer as much of the gain as possible, what is the recognized gain, the basis for the new office building, and the basis for the machinery acquired?

I:12-39 *Involuntary Conversion: Replacement Period.* The Madison Corporation paid $3,000 for several acres of land in 1993 to use in its business. The land is condemned and taken by the state in March 2015. The company receives $25,000 from the state. Whenever possible, the corporation elects to minimize taxable income. For each of the following independent cases, what is the recognized gain or loss in 2015 on the conversion and the tax basis of the replacement property (replacement land will be purchased in July)?
a. 2016 for $22,500.
b. 2017 for $28,500.
c. 2018 for $23,600.

I:12-40 *Involuntary Conversion of Real Property.* On April 27, 2015, an office building owned by Newark Corporation, an offshore drilling company that is a calendar-year taxpayer, is destroyed by a hurricane. The basis of the office building is $600,000, and the corporation receives $840,000 from the insurance company.
a. To defer the entire gain due to the involuntary conversion, what amount must the corporation pay for replacement property?
b. To defer the gain due to the involuntary conversion, by what date must the corporation replace the converted property?
c. If Newark replaces the office building by purchasing a 900,000 gallon storage tank for $810,000, may it defer any of the gain due to the involuntary conversion?
d. Will answers to Parts b and c change if the office building had been condemned by the state? Explain.

I:12-41 *Involuntary Conversion: Different Methods of Replacement.* On September 3, 2015, Federal Corporation's warehouse is totally destroyed by fire. $800,000 of insurance proceeds are received, and the realized gain is $300,000. Whenever possible, Federal elects to defer gains. For each of the following independent situations, what is the amount of gain recognized? Explain why the gain is not deferred, if applicable.
a. On October 23, 2015, Federal purchases a warehouse for $770,000.
b. On February 4, 2016, Federal purchases 100% of the Park Corporation, which owns a warehouse. Federal pays $895,000 for the stock.
c. On November 20, 2017, Federal purchases an apartment complex for $900,000.
d. On March 26, 2018, Federal purchases a warehouse for $888,000.

I:12-42 *Severance Damages.* Twelve years ago, Marilyn purchased two lots in an undeveloped subdivision as an investment. Each lot has a $10,000 basis and a $40,000 FMV when the city condemns one lot for use as a municipal sewage treatment plant. As a result of the condemnation, Marilyn receives $40,000 from the city. Because the value of the other lot is reduced, the city pays $7,500 severance damages. She does not plan to replace the condemned lot. What is her:
a. recognized gain due to the condemnation?
b. recognized gain from the receipt of the severance damages?
c. basis for the lot she continues to own?

I:12-43 *Sale of a Principal Residence.* Marc, age 45, sells his personal residence on May 15, 2015, for $180,000. He pays $8,000 in selling expenses and $900 in repair expenses to help sell the residence. He has lived in the residence since 1980, when he purchased it for $55,000. In 1996, he paid $6,000 to install central air conditioning. If Marc purchases a new principal residence in December of the current year for $162,000, what is the realized gain, recognized gain, and the basis for the new residence?

I:12-44 *Sale of a Principal Residence.* Mr. and Mrs. Rusbarsky purchased a residence on June 12, 2012, for $200,000. On March 12, 2015, they sell the residence for $300,000, and selling expenses amount to $11,000. They purchase another house in a new subdivision for $275,000. Determine the gain realized and recognized.

I:12-45 *Sale of a Principal Residence.* On January 10, 2015, Kirsten married Joe. Joe sold his personal residence on October 25, 2014, and excluded the entire gain of $175,000. Although they had originally planned to live in the house that Kirsten had received as a gift from her parents in 2006, they decided to purchase a larger house, and Kirsten sold her house 60 days after their wedding and realized a $370,000 gain.

a. If they file a joint return, how much of the $370,000 gain may be excluded?

b. If Kirsten files as married filing separately, how much of the $370,000 gain may be excluded?

I:12-46 *Involuntary Conversion of Principal Residence.* Mr. and Mrs. Snell own and live in a house, with an adjusted basis of $300,000, that was purchased in 1994. The house is destroyed by a tornado on March 10 of the current year, and the Snells receive insurance proceeds of $410,000. They purchase another residence for $480,000 four months later.

a. May they exclude the $110,000 gain, and if so, what is the basis of the residence purchased in July?

b. May they defer the $110,000 gain, and if so, what is the basis of the residence purchased in July?

I:12-47 *Sale of a Principal Residence.* Mr. and Mrs. Kitchens purchased their first home in Ohio for $135,000 on October 1, 2014. Because Mr. Kitchens' employer transferred him to Utah, they sold the house for $160,000 on January 10, 2015. How much of the gain is recognized?

I:12-48 *Sale or Other Disposition of a Principal Residence.* In 1970, Mr. and Mrs. Self purchased their first principal residence for $80,000. In 1995, they sold the house for $300,000 and purchased a new residence for $1.5 million. At that time, the Selfs were allowed to defer the $220,000 gain because they purchased a more expensive residence, but the basis of the residence was reduced by the gain deferred. The Taxpayer Relief Act of 1997 eliminated this deferral provision and made it easier for taxpayers who sell a principal residence to exclude the gain resulting from the sale even if they do not purchase a replacement residence.

In 2001, the Selfs spent $200,000 to add a porch to their house that overlooks the small pond behind their house. In 2004, they hired painters to paint the entire house at a cost of $18,000. They estimate that $20,000 has been spent on routine repairs since 1995, but insurance of $11,000 was collected for the repairs resulting from a small tornado in 2008. No casualty loss deduction was allowed. They hold the residence as joint tenants.

1. What is the current adjusted basis of the house?
2. Mrs. Self is an employee of Bulldog Consulting and has a nice office on the business premises; however, she finds it helpful to use one of the bedrooms as an office to do work in the evenings and on weekends. May the Selfs claim a deduction for depreciation?
3. Determine their recognized gain and character if they sell the house today for $2.8 million.
4. If the property is owned by Mrs. Self instead of owned jointly, determine their recognized gain and character if they sell the house today for $2.8 million.
5. If the property is owned by Mrs. Self instead of owned jointly and Mr. Self dies, will the basis of the house be increased?
6. Determine their recognized gain if they exchange the house today for an apartment complex valued at $2.8 million. The Selfs will purchase another house and hire someone to manage the apartment complex.
7. If the house is destroyed by a fire when its FMV is $2.8 million and the Selfs receive $2.6 million, determine their casualty loss deduction and gain recognized, if any. The Selfs do not plan to purchase another residence.
8. If the Selfs want to purchase another principal residence after collecting the insurance in question #7 above, what is the minimum amount they would have to pay for the new residence to avoid recognizing any gain?

I:12-49 *Unqualified Use.* Sherron, who is single, purchased a house to use as rental property on April 1, 2007, for $300,000. He moved into the house on June 1, 2014, and used it as a personal residence until August 1, 2015, when he sells the house for $500,000. Depreciation allowed while property was used as rental property amounts to $25,000. Determine his:
a. realized gain on the sale
b. recognized gain on the sale
c. recognized gain on the sale if the house is not sold until August 1, 2016, for $500,000

I:12-50 *Sale of a Principal Residence: Rental Property.* For the last five years, Mr. and Mrs. Cockrell rented their furnished basement to local college students. When determining their taxable income each year, they deducted a portion of the utilities, property taxes, interest, and depreciation based on the fact that 15% of the house is used for rental purposes. The original basis of the property is $100,000, and depreciation of $4,000 has been allowed on the rental portion of the property. During the current year, Mr. and Mrs. Cockrell sell the house for $300,000. No selling expenses or fixing-up expenses are incurred. Determine:
a. realized gain on the sale.
b. recognized gain on the sale.

I:12-51 *Multiple Sales of a Principal Residence.* Consider the following information for Mr. and Mrs. Di Palma:

- On June 10, 2014, they sold their principal residence for $80,000 and incur $6,000 of selling expenses. The basis of the residence, acquired in 2004, is $50,000.
- On June 25, 2014, they purchased a new principal residence for $90,000 and occupied it immediately.
- On May 10, 2015, they purchase their neighbor's residence for $115,000 and occupy the residence immediately.
- On August 29, 2015, they sell the residence purchased on June 25, 2014, for $148,000. They pay $7,000 of selling expenses. Determine:

a. realized gain on the sale of the residence in 2014.
b. recognized gain on the sale of the residence in 2014.
c. realized gain on the sale of the residence in 2015.
d. recognized gain on the sale of the residence in 2015.

I:12-52 *Multiple Sales of a Principal Residence.* Consider the following information for Mr. and Mrs. Gomez:

- On May 26, 2014, they sold their principal residence, acquired in 1999, for $200,000. They paid $8,000 of selling expenses. Their basis in the residence was $70,000.
- On July 25, 2014, they purchased a new principal residence for $250,000.
- On June 2, 2015, Mr. Gomez, a bank officer, is transferred to another bank in the northern part of the state and they vacate their house.
- On July 1, 2015, they purchase a new principal residence for $420,000.
- On October 6, 2015, they sell the residence that was purchased on July 25, 2013, for $520,000. They pay $30,000 of selling expenses. Determine:

a. realized gain on the sale of the residence in 2014.
b. recognized gain on the sale of the residence in 2014.
c. realized gain on the sale of the residence in 2015.
d. recognized gain on the sale of the residence in 2015.

COMPREHENSIVE PROBLEM

I:12-53 Paden, who is single and has been employed as an accountant for 27 years with Harper, Inc., lost his job due to company downsizing. His last day of employment is July 31, 2015, and Harper provides a $9,000 severance payment. The severance payments are based on an employee's time of employment. During the year, Paden received a salary from Harper of $36,000. Harper also paid $1,500 of Paden's medical insurance premiums.

In May 2015, Paden, who had always wanted to be associated with a football team, applied for the head coaching job at Hawk University in Iowa and, much to his surprise, received the job beginning on August 1. In June and July, Paden paid $4,500 to take courses in sports management at the local university. Hawk University is substantially short of funding and Paden paid $2,000 for entertainment expenses related to his job and $500 for supplies. No reimbursement was received.

His salary from Hawk is $4,000 per month payable at the end of each month. His salary for December was not received until January 6, 2016.

On August 1, he sold his house for $329,000 in Texas and paid a sales commission of $14,000. He inherited the house 20 years ago when his mother died. Her basis for the house was $37,000 and the FMV when she died was $50,000. Property taxes for the 2015 calendar year amount to $3,600, and property taxes were apportioned at the closing. Property taxes are payable on October 1. He paid $12,000 of interest on home equity debt of $150,000.

To move to Iowa, he drove 700 miles and spent $45 for meals during the trip in July. Movers charged $4,150 to move his household items. Use the standard mileage rate for moving expenses for 2015 which is 23 cents per mile. He purchased a new house in Iowa for $150,000 on August 15 and borrowed $110,000. He also agreed to pay all property taxes for 2015. Real property taxes for the home in Iowa will be paid on January 30, 2016, and amount to $1,500. Interest on the $110,000 debt during the current year is $1,475. To obtain the loan, Paden paid points of $1,000.

He contributed common stock (basis of $1,000 and FMV of $6,000) held as an investment for three years to Hawk University. He also paid state income taxes of $1,765 (which was greater than state sales taxes for the year) as well as personal property taxes of $435 for his car.

Paden sold 200 shares of Dell Corporation stock on April 10 for $100 per share. His basis was $145 per share. On May 1, he purchased 300 shares of Dell at $89 per share.

Determine:

1. gross income without considering the sale of his house or the Dell Corporation stock.
2. recognized gain due to the sale of his house.
3. net capital gain.
4. adjusted gross income.
5. total amount of itemized deductions.
6. taxable income.
7. basis of his house in Iowa.
8. if the sales price for his home was $470,000 instead of $370,000, would his taxable income increase by more than $100,000. If yes, explain.

TAX STRATEGY PROBLEM

I:12-54 *Sale of a Principal Residence.* Ray and Ellie have each owned a principal residence used for more than five years. Ray's residence has an adjusted basis of $100,000 and a FMV of $325,000, while Ellie's residence has an adjusted basis of $300,000 and a FMV of $490,000. They plan to marry and will purchase another house.

a. Should they sell their houses before the marriage in order to minimize their taxes?
b. Will your answer to Part a change if the FMV of Ellie's house is $690,000?
c. In Part b, what tax strategy should Ray and Ellie consider?

TAX FORM/RETURN PREPARATION PROBLEMS

I:12-55 On October 29, 2014, Miss Joan Seely (SSN 123-45-6789) sells her principal residence for $150,000 cash. She purchased the residence on May 12, 2005, for $85,000. She spent $12,000 for capital improvements in 2005. To help sell the house, she pays $300 for minor repairs. The realtor's commission amounts to $7,500. Her old residence is never rented out or used for business. Complete the worksheet on page 12-24 for Miss Seely for 2014.

I:12-56 At the beginning of 2014, Donna Harp was employed as a cinematographer by Farah Movie, Inc., a motion picture company in Los Angeles, California. In June, she accepted a new job with Ocala Production in Orlando, Florida. Donna is single and her Social Security number is 000-00-1111. She sold her house in California on August 10 for $500,000. She paid a $14,000 sales commission. The house was acquired on March 23, 1987, for $140,000.

The cost of transporting her household goods and personal effects from California to Orlando amounted to $2,350. To travel from California to Florida, she paid travel and lodging costs of $370 and $100 for meals.

On July 15, she purchased a house for $270,000 on 1225 Minnie Lane in Orlando. To purchase the house, she incurred a 20-year mortgage for $170,000. To obtain the loan, she paid points of $3,400. The $3,600 of property taxes for the house in Orlando were prorated with $1,950 being apportioned to the seller and $1,650 being apportioned to the buyer. In December of the current year she paid $3,600 for property taxes.

Other information related to her return:

Salary from Farah Movie, Inc.	$30,000
Salary from Ocala Production, Inc.	70,000
Federal income taxes withheld by Farah	6,000
Federal income taxes withheld by Ocala	22,000
FICA taxes withheld by Farah	2,295
FICA taxes withheld by Ocala	5,355
Interest income from Sun National Bank	1,800
Dividend income	10,000
Interest paid for mortgage:	
Home in California	6,780
Home in Orlando	3,800
Property taxes paid in California	4,100
Sales taxes paid in California and Florida	3,125
State income taxes paid in California	2,900

Prepare Form 1040 including Schedules A, B, and D. Prepare Form 3903 and Form 8960. Use the worksheet on page 12-24 to determine the amount of recognized gain on the sale of the residence.

I:12-57 Jim Sarowski (SSN 000-00-2222) is 70 years old and single. He received Social Security benefits of $16,000. He works part-time as a greeter at a local discount store and received wages of $7,300. Federal income taxes of $250 were withheld from his salary. Jim lives at Rt. 7 in Daingerfield, Texas.

In March of 2014, he purchased a duplex at 2006 Tennessee Street to use as rental property for $100,000, with 20% of the price allocated to land. During the year, he had the following receipts and expenditures with respect to the duplex:

Rent receipts	$8,800
Interest paid	5,900
Property taxes	1,400
Insurance	800
Maintenance	300

Other expenditures during the year:

Contributions to the church	$2,600
Personal property taxes	225
Sales tax	345

On July 24, he exchanged ten acres of land for a car with a $16,500 FMV to be held for personal use. The land was purchased on November 22, 1991, for $18,000 as an investment. Because of pollution problems in the area, the value of the land declined.

On December 1, he sold his residence, which had been his home for 30 years, for $475,000. Sales commissions of $16,000 were paid, and the adjusted basis for his home is $110,000. He plans to rent an apartment and does not plan to purchase another home. His only other sale of a principal residence occurred 32 years ago.

Prepare Forms 1040 and 4562 and Schedules D and E. Use the worksheet on page 12-24 to determine the amount of recognized gain on the sale of the residence.

CASE STUDY PROBLEM

I:12-58 The Electric Corporation, a publicly held corporation, owns land with a $1,600,000 basis that is being held for investment. The company is considering exchanging the land for two assets owned by the Quail Corporation: land with a FMV of $4,000,000 and marketable securities with a $1,000,000 FMV. Both assets will be held by the Electric Corporation for investment, although the corporation is considering the possibility of developing the land and building residential houses. The president of the corporation has hired you to prepare a report explaining how the exchange will affect the corporation's reported net income and its tax liability. The corporation has a tax rate of 34%.

TAX RESEARCH PROBLEMS

I:12-59 For the last nine years, Mr. and Mrs. Orchard live in a residence located on eight acres. In January of the current year they sell the home and two acres of land. The purchaser of the residence does not wish to own the entire eight acres of land. In December they sell the remaining six acres of land to another individual for $60,000. The house and the land have never been used by the Orchards in a trade or business or held for investment. The realized gains resulting from the two sales are computed as follows:

	House and Two Acres January Sales	*Eight Acres December Sale*
Selling price	$140,000	$60,000
Minus: Selling expenses	(8,000)	(3,000)
Amount realized	$132,000	$57,000
Minus: Basis	(80,000)	(18,000)
Realized gain	$ 52,000	$39,000

As a result of the sales described above, what is the amount of realized gain that must be recognized during the current year?

A partial list of research sources is:

- Reg. Sec. 1.121-1(b)

I:12-60 George, age 68, decides to retire from farming and is considering selling his farm. The farm has a $100,000 basis and a $400,000 FMV. George's two sons are not interested in farming. Both sons have large families and would like to own houses suitable for their needs. The Iowa Corporation is willing to purchase George's farm. George's tax advisor suggests that Iowa Corporation should buy the two houses the sons want to own for $400,000 and then exchange the houses for George's farm. After the exchange, George could make a gift of the houses to the sons.

a. If the transactions are executed as suggested by the tax advisor, George's recognized gain will be $300,000. Explain why the transaction does not qualify as a like-kind exchange.

b. George wants the exchange to qualify as a like-kind exchange and still help his sons obtain the houses. What advice do you have for him?

A partial list of research sources is:

- *Dollie H. Click*, 78 T.C. 225 (1982)
- *Fred S. Wagensen*, 74 T.C. 653 (1980)

I:12-61 On March 10, 2012, Elizabeth, a college professor, purchased a house for $300,000. She did not move into the house until August 8, 2012. On August 1, 2013, she accepted a position as a visiting professor at Hogwatts University for one year and moved to Liverpool where she rented an apartment. While away at Hogwatts, two of her former students lived in the house but did not pay rent. She returned to the house on August 1, 2014, and lived in the house until July 15, 2015, when she sold the house for $500,000. The realtor's commission was $35,000. Determine her recognized gain.

A partial list of research sources is:

- Reg. Sec. 1.121-1(c)

I:12-62 Mr. and Mrs. Hattan have lived in their residence for 20 years and purchased the house for $100,000 as joint tenants with right of survivorship. Mr. Hattan died in May of the current year when the house's FMV was $800,000. Mrs. Hattan wants to sell the house. What is the tax effect of selling the house this year for $825,000 or next year for $830,000?

A partial list of research sources is:

- Sections 121 and 1014

I:12-63 Joseph Allen, who is single, purchased his first house in Orono, ME one year ago for $200,000. Katahdin wants to purchase the house for $360,000. Refer to the regulations to determine if he may exclude part of the gain in the following independent cases:

a. He has been unemployed for 16 months and has a chance to start work for Penobscot Manufacturing whose plant is located 62 miles from Joseph's home in Orono.

b. His dependent son, Ryan, has chronic asthma, and the son's doctor has advised Joseph that Ryan should live in a warm, dry climate to mitigate the chronic asthma. Joseph and Ryan move to Nevada.

c. Joseph has become increasingly annoyed at the amount of traffic in his neighborhood although the amount of traffic has not increased much compared to the traffic when he purchased the house.

A partial list of research sources is:

- Reg. Sec. 1.121-3(c), (d) and (e)

CHAPTER

13

PROPERTY TRANSACTIONS: SECTION 1231 AND RECAPTURE

LEARNING OBJECTIVES

After studying this chapter, you should be able to

1. Understand the basic tax treatment for Sec. 1231 transactions
2. Identify Sec. 1231 property
3. Understand the tax treatment for Sec. 1231 transactions
4. Apply the recapture provisions of Sec. 1245
5. Apply the recapture provisions of Sec. 1250
6. Understand recapture provisions for corporations
7. Describe other recapture applications
8. Describe tax planning considerations for Sec. 1231 assets
9. Describe compliance and procedural considerations for Sec. 1231 assets

CHAPTER OUTLINE

Chapter I:5 states that all recognized gains and losses must eventually be designated as either capital or ordinary. However, gains or losses on certain types of property are designated as Sec. 1231 gains or losses, which are given preferential treatment under the tax law. Section 1231 property primarily is business property, either real or depreciable property used in a trade or business.[1] A net Sec. 1231 loss, defined as the excess of Sec. 1231 losses over Sec. 1231 gains, is treated as an ordinary loss.[2] Net Sec. 1231 gain, the excess of Sec. 1231 gains over Sec. 1231 losses, is generally treated as long-term capital gain.[3] However, the preferential treatment of Sec. 1231 gains is diminished, principally by the so-called depreciation recapture rules and the five-year lookback rule. This chapter discusses the important rules dealing with Sec. 1231 gains and losses and depreciation recapture.

HISTORY OF SEC. 1231

During the depressed economy of the early and mid-1930s, business property was classified as a capital asset. Many business properties were worth less than their adjusted basis. Instead of selling business properties, taxpayers found it advantageous to retain assets that had declined in value because they could recover the full cost as depreciation. Capital losses had only limited deductibility during this period. To encourage the mobility of capital (i.e., the replacement of business fixed assets), the Revenue Act of 1938 added business property to the list of properties not considered to be capital assets.

KEY POINT

Taxpayers normally prefer to have gains treated as capital gains, and losses treated as ordinary losses. Because Sec. 1231 property receives the preferable treatment for both net gains and losses, it has been said that this property enjoys the best of both worlds.

From 1938 to 1942, gains and losses on the sale or exchange of business property were treated as ordinary gains and losses. Favorable capital gain treatment was eliminated and taxpayers with appreciated business properties were reluctant to sell the assets because of the high tax cost. This restriction on the mobility of capital was more significant than usual because business assets had to be shifted into industries that were heavily involved in the production of military goods. Furthermore, taxpayers were often forced to recognize ordinary gains because the government used the condemnation process to obtain business property for the war effort. In 1942, Congress created the predecessor of Sec. 1231, which allowed taxpayers to treat net gains from the sale of business property as capital gains and net losses as ordinary losses. Before 1987, only 40% of an individual's net capital gain might be subject to tax because of the 60% long-term capital gain deduction.

ADDITIONAL COMMENT

Beginning in 2013, higher-income taxpayers also have to pay an additional 3.8% tax on net investment income, which includes capital gains. Generally, for this provision, higher-income taxpayers are defined as those with modified AGI of greater than $200,000 if single or head of household and $250,000 if married, filing jointly. More information on this additional tax can be found in Chapter I:5.

The Tax Reform Act of 1986 eliminated the 60% long-term capital gain deduction for net capital gains. Favorable long-term capital gain treatment was reinstated into the tax law in 1991 in the form of a 28% maximum tax rate applying to net capital gains for noncorporate taxpayers. The Taxpayer Relief Act of 1997 significantly increased the preferential tax treatment by reducing the maximum rate to 20% for net capital gain that is adjusted net capital gain. The maximum rate was reduced by the Jobs and Growth Tax Relief Reconciliation Act of 2003 (2003 Tax Act) to 15%, for sales after May 5, 2003. The American Tax Relief Act of 2012 increased the maximum rate to 20% starting in 2013 for unmarried taxpayers with taxable income above $400,000 ($413,200 in 2015) and $450,000 ($464,850 in 2015) for married taxpayers (i.e., those taxpayers with a marginal tax rate of 39.6%).

It may also be advantageous to have gains classified as capital or Sec. 1231 if taxpayers have capital losses or capital loss carryovers because of the limitations imposed on the deductibility of capital losses. Furthermore, there are other situations where it may be important for the property to be Sec. 1231 property (e.g., a contribution of appreciated property to a charitable organization).

[1] (See page I:13-5 for a more complete definition of Sec. 1231 property.)
[2] Secs. 1231(c)(4) and (a)(2).
[3] Secs. 1231(c)(3) and (a)(1). There are several exceptions to this rule that are covered later in this chapter.

Overview of Basic Tax Treatment for Sec. 1231

OBJECTIVE 1

Understand the basic tax treatment for Sec. 1231 transactions

NET GAINS

At the end of the tax year, Sec. 1231 gains are netted against Sec. 1231 losses. If the overall result is a net Sec. 1231 gain, the gains and losses are treated as long-term capital gains (LTCGs) and long-term capital losses (LTCLs), respectively.[4] For the sake of expediency, it is often stated that a net Sec. 1231 gain is treated as a LTCG. However, a portion or all of the net Sec. 1231 gain may be treated as ordinary income because of a special five-year lookback rule (see discussion below).

EXAMPLE I:13-1 ▶ Dawn owns a business that has $20,000 of Sec. 1231 gains and $12,000 of Sec. 1231 losses during the current year. Because the Sec. 1231 gains exceed the Sec. 1231 losses, the gains and losses are treated as LTCGs and LTCLs. After the gains and losses are offset, there is an $8,000 net long-term capital gain (NLTCG). ◀

EXAMPLE I:13-2 ▶ Assume the same facts as in Example I:13-1 except that Dawn also recognizes a $7,000 LTCG from the sale of a capital asset. After considering the $8,000 net Sec. 1231 gain, which is treated as a LTCG, Dawn has a $15,000 NLTCG ($8,000 + $7,000). ◀

NET LOSSES

If the netting of Sec. 1231 gains and losses at the end of the year results in a net Sec. 1231 loss, the Sec. 1231 gains and losses are treated as ordinary gains and losses.[5] For expediency, it is often stated that the net Sec. 1231 loss is treated as an ordinary loss.

EXAMPLE I:13-3 ▶ David owns an unincorporated business and has $30,000 of Sec. 1231 gains and $40,000 of Sec. 1231 losses in the current year. Because the losses exceed the gains, they are treated as ordinary losses and gains. ◀

EXAMPLE I:13-4 ▶ Assume the same facts as in Example I:13-3 except that David receives a $67,000 salary as a corporate employee. David has no other income, losses, or deductions affecting his adjusted gross income (AGI). The Sec. 1231 gains and losses are treated as ordinary gains and losses, and David's AGI is $57,000 ($67,000 salary − $10,000 of ordinary loss). The $40,000 of ordinary losses offsets the $30,000 of ordinary gains and $10,000 of David's salary. ◀

TYPICAL MISCONCEPTION

It is sometimes erroneously thought that each Sec. 1231 gain should be treated as a LTCG and each Sec. 1231 loss as an ordinary loss. However all Sec. 1231 gains and losses must be combined to determine whether the Sec. 1231 gains and losses are LTCGs and LTCLs or ordinary gains and losses.

One important advantage of Sec. 1231 is illustrated in Example I:13-4. Because the Sec. 1231 gains and losses are treated as ordinary, the $10,000 net Sec. 1231 loss is fully deductible in the current year. If the gains and losses were classified as long-term capital gains and losses, David would have a $10,000 net long-term capital loss (NLTCL). Only $3,000 of the $10,000 NLTCL would have been deductible against David's other income. As explained in Chapter I:5, only $3,000 of net capital losses may be deducted from non-capital gain income per year for individual taxpayers.

ADDITIONAL COMMENT

A taxpayer's share of a Sec. 1231 loss from a partnership or S Corporation may be subject to the passive activity loss rules.

Five-Year Lookback Rule Beginning in 1985, the benefits of Sec. 1231 were reduced. For tax years beginning after 1984, any net Sec. 1231 gain is ordinary gain to the extent of any nonrecaptured net Sec. 1231 losses from the previous five years.[6] This provision is referred to as the *five-year lookback rule*. In essence, net Sec. 1231 losses previously deducted as ordinary losses are recaptured by changing what would otherwise be a LTCG into ordinary income.

EXAMPLE I:13-5 ▶ In 2015, Craig recognizes $25,000 of Sec. 1231 gains and $15,000 of Sec. 1231 losses. In 2011, Craig reported $14,000 of Sec. 1231 losses and no Sec. 1231 gains. No other Sec. 1231 gains or losses were recognized by Craig during the five-year period, 2010–2014. The $10,000

[4] Sec. 1231(a)(1).
[5] Sec. 1231(a)(2).
[6] Sec. 1231(c)(1).

HISTORICAL NOTE

Congress reduced the benefits of Sec. 1231 by requiring the recapture of any nonrecaptured net Sec. 1231 loss. This recapture is required because taxpayers have a certain amount of control over the timing of the recognition of Sec. 1231 gains or losses. Taxpayers attempted to recognize Sec. 1231 losses in one year and Sec. 1231 gains in another year to avoid the netting process.

($25,000 − $15,000) of net Sec. 1231 gain in 2015 is treated as ordinary income due to the $14,000 of nonrecaptured net Sec. 1231 losses. ◀

To determine the amount of nonrecaptured net Sec. 1231 losses, compare the aggregate amount of net Sec. 1231 losses for the most recent preceding five tax years with the amount of such losses recaptured as ordinary income for those preceding tax years. The excess of the aggregate amount of net Sec. 1231 losses over the previously recaptured loss is the nonrecaptured net Sec. 1231 loss. In Example I:13-5, the remaining $4,000 of nonrecaptured net Sec. 1231 losses could be recaptured in 2016. In 2016, the preceding five-year period includes 2011 through 2015.

TAX RATE FOR NET SEC. 1231 GAIN

In general, net Sec. 1231 gains are taxed similarly to net long-term capital gains. Thus, a Sec. 1231 gain may be taxed at a rate of 15% (or zero if the taxpayer's regular tax rate is 15% or less) or 20% if taxable income is above $413,200 for unmarried taxpayers and $464,850 for married taxpayers. Section 1231 property must have a holding period of more than one year. Recall from Chapter I:5 that adjusted net capital gain (ANCG) is net capital gain (NCG) determined *without* regard to:

(1) the 28% rate gain, and
(2) unrecaptured Sec. 1250 gain, which is taxed at no more than 25% as explained later.

ANCG might be taxed at 15% or zero. The tax rate on ANCG for taxpayers in the 10% or 15% tax brackets is 0%. If Sec. 1231 property is sold at a gain, the Sec. 1231 gain is LTCG if there are no Sec. 1231 losses or nonrecaptured net Sec. 1231 losses. However, all or part of this gain is unrecaptured Section 1250 gain if the asset is a building. Thus, net Sec. 1231 gain might be taxed today at 15%, 20%, or 25% depending on the taxpayer's tax rate and whether or not the gain is unrecaptured section 1250 gain. Part or all of Sec. 1231 gain due to the sale of real property subject to depreciation that is unrecaptured Sec. 1250 gain is taxed at a maximum of 25%.

EXAMPLE I:13-6 ▶ Savannah, whose tax rate is 28% and AGI is less than $413,200, sells land at a gain of $10,000 and other land at a gain of $15,000. Both tracts of land qualify as Sec. 1231 property. She has no other transactions involving capital assets or 1231 property and no nonrecaptured net Sec. 1231 losses. Savannah has net Sec. 1231 gain of $25,000 that is NLTCG and her NCG is $25,000. Her ANCG is $25,000 taxed at a rate of 15%. ◀

EXAMPLE I:13-7 ▶ Assume the same facts as in Example I:13-6 except Savannah also has a $7,000 loss from the sale of a third tract of land that is Sec. 1231 property. Her net Sec. 1231 gain is $18,000. Her NCG is $18,000 and her ANCG is $18,000 taxed at a rate of 15%. ◀

EXAMPLE I:13-8 ▶ Grace, whose tax rate is 15% or less, sells land that is Sec. 1231 property at a gain of $2,000. She has no other transactions involving capital assets or 1231 property and no nonrecaptured net Sec. 1231 losses. The $2,000 gain is not taxed since her tax rate for ANCG is zero. ◀

ADDITIONAL COMMENT

Because Sec. 1231 property in Examples I:13-6, I:13-7, and I:13-8 is land, none of the gain is unrecaptured Section 1250 gain.

Applying the Five-Year Lookback Rule. As explained earlier, net Sec. 1231 gain is ordinary income to the extent of nonrecaptured net Sec. 1231 losses. Net Sec. 1231 gain is recharacterized as ordinary income under the five-year lookback rule in the following order:

(1) Net Sec. 1231 gain in the 25% group (unrecaptured Sec. 1250 gain)
(2) Net Sec. 1231 gain in the 20% or 15% group

EXAMPLE I:13-9 ▶ Chris, whose tax rate is 33%, has nonrecaptured net Sec. 1231 losses of $20,000 at the beginning of the current year when he recognizes gains from the sale of two assets used in his trade or business and held more than one year. Asset #1 is a building and the entire $14,000 Sec. 1231 gain is unrecaptured Sec. 1250 gain. Asset #2 is land and the Sec. 1231 gain is $15,000. All gain resulting from the sale of asset #1 is ordinary income and $6,000 of the gain from the sale of asset #2 is ordinary income because of the five-year lookback rule. The remaining $9,000 gain from the sale of asset #2 (land) is taxed at 15%. ◀

Section 1231 Property

OBJECTIVE 2

Identify Sec. 1231 property

SECTION 1231 PROPERTY DEFINED

Section 1231 property includes the following types of property:

- Real property or depreciable property used in a trade or business with a holding period of more than one year
- Timber, coal, or domestic iron ore
- Livestock
- Unharvested crops

Each of these types of Sec. 1231 assets are discussed below.

REAL OR DEPRECIABLE PROPERTY USED IN TRADE OR BUSINESS

KEY POINT

Inventory, free publications of the U.S. government, and copyrights, as well as literary, musical, or artistic compositions are not capital assets.

As noted in Chapter I:5, the IRC does not provide a definition of a capital asset. Instead, Sec. 1221 provides a list of noncapital assets. This list includes both depreciable property and real property used in a trade or business.[7] These properties are treated as Sec. 1231 properties if held for more than one year. Depreciable property and real property used in a trade or business and held for **one year or less** are neither capital assets nor Sec. 1231 property. Any gain or loss resulting from the disposition of such assets is ordinary.

EXAMPLE I:13-10 ► The Prime Corporation owns land held as an investment and land used as an employee parking lot. The land held as an investment is a capital asset. The land used as a parking lot is real property used in a trade or business and is not a capital asset. The land used as a parking lot is a Sec. 1231 asset if held for more than one year. ◄

EXAMPLE I:13-11 ► Dale, a self-employed plumber, owns an automobile held for personal use and a truck used in his trade. The automobile is a capital asset, but the truck is a Sec. 1231 asset if held for more than one year. As described later, a portion or all of any gain realized on the sale of the truck may be taxed as ordinary income due to the Sec. 1245 depreciation recapture provisions which are explained on page 8. ◄

KEY POINT

Only property used in a trade or business is included in the definition of Sec. 1231 property. Gains and losses on property held for investment may be included only if the result of a condemnation or casualty.

Certain types of property do not qualify as Sec. 1231 property, even if used in a trade or business. For example, inventory is not Sec. 1231 property. Thus, a sale of inventory results in ordinary gain or loss. Publications of the U.S. Government received other than by purchase at its regular sale price; a copyright; literary, musical, or artistic compositions; letters or memorandums; or similar properties held by certain taxpayers, such as their creator, are not classified as Sec. 1231 property.[8]

EXAMPLE I:13-12 ► Carl, who owns a recording studio, writes a musical composition and obtains a copyright that is sold to a record company. Because the musical composition is created by the personal efforts of the taxpayer, the musical composition is not Sec. 1231 property, and the sale results in ordinary gain from the sale of an ordinary asset. ◄

KEY POINT

The record company in example I:13-12 may amortize the cost of the copyright. The copyright is Sec. 1231 property if held more than one year.

Timber. Section 631 allows taxpayers to elect to treat the cutting of timber as a sale or exchange of such timber. To be eligible to make this election, the taxpayer must own the timber or hold the contract right on the first day of the year and for more than one year. Furthermore, the timber must be cut for sale or for use in the taxpayer's trade or business.[9]

REAL-WORLD EXAMPLE

Christmas trees can be included in the definition of Sec. 1231 property.

The gain or loss is determined by comparing the timber's adjusted basis for depletion with its fair market value (FMV) on the first day of the tax year in which it is cut. If the timber is eventually sold for more or less than its FMV (determined on the first day of the year the timber is cut), the difference is ordinary gain or loss.

[7] Sec. 1221(2).
[8] Sec. 1231(b)(1).
[9] Sec. 631(a) and Reg. Sec. 1.631-1.

EXAMPLE I:13-13 ▶ Vermont Corporation owns timber with a $60,000 basis for depletion. The timber, acquired four years ago, is cut during the current year for use in the corporation's business. The FMV of the timber on the first day of the current year is $200,000. Vermont Corporation may elect to treat the cutting of the timber as a sale or exchange and recognize a $140,000 ($200,000 − $60,000) gain. ◀

SELF-STUDY QUESTION

Is the possible inclusion of timber and coal or domestic iron ore in the definition of Sec. 1231 property favorable to the taxpayers who produce these items?

ANSWER

Yes, it can result in income being taxed at rates applicable for LTCG instead of ordinary income from the sale of inventory.

ADDITIONAL COMMENT

Livestock includes cattle, hogs, horses, mules, donkeys, sheep, goats, fur-bearing animals, and other mammals but excludes poultry, fish, frogs, and reptiles.

ADDITIONAL COMMENT

The treatment of unharvested crops as a Sec. 1231 asset is largely a rule of convenience. If the taxpayer were not permitted to treat the crops in this fashion, it would be necessary to allocate the selling price between the land and crops.

If the election is made to treat the cutting of timber as a sale or exchange, the timber is considered Sec. 1231 property.[10] Thus, the $140,000 gain in Example I:13-13 is Sec. 1231 gain. If the taxpayer does not make the election, the character of any gain or loss depends on whether the timber is held for sale in the ordinary course of the taxpayer's trade or business, held for investment, or held for use in a trade or business.

Coal or Domestic Iron Ore. An owner who disposes of coal (including lignite) or domestic iron ore while retaining an economic interest in it must treat the disposal as a sale.[11] The coal or iron ore is considered Sec. 1231 property.[12] The owner must own and retain an economic interest in the coal or iron ore in place.[13] An economic interest is owned when one acquires by investment any interest in mineral in place and seeks a return of capital from income derived from the extraction of the mineral.

Livestock. Livestock held by the taxpayer for draft, breeding, dairy, or sporting purposes is considered Sec. 1231 property if held for 12 months or more from the date of acquisition. However, cattle and horses must be held for 24 months or more from the date of acquisition to qualify as Sec. 1231 property.[14]

Unharvested Crops and Land. An unharvested crop growing on land used in a trade or business is considered Sec. 1231 property if the crop and the land are both sold at the same time to the same person and the land is held more than one year.[15] Section 1231 does not apply to the sale or exchange of an unharvested crop if the taxpayer retains any right or option to reacquire the land.[16]

If Sec. 1231 applies to the sale or exchange of an unharvested crop sold with the land, no deductions are allowed for expenses attributable to the production of the unharvested crop.[17] Instead, costs of producing the crop must be capitalized.

INVOLUNTARY CONVERSIONS

Gains and losses from involuntary conversions of property used in a trade or business generally are classified as Sec. 1231 gains and losses. Involuntary conversions of capital assets that are held in connection with a trade or business or in a transaction entered into for profit also generally qualify for Sec. 1231 treatment. The property that is involuntarily converted must be held more than one year. Certain involuntary conversions are treated differently for income tax purposes. For example, the tax rules are different for condemnations and casualties, even though both are involuntary conversions of property.

CONDEMNATIONS

Gains and losses resulting from condemnations of Sec. 1231 property and capital assets held more than one year are classified as Sec. 1231 gains and losses. As indicated above, the capital assets must be held in connection with a trade or business or with a transaction entered into for profit.[18]

EXAMPLE I:13-14 ▶ Kathryn owns land with a $20,000 basis and a $30,000 FMV as well as a building with a $40,000 adjusted basis and a $26,000 FMV. Both assets are used in her trade or business and have been held for more than one year. As a result of the state exercising its powers of requisition or

[10] Sec. 1231(b)(2) and Reg. Sec. 1.631-1(d)(4).
[11] Sec. 631(c) and Reg. Sec. 1.631-3(a)(1).
[12] Sec. 1231(b)(2) and Reg. Sec. 1.631-3(a)(2).
[13] Reg. Sec. 1.631-3(b)(4).
[14] Sec. 1231(b)(3).
[15] Sec. 1231(b)(4) and Reg. Secs. 1.1231-1(c)(5) and 1(f).
[16] Reg. Sec. 1.1231-1(f).
[17] Sec. 268 and Reg. Sec. 1.268-1.
[18] Secs. 1231(a)(3)(A) and (4)(B).

condemnation, Kathryn is required to transfer both properties to the state for cash equal to their FMVs. No other transfers of assets occur during the current year. The $10,000 gain due to condemnation of the land is a Sec. 1231 gain and the $14,000 loss due to condemnation of the building is a Sec. 1231 loss. ◀

OTHER INVOLUNTARY CONVERSIONS

TYPICAL MISCONCEPTION

The inclusion of gains and losses from condemnations in the netting of the other involuntary conversions is a common error.

Gains or losses resulting from an involuntary conversion arising from fire, storm, shipwreck, other casualty, or theft are not classified as Sec. 1231 gains or losses if the recognized losses from such conversions exceed the recognized gains.[19] In such a case, the involuntary conversions are treated as ordinary gains and losses. However, if the gains from such involuntary conversions exceed the losses, both are classified as Sec. 1231 gains and losses.

EXAMPLE I:13-15 ▶ Jose owns equipment having a $50,000 adjusted basis and a $42,000 FMV and a building having a $30,000 adjusted basis and a $35,000 FMV which are used in Jose's trade or business. The straight-line method of depreciation is used for the building. Both assets are held for more than a year. As a result of a fire, both assets are destroyed, and Jose collects insurance proceeds equal to the assets' FMV. No other transfers of assets occur during the current year. Because the $8,000 ($42,000 − $50,000) recognized loss exceeds the $5,000 ($35,000 − $30,000) recognized gain, the recognized loss and gain are both treated as ordinary. ◀

PROCEDURE FOR SEC. 1231 TREATMENT

OBJECTIVE 3

Understand the tax treatment for Sec. 1231 transactions

After determining the recognized gains and losses from transfers of property qualifying for Sec. 1231 treatment, it is necessary to determine whether any gain must be recaptured as ordinary income under Secs. 1245 and 1250. The recaptured gain, discussed later in this chapter, is not eligible for Sec. 1231 treatment. After eliminating the gain recaptured as ordinary income due to the recapture of depreciation, the procedure for analyzing Sec. 1231 transactions is as follows:

STEP 1. Determine all gains and losses resulting from casualties or thefts of Sec. 1231 property and non–personal-use capital assets held for more than one year. Gains and losses are netted and the net gain is treated as Sec. 1231 gain if the gains exceed the losses. If the losses exceed the gains, both are treated as ordinary losses and gains and do not, therefore, enter into the Sec. 1231 netting procedure. Recall from Chapter I:7 that business casualty losses are deductible *for* AGI and other casualty losses are deductible *from* AGI.

KEY POINT

Gains that are recaptured under Secs. 1245 and 1250 are not eligible for Sec. 1231 treatment.

STEP 2. Combine the following gains and losses to determine whether Sec. 1231 gains exceed Sec. 1231 losses or vice versa:

- Net casualty and theft *gains* resulting from Step 1, if any
- Gains and losses resulting from the sale or exchange of Sec. 1231 property
- Gains and losses resulting from the condemnation of Sec. 1231 property and non–personal-use capital assets held more than one year.

If a net Sec. 1231 loss is the result, the losses and gains are treated as ordinary losses and gains. If a net Sec. 1231 gain is the result, the gains and losses are treated as LTCGs and LTCLs, although a portion or all of the capital gain may be recaptured as ordinary income as outlined in Step 3 (five-year lookback rule) below.

STEP 3. If a net Sec. 1231 gain is the result of Step 2, determine if the taxpayer has any nonrecaptured net Sec. 1231 losses. Nonrecaptured net Sec. 1231 losses are the excess of aggregate net Sec. 1231 losses for the preceding five years over losses previously recaptured as ordinary income due to the recapture provision of Sec. 1231. Net Sec. 1231 gains to the extent of any nonrecaptured net Sec. 1231 losses are treated as ordinary income. Section 1231 gain that is unrecaptured Sec. 1250 gain is first treated as ordinary income to the extent of nonrecaptured net Sec. 1231 losses. Any net Sec. 1231 gain in excess of nonrecaptured net Sec. 1231 loss is treated as a LTCG.

---

[19] Sec. 1231(a)(4)(C).

EXAMPLE I:13-16 ▶ The following gains and losses pertain to Danielle's business assets that qualify as Sec. 1231 property. Danielle does not have any nonrecaptured net Sec. 1231 losses from previous years, and the portion of gain recaptured as ordinary income due to the depreciation recapture provisions has been considered.

Gain due to an insurance reimbursement for fire damage	$10,000
Loss due to condemnation	(19,000)
Gain due to the sale of Sec. 1231 property	22,000

The $10,000 casualty gain is classified as a Sec. 1231 gain because gains resulting from casualties or thefts of Sec. 1231 property exceed losses. Danielle has $32,000 ($10,000 + $22,000) of Sec. 1231 gains and a $19,000 Sec. 1231 loss. Danielle's $13,000 net Sec. 1231 gain is treated as a LTCG. No portion of the $13,000 LTCG is recaptured as ordinary income because Danielle does not have any nonrecaptured net Sec. 1231 losses during the preceding five-year period. ◀

ADDITIONAL COMMENT

If Danielle has AGI of $80,000 without considering the gains and losses in Example I:13-16, her AGI is $93,000.

EXAMPLE I:13-17 ▶ Assume the same facts as in Example I:13-16 except that Danielle has a $10,000 loss because of the fire instead of a $10,000 gain. The $10,000 casualty loss is an ordinary loss, not a Sec. 1231 loss because losses resulting from casualties or thefts of Sec. 1231 property exceed gains. Because the loss is a business loss, it is deductible *for* AGI. Due to the $19,000 condemnation loss and the $22,000 of Sec. 1231 gain, she has a $3,000 net Sec. 1231 gain that is treated as a LTCG. ◀

EXAMPLE I:13-18 ▶ The following gains and losses recognized in 2015 pertain to Fred's business assets that were held for more than one year. The assets qualify as Sec. 1231 property.

Gain due to an insurance reimbursement for a casualty	$15,000
Gain due to a condemnation	25,000
Loss due to the sale of Sec. 1231 property	(12,000)

A summary of Fred's net Sec. 1231 gains and losses for the previous five-year period is as follows:

Year	*Sec. 1231 Gain*	*Sec. 1231 Loss*	*Cumulative Nonrecaptured Net Sec. 1231 Losses (from five prior years)*
2010	$ 5,000		–0–
2011		$2,000	$2,000
2012		6,000	8,000
2013	13,000		–0–
2014		9,000	9,000

The $15,000 gain due to the insurance reimbursement for a casualty is treated as a Sec. 1231 gain. The $25,000 gain from the condemnation is also a Sec. 1231 gain. Fred's net Sec. 1231 gain in 2015 is $28,000 [($15,000 + $25,000) − $12,000]. However, $9,000 of the Sec. 1231 gain is recaptured as ordinary income due to the $9,000 of nonrecaptured net Sec. 1231 loss existing at the end of 2014. The remaining $19,000 of net Sec. 1231 gain is a LTCG. ◀

ADDITIONAL COMMENT

If Danielle has AGI of $80,000 without considering the gains and losses in Example I:13-17, her AGI is $73,000.

RECAPTURE PROVISIONS OF SEC. 1245

OBJECTIVE 4

Apply the recapture provisions of Sec. 1245

In 1962, Congress enacted Sec. 1245, which substantially reduced the advantages of Sec. 1231. A gain from the disposition of Sec. 1245 property is treated as ordinary income to the extent of the total amount of depreciation (or cost-recovery) deductions allowed since January 1, 1962. The gain recaptured as ordinary income cannot exceed the amount of the realized gain.

EXAMPLE I:13-19 ▶ Adobe Corporation sells equipment used in its trade or business for $95,000. The equipment was acquired several years ago for $110,000 and is Sec. 1245 property.[20] The equipment's adjusted basis is $60,000 because $50,000 of depreciation was deducted. The entire $35,000 ($95,000 − $60,000) gain is treated as ordinary income because the total amount of depreciation taken ($50,000) is greater than the $35,000 realized gain. ◀

---

20 Throughout this chapter, property is considered to be placed in service when it is purchased or acquired. The term *Sec. 1245 property* is used here to refer to either recovery property under the ACRS or MACRS rules or nonrecovery property that falls outside of the ACRS or MACRS rules.

TYPICAL MISCONCEPTION

It is sometimes thought that only tangible property is subject to Sec. 1245 recapture. In fact, both tangible and intangible personal property are included.

The recapture provisions of Sec. 1245 apply to the total amount of depreciation (or cost recovery) allowed or allowable for Sec. 1245 property. It makes no difference which method of depreciation is used.[21]

Generally, the entire gain from the disposition of Sec. 1245 property is recaptured as ordinary income because the total amount of depreciation (or cost recovery) is greater than the gain realized. A portion of the gain will receive Sec. 1231 treatment if the realized gain exceeds total depreciation or cost recovery.

EXAMPLE I:13-20 ▶ Assume the same facts as in Example I:13-19 except that the asset is sold for $117,000. Because the $57,000 ($117,000 − $60,000) realized gain is greater than the $50,000 of total depreciation, $50,000 of the gain is ordinary income and the remaining $7,000 is a Sec. 1231 gain. ◀

ADDITIONAL COMMENT

Section 1245 does not apply to losses because in these cases the taxpayers have not taken more depreciation than the asset's decline in value.

PURPOSE OF SEC. 1245

The purpose of Sec. 1245 is to eliminate any advantage taxpayers would have if they were able to reduce ordinary income by deducting depreciation and subsequently receive Sec. 1231 treatment when the asset was sold. For individuals, Sec. 1245 recapture prevents net Sec. 1231 gain from being treated as LTCG. The conversion of Sec. 1231 gain to Sec. 1245 ordinary income also prevents taxpayers from possibly using capital losses.

EXAMPLE I:13-21 ▶ During the current year, Coastal Corporation has capital losses of $50,000 and no capital gains for the current year or the preceding three years. The corporation owns equipment purchased several years ago for $90,000, and depreciation deductions of $48,000 have been allowed. If Coastal sells the equipment for $72,000, the entire $30,000 ($72,000 − $42,000) gain, which is due to the depreciation deductions, is Sec. 1245 ordinary income. Without Sec. 1245, the $30,000 gain is a Sec. 1231 gain that could be offset by $30,000 of the corporation's capital loss if Coastal has net Sec. 1231 gain. ◀

KEY POINT

On the sale of Sec. 1245 property, a portion of the gain is treated as Sec. 1231 gain only if the property is sold for more than the original cost. This is very unlikely for factory equipment, trucks, office equipment, and other Sec. 1245 property.

Note that Sec. 1245 does not apply to losses. If Coastal Corporation sells the equipment in Example I:13-21 for $40,000, a $2,000 ($40,000 − $42,000 basis) Sec. 1231 loss is recognized.

KEY POINT

Property must be depreciable or amortizable to be considered Sec. 1245 property.

Section 1245 Property. **Section 1245 property** is certain property subject to depreciation and, in some cases, amortization. The most common example of Sec. 1245 property is depreciable personal property such as equipment. Automobiles, livestock, railroad grading, and single-purpose agricultural or horticultural structures are Sec. 1245 properties as well as intangible assets subject to amortization under Sec. 197 (see Chapter I:10).[22] Except for certain buildings placed in service after 1980 and before 1987, buildings and structural components generally are not Sec. 1245 property.[23]

EXAMPLE I:13-22 ▶ Buckeye Corporation owns the following assets acquired in 2009: equipment, a patent, an office building (including structural components), and land. The equipment and patent are Sec. 1245 property. The office building and the land are not Sec. 1245 property. ◀

REAL-WORLD EXAMPLE

Pipelines, electric transmission towers, blast furnaces, greenhouses, and oil tanks are examples of real property that are included in the definition of Sec. 1245 property.

In many cases, taxpayers are allowed preferential treatment with respect to amortizing certain costs. For example, taxpayers may elect to expense up to $15,000 of the cost of making any business facility more accessible to handicapped and elderly people,[24] or to amortize pollution control facilities over 60 months[25] and reforestation expenditures over 84 months.[26] If taxpayers have amortized the costs of any real property under the special provisions, Sec. 1245 applies to the gain resulting from the disposition of such property.[27]

If taxpayers elect to expense certain depreciable property under Sec. 179, the amount deducted is treated as a depreciation deduction for purposes of the Sec. 1245 recapture provisions.[28]

---

21 As explained later in this chapter, the method of cost recovery used determines whether certain real property is treated as Sec. 1245 recovery property.

22 Sec. 1245(a)(3).

23 Sec. 1245(a)(3)(B)(i). Tangible real property "used as an integral part of the manufacturing, production, extraction, or furnishing of transportation, communication, electrical energy, gas, water, or sewage disposal services" is Sec. 1245 property.

24 Sec. 190.

25 Sec. 169(a).

26 Sec. 194(a).

27 Sec. 1245(a)(3)(C). The Sec. 1245 rules recapture amortization deductions claimed on real property under Secs. 169, 179, 185, 188, 190, 193, and 194.

28 Sec. 1245(a)(2)(C). The maximum amount deductible under Sec. 179 is $25,000 in 2015 unless Congress decides to increase the amount, $500,000 in 2010–2014, $250,000 in 2008–2009, $125,000 in 2007, $108,000 in 2006, and $105,000 in 2005.

EXAMPLE I:13-23 ▶ Compact Corporation purchased $90,000 of five-year equipment on March 10, 2014, and elected to expense $20,000 of the cost under Sec. 179. Compact sells the equipment on July 30, 2015, for $95,000. Regular depreciation allowed under MACRS for 2014 and 2015 is $14,000 and $11,200 (1/2 year), respectively. The adjusted basis of the equipment on the date of sale is $44,800 ($90,000 − $20,000 − $25,200 depreciation). The realized gain is $50,200 ($95,000 − $44,800), and $45,200 ($20,000 + $25,200) of the gain is Sec. 1245 ordinary income. The remaining $5,000 is Sec. 1231 gain. ◀

TYPICAL MISCONCEPTION

The categorization of nonresidential real estate acquired between 1981 and 1986 on which an accelerated depreciation method was used as Sec. 1250 property rather than as Sec. 1245 property is a common error.

Application of Sec. 1245 to Nonresidential Real Estate. Most real property is not affected by Sec. 1245. However, Sec. 1245 does apply to nonresidential real estate that qualified as recovery property under the ACRS rules (i.e., placed in service after 1980 and before 1987) unless the taxpayer elected to use the straight-line method of cost recovery.[29] Section 1245 does not apply to depreciable real estate acquired after 1986.

EXAMPLE I:13-24 ▶ Brad sells two warehouses during the current year that are totally depreciated because their recovery period is 19 years.

HISTORICAL NOTE

Taxpayers acquiring nonresidential real property between 1981 and 1986 were confronted with choosing between straight-line ACRS and ACRS using the statutory rates. In making the decision, these taxpayers should have considered the number of years the property would be held, the estimated selling price, the present value of the tax savings due to deducting depreciation sooner, and any preferential treatment for net capital gains.

	Warehouse 1	*Warehouse 2*
Year of purchase	1985	1985
Cost*	$720,000	$900,000
Cost recovery—straight line ACRS	720,000	
Cost recovery—ACRS statutory rates (accelerated)		900,000
Adjusted basis	0	0
Selling price	700,000	800,000

*does not consider the cost of land

Both warehouses were placed in service after 1980 and before 1987 and qualify as recovery property under ACRS. The $700,000 ($700,000 − $0) gain on the sale of Warehouse 1 is a Sec. 1231 gain. Section 1245 does not apply because Brad elected to use the straight-line method of cost recovery. Section 1245 applies to the sale of Warehouse 2 because ACRS was used and the property is nonresidential real estate placed in service after 1980 and before 1987. Therefore, the $800,000 ($800,000 − $0) gain is Sec. 1245 ordinary income because the $800,000 gain is less than the $900,000 total ACRS cost-recovery allowance. ◀

As illustrated in the example above, nonresidential buildings placed in service after 1980 and before 1987 are Sec. 1245 property if an accelerated method of cost recovery was used.

If the properties in Example I:13-24 were acquired before 1981 or after 1986, they would not be subject to the Sec. 1245 recapture rules regardless of the method of depreciation used.

The Sec. 1245 recapture rules are summarized in Topic Review I:13-1.

RECAPTURE PROVISIONS OF SEC. 1250

OBJECTIVE 5

Apply the recapture provisions of Sec. 1250

In 1964, Sec. 1250 was enacted to extend the recapture concept to include most depreciable real property. Unlike Sec. 1245, where the recapture is based upon the total amount of depreciation (or cost recovery) allowed, Sec. 1250 applies solely to additional depreciation. **Additional depreciation**, also referred to as **excess depreciation**, is the excess of the actual amount of accelerated depreciation (or cost-recovery deductions under ACRS) over

[29] Sec. 1245(a)(5).

TOPIC REVIEW I:13-1

Section 1245 Recapture

- Section 1245 affects the character of the gain, not the amount of gain. Character refers to gain being classified as either ordinary income or Sec. 1231 gain.
- Section 1245 does not apply to assets sold or exchanged at a loss.
- Section 1245 ordinary income is never more than the realized gain.
- Section 1245 recapture applies to the total depreciation or amortization allowed or allowable but not more than the realized gain.
- Section 1245 property includes depreciable personal property and amortizable intangible assets (e.g., a patent).
- Section 1245 property includes nonresidential real estate placed in service after 1980 and before 1987 under the ACRS rules *unless* the taxpayer elected to use the straight-line method of cost recovery.
- Section 1245 does not apply to any buildings placed in service after 1986.

the amount of depreciation that would be deductible under the straight-line method. Any gain due to excess depreciation is Sec. 1250 ordinary income.

EXAMPLE I:13-25 ► Wyatt sells a building that was placed in service before 1981 and the gain is $50,000. Accelerated depreciation was used and excess depreciation amounts to $74,000. All $50,000 of the gain is Sec. 1250 ordinary income. If the gain is $90,000, $74,000 is Sec. 1250 ordinary income and $16,000 is Sec. 1231 gain. ◄

ADDITIONAL COMMENT

Since buildings generally must be depreciated on a straight-line basis since 1987, Sec. 1250 depreciation recapture becomes less and less applicable as time passes.

PURPOSE OF SEC. 1250

Section 1250 has the effect of converting a portion of the Sec. 1231 gain into ordinary income when real property is sold or exchanged. The incremental benefits from using accelerated depreciation or ACRS cost recovery may be recaptured when the property is sold. Noncorporate taxpayers can avoid Sec. 1250 recapture by either using the straight-line method of depreciation or cost recovery or holding the Sec. 1250 property for its entire useful life or recovery period.

The Sec. 1250 recapture rules are applied solely to the additional depreciation amount instead of total depreciation allowable as is the case for Sec. 1245 property. Sec. 1250 provides for less depreciation recapture than Sec. 1245.

ADDITIONAL COMMENT

Elevators and escalators are Sec. 1245 property if placed in service before 1987, but Sec. 1250 property if placed in service after 1986.

SECTION 1250 PROPERTY DEFINED

Section 1250 property is any depreciable real property other than Sec. 1245 property.[30] As stated on page 10, nonresidential real estate placed in service after 1980 and before 1987 is Sec. 1245 property unless the straight-line method of cost recovery is elected. The property is Sec. 1250 property if straight-line cost recovery is elected.

Depreciation recapture is not required on real property placed in service after 1986 because such property must be depreciated under the straight-line MACRS rules.[31]

KEY POINT

An apartment building is the most common type of property classified as residential real estate.

EXAMPLE I:13-26 ► Frances, whose marginal tax rate is less than 39.6%, sells an office building during the current year for $800,000. The office building was purchased before 1981 for $700,000* and depreciation of $500,000 has been allowed using an accelerated method of depreciation. If the straight-line method was used, depreciation would be $420,000. The office building is Sec. 1250 property. Her recognized gain is $600,000 and $80,000 is Sec. 1250 ordinary income due to excess depreciation ($500,000 − $420,000). The remaining $520,000 gain is Sec. 1231 gain.

If Frances purchased the building after 1986, she was required to use the straight-line method. Thus her recognized gain is $520,000 ($800,000 − $280,000) with straight-line depreciation being $420,000. None of the gain is Sec. 1250 ordinary income. The gain is Sec. 1231 gain. ◄

*does not consider the cost of land

ADDITIONAL COMMENT

If the building in Example I:13-26 was placed in service after 1980 and before 1987, the building is Sec. 1245 property if Frances uses accelerated cost recovery and not the straight-line method.

[30] Sec. 1250(c).

[31] As explained in the Additional Recapture for Corporations section in this chapter, corporations may have depreciation recapture under Sec. 291(a) despite the use of straight-line depreciation.

SELF-STUDY QUESTION

In Example I:13-24, how much of the $700,000 Sec. 1231 gain resulting from the sale of warehouse #1 is unrecaptured Sec. 1250 gain?

ANSWER

All $700,000

HISTORICAL NOTE

Prior to the Taxpayer Relief Act of 1997, all LTCGs were taxed at a maximum rate of 28%. When the maximum rate was reduced to 20% (now 15% unless taxable income exceeds threshold amounts when the rate is 20%). Congress did not extend this favorable treatment to depreciable real estate. The maximum rate on this type of property was reduced from 28% to 25%.

As explained below, $420,000 of the Sec. 1231 gain in Example 13-26 is taxed at a maximum rate of 25% and $100,000 is taxed at 20% if there are no Sec. 1231 losses, nonrecaptured net Sec. 1231 losses, and no capital gains and losses from other transactions. Recall from Chapter I:5 that the tax rate on adjusted net capital gain may be 20%, 15%, or zero.

UNRECAPTURED SECTION 1250 GAIN

For sales of real property, some or all of the Sec. 1231 gain may be LTCG that is unrecaptured Sec. 1250 gain taxed at a maximum rate of 25%. Unrecaptured Sec. 1250 gain is the amount of LTCG which would be taxed as ordinary if Sec. 1250 provided for the recapture of all depreciation instead of additional (excess) depreciation. When a taxpayer sells Sec. 1250 property (e.g., an office building) at a gain, any gain due to excess depreciation is ordinary income. Any remaining gain is Sec. 1231 gain and may be LTCG; however, any of the LTCG due to depreciation other than excess depreciation is unrecaptured Sec. 1250 gain taxed at a maximum rate of 25%.

An individual taxpayer who uses straight-line depreciation for Sec. 1250 property does not have any additional depreciation that would be recaptured as ordinary gain under Sec. 1250. Therefore, for buildings placed in service after 1986, all of the Sec. 1231 gain to the extent of the depreciation is unrecaptured Sec. 1250 gain subject to a maximum tax rate of 25% because only straight-line depreciation may be used.

EXAMPLE I:13-27 ▶ Linnie owns a building used in her trade or business that was placed in service in 1995. She has no Sec. 1231 losses, nonrecaptured net Sec. 1231 losses or capital gains and losses. The building cost $400,000* and depreciation-to-date amounts to $172,000. If she sells the building for $350,000, her $122,000 gain ($350,000−$228,000) is Sec. 1231 gain and there is no depreciation recapture under Sec. 1250 because straight-line depreciation was allowed. The $122,000 Sec. 1231 gain is LTCG taxed at a maximum rate of 25% because it is unrecaptured Sec. 1250 gain. ◀

*does not consider the cost of land

STOP & THINK

Question: What is the difference between *Sec. 1250 depreciation recapture* and *unrecaptured Sec. 1250 gain*?

Solution: Section 1250 depreciation recapture is the recharacterization of some or all of the Sec. 1231 gain on a building to ordinary income. Section 1250 depreciation recapture only applies to a noncorporate taxpayer if accelerated depreciation was used. Because accelerated depreciation is not allowed after 1986, this provision does not apply to noncorporate taxpayers for buildings placed in service after 1986. Unrecaptured Sec. 1250 gain is taxed at a maximum rate of 25% and occurs when there is a sale or an exchange of a building that is not Sec. 1245 property. If straight-line depreciation is used for a building, the gain is Sec. 1231 gain and the portion of the gain due to depreciation is unrecaptured Sec. 1250 gain. Part or all of the Sec. 1231 gain is taxed at a maximum rate of 25% with any excess taxed at 15% (or 20% if regular marginal tax rate is 39.6%).

EXAMPLE I:13-28 ▶ Assume the same facts as in Example I:13-27 except Linnie has a marginal tax rate less than 39.6% and sells the building for $500,000. Her Sec. 1231 gain is $272,000 ($500,000−$228,000), and $172,000 of the gain is taxed at 25% because it is unrecaptured Sec. 1250 gain. The remaining $100,000 of gain is taxed at 15%. ◀

ADDITIONAL COMMENT

When a building is sold at a gain, different tax rates might apply to portions of the gain: rate for ordinary income, 25% for unrecaptured Sec. 1250 gain, and zero, 15%, or 20% for ANCG.

TAXATION OF GAINS ON SALE OR EXCHANGE OF DEPRECIABLE REAL PROPERTY

Noncorporate taxpayers who placed real property in service after 1963 and before 1981 may have to recognize Sec. 1250 ordinary income if they used a depreciation method greater than straight-line. Only noncorporate taxpayers may have gain treated as unrecaptured Sec. 1250 gain and the amount of unrecaptured Sec. 1250 gain is not greater than the amount of depreciation allowed.

There is a difference between Sec. 1250 ordinary income and unrecaptured Sec. 1250 gain. Section 1250 ordinary income could be taxed at 39.6% after 2012 for noncorporate taxpayers while unrecaptured Sec. 1250 gain is taxed at a maximum rate of 25%. To have unrecaptured Sec. 1250 gain, the property must have a holding period greater than one year.

EXAMPLE I:13-29 ▶ Erin, whose tax rate is 35%, owns an office building purchased for $1 million* on April 10 of last year. The building is sold on March 28 of the current year for $990,000 when its adjusted basis is $966,850. The $23,150 gain is not Sec. 1231 gain and none of the gain is unrecaptured Sec. 1250 gain because the holding period is not more than one year. The $23,150 gain is ordinary taxed at 35%. If the holding period was more than one year, the Sec. 1231 gain of $23,150 is LTCG that is unrecaptured Sec. 1250 gain taxed at 25%. ◀

*does not consider the cost of land

The proper tax treatment for depreciable real estate depends on the method of depreciation, when the property was placed in service, and how the property is used. Section 1245 applies to a building placed in service after 1980 and before 1987 if accelerated cost recovery is allowed and the building is not used as residential rental property.

Real property used as residential rental property placed in service before 1987 may be taxed more favorably than other types of real property because the Sec. 1250 recapture of excess depreciation rules apply only to additional depreciation allowed after 1975 for residential rental property. Also, buildings used as residential rental property are never subject to the Sec. 1245 recapture rules.

For a building or structure to qualify as residential rental property, 80% or more of the gross rental income from the building or structure must be rental income from dwelling units. Residential rental property does not include any unit in a hotel, motel, inn, or other establishment if more than one-half of the units are used on a transient basis.[32]

When a building is sold at a gain, different tax rates may apply to portions of the gain:

Rate for ordinary income − Sec. 1250 due to recapture of excess depreciation or 1245 due to recapture of depreciation
25% − unrecaptured Sec. 1250 gain
20%, 15%, or zero − portion of Sec. 1231 gain that becomes adjusted net capital gain

Depreciable Real Property Placed in Service Before 1981. Taxpayers who elected to use accelerated depreciation on real property placed in service before 1981 may have some or all of their gain treated as Sec. 1250 ordinary income. Gain due to excess depreciation allowed after 1963 is Sec. 1250 ordinary income unless the building is used as residential rental property where gain due to excess depreciation after 1975 is ordinary income. The Sec. 1250 recapture rules are the same for residential rental property and other real property placed in service after 1975.

EXAMPLE I:13-30 ▶ Buddy sells an apartment complex used as residential rental property and placed in service on January 1, 1977. The cost of the apartment complex is $900,000,* and the complex is sold on January 1, 2015, for $700,000. Depreciation claimed by Buddy on the property is as follows:

Time Period	*Depreciation Allowed*	*Straight-Line Depreciation*	*Excess Depreciation*
Jan. 1, 1977–Jan. 1, 2015	$800,000	$710,000	$90,000

On the date of sale, the adjusted basis of the apartment is $100,000 ($900,000 − $800,000) and the realized gain is $600,000 ($700,000 − $100,000). All $90,000 of excess depreciation allowed is recaptured as Sec. 1250 ordinary income because the excess depreciation is less than the realized gain. The remaining $510,000 ($600,000 − $90,000) of gain is a Sec. 1231 gain. The Sec. 1231 gain is LTCG if 1231 gains exceed 1231 losses and is taxed at 25% because it is unrecaptured Sec. 1250 gain. ◀

*does not consider the cost of land

ADDITIONAL COMMENT

If the selling price in Example I:13-30 is $172,000, all of the gain is Sec. 1250 ordinary income.

Selling Price	$172,000
Adjusted Basis	100,000
Realized Gain	$ 72,000
Ordinary Gain	$ 72,000

32 Reg. Sec. 1.167(j)-3(b)(1)(i).

EXAMPLE I:13-31 ▶ Assume the same facts as in Example I:13-30 except the building is nonresidential real estate such as a warehouse, manufacturing plant or an office building. The tax treatment is the same for both examples. Buddy has $90,000 of ordinary income and Sec. 1231 gain of $510,000. The Sec. 1231 gain is LTCG if 1231 gains exceed 1231 losses and is taxed at 25% because it is unrecaptured Sec. 1250 gain. ◀

There is no excess depreciation, and thus no Sec. 1250 ordinary income if the building is fully depreciated when sold or exchanged. As each year passes, noncorporate shareholders are increasingly less likely to have Sec. 1250 ordinary income.

EXAMPLE I:13-32 ▶ Assume the same facts as in Examples 30 and 31 except the buildings are fully depreciated and the selling price is $720,000. For both buildings, the realized gain of $720,000 is Sec. 1231 gain and is unrecaptured Sec. 1250 gain taxed at a maximum rate of 25%. ◀

Depreciable Real Property Placed in Service After 1980 and Before 1987. Gain due to excess depreciation for buildings used as residential rental property placed in service after 1980 and before 1987 is Sec. 1250 ordinary income. Because the recovery period for buildings placed in service during this period is 15, 18 or 19 years, all such buildings will be fully depreciated if sold in 2015, thus there is no excess depreciation and no Sec. 1250 ordinary income.

The method of depreciation used for other buildings placed in service during this period is a critical factor in determining the tax treatment when sold. If accelerated cost recovery was used, the nonresidential real estate is Sec. 1245 property where all gain due to depreciation is ordinary income. If the straight-line method is used, the property is Sec. 1250 property and none of the gain is ordinary income for noncorporate taxpayers.

EXAMPLE I:13-33 ▶ Ford purchased three buildings (A, B and C) in 1982 for $500,000 each*. The recovery period for each building is 15 years, so each building is fully depreciated when he sells the buildings during the current year for $400,000 each.

*does not consider the cost of land

Building	*Use of Property*	*Method of Cost Recovery (Depreciation)*
A	residential rental property	accelerated or straight-line
B	office building	accelerated
C	warehouse	straight-line

Building B is Sec. 1245 property, and the $400,000 gain is Sec. 1245 ordinary income. For buildings A and C, the $400,000 gain is Sec. 1231 gain and is unrecaptured Sec. 1250 gain because the gain is due to depreciation. ◀

EXAMPLE I:13-34 ▶ Assume the same facts as in Example I:13-33 except the selling price is $570,000. For building B, Ford must recognize $500,000 of Sec. 1245 ordinary income and $70,000 of Sec. 1231 gain taxed at 15% or 20%. For buildings A and C, the $570,000 gain is Sec. 1231 gain with $500,000 taxed at 25% and $70,000 taxed at 15% or 20%. ◀

Depreciable Real Property Placed in Service After 1986. The straight-line method of depreciation is the only method of depreciation allowed for buildings placed in service after 1986, and thus noncorporate taxpayers will not have any Sec. 1250 ordinary income when they sell or exchange buildings placed in service after 1986. Gain due to depreciation is unrecaptured Sec. 1250 gain subject to a maximum tax rate of 25%.

The tax treatment for residential rental property and other real property placed in service after 1986 is the same, but taxpayers may depreciate residential rental property over 27.5 years and other real property placed in service after May 12, 1993, over 39 years.

EXAMPLE I:13-35 ▶ Stella purchased an apartment complex on October 10, 2008, for $275,000 (exclusive of land) while Mack purchased an office building for $275,000 on the same day. Stella and Mack sell the

▼ **TABLE I:13-1**
CHARACTER OF GAIN ON SALE OR EXCHANGE OF DEPRECIABLE REAL PROPERTY FOR NONCORPORATE TAXPAYERS

	Sec. 1245 Ordinary	Sec. 1250 Ordinary	Sec. 1231	Unrecaptured Sec. 1250 (Maximum rate of 25%)
RESIDENTIAL RENTAL				
Placed in Service Before 1981				
Use straight-line depreciation	No	No	Yes	Yes
Use accelerated depreciation	No	Yes*	Yes**	Yes
Placed in Service After 1980 & Before 1987				
Use straight-line depreciation	No	No	Yes	Yes
Use accelerated depreciation	No	Yes*	Yes**	Yes
Placed in Service After 1986				
Use straight-line depreciation	No	No	Yes	Yes
NONRESIDENTIAL				
Placed in Service Before 1981				
Use straight-line depreciation	No	No	Yes	Yes
Use accelerated depreciation	No	Yes*	Yes**	Yes
Placed in Service After 1980 & Before 1987				
Use straight-line depreciation	No	No	Yes	Yes
Use accelerated depreciation	Yes	No	Yes***	No
Placed in Service After 1986				
Use straight-line depreciation	No	No	Yes	Yes

* Portion of gain due to excess depreciation
** To extent gain is greater than excess depreciation
*** To extent gain is greater than total depreciation

buildings on April 22, 2015, for $250,000. At the date of sale, Stella's adjusted basis in the apartment complex is $210,005 based on a 27.5 year recovery period and Mack's adjusted basis in the office building is $229,166 based on a 39 year recovery period. Stella has a Sec. 1231 gain of $39,995 [$250,000 − $210,005 adjusted basis], and all of the gain is unrecaptured Sec. 1250 gain. Mack has a Sec. 1231 gain of $20,834 [$250,000 − $229,166 adjusted basis], and all of the gain is unrecaptured Sec. 1250 gain. ◀

LOW-INCOME HOUSING

Congress has provided incentives for the construction and rehabilitation of low-income housing. For tax years after 1986, a low-income housing credit is available to owners of qualified low-income housing projects.[33]

If the low-income housing unit is held for 16 years and 8 months, none of the additional depreciation is subject to recapture as ordinary income.[34] Thus noncorporate taxpayers will not have any Sec. 1250 ordinary income if the low-income housing is sold after 2002.

The Sec. 1250 recapture rules for noncorporate taxpayers are summarized in Topic Review I:13-2.

[33] Sec. 42.

[34] Secs. 1250(a)(1)(B)(i), (ii), (iii), and (iv).

TOPIC REVIEW I:13-2

Section 1250 Recapture for Noncorporate Taxpayers

- Section 1250 affects the character of the gain, not the amount of gain.
- Section 1250 does not apply to assets sold or exchanged at a loss.
- Section 1250 ordinary income is never more than the realized gain.
- Section 1250 ordinary income is never more than the *additional* (excess) depreciation allowed. (Note, that this statement is not true for corporate taxpayers.)
- Section 1250 property includes depreciable real property unless the real property is nonresidential real estate placed in service in 1980 and before 1987 under the ACRS rules and the straight-line method is not elected.
- Section 1250 ordinary income does not exist if the straight-line method of depreciation is used. (This statement is not true for corporate taxpayers because of the additional recapture requirements under Sec. 291.)

ADDITIONAL RECAPTURE FOR CORPORATIONS

OBJECTIVE 6

Understand recapture provisions for corporations

KEY POINT

Section 291 has no effect on Sec. 1245 property because gain is already recaptured to the extent of all depreciation.

ADDITIONAL COMMENT

Corporations are subject to an additional 20% depreciation recapture rule under Sec. 291 on sales of Sec. 1250 property.

SELF-STUDY QUESTION

If the taxpayer in Example I:13-36 is a noncorporate taxpayer, how much of the gain is Sec. 1250 ordinary income?

ANSWER

$60,000

Corporations are subject to additional recapture rules under Sec. 291 if depreciable real estate is sold or otherwise disposed of. This recapture is in addition to the normal recapture rules under Sec. 1250. The additional ordinary income that is recaptured effectively reduces the amount of the Sec. 1231 gain.

The additional recapture amount under Sec. 291 is equal to 20% of the difference between the amount that would be recaptured if the property was Sec. 1245 property and actual recapture amount under Sec. 1250.[35]

EXAMPLE I:13-36 ▶ In 1980, Orlando Corporation purchased an office building for $500,000* for use in its business. The building is sold during the current year for $480,000. Pertinent details relating to depreciation of the building and realized gain on the sale are below:

- Total depreciation allowed for the building is $420,000.
- If straight-line depreciation had been used, depreciation allowed would have been $360,000.
- Building's adjusted basis is $80,000 ($500,000 − $420,000).
- Realized and recognized gain is $400,000 ($480,000 − $80,000).

To determine the character of the $400,000 gain, the following analysis must be made:

- Excess depreciation is $60,000 ($420,000 − $360,000). Gain to the extent of excess depreciation is recaptured as Sec. 1250 ordinary income.
- Section 291 depreciation recapture applies because the taxpayer is a corporation. If the property was Sec. 1245 property, $400,000 of the gain would be ordinary income.
- Because of Sec. 291, Orlando has more Sec. 1250 ordinary income: $68,000 [0.20 × ($400,000 − $60,000)].

In summary, $128,000 of the total recognized gain of $400,000 is recaptured as ordinary income ($60,000 + $68,000) and the remaining $272,000 ($400,000 − $128,000) is Sec. 1231 gain. ◀

*does not consider the cost of land

EXAMPLE I:13-37 ▶ Pacific Corporation purchased an office building in 1981 for $800,000* for use in its trade or business. The building is sold during the current year for $850,000. Pacific elected to use the straight-line method of cost recovery and $800,000 cost-recovery deductions have been allowed. The realized gain is $850,000 ($850,000 − 0). None of the gain is ordinary income under Sec. 1250 if Sec. 291 is not considered. If the building were instead Sec. 1245 recovery property, $800,000 of the gain would be treated as ordinary income.

[35] Sec. 291(a)(1).

SELF-STUDY QUESTION

If the taxpayer in Example I:13-37 is a noncorporate taxpayer, how much of the gain is Sec. 1250 ordinary income?

ANSWER

Zero

The $850,000 gain is Sec. 1231 gain and $800,000 is unrecaptured Sec. 1250 gain subject to a maximum tax rate of 25%.

The amount of Sec. 1250 ordinary income under Sec. 291 for a corporate taxpayer is $160,000 [0.20 × ($800,000 − $0)]. The remaining $690,000 ($850,000 − $160,000) gain is Sec. 1231 gain. ◀

*does not consider the cost of land

For corporations, none of the Sec. 1231 gain is unrecaptured Sec. 1250 gain.

SUMMARY OF SECS. 1231, 1245, AND 1250 GAINS

Section 1231 property is depreciable property and nondepreciable real property used in one's trade or business and held for more than one year. Net Sec. 1231 gain, the excess of Sec. 1231 gain over Sec. 1231 loss, is LTCG unless the five-year lookback rule applies in which case the gain is ordinary to the extent of the nonrecaptured net Sec. 1231 loss. Net Sec. 1231 loss, the excess of Sec. 1231 loss over Sec. 1231 gain, is ordinary.

Section 1245 applies to depreciable personal property and amortizable intangible assets. It also applies to certain nonresidential real property placed in service during ACRS (after 1980 and before 1987) if accelerated cost recovery is used. Gain to the extent of depreciation is ordinary income. All of the gain resulting from the sale of Sec. 1245 property is ordinary income unless the asset is sold for more than its original basis.

Section 1250 property is depreciable real property, and gain is ordinary income to the extent of excess depreciation, the excess of accelerated depreciation over straight-line. After 1986, the straight-line method must be used for real property and thus noncorporate taxpayers will not have any Sec. 1250 ordinary income on the sale of depreciable real property placed in service after 1986. Unfortunately, Congress made the sale and exchange of buildings more complicated in 1997 when it created the concept of unrecaptured Sec. 1250 gain that is taxed at 25%. When a noncorporate taxpayer sells depreciated buildings at a gain, any gain to the extent of straight-line depreciation is Sec. 1231 gain but is taxed at a rate no higher than 25% because it is unrecaptured Sec. 1250 gain.

To further illustrate Sec. 1231, 1245, and 1250, refer to Topic Review I:13-3 where a noncorporate taxpayer with a 35% tax rate sells various assets during the current year. Each asset was purchased in 1997 and the selling price is $450,000 for each of the first three assets. All assets are used in a trade or business. There are no other gains and losses and no nonrecaptured net Sec. 1231 losses.

TOPIC REVIEW I:13-3

Sections 1231, 1245, and 1250—Comparison of Various Assets

The taxpayer is a noncorporate taxpayer with a 35% tax rate who sells each of the first three assets for $450,000. Each asset was purchased in 1997 and is used in a trade or business. The difference between the original basis and the adjusted basis of the equipment and building is attributable to depreciation. There are no other gains and losses and no nonrecaptured net Sec. 1231 losses, thus the Sec. 1231 gain becomes LTCG.

	Original Basis	Adjusted Basis	Tax Treatment
1. Land	$400,000	$400,000	$50,000 Sec. 1231 gain taxed at 15%.*
2. Equipment	600,000	400,000	$50,000 Sec. 1245 ordinary income taxed at 35%. All gain is due to depreciation.
3. Building	500,000	400,000	$50,000 Sec. 1231 gain which is unrecaptured Sec. 1250 gain taxed at 25%.
For assets 4, 5, & 6, assume the selling price is $700,000.			
4. Land	$400,000	$400,000	$300,000 Sec. 1231 gain taxed at 15%.*
5. Equipment	600,000	400,000	$200,000 Sec. 1245 ordinary income taxed at 35% and $100,000 Sec. 1231 gain taxed at 15%.*
6. Building	500,000	400,000	$300,000 Sec. 1231 gain with $100,000 of unrecaptured Sec. 1250 gain taxed at 25% and $200,000 taxed at 15%.*

* 20% if unmarried with taxable income above $413,200 or married with taxable income above $464,850.

RECAPTURE PROVISIONS—OTHER APPLICATIONS

OBJECTIVE 7

Describe other recapture applications

Sections 1245 and 1250 recapture provisions take precedence over other provisions of the tax law.[36] Unless an exception or limitation is specifically stated in Secs. 1245 or 1250, gain is recognized under Secs. 1245 or 1250 despite the existence of provisions elsewhere in the IRC that allow nonrecognition of gain.[37]

GIFTS OF PROPERTY SUBJECT TO RECAPTURE

A gift of appreciated depreciable property does not result in the recapture of depreciation or cost-recovery deductions under Secs. 1245 or 1250.[38] The donee must consider the recapture potential when disposing of the property. The recapture amount for the donee is computed by including the recaptured amount attributable to the donor.[39]

EXAMPLE I:13-38 ▶ Ashley makes a gift of equipment with an $8,200 FMV to Helmut. Ashley paid $10,000 for the equipment and deducted $4,000 of depreciation before making the gift. Ashley does not have to recapture any depreciation when making the gift. Helmut's basis for the equipment is $6,000 and the potential depreciation recapture carries over to Helmut. ◀

EXAMPLE I:13-39 ▶ Assume the same facts as in Example I:13-38 except that Helmut uses the equipment in a trade or business, deducts $1,500 of depreciation, and sells the equipment for $7,100. When determining the amount of depreciation subject to recapture, Helmut must also consider the depreciation allowed to Ashley. The entire $2,600 [$7,100 − ($6,000 − $1,500)] gain is recaptured as ordinary income because it is less than the $5,500 ($4,000 + $1,500) of depreciation claimed. ◀

ADDITIONAL COMMENT

If the taxpayer in Topic Review I:13-3 is a corporation, the character of the gain is the same for assets 1, 2, 4, and 5. For asset 3, $10,000 of the gain is Sec. 1250 ordinary income because of Sec. 291 and $40,000 is Sec. 1231 gain. For asset 6, $20,000 is Sec. 1250 ordinary income because of Sec. 291 and $280,000 is Sec. 1231 gain.

TRANSFER OF PROPERTY SUBJECT TO RECAPTURE AT DEATH

The transfer of appreciated property at death does not cause a recapture of depreciation deductions to the decedent's estate under Secs. 1245 and 1250.[40] In addition, recapture potential does not carry over to the person who receives the property from the decedent.

EXAMPLE I:13-40 ▶ Jackie dies while owning a building with a $900,000 FMV. The building is Sec. 1245 property acquired in 1985 for $800,000* on which cost-recovery deductions of $800,000 have been claimed. Pam inherits the building from Jackie. Pam's basis for the building is $900,000, and the $800,000 of cost-recovery deductions are not recaptured. If Pam immediately sells the building, there is no depreciation recapture attributable to the $800,000 of cost-recovery deductions taken by the decedent. ◀

*does not include cost of land

KEY POINT

Death is one of the few ways to avoid the recapture provisions.

CHARITABLE CONTRIBUTIONS

As discussed in Chapter I:7, the deduction for a charitable contribution of appreciated ordinary income property is generally limited to its adjusted basis (i.e., the amount of the contribution deduction is equal to the FMV of the property less the amount of gain that would not have been LTCG [or Sec. 1231 gain] if the contributed property had been sold by the taxpayer at its FMV).[41] Thus, the contribution deduction for recapture property is reduced to reflect the ordinary income that would be recognized if the property were sold rather than contributed to the charity.

EXAMPLE I:13-41 ▶ Ralph makes a gift of an organ to a church. The organ is used in Ralph's trade or business and has a $6,300 FMV. Ralph paid $10,000 for the organ, and $8,000 depreciation has been claimed. If the organ were sold for its $6,300 FMV, the realized and recognized gain would be $4,300 ($6,300 − $2,000) and all of the gain would be ordinary income due to the recapture of depreciation under Sec. 1245. The charitable contribution deduction is limited to $2,000 ($6,300 − $4,300), because none of the $4,300 gain would be taxed as a LTCG if the organ were sold. ◀

---

36 Secs. 1245(d) and 1250(i).
37 Reg. Secs. 1.1245-6(a) and 1.1250-1(c)(1).
38 Secs. 1245(b)(1) and 1250(d)(1).
39 Reg. Secs. 1.1245-2(a)(4) and 1.1250-2(d).
40 Secs. 1245(b)(2) and 1250(d)(2).
41 Sec. 170(e)(1)(A).

ADDITIONAL COMMENT

If the FMV of the organ in Example I:13-41 is $11,000, the charitable contribution deduction is limited to $3,000, the $11,000 FMV less $8,000. If the organ is sold for $11,000, $8,000 of the gain is ordinary income.

LIKE-KIND EXCHANGES

A taxpayer who receives boot (i.e., non–like-kind property) in a transaction that otherwise qualifies as a like-kind exchange recognizes gain equal to the lesser of the realized gain or the amount of boot received. If the property is Sec. 1245 or 1250 property, the gain is first considered to be ordinary income up to the maximum amount of the gain that is subject to the recapture provisions.

EXAMPLE I:13-42 ▶ The Krider Corporation owns a purebred bull used in its trade or business that cost $300,000 two years ago. During the current year, the bull is exchanged when its adjusted basis is $115,000 for another bull with an FMV of $187,000 and $200,000 of cash. Gain realized on the exchange is $272,000 [($187,000 + $200,000) − $115,000], and gain recognized is the lesser of the $200,000 boot received or the $272,000 gain realized. Because the $200,000 recognized gain is greater than depreciation allowed of $185,000, $185,000 is Sec. 1245 ordinary income and $15,000 is Sec. 1231 gain. ◀

REAL-WORLD EXAMPLE

A taxpayer's exchange of yachts used for business was a nontaxable transaction under Sec. 1031. Because no gain was recognized on the transaction, no gain could be subject to the recapture rules. *J. Wade Harris,* 1975 PH T.C. Memo ¶75,276, 34 TCM 1192.

If gain is not recognized in a like-kind exchange, the recapture potential carries over to the replacement property (i.e., any recapture potential associated with the property exchanged attaches to the property received in the exchange).[42]

EXAMPLE I:13-43 ▶ Melissa owns a Chevrolet pickup truck used in her trade or business that cost $10,000 and has a $6,000 adjusted basis due to $4,000 in depreciation deductions she has claimed. The truck is exchanged for a Ford pickup truck with a $9,000 FMV. The Ford truck is used in Melissa's business. Melissa does not recognize any portion of the $3,000 realized gain because the exchange qualifies as a like-kind exchange and no boot is received. Her basis for the Ford truck is $6,000 (i.e., a substituted basis).

After deducting $2,000 of depreciation, Melissa sells the Ford truck for $7,300. All of the recognized gain of $3,300 ($7,300 − $4,000) is ordinary income. The depreciation recapture amount under Sec. 1245 is equal to the total $6,000 in depreciation (including $4,000 on the Chevrolet pickup truck) but the recognized gain is only $3,300.[43] ◀

INVOLUNTARY CONVERSIONS

If an involuntary conversion of Sec. 1245 property occurs and all or a portion of the gain is not recognized,[44] the amount of gain considered to be Sec. 1245 ordinary income is limited and cannot be more than the recognized gain.[45] A similar provision exists for the involuntary conversion of Sec. 1250 property.[46]

EXAMPLE I:13-44 ▶ The Ryan Corporation's printing equipment with original cost of $600,000 and adjusted basis of $200,000 is destroyed by fire. Ryan, Inc. receives $550,000 of insurance proceeds and purchases $510,000 of printing equipment. If the corporation elects to defer gain, it must recognize a $40,000 gain which is Sec. 1245 ordinary income. The basis of the printing equipment acquired is $200,000. ◀

REAL-WORLD EXAMPLE

Taxpayer received insurance proceeds in excess of the adjusted basis of a business automobile upon the destruction of the auto in an accident. The taxpayer did not use Sec. 1033 to defer the gain and the court held that the gain was subject to recapture under Sec. 1245. *Anthony Astone,* 1983 PH T.C. Memo ¶83,747, 47 TCM 632.

INSTALLMENT SALES

As discussed in Chapter I:11, gain resulting from an installment sale is generally recognized as payments are received. Thus, the gain may be spread over more than one accounting period. An installment sale of depreciable property may result in all of the recaptured gain being taxed in the year of the sale.[47] Recapture income is "the aggregate amount which would be treated as ordinary income under Sec. 1245 or 1250 for the taxable year of the disposition if all payments to be received were received in the taxable year of disposition."[48] Recapture income must be recognized in the year of sale, even if no payments are received.

---

[42] Reg. Sec. 1.1245-2(c)(4).

[43] Reg. Sec. 1.1245-2(a)(4).

[44] As discussed in Chapter I:12, one may elect to defer recognition of the gain if the Sec. 1033 requirements are satisfied.

[45] Sec. 1245(b)(4) and Reg. Sec. 1.1245-4(d)(1).

[46] Sec. 1250(d)(4) and Reg. Sec. 1.1250-3(d).

[47] Sec. 453(i)(1).

[48] Sec. 453(i)(2).

EXAMPLE I:13-45 ▶ Pat owns equipment with a $100,000 acquisition cost and a $42,000 adjusted basis. During the current year, Pat sells the property for $30,000 cash and a $60,000 interest-bearing note to be paid over a ten-year period. The realized gain is $48,000 ($90,000 − $42,000), and the recapture income amount is $48,000 (the lesser of total depreciation deductions of $58,000 or the $48,000 realized gain). The $48,000 gain is all recognized as ordinary income in the current year, despite the fact that the transaction qualifies as an installment sale and only $30,000 of cash is received in the year of sale. ◀

KEY POINT

In the case of an installment sale of Sec. 1245 or 1250 property, it is possible to report a large taxable gain even though the taxpayer has not yet received the cash to pay the tax on such gain.

If gain realized from the installment sale exceeds the recapture income, the excess gain is reported under the installment method.[49] The amount of recapture income recognized is added to the adjusted basis to determine the gross profit ratio.

EXAMPLE I:13-46 ▶ Bob owns an office building acquired for $700,000* in 1986 and subject to the Sec. 1245 recapture rules. After claiming $700,000 of cost recovery deductions, Bob sells the building to Janet in 2015 for $1 million. Bob receives $200,000 in cash and an $800,000 interest-bearing note. The note is to be paid with annual principal payments of $100,000 and interest on the unpaid balance beginning in 2016. The total amount of realized gain is $1 million ($1,000,000 − 0). In 2015, Bob recognizes $700,000 of Sec. 1245 ordinary income. The gross profit ratio is determined by adding $700,000 recapture income to the $0 basis. The gross profit ratio is 30% [($1,000,000 − $700,000) ÷ $1,000,000]. In addition to recognizing $700,000 of ordinary income, Bob recognizes $60,000 (0.30 × $200,000) Sec. 1231 gain in 2015 because a $200,000 cash down payment was received in the year of the sale. In 2016 and in each subsequent year, $30,000 (0.30 × $100,000) of Sec. 1231 gain is recognized as the cash payments on the principal are received. ◀

*does not include cost of land

SELF-STUDY QUESTION

What method of cost recovery did Bob use in Example I:13-46?

ANSWER

Accelerated cost recovery. The office building is subject to Sec. 1245 recapture.

SECTION 179 EXPENSING ELECTION

In lieu of capitalizing the cost of new or used tangible personal business property, taxpayers may elect to expense up to $25,000 of the acquisition cost in 2015.[50] (see Chapter I:10). If the property is subsequently converted to nonbusiness use, previous tax benefits derived from the immediate expensing election must be recaptured and added to the taxpayer's gross income in the year of the conversion.[51] The recaptured amount equals the difference between the amount expensed under Sec. 179 and the total depreciation that would otherwise have been claimed for the period of business use.

EXAMPLE I:13-47 ▶ Behren purchased business equipment (a five-year recovery period) in 2014 for $18,100 and elected to expense the entire amount under Sec. 179. In 2015, he converts the equipment to nonbusiness use. Depreciation of $3,620 (0.20 × $18,100) under the MACRS rules would have been allowed during the period the equipment was held for business use if Behren had not elected to expense the $18,100 cost. Behren must recognize $14,480 ($18,100 − $3,620) of Sec. 1245 ordinary income in 2015. ◀

SELF-STUDY QUESTION

If Behren in Example I:13-47 sells the equipment for $15,000 instead of converting it to a nonbusiness use, what is the character of the gain?

ANSWER

$15,000 of Sec. 1245 ordinary income

CONSERVATION AND LAND CLEARING EXPENDITURES

Taxpayers engaged in the business of farming may deduct expenditures paid or incurred during the taxable year for soil and water conservation or the prevention of erosion. The expenditures must be made with respect to land used in farming and would be capital expenditures except for this provision.[52]

The deductions for conservation expenditures may be partially or fully recaptured as ordinary income if the farmland is disposed of before the land is held for more than nine years.[53] The amount of deductions recaptured as ordinary income under Sec. 1252 is a percentage of the aggregate deductions allowed for conservation expenditures. The amount of ordinary income recognized under Sec. 1252 is limited to the lesser of the taxpayer's realized gain or the applicable recapture percentage times the total conservation expenditures.

---

49 Sec. 453(i)(1)(B).0.

50 Secs. 179(a) and (b)(1). In 2015, the maximum Sec. 179 deduction is $25,000 with a dollar for dollar reduction when the cost of qualifying property placed in service exceeds $200,000. In recent years, Congress has changed the law to allow for a larger deduction ($500,000 in 2014).

51 Sec. 179(d)(10) and Reg. Sec. 1.179-1(e).

52 Sec. 175(a).

53 Sec. 1252(a)(1).

WHAT WOULD YOU DO IN THIS SITUATION?

You recently graduated with an advanced degree in taxation and have accepted a job with a CPA firm in the tax department. One of the firm's clients, a wealthy individual, was in need of cash and decided to sell some assets to raise the cash. The client asked the firm to advise him, from a tax standpoint, which assets he should sell. The client is in the 35% tax bracket. You suggested in a written memo that the client sell one of the client's jet airplanes. The plane you recommended to be sold had originally cost $16 million and now had an adjusted basis of $5 million. A buyer had offered to buy the plane for $12 million on the installment basis, paying $4 million per year for three years plus interest at 9%. The principal reason for selling that particular plane is that it would raise $12 million over three years, but the tax could be spread over three years by using the installment sale method. The client took your advice and sold the plane in the current year.

Later, when preparing the client's tax return, you realize that gain due to depreciation of the airplane must be recognized in the year of sale, even if the property is sold under the installment sale method. Thus, *all* of the gain on the sale of the plane must be recognized in the year of sale, not spread over three years. You go to your manager and tell him about your major mistake. Your manager, who reviewed your original memo, indicates that he thinks that the two of you should not tell anyone about the mistake as it will negatively impact both of your careers. The manager thinks that because the client has such a large amount of income, reporting the entire gain on the sale of the plane on the client's return might not be detected by the client. Thus, the manager instructs you to prepare the current year return with the entire $7 million of gain and not tell anyone about the mistake. What should you do in this situation?

KEY POINT
There is no recapture of conservation costs if the farmland is held for at least 10 years.

The recapture percentage is 100% if the farmland is disposed of within five years after the date it is acquired. The percentage declines by 20 percentage points for each additional year the property is held. If the land is disposed of after being held for more than nine years, none of the expenses are recaptured.[54]

EXAMPLE I:13-48 ▶ Paula owns farmland with a $400,000 basis. She has deducted $50,000 for soil and water conservation expenditures. After farming the land for six years and five months, Paula sells the land for $520,000. The realized gain is $120,000 ($520,000 − $400,000) and the recapture percentage is 60%, because the farmland is disposed of within the seventh year after it was acquired. The amount of ordinary income due to recapture under Sec. 1252 is $30,000, the lesser of the $120,000 realized gain or the $30,000 (0.60 × $50,000) recapture amount. ◀

ADDITIONAL COMMENT
Intangible drilling and development costs represent the major cost of operations and can provide investors with working interests in oil and gas properties with a first-year write-off of substantially all of their investment.

INTANGIBLE DRILLING COSTS AND DEPLETION

Taxpayers may elect to either expense or capitalize intangible drilling and development costs (IDC).[55] If the election to expense is not made, the costs are capitalized and recovered through additional depletion deductions. Intangible drilling and development costs include "all expenditures made by an operator for wages, fuel, repairs, hauling, supplies, etc., incident to and necessary for the drilling of wells and the preparation of wells for the production of oil or gas."[56]

Part or all of the gain from the sale of oil and gas properties may be recaptured as ordinary income due to the recapture of the IDC deduction and the deduction for depletion. However, the amount of ordinary income recognized from the recapture of IDC and depletion is limited to the gain realized from disposition of the property.[57]

EXAMPLE I:13-49 ▶ In 2008, Marty purchased undeveloped property to drill for oil and gas. Intangible drilling and development costs of $400,000 were paid in 2008, and Marty elected to expense the IDC. During the current year, Marty sells the property and realizes a $900,000 gain. $300,000 of cost depletion was also allowed. Marty must recognize $700,000 of ordinary income because of the recapture of IDC ($400,000) and the recapture of depletion ($300,000). The remaining $200,000 ($900,000 − $700,000) gain is Sec. 1231 gain. ◀

---

54 Sec. 1252(a)(3).
55 Sec. 263(c).
56 Reg. Sec. 1.612-4(a).
57 Sec. 1254(a)(1).

EXAMPLE I:13-50 ▶ In 2007, Tina acquired oil and gas properties for $700,000 and paid $200,000 for intangible drilling costs. During 2007, she elected to expense the $200,000 of IDC. Total depletion allowed was $80,000. During the current year, Tina sells the property for $840,000 and realizes a $220,000 [$840,000 − ($700,000 − $80,000)] gain. The amount of ordinary income due to recapture is $220,000, because both IDC and depletion must be recaptured only to the extent of the gain. ◀

SELF-STUDY QUESTION

If Tina in Example I:13-50 sells the properties for $990,000, what is the character of her gain?

ANSWER

$280,000 of ordinary income and $90,000 of Sec. 1231 gain

GAIN ON SALE OF DEPRECIABLE PROPERTY BETWEEN RELATED PARTIES

All gain recognized on the sale or exchange of property between related parties is ordinary income if the property is subject to depreciation in the hands of the transferee (i.e., the person who purchases the property). The sale or exchange may be direct or indirect.[58]

EXAMPLE I:13-51 ▶ Phil owns a building with a $500,000 adjusted basis and $800,000 FMV. The building, which cost $700,000, is used in his business, and the straight-line method of depreciation is used. $200,000 of depreciation deductions were allowed. If the building is sold to Phil's 100%-owned corporation for $800,000, the $300,000 realized gain ($800,000 − $500,000) is treated as ordinary income under Sec. 1239, because the property is subject to depreciation in the hands of the transferee and the corporation and Phil are related parties. ◀

SELF-STUDY QUESTION

If Phil sells the building in Example I:13-51 to an unrelated party, what is the character of the gain?

ANSWER

$300,000 of Sec. 1231 gain. If the Sec. 1231 gain becomes LTCG, $200,000 of the gain is unrecaptured Sec. 1250 gain taxed at a maximum rate of 25%

A sale or exchange of property could be subject to depreciation recapture under Sec. 1245 or 1250 as well as the Sec. 1239 related party rules. If so, recapture under Sec. 1245 or 1250 is considered before recapture under Sec. 1239.[59]

EXAMPLE I:13-52 ▶ Assume the same facts as in Example I:13-51 except that Phil sells equipment to the corporation instead of a building. All of the $300,000 realized gain is treated as ordinary income. The recapture amount under Sec. 1245 is $200,000, and Sec. 1239 applies to the remaining $100,000 gain. ◀

REAL-WORLD EXAMPLE

A taxpayer sold a secret formula for typing correction fluid to a corporation that was a related party. The gain on the sale was treated as a capital gain, not as ordinary income under Sec. 1239, because the secret formula was not depreciable. *Bette C. Graham v. U.S.*, 43 AFTR 2d 79-1013, 79-1 USTC ¶9274 (D.C. Tx., 1979).

Purpose of Sec. 1239. Without Sec. 1239, a taxpayer could transfer appreciated depreciable property to a related party and recognize a Sec. 1231 gain on the sale. Net Sec. 1231 gain is treated as LTCG. The related purchaser of the property would receive a step up in the depreciable basis of the property to its FMV and be able to claim a larger amount of depreciation. In Example I:13-51, Phil might prefer to recognize a $300,000 Sec. 1231 gain if the 100%-owned corporation was able to obtain a step-up in the property's basis to $800,000. Because Sec. 1239 applies, Phil must recognize $300,000 of ordinary income rather than Sec. 1231 gain. This rule prevents an individual taxpayer from receiving favorable Sec. 1231 gain treatment and prevents all taxpayers having large capital loss carryovers from using a related party to recognize a Sec. 1231 or capital gain which can be offset against their capital losses.

Related Parties. A person is related (1) to any corporation if the individual owns (directly or indirectly) more than 50% of the value of the outstanding stock and (2) to any partnership in which the person has a capital or profits interest of more than 50%.[60] Constructive ownership rules apply when determining whether the person owns more than 50% of the corporation or has more than a 50% interest in the partnership. Thus, an individual is considered to own stock owned by other family members and related entities (e.g., corporations, partnerships, estates, and trusts).

EXAMPLE I:13-53 ▶ Tony sells a truck used for nonbusiness purposes to the Able Corporation for $15,000 when its original cost basis is $12,000. Tony owns 30% of Able and his spouse owns 40% of Able. Tony and Able are related parties because Tony is deemed to own 70% of Able under the constructive ownership rules and $3,000 of ordinary income must be recognized under Sec. 1239. ◀

A person is related to any trust in which such a person or the person's spouse is a beneficiary.[61] Section 1239 also applies to a sale or exchange of depreciable property between two corporations if the same individual owns more than 50% of each corporation.[62]

---

[58] Sec. 1239(a).
[59] Reg. Sec. 1.1245-6(f).
[60] Sec. 1239(c).
[61] Sec. 1239(b)(2).
[62] Rev. Rul. 79-157, 1979-1 C.B. 281.

TAX PLANNING CONSIDERATIONS

OBJECTIVE 8

Describe tax planning considerations for Sec. 1231 assets

For noncorporate taxpayers, net Sec. 1231 gains are generally preferable to ordinary gains because of the possible lower tax rate applicable to net capital gains. The tax rate could be zero, 15%, 20%, or 25%. For corporate taxpayers, however, after 1986 it usually does not make any difference whether a gain is classified as Sec. 1231 or ordinary unless the corporation has capital losses. Corporations do not have preferential tax rates on net capital gains.

EXAMPLE I:13-54 ▶ Western Corporation has taxable income of $550,000 without considering the sale of equipment for $400,000 during the current year. The equipment originally cost $500,000 and has a $350,000 adjusted basis after deducting depreciation. The corporation has no other gains and losses during the year or any capital loss carryovers from previous years. For Western Corporation, it does not make any difference whether the gain is Sec. 1245 ordinary income or Sec. 1231 gain. The effect on the corporation's taxable income and tax liability is the same regardless of whether the gain is classified as capital or ordinary. ◀

The avoidance of the recapture provisions is important to both corporate and noncorporate taxpayers if capital loss carryovers exist. For example, if Western Corporation has a capital loss carryforward of $40,000 in Example I:13-54, the corporation's taxable income is increased by $10,000 ($50,000 − $40,000) if the $50,000 gain is Sec. 1231 gain. However, because the gain is Sec. 1245 ordinary income, the corporation's taxable income is increased by $50,000. The $40,000 capital loss carryforward is deductible only if Western has capital gain or net Sec. 1231 gain which becomes capital gain.

AVOIDING THE RECAPTURE PROVISIONS

In view of the pervasiveness of the recapture provisions discussed in this chapter, recapture is difficult to avoid. In some cases, recapture can be avoided by holding the property a specific length of time before disposing of it (e.g., the recapture of conservation and land clearing expenses can be avoided by holding the farmland for more than nine years).[63] Contributing appreciated property to a qualified charitable organization cannot be used to circumvent the recapture provisions because in such case the amount of the charitable contribution is reduced by the amount of the gain that would not be a LTCG if the property were sold by the taxpayer.[64]

Although it is often difficult to avoid the recapture provisions, taxpayers may dispose of the property and defer recapture if the disposition is a nontaxable exchange. In a like-kind exchange where no boot is received, the recapture potential is carried over to the property received in the exchange.

Proper timing of the asset's disposition may be advantageous. Disposition may be delayed until the taxpayer's tax rate is low or the property can be sold in the same year that the taxpayer has an NOL that is about to expire.

Taxpayers can shift the recapture potential to other taxpayers by making a gift of property subject to recapture. The recapture potential remains with the property and must be considered when the donee disposes of the property.

Transfer Property at Death. One way to avoid the recapture provisions is to transfer the property at death. No recapture occurs at the time of the transfer, and the basis of property received from a decedent is generally the FMV of the property at the date of the decedent's death.[65] The property's recapture potential does not carry over to the beneficiary as in the case of a gift made to a donee.

[63] Sec. 1252(a)(1).
[64] Sec. 170(e)(1)(A).
[65] Sec. 1014(a). For property inherited in 2010, it is possible that carryover basis rules might be used.

Compliance and Procedural Considerations

OBJECTIVE 9

Describe compliance and procedural considerations for Sec. 1231 assets

ADDITIONAL COMMENT

Form 4797 has four major parts. In completing this form one should normally begin with Part III on page 2, where the recapture of depreciation is calculated. Note that the total amount recaptured from line 31 is carried forward to Part II, where it is combined with other ordinary gains and losses. Any unrecaptured gain from line 32 is carried forward to Part I, where it is netted with other Sec. 1231 gains and losses.

Form 4797, Supplemental Schedule of Gains and Losses, is used to report gains and losses from sales or exchanges of assets used in a trade or business (see Figures I:13-1 through I:13-3). The form is also used to report gains or losses resulting from involuntary conversions, other than casualties or thefts, of property used in the trade or business and capital assets held more than a year. If gains or losses due to casualties or thefts of property used in a trade or business or property held to produce income are recognized, they are reported on Form 4684, Casualties and Thefts (see Figure I:13-3). If such casualties or thefts occur, Form 4684 is prepared either before or at the same time as Form 4797.

Reporting Sec. 1231 Gains and Losses on Form 4797

Part I of Form 4797, which is reproduced in Figure I:13-1, is used to report gains and losses resulting from

- The sale or exchange of Sec. 1231 property
- An involuntary conversion, other than a casualty or theft, of Sec. 1231 property
- An involuntary conversion, other than a casualty or theft, of capital assets held more than one year and used to produce income.

As indicated on lines 3 through 6 in Part I of Form 4797, gains and losses recorded on other forms and in Part III of Form 4797 are reported in Part I. The netting of Sec. 1231 gains and losses occurs in Part I of Form 4797. All gains and losses are recorded in column (g). If line 7(g) has a loss, Sec. 1231 losses exceed Sec. 1231 gains and the net loss is reported on line 11 as ordinary loss. If there is no nonrecaptured net section 1231 losses, all gain reported on line 7(g) is transferred to Schedule D. If the taxpayer does have nonrecaptured net Sec. 1231 losses, that amount is reported on line 8. Gains reported on line 7(g) will be recharacterized as ordinary income to the extent of the nonrecaptured net Sec. 1231 losses and reported as ordinary income on line 12.

Ordinary gains and losses recognized including those recorded on other forms and in Parts I and III of Form 4797 are reported on lines 11 through 17 in Part II of Form 4797.

Reporting Gains Recaptured as Ordinary Income on Form 4797

Part III of Form 4797 for 2014, reproduced in Figure I:13-2, is completed before Parts I and II to determine and report ordinary income due to the recapture provisions of Secs. 1245, 1250, 1252, 1254, and 1255. To illustrate the use of Part III, assume an individual sells equipment (7-year recovery) used in a trade or business for $60,000 on April 30, 2014. The equipment cost $58,000 on March 10, 2012, and depreciation deductions through the date of sale of $27,565 were allowed. The $29,565 ($60,000 − $30,435) total gain is reported on line 24. On line 30, total gains resulting from the sale of all properties ($29,565 in this illustration) reported in Part III are combined. The total amount of ordinary income due to the recapture provisions ($27,565 in this illustration) is reported on line 31 and then reported as ordinary income on line 13 in Part II. The excess of the gain over the amount of ordinary income is reported on line 32. The portion of this gain not due to casualty or theft ($2,000 in this illustration) is a Sec. 1231 gain and is reported on line 6 of Part I of Form 4797. If any of the gain is due to casualty or theft, that portion of the gain is reported on Section B of Form 4684.

Reporting Casualty or Theft Gain or Loss on Form 4684

Section A of Form 4684 is used to report gains and losses resulting from a casualty or theft of personal-use property. These gains and losses are not Sec. 1231 transactions, and Sec. A of Form 4684 is not discussed in this chapter.

Section B of Form 4684, reproduced in Figure I:13-3, is used to report gains and losses resulting from a casualty or theft of property used in a trade or business or held for the

Form **4797**

Department of the Treasury
Internal Revenue Service

Sales of Business Property

(Also Involuntary Conversions and Recapture Amounts Under Sections 179 and 280F(b)(2))

▶ Attach to your tax return.

▶ Information about Form 4797 and its separate instructions is at *www.irs.gov/form4797*.

OMB No. 1545-0184

2014

Attachment Sequence No. 27

Name(s) shown on return	Identifying number

1	Enter the gross proceeds from sales or exchanges reported to you for 2014 on Form(s) 1099-B or 1099-S (or substitute statement) that you are including on line 2, 10, or 20 (see instructions)	1	

Part I **Sales or Exchanges of Property Used in a Trade or Business and Involuntary Conversions From Other Than Casualty or Theft—Most Property Held More Than 1 Year** (see instructions)

2 (a) Description of property	(b) Date acquired (mo., day, yr.)	(c) Date sold (mo., day, yr.)	(d) Gross sales price	(e) Depreciation allowed or allowable since acquisition	(f) Cost or other basis, plus improvements and expense of sale	(g) Gain or (loss) Subtract (f) from the sum of (d) and (e)

3	Gain, if any, from Form 4684, line 39	3	
4	Section 1231 gain from installment sales from Form 6252, line 26 or 37	4	
5	Section 1231 gain or (loss) from like-kind exchanges from Form 8824	5	
6	Gain, if any, from line 32, from other than casualty or theft	6	2,000
7	Combine lines 2 through 6. Enter the gain or (loss) here and on the appropriate line as follows:	7	2,000
	Partnerships (except electing large partnerships) and S corporations. Report the gain or (loss) following the instructions for Form 1065, Schedule K, line 10, or Form 1120S, Schedule K, line 9. Skip lines 8, 9, 11, and 12 below.		
	Individuals, partners, S corporation shareholders, and all others. If line 7 is zero or a loss, enter the amount from line 7 on line 11 below and skip lines 8 and 9. If line 7 is a gain and you did not have any prior year section 1231 losses, or they were recaptured in an earlier year, enter the gain from line 7 as a long-term capital gain on the Schedule D filed with your return and skip lines 8, 9, 11, and 12 below.		
8	Nonrecaptured net section 1231 losses from prior years (see instructions)	8	
9	Subtract line 8 from line 7. If zero or less, enter -0-. If line 9 is zero, enter the gain from line 7 on line 12 below. If line 9 is more than zero, enter the amount from line 8 on line 12 below and enter the gain from line 9 as a long-term capital gain on the Schedule D filed with your return (see instructions)	9	

Part II **Ordinary Gains and Losses** (see instructions)

10 Ordinary gains and losses not included on lines 11 through 16 (include property held 1 year or less):

11	Loss, if any, from line 7	11	( )
12	Gain, if any, from line 7 or amount from line 8, if applicable	12	
13	Gain, if any, from line 31	13	27,565
14	Net gain or (loss) from Form 4684, lines 31 and 38a	14	
15	Ordinary gain from installment sales from Form 6252, line 25 or 36	15	
16	Ordinary gain or (loss) from like-kind exchanges from Form 8824	16	
17	Combine lines 10 through 16	17	27,565
18	For all except individual returns, enter the amount from line 17 on the appropriate line of your return and skip lines a and b below. For individual returns, complete lines a and b below:		
a	If the loss on line 11 includes a loss from Form 4684, line 35, column (b)(ii), enter that part of the loss here. Enter the part of the loss from income-producing property on Schedule A (Form 1040), line 28, and the part of the loss from property used as an employee on Schedule A (Form 1040), line 23. Identify as from "Form 4797, line 18a." See instructions	18a	
b	Redetermine the gain or (loss) on line 17 excluding the loss, if any, on line 18a. Enter here and on Form 1040, line 14	18b	27,565

For Paperwork Reduction Act Notice, see separate instructions. Cat. No. 13086I Form **4797** (2014)

FIGURE I:13-1 ▶ PART I AND PART II OF FORM 4797

Part III **Gain From Disposition of Property Under Sections 1245, 1250, 1252, 1254, and 1255** (see instructions)

19 (a) Description of section 1245, 1250, 1252, 1254, or 1255 property:	(b) Date acquired (mo., day, yr.)	(c) Date sold (mo., day, yr.)
A Equipment	3-10-12	4-30-14
B		
C		
D		

These columns relate to the properties on lines 19A through 19D. ▶		Property A	Property B	Property C	Property D
20 Gross sales price (**Note:** *See line 1 before completing.*)	20	60,000			
21 Cost or other basis plus expense of sale	21	58,000			
22 Depreciation (or depletion) allowed or allowable	22	27,565			
23 Adjusted basis. Subtract line 22 from line 21	23	30,435			
24 Total gain. Subtract line 23 from line 20	24	29,565			
25 **If section 1245 property:**					
a Depreciation allowed or allowable from line 22	25a	27,565			
b Enter the **smaller** of line 24 or 25a	25b	27,565			
26 **If section 1250 property:** If straight line depreciation was used, enter -0- on line 26g, except for a corporation subject to section 291.					
a Additional depreciation after 1975 (see instructions)	26a				
b Applicable percentage multiplied by the **smaller** of line 24 or line 26a (see instructions)	26b				
c Subtract line 26a from line 24. If residential rental property **or** line 24 is not more than line 26a, skip lines 26d and 26e	26c				
d Additional depreciation after 1969 and before 1976	26d				
e Enter the **smaller** of line 26c or 26d	26e				
f Section 291 amount (corporations only)	26f				
g Add lines 26b, 26e, and 26f	26g				
27 **If section 1252 property:** Skip this section if you did not dispose of farmland or if this form is being completed for a partnership (other than an electing large partnership).					
a Soil, water, and land clearing expenses	27a				
b Line 27a multiplied by applicable percentage (see instructions)	27b				
c Enter the **smaller** of line 24 or 27b	27c				
28 **If section 1254 property:**					
a Intangible drilling and development costs, expenditures for development of mines and other natural deposits, mining exploration costs, and depletion (see instructions)	28a				
b Enter the **smaller** of line 24 or 28a	28b				
29 **If section 1255 property:**					
a Applicable percentage of payments excluded from income under section 126 (see instructions)	29a				
b Enter the **smaller** of line 24 or 29a (see instructions)	29b				

Summary of Part III Gains. Complete property columns A through D through line 29b before going to line 30.

30 Total gains for all properties. Add property columns A through D, line 24	30	29,565
31 Add property columns A through D, lines 25b, 26g, 27c, 28b, and 29b. Enter here and on line 13	31	27,565
32 Subtract line 31 from line 30. Enter the portion from casualty or theft on Form 4684, line 33. Enter the portion from other than casualty or theft on Form 4797, line 6	32	2,000

Part IV **Recapture Amounts Under Sections 179 and 280F(b)(2) When Business Use Drops to 50% or Less** (see instructions)

		(a) Section 179	(b) Section 280F(b)(2)
33 Section 179 expense deduction or depreciation allowable in prior years	33		
34 Recomputed depreciation (see instructions)	34		
35 Recapture amount. Subtract line 34 from line 33. See the instructions for where to report	35		

Form **4797** (2014)

FIGURE I:13-2 ▶ PART III OF FORM 4797

Name(s) shown on tax return. Do not enter name and identifying number if shown on other side. | **Identifying number**

SECTION B—Business and Income-Producing Property

Part I Casualty or Theft Gain or Loss (Use a separate Part I for each casualty or theft.)

19 Description of properties (show type, location, and date acquired for each property). Use a separate line for each property lost or damaged from the same casualty or theft. **See instructions if claiming a loss due to a Ponzi-type investment scheme and Section C is not completed.**

Property **A** ____________

Property **B** ____________

Property **C** ____________

Property **D** ____________

		Properties A	Properties B	Properties C	Properties D
20 Cost or adjusted basis of each property	20				
21 Insurance or other reimbursement (whether or not you filed a claim). See the instructions for line 3	21				
Note: *If line 20 is* ***more*** *than line 21, skip line 22.*					
22 Gain from casualty or theft. If line 21 is **more** than line 20, enter the difference here and on line 29 or line 34, column (c), except as provided in the instructions for line 33. Also, skip lines 23 through 27 for that column. See the instructions for line 4 if line 21 includes insurance or other reimbursement you did not claim, or you received payment for your loss in a later tax year	22				
23 Fair market value **before** casualty or theft	23				
24 Fair market value **after** casualty or theft	24				
25 Subtract line 24 from line 23	25				
26 Enter the **smaller** of line 20 or line 25	26				
Note: *If the property was totally destroyed by casualty or lost from theft, enter on line 26 the amount from line 20.*					
27 Subtract line 21 from line 26. If zero or less, enter -0-	27				

28 Casualty or theft loss. Add the amounts on line 27. Enter the total here and on line 29 **or** line 34 (see instructions) | 28 |

Part II Summary of Gains and Losses (from separate Parts I)

(a) Identify casualty or theft		(b) Losses from casualties or thefts (i) Trade, business, rental or royalty property	(b) (ii) Income-producing and employee property	(c) Gains from casualties or thefts includible in income
Casualty or Theft of Property Held One Year or Less				
29		( )	( )	
		( )	( )	
30 Totals. Add the amounts on line 29	30	( )	( )	
31 Combine line 30, columns (b)(i) and (c). Enter the net gain or (loss) here and on Form 4797, line 14. If Form 4797 is not otherwise required, see instructions			31	
32 Enter the amount from line 30, column (b)(ii) here. Individuals, enter the amount from income-producing property on Schedule A (Form 1040), line 28, or Form 1040NR, Schedule A, line 14, and enter the amount from property used as an employee on Schedule A (Form 1040), line 23, or Form 1040NR, Schedule A, line 9. Estates and trusts, partnerships, and S corporations, see instructions			32	
Casualty or Theft of Property Held More Than One Year				
33 Casualty or theft gains from Form 4797, line 32			33	
34		( )	( )	
		( )	( )	
35 Total losses. Add amounts on line 34, columns (b)(i) and (b)(ii)	35	( )	( )	
36 Total gains. Add lines 33 and 34, column (c)			36	
37 Add amounts on line 35, columns (b)(i) and (b)(ii)			37	

38 If the loss on line 37 is **more** than the gain on line 36:

a Combine line 35, column (b)(i) and line 36, and enter the net gain or (loss) here. Partnerships (except electing large partnerships) and S corporations, see the note below. All others, enter this amount on Form 4797, line 14. If Form 4797 is not otherwise required, see instructions | 38a |

b Enter the amount from line 35, column (b)(ii) here. Individuals, enter the amount from income-producing property on Schedule A (Form 1040), line 28, or Form 1040NR, Schedule A, line 14, and enter the amount from property used as an employee on Schedule A (Form 1040), line 23, or Form 1040NR, Schedule A, line 9. Estates and trusts, enter on the "Other deductions" line of your tax return. Partnerships (except electing large partnerships) and S corporations, see the note below. Electing large partnerships, enter on Form 1065-B, Part II, line 11 | 38b |

39 If the loss on line 37 is **less** than or **equal** to the gain on line 36, combine lines 36 and 37 and enter here. Partnerships (except electing large partnerships), see the note below. All others, enter this amount on Form 4797, line 3 | 39 |

Note: *Partnerships, enter the amount from line 38a, 38b, or line 39 on Form 1065, Schedule K, line 11. S corporations, enter the amount from line 38a or 38b on Form 1120S, Schedule K, line 10.*

Form **4684** (2014)

FIGURE I:13-3 ▶ SECTION B OF FORM 4684

production of income. Note that a separate Part I is used for each different casualty or theft. Gains are reported on line 26, and losses are reported on line 32. For properties held a year or less, the gains and losses are reported on lines 33 through 36 of Part II. These gains and losses are either recorded as ordinary gains and losses on line 14 of Part II of Form 4797 or as itemized deductions on Schedule A of Form 1040.

For properties held more than a year, the gains and losses are reported on lines 40 and 41. If gains exceed losses, the net gain is reported on line 43 and then on line 3 of Part I of Form 4797 (i.e., the gains and losses are treated as Sec. 1231 gains and losses). If the losses exceed the gains, all or part of the gains and losses are reported as ordinary in Part II of Form 4797 and/or on Schedule A of Form 1040.

PROBLEM MATERIALS

DISCUSSION QUESTIONS

I:13-1 Explain how the gain on the sale or exchange of land could be classified as either ordinary income, a Sec. 1231 gain, or a LTCG, depending on the facts and circumstances.

I:13-2 Why were taxpayers reluctant to sell appreciated business property between 1938 and 1942? What effect did this reluctance have on the tax law?

I:13-3 Alice owns timber, purchased six years ago, with an adjusted basis of $50,000. The timber is cut for use in her furniture business on October 1, when the FMV of the timber is $200,000. The FMV of the timber on January 1 is $190,000. May Alice treat any of the gain as Sec. 1231 gain? If so, how much?

I:13-4 Explain how the gain from an involuntary conversion of business property held more than one year is taxed if the involuntary conversion is the result of a condemnation. Explain the tax treatment if the involuntary conversion is due to a casualty.

I:13-5 When is livestock considered Sec. 1231 property?

I:13-6 When is a net Sec. 1231 gain treated as ordinary income?

I:13-7 Carlie who is single has a Sec. 1231 gain of $10,000 and no Sec. 1231 losses during the current year. Explain why the gain might be taxed at (a) 15%, (b) 39.6%, (c) 25%, (d) 20%, or (e) zero.

I:13-8 Why is it unlikely that gains due to the sale of equipment will be treated as Sec. 1231 gains?

I:13-9 Hank sells equipment used in a trade or business for $25,000. The equipment costs $30,000 and has an adjusted basis of $25,500. Why is it important to know the holding period?

I:13-10 Jackie purchases equipment during the current year for $800,000 that has a seven-year MACRS recovery period. She expects to sell the property after three years. Jackie anticipates that her marginal tax rate in the year of sale will be significantly higher than her current marginal tax rate. Why might it be advantageous for her to use the straight-line method of depreciation?

I:13-11 Karen purchased a computer three years ago for $15,300 to use exclusively in her business. She expensed the entire cost of the computer under Sec. 179. If she sells the computer during the current year for $3,721, what is the amount and character of her recognized gain?

I:13-12 Sheila owns a motel that is used in a trade or business. If she sells the motel, the gain will be Sec. 1245 ordinary income. During what period of time was the motel placed into service?

I:13-13 Will an individual taxpayer ever have to recognize Sec. 1250 ordinary income on the sale of a building used for business and placed in service after 1986? Explain.

I:13-14 Marty sells his fully depreciated building at a gain to an unrelated party. The building is purchased before 1981. Is any of the gain taxed as ordinary income?

I:13-15 Which of the following assets (assume all assets have a holding period of more than one year) do not qualify as Sec. 1231 property: inventory, a pig held for breeding, land used as a parking lot for customers, and marketable securities?

I:13-16 When is an office building subject to the depreciation recapture rules of Sec. 1245?

I:13-17 Does a building that is 60% rented for residential use and 40% for commercial use qualify as residential rental property?

I:13-18 Roger owns an apartment complex with a FMV of $2 million. If he sells the apartment complex, $700,000 of the gain is Sec. 1231 gain with $600,000 taxed at 25% because it is unrecaptured Sec. 1250 gain. If he dies before selling the apartment complex and his estate sells the property for $2 million, how much ordinary income must the estate recognize?

I:13-19 Rashad owns a duplex used 100% as residential rental property. Under what conditions, if any, will any gain that he recognizes be Sec. 1245 ordinary income?

I:13-20 John and Karen are unrelated individuals. John sold land that is Sec. 1231 property held for three years and recognized a $50,000 gain. Karen sold a building that is Sec. 1231 property held for three years and recognized a $50,000 gain. Straight-line depreciation was used. John and Karen both have a 33% tax rate, no other transactions involving capital assets or 1231 assets, and no nonrecaptured Sec. 1231 losses. Except for the sales of different assets, their tax situation is exactly the same. As a result of selling his Sec. 1231 property, will John pay more, less or the same amount of taxes than Karen as a result of selling her Sec. 1231 property? Explain.

I:13-21 Why may a corporation recognize a greater amount of ordinary income due to the sale of Sec. 1250 property than a noncorporate taxpayer?

I:13-22 Assume a taxpayer sells equipment used in a trade or business for a gain that is less than the depreciation allowed. If the taxpayer is a corporation, will a greater amount of Sec. 1245 income be recognized than if the taxpayer is an individual? Explain.

I:13-23 Dale owns business equipment with a $100,000 FMV and an adjusted basis of $60,000. The property was originally acquired for $150,000. Which one of the following transactions would result in recognition of $40,000 ordinary income by Dale due to the depreciation recapture rules of Sec. 1245?

a. He makes a gift of the property to a daughter.

b. He contributes the property to a qualified charitable organization.

c. He disposes of the equipment in an installment sale and receives $10,000 cash in the year of sale.

I:13-24 Carlos owns equipment with an $800,000 acquisition cost, a $270,000 adjusted basis, and a $500,000 FMV. Carlos makes a gift of the equipment to a charitable organization. The equipment is used by the charity in its exempt function. What is the amount of his charitable contribution deduction?

I:13-25 Ted owns a warehouse that cost $850,000 in 1984 and is subject to depreciation recapture under Sec. 1245. The warehouse, which has an adjusted basis of zero, is destroyed by a tornado and Ted receives $580,000 from the insurance company. Within nine months, he pays $500,000 for a new warehouse and an election is made to defer the gain under Sec. 1033. What is the amount and character of Ted's recognized gain?

I:13-26 When a taxpayer disposes of oil, gas, or geothermal property, part or all of the gain may be recaptured as ordinary income. Explain how the recapture amount is determined for oil and gas and geothermal properties.

I:13-27 William owns two appreciated assets, land and a building, which have been used in his trade or business since purchased in 1990. If he sells the two assets to his 100%-owned corporation, will William have to recognize any ordinary income? Explain.

ISSUE IDENTIFICATION QUESTIONS

I:13-28 Six years ago Joelle started raising chinchillas. She separates her chinchillas into two groups, a breeding group and a market group. During the year, she had the following sales of chinchillas from her market group: 400 to producers of fur products; 100 to pet stores; and 25 to individuals to use as pets. From her breeding stock, she sold six chinchillas to Rebecca, an individual who is starting a chinchilla ranch, and five to Fur Pelts, a producer of fur products. All 11 chinchillas from the breeding group have been held for at least 22 months, and the five sold to Fur Pelts were poor performers.

I:13-29 Green Acres, Inc., owns 1,400 acres adjacent to land owned by the U.S. government. The government, wanting to sell timber from its land, had to assure prospective bidders of access to the timber. The government entered into an agreement with Green Acres for a logging road easement across land owned by Green Acres. The government agreed to pay $2 per thousand board feet of timber removed up to a maximum of $130,000. Bidders for the rights to obtain the government's timber had to agree to pay the fee to Green Acres as part of their bids for the timber. Stanley Lumberyard, Inc. provided the highest bid and paid $80,000 to Green Acres during the first year of cutting and removing the timber and $50,000 during the second year. What tax issues should Green Acres and Stanley Lumberyard consider?

I:13-30 Sarah, who has been in the business of erecting, maintaining, and renting outdoor advertising displays for 18 years, has an offer to purchase her business. Two basic types of advertising displays are used in her business: structure X and structure Y. Structure X consists of a single sign face nailed to a wooden support frame and attached to wooden poles 30 feet long. Its structure is rather easy to dismantle and move from one location to another. In contrast, structure Y is a permanent sign that is designed to withstand winds of up to 100 miles per hour. None of the Structure Y signs have ever been moved. What tax issues should Sarah consider?

I:13-31 Sylvester owns and operates an unincorporated pizza business that delivers pizza to customers. Three years ago, he acquired an automobile for $10,000 to provide delivery service. Recently, Sylvester hired an employee who prefers to use his personal automobile to make the deliveries. Thus, Sylvester decided to permit his 18-year old daughter to use the automobile for her personal use. The automobile's adjusted basis is $3,080 and its FMV is $4,700. What tax issues should Sylvester consider?

PROBLEMS

I:13-32 *Secs. 1231, 1245, and 1250 Transactions.* All assets listed below have been held for more than one year. Which assets might be classified as Sec. 1231, Sec. 1245, or Sec. 1250 property? An asset may be classified as more than one type of property.

a. Land on which a factory is located
b. Equipment used in the factory
c. Raw materials inventory
d. Patent purchased to allow use of a manufacturing process
e. Land held primarily for sale
f. Factory building acquired in 1986 (the straight-line ACRS recovery method is used)

I:13-33 *Sec. 1231 Gains and Losses.* Vivian's AGI is $40,000 without considering the gains and losses below. Determine her revised AGI after the inclusion of any applicable gains or losses for the following independent cases. Assume she has no nonrecaptured net Sec. 1231 losses at the beginning of the year.

	Case A	*Case B*	*Case C*	*Case D*
Sec. 1231 gain	$19,000	$10,000	$30,000	$ 5,000
Sec. 1231 loss	5,000	22,000	39,000	12,000
LTCG	–0–	–0–	6,300	–0–
LTCL	–0–	–0–	–0–	4,200

I:13-34 *Sec. 1231 Gains and Losses.* Edith, who has no other sales or exchanges and no nonrecaptured Sec. 1231 losses, sells three tracts of land that are used in her trade or business. Edith is single, and her regular income tax rate is 33%.

Asset #1—$15,000 gain and holding period of 20 months
Asset #2—$17,000 loss and holding period of 25 months
Asset #3—$ 5,000 gain and holding period of 13 months

a. What is the increase in her taxes as a result of the three sales?
b. If the holding period for Asset #2 is nine months, what is the decrease in her taxes as a result of the three sales?
c. Same as part a except her tax rate is 39.6%.

I:13-35 *Sec. 1231 Transactions.* Which of the following transactions or events is treated as a Sec. 1231 gain or loss? All assets are held for more than one year.

a. Theft of uninsured diamond ring, with an $800 basis and a $1,000 FMV.
b. Gain due to condemnation of land used in business.
c. Loss on the sale of a warehouse.
d. Gain of $4,000 on the sale of equipment. Depreciation deductions allowed amount to $10,000.

I:13-36 *Capital Loss Versus Sec. 1231 Loss.* Vicki has an AGI of $70,000 without considering the sale of a nondepreciable asset for $23,000. The asset was acquired six years ago and has an adjusted basis of $35,000. She has no other sales or exchanges. Determine her AGI for the following independent situations when the asset is:

a. A capital asset.
b. Sec. 1231 property.

I:13-37 *Ordinary Income Versus Sec. 1231 Gain.* At the beginning of 2015, Silver Corporation has a $95,000 capital loss carryforward from 2014. During 2015, the corporation sells land, held for four years, and realizes an $80,000 gain. Silver has no unrecaptured net Sec. 1231 losses, and it made no other sales during the current year. Determine the amount of capital loss carryforward that Silver can use in 2015 if the land is:

a. Sec. 1231 property.
b. Not a capital asset or Sec. 1231 property.

I:13-38 *Sec. 1231 Transactions.* During the current year, Sean's office building is destroyed by fire. After collecting the insurance proceeds, Sean has a $50,000 recognized gain. The building was acquired in 1998, and the straight-line method of depreciation has been used. He does not plan to acquire a replacement building. In addition to the gain on the building, consider the following independent cases and determine his total net capital gain. For each case, include the $50,000 casualty gain described above.

a. Land used in his trade or business and held more than a year is condemned by the state. The recognized gain is $60,000.
b. Assume the same facts as in Part a, except the condemnation results in a $60,000 loss.
c. An apartment building used as residential rental property and held more than one year is destroyed by a sudden, unexpected mudslide. The building is not insured, and the loss amounts to $200,000.

I:13-39 *Nonrecaptured Net Sec. 1231 Losses.* Consider the following summary of Sec. 1231 gains and losses recognized by Janet during the period 2010–2015. Janet had no nonrecaptured Sec. 1231 losses at the beginning of 2010. If Janet has no capital gains and losses during the six-year period, determine her net capital gain for each year.

	Sec. 1231 Gains	*Sec. 1231 Losses*
2010	$ 9,000	$ 7,000
2011	20,000	24,000
2012	12,000	19,000
2013	9,000	4,000
2014	25,000	13,200
2015	10,000	17,000

I:13-40 *Nonrecaptured Net Sec. 1231 Losses.* Dillion whose taxable income is less than $300,000 has a tax rate of 33% on his ordinary income and $40,000 of net nonrecaptured Sec. 1231 losses at the start of the year. During the year, he recognizes a Sec. 1231 gain of $53,000 from the sale of land. As a result of the sale, how much does Dillion's tax liability increase?

I:13-41 *Sec. 1245.* The Pear Corporation owns equipment with a $300,000 adjusted basis. The equipment was purchased six years ago for $650,000. If Pear sells the equipment for the selling prices given in the three independent cases below, what are the amount and character of Pear's recognized gain or loss?

Case	*Selling Price*
A	$407,000
B	752,000
C	245,000

I:13-42 *Sec. 1245.* Elizabeth owns equipment that cost $500,000 and has an adjusted basis of $230,000. If the straight-line method of depreciation had been used, the adjusted basis would be $300,000.

a. What is the maximum selling price that she could sell the equipment for without having to recognize Sec. 1245 ordinary income?
b. If she sold the equipment and had to recognize $61,000 of Sec. 1245 ordinary income, what was the selling price?

I:13-43 *Sale of Business and Personal-Use Property.* Arnie, a college student, purchased a truck in 2013 for $6,000. He used the truck 70% of the time as a distributor for the local newspaper and 30% of the time for personal use. The truck has a five-year recovery period, and he claimed depreciation deductions of $840 in 2013 and $1,344 in 2014. Arnie sells the truck on June 20, 2015, for $3,000.

a. What is the amount of allowable depreciation in 2015?
b. Determine Arnie's realized and recognized gain or loss and its character.

I:13-44 *Like-Kind Exchange of Sec. 1245 Property.* General Corporation owns equipment which cost $70,000 and has a $44,000 adjusted basis. General exchanges the equipment for other equipment ($42,000 FMV) and marketable securities ($30,000 FMV). Determine the following:

a. Realized gain
b. Recognized gain
c. Gain treated as ordinary income
d. Gain treated as Sec. 1231 gain
e. Basis of marketable securities received
f. Basis of equipment received

I:13-45 *Like-Kind Exchange of Sec. 1245 Property.* Leroy owns a truck used in his trade or business that cost $50,000 and has an adjusted basis of $34,000. The truck is exchanged for a new truck that is like-kind property with a FMV of $40,000. Prior to selling the new truck two years later, Leroy is allowed depreciation of $13,000 for the new truck. Determine:

a. Realized gain on the exchange
b. Recognized gain on the exchange
c. Basis of truck received
d. Recognized gain, and the character of the gain, if the sales price of the truck is $41,000
e. Recognized gain, and the character of the gain, if the sale price of the truck is $52,000

I:13-46 *Purpose of Sec. 1245.* Martin owns equipment used in his trade or business purchased four years ago for $200,000. Martin sells the equipment in the current year for $110,000 when its adjusted basis is $52,000. No other sales or exchanges are made this year or the preceding five years. His tax rate is 35% for all years since the year of purchase.

a. Determine the increase in Martin's AGI for the current year as a result of the sale if Sec. 1245 did not exist.
b. Determine the increase in Martin's AGI for the current year as a result of the sale if Sec. 1245 does exist.
c. Given that Sec. 1245 does exist, how much higher is his tax in (b) than in (a)?

I:13-47 *Secs. 1231 and 1250-Real Property Placed in Service Before 1981.* Charles owns an office building and land that are used in his trade or business. The office building and land were acquired in 1978 for $800,000 and $100,000, respectively. During the current year, the properties are sold for $900,000 with 20% of the selling price being allocated to the land. The assets as shown on the taxpayer's books before their sale are as follows:

Building	$800,000	
Accumulated depreciation	690,000[a]	$110,000
Land		100,000

[a]If the straight-line method of depreciation had been used, the accumulated depreciation would be $560,000.

a. What is the recognized gain due to the sale of the building?
b. What is the character of the recognized gain due to the sale of the building?
c. What is the recognized gain and character of the gain due to the sale of the land?

I:13-48 Assume the same facts as in Problem I:13-47 except the taxpayer is a corporation and answer the same questions.

I:13-49 *Secs. 1231, 1245, and Unrecaptured Sec. 1250.* Brigham is single and is in the 33% marginal income tax bracket. He has the sales or exchanges below. At the beginning of the year, he has nonrecaptured net Sec. 1231 losses of $10,000. Determine the increase or decrease in Brigham's tax liability as a result of the following independent sales or exchanges.

a. Sells equipment used in his trade or business for $40,000. The equipment was purchased for $100,000 and depreciation allowed amounts to $72,000.
b. Sells land used in his trade or business for $80,000. The land was purchased four years ago for $61,000.
c. He sells a building used in his trade or business for $163,000. The building was purchased in 1988 for $250,000 and depreciation allowed amounts to $110,000.
d. Same as Part c except he sells the building for $127,000.

I:13-50 *Secs. 1245 and 1231.* The LaPoint Corporation placed in service $350,000 of used equipment (7-year recovery property) on June 3, 2014 and elected to expense $250,000 as Sec. 179 depreciation expense. LaPont sold the equipment for $150,000 on November 22, 2015. Determine the following:

a. Depreciation allowed in 2014
b. Depreciation allowed during 2015
c. Amount of gain or loss and character

I:13-51 *Unrecaptured Sec. 1250 Gain and 1231.* Mr. Briggs purchased an apartment complex on January 10, 2013, for $2 million with 10% of the price allocated to land. He sells the complex on October 22, 2015, for $2.5 million. Assume that 10% of the $2.5 million selling price is allocated to land and 90% is allocated to the building.

a. How much depreciation was allowed for 2013?
b. How much depreciation is allowed for 2015?
c. Will any of the gain be ordinary income?
d. What is the amount of gain and the character of the gain on the sale of the building?

e. What is the amount of gain and the character of the gain on the sale of the land?
f. Will any of the gain be taxed at 25%?

I:13-52 *Sec. 1250 Residential Rental Property-Placed in Service After 1981 and Before 1987.* Jesse owns a duplex used as residential rental property. The duplex cost $100,000 in 1986, and 10% of the cost was allocated to the land. Total cost-recovery deductions allowed amount to $90,000. The statutory percentages were used to compute cost-recovery deductions. If the straight-line method of cost recovery were used instead, $90,000 of cost-recovery deductions would have been allowed.
a. What is the amount of recognized gain and the character of the gain if Jesse sells the duplex for $125,000 with 10% of the price allocated to land?
b. Same as (a) except the building is an office building.

I:13-53 *Sec. 1250-Real Property Placed in Service Before 1981.* Rosemary owns an office building placed in service in 1980 that cost $625,000 and has an adjusted basis of $227,000. If the straight-line method of depreciation were used, the adjusted basis would be $300,000.
a. What is the maximum selling price that she could sell the building for without having to recognize Sec. 1250 ordinary income?
b. If she sold the building and had to recognize $51,000 of Sec. 1250 ordinary income, what was the selling price?

I:13-54 *Nonresidential Real Property-Noncorporate Taxpayer.* Consider three office buildings placed in service as shown below and answer the following true-false questions. Assume all assets are sold by a noncorporate taxpayer at a gain and there are no other sales or exchanges or nonrecaptured Sec. 1231 loss unless told otherwise. None of the buildings are fully depreciated when sold and the taxpayer's tax rate is more than 25%.

	Placed in Service
Building #1	Before 1981
Building #2	After 1980 and before 1987
Building #3	After 1986

1. Some or all of the gain on sale of #1 is ordinary if accelerated depreciation was used.
2. If the straight-line method of depreciation was used for #1, some or all of the gain may be taxed at 25%.
3. Gain on the sale of #2 could be Sec. 1245 ordinary income.
4. Gain on the sale of #2 could be Sec. 1231 gain.
5. Part of the gain on the sale of #2 could be Sec. 1245 ordinary income and part could be Sec. 1231 gain.
6. If the straight-line method of depreciation was used for #2, some or all of the gain may be taxed at 25%.
7. Some or all of the gain on the sale of #3 could be Sec. 1245 ordinary income.
8. Some or all of the gain on the sale of #3 could be taxed at 25%.
9. Some of the gain on the sale of #3 could be Sec. 1250 ordinary income.
10. If the taxpayer has a nonrecaptured Sec. 1231 loss of $30,000 and the gain on the sale of #3 is $40,000, all $40,000 of the gain is taxed as ordinary income.

I:13-55 *Nonresidential Real Property-Corporate Taxpayer.* Assume the same facts as in Problem I:13-54 except the taxpayer is a corporate taxpayer with a 34% tax rate and answer the ten true-false questions.

I:13-56 *Secs. 1231 and 1250-Placed in Service After 1986.* Molly, whose tax rate is 39.6% , sells an apartment complex for $4.5 million with 10% of the price allocated to land. The apartment complex was purchased in 1993. She has no other sales or exchanges during the year and no nonrecaptured net Sec. 1231 losses. Information about the assets at the time of sale is:

	Building	*Land*
Original Cost	$2,700,000	$300,000
Accumulated Depreciation	1,000,000	0

a. What is the recognized gain on the sale of the building and the character of the gain?
b. What is the recognized gain on the sale of the land and the character of the gain?
c. How much of the Sec. 1231 gain is taxed at 25%?
d. If Molly has NSTCL of $50,000, will the capital loss reduce the Sec. 1231 gain taxed at 25% or 20%?

I:13-57 *Secs. 1231 and 1250 for Corporate Taxpayer.* Assume the same facts as in Problem I:13-56 except the taxpayer is a corporation instead of an individual.

a. What is the recognized gain on the sale of the building and the character of the gain?
b. What is the recognized gain on the sale of the land and the character of the gain?
c. How much of the Sec. 1231 gain is taxed at 25%?

I:13-58 *Charitable Contribution of Sec. 1231 Property.* Raquel owns land used in her trade or business for more than one year. The basis is $10,000 and its FMV is $40,000. Her tax rate is 33% and her AGI is $250,000. She makes no other charitable contributions except for the ones considered below.

a. If she gives the land to a university, determine her tax savings.
b. If she sells the land for $40,000, pays the tax and then contributes the remainder of the cash to the charity, determine her tax savings because of the contribution and the amount that the university receives. Assume that she has no other sales or exchanges during the year.

I:13-59 *Secs. 1231, 1245 and 1250.* Glen, whose tax rate is 33%, sells each of the following assets for $200,000. Each case is an independent case.

	Sec. 1231 Gain (Loss)	*Ordinary Income*	*Taxed at 33%*	*Taxed at 25%*	*Taxed at 20%*	*Taxed at 15%*
Building purchased in 1999 for $220,000 with adjusted basis of $165,000	_____	_____	_____	_____	_____	_____
Equipment purchased in 2011 for $300,000 with adjusted basis of $144,000	_____	_____	_____	_____	_____	_____
Land purchased in 1992 for $30,000 to use as a building site	_____	_____	_____	_____	_____	_____
Building purchased in 1997 for $150,000 with adjusted basis of $112,000	_____	_____	_____	_____	_____	_____
Equipment purchased in 2012 for $180,000 with adjusted basis of $140,000	_____	_____	_____	_____	_____	_____

I:13-60 *Recapture of Soil and Water Conservation Expenditures.* Bob owns farmland with a $600,000 basis, and he elects to expense $100,000 of expenditures incurred for soil and water conservation purposes. Bob sells the farmland after farming for seven years and four months. What is the amount of the recognized gain and the character of the gain if the selling price is

a. $825,000
b. $615,000

I:13-61 *Recapture of Intangible Drilling Costs.* Jeremy purchased undeveloped oil and gas property five years ago. He paid $300,000 for intangible drilling and development costs and elected to expense the $300,000. During the current year, Jeremy sells the property, which has an $800,000 adjusted basis, for $900,000. What is the amount of gain treated as ordinary income under Sec. 1254 because of the election to expense intangible drilling and development costs?

I:13-62 *Recapture of Intangible Drilling Costs and Depletion.* In 2009, Jack purchased undeveloped oil and gas property for $900,000 and paid $170,000 for intangible drilling and development costs. He elected to expense the intangible drilling and development costs. During the current year he sells the property for $950,000 when the property's adjusted basis is $700,000. Depletion of $200,000 was allowed on the property.

a. What is the realized gain and how much of the gain is ordinary income?
b. For Jack to have a Sec. 1231 gain, the selling price must exceed what amount?

I:13-63 *Related Party Transactions.* Ed operates a storage business as a sole proprietorship and owns the following assets acquired in 1996:

Warehouse	$400,000
Minus: Accumulated depreciation	(230,000)

Adjusted basis	$170,000
Land	65,000

The FMV of the warehouse and the land are $500,000 and $200,000, respectively. Ed owns 75% of the stock of the Crane Corporation. If he sells the two assets to Crane at a price equal to the FMV of the assets, determine the recognized gain and its character due to the sale of the:

a. Building
b. Land

COMPREHENSIVE PROBLEM

I:13-64 Betty, whose tax rate is 33%, is in the business of breeding and racing horses. Except for the transactions below, she has no other sales or exchanges and she has no unrecaptured net Sec. 1231 losses. Consider the following transactions that occur during the year:

- A building with an adjusted basis of $300,000 is destroyed by fire. Insurance proceeds of $500,000 are received, but Betty does not plan to replace the building. The building was built 12 years ago at a cost of $430,000 and used to provide lodging for her employees. Straight-line depreciation has been used.
- Four acres of the farm are condemned by the state to widen the highway and Betty receives $50,000. The land was inherited from her mother 15 years ago when its FMV was $15,000. Her mother purchased the land for $10,300. Betty does not plan to purchase additional land.
- A racehorse purchased four years ago for $200,000 was sold for $550,000. Total depreciation allowed using the straight-line method amounts to $160,000.
- Equipment purchased three years ago for $200,000 is exchanged for $100,000 of IBM common stock. The adjusted basis of the equipment is $120,000. If straight-line depreciation had been used, the adjusted basis would be $152,000.
- An uninsured pony, with an adjusted basis of $20,000 and FMV of $35,000, that her daughter uses only for personal use is injured while attempting a jump. Because of the injury, the uninsured pony has to be destroyed by a veterinarian.

a. What amount of Sec. 1245 ordinary income must be recognized?
b. What amount of Sec. 1250 ordinary income must be recognized?
c. Will the loss resulting from the destruction of her daughter's pony be used to determine net Sec. 1231 gains or losses?
d. What is the amount of the net Sec. 1231 gain or loss?
e. After all of the netting of gains or losses is completed, will the gain resulting from the involuntary conversion of the building be treated as LTCG?
f. What is the amount of her Sec. 1231 gain that is unrecaptured Sec. 1250 gain?

TAX STRATEGY PROBLEMS

I:13-65 Russ has never recognized any Sec. 1231 gains or losses. In December 2015, Russ is considering the sale of two Sec. 1231 assets. The sale of one asset will result in a $20,000 Sec. 1231 gain while the sale of the other asset will result in a $20,000 Sec. 1231 loss. Russ has no other capital or Sec. 1231 gains and losses in 2015 and does not expect to have any other capital or Sec. 1231 gains and losses in 2015. He is aware that it might be advantageous to recognize the Sec. 1231 gain and the Sec. 1231 loss in different tax years. However, he does not know whether he should recognize the Sec. 1231 gain in 2015 and the Sec. 1231 loss in 2016 or vice versa. His marginal tax rate for each year is expected to be 33%. Advise the taxpayer with respect to these two alternatives:

a. Recognize the $20,000 Sec. 1231 loss in 2015 and the $20,000 Sec. 1231 gain in 2016.
b. Recognize the $20,000 Sec. 1231 gain in 2015 and the $20,000 Sec. 1231 loss in 2016.

I:13-66 Holly has recognized a $9,000 STCL. She has no other recognized capital gains and losses in 2015. She is considering the sale of a Sec. 1231 asset held for four years at a $5,000 gain in 2015. She had not recognized any Sec. 1231 losses during the previous five years and does not expect to have any other Sec. 1231 transactions in 2015. Her marginal tax rate for 2015 is 33%. What is the amount of increase in her 2015 taxes if Holly recognizes the $5,000 Sec. 1231 gain in 2015?

TAX FORM/RETURN PREPARATION PROBLEMS

I:13-67 George Buckner sells an apartment building on October 10 for $1.75 million. The building was purchased on January 1, 1995, for $2 million. Depreciation of $420,000 has been taken. The figures given above do not include the purchase price or the selling price of the land. Mr. Buckner's adjusted basis for the land is $200,000, and the sales price is $350,000. Mr. Buckner, who owns and operates a taxi business, sells one of the automobiles for $1,800 on November 14th. The automobile's adjusted basis is zero, and the original cost is $15,000. The automobile was purchased on April 25, 2006. Mr. Buckner has no other gains and losses during the year, and nonrecaptured net Sec. 1231 losses amount to $32,000. Prepare Form 4797.

I:13-68 Julie Hernandez is single and has no dependents. She operates a dairy farm and her Social Security number is 000-00-1111. She lives at 1325 Vermont Street in Costa, Florida. Consider the following information for the current year:

- Schedule C was prepared by her accountant and the net profit from the dairy operations is $48,000.
- Itemized deductions amount to $4,185.
- Dividend income (qualified dividend) amounts to $280.
- State income tax refund received during the year is $125. She did not itemize last year.
- In June, a burglar broke into her house and stole the following two assets, which were acquired in 1988:

	Basis	*FMV*	*Insurance Proceeds Received*
Painting	$2,000	$10,000	$9,000
Sculpture	1,700	1,500	0

The following assets used in her business were sold during the year:

	Acquisition Date	*Original Cost*	*Depreciation to Date of Sale*	*Date of Sale*	*Selling Price*
Tractor	June 10, 2004	$25,000	$25,000	Oct. 20	$ 8,300
Barn	May 23, 1994	90,000	61,000	May 13	87,000
Land	May 23, 1994	15,000	–0–	May 13	27,000
Cows	Sept. 7, 2012	20,000	13,000	Nov. 8	21,000

In August, three acres of the farm were taken by the state under the right of eminent domain for the purpose of building a highway. The basis of the three acres is $1,500, and the state paid the FMV, $22,000, on February 10. The farm was purchased on August 12, 1976.

Nonrecaptured net Section 1231 losses from the five most recent tax years preceding the current year amount to $7,000. Estimated taxes paid during the year amount to $32,000.

Prepare Forms 1040, 4684 Section A, 4797, and Schedule D. (Do not consider the alternative minimum tax or self-employment taxes discussed in Chapter I:14.)

CASE STUDY PROBLEMS

I:13-69 Your client, Kent Earl, whose tax rate is 35%, owns a bowling alley and has indicated that he wants to sell the business for $1 million and purchase a minor league baseball franchise. His business consists of the following tangible assets:

	Acquisition Date	*Original Cost*	*Adjusted Basis*
Equipment	2003	$600,000	$150,000
Building	2003	900,000	494,000
Land	1988	100,000	100,000
Inventory	Current year	50,000	50,000

Because you have another client, Tom Quick, who is interested in purchasing a business, you informed Tom of Kent's interest in selling. Tom wants to purchase the bowling alley, and the price sounds right to him. The bowling alley business has been very profitable in the last few years because Kent has developed a loyal group of customers by promoting bowling leagues during the week days and a special Saturday afternoon session for children in the elementary school grades. Kent and Tom have come to you and want to know how the transaction should be handled for the best tax results. You know that the $1 million purchase price will have to be allocated among the assets and it will be necessary to estimate the FMV of all assets. Because FMV is often subjective, Kent and Tom recognize that some flexibility might exist in allocating the purchase price. For example, it might be just as easy to justify a FMV of $300,000 or $325,000 for the equipment.

a. What advice do you have for Kent with respect to the allocation (i.e., should he be interested in allocating more to some assets than others)? Explain the reasoning for your advice.

b. Would your advice to Kent be different if he had a large amount of capital losses and no nonrecaptured net Sec. 1231 losses?

c. What advice do you have for Tom with respect to the allocation (i.e., should he be interested in allocating more of the purchase price to some assets than to others)? Explain the reasoning for your advice.

d. What advantages might result from having Kent sign an agreement not to compete (i.e., operate a bowling alley)?

e. Should you have a concern about the ethical implications of advising both Kent and Tom?

I:13-70 Assume the same facts as in Case Study Problem I:13-69 except you have the following market values as a result of an appraisal:

Equipment	$ 250,000
Building	500,000
Land	140,000
Inventory	110,000
Total	$1,000,000

Tom insists that $150,000 of the purchase price should be allocated to inventory and $100,000 should be allocated to land. He refuses to complete the purchase unless the allocation is made as he requests. What action should you take with respect to Tom's request? (See Chapter I:10 for a discussion of valuation issues in the purchase and sale of a business.)

TAX RESEARCH PROBLEM

I:13-71 Berkeley Corporation has a policy of furnishing new automobiles to the athletic department of the local university. The automobiles are used for short periods of time by the extremely popular head basketball coach. When the automobiles are returned to Berkeley Corporation, they are sold to regular customers. The owner of Berkeley Corporation maintains that any such cars held for more than one year should qualify as Sec. 1231 property. Do you agree?

Research sources include:

- Rev. Rul. 75-538, 1975-2 C.B. 34

CHAPTER 14

SPECIAL TAX COMPUTATION METHODS, TAX CREDITS, AND PAYMENT OF TAX

LEARNING OBJECTIVES

After studying this chapter, you should be able to

1. Calculate the alternative minimum tax
2. Describe self-employment income and compute the self-employment tax
3. Describe the various business and personal tax credits
4. Describe and compute the premium tax credit and the shared responsibility payment
5. Explain the mechanics of the federal withholding tax system and the requirements for making estimated tax payments
6. Describe tax planning considerations for AMT, tax credits, and payment of taxes
7. Describe compliance and procedural considerations for AMT, tax credits, and payment of taxes

CHAPTER OUTLINE

Chapter I:2 discussed the basic tax computation for individuals using the tax table and tax rate schedules. This chapter completes the discussion of the tax computation by examining three principal topics:

1. Two additional taxes: the alternative minimum tax and self-employment tax;
2. Various tax credits that reduce tax liability; and
3. Methods for prepayment of an individual's tax liability, including wage withholding and estimated tax payments.

ALTERNATIVE MINIMUM TAX

OBJECTIVE 1

Calculate the alternative minimum tax

Over the years, Congress has used the income tax law for a variety of purposes beyond raising revenue to fund government operations, such as enacting provisions to promote economic and social goals. As the number of special tax provisions increased, many taxpayers were able to plan their financial affairs to substantially reduce or eliminate their income tax liability. As a result, in 1969, Congress passed a new set of rules to ensure that all taxpayers would pay at least a minimum amount of income tax. Thus was born what is known today as the **alternative minimum tax** (**AMT**).

The present AMT system operates as a separate tax system, parallel to the regular income tax system. Taxpayers first determine their regular income tax liability and then determine their tax liability under the AMT system. They must pay the *greater* of the regular income tax or their tax under the AMT system.

The AMT system applies to individuals, corporations, estates, and trusts.[1] It requires taxpayers to modify the amount of their regular taxable income for a number of adjustments and preferences and to subtract an AMT exemption, with the result being the tax base for the AMT system. AMT tax rates are applied to compute the tax, which is called the Tentative Minimum Tax (TMT).

Few individual taxpayers pay the AMT. Only approximately 1 percent of taxpayers were subject to AMT during the late 1990s, but that number has increased, with almost 3 percent of taxpayers paying AMT in 2012.[2]

EXAMPLE I:14-1 ▶ Ricardo and Sue are married and file a joint return for 2015 with regular taxable income of $50,000 and tax preferences and adjustments of $12,000. Their alternative minimum taxable income (AMTI) is $62,000 ($50,000 + $12,000), but the alternative minimum tax base is zero because of the $83,400 exemption. Thus, their tax liability is based on the regular tax computation, and they owe no AMT liability. ◀

EXAMPLE I:14-2 ▶ Assume the same facts for Ricardo and Sue as in Example I:14-1 except they have tax preferences and adjustments of $61,000. Their alternative minimum taxable income (AMTI) is $111,000. Their tentative minimum tax (TMT) is $7,176 [($111,000 − $83,400) = $27,600 × 0.26 = $7,176.] Regular tax on taxable income of $50,000 is $6,578. Ricardo and Sue must pay the TMT of $7,176 because it exceeds the regular tax of $6,578. ◀

---

[1] The AMT applicable to corporations is discussed in Chapter C:5 of *Prentice Hall's Federal Taxation: Corporations, Partnerships, Estates, and Trusts* text and in the *Comprehensive* volume.

[2] IRS, *Statistics of Income Bulletin*, Fall 2014.

HISTORICAL NOTE

The original add-on minimum tax, enacted in 1969, was 10% of the taxpayer's tax preferences in excess of a $30,000 statutory exemption.

ADDITIONAL COMMENT

Some tax advisors recommend accelerating income into a year in which the taxpayer is subject to the AMT because the income will be taxed at a 26% or a 28% rate rather than a possibly higher rate in a later year.

AMT COMPUTATION

The individual AMT uses the approach outlined below to determine the AMT tax base and the amount of AMT imposed, if any.[3]

TAXABLE INCOME (determined under the regular income tax system)
Plus: AMT preference items
Plus or minus: AMT adjustments

=ALTERNATIVE MINIMUM TAXABLE INCOME (AMTI)
Minus: AMT exemption amount (see table below)

=ALTERNATIVE MINIMUM TAX BASE
Multiplied by AMT tax rates[4]

=TENTATIVE MINIMUM TAX
Minus: Regular income tax

ALTERNATIVE MINIMUM TAX

From 2001 to 2011, three elements in the AMT computation—the AMT exemption amount, the AMT exemption phase-out range, and the AMT tax brackets—were not automatically adjusted for annual inflation. Almost annually, Congress acted to "patch" the amount of the AMT exemption. In the American Taxpayer Relief Act of 2012, Congress provided for future years with a provision for automatic annual inflation adjustments for all three elements (Sec. 55(d)(4)). The inflation adjusted amounts for the 2015's AMT exemption and phase-out range appear in the table below.

AMT TAX RATES AND BRACKETS

The AMT for 2015 (2014) is imposed on the AMT base at 26% of the first $185,400 ($182,500) and at 28% on AMTI over $185,400 ($182,500).

AMT EXEMPTION AMOUNT

The AMT exemption operates as a buffer to reduce the impact of AMT. The buffer is ineffective for high-income taxpayers both because of the limited amount of the basic exemption and because the exemption amount is disallowed (phased-out) as income rises over a threshold amount. The exemption is reduced by 25 cents per dollar of AMTI over the threshold: Exemption allowed = Basic exemption amount – 25% (AMTI – Threshold). The phase-out concludes when the amount of AMTI is sufficient to reduce the exemption allowed to $0.

Filling Status	*2015 Basic Exemption*	*2014 Basic Exemption*	*2015 Phaseout Threshold*	*2014 Phaseout Threshold*
Married jointly	$83,400	$82,100	$158,900	$156,500
Single	$53,600	$52,800	$119,200	$117,300
Married separately	$41,700	$41,050	$ 79,450	$ 78,250

[3] Sec. 55(b)(1).

[4] The AMT rate on net capital gains corresponds with the reduced rates on net capital gains and qualified dividends for regular tax purposes: 20% if the taxpayer's top regular tax rate is 39.6%; 15% if the taxpayer's top regular tax rate is 25%, 28%, 33%, or 35%; and 0% if the taxpayer's top regular tax rate is 15%. (Sec. 1(h)(1)).

EXAMPLE I:14-3 ▶

Rita, an unmarried taxpayer filing single, has regular taxable income of $185,000 in 2015, a regular tax liability after credits of $43,271 ($44,871 − $1,600), a positive AMT adjustment (due to limitations on itemized deductions) of $25,300, and tax preferences of $10,000. Rita's nonrefundable tax cedits were an adoption credit of $1,000 and a dependent care credit of $600. Rita's alternative minimum tax is calculated as follows:

Taxable income	$185,000
Plus: Tax preferences	10,000
Plus: AMT Adjustment for itemized deductions	25,300
Plus: AMT Adjustment for personal exemption	4,000
Alternative minimum taxable income (AMTI)	$224,300
Minus: Exemption amount ($53,600 − $26,275)[a]	(27,325)
Alternative minimum tax base	$196,975
Tax on first $185,400: ($185,400 × 0.26)	$ 48,204
Tax on excess over $185,400: ($11,575 × 0.28)	3,241
Tentative minimum tax	$ 51,445
Minus: Nonrefundable tax credits	$ (1,600)
Regular tax	(43,271)
Alternative minimum tax (AMT)	$ 6,574

[a]Exemption phaseout: [0.25 × ($224,300 − $119,200)] = $26,275 ◀

KEY POINT

For purposes of the alternative minimum tax, no deduction is allowed personal exemptions or the standard deduction.

HISTORICAL NOTE

In the Revenue Reconciliation Act of 1993, Congress created a two-tier alternative minimum tax schedule in order to make the individual income tax system more progressive.

AMT TAX PREFERENCE ITEMS

Certain provisions in the Internal Revenue Code grant favorable treatment to taxpayers. However, because of concern that some taxpayers may overuse these favorable provisions, Congress has classified them as tax preferences (IRC Sec. 57). For example, though the regular tax system allows deductions for depletion in excess of the property's basis, the AMT system limits depletion deductions to the property's basis. So, an AMT preference item (equal to depletion deducted in excess of basis) is a required addition. All AMT tax preference items are additions toward AMTI. However, only certain items receiving preferential regular tax treatment are tax preference items.

To compute the AMT tax base, the tax preferences designated in Sec. 57 must be added to regular taxable income. Some common tax preference items designated in Sec. 57 include:

- The excess of accelerated depreciation expense over a hypothetical straight-line depreciation amount for real property placed in service before 1987 (computed on an item-by-item basis).
- Tax-exempt interest on certain private activity bonds. In general, private activity bonds are state or local bonds that are issued to help finance a private business.
- The excess of depletion expense over the adjusted basis of the underlying natural resource asset.

ADDITIONAL COMMENT

Most taxpayers will not have tax preference items. Over the years, tax preference items have diminished in importance while adjustments have increased in impacting AMT liabilities.

ADDITIONAL COMMENT

Under the American Recovery and Reinvestment Act of 2009, interest on private activity bonds issued in 2009 or 2010 is not treated as a tax preference item.

EXAMPLE I:14-4 ▶

Richard, a single taxpayer, has the following tax preference items for the current year:

- $15,000 ACRS cost-recovery deduction on real property placed in service before 1987 and held for investment. The straight-line ACRS deduction would have been $10,000.
- $10,000 of tax-exempt interest on private activity bonds.

Richard's total tax preferences are $15,000, consisting of $5,000 excess cost recovery deductions and $10,000 tax-exempt interest on the private activity bonds. ◀

AMT ADJUSTMENTS

For most individual taxpayers, adjustments fall into three categories: (1) regular tax itemized deductions disallowed in computing AMTI, (2) the AMT system's disallowance of the standard deduction (if taken) and personal exemptions, and (3) timing differences relating to the deferral of income or the acceleration of deductions under the regular tax rules.

ADDITIONAL COMMENT

Some tax advisors recommend that cash basis taxpayers prepay their local property taxes or state income taxes before the end of the year to reduce the current year's tax liability. However, if the taxpayer is subject to the AMT, this may not be effective in reducing the current tax liability.

Itemized Deductions. Only certain itemized deductions are allowed in computing AMTI. The more significant itemized deductions that *are not deductible* for the AMT include:

- Miscellaneous itemized deductions.
- State, local and foreign income taxes and real and personal property taxes.
- Home mortgage interest expense that is *not* "qualified housing interest." Qualified housing interest includes only interest on debt incurred to acquire/build/improve taxpayers' principal residence or second home, and
- Medical and dental expenses that exceed the AGI ceiling for regular tax but do not exceed the AGI ceiling for AMT. For most taxpayers, the AGI ceiling is 10% for both regular tax and the AMT. However, for tax years 2013–2016, taxpayers who are age 65 or over have a 7.5% AGI ceiling for regular tax but a 10% AGI ceiling for AMT.

Standard Deduction and Personal Exemptions. Although allowed for regular tax, a standard deduction is not allowed for AMTI. In addition, personal and dependency exemptions are not allowed as deductions in determining AMTI.

EXAMPLE I:14-5 ▶ Robin, a single taxpayer with no dependents, has AGI of $100,000 and the following itemized deductions for the current tax year:

Charitable contributions	4,000
Medical expenses, net of insurance	10,500
Mortgage interest on Robin's personal residence	18,400
Real estate taxes	4,000
State income taxes	6,000
Personal casualty loss, net of insurance	$15,000

From the information above, Robin's regular taxable income would be:

AGI			$100,000
Itemized deductions:			
Charitable contributions		$ 4,000	
Medical expenses	$10,500		
Less 10.0% of AGI	(10,000)	500	
Mortgage interest (100% qualified housing interest)		18,400	
Real estate taxes		4,000	
State income taxes		6,000	
Personal casualty loss	$15,000		
Less $100 floor	(100)		
Less 10% of AGI	(10,000)	4,900	(37,800)
Personal exemption			(4,000)
Taxable income			$58,200

To compute her AMTI, Robin must make adjustments to her regular taxable income. Assume that Robin also has $20,000 of tax preferences. Her AMTI would be computed as follows:

Taxable income	$58,200
Tax preferences	20,000
AMT adjustments:	
Medical expenses: ($500 allowed for regular taxable income and for AMTI)	0
Real estate and state income taxes (not allowed for AMTI)	10,000
Personal exemption (not allowed for AMTI)	4,000
AMTI	$92,200 ◀

Timing Differences. Other adjustments are required when the rules for calculating regular taxable income permit the taxpayer temporarily to defer the recognition of income or to accelerate deductions (timing differences). The most common AMT adjustments for timing differences include:

- For personal property placed in service after 1998, the difference between the MACRS depreciation deduction and the hypothetical amount determined by using the 150%

declining balance method over the recovery period used for regular tax purposes. Bonus depreciation, where applicable, is allowed in full for purposes of the AMT.

- For real property placed in service after 1986 and before January 1, 1999, the difference between the MACRS depreciation claimed using the property's actual recovery period and a hypothetical straight-line depreciation amount calculated using a 40-year life (see Chapter I:10 for a discussion of the alternative depreciation system).[5]
- For incentive stock options, the excess of the option's fair market value over the price paid by the individual for the option. This adjustment is measured on the date the rights to the underlying stock are freely transferable or are not subject to a substantial risk of forfeiture.
- For research and experimental (R&E) expenditures, the difference between the regular tax deduction and the deduction that would have been allowed if the expenditures were capitalized and amortized over a ten-year period.[6]

EXAMPLE I:14-6 Rob has the following AMT adjustments caused by timing differences in 2015:

- Depreciation of $3,636 on residential rental property costing $100,000 and placed in service in January 1998 (using the straight-line method and a 27 1/2-year recovery period under MACRS). Depreciation for AMT purposes is $2,500 (using the straight-line method and a 40-year recovery period under the alternative depreciation system). Thus, the positive AMT adjustment is $1,136 ($3,636 − $2,500).
- Depreciation is $2,000 on a computer used in business costing $10,000 and placed in service in January 2015 based on MACRS rules. Depreciation for AMT purposes is $1,500 based on the alternative depreciation system (i.e., 150% DB method, half-year convention, and a five-year recovery period). Thus, the positive AMT adjustment is $500 ($2,000 − $1,500).
- R&E expenditures amounting to $50,000 are expensed in the current year. For AMT purposes, the R&E deduction would be $5,000 ($50,000 ÷ 10 years) since the expenditures are capitalized and amortized over a 10-year period. Thus, the positive AMT adjustment is $45,000 ($50,000 − $5,000).

Rob's total positive AMT adjustment to taxable income to arrive at AMTI is $46,636 ($1,136 + $500 + $45,000). ◀

ADDITIONAL COMMENT

For corporate taxpayers only, there is a 0.12% environmental tax imposed on the excess of the corporation's modified alternative minimum taxable income over $2 million. This additional tax levy is primarily imposed on corporations larger than "mom and pop" entities.

AMT CREDITS

Credits that Reduce AMT. As discussed later in this chapter, a number of credits are allowed to reduce a taxpayer's regular tax liability. However, only the foreign tax credit and nonrefundable personal credits are allowed to reduce AMT. The foreign tax credit that applies to the AMT is a specially computed credit, called the "alternative minimum tax foreign tax credit" and is beyond the scope of this text. Nonrefundable personal tax credits are allowed against both regular tax and the AMT. They are discussed on pp. I:14-10–19 and are summarized in Topic Review I:14-2.

STOP & THINK

Question: What are the most common characteristics of taxpayers who are subject to the AMT?

Solution: While each situation is unique, certain taxpayers are more likely to be subject to the AMT. First, taxpayers who have materially invested in real estate before January 1, 1999 are likely candidates for the AMT because they will have a large positive adjustment caused from differences in depreciation. Second, as discussed above, taxpayers who use credits to reduce their regular tax liability may be subject to the AMT because only certain credits reduce the AMT. Third, taxpayers who have very large itemized deductions, primarily from large state and local tax liabilities, may be subject to the AMT because state and

[5] For real property being depreciated under the straight-line method and placed in service after 1998, the Taxpayer Relief Act of 1997 eliminates this adjustment.

[6] Sec. 56(b)(2). However, this adjustment does not apply if the taxpayer materially participates in the activity, Sec. 56(b)(2)(D).

ADDITIONAL COMMENT

The American Recovery and Reinvestment Act of 2009 allows taxpayers with deferred credits from tax years beginning before 2006 (deferred research credits or deferred AMT credits) to turn these into refundable credits in lieu of taking bonus and accelerated depreciation on qualified eligible property (see Chapter I:10.)

local taxes are not deductible for AMT purposes. Fourth, taxpayers who have numerous personal exemptions (large families) may be subject to the AMT.

Minimum Tax Credit (MTC) Under Sec. 53, individual taxpayers are allowed a credit for AMT paid in past years against future years' *regular tax liability*. The logic is as follows: the AMT may be caused by adjustments that will reverse in the future, and the taxpayer will actually pay a higher regular tax in those future years. Thus, the combination of a prior year AMT and current year regular tax essentially constitutes double taxation. A taxpayer who paid AMT in prior years but is not subject to AMT in the current year may be entitled to an MTC against his regular tax liability in the current year.[7]

SUMMARY ILLUSTRATION OF THE AMT COMPUTATION

EXAMPLE I:14-7 ▶ Roger and Kate are married, file a joint return, and have four dependent children. All the children are under age 17. The following items were used to compute regular taxable income for the current year:

ADDITIONAL COMMENT

In some circumstances, the AMT applies to unsuspecting taxpayers. In a classic case, *D.R. Klaassen*, T.C. Memo 1998-241 (affd, CA-10), the taxpayers had 12 personal exemptions and were subject to the AMT even though they had no tax preferences or other adjustments.

Gross income:		
Salary		$ 70,000
Interest income		10,000
Business income		30,000[a]
AGI		$110,000
Itemized deductions:		
State and local taxes	$9,400	
Mortgage interest (100% qualified housing interest)	12,000	
Charitable contributions	3,000	(24,400)
Personal and dependency exemptions ($4,000 × 6)		(24,000)
Taxable income		$ 61,600
Regular tax		$8,318
Child tax credit		(4,000)
Net regular tax		$ 4,318

[a]MACRS depreciation deductions of $75,000 on personal property placed in service after 1986 were claimed in arriving at business income. Only $50,000 of depreciation would be claimed under the alternative depreciation system using the 150% declining balance method.

Their AMT is computed as follows:		
Taxable income		$ 61,600
AMT adjustments:		
Personal and dependency exemptions	$24,000	
Excess depreciation ($75,000 − $50,000)	25,000	
State and local taxes	9,400	58,400
AMTI		$120,000
AMT exemption		(83,400)
Alternative Minimum Tax base		$ 36,600
Tax rate		× 0.26
Tentative minimum tax before credit		$ 9,516
Child tax credit		(4,000)
Tentative minimum tax		$ 5,516
Net regular tax after child tax credit		(4,318)
Alternative minimum tax		$ 1,198[b]

The total tax liability for Roger and Kate is $5,516 ($4,318 + $1,198).

[b]An AMT credit may be available in future years to offset regular tax. However, the AMT credit applies only to the AMT that results from timing differences (e.g., depreciation adjustments) and not from exclusions (e.g., personal exemptions and taxes). ◄

[7] The Minimum Tax Credit applies to timing adjustments rather than permanent adjustments. A detailed discussion of the rules for computing this credit for individuals is beyond the scope of this book.

SELF-EMPLOYMENT TAX

OBJECTIVE 2

Describe self-employment income and compute the self-employment tax

An individual may work either as an employee or as an independent contractor. The distinction generally hinges on the degree of influence and control an individual has over his work.[8] The classification is important in determining the responsible party for employment taxes imposed under the Federal Insurance Contribution Act (FICA). FICA includes old-age, survivors, and disability insurance (OASDI, commonly referred to as Social Security) and hospital insurance (Medicare).

Individuals classified as *employees* pay the employee part of FICA on their earnings as they are earned through withholding, and their employers pay the employer part of employment taxes on the same earnings. Because employers report and remit both the withheld employee portion and the employer portion of FICA taxes to the U.S. Treasury, it is not necessary for employees to report employment taxes within their federal income tax returns.

Individuals classified as *self-employed* are responsible for paying both the employee share and employer share of employment taxes. This tax is called the self-employment (SE) tax, and it is imposed on net earnings from self-employment (defined below). It is reported as part of the self-employed individual's federal income tax return.

A combined FICA rate of 15.3% applied for the years 1989 through 2010 and will hold for years after 2012. The rate includes the following:

1) Social Security tax imposed at a rate of 12.4% on wages (6.2% by withholding for the employee portion and 6.2% for the employer portion) and on net earnings from self-employment (SE);[9] and,
2) Medicare tax imposed at a rate of 2.9% on wages (1.45% by withholding for the employee portion and 1.45% for the employer portion) and on net earnings from self-employment. (See next page for separate discussion of the Additional Medicare Tax)

Social Security tax is imposed on wages and net earnings from SE up to a ceiling amount (adjusted for inflation annually). For 2015, the ceiling equals $118,500 ($117,000 for 2014). The regular Medicare tax is imposed on all wages and net earnings from SE—without limit.

Net earnings from SE is defined as 92.35% of self-employment income The SE tax is imposed only if net earnings from SE equals or exceeds $400.

Self employed individuals are entitled to deduct—*for* AGI—50% of the employer portion of their SE tax.[10]

EXAMPLE I:14-8 ▶ Robert, a cabinet maker, works as a sole proprietor. For 2015, his self-employment earnings totaled $75,000. His net earnings from SE equal $69,263 ($75,000 × 0.9235). His SE tax of $10,596 includes Social Security tax and Medicare tax. His deduction for SE tax equals $5,298.

Social Security tax: 0.124 × ($69,263) = $8,589
Medicare tax: 0.029 × ($69,263) = $2,009
SE tax deduction: 0.50 × ($8,589 + $2,009) = $5,299. ◀

EXAMPLE I:14-9 ▶ The facts are identical to I:14-8 except Robert's self-employment earnings totaled $175,000. His net earnings from SE equal $161,613 (0.9235 × 175,000).

His SE tax of $19,381 includes Social Security tax and Medicare tax. His deduction for SE tax equals $9,691.

Social Security tax: 0.124 ($118,500 ceiling) = $14,694
Medicare tax: 0.029 ($161,613) = $4,687
SE tax deduction: 0.50 ($14,694 + $4,687) = $9,691 ◀

Individuals who work as employees but also operate a business are subject to self-employment tax on net earnings from self-employment (SE). For Social Security tax, the tax base

[8] Rev. Rul. 87-41 provides a list of twenty factors to be considered in evaluating whether an employer-employee relationship exists.

[9] PL 112-78. During 2011 and 2012, a temporary payroll tax holiday applied, reducing the OASDI rate for employees to 4.2% (OASDI rate of 10.4% and combined FICA rate of 13.3%).

[10] In 2011 and 2012, the deductible portion of Social Security tax was based on the employer portion (6.2%/(4.2% + 6.2%) = 59.6%), and 50% of the Medicare tax was deductible.

equals the lesser of (1) net earnings from self-employment or (2) the Social Security tax ceiling reduced by the individual's earnings as an employee. The Medicare tax is imposed on net earnings from SE (without limit).

EXAMPLE I:14-10 ▶ In the current year, Sandy earns $75,000 in employee wages. In addition, from her small consulting practice, she earns $10,000 of income from self-employment. The tax base for her Social Security tax equals the smaller of $9,235 (0.9235 × $10,000) or $43,500 ($118,500 − $75,000). Sandy's SE tax equals $1,413, including Social Security tax of $1,145 ($9,235 × 0.124), and Medicare tax of $268 ($9,235 × 0.029). Her deduction for SE tax equals $707 (0.50 × $1,413). ◀

EXAMPLE I:14-11 ▶ Assume the facts in Example 14-10 apply except that Sandy earns $125,000 in employee wages. The tax base for her Social Security tax equals $0 because her employee earnings exceed the Social Security tax ceiling (more precisely, the tax base equals the smaller of $9,235 [0.9235 × $10,000] or $0 [$118,500 − $125,000]). The Medicare tax (and the SE tax) totals $268 ($9,235 × 0.029). Her deduction for SE tax equals $134 (0.50 × $268). ◀

For tax years after 2012, a new hospital insurance tax (Additional Medicare Tax) of 0.9% applies to self-employment income (Sec. 1401(b)(2)) of individuals whose earned income exceeds threshold amounts (table below). Unlike the regular Medicare Tax of 2.9%, the Additional Medicare Tax is *not* included in the "for AGI" deduction allowed to self-employed taxpayers for the employer portion of SE tax (Sec. 164(f)(1)).

ADDITIONAL COMMENT

For some self-employed taxpayers, the amount of SE tax exceeds the amount of income tax for the year. For example, a married couple with two children and $17,000 of self-employment income would not owe any income tax, but would have a $2,402 (17,000 × .9235 × 15.3%) SE tax liability.

Filing Status	Threshold Amount
Married Jointly	$250,000
Single	$200,000
Married Separately	$125,000

Because the new tax applies to all earned income, in determining the amount of earned income subject to the new tax, the threshold amount is used first against employee compensation, and any remainder used against self-employment income.

EXAMPLE I:14-12 ▶ Henry, an unmarried taxpayer filing single for 2015, earns a salary of $130,000 plus self-employment income of $145,000 in consulting fees. His net SE income is $133,908 ($145,000 × .9235).

For regular SE tax, Henry will not pay Social Security tax on his SE income from consulting (his salary subject to this tax exceeds the $118,500 ceiling). He will pay Medicare tax of $3,883 ($133,908 × .029). One-half of the Medicare tax, $1,942, is allowed as a for AGI deduction.

Henry will pay the Additional Medicare Tax because his earned income exceeds $200,000. The $200,000 threshold first will exempt his salary from the additional tax ($200,000 threshold − $130,000 = $70,000 remaining), and the remainder will exempt all but $63,908 of his self-employment income ($133,908 − $70,000 remaining threshold = $63,908).

The Additional Medicare tax imposed will equal $575 ($63,908 × 0.009). A deduction for AGI is not allowed for the Additional Medicare Tax. ◀

ADDITIONAL COMMENT

If an individual works for more than one employer during the year and earns (in total) more than the Social Security tax ceiling, the employers will have withheld more than the employee's required Social Security tax. The taxpayer is entitled to a credit (or refund) for the overpaid tax against his regular income tax liability.

WHAT CONSTITUTES SELF-EMPLOYMENT INCOME

Individuals who carry on a trade or business as a proprietor or partnership are subject to the SE tax. If an individual has two separate self-employment activities, the *net* earnings from each activity are aggregated. However, where a husband and wife file a joint return and both have self-employment income, the SE tax must be computed for each individual separately.

EXAMPLE I:14-13 ▶ Bob and Ruth are married and file a joint return. Bob has $93,000 net earnings from a consulting business and a $4,000 net loss from a retail store that he operates as a sole proprietorship. Ruth has wages of $50,000 from her employer that are subject to FICA taxes. Bob's net earnings from self-employment are $82,192 ($89,000 × 0.9235). No reduction in Bob's SE tax base is allowed for Ruth's wages. The SE tax is computed separately for Bob and Ruth. ◀

KEY POINT

In the case of married taxpayers filing joint returns, it is important on Schedule SE of Form 1040 to fill in the name and Social Security number of the spouse with the self-employment income. This information is used to establish specific benefit eligibility.

Among the items that constitute earnings subject to the SE tax are:

- Net earnings from a sole proprietorship

- Director's fees[11]
- Taxable research grants
- Distributive share of partnership income plus guaranteed payments from the partnership[12]

The self-employment tax is computed on Schedule SE of Form 1040 (see Appendix B). The rules for computing the SE tax are summarized in Topic Review I:14-1.

TOPIC REVIEW I:14-1

Self-Employment Tax Summary

- The tax base is generally net earnings from SE which equals 92.35% of self-employment income.
- The Social Security tax is imposed at 12.4% of net earnings from SE, and the Medicare tax is imposed at 2.9% of net earnings from SE.
- For years after 2012, an Additional Medicare Tax is imposed on earnings from employment (employee and self-employed). The tax is imposed at a rate of 0.9% on earnings in excess of a threshold amount.
- In 2015, a ceiling of $118,500 applies to the amount of SE earnings subject to Social Security tax. No ceiling applies to the Medicare portion of the tax.
- SE tax is computed separately for each spouse for married individuals filing joint returns.

PERSONAL AND BUSINESS TAX CREDITS

OBJECTIVE 3

Describe the various business and personal tax credits

USE AND IMPORTANCE OF TAX CREDITS

Tax credits often serve as incentives for activities supporting broader policy objectives. For example, tax credits may help to increase employment, encourage energy conservation and research and experimental activities, and provide tax relief for low-income taxpayers. Tax credits are also used to mitigate the effects of double taxation on income from foreign countries. Thus, tax credits are an important part of the income tax law.

Credits are classified into two broad categories, **nonrefundable** and **refundable**. Nonrefundable credits only offset tax liability. Refundable credits, on the other hand, not only offset tax liability but if the credits exceed the tax liability, the excess will be paid (refunded) directly to the taxpayer. At the end of the section, Topic Review I:14-2 provides a summary of selected tax credits and the rationale for their inclusion in the tax law. Taxes withheld from employee wages are prepayments of tax, but are also referred to as refundable credits.

VALUE OF A CREDIT VERSUS A DEDUCTION

As discussed in Chapter I:2, tax credits reduce tax liability on a dollar-for-dollar basis. This is in contrast to tax deductions, which reduce taxable income. The value of a tax deduction increases with the taxpayer's marginal tax rate, so tax deductions are more valuable to high-income taxpayers than to lower-income taxpayers. Tax credits, however, benefit all taxpayers in the same amount regardless of their marginal tax rate.

ADDITIONAL COMMENT

The American Recovery and Reinvestment Act of 2009 has expanded and increased both nonrefundable and refundable credits.

EXAMPLE I:14-14 ▶ Tasha and Sean are both single taxpayers. Each has an $800 expenditure that qualifies as either a tax deduction or a 20% credit. Tasha is in the 15% marginal tax bracket while Sean is in the 33% marginal tax bracket. If the $800 is claimed as a deduction, Tasha would receive a tax benefit of $120 ($800 × 15%) whereas Sean would receive a tax benefit of $264 ($800 × 33%). Conversely, if the credit is claimed, Tasha and Sean would benefit equally from a $160 credit ($800 × 20%). In this case, Tasha would prefer the credit while Sean would prefer the tax deduction. ◀

---

[11] Rev. Rul. 57-246, 1957-1 C.B. 338. It is a factual question whether an officer who also serves as a director is performing services as an employee or as an independent contractor. The courts have recognized that an individual can perform services as a director and also perform employment-related services, but the director fees may be recharacterized by the courts if the fees are in reality compensation for services rendered as an employee. (See *Peter H. Jacobs*, 1993 RIA T.C. Memo ¶ 93, 570, 66 TCM 1470.)

[12] A limited partner's share of partnership income is not considered SE income (Sec. 1402(a) (13)) given the inability of limited partners to participate in managing the partnership. LLPs and LLCs developed as business entities long after 1977, when Sec. 1402(a)(13) was added to the law. Individuals are considered members of LLCs, and they participate in management (like general partners). But, they have limited liability. Thus, determination of whether LLC (and LLP) earnings are considered SE income is unsettled.

NONREFUNDABLE PERSONAL TAX CREDITS

As a result of tax legislation in the last few years, the number of personal tax credits for individual taxpayers has increased significantly. For tax years after 2010, nonrefundable personal credits offset an individual's regular tax and AMT.[13] The more important nonrefundable personal tax credits are discussed below.

ADDITIONAL COMMENT

The dollar amount of the child and dependent care credit amounted to $3.4 billion in 2011.

Child and Dependent Care Credit. The child and dependent care credit provides tax savings for taxpayers who incur child and dependent care expenses because of employment activities. To qualify for the credit, an individual must meet two requirements: (1) expenses for the care of a qualifying individual are incurred to enable the taxpayer to be gainfully employed, and (2) the qualifying individual is either a qualifying child under age 13 or an incapacitated dependent or spouse who lived with the taxpayer for more than one-half of the year. The credit equals 35% of qualified expenditures.

EXAMPLE I:14-15 ▶ Tim and Tina are married and have two children under age 13. They incur child care expenses (e.g., a housekeeper and nurse) to enable both Tim and Tina to work on a full-time basis. These expenditures are eligible for the child and dependent care credit because Tim and Tina incurred them for qualifying individuals and to be gainfully employed. Alternatively, if Tina were not employed, but incurred the child care expenses to volunteer at the city library, the expenditures would not be eligible for the credit. ◀

ADDITIONAL COMMENT

Qualifying child care expenses include amounts spent to send a child to nursery school or kindergarten, but not first grade.

Qualifying Employment-Related Expenses. Eligible expenses include amounts paid for care inside the home or outside the home for a qualifying individual. If care is provided in the home, amounts paid for care and household maintenance (e.g., housekeeper who cares for the child, and serves as maid and cook) are qualifying expenses. If the care is provided outside the home by a dependent care facility (e.g., a day care facility), the amounts will be eligible expenses only if the dependent care facility operates in compliance with federal, state and local law.[14] Amounts paid for services outside of the taxpayer's household (e.g., adult day care) that are spent for the care of an incapacitated dependent or spouse qualify only if the individual lives in the taxpayer's home for at least eight hours a day.

EXAMPLE I:14-16 ▶ Tony is divorced and has two children under age 13. He is employed and incurs child care expenses at a preschool nursery for one of the children. He also relies on a live-in nanny who cares for both children and provides housekeeping services and a gardener to care for his yard. All of the expenditures for the preschool nursery and the nanny qualify because these services constitute eligible household services, and care of qualifying individuals. However, the payments to the gardener are not eligible because they do not constitute qualifying household services. ◀

The following additional limitations apply:

1) Ceiling on qualifying expenses: The maximum amount of child and dependent care expenses that qualify for the credit equals $3,000 for one qualifying individual and $6,000 for two or more qualifying individuals. No carryover is permitted for expenses in excess of the maximum amounts.
2) Earned income limit: Maximum qualifying expenses cannot exceed the taxpayer's earned income. For married individuals, the limitation is applied to the earned income of the spouse with the smaller earned income. Gratuitous services performed by the taxpayer for charitable organizations are not considered gainful employment.[15] A spouse who is a full-time student or incapacitated is deemed to have an earned income of $250 per month ($500 per month if there are two or more qualifying individuals in the household).[16]
3) Payments to a relative are qualifying expenses unless the relative is a dependent or a child (under age 19) of the taxpayer.[17]
4) The credit will not be allowed unless the qualifying individual's Social Security number and the dependent care provider's social security number (or employer ID number) are reported on the return on which the credit is claimed.

EXAMPLE I:14-17 ▶ Troy and Tracy are married and incur qualifying child care expenses of $4,000 to take care of their two children, ages 1 and 3. Tracy's earned income is $20,000, and Troy's earned income

[13] Before 2011, these credits could offset a taxpayer's AMT liability only to the extent of tentative minimum tax over regular tax (the AMT).

[14] Employment-related expenses do not include amounts paid for services outside of the taxpayer's household at an overnight-stay camp.

[15] Rev. Rul. 73-597, 1973-2 CB 69.

[16] Sec. 21(d)(2). To qualify as a full-time student, the individual must enroll in an educational institution on a full-time basis for at least five calendar months of the year (Reg. Sec. 1.44A-2(b)(3)(B)(ii)).

[17] Sec. 21(e)(6).

KEY POINT

The percentage used to calculate the credit varies from 20% to 35% depending on the taxpayer's AGI.

from a part-time job is $3,500. Although their expenses do not exceed the overall qualifying expense limitation of $6,000, the earned income limitation applies because Troy's earned income ($3,500) is less than the child care expenses ($4,000). Therefore, the amount of child care expenses eligible for the credit is limited to $3,500. ◀

Credit Rate and Amount. Though generally, the credit equals 35% of qualifying expenses, the credit rate is reduced by one percentage point for each $2,000 (or fraction thereof) of adjusted gross income in excess of $15,000. The rate goes no lower than 20%.

Credit rates for the child care credit across AGI levels

Adjusted Gross Income	Applicable Percentage	Adjusted Gross Income	Applicable Percentage
$ 0 to $15,000	35%	29,001 to 31,000	27%
15,001 to 17,000	34	31,001 to 33,000	26
17,001 to 19,000	33	33,001 to 35,000	25
19,001 to 21,000	32	35,001 to 37,000	24
21,001 to 23,000	31	37,001 to 39,000	23
23,001 to 25,000	30	39,001 to 41,000	22
25,001 to 27,000	29	41,001 to 43,000	21
27,001 to 29,000	28	43,001 and above	20

EXAMPLE I:14-18 ▶ Mark and Vicki are married, file a joint return, and have three children under age 13. Mark and Vicki's employment-related earnings are $25,000 and $10,000, respectively. Including all sources of income, their AGI is $36,000. They incur $8,000 of child care expenses during the year. First, their eligible child care expenses are limited to $6,000 because Mark and Vicki have more than one qualifying child. Second, the credit rate equals 24%, computed as follows:

Adjusted gross income (AGI)	$36,000
Base amount	(15,000)
Excess	21,000
Divided by $2,000	10.5
Rounded up to	11
Applicable credit (35% − 11%)	24%

Mark and Vicki's child and dependent care credit for the year is $1,440 ($6,000 × 0.24). ◀

Other Sources of Tax Benefits for Dependent Care. Employees may be eligible for two types of employer supported dependent care assistance that exclude from employees' gross income payments made by their employer for the provision for dependent care. The assistance is through dependent care assistance programs (IRC Section 129)[18] and employee funding of flexible spending arrangement (IRC Section 125). Qualifying employment-related expenses for purposes of the child and dependent care credit are reduced to the extent dependent care costs are funded through either of these types of plans.

EXAMPLE I:14-19 ▶ Assume the same facts as in Example I:14-18 except that Mark was reimbursed $4,100 by his employer under a qualified dependent care assistance program and this amount was excluded from his gross income. Thus, expenses eligible for the child and dependent care credit are reduced to $1,900 ($6,000 − $4,100) and the child care credit is $456 ($1,900 × 0.24). ◀

ADDITIONAL COMMENT

The tax credit for the elderly or disabled has been declining in recent years and amounted to only $16.2 million in 2011.

Tax Credit for the Elderly and Disabled. A limited credit is provided for certain low-income individuals who have attained age 65 before the end of the tax year or who retired because of a permanent and total disability.

The maximum credit is 15% of an initial amount of $5,000 ($7,500 for married individuals filing jointly if both spouses qualify).[19] This initial amount is reduced by:

---

18 Sec. 129. (See Chapter I:4 for a discussion of the requirements for exclusion.)

19 Sec. 22(c)(2).

1) Nontaxable Social Security, railroad retirement, or Veterans Administration pension or annuity benefits, and
2) One-half of AGI in excess of $7,500 for a single individual ($10,000 (MFJ)).[20]

Most elderly or disabled taxpayers are ineligible for the credit because they either receive Social Security benefits in excess of ceiling limitations or they have AGI amounts in excess of the limitations, which effectively reduces or eliminates the allowable credit.

EXAMPLE I:14-20 ▶ Wayne and Tammy are both 67 years old and file a joint return. They have AGI of $11,000 and receive nontaxable Social Security benefits of $3,000 during the current year. Their tax credit for the elderly is computed as follows:

Initial ceiling amount		$7,500
Minus: Nontaxable social security benefits	$3,000	
One-half of excess AGI (0.50 × [$11,000 − $10,000])	500	(3,500)
Total credit base		$4,000
		× 0.15
Tax credit		$ 600

◀

Adoption Credit. A nonrefundable credit is allowed for qualified adoption expenses in 2015 of up to $13,400 for adoption of an eligible child ($13,190 in 2014).[21] The credit generally is allowable in the year the adoption is finalized. If adoption expenses are paid prior to the year in which the adoption is finalized, such expenses are not eligible for the credit until the year the adoption is finalized. If expenses are paid during or after the year the adoption is finalized, the credit is allowable in the year the expenses are paid or incurred.

The credit is phased out (ratably over a $40,000 range) for high income taxpayers. The 2015 phaseout begins at AGI of $201,010 (2014 at $197,880).[22]

Qualified adoption expenses include reasonable and necessary adoption fees, court costs, attorney fees, and other expenses that are directly related to the legal adoption of an eligible child. Qualified adoption expenses are reduced by any reimbursements from an employer plan. An eligible child is defined as a child who has not reached 18 years old when the adoption takes place, or one who is physically or mentally incapable of self-care.

Taxpayers adopting a special needs child are treated as having incurred qualified adoption expenses of the maximum credit amount even if actual expenses are less.

EXAMPLE I:14-21 ▶ Oscar and Betty began proceedings in June 2014 to adopt a child. They incurred $7,000 of attorney fees and adoption agency fees in 2014. In 2015, they incurred an additional $8,000 of qualified adoption expenses, and the adoption became final. Oscar and Betty's AGI in 2015 equals $215,000. The adoption credit is allowable in 2015, computed as follows:

Total qualified adoption expenses	$15,000
Maximum credit (lesser of $15,000 or $13,400)	13,400
Phase-out percentage [($215,000 − $201,010) / $40,000] = 34.98%	
Amount of credit disallowed ($13,400 × 34.98%)	(4,687)
Amount of credit allowed	$ 8,713

[20] The AGI ceiling is $5,000 for married individuals filing a separate return.

[21] The credit as well as the AGI phaseout amounts are adjusted for inflation each year.

[22] For purposes of the phase-out, AGI is modified and determined without regard to the exclusions from gross income for foreign earned income, after the application of the rules relating to the taxation of Social Security, and other items. (See Sec. 36B(2).)

Oscar and Betty can take a credit for $8,713 of expenses and must claim the credit in 2015, the year the adoption becomes final. ◀

Child Tax Credit. Taxpayers are allowed a credit of $1,000 for each qualifying child. The definition of qualifying child for the child tax credit requires that the child is the taxpayer's dependent based on the category "qualifying child" under the conditions for the dependency exemption,[23] and that the child is under age 17.

The credit begins to phase out when modified AGI[24] reaches a threshold amount ($110,000 (MFJ), $75,000 (Single), or $55,000 (MFS)). The credit lost to phaseout is determined by the following.

[(Modified AGI − Threshold)/$1,000]* × $50

*rounded up to the next whole number

Thus, a married couple filing jointly with one qualifying child and modified AGI of $123,500 will have a tentative child tax credit of $1,000. The credit will be subject to a phaseout of $700 [($123,500 − $110,000) ÷ $1,000 = 13.5 and 14 × $50 = $700]. Their allowable credit will be $300.

ADDITIONAL COMMENT

For taxpayers with three or more qualifying children, the refundable child tax credit equals the lesser of (1) the unclaimed portion of the credit or (2) the greater of a) 15% of the taxpayers earned income in excess of $3,000 or b) the taxpayer's social security taxes in excess of the taxpayer's earned income credit.

The child tax credit is generally *nonrefundable*. However, for tax years 2009–2017, if a taxpayer's tentative child tax credit is greater than the total tax liability, part of the credit (the "additional" child tax credit) is *refundable*. The refundable portion is the lesser of (1) the unclaimed portion of the credit or (2) 15% of taxpayer's earned income in excess of $3,000. Form 8812 is used to compute the refundable portion of the child tax credit.

Higher Education Costs Tax Credits. Two credits are available to taxpayers who incur higher education expenses. The two credits are the "American Opportunity Tax Credit (AOTC)" and the "Lifetime Learning Credit (LLC)."[25]

American Opportunity Tax Credit.[26] Under the AOTC, taxpayers are allowed a credit for up to $2,500 for qualified tuition and related expenses paid during the taxable year for each eligible student. The credit allowed equals 100% of the first $2,000 of qualified expenses plus 25% of up to $2,000 of qualified expenses in excess of the first $2,000 ($2,000 + 25%($2,000)) = $2,500, maximum credit amount).

Qualified tuition and related expenses include tuition and fees required for enrollment and course materials, including textbooks. They do not include room and board, student activity fees, and other expenses unrelated to an individual's academic coursework. Qualified expenses are limited to those paid for the first four years of postsecondary education. This requirement is based on whether the educational institution has awarded the student four years of academic credit as of the *beginning* of the tax year. Qualified expenses include those paid during the tax year for an eligible student, including the taxpayer, the taxpayer's spouse, or the taxpayer's dependent. An eligible student must (1) be enrolled in or attending an eligible education institution and (2) be taking courses on at least one-half of a full-time load for at least one academic term at that educational institution. Students are considered ineligible if they have been convicted of a federal or state felony drug offense by the end of tax year.

ADDITIONAL COMMENT

In addition to the AOTC and Lifetime Learning credits, there have been a plethora of new tax laws that encourage education, including:

(1) Sec. 529 plans;
(2) Improved student loan interest deduction rules;
(3) Increased limits for Coverdell Education IRAs.

Other requirements include the following items.

- If a taxpayer pays qualified expenses in one year but the expenses relate to an academic period that begins during January, February, or March of the next taxable year, the academic period is treated as beginning during the taxable year in which the payment is made. Thus, a payment of tuition in December 2014 for the Spring Semester, 2015 (which begins in January 2015) would be eligible for the AOTC in 2014.

---

23 Under IRC Section 152(c) for the dependency exemption, a qualifying child must 1) be a relative of the taxpayer (descendent, sibling, or descendent of a sibling), 2) reside in the taxpayer's household for more than one-half of the year, 3) be supported by the taxpayer, 4) not file a joint return with a spouse, and 5) be younger than the taxpayer and under age 19 (or a student under age 24). For the child tax credit, the age requirement in the dependency exemption is modified to under age 17.

24 Modified AGI means AGI increased by any amount excluded from gross income under Secs. 911, 931, or 933. Sec. 911, 931, and 933 are special exclusions in the international tax area.

25 Sec. 25A.

26 The provisions discussed for the AOTC apply for tax years 2009–2017, and represent those of the "expanded" Hope Scholarship credit.

- Qualified tuition and related expenses eligible for the AOTC must be reduced by amounts received under other sections of the tax law, such as scholarships (Sec. 117), employer-sponsored educational reimbursement plans (Sec. 127), education IRAs (Sec. 530), or other provisions of the tax law.

The allowable credit is phased out for high income taxpayers. The phase-out occurs over a $20,000 range (for married filing joint taxpayers) and begins when modified AGI is $160,000 as follows:

$$\text{Tentative AOTC} \times \frac{\text{Modified AGI} - \$160{,}000}{\$20{,}000} = \text{Phaseout for MFJ taxpayers}$$

For taxpayers other than joint filers, phase-out occurs over a $10,000 range, beginning at $80,000 of modified AGI. Modified AGI is AGI before exclusions for foreign earned income and foreign housing costs.

It is important to understand that the AOTC applies to each student. Thus, parents who have two children in their first four years of college may claim up to $2,500 for each child. For tax years 2009 through 2017, up to 40% of the allowable AOTC is refundable.

ADDITIONAL COMMENT

The education expenses for the AOTC and lifetime learning credits must be incurred at an educational institution that is eligible to participate in Department of Education student aid programs.

Lifetime Learning Credit. The LLC allowed equals 20% of up to $10,000 of qualified education expenses paid (per year). Education expenses of students eligible for AOTC must first be considered for AOTC. None of the expenses of a student for whom an AOTC credit is allowed are eligible for the LLC (LLC cannot be combined with AOTC to yield LLC on expenses in excess of those yielding maximum AOTC).

Like AOTC, qualified education expenses include those paid during the tax year for an eligible student, who may be the taxpayer, the taxpayer's spouse, or the taxpayer's dependent. However, for LLC, qualified education expenses include only tuition and academic fees, not course materials.

In some aspects, the LLC is more expansive than the AOTC: qualified expenses for LLC include those paid for any year (not limited to the first four years of postsecondary education), whether taken as part of a postsecondary degree program or to acquire or improve job skills. The expenses of a student with a record of conviction a felony drug offense qualify for LLC.

In other ways, the LLC is more restrictive than AOTC. Importantly, the $10,000 limitation on qualified expenses for LLC applies at the "family" level. For example, assuming a family pays $12,000 of qualified tuition, $6,000 for each of two dependent children who are eligible students. If the expenses qualify only for LLC, the maximum credit allowed equals $2,000. Had the expenses qualified for AOTC, the AOTC credit would equal $5,000 (2 students × $2,500 each). The LLC phases out more quickly for high-income taxpayers because the phase-out range begins at lower income levels and is indexed for inflation. For 2015, the LLC phase-out occurs for married taxpayers over a $20,000 range, beginning at $110,000 (at $108,000 in 2014) and for single taxpayers, phase-out occurs over a $10,000 range, beginning at $55,000 (at $54,000 in 2014).[27] Finally, the LLC is nonrefundable.

EXAMPLE I:14-22 ▶ Mark and Jane Green are married, file a joint return, and have three dependent children in college, Ron, Susan, and Bill. Ron and Susan attend State University and Bill attends Private University. The Greens' modified AGI in 2015 is $164,000. Details are as follows:

	Spring Semester 2015 (Paid in January 2015)	Fall Semester 2015 (Paid in August 2015)	AOTC Eligible Expenses
Ron:	Senior	5th year Senior	
Tuition and fees	$1,500	$1,550	$3,050
Course materials (books)	300	300	600
Room and board	3,500	3,700	—

[27] Note that inflation adjustments apply only to the phase-outs under LLC, not AOTC.

Susan:	Junior	Senior	
Tuition and fees	$1,500	$1,550	$3,050
Course materials (books)	300	300	600
Room and board	3,500	3,700	—
Bill:		Freshman	
Tuition and fees	—	$3,700	$3,700
Course materials (books)	—	300	300
Room and board	—	3,700	—

In 2015, the Greens are allowed to claim the American Opportunity Tax credit (AOTC) and the Lifetime Learning Credit (LLC) as follows:

Ron has not completed four years of postsecondary education at the beginning of 2015, so he qualifies as an eligible student for *all* of 2015. Assuming the AOTC has not been used for Ron in four prior tax years, his 2015 qualifying education expenses include his tuition and fees and course materials, totaling $3,650 ($1,500 + $1,550 + $300 + $300).

Ron's tentative AOTC equals $2,413 ((100% × $2,000) + (25% × $1,650)).

Susan qualifies for the AOTC in both semesters. Her tentative AOTC is $2,413 [(100% × $2,000) + ($1,650 × 25%)]. Bill qualifies for the AOTC only in Fall 2015 because he began postsecondary education in that semester. His tentative credit is $2,500 [(100% × $2,000) + (the next $ 2,000 x 25%)], based on qualifying expenses of $4,000.

The Greens' total tentative AOTC is $7,326 ($2,413 + $2,413 + $2,500). The phaseout is $1,465 ($7,326 × ($164,000 – $160,000)/$20,000). Thus, the Greens' total allowable AOTC is $5,861 ($7,326 – $1,465).

Note: If the AOTC has been used for Ron in four prior tax years, the Greens' total allowable AOTC is $3,930. Their total tentative AOTC is $4,913 ($0 + $2,413 + $2,500), and their phaseout is $983 ($4,913 × ($164,000 – $160,000)/$20,000).

If the AOTC has already been claimed for Ron for four years, Ron qualifies for the LLC in 2015 because the LLC is not limited to four years of postsecondary education. His qualified education expenses for 2015 total $3,050, so the Greens' tentative LLC is $610 ($3,050 × 20%). The phaseout is $610 ($610 × ($164,000 – $110,000)/$20,000). Thus, the Greens' total allowable LLC is zero. ◀

Residential Energy Credits. Congress has enacted a wide range of incentives for both individuals and businesses to promote domestic energy production and conservation. Most of these incentives are in the form of tax credits. Two major credits for individual taxpayers are (1) the nonbusiness energy property credit, and (2) the residential energy efficient property credit.

Nonbusiness Energy Property Credit. Individuals are allowed a nonrefundable tax credit for nonbusiness residential energy property (qualified windows, exterior doors, insulation, heat pumps, furnaces, central air conditioners, and water heaters). The credit equals 10% of the cost of building components (exterior doors and insulation, for example) plus the cost of energy property (water heaters and furnaces, for example). The credit's lifetime limit is $500 per taxpayer. It applies to property placed into service after December 31, 2008, and before January 1, 2015.[28]

Residential Energy Efficient Property (REEP) Credit. For tax years beginning after December 31, 2005 and before January 1, 2017, a tax credit is allowed for several types of energy efficient property installed on a taxpayer's principal residence:[29] Solar hot water heaters, Qualified solar electric property, Fuel cell property, Residential wind property, and Geothermal heat pumps.

The credit is 30% of the cost of eligible property. Other features of the REEP credit are:

- Labor costs to install the property are included in the qualified cost of the property.
- Second homes or vacation homes do not qualify for some parts of the credit.

[28] Sec. 25C(g), as amended by the Tax Increase Prevention Act of 2014.

[29] Sec. 25D, as amended by the American Recovery and Reinvestment Act of 2009.

- If less than 80% of the use of the dwelling is for nonbusiness use, then only the percentage of nonbusiness use can be taken into account.
- The taxpayer's basis in the property is reduced by the amount of the credit.
- The credit is not available for use with swimming pools or hot tubs.
- Credits earned but not used in the current year can be carried forward to the next year.

Alternative Motor Vehicle Credit. Congress has enacted several nonrefundable personal credits to encourage taxpayers to invest in alternative vehicles. The comprehensive alternative motor vehicle credit (AMVC) contains the: Qualified fuel cell credit, Advanced lean-burn technology credit, Qualified hybrid credit, Qualified alternative fuel refueling property credit, Plug-in conversion credit, Plug-in electric vehicle credit. Under current law, only the provision for the credit for a fuel cell motor vehicle is active. It is allowed for qualifying vehicles purchased before January 1, 2015. Details on these credits are beyond the scope of this text.

Qualified Retirement Savings Contributions Credit ("Saver's Credit"). To encourage low and middle income taxpayers to save for retirement, a *permanent*, nonrefundable credit for contributions or deferrals to qualified retirement plans has been established for tax years beginning after December 31, 2001.[30] The saver's credit is allowed *in addition* to otherwise allowable exclusions or deductions from gross income for retirement plan contributions or deferrals.

To be eligible for the credit, a taxpayer must be at least 18 years of age as of the close of the tax year, must not be claimed as a dependent on another taxpayer's tax return, and must not be a full-time student[31] for purposes of the dependency exemption (full-time student for at least 5 calendar months).

The saver's credit is computed by multiplying the amount contributed (maximum $2,000 per eligible individual per year) by an applicable percentage. The percentage for 2015 depends on the taxpayer's adjusted gross income, as shown in the following table:

Applicable	*MFJ*		*Head of Household*		*All Other Statuses*	
Percentage	*AGI Over*	*Not Over*	*AGI Over*	*Not Over*	*AGI Over*	*Not Over*
50%	$ 0	$36,500	$ 0	$27,375	$ 0	$18,250
20%	36,500	39,500	27,375	29,625	18,250	19,750
10%	39,500	61,000	29,625	45,750	19,750	30,500
0%	61,000		45,750		30,500	

Annual qualified retirement savings contribution equals the sum of contributions or deferrals by the taxpayer to specified retirement plans, including IRAs (Roth and Traditional), 401(k) plans, 403(b) plans, and certain other plans, reduced by any distributions from such plans. The maximum contribution eligible for the credit for each individual is $2,000 per year.

EXAMPLE I:14-23 ▶ Steve is 20 years old, unmarried, filing single and has AGI of $17,000 in 2015. During the year, he contributes $2,000 to his Roth IRA. Steve is eligible for a Qualified Retirement Savings Contributions Credit in the amount of $1,000 ($2,000 × 50%). The credit would be the same if he contributed $2,000 to a traditional IRA, but in addition to the $1,000 credit, Steve would be permitted to deduct the $2,000 contribution to the traditional IRA on his individual return. ◀

Limitation on Nonrefundable Personal Credits. Nonrefundable personal credits may not exceed the regular tax liability minus foreign tax credit. After passage of the 2012 American Taxpayer Relief Act, these credits may offset AMT as well.

---

30 Sec. 25B. The Pension Protection Act of 2006 made the credit permanent.

31 Sec. 152(f)(2).

KEY POINT

The foreign tax credit is available only on income, war profits, and excess profits taxes or taxes paid in lieu of such taxes. It is sometimes difficult to determine whether a particular foreign tax falls into the qualifying category.

FOREIGN TAX CREDIT

U.S. citizens, resident aliens, and U.S. corporations are subject to U.S. taxation on their worldwide income.[32] The foreign-source portion of worldwide income is also subject to taxation by the foreign country. To reduce possible double taxation, U.S. tax law provides a foreign tax credit (FTC) for income taxes paid or accrued to a foreign country or a U.S. possession.

In lieu of the FTC, taxpayers may elect to take a deduction for foreign taxes paid or accrued.[33] In general, the FTC results in a greater tax benefit because (as previously discussed) a credit is fully offset against the tax liability, while a deduction merely reduces taxable income. Finally, in lieu of the FTC, taxpayers may elect to exclude foreign earned income from U.S. gross income (Sec. 911). (See chapter I:4 for more information).

ADDITIONAL COMMENT

In 2011, 6.9 million tax returns of individual taxpayers claimed $16.4 billion in foreign tax credits.

Computation of Allowable Credit. The FTC equals the lesser of (1) foreign tax paid or accrued, or (2) the portion of U.S. income tax liability attributable to income earned in all foreign countries (FTC limitation).[34] This limitation restricts claiming the benefit from foreign tax credit if the effective foreign tax rate on foreign earnings exceeds the effective U.S. tax rate on these earnings. The FTC limitation is computed using the following formula:

$$\frac{\text{Foreign source taxable income}}{\text{Worldwide taxable income}} \times \text{U.S. income tax before credits} = \text{FTC limitation}$$

EXAMPLE I:14-24 ▶ Robert Albertson has $200,000 of U.S. source taxable income and $100,000 of foreign source taxable income from country A. Robert's worldwide taxable income is $300,000 ($200,000 + $100,000). Country A levies $40,000 in foreign income taxes on the foreign source taxable income (i.e., a 40% effective tax rate). His U.S. tax before credits is $100,250 on the $300,000 of worldwide taxable income. Using the formula given above, the overall FTC limitation is computed as follows:[35]

$$\frac{\$100{,}000}{\$300{,}000} \times \$100{,}250 = \$33{,}417$$

Because the foreign tax payments ($40,000) exceed the U.S. tax attributable to the foreign source income ($33,417), the limitation applies. Thus, Robert's net U.S. tax equals $66,833 ($100,250 − $33,417) and, $6,583 ($40,000 − $33,417) of FTC cannot be used in the current year. ◀

STOP & THINK

Question: Since a credit is generally more valuable than a deduction, under what circumstances would it be beneficial for a taxpayer to take a deduction for foreign taxes in lieu of the foreign tax credit?

Solution: If a taxpayer has foreign source taxable income from one country and an equal loss from another foreign country, the foreign tax credit limitation is zero because the net foreign-source taxable income is zero. Because none of the taxes paid in the foreign country in which taxable income was produced can be claimed as a credit, the taxpayer may choose to deduct them (unless the unused credits can be carried back or forward.)

---

[32] Certain exceptions are provided by treaty agreements between the United States and foreign countries whereby certain types of foreign-source income may be exempt from taxation or taxed at a reduced tax rate in the foreign country.

[33] Sec. 164(a)(3).

[34] Sec. 904.

[35] Two types of income have a separate foreign tax credit limitation: passive income and all other income. (See Chapter C:16 of *Prentice Hall's Federal Taxation: Corporations, Partnerships, Estates, and Trusts* for a more detailed discussion of these separate limitations.)

Treatment of Unused Credits. Unused foreign tax credits may be carried back one year and then forward for ten years to tax years where the limitation is not exceeded (i.e., the foreign tax payment is lower than the U.S. taxes attributable to the foreign-source income in the carryback or carryover years). Unused credits are lost if they are not used by the end of the ten-year carryover period.

BUSINESS RELATED TAX CREDITS

General Business Credits. The tax credits commonly available to businesses are grouped into a special category called **general business credits.** These credits are combined for the purpose of computing an overall dollar limitation based on the taxpayer's tax liability (discussed in more detail on page I:14-23). If the general business credits earned in the current year exceed the limitation, the excess may be carried back one year and carried forward 20 years. The credits are used in order of time generated with carryforward credits used first, current year credits next, and then carryback credits.[36]

EXAMPLE I:14-25 ▶ Eastern Corporation had unused general business tax credits of $10,000 in 2014 that are carried forward to 2015. Eastern earns $5,000 of additional credits in 2015 and computes an overall credit limitation of $12,000 for the year. The allowable $12,000 credit consists of the $10,000 carryover and $2,000 from 2015. The $3,000 of unused 2015 credit ($5,000 − $2,000) is carried forward to 2016. ◀

The more important general business credits are discussed below. All are nonrefundable.

Tax Credit for Rehabilitation Expenditures. Congress provides a credit for investments in the rehabilitation of older industrial and commercial buildings and certified historic structures.[37]

REAL-WORLD EXAMPLE

Taxpayers incurred substantial rehabilitation expenditures on an old factory building, but the tax credit was not allowed because the taxpayers did not use the straight-line depreciation method. *Frank DeMarco,* 87 T.C. 518 (1986).

The credit equals 10% of qualified rehabilitation expenditures (QRE) for buildings originally placed in service before 1936 and 20% of QRE for certified historic structures. The credit applies only to depreciable trade or business property and depreciable property held for investment. Residential rental property does not qualify unless the building is a certified historic structure. Rehabilitation includes renovation, restoration, or construction of a building, but not an enlargement or new construction. For buildings other than certified historic structures, a rehabilitation project must meet certain structural tests and must be substantial (QRE exceed the greater of $5,000 or the building's adjusted basis).[38]

The following additional provisions apply.

- For certified historic structures, the total rehabilitation must be certified by the Department of the Interior as being consistent with the historic character of the building.
- Straight-line depreciation generally must be used with the applicable Sec. 168 recovery periods with respect to rehabilitation expenditures. The regular MACRS depreciation rules apply to the portion of the property's basis that is not eligible for the credit.
- The basis of the property for depreciation is reduced by the full amount of the credit taken.[39]
- The rehabilitation credit is recaptured at a rate of 20% per year if the property is disposed of within five years of the date placed in service.

---

[36] Sec. 38(d).

[37] Secs. 47(a)(1) and (2). A certified historic structure must be certified by the Department of the Interior and must be located in a registered historic district or listed in the *National Register.*

[38] Sec. 47(c)(1)(A).

[39] Sec. 50(c)(1).

EXAMPLE I:14-26 ▶ During the current year, Ted incurs $40,000 of qualified rehabilitation expenditures (QRE) in connection with a certified historic structure used in his business. The adjusted basis of the certified historic structure was $38,000 at the time the rehabilitation began. The property qualifies for the rehabilitation credit because:

- It is used in Ted's trade or business and is depreciable.
- The property is a certified historic structure.
- The amount of the QRE exceeds the greater of the property's $38,000 adjusted basis or the $5,000 statutory minimum.

Thus, the credit is $8,000 ($0.20 \times$ $40,000). The building's depreciable basis attributable to the $40,000 of QRE rehabilitation expenditures is reduced by the full amount of the credit to $32,000 ($40,000 − $8,000). If the property is disposed of after one year, $6,400 of the credit ($8,000 − $1,600) is recaptured. ◀

ADDITIONAL COMMENT

The American Recovery and Reinvestment Act of 2009 expanded or added several new business energy tax credits.

Business Energy Tax Credits. To encourage energy conservation measures, credits are available to businesses that invest in energy-conserving properties (e.g., solar and geothermal property).[40] The credit for geothermal energy property is 10% of the property's basis. The credit for solar energy property and qualified fuel cell property purchased in tax years ending after December 31, 2005 and before January 1, 2016 is 30% of the property's basis. Construction, reconstruction, or erection of the property must be completed by the taxpayer, and its original use must begin with the taxpayer.

Recent tax law changes have set up a complex interaction among the energy credit, renewable energy grants, and an electricity production credit. Details are beyond the scope of this text, but essentially, taxpayers must choose to receive grants or take credits, but not both.

Employer-Provided Child Care Credit. The employer-provided child care credit is an incentive for businesses to provide child care for their employees. The credit is the *sum* of the following two amounts:

- 25% of qualified child care expenses. These expenses are amounts paid to acquire, construct, rehabilitate, expand, and operate a qualified child care facility or paid under contract to a qualified child care facility for services to employees; plus
- 10% of qualified child care resources and referral expenditures. These are expenses paid or incurred by a taxpayer under a contract to provide child care resource and referral services to employees.

These are several special rules with regard to the credit, including:

- The total credit amount allowed for any given year cannot exceed $150,000.
- Employers claiming this credit cannot claim a deduction for child care expenses and also claim the credit. Expenses that would be otherwise deductible must be reduced by the amount of the credit claimed.
- If, within 10 years of the year in which a child care facility is placed in service, an employer terminates its use as a qualified child care facility, the credit must be recaptured. The recapture rate begins at 100% (terminate within the first three years), and declines steadily as the years of facility use increase.

This credit is part of, and is subject to, the limitations of the general business credit.

EXAMPLE I:14-27 ▶ Gamechicken Partnership began a child care facility for its employees during the current year. The business incurred the following expenses:

Rent on facility	$ 25,000
Leasehold improvements	60,000
Equipment, toys, etc.	18,000
Salaries of child care employees	30,000
Other operating expenses of facility	12,000
Qualified child care referral fees*	8,000
Total expenses	$153,000

*Fees paid to a firm to place children in other facilities.

[40] Sec. 48(a)(2).

Gamechicken's credit for the year would be $37,050 [($145,000 × 25%) + ($8,000 × 10%)]. All of the above amounts are also deductible after reduction by the amount of the credit. So, the rent, salaries, and operating expenses of $67,000 ($25,000 + $30,000 + $12,000) must be reduced by a total of $16,750 ($67,000 × 25%), the referral fees must be reduced by $800 ($8,000 × 10%), and the basis of the leasehold improvements and equipment must be reduced by $19,500 ($78,000 × 25%). ◀

Disabled Access Credit. A nonrefundable tax credit is available to eligible small businesses for expenditures incurred to make existing business facilities accessible to disabled individuals. The disabled access credit equals 50% of eligible expenditures that exceed $250 but do not exceed $10,250.[41] Thus, the annual credit limitation is $5,000 [0.50($10,250 − $250)].

Eligible expenditures include payments for removing architectural, communication, physical, or transportation barriers that prevent a business from being accessible. Expenditures made in connection with *new facility* construction are not eligible for the credit. The allowed credit reduces the deduction for eligible expenses. An eligible small business is any business that either (1) had gross receipts of $1 million or less in the preceding year or, (2) in the case of a business failing the first test, had no more than 30 full-time employees in the preceding year and makes a timely election to claim the credit.

EXAMPLE I:14-28 ▶ In the previous year, Crane Corporation (an S Corp) had 14 employees and $2 million of gross receipts. During the current year, Crane installed concrete access ramps at a total cost of $14,000. Crane is an eligible small business because the company had 30 or fewer full-time employees during the preceding year. Only $10,000 of eligible expenditures qualify for the credit, thereby limiting the credit to $5,000 ($10,000 × 0.50). The depreciable basis of the property must be reduced by the credit amount to $9,000 ($14,000 − $5,000). ◀

Credit for Increased Research Activities. To encourage businesses to conduct research and experimentation, a credit is allowed under Sec. 41. The research credit is equal to the sum of the regular research credit, the university basic research credit, and the energy research consortium credit. The last two are beyond the scope of this book.

This credit is allowed for increased research expenses and at a rate of 20% of the excess of qualified research expenses over the base amount. It applies to qualified expenses incurred before January 1, 2015. Qualified research expenses (QRE) are defined as internal and external research expenses that are incident to the development or improvement of a product or component. Only incremental expenditures (the excess over a base amount) are eligible for the credit. Research conducted after the start of commercial production does not qualify for the credit, nor do marketing, advertising, or production expenses.

The base amount equals the greater of (1) the product of the taxpayer's fixed-base percentage and average annual gross receipts over the four years prior to the credit year, and (2) 50% of credit year qualified research expenditures. The fixed-base percentage is the historical ratio of qualified research expenditures to gross receipts and is limited to 16%. The table below specifies the historical period used based on the years in which the taxpayer incurred qualified research expenses, assuming the taxpayer is considered a start-up company.[42]

---

[41] Sec. 44.

[42] Sec. 41(c)(3)(B)

History of Incurred QREs	*Fixed base percentage*
First year through fifth year	3%
Sixth year	1/6*(QRE /gross receipts for years 4 & 5)
Seventh year	1/3*(QRE /gross receipts for years 5 & 6)
Eighth year	1/2*(QRE /gross receipts for years 5, 6 & 7)
Ninth year	2/3*(QRE /gross receipts for years 5, 6, 7 & 8)
Tenth year	5/6*(QRE /gross receipts for years 5, 6, 7, 8 & 9)

After the tenth year in which the taxpayer incurs QREs, the fixed base percentage equals the ratio of QRE accumulated across any five years in the year 5 to year 10 range divided by the gross receipts for the same five year range.

EXAMPLE I:14-29 ▶ Northern Inc. (an S Corp). began operations in 2010 and had the following gross receipts for the previous four-year period.

2010	$4,500,000
2011	7,000,000
2012	8,000,000
2013	8,500,000

Northern's average annual gross receipts for the four-year prior period is $7,000,000. In 2014, Northern incurred $500,000 of qualified research expenditures. Assuming Northern Inc. uses a fixed-base percentage of 3%, the corporation's base amount equals the greater of (1) $210,000 ($7,000,000 × 3%) or (2) $250,000 ($500,000 × 50%). The 2014 regular research credit would be $50,000 [($500,000 − $250,000) × 20%]. ◀

Taxpayers may elect a simplified credit in lieu of the regular credit, effective for tax years ending after December 31, 2006. This simplified credit is not based on historical gross receipts, thus opening the research credit to new businesses. The base and credit percentage is computed as follows:

- ▶ For tax years after 2008, 14% of the excess of qualified research expenses of the current year over 50 percent of the average qualified research expenses for the three preceding taxable years; or
- ▶ 6% of qualified research expenses of the current year if the taxpayer has no qualified research expenses in any one of the three preceding taxable years.

EXAMPLE I:14-30 ▶ Howell Company is a calendar year taxpayer. In 2014, it incurs $175,000 of qualified research expenses. In the three preceding tax years, Howell's qualified research expenses averaged $40,000 per year. Howell can elect a simplified research credit of $21,700 [($175,000 − 50% ($40,000) × 0.14)]. If Howell had no qualified research expenses in the three preceding years, its credit would be $10,500 ($175,000 × .06). ◀

A business deduction is allowed for research and experimentation expenditures under Sec. 174. This deduction must be reduced by the amount of the research credit.[43]

General Business Credit Overall Limitation. There is an overall dollar limitation of the general business credit based on tax liability. The general business credit may not exceed the smaller of:[44]

[43] Sec. 280(c)(2).

[44] The limitation discussed above must be separated into two parts: (1) all general business credits other than the empowerment zone and New York Liberty Zone employment credits and (2) the empowerment zone and New York Liberty Zone employment credits. Only the first part is covered here. The second part allows these credits to reduce, in whole or part, the AMT. (See Sec. 38(c) for details.)

1. Net income tax – Tentative AMT, and
2. Net income tax – 0.25 (Net regular tax – $25,000)

Net income tax means the sum of the net regular tax liability and the AMT, reduced by the nonrefundable personal credits and the foreign tax credit. *Net regular tax liability* means the regular tax reduced by nonrefundable personal credits and the foreign tax credit. The limitation also prevents a taxpayer from claiming a general business credit in the same tax year that the taxpayer has alternative minimum tax. The overall credit limitation is demonstrated in the example below.

EXAMPLE I:14-31 ► Steve's general business tax credit before limitation is $50,000 (a $50,000 research credit). Steve's regular tax liability (before credits) is $45,000, and his tentative minimum tax is $10,000. His nonrefundable tax credits also include a $1,200 child and dependent care credit and an $1,800 foreign tax credit. Steve's general business tax credit is initially limited to the smaller of (A) and (B) below. Thus, the limitation on the $50,000 of general business tax credit is $32,000, and Steve's general business credit is limited to $32,000. This credit reduces his tax liablity to $13,000,

A) Net income tax – Tentative AMT
[($45,000 – $1,200 – $1,800) – ($10,000)] = $32,000
B) Net income tax – $25% (Net regular tax – $25,000)
{($45,000 – $1,200 – $1,800) – 25% [($45,000 – $1,200 – $1,800) – $25,000] = $37,750} ◄

REFUNDABLE PERSONAL CREDITS

As mentioned earlier, refundable credits not only offset a taxpayer's income tax liability but can create a refund. If the refundable credits exceed the tax liability, such excess will be refunded to the taxpayer.

HISTORICAL NOTE

The earned income credit was claimed on 24.6 million tax returns in 2011 and amounted to $55.3 billion. This compares with 19.4 million returns and $32.5 billion in 2000.

Earned Income Credit. The earned income credit (EIC) is a special type of "negative income tax" designed to encourage individuals to become employed or to continue work despite low earnings.[45] The credit is based on earned income, which includes wages, salaries, tips, and other employee compensation plus net earnings from self-employment. Earned income does not include any form of employee compensation that is not includible in the taxpayer's income for the year.

The EIC is not available to taxpayers whose "disqualified income" exceeds $3,400 in 2015 ($3,350 in 2014). Disqualified income includes taxable interest income and dividends, tax-exempt interest income, net income from nonbusiness rents or royalties, net capital gains, and net passive activity income.

The credit is available to individuals with qualifying children[46] (see Chapter I:2 for the uniform definition of a qualifying child) and to individuals without children.[47] Individuals without children are eligible only if the following requirements are met:

- The individual's principal place of abode is in the United States for more than one-half of the tax year.
- The individual (or spouse if married) is at least age 25 and not more than age 64 at the end of the tax year.
- The individual is not a dependent or qualifying child of another taxpayer for the tax year.[48]

Married taxpayers must file a joint return to be eligible for the credit. Earned income credit percentages and the maximum amount of earned income allowed for the credit in

---

[45] (See Chapter I:2 for a discussion of the relationship between the child tax credit and the earned income credit.)

[46] Any qualifying child's name, age, and taxpayer identification number must be reported on the tax return.

[47] Sec. 32(c).

[48] Sec. 32(c)(1)(A), as amended by the 2008 Adoption Act.

2015 are summarized in Table I:14-1. These vary by the number of qualifying children and the taxpayer's filing status. The allowable credit phases out when the taxpayer's AGI or earned income (whichever is greater) exceeds a specified amount (Table I:14-1).[49]

EXAMPLE I:14-32 ▶ Vivian is not married, has one qualifying child, and is eligible for the earned income credit in 2015. Vivian's AGI is $19,500 ($15,900 of wages and $3,600 of alimony). The wages are considered earned income; the alimony is not earned income. The tentative credit is $3,359 (0.34 × $9,880). The phaseout is $222 [15.98% × ($19,500 AGI − $18,110)]. The allowable credit is therefore $3,137 ($3,359 − 222), and this amount is refundable to Vivian. ◀

▼ TABLE I:14-1
2015 Earned Income Credit Table

Number of Qualifying Children	Credit Rate	Credit Base (Earned Income)	Maximum Credit	Phase-out Rate*	Phase-out Threshold for Taxpayers Married Filing Joint (Not Married Filing Joint)
0	7.65%	$ 6,580	$ 503	7.65%	$13,750 ($8,240)
1	34%	$ 9,880	$3,359	15.98%	$23,630 ($18,110)
2	40%	$13,870	$5,548	21.06%	$23,630 ($18,110)
3 or more	45%	$13,870	$6,242	21.06%	$23,630 ($18,110)

[a]applied to Earned Income (or AGI if larger) in excess of phase-out threshold.

PROVISIONS RELATED TO HEALTH INSURANCE

OBJECTIVE 4

Describe and compute the premium tax credit and the shared responsibility payment

HEALTH INSURANCE PREMIUM ASSISTANCE CREDIT (ALSO KNOWN AS PREMIUM TAX CREDIT)

For years after 2013, a credit is allowed for a portion of taxpayers' health insurance premiums (Sec. 36B). The credit allowed equals the excess of qualifying premiums over the premium amount deemed affordable based on the taxpayer's household income. Qualifying premiums are based on the purchase of health insurance through a state American Health Benefit exchange or a federal exchange. The qualifying premiums are calibrated to premiums in the taxpayer's residential area. Plans are categorized by the portion of cost of benefits covered by the plan, and they range from Bronze to Silver to Gold to Platinum. Qualifying premiums for the credit are set at the cost of premiums for the second-lowest-cost Silver plan. Premium amounts are reported by state and family characteristics on the federal website HealthCare.gov (https://www.healthcare.gov/health-plan-information/).

Credit-eligible taxpayers (1) must not have access through employer health insurance or other government sponsored plans to minimum affordable essential coverage (affordable: premiums ≤ 9.56% of household income and essential: plan covers 60% or more of the cost of allowed plan benefits), (2) must file jointly if married, and (3) may not be eligible as a dependent of another taxpayer. Furthermore, to be eligible for the credit, the taxpayer must have household income that falls between 100% and 400% of the federal poverty line (FPL).[50] Household income is a taxpayer's modified AGI plus the AGI of dependent family members required to file a federal income tax return.[51] The 2015 FPL minimums for the 48 contiguous U.S. states are outlined in the following table:

[49] The percentages are adjusted annually for inflation.

[50] THE FPL is defined in Sec. 36B(d)(3) based on its definition in the Social Security Act (42 USC 1397jj(c)(5)). The U.S. Department of Health and Human Services publishes these guidelines annually.

[51] Section 36B(d)(2). Modified AGI includes nontaxable Social Security benefits, tax-exempt interest income, and any excluded foreign earned income.

▼ **TABLE I:14-2**
2015 Federal Poverty Guidelines[52]

People in Household	Poverty Guideline (100%)	People in Household	Poverty Guideline (100%)
1	\$11,770	5	\$28,410
2	\$15,930	6	\$32,570
3	\$20,090	7	\$36,730
4	\$24,250	8	\$40,890
Beyond 8, add \$4,160 for each additional person beyond 8			

▼ **TABLE I:14-3**
Premium Levels Deemed Affordable as a Percent of Household Income–2015

Categories of Household Income Relative to the FPL	Affordable Premium as a Percent of Household Income	
	Initial %	Final %
100% up to 133% FPL	2.01%	2.01%
Over 133% up to150% FPL	3.02%	4.02%
Over 150% up to 200% FPL	4.02%	6.34%
Over 200% up to 250% FPL	6.34%	8.10%
Over 250% up to 300% FPL	8.10%	9.56%
Over 300% up to 400% FPL	9.56%	9.56%

EXAMPLE I:14-33 ▶ Bryan and Heather Delane (27 and 26 years old, respectively) are eligible taxpayers and have household income of \$29,600. Their income and household size put them at 186% (\$29,600/\$15,930) of the FPL. ◀

Neither has available coverage from their employers. For 2015, the Delanes enroll in the second-lowest-cost Silver plan available through their state's health care exchange, for which total premiums will cost \$5,500. Determine the amount of the Delanes' health insurance premium tax credit.

1st: Affordable premium

The Delanes' household income relative to the FPL equals 186% and falls in the 150%–200% range of the FPL. The share of the premium deemed affordable for them must be based on the initial rate (4.02%) plus a prorated portion of the distance to the final rate (6.34%).

FPL range: 200% − 150% = 50 Distance from initial range = 186% − 150% = 36

Range of rates within FPL range: 6.34% − 4.02% = 2.32%

Delanes' rate = Initial rate + prorated portion of range of rates
= 4.02% + 36/50 (2.32%) = 5.69%

Delanes' affordable premiums = 5.69% (\$29,600 household income) = \$1,684

2nd: Credit amount

Premium tax credit = cost of coverage (total premiums) − personal share (affordable premiums) = \$5,500 − \$1,684 = \$3,816

This credit may be available as an advance payment directly from the U.S. Treasury to the issuer of the health insurance plan. This approach reduces the taxpayer's periodic payment required for the personal share of the total premiums. The tax credit reported on the taxpayer's individual income tax return reflects the computed credit reduced by advance

[52] http://aspe.hhs.gov/poverty/15poverty.cfm.

payments of the credit (Sec. 36B(f)). Any excess of the credit over advance payments represents an additional credit. Any shortfall is an additional tax liability.

SHARED RESPONSIBILITY PAYMENT

After 2013, individuals without the required minimum essential health insurance coverage (for taxpayer and dependents) must pay an excise tax commonly referred to as the "shared responsibility payment" (Sec. 5000A). The shared responsibility payment equals the lesser of (1) the cost of bronze level insurance coverage in a health plan ($207 per month or $2,484 per individual for 2015) or (2) the calculated penalty. The calculated penalty equals the greater of (1) the applicable dollar amount ($325 for 2015) or (2) 2% of household income in excess of the filing threshold. The filing threshold is the sum of the deduction for exemptions and the standard deduction amount for non-itemizers.

EXAMPLE I:14-34 ▶ In 2015, Robert Dice is single, has no dependents, has no health insurance, and has gross income of $75,000. The annual cost of qualified health insurance for him at the bronze level would have been $2,484. The penalty for Robert will equal the greater of (a) $325, the flat dollar amount for a single person with no dependents, or (b) $1,294, the excess income amount based on 2.0% of Robert's household income in excess of his filing threshold ($75,000 − $4,000 personal exemption − $6,300 standard deduction). Robert's shared responsibility payment will equal $1,294, the lesser of the annual cost of insurance, $2,484 or the penalty amount, $1,294. ◀

TOPIC REVIEW I:14-2

Summary of Selected Tax Credits Discussed in Chapter 14

Tax Credit Item	Rationale for Inclusion in Tax Law
NONREFUNDABLE PERSONAL CREDITS:	
Adoption credit (Sec. 23)	Provides relief for taxpayers who incur expenses in the adoption of children
Child tax credit (Sec. 24)	Reduces the tax burden on families with dependent children
Child and Dependent care credit (Sec. 21)	Provides relief for employed parents and other individuals who incur expenses for dependent care
Elderly and Disabled credit (Sec. 22)	Provides relief for elderly taxpayers who are not substantially covered by Social Security
American Opportunity Tax Credit and Lifetime Learning Credit (Sec. 25A)	Assists students and families with the cost of post-secondary education
Qualified retirement savings contributions credit (Sec. 25B)	Encourages low- and middle-income taxpayers to save for retirement
Residential energy credits (Sec. 25C & D)	Encourages energy conservation measures on principal residences
MISCELLANEOUS CREDITS:	
Foreign tax credit (Sec. 27)	Mitigates the effects of double taxation on foreign-source income
GENERAL BUSINESS CREDITS:	
Business energy credits (Sec. 48)	Encourages energy conservation measures
Disabled access credit (Sec. 44)	Encourages small businesses to provide access for disabled persons
Employer-provided child care credit (Sec. 45F)	Provides incentive for businesses to provide child care for employees
Rehabilitation expenditures credit (Sec. 21)	Encourages the rehabilitation of older buildings
Research credit (Sec. 41)	Encourages research and experimental activities
REFUNDABLE PERSONAL CREDITS:	
Earned income credit (Sec. 32)	Provides incentive for low-income individuals to work
Overpayment of social security taxes (Sec. 31)	Provides a credit or refund for social security taxes overpaid when a taxpayer has multiple employers
Taxes withheld from wages and other income (Sec. 31)	Recognizes taxpayer's prepayment of tax
Premium Tax Credit (Sec. 36B)	Reduces the cost of health insurance for households with low and modest incomes.

PAYMENT OF TAXES

OBJECTIVE 5

Explain the mechanics of the federal withholding tax system and the requirements for making estimated tax payments

The IRS collects federal income taxes during the year ("pay as you go") through withholding on wages and quarterly estimated tax payments. If the total of withholdings and estimated taxes is less than the amount of tax liability, the taxpayer must pay the balance of the tax due when the tax return is filed. If there has been an overpayment of tax, the taxpayer may either request a refund or apply the overpayment to the following year's estimated tax.

Substantial penalties are imposed if an employer fails to withhold federal income tax and pay such amounts to the IRS.[53] In addition, taxpayers may be subject to penalties for underpayment of estimated tax.[54]

WITHHOLDING OF TAXES

REAL-WORLD EXAMPLE

A teacher claimed a credit for Social Security taxes that had been withheld from his salary. He believed that the Social Security tax was illegally withheld because he did not authorize the collection of the tax. The Tax Court held that the Social Security tax is mandatory for designated employees and does not allow a person to elect not to contribute. *Richard L. Feldman,* 1967 PH T.C. Memo ¶67,091, 26 TCM 444.

HISTORICAL NOTE

The withholding of federal income taxes by employers began during World War II.

Employers must withhold federal income taxes and FICA taxes from an employee's wages. No withholdings are required if an employer-employee relationship does not exist (e.g., an individual who performs services as an independent contractor). Generally, unless a specific exemption is provided, withholding is required on all forms of employee compensation (salaries, fees, bonuses, dismissal payments, commissions, vacation pay, and taxable fringe benefits).[55] Below are some special rules relating to withholding of federal taxes:

- *More than one employer during the same year.* Each employer must withhold FICA and federal income taxes without regard to the fact that the employee has more than one employer. As mentioned on page I:14-9, this may cause an overwithholding of FICA taxes if the employee's wages exceed the ceiling amount on the OASDI portion of the tax. In the event of overwithholding of FICA taxes, the employee may credit the excess amount as an additional payment of tax. However, the matching employer excess FICA contributions are not refundable or creditable against the tax liabilities of either employer or employee.
- *Overall exemption.* Taxpayers are exempt from income tax withholding in the current year if they (1) had no tax liability in the prior year; (2) expect no tax liability in the current year; and (3) can be claimed as dependent by another taxpayer and report no more than $950 total income, no more than $300 of which is unearned. The earnings of such individuals are still fully taxable, and an employer may be liable for FICA tax payments on these earnings.
- *Exemption for certain employment activities.* Certain employees, such as agricultural laborers, ministers, household employees, newspaper carriers under age 18, and those earning tips of less than $20 per month from an employer, are exempt from withholding. The earnings of such individuals are still fully taxable, and an employer may be liable for matching FICA tax payments on these earnings.[56]
- *Special rules for supplemental wage payments.* Supplemental wages payments include items such as bonuses, commissions, overtime, accumulated sick pay, severance pay, awards, prizes, back pay, and retroactive pay increases. If an employee receives supplemental wage payments, the federal income tax withholding amount is determined under either of two methods:[57]

---

[53] Sec. 3403. Employers are liable for payment of the full amount that must be withheld and paid to the IRS. In addition, responsible individuals (e.g., corporate officers, directors, and consultants) may be held personally liable for payment of the tax. (See *Renate Schiff v. U.S.,* 69 AFTR 2d 92-804, 92-1 USTC ¶50,248 (D.C. NV, 1992), *Ted E. Tsouprake v. U.S.,* 69 AFTR 2d 92-821, 92-1 USTC ¶50,249 (D.C. FL, 1992), and *Ralph M. Guito, Jr. v. U.S.,* 67 AFTR 2d 91-1066, 92-1 USTC ¶ 50,231 (D.C. FL, 1991).)

[54] Sec. 6654.

[55] Reg. Sec. 31.3401(a)-1(a)(2).

[56] Reg. Sec. 31.3401(a)(10)-1(a). An employer is liable for FICA tax payments for domestic servants if $1,400 or more is paid to an individual in any calendar year.

[57] Reg. Sec. 31.3402(g)-1(a).

- Concurrent payments—if the supplemental wages are included in the payment of regular wages, the tax is withheld as if the combined wages were a single wage payment for the payroll period.
- Separate payments—if the supplemental wages are paid separately, the tax withheld is either a flat 25%, or the percentage that applies to the aggregate of the supplemental wage payment with wages paid within the same calendar year for the last preceding payroll period or the current payroll period.

▶ *Backup withholding.* Backup withholding rules were enacted to prevent abusive noncompliance situations, such as not providing the payor of a dividend with the payee's Social Security number. A 28% withholding rate is required on most types of payments that are reported on Form 1099 (e.g., interest, dividends, royalties, etc.) where a proper taxpayer identification number is not provided.

▶ *Other special rules.* There are many other special rules on withholding in certain circumstances, such as for fringe benefits, pension and annuity payments, etc. that are beyond the scope of this text.

REAL-WORLD EXAMPLE

It has been held that the employer's withholding of federal income taxes is not an improper taking of property without due process in violation of the Fifth Amendment. *Michael O. Campbell v. Amax Coal Co.*, 610 F.2d 701, 45 AFTR 2d 80-564, 80-1 USTC ¶9185 (10th Cir., 1980).

Withholding Allowances and Methods. On beginning a new job, each employee must file with his/her employer an employee's withholding allowance certificate (Form W-4), which lists the employee's marital status and number of withholding allowances. The W-4 provides the employer with the information needed to determine the amount of federal income tax to be withheld from the employee's earnings. If an employee's circumstances change (e.g., a married taxpayer is divorced during the year), an amended Form W-4 must be provided to the employer within 10 days.

The number of withholding allowances claimed on Form W-4 is typically the same as the number of personal and dependency exemptions that will be taken on the employee's tax return for the year. An additional withholding allowance (reflecting the standard deduction) may be claimed by a taxpayer who has one job or, if married, has a spouse who is unemployed.[58] Further additional withholding allowances may be claimed if an individual has deductions, losses, or credits from a wide variety of sources, including itemized deductions, alimony payments, moving expenses, and losses from a trade or business, rental property, or a farm. Form W-4 contains tables and a worksheet to help employees compute the number of additional withholding allowances.[59]

EXAMPLE I:14-35 ▶ Sam and Sally are married and have three dependent children. They file a joint tax return. Sally is not employed, and Sam does not claim additional withholding allowances for unusually large deductions or tax credits. Sam may claim six allowances (two personal exemptions [for Sam and Sally] plus three dependency exemptions, plus one special allowance to reflect the standard deduction). The special allowance is available because Sally is not employed and Sam has only one job. ◀

? STOP & THINK

Question: Many taxpayers believe that they must claim the same number of withholding allowances for withholding purposes as the number of personal exemptions on their income tax return. Why is this not correct?

Solution: While the starting point for determining withholding allowances is the taxpayer's marital status and number of exemptions, taxpayers are allowed to claim more or fewer withholding allowances based on their individual situation. Taxpayers may claim additional withholding allowances for two principal reasons: (1) a taxpayer has high deductions, losses, or credits; or (2) an unmarried taxpayer qualifies

---

[58] Sec. 3402(f)(1)(E).

[59] Married taxpayers who are both employed may allocate withholding allowances between them as they see fit as long as the same allowance is not claimed more than once.

for head of household filing status. The withholding tables are constructed assuming that the taxpayer will use the standard deduction. Therefore, if a taxpayer has much higher itemized deductions than the standard deduction, the withholding tables may prescribe too much withholding, and the taxpayer would have a large refund at the end of the year. To alleviate this situation, taxpayers are allowed to claim additional withholding allowances. Similarly, the withholding tables only have two categories for marital status, single or married. Thus, if an unmarried taxpayer qualifies for head of household status, the "single" withholding tables may cause over-withholding of tax.

Computation of Federal Income Tax Withheld. Employers use either wage bracket tables or an optional percentage method to compute the actual amount of withholding. The two methods produce approximately the same results. Wage bracket tables are available for daily, weekly, biweekly, and monthly payroll periods. Separate tables are used for single (including heads-of-household) and married individuals. Partial wage bracket tables for married and single persons using a monthly payroll period for wages are located in the Tax Tables and Rate Schedules in the Tables beginning on page T-15.

EXAMPLE I:14-36 ▶ Henry is married and claims four withholding allowances. His monthly salary is $3,000. The federal income tax, Social Security tax and Medicare tax withheld per month for 2015 using the wage bracket table on page T-17 is $328.03. ◀

ESTIMATED TAX PAYMENTS

ADDITIONAL COMMENT

The IRS does not mail reminder statements for the required quarterly estimated payments.

Certain types of income are not subject to withholding (e.g., investment income, rents, income from self-employment, and capital gains). Taxpayers who earn this type of income must make quarterly estimated tax payments.

The purpose of the estimated tax payment system is to ensure that all taxpayers have pre-paid enough tax by the end of the tax year to cover most of their tax liability. Thus, estimated tax payments may also be required if insufficient tax is being withheld from an individual's salary, pension, or other income (although many taxpayers prefer to file an amended Form W-4 to reduce the number of withholding allowances). The amount of estimated tax is the taxpayer's estimated tax liability (including self-employment tax and alternative minimum tax) reduced by withholdings and tax credits.

Required Estimated Tax Payments. For calendar-year individuals, required quarterly payments are due by April 15, June 15, September 15 of the current year, and January 15 of the following year. To avoid an underpayment penalty,[60] total estimated tax payments must equal or exceed any of the following three "safe harbor" amounts:

1) 90% of current year tax liability;
2) 100% of the prior year tax liability shown if the taxpayer's AGI in the prior year was $150,000 or less.

   110% of the prior year tax liability if the taxpayer's AGI in the prior year was more than $150,000.
3) 90% of current year tax liability computed on an annualized basis (helpful for taxpayers who do not earn taxable income evenly through the year).

In addition, no penalty is imposed if (1) the estimated tax for the current year is less than $1,000, or (2) the individual had no tax liability for the prior year.

---

[60] Sec. 6654.

WHAT WOULD YOU DO IN THIS SITUATION?

THE NANNY TAX: DON'T PAY NOW, WORRY LATER

You are a CPA engaged in tax practice, and one of your clients is Mr. Throckmorton D. Princeton, J.D. He is a senior partner in the prestigious employment litigation firm of Huey, Dewey and Fooey. Mr. Princeton is known for his ruthless litigation style.

Things were rosy for Mr. Princeton until last week, when there was some speculation in the press about his being appointed to a cabinet-level position by the President. A TV news magazine show looked into Mr. Princeton's domestic worker situation. It appears that Mr. Princeton has long engaged in the practice of hiring part-time workers in his household to clean his house, tend to his gardens, walk his dogs, cook his meals, service his car, and nurse him when he is ill. All told, he used over twenty-five people at one time or another in the past year. These workers were paid as little as possible, and all were asked to sign a contract with Mr. Princeton stating that they were to be classified as independent contractors. The total amount paid to these workers was $50,000. Mr. Princeton paid no payroll taxes, although he did file Forms 1099 with the IRS. What tax and ethical issues should be considered?

EXAMPLE I:14-37 ▶ Sarah does not make quarterly estimated tax payments for 2015, even though she has a substantial amount of income not subject to withholding. Her taxable income is $140,000. Her actual tax liability (including self-employment taxes and the alternative minimum tax) for the current year is $40,000. Withholdings from her salary are $30,000. She pays the $10,000 balance due to the IRS when she files her return on April 3, 2016. Sarah's tax liability for the prior year was $28,000. No underpayment penalty is imposed because she meets the second exception: the $30,000 of withholdings is more than 100% of her $28,000 prior year tax liability. ◀

EXAMPLE I:14-38 ▶ Assume the same facts in Example I:14-37 except Sarah's AGI in the prior year was $180,000. Since her AGI exceeded $150,000, the second safe harbor amount is 110% (instead of 100%) of the prior year's tax or $30,800 ($28,000 × 1.10). Because the $30,000 of withholding for 2015 is less than 110% of her previous year tax liability, Sarah would not meet either exception and would be subject to the underpayment penalty. ◀

Form 2210 (see Appendix B) should be completed and submitted with the tax return if a possible underpayment of tax is indicated. This form is used to determine whether one of the exceptions applies and, if not, to compute the amount of the underpayment penalty. Topic Review I:14-3 summarizes the withholding tax and estimated payment requirements.

TAX PLANNING CONSIDERATIONS

OBJECTIVE 6

Describe tax planning considerations for AMT, tax credits, and payment of taxes

AVOIDING THE ALTERNATIVE MINIMUM TAX

Taxpayers with substantial amounts of tax preference items and/or positive AMT adjustments and a correspondingly low regular tax liability may be subject to the AMT. These taxpayers need to engage in tax planning to minimize or avoid the AMT.

A liberal AMT exemption is provided for most individuals, so taxpayers can plan for full use of the exemption by timing certain income and deduction items each year. For example, the AMT may be avoided by delaying payment of certain itemized deductions (e.g., state and local taxes) that reduce the regular income tax but do not reduce the AMT. A cash method taxpayer who defers payment of state income taxes into the

TOPIC REVIEW I:14-3

Withholding Taxes and Estimated Payments

EMPLOYER WITHHOLDING OF TAXES:

	FICA	INCOME TAX
Subject to withholding:	For Social Security tax, all employee earnings up to $118,500 in 2015 per employer. No ceiling applies to Medicare portion.	All employee compensation including wages, salaries, fees, bonuses, commissions, taxable fringe benefits.[a]
Withholding amounts:	7.65% of FICA wages including 6.2% on Social Security earnings and 1.45% on Medicare earnings.	Determined using withholding tables or the percentage method based on an individual's filing status and number of withholding allowances.

[a]Exceptions are provided for certain nontaxable fringe benefits.

ESTIMATED TAX PAYMENTS:

- To avoid an underpayment penalty, estimated tax payments and withholdings for the year must equal or exceed: 90% of the current year tax liability; or 100% of the prior year tax liability (110% if prior year AGI exceeds $150,000); or 90% of the current year tax liability computed on an annualized basis.
- The underpayment penalty is not deductible for income tax purposes.
- Form 2210 is used to determine the underpayment penalty amount.

KEY POINT

The alternative minimum tax can be avoided or its impact lessened by various tax strategies.

following year, triggers an increase in the regular tax for the current year. This increase can eliminate the AMT liability. However, it is necessary to consider tax effects for both the current and following years, because state income taxes are deductible for purposes of the regular tax calculation when payment is made in the following year. This reduction may affect the AMT calculation in the following year and increase the amount of tax owed then.

Certain tax-exempt investments, such as interest on private activity bonds, generate additional tax preferences for the investor. Before acquiring such investments, an investor should determine the potential AMT impact.

AVOIDING THE UNDERPAYMENT PENALTY FOR ESTIMATED TAX

Many taxpayers find it difficult to estimate their taxes for the purposes of making quarterly estimated payments and are uncertain whether their withholdings and estimated tax will equal or exceed 90% or more of their actual tax liability for the year. A common planning technique to avoid a possible underpayment tax penalty is to make estimated tax payments and withholdings in an amount that is at least 100% (or 110% if AGI was in excess of $150,000 for the prior year) of the actual tax liability for the prior year, thereby meeting one of the exceptions that prevents the underpayment penalty from being imposed.

EXAMPLE I:14-39 ▶ Yong expects his 2015 federal income tax withholdings to total $14,000 and estimates that his income tax liability will be $24,000. Yong's actual federal income taxes in the prior year were $20,000. If estimated taxes of at least $6,000 are paid during 2015, Yong's estimated taxes plus withholding will be at least 100% of his prior year's tax liability ($14,000 + $6,000 = $20,000), and no underpayment penalty will be imposed, despite the $4,000 ($24,000 − $20,000) balance due on the 2015 return. If Yong's prior year AGI exceeded $150,000, his estimated taxes plus withholding must be at least 110% of his prior year tax liability or $22,000 (1.10 × $20,000) to avoid the underpayment penalty. Thus, his estimated tax payments must total at least $8,000. ◄

KEY POINT

A taxpayer should avoid making estimated payments that exceed the actual tax liability because the taxpayer is making an interest-free loan to the IRS. Nevertheless, many taxpayers deliberately have excess amounts withheld from their wages or make excessive estimated payments to receive a refund. These taxpayers view this strategy as a forced saving plan.

CASH-FLOW CONSIDERATIONS

Assuming that the underpayment penalty can be avoided, it is generally preferable to have a balance due to the government at the time for filing the return rather than to receive a refund of an overpayment of tax. No interest is paid on a refund if the IRS pays the refund within 45 days from the later of the due date of the return or its filing date.[61] In addition, the IRS has, in effect, received an interest-free loan from the taxpayer during the period such overpayment exists. To avoid an overpayment, a taxpayer may file an amended W-4 form and claim additional withholding allowances if the requirements are met (e.g., the taxpayer has unusually large itemized deductions, tax credits, alimony payments, etc.).

If an individual anticipates that her combined estimated tax payments and withholdings will be insufficient to avoid the underpayment penalty, it may be preferable to increase amounts withheld near the end of the tax year rather than increase the estimated tax payments.[62] This technique may be advantageous because the penalty's quarterly calculation treats withholdings as made evenly over the year, even when withholding amounts are increased near the end of the year. Another way to avoid the underpayment penalty is to accelerate certain deductions (e.g., real estate taxes on a personal residence) by paying such amounts before the end of the current tax year. Additionally, otherwise deductible contributions to an IRA made after the end of the tax year but by the due date for the tax return may be treated as a deduction for the prior year, thereby avoiding the underpayment penalty (see Chapter I:9).

USE OF GENERAL BUSINESS TAX CREDITS

Taxpayers must consider the priority and interrelated aspects of credits to ensure that a particular credit is fully used. For example, an individual's nonrefundable personal tax credits reduce tax liability before the foreign tax credit limitation is applied. Then, the nonrefundable personal tax credits and foreign tax credit are deducted from the individual's tax liability before limitations are applied to the general business tax credit.

FOREIGN TAX CREDITS AND THE FOREIGN EARNED INCOME EXCLUSION

Individuals who accept foreign job assignments should consider federal income tax implications, because U.S. citizens are subject to U.S. tax on their worldwide income. Assuming that certain requirements and limitations are met, an individual may elect to take either a foreign tax credit or a foreign-earned income exclusion of $100,800 in 2015 ($99,200 in 2014) with respect to salaries, allowances, and other forms of earned income that are earned while on extended non-U.S. assignments.[63] Any taxes paid or accrued with respect to the excluded income are not available as a foreign tax credit. In general, when the effective foreign tax rate is less than the effective U.S. tax rate, the exclusion is preferable because the foreign tax credit that can be claimed does not equal the gross U.S. tax owed on the income. When the effective foreign tax rate exceeds the effective U.S. tax rate, U.S. taxpayers ordinarily elect not to use the exclusion. Instead, the excess tax credits on earned income are used to offset the U.S. taxes owed on other types of foreign income. Detailed coverage of the interaction between foreign tax credits and the exclusion is contained in Chapter C:16 of the *Prentice Hall's Federal Taxation: Corporations, Partnerships, Estates & Trusts* text.

[61] Sec. 6611(e).

[62] To completely avoid the underpayment penalty, the tax law generally requires the estimated payments to be made equally on the four installment dates.

[63] Sec. 911(a). The foreign income exclusion requirements are discussed in Chapter I:4.

COMPLIANCE AND PROCEDURAL CONSIDERATIONS

OBJECTIVE 7

Describe compliance and procedural considerations for AMT, tax credits, and payment of taxes

ALTERNATIVE MINIMUM TAX (AMT) FILING PROCEDURES

Individual taxpayers use Form 6251 to compute the AMT, and corporations use Form 4626 (see Appendix B for both forms). Form 6251 must be completed and attached to an individual's income tax return in any of the following situations:

- An AMT tax liability actually exists.
- The taxpayer has tax credits that are limited by the tentative minimum tax.
- The AMT base exceeds the AMT exemption amounts, and the individual has AMT adjustment or tax preference items.

WITHHOLDINGS AND ESTIMATED TAX PAYMENTS

Taxpayers who have income taxes withheld from wages, pensions, and other income should receive a Form W-2 (or Form 1099-R for pensions) from the employer by January 31. These forms should be attached to the individual's tax return to substantiate the amount of withholdings.

Taxpayers who make quarterly estimated tax payments may not file Form 1040A or Form 1040EZ. Married individuals may make either joint or separate estimated tax payments. If joint estimated tax payments are made and the married individuals subsequently file separate returns (e.g., in the case of a divorce that is pending or a divorce completed before the end of the year), the joint estimated tax payments are divided in proportion to each spouse's individual tax if no agreement is reached concerning an appropriate division.

EXAMPLE I:14-40 ▶ George and Alice are married and make joint estimated tax payments of $10,000 during 2015. George and Alice are separated in February 2016 and Alice refuses to file a joint return with George. George's tax liability for 2015 on his separate return is $20,000 and Alice's tax liability on her separate return is $5,000. If no agreement is reached concerning the allocation of the joint estimated payments of $10,000, Alice is entitled to claim $2,000 of the estimated tax payments on her return [($5,000/($20,000 + $5,000) × $10,000]. The remaining $8,000 is apportioned to George. ◀

GENERAL BUSINESS TAX CREDITS

The computation of the business energy credit is made on Form 3468. Form 3800 must be filed if any other general business credits are claimed.

NONREFUNDABLE PERSONAL TAX CREDITS

KEY POINT

The earned income credit is available even in cases where the taxpayer has no tax liability. The refund of taxes not paid or incurred is often called a negative income tax.

Nonrefundable personal tax credits are deducted from the taxpayer's tax liability before other credits. The credits section on page 2 of Form 1040 limits the deduction for nonrefundable personal tax credits to the amount of tax due. Form 2441 (see Appendix B) must be filed to claim the child and dependent care credit. Taxpayers who claim the child and dependent care credit must also include the care provider's name, address, and taxpayer identification number on their tax return. If the caregiver will not provide the required information, the taxpayer has the option to supply the name and address of the caregiver on Form 2441 and attach a statement explaining that the caregiver has refused to provide his or her taxpayer identification number (TIN). Schedule R of Form 1040 is filed to claim the credit for the elderly and disabled. An eligible individual may elect to have the IRS compute the tax and the amount of the tax credit.[64]

---

[64] Sec. 6014. (See Form 1040 instructions for more reporting details.)

The earned income tax credit is refundable to an individual even if no income tax is owed. The IRS will automatically compute the credit amount.[65] However, helpful tax tables are included in the IRS instructions to Forms 1040, 1040A and 1040 EZ. Schedule EIC is filed if the taxpayer has a qualifying child for the earned income credit.

The foreign tax credit for individuals is computed on Form 1116.

PROBLEM MATERIALS

DISCUSSION QUESTIONS

I:14-1 Why are most taxpayers not subject to the alternative minimum tax (AMT)?

I:14-2 Does the AMT apply if an individual's tax liability as computed under the AMT rules is less than his or her regular tax amount?

I:14-3 Which of the following are tax preference items for purposes of computing the individual AMT?
a. Net long-term capital gain
b. Excess depreciation for real property placed in service before 1987
c. Straight-line depreciation on residential real estate acquired in 1992
d. Appreciated portion of the value of capital gain real property contributed to charity

I:14-4 Which of the following are individual AMT adjustments?
a. Itemized deductions that are allowed for regular tax purposes but not allowed in computing AMTI.
b. Excess of MACRS depreciation over depreciation computed under the alternative depreciation system for real property placed in service after 1986 and before 1999.
c. Excess of MACRS depreciation over depreciation computed under the alternative depreciation system for personal property placed in service after 1986.
d. Tax-exempt interest earned on State of Michigan bonds.

I:14-5 Which of the following itemized deductions are deductible when computing the alternative minimum tax for individuals?
a. Charitable contributions
b. Mortgage interest on a loan used to acquire a personal residence
c. State and local income taxes
d. Interest related to an investment in undeveloped land where the individual has no investment income
e. Medical expenses amounting to 9% of AGI

I:14-6 Why are most individuals not subject to the self-employment tax?

I:14-7 Tony, who is single and 58 years old, is considering early retirement from his salaried job. He currently has $70,000 salary and also earns $50,000 profit from a consulting business. What advice would you give Tony relative to the need to make Social Security tax payments if he retires and continues to be actively engaged as a consultant during his retirement?

I:14-8 Theresa is a college professor who wants to work for a consulting firm during the summer. She will be working on special projects relating to professional development programs. What advantages might accrue to the consulting firm if the engagement is set up as a consulting arrangement rather than an employment contract?

I:14-9 Brian and Jennifer are a married couple who believe they may be subject to the AMT this year. Currently, they calculate their alternative minimum taxable income (AMTI) to be $160,000.
a. What is their AMT exemption amount?
b. They are considering an opportunity that would allow them to earn additional income this year. As a result of this additional income, they believe that their AMTI will increase by $200,000. What will their AMT exemption be if they recognize the additional income?

---

[65] Sec. 6695(g) requires preparers to meet due diligence requirements with respect to the earned income tax credit (EIC). If the EIC is incorrectly computed or overlooked, the *preparer* could be subject to a $100 penalty.

I:14-10 Discuss the underlying rationale for the following tax credit items:
a. Foreign tax credit
b. Research credit
c. Business energy credit
d. Premium tax credit
e. Dependent care credit
f. Earned income credit
g. American Opportunity credit
h. Adoption credit

I:14-11 If Congress is considering a tax credit or deduction as an incentive to encourage certain activities, is a $40 tax credit more valuable than a $200 tax deduction for a taxpayer with a 15% marginal rate? a 25% marginal rate?

I:14-12 What are the more significant tax credit items included in the computation of the general business tax credit?

I:14-13 Discuss the limitations that have been imposed on the general business tax credit, including the following:
a. Overall ceiling limitation based on the tax liability
b. Priority of general business and personal credits
c. Carryback and carryover of unused credits (including the application of the FIFO method)

I:14-14 Sarah, a married taxpayer who files a joint return, is considering a foreign assignment for two years. In 2015, she will earn $120,000 in the foreign country. Sarah has no other income. She will be eligible for either the foreign tax credit or the foreign-earned income exclusion. The average tax rate on Sarah's earnings if fully taxable under U.S. law would be 30%. The average tax rate for the foreign salary is 20% under the foreign country's laws.
a. Discuss in general terms the computation of the foreign tax credit and its limitation.
b. Would Sarah be better off electing the foreign tax credit or the foreign earned income exclusion? Explain.

I:14-15 Although it became law in 2010, one of the key features of the Affordable Care Act, the Premium Assistance Credit, became effective in 2014. Describe the tax costs to a taxpayer who does not purchase health insurance coverage for 2015. Assume the taxpayer is single, 40 years old, has no dependents, has household income of $55,000, and does not meet any of the conditions to be exempt from the tax.

I:14-16 Queen Corporation has been in business since 1989. During the preceding year, the company had 25 full-time employees and gross receipts of $8,000,000. During the current year, Queen spent $15,000 to install access ramps for disabled individuals. Is Queen Corporation eligible for the disabled access credit? If so, what is the credit amount and the basis reduction (if any) for the depreciable property?

I:14-17 Discuss the special tax rules that apply to the tax credit for rehabilitation expenditures including the following:
a. Types of eligible expenditures
b. Applicable tax credit rates
c. Calculation of basis for expenditures
d. Restrictions on depreciation methods
e. Potential recapture of the credit

I:14-18 What types of business property qualify for the business energy credit?

I:14-19 What are the underlying reason for enactment of many of the personal tax credits?

I:14-20 Discuss the difference between a refundable tax credit and a nonrefundable tax credit. Give at least one example of each type of credit.

I:14-21 If an individual is not employed and has no earned income, is it possible to take a child and dependent care credit for otherwise qualifying child and dependent care expenses? Explain.

I:14-22 Discuss the major differences between the American Opportunity credit and the Lifetime Learning credit. Include in your discussion the type of taxpayers who would likely qualify for each of the credits.

I:14-23 What is the maximum child and dependent care credit available to an employed individual who has $8,000 of qualifying child care expenses and two or more qualifying dependents?

I:14-24 Vivian is a single taxpayer with two children who qualify for the child and dependent care credit. She incurred $7,000 of qualifying child care expenses during the current year. She also received $4,000 in reimbursements from her employer from a qualified employee dependent care assistance program. What is the maximum child and dependent care credit available to Vivian if her AGI is $24,500?

I:14-25 The adoption credit is intended to assist taxpayers with the financial burden of adopting children.
a. Discuss how the credit is computed.
b. Why did Congress impose a phase-out of the credit for taxpayers based on AGI?

I:14-26 Alice is a single mother, 37 years old, and has two qualifying children, ages 3 and 6. She receives $3,600 alimony and earns $18,000 in wages resulting in $21,600 of AGI in 2015. Is Alice eligible for the earned income credit? If so, is it possible for her to receive advance payments of the credit rather than receiving a tax refund when her tax return is filed?

I:14-27 Why are most elderly people unable to qualify for the tax credit for the elderly?

I:14-28 If an employer fails to withhold federal income taxes and FICA taxes on wages or fails to make payment to the IRS, what adverse tax consequences may result? May corporate officers or other corporate officials be held responsible for the underpayment?

I:14-29 Taxpayers are permitted to contribute money to qualified retirement plans and receive very favorable tax benefits. Congress has provided further incentives to contribute money to such plans by enacting the Qualified Retirement Savings Contributions Credit.

a. Why did Congress enact this credit when such contributions already receive favorable tax treatment?

b. Briefly describe how the credit is computed.

I:14-30 The credit for employer-provided child care has two major components, a credit for qualified child care expenses and a credit for qualified child care resources and referral expenditures.

a. Discuss each of the two components. What type of expenses are included in each component?

b. The two components are added together to compute the credit for employer-provided child care. Discuss the rates for each component, the limitation for the credit, and the tax result if the employer ceases to offer child care operations within the first three years after claiming the credit.

I:14-31 A credit is allowed to encourage businesses to conduct research and experimentation. One feature of the research credit is that only incremental expenditures are eligible. Explain the concept that the credit is allowed for *increasing* research activities.

I:14-32 Although Virginia is entitled to five personal and dependency exemptions on her income tax return, she claims only one withholding allowance on Form W-4.

a. Is it permissible to claim fewer allowances than an individual is entitled to?

b. Why would an individual claim fewer allowances?

c. Is it possible for Virginia to claim more than five withholding allowances?

I:14-33 Mario is a college student who had no income tax liability in the prior year and expects to have no tax liability for the current year.

a. What steps should Mario take to avoid having amounts withheld from his summer employment wages?

b. What are the cash-flow implications to Mario if the employer withholds federal income taxes?

I:14-34 What is backup withholding? What is its purpose?

I:14-35 In March 2016, Vincent anticipates that his actual tax liability for the tax year 2015 will be $12,000 and that federal income taxes withheld from his salary will be $9,000. Thus, when he files his income tax return in early 2016, he will have a $3,000 balance due. In the previous year, his actual federal income tax liability was $8,000 and his AGI was less than $150,000.

a. Is Vincent required to make estimated tax payments in 2015?

b. If no estimated tax payments are made, will Vincent be subject to an underpayment penalty if the actual tax liability for 2015 is $12,000? Why or why not?

c. Will Vincent be subject to an underpayment penalty if his 2014 AGI was $175,000? Why?

I:14-36 An individual has increasing levels of income each year and is uncertain regarding the amount of his estimated taxable income for any given year. What tax planning strategy can you suggest to avoid the penalty for underpayment of estimated tax?

I:14-37 From a cash-flow perspective, why is it generally preferable to have an underpayment of tax (assuming no underpayment penalty is imposed) rather than an overpayment of tax?

I:14-38 Why do many taxpayers intentionally overpay their tax through withholdings to obtain a tax refund?

ISSUE IDENTIFICATION QUESTIONS

I:14-39 Daryl is an executive who has an annual salary of $120,000. He is considering early retirement so he can pursue a career as a management consultant. Daryl estimates that he could earn approximately $80,000 annually from his consulting business. What tax issues should Daryl consider?

I:14-40 Jennifer recently received a check for $30,000 and securities with an FMV of $200,000 from her former husband pursuant to a divorce. The $30,000 represents alimony and the securities were transferred pursuant to the property settlement. The property settlement is nontaxable to Jennifer. Assuming the alimony is taxable and no income taxes are withheld, what tax issues should Jennifer consider?

I:14-41 Dale Eisen is saving as much as possible to fund a down payment on his first home. He is young (25 years old) and healthy, and has declined health insurance coverage offered by his employer because he would have to pay one-third of the cost (another $100 would be withheld from his monthly paycheck). He earns $65,000 per year. He received a notice from his employer indicating that unless he declined coverage, he would automatically be enrolled in the employer's basic health insurance plan ($5,000 deductible, employee pays one-third of the premium or $100 per month). Dale made an appointment with the human resources (HR) manager, intending to decline coverage. Assume you are the HR manager, and explain the costs to Dale of accepting coverage and declining coverage.

Notes: Remember that the $200 of cost paid by the employer is not treated as taxable income to Dale. For simplicity, assume any health insurance premiums paid by Dale do not exceed the 10% floor to become itemized deductions.

PROBLEMS

I:14-42 ***AMT Computation.*** William and Maria Smith are a married couple filing jointly. They have no children and report the following items in 2015:

Taxable income	$70,000
Tax preferences	20,000
AMT adjustments related to itemized deductions	15,000
Regular tax liability	9,578

a. What is the Smith's AMT liability?
b. What would be William's AMT liability if he were an unmarried taxpayer filing single with a regular tax liability of $13,294?

I:14-43 ***AMT Computation.*** Jose, an unmarried taxpayer filing single with no dependents, has AGI of $200,000 and reports the following items in 2015:

Taxable income	$160,000
Tax preferences	10,000
AMT adjustments related to itemized deductions	30,000
Regular tax liability	37,871

What is Jose's AMT liability for 2015?

I:14-44 ***AMT Computation.*** Harry and Mary Prodigious are married filing jointly and have 12 dependent children. Six of the children are under age 17. With the large number of children, they live in a very austere manner. Harry, in his spare time, works a large garden that provides most of their food. Mary makes all the children's clothes. Harry works for a local engineering firm and earns a salary of $100,000 annually. Mary does not work outside the home. The only other income is taxable interest in the amount of $8,000. For 2015, they claim the standard deduction and have no tax preferences or adjustments for purposes of the AMT.

a. Compute Harry and Mary's regular tax and AMT under the facts above.
b. Comment on the tax policy implications of your answer in Part a above.

I:14-45 ***AMT Adjustments and Computation of Tax.*** Allen, an unmarried taxpayer filing single, has no dependents and reports the following items on his 2015 federal income tax return:

Adjusted gross income	$82,450
Taxable income	47,950
Regular tax liability	7,781
Tax preferences	20,000
Itemized deductions including:	
Charitable contributions	7,500
Medical expenses (before AGI floor)	10,000
Mortgage interest on personal residence	10,000
State income taxes	5,000
Real estate taxes	8,000

a. What is the amount of Allen's AMT adjustments related to itemized deductions?
b. What is Allen's AMT liability for 2015?

I:14-46 ***Self-Employment Tax.*** Amelia has wages of $45,000 and net income from a small unincorporated business of $70,000 for 2015.

a. What is the amount of Amelia's self-employment (SE) tax and deduction *for* AGI for her SE tax?
b. How would your answer to Part a change if Amelia's wages were $120,000 rather than $45,000?

I:14-47 ***Self-Employment Tax.*** Arnie and Angela are married and file a joint return in 2015. Arnie is a partner in a public accounting firm. His share of the partnership's income in the current year is $40,000, and he receives guaranteed payments of $35,000. Angela receives wages of $50,000 from a large corporation. What is each taxpayer's self-employment tax amount? (Hint: Guaranteed payments received from a partnership are considered self-employment income.)

I:14-48 ***Self-Employment Tax.*** Anita, a single taxpayer, reports the following items for 2015:

Salary (subject to withholding)	$20,000
Income for serving on the Board of Directors for XYZ Corporation	11,000
Consulting gross income	9,000
Expenses related to consulting practice	(15,000)

a. What is the amount of Anita's self-employment tax?
b. How would your answer to Part a change if Anita's salary were $120,000?

I:14-49 *Computation of Tax Credits.* During the current year, Becky has personal credits (P) as well as business credits (B) related to her sole proprietorship. Her tentative tax credits for the current year include the following:

Child tax credit	$ 2,000 P
Disabled access credit	$ 900 B
Child and dependent care credit	1,200 P
Business energy credit	600 B

Becky's regular tax liability before credits is $4,000. Assume that she has no alternative minimum tax liability.
a. What is the amount of allowable personal tax credits?
b. What is the amount of allowable business tax credits?
c. What treatment is accorded to the unused tax credits for the current year?

I:14-50 *Child and Dependent Care Credit.* In each of the following independent situations, determine the amount of the child and dependent care tax credit. (Assume that both taxpayers are employed and the year is 2015).
a. Brad and Bonnie are married and file a joint return, with earned income of $40,000 and $14,000, respectively. Their combined AGI is $52,000. They have two children, ages 10 and 12, and employ a live-in nanny at an annual cost of $9,000.
b. Assume the same facts as in Part a, except that Brad and Bonnie employ Bonnie's mother, who is not their dependent, as the live-in nanny.
c. Bruce is divorced and has two children, ages 10 and 16. He has AGI and earned income of $27,000. Bruce incurs qualifying child care expenses of $8,000 during the year, incurred equally for both children. Bruce's employer maintains an employee dependent care assistance program. $1,000 was paid to Bruce from this program and excluded from Bruce's gross income.
d. Buddy and Candice are married and file a joint return. Their combined AGI is $50,000. Buddy earns $46,000, and Candice's salary from a part-time job is $4,000. They incur $5,000 of qualifying child care expenses for a day-care facility for their two children, ages 2 and 4.
e. Ben and Bunny are married and file a joint return. Their AGI is $75,000, all earned by Bunny. Ben was a full-time student for two semesters (10 months) at State University during the year. They incur $7,000 of qualifying child care expenses for their two children, ages 6 and 4.

I:14-51 *Adoption Credit.* Brad and Valerie decided to adopt a child and contacted an adoption agency in August 2014. After extensive interviews and other requirements (such as financial status, etc.), Brad and Valerie were approved as eligible parents to adopt a child. The agency indicated that it might take up to two years to find a proper match. In March 2015, the adoption became final, and Brad and Valerie adopted an infant daughter (not a special needs child). Below is a list of expenses that they incurred:

2014:	Agency fees (first installment)	$5,000
	Travel expenses for interviews, etc.	1,500
	Publications for prospective adoptive parents	300
	Legal fees connected with the adoption	1,000
	Kennel fees for dog while on adoption trips	250
2015:	Agency fees (final installment)	$4,000
	Travel expenses	400
	Court costs for adoption	1,500
	Kennel fees	100
	Nursery furniture (baby's room) and supplies	2,000

Brad and Valerie's AGI in 2014 was $70,000, and in 2015 was $90,000.

a. Compute Brad and Valerie's qualified adoption expenses for 2014 and 2015

b. Compute Brad and Valerie's adoption credit. In which year(s) may the credit be taken?

c. Would your answer to Part b change if the adopted child was a special needs child and if a grant covered all adoption cost except for legal fees?

I:14-52 *American Opportunity Tax Credit and Lifetime Learning Credit.* Lou and Stella North are married, file a joint return, and have two dependent children in college, Phil and Jaci. Phil attends a State University in a neighboring state, and Jaci attends a State University in their home state. Neither receives any type of financial assistance. The Norths' modified AGI in 2015 is $112,000. The children's classifications and expenses are as follows:

	Spring Semester 2015 (paid in January 2015)	Fall Semester 2015 (paid in July 2015)
Phil:	Senior	Master's candidate
Tuition	$7,500	$8,000
Laboratory fees	500	500
Student activity fees	100	100
Course materials (books)	400	450
Room and board	3,200	3,200
Jaci:	Sophomore	Junior
Tuition	$1,600	$1,750
Student activity fees	100	100
Course materials (books)	250	300
Room and board	3,500	3,700

a. Compute any education credits that the Norths may claim in 2015.

b. How would your answer in Part a change if Phil received an academic scholarship of $3,000 (excluded from gross income) for each semester in 2015?

c. How would your answer in Part a change if Lou and Stella's modified AGI for 2015 was $175,000?

d. How would your answer in Part a change if Phil had been a junior during Spring semester 2015 and a senior during Fall semester 2015?

I:14-53 *Tax Credit for the Elderly.* Caroline, age 66 and filing single as a dependent of another, received the following income items for 2015:

Social Security benefits (nontaxable)	$ 3,000
Pension benefits (taxable)	6,450
Interest income (taxable)	2,050
Total	$11,500

Caroline's tax liability (before credits) is $200.

a. What is Caroline's tentative tax credit for the elderly (before the tax liability limitation is applied)?

b. What is Caroline's allowable tax credit?

I:14-54 *General Business Tax Credit Limitation.* During the current year, Joule Company, a sole proprietorship, earned general business tax credits of $30,000 for energy conservation and rehabilitation expenditures. The owner, Mark Joule, knows that the overall credit will be limited. He provides you with the following information for the current year: regular tax (before credits) = $37,500; tentative minimum tax = $20,200; alternative minimum tax = $0; foreign tax credit = $4,500; other nonrefundable credits = $6,100. Mark also has a $3,000 carryforward of general business credit from the prior year.

a. What is the current year limitation on Mark's general business credit?

b. What is Mark's allowable general business credit in the current year and where does it come from?

c. What is Mark's general business credit carryover?

I:14-55 *Foreign Tax Credit.* Laser Corporation, a U.S. corporation, has a foreign office that conducts business in France. Laser pays foreign taxes of $74,000 on foreign-source taxable income of $185,000. Its U.S.-source taxable income is $320,000, total U.S. taxable income (worldwide) of $505,000, and U.S. tax liability (before reductions for the foreign tax credit) is $171,700. What is Laser's foreign tax credit? What is Laser's foreign tax credit carryback or carryover?

I:14-56 *Premium Tax Credit.* Randall and Dianne Wall live in St. Louis, Missouri. Randall and Dianne are each 30 years old, neither smokes, and they have no children or other dependents.

Randall is attending law school full time and working part time (2015 earnings = $9,000). Dianne works full time (2015 earnings = $38,200). Their 2015 household income is more than 200% of the FPL (but not more than 300% of the FPL).

Dianne's employer does not offer employee health insurance coverage. The Walls choose to purchase insurance through the federal exchange operating in Missouri. They are credit eligible for all 12 months in 2015.

Their premiums for coverage vary by the type of plan.

- Under a Gold plan, monthly premiums are $585 (covers 2) per month, so the annual cost of coverage is $7,020.
- The second-least-expensive Silver plan (the benchmark plan) involves premiums of $468 per month (covers 2), or $5,616 per year.
- Under a Bronze plan, monthly premiums are $390 (covers 2) per month, so the annual cost of coverage is $4,680.

What is the 2015 after-tax-credit cost of health insurance for the Walls under each of the plans described above?

I:14-57 *Rehabilitation Tax Credit.* Bob acquired a certified historic structure and placed it in service August of the current year, as an office for his business. He paid $20,000 for the building (exclusive of the land) and spent $40,000 for renovation costs.

a. What is the rehabilitation tax credit (before limitations)?
b. What is the basis of the building for MACRS depreciation purposes?
c. Compute the depreciation that Bob can take on the building for the current year.

I:14-58 *Research Credit.* Pharm Inc. is a small pharmaceutical company (organized four years ago) that is heavily involved in drug research. During the current year, Pharm Inc. incurred the following expenditures related to the company's research efforts:

Salaries of research scientists and technicians	$180,000
Supplies and materials	162,000
Depreciation on research equipment	30,000

For the previous four years, Pharm Inc. had average gross receipts of $5,000,000. The company's fixed-base percentage is 3%. Compute Pharm Inc.'s current year credit for research activities. Is Pharm Inc. entitled to claim any deduction for research and experimentation expenses for the current year?

I:14-59 *Earned Income Credit.* Carolyn is unmarried and has one dependent child, age 6, who lived with her for the entire year. In 2015, she has income of $16,000 in wages and $6,000 in alimony. Her AGI is $22,000.

a. What is Carolyn's tentative earned income credit (before phaseout)?
b. What is Carolyn's allowable earned income credit?
c. If Carolyn has no income tax liability (before the earned income credit is subtracted), is she entitled to a refund in the current year?
d. How will your answers to Parts a and b change if Carolyn is married filing a joint return?

I:14-60 *Earned Income Credit.* Jose is unmarried with no qualifying children. He has $8,300 of 2015 wages and is otherwise eligible for the earned income credit. Jose has $200 of interest income and no *for* AGI deductions.

a. What is Jose's tentative earned income credit before phaseout?
b. What is Jose's allowable earned income credit?
c. If Jose has no income tax liability (before the earned income credit is subtracted), is he entitled to a refund for the current year?
d. Would your answer to Part b change if Jose had dividend and interest income of $3,700 during the taxable year?

I:14-61 *Refundable Credits.* Latisha is an unmarried taxpayer, filing head of household. She has two dependent children (7 year old twins) who lived with her all year. Her 2015 earned income was $18,600, her AGI was $22,700, and she uses the standard deduction. Determine her:

1. Taxable income and regular tax before credits
2. Earned income credit (EIC).
3. Balance due or refund.

I:14-62 *Penalties for Nonpayment of Withholding and FICA Taxes.* Lake Corporation has some severe cash-flow problems. You are the company's financial and tax consultant. The treasurer of the company has informed you that the company has failed to make FICA and federal income tax withholding payments to the IRS (both the employer and employee contributions) for a period of approximately six months.

a. What advice can you give to the company treasurer regarding the nonpayment of taxes?
b. Can the liability for payment of the taxes extend to parties other than the corporation? Explain.

I:14-63 *Exemptions from Withholding.* Which of the following categories of individuals or income are exempt from the federal income tax withholding requirements?

a. Household employees
b. Independent contractors
c. Newspaper carriers over age 18
d. Bonuses
e. Commissions
f. Vacation pay
g. Tips under $20 per month from a single employer

I:14-64 *Withholding Exemptions.* Barry is a college student who is employed as a waiter during the summer. He earns approximately $1,500 during the summer and estimates that he will not be required to file a tax return and will have no federal income tax liability. Last year, however, he made $6,000 and was required to file a return and pay $400 in taxes. Barry is unmarried and is supported by his parents. He has no dependents and does not have any other sources of income or deductions.

a. Can Barry claim exempt status on Form W-4 for withholding purposes?
b. Can Barry claim more than one exemption on Form W-4 (e.g., additional withholding allowances or the standard deduction allowance) to minimize the amount withheld? Explain.

I:14-65 *Withholding Allowances.* Bart and Jane Lee are married, file a joint return and have two dependent children. Bart begins a new job in 2015 and is asked to fill out a Form W-4. His monthly gross earnings will be $3,200. Jane does not work outside their home. Bart can claim three additional withholding allowances because he will have a large for-AGI deduction for substantial alimony paid to his ex-wife, Sue.

a. What is the correct number of withholding allowances on Form W-4?
b. What is the federal income tax, FICA and Medicare tax to be withheld using the wage bracket tables (see withholding table on page T-15)?
c. What disclosure procedures must Bart's employer follow if Bart claims more than ten allowances?

I:14-66 *Estimated Tax Requirements.* Anna does not make quarterly estimated tax payments even though she has substantial amounts of income that are not subject to withholding. In the previous year, Anna's tax liability was $18,000 and her AGI was $ 135,000. In the current year, Anna's actual tax liability is $30,000, and $18,200 was withheld from her salary.

a. Is Anna subject to the underpayment penalty? Why?
b. If Anna's withholdings were only $15,000, would she be subject to the underpayment penalty? Why?
c. If Anna is subject to an underpayment penalty, can she deduct this amount as interest? Explain.

I:14-67 *Estimated Tax Underpayment Penalty.* Jane's estimated tax payments for the current year total $14,000, and federal income taxes withheld from her salary amount to $12,000. Jane's actual tax liability for the current year is $30,000. Her income was earned evenly throughout the current year. Jane's AGI for the prior year was $160,000 and her tax liability was $25,000. Is Jane subject to the underpayment penalty? Explain.

COMPREHENSIVE PROBLEM

I:14-68 Mike Webb, married to Nancy Webb, is employed by a large pharmaceutical company and earns a salary. In addition, Mike is an entrepreneur and has two small businesses on the side, both of which operate as sole proprietorships. One is a profitable consulting business where Mike provides financial and retirement advice to pharmacists. The other involves the manufacture of Christmas novelties in China, selling the products in gift shops in the U.S. This business is struggling. However, Mike feels the Christmas novelty business has great potential. Mike reports the following for 2015:

Salary			$150,000
Consulting practice:	Revenues	$65,000	
	Ordinary expenses	12,000	53,000
Sole proprietorship:	Revenues	$22,000	
	Ordinary Expenses	40,000	(18,000)
Interest (none tax-exempt)			3,000
Dividends, qualified			9,000
LTCG		$24,000	
STCL		(4,000)	20,000
Itemized deductions:			
State and local taxes		$14,000	
Real estate taxes		8,000	
Mortgage interest on personal residence		7,000	
Charitable contributions		8,000	37,000
Child care expenses:			
The Webb's have two dependent children, ages 13 and 11, and pay child care expenses of $4,000 per year for each child. Nancy is not employed, but is a full-time student (all of 2015) at State University, majoring in Accounting.			
Federal income tax withheld from salary			$21,000
Estimated taxes paid for 2015			14,000

For 2014, Mike and Nancy's AGI was $175,000 and their actual federal income tax liability was $29,000.

a. Compute the Webbs regular federal income tax liability for 2015, including self-employment taxes.
b. Are the Webbs subject to AMT in 2015?
c. Are the Webbs due a refund for 2015?
d. Are the Webbs subject to any underpayment penalties for 2015?

TAX STRATEGY PROBLEM

I:14-69 Jeff and Linda Foley are married and file a joint income tax return. Jeff is a lawyer and a partner in the firm of Foley & Looby, Attorneys at Law. Jeff is a 50% partner in the firm along with his partner, John Looby who is the other 50% partner. Foley & Looby (F&L) currently rent office space in a prestigious building and pay rent of $6,000 per month or $72,000 per year for their 4,000 square foot office. Thus, the firm pays $18 per square foot per year. As no equity is being generated by paying rent, Jeff and John are considering buying an office building. They have two buildings under consideration, as follows:

Building #1

Building #1 is a relatively new building and has 10,000 square feet of space. The new building can be purchased for a total price of $1,000,000. F&L would only use 4,000 square feet of the space and have other businesses that would rent the other 6,000 square feet from F&L for $15 per square foot per year, a total of $90,000 per year. Maintenance costs would amount to approximately $10 per square foot per year. The building is in excellent condition and is ready to be moved into immediately and would require very few other outlays by F&L.

Building #2

Building #2 is located in the downtown area in a certified historic district and would qualify as a certified historic structure. This building, nearly 80 years old, also has 10,000 square feet and, like Building #1, the other 6,000 square feet can be rented to other tenants at $15 per square foot per year, a total of $90,000 per year. However, Building #2 is not in as good condition as Building #1. The purchase price of the building would be $400,000, and Jeff and John estimate that approximately $600,000 would have to be invested in capital expenditures to make the building suitable for their business. After the significant capital expenditures, F&L estimates the maintenance costs to be similar to Building #1, or $10 per square foot per year.

Both buildings can be 100% financed at 8% annual interest rate for 15 years. The annual cash payment on the $1,000,000 mortgage would be $117,000. Assume both buildings will appreciate at a rate of 8% per year.

Jeff and John have come to you as their financial and tax advisor to help them make the decision as to which building to purchase. If the buildings are equally desirable from a non-financial and non-tax standpoint, what is the best decision for them? That is, should they stay where they are and rent, or purchase one of the two buildings? Assume both Jeff and John are in the top 35% marginal tax bracket.

TAX FORM/RETURN PREPARATION PROBLEMS

I:14-70 Len and Christy Vole, ages 42 and 39 respectively, are married and file jointly in 2014. Len is a contractor operating as a sole proprietorship (EIN 11-1111111). Christy is employed, earning $24,000 as a part-time paralegal. They have two dependent children, Jill, age 8 and Lee, age 5. In 2014, they received $4,550 from Good Bank in taxable interest income. Their allowable itemized deductions include state income tax $3,700; home mortage interest $6,000; and charity $5,000. Federal income tax withholding was $7,500 and estimated tax payments were $13,000. The Voles also incurred $7,000 of qualifying child care expenses to enable them to work ($3,500 for each child). It was paid to HiTop Daycare, 327 Fowler St., Indianapolis, IN 46802 (EIN 22-2222222).

Len earns $95,000 in profit in a sole proprietorship. He incurred the following expenses that qualify for the general business credit: $6,000 for disabled access. No adjustments are required to this credit and there are no carrybacks or carryforwards.

Social security numbers are: Len, 111-11-1111; Christy, 222-22-2222; Jill, 333-33-3333; Lee, 444-44-4444.

Complete the Voles' Form 1040 for 2014, along with supporting Schedules A, B, C, and SE, Form 2441 (child and dependent care credit), Form 3800 (general business credit), Form 8826 (disabled access credit), and Form 5884 (work opportunity credit). Show detail of the child tax credit computation (with any phaseout) at the bottom of Form 1040, page 2.

I:14-71 Harold J. Milton (SSN 000-22-1111) is 45 years old and unmarried, filing single with no dependents. He had the following income and deductions for 2014:

Salary	$177,000	State income taxes	$18,000
Interest income from State Bank	12,000	Mortgage interest expense on residence (100% acquisition debt)	19,000
Dividend income (qualified)	18,000	Interest expense on car loan	3,000
Deductible IRA contribution	5,000	Real estate taxes on residence	2,000
Tax-exempt interest income from municipal bonds	24,000	Miscellaneous deductions—other (before the 2% AGI floor)	7,000
Charitable contributions	27,000	Income taxes withheld	20,000
		Estimated tax payments ($2,500 per quarter)	10,000

Complete Milton's 2014 Form 1040, Schedule A, B, D, and Form 6251. In 2013, Milton had AGI of $200,000 and his income tax liability was $46,000.

CASE STUDY PROBLEMS

I:14-72 Barbara was divorced in 2012. However, the final property settlement and determination of alimony payments was not made until February 2015 because of extended litigation. Barbara received a $20,000 payment of back alimony in March 2015 and will receive monthly alimony payments of $2,000 for the period April through December 2015.

Last year, Barbara's income consisted of $15,000 salary and $2,000 of taxable interest income, and her tax liability was $1,900. She expects to continue working at an annual salary of $15,000 and will have $2,000 of interest income. Federal income taxes withheld from her salary in 2015 will be $1,500. Her monthly alimony payments of $2,000 are also expected to continue for an indefinite period.

In early April 2015 Barbara requests your advice regarding the payment of quarterly estimated taxes for 2015. Prepare a memo to your client that discusses these requirements, including any possible penalties for not making quarterly payments and nontax issues such as cash-flow and investment income decisions.

I:14-73 Chips-R-Us is a computer technology corporation that designs hardware and software for use in large businesses. The corporation regularly pays individuals to install programs and give advice to companies that buy their software. In the current year, Simone, a computer expert, was sent to a customer of Chips-R-Us to perform computer services. Simone is not a regular employee of the corporation and the corporation did not train Simone for the task. Simone keeps track of the time spent on the job at the customer and reports to the corporation, which pays Simone for her services. The corporation specifies the work to be done for their client. The corporation can also replace Simone with another individual if her work is not satisfactory. Chips-R-Us treats Simone as an independent contractor for employment tax purposes.

In the current year the IRS challenges the corporation that it has failed to remit FICA taxes and income taxes that should have been withheld with respect to Simone's employment. Chips-R-Us refuses to pay the amount, stating that it is not required to do so because Simone is not an employee of the corporation. What will be the likely outcome of the IRS's challenge concerning Simone's status as an employee or independent contractor? Who may be liable for payment of the employment taxes, interest, and penalties to the government? What ethical responsibilities should be followed in the remittance of withheld employee taxes?

TAX RESEARCH PROBLEM

I:14-74 Lean Corporation was incorporated in 1981 by Bruce Smith, who has served as an officer and member of the Board of Directors. Carl Jones has served as the secretary-treasurer of the company as a convenience to his friend Bruce. Carl acted as a part-time bookkeeper but did not run the everyday business affairs and paid only the bills he was instructed to pay. Carl was an authorized signatory for the corporate bank accounts but had no final control over expenditures.

Beginning in the last quarter of 2012, the company failed to pay all of the taxes withheld from employees and the employer's share of FICA taxes to the IRS. Despite this delinquency, the corporation continued to pay other creditors, including its employees, in preference to the IRS.

In January, 2014 Lean Corporation entered into an installment agreement with the IRS to keep current on its withholding taxes and to make payments on the past due balance until paid in full. The company subsequently defaulted on the agreement in April 2014. During this period, Bruce Smith was serving as chief financial officer and was a member of the board of directors. He had the authority to make policy decisions. He was responsible for negotiating the installment agreement with the IRS and the decision to default on the agreement.

Who is liable for the penalty for the nonpayment of the payroll tax withholdings?

A partial list of research sources is:

- Sec. 6672
- *Ernest W. Carlson v. U.S.*, 67 AFTR 2d 91-1104, 91-1 USTC ¶50,262 (D.C. UT, 1991)

CHAPTER

1

TAX RESEARCH

LEARNING OBJECTIVES

After studying this chapter, you should be able to

1. Distinguish between closed fact and open fact tax situations
2. Describe the steps in the tax research process
3. Explain how the facts influence tax consequences
4. Identify the sources of tax law and assess the authoritative value of each
5. Consult tax services to research an issue
6. Apply the basics of Internet-based tax research
7. Use a citator to assess tax authorities
8. Describe the professional guidelines that CPAs in tax practice should follow
9. Prepare work papers and communicate to clients

CHAPTER OUTLINE

This chapter introduces the reader to the tax research process. Its major focus is the sources of the tax law (i.e., the Internal Revenue Code and other tax authorities) and the relative weight given to each source. The chapter describes the steps in the tax research process and places particular emphasis on the importance of the facts to the tax consequences. It also describes the features of frequently used tax services and computer-based tax research resources. Finally, it explains how to use a citator.

The end product of the tax research process—the communication of results to the client—also is discussed. This text uses a hypothetical set of facts to provide a comprehensive illustration of the process. Sample work papers demonstrating how to document the results of research are included in Appendix A. The text also discusses two types of professional guidelines for CPAs in tax practice: the American Institute of Certified Public Accountants' (AICPA's) *Statements on Standards for Tax Services* (reproduced in Appendix E) and Treasury Department *Circular 230*.

OVERVIEW OF TAX RESEARCH

OBJECTIVE 1

Distinguish between closed fact and open fact tax situations

Tax research is the process of solving tax-related problems by applying tax law to specific sets of facts. Sometimes it involves researching several issues and often is conducted to formulate tax policy. For example, policy-oriented research would determine how far the level of charitable contributions might decline if such contributions were no longer deductible. Economists usually conduct this type of tax research to assess the effects of government policy.

Tax research also is conducted to determine the tax consequences of transactions to specific taxpayers. For example, client-oriented research would determine whether Smith Corporation could deduct a particular expenditure as a trade or business expense. Accounting and law firms generally engage in this type of research on behalf of their clients.

ADDITIONAL COMMENT

Closed-fact situations afford the tax advisor the least amount of flexibility. Because the facts are already established, the tax advisor must develop the best solution possible within certain predetermined constraints.

This chapter deals only with client-oriented tax research, which occurs in two contexts:

1. **Closed fact or tax compliance situations:** The client contacts the tax advisor after completing a transaction or while preparing a tax return. In such situations, the tax consequences are fairly straightforward because the facts cannot be modified to obtain different results. Consequently, tax saving opportunities may be lost.

EXAMPLE C:1-1 ▶ Tom informs Carol, his tax advisor, that on November 4 of the current year, he sold land held as an investment for $500,000 cash. His basis in the land was $50,000. On November 9, Tom reinvested the sales proceeds in another plot of investment property costing $500,000. This is a closed fact situation. Tom wants to know the amount and the character of the gain (if any) he must recognize. Because Tom solicits the tax advisor's advice after the sale and reinvestment, the opportunity for tax planning is limited. For example, the possibility of deferring taxes by using a like-kind exchange or an installment sale is lost. ◀

ADDITIONAL COMMENT

Open-fact or tax-planning situations give a tax advisor flexibility to structure transactions to accomplish the client's objectives. In this type of situation, a creative tax advisor can save taxpayers dollars through effective tax planning.

2. **Open fact or tax planning situations:** Before structuring or concluding a transaction, the client contacts the tax advisor to discuss tax planning opportunities. Tax-planning situations generally are more difficult and challenging because the tax advisor must consider the client's tax and nontax objectives. Most clients will not engage in a transaction if it is inconsistent with their nontax objectives, even though it produces tax savings.

EXAMPLE C:1-2 ▶ Diane is a widow with three children and five grandchildren and at present owns property valued at $30 million. She seeks advice from Carol, her tax advisor, about how to minimize her estate taxes and convey the greatest value of property to her descendants. This is an open-fact situation. Carol could advise Diane to leave all but $5 million of her property to a charitable organization so that her estate would owe no estate taxes. Although this recommendation would eliminate Diane's estate taxes, Diane is likely to reject it because she wants her children or grandchildren to be her primary beneficiaries. Thus, reducing estate taxes to zero is inconsistent with her objective of allowing her descendants to receive as much after-tax wealth as possible.

TAX STRATEGY TIP

Taxpayers should make investment decisions based on after-tax rates of return or after-tax cash flows.

When conducting research in a tax planning context, the tax professional should keep a number of points in mind. First, the objective is not to minimize taxes per se but rather to maximize a taxpayer's after-tax return. For example, if the federal income tax rate is a constant 30%, an investor should not buy a tax-exempt bond yielding 5% when he or she could buy a corporate bond of equal risk that yields 9% before tax and 6.3% after tax. This is the case even though his or her explicit taxes (actual tax liability) would be minimized by investing in the tax-exempt bond.[1] Second, taxpayers typically do not engage in unilateral or self-dealing transactions; thus, the tax ramifications for all parties to the transaction should be considered. For example, in the executive compensation context, employees may prefer to receive incentive stock options (because they will not recognize income until they sell the stock), but the employer may prefer to grant a different type of option (because the employer cannot deduct the value of incentive stock options upon issuance). Thus, the employer might grant a different number of options if it uses one type of stock option versus another type as compensation. Third, taxes are but one cost of doing business. In deciding where to locate a manufacturing plant, for example, factors more important to some businesses than the amount of state and local taxes paid might be the proximity to raw materials, good transportation systems, the cost of labor, the quantity of available skilled labor, and the quality of life in the area. Fourth, the time for tax planning is not restricted to the beginning date of an investment, contract, or other arrangement. Instead, the time extends throughout the duration of the activity. As tax rules change or as business and economic environments change, the tax advisor must reevaluate whether the taxpayer should hold onto an investment and must consider the transaction costs of any alternatives.

ADDITIONAL COMMENT

It is important to consider nontax as well as tax objectives. In many situations, the nontax considerations outweigh the tax considerations. Thus, the plan eventually adopted by a taxpayer may not always be the best when viewed strictly from a tax perspective.

One final note: the tax advisor should always bear in mind the financial accounting implications of proposed transactions. An answer that may be desirable from a tax perspective may not always be desirable from a financial accounting perspective. Though interrelated, the two fields of accounting have different orientations and different objectives. Tax accounting is oriented primarily to the Internal Revenue Service (IRS). Its objectives include calculating, reporting, and predicting one's tax liability according to legal principles. Financial accounting is oriented primarily to shareholders, creditors, managers, and employees. Its objectives include determining, reporting, and predicting a business's financial position and operating results according to Generally Accepted Accounting Principles. Because tax and financial accounting objectives may differ, planning conflicts could arise. For example, management might be reluctant to engage in tax reduction strategies that also reduce book income and reported earnings per share. Success in any tax practice, especially at the managerial level, requires consideration of both sets of objectives and orientations.

STEPS IN THE TAX RESEARCH PROCESS

OBJECTIVE 2

Describe the steps in the tax research process

In both open- and closed-fact situations, the tax research process involves six basic steps:

1. Determine the facts.
2. Identify the issues (questions).
3. Locate the applicable authorities.
4. Evaluate the authorities and choose those to follow where the authorities conflict.
5. Analyze the facts in terms of the applicable authorities.
6. Communicate conclusions and recommendations to the client.

[1] For an excellent discussion of explicit and implicit taxes and tax planning see M. S. Scholes, M. A. Wolfson, M. Erickson, L. Maydew, and T. Shevlin, *Taxes and Business Strategy: A Planning Approach*, fourth edition (Upper Saddle River, NJ: Pearson Prentice Hall, 2008). Also see Chapter I:18 of the *Individuals* volume. An example of an implicit tax is the excess of the before-tax earnings on a taxable bond over the risk-adjusted before-tax earnings on a tax-favored investment (e.g., a municipal bond).

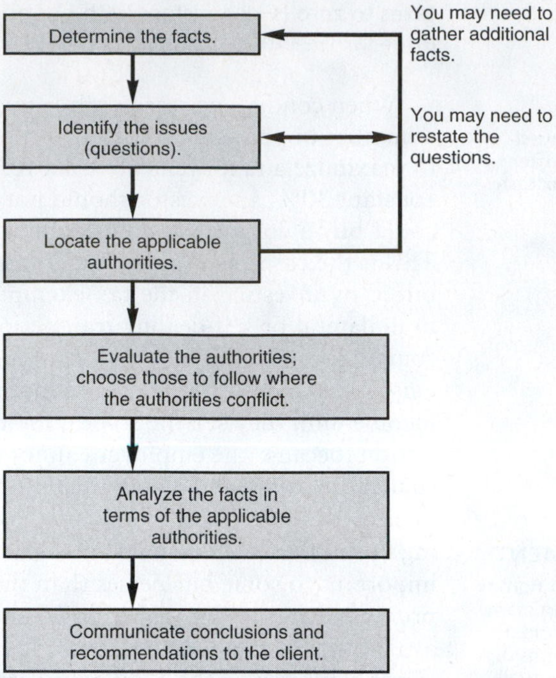

FIGURE C:1-1 ▶ STEPS IN THE TAX RESEARCH PROCESS

ADDITIONAL COMMENT

The steps of tax research provide an excellent format for a written tax communication. For example, a good format for a client memo includes (1) statement of facts, (2) list of issues, (3) discussion of relevant authority, (4) analysis, and (5) recommendations to the client of appropriate actions based on the research results.

TYPICAL MISCONCEPTION

Many taxpayers think the tax law is all black and white. However, most tax research deals with gray areas. Ultimately, when confronted with tough issues, the ability to develop strategies that favor the taxpayer and then to find relevant authority to support those strategies will make a successful tax advisor. Thus, recognizing planning opportunities and avoiding potential traps is often the real value added by a tax advisor.

Although the above outline suggests a linear approach, the tax research process often is circular. That is, it does not always proceed step-by-step. Figure C:1-1 illustrates a more accurate process, and Appendix A provides a comprehensive example of this process.

In a closed-fact situation, the facts have already occurred, and the tax advisor's task is to analyze them to determine the appropriate tax treatment. In an open-fact situation, by contrast, the facts have not yet occurred, and the tax advisor's task is to plan for them or shape them so as to produce a favorable tax result. The tax advisor performs the latter task by reviewing the relevant legal authorities, particularly court cases and IRS rulings, all the while bearing in mind the facts of those cases or rulings that produced favorable results compared with those that produced unfavorable results. For example, if a client wants to realize an ordinary loss (as opposed to a capital loss) on the sale of several plots of land, the tax advisor might consult cases involving similar land sales. The advisor might attempt to distinguish the facts of those cases in which the taxpayer realized an ordinary loss from the facts of those cases in which the taxpayer realized a capital loss. The advisor then might recommend that the client structure the transaction based on the fact pattern in the ordinary loss cases.

Often, tax research involves a question to which no clearcut, unequivocally correct answer exists. In such situations, probing a related issue might lead to a solution pertinent to the central question. For example, in researching whether the taxpayer may deduct a loss as ordinary instead of capital, the tax advisor might research the related issue of whether the presence of an investment motive precludes classifying a loss as ordinary. The solution to that issue might be relevant to the central question of whether the taxpayer may deduct the loss as ordinary.

Identifying the issue(s) to be researched often is the most difficult step in the tax research process. In some instances, the client defines the issue(s) for the tax advisor, such as where the client asks, "May I deduct the costs of a winter trip to Florida recommended by my physician?" In other instances, the tax advisor, after reviewing the documents submitted to him or her by the client, identifies and defines the issue(s) himself or herself. Doing so presupposes a firm grounding in tax law.[2]

[2] Often, in an employment context, supervisors define the questions to be researched and the authorities that might be relevant to the tax consequences.

Once the tax advisor locates the applicable legal authorities, he or she might have to obtain additional information from the client. Example C:1-3 illustrates the point. The example assumes that all relevant tax authorities are in agreement.

EXAMPLE C:1-3 ▶ Mark calls his tax advisor, Al, and states that he (1) incurred a loss on renting his beach cottage during the current year and (2) wonders whether he may deduct the loss. He also states that he, his wife, and their minor child occupied the cottage only eight days during the current year.

This is the first time Al has dealt with the Sec. 280A vacation home rules. On reading Sec. 280A(d), Al learns that a loss is *not* deductible if the taxpayer used the residence for personal purposes for longer than the greater of (1) 14 days or (2) 10% of the number of days the unit was rented at a fair rental value. He also learns that the property is *deemed* to be used by the taxpayer for personal purposes on any days on which it is used by any member of his or her family (as defined in Sec. 267(c)(4)). The Sec. 267(c)(4) definition of family members includes brothers, sisters, spouse, ancestors (e.g., parents and grandparents), or lineal descendants (e.g., children and grandchildren).

Mark's eight-day use is not long enough to make the rental loss nondeductible. However, Al must inquire about the number of days, if any, Mark's brothers, sisters, or parents used the property. (He already knows about use by Mark, his spouse, and his lineal descendants.) In addition, Al must find out how many days the cottage was rented to other persons at a fair rental value. Upon obtaining the additional information, Al proceeds to determine how to calculate the deductible expenses. Al then derives his conclusion concerning the deductible loss, if any, and communicates it to Mark. (This example assumes the passive activity and at-risk rules restricting a taxpayer's ability to deduct losses from real estate activities will not pose a problem for Mark. See Chapter I:8 for a comprehensive discussion of these topics.) ◀

Many firms require that a researcher's conclusions be communicated to the client in writing. Members or employees of such firms may answer questions orally, but their oral conclusions should be followed by a written communication. According to the AICPA's *Statements on Standards for Tax Services* (reproduced in Appendix E),

> Although oral advice may serve a client's needs appropriately in routine matters or in well-defined areas, written communications are recommended in important, unusual, substantial dollar value, or complicated transactions. The member may use professional judgment about whether, subsequently, to document oral advice.[3]

In addition, Treasury Department *Circular 230* covers all written advice communicated to clients. These requirements are more fully discussed at the end of this chapter and in Chapter C:15.

IMPORTANCE OF THE FACTS TO THE TAX CONSEQUENCES

OBJECTIVE 3

Explain how the facts influence tax consequences

Many terms and phrases used in the Internal Revenue Code (IRC) and other tax authorities are vague or ambiguous. Some provisions conflict with others or are difficult to reconcile, creating for the researcher the dilemma of deciding which rules are applicable and which tax results are proper. For example, as a condition to claiming another person as a dependent, the taxpayer must provide a certain level of support for such person.[4] Neither the IRC nor the Treasury Regulations define "support." This lack of definition could be problematic. For example, if the taxpayer purchased a used automobile costing $8,000 for an elderly parent whose only source of income is $7,800 in Social Security benefits, the question of whether the expenditure constitutes support would arise. The tax advisor would have to consult court opinions, revenue rulings, and other IRS pronouncements to ascertain the legal meaning of the term "support." Only after thorough research would the meaning of the term become clear.

[3] AICPA, *Statement on Standards for Tax Services*, No. 7, "Form and Content of Advice to Taxpayers," 2010, Para. 6.

[4] Sec. 152(e)(1)(A) and Sec. 152(d)(1)(C).

In other instances, the legal language is quite clear, but a question arises as to whether the taxpayer's transaction conforms to a specific pattern of facts that gives rise to a particular tax result. Ultimately, the peculiar facts of a transaction or event determine its tax consequences. A change in the facts can significantly change the consequences. Consider the following illustrations:

Illustration One

Facts: A holds stock, a capital asset, that he purchased two years ago at a cost of $1,000. He sells the stock to B for $920. What are the tax consequences to A?
Result: Under Sec. 1001, A realizes an $80 capital loss. He recognizes this loss in the current year. A must offset the loss against any capital gains recognized during the year. Any excess loss is deductible from ordinary income up to a $3,000 annual limit.
Change of Facts: A is B's son.
New Result: Under Sec. 267, A and B are related parties. Therefore, A may not recognize the realized loss. However, B may use the loss if she subsequently sells the stock at a gain.

Illustration Two

Facts: C donates to State University ten acres of land that she purchased two years ago for $10,000. The fair market value (FMV) of the land on the date of the donation is $25,000. C's adjusted gross income is $100,000. What is C's charitable contribution deduction?
Result: Under Sec. 170, C is entitled to a $25,000 charitable contribution deduction (i.e., the FMV of the property unreduced by the unrealized long-term gain).
Change of Facts: C purchased the land 11 months ago.
New Result: Under the same IRC section, C is entitled to only a $10,000 charitable contribution deduction (i.e., the FMV of the property reduced by the unrealized short-term gain).

Illustration Three

Facts: Acquiring Corporation pays Target Corporation's shareholders one million shares of Acquiring voting stock. In return, Target's shareholders tender 98% of their Target voting stock. The acquisition is for a bona fide business purpose. Acquiring continues Target's business. What are the tax consequences of the exchange to Target's shareholders?
Result: Because the transaction qualifies as a reorganization under Sec. 368(a)(1)(B), Target's shareholders are not taxed on the exchange, which is solely for Acquiring voting stock.
Change of Facts: In the transaction, Acquiring purchases the remaining 2% of Target's shares with cash.
New Result: Under the same IRC provision, Target's shareholders are now taxed on the exchange, which is not solely for Acquiring voting stock.

CREATING A FACTUAL SITUATION FAVORABLE TO THE TAXPAYER

TYPICAL MISCONCEPTION

Many taxpayers believe tax practitioners spend most of their time preparing tax returns. In reality, providing tax advice that accomplishes the taxpayer's objectives is one of the most important responsibilities of a tax advisor. This latter activity is tax consulting as compared to tax compliance.

Based on his or her research, a tax advisor might recommend to a taxpayer how to structure a transaction or plan an event so as to increase the likelihood that related expenses will be deductible. For example, suppose a taxpayer is assigned a temporary task in a location (City Y) different from the location (City X) of his or her permanent employment. Suppose also that the taxpayer wants to deduct the meal and lodging expenses incurred in City Y as well as the cost of transportation thereto. To do so, the taxpayer must establish that City X is his or her tax home and that he or she temporarily works in City Y. (Section 162 provides that a taxpayer may deduct travel expenses while "away from home" on business. A taxpayer is deemed to be "away from home" if his or her employment at the new location does not exceed one year, i.e., it is "temporary.") Suppose the taxpayer wants to know the tax consequences of his or her working in City Y for ten months and then, within that ten-month period, finding permanent employment in City Y. What is tax research likely to reveal?

Tax research will lead to an IRS ruling stating that, in such circumstances, the employment will be deemed to be temporary until the date on which the realistic expectation about the temporary nature of the assignment changes.[5] After this date, the employment

[5] Rev. Rul. 93-86, 1993-2 C.B. 71.

will be deemed to be permanent, and travel expenses relating to it will be nondeductible. Based on this finding, the tax advisor might advise the taxpayer to postpone his or her permanent job search in City Y until the end of the ten-month period and simply treat his or her assignment as temporary. So doing would lengthen the time he or she is deemed to be "away from home" on business and thus increase the amount of meal, lodging, and transportation costs deductible as travel expenses. The taxpayer should compare the tax savings to any additional personal costs of maintaining two residences.

THE SOURCES OF TAX LAW

OBJECTIVE 4

Identify the sources of tax law and assess the authoritative value of each

The language of the IRC is general; that is, it prescribes the tax treatment of broad categories of transactions and events. The reason for the generality is that Congress can neither foresee nor provide for every conceivable transaction or event. Even if it could, doing so would render the statute narrow in scope and inflexible in application. Accordingly, interpretations of the IRC—both administrative and judicial—are necessary. Administrative interpretations are provided in Treasury Regulations, revenue rulings, revenue procedures, and several other pronouncements discussed later in this chapter. Judicial interpretations are presented in court opinions. The term *tax law* as used by most tax advisors encompasses administrative and judicial interpretations in addition to the IRC. It also includes the meaning conveyed in reports issued by Congressional committees involved in the legislative process.

THE LEGISLATIVE PROCESS

Tax legislation begins in the House of Representatives. Initially, a tax proposal is incorporated in a bill. The bill is referred to the House Ways and Means Committee, which is charged with reviewing all tax legislation. The Ways and Means Committee holds hearings in which interested parties, such as the Treasury Secretary and IRS Commissioner, testify. At the conclusion of the hearings, the Ways and Means Committee votes to approve or reject the measure. If approved, the bill goes to the House floor where it is debated by the full membership. If the House approves the measure, the bill moves to the Senate where it is taken up by the Senate Finance Committee. Like Ways and Means, the Finance Committee holds hearings in which Treasury officials, tax experts, and other interested parties testify. If the committee approves the measure, the bill goes to the Senate floor where it is debated by the full membership. Upon approval by the Senate, it is submitted to the President for his or her signature. If the President signs the measure, the bill becomes public law. If the President vetoes it, Congress can override the veto by at least a two-thirds majority vote in each chamber.

Generally, at each stage of the legislative process, the bill is subject to amendment. If amended, and if the House version differs from the Senate version, the bill is referred to a House-Senate conference committee.[6] This committee attempts to resolve the differences between the House and Senate versions. Ultimately, it submits a compromise version of the measure to each chamber for its approval. Such referrals are common. For example, in 1998 the House and Senate disagreed over what the taxpayer must do to shift the burden of proof to the IRS. The House proposed that the taxpayer assert a "reasonable dispute" regarding a taxable item. The Senate proposed that the taxpayer introduce "credible evidence" regarding the item. A conference committee was appointed to resolve the differences. This committee ultimately adopted the Senate proposal, which was later approved by both chambers.

ADDITIONAL COMMENT

Committee reports can be helpful in interpreting new legislation because they indicate the intent of Congress. With the proliferation of tax legislation, committee reports have become especially important because the Treasury Department often is unable to draft the needed regulations in a timely manner.

After approving major legislation, the Ways and Means Committee and Senate Finance Committee usually issue official reports. These reports, published by the U.S. Government Printing Office (GPO) as part of the *Cumulative Bulletin* and as separate documents, explain the committees' reasoning for approving (and/or amending) the legislation.[7] In addition, the GPO publishes both records of the committee hearings and transcripts of the floor debates. The records are published as separate House or Senate documents. The transcripts are incorporated in the *Congressional Record* for the day of the

[6] The size of a conference committee can vary. It is made up of an equal number of members from the House and the Senate.

[7] The *Cumulative Bulletin* is described in the discussion of revenue rulings on page C:1-12.

debate. In tax research, these records, reports, and transcripts are useful in deciphering the meaning of the statutory language. Where this language is ambiguous or vague, and the courts have not interpreted it, the documents can shed light on **Congressional intent**, i.e., what Congress *intended* by a particular term, phrase, or provision.

EXAMPLE C:1-4 ▶ In 1998, Congress passed legislation concerning shifting the burden of proof to the IRS. This legislation was codified in Sec. 7491. The question arises as to what constitutes "credible evidence" because the taxpayer must introduce such evidence to shift the burden of proof to the IRS. Section 7491 does not define the term. Because the provision was relatively new, few courts had an opportunity to interpret what "credible evidence" means. In the absence of relevant statutory or judicial authority, the researcher might have looked to the committee reports to ascertain what Congress intended by the term. Senate Report No. 105-174 states that "credible evidence" means evidence of a quality, which, "after critical analysis, the court would find sufficient upon which to base a decision on the issue if no contrary evidence were submitted."[8] This language suggests that Congress intended the term to mean evidence of a kind sufficient to withstand judicial scrutiny. Such a meaning should be regarded as conclusive in the absence of other authority. ◀

THE INTERNAL REVENUE CODE

The IRC, which comprises Title 26 of the United States Code, is the foundation of all tax law. First codified (i.e., organized into a single compilation of revenue statutes) in 1939, the tax law was recodified in 1954. The IRC was known as the Internal Revenue Code of 1954 until 1986, when its name was changed to the Internal Revenue Code of 1986. Whenever changes to the IRC are approved, the old language is deleted and new language added. Thus, the IRC is organized as an integrated document, and a researcher need not read through the relevant parts of all previous tax bills to find the current version of the law. Nevertheless, a researcher must be sure that he or she is working with the law in effect when a particular transaction occurred.

ADDITIONAL COMMENT

The various tax services, discussed later in this chapter, provide IRC histories for researchers who need to work with prior years' tax law.

The IRC contains provisions dealing with income taxes, estate and gift taxes, employment taxes, alcohol and tobacco taxes, and other excise taxes. Organizationally, the IRC is divided into subtitles, chapters, subchapters, parts, subparts, sections, subsections, paragraphs, subparagraphs, and clauses. Subtitle A contains rules relating to income taxes, and Subtitle B deals with estate and gift taxes. A set of provisions concerned with one general area constitutes a subchapter. For example, the topics of corporate distributions and adjustments appear in Subchapter C, and topics relating to partners and partnerships appear in Subchapter K. Figure C:1-2 presents the organizational scheme of the IRC.

An IRC section contains the operative provisions to which tax advisors most often refer. For example, they speak of "Sec. 351 transactions," "Sec. 306 stock," and "Sec. 1231 gains and losses." Although a tax advisor need not know all the IRC sections, paragraphs, and parts, he or she must be familiar with the IRC's organizational scheme to read and interpret it correctly. The language of the IRC is replete with cross-references to titles, paragraphs, subparagraphs, and so on.

EXAMPLE C:1-5 ▶ Section 7701, a definitional section, begins, "When used in this title . . ." and then provides a series of definitions. Because of this broad reference, a Sec. 7701 definition applies for all of Title 26; that is, it applies for purposes of the income tax, estate and gift tax, excise tax, and other taxes governed by Title 26. ◀

EXAMPLE C:1-6 ▶ Section 302(b)(3) allows taxpayers whose stock holdings are completely terminated in a redemption (a corporation's purchase of its stock from one or more of its shareholders) to receive capital gain treatment on the excess of the redemption proceeds over the stock's basis instead of ordinary income treatment on the entire proceeds. Section 302(c)(2)(A) states, "In the case of a distribution described in subsection (b)(3), section 318(a)(1) shall not apply if. . . ." Further, Sec. 302(c)(2)(C)(i) indicates "Subparagraph (A) shall not apply to a distribution to any entity unless. . . ." Thus, in determining whether a taxpayer will receive capital gain treatment in a stock redemption, a tax advisor must be able to locate and interpret various cross-referenced IRC sections, subsections, paragraphs, subparagraphs, and clauses. ◀

[8] S. Rept. No. 105-174, 105th Cong., 1st Sess. (unpaginated) (1998).

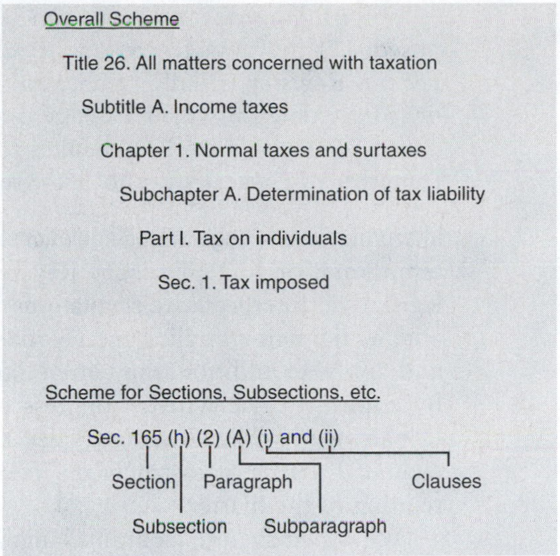

FIGURE C:1-2 ▶ ORGANIZATIONAL SCHEME OF THE INTERNAL REVENUE CODE

TREASURY REGULATIONS

The Treasury Department issues regulations that expound upon the IRC. Treasury Regulations often provide examples with computations that assist the reader in understanding how IRC provisions apply. Treasury Regulations are formulated on the basis of Treasury Decisions (T.D.s). The numbers of the Treasury Decisions that form the basis of a Treasury Regulation usually are found in the notes at the end of the regulation.

Because of frequent IRC changes, the Treasury Department does not always update the regulations in a timely manner. Consequently, when consulting a regulation, a tax advisor should check its introductory or end note to determine when the regulation was adopted. If the regulation was adopted before the most recent revision of the applicable IRC section, the regulation should be treated as authoritative to the extent consistent with the revision. Thus, for example, if a regulation issued before the passage of an IRC amendment specifies a dollar amount, and the amendment changed the dollar amount, the regulation should be regarded as authoritative in all respects except for the dollar amount.

Proposed, Temporary, and Final Regulations. A Treasury Regulation is first issued in proposed form to the public, which is given an opportunity to comment on it. Parties most likely to comment are individual tax practitioners and representatives of organizations such as the American Bar Association, the Tax Division of the AICPA, and the American Taxation Association. The comments may suggest that the proposed rules could affect taxpayers more adversely than Congress had anticipated. In drafting a final regulation, the Treasury Department generally considers the comments and may modify the rules accordingly. If the comments are favorable, the Treasury Department usually finalizes the regulation with minor revisions. If the comments are unfavorable, it usually finalizes the regulation with major revisions or allows the proposed regulation to expire.

Proposed regulations are just that—proposed. Consequently, they carry no more authoritative weight than do the arguments of the IRS in a court brief. Nevertheless, they represent the Treasury Department's official interpretation of the IRC. By contrast, **temporary regulations** are binding on the taxpayer. Effective as of the date of their publication, they often are issued immediately after passage of a major tax act to guide taxpayers and their advisors on procedural or computational matters. Regulations issued as temporary are concurrently issued as proposed. Because their issuance is not preceded by a public comment period, they are regarded as somewhat less authoritative than final regulations.

Once finalized, regulations can be effective the earliest of (1) the date they were proposed; (2) the date temporary regulations preceding them were first published in the *Federal Register*, a daily publication that contains federal government pronouncements; or (3) the date on which a notice describing the expected contents of the regulation was issued to the public.[9] For changes to the IRC enacted after July 29, 1996, the Treasury Department generally cannot issue regulations with retroactive effect.

Interpretative and Legislative Regulations. In addition to being officially classified as proposed, temporary, or final, Treasury Regulations are unofficially classified as interpretative or legislative. **Interpretative regulations** are issued under the general authority of Sec. 7805 and, as the name implies, merely make the IRC's statutory language easier to understand and apply. In addition, they often illustrate various computations. **Legislative regulations,** by contrast, arise where Congress delegates its rule-making authority to the Treasury Department. When Congress believes it lacks the expertise necessary to deal with a highly technical matter, it instructs the Treasury Department to set forth substantive tax rules relating to the matter.

Whenever the IRC contains language such as "The Secretary shall prescribe such regulations as he may deem necessary" or "under regulations prescribed by the Secretary," the regulations interpreting the IRC provision are legislative. The consolidated tax return regulations are an example of legislative regulations. In Sec. 1502, Congress delegated to the Treasury Department authority to issue regulations that determine the tax liability of a group of affiliated corporations filing a consolidated tax return. As a precondition to filing such a return, the corporations must consent to follow the consolidated return regulations.[10] Such consent generally precludes the corporations from later arguing in court that the regulatory provisions are invalid.

Authoritative Weight. Final Treasury Regulations are presumed to be valid and have almost the same authoritative weight as the IRC. Despite this presumption, taxpayers occasionally argue that a regulation is invalid and, consequently, should not be followed.

Prior to 2011, courts held interpretive and legislative regulations to different standards, giving more authority to legislative regulations that Congress specifically delegated to the Treasury Department to draft. The difference in authoritative weight largely disappeared, however, in 2011 with the Supreme Court decision in *Mayo Foundation.*[11] Going forward, both types of regulations will have the same authoritative weight and will be overturned only in very limited cases such as when, in the Court's opinion, the regulations exceed the scope of power delegated to the Treasury Department,[12] are contrary to the IRC,[13] or are unreasonable.[14]

KEY POINT

The older a Treasury Regulation becomes, the less likely a court is to invalidate the regulation. The legislative reenactment doctrine holds that if a regulation did not reflect the intent of Congress, lawmakers would have changed the statute in subsequent legislation to obtain their desired objectives.

In assessing the validity of long-standing Treasury Regulations, some courts apply the **legislative reenactment doctrine**. Under this doctrine, a regulation is deemed to receive congressional approval whenever the IRC provision under which the regulation was issued is reenacted without amendment.[15] Underlying this doctrine is the rationale that, if Congress believed that the regulation offered an erroneous interpretation of the IRC, it would have amended the IRC to conform to its belief. Congress's failure to amend the IRC signifies approval of the regulation.[16] This doctrine is predicated on Congress's constitutional authority to levy taxes. This authority implies that, if Congress is dissatisfied with the manner in which either the executive or the judiciary has interpreted the IRC, it can invalidate these interpretations through new legislation.

? STOP & THINK

Question: You are researching the manner in which a deduction is calculated. You consult Treasury Regulations for guidance because the IRC states that the calculation is to be done "in a manner prescribed by the Secretary." After reviewing these authorities, you

---

[9] Sec. 7805(b).
[10] Sec. 1501.
[11] *Mayo Foundation for Medical Education & Research, et al. v. U.S.,* 107 AFTR 2d 2011-341, 131 S.Ct. 704 (2011).
[12] *McDonald v. CIR,* 56 AFTR 2d 85-5318, 85-2 USTC ¶9494 (5th Cir., 1985).
[13] *Jeanese, Inc. v. U.S.,* 15 AFTR 2d 429, 65-1 USTC ¶9259 (9th Cir., 1965).
[14] *United States v. Vogel Fertilizer Co.,* 49 AFTR 2d 82-491, 82-1 USTC ¶9134 (USSC, 1982).
[15] *United States v. Homer O. Correll,* 20 AFTR 2d 5845, 68-1 USTC ¶9101 (USSC, 1967).
[16] One can rebut the presumption that Congress approved of the regulation by showing that Congress was unaware of the regulation when it reenacted the statute.

conclude that another way of doing the calculation arguably is correct under an intuitive approach. This approach would result in a lower tax liability for the client. Should you follow the Treasury Regulations, or should you use the intuitive approach and argue that the regulations are invalid?

Solution: Because of the language "in a manner prescribed by the Secretary," the Treasury Regulations dealing with the calculation are legislative. Whenever Congress calls for legislative regulations, it explicitly authorizes (directs) the Treasury Department to write the "rules." Thus, a challenge based on the existence of a reasonable alternative method is unlikely to succeed in court. Under the *Mayo Foundation* decision, you should reach the same conclusion even if dealing with an interpretive Treasury Regulation.

ADDITIONAL COMMENT

Citations serve two purposes in tax research: first, they substantiate propositions; second, they enable the reader to locate underlying authority.

Citations. Citations to Treasury Regulations are relatively easy to understand. One or more numbers appear before a decimal place, and several numbers follow the decimal place. The numbers immediately following the decimal place indicate the IRC section being interpreted. The numbers preceding the decimal place indicate the general subject of the regulation. Numbers that often appear before the decimal place and their general subjects are as follows:

Number	*General Subject Matter*
1	Income tax
20	Estate tax
25	Gift tax
301	Administrative and procedural matters
601	Procedural rules

The number following the IRC section number indicates the numerical sequence of the regulation, such as the fifth regulation. No relationship exists between this number and the subsection of the IRC being interpreted. An example of a citation to a final regulation is as follows:

Reg. Sec. 1.165 – 5

Income tax (1) — IRC section (165) — Fifth regulation (5)

Citations to proposed or temporary regulations follow the same format. They are referenced as Prop. Reg. Sec. or Temp. Reg. Sec. For temporary regulations the numbering system following the IRC section number always begins with the number of the regulation and an upper case T (e.g., -1T).

Section 165 addresses the broad topic of losses and is interpreted by several regulations. According to its caption, the topic of Reg. Sec. 1.165-5 is worthless securities, which also is addressed in subsection (g) of IRC Sec. 165. Parenthetical information following the text of the Treasury Regulation indicates that the regulation was last revised on March 11, 2008, by Treasury Decision (T.D.) 9386. Section 165(g) was last amended in 2000. A researcher must always check when the regulations were last amended and be aware that an IRC change may have occurred after the most recent regulation amendment, potentially making the regulation inapplicable.

When referencing a regulation, the researcher should fine-tune the citation to indicate the precise passage that supports his or her conclusion. An example of such a detailed citation is Reg. Sec. 1.165-5(j), Ex. 2(i), which refers to paragraph (i) of Example 2, found in paragraph (j) of the fifth regulation interpreting Sec. 165.

ADMINISTRATIVE PRONOUNCEMENTS

The IRS interprets the IRC through **administrative pronouncements**, the most important of which are discussed below. After consulting the IRC and Treasury Regulations, tax advisors are likely next to consult these pronouncements.

TYPICAL MISCONCEPTION

Even though revenue rulings do not have the same weight as Treasury Regulations or court cases, one should not underestimate their importance. Because a revenue ruling is the official published position of the IRS, in audits the examining agent will place considerable weight on any applicable revenue rulings.

Revenue Rulings. In **revenue rulings**, the IRS indicates the tax consequences of specific transactions encountered in practice. For example, in a revenue ruling, the IRS might indicate whether the exchange of stock for stock derivatives in a corporate acquisition is tax-free.

The IRS issues more than 50 revenue rulings a year. These rulings do not rank as high in the hierarchy of authorities as do Treasury Regulations or federal court cases. They simply represent the IRS's view of the tax law. Taxpayers who do not follow a revenue ruling will not incur a substantial understatement penalty if they have substantial authority for different treatment.[17] Nonetheless, the IRS presumes that the tax treatment specified in a revenue ruling is correct. Consequently, if an examining agent discovers in an audit that a taxpayer did not adopt the position prescribed in a revenue ruling, the agent will contend that the taxpayer's tax liability should be adjusted to reflect that position.

Soon after it is issued, a revenue ruling appears in the weekly *Internal Revenue Bulletin* (cited as I.R.B.), published by the U.S. Government Printing Office (GPO). Revenue rulings later appear in the *Cumulative Bulletin* (cited as C.B.), a bound volume issued semiannually by the GPO. An example of a citation to a revenue ruling appearing in the *Cumulative Bulletin* is as follows:

Rev. Rul. 97-4, 1997-1 C.B. 5.

This is the fourth ruling issued in 1997, and it appears on page 5 of Volume 1 of the 1997 *Cumulative Bulletin.* Before the GPO publishes the pertinent volume of the *Cumulative Bulletin,* researchers should use citations to the *Internal Revenue Bulletin.* An example of such a citation follows:

Rev. Rul. 2013-8, 2013-15 I.R.B. 763.

For revenue rulings (and other IRS pronouncements) issued after 1999, the full four digits of the year of issuance are set forth in the title. For revenue rulings (and other IRS pronouncements) issued before 2000, only the last two digits of the year of issuance are set forth in the title. The above citation represents the eighth ruling for 2013. This ruling is located on page 763 of the *Internal Revenue Bulletin* for the fifteenth week of 2013. Once a revenue ruling is published in the *Cumulative Bulletin,* only the citation to the *Cumulative Bulletin* should be used. Thus, a citation to the I.R.B. is temporary.

Revenue Procedures. As the name suggests, **revenue procedures** are IRS pronouncements that usually deal with the procedural aspects of tax practice. For example, one revenue procedure deals with the manner in which tip income should be reported. Another revenue procedure describes the requirements for reproducing paper substitutes for informational returns such as Form 1099.

As with revenue rulings, revenue procedures are published first in the *Internal Revenue Bulletin,* then in the *Cumulative Bulletin.* An example of a citation to a revenue procedure appearing in the *Cumulative Bulletin* is as follows:

SELF-STUDY QUESTION

Are letter rulings of precedential value for third parties?

ANSWER

No. A letter ruling is binding only on the taxpayer to whom the ruling was issued. Nevertheless, letter rulings can be very useful to third parties because they provide insight as to the IRS's opinion about the tax consequences of various transactions.

Rev. Proc. 97-19, 1997-1 C.B. 644.

This pronouncement is found in Volume 1 of the 1997 *Cumulative Bulletin* on page 644. It is the nineteenth revenue procedure issued in 1997.

In addition to revenue rulings and revenue procedures, the *Cumulative Bulletin* contains IRS notices, as well as the texts of proposed regulations, tax treaties, committee reports, and U.S. Supreme Court decisions.

Letter Rulings. **Letter rulings** are initiated by taxpayers who ask the IRS to explain the tax consequences of a particular transaction.[18] The IRS provides its explanation in the form of a letter ruling, a response personal to the taxpayer requesting an answer. Only the

---

[17] Chapter C:15 discusses the authoritative support taxpayers and tax advisors should have for positions they adopt on a tax return.

[18] Chapter C:15 further discusses letter rulings.

taxpayer to whom the ruling is addressed may rely on it as authority. Nevertheless, letter rulings are relevant for other taxpayers and tax advisors because they offer insight into the IRS's position on the tax treatment of particular transactions.

Originally the public did not have access to letter rulings issued to other taxpayers. As a result of Sec. 6110, enacted in 1976, letter rulings (with confidential information deleted) are accessible to the general public and have been reproduced by major tax services. An example of a citation to a letter ruling appears below:

Ltr. Rul. 200130006 (July 30, 2001).

The first four digits (two if issued before 2000) indicate the year in which the ruling was made public, in this case, 2001.[19] The next two digits denote the week in which the ruling was made public, here the thirtieth. The last three numbers indicate the numerical sequence of the ruling for the week, here the sixth. The date in parentheses denotes the date of the ruling.

ADDITIONAL COMMENT

A technical advice memorandum is published as a letter ruling. Whereas a taxpayer-requested letter ruling deals with prospective transactions, a technical advice memorandum deals with past or consummated transactions.

Other Interpretations

Technical Advice Memoranda. When the IRS audits a taxpayer's return, the IRS agent might ask the IRS national office for advice on a complicated, technical matter. The national office will provide its advice in a **technical advice memorandum**, released to the public in the form of a letter ruling.[20] Researchers can identify which letter rulings are technical advice memoranda by introductory language such as, "In response to a request for technical advice. . . ." An example of a citation to a technical advice memorandum is as follows:

T.A.M. 9801001 (January 2, 1998).

This citation refers to the first technical advice memorandum issued in the first week of 1998. The memorandum is dated January 2, 1998.

Information Releases. If the IRS wants to disseminate information to the general public, it will issue an **information release**. Information releases are written in lay terms and are dispatched to thousands of newspapers throughout the country. The IRS, for example, may issue an information release to announce the standard mileage rate for business travel. An example of a citation to an information release is as follows:

I.R. 86-70 (June 12, 1986).

This citation is to the seventieth information release issued in 1986. The release is dated June 12, 1986.

ADDITIONAL COMMENT

Announcements are used to summarize new tax legislation or publicize procedural matters. Announcements generally are aimed at tax practitioners and are considered to be "substantial authority" [Rev. Rul. 90-91, 1990-2 C.B. 262].

Announcements and Notices. The IRS also disseminates information to tax practitioners in the form of **announcements** and **notices**. These pronouncements generally are more technical than information releases and frequently address current tax developments. After passage of a major tax act, and before the Treasury Department has had an opportunity to issue proposed or temporary regulations, the IRS may issue an announcement or notice to clarify the legislation. The IRS is bound to follow the announcement or notice just as it is bound to follow a revenue procedure or revenue ruling. Examples of citations to announcements and notices are as follows:

Announcement 2007-3, 2007-1 C.B. 376.
Notice 2007-9, 2007-1 C.B. 401.

The first citation is to the third announcement issued in 2007. It can be found on page 376 of the first *Cumulative Bulletin* for 2007. The second citation is to the ninth

[19] Sometimes a letter ruling is cited as PLR (private letter ruling) instead of Ltr. Rul.

[20] Technical advice memoranda are discussed further in Chapter C:15.

notice issued in 2007. It can be found on page 401 of the first *Cumulative Bulletin* for 2007. Notices and announcements appear in both the *Internal Revenue Bulletin* and the *Cumulative Bulletin*.

JUDICIAL DECISIONS

Judicial decisions are an important source of tax law. Judges are reputed to be unbiased individuals who decide questions of fact (the existence of a fact or the occurrence of an event) or questions of law (the applicability of a legal principle or the proper interpretation of a legal term or provision). Judges do not always agree on the tax consequences of a particular transaction or event. Therefore, tax advisors often must derive conclusions against a background of conflicting judicial authorities. For example, a U.S. district court might disagree with the Tax Court on the deductibility of an expense. Likewise, one circuit court might disagree with another circuit court on the same issue.

Overview of the Court System. A taxpayer may begin tax litigation in any of three courts: the U.S. Tax Court, the U.S. Court of Federal Claims (formerly the U.S. Claims Court), or U.S. district courts. Court precedents are important in deciding where to begin such litigation (see page C:1-21 for a discussion of precedent). Also important is when the taxpayer must pay the deficiency the IRS contends is due. A taxpayer who wants to litigate either in a U.S. district court or in the U.S. Court of Federal Claims must first pay the deficiency. The taxpayer then files a claim for refund, which the IRS is likely to deny. Following this denial, the taxpayer must petition the court for a refund. If the court grants the taxpayer's petition, he or she receives a refund of the taxes in question plus accrued interest. If the taxpayer begins litigation in the Tax Court, on the other hand, he or she need not pay the deficiency unless and until the court decides the case against him or her. In that event, the taxpayer also must pay interest and penalties.[21] A taxpayer who believes that a jury would be sympathetic to his or her case should litigate in a U.S. district court, the only forum where a jury trial is possible.

SELF-STUDY QUESTION

What are some of the factors that a taxpayer should consider when deciding in which court to file a tax-related claim?

ANSWER

(1) Each court's published precedent pertaining to the issue, (2) desirability of a jury trial, (3) tax expertise of each court, and (4) when the deficiency must be paid.

If a party loses at the trial court level, it can appeal the decision to a higher court. Appeals of Tax Court and U.S. district court decisions are made to the court of appeals for the taxpayer's circuit. The appeals court system is comprised of 11 geographical circuits designated by numbers, the District of Columbia Circuit, and the Federal Circuit.[22] Table C:1-1 shows the states that lie in the various circuits. California, for example, lies in the Ninth Circuit. When referring to these appellate courts, instead of saying, for example, "the Court of Appeals for the Ninth Circuit," one generally says "the Ninth Circuit." All decisions of the U.S. Court of Federal Claims are appealable to one court—the Court of Appeals for the Federal Circuit—irrespective of where the taxpayer resides or does business.[23] The only cases the Federal Circuit hears are those that originate in the U.S. Court of Federal Claims.

The party losing at the appellate level can petition the U.S. Supreme Court to review the case under a **writ of certiorari**. If the Supreme Court agrees to hear the case, it grants certiorari.[24] If it refuses to hear the case, it denies certiorari. In recent years, the Court has granted certiorari in only about six to ten tax cases per year. Figure C:1-3 and Table C:1-2 provide an overview and summary of the court system with respect to tax matters.

ADDITIONAL COMMENT

Because the Tax Court deals only with tax cases, it presumably has a higher level of tax expertise than do other courts. Tax Court judges are appointed by the President, in part, due to their considerable tax experience. The Tax Court typically maintains a large backlog of tax cases, sometimes numbering in the tens of thousands.

The U.S. Tax Court. The U.S. Tax Court was created in 1942 as a successor to the Board of Tax Appeals. It is a court of national jurisdiction that hears only tax-related cases. All taxpayers, regardless of their state of residence or place of business, may litigate in the Tax Court. It has 19 judges, including one chief judge.[25] The President, with the consent of the Senate, appoints the judges for a 15-year term and may reappoint them for an additional

---

[21] Revenue Procedure 2005-18, 2005-1 C.B. 798, provides procedures for taxpayers to make remittances or apply overpayments to stop the accrual of interest on deficiencies.

[22] The Federal Circuit has nationwide jurisdiction to hear appeals in specialized cases, such as those involving patent laws.

[23] The Court of Claims was reconstituted as the United States Court of Claims in 1982. In 1992, this court was renamed the U.S. Court of Federal Claims.

[24] The granting of certiorari signifies that the Supreme Court is granting an appellate review. The denial of certiorari does not necessarily mean that the Supreme Court endorses the lower court's decision. It simply means the court has decided not to hear the case.

[25] The Tax Court also periodically appoints, depending on budgetary constraints, a number of trial judges and senior judges who hear cases and render decisions with the same authority as the regular Tax Court judges.

▼ TABLE C:1-1
Federal Judicial Circuits

Circuit	States Included in Circuit
First	Maine, Massachusetts, New Hampshire, Rhode Island, Puerto Rico
Second	Connecticut, New York, Vermont
Third	Delaware, New Jersey, Pennsylvania, Virgin Islands
Fourth	Maryland, North Carolina, South Carolina, Virginia, West Virginia
Fifth	Louisiana, Mississippi, Texas
Sixth	Kentucky, Michigan, Ohio, Tennessee
Seventh	Illinois, Indiana, Wisconsin
Eighth	Arkansas, Iowa, Minnesota, Missouri, Nebraska, North Dakota, South Dakota
Ninth	Alaska, Arizona, California, Hawaii, Idaho, Montana, Nevada, Oregon, Washington, Guam, Northern Marina Islands
Tenth	Colorado, Kansas, New Mexico, Oklahoma, Utah, Wyoming
Eleventh	Alabama, Florida, Georgia
D.C.	District of Columbia
Federal	All jurisdictions (for taxpayers appealing from the U.S. Court of Federal Claims)

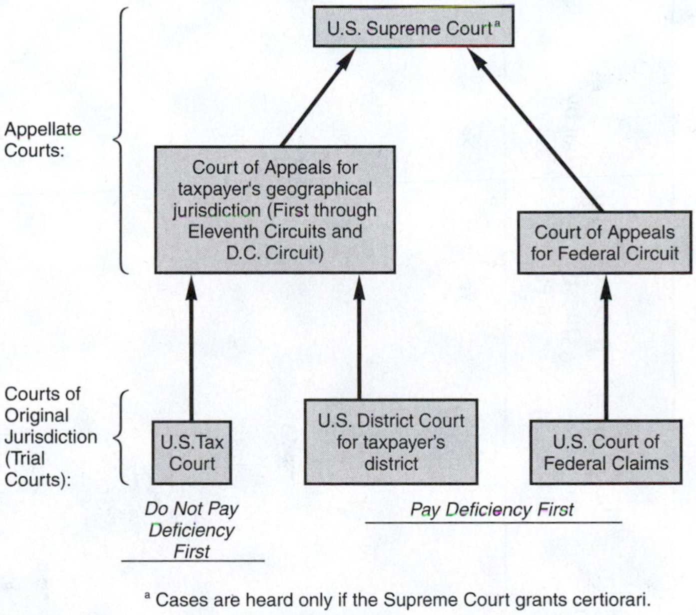

FIGURE C:1-3 ▶ OVERVIEW OF COURT SYSTEM—TAX MATTERS

term. The judges, specialists in tax-related matters, periodically travel to roughly 100 cities throughout the country to hear cases. In most instances, only one judge hears a case.

The Tax Court issues both regular and memorandum (memo) decisions. Generally, the first time the Tax Court decides a legal issue, its decision appears as a **regular decision. Memo decisions**, on the other hand, usually deal with factual variations of previously decided cases. Nevertheless, regular and memo decisions carry the same authoritative weight.

At times, the chief judge determines that a particular case concerns an important issue that the entire Tax Court should consider. In such a situation, the words *reviewed by the court* appear at the end of the majority opinion. Any concurring or dissenting opinions follow the majority opinion. A judge who issues a concurring opinion agrees with the basic outcome of the majority's decision but not with its rationale. A judge who issues a dissenting opinion believes the majority reached an erroneous conclusion.

▼ **TABLE C:1-2**
Summary of Court System—Tax Matters

Court(s) (Number of)	Number of Judges on Each	Personal Jurisdiction	Subject Matter Jurisdiction	Determines Questions of Fact	Trial by Jury	Precedents Followed	Where Opinions Published
U.S. district courts (over 95)	1–28*	Local	General	Yes	Yes	Same court Court for circuit where situated U.S. Supreme Court	*Federal Supplement* *American Federal Tax Reports* *United S tates Tax Cases*
U.S. Tax Court (1)	19	National	Tax	Yes	No	Same court Court for taxpayer's circuit U.S. Supreme Court	*Tax Court of the U.S. Reports* *CCH Tax Court Memorandum Decisions* *RIA Tax Court Memorandum Decisions*
U.S. Court of Federal Claims (1)	16	National	Claims against U.S. Government	Yes	No	Same court Federal Circuit Court U.S. Supreme Court	*Federal Reporter* (pre-1982) *U.S. Court of Federal Claims* *American Federal Tax Reports* *United States Tax Cases*
U.S. Courts of Appeals (13)	About 20	Regional	General	No	No	Same court U.S. Supreme Court	*Federal Reporter* *American Federal Tax Reports* *United States Tax Cases*
U.S. Supreme Court (1)	9	National	General	No	No	Same court	*U.S. Supreme Court Reports* *Supreme Court Reporter* *United States Reports, Lawyers' Edition* *American Federal Tax Reports* *United States Tax Cases*

*Although the number of judges assigned to each court varies, only one judge hears a case.

Another phrase sometimes appearing at the end of a Tax Court opinion is *Entered under Rule 155*. This phrase signifies that the court has reached a decision concerning the tax treatment of an item but has left computation of the deficiency to the two litigating parties.

SELF-STUDY QUESTION

What are some of the considerations for litigating under the small cases procedure of the Tax Court?

ANSWER

The small cases procedure gives the taxpayer the advantage of having his or her "day in court" without the expense of an attorney. But if the taxpayer loses, the decision cannot be appealed.

Small Cases Procedure. Taxpayers have the option of having their cases heard under the **small cases procedure** of the Tax Court if the amount in controversy on an annual basis does not exceed $50,000.[26] This procedure is less formal than the regular Tax Court procedure, and taxpayers can represent themselves without an attorney.[27] The cases are heard by special commissioners instead of by one of the 19 Tax Court judges. A disadvantage of the small cases procedure for the losing party is that the decision cannot be appealed. The opinions of the commissioners generally are not published and have no precedential value.

Acquiescence Policy. The IRS has adopted a policy of announcing whether, in future cases involving similar facts and similar issues, it will follow federal court decisions that are adverse to it. This policy is known as the IRS **acquiescence policy**. If the IRS wants taxpayers to know that it will follow an adverse decision in future cases involving similar facts and issues, it will announce its "acquiescence" in the decision. Conversely, if it wants taxpayers to know that it will not follow the decision in such future cases, it will announce its "nonacquiescence." The IRS does not announce its acquiescence or nonacquiescence in every decision it loses.

The IRS publishes its acquiescences and nonacquiescences as "Actions on Decision" first in the *Internal Revenue Bulletin,* then in the *Cumulative Bulletin*. Before 1991, the IRS acquiesced or nonacquiesced in regular Tax Court decisions only. In 1991, it broadened the scope of its policy to include adverse U.S. Claims Court, U.S. district court, and U.S. circuit court decisions.

ADDITIONAL COMMENT

The only cases with respect to which the IRS will acquiesce or nonacquiesce are decisions that the government loses. Because the majority of cases, particularly Tax Court cases, are won by the government, the IRS will potentially acquiesce in only a small number of cases.

In cases involving multiple issues, the IRS may acquiesce in some issues but not others. In decisions supported by extensive reasoning, it may acquiesce in the result but not the rationale (*acq. in result*). Furthermore, it may retroactively revoke an acquiescence or nonacquiescence. The footnotes to the relevant announcement in the *Internal Revenue Bulletin* and *Cumulative Bulletin* indicate the nature and extent of IRS acquiescences and nonacquiescences.

These acquiescences and nonacquiescences have important implications for taxpayers. If a taxpayer bases his or her position on a decision in which the IRS has nonacquiesced, he or she can expect an IRS challenge in the event of an audit. In such circumstances, the taxpayer's only recourse may be litigation. On the other hand, if the taxpayer bases his or her position on a decision in which the IRS has acquiesced, he or she can expect little or no challenge. In either case, the examining agent will be bound by the IRS position.

ADDITIONAL COMMENT

If a particular case is important, the chief judge will instruct the other judges to review the case. If a case is reviewed by the entire court, the phrase *reviewed by the court* is inserted immediately after the text of the majority opinion. A reviewed decision provides an opportunity for Tax Court judges to express their dissenting opinions.

Published Opinions and Citations. Regular Tax Court decisions are published by the U.S. Government Printing Office in a bound volume known as the *Tax Court of the United States Reports*. Soon after a decision is made public, Research Institute of America (RIA) and Commerce Clearing House (CCH) each publish the decision in its respective reporter of Tax Court decisions. An official citation to a Tax Court decision is as follows:[28]

MedChem Products, Inc., 116 T.C. 308 (2001).

The citation indicates that this case appears on page 308 in Volume 116 of *Tax Court of the United States Reports* and that the case was decided in 2001.

---

[26] Sec. 7463. The $50,000 amount includes penalties and additional taxes but excludes interest.

[27] Taxpayers also can represent themselves in regular Tax Court proceedings even though they are not attorneys. Where taxpayers represent themselves, the words *pro se* appear in the opinion after the taxpayer's name. The Tax Court is the only federal court before which non-attorneys, including CPAs, may practice.

[28] In a citation to a case decided by the Tax Court, only the name of the plaintiff (taxpayer) is listed. The defendant is understood to be the Commissioner of Internal Revenue whose name usually is not shown in the citation. In cases decided by other courts, the name of the plaintiff is listed first and the name of the defendant second. For non-Tax Court cases, the Commissioner of Internal Revenue is referred to as *CIR* in our footnotes and text.

From 1924 to 1942, regular decisions of the Board of Tax Appeals (predecessor of the Tax Court) were published by the U.S. Government Printing Office in the *United States Board of Tax Appeals Reports*. An example of a citation to a Board of Tax Appeals case is as follows:

J.W. Wells Lumber Co. Trust A., 44 B.T.A. 551 (1941).

This case is found in Volume 44 of the *United States Board of Tax Appeals Reports* on page 551. It is a 1941 decision.

ADDITIONAL COMMENT

Once the IRS has acquiesced in a federal court decision, other taxpayers generally will not need to litigate the same issue. However, the IRS can change its mind and revoke a previous acquiescence or nonacquiescence. References to acquiescences or nonacquiescences in federal court decisions can be found in the citators.

If the IRS has acquiesced or nonacquiesced in a federal court decision, the IRS's action should be denoted in the citation. At times, the IRS will not announce its acquiescence or nonacquiescence until several years after the date of the decision. An example of a citation to a decision in which the IRS has acquiesced is as follows:

Security State Bank, 111 T.C. 210 (1998), *acq.* 2001-1 C.B. xix.

The case appears on page 210 of Volume 111 of the *Tax Court of the United States Reports* and the acquiescence is reported on page xix of Volume 1 of the 2001 *Cumulative Bulletin*. In 2001, the IRS acquiesced in this 1998 decision. A citation to a decision in which the IRS has nonacquiesced is as follows:

Estate of Algerine Allen Smith, 108 T.C. 412 (1997), *nonacq.* 2000-1 C.B. xvi.

KEY POINT

To access all Tax Court cases, a tax advisor must refer to two different publications. The regular opinions appear in the *Tax Court of the United States Reports*, published by the U.S. Government Printing Office, and the memo decisions are published by both RIA (formerly PH) and CCH in their own court reporters.

The case appears on page 412 of Volume 108 of the *Tax Court of the United States Reports*. The nonacquiescence is reported on page xvi of Volume 1 of the 2000 *Cumulative Bulletin*. In 2000, the IRS nonacquiesced in this 1997 decision.

Tax Court memo decisions are not published by the U.S. Government Printing Office. They are, however, published by RIA in *RIA T.C. Memorandum Decisions* and by CCH in *CCH Tax Court Memorandum Decisions*. In addition, shortly after its issuance, an opinion is made available electronically and in loose-leaf form by RIA and CCH in their respective tax services. The following citation is to a Tax Court memo decision:

Edith G. McKinney, 1981 PH T.C. Memo ¶81,181 (T.C. Memo 1981-181), 41 TCM 1272.

ADDITIONAL COMMENT

In its Internet-based tax service (see Page C:1-26), RIA uses a different format for its Tax Court Memorandum Decisions, which in this textbook appear in parentheses after the "official" RIA citation.

McKinney is found at Paragraph 81,181 of Prentice Hall's (now RIA's)[29] 1981 *PH T.C. Memorandum Decisions* reporter, and in Volume 41, page 1272, of CCH's *Tax Court Memorandum Decisions*. The 181 in the PH citation indicates that the case is the Tax Court's 181st memo decision of the year. A more recent citation is formatted in the same way but refers to RIA memo decisions.

Paul F. Belloff, 1992 RIA T.C. Memo ¶92,346 (T.C. Memo 1992-346), 63 TCM 3150.

U.S. District Courts. Each state has at least one U.S. district court, and more populous states have more than one. Each district court is independent of the others and is thus free to issue its own decisions, subject to the precedential constraints discussed later in this chapter. Different types of cases—not just tax-related—are adjudicated in this forum. A district court is the only forum in which the taxpayer may have a jury decide questions of fact. Depending on the circumstances, a jury trial might be advantageous for the taxpayer.[30]

District court decisions are officially reported in the *Federal Supplement* (cited as F. Supp.) published by West®. Some decisions are not officially reported and are referred

[29] Several ownership changes have occurred for publishers of tax service materials. Thomson Reuters added the former Prentice Hall tax materials to the product line of its RIA tax publishing division. RIA and West® are members of Thomson Reuters, Tax and Accounting Division, and CCH is a member of the Wolters Kluwer Tax, Accounting and Legal Division.

[30] Taxpayers might prefer to have a jury trial if they believe a jury will be sympathetic to their case.

to as **unreported decisions**. Decisions by U.S. district courts on the topic of taxation also are published by RIA and CCH in secondary reporters that contain only tax-related opinions. RIA's reporter is *American Federal Tax Reports* (cited as AFTR).[31] CCH's reporter is *U.S. Tax Cases* (cited as USTC). A case not offically reported nevertheless might be published in the AFTR and USTC. An example of a complete citation to a U.S. district court decision is as follows:

> *Alfred Abdo, Jr. v. IRS,* 234 F. Supp. 2d 533, 90 AFTR 2d 2002-7484, 2003-1 USTC ¶50,107 (DC North Carolina, 2002).

ADDITIONAL COMMENT

A citation, at a minimum, should contain the following information: (1) the name of the case, (2) the reporter that publishes the case along with both a volume and page (or paragraph) number, (3) the year the case was decided, and (4) the court that decided the case.

In the example above, the **primary citation** is to the *Federal Supplement.* The case appears on page 533 of Volume 234 of the second series of this reporter. **Secondary citations** are to *American Federal Tax Reports* and *U.S. Tax Cases.* The same case is found in Volume 90 of the second series of the AFTR, page 2002-7484 (meaning page 7484 in the volume containing 2002 cases) and in Volume 1 of the 2003 USTC at Paragraph 50,107. The parenthetical information indicates that the case was decided in 2002 by the U.S. District Court for North Carolina. Because some judicial decisions have greater precedential weight than others (e.g., a Supreme Court decision versus a district court decision), information relating to the identity of the adjudicating court is useful in evaluating the authoritative value of the decision.

ADDITIONAL COMMENT

The U.S. Court of Federal Claims adjudicates claims (including suits to recover federal income taxes) against the U.S. Government. This court usually hears cases in Washington, D.C., but will hold sessions in other locations as the court deems necessary.

U.S. Court of Federal Claims. The U.S. Court of Federal Claims, another court of first instance that addresses tax matters, has nationwide jurisdiction. Originally, this court was called the U.S. Court of Claims (cited as Ct. Cl.), and its decisions were appealable to the U.S. Supreme Court only. In a reorganization, effective October 1, 1982, the reconstituted court was named the U.S. Claims Court (cited as Cl. Ct.), and its decisions became appealable to the Circuit Court of Appeals for the Federal Circuit. In October 1992, the court's name was again changed to the U.S. Court of Federal Claims (cited as Fed. Cl.).

Beginning in 1982, U.S. Claims Court decisions were reported officially in the *Claims Court Reporter,* published by West® from 1982 to 1992.[32] An example of a citation to a U.S. Claims Court decision appears below:

> *Benjamin Raphan v. U.S.,* 3 Cl. Ct. 457, 52 AFTR 2d 83-5987, 83-2 USTC ¶9613 (1983).

The *Raphan* case appears on page 457 of Volume 3 of the *Claims Court Reporter*. Secondary citations are to Volume 52, page 83-5987 of the AFTR, Second Series, and to Volume 2 of the 1983 USTC at Paragraph 9613.

Effective with the 1992 reorganization, decisions of the U.S. Court of Federal Claims are now reported in the *Federal Claims Reporter.* An example of a citation to an opinion published in this reporter is presented below:

> *Jeffrey G. Sharp v. U.S.,* 27 Fed. Cl. 52, 70 AFTR 2d 92-6040, 92-2 USTC ¶50,561 (1992).

The *Sharp* case appears on page 52 of Volume 27 of the *Federal Claims Reporter,* on page 6040 of the 70th volume of the AFTR, Second Series, and at Paragraph 50,561 of Volume 2 of the 1992 USTC reporter. Note that, even though the name of the reporter published by West® has changed, the volume numbers continue in sequence as if no name change had occurred.

---

[31] The *American Federal Tax Reports* (AFTR) is published in two series. The first series, which includes opinions issued up to 1957, is cited as AFTR. The second series, which includes opinions issued after 1957, is cited as AFTR 2d. The *Alfred Abdo, Jr.* decision cited as an illustration of a U.S. district court decision appears in the second *American Federal Tax Reports* series.

[32] Before the creation in 1982 of the U.S. Claims Court (and the *Claims Court Reporter*), the opinions of the U.S. Court of Claims were reported in either the *Federal Supplement* (F. Supp.) or the *Federal Reporter, Second Series* (F.2d). The *Federal Supplement* is the primary source of U.S. Court of Claims opinions from 1932 through January 19, 1960. Opinions issued from January 20, 1960, to October 1982 are reported in the *Federal Reporter, Second Series.*

Circuit Courts of Appeals. Lower court decisions are appealable by the losing party to the court of appeals for the circuit in which the litigation originated. Generally, if the case began in the Tax Court or a U.S. district court, the case is appealable to the circuit for the individual's residence as of the appeal date. For a corporation, the case is appealable to the circuit for the corporation's principal place of business. The Federal Circuit hears all appeals of cases originating in the U.S. Court of Federal Claims.

As mentioned earlier, there are 11 geographical circuits designated by numbers, the District of Columbia Circuit, and the Federal Circuit. In October 1981, the Eleventh Circuit was created by moving Alabama, Georgia, and Florida from the Fifth to a new geographical circuit. The Eleventh Circuit has adopted the policy of following as precedent all decisions of the Fifth Circuit during the time the states currently constituting the Eleventh Circuit were part of the Fifth Circuit.[33]

EXAMPLE C:1-7 ▶ In the current year, the Eleventh Circuit first considered an issue in a case involving a Florida taxpayer. In 1980, the Fifth Circuit had ruled on the same issue in a case involving a Louisiana taxpayer. Because Florida was part of the Fifth Circuit in 1980, under the policy adopted by the Eleventh Circuit, it will follow the Fifth Circuit's earlier decision. Had the Fifth Circuit's decision been rendered in 1982—after the creation of the Eleventh Circuit—the Eleventh Circuit would not have been bound by the Fifth Circuit's decision. ◀

As the later discussion of precedent points out, different circuits may reach different conclusions concerning similar facts and issues.

Circuit court decisions—regardless of topic (e.g., civil rights, securities law, and taxation)—are now reported officially in the *Federal Reporter, Third Series* (cited as F.3d), published by West®. The third series was created in October 1993 after the volume number for the second series reached 999. The primary citation to a circuit court opinion should be to the *Federal Reporter*. Tax decisions of the circuit courts also appear in the *American Federal Tax Reports* and *U.S. Tax Cases*. Below is an example of a citation to a 1994 circuit court decision:

> *Leonard Greene v. U.S.*, 13 F.3d 577, 73 AFTR 2d 94-746, 94-1 USTC ¶50,022 (2nd Cir., 1994).

The *Greene* case appears on page 577 of Volume 13 of the *Federal Reporter, Third Series*. It also is published in Volume 73, page 94-746 of the AFTR, Second Series, and in Volume 1, Paragraph 50,022, of the 1994 USTC. The parenthetical information indicates that the Second Circuit decided the case in 1994. (A *Federal Reporter, Second Series* reference is found in footnote 33 of this chapter.)

ADDITIONAL COMMENT

A judge is not required to follow judicial precedent beyond his or her jurisdiction. Thus, the Tax Court, the U.S. district courts, and the U.S. Court of Federal Claims are not required to follow the others' decisions, nor is a circuit court required to follow the decision of a different circuit court.

U.S. Supreme Court. Whichever party loses at the appellate level can request that the U.S. Supreme Court hear the case. The Supreme Court, however, hears very few tax cases. Unless the circuits are divided on the tax treatment of an item, or the issue is deemed to be of great significance, the Supreme Court probably will not hear the case.[34] Supreme Court decisions are the law of the land and take precedence over all other court decisions, including the Supreme Court's earlier decisions. As a practical matter, a Supreme Court interpretation of the IRC is almost as authoritative as an act of Congress. If Congress does not agree with the Court's interpretation, it can amend the IRC to achieve a different result and has in fact done so on a number of occasions. If the Supreme Court declares a tax statute to be unconstitutional, the statute is invalid.

All Supreme Court decisions, regardless of subject, are published in the *United States Supreme Court Reports* (cited as U.S.) by the U.S. Government Printing Office, the *Supreme Court Reporter* (cited as S. Ct.) by West®, and the *United States Reports, Lawyers' Edition* (cited as L. Ed.) by LexisNexis®. In addition, the AFTR and USTC

---

[33] *Bonner v. City of Prichard*, 661 F.2d 1206 (11th Cir., 1981).

[34] *Vogel Fertilizer Co. v. U.S.*, 49 AFTR 2d 82-491, 82-1 USTC ¶9134 (USSC, 1982), is an example of a case the Supreme Court heard to settle a split in judicial authority. The Fifth Circuit, the Tax Court, and the Court of Claims had reached one conclusion on an issue, while the Second, Fourth, and Eighth Circuits had reached another.

reporters published by RIA and CCH, respectively, contain Supreme Court decisions concerned with taxation. An example of a citation to a Supreme Court opinion appears below:

> *Boeing Company v. U.S.*, 537 U.S. 437, 91 AFTR 2d 2003-1088, 2003-1 USTC ¶50,273 (USSC, 2003).

According to the primary citation, this case appears in Volume 537, page 437, of the *United States Supreme Court Reports*. According to the secondary citation, it also appears in Volume 91, page 2003-1088, of the AFTR, Second Series, and in Volume 1, Paragraph 50,273, of the 2003 USTC.

Table C:1-3 provides a summary of how the IRC, court decisions, revenue rulings, revenue procedures, and other administrative pronouncements should be cited. Primary citations are to the reporters published by West® or the U.S. Government Printing Office, and secondary citations are to the AFTR and USTC.

SELF-STUDY QUESTION

Is it possible for the Tax Court to intentionally issue conflicting decisions?

ANSWER

Yes. If the Tax Court issues two decisions that are appealable to different circuit courts and these courts have previously reached different conclusions on the issue, the Tax Court follows the respective precedent in each circuit and issues conflicting decisions. This is a result of the *Golsen* Rule.

Precedential Value of Various Decisions.

Tax Court. The Tax Court is a court of national jurisdiction. Consequently, it generally rules uniformly for all taxpayers, regardless of their residence or place of business. It follows U.S. Supreme Court decisions and its own earlier decisions. It is not bound by cases decided by the U.S. Court of Federal Claims or a U.S. district court, even if the district court has jurisdiction over the taxpayer.

In 1970, the Tax Court adopted what is known as the *Golsen* Rule.[35] Under this rule, the Tax Court departs from its general policy of adjudicating uniformly for all taxpayers and instead follows the decisions of the court of appeals to which the case in question is appealable. Stated differently, the *Golsen* Rule mandates that the Tax Court rule consistently with decisions of the court for the circuit where the taxpayer resides or does business.

EXAMPLE C:1-8 ► In the year in which an issue was first litigated, the Tax Court decided that an expenditure was deductible. The government appealed the decision to the Tenth Circuit Court of Appeals and won a reversal. This is the only appellate decision regarding the issue. If and when the Tax Court addresses this issue again, it will hold, with one exception, that the expenditure is deductible. The exception applies to taxpayers in the Tenth Circuit. Under the *Golsen* Rule, these taxpayers will be denied the deduction. ◄

U.S. District Court. Because each U.S. district court is independent of the other district courts, the decisions of each have precedential value only within its own jurisdiction (i.e., only with respect to subsequent cases brought before that court). District courts must follow decisions of the U.S. Supreme Court, the circuit court to which the case is appealable, and the district court's own earlier decisions regarding similar facts and issues.

EXAMPLE C:1-9 ► The U.S. District Court for Rhode Island, the Tax Court, and the Eleventh Circuit have decided cases involving similar facts and issues. Any U.S. district court within the Eleventh Circuit must follow that circuit's decision in future cases involving similar facts and issues. Likewise, the U.S. District Court for Rhode Island must decide such cases consistently with its previous decision. Tax Court decisions are not binding on the district courts. Thus, all district courts other than the one for Rhode Island and those within the Eleventh Circuit are free to decide such cases independently. ◄

U.S. Court of Federal Claims. In adjudicating a case, the U.S. Court of Federal Claims must rule consistently with U.S. Supreme Court decisions, decisions of the Circuit Court of Appeals for the Federal Circuit, and its own earlier decisions, including those rendered when the court had a different name. It need not follow decisions of other circuit courts, the Tax Court, or U.S. district courts.

[35] The *Golsen* Rule is based on the decision in *Jack E. Golsen*, 54 T.C. 742 (1970).

▼ **TABLE C:1-3**

Summary of Tax-related Primary Sources—Statutory and Administrative

Source Name	Publisher	Materials Provided	Citation Example
U.S. Code, Title 26	Government Printing Office	Internal Revenue Code	Sec. 441(b)
Code of Federal Regulations, Title 26	Government Printing Office	Treasury Regulations (final)	Reg. Sec. 1.461-1(c)
		Treasury Regulations (temporary)	Temp. Reg. Sec. 1.62-1T(e)
Internal Revenue Bulletin	Government Printing Office	Treasury Regulations (proposed)	Prop. Reg. Sec. 1.671-1(h)
		Treasury decisions	T.D. 8756 (January 13, 1998)
		Revenue rulings	Rev. Rul. 2009-33, 2009-40 I.R.B. 447
		Revenue procedures	Rev. Proc. 2009-52, 2009-49 I.R.B. 744
		Committee reports	S.Rept. No. 105-33, 105th Cong., 1st Sess., p. 308 (1997)
		Public laws	P.L. 105-34, Sec. 224(a), enacted August 6, 1997
		Announcements	Announcement 2007-3, 2007-4 I.R.B. 376
		Notices	Notice 2009-21, 2009-13 I.R.B. 724
Cumulative Bulletin	Government Printing Office	Treasury Regulations (proposed)	Prop. Reg. Sec. 1.671-1(h)
		Treasury decisions	T.D. 8756 (January 12, 1998)
		Revenue rulings	Rev. Rul. 84-111, 1984-2 C.B. 88
		Revenue procedures	Rev. Proc. 77-28, 1977-2 C.B. 537
		Committee reports	S.Rept. No. 105-33, 105th Cong., 1st Sess., p. 308 (1997)
		Public laws	P.L. 105-34, Sec. 224(a), enacted August 6, 1997
		Announcements	Announcement 2006-8, 2006-1 C.B. 344
		Notices	Notice 88-74, 1988-2 C.B. 385

Summary of Tax-related Primary and Secondary Sources—Judicial

Reporter Name	Publisher	Decisions Published	Citation Example
U.S. Supreme Court Reports	Government Printing Office	U.S. Supreme Court	*Boeing Company v. U.S.*, 537 U.S. 437 (2003)
Supreme Court Reports	Thomson Reuters/West	U.S. Supreme Court	*Boeing Company v. U.S.*, 123 S. Ct. 1099 (2003)
Federal Reporter (1st–3rd Series)	Thomson Reuters/West	U.S. Court of Appeal Pre-1982 Court of Claims	*Leonard Greene v. U.S.*, 13 F.3d 577 (2nd Cir., 1994)
Federal Supplement Series	Thomson Reuters/West	U.S. District Court	*Alfred Abdo, Jr. v. IRS*, 234 F. Supp. 2d 553 (DC North Carolina, 2002)
U.S. Court of Federal Claims	Thomson Reuters/West	Court of Federal Claims	*Jeffery G. Sharp v. U.S.*, 27 Fed. Cl. 52 (1992)
Tax Court of the U.S. Reports	Government Printing Office	U.S. Tax Court regular	*Security State Bank*, 111 T.C. 210 (1998), acq. 2001-1 C.B. xix
Tax Court Memorandum Decisions	Wolters Kluwer/CCH	U.S. Tax Court memo	*Paul F. Belloff*, 63 TCM 3150 (1992)
RIA Tax Court Memorandum Decisions	Thomson Reuters/RIA	U.S. Tax Court memo	*Paul F. Belloff*, 1992 RIA T.C. Memo ¶92,346 (T.C. Memo 1992-346)
American Federal Tax Reports	Thomson Reuters/RIA	Tax: all federal courts except Tax Court	*Boeing Company v. U.S.*, 91 AFTR 2d 2003-1 (USSC, 2003)
U.S. Tax Cases	Wolters Kluwer/CCH	Tax: all federal courts except Tax Court	*Ruddick Corp. v. U.S.*, 81-1 USTC ¶9343 (Ct. Cls., 1981)

EXAMPLE C:1-10 ▶ Assume the same facts as in Example C:1-9. In a later year, a case involving similar facts and issues is heard by the U.S. Court of Federal Claims. This court is not bound by precedents set by any of the other courts. Thus, it may reach a conclusion independently of the other courts. ◀

Circuit Courts of Appeals. A circuit court is bound by U.S. Supreme Court decisions and its own earlier decisions. If neither the Supreme Court nor the circuit in question has already decided an issue, the circuit court has no precedent that it must follow, regardless of whether other circuits have ruled on the issue. In such circumstances, the circuit court is said to be writing on a clean slate. In rendering a decision, the judges of that court may adopt another circuit's view, which they are likely to regard as relevant.

EXAMPLE C:1-11 ▶ Assume the same facts as in Example C:1-9. Any circuit other than the Eleventh would be writing on a clean slate if it adjudicated a case involving similar facts and issues. After reviewing the Eleventh Circuit's decision, another circuit might find it relevant and rule in the same way. ◀

In such a case of "first impression," when the court has had no precedent on which to base a decision, a tax practitioner might look at past opinions of the court to see which other judicial authority the court has found to be "persuasive."

Forum Shopping. Not surprisingly, courts often disagree on the tax treatment of the same item. This disagreement gives rise to differing precedents within the various jurisdictions (what is called a "split in judicial authority"). Because taxpayers have the flexibility of choosing where to file a lawsuit, these circumstances afford them the opportunity to **forum shop.** Forum shopping involves choosing where among the courts to file a lawsuit based on differing precedents.

An example of a split in judicial authority concerned the issue of when it became too late for the IRS to question the tax treatment of items that "flowed through" an S corporation's return to a shareholder's return. The key question was this: if the time for assessing a deficiency (limitations period) with respect to the corporation's, but not the shareholder's, return had expired, was the IRS precluded from collecting additional taxes from the shareholder? In *Kelley,*[36] the Ninth Circuit Court of Appeals ruled that the IRS would be barred from collecting additional taxes from the shareholder if the limitations period for the *S corporation's* return had expired. In *Bufferd,*[37] *Fehlhaber,*[38] and *Green,*[39] three other circuit courts ruled that the IRS would be barred from collecting additional taxes from the shareholder if the limitations period for the *shareholder's* return had expired. The Supreme Court affirmed the *Bufferd* decision,[40] establishing that the statute of limitations for the shareholder's return governed. This action brought about certainty and uniformity within the judicial system.

Dictum. At times, a court may comment on an issue or a set of facts not central to the case under review. A court's remark not essential to the determination of a disputed issue, and therefore not binding authority, is called *dictum.* An example of dictum is found in *Central Illinois Public Service Co.*[41] In this case, the U.S. Supreme Court addressed whether lunch reimbursements received by employees constitute wages subject to withholding. Justice Blackman remarked in passing that earnings in the form of interest, rents, and dividends are not wages. This remark is dictum because it is not essential to the determination of whether lunch reimbursements are wages subject to withholding. Although not authoritative, dictum may be cited by taxpayers to bolster an argument in favor of a particular tax result.

---

[36] *Daniel M. Kelley v. CIR,* 64 AFTR 2d 89-5025, 89-1 USTC ¶9360 (9th Cir., 1989).

[37] *Sheldon B. Bufferd v. CIR,* 69 AFTR 2d 92-465, 92-1 USTC ¶50,031 (2nd Cir., 1992).

[38] *Robert Fehlhaber v. CIR,* 69 AFTR 2d 92-850, 92-1 USTC ¶50,131 (11th Cir., 1992).

[39] *Charles T. Green v. CIR,* 70 AFTR 2d 92-5077, 92-2 USTC ¶50,340 (5th Cir., 1992).

[40] *Sheldon B. Bufferd v. CIR,* 71 AFTR 2d 93-573, 93-1 USTC ¶50,038 (USSC, 1993).

[41] *Central Illinois Public Service Co. v. CIR,* 41 AFTR 2d 78-718, 78-1 USTC ¶9254 (USSC, 1978).

STOP & THINK *Question:* You have been researching whether an amount received by your new client can be excluded from her gross income. The IRS is auditing the client's prior year tax return, which another firm prepared. In a similar case decided a few years ago, the Tax Court allowed an exclusion, but the IRS nonacquiesced in the decision. The case involved a taxpayer in the Fourth Circuit. Your client is a resident of Maine, which is in the First Circuit. Twelve years ago, in a case involving another taxpayer, the federal court for the client's district ruled that this type of receipt is not excludable. No other precedent exists. To sustain an exclusion, must your client litigate? Explain. If your client litigates, in which court of first instance should she begin her litigation?

Solution: Because of its nonacquiescence, the IRS is likely to challenge your client's tax treatment. Thus, she may be compelled to litigate. She would not want to litigate in her U.S. district court because it would be bound by its earlier decision, which is unfavorable to taxpayers generally. A good place to begin would be the Tax Court because it is bound by appellate court, but not district court, decisions and because of its earlier pro-taxpayer position. No one can predict how the U.S. Court of Federal Claims would rule because no precedent that it must follow exists.

ADDITIONAL COMMENT

A tax treaty carries the same authoritative weight as a federal statute (IRC). A tax advisor should be aware of provisions in tax treaties that will affect a taxpayer's worldwide tax liability.

TAX TREATIES

The United States has concluded **tax treaties** with numerous foreign countries. These treaties address the alleviation of double taxation and other matters. A tax advisor exploring the U.S. tax consequences of a U.S. corporation's operations in another country should determine whether a treaty between that country and the United States exists. If one does, the tax advisor should ascertain the applicable provisions of the treaty. (See Chapter C:16 of this text for a more extensive discussion of treaties.)

KEY POINT

Tax articles can be used to help *find* answers to tax questions. Where possible, the underlying statutory, administrative, or judicial sources referenced in the tax article should be cited as authority and not the author of the article. The courts and the IRS will place little, if any, reliance on mere editorial opinion.

TAX PERIODICALS

Tax periodicals assist the researcher in tracing the development of, and analyzing tax law. These periodicals are especially useful when they discuss the legislative history of a recently enacted IRC statute that has little or no administrative or judicial authority on point.

Tax experts write articles on landmark court decisions, proposed regulations, new tax legislation, and other matters. Frequently, those who write articles of a highly technical nature are attorneys, accountants, or professors. Among the periodicals that provide in-depth coverage of tax-related matters are the following:

The Journal of Taxation
The Tax Adviser
Practical Tax Strategies
Taxes—The Tax Magazine
Tax Law Review
Tax Notes
Corporate Taxation
Business Entities
Real Estate Taxation
Estate Planning

The first six journals are generalized; that is, they deal with a variety of topics. As their titles suggest, the next four are specialized; they deal with specific subjects. All these publications (other than *Tax Notes,* which is published weekly) are published either monthly or quarterly. Daily newsletters, such as the *Daily Tax Report,* published by Bloomberg BNA in print and electronic formats, are used by tax professionals when they need updates more timely than can be provided by monthly or quarterly publications.

Tax periodicals and tax services are secondary authorities. The IRC, Treasury Regulations, IRS pronouncements, and court opinions are primary authorities. In presenting research results, the tax advisor should always cite primary authorities.

Tax Services

OBJECTIVE 5

Consult tax services to research an issue

Various publishers provide multivolume commentaries on the tax law in what are familiarly referred to as **tax services.** Researchers often consult tax services at the beginning of the research process because a tax service helps identify the tax authorities pertaining to a particular tax issue. The actual tax authorities (e.g., IRC, Treasury Regulations, IRS pronouncements, and court cases), and not the tax services, are generally cited as support for a particular tax position. The services are available in print form via the publishers and electronic form via the Internet. (See further discussion at "The Internet as a Research Tool" later in this chapter). Although each major tax service is an outstanding resource, significant differences exist in the content and organizational scheme from one publisher to the next. For example, each service has its own special features and editorial approach to tax issues along with a great deal of proprietary content. The best way to acquaint oneself with the various tax services and the advantages and disadvantages of each is to use them in researching hypothetical or actual problems.

Organizationally, tax services fall into two types: annotated and topical (although this distinction has become somewhat blurred in the Internet version of these services). An **annotated tax service** is organized by IRC section. The IRC-arranged subdivisions of this service are likely to encompass several topics. The annotations accompany editorial commentaries and include digests or summaries of IRS pronouncements and court opinions that interpret a particular IRC section. They are classified by subtopic and cite pertinent primary authorities. A **topical tax service**, on the other hand, is organized by broad topic, including income taxes, estate and gift taxes, and excise taxes. The topically arranged subdivisions of this service are likely to encompass several IRC sections.

Annotated tax services include the *United States Tax Reporter* and the *Standard Federal Income Tax Reporter* services, both of which are organized by IRC section. Many tax advisors find these reporters easy to use because of their extensive indexing system. Topical tax services include RIA's *Federal Tax Coordinator 2d* and Bloomberg BNA's *Tax Management Portfolios. Tax Management Portfolios* are popular with many tax advisors because they are very readable yet still provide a comprehensive discussion of a broad range of tax issues. Each portfolio (e.g., Passive Loss Rules, Portfolio 549) covers a particular topic in great detail. However, because the published portfolios do not cover all areas of the tax law, another service may be necessary to supplement the gaps in a portfolio's coverage. Table C:1-4 summarizes the organization and key features of the major tax services.

▼ TABLE C:1-4
Summary of Key Features of Tax Services

Name	Publisher	Organization	Key Features
United States Tax Reporter	Thomson Reuters/RIA	IRC section number	• Editorial commentary • Index and findings list • Annotations
Standard Federal Income Tax Reporter	Wolters Kluwer/CCH	IRC section number	• Editorial commentary • Index and findings list • Annotations
Federal Tax Coordinator 2d	Thomson Reuters/RIA	Tax topic (income tax by topic, estate and gift taxes, excise taxes)	• Commentary organized by topic with references to primary authority and tabbed access to IRC and Treasury Regulations.
Tax Management Portfolios	Bloomberg BNA	U.S. income, foreign income, state tax, estate and gift tax	• Over 400 specialized booklets with extensive commentary by topic, heavily footnoted and referenced to primary authority.

THE INTERNET AS A RESEARCH TOOL

OBJECTIVE 6

Apply the basics of Internet-based tax research

Internet databases are rapidly replacing print-based services as the principal source of tax related information. These databases encompass not only the IRC, Treasury Regulations, court cases, state laws, and other primary authorities, but also citators and secondary sources such as tax service reporters, treatises, journals, and newsletters. The principal advantages of using Internet-based tax services are ease and speed of access. These services eliminate the need for searching through several volumes of text, the need for consulting numerous cumulative supplements, and the time required to regularly update a print-based library. In addition, Internet based research tools put a vast amount of information in the hands of a tax practitioner without the cost and space requirements of a well equipped print-based tax library.

ADDITIONAL COMMENT

To apply the online research tools discussed in this chapter, textbook users must have access to the described Internet-based tax services at their institution.

Because of these advantages, the Internet has become the principal medium for conveying tax related information to professionals. The most widely used Internet-based research services are RIA's Checkpoint™ (hereafter CHECKPOINT), accessible at *checkpoint.riag.com*, and CCH IntelliConnect™ (hereafter INTELLICONNECT), accessible at *intelliconnect.cch.com*. Westlaw®[42] and LexisNexus are online legal research services that are predominately used by legal professionals.[43] This chapter limits its discussion to CHECKPOINT and INTELLICONNECT. Both subscription-based services are updated continuously and store information in databases, called libraries, principal among which are the following:[44]

CHECKPOINT	*INTELLICONNECT*
Newsstand	Tax News, Journals, and Newsletters
Federal	Federal Tax
State and Local	State Tax
International	International Tax
Estate Planning	Financial and Estate Planning
Pension and Benefits	Pension
Payroll	Payroll

Newsstand on CHECKPOINT and *Tax News, Journals, and Newsletters* on INTELLICONNECT provide daily updates on recent tax developments. The *Federal* library on both series contains the text of the IRC, Treasury Regulations, IRS pronouncements, court opinions, and other primary sources. In addition to primary sources, the *Federal* library on CHECKPOINT contains the RIA citator, *Federal Tax Coordinator 2d*, and *United States Tax Reporter* annotations and explanations. The *Federal* library on INTELLICONNECT contains the *Standard Federal Income Tax Reporter* and the *Standard Federal Income Tax Reporter Explanations*. Tax reporters for all 50 states as well as multistate tax guides are found in the *State and Local* library on CHECKPOINT and the *State Tax* library on INTELLICONNECT. International tax treaties are found in the *International* library of both services. CHECKPOINT's *Estate Planning* offers the text of estate tax treaties, newsletters, journals, and Warren, Gorham & Lamont tax treatises. INTELLICONNECT's *Financial and Estate Planning* library supplies the *Federal Estate and Gift Tax Reporter*, as well as the text of estate and gift tax statutes, cases, and rulings. Finally, *Pension and Benefits* on CHECKPOINT and *Pension* on INTELLICONNECT contain the text of the Employee Retirement Income Security Act (ERISA), related Treasury Regulations, and Congressional committee reports, while *Payroll* provides the text of state and federal employment regulations and current withholding tables.

[42] Westlaw® is owned by Thomson Reuters.

[43] The research products discussed in this section (e.g., CHECKPOINT, INTELLICONNECT, Westlaw®, and LexisNexus) generally are available only to paid subscribers.

[44] INTELLICONNECT has numerous other databases, including Accounting and Audit, Banking, Corporate Government, Energy & Natural Resources, Health Care Compliance and Reimbursement. These specialty areas generally fall outside the tax arena and therefore are not described in this chapter.

CHECKPOINT and INTELLICONNECT libraries and databases can be searched in four basic ways:

- By keyword
- By index
- By citation
- By content

EXAMPLE C:1-12 ▶ Rhonda Researcher's client is a real estate developer and wants to exchange an office building for a residential condominium in the same town. The client wants to know if he can structure the transaction in a tax advantaged way. Rhonda immediately recognizes the situation as a potential like-kind exchange of real property. Therefore, she undertakes a keyword search of INTELLICONNECT using the term *like kind exchange* to quickly uncover potentially applicable documents. She also knows that Sec. 1031 is the relevant IRC section and can search the IRC or Treasury Regulations by citation. On the other hand, if she were unfamiliar with the topic, she could employ several other options. For example, INTELLICONNECT's Federal Tax editorial content has a heading for Standard Federal Tax Reporter topical index. The "Exchange of property" term in the topical index directs Rhonda to "See Like-kind Exchanges; Sales and Exchanges; and Tax-free Exchanges." The index entries under these headings direct Rhonda to a number of entries potentially applicable to the transaction. Rhonda also conducts a similar research procedure on CHECKPOINT to see whether this alternative service provides any additional information. In particular, she searches in the *Federal Tax Coordinator 2d,* which is RIA's topical service. ◄

KEY WORD SEARCHES

Searching CHECKPOINT and INTELLICONNECT by keyword is relatively simple, particularly if the researcher is familiar with the Internet. The first step is to activate a database or multiple databases, perform an initial keyword search, and refine the results after the initial query. The researcher can choose to search across any combination of the available databases. The CHECKPOINT Federal databases include primary sources such as the Internal Revenue Code, Treasury Regulations, and Federal Tax Cases along with editorial databases such as RIA's *Federal Tax Coordinator 2d*. Similar choices exist for INTELLICONNECT. Deciding which database to include in the search depends partly on the expected complexity of the research question and on the researcher's familiarity with the topic.

The search engines within the services look for the terms selected and many variations of the terms. For example, the search for *auto* will return documents with auto, car, automobile, motor vehicle, passenger vehicle, sedan, and others.[45] Searches will include both singular and plural variations. Any document with the term or terms is returned and ranked by best match according to the search. If two terms are used, the best matches generally are documents where the terms are close together. Picking key words and search terms is critical to success. The search must be broad enough to include relevant documents but not so broad to include hundreds or thousands of documents unlikely to be on point.

For example, if the researcher selects only the INTELLICONNECT Cases database, the term *property exchange* returns thousands of results that have both the words *property* and *exchange* somewhere in the document. Clearly this outcome is too broad for a researcher just beginning his or her research. Fortunately, several methods of narrowing the search exist. For example, the search for *property exchange* can be limited to all terms, any terms, near phrase, or exact phrase. Specifically, the keyword search "property exchange" that uses quotation marks around the search phrase will return documents only with that exact phrase. Thus, quotation marks should be used sparingly and only when the researcher knows the precise phrase. Using Boolean connectors is helpful as well. These connectors force the search engine to narrow the search based on the parameters set. Table C:1-5 provides a partial list of connectors available in CHECKPOINT and INTELLICONNECT.

Another way to narrow a search is to focus on terms unique to the research question at hand. The goal is to identify tax related terms likely to appear only in relevant tax

[45] Both CHECKPOINT and INTELLICONNECT provide a thesaurus tool, which can identify synonyms and suggest alternative terms related to search terms used by the researcher. The search engine automatically searches for synonyms unless the researcher restricts the search to specific terms using Boolean connectors or quotation marks. For example, a search for the specific phrase "automobile depreciation" will not return documents that refer to *auto*, *car*, or *vehicle*.

▼ **TABLE C:1-5**
Connectors Used in INTELLICONNECT and CHECKPOINT

INTELLICONNECT	CHECKPOINT	Description	Examples
and	&, and	Retrieves documents with both terms.	INTELLICONNECT: property and exchange CHECKPOINT: property & exchange
or	|, or	Retrieves documents with either term.	INTELLICONNECT: property or exchange CHECKPOINT: property | exchange
not	^, not	Retrieves documents with one term but not the other.	INTELLICONNECT: property not exchange CHECKPOINT: property ^ exchange
w/n	/n	Retrieves documents in which the first term is separated from the second term by no more than n number of words.	INTELLICONNECT: property w/5 exchange CHECKPOINT: property /5 exchange Locates property within 5 words of exchange
w/sen	/s	Retrieves documents that contain the first term within 20 words of the second term (or within the same sentence for RIA).	INTELLICONNECT: property w/sen exchange CHECKPOINT: property /s exchange
w/par	/p	Retrieves documents that contain the first term within 80 words of the second term (or within the same paragraph for RIA).	INTELLICONNECT: property w/par exchange CHECKPOINT: property /p exchange
" "	" "	Exact phrase.	INTELLICONNECT and CHECKPOINT: "property exchange"
*	*	Keyword variation.	Deprecia* returns depreciation, depreciate, depreciated, depreciating
?	?	Keyword variation.	Advis?r returns advisor and adviser

authorities. For example, stamps are a type of collectible, but the term also will appear in documents discussing taxation of distilled spirits, food stamps, and store stamps and coupons. The researcher should begin the search with limiting terms such as *collectible* rather than the broader term *stamps*. Also, researchers with a good working knowledge of the IRC quickly learn that using IRC sections in search terms is a great way to obtain relevant documents.

Searching using key words is a skill that improves with practice. Researchers becoming familiar with using the databases will learn to craft search terms that include the most relevant elements of the question at hand. Once the researcher finds a document on point, the information within that document often can be used to narrow future searches. The search can be repeated by adding terms, or the documents returned originally can be searched using a new set of terms. Also, the "search within results" feature offered by both CHECKPOINT and INTELLICONNECT is helpful when the search returns too many documents. However, if searches by key word search do not return the desired results, other options exist.

SEARCH BY INDEX

Both CHECKPOINT and INTELLICONNECT offer traditional indexes. With INTELLICONNECT, the user can click on most databases to see an index of the contents. For example, clicking on the *Standard Federal Income Tax Reporter* Topical Index listed in the Federal Tax Editorial content database reveals a list from A to Z, and the researcher can easily click on a hyperlink for any letter and scroll through the alphabetized topics list. As an example, one can find the letter C, then scroll through the screens and find the topic "casualty losses" that directs the researcher to a variety of subheadings. CHECKPOINT has an Indexes option under the GO TO area of the Search tab. In CHECKPOINT, the researcher can choose the *Federal Tax Coordinator 2d* Topic Index database. Again, the researcher will find the letter C and scroll through the topics to find "casualty losses," which leads the researcher to subheadings with hyperlinks to CHECKPOINT's editorial materials.

In addition, both INTELLICONNECT and CHECKPOINT have topical indexes that use hyperlinks to the Internal Revenue Code. In INTELLICONNECT, the researcher begins with the Topical Index option located under Federal Tax Primary Sources, selects the Current Internal Revenue Code Topical Index, and begins his or her research with an A to Z list. In CHECKPOINT, the researcher selects the Current Code Topic Index located in the Indexes link on the Search tab.

SEARCH BY CITATION

Often the desired document is a specific IRC section, Treasury Regulation, court case, IRS pronouncement, or other document. If so, both services offer searches by specific citation. Researchers must be careful to use exact citations using this tool because close matches will not return the desired document.

Both CHECKPOINT and INTELLICONNECT citation search tools provide dedicated boxes in which to type the specific type of document requested. For example, to search for IRC Sec. 267, the researcher simply types 267 in the box labeled Current Code in CHECKPOINT under the "Find by Citation" link, or IRC Code & Hist. Sec. in INTELLICONNECT under the "Citations" link. Specific boxes also exist for various court decisions, revenue rulings, revenue procedures, and other IRS pronouncements.

SEARCH BY CONTENT

Each database also can be searched by content. Clicking on the hyperlink for each database will return a table of contents. Clicking through an entry will take the researcher further into the table of contents. For example, in INTELLICONNECT, several documents discussing adoption credits can be located by clicking on the following series of hyperlinks:

- Federal Tax
  - Federal Tax Editorial Content
    - Standard Federal Tax Reporter
      - Credits
        - Adoption expenses – Sec. 23

CHECKPOINT also has a Table of Contents tab. Documents discussing adoption credits may be found by clicking on the following series of hyperlinks:

- Federal Library
  - Federal Editorial Materials
    - Federal Tax Coordinator 2d
      - Chapter A Individuals and Self-Employment Tax
        - A-4400 Adoption Expense Credit

NONCOMMERCIAL INTERNET SERVICES

Many noncommercial institutions, such as governments and universities, allow access to their tax-related databases via the Internet. In "tax-surfing" the Internet, the researcher might first visit the IRS site located at *www.irs.gov*. Although oriented to the layman, this site contains a wealth of information useful to the tax professional. Such information includes guidelines for electronic filing, IRS forms and instructions, the full text of Treasury Regulations, and recent issues of the *Internal Revenue Bulletin*. Other useful sites include those maintained by the Library of Congress at *www.loc.gov* and the U.S. Government Printing Office Federal Digital System at *www.gpo.gov/fdsys/*. From these sites, the researcher can retrieve the text of recent court opinions, tax legislation, committee reports, state and federal tax laws, and much more.

An excellent gateway for starting tax related research is the Tax, Accounting, and Payroll Sites Directory at *www.taxsites.com*, maintained by AccountantsWorld,

LLC. This site provides hundreds of hyperlinks to federal, state, and international tax law and tax form databases. Instrumental in financial accounting searches is the Electronic Data Gathering, Analysis, and Retrieval (EDGAR) site at *www.sec.gov/edgar.shtml*. EDGAR is a document filing and retrieval service sponsored by the U.S. Securities and Exchange Commission (SEC). It provides access to the full text of documents filed with the SEC by publicly traded companies. These documents include annual financial statements on Form 10-K, quarterly financial statements on Form 10-Q, proxy statements, and prospectuses. The EDGAR database extends from January 1994 to the present and is accessible by company name, central index key, document file number, and keyword.

Citators

OBJECTIVE 7

Use a citator to assess tax authorities

Citators serve two functions. First, they trace the judicial history of a particular case (e.g., if the case under analysis is an appeals court decision, the citator indicates the lower court that heard the case and whether the Supreme Court reviewed the case). Second, they list other authorities (e.g., cases and IRS pronouncements) that cite the case or authority in question. These listed authorities are called *citing cases* or *citing rulings*. The judicial history also indicates whether the case is affirmed, reversed or remanded.[46]

Because tax law relies heavily on precedent, the citator provides an index of citing cases and rulings that help the researcher determine the strength of the case or ruling he or she is evaluating. The citator gives full citations for the citing case and lists where the citing cases can be found. It is important to note that the same case may have as many as three decisions (i.e., lower court, court of appeals, and Supreme Court) with each listing having its own list of citing cases. Therefore, if a citing case cites only the Supreme Court decision, the citator will list it only under the Supreme Court cite.

Two principal tax related commercial citators are those in INTELLICONNECT and CHECKPOINT. Both citators allow the researcher to enter case names or case citations. The discussion in this section focuses on the electronic version of the citators, although both CCH and RIA offer print versions as well.

The INTELLICONNECT citator analyzes every decision reported in the *Standard Federal Income Tax Reporter*, the *Excise Tax Reporter*, and the *Federal Estate and Gift Tax Reporter* and selectively lists cases that cite the decision under analysis. INTELLICONNECT lists only the citing cases that its editors believe will influence the precedential weight of the decision under analysis.

The CHECKPOINT citator also provides the history of each authority and lists the cases and pronouncements that have cited the authority. This citator, however, differs from the INTELLICONNECT citator in a couple of important ways. First, CHECKPOINT lists all citing cases, and not just those that the editors believe will serve as relevant precedent. Second, the CHECKPOINT citator provides additional information about the citing case, showing whether the citing authorities comment favorably or unfavorably on the cited case or whether they can be distinguished from the cited case.[47]

In addition to tax cases, the CHECKPOINT and INTELLICONNECT citators evaluate revenue rulings and other IRS pronouncements and lists any status changes. Before relying on a revenue ruling or pronouncement, a researcher must confirm that the pronouncement reflects the current position of the IRS. For example, a revoked ruling is

[46] If a case is *affirmed*, the decision of the lower court is upheld. *Reversed* means the higher court invalidated the decision of the lower court because it reached a conclusion different from that derived by the lower court. *Remanded* signifies that the higher court sent the case back to the lower court with instructions to address matters consistent with the higher court's ruling.

[47] When a court distinguishes the facts of one case from those of an earlier case, it suggests that its departure from the earlier decision is justified because the facts of the two cases are different.

▼ **TABLE C:1-6**
Terms to Describe Status Changes to IRS Rulings

Term	Description of Term
Amplified	No change in the prior published position has occurred, but the prior position is extended to cover a variation of the fact situation previously addressed.
Clarified	Language used in a prior published position is being made clear because the previous language has caused or could cause confusion.
Distinguished	The ruling mentions a prior ruling but points out an essential difference between the two rulings.
Modified	The substance of a previously published ruling is being changed, but the prior ruling remains in effect.
Obsoleted	A previously published ruling is no longer determinative with respect to future transactions, e.g., because laws or regulations have changed, or the substance of the ruling has been adopted into regulations.
Revoked	A previously published ruling has been determined to be incorrect, and the correct position is being stated in the new ruling.
Superseded	The new ruling merely restates the substance of a previously published ruling or series of rulings.
Supplemented	The ruling expands a previous ruling, e.g., by adding items to a list.
Suspended	The previously published ruling will not be applied pending some future action, such as the issuance of new or amended regulations.

Source: www.irs.gov.

one in which the ruling is no longer correct and the correct position is being stated in the new ruling. The IRS does not remove the old ruling from the *Internal Revenue Bulletin* or *Cumulative Bulletin*, but the old ruling does not have authority regarding a transaction occurring after the revocation. Thus, failure to confirm its status could result in an incorrect conclusion. Table C:1-6 provides a list of terms the IRS uses to describe changes in the status of a ruling.

USING THE CITATOR

Internet-based versions of the citators are easier to use than print-based citators. For example, assume the researcher is currently reading *Leonarda C. Diaz v. Commissioner of Internal Revenue*, 70 TC 1067 (1978). Using INTELLICONNECT, the researcher can click on the Citator button in the left column at the top left of the page, and the service opens up a new tab with a summary of activity of the case. The information in bold print with bullets to the left denotes that the *Diaz* case was first decided by the Tax Court (i.e., TC), and then by the Second Circuit Court of Appeals (i.e., CA-2). It shows that the Second Circuit affirmed (upheld) the Tax Court's decision. The four cases underneath the Second Circuit decision cite the *Diaz* decision and might be useful for the researcher to better understand the impact of the case. The seven cases listed beneath the Tax Court decision cite the Tax Court's opinion.

The CHECKPOINT citator is similarly easy to use. Once again, if the researcher is reading the *Diaz* case, he or she simply clicks on the Citator button at the top of the case window. The two main decisions (Tax Court and Second Circuit) appear in a list. Clicking on either case brings up the court decisions that have cited the *Diaz* decision. CHECKPOINT sometimes lists more cases than does INTELLICONNECT. In this example, CHECKPOINT lists 11 cases that have cited the *Diaz* Second Circuit decision and 26 cases that have cited the Tax Court decision. CHECKPOINT also adds a brief description of the type of citation—cited favorably, cited unfavorable, case distinguished, or reasoning followed.

Professional Guidelines for Tax Services

Objective 8

Describe the professional guidelines that CPAs in tax practice should follow

Professional guidelines for tax services are contained in both government-imposed and professional-imposed tax standards. The following sections briefly describe two types of guidelines—Treasury Department ***Circular 230*** (Rev. 8-2011) and the American Institute of Certified Public Accountants (AICPA) ***Statements on Standards for Tax Services (SSTSs)***. A fuller discussion of these standards appears in Chapter C:15.

TREASURY DEPARTMENT *CIRCULAR 230*

Circular 230 sets forth rules to practice before the Internal Revenue Service and pertains to certified public accountants, attorneys, enrolled agents, and other persons representing taxpayers before the IRS. It presents the duties and restrictions relating to such practice and prescribes sanctions and disciplinary proceedings for violating these regulations.

Circular 230 rules, however, are not ethical standards. Instead, the document focuses on the right to represent clients before the IRS. These standards differ from the AICPA's SSTSs in the following ways:

- They apply only to federal tax issues and not state authorities.
- They generally apply only to federal income tax practice.
- They do not provide the depth of guidance found in the SSTSs.
- They give the government the authority to impose monetary penalties for violations of the rules.

Circular 230 provides guidelines for written advice to taxpayers. In June 2014, the IRS substantially revised and simplified the rules and eliminated the distinction between covered opinions and other written advice. Under the new rules, all written advice is held to a "reasonable practitioner standard" that will vary based on the nature and extent of the advice. An email to a client answering a routine tax question will be held to a different standard than will an opinion on the tax effects of a complex transaction. The written advice rules do not apply to training or educational presentations but do apply to marketing and sales presentations.

For all written advice, the practitioner is expected to base the advice on reasonable assumptions, consider relevant facts and circumstances, identify the facts relevant to the advice, be properly skeptical of representations by the taxpayer and others, relate applicable law and authority to the facts, and not base an opinion on the chances that a transaction will or will not be identified by IRS and subject to audit. The revised Section 10.37 of *Circular 230* does note that the IRS representative will consider the "additional risk" associated with opinions related to tax shelters.

AICPA'S STATEMENTS ON TAX STANDARDS

Tax advisors confronted with ethical issues frequently turn to a professional organization for guidance. Although the guidelines set forth by such organizations are not *legally* enforceable, they carry significant moral weight, and may be cited in a negligence lawsuit as the proper "standard of care" for tax practitioners. They also may provide grounds for the termination or suspension of one's professional license. One such set of guidelines is the *Statements on Standards for Tax Services* (SSTSs),[48] issued by the American Institute of Certified Public Accountants (AICPA) and reproduced in Appendix E.

The SSTSs provide an ethical framework to govern the normative relationship between a tax advisor and his or her client, where, unlike an auditor, a tax advisor acts as the client's advocate. Thus, his or her primary duty is to the client, not the IRS. In

---

[48] AICPA, *Statements on Standards for Tax Services*, 2009, effective January 1, 2010.

fulfilling this duty, the advisor is bound by the highest standards of care. The most recent version of the SSTSs includes seven standards that provide guidance for AICPA members in their professional tax practice.

SSTS No. 1—Tax Return Positions. Tax professionals often provide tax advice in situations where the authority is unclear or evolving. Frequently this advice involves recommending positions that could be reversed upon audit. This statement describes the minimum level of confidence a CPA must achieve to recommend a tax return position to a taxpayer. Members first must determine and comply with all standards imposed by the various taxing authorities. Regardless of those standards, a member should not recommend a position unless he or she has a good faith belief that the position has a "realistic possibility" of being sustained administratively or judicially on its merits if challenged. Members are not permitted to take the probability of audit into account.

If the position does not meet the realistic probability standard, a member still may recommend a tax return position if he or she concludes that the position has a "reasonable basis" and the position is properly disclosed. When recommending a tax return position and when preparing or signing a return on which a tax return position is taken, a member should, when relevant, advise the taxpayer regarding potential penalty consequences of such tax return position and the opportunity, if any, to avoid such penalties through disclosure. The member also may consider any GAAP requirements to disclose aggressive tax positions under the portion of Accounting Standards Codification 740 formerly known as FIN 48.

The standard highlights the dual responsibility of the member. The U.S. tax system can function only when taxpayers file "true, correct, and complete" returns, but taxpayers also have no obligation to pay more in tax than they legally owe. The tax professional's duty is to meet his or her responsibilities to both the tax system and the taxpayer client.

SSTS No. 2—Answers to Questions on Returns. Return preparers often must sign a declaration that the return is "true, correct, and complete." A member should make a reasonable effort to obtain from the taxpayer the information necessary to provide appropriate answers to all questions on a tax return before signing as preparer. However, in certain circumstances, questions or information applicable to the taxpayer may be omitted. Reasonable grounds include the following situtations:

- ► The omitted information is not readily available or is immaterial and has little effect on taxable income or loss or the tax liability.
- ► The meaning of the question as it relates to the taxpayer is uncertain.
- ► The requested information is voluminous, in which case the taxpayer can attach a statement indicating that the requested information will be supplied upon request.

SSTS No. 3—Certain Procedural Aspects of Preparing Returns. Tax returns are based on information provided by the client. This statement sets forth the applicable standards for members concerning this information. Specifically, in preparing or signing a return, members are not required to examine or verify a client's supporting data. A member may rely on information supplied by the taxpayer unless the information appears to be incorrect, incomplete, inconsistent, or unreasonable under the circumstances. However, if the applicable law or regulations impose a specific record keeping requirement to claim a deduction, the member should inquire and satisfy himself or herself that the required records do exist.

Members are specifically encouraged to make use of a taxpayer's returns for one or more prior years in preparing the current return, whenever feasible. The practice should help avoid the omission or duplication of items and provide a basis for the treatment of similar or related transactions.

SSTS No. 4—Use of Estimates. For various reasons, precise information about an amount required on a tax return might not be available at the time the tax return is prepared. For example, the taxpayer might not have a record of small transactions or might be missing certain records. In such cases, a member may advise on estimates used in the preparation of the tax return, but the taxpayer has the responsibility to provide the estimated data. Appraisals and valuations are not considered estimates.

If estimates are used, they generally need not be labeled as estimates, but they should not be presented in a manner that provides a misleading impression about the degree of factual accuracy. However, disclosure that estimates were used should be made in some unusual situations, including:

- A taxpayer has died or is ill at the time the return is prepared.
- A taxpayer has not received a schedule K-1 at the time the tax return is to be filed.
- Litigation is pending that affects the return.
- Fire, computer failure, or a natural disaster has destroyed the relevant records.

Notwithstanding this statement, the tax practitioner may not use estimates when such use is implicitly prohibited by the IRC. For example, Sec. 274(d) disallows deductions for certain expenses (e.g., meals and entertainment) unless the taxpayer can substantiate the expenses with adequate records or sufficient corroborating information. The documentation requirement effectively precludes the taxpayer from estimating such expenses and the practitioner from using such estimates.

SSTS No. 5—Departure from a Position Previously Concluded in an Administrative Proceeding or Court Decisions. Members can take positions that differ from a position determined in an administrative proceeding with respect to the taxpayer's prior return (such as an IRS audit, IRS appeals conference, or a court decision.) Departure might be warranted because of a change in the law or regulations, or favorable court decisions. In any event, if the member can otherwise meet the standards of SSTS No. 1, departure from previous positions is permissible.

SSTS No. 6—Knowledge of Error: Return Preparation and Administrative Proceedings. For purposes of this standard, the definition of an error has the common meaning, including a mathematical error, but the definition also encompasses any position that does not meet the standards of SSTS No. 1. A position also qualifies as an error if it met the standard when a return was originally filed but no longer does because of a retroactive legislative or legal proceeding. An error for this purpose does not include immaterial items.

A member should inform the taxpayer promptly upon becoming aware of (1) an error in a previously filed return, (2) an error in a return that is the subject of an administrative proceeding (e.g., an IRS audit or appeals conference), or (3) a taxpayer's failure to file a required return. A member should advise the taxpayer of the potential consequences of the error and recommend corrective measures to be taken. This advice can be given orally. The member is not obligated to inform the taxing authority of an error and, in fact, may not do so without the taxpayer's permission except when required by law.

However, if the taxpayer requests that a member prepare the current year's return and the taxpayer has not taken appropriate action to correct an error in a prior year's return, the member should consider whether to withdraw from preparing the return and whether to continue a professional or employment relationship with the taxpayer.

The standard recognizes that conflicts can arise between the member's interests and those of the client. For example, withdrawal from an engagement could have an adverse impact on the taxpayer. In some situations, the member should consult his or her own legal counsel before deciding on recommendations to the taxpayer and whether to continue the engagement. In situations involving potential fraud or criminal charges, the member should advise the client to consult with an attorney before taking any action.

SSTS No. 7—Form and Content of Advice to Taxpayers. A member should use professional judgment to ensure that tax advice provided to a taxpayer reflects competence and appropriately serves the taxpayer's needs. The advice can be communicated in writing or orally. When communicating tax advice to a taxpayer in writing, a member should comply with relevant taxing authorities' standards applicable to written tax advice. A member should use professional judgment about any need to document oral advice.

In deciding on the form of advice provided to a taxpayer, a member should consider factors such as:

- The importance of the transaction and the amounts involved
- The technical complexity involved
- The existence of authorities and precedents
- The tax sophistication of the taxpayer
- The need to seek other professional advice
- The potential penalty consequences of a tax return position and whether any penalties can be avoided through disclosure

This statement implies that practitioner-taxpayer dealings should not be casual, nonconsensual, or open ended. Rather, they should be professional, contractual, and definite. Oral advice may be appropriate in routine matters, but written communications are recommended in important, complicated, or significant dollar value transactions.

In addition to these obligations, the tax advisor has a strict duty of confidentiality to the client. Although not encompassed under the SSTSs, this duty is implied in the accountant client privilege. (For a discussion of this privilege, see Chapter C:15.)

STOP & THINK

Question: As described in the Stop & Think box on pages C:1-10 and C:1-11, you are researching the manner in which a deduction is calculated. The IRC states that the calculation is to be made "in a manner prescribed by the Secretary." After studying the IRC, Treasury Regulations, and committee reports, you conclude that another way of doing the calculation is arguably correct under an intuitive approach. This approach would result in a lower tax liability for the client. According to the *Statements on Standards for Tax Services,* may you take a position contrary to final Treasury Regulations based on the argument that the regulations are not valid?

Solution: You should not take a position contrary to the Treasury Regulations unless you have a "good-faith belief that the position has a realistic possibility of being sustained administratively or judicially on its merits." However, you can take a position that does not meet the above standard, provided you adequately disclose the position, and the position has a reasonable basis. Whether or not you have met the standard depends on all the facts and circumstances. Chapter C:15 discusses tax return preparer positions contrary to Treasury Regulations.

WHAT WOULD YOU DO IN THIS SITUATION?

Regal Enterprises and Macon Industries, unaffiliated corporations, have hired you to prepare their respective income tax returns. In preparing Regal's return, you notice that Regal has claimed a depreciation deduction for equipment purchased from Macon on February 22 at a cost of $2 million. In preparing Macon's return, you notice that Macon has reported sales proceeds of $1.5 million from the sale of equipment to Regal on February 22. One of the two figures must be incorrect. How do you proceed to correct it? Hint: See SSTS No. 3 in Appendix E.

Sample work papers and client letter

OBJECTIVE 9

Prepare work papers and communicate to clients

Appendix A presents a set of sample work papers, including a draft of a client letter and a memo to the file. The work papers indicate the issues to be researched, the authorities addressing the issues, and the researcher's conclusions concerning the appropriate tax treatment, with rationale therefor.

The format and other details of work papers differ from firm to firm. The sample in this text offers general guidance concerning the content of work papers. In practice, work papers may include less detail.

Problem materials

Note: To complete the online research problems for this chapter, textbook users must have access to the Internet-based services described in the chapter.

DISCUSSION QUESTIONS

C:1-1 Explain the difference between closed-fact and open-fact situations.

C:1-2 According to the AICPA's *Statements on Standards for Tax Services,* what duties does the tax practitioner owe the client?

C:1-3 Explain what is encompassed by the term *tax law* as used by tax advisors.

C:1-4 The U.S. Government Printing Office publishes both hearings on proposed legislation and committee reports. Distinguish between the two.

C:1-5 Explain how committee reports can be used in tax research. What do they indicate?

C:1-6 A friend notices that you are reading the Internal Revenue Code of 1986. Your friend inquires why you are consulting a 1986 publication, especially when tax laws change so frequently. What is your response?

C:1-7 Does Title 26 contain statutory provisions dealing only with income taxation? Explain.

C:1-8 Refer to IRC Sec. 301.
- a. Which subsection discusses the general rule for the tax treatment of a property distribution?
- b. Where should one look for exceptions to the general rule?
- c. What type of Treasury Regulations would relate to subsection (e)?

C:1-9 Why should tax researchers note the date on which a Treasury Regulation was adopted?

C:1-10
- a. Distinguish between proposed, temporary, and final Treasury Regulations.
- b. Distinguish between interpretative and legislative Treasury Regulations.

C:1-11 Which type of regulation is more difficult for a taxpayer to successfully challenge, and why?

C:1-12 Explain the legislative reenactment doctrine.

C:1-13
- a. Discuss the authoritative weight of revenue rulings.
- b. As a practical matter, what consequences are likely to ensue if a taxpayer does not follow a revenue ruling and the IRS audits his or her return?

C:1-14
- a. In which courts may litigation dealing with tax matters begin?
- b. Discuss the factors that might be considered in deciding where to litigate.
- c. Describe the appeals process in tax litigation.

C:1-15 May a taxpayer appeal a case litigated under the Small Cases Procedure of the Tax Court?

C:1-16 Explain whether the following decisions are of the same precedential value: (1) Tax Court regular decisions, (2) Tax Court memo decisions, (3) decisions under the Small Cases Procedures of the Tax Court.

C:1-17 Does the IRS acquiesce in decisions of U.S. district courts?

C:1-18 The decisions of which courts are reported in the AFTR? In the USTC?

C:1-19 Why do some revenue ruling citations refer to the *Internal Revenue Bulletin* (I.R.B.) and others to a *Cumulative Bulletin* (C.B.)?

C:1-20 Explain the *Golsen* Rule. Give an example of its application.

C:1-21 Assume that the only precedents relating to a particular issue are as follows:

Tax Court—decided for the taxpayer
Eighth Circuit Court of Appeals—decided for the taxpayer (affirming the Tax Court)
U.S. District Court for Eastern Louisiana—decided for the taxpayer
Fifth Circuit Court of Appeals—decided for the government (reversing the U.S. District Court of Eastern Louisiana)

- a. Discuss the precedential value of the foregoing decisions for your client, who is a California resident.

b. If your client, a Texas resident, litigates in the Tax Court, how will the court rule? Explain.

C:1-22 Which official publication(s) contain(s) the following:
a. Transcripts of Senate floor debates
b. IRS announcements
c. Tax Court regular opinions
d. Treasury decisions
e. U.S. district court opinions
f. Technical advice memoranda

C:1-23 Under what circumstances might a tax advisor find the provisions of a tax treaty useful?

C:1-24 What two functions does a citator serve?

C:1-25 Describe two ways that the information available from the CHECKPOINT citator differs from that available from the INTELLICONNECT citator.

C:1-26 List four methods of searching the CHECKPOINT and INTELLICONNECT databases.

C:1-27 Access INTELLICONNECT at *http://intelliconnect.cch.com* and RIA CHECKPOINT™ at *http://checkpoint.riag.com*. Then answer the following questions:
a. What are the principal primary sources found in both Internet tax services?
b. What are the principal secondary sources found in each Internet tax service?

C:1-28 Compare the features of the computerized tax services with those of Internet sites maintained by noncommercial institutions. What are the relative advantages and disadvantages of each? Could the latter sites serve as a substitute for a commercial tax service?

C:1-29 According to the *Statements on Standards for Tax Services,* what belief should a CPA have before taking a pro-taxpayer position on a tax return?

C:1-30 List an advisor's duties that are excluded under the AICPA's *Statements on Standards for Tax Services*.

C:1-31 List three requirements that apply to written advice under Treasury Department *Circular 230*.

C:1-32 Explain how Treasury Department *Circular 230* differs from the AICPA's *Statements on Standards for Tax Services*.

PROBLEMS

C:1-33 *Interpreting the IRC.* Under a divorce agreement executed in the current year, an ex-wife receives from her former husband cash of $25,000 per year for eight years. The agreement does not explicitly state that the payments are excludable from gross income.
a. Does the ex-wife have gross income? If so, how much?
b. Is the former husband entitled to a deduction? If so, is it for or from AGI?
Refer only to the IRC in answering this question. Start with Sec. 71.

C:1-34 *Interpreting the IRC.* Refer to Sec. 385 and answer the questions below.
a. Whenever Treasury Regulations are issued under this section, what type are they likely to be: legislative or interpretative? Explain.
b. Assume Treasury Regulations under Sec. 385 have been finalized. Will they be relevant to estate tax matters? Explain.

C:1-35 *Using IRS Rulings.* Locate PLR 8733007 and Rev. Rul. 81-219.
a. Briefly summarize the tax issue and conclusion of each ruling.
b. Under what circumstances can a researcher rely on the private letter ruling?
c. Under what circumstances can a researcher rely on the revenue ruling?

C:1-36 *Using Treasury pronouncements.* Which IRC section(s) does Rev. Rul. 2001-29 interpret? (Hint: consult the official pronouncement of the IRS.)

C:1-37 *Using CHECKPOINT for a Keyword Search.* The objective is to locate a general overview of available home office deductions. On the main research tab, select the *United States Tax Reporter—Explanations (RIA)* library. How many results does CHECKPOINT return for each search term if the terms and connectors option is selected?
a. Search term: home office deduction.
b. Search term: "home office" deduction.
c. Search term: "home office" /5 deduction.
d. Perform the search in Part a above. Select *Sort by Relevance*. How does this sort change the results? Does the sort make it easier to locate relevant documents?
e. How do your answers change to Parts a–c if you use the intuitive search?

C:1-38 *Using INTELLICONNECT for a Keyword Search.* The search objective is to determine the amount generally excludable on the sale of a married couple's home. Using Browse, locate the *Standard Federal Tax Reporter—Explanations* library. How many results does INTELLICONNECT return for each search term?
a. Search term: home sale gain exclusion.
b. Search term: "home sale" gain exclusion and turn off "apply thesaurus" under Advanced Search.

c. Does limiting the results to only those documents containing the specific term "home sale" improve your results?
d. How do most tax documents refer to a person's home?

C:1-39 *Determining Acquiescence.*
a. What official action (acquiescence or nonacquiescence) did the IRS Commissioner take regarding the 1985 Tax Court decision in *John McIntosh,* 85 T.C. 31 (1985)? (Hint: Consult Actions on Decisions.)
b. Did this action concern *all* issues in the case? If not, explain. (Before answering this question, consult the headnote to the court opinion.)

C:1-40 *Determining Acquiescence.*
a. What original action (acquiescence or nonacquiescence) did the IRS Commissioner take regarding the 1952 Tax Court decision in *Streckfus Steamers, Inc.*, 19 T.C.1 (1952)? (Hint: Consult Actions on Decisions.)
b. Was the action complete or partial?
c. Did the IRS Commissioner subsequently change his mind? If so, when?

C:1-41 *Determining Acquiescence.*
a. What original action (acquiescence or nonacquiescence) did the IRS Commissioner take regarding the 1982 Tax Court decision in *Doyle, Dane, Bernbach, Inc.*, 79 T.C. 101 (1982)? (Hint: Consult Actions on Decisions.)
b. Did the IRS Commissioner subsequently change his mind? If so, when?

C:1-42 *Evaluating a Case.* Look up *James E. Threlkeld,* 87 T.C. 1294 (1988) and answer the questions below.
a. Was the case reviewed by the court? If so, was the decision unanimous? Explain.
b. Was the decision entered under Rule 155?
c. Consult a citator. Was the case reviewed by an appellate court? If so, which one?

C:1-43 *Evaluating a Case.* Look up *Bush Brothers & Co.,* 73 T.C. 424 (1979) and answer the questions below.
a. Was the case reviewed by the court? If so, was the decision unanimous? Explain.
b. Was the decision entered under Rule 155?
c. Consult a citator. Was the case reviewed by an appellate court? If so, which one?

C:1-44 *Writing Citations.* Provide the proper citations (including both primary and secondary citations where applicable) for the authorities listed below. (For secondary citations, reference both the AFTR and USTC.)
a. *National Cash Register Co.,* a 6th Circuit Court decision
b. *Thomas M. Dragoun v. CIR,* a Tax Court memo decision
c. *John M. Grabinski v. U.S.,* a U.S. district court decision
d. *John M. Grabinski v. U.S.,* an Eighth Circuit Court decision
e. *Rebekah Harkness,* a 1972 Court of Claims decision
f. *Hillsboro National Bank v. CIR,* a Supreme Court decision
g. Rev. Rul. 78-129

C:1-45 *Writing Citations.* Provide the proper citations (including both primary and secondary citations where applicable) for the authorities listed below. (For secondary citations, reference both the AFTR and USTC.)
a. Rev. Rul. 99-7
b. *Frank H. Sullivan,* a Board of Tax Appeals decision
c. *Tate & Lyle, Inc.,* a 1994 Tax Court decision
d. *Ralph L. Rogers v. U.S.,* a U.S. district court decision
e. *Norman Rodman v. CIR,* a Second Circuit Court decision

C:1-46 *Interpreting Citations.* Indicate which courts decided the cases cited below. Also indicate on which pages and in which publications the authority is reported.
a. *Lloyd M. Shumaker v. CIR,* 648 F.2d 1198, 48 AFTR 2d 81-5353 (9th Cir., 1981)
b. *Xerox Corp. v. U.S.,* 14 Cl. Ct. 455, 88-1 USTC ¶9231 (1988)
c. *Real Estate Land Title & Trust Co. v. U.S.,* 309 U.S. 13, 23 AFTR 816 (USSC, 1940)
d. *J. B. Morris v. U.S.,* 441 F. Supp. 76, 41 AFTR 2d 78-335 (DC TX, 1977)
e. Rev. Rul. 83-3, 1983-1 C.B. 72
f. *Malone & Hyde, Inc. v. U.S.,* 568 F.2d 474, 78-1 USTC ¶9199 (6th Cir., 1978)

C:1-47 *Using a Tax Service.* Use the topical index of the *United States Tax Reporter* to locate authorities dealing with the deductibility of the cost of a facelift.
a. In which paragraph(s) does the *United States Tax Reporter* summarize and cite these authorities?
b. List the authorities.
c. May a taxpayer deduct the cost of a facelift paid in the current year? Explain.

C:1-48 *Using a Tax Service.* Locate Reg. Sec. 1.302-1 using either CHECKPOINT or INTELLICONNECT. Does this Treasury Regulation reflect recent amendments to the IRC? Explain.

C:1-49 *Using a Tax Service.* Using the topical index of the *Standard Federal Income Tax Reporter* in INTELLICONNECT, locate authorities addressing whether termite damage constitutes a casualty loss.
a. In which paragraph(s) does the *Standard Federal Income Tax Reporter* summarize and cite these authorities?
b. List three authorities cited by the Reporter.

C:1-50 *Using a Tax Service.*
a. Using the *Standard Federal Income Tax Reporter* in INTELLICONNECT, locate where Sec. 303(b)(2)(A) appears. This provision states that Sec. 303(a) applies only if the stock in question meets a certain percentage test. What is the applicable percentage?
b. Locate Reg. Sec. 1.303-2(a) in the same service. Does this Treasury Regulation reflect recent amendments to the IRC with respect to the percentage test addressed in Part a? Explain.

C:1-51 *Using a Tax Service.* Using the BNA tax service, identify the number of the BNA portfolio for the following subjects.
a. Innocent spouse relief.
b. Accounting methods.
c. Involuntary conversions.
d. IRAs.
e. Deductibility of legal and accounting fees, bribes, and illegal payments.

C:1-52 *Using a Tax Service.* This problem deals with CHECKPOINT's *Federal Tax Coordinator 2d.* Use the topical index CHECKPOINT to locate authorities dealing with the deductibility of the cost of work clothing by ministers (clergymen). List the authorities.

C:1-53 *Using a Citator.* Trace *Biltmore Homes, Inc.,* a 1960 Tax Court memo decision, in both the INTELLICONNECT and CHECKPOINT citators.
a. According to the CHECKPOINT citator, how many times has the Tax Court decision been cited by other courts on Headnote Number 5?
b. How many issues did the lower court address in its opinion? (Hint: Refer to the case headnote numbers.)
c. Did an appellate court review the case? If so, which one?
d. According to the INTELLICONNECT citator, how many times has the Tax Court decision been cited by other courts?
e. According to the INTELLICONNECT citator, how many times has the circuit court decision been cited by other courts on Headnote Number 5?

C:1-54 *Using a Citator.* Trace *Stephen Bolaris,* 776 F.2d 1428, in both the INTELLICONNECT and CHECKPOINT citators.
a. According to the CHECKPOINT citator, how many times has the Ninth Circuit's decision been cited?
b. Did the decision address more than one issue? Explain.
c. Was the decision ever cited unfavorably? Explain.
d. According to the INTELLICONNECT citator, how many times has the Ninth Circuit's decision been cited?
e. According to the INTELLICONNECT citator, how many times has the Tax Court's decision been cited on Headnote Number 1?

C:1-55 ***Interpreting a Case.*** Using either CHECKPOINT or INTELLICONNECT refer to the *Holden Fuel Oil Company,* RIA T.C. Memo ¶72,045 (T.C. Memo 1972-45), 31 TCM 184.
a. In which year was the case decided?
b. What controversy was litigated?
c. Who won the case?
d. Was the decision reviewed at the lower court level?
e. Was the decision appealed?
f. Has the decision been cited in other cases?

C:1-56 ***Internet Research.*** Access the IRS Internet site at *www.irs.gov* and answer the following questions:
a. How does one file a tax return electronically?
b. How can the taxpayer transmit funds electronically?
c. What are the advantages of electronic filing?

C:1-57 *Internet Research.* Access the IRS Internet site at *www.irs.gov* and indicate the titles of the following IRS forms:
a. Form 4506
b. Form 973
c. Form 8725

C:1-58 *Internet Research.* Access the Federation of Tax Administrators Internet site at *www.taxadmin.org/fta/link/forms.html* and indicate the titles of the following state tax forms and publications:
a. Minnesota Form M-100
b. Illinois Individual Schedule CR
c. New York State Corporate Form CT-3-C

C:1-59 *Internet Research.* Access the Urban Institute and Brookings Institution Tax Policy Center at *taxpolicycenter.org*. On the home page, search for *state individual income tax rates* and locate the Tax Policy Center's latest summary of each state's rates. Researchers also can locate the file by looking under the TAX FACTS tab and then the *State* tab, *Main Features of State Tax Systems*.
a. How many states do not have a state individual income tax?
b. How many states tax only interest and dividends for individuals?
c. What is the top marginal individual income tax rate in Oregon?
d. Of those that do impose an income tax, which state's top marginal rate is lowest?

COMPREHENSIVE PROBLEM

C:1-60 Your client, a physician, recently purchased a yacht on which he flies a pennant with a medical emblem on it. He recently informed you that he purchased the yacht and flies the pennant to advertise his occupation and thus attract new patients. He has asked you if he may deduct as ordinary and necessary business expenses the costs of insuring and maintaining the yacht. In search of an answer, consult either INTELLICONNECT's *Standard Federal Income Tax Reporter* or CHECKPOINT's *United States Tax Reporter*. Explain the steps taken to find your answer.

TAX STRATEGY PROBLEM

C:1-61 Your client, Home Products Universal (HPU), distributes home improvement products to independent retailers throughout the country. Its management wants to explore the possibility of opening its own home improvement centers. Accordingly, it commissions a consulting firm to conduct a feasibility study, which ultimately persuades HPU to expand into retail sales. The consulting firm bills HPU $150,000, which HPU deducts on its current year tax return. The IRS disputes the deduction, contending that, because the cost relates to entering a new business, it should be capitalized. HPU's management, on the other hand, firmly believes that, because the cost relates to expanding HPU's existing business, it should be deducted. In contemplating legal action against the IRS, HPU's management considers the state of judicial precedent: The federal court for HPU's district has ruled that the cost of expanding from distribution into retail sales should be capitalized. The appellate court for HPU's circuit has stated in *dictum* that, although in some circumstances switching from product distribution to product sales entails entering a new trade or business, improving customer access to one's existing products generally does not. The Federal Circuit Court has ruled that wholesale distribution and retail sales, even of the same product, constitute distinct businesses. In a case involving a taxpayer from another circuit, the Tax Court has ruled that such costs invariably should be capitalized. HPU's Chief Financial Officer approaches you with the question, "In which judicial forum should HPU file a lawsuit against the IRS: (1) U.S. district court, (2) the Tax Court, or (3) the U.S. Court of Federal Claims?" What do you tell her?

CASE STUDY PROBLEM

C:1-62 A client, Mal Manley, fills out his client questionnaire for the previous year and on it provides information for the preparation of his individual income tax return. The IRS has never audited Mal's returns. Mal reports that he made over 100 relatively small cash contributions totaling $24,785 to charitable organizations. In the last few years, Mal's charitable contributions have averaged about $15,000 per year. For the previous year, Mal's adjusted gross income was roughly $350,000, about a 10% increase from the year before.

Required: Applying *Statements on Standards for Tax Services* No. 3, determine whether you can accept at face value Mal's information concerning his charitable contributions. Now assume that the IRS recently audited Mal's tax return for two years ago and denied 75% of that year's charitable contribution deduction because the deduction was not substantiated. Assume also that Mal indicates that, in the previous year, he contributed $25,000 (instead of $24,785). How do these changes of fact affect your earlier decision?

TAX RESEARCH PROBLEMS

C:1-63 The purpose of this problem is to enhance your skills in interpreting the authorities that you locate in your research. In answering the questions that follow, refer only to *Thomas A. Curtis, M.D., Inc.*, 1994 RIA TC Memo ¶94,015 (T.C. Memo 1994-15), 67 TCM 1958.

a. What was the principal controversy litigated in this case?
b. Which party—the taxpayer or the IRS—won?
c. Why is the corporation instead of Dr. and/or Ms. Curtis listed as the plaintiff?
d. What is the relationship between Ellen Barnert Curtis and Dr. Thomas A. Curtis?
e. Approximately how many hours a week did Ms. Curtis work, and what were her credentials?
f. For the fiscal year ending in 1989, what salary did the corporation pay Ms. Curtis? What amount did the court decide was reasonable?
g. What dividends did the corporation pay for its fiscal years ending in 1988 and 1989?
h. To which circuit would this decision be appealable?
i. According to *Curtis*, what five factors did the Ninth Circuit mention in *Elliotts, Inc.* as relevant in determining reasonable compensation?

C:1-64 Josh contributes $5,000 toward the support of his widowed mother, aged 69, a U.S. citizen and resident. She earns gross income of $2,000 and spends it all for her own support. In addition, Medicare pays $3,200 of her medical expenses. She does not receive financial support from sources other than those described above. Must the Medicare payments be included in the support that Josh's mother is deemed to provide for herself?

Prepare work papers and a client letter (to Josh) dealing with the issue.

C:1-65 Amy owns a vacation cottage in Maine. She predicts that the time during which the cottage will be used in the current year is as follows:

By Amy, solely for vacation	12 days
By Amy, making repairs ten hours per day and vacationing the rest of the day	2 days
By her sister, who paid fair rental value	8 days
By her cousin, who paid fair rental value	4 days
By her friend, who paid a token amount of rent	2 days
By three families from the Northeast, who paid fair rental value for 40 days each	120 days
Not used	217 days

Calculate the ratio for allocating the following expenses to the rental income expected to be received from the cottage: interest, taxes, repairs, insurance, and depreciation. The ratio will be used to determine the amount of expenses that are deductible and, thus, Amy's taxable income for the year.

For the tax manager to whom you report, prepare work papers in which you discuss the calculation method. Also, draft a memo to the file dealing with the results of your research.

C:1-66 Look up *Summit Publishing Company*, 1990 PH T.C. Memo ¶90,288, 59 (T.C. Memo 1990-288) TCM 833, and *J.B.S. Enterprises*, 1991 PH T.C. Memo ¶91,254, (T.C. Memo 1991-254) 61 TCM 2829, and answer the following questions:

a. What was the principal issue in these cases?
b. What factors did the Tax Court consider in resolving the central issue?
c. How are the facts of these cases similar? How are they dissimilar?

C:1-67 Your supervisor would like to set up a single Sec. 401(k) plan exclusively for the managers of your organization. Concerned that this arrangement might not meet the requirements for a qualified plan, he has asked you to request a determination letter from the IRS. In a brief memorandum, address the following issues:

a. What IRS pronouncements govern requests for determination letters?
b. What IRS forms must be filed with the request?
c. What information must be provided in the request?
d. What actions must accompany the filing?
e. Where must the request be filed?

CHAPTER 2

CORPORATE FORMATIONS AND CAPITAL STRUCTURE

LEARNING OBJECTIVES

After studying this chapter, you should be able to

1. Discuss the tax advantages and disadvantages of alternative business forms
2. Apply the check-the-box regulations to partnerships, corporations, and trusts
3. Recognize the legal requirements and tax considerations related to forming a corporation
4. Discuss the requirements for deferring gain or loss upon incorporation
5. Explain the tax implications of alternative capital structures
6. Determine the tax consequences of worthless stock or debt obligations
7. Identify tax planning opportunities in corporate formations
8. Comply with procedural rules for corporate formations

CHAPTER OUTLINE

When starting a business, entrepreneurs must decide whether to organize it as a sole proprietorship, partnership, corporation, limited liability company, or limited liability partnership. This chapter discusses the advantages and disadvantages of each form of business association. Because many entrepreneurs find organizing their business as a corporation advantageous, the chapter looks at the definition of a corporation for federal income tax purposes. It also discusses the tax consequences of incorporating a business. The chapter closes by examining the tax implications of capitalizing a corporation with equity and/or debt and describing the advantages and disadvantages of alternative capital structures.

This textbook takes a life-cycle approach to corporate taxation. The corporate life cycle starts with corporate formation, discussed in this chapter. Once formed and operating, the corporation generates taxable income (or loss), incurs federal income tax and other liabilities, and makes distributions to its shareholders. Finally, at some point, the corporation might outlive its usefulness and be liquidated and dissolved. The corporate life cycle is too complex to discuss in one chapter. Therefore, additional coverage follows in Chapters C:3 through C:8.

ORGANIZATION FORMS AVAILABLE

OBJECTIVE 1

Discuss the tax advantages and disadvantages of alternative business forms

Businesses can be organized in several forms including

- Sole proprietorships
- Partnerships
- Corporations
- Limited liability companies
- Limited liability partnerships

A discussion of the tax implications of each form is presented below.

ADDITIONAL COMMENT

The income/loss of a sole proprietorship reported on Schedule C carries to page 1 of Form 1040 and is included in the computation of the individual's taxable income. Net income, if any, also carries to Schedule SE of Form 1040 for computation of the sole proprietor's self-employment tax.

SOLE PROPRIETORSHIPS

A **sole proprietorship** is an unincorporated business owned by one individual. It often is selected by entrepreneurs who are beginning a new business with a modest amount of capital. From a tax and legal perspective, a sole proprietorship is not a separate entity. Rather, it is a legal extension of its individual owner. Thus, the individual owns all the business assets and reports income or loss from the sole proprietorship directly on his or her individual tax return. Specifically, the individual owner (proprietor) reports all the business's income and expenses for the year on Schedule C (Profit or Loss from Business) or Schedule C-EZ (Net Profit from Business) of Form 1040. A completed Schedule C is included in Appendix B, where a common set of facts (with minor modifications) illustrates the similarities and differences in sole proprietorship, C corporation, partnership, and S corporation tax reporting.

If the business is profitable, the profit is included in the proprietor's other income.

EXAMPLE C:2-1 ► John, a single taxpayer, starts a new computer store, which he operates as a sole proprietorship. John reports a $15,000 profit from the business in its first year of operation. Assuming his marginal tax rate is 33%, John's tax on the $15,000 of profit from the business is $4,950 (0.33 × $15,000).[1] ◄

If the business is unprofitable, the loss reduces the proprietor's total taxable income, thereby generating tax savings.

EXAMPLE C:2-2 ► Assume the same facts as in Example C:2-1 except John reports a $15,000 loss instead of a $15,000 profit in the first year of operation. Assuming he still is taxed at a 33% marginal tax rate, the $15,000 loss produces tax savings of $4,950 (0.33 × $15,000). ◄

[1] The $15,000 Schedule C profit in Example C:2-1 will increase adjusted gross income (AGI). The AGI level affects certain deduction calculations (e.g., medical, charitable contributions, and miscellaneous itemized) and, because of limitations, may result in a taxable income increase different from the $15,000 AGI increase.

ADDITIONAL COMMENT

Although this chapter emphasizes the tax consequences of selecting the entity in which a business will be conducted, other issues also are important in making such a decision. For example, the amount of legal liability assumed by an owner is important and can vary substantially among the different business entities.

Tax Advantages. The tax advantages of conducting business as a sole proprietorship are as follows:

- The sole proprietorship is not subject to taxation as a separate entity. Rather, the sole proprietor, as an individual, is taxed at his or her marginal rate on income earned by the business.
- The proprietor's marginal tax rate may be lower than the marginal tax rate that would have applied had the business been organized as a corporation.
- The owner may contribute cash to, or withdraw profits from, the business without tax consequences.
- Although the owner usually maintains separate books, records, and bank accounts for the business, the money in these accounts belongs to the owner personally.
- The owner may contribute property to, or withdraw property from, the business without recognizing gain or loss.
- Business losses may offset nonbusiness income, such as interest, dividends, and any salary earned by the sole proprietor or his or her spouse, subject to the passive activity loss rules.

Tax Disadvantages. The tax disadvantages of conducting business as a sole proprietorship are as follows:

- The profits of a sole proprietorship are currently taxed to the individual owner, whether or not the profits are retained in the business or withdrawn for personal use. By contrast, the profits of a corporation are taxed to its shareholders only if and when the corporation distributes the earnings as dividends.
- At times, corporate tax rates have been lower than individual tax rates. In such times, businesses conducted as sole proprietorships have been taxed more heavily than businesses organized as corporations.
- A sole proprietor must pay the full amount of Social Security taxes because he or she is not considered to be an employee of the business. By contrast, shareholder-employees must pay only half their Social Security taxes; the corporate employer pays the other half. (The employer, however, might pass this half onto employees in the form of lower wages or fewer employees hired.)
- Sole proprietorships may not deduct compensation paid to owner-employees. By contrast, corporations may deduct compensation paid to shareholder-employees.
- Certain tax-exempt benefits (e.g., premiums for group term life insurance) available to shareholder-employees are not available to owner-employees.[2]
- A sole proprietor must use the same accounting period for business and personal purposes. Thus, he or she cannot defer income by choosing a business fiscal year that differs from the individual's calendar year. By contrast, a corporation may choose a fiscal year that differs from the shareholders' calendar years.

ADDITIONAL COMMENT

In 2014 and 2015, the employee's half of Social Security taxes is 6.2%, and the employee's half of the Medicare tax is 1.45%, for a total of 7.65%. The employer pays the same percentages for its half of these items. In addition, the employee (but not the employer) is subject to an additional 0.9% Medicare tax if the employee's wages exceed a threshold amount ($200,000 unmarried; $250,000 for married filing jointly; $125,000 for married filing separately).

PARTNERSHIPS

A **partnership** is an unincorporated business carried on by two or more individuals or entities for profit. The partnership form often is used by friends or relatives who engage in a business and by groups of investors who want to share the profits, losses, and expenses of an investment such as a real estate project.

A partnership is a tax reporting, but not taxpaying, entity. The partnership acts as a conduit for its owners. Its income, expenses, losses, credits, and other tax-related items pass through to the partners who report these items on their separate tax returns.

Each year a partnership must file a tax return (Form 1065—U.S. Partnership Return of Income) to report the results of its operations. When the partnership return is filed, the preparer must send each partner a statement (Schedule K-1, Form 1065) that reports the

REAL-WORLD EXAMPLE

Entities filed the following number of tax returns in 2013:

Entity	Number
Partnership	3.7 million
C corporation	2.2 million
S corporation	4.6 million

---

[2] Section 162(l) permits self-employed individuals to deduct as a trade or business expense all of the health insurance costs incurred on behalf of themselves, their spouses, and their dependents.

partner's allocable share of partnership income, expenses, losses, credits, and other tax-related items. The partner then must report these items on his or her separate tax return. As with a sole proprietorship, the partner's allocable share of business profits is added to the partner's other income and taxed at that partner's marginal tax rate. A completed Form 1065 appears in Appendix B.

EXAMPLE C:2-3 ▸ Bob, a single taxpayer, owns a 50% interest in the BT Partnership, a calendar year entity. The BT Partnership reports a $30,000 profit in its first year of operation. Bob's $15,000 share passes through from the partnership level to Bob's individual tax return. Assuming Bob is taxed at a 33% marginal rate, his tax on the $15,000 is $4,950 (0.33 × $15,000). Bob must pay the $4,950 tax whether or not the BT Partnership distributes any of its profits to him. ◂

If a partnership reports a loss, the partner's allocable share of the loss reduces that partner's other income and provides tax savings based on the partner's marginal tax rate. The passive activity loss rules, however, may limit the amount of any loss deduction available to the partner. (For a discussion of these rules, see Chapter C:9 of this textbook.)

EXAMPLE C:2-4 ▸ Assume the same facts as in Example C:2-3 except that, instead of a profit, the BT Partnership sustains a $30,000 loss in its first year of operation. Assuming Bob is taxed at a 33% marginal rate, his $15,000 share of the first year loss produces a tax savings of $4,950 (0.33 × $15,000). ◂

TAX STRATEGY TIP

In a limited partnership, the general partner could be a corporation, thereby affording the general owners (shareholders) of the corporation added liability protection.

Organizationally, a partnership can be either general or limited. In a general partnership, the liability of each partner for partnership debts is unlimited. Thus, these partners are at risk for more than the amount of their capital investment in the partnership. In a limited partnership, at least one partner must be a general partner, and at least one partner must be a limited partner. As in a general partnership, the general partners are liable for all partnership debts, and the limited partners are liable only to the extent of their capital investment in the partnership, plus any amount they are obligated to contribute under their partnership agreement. Unless specified in that agreement, limited partners generally may not participate in the management of the partnership business.

Tax Advantages. The tax advantages of doing business as a partnership are as follows:

- The partnership as an entity pays no tax. Rather, the income of the partnership passes through to the separate returns of the partners and is taxed directly to them.
- A partner's tax rate may be lower than a corporation's tax rate for the same level of taxable income.
- Partnership income is not subject to double taxation. Although partnership profits are accounted for at the partnership level, they are taxed only at the partner level.
- Additional taxes generally are not imposed on distributions to the partners. With limited exceptions, partners can contribute money or property to, or withdraw money or property from, the partnership without recognizing gain or loss.
- Subject to limitations, partners can use losses to offset income from other sources.
- A partner's basis in a partnership interest is increased by his or her share of partnership income. This basis adjustment reduces the amount of gain recognized when the partner sells his or her partnership interest, thereby avoiding double taxation.

ADDITIONAL COMMENT

If two or more owners exist, a business cannot be conducted as a sole proprietorship. From a tax compliance and recordkeeping perspective, conducting a business as a partnership is more complicated than conducting the business as a sole proprietorship.

Tax Disadvantages. The tax disadvantages of doing business as a partnership are as follows:

- All the partnership's profits are taxed to the partners when earned, even if not distributed.
- A partner's tax rate could be higher than a corporation's tax rate for the same level of taxable income.
- A partner is not considered to be an employee of the partnership. Therefore, he or she must pay the full amount of self-employment taxes on his or her share of partnership

income. Some tax-exempt fringe benefits (e.g., premiums for group term life insurance) are not available to partners.[3]

- Partners generally cannot defer income by choosing a fiscal year for the partnership that differs from the tax year of the principal partner(s). However, if the partnership demonstrates a business purpose, or if it makes a special election, it may use a fiscal year in general.

Chapters C:9 and C:10 of this volume discuss partnerships in greater detail.

CORPORATIONS

Corporations fall into two categories: C corporations and S corporations. Both have limited liability. A C corporation is subject to double taxation. Its earnings are taxed first at the corporate level when earned, then again at the shareholder level when distributed as dividends. An S corporation, by contrast, is subject to single-level taxation, much like a partnership. Its earnings are accounted for at the corporate level but are taxed only at the shareholder level.

ADDITIONAL COMMENT

Unlike a sole proprietorship and a partnership, a C corporation is a separate taxpaying entity. This form can be advantageous because corporate rates start at 15%, which may be much lower than an individual shareholder's rate, which might be as high as 39.6%.

C Corporations. A C **corporation** is a separate entity taxed on its income at rates ranging from 15% to 35%.[4] A C corporation must report all its income and expenses and compute its tax liability on Form 1120 (U.S. Corporation Income Tax Return). A completed Form 1120 appears in Appendix B. Shareholders are not taxed on the corporation's earnings unless these earnings are distributed as dividends. After 2012, the applicable capital gains tax rate for net capital gains and qualified dividends of noncorporate taxpayers is 0% for taxpayers in tax brackets of 15% and below, 15% for taxpayers in the 25% through 35% tax brackets, and 20% for taxpayers in the 39.6% tax bracket. Also, 25% and 28% rates apply for gains on certain types of property. In addition, an incremental 3.8% rate applies to net investment income for taxpayers whose modified AGI exceeds $200,000 ($250,000 for married filing jointly). Net investment income includes, among other things, interest, dividends, annuities, royalties, rents, and net gains from the disposition of property not used in a trade or business, all reduced by deductions allocable to such income or gains.

EXAMPLE C:2-5 ▶ Jane owns 100% of York Corporation stock. York reports taxable income of $50,000 for the current year. The first $50,000 of taxable income is taxed at a 15% rate, so York pays a corporate income tax of $7,500 (0.15 × $50,000). If the corporation distributes none of its earnings to Jane during the year, she pays no tax on York's earnings. However, if York distributes its current after-tax earnings to Jane, she must pay tax on $42,500 ($50,000 − $7,500) of dividend income. Assuming Jane's capital gains tax rate is 15%, her tax on the dividend income is $6,375 (0.15 × $42,500). The total tax on York's $50,000 of profits is $13,875 ($7,500 paid by York + $6,375 paid by Jane). ◀

TAX STRATEGY TIP

If a shareholder is also an employee of the corporation, the corporation can avoid double taxation by paying a deductible salary instead of a dividend. The salary, however, must be reasonable in amount. See Tax Planning Considerations in Chapter C:3 for further discussion of this technique along with an example demonstrating how the lower tax rate on dividends reduces the difference between salary and dividend payments.

Even when a corporation does not distribute its profits, double taxation may result. The profits are taxed to the corporation when they are earned. Then, effectively, they may be taxed a second time (as capital gains) when the shareholder sells appreciated stock or when the corporation liquidates.

EXAMPLE C:2-6 ▶ On January 2 of the current year, Carl purchases 100% of York Corporation stock for $60,000. In the same year, York reports taxable income of $50,000, on which it pays tax of $7,500. The corporation distributes none of the remaining $42,500 to Carl. On January 3 of the next year, Carl sells his stock to Mary for $102,500 (his initial investment plus the current year's accumulated earnings). Carl must report a capital gain of $42,500 ($102,500 − $60,000). Thus, York's profit is effectively taxed twice—first at the corporate level when earned and again at the shareholder level when Carl sells the appreciated stock at a gain. ◀

TAX STRATEGY TIP

By having a corporation retain earnings instead of paying dividends, the shareholder converts current ordinary income into deferred capital gains. The corporation, however, must avoid the accumulated earnings tax (see Chapter C:5).

Tax Advantages. The tax advantages of doing business as a C corporation are as follows:

- A C corporation is an entity separate and distinct from its owners. Its marginal tax rate may be lower than its owners' marginal tax rates. So long as these earnings are not distributed and taxed to both the shareholders and the corporation, aggregate tax savings may result. If retained in the business, the earnings may be used for reinvestment and the retirement of debt. This advantage, however, may be limited by the accumulated earnings tax and the personal holding company tax. (See Chapter C:5 for a discussion of these two taxes.)

[3] Partners are eligible to deduct their health insurance costs in the same manner as a sole proprietor. See footnote 2 for details.

[4] As discussed in Chapter C:3, the corporate tax rate is 39% and 38% for certain levels of taxable income.

- Shareholders employed by the corporation are considered to be employees for tax purposes. Consequently, they are liable for only half their Social Security taxes, while their corporate employer is liable for the other half.
- Shareholder-employees are entitled to nontaxable fringe benefits (e.g., premiums paid on group term life insurance and accident and health insurance). The corporation can provide these benefits with before-tax dollars (instead of after-tax dollars). By contrast, because sole proprietors and partners are not considered to be employees for tax purposes, they are ineligible for certain tax-free fringe benefits, although they are permitted to deduct their health insurance premiums.
- A corporation may deduct as an ordinary and necessary business expense compensation and certain benefits paid to shareholder-employees. Within reasonable limits, it may adjust this compensation and these benefits upward to shelter corporate taxable income.
- A C corporation can use a fiscal instead of a calendar year as its reporting period. A fiscal year could permit a corporation to defer income to a later reporting period. (A personal service corporation, however, generally must use a calendar year as its tax year.[5])
- Special rules allow a shareholder to exclude 50% of the gain realized on the sale or exchange of stock held more than five years, provided the corporation meets certain requirements.

SELF-STUDY QUESTION

How are corporate earnings subject to double taxation?

ANSWER

Corporate earnings initially are taxed to the corporation. In addition, once these earnings are distributed to the shareholders as dividends, they are taxed again. Because the corporation does not receive a deduction for the distribution, these earnings have been taxed twice. Also, double taxation can occur when a shareholder sells his or her stock at a gain. In either case, the dividends or capital gains are taxed at the applicable capital gains rate.

Tax Disadvantages. The tax disadvantages of doing business as a C corporation are as follows:

- Double taxation of income results when the corporation distributes its earnings as dividends to shareholders or, effectively, when shareholders sell or exchange appreciated stock.
- Shareholders generally cannot withdraw money or property from the corporation without recognizing income. A distribution of cash or property to a shareholder generally is taxable as a dividend if the corporation has sufficient earnings and profits (E&P). (See Chapter C:4 for a discussion of E&P.)
- Net operating losses confer no tax benefit to the owners in the year the corporation incurs them. They can be carried back or carried forward to offset the corporation's income in other years. For start-up corporations, these losses provide no tax benefit until the corporation earns a profit in a subsequent year. Shareholders cannot use these losses to offset income from other sources.
- Capital losses confer no tax benefit to the owners in the year the corporation incurs them. They cannot offset the ordinary income of either the corporation or its shareholders. These losses must be carried back or carried forward to offset corporate capital gains realized in other years.

S Corporations. An **S corporation** is so designated because special rules governing its tax treatment are found in Subchapter S of the IRC. Nevertheless, the general corporate tax rules apply unless overridden by the Subchapter S provisions. Like a partnership, an S corporation is a pass-through entity. Income, deductions, losses, and credits are accounted for by the S corporation, which generally is not subject to taxation. They pass through to the separate returns of its owners, who generally are subject to taxation. An S corporation offers its owners less planning flexibility than does a partnership. For example, the number and type of S corporation shareholders are limited, and the shareholders cannot allocate income, deductions, losses, and credits in a way that differs from their proportionate ownership. As mentioned before, like C corporation shareholders, S corporation shareholders enjoy limited liability.

To obtain S corporation status, a corporation must make a special election, and its shareholders must consent to that election. Each year, an S corporation files an information return, Form 1120S (U.S. Income Tax Return for an S Corporation), which reports the results of its operations and indicates the items of income, deduction, loss, and credit that pass through to the separate returns of its shareholders.

---

[5] Sec. 441. See Chapter C:3 for the special tax year restrictions applying to personal service corporations.

EXAMPLE C:2-7 ▶ Chuck owns 50% of the stock in Maine, an S corporation that uses the calendar year as its tax year. In its first year of operation, Maine reports $30,000 of taxable income, all ordinary in character. Maine pays no corporate income tax. Chuck, however, must pay tax on his $15,000 (0.50 × $30,000) share of Maine's income whether or not the corporation distributes this income to him. If his marginal rate is 33%, Chuck pays a tax of $4,950 (0.33 × $15,000) on this share. If Maine instead reports a $30,000 loss, Chuck's $15,000 share of the loss reduces his tax liability by $4,950 (0.33 × $15,000). ◀

TAX STRATEGY TIP

If a corporation anticipates losses in its early years, it might consider operating as an S corporation so that the losses pass through to the shareholders. When the corporation becomes profitable, it can revoke the S election if it wishes to accumulate earnings for growth.

Tax Advantages. The tax advantages of doing business as an S corporation are as follows:

- S corporations generally pay no tax. Instead, corporate income passes through and is taxed to the shareholders.
- The shareholders' marginal tax rates may be lower than a C corporation's marginal tax rate, thereby producing overall tax savings.
- Corporate losses flow through to the separate returns of the shareholders and may be used to offset income earned from other sources. (Passive loss and basis rules, however, may limit loss deductions to shareholders. See Chapter C:11.) This treatment can be beneficial to owners of start-up corporations that generate losses in their early years of operation.
- Because capital gains, as well as other tax-related items, retain their character when they pass through to the separate returns of shareholders, the shareholders are taxed on these gains as though they directly realized them. Consequently, they can offset the gains against capital losses from other sources. Furthermore, they are taxed on these gains at their own capital gains rates.
- Shareholders generally can contribute money to or withdraw money from an S corporation without recognizing gain.
- Corporate profits are taxed only at the shareholder level in the year earned. Generally, the shareholders incur no additional tax liability when the corporation distributes the profits.
- A shareholder's basis in S corporation stock is increased by his or her share of corporate income. This basis adjustment reduces the shareholder's gain when he or she later sells the stock, thereby avoiding double taxation.

TAX STRATEGY TIP

Relatively low individual tax rates may increase the attractiveness of an S corporation relative to the C corporation form of doing business.

Tax Disadvantages. The tax disadvantages of doing business as an S corporation are as follows:

- Shareholders are taxed on all of an S corporation's current year profits whether or not the corporation distributes these profits and whether or not the shareholders have the wherewithal to pay the tax on these profits.
- If the shareholders' marginal tax rates exceed those for a C corporation, the overall tax burden may be heavier, and the after-tax earnings available for reinvestment and debt retirement may be reduced.
- Nontaxable fringe benefits generally are not available to S corporation shareholder-employees.[6] Ordinarily, fringe benefits provided by an S corporation are deductible by the corporation and taxable to the shareholder. On the other hand, S corporation shareholder-employees pay half of Social Security taxes while the S corporation employer pays the other half.
- S corporations generally cannot defer income by choosing a fiscal year other than a calendar year unless the S corporation can establish a legitimate business purpose for a fiscal year or unless it makes a special election.

Chapter C:11 discusses S corporations in greater detail. In addition, Appendix F compares the tax treatment of C corporations, partnerships, and S corporations.

---

[6] S corporation shareholders may deduct their health insurance costs in the same manner as sole proprietors and partners. See footnotes 2 and 3 for details.

ADDITIONAL COMMENT

All 50 states have adopted statutes providing for LLCs.

LIMITED LIABILITY COMPANIES

A **limited liability company** (LLC) combines the best features of a partnership with those of a corporation even though, from a legal perspective, it is neither. While offering its owners the limited liability of a corporation, an LLC with more than one owner generally is treated as a partnership for tax purposes. This limited liability extends to all the LLC's owners. In this respect, the LLC is analogous to a limited partnership with no general partners. Unlike an S corporation, an LLC may have an unlimited number of owners who can be individuals, corporations, estates, and trusts. As discussed below, under the check-the-box regulations, the LLC may elect to be taxed as a corporation or be treated by default as a partnership. If treated as a partnership, the LLC files Form 1065 (U.S. Partnership Return of Income) with the IRS.

REAL-WORLD EXAMPLE

All the Big 4 accounting firms have converted general partnerships into LLPs.

LIMITED LIABILITY PARTNERSHIPS

Many states allow a business to operate as a **limited liability partnership** (LLP). This business form is attractive to owners of professional service organizations, such as public accounting firms, that adopt LLP status primarily to limit their legal liability. Under state LLP laws, partners are liable for their own acts and omissions as well as the acts and omissions of individuals under their direction. On the other hand, LLP partners are not liable for the negligence or misconduct of the other partners. Thus, from a legal liability perspective, an LLP partner is like a limited partner with respect to other partners' acts but like a general partner with respect to his or her own acts, as well as the acts of his or her agents. Like a general partnership or LLC with more than one owner, an LLP can elect to be taxed as a corporation under the check-the-box regulations. If treated as a partnership by default, the LLP files Form 1065 (U.S. Partnership Return of Income) with the IRS.

CHECK-THE-BOX REGULATIONS

OBJECTIVE 2

Apply the check-the-box regulations to partnerships, corporations, and trusts

Most unincorporated businesses may choose to be taxed as a partnership or a corporation under rules commonly referred to as the **check-the-box regulations**. According to these regulations, an unincorporated business with two or more owners is treated by default as a partnership for tax purposes unless it elects to be taxed as a corporation. An unincorporated business with one owner is disregarded as a separate entity and thus treated as a sole proprietorship by default unless it elects to be taxed as a corporation.[7]

An eligible entity (i.e., an unincorporated business) may elect its classification by filing Form 8832 (Entity Classification Election) with the IRS. The form must be signed by each owner of the entity, or any officer, manager, or owner of the entity authorized to make the election. The signatures must specify the date on which the election will be effective. The effective date cannot be more than 75 days before or 12 months after the date the entity files Form 8832. A copy of the form must be attached to the entity's tax return for the election year.

TAX STRATEGY TIP

When applying the federal check-the-box regulations, taxpayers also must check to see whether or not their state will treat the entity in a consistent manner for state tax purposes.

EXAMPLE C:2-8 ▶ On January 10 of the current year, a group of ten individuals organizes an LLC to conduct a bookbinding business in Texas. In the current year, the LLC is an eligible entity under the check-the-box regulations and thus may elect (with the owners' consent) to be taxed as a corporation. If the LLC does not make the election, the LLC, for tax purposes, will be treated as a partnership by default. ◀

EXAMPLE C:2-9 ▶ Assume the same facts as in Example C:2-8 except only one individual organized the LLC. Unless the LLC elects to be taxed as a corporation, the LLC, For tax purposes, will be disregarded by default. Consequently, its income will be taxed directly to the owner as if it were a sole proprietorship. ◀

---

[7] This rule does not apply to corporations, trusts, or certain special entities such as real estate investment trusts, real estate mortgage investment conduits, or publicly traded partnerships. Reg. Sec. 301.7701-2(b)(8). Publicly traded partnerships are discussed in Chapter C:10. Special check-the-box rules apply to foreign corporations. These rules are beyond the scope of this text.

If an entity elects to change its tax classification, it cannot make another election until 60 months after the effective date of the initial election. Following the election, certain tax consequences ensue. For example, following a partnership's election to be taxed as a corporation, the partnership is deemed to distribute its assets to the partners, who are then deemed to contribute the assets to a new corporation in a nontaxable exchange for stock. If an eligible entity that previously elected to be taxed as a corporation subsequently elects to be treated as a partnership or a disregarded entity, it is deemed to have distributed its assets and liabilities to its owner(s) in a liquidation as described in Chapter C:6. In the case of a partnership, the deemed distribution is followed by a deemed contribution of assets and liabilities to a newly formed partnership.[8]

LEGAL REQUIREMENTS AND TAX CONSIDERATIONS RELATED TO FORMING A CORPORATION

OBJECTIVE 3

Recognize the legal requirements and tax considerations related to forming a corporation

LEGAL REQUIREMENTS

State or jurisdictional laws dictate the legal requirements for forming a corporation. These requirements usually include

- Investing a minimum amount of capital
- Filing articles of incorporation
- Issuing stock
- Paying incorporation fees to the state or other jurisdiction

One of the first decisions an entrepreneur must make when organizing a corporation is choosing a state of incorporation. Although most entrepreneurs incorporate in the state where they conduct business, many incorporate in other states with more favorable corporation laws. Such laws might provide for little or no income, sales, or use taxes; low minimum capital requirements; and modest incorporation fees. Regardless of the state of incorporation, the entrepreneur must follow the incorporation procedure set forth in the applicable state statute. Typically, under this procedure, the entrepreneur must file articles of incorporation with the appropriate state agency. The articles must specify certain information, such as the formal name of the corporation; its purpose; the par value, number of shares, and classes of stock it is authorized to issue; and the names of the individuals who will initially serve on the corporation's board of directors. The state usually charges a fee for incorporation or filing. In addition, it periodically may assess a franchise tax for the privilege of doing business in the state. These fees and taxes could be substantial.

ADDITIONAL COMMENT

States are not consistent in how they tax corporations. Certain states have no state income taxes. Other states do not recognize an S corporation election, thereby taxing an S corporation as a C corporation.

TAX CONSIDERATIONS

Once the entrepreneur decides on the corporate form, he or she must transfer cash, property (e.g., equipment, furniture, inventory, and receivables), or services (e.g., accounting, legal, or architectural services) to the corporation in exchange for its debt or equity. These transfers may have tax consequences for both the transferor investor and the transferee corporation. For instance, the sale of property for stock usually is taxable to the transferor.[9] However, if Sec. 351(a) (which treats an investor's interest in certain transferred business assets to be "changed in form" rather than "disposed of") applies, any gain or loss realized on the exchange may be deferred. In determining the tax consequences of incorporation, one must answer the following questions:

- What property should be transferred to the corporation?
- What services should the transferors or third parties provide for the corporation?

[8] Reg. Sec. 301.7701-3(g). An alternative way for a corporation to be taxed as a pass-through entity is to make an election to be taxed as an S corporation. See Chapter C:11.

[9] Sec. 1001.

- What liabilities, in addition to property, should be transferred?
- How should the property be transferred (e.g., sale, contribution to capital, or loan)?

Example C:2-10 and Table C:2-1 compare the tax consequences of taxable and nontaxable property transfers.

EXAMPLE C:2-10 ▶ For several years Brad has operated a successful manufacturing business as a sole proprietorship. To limit his liability, he decides to incorporate his business as Block Corporation. Immediately preceding the incorporation, he reports the following balance sheet for his sole proprietorship, which uses the accrual method of accounting:

		Adjusted Basis	*Fair Market Value*
Assets:			
Cash		$ 10,000	$ 10,000
Accounts receivable		15,000	15,000
Inventory		20,000	25,000
Equipment	$120,000		
Minus: Depreciation	(35,000)	85,000	100,000
Total		$130,000	$150,000
Liabilities and owner's equity:			
Accounts payable		$ 30,000	$ 30,000
Note payable on equipment		50,000	50,000
Owner's equity		50,000	70,000
Total		$130,000	$150,000

When Brad transfers the assets to Block in exchange for its stock, he realizes a gain because the value of the stock received exceeds his basis in the assets. If the exchange is taxable, Brad recognizes $5,000 of ordinary income on the transfer of the inventory ($25,000 FMV – $20,000 basis) and, because of depreciation recapture, $15,000 of ordinary income on the transfer of the equipment ($100,000 FMV – $85,000 basis). However, if the exchange meets the requirements of Sec. 351(a), it is nontaxable. In other words, Brad recognizes none of the income or gain realized on the transfer of assets and liabilities to Block. ◀

? STOP & THINK

Question: Joyce has conducted a business as a sole proprietorship for several years. She needs additional capital and wants to incorporate her business. The assets of her business (building, land, inventory, etc.) have a $400,000 adjusted basis and a $1.5 million FMV. Joyce is willing to exchange the assets for 1,500 shares of Ace Corporation stock, each having a $1,000 fair market value. Bill and John each are willing to invest $500,000 in Joyce's business for 500 shares of stock. Why is Sec. 351 relevant to Joyce? Does it matter to Bill and John?

Solution: If not for Sec. 351, Joyce would recognize gain on the incorporation of her business. She realizes a gain of $1.1 million ($1,500,000 – $400,000) on her contribution of proprietorship assets to a new corporation in exchange for 60% of its outstanding shares (1,500 ÷ [1,500 + 500 + 500] = 0.60). However, she recognizes none of this gain because she meets the requirements of Sec. 351. Section 351 does not affect Bill or John because each is simply purchasing 20% of the new corporation's stock for $500,000 cash. They will not realize or recognize gain or loss unless they subsequently sell their stock at a price above or below the $500,000 cost.

If all exchanges of property for corporate stock were taxable, many entrepreneurs would find the tax cost of incorporating their business prohibitively high. In Example C:2-10, for example, Brad would recognize a $20,000 gain on the exchange of his assets for the corporate stock. Moreover, because losses also are realized in an exchange, without special rules, taxpayers could exchange loss property for stock and recognize the loss while maintaining an equity interest in the property transferred.

▼ **TABLE C:2-1**
Overview of Corporate Formation Rules

Tax Treatment for:	Taxable Property Transfer	Nontaxable Property Transfer
Transferors: 1. Gain realized	FMV of stock received Money received FMV of noncash boot property (including securities) received Amount of liabilities assumed by transferee corporation Minus: Adjusted basis of property transferred Realized gain (Sec. 1001(a))	Same as in a taxable transaction
2. Gain recognized	Transferors recognize the entire amount of realized gain (Sec. 1001(c)) Losses may be disallowed under related party rules (Sec. 267(a)(1)) Installment sale rules may apply to the realized gain (Sec. 453)	Transferors recognize none of the realized gain unless one of the following exceptions applies (Sec. 351(a)): a. Boot property is received (Sec. 351(b)) b. Liabilities are transferred to the corporation for a nonbusiness or tax avoidance purpose (Sec. 357(b)) c. Liabilities exceeding basis are transferred to the corporation (Sec. 357(c)) d. Services, certain corporate indebtedness, and interest claims are transferred to the corporation (Sec. 351(d)) The installment method may defer recognition of gain when a shareholder receives a corporate note as boot (Sec. 453)
3. Basis of property received	FMV (Cost) (Sec. 1012)	Basis of property transferred to the corporation Plus: Gain recognized Minus: Money received (including liabilities treated as money) FMV of noncash boot property Total basis of stock received (Sec. 358(a)) Allocation of total stock basis is based on relative FMVs Basis of noncash boot property is its FMV
4. Holding period of property received	Day after the exchange date	Holding period of stock received includes holding period of Sec. 1231 property or capital assets transferred; otherwise it begins the day after the exchange date
Transferee Corporation: 1. Gain recognized	The corporation recognizes no gain or loss on the receipt of money or other property in exchange for its stock (including treasury stock) (Sec. 1032)	Same as taxable transaction except the corporation may recognize gain under Sec. 311 if it transfers appreciated noncash boot property (Sec. 351(f))
2. Basis	FMV (Cost) (Sec. 1012)	Generally, same as in transferor's hands plus any gain recognized by transferor (Sec. 362) If the total adjusted basis of all transferred property exceeds the total FMV of the property, the total basis to the transferor is limited to the property's total FMV
3. Holding period	Day after the exchange date	Transferor's carryover holding period for the property transferred regardless of the property's character (Sec. 1223(2)) Day after the exchange date if basis is reduced to FMV

To allow taxpayers to incorporate without incurring a high tax cost and to prevent taxpayers from recognizing losses while maintaining an equity claim to the loss assets, Congress enacted Sec. 351.

SECTION 351: DEFERRING GAIN OR LOSS UPON INCORPORATION

OBJECTIVE 4

Discuss the requirements for deferring gain or loss upon incorporation

Section 351(a) provides that transferors recognize no gain or loss when they transfer property to a corporation solely in exchange for the corporation's stock if immediately after the exchange, the transferors are in control of the corporation. Section 351 does not apply to a transfer of property to an investment company, nor does it apply in certain bankruptcy cases.

This rule is based on the premise that, when property is transferred to a controlled corporation, the transferors merely exchange direct ownership for indirect ownership through stock in the transferee corporation, which gives them an equity interest in the underlying assets. In other words, the transferors maintain a continuity of interest in the transferred property. Furthermore, if the only consideration the shareholders receive is stock, they have not generated cash with which to pay their taxes. If the transferors of property receive other consideration in addition to stock, such as cash or debt instruments, they will have the wherewithal to pay taxes and, under Sec. 351(b), may have to recognize some or all of their realized gain.

TAX STRATEGY TIP

A transferor who wishes to recognize gain or loss must take steps to avoid Sec. 351 by deliberately failing at least one of its requirements or by engaging in sales transactions. See Tax Planning Considerations at the end of this chapter for details.

A transferor's realized gain or loss that is unrecognized for tax purposes is not exempt from taxation. It is only *deferred* until the shareholder sells or exchanges the stock received in the Sec. 351 exchange. Shareholders who receive stock in such an exchange take a stock basis that reflects the deferred gain or loss. For example, if a shareholder receives stock in exchange for property and recognizes no gain or loss, the stock basis equals the basis of property transferred less liabilities assumed by the corporation (see Table C:2-1). This tax treatment is discussed later in this chapter. Under an alternative approach, the stock basis can be calculated as follows: FMV of qualified stock received, minus any deferred gain (or plus any deferred loss). This latter approach highlights the deferral aspect of this type of transaction. If the shareholder later sells the stock, he or she will recognize the deferred gain or loss inherent in the basis adjustment.

EXAMPLE C:2-11 ▶ Assume the same facts as in Example C:2-10. If Brad satisfies the conditions of Sec. 351, he will not recognize the $20,000 realized gain ($15,000 gain on equipment + $5,000 gain on inventory) when he transfers the assets and liabilities of his sole proprietorship to Block Corporation. Under the alternative approach, Brad's basis in the Block stock is decreased to reflect the deferred gain. Thus, Brad's basis in the Block stock is $50,000 ($70,000 FMV − $20,000 deferred gain). If Brad later sells his stock for its $70,000 FMV, he will recognize the $20,000 gain at the time of sale. ◀

The specific requirements for deferral of gain and loss under Sec. 351(a) are

- The transferors must transfer property to the corporation.
- They must receive stock of the transferee corporation in exchange for their property.
- They must be in control of the corporation immediately after the exchange.

Each of these requirements is explained below.

THE PROPERTY REQUIREMENT

The rule of gain or loss nonrecognition applies only to transfers of property to a corporation in exchange for the corporation's stock. Section 351 does not define the term *property*. However, the courts and the IRS have defined *property* to include cash and almost any other asset, including installment obligations, accounts receivable, inventory, equipment, patents and other intangibles representing know-how, trademarks, trade names, and computer software.[10]

Excluded from the statutory definition of property are[11]

- Services (such as legal or accounting services) rendered to the corporation in exchange for its stock
- Indebtedness of the transferee corporation not evidenced by a security
- Interest on transferee corporation debt that accrued on or after the beginning of the transferor's holding period for the debt

The first of these exclusions perhaps is the most important. A person receiving stock in compensation for services must recognize the stock's FMV as ordinary income for tax purposes. In other words, an exchange of services for stock is a taxable transaction even where concurrent transfers of property for stock are nontaxable under Sec. 351.[12] A shareholder's basis in the stock received in compensation for services is the stock's FMV (not necessarily the FMV of the services).

EXAMPLE C:2-12 ► Amy and Bill form West Corporation. Amy exchanges property for 90 shares (90% of the outstanding shares) of West stock. Amy's exchange is nontaxable because Amy has exchanged property for stock and controls West immediately after the exchange. Bill performs accounting services that he normally bills for $12,000 in exchange for ten shares of West stock worth $10,000. Bill's exchange is taxable because he has provided services in exchange for stock. Thus, Bill recognizes $10,000 of ordinary income—the FMV of the stock—as compensation for his services. Bill's basis in the stock is its $10,000 FMV. ◄

THE CONTROL REQUIREMENT

Section 351 requires the transferors, as a group, to be in control of the transferee corporation immediately after the exchange. A transferor may be an individual or any type of entity (such as a partnership, another corporation, or a trust). Section 368(c) defines *control* as ownership of at least 80% of the total combined voting power of all classes of stock entitled to vote and at least 80% of the total number of shares of all other classes of stock (e.g., nonvoting preferred stock).[13] The minimum ownership levels for nonvoting stock apply to each class of stock rather than to the nonvoting stock in total.[14]

EXAMPLE C:2-13 ► Dan exchanges property having a $22,000 adjusted basis and a $30,000 FMV for 60% of newly created Sun Corporation's single class of stock. Ed exchanges $20,000 cash for the remaining 40% of Sun stock. The transaction qualifies as a nontaxable exchange under Sec. 351 because the transferors, Dan and Ed, together own at least 80% of the Sun stock immediately after the exchange. Therefore, Dan defers recognition of his $8,000 ($30,000 − $22,000) realized gain. (Ed realizes no gain because he contributes cash.) ◄

Because services do not qualify as property, stock received by a person who exclusively provides services does not count toward the 80% control threshold. Unless transferors of property own at least 80% of the corporation's stock immediately after the exchange, the control requirement will not be met, and the entire transaction will be taxable.

EXAMPLE C:2-14 ► Dana transfers property having an $18,000 adjusted basis and a $35,000 FMV to newly created York Corporation for 70 shares of York stock. Ellen provides legal services for the remaining 30 York shares valued at $15,000. Because Ellen does not transfer property to York, her stock is not counted toward the 80% ownership threshold. On the other hand, because Dana transfers property to York, his stock is counted toward this threshold. However, Dana is not in control of York immediately after the exchange because he owns only 70% of York stock. Therefore, Dana recognizes all $17,000 ($35,000 − $18,000) of his gain realized on the exchange. Dana's basis in his York stock is its $35,000 FMV. Ellen recognizes $15,000 of ordinary income, the FMV of stock received for her services. Ellen's basis in her York stock is $15,000. The tax consequences to Ellen are the same whether or not Dana meets the control requirement. ◄

---

[10] For an excellent discussion of the definition of *property*, see footnote 6 of *D.N. Stafford v. U.S.*, 45 AFTR 2d 80-785, 80-1 USTC ¶9218 (5th Cir., 1980).

[11] Sec. 351(d).

[12] Secs. 61 and 83.

[13] In determining whether the 80% requirements are satisfied, the constructive ownership rules of Sec. 318 do not apply (see Rev. Rul. 56-613, 1956-2 C.B. 212). See Chapter C:4 for an explanation of Sec. 318.

[14] Rev. Rul. 59-259, 1959-2 C.B. 115, as modified by Rev. Rul. 81–17, 1981-1 C.B. 75.

If the property transferors own at least 80% of the stock immediately after the exchange, they, but not the provider of services, will be in control of the transferee corporation.

EXAMPLE C:2-15 ▶ Assume the same facts as in Example C:2-14, except a third individual, Fred, contributes $35,000 in cash for 70 shares of York stock. Now Dana and Fred together own more than 80% of the York stock (140 ÷ 170 = 0.82) immediately after the exchange. Therefore, the transaction meets the Sec. 351 control requirement, and neither Dana nor Fred recognizes gain on the exchange. Ellen still must recognize $15,000 of ordinary income, the FMV of the stock she receives for her services. ◀

Transferors of Both Property and Services. If a person transfers both services *and* property to a corporation in exchange for the corporation's stock, all the stock received by that person, including stock received in exchange for services, is counted toward the 80% control threshold.[15]

EXAMPLE C:2-16 ▶ Assume the same facts as in Example C:2-14 except that, in addition to providing legal services in exchange for stock worth $15,000, Ellen contributes property worth at least $1,500. In this case, all of Ellen's stock counts toward the 80% ownership threshold. Because Dana and Ellen together own 100% of the York stock, the exchange meets the Sec. 351 control requirement. Therefore, Dana recognizes no gain on his property exchange. However, Ellen still must recognize $15,000 of ordinary income, the FMV of the stock received as compensation for services. ◀

When a person transfers both property and services in exchange for a corporation's stock, the property must have more than nominal value for that person's stock to count toward the 80% control threshold.[16] The IRS generally requires that the FMV of the stock received for transferred property be at least 10% of the value of the stock received for services provided. If the value of the stock received for the property is less than 10% of the value of the stock received for the services, the IRS will not issue an advance ruling to the effect that the transaction meets the requirements of Sec. 351.[17]

EXAMPLE C:2-17 ▶ Assume the same facts as in Example C:2-16 except that Ellen contributes only $1,000 worth of property in addition to the legal services. In this case, the IRS will not issue an advance ruling that the transaction meets the Sec. 351 requirements because the FMV of stock received for the property ($1,000) is less than 10% of the value of the stock received for the services ($1,500 = 0.10 × $15,000). Consequently, if the IRS audits Ellen's tax return for the year of transfer, it probably will challenge Dana's and Ellen's position that the transfer is nontaxable under Sec. 351. ◀

Transfers to Existing Corporations. Section 351 applies to transfers to an existing corporation as well as transfers to a newly created corporation. The same requirements must be met in both cases. Property must be transferred in exchange for stock, and the property transferors must be in control of the corporation immediately after the exchange.

EXAMPLE C:2-18 ▶ Jack and Karen own 75 and 25 shares, respectively, of Texas Corporation stock. Jack transfers property with a $15,000 adjusted basis and a $25,000 FMV to the corporation in exchange for an additional 25 shares of Texas stock. The transaction meets the Sec. 351 control requirement because, immediately after the exchange, Jack owns 80% (100 ÷ 125 = 0.80) of Texas stock. Therefore, Jack recognizes no gain. ◀

If a shareholder transfers property to an existing corporation for additional stock but does not own at least 80% of the stock immediately after the exchange, the control requirement is not met. Thus, Sec. 351 denies tax-free treatment for many transfers of property to an existing corporation by a new shareholder. A new shareholder's transfer of property to an existing corporation is nontaxable only if that shareholder acquires at least 80% of the corporation's stock, or if enough existing shareholders also transfer additional property so that the transferors as a group, including the new shareholder, control the corporation immediately after the exchange.

[15] Reg. Sec. 1.351-1(a)(2), Ex. (3).
[16] Reg. Sec. 1.351-1(a)(1)(ii).
[17] Rev. Proc. 77-37, 1977-2 C.B. 568, Sec. 3.07, as modified by T.D. 8761, 1998-1 C.B. 812.

EXAMPLE C:2-19 ▶ Alice owns all 100 shares of Local Corporation stock, valued at $100,000. Beth owns property with a $15,000 adjusted basis and a $100,000 FMV. Beth contributes the property to Local in exchange for 100 shares of newly issued Local stock. The transaction does not meet the Sec. 351 control requirement because Beth owns only 50% of Local stock immediately after the exchange. Consequently, Beth recognizes an $85,000 ($100,000 − $15,000) gain. ◀

If an existing shareholder exchanges property for additional stock to enable another shareholder to qualify for tax-free treatment under Sec. 351, the stock received must be of more than nominal value.[18] For advance ruling purposes, the IRS requires that this value be at least 10% of the value of the stock already owned.[19]

EXAMPLE C:2-20 ▶ Assume the same facts as in Example C:2-19 except that Alice transfers additional property worth $10,000 for an additional ten shares of Local stock. Now both Alice and Beth are transferors, thereby satisfying the Sec. 351 control requirement. Consequently, neither Alice nor Beth recognizes gain on the exchange. If Alice receives fewer than ten shares, the IRS will not issue an advance ruling that the exchange is tax-free under Sec. 351. ◀

? STOP & THINK

Question: Matthew and Michael each own 50 shares of Main Corporation stock having a $250,000 FMV. Matthew wants to transfer property with a $40,000 adjusted basis and a $100,000 FMV to Main in exchange for an additional 20 shares. Can Matthew avoid recognizing $60,000 ($100,000 − $40,000) of the gain realized on the transfer?

Solution: If Matthew simply exchanges the property for additional stock, he must recognize the gain. The Sec. 351 control requirement will not have been met because Matthew will own only 70 of the 120 outstanding shares (or 58.33%) immediately after the exchange.

Gain recognition can be avoided in two ways:

1. Matthew can transfer sufficient property (i.e., $750,000 worth) to Main to receive 150 additional shares so that, immediately after the exchange, he will own 80% (200 out of 250 shares) of Main stock.
2. Alternatively, Michael also can contribute additional property to qualify as a transferor. Specifically, he can contribute to the corporation at least $25,000, or 10% of the $250,000 value of the Main stock that he already owns so that together the two transferors will own 100% of Main stock immediately after the exchange.

Disproportionate Exchanges of Property and Stock. Section 351 does not require that the value of the stock received by the transferors be proportionate to the value of the property transferred. However, if the value of the stock received is *not* proportionate to the value of the property transferred, the exchange may be treated in accordance with its economic effect, that is, a proportional exchange followed by a constructive gift, compensation payment, or extinguishment of a liability owed by one shareholder to another.[20] If the deemed effect of the transaction is a gift from one transferor to another, for example, the "donor" will be treated as though he or she received stock equal in value to that of the property contributed and then gave some of the stock to the "donee."

EXAMPLE C:2-21 ▶ Don and his son John transfer property worth $75,000 (adjusted basis of $42,000 to Don) and $25,000 (adjusted basis of $20,000 to John), respectively, to newly formed Star Corporation in exchange for all 100 shares of Star stock. Don and John receive 25 and 75 Star shares, respectively. Because Don and John are in control of Star immediately after the exchange, they recognize no gain or loss. However, because Don and John did not receive the stock in proportion to the FMV of their respective property contributions, Don might be deemed to have received 75 shares (worth $75,000), then to have given 50 shares (worth $50,000) to John. If the IRS deems such a gift, it might require Don to pay gift taxes. Don's basis in his remaining 25 shares is $14,000 [(25 ÷ 75) × $42,000 basis in the property transferred]. John's basis in the 75 shares is $48,000 [$20,000 basis in the property transferred by John + ($42,000 − $14,000) basis in the shares deemed to have been gifted by Don]. ◀

---

[18] Reg. Sec. 1.351-1(a)(1)(ii).

[19] Rev. Proc. 77-37, 1977-2 C.B. 568, Sec. 3.07, as modified by T.D. 8761, 1998-1 C.B. 812.

[20] Reg. Sec. 1.351-1(b)(1).

Immediately after the Exchange. Section 351 requires that the transferors be in control of the transferee corporation "immediately after the exchange." This requirement does not mean that all transferors must simultaneously exchange their property for stock. It does mean, however, that all the exchanges must be agreed to beforehand, and the agreement must be executed in an expeditious and orderly manner.[21]

EXAMPLE C:2-22 ▶ Art, Beth, and Carlos form New Corporation. Art and Beth each transfer noncash property worth $25,000 in exchange for one-third of the New stock. Carlos contributes $25,000 cash for another one-third of the New stock. On January 10, Art and Carlos transfer their property and cash, respectively. Beth transfers her property on March 3. Because all three transfers are part of the same prearranged transaction, the transferors are deemed to be in control of the corporation immediately after the exchange. ◀

TAX STRATEGY TIP

If one shareholder has a prearranged plan to dispose of his or her stock, and the disposition reduces the ownership of the transferor shareholders below the required 80% control, such disposition can disqualify the Sec. 351 transaction for all the shareholders. As a precaution, all shareholders should provide a written representation that they do not currently have a plan to dispose of their stock.

Section 351 does not require the transferors to retain control of the transferee corporation for any specific length of time after the exchange. Control is required only "immediately after the exchange." The IRS has interpreted this phrase to mean that the transferors must not have a prearranged plan to dispose of their stock outside the control group. If they do have such a plan, they are not considered to be in control immediately after the exchange.[22]

EXAMPLE C:2-23 ▶ Amir, Bill, and Carl form White Corporation. Each contributes to White appreciated property worth $25,000 in exchange for one-third of White stock. Before the exchange, Amir arranges to sell his stock to Dana as soon as he receives it. This prearranged plan implies that Amir, Bill, and Carl do *not* have control immediately after the exchange because Bill and Carl own only 66.7% of the stock while Amir has disposed of his interest. Therefore, each must recognize gain on the exchange. ◀

THE STOCK REQUIREMENT

Under Sec. 351, transferors who exchange property solely for transferee corporation stock recognize no gain or loss if they control the corporation immediately after the exchange. For this purpose, stock may be voting or nonvoting. On the other hand, nonqualified preferred stock is treated as boot. Preferred stock generally has a preferred claim to dividends and liquidating distributions. Such stock is nonqualified if

- The shareholder can require the corporation to redeem it,
- The corporation either is required to redeem the stock or is likely to exercise a right to redeem it, or
- The dividend rate on the stock varies with interest rates, commodity prices, or other similar indices.

These features render the preferred stock more like cash or debt than like equity. Thus, it is treated as boot subject to the rules discussed below. In addition, stock rights or stock warrants are not considered stock for purposes of Sec. 351.[23]

Topic Review C:2-1 summarizes the major requirements for a nontaxable exchange under Sec. 351.

EFFECT OF SEC. 351 ON THE TRANSFERORS

If all Sec. 351 requirements are met, the transferors recognize no gain or loss on the exchange of their property for stock in the transferee corporation. The receipt of property other than stock does not necessarily render the entire transaction taxable. Rather, it could result in the recognition of all or part of the transferors' realized gain.

Receipt of Boot. If a transferor receives any money or property other than stock in the transferee corporation, the additional money or property is considered to be **boot**. Boot may include cash, notes, securities, or stock in another corporation. Upon receiving boot, the transferor recognizes gain to the extent of the lesser of the transferor's realized

[21] Reg. Sec. 1.351-1(a)(1).
[22] Rev. Rul. 79-70, 1979-1 C.B. 144.
[23] Reg. Sec. 1.351-1(a)(1)(ii).

TOPIC REVIEW C:2-1

Major Requirements of Sec. 351

1. The nonrecognition of gain or loss rule applies only to transfers of property in exchange for a corporation's stock. It does not apply to an exchange of services for stock.
2. The property transferors must be in control of the transferee corporation immediately after the exchange. Control means ownership of at least 80% of the voting power and at least 80% of the total number of shares of all other classes of stock. Stock disposed of after the exchange pursuant to a prearranged plan does not meet the "immediately after the exchange" requirement.
3. The nonrecognition rule applies only to the gain realized in an exchange of property for stock. If the transferor receives property other than stock, such property is considered to be boot. The transferor recognizes gain to the extent of the lesser of the FMV of any boot received or the realized gain.

gain or the FMV of the boot property received.[24] A transferor never recognizes a loss in an exchange qualifying under Sec. 351 whether or not he or she receives boot.

The character of the recognized gain depends on the type of property transferred. For example, if the shareholder transfers a capital asset such as stock in another corporation, the recognized gain is capital in character. If the shareholder transfers Sec. 1231 property, such as equipment or a building, the recognized gain is ordinary in character to the extent of any depreciation recaptured under Sec. 1245 or 1250.[25] Thus, depreciation is not recaptured unless the transferor receives boot and recognizes a gain on the depreciated property transferred.[26] If the shareholder transfers inventory, the recognized gain is entirely ordinary in character.

EXAMPLE C:2-24 ▶ Pam, Rob, and Sam form East Corporation and transfer the following property:

Transferor	*Asset*	*Transferor's Adj. Basis*	*FMV*	*Consideration Received*
Pam	Machinery	$ 10,000	$12,500	25 shares East stock
Rob	Land	18,000	25,000	40 shares East stock and $5,000 East note
Sam	Cash	17,500	17,500	35 shares East stock

The machinery is Sec. 1231 property, and the land is a capital asset. The exchange meets the requirements of Sec. 351 except that, in addition to East stock, Rob receives boot of $5,000 (the FMV of the note). Rob realizes a $7,000 ($25,000 − $18,000) gain, of which he recognizes $5,000—the lesser of the $7,000 realized gain or the $5,000 boot received. The gain is capital in character because the property transferred was a capital asset in Rob's hands. Pam realizes a $2,500 gain on her exchange of machinery. However, even though Pam would have been required to recapture depreciation had she sold or exchanged the machinery, she recognizes no gain because she received no boot. Sam neither realizes nor recognizes gain on his cash purchase of East stock. ◀

ADDITIONAL COMMENT

If multiple assets were aggregated into one computation, any built-in losses would be netted against the gains. Such a result is inappropriate because losses cannot be recognized in a Sec. 351 transaction.

Computing Gain when Several Assets are Transferred. Revenue Ruling 68-55 adopts a "separate properties approach" for computing gain or loss when a shareholder transfers more than one asset to a corporation.[27] Under this approach, the gain or loss realized and recognized is computed separately for each property transferred. The transferor is deemed to have received a proportionate share of stock, securities, and boot in exchange for each property transferred, based on the assets' relative FMVs.

EXAMPLE C:2-25 ▶ Joan transfers two assets to newly formed North Corporation in a transaction qualifying in part for tax-free treatment under Sec. 351. The total FMV of the assets is $100,000. The consideration

[24] Sec. 351(b).

[25] Section 1239 also may require some gain to be characterized as ordinary income. Section 1250 ordinary depreciation recapture will not apply to real property placed in service after 1986 because MACRS mandates straight-line depreciation.

[26] Secs. 1245(b)(3) and 1250(c)(3).

[27] 1968-1 C.B. 140, as amplified by Rev. Rul. 85-164, 1985-2 C.B. 117.

received by Joan consists of $90,000 of North stock and $10,000 of North notes. The following data illustrate how Joan determines her realized and recognized gain under the procedure set forth in Rev. Rul. 68-55.

	Asset 1	*Asset 2*	*Total*
Asset's FMV	$40,000	$60,000	$100,000
Percent of total FMV	40%	60%	100%
Consideration received in exchange for asset:			
Stock (Stock × percent of total FMV)	$36,000	$54,000	$ 90,000
Notes (Notes × percent of total FMV)	4,000	6,000	10,000
Total proceeds	$40,000	$60,000	$100,000
Minus: Adjusted basis	(65,000)	(25,000)	(90,000)
Realized gain (loss)	($25,000)	$35,000	$ 10,000
Boot received	$ 4,000	$ 6,000	$ 10,000
Recognized gain (loss)	None	$ 6,000	$ 6,000

Under the separate properties approach, the loss realized on the transfer of Asset 1 does not offset the gain realized on the transfer of Asset 2. Therefore, Joan recognizes $6,000 of the total $10,000 realized gain, even though she receives $10,000 of boot. Joan's selling Asset 1 to North so as to recognize the loss might be advisable. However, the Sec. 267 loss limitation rules may apply to Joan if she is a controlling shareholder (see pages C:2-34 and C:2-35). ◀

Computing a Shareholder's Basis.

Boot Property. A transferor's basis in any boot property received is the property's FMV.[28]

Stock. A shareholder computes his or her adjusted basis in stock received in a Sec. 351 exchange as follows:[29]

Adjusted basis of property transferred to the corporation	
Plus:	Any gain recognized by the transferor
Minus:	FMV of boot received from the corporation
	Money received from the corporation
	Liabilities assumed by the corporation
Adjusted basis of stock received	

EXAMPLE C:2-26 ▶ Bob transfers a capital asset having a $50,000 adjusted basis and an $80,000 FMV to South Corporation. He acquired the property two years ago. Bob receives all 100 shares of South stock, having a $70,000 FMV, plus a $10,000 90-day South note (boot property). Bob realizes a $30,000 gain on the exchange, computed as follows:

FMV of stock received	$70,000
Plus: FMV of 90-day note	10,000
Amount realized	$80,000
Minus: Adjusted basis of property transferred	(50,000)
Realized gain	$30,000

Bob's recognized gain is $10,000, i.e., the lesser of the $30,000 realized gain or the $10,000 FMV of the boot property. This gain is long-term and capital in character. The Sec. 351 rules effectively require Bob to defer $20,000 ($30,000 – $10,000) of his realized gain. Bob's basis in the South stock is $50,000, computed as follows:

Adjusted basis of property transferred	$50,000
Plus: Gain recognized by Bob	10,000
Minus: FMV of boot received	(10,000)
Adjusted basis of Bob's stock	$50,000 ◀

ADDITIONAL COMMENT

Because Sec. 351 is a deferral provision, any unrecognized gain must be reflected in the basis of the stock received by the transferor shareholder and is accomplished by substituting the shareholder's basis in the property transferred for the basis of the stock received. This substituted basis may be further adjusted by gain recognized and boot received.

SELF-STUDY QUESTION

What is an alternative method for determining the basis of the assets received by the transferor shareholder? How is this method applied to Bob in Example C:2-26?

[28] Sec. 358(a)(2).

[29] Sec. 358(a)(1).

If a transferor receives more than one class of qualified stock, his or her basis must be allocated among the classes according to their relative FMVs.[30]

EXAMPLE C:2-27 ▶ Assume the same facts as in Example C:2-26 except Bob receives 100 shares of South common stock with a $45,000 FMV, 50 shares of South qualified preferred stock with a $25,000 FMV, and a 90-day South note with a $10,000 FMV. The total adjusted basis of the stock is $50,000 ($50,000 basis of property transferred + $10,000 gain recognized − $10,000 FMV of boot received). This basis must be allocated between the common and qualified preferred stock according to their relative FMVs, as follows:

$$\text{Basis of common stock} = \frac{\$45{,}000}{\$45{,}000 + \$25{,}000} \times \$50{,}000 = \$32{,}143$$

$$\text{Basis of preferred stock} = \frac{\$25{,}000}{\$45{,}000 + \$25{,}000} \times \$50{,}000 = \$17{,}857$$

Bob's basis in the note is its $10,000 FMV. ◀

ANSWER

The basis of all boot property is its FMV, and the basis of stock received is the stock's FMV minus any deferred gain or plus any deferred loss. Bob's stock basis under the alternative method is $50,000 ($70,000 FMV of stock − $20,000 deferred gain).

Transferor's Holding Period. The transferor's holding period for any stock received in exchange for a capital asset or Sec. 1231 property includes the holding period of the property transferred.[31] If the transferor exchanged any other kind of property (e.g., inventory) for the stock, the transferor's holding period for the stock begins on the day after the exchange. Likewise, the holding period for boot property begins on the day after the exchange.

EXAMPLE C:2-28 ▶ Assume the same facts as in Example C:2-26. Bob's holding period for the stock includes the holding period of the capital asset transferred. His holding period for the note starts on the day after the exchange. ◀

STOP & THINK

Question: The holding period for stock received in exchange for a capital asset or Sec. 1231 property includes the holding period of the transferred item. The holding period for inventory or other assets begins on the day after the exchange. Why the difference?

Solution: Because stock received in a Sec. 351 exchange represents a "continuity of interest" in the property transferred, logically the stock should not only be valued and characterized in the same manner as the asset exchanged for the equity claim, but also accorded the same tax attributes. Because the holding period of a capital asset is relevant in determining the character of gain or loss realized (i.e., long-term or short-term) on the asset's subsequent sale, stock received in a tax-free exchange of the asset should be accorded the same holding period for the purpose of determining the character of gain or loss realized on the stock's subsequent sale. By the same token, because the holding period of a noncapital asset is less relevant in determining the character of gain or loss realized on the asset's subsequent sale, stock received in a tax-free exchange of the asset need not be accorded the same holding period for the purpose of determining the character of gain or loss realized on the stock's subsequent sale. Given the very nature of a noncapital asset, this gain or loss generally is ordinary in character, in any event. Moreover, if stock received in exchange for a noncapital asset were accorded a holding period that includes that of the transferred property, a transferor could sell the stock in a short time to realize a long-term capital gain, thereby converting ordinary income (potentially from the sale of the noncapital asset) into capital gain from the sale of stock.

Topic Review C:2-2 summarizes the tax consequences of a Sec. 351 exchange to the transferor(s) and the transferee corporation.

[30] Sec. 358(b)(1) and Reg. Sec. 1.358-2(b)(2).

[31] Sec. 1223(1). Revenue Ruling 85-164 (1985-2 C.B. 117) provides that a single share of stock may have two holding periods: a carryover holding period for the portion of such share received in exchange for a capital asset or Sec. 1231 property and a holding period that begins on the day after the exchange for the portion of such share received for inventory or other property. The split holding period is relevant only if the transferor sells the stock received within one year of the transfer date.

TOPIC REVIEW C:2-2

Tax Consequences of a Sec. 351 Exchange

TO TRANSFEROR(S):

1. Transferors recognize no gain or loss when they exchange property for stock. Exception: A transferor recognizes gain equal to the lesser of the realized gain or the sum of any money received plus the FMV of any non-cash property received. The character of the gain depends on the type of property transferred.
2. The basis of the stock received equals the adjusted basis of the property transferred plus any gain recognized by the transferor minus the FMV of any boot property received minus any money received (including liabilities assumed or acquired by the transferee corporation).
3. The holding period of stock received in exchange for capital assets or Sec. 1231 property includes the holding period of the transferred property. The holding period of stock received in exchange for any other property begins on the day after the exchange.

TO TRANSFEREE CORPORATION:

1. A corporation recognizes no gain or loss when it exchanges its own stock for property or services.
2. The corporation's basis in property received is the transferor's basis plus any gain recognized by the transferor. However, if the total adjusted basis of all transferred property exceeds the total FMV of the property, the total basis to the transferee is limited to the property's total FMV.
3. The corporation's holding period for property received includes the transferor's holding period.

ADDITIONAL COMMENT

The nonrecognition rule for corporations that issue stock for property applies whether or not the transaction qualifies the transferor shareholder for Sec. 351 treatment.

TAX CONSEQUENCES TO TRANSFEREE CORPORATION

A corporation that issues stock or debt for property or services is subject to various IRC rules for determining the tax consequences of that exchange.

Gain or Loss Recognized by the Transferee Corporation. Corporations recognize no gain or loss when they issue their own stock in exchange for property or services.[32] This result ensues whether or not Sec. 351 governs the exchange and whether or not the corporation issues new stock or treasury stock.

EXAMPLE C:2-29 ▶ West Corporation pays $10,000 to acquire 100 shares of its own stock from existing shareholders. The next year, West reissues these 100 treasury shares in exchange for land having a $15,000 FMV. West realizes a $5,000 ($15,000 − $10,000) gain on the exchange but recognizes none of this gain. ◀

Corporations also recognize no gain or loss when they exchange their own debt instruments for property or services. On the other hand, a corporation recognizes gain (but not loss) if it transfers appreciated property to a transferor as part of a Sec. 351 exchange. The amount and character of the gain are determined as though the property had been sold by the corporation immediately before the transfer.

EXAMPLE C:2-30 ▶ Alice, who owns 100% of Ace Corporation stock, transfers to Ace land having a $100,000 FMV and a $60,000 adjusted basis. In exchange, Alice receives 75 additional shares of Ace common stock having a $75,000 FMV, and Zero Corporation common stock having a $25,000 FMV. Ace's basis in the Zero stock, a capital asset, is $10,000. Alice realizes a $40,000 gain [($75,000 + $25,000) − $60,000] on the land transfer, of which she recognizes $25,000 (i.e., the FMV of the boot property received). In addition, Ace recognizes a $15,000 capital gain ($25,000 − $10,000) upon transferring the Zero stock to Alice. ◀

Transferee Corporation's Basis for Property Received. A corporation that acquires property in exchange for its stock in a transaction that is taxable to the transferor takes a current cost (i.e., its FMV) basis in the property. On the other hand, if

[32] Sec. 1032.

ADDITIONAL COMMENT

If a shareholder transfers built-in gain property in a Sec. 351 transaction, the built-in gain actually is duplicated. This duplication occurs because the transferee corporation assumes the potential gain through its carryover basis in the assets it receives, and the transferor shareholder assumes the potential gain through its substituted basis in the transferee corporation stock. A similar duplication occurs for built-in loss property. This result reflects the double taxation characteristic of C corporations.

the exchange qualifies for nonrecognition treatment under Sec. 351 and is wholly or partially tax-free to the transferor, the corporation's basis in the property is computed as follows:[33]

Transferor's adjusted basis in property transferred to the corporation
Plus: Gain (if any) recognized by transferor
Minus: Reduction for loss property (if applicable)

Transferee corporation's basis in property

The transferee corporation's holding period for property acquired in a transaction satisfying the Sec. 351 requirements includes the period during which the property was held by the transferor.[34] This general rule applies to all types of property without regard to their character in the transferor's hands or the amount of gain recognized by the transferor. However, if the corporation reduces a property's basis to its FMV under the loss property limitation rule discussed below, the holding period will begin the day after the exchange date because no part of the new basis references the transferor's basis.

EXAMPLE C:2-31 ▶ Top Corporation issues 100 shares of its stock for land having a $15,000 FMV. Tina, who transferred the land, had a $12,000 basis in the property. If the exchange satisfies the Sec. 351 requirements, Tina recognizes no gain on the exchange. Top's basis in the land is $12,000, the same as Tina's. Top's holding period includes Tina's holding period. However, if the exchange does *not* satisfy the Sec. 351 requirements, Tina recognizes $3,000 of gain. Top's basis in the land is its $15,000 acquisition cost, and its holding period begins on the day after the exchange date. ◀

Reduction for Loss Property. Section 362(e)(2) prevents shareholders from generating double losses by transferring loss property to a corporation. The double loss potential exists because the corporation would hold property with a built-in loss, and the shareholders would hold stock with a built-in loss. Accordingly, if a corporation's total adjusted basis (including any increase for gain recognized by the shareholder) for all properties transferred by the shareholder exceeds the properties' total FMV, the basis to the corporation of the properties must be reduced by this excess. The reduction in basis is allocated among the properties in proportion to their respective built-in losses. The limitation applies on a shareholder-by-shareholder basis. In other words, the property values and built-in losses of all shareholders are not aggregated.

EXAMPLE C:2-32 ▶ John transfers the following assets to Pecan Corporation in exchange for all of Pecan's stock worth $26,000.

Assets	*Adjusted Basis to John*	*FMV*
Inventory	$ 5,000	$ 8,000
Equipment	15,000	11,000
Furniture	9,000	7,000
Total	$29,000	$26,000

Although the transaction meets the requirements of Sec. 351, the total basis of the assets transferred ($29,000) exceeds their total FMV. Consequently, the total basis to Pecan is limited to the assets' FMV ($26,000). The $3,000 ($29,000 − $26,000) reduction in basis must be allocated among the assets in proportion to their respective built-in losses as follows:

Assets	*Built-in Losses*	*Allocated Reduction*
Equipment	$4,000	$2,000
Furniture	2,000	1,000
Total	$6,000	$3,000

[33] Sec. 362.

[34] Sec. 1223(2).

Thus, Pecan's bases for the assets transferred by John are:

Inventory	$ 5,000
Equipment ($15,000 − $2,000)	13,000
Furniture ($9,000 − $1,000)	8,000
Total	$26,000

Because each property's basis was not reduced to the property's FMV, the holding period of each property includes the transferor's holding period. ◀

A corporation subject to the basis reduction rules described above can avoid this result if the corporation and all its shareholders so elect. Under the election, the corporation need not reduce the bases of the assets received, but the affected shareholder's basis in stock received for the property is reduced by the amount by which the corporation would have reduced its basis absent the election.

EXAMPLE C:2-33 ▶ Assume the same facts as in Example C:2-32 except John and Pecan elect not to reduce the bases of the assets Pecan received. Under the election, John's basis in his Pecan stock is reduced to $26,000 ($29,000 − $3,000). ◀

A corporation and its shareholders can avoid the basis reduction rules altogether if each shareholder transfers enough appreciated property to offset any built-in losses of other property transferred. This avoidance opportunity exists because in making the comparison, each shareholder aggregates the adjusted bases and FMVs of his or her property transferred.

EXAMPLE C:2-34 ▶ Assume the same facts as in Example C:2-32 except the inventory's FMV is $12,000. In this case, total basis equals $29,000 and total FMV equals $30,000. Because total basis does not exceed total FMV, the limitation does not apply. Consequently, the corporation takes a carryover basis in each asset even though some assets have built-in losses. ◀

ASSUMPTION OF THE TRANSFEROR'S LIABILITIES

When a shareholder transfers property to a controlled corporation, the corporation often assumes the transferor's liabilities. The question arises as to whether the transferee corporation's assumption of liabilities is equivalent to a cash (boot) payment to the transferor. In certain types of transactions, the transferee's assumption of a transferor's liability is treated as a payment of cash to the transferor. For example, in a like-kind exchange, if a transferee assumes a transferor's liability, the transferor is treated as though he or she received a cash payment equal to the amount of the liability assumed. By contrast, if a transaction satisfies the Sec. 351 requirements, Sec. 357 provides relief from such treatment.

General Rule—Sec. 357(a). For the purpose of determining gain recognition, the transferee corporation's assumption of liabilities in a property transfer qualifying under Sec. 351 is *not* considered equivalent to the transferor's receipt of money. Consequently, the transferee corporation's assumption of liabilities does not result in the transferor's recognizing part or all of his or her realized gain. For the purpose of calculating the transferor's stock basis, however, the transferee corporation's assumption of liabilities *is* treated as money received and thus decreases the transferor's stock basis. Moreover, for the purpose of calculating the transferor's *realized* gain, the transferee corporation's assumption of liabilities is treated as part of the transferor's amount realized.[35]

EXAMPLE C:2-35 ▶ Roy and Eduardo transfer the following assets and liabilities to newly formed Palm Corporation:

[35] Sec. 358(d)(1).

Transferor	*Asset/ Liability*	*Transferor's Adj. Basis*	*FMV*	*Consideration Received*
Roy	Machinery	$15,000	$32,000	50 shares Palm stock
	Mortgage	8,000	—	Assumed by Palm
Eduardo	Cash	24,000	24,000	50 shares Palm stock

The transaction meets the requirements of Sec. 351. Roy's recognized gain is determined as follows:

FMV of stock received	$24,000
Plus: Palm's assumption of the mortgage liability	8,000
Amount realized	$32,000
Minus: Basis of machinery	(15,000)
Realized gain	$17,000
Boot received	$ –0–
Recognized gain	$ –0–

Although Palm's assumption of the mortgage liability increases Roy's amount realized, Roy recognizes none of his realized gain because the mortgage assumption is not considered to be boot (i.e., a cash equivalent). Eduardo recognizes no gain because he transferred only cash. Roy's stock basis is $7,000 ($15,000 basis of property transferred − $8,000 liability assumed by Palm). Eduardo's stock basis is $24,000. ◀

ADDITIONAL COMMENT

If any of the assumed liabilities are created for tax avoidance purposes, *all* the assumed liabilities are tainted.

The general rule of Sec. 357(a), however, has two exceptions. These exceptions, discussed below, relate to (1) transfers for the purpose of tax avoidance or without a bona fide business purpose and (2) transfers where the liabilities assumed by the corporation exceed the total basis of the property transferred.

ETHICAL POINT

Information about any transferor liabilities assumed by the transferee corporation must be reported with the transferee and transferor's tax returns for the year of transfer (see page C:2-36). Where a client asks a tax practitioner to ignore the fact that tax avoidance is the primary purpose for transferring a liability to a corporation, the tax practitioner must examine the ethical considerations of continuing to prepare returns and provide tax advice for the client.

Tax Avoidance or no Bona Fide Business Purpose—Sec. 357(b). All liabilities assumed by a controlled corporation *are* considered to be money received by the transferor, and therefore boot, if the principal purpose of the transfer of any portion of such liabilities is tax avoidance or if the liability transfer has no bona fide business purpose.

The transfer of liabilities might be considered to be motivated principally by tax avoidance where the transferor incurred the liabilities shortly before the transfer. Thus, the most important factor in determining whether a tax avoidance purpose exists may be the length of time between the incurrence of the liability and its transfer to, or assumption by, the corporation.

The assumption of liabilities normally is considered to have a business purpose if the transferor incurred the liabilities in the normal course of business or in the course of acquiring business property. Examples of liabilities without a bona fide business purpose and whose transfer would cause *all* liabilities transferred to be considered boot are personal obligations of the transferor, including a home mortgage or any other loans of a personal nature.

EXAMPLE C:2-36 ▶ David owns land having a $100,000 FMV and a $60,000 adjusted basis. The land is not encumbered by any liabilities. To obtain cash for his personal use, David transfers the land to his wholly owned corporation in exchange for additional stock and $25,000 cash. Because the cash is considered to be boot, David must recognize $25,000 of gain. Assume instead that David mortgages the land for $25,000 to obtain the needed cash. If shortly thereafter David transfers the land and the mortgage to his corporation for additional stock, the $25,000 mortgage assumed by the corporation will be considered to be boot because the transfer of the mortgage appears to have no bona fide business purpose. David's recognized gain will be $25,000, i.e., the lesser of the boot received ($25,000) or his realized gain ($40,000). This special liability rule prevents David from obtaining cash without boot recognition. ◀

Liabilities in Excess of Basis—Sec. 357(c). Under Sec. 357(c), if the total amount of liabilities transferred to a controlled corporation exceeds the total adjusted basis of all property transferred, the excess liability is taxed as a gain to the transferor.

This rule applies regardless of whether the transferor realizes any gain or loss. The rationale for the rule is that the transferor has received a benefit (in the form of a release from liabilities) that exceeds his or her original investment in the transferred property. Therefore, the transferor should be taxed on this benefit. The character of the recognized gain depends on the type of property transferred to the corporation. The transferor's basis in any stock received is zero.

EXAMPLE C:2-37 ▶ Judy transfers $10,000 cash and land, a capital asset, to Duke Corporation in exchange for all its stock. At the time of the exchange, the land has a $70,000 adjusted basis and a $125,000 FMV. Duke assumes a $100,000 mortgage on the land for a bona fide business purpose. Although Judy receives no boot, Judy must recognize a $20,000 ($100,000 − $80,000) capital gain, the amount by which the liabilities assumed by Duke exceed the basis of the land and the cash. Judy's basis in the Duke stock is zero, computed as follows:

Judy's basis in the land transferred		$ 70,000
Plus:	Cash transferred	10,000
	Gain recognized	20,000
Minus:	Liabilities assumed by Duke	(100,000)
Judy's basis in the Duke stock		$ -0-

Note that, without the recognition of the $20,000 gain, Judy's basis in the Duke stock would be a negative $20,000 ($80,000 – $100,000). ◀

STOP & THINK

Question: What are the fundamental differences between the liability exceptions of Sec. 357(b) and Sec. 357(c)?

Solution: Section 357(b) treats all "tainted" liabilities as boot so that gain recognition is the lesser of gain realized or the amount of boot. Excess liabilities under Sec. 357(c) are not treated as boot; they require gain recognition whether or not the transferor realizes any gain. Section 357(b) tends to be punitive in that the "tax avoidance" liabilities cause all the "offending" shareholder's transferred liabilities to be treated as boot even if the transfer of some liabilities do not have a tax avoidance purpose. Section 357(c) is not intended to be punitive. It recognizes that the shareholder has received an economic benefit to the extent of excess liabilities, and it prevents the occurrence of a negative stock basis. In short, Section 357(b) deters or punishes tax avoidance while Sec. 357(c) taxes an economic gain.

KEY POINT

Because of the "liabilities in excess of basis" exception, many cash basis transferor shareholders might inadvertently create recognized gain in a Sec. 351 transaction. However, a special exception exists that protects cash basis taxpayers. This exception provides that liabilities that would give rise to a deduction when paid are not treated as liabilities for purposes of Sec. 357(c).

Liabilities of a Cash Method Taxpayer—Sec. 357(c)(3). In a Sec. 351 tax-free exchange, special problems arise when a taxpayer using the cash or hybrid method of accounting transfers property and liabilities of an ongoing business to a corporation.[36] Often, the principal assets transferred are accounts receivable having a zero basis. Liabilities usually are transferred as well. Consequently, the amount of liabilities transferred may exceed the total basis (but not the FMV) of the property transferred.

Under the general rule of Sec. 357(c), the transferor recognizes gain equal to the amount by which the liabilities assumed exceed the total basis of the property transferred. Section 357(c)(3), however, provides that, in applying the general rule, the term *liabilities* does *not* include any amount that would give rise to a deduction when paid (e.g., accounts payable of a cash basis taxpayer). These amounts also are not considered liabilities for the purpose of determining the shareholder's basis in stock received.[37] Therefore, they generally do not reduce this basis. However, if after all other adjustments the stock's basis exceeds its FMV, these liabilities could reduce stock basis, but not below the stock's FMV.[38]

EXAMPLE C:2-38 ▶ Tracy operates a cash basis accounting practice as a sole proprietorship. She transfers the assets of her practice to Prime Corporation in exchange for all the Prime stock. The balance sheet for the transferred practice is as follows:

[36] Sec. 357(c)(3).
[37] Sec. 358(d)(2).
[38] Sec. 358(h)(1).

Assets and Liabilities	*Adjusted Basis*	*FMV*
Cash	$ 5,000	$ 5,000
Furniture	5,000	8,000
Accounts receivable	–0–	50,000
Total	$10,000	$63,000
Accounts payable (deductible expenses)	$ –0–	$25,000
Note payable (on office furniture)	2,000	2,000
Owner's equity	8,000	36,000
Total	$10,000	$63,000

If, for purposes of Sec. 357(c), the accounts payable were considered liabilities, the $27,000 of liabilities transferred (i.e., the $25,000 of accounts payable and the $2,000 note payable) would exceed the $10,000 total basis of assets transferred, and Troy would recognize a $17,000 gain. Because paying the $25,000 of accounts payable gives rise to a deduction, however, they are not considered liabilities for purposes of Sec. 357(c). On the other hand, the $2,000 note payable *is* considered a liability for this purpose because paying it would not give rise to a deduction. Thus, the total liabilities transferred to Prime amount to only $2,000. Because that amount does not exceed the $10,000 total basis of the assets transferred, Tracy recognizes no gain. Moreover, the accounts payable are not considered liabilities for purposes of computing Tracy's basis in her stock because the stock's basis ($8,000) does not exceed its FMV ($36,000). Thus, her basis in the Prime stock is $8,000 ($10,000 – $2,000). ◄

Topic Review C:2-3 summarizes the liability assumption and acquisition rules of Sec. 357.

OTHER CONSIDERATIONS IN A SEC. 351 EXCHANGE

Recapture of Depreciation. If a Sec. 351 exchange is completely nontaxable (i.e., the transferor receives no boot), no depreciation is recaptured. Instead, the corporation inherits the entire amount of the transferor's recapture potential. Where the transferor recognizes some depreciation recapture as ordinary income (e.g., because of boot recognition), the transferee inherits the remaining recapture potential. If the transferee corporation subsequently disposes of the depreciated property, the corporation is subject to recapture rules on depreciation it claimed subsequent to the transfer, plus the recapture potential it inherited from the transferor.

EXAMPLE C:2-39 ► Azeem transfers machinery having a $25,000 original cost, an $18,000 adjusted basis, and a $35,000 FMV for all 100 shares of Wheel Corporation stock. Before the transfer, Azeem used the machinery in his business and claimed $7,000 of depreciation. In the transfer, Azeem recaptures no depreciation, and Wheel inherits the $7,000 recapture potential. After claiming an additional $2,000 of depreciation, Wheel has a $16,000 adjusted basis in the machinery. If

TOPIC REVIEW C:2-3

Liability Assumption and Acquisition Rules of Sec. 357

1. *General Rule (Sec. 357(a)):* A transferee corporation's assumption of liabilities in a Sec. 351 exchange is not treated as boot by the shareholder for gain recognition purposes. On the other hand, the assumption of liabilities is treated as the receipt of money for purposes of determining the transferor's stock basis and amount realized.
2. *Exception 1 (Sec. 357(b)):* All liabilities assumed by a transferee corporation are considered to be money/boot received by the transferor if the principal purpose of the transfer of any of the liabilities is tax avoidance or if no bona fide business purpose exists for the transfer.
3. *Exception 2 (Sec. 357(c)):* If the total amount of liabilities assumed by a transferee corporation exceeds the total basis of property transferred, the transferor recognizes the excess as gain.
4. *Special Rule (Sec. 357(c)(3)):* For purposes of Exception 2, the term liabilities for a transferor using a cash or hybrid method of accounting does not include any amount that would give rise to a deduction when paid.

Wheel now sells the machinery for $33,000, it must recognize a $17,000 ($33,000 − $16,000) gain. Of this gain, $9,000 is ordinary income recaptured under Sec. 1245. The remaining $8,000 is a Sec. 1231 gain. ◀

Computing Depreciation. When a shareholder transfers depreciable property to a corporation in a nontaxable Sec. 351 exchange and the shareholder has not fully depreciated the property, the corporation must use the depreciation method and recovery period used by the transferor.[39] For the year of the transfer, the depreciation must be allocated between the transferor and the transferee corporation according to the number of months each party held the property. The transferee corporation is assumed to have held the property for the entire month in which the property was transferred.[40]

EXAMPLE C:2-40 ▶ On June 10 of Year 1, Carla paid $6,000 for a computer (five-year property for MACRS purposes), which she used in her sole proprietorship business. In Year 1, she claimed $1,200 (0.20 × $6,000) of depreciation. She did not elect Sec. 179 expensing and did not claim any bonus depreciation. On February 10 of Year 2, she transfers the computer and other sole proprietorship assets to King Corporation in exchange for King stock. Because Sec. 351 applies, she recognizes no gain or loss. King must use the same MACRS recovery period and method that Carla used. Depreciation for Year 2 is $1,920 (0.32 × $6,000). That amount must be allocated between Carla and King. The computer is considered to have been held by Carla for one month and by King for 11 months (including the month of transfer). The Year 2 depreciation amounts claimed by Carla and King are calculated as follows:

Carla	$6,000 × 0.32 × 1/12 = $ 160
King Corporation	$6,000 × 0.32 × 11/12 = $1,760

King's basis in the computer is calculated as follows:

Original cost	$6,000
Minus: Year 1 depreciation claimed by Carla	(1,200)
Year 2 depreciation claimed by Carla	(160)
Adjusted basis on transfer date	$4,640

King's depreciation for Year 2 and subsequent years is as follows:

Year 2 (as computed above)	$1,760
Year 3 ($6,000 × 0.1920)	1,152
Year 4 ($6,000 × 0.1152)	691
Year 5 ($6,000 × 0.1152)	691
Year 6 ($6,000 × 0.0576)	346
Total	$4,640 ◀

If the transferee corporation's basis in the depreciable property exceeds the transferor's basis (e.g., as a result of an upward adjustment to reflect gain recognized by the transferor), the corporation treats the excess amount as newly purchased MACRS property and uses the recovery period and method applicable to the class of property transferred.[41]

EXAMPLE C:2-41 ▶ Assume the same facts as in Example C:2-40 except that, in addition to King stock, Carla receives a King note. Consequently, she must recognize $1,000 of gain on the transfer of the computer. King's basis in the computer is calculated as follows:

Original cost	$6,000
Depreciation claimed by Carla	(1,360)
Adjusted basis on transfer date	$4,640
Plus: Gain recognized by Carla	1,000
Basis to King on transfer date	$5,640

The additional $1,000 of basis is depreciated as though it were separate, newly purchased five-year MACRS property. Thus, King claims depreciation of $200 (0.20 × $1,000) on this portion of

[39] Sec. 168(i)(7).
[40] Prop. Reg. Secs. 1.168-5(b)(2)(i)(B), 1.168-5(b)(4)(i), and 1.168-5(b)(8).
[41] Prop. Reg. Sec. 1.168-5(b)(7).

ADDITIONAL COMMENT

Currently, we have no clear guidance on how the corporation depreciates transferred property that has a reduced basis under the loss property limitation rule discussed on page C:2-21. For now, taxpayers probably should rely on Prop. Reg. 1.168-2(d)(3), which provides a method for calculating depreciation when the transferee's basis is less than the transferor's basis.

the basis in addition to the $1,760 of depreciation on the $4,640 carryover basis. Alternatively, King could elect to expense the $1,000 "new" basis under Sec. 179. ◄

Assignment of Income Doctrine. The **assignment of income doctrine** holds that income is taxable to the person who earned it and that it may not be assigned to another person for tax purposes.[42] The question arises as to whether the assignment of income doctrine applies where a cash method taxpayer transfers uncollected accounts receivable to a corporation in a Sec. 351 exchange. Specifically, who must recognize the income when it is collected—the taxpayer who transferred the receivable or the corporation that now owns and collects on the receivable? The IRS has ruled that the doctrine does *not* apply in a Sec. 351 exchange if the taxpayer transfers substantially all the business assets and liabilities, and a bona fide business purpose exists for the transfer. Instead, the accounts receivable take a zero basis in the corporation's hands, and the corporation includes their value in its income when it collects on the receivables.[43]

EXAMPLE C:2-42 ► For a bona fide business purpose, Ruth, a cash basis taxpayer, transfers all the assets and liabilities of her legal practice to Legal Services Corporation in exchange for all of Legal Services stock. The assets include $30,000 of accounts receivable that will generate earnings that Ruth has not included in her gross income. Because Ruth transfers substantially all the business assets and liabilities for a bona fide business purpose, the assignment of income doctrine does not apply to the receivables transferred, and Legal Services takes a zero basis in the receivables. Subsequently, Legal Services includes the value of the receivables in its income as it collects on them. ◄

The question of whether a transferee corporation can deduct the accounts payable transferred to it in a nontaxable transfer has frequently been litigated.[44] Most courts have held that ordinarily expenses are deductible only by the party that incurred those liabilities in the course of its trade or business. However, the IRS has ruled that in a nontaxable exchange the transferee corporation may deduct the payments it makes to satisfy the transferred accounts payable even though they arose in the transferor's business.[45]

CHOICE OF CAPITAL STRUCTURE

OBJECTIVE 5

Explain the tax implications of alternative capital structures

When a corporation is formed, the way it is financed will determine its capital structure. The corporation may obtain capital from shareholders, nonshareholders, and creditors. In exchange for their capital, shareholders may receive common or preferred stock; nonshareholders may receive benefits such as employment or special rates on products sold by the corporation; and creditors may receive long- or short-term debt. As explained below, each of these alternatives has tax advantages and disadvantages for the shareholders, creditors, and corporation.

CHARACTERIZATION OF OBLIGATIONS AS DEBT OR EQUITY

The deductibility of interest payments creates an incentive for corporations to incur as much debt as possible. Because debt financing often resembles equity financing (e.g., preferred stock), the IRS and the courts have refused to accept the form of the security as controlling.[46] In some cases, debt obligations that possess equity characteristics have been treated as common or preferred stock for tax purposes. In determining the appropriate tax treatment, the courts have relied on a number of factors.

[42] See, for example, *Lucas v. Guy C. Earl,* 8 AFTR 10287, 2 USTC ¶496 (USSC, 1930).

[43] Rev. Rul. 80-198, 1980-2 C.B. 113.

[44] See, for example, *Wilford E. Thatcher v. CIR,* 37 AFTR 2d 76-1068, 76-1 USTC ¶9324 (9th Cir., 1976), and *John P. Bongiovanni v. CIR,* 31 AFTR 2d 73-409, 73-1 USTC ¶9133 (2nd Cir., 1972).

[45] Rev. Rul. 80-198, 1980-2 C.B. 113.

[46] See, for example, *Aqualane Shores, Inc. v. CIR,* 4 AFTR 2d 5346, 59-2 USTC ¶9632 (5th Cir., 1959) and *Sun Properties, Inc. v. U.S.,* 47 AFTR 273, 55-1 USTC ¶9261 (5th Cir., 1955).

Congress enacted Sec. 385 to establish a standard for determining whether a security is debt or equity. Section 385 provides that the following factors be considered in the determination:

- Whether there is a written unconditional promise to pay on demand or on a specified date a certain sum of money in return for adequate consideration in the form of money or money's worth, in addition to an unconditional promise to pay a fixed rate of interest
- Whether the debt is subordinate to, or preferred over, other indebtedness of the corporation
- The ratio of corporate debt to equity
- Whether the debt is convertible into stock of the corporation
- The relationship between holdings of stock in the corporation and holdings of the interest in question[47]

HISTORICAL NOTE

The Treasury Department at one time issued proposed and final regulations covering Sec. 385. These regulations were the subject of so much criticism that the Treasury Department eventually withdrew them. Section 385, however, makes it clear that Congress wants the Treasury Department to make further attempts at clarifying the debt-equity issue. So far, the Treasury Department has issued no "new" proposed or final regulations.

DEBT CAPITAL

Various provisions govern the tax treatment of (1) the issuance of debt; (2) the payment of interest on debt; and (3) the extinguishment, retirement, or worthlessness of debt. The tax implications of each of these events are examined below.

SELF-STUDY QUESTION

From a tax perspective, why is the distinction between debt and equity important?

ANSWER

Interest paid with respect to a debt instrument is deductible by the payor corporation. Dividends paid with respect to an equity instrument are not deductible by the payor corporation. Thus, the determination of whether an instrument is debt or equity can provide different results to the payor corporation. Different results apply to the payee as well. Qualified dividends are subject to the applicable capital gains tax rate while interest is taxed as ordinary income.

Issuance of Debt. If a transferor transfers appreciated property in exchange for stock, the transfer will be nontaxable, provided the Sec. 351 requirements have been met. On the other hand, if the transferor transfers appreciated property in exchange for corporate debt as part of a Sec. 351 exchange, the FMV of the debt received will be treated as boot, possibly leading to gain recognition.

Payment of Interest. Interest paid on indebtedness is deductible by the corporation in deriving its taxable income.[48] Moreover, a corporation is not subject to the investment interest deduction limitation applicable to individual taxpayers. By contrast, the corporation cannot deduct dividends paid on equity securities.

If a corporation issues a debt instrument at a discount, Sec. 1272 requires the holder to amortize the original issue discount over the term of the obligation and treat the accrual as interest income. The debtor corporation amortizes the original issue discount over the term of the obligation and treats the accrual as an additional cost of borrowing.[49] If the corporation repurchases the debt instrument for more than the issue price (plus any original issue discount deducted as interest), the corporation deducts the excess of the purchase price over the issue price (adjusted for any amortization of original issue discount) as interest expense.[50]

Under Sec. 171, if a corporation issues a debt instrument at a premium, the holder may elect to amortize the premium over the term of the obligation and treat the accrual as a reduction in interest income earned on the obligation. For the debtor corporation, the premium reduces the amount of deductible interest.[51] If the corporation repurchases the debt instrument at a price greater than the issue price (minus any premium treated as income), the corporation deducts the excess of the purchase price over the issue price (adjusted for any amortization of premium) as interest expense.[52]

Extinguishment of Debt. Generally, the retirement of debt is not a taxable event. Thus, a debtor corporation's extinguishing an obligation at face value does not result in the creditor's recognizing gain or loss. However, amounts received by the holder

[47] See also *O.H. Kruse Grain & Milling v. CIR*, 5 AFTR 2d 1544, 60-2 USTC ¶9490 (9th Cir., 1960), which lists additional factors that the courts might consider.

[48] Sec. 163(a).

[49] Sec. 163(e).

[50] Reg. Sec. 1.163-7(c).

[51] Reg. Sec. 1.163-12.

[52] Reg. Sec. 1.163-7(c).

of a debt instrument (e.g., note, bond, or debenture) at the time of its retirement are deemed to be "in exchange for" the obligation. Thus, if the obligation is a capital asset in the holder's hands, the holder must recognize a capital gain or loss if the amount received differs from its face value or adjusted basis, unless the difference is due to original issue or market discount.

EXAMPLE C:2-43 ► Titan Corporation issues a ten-year note at its $1,000 face amount. On the date of issuance, Rick purchases the note for $1,000. Because of a decline in interest rates, Titan calls the note at a price of $1,050 payable to each note holder. Rick reports the premium as a $50 capital gain, and Titan deducts as interest expense total premiums paid to all its note holders. ◄

ADDITIONAL COMMENT

Even though debt often is thought of as a preferred instrument because of the deductibility of the interest paid, the debt must be repaid at its maturity, whereas stock has no specified maturity date. Also, interest usually must be paid at regular intervals, whereas dividends do not have to be declared if sufficient funds are not available to pay them or if the corporation needs to retain funds for operations or growth.

Table C:2-2 presents a comparison of the tax advantages and disadvantages of a corporation's using debt in its capital structure.

EQUITY CAPITAL

Corporations can raise equity capital through the issuance of various types of stock. Some corporations issue only a single class of stock, whereas others issue numerous classes of stock. Reasons for the use of multiple classes of stock include

- Permitting nonfamily employees of family owned corporations to obtain an equity interest in the business while keeping voting control in the hands of family members.
- Financing a **closely held corporation** through the issuance of preferred stock to an outside investor, while leaving voting control in the hands of existing common stockholders.

Table C:2-3 lists some of the major tax advantages and disadvantages of using common and preferred stock in a corporation's capital structure.

SELF-STUDY QUESTION

Does the transferee corporation recognize gain on the receipt of appreciated property from a shareholder?

ANSWER

No. A corporation does not recognize gain when it receives property from its shareholders, whether or not it exchanges its own stock. However, the transfer must qualify as a Sec. 351 exchange or the transaction will be taxable to the shareholders.

CAPITAL CONTRIBUTIONS BY SHAREHOLDERS

A corporation recognizes no income when it receives cash or noncash property as a capital contribution from a shareholder.[53] If the shareholders make voluntary pro rata payments to a corporation but do not receive any additional stock, the payments are treated as additional consideration for the stock already owned.[54] The shareholders' respective bases in their stock are increased by the amount of cash contributed, plus the basis of any noncash property contributed, plus any gain recognized by the shareholders. The

▼ TABLE C:2-2
Tax Advantages and Disadvantages of Using Debt in a Corporation's Capital Structure

Advantages:
1. A corporation can deduct interest paid on a debt obligation.
2. Shareholders do not recognize income in a debt retirement as they would in a stock redemption.

Disadvantages:
1. If at the time the corporation is formed or later when a shareholder makes a capital contribution, the shareholder receives a debt instrument in exchange for property, the debt is treated as boot, and the shareholder recognizes gain to the extent of the lesser of the boot's FMV or the realized gain.
2. If debt becomes worthless or is sold at less than its face value, the loss generally is a nonbusiness bad debt (treated as a short-term capital loss) or a capital loss. Section 1244 ordinary loss treatment applies only to stock (see pages C:2-32 and C:2-33).

[53] Sec. 118(a).

[54] Reg. Sec. 1.118-1.

▼ **TABLE C:2-3**

Tax Advantages and Disadvantages of Using Equity in a Corporation's Capital Structure

Advantages:

1. A 70%, 80%, or 100% dividends-received deduction is available to a corporate shareholder who receives dividends. A similar deduction is not available for the receipt of interest (see Chapter C:3).
2. A shareholder can receive common and preferred stock in a tax-free corporate formation under Sec. 351 or a nontaxable reorganization under Sec. 368 without recognizing gain (see Chapters C:2 and C:7, respectively). Receipt of debt securities in each of these two types of transactions generally results in the shareholder's recognizing gain.
3. Common and preferred stock can be distributed tax-free to the corporation's shareholders as a stock dividend. Some common and preferred stock distributions, however, may be taxable as dividends under Sec. 305(b). Distributions of debt obligations generally are taxable as a dividend (see Chapter C:4).
4. Under Sec. 1244, common or preferred stock that the shareholder sells or exchanges or that becomes worthless is eligible for ordinary loss treatment, subject to limitations (see pages C:2-32 and C:2-33). The loss recognized on similar transactions involving debt securities generally is treated as capital in character.
5. Section 1202 excludes 50% of capital gains realized on the sale or exchange of qualified small business (C) corporation stock that has been held for more than five years. For qualified stock acquired after February 17, 2009 and before September 28, 2010, the exclusion is 75%, and for qualified stock acquired after September 27, 2010 and before January 1, 2015, the exclusion is 100%.
6. Qualified dividends are taxed at the applicable capital gains rate.

Disadvantages:

1. Dividends are not deductible in determining a corporation's taxable income.
2. Redemption of common or preferred stock generally is taxable to the shareholders as a dividend. Under the general rule, none of the redemption distribution offsets the shareholder's basis for the stock investment. Redemption of common and preferred stock is eligible for exchange treatment only in situations specified in Secs. 302 and 303 (see Chapter C:4).
3. Preferred stock issued to a shareholder as a dividend might meet the definition of Sec. 306 stock. Sale, exchange, or redemption of such stock can result in the recognition of ordinary income instead of capital gain (see Chapter C:4). This ordinary income is taxed as a "deemed dividend" at the applicable capital gains rate.

TYPICAL MISCONCEPTION

The characteristics of preferred stock can be similar to those of a debt security. Often, a regular dividend is required at a stated rate, much like what would be required with respect to a debt obligation. The holder of preferred stock, like a debt holder, may have preferred liquidation rights over holders of common stock. Also, preferred stock is not required to possess voting rights. However, differences remain. A corporation can deduct its interest expense but not dividends. Interest income is ordinary income to shareholders, but qualified dividends are subject to the applicable capital gains tax rate.

corporation's basis in any property received as a capital contribution from a shareholder equals the shareholder's basis, plus any gain recognized by the shareholder.[55] Normally, the shareholders recognize no gain when they transfer property to a controlled corporation as a capital contribution.

EXAMPLE C:2-44 ▶ Dot and Fred each own 50% of the stock in Trail Corporation, and each has a $50,000 basis in that stock. Later, as a voluntary contribution to Trail's capital, Dot contributes $40,000 in cash and Fred contributes property having a $25,000 basis and a $40,000 FMV. As a result of the contributions, Trail recognizes no income. Dot's basis in her stock is increased to $90,000 ($50,000 + $40,000), and Fred's basis in his stock is increased to $75,000 ($50,000 + $25,000). Trail's basis in the property contributed by Fred is $25,000—the same as Fred's basis in the property. ◀

If a shareholder-lender gratuitously forgives corporate debt, the debt forgiveness might be treated as a capital contribution equal to the principal amount of the forgiven debt. A determination of whether debt forgiveness is a capital contribution is based on the facts and circumstances surrounding the event.

[55] Sec. 362(a).

WHAT WOULD YOU DO IN THIS SITUATION?

Your corporate client wants to issue 100-year bonds. The corporation's CEO reads *The Wall Street Journal* regularly and has observed that similar bonds have been issued by several companies, including several Fortune 500 companies. He touts the fact that the interest rate on these bonds is slightly more than that for 30-year U.S. Treasury bonds. In addition, he expresses the belief that interest on the bonds would be deductible, whereas dividends on preferred or common stock would be nondeductible. You are concerned that the IRS might treat the bonds as equity because of their extraordinarily long term. If the IRS does treat the bonds as such, it might recharacterize the "interest" as dividends and deny your client an interest deduction.

What advice would you give the client now regarding the bond issue? What advice would you give it when it prepares its tax return after the new bonds have been issued?

CAPITAL CONTRIBUTIONS BY NONSHAREHOLDERS

BOOK-TO-TAX ACCOUNTING COMPARISON

The IRC requires capital contributions of property other than money made by a nonshareholder to be reported at a zero basis. Financial accounting rules, however, require donated capital to be reported at the FMV of the asset on the financial accounting books. Neither set of rules requires the property's value to be included in income.

Nonshareholders sometimes contribute capital to a corporation in the form of cash or other property. For example, a city government might contribute land to a corporation to induce the corporation to locate within the city and provide jobs for citizens of the municipality. Such contributions are excluded from the corporation's gross income if the money or property contributed is neither a payment for goods or services nor a subsidy to induce the corporation to limit production.[56]

If a nonshareholder contributes noncash property to a corporation, the corporation's basis in such property is zero.[57] The zero basis precludes the corporation from claiming either a depreciation deduction or capital recovery offset with respect to the contributed property.

If a nonshareholder contributes cash, the basis of any property acquired with the cash during a 12-month period beginning on the day the corporation received the contribution is reduced by the cash amount. This rule limits the corporation's deduction to the amount of funds it invested in the property. The amount of any cash received from nonshareholders that the corporation did not spend to purchase property during the 12-month period reduces the basis of any noncash property held by the corporation on the last day of the 12-month period.[58]

The basis reduction applies to the corporation's property in the following order:

1. Depreciable property
2. Amortizable property
3. Depletable property
4. All other property

In the sequence of these downward adjustments, however, a property's basis may not be reduced below zero.

EXAMPLE C:2-45 ▶ To induce the company to locate in the municipality, the City of San Antonio contributes to Circle Corporation $100,000 in cash and a tract of land having a $500,000 FMV. Because of a downturn in Circle's business, the company spends only $70,000 of the contributed funds over a 12-month period. Circle recognizes no income as a result of the contribution. Circle's bases in the land and other property purchased with the contributed funds are zero. The basis of Circle's remaining assets, starting with its depreciable property, must be reduced by the $30,000 ($100,000 − $70,000) contributed but not spent. ◀

---

56 Reg. Sec. 1.118-1.

57 Sec. 362(c)(1).

58 Sec. 362(c)(2).

Worthlessness of Stock or Debt Obligations

OBJECTIVE 6

Determine the tax consequences of worthless stock or debt obligations

Investors who purchase stock in, or lend money to, a corporation usually want to earn a profit and recover their investment. Some investments, however, do not offer an adequate return on capital, and an investor may lose part or all of the investment. In this event, the securities evidencing the investment become worthless. This section examines the tax consequences of stock or debt securities becoming worthless.

SECURITIES

A debt or equity **security** that becomes worthless results in a capital loss for the investor as of the last day of the tax year in which the security becomes worthless. For purposes of this rule, the term *security* includes (1) a share of stock in a corporation; (2) a right to subscribe for, or the right to receive, a share of stock in a corporation; or (3) a bond, debenture, note, or other evidence of indebtedness with interest coupons or in registered form issued by a corporation.[59]

TYPICAL MISCONCEPTION

Probably the most difficult aspect of deducting a loss on a worthless security is establishing that the security is actually worthless. A mere decline in value is not sufficient to create a loss. The burden of proof of establishing total worthlessness rests with the taxpayer.

In some situations, investors recognize an ordinary loss when a security becomes worthless. Investors who contribute capital, either in the form of equity or debt to a corporation that later fails, generally prefer ordinary losses because such losses are deductible against ordinary income. Ordinary losses that generate an NOL can be carried back two years or forward up to 20 years. In general, ordinary loss treatment is available in the following circumstances:

- *Securities that are noncapital assets.* An ordinary loss occurs when a security that is a noncapital asset in the hands of the taxpayer is sold or exchanged or becomes totally worthless. Securities in this category include those held as inventory by a securities dealer.
- *Affiliated corporations.* A domestic corporation can claim an ordinary loss for any affiliated corporation's security that becomes worthless during the tax year. The domestic corporation must own at least 80% of the total voting power of all classes of stock entitled to vote, and at least 80% of each class of nonvoting stock (other than stock limited and preferred as to dividends). At least 90% of the aggregate gross receipts of the loss corporation for all tax years must have been derived from nonpassive income sources.
- *Section 1244 stock.* Section 1244 permits a shareholder to claim an ordinary loss if qualifying stock issued by a small business corporation is sold or exchanged or becomes worthless. This treatment is available only to an individual who was issued the qualifying stock or who was a partner in a partnership at the time the partnership acquired the qualifying stock. In the latter case, the partner's distributive share of partnership losses includes the loss sustained by the partnership on such stock. Ordinary loss treatment is not available for stock inherited, received as a gift, or purchased from another shareholder. The ordinary loss is limited to $50,000 per year (or $100,000 if the taxpayer is married and files a joint return). Losses exceeding the dollar ceiling in any given year are considered capital in character.

SELF-STUDY QUESTION

Why would a shareholder want his or her stock to qualify as Sec. 1244 stock?

ANSWER

Section 1244 is a provision that may help the taxpayer but that can never hurt. If the Sec. 1244 requirements are satisfied, the individual shareholders of a small business corporation may treat losses from the sale or worthlessness of their stock as ordinary rather than capital in character. If the Sec. 1244 requirements are not satisfied, such losses generally are treated as capital in character.

EXAMPLE C:2-46 ▶ For $175,000, Tammy and her husband Cole purchased 25% of Minor Corporation's initial offering of a single class of stock. Minor is a small business corporation, and the Minor stock satisfies all Sec. 1244 requirements. On September 1 of the current year, Minor filed for bankruptcy. Two years later, the bankruptcy court notifies shareholders that the Minor stock is worthless. In that year, Tammy and Cole can deduct $100,000 of their initial investment as an ordinary loss. The remaining $75,000 loss is treated as capital in character. ◀

If a corporation issues Sec. 1244 stock for property whose adjusted basis exceeds its FMV immediately before the exchange, the stock's basis is reduced to the property's FMV for the purpose of determining the ordinary loss amount.

[59] Sec. 165(g).

EXAMPLE C:2-47 ▶ In a Sec. 351 nontaxable exchange, Penny transfers to Small Corporation property having a $40,000 adjusted basis and a $32,000 FMV for 100 shares of Sec. 1244 stock. Ordinarily, Penny's basis in the stock would be $40,000. However, for Sec. 1244 purposes, her stock basis is the property's FMV, or $32,000. If Penny sells the stock for $10,000, her recognized loss is $30,000 ($10,000 − $40,000). Her ordinary loss under Sec. 1244 is $22,000 ($10,000 − $32,000 Sec. 1244 basis). The remaining $8,000 loss is treated as capital in character. (Note also that, under Sec. 362(e)(2), Small would reduce its basis in the transferred property to its $32,000 FMV.) ◀

Section 1244 loss treatment requires no special election. Investors, however, should be aware that, if they fail to satisfy certain requirements, ordinary loss treatment will be unavailable, and their loss will be treated as capital in character. The requirements are as follows:

- The issuing corporation must be a small business corporation at the time it issues the stock. A small business corporation is a corporation that receives in the aggregate $1 million or less in money or noncash property (other than stock and securities) in exchange for its stock.[60]
- The issuing corporation must have derived more than 50% of its aggregate gross receipts from "active" sources (i.e., other than royalties, rents, dividends, interest, annuities, and gains on sales of stock and securities) during the five most recent tax years ending before the date on which the shareholder sells or exchanges the stock or the stock becomes worthless.

TAX STRATEGY TIP

If a shareholder contributes additional money or property to an existing corporation, he or she should be sure to receive additional stock in the exchange so that it will qualify for Sec. 1244 treatment if all requirements are met. If the shareholder does not receive additional stock, the increased basis of existing stock resulting from the capital contribution will not qualify for Sec. 1244 treatment.

If a shareholder contributes additional cash or property to a corporation after acquiring Sec. 1244 stock, the amount of ordinary loss recognized on the sale, exchange, or worthlessness of the Sec. 1244 stock is limited to the shareholder's capital contribution at the time the corporation issued the stock.

UNSECURED DEBT OBLIGATIONS

In addition to holding an equity interest, shareholders may lend funds to the corporation. The type of loss allowed if the corporation does not repay the borrowed funds depends on the nature of the loan or advance.

If the unpaid loan was not evidenced by a security (i.e., an unsecured debt obligation), it is considered to be either business or nonbusiness bad debt. Nonbusiness bad debts are treated less favorably than business bad debts. Under Sec. 166, nonbusiness bad debts are deductible as short-term capital losses (up to the $3,000 annual limit for net capital losses) when they become totally worthless. Business bad debts are deductible as ordinary losses without limitation when they become either partially or totally worthless. The IRS generally treats a loan made by a shareholder to a corporation in connection with his or her stock investment as nonbusiness in character.[61] It is understandable why a shareholder might attempt to rebut this presumption with the argument that a business purpose exists for the loan.

An advance in connection with the shareholder's trade or business, such as a loan to protect the shareholder's employment at the corporation, may be treated as an ordinary loss under the business bad debt rules. Regulation Sec. 1.166-5(b) states that whether a bad debt is business or nonbusiness related depends on the taxpayer's motive for making the advance. The debt is business related if the necessary relationship between the loss and the conduct of the taxpayer's trade or business exists at the time the debt was incurred, acquired, or became worthless.

In *U.S. v. Edna Generes,* the U.S. Supreme Court held that where multiple motives exist for advancing funds to a corporation, such as where a shareholder-employee advances funds to protect his or her employment, determining whether the advance is business or nonbusiness related must be based on the "dominant motivation" for the

[60] Regulation Sec. 1.1244(c)-2 provides special rules for designating which shares of stock are eligible for Sec. 1244 treatment when the corporation has issued more than $1 million of stock.

[61] Here, it is assumed that the loan is not considered to be an additional capital contribution. In such a case, the Sec. 165 worthless security rules apply instead of the Sec. 166 bad debt rules.

KEY POINT

In many closely held corporations, the shareholders are also employees. Thus, when a shareholder-employee makes a loan to the corporation, a question arises as to whether the loan is being made in the individual's capacity as an employee or a shareholder. The distinction is important because an employee loan that is worthless is entitled to ordinary loss treatment, whereas a shareholder loan that is worthless is treated as a nonbusiness bad debt (short-term capital loss).

advance.[62] If the advance is only "significantly motivated" by considerations relating to the taxpayer's trade or business, such motivation will not establish a proximate relationship between the bad debt and the taxpayer's trade or business. Therefore, it may result in a nonbusiness bad debt characterization. On the other hand, if the advance is "dominantly motivated" by considerations relating to the taxpayer's trade or business, such motivation usually is sufficient to establish such a proximate relationship. Therefore, it may result in a business bad debt characterization.

Factors deemed important in determining the character of bad debt include the taxpayer's equity in the corporation relative to compensation paid by the corporation. For example, a modest salary paid by the corporation relative to substantial stockholdings in the corporation suggests an investment motive for the advance. Conversely, a substantial salary paid by the corporation relative to modest stockholdings suggests a business motive for the advance. The business motive at issue is the protection of the employee-lender's employment because the advance may help save the business from failing. Reasonable minds may differ on what is substantial and what is modest, and monetary stakes often are high in these cases. Consequently, the determination frequently involves litigation.

EXAMPLE C:2-48 ▶

Top Corporation employs Mary as its legal counsel. It pays Mary an annual salary of $100,000. In March of the current year, Mary advances the corporation $50,000 to assist it financially. In October of the current year, Top declares bankruptcy and liquidates. In the liquidation, Mary and other investors receive 10 cents on every dollar advanced. If Mary can show that her advance was dominantly motivated by a desire to preserve her employment, her $45,000 ($50,000 × 0.90) loss will be treated as business bad debt, ordinary in character, and fully deductible in the current year. On the other hand, if Mary shows that the advance was only significantly motivated by a desire to preserve her employment, her $45,000 loss will be treated as nonbusiness bad debt, capital in character, and deductible in this year and in subsequent years only to the extent of $3,000 in excess of any capital gains she recognizes. ◀

ADDITIONAL COMMENT

For the act of lending money to a corporation to be considered the taxpayer's trade or business, the taxpayer must show that he or she was individually in the business of seeking out, promoting, organizing, and financing business ventures. *Ronald L. Farrington v. CIR,* 65 AFTR 2d 90-616, 90-1 USTC ¶50,125 (DC Okla., 1990).

A loss sustained by a shareholder who guarantees a loan made by a third party to the corporation generally is treated as a nonbusiness bad debt. The loss can be claimed only to the extent the shareholder actually pays the third party and is unable to recover the payment from the debtor corporation.[63] Occasionally, the IRS treats the amount of a shareholder advance as additional paid-in capital. In such circumstances, any worthless security loss the shareholder claims for his or her equity investment may be increased by this amount.

TAX PLANNING CONSIDERATIONS

OBJECTIVE 7

Identify tax planning opportunities in corporate formations

AVOIDING SEC. 351

Section 351 is not an elective provision. If its conditions are met, a corporate formation is tax-free, even if the taxpayer does not want it to be. Most often, taxpayers desire Sec. 351 treatment because it allows them to defer gains when transferring appreciated property to a corporation. In some cases, however, shareholders find such treatment disadvantageous because they would like to recognize gain or loss on the property transferred.

Avoiding Nonrecognition of Losses Under Sec. 351. If a shareholder transfers to a corporation property that has declined in value, the shareholder may want to recognize the loss so it can offset income from other sources. The shareholder can recognize the loss only if the Sec. 351 nonrecognition rules and the Sec. 267 related party rules do not apply to the exchange.

Avoiding Sec. 351 treatment requires that one or more of its requirements not be met. The simplest way to accomplish this objective is to ensure that the transferors of property do not receive 80% of the voting stock.

[62] 29 AFTR 2d 72-609, 72-1 USTC ¶9259 (USSC, 1972).

[63] Reg. Sec. 1.166-8(a).

Even if a shareholder avoids Sec. 351 treatment, he or she still may not be able to recognize the losses because of the Sec. 267 related party loss rules. Under Sec. 267(a)(1), if the shareholder owns more than 50% of the corporation's stock, directly or indirectly, he or she is a related party and therefore cannot recognize loss on an exchange of property for the corporation's stock or other property. If the transferors of property receive less than 80% of the corporation's voting stock and if the transferor of loss property does not own more than 50% of the stock, the transferor of loss property may recognize the loss.

EXAMPLE C:2-49 ▶ Lynn owns property having a $100,000 basis and a $60,000 FMV. If Lynn transfers the property to White Corporation in a nontaxable exchange under Sec. 351, she will not recognize a loss, which will be deferred until she sells her White stock. If the Sec. 351 requirements are not met, she will recognize a $40,000 loss in the year she transfers the property. If Lynn receives 50% of the White stock in exchange for her property, Cathy, an unrelated individual, receives 25% of the stock in exchange for $30,000 cash, and John, another unrelated individual, receives the remaining 25% for services performed, the Sec. 351 control requirement will not be met because the transferors of property acquire less than 80% of the White stock. Moreover, Lynn will not be a related party under Sec. 267 because she will not own more than 50% of the stock either directly or indirectly. Therefore, Lynn will recognize a $40,000 loss on the exchange. ◀

SELF-STUDY QUESTION

Which tax provisions may potentially limit a transferor shareholder from recognizing a loss on the transfer of property to a corporation?

ANSWER

Such transfer cannot be to a controlled corporation, or Sec. 351 will defer the loss. Even if Sec. 351 can be avoided, losses on sales between a corporation and a more-than-50% shareholder are disallowed under Sec. 267. Thus, to recognize a loss on the sale of property, such shareholder must, directly or indirectly, own 50% or less of the transferee corporation's stock.

Avoiding Nonrecognition of Gain Under Sec. 351. Sometimes a transferor would like to recognize gain when he or she transfers appreciated property to a corporation so the transferee corporation can get a stepped-up basis in the transferred property. Some other reasons for recognizing gain are as follows:

- If the transferor's gain is capital in character, he or she can offset this gain with capital losses from other transactions.
- Individual long-term capital gains are taxed at the applicable capital gains rate, which may be lower than the 35% top tax rate applicable to corporate-level capital gains.
- The corporation's marginal tax rate may be higher than a noncorporate transferor's marginal tax rate. In such case, it might be beneficial for the transferor to recognize gain so the corporation can get a stepped-up basis in the property. A stepped-up basis would either reduce the corporation's gain when it later sells the property or allow the corporation to claim greater depreciation deductions when it uses the property.

ADDITIONAL COMMENT

Any potential built-in gain on property transferred to the transferee corporation is duplicated because such gain may be recognized at the corporate level and at the shareholder level. This double taxation may be another reason for avoiding the nonrecognition of gain under Sec. 351.

A transferor who wishes to recognize gain on the transfer of appreciated property to a corporation can avoid Sec. 351 treatment through one of the following planning techniques:

- The transferor can sell the property to the controlled corporation for cash.
- The transferor can sell the property to the controlled corporation for cash and debt. This transaction involves relatively less cash than the previous transaction. However, the sale may be treated as a nontaxable exchange if the IRS recharacterizes the debt as equity.[64]
- The transferor can sell the property to a third party for cash and have the third party contribute the property to the corporation for stock.
- The transferor can have the corporation distribute sufficient boot property so that, even if Sec. 351 applies to the transaction, he or she will recognize gain.
- The transferors can fail one or more of the Sec. 351 tests. For example, if the transferors do not own 80% of the voting stock immediately after the exchange, the Sec. 351 control requirement will not have been met, and they will recognize gain.
- To trigger gain recognition under Sec. 357(c), the transferors may transfer to the corporation debt that exceeds the basis of all property transferred.

[64] See, for example, *Aqualane Shores, Inc. v. CIR,* 4 AFTR 2d 5346, 59-2 USTC ¶9632 (5th Cir., 1959) and *Sun Properties, Inc. v. U.S.,* 47 AFTR 273, 55-1 USTC ¶9261 (5th Cir., 1955).

EXAMPLE C:2-50 ▶ Ten years ago, James purchased land as an investment for $100,000. The land is now worth $500,000. James plans to transfer the land to Bell Corporation in exchange for all its stock. Bell will subdivide the land and sell individual tracts. Because the land is inventory, Bell's gain on the land sales will be ordinary income. James has realized a large capital loss in the current year and would like to recognize capital gain on the transfer of the land to Bell. One way for James to accomplish this objective is to transfer the land to Bell in exchange for all the Bell stock plus a note for $400,000. Because the note is boot, James will recognize $400,000 of gain even though Sec. 351 applies to the exchange. However, if the note is due in a subsequent year, James's gain will be deferred until collection unless he elects out of the installment method. ◀

Compliance and Procedural Considerations

OBJECTIVE 8

Comply with procedural rules for corporate formations

Reporting Requirements Under Sec. 351

A taxpayer who receives stock or other property in a Sec. 351 exchange must attach a statement to his or her tax return for the period encompassing the date of the exchange.[65] The statement must include all facts pertinent to the exchange, including:

- A description of the property transferred and its adjusted basis to the transferor
- A description of the stock received in the exchange, including its type, number of shares, and FMV
- A description of any other securities received in the exchange, including principal amount, terms, and FMV
- The amount of money received
- A description of any other property received, including its FMV
- A statement of the liabilities transferred to the corporation, including the nature of the liabilities, when and why they were incurred, and the business reason for their transfer

ADDITIONAL COMMENT

The required information provided to the IRS by both the transferor-shareholders and the transferee corporation should be consistent. For example, the FMVs assigned to the stock and other properties included in the exchange should be the same for all parties to the transaction.

The transferee corporation must attach a statement to its tax return for the year in which the exchange took place. The statement must include

- A complete description of all property received from the transferors
- The transferors' adjusted bases in the property
- A description of the stock issued to the transferors
- A description of any other securities issued to the transferors
- The amount of money distributed to the transferors
- A description of any other property distributed to the transferors
- Information regarding the transferor's liabilities assumed by the corporation

[65] Reg. Sec. 1.351-3.

Problem Materials

DISCUSSION QUESTIONS

C:2-1 What entities or business forms are available for a new enterprise? Explain the advantages and disadvantages of each.

C:2-2 Alice and Bill plan to go into business together. For the first two or three years of operations, they anticipate losses, which they would like to use to offset income from other sources. They also are concerned about exposing their personal assets to business liabilities. Advise Alice and Bill as to what business form would best meet their needs.

C:2-3 Bruce and Bob organize Black LLC on May 10 of the current year. What is the entity's default tax classification? Are any alternative classification(s) available? If so, (1) how do Bruce and Bob elect the alternative classification(s) and (2) what are the tax consequences of doing so?

C:2-4 John and Wilbur form White Corporation on May 3 of the current year. What is the entity's default tax classification? Are any alternative classification(s) available? If so, (1) how do John and Wilbur elect the alternative classification(s) and (2) what are the tax consequences of doing so?

C:2-5 Barbara organizes Blue LLC on May 17 of the current year. What is the entity's default tax classification? Are any alternative classification(s) available? If so, (1) how does Barbara elect the alternative classification(s) and (2) what are the tax consequences of doing so?

C:2-6 Debate the following proposition: All corporate formation transactions should be taxable events.

C:2-7 What are the tax consequences for the transferor and transferee when property is transferred to a newly created corporation in an exchange qualifying as nontaxable under Sec. 351?

C:2-8 What items are considered to be property for purposes of Sec. 351(a)? What items are not considered to be property?

C:2-9 How is "control" defined for purposes of Sec. 351(a)?

C:2-10 Explain how the IRS has interpreted the phrase "in control immediately after the exchange" for purposes of a Sec. 351 exchange.

C:2-11 John and Mary each exchange property worth $50,000 for 100 shares of New Corporation stock. Peter exchanges services for 98 shares of New stock and $1,000 in cash for two shares of New stock. Are the Sec. 351 requirements met? Explain why or why not. What advice would you give the shareholders?

C:2-12 Does Sec. 351 require shareholders to receive stock equal in value to the property transferred? Suppose Fred and Susan each transfer property worth $50,000 to Spade Corporation. In exchange, Fred receives 25 shares of Spade stock and Susan receives 75 shares. Are the Sec. 351 requirements met? Explain the tax consequences of the exchange.

C:2-13 Does Sec. 351 apply to property transfers to an existing corporation? Suppose Carl and Lynn each own 50 shares of North Corporation stock. Carl transfers property worth $50,000 to North for an additional 25 shares. Does Sec. 351 apply? Explain why or why not. If not, what can be done to qualify the transaction for Sec. 351 treatment?

C:2-14 How are a transferor's basis and holding period determined for stock and other property (boot) received in a Sec. 351 exchange? How does the transferee corporation's assumption of liabilities affect the transferor's basis in the stock?

C:2-15 Under what circumstances is a corporation's assumption of liabilities considered boot in a Sec. 351 exchange?

C:2-16 What factor(s) would the IRS likely consider to determine whether the transfer of a liability to a corporation in a Sec. 351 exchange was motivated by a business purpose?

C:2-17 Mark transfers all the property of his sole proprietorship to newly formed Utah Corporation in exchange for all the Utah stock. Mark has claimed depreciation on some of the property. Under what circumstances is Mark required to recapture previously claimed depreciation deductions? How is the depreciation deduction for the year of transfer calculated? What are the tax consequences if Utah sells the depreciable property?

C:2-18 How does the assignment of income doctrine apply to a Sec. 351 exchange?

C:2-19 What factors did Congress mandate to be considered in determining whether indebtedness is classified as debt or equity for tax purposes?

C:2-20 What are the advantages and disadvantages of using debt in a firm's capital structure?

C:2-21 What are the advantages of Sec. 1244 loss treatment when a stock investment becomes worthless? What conditions must be met to qualify for this treatment?

C:2-22 What are the advantages of business bad debt treatment when a shareholder's loan or advance to a corporation cannot be repaid? What must the debtholder show to claim a business bad debt deduction?

C:2-23 Why might shareholders avoid Sec. 351 treatment? Explain three ways they can accomplish this end.

C:2-24 What are the Sec. 351 reporting requirements?

ISSUE IDENTIFICATION QUESTIONS

C:2-25 Peter Jones has owned all 100 shares of Trenton Corporation stock for the past five years. This year, Mary Smith contributes property with a $50,000 basis and an $80,000 FMV for 80 newly issued Trenton shares. At the same time, Peter contributes $15,000 in cash for 15 newly issued Trenton shares. What tax issues regarding the exchanges should Mary and Peter consider?

C:2-26 Carl contributes equipment with a $50,000 adjusted basis and an $80,000 FMV to Cook Corporation for 50 of its 100 shares of stock. His son, Carl Jr., contributes $20,000 cash for the remaining 50 Cook shares. What tax issues regarding the exchanges should Carl and his son consider?

C:2-27 Several years ago, Bill acquired 100 shares of Bold Corporation stock directly from the corporation for $100,000 in cash. This year, he sold the stock to Sam for $35,000. What tax issues regarding the stock sale should Bill consider?

PROBLEMS

C:2-28 *Organizational Forms Available.* Lucia, a single taxpayer, operates a florist business. She is considering either continuing the business as a sole proprietorship or reorganizing it as either a C corporation or an S corporation. Her goal is to withdraw $20,000 of profits from the business annually while minimizing her total tax liability. She expects the business to generate annually $50,000 of taxable income before considering a deductible salary expense (see below). Which business form(s) can best achieve Lucia's goals? Remember that a shareholder is taxed on S corporation income whether withdrawn or not and is not taxed on the actual withdrawals or distributions. Assume that the C corporation is in the 15% corporate tax bracket, Lucia is in the 25% individual tax bracket for ordinary income, and Lucia is taxed at 15% on dividend income. When considering either corporate option, perform the analysis first by treating any withdrawals as deductible salary payments of the corporation. Then do the analysis by treating them as nondeductible dividends or distributions. Ignore employment taxes.

C:2-29 *Transfer of Property and Services to a Controlled Corporation.* In 2015, Dick, Evan, and Fran form Triton Corporation. Dick contributes land (a capital asset) having a $50,000 FMV in exchange for 50 shares of Triton stock. He purchased the land in 2013 for $60,000. Evan contributes machinery (Sec. 1231 property purchased in 2012) having a $45,000 adjusted basis and a $30,000 FMV in exchange for 30 shares of Triton stock. Fran contributes services worth $20,000 in exchange for 20 shares of Triton stock.

a. What is the amount of Dick's recognized gain or loss?
b. What is Dick's basis in his Triton shares? When does his holding period begin?
c. What is the amount of Evan's recognized gain or loss?
d. What is Evan's basis in his Triton shares? When does his holding period begin?
e. How much income, if any, does Fran recognize?
f. What is Fran's basis in her Triton shares? When does her holding period begin?
g. What is Triton's basis in the land and the machinery? When does its holding period begin? How does Triton treat the amount paid to Fran for her services?

C:2-30 *Transfer of Property and Services to a Controlled Corporation.* In 2015, Ed, Fran, and George form Jet Corporation. Ed contributes land (a capital asset) having a $35,000 FMV purchased as an investment in 2011 for $15,000 in exchange for 35 shares of Jet stock. Fran contributes machinery (Sec. 1231 property) purchased in 2011 and used in her business in exchange for 35 shares of Jet stock. Immediately before the exchange, the machinery had a $45,000 adjusted basis and a $35,000 FMV. George contributes services worth $30,000 in exchange for 30 shares of Jet stock.

a. What is the amount of Ed's recognized gain or loss?
b. What is Ed's basis in his Jet shares? When does his holding period begin?
c. What is the amount of Fran's recognized gain or loss?
d. What is Fran's basis in her Jet shares? When does her holding period begin?
e. How much income, if any, does George recognize?
f. What is George's basis in his Jet shares? When does his holding period begin?
g. What is Jet's basis in the land and the machinery? When does its holding period begin? How does Jet treat the amount paid to George for his services?
h. How would your answers to Parts a through g change if George instead contributed $5,000 in cash and services worth $25,000 for his 30 shares of Jet stock?

C:2-31 ***Control Requirement.*** In which of the following independent situations is the Sec. 351 control requirement met?

a. Olive transfers property to Quick Corporation for 75% of Quick stock, and Mary provides services to Quick for the remaining 25% of Quick stock.
b. Pete transfers property to Target Corporation for 60% of Target stock, and Robert transfers property worth $15,000 and performs services worth $25,000 for the remaining 40% of Target stock.
c. Herb and his wife, Wilma, each have owned 50 of the 100 outstanding shares of Vast Corporation stock since it was formed three years ago. In the current year, their son, Sam, transfers property to Vast for 50 newly issued shares of Vast stock.
d. Charles and Ruth develop a plan to form Tiny Corporation. On June 3 of this year, Charles transfers property worth $50,000 for 50 shares of Tiny stock. On August 1, Ruth transfers $50,000 cash for 50 shares of Tiny stock.
e. Assume the same facts as in Part d except that Charles has a prearranged plan to sell 30 of his shares to Sam on October 1.

C:2-32 ***Control Requirement.*** In which of the following unrelated exchanges is the Sec. 351 control requirement met? If the transaction does not meet the Sec. 351 requirements, suggest ways in which the transaction can be structured so as to meet these requirements.

a. Fred exchanges property worth $50,000 and services worth $50,000 for 100 shares of New Corporation stock. Greta exchanges $100,000 cash for the remaining 100 shares of New stock.
b. Maureen exchanges property worth $2,000 and services worth $48,000 for 100 shares of Gemini Corporation stock. Norman exchanges property worth $50,000 for the remaining 100 shares of Gemini stock.

C:2-33 ***Control Requirement.*** Sam and Veronica own 300 and 200 shares, respectively, of Poly-Electron Corporation stock, which represent all the shares outstanding. The current market value per share is $25. Poly-Electron needs capital to expand its operations, and Veronica is willing to contribute to Poly-Electron silver bullion against which the corporation can borrow operating funds. Veronica purchased the bullion 12 years ago, when its cost was a fraction of its current market value. If Veronica wants to avoid recognizing a gain upon transferring the bullion to the corporation, how many additional shares must she receive in exchange for the bullion, and what value of silver bullion should she contribute to Poly-Electron in exchange for additional shares? Hint: Veronica needs to achieve 80% control of the corporation.

C:2-34 ***Sec. 351 Requirements.*** Al, Bob, and Carl form West Corporation and transfer the following items to West:

	Item Transferred			
Transferor	*Item*	*Transferor's Basis*	*FMV*	*Shares Received by Transferor*
Al	Patent	–0–	$25,000	1,000 common
Bob	Cash	$25,000	25,000	250 preferred
Carl	Services	–0–	7,500	300 common

The common stock has voting rights. The preferred stock does not.

a. Is the exchange nontaxable under Sec. 351? Explain the tax consequences of the exchange to Al, Bob, Carl, and West.

b. How would your answer to Part a change if Bob instead had received 200 shares of common stock and 200 shares of preferred stock?
c. How would your answer to Part a change if Carl instead had contributed $800 cash as well as services worth $6,700?

C:2-35 ***Incorporating a Sole Proprietorship.*** Tom incorporates his sole proprietorship as Total Corporation and transfers its assets to Total in exchange for all 100 shares of Total stock and four $10,000 interest-bearing notes. The stock has a $125,000 FMV. The notes mature consecutively on the first four anniversaries of the incorporation date. The assets transferred are as follows:

Assets		*Adjusted Basis*	*FMV*
Cash		$ 5,000	$ 5,000
Equipment	$130,000		
Minus: Accumulated depreciation	(70,000)	60,000	90,000
Building	$100,000		
Minus: Accumulated depreciation	(49,000)	51,000	40,000
Land		24,000	30,000
Total		$140,000	$165,000

a. What are the amounts and character of Tom's recognized gains or losses?
b. What is Tom's basis in the Total stock and notes?
c. What is Total's basis in the property received from Tom?

C:2-36 ***Transfer to an Existing Corporation.*** For the last five years, Ann and Fred each have owned 50 of the 100 outstanding shares of Zero Corporation stock. Ann transfers land having a $10,000 basis and a $25,000 FMV to Zero for an additional 25 shares of Zero stock. Fred transfers $1,000 cash to Zero for one additional share of Zero stock. What amount of the gain or loss must Ann recognize on the exchange? If the transaction does not meet the Sec. 351 requirements, suggest ways in which it can be structured so as to meet these requirements.

C:2-37 ***Transfer to an Existing Corporation.*** For the last three years, Lucy and Marvin each have owned 50 of the 100 outstanding shares of Lucky Corporation stock. Lucy transfers property having an $8,000 basis and a $12,000 FMV to Lucky for an additional ten shares of Lucky stock. How much gain or loss must Lucy recognize on the exchange? If the transaction does not meet the Sec. 351 requirements, suggest ways in which it can be structured so as to meet these requirements.

C:2-38 ***Disproportionate Receipt of Stock.*** Jerry transfers property with a $28,000 adjusted basis and a $50,000 FMV to Texas Corporation for 75 shares of Texas stock. Frank, Jerry's father, transfers property with a $32,000 adjusted basis and a $50,000 FMV to Texas for the remaining 25 shares of Texas stock.
a. What is the amount of each transferor's recognized gain or loss?
b. What is Jerry's basis in his Texas stock?
c. What is Frank's basis in his Texas stock?

C:2-39 ***Sec. 351: Boot Property Received.*** Sara transfers land (a capital asset) having a $30,000 adjusted basis to Temple Corporation in a Sec. 351 exchange. In return, Sara receives the following consideration:

Consideration	*FMV*
100 shares of Temple common stock	$100,000
50 shares of Temple qualified preferred stock	50,000
Temple note due in three years	20,000
Total	$170,000

a. What are the amount and character of Sara's recognized gain or loss?
b. What is Sara's basis in her common stock, preferred stock, and note?
c. What is Temple's basis in the land?

C:2-40 ***Receipt of Bonds for Property.*** Joe, Karen, and Larry form Gray Corporation. Joe contributes land (a capital asset) having an $8,000 adjusted basis and a $15,000 FMV to

Gray in exchange for Gray ten-year notes having a $15,000 face value. Karen contributes equipment (Sec. 1231 property) having an $18,000 adjusted basis and a $25,000 FMV for 50 shares of Gray stock. She previously claimed $10,000 of depreciation on the equipment. Larry contributes $25,000 cash for 50 shares of Gray stock.

a. What are the amount and character of Joe's, Karen's, and Larry's recognized gains or losses?
b. What basis do Joe, Karen, and Larry take in the stock or notes they receive?
c. What basis does Gray take in the land and equipment? What happens to the $10,000 of depreciation recapture potential on the equipment?

C:2-41 *Transfer of Depreciable Property.* Nora transfers to Needle Corporation depreciable machinery originally costing $18,000 and now having a $15,000 adjusted basis. In exchange, Nora receives all 100 shares of Needle stock having an $18,000 FMV and a three-year Needle note having a $4,000 FMV.

a. What are the amount and character of Nora's recognized gain or loss?
b. What are Nora's bases in the Needle stock and note?
c. What is Needle's basis in the machinery?

C:2-42 *Transfer of Personal Liabilities.* Jim owns 80% of Gold Corporation stock. He transfers a business automobile to Gold in exchange for additional Gold stock worth $5,000 and Gold's assumption of both his $1,000 automobile debt and his $2,000 education loan. The automobile originally cost Jim $12,000 and, on the transfer date, has a $4,500 adjusted basis and an $8,000 FMV.

a. What are the amount and character of Jim's recognized gain or loss?
b. What is Jim's basis in his additional Gold shares?
c. When does Jim's holding period for the additional shares begin?
d. What basis does Gold take in the automobile?

C:2-43 *Liabilities in Excess of Basis.* Barbara transfers to Moore Corporation $10,000 cash and machinery having a $15,000 basis and a $35,000 FMV in exchange for 50 shares of Moore stock. The machinery was used in Barbara's business, originally cost Barbara $50,000, and is subject to a $28,000 liability, which Moore assumes. Sam exchanges $17,000 cash for the remaining 50 shares of Moore stock.

a. What are the amount and character of Barbara's recognized gain or loss?
b. What is Barbara's basis in the Moore stock?
c. What is Moore's basis in the machinery?
d. What are the amount and character of Sam's recognized gain or loss?
e. What is Sam's basis in the Moore stock?
f. When do Barbara and Sam's holding periods for their stock begin?
g. How would your answers to Parts a through f change if Sam received $17,000 of Moore stock for legal services (instead of cash)?

C:2-44 *Transfer of Business Properties.* Jerry transfers to Emerald Corporation property having a $32,000 adjusted basis and a $50,000 FMV in exchange for all of Emerald's stock worth $15,000 and Emerald's assumption of a $35,000 mortgage on the property.

a. What is the amount of Jerry's recognized gain or loss?
b. What is Jerry's basis in the Emerald stock?
c. What is Emerald's basis in the property?
d. How would your answers to Parts a through c change if the mortgage assumed by Emerald were $15,000 and the Emerald stock were worth $35,000?

C:2-45 *Incorporating a Cash Basis Proprietorship.* Ted decides to incorporate his medical practice. He uses the cash method of accounting. On the date of incorporation, the practice reports the following balance sheet:

	Basis	*FMV*
Assets:		
Cash	$ 5,000	$ 5,000
Accounts receivable	–0–	65,000
Equipment (net of $15,000 depreciation)	35,000	40,000
Total	$40,000	$110,000

Liabilities and Owner's Equity:		
Current liabilities	$ –0–	$ 35,000
Note payable on equipment	15,000	15,000
Owner's equity	25,000	60,000
Total	$40,000	$110,000

All the current liabilities would be deductible by Ted if he paid them. Ted transfers all the assets and liabilities to a professional corporation in exchange for all of its stock.

a. What are the amount and character of Ted's recognized gain or loss?
b. What is Ted's basis in the stock?
c. What is the corporation's basis in the property?
d. Who recognizes income on the receivables upon their collection? Can the corporation obtain a deduction for the liabilities when it pays them?

C:2-46 *Transfer of Depreciable Property.* On January 10, 2015, Mary transfers to Green Corporation a machine purchased on March 3, 2012, for $100,000. On the transfer date, the machine has a $60,000 adjusted basis and a $110,000 FMV. Mary receives all 100 shares of Green stock, worth $100,000, and a two-year Green note worth $10,000.

a. What are the amount and character of Mary's recognized gain or loss?
b. What is Mary's basis in the stock and note? When does her holding period begin?
c. What are the amount and character of Green's gain or loss?
d. What is Green's basis in the machine? When does Green's holding period begin?

C:2-47 *Contribution to Capital by a Nonshareholder.* The City of Omaha donates land worth $500,000 to Ace Corporation to induce it to locate in Omaha and create an estimated 2,000 jobs for its citizens.

a. How much income, if any, must Ace report on the land contribution?
b. What basis does Ace take in the land?
c. Assume the same facts except the City of Omaha also donated to Ace $100,000 cash, which the corporation used to pay a portion of the $250,000 cost of equipment that it purchased six months later. How much income, if any, must Ace report on the cash contribution? What basis does Ace take in the equipment?

C:2-48 *Choice of Capital Structure.* Kobe transfers $500,000 in cash to newly formed Bryant Corporation for 100% of Bryant's stock. In the first year of operations, Bryant's taxable income before any payments to Kobe is $120,000. What total amount of taxable income must Kobe and Bryant each report in the following two scenarios?

a. Bryant pays a $70,000 dividend to Kobe.
b. Assume that when Bryant was formed, Kobe transferred his $500,000 to the corporation for $250,000 of Bryant stock and $250,000 in Bryant notes. The notes are repayable in five annual installments of $50,000 plus 8% annual interest on the unpaid balance. During the current year, Bryant gives Kobe $50,000 in repayment of the first note plus $20,000 interest.

C:2-49 *Worthless Stock or Securities.* Tom and Vicki are married and file a joint income tax return. They each purchase 50% of the stock in Guest Corporation from Al for $75,000. Tom is employed full-time by Guest and earns $100,000 in annual salary. Because of Guest's financial difficulties, Tom and Vicki each lend Guest an additional $25,000. The $25,000 is secured by bonds and is repayable in five years, with interest accruing at the prevailing market rate. Guest's financial difficulties escalate, and it eventually declares bankruptcy. Tom and Vicki receive nothing for their Guest stock or Guest bonds.

a. What are the amount and character of each shareholder's loss on the worthless stock and bonds?
b. How would your answer to Part a change if the liability were not secured by bonds?
c. How would your answer to Part a change if Tom and Vicki had purchased their stock for $75,000 each at the time Guest was formed?

C:2-50 *Worthless Stock.* Duck Corporation is owned equally by Harry, Susan, and Big Corporation. Harry and Susan are single. In 2007, Harry, Tom, and Big, the original investors in Duck, each paid $125,000 for their Duck stock. Susan purchased her stock from Tom in 2010 for $175,000. No adjustments to basis occur after the stock acquisition date. Duck encounters financial difficulties as a result of a lawsuit brought by a customer who suffered personal injuries from using a defective product. Duck files for bankruptcy, and uses all its assets to pay its creditors in 2015. What are the amount and character of each shareholder's loss?

C:2-51 ***Sale of Sec. 1244 Stock.*** Lois, who is single, transfers property with an $80,000 basis and a $120,000 FMV to Water Corporation in exchange for all 100 shares of Water stock. The shares qualify as Sec. 1244 stock. Two years later, Lois sells the shares for $28,000.

a. What are the amount and character of Lois's recognized gain or loss?
b. How would your answer to Part a change if the FMV of the property were $70,000?

C:2-52 ***Transfer of Sec. 1244 Stock.*** Assume the same facts as in Problem C:2-51 except that Lois gave the Water stock to her daughter, Sue, six months after she received it. The stock had a $120,000 FMV when Lois acquired it and when she made the gift. Sue sold the stock two years later for $28,000. How is the loss treated for tax purposes?

C:2-53 ***Avoiding Sec. 351 Treatment.*** Six years ago, Donna purchased land as an investment. The land cost $150,000 and is now worth $480,000. Donna plans to transfer the land to Development Corporation, which will subdivide it and sell individual tracts. Development's income on the land sales will be ordinary in character.

a. What are the tax consequences of the asset transfer and land sales if Donna contributes the land to Development in exchange for all its stock?
b. In what alternative ways can the transaction be structured to achieve more favorable tax results? Assume Donna's marginal tax rate is 39.6%, and Development's marginal tax rate is 34%.

COMPREHENSIVE PROBLEMS

C:2-54 On March 1 of the current year, Alice, Bob, Carla, and Dick form Bear Corporation and transfer the following items:

	Property Transferred			
Transferor	*Asset*	*Basis to Transferor*	*FMV*	*Number of Common Shares Issued*
Alice	Land	$12,000	$30,000	
	Building	38,000	70,000	400
	Mortgage on the land and building	60,000	60,000	
Bob	Equipment	25,000	40,000	300
Carla	Van	15,000	10,000	50
Dick	Accounting services	–0–	10,000	100

Alice purchased the land and building several years ago for $12,000 and $50,000, respectively. Alice has claimed straight-line depreciation on the building. Bob also receives a Bear note for $10,000 due in three years. The note bears interest at the prevailing market rate. Bob purchased the equipment three years ago for $50,000. Carla also receives $5,000 cash. Carla purchased the van two years ago for $20,000.

a. Does the transaction satisfy the requirements of Sec. 351?
b. What are the amount and character of the gains or losses recognized by Alice, Bob, Carla, Dick, and Bear?
c. What is each shareholder's basis in his or her Bear stock? When does the holding period for the stock begin?
d. What is Bear's basis in its property and services? When does the holding period for each property begin?

C:2-55 On June 3 of the current year, Eric, Florence, and George form Wildcat Corporation and transfer the following items:

	Item Transferred			
Transferor	*Asset*	*Basis to Transferor*	*FMV*	*Number of Common Shares Issued*
Eric	Land	$200,000	$50,000	500
Florence	Equipment	–0–	25,000	250
George	Legal services	–0–	25,000	250

Eric purchased the land (a capital asset) five years ago for $200,000. Florence purchased the equipment three years ago for $48,000. The equipment has been fully depreciated.

a. Does the transaction meet the requirements of Sec. 351?
b. What are the amount and character of the gains or losses recognized by Eric, Florence, George, and Wildcat?
c. What is each shareholder's basis in his or her Wildcat stock? When does the holding period for the stock begin?
d. What is Wildcat's basis in the land, equipment, and services? When does the holding period for each property begin?

TAX STRATEGY PROBLEMS

C:2-56 Assume the same facts as in Problem C:2-55.

a. Under what circumstances is the tax result in Problem C:2-55 beneficial, and for which shareholders? Are the shareholders likely to be pleased with the result?
b. If the shareholders decide that meeting the Sec. 351 requirements would generate a greater tax benefit, how might they proceed?

C:2-57 Paula Green owns and operates the Green Thumb Nursery as a sole proprietorship. The business has total assets with a $260,000 adjusted basis and a $500,000 FMV. Paula wants to expand into the landscaping business. She views this expansion as risky and therefore wants to incorporate so as not to put her personal assets at risk. Her friend, Mary Brown, is willing to invest $250,000 in the enterprise.

Although Green Thumb has earned approximately $55,000 per year, Paula and Mary expect that, when the landscaping business is launched, the new corporation will incur annual losses of $50,000 for the next two years. They expect profits of at least $80,000 annually, beginning in the third year. Paula and Mary earn approximately $50,000 from other sources. They are considering the following alternative capital structures and elections:

a. Green Thumb issues 50 shares of common stock to Paula and 25 shares of common stock to Mary.
b. Green Thumb issues 50 shares of common stock to Paula and a $250,000 ten-year note bearing interest at 8% to Mary.
c. Green Thumb issues 40 shares of common stock to Paula plus a $100,000 ten-year note bearing interest at 6% and 15 shares of common stock to Mary, plus a $100,000 ten-year note bearing interest at 6%.
d. Green Thumb issues 50 shares of common stock to Paula and 25 shares of preferred stock to Mary. The preferred stock is nonparticipating but pays a cumulative preferred dividend at 8% of its $250,000 stated value.

What are the advantages and disadvantages of each of these alternatives? What considerations are relevant for determining the best alternative?

C:2-58 Assume the same facts as in Problem C:2-57.

a. Given the nursery's operating prospects, what business forms might Paula and Mary consider and why?
b. In light of their proposed use of debt and equity, how might Paula and Mary structure a partnership to achieve their various business and investment objectives?

CASE STUDY PROBLEMS

C:2-59 Bob Jones has a small repair shop that he has run for several years as a sole proprietorship. The proprietorship uses the cash method of accounting and the calendar year as its tax year. Bob needs additional capital for expansion and knows two people who might be interested in investing in the business. One would like to work for the business. The other would only invest.

Bob wants to know the tax consequences of incorporating the business. His business assets include a building, equipment, accounts receivable, and cash. Liabilities include a mortgage on the building and a few accounts payable, which are deductible when paid. Assume that Bob's ordinary tax rate is greater than 25%.

Required: Write a memorandum to Bob explaining the tax consequences of the incorporation. As part of your memorandum examine the possibility of having the corporation issue common and preferred stock and debt for the shareholders' property and money.

C:2-60 Eric Wright conducts a dry cleaning business as a sole proprietorship. The business operates in a building that Eric owns. Last year, Eric mortgaged for $150,000 the building and the land on which the building sits. He used the money for a down payment on his personal residence and college expenses for his two children. He now wants to incorporate his business and transfer the building and the mortgage to a new corporation, along with other assets and some accounts payable. The amount of the unpaid mortgage balance will not exceed Eric's adjusted basis in the land and building at the time he transfers them to the corporation. Eric is aware that Sec. 357(b) could impact the tax consequences of the transaction because no bona fide business purpose exists for the mortgage transfer, which the IRS might consider to have been for a tax avoidance purpose. However, Eric refuses to acknowledge this possibility when you confront him. He maintains that many taxpayers play the audit lottery and that, in the event of an audit, invoking this issue could be a bargaining ploy.

Required: What information about the transaction must be provided with the transferor and transferee's tax returns for the year in which the transfer takes place? Discuss the ethical issues raised by the AICPA's *Statements on Standards for Tax Services No. 1, Tax Return Positions* (which can be found in Appendix E) as it relates to this situation. Should the tax practitioner act as an advocate for the client? Should the practitioner sign the return?

TAX RESEARCH PROBLEMS

C:2-61 Anne and Michael own and operate a successful mattress business. They have decided to take the business public. They contribute all the assets of the business to newly formed Spring Corporation each in exchange for 20% of the stock. The remaining 60% is issued to an underwriting company that will sell the stock to the public and charge 10% of the sales proceeds as a commission. Prepare a memorandum for your tax manager explaining whether or not this transaction meets the tax-free requirements of Sec. 351.

C:2-62 Bob and Carl transfer property to Stone Corporation for 90% and 10% of Stone stock, respectively. Pursuant to a binding agreement concluded before the transfer, Bob sells half of his stock to Carl. Prepare a memorandum for your tax manager explaining why the exchange does or does not meet the Sec. 351 control requirement. Your manager has suggested that, at a minimum, you consult the following authorities:

- IRC Sec. 351
- Reg. Sec. 1.351-1

C:2-63 In an exchange qualifying for Sec. 351 tax-free treatment, Greta receives 100 shares of White Corporation stock plus a right to receive another 25 shares. The right is contingent on the valuation of a patent contributed by Greta. Because the patent license is pending, the patent cannot be valued for several months. Prepare a memorandum for your tax manager explaining whether the underlying 25 shares are considered "stock" for purposes of Sec. 351 and what tax consequences ensue from Greta's receipt of the 100 shares now and 25 shares later upon exercise of the right.

TAX & FINANCIAL ACCOUNTING

C:2-64 Your clients, Lisa and Matthew, are planning to form Lima Corporation. Lisa will contribute $50,000 cash to Lima for 50 shares of its stock. Matthew will contribute land having a $35,000 adjusted basis and a $50,000 FMV for 50 shares of Lima stock. Lima will borrow additional capital from a bank and then will subdivide and sell the land. Prepare a memorandum for your tax manager outlining the tax treatment of the corporate formation. In your memorandum, compare tax and financial accounting for this transaction. References:

- IRC Sec. 351
- Accounting Standards Codification (ASC) 845 (Nonmonetary Transactions), formerly APB No. 29

C:2-65 John plans to transfer the assets and liabilities of his business to Newco in exchange for all of Newco's stock. The assets have a $250,000 basis and an $800,000 FMV. John also plans to transfer $475,000 of business related liabilities to Newco. Under Sec. 357(c), can John avoid recognizing a $175,000 gain (the excess of liabilities over the basis of assets transferred) by transferring a $175,000 personal promissory note along with the assets and liabilities?

C:2-66 Six years ago, Leticia, Monica, and Nathaniel organized Lemona Corporation to develop and sell computer software. Each individual contributed $10,000 to Lemona in exchange for 1,000 shares of Lemona stock (for a total of 3,000 shares issued and outstanding). The corporation also borrowed $250,000 from Venture Capital Associates to finance operating costs and capital expenditures.

Because of intense competition, Lemona struggled in its early years of operation and sustained chronic losses. This year, Leticia, who serves as Lemona's president, decided to seek additional funds to finance Lemona's working capital.

Venture Capital Associates declined Leticia's request for additional capital because of the firm's already high credit exposure to the software corporation. Hi-Tech Bank proposed to lend Lemona $100,000, but at a 10% premium over the prime rate. (Other software manufacturers in the same market can borrow at a 3% premium.) Investment Managers LLC proposed to inject $50,000 of equity capital into Lemona, but on the condition that the investment firm be granted the right to elect five members to Lemona's board of directors. Discouraged by the "high cost" of external borrowing, Leticia turned to Monica and Nathaniel.

She proposed to Monica and Nathaniel that each of the three original investors contribute an additional $25,000 to Lemona, each in exchange for five 20-year debentures. The debentures would be unsecured and subordinated to Venture Capital Associates debt. Annual interest on the debentures would accrue at a floating 5% premium over the prime rate. The right to receive interest payments would be cumulative; that is, each debenture holder would be entitled to past and current interest payents before Lemona's board could declare a common stock dividend. The debentures would be both nontransferable and noncallable.

Leticia, Monica, and Nathaniel have asked you, their tax accountant, to advise them on the tax implications of the proposed financing arrangement. After researching the issue, set forth your advice in a client letter. At a minimum, you should consult the following authorities:

- IRC Sec. 385
- *Rudolph A. Hardman*, 60 AFTR 2d 87-5651, 87-2 USTC ¶9523 (9th Cir., 1987)
- *Tomlinson v. The 1661 Corporation*, 19 AFTR 2d 1413, 67-1 USTC ¶9438 (5th Cir., 1967)

CHAPTER

3

THE CORPORATE INCOME TAX

LEARNING OBJECTIVES

After studying this chapter, you should be able to

1. Select tax years and accounting methods for C corporations
2. Calculate deductions particular to corporations and arrive at corporate taxable income
3. Compute a corporation's regular income tax liability
4. Recognize what a controlled group is and determine the tax consequences of being a controlled group
5. Identify planning strategies to reduce taxes for corporations and their shareholders
6. Comply with corporate tax filing requirements
7. Determine the financial statement implications of corporate federal income taxes

CHAPTER OUTLINE

A **corporation** is a separate taxpaying entity that must file an annual tax return even if it has no income or loss for the year. This chapter covers the tax rules for **domestic corporations** (i.e., corporations incorporated in one of the 50 states or under federal law) and other entities taxed as domestic corporations under the check-the-box regulations.[1] It explains the rules for determining a corporation's taxable income, loss, and tax liability and for filing corporate tax returns. See Table C:3-1 for the general formula for determining the corporate tax liability. It also discusses the financial implications of federal income taxes. Some of these implications appear briefly in the Book-to-Tax Accounting Comparisons, and a more detailed discussion appears at the end of this chapter.

The corporations discussed in this chapter are sometimes referred to as regular or C corporations because Subchapter C of the Internal Revenue Code (IRC) dictates much of their tax treatment. Corporations that have a special tax status include S corporations (see Chapter C:11) and affiliated groups of corporations that file consolidated returns (see Chapter C:8). A comparison of the tax treatments of C corporations, partnerships, and S corporations appears in Appendix F.

CORPORATE ELECTIONS

OBJECTIVE 1

Select tax years and accounting methods for C corporations

Once formed, a corporation must make certain elections, such as selecting its **tax year** and its accounting methods. The corporation makes these elections on its first tax return. They are important and should be considered carefully because, once made, they generally can be changed only with permission from the Internal Revenue Service (IRS).

CHOOSING A CALENDAR OR FISCAL YEAR

A new corporation may elect to use either a calendar year or a fiscal year as its accounting period. The corporation's tax year must be the same as the annual accounting period used for financial accounting purposes. The corporation makes the election by filing its first tax return for the selected period. A calendar year is a 12-month period ending on December 31. A fiscal year is a 12-month period ending on the last day of any month other than December. Examples of acceptable fiscal years are February 1, 2015, through January 31, 2016, and October 1, 2015, through September 30, 2016. A fiscal year that runs from September 16, 2015, through September 15, 2016, however, is not an acceptable tax year because it does not end on the last day of the month. The IRS requires that a corporation using an unacceptable tax year change to a calendar year.[2]

KEY POINT

Whereas partnerships and S corporations generally must adopt a calendar year, C corporations (other than personal service corporations) have the flexibility of adopting a fiscal year. The fiscal year must end on the last day of the month.

Short Tax Period. A corporation's first tax year might not cover a full 12-month period. If, for example, a corporation begins business on March 10, 2015, and elects a fiscal year ending on September 30, its first tax year covers the period from March 10, 2015, through September 30, 2015. Its second tax year covers the period from October 1, 2015, through September 30, 2016. The corporation must file a **short-period tax return** for its first tax year.[3] From then on, its tax returns will cover a full 12-month period. The last year of a corporation's life, however, also may be a short period covering the period from the beginning of the last tax year through the date the corporation ceases to exist.

Restrictions on Adopting a Tax Year. A corporation may be subject to restrictions in its choice of a tax year. For example, an S corporation generally must use a calendar year (see Chapter C:11), and members of an affiliated group filing a consolidated return must use the same tax year as the group's parent corporation (see Chapter C:8).

A **personal service corporation** (PSC) generally must use a calendar year as its tax year. This restriction prevents a personal service corporation with, for example, a January 31 year-end from distributing a large portion of its income earned during the February through December portion of 2015 to its calendar year shareholder-employees in January

[1] Sec. 7701(a)(4). Corporations that are not classified as domestic are foreign corporations. Foreign corporations are taxed like domestic corporations if they conduct a trade or business in the United States.

[2] Sec. 441. Section 441 also permits accounting periods of either 52 or 53 weeks that always end on the same day of the week (such as Friday).

[3] Sec. 443(a)(2).

▼ TABLE C:3-1
General Rules for Determining the Corporate Tax Liability

Income Tax	Alternative Minimum Tax (AMT)
Gross income Minus: Deductions and losses	
Taxable income before special deductions Minus: Special deductions	
Taxable income →	Taxable income before NOL deduction Plus or minus: Adjustments to taxable income Plus: Tax preference items Minus: Alternative tax NOL deduction
Times: Corporate tax rates	Alternative minimum taxable income Minus: Statutory exemption
Regular tax before credits and other taxes Minus: Foreign tax credit and possessions tax credit	Tax base Times: 20% tax rate
Regular tax (→ to AMT "Minus: Regular (income) tax") Minus: Other tax credits Plus: Recapture of previously claimed tax credits	Tentative minimum tax before credits Minus: AMT foreign tax credit
Income (regular) tax liability	Tentative minimum tax → Minus: Regular (income) tax
	Alternative minimum tax (if greater than zero) (See Table C:5-1)

Income (regular) tax liability
Plus: Alternative minimum tax ←
Special taxes (if applicable):
Accumulated earnings tax
Personal holding company tax

Total tax liability
Minus: Estimated tax payments

Net tax due (or refund)

2016, thereby deferring income largely earned in 2015 to 2016. For this purpose, the IRC defines a PSC as a corporation whose principal activity is the performance of personal services by its employee-owners who own more than 10% of the stock (by value) on any day of the year.[4]

A PSC, however, may adopt a fiscal tax year if it can establish a business purpose for such a year. For example, it may be able to establish a natural business year and use that year as its tax year.[5] Deferral of income by shareholders is not an acceptable business purpose. Even when no business purpose exists, a new PSC may elect to use a September 30, October 31, or November 30 year-end if it meets minimum distribution requirements to employee-owners during the deferral period.[6] If it fails to meet these distribution requirements, the PSC may have to defer to its next fiscal year the deduction for amounts paid to employee-owners.[7]

[4] Sec. 441(i).
[5] The natural business year rule requires that the year-end used for tax purposes coincide with the end of the taxpayer's peak business period. (See the partnership and S corporation chapters and Rev. Proc. 2006-46, 2006-2 C.B. 859, for a further explanation of this exception.)
[6] Sec. 444.
[7] Sec. 280H.

EXAMPLE C:3-1 ▶ Alice and Bob form Cole Corporation with each shareholder owning 50% of its stock. Alice and Bob use the calendar year as their tax year. Alice and Bob are both active in the business and are the corporation's primary employees. The new corporation performs engineering services for the automotive industry. Cole must use a calendar year as its tax year unless it qualifies for a fiscal year based on a business purpose exception. Alternatively, it may adopt a fiscal year ending on September 30, October 31, or November 30, provided it complies with certain minimum distribution requirements. ◀

Changing the Annual Accounting Period. A corporation that desires to change its annual accounting period must obtain the prior approval of the IRS unless Treasury Regulations specifically authorized the change or IRS procedures allow an automatic change. A change in accounting period usually results in a short period running from the end of the old annual accounting period to the beginning of the new accounting period. A corporation must request approval of an accounting period change by filing Form 1128 (Application for Change in Annual Accounting Period) on or before the fifteenth day of the third calendar month following the close of the short period. The IRS usually will approve a request for change if a substantial business purpose exists for the change and if the taxpayer agrees to the IRS's prescribed terms, conditions, and adjustments necessary to prevent any substantial distortion of income. A substantial distortion of income includes, for example, a change that causes the "deferral of a substantial portion of the taxpayer's income, or shifting of a substantial portion of deductions, from one taxable year to another."[8]

Under IRS administrative procedures, a corporation may change its annual accounting period without prior IRS approval if it meets the following conditions:

- The corporation files a short-period tax return for the year of change and annualizes its income when computing its tax for the short period.
- The corporation files full 12-month returns for subsequent years ending on the new year-end.
- The corporation closes its books as of the last day of the short-period and subsequently computes its income and keeps its books using the new tax year.
- If the corporation generates an NOL or capital loss in the short period, it may not carry back the losses but must carry them over to future years. However, if the loss is $50,000 or less, the corporation may carry it back.
- The corporation must not have changed its accounting period within the previous 48 months (with some exceptions).
- The corporation must not have an interest in a pass-through entity as of the end of the short period (with some exceptions).
- The corporation is not an S corporation, personal service corporation, tax-exempt organization, or other specialized corporation.[9]

BOOK-TO-TAX ACCOUNTING COMPARISON

Treasury Regulations literally require taxpayers to use the same overall accounting method for book and tax purposes. However, the courts have allowed different methods if the taxpayer maintains adequate reconciling workpapers. The IRS has adopted the courts' position on this issue.

ACCOUNTING METHODS

A new corporation must select the overall **accounting method** it will use for tax purposes. The method chosen must be indicated on the corporation's initial return. The three possible accounting methods are: accrual, cash, and hybrid.[10]

Accrual Method. Under the accrual method, a corporation reports income in the year it earns the income and reports expenses in the year it incurs the expenses. A corporation must use the accrual method unless it qualifies under one of the following exceptions:

- It qualifies as a family farming corporation.[11]

---

[8] Reg. Sec. 1.442-1(b)(3). Also see Rev. Proc. 2002-39, 2002-1 C.B. 1046.
[9] Rev. Proc. 2006-45, 2006-2 C.B. 851. For automatic change procedures for S corporations and personal service corporations, see Rev. Proc. 2006-46, 2006-2 C.B. 859.
[10] Sec. 446.
[11] Sec. 448. Certain family farming corporations having gross receipts of less than $25 million may use the cash method of accounting. Section 447 requires farming corporations with gross receipts over $25 million to use the accrual method of accounting.

- It qualifies as a personal service corporation, which is a corporation substantially all of whose activities involve the performance of services in the fields of health, law, engineering, architecture, accounting, actuarial science, performing arts, or consulting; and substantially all of whose stock is held by current (or retired) employees performing the services listed above, their estates, or (for two years only) persons who inherited their stock from such employees.[12]
- It meets a $5 million gross receipts test for all prior tax years beginning after December 31, 1985. A corporation meets this test for any prior tax year if its average gross receipts for the three-year period ending with that prior tax year do not exceed $5 million. If the corporation was not in existence for the entire three-year period, the period during which the corporation *was* in existence may be used.
- It has elected S corporation status.

ADDITIONAL COMMENT

Whereas partnerships and S corporations are generally allowed to be cash method taxpayers, most C corporations must use the accrual method of accounting. This restriction can prove inconvenient for many small corporations (with more than $5 million of gross receipts) that would rather use the less complicated cash method of accounting.

If a corporation meets one of the exceptions listed above, it may use either the accrual method or one of the following two methods.

Cash Method. Under the cash method, a corporation reports income when it actually or constructively receives the income and reports expenses when it pays them. Corporations in service industries such as engineering, medicine, law, and accounting generally use this method because they prefer to defer recognition until they actually receive the income. This method may not be used if inventories are a material income-producing factor. In such case, the corporation must use either the *accrual* method or the *hybrid* method of accounting.

Hybrid Method. Under the hybrid method, a corporation uses the accrual method of accounting for sales, cost of goods sold, inventories, accounts receivable, and accounts payable, and uses the cash method of accounting for all other income and expense items. Small businesses with inventories (e.g., retail stores) often use this method. Although they must use the accrual method of accounting for sales-related income and expense items, they often find the cash method less burdensome to use for other income and expense items, such as utilities, rents, salaries, and taxes.

DETERMINING A CORPORATION'S TAXABLE INCOME

OBJECTIVE 2

Calculate deductions particular to corporations and arrive at corporate taxable income

Each year, C corporations must determine their corporate income (or regular) tax liability. In addition to the income tax, a C corporation may owe the corporate alternative minimum tax and possibly either the accumulated earnings tax or the personal holding company tax. A corporation's total tax liability equals the sum of its regular income tax liability plus any additional taxes that it owes.

This chapter explains how to compute a corporation's income (or regular) tax liability. Chapter C:5 explains the computation of the corporate alternative minimum tax, personal holding company tax, and accumulated earnings tax.

[12] The personal service corporation definition for the tax year election [Sec. 441(i)] is different from the personal service corporation definition for the cash accounting method election [Sec. 448].

Like an individual, a corporation is a taxpaying entity with gross income and deductions. However, a number of differences arise between individual and corporate taxation as summarized in Figure C:3-1. This section of the text expands on some of these items and discusses other tax aspects particular to corporations.

SALES AND EXCHANGES OF PROPERTY

Sales and exchanges of property generally are treated the same way for corporations as for an individual. However, special rules apply to capital gains and losses, and corporations are subject to an additional 20% depreciation recapture rule under Sec. 291 on sales of Sec. 1250 property.

1. **Gross income:** Generally, the same gross income definition applies to individuals and corporations. Certain exclusions are available to individuals but not to corporations (e.g, fringe benefits); other exclusions are available to corporations but not to individuals (e.g., capital contributions).
2. **Deductions:** Individuals have above-the-line deductions (for AGI), itemized deductions (from AGI), and personal exemptions. Corporations do not compute AGI, and their deductions are presumed to be ordinary and necessary business expenses.
3. **Charitable contributions:** Individuals are limited to 50% of AGI (30% for capital gain property). Corporations are limited to 10% of taxable income computed without regard to the dividends-received deductions, the U.S. production activities deduction, NOL and capital loss carrybacks, and the contribution deduction itself. Individuals deduct a contribution only in the year they pay it. Accrual basis corporations may deduct contributions in the year of accrual if the board of directors authorizes the contribution by year-end, and the corporation pays it by the fifteenth day of the third month of the next year.
4. **Depreciation on Sec. 1250 property:** Individuals generally do not recapture depreciation under the MACRS rules because straight-line depreciation applies to real property. Corporations must recapture 20% of the amount that would be recaptured under Sec. 1245. Individuals are subject to a 25% (and possibly an incremental 3.8%) tax rate on unrecaptured Sec. 1250 gains. Corporations are not subject to this rate.
5. **Net capital gains:** The applicable capital gains tax rate for net capital gains and qualified dividends of noncorporate taxpayers is 0% for taxpayers in tax brackets of 15% and below, 15% for taxpayers in the 25% through 35% tax brackets, and 20% for taxpayers in the 39.6% tax bracket. Also, 25% and 28% rates apply for gains on certain types of property. In addition, an incremental 3.8% rate applies to net investment income for taxpayers whose modified AGI exceeds $200,000 ($250,000 for married filing jointly). Net investment income includes, among other things, interest, dividends, annuities, royalties, rents, and net gains from the disposition of property not used in a trade or business, all reduced by deductions allocable to such income or gains. Corporate capital gains are taxed at the regular corporate tax rates.
6. **Capital losses:** Individuals can deduct up to $3,000 of net capital losses to offset ordinary income. Individual capital losses carry over indefinitely. Corporations cannot offset any ordinary income with capital losses. However, capital losses carry back three years and forward five years and offset capital gains in those years.
7. **Dividends-received deduction:** This deduction is not available to individuals. Corporations receive a 70%, 80%, or 100% special deduction depending on the percentage of stock ownership.
8. **NOLs:** Individuals must make many adjustments to arrive at the NOL they are allowed to carry back or forward. A corporation's NOL is simply the excess of its deductions over its income for the year. The NOL carries back two years (or an extended period if applicable) and forward 20 years for individuals and corporations, or the taxpayer can elect to forgo the carryback and only carry the NOL forward.
9. For individuals, the U.S. production activities deduction is based on the lesser of qualified production activities income or AGI. For corporations, the deduction is based on the lesser of qualified production activities income or taxable income.
10. **Tax rates:** Individual's ordinary tax rates range from 10% to 39.6% (in 2015). Corporate tax rates range from 15% to 39%.
11. **AMT:** Individual AMT rates are 26% or 28%. The corporate AMT rate is 20%. Corporations are subject to a special AMTI adjustment, called adjusted current earnings (ACE), that does not apply to individuals.
12. **Passive Losses:** Passive loss rules apply to individuals, partners, S corporation shareholders, closely held C corporations, and personal service corporations. They do not apply to widely held C corporations.
13. **Casualty losses:** Casualty losses are deductible in full by a corporation because all corporate casualty losses are considered to be business related. Moreover, they are not reduced by a $100 offset, nor are they restricted to losses exceeding 10% of AGI, as are an individual's nonbusiness casualty losses.

FIGURE C:3-1 ▶ DIFFERENCES BETWEEN INDIVIDUAL AND CORPORATE TAXATION

Capital Gains and Losses. A corporation has a capital gain or loss if it sells or exchanges a capital asset. As with individuals, a corporation must net all its capital gains and losses to obtain its net capital gain or loss position.

Net Capital Gain. A corporation includes all its net capital gains (net long-term capital gains in excess of net short-term capital losses) for the tax year in gross income. Unlike with individuals, a corporation's capital gains receive no special tax treatment and are taxed in the same manner as any other ordinary income item.

EXAMPLE C:3-2 ► Beta Corporation has a net capital gain of $40,000, gross profits on sales of $110,000, and deductible expenses of $28,000. Beta's gross income is $150,000 ($40,000 + $110,000). Its taxable income is $122,000 ($150,000 − $28,000). The $40,000 of net capital gain receives no special treatment and is taxed using the regular corporate tax rates described below. ◄

Net Capital Losses. If a corporation incurs a net capital loss, it cannot deduct the net loss in the current year. A corporation's capital losses can offset only capital gains. They never can offset the corporation's ordinary income.

A corporation must carry back a net capital loss as a short-term capital loss to the three previous tax years and offset capital gains in the earliest year possible (i.e., the losses carry back to the third previous year first). If the loss is not totally absorbed as a carryback, the remainder carries over as a short-term capital loss for five years. Any unused capital losses remaining at the end of the carryover period expire.

EXAMPLE C:3-3 ► In 2015, East Corporation reports gross profits of $150,000, deductible expenses of $28,000, and a net capital loss of $10,000. East reported the following capital gain net income (excess of gains from sales or exchanges of capital assets over losses from such sales or exchanges) during 2012 through 2014:

Year	*Capital Gain Net Income*
2012	$6,000
2013	-0-
2014	3,000

East has gross income of $150,000 and taxable income of $122,000 ($150,000 − $28,000) for 2015. East also has a $10,000 net capital loss that carries back to 2012 first and offsets the $6,000 capital gain net income reported in that year. East receives a refund for the taxes paid in 2012 on the $6,000 of capital gains. The $4,000 ($10,000 − $6,000) remainder of the loss carryback carries to 2014 and offsets East's $3,000 capital gain net income reported in that year. East still has a $1,000 net capital loss carryover to 2016. ◄

ADDITIONAL COMMENT

A corporation accomplishes the net capital loss carryback by filing either Form 1139, Corporation Application for Tentative Refund, or Form 1120X, Amended U.S. Corporation Income Tax Return. Form 1139 usually results in a quicker refund than does Form 1120X but must be filed within one year after the end of the year in which the net capital loss occurred.

Sec. 291: Tax Benefit Recapture Rule. If a taxpayer sells Sec. 1250 property at a gain, Sec. 1250 requires that the taxpayer report the recognized gain as ordinary income to the extent the depreciation taken exceeds the depreciation that would have been allowed had the taxpayer used the straight-line method. This ordinary income is known as Sec. 1250 depreciation recapture. For individuals, any remaining gain is characterized as a combination of unrecaptured Sec. 1250 gain and Sec. 1231 gain. Corporations, however, must recapture as ordinary income an amount equal to 20% of the ordinary income that would have been recognized had the property been Sec. 1245 property instead of Sec. 1250 property.

ADDITIONAL COMMENT

Under the modified accelerated cost recovery system (MACRS), Sec. 1250 depreciation recapture seldom, if ever, occurs for individuals because MACRS requires straight-line depreciation for Sec. 1250 property. Nevertheless, individuals would be subject to the 25% tax rate on unrecaptured Sec. 1250 gains.

EXAMPLE C:3-4 ► Texas Corporation purchased residential real estate several years ago for $125,000, of which $25,000 was allocated to the land and $100,000 to the building. Texas took straight-line MACRS depreciation deductions of $10,606 on the building during the period it held the building. In December of the current year, Texas sells the property for $155,000, of which $45,000 is allocated to the land and $110,000 to the building. Texas has a $20,000 ($45,000 − $25,000) gain on the land sale, all of which is Sec. 1231 gain. This gain is not affected by Sec. 291 because land is not Sec. 1250 property. Texas has a $20,606 [$110,000 sales price − ($100,000 original cost − $10,606 depreciation)] gain on the sale of the building. If Texas were an individual taxpayer, $10,606 would be an unrecaptured Sec. 1250 gain subject to a 25% tax rate, and the remaining

ADDITIONAL COMMENT

Section 291 results in the recapture, as ordinary income, of up to 20% of the gain on sales of Sec. 1250 property. This recapture requirement reduces the amount of net Sec.1231 gains that can be offset by corporate capital losses.

ADDITIONAL COMMENT

If an individual sold the same business property as in Example C:3-4, he or she would recognize $10,606 of nonrecaptured Sec. 1250 gain, $30,000 of Sec. 1231 gain, and no ordinary income.

$10,000 would be a Sec. 1231 gain. However, a corporate taxpayer reports $2,121 of gain as ordinary income. These amounts are summarized below:

	Land	Building	Total
Amount of gain:			
Sales price	$45,000	$110,000	$155,000
Minus: Adjusted basis	(25,000)	(89,394)	(114,394)
Recognized gain	$20,000	$ 20,606	$ 40,606
Character of gain:			
Ordinary income	$ -0-	$ 2,121[a]	$ 2,121
Sec. 1231 gain	20,000	18,485	38,485
Recognized gain	$20,000	$ 20,606	$ 40,606

[a]0.20 × lesser of $10,606 depreciation claimed or $20,606 recognized gain. ◀

BUSINESS EXPENSES

Corporations are allowed deductions for ordinary and necessary business expenses, including salaries paid to officers and other employees of the corporation, rent, repairs, insurance premiums, advertising, interest, taxes, losses on sales of inventory or other property, bad debts, and depreciation. No deductions are allowed, however, for interest on amounts borrowed to purchase tax-exempt securities, illegal bribes or kickbacks, fines or penalties imposed by a government, or insurance premiums incurred to insure the lives of officers and employees when the corporation is the beneficiary.

Organizational Expenditures. When formed, a corporation may incur some organizational expenditures such as legal fees and accounting fees incident to the incorporation process. These expenditures normally must be capitalized. Nevertheless, under Sec. 248, a corporation may elect to deduct the first $5,000 of organizational expenditures. However, the corporation must reduce the $5,000 by the amount by which cumulative organizational expenditures exceed $50,000 although the $5,000 cannot be reduced below zero. The corporation can amortize the remaining organizational expenditures over a 180-month period beginning in the month it begins business.

EXAMPLE C:3-5 ▶ Sigma Corporation incorporates on January 10 of the current year, and begins business on March 3. Sigma elects a September 30 year-end. Thus, it conducts business for seven months during its first tax year. During the period January 10 through September 30, Sigma incurs $52,000 of organizational expenditures. Because these expenditures exceed $50,000, Sigma must reduce the first $5,000 by $2,000 ($52,000 − $50,000), leaving a $3,000 deduction. Sigma amortizes the remaining $49,000 ($52,000 − $3,000) over 180 months beginning in March of its first year. This portion of the deduction equals $1,906 ($49,000/180 × 7 months). Accordingly, its total first-year deduction is $4,906 ($3,000 + $1,906). ◀

WHAT WOULD YOU DO IN THIS SITUATION?

You are a CPA with a medium-size accounting firm. One of your corporate clients is an electrical contractor in New York City. The client is successful and had $10 million of sales last year. The contracts involve private and government electrical work. Among the corporation's expenses are $400,000 of kickbacks paid to people working for general contractors who award electrical subcontracts to the corporation, and $100,000 of payments to individuals in the electricians' union. Technically, these payments are illegal. However, your client says that everyone in this business needs to pay kickbacks to obtain contracts and to have enough electricians to finish the projects in a timely manner. He maintains that it is impossible to stay in business without making these payments. In preparing its tax return, your client wants you to deduct these expenses. What is your opinion concerning the client's request?

BOOK-TO-TAX ACCOUNTING COMPARISON

Most corporations amortize organizational expenditures for tax purposes over the specified period. For financial accounting purposes, they are expensed currently under ASC 720-15. Thus, the differential treatment creates a deferred tax asset.

For organizational expenditures paid or incurred after August 16, 2011, a corporation is deemed to have made the Sec. 248 election for the tax year the corporation begins business.[13] A corporation also can apply the amortization provisions for expenditures made after October 22, 2004, provided the statute of limitations is still open for the particular year. If the corporation chooses to forgo the deemed election, it can elect to capitalize the expenditures (without amortization) on a timely filed tax return for the tax year the corporation begins business. Either election, to amortize or capitalize, is irrevocable and applies to all organizational expenditures of the corporation.

A corporation begins business when it starts the business operations for which it was organized. Merely coming into existence is not sufficient. For example, obtaining a corporate charter does not in itself establish the beginning of business. However, acquiring assets necessary for operating the business may be sufficient.

Organizational expenditures include expenditures (1) incident to the corporation's creation; (2) chargeable to the corporation's capital account; and (3) of a character that, if expended incident to the creation of a corporation having a limited life, would be amortizable over that life.

Specific organizational expenditures include

- ▶ Legal services incident to the corporation's organization (e.g., drafting the corporate charter and bylaws, minutes of organizational meetings, and terms of original stock certificates)
- ▶ Accounting services necessary to create the corporation
- ▶ Expenses of temporary directors and of organizational meetings of directors and stockholders
- ▶ Fees paid to the state of incorporation[14]

Organizational expenditures do not include expenditures connected with issuing or selling the corporation's stock or other securities (e.g., commissions, professional fees, and printing costs) and expenditures related to the transfer of assets to the corporation.

EXAMPLE C:3-6 ▶ Omega Corporation incorporates on July 12 of the current year, starts business operations on August 10, and elects a tax year ending on September 30. Omega incurs the following expenditures while organizing the corporation:

Date	*Type of Expenditure*	*Amount*
June 10	Legal expenses to draft charter	$ 2,000
July 17	Commission to stockbroker for issuing and selling stock	40,000
July 18	Accounting fees to set up corporate books	2,400
July 20	Temporary directors' fees	1,000
August 25	Directors' fees	1,500

Omega's first tax year begins July 12 and ends on September 30. Omega has organizational expenditures of $5,400 ($2,000 + $2,400 + $1,000). The commission for selling the Omega stock is treated as a reduction in the amount of Omega's paid-in capital. Omega deducts the directors' fees incurred in August as a trade or business expense under Sec. 162 because Omega had begun business operations by that date. Assuming a deemed election to amortize its organizational expenditures, Omega can deduct $5,000 in its first tax year and amortize the remaining $400 over 180 months. Thus, its first year deduction is $5,004 [$5,000 + ($400/180) × 2 months].

The following table summarizes the classification of expenditures:

			Type of Expenditure		
Date	*Expenditure*	*Amount*	*Organizational*	*Capital*	*Business*
June 10	Legal	$ 2,000	$2,000		
July 17	Commission	40,000		$40,000	
July 18	Accounting	2,400	2,400		
July 20	Temporary directors' fees	1,000	1,000		
August 25	Directors' fees	1,500			$1,500
	Total	$46,900	$5,400	$40,000	$1,500 ◀

[13] Reg. Sec. 1.248-1(c) and 1(f).

[14] Reg. Sec. 1.248-1(b)(2).

BOOK-TO-TAX ACCOUNTING COMPARISON

For tax purposes, a corporation amortizes start-up expenditures over 180 months (after the initial deduction). ASC 915 holds that the financial accounting practices and reporting standards used for development stage businesses should be no different for an established business. The two different sets of rules can lead to different reporting for tax and book purposes.

Start-Up Expenditures. A distinction must be made between a corporation's organizational expenditures and its start-up expenditures. Start-up expenditures are ordinary and necessary business expenses paid or incurred by an individual or corporate taxpayer

- To investigate the creation or acquisition of an active trade or business
- To create an active trade or business
- To conduct an activity engaged in for profit or the production of income before the time the activity becomes an active trade or business

Examples of start-up expenditures include the costs for a survey of potential markets; an analysis of available facilities; advertisements relating to opening the business; the training of employees; travel and other expenses for securing prospective distributors, suppliers, or customers; and the hiring of management personnel and outside consultants. The expenditures must be such that, if incurred in connection with the operation of an existing active trade or business, they would be allowable as a deduction in the year paid or incurred.

Under Sec. 195, a corporation may elect to deduct the first $5,000 of start-up expenditures. However, this amount is reduced (but not below zero) by the amount by which the cumulative start-up expenditures exceed $50,000. The corporation can amortize the remaining start-up expenditures over a 180-month period beginning in the month it begins business.

For start-up expenditures paid or incurred after August 16, 2011, a corporation is deemed to have made the Sec. 195 election for the tax year the business to which the expenditures relate begins.[15] A corporation also can apply the amortization provisions for expenditures made after October 22, 2004, provided the statute of limitations is still open for the particular year. If the corporation chooses to forgo the deemed election, it can elect to capitalize the expenditures (without amortization) on a timely filed tax return for the tax year the business to which the expenditures relate begins. Either election, to amortize or capitalize, is irrevocable and applies to all start-up expenditures related to the business.

? STOP & THINK

Question: What is the difference between an organizational expenditure and a start-up expenditure?

Solution: Organizational expenditures are outlays made in forming a corporation, such as fees paid to the state of incorporation for the corporate chapter and fees paid to an attorney to draft the documents needed to form the corporation. Start-up expenditures are outlays that otherwise would be deductible as ordinary and necessary business expenses but that are capitalized because they were incurred prior to the start of the corporation's business activities.

A corporation may elect to deduct the first $5,000 of organizational expenditures and the first $5,000 of start-up expenditures. The corporation can amortize the remainder of each set of expenditures over 180 months. Like a corporation, a partnership can deduct and amortize its organizational and start-up expenditures. A sole proprietorship may incur start-up expenditures, but sole proprietorships do not incur organizational expenditures.

Limitation on Deductions for Accrued Compensation. If a corporation accrues an obligation to pay compensation, the corporation must make the payment within 2½ months after the close of its tax year. Otherwise, the deduction cannot be taken until the year of payment.[16] The reason is that, if a payment is delayed beyond 2½ months, the IRS treats it as a deferred compensation plan. Deferred compensation cannot be deducted until the year the corporation pays it and the recipient includes the payment in income.[17]

EXAMPLE C:3-7 ▶ On December 10 of the current year, Bell Corporation, a calendar year taxpayer, accrues an obligation for a $100,000 bonus to Marge, a sales representative who has had an outstanding year. Marge owns no Bell stock. Bell must make the payment by March 15 of next year. Otherwise, Bell Corporation cannot deduct the $100,000 in its current year tax return but must wait until the year it pays the bonus. ◀

[15] Reg. Sec. 1.195-1(b) and 1(d).
[16] Temp. Reg. Sec. 1.404(b)-1T.
[17] Sec. 404(b).

Charitable Contributions. The treatment of charitable contributions by individual and corporate taxpayers differs in three ways: the timing of the deduction, the amount of the deduction permitted for the contribution of certain noncash property, and the maximum deduction permitted in any given year.

Timing of the Deduction. Corporations may deduct contributions to qualified charitable organizations. Generally, the contribution must have been *paid* during the year (not just pledged) for a deduction to be allowed for a given year. A special rule, however, applies to corporations using the accrual method of accounting (corporations using the cash or hybrid methods of accounting are not eligible).[18] These corporations may elect to treat part or all of a charitable contribution as having been made in the year it accrued (instead of the year paid) if

- The board of directors authorizes the contribution in the year it accrued
- The corporation pays the contribution on or before the fifteenth day of the third month following the end of the accrual year.

The corporation makes the election by deducting the contribution in its tax return for the accrual year and by attaching a copy of the board of director's resolution to the return. Any portion of the contribution for which the corporation does not make the election is deducted in the year paid.

EXAMPLE C:3-8 ► Echo Corporation is a calendar year taxpayer using the accrual method of accounting. In the current year, its board of directors authorizes a $10,000 contribution to the Girl Scouts. Echo pays the contribution on March 10 of next year. Echo may elect to treat part or all of the contribution as having been paid in the current year. If the corporation pays the contribution after March 15 of next year, it may not deduct the contribution in the current year but may deduct it next year. ◄

TAX STRATEGY TIP

The tax laws do not require a corporation to recognize a gain when it contributes appreciated property to a charitable organization. Thus, except for inventory and limited other properties, a corporation can deduct the FMV of its donation without having to recognize any appreciation in its gross income. On the other hand, a decline in the value of donated property is not deductible. Thus, the corporation should sell the loss property to recognize the loss and then donate the sales proceeds to the chariable organization.

Deducting Contributions of Nonmonetary Property. If a taxpayer donates money to a qualified charitable organization, the amount of the charitable contribution deduction equals the amount of money donated. If the taxpayer donates property, the amount of the charitable contribution deduction generally equals the property's fair market value (FMV). However, special rules apply to donations of appreciated nonmonetary property known as ordinary income property and capital gain property.[19]

In this context, **ordinary income property** is property whose sale would have resulted in a gain other than a long-term capital gain (i.e., ordinary income or short-term capital gain). Examples of ordinary income property include investment property held for one year or less, inventory property, and property subject to depreciation recapture under Secs. 1245 and 1250. The deduction allowed for a donation of such property is limited to the property's FMV minus the amount of ordinary income or short-term capital gain the corporation would have recognized had it sold the property.

In three special cases, a corporation may deduct the donated property's adjusted basis plus one-half of the excess of the property's FMV over its adjusted basis (not to exceed twice the property's adjusted basis). This special rule applies to inventory if

1. The use of the property is related to the donee's exempt function, and it is used solely for the care of the ill, the needy, or infants;
2. The property is not transferred to the donee in exchange for money, other property, or services; and
3. The donor receives a statement from the charitable organization stating that conditions (1) and (2) will be complied with.

A similar rule applies to contributions of scientific research property if the corporation created the property and contributed it to a college, university, or tax-exempt scientific research organization for its use within two years of creating the property.

EXAMPLE C:3-9 ► King Corporation donates inventory having a $26,000 adjusted basis and a $40,000 FMV to a qualified public charity. A $33,000 [$26,000 + (0.50 × $14,000)] deduction is allowed for the

[18] Sec. 170(a).

[19] Sec. 170(e).

contribution of the inventory if the charitable organization will use the inventory for the care of the ill, needy, or infants, or if the donee is an educational institution or research organization that will use the scientific research property for research or experimentation. Otherwise, the deduction is limited to the property's $26,000 adjusted basis. If instead the inventory's FMV is $100,000 and the donation meets either of the two sets of requirements outlined above, the charitable contribution deduction is limited to $52,000, the lesser of the property's adjusted basis plus one-half of the appreciation [$63,000 = $26,000 + (0.50 × $74,000)] or twice the property's adjusted basis ($52,000 = $26,000 × 2). ◀

When a corporation donates appreciated property whose sale would result in long-term capital gain (also known as **capital gain property**) to a charitable organization, the amount of the contribution deduction generally equals the property's FMV. However, special restrictions apply if

- ▶ The corporation donates a patent, copyright, trademark, trade name, trade secret, know-how, certain software, or other similar property;
- ▶ A corporation donates tangible personal property to a charitable organization and the organization's use of the property is unrelated to its tax-exempt purpose; or
- ▶ A corporation donates appreciated property to certain private nonoperating foundations.[20]

In these cases, the amount of the corporation's contribution is limited to the property's FMV minus the long-term capital gain that would have resulted from the property's sale.

EXAMPLE C:3-10 ▶ Fox Corporation donates artwork to the MacNay Museum. The artwork, purchased two years earlier for $15,000, is worth $38,000 on the date Fox donates it. At the time of the donation, the museum's directors intend to sell the work to raise funds to conduct museum activities. Fox's deduction for the gift is limited to $15,000. If the museum plans to display the artwork to the public, the entire $38,000 deduction is permitted. Fox can avoid losing a portion of its charitable contribution deduction by, as a condition of the donation, placing restrictions on the sale or use of the property. ◀

Substantiation Requirements. Section 170(f)(11) imposes substantiation requirements for noncash charitable contributions. If the corporation does not comply, it will lose the charitable contribution deduction. The requirements are as follows:

ADDITIONAL COMMENT

The $500, $5,000, and $500,000 thresholds apply on an aggregate basis for similar property donated to one or more donees.

- ▶ If the contribution deduction exceeds $500, the corporation must include with its tax return a description of the property and any other information required by Treasury Regulations.
- ▶ If the contribution deduction exceeds $5,000, the corporation must obtain a qualified appraisal and include with its tax return any information and appraisal required by Treasury Regulations.
- ▶ If the contribution deduction exceeds $500,000, the corporation must attach a qualified appraisal to the tax return.

The second and third requirements, however, do not apply to contributions of cash; publicly traded securities; inventory; or certain motor vehicles, boats, or aircraft the donee organization sells without any intervening use or material improvement. With regard to these vehicles, the donor corporation's deduction is limited to the amount of gross proceeds the donee organization receives on the sale.

Maximum Deduction Permitted. A limit applies to the amount of charitable contributions a corporation can deduct in a given year. The limit is calculated differently for corporations than for individuals. Contribution deductions by corporations are limited to 10% of adjusted taxable income. Adjusted taxable income is the corporation's taxable income computed without regard to any of the following amounts:

[20] Sec. 170(e)(5). The restriction on contributions of appreciated property to private nonoperating foundations does not apply to contributions of stock for which market quotations are readily available.

BOOK-TO-TAX ACCOUNTING COMPARISON

For financial accounting purposes, all charitable contributions can be claimed as an expense without regard to the amount of profits reported. For tax purposes, however, the charitable contribution deduction may be limited. Thus, the charitable contribution carryover for tax purposes creates a deferred tax asset, possibly subject to a valuation allowance.

- The charitable contribution deduction
- An NOL carryback
- A capital loss carryback
- The dividends-received deduction[21]
- The U.S. production activities deduction

Contributions that exceed the 10% limit are not deductible in the current year. Instead, they carry forward to the next five tax years. Any excess contributions not deducted within those five years expire. The corporation may deduct excess contributions in the carryover year only after it deducts any contributions made in that year. The total charitable contribution deduction (including any deduction for contribution carryovers) is limited to 10% of the corporation's adjusted taxable income in the carryover year.[22]

EXAMPLE C:3-11 ▶ Golf Corporation reports the following results in Year 1 and Year 2:

	Year 1	*Year 2*
Adjusted taxable income	$200,000	$300,000
Charitable contributions	35,000	25,000

Golf's Year 1 contribution deduction is limited to $20,000 (0.10 × $200,000). Golf has a $15,000 ($35,000 − $20,000) contribution carryover to Year 2. The Year 2 contribution deduction is limited to $30,000 (0.10 × $300,000). Golf's deduction for Year 2 is composed of the $25,000 donated in Year 2 and $5,000 of the Year 1 carryover. The remaining $10,000 carryover from Year 1 carries over to the next four years. ◀

Topic Review C:3-1 summarizes the basic corporate charitable contribution deduction rules.

TOPIC REVIEW C:3-1

Corporate Charitable Contribution Rules

1. Timing of the contribution deduction
   a. General rule: A deduction is allowed for contributions paid during the year.
   b. Accrual method corporations can accrue contributions approved by their board of directors prior to the end of the accrual year and paid within 2½ months of that year-end.
2. Amount of the contribution deduction
   a. General rule: A deduction is allowed for the amount of money and the FMV of other property donated.
   b. Exceptions for ordinary income property:
      1. If donated property would result in ordinary income or short-term capital gain if sold, the deduction is limited to the property's FMV minus this potential ordinary income or short-term capital gain. Thus, for gain property the deduction equals the property's cost or adjusted basis.
      2. Special rule: For donations of (1) inventory used for the care of the ill, needy, or infants, or (2) scientific research property or computer technology and equipment to certain educational institutions, a corporate donor may deduct the property's basis plus one-half of the excess of the property's FMV over its adjusted basis. The deduction may not exceed twice the property's adjusted basis.
   c. Exceptions for capital gain property: If the corporation donates tangible personal property to a charitable organization for a use unrelated to its tax-exempt purpose, or the corporation donates appreciated property to a private nonoperating foundation, the corporation's contribution is limited to the property's FMV minus the long-term capital gain that would result if the corporation sold the property.
3. Limitation on contribution deduction
   a. The contribution deduction is limited to 10% of the corporation's taxable income computed without regard to the charitable contribution deduction, any NOL or capital loss carryback, the dividends-received deduction, and the U.S production activities deduction.
   b. Excess contributions carry forward for a five-year period.

[21] Sec. 170(b)(2).

[22] Sec. 170(d)(2).

SPECIAL DEDUCTIONS

C corporations are allowed three special deductions: the U.S. production activities deduction, the dividends-received deduction, and the NOL deduction.

ADDITIONAL COMMENT

While discussed in this text under special deductions, the U.S. production activities deduction actually appears before Line 28 on Form 1120. This deduction also is referred to as the domestic production activities deduction or the manufacturing deduction.

U.S. Production Activities Deduction. Section 199 allows a **U.S. production activities deduction** equal to 9% times the lesser of (1) qualified production activities income for the year or (2) taxable income before the U.S. production activities deduction. The deduction, however, cannot exceed 50% of the corporation's W-2 wages allocable to qualifying U.S. production activities for the year.

Qualified production activities income is the taxpayer's domestic production gross receipts less the following amounts:

- Cost of goods sold allocable to these receipts;
- Other deductions, expenses, and losses directly allocable to these receipts; and
- A ratable portion of other deductions, expenses, and losses not directly allocable to these receipts or to other classes of income.

BOOK-TO-TAX ACCOUNTING COMPARISON

The U.S. production activities deduction is not expensed for financial accounting purposes. Thus, it creates a permanent difference that affects the corportion's effective tax rate but not its deferred taxes.

Domestic production gross receipts include receipts from the following taxpayer activities:

- The lease, rental, license, sale, exchange, or other disposition of (1) qualified production property (tangible property, computer software, and sound recordings) manufactured, produced, grown, or extracted in whole or significant part within the United States; (2) qualified film production; or (3) electricity, natural gas, or potable water produced within the United States
- Construction performed in the United States
- Engineering or architectural services performed in the United States for construction projects in the United States

ADDITIONAL COMMENT

In addition to providing a benefit, the U.S. production activities deduction will increase a corporation's compliance costs because of the time necessary to determine what income and deductions pertain to U.S. production activities.

Domestic production gross receipts, however, do not include receipts from the sale of food and beverages the taxpayer prepares at a retail establishment and do not apply to the transmission of electricity, natural gas, or potable water.

The U.S. production activities deduction has the effect of reducing a corporation's marginal tax rate on qualifying taxable income. For example, a 9% deduction for a corporation in the 35% tax bracket decreases the corporation's marginal tax rate by about 3% ($0.09 \times 35\% = 3.15\%$).

EXAMPLE C:3-12 ▶ Gamma Corporation earns domestic production gross receipts of $1 million and incurs allocable expenses of $400,000. Thus, its qualified production activities income is $600,000. In addition, Gamma has $200,000 of income from other sources, resulting in taxable income of $800,000 before the U.S. production activities deduction. Its U.S. production activities deduction, therefore, is $54,000 ($600,000 × 0.09), and its taxable income is $746,000 ($800,000 − $54,000). ◀

EXAMPLE C:3-13 ▶ Assume the same facts as in Example C:3-12 except Gamma has $100,000 of losses from other sources rather than $200,000 of other income, resulting in taxable income of $500,000 before the U.S. production activities deduction. In this case, its U.S. production activities deduction is $45,000 ($500,000 × 0.09), and its taxable income is $455,000 ($500,000 − $45,000). ◀

Dividends-Received Deduction. A corporation must include in its gross income any dividends received on stock it owns in another corporation. As described in Chapter C:2, the taxation of dividend payments to a shareholder generally results in double taxation. When a distributing corporation pays a dividend to a corporate shareholder and the recipient corporation subsequently distributes these earnings to its shareholders, potential triple taxation of the earnings can result.

EXAMPLE C:3-14 ▶ Adobe Corporation owns stock in Bell Corporation. Bell reports taxable income of $100,000 and pays federal income taxes on its income. Bell distributes its after-tax income to its shareholders. The dividend Adobe receives from Bell must be included in its gross income and, to the extent it reports a profit for the year, Adobe will pay taxes on the dividend. Adobe distributes its remaining after-tax income to its shareholders. The shareholders must include Adobe's dividends in their gross income and pay federal income taxes on the distribution. Thus, Bell's income in this example potentially is taxed three times. ◀

BOOK-TO-TAX ACCOUNTING COMPARISON

A corporation includes dividends in its financial accounting income but does not subtract a dividends-received deduction in determining its book net income. Thus, the dividends-received deduction creates a permanent difference that affects the corporation's effective tax rate but not its deferred taxes.

To partially mitigate the effects of multiple taxation, corporations are allowed a **dividends-received deduction** for dividends received from other domestic corporations and from certain foreign corporations.

General Rule for Dividends-Received Deduction. Corporations that own less than 20% of the distributing corporation's stock may deduct 70% of the dividends received. If the shareholder corporation owns 20% or more of the distributing corporation's stock (both voting power and value) but less than 80% of such stock, it may deduct 80% of the dividends received.[23]

EXAMPLE C:3-15 ▶ Hale Corporation reports the following results in the current year:

Gross income from operations	$300,000
Dividends from 15%-owned domestic corporation	100,000
Operating expenses	280,000

Gross income from operations and expenses both pertain to qualified production activities, so Hale's qualified production activities income is $20,000 ($300,000 − $280,000). Hale's dividends-received deduction is $70,000 (0.70 × $100,000). Thus, Hale's taxable income is computed as follows:

Gross income	$400,000
Minus: Operating expenses	(280,000)
Taxable income before special deductions	$120,000
Minus: Dividends-received deduction	(70,000)
Taxable income before the U.S. production activites deduction	$ 50,000
Minus: U.S. production activities deduction ($20,000 × 0.09)	(1,800)
Taxable income	$ 48,200 ◀

Limitation on Dividends-Received Deduction. In the case of dividends received from corporations that are less than 20% owned, the deduction is limited to the lesser of 70% of dividends received or 70% of taxable income computed without regard to any NOL deduction, any capital loss carryback, the dividends-received deduction itself, or the U.S. production activities deduction.[24] In the case of dividends received from a 20% or more owned corporation, the dividends-received deduction is limited to the lesser of 80% of dividends received or 80% of taxable income computed without regard to the same deductions.

EXAMPLE C:3-16 ▶ Assume the same facts as in Example C:3-15 except Hale Corporation's operating expenses for the year are $310,000 and that qualified production activities income is zero (or negative). Thus, the corporation cannot claim the U.S. production activities deduction. Hale's taxable income before the dividends-received deduction is $90,000 ($300,000 + $100,000 − $310,000). The dividends-received deduction is limited to the lesser of 70% of dividends received ($70,000 = $100,000 × 0.70) or 70% of taxable income before the dividends-received deduction ($63,000 = $90,000 × 0.70). Thus, the dividends-received deduction is $63,000. Hale's taxable income is $27,000 ($90,000 − $63,000). ◀

A corporation that receives dividends eligible for both the 80% dividends-received deduction and the 70% dividends-received deduction must compute the 80% dividends-received deduction first and then reduce taxable income by the aggregate amount of dividends eligible for the 80% deduction before computing the 70% deduction.

[23] Secs. 243(a) and (c).

[24] Sec. 246(b).

EXAMPLE C:3-17 ▶ Assume the same facts as in Example C:3-16 except Hale Corporation receives $75,000 of the dividends from a 25%-owned corporation and the remaining $25,000 from a 15%-owned corporation. The tentative dividends-received deduction from the 25%-owned corporation is $60,000 ($75,000 × 0.80), which is less than the $72,000 ($90,000 × 0.80) limitation. Thus, Hale can deduct the entire $60,000. The tentative dividends-received deduction from the 15%-owned corporation is $17,500 ($25,000 × .70). The limitation, however, is $10,500 [($90,000 − $75,000) × 0.70]. Note that, in computing this limitation, Hale reduces its taxable income by the entire $75,000 dividend received from the 25%-owned corporation. Thus, Hale can deduct only $10,500 of the $17,500 amount. Hale's taxable income is $19,500 ($90,000 − $60,000 − $10,500). ◀

Exception to the Limitation. The taxable income limitation on the dividends-received deduction does not apply if the tentative dividends-received deduction creates or increases an NOL for the year.

EXAMPLE C:3-18 ▶ Assume the same facts as in Example C:3-16 except Hale Corporation's operating expenses for the year are $331,000. Hale's taxable income before the dividends-received deduction is $69,000 ($300,000 + $100,000 − $331,000). The tentative dividends-received deduction is $70,000 ($100,000 × 0.70). Hale's dividends-received deduction is not restricted by the limitation of 70% of taxable income before the dividends-received deduction because, after taking into account the tentative $70,000 dividends-received deduction, the corporation has a $1,000 ($69,000 − $70,000) NOL for the year. If Hale's operating expenses were $410,000 instead of $331,000, it would have a $10,000 NOL before the dividends-received deduction ($300,000 + $100,000 − $410,000). Again, the dividends-received deduction is not restricted by the limitation because it increases the NOL. In this case, the corporation has an $80,000 [$(10,000) − $70,000] NOL for the year. ◀

ADDITIONAL COMMENT

When the dividends-received deduction creates (or increases) an NOL, the corporation gets the full benefit of the deduction because it can carry back or carry forward the NOL.

TAX STRATEGY TIP

A corporation can avoid the dividends-received deduction limitation either by (1) increasing its taxable income before the dividends-received deduction so the limitation exceeds the tentative dividends-received deduction or (2) decreasing its taxable income before the dividends-received deduction so the tentative dividends-received deduction creates an NOL.

The following table compares the results of Examples C:3-15, C:3-16, and C:3-18:

	Example C:3-15	*Example C:3-16*	*Example C:3-18*	
Gross income	$400,000	$400,000	$400,000	$400,000
Minus: Operating expenses	(280,000)	(310,000)	(331,000)	(410,000)
Taxable income (NOL) before special deductions	$120,000	$ 90,000	$ 69,000	$(10,000)
Minus: Dividends-received deduction	(70,000)	(63,000)	(70,000)	(70,000)
U.S. production activities deduction	(1,800)	–0–	–0–	–0–
Taxable income (NOL)	$ 48,200	$ 27,000	$ (1,000)	$(80,000)

Of these three examples, the only case where the dividends-received deduction does not equal the full 70% of the $100,000 dividend is Example C:3-16. In that case, the deduction is limited to $63,000 because taxable income before special deductions is less than the $100,000 dividend *and* because the full $70,000 deduction would not create an NOL. The special exception to the dividends-received deduction can create interesting situations. For example, the additional $21,000 of deductions incurred in Example C:3-18 (as compared to Example C:3-16) resulted in a $28,000 reduction in taxable income. Corporate taxpayers should be aware of these rules and consider deferring income or recognizing expenses to ensure being able to deduct the full 70% or 80% dividends-received deduction. If the taxable income limitation applies, the corporation loses the unused dividends-received deduction.

ADDITIONAL COMMENT

If the affiliated group files a consolidated tax return, the recipient of the dividend does not claim the 100% dividends received deduction because the intercompany dividend gets eliminated in the consolidation (see Chapter C:8).

Members of an Affiliated Group. Members of an affiliated group of corporations can claim a 100% dividends-received deduction with respect to dividends received from other group members.[25] A group of corporations is affiliated if a parent corporation owns at least 80% of the stock (both voting power and value) of at least one subsidiary corporation, and at least 80% of the stock (both voting power and value) of each other corporation is owned by other group members. The 100% dividends-received deduction is not subject to a taxable income limitation and is taken before the 80% or 70% dividends-received deduction.[26]

[25] Sec. 243(a)(3).

[26] Secs. 243(b)(5) and 1504.

EXAMPLE C:3-19 ▶ Hardy Corporation reports the following results for the current year:

Gross income from operations	$520,000
Dividend received from an 80%-owned affiliated corporation	100,000
Dividend received from a 20%-owned corporation	250,000
Operating expenses	550,000

Hardy does not file a consolidated tax return with the 80%-owned affiliate. Because Hardy's qualified production activities income is negative, it cannot claim the U.S. production activities deduction. Hardy's taxable income before any dividends-received deduction is $320,000 ($520,000 + $100,000 + $250,000 − $550,000). Hardy can deduct the entire dividend received from the 80%-owned affiliate without limitation. The tentative dividends-received deduction from the 20%-owned corporation is $200,000 ($250,000 × 0.80). The limitation, however, is $176,000 [($320,000 − $100,000) × 0.80]. Note that, in computing this limitation, Hardy first reduces its taxable income by the $100,000 dividend received from the 80%-owned affiliate. Thus, Hardy can deduct only $176,000 of the $200,000 amount. Hardy's taxable income is $44,000 ($320,000 − $100,000 − $176,000). ◀

Dividends Received from Foreign Corporations. The dividends-received deduction applies primarily to dividends received from domestic corporations. The dividends-received deduction does not apply to dividends received from a foreign corporation because the U.S. Government does not tax its income. Thus, that income is not subject to the multiple taxation illustrated above.[27]

ADDITIONAL COMMENT

Stock purchased on which a dividend has been declared has an increased value. This value will drop when the corporation pays the dividend. If the dividend is eligible for a dividends-received deduction and the drop in value also creates a capital loss, corporate shareholders could use this event as a tax planning device. To avoid this result, no dividends-received deduction is available for stock held 45 days or less.

Stock Held 45 Days or Less. A corporation may not claim a dividends-received deduction if it holds the dividend paying stock for less than 46 days during the 91-day period that begins 45 days before the stock becomes ex-dividend with respect to the dividend.[28] This rule prevents a corporation from claiming a dividends-received deduction if it purchases stock shortly before an ex-dividend date and sells the stock shortly thereafter. (The ex-dividend date is the first day on which a purchaser of stock is not entitled to a previously declared dividend.) Absent this rule, such a purchase and sale would allow the corporation to receive dividends at a low tax rate—a maximum of a 10.5% [(100% − 70%) × 0.35] effective tax rate—and to recognize a capital loss on the sale of stock that could offset capital gains taxed at a 35% corporate tax rate.

EXAMPLE C:3-20 ▶ Theta Corporation purchases 100 shares of Maine Corporation's stock for $100,000 one day before Maine's ex-dividend date. Theta receives a $5,000 dividend on the stock and then sells the stock for $95,000 shortly after the dividend payment date. Because the stock is worth $100,000 immediately before the $5,000 dividend payment, its value drops to $95,000 ($100,000 − $5,000) immediately after the dividend. The sale results in a $5,000 ($100,000 − $95,000) capital loss that may offset a $5,000 capital gain. Assuming a 35% corporate tax rate, the following table summarizes the profit (loss) to Theta with and without the 45-day rule.

	If Deduction Is Allowed	*If Deduction Is Not Allowed*
Dividends	$5,000	$5,000
Minus: 35% tax on dividend	(525)[a]	(1,750)
Dividend (after taxes)	$4,475	$3,250
Capital loss	$5,000	$5,000
Minus: 35% tax savings on loss	(1,750)	(1,750)
Net loss on stock	$3,250	$3,250
Dividend (after taxes)	$4,475	$3,250
Minus: Net loss on stock[b]	(3,250)	(3,250)
Net profit (loss)	$1,225	$ -0-

[a] [$5,000 − (0.70 × $5,000)] × 0.35 = $525
[b] This example assumes the corporation has capital gains against which to deduct this capital loss.

[27] Sec. 245. A limited dividends-received deduction is allowed on dividends received from a foreign corporation that earns income by conducting a trade or business in the United States and, therefore, is subject to U.S. taxes.

[28] Sec. 246(c)(1).

ADDITIONAL COMMENT

Borrowing money with deductible interest to purchase a tax-advantaged asset, such as stock eligible for the dividends-received deduction, is an example of "tax arbitrage." Many provisions in the IRC, such as the limits on debt-financial stock, are aimed at curtailing tax arbitrage transactions.

The profit is not available if Theta sells the stock shortly after receiving the dividend because Theta must hold the Maine stock for at least 46 days to obtain the dividends-received deduction. ◀

Debt-Financed Stock. The dividends-received deduction is not allowed to the extent the corporation borrows money to acquire the dividend paying stock.[29] This rule prevents a corporation from deducting interest paid on money borrowed to purchase the stock, while paying little or no tax on the dividends received on the stock.

EXAMPLE C:3-21 ▶ Palmer Corporation, whose marginal tax rate is 35%, borrows $100,000 at a 10% interest rate to purchase 30% of Sun Corporation's stock. The Sun stock pays an $8,000 annual dividend. If a dividends-received deduction were allowed for this investment, Palmer would have a net profit of $940 annually on owning the Sun stock even though the dividend received is less than the interest paid. The following table summarizes the profit (loss) to Palmer with and without the debt-financing rule.

REAL-WORLD EXAMPLE

Although sound in theory, the debt-financed stock limitation may be difficult to apply in practice. This difficulty became particularly apparent in a district court case, *OBH, Inc. v. U.S.*, 96 AFTR 2d, 2005-6801, 2005-2 USTC ¶50,627 (DC NB, 2005), where the IRS failed to establish that a corporation's debt proceeds were directly traceable to the acquisition of dividend paying stock.

	If Deduction Is Allowed	*If Deduction Is Not Allowed*
Dividends	$ 8,000	$ 8,000
Minus: 35% tax on dividend	(560)[a]	(2,800)
Dividend (after taxes)	$ 7,440	$ 5,200
Interest paid	$10,000	$10,000
Minus: 35% tax savings on deduction	(3,500)	(3,500)
Net cost of borrowing	$ 6,500	$ 6,500
Dividend (after taxes)	$ 7,440	$ 5,200
Minus: Net cost of borrowing	(6,500)	(6,500)
Net profit (loss)	$ 940	$ (1,300)

[a] [$8,000 − ($8,000 × 0.80)] × 0.35 = $560

This example illustrates how the rule disallowing the dividends-received deduction on debt-financed stock prevents corporations from making an after-tax profit by borrowing funds to purchase stocks paying dividends that are less than the cost of the borrowing. ◀

Net Operating Losses (NOLs). If a corporation's deductions exceed its gross income for the year, the corporation has a **net operating loss** (NOL). The NOL is the amount by which the corporation's deductions (including any dividends-received deduction) exceed its gross income.[30] In computing an NOL for a given year, no deduction is permitted for a carryover or carryback of an NOL from a preceding or succeeding year. However, unlike an individual's NOL, no other adjustments are required to compute a corporation's NOL. If the corporation has an NOL, it also would not be allowed a U.S. production activities deduction because it has no positive taxable income.

A corporation's NOL carries back two years and carries over 20 years. It carries to the earliest of the two preceding years first and offsets taxable income reported in that year. If the loss cannot be used in that year, it carries to the immediately preceding year, and then to the next 20 years in chronological order. The corporation may elect to forgo the carryback period entirely and instead carry over the entire loss to the next 20 years.[31]

EXAMPLE C:3-22 ▶ In 2015, Gray Corporation, a calendar year taxpayer, has gross income of $150,000 (including $100,000 from operations and $50,000 in dividends from a 30%-owned domestic corporation) and $180,000 of expenses. Gray has a $70,000 [$150,000 − $180,000 − (0.80 × $50,000)] NOL. The NOL carries back to 2013 unless Gray elects to forego the carryback period. If Gray had

[29] Sec. 246A.
[30] Sec. 172(c).

[31] Various other carryback and carryover periods have applied in past years.

$20,000 of taxable income in 2013, $20,000 of Gray's 2015 NOL offsets that income. Gray receives a refund of all taxes paid in 2013. Gray carries the remaining $50,000 of the 2015 NOL to 2014. Any of the NOL not used in 2014 carries over to 2016. ◀

BOOK-TO-TAX ACCOUNTING COMPARISON

An NOL carryover for tax purposes creates a deferred tax asset, possibly subject to a valuation allowance.

A corporation might elect not to carry an NOL back because its income was taxed at a low marginal tax rate in the carryback period and the corporation anticipates income being taxed at a higher marginal tax rate in later years or because it used tax credit carryovers in the earlier year that were about to expire. The corporation must make this election for the entire carryback by the due date (including extensions) for filing the return for the year in which the corporation incurred the NOL. The corporation makes the election by checking a box on Form 1120 when it files the return. Once made for a tax year, the election is irrevocable.[32] However, if the corporation incurs an NOL in another year, the decision as to whether that NOL should be carried back is a separate decision. In other words, each year's NOL is treated separately and is subject to a separate election.

To obtain a refund due to carrying an NOL back to a preceding year, a corporation files Form 1139 (Corporation Application for a Tentative Refund) if one year or less has elapsed since the year in which the NOL occurred. If a longer period has elapsed, the corporation files Form 1120X (Amended U.S. Corporation Income Tax Return).

The Sequencing of the Deduction Calculations. The rules for charitable contributions, dividends-received, NOL, and U.S. production activities deductions require that these deductions be calculated in the following sequence:

1. All deductions other than the charitable contributions deduction, the dividends-received deduction, the NOL deduction, and the U.S. production activities deduction
2. The charitable contributions deduction
3. The dividends-received deduction
4. The NOL deduction
5. The U.S. production activities deduction

As stated previously, the charitable contributions deduction is limited to 10% of taxable income before the charitable contributions deduction, any NOL or capital loss carryback, the dividends-received deduction, or the U.S. production activities deduction, but *after* any NOL carryover deduction. Once the corporation determines its charitable contributions deduction, it adds back any NOL carryover deduction and subtracts the charitable contributions deduction before computing the dividends-received deduction. The corporation then subtracts the NOL deduction, if any, before determining its U.S. production activities deduction.

EXAMPLE C:3-23 ▶ East Corporation reports the following results for the current year:

Gross income from operations	$150,000
Dividends from 30%-owned domestic corporation	100,000
Operating expenses	100,000
Charitable contributions	35,000

These results include $50,000 of qualified production activities income in the current year ($150,000 gross income from operations – $100,000 operating expenses). East also has a $40,000 NOL carryover from the previous year. East's charitable contributions deduction is computed as follows:

Gross income from operations	$150,000
Plus: Dividends	100,000
Gross income	$250,000
Minus: Operating expenses	(100,000)
NOL carryover	(40,000)
Base for charitable contributions limitation (adjusted taxable income)	$110,000

East's charitable contributions deduction is limited to $11,000 ($110,000 × 0.10). The $11,000 limitation means that East has a $24,000 ($35,000 − $11,000) excess contribution that carries over for five years. East Corporation computes its taxable income as follows:

[32] Sec. 172(b)(3)(C).

ADDITIONAL COMMENT

The U.S. production activities deduction is last in the ordering of deductions because it is limited to taxable income after all other deductions. However, on the corporate tax return, it appears after the charitable contributions deduction but before the dividends-received and NOL deductions. Specifically, it appears on Form 1120, Line 25, before Line 28.

Gross income	$250,000
Minus: Operating expenses	(100,000)
Charitable contributions deduction	(11,000)
Taxable income before special deductions	$139,000
Minus: Dividends-received deduction ($100,000 × 0.80)	(80,000)
NOL carryover deduction	(40,000)
Taxable income before the U.S. production activities deduction	$ 19,000
Minus: U.S. production activities deduction ($19,000 × 0.09)	(1,710)
Taxable income	$ 17,290 ◀

Note that, if an NOL carries *back* from a later year, it is *not* taken into account in computing a corporation's charitable contributions limitation. In other words, the contribution deduction remains the same as in the year of the original return.

EXAMPLE C:3-24 ▶ Assume the same facts as in Example C:3-23, except the facts pertain to a prior year, and East carries back a $40,000 NOL to that year. East's base for calculation of the charitable contributions limitation was computed as follows when it filed the original prior year return:

ADDITIONAL COMMENT

These computations in the carryback year are done on an amended return or an application for refund.

Gross income from operations	$150,000
Plus: Dividends	100,000
Gross income	$250,000
Minus: Operating expenses	(100,000)
Adjusted taxable income	$150,000

East's charitable contributions deduction was limited to $15,000 ($150,000 × 0.10). The $15,000 limitation means that East had a $20,000 ($35,000 − $15,000) contribution carryover from the prior year. East Corporation computes its taxable income after the NOL carryback as follows:

Gross income ($150,000 + $100,000)	$250,000
Minus: Operating expenses	(100,000)
Charitable contributions deduction	(15,000)
Taxable income before special deductions	$135,000
Minus: Dividends-received deduction ($100,000 × 0.80)	(80,000)
NOL carryback deduction	(40,000)
Taxable income before the U.S. production activities deduction	$ 15,000
Minus: U.S. production activities deduction ($15,000 × 0.09)	(1,350)
Taxable income as recomputed	$ 13,650

Thus, East's prior year charitable contributions deduction remains the same as originally claimed. ◀

STOP & THINK

Question: Why does a corporation's NOL or capital loss carryback not affect its charitable contributions deduction, but yet the corporation must take into account an NOL or capital loss carryover when calculating its charitable contribution limitation?

Solution: A carryback affects a tax return already filed in a prior year. If a carryback had to be taken into account when calculating the charitable contribution deduction limitation in the prior year, it might change the amount of the allowable charitable contribution. This change in turn might affect other items such as the carryback year's dividends-received deduction and some later years' deductions as well. For example, assume Alpha Corporation has a $10,000 NOL in 2015 that it carries back to 2013. If the NOL were permitted to reduce Alpha's allowable charitable contribution for 2013 by $1,000, Alpha's dividends-received deduction for 2013 and its charitable contribution deduction for 2014 as well might change.

To avoid these complications, the law states that carrybacks are not taken into account in calculating the charitable contribution deduction limitation. Also, in the prior year, management made its charitable contribution decisions without knowledge of future NOLs. Altering the result of those prior decisions with future events might be unfair.

EXCEPTIONS FOR CLOSELY HELD CORPORATIONS

Congress has placed limits on certain transactions to prevent abuse in situations where a corporation is closely held. Some of these restrictions are explained below.

Transactions Between a Corporation and its Shareholders. Special rules apply to transactions between a corporation and a controlling shareholder. Section 1239 may convert a capital gain realized on the sale of depreciable property between a corporation and a controlling shareholder into ordinary income. Section 267(a)(1) denies a deduction for losses realized on property sales between a corporation and a controlling shareholder. Section 267(a)(2) defers a deduction for accrued expenses and interest on certain transactions involving a corporation and a controlling shareholder.

In all three of the preceding situations, a controlling shareholder is one who owns more than 50% (in value) of the corporation's stock.[33] In determining whether a shareholder owns more than 50% of a corporation's stock, certain constructive stock ownership rules apply.[34] Under these rules, a shareholder is considered to own not only his or her own stock, but stock owned by family members (e.g., brothers, sisters, spouse, ancestors, and lineal descendants) and entities in which the shareholder has an ownership or beneficial interest (e.g., corporations, partnerships, trusts, and estates).

Gains on Sale or Exchange Transactions. If a controlling shareholder sells depreciable property to a controlled corporation (or vice versa) and the property is depreciable in the purchaser's hands, any gain on the sale is treated as ordinary income under Sec. 1239(a).

EXAMPLE C:3-25 ▶ Ann owns all of Cape Corporation's stock. Ann sells a building to Cape and recognizes a $25,000 gain, which usually would be Sec. 1231 gain or unrecaptured Sec. 1250 gain taxed at the applicable capital gains rates. However, because Ann owns more than 50% of the Cape stock and the building is a depreciable property in Cape's hands, Sec. 1239 requires that Ann recognize the entire $25,000 gain as ordinary income. ◀

BOOK-TO-TAX ACCOUNTING COMPARISON

The denial of deductions for losses involving related party transactions is unique to the tax area. Financial accounting rules contain no such disallowance provision.

Losses on Sale or Exchange Transactions. Section 267(a)(1) denies a deduction for losses realized on a sale of property by a corporation to a controlling shareholder or on a sale of property by the controlling shareholder to the corporation. If the purchaser later sells the property to another party at a gain, that seller recognizes gain only to the extent it exceeds the previously disallowed loss.[35] Should the purchaser instead sell the property at a loss, the previously disallowed loss is never recognized.

EXAMPLE C:3-26 ▶ Quattros Corporation sells an automobile to Juan, its sole shareholder, for $6,500. The corporation's adjusted basis for the automobile is $8,000. Quattros realizes a $1,500 ($6,500 − $8,000) loss on the sale. Section 267(a)(1), however, disallows the loss to the corporation. If Juan later sells the auto for $8,500, he realizes a $2,000 ($8,500 − $6,500) gain. He recognizes only $500 of that gain, the amount by which his $2,000 gain exceeds the $1,500 loss previously disallowed to Quattros. If Juan instead sells the auto for $7,500, he realizes a $1,000 ($7,500 − $6,500) gain but recognizes no gain or loss. The previously disallowed loss reduces the gain to zero but may not create a loss. Finally, if Juan instead sells the auto for $4,000, he realizes and may be able to recognize a $2,500 ($4,000 − $6,500) loss. However, the $1,500 loss previously disallowed to Quattros is permanently lost. ◀

KEY POINT

Section 267(a)(2) is primarily aimed at the situation involving an accrual method corporation that accrues compensation to a cash method shareholder-employee. This provision forces a matching of the income and expense recognition by deferring the deduction to the year the shareholder recognizes the income.

Corporation and Controlling Shareholder Using Different Accounting Methods. Section 267(a)(2) defers a deduction for accrued expenses or interest owed by a corporation to a controlling shareholder or by a controlling shareholder to a corporation when the two parties use different accounting methods and the payee thereby includes the amount in gross income later than when the payer accrues the deduction. Under this rule, accrued expenses or interest owed by a corporation to a controlling shareholder may not be deducted until the shareholder includes the payment in gross income.

---

[33] Sec. 267(b)(2).

[34] Sec. 267(e)(3).

[35] Sec. 267(d).

EXAMPLE C:3-27 ▶ Hill Corporation uses the accrual method of accounting. Hill's sole shareholder, Ruth, uses the cash method of accounting. Both taxpayers use the calendar year as their tax year. The corporation accrues a $25,000 interest payment to Ruth on December 20 of the current year. Hill makes the payment on March 20 of next year. Hill, however, cannot deduct the interest in the current year but must wait until Ruth reports the income next year. Thus, the expense and income are matched. ◀

Loss Limitation Rules

At-Risk Rules. If five or fewer shareholders own more than 50% (in value) of a C corporation's outstanding stock at any time during the last half of the corporation's tax year, the corporation is subject to the at-risk rules.[36] In such case, the corporation can deduct losses pertaining to an activity only to the extent the corporation is at risk for that activity at year-end. Any losses not deductible because of the at-risk rules must be carried over and deducted in a succeeding year when the corporation's risk with respect to the activity increases. (See Chapter C:9 for additional discussion of the at-risk rules.)

Passive Activity Limitation Rules. Personal service corporations (PSCs) and **closely held C corporations** (those subject to the at-risk rules described above) also may be subject to the **passive activity limitations.**[37] If a PSC does not meet the material participation requirements, its net **passive losses** and credits must be carried over to a year when it has **passive income.** In the case of closely held C corporations that do not meet material participation requirements, passive losses and credits are allowed to offset the corporation's net active income but not its portfolio income (i.e., interest, dividends, annuities, royalties, and capital gains on the sale of investment property).[38]

COMPUTING A CORPORATION'S INCOME TAX LIABILITY

OBJECTIVE 3

Compute a corporation's regular income tax liability

Once a corporation determines its taxable income, it then must compute its tax liability for the year. Table C:3-2 outlines the steps for computing a corporation's regular (income) tax liability. This section explains the steps involved in arriving at a corporation's income tax liability in detail.

▼ TABLE C:3-2

Computation of the Corporate Regular (Income) Tax Liability

Taxable income	
Times:	Income tax rates
Regular tax liability	
Minus:	Foreign tax credit (Sec. 27)
Regular tax	
Minus:	General business credit (Sec. 38)
	Minimum tax credit (Sec. 53)
	Other allowed credits
Plus:	Recapture of previously claimed tax credits
Income (regular) tax liability	

[36] Sec. 465(a).

[37] Secs. 469(a)(2)(B) and (C).

[38] Sec. 469(e)(2).

GENERAL RULES

REAL-WORLD EXAMPLE

In 2013, the IRS collected $312 billion from corporations, which was 10.9% of the $2.86 trillion collected by the IRS. This percentage is down from 11.1% in 2012.

All C corporations (other than members of controlled groups of corporations and personal service corporations) use the same tax rate schedule to compute their **regular tax** liability. The following table shows these rates, which also are reproduced on the inside back cover of this textbook.

Taxable Income Over	*But Not Over*	*The Tax Is*	*Of the Amount Over*
$ –0–	$ 50,000	15%	$ –0–
50,000	75,000	$ 7,500 + 25%	50,000
75,000	100,000	13,750 + 34%	75,000
100,000	335,000	22,250 + 39%	100,000
335,000	10,000,000	113,900 + 34%	335,000
10,000,000	15,000,000	3,400,000 + 35%	10,000,000
15,000,000	18,333,333	5,150,000 + 38%	15,000,000
18,333,333	—	6,416,667 + 35%	18,333,333

EXAMPLE C:3-28 ▶ Copper Corporation reports taxable income of $100,000. Copper's regular tax liability is computed as follows:

Tax on first $50,000:	0.15 × $50,000 =	$7,500
Tax on second $25,000:	0.25 × 25,000 =	6,250
Tax on remaining $25,000:	0.34 × 25,000 =	8,500
Regular tax liability		$22,250

This tax liability also can be determined from the above tax rate schedule. ◀

If taxable income exceeds $100,000, a 5% surcharge applies to the corporation's taxable income exceeding $100,000. The surcharge phases out the lower graduated tax rates that apply to the first $75,000 of taxable income for corporations earning between $100,000 and $335,000 of taxable income. The maximum surcharge is $11,750 [($335,000 − $100,000) × 0.05]. The above tax rate schedule incorporates the 5% surcharge by imposing a 39% (34% + 5%) rate on taxable income from $100,000 to $335,000.

EXAMPLE C:3-29 ▶ Delta Corporation reports taxable income of $200,000. Delta's regular tax liability is computed as follows:

Tax on first $50,000:	0.15 × $ 50,000 =	$ 7,500
Tax on next $25,000:	0.25 × 25,000 =	6,250
Tax on remaining $125,000:	0.34 × 125,000 =	42,500
Surcharge (income over $100,000):	0.05 × 100,000 =	5,000
Regular tax liability		$61,250

Alternatively, from the above tax rate schedule, the tax is $22,250 + [0.39 × ($200,000 − $100,000)] = $61,250. ◀

If taxable income is at least $335,000 but less than $10 million, the corporation pays a flat 34% tax rate on all of its taxable income. A corporation whose income is at least $10 million but less than $15 million pays $3.4 million plus 35% of the income above $10 million.

EXAMPLE C:3-30 ▶ Elgin Corporation reports taxable income of $350,000. Elgin's regular tax liability is $119,000 (0.34 × $350,000). If Elgin's taxable income is instead $12 million, its tax liability is $4.1 million [$3,400,000 + (0.35 × $2,000,000)]. ◀

If a corporation's taxable income exceeds $15 million, a 3% surcharge applies to the corporation's taxable income exceeding $15 million (but not exceeding $18,333,333). The surcharge phases out the one percentage point lower rate (34% vs. 35%) that applies to the first $10 million of taxable income. The maximum surcharge is $100,000 [($18,333,333 − $15,000,000) × 0.03]. The above tax rate schedule incorporates the 3%

surcharge by imposing a 38% (35% + 3%) rate on taxable income from $15 million to $18,333,333. A corporation whose taxable income exceeds $18,333,333 pays a flat 35% tax rate on all its taxable income.

? STOP & THINK

Question: Planner Corporation has an opportunity to realize $50,000 of additional income in either the current year or next year. Planner has some discretion as to the timing of this additional income. Not counting the additional income, Planner's current year taxable income is $200,000, and it expects next year's taxable income to be $500,000. In what year should Planner recognize the additional $50,000?

Solution: Even though Planner's current year taxable income is lower than next year's expected taxable income, Planner will have a lower marginal tax rate next year. The current year's marginal tax rate is 39% because Planner's taxable income is in the 5% surtax range (or 39% "bubble"). Next year's taxable income is beyond the 39% bubble and is in the flat 34% range. Thus, Planner can save $2,500 ($0.05 \times \$50,000$) in taxes by deferring the $50,000 until next year.

PERSONAL SERVICE CORPORATIONS

Personal service corporations are denied the benefit of the graduated corporate tax rates. Thus, all the income of personal service corporations is taxed at a flat 35% rate.

Section 448(d) defines a personal service corporation as a corporation that meets the following two tests:

- Substantially all its activities involve the performance of services in the fields of health, law, engineering, architecture, accounting, actuarial science, performing arts, and consulting.
- Substantially all its stock (by value) is held directly or indirectly by employees performing the services or retired employees who performed the services in the past, their estates, or persons who hold stock in the corporation by reason of the death of an employee or retired employee within the past two years.

This rule encourages employee-owners of personal service corporations either to withdraw earnings from the corporation as deductible salary (rather than have the corporation retain them) or make an S election.

CONTROLLED GROUPS OF CORPORATIONS

OBJECTIVE 4

Recognize what a controlled group is and determine the tax consequences of being a controlled group

Special tax rules apply to corporations under common control to prevent them from avoiding taxes that otherwise would be due. The rules apply to corporations that meet the definition of a controlled group. This section explains why special rules apply to controlled groups, how the IRC defines controlled groups, and what special rules apply to controlled groups.

WHY SPECIAL RULES ARE NEEDED

Special controlled group rules prevent shareholders from using multiple corporations to avoid having corporate income taxed at a 35% rate. If these rules were not in effect, the owners of a corporation could allocate the corporation's income among two or more corporations and take advantage of the lower 15%, 25%, and 34% rates on the first $10 million of corporate income for each corporation.

The following example demonstrates how a group of shareholders could obtain a significant tax advantage by dividing a business enterprise among several corporate entities. Each corporation then could take advantage of the graduated corporate tax rates. To prevent a group of shareholders from using multiple corporations to gain such tax advantages, Congress enacted laws that limit the tax benefits of multiple corporations.[39]

[39] Secs. 1561 and 1563.

EXAMPLE C:3-31 ▶ Axle Corporation reports taxable income of $450,000. Axle's regular tax liability on that income is $153,000 (0.34 × $450,000). If Axle could divide its taxable income equally among six corporations ($75,000 apiece), each corporation's federal income tax liability would be $13,750 [(0.15 × $50,000) + (0.25 × $25,000)], or an $82,500 total regular tax liability for all the corporations. Thus, Axle could save $70,500 ($153,000 − $82,500) in federal income taxes. ◀

The law governing controlled corporations requires special treatment for two or more corporations controlled by the same shareholder or group of shareholders. The most important restrictions on a controlled group of corporations are that the group must share the benefits of the progressive corporate tax rate schedule and pay a 5% surcharge on the group's taxable income exceeding $100,000, up to a maximum surcharge of $11,750, and also pay a 3% surcharge on the group's taxable income exceeding $15 million, up to a maximum surcharge of $100,000.

EXAMPLE C:3-32 ▶ White, Blue, Yellow, and Green Corporations belong to a controlled group. Each corporation reports $100,000 of taxable income (a total of $400,000). Only one $50,000 amount is taxed at 15% and only one $25,000 is taxed at 25%. Furthermore, the group is subject to the maximum $11,750 surcharge because its total taxable income exceeds $335,000. This surcharge is levied on the group member(s) that received the benefit of the 15 and 25% rates. Therefore, the group's total regular tax liability is $136,000 (0.34 × $400,000), as though one corporation earned the entire $400,000. Each corporation would be allocated $34,000 of this tax liability. ◀

WHAT IS A CONTROLLED GROUP?

A **controlled group** is comprised of two or more corporations owned directly or indirectly by the same shareholder or group of shareholders. Controlled groups fall into three categories: a parent-subsidiary controlled group, a brother-sister controlled group, and a combined controlled group. Each of these groups is subject to the limitations described above.

ADDITIONAL COMMENT

For purposes of the Sec. 179 expense dollar limitation, a more-than-50% threshold replaces the at-least-80% threshold in defining a parent-subsidiary controlled group.

Parent-Subsidiary Controlled Groups. In a **parent-subsidiary controlled group**, one corporation (the parent corporation) must directly own at least 80% of the voting power of all classes of voting stock, or 80% of the total value of all classes of stock, of a second corporation (the subsidiary corporation).[40] The group can contain more than one subsidiary corporation. If the parent corporation, the subsidiary corporation, or any other members of the controlled group in total own at least 80% of the voting power of all classes of voting stock, or 80% of the total value of all classes of stock, of another corporation, that other corporation also is included in the parent-subsidiary controlled group.

EXAMPLE C:3-33 ▶ Parent Corporation owns 80% of Axle Corporation's single class of stock and 40% of Wheel Corporation's single class of stock. Axle also owns 40% of Wheel's stock. (See Figure C:3-2.) Parent, Axle, and Wheel are members of the same parent-subsidiary controlled group because Parent directly owns 80% of Axle's stock and therefore is its parent corporation, and Wheel's stock is 80% owned by Parent (40%) and Axle (40%).

If Parent and Axle together owned only 70% of Wheel's stock and an unrelated shareholder owned the remaining 30%, Wheel would not be included in the parent-subsidiary group. The controlled group then would consist only of Parent and Axle. ◀

EXAMPLE C:3-34 ▶ Beta Corporation owns 70% of Spectrum Corporation's single class of stock and 60% of Red Corporation's single class of stock. Blue Corporation owns the remaining stock of Spectrum (30%) and Red (40%). No combination of these corporations forms a parent-subsidiary group because no corporation has direct stock ownership of at least 80% of any other corporation's stock. ◀

[40] Sec. 1563(a)(1). Section 1563(d)(1) requires that certain attribution rules apply to determine stock ownership for parent-subsidiary controlled groups. If any person has an option to acquire stock, such stock is considered owned by the person having the option. Section 1563(c) excludes certain types of stock from the controlled group definition of stock.

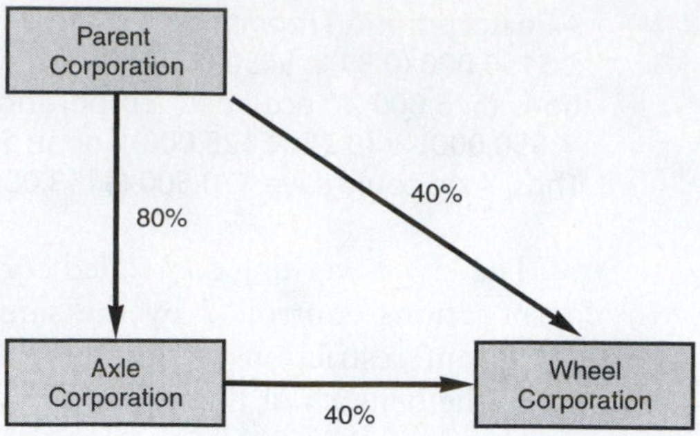

FIGURE C:3-2 ▶ PARENT-SUBSIDIARY CONTROLLED GROUP (EXAMPLE C:3-33)

Brother-Sister Controlled Groups. The IRC contains two definitions of a **brother-sister controlled group.** This textbook will refer to them as the 50%-80% definition and the 50%-only definition. Under the 50%-80% definition, a group of two or more corporations is a brother-sister controlled group if five or fewer individuals, trusts, or estates meet both of the following conditions:

- More than 50% of the voting power of all classes of stock (or more than 50% of the total value of the outstanding stock) of each corporation, taking into account only the stock ownership that is common with respect to each corporation.[41] A common ownership is the percentage of stock a shareholder owns that is common or identical in each of the corporations. For example, if a shareholder owns 30% of New Corporation and 70% of Old Corporation, his or her common ownership is 30%.
- At least 80% of the voting power of all classes of voting stock (or at least 80% of the total value of the outstanding stock) of each corporation.

Thus, under the 50%-80% definition, the five or fewer shareholders not only must have more than 50% common ownership in the corporations, they also must own at least 80% of the stock of each corporation in the brother-sister group. This definition is narrow because the shareholders must meet two tests.

The 50%-only definition, on the other hand, is broader than the 50%-80% definition in that the five or fewer shareholders must satisfy only the 50% common ownership test described above. Consequently, in situations where the 50%-only definition applies, more corporations may be pulled into the controlled group than under the 50%-80% definition. Table C:3-3 on page C:3-29 indicates which definition applies to specific situations.

EXAMPLE C:3-35 ▶ North and South Corporations have only one class of stock outstanding, owned by the following individuals:

	Stock Ownership Percentages		
Shareholder	*North Corp.*	*South Corp.*	*Common Ownership*
Walt	30%	70%	30%
Gail	70%	30%	30%
Total	100%	100%	60%

Five or fewer individuals (Walt and Gail) together own at least 80% (actually 100%) of each corporation's stock, and the same individuals own more than 50% (actually 60%) of the corporations' stock taking into account only their common ownership in each corporation. Because

[41] Sec. 1563(a)(2). Section 1563(d)(2) requires that certain attribution rules apply to determine stock ownership for brother-sister controlled groups. If any person has an option to acquire stock, such stock is considered to be owned by the person having the option. A proportionate amount of stock owned by a partnership, estate, or trust is attributed to partners having an interest of 5% or more in the capital or profits of the partnership or beneficiaries having a 5% or more actuarial interest in the estate or trust. A proportionate amount of stock owned by a corporation is attributed to shareholders owning 5% or more in value of the corporate stock. Family attribution rules also can cause an individual to be considered to own the stock of a spouse, child, grandchild, parent, or grandparent.

their ownership satisfies both tests, North and South are a brother-sister controlled group under the 50%-80% definition. (See Figure C:3-3.) ◀

EXAMPLE C:3-36 ▶ East and West Corporations have only one class of stock outstanding, owned by the following individuals:

Shareholder	East Corp.	West Corp.	Common Ownership
	Stock Ownership Percentages		
Javier	80%	25%	25%
Sara	20%	75%	20%
Total	100%	100%	45%

Five or fewer individuals (Javier and Sara) together own at least 80% (actually 100%) of each corporation's stock. However, those same individuals own only 45% of the corporations' stock taking into account only their common ownership. Because their ownership does not satisfy the more-than-50% test, East and West are not a brother-sister controlled group under either the 50%-80% or the 50%-only definition. Consequently, each corporation is taxed on its own income without regard to the earnings of the other. ◀

An individual's stock ownership can be counted for the 80% test only if that individual owns stock in each and every corporation in the controlled group.[42]

EXAMPLE C:3-37 ▶ Long and Short Corporations each have only a single class of stock outstanding, owned by the following individuals:

Shareholder	Long Corp.	Short Corp.	Common Ownership
	Stock Ownership Percentages		
Al	50%	40%	40%
Beth	20%	60%	20%
Carol	30%	—	—
Total	100%	100%	60%

Carol's stock does not count for purposes of Long's 80% stock ownership requirement because she owns no stock in Short. Only Al's and Beth's stock holdings count, and together they own only 70% of Long's stock. Thus, the 80% test fails. Consequently, Long and Short are not a brother-sister controlled group under the 50%-80% defintion, but they are a brother-sister controlled group under the 50%-only definition. ◀

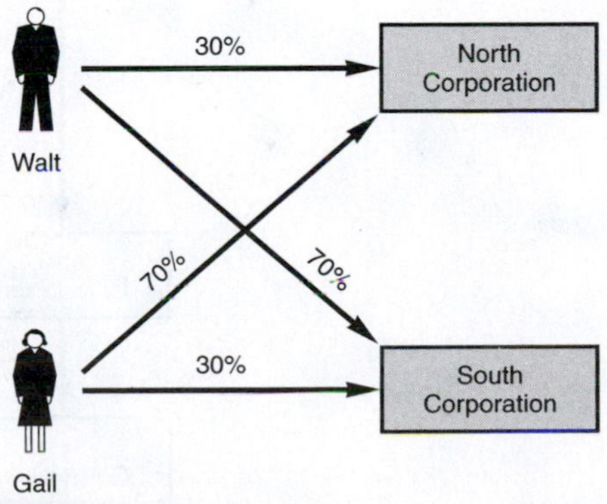

FIGURE C:3-3 ▶ BROTHER-SISTER CONTROLLED GROUP (EXAMPLE C:3-35)

[42] Reg. Sec. 1.1563-1(a)(3).

Combined Controlled Groups. A **combined controlled group** is comprised of three or more corporations meeting the following criteria:

- Each corporation is a member of a parent-subsidiary controlled group or a brother-sister controlled group.
- At least one of the corporations is both the parent corporation of a parent-subsidiary controlled group and a member of a brother-sister controlled group.[43]

KEY POINT

The combined controlled group definition does just what its name implies: It combines a parent-subsidiary controlled group and a brother-sister controlled group. Thus, instead of trying to apply the controlled group rules to two different groups, the combined group definition eliminates the issue by combining the groups into one controlled group.

EXAMPLE C:3-38 ▶ Able, Best, and Coast Corporations each have a single class of stock outstanding, owned by the following shareholders:

	Stock Ownership Percentages		
Shareholder	*Able Corp.*	*Coast Corp.*	*Best Corp.*
Art	50%	50%	—
Barbara	50%	50%	—
Able Corp.	—	—	100%

Able and Coast are a brother-sister controlled group under the 50%-80% definition because Art's and Barbara's ownership satisfy both the 80% and 50% tests. Able and Best are a parent-subsidiary controlled group because Able owns all of Best's stock. Each of the three corporations is a member of either the parent-subsidiary controlled group (Able and Best) or the brother-sister controlled group (Able and Coast), and the parent corporation (Able) of the parent-subsidiary controlled group also is a member of the brother-sister controlled group. Therefore, Able, Best, and Coast Corporations are members of a combined controlled group. (See Figure C:3-4.) ◀

APPLICATION OF THE CONTROLLED GROUP TEST

Controlled group status generally is tested on December 31. A corporation is included in a controlled group if it is a group member on December 31 and has been a group member on at least one-half of the days in its tax year that precede December 31. A corporation that is not a group member on December 31, nevertheless, is considered a member for the tax year if it has been a group member on at least one-half the days in its tax year that precede December 31. Corporations are excluded from the controlled group if they were members for less than one-half the days in their tax year that precede December 31 or if they retain certain special tax statuses such as being a tax-exempt corporation.

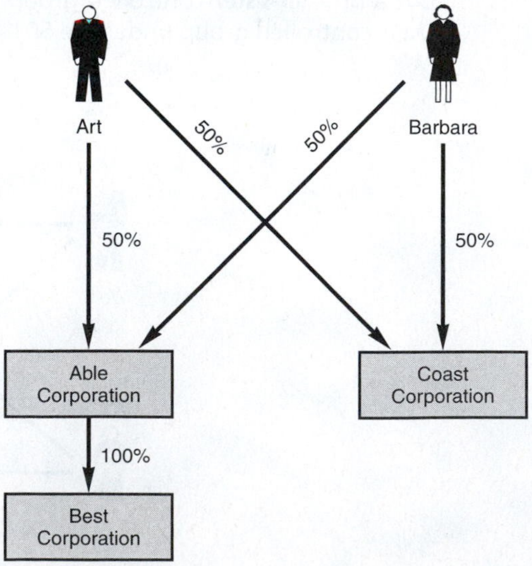

FIGURE C:3-4 ▶ COMBINED CONTROLLED GROUP (EXAMPLE C:3-38)

[43] Sec. 1563(a)(3).

▼ TABLE C:3-3
Items that Must be Apportioned if a Controlled Group Exists

Item	Brother-Sister 50%-Only	Brother-Sister 50%–80%	Parent-Subsidiary ≥ 80%	Parent-Subsidiary > 50%
Low-bracket tax rates	x	x	x	
AMT exemption	x	x	x	
Minimum accumulated earnings tax credit	x	x	x	
Section 179 expense limitation		x	x	x
General business tax credit limitation		x	x	

EXAMPLE C:3-39 ▶ Ace and Copper Corporations are members of a parent-subsidiary controlled group of which Ace is the common parent. Both corporations are calendar year taxpayers and have been group members for the entire year. They do not file a consolidated return. Bell Corporation, which has a fiscal year ending on August 31, becomes a group member on December 1 of the current year. Although Bell is a group member on December 31 of the current year, it has been a group member for less than half the days in its tax year that precede December 31—only 30 of 121 days starting on September 1. Therefore, Bell is not a member of the Ace-Copper *controlled* group for its tax year beginning on September 1 of the current year. ◀

TAX STRATEGY TIP

A controlled group of corporations should elect to apportion the tax benefits in a manner that maximizes the tax savings from the tax benefits. See Tax Planning Considerations later in this chapter for details.

SPECIAL RULES APPLYING TO CONTROLLED GROUPS

As discussed earlier, if two or more corporations are members of a controlled group, the member corporations are limited to a total of $50,000 taxed at 15%, $25,000 being taxed at 25%, and $9,925,000 million being taxed at 34%. For brother-sister corporations, the broader 50%-only definition applies for limiting the reduced tax rates.

In addition, a controlled group must apportion certain other items among its group members, some of which are shown in Table C:3-3. For purposes of apportioning the Sec. 179 expense dollar limitation in a parent-subsidiary situation, the corporations are considered a controlled group if the ownership percentage is more than 50% rather than at least 80%.[44]

In addition to the above restrictions, Sec. 267(a)(1) allows no deduction for any loss on the sale or exchange of property between two members of the same controlled group, with control defined as more than 50% rather than as at least 80%. However, in contrast to losses between a corporation and controlling shareholder described earlier in this chapter, a loss realized on a transaction between members of a controlled group is deferred (instead of being disallowed). The original selling member recognizes the deferred loss when the property sold or exchanged in the intragroup transaction is sold outside the controlled group.

Section 267(a)(2) allows no deduction for certain accrued expenses or interest owed by one member of a controlled group to another member of the same controlled group when the two corporations use different accounting methods so that the payments would be reported in different tax years. (See page C:3-21 for a detailed discussion of Sec. 267.) The Sec. 1239 rules that convert capital gain into ordinary income on depreciable property sales between related parties also apply to sales or exchanges involving two members of the same controlled group. Sections 267 and 1239, however, provide special definitions of controlled groups that differ somewhat from those described above. These details are beyond the scope of this textbook.

TYPICAL MISCONCEPTION

The definitions of a parentsubsidiary controlled group and an affiliated group are similar, but not identical. For example, the 80% stock ownership test for controlled group purposes is satisfied if 80% of the voting power *or* 80% of the FMV of a corporation's stock is owned. For purposes of an affiliated group, 80% of both the voting power *and* the FMV of a corporation's stock must be owned.

CONSOLIDATED TAX RETURNS

Who can File a Consolidated Return. Some groups of related corporations (i.e., affiliated groups) may elect to file a single income tax return called a **consolidated tax return.** An **affiliated group** is one or more chains of includible corporations connected through stock ownership with a common parent. In general, includible corporations are those other than foreign corporations, certain insurance companies, tax-exempt organizations,

[44] Secs. 179(d)(6) and (7).

S corporations, and a few other specially defined corporations. The required ownership criteria are as follows:

- The common parent must directly own stock with at least 80% of the voting power *and* 80% of the value of at least one includible corporation.
- One or more group members must directly own stock with at least 80% of the voting power *and* 80% of the value of each other corporation included in the affiliated group.[45]

BOOK-TO-TAX ACCOUNTING COMPARISON

The corporations included in a consolidated tax return may differ from those included in consolidated financial statements. Page 1 of Schedule M-3 reconciles financial statement worldwide consolidated net income to financial statement net income (loss) of corporations included in the consolidated tax return.

Many parent-subsidiary controlled groups also qualify as affiliated groups and thus are eligible to file a consolidated return in place of separate tax returns for each corporation. The parent-subsidiary portion of a combined group also can file a consolidated tax return if it also qualifies as an affiliated group. Brother-sister controlled groups, however, are not eligible to file consolidated returns because the requisite parent-subsidiary relationship does not exist.

An affiliated group elects to file a consolidated tax return by filing Form 1120, which includes all the income and expenses of each of its members. Each corporate member of the affiliated group must consent to the original election. Thereafter, any new member of the affiliated group must join in the consolidated return.

SELF-STUDY QUESTION

What is probably the most common reason for making a consolidated return election?

ANSWER

Filing consolidated returns allows the group to offset losses of one corporation against the profits of other members of the group.

Advantages of Filing a Consolidated Return. A consolidated return, in effect, is one tax return for the entire affiliated group of corporations. The main advantages of filing a consolidated return are

- Losses of one member of the group can offset profits of another member of the group.
- Capital losses of one member of the group can offset capital gains of another member of the group.
- Profits or gains realized on intercompany transactions are deferred until a sale outside the group occurs (i.e., if one member sells property to another member, the gain is postponed until the member sells the property to someone outside the affiliated group).

In contrast, if the group members file separate returns, members with NOLs or capital losses must either carry back these losses to earlier years or carry them over to future years rather than offset another member's profits or gains.

Although the losses of one group member can offset the profits of another group member when the group files a consolidated return, some important limitations apply to the use of a member corporation's NOL. These limitations prevent one corporation from purchasing another corporation's NOL carryovers to offset its own taxable income or purchasing a profitable corporation to facilitate the use of its own NOL carryovers. (See Chapters C:7 and C:8.)

The following example illustrates the advantage of a consolidated return election.

EXAMPLE C:3-40 ▶ Parent Corporation owns 100% of Subsidiary Corporation's stock. Parent reports $110,000 of taxable income, including a $10,000 capital gain. Subsidiary incurs a $100,000 NOL and a $10,000 capital loss. If Parent and Subsidiary file separate returns, Parent has a $26,150 [$22,250 + 0.39 × ($110,000 − $100,000)] tax liability. Subsidiary has no tax liability but may be able to use its $100,000 NOL and $10,000 capital loss to offset taxable income in other years. On the other hand, if Parent and Subsidiary file a consolidated return, the group's consolidated taxable income is zero and the group has no tax liability. By filing a consolidated return, the group saves $26,150 in taxes for the year. ◀

Disadvantages of Filing a Consolidated Return. The main disadvantages of a consolidated return election are

- The election is binding on all subsequent tax years unless the IRS grants permission to discontinue filing consolidated returns or the affiliated group terminates.
- Losses on intercompany transactions are deferred until a sale outside the group takes place.
- One member's Sec. 1231 loss offsets another member's Sec. 1231 gain instead of being reported as an ordinary loss.
- Losses of an unprofitable member of the group may reduce the deduction or credit limitations of the group below what would be available had the members filed separate tax returns.

ADDITIONAL COMMENT

Under Sec. 267 discussed earlier, intercompany losses may be deferred even if the corporations file separate tax returns.

---

[45] Sec. 1504(a).

- The group may incur additional administrative costs in maintaining the records needed to file a consolidated return.

Determining whether to make a consolidated tax return election is a complex decision because of the various advantages and disadvantages and because the election is so difficult to revoke once made. Chapter C:8 provides detailed coverage of the consolidated return rules.

TAX PLANNING CONSIDERATIONS

OBJECTIVE 5

Identify planning strategies to reduce taxes for corporations and their shareholders

COMPENSATION PLANNING FOR SHAREHOLDER-EMPLOYEES

Compensation paid to a shareholder-employee in the form of salary has the advantage of single taxation because, while taxable to the employee, salary is deductible by the corporation. Dividend payments, on the other hand, are taxed twice. The corporation is taxed on its income when earned, and the shareholder is taxed on profits distributed as dividends. Double taxation occurs because the corporation may not deduct dividend payments. The applicable capital gains tax rate on dividends, however, makes the difference between salary and dividends less substantial than it would be if dividends were taxed at ordinary rates.

EXAMPLE C:3-41 ▶ Delta Corporation earns $100,000 and wishes to distribute $100,000 or as much of the $100,000 as possible to Mary, its sole shareholder and CEO. Mary's ordinary tax rate is 39.6%, her capital gains rate is 23.8% (20% plus the 3.8% rate on net investment income), and the corporation's marginal tax rate is 34%. Ignoring payroll taxes, the following table compares salary and dividend payments to Mary with respect to the $100,000 of partial earnings:

	Salary	*Dividend at Capital Gains Tax Rate*
1. Corporate earnings (partial)	$100,000	$100,000
2. Minus: Salary deduction	(100,000)	-0-
3. Corporate taxable income (partial)	$ -0-	$100,000
4. Times: Corporate tax rate	0.34	0.34
5. Corporate income tax (on partial income)	$ -0-	$ 34,000
6. Dividend to Mary (Line 1 – Line 5)	$100,000	$ 66,000
7. Times: Mary's tax rate	0.396	0.238
8. Mary's tax	$ 39,600	$ 15,708
9. Total tax (Line 5 + Line 8)	$ 39,600	$ 49,708
10. Overall tax rate (Line 9 ÷ Line 1)	39.6%	49.7%

Thus, in this situation, the double taxation due to paying nondeductible dividends instead of deductible salary increases Mary's overall tax rate from 39.6% to 49.7%. ◀

To avoid double taxation, some owners of closely held corporations prefer to be taxed under the rules of Subchapter S (see Chapter C:11). Other owners of closely held corporations retain C corporation status to use the 15% and 25% marginal corporate tax rates and to benefit from nontaxable fringe benefits such as health and accident insurance. These fringe benefits are nontaxable to the employee and deductible by the corporation. For both tax and nontax reasons, closely held corporations must determine the appropriate level of earnings to be withdrawn from the business in the form of salary and fringe benefits and the amount of earnings to be retained in the business.

Advantage of Salary Payments. If a corporation distributes all its profits as deductible salary and fringe benefit payments, it will eliminate double taxation. However, the following considerations limit such tax planning opportunities:

ADDITIONAL COMMENT

Reasonableness of a salary payment is a question of fact to be determined in each case. No formula can be used to determine a reasonable amount.

- Regulation Sec. 1.162-7(a) requires salary or fringe benefit payments to be reasonable in amount and to be paid for services rendered by the employee. If the IRS deems compensation to be unreasonable, it may disallow the portion of the salary it deems unreasonable while still requiring the employee to include all compensation in gross income (see Chapter C:4). This disallowance will result in double taxation. The reasonable compensation restriction primarily affects closely held corporations.
- A corporation may not deduct compensation paid to an executive of a publicly traded corporation that exceeds $1 million. However, this limitation does not apply to compensation paid to an executive other than the corporation's top five officers, or to performance-based compensation.[46]
- A corporation is a taxpaying entity independent of its owners. The first $75,000 of a corporation's earnings is taxed at 15% and 25% corporate tax rates. These rates are lower than the marginal tax rate that may apply to an individual taxpayer and provides an incentive to retain some earnings in the corporation instead of paying them out as salaries.
- A combined employee–employer Social Security tax rate of 15.3% generally applies Employers and employees were each liable for 6.2% of old age security and disability insurance tax, or a total of 12.4% on wages up to the salary cap ($117,000 in 2014; 118,500 in 2015). Employers and employees also are each liable for a 1.45% Medicare hospital insurance tax, for a total of 2.9% of all wages. An additional 0.9% for the Medicare hospital insurance tax applies to the employee's portion of wages exceeding $200,000 ($250,000 for married filing jointly). In addition to these taxes, state and federal unemployment taxes may be imposed on a portion of wages paid.

TAX STRATEGY TIP

A fringe benefit probably is the most cost effective form of compensation because the amount of the benefit is deductible by the employer and never taxed to the employee. Thus, where possible, fringe benefits are an excellent compensation planning tool. For closely held corporations, however, the tax savings to shareholder-employees are reduced because the fringe benefit must be offered to all employees without discrimination.

Advantage of Fringe Benefits. Fringe benefits provide two types of tax advantages: a tax deferral or an exclusion. Qualified pension, profit-sharing, and stock bonus plans provide a tax deferral; that is, the corporation's contribution to such a plan is not taxable to the employees when the corporation makes the contribution. Instead, employees are taxed on the benefits when they receive them. Other common fringe benefits, such as group term life insurance, accident and health insurance, and disability insurance, are exempt from tax altogether; that is, the employee never is taxed on the value of these fringe benefits.

Because the employee excludes the value of fringe benefits from gross income, the marginal individual tax rate applicable to these benefits is zero. Thus, conversion of salary into a fringe benefit provides tax savings for the shareholder-employee equal to the amount of the converted salary times the employee's marginal tax rate, assuming the shareholder-employee could not purchase the same fringe benefit and deduct its cost on his or her individual tax return.

SPECIAL ELECTION TO ALLOCATE REDUCED TAX RATE BENEFITS

A controlled group may elect to apportion the tax benefits of the 15%, 25%, and 34% tax rates to the member corporations in any manner it chooses. If the corporations elect no special apportionment plan, the $50,000, $25,000, and $9,925,000 amounts allocated to the three reduced tax rate brackets are divided equally among all the corporations in the group.[47] If a controlled group has one or more group members that report little or no taxable income, the group should elect special apportionment of the reduced tax benefits to obtain the full tax savings resulting from the reduced rates. The following steps outline a set of procedures for apportioning tax rates for taxable income levels at or below $10 million.[48]

1. If aggregate positive taxable income is $100,000 or less, apportion the 15%, 25%, and 34% rates to members that have positive taxable income so as to maximize their benefit.
   a. To avoid "wasting" low tax rates on loss members, elect special apportionment of tax benefits.

[46] Sec. 162(m).
[47] Sec. 1561(a).
[48] For the sake of simplicity, we do not extend the procedures to taxable income exceeding $10 million but similar procedures apply.

b. Summing the members' taxes results in the same total tax as would occur by applying the corporate tax rate schedule to the group's aggregate positive taxable income.

2. If aggregate positive taxable income is between $100,000 and $335,000, apportion the 15%, 25%, and 34% brackets as in Step 1 above. Follow the next steps to apportion the 5% surtax.

ADDITIONAL COMMENT

This apportionment method for the 5% surtax is one of two possible methods available. It apportions the surtax first to the corporation using the 15% bracket and then to the corporation using the 25% bracket. Hence, it is referred to as the FIFO method. The other method is called the proportionate method. See the Additional Comment next to Example C:3-43.

a. Calculate the surtax as 5% times (aggregate positive taxable income − $100,000).
b. If the calculated surtax is $9,500 or less, apportion the calculated surtax in proportion to the way the corporations apportioned the 15% bracket.
c. If the surtax is greater than $9,500 ($11,750 maximum), apportion the first $9,500 as in Step 2b, and apportion the excess in proportion to the way the corporations apportioned the 25% bracket in Step 1 above.
d. Summing the members' taxes results in the same total tax as would occur by applying the corporate tax rate schedule to the group's aggregate positive taxable income.

3. If aggregate positive taxable income is from $335,000 to $10,000,000, the 15% and 25% tax brackets are fully phased out, so each member's tax equals a flat 34% of its taxable income, and the group's total tax equals 34% of aggregate positive taxable income.

EXAMPLE C:3-42 ▶ North and South Corporations are members of a controlled group. The corporations file separate tax returns for the current year and report the following results:

Corporation	*Taxable Income (NOL)*
North	$(25,000)
South	100,000

If they elect no special apportionment plan, North and South are limited to $25,000 each taxed at a 15% rate and to $12,500 each taxed at a 25% rate. The tax liability for each corporation is determined as follows:

Corporation	*Calculation*	*Tax*
North		$ -0-
South	15% tax bracket: 0.15 × $25,000	$ 3,750
	25% tax bracket: 0.25 × $12,500	3,125
	34% tax bracket: 0.34 × $62,500	21,250
	Subtotal for South Corporation	$28,125
Total for North-South controlled group		$28,125

If the corporations elect a special apportionment plan, the group may apportion the full $50,000 and $25,000 amounts for each of the reduced tax rate brackets to South. The tax liability for each corporation is determined as follows:

Corporation	*Calculation*	*Tax*
North		$ -0-
South	15% tax bracket: 0.15 × $50,000	$ 7,500
	25% tax bracket: 0.25 × $25,000	6,250
	34% tax bracket: 0.34 × $25,000	8,500
	Subtotal for South Corporation	$22,250
Total for North-South controlled group		$22,250

By shifting the benefit of low tax brackets away from a corporation that cannot use it (North) to a corporation that can (South), the special apportionment election reduces the total tax liability for the North-South controlled group by $5,875 ($28,125 − $22,250). ◀

If a controlled group's total taxable income exceeds $100,000 ($15 million), a 5% (3%) surcharge recaptures the benefits of the reduced tax rates. The component member (or members) that took advantage of the lower tax rates pays this additional tax.

EXAMPLE C:3-43 ▶ Alpha, Beta, and Gamma Corporations are members of a controlled group and report the following results:

Corporation	*Taxable Income (Loss)*
Alpha	$ 80,000
Beta	(25,000)
Gamma	230,000

The group, which has aggregate taxable income of $310,000 ($80,00 + $230,000), elects special apportionment. They apportion the 15% tax bracket to Alpha with the balance of Alpha's income taxed at 34% (before the surtax apportionment), and they apportion the 25% tax bracket to Gamma with the balance of Gamma's income taxed at 34% (before the surtax apportionment). The surtax in this case is $10,500 (0.05 × ($310,000 − $100,000)). Using the procedures outlined above, the members apportion $9,500 of the surtax to Alpha because that corporation received the entire 15% tax bracket, and they apportion the remaining $1,000 surtax to Gamma because that corporation received the entire 25% tax bracket. Accordingly, the tax liability for each corporation is as follows:

ADDITIONAL COMMENT

If the group used the proportionate method, the surtax would be apportioned based on the relative tax benefit of the lower brackets. The tax benefit of the 15% bracket is $9,500 [$50,000 × (0.34 − 0.15)], and the tax benefit of the 25% bracket is $2,250 [$25,000 × (0.34 − 0.25)]. Thus, $8,489 of the surtax would be allocated to Alpha, calculated as $10,500 × ($9,500/$11,750), and $2,011 would be allocated to Gamma, calculated as $10,500 × ($2,250/$11,750).

Alpha:		
Tax on $50,000 at 15%	$ 7,500	
Tax on $30,000 at 34%	10,200	
Surtax	9,500	
Total for Alpha		$27,200
Beta		–0–
Gamma:		
Tax on $25,000 at 25%	$ 6,250	
Tax on $205,000 at 34%	69,700	
Surtax	1,000	
Total for Alpha		76,950
Total for the group		$104,150

The total tax for the group is the same as if they applied the corporate tax rate schedule to the $310,000 aggregate positive taxable income as follows: $22,250 + ($210,000 × 0.39) = $104,150. ◀

EXAMPLE C:3-44 ▶ Hill, Jet, and King Corporations are members of a controlled group and report the following results:

Corporation	*Taxable Income*
Hill	$300,000
Jet	(50,000)
King	100,000

The group's aggregate positive taxable income is $400,000 ($300,000 + $100,000), which exceeds $335,000. Therefore, with special apportionment, Hill's and King's tax equals 34% of each corporation's taxable income as follows:

Hill ($300,000 × 0.34)	$102,000
Jet	–0–
King ($100,000 × 0.34)	34,000
Total for the group ($400,000 × 0.34)	$136,000 ◀

TAX STRATEGY TIP

A corporation may want to elect to forgo the NOL carryback when tax credit carryovers are being used in the earlier years. If the NOLs are carried back, the tax credits may expire. Thus, before deciding to carry back NOLs, the prior tax returns should be carefully examined to ensure that expiring tax credits do not exist.

USING NOL CARRYOVERS AND CARRYBACKS

When a corporation incurs an NOL for the year, it has two choices:

- Carry the NOL back to the second and first preceding years in that order (assuming no extended carryback period), and then forward to the succeeding 20 years in chronological order until the NOL is exhausted.
- Forgo any carryback and just carry the NOL forward to the 20 succeeding years.

A corporation might elect to forgo an NOL carryback if it would offset income at a low tax rate, resulting in a small tax refund compared to a greater anticipated benefit if the NOL instead were carried over to a high tax rate year.

EXAMPLE C:3-45 ▶ Boyd Corporation, a calendar year taxpayer, incurs a $30,000 NOL in 2015. Boyd's 2013 taxable income was $50,000. If Boyd carries the NOL back to 2013, Boyd's tax refund is computed as follows:

Original tax on $50,000 (using 2013 rates)	$7,500
Minus: Recomputed tax on $20,000 [($50,000 − $30,000) × 0.15]	(3,000)
Tax refund	$4,500

If Boyd anticipates taxable income (after reduction for any NOL carryovers) of $75,000 or more in 2016, carrying over the NOL will result in the entire loss offsetting taxable income that otherwise would be taxed at a 34% or higher marginal tax rate. The tax savings is computed as follows:

Tax on $105,000 of expected taxable income	$24,200
Minus: Tax on $75,000 ($105,000 − $30,000)	(13,750)
Tax savings in 2016	$10,450

Thus, if Boyd expects taxable income to be $105,000 in 2016, it might elect to forgo the NOL carryback and obtain the additional $5,950 ($10,450 − $4,500) tax benefit. Of course, by carrying the NOL over to 2016, Boyd loses the value of having the funds immediately available. However, Boyd may use the NOL to reduce its estimated tax payments for 2016. If the corporation expects the NOL carryover benefit to occur at an appreciably distant point in the future, the corporation would have to determine the benefit's present value to make it comparable to a refund from an NOL carryback. This example ignores the effect the NOL carryover has on the U.S. production activities deduction in the carryover year. ◀

ETHICAL POINT

When tax practitioners take on a new client, they should review the client's prior year tax returns and tax elections for accuracy and completeness. Tax matters arising in the current year, such as an NOL, can affect prior year tax returns prepared by another tax practitioner. Positions taken or errors discovered in a prior year return may have ethical consequences for a practitioner who takes on a new client.

COMPLIANCE AND PROCEDURAL CONSIDERATIONS

OBJECTIVE 6

Comply with corporate tax filing requirements

ESTIMATED TAXES

Every corporation that expects to owe more than $500 in tax for the current year must pay four installments of estimated tax, each equal to 25% of its required annual payment.[49] For corporations that are not large corporations (defined below), the required annual payment is the lesser of 100% of the tax shown on the current year return or 100% of the tax shown on the preceding year return. A corporation may not base its required estimated tax amount on the tax shown on the preceding year return if the preceding year tax return showed a zero tax liability.[50] The estimated tax amount is the sum of the corporation's income tax and alternative minimum tax liabilities that exceeds its tax credits. The amount of estimated tax due may be computed on Schedule 1120-W (Estimated Tax for Corporations).

Estimated Tax Payment Dates. A calendar year corporation must deposit estimated tax payments in a Federal Reserve bank or authorized commercial bank on or before April 15, June 15, September 15, and December 15.[51] This schedule differs from that of an individual taxpayer. The final estimated tax installment for a calendar year corporation is due in December of the tax year rather than in January of the following tax year, as is the case for individual taxpayers. For a fiscal year corporation, the due dates are the fifteenth day of the fourth, sixth, ninth, and twelfth months of the tax year.

[49] Sec. 6655.

[50] Rev. Rul. 92-54, 1992-2 C.B. 320.

[51] Sec. 6655(c)(2). Fiscal year corporations must deposit their taxes on or before the fifteenth day of the fourth, sixth, ninth, and twelfth month of their tax year. If the fifteenth falls on a weekend or holiday, a payment made on the next business day is considered made on the fifteenth due date. If April 15 falls on Sunday, April 16 also is a nonfiling day because April 16 is Emancipation Day, which is a holiday in Washington, D.C. In this case, a return will be due on April 17.

EXAMPLE C:3-46 ▶ Garden Corporation, a calendar year taxpayer, expects to report the following results for the current year:

Regular tax	$119,000
Alternative minimum tax	25,000

Garden's current year estimated tax liability is $144,000 ($119,000 regular tax liability + $25,000 AMT liability). Garden's tax liability last year was $120,000. Assuming Garden is not a large corporation, its required annual payment for the current year is $120,000, the lesser of its prior year liability ($120,000) or its current year tax return liability ($144,000). Garden will not incur a penalty if it deposits four equal installments of $30,000 ($120,000 ÷ 4) on or before April 15, June 15, September 15, and December 15 of the current year. ◀

TYPICAL MISCONCEPTION

The easiest method of determining a corporation's estimated tax payments is to pay 100% of last year's tax liability. Unfortunately, for "large corporations," other than for its first quarterly payment, last year's tax liability is not an acceptable method of determining the required estimated tax payments. Also, last year's tax liability cannot be used if no tax liability existed in the prior year or if the corporation filed a short-year return for the prior year.

Different estimated tax payment rules apply to large corporations. A large corporation's required annual payment is 100% of the tax shown on the current year return. A large corporation's estimated tax payments cannot be based on the prior year's tax liability except the first installment. If a large corporation bases its first estimated tax installment on the prior year's liability, any shortfall between the required payment based on the current year's tax liability and the actual payment must be made up with the second installment.[52] A large corporation is one whose taxable income was $1 million or more in any of its three immediately preceding tax years. Controlled groups of corporations must allocate the $1 million amount among its group members.

EXAMPLE C:3-47 ▶ Assume the same facts as in Example C:3-46 except Garden is a large corporation (i.e., it had more than $1 million of taxable income in one of its prior three years). Garden can base its first estimated tax payment on either 25% of its current year tax liability or 25% of last year's tax liability. Garden should elect to use its prior year tax liability as the basis for its first installment because it can reduce the needed payment from $36,000 (0.25 × $144,000) to $30,000 (0.25 × $120,000). However, it must recapture the $6,000 ($36,000 − $30,000) shortfall when it pays its second installment. Therefore, the total second installment is $42,000 ($36,000 second installment + $6,000 recapture from first installment). The third and fourth installments are $36,000 each. ◀

KEY POINT

The amount of penalty depends on three factors: the applicable underpayment rate, the amount of the underpayment, and the amount of time that lapses until the corporation makes the payment.

Penalites for Underpayment of Estimated Tax. The IRS will assess a nondeductible penalty if a corporation does not deposit its required estimated tax installment on or before the due date for that installment. The penalty is the underpayment rate found in Sec. 6621 times the amount by which the installment due by a payment date exceeds the payment actually made.[53] The penalty accrues from the payment due date for the installment until the earlier of the actual date of the payment or the due date for the tax return (excluding extensions).

EXAMPLE C:3-48 ▶ Globe Corporation is a calendar year taxpayer that reported a $100,000 tax liability for 2014. Globe's tax liability for 2013 was $125,000. It should have made estimated tax payments of $25,000 ($100,000 ÷ 4) on or before April 15, June 15, September 15, and December 15, 2014. If any of these dates fall on a weekend or holiday, a payment made on the next business day is considered to have been made on the due date. No penalty is assessed if Globe deposited or is considered to have deposited the requisite amounts on or before each of those dates. However, if Globe deposited only $16,000 ($9,000 less than the required $25,000) on April 16, 2014, and did not deposit the remaining $9,000 before the due date for the 2014 return, the corporation must pay a penalty on the $9,000 underpayment for the period of time from April 16, 2014, through March 15, 2015. If Globe deposits, or is considered to have deposited, $34,000 on the second installment date (June 15, 2014), so that it has paid a total of $50,000 by the second installment due date, the penalty runs only from April 16, 2014, through June 15, 2014.

ADDITIONAL COMMENT

This illustration pertains to 2014 because tax forms for that year are the latest available at the time this textbook was published.

Now assume that Globe instead made, or is considered to have made, the following estimated tax payments in 2014:

---

[52] Sec. 6655(d)(2)(B). A revision to the required estimated tax payment amount also may be needed if the corporation is basing its quarterly payments on the current year's tax liability. Installments paid after the estimate of the current year's liability has been revised must take into account any shortage or excess in previous installment payments resulting from the change in the original estimate.

[53] Sec. 6621. This interest rate is the short-term federal rate as determined by the Secretary of the Treasury plus three percentage points. It is subject to change every three months. The interest rate for large corporations is the short-term federal rate plus five percentage points. This higher interest rate begins 30 days after the issuance of either a 30-day or 90-day deficiency notice.

Date	Amount
April 15	$16,000
June 15	16,000
September 15	21,000
December 15	35,000

Form 2220 in Appendix B calculates the underpayments and resultant penalty given this pattern of payments. ◀

Special Computation Methods. In lieu of the current year and prior year methods, corporations can use either of two special methods for calculating estimated tax installments:

- ▶ The annualized income method
- ▶ The adjusted seasonal income method

The Annualized Income Method. This method is useful if a corporation's income is likely to increase a great deal toward the end of the year. It allows a corporation to base its first and second quarterly estimated tax payments on its annualized taxable income for the first three months of the year. The corporation then bases its third payment on its annualized taxable income for the first six months of the year and its fourth payment on annualized taxable income for the first nine months of the year. (Two other options for the number of months used for each installment also are available.)

TAX STRATEGY TIP

Both the "annualized income exception" and the "adjusted seasonal income exception" are complicated computations. However, due to the large amounts of money involved in making corporate estimated tax payments along with the possible underpayment penalties, the time and effort spent in determining the least amount necessary for a required estimated tax payment are often worthwhile.

EXAMPLE C:3-49 ▶ Erratic Corporation, a calendar year taxpayer, reports taxable income of: $10,000 in each of January, February, and March; $20,000 in each of April, May, and June; and $50,000 in each of the last six months of the current year. Erratic's annualized taxable income and annualized tax are calculated as follows:

Through	Cumulative Taxable Income	Annualization Factor	Annualized Taxable Income	Tax on Annualized Taxable Income
Third month	$ 30,000	12/3	$120,000	$ 30,050
Sixth month	90,000	12/6	180,000	53,450
Ninth month	240,000	12/9	320,000	108,050

Assuming Erratic uses the annualized method for all four estimated tax payments, its installments will be as follows:

Installment Number	Annualized Tax	Applicable Percentage	Installment Amount	Cumulative Installment
One	$ 30,050	25%	$ 7,513[a]	$ 7,513
Two	30,050	50	7,512[b]	15,025
Three	53,450	75	25,063[c]	40,088
Four	108,050	100	67,962[d]	108,050

[a]$30,050 × 0.25
[b]($30,050 × 0.50) – $7,513
[c]($53,450 × 0.75) – $15,025
[d]($108,050 × 1.00) – $40,088 ◀

A corporation may use the annualized income method for an installment payment only if it is less than the regular required installment (including the recapture described in the next sentence). It must recapture any reduction in an earlier required installment resulting from use of the annualized income method by increasing the amount of the next installment that does not qualify for the annualized income method.

For small corporations, the sure way to avoid a penalty for the underpayment of estimated tax is to base the current year's estimated tax payments on 100% of last year's tax. This approach is not possible, however, for large corporations or for corporations that owed no tax in the prior year or that filed a short period tax return for the prior year. This approach also is not advisable if the corporation had a high tax liability in the prior year and expects a low tax liability in the current year.

Adjusted Seasonal Income Method. A corporation may base its installments on its adjusted seasonal income. This method permits corporations that earn seasonal income to annualize their income by assuming income earned in the current year is earned in the same pattern as in preceding years. As in the case of the annualized income exception, a corporation can use the seasonal income exception only if the resulting installment payment is less than the regular required installment. Once the exception no longer applies, any savings resulting from its use for prior installments must be recaptured.

Reporting the Underpayment. A corporation reports its underpayment of estimated taxes and the amount of any penalty on Form 2220 (Underpayment of Estimated Tax by Corporations). A completed Form 2220 using the facts from Example C:3-48 appears in Appendix B.

Paying the Remaining Tax Liability. A corporation must pay its remaining tax liability for the year when it files its corporate tax return. An extension of time to file the tax return, however, does *not* extend the time to pay the tax liability. If any tax remains unpaid after the original due date for the tax return, the corporation must pay interest at the underpayment rate prescribed by Sec. 6621 from the due date until the corporation pays the tax. In addition to interest, the IRS assesses a penalty if the corporation does not pay the tax on time and cannot show reasonable cause for the failure to pay. The IRS presumes that reasonable cause exists if the corporation requests an extension of time to file its tax return and the amount of tax shown on the request for extension (Form 7004) or the amount of tax paid by the original due date of the return is at least 90% of the corporation's tax shown on its Form 1120.[54] A discussion of the failure-to-pay penalty and the interest calculation can be found in Chapter C:15.

STOP & THINK

Question: Why does the tax law permit a corporation to use special methods such as the annualized income method to calculate its required estimated tax installments?

Solution: A large corporation whose income varies widely may not be able to estimate its taxable income for the year until late in the year, and it is not allowed to base its estimates on last year's income. If, for example, a calendar year corporation earns income of $100,000 per month during the first six months of its year, it might estimate its first two installments on the assumption that it will earn a total taxable income of $1.2 million for the year. But if its income unexpectedly increases to $500,000 per month in the seventh month, it would need an annualized method to avoid an underpayment penalty for the first two installments. Were it not for the ability to use the annualized method, the corporation would have no way to avoid an underpayment penalty even though it could not predict its taxable income for the year when it made the first two installment payments.

REQUIREMENTS FOR FILING AND PAYING TAXES

A corporation must file a tax return, Form 1120 (U.S. Corporation Income Tax Return), even if it has no taxable income for the year.[55] If the corporation did not exist for its entire annual accounting period (either calendar year or fiscal year), it must file a short period return for the part of the year it did exist. For tax purposes, a corporation's existence ends when it ceases business and dissolves, retaining no assets, even if state law treats the corporation as continuing for purposes of winding up its affairs.[56]

A completed Form 1120 corporate income tax return appears in Appendix B. A spreadsheet that converts book income into taxable income for the Johns and Lawrence business enterprise (introduced in Chapter C:2) is presented with the C corporation tax return.

[54] Reg. Sec. 301.6651-1(c)(4).
[55] Sec. 6012(a)(2).
[56] Reg. Sec. 1.6012-2(a)(2).

WHEN THE RETURN MUST BE FILED

Corporations must file their tax returns by the fifteenth day of the third month following the close of their tax year.[57] A corporation can obtain an automatic six-month extension to file its tax return by filing Form 7004 (Application for Automatic Extension of Time to File Certain Business Tax, Information, and Other Returns) by the original due date for the return. Corporations that fail to file a timely tax return are subject to the failure-to-file penalty. Chapter C:15 discusses this penalty in some detail.

EXAMPLE C:3-50 ▶ Palmer Corporation's fiscal tax year ends on September 30. Its corporate tax return for the year ending September 30, 2015, is due on or before December 15, 2015. If Palmer files Form 7004 by December 15, 2015, it can obtain an automatic extension of time to file until June 15, 2016. Assuming Palmer expects its tax liability for the year ending September 30, 2015 to be $72,000 and it has paid $68,000 in estimated tax during the year, it must pay the remaining $4,000 by December 15, 2015. A completed Form 7004 appears in Appendix B. ◀

ADDITIONAL COMMENT

The IRS will not assess a late payment penalty if the corporation extends its due date and pays 90% of its total tax liability by the unextended due date and pays the balance by the extended due date.

Additional extensions beyond the automatic six-month period are not available. The IRS can rescind the extension period by mailing a ten-day notice to the corporation before the end of the six-month period.[58]

TAX RETURN SCHEDULES

BOOK-TO-TAX ACCOUNTING COMPARISON

Schedule L (of Form 1120) requires a financial accounting (book) balance sheet rather than a tax balance sheet.

Schedule L (of Form 1120): The Balance Sheet. Schedule L of Form 1120 requires a balance sheet showing the financial accounting results at the beginning and end of the tax year.

Reconciliation Schedules. The IRS also requires the reconciliation of the corporation's financial accounting income (also known as book income) and its taxable income (before special deductions). Book income is calculated according to generally accepted accounting principles (GAAP) including rules promulgated by the Financial Accounting Standards Board (FASB). On the other hand, taxable income must be calculated using tax rules. Therefore, book income and taxable income usually differ.

Some small corporations that do not require audited statements keep their books on a tax basis. For example, they may calculate depreciation for book purposes the same way they do for tax purposes. Income tax expense for book purposes may simply reflect the federal income tax liability. Most corporations, however, must use GAAP to calculate net income per books. For such corporations, taxable income and book income may differ significantly. The reconciliation of book income and taxable income provides the IRS with information that helps it audit a corporation's tax return.

ADDITIONAL COMMENT

For examples of Schedules M-1, M-2, and M-3 (of Form 1120), see Figure C:3-5, Figure C:3-6, and tax forms in Appendix B.

For many corporations, the reconciliation must be provided on Schedule M-1 of Form 1120. Corporations with total assets of $10 million or more on the last day of the tax year, however, must complete Schedule M-3 instead of Schedule M-1. This schedule provides the IRS with much more detailed information on differences between book income and taxable income than does Schedule M-1. This additional transparency of corporate transactions will increase the IRS's ability to audit corporate tax returns. Form 1120 also requires an analysis of unappropriated retained earnings on Schedule M-2.

BOOK-TO-TAX ACCOUNTING COMPARISON

The Internal Revenue Code and related authorities determine the treatment of items in the tax return while Accounting Standards Codification (ASC) 740 (Income Taxes) dictates the treatment of tax items in the financial statements.

Book-Tax Differences. A corporation's book income usually differs from its taxable income for a large number of transactions. Some of these differences are permanent. **Permanent differences** arise because:

- Some book income is never taxed. Examples include:
  1. Tax-exempt interest received on state and municipal obligations
  2. Proceeds of life insurance carried by the corporation on the lives of key officers or employees
- Some book expenses are never deductible for tax purposes. Examples include:
  1. Expenses incurred in earning tax-exempt interest

[57] Sec. 6072(b).

[58] Reg. Sec. 1.6081-3.

SELF-STUDY QUESTION

Why might the IRS be interested in reviewing a corporation's Schedule M-1 or M-3?

ANSWER

Schedule M-1 or M-3 adjustments reconcile book income to taxable income. Thus, these schedules can prove illuminating to an IRS agent who is auditing a corporate return. Because Schedule M-1 or M-3 highlights each departure from the financial accounting rules, the schedules sometimes help the IRS identify tax issues it may want to examine further.

2. Premiums paid for life insurance carried by the corporation on the lives of key officers or employees
3. Fines and expenses resulting from a violation of law
4. Disallowed travel and entertainment costs
5. Political contributions
6. Federal income taxes per books, which is based on GAAP (ASC 740)

▶ Some tax deductions are never taken for book purposes. Examples include:
1. The dividends-received deduction
2. The U.S. production activities deduction
3. Percentage depletion of natural resources in excess of their cost

Some of the differences are temporary. **Temporary differences** arise because:

▶ Some revenues or gains are recognized for book purposes in the current year but not reported for tax purposes until later years. Examples include:
1. Installment sales reported in full for book purposes in the year of sale but reported over a period of years using the installment method for tax purposes
2. Gains on involuntary conversions recognized currently for book purposes but deferred for tax purposes

▶ Some revenues or gains are taxable before they are reported for book purposes. These items are included in taxable income when received but are included in book income as they accrue. Examples include:
1. Prepaid rent or interest income
2. Advance subscription revenue

▶ Some expenses or losses are deductible for tax purposes after they are recognized for book purposes. Examples include:
1. Excess of capital losses over capital gains, which are expensed for book purposes but carry back or over for tax purposes
2. Book depreciation in excess of tax depreciation
3. Charitable contributions exceeding the 10% of taxable income limitation, which are currently expensed for book purposes but carry over for tax purposes
4. Bad debt accruals using the allowance method for book purposes and the direct write-off method for tax purposes
5. Organizational and start-up expenditures, which are expensed currently for book purposes but partially deducted and amortized for tax purposes
6. Product warranty liabilities expensed for book purposes when estimated but deducted for tax purposes when the liability becomes fixed
7. Net operating losses (NOLs) that, for tax purposes, carry back two years (or extended period if applicable) and carry over 20 years

▶ Some expenses or losses are deductible for tax purposes before they are recognized for book purposes. Examples include:
1. Tax depreciation in excess of book depreciation
2. Prepaid expenses deducted on the tax return in the period paid but accrued over a period of years for book purposes

For book purposes, temporary differences listed under the first and fourth bullets create deferred tax liabilities while those listed under the second and third bullets create deferred tax assets. The Financial Statement Implications section later in this chapter discusses the financial accounting treatment of book-tax differences.

Schedule M-1 (of Form 1120). The Schedule M-1 reconciliation of book to taxable income begins with net income per books and ends with taxable income before special deductions, which corresponds with Line 28 of Form 1120. Thus, some book-tax differences enumerated above do not appear in the reconciliation, for example, the dividends-received deduction and the net operating loss deduction.

The left side of Schedule M-1 contains items the corporation adds back to book income. These items include the following categories:

▶ Federal income tax expense (per books)

▶ Excess of capital losses over capital gains

- Income subject to tax but not recorded on the books in the current year
- Expenses recorded on the books but not deductible for tax purposes in the current year

The right side of the schedule contains items the corporation deducts from book income. These items include the following categories:

- Income recorded on the books in the current year that is not taxable in the current year
- Deductions or losses claimed in the tax return that do not reduce book income in the current year

These categorizations, however, do not distinguish between permanent and temporary differences as does Schedule M-3 discussed below. The following example illustrates a Schedule M-1 reconciliation.

EXAMPLE C:3-51 ▶ Valley Corporation reports the following items for book and tax purposes in its first year of operations (Year 1):

	Book	*Tax*	*Difference*
Gross receipts	$1,500,000	$1,500,000	
MInus: Cost of goods sold	(550,000)	(550,000)	
Gross profit from operations	$ 950,000	$950,000	
Plus: Dividends from less than 20%-owned corporations	10,000	10,000	
Tax-exempt income	3,000	–0–	$ (3,000)
Prepaid rental income	–0–	8,000	8,000
Minus: Operating expenses	(300,000)	(300,000)	
Depreciation	(60,000)	(170,000)	(110,000)
Bad debt expense	(25,000)	(16,000)	9,000
Business interest expense	(75,000)	(75,000)	
Insurance premiums on life for key employee (Valley is the beneficiary)	(2,800)	–0–	2,800
Net capital loss disallowed for tax purposes	(12,000)	–0–	12,000
U.S. production activities deduction (rounded)	–0–	(35,000)	(35,000)
Net income before federal income taxes	$ 488,200		
Taxable income before special deductions		$372,000	
Minus: Federal income tax expense per books	(151,640)	–0–	151,640
Dividends-received deduction	–0–	(7,000)	(7,000)
Net income per books / Taxable income	$ 336,560	$365,000	
Federal tax liability ($365,000 × 0.34)		$124,100	
Effective tax rate ($151,640/$488,200)	31.06%		

Valley's Schedule M-1 reconciliation appears in Figure C:3-5.[59] ◀

BOOK-TO-TAX COMPARISON

Schedules M-1 and M-3 adjustments highlight the fact that financial accounting and tax accounting differ in many ways. A review of Schedule M-1 or M-3 is an excellent way to compare the financial accounting and tax accounting differences in a corporation.

Schedule M-3 (of Form 1120). Schedule M-3 requires extensive detail in its reconciliation. Moreover, the schedule has the corporation distinguish between its permanent and temporary differences. The schedule contains three parts. Part I adjusts worldwide income per books to worldwide book income for only includible corporations. As described in Chapter C:8, some corporations may be included in the financial statement consolidation that might be excluded from the tax consolidated tax return. This resulting figure is then reconciled to taxable income before special deductions (again Line 28 of Form 1120). Part II enumerates the corporation's income and loss items, and Part III enumerates the expense and deduction items. The total items from Part III carry over to Part II for the final reconciliation. Both Parts II and III contain the following four columns: (a) book items, (b) temporary differences, (c) permanent differences, and (d) tax items.

[59] A worksheet for converting book income to taxable income for a sample Form 1120 return is provided in Appendix B with that return.

1	Net income (loss) per books	336,560	7	Income recorded on books this year not included on this return (itemize):	
2	Federal income tax per books	151,640			
3	Excess of capital losses over capital gains	12,000	a	Tax-exempt interest $ 3,000	
4	Income subject to tax not recorded on books this year (itemize):		b	Other (itemize):	
					3,000
	Prepaid rent	8,000	8	Deductions on this return not charged against book income this year (itemize):	
5	Expenses recorded on books this year not deducted on this return (itemize):				
a	Depreciation $		a	Depreciation $ 110,000	
b	Charitable contributions $		b	Charitable contributions $	
c	Travel and entertainment $		c	Other (itemize): U.S. prod. act. ded. 35,000	
d	Other (itemize): Bad debt expense 9,000				145,000
	Premiums on life insurance 2,800	11,800	9	Add lines 7 and 8	148,000
6	Add lines 1 through 5	520,000	10	Income—line 6 less line 9	372,000

FIGURE C:3-5 ▶ VALLEY CORPORATION'S FORM 1120 SCHEDULE M-1 (EXAMPLE C:3-51)

Appendix B provides an example of Schedule M-3 using the data from Example C:3-51. Valley Corporation in that example is too small to be required to use Schedule M-3 although it may elect to do so. Nevertheless, that data is used to allow for comparison of Schedules M-1 and M-3. Note that Lines 1 and – of Schedule M-3, Part III, break the \$151,640 federal income tax expense into its current and deferred components. In this example, the current expense ties to the current tax liability (\$124,100), and the deferred expense ties to the change in net deferred tax liabilities and assets arising from temporary differences, specifically, depreciation, net capital loss, prepaid rent, and bad debt expense [\$27,540 = 0.34 × (\$110,000 − \$12,000 − \$8,000 − \$9,000)]. These temporary differences appear in Column b of Schedule M-3, Parts II and III.

Schedule M-2 (of Form 1120). Schedule M-2 of Form 1120 requires an analysis of changes in unappropriated retained earnings from the beginning of the year to the end of the year. The schedule supplies the IRS with information regarding dividends paid during the year and any special transactions that caused a change in retained earnings for the year.

BOOK-TO-TAX ACCOUNTING COMPARISON

Schedule M-2 requires an analysis of a corporation's retained earnings. Retained earnings is a financial accounting number that has little relevance to tax accounting. A more relevant analysis for tax purposes is one of current and accumulated earnings and profits (E&P). If a corporation distributes more than its E&P, the excess is a nondividend distribution. In this case, the corporation must file Form 5452, Corporate Report of Nondividend Distributions, which requires an analysis of E&P along with other supporting information.

Schedule M-2 starts with the balance in the unappropriated retained earnings account at the beginning of the year. The following items, which must be added to the beginning balance amount, are listed on the left side of the schedule:

- Net income per books
- Other increases (e.g., refund of federal income taxes paid in a prior year taken directly to the retained earnings account instead of used to reduce federal income tax expense)

The following items, which must be deducted from the beginning balance amount, are listed on the right side of the schedule:

- Dividends (e.g., cash or property)
- Other decreases (e.g., appropriation of retained earnings made during the tax year)

The result is the amount of unappropriated retained earnings at the end of the year.

EXAMPLE C:3-52 ▶ In the current year, Beta Corporation reports net income and other capital account items as follows:

Unappropriated retained earnings, January 1, current year	\$400,000
Net income	350,000
Federal income tax refund for capital loss carryback	15,000
Cash dividends paid in the current year	250,000
Unappropriated retained earnings, December 31, current year	515,000

Beta Corporation's Schedule M-2 appears in Figure C:3-6. ◀

Topic Review C:3-2 summarizes the requirements for paying the taxes due and filing the corporate tax return.

Schedule M-2 **Analysis of Unappropriated Retained Earnings per Books**

1	Balance at beginning of year	400,000	5	Distributions: a Cash	250,000
2	Net income (loss) per books	350,000		b Stock	
3	Other increases (itemize):			c Property	
			6	Other decreases (itemize):	
	Federal tax refund	15,000	7	Add lines 5 and 6	250,000
4	Add lines 1, 2, and 3	765,000	8	Balance at end of year (line 4 less line 7)	515,000

FIGURE C:3-6 ▶ BETA CORPORATION'S FORM 1120 SCHEDULE M-2 (EXAMPLE C:3-52)

FINANCIAL STATEMENT IMPLICATIONS

OBJECTIVE 7

Determine the financial statement implications of corporate federal income taxes

The book-tax differences discussed on pages C:3-39 and C:3-40 have implications not only for preparing the reconciliation Schedules M-1 and M-3 but also affect how a firm's financial statements present income taxes. Income taxes impact both the income statement and balance sheet. For example, the tax section of the income statement might appear as follows:

Net income before federal income taxes
Minus: Federal income tax expense
Net income

Moreover, the **income tax expense** (also called the total tax provision) usually breaks down into a current component and a deferred component. The current component ties into the taxes payable for the current year, and the deferred component arises from book-tax temporary differences. The income tax expense also can contain state and foreign tax components. For this textbook, however, we focus primarily on federal income taxes. Financial statements usually publish details concerning its tax provision in a footnote to the financial statements. Temporary differences also create **deferred tax liabilities** and **deferred tax assets,** which appear on the balance sheet.

The primary standard that dictates financial statement treatment is Accounting Standards Codification (ASC) 740, issued by the Financial Accounting Standards Board (FASB). This section first describes the basic principles of ASC 740 and then presents a comprehensive example to demonstrate its application.

TOPIC REVIEW C:3-2

Requirements for Paying Taxes Due and Filing Tax Returns

1. Estimated Tax Requirement
   a. Corporations that expect to owe more than $500 in tax for the current year must pay four installments of estimated tax, each equal to 25% of its required annual payment.
   b. Taxes for which estimated payments are required of a C corporation include regular tax and alternative minimum tax, minus any tax credits.
   c. If a corporation is not a large corporation, its required annual payment is the lesser of 100% of the tax shown on the current year's return or 100% of the tax shown on the preceding year's return.
   d. If a corporation is a large corporation, its required annual payment is 100% of the tax shown on the current year's return. Its first estimated tax payment may be based on the preceding year's tax liability, but any shortfall must be made up when the second installment is due.
   e. Special rules apply if the corporation bases its estimated tax payments on the annualized income or adjusted seasonal income method.
2. Filing Requirements
   a. The corporate tax return is due by the fifteenth day of the third month after the end of the tax year.
   b. A corporate taxpayer may request an automatic six-month extension to file its tax return (but not to pay its tax due).

SCOPE, OBJECTIVES, AND PRINCIPLES OF ASC 740

ASC 740 establishes principles of accounting for current income taxes and for deferred taxes arising from temporary differences. Specifically, ASC 740 addresses the financial statement consequences of the following events:

- Revenues, expenses, gains, or losses recognized for tax purposes in an earlier or later year than recognized for financial statement purposes
- Other events that create differences between book and tax bases of assets and liabilities
- Operating loss and tax credit carrybacks or carryforwards

ASC 740 sets out two objectives: (1) to recognize current year taxes payable or refundable and (2) to recognize deferred tax liabilities and assets for the future tax consequences of events recognized in a firm's financial statements or tax return. To implement these objectives, ASC 740 applies the following principles:

- Recognize a current tax liability or asset for taxes payable or refundable on current year tax returns
- Recognize a deferred tax liability or asset for future tax effects attributable to temporary differences and carryforwards
- Measure current and deferred tax liabilities and assets using only enacted tax law, not anticipated future changes
- Reduce deferred tax assets by the amount of tax benefits the firm does not expect to realize, based on available evidence and adjusted via a valuation allowance
- Establish a liability for uncertain tax positions if necessary

Interestingly, the only comment ASC 740 makes about permanent differences is that "[s]ome events do not have tax consequences. Certain revenues are exempt from taxation and certain expenses are not deductible." In this context, ASC 740 does not mention certain events that do have tax consequences but, nevertheless, create permanent differences, for example, the dividends-received deduction and the U.S. production activities deduction. As we show later, permanent differences do not affect deferred taxes, but they do impact the firm's effective tax rate.

TEMPORARY DIFFERENCES

Similarly to the discussion on pages C:3-39 and C:3-40, the following lists describe events that generate (1) taxable temporary differences and thus deferred tax liabilities and (2) deductible temporary differences and thus deferred tax assets. Deferred tax liabilities and assets appear on a firm's balance sheet.

Taxable temporary differences and deferred tax liabilities occur when:

- Revenue or gains are recognized earlier for book purposes than for tax purposes
- Expenses or losses are deductible earlier for tax purposes than for book purposes
- Tax basis of an asset is less than its book basis
- Tax basis of a liability exceeds its book basis

Deductible temporary differences and deferred tax assets occur when:

- Revenue or gains are recognized earlier for tax purposes than for book purposes
- Expenses or losses are deductible earlier for book purposes than for tax purposes
- Tax basis of an asset exceeds its book basis
- Tax basis of a liability is less than its book basis
- Operating loss or tax credit carryforwards exist

DEFERRED TAX ASSETS AND THE VALUATION ALLOWANCE

A deferred tax asset indicates that a firm will realize the tax benefit of an event some time in the future. For example, if the firm generates a net operating loss in the current year and, for tax purposes carries the loss forward, the firm will realize a tax benefit only if it earns sufficient future income to use the carryover before it expires. If the firm likely will not realize the entire tax benefit, it must record a **valuation allowance** to reflect the unrealizable portion. The valuation allowance is a contra-type account that reduces the deferred tax asset.

EXAMPLE C:3-53 ▶ Delta Corporation's NOL carryover is $200,000, and it expects to realize (deduct) the entire carryover at a 34% tax rate. Thus, Delta's deferred tax asset is $68,000 ($200,000 × 0.34), and it makes the following book journal entry:

Deferred tax asset	68,000	
Federal income tax expense (benefit)		68,000

Consequently, the deferred tax asset reduces the income tax expense or creates an income tax benefit.

If Delta determines that it likely will realize (deduct) only $150,000 of the NOL carryover, it must record a $17,000 ($50,000 × 0.34) valuation allowance. Accordingly, Delta makes the following book journal entry:

Deferred tax asset	68,000	
Valuation allowance		17,000
Federal income tax expense (benefit)		51,000

◀

ASC 740 specifically states that a deferred tax asset must be reduced by a valuation allowance if, based on the weight of evidence available, the firm *more likely than not* will fail to realize the benefit of the deferred tax asset. For this purpose, the term *more likely than not* means a greater than 50% likelihood. In assessing this likelihood, a firm must consider both negative and positive evidence, where negative evidence leads toward establishing a valuation allowance while positive evidence helps avoid a valuation allowance. ASC 740 lists several examples of each type of evidence. Examples of negative evidence include the following items:

- ▶ Cumulative losses in recent years
- ▶ A history of expiring loss or credit carryforwards
- ▶ Expected losses in the near future
- ▶ Unfavorable contingencies with future adverse effects
- ▶ Short carryback or carryover periods that might limit realization of the deferred tax asset

Examples of positive evidence include the following items:

- ▶ Existing contracts or sales backlogs that will produce sufficient income to realize the deferred tax asset
- ▶ Excess of appreciated asset value over tax basis (i.e., built-in gain) sufficient to realize the deferred tax asset
- ▶ A strong earnings history aside from the event causing the deferred tax asset along with evidence that the event is an aberration

In essence, a firm can realize (deduct) a deferred tax asset if it has sufficient taxable income to offset the deduction. ASC 740 suggests the following potential sources of such income:

- ▶ Future reversals of deferred tax liabilities
- ▶ Future taxable income other than reversing deferred tax liabilities
- ▶ Taxable income in carryback years assuming the tax law allows a carryback
- ▶ Taxable income from prudent and feasible tax planning strategies that a firm ordinarily would not take but nevertheless would pursue to realize an otherwise expiring deferred tax asset

ACCOUNTING FOR UNCERTAIN TAX POSITIONS

ADDITIONAL COMMENT

This financial statement standard used to be referred to as FIN 48, a pre-codification designation. Many practitioners, however, still use the FIN 48 terminology.

ASC 740 also prescribes acceptable accounting for uncertain tax positions. This standard addresses the following basic situation: For tax purposes, a firm may take a position in claiming a tax benefit that might not be sustained under IRS scrutiny. The FASB, however, believes that, for determining the financial statement tax provision, such uncertain tax positions either should not be recognized or should be recognized only partially.

REAL-WORLD EXAMPLE

The IRS has developed Schedule UTP for inclusion in Form 1120. This schedule requires certain taxpayers to provide information about their uncertain tax positions. The required information will provide the IRS a road map for auditing the tax return.

In applying the tax position standard, a firm takes a two-step approach. First, the firm determines whether the tax position has a *more likely than not* (greater than 50%) probability of being sustained upon an IRS examination. This determination requires substantial judgment and necessitates careful documentation for the financial statement audit and any IRS examination. If the tax position does not exceed this threshold, the firm cannot recognize the tax benefit for financial reporting purposes until one of the following three events occur:

- The position subsequently meets the *more likely than not* threshold.
- The firm favorably settles the tax issue with the IRS or in court.
- The statute of limitations on the transaction expires.

If the firm determines that a tax position meets the *more like than not* threshold, it then must measure the amount of benefit it can recognize for financial reporting purposes. This measure is the largest amount of tax benefit that exceeds a 50% probability of realization upon settlement with the taxing authorities. Further details of this measurement process and other procedures under the tax position standard become quite complex and are beyond the scope of this textbook.

EXAMPLE C:3-54 ▶ Lambda Corporation claims a $1 million deduction on its tax return, which provides a $350,000 tax savings, assuming a 35% tax rate. After some analysis and judgment, management determines the deduction has only a 45% chance of being allowed should the IRS audit Lambda's tax return. Assume for simplicity that Lambda has no deferred tax assets or liabilities. Assume further that Lambda's pretax book income and taxable income equal $20 million after taking the $1 million deduction. Thus, Lambda's tax liability is $7 million. Under the tax position standard, Lambda makes the following journal entry (ignoring potential penalties and interest):

Federal income tax expense	7,350,000	
Liability for unrecognized tax benefits		350,000
Federal income taxes payable		7,000,000

Suppose in a subsequent period Lambda negotiates a settlement with the IRS that allows $200,000 of the deduction, and Lambda pays $280,000 tax on the $800,000 disallowed portion. Ignoring penalties and interest, Lambda would make the following journal entry:

Liability for unrecognized tax benefits	350,000	
Cash		280,000
Federal income tax expense		70,000

◀

EXAMPLE C:3-55 ▶ Assume the same facts as in Example C:3-54 except Lambda meets the *more likely than not* threshold. Lambda then measures the benefit more than 50% likely to be realized as $600,000 of the $1 million deduction taken. Thus, Lambda may not recognize $400,000 in determining its federal income tax expense for financial reporting purposes and, accordingly, makes the following journal entry:

Federal income tax expense	7,140,000	
Liability for unrecognized tax benefits		140,000
Federal income taxes payable		7,000,000

◀

BALANCE SHEET CLASSIFICATION

ADDITIONAL COMMENT

According to an internal memorandum, the FASB is considering a change to its accounting standards that would require that all deferred assets and liabilities be presented as noncurrent in classified financial statements.

Deferred tax liabilities and assets must be classified as either current or noncurrent. If related to another asset or liability, the classification is the same as the related asset. For example, a deferred tax asset pertaining to a difference between book and tax bad debt expense is current because it relates to accounts receivable. On the other hand, a deferred tax liability pertaining to a difference between book and tax depreciation is noncurrent because it relates to fixed assets. If a deferred tax liability or asset does not relate to a particular asset or liability, it is classified as current or noncurrent depending on its expected reversal date. Once classified as current and noncurrent, all current deferred tax liabilities and assets must be netted and presented as one amount. Similarly, all noncurrent deferred tax liabilities and assets must be netted and presented as another amount.

TAX PROVISION PROCESS

The following steps outline the approach used in this chapter to provide for income taxes in the financial statements. This process addresses only federal income taxes.

1. Identify temporary differences by comparing the book and tax bases of assets and liabilities, and identify tax carryforwards.
2. Prepare "roll forward" schedules of temporary differences that tabulate cumulative differences and current-year changes.
3. In the roll forward schedules, apply the appropriate statutory tax rates to determine the ending balances of deferred tax assets and liabilities.
4. Adjust deferred tax assets by a valuation allowance if necessary.
5. Adjust the income tax expense for uncertain tax positions if necessary.
6. Determine current federal income taxes payable, which, in many cases, also is the current federal income tax expense for book purposes.
7. Determining the total federal income tax expense (benefit).
8. Prepare and record tax related journal entries.
9. Prepare a tax provision reconciliation.
10. Prepare the tax rate reconciliation.
11. Prepare financial statements.

ADDITIONAL COMMENT

Determining the valuation allowance and uncertain tax position adjustments requires a great deal of professional judgment.

In practice, various firms may use slightly different approaches. For this chapter, however, the above steps provide a logical and systematic approach.

COMPREHENSIVE EXAMPLE – YEAR 1

ADDITIONAL COMMENT

The format used in this example is a basic framework. Each firm preparing or reviewing the tax provision will have its own workpaper format for this process.

To provide comprehensiveness, this example continues with the facts set forth in Example C:3-51. Thus, when completed, the two examples together provide the financial statement implications of federal income taxes as well as the tax return reporting in Schedules M-1 and M-3 for Year 1. We then continue the example with events occurring in Year 2.

In addition to the facts stated in Example C:3-51, Valley reports the following book and tax balance sheet items at the end of Year 1, prior to adjustment for tax related items. Step 11 below presents the completed book balance sheet after making tax related journal entries.

Assets:	*Book*	*Tax*	*Difference*
Cash	$ 230,200	$ 230,200	
Accounts receivable	300,000	300,000	
Minus: Allowance for bad debts	(9,000)	–0–	
Net accounts receivable	291,000	300,000	$ 9,000
Investment in corporate stock	90,000	90,000	
Investment in tax-exempt bonds	50,000	50,000	
Inventory	500,000	500,000	
Fixed assets	1,200,000	1,200,000	
Minus: Accumulated depreciation	(60,000)	(170,000)	
Net fixed assets	1,140,000	1,030,000	110,000
Liabilities and stock equity:			
Accounts payable	225,000	225,000	
Unearned rental income	8,000	–0–	8,000
Long-term liabilities	930,000	930,000	
Common stock	650,000	650,000	

Steps 1 through 3.

The book and tax balance sheets above indicate the items where the book and tax bases differ, thereby indicating temporary differences. In addition, the facts from Example C:3-51 indicates a nondeductible net capital loss, which creates a carryforward.

The following three roll forward schedules calculate the deferred tax assets and deferred tax liability associated with these temporary differences. The beginning and ending balances for the balance sheet items reflect the differences between the book and tax bases for these assets and liabilities. In the first schedule, the deferred tax asset for the net accounts receivable is current because it relates to a current asset. The deferred tax asset for the unearned rental income is current because Valley expects to earn that income in the next year. In the second schedule, the example assumes Valley does not expect to have sufficient capital gains to offset the capital loss carryover until three years from now. Therefore, this deferred tax asset will not reverse next year and is considered noncurrent. In the third schedule, the deferred tax liability pertaining to fixed assets is noncurrent because it relates to a noncurrent asset.

Current deferred tax asset:	*Beg. of Year 1*	*End of Year 1*	*Change*
Net accounts receivable	$ -0-	$ 9,000	$ 9,000
Unearned rental income	-0-	8,000	8,000
Total	$ -0-	$ 17,000	$ 17,000
Times: Tax rate	0.34	0.34	
Current deferred tax asset	$ -0-	$ 5,780	$ 5,780

Noncurrent deferred tax asset:	*Beg. of Year 1*	*End of Year 1*	*Change*
Net capital loss	$ -0-	$ 12,000	$ 12,000
Times: Tax rate	0.34	0.34	
Noncurrent deferred tax asset	$ -0-	$ 4,080	$ 4,080

Noncurrent deferred tax liability:	*Beg. of Year 1*	*End of Year 1*	*Change*
Net fixed assets	$ -0-	$110,000	$110,000
Times: Tax rate	0.34	0.34	
Noncurrent deferred tax liability	$ -0-	$ 37,400	$ 37,400

The amounts in the change column also appear as book-tax differences in the book and tax income schedules in Example C:3-51. In those schedules, the differences occur in the related income or expense accounts, specifically, bad debt expense, prepaid rental income, and depreciation.

One last aspect of these schedules needs mentioning. Specifically, the changes in the deferred tax assets and liabilities also represent the deferred federal tax expense or benefit for the current year. See Step 7 below.

Step 4.
Assuming evidence supports that Valley will realize the entire amount of its deferred tax assets, Valley need not establish a valuation allowance.

Step 5.
Assume that Valley requires no adjustments for uncertain tax positions.

Step 6.
As provided in Example C:3-51, current federal income taxes payable is $124,100. In this example, the current payable amount also is the current federal income tax expense for book purposes. (The equality of the current payable amount and the federal income tax expense may not occur, however, under some uncertain tax position situations and in other special circumstances.)

Step 7.

The net deferred federal tax expense from the roll forward schedules equals $27,540 ($37,400 − $5,780 − $4,080). Therefore, the total federal income tax expense for this year can be calculated as follows:

Current federal income tax expense	$124,100
Deferred income tax expense	27,540
Total federal income tax expense	$151,640

Step 8.

Given the amounts determined in previous steps, Valley makes the following book journal entry:

Current federal income tax expense	124,100	
Deferred federal income tax expense	27,540	
Current deferred tax asset	5,780	
Noncurrent deferred tax asset	4,080	
Noncurrent deferred tax liability		37,400
Federal income taxes payable		124,100

Alternatively, Valley could make the following combined book journal entry:

Total federal income tax expense	151,640	
Current deferred tax asset	5,780	
Net noncurrent deferred tax liability (37,400 − 4,080)		33,320
Federal income taxes payable		124,100

Step 9.

As a cross check on the previous steps, Valley can prepare the following tax provision reconciliation:

Net income before federal income taxes (FIT)	$488,200
Permanent differences:	
Nondeductible insurance premiums	2,800
Tax-exempt income	(3,000)
U.S. production activities deduction	(35,000)
Dividends-received deduction	(7,000)
Net income after permanent differences	$446,000
Temporary differences:	
Unearned rental income	8,000
Net capital loss disallowed for tax	12,000
Net accounts receivable (bad debt expense)	9,000
Net fixed assets (depreciation)	(110,000)
Taxable income	$365,000

ADDITIONAL COMMENT

This approach and the balance sheet approach may not always lead to the same result when enacted tax rates change, under some uncertain tax position situations, and in other special circumstances.

Assuming no enacted change in future tax rates, net income after permanent differences times the tax rate results in the total federal income tax expense. Specifically, $446,000 × 0.34 = $151,640. Similarly, taxable income times the tax rate results in current federal income taxes payable. Specifically, $365,000 × 0.34 = $124,100.

ADDITIONAL COMMENT

Remember that we are looking only at federal income taxes in these examples. Foreign, state, and local taxes also can affect a firm's effective tax rate.

Step 10.

A firm's effective tax rate is its income tax expense divided by its pretax book income. Because the income tax expense is based on net income after adjustment for permanent differences (see Step 9), these differences cause a firm's effective tax rate to differ from the statutory tax rate. In the footnotes to financial statements, firms reconcile the statutory tax rate to their effective tax rate. Accordingly, Valley's effective tax rate reconciliation is as follows:

Statutory tax rate	34.00%
Nondeductible insurance premiums ($2,800/$488,200 × 34%)	0.20%
Tax-exempt income [($3,000)/$488,200 × 34%]	(0.21)%
U.S. production activities deduction [($35,000)/$488,200 × 34%]	(2.44)%
Dividends-received deduction [($7,000)/$488,200 × 34%]	(0.49)%
Effective tax rate ($151,640/$488,200)	31.06%

In practice, a firm would not disclose the detail shown here but would aggregate small percentage amounts into an "other" category. Also, if the enacted future tax rate changes, that change also would be reflected in this schedule.

Step 11.

At this point, Valley can complete its financial statements. The income statement appears in Example C:3-51, but the tax portion is repeated here.

Partial income statement:	
Net income before federal income taxes	$488,200
Minus: Federal income tax expense	(151,640)
Net income	$336,560
Effective tax rate ($151,640/$488,200)	31.06%

As shown in Step 7, the total federal income tax expense has two components as follows:

Current federal income tax expense	$124,100
Deferred income tax expense	27,540
Total federal income tax expense	$151,640

The book balance sheet for Year 1 is as follows:

Assets:		
Cash		$ 230,200
Accounts receivable	$ 300,000	
Minus: Allowance for bad debts	(9,000)	291,000
Investment in corporate stock		90,000
Investment in tax-exempt bond		50,000
Inventory		500,000
Current deferred tax asset		5,780
Fixed assets	$1,200,000	
Minus: Accumulated depreciation	(60,000)	1,140,000
Total assets		$2,306,980
Liabilities and equity:		
Accounts payable		$ 225,000
Unearned rental income		8,000
Federal income taxes payable		124,100
Noncurrent deferred liability ($37,400 − $4,080)		33,320
Long-term liabilities		930,000
Common stock		650,000
Retained earnings		336,560
Total liabilities and equity		$2,306,980

ADDITIONAL COMMENT

This example ignores estimated tax payments, so that the entire amount of federal income taxes payable appears on the balance sheet.

COMPREHENSIVE EXAMPLE – YEAR 2

Valley reports the following book and tax balance sheet items at the end of Year 2, prior to adjustment for tax related items. Pertinent to the temporary differences, in Year 2 Valley earned the rental income that was prepaid in Year 1 and did not collect additional amounts. It also adjusted its allowance for bad debts and claimed additional depreciation on fixed assets. It did not recognize any capital gains to offset the capital loss carryover. Step 11 below presents the completed book balance sheet after making tax related journal entries.

Assets:	*Book*	*Tax*	*Difference*
Cash	$ 318,800	$ 318,800	
Accounts receivable	400,000	400,000	
Allowance for bad debts	(37,000)	–0–	
Net accounts receivable	363,000	400,000	$ 37,000
Investment in corporate stock	90,000	90,000	
Investment in tax-exempt bonds	50,000	50,000	
Inventory	600,000	600,000	
Fixed assets	1,200,000	1,200,000	
Accumulated depreciation	(180,000)	(465,000)	
Net fixed assets	1,020,000	735,000	285,000
Liabilities and stock equity:			
Accounts payable	295,000	295,000	
Unearned rental income	–0–	–0–	
Long-term liabilities	530,000	530,000	
Common stock	650,000	650,000	

Valley also reports the following book income statement through net income before federal income taxes and tax return schedule through taxable income. The tax portion of the book income statement appears in Step 11.

	Book	*Tax*	*Difference*
Gross receipts	$2,000,000	$2,000,000	
Minus: Cost of goods sold	(700,000)	(700,000)	
Gross profit from operations	$1,300,000	$1,300,000	
Plus: Dividends from less than 20%-owned corporations	15,000	15,000	
Tax-exempt income	3,200	–0–	$ (3,200)
Prepaid rental income	8,000	–0–	(8,000)
Minus: Operating expenses	(500,000)	(500,000)	
Depreciation	(120,000)	(295,000)	(175,000)
Bad debt expense	(40,000)	(12,000)	28,000
Business interest expense	(60,000)	(60,000)	
Insurance premiums on life insurance for key employee (Valley is the beneficiary)	(3,500)	–0–	3,500
U.S. production activities deduction (rounded)	–0–	(39,000)	(39,000)
Dividends-received deduction	–0–	(10,500)	(10,500)
Net income before federal income taxes	$ 602,700		
Taxable income		$ 398,500	

Steps 1 through 3.

The book and tax balance sheets above indicate the items where the book and tax bases differ, thereby indicating temporary differences. In addition, the net capital loss carryforward remains unused.

The following three roll forward schedules calculate the deferred tax assets and deferred tax liability associated with these temporary differences. The beginning and ending balances for the balance sheet items reflect the differences between the book and tax bases for these assets and liabilities. In the first schedule, the net accounts receivable temporary difference increases, and the unearned rental income item reverses. In the second schedule, Valley has not realized the deferred tax asset because it recognized no capital gains in Year 2. Therefore, this deferred tax asset has not yet reversed. In the third schedule, the fixed asset temporary difference increases.

Current deferred tax asset:	Beg. of Year 2	End of Year 2	Change
Net accounts receivable	$ 9,000	$ 37,000	$ 28,000
Unearned rental income	8,000	–0–	(8,000)
Total	$ 17,000	$ 37,000	$ 20,000
Times: Tax rate	0.34	0.34	
Current deferred tax asset	$ 5,780	$ 12,580	$ 6,800

Noncurrent deferred tax asset:	Beg. of Year 2	End of Year 2	Change
Net capital loss	$ 12,000	$ 12,000	$ –0–
Times: Tax rate	0.34	0.34	
Noncurrent deferred tax asset	$ 4,080	$ 4,080	$ –0–

Noncurrent deferred tax liability:	Beg. of Year 2	End of Year 2	Change
Net fixed assets	$110,000	$285,000	$175,000
Times: Tax rate	0.34	0.34	
Noncurrent deferred tax liability	$ 37,400	$ 96,900	$ 59,500

The amounts in the change column also appear as book-tax differences in the above book and tax income schedules. In those schedules, the differences occur in the related income or expense accounts, specifically, bad debt expense, prepaid rental income, and depreciation.

As before, the changes in the deferred tax assets and liabilities also represent the deferred federal tax expense or benefit for the current year. See Step 7 below.

Step 4.
Assuming evidence supports that Valley still will realize the entire amount of its deferred tax assets, Valley need not establish a valuation allowance.

Step 5.
Assume again that Valley requires no adjustments for uncertain tax positions.

Step 6.
As provided in the schedule above, taxable income is $398,500. Therefore, current federal income taxes payable is $135,490 ($398,500 × 0.34). In this example, the current payable amount also is the current federal income tax expense for book purposes. (The equality of the current payable amount and the federal income tax expense may not occur, however, under some uncertain tax position situations and in other special circumstances.)

Step 7.
The net deferred federal tax expense from the roll forward schedules equals $52,700 ($59,500 − $6,800). Therefore, the total federal income tax expense for this year can be calculated as follows:

Current federal income tax expense	$135,490
Deferred income tax expense	52,700
Total federal income tax expense	$188,190

Step 8.
Given the amounts determined in previous steps, Valley makes the following book journal entry:

Current federal income tax expense	135,490	
Deferred federal income tax expense	52,700	
Current deferred tax asset	6,800	
Noncurrent deferred tax liability		59,500
Federal income taxes payable		135,490

Alternatively, Valley could make the following combined book journal entry:

Total federal income tax expense	188,190	
Current deferred tax asset	6,800	
Noncurrent deferred tax liability		59,500
Federal income taxes payable		135,490

Step 9.
As a cross check on the previous steps, Valley can prepare the following tax provision reconciliation:

Net income before federal income taxes (FIT)	$602,700
Permanent differences:	
Nondeductible insurance premiums	3,500
Tax-exempt income	(3,200)
U.S. production activities deduction	(39,000)
Dividends-received deduction	(10,500)
Net income after permanent differences	$553,500
Temporary differences:	
Unearned rental income	(8,000)
Net accounts receivable (bad debt expense)	28,000
Net fixed assets (depreciation)	(175,000)
Taxable income	$398,500

ADDITIONAL COMMENT
This approach and the balance sheet approach may not always lead to the same result when enacted tax rates change, under some uncertain tax position situations, and in other special circumstances.

Assuming no enacted change in future tax rates, net income after permanent differences times the tax rate results in the total federal income tax expense. Specifically, $553,500 × 0.34 = $188,190. Similarly, taxable income times the tax rate results in current federal income taxes payable. Specifically, $398,500 × 0.34 = $135,490.

Step 10.
Valley's Year 2 effective tax rate is its income tax expense divided by its pretax book income, or $188,190/$602,700 = 31.23% (rounded up). Accordingly, Valley's effective tax rate reconciliation is as follows:

Statutory tax rate	34.00%
Nondeductible insurance premiums ($3,500/$602,700 × 34%)	0.20%
Tax-exempt income [($3,200)/$602,700 × 34%]	(0.18)%
U.S. production activities deduction [($39,000)/$602,700 × 34%]	(2.20)%
Dividends-received deduction [($10,500)/$602,700 × 34%]	(0.59)%
Effective tax rate ($188,190/$602,700)	31.23%

Step 11.
At this point, Valley can complete its financial statements. The first part of the income statement appears in the schedule appearing before Steps 1 through 3, and the tax portion is as follows:

Partial income statement:	
Net income before federal income taxes	$602,700
Minus: Federal income tax expense	(188,190)
Net income	$414,510
Effective tax rate ($188,190/$602,700)	31.23%

As shown in Step 7, the federal income tax expense has two components as follows:

Current federal income tax expense	$135,490
Deferred income tax expense ($59,500 − $6,800)	52,700
Total federal income tax expense	$188,190

The book balance sheet for Year 2 is as follows:

Assets:		
Cash		$ 318,800
Accounts receivable	$ 400,000	
Minus: Allowance for bad debts	(37,000)	363,000
Investment in corporate stock		90,000
Investment in tax-exempt bond		50,000
Inventory		600,000
Current deferred tax asset		12,580
Fixed assets	$1,200,000	
Minus: Accumulated depreciation	(180,000)	1,020,000
Total assets		$2,454,380
Liabilities and equity:		
Accounts payable		$ 295,000
Unearned rental income		–0–
Federal income taxes payable		135,490
Noncurrent deferred liability ($96,900 − $4,080)		92,820
Long-term liabilities		530,000
Common stock		650,000
Retained earnings		751,070
Total liabilities and equity		$2,454,380

ADDITIONAL COMMENT

This example ignores estimated tax payments, so the entire amount of federal income taxes payable appears on the balance sheet.

OTHER TRANSACTIONS

Chapters C:5, C:7, C:8, and C:16 describe the financial statement implications of other transactions, for example, the alternative minimum tax (Chapter C:5), corporate acquisitions (Chapter C:7), intercompany transactions (Chapter C:8), and the foreign tax credit and deferred foreign earnings (Chapter C:16). Also, Problem C:3-64 provides a comprehensive tax return and financial accounting exercise.

PROBLEM MATERIALS

DISCUSSION QUESTIONS

C:3-1 High Corporation incorporates on May 1 and begins business on May 10 of the current year. What alternative tax years can High elect to report its initial year's income?

C:3-2 Port Corporation wants to change its tax year from a calendar year to a fiscal year ending June 30. Port is a C corporation owned by 100 shareholders, none of whom own more than 5% of the stock. Can Port change its tax year? If so, how can it accomplish the change?

C:3-3 Stan and Susan, two calendar year taxpayers, are starting a new business to manufacture and sell digital circuits. They intend to incorporate the business with $600,000 of their own capital and $2 million of equity capital obtained from other investors. The company expects to incur organizational and start-up expenditures of $100,000 in the first year. Inventories are a material income-producing factor. The company also expects to incur losses of $500,000 in the first two years of operations and substantial research and development expenses during the first three years. The company expects to break even in the third year and be profitable at the end of the fourth year, even though the nature of the digital circuit business will require continual research and development activities. What accounting methods and tax elections must Stan and Susan consider in their first year of operation? For each method and election, explain the possible alternatives and the advantages and disadvantages of each alternative.

C:3-4 Compare the tax treatment of capital gains and losses by a corporation and by an individual.

C:3-5 What are organizational expenditures? How are they treated for tax purposes?

C:3-6 What are start-up expenditures? How are they treated for tax purposes?

C:3-7 Describe three ways in which the treatment of charitable contributions by individual and corporate taxpayers differ.

C:3-8 Carver Corporation uses the accrual method of accounting and the calendar year as its tax year. Its board of directors authorizes a cash contribution on November 3 of Year 1, that the corporation pays on March 9 of Year 2. In what year(s) is it deductible? What happens if the corporation does not pay the contribution until April 20 of Year 2?

C:3-9 Zero Corporation contributes inventory (computers) to State University for use in its mathematics program. The computers have a $1,225 cost basis and an $2,800 FMV. How much is Zero's charitable contribution deduction for the computers? (Ignore the 10% limit.)

C:3-10 Why are corporations allowed a dividends-received deduction? What dividends qualify for this special deduction?

C:3-11 Why is a dividends-received deduction disallowed if the stock on which the corporation pays the dividend is debt-financed?

C:3-12 Crane Corporation incurs a $75,000 NOL in the current year. In which years can Crane use this NOL if it makes no special elections? When might a special election to forgo the carryback of the NOL be beneficial for Crane?

C:3-13 What special restrictions apply to the deduction of a loss realized on the sale of property between a corporation and a shareholder who owns 60% of the corporation's stock? What restrictions apply to the deduction of expenses accrued by a corporation at year-end and owed to a cash method shareholder who owns 60% of the corporation's stock?

C:3-14 Deer Corporation is a C corporation. Its taxable income for the current year is $200,000. What is Deer Corporation's income tax liability for the year?

C:3-15 Budget Corporation is a personal service corporation. Its taxable income for the current year is $75,000. What is Budget's income tax liability for the year?

C:3-16 Describe the three types of controlled groups.

C:3-17 Why do special restrictions on using the progressive corporate tax rates apply to controlled groups of corporations? List five restrictions on claiming multiple tax benefits that apply to controlled groups of corporations.

C:3-18 What are the major advantages and disadvantages of filing a consolidated tax return?

C:3-19 What are the tax advantages of substituting fringe benefits for salary paid to a shareholder-employee?

C:3-20 Explain the tax consequences to both the corporation and a shareholder-employee if an IRS agent determines that a portion of the compensation paid in a prior tax year exceeds a reasonable compensation level.

C:3-21 What is the advantage of a special apportionment plan for the benefits of the 15%, 25%, and 34% tax rates to members of a controlled group?

C:3-22 What corporations must pay estimated taxes? When are the estimated tax payments due?

C:3-23 What is a "large" corporation for purposes of the estimated tax rules? What special rules apply to such large corporations?

C:3-24 What penalties apply to the underpayment of estimated taxes? The late payment of the remaining tax liability?

C:3-25 Describe the situations in which a corporation must file a tax return.

C:3-26 When is a corporate tax return due for a calendar-year taxpayer? What extension(s) of time in which to file the return are available?

C:3-27 List four types of differences that can cause a corporation's book income to differ from its taxable income.

ISSUE IDENTIFICATION QUESTIONS

C:3-28 X-Ray Corporation received a $100,000 dividend from Yancey Corporation this year. X-Ray owns 10% of the Yancey's single class of stock. What tax issues should X-Ray consider with respect to its dividend income?

C:3-29 Williams Corporation sold a truck with an adjusted basis of $100,000 to Barbara for $80,000. Barbara owns 25% of the Williams stock. What tax issues should Williams and Barbara consider with respect to the sale/purchase?

C:3-30 You are the CPA who prepares the tax returns for Don, his wife, Mary, and their two corporations. Don owns 100% of Pencil Corporation's stock. Pencil's current year taxable income is $100,000. Mary owns 100% of Eraser Corporation's stock. Eraser's current year taxable income is $150,000. Don and Mary file a joint federal income tax return. What issues should Don and Mary consider with respect to the calculation of the three tax return liabilities?

C:3-31 Rugby Corporation has a $50,000 NOL in the current year. Rugby's taxable income in each of the previous two years was $25,000. Rugby expects its taxable income for next year to exceed $400,000. What issues should Rugby consider with respect to the use of the NOL?

PROBLEMS

C:3-32 ***Depreciation Recapture.*** Young Corporation purchased residential real estate several year ago for $225,000, of which $25,000 was allocated to the land and $200,000 was allocated to the building. Young took straight-line MACRS deductions of $30,000 during the years it held the property. In the current year, Young sells the property for $285,000, of which $60,000 is allocated to the land and $225,000 is allocated to the building. What are the amount and character of Young's recognized gain or loss on the sale?

C:3-33 ***Depreciation Recapture, Sec. 1231, and Capital Gains and Losses.*** Gamma Corporation sold the following property on March 3 of the current year:

	Securities	*Equipment*	*Building*	*Land*
Selling price	$ 65,000	$210,000	$385,000	$175,000
Cost	$100,000	$200,000	$400,000	$190,000
Accumulated depreciation	–0–	(125,000)	(120,000)	–0–
Adjusted basis	$100,000	$ 75,000	$280,000	$190,000
Gain (loss)	$ (35,000)	$135,000	$105,000	$(15,000)

The corporation used the equipment, building, and land in its business and has held all the property for more than one year. Aside from these transactions, Alpha had $720,000 of operating net income during the current year. Gamma has a $24,000 nonrecaptured Sec. 1231 loss from prior years. Determine the character of the gains and losses, and calculate the corporation's taxable income. Ignore the U.S. production activities deduction.

C:3-34 ***Organizational and Start-up Expenditures.*** Delta Corporation incorporates on January 7, begins business on July 10, and elects to have its initial tax year end on October 31. Delta incurs the following expenses between January and October related to its organization during the current year:

Date	*Expenditure*	*Amount*
January 30	Travel to investigate potential business site	$2,000
May 15	Legal expenses to draft corporate charter	2,500
May 30	Commissions to stockbroker for issuing and selling stock	4,000
May 30	Temporary directors' fees	2,500
June 1	Expense of transferring building to Delta	3,000
June 5	Accounting fees to set up corporate books	1,500
June 10	Training expenses for employees	5,000
June 15	Rent expense for June	1,000
July 15	Rent expense for July	1,000

a. What alternative treatments are available for Delta's expenditures?
b. What amount of organizational expenditures can Delta Corporation deduct on its first tax return for the fiscal year ending October 31?
c. What amount of start-up costs can Delta Corporation deduct on its first tax return?

C:3-35 ***Charitable Contribution of Property.*** Yellow Corporation donates the following property to the State University:

- ABC Corporation stock purchased two years ago for $18,000. The stock, which trades on a regional stock exchange, has a $25,000 FMV on the contribution date.
- Inventory with a $17,000 adjusted basis and a $22,000 FMV. State will use the inventory for scientific research that qualifies under the special Sec. 170(e)(4) rules.
- An antique vase purchased two years ago for $10,000 and having an $18,000 FMV. State University plans to sell the vase to obtain funds for educational purposes.

Yellow Corporation's taxable income before any charitable contributions deduction, NOL or capital loss carryback, or dividends-received deduction is $250,000.
a. What is Yellow Corporation's charitable contributions deduction for the current year?
b. What is the amount of its charitable contributions carryover (if any)?

C:3-36 ***Charitable Contributions of Property.*** Blue Corporation donates the following property to Johnson Elementary School:

- XYZ Corporation stock purchased two years ago for $25,000. The stock has a $19,000 FMV on the contribution date.
- ABC Corporation stock purchased three years ago for $2,000. The stock has a $16,000 FMV on the contribution date.
- PQR Corporation stock purchased six months ago for $12,000. The stock has an $18,000 FMV on the contribution date.

The school will sell the stock and use the proceeds to renovate a classroom to be used as a computer laboratory. Blue's taxable income before any charitable contribution deduction, dividends-received deduction, or NOL or capital loss carryback is $400,000.

a. What is Blue's charitable contributions deduction for the current year?
b. What is Blue's charitable contribution carryback or carryover (if any)? In what years can it be used?
c. What would have been a better tax plan concerning the XYZ stock donation?

C:3-37 ***Charitable Contribution Deduction Limitation.*** Zeta Corporation reports the following results for Year 1 and Year 2:

	Year 1	*Year 2*
Adjusted taxable income	$180,000	$125,000
Charitable contributions (cash)	20,000	12,000

The adjusted taxable income is before Zeta claims any charitable contributions deduction, NOL or capital loss carryback, dividends-received deduction, or U.S. production activities deduction.

a. How much is Zeta's charitable contributions deduction in Year 1? In Year 2?
b. What is Zeta's contribution carryover to Year 3, if any?

C:3-38 ***Taxable Income Computation.*** Omega Corporation reports the following results for the current year:

Gross profits on sales	$120,000
Dividends from less-than-20%-owned domestic corporations	40,000
Operating expenses	100,000
Charitable contributions (cash)	11,000

a. What is Omega's charitable contributions deduction for the current year and its charitable contributions carryover to next year, if any?
b. What is Omega's taxable income for the current year, assuming qualified production activities income is $20,000?

C:3-39 ***Dividends-Received Deduction.*** Theta Corporation reports the following results for the current year:

Gross profits on sales	$220,000
Dividends from less-than-20%-owned domestic corporations	100,000
Operating expenses	218,000

a. What is Theta's taxable income for the current year, assuming qualified production activities income is $2,000?
b. How would your answer to Part a change if Theta's operating expenses are instead $234,000, assuming qualified production activities income is zero or negative?
c. How would your answer to Part a change if Theta's operating expenses are instead $252,000, assuming qualified production activities income is zero or negative?
d. How would your answers to Parts a, b, and c change if Theta received $75,000 of the dividends from a 20%-owned corporation and the remaining $25,000 from a less-than-20%-owned corporation?

C:3-40 ***Stock Held 45 Days or Less.*** Beta Corporation purchased 100 shares of Gamma Corporation common stock (less than 5% of the outstanding stock) two days before the ex-dividend date for $200,000. Beta receives a $10,000 cash dividend from Gamma. Beta sells the Gamma stock one week after purchasing it for $190,000. What are the tax consequences of these three events?

C:3-41 ***Debt-financed Stock.*** Cheers Corporation purchased for $500,000 5,000 shares of Beer Corporation common stock (less than 5% of the outstanding Beer stock) at the beginning of the current year. It used $400,000 of borrowed money and $100,000 of its own cash to make this purchase. Cheers paid $50,000 of interest on the debt this year. Cheers received a $40,000 cash dividend on the Beer stock on September 1 of the current year.

a. What amount can Cheers deduct for the interest paid on the loan?

b. What dividends-received deduction can Cheers claim with respect to the dividend?

C:3-42 ***Net Operating Loss Carrybacks and Carryovers.*** In 2015, Ace Corporation reports gross income of $200,000 (including $150,000 of profit from its operations and $50,000 in dividends from less-than-20%-owned domestic corporations) and $220,000 of operating expenses. Ace's 2013 taxable income (all ordinary income) was $75,000, on which it paid taxes of $13,750.

a. What is Ace's NOL for 2015?

b. What is the amount of Ace's tax refund if Ace carries back the 2015 NOL to 2013?

c. Assume that Ace expects 2016's taxable income to be $400,000. Ignore the U.S. production activities deduction. What election could Ace make to increase the tax benefit from its NOL? What is the dollar amount of the expected benefit (if any)? Assume a 10% discount rate as a measure of the time value of money.

C:3-43 ***Ordering of Deductions.*** Beta Corporation reports the following results for the current year:

Gross income from operations	$180,000
Dividends from less-than-20%-owned domestic corporations	100,000
Operating expenses	150,000
Charitable contributions	20,000

In addition, Beta has a $50,000 NOL carryover from the preceding tax year, and its qualified production activities income is $30,000.

a. What is Beta's taxable income for the current year?

b. What carrybacks or carryovers are available to other tax years?

C:3-44 ***Sale to a Related Party.*** Union Corporation sells a truck for $18,000 to Jane, who owns 70% of its stock. The truck has a $24,000 adjusted basis on the sale date. Jane sells the truck to an unrelated party, Mike, for $28,000 two years later after claiming $5,000 in depreciation.

a. What is Union's realized and recognized gain or loss on selling the truck?

b. What is Jane's realized and recognized gain or loss on selling the truck to Mike?

c. How would your answers to Part b change if Jane instead sold the truck for $10,000?

C:3-45 ***Payment to a Cash Basis Employee-Shareholder.*** Value Corporation is a calendar year taxpayer that uses the accrual method of accounting. On December 10 of the current year, Value accrues a bonus payment of $100,000 to Brett, its president and sole shareholder. Brett is a calendar year taxpayer who uses the cash method of accounting.

a. When can Value deduct the bonus if it pays it to Brett on March 11 of next year? On March 18 of next year?

b. How would your answers to Part a change if Brett were an employee of Value who owns no stock in the corporation?

C:3-46 ***Capital Gains and Losses.*** Western Corporation reports the following results for the current year:

Gross profits on sales	$150,000
Long-term capital gain	8,000
Long-term capital loss	15,000
Short-term capital gain	10,000
Short-term capital loss	2,000
Operating expenses	61,000

a. What are Western's taxable income and income tax liability for the current year, assuming qualified production activities income is $89,000?

b. How would your answers to Part a change if Western's short-term capital loss is $5,000 instead of $2,000?

C:3-47 ***Corporate Taxable Income and Tax Liability.*** Alpha Corporation has been in business for two years. It incurred the following items last year (Year 1):

Gross profits on sales	$240,000
Operating expenses	100,000
Long-term capital gain	8,000
Short-term capital loss	12,000

Omega reported the following items this year (Year 2):

Gross profits on sales	$600,000
Operating expenses	165,000
Long-term capital gain	10,000

Assume that qualified production activities income in each year equals gross profit minus operating expenses. Compute Alpha's taxable income and tax liability for Year 1 and Year 2.

C:3-48 ***Computing the Corporate Income Tax Liability.*** What is Beta Corporation's income tax liability assuming its taxable income is (a) $94,000, (b) $300,000, and (c) $600,000. How would your answers change if Beta were a personal service corporation?

C:3-49 ***Computing the Corporate Income Tax Liability.*** Fawn Corporation, a C corporation, paid no dividends and recognized no capital gains or losses in the current year. What is its income tax liability assuming its taxable income for the year is

a. $50,000
b. $14,000,000
c. $18,000,000
d. $34,000,000

C:3-50 ***Computing Taxable Income and Income Tax Liability.*** Pace Corporation reports the following results for the current year:

Gross profit on sales	$120,000
Long-term capital loss	10,000
Short-term capital loss	5,000
Dividends from 40%-owned domestic corporation	30,000
Operating expenses	65,000
Charitable contributions	10,000

a. What are Pace's taxable income and income tax liability, assuming qualified production activities income is $55,000?
b. What carrybacks and carryovers (if any) are available and to what years must they be carried?

C:3-51 ***Computing Taxable Income and Income Tax Liability.*** Roper Corporation reports the following results for the current year:

Gross profits on sales	$80,000
Short-term capital gain	40,000
Long-term capital gain	25,000
Dividends from 25%-owned domestic corporation	15,000
NOL carryover from the preceding tax year	9,000
Operating expenses	45,000

What are Roper's taxable income and income tax liability, assuming qualified production activities income is $35,000?

C:3-52 ***Controlled Groups.*** Which of the following groups constitute controlled groups? (Any stock not listed below is held by unrelated individuals each owning less than 1% of the outstanding stock.) For brother-sister corporations, which definition applies?

a. Judy owns 100% of the single classes of stock of Hot and Ice Corporations.
b. Jones and Kane Corporations each have only a single class of stock outstanding. The two controlling individual shareholders own the stock as follows:

	Stock Ownership Percentages	
Shareholder	*Jones Corp.*	*Kane Corp.*
Tom	60%	100%
Mary	40%	

c. Link, Model, and Name Corporations each have a single class of stock outstanding. The stock is owned as follows:

	Stock Ownership Percentages	
Shareholder	*Model Corp.*	*Name Corp.*
Link Corp.	80%	50%
Model Corp.		40%
Unrelated individuals	20%	10%

Link Corporation's stock is widely held by over 1,000 shareholders, none of whom owns directly or indirectly more than 1% of Link's stock.

d. Oat, Peach, Rye, and Seed Corporations each have a single class of stock outstanding. The stock is owned as follows:

	Stock Ownership Percentages			
Shareholder	*Oat Corp.*	*Peach Corp.*	*Rye Corp.*	*Seed Corp.*
Bob	100%	90%		
Oat Corp.			80%	30%
Rye Corp.				60%
Unrelated individuals		10%	20%	10%

C:3-53 ***Controlled Groups of Corporations.*** Sally owns 100% of the outstanding stock of Eta, Theta, Phi, and Gamma Corporations, each of which files a separate return for the current year. During the current year, the corporations report taxable income as follows:

Corporation	*Taxable Income*
Eta	$40,000
Theta	(25,000)
Phi	50,000
Gamma	10,000

a. What is each corporation's separate tax liability, assuming the corporations do not elect a special apportionment plan for allocating the corporate tax rates?

b. What is each corporation's separate tax liability, assuming the corporations make a special election to apportion the reduced corporate tax rates in such a way that minimizes the group's total tax liability? Note: More than one plan can satisfy this goal.

c. How does the result in Part b change if Gamma's income is $30,000 instead of $10,000?

C:3-54 ***Compensation Planning.*** Marilyn owns all of Bell Corporation's stock. Bell is a C corporation and employs 40 people. Marilyn is married, has two dependent children, and files a joint tax return with her husband. She projects that Bell will report $400,000 of pretax profits for the current year. Marilyn is considering five salary levels as shown below. Ignore the U.S. production activities deduction for this problem.

			Tax Liability		
Total Income	*Salary Paid to Marilyn*	*Earnings Retained by Bell Corporation*	*Marilyn*	*Bell Corporation*	*Total*
$300,000	$ -0-	$300,000			
300,000	$100,000	200,000			
300,000	200,000	100,000			
300,000	400,000	-0-			

a. Determine the total tax liability for Marilyn and Bell for each of the four proposed salary levels. Assume no other income for Marilyn's family, and assume that Marilyn and her husband claim a combined itemized deduction and personal exemption of $30,000. Ignore employment taxes.

b. What recommendations can you make about a salary level for Marilyn that will minimize the total tax liability? Assume salaries paid up to $300,000 are considered reasonable compensation.

c. What is the possible disadvantage to Marilyn if Bell retains funds in the business and distributes some of the accumulated earnings as a dividend in a later tax year?

C:3-55 ***Fringe Benefits.*** Refer to the facts in Problem C:3-54. Marilyn has read an article explaining the advantages of paying nontaxable fringe benefits (premiums on group term life insurance, accident and health insurance, etc.) and having deferred compensation plans (e.g., qualified pension and profit-sharing plans). Provide Marilyn with information on the tax savings associated with converting $3,000 of her salary into nontaxable fringe benefits. What additional costs might Bell Corporation incur if it adopts a fringe benefit plan?

C:3-56 ***Estimated Tax Requirement.*** Zeta Corporation's taxable income for 2014 was $1.5 million, on which Zeta paid federal income taxes of $510,000. Zeta estimates calendar year 2015's taxable income to be $2 million, on which it will owe $680,000 in federal income taxes.

a. What are Zeta's minimum quarterly estimated tax payments for 2015 to avoid an underpayment penalty?

b. When is Zeta's 2015 tax return due?

c. When are any remaining taxes due? What amount of taxes are due when Zeta files its return assuming Zeta timely pays estimated tax payments equal to the amount determined in Part a?

d. If Zeta obtains an extension to file, when is its tax return due? Will the extension permit Zeta to delay making its final tax payments?

C:3-57 ***Filing the Tax Return and Paying the Tax Liability.*** Wright Corporation's taxable income for calendar years 2012, 2013, and 2014 was $120,000, $150,000, and $100,000, respectively. Its total tax liability for 2014 was $22,250. Wright estimates that its 2015 taxable income will be $500,000, on which it will owe federal income taxes of $170,000. Assume Wright earns its 2015 taxable income evenly throughout the year.

a. What are Wright's minimum quarterly estimated tax payments for 2015 to avoid an underpayment penalty?

b. When is Wright's 2015 tax return due?

c. When are any remaining taxes due? What amount of taxes are due when Wright files its return assuming it timely paid estimated tax payments equal to the amount determined in Part a?

d. How would your answer to Part a change if Wright's tax liability for 2014 had been $200,000?

C:3-58 ***Converting Book Income to Taxable Income.*** The following income and expense accounts appeared in the book accounting records of Rocket Corporation, an accrual basis taxpayer, for the current calendar year.

	Book Income	
Account Title	*Debit*	*Credit*
Net sales		$3,230,000
Dividends		10,000 (1)
Interest		18,000 (2)
Gain on sale of stock		9,000 (3)
Key-person life insurance proceeds		100,000
Cost of goods sold	$2,000,000	
Salaries and wages	500,000	
Bad debts	13,000 (4)	
Payroll taxes	62,000	
Interest expense	12,000 (5)	
Charitable contributions	50,000 (6)	
Depreciation	70,000 (7)	
Other expenses	40,000 (8)	
Federal income taxes	166,000	
Net income	454,000	
Total	$3,367,000	$3,367,000

The following additional information applies.

1. Dividends were from Star Corporation, a 30%-owned domestic corporation.
2. Interest revenue consists of interest on corporate bonds, $15,000; and municipal bonds, $3,000.
3. The stock is a capital asset held for three years prior to sale.
4. Rocket uses the specific writeoff method of accounting for bad debts.
5. Interest expense consists of $11,000 interest incurred on funds borrowed for working capital and $1,000 interest on funds borrowed to purchase municipal bonds.
6. Rocket paid all contributions in cash during the current year to State University.
7. Rocket calculated depreciation per books using the straight-line method. For income tax purposes, depreciation amounted to $95,000.
8. Other expenses include premiums of $5,000 on the key-person life insurance policy covering Rocket's president, who died in December.
9. Qualified production activities income is $300,000.
10. Rocket has a $90,000 NOL carryover from prior years.

Required:

a. Prepare a worksheet reconciling Rocket's book income with its taxable income (before special deductions). Six columns should be used—two (one debit and one credit) for each of the following three major headings: book income, Schedule M-1 adjustments, and taxable income. (See the sample worksheet with Form 1120 in Appendix B if you need assistance).

b. Prepare a tax provision reconciliation as in Step 9 of the Tax Provision Process. Assume a 34% corporate tax rate.

C:3-59 ***Reconciling Book Income and Taxable Income.*** Omega Corporation reports the following results for the current year:

Net income per books (before federal income taxes)	$738,000
Federal income tax expense per books	(231,540)
Net income per books (after federal income taxes)	$506,460
Tax-exempt interest income	10,000
Interest on loan to purchase tax-exempt bonds	7,000
MACRS depreciation exceeding book depreciation	40,000
Net capital loss	8,000
Insurance premium on life of corporate officer where Omega is the beneficiary	9,000
Excess charitable contributions carried over to next year	4,000
U.S. production activities deduction ($700.0000 × 0.09)*	63,000

* Assume that qualified production activities income is $700,000.

a. Prepare a reconciliation of Omega's taxable income before special deductions with its book income.

b. Prepare a tax provision reconciliation as in Step 9 of the Tax Provision Process.

C:3-60 ***Reconciling Unappropriated Retained Earnings.*** White Corporation's financial accounting records disclose the following results for the period ending December 31 of the current year:

Retained earnings balance on January 1	$246,500
Net income for year	259,574
Contingency reserve established on December 31	60,000
Cash dividend paid on July 23	23,000

What is White's unappropriated retained earnings balance on December 31 of the current year?

C:3-61 ***Tax Reconciliation Process.*** Omega Corporation, a regular C corporation, presents you with the following partial *book* income statement for the current year:

Sales	$1,900,000	
Cost of goods sold	(1,100,000)	
Gross profit		$800,000
Operating expenses:		
Depreciation	$ 80,000	
Interest expense	18,000	
Warranty expense	12,000	
Fines and penalties	10,000	
Other business expenses	220,000	(340,000)
Net operating income		$460,000
Other income (losses):		
Interest received on municipal bonds	$ 1,000	
Income on installment sale	9,000	
Net losses on stock sales	(20,000)	(10,000)
Net income before federal income taxes		$450,000

Omega also provides the following partial balance sheet information:

	Book		*Tax*	
	Beg. of Year	*End of Year*	*Beg. of Year*	*End of Year*
Installment note receivable	$ –0–	$ 30,000	$ –0–	$ 30,000
Minus: Unrecognized income on note	–0–	–0–	–0–	(9,000)
Net basis of note receivable	–0–	30,000	–0–	21,000
Tax-exempt bonds	18,000	18,000	18,000	18,000
Current deferred asset	5,100	?	–0–	–0–
Investment stocks	100,000	40,000	100,000	40,000

Fixed assets	400,000	400,000	400,000	400,000
Minus: Accumulated depreciation	(40,000)	(120,000)	(80,000)	(208,000)
Net basis of fixed assets	360,000	280,000	320,000	192,000
Liability for warranties	–0–	12,000	–0–	–0–
Noncurrent deferred tax liability	13,600	?	–0–	–0–

You have gathered the following additional information:

1. Depreciation for tax purposes is $128,000.
2. Of the $18,000 interest expense, $2,000 is allocable to a loan used to purchase the municipal bonds.
3. The warranty expense is an estimated amount for book purposes. Omega expects actual claims on these warranties to be filed and paid next year.
4. Your research determines that the fines and penalties are not deductible for tax purposes.
5. In the current year, Omega sold property using the installment method as follows:

Selling price	$30,000
Adjusted basis	(21,000)
Gain	$9,000

Omega obtains a $30,000 installment note receivable this year and will receive the $30,000 sales proceeds next year. For book purposes, Omega recognizes the $9,000 gain in the current year. For tax purposes, Omega will recognize the $9,000 gain next year when it receives the $30,000 sales proceeds.

6. Omega sold a significant portion of its stock portfolio in the current year. The $20,000 net loss per books from these stock sales includes the following components:

Long-term capital gain	$15,000
Long-term capital loss	(38,000)
Short-term capital gain	3,000

Omega had no capital gains in prior years, so it cannot carry the net capital losses back.

7. Omega does not expect to realize capital gains next year, but it does expect sufficient capital gains within the next five years so that it can use the capital loss carryover before it expires. Thus, Omega determines that it needs no valuation allowance.
8. Omega has a $15,000 net operating loss carryover from last year, which it then expected to use in the next year (now the current year).
9. Qualified production activities income for the current year equals $300,000, which is less than taxable income before the U.S. production activities deduction. The applicable percentage is 9%.
10. Omega's tax rate is 34% and will remain so in future years.
11. The beginning deferred tax asset pertains to the NOL carryover, and the beginning deferred tax liability pertains to fixed assets. Other deferred tax assets and deferred tax liabilities may arise in the current year.
12. Omega determines that it needs no adjustment for uncertain tax positions.

Required: Perform the tax provision process steps as outlined in the text. For Step 11, just present partial income statement and balance sheet disclosures as allowed by the given facts.

C:3-62 *Valuation Allowance.* In the current year, Alpha Corporation generated $500,000 of ordinary operating income and incurred a $20,000 capital loss on the sale of marketable securities from its investment portfolio. Alpha expects to generate $500,000 of ordinary operating income in each of the next five years. Alpha incurred no capital gains in its previous three years, so it must carry over the $20,000 capital loss for up to five years. Alpha estimates that its remaining marketable securities would produce a $12,000 capital gain if sold. Thus, Alpha determines that, more likely than not, the corporation will not realize (deduct) $8,000 of the current year capital loss. Alpha has no other book-tax differences and is subject to a 34% tax rate.

Required:

a. Determine Alpha's deferred tax asset and valuation allowance for the current year.
b. Determine Alpha's current federal income tax expense, deferred federal income tax expense (benefit), total federal income tax expense, and federal income taxes payable.

c. Prepare the journal entry necessary to record the above amounts.
d. Prepare a tax provision reconciliation and effective tax rate reconciliation for the current year.

C:3-63 *Uncertain Tax Positions.* In the current year, Kappa Corporation earned $1 million of net income before federal income taxes. This amount of book income includes a $100,000 expense for what the company considers an ordinary and necessary business expense. Kappa also deducted the entire $100,000 for tax purposes. In assessing the expense for its tax provision, Kappa determines that it has a more-likely-than-not probability of sustaining some portion of the deduction upon an IRS examination. However, some uncertainty remains as to whether the entire amount is deductible. Any amount ultimately disallowed by the IRS would be a permanent disallowance and not merely a temporary item that could be amortized over time. Upon further analysis, Kappa measures the benefit that is more than 50% likely to be realized as $70,000. Thus, Kappa may not recognize $30,000 of the expense in determining its federal income tax provision. In addition, Kappa has a $25,000 temporary difference that decreases its taxable income to $975,000 and increases its deferred tax liability.

Required:
a. Determine Kappa's liability for unrecognized tax benefits, total federal income tax expense, deferred federal income tax expense, current federal income tax expense, increase in deferred tax liability, and federal income taxes payable.
b. Prepare the journal entry necessary to record the current year tax provision.

COMPREHENSIVE PROBLEM

C:3-64 Jackson Corporation prepared the following *book* income statement for its year ended December 31, 2015:

Sales			$950,000
Minus:	Cost of goods sold		(450,000)
Gross profit			$500,000
Plus:	Dividends received on Invest Corporation stock	$ 3,000	
	Gain on sale of Invest Corporation stock	30,000	
	Total dividends and gain		33,000
Minus:	Depreciation ($7,500 + $52,000)	$ 59,500	
	Bad debt expense	22,000	
	Other operating expenses	105,500	
	Loss on sale of Equipment 1	70,000	
	Total expenses and loss		(257,000)
Net income per books before taxes			$276,000
Minus:	Federal income tax expense		(90,000)
Net income per books			$ 186,000

Information on equipment depreciation and sale:

Equipment 1:

- Acquired March 3, 2013 for $180,000
- For books: 12-year life; straight-line depreciation
- Sold February 17, 2015 for $80,000

Sales price				$ 80,000
Cost			$180,000	
Minus:	Depreciation for 2013 (½ year)	$ 7,500		
	Depreciation for 2014 ($180,000/12)	15,000		
	Depreciation for 2015 (½ year)	7,500		
	Total book depreciation		(30,000)	
Book value at time of sale				(150,000)
Book loss on sale of Equipment 1				$(70,000)

- For tax: Seven-year MACRS property for which the corporation made no Sec. 179 election in the acquisition year and elected out of bonus depreciation.

Equipment 2:

- Acquired February 16, 2014 for $624,000
- For books: 12-year life; straight-line depreciation
- Book depreciation in 2015: $624,000/12 = $52,000
- For tax: Seven-year MACRS property for which the corporation made the Sec. 179 election in 2014 but elected out of bonus depreciation.

Other information:

- Under the direct writeoff method, Jackson deducts $15,000 of bad debts for tax purposes.
- Jackson has a $40,000 NOL carryover and a $6,000 capital loss carryover from last year.
- Jackson purchased the Invest Corporation stock (less than 20% owned) on June 21, 2013, for $25,000 and sold the stock on December 23, 2015, for $55,000.
- Jackson Corporation has qualified production activities income of $120,000.

Required:

a. For 2015, calculate Jackson's tax depreciation deduction for Equipment 1 and Equipment 2, and determine the tax loss on the sale of Equipment 1.
b. For 2015, calculate Jackson's taxable income and tax liability.
c. Prepare a schedule reconciling net income per books to taxable income before special deductions (Form 1120, line 28).

TAX STRATEGY PROBLEM

C:3-65 Mike Barton owns Barton Products, Inc. The corporation has 30 employees. Barton Corporation expects $800,000 of net income before taxes in 2015. Mike is married and files a joint return with his wife, Elaine, who has no earnings of her own. They have one dependent son, Robert, who is 16 years old. Mike and Elaine have no other income and do not itemize. Mike's salary is $180,000 per year (already deducted in computing Barton Corporation's $800,000 net income). Assume that variations in salaries will not affect the U.S. production activities deduction already reflected in taxable income.

a. Should Mike increase his salary from Barton by $50,000 to reduce the overall tax burden to himself and Barton Products? Because of the Social Security cap, the corporation and Mike each would incur a 1.45% payroll tax with the corporate portion being deductible.
b. Should Barton employ Mike's wife Elaine for $50,000 rather than increase Mike's salary? Take into consideration employment taxes as well as federal income taxes. Note, that Elaine's salary would be well below the Social Security cap, so that she and the corporation each would incur the full amount of payroll taxes with the corporate portion being deductible. Both Elaine's and the corporation's portion is 7.65%.

TAX FORM/RETURN PREPARATION PROBLEMS

C:3-66 Melodic Musical Sales, Inc. is located at 5500 Fourth Avenue, City, ST 98765. The corporation uses the calendar year and accrual basis for both book and tax purposes. It is engaged in the sale of musical instruments with an employer identification number (EIN) of XX-2016014. The company incorporated on December 31, 2010, and began business on January 2, 2011. Table C:3-4 contains balance sheet information at January 1, 2014, and December 31, 2014. Table C:3-5 presents an income statement for 2014. These schedules are presented on a book basis. Other information follows the tables.

Estimated Tax Payments (Form 2220):
The corporation deposited estimated tax payments as follows:

April 15, 2014	$105,000
June 15, 2014	210,000
September 15, 2014	252,000
December 15, 2014	252,000
Total	$819,000

Although June 15 falls on a weekend, a deposit made on the next business day is considered made on the due date, June 15. Taxable income in 2013 was $1.5 million, and the

▼ TABLE C:3-4
Melodic Musical Sales, Inc.—Book Balance Sheet Information

Account	January 1, 2014 Debit	January 1, 2014 Credit	December 31, 2014 Debit	December 31, 2014 Credit
Cash	$ 242,794		$ 433,399	
Accounts receivable	360,000		450,000	
Allowance for doubtful accounts		$ 18,000		$ 22,500
Inventory	2,250,000		3,150,000	
Investment in corporate stock	285,000		50,000	
Investment in municipal bonds	32,000		32,000	
Net current deferred tax asset	12,920		7,650	
Cash surrender value of insurance policy	50,000		70,000	
Land	250,000		250,000	
Buildings	1,500,000		1,500,000	
Accumulated depreciation—Buildings		75,000		105,000
Equipment	1,200,000		2,400,000	
Accumulated depreciation—Equipment		200,000		266,667
Trucks	200,000		200,000	
Accumulated depreciation—Trucks		60,000		100,000
Accounts payable		320,000		288,000
Notes payable (short-term)		600,000		480,000
Accrued payroll taxes		13,500		16,875
Accrued state income taxes		8,100		13,500
Accrued federal income taxes		-0-		110,866
Bonds payable (long-term)		2,200,000		2,200,000
Net noncurrent deferred tax liability		188,114		308,713
Capital stock—Common		900,000		900,000
Retain earnings—Unappropriated		1,800,000		3,730,928
Totals	$6,382,714	$6,382,714	$8,543,049	$8,543,049

2013 tax was $510,000. The corporation earned its 2014 taxable income evenly throughout the year. Therefore, it does not use the annualization or seasonal methods.

Inventory and Cost of Goods Sold (Form 1125-A):
The corporation uses the periodic inventory method and prices its inventory using the lower of FIFO cost or market. Only beginning inventory, ending inventory, and purchases should be reflected on Form 1125-A. No other costs or expenses are allocated to cost of goods sold. Note: the corporation is exempt from the uniform capitalization (UNICAP) rules because average gross income for the previous three years was less than $10 million.

Line 9 (a)	Check (ii)
(b), (c) & (d)	Not applicable
(e) & (f)	No

Compensation of Officers (Form 1125-E):

(a)	(b)	(c)	(d)	(f)
Mary Travis	XXX-XX-XXXX	100%	50%	$265,000
John Willis	XXX-XX-XXXX	100%	25%	160,000
Chris Parker	XXX-XX-XXXX	100%	25%	160,000
Total				$585,000

Bad Debts:
For tax purposes, the corporation uses the direct writeoff method of deducting bad debts. For book purposes, the corporation uses an allowance for doubtful accounts. During 2014, the corporation charged $36,000 to the allowance account, such amount representing actual writeoffs for 2014.

▼ TABLE C:3-5

Melodic Musical Sales, Inc.—Book Income Statement 2014

Sales		$ 9,000,000
Returns		(225,000)
Net sales		$ 8,775,000
Beginning inventory	$2,250,000	
Purchases	4,950,000	
Ending inventory	(3,150,000)	
Cost of goods sold		(4,050,000)
Gross profit		$ 4,725,000
Expenses:		
Amortization	$ -0-	
Depreciation	216,667	
Repairs	18,720	
General insurance	49,500	
Net premium-Officers' life insurance	40,500	
Officers' compensation	585,000	
Other salaries	360,000	
Utilities	64,800	
Advertising	43,200	
Legal and accounting fees	45,000	
Charitable contributions	27,000	
Payroll taxes	56,250	
Interest expense	189,000	
Bad debt expense	40,500	
Total expenses		(1,736,137)
Gain on sale of equipment		105,000
Interest on municipal bonds		4,500
Net gain on stock sales		35,000
Dividend income		10,800
Net income before income taxes		$ 3,144,163
Federal income tax expense		(1,055,735)
State income tax expense		(67,500)
Net income		$ 2,020,928

Additional Information (Schedule K):

1 b	Accrual	8	Do not check box
2 a	451140	9	Fill in the correct amount
b	Retail sales	10	3
c	Musical instruments	11	Do not check box
3	No	12	Not applicable
4 a	No	13-14	No
b	Yes; omit Schedule G		
5 a	No	15a	No
b	No	b	Not applicable
6-7	No	16-18	No

Organizational Expenditures:
The corporation incurred $11,000 of organizational expenditures on January 2, 2010. For book purposes, the corporation expensed the entire expenditure. For tax purposes, the corporation elected under Sec. 248 to deduct $5,000 in 2011 and amortize the remaining $6,000 amount over 180 months, with a full month's amortization taken for January 2011. The corporation reports this amortization in Part VI of Form 4562 and includes it in "Other Deductions" on Form 1120, Line 26.

Capital Gains and Losses:
The corporation sold 100 shares of PDQ Corp. common stock on October 7, 2014, for $150,000. The corporation acquired the stock on December 16, 2013, for $100,000. The corporation also sold 75 shares of JSB Corp. common stock on June 17, 2014, for $120,000. The corporation acquired this stock on September 18, 2012, for $135,000. The corporation has a $20,000 capital loss carryover from 2013. These transactions were not reported to the corporation on Form 1099-B.

Fixed Assets and Depreciation:
For book purposes: The corporation uses straight-line depreciation over the useful lives of assets as follows: Store building, 50 years; Equipment, 15 years (old) and ten years (new); and Trucks, five years. The corporation takes a half-year's depreciation in the year of acquisition and the year of disposition and assumes no salvage value. The book financial statements in Tables C:3-4 and C:3-5 reflect these calculations.

For tax purposes: All assets are MACRS property as follows: Store building, 39-year nonresidential real property; equipment, seven-year property; and trucks, five-year property. The corporation acquired the store building for $1.5 million and placed it in service on January 2, 2011. The corporation acquired two pieces of equipment for $400,000 (Equipment 1) and $800,000 (Equipment 2) and placed them in service on January 2, 2011. The corporation acquired the trucks for $200,000 and placed them in service on July 18, 2012. The trucks are not listed property and are not subject to the limitation on luxury automobiles. The corporation did not make the expensing election under Sec. 179 or take bonus depreciation on any property acquired before 2014. Accumulated tax depreciation through December 31, 2013, on these properties is as follows:

Store building	$113,835
Equipment 1	225,080
Equipment 2	450,160
Trucks	104,000

On October 16, 2014, the corporation sold for $425,000 Equipment 1 that originally cost 400,000 on January 2, 2011. The corporation had no Sec. 1231 losses from prior years. In a separate transaction on October 17, 2014, the corporation acquired and placed in service a piece of equipment costing $1.6 million. Assume these two transactions do not qualify as a like-kind exchange. The new equipment is seven-year property. The corporation made the Sec. 179 expensing election with regard to the new equipment but elected out of bonus depreciation. Where applicable, use published IRS depreciation tables to compute 2014 depreciation (reproduced in Appendix C of this text).

Other Information:

- The corporation's activities do not qualify for the U.S. production activities deduction.
- Ignore the AMT and accumulated earnings tax.
- The corporation received dividends (see Income Statement in Table C:3-5) from taxable, domestic corporations, the stock of which Melodic Musical Sales, Inc. owns less than 20%.
- The corporation paid $90,000 in cash dividends to its shareholders during the year and charged the payment directly to retained earnings.
- The state income tax in Table C:3-5 is the exact amount of such taxes incurred during the year.
- The corporation is not entitled any credits.
- Ignore the financial statement impact of any underpayment penalties incurred on the tax return.

Required: Prepare the 2014 corporate tax return for Melodic Musical Sales, Inc. along with any necessary supporting schedules.

Optional: Prepare both Schedule M-3 (but omit Schedule B and Form 8916-A) and Schedule M-1 even though the IRS does not require both Schedule M-1 and Schedule M-3.

Note to Instructor: See solution in the Instructor's Guide for other optional information to provide to students.

C:3-67 Permtemp Corporation formed in 2013 and, for that year, reported the following book income statement and balance sheet, excluding the federal income tax expense, deferred tax assets, and deferred tax liabilities:

Sales		$20,000,000
Cost of goods sold		(15,000,000)
Gross profit		$ 5,000,000
Dividend income		50,000
Tax-exempt interest income		15,000
Total income		$ 5,065,000
Expenses:		
Depreciation	$ 800,000	
Bad debts	400,000	
Charitable contributions	100,000	
Interest	475,000	
Meals and entertainment	45,000	
Other	3,855,000	
Total expenses		(5,675,000)
Net loss before federal income taxes		$ (610,000)
Cash		$ 500,000
Accounts receivable	$ 2,000,000	
Allowance for doubtful accounts	(250,000)	1,750,000
Inventory		4,000,000
Fixed assets	$10,000,000	
Accumulated depreciation	(800,000)	9,200,000
Investment in corporate stock		1,000,000
Investment in tax-exempt bonds		50,000
Total assets		$16,500,000
Accounts payable		$2,610,000
Long-term debt		8,500,000
Common stock		6,000,000
Retained earnings		(610,000)
Total liabilities and equity		$16,500,000

Additional information for 2013:

- The investment in corporate stock is comprised of less-than-20%-owned corporations.
- Depreciation for tax purposes is $1.4 million under MACRS.
- Bad debt expense for tax purposes is $150,000 under the direct writeoff method.
- Limitations to charitable contribution deductions and meals and entertainment expenses must be tested and applied if necessary.
- Qualified production activities income is zero.

Required for 2013:

a. Prepare page 1 of the 2013 Form 1120, computing the corporation's NOL.
b. Determine the corporation's deferred tax asset and deferred tax liability situation, and then complete the income statement and balance sheet to reflect proper GAAP accounting under ASC 740. Use the balance sheet information to prepare Schedule L of the 2013 Form 1120.
c. Prepare the 2013 Schedule M-3 for Form 1120.
d. Prepare a schedule that reconciles the corporation's effective tax rate to the statutory 34% tax rate.

Note: For 2013 forms, go to forms and publications, previous years, at the IRS website, *www.irs.gov*.

For 2014, Permtemp reported the following book income statement and balance sheet, excluding the federal income tax expense, deferred tax assets, and deferred tax liabilities:

Sales		$33,000,000
Cost of goods sold		(22,000,000)
Gross profit		$11,000,000
Dividend income		55,000
Tax-exempt interest income		15,000
Total income		$11,070,000
Expenses:		
Depreciation	$ 800,000	
Bad debts	625,000	
Charitable contributions	40,000	
Interest	455,000	
Meals and entertainment	60,000	
Other	4,675,000	
Total expenses		(6,655,000)
Net income before federal income taxes		$ 4,415,000

Cash		$ 2,125,000
Accounts receivable	$ 3,300,000	
Allowance for doubtful accounts	(450,000)	2,850,000
Inventory		6,000,000
Fixed assets	$10,000,000	
Accumulated depreciation	(1,600,000)	8,400,000
Investment in corporate stock		1,000,000
Investment in tax-exempt bonds		50,000
Total assets		$20,425,000
Accounts payable		$ 2,120,000
Long-term debt		8,500,000
Common stock		6,000,000
Retained earnings		3,805,000
		$20,425,000

Additional information for 2014:

- Depreciation for tax purposes is $2.45 million under MACRS.
- Bad debt expense for tax purposes is $425,000 under the direct writeoff method.
- Qualified production activities income is $3 million.

Required for 2014:

a. Prepare page 1 of the 2014 Form 1120, computing the corporation's taxable income and tax liability.

b. Determine the corporation's deferred tax asset and deferred tax liability situation, and then complete the income statement and balance sheet to reflect proper GAAP accounting ASC 740. Use the balance sheet information to prepare Schedule L of the 2014 Form 1120.

c. Prepare the 2014 Schedule M-3 for Form 1120.

d. Prepare a schedule that reconciles the corporation's effective tax rate to the statutory 34% tax rate.

CASE STUDY PROBLEMS

C:3-68 Marquette Corporation, a tax client since its creation three years ago, has requested that you prepare a memorandum explaining its estimated tax requirements for the current year. The corporation is in the fabricated steel business. Its earnings have been growing each year. Marquette's taxable income for the last three tax years has been $500,000, $1.5 million, and $2.5 million, respectively. The Chief Financial Officer expects its taxable income in the current year to be approximately $3 million.

Required: Prepare a one-page client memorandum explaining Marquette's estimated tax requirements for the current year, providing the necessary supporting authorities.

C:3-69 Susan Smith accepted a new corporate client, Winter Park Corporation. One of Susan's tax managers conducted a review of Winter Park's prior year tax returns. The review revealed that an NOL for a prior tax year was incorrectly computed, resulting in an overstatement of NOL carrybacks and carryovers to prior tax years. Apply the Statements on Standards for Tax Services (SSTSs) to the following situtations. The SSTSs are in Appendix E of this text.

a. Assume the incorrect NOL calculation does not affect the current year's tax liability. What recommendations (if any) should Susan make to the new client? See SSTS No. 6.

b. Assume the IRS is currently auditing a prior year. What are Susan's responsibilities in this situation? See SSTS No. 6.

c. Assume the NOL carryover is being carried to the current year, and Winter Park does not want to file amended tax returns to correct the error. What should Susan do in this situation? See SSTS No. 1.

C:3-70 The Chief Executive Officer of a client of your public accounting firm saw the following advertisement in a financial newspaper:

> DONATIONS WANTED
> The Center for Restoration of Waters
> A Nonprofit Research and Educational Organization
> Needs Donations—Autos, Boats, Real Estate, Etc.
> ALL DONATIONS ARE TAX-DEDUCTIBLE

Prepare a memorandum to your client Phil Nickelson explaining how the federal income tax laws regarding donations of cash, automobiles, boats, and real estate apply to corporate taxpayers.

TAX RESEARCH PROBLEMS

C:3-71 Wicker Corporation made estimated tax payments of $6,000 in Year 1. On March 12 of Year 2, it filed its Year 1 tax return showing a $20,000 tax liability, and it paid the $14,000 balance at that time. On April 20 of Year 2, it discovers an error and files an amended return for Year 1 showing a reduced tax liability of $8,000. Prepare a memorandum for your tax manager explaining whether Wicker can base its estimated tax payments for Year 2 on the amended $8,000 tax liability for Year 1, or whether it must use the $20,000 tax liability reported on its original Year 1 return. Your manager has suggested that, at a minimum, you consult the following resources:

- IRC Sec. 6655(d)(1)
- Rev. Rul. 86-58, 1986-1 C.B. 365

C:3-72 Alice, Bill, and Charles each received an equal number of shares when they formed King Corporation a number of years ago. King has used the cash method of accounting since its inception. Alice, Bill, and Charles, the shareholder-employees, operate King as an environmental engineering firm with 57 additional employees. King had gross receipts of $4.3 million last year. Gross receipts have grown by about 15% in each of the last three years and were just under $5 million in the current year. The owners expect the 15% growth rate to continue for at least five more years. Outstanding accounts receivable average about $600,000 at the end of each month. Forty-four employees (including Alice, Bill, and Charles) actively engage in providing engineering services on a full-time basis. The remaining 16 employees serve in a clerical and support capacity (secretarial staff, accountants, etc.). Bill has read about special restrictions on the use of the cash method of accounting and requests information from you about the impact these rules might have on King's continued use of that method. Prepare a memorandum for your tax manager addressing the following issues: (1) If the corporation changes to the accrual method of accounting, what adjustments must it make? (2) Would an S election relieve King from having to make a change? (3) If the S election relieves King from having to make a change, what factors should enter into the decision about whether King should make an S election?

Your manager has suggested that, at a minimum, you should consult the following resources:

- IRC Secs. 446 and 448
- Temp. Reg. Sec. 1.448-1T
- H. Rept. No. 99-841, 99th Cong., 2d Sess., pp. 285–289 (1986)

TAX & FINANCIAL ACCOUNTING

C:3-73 James Bowen owns 100% of Bowen Corporation stock. Bowen is a calendar year, accrual method taxpayer. During the current year, Bowen made three charitable contributions:

Donee	*Property Donated*	*FMV of Property*
State University	Bates Corporation stock	$110,000
Red Cross	Cash	5,000
Girl Scouts	Pledge to pay cash	25,000

Bowen purchased the Bates stock three years ago for $30,000. Bowen holds a 28% interest, which it accounts for under GAAP using the equity method of accounting. The current carrying value for the Bates stock for book purposes is $47,300. Bowen will pay the pledge to the Girl Scouts by check on March 3 of next year. Bowen's taxable income for the current year before the charitable contributions deduction, dividends-received deduction, NOL deduction, and U.S. production activities deduction is $600,000. Your tax manager has asked you to prepare a memorandum explaining how these transactions are to be treated for tax purposes and for accounting purposes. Your manager has suggested that, at a minimum, you should consult the following resources:

- IRC Sec. 170
- Accounting Standards Codification (ASC) 720

C:3-74 Production Corporation owns 70% of Manufacturing Corporation's common stock and Rita Howard owns the remaining 30%. Each corporation operates and sells its product within the United States, and the corporations engaged in no intercompany transactions. Production's Chief Financial Officer (CFO) presents you with the following information pertaining to current year operations:

	Production Corporation	*Manufacturing Corporation*
Gross profit on sales	$500,000	$225,000
Minus: Operating expenses	(200,000)	(100,000)
Qualified production activities income	$300,000	$125,000
Plus: Dividends received from 20%-owned corporations	20,000	–0–
Minus: Dividends-received deduction	(16,000)	–0–
NOL carryover deduction	–0–	(15,000)
Taxable income before the U.S. production activities deduction	$304,000	$110,000

Operating expenses include W-2 wages allocable to U.S. production activities of $75,000 and $35,000 for Production and Manufacturing, respectively. Given this information, the CFO asks you to determine each corporation's qualified production activities deduction. The applicable deduction percentage is 9%. At a minimum, you should consult the following resources:

- IRC Sec. 199
- Reg. Sec. 1.199-7

CHAPTER

4

CORPORATE NONLIQUIDATING DISTRIBUTIONS

LEARNING OBJECTIVES

After studying this chapter, you should be able to

1. Ask the key questions pertaining to corporate liquidations
2. Calculate a corporation's earnings and profits (E&P)
3. Determine the tax consequences of nonliquidating distributions
4. Determine the tax consequences of stock dividends and the issuance of stock rights
5. Decide whether a stock redemption should be treated as a sale or a dividend
6. Explain the tax treatment of preferred stock bailouts
7. Assess the applicability and tax consequences of Sec. 304 to stock sales
8. Identify tax planning opportunities in nonliquidating distributions
9. Comply with procedural rules for nonliquidating distributions

CHAPTER OUTLINE

A corporation may distribute money, property, or stock to its shareholders. Shareholders who receive such distributions might have to recognize ordinary income, capital gain, or no taxable income at all. The distributing corporation might be required to recognize gain or loss when making the distribution. How the corporation and its shareholders treat distributions for tax purposes depends on not only what the corporation distributes but also the circumstances surrounding the distribution. Was the corporation in the process of liquidating? Was the distribution made in exchange for some of the shareholder's stock?

This chapter addresses distributions made when a corporation is not in the process of liquidating. It discusses the tax consequences of the following types of distributions:

- Distributions of cash or other property where the shareholder does not surrender any stock
- Distributions of stock or rights to acquire stock of the distributing corporation
- Distributions of property in exchange for the corporation's own stock (i.e., stock redemptions)

Chapter C:6 discusses **liquidating distributions**, and Chapter C:7 discusses distributions associated with corporate reorganizations.

Nonliquidating Distributions in General

OBJECTIVE 1

Ask the key questions pertaining to corporate liquidations

When a corporation makes a nonliquidating distribution to a shareholder, the shareholder must answer the following three questions:

- What is the amount of the distribution?
- To what extent is this amount treated as a dividend?
- What is the basis of the distributed property, and when does its holding period begin?

In addition, the distributing corporation must answer the following two questions:

- What are the amount and character of gain or loss the corporation must recognize?
- What effect does the distribution have on the distributing corporation's earnings and profits (E&P) account?

SELF-STUDY QUESTION

How does a shareholder classify a distribution for tax purposes?

ANSWER

Distributions are treated as follows: (1) dividends to the extent of corporate E&P, (2) return of capital to the extent of the shareholder's stock basis, and (3) gain from the sale of stock.

A brief summary of the rules for determining the taxability of a distribution follows, along with a simple example.

Section 301 requires a shareholder to include in gross income the amount of any corporate distribution to the extent it is treated as a dividend. Qualified dividends received by a noncorporate shareholder are subject to a maximum 20% tax rate. Section 316(a) defines **dividend** as a distribution of property made by a corporation out of its earnings and profits (E&P), which are discussed in the next section of this chapter. Section 317(a) defines **property** broadly to include money, securities, and any other property except stock or stock rights of the distributing corporation. Distributed amounts that exceed a corporation's E&P are treated as a return of capital that reduces the shareholder's basis in his or her stock (but not below zero). Distributions exceeding the shareholder's basis are treated as gain from the sale of the stock. If the stock is a capital asset in the shareholder's hands, the gain is capital in character.

EXAMPLE C:4-1 ▶ On March 1, Gamma Corporation distributes $60,000 in cash to each of its two equal shareholders, Ellen and Bob. At the time of the distribution, Gamma's E&P is $80,000. Ellen's basis in her stock is $25,000, and Bob's basis in his stock is $10,000. Ellen and Bob each recognize $40,000 (0.50 × $80,000) of dividend income. This portion of the distribution reduces Gamma's E&P to zero. The additional $20,000 that each shareholder receives is treated first as a return of capital and then as a capital gain. The following table illustrates the relevant calculations:

	Ellen	*Bob*	*Total*
Distribution	$60,000	$60,000	$120,000
Dividend income[a]	(40,000)	(40,000)	(80,000)
Remaining distribution	$20,000	$20,000	$ 40,000
Return of capital[b]	(20,000)	(10,000)	(30,000)
Capital gain[c]	$ –0–	$10,000	$ 10,000

[a]Smaller of E&P allocable to the distribution or the distribution amount.
[b]Smaller of remaining distribution amount to the shareholder or his or her stock basis.
[c]Any amount that exceeds the shareholder's basis in his or her stock. ◀

EARNINGS AND PROFITS (E&P)

OBJECTIVE 2

Calculate a corporation's earnings and profits (E&P)

The term E&P is not defined in the IRC. Its meaning must be gleaned from judicial opinions, Treasury Regulations, and IRC provisions relating to how certain transactions affect E&P.

To some extent, E&P measures a corporation's economic ability to pay dividends to its shareholders. Distributions are presumed to be made out of the corporation's E&P, unless the corporation reports no E&P.

CURRENT EARNINGS AND PROFITS

TYPICAL MISCONCEPTION

Because E&P is such an important concept in many corporate transactions, one would assume that corporations know exactly what their E&P is. However, many corporations do not compute their E&P on a regular basis.

A corporation's E&P falls into two categories: current and accumulated. As explained below, **Current E&P** is calculated annually. **Accumulated E&P** is the sum of undistributed current E&P balances for all previous years reduced by the sum of all previous current E&P deficits and any distributions the corporation made out of accumulated E&P. Distributions are deemed to have been made first out of current E&P and then out of accumulated E&P to the extent that current E&P is insufficient.

EXAMPLE C:4-2 ▶ Zeta Corporation was formed in Year 1. Its current E&P balance (or deficit) and distributions for each year through Year 4 are as follows:

Year	*Current E&P (Deficit)*	*Distributions*
1	$(10,000)	–0–
2	15,000	–0–
3	18,000	$9,000
4	8,000	–0–

The corporation is deemed to have made the $9,000 distribution out of its Year 3 current E&P balance. At the beginning of Year 4, Zeta's accumulated E&P balance is $14,000 (− $10,000 + $15,000 + $18,000 − $9,000). At the beginning of Year 5, Zeta's accumulated E&P balance is $22,000 ($14,000 + $8,000). ◀

Computing Current E&P. A corporation computes its current E&P on an annual basis at the end of each year. The starting point for computing current E&P is the corporation's taxable income or net operating loss (NOL) for the year. Taxable income or the NOL must be adjusted to derive the corporation's economic income or loss (current E&P) for the year. For example, federal income taxes must be deducted from taxable income to derive E&P. Because the corporation must pay these taxes to the U.S. government, they reduce the amount available to pay dividends to shareholders. On the other hand, tax-exempt income must be added to taxable income (or the NOL) because, even though not taxable, such income increases the corporation's ability to pay dividends.

Table C:4-1 lists some of the adjustments a corporation must make to taxable income (NOL) to derive current E&P. Some of these adjustments are explained below.[1]

[1] The adjustments are based on rules set forth in Sec. 312 and related Treasury Regulations.

▼ **TABLE C:4-1**
Computation of Current E&P

Taxable income	
Plus:	*Income excluded from taxable income but included in E&P*
	Tax-exempt interest
	Proceeds from a life insurance contract in which the corporation is named as the beneficiary
	Recoveries of bad debts and other deductions from which the corporation received no tax benefit
	Federal income tax refunds from prior years
Plus:	*Income deferred to a later year when computing taxable income but included in E&P in the current year*
	Deferred gain on installment sales. Such gain is included in E&P in the year of sale.
Plus or minus:	*Income and deduction items that must be recomputed for E&P purposes*
	Income on long-term contracts based on the percentage of completion rather than the completed contract method
	Depreciation on personal and real property based on:
	The straight-line method for other than MACRS property
	The alternative depreciation system for MACRS property
	Excess of percentage depletion over cost depletion
Plus:	*Deductions that are allowed for taxable income purposes but denied for E&P purposes*
	Dividends-received deduction
	NOL carryovers, charitable contribution carryovers, and capital loss carryovers applied in the current year
	U.S. production activities deduction
Minus:	*Expenses and losses that are denied for taxable income purposes but allowed for E&P purposes*
	Federal income taxes
	Premiums on life insurance contracts in which the corporation is named as the beneficiary
	Excess capital losses that are not currently deductible
	Excess charitable contributions that are not currently deductible
	Expenses related to the production of tax-exempt income
	Nondeductible losses on sales to related parties
	Nondeductible penalties and fines
	Nondeductible political contributions and lobbying expenses
Current E&P balance (or deficit)	

Income Excluded from Taxable Income but Included in E&P. Although certain items of income are excluded from taxable income, these items must be included in E&P if they increase the corporation's ability to pay dividends. For example, a corporation's current E&P includes both tax-exempt interest and life insurance proceeds. Current E&P also includes the recovery of an item deducted in a previous year if the deduction produced no tax benefit for the corporation and therefore was excluded from its taxable income.

EXAMPLE C:4-3 ▶ Ace Corporation deducted $10,000 of bad debts in Year 1. In the same year, Ace generated an NOL that it could not carry back. Consequently, it derived no tax benefit from the deduction. In Year 2, Ace recovers $8,000 of the debt owed to it. Ace excludes the $8,000 from its gross income for Year 2 because it derived no tax benefit from the bad debt deduction in Year 1. However, Ace must add the $8,000 to its taxable income when computing current E&P for Year 2 because the NOL reduced current E&P in Year 1. (Ace also reduces its NOL carryover by $8,000 because of the recovery.) ◀

Income Deferred to a later Year when Computing Taxable Income but Included in E&P in the Current Year. Gains and losses on property transactions generally are included in E&P in the same year they are recognized for taxable income purposes.

EXAMPLE C:4-4 ▶ Stone Corporation exchanges investment property with a $12,000 basis and an $18,000 fair market value (FMV) for $1,000 cash and investment property worth $17,000. Stone recognizes a $1,000 gain—the amount of boot received—in the like-kind exchange and defers the remaining $5,000 of realized gain. Stone includes the recognized gain in both taxable income and current E&P. It does not include the deferred gain in either taxable income or current E&P. ◀

In the case of an installment sale, the entire realized gain must be included in current E&P in the year of the sale. This rule applies to sales made by dealers and nondealers.

EXAMPLE C:4-5 ▶ In the current year, Tally Corporation sells land with a $12,000 basis and $20,000 FMV to Rick, an unrelated individual. Rick makes a $5,000 down payment this year and promises to pay Tally, in each of the next three years, an additional $5,000 plus interest at the prevailing market rate on the unpaid balance. Tally's realized gain is $8,000 ($20,000 − $12,000). For taxable income purposes, Tally currently recognizes $2,000 of gain [($8,000 ÷ $20,000) × $5,000] under the installment method for nondealers. For E&P purposes, Tally includes all $8,000 of its realized gain in current E&P. Thus, in computing current E&P, Tally increases taxable income by $6,000. As it receives the installments over the next three years, Tally will recognize the remaining $6,000 of gain ($2,000 per year) for taxable income purposes. It will reduce E&P by $2,000 in each of those years because it included in E&P all $8,000 in the current year. ◀

SELF-STUDY QUESTION

In computing taxable income and E&P, different depreciation methods are often used. What happens when the taxpayer sells such assets?

ANSWER

The taxpayer must calculate gain or loss for taxable income and E&P purposes separately. This difference is an added complexity in making E&P calculations.

Income and Deduction Items that Must be Recomputed for E&P Purposes. Some deductions are computed differently for E&P purposes than for taxable income purposes, thereby requiring adjustments.

- E&P must be computed under the percentage of completion method even where the corporation uses the completed contract method for taxable income purposes.
- Depreciation must be recomputed under the alternative depreciation system of Sec. 168(g). Also, the cost of property expensed under Sec. 179 must be recovered ratably over a five-year period starting with the month in which it was expensed. Other personal property must be depreciated over the property's class life under the half-year convention. Real property must be depreciated over a 40-year period under the straight-line method and mid-month convention.

EXAMPLE C:4-6 ▶ In January of last year, Radon Corporation placed in service equipment costing $500,000. For regular tax purposes, the corporation expensed the $500,000 under Sec. 179. However, for E&P purposes, the corporation expensed only $100,000 ($500,000/5). Thus, in last year's E&P calculation, the corporation would have increased its taxable income amount by $400,000 ($500,000 − $100,000) to derive last year's current E&P (a positive adjustment). In the current year's E&P calculation (and for the next three years), the corporation reduces its taxable income amount by $100,000 to derive its current E&P balance (a negative adjustment). ◀

- Cost depletion must be used for E&P purposes even where percentage depletion is used for taxable income purposes.
- Intangible drilling costs must be capitalized and amortized over 60 months.

BOOK-TO-TAX ACCOUNTING COMPARISION

Many corporations use retained earnings to measure the taxability of their dividend payments. However, because retained earnings are based on financial accounting concepts, E&P may represent a different amount and may provide a different measure of the corporation's economic ability to pay dividends.

Deductions Allowed for Taxable Income Purposes but Denied for E&P Purposes. Some deductions allowed for taxable income purposes are not allowed for E&P purposes.

- The dividends-received deduction is denied for E&P purposes because it does not reduce the corporation's ability to pay dividends. In the computation of E&P, this deduction must be added back to taxable income.
- NOL, charitable contribution, and capital loss carryovers that reduce current taxable income cannot be deducted to derive E&P. These excess losses or deductions reduce E&P in the year they are incurred or taken.
- The U.S. production activities deduction is disallowed for E&P purposes because it does not reduce the corporation's ability to pay dividends. It must be added back to taxable income to derive E&P.
- Deduction and amortization of organizational expenses are disallowed for E&P purposes.

EXAMPLE C:4-7 ▶ Thames Corporation's taxable income is $500,000 after deductions for the following items: a $10,000 NOL carryover from two years ago, $20,000 for dividends received, and $8,000 for U.S. production activities. To compute current E&P, Thames must add these items (totaling $38,000) back to its taxable income. As a result, current E&P is $538,000. ◀

Expenses and Losses Denied for Taxable Income Purposes but Allowed for E&P Purposes. Some expenses and losses that are not deductible for taxable income purposes are deductible for E&P purposes.

- For taxable income purposes, federal income taxes are not deductible. For E&P purposes, however, federal income taxes are deductible in the year they accrue if the corporation uses the accrual method and in the year they are paid if the corporation uses the cash method.

EXAMPLE C:4-8 ▶ Perch Corporation, an accrual basis taxpayer, earns taxable income of $100,000 on which it owes $22,250 of federal income taxes. In computing current E&P, Perch reduces taxable income by the amount of these taxes, or $22,250. ◀

- For E&P purposes, charitable contributions are fully deductible. Thus, when current E&P is computed, taxable income must be reduced by any charitable contributions disallowed because of the 10% limitation.

EXAMPLE C:4-9 ▶ Dot Corporation computes $25,000 of taxable income before any charitable contribution deduction. Dot contributed $10,000 to the Red Cross. For taxable income purposes, Dot's charitable contribution deduction is limited to $2,500 because of the 10% limitation. However, Dot deducts the entire $10,000 in computing current E&P. In this computation, it must subtract the remaining $7,500 from taxable income of $22,500 ($25,000 − $2,500). In a later year, when the corporation deducts the $7,500 carryover to compute taxable income, it must add that amount back to taxable income to derive current E&P. ◀

- Premiums paid on insurance policies covering the lives of key corporate personnel (net of any increase in the cash surrender value) are not deductible when computing taxable income but are deductible when computing E&P.
- Capital losses exceeding capital gains cannot be deducted when computing taxable income but can be deducted when computing current E&P.
- Nondeductible expenses related to the production of tax-exempt income (e.g., interest charges to borrow money to purchase tax-exempt securities) are deductible when computing E&P.
- Losses on related party sales that are disallowed under Sec. 267 are allowed when computing E&P.
- Fines, penalties, and political contributions that are nondeductible for taxable income purposes are deductible for E&P purposes.

The foregoing items constitute only a partial list of adjustments that must be made to taxable income to compute current E&P. The basic rule is that an adjustment to taxable income must be made so that current E&P reflects the corporation's economic ability to pay dividends.

DISTINCTION BETWEEN CURRENT AND ACCUMULATED E&P

A distinction must be made between current and accumulated E&P. A nonliquidating distribution is taxed as a dividend if made out of either current or accumulated E&P. Corporate distributions are deemed to be made first out of current E&P and then out of accumulated E&P to the extent that current E&P is insufficient.[2] If current E&P is sufficient to cover all distributions during the year, each distribution is treated as a taxable

[2] The distinction between current and accumulated E&P is explained in Reg. Sec. 1.316-2.

dividend. This rule applies even where the corporation reports a deficit in its beginning accumulated E&P account. Current E&P is computed as of the last day of the tax year without reduction for distributions during the year.

EXAMPLE C:4-10 ▶ At the beginning of the current year, Water Corporation has a $30,000 accumulated E&P deficit. For the entire year, Water generates current E&P of $15,000. During the year, Water distributes $10,000 in cash to its shareholders. The $10,000 distribution is treated as a taxable dividend to the shareholders because it is deemed to be made entirely out of current E&P. At the beginning of the next tax year, Water's accumulated E&P deficit is $25,000 ($30,000 E&P deficit reduced by $5,000 of undistributed current E&P) computed as of the last day of the previous year. ◀

TAX STRATEGY TIP

A corporation with an accumulated E&P deficit and current E&P balance may want to postpone distributions to a later year to avoid dividend treatment in the current year. See Example C:4-53 later in this chapter.

If distributions during the year exceed current E&P, current E&P is allocated on a pro rata basis regardless of when during the year the distributions occurred. Distributions exceeding current E&P are deemed to be made in chronological order out of accumulated E&P (if any). Distributions exceeding current and accumulated E&P are treated as a return of capital and reduce the shareholder's stock basis. However, such distributions cannot create an E&P deficit, which results only from losses. These rules are particularly relevant if stock changes hands during the year and total E&P is insufficient to cover all distributions.

EXAMPLE C:4-11 ▶ At the beginning of the current year, Cole Corporation has $20,000 of accumulated E&P. For the entire year, Cole's current E&P is $30,000. On April 10, Cole distributes $20,000 in cash to Bob, its sole shareholder. On July 15, Cole distributes an additional $24,000 in cash to Bob. On August 1, Bob sells all of his Cole stock to Lynn. On September 15, Cole distributes $36,000 in cash to Lynn. Cole's current and accumulated E&P must be allocated among the three distributions as follows:

Date	Distribution Amount	Current E&P	Accumulated E&P	Dividend Income	Return of Capital
April 10	$20,000	$ 7,500	$12,500	$20,000	$ –0–
July 15	24,000	9,000	7,500	16,500	7,500
September 15	36,000	13,500	–0–	13,500	22,500
Total	$80,000	$30,000	$20,000	$50,000	$30,000

The current E&P allocated to the April 10 distribution is calculated as follows:

$$\$30,000\ (\text{Current E\&P}) \times \frac{\$20,000\ (\text{April 10 distribution})}{\$80,000\ (\text{Total distributions})}$$

Note that the total amount of dividends paid by Cole equals $50,000, the sum of $30,000 of current E&P and $20,000 of accumulated E&P. Current E&P is allocated among all three distributions on a pro rata basis, whereas accumulated E&P is reduced first by the April 10 distribution ($12,500), then by the July 15 distribution, so that no accumulated E&P is available for the September 15 distribution. Thus, Bob's dividend income from Cole is $36,500 ($20,000 + $16,500). He also receives a $7,500 return of capital that reduces his stock basis accordingly. Lynn's dividend income from Cole is $13,500. She also receives a $22,500 return of capital that reduces her stock basis accordingly. Bob cannot determine his gain on the stock sale until after the end of the year. He must wait until he knows the extent to which the April 10 and July 15 distributions reduce his stock basis. ◀

If the corporation generates both a current E&P deficit and an accumulated E&P deficit, none of the distributions is treated as a dividend. Instead, all distributions are treated as a return of capital to the extent of the shareholder's stock basis. Distributions exceeding this basis are taxed as a capital gain.

EXAMPLE C:4-12 ▶ At the beginning of the current year, Rose Corporation has a $15,000 accumulated E&P deficit. Rose's current E&P deficit is $20,000. Rose distributes $10,000 on July 1. The distribution is treated not as a dividend but rather as a return of capital to the extent of the shareholder's stock basis. Any amount exceeding stock basis is taxed as a capital gain. Rose's accumulated E&P deficit on January 1 of next year is $35,000 because the distribution was not made out of E&P and because the negative balance in the current E&P account is transferred to the accumulated E&P account at the end of the current year. ◀

SELF-STUDY QUESTION

When is E&P measured for purposes of determining whether a distribution is a dividend?

ANSWER

Usually at year-end. However, if a current deficit exists, the E&P available for measuring dividend income is determined at the distribution date.

If the corporation has a current E&P deficit and a positive accumulated E&P balance, it must net the two accounts at the time of the distribution to determine the dividend amount.[3] The deficit in current E&P that has accrued up through the day before the distribution reduces the accumulated E&P balance on that date. If the balance remaining after the reduction is positive, the distribution is treated as a dividend to the extent of the lesser of the distribution amount or the E&P balance. If the E&P balance is zero or negative, the distribution is treated as a return of capital. If the actual deficit in current E&P to the date of distribution cannot be determined, the current E&P deficit is prorated on a daily basis to the day before the distribution.

EXAMPLE C:4-13 ▶ Assume the same facts as in Example C:4-12 except that Rose Corporation has a $15,000 accumulated E&P balance. Unless information indicates otherwise, the current E&P deficit of $20,000 accrues on a daily basis. The amount of the July 1 distribution treated as a dividend is calculated as follows:

Date	*Distribution Amount*	*Accumulated E&P*	*Dividend Income*	*Return of Capital*
January 1	$ –0–	$15,000	–0–	–0–
July 1	10,000	(9,918)[a]	$5,082	$4,918
Total	$10,000	$ 5,082[b]	$5,082	$4,918

[a] 181/365 × $(20,000) = $(9,918)—the current E&P deficit accrued up to the distribution date. (The denominator in the 181/365 fraction assumes that the current year is not a leap year.)

[b] $15,000 − $9,918 = $5,082—accumulated E&P at beginning of year minus the current E&P deficit accrued up to the distribution date. ◀

STOP & THINK

Question: Why is it necessary to keep separate balances for current and accumulated E&P, and why is it necessary to track E&P to individual distributions?

Solution: Separate balances are necessary because of the way dividends are accounted for. If total current and accumulated E&P is less than the total distributions to the shareholders, E&P must be allocated to all distributions during the year to determine the amount of each distribution that should be treated as a dividend. When no change in the shareholder's stock ownership occurs during the year and all distributions are proportional to stock ownership, an E&P allocation is needed only to track each shareholder's stock basis. Tracking E&P to individual distributions is necessary to determine the taxability of a particular distribution when a change in a shareholder's stock ownership occurs because current E&P is allocated on a pro rata basis and accumulated E&P is allocated chronologically. As a result of the chronological allocation, a greater portion of distributions early in a tax year may be taxed as a dividend relative to distributions later in the year. On the other hand, because accrued current E&P deficits offset accumulated E&P balances, a smaller portion of distributions later in a tax year may be taxed as a dividend relative to distributions earlier in the year.

NONLIQUIDATING PROPERTY DISTRIBUTIONS

OBJECTIVE 3

Determine the tax consequences of nonliquidating distributions

CONSEQUENCES OF NONLIQUIDATING PROPERTY DISTRIBUTIONS TO THE SHAREHOLDERS

Property includes cash, securities, and any other property except stock in the corporation making the distribution (or rights to acquire such stock).[4] When a corporation distributes property to its shareholders, the following three questions must be answered:

[3] Reg. Sec. 1.316-2(b).

[4] Sec. 317(a).

KEY POINT

The amount of the distribution is measured by the FMV of the property less liabilities assumed (but not below zero) because this net amount represents the real economic value received by the shareholder.

- What is the amount of the distribution?
- To what extent is this amount treated as a dividend?
- What is the basis of the property to the shareholder, and when does its holding period begin?

For cash distributions, these questions are easy to answer. The distribution is the amount of cash distributed, which is treated as a dividend to the extent of the corporation's current and accumulated E&P. The E&P account is reduced by the amount distributed, and the shareholder's basis in the cash received is its face value. The distributing corporation recognizes no gain or loss on cash distributions.

When the corporation distributes property, such as land or inventory, these questions are more difficult to answer. Neither the distribution amount nor the shareholder's basis in the property is immediately apparent. The corporation must recognize gain (but not loss) on the distribution, and the impact of the distribution on the corporation's E&P, as well as the taxability of the distribution, must be ascertained. The following sections set forth rules that address these issues.

When the corporation distributes property to a shareholder, the distribution amount is the property's FMV, determined as of the distribution date.[5] The amount of any liability assumed by the shareholder in the distribution, or to which the distributed property is subject, reduces the distribution amount, but never below zero. The distribution amount is treated as a dividend to the extent of the distributing corporation's E&P.

The shareholder takes a FMV basis in any property received. This basis is not reduced by any liabilities assumed by the shareholder or to which the property is subject.[6] The holding period for the property begins on the day after the distribution date and does not include the distributing corporation's holding period.

EXAMPLE C:4-14 ► Post Corporation has $100,000 of current and accumulated E&P. On March 1, Post distributes to Meg, its sole shareholder, land with a $60,000 FMV and a $35,000 adjusted basis. The land is subject to a $10,000 liability, which Meg assumes. The distribution amount is $50,000 ($60,000 − $10,000), all of which is treated as a dividend to Meg because it does not exceed Post's E&P balance. Meg's basis in the property is its $60,000 FMV, and her holding period for the property begins on March 2. ◄

STOP & THINK

Question: When a corporation distributes property, why do liabilities reduce the amount of income realized by the shareholder but not the shareholder's adjusted basis in the property?

Solution: The liabilities reduce the amount of income realized, but not the shareholder's adjusted basis, because the distribution is analogous to the corporation's transferring an asset that it has financed with debt. Recall that financing the purchase of an asset has no bearing on the asset's cost basis. On the other hand, assuming a liability is tantamount to the transferee's settling the liability with the transferee's own funds, and thus receiving less value from the transferor.

Topic Review C:4-1 summarizes the tax consequences of a nonliquidating distribution to the shareholders.

CONSEQUENCES OF PROPERTY DISTRIBUTIONS TO THE DISTRIBUTING CORPORATION

KEY POINT

Property distributions may trigger income at both the shareholder and the distributing corporation level. This result is another example of the double taxation that exists in our corporate tax system.

Two questions must be answered with respect to a corporation that distributes property:

- What amount and character of gain or loss must the distributing corporation recognize?
- What effect does the distribution have on the corporation's E&P?

[5] Sec. 301(b).

[6] Sec. 301(d).

TOPIC REVIEW C:4-1

Tax Consequences of a Nonliquidating Distribution to the Shareholders

1. The amount of a distribution equals cash received plus the FMV of any noncash property received reduced by any liabilities assumed or acquired by the shareholder.
2. The distribution is treated as a dividend to the extent of the distributing corporation's current and accumulated E&P. Any distribution amount exceeding E&P is treated as a return of capital that reduces the shareholder's stock basis (but not below zero). Any additional excess is treated as a capital gain.
3. The shareholder's basis in the property received is its FMV.
4. The shareholder's holding period for the property begins on the day after the distribution date.

Corporate Gain or Loss on Property Distributions. When a corporation distributes property that has appreciated in value, the corporation must recognize gain as though the corporation had sold the property for its FMV. On the other hand, a corporation does not recognize loss when it distributes property that has depreciated in value even though the corporation would have recognized a loss upon selling the property.[7]

EXAMPLE C:4-15 ▶ Silver Corporation distributes to Mark, a shareholder, land (a capital asset) worth $60,000. Silver's adjusted basis in the land is $20,000. Upon distributing the land, Silver recognizes a $40,000 ($60,000 − $20,000) capital gain, as if Silver had sold the property. If the land instead had a $12,000 FMV, Silver would not have recognized a loss. ◀

TAX STRATEGY TIP

Rather than distribute loss property, the corporation should consider selling it and distributing the proceeds. The sale will allow the corporation to deduct the loss.

If the distributed property is subject to a liability or the shareholder assumes a liability in the distribution, for the purpose of calculating gain, the property's FMV is deemed to be no less than the amount of the liability.[8]

EXAMPLE C:4-16 ▶ Assume the same facts as in Example C:4-15 except the land's FMV instead is $25,000, and the land is subject to a $35,000 mortgage. For the purpose of calculating gain, the land's FMV is deemed to be $35,000 because this value cannot be less than the liability amount. Thus, Silver Corporation's gain is $15,000 ($35,000 – $20,000), the extent to which the land's deemed FMV exceeds its adjusted basis.[9] ◀

TAX STRATEGY TIP

If possible, a corporation should avoid distributing property subject to a liability exceeding the property's FMV because of the potential gain recognition caused by the excess liability.

Effect of Property Distributions on the Distributing Corporation's E&P. Distributions have two effects on E&P:[10]

- When a corporation distributes appreciated property to its shareholders, it must increase E&P by the **E&P gain**, which is the excess of the property's FMV over its adjusted basis for E&P purposes. Because a property's **E&P adjusted basis** may differ from its tax basis (as discussed earlier in this chapter), this E&P gain may differ from the corporation's recognized gain for taxable income purposes.
- If the E&P adjusted basis of the noncash asset distributed equals or exceeds its FMV, E&P is reduced by the asset's E&P adjusted basis. If the FMV of the asset distributed exceeds its E&P adjusted basis, E&P is reduced by the asset's FMV. In either case, the E&P reduction is net of any liability to which the asset is subject or that the shareholder assumes in the distribution. E&P also is reduced by the income tax liability incurred on any gain recognized.[11]

---

[7] Sec. 311(a).

[8] Sec. 311(b)(2).

[9] The tax treatment of the shareholder is not entirely clear. Section 336(b), which Sec. 311(b)(2) makes applicable to nonliquidating distributions, specifically states that this liability rule applies only for determining the corporation's gain or loss. Thus, its applicability does not seem to extend to Sec. 301(d), which gives the shareholder a FMV basis in the distributed property. Some commentators have suggested that a strict interpretation of the statutory provision that gives the shareholder an actual FMV basis, rather than the greater liability basis, produces an illogical result. (See B. C. Randall and D. N. Stewart, "Corporate Distributions: Handling Liabilities in Excess of the Fair Market Value of Property Remains Unresolved," *The Journal of Corporate Taxation*, 1992, pp. 55–64.) Also, in principle, given that the liability exceeds the distributed property's FMV, the shareholder's amount distributed should be zero, resulting in no dividend.

[10] Secs. 312(a) and (b).

[11] Secs. 312(a) and (c).

EXAMPLE C:4-17 ► Brass Corporation distributes to its shareholder, Joan, property with a $25,000 adjusted basis for taxable income purposes, a $22,000 adjusted basis for E&P purposes, and a $40,000 FMV. The property is subject to a $12,000 mortgage, which Joan assumes. In the distribution, Brass recognizes a $15,000 ($40,000 FMV − $25,000 tax adjusted basis) gain for taxable income purposes. For E&P purposes, Brass's E&P is increased by an $18,000 ($40,000 FMV − $22,000 E&P adjusted basis) gain and reduced by the amount of income taxes paid or accrued by Brass on the $15,000 tax gain. E&P is further reduced by the $28,000 ($40,000 FMV − $12,000 liability) net value of the distribution. ◄

A special rule applies when a corporation distributes its own obligations (e.g., its notes, bonds, or debentures) to a shareholder. In such case, the distributing corporation's E&P is reduced by the principal amount, not the fair market value, of the obligations.[12]

BOOK-TO-TAX ACCOUNTING COMPARISON

The distributing corporation reports dividends-in-kind at their FMV for financial accounting (book) purposes. For book purposes, the distributing corporation recognizes the difference between the property's FMV and its carrying value as a gain or loss. For tax purposes, however, the corporation recognizes gains but not losses.

Topic Review C:4-2 summarizes the tax consequences of a nonliquidating distribution to the distributing corporation.

CONSTRUCTIVE DIVIDENDS

A **constructive dividend** (or deemed distribution) is the manner in which the IRS or the courts might recharacterize an excessive corporate payment to a shareholder to reflect the true economic benefit conferred upon the shareholder. As a result of the recharacterization, the IRS or courts usually recast a corporate-shareholder transaction as an E&P distribution, deny the corporation an offsetting deduction, and treat all or a portion of the income recognized by the shareholder as a dividend. Ordinarily, a corporate dividend involves a direct, pro rata distribution to all shareholders and is declared by the board of directors. By contrast, a constructive dividend need not be direct or pro rata, nor be declared by the board of directors.

Constructive dividends generally are deemed to be paid in the context of a closely held corporation where the shareholders (or relatives of shareholders) and management groups overlap. In such situations, the dealings between the corporation and its shareholders are likely to be less formal and subject to closer review than dealings between a publicly held corporation and its shareholders. Constructive dividends also may occur in the context of a publicly held corporation.

ADDITIONAL COMMENT

The incentive to disguise dividends as salary, however, is somewhat diminished with the reduced tax rate on dividends.

Intentional Efforts to Avoid Dividend Treatment. The IRS's recharacterization of a payment as a constructive dividend often is in response to a shareholder's attempt either to bail out E&P without subjecting the corporate income to taxation at the shareholder level or to obtain a deduction at the corporate level that otherwise would be disallowed. If a corporation generates sufficient E&P, dividend distributions are fully taxable to the shareholder but are not deductible by the distributing corporation. For this reason,

TOPIC REVIEW C:4-2

Tax Consequences of a Nonliquidating Property Distribution to the Distributing Corporation

1. When a corporation distributes appreciated property, it must recognize gain as if it sold the property for its FMV immediately before the distribution.
2. For gain recognition purposes, a property's FMV is deemed to be at least equal to any liability to which the property is subject or that the shareholder assumes in connection with the distribution.
3. A corporation recognizes no loss when it distributes to its shareholders property that has depreciated in value.
4. A corporation's E&P is increased by any E&P gain resulting from a distribution of appreciated property.
5. A corporation's E&P is reduced by (a) the amount of money distributed plus (b) the greater of the FMV or E&P adjusted basis of any noncash property distributed, minus (c) any liabilities to which the property is subject or that the shareholder assumes in connection with the distribution. E&P also is reduced by taxes paid or incurred on the corporation's recognized gain, if any.

[12] Sec. 312(a)(2).

shareholders may try to disguise a dividend as a salary payment. Without recharacterization, the payment would be taxable to the shareholder-employee and deductible by the distributing corporation as long as the payment is reasonable in amount. Shareholders also may try to disguise dividends as loans to themselves. Without recharacterization, a loan would be neither deductible by the corporation nor taxable to the shareholder. If the IRS recharacterizes either payment as a dividend, the payment is taxable to the shareholder and nondeductible by the corporation.

ETHICAL POINT

A CPA should always be an advocate for his or her client if the question of whether a constructive dividend has been paid is in doubt (i.e., when the facts and the law are sufficiently gray and the taxpayer's position has reasonable support).

Unintentional Constructive Dividends. Some constructive dividends are inadvertent. Shareholders may not realize that the benefits they receive from the corporation are effectively taxable dividends until a tax advisor or the IRS examines the transactions. If a payment in the form of a salary, loan, lease, etc. is recast as a dividend, corresponding adjustments must be made at the corporate and shareholder levels. These adjustments may increase the shareholder's taxable income (e.g., because the distribution has been recharacterized as a dividend rather than a loan) or increase the distributing corporation's taxable income (i.e., because dividends are not deductible). Transactions most likely to be recast and treated as dividends are described below.

ADDITIONAL COMMENT

The government requires that, when loans exist between a corporation and its shareholders, the loans must bear a reasonable interest rate. If a "below-market" interest rate loan exists, the IRS will impute a reasonable rate of interest (Sec. 7872).

Loans to Shareholders. Loans to shareholders may be viewed as disguised dividends unless the shareholders can prove that the loans are bona fide. Whether a loan is bona fide ordinarily depends on the shareholder's intent at the time he or she makes the loan. To prove that the loan is bona fide (and thus to avoid recharacterization of the loan as a dividend), the shareholder must show that he or she intends to repay the loan. Factors indicative of an intent to repay include

- Recording the loan on the corporate books
- Evidencing the loan with a written note
- Charging a reasonable rate of interest
- Scheduling regular payment of principal and interest

Factors that suggest the loan is *not* bona fide include

- Borrowing on "open account" (i.e., the shareholder borrows from the corporation with no fixed repayment schedule, whenever he or she needs cash)
- Failing to charge a market rate of interest
- Failing to enforce the regular payment of interest and principal
- Paying advances in proportion to stockholdings
- Paying advances to a controlling shareholder

If the corporation lends money to a shareholder and then, after a period of time, cancels the loan, the amount cancelled might be treated as a dividend to the extent of the corporation's E&P. If the corporation charges a below market interest rate, the IRS could impute interest on the loan. In such case, the corporation would be deemed to have earned interest income on the loan, and the shareholder would be allowed a deduction for interest deemed paid.

Excessive Compensation Paid to Shareholder-Employees. Shareholders may be compensated for services in the form of salary, bonus, or fringe benefits. Ordinarily, the corporate employer may deduct such compensation as long as it represents an ordinary and necessary business expense and is reasonable in amount. However, if the IRS finds the compensation to be excessive, the excess amount will not be deductible by the corporation but still will be taxable to the shareholder. Depending upon the circumstances, this amount may be treated as a dividend or simply be included in the gross income of the recipient. No hard and fast rules offer guidance for determining when compensation is excessive. As a result, the issue frequently is litigated.

Before 2003, the IRS's main focus was the corporation's deducting the excess amount. The shareholder-employee recognized ordinary income regardless of whether the excess was characterized as compensation or a dividend. Because the tax rate on qualified dividends is now lower than the tax rate on salaries and wages, the corporation still will lose the deduction for excess compensation, but the IRS is unlikely to classify the excess as a dividend. Instead, the IRS probably will treat the excess as compensation to the shareholder-employee even though the corporation is not allowed to deduct it.[13]

Excessive Compensation Paid to Shareholders for the use of Shareholder Property. As with compensation, corporate payments to shareholders for the use of property (i.e., rents, interest, and royalties) are deductible under Sec. 162(a) if they are ordinary, necessary, and reasonable in amount. The corporation may not deduct any amount exceeding what it would have paid to an unrelated party in an arm's-length transaction.

Corporate Payments for the Shareholder's Benefit. If a corporation pays the personal obligation of a shareholder, the corporate payment may result in gross income to the shareholder. Such a payment may cover the shareholder's personal debt, expenses in connection with the shareholder's personal residence, expenses incurred for the improvement of the shareholder's real property, or an obligation personally guaranteed by the shareholder.

In addition, if the IRS denies a corporate deduction, the disallowed deduction may result in gross income to the shareholder if the expenditure associated with the deduction conferred an economic benefit upon the shareholder. Examples of such expenditures are unsubstantiated travel and entertainment expenses; club dues; and automobile, airplane, and yacht expenses related to the shareholder-employee's personal use.

Bargain Purchase of Corporate Property. If a shareholder purchases corporate property at a discount relative to the property's FMV, the discount may be treated as a constructive dividend to the shareholder.

Shareholder Use of Corporate Property. If a shareholder uses corporate property (such as a hunting lodge, yacht, or airplane) without paying adequate consideration to the corporation, the fair rental value of such property (minus any amounts paid) may be treated as a constructive dividend to the shareholder.

Stock Dividends and Stock Rights

OBJECTIVE 4

Determine the tax consequences of stock dividends and the issuance of stock rights

In 1919, the Supreme Court held in *Eisner v. Macomber* that a stock dividend is not income to the shareholder because it takes no property from the corporation and adds no property to the shareholder.[14] Subsequently, Congress enacted the Revenue Act of 1921, which provides that stock dividends are nontaxable. Although this general rule still applies today, Congress has carved out several exceptions to prevent abuses.

Section 305(a) states, "Except as otherwise provided in this section, gross income does not include the amount of any distribution of the stock of a corporation made by such corporation to its shareholders with respect to its stock." Thus, a distribution of additional common stock with respect to a shareholder's pre-existing common stock holdings represents a nontaxable stock dividend. However, whenever a stock dividend changes or has the potential to change the shareholders' proportionate interest in the distributing corporation, the distribution will be taxable. Taxable stock distributions include those where

- Any shareholder can elect to receive either stock of the distributing corporation or other property (e.g., cash).
- Some shareholders receive property and other shareholders receive an increase in their proportionate interest in the distributing corporation's assets or E&P.

TYPICAL MISCONCEPTION

Stock dividends generally are nontaxable as long as a shareholder's proportionate interest in the corporation do not increase. If a shareholder's stock interest increases, Sec. 305(b) causes the dividend to be taxable.

[13] *Sterno Sales Corp. v. U.S.*, 15 AFTR 2d 979, 65-1 USTC ¶9419 (Ct. Cl., 1965).

[14] *Eisner v. Myrtle H. Macomber*, 3 AFTR 3020, 1 USTC ¶32 (USSC, 1919).

- Some holders of common stock receive preferred stock and others receive additional common stock.
- The underlying stock is preferred unless the distribution involves a change in the conversion ratio of convertible preferred stock to take into account a common stock dividend or a common stock split.
- The distributed stock is convertible preferred, unless it can be established that the distribution will have no disproportionate effect.

The following example illustrates one such exception.

EXAMPLE C:4-18 ▶ Two shareholders, Al and Beth, each own 100 of the 200 outstanding shares of Peach Corporation stock. Because Al's marginal tax rate is high, he does not want to recognize any additional income in the current year. Beth has a low marginal tax rate and needs additional cash. Peach, whose current E&P is $100,000, declares a dividend payable in stock or cash. Each taxpayer can receive one share of Peach stock (valued at $100) or $100 in cash for each share of Peach stock already owned. Al, who elects to receive stock, receives 100 additional Peach shares. Beth, who elects to receive cash, receives $10,000. Beth's distribution is taxable as a dividend. Absent any exceptions to Sec. 305, Al's dividend would be nontaxable because it was paid in Peach stock. After the distribution, however, Al owns two-thirds of the outstanding shares of Peach stock, whereas before the distribution he owned only one-half of Peach's outstanding shares. In this case, an exception to the general rule of Sec. 305(a) applies so that Al is deemed to have received a taxable dividend equal to the value of the additional shares he received. Even if both shareholders elected to receive a stock dividend, this dividend would be taxable because each shareholder had the option to receive cash. In this example, Al and Beth each recognize $10,000 of dividend income. Al's basis in his new shares is their $10,000 FMV. His basis in his original shares is unchanged. Peach reduces its E&P by $20,000, the amount of the taxable dividend to Al and Beth. ◀

NONTAXABLE STOCK DIVIDENDS

If a **stock dividend** is nontaxable, the basis of the stock with respect to which the distribution was made must be allocated between the old and new shares.[15] The holding period for the new shares includes the holding period for the old shares.[16]

If the old and new shares are identical, the basis of each share is determined by dividing the basis of the old shares by the total number of shares held by the shareholder after the distribution.

EXAMPLE C:4-19 ▶ Barbara owns 1,000 shares of Axle Corporation common stock having a $66,000 basis ($66 per share). Barbara receives a nontaxable 10% common stock dividend and now owns 1,100 Axle common shares. Her basis in each share becomes $60 ($66,000 ÷ 1,100). ◀

If the old and new shares are not identical, the basis of the old shares is allocated according to the relative FMVs of the old and new shares on the distribution date.

EXAMPLE C:4-20 ▶ Mark owns 1,000 shares of Axle Corporation common stock having a $60,000 basis. In a nontaxable distribution, Mark receives 50 shares of Axle preferred stock. At the time of the distribution, the FMV of the common stock is $90,000 ($90 × 1,000 shares), and the FMV of the preferred stock is $10,000 ($200 × 50 shares). After the distribution, $6,000 [($10,000 ÷ $100,000) × $60,000] of the common stock basis is allocated to the preferred stock, and the basis of the common stock is reduced from $60,000 to $54,000. ◀

REAL-WORLD EXAMPLE

Tracking the effects of nontaxable dividends, stock splits, stock dividends, and stock rights distributions on the basis of a stock investment can be difficult and time consuming. A number of publishers offer capital change reporters that provide a complete history of these four types of events for publicly traded companies. These reporters greatly simplify the stock basis calculations.

NONTAXABLE STOCK RIGHTS

Under Sec. 305, a distribution of **stock rights** is nontaxable unless it changes, or has the potential to change, the shareholders' proportionate interest in the distributing corporation. The same Sec. 305(b) exceptions to the nontaxability of stock dividends also apply to distributions of stock rights.

If the value of the stock rights is less than 15% of the value of the stock with respect to which the rights were distributed (i.e., the underlying stock), the basis of the rights is zero unless the shareholder elects to allocate stock basis to the rights.[17] If the taxpayer intends to sell the

[15] Sec. 307(a) and Reg. Secs. 1.307-1 and -2.
[16] Sec. 1223(5).
[17] Sec. 307(b)(1).

rights, an allocation of his or her stock basis to the rights might be advisable so as to minimize the amount of gain recognized on the sale. The election to allocate stock basis to the rights must be made in a statement attached to the shareholder's return for the year in which the rights are received. The allocation must be based on the relative FMVs of the stock and the stock rights. The holding period for the rights includes the holding period for the underlying stock.[18]

EXAMPLE C:4-21 ▶ Linda owns 100 shares of Yale Corporation common stock having a $27,000 basis and a $50,000 FMV. Linda receives 100 nontaxable stock rights with a $4,000 FMV. Because the FMV of the stock rights is less than 15% of the FMV of the underlying stock (0.15 × $50,000 = $7,500), the basis of the stock rights is zero unless Linda elects to allocate the $27,000 stock basis between the stock and the stock rights. If Linda makes the election, the basis of the rights is $2,000 [($4,000 ÷ $54,000) × $27,000], and the basis of the stock is $25,000 ($27,000 − $2,000). ◀

If the value of the stock rights is 15% or more of the value of the underlying stock, the shareholder must allocate the basis of the underlying stock between the stock and the stock rights. This provision is mandatory, not elective.

EXAMPLE C:4-22 ▶ Kay owns 100 shares of Minor Corporation common stock having a $14,000 basis and a $30,000 FMV. Kay receives 100 stock rights with a total FMV of $5,000. Because the FMV of the stock rights is at least 15% of the stock's FMV (0.15 × $30,000 = $4,500), the $14,000 basis must be allocated between the stock rights and the underlying stock based on their relative FMVs. The basis of the stock rights is $2,000 [($5,000 ÷ $35,000) × $14,000], and the basis of the underlying stock is $12,000 [($30,000 ÷ $35,000) × $14,000]. ◀

TYPICAL MISCONCEPTION

Taxpayers often get confused about what happens to a stock right. A stock right may be sold or exercised, which means the actual stock is acquired. If the rights are not sold or exercised, they eventually will lapse.

If the taxpayer sells the stock rights, he or she calculates gain or loss by subtracting the allocated basis of the rights (if any) from the sale price. A shareholder cannot claim a loss if the stock rights expire. If the stock rights do expire, the basis of the allocated rights is added back to the basis of the underlying stock. If the taxpayer exercises the rights before they expire, the basis of the allocated rights is added to the basis of the stock acquired through the exercise of the rights.[19] The holding period for the stock acquired begins on the exercise date.[20]

EXAMPLE C:4-23 ▶ In a nontaxable distribution, Jeff receives ten stock rights to which no stock basis is allocated. Each stock right entitles Jeff to acquire one share of Jackson stock for $20. If Jeff exercises all ten rights, the Jackson stock acquired will have a $200 (10 rights × $20) basis. If instead Jeff sells the ten rights for $30 each, he will recognize a gain of $300 [($30 × 10 rights) − 0 basis]. If the rights expire, Jeff may not claim a loss. ◀

EFFECT OF NONTAXABLE STOCK DIVIDENDS ON THE DISTRIBUTING CORPORATION

BOOK-TO-TAX ACCOUNTING COMPARISON

For financial accounting purposes, stock dividends reduce retained earnings. However, for tax purposes, nontaxable stock dividends have no effect on a corporation's E&P.

From a tax perspective, nontaxable distributions of stock and stock rights have no tax effect on the distributing corporation. The corporation recognizes no gain or loss and does not reduce its E&P balance.[21]

TAXABLE STOCK DIVIDENDS AND STOCK RIGHTS

If a distribution of stock or stock rights is taxable, the distribution amount equals the FMV of the stock or stock rights on the distribution date. The distribution is treated in the same way as any other property distribution. It is a dividend to the extent of the distributing corporation's E&P, and the recipient takes a FMV basis in the stock or stock rights received.[22] The holding period for the stock or stock rights begins on the day after the distribution date. No adjustment is made to the basis of the underlying stock. The distributing corporation recognizes no gain or loss on the distribution,[23] and the corporation reduces its E&P by the FMV of the stock or stock rights on the distribution date.

Topic Review C:4-3 summarizes the tax consequences of a stock dividend.

[18] Sec. 1223(5).
[19] Reg. Sec. 1.307-1(b).
[20] Sec. 1223(6).
[21] Secs. 311(a) and 312(d).
[22] Reg. Sec. 1.301-1(h)(2)(i).
[23] Sec. 311(a). Gain may be recognized when the shareholder can elect to receive either appreciated property or stock or stock rights of the distributing corporation.

TOPIC REVIEW C:4-3

Tax Consequences of a Stock Dividend

SHAREHOLDERS:

1. A stock dividend is nontaxable except where (1) a shareholder can elect to receive other property in lieu of the stock dividend; (2) some shareholders receive property and other shareholders increase their proportionate equity interest; (3) some common shareholders receive preferred and others receive common stock; (4) the underlying stock is preferred stock, unless the conversion ratio, if any, is adjusted to account for a common stock split or dividend; or (5) the distributed stock is convertible preferred, and the distribution has a disproportionate effect.
2. If the stock dividend meets one of the exceptions to nontaxable treatment, the stock dividend is treated as a property distribution under Sec. 301, where the FMV of the distribution is a taxable dividend to the extent of the distributing corporation's E&P.
3. If the stock dividend is nontaxable, (1) the basis of the underlying stock (old shares) is allocated among the old and new shares according to relative FMVs, and (2) the holding period for the new shares includes the holding period for the old shares.
4. If the stock dividend is taxable, (1) the distributed stock takes a basis equal to its FMV on the distribution date, and (2) the holding period begins the after the distribution date.

DISTRIBUTING CORPORATION:

1. The distributing corporation recognizes no gain or loss on the stock dividend, whether it is nontaxable or taxable.
2. If the stock dividend is nontaxable, the distributing corporation does not reduce its E&P.
3. If the stock dividend is taxable, the distributing corporation reduces its E&P to the extent the distribution is treated as a taxable dividend.

STOCK REDEMPTIONS

OBJECTIVE 5

Decide whether a stock redemption should be treated as a sale or a dividend

A **stock redemption** is a corporation's acquiring its own stock in exchange for corporate property. This property may be cash, securities of other corporations, or any other consideration the corporation uses to acquire its own stock.[24] The corporation may cancel the acquired stock, retire it, or hold it as treasury stock.

A stock redemption may be desirable for the following reasons:

- A shareholder may want to withdraw from the corporate business and sell his or her equity interest. In such a case, the shareholder may prefer that the corporation, rather than an outsider, purchase his or her stock so that the remaining shareholders (who may be family members) retain complete control and ownership of the corporation after his or her withdrawal from the business.
- A shareholder may be required to sell stock to the corporation under the terms of a stock purchase agreement with the issuing corporation.
- A shareholder may want to reduce his or her equity interest in a corporation but may be unwilling or unable to sell stock to outsiders. For example, no market may exist for the shares, or sales to outsiders may be restricted.
- A shareholder may want to withdraw assets from a corporation before a sale of the corporation's business. A potential purchaser may not be interested in acquiring all the assets or be able to pay full value for all outstanding shares. A withdrawal of some assets by the seller in exchange for some of his or her shares allows the purchaser to acquire the remaining shares and business assets at a lower total price.
- After the death of a major shareholder, a corporation may agree to purchase the decedent's stock from either the estate or a beneficiary to provide sufficient funds to pay estate and inheritance taxes and funeral and administrative expenses.
- Management may believe that the corporation's stock is selling at a low price and that, to increase share value, the corporation should acquire some of its stock in the open market.

[24] Sec. 317.

Whatever the reason for the redemption, the shareholder must answer the following questions:

- What are the amount and character of the income, gain, or loss recognized as a result of the redemption?
- What basis does the shareholder take in any property received in exchange for his or her stock?
- When does the holding period for the property begin?
- What basis does the shareholder take in any distributing corporation stock held after the redemption?

The distributing corporation must answer the following questions:

- What amount and character of gain or loss, if any, must the corporation recognize when it redeems stock with noncash property?
- What effect does the redemption have on the corporation's E&P?[25]

TAX CONSEQUENCES OF THE REDEMPTION TO THE SHAREHOLDER

KEY POINT

As far as a shareholder is concerned, the basic issue in a stock redemption is whether the redemption is treated as a dividend or a sale.

As a general rule, when a shareholder sells or exchanges corporate stock, any gain or loss in the transaction is capital in character. In some cases, a redemption is treated as a stock sale. In other cases, it is treated as a dividend. The reason for this difference is that some redemptions resemble a stock sale to a third party, whereas others are essentially equivalent to a dividend. The following two examples illustrate the difference between a redemption resembling a dividend and a redemption resembling a sale. (The IRC refers to a "sale or exchange," but for simplicity in this chapter, we will use only the term "sale.")

EXAMPLE C:4-24 ▶ John owns all 100 outstanding shares of Tango Corporation stock. John's basis in his shares is $50,000, and Tango's E&P is $100,000. If Tango redeems 25 of John's shares for $85,000, John still owns 100% of Tango stock. Because John's proportionate ownership of Tango has not changed as a result of the redemption, the redemption resembles a dividend (i.e., a distribution of corporate earnings). Accordingly, for tax purposes, John is deemed to have received an $85,000 dividend. ◀

EXAMPLE C:4-25 ▶ Carol has owned three of the 1,000 outstanding shares of Water Corporation stock for two years. Her basis in the shares is $1,000, and Water's E&P is $100,000. If Water redeems all three of Carol's shares for $5,000, Carol is essentially in the same position as a seller of stock to a third party. She has received $5,000 for her stock and has no further ownership interest in the corporation. Thus, the redemption resembles a sale and is not essentially equivalent to a dividend. Accordingly, Carol recognizes a $4,000 ($5,000 − $1,000) capital gain. ◀

Example C:4-24 is an extreme case involving a redemption that clearly should be treated as a dividend to the shareholder. Example C:4-25 also is an extreme case involving a redemption that clearly should be treated as a sale of stock by the shareholder. Many cases, however, fall between the two extremes, and the way the redemption should be treated is not immediately apparent. The problem for Congress and the courts has been how to distinguish redemptions that should be treated as sales from those that should be treated as dividends. Under current law, a redemption qualifies for sale treatment if it satisfies one of the following conditions:

- The redemption is substantially disproportionate.
- The redemption is a complete termination of the shareholder's interest.
- The redemption is not essentially equivalent to a dividend.
- The redemption involves a partial liquidation of the corporation in conjunction with its redeeming stock from a noncorporate shareholder.
- The redemption provides funds for an estate to pay death taxes.

If a redemption qualifies as a sale, the transaction is treated as though the shareholder sold stock to a third party. The shareholder recognizes gain or loss equal to the FMV of

[25] This discussion concerns the redemption of C corporation stock. Different rules apply to the redemption of S corporation stock.

the property received less the shareholder's adjusted basis in the stock surrendered. The gain or loss is capital in character if the stock is a capital asset in the hands of the shareholder. The shareholder's basis in any property received is its FMV. The holding period for the property begins on the day following the exchange date.

A redemption that does not satisfy any of the five conditions necessary for sale treatment is regarded as a property distribution under Sec. 301. Accordingly, the entire amount of the distribution is treated as a dividend to the extent of the distributing corporation's E&P.[26] The shareholder's stock basis is not taken into account in determining the dividend amount. Generally, this basis is added to the basis of any remaining shares owned by the shareholder. If all the shareholder's stock has been redeemed, the basis of the redeemed shares is added to the basis of shares owned by those individuals whose ownership is attributed to the shareholder under attribution rules described below.[27]

EXAMPLE C:4-26 ▶ Amy and Rose each own 50 of the 100 outstanding shares of stock in York Corporation, which reports $100,000 of E&P. On May 10, York redeems 20 of Amy's shares with property worth $25,000. Amy's adjusted basis in those shares is $20,000. If the redemption satisfies one of the conditions necessary for sale treatment, Amy recognizes a capital gain of $5,000 ($25,000 − $20,000). Her basis in the property received is its $25,000 FMV, and its holding period begins on May 11. If the redemption does not satisfy any of the conditions necessary for sale treatment, Amy recognizes $25,000 of dividend income. Her $20,000 basis in the surrendered shares is added to the basis of her remaining 30 shares. ◀

ADDITIONAL COMMENT

Because capital gains and qualified dividends are taxed at the same rate, the difference in tax between exchange treatment and dividend treatment is primarily a function of the taxpayer's basis in the redeemed stock. Another difference is that dividends cannot offset capital losses.

Structuring a stock redemption as a sale offers two advantages. First, capital gains may be offset by capital losses. Second, in a sale, the basis of the shares redeemed reduces the amount of income recognized. By contrast, if a redemption is treated as a dividend, the basis of the shares redeemed does not reduce the dividend amount. Instead, the basis shifts to the shareholder's remaining stock, which reduces the gain (or increases the loss) recognized in a later sale of this stock.

Topic Review C:4-4 summarizes the tax consequences of stock redemptions to both the shareholder and the distributing corporation.

ATTRIBUTION RULES

Three of the five tests for determining how a redemption should be treated (i.e., as a sale or dividend) are based on stock ownership before and after the redemption. The tests measure the extent to which the shareholder's proportionate interest in the corporation has been reduced as a result of the exchange. In general, if the shareholder's proportionate interest has been substantially reduced, the redemption is treated as a sale. On the other hand, if this

TOPIC REVIEW C:4-4

Tax Consequences of Stock Redemptions

SHAREHOLDERS:

General Rule: The distribution amount received by a shareholder in exchange for his or her stock is treated as a dividend to the extent of the distributing corporation's E&P. The basis of the surrendered stock is added to the basis of the shareholder's remaining stock.

Sale Exception: If the redemption meets specific requirements, the distribution amount received by the shareholder is offset by the adjusted basis of the shares surrendered. The difference generally is treated as a capital gain or loss. No basis adjustment occurs.

DISTRIBUTING CORPORATION:

Gain/Loss Recognition: Under either the general rule or sale exception, the corporation recognizes gain (but not loss) as though it had sold distributed noncash property for its FMV immediately before the redemption.

Earnings and Profits Adjustment: For a redemption treated as a dividend, E&P is reduced in the same manner as for a regular dividend (e.g., by the amount of any money or the FMV of any property distributed). For a redemption treated as a sale, E&P is reduced by the portion of current and accumulated E&P attributable to the redeemed stock. Any distribution amount exceeding this portion reduces the corporation's paid-in capital.

---

[26] Sec. 302(d).

[27] Reg. Sec. 1.302-2(c).

interest remains essentially the same or increases, the redemption is treated as a dividend (assuming sufficient E&P).

For the purpose of applying these tests, stock ownership is determined under the constructive ownership or attribution rules of Sec. 318.[28] According to these rules, a shareholder owns not only the shares he or she directly owns but also shares owned by his or her spouse, other immediate family members, and related entities. In addition, corporations, partnerships, trusts, and estates are considered to constructively own shares owned by their shareholders, partners, and beneficiaries.

The attribution rules prevent shareholders from taking advantage of favorable tax rules or avoiding unfavorable tax rules by transferring to family members or related entities stock that the shareholder previously owned. The proportionate stock ownership tests would be subject to abuse if only direct ownership were considered.

Section 318(a) sets forth four types of attribution rules: attribution among family members, attribution from entities, attribution to entities, and option attribution. These rules are discussed below.

ADDITIONAL COMMENT

The family attribution rules of Sec. 318 are not as inclusive as the family attribution rules of Sec. 267 (covered in Chapter C:3). For example, siblings and grandparents are not considered family members by Sec. 318 but are included under Sec. 267.

Family Attribution. Under the first set of rules, an individual is considered to own constructively all stock owned by or for his or her spouse, children, grandchildren, and parents. An individual is not considered to own stock owned by his or her brothers, sisters, or grandparents.

Once attributed to an individual under one set of attribution rules, stock ownership may not be reattributed to another individual under the same set of rules. Thus, stock ownership attributed to one family member under the family attribution rules may not be reattributed to a second family member under the same set of rules. However, once attributed to an individual under one set of attribution rules, stock ownership may be reattributed to another individual under a different set of attribution rules. For example, stock ownership attributed from a corporation to its shareholder under the corporate attribution rules may be reattributed to the shareholder's spouse under the family attribution rules.

EXAMPLE C:4-27 ▶

Harry; his wife, Wilma; their son, Steve; and Harry's father, Frank, each own 25 of the 100 outstanding shares of Strong Corporation stock. Under the family attribution rules, Harry is considered to own all 100 Strong shares (25 directly plus constructively the shares owned by Wilma, Steve, and Frank). Wilma is considered to own 75 shares (25 directly plus constructively the 50 shares owned by Harry and Steve). Ownership of Frank's shares is neither directly attributed to Wilma nor reattributed to Wilma through Harry. Steve is considered to own 75 shares (25 directly plus constructively the 50 shares owned by his parents Harry and Wilma). Ownership of Frank's shares is neither directly attributed to Steve nor reattributed to Steve through Harry. Frank is considered to own 75 shares (25 directly plus constructively the shares owned by Harry and Steve (his grandson)). Ownership of Wilma's shares is neither directly attributed to Frank nor reattributed to Frank through Harry.

The diagram below illustrates the constructive stock ownership of the four shareholders. The arrows indicate the direction(s) of ownership attribution.

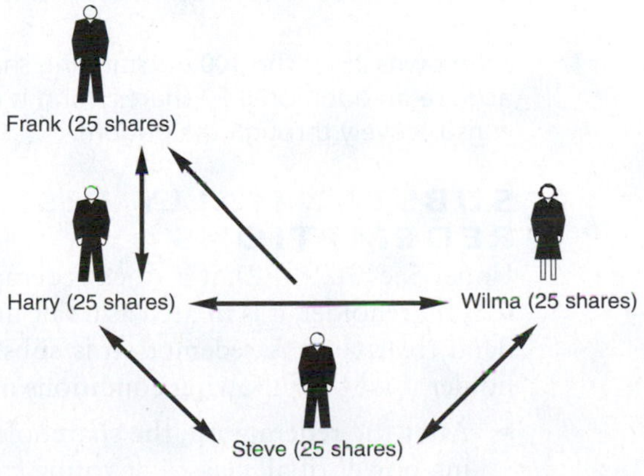

[28] Sec. 302(c).

The table below shows each shareholder's direct and constructive stock ownership. Note that the total number of shares owned directly and constructively by all shareholders may exceed the total number of actual shares issued and outstanding.

		Shares Constructively Owned From:				
Shareholder	*Direct Ownership*	*Spouse*	*Child*	*Grandchild*	*Parent(s)*	*Total*
Frank	25		25	25		75
Harry	25	25	25		25	100
Wilma	25	25	25			75
Steve	25				50	75
	100					

Attribution From Entities. Under the second set of attribution rules, stock owned by or for a partnership is considered to be owned proportionately by the partners. Stock owned by or for an estate is considered to be owned proportionately by the beneficiaries. Stock owned by or for a trust is considered to be owned by the beneficiaries in proportion to their actuarial interests. Stock owned by or for a C corporation is considered to be owned proportionately only by shareholders owning (directly or indirectly) 50% or more of the corporation's stock value.[29]

EXAMPLE C:4-28 ▶ Bill, who is married to Nancy, owns a 50% interest in Partnership A. Partnership A owns 40 of the 100 outstanding shares of Yellow Corporation stock, and Bill owns the remaining 60 shares. Under the entity attribution rules, Bill is considered to own 80 shares, 60 directly and 20 (0.50 × 40 shares) constructively. In addition, the stock ownership attributed to Bill under the entity attribution rules is reattributed to Nancy under the family attribution rules. ◀

Attribution to Entities. Under the third set of attribution rules, all stock owned by or for a partner is considered to be constructively owned by the partnership. All stock owned by or for a beneficiary of an estate or a trust is considered to be constructively owned by the estate or trust. All stock owned by or for a shareholder who owns (directly or indirectly) 50% or more of a C corporation's stock value is considered to be constructively owned by the corporation.

Stock ownership attributed to a partnership, estate, trust, or corporation from a partner, beneficiary, or shareholder is not reattributed from the entity to another partner, beneficiary, or shareholder.

EXAMPLE C:4-29 ▶ Assume the same facts as in Example C:4-28. The partnership in which Bill is a partner is considered to own all 100 shares of Yellow stock (40 directly and 60 constructively through Bill). Bill's stock ownership attributed to the partnership cannot be reattributed from the partnership to Bill's partners. ◀

Option Attribution. Under the last set of attribution rules, a person who holds an option to purchase stock is considered to own the underlying stock.

EXAMPLE C:4-30 ▶ John owns 25 of the 100 outstanding shares of Yard Corporation stock. He holds an option to acquire an additional 50 shares. John is considered to own 75 Yard shares (25 directly plus 50 constructively through the option). ◀

SUBSTANTIALLY DISPROPORTIONATE REDEMPTIONS

Under Sec. 302(b)(2), if a stock redemption is substantially disproportionate with respect to a shareholder, it is treated as a sale and thus qualifies for capital gain as opposed to dividend treatment. A redemption is substantially disproportionate with respect to a shareholder if all the following conditions are met:

- After the redemption, the shareholder owns less than 50% of the total combined voting power of all classes of voting stock.

[29] For purposes of the attribution rules, S corporations are treated as partnerships, not corporations. Thus, attribution occurs to and from shareholders owning less than 50% of the S corporation stock. Unless otherwise stated, all corporations in the examples are C corporations.

- After the redemption, the shareholder owns less than 80% of his or her percentage ownership of voting stock before the redemption.
- After the redemption, the shareholder owns less than 80% of his or her percentage ownership of common stock (whether voting or nonvoting) before the redemption.

TAX STRATEGY TIP

If possible, taxpayers should structure a redemption to meet the substantially disproportionate test rather than the subjective "not equivalent to a dividend" test (discussed on page C:4-23), thereby obtaining certainty of results.

These tests are applied mechanically to each shareholder's ownership interest. The 50% test precludes shareholders from qualifying for capital gains treatment if they own a controlling interest in the distributing corporation after the redemption. The 80% tests define a degree of change in the shareholder's proportionate interest that constitutes a substantial reduction in that interest. A redemption may be substantially disproportionate with respect to one shareholder but not another. If only one class of stock is outstanding, the second and third requirements are essentially the same.

EXAMPLE C:4-31 ▶ Long Corporation has issued 400 shares of common stock and plans to redeem 100 of these shares. Before the redemption, Ann, Bob, Carl, and Dana (all unrelated) own 100 shares each. Long redeems 55 shares from Ann, 25 shares from Bob, and 20 shares from Carl. The following table illustrates ownership before and after the redemption.

ADDITIONAL COMMENT

In calculating the percentage of stock owned *after* a redemption note that the denominator used is the number of shares outstanding *after* the redemption.

	Before Redemption			*After Redemption*	
Shareholder	*No. of Shares Owned*	*Percentage of Ownership*	*Shares Redeemed*	*No. of Shares Owned*	*Percentage of Ownership*
	(1)	(1) ÷ 400	(2)	(1) − (2)	[(1) − (2)] ÷ 300
Ann	100	25%	55	45	15.00%
Bob	100	25%	25	75	25.00%
Carl	100	25%	20	80	26.67%
Dana	100	25%	—	100	33.33%
Total	400	100%	100	300	100.00%

The redemption is substantially disproportionate with respect to Ann because, after the redemption, she owns less than 50% of Long's stock, and her stock ownership percentage (15%) is less than 80% of her stock ownership percentage before the redemption (0.80 × 25% = 20%). The redemption is not substantially disproportionate with respect to Bob because the percentage reduction in his stock ownership is not less than 80% of his pre-redemption ownership percentage. In fact, Bob owns the same percentage of stock (25%) after the redemption as he did before the redemption (25%). The redemption also is not substantially disproportionate with respect to Carl because his stock ownership percentage increases from 25% to 26.67%. Thus, only the redemption of Ann's shares is treated as a sale and qualifies for capital gains treatment. ◀

The constructive ownership rules of Sec. 318(a) apply in determining whether the shareholder has met the three conditions for a substantially disproportionate redemption.[30]

EXAMPLE C:4-32 ▶ Assume the same facts as in Example C:4-31 except that Ann is Bob's mother. In this case, the redemption is not substantially disproportionate with respect to either Ann or Bob because, before the redemption, each directly and constructively owns 200 shares, or 50% of the Long stock, and after the redemption each directly and constructively owns 120 shares, or 40% of the stock. Although the 50% test is met, neither Ann nor Bob satisfies the 80% test. After the redemption each directly and constructively owns *exactly* 80% of the percentage owned before the redemption (0.80 × 50% = 40%). ◀

COMPLETE TERMINATION OF THE SHAREHOLDER'S INTEREST

Under Sec. 302(b)(3), if a stock redemption completely terminates a shareholder's interest in the corporation, the redemption also is treated as a sale. At first glance, this rule does not offer a route to sale treatment that is not already provided by the other Sec. 302 rules. If a corporation redeems all of a shareholder's stock, in most cases the requirements for a substantially disproportionate redemption under Sec. 302(b)(2) would have been satisfied.

30 Reg. Sec. 1.302-3(a).

However, the complete termination rule extends sale treatment to two redemptions not covered by the substantially disproportionate redemption rules:

- If a shareholder's interest in a corporation consists exclusively of nonvoting stock, a redemption of all the stock could not qualify as substantially disproportionate under Sec. 302(b)(2) because no reduction of voting power occurs. However, it could qualify as a complete termination of the shareholder's interest under Sec. 302(b)(3) because the interest need not consist of voting stock.
- If a shareholder owns some voting stock and the redemption terminates his or her entire interest in the corporation, the family attribution rules of Sec. 318(a)(1) may be waived. Consequently, the redemption could qualify for sale treatment even though other family members continue to own some or all of the corporation's stock.[31]

To have the family attribution rules waived, the shareholder must meet all of the following conditions:

- After the redemption, the shareholder must not retain any interest in the corporation except as a creditor. This restriction includes any interest as an officer, director, or employee.
- The shareholder must not acquire any such interest (other than by bequest or inheritance) for at least ten years from the date of the redemption.
- The shareholder must file a written agreement with the IRS that he or she will notify the IRS upon acquiring any prohibited interest.

The written agreement authorizes the IRS to assess additional taxes for the year of the redemption if the prohibited interest is acquired, even when the basic three-year limitations period has expired.

EXAMPLE C:4-33 ▶ Father and Son each own 50 of the 100 outstanding shares of Short Corporation stock. Short redeems all of Father's shares. Under the family attribution rules, Father is considered to own directly and constructively 100% of the Short stock both before and after the redemption. Thus, the redemption is not substantially disproportionate with respect to him. However, if Father agrees not to retain or acquire any interest in Short for ten years (except as a creditor, devisee, or heir), the family attribution rules may be waived. Consequently, the redemption could qualify as a complete termination of Father's interest and be treated as a sale. ◀

Waiver of the family attribution rules is not permitted in the following two situations involving related parties:

- Within the ten-year period ending on the distribution date, the distributee acquired, directly or indirectly, part or all of the redeemed stock from a person whose stock ownership would be attributable (at the time of the distribution) to the distributee under Sec. 318.
- Any person owns (at the time of the distribution) stock of the redeeming corporation the ownership of which is attributable to the distributee under Sec. 318, and such person acquired any stock in the redeeming corporation, directly or indirectly, from the distributee within the ten-year period ending on the distribution date.

The first restriction is aimed at an individual who transfers stock to a related party (e.g., family member or controlled entity) purportedly to enable the related party to invoke the complete termination provision so as to recognize a capital gain when the corporation redeems the transferred stock. The second restriction is aimed at an individual who transfers some of his or her stock to a related party purportedly to invoke the complete termination provision so as to recognize a capital gain when the corporation redeems his or her remaining stock. These prohibitions against waiving the family attribution rules do not apply if the shareholder transferred the stock more than ten years before the redemption or if the distributee can show that the acquisition or disposition of the stock did not have tax avoidance as one of its principal purposes. In the second situation above, the family attribution rules also can be waived if the corporation redeems as part of the same transaction stock previously transferred to the related party.

Note that only the family attribution rules can be waived. Entities may have the family attribution rules waived if both the entity and the individual whose stock is attributed to the entity agree not to acquire any prohibited interest in the corporation for at least ten years.

[31] Section 302(c)(2) provides for the waiver of family attribution rules.

EXAMPLE C:4-34 ► Andrew created the A Trust, which owns 30% of Willow Corporation stock. Andrew's wife, Wanda, is the sole beneficiary of the trust. Their son, Steve, owns the remaining 70% of Willow stock. Willow redeems all of its stock owned by the A Trust. At first glance, the redemption does not qualify for sale treatment because the trust is deemed to own all the stock owned by Wanda, and Wanda is deemed to own all the stock owned by Steve. However, if both A Trust and Wanda agree not to acquire any interest in the corporation for ten years, the family attribution rules may be waived. Consequently, the redemption will be treated as a complete termination of the trust's interest in Willow and will be eligible for sale treatment. ◄

REDEMPTIONS NOT ESSENTIALLY EQUIVALENT TO A DIVIDEND

KEY POINT

Section 302(b)(1) has generally been interpreted to require that a shareholder incur a "meaningful reduction" of its stock interest. What constitutes a "meaningful reduction" remains unsettled.

Section 302(b)(1) provides that a redemption will be treated as a sale if it is not essentially equivalent to a dividend. The tax law sets forth no mechanical test for determining when a redemption is not essentially equivalent to a dividend. Instead, it implies that a determination should be based on the facts and circumstances of each case.[32] Sec. 302(b)(1) does not provide a safe harbor similar to the rules for substantially disproportionate redemptions or redemptions that are a complete termination of a shareholder's interest. On the other hand, the provision prevents the redemption rules from being too restrictive, especially in the case of transactions involving preferred stock.

The Supreme Court's decision in *Maclin P. Davis* sets forth guidelines for determining when a redemption is not essentially equivalent to a dividend.[33] The Supreme Court held that (1) in this determination, a business purpose is irrelevant; (2) the Sec. 318 attribution rules must be applied to establish dividend equivalency; and (3) a redemption of part of a sole shareholder's stock is always essentially equivalent to a dividend. The Court further held that for Sec. 302(b)(1) purposes, there must be a "meaningful reduction" in the shareholder's proportionate interest in the corporation after taking into account the constructive ownership rules of Sec. 318(a). Despite this holding, the definition of "a meaningful reduction in interest" remains unclear.

Because of this lack of clarity, Sec. 302(b)(1) generally applies to a redemption of nonvoting preferred stock only where the shareholder does not own any common stock,[34] or to redemptions resulting in a substantial reduction in the shareholder's rights to vote and exercise control over the corporation, participate in earnings, and share in net assets upon liquidation. Generally, the IRS allows sale treatment if a controlling shareholder reduces his or her interest to a noncontrolling position,[35] or a noncontrolling shareholder further reduces his or her minority interest.[36] A shareholder does not qualify for sale treatment if he or she maintains control both before and after the redemption,[37] or if he or she assumes a controlling position.

EXAMPLE C:4-35 ► Four unrelated individuals own all of Thyme Corporation's single class of stock as follows: Alan, 27%; Betty, 24.33%; Clem, 24.33%; and David, 24.33%. Thyme redeems some of Alan's stock holdings, resulting in a reduction of Alan's interest to 22.27%. Betty, Clem, and David own equally the remaining 77.73% of Thyme stock. The redemption of Alan's stock does not qualify as substantially disproportionate because Alan's interest is not reduced below 21.6% ($0.80 \times 27\% = 21.6\%$). Nor does the redemption qualify as a complete termination of Alan's interest because Alan still owns Thyme shares. However, the redemption might be treated as a sale under Sec. 302(b)(1) because the transaction results in a meaningful reduction of Alan's noncontrolling interest in Thyme. ◄

PARTIAL LIQUIDATIONS

Under Sec. 302(b)(4), a redemption of a noncorporate shareholder's stock qualifies for sale treatment if the redemption is in **partial liquidation** of the corporation. A partial liquidation occurs when a corporation discontinues one line of business, distributes assets used in that business to its shareholders, and continues at least one other line of business.[38] A distribution

[32] Reg. Sec. 1.302-2(b).

[33] *U.S. v. Maclin P. Davis*, 25 AFTR 2d 70-827, 70-1 USTC ¶9289 (USSC, 1970).

[34] Reg. Sec. 1.302-2(a).

[35] In Rev. Rul. 75-502, 1975-2 C.B. 111, a reduction in stock ownership from 57% to 50% where the shareholder no longer had control was considered a meaningful reduction in interest.

[36] In Rev. Rul. 76-364, 1976-2 C.B. 91, a reduction in stock ownership from 27% to 22% was considered a meaningful reduction in interest.

[37] See *Jack Paparo*, 71 T.C. 692 (1979), where reductions in stock ownership from 100% to 81.17% and from 100% to 74.15% were not considered meaningful reductions in interest.

[38] A partial liquidation also can occur when a corporation sells one line of business, distributes the sales proceeds (after paying taxes on any gain from the sale), and continues at least one other line of business. See Rev. Rul. 79-275, 1979-2 C.B. 137.

in partial liquidation qualifies for sale treatment if it is not essentially equivalent to a dividend. The distribution must be made within the tax year in which a plan of partial liquidation has been adopted or within the succeeding tax year.

Determination Made at the Corporate Level. For purposes of Sec. 302(b)(4), whether a distribution is not essentially equivalent to a dividend is determined at the corporate level.[39] The distribution must result from a bona fide contraction of the corporate business. In relevant Treasury Regulations and revenue rulings, the government provides guidance as to what constitutes a bona fide business contraction. Examples include

- The distribution of insurance proceeds received as a result of a fire that destroys part of a business.[40]
- Termination of a contract representing 95% of a domestic corporation's gross income.[41]
- Change in a corporation's business from a full-line department store to a discount apparel store, which results in the elimination of certain units; the elimination of most forms of credit; and a reduction in inventory, floor space, and employees.[42]

Safe Harbor Rule. Under Sec. 302(e)(2), a distribution satisfies the not-essentially-equivalent-to-a-dividend requirement and qualifies as a partial liquidation if

- The distribution is attributable to the distributing corporation's ceasing to conduct a qualified trade or business, or consists of the assets of a qualified trade or business; and
- Immediately after the distribution, the distributing corporation is engaged in the active conduct of at least one qualified trade or business.

A qualified trade or business is any trade or business that

- Has been actively conducted throughout the five-year period ending on the date of the redemption, and
- Was not acquired by the corporation within such five-year period in a partially or wholly taxable transaction.

The definition of an active trade or business is the same as that used for Sec. 355 (corporate division) purposes, as discussed in Chapter C:7.

EXAMPLE C:4-36 ▶ Sage Corporation has manufactured hats and gloves for the past five years. In the current year, Sage discontinues hat manufacturing, sells all of its hat manufacturing machinery, and distributes the proceeds to its shareholders in redemption of some of their Sage shares. The corporation continues glove manufacturing. The distribution is pursuant to a partial liquidation and thus qualifies for sale treatment. ◀

Tax Consequences of a Partial Liquidation to the Shareholders. If a distribution is in partial liquidation of the corporation, a noncorporate shareholder treats the redemption of his or her stock as a sale, whether or not the distribution is pro rata. In contrast, a corporate shareholder treats the redemption distribution as a dividend unless the corporation meets one of the other tests for sale treatment (i.e., Sec. 302(b)(1)-(3) or Sec. 303). For a corporate shareholder, dividend treatment may be more advantageous than sale treatment because a corporation receives no preferential tax rate on capital gains, but may be eligible for a 70%, 80%, or 100% dividends-received deduction. In determining whether stock is owned by a corporate or noncorporate shareholder, stock held by a partnership, trust, or estate is considered to be held proportionately by its partners or beneficiaries.

EXAMPLE C:4-37 ▶ Assume the same facts as in Example C:4-36 except Sage Corporation is owned by Ted and Jolly Corporation. Each shareholder owns 50 shares of Sage stock with a $20,000 basis and has owned the stock since Sage's inception. Sage reports $100,000 of current and accumulated E&P. Sage distributes $18,000 to each shareholder in redemption of ten shares of stock worth $18,000. Because the redemption involves a partial liquidation, Ted treats

[39] Sec. 302(e)(1)(A).
[40] Reg. Sec. 1.346-1.
[41] Rev. Rul. 75-3, 1975-1 C.B. 108.
[42] Rev. Rul. 74-296, 1974-1 C.B. 80.

the transaction as a sale and recognizes a capital gain of $14,000 ($18,000 − $4,000). Jolly, however, cannot treat the transaction as a sale because Jolly is a corporate shareholder and thus must recognize $18,000 of dividend income. On the other hand, Jolly is eligible for a $14,400 (0.80 × $18,000) dividends-received deduction. Jolly's $4,000 basis in the ten redeemed shares is added to the basis of its 40 remaining shares, resulting in a $20,000 basis in those shares. ◄

STOP & THINK

Question: Why is a distribution in partial liquidation of a corporation treated as a sale by its noncorporate shareholders and as a dividend by its corporate shareholders?

Solution: The different tax treatment probably reflects different tax advantages. Noncorporate shareholders benefit most from sale treatment because they can offset their stock basis against any amount realized in the distribution. Corporate shareholders benefit most from dividend treatment because they can take the dividends-received deduction, thereby reducing the dividend tax burden. These disparate advantages stem from the different tax status of corporations, other entities, and individuals.

TAX STRATEGY TIP

An estate with liquidity problems owing to large holdings of a closely held business also may want to consider installment payment of the estate tax under Sec. 6166. See Chapter C:13 for further details.

REDEMPTIONS TO PAY DEATH TAXES

If corporate stock represents a substantial portion of a decedent's gross estate, a redemption of the stock from the estate or its beneficiaries may be eligible for sale treatment under Sec. 303. This IRC section helps shareholders who inherit stock in a closely held corporation pay estate and inheritance taxes and funeral and administrative expenses. If the stock is not readily marketable, a stock redemption may be the only way to provide the estate and its beneficiaries with sufficient liquidity to defray the costs of estate administration. Under the substantially disproportionate or complete termination rules, ownership attribution would disqualify the redemption from sale treatment. Consequently, the redemption would be treated as a dividend. Under Sec. 303, ownership attribution does not apply to the portion of a stock redemption that meets certain requirements.

Section 303 provides that a redemption of stock that was included in a decedent's gross estate is treated as a stock sale by the shareholder (i.e., either the estate or the beneficiary of the estate) if the following conditions are met:

1. The value of the redeeming corporation's stock included in the decedent's gross estate is more than 35% of the adjusted gross estate. The adjusted gross estate consists of the FMV of all property on the date of the decedent's death less allowable deductions for funeral and administrative expenses, claims against the estate, debts, and casualty and other losses.

EXAMPLE C:4-38 ► A decedent's gross estate, valued at $5.8 million, includes $3.4 million in cash and Pepper Corporation stock worth $2.4 million. Funeral and other deductible estate expenses amount to $1.8 million. Thus, the decedent's adjusted gross estate is $4 million ($5,800,000 − $1,800,000). Because the $2.4 million value of the Pepper stock included in the gross estate exceeds 35% of the adjusted gross estate ($1.4 million = 0.35 × $4,000,000), a redemption of this stock qualifies for sale treatment under Sec. 303. ◄

2. The maximum amount of the redemption distribution that can qualify for sale treatment is the sum of all federal and state estate and inheritance taxes, plus any interest due on those taxes, and all funeral and administrative expenses allowable as deductions in computing the federal estate tax. The redemption must be of stock held by the estate or by the decedent's heirs who are liable for estate taxes and other administrative expenses.

3. Section 303 applies to a redemption distribution only to the extent the shareholder's interest in the estate is reduced by the payment of death taxes and funeral and administration expenses. The maximum distribution eligible for sale treatment is the amount of estate taxes and expenses the shareholder is obligated to bear.

EXAMPLE C:4-39 ► Assume the same facts as in Example C:4-38 except that, before the decedent's death, all the stock was gifted to the decedent's son, Sam. The remaining assets were bequeathed to the decedent's wife, Wilma, who as beneficiary is indirectly liable for all estate taxes and administrative expenses. Section 303 sale treatment is not available to Sam because he is not liable for estate taxes or administrative expenses. If instead $1.6 million in nonstock assets had been gifted to Wilma before the decedent's death, and the remaining assets bequeathed to Sam, Sam as beneficiary would be indirectly liable for all estate taxes and administrative expenses. In such case, he could use Sec. 303 to obtain sale treatment for the redemption of enough of his stock to pay estate taxes and administrative expenses. ◀

4. Section 303 applies only to distributions within certain time limits.

a. In general, the redemption must occur not later than 90 days after the expiration of the period for assessing the federal estate tax. Because the limitations period for the federal estate tax expires three years after the estate tax return is due and because the return is due nine months after the date of death, the redemption generally must occur within four years after the date of death.

b. If a petition for redetermination of an estate tax deficiency is filed with the Tax Court, the distribution period is extended to 60 days after the Tax Court's decision becomes final.

c. If the taxpayer made a valid election under Sec. 6166 to defer paying of federal estate taxes under an installment plan, the distribution period is extended to the time the installment payments are due.

5. The stock of two or more corporations may be aggregated to meet the 35% threshold, provided that 20% or more of the value of each corporation's outstanding stock is included in the gross estate.

EXAMPLE C:4-40 ▶ A decedent's gross estate, valued at $5.8 million, includes 80% of the stock in Curry Corporation, valued at $800,000, and 90% of the stock in Brodie Corporation, valued at $900,000. Deductible funeral and administrative expenses amount to $1.8 million. Thus, the decedent's adjusted gross estate is $4 million. Although the value of neither the Curry stock nor the Brodie stock exceeds 35% of the $4 million adjusted gross estate, the total value of both corporations' stock ($1.7 million = $800,000 + $900,000) exceeds 35% of the adjusted gross estate ($1.4 million = 0.35 × $4,000,000). Therefore, a redemption of sufficient Curry stock and/or Brodie stock to pay estate taxes and funeral and administrative expenses qualifies for sale treatment under Sec. 303. ◀

Although the legislative intent behind Sec. 303 is to provide liquidity for the payment of estate taxes and administrative expenses where a significant portion of the estate consists of stock in a closely held corporation, a redemption can qualify for Sec. 303 sale treatment even where the estate includes sufficient liquid assets to pay estate taxes and defray administrative costs. The redemption proceeds need not be used for these purposes.

The advantage of a Sec. 303 redemption is that the redeeming shareholder usually realizes little or no capital gain because his or her basis in the redeemed stock is the stock's FMV on date of the decedent's death (or an alternate valuation date, if applicable). If the redemption does *not* qualify as a sale, the redeeming shareholder recognizes dividend income equal to the distribution proceeds received in redemption of the stock.

EXAMPLE C:4-41 ▶ Chili Corporation pays $105,000 to redeem 100 shares of stock from Art, who inherited the stock from his father, Fred. The stock's FMV on Fred's date of death was $100,000. Chili reports an E&P balance of $500,000. If the redemption qualifies for sale treatment under Sec. 303, Art recognizes a $5,000 ($105,000 − $100,000) capital gain. On the other hand, if the redemption does not qualify for sale treatment under Sec. 303 or one of the other redemption provisions, Art recognizes $105,000 of dividend income. Although both the capital gain and the dividend income are subject to the applicable capital gains tax rate, the dividend amount significantly exceeds the capital gain amount. ◀

SELF-STUDY QUESTION

How much gain is the redeeming shareholder likely to recognize in a qualifying Sec. 303 redemption?

ANSWER

Probably little or none. The basis in the redeemed stock equals its FMV at the decedent's date of death (or an alternate valuation date). The recognized gain generally is only the post-death appreciation.

EFFECT OF REDEMPTIONS ON THE DISTRIBUTING CORPORATION

As in the case of property distributions that are not in redemption of stock, two questions relating to property distributions in redemption of stock must be answered:

- What amount and character of gain or loss must the distributing corporation recognize?
- What effect does the distribution have on the corporation's E&P?

Each of these questions is addressed below.

Corporate Gain or Loss on Property Distributions. The rules for gain or loss recognition for a corporation that distributes property in redemption of its stock are the same as the Sec. 311 rules pertaining to property distributions not in redemption of stock.

- The corporation recognizes gain when it redeems its stock by distributing property that has appreciated in value. The character of the gain depends on the character of the property distributed.
- The corporation recognizes no loss when it redeems its stock by distributing property that has declined in value.

Effect of Redemptions on E&P. A stock redemption affects a corporation's E&P in two ways. First, if the corporation distributes appreciated property, the excess of the property's FMV over its E&P adjusted basis increases the balance in the E&P account. Second, if the corporation distributes cash, or other property, the corporation's E&P balance is reduced accordingly. The extent of the reduction depends on whether the shareholder treats the redemption as a sale or a dividend.

If the redemption is treated as a dividend, the corporation reduces its E&P by the amount of any cash, the principal amount of any obligations, and the greater of the adjusted basis or FMV of any other property distributed, in the same way as it does for a property distribution not in redemption of stock.

If the redemption is treated as a sale, the corporation reduces its E&P by the portion of its current and accumulated E&P attributable to the redeemed stock. In other words, E&P is reduced by the percentage of the total outstanding shares redeemed, not to exceed the actual distribution amount. Any distribution amount exceeding this percentage reduces the corporation's tax basis paid-in capital.[43] Ordinary dividend amounts are subtracted from current E&P before the subtraction of stock redemption amounts. No such sequencing exists for accumulated E&P. Both ordinary dividend distributions and redemption distributions reduce accumulated E&P in chronological order.

EXAMPLE C:4-42 ► Apex Corporation has 100 shares of stock outstanding, 30 of which are owned by Mona. On December 31, Apex pays $36,000 to redeem all 30 of Mona's shares in a redemption qualifying as a sale. At the time of the redemption, Apex has $60,000 in paid-in capital and $40,000 of E&P. Because Apex redeemed 30% of its outstanding stock, the distribution reduces Apex's E&P by $12,000 (0.30 × $40,000). The remaining $24,000 ($36,000 − $12,000) reduces Apex's tax basis paid-in capital to $36,000 ($60,000 − $24,000).[44] ◄

PREFERRED STOCK BAILOUTS

OBJECTIVE 6

Explain the tax treatment of preferred stock bailouts

The stock redemption rules permit sale treatment in certain situations and require dividend treatment in all others. Generally, taxpayers prefer sale treatment for two reasons. First, sale treatment allows taxpayers to offset their stock basis against the distribution proceeds. Second, gain on a stock sale generally is long-term and capital in character. This gain may be entirely offset by the taxpayer's capital losses and thus not be taxed at all. With these results in mind, taxpayers have attempted various schemes to obtain sale rather than dividend treatment.

[43] Sec. 312(n)(7). This adjustment to paid-in capital might be necessary for companies that maintain tax basis balance sheets, for example, to determine book-tax differences in complying with ASC 740, Income Taxes, which is the FASB Accounting Standards Codification for SFAS No. 109.

[44] Distributions during the year require a different calculation, which is beyond the scope of this text.

ADDITIONAL COMMENT

When the term *bailout* is used in the corporate context, it generally refers to a scheme that allows a corporation to make a dividend distribution that for tax purposes is treated as a sale of a capital asset.

One such method is a **preferred stock bailout**. Prior to Congress' enacting anti-tax avoidance measures, a preferred stock bailout typically proceeded as follows:

1. A corporation issued a nontaxable dividend of nonvoting preferred stock to its common shareholders. Under the rules relating to nontaxable stock dividends, a portion of the common stock basis was allocated to the preferred stock. Its holding period included the holding period for the common stock.

2. The recipient shareholder then sold the preferred stock at its FMV to an unrelated third party. As a result of the sale, the shareholder recognized a capital gain equal to the difference between the preferred stock's sale price and its allocated basis.

3. Next, the corporation redeemed the preferred stock from the third-party (usually at a small premium to reward the third party for his or her cooperation in the scheme).

4. As an alternative to steps 2 and 3, the corporation redeemed the preferred stock directly from the shareholder.

As a result of this preferred stock bailout, the shareholder extracted the corporation's E&P and converted what otherwise would have been a dividend into a long-term capital gain without changing his or her equity position. To deter such tax avoidance, Congress enacted Sec. 306, which "taints" certain stock (usually preferred stock) when distributed to a shareholder in a nontaxable stock dividend. Section 306 treats the distribution proceeds as a dividend if the corporation redeems the tainted stock directly from the shareholder and treats the amount realized as ordinary income if the shareholder sells the stock to a third party. Either way, Sec. 306 prevents shareholders from using a preferred stock bailout to convert ordinary income into capital gain.

Recent tax acts, however, have taken the "sting" out of Sec. 306 by taxing dividends at the same rate as capital gains. Thus, both the dividend recognized on a direct redemption of Sec. 306 stock and the "deemed" dividend recognized on a third-party sale of the stock are taxed at the applicable capital gains rate. Nevertheless, the Sec. 306 taint is still disadvantageous because, even though subject to the preferential capital gains tax rate, dividends cannot offset capital losses as can "real" capital gains. Also, if Sec. 306 recasts the redemption as a dividend, the shareholder is taxed on the entire amount of distribution proceeds rather than just the net gain.

SEC. 306 STOCK DEFINED

Section 306 stock is defined as follows:[45]

- Stock (other than common issued with respect to common) received in a nontaxable stock dividend
- Stock (other than common) received in a nontaxable corporate reorganization or corporate division if the effect of the transaction was substantially the same as the receipt of a stock dividend, or if the stock was received in exchange for Sec. 306 stock
- Stock that has a basis determined by reference to the basis of Sec. 306 stock (i.e., a substituted or transferred basis)
- Stock (other than common) acquired in an exchange to which Sec. 351 applies if the receipt of money (in lieu of the stock) would have been treated as a dividend

Preferred stock issued by a corporation with no current or accumulated E&P in the year the stock is issued is not Sec. 306 stock. Also, inherited stock is not Sec. 306 stock because the basis of such stock is its FMV on the date of the decedent's death (or alternate valuation date) and, therefore, is not determined by reference to the decedent's basis.[46]

TYPICAL MISCONCEPTION

Although the amount of deemed dividend income recognized on a sale of Sec. 306 stock is measured by the E&P existing in the year the Sec. 306 stock was distributed, the E&P of the distributing corporation is not reduced by the amount of the deemed dividend.

DISPOSITIONS OF SEC. 306 STOCK

If a shareholder sells or otherwise disposes of Sec. 306 stock (except in a redemption), the amount realized is treated as a deemed dividend to the extent the shareholder would have recognized a dividend at the time of the distribution had cash equal to the stock's FMV, instead of stock, been distributed. The shareholder's deemed dividend is measured by

[45] Sec. 306(c).

[46] Reg. Sec. 1.306-3(e).

reference to the corporation's E&P in the year the Sec. 306 stock was issued, although the corporation does not reduce its E&P upon the sale. Any additional amount received for the Sec. 306 stock generally is treated as a return of capital. If the additional amount exceeds the shareholder's basis in the Sec. 306 stock, the excess is treated as a capital gain. If the additional amount is less than the shareholder's basis, the unrecovered basis is not treated as a loss. Rather, it is added back to the shareholder's basis in his or her common shares.

EXAMPLE C:4-43 ▶ Carlos owns all 100 outstanding shares of Adobe Corporation common stock. His basis in the shares is $100,000. Adobe, which has $150,000 of E&P, distributes 50 shares of nonvoting preferred to Carlos in a nontaxable stock dividend. On the distribution date, the FMV of the preferred stock is $50,000, and the FMV of the common stock is $200,000. Carlos must allocate his $100,000 common stock basis between the common and preferred shares according to their relative FMVs as follows:

	FMV	*Basis*
Common stock	$200,000	$ 80,000[a]
Preferred stock	50,000	20,000[b]
Total	$250,000	$100,000

[a] $\frac{\$200{,}000}{\$250{,}000} \times \$100{,}000$ [b] $\frac{\$50{,}000}{\$250{,}000} \times \$100{,}000$

Carlos subsequently sells the preferred stock to Dillon for $50,000. The $50,000 sales proceeds are treated as a deemed dividend because Adobe's E&P in the year the corporation distributed the preferred stock exceeded the stock's FMV. Carlos's $20,000 basis in the preferred shares is added back to his basis in the common shares, thereby restoring his common stock basis to $100,000. If instead Carlos sells the preferred stock for $80,000, he recognizes a $50,000 deemed dividend, a $20,000 return of capital, and a $10,000 capital gain computed as follows:

Sales proceeds	$80,000
Minus: Deemed dividend income[a]	(50,000)
Remaining sales proceeds	$30,000
Minus: Return of capital[b]	(20,000)
Capital gain[c]	$10,000

[a] Smaller of E&P in year stock was issued or stock's FMV on the distribution date.
[b] Smaller of remaining sales proceeds or stock adjusted basis.
[c] Sales proceeds received in excess of stock adjusted basis. ◀

REDEMPTIONS OF SEC. 306 STOCK

KEY POINT

The amount realized in a redemption of Sec. 306 stock is a dividend to the extent of E&P existing in the year of redemption. Unlike a sale of Sec. 306 stock, E&P is reduced as a result of a redemption.

If the issuing corporation redeems Sec. 306 stock, the shareholder's total amount realized is treated as a distribution to which the Sec. 301 dividend rules apply. Specifically, it is treated as a dividend to the extent of the redeeming corporation's current and accumulated E&P measured *in the year of the redemption* and reduces corporate E&P accordingly. Amounts received in excess of the corporation's E&P are treated as a recovery of the shareholder's basis in his or her Sec. 306 stock, and then as a capital gain to the extent such amounts exceed basis. If all or a portion of the shareholder's basis in the redeemed stock is not recovered, the unrecovered amount increases the basis of the shareholder's common stock.

EXAMPLE C:4-44 ▶ Don owns all 100 shares of Brigham Corporation common stock having a $300,000 adjusted basis. Four years ago, Brigham issued 50 shares of preferred stock to Don. On the distribution date, the FMVs of the preferred stock and common stock were $100,000 and $400,000, respectively. Brigham's E&P in the distribution year was $200,000. Don's allocated basis in the preferred stock was $60,000 {[$100,000 ÷ ($100,000 + $400,000)] × $300,000}. The basis of Don's common stock was reduced to $240,000 ($300,000 − $60,000) as a result of this allocation. On January 2 of the current year, Brigham redeems the preferred shares for $250,000. In the redemption year, Brigham's total E&P is $400,000. Thus, Don recognizes dividend income of $250,000. If Brigham's total E&P instead had been $200,000 in the redemption year, Don would have recognized $200,000 of dividend income and a $50,000 nontaxable return of capital.

Because Don's basis in his preferred stock is $60,000, the $10,000 unrecovered basis would have increased his basis in the common stock to $250,000 ($240,000 + $10,000). ◀

EXCEPTIONS TO SEC. 306 TREATMENT

Section 306 does not apply in the following situations.

- A shareholder sells all of his or her common and preferred stock, thereby completely terminating his or her interest in the issuing corporation.
- The corporation redeems all the shareholder's common and preferred stock, completely terminating the shareholder's interest in the corporation.
- The corporation redeems an individual shareholder's stock in a partial liquidation qualifying for sale treatment under Sec. 302(b)(4).
- A shareholder disposes of Sec. 306 stock in a way that triggers no gain or loss recognition (e.g., a gift). Although the donor recognizes no income when he or she disposes of Sec. 306 stock by gift, the stock retains its taint and remains Sec. 306 stock in the donee's hands. On the other hand, because heirs and devisees take a FMV basis in estate assets, the taint disappears when they inherit the stock.
- Section 306 does not apply if the taxpayer demonstrates to the IRS's satisfaction that the distribution and subsequent disposition of Sec. 306 stock did not have tax avoidance as a principal purpose.

TAX STRATEGY TIP

A taxpayer owning a portfolio of stock that includes Sec. 306 stock may want to retain the Sec. 306 stock and pass it on to his or her heirs, thereby eliminating the Sec. 306 taint. Market conditions, however, will dictate whether retaining the stock is a good investment strategy.

STOCK REDEMPTIONS BY RELATED CORPORATIONS

OBJECTIVE 7

Assess the applicability and tax consequences of Sec. 304 to stock sales

If a shareholder sells stock in one corporation (the issuing corporation) to a second corporation (the acquiring corporation), the shareholder usually recognizes a capital gain or loss. However, if the shareholder controls both corporations, he or she may have to recognize dividend income because the net result may resemble a dividend more than a sale.

To prevent shareholders from using two corporations they commonly control to convert what is essentially a dividend into a capital gain, Sec. 304 requires that a sale of stock of one controlled corporation to a second controlled corporation be treated as a stock redemption. If the redemption meets the requirements for sale treatment (e.g., if the redemption is substantially disproportionate), the transaction will be treated as a sale. Otherwise, the redemption will be treated as a dividend to the extent of E&P. As in the case of Sec. 306 preferred stock bailouts, because individuals pay the applicable capital gains tax rate on qualified dividends and capital gains, Sec. 304 does not deliver a major "sting." Nevertheless, when it does apply, shareholders may have to recognize dividend income rather than capital gain and cannot offset either stock basis or capital losses against this dividend income.

Section 304 applies to two types of sales. The first is a sale of stock involving two brother-sister corporations. The second is a sale of a parent corporation's stock to one of its subsidiaries. The following sections define brother-sister and parent-subsidiary corporations and explain how Sec. 304 applies to each group.

BROTHER-SISTER CORPORATIONS

ADDITIONAL COMMENT

The definition of brother-sister corporations for Sec. 304 differs from the definition for controlled groups discussed in Chapter C:3.

Two corporations are called brother-sister corporations when one or more shareholders control each of the corporations and a parent-subsidiary relationship does not exist. Control means ownership of at least 50% of the voting power or 50% of the total value of all the corporation's stock. The shareholder(s) who acquired such ownership are called controlling shareholders. If a controlling shareholder (or shareholders) transfers stock in one corporation to the other corporation in exchange for property, the exchange must be recast as a redemption.

To determine whether the redemption is treated as a sale or a dividend, reference is made to the shareholder's stock ownership in the issuing corporation. For purposes of this determination, the attribution rules of Sec. 318(a) apply.[47]

Redemption Treated as a Distribution. If the redemption does not qualify for sale treatment, it is treated as a dividend paid first by the acquiring corporation to the extent of its E&P, and then by the issuing corporation to the extent of its E&P. The shareholder's basis in the issuing corporation's stock sold is added to his or her basis in the acquiring corporation's stock. The acquiring corporation takes the same basis in the issuing corporation's stock as the shareholder's.

EXAMPLE C:4-45 ▶ Bert owns 60 of the 100 outstanding shares of First Corporation stock and 60 of the 100 outstanding shares of Second Corporation stock (see Figure C:4-1). First and Second have $50,000 and $20,000 of E&P, respectively. Bert sells to Second for $20,000 20 shares of First stock with an adjusted basis of $10,000. Because Bert owns at least 50% of each corporation's stock, Bert is deemed to control both First and Second, and Sec. 304 governs the transaction. Accordingly, the sale is recast as a redemption. To determine whether the redemption qualifies for sale treatment, reference is made to Bert's percentage ownership of First stock. Before the redemption, Bert owned 60% of First stock. After the redemption, Bert owns 52% of First stock (40 shares directly and 12 [0.60 × 20] shares constructively through Second). Because the redempton satisfies none of the Sec. 302 tests for sale treatment, Sec. 301 governs the outcome. Under this provision, the entire distribution is treated as a dividend because it does not exceed First's and Second's total E&P of $70,000. All $20,000 of the distribution is deemed to have been made out of Second's E&P because it is sufficient to cover the distribution amount. Second's basis in the First stock is $10,000, the same as Bert's. Bert increases his basis in Second stock by $10,000, his basis in the First stock he is deemed to have contributed to Second. ◀

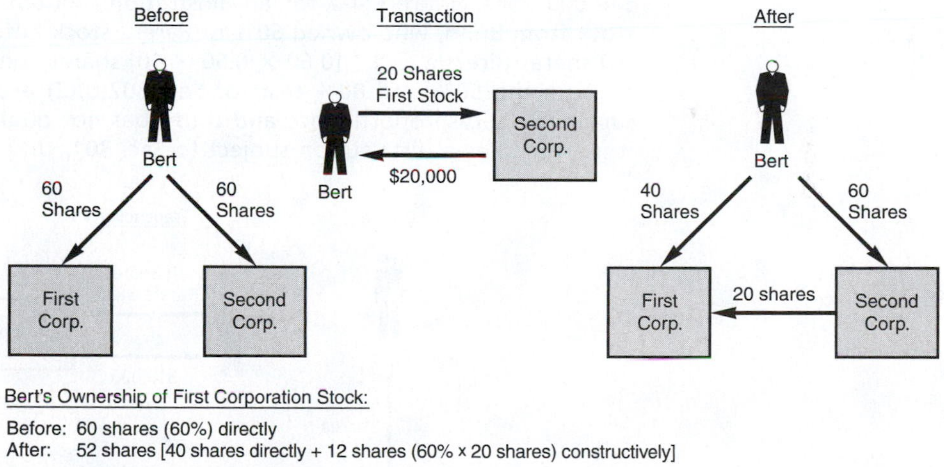

FIGURE C:4-1 ▶ ILLUSTRATION OF A BROTHER-SISTER REDEMPTION (EXAMPLE C:4-45)

Redemption Treated as a Sale. If the redemption qualifies for sale treatment, the shareholder's recognized gain or loss equals the difference between the amount received from the acquiring corporation and the shareholder's basis in the surrendered shares. The acquiring corporation is treated as having purchased the issuing corporation's shares and thus takes a cost basis in such shares.

EXAMPLE C:4-46 ▶ Assume the same facts as in Example C:4-45 except Bert sells to Second Corporation for $40,000 40 shares of First stock having an adjusted basis of $20,000. After the redemption, Bert owns

[47] For Sec. 304 purposes, the attribution rules of Sec. 318(a) are modified so that a shareholder is considered to own an amount of stock proportionate to that owned by any corporation of which he or she owns 5% or more (instead of 50% or more) of the value of the stock.

44 shares of First stock (20 shares directly and 24 [0.60 × 40] shares constructively through Second). Therefore, he meets both the 50% and the 80% tests for a substantially disproportionate redemption, treats the redemption as a sale, and recognizes a capital gain of $20,000 ($40,000 received from Second − $20,000 adjusted basis in the First shares). Second's basis in the First shares acquired from Bert equals the $40,000 stock purchase price. ◀

ADDITIONAL COMMENT

The definition of a parent-subsidiary relationship for Sec. 304 differs from the definition for controlled groups or affiliated corporations discussed in Chapter C:3.

PARENT-SUBSIDIARY CORPORATIONS

If a shareholder sells stock in a parent corporation to a subsidiary of the parent, the sale is treated as a distribution in redemption of part or all of the shareholder's parent stock. A parent-subsidiary relationship exists if one corporation owns at least 50% of the voting power or 50% of the total value of all stock in another corporation.

To determine whether the redemption is treated as a sale or a dividend, reference is made to the shareholder's ownership of parent stock before and after the redemption. In this determination, the constructive ownership rules of Sec. 318 apply.

Redemption Treated as a Dividend. If the redemption does not qualify for sale treatment, the distribution is treated as a dividend, first from the subsidiary to the extent of its E&P and then from the parent to the extent of its E&P. This rule effectively sets the combined E&P of both corporations as the standard for measuring the amount of the distribution that constitutes a dividend. The shareholder's basis in his or her remaining parent shares is increased by his or her basis in the shares transferred to the subsidiary. The subsidiary's basis in the parent stock is the amount the subsidiary paid for the stock.[48]

EXAMPLE C:4-47 ▶ Of the 100 shares of Parent Corporation stock, Brian owns 60 shares with a $15,000 basis. Parent owns 60 of the 100 shares of Subsidiary stock. Parent and Subsidiary have $10,000 and $30,000 of E&P, respectively. Brian sells ten of his Parent shares to Subsidiary for $12,000. (See Figure C:4-2 for an illustration.) Parent is deemed to have redeemed its stock from Brian, who owned 60% of Parent stock before the redemption and 53 shares (50 shares directly and 3 [0.60 × 0.50 × 10] shares constructively) after the redemption. Because the 50% and 80% tests of Sec. 302(b)(2) are not met, the redemption is not substantially disproportionate and thus does not qualify for sale treatment. Therefore, it is treated as a distribution subject to Sec. 301. Under this provision, Brian recognizes

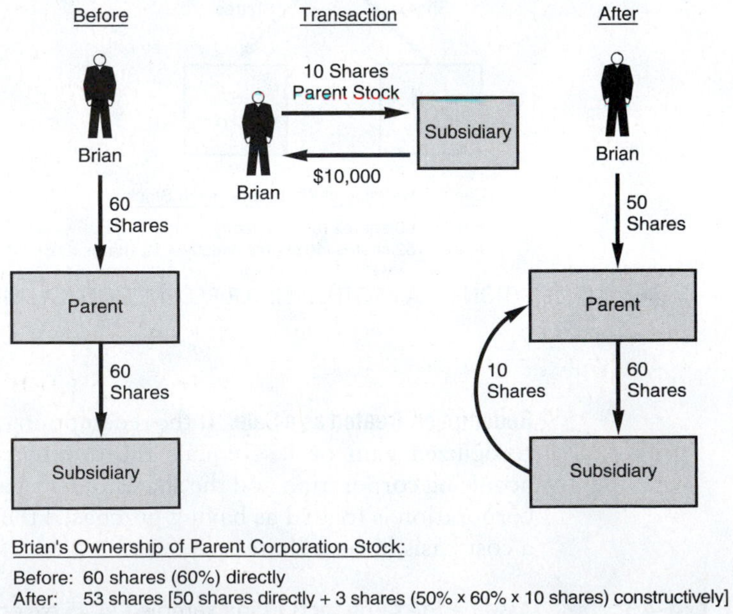

FIGURE C:4-2 ▶ ILLUSTRATION OF A PARENT-SUBSIDIARY REDEMPTION (EXAMPLE C:4-47)

[48] Rev. Rul. 80-189, 1980-2 C.B. 106.

a $12,000 dividend. This dividend is deemed to have been paid out of Subsidiary's E&P, which is sufficient to cover the entire distribution amount. Brian's $2,500 basis in the redeemed shares increases his $12,500 basis in his remaining Parent shares, so that his total basis in those shares remains $15,000. Subsidiary's basis in the ten Parent shares acquired from Brian is $12,000, the amount that Subsidiary paid for the shares. ◀

Redemption Treated as a Sale. If the redemption of the parent's stock qualifies for sale treatment, the basis of the stock transferred to the subsidiary is subtracted from the amount realized in the distribution to derive the shareholder's recognized gain or loss.

EXAMPLE C:4-48 ▶ Assume the same facts as in Example C:4-47 except Brian sells 40 shares of Parent stock to Subsidiary for $48,000. Because Brian owns 60% of Parent stock before the redemption and 24.8% (20 shares directly and 4.8 [$0.60 \times 0.20 \times 40$] shares constructively) after the redemption, the redemption meets the Sec. 302(b)(2) 50% and 80% tests for a substantially disproportionate redemption. Consequently, Brian recognizes a capital gain of $38,000 ($48,000 selling price − $10,000 adjusted basis in the 40 shares sold). Brian's adjusted basis in his remaining 20 shares of Parent stock is $5,000. Subsidiary's basis in the 40 Parent shares purchased from Brian is $48,000, the amount that Subsidiary paid for the shares. ◀

Topic Review C:4-5 summarizes the alternative treatments of stock redemptions.

TOPIC REVIEW C:4-5

Alternative Treatments of Stock Redemptions

General Rule: A distribution in redemption of stock generally is treated as a dividend (Secs. 302(d) and 301).
Exception: The following transactions qualify for sale (i.e., capital gains) treatment:

1. Redemptions that are not essentially equivalent to a dividend (Sec. 302(b)(1))
2. Substantially disproportionate redemptions (Sec. 302(b)(2))
3. Complete terminations of a shareholder's interest (Sec. 302(b)(3))
4. Partial liquidations in redemption of a noncorporate shareholder's stock (Sec. 302(b)(4))
5. Redemptions to pay death taxes (Sec. 303)

Special Redemption Rules

1. Redemptions of Sec. 306 preferred stock generally are taxed as dividends to the shareholder (Sec. 306).
2. A sale of stock in one controlled corporation to another controlled corporation is treated as a redemption (Sec. 304).

TAX PLANNING CONSIDERATIONS

OBJECTIVE 8

Identify tax planning opportunities in nonliquidating distributions

AVOIDING UNREASONABLE COMPENSATION

Chapter C:3 discussed the use of salary and fringe benefits to permit a shareholder of a closely held corporation to withdraw funds from the corporation and be subject to a single level of taxation. If a corporation pays too large a salary to a shareholder-employee, some of the salary may be disallowed as a corporate deduction while still taxed to the shareholder-employee as a constructive dividend. In such case, double taxation of the disallowed portion results.

Corporations can avoid this result by entering into a **hedge agreement** with a shareholder-employee. This agreement obligates the shareholder-employee to repay any portion of salary the IRS disallows as a corporate deduction. Under Sec. 162, the shareholder-employee may deduct this amount in the year he or she repays it, provided state law imposes a legal obligation to repay.[49] If a hedge agreement is not in effect, voluntary repayment of the salary is not deductible by the shareholder-employee.[50]

EXAMPLE C:4-49 ▶ Theresa owns one-half the stock in Marine Corporation and serves as its president. The remaining Marine stock is owned by eight investors, none of whom owns more than 10% of the outstanding shares. In Year 1, Theresa and Marine conclude a hedge agreement requiring Theresa to repay all compensation the IRS declares unreasonable. In Year 3, Marine pays Theresa a salary and bonus of $750,000. The IRS subsequently claims that $300,000 of the salary is unreasonable and thus nondeductible by Marine. After protracted negotiations, Marine and the IRS settle on $180,000 as unreasonable and nondeductible by Marine. Theresa repays the $180,000 in Year 6. The entire $750,000 is taxable to Theresa in Year 3. However, she can deduct the $180,000 as a trade or business expense in Year 6. ◀

Hedge agreements also have been used in connection with other payments between a corporation and its shareholders (e.g., travel and entertainment expenses). Some employers are averse to hedge agreements because the IRS might consider the very existence of such an agreement as evidence of unreasonable compensation.

BOOTSTRAP ACQUISITIONS

A prospective purchaser who wants to acquire stock in a corporation may not have sufficient cash to do so. To facilitate the purchase, corporate funds could be used in the following way: a shareholder sells part of his or her stock to the purchaser and then causes the corporation to redeem the shareholder's remaining shares. Such an arrangement is called a **bootstrap acquisition**.

EXAMPLE C:4-50 ▶ Ted owns all 100 shares of Dragon Corporation stock having a $100,000 FMV. Vickie wants to purchase the stock from Ted but has only $60,000 in cash. Dragon has a large cash balance, which it does not need for its operations. Ted sells Vickie 60 Dragon shares for $60,000 and then causes Dragon to redeem his remaining shares for $40,000. The redemption qualifies as a complete termination of Ted's interest under Sec. 302(b)(3) and, therefore, is eligible for sale treatment. ◀

Court cases have held that such redemptions qualify for sale treatment as long as the third-party sale and redemption are part of an integral plan to terminate the seller's entire corporate interest. Whether the redemption precedes the sale is immaterial.[51] The purchaser, however, must carefully avoid generating a dividend, actual or constructive. For example, a purchaser who contracts to acquire all the stock in a corporation on an installment basis and then causes the corporation to pay the installment obligations will recognize dividend income. The use of corporate funds results in a constructive dividend to the purchaser where the corporation discharges the purchaser's legal obligation. Even if the corporation uses its own funds to redeem the seller's shares, a purchaser who was legally obligated to purchase the shares is considered to have received a constructive dividend.[52]

EXAMPLE C:4-51 ▶ Assume the same facts as in Example C:4-50 except that, after Vickie purchases the 60 shares from Ted, she becomes legally obligated to purchase Ted's remaining 40 shares. After entering into the contract, Vickie causes Dragon Corporation to redeem the 40 shares. Because Dragon has extinguished Vickie's legal obligation, the corporation is deemed to have paid Vickie a $40,000 constructive dividend. No constructive dividend would have resulted had Vickie been legally obligated to purchase only 60 shares from Ted. ◀

Rev. Rul. 69-608 provides guidance to a bootstrap acquirer on how to avoid constructive dividend treatment.[53] According to this ruling, when the corporation redeems some of the seller's shares, the buyer will not be deemed to have received a constructive dividend as

---

[49] Rev. Rul. 69-115, 1969-1 C.B. 50, and *Vincent E. Oswald*, 49 T.C. 645 (1968), *acq.* 1968-2 C.B. 2.

[50] *Ernest H. Berger*, 37 T.C. 1026 (1962), and *John G. Pahl*, 67 T.C. 286 (1976).

[51] See, for example, *U.S. v. Gerald Carey*, 7 AFTR 2d 1301, 61-1 USTC ¶9428 (8th Cir., 1961).

[52] *H. F. Wall v. U.S.*, 36 AFTR 423, 47-2 USTC ¶9395 (4th Cir., 1947).

[53] Rev. Rul. 69-608, 1969-2 C.B. 42.

WHAT WOULD YOU DO IN THIS SITUATION?

One of the most cherished traditions observed by many professional firms centers around the year-end bonus. Legal, medical, business, and accounting administrators often use bonus compensation to clear the books at the end of the year. In partnerships, bonuses are characterized as distributive shares or a form of compensation. As such, they are taxed only once as income paid to professionals for services rendered, net of appropriate accounting adjustments.

With the advent of the professional corporation, an entity intended to limit personal liability, many professionals have opted to do business as shareholders. The continued use of the year-end bonus in the professional corporation has come under close IRS scrutiny. The position taken by the IRS is clear. If the payments to the shareholder-professional are in exchange for his or her services rendered to the firm, the corporation may deduct them as salaries (assuming they are reasonable in amount). On the other hand, if they are a disguised bailout of owners' profits, the corporation cannot deduct them. As a result, the corporation's taxable income will be increased by the amount of the disallowed deduction. The shareholder who receives the bonus must treat it as a dividend rather than salary. However, treating the bonus as a dividend generally results in less tax paid by the shareholder because dividends are taxed at a maximum rate of 23.8% (including the 3.8% net investment tax rate) as opposed to 39.6% for salary. The consequences are negative only to the corporation, which may not deduct the dividend payment.

This principle is illustrated in a case, *Rapco, Inc. v. CIR,* 77 AFTR 2d 2405, 96-1 USTC ¶50,297 (CA-2, 1996), decided by the Second Circuit. In *Rapco,* the court denied a deduction for bonus payments to the president of the company, even though he played a significant role in the company's rapid growth and had guaranteed third party loans to Rapco. Reasons cited by the court were that Rapco's compensation scheme was "bonus-heavy and salary light," suggesting dividend avoidance; Rapco had ignored its own bonus policy set forth in its preincorporation minutes; the corporation had a history of never paying dividends; the shareholder who determined the amount of his own salary owned 95% of the corporation's stock; and Rapco's own expert testified that $400,000 to $500,000 was fair compensation for the president's services. (The IRS allowed a salary deduction of $405,000).

Assuming your CPA firm is acting as a tax advisor to several similarly situated professional corporations, what advice that complies with the IRC, Treasury Regulations, and the AICPA's *Statements on Standards for Tax Services* would you give?

long as he or she does not have a primary and unconditional obligation to purchase the shares, and the corporation pays no more for the redeemed shares than their FMV. Furthermore, a purchaser who has an option—not a legal obligation—to purchase the seller's remaining shares, and who assigns the option to the redeeming corporation, is unlikely to generate a constructive dividend.[54]

TIMING OF DISTRIBUTIONS

Dividends can be paid only out of a corporation's E&P. Therefore, if a distribution can be made when the corporation has little or no E&P, it will be treated as a return of capital rather than as a dividend.

If a corporation generates a current E&P deficit, the deficit reduces accumulated E&P evenly throughout the year unless the corporation can demonstrate that it incurred the deficits on particular dates. Thus, if a corporation with a current E&P deficit, but a positive accumulated E&P balance, makes a distribution in the current year, the timing of the distribution will be critical in determining whether the distribution should be treated as a dividend or as a return of capital.

EXAMPLE C:4-52 ► Major Corporation has a $30,000 accumulated E&P balance at the beginning of the year and incurs a $50,000 deficit during the year. Because of its poor operating performance, Major pays to its sole shareholder only two of its four $5,000 quarterly dividends, specifically those usually paid on March 31 and June 30. The tax treatment of the two distributions is determined as follows:

[54] *Joseph R. Holsey v. CIR,* 2 AFTR 2d 5660, 58-2 USTC ¶9816 (3rd Cir., 1958).

E&P balance, January 1		$30,000
Minus:	Reduction for first quarter loss	(12,500)
	Reduction for March 31 distribution	(5,000)
E&P balance, April 1		$12,500
Minus:	Reduction for second quarter loss	(12,500)
E&P balance, June 30		$ –0–

The first and second quarter losses each are $12,500 [($50,000) × 0.25 = ($12,500)].

The operating loss reduces the accumulated E&P balance evenly throughout the year. All of the March 31 distribution is taxable because the corporation did not incur sufficient losses to offset the positive accumulated E&P balance at the beginning of the year. The second quarter loss results in return of capital treatment for the June 30 distribution and any other distributions before year-end (assuming that the shareholder's basis in his or her stock exceeds the distribution amount). Delaying all the distributions until late in the year could result in a nontaxable return of capital. ◀

The timing of a distribution also can be critical if the distributing corporation has an accumulated E&P deficit and a positive current E&P balance.

EXAMPLE C:4-53 ▶ At the beginning of Year 1, Yankee Corporation has an accumulated E&P deficit of $250,000. During Year 1 and Year 2, Yankee reports the following current E&P balances and makes the following distributions to Joe, its sole shareholder:

Year	*Current E&P*	*Distributions*	*Distribution Date*
1	$100,000	$75,000	December 31
2	–0–	–0–	None

The $75,000 distribution in Year 1 is taxable as a dividend. The $25,000 of current E&P that is not distributed reduces Yankee's accumulated E&P deficit to $225,000. Had Yankee delayed distributing the $75,000 until sometime in Year 2, the distribution would have been treated as a nontaxable return of Joe's capital. ◀

COMPLIANCE AND PROCEDURAL CONSIDERATIONS

OBJECTIVE 9

Comply with procedural rules for nonliquidating distributions

CORPORATE REPORTING OF NONDIVIDEND DISTRIBUTIONS

A corporation that makes a nondividend distribution to its shareholders must file with its income tax return Form 5452 (Corporate Report of Nondividend Distributions), along with supporting computations. Form 5452 reports the distributing corporation's E&P so as to enable the IRS to verify the tax treatment of the distribution. Form 5452 requires the following information: current and accumulated E&P, distribution amounts paid to shareholders during the tax year, the percentage of each payment that is taxable and nontaxable, and a detailed computation of E&P from the date of incorporation.

ADDITIONAL COMMENT

Information on basis adjustments for nontaxable dividends, stock splits, stock dividends, etc. for individual firms can be found in special tax services.

AGREEMENT TO TERMINATE INTEREST UNDER SEC. 302(b)(3)

As mentioned earlier, if a redemption completely terminates a shareholder's interest in a corporation, the family attribution rules of Sec. 318(a)(1) may be waived. To have the rules waived, the shareholder must agree in writing that he or she will notify the IRS upon acquiring any prohibited interest within the ten-year period following the redemption. A copy of this agreement (in the form of a signed statement in duplicate) must be attached to the first return filed by the shareholder for the tax year in which the redemption occurs. If the agreement cannot be filed on time, the IRS may grant an extension. Regulation Sec. 1.302-4(a) provides that an extension will be granted only if reasonable cause exists for

KEY POINT

The limitations period extends to one year beyond the date a shareholder notifies the IRS that a forbidden interest has been acquired. Otherwise, it would be almost impossible for the IRS to administer this provision.

failure to timely file the agreement and if the request for such an extension is filed within such time as the appropriate IRS official considers reasonable in the circumstances.

Treasury Regulations do not indicate what constitutes reasonable cause for failure to file or what constitutes a reasonable extension of time. In *Edward J. Fehrs* the U.S. Court of Claims held that late filing of a ten-year agreement was permissible where a taxpayer could not reasonably have expected that a filing would be necessary, where the taxpayer filed the agreement promptly after receiving notice that it was required, and where the agreement was filed before the issues in question were presented for trial.[55] However, in *Robin Haft Trust,* an agreement was filed *after* an adverse court ruling. In an appeal for a rehearing, the judge ruled that the filing of the agreement after the case was brought to trial was too late. Consequently, the judge denied the appeal for a rehearing.[56]

If the shareholder acquires a prohibited interest within the ten-year period following the redemption, the IRS may assess additional taxes. Such an acquisition ordinarily results in recasting the redemption as a dividend rather than a sale. The limitations period for assessing additional taxes extends to one year after the date the shareholder files with the IRS notice of acquiring the prohibited interest.[57]

PROBLEM MATERIALS

DISCUSSION QUESTIONS

C:4-1 Explain how a corporation computes its current and accumulated E&P balances.

C:4-2 Why is it necessary to distinguish between current and accumulated E&P?

C:4-3 Describe the effect of a $100,000 cash distribution paid on January 1 to the sole shareholder of a calendar year corporation whose stock basis is $25,000 when the corporation has

a. $100,000 of current E&P and $100,000 of accumulated E&P

b. A $50,000 accumulated E&P deficit and a $60,000 current E&P balance

c. A $60,000 accumulated E&P deficit and a $60,000 current E&P deficit

d. An $80,000 current E&P deficit and a $100,000 accumulated E&P balance

Answer Parts a through d again, assuming instead that the corporation makes the distribution on October 1 in a nonleap year.

C:4-4 Pecan Corporation distributes land to a noncorporate shareholder. Explain how the following items are determined:

a. The amount of the distribution

b. The amount of the dividend

c. The shareholder's basis in the land

d. When the holding period for the land begins.

How would your answers change if the distribution were made to a corporate shareholder?

C:4-5 What effect do the following transactions have on the calculation of Young Corporation's current E&P? Assume that the starting point for the calculation is Young's taxable income for the current year.

a. The corporation earns tax-exempt interest income of $10,000.

b. Taxable income includes a $10,000 dividend and is reduced by a $7,000 dividends-received deduction.

c. A $5,000 capital loss carryover from the preceding tax year offsets $5,000 of capital gains.

d. The corporation accrued federal income taxes of $25,280.

e. The corporation took a U.S. production activities deduction of $3,000.

C:4-6 Badger Corporation was incorporated in the current year. It reports an $8,000 NOL on its initial tax return. Badger distributes $2,500 to its shareholders. Is it possible for this distribution to be taxed as a dividend to Badger's shareholders? Explain.

C:4-7 Does the timing of a distribution matter as to whether it is taxed as a dividend or treated as a return of capital? Explain.

C:4-8 Hickory Corporation owns a building with a $160,000 adjusted basis and a $120,000 FMV. Hickory's E&P is $200,000. Should the

---

[55] *Edward J. Fehrs v. U.S.*, 40 AFTR 2d 77-5040, 77-1 USTC ¶9423 (Ct. Cl., 1977).

[56] *Robin Haft Trust,* 62 T.C. 145 (1974).

[57] Sec. 302(c)(2)(A).

corporation sell the building and distribute the sales proceeds to its shareholders or distribute the property to its shareholders and let them sell it? Why?

C:4-9 Walnut Corporation owns a building with a $120,000 adjusted basis and a $160,000 FMV. Walnut's E&P is $200,000. Should the corporation sell the building and distribute the sales proceeds to its shareholders or distribute the building to its shareholders and let them sell it? Why?

C:4-10 What is a constructive dividend? Under what circumstances is the IRS likely to argue that a constructive dividend has been paid?

C:4-11 Why are stock dividends generally nontaxable? Under what circumstances are stock dividends taxable?

C:4-12 What is a stock redemption? What are some reasons for redeeming stock? Why are some redemptions treated as sales and others as dividends?

C:4-13 Field Corporation redeems 100 shares of its stock from Andrew for $10,000. Andrew's basis in the shares is $8,000. Explain possible alternative tax treatments of Andrew's receiving the $10,000.

C:4-14 What conditions must be met for a redemption to be treated as a sale by the redeeming shareholder?

C:4-15 Explain the purpose of the attribution rules in determining stock ownership in a redemption. Describe the four types of attribution rules that apply to redemptions.

C:4-16 Abel, the sole shareholder of Ace Corporation, has an opporunity to purchase the assets of a sole proprietorship for $50,000 in cash. Ace has a substantial E&P balance. Abel does not have sufficient cash to personally make the purchase. If Abel obtains the needed $50,000 from Ace via a nonliquidating distribution, Abel will have to recognize dividend income. Alternatively, would Ace's purchase of the assets of the sole proprietorship followed by their distribution to Abel in redemption of part of his stock holdings constitute a partial liquidation? Explain.

C:4-17 Why does a redemption that qualifies for sale treatment under Sec. 303 usually result in the shareholder's recognizing little or no gain or loss?

C:4-18 Under what circumstances does a corporation recognize gain or loss when it distributes noncash property in redemption of its stock? What effect does a redemption distribution have on the distributing corporation's E&P?

C:4-19 What is a preferred stock bailout? How does Sec. 306 operate to prevent a shareholder from realizing the otherwise available tax benefits of a preferred stock bailout?

C:4-20 Explain the tax consequences, to both the corporation and a shareholder-employee, of an IRS determination that a portion of the compensation paid in a prior tax year is unreasonable. What steps can the corporation and shareholder-employee take to avoid the double taxation usually associated with such a determination?

C:4-21 What is a bootstrap acquisition? What are the tax consequences of such a transaction?

ISSUE IDENTIFICATION QUESTIONS

C:4-22 Marsha receives a $10,000 cash distribution from Dye Corporation in April of the current year. At the beginning of the year, Dye has $4,000 of accumulated E&P and $8,000 of current E&P. Dye also distributed $10,000 in cash to Barbara, who purchased all 200 shares of Dye stock from Marsha in June of the current year. What tax issues should be considered with respect to the distributions to Marsha and Barbara?

C:4-23 Neil purchased land from Spring Harbor, his 100%-owned corporation, for $275,000. The corporation purchased the land three years ago for $300,000. Similar tracts of land located nearby have sold for $400,000 in recent months. What tax issues should be considered with respect to the corporation's sale of the land?

C:4-24 Price Corporation has 100 shares of common stock outstanding. Price repurchased all of Penny's 30 shares for $35,000 cash during the current year. Three years ago, Penny received the shares as a gift from her mother. Her basis in the shares is $16,000. Price has $100,000 of current and accumulated E&P. Penny's mother owns 40 of the remaining shares; unrelated individuals own the other 30 shares. What tax issues should be considered with respect to the corporation's purchase of Penny's shares?

C:4-25 George owns all 100 shares of Gumby's Pizza Corporation. The shares are worth $200,000, while George's basis is only $70,000. Mary and George have reached a tentative agreement under which George will sell all his shares to Mary. However, Mary is unwilling to pay more than $150,000 for the stock because the corporation currently has an excess cash balance. They have agreed that George can withdraw $50,000 in cash from Gumby's before the stock sale. What tax issues should be considered with respect to George and Mary's agreement?

PROBLEMS

C:4-26 *Current E&P Calculation.* Alabre Corporation has 150,000 shares of common stock outstanding and pays quarterly dividends of $0.15 per share. At the beginning of the current year, the balance in its accumulated E&P account is $23,000. Alabre would like to have sufficient E&P to pay its dividends in the current year. To do so, what minimum amount of E&P must the corporation generate in the current year?

C:4-27 *Current E&P Calculation.* Beach Corporation, an accrual basis taxpayer, reports the following results for the current year:

Income:	
Gross profit from manufacturing operations	$250,000
Dividends received from 25%-owned domestic corporation	20,000
Interest income: Corporate bonds	10,000
Municipal bonds	12,000
Proceeds from life insurance policy on key employee	100,000
Section 1231 gain on sale of land	8,000
Expenses:	
Administrative expenses	110,000
Bad debts	5,000
Depreciation:	
Financial accounting	68,000
Taxable income	86,000
Alternative depreciation system (for E&P)	42,000
NOL carryover	40,000
Charitable contributions: Current year	8,000
Carryover from last year	3,500
Capital loss on sale of stock	1,200
U.S. production activities deduction	1,500
Penalty on late payment of federal taxes	450

a. What is Beach's taxable income?
b. What is Beach's current E&P?

C:4-28 *Current E&P Computation.* Water Corporation reports $500,000 of taxable income for the current year. The following additional information is available:

- For the current year, Water reports an $80,000 long-term capital loss and no capital gains.
- Taxable income includes $80,000 of dividends from a 10%-owned domestic corporation.
- Water paid fines and penalties of $6,000 that were not deducted in computing taxable income.
- In computing this year's taxable income, Water deducted a $20,000 NOL carryover from a prior tax year.
- Water claimed a $10,000 U.S. production activities deduction.
- Taxable income includes a deduction for $40,000 of depreciation that exceeds the depreciation allowed for E&P purposes.

Assume a 34% corporate tax rate. What is Water's current E&P for this year?

C:4-29 *Calculating Accumulated E&P.* Investors formed Peach Corporation in Year 1. Its current E&P (or current E&P deficit) and distributions for Years 1 through 4 are as follows:

Year	*Current E&P (Deficit)*	*Distributions*
1	$ (8,000)	$ 2,000
2	(12,000)	–0–
3	10,000	5,000
4	14,000	17,000

What is Peach's accumulated E&P at the beginning of Years 1 through 4?

C:4-30 *Consequences of a Single Cash Distribution.* Clover Corporation is a calendar year taxpayer. Connie owns all of its stock. Her basis in the stock is $10,000. On April 1 of the current (non-leap) year Clover distributes $52,000 to Connie. Determine the tax consequences of the cash distribution in each of the following independent situations:
a. Current E&P of $15,000; accumulated E&P of $25,000.
b. Current E&P of $30,000; accumulated E&P deficit of ($20,000).
c. Current E&P deficit of ($73,000); accumulated E&P of $50,000.
d. Current E&P deficit of ($20,000); accumulated E&P deficit of ($15,000).

C:4-31 *Consequences of a Single Cash Distribution.* Pink Corporation is a calendar year taxpayer. Pete owns one-third (100 shares) of Pink stock. His basis in the stock is $25,000. Cheryl owns two-thirds (200 shares) of Pink stock. Her basis in the stock is $40,000. On June 10 of the current year, Pink distributes $40,000 to Pete and $80,000 to Cheryl. Determine the tax consequences of the cash distributions to Pete and Cheryl in each of the following independent situations:
a. Current E&P of $60,000; accumulated E&P of $100,000.
b. Current E&P of $36,000; accumulated E&P of $30,000.

C:4-32 *Consequences of Multiple Cash Distributions.* At the beginning of the current (non-leap) year, Charles owns all of Pearl Corporation's outstanding stock. His basis in the stock is $80,000. On July 1, he sells all his stock to Donald for $125,000. During the year, Pearl, a calendar year taxpayer, makes two cash distributions: $60,000 on March 1 to Charles and $90,000 on September 1 to Donald. How are these distributions treated in the following independent situations? What are the amount and character of Charles' gain on his sale of stock to Donald? What is Donald's basis in his Pearl stock at the end of the year?
a. Current E&P of $40,000; accumulated E&P of $30,000.
b. Current E&P of $100,000; accumulated E&P (deficit) of ($50,000).
c. Current E&P (deficit) of ($36,500); accumulated E&P of $120,000.

C:4-33 *Distribution of Appreciated Property.* In the current year, Sedgwick Corporation has $100,000 of current and accumulated E&P. On March 3, Sedgwick distributes to its shareholder Dina a parcel of land (a capital asset) having a $56,000 FMV. The land has a $40,000 adjusted basis (for both taxable income and E&P purposes) to Sedgwick and is subject to an $8,000 mortgage, which Dina assumes. Assume a 34% marginal corporate tax rate.
a. What are the amount and character of the income Dina recognizes as a result of the distribution?
b. What is Dina's basis in the land?
c. What are the amount and character of Sedgwick's gain or loss as a result of the distribution?
d. What effect does the distribution have on Sedgwick's E&P?

C:4-34 *Distribution of Property Subject to a Liability.* On May 10 of the current year, Stowe Corporation distributes to its shareholder Arlene $20,000 in cash and land (a capital asset) having a $50,000 FMV. The land has a $15,000 adjusted basis (for both taxable income and E&P purposes) and is subject to a $60,000 mortgage, which Arlene assumes. Stowe has an E&P balance exceeding the amount distributed and is subject to a 34% marginal corporate tax rate.
a. What are the amount and character of the income Arlene recognizes as a result of the distribution?
b. What is Arlene's basis in the land?
c. What are the amount and character of Stowe's gain or loss as a result of the distribution?

C:4-35 *Distribution of Depreciable Property.* On May 15 of the current year, Quick Corporation distributes to its shareholder Calvin a building having a $250,000 FMV and used in Quick's business. The building originally cost $180,000. Quick claimed $30,000 of straight-line depreciation, so that the adjusted basis of the building on the date of distribution for taxable income purposes is $150,000. The adjusted basis of the building for E&P purposes is $160,000. The building is subject to an $80,000 mortgage, which Calvin assumes. Quick has an E&P balance exceeding the amount distributed and is subject to a 34% marginal tax rate.
a. What are the amount and character of the income Calvin recognizes as a result of the distribution?
b. What is Calvin's basis in the building?

c. What are the amount and character of Quick's gain or loss as a result of the distribution?
d. What effect does the distribution have on Quick's E&P?

C:4-36 *Distribution of Various Types of Property.* During the current year, Zeta Corporation distributes the assets listed below to its sole shareholder, Susan. For each asset listed, determine the gross income recognized by Susan, her basis in the asset, the amount of gain or loss recognized by Zeta, and the effect of the distribution on Zeta's E&P. Assume that Zeta has an E&P balance exceeding the amount distributed and is subject to a 34% marginal tax rate. Unless stated otherwise, adjusted bases for taxable income and E&P purposes are the same.
a. A parcel of land used in Zeta's business that has a $200,000 FMV and a $125,000 adjusted basis.
b. Assume the same facts as in Part a except that the land is subject to a $140,000 mortgage.
c. FIFO inventory having a $25,000 FMV and an $18,000 adjusted basis.
d. A building used in Zeta's business having an original cost of $225,000, a $450,000 FMV, and a $150,000 adjusted basis for taxable income purposes. Zeta has claimed $75,000 of depreciation for taxable income purposes under the straight-line method. Depreciation for E&P purposes is $60,000.
e. An automobile used in Zeta's business having an original cost of $12,000, an $8,000 FMV, and a $5,760 adjusted basis. For taxable income purposes, Zeta has claimed $6,240 of MACRS depreciation on the automobile. For E&P purposes, depreciation is $5,200.
f. Installment obligations having a $35,000 face amount (and FMV) and a $24,500 adjusted basis. The obligations were created when Zeta sold a Sec. 1231 asset.

C:4-37 *Disguised Dividends.* King Corporation is a profitable manufacturing concern with $800,000 of E&P. It is owned in equal shares by Harry and Wilma, husband and wife. Both individuals are actively involved in the business. Determine the tax consequences of the following independent events:
a. In reviewing a prior year tax return for King, the IRS determines that the $500,000 of salary and bonuses paid to Wilma is unreasonable and that reasonable compensation is $280,000.
b. King loaned Harry $400,000 over the past three years. None of the money has been repaid. Harry does not pay interest on the loans.
c. King sells a building to Wilma for $150,000 in cash. The property has an adjusted basis of $90,000 and is subject to a $60,000 mortgage, which Wilma assumes. The FMV of the building is $350,000.
d. Harry leases a warehouse to King for $50,000 per year. According to an IRS auditor, similar warehouses can be leased for $35,000 per year.
e. Wilma sells to King for $250,000 land on which King intends to build a factory. According to a recent appraisal, the FMV of the land is $185,000.
f. The corporation owns an airplane that it uses to fly executives to business meetings. When the airplane is not being used for business, Harry and Wilma use it to travel to their ranch in Idaho for short vacations. The approximate cost of their trips to the ranch in the current year is $8,000.

C:4-38 *Unreasonable Compensation.* Forward Corporation is owned by a group of 15 shareholders. During the current year, Forward pays $550,000 in salary and bonuses to Alvin, its president and controlling shareholder. The corporation's marginal tax rate is 34%, and Alvin's marginal tax rate is 39.6%. The IRS audits Forward's tax return and determines that reasonable compensation for Alvin is $350,000. Forward agrees to the adjustment. What effect does the disallowance of part of the salary and bonus deduction have on Forward's and Alvin's respective tax positions? Ignore payroll taxes, such as FICA.

C:4-39 *Stock Dividend Distribution.* Wilton Corporation has a single class of common stock outstanding. Robert owns 100 shares, which he purchased in 2009 for $100,000. In 2015, when the stock is worth $1,200 per share, Wilton declares a 10% dividend payable in common stock. On December 10, 2015, Robert receives ten additional shares. On January 30, 2016, he sells five of the ten shares for $7,000.
a. How much income must Robert recognize when he receives the stock dividend?
b. How much gain or loss must Robert recognize when he sells the common stock?
c. What is Robert's basis in his remaining common shares? When does his holding period in the new common shares begin?

C:4-40 ***Stock Dividend Distribution.*** Moss Corporation has a single class of common stock outstanding. Tillie owns 1,000 shares, which she purchased in 2011 for $100,000. Moss declares a stock dividend payable in 8% preferred stock having a $100 par value. Each shareholder receives one share of preferred stock for ten shares of common stock. On the distribution date—December 10, 2015—the common stock was worth $180 per share, and the preferred stock was worth $100 per share. On April 1, 2015, Tillie sells half of her preferred stock for $5,000.

a. How much income must Tillie recognize when she receives the stock dividend?
b. How much gain or loss must Tillie recognize when she sells the preferred stock? (Ignore the implications of Sec. 306.)
c. What is Tillie's basis in her remaining common and preferred shares after the sale? When does her holding period for the preferred shares begin?

C:4-41 ***Stock Rights Distribution.*** Trusty Corporation has a single class of common stock outstanding. Jim owns 200 shares, which he purchased for $50 per share two years ago. On April 10 of the current year, Trusty distributes to its common shareholders one right to purchase for $60 one common share for each common share owned. At the time of the distribution, each common share is worth $75, and each right is worth $15. On September 10, Jim sells 100 rights for $2,000 and exercises the remaining 100 rights. On November 10, he sells for $80 each 60 of the shares acquired through exercise of the rights.

a. What are the amount and character of income Jim recognizes upon receiving the rights?
b. What are the amount and character of gain or loss Jim recognizes upon selling the rights?
c. What are the amount and character of gain or loss Jim recognizes upon exercising the rights?
d. What are the amount and character of gain or loss Jim recognizes upon selling the newly acquired common shares?
e. What basis does Jim take in his remaining shares?

C:4-42 ***Attribution Rules.*** George owns 100 of the 1,000 outstanding shares of Polar Corporation common stock. Under the Sec. 318 family attribution rules, to which of the following individuals will ownership of George's stock be attributed? In other words, who is deemed to constructively own George's stock?

a. George's wife
b. George's father
c. George's brother
d. George's mother-in-law
e. George's daughter
f. George's son-in-law
g. George's grandfather
h. George's grandson
i. George's mother's brother (his uncle)

C:4-43 ***Attribution Rules.*** Moose Corporation's 400 shares of outstanding stock are owned as follows:

Name	*Shares*
Lara (an individual)	60
LMN Partnership (Lara is a 20% partner)	50
LST Partnership (Lara is a 70% partner)	100
Lemon Corporation (Lara is a 30% shareholder)	100
Lime Corporation (Lara is a 60% shareholder)	90
Total	400

How many shares is Lara deemed to own under the Sec. 318 attribution rules?

C:4-44 ***Redemption from a Sole Shareholder.*** Paul owns all 100 shares of Presto Corporation stock. His basis in the stock is $10,000. Presto has $100,000 of E&P. Presto redeems 25 of Paul's shares for $30,000. What are the tax consequences of the redemption to Paul and to Presto?

C:4-45 ***Multiple Redemptions.*** Four unrelated shareholders own Benton Corporation's 400 shares of outstanding stock. As indicated below, Benton redeems a total of 100 shares for $500 per share from three of its shareholders. Each shareholder has a $230 per share basis in his or her stock. Benton's current and accumulated E&P at the end of the tax year is $150,000.

Shareholder	*Shares Held Before the Redemption*	*Shares Redeemed*
Ethel	200	40
Fran	100	30
Georgia	50	30
Henry	50	–0–
Total	400	100

a. What are the tax consequences (e.g., basis of remaining shares and amount and character of recognized income, gain, or loss) of the redemptions to Ethel, Fran, and Georgia?
b. How would your answer to Part a change if Ethel were Georgia's mother?

C:4-46 *Redemption Requirements for Sale Treatment.* Of the 9,500 shares of Favor Corporation stock outstanding, Olsen owns 6,100 shares. Unrelated parties own the remaining shares. To bolster its stock price, Favor plans to reduce the total number of shares outstanding by redeeming some of the shares held by Olsen.
a. To qualify the redemption as "substantially disproportionate" and thereby make it eligible for sale treatment, how many of Olsen's shares must Favor redeem?
b. How would your answer change if Olsen owns only 5,800 out of 9,500 shares before the redemption?

C:4-47 *Partial Liquidation.* Unrelated parties Amy, Beth, Carla, and Delta Corporation each own 25 of the 100 outstanding shares of Axle Corporation stock. In a transaction that qualifies as a partial liquidation, Axle distributes $20,000 cash to each shareholder in exchange for five Axle shares. Each redeemed share has a $1,000 basis to the shareholder and a $4,000 FMV. How does each shareholder treat the distribution for tax purposes?

C:4-48 *Redemption to Pay Death Taxes.* John died on March 3. His gross estate of $2.5 million includes First Corporation stock (400 of the 1,000 outstanding shares) worth $1.5 million. John's wife, Myra, owns the remaining 600 shares. Deductible funeral and administrative expenses total $250,000. John, Jr. is the sole beneficiary of John's estate. Estate taxes amount to $350,000.
a. Does a redemption of First stock from John's estate, John, Jr., or John's wife qualify for sale treatment under Sec. 303?
b. On September 10, First Corporation redeems 200 shares of its stock from John's estate for $800,000. How does the estate treat this redemption for tax purposes?

C:4-49 *Effect of Redemption on E&P.* White Corporation has 100 shares of stock outstanding. Ann owns 40 of these shares, and unrelated individuals own the remaining 60 shares. White redeems 30 of Ann's shares for $30,000. In the year of the redemption, White has $30,000 of paid-in capital and $80,000 of E&P.
a. How does the redemption affect White's E&P balance if the redemption qualifies for sale treatment?
b. How does the redemption affect White's E&P balance if the redemption does *not* qualify for sale treatment?

C:4-50 *Various Redemption Issues.* Alan, Barbara, and Dave are unrelated. Each has owned 100 shares of Time Corporation stock for five years and each has a $60,000 basis in those shares. Time's E&P is $240,000. Time redeems all 100 of Alan's shares for their $100,000 FMV.
a. What are the amount and character of Alan's recognized gain or loss? What basis do Barbara and Dave take in their remaining shares? What effect does the redemption have on Time's E&P?
b. If Alan were Barbara's son, how would your answers to the questions in Part a change?
c. Assume the same facts as in Part b except Alan agrees with the IRS to waive the family attribution rules. Based on this assumption, how would your answers to the questions in Part a again change?

C:4-51 ***Various Redemption Issues.*** Andrew, Bea, Carl, and Carl, Jr. (Carl's son), and Tetra Corporation own all of the single class of Excel Corporation stock as follows:

Shareholder	*Shares Held*	*Adjusted Basis*
Andrew	20	$3,000
Bea	30	6,000
Carl	25	4,000
Carl, Jr.	15	3,000
Tetra Corporation	10	2,000
Total	100	

Andrew, Bea, and Carl are unrelated. Bea owns 75% of the Tetra stock, and Andrew owns the remaining 25%. Excel's E&P is $100,000. Determine the tax consequences of the following independent transactions to the shareholders and Excel:

a. Excel redeems 25 of Bea's shares for $30,000.
b. Excel redeems 10 of Bea's shares for $12,000.
c. Excel redeems all of Carl's shares for $30,000.
d. Assume the same facts as in Part c except the stock is redeemed from Carl's estate to pay death taxes, and the entire redemption qualifies for sale treatment under Sec. 303. The stock has a $28,000 FMV on the date of Carl's death. The alternate valuation date is not elected.
e. Excel redeems all of Andrew's shares for Excel land having a $6,000 basis for both taxable income and E&P purposes and a $24,000 FMV. Assume a 34% marginal corporate tax rate.
f. Assume that Carl owns 25 shares of Excel stock and that Carl, Jr. owns the remaining 75 shares. Determine the tax consequences to Carl and Excel if Excel redeems all 25 of Carl's shares for $30,000.

C:4-52 ***Comparison of Dividends and Redemptions.*** Bailey is one of four equal unrelated shareholders of Checker Corporation. Bailey has held Checker stock for four years and has a basis in her stock of $40,000. Checker has $280,000 of current and accumulated E&P and distributes $100,000 to Bailey.

a. What are the tax consequences to Checker and to Bailey if Bailey is an individual and the distribution is treated as a dividend?
b. In Part a, what would be the tax consequences if Bailey were a corporation?
c. What are the tax consequences to Checker and to Bailey (an individual) if Bailey surrenders all her stock in a redemption qualifying for sale treatment?
d. In Part c, what would be the tax consequences if Bailey were a corporation?
e. Which treatment would Bailey prefer if Bailey were an individual? Which treatment would Bailey Corporation prefer?

C:4-53 ***Preferred Stock Bailout.*** Does Sec. 306 apply in each of the following independent situations? If so, what is its effect?

a. Beth sells her Sec. 306 stock to Marvin in a year in which the issuing corporation has no E&P.
b. Zero Corporation redeems Sec. 306 stock from Jim in a year in which it has no E&P.
c. Zero Corporation redeems Sec. 306 stock from Ruth in a year in which it has a large E&P balance.
d. Joan gives 100 shares of her Sec. 306 stock to her nephew, Barry.
e. Ed completely terminates his interest in Zero Corporation by having Zero redeem all his common shares and Sec. 306 preferred stock.
f. Carl inherits 100 shares of Sec. 306 stock from his uncle Ted.

C:4-54 ***Preferred Stock Bailout.*** Fran owns all 100 shares of Star Corporation stock. Her stock basis is $60,000. On December 1 of the current year, Star distributes 50 shares of preferred stock to Fran in a nontaxable distribution. In the year of the distribution, Star's total E&P is $100,000, the preferred shares are worth $150,000, and the common shares are worth $300,000.

a. What are the tax consequences to Fran and to Star if Fran sells her preferred stock to Ken for $200,000 on January 10 of the following year? In that year, Star's current E&P is $75,000 (in addition to the $100,000 balance from the prior year).

b. How would your answer to Part a change if Fran sells her preferred stock to Ken for $110,000 instead of $200,000?
c. How would your answer to Part a change if Star redeems Fran's preferred stock for $200,000 on January 10 of the following year?

C:4-55 ***Brother-Sister Redemptions.*** Bob owns 60 of the 100 outstanding shares of Dazzle Corporation stock and 80 of the 100 outstanding shares of Razzle Corporation stock. Bob's basis in his Dazzle shares is $12,000, and his basis in his Razzle shares is $8,000. Bob sells 30 of his Dazzle shares to Razzle for $50,000. At the end of the year of sale, Dazzle and Razzle have E&P of $25,000 and $40,000, respectively.
a. What are the amount and character of Bob's recognized gain or loss on the sale?
b. What is Bob's basis in his remaining shares of the Dazzle and Razzle stock?
c. How does the sale affect the E&P of Dazzle and Razzle?
d. What basis does Razzle take in the Dazzle shares it purchases?
e. How would your answer to Part a change if Bob owns only 50 of the 100 outstanding shares of Razzle stock?

C:4-56 ***Parent-Subsidiary Redemptions.*** Jane owns 150 of the 200 outstanding shares of Parent Corporation stock. Parent owns 160 of the 200 outstanding shares of Subsidiary Corporation stock. Jane sells 50 shares of her Parent stock to Subsidiary for $40,000. Jane's basis in her Parent shares is $15,000 ($100 per share). At the end of the year of sale, Subsidiary and Parent have E&P of $60,000 and $25,000, respectively.
a. What are the amount and character of Jane's recognized gain or loss on the sale?
b. What is Jane's basis in her remaining shares of Parent stock?
c. How does the sale affect the E&P of Parent and Subsidiary?
d. What basis does Subsidiary take in the Parent shares it purchases?
e. How would your answer to Part a change if Jane instead sells 100 of her Parent shares to Subsidiary for $80,000?

C:4-57 ***Bootstrap Acquisition.*** Jana owns all 100 shares of Stone Corporation stock having a $1 million FMV. Her basis in the stock is $400,000. Stone's E&P balance is $600,000. Michael would like to purchase the stock but wants only the corporation's non-cash assets valued at $750,000. Michael is willing to pay $750,000 for these assets.
a. What are the tax consequences to Jana, Michael, and Stone if Michael purchases 75 shares of Stone stock for $750,000 and Stone redeems Jana's remaining 25 shares for $250,000 cash?
b. How would your answer to Part a change (if at all) if Stone first redeems 25 shares of Jana's stock for $250,000 and then Michael purchases the remaining 75 shares from Jana for $750,000?

COMPREHENSIVE PROBLEM

C:4-58 Several years ago, Brian formed Sigma Corporation, a retail company ineligible for the U.S. production activities deduction. Sigma uses the accrual method of accounting. In 2015, the corporation reported the following items:

Gross profit	$290,000
Long-term capital gain	20,000
Tax-exempt interest received	7,000
Salary paid to Brian	80,000
Payroll tax on Brian's salary (Sigma's share)	6,120
Depreciation	25,000 ($21,000 for E&P purposes)
Other operating expenses	89,000
Dividend distribution to Brian	60,000

In addition to owning 100% of Sigma's stock, Brian manages Sigma's business and earns the $80,000 salary listed above. This salary is an ordinary and necessary business expense of the corporation and is reasonable in amount. The payroll tax on Brian's $80,000 salary is $12,240, $6,120 of which Sigma pays and deducts, and the other $6,120 of which Brian pays through Social Security withholding. Brian is single with no dependents and claims the standard deduction.
a. Calculate Sigma's and Brian's 2015 taxable income and total tax liability, as well as their combined tax liability. Also, calculate the corporation's current E&P after the dividend distribution.

b. Assume instead that Brian operates Sigma as a sole proprietorship. In the current year, the business reports the same operating results as above, and Brian withdraws $140,000 in lieu of the salary and dividend. Brian's self-employment tax is $19,408. Compute Brian's total tax liability for 2015.

c. Assume a C corporation such as in Part a distributes all of its after-tax earnings. Compare the tax treatment of long-term capital gains, tax-exempt interest, and operating profits if earned by a C corporation with the tax treatment of these items if earned by a sole proprietorship.

TAX STRATEGY PROBLEM

C:4-59 John owns all 100 shares of stock in Jamaica Corporation, which has $100,000 of current E&P. John would like to receive a $50,000 distribution from the corporation. Jamaica owns several assets that it could distribute to John. What are the tax consequences of Jamaica's distributing each of the following assets? Assume Jamaica has a 34% marginal tax rate and, unless stated otherwise, its bases for E&P and taxable income purposes are the same.

a. $50,000 cash.
b. 100 shares of XYZ stock purchased two years ago for $10,000 and now worth $50,000.
c. 100 shares of ABC stock purchased one year ago for $72,000 and now worth $50,000.
d. Equipment purchased four years ago for $120,000 that now has a tax adjusted basis of $22,000 and an E&P adjusted basis of $40,000. John would assume a liability of $31,000 on the equipment. The equipment is now worth $81,000.
e. An installment obligation with a face value of $50,000 and a basis of $32,000. Jamaica acquired this obligation three years ago when it sold land held as an investment.
f. Would your answers in Parts a–e change if Jamaica redeems 50 of John's shares for each of the properties listed?
g. Based on the foregoing results, which distribution would you recommend? Which distribution(s) should be avoided?
h. Would your answers in Parts a–e change if John's 100 shares represented one third of Jamaica's outstanding shares, unrelated parties owned the remaining 200 shares, and Jamaica exchanged all of John's shares for each of the properties listed?
i. If John were an investor, would treating the distribution as a sale be preferable to treating the distribution as a dividend? Why or why not?

CASE STUDY PROBLEMS

C:4-60 Amy, Beth, and Meg each own 100 of the 300 outstanding shares of Theta Corporation stock. Amy wants to sell her shares, which have a $40,000 basis and a $100,000 FMV. Either Beth and/or Meg can purchase Amy's shares (50 shares each) or Theta can redeem all of them. Theta has a $150,000 E&P balance.

Required: Write a memorandum comparing the tax consequences of the two options to the three sisters, who actively manage Theta.

C:4-61 Maria Garcia is a CPA whose firm has prepared the tax returns of Stanley Corporation for many years. A review of Stanley's last three tax returns by a new staff accountant, who has been assigned to the client for the first time, reveals that the corporation may be paying excessive compensation to one of its key officers. The staff accountant feels that the firm should inform the IRS and/or report the excess amount as a nondeductible dividend. Although the facts are ambiguous, they tend to support the contention that the compensation paid in current and prior years is reasonable.

Required: In a client letter, discuss Maria's role as an advocate for Stanley, and discuss the possible tax consequences resulting from a subsequent audit.

TAX RESEARCH PROBLEMS

C:4-62 Fifteen years ago, husband and wife Stuart and Marsha Widell organized Widell Engineering Associates (WEA), a Delaware corporation that builds, repairs, and manages waste treatment plants throughout the Southwest. The Widells capitalized WEA with cash of $500,000 and industrial equipment having an adjusted basis of $4.5 million, each in exchange for 2,500 shares of WEA common stock. Three years later, Stuart and Marsha each gifted 500 shares of their WEA stock to their son Weymouth.

As a result of a sharp upswing in the economy, WEA's profits swelled under the joint management of Stuart and Weymouth. After ten years of joint control, however, and because of irreconcilable differences with his father, Weymouth decided to leave WEA and organize his own engineering firm, Fortunelle.

To keep WEA's business in the family and to give Stuart complete WEA management control, Stuart, Marsha, and Weymouth agreed that WEA would redeem all of Weymouth's 1,000 shares with waste treatment property worth $8.5 million. To ensure capital gains treatment, Weymouth obtained a waiver of the family attribution rules in return for an agreement with the IRS not to acquire an equity interest in WEA for ten years and to notify the IRS if he does so. Following the redemption, Weymouth transferred the property to Fortunelle in exchange for all 8,500 shares of Fortunelle common stock.

Last year, Stuart suffered a heart attack. He now has proceeded to reconcile his differences with Weymouth. To retain Widell family control of WEA's business, Stuart, Marsha, and Weymouth propose that WEA and Fortunelle conclude an "arms length" agreement under which Fortunelle would manage WEA's waste treatment plants in return annually for 20% of WEA's gross rental revenues, but no equity interest. The Widells are convinced that the proposed arrangement does not violate either the Sec. 302 waiver rules or Weymouth's agreement with the IRS. They have asked you to draft a letter that confirms this understanding. In researching the issue, consult at a minimum the following authorities:

- IRC Sec. 302(c)(2)
- Rev. Rul. 70-104, 1970 C.B. 66
- *Chertkof v. Commissioner*, 48 AFTR 2d 81-5194, 81-1 USTC ¶9462 (4th Cir, 1981)

C:4-63 When the IRS audited Winter Corporation's current year tax return, the IRS disallowed $10,000 of travel and entertainment expenses incurred by Charles, an officer-shareholder, because of inadequate documentation. The IRS asserted that the $10,000 expenditure was a constructive dividend to Charles, who maintained that the expense was business related. Charles argued that he derived no personal benefit from the expenditure and therefore received no constructive dividend. Prepare a memorandum for your tax manager explaining whether the IRS's assertion or Charles's assertion is correct. Your manager has suggested that, at a minimum, you consult the following resources:

- IRC Secs. 162 and 274
- Reg. Secs. 1.274-1 and -2

C:4-64 Scott and Lynn Brown each own 50% of Benson Corporation stock. During the current year, Benson made the following distributions to its shareholders:

Shareholder	*Property Distributed*	*Adjusted Basis to Corporation*	*Property's FMV*
Scott Brown	Land parcel A	$ 40,000	$75,000
Lynn Brown	Land parcel B	120,000	75,000

Benson had E&P of $250,000 immediately before the distributions. Prepare a memorandum for your tax manager explaining how Benson should treat these transactions for tax and financial accounting purposes. How will the two shareholders report the distributions? Assume Benson's marginal tax rate is 34%. Your manager has suggested that, at a minimum, you consult the following resources:

- IRC Sec. 301
- IRC Sec. 311
- IRC Sec. 312
- Accounting Standards Codification (ASC) 845, formerly APB No. 29

C:4-65 John and Jean own 80% and 20%, respectively, of Plum Corporation stock. Thanks to their hard work, Plum's software sales have sky rocketed. In its first year of operation Plum's earnings were minimal, but four years later, Plum grossed $10 million. Plum compensated John and Jean as follows: John received a bonus of 76% of net profits and Jean received a bonus of 19% of net profits at the end of each year. Plum never paid any dividends. Can Plum deduct any or all of the "salaries" paid to John and Jean?

C:4-66 Sara owns 60% of Mayfield Corporation's single class of stock. A group of five family members and three key employees own the remaining 40%. Mayfield is a calendar year taxpayer that uses the accrual method of accounting. Sara is a Mayfield officer and director and uses the cash method of accounting. During the period Year 1 through Year 3, Sara received the following amounts as salary and nontaxable fringe benefits from Mayfield: Year 1, $160,000; Year 2, $240,000; and Year 3, $290,000. She earned these amounts evenly throughout the tax years in question. In Year 4, upon auditing Mayfield's tax returns for Year 1 through Year 3, a revenue agent determined that reasonable compensation for Sara's services for the three years in question is $110,000, $165,000, and $175,000, respectively. The bylaws of Mayfield were amended on December 15, Year 2, to provide that:

> Any payments made to an officer of the corporation, including salary, commissions, bonuses, other forms of compensation, interest, rent, or travel and entertainment expenses incurred, and which shall be disallowed in whole or in part as a deductible expense by the Internal Revenue Service, shall be reimbursed by such officer to the corporation to the full extent of such disallowance.

Following the disallowance of $240,000 of the total salary expense, the board of directors met and requested that Sara reimburse Mayfield for the portion of her salary deemed to be excessive. Because of the large amount of money involved, the board of directors approved an installment plan whereby Sara would repay the $240,000 in five annual installments of $48,000 each over the period Year 5 through Year 9. The corporation would not charge Sara interest on the unpaid balance of $240,000. Prepare a memorandum for your tax manager explaining what salary and fringe benefits are taxable to Sara in the period Year 1 through 3 and what reimbursements Sara can deduct during the period Year 5 through Year 9.

CHAPTER

5

OTHER CORPORATE TAX LEVIES

LEARNING OBJECTIVES

After studying this chapter, you should be able to

1. Determine whether a corporation is subject to the alternative minimum tax (AMT) and, if so, calculate the AMT
2. Determine whether a corporation is a personal holding company (PHC) and, if so, calculate the PHC tax
3. Establish whether a corporation is subject to the accumulated earnings tax and, if so, calculate the tax
4. Identify tax planning opportunities to minimize the AMT and to avoid the PHC and accumulated earnings taxes
5. Comply with AMT, PHC tax, and accumulated earnings tax procedures
6. Describe the financial statement implications of the AMT

CHAPTER OUTLINE

Chapter C:3 examines a corporation's regular income tax and the procedures for calculating, reporting, and paying this tax. Chapter C:5 focuses on the following three additional taxes the tax law may impose on a C corporation: (1) the alternative minimum tax, (2) the personal holding company tax, and (3) the accumulated earnings tax. For a specific taxable year, a corporation could be liable for none, one, or two of these three taxes (as is discussed later in the chapter, a corporation cannot be liable for the personal holding company tax and accumulated earnings tax for the same taxable year). A corporation pays these additional taxes, if any, in addition to its regular tax liability. For each of these additional taxes, this chapter examines the requirements for the tax to be imposed, the calculation of the tax imposed, and the measures a corporation can take to avoid it.

THE ALTERNATIVE MINIMUM TAX

OBJECTIVE 1

Determine whether a corporation is subject to the alternative minimum tax (AMT) and, if so, calculate the AMT

THE GENERAL FORMULA

The **alternative minimum tax (AMT)** is Congress' attempt to ensure that taxpayers with substantial economic income cannot use exclusions, deductions, and credits to avoid a significant part of their tax liability.[1] Chapter I:14 discusses the AMT as it applies to individuals. Some aspects of the AMT apply to corporations and individuals in the same way, but other aspects of the AMT apply to these two types of taxpayers in different ways.

Table C:5-1 summarizes the calculation of a corporation's AMT. Starting with its regular taxable income, the corporation adds AMT preference items and adds and/or subtracts AMT adjustment items, all of which results in **alternative minimum taxable income (AMTI)**. AMT preferences and adjustments are income and deduction items that are treated differently for regular tax and AMT purposes and are discussed more fully later in this chapter. The tax base for the AMT equals AMTI minus an AMT exemption amount. The corporation multiplies this tax base by a 20% tax rate and subtracts an AMT foreign tax credit to determine its **tentative minimum tax (TMT)**. AMT, then, is the amount by which the TMT exceeds the corporation's regular tax.[2]

ADDITIONAL COMMENT

When AMTI exceeds $150,000 and is less than $310,000, the effective marginal AMT tax rate is 25% due to the AMT exemption amount phase-out [20% + (0.25 × 20%) = 25%].

The AMT exemption amount for corporations is $40,000 reduced by 25% of the amount by which AMTI exceeds $150,000. Thus, the AMT exemption amount is completely phased out if AMTI is $310,000 or more. If two or more corporations comprise a controlled group, they apportion among themselves one $40,000 AMT exemption amount (see Chapter C:3). In addition, the controlled group phases out its AMT exemption amount based on its members' combined AMTIs.

EXAMPLE C:5-1 ▶ Yellow Corporation's AMTI is $200,000. Because its AMTI is more than $150,000 but less than $310,000, Yellow's AMT exemption amount is less than $40,000 but more than $0. Specifically, its AMT exemption equals $27,500 {$40,000 – [0.25 × ($200,000 – $150,000)]}.[3] ◀

EXAMPLE C:5-2 ▶ Badger Corporation's regular taxable income is $400,000. It also has $350,000 of AMT preference items, $285,000 of positive AMT adjustment items, $35,000 of negative AMT adjustment items, and no tax credits. Badger's regular tax is $136,000 (0.34 × $400,000). Badger's AMTI is $1 million ($400,000 + $350,000 + $285,000 − $35,000). Its AMT exemption amount is zero because its AMTI exceeds $310,000. Thus, Badger's AMT tax base is $1 million ($1,000,000 AMTI − $0 AMT exemption amount), and its TMT is $200,000 (0.20 × $1,000,000 AMT tax base). Badger's AMT is $64,000 ($200,000 − $136,000). In total, Badger pays $200,000 ($136,000 + $64,000) of total federal income tax. ◀

ADDITIONAL COMMENT

The AMT is a small part of corporate taxes. In 2011, the federal government collected $3.4 billion of AMT from corporations compared to $221 billion of regular income tax net of tax credits. Of the 1.6 million corporate tax returns (Form 1120) filed in 2011, only 11,374 reported any AMT.

A corporation is liable for any amount of positive AMT, no matter how small. Thus, a corporation needs to calculate its AMT every year (unless it is exempt from the AMT, a topic discussed later).

---

[1] S corporations are not subject to the AMT (Sec. 1363(a)). Instead, an S corporation's AMT preference and adjustment items pass through to their shareholders.

[2] The regular tax is the tax imposed on regular taxable income (see Chapter C:3), reduced by the regular foreign tax credit, the possessions tax credit, and the Puerto Rico economic activity credit. The regular tax does not include any accumulated earnings tax or personal holding company tax, which are discussed later in the chapter, and it does not include any AMT.

[3] In the examples, assume that all corporations are C corporations not exempt from the AMT.

▼ **TABLE C:5-1**
Calculation of a Corporation's Alternative Minimum Tax Liability

Regular taxable income or loss before the NOL deduction	
Plus:	Tax preference items
Plus or minus:	AMT adjustment items other than the ACE adjustment and the alternative tax NOL deduction
Preadjustment AMTI	
Plus or minus:	75% of the difference between pre-adjustment AMTI and adjusted current earnings (ACE)
Minus:	Alternative tax NOL deduction
Alternative minimum taxable income (AMTI)	
Minus:	AMT exemption amount
Tax base for the AMT	
Times:	0.20 tax rate
Tentative minimum tax before credits	
Minus:	AMT foreign tax credit
Tentative minimum tax (TMT)	
Minus:	Regular (income) tax
Alternative minimum tax (AMT, not less than zero)	

STOP & THINK

Question: In Example C:5-2, Badger Corporation pays both the regular tax and the AMT because its TMT exceeds its regular tax. How is this result possible if the regular tax rate for corporations with \$335,000 to \$10 million of taxable income is 34% while the AMT rate is a flat 20%?

Solution: The result is possible because different tax bases are used to calculate the two taxes. The regular tax is based on regular taxable income while the TMT is based on AMTI minus the AMT exemption amount. The circumstances in which the TMT will exceed the regular tax can be expressed as follows (assuming the AMT exemption amount is completely phased out):

$$[\text{Regular taxable Income (RTI)} + \text{Preferences (P)} \pm \text{Adjustments (A)}] \times 0.20 > \text{RTI} \times 0.34$$

The inequality can be simplified as follows:

$$0.20 \times (P \pm A) > 0.14 \times \text{RTI}$$
$$(P \pm A) > 0.70 \times \text{RTI}$$

For Example C:5-2, the inequality indicates that Badger will incur an AMT if its total AMT preference and adjustment items exceed \$280,000 (0.70 × \$400,000 regular taxable income). Badger's \$600,000 (\$350,000 + \$285,000 − \$35,000) of total AMT preference and adjustment items exceed \$280,000, so the inequality correctly indicates that Badger incurs an AMT. If Badger's total AMT preference and adjustment items were \$280,000, its AMTI would be \$680,000 (\$400,000 + \$280,000), its TMT would be \$136,000 (0.20 × \$680,000), and its AMT would be zero because its TMT would not exceed its \$136,000 regular tax.[a]

[a] The inequality will be different if the corporation's marginal regular tax rate is different than 34% as used above (i.e., it is 15%, 25%, 35%, 38%, or 39%) or if the AMT exemption amount is more than zero.

EXEMPTION FROM THE AMT FOR SMALL CORPORATIONS AND FIRST-YEAR CORPORATIONS

A qualifying small corporation is exempt from the AMT. To qualify, the corporation's average gross receipts generally must be \$7.5 million or less for all three-taxable-year periods before the taxable year for which the corporation is determining qualification.[4] A corporation that did not exist for a full three-year period calculates its average gross receipts for the period it existed. For the corporation's second year of existence, it has only its first taxable year to use when applying the gross receipts test, and it applies the test using $5 million instead of $7.5 million as the threshold. At this point, the corporation will have tested its first three-year period (or, in this case, a portion thereof). For its third year, the corporation applies the gross receipts test using its first and second years, subject to the $7.5 million threshold. For its fourth and subsequent years, the corporation applies the $7.5 million threshold to the average gross receipts of the immediately preceding three years. A corporation generally is exempt from the AMT for its first year of existence, regardless of its gross receipts. If a corporation does not qualify for exemption from the AMT, it is subject to the AMT for the year it does not so qualify and all subsequent years.[5]

EXAMPLE C:5-3 ▶ Kiho Corporation forms on January 1 of Year 1 and has gross receipts as follows:

Year 1	$4,500,000	Year 4	8,400,000
Year 2	6,000,000	Year 5	7,650,000
Year 3	7,800,000	Year 6	6,300,000

Kiho is exempt from the AMT for Year 1 because it is the first year the corporation exists. For each subsequent year, Kiho calculates its average gross receipts and determines whether it is exempt from the AMT as follows:

Year 2: For its second year of existence, Kiho applies the test using only its Year 1 gross receipts and a $5 million threshold. The Year 1 gross receipts of $4.5 million is less than or equal to $5 million, so Kiho is exempt from the AMT for Year 2.

Year 3: For its third year of existence, Kiho applies the test using its average gross receipts for Years 1 and 2. This $5.25 million [($4,500,000 + $6,000,000) ÷ 2] average is less than or equal to the $7.5 million threshold that applies after the second year of existence, so Kiho is exempt from the AMT for Year 3.

Year 4: Kiho averages its gross receipts for Years 1 through 3. This $6.1 million [($4,500,000 + $6,000,000 + $7,800,000) ÷ 3] average is less than or equal to $7.5 million, so Kiho is exempt from the AMT for Year 4.

Year 5: Kiho averages its gross receipts for Years 2 through 4. This $7.4 million [($6,000,000 + $7,800,000 + $8,400,000) ÷ 3] average is less than or equal to $7.5 million, so Kiho is exempt from the AMT for Year 5.

Year 6: Kiho averages its gross receipts for Years 3 through 5. This $7.95 million [($7,800,000 + $8,400,000 + $7,650,000) ÷ 3] average is greater than $7.5 million, so Kiho is not exempt from the AMT for Year 6. However, Kiho's failure to qualify for exemption from the AMT does not necessarily mean it will pay any AMT for Year 6. Kiho would not pay any AMT if its TMT were less than its regular tax for Year 6.

Year 7: Kiho is not exempt from the AMT because it failed to so qualify in a prior year. It is irrelevant that Kiho's $7.45 million [($8,400,000 + $7,650,000 + $6,300,000) ÷ 3] average gross receipts for Years 4 through 6 is less than $7.5 million. ◀

Additional rules determine whether a corporation is exempt from the AMT:

- Gross receipts include total sales and amounts received for services. Gross receipts are not reduced for cost of goods sold and expenses. Gross receipts differ from gross income, gross profit, and taxable income. Thus, even though a corporation may have low gross profit or taxable income, it still may not qualify for exemption if it has high gross receipts.
- For any short taxable year (e.g., a corporation's initial year of existence), gross receipts are annualized.
- Gross receipts of a controlled group of corporations are aggregated. For example, if two corporations each have $4 million of average gross receipts and comprise a controlled group, the corporations will not be exempt from the AMT because their $8 million aggregate average gross receipts exceeds $7.5 million (or $5 million, if applicable).

ADDITIONAL COMMENT

Only a small fraction of corporations are subject to the AMT because most corporations' average gross receipts are less than $5 million.

---

[4] Sec. 55(e). To determine average gross receipts, the corporation takes into account only taxable years beginning after 1993.

[5] A corporation losing its exemption from the AMT applies the AMT on a prospective basis. For example, the AMT adjustment item for depreciation, discussed later, does not apply for property placed into service while the corporation is exempt from the AMT but whose recovery period includes years the corporation is subject to the AMT. This rule and similar rules for other AMT preference and adjustment items are beyond the scope of this chapter.

- A corporation that is a successor to another entity aggregates its gross receipts with those of its predecessor (e.g., a newly created subsidiary's gross receipts include those of its parent corporation).

TAX PREFERENCE ITEMS

A corporation adds **tax preference items** to its regular taxable income when calculating preadjustment AMTI. Tax preference items always increase a corporation's AMTI. Tax preference items include:[6]

- The depletion deduction allowable for the tax year in excess of the depletable property's adjusted basis at the end of the tax year (before reducing the adjusted basis for the current year's depletion deduction).[7]
- The amount by which excess intangible drilling and development costs (IDCs) incurred in connection with oil, gas, and geothermal wells exceeds 65% of the net income from such property.[8]
- Tax-exempt interest on private activity bonds. A private activity bond is a bond issued by a state or local government whose proceeds are used wholly or partially for private business activities (e.g., the bond proceeds are used to construct a stadium used by professional sports teams).

ADDITIONAL COMMENT

Tax-exempt interest on private activity bonds issued before August 8, 1986 or in 2009 or 2010 is not treated as a tax preference item.

EXAMPLE C:5-4 ▶ Duffy Corporation mines iron ore. The adjusted basis for one of its properties is zero due to previous years' depletion deductions. Duffy earns $125,000 of gross income and $45,000 of taxable income from the sale of iron ore extracted from this property in the current year. The iron ore depletion percentage is 15%. Duffy's percentage deduction for regular taxable income before any reduction is $18,750 ($125,000 × 0.15), but Duffy reduces this deduction by $3,750 ($18,750 × 0.20) under Sec. 291(a)(2). Duffy's $15,000 ($18,750 − $3,750) deduction is less than the $22,500 ($45,000 × 0.50) maximum deduction. For AMT purposes, the $15,000 deduction for regular taxable income in excess of the property's zero adjusted basis is a tax preference item, which effectively disallows the $15,000 deduction for preadjustment AMTI. ◀

EXAMPLE C:5-5 ▶ Salek Corporation earns the following interest income in the current year:

Source	*Amount*
IBM Corporation bonds	$25,000
Madison County School District bonds	30,000
City of Franklin bonds	15,000

The interest on the IBM bonds is taxable because the bonds are not issued by a state or local government, so Salek includes the $25,000 in its regular taxable income. The Madison County School District issued its bonds to renovate school facilities. Thus, the bonds' proceeds were not used for private business activities and are not private activity bonds. Salek does not include the $30,000 in its regular taxable income, and it is not a tax preference item. The City of Franklin issued its bonds in 2008 to finance a parking garage, where 35% of the space is leased exclusively to a nonexempt corporation. Thus, the bonds are private activity bonds. Salek does not include the $15,000 in its regular taxable income but adds the $15,000 to its regular taxable income when calculating preadjustment AMTI. ◀

AMT ADJUSTMENT ITEMS

Although tax preference items always *increase* AMTI, **AMT adjustment items** can either *increase* or *decrease* AMTI. Common AMT adjustment items are discussed below.[9]

Depreciation. Taxpayers calculate depreciation on some property differently for preadjustment AMTI than for regular taxable income (see Chapter I:10 for depreciation rules for

[6] Sec. 57(a).

[7] Independent producers and royalty owners are not required to treat the oil and gas depletion deduction in excess of the depletable property's adjusted basis as a tax preference item, so this tax preference item applies almost exclusively to integrated oil companies.

[8] Excess IDCs are the amount by which IDCs in the tax year exceed the deduction that would have been allowable if the IDCs had been capitalized and amortized over a ten-year period. The oil and gas excess IDC preference applies to a more limited extent for independent oil companies than it does for integrated oil companies.

[9] Sec. 56(a).

regular tax purposes). These AMT depreciation rules apply to individual and corporate taxpayers. For simplicity, this chapter discusses rules for property placed in service after 1998.[10]

Personal Property Placed in Service After 1998. For AMT purposes, the taxpayer uses the same recovery period (e.g., MACRS recovery period) and same convention (i.e., half-year or mid-quarter) for AMT purposes as it uses for regular tax purposes. However, the taxpayer generally uses the 150% declining balance method to calculate AMT depreciation but uses the 200% declining balance method to calculate regular tax depreciation.[11] The AMT adjustment equals the difference between AMT and regular tax depreciation, and the adjustment could be positive or negative. For property depreciated under the half-year convention, see Table 1 in Appendix C for the regular tax depreciation rates and Table 10 for the AMT depreciation rates.

EXAMPLE C:5-6 ▶ In Year 1, Euclid Corporation places into service used office furniture costing $10,000. The property has a seven-year MACRS recovery period, and the half-year convention applies to it. Euclid does not elect Sec. 179 expensing for the property, and it does not qualify for bonus depreciation because it is not new property. In Year 1, regular tax depreciation is $1,429 ($10,000 × 0.1429), and AMT depreciation is $1,071 ($10,000 × 0.1071). Euclid adds the $358 ($1,429 − $1,071) difference in the depreciation amounts when calculating preadjustment AMTI. This AMT adjustment is positive because regular taxable income, which is the starting point for the preadjustment AMTI calculation, includes a larger depreciation deduction than is allowed for AMT purposes.

Toward the end of the recovery period, the depreciation adjustment becomes negative. For example, in Year 6, regular tax depreciation is $892 ($10,000 × 0.0892) while AMT depreciation is $1,225 ($10,000 × 0.1225). Thus, Euclid makes a negative $333 ($892 − $1,225) adjustment in Year 6. ◀

Any amount the taxpayer elects to expense under Sec. 179 for regular tax purposes also is allowed for AMT purposes.

EXAMPLE C:5-7 ▶ Assume the same facts as in Example C:5-6, except Euclid elects Sec. 179 expensing for $6,000 of the property's cost. In Year 1, Euclid's regular tax depreciation is $6,572 [$6,000 + (0.1429 × ($10,000 − $6,000))], and its AMT tax depreciation is $6,428 [$6,000 + (0.1071 × ($10,000 − $6,000))]. Euclid makes a $144 ($6,572 − $6,428) positive AMT adjustment in the current year. ◀

Bonus Depreciation for Personal Property. For regular tax purposes, depreciation on *new* personal property acquired and placed in service in 2008 through September 8, 2010 and in 2012 through 2014 generally is eligible for 50% bonus depreciation. For property acquired and place in service after September 8, 2010 and before January 1, 2012, bonus depreciation of 100% applies.[12] Bonus depreciation allows the taxpayer to deduct 50% (or 100%, if applicable) of the cost of qualified property in the year the taxpayer places the property in service. Qualified property is primarily computer software and personal property with a MACRS recovery period of 20 years or less. Any Sec. 179 expensing the taxpayer elects with respect to qualified property applies before applying bonus depreciation. Then, the taxpayer applies 50% (or 100%, if applicable) bonus depreciation to the property's cost minus the amount expensed under Sec. 179. Finally, the MACRS depreciation percentages apply to the remaining cost, if any. Property to which bonus depreciation applies is depreciated the same way for AMT purposes as it is for regular tax purposes. Thus, no AMT depreciation adjustment is required. However, a taxpayer can elect out of bonus

---

[10] AMT depreciation rules different than those discussed in the text apply to personal property and real property placed in service before 1999. For such property, the AMT adjustment usually differs from that which would apply to property placed in service after 1998.

[11] If a taxpayer elects to use the straight-line or 150% declining balance method of depreciation for personal property for regular tax purposes, AMT depreciation is the same as regular tax depreciation, so the taxpayer makes no AMT adjustment for depreciation.

[12] Sec. 168(k)(5). Fifty percent bonus depreciation also was allowed for new personal property acquired and placed in service after May 5, 2003 but before January 1, 2005, and 30% bonus depreciation was allowed for new personal property acquired and placed in service after September 11, 2001 but before May 6, 2003.

depreciation, in which case the taxpayer calculates AMT depreciation using the 150% declining balance method discussed above.[13]

EXAMPLE C:5-8 ► On August 25, 2014, Brighton Corporation purchased and placed in service $700,000 of new MACRS five-year property. For 2014, Brighton expensed $500,000 under Sec. 179. In addition, it claimed $100,000 [0.50 × ($700,000 − $500,000)] of bonus depreciation on the cost that remained after Sec. 179 expensing. The corporation also claimed $20,000 [0.20 × ($700,000 − $500,000 − $100,000)] of regular MACRS depreciation on the cost that remained after subtracting Sec. 179 expensing and bonus depreciation. Thus, for regular tax purposes, total 2014 depreciation was $620,000 ($500,000 + $100,000 + $20,000). This $620,000 also was 2014 AMT depreciation for the property, so Brighton had no AMT adjustment for depreciation on this property in 2014 or subsequent years. If instead Brighton had purchased the property and placed it in service sometime from September 9, 2010 through December 31, 2011, Brighton could have deducted the entire $700,000 cost as bonus depreciation and would not have had to elect Sec. 179 expensing for this property. ◄

ADDITIONAL COMMENT

When a taxpayer claims Sec. 179 expensing and/or bonus depreciation, all subsequent cost recovery years are affected because, in the first year, these amounts reduce the basis of the property subject to MACRS depreciation in subsequent years.

Real Property Placed in Service After 1998. Depreciation on real property is the same for preadjustment AMTI as it is for regular taxable income. Thus, the taxpayer makes no AMT adjustment for it.

Basis Calculations. For regular tax purposes, a taxpayer reduces the adjusted basis of property for depreciation allowed for regular tax purposes. Similarly, a taxpayer reduces a property's AMT adjusted basis for allowable AMT depreciation. Thus, a property's adjusted basis for regular tax and AMT purposes will differ if these depreciation amounts differ. When selling such property, the taxpayer calculates separate amounts of gain or loss for regular tax and AMT purposes. Typically, a property's AMT adjusted basis will be more than its regular tax adjusted basis because regular tax depreciation is more accelerated than AMT depreciation, so the taxpayer has a smaller gain (or larger loss) for AMT purposes than it has for regular tax purposes. When calculating preadjustment AMTI, the taxpayer typically subtracts the regular tax gain in excess of the AMT gain (or subtracts the AMT loss in excess of the regular tax loss). These gain difference are a result of the differing regular tax and AMT bases.

EXAMPLE C:5-9 ► Assume the same facts as in Example C:5-6 except, on February 1 of Year 4, Euclid Corporation sells the property for $6,000. Euclid claims the following depreciation amounts each year for regular tax and AMT purposes.

Year	*Regular Tax Depreciation (1)*[a]		*AMT Depreciation (2)*[b]		*AMT Adj. (1) − (2)*
Year 1	$10,000 × 0.1429	$1,429	$10,000 × 0.1071	$1,071	$ 358
Year 2	$10,000 × 0.2449	2,449	$10,000 × 0.1913	1,913	536
Year 3	$10,000 × 0.1749	1,749	$10,000 × 0.1503	1,503	246
Year 4	$10,000 × 0.1249 × 0.5	625	$10,000 × 0.1225 × 0.5	613	12
Total		$6,252	Total	$5,100	$1,152

[a] See Table 1, Appendix C for depreciation percentages.
[b] See Table 10, Appendix C for depreciation percentages.

Because the mid-year convention applies to the property, Euclid claims a half-year of depreciation in Year 4, the year it sells the property. When Euclid sells the property, its adjusted basis for regular tax purposes is $3,748 ($10,000 – $6,252), and its adjusted basis for AMT purposes is $4,900 ($10,000 – $5,100). Thus, Euclid's gain when it sells the property is $2,252 ($6,000 – $3,748) for regular tax purposes and $1,100 ($6,000 – $4,900) for AMT purposes. Euclid makes a $1,152 ($2,252 – $1,100) negative AMT adjustment in Year 4 because the gain it includes in regular taxable income is $1,152 more than the gain it has for AMT purposes. This $1,152 difference is attributable to the regular tax depreciation in excess of the AMT depreciation for Years 1 through 4. For Year 4, Euclid's net AMT adjustment for the property is a negative $1,140 ($12 positive adjustment for depreciation minus $1,152 negative adjustment for the gain (basis) difference). ◄

ADDITIONAL COMMENT

In Example C:5-9, the $1,152 adjustment also can be calculated by subtracting the tax adjusted basis from the AMT adjusted basis ($4,900 − $3,748 = $1,152).

[13] Sec. 168(k)(2)(D)(iii) and Reg. Sec.1.168(k)-1(e)(6).

ADDITIONAL COMMENT

Because of the AMT small corporation exemption, many corporations that can use the completed contract method for regular tax purposes because their average gross receipts are $10 million or less do not have to make an AMT adjustment for long-term contracts.

Long-Term Contracts. For regular tax purposes, taxpayers generally use the percentage of completion method to account for long-term contracts (e.g., a contract to construct a building). However, a taxpayer may use the completed contract method for construction contracts it expects to complete within two years if its average gross receipts for the three preceding tax years is $10 million or less. A taxpayer also may use the completed contract method for home construction contracts (see Chapter I:11). For AMT purposes, the completed contract method is allowed for home construction contracts, but the percentage of completion method must be used for other long-term contracts.

U.S. Production Activites Deduction. A special rule applies for the U.S. production activities deduction. For regular tax purposes, the deduction is 9% of qualified production activities income but is limited to 9% of taxable income before this deduction (see Chapter C:3). For AMT purposes, the deduction is limited to 9% of AMTI before the deduction, but the taxpayer does not have to recompute qualified production activities income based on the AMT rules.[14] Thus, the taxpayer usually will have an AMT adjustment for this deduction if its qualified production activities income is more than its regular taxable income and/or AMTI (both before the deduction). However, if qualified production activities income is less than regular taxable income and also is less than AMTI (both before the deduction), the taxpayer usually will not have to make an AMT adjustment for this deduction because the deduction will be 9% of qualified production activities income for both purposes.

NOL Deduction. For AMT purposes, a taxpayer claims the alternative tax NOL deduction instead of the regular tax NOL deduction. Similar to the regular tax NOL, the alternative tax NOL is the excess of deductions over gross income, but it is based on deductions and gross income determined under the AMT rules. The alternative tax NOL deduction is limited to 90% of AMTI before this deduction and the U.S. production activities deduction. A taxpayer generally carries its alternative tax NOL back two years and forward 20 years, but it foregoes the two-year carryback period for AMT purposes if it elects to do so for regular tax purposes.[15]

The following example illustrates the computation of **preadjustment AMTI** (see Table C:5-1). Preadjustment AMTI is a component of the ACE and AMTI calculations presented later.

EXAMPLE C:5-10 ▶ In the current year, Marion Corporation reports $300,000 of regular taxable income. The $300,000 includes a $70,000 deduction for percentage depletion (the $70,000 is after the 20% reduction under Sec. 291(a)(2)). The depletable property's adjusted basis at the beginning of the year is $40,000. Regular taxable income also includes an $80,000 deduction for MACRS depreciation. For AMT purposes, depreciation for the depreciable property is $55,000.

Regular taxable income	$300,000
Plus: Percentage depletion in excess of basis ($70,000 – $40,000)	30,000
AMT depreciation adjustment ($80,000 – $55,000)	25,000
Preadjustment AMTI	$355,000

◀

Application of Other Regular Tax Rules. As discussed above, the IRC treats many income and deduction items differently for regular tax and AMT purposes. In addition, for AMT purposes, a corporation recomputes income and deduction items for which the regular tax and AMT rules do not differ, based on the regular tax rules and the AMT amounts.[16] For example, for regular tax purposes, the charitable contributions deduction is limited to 10% of taxable income before deducting certain items (see Chapter C:3). For AMT purposes, this limitation is 10% of AMTI before deducting those items. Similarly,

[14] Sec. 199(d)(6).

[15] Instructions for Form 4626, Alternative Minimum Tax—Corporations.

[16] Reg. Sec. 1.55-1(a). However, Reg. Sec. 1.56(g)-1(r) allows the taxpayer to elect to use a simplified inventory method for AMT purposes.

closely held corporations and personal service corporations recalculate their at-risk and passive activity losses, taking into account their AMT preference and adjustment items.

ADDITIONAL COMMENT

In 2011, corporations' ACE adjustments totaled $13.8 billion while other AMT preference and adjustment items were a net positive $11.5 billion.

ADJUSTED CURRENT EARNINGS (ACE) ADJUSTMENT

Congress added the ACE adjustment in an attempt to bring the AMT tax base closer to a corporation's economic income. The IRC requires C corporations, but not individuals and S corporations, to make the ACE adjustment when calculating the AMT.[17] The ACE adjustment generally equals 75% of ACE minus preadjustment AMTI. ACE is similar to the concept of earnings and profits (E&P) that determines whether a corporate distribution is a dividend (see Chapter C:4), but ACE is not exactly the same as E&P because the tax law treats some items differently for ACE purposes than for E&P purposes. ACE equals preadjustment AMTI plus and/or minus adjustments for items whose treatment differs for the two purposes. These differences are discussed below.

The ACE adjustment generally can be positive or negative. However, a corporation's negative ACE adjustment is limited to the cumulative net amount of its positive and negative ACE adjustment in all prior years. A corporation cannot carry over to another year any negative ACE adjustment that exceeds this limitation.

EXAMPLE C:5-11 ▶ Kantro Corporation's ACE adjustments prior to Year 1 net to a positive $10,000. Kantro reports the following ACE and preadjustment AMTI amounts for Years 1 through 3:

	Year 1	*Year 2*	*Year 3*
ACE	$600,000	$535,000	$570,000
Preadjustment AMTI	500,000	575,000	650,000

Kantro makes a positive $75,000 [0.75 × ($600,000 – $500,000)] ACE adjustment in Year 1 and a negative $30,000 [0.75 × ($535,000 – $575,000)] ACE adjustment in Year 2. Kantro's Year 2 negative ACE adjustment is limited to $85,000 ($10,000 + $75,000), so Kantro is allowed all $30,000 of the negative ACE adjustment. Kantro's Year 3 ACE adjustment is negative $60,000 [0.75 × ($570,000 – $650,000)] before considering the limitation on it. This negative adjustment is limited to $55,000 ($10,000 + $75,000 – $30,000), so Kantro's Year 3 ACE adjustment is negative $55,000. The total ACE adjustments over the three years is negative $10,000 ($75,000 – $30,000 – $55,000). ◀

ADDITIONAL COMMENT

Under the American Recovery and Reinvestment Act of 2009, interest on tax-exempt bonds issued in 2009 or 2010 is not treated as an adjustment for ACE purposes.

The following rules apply for determining ACE.[18]

- Any income or gains permanently excluded from gross income for preadjustment AMTI purposes but increase E&P are included in gross income for ACE purposes (e.g., interest on tax-exempt bonds that are not private activity bonds and life insurance proceeds).[19] A corporation adds these items to its preadjustment AMTI when calculating its ACE.
- Any expenses or losses deductible for preadjustment AMTI purposes but not deductible for E&P are not deductible for ACE purposes (e.g.,70% dividends-received deduction). A corporation adds these items to its preadjustment AMTI when calculating its ACE. The 80% and 100% dividends-received deductions and the U.S. production activities deduction are exceptions to this rule. These two deductions are allowed for ACE purposes even though they are not deductible for E&P.
- Any expenses or losses not deductible for preadjustment AMTI purposes but deductible for E&P are not deductible for ACE purposes (e.g., federal income taxes). A corporation does not adjust for these items when calculating ACE because they are not deductible for preadjustment AMTI or ACE.

---

[17] Sec. 56(c)(1) and (g)(6).

[18] Sec. 56(g)(4) and Reg. Sec. 1.56(g)-1. Depreciation on property placed in service before 1994 is calculated differently for ACE purposes than it is for preadjustment AMTI purposes. A corporation makes an adjustment for such property when calculating ACE. For property placed in service after 1993, depreciation for ACE purposes is that same as that for preadjustment AMTI purposes, so a corporation does not make any adjustment for such property when calculating ACE.

[19] The items are reduced by any deduction that would be allowable in computing preadjustment AMTI if the income were includible in preadjustment AMTI. No adjustment is made for timing differences (e.g., income or gains that are included in preadjustment AMTI and E&P but in different taxable years).

- The installment method generally is not allowed for ACE purposes. A corporation with a sale to which the installment method applies makes a positive adjustment to preadjustment AMTI to calculate ACE in the year of sale, and it makes a negative adjustment in the year(s) it receives the sales proceeds.
- Organizational expenditures are not deductible for ACE purposes. A corporation adds such a deduction to its preadjustment AMTI when calculating its ACE. Any organizational expenditures deducted for regular tax purposes are also deductible for preadjustment AMTI purposes, so a corporation makes no adjustment when calculating preadjustment AMTI.
- The increase or decrease in the annual LIFO recapture amount increases or decreases ACE. The LIFO recapture amount is the amount by which ending inventory under the first-in, first-out (FIFO) method exceeds ending inventory under the last-in, first-out (LIFO) method. This adjustment effectively converts the corporation's inventory method from LIFO to FIFO for ACE purposes.
- Depletion is determined under the cost method. For ACE purposes, a corporation amortizes intangible drilling costs over 60 months beginning with the month in which it pays or incurs them.
- For ACE purposes, a corporation recomputes income and deductions for which the preadjustment AMTI and ACE rules do not differ, based on the preadjustment AMTI rules and the ACE amounts.[20] For example, a corporation recalculates the charitable contribution and percentage depletion deduction limitations. For many corporations, recalculating the charitable contribution deduction limitation results in no adjustment to preadjustment AMTI because their charitable contributions are less than the limit for both preadjustment AMTI and ACE purposes.

Topic Review C:5-1 summarizes the ACE calculation.

Comprehensive Example. Glidden Corporation does not qualify for the first year or small corporation exemption from the AMT. Glidden calculates its regular taxable income and regular tax as follows:

Gross profit from sales	$300,000
Dividends: From 30%-owned corporation	10,000
From 10%-owned corporation	20,000
Gain on sale of machine	12,778
Gain on installment sale of land	25,000
Gross income	$367,778
Operating expenses (other than depreciation)	(175,000)
Depreciation	(40,000)
Deduction for organizational expenditures	(500)
Dividends-received deduction	(22,000)
Total deductions	($237,500)
Taxable income	$130,278
Regular tax	$ 34,058

Assume the following additional facts:

- Glidden receives $15,000 of tax-exempt bond interest. The bonds are not private activity bonds and were not issued in 2009 or 2010.
- Glidden receives $100,000 of life insurance proceeds upon the death of one of its executives.
- Glidden sells land for a $77,000 gain, $25,000 of which it reports in the current year for regular tax purposes under the installment method.
- The gain on the machine sale for AMT purposes is $5,860.

[20] Reg. Sec. 1.56(g)-1(a)(5).

TOPIC REVIEW C:5-1

Summary of Common Alternative Minimum Tax Preference and Adjustment Items

Income/Expense Item	Typical Adjustment to: Regular Taxable Income to Calculate Preadjustment AMTI	Typical Adjustment to: Preadjustment AMTI to Calculate ACE
Tax-exempt interest:		
Private activity bonds	Increase[a]	None
Other bonds	None	Increase[a]
Life insurance proceeds	None	Increase
Deferred gain on installment method sale:		
Year of sale	None	Increase
Subsequent years' proceeds received	None	Decrease
LIFO inventory adjustment	None	Increase or decrease
Depreciation	Increase or decrease	None[b]
"Basis adjustment" on asset sale	Decrease	None[c]
Excess charitable contributions:		
Year of contribution	Decrease	Decrease
Carryover year	Increase	Increase
Excess capital losses	None	None
Dividends-received deduction:		
80% and 100% DRD	None	None
70% DRD	None	Increase
U.S. production activities deduction	Decrease or None	None
Organizational expenditure deduction	None	Increase
Federal income taxes	None	None
Penalties and fines	None	None
Disallowed travel and entertainment expenses and club dues	None	None

[a] Except for bonds issued in 2009 or 2010.
[b] Increase or none for property placed into service before 1994.
[c] Decrease or none for property placed into service before 1994.

- Depreciation for AMT purposes is $32,500.
- Glidden incurred $12,500 of organizational expenditures three years ago. It expensed $5,000 of these expenditures in that year and is amortizing the remaining $7,500 over 180 months. The deduction for the current year is $500.
- Glidden's ACE adjustments for prior years are a net positive $311,296.

Based on the above facts, Glidden calculates its preadjustment AMTI as follows:

Taxable income	$130,278
Plus: Depreciation adjustment	7,500[a]
Minus: Basis adjustment on machine sale	(6,918)[b]
Preadjustment AMTI	$130,860

[a] $40,000 − $32,500 = $7,500.
[b] $5,860 − $12,778 = $(6,918).

Glidden makes the $7,500 depreciation adjustment because the depreciation method it uses for regular tax purposes differs from that for AMT purposes. Similarly, Glidden's gain on the machine sale differs for regular tax and AMT purposes because the different depreciation methods result in different adjusted bases for the property for these two purposes. Glidden makes no adjustment for preadjustment AMTI for the tax-exempt interest because it is not earned on private activity bonds, so Glidden treats the interest in the same manner for regular tax and preadjustment AMTI purposes. Likewise, Glidden makes no adjustment for the life insurance proceeds, the installment sale gain, or the organizational expenditures because it treats these items in the same manner to calculate regular taxable income and preadjustment AMTI.

Glidden calculates its ACE as follows:

Preadjustment AMTI	$130,860
Plus: Tax-exempt bond interest	15,000
Life insurance proceeds	100,000
Deferred gain on installment sale	52,000[a]
Deduction for organizational expenditures	500
Dividends-received deduction	14,000[b]
Adjusted current earnings	$312,360

[a] $77,000 − $25,000 = $52,000.
[b] $20,000 × 70% = $14,000.

The tax-exempt interest and life insurance proceeds are not included in regular taxable income and preadjustment AMTI but are included in ACE, so Glidden adds these items to preadjustment AMTI when calculating ACE. The portion of the installment sale gain whose taxation is deferred for regular tax and preadjustment AMTI purposes is not deferred for ACE purposes, so Glidden makes a positive adjustment for it. (Glidden will make negative adjustments in subsequent years as this deferred gain is recognized for regular tax and preadjustment AMTI purposes but not for ACE purposes.) Glidden adds the organizational expenditures and 70% dividends-received deductions because they are not allowed for ACE purposes.

Glidden calculates its AMT as follows:

Preadjustment AMTI		$130,860
ACE adjustment:		
ACE	$312,360	
Minus: Preadjustment AMTI	(130,860)	
Difference	$181,500	
Times: 75%	× 0.75	136,125
Alternative minimum taxable income (AMTI)		$266,985
Minus: AMT exemption amount		(10,754)[a]
AMT base		$256,231
Times: 20% tax rate		× 0.20
Tentative minimum tax (TMT)		$ 51,246
Minus: Regular tax		(34,058)[b]
Alternative minimum tax (AMT)		17,188

[a] $40,000 − [0.25 × ($266,985 − $150,000)] = $10,754.
[b] $22,250 + [0.39 × ($130,278 − $100,000)] = $34,058.

Glidden reduces its AMT exemption amount, but not to zero, because its AMTI is more than $150,000 and less than $310,000. Glidden's total federal income tax is $51,246 ($34,058 regular tax + $17,188 AMT), which equals its TMT. A completed Form 4626 for this comprehensive example appears in Appendix B.

MINIMUM TAX CREDIT

If applicable, a corporation incurs the AMT in addition to its regular tax. The AMT also creates a **minimum tax credit**, which the corporation may use to offset future regular taxes. The amount of unused minimum tax credits from prior years a corporation can use in a tax year is limited to the extent its regular tax (minus all credits other than refundable credits) exceeds its TMT. That is, a corporation's unused minimum tax credits can offset its regular tax but not its AMT. Also, the limitation prevents the minimum tax credit from reducing the regular tax below the TMT in a given year. A corporation's unused minimum tax credits carry forward indefinitely. Because of the minimum tax credit, the AMT generally accelerates a corporation's tax liability rather than permanently increasing it.[21] In effect, the AMT is a prepaid tax on corporate preferences and AMT adjustments.

[21] Sec. 53. Several of the differences between regular taxable income and AMTI are timing differences (e.g., depreciation). If no minimum tax credit were allowed, a corporation might incur AMT in one year when such a timing difference results in a positive AMT adjustment that causes its TMT to exceed its regular tax, but the corporation might not save AMT when the timing difference reverses and results in a negative AMT adjustment because its regular tax exceeds its TMT that year. Regular taxable income and AMTI can differ due to permanent differences that will never reverse (e.g., tax-exempt interest on private activity bonds or an ACE adjustment resulting from the 70% dividends-received deduction). A corporation generally is allowed a minimum tax credit for all of its AMT, whether it is due to timing or permanent differences. This treatment differs from that for individuals, who are allowed a minimum tax credit only for the AMT attributable to certain AMT preference and adjustment items (see Chapter I:14).

EXAMPLE C:5-12 ► For the current year, Woodford Corporation's regular tax is $59,300, and its TMT is $70,000. Thus, Woodford's AMT is $10,700 ($70,000 − $59,300). This $10,700 of AMT generates a $10,700 minimum tax credit for Woodford. Woodford's total tax is $70,000 ($59,300 + $10,700).

In the next year, Woodford's regular tax is $86,600, and its TMT is $75,000. Thus, Woodford's AMT is zero. Woodford claims all $10,700 of its unused minimum tax credit because its use is limited to $11,600 ($86,600 − $75,000). Woodford's net tax for the next year is $75,900 ($86,600 − $10,700). If Woodford's regular tax in the next year had been $83,000 instead of $86,600, it could have taken only $8,000 ($83,000 − $75,000) of the minimum tax credit that year with $2,700 carrying forward to a subsequent year. ◄

ADDITIONAL COMMENT

In Example C:5-12, the $145,900 ($70,000 + $75,900) total tax that Woodford pays in the current year and next year equals the $145,900 ($59,300 + $86,600) total regular tax that Woodford pays in those years. This equality illustrates that the AMT generally accelerates a corporation's tax liability rather than permanently increasing it. With discounting, the total present value of the $70,000 and $75,900 amounts exceeds the total present value of the $59,300 and $86,600 amounts, demonstating the time value of money.

TAX CREDITS AND THE AMT

AMT and the General Business Credit. The general business credit is the sum of many business credits, such as the credit for research activities (see Chapter I:14). The IRC limits the general business credit a taxpayer may claim for regular tax purposes, which the following points describe:[22]

- A taxpayer's general business credit limitation is:
  - a. Net income tax in excess of
  - b. Greater of:
    - i. TMT, or
    - ii. 25% of its net regular tax in excess of $25,000.
- The net income tax is the sum of the regular tax and AMT, reduced by the foreign tax credit, possessions tax credit, and Puerto Rico economic activity credit.
- The net regular tax is regular tax reduced by the same credits that reduce the net income tax.
- A small corporation exempt from the AMT is treated as having a zero TMT.
- The taxpayer can carry back one year and forward 20 years any general business credit that cannot be used in the current year because of the credit limitation.[23]

ADDITIONAL COMMENT

Because the general business credit limitation depends on the TMT, *every* corporation not exempt from the AMT needs to compute its TMT, even if it owes no AMT.

The effect of this limitation is that the general business credit can offset, at most, only the portion of the regular tax that exceeds the TMT, and it cannot offset any AMT.

EXAMPLE C:5-13 ► In the current year, Keene Corporation's regular tax before credits is $165,000, its TMT is $120,000, and the only available credit it has is a $55,000 general business credit. Keene's AMT is zero because its TMT does not exceed its regular tax. Keene calculates its general business credit limitation as follows:

Net income tax		$165,000
Minus: Greater of:		
(1) Tentative minimum tax, or	$120,000	
(2) 25% of regular tax (reduced by certain other credits) in excess of $25,000 [0.25 × ($165,000 − $25,000)]	$ 35,000	(120,000)
General business credit limitation		$ 45,000

Keene may claim $45,000 of its general business credit in the current year, so its regular tax (net of credits) is $120,000 ($165,000 − $45,000). Keene's general business credit in excess of the limitation is $10,000 ($55,000 − $45,000), which it carries back one year and forward 20 years. ◄

AMT and the Foreign Tax Credit. A taxpayer may reduce its TMT by a modified version of the foreign tax credit. For regular tax purposes, the foreign tax credit is limited to the regular tax before credits multiplied by the ratio of foreign source regular taxable income to worldwide regular taxable income (see Chapter I:14). For AMT

[22] Sec. 38(c). Special rules apply for certain credits that comprise the general business credit, such as the empowerment zone employment credit.

[23] Sec. 39.

TOPIC REVIEW C:5-2

Alternative Minimum Tax (AMT) for Corporations

1. Qualifying small corporations are exempt from the AMT. To qualify, a corporation's average gross receipts generally must be $7.5 million or less. Also, first-year corporations generally are exempt from the AMT. S corporations are exempt from the AMT and, instead, pass through their AMT preference and adjustment items to their shareholders.
2. The starting point for calculating preadjustment alternative minimum taxable income (AMTI) is regular taxable income. A taxpayer increases this amount for tax preference items and increases and/or decreases it for AMT adjustment items (other than the adjusted current earnings (ACE) adjustment and the alternative tax net operating loss (NOL) deduction). The resulting amount is preadjustment AMTI.
3. The ACE adjustment generally equals 75% of ACE minus preadjustment AMTI. ACE is a modified version of preadjustment AMTI.
4. AMTI equals preadjustment AMTI, plus or minus the ACE adjustment, and minus the alternative tax NOL deduction.
5. The AMT tax base is AMTI minus a $40,000 AMT exemption amount. The $40,000 amount phases out as AMTI increases from $150,000 to $310,000.
6. A corporation's tentative minimum tax (TMT) equals 20% of its AMT tax base. It is reduced by the AMT foreign tax credit allowed. The TMT can limit the amount of general business credit allowed for regular tax purposes.
7. The AMT is the excess of the TMT over the regular tax, and it is levied in addition to the regular tax.
8. A corporation's AMT generates an equal amount of minimum tax credit, which the corporation can carry forward indefinitely to offset future regular taxes. Minimum tax credits can be used only to the extent the regular tax exceeds the TMT.
9. When determining its quarterly estimated tax payments, a taxpayer includes its regular tax and AMT.

purposes, a taxpayer calculates its credit limitation by substituting the TMT (before subtracting any AMT foreign tax credit) for the regular tax and by substituting AMTI for regular taxable income.[24]

Topic Review C:5-2 presents an overview of the AMT for corporations. Also see the financial statement implications of the AMT later in this chapter.

PERSONAL HOLDING COMPANY TAX

OBJECTIVE 2

Determine whether a corporation is a personal holding company (PHC) and, if so, calculate the PHC tax

A corporation that meets both a stock ownership test and a passive income test is classified as a **personal holding company** (**PHC**) for the tax year. Congress enacted the PHC tax to prevent taxpayers from using closely held corporations to shelter passive income from the higher individual tax rates. The PHC tax is 20% of the PHC tax base (called undistributed personal holding company income and discussed later in the chapter). A corporation subject to the PHC tax pays this tax in addition to the regular tax and the alternative minimum tax. Corporations, however, can escape the PHC tax by intentionally failing either the stock ownership test or passive income test or through dividend distributions that reduce UPHCI to zero.

The significance of the PHC tax has been diminished since Congress reduced the PHC tax rate to match the top tax rate on qualified dividends (15% from 2003 through 2012 and 20% in 2013 and after). Prior to 2003, the PHC tax rate was the same rate as the top corporate tax rate.

[24] Sec. 59(a). A taxpayer may elect to use a simplified AMT foreign tax credit limitation, which uses the ratio of foreign source regular taxable income to worldwide AMTI rather than the ratio of foreign source AMTI to worldwide AMTI.

ADDITIONAL COMMENT

The Congressional intent behind enacting the personal holding company and accumulated earnings taxes was not to produce large amounts of tax revenues. However, the presence of these taxes in the IRS's arsenal prevents substantial revenue losses from certain tax-motivated transactions involving closely held corporations.

PERSONAL HOLDING COMPANY DEFINED

A personal holding company is any corporation that (1) has five or fewer individual shareholders who own more than 50% of the corporation's outstanding stock at any time during the last half of its tax year and (2) has personal holding company income that is at least 60% of its adjusted ordinary gross income for the tax year.[25]

Corporations with special tax status generally are excluded from the PHC definition. Among these are S corporations and tax-exempt organizations.

STOCK OWNERSHIP REQUIREMENT

Section 542(a)(2) provides that a corporation satisfies the PHC stock ownership requirement if more than 50% of the value of its outstanding stock is directly or indirectly owned by five or fewer individuals at any time during the last half of its tax year.[26] Any corporation with fewer than ten individual shareholders at any time during the last half of its tax year, which is not an excluded corporation, will meet the stock ownership requirement.[27]

For purposes of determining whether the 50% requirement is satisfied, stock owned directly or indirectly by or for an individual is considered to be owned by that individual. The Sec. 544 stock attribution rules provide that

ADDITIONAL COMMENT

The Sec. 544 stock attribution rules are similar to the Sec. 318 stock attribution rules discussed in Chapter C:4, but they are not identical. For example, family members include brothers and sisters for the Sec. 544 rules but not for the Sec. 318 rules.

- Stock owned by a family member is considered to be owned by the other members of his or her family. Family members include a spouse, brothers and sisters, ancestors, and lineal descendants.
- Stock owned directly or indirectly by or for a corporation, partnership, estate, or trust is considered to be owned proportionately by its shareholders, partners, or beneficiaries.
- A person who holds an option to acquire stock is considered to own such stock whether or not the individual intends to exercise the option.
- Stock owned by a partnership's partner is considered to be owned by his or her partners.
- The family, partnership, and option rules can be used only to make a corporation a PHC. They cannot be used to prevent a corporation from acquiring PHC status.[28]

PASSIVE INCOME REQUIREMENT

A corporation whose shareholders satisfy the stock ownership requirement is not a PHC unless the corporation also earns predominantly passive income. The passive income requirement is met if at least 60% of the corporation's **adjusted ordinary gross income (AOGI)** for the tax year is personal holding company income (PHCI). The following text sections define AOGI and PHCI and outline ways in which a corporation can sidestep the passive income requirements.

KEY POINT

To be deemed a PHC, a corporation must satisfy two tests: a stock ownership test and a passive income test. Because most closely held corporations satisfy the stock ownership test, the passive income test usually is decisive.

Adjusted Ordinary Gross Income Defined. The first step toward determining AOGI is calculating the corporation's gross income (see Figure C:5-1). Gross income is determined under the same accounting method used to compute taxable income. Thus, an income item excluded from gross income also is excluded from AOGI. Gross receipts from sales are reduced by the corporation's cost of goods sold.

The next step toward determining AOGI is calculating the corporation's **ordinary gross income (OGI)**. To do this, the corporation's gross income is reduced by the amount of its capital gains and Sec. 1231 gains.[29] These items are neutral in determining whether a corporation is a PHC; that is, the realization and recognition of a large Sec. 1231 or capital gain cannot make a corporation a PHC.

[25] Sec. 542(a).

[26] The PHC stock ownership test also is used to determine whether a closely held C corporation is subject to the at-risk rules (Sec. 465) or the passive activity loss and credit limitation rules (Sec. 469). Thus, a closely held corporation that is not a PHC may be subject to certain restrictions because of the PHC stock ownership rules.

[27] This statement may not be valid if entities own stock that might be attributed to the individual owners.

[28] Sec. 544(a)(4)(A).

[29] Sec. 543(b)(1).

▼ **FIGURE C:5-1**
Determining Adjusted Ordinary Gross Income

Gross income (GI) reported for taxable income and PHC purposes
Minus: Gross gains on the sale of capital assets
Gross gains on the sale of Sec. 1231 property

Ordinary gross income (OGI)
Minus: Certain expenses relating to gross income from rents; mineral, oil, and gas royalties; and working interests in oil or gas wells
Interest earned on certain U.S. obligations held for sale to customers by dealers
Interest on condemnation awards, judgments, or tax refunds
Certain expenses relating to rents from tangible personal property manufactured or produced by the corporation, provided it has engaged in substantial manufacturing or production of the same type of personal property in the current tax year

Adjusted ordinary gross income (AOGI)

Next, OGI is reduced by certain expenses. These expenses relate to the generation of rental income; mineral, oil, and gas (M, O, & G) royalties; and income from working interests in oil or gas wells.[30] The rental income adjustment is described below.

Reduction by Rental Income Expenses. Gross income from rents is reduced by deductions for depreciation or amortization, property taxes, interest, and rental payments. This net amount is known as **adjusted income from rents (AIR)**.[31] No other Sec. 162 expenses incurred in the generation of rental income reduce OGI. The expense adjustment cannot exceed total gross rental income.

EXAMPLE C:5-14 ▶ Ingrid owns all of Keno Corporation's single class of stock. Both Ingrid and Keno use the calendar year as their tax year. Keno reports the following results for the current year:

Rental income	$100,000
Depreciation	15,000
Interest expense	9,000
Real estate taxes	4,000
Maintenance expenses	8,000
Administrative expenses	12,000

Keno's AIR is $72,000 ($100,000 − $15,000 − $9,000 − $4,000). The maintenance and administrative expenses are deductible in determining taxable income and, consequently, UPHCI, but do not reduce the AIR amount. ◀

ADDITIONAL COMMENT

Income not included in AOGI cannot be PHCI. In calculating the 60% passive income test, PHCI is the numerator and AOGI is the denominator. Because the passive income test is purely objective, both the numerator and denominator can be manipulated. When the ratio is close to 60%, one planning opportunity is to accelerate the recognition of income that is AOGI but not PHCI.

Personal Holding Company Income Defined. **Personal holding company income** includes dividends, interest, annuities, adjusted income from rents, royalties, produced film rents, income from personal service contracts involving a 25% or more shareholder, rental income from corporate property used by a 25% or more shareholder, and distributions from estates or trusts.

PHCI is determined according to the following general rules:

- *Dividends:* Includes only distributions out of E&P. Any amounts that are tax exempt (e.g., return of capital distributions) or eligible for capital gain treatment (e.g., liquidating distributions) are excluded from PHCI.[32]
- *Interest income:* Includes interest included in gross income. Interest excluded from gross income also is excluded from PHCI.[33]

[30] Sec. 543(b)(2).
[31] Sec. 543(b)(3).
[32] Reg. Sec. 1.543-1(b)(1).
[33] Reg. Sec. 1.543-1(b)(2).

- *Annuity proceeds:* Includes only annuity amounts included in gross income. Annuity amounts excluded from gross income (for example, as a return of capital) also are excluded from PHCI.[34]
- *Royalty income:* Includes amounts received for the use of intangible property (e.g., patents, copyrights, and trademarks). Special rules apply to copyright royalties, mineral, oil, and gas royalties, active business computer software royalties, and produced film rents. Each of these four types of income constitutes a separate PHCI category that may be excluded under one of the exceptions discussed below and set forth in Table C:5-2.[35]
- *Distributions from an estate or trust:* Included in PHCI.[36]

In the calculation of PHCI, special rules apply that could result in the exclusion of rents; mineral, oil, and gas royalties; copyright royalties; produced film rents; rental income from the use of property by a 25% or more shareholder; and active business computer software royalties from PHCI. These rules, summarized in Table C:5-2, reduce the likelihood that a corporation will be deemed a PHC. The two most frequently encountered exclusions, for rental income and personal service contract income, are explained in the next two sections.

ADDITIONAL COMMENT

Without the exception for royalties on computer software, many closely held computer software companies would qualify as PHCs.

SELF-STUDY QUESTION

What is the effect of the two-pronged test that allows the exclusion from PHCI of certain AIR?

ANSWER

This two-pronged test makes it difficult to use rents to shelter other passive income. For example, the 50% test would require at least $100 of AIR to shelter $100 of interest income. The 10% test is even more restrictive. To satisfy this test, it would be necessary to generate $900 of OGI (AIR and other items) to shelter the same $100 of interest income.

Exclusion for Rents. Adjusted income from rents (AIR) is included in PHCI unless a special exception applies for corporations earning predominantly rental income. PHCI does not include rents if (1) AIR is at least 50% of AOGI and (2) the dividends-paid deduction equals or exceeds the amount by which nonrental PHCI exceeds 10% of OGI.[37] The special exception permits corporations earning predominantly rental income and very little nonrental PHCI to avoid PHC status. The dividends-paid deduction is available for (1) dividends paid during the tax year, (2) dividends paid within 2½ months of the end of the tax year for which the PHC makes a special throwback election to treat the distribution as

TAX STRATEGY TIP

Taxpayers potentially liable for the PHC tax should carefully monitor the PHC exclusion requirements to avoid having to pay the tax or having to make a deficiency dividend payment.

▼ TABLE C:5-2
Tests to Determine Exclusions from Personal Holding Company Income

	A PHCI Category Is Excluded If:		
PHCI Category	**Income in the Category Is:**	**Other PHCI Is:**	**Business Expenses Are:**
Rents	≥50% of AOGI[a]	≤10% of OGI (unless reduced by distributions)	—
Mineral, oil, and gas royalties	≥50% of AOGI[a]	≤10% of OGI	≥15% of AOGI
Copyright royalties	≥50% of OGI	≤10% of OGI	≥25% of OGI
Produced film rents	≥50% of OGI	—	—
Compensation for use of property by a shareholder owning at least 25% of the outstanding stock	—	≤10% of OGI	—
Active business computer software royalties	≥50% of OGI	≤10% of OGI (unless reduced by distributions)	≥25% of OGI[b]
Personal services contract income	—[c]	—	—

[a] Measured in terms of adjusted income from rents or mineral, oil, and gas royalties, respectively.
[b] The deduction test can apply to either the single tax year in question or the five-year period ending with the tax year in question.
[c] Personal services income is excluded from PHCI if the corporation has the right to designate the person who is to perform the services or if the person performing the services owns less than 25% of the corporation's outstanding stock.

[34] Reg. Sec. 1.543-1(b)(4).
[35] Reg. Sec. 1.543-1(b)(3). Royalties include mineral, oil, and gas royalties, royalties on working interests in oil or gas wells, computer software royalties, copyright royalties, and all other royalties.
[36] Sec. 543(a)(8).
[37] Sec. 543(a)(2). AIR excludes rental income earned from leasing property to a shareholder owning 25% or more of the corporation's stock. Such income is included in PHCI as a separate category.

having been paid on the last day of the preceding tax year, and (3) consent dividends (see page C:5-21). Nonrental PHCI includes all PHCI (determined without regard to the exclusions for copyright royalties and mineral, oil, and gas royalties) *other than* adjusted income from rents and rental income earned from leasing property to a shareholder owning 25% or more of the corporation's stock.

EXAMPLE C:5-15 ▶ Karen owns all of Texas Corporation's single class of stock. Both Karen and Texas use the calendar year as their tax year. Texas reports the following results for the current year:

Rental income	$100,000
Operating profit from sales	40,000
Dividend income	15,000
Interest income on corporate bonds	10,000
Rental expenses:	
Depreciation	15,000
Interest	9,000
Real estate taxes	4,000
Other expenses	20,000

Texas pays no dividends during the current year or during the 2½-month throwback period following year-end. Because one shareholder owns all the Texas stock, Texas satisfies the stock ownership requirement. Texas's AOGI is calculated as follows:

Rental income		$100,000
Operating profit from sales		40,000
Dividends		15,000
Interest income		10,000
Gross income and OGI		$165,000
Minus: Depreciation	$15,000	
Interest expense	9,000	
Real estate taxes	4,000	(28,000)
AOGI		$137,000

The two AIR tests are illustrated as follows:

Test 1: Rental income	$100,000
Minus: Depreciation	(15,000)
Interest expense	(9,000)
Real estate taxes	(4,000)
AIR	$ 72,000
50% of AOGI (0.50 × $137,000 AOGI) [Test passed]	$ 68,500
Test 2: Dividends	$ 15,000
Interest income	10,000
Nonrental income	$ 25,000
Minus: 10% of OGI (0.10 × $165,000)	(16,500)
Minimum amount of distributions	$8,500
Actual dividends paid [Test failed]	$ –0–

AIR exceeds the 50% threshold, so Texas passes Test 1. Because Texas paid no dividends, its dividends-paid deduction is less than the nonrental income ceiling, and Texas fails Test 2. AIR is included in PHCI because Texas passed only one of the two tests. Application of the 60% PHC income test is illustrated below:

AIR	$ 72,000
Dividends	15,000
Interest income	10,000
PHCI	$ 97,000
AOGI	$137,000
Times: AOGI threshold	0.60
AOGI ceiling [Test passed]	$ 82,200

Texas is a PHC because PHCI exceeds 60% of AOGI and because it satisfies the stock ownership requirement.

Texas could have avoided PHC status by paying sufficient cash dividends during the current year or a consent dividend following year-end. The amount of dividends required to avoid PHC status is the excess of nonrental PHCI ($25,000) over 10% of OGI ($16,500), or $8,500. Thus, an $8,500 cash dividend paid during the current year or during the 2½-month throwback period in the next year or an $8,500 consent dividend would have permitted Texas to exclude the $72,000 of AIR from PHCI. PHCI then would have been $25,000 ($15,000 + $10,000), which is less than 60% of AOGI ($82,200). (Throwback dividends and consent dividends are discussed on page C:5-21.) ◄

ADDITIONAL COMMENT

Congress enacted the provision for personal service contracts to prevent entertainers, athletes, and other highly compensated professionals from incorporating their activities and, after paying themselves a below-normal salary, having the rest of the income taxed at the corporate rates. Even if it is apparent that a 25%-shareholder will perform the services, as long as no one other than the corporation has the right to designate who performs the services, the income is not PHCI. Thus, the careful drafting of contracts is important.

Exclusion for Personal Service Contracts. Income earned from contracts under which the corporation is obligated to perform personal services, as well as income earned on the sale of such contracts, is included in PHCI if the following two conditions are met:

- A person other than the corporation has the right to designate (by name or by description) the individual who is to perform the services, or the individual who is to perform the services is designated (by name or by description) in the contract.
- 25% or more of the value of the corporation's outstanding stock is directly or indirectly owned by the person who has performed, is to perform, or may be designated as the person to perform the services.[38]

The 25% or more requirement must be satisfied at some point during the tax year and is determined under the Sec. 544 constructive stock ownership rules. Congress enacted this provision to prevent professionals, entertainers, and sports figures from incorporating their activities, paying themselves a substandard salary, and sheltering at the lower corporate tax rates the difference between their actual earnings and their substandard salary.

EXAMPLE C:5-16 ►

Dr. Kellner owns all the stock in a professional corporation that provides medical services. The professional corporation concludes with Dr. Kellner an exclusive employment contract that specifies the terms of his employment and that provides for the hiring of a qualified substitute when Dr. Kellner is off duty. The corporation provides office space for Dr. Kellner and employs office staff to enable Dr. Kellner to perform medical services. The income earned by Dr. Kellner does not constitute PHCI because (1) the normal patient–physician relationship generally does not involve a contract that designates a doctor who will perform the services, nor will the patient generally be permitted to designate a doctor who will perform the services, and (2) the professional corporation will be able to appoint a qualified substitute when Dr. Kellner is not on duty (for example, when he is on vacation or not on call).[39]

The income earned by the corporation in connection with Dr. Kellner's services would constitute PHCI if the contract with the patient specified that only Dr. Kellner would provide the services or if the services provided by Dr. Kellner were so unique that only he could provide them. Any portion of the corporation's income from the personal service contract attributable to "important and essential" services provided by persons other than Dr. Kellner is not included in PHCI.[40] ◄

CALCULATING THE PHC TAX

The PHC tax is calculated in two basic steps. First, the corporation determines the amount of its undistributed personal holding company income (UPHCI). It then applies the 20% PHC tax rate (for 2013 and later years) to UPHCI. If the corporation owes the PHC tax, it can avoid paying the tax by making a timely consent or deficiency dividend distribution.

Calculating UPHCI. The starting point for calculating UPHCI is the corporation's taxable income. A series of adjustments are made to taxable income to derive UPHCI. The most important of these adjustments are outlined in Figure C:5-2 and discussed in the following paragraphs.

---

[38] Sec. 543(a)(7).

[39] Rev. Rul. 75-67, 1975-1 C.B. 169. See also Rev. Ruls. 75-249, 1975-1 C.B. 171 (relating to a composer), and 75-250, 1975-1 C.B. 172 (relating to an accountant).

[40] Reg. Sec. 1.543-1(b)(8)(ii).

TYPICAL MISCONCEPTION

The PHC tax applies to any corporation deemed to be a personal holding company based on objective criteria. No improper intent is necessary. Thus, the PHC tax truly fits into the category of "a trap for the unwary."

KEY POINT

The PHC tax is in addition to the corporate income tax. Thus, the existence of both taxes reduces any advantage obtained by interposing a corporation between the taxpayer and his or her income-producing assets.

▼ FIGURE C:5-2

Calculating the Personal Holding Company Tax

Regular taxable income
Plus: Positive adjustments
1. Dividends-received deduction
2. NOL deduction
3. Excess charitable contributions carried over from a preceding tax year and deducted in current year in determining regular taxable income
4. Net loss attributable to the operation or maintenance of certain property owned or operated by the corporation

Minus: Negative adjustments
1. Accrued U.S. and foreign income taxes
2. Current year charitable contributions that exceed the 10% corporate limitation
3. NOL (computed without regard to the dividends-received deduction) incurred in the immediately preceding tax year
4. Net capital gain minus the amount of any income taxes attributed to it

Minus: Dividends-paid deduction

Undistributed personal holding company income (UPHCI)
Times: 0.20

Personal holding company tax

Positive Adjustments to Taxable Income. The dividends-received deduction is not allowed for UPHCI. Thus, a PHC adds any dividends-received deduction to its regular taxable income when calculating its UPHCI.[41] Rental expenses that exceed rental income also are added back to taxable income to derive UPHCI.

Because PHCs may deduct only the NOL for the immediately preceding tax year, two NOL compensating adjustments must be made. First, the amount of the NOL deduction claimed in determining taxable income must be added back to taxable income. Second, the entire amount of the corporation's NOL (computed without regard to the dividends-received deduction) for the immediately preceding tax year must be subtracted from taxable income.[42] The U.S. production activities deduction, however, is not added back to taxable income.

KEY POINT

The negative adjustments made to taxable income in deriving UPHCI (e.g., federal income taxes) represent items that do not reduce taxable income but reduce the earnings available for distribution to the shareholders. In contrast, positive adjustments made to taxable income (e.g., the dividends-received deduction) are not allowed in deriving UPHCI because they do not represent a reduction in earnings available for distribution to the shareholders.

TYPICAL MISCONCEPTION

A PHC does not adjust its taxable income for all items that affect taxable income differently than they affect the earnings available for distribution to its shareholders (e.g., no adjustment is required for tax-exempt interest and the U.S. production activities deduction).

Negative Adjustments to Taxable Income. Charitable contributions made by corporations are deductible for regular taxable income purposes up to 10% of taxable income without regard to the charitable contribution deduction, an NOL carryback, a capital loss carryback, the dividends-received deduction, and the U.S. production activities deduction. Charitable contributions made by individuals are deductible up to 20%, 30%, or 50% of adjusted gross income, depending on the type of contribution and type of donee. For purposes of a corporation's PHC tax, the deduction limitation is expanded from 10% to 20%, 30%, or 50% of taxable income (without regard to the same five items as for the 10% limitation), depending on the type of contribution and type of donee. Thus, a PHC has two adjustments for charitable contributions when calculating its UPHCI: (1) subtracting the amount of current year charitable contributions exceeding the 10% corporate limitation, but not exceeding the 20%, 30%, or 50% limitation, and (2) adding back charitable contribution carryovers deducted in the current year for regular tax purposes, but in an earlier year for PHC tax purposes.[43]

Income taxes (i.e., federal income taxes, the AMT, foreign income taxes, and U.S. possessions' income taxes) accrued by the corporation reduce UPHCI.[44]

---

[41] Sec. 545(b)(3).

[42] Sec. 545(b)(4) and Rev. Rul. 79-59, 1979-1 C.B. 209.

[43] Sec. 545(b)(2).

[44] Sec. 545(b)(1).

A PHC is allowed to deduct for UPHCI its net capital gain (i.e., net long-term capital gain over net short-term capital loss) minus income taxes attributable to the net capital gain.[45] The portion of federal income taxes attributable to the net capital gain equals the tax imposed on the corporation's taxable income minus the tax imposed on the corporation's taxable income excluding the net capital gain. The tax offset eliminates the possibility of a double benefit for federal income taxes, which are deductible in determining UPHCI.

The capital gains adjustment precludes a corporation from being classified as a PHC because of a large capital gain. Even where the corporation is classified as a PHC, the capital gains adjustment allows it to avoid the PHC tax on its long-term (but not short-term) capital gains.

ADDITIONAL COMMENT

The intent behind the PHC rules is not to collect taxes from a corporation. Instead, the rules are meant to compel the distribution of income by a closely held corporation so that such income will be taxed at the shareholders' individual tax rates. This purpose is evidenced by the flexibility of the dividends-paid deduction.

AVOIDING THE PHC DESIGNATION AND TAX LIABILITY BY MAKING DIVIDEND DISTRIBUTIONS

The PHC can claim a **dividends-paid deduction** for distributions made during the current year if they are made out of the corporation's current or accumulated E&P.[46] A dividends-paid deduction is not available for **preferential dividends**. A dividend is preferential when (1) the amount distributed to a shareholder exceeds his or her ratable share of the distribution as determined by the number of shares of stock owned or (2) the amount received by a class of stock is greater or less than its rightful amount.[47] In either case, the entire distribution (and not just any excess distributions) is considered to be a preferential dividend.

TYPICAL MISCONCEPTION

Do not confuse the dividends-paid deduction with the dividends-received deduction that is allowed for regular taxable income.

Throwback dividends are distributions made in the first 2½ months after the close of the tax year. A dividend paid in the first 2½ months of the next tax year is treated as a throwback distribution in the preceding tax year only if the PHC makes the appropriate election.[48] Otherwise, the dividends-paid deduction is allowable only in the tax year in which the PHC actually makes the distribution. Throwback dividends paid by a PHC are limited to the lesser of the PHC's UPHCI or 20% of the amount of any dividends (other than consent dividends) paid during the tax year. Thus, a PHC that fails to make any dividend distributions during its tax year is precluded from paying a throwback dividend.

TAX STRATEGY TIP

If the corporation does not have the cash to pay a throwback dividend, it should consider a consent dividend. The consent dividend is not subject to the 20% limitation on throwback dividends and may be elected up to the extended due date for the corporation's tax return.

Consent dividends are hypothetical dividends deemed to have been paid to shareholders on the last day of the corporation's tax year. Consent dividends permit a corporation to reduce its PHC tax liability when it cannot make an actual dividend distribution because of a lack of cash, a restrictive loan covenant, or other financial or legal constraints. Any shareholder who owns stock on the last day of the corporation's tax year can elect to be treated as having received a consent dividend.[49] For PHC tax purposes, the election results in a hypothetical cash dividend on the last day of the PHC's tax year for which the dividends-paid deduction is claimed. The shareholder treats the consent dividend as received on the distribution date and then immediately contributed by the shareholder to the distributing corporation's capital account. The contribution increases the shareholder's stock basis. The shareholder can make the consent dividend election through the due date for the corporation's income tax return (including any permitted extensions).

TAX STRATEGY TIP

A deficiency dividend can be beneficial if a corporation fails to eliminate its UPHCI, either under the erroneous assumption that it was not a PHC or due to a miscalculation of its UPHCI. If certain requirements are satisfied, a deficiency dividend can be retroactively paid and thus be deductible from UPHCI earned in a previous year.

Dividend Carryovers. Dividends paid in the preceding two tax years may be used as a dividend carryover to reduce the amount of the current year's PHC tax liability.[50] Section 564 permits a PHC to deduct the amount by which its dividend distributions eligible for a dividends-paid deduction in each of the two preceding tax years exceed the corporation's UPHCI for such year.

Liquidating Dividends. Section 562 allows a dividends-paid deduction for liquidating distributions made by a PHC within 24 months of adopting a plan of liquidation.[51]

Deficiency Dividends. Under Sec. 547, a corporation liable for the PHC tax can avoid paying the tax by electing to pay a deficiency dividend. The deficiency dividend provisions

[45] Sec. 545(b)(5).
[46] Secs. 561(a) and 562(a).
[47] Sec. 562(c).
[48] Sec. 563(b).
[49] Sec. 565.
[50] Sec. 561(a)(3).
[51] Sec. 562(b).

substitute a tax on the dividend at the shareholder level for the PHC tax at the corporate level. The distributing corporation's shareholders must include the deficiency dividend in their gross income in the tax year in which it is received, not the tax year for which the PHC claims a dividends-paid deduction. Payment of a deficiency dividend does not relieve the PHC from liability for interest and penalties relating to the PHC tax.

To claim a dividends-paid deduction for a deficiency dividend, a PHC must meet the following requirements:

- Obtain a determination (e.g., judicial decision or IRS agreement) that establishes the amount of the PHC tax liability.
- Pay a dividend within 90 days after this determination.
- File a claim for a dividends-paid deduction within 120 days of the determination date.[52]

EXAMPLE C:5-17 ▶ On its current year return, Boston Corporation characterizes a $200,000 distribution received pursuant to a stock redemption as a capital gain. Upon audit, the IRS and Boston agree that the distribution should be recharacterized as a dividend and that Boston is liable for the PHC tax. Boston can extinguish its PHC tax liability if it pays a deficiency dividend that is large enough to reduce its UPHCI to zero within 90 days after signing the agreement and if Boston files a timely claim. ◀

PHC TAX CALCULATION

The following example illustrates how UPHCI is calculated and how a corporation's regular tax and PHC tax liabilities are determined.

EXAMPLE C:5-18 ▶ In the current year, Marlo Corporation qualifies as a PHC, contributes $60,000 to charities, and pays $50,000 in dividends in August. It reports $226,000 of taxable income as follows:

Operating profit	$100,000
Long-term capital gain	60,000
Short-term capital gain	30,000
Dividends (20%-owned corporation)	200,000
Interest	100,000
Gross income	$490,000
Salaries	(40,000)
General and administrative expenses	(20,000)
Charitable contributions	(43,000)[a]
Dividends-received deduction	(160,000)[b]
U.S. production activities deduction	(1,000)
Taxable income	$226,000

[a] $43,000 limit = 0.10 × ($490,000 − $40,000 − $20,000).
[b] $200,000 × 0.80

Marlo's regular income tax is $71,390 [$22,250 + 0.39 × ($226,000 − $100,000)]. Assuming its AMT is zero, Marlo's PHC tax is calculated as follows:

Taxable income			$226,000
Plus:	Dividends-received deduction		160,000
Minus:	Excess charitable contributions		(17,000)[c]
	Federal income taxes		(71,390)
	Dividends-paid deduction		(50,000)
	Net capital gain (NCG)	$60,000	
	Minus: Federal income taxes on the NCG	(23,400)[d]	
	NCG adjustment		(36,600)
Undistributed personal holding company income (UPHCI)			$211,010
Times:	Tax rate		× 0.20
Personal holding company tax			$ 42,202

[c] $60,000 total contributions − $43,000 deducted.
[d] Because Marlo is in the 39% tax bracket with and without the LTCG, it calculates the applicable federal income tax as 0.39 × $60,000 = $23,400.

ADDITIONAL COMMENT

Net capital gain is defined as the excess of net long-term capital gain over net short-term capital loss.

[52] Secs. 547(c) through (e).

WHAT WOULD YOU DO IN THIS SITUATION?

Shareholders formed Taylor Corporation on July 1 of the previous year, contributing $1 million of capital to the corporation. Because of delays in procuring manufacturing equipment, Taylor did not begin business until January of the current year. During the last six months of the previous year, the corporation earned $50,000 of taxable interest and incurred $20,000 of deductible expenses. A second-year accountant in a small accounting firm was assigned to prepare the Taylor corporate tax return. All of his previous assignments were for individual tax returns. The senior accountant responsible for the assignment told him that the return "would be simple and that all you need to do is input the interest and expense information into the Form 1120 software." Because of the rush to finish and deliver the return to the client by March 15, no one in the office noticed during the review process that Taylor might be a personal holding company (PHC) in the previous year. The corporation filed its return on March 15 without paying any PHC tax. Another Taylor corporate issue arose in August of the current year and was assigned to you. When you considered the issue, you asked yourself, "Does Taylor have a PHC tax problem?" If so, what can Taylor and/or you do to resolve the problem?

Marlo's total federal tax liability is $113,592 ($71,390 + $42,202). Marlo can avoid the $42,202 PHC tax by timely paying a deficiency dividend of $211,010, which equals the amount of UPHCI in the current year. ◀

Topic Review C:5-3 presents an overview of the personal holding company tax.

ACCUMULATED EARNINGS TAX

OBJECTIVE 3

Establish whether a corporation is subject to the accumulated earnings tax and, if so, calculate the tax

Corporations not subject to the personal holding company tax may be subject to the accumulated earnings tax. The **accumulated earnings tax** attempts "to compel the company to distribute any profits not needed for the conduct of its business so that, when so distributed, individual stockholders will become liable" for taxes on the dividends received.[53] Unlike its name, the tax is not levied on the corporation's total accumulated earnings balance but only on its current year addition to the balance. In other words, the tax is levied on current earnings that are not needed for a reasonable business purpose, such as excessive earnings invested by a corporation in speculative securities. Note, however, that the 23.8% (20% + 3.8% net investment tax rate) maximum tax rate on qualified dividends for 2013 and later years reduces somewhat the negative effect of double taxation, and the 0% and 15% tax rates applicable to qualified dividends of lower-bracket taxpayers eliminate or reduce the negative effect even further.

ADDITIONAL COMMENT

The accumulated earnings tax is a penalty tax imposed on corporations that accumulate unreasonable amounts of earnings for the purpose of avoiding shareholder-level taxes. When corporate tax rates are lower than individual rates, tax incentives exist for accumulating earnings inside a corporation. These opportunities should lead to the IRS imposing the accumulated earnings tax.

CORPORATIONS SUBJECT TO THE PENALTY TAX

Section 532(a) states that the accumulated earnings tax applies "to every corporation . . . formed or availed of for the purpose of avoiding the income tax with respect to its shareholders . . . by permitting earnings and profits to accumulate instead of being divided or distributed." Certain corporate forms are excluded from the accumulated earnings tax, including the following:

- Personal holding companies
- Corporations exempt from tax under Secs. 501 through 530
- S corporations[54]

[53] *Helvering v. Chicago Stock Yards Co.*, 30 AFTR 1091, 43-1 USTC ¶9379 (USSC, 1943).

[54] Secs. 532(b) and 1363(a).

TOPIC REVIEW C:5-3

Personal Holding Company (PHC) Tax

1. The PHC tax applies only to corporations deemed to be PHCs. A PHC has (1) five or fewer individual shareholders owning more than 50% in value of the corporation's stock at any time during the last half of the tax year and (2) PHCI that is at least 60% of its adjusted ordinary gross income for the tax year.
2. Two special exceptions to the PHC test may apply. First, certain types of corporations (e.g., S corporations) are excluded from the tax. Second, certain categories of income (e.g., rents and active business computer software royalties) are excluded if conditions relating to percentage of income, maximum level of other PHC income, and minimum level of business expenses are met. Table C:5-2 on page C:5-17 summarizes the excludable categories of income and related requirements.
3. The PHC tax equals 20% times UPHCI. UPHCI equals taxable income plus certain positive adjustments (e.g., dividends-received deduction) and minus certain negative adjustments (e.g., federal income taxes, excess charitable contributions, and net capital gain reduced by federal income taxes attributable to the gain).
4. UPHCI can be reduced by a deduction for cash and property dividends paid during the tax year, as well as consent and throwback dividends distributed after year-end.
5. A PHC tax liability (but not liability for related interest and penalties) can be extinguished through payment of a deficiency dividend. Deficiency dividend provisions effectively substitute an income tax levy at the shareholder level for the corporate-level PHC tax.

In principle, the accumulated earnings tax applies to both large and small corporations.[55] In practice, however, it applies primarily to closely held corporations where management can implement a corporate dividend policy to reduce the tax liability of the shareholder group.

PROVING A TAX-AVOIDANCE PURPOSE

Section 533(a) provides that the accumulation of E&P by a corporation beyond the reasonable needs of the business indicates a tax-avoidance purpose unless the corporation can prove that it is not accumulating the earnings merely to avoid taxes. In limited circumstances, this burden of proof may be shifted to the IRS under rules set forth in Sec. 534.

The existence of a tax-avoidance purpose may be inferred from all pertinent facts and circumstances. Regulation Sec. 1.533-1(a)(2) lists the following specific circumstances that suggest a tax-avoidance purpose:

- Dealings between the corporation and its shareholders (e.g., loans made by the corporation to its shareholders or funds expended by the corporation for the shareholders' personal benefit).
- Investments of undistributed earnings in assets having no reasonable connection to the corporation's business.
- The extent to which the corporation has distributed its E&P (e.g., a low dividend payout rate, low salaries, and substantial earnings accumulation may indicate a tax-avoidance purpose).

TAX STRATEGY TIP

When the IRS determines that the accumulation of earnings is unreasonable, it presumes that its determination is correct. To rebut this presumption, the taxpayer must show by a preponderance of the evidence that the IRS's determination is improper. Thus, periodic updating of the plans to use corporate earnings should be undertaken to reduce accumulated earnings tax problems.

Holding or investment companies are held to a standard different from that which applies to operating companies. Section 533(b) provides that holding or investment company status is prima facie evidence of a tax-avoidance purpose.[56] A holding company, like an operating company, can rebut this presumption by showing that it was neither formed nor availed of to avoid shareholder income taxes.

A tax-avoidance purpose may be only one of several reasons for the corporation's accumulation of earnings. In *U.S. v. The Donruss Company,* the Supreme Court held that tax avoidance does not have to be the dominant motive for the accumulation of earnings, which could lead to imposition of the accumulated earnings tax. According to the court,

[55] Sec. 532(c). See, however, *Technalysis Corporation v. CIR* [101 T.C. 397 (1993)] where the Tax Court held that the accumulated earnings tax can be imposed on a publicly held corporation regardless of the concentration of ownership or whether the shareholders are actively involved in corporate operations.

[56] Regulation Sec. 1.533-1(c) defines a holding or investment company for this purpose as "a corporation having practically no activities except holding property and collecting income therefrom or investing therein."

for a tax avoidance purpose to exist, the corporation must know about the tax consequences of accumulating earnings.[57] Such knowledge need not be the dominant motive or purpose for the accumulation of the earnings.

EVIDENCE CONCERNING THE REASONABLENESS OF AN EARNINGS ACCUMULATION

The courts have not specified any single factor that indicates an unreasonable level of accumulated earnings. Instead, they have alluded to several factors that suggest a tax-avoidance purpose. The IRS and the courts have cited other factors that indicate reasonable business needs for the legitimate accumulation of earnings and profits.

TYPICAL MISCONCEPTION

The IRC refers to the existence of a tax-avoidance purpose, which would appear to involve a subjective test. However, the existence of the tax-avoidance purpose really hinges on the objective determination of whether a corporation has accumulated earnings beyond the reasonable needs of the business.

Evidence of a Tax-Avoidance Purpose. A corporation that wants to avoid liability for the accumulated earnings tax should act defensively. It can minimize this liability by avoiding or restricting the following transactions:

- Loans to shareholders
- Corporate expenditures for the personal benefit of shareholders
- Loans having no reasonable relation to the conduct of business (e.g., loans to relatives or friends of shareholders)
- Loans to a corporation controlled by the same shareholders that control the lending corporation
- Investments in property or securities unrelated to the activities of the corporation
- Insuring against unrealistic hazards[58]

Loans to shareholders or corporate expenditures for the personal benefit of shareholders are viewed as as substitutes for dividend payments to shareholders. Similarly, corporate loans made to relatives or friends of shareholders are viewed as substitutes for dividend payments to shareholders, who then make personal loans to their friends and relatives. All three measures suggest an unreasonable accumulation of corporate earnings, which should have been distributed as dividends.

Likewise, loans or corporate expenditures made for the benefit of a second corporation controlled by the shareholder (or the shareholder group) who also controls the first corporation may be considered to have a tax-avoidance purpose. Theoretically, the first corporation instead could have paid a dividend to the shareholder who in turn could have paid income taxes on the dividend and then contributed after-tax funds to the second corporation.

Another factor indicative of a tax-avoidance motive, but not mentioned in Treasury Regulations, is operating a corporation as a holding or investment company that pays little or no dividends.

? STOP & THINK

Question: In 2015, an IRS auditor examines Baylor Corporation's 2012 C corporation tax return. What items might the auditor scrutinize to assertain excess accumulated earnings?

Solution: The auditor might look first at the retained earnings accounts in the beginning and year-end balance sheets (Schedule L of Form 1120). Then, the auditor might review Schedule M-2 (Analysis of Unappropriated Retained Earnings per Books) for current year earnings, the amount of earnings distributed as dividends, and the manner in which the corporation used the undistributed earnings. Next, the auditor might examine the beginning and year-end balance sheets for evidence of transactions suggesting a tax-avoidance motive. Such transactions might include loans to shareholders (Schedule L, Line 7), loans to persons other than shareholders (Schedule L, Lines 6 and 14), and portfolio investments

---

57 *U.S. v. The Donruss Company,* 23 AFTR 2d 69-418, 69-1 USTC ¶9167 (USSC, 1969).

58 Reg. Sec. 1.537-2(c).

(Schedule L, Lines 4, 5, 6, and 9). Information about expenditures of corporate funds made for the personal benefit of shareholders might be found in the noncurrent asset section of the balance sheets (e.g., corporate ownership of a boat, airplane, or second home of a major shareholder).

Reasonable Needs of the Business. Section 537 identifies several needs as being among the reasonable needs of the business. Two of these are:

- The reasonably anticipated needs of the business, which are discussed in more detail below.
- The amount needed (or reasonably anticipated to be needed) for stock redemptions qualifying under Sec. 303. This IRC section treats certain redemptions to pay death taxes as a sale of stock rather than a Sec. 301 distribution (see Chapter C:4).[59]

The terms "reasonable" and "reasonably" appear frequently with respect to the accumulated earnings tax. Treasury Regulations specify a "prudent businessman" standard for determining reasonableness.[60] Applying this standard to a specific corporation requires much judgment and attention to its particular facts and circumstances, but the courts generally are reluctant to substitute their judgment for that of corporate management.

The Treasury Regulations and the courts have identified several circumstances for which accumulations of earnings are likely to be for reasonable needs:[61]

- Expansion of business or replacement of plant.
- Acquiring a business enterprise. This activity might involve extending the corporation's current business or expanding into a new business, and it could occur through purchasing the stock or the assets of the enterprise conducting the acquired business. The corporation should be careful to acquire a sufficient interest so it will be considered the corporation's business activity and not a passive investment.
- Debt retirement.
- Working capital build-up, such as for the purchase of inventories. This topic is discussed in more detail below.
- Loans to suppliers or customers.
- Business contingencies. The courts and the IRS have accepted earnings accumulations for business contingencies, such as actual or potential litigation, a likely decline in business activities following the loss of a major customer, insuring against a potential loss, providing for a threatened strike, and funding an employee retirement plan.[62]

Reasonably Anticipated Needs of the Business. Corporations operate in business settings that change over time, making their future business needs uncertain. As discussed, a prudent businessman standard is used to determine reasonableness. Treasury Regulations identify several other factors to be taken into account when determining a corporation's reasonably anticipated business needs.[63]

Need for Accumulation. Some evidence must indicate that the future needs of the business require the accumulation of earnings.

[59] Sec. 537(a)(3) also treats as a reasonable need of the business any excess business holdings redemption needs, meaning the amount needed (or reasonably anticipated to be needed) to redeem stock from a private foundation that meets certain conditions.

[60] Reg. Sec. 1.537-1(a). This standard is "the amount that a prudent businessman would consider appropriate for the present business purposes and for the reasonably anticipated future needs of the business." The Regulation's use of the term "businessman" also includes a businesswoman.

[61] Reg. Sec. 1.537-2(b).

[62] Sec. 537(b)(4) treats the accumulation of reasonable amounts for reasonably anticipated product liability losses as being accumulated for the reasonably anticipated needs of the business.

[63] Reg. Sec. 1.537-1(b).

Specific, Definite, and Feasible Plans. The corporation must have specific, definite, and feasible plans for using earnings accumulated for its reasonably anticipated business needs. The plans should not be uncertain or vague.[64] The plans need not be written, but written documentation helps to establish the plans' existence.

No Specific Time Limitations. The corporation need not use the accumulated earnings immediately nor within a short period after the close of the tax year. However, the plans must provide that the corporation will use the accumulated earnings within a reasonable period of time, which depends on the facts and circumstances relating to the future business needs.

Impact of Subsequent Events. The facts and circumstances at the close of the tax year should be used to determine the corporation's reasonably anticipated business needs. Subsequent events also may be used to determine such facts and circumstances but only for such purposes. For example, events in Year 2 may indicate that, as of the close of Year 1, the corporation did not intend to use the accumulated earnings within a reasonable period of time. In this case, the subsequent events should be taken into account. On the other hand, events in Year 2 may indicate the infeasibility of plans that appeared to be feasible as of the close of Year 1. In this case, the subsequent events should not be taken into account for Year 1.

Working Capital: The *BARDAHL* Formula. Firms need to spend cash to generate sales. For example, some firms need to purchase raw materials or already-manufactured items to sell goods to their customers. In addition, a firm's sales may be on credit, so it does not receive cash immediately but instead has accounts receivable. The operating cycle is the amount of time from the corporation's acquisition of inventory to the collection of cash from its sale. The need for working capital for one operating cycle is a reasonable need of the business.

The *Bardahl* formula is an estimate of the working capital needed for an operating cycle.[65] The formula is comprised of three financial statement ratios:

- Inventory cycle: This ratio equals an inventory amount divided by annual cost of goods sold. It is the average time from the purchase of raw materials or merchandise inventory to the sale of goods to customers, expressed as a fraction of a year. This ratio is similar to the inverse of the inventory turnover ratio used in financial statement analysis.
- Accounts receivable cycle: This ratio equals an accounts receivable amount divided by annual sales. It is the average time from the sale of goods to customers to the collection of cash from those sales. This ratio is similar to the inverse of the receivables turnover ratio used in financial statement analysis.
- Credit cycle: This ratio equals a trade accounts payable amount divided by annual operating expenses and inventory purchases. It is the average time from the occurrence of these expenses and purchases to their payment. The annual operating expenses are reduced by noncash expenses, such as depreciation. The credit cycle reduces the operating cycle because the corporation can incur these expenses and purchases without paying them for the length of the credit cycle.

[64] See, for example, *Myron's Enterprises v. U.S.*, 39 AFTR 2d 77-693, 77-1 USTC ¶9253 (9th Cir., 1977) and *Atlas Tool Co., Inc. v. CIR*, 45 AFTR 2d 80-645, 80-1 USTC ¶9177 (3rd Cir., 1980).

[65] *Bardahl Manufacturing Corp.*, 1965 PH T.C. Memo ¶65,200, 24 TCM 1030 and *Bardahl International Corp.*, 1966 PH T.C. Memo ¶66,182, 25 TCM 935.

These ratios are used to determine the operating cycle, which equals the inventory cycle, plus the accounts receivable cycle, minus the credit cycle. The operation cycle, in turn, is used to estimate the corporation's working capital needs as follows:

$$\text{Operating cycle (as a fraction of a year)} \times \left[\text{Cost of goods sold} + \text{Operating expenses minus noncash expenses} \right] = \text{Estimated working capital needed}$$

Cost of goods sold takes into account both direct and indirect expenses. Operating expenses include federal income taxes, for example, quarterly estimated tax payments.[66]

Working capital typically is defined as the excess of current assets over current liabilities. Any estimated working capital needed in excess of actual working capital at year-end is deemed to be a reasonable need of the business. Any actual working capital at year-end in excess of estimated working capital needed is deemed not to be a reasonable need of the business unless the accumulation otherwise is reasonable (for example, for plant replacement).

EXAMPLE C:5-19 ▶ Austin Corporation's records contain the following information pertaining to the current year:

Average accounts receivable	$ 750,000
Average inventory	675,000
Average trade accounts payable	350,000
Cost of goods sold	2,700,000
Estimated federal income tax payments	100,000
Inventory purchases	3,000,000
Operating expenses (including $75,000 of depreciation)	875,000
Sales (all on account)	6,000,000
Working capital on December 31	825,000

Using the *Bardahl* formula, Austin's operating cycle is calculated as follows:

Inventory cycle:	$675,000 ÷ $2,700,000 = 0.2500
Accounts receivable cycle:	$750,000 ÷ $6,000,000 = 0.1250
Credit cycle:	$350,000 ÷ ($875,000 + $3,000,000 − $75,000) = 0.0921
Operating cycle:	0.2500 + 0.1250 − 0.0921 = 0.2829

Austin's estimated working capital needed is:

0.2829 × ($2,700,000 + $875,000 − $75,000 + $100,000) = $1,018,440

The $1,018,440 is $193,440 more than the $825,000 of actual working capital on December 31. Accordingly, Austin can justify accumulating $193,440 of its current earnings for reasonable needs of the business, plus the amount it can justify for other reasons (e.g., for plant replacement). ◀

The *Bardahl* formula can provide a false sense of mathematical precision. In practice, it often is modified to better fit a corporation's specific facts and circumstances. For instance, in Example C:5-19, the average inventory was used to determine the inventory cycle (and likewise for the accounts receivable and credit cycles). Some courts have used peak amounts instead of average amounts, reasoning that the corporation needs to accumulate earnings for its peak working capital needs and not its average needs.[67] Using

[66] *Doug-Long, Inc.*, 72 T.C. 158 (1979).
[67] *State Office Supply, Inc.*, 1982 PH T.C. Memo ¶82,292, 43 TCM 1481.

peak amounts usually results in a larger amount of estimated working capital needs than does using average amounts. Another modification sometimes applied is the use of estimates for the following year rather than actual amounts for the current year. For example, if a corporation has expanding operations, its working capital needs will tend to increase from the current to the following year. If the *Bardahl* formula is applied using current-year amounts, it may produce an estimate of working capital needs that is too low. As a result of factors such as these, disputes have arisen between the IRS and corporations over what constitutes working capital needs.

TYPICAL MISCONCEPTION

No exact method exists for determining a corporation's working capital needs. The *Bardahl* formula is merely a rule of thumb adopted by several courts. Modifications to the *Bardahl* formula, as well as other factors, may be used by a court as it deems appropriate.

The *Bardahl* formula can be applied to a corporation whose business activities involve services (e.g., engineering), but it is applied differently than for manufacturing or merchandising companies because a service company generally holds little or no inventory. Like nonservice companies, service companies often have accounts receivable, but salaries are an important working capital need for these types of businesses. Their principal asset is their workforce, and they need to retain employees when a below-normal level of business occurs. Some amount may be added to working capital to cover the cost of retaining personnel during such times.[68]

CALCULATING THE ACCUMULATED EARNINGS TAX

The accumulated earnings tax calculation is set forth in Figure C:5-3. As with the PHC tax, a corporation can reduce its tax liability by paying dividends. However, corporations generally do not avail themselves of this tax planning device because they often pay only a nominal dividend or no dividend at all. Also, IRS auditors generally do not raise the accumulated earnings tax issue until one or more years after the corporation has filed its tax return. Unlike the PHC tax liability, the accumulated earnings tax liability cannot be extinguished through the payment of deficiency dividends.

ADDITIONAL COMMENT

Accumulated taxable income should not be confused with current E&P. In fact, the accumulated earnings tax has been assessed in years where no increase in the corporation's E&P had occurred.

Accumulated Taxable Income. The starting point for calculating **accumulated taxable income** is the corporation's regular taxable income. A series of positive and negative adjustments to regular taxable income are made to derive accumulated taxable income.

ADDITIONAL COMMENT

The accumulated earnings tax adjustments derive an amount that more closely corresponds to the corporation's economic income and thus better measures the dividend-paying capability of the corporation than does taxable income.

Positive Adjustments to Regular Taxable Income. A corporation may not claim a dividends-received deduction. Thus, regular taxable income must be increased by the amount of this deduction in a manner similar to that under the PHC tax rules.[69] The U.S. production activities deduction, however, is not added back to regular taxable income to derive accumulated taxable income. Any NOL deduction claimed must be added back to regular taxable income. The IRC allows no special deduction for an NOL incurred in the immediately preceding year, as it does under the PHC tax rules.

---

[68] See, for example, *Simons-Eastern Co. v. U.S.*, 31 AFTR 2d 73-640, 73-1 USTC ¶9279 (D.C. GA, 1972).

[69] Sec. 535(b)(3).

▼ **FIGURE C:5-3**

Calculating the Accumulated Earnings Tax

Regular taxable income
Plus: Positive adjustments
1. Dividends-received deduction
2. NOL deduction
3. Excess charitable contributions carried over from a preceding tax year and deducted in determining current year regular taxable income
4. Excess capital losses carried over from another tax year and deducted when calculating current year regular taxable income

Minus: Negative adjustments
1. Accrued U.S. and foreign income taxes
2. Current year charitable contributions that exceed the 10% corporate limitation
3. Net capital losses (where capital losses for the year exceed capital gains)
4. Net capital gain minus the amount of any associated income taxes

Minus: Dividends-paid deduction
Minus: Accumulated earnings credit

Accumulated taxable income
Times: 0.20

Accumulated earnings tax

TYPICAL MISCONCEPTION

A corporation incurring the accumulated earnings tax does not adjust its taxable income for all items that affect its taxable income differently than they affect the earnings available for distribution to its shareholders (e.g., no adjustment is required for tax-exempt interest and the U.S. production activities deduction).

Negative Adjustments to Taxable Income. Charitable contributions are deductible without regard to any percentage limitation. Thus, two adjustments are required for charitable contributions when calculating accumulated taxable income: (1) subtracting the amount of current year charitable contributions exceeding the 10% limitation, and (2) adding back charitable contribution carryovers deducted in the current year for regular tax purposes but in an earlier tax year for accumulated earnings tax purposes.

U.S. and foreign income taxes accrued by the corporation reduce accumulated taxable income whether the corporation uses the accrual or cash method of accounting. A corporation may deduct the amount of its net capital gain (i.e., net long-term capital gain over net short-term capital loss), minus income taxes attributable to this gain. The capital gains adjustment prevents a corporation with substantial capital gains from paying the accumulated earnings tax on that portion of the gains retained in the business. Net capital losses (the excess of capital losses over capital gains for the year) represent a negative adjustment to regular taxable income.

WHAT WOULD YOU DO IN THIS SITUATION?

Magnum Corporation, your client, has manufactured handguns and rifles for years. Because of competition from foreign manufacturers, demand for U.S. manufactured guns has recently declined. The total historical cost of Magnum's operating assets at the end of its most recent fiscal year is $10 million. Total gross operating revenues are $18 million. Over the years, the company accumulated $2.5 million of earnings that Magnum's CEO Allen Blay invested in securities. The investment portfolio consists primarily of growth stocks, debt instruments, and Internet stocks. Along with his other duties as CEO, Allen manages this portfolio. With the recent surge in the stock market, the value of Magnum's investment securities have increased to more than $12 million. The portfolio took a small "hit" in the Fall of the previous year. The dividend and interest income earned on the portfolio represents only a small portion of Magnum's gross income. During a meeting with you, Allen brings to your attention this investment and its stellar performance. Is Magnum liable for the accumulated earnings tax? What action(s) do you recommend that the corporation take?

TYPICAL MISCONCEPTION

Do not confuse the dividends-paid deduction with the dividends-received deduction allowed for regular taxable income.

Dividends-Paid Deduction. A deduction is allowed for four types of dividends paid:

- Regular dividends
- Throwback dividends
- Consent dividends
- Liquidating distributions

With minor exceptions, the rules for the dividends-paid deduction are the same in the accumulated earnings tax calculation as in the PHC tax calculation. Nonliquidating distributions paid during the tax year are eligible for the dividends-paid deduction only if paid out of the corporation's E&P. A dividends-paid deduction is not available for preferential dividends.[70]

Throwback dividends are distributions made out of E&P in the first 2½ months following the close of the tax year. The accumulated earnings tax rules require that any distribution made in the first 2½ months following the close of the tax year be treated as if paid on the last day of the preceding tax year without regard to the amount of dividends actually paid during the preceding tax year.[71] Because the IRS generally does not raise the accumulated earnings tax issue until after it has audited a corporation's tax return, throwback and consent dividends are of limited use in avoiding the accumulated earnings tax. Liquidating distributions eligible for the dividends-paid deduction include those made in connection with a complete liquidation, a partial liquidation, or a stock redemption.[72]

ADDITIONAL COMMENT

The minimum accumulated earnings credit is $250,000 ($150,000 for certain personal service corporations) reduced by accumulated E&P at the close of the preceding year. In many situations, corporations that have been in existence for some time have accumulated E&P exceeding $250,000. Thus, the minimum credit is of little practical significance for them.

Unlike the PHC tax, a corporation liable for the accumulated earnings tax cannot reduce the tax by electing to pay a deficiency dividend. Thus, if a determination (e.g., judicial decision or IRS agreement) establishes the amount of accumulated earnings tax, the corporation must pay the tax, as well as any related interest and penalties.

Accumulated Earnings Credit. The accumulated earnings credit permits a corporation to accumulate E&P up to either a minimum amount ($250,000 for most C corporations) or the level of its earnings accumulated for the reasonable needs of the business. Unlike other credits, the **accumulated earnings credit** does not offset the accumulated earnings tax liability on a dollar-for-dollar basis. Instead, it is like a deduction because it reduces accumulated taxable income. Different rules for the accumulated earnings credit exist for operating companies, service companies, and holding or investment companies.[73]

TYPICAL MISCONCEPTION

The maximum accumulated earnings credit is the amount of current E&P retained to meet the reasonable needs of the business minus an adjustment for net capital gains. This amount does not include the entire accumulation for business needs but only the accumulation in the current tax year. Thus, to calculate the maximum credit, it is necessary to determine how much of prior accumulations are retained for reasonable business needs.

- Operating companies can claim a credit equal to the greater of (1) $250,000 minus accumulated E&P at the end of the preceding tax year[74] or (2) current E&P retained to meet the reasonable needs of the business.
- The accumulated E&P balance mentioned in the previous bullet point is reduced by the amount of any current year throwback distributions treated as having been made out of the preceding year's E&P.
- Current E&P is reduced by the dividends-paid deduction. Any net capital gains (reduced by federal taxes attributable to the gains) reduce the amount of current E&P retained for business needs.
- Special rules apply to personal service companies operating primary in the fields of health, law, engineering, architecture, accounting, actuarial science, performing arts, and consulting. For these companies, the basic calculation set forth above applies, but the $250,000 minimum credit is reduced to $150,000.
- Holding and investment companies may claim a credit equal to $250,000 minus accumulated E&P at the end of the preceding tax year. An increased credit based on the reasonable needs of the business is not available to a holding or investment company.

EXAMPLE C:5-20 ► Midway Corporation reports accumulated E&P, current E&P, and current E&P retained for business needs as shown in the table below. The corporation paid no dividends during the current year. Midway is a C corporation that is not a personal service or investment company. Its minimum credit is $250,000.

---

[70] Sec. 562(c). See page C:5-21 for a more detailed discussion.

[71] Sec. 563(a). Personal holding companies, on the other hand, may elect throwback treatment for dividends paid in the 2½ month period following the end of the tax year, but a throwback dividend is limited to the lesser of the PHC's UPHCI or 20% of any dividends paid during the year (other than consent dividends).

[72] Sec. 562(b)(1)(B).

[73] Sec. 535(c).

[74] Section 1561(a)(2) limits a controlled group of corporations to a single $250,000 amount for the accumulated earnings credit.

TYPICAL MISCONCEPTION

Although called a *credit*, the accumulated earnings credit actually is a *deduction* in deriving accumulated taxable income.

Tax Items	*Scenario One*	*Scenario Two*
1. Accumulated E&P	$ 75,000	$ 75,000
2. Lifetime minimum credit	250,000	250,000
2a. Current year minimum credit (2a = 2 − 1)	175,000	175,000
3. Current E&P	400,000	400,000
3a. Current E&P retained for business needs	300,000	50,000
3b. Current E&P exceeding business needs (3b = 3 − 3a)	100,000	350,000
4. Accumulated earnings credit (Greater of 2a or 3a)	300,000	175,000

In both scenarios, $175,000 of the minimum credit is available. In Scenario One, because the available $175,000 minimum credit is less than $300,000 of E&P retained for business needs, the accumulated earnings credit is $300,000. In Scenario Two, because the available $175,000 minimum credit is greater than the $50,000 of E&P retained for business needs, the accumulated earnings credit is $175,000. In both scenarios, no minimum credit is available in future years. All future accumulated earnings credits are based on E&P retained for business needs. ◀

COMPREHENSIVE EXAMPLE

The following example illustrates the calculation of accumulated taxable income and the accumulated earnings tax liability.

EXAMPLE C:5-21 ▶ Pasadena is a closely held C corporation that is not a personal holding company. Pasadena has conducted a successful manufacturing business for several years. On January 1 of the current year, Pasadena reports a $750,000 accumulated E&P balance. The following information pertains to current year operations:

Operating profit	$650,000
Long-term capital gain	30,000
Dividends received from a 20%-owned corporation	150,000
Interest	70,000
Gross income	$900,000
Salaries	(100,000)
General and administrative expenses	(200,000)
Charitable contribution deduction	(60,000)[a]
Dividends-received deduction	(120,000)
U.S. production activities deduction	(10,000)
Regular taxable income	$410,000

[a] $60,000 = 0.10 × [$900,000 − ($100,000 + $200,000)].

Federal income taxes accrued by Pasadena are $139,400 ($410,000 × 0.34). Actual charitable contributions are $75,000. On June 30, the corporation pays cash dividends of $20,000. Pasadena's current E&P retained for the reasonable needs of the business (after the dividends-paid deduction) is $160,000.

If the IRS determines that Pasadena has accumulated earnings exceeding the reasonable needs of its business, Pasadena's accumulated earnings tax liability would be calculated as follows:

Regular taxable income		$410,000
Plus: Dividends-received deduction		120,000
Minus: Excess charitable contributions		(15,000)[a]
Federal income taxes		(139,400)
Net capital gain (NCG)	$ 30,000	
Minus: Federal income taxes on the NCG	(10,200)[b]	(19,800)
Dividends-paid deduction		(20,000)
Accumulated earnings credit:		
Increase in current year reasonable needs	$160,000	
Minus: Long-term capital gain (net of taxes)	(19,800)	(140,200)

ADDITIONAL COMMENT

Net capital gain is defined as the excess of net long-term capital gain over net short-term capital loss.

Accumulated taxable income	$195,600
Times: Tax rate	× 0.20
Accumulated earnings tax liability	$ 39,120

[a] $75,000 total contributions − $60,000 limitation = $15,000 excess contributions.
[b] $10,200 = $30,000 × 0.34

Pasadena's accumulated earnings credit is based on its current E&P retained for reasonable business needs (minus its net capital gain, net of taxes) because its $750,000 accumulated E&P exceeds the $250,000 minimum credit.

Assuming the corporation owes no AMT, Pasadena's total federal tax liability for the current year would be $178,520 ($139,400 + $39,120). ◀

Topic Review C:5-4 presents an overview of the accumulated earnings tax.

Tax Planning Considerations

OBJECTIVE 4

Identify tax planning opportunities to minimize the AMT and to avoid the PHC and accumulated earnings taxes

This section examines five areas of tax planning: special accounting method elections for AMT purposes, eliminating the ACE adjustment, multiyear effects of the AMT, avoiding the PHC tax, and avoiding the accumulated earnings tax.

DEPRECIATION ELECTION

Personal property generally is depreciated using the 200% declining balance method for regular tax purposes but using the 150% declining balance method for AMT purposes. For regular tax purposes, a taxpayer can elect to use the same depreciation method used for AMT purposes.[75] Such an election can reduce a taxpayer's AMT compliance burden by eliminating the need to keep an additional set of depreciation records to determine the AMT depreciation adjustment, as well as the AMT adjustment that arises when the taxpayer sells depreciable property. This election usually will reduce a taxpayer's AMT but also increase its regular tax. The reduced AMT and increased regular tax often will exactly offset each other.

TOPIC REVIEW C:5-4

Accumulated Earnings Tax

1. The accumulated earnings tax rules apply to all but certain types of corporations. As a practical matter, the tax is assessed primarily on closely held corporations (other than S corporations and personal holding companies).
2. Certain transactions generally lead IRS auditors to believe that an accumulated earnings tax problem exists. These transactions include loans made by the corporation to its shareholders, the expenditure of corporate funds for the personal benefit of shareholders, and investments in property or securities unrelated to the corporation's principal activities.
3. Earnings accumulated for the reasonable needs of the business are exempt from the accumulated earnings tax. Among such needs are a business acquisition, debt retirement, and the build up of working capital. A $250,000 minimum credit is available to reduce accumulated taxable income. The credit amount declines to $150,000 for certain personal service corporations.
4. The accumulated earnings tax is 20% of accumulated taxable income. Accumulated taxable income is regular taxable income plus certain positive adjustments (e.g., dividends-received deduction) and minus certain negative adjustments (e.g., federal income taxes, excess charitable contributions, and a portion of net capital gains). An accumulated earnings credit equal to the greater of a fixed dollar amount or earnings accumulated during the year for the reasonable needs of the business also is available.
5. Accumulated taxable income can be reduced by cash and property dividends paid during the year as well as consent and throwback dividends paid after year-end. Deficiency dividends, available for PHC tax purposes, are not available for accumulated earnings tax purposes.

[75] Sec. 168(b)(2) and (5).

For any tax year, a taxpayer may make this election with respect to one or more classes of property. The election applies to all property in such class(es) placed in service during the tax year. The taxpayer must make the election by the due date for that year's tax return (including permissible extensions). Depreciation for real property generally is the same for regular tax and AMT purposes, so the election is not relevant for such property.

ELIMINATING THE ACE ADJUSTMENT

C corporations make the ACE adjustment, which substantially increases AMTI for many C corporations. A C corporation can eliminate the ACE adjustment by electing to be taxed as an S corporation, assuming it qualifies to make the election (see Chapter C:11). S corporations are not subject to the AMT but pass through their tax preference and AMT adjustment items to their shareholders. On the other hand, a corporation that qualifies to make an S election also may have average gross receipts that qualify it to be exempt from the AMT. If such a corporation were taxed as a C corporation, it would incur no AMT and would not pass through any preference and adjustment items to its shareholders.

MULTIYEAR EFFECTS OF AMT

A corporation pays any AMT in addition to its regular tax, which increases its current tax liability. However, its AMT also generates the same amount of minimum tax credit, which can reduce its future regular tax liabilities. A corporation's tax planning with respect to the AMT should take into account the multiyear effects on its regular tax and AMT.

STOP & THINK

Question: Flair Corporation is considering investing in municipal bonds. Flair's Chief Financial Officer (CFO) thought that the interest earned on these bonds is tax-exempt, but she was surprised to learn that it could be taxed by the federal government at a rate of up to 20% if earned by a corporation. Can such tax-exempt interest be taxed at a rate of up to 20%?

Solution: If the bond is a private activity bond not issued in 2009 or 2010, the interest income is a tax preference item. Assuming its inclusion in AMTI does not affect the phase out of Flair's AMT exemption amount, each $1 of interest income on a private activity bond increases Flair's AMTI by $1 and its TMT by $0.20. The effect this $0.20 increase has on Flair's total income tax depends on its TMT versus its regular tax.

TMT < regular tax with and without the tax-exempt interest income: The tax-exempt interest income does not increase Flair's total income tax because it has zero AMT.

TMT > regular tax with and without the tax-exempt interest income: Each $1 of private activity bond interest income increases Flair's current year tax by $0.20 because it increases Flair's AMT by $0.20. However, this increased AMT also generates $0.20 of minimum tax credit that Flair can carry forward. Assuming Flair can use the credit in the subsequent year and it discounts cash flows at an 11% rate, the $0.20 of tax Flair saves has a $0.18 ($0.20 ÷ 1.11) present value. Thus, the net increase in the present value of Flair's taxes is $0.02 ($0.20 − $0.18). If Flair cannot use the $0.20 minimum tax credit until after the subsequent year, the net increase in the present value of Flair's taxes will be greater than $0.02 but less than $0.20, depending on the number of years until Flair can use the credit.

TMT < regular tax without tax-exempt interest income but TMT > regular tax with it: Each $1 of private activity bond interest income increases Flair's tax by less than $0.20 because part of the interest income merely increases its TMT up to its regular tax, but Flair's tax does increase because the rest of the interest income generates some AMT. This AMT creates an equal amount of minimum tax credit that Flair can carry forward. Thus, Flair should consider the present value of these future tax savings.

AVOIDING THE PERSONAL HOLDING COMPANY TAX

Five tax planning techniques can be used to avoid the PHC tax.

Changes in the Corporation's Stock Ownership. To circumvent the stock ownership rules, a potential PHC can issue additional stock to unrelated parties. The stock may be either common or preferred. The issuance of nonvoting preferred stock to unrelated parties permits the corporation to distribute stock ownership among a larger number of individuals without diluting the voting power of the current common shareholder group.

Changing the Amount and Type of Income Earned by the Corporation. A corporation can change the amount and type of its income in the following ways:

- Adding "operating" activities to its business to decrease the proportion of passive or investment earnings in its total income.
- Converting taxable interest or dividends earned on an investment portfolio into non-taxable interest or long-term capital gains. Nontaxable interest and long-term capital gains are excluded from PHCI.
- Generating passive income of a type that is excludible from PHCI or in an amount that diminishes the proportion of other items includible in PHCI. For example, a corporation might attempt to increase the proportion of its rental income to more than 50% of AOGI so as to exclude from PHCI adjusted income from rents.

KEY POINT

One of the easiest ways to avoid the PHC penalty tax is a dividend distribution. If a corporation lacks the funds to pay a cash dividend, its shareholders can elect a consent dividend (which is a hypothetical dividend). In addition, throwback and consent dividends can be declared after year-end in after-the-fact tax planning.

Dividend Distributions. Dividend payments reduce the PHC tax base. A corporation can exclude certain categories of income (e.g., adjusted income from rents) from PHCI through the payment of dividends sufficient to reduce the amount of other PHCI to 10% or less of OGI. Some of these dividends (e.g., throwback and consent) can be declared after year-end, thereby allowing last-minute tax planning.

Making an S Corporation Election. As mentioned earlier, an S corporation election eliminates liability for the PHC tax because S corporations are exempt from this tax. The election also eliminates the double taxation of corporate earnings distributed as dividends (see Chapter C:11). Such an election is advantageous where corporate tax rates exceed individual tax rates. The LLC form offers many of the same tax and nontax benefits offered by the S corporation form.

Liquidating the Corporation. A PHC could liquidate and distribute its assets to the shareholders. Liquidating distributions made out of E&P are eligible for the dividends-paid deduction and thus can reduce UPHCI. This alternative, however, may be unattractive where top individual tax rates exceed corporate tax rates.

AVOIDING THE ACCUMULATED EARNINGS TAX

The primary defense against an IRS argument that the corporation has accumulated an unreasonable amount of earnings is that the earnings accumulations are necessary to meet the future needs of the business. Business plans in support of this defense should be documented and revised periodically. The plans should describe completed, but not abandoned, projects in sufficient detail. In the event of an IRS challenge, a tentative timetable for the completion of current projects should be set forth. Such plans might be incorporated into the minutes of one or more board meetings.

Transactions suggesting an unreasonable earnings accumulation (e.g., loans to shareholders or large investment portfolios) should be avoided. The business purpose for major transactions should be thoroughly documented.

Corporations potentially liable for the accumulated earnings tax should consider making an S corporation election. S corporations avoid accumulated earnings tax liability on a prospective basis. By implication, an S corporation election will not eliminate potential exposure to the accumulated earnings tax for tax years prior to the year in which the election becomes effective.

COMPLIANCE AND PROCEDURAL CONSIDERATIONS

OBJECTIVE 5

Comply with AMT, PHC tax, and accumulated earnings tax procedures

ALTERNATIVE MINIMUM TAX

A corporation reports its AMT calculation on Form 4626 (Alternative Minimum Tax—Corporations). A completed Form 4626, based on the facts in the comprehensive example on pages C:5-10 through C:5-12, appears in Appendix B. The instructions for Form 4626 include a worksheet for calculating ACE. A corporation uses Form 8827 (Credit for Prior Year Minimum Tax—Corporations) to calculate the minimum tax credit it claims, as well as the minimum tax credit it carries forward to the subsequent year.

Section 6655(g) provides that a corporation's required quarterly estimated tax payments take into account its regular tax and AMT. A corporation whose estimated tax payments are not large enough incurs an underpayment penalty, which is discussed in Chapter C:3.

ETHICAL POINT

A tax practitioner has a responsibility to advise his or her client early in the year about potential PHC problems and steps that can be taken to avoid the penalty tax. Because the PHC tax is self-assessed, a Schedule PH must be filed with Form 1120 even if the corporation owes no PHC tax.

PERSONAL HOLDING COMPANY TAX

Filing Requirements for Tax Returns. A PHC must file a corporate income tax return (Form 1120). Schedule PH must accompany the return. Schedule PH incorporates the tests for determining whether a corporation is a PHC and includes the UPHCI and PHC tax calculations. Section 6501(f) extends from three to six years the limitations period for the PHC tax if a PHC fails to file Schedule PH, even if the corporation owes no additional tax.

Payment of the Tax, Interest, and Penalties. Corporations ordinarily pay the PHC tax when they file Form 1120 and Schedule PH, or when the IRS or the courts determine that the corporation owes the tax. Unlike the AMT, the PHC tax is not included in the corporation's required estimated tax payments. Corporations that pay the PHC tax after the due date for filing their return (without regard to extensions) generally will also owe interest and penalties on the unpaid PHC tax balance. Interest will accrue from the date the return is originally due (without regard to extensions) until the entire tax is paid.[76]

ETHICAL POINT

Notwithstanding the tax practitioner's responsibility to advise his or her client about potential accumulated earnings tax problems, because the tax is not self-assessed, the CPA or the client are under no duty to notify the IRS of the tax problem.

ACCUMULATED EARNINGS TAX

No schedule or return is required for reporting the accumulated earnings tax. Because of the ad hoc nature of this tax, a corporation generally will not pay it until some time after the IRS has audited its tax return. Sec. 6601(b) requires the charging of interest on the accumulated earnings tax balance from the original due date for the return (without regard to extensions) until the date the IRS receives full tax payment.[77] The IRS also may impose a penalty for negligent underpayment of an accumulated earnings tax.[78]

[76] *Hart Metal Products Corp. v. U.S.*, 38 AFTR 2d 76-6118, 76-2 USTC ¶9781 (Ct. Cls., 1976).

[77] Rev. Rul. 87-54, 1987-1 C.B. 349.

[78] Rev. Rul. 75-330, 1975-2 C.B. 496.

FINANCIAL STATEMENT IMPLICATIONS

OBJECTIVE 6

Describe the financial statement implications of the alternative minimum tax

ALTERNATIVE MINIMUM TAX

When a corporation pays AMT, it also obtains a minimum tax credit that it can carryforward indefinitely. Accounting Standards Codification (ASC) 740 prescribes the following rules for accounting for income taxes in financial statements when a firm pays AMT:

- For a firm's temporary differences and carryforwards, calculate its deferred tax assets and liabilities for regular tax temporary differences using the regular tax rate and the difference between the book basis and regular tax basis of its assets and liabilities.
- Include in a firm's deferred tax assets its minimum tax credit carryforwards, which may be comprised of minimum tax credits arising from AMT in the current year and unused minimum tax credits from prior years. As with other deferred tax assets, reduce the deferred tax asset for the minimum tax credit by a valuation allowance if, based on available evidence, it is more likely than not (i.e., greater than 50%) that all or some of the deferred asset will not be realized.

EXAMPLE C:5-22 ► In the current year, Alpha Corporation's regular tax is $40,000, and its tentative minimum tax is $50,000. Alpha's current year AMT of $10,000 ($50,000 − $40,000) generates a $10,000 minimum tax credit. Alpha assesses a more than 50% probability that it will realize (use) the entire credit in future years. Therefore, it need not establish a valuation allowance. Assuming Alpha has no book-tax differences, the minimum tax credit carryover is its only deferred tax asset or liability item. Accordingly, Alpha makes the following book journal entry:

Federal income tax expense	40,000	
Deferred tax asset	10,000	
Taxes payable		50,000

In the above entry, Alpha's taxes payable includes its $40,000 regular tax plus the $10,000 AMT. Alpha's $40,000 current year federal income tax expense for its financial statements equals its current year regular tax. This result occurs because Alpha pays $10,000 of AMT in the current year but expects to recover all $10,000 in subsequent years by using its minimum tax credit.

In the subsequent year, Alpha's regular tax is $90,000, and its tentative minimum tax is $70,000. Thus, its AMT is zero, and it can realize (use) the entire minimum tax credit because the regular tax exceeds its tentative minimum tax by more than $10,000. Alpha's net tax liability is $80,000 ($90,000 − $10,000). Accordingly, it makes the following book journal entry:

Federal income tax expense	90,000	
Deferred tax asset		10,000
Taxes payable		80,000

◄

See Chapter C:3 for a general discussion of financial implications of federal income taxes.

Problem Materials

DISCUSSION QUESTIONS

C:5-1 Explain Congress' intent for enacting the AMT.

C:5-2 Define the following terms relating to the AMT:
a. Tax preference item
b. AMT adjustment item
c. Adjusted current earnings
d. Alternative minimum taxable income
e. AMT exemption amount
f. Tentative minimum tax
g. Minimum tax credit

C:5-3 Dunn Corporation is not a small corporation exempt from the AMT. Dunn's CPA does not calculate the AMT because he knows that Dunn's taxable income is less than the $40,000 AMT exemption amount allowed to corporations. Is the CPA correct in his belief? Explain.

C:5-4 What special rules (if any) apply to the AMT calculation for the following entities:
a. Corporations, particularly small ones
b. Controlled groups
c. S corporations

C:5-5 Agnew Corporation operates a small manufacturing business. During Year 1 (its first tax year, which is 12 months long), Agnew sells goods for $3.8 million for which the cost of goods sold is $2.8 million. Agnew's owner estimates that future sales and cost of goods sold will grow by 25% each year. Agnew is not related to any other corporations. Is Agnew exempt from the AMT in Year 1? In any of the next five years? Explain.

C:5-6 Menifee Corporation has conducted business for several years, and its annual gross receipts never have been more than $4 million. Jackie, who has owned all of Menifee's stock since she incorporated it, purchases all of Estill Corporation's stock in the current year. Estill's annual gross receipts have been approximately $6 million in recent years. Explain to Jackie how her acquisition of Estill's stock will affect the AMT that Menifee pays.

C:5-7 Determine whether the following statements relating to the AMT for a corporation are true or false. If false, explain why.
a. Tax preference items only increase AMTI.
b. A corporation uses the same NOL carryover amount for regular tax and AMT purposes.
c. A corporation is allowed a tax credit for the excess of its AMT over its regular tax.
d. The general business credit can reduce a corporation's regular tax and also its AMT.
e. The ACE adjustment only increases AMTI.
f. An S corporation is exempt from the AMT, regardless of its gross receipts.

C:5-8 Identify each of the following as a tax preference item (PREF), an AMT adjustment item to calculate preadjustment AMTI (ADJ), an item to adjust from preadjustment AMTI to ACE (ACE), or none of these (NONE):
a. Percentage depletion in excess of a property's adjusted basis at the beginning of the tax year
b. MACRS depreciation deducted on a machine placed in service in the current year
c. Sec. 179 expense deducted on delivery trucks placed in service in the current year
d. Gain or loss realized on the sale of a machine placed in service four years ago
e. Tax-exempt interest earned on State of Michigan private activity bonds
f. Tax-exempt interest earned on State of Michigan general revenue bonds
g. Long-term contract for which the taxpayer uses the completed contract method

C:5-9 What adjustment does a corporation make if ACE is more than preadjustment AMTI? If ACE is less than preadjustment AMTI?

C:5-10 Florida Corporation incurs AMT for the first time in the current year. The main reason for incurring the AMT is a $2 million gain on a current year installment sale that Florida is recognizing over ten years for regular tax purposes. Explain to Florida's president how the installment sale can cause Florida to incur the AMT, how its treatment for ACE is similar to and different from the E&P treatment with which she is familiar, and whether its ACE treatment will partially or completely reverse in future years.

C:5-11 Some tax scholars say tax-exempt interest on state or local bonds that are not private activity bonds can, because of the ACE adjustment, produce three different effective tax rates depending on the corporation's tax situation: (1) a 0% effective tax rate, (2) a 15% effective tax rate, or (3) between a 0% and 15% effective tax rate. Explain what the tax scholars mean.

C:5-12 Indicate whether the following items are includible in regular taxable income, preadjustment AMTI, and/or ACE. Also indicate whether a corporation must make a positive, negative, or zero adjustment when calculating preadjustment AMTI and when calculating ACE.

a. Tax-exempt interest on private activity bonds (not issued in 2009 or 2010)
b. Tax-exempt interest on a state's general revenue bonds (not issued in 2009 or 2010)
c. Proceeds from a life insurance policy (with no cash surrender value) paid on account of a corporate officer's death
d. Gain on a current year sale of property for which a corporation uses the installment method
e. Gain on a previous year sale of property for which a corporation uses the installment method
f. Deduction of organizational expenditures made in the previous year
g. Deduction for a dividend received from a 25%-owned domestic corporation
h. Deduction for a dividend received from a 5%-owned domestic corporation

C:5-13 Discuss the regular tax and AMT depreciation rules applicable to the following types of property acquired in the current year.

a. Section 1250 property—a factory building
b. Section 1245 property—a drill press

C:5-14 In the current year, Burbank Corporation incurs an AMT for the first time. Its AMT is due to an ACE adjustment resulting from Burbank's receiving $4 million of life insurance proceeds upon the death of the corporation's chief executive officer. The policy had no cash surrender value. Explain to Burbank's chief financial officer whether Burbank can reduce its future regular taxes by the AMT paid in the current year.

C:5-15 The personal holding company tax and the accumulated earnings tax reflect efforts to prevent use of the corporate entity to avoid taxation. Explain the congressional intent behind these two tax measures.

C:5-16 Which of the following corporate forms are exempt from the PHC tax? The accumulated earnings tax?

a. Closely held corporations
b. S corporations
c. Professional corporations
d. Tax-exempt organizations
e. Publicly held corporations
f. Corporations filing a consolidated tax return
g. Limited liability companies

C:5-17 Because of its quality investments, Carolina Corporation has always generated 30% to 40% of its gross income from passive sources. In the current year, Carolina sold a block of stock in a company it acquired several years ago. As a result of the sale, the corporation realized a substantial long-term capital gain that will increase this year's investment income from 40% to 70% of gross income. Explain to Carolina's president why she should or should not be worried about the personal holding company tax.

C:5-18 Which of the following income items, when received by a corporation, are included in personal holding company income (PHCI)? Indicate whether any special circumstances would exclude an income item that is generally includible in PHCI.

a. Dividends
b. Interest on a corporate bond
c. Interest on a general revenue bond issued by a state government
d. Rental income from a warehouse leased to a third party
e. Rental income from a warehouse leased to the corporation's sole shareholder
f. Royalty income on a book whose copyright is owned by the corporation
g. Royalty income on a computer software copyright developed by the corporation and leased to a software marketing firm
h. Accounting fees earned by a professional corporation owned by three equal shareholders, which offers public accounting services to various clients
i. Long-term capital gain on the sale of a stock investment

C:5-19 Which of the following dividends are eligible for the dividends-paid deduction in the calculation of the PHC tax? The accumulated earnings tax?

a. Cash dividend paid on common stock during the tax year
b. Annual cash dividend paid on preferred stock where no dividend is paid to the common shareholders
c. Dividend payable in the stock of an unrelated corporation
d. Stock dividend payable on the single class of stock of the distributing corporation
e. Cash dividend paid two months after the close of the tax year

C:5-20 Define the term *consent dividend*. How can a consent dividend be used to avoid the PHC and accumulated earnings taxes? In each case, what requirements must be met by the distributing corporation and/or its shareholders to qualify a consent dividend for the dividends-paid deduction? What are the tax consequences of a consent dividend to the shareholders and the distributing corporation?

C:5-21 Explain the advantages of a deficiency dividend. What requirements must a PHC and its shareholders meet to use a deficiency dividend to reduce or eliminate the PHC tax liability? Can a deficiency dividend eliminate interest and penalties, in addition to the PHC tax liability?

C:5-22 Determine whether the following statements regarding the PHC tax are true or false:

a. In a given tax year, a corporation might not owe the PHC tax even though it is deemed to be a PHC.
b. A sale of a large tract of land held for investment can make a manufacturing corporation a PHC.
c. Federal income taxes (including the alternative minimum tax) accrued by the PHC reduce UPHCI for the tax year.
d. To reduce UPHCI, the corporation's shareholders can elect to be treated as having received consent dividends. They can make this election any time from the first day of the corporation's tax year through the due date for the corporation's tax return (including extensions).
e. The payment of a deficiency dividend permits a PHC to eliminate its PHC tax liability, as well as related interest and penalties.
f. A corporation deemed to be a PHC for a particular tax year also can be liable for the accumulated earnings tax for that year.
g. A PHC can be subject to the alternative minimum tax.

C:5-23 Explain the implication of the following statement: "Like many dogs, the threat (bark) of the PHC tax is much worse than the actual penalties assessed in connection with its (bite)."

C:5-24 Explain the following statement: "Although the accumulated earnings tax can be imposed on both publicly held and closely held corporations, the tax is likely to be imposed primarily on closely held corporations."

C:5-25 The accumulated earnings tax is imposed only when the corporation is "formed or availed of for the purpose of avoiding the income tax." Does tax avoidance have to occur at the corporate or the shareholder level for the accumulated earnings tax to be imposed? Does tax avoidance have to be the sole motive for earnings accumulation before such imposition?

C:5-26 How, in its first year of operation, can a newly formed corporation be subject to the PHC tax but not the AMT and the accumulated earnings tax?

C:5-27 Gamma Corporation has generated substantial cash flows from its manufacturing activities. It has only a moderate need to reinvest its earnings in existing facilities or for expansion. In recent years, the corporation has amassed a large investment portfolio due to management's unwillingness to pay dividends. The corporation is unlikely to be deemed a PHC but is concerned about its exposure to the accumulated earnings tax. Explain to Gamma's president what steps he can take to avoid liability for the accumulated earnings tax in the current year? In future tax years? Do these steps require the payment of a cash dividend?

C:5-28 Explain the *Bardahl* formula. Why have some tax authorities said that this formula implies a greater degree of mathematical precision than is actually the case? Does the *Bardahl* formula apply to service companies?

C:5-29 Different rules for calculating the accumulated earnings credit apply to operating companies, holding and investment companies, and service companies. Explain the differences.

C:5-30 Determine whether the following statements about the accumulated earnings tax are true or false:

a. Before the IRS can impose the accumulated earnings tax, it need only show that tax avoidance was one of the motives for the corporation's unreasonable accumulation of earnings.
b. Long-term capital gains are included in the accumulated earnings tax base.
c. Each corporate member of a controlled group can claim a separate $150,000 or $250,000 accumulated earnings credit.
d. A dividends-paid deduction can be claimed for both cash and property distributions (other than nontaxable stock dividends) made by a corporation. This deduction reduces both regular taxable income and accumulated taxable income.
e. The accumulated earnings tax liability cannot be eliminated by paying a deficiency dividend.
f. Interest and penalties on the accumulated earnings tax deficiency accrue only from the date the IRS or the courts determine that the tax is owed.
g. The accumulated earnings tax is self-reported on Form 1120-AET that is filed along with the corporate tax return.

C:5-31 For each of the following statements, indicate whether the statement is true for the PHC tax only (P), the accumulated earnings tax only (A), both taxes (B), or neither tax (N).

a. The tax is imposed only if the corporation satisfies certain stock ownership and income requirements.
b. The tax applies to both closely held and publicly traded corporations.
c. The tax is ad hoc in nature (i.e., assessed in the course of an audit).
d. Long-term capital gains are a neutral factor in determining the amount of the tax liability.
e. Tax-exempt interest income is excluded from the tax base.
f. A credit that reduces the tax liability on a dollar-for-dollar basis is available.
g. Throwback dividends may be paid without limit.
h. Consent dividends are eligible for a dividends-paid deduction.
i. Throwback and consent dividends are effective in reducing or eliminating the tax liability.
j. The tax can be avoided by paying a deficiency dividend.
k. The tax applies to S corporations.

ISSUE IDENTIFICATION QUESTIONS

C:5-32 Bird Corporation purchases machinery for $3 million and places it in service in June 2014. Installation costs are $75,000. The machine replaces an old machine that Bird purchased several years ago, which Bird sells at a $125,000 financial accounting profit. What issues must you, as Bird's director of taxes, address because of the sale of the old machine and purchase of the new machine?

C:5-33 Parrish is a closely held C corporation. Robert and Kim Parrish own all its stock. The corporation, now in its second month of operation, expects to earn $200,000 of gross income in the current tax year. This income is expected to consist of approximately 40% dividends, 30% corporate bond interest, and 30% net real estate rentals (after interest expense, property taxes, and depreciation). Administrative expenses are estimated to be $40,000. What special problems does Parrish Corporation's earning substantial passive income present to you as its CPA?

C:5-34 McHale is a C corporation owned by eight individuals, three of whom own 51% of the stock and comprise the board of directors. The corporation operates a successful automobile repair parts manufacturing business. It has accumulated $2 million of E&P and expects to accumulate another $300,000 annually. Annual dividends are $30,000. Because Americans retain their vehicles longer than they did 20 years ago, demand for McHale's repair parts has been strong for the past five years. However, little expansion or replacement of the current plant is projected for three to five years. Management has invested $200,000 annually in growth stocks. Its current investment portfolio, which is held primarily as protection against a business downturn, is valued at $1.2 million. Loans to shareholder-employees currently amount to $400,000. As McHale's tax return preparer, what tax issues should you have your client consider?

PROBLEMS

C:5-35 *General Formula for AMT.* In the current year, Whitaker Corporation has taxable income of $700,000 and tax preference items of $100,000. It also has $250,000 of positive AMT adjustment items and $80,000 of negative AMT adjustment items (neither of which includes the ACE adjustment). Whitaker's ACE amount is $1.3 million. Whitaker is not a small corporation exempt from the AMT. Determine the following for Whitaker:

a. AMTI
b. Tentative minimum tax (TMT)
c. AMT
d. Minimum tax credit
e. How much smaller would Whitaker's tax preference and AMT adjustment items have to be for its AMT to be zero?

C:5-36 *General Formula for AMT.* Westwood Corporation has $100,000 of taxable income and $20,000 of tax preference items in the current year. Westwood's positive and negative AMT adjustment items (other than the ACE adjustment) are $38,000 and $45,000, respectively, and its ACE amount is $175,000. Westwood is not a small corporation exempt from the AMT. Determine Westwood's AMT for the current year.

C:5-37 *Small Corporation Exemption from AMT.* Willis Corporation is a calendar year corporation that forms on April 1 of Year 1. Willis Corporation reports the following gross receipts:

Year	*Gross Receipts*
1	$ 3,000,000
2	5,400,000
3	7,400,000
4	8,800,000
5	10,500,000
6	12,400,000

Willis is not a member of a controlled group and is not a successor to another corporation. In which year(s) is Willis exempt from the AMT?

C:5-38 *AMT Depreciation.* On June 1 of Year 1, Water Corporation places into service a machine costing $10,000. The machine is seven-year property under the MACRS rules and has a 12-year class life. Water does not elect Sec. 179 expensing, and assume that bonus depreciation is not available for the property. Based on the half-year convention, calculate each year's depreciation deductions for regular tax and AMT purposes, and determine the amount of Water's AMT depreciation adjustment each year.

C:5-39 *AMT Gain or Loss.* Assume the same facts as in Problem C:5-38 except Water Corporation sells the machine for $9,000 on August 31 of Year 3. Determine the following:

a. Water's gain or loss on the machine's sale for regular tax and AMT purposes.

b. The amount of Water's AMT adjustments for Year 3.

C:5-40 *AMT Depreciation and Gain or Loss.* Wabash Corporation, a calendar year taxpayer, purchases and places into service $400,000 of equipment in Year 1. The equipment is seven-year MACRS property, and the half-year convention applies to it. Wabash sells the equipment for $245,000 in Year 3. Assume that 50% bonus depreciation is available in Year 1. For each of the following two independent cases, determine Wabash's gain or loss on the equipment's sale for regular tax and AMT purposes, and determine the amount of Wabash's AMT adjustments for Years 1, 2, and 3.

a. Wabash elects to expense $120,000 of the equipment's cost under Sec. 179 and does not elect out of bonus depreciation for Year 1.

b. Wabash does not elect to expense any of the equipment's cost under Sec. 179 and elects out of bonus depreciation for Year 1.

C:5-41 *ACE Adjustment.* Towne Corporation has the following amounts of ACE and preadjustment AMTI for Years 1 through 5:

	Year				
	1	*2*	*3*	*4*	*5*
ACE	$ 700	$ 700	$ 700	$700	$(700)
Preadjustment AMTI	(100)	1,300	1,000	–0–	(200)

Towne's net ACE adjustments prior to Year 1 are zero. Calculate Towne's ACE adjustment and AMTI for each year.

C:5-42 *Municipal Bond Interest and AMT.* Maple Corporation reports $500,000 of regular taxable income for the current year. Maple also reports the following amounts of interest income earned during the current year (reflected in regular taxable income, if applicable):

Franklin County bonds	$5,000
Omega Corporation bonds	4,400
Springfield School District bonds	3,700
U.S. Treasury bonds	2,100

The Springfield School District bonds are general obligation bonds and are not private activity bonds. The Franklin County bonds were issued to finance redevelopment activities and are private activity bonds. Maple's preference and adjustment items (other than those relating to interest income) are a net positive $100,000, and its items to adjust from preadjustment AMTI to adjusted current earnings (other than those relating to interest income) are a net positive $125,000.

a. Assuming none of the bonds were issued in 2009 or 2010, determine Maple's alternative minimum taxable income for the current year.

b. How would your answer to Part a change if the Franklin County bonds were issued in 2010?

C:5-43 *Regular Tax and AMT Calculations.* Bronze Corporation reports the following data for the current year:

Net profit from recurring operations	$278,000
Other income and expenses not included in the $278,000 amount:	
Dividend from 10%-owned corporation	40,000
Life insurance proceeds received upon death of a Bronze officer	500,000
Tax-exempt interest on private activity bonds	25,000
Tax-exempt interest on general revenue bonds	30,000
Installment sale in current year:	
Total realized gain	400,000
Portion of gain on installment collections in current year	32,000

Depreciation:	
For regular tax purposes	120,000
For AMT purposes	85,000
Sec. 1245 property sold in current year:	
Gain for regular tax purposes	30,000
Basis for regular tax purposes	54,000
Basis for AMT purposes	60,000

Bronze is not a small corporation exempt from the AMT and has no AMT adjustment for the U.S. production activities deduction. The tax-exempt bonds were not issued in 2009 or 2010.

a. What is Bronze's regular taxable income and regular tax?
b. What is Bronze's preadjustment AMTI?
c. What is Bronze's ACE?
d. What is Bronze's AMTI?
e. What is Bronze's AMT?
f. What minimum tax credit does Bronze obtain in the current year? In what year(s) can Bronze use it?
g. Does Bronze have to include the AMT when determining its estimated tax payments and any tax underpayment penalty for the current year?

C:5-44 ***Regular Tax and AMT Calculations.*** Campbell Corporation reports regular taxable income of $210,000 in the current year. Campbell takes into account the following facts when calculating the $210,000 amount.

- Campbell deducts $100,000 of MACRS depreciation for regular tax purposes. Depreciation for AMT purposes is $75,000.
- Campbell recognizes a $12,000 Sec. 1245 gain on the sale of an asset. The asset's regular tax basis at the time of sale is $9,000 less than its AMT basis.
- Campbell's ACE is $290,000.

Campbell is not a small corporation exempt from the AMT and has no AMT adjustment for the U.S. production activities deduction.

a. What is Campbell's AMTI?
b. What is Campbell's AMT?
c. What minimum tax credit does Campbell obtain in the current year? In what year(s) can Campbell use it?
d. Does Campbell have to include the AMT when determining its estimated tax payments and any tax underpayment penalty for the current year?

C:5-45 ***Regular Tax and AMT Calculations.*** Sheldon Corporation reports regular taxable income of $150,000 in the current year. Its regular tax is $41,750. Sheldon takes into account the following facts when calculating the $150,000 amount.

- Sheldon deducts $90,000 of MACRS depreciation for regular tax purposes. Depreciation for AMT purposes is $60,000.
- Sheldon sells equipment for $28,000. The equipment's regular tax basis at the time of sale is $16,000, and its AMT basis is $25,000.
- Sheldon's ACE is $340,000.

Sheldon is not a small corporation exempt from the AMT and has no AMT adjustment for the U.S. production activities deduction.

a. What is Sheldon's AMT?
b. What minimum tax credit does Sheldon obtain in the current year? In what year(s) can Sheldon use it?

C:5-46 ***Regular Tax and AMT Calculations.*** Subach Corporation reports $600,000 of regular taxable income for the current year. Subach also reports the following information (reflected in regular taxable income, if applicable):

Depreciation:	
For regular tax purposes	$440,000
For AMT purposes	410,000
Tax-exempt interest:	
On general revenue bonds	100,000
On private activity bonds	75,000

Current year installment sale:	
Total realized gain	150,000
Portion of gain on current year installment collections	25,000
Prior year installment sale:	
Total realized gain	140,000
Portion of gain on current year installment collections	35,000
Life insurance proceeds received upon the death of a Subach executive	500,000
Organizational expenditures deducted in current year	5,000
Dividend received from 25%-owned corporation	90,000

Subach is not a small corporation exempt from the AMT and has no AMT adjustment for the U.S. production activities deduction. The general revenue bonds and private activity bonds were not issued in 2009 or 2010. What is Subach's total current year federal income tax?

C:5-47 *Regular Tax and AMT Calculations.* Alabama Corporation conducts a copper mining business. During the current year, it reports regular taxable income of $400,000, which includes a $100,000 deduction for percentage depletion. The depletable property's adjusted basis at year-end (before reduction for current year depletion) is $40,000. Cost depletion, had Alabama deducted it, would have been $30,000. Depreciation for other property is $140,000 for regular tax purposes and $90,000 for AMT purposes. Alabama sold an asset for which it included a $12,000 gain in regular taxable income. The asset's adjusted basis is $10,000 higher for AMT purposes than for regular tax purposes. Alabama's adjusted current earnings are $800,000. Alabama is not a small corporation exempt from the AMT and has no AMT adjustment for the U.S. production activities deduction.

a. What is Alabama's AMTI and AMT?
b. What minimum tax credit does Alabama obtain in the current year? In what year(s) can Alabama use it?

C:5-48 *Regular Tax and AMT Calculations.* What is Middle Corporation's regular tax, AMT, total federal income tax, and minimum tax credit generated in each of the following scenarios? Assume that Middle's ACE adjustments in prior years net to a positive $120,000 and that Middle is not a small corporation exempt from the AMT.

	Scenario 1	*Scenario 2*	*Scenario 3*
Regular taxable income	$200,000	$ 50,000	$300,000
AMT preference and adjustment items (other than the ACE adjustment)	100,000	25,000	160,000
Adjusted current earnings	500,000	150,000	400,000

C:5-49 *Regular tax and AMT Calculations.* For the current year, Delta Corporation reports taxable income of $2 million, tax preference items of $100,000, net positive AMT adjustment items (other than the ACE adjustment) of $600,000, and adjusted current earnings of $4 million. Delta is not a small corporation exempt from the AMT and has no AMT adjustment for the U.S. production activities deduction.

a. What is Delta's regular tax?
b. What is Delta's AMT?
c. What is Delta's total tax?
d. What minimum tax credit does Delta obtain? In what year(s) can Delta use it?
e. Suppose Delta qualified as a small corporation exempt from the AMT. How would your answers to Parts a, b, and c change?

C:5-50 *Regular Tax and AMT Calculations.* Jones Corporation has $550,000 of regular taxable income, $120,000 of tax preference items, $240,000 of net positive AMT adjustment items (other than the ACE adjustment), and $970,000 of adjusted current earnings. Jones is not a small corporation exempt from the AMT and has no AMT adjustment for the U.S. production activities deduction.

a. What is Jones' total federal income tax?
b. What minimum tax credit does Jones obtain? In what year(s) can Jones use it?
c. Suppose Jones qualifies as a small corporation that is exempt from the AMT. How would your answers to Parts a and b change?

C:5-51 *Installment Sale and AMT.* Duncan Corporation sells land in the current year (Year 1) for $900,000. The land is Sec. 1231 property having a $360,000 adjusted basis. The purchaser of the land pays Duncan $300,000 in the current year and in each of the next two years. Duncan charges the purchaser a market interest rate on the unpaid balance. Duncan's CEO asks you to prepare a year-by-year analysis of the impact of this land sale on the firm's tax position. By how much will the land sale affect Duncan's regular tax and AMT each year? In your calculation, you can ignore the interest Duncan charges the purchaser. Assume that Duncan is not a small corporation exempt from the AMT, has no AMT adjustment for the U.S. production activities deduction, and has a 34% regular tax rate. Also assume that Duncan has AMT in each year whether or not it takes the land sale into consideration.

C:5-52 ***Minimum Tax Credit.*** Gulf Corporation reports the following amounts for Years 1 through 4:

Type of Tax	*Year 1*	*Year 2*	*Year 3*	*Year 4*
Regular tax	$75,000	$100,000	$120,000	$144,000
Tentative minimum tax	40,000	150,000	105,000	95,000

Gulf is not a small corporation exempt from the AMT. In what year(s) does Gulf obtain a minimum tax credit? In what year(s) can Gulf use the minimum tax credit?

C:5-53 ***General Business Credit.*** In the current year, Edge Corporation's regular tax before credits is $165,000. Its tentative minimum tax is $100,000, and its only available tax credit is a $200,000 general business credit relating to research expenditures.

a. What amount of general business credit may Edge claim for the current year?
b. To what year(s) may Edge carry any unused general business credit from the current year?

C:5-54 ***General Business Credit.*** In the current year, Harden Corporation has $700,000 of regular taxable income, $60,000 of tax preference items, $140,000 of net positive AMT adjustment items (other than the ACE adjustment), and $1 million of adjusted current earnings. Harden's only available tax credit is a $45,000 general business credit relating to research expenditures.

a. What is Harden's AMT for the current year?
b. What amount of general business credit may Harden claim for the current year?
c. To what year(s) may Harden carry any unused general business credit from the current year?

C:5-55 ***Estimated Tax Payments and AMT.*** Ajax Corporation expects to have a $100,000 regular tax and a $70,000 AMT for the current year. Last year, it had a $200,000 regular tax and no AMT. What minimum quarterly estimated tax payment must Ajax make for the current year?

C:5-56 ***Estimated Tax Payments and AMT.*** Dallas Corporation reports the following amounts for Years 1 and 2:

Type of Tax	*Year 1*	*Year 2*
Regular tax	$100,000	$150,000
AMT	–0–	25,000

Each tax year is a 12-month period. Dallas qualifies as a small corporation for purposes of estimated tax payments, but it does not qualify as a small corporation exempt from the AMT. Dallas makes $23,000 of estimated tax payments for each quarter of Year 2.

a. How much tax will Dallas owe when it files its Year 2 tax return?
b. Is Dallas liable for any estimated tax underpayment penalty? If so, how much did Dallas underpay in each quarter?

C:5-57 ***Stock Ownership and Passive Income Requirements.*** Zhao (an individual) and nine other unrelated individuals own all of Duck Corporation's stock. The following information pertains to Duck for the current year:

Adjusted ordinary gross income	$390,000
Ordinary gross income	450,000
Personal holding company income	284,000
Taxable income	195,000

In each of the following independent cases, determine whether Duck qualifies as a personal holding company for the current year.

a. Zhao owns 19% of Duck's stock and each of the nine other individuals owns 9% of Duck's stock.
b. Zhao owns 10% of Duck's stock and each of the nine other individuals owns 10% of Duck's stock.
c. Zhao owns 9.1% of Duck's stock and each of the nine other individuals owns 10.1% of Duck's stock.

C:5-58 ***PHC Definition.*** In which of the following situations will Small Corporation be deemed to be a PHC? Assume that personal holding company income comprises more than 60% of Small's adjusted ordinary gross income.

a. Art owns 100% of Parent Corporation stock, and Parent owns 100% of Small's stock. Parent and Small file separate tax returns.

b. Art owns one-third of Small's stock. The PRS Partnership, of which Phil, Robert, and Sue each have a one-third capital and profits interest, also owns one-third of Small's stock. The remaining shares of Small's stock are owned by 50 individuals unrelated to Art, Phil, Robert, and Sue.

c. Art and his wife, Becky, each own 20% of Small's stock. The remaining shares of Small's stock are owned by the Whitaker Family Trust. Becky and her three sisters each have a one-fourth beneficial interest in the trust.

C:5-59 ***Personal Holding Company Status.*** In each of the following four scenarios, determine whether the corporation is a personal holding company. Assume the corporation's outstanding stock is owned equally by three individuals.

Item	*Scenario 1*	*Scenario 2*	*Scenario 3*	*Scenario 4*
Gross profit from sales	$40,000	$ 80,000	$40,000	$ 60,000
Capital gains	–0–	10,000	5,000	10,000
Taxable interest income	15,000	15,000	10,000	20,000
Dividends received	10,000	10,000	2,000	–0–
Rental income	80,000	150,000	–0–	–0–
Copyright royalties	–0–	5,000	80,000	–0–
Personal service income	–0–	–0–	–0–	100,000
Rent-related expenses	20,000	30,000	–0–	–0–
Copyright-related expenses	–0–	–0–	25,000	–0–
Dividends paid	8,000	10,000	5,000	10,000

C:5-60 ***PHC Tax.*** In the current year, Moore Corporation is deemed to be a PHC and reports the following results:

Taxable income	$200,000
Dividend received from an 18%-owned domestic corporation	50,000
Dividends paid	75,000

a. What is Moore's regular tax liability (ignoring any AMT implications)?

b. What is Moore's PHC tax liability?

c. What measures can Moore take to eliminate its PHC tax liability after year-end and before it files its tax return? After it files its tax return?

C:5-61 ***PHC Tax.*** In the current year, Kennedy Corporation is deemed to be a PHC and reports the following results:

Taxable income	$400,000
Federal income taxes	136,000
Dividends paid to Marlene, Kennedy's sole shareholder	75,000

The following information is available:

- The corporation received $100,000 of dividends from a 25%-owned domestic corporation.
- The corporation received $30,000 of tax-exempt interest income.
- The corporation recognized a $175,000 Sec. 1231 gain on the sale of land.

a. What is Kennedy's PHC tax liability?

b. What measures can Kennedy take to eliminate the PHC tax liability after year-end and before Kennedy files its tax return? After Kennedy files its tax return?

C:5-62 ***PHC Tax.*** Alice and Barry own all the shares of Alpha Corporation. For the current year, the corporation reports the following income and expenses:

Rental income		$ 750,000
Dividend income from less than 20%-owned corporations		200,000
Tax-exempt interest income		40,000
Gross profit on sale of merchandise		50,000
Long-term capital gain on the sale of stocks		200,000
Total income		$1,240,000
Minus: Rent related expenses:		
Interest expense	$140,000	
Depreciation expense	150,000	
Property taxes	175,000	
Other Sec. 162 expenses	165,000	(630,000)
Minus: Administrative expenses		(90,000)
Pre-tax profit		$ 520,000

During the current year, Alpha Corporation paid $50,000 in dividends to its shareholders. Assume Alpha is not eligible for the U.S. production activities deduction.

a. Is Alpha a personal holding company?

b. What is Alpha's regular tax liability?

c. What is Alpha's personal holding company tax liability (if any)?

C:5-63 ***Unreasonable Accumulation of Earnings.*** In each of the following scenarios, indicate why Adobe Corporation's accumulation of earnings might be unreasonable relative to its business needs. Provide one or more arguments the corporation might put forth to support its position that the accumulation is reasonable. Assume that Tess owns all the Adobe stock.

a. Ten years ago, Adobe established a sinking fund to retire its ten-year notes and has added cash to the fund annually. Six months ago, the corporation decided to refinance the notes at maturity at a lower interest rate through the issuance of a new series of bonds sold to an insurance company. The sinking fund balance is invested in stocks and commercial paper. A general plan exists to use the balance to purchase operating assets. No definite plans have been established by year-end.

b. Adobe regularly lends money to Tess at a rate slightly below the rate charged by a commercial bank. Tess has repaid about 20% of these loans. The current balance on the loans is $500,000, which approximates one year's net income for Adobe.

c. Adobe has heavily invested in stocks and bonds. The current market value of its investments is $2 million. The investment portfolio comprises approximately one-half of Adobe's assets.

d. Tess owns three other corporations, which, together with Adobe, form a brother-sister controlled group. Adobe regularly lends funds to Tess's three other corporations. Current loans amount to $500,000. The interest rate charged approximates the commercial rate for similar loans.

C:5-64 ***Bardahl Formula.*** Lion Corporation is concerned about a potential accumulated earnings tax liability. It accumulates E&P for working capital necessary to conduct its manufacturing business. The following data appear in its current year balance sheets.

Account	*Beginning Balance*	*Ending Balance*	*Peak Balance for the Year*
Accounts receivable	$300,000	$400,000	$400,000
Inventory	240,000	300,000	375,000
Accounts payable	150,000	200,000	220,000

Lion reports the following data in its current year income statement:

Sales	$3,200,000
Cost of goods sold	1,500,000
Purchases	1,200,000
Operating expenses (other than cost of goods sold)	1,000,000

Included in operating expenses are depreciation of $150,000 and federal income taxes of $100,000 (assume paid at one time rather than in installments).

a. What is Lion's operating cycle in days? As a decimal?

b. What is Lion's reasonable working capital amount as determined under the *Bardahl* formula?

c. What steps must Lion take to justify accumulating earnings that exceed the amount prescribed under the *Bardahl* formula?

C:5-65 ***Accumulated Earnings Credit.*** In each of the following scenarios, calculate the accumulated earnings credit. Assume the corporation uses a calendar year as its tax year. Also assume that it realizes no current year capital gains.

a. Frank Corporation, a manufacturer of plastic toys, started business last year and reported E&P of $50,000. In the current year, the corporation reports E&P of $150,000 and pays no dividends. Of the $150,000 current E&P, the corporation retains $130,000 to meet its business needs.

b. How would your answer to Part a change if Frank were a service company that provides accounting services?

c. Hall Corporation's accumulated E&P balance at January 1 of the current year is $200,000. During the year, Hall, a glass container manufacturer, reports $100,000 of current E&P, all of which is retained to meet the reasonable needs of the business. Hall pays no dividends.

C:5-66 ***Accumulated Earnings Tax.*** Century Cleaning, Inc. provides cleaning services in Atlanta, Georgia. It is not a member of a controlled or an affiliated group. Century reports the following results for the current year:

Taxable income	$500,000
Federal income taxes (at 34%)	170,000
Dividends paid in August of the current year	75,000

Included in taxable income are the following items that may require special treatment:

Long-term capital gains	$ 30,000
Short-term capital gains	10,000
Dividends from 21%-owned domestic corporation	100,000
Excess charitable contributions from last year that are deductible in the current year	25,000

Century's accumulated E&P balance and its reasonable business needs on January 1 of the current year, were $125,000. The firm can justify the retention of $90,000 of current E&P to meet its reasonable business needs. Assume the corporation is not eligible for the U.S. production activities deduction.

a. What is Century's accumulated taxable income?

b. What is Century's accumulated earnings tax liability?

C:5-67 ***Accumulated Earnings Tax.*** Howard Corporation conducts a manufacturing business and has a compelling need to accumulate earnings. Its January 1, E&P balance is $600,000. It reports the following operating results for the current year:

Taxable income		$700,000
Federal income taxes		238,000
Dividends paid:	July 15 of the current year	50,000
	February 10 of the following year	100,000

Other information relating to Howard's current year operations is as follows:

NOL carryover from last year deducted in the current year	$100,000
Net capital gain	100,000
Dividends received from 10%-owned domestic corporation	75,000

Current year E&P before dividend payments is $400,000. Howard can justify the retention of $120,000 of current E&P to meet the reasonable needs of its business.

a. What is Howard's accumulated taxable income?

b. What is Howard's accumulated earnings tax liability?

C:5-68 *Financial Statement Implications.* Woodland Corporation reports the following financial accounting results and other depreciation information for the current year:

Sales revenue	$ 2,000,000
Plus: Interest income on municipal bonds	300,000
Minus: Depreciation for financial accounting purposes	(92,000)
Other operating expenses	(1,500,000)
Financial accounting net income before federal income taxes	$ 708,000
Depreciation for:	
For regular tax purposes	$ 152,000
For AMT purposes	114,000

Woodland's sales revenue and other operating expenses are the same for financial accounting, regular tax, and AMT purposes. The municipal bonds are not private activity bonds and were not issued in 2009 or 2010. The depreciation pertains to $900,000 of property Woodland acquired and placed in service during the current year. Assume that Woodland is not exempt from the AMT and has zero deferred tax assets and liabilities at the beginning of the current year. Also assume that Woodland does not have to establish a valuation allowance for any of its deferred tax assets and that the enacted tax rate for all future years is 34%.

a. Determine Woodland's regular taxable income, preadjustment AMTI, and ACE.
b. Determine Woodland's regular tax and AMT.
c. Prepare the journal entry to record Woodland's federal income tax expense, and determine Woodland's financial accounting net income.

COMPREHENSIVE PROBLEM

C:5-69 Stock in Random Corporation is owned equally by two individual shareholders. During the current year, Random reports the following results:

Income:	Rentals	$200,000
	Dividend (from a 25%-owned domestic corporation)	30,000
	Taxable interest	15,000
	Short-term capital gains	3,000
	Long-term capital gains	17,000
Expenses related to rental income:		
	Interest	30,000
	Depreciation	32,000
	Property taxes	11,000
	Other Sec. 162 expenses	50,000
General and administrative expenses		10,000
Dividend paid on June 30		15,000

a. What is Random's gross income?
b. What is Random's ordinary gross income?
c. What is Random's adjusted income from rents?
d. What is Random's adjusted ordinary gross income?
e. What is Random's personal holding company income?
f. Is Random a PHC?
g. What is Random's regular taxable income and regular tax liability?
h. What is Random's undistributed PHC income (UPHCI) and PHC tax liability?
i. What measures can Random take before year-end to avoid the PHC tax? Alternatively, what can Random do after year-end but before the corporation files its tax return? If the corporation takes no action before or after filing its return, what remedy does it have after filing?
j. Assume that Random's income and expense items will be similar in future years unless management changes Random's asset mix. What changes can management make to reduce the corporation's PHC exposure in future years?
k. If Random is a PHC, can it also be subject to the accumulated earnings tax?

TAX STRATEGY PROBLEMS

C:5-70 Galadriel and John, married with no children, own all the stock in Marietta Horse Supplies. The couple's C corporation has been in business for ten years. The business has been successful, permitting both owners to pay themselves a reasonable salary from its revenues. Although the salaries cover life's necessities, a review of industry statistics shows that the salary of each owner is about one-half or two-thirds of salaries paid by similar-sized horse supply businesses. The reason for the low salaries is that, for a number of years, the owners felt continual pressure to retain as much of the profits in the business as possible to have sufficient working capital to finance inventories and other business needs. In the past two years, the firm has established lines of credit with two local banks that have alleviated much of this pressure. However, the couple has never had time to review the level of their compensation. Recently, an IRS agent asked the couple about items reported in a previously filed tax return. The agent reviewed all three open years and proposed a settlement for the items in question. While in the office, the IRS agent indicated to you as the couple's CPA that, in her opinion, the company had unreasonably accumulated earnings and that she would be investigating the issue before closing the audit. What advice can you give the couple about their salaries and potential liability for the accumulated earnings tax?

C:5-71 Steve and Andrew write music and lyrics for popular songs. Two years ago, they organized S&A Music Corporation, each brother owning one-half of its stock. Through the end of the current year, they contributed a total of $250,000 in capital to the business. The songs that Steve and Andrew write and promote have been successful. Annually, the firm earns $300,000 of royalties from the copyrights that it owns. With the aid of their aunt who operates a local bookkeeping service, Steve and Andrew organized their business as a C corporation. The brothers decide that, with the success of their music business, perhaps they should move their accounting services to an accounting firm that specializes in providing tax advice for small- and medium-sized businesses. As a staff member of this accounting firm, what advice can you provide the brothers about possible tax problems and potential tax strategies?

TAX FORM/RETURN PREPARATION PROBLEM

C:5-72 King Corporation, an accrual method taxpayer, reports the following results for 2014:

Regular taxable income before regular tax NOL deduction	$800,000
Minus: Regular tax NOL deduction	(200,000)
Regular taxable income	$600,000
Alternative tax NOL deduction	$175,000
AMT depreciation adjustment	148,000
Personal property acquired eight years ago and sold this year:	
Acquisition cost	50,000
Regular tax depreciation	38,845
AMT depreciation	26,845
Increase in LIFO recapture amount	75,000
Tax-exempt interest income:	
Private activity bonds (not issued in 2009 or 2010)	31,000
Other bonds (not issued in 2009 or 2010)	33,000
Dividends received (less than 1% ownership)	120,000
Dividends paid	110,000

King is not a small corporation exempt from the AMT, and it has no AMT adjustment for the U.S. production activities deduction. Regular taxable income includes $35,000 of Sec. 1231 gain from a prior year installment sale on which King's total realized gain was $350,000. Regular taxable income also includes $39,000 of Sec. 1231 gain from a 2014 installment sale on which King's total realized gain is $195,000. King's ACE adjustments for prior years are a net positive $500,000. Prepare Form 4626 for King Corporation to report its 2014 AMT liability (if any).

CASE STUDY PROBLEMS

C:5-73 Eagle Corporation operates a family business established by Edward Eagle, Sr. ten years ago. Edward Eagle, Sr. died, and the Eagle stock passed to his children. The corporation operates rental property and also invests in dividend paying stock and corporate bonds. Eagle's tax advisor made the following profit projection for the current year:

Rentals	$260,000
Dividend income (from a 40%-owned domestic corporation)	90,000
Interest income	20,000
Gross income	$370,000
Rental expenses:	
Depreciation expense	$ 70,000
Interest expense	100,000
Property taxes	10,000
Other Sec. 162 expenses	20,000
General and administrative expenses	15,000
Total expenses	$215,000
Net profit	$155,000

Eagle paid dividends of $40,000 in each of the past three years. Eagle was not a PHC in prior years.

Required: Prepare a memorandum to Edward Eagle, Jr. regarding potential liability for the PHC tax. In your memorandum, discuss the following two questions:

a. Is Eagle likely to be deemed a PHC for the current year?

b. If Eagle is likely to be deemed a PHC for the current year, what measures (if any) should be taken before year-end to eliminate the PHC tax liability? After year-end?

C:5-74 Goss Corporation is a leading manufacturer of hangers for the laundry and dry cleaning industry. The family-owned business has prospered for many years and has generated approximately $100 million of sales and $8 million in after-tax profits. Your accounting firm has performed the audit and tax work for Goss and its executives since the company was created many years ago. The advent of plastic hangers and improved fabrics has kept the company's market share constant, and the corporation plans no major plant expansions or additions. Salaries paid to corporate executives, most of whom are family members, are above the national averages for similar officers. Dividend payments in recent years have not exceeded 10% of the after-tax profits. On December 1 of the current year, you were assigned to oversee the preparation of the current year Goss tax return. In undertaking the assignment, you review Goss tax returns for the past three years. You note from Schedule L (the balance sheet) that, during this period, the corporation made about $1.5 million in loans to three executives and regularly increased the size of its stock portfolio. This increase leads you to believe that Goss may be liable for the accumulated earnings tax in the current year and prior years.

Required:

a. What responsibility do you have to make Goss or the partner in charge of the Goss account aware of the potential accumulated earnings tax liability?

b. Should you advise the IRS of the potential liability for prior years? Should you disclose the potential liability on the current year return?

c. Prepare a list of measures that can be taken to reduce or eliminate Goss' liability for the accumulated earnings tax.

TAX RESEARCH PROBLEMS

C:5-75 Broadway Corporation is a C corporation not exempt from the AMT. During the current year, Broadway contributed significant amounts of cash to various charitable organizations. Should Broadway make any adjustment for its charitable contributions when calculating its alternative minimum taxable income and/or adjusted current earnings?

A partial list of sources is:

- IRC Sec. 170(b)(1) and (2)
- Reg. Sec. 1.55-1(a)

- Reg. Sec. 1.56(g)-1(a)(5)
- Ltr. Rul. 9320003 (February 1, 1993)
- Ltr. Rul. 9321063 (March 2, 1993)

C:5-76 Camp Corporation is owned by Hal and Ruthie, who have owned their stock since the corporation was formed fourteen years ago. The corporation uses the calendar year as its tax year and the accrual method of accounting. In Year 1, Camp borrowed $4 million from a local bank. The loan is secured by a lien on its machinery. Camp loaned 90% of the borrowings to Vickers Corporation at the same annual rate as the rate on the bank loan. Vickers also is owned equally by Hal and Ruthie. Vickers sells to the automobile industry parts that are manufactured by Camp and unrelated companies. Camp's operating results suffered as a result of a slowdown in the automobile industry. The gross margin on its sales declined from $1 million in Year 1 to $200,000 in Year 2. Interest earned by Camp on the loan to Vickers is $432,000 in Year 2. Other passive income earned by Camp is $40,000. Camp's accountant believes that the corporation is not a PHC because the interest income Camp earns can be netted against the $432,000 interest expense paid to the bank for the loan to Vickers. Is he correct in his belief?

A partial list of sources is

- IRC Secs. 542(a) and 543(a)(1)
- Reg. Sec. 1.543-1(b)(2)
- *Bell Realty Trust,* 65 T.C. 766 (1976)
- *Blair Holding Co., Inc.,* 1980 PH T.C. Memo ¶80,079, 39 TCM 1255

C:5-77 William Queen owns all the stock in Able and Baker Corporations. Able, a successful enterprise, has generated excess working capital of $3 million. Baker is still in its developmental stages and has had substantial capital needs. To meet some of these needs, William had Able lend Baker $2 million during Year 1 and Year 2. These loans are secured by Baker notes, but not other Baker property. Able has charged Baker interest at a rate ordinarily charged by a commercial lender. Upon reviewing Able's books in the audit of its Year 1 tax return, an IRS agent indicates that Able is liable for the accumulated earnings tax because of its build up of excess working capital and its loans to Baker. Later this week, you will meet with the agent for a third time. Before this meeting, you must research whether loans to a related corporation to finance its working capital meet a reasonable need of the business. At a meeting to discuss this problem, William asks whether filing a consolidated tax return would eliminate this potential problem and, if so, how must the ownership structure change to accomplish this objective.

A partial list of research sources is

- IRC Secs. 532 and 537
- Reg. Secs. 1.537-2(c) and -3(b) and 1.1502-43
- *Latchis Theatres of Keene, Inc. v. CIR,* 45 AFTR 1836, 54-2 USTC ¶9544 (1st Cir., 1954)
- *Bremerton Sun Publishing Co.,* 44 T.C. 566 (1965)

CHAPTER

6

CORPORATE LIQUIDATING DISTRIBUTIONS

LEARNING OBJECTIVES

After studying this chapter, you should be able to

1. Discuss the issues involved in corporate liquidations
2. Determine the tax consequences to the shareholders and liquidating corporation when the general liquidation rules apply
3. Determine the tax consequences when a parent corporation liquidates a controlled subsidiary
4. Recognize special reporting issues pertaining to shareholders and the liquidating corporation
5. Assess when a liquidating corporation recognizes gains and losses on the retirement of debt
6. Identify tax planning opportunities in corporate liquidations
7. Comply with procedural rules for corporate liquidations

CHAPTER OUTLINE

As part of the corporate life cycle, management may decide to discontinue the operations of a profitable or unprofitable corporation by liquidating it. As a result of this decision, the shareholders may receive liquidating distributions of the corporation's assets. Preceding the formal liquidation of the corporation, management may sell part or all the corporation's assets, which the shareholders may not want to receive in a liquidating distribution. An asset sale also generates cash to pay the corporation's liabilities (including federal income taxes incurred on the liquidation).

Ordinarily, the liquidation is motivated by a combination of tax and business reasons. However, sometimes it is undertaken principally for tax reasons.

- If the corporation liquidates and its shareholders hold the assets in an unincorporated form (e.g., sole proprietorship or partnership), the marginal tax rate may be reduced from the 35% top corporate rate to a lower rate for individuals in tax brackets less than 35%. For example, even low amounts of taxable income are taxed at 35% in a personal service corporation and thus could be taxed at a lower rate in noncorporate form.
- If the assets are producing losses, the shareholders may prefer to hold them in an unincorporated form and deduct the losses on their personal tax returns.
- Corporate earnings are taxed once under the corporate income tax rules and a second time when the corporation distributes the earnings as dividends or when the shareholder sells or exchanges the corporate stock at a gain. Liquidation of the corporation permits the assets to be held in an unincorporated form, thereby avoiding double taxation of subsequent earnings.

Liquidating a corporation carries a tax cost, however. The liquidating corporation is taxed as though it sold its assets, and the shareholders receiving liquidating distributions are taxed as though they sold their stock. A C corporation cannot simply elect to be treated as a pass-through entity under the check-the-box regulations (see Chapter C:2). Thus, the only route to converting a C corporation into a sole proprietorship, partnership, limited liability company, or limited liability partnership is via a taxable corporate liquidation followed by formation of the desired entity. Alternatively, a C corporation could obtain pass-through status without liquidating if it elects S corporation status. Even with this approach, the S corporation faces potential taxation on its built-in gains (see Chapter C:11).

This chapter explains the tax consequences of corporate liquidations to both the liquidating corporation and its shareholders. In so doing, the chapter presents two sets of liquidation rules. The general liquidation rules apply to liquidations of corporations not controlled by a parent corporation. Special rules apply to the liquidation of a controlled subsidiary.

ADDITIONAL COMMENT

The applicable capital gains tax rate for net capital gains and qualified dividends of noncorporate taxpayers is 0% for taxpayers in tax brackets of 15% and below, 15% for taxpayers in the 25% through 35% tax brackets, and 20% for taxpayers in the 39.6% tax bracket. Also, 25% and 28% rates apply for gains on certain types of property. In addition, an incremental 3.8% rate applies to net investment income for taxpayers whose modified AGI exceeds $200,000 ($250,000 for married filing jointly). Net investment income includes, among other things, interest, dividends, annuities, royalties, rents, and net gains from the disposition of property not used in a trade or business, all reduced by deductions allocable to such income or gains. Thus, dividends and capital gains receive comparable tax rate treatment except that capital gain taxation is deferred until sale of the stock or liquidation of the corporation.

OVERVIEW OF CORPORATE LIQUIDATIONS

OBJECTIVE 1

Discuss the issues involved in corporate liquidations

This chapter initially presents an overview of the tax and nontax consequences of a corporate liquidation to both the shareholders and the distributing corporation.

THE SHAREHOLDER

Determining the tax consequences of the liquidation to each of the liquidating corporation's shareholders entails several questions:

- What are the amount, timing, and character of the shareholder's recognized gain or loss?
- What is the shareholder's adjusted basis of each property received?
- When does the holding period begin for each property received by the shareholder?

When a corporation liquidates under the general rules, a shareholder treats the liquidating distribution as an amount received in exchange for his or her stock. The shareholder recognizes a capital gain or loss equal to the excess of any money received plus the FMV of any noncash property received over the adjusted basis of his or her stock. The basis of each property received is stepped-up or stepped-down to the property's FMV on the liquidation date. The holding period for the asset begins the day after the liquidation date.

If a parent corporation liquidates a controlled subsidiary under special rules, however, the parent corporation (shareholder) recognizes no gain or loss. In addition, the bases and holding periods of the subsidiary's assets carry over to the parent.

TAX STRATEGY TIP

Although the shareholders and corporation usually incur no tax cost upon forming a corporation, the tax costs of liquidating a corporation (other than a controlled subsidiary) may be substantial. The tax consequences of liquidating a corporation should be a consideration in the initial decision to use the corporate form. For example, assuming a 34% corporate tax rate and a 15% capital gains rate at the shareholder level, the effective tax cost of a complete liquidation is approximately 43.9% {34% + [(1 − 0.34) × 15%]}. The effective tax increases accordingly for shareholders facing a capital gains tax rate higher than 15%.

THE CORPORATION

Two questions must be answered to determine the tax consequences of the liquidation transaction for the liquidating corporation:

- What are the amount and character of the corporation's recognized gain or loss?
- What happens to the corporation's tax attributes upon liquidation?

When a liquidation occurs under the general rules, the liquidating corporation recognizes gain or loss on the distribution of property to its shareholders. The recognized gain or loss is the same as what the corporation would recognize had it sold the distributed property to its shareholders. Some restrictions (discussed later in the chapter) limit loss recognition in certain potentially abusive situations. Also, tax attributions, such as net operating loss (NOL) carryovers and earnings and profits, disappear when the corporation liquidates under the general rules.

If the liquidating corporation is an 80%-controlled subsidiary of the parent corporation, the liquidating corporation recognizes no gain or loss under special rules. In this case, the subsidiary's tax attributes carry over to the parent corporation.

EXAMPLE C:6-1 ► Randy Jones owns Able Corporation, a C corporation. Randy's basis for his Able stock is \$100,000. The corporation's assets are summarized below. In addition, Able Corporation owes \$60,000 to its creditors.

Assets	*Adjusted Basis*	*Fair Market Value*
Cash	\$ 50,000	\$ 50,000
General stock	75,000	125,000
Machinery	115,000	200,000
Total	\$240,000	\$375,000

See Figure C:6-1 for an illustration of the corporate liquidation. In step 1, Able sells its machinery to an unrelated purchaser for \$200,000 cash. The machinery originally cost \$250,000, and Able has claimed \$135,000 of depreciation on the machinery. Able recognizes a total gain on the machinery sale of \$85,000 (\$200,000 − \$115,000). Because depreciation taken exceeds the amount of gain, the entire gain is Sec.1245 recapture (ordinary income). In step 2, Able uses \$60,000 in cash to pay its creditors. In step 3, Able distributes remaining cash and the General stock, a capital asset, to Randy. Able recognizes a \$50,000 (\$125,000 − \$75,000) capital gain on the General stock distribution. Assuming a 34% marginal tax rate, Able must pay \$45,900 [(\$85,000 + \$50,000) × 0.34] in federal income taxes on the distribution of the General stock and the sale of the machinery (step 4). The tax payment reduces Able's remaining cash to \$144,100 (\$50,000 + \$200,000 sale proceeds − \$60,000 paid to creditors − \$45,900 paid in federal income taxes). Thus, Randy recognizes a \$169,100 (\$144,100 cash + \$125,000 securities − \$100,000 basis for stock) long-term capital gain on the liquidating distribution. The same federal income taxes would have occurred had Able sold both the General stock and machinery to unrelated purchasers, or had Able distributed both the stock and machinery to Randy because each of Able's noncash assets have FMVs exceeding their adjusted bases.[1] ◄

DEFINITION OF A COMPLETE LIQUIDATION

The term *complete liquidation* is not defined in the IRC, but Reg. Sec. 1.332-2(c) indicates that distributions made by a liquidating corporation must either completely cancel or redeem all its stock in accordance with a plan of liquidation or be one of a series of distributions that completely cancels or redeems all its stock in accordance with a plan of liquidation (see page C:6-20 for a discussion of plans of liquidation). When more than one distribution occurs, the corporation must be in a liquidation status when it makes the first

[1] The corporation's recognized gains and losses might be different if one or more of the properties had declined in value. Under some circumstances, the loss might be disallowed if the property were distributed to Randy Jones, where it would be recognized if the property had been sold to an unrelated purchaser.

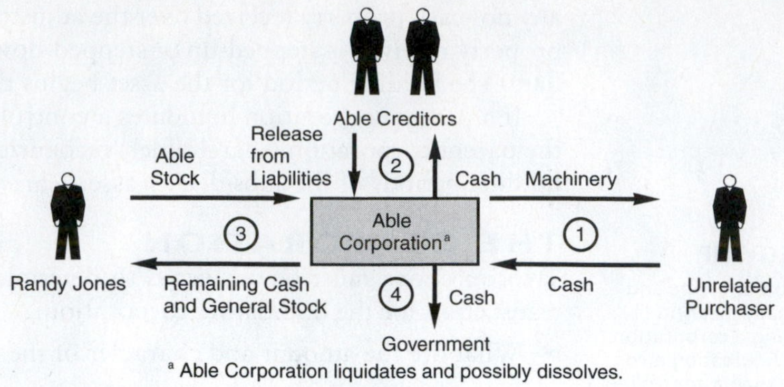

FIGURE C:6-1 ▶ ILLUSTRATION OF CORPORATE LIQUIDATION (EXAMPLE C:6-1)

liquidating distribution under the plan, and such status must continue until the liquidation is completed. A distribution made before the corporation adopts a plan of liquidation is taxed to the shareholders as a dividend distribution or stock redemption (see Chapter C:4).

Liquidation status exists when the corporation ceases to be a going concern and its activities are for the purpose of winding up its affairs, paying its debts, and distributing any remaining property to its shareholders. A liquidation is completed when the liquidating corporation has divested itself of substantially all property. Retention of a nominal amount of assets (e.g., to retain the corporation's name) does not prevent a liquidation from occurring under the tax rules.

The liquidation of a corporation does not mean the corporation has undergone dissolution. **Dissolution** is a legal term that implies the corporation has surrendered the charter it received from the state. A corporation may complete its liquidation before surrendering its charter to the state and undergoing dissolution. Dissolution may never occur if the corporation retains its charter to protect the corporate name from being acquired by another party.

EXAMPLE C:6-2 ▶ Thompson Corporation adopts a plan of liquidation in December of the current year. The corporation distributes all but a nominal amount of assets to its shareholders in January of the next year. The nominal assets retained are the minimum amount needed to preserve the corporation's existence under state law and to prevent others from acquiring its name. Despite the retention of a nominal amount of assets, Thompson Corporation has liquidated for tax purposes even though it has not dissolved. ◀

? STOP & THINK

Question: Peter Jenkins, age 58, is considering forming a new business entity to operate the rental real estate activities that he and his wife have owned personally for a number of years. He has heard about corporations and limited liability companies from reading various real estate journals. Because of their level of personal wealth and the liability protection afforded by the corporate form of doing business, Peter wants to use a corporation to own and operate their real estate. The assets Peter and his wife plan to transfer to the corporation have a $600,000 FMV and a $420,000 adjusted basis. As Peter's CPA, why should you consider the tax cost of liquidating the corporation as part of the overall analysis of the business entity selection decision?

Solution: A transfer of real estate by Peter and his wife to a corporation is nontaxable. A subsequent liquidation of the corporation is taxable, however, because both the corporation and the shareholder may recognize gain or loss. Peter and his wife have $180,000 ($600,000 − $420,000) of appreciation in their real estate. Even if no change in value occurs, liquidation of the real estate corporation at a later date will cause gain to be taxed twice, once at the corporate level and again at the shareholder level. On the other hand, creation and liquidation of a limited liability company are not taxable events to the entity or its owners. Thus, the difference in liquidation treatment at a future date is one of many differences the owners must consider when forming an entity. More information on liquidating a limited liability company can be found in Chapter C:10.

GENERAL LIQUIDATION RULES

OBJECTIVE 2

Determine the tax consequences to the shareholders and liquidating corporation when the general liquidation rules apply

This chapter section presents the general liquidation rules. These rules are considered in two parts: the effects of liquidating on the shareholders and the effects of liquidating on the corporation.

EFFECTS OF LIQUIDATING ON THE SHAREHOLDERS

Three aspects of the general liquidation rules are discussed below: amount and timing of gain or loss recognition, character of the recognized gain or loss, and basis and holding period of property received in the liquidation. Table C:6-1 summarizes the liquidation rules applying to shareholders under both the general liquidation rules and the controlled subsidiary corporation exception.

Amount of Recognized Gain or Loss. Section 331(a) requires that liquidating distributions received by a shareholder be treated as full payment in exchange for his or her stock. The shareholder's recognized gain or loss equals the difference between the amount realized (the FMV of the assets received from the corporation plus any money) and his or her basis in the stock. If a shareholder assumes or acquires liabilities of the liquidating corporation, the amount of these liabilities reduces the shareholder's amount realized.

EXAMPLE C:6-3 ▶ Gamma Corporation liquidates, with Joseph receiving $10,000 in cash plus other property having a $12,000 FMV. Joseph's basis in his Gamma stock is $16,000. Joseph's amount realized is $22,000 ($12,000 + $10,000). Therefore, he recognizes a $6,000 ($22,000 − $16,000) gain on the liquidation. ◀

EXAMPLE C:6-4 ▶ Assume the same facts as in Example C:6-3 except Joseph also assumes a $2,000 mortgage attaching to the other property. The $2,000 liability assumed reduces Joseph's amount realized to $20,000 ($22,000 − $2,000). His recognized gain on the liquidation is $4,000 ($20,000 − $16,000). ◀

▼ **TABLE C:6-1**
Tax Consequences of a Liquidation to the Shareholders

	Amount of Gain or Loss Recognized	Character of Gain or Loss Recognized	Adjusted Basis of Property Received	Holding Period of Property Received
General rule	Shareholders recognize gain or loss (money + FMV of noncash property received − adjusted basis of stock) upon liquidation (Sec. 331).	Long-term or short-term capital gain or loss (Sec. 1222). Limited ordinary loss treatment available (Sec. 1244).	FMV of the property (Sec. 334(a)).	Begins on the day after the liquidation date (Sec. 1223(1)).
Controlled subsidiary corporation rule	Parent corporation recognizes no gain or loss when an 80% controlled subsidiary corporation liquidates into the parent corporation (Sec. 332).[a]	Not applicable.[a]	Carryover basis for property received from subsidiary corporation (Sec. 334(b)).[a]	Includes subsidiary corporation's holding period for the assets (Sec. 1223(2)).[a]

[a] Minority shareholders use the general rule.

Impact of Accounting Method. Shareholders who use the accrual method of accounting recognize gain or loss when all events have occurred that fix the amount of the liquidating distribution and the time the shareholders are entitled to receive the distribution upon surrender of their shares. Shareholders who use the cash method of accounting report the gain or loss when they have actual or constructive receipt of the liquidating distribution(s).[2]

ADDITIONAL COMMENT

Calculating the gain or loss separately on each block may result in (1) both gains and losses existing in the same liquidating distribution and (2) the character of the various gains or losses being different.

When Stock Is Acquired. A shareholder may have acquired his or her stock at different times or for different per-share amounts. In this case, the shareholder must compute the gain or loss separately for each share or block of stock owned.[3]

Character of the Recognized Gain or Loss. Generally, the liquidating corporation's stock is a capital asset in the shareholder's hands. The gain or loss recognized, therefore, is a capital gain or loss for most shareholders. Two exceptions to these rules are indicated below.

- Loss recognized by an individual shareholder on Sec. 1244 stock is an ordinary loss, within limits (see Chapter C:2).
- Loss recognized by a corporate shareholder on the worthlessness of the controlled subsidiary's stock is an ordinary loss under Sec. 165(g)(3) (see Chapter C:2).

Basis and Holding Period of Property Received in the Liquidation. Section 334(a) provides that the shareholder's basis of property received under the general liquidation rules is its FMV on the distribution date. The holding period for the property starts on the day after the distribution date.

EFFECTS OF LIQUIDATING ON THE LIQUIDATING CORPORATION

Two aspects of the general liquidation rules are discussed below: (1) the recognition of gain or loss by the liquidating corporation when it distributes property in redemption of its stock and (2) the special valuation rules used when the liabilities assumed or acquired by the shareholder exceed the property's adjusted basis in the liquidating corporation's hands. Table C:6-2 summarizes rules applying to the liquidating corporation.

Recognition of Gain or Loss When Corporation Distributes Property in Redemption of Stock. Section 336(a) provides that the liquidating corporation must recognize gain or loss when it distributes property in a complete liquidation. The amount and character of the gain or loss are determined as if the corporation sold the property to the shareholder at its FMV.

EXAMPLE C:6-5 ▶ Under a plan of liquidation, West Corporation distributes land to one of its shareholders, Arnie. Arnie's basis in his stock is $70,000. The land, which is used in West's trade or business, has a $40,000 adjusted basis and a $120,000 FMV on the distribution date. West recognizes an $80,000 ($120,000 − $40,000) Sec. 1231 gain when it makes the liquidating distribution. Arnie recognizes a $50,000 ($120,000 − $70,000) capital gain on the distribution, and his basis for the land is its $120,000 FMV. A nonliquidating distribution would have produced similar results for the corporation. However, for the shareholder, the entire FMV would have been a dividend instead of a capital gain assuming sufficient E&P. Thus, both liquidating and nonliquidating distributions produce double taxation although the amount and character of the shareholder's gain or income differ. (Also, see Example C:6-1 for another illustration.) ◀

With limited exceptions, the liquidating corporation can recognize a loss when it distributes property that has declined in value to its shareholders. This rule eliminates the need for a liquidating corporation to sell property that has declined in value to recognize its losses.

EXAMPLE C:6-6 ▶ Assume the same facts as in Example C:6-5 except the land's FMV is instead $10,000. West recognizes a $30,000 ($10,000 − $40,000) Sec. 1231 loss when it distributes the land to Arnie. Arnie recognizes a $60,000 ($10,000 − $70,000) capital loss, and his basis for the land is $10,000. ◀

---

[2] Rev. Rul. 80-177, 1980-2 C.B. 109.

[3] Reg. Sec. 1.331-1(e).

▼ **TABLE C:6-2**

Tax Consequences of a Liquidation to the Liquidating Corporation

	Amount and Character of Gain, Loss, or Income Recognized	Treatment of the Liquidating Corporation's Tax Attributes
General rule	The liquidating corporation recognizes gain or loss when it distributes property as part of a complete liquidation (Sec. 336(a)).	Tax attributes disappear when the liquidation is completed.
Controlled subsidiary corporation rules	1. The liquidating subsidiary corporation recognizes no gain or loss upon a distribution of property to its parent corporation when the Sec. 332 nonrecognition rules apply to the parent corporation (Sec. 337(a)). 2. The liquidating subsidiary corporation recognizes no loss upon a distribution of property to minority shareholders when the Sec. 332 nonrecognition rules apply to the parent corporation (Sec. 336(d)(3)). It does recognize gains, however.	Tax attributes of a subsidiary corporation carry over to the parent corporation when the Sec. 332 rules apply (Sec. 381(a)).
Related party rule	The liquidating subsidiary corporation recognizes no loss upon a distribution of property to a related person unless the corporation distributes such property ratably to all shareholders *and* the liquidating corporation did not acquire the property in a Sec. 351 transaction or as a capital contribution during the five years preceding the distribution (Sec. 336(d)(1)).	
Tax avoidance rule	The liquidating subsidiary corporation recognizes no loss when a sale, exchange, or distribution of property occurs and the liquidating corporation acquired such property in a Sec. 351 transaction or as a capital contribution having as a principal purpose the recognition of loss (Sec. 336(d)(2)).	

TAX STRATEGY TIP

If possible, a corporation should avoid distributing property subject to a mortgage that exceeds the property's FMV. Such distributions cause excessive corporate gain recognition and uncertainty of results at the shareholder level.

Liabilities Assumed or Acquired by the Shareholders. As described earlier, for purposes of determining the amount of gain or loss recognized under Sec. 336, property distributed by the liquidating corporation is treated as having been sold to the shareholder for its FMV on the distribution date. Section 336(b) contains a special restriction on valuing a liquidating property distribution when the shareholders assume or acquire liabilities. According to this rule, the FMV of the distributed property cannot be less than the amount of the liability assumed or acquired. Congress enacted Sec. 336(b) because the corporation realizes an economic gain or benefit equal to the amount of the liability the shareholder assumes or acquires (and not just the lower FMV of the property distributed) as part of the liquidation. Treatment at the shareholder level is not completely clear. Section 336(b) specifically states that this liability rule applies only for determining the corporation's gain or loss. Thus, it does not seem to extend to Sec. 334(a), which requires the shareholder to take a FMV basis in the distributed property. Some commentators have suggested that the strict statutory interpretation of giving the shareholders the actual FMV basis, rather than the greater liability basis, produces an illogical result.[4] Also, given that the liability exceeds the distributed property's FMV, the shareholder's amount realized should be zero, resulting in a capital loss equal to the shareholder's stock basis.

[4] For a detailed discussion, see B. C. Randall and D. N. Stewart, "Corporate Distributions: Handling Liabilities in Excess of the Fair Market Value of Property Remains Unresolved," *The Journal of Corporate Taxation*, Spring 1992, pp. 55–64.

EXAMPLE C:6-7 ▶ Jersey Corporation owns an apartment complex originally costing $3 million and, after depreciation, having a $2.4 million adjusted basis. The property is secured by a $2.7 million mortgage. Pursuant to a plan of liquidation, Jersey distributes the property and the mortgage to Rex, Jersey's sole shareholder, at a time when the property's FMV is $2.2 million. Rex's stock basis is $500,000. Jersey recognizes a $300,000 ($2,700,000 − $2,400,000) gain on distributing the property because its FMV cannot be less than the $2.7 million mortgage. The shareholder recognizes a $500,000 capital loss on the corporate stock and takes either a $2.2 million or $2.7 million basis in the property, depending on which interpretation applies. ◀

Exceptions to the General Gain or Loss Recognition Rule. The IRC provides four exceptions to the general recognition rule of Sec. 336(a). Two of these exceptions apply to liquidations of controlled subsidiary corporations and are covered later. The other two exceptions prevent certain abusive practices (e.g., the manufacturing of losses) from being accomplished and are examined below. Also, Sec 362(e)(2) may reduce a liquidating corporation's loss recognition. Specifically, for property contributed to a controlled corporation, the corporation must reduce the basis of loss property if the total adjusted basis of property contributed by a shareholder exceeds the total FMV of that property (see Chapter C:2 for details). Consequently, upon a later liquidating distribution, the corporation will realize a smaller loss or no loss at all.[5]

ADDITIONAL COMMENT

The disqualified property rule prohibits a shareholder from infusing loss property into the liquidating corporation and generating losses at both the corporate and shareholder levels by liquidating the corporation.

Distributions to Related Persons. Section 336(d)(1)(A) prevents loss recognition in connection with property distributions to a related person if (1) the distribution of loss property is other than pro rata to all shareholders based on their stock ownership or (2) the distributed property is disqualified property. Section 267(b) defines a related person as including, for example, an individual and a corporation whose stock is more than 50% owned (in terms of value) by such individual, as well as two corporations that are members of the same controlled group. Section 336(d)(1)(B) defines disqualified property as (1) any property acquired by the liquidating corporation in a transaction to which Sec. 351 applies, or as a contribution to capital, during the five-year period ending on the distribution date or (2) any property having an adjusted basis that carries over from disqualified property.

EXAMPLE C:6-8 ▶ Lei owns 60% and Betty owns 40% of Mesa Corporation's stock. Pursuant to a plan of liquidation, Mesa distributes Beta stock to Lei that Mesa purchased two years ago. The Beta stock, which is not disqualified property, has a $40,000 FMV and a $100,000 adjusted basis. Betty receives only cash in the liquidation. The non–pro rata distribution of the Beta stock (the loss property), however, prevents Mesa from claiming a $60,000 capital loss when it makes the distribution. If Mesa instead distributes the Beta stock 60% to Lei and 40% to Betty, Mesa deducts the entire capital loss, assuming Mesa has offsetting capital gains. ◀

EXAMPLE C:6-9 ▶ Assume the same facts as in Example C:6-8 except Mesa acquired the Beta stock two years ago as a capital contribution from Lei when the Beta stock basis was $100,000 and its FMV was $105,000. Thus, the stock was not subject to the Sec. 362(e)(2) basis reduction rule when contributed, and Mesa took a $100,000 carryover basis in the stock. The stock's FMV now is $40,000, and the corporation distributes it to Lei upon liquidation of the corporation. The Beta stock in this case is disqualified property. The $60,000 realized loss is disallowed because Lei is a related party under Sec. 267(b). If Mesa instead distributes the Beta stock 60% to Lei and 40% to Betty, Mesa still is prohibited from deducting the portion of the $60,000 capital loss attributable to the stock distributed to the related party even though Mesa distributed it ratably to Lei and Betty. Mesa can deduct only the $24,000 ($60,000 × 0.40) capital loss attributable to the Beta stock distributed to Betty because she is not a related party. Alternatively, a sale of the disqualified property to an unrelated purchaser permits Mesa to recognize the entire $60,000 loss, again assuming offsetting capital gains exist. ◀

EXAMPLE C:6-10 ▶ Assume the same facts as in Example C:6-9 except the Beta stock had an $85,000 FMV when contributed, and Mesa had to reduce its basis in the stock to $85,000 at that time. Upon

[5] For a detailed discussion, see B. C. Randall, B. C. Spilker, and J. M. Werlhof, "The Interaction of New Section 362(e)(2) With the Loss Disallowance Rules in Corporate Liquidations," *Corporate Taxation*, September/October 2005.

liquidation and distribution to Lei, Mesa realizes a $45,000 ($40,000 − $85,000) loss, which is disallowed under the related person, disqualified property rule. If instead Mesa distributes the Beta stock ratably to Lei and Betty, Mesa can deduct $18,000 ($45,000 × 0.40) of the loss attributable to the stock distributed to Betty, again assuming Mesa recognizes offsetting gains on other property. ◀

Sales Having a Tax-Avoidance Purpose. Section 336(d)(2) restricts loss recognition with respect to the sale, exchange, or distribution of property acquired in a Sec. 351 transaction, or as a contribution to capital, where the liquidating corporation acquired the property as part of a plan having the principal purpose of loss recognition by the corporation in connection with its liquidation. This loss limitation prevents a shareholder from transferring loss property into a corporation to reduce or eliminate the gain the liquidating corporation otherwise would have recognized from the distribution of other appreciated property.

TAX STRATEGY TIP

To avoid loss disallowance under Sec. 336(d)(2), a corporation should delay adopting a plan of liquidation until two years after receiving loss property in a Sec. 351 transaction.

TAX STRATEGY TIP

If the corporation made a basis reduction for contributed loss property under Sec. 362(e)(2), it might argue that no tax avoidance purpose existed, thereby making a Sec. 336(d) disallowance inapplicable. See article referenced in footnote 5.

Property acquired by the liquidating corporation in any Sec. 351 transaction or as a contribution to capital within two years of the date on which a plan of complete liquidation is adopted are treated as part of a plan having a tax-avoidance purpose unless exempted by forthcoming regulations. Treasury Regulations, when issued, should not prevent corporations from deducting losses associated with dispositions of assets that are contributed to the corporation and used in a trade or business (or a line of business), or dispositions occurring during the first two years of a corporation's existence.[6]

The basis of the contributed property for loss purposes equals its adjusted basis to the corporation at the time of liquidation reduced (but not below zero) by the excess (if any) of the property's adjusted basis over its FMV immediately after its contribution to the corporation. This adjusted basis already may include a reduction under Sec. 362(e)(2) for contributed loss property. No adjustment occurs to the contributed property's adjusted basis when determining the corporation's recognized gain.

EXAMPLE C:6-11 ▶ Terry contributed a widget maker having a $1,000 adjusted basis and a $100 FMV to Pirate Corporation in exchange for additional stock on January 10 of Year 2. At the same time, Terry contributed a second property having a $2,000 FMV and a $900 adjusted basis. Because the total FMV of Terry's contributed property ($2,100) exceeded the total adjusted basis of that property ($1,900), the corporation did not reduce the loss property's basis under Sec. 362(e)(2) at that time. On April 1 of Year 3, Pirate adopts a plan of liquidation. Between January 10 of Year 2, and April 1 of Year 3, Pirate does not use the widget maker in its trade or business. Liquidation occurs on July 1 of Year 3, and Pirate distributes the widget maker and a second property that has a $2,500 FMV and a $900 adjusted basis. Because Terry contributed the widget maker to Pirate after April 1 of Year 1 (two years before Pirate adopted its plan of liquidation), and the widget maker is not used in Pirate's trade or business, its acquisition and distribution are presumed to be motivated by a desire to recognize the $900 loss. Unless Pirate can establish otherwise (e.g., by arguing that Sec. 362(e)(2) precludes a tax avoidance purpose), Sec. 336(d)(2) will apply to the distribution of the widget maker. Pirate's basis for determining its loss will be $100 [$1,000 − ($1,000 − $100)]. Thus, Pirate cannot claim a loss upon distributing the widget maker. This rule prevents Pirate from offsetting the $1,600 ($2,500 − $900) gain recognized on distributing the second property by the $900 loss realized on distributing the widget maker. ◀

The basis adjustment also affects sales, exchanges, or distributions of property made before the adoption of the plan of liquidation or in connection with the liquidation. Thus, losses claimed in a tax return filed before the adoption of the plan of liquidation may be restricted by Sec. 336(d)(2). The liquidating corporation may recapture these losses in the tax return for the tax year in which the plan of liquidation is adopted, or it can file an amended tax return for the tax year in which it originally claimed the loss.

EXAMPLE C:6-12 ▶ Assume the same facts as in Example C:6-11 except Pirate sells the widget maker for $200 on July 10 of Year 2. Pirate reports an $800 loss ($200 − $1,000) on its Year 2 tax return. The adoption of the plan of liquidation on April 1 of Year 3, causes the loss on the sale of the widget maker to be

[6] H. Rept. No. 99-841, 99th Cong., 2d Sess., p. II-201 (1986). The Conference Committee Report for the 1986 Tax Act indicates that property transactions occurring more than two years in advance of the adoption of the plan of liquidation will be disregarded unless no clear and substantial relationship exists between the contributed property and the conduct of the corporation's current or future business enterprises.

covered by the Sec. 336(d)(2) rules, again assuming a tax avoidance purpose exists. Pirate can file an amended Year 2 tax return showing the $800 loss being disallowed, or it can file its Year 3 tax return reporting $800 of income under the loss recapture rules.[7] ◀

Topic Review C:6-1 summarizes the general corporate liquidation rules.

TOPIC REVIEW C:6-1

Tax Consequences of a Corporate Liquidation

General Corporate Liquidation Rules

1. The shareholder's recognized gain or loss equals the amount of cash plus the FMV of the other property received minus the adjusted basis of stock surrendered. Corporate liabilities assumed or acquired by the shareholder reduce the amount realized.
2. The gain or loss is capital if the stock investment is a capital asset. If the shareholder recognizes a loss on the liquidation, Sec. 1244 permits ordinary loss treatment (within limits) for qualifying individual shareholders.
3. The adjusted basis of the property received is its FMV on the distribution date.
4. The shareholder's holding period for the property begins the day after the distribution date.
5. With certain limited exceptions, the distributing corporation recognizes gain or loss when making the distribution. The amount and character of the gain or loss are determined as if the corporation sold the property for its FMV immediately before the distribution. Special rules apply when the shareholders assume or acquire corporate liabilities and the amount of such liabilities exceeds the property's FMV.
6. The liquidated corporation's tax attributes disappear upon liquidation.

Liquidation of a Controlled Subsidiary

OBJECTIVE 3

Determine the tax consequences when a parent corporation liquidates a controlled subsidiary

After a brief overview, the discussion of the controlled subsidiary exception is divided into three parts: the requirements for using the exception, the effects of liquidating on the parent corporation, and the effects of liquidating on the subsidiary corporation.

Overview

Section 332(a) provides that the parent corporation recognizes no gain or loss when a controlled subsidiary corporation liquidates into its parent corporation. This liquidation rule permits a corporation to modify its corporate structure without incurring any adverse tax consequences. Section 332 applies only to the parent corporation. Other shareholders owning a minority interest are taxed under the general liquidation rules of Sec. 331. When Sec. 332 applies to the parent corporation, Sec. 337 permits the liquidating corporation to recognize no gains or losses on the assets distributed to the parent corporation. The liquidating corporation, however, recognizes gains (but not losses) on distributions made to shareholders holding a minority interest. The nonrecognition of gain or loss rule is logical for the distribution to the parent corporation because the assets remain within the corporate group following the distribution. Thus, the subsidiary corporation can be liquidated and operated as a division of its parent corporation without gain or loss recognition.

EXAMPLE C:6-13 ▶ Parent Corporation owns all of Subsidiary Corporation's stock. Subsidiary's assets have a $1 million FMV and a $400,000 adjusted basis. Parent's basis for its Subsidiary stock is $250,000. The liquidation of Subsidiary results in a $600,000 ($1,000,000 − $400,000) realized gain for Subsidiary on the distribution of its assets, none of which is recognized. Parent

[7] The property has a $1,000 basis when determining Pirate's gain on the sale and a $100 ($1,000 − $900) basis when determining its loss on the sale. Therefore, Pirate recognizes no gain or loss because the $200 sale price lies between the gain and loss basis amounts.

has a $750,000 ($1,000,000 − $250,000) realized gain on surrendering its Subsidiary stock, none of which is recognized. If Secs. 332 and 337 were not available, both Subsidiary and Parent would recognize their realized gains. In this case, Parent's gain would be reduced by the taxes paid by Subsidiary on its gain because Subsidiary's taxes reduce the amount available for distribution to Parent. ◀

REQUIREMENTS

TAX STRATEGY TIP

A parent corporation that does not own the requisite 80% should consider purchasing additional subsidiary stock from minority shareholders or consider having the subsidiary redeem shares from its minority shareholders. In either case, the strategy to attain 80% ownership must be applied before the corporations adopt a plan of liquidation. See Tax Planning Considerations for further details.

All the following requirements must be met for a liquidation to qualify for the Sec. 332 nonrecognition rules:

- The parent corporation must own at least 80% of the total combined voting power of all classes of stock entitled to vote and 80% of the total value of all classes of stock (other than certain nonvoting preferred stock) from the date on which the plan of liquidation is adopted until receipt of the subsidiary corporation's property.[8]
- The property distribution must be in complete cancellation or redemption of all the subsidiary corporation's stock.
- Distribution of the property must occur within a single tax year or be one of a series of distributions completed within three years of the close of the tax year during which the subsidiary makes the first of the series of liquidating distributions.

If the corporations meet all these requirements, the Sec. 332 nonrecognition rules are mandatory. If one or more of the conditions listed above are not met, the parent corporation is taxed under the previously discussed general liquidation rules.

TYPICAL MISCONCEPTION

The 80% stock ownership requirement of Sec. 332 is not the same stock ownership requirement for corporate formations in Chapter C:2. Instead, the Sec. 332 ownership requirement is the same one used for affiliated groups filing consolidated tax returns (see Chapter C:8).

Stock Ownership. For Sec. 332 to apply, the parent corporation must own the requisite amount of voting and nonvoting stock. In applying this requirement, the Sec. 318 attribution rules for stock ownership do not apply (see Chapter C:4).[9] The parent corporation must own the requisite 80% of voting and nonvoting stock from the date on which the plan of liquidation is adopted until the liquidation is completed. Failure to satisfy this requirement denies the transaction the benefits of Secs. 332 and 337.

Cancellation of the Stock. The subsidiary corporation must distribute its property in complete cancellation or redemption of all its stock in accordance with a plan of liquidation. When more than one liquidating distribution occurs, the subsidiary corporation must have adopted a plan of liquidation and be in a status of liquidation when it makes the first distribution. This status must continue until the liquidation is completed. Regulation Sec. 1.332-2(c) indicates that a liquidation is completed when the liquidating corporation has divested itself of all its property. The liquidating corporation, however, may retain a nominal amount of property to permit retention or sale of the corporate name.

Timing of the Distributions. The distribution of all the subsidiary corporation's assets within one subsidiary tax year in complete cancellation or redemption of all its stock is considered a complete liquidation.[10] Although a formal plan of liquidation can be adopted, the shareholders' adoption of a resolution authorizing the distribution of the corporation's assets in complete cancellation or redemption of its stock is considered to be the adoption of a plan of liquidation when the distribution occurs within a single tax year. The tax year in which the liquidating distribution occurs does not have to be the same as the one in which the plan of liquidation is adopted.[11]

The subsidiary corporation can carry out the plan of liquidation by making a series of distributions that extend over a period of more than one tax year to cancel or redeem its stock. In this case, however, a formal plan of liquidation must be adopted, and the liquidation must be completed within three years of the close of the tax year in which the subsidiary makes the first distribution under the plan.[12]

[8] The stock definition used for Sec. 332 purposes excludes any stock that is not entitled to vote, is limited and preferred as to dividends and does not participate in corporate growth to any significant extent, has redemption and liquidation rights that do not exceed its issue price (except for a reasonable redemption or liquidation premium), and is not convertible into another class of stock.

[9] Sec. 332(b)(1).

[10] Sec. 332(b)(2) and Reg. Sec. 1.332-3.

[11] Rev. Rul. 76-317, 1976-2 C.B. 98.

[12] Sec. 332(b)(3) and Reg. Sec. 1.332-4.

EFFECTS OF LIQUIDATING ON THE SHAREHOLDERS

Recognition of Gain or Loss to Parent Corporation. The Sec. 332(a) nonrecognition rules apply only to a parent corporation that receives a liquidating distribution from a solvent subsidiary. Section 332(a) does not apply to a parent corporation that receives a liquidating distribution from an insolvent subsidiary, to minority shareholders who receive liquidating distributions, or to a parent corporation that receives a payment to satisfy the subsidiary's indebtedness to the parent. All of these exceptions are discussed below.

SELF-STUDY QUESTION

What are the tax consequences if the liquidating subsidiary is insolvent?

ANSWER

The parent generally is entitled to an ordinary loss deduction under Sec. 165(g)(3) when it fails to receive any liquidation proceeds because the subsidiary is insolvent. The parent also may have a bad debt deduction under Sec. 166.

Section 332 does not apply if the subsidiary corporation is insolvent at the time of the liquidation because the parent corporation does not receive the distributions in exchange for its stock investment. An insolvent subsidiary is one whose liabilities exceed the FMV of its assets. Regulation Sec. 1.332-2(b) requires that the parent corporation receive at least partial payment for the stock it owns in the subsidiary corporation to qualify for nonrecognition under Sec. 332. If the subsidiary is insolvent, however, the special worthless security rules of Sec. 165(g)(3) for affiliated corporations and the bad debt rules of Sec. 166 permit the parent corporation to recognize an ordinary loss with respect to its investment in the subsidiary's stock or debt obligations (see Chapter C:2).

EXAMPLE C:6-14 ▶ Parent Corporation owns all of Subsidiary Corporation's stock. Parent established Subsidiary to produce and market a product that proved unsuccessful. Parent has a $1.5 million basis in its Subsidiary stock. In addition, it made a $1 million advance to Subsidiary that is not secured by a note. Under a plan of liquidation, Subsidiary distributes all its assets, having a $750,000 FMV, to Parent in partial satisfaction of the advance after having paid all third-party creditors. No assets remain to pay the remainder of the advance or to redeem the outstanding stock. Because Subsidiary is insolvent immediately before the liquidating distribution, it distributes none of its assets in redemption of the Subsidiary stock. Therefore, the liquidation cannot qualify under the Sec. 332 rules. Parent, therefore, claims a $250,000 business bad debt with respect to the unpaid portion of the advance and a $1.5 million ordinary loss for its stock investment. ◀

TYPICAL MISCONCEPTION

Section 332 applies only to the parent corporation. If a minority interest exists, the general liquidation rules of Sec. 331 apply to the minority shareholders.

STOP & THINK

Question: In Example C:6-14, assume Subsidiary Corporation had a $3 million net operating loss (NOL) carryover, which would disappear upon liquidation because Sec. 332 did not apply. To prevent this disappearance, Parent Corporation proposes to cancel the $1 million advance as a contribution to Subsidiary's capital. Thus, Parent would have a $2.5 million basis in its Subsidiary stock prior to the liquidation and no advances receivable. Now when Parent liquidates Subsidiary, all of Subsidiary's assets redeem Subsidiary's outstanding stock, and the transaction seems to qualify for Sec. 332 treatment. Under these circumstances, the $3 million NOL would carry over to Parent under Sec. 381, giving Parent $3 million worth of NOL deductions rather than $1.75 million worth of bad debt and worthless stock deductions under the original transaction. Do you think the IRS would condone this proposed transaction?

Solution: No. In Rev. Rul. 68-602, 1968-2 C.B. 135, the IRS held under similar circumstances that, because the cancellation "was an integral part of the liquidation and had no independent significance other than to secure the tax benefits of [Subsidiary's] net operating loss carryover, such step will be considered transitory and, therefore, disregarded." Thus, if Parent proceeded with the proposed transaction, the IRS would ignore it and treat the liquidation the same as originally done in Example C:6-14.

Treatment of Minority Shareholders. Liquidating distributions made to minority shareholders are taxed under the Sec. 331 general liquidation rules. These rules require the minority shareholders to recognize gain or loss—which generally is capital—upon the redemption of their stock in the subsidiary corporation.

EXAMPLE C:6-15 ▶ Parent Corporation and Jane own 80% and 20%, respectively, of Subsidiary Corporation's single class of stock. Parent and Jane have adjusted bases of $100,000 and $15,000, respectively, for their stock interests. Subsidiary adopts a plan of liquidation on May 30 and makes liquidating

SELF-STUDY QUESTION

What bases do both the parent and minority shareholders take in the assets received in a Sec. 332 liquidation?

ANSWER

Because the parent corporation recognizes no gain or loss in the transaction, the parent corporation takes a carryover basis in its assets. However, because the minority shareholders are involved in a taxable exchange, they take a FMV basis in their assets.

distributions of two parcels of land having $250,000 and $62,500 FMVs to Parent and Jane, respectively, on November 1 in exchange for their stock. Parent does not recognize its $150,000 ($250,000 − $100,000) gain because of Sec. 332. Jane recognizes a $47,500 ($62,500 − $15,000) capital gain under Sec. 331. (Subsidiary also faces gain recognition on the distribution of appreciated property to its minority shareholder as demonstrated in Example C:6-18.) ◀

Basis of Property Received. Under Sec. 334(b)(1), the parent corporation's basis for property received in the liquidating distribution is the same as the subsidiary corporation's basis prior to the distribution. This carryover basis rule reflects the principle that the liquidating corporation recognizes no gain or loss when it distributes the property and that the property's tax attributes (e.g., the depreciation recapture potential) carry over from the subsidiary corporation to the parent corporation. The parent corporation's basis for its stock investment in the subsidiary corporation is ignored in determining the basis for the distributed property and disappears once the parent surrenders its stock in the subsidiary. Property received by minority shareholders takes a basis equal to its FMV.

EXAMPLE C:6-16 ▶ Assume the same facts as in Example C:6-15 and that the two parcels of land received by Parent Corporation and Jane have adjusted bases of $175,000 and $40,000, respectively, to Subsidiary. Parent takes a $175,000 carryover basis for its land, and Jane takes a $62,500 FMV basis for her land. ◀

A special rule prevents the importation of built-in losses upon the liquidation of a foreign subsidiary. Specifically, the parent takes a FMV basis in each transferred property if the following three conditions prevail: (1) the parent is a U.S. corporation, (2) the liquidating subsidiary is a foreign corporation, and (3) the aggregate adjusted basis of the transferred property exceeds the aggregate FMV.

STOP & THINK

Question: Why should a corporation that is 100%-owned by another corporation be treated differently when it liquidates than a corporation that is 100%-owned by an individual?

Solution: A corporation that is 100%-owned by another corporation can file a consolidated tax return (see Chapters C:3 and C:8). As a result, the parent and its subsidiary corporations are treated as a single entity. This result is the same as if the subsidiary were one of a number of divisions of a single corporation. An extension of the single-entity concept is that a subsidiary corporation can be liquidated tax-free into its parent corporation. An individual and his or her corporation are treated as two separate tax entities when calculating their annual tax liabilities. As separate entities, nonliquidating distributions (e.g., ordinary distributions and stock redemptions) from the corporation to its shareholder(s) are taxable. The same principle applies to liquidating distributions.

EFFECTS OF LIQUIDATING ON THE SUBSIDIARY CORPORATION

Recognition of Gain or Loss. Section 337(a) provides that the liquidating corporation recognizes no gain or loss on the distribution of property to the 80% distributee in a complete liquidation to which Sec. 332 applies.[13] The term 80% distributee refers to a corporation that meets the 80% stock ownership requirement described on page C:6-11.

EXAMPLE C:6-17 ▶ Parent Corporation owns all the stock of Subsidiary Corporation. Pursuant to a plan of complete liquidation, Subsidiary distributes land having a $200,000 FMV and a $60,000 basis to Parent. Subsidiary recognizes no gain with respect to the distribution. Parent takes a $60,000 basis for the land. ◀

[13] Section 336(e) permits a corporation to sell, exchange, or distribute the stock of a subsidiary corporation and to elect to treat such a transaction as a disposition of all the subsidiary corporation's assets. The parent corporation recognizes no gain or loss on the sale, exchange, or distribution of the stock. The economic consequences of making this election for a stock sale are essentially the same as if the parent corporation instead liquidates the subsidiary in a transaction to which Sec. 332 applies and then immediately sells the properties to the purchaser.

TAX STRATEGY TIP

A corporation that sells, exchanges, or distributes the stock of a subsidiary may elect to treat the sale of the stock as a sale of the subsidiary's assets. This election could prove beneficial when a sale of the subsidiary stock occurs and the assets of the subsidiary corporation are substantially less appreciated than the subsidiary stock itself.

The depreciation recapture provisions in Secs. 1245, 1250, and 291 do not override the Sec. 337(a) nonrecognition rule if a controlled subsidiary corporation liquidates into its parent corporation. Instead, the parent corporation assumes the depreciation recapture potential associated with the distributed property, and recapture occurs when the parent corporation sells or exchanges the property.[14]

The Sec. 337(a) nonrecognition rule applies only to distributions to the parent corporation. Liquidating distributions to minority shareholders are not eligible for nonrecognition under Sec. 337(a). Consequently, the liquidating corporation must recognize gain under Sec. 336(a) when it distributes appreciated property to the minority shareholders. Section 336(d)(3), however, prevents the subsidiary corporation from recognizing loss on distributions made to minority shareholders. Thus, for the subsidiary, liquidating distributions made to minority shareholders are treated the same way as nonliquidating distributions.

EXAMPLE C:6-18 ▶ Assume the same facts as in Example C:6-17 except Parent owns 80% of the Subsidiary stock, Chuck owns the remaining 20% of such stock, and Subsidiary distributes two parcels of land to Parent and Chuck. The parcels have FMVs of $160,000 and $40,000, and adjusted bases of $50,000 and $10,000, respectively. Subsidiary does not recognize the $110,000 ($160,000 − $50,000) gain realized on the distribution to Parent. However, Subsidiary does recognize the $30,000 ($40,000 − $10,000) gain realized on the distribution to Chuck because the Sec. 337(a) nonrecognition rule applies only to distributions to the 80% distributee. Assume that the land distributed to Chuck instead has a $40,000 FMV and a $50,000 adjusted basis. Subsidiary can deduct none of the $10,000 loss because it distributed the land to a minority shareholder. ◀

Tax Attribute Carryovers. The tax attributes of the liquidating corporation disappear when the liquidation is completed under the general rules. They carry over, however, in the case of a controlled subsidiary corporation liquidated into its parent corporation under Sec. 332.[15] The following items are included among the carried-over attributes:

- NOL carryovers
- Earnings and profits
- Capital loss carryovers
- General business and other tax credit carryovers

The carryover amount is determined as of the close of the day on which the subsidiary corporation completes the distribution of all its property. Chapter C:7 contains further discussion of these rules.

Topic Review C:6-2 summarizes the special rules applicable to the liquidation of a controlled subsidiary corporation.

TOPIC REVIEW C:6-2

Tax Consequences of a Corporate Liquidation

TAX CONSEQUENCES OF LIQUIDATING A CONTROLLED SUBSIDIARY CORPORATION

1. Specific requirements must be met with respect to (a) stock ownership, (b) distribution of the property in complete cancellation or redemption of all the subsidiary's stock, and (c) distribution of all property within a single tax year or within a three-year period. To satisfy the stock ownership requirement, the parent corporation must own at least 80% of the total voting power of all voting stock and at least 80% of the total value of all stock.
2. The parent corporation recognizes no gain or loss when it receives distributed property from the liquidating subsidiary. Section 332 does not apply to liquidations of insolvent subsidiaries and distributions to minority shareholders.
3. The basis of the distributed property carries over from the subsidiary corporation to the parent corporation.
4. The parent corporation's holding period for the assets includes the subsidiary corporation's holding period.
5. The subsidiary corporation recognizes no gain or loss when making a distribution to an 80% distributee (parent). The liquidating subsidiary recognizes gain (but not loss) on distributions to minority shareholders. Also, the liquidating subsidiary recognizes no gain when it distributes appreciated property to satisfy certain subsidiary debts owed to the parent corporation.
6. The subsidiary corporation's tax attributes carry over to the parent corporation as part of the liquidation.

[14] Secs. 1245(b)(3) and 1250(d)(3).

[15] Sec. 381(a).

SPECIAL REPORTING ISSUES

PERTAINING TO SHAREHOLDERS

OBJECTIVE 4

Recognize special reporting issues pertaining to shareholders and the liquidating corporation

Four special shareholder reporting rules apply to liquidation transactions described below. These rules add different degrees of complexity to the general liquidation rules outlined above.

Partially Liquidating Distributions. Shareholders often receive a series of partially liquidating distributions that culminate in the redemption of all the corporation's stock. Section 346(a) treats this situation as a complete liquidation. Consequently, the distributions received are taxed under the Sec. 331 liquidation rules instead of under the Sec. 302 rules applying to redemptions in partial liquidation. The IRS permits the shareholder's basis to be recovered first and requires the recognition of gain once the shareholder fully recovers the basis of a particular share or block of stock. The shareholder cannot recognize a loss with respect to a share or block of stock until he or she receives the final liquidating distribution, or until it becomes clear that no more liquidating distributions will occur.[16]

EXAMPLE C:6-19 ▶ Diane owns 1,000 shares of Adobe Corporation stock, which she acquired five years ago. Her basis in the stock is $40,000. Recently, she initiated a series of liquidating distributions from Adobe to be received over a three-year period (Years 1–3) as follows: $25,000 on July 23 of Year 1, $17,000 on March 12 of Year 2, and $10,000 on April 5 of Year 3. Diane recognizes no gain in Year 1 because she has not fully recovered her $40,000 basis by year-end. The $15,000 ($40,000 − $25,000) unrecovered basis remaining after the first distribution is less than the $17,000 liquidating distribution received on March 12 of Year 2, so Diane recognizes a $2,000 gain in Year 2. She recognizes an additional $10,000 gain in Year 3 when she receives the final liquidating distribution. ◀

EXAMPLE C:6-20 ▶ Assume the same facts as in Example C:6-19 except Diane paid $60,000 for her Adobe stock. The receipt of each of the liquidating distributions is nontaxable because Diane's $60,000 basis exceeds the $52,000 ($25,000 + $17,000 + $10,000) total of the distributions. Diane recognizes an $8,000 ($52,000 − $60,000) loss in Year 3 when she receives the final liquidating distribution. ◀

SELF-STUDY QUESTION

If a cash method shareholder is subsequently obligated to pay a contingent liability of the liquidated corporation, what are the tax consequences of such a payment?

ANSWER

First, the prior tax year return is not amended. The additional payment results in a loss recognized in the year of payment. The character of the loss depends on the nature of the gain or loss recognized by the shareholder in the year of liquidation.

Subsequent Assessments. At some date after the liquidation, the shareholders may be required to pay a contingent liability of the corporation or a liability not anticipated at the time of the liquidating distribution (e.g., an income tax deficiency determined after the liquidation occurs or a judgment that is contingent when the corporation makes the final liquidating distribution). The additional payment does not affect the reporting of the initial liquidation. The tax treatment for the additional payment depends on the nature of the gain or loss originally reported by the shareholder and not on the type of loss or deduction the liquidating corporation would have reported had it paid the liability.[17] If the liquidation results in a recognized capital gain or loss, a cash method shareholder treats the additional payment as a capital loss in the year of payment (i.e., the shareholder does not file an amended tax return for the year in which he or she originally reported the gain or loss from the liquidation). An accrual method shareholder recognizes the capital loss when he or she incurs the liability.

EXAMPLE C:6-21 ▶ Coastal Corporation liquidated three years ago with Tammy, a cash method taxpayer, reporting a $30,000 long-term capital gain on the exchange of her Coastal stock. In the current year, Tammy pays $5,000 as her part of the settlement of a lawsuit against Coastal. All shareholders pay an additional amount because the settlement exceeds the amount of funds that Coastal placed into an escrow account as a result of the litigation. The amount placed into the escrow account was not included in the amount Tammy realized from the liquidating distribution

[16] Rev. Ruls. 68-348, 1968-2 C.B. 141, 79-10, 1979-1 C.B. 140, and 85-48, 1985-1 C.B. 126.

[17] *F. Donald Arrowsmith v. CIR*, 42 AFTR 649, 52-2 USTC ¶9527 (USSC, 1952).

three years ago. Because Tammy had not been taxed on the cash placed in the escrow account, she cannot deduct the amount of the payment made from the escrow account in the current year. Nevertheless, Tammy treats the $5,000 paid from her personal funds as a long-term capital loss in the current year. ◀

Open Versus Closed Transactions. Sometimes the value of property received in a corporate liquidation cannot be determined by the usual valuation techniques. Property that can be valued only on the basis of uncertain future payments falls into this category. In such a case, the shareholders may attempt to rely on the **open transaction doctrine** of *Burnet v. Logan* and treat the liquidation as an open transaction.[18] Under this doctrine, the shareholder's gain or loss from the liquidation is not determined until the assets that cannot be valued are subsequently sold, collected, or able to be valued. Any assets that cannot be valued are assigned a zero value. The IRS's position is that the FMV of almost any asset should be ascertainable. Thus, the IRS assumes that the open transaction method should be used only in extraordinary circumstances. For example, an open transaction cannot be used merely because a market valuation for an investment in a closely held corporation is not readily available through market quotations for the stock.

ETHICAL POINT

A tax practitioner needs to ensure that the client obtains appropriate appraisals to support the values assigned to property distributed to shareholders in a corporate liquidation. A 20% substantial underpayment penalty may be imposed on corporations and shareholders that substantially understate their income tax liabilities.

Installment Obligations. Shareholders who receive an installment obligation as part of their liquidating distribution ordinarily report the FMV of their obligation as part of the consideration received to calculate the amount of the recognized gain or loss. Shareholders who receive an installment obligation that was acquired by the liquidating corporation in connection with the sale or exchange of its property are eligible for special treatment in reporting their gain on the liquidating transaction if the sale or exchange takes place during the 12-month period beginning on the date a plan of complete liquidation is adopted and the liquidation is completed during such 12-month period. These shareholders may report their gain as they receive the installment payments.[19]

PERTAINING TO THE LIQUIDATING CORPORATION

Expenses of the Liquidation. The corporation can deduct the expenses incurred in connection with the liquidation. These expenses include attorneys' and accountants' fees, costs incurred in drafting the plan of liquidation and obtaining shareholder approval, and so on.[20] Such amounts ordinarily are deductible in the liquidating corporation's final tax return.

A liquidating corporation treats expenses associated with selling its property as an offset against the sales proceeds. When a corporation sells an asset pursuant to its liquidation, the selling expenses reduce the amount of gain or increase the amount of loss reported by the corporation.[21]

EXAMPLE C:6-22 ▶ Madison Corporation adopts a plan of liquidation on July 15 and shortly thereafter sells a parcel of land on which it realizes a $60,000 gain (excluding the effects of a $6,000 sales commission). Madison pays its legal counsel $1,500 to draft the plan of liquidation. Madison distributes all its remaining properties to its shareholders on December 15. The $1,500 paid to legal counsel is deductible as a liquidation expense in Madison's current year income tax return. The sales commission reduces the $60,000 gain realized on the land sale, so that Madison's recognized gain is $54,000 ($60,000 − $6,000). ◀

---

[18] *Burnet v. Edith A. Logan*, 9 AFTR 1453, 2 USTC ¶736 (USSC, 1931).

[19] Sec. 453(h)(1)(A). A tax deferral is available only with respect to the gain realized by the shareholder. The liquidating corporation must recognize the deferred gain when it distributes the installment obligation to the shareholder as if it had sold the obligation immediately before the distribution.

[20] *Pridemark, Inc. v. CIR*, 15 AFTR 2d 853, 65-1 USTC ¶9388 (4th Cir., 1965).

[21] See, for example, *J. T. Stewart III Trust*, 63 T.C. 682 (1975), *acq.* 1977-1 C.B. 1.

Any capitalized expenditures unamortized at the time of liquidation should be deducted if they have no further value to the corporation (e.g., unamortized organizational costs).[22] Capitalized expenditures that have value must be allocated to the shareholders receiving the benefit of such an outlay (e.g., prepaid insurance and prepaid rent).[23] Expenses related to issuing the corporation's stock are nondeductible, even at the time of liquidation, because they are treated as a reduction of paid-in capital. Unamortized bond premiums, however, are deductible at the time the corporation retires the bonds.

TAX STRATEGY TIP

If a liquidating corporation creates an NOL in the year of liquidation or already has NOL carryovers, these losses may disappear with the liquidated corporation. If the liquidation qualifies under Sec. 332, however, the parent corporation acquires the NOL. If the liquidation falls under the general liquidation rules, the liquidating corporation may want to consider an S election for the liquidation year so any NOLs created in that year can pass through to the shareholders.

Treatment of Net Operating Losses. If the liquidating corporation reports little or no income in its final income tax return, the corporation may create an NOL when it deducts its liquidating expenses and any remaining capitalized expenditures. The NOL carries back to reduce corporate taxes paid in prior years. The resultant federal income tax refund increases (decreases) the gain (loss) previously reported by the shareholder. Alternatively, the shareholders might consider having the corporation make an S election for the liquidation year and have the flow-through loss reported on the shareholders' tax returns. (See Chapter C:11 for the tax treatment of S corporations.)

The need for a liquidating corporation to recognize gains when distributing appreciated property can be partially or fully offset by expenses incurred in carrying out the liquidation or by any available NOL carryovers. Losses recognized by the liquidating corporation when distributing property that has declined in value can offset operating profits or capital gains earned in the liquidation year. Should such losses produce an NOL or net capital loss, the losses may be carried back to provide a refund of taxes paid in a prior year, or they may be passed through to the corporation's shareholders if the corporation makes an S corporation election for the tax year.

RECOGNITION OF GAIN OR LOSS WHEN PROPERTY IS DISTRIBUTED IN RETIREMENT OF DEBT

OBJECTIVE 5

Assess when a liquidating corporation recognizes gains and losses on the retirement of debt

GENERAL RULE

A shareholder recognizes no gain or loss when the liquidating corporation pays off an unsecured debt obligation it owes to the shareholder. However, when the corporation retires a security at an amount different from the shareholder's adjusted basis for the obligation, the shareholder recognizes gain or loss for the difference. These rules apply whether the debtor corporation pays or retires the debt as part of its operations or as part of its liquidation. The debtor corporation recognizes no gain or loss when it uses cash to satisfy its debt obligations. However, the debtor corporation recognizes gain when it uses appreciated noncash property to satisfy its debt obligations. Similarly, a debtor corporation recognizes a loss when it uses noncash property that has declined in value to satisfy its debt obligations.

SATISFACTION OF THE SUBSIDIARY'S DEBT OBLIGATIONS

The Sec. 332(a) nonrecognition rules apply only to amounts received by the parent corporation in its role as a shareholder. The parent corporation, however, does recognize gain or loss upon receipt of property in payment of a subsidiary corporation indebtedness if the payment differs from the parent's basis in the debt.[24]

As mentioned above, the use of property to satisfy an indebtedness generally results in the debtor recognizing gain or loss at the time it transfers the property.[25] Section 337(b), however, prevents a liquidating subsidiary corporation from recognizing gain or loss

[22] Reg. Sec. 1.248-1(b)(3).

[23] *Koppers Co., Inc. v. U.S.*, 5 AFTR 2d 1597, 60-2 USTC ¶9505 (Ct. Cls., 1960).

[24] Sec. 1001(c). This general IRC section requires realized gains or losses to be recognized unless otherwise excluded or disallowed.

[25] Ibid.

WHAT WOULD YOU DO IN THIS SITUATION?

Andrea has operated her trendy, upscale clothing store as a C corporation for a number of years. Annually, the corporation earns $200,000 in pre-tax profits. Andrea's stock is worth about $800,000. Her stock basis is $125,000. One of her good friends, Jenna, has opened a clothing store as a limited liability company and has been telling Andrea about the advantage of not having to pay the corporate income tax. She also hears about the check-the-box regulations that permit corporations to elect to be taxed as partnerships and limited liability companies. She calls and tells you that she wants you to file the necessary paperwork with the IRS to make the change from being taxed as a C corporation to being taxed as a flow-through entity. What advice should you provide Andrea in this situation?

when it transfers noncash property to its parent corporation in satisfaction of an indebtedness. The IRC provides this exception because the property remains within the economic unit of the parent-subsidiary group.

Section 337(b) applies only to the subsidiary's indebtedness owed to the parent corporation on the date the plan of liquidation is adopted and that is satisfied by the transfer of property pursuant to a complete liquidation of the subsidiary corporation. It does not apply to liabilities owed to other shareholders or third-party creditors, or to liabilities incurred after the plan of liquidation is adopted. In addition, if the subsidiary corporation satisfies the indebtedness for less than its face amount, it may have to recognize income from the discharge of an indebtedness.

EXAMPLE C:6-23 ▶ Parent Corporation owns all of Subsidiary Corporation's single class of stock. When Parent acquired the Subsidiary stock, it also purchased $1 million of Subsidiary bonds at their face amount. Subsequently, Parent and Subsidiary adopt a plan of liquidation, and Subsidiary distributes to Parent property having a $1 million FMV and a $400,000 adjusted basis in cancellation of the bonds. Subsidiary also distributes its remaining property to Parent in exchange for all of its outstanding stock. Subsidiary recognizes no gain on the transfer of the property in cancellation of its bonds. Parent recognizes no gain on receipt of the property because the property's FMV equals Parent's adjusted basis of the bonds. Parent takes a $400,000 carryover basis for the noncash property it receives in cancellation of the bonds. ◀

TAX PLANNING CONSIDERATIONS

OBJECTIVE 6

Identify tax planning opportunities in corporate liquidations

TIMING THE LIQUIDATION TRANSACTION

Sometimes corporations adopt a plan of liquidation in one year but do not complete the liquidation until a subsequent year. Corporations planning to distribute properties that have both increased in value and decreased in value may find it advantageous to sell or distribute property that has declined in value in a tax year in which they also conducted business activities. As such, the loss recognized when selling or distributing the property can offset profits that are taxed at higher rates. Deferring the sale or distribution of property that has appreciated in value may delay the recognition of gain for one tax year and also place the gain in a year in which the marginal tax rate is lower.

EXAMPLE C:6-24 ▶ Miami Corporation adopts a plan of liquidation in November of the current year, a tax year in which it earns $150,000 in operating profits. Miami discontinues its operating activities before the end of the current year. Pursuant to the liquidation, it distributes assets, producing $40,000 of recognized ordinary losses. In January of next year, Miami distributes assets that have appreciated in value, producing $40,000 of recognized ordinary income. Distributing the loss property in the current year results in a $15,600 tax savings ($40,000 × 0.39). Only $6,000 ($40,000 × 0.15) in taxes result from distributing the appreciated property next year. The rate differential provides a $9,600 ($15,600 − $6,000) net savings to Miami. ◀

TAX STRATEGY TIP

Timing the distribution of loss property so that the losses may be used to offset high-bracket taxable income at the corporate level makes good tax sense if the general liquidation rules are applicable. However, this planning opportunity would not exist in a Sec. 332 parent-subsidiary liquidation because the liquidating subsidiary does not recognize losses.

Timing the liquidating distributions should not proceed without the planner also considering the tax position of the various shareholders. Taxpayers should be careful about timing the liquidating distributions to avoid creating a short-term capital gain taxed at ordinary rates rather than long-term capital gains taxed at the lower capital gains rate. If the liquidation results in a recognized loss, shareholders should take advantage of the opportunity to offset the loss against capital gains plus $3,000 of ordinary income, as well as attempt to increase the portion of the loss eligible for ordinary loss treatment under Sec. 1244 (see next section).

RECOGNITION OF ORDINARY LOSSES WHEN A LIQUIDATION OCCURS

Shareholders sometimes recognize losses when a liquidation occurs. Individual shareholders should be aware that, because a complete liquidation is treated as an exchange transaction, Sec. 1244 ordinary loss treatment is available when a small business corporation liquidates. This treatment permits the shareholder to claim $50,000 of ordinary loss when he or she surrenders the stock ($100,000 if the taxpayer is married and files a joint return).

Ordinary loss treatment also is available for a domestic corporation that owns stock or debt securities in a subsidiary corporation. Because the rules in Sec. 332 regarding nonrecognition of gain or loss do not apply when a subsidiary corporation is insolvent (see page C:6-12), the parent corporation can recognize a loss when the subsidiary corporation's stocks and debt securities are determined to be worthless. This loss is an ordinary loss (instead of a capital loss) if the domestic corporation owns at least 80% of the voting stock and 80% of each class of nonvoting stock, and more than 90% of the liquidating corporation's gross income for all tax years has been other than passive income.[26]

OBTAINING 80% OWNERSHIP TO ACHIEVE SEC. 332 BENEFITS

The 80% stock ownership requirement provides tax planning opportunities when a subsidiary corporation liquidates. A parent corporation seeking nonrecognition under Sec. 332 may acquire additional shares of the subsidiary corporation's stock *before* the adoption of the plan of liquidation. This acquisition helps the parent corporation meet the 80% minimum and avoids gain recognition on the liquidation. If the parent corporation purchases these additional shares of stock from other shareholders to satisfy the 80% minimum *after* adopting the plan of liquidation, Sec. 332 will not apply.[27]

EXAMPLE C:6-25 ▶ Parent Corporation owns 75% of Subsidiary Corporation's single class of stock. On March 12, Parent purchases for cash the remaining 25% of the Subsidiary stock from three individual shareholders pursuant to a tender offer. Parent and Subsidiary adopt a plan of liquidation on October 1, and Subsidiary distributes its assets to Parent on December 1 in exchange for all of Subsidiary's outstanding stock. Parent recognizes no gain or loss on the liquidation of Subsidiary because all the Sec. 332 requirements had been satisfied prior to adoption of the plan of liquidation. ◀

Alternatively, the parent corporation might cause the subsidiary corporation to redeem some of its shares held by minority shareholders before the plan of liquidation is adopted. The IRS originally held that the intention to liquidate is present once the subsidiary corporation agrees to redeem the shares of the minority shareholders. Thus, redemption of a 25% minority interest did not permit Sec. 332 to be used even though the parent corporation owned 100% of the outstanding stock after the redemption.[28]

In *George L. Riggs, Inc.*, however, the Tax Court held that a parent corporation's tender offer to minority shareholders and the calling of the subsidiary's preferred stock do not invalidate the Sec. 332 liquidation because "the formation of a conditional intention to liquidate in the future is not the adoption of a plan of liquidation."[29] The IRS has acquiesced to the *Riggs* decision.

[26] Sec. 165(g)(3).
[27] Rev. Rul. 75-521, 1975-2 C.B. 120.
[28] Rev. Rul. 70-106, 1970-1 C.B. 70.
[29] *George L. Riggs, Inc.*, 64 T.C. 474 (1975), *acq.* 1976-2 C.B. 2.

Thus, careful planning can help both the parent corporation and subsidiary corporation avoid gain recognition under Secs. 332 and 337. Nonrecognition, however, does not extend to minority shareholders as discussed earlier.

EXAMPLE C:6-26 ▶ Parent Corporation owns 80% of Subsidiary Corporation's stock. Anthony owns the remaining 20% of Subsidiary stock. Parent and Anthony have adjusted bases of $200,000 and $60,000, respectively, for their Subsidiary stock. Subsidiary distributes land having a $250,000 adjusted basis and a $400,000 FMV to Parent and $100,000 in cash to Anthony. Subsidiary recognizes no gain or loss on the distribution of the land or the cash. Parent recognizes no gain on the liquidation and takes a $250,000 basis for the land. Anthony recognizes a $40,000 ($100,000 − $60,000) capital gain on the receipt of the money. Alternatively, distribution of the land and cash ratably to Parent and Anthony would require Subsidiary to recognize as gain the appreciation on the portion of land distributed to Anthony. ◀

AVOIDING SEC. 332 TO RECOGNIZE LOSSES

ADDITIONAL COMMENT

The parent corporation, however, would not acquire the subsidiary's tax attributes if a taxable liquidation occurs.

A parent corporation may want to avoid the Sec. 332 nonrecognition rules to recognize a loss when a solvent subsidiary corporation liquidates. Because the stock ownership requirement must be met during the entire liquidation process, the parent corporation apparently can sell some of its stock in the subsidiary corporation to reduce its stock ownership below the 80% level at any time during the liquidation process and be able to recognize the loss.[30] Such a sale permits the parent corporation to recognize a capital loss when it surrenders its stock interest in the subsidiary corporation. The parent corporation may desire this capital loss if it has offsetting capital gains.

The sale of a portion of the subsidiary's stock after the plan of liquidation is adopted prevents Sec. 332 from applying to the parent corporation. The Sec. 337 rules, which prevent the subsidiary corporation from recognizing gain or loss when making a liquidating distribution to an 80% distributee, also do not apply because nonrecognition is contingent on Sec. 332 applying to the distributee. Thus, the subsidiary corporation also can recognize a loss when it distributes property that has declined in value.

COMPLIANCE AND PROCEDURAL CONSIDERATIONS

OBJECTIVE 7

Comply with procedural rules for corporate liquidations

GENERAL LIQUIDATION PROCEDURES

Section 6043(a) requires a liquidating corporation to file Form 966 (Corporate Dissolution or Liquidation) within 30 days after the adoption of any resolution or plan calling for the liquidation or dissolution of the corporation. The liquidating corporation files this form with the District Director of the IRS for the district in which it files its income tax return. Any amendment or supplement to the resolution or plan must be filed on an additional Form 966 within 30 days of making the amendment or supplement. The liquidating corporation must file Form 966 whether the shareholders' realized gain is recognized or not. The information included with Form 966 is described in Reg. Sec. 1.6043-1(b).

Regulation Sec. 1.6043-2(a) requires every corporation that makes a distribution of $600 or more during a calendar year to any shareholder in liquidation of part or all of its capital stock to file Form 1099-DIV (Dividends and Distributions). A separate Form 1099-DIV is required for each shareholder. The information that must be included with the Form 1099-DIV is described in Reg. Secs. 1.6043-2(a) and (b).

Regulation Sec. 1.6012-2(a)(2) requires a corporation that exists for part of a year to file a corporate tax return for the portion of the tax year that it existed. A corporation that ceases business and dissolves, while retaining no assets, is not considered to be in existence for federal tax purposes even though under state law it may be considered for certain purposes to be continuing its affairs (e.g., for purposes of suing or being sued).

[30] *CIR v. Day & Zimmerman, Inc.*, 34 AFTR 343, 45-2 USTC ¶9403 (3rd Cir., 1945).

ADDITIONAL COMMENT

As evidenced in this chapter, the compliance and procedural requirements of complete liquidations are formidable. Any taxpayer contemplating this type of corporate transactions should consult competent tax and legal advisors to ensure that the technical requirements of the proposed transaction are satisfied.

SECTION 332 LIQUIDATIONS

Regulation Sec. 1.332-6 requires every corporation receiving distributions in a Sec. 332 complete liquidation to maintain permanent records. A complete statement of all facts pertinent to the nonrecognition of gain or loss must be included in the corporate distributee's return for the tax year in which it receives a liquidating distribution. This statement includes the following: a certified copy of the plan of liquidation, a list of all property received upon the distribution, a statement of any indebtedness of the liquidating corporation to the recipient corporation, and a statement of stock ownership.

Treasury Regulations require a special waiver of the general three-year statute of limitations when the liquidation covers more than one tax year.[31] The distributee corporation must file a waiver of the limitations period on assessment for each of its tax years that falls partially or wholly within the liquidation period. The distributee corporation files this waiver at the time it files its income tax return. This waiver must extend the assessment period to a date at least one year after the last date of the period for assessment of such taxes for the last tax year in which the liquidation may be completed under Sec. 332.

PLAN OF LIQUIDATION

A **plan of liquidation** is a written document detailing the steps to be undertaken while carrying out the complete liquidation of the corporation. Although a formal plan of liquidation is not required, it may assist the corporation in determining when it enters a liquidation status and, therefore, when distributions to the shareholders qualify for exchange treatment under Sec. 331 (instead of possibly being treated as a dividend under Sec. 301). The adoption of a formal plan of liquidation can provide the liquidating corporation or its shareholders additional benefits under the tax laws. For example, the adoption of a plan of liquidation permits a parent corporation to have a three-year time period (instead of one tax year) to carry out the complete liquidation of a subsidiary corporation.

PROBLEM MATERIALS

DISCUSSION QUESTIONS

C:6-1 What is a complete liquidation? A partial liquidation? Explain the difference in the tax treatment accorded these two different events.

C:6-2 Summitt Corporation has manufactured and distributed basketball equipment for 20 years. Its owners would like to avoid the corporate income tax and are considering becoming a limited liability company (LLC). What tax savings may result from electing to be treated as an LLC? What federal tax costs will be incurred to make the change from a C corporation to an LLC? Would the same transaction costs be incurred if instead the corporation made an S election? Would the transaction costs be incurred had LLC status been adopted when the entity was initially organized?

C:6-3 Explain why tax advisors caution people who are starting a new business that the tax costs of incorporating a business may be low while the tax costs of liquidating a business may be high.

C:6-4 Explain the following statement: A corporation may be liquidated for tax purposes even though dissolution has not occurred under state corporation law.

C:6-5 Compare the tax consequences to the shareholder and the distributing corporation of the following three kinds of corporate distributions: ordinary dividends, stock redemptions, and complete liquidations.

C:6-6 What event or occurrence determines when a cash or accrual method of accounting taxpayer reports a liquidating distribution?

C:6-7 Explain why a shareholder receiving a liquidating distribution would prefer to receive either capital gain treatment or ordinary loss treatment.

C:6-8 A liquidating corporation could either (1) sell its assets and then distribute remaining cash to its shareholders or (2) distribute its assets directly to

[31] Reg. Sec. 1.332-4(a)(2).

the shareholders who then sell the distributed assets. Do the tax consequences of these alternatives differ?

C:6-9 Explain the circumstances in which a liquidating corporation does not recognize gain and/or loss when making a liquidating distribution.

C:6-10 Kelly Corporation makes a liquidating distribution. Among other property, it distributes land subject to a mortgage. The mortgage amount exceeds both the adjusted basis and FMV for the land. Explain to Kelly Corporation's president how the amount of its recognized gain or loss on the distribution and the shareholder's basis for the land are determined.

C:6-11 Explain the congressional intent behind the enactment of the Sec. 332 rules regarding the liquidation of a subsidiary corporation.

C:6-12 What requirements must be satisfied for the Sec. 332 rules to apply to a corporate shareholder?

C:6-13 Compare the general liquidation rules with the Sec. 332 rules for liquidation of a subsidiary corporation with respect to the following items:

a. Recognition of gain or loss by the distributee corporation
b. Recognition of gain or loss by the liquidating corporation
c. Basis of assets in the distributee corporation's hands
d. Treatment of the liquidating corporation's tax attributes

C:6-14 Parent Corporation owns 80% of the stock of Subsidiary Corporation, which is insolvent. Tracy owns the remaining 20% of the stock. The courts determine Subsidiary to be bankrupt. The shareholders receive nothing for their investment. How do they report their losses for tax purposes?

C:6-15 Parent Corporation owns all the stock of Subsidiary Corporation and a substantial amount of Subsidiary Corporation bonds. Subsidiary proposes to transfer appreciated property to Parent in redemption of its bonds pursuant to the liquidation of Subsidiary. Explain the tax consequences of the redemption of the stock and bonds to Parent and Subsidiary.

C:6-16 Explain the differences in the tax rules applying to distributions made to the parent corporation and a minority shareholder when a controlled subsidiary corporation liquidates.

C:6-17 Parent Corporation owns 80% of Subsidiary Corporation's stock. Sally owns the remaining 20% of the Subsidiary stock. Subsidiary plans to distribute cash and appreciated property pursuant to its liquidation. It has more than enough cash to redeem all of Sally's stock. What strategy for distributing the cash and appreciated property would minimize the gain recognized by Subsidiary on the distribution? Does the substitution of appreciated property for cash change the tax consequences of the liquidating distribution for Sally?

C:6-18 Parent Corporation owns 70% of Subsidiary Corporation's stock. The FMV of Subsidiary's assets is significantly greater than their basis to Subsidiary. The FMV of Parent's interest in the assets also substantially exceeds Parent's basis for the Subsidiary stock. Also, Parent's basis in its Subsidiary stock exceeds Subsidiary's basis in its assets. On January 30, Parent acquired an additional 15% of Subsidiary stock from one of Subsidiary's shareholders who owns none of the Parent stock. Subsidiary adopts a plan of liquidation on March 12. The liquidation is completed before year-end. What advantages accrue to Parent with respect to the liquidation by acquiring the additional Subsidiary stock?

C:6-19 Texas Corporation liquidates through a series of distributions to its shareholders after a plan of liquidation has been adopted. How are these distributions taxed?

C:6-20 Able Corporation adopts a plan of liquidation. Under the plan, Robert, who owns 60% of the Able stock, is to receive 2,000 acres of land in an area where a number of producing oil wells have been drilled. No wells have been drilled on Able's land. Discussions with two appraisers have produced widely differing market values for the land, both of which are above Able's basis for the land and Robert's basis for the Able stock. Explain the alternatives available to Able and Robert for reporting the liquidating distribution.

C:6-21 Explain the IRS's position regarding whether a liquidation transaction will be considered open or closed.

C:6-22 For a corporation that intends to liquidate, explain the tax advantages to the shareholders of having the corporation (1) adopt a plan of liquidation, (2) sell its assets in an installment sale, and then (3) distribute the installment obligations to its shareholders.

C:6-23 Cable Corporation is 60% owned by Anna and 40% owned by Jim, who are unrelated. It has noncash assets, which it sells to an unrelated purchaser for $100,000 in cash and $900,000 in installment obligations due 50% in the current year and 50% in the following year. Cable will distribute its remaining cash, after payment of the federal income taxes on the sale and other corporate obligations, to Jim and Anna along with the installment obligations. Explain to the two shareholders the alternatives for reporting the gain realized on their receipt of the installment obligations.

C:6-24 Describe the tax treatment accorded the following expenses associated with a liquidation:

a. Commissions paid on the sale of the liquidating corporation's assets
b. Accounting fees paid to prepare the corporation's final income tax return
c. Unamortized organizational expenditures
d. Prepaid rent for office space occupied by one of the shareholders following the liquidation (Assume the prepaid rent was deducted in the preceding year's corporate tax return.)

C:6-25 Yancy owns 70% of Andover Corporation stock. At the beginning of the current year, the corporation has $400,000 of NOLs. Yancy plans to liquidate the corporation and have it distribute assets having a $600,000 FMV and a $350,000 adjusted basis to its shareholders. Explain to Yancy the tax consequences of the liquidation to Andover Corporation.

C:6-26 Nils Corporation, a calendar year taxpayer, adopts a plan of liquidation on April 1 of the current year. The final liquidating distribution occurs on January 5 of next year. Must Nils Corporation file a tax return for the current year? For next year?

C:6-27 What is a plan of liquidation? Why is it advisable for a corporation to adopt a formal plan of liquidation?

C:6-28 Indicate whether each of the following statements about a liquidation is true or false. If the statement is false, explain why.

a. Liabilities assumed by a shareholder when a corporation liquidates reduce the amount realized by the shareholder on the surrender of his or her stock.
b. The loss recognized by a shareholder on a liquidation generally is characterized as an ordinary loss.
c. A shareholder's basis for property received in a liquidation is the same as the property's basis in the liquidating corporation's hands.
d. The holding period for property received in a liquidation includes the period of time it is held by the liquidating corporation.
e. The tax attributes of a liquidating corporation are assumed ratably by its shareholders.
f. A parent corporation can elect to recognize gain or loss when it liquidates a controlled subsidiary corporation.
g. A liquidating subsidiary recognizes no gain or loss when it distributes its property to its parent corporation.
h. A parent corporation's basis for the assets received in a liquidation where gain is not recognized remains the same as it was to the liquidating subsidiary corporation.

ISSUE IDENTIFICATION QUESTIONS

C:6-29 Cable Corporation, which operates a fleet of motorized trolley cars in a resort city, is undergoing a complete liquidation. John, who owns 80% of the Cable stock, plans to continue the business in another city, and will receive the cable cars, two support vehicles, the repair parts inventory, and other tools and equipment. Peter, who owns the remaining 20% of the Cable stock, will receive a cash distribution. The corporation will incur $15,000 of liquidation expenses to break its lease on its office and garage space and cancel other contracts. What tax issues should Cable, John, and Peter consider with respect to the liquidation?

C:6-30 Parent Corporation, which operates an electric utility, created a 100%-owned corporation, Subsidiary, that built and managed an office building. Assume the two corporations have filed separate tax returns for a number of years. The utility occupied two floors of the office building, and Subsidiary offered the other ten floors for lease. Only 25% of the total rental space was leased because of the high crime rate in the area surrounding the building. Rental income was insufficient to cover the mortgage payments, and Subsidiary filed for bankruptcy because of the poor prospects. Subsidiary's assets were taken over by the mortgage lender. Parent lost its entire $500,000 investment. Another $100,000 of debts remained unpaid for the general creditors, which included a $35,000 account payable to Parent, at the time Subsidiary was liquidated. What tax issues should Parent and Subsidiary consider with respect to the bankruptcy and liquidation of Subsidiary?

C:6-31 Alpha Corporation is a holding company owned equally by Harry and Rita. They acquired the Alpha stock many years ago when the corporation was formed. Alpha has its money invested almost entirely in stocks, bonds, rental real estate, and land. Market quotations are available for all of its stock and bond investments except for 10,000 shares of Mayfair Manufacturing Corporation stock. Mayfair is privately held with 40 individuals owning all 100,000 outstanding shares. Last year, Mayfair reported slightly more than $3 million in net income. In a discussion with Harry and Rita, you find that they plan to liquidate Alpha Corporation in the next six months to avoid the personal holding company tax. What tax issues should Harry and Rita consider with respect to this pending liquidation?

PROBLEMS

C:6-32 *Shareholder Gain or Loss Calculation.* For seven years, Monaco Corporation has been owned entirely by Stacy and Monique, who are husband and wife. Stacy and Monique have a $165,000 basis in their jointly owned Monaco stock. The Monaco stock is Sec. 1244 stock. They receive the following assets in liquidation of their corporation: accounts receivable, $25,000 FMV; a car, $16,000 FMV; office furniture, $6,000 FMV; and $5,000 cash.

a. What are the amount and character of their gain or loss?
b. How would your answer change if the accounts receivable instead had a $140,000 FMV?
c. What is the Monaco's basis for each property received in the liquidation in Parts a and b?

C:6-33 *Shareholder Gain or Loss Calculation.* For three years, Diamond Corporation has been owned equally by Arlene and Billy. Arlene and Billy have $40,000 and $20,000 adjusted bases, respectively, in their Diamond stock. Arlene receives a $30,000 cash liquidating distribution in exchange for her Diamond stock. Billy receives as a liquidating distribution a parcel of land having a $70,000 FMV and subject to a $45,000 mortgage, which he assumes, and $5,000 of cash in exchange for his Diamond stock.

a. What are the amount and character of each shareholder's gain or loss?
b. What is each shareholder's basis for the property received in the liquidation?

C:6-34 *Timing of Gain/Loss Recognition.* Peter owns 25% of Crosstown Corporation stock in which he has a $200,000 adjusted basis. In each of the following situations, what amount of gain/loss will Peter report in the current year? In the next year?

a. Peter is a cash method of accounting taxpayer. Crosstown determines on December 24 of the current year that it will make a $260,000 liquidating distribution to Peter. Crosstown pays the liquidating distribution on January 3 of the next year.
b. Assume the same facts as in Part a except that Peter is an accrual method of accounting taxpayer.

C:6-35 *Corporate Formation/Corporate Liquidation.* Len Wallace contributed assets with a $100,000 adjusted basis and a $400,000 FMV to Ace Corporation in exchange for all of its single class of stock. The corporation conducted operations for five years and was liquidated. Len received a liquidating distribution of $500,000 cash (less federal income taxes owed on the liquidation by the corporation) and the assets that he had contributed, which now have a $100,000 adjusted basis and a $500,000 FMV. Assume a 34% corporate tax rate.

a. What are the tax consequences of the corporate formation transaction?
b. What are the tax consequences of the corporate liquidation transaction?
c. Would your answers to Parts a and b remain the same if instead the assets had been contributed by Wallace Corporation to Ace Corporation? If not, explain how your answer(s) would change?

C:6-36 *Gain or Loss on Making a Liquidating Distribution.* What are the amount and character of the gain or loss recognized by the distributing corporation when making liquidating distributions in the following situations? What is the shareholder's basis for the property received? In any situation where a loss is disallowed, indicate what changes would be necessary to improve the tax consequences of the transaction.

a. Best Corporation distributes land having a $200,000 FMV and a $90,000 adjusted basis to Tanya, its sole shareholder. The land, a capital asset, is subject to a $40,000 mortgage, which Tanya assumes.
b. Wilkins Corporation distributes depreciable property to its two equal shareholders. Robert receives a milling machine having a $50,000 adjusted basis and a $75,000 FMV. The corporation claimed $30,000 depreciation on the machine. The corporation purchased the milling machine from an unrelated seller four years ago. Sharon receives an automobile that originally cost $40,000 two years earlier and has a $26,000 FMV. The corporation claimed $25,000 depreciation on the automobile.
c. Jordan Corporation distributes marketable securities having a $100,000 FMV and a $175,000 adjusted basis to Brad, a 66.67% shareholder. Jordan purchased the marketable securities three years ago. Jordan distributes $50,000 cash to Ann, a 33.33% shareholder.
d. Assume the same facts as in Part c except the securities and cash are instead each distributed two-thirds to Brad and one-third to Ann.

C:6-37 *Gain or Loss Recognition by a Distributing Corporation.* Melon Corporation, which is owned equally by four individual shareholders, adopts a plan of liquidation for distributing the following property:

- Land (a capital asset) having a $30,000 FMV and a $12,000 adjusted basis.
- Depreciable personal property having a $15,000 FMV and a $9,000 adjusted basis. Melon has claimed depreciation of $10,000 on the property during the three years since its acquisition.
- Installment obligations having a $30,000 FMV and face amount and a $21,000 adjusted basis, acquired when Melon sold a Sec. 1231 property.
- Supplies that cost $6,000 and were expensed in the preceding tax year. The supplies have a $7,500 FMV.
- Marketable securities having a $15,000 FMV and an $18,000 adjusted basis. Melon purchased the marketable securities from a broker 12 months ago.

a. Which property, when distributed by Melon Corporation to one of its shareholders, will require the distributing corporation to recognize gain or loss?
b. How will your answer to Part a change if the distribution instead is made to Melon's parent corporation as part of a complete liquidation meeting the Sec. 332 requirements?
c. How will your answer to Part b change if the distribution instead is made to a minority shareholder?

C:6-38 ***Distribution of Property Subject to a Mortgage.*** Titan Corporation adopts a plan of liquidation. It distributes an apartment building having a $3 million FMV and a $1.8 million adjusted basis, and land having a $1 million FMV and a $600,000 adjusted basis, to MNO Partnership in exchange for all the outstanding Titan stock. MNO Partnership has an $800,000 basis in its Titan stock. Titan has claimed $600,000 of MACRS depreciation on the building. MNO Partnership agrees to assume the $3 million mortgage on the land and building. All of Titan's assets other than the building and land are used to pay its federal income tax liability.

a. What are the amount and character of Titan's recognized gain or loss on the distribution?
b. What are the amount and character of MNO Partnership's gain or loss on the liquidation? What is its basis for the land and building?
c. How would your answer to Parts a and b change if the mortgage instead was $4.5 million?

C:6-39 ***Sale of Loss Property by a Liquidating Corporation.*** In March of Year 2, Mike contributed the following two properties, which he acquired in February of Year 1, to Kansas Corporation in exchange for additional Kansas stock: (1) land having a $50,000 FMV and a $75,000 basis and (2) another property having an $85,000 FMV and a $70,000 adjusted basis. Kansas' employees use the land as a parking lot until Kansas sells it in March of Year 3 for $45,000. One month after the sale, in April of Year 3, Kansas adopts a plan of liquidation.

a. What is Kansas' adjusted basis in the land immediately after its contribution in March of Year 2?
b. What is Kansas' recognized gain or loss on the subsequent land sale?
c. How would your answer to Part b change if the land were not used in Kansas' trade or business?
d. How would your answer to Part c change if Mike contributed the land and other property in March of Year 1 instead of March of Year 2?
e. How would your answer to Part c change if the corporation sold the land (contributed in March of Year 2) for $80,000 instead of $45,000?

C:6-40 ***Tax Consequences of a Corporate Liquidation.*** Marsha owns 100% of Gamma Corporation's common stock. Gamma is an accrual basis, calendar year corporation. Marsha formed the corporation six years ago by transferring $250,000 of cash in exchange for the Gamma stock. Thus, she has held the stock for six years and has a $250,000 adjusted basis in the stock. Gamma's balance sheet at January 1 of the current year is as follows:

Assets	*Basis*	*FMV*
Cash	$ 400,000	$ 400,000
Marketable securities	50,000	125,000
Inventory	300,000	350,000
Equipment	200,000	275,000
Building	500,000	750,000
Total	$1,450,000	$1,900,000

Liabilities and Equity		
Accounts payable	$ 175,000	$ 175,000
Common stock	250,000	1,725,000
Retained earnings (and E&P)	1,025,000	
Total	$1,450,000	$1,900,000

Gamma has held the marketable securities for two years. In addition, Gamma has claimed $60,000 of MACRS depreciation on the machinery and $90,000 of straight-line depreciation on the building. On January 2 of the current year, Gamma liquidates and distributes all property to Marsha except that Gamma retains cash to pay the accounts payable and any tax liability resulting from Gamma's liquidation. Assume that Gamma has no other taxable income or loss. Determine the tax consequences to Gamma and Marsha. Assume a 34% corporate tax rate.

C:6-41 ***Sale of Assets Followed by a Corporation Liquidation.*** Assume the same facts as in Problem C:6-40 except, on January 2 of the current year, Gamma Corporation sells all property other than cash to Acquiring Corporation for FMV. Gamma pays off the accounts payable and retains cash to pay any tax liability resulting from Gamma's liquidation. Gamma then liquidates and distributes all remaining cash to Marsha. Assume that Gamma has no other taxable income or loss. Determine the tax consequence to Gamma, Acquiring, and Marsha. How do these results compare to those in Problem C:6-40?

C:6-42 ***Tax Consequences of a Corporate Liquidation.*** Pamela owns 100% of Sigma Corporation's stock. She purchased her stock ten years ago, and her current basis for the stock is $300,000. On June 10, Pamela decided to liquidate Sigma. Sigma's balance sheet prior to the sale of the assets, payment of the liquidation expenses, and payment of federal income taxes is as follows:

Assets	*Basis*	*FMV*
Cash	$240,000	$ 240,000
Marketable securities	90,000	80,000
Equipment	150,000	200,000
Land	320,000	680,000
Total	$800,000	$1,200,000
Equity		
Common stock	$300,000	$1,200,000
Retained earnings (and E&P)	500,000	
Total	$800,000	$1,200,000

- The corporation has claimed depreciation of $150,000 on the equipment.
- The corporation received the marketable securities as a capital contribution from Pamela three years earlier at a time when their adjusted basis was $90,000 and their FMV was $70,000.
- Sigma incurred $20,000 in liquidation expenses in its final tax year.

a. What are the tax consequences of the liquidation to Pamela and Sigma Corporation? Assume a 34% corporate tax rate.

b. How would your answer change if Pamela contributed the marketable securities six years ago?

C:6-43 ***Liquidation of a Subsidiary Corporation.*** Parent Corporation owns 100% of Subsidiary Corporation's stock. The adjusted basis of its stock investment is $175,000. A plan of liquidation is adopted, and Subsidiary distributes to Parent assets having a $400,000 FMV and a $300,000 adjusted basis (to Subsidiary), and liabilities in the amount of $60,000. Subsidiary has a $150,000 E&P balance.

a. What are the amount and character of Subsidiary's recognized gain or loss on the distribution?

b. What are the amount and character of Parent's recognized gain or loss on the surrender of the Subsidiary stock?

c. What basis does Parent take in the assets?

d. What happens to Parent's basis in the Subsidiary stock and to Subsidiary's tax attributes?

C:6-44 ***Liquidation of a Subsidiary Corporation.*** Parent Corporation owns 100% of Subsidiary Corporation's single class of stock. Its adjusted basis for the stock is $175,000. After adopting a plan of liquidation, Subsidiary distributes the following property to Parent: money, $20,000; LIFO inventory, $200,000 FMV; and equipment, $150,000 FMV. The inventory has a $125,000 adjusted basis. The equipment originally cost $280,000. Subsidiary has claimed depreciation of $160,000 on the equipment. Subsidiary has a $150,000 E&P balance and a $40,000 NOL carryover on the liquidation date.

a. What are the amount and character of Subsidiary's recognized gain or loss when it makes the liquidating distributions?

b. What are the amount and character of Parent's recognized gain or loss on its surrender of the Subsidiary stock?

c. What is Parent's basis in each noncash property?

d. What happens to Subsidiary's E&P balance and NOL carryover following the liquidation?

e. What happens to Parent's $175,000 basis in the Subsidiary stock?

C:6-45 ***Liquidation of a Subsidiary Corporation.*** Parent Corporation owns 100% of Subsidiary Corporation's single class of stock and $2 million of Subsidiary debentures. Parent purchased the debentures in small blocks from various unrelated parties at a $100,000 discount from their face amount. Parent has a $1.3 million basis in the Subsidiary stock. Subsidiary adopts a plan of liquidation whereby it distributes property having a $4 million FMV and a $2.4 million adjusted basis in redemption of the Subsidiary stock. The debentures are redeemed for Subsidiary property having a $2 million FMV and a $2.2 million adjusted basis.

a. What income or gain does Subsidiary recognize as a result of making the liquidating distributions?

b. What gain or loss does Parent recognize on the surrender of the Subsidiary stock? The Subsidiary debentures?

c. What is Parent's basis for the property received from Subsidiary?

C:6-46 ***Comparison of Liquidations.*** Shareholder owns 100% of Lambda Corporation stock and has a $700,000 basis in that stock. Shareholder has owned the stock for several years. Prior to liquidating, Lambda had the following balance sheet:

Assets	*Basis*	*FMV*
Cash	$200,000	$ 200,000
Property	600,000	1,000,000
Total	$800,000	$1,200,000
Equity		
Common stock	$700,000	$1,200,000
Retained earnings (and E&P)	100,000	
Total	$800,000	$1,200,000

For Parts a and b below, determine the following results for the liquidating corporation (Lambda): Gain realized, gain recognized, corporate tax, and disposition of E&P. For Shareholder, determine the following results: Total distribution, gain realized, gain recognized, and basis of noncash property received. Assume a 34% corporate tax rate and that the liquidating corporation pays any necessary taxes resulting from the liquidation. Also, assume no other transactions for the year of liquidation.

a. Shareholder is an individual.

b. Shareholder is a parent corporation of Lambda.

C:6-47 ***Liquidation of an Insolvent Subsidiary.*** Subsidiary Corporation is a wholly owned subsidiary of Parent Corporation. The two corporations have the following balance sheets:

Assets	*Parent*	*Subsidiary*
General assets	$1,500,000	$ 750,000
Investment in Subsidiary stock	200,000	
Note receivable from Subsidiary	1,000,000	
Total	$2,700,000	$ 750,000

Liabilities & Equity		
General liabilities	$1,500,000	$ 150,000
Note payable to Parent		1,000,000
Common Stock	300,000	200,000
Retained earnings (deficit)	900,000	(600,000)
Total	$2,700,000	$ 750,000

Other Facts:

- Parent's basis in its Subsidiary stock is $200,000, which corresponds to the $200,000 common stock on Subsidiary's balance sheet.
- The $1 million note payable on Subsidiary's balance sheet is payable to Parent and corresponds to the note receivable on Parent's balance sheet.
- The corporations do not file consolidated tax returns.
- Subsidiary has $600,000 of net operating loss (NOL) carryovers.
- The FMV and adjusted basis of Subsidiary's assets are the same amount.
- Just prior to the liquidation, Subsidiary uses $150,000 of its assets to pay off its general liabilities.
- Subsidiary transfers all its assets and liabilities to Parent upon a complete liquidation.

Determine the tax consequences to Parent and Subsidiary upon Subsidiary's liquidation.

C:6-48 ***Liquidation of a Subsidiary Corporation.*** Majority Corporation owns 90% of Subsidiary Corporation's stock and has a $45,000 basis in that stock. Mindy owns the other 10% and has a $5,000 basis in her stock. Subsidiary holds $20,000 cash and other assets having a $110,000 FMV and a $40,000 adjusted basis. Pursuant to a plan of liquidation, Subsidiary (1) distributes to Mindy assets having an $11,000 FMV and a $4,000 adjusted basis prior to the liquidation, (2) distributes to Majority assets having a $99,000 FMV and a $36,000 adjusted basis prior to the liquidation, and (3) distributes ratably to the two shareholders any cash remaining after taxes. Assume a 34% corporate tax rate and a 15% capital gains tax rate.

a. What are the tax consequences of the liquidation to Majority Corporation, Subsidiary Corporation, and Mindy?

b. Can you recommend a different distribution of assets that will produce better tax results than in Part a?

C:6-49 ***Tax Consequences of a Corporate Liquidation.*** Gabriel Corporation is owned 90% by Zeier Corporation and 10% by Ray Goff, a Gabriel employee. A preliquidation balance sheet for Gabriel is presented below:

Assets	*Basis*	*FMV*
Cash	$ 100,000	$ 100,000
Inventory	420,000	700,000
Equipment	80,000	100,000
Land	400,000	300,000
Total	$1,000,000	$1,200,000
Liabilities & Equity		
Accounts payable	$ 100,000	$ 100,000
Bonds payable	500,000	500,000
Common stock	100,000	600,000
Retained earnings (and E&P)	300,000	
Total	$1,000,000	$1,200,000

Gabriel has claimed $150,000 of MACRS depreciation on the equipment. Gabriel purchased the land three years ago as a potential plant site. Plans to build the plant never were consummated, and Gabriel has held the land since then as an investment. Zeier and Ray Goff have $90,000 and $10,000 bases, respectively, in their Gabriel stock. Both shareholders have held their stock since the corporation's inception ten years ago. Zeier purchased the Gabriel bonds from an insurance company two years ago for $20,000 above their face amount. Gabriel adopts a plan of liquidation. Gabriel transfers $500,000 of inventory to Zeier to retire the bonds. The shareholders receive their share of Gabriel's remaining assets and assume their share of Gabriel's liabilities (other than federal income taxes). Gabriel pays federal income taxes owed on the liquidation. Assume a 34% corporate tax rate. What are the tax consequences of the liquidation to Ray Goff, Zeier Corporation, and Gabriel Corporation?

C:6-50 *Tax Consequences of a Corporate Liquidation.* Art owns 80% of Pueblo Corporation stock, and Peggy owns the remaining 20%. Art and Peggy have $320,000 and $80,000 adjusted bases, respectively, for their Pueblo stock. Pueblo owns the following assets: cash, $25,000; inventory, $150,000 FMV and $100,000 adjusted basis; marketable securities, $100,000 FMV and $125,000 adjusted basis; and equipment, $325,000 FMV and $185,000 adjusted basis. Pueblo purchased the equipment four years ago and subsequently claimed $215,000 of MACRS depreciation. The securities are not disqualified property. On July 1 of the current year, Pueblo adopts a plan of liquidation at a time when it has $250,000 of E&P and no liabilities. Pueblo distributes the equipment, $50,000 of inventory, the marketable securities, and $5,000 of money to Art before year-end as a liquidating distribution. Pueblo also distributes $20,000 of cash and $100,000 of inventory to Peggy before year-end as a liquidating distribution.

a. What are the gain and loss tax consequences of the liquidation to Pueblo Corporation and to Art and Peggy?
b. Can you offer any suggestions to Pueblo's management that could improve the tax consequences of the liquidation? Explain.
c. How would your answers to Parts a and b change if Art and Peggy instead were domestic corporations rather than individuals?

C:6-51 *Tax Attribute Carryovers.* Bell Corporation is 100% owned by George, who has a $400,000 basis in his Bell stock. Bell's operations have been unprofitable in recent years, and it has incurred small NOLs. Its operating assets currently have a $300,000 FMV and a $500,000 adjusted basis. George is approached by Time Corporation, which wants to purchase Bell's assets for $300,000. Bell expects to have approximately $200,000 in cash after the payment of its liabilities.

a. What are the tax consequences of the transaction if Bell adopts a plan of liquidation, sells the assets, and distributes the cash in redemption of the Bell stock within a 12-month period?
b. What advantages (if any) would accrue to Bell and George if the corporation remains in existence and uses the $200,000 of cash that remains after payment of the liabilities to conduct a new trade or business?

C:6-52 *Series of Liquidating Distributions.* Union Corporation is owned equally by Ron and Steve. Ron and Steve purchased their stock several years ago and have adjusted bases for their Union stock of $15,000 and $27,500, respectively. Each shareholder receives two liquidating distributions. The first liquidating distribution, made in the current year, results in each shareholder receiving a one-half interest in a parcel of land that has a $40,000 FMV and an $18,000 adjusted basis to Union Corporation. The second liquidating distribution, made in the next year, results in each shareholder receiving $20,000 in cash.

a. What are the amount and character of Ron and Steve's recognized gain or loss for the current year? For the next year?
b. What is the basis of the land in Ron and Steve's hands?
c. How would your answers to Parts a and b change if the land has a $12,000 FMV instead of a $40,000 FMV?

C:6-53 *Subsequent Assessment on the Shareholders.* Meridian Corporation originally was owned equally by five individual shareholders. Four years ago, Meridian adopted a plan of liquidation, and each shareholder received a liquidating distribution. Tina, a cash method taxpayer, reported a $30,000 long-term capital gain in the prior liquidation year on the redemption of her stock. Pending the outcome of a lawsuit in which Meridian is one of the defendents, $5,000 of Tina's liquidating distribution was held back and placed in escrow. Settlement of the lawsuit in the current year requires that the escrowed funds plus the interest earned on these funds be paid out to the plaintiff and that each shareholder pay an additional $2,500. Tina pays the amount due in the next year. How does Tina report the settlement of the lawsuit and the payment of the additional amount?

COMPREHENSIVE PROBLEM

C:6-54 The following facts pertain to Lifecycle Corporation:

- Able owns a parcel of land (Land A) having a $30,000 FMV and $16,000 adjusted basis. Baker owns an adjacent parcel of land (Land B) having a $20,000 FMV and $22,000 adjusted basis. On January 2, 2015, Able and Baker contribute their parcels of land to newly formed Lifecycle Corporation in exchange for 60% of the corporation's stock for Able and 40% of the corporation's stock for Baker. The corporation elects a calendar tax year and the accrual method of accounting.
- On January 2, 2015, the corporation borrows $2 million and uses the loan proceeds to build a factory ($1 million), purchase equipment ($500,000), produce inventory ($450,000), pay other operating expenses ($30,000), and retain working cash ($20,000). Assume the corporation sells all inventory produced and collects on all sales immediately so that, at the end of any year, the corporation has no accounts receivable or inventory balances.
- Operating results for 2015 are as follows:

Sales	$964,000	
Cost of goods sold	450,000	
Interest paid on loan	140,000	
Depreciation:		
Equipment	70,000	($25,000 for E&P)
Building	24,000	($24,000 for E&P)
Operating expenses	30,000	

Of these amounts, $250,000 is qualified production activities income. The deduction percentage is 9%.

- In 2016, Lifecycle Corporation invests $10,000 of excess cash in Macro Corporation stock (less than 20% owned) and $20,000 in tax-exempt bonds. In addition, the corporation pays Able a $12,000 salary and distributes an additional $42,000 to Able and $28,000 to Baker. The corporation also makes a $100,000 principal payment on the loan.
- Results for 2016 are as follows:

Sales	$990,000	
Cost of goods sold	500,000	
Interest paid on loan	130,000	
Depreciation:		
Equipment	125,000	($50,000 for E&P)
Building	25,000	($25,000 for E&P)
Operating expenses	40,000	
Salary paid to Able	12,000	
Dividend received on Macro Corporation stock	2,000	
Short-term capital gain on sale of portion of Macro Corporation stock holdings ($4,000 − $3,000)	1,000	
Tax-exempt interest received	1,500	
Charitable contributions	500	

Of these amounts, $158,000 is qualified production activities income. The deduction percentage is 9%.

- In 2017, the corporation did not pay a salary to Able and made no distributions to the shareholders. The corporation, however, made a $30,000 principal payment on the loan.
- Results for 2017 are as follows:

Sales	$500,000
Cost of goods sold	280,000
Interest paid on loan	125,000

Depreciation:		
Equipment	90,000	($50,000 for E&P)
Building	25,000	($25,000 for E&P)
Operating expenses	60,000	
Long-term capital gain on sale of remaining Macro Corporation stock ($9,000 − $7,000)	2,000	
Long-term capital gain on sale of tax-exempt bond ($21,000 − $20,000)	1,000	

Of these amounts, qualified production activities income is zero (because it is negative).

- On January 2, 2018, the corporation receives a refund for the 2017 NOL carried back to 2015. When carrying back the NOL, remember to recalculate the U.S. production activities deduction in the carryback year because of the reduced taxable income resulting from carryback. In addition, the corporation sells its assets, pays taxes on the gain, and pays off the $1.87 million remaining debt.

	Sales Price	*Tax Adj. Basis**	*E&P Adj. Basis*
Equipment	$ 250,000	$ 215,000	$ 375,000
Building	986,000	926,000	926,000
Land A	80,000	16,000	16,000
Land B	50,000	20,000	20,000
Total	$1,366,000	$1,177,000	$1,337,000

*Note: Technically, the equipment should be depreciated for 1/2 year in the year of disposition, and the building should be depreciated for 1/2 month (because of the January disposition). However, for simplicity, the above calculations ignore depreciation deductions in the disposition year, which creates an offsetting overstatement of adjusted basis. Section 362(e)(2) limits Land B basis to the FMV.

Immediately after these transactions, the corporation makes a liquidating distribution of the remaining cash to Able and Baker. The remaining cash is $348,639, which the corporation distributes in proportion to the shareholders' ownership (60% and 40%). Assume that the shareholder's long-term capital gains will be taxed in 2018 at 23.8% (the 20% maximum capital gains rate plus the 3.8% rate on net investment income).

Required:

a. Determine the tax consequences of the corporate formation to Able, Baker, and Lifecycle Corporation.
b. For 2015 through 2017, prepare schedules showing corporate taxable income, taxes, and E&P activity. Assume that Lifecycle pays its taxes in the same year they accrue.
c. For 2018, prepare a schedule showing the results of this year's transactions on Lifecycle Corporation, Able, and Baker.

Note: See Problem C:10-56 for a partnership variation of this problem.

TAX STRATEGY PROBLEMS

C:6-55 Sarah plans to invest $1 million in a business venture that will last five years. She is debating whether to operate the business as a C corporation or a sole proprietorship. If a C corporation, she will liquidate the corporation at the end of the five-year period. She expects the business to generate taxable income as follows:

Year	*Taxable Income*
1	$ 40,000
2	70,000
3	90,000
4	150,000
5	350,000

If incurred in corporate form, these taxable income amounts will be subject to the corporate tax rate schedule. If in proprietorship form, they will be subject to Sarah's 39.6% marginal tax rate because she has income from other sources that puts her in the top individual tax bracket. Any capital gain upon corporate liquidation will be taxed at 23.8% (the 20% maximum capital gain rate plus the 3.8% rate on net investment income). Assume that Sec. 1202 does not apply.

Required: Determine the after-tax amount Sarah will have at the end of five years under each alternative. Which alternative do you recommend?

C:6-56 One way to compare the accumulation of income by alternative business entity forms is to use mathematical models. The following models express the investment after-tax accumulation calculation for a particular entity form:

Flow-through entities and sole proprietorships: $\text{Contribution} \times [1 + R(1 - t_p)]^n$
C corporation: $\text{Contribution} \times \{[1 + R(1 - t_c)]^n(1 - t_g) + t_g\}$

Where: ATA = after-tax accumulation in n years
R = before-tax rate of return for the business entity
t_p = owner's marginal tax rate on ordinary income
t_c = corporation's marginal tax rate
t_g = owner's tax rate on capital gains
n = number of periods

In the C corporation model, the corporation operates for n years, paying taxes currently and distributing no dividends. At the end of its existence, the corporation liquidates, causing the shareholder to recognize a capital gain. In the flow-through model, the entity or sole proprietorship distributes just enough cash for the owner or owners to pay individual taxes, and the entity reinvests the remaining after-tax earnings in the business. (See Chapter I:18 of the *Individuals* volume for a detailed explanation of these models. The *Comprehensive* volume, however, does not contain Chapter I:18.)

Now consider the following facts. Twelve years ago, your client formed a C corporation with a \$100,000 investment (contribution). The corporation's before-tax rate of return (R) has been and will continue to be 10%. The corporate tax rate (t_c) has been and will continue to be 35%. The corporation pays no dividends and reinvests all after-tax earnings in its business. Thus, the corporation's value grows at its after-tax rate of return. Your client's marginal ordinary tax rate (t_p) has been 33%, and her capital gains rate (t_g) has been 15%. Your client expects her ordinary tax rate to drop to 25% at the beginning of this year and stay at that level indefinitely. Her capital gains tax rate will remain at 15%. Assume the corporate stock does not qualify for the Sec. 1202 exclusion.

Your client wants you to consider two alternatives:

(1) Continue the business in C corporation form for the next 20 years and liquidate at that time (32 years in total).

(2) Liquidate the C corporation at the end of the 12-year period, invest the after-tax proceeds in a sole proprietorship, and operate as a sole proprietorship for the next 20 years.

The sole proprietorship's before-tax rate of return (R) also will be 10% for the next 20 years. Earnings from the sole proprietorship will be taxed currently at your client's ordinary tax rate, and your client will withdraw just enough earnings from the business to pay her taxes on the business's income. The remaining after-tax earnings will remain in the business until the end of the investment horizon (20 years from now).

Required: Show the results of each alternative along with supporting models and calculations. Ignore self employment taxes and the accumulated earnings tax. Which alternative should your client adopt?

Note: See Problem C:11-61 for a third alternative to consider.

CASE STUDY PROBLEMS

C:6-57 Paul, a long-time client of yours, has operated an automobile repair shop (as a C corporation) for most of his life. The shop has been fairly successful in recent years. His children are not interested in continuing the business. Paul is age 62 and has accumulated approximately \$500,000 in assets outside of his business, most of which are in his personal residence and retirement plan. A recent balance sheet for the business shows the following amounts:

Assets	*Adjusted Basis*	*FMV*	*Liabilities & Equity*	*Amount*
Cash	$ 25,000	$ 25,000	Accounts payable	$ 30,000
Inventory	60,000	75,000	Mortgage payable	70,000
Equipment	200,000	350,000	Paid-in capital	120,000
Building	100,000	160,000	Retain earnings	205,000
Land	40,000	60,000		
Goodwill	–0–	100,000		
Total	$425,000	$770,000	Total	$425,000

The inventory is accounted for using the first-in, first-out inventory method. The corporation has claimed depreciation of $250,000 on the equipment. The corporation acquired the building 11 years ago and has claimed $25,000 of depreciation under the MACRS rules. The goodwill is an estimate that Paul feels reflects the value of his business over and above the other tangible assets.

Paul has received an offer of $775,000 from a competing automobile repair company for the noncash assets of his business, which will be used to establish a second location for the competing company. The corporation will sell the assets within 60 days and distribute remaining cash to Paul in liquidation of the corporation. The purchaser has obtained the necessary bank financing to make the acquisition. Paul's basis in his stock is $300,000.

Required: Prepare a memorandum for Paul outlining the tax consequences of the sale transaction and liquidation of the corporation.

C:6-58 Your accounting firm has done the audit and tax work for the Peerless family and their business entities for 20 years. Approximately 25% of your accounting and tax practice billings come from Peerless family work. Peerless Real Estate Corporation owns land and a building (MACRS property) having a $4.5 million FMV and a $1.0 million adjusted basis. The corporation owes a $1.3 million mortgage balance on the building. The corporation used substantial leverage to acquire the building so Myron Peerless and his brother Mark Peerless, who are equal shareholders in Peerless Real Estate, each have only $200,000 adjusted bases in their stock. Cash flows are good from the building, and only a small portion of the annual profits is needed for reinvestment in the building. Myron and Mark have decided to liquidate the corporation to avoid the federal and state corporate income taxes and continue to operate the business as a partnership. They want the MM Partnership, which has Mark and Myron equally sharing profits, losses, and liabilities, to purchase the building from the corporation for $400,000 cash plus their assumption of the $1.3 million mortgage. Mark knows a real estate appraiser who, for the right price, will provide a $1.7 million appraisal. Current corporate cash balances are sufficient to pay any federal and state income taxes owed on the sale of the building. Mark and Myron each would receive $200,000 from the corporation in cancellation of their stock.

Required: Prepare notes on the points you will want to cover with Myron and Mark Peerless about the corporate liquidation and the Peerless' desire to avoid federal and state corporate income taxes at your meeting tomorrow.

TAX RESEARCH PROBLEMS

C:6-59 Parent Corporation owns 85% of the common stock and 100% of the preferred stock of Subsidiary Corporation. The common stock and preferred stock have adjusted bases of $500,000 and $200,000, respectively, to Parent. Subsidiary adopts a plan of liquidation on July 3 of the current year, when its assets have a $1 million FMV. Liabilities on that date amount to $850,000. On November 9, Subsidiary pays off its creditors and distributes $150,000 to Parent with respect to its preferred stock. No cash remains to be paid to Parent with respect to the remaining $50,000 of its liquidation preference for the preferred stock, or with respect to any of the common stock. In each of Subsidiary's tax years, less than 10% of its gross income has been passive income. What are the amount and character of Parent's loss on the preferred stock? The common stock?

A partial list of research sources is

- IRC Secs. 165(g)(3) and 332(a)
- Reg. Sec. 1.332-2(b)
- *Spaulding Bakeries, Inc.*, 27 T.C. 684 (1957)
- *H. K. Porter Co., Inc.*, 87 T.C. 689 (1986)

C:6-60 Parent Corporation has owned 60% of Subsidiary Corporation's single class of stock for a number of years. Tyrone owns the remaining 40% of the Subsidiary stock. On August 10 of the current year, Parent purchases Tyrone's Subsidiary stock for cash. On September 15, Subsidiary adopts a plan of liquidation. Subsidiary then makes a single liquidating distribution on October 1. The activities of Subsidiary continue as a separate division of Parent. Does the liquidation of Subsidiary qualify for nonrecognition treatment under Secs. 332 and 337? Must Parent assume Subsidiary's E&P balance?

A partial list of research sources is

- IRC Secs. 332(b) and 381
- Reg. Sec. 1.332-2(a)

CHAPTER

7

CORPORATE ACQUISITIONS AND REORGANIZATIONS

LEARNING OBJECTIVES

After studying this chapter, you should be able to

1. Identify types of taxable acquisitions and determine the consequences of a Sec. 338 deemed sale election
2. Distinguish between taxable and nontaxable acquisitions
3. Recognize the types of nontaxable reorganizations and determine their tax consequences
4. Describe the structure and requirements of each type of acquisitive reorganization
5. Describe the structure and requirements of divisive reorganizations
6. Define other types of reorganizations
7. Explain judicial doctrines pertaining to corporate reorganizations
8. Assess what happens to NOL carryovers and other tax attributes in a reorganization
9. Identify tax planning opportunities in taxable acquisitions and reorganizations
10. Comply with procedural rules for taxable acquisitions and reorganizations
11. Determine the financial statement implications of corporate acquisitions

CHAPTER OUTLINE

A corporation's directors or shareholders may decide to acquire a second corporation either directly or indirectly. Alternatively, they may decide to divest the corporation of part or all of its assets, such as the assets of an operating division or stock in a subsidiary. Depending on the transactional structure, these acquisitions or divestitures can be either taxable or nontaxable. In a taxable transaction, the entire realized gain or loss is recognized. To qualify as nontaxable, the transaction must meet certain statutory and judicial requirements. If the transaction meets these requirements, part or all of the realized gain or loss generally goes unrecognized. This unrecognized gain or loss is deferred until the assets or stock exchanged are sold or disposed of in a taxable transaction. The nontaxable reorganization rules embody the continuity of interest doctrine, which holds that no tax is imposed if the taxpayer retains a continuing interest in the acquired corporation via an equity interest in the acquiring corporation. A tax is imposed, however, where the taxpayer receives cash or property other than stock or securities.[1] On the other hand, taxpayers are likely to engage in a taxable transaction (instead of a nontaxable reorganization) where they prefer to recognize loss on an asset sale or stock disposition.

This chapter presents an overview of taxable and nontaxable acquisitions and divestitures. It also examines the statutory provisions and judicial doctrines that determine the tax consequences of these types of transactions.

TAXABLE ACQUISITION TRANSACTIONS

OBJECTIVE 1

Identify types of taxable acquisitions and determine the consequences of a Sec. 338 deemed sale election

In taxable acquisitions, corporations acquire a **target corporation** in two principal ways.[2] First, they purchase target assets directly from the target corporation. Second, they acquire target corporation stock directly from target shareholders or target's parent corporation. Two options exist once the acquiring corporation has purchased the target stock.

- The acquiring corporation and its new subsidiary can exist as separate entities.
- The acquiring corporation can liquidate its new subsidiary in a nontaxable transaction. Following the liquidation, the parent corporation retains a direct interest in target corporation assets.

Under the first option, the acquiring corporation can make a Sec. 338 election, which adjusts the aggregate basis of subsidiary assets to the price the acquiring corporation paid for the subsidiary stock, plus the amount of any subsidiary liabilities.

The principal asset and stock acquisitions are examined below. Table C:7-1 summarizes the tax consequences of these transactions.

ASSET ACQUISITIONS

From a tax perspective, accounting for an asset purchase is straightforward. The selling corporation simply calculates the gain or loss recognized on the sale of each asset. Sales of depreciable assets (e.g., Sec. 1245 and 1250 property) may result in the recapture of previously claimed depreciation.

The purchaser's bases in the acquired assets equal their acquisition cost.[3] The purchaser eventually can claim depreciation deductions based on the acquisition cost of depreciable property.

A taxable asset acquisition provides the purchaser with two major advantages. First, a significant portion of the acquisition cost can be debt-financed. Interest accruing on the debt is deductible for federal income tax purposes. By contrast, in a nontaxable asset acquisition, the use of debt is either prohibited or restricted. Second, only assets and liabilities specified in the purchase-sale agreement are acquired. The purchaser need not acquire all or substantially all the target corporation's assets, as in the case of a taxable or

TAX STRATEGY TIP

Three types of state taxes may arise in an *asset* sale—transfer taxes, state income taxes, and sales taxes (some state sales tax laws allow certain bulk-sale exceptions). These taxes need to be taken into account by both the buyer and seller when drafting the sales agreement. When a *stock* sale occurs, these taxes can be avoided because the assets remain inside the same entity before and after the stock sale.

---

[1] The tax deferral can be permanent if the stock and securities are held until death. At death, the carryover or substituted basis is stepped up to its fair market value (FMV) without income tax consequences.

[2] The terms *target* and *acquired corporation* are used interchangeably here.

[3] Sec. 1012.

▼ TABLE C:7-1
Comparison of Taxable Acquisition Transactions

		Taxable Stock Acquisition with:		
	Taxable Asset Acquisition	**No Liquidation of Target**	**Nontaxable Liquidation of Target**	**Sec. 338 Election for Target**
Acquiring corporation's basis in stock	N/A	Cost basis	Cost basis initially; disappears upon liquidation of target corporation	Cost basis
Parent-subsidiary relationship created	No	Yes	Yes, until liquidation occurs	Yes
Consolidated tax return election available	No	Yes	Yes, until liquidation occurs	Yes
Gain/loss recognized by target corporation on asset sale	Yes	No	No	Yes, on deemed sale of assets by target corporation
Gain/loss recognized by target corporation upon liquidating	Yes, if target elects to liquidate before or after the asset sale	N/A	No	No
Gain recognized by acquiring corporation in liquidating distribution	N/A	N/A	No	No
Acquiring corporation's basis in assets acquired	Cost basis to acquiring corporation	No change in basis of target corporation's assets	Carryover basis upon liquidation	Cost basis in target stock acquired plus amount of target liabilities
Transfer of tax attributes to acquiring corporation	Remain with target corporation	Remain with target corporation	Carryover to acquiring corporation upon liquidation	Disappear upon deemed sale of assets by old target corporation

N/A = Not applicable.

ADDITIONAL COMMENT

In specific examples and some problems, we will use Alpha Corporation to designate the acquiring corporation and Theta Corporation to designate the target corporation.

nontaxable stock acquisition or a nontaxable asset acquisition. Similarly, the purchaser assumes only liabilities specified in the purchase-sale agreement. Contingent or unknown liabilities generally remain the responsibility of the seller.

The target (acquired) corporation recognizes gain or loss on the sale of assets and may subsequently liquidate. If it liquidates, any property retained by the target corporation is distributed to the shareholders as part of the liquidation. The liquidating corporation recognizes gain or loss on the distribution as if such property had been sold. Upon receiving the liquidating distribution, the target corporation's shareholders each recognize capital gain or loss depending on his or her respective stock basis (see Chapter C:6).

EXAMPLE C:7-1 ▶ Six years ago, Ann, Bob, and Cathy each acquired one-third of Theta Corporation stock. Each shareholder has a $20,000 basis in his or her stock. Alpha Corporation purchases Theta's noncash assets for $100,000 in cash and $300,000 in Alpha debt obligations (three notes at $100,000 each). Theta retains its $50,400 of cash. On the sale date, Theta's noncash assets have a $280,000 adjusted basis and a $400,000 FMV. Its liabilities total $100,000 on the sale date. Theta recognizes a $120,000 aggregate gain [($100,000 + $300,000) − $280,000]. The character of its separate asset gains and losses depends on the type of properties sold. Based on a 34% corporate tax rate, Theta's tax liability on the sale is $40,800 ($120,000 × 0.34). Alpha takes a

$400,000 basis in the noncash assets acquired. After Theta pays its income tax and other liabilities, Theta has remaining cash of $9,600 ($50,400 retained cash + $100,000 cash received − $100,000 liabilities paid − $40,800 tax paid) and holds the three $100,000 notes received. Ann, Bob, and Cathy then decide to liquidate Theta with each receiving $3,200 cash ($9,600 ÷ 3) plus a $100,000 note. Thus, each shareholder recognizes a capital gain of $83,200 ($103,200 − $20,000 stock basis). ◀

Sometimes a target corporation liquidates before it sells its assets. In this case the target corporation distributes the assets to the shareholders who then sell them. The tax consequences of the liquidation are set forth in Chapter C:6. In general, the total tax liability of the corporation and its shareholders are the same whether the liquidation of the target corporation precedes or follows the asset sale.

STOCK ACQUISITIONS

KEY POINT

In a stock acquisition, only the shareholders of the target corporation recognize gain. In an asset acquisition, both the target corporation and its shareholders may recognize gain.

Stock Acquisition with No Liquidation. A stock purchase is the simplest of acquisition transactions. Gain recognized on the sale is capital in character if the stock is a capital asset in the seller's hands. If payment of part or all of the consideration is deferred to a later year, the seller can defer gain recognition under the installment method of accounting.[4] If part of the total amount received by the seller represents consideration for a promise not to compete with the purchaser, this portion is taxed as ordinary income.[5]

The purchaser's basis in the stock is its acquisition cost.[6] The target corporation's basis in its assets ordinarily does not change as a result of the stock sale. Any potential for depreciation recapture that exists on the transaction date remains with the target corporation's assets and, therefore, is assumed by the purchaser. If the target corporation has loss or credit carryovers, these carryovers can be subject to special limitations in the post-acquisition tax years (see pages C:7-43 through C:7-46).

ADDITIONAL COMMENT

A shareholder's basis in stock sometimes is referred to as "outside basis" as opposed to "inside basis," which is the corporation's basis in its assets.

Stock sales are popular with sellers because they often are less costly than asset sales due to a single level of taxation. No adjustment to the bases of the target corporation's assets is made after a stock sale even though the basis of the stock acquired may be substantially higher than the aggregate basis of these assets. Thus, one of the tax advantages of purchasing target corporation assets—a higher asset basis—is not available in a stock purchase unless the purchasing corporation makes a Sec. 338 deemed sale election (discussed later in this chapter).

EXAMPLE C:7-2 ▶ Assume the same facts as in Example C:7-1 except Alpha offers to purchase Theta stock for $50 per share. Ann, Bob, and Cathy tender their 7,000 Theta shares in response to Alpha's offer. Alpha's $350,000 (7,000 shares × $50/share) purchase price equals Theta's net asset value ($450,000 − $100,000 liabilities). Ann, Bob, and Cathy each recognize a long-term capital gain on the sale of their stock. Theta becomes a wholly-owned subsidiary of Alpha and, without a Sec. 338 election, does not adjust the bases of its assets. ◀

KEY POINT

In Example C:7-2, the built-in gain in Theta's assets is not recognized in a stock acquisition. Likewise, the bases of Theta's assets are not stepped-up even though Alpha pays their full $350,000 FMV for the Theta stock.

If the purchasing corporation is a member of an affiliated group that files a consolidated tax return, the new subsidiary must join in the consolidated return election if the purchasing corporation owns at least 80% of the subsidiary's stock and if the subsidiary is an includible corporation (see Chapter C:8). Otherwise, the parent and subsidiary may make an initial consolidated return election.

TYPICAL MISCONCEPTION

Taxpayers often do not understand that the parent's basis in its subsidiary's stock disappears in a Sec. 332 liquidation. Instead, the subsidiary's bases in the liquidated assets carry over to the parent.

Stock Acquisition Followed by a Liquidation. The type of stock acquisition discussed in the preceding section can be followed by a liquidation of the acquired (subsidiary) corporation into its acquiring (parent) corporation. If the parent owns at least 80% of subsidiary stock, the liquidation is nontaxable under the Sec. 332 and 337 rules outlined in Chapter C:6.[7] The bases of the subsidiary's assets carry over to the parent. If the parent paid a premium for the assets (i.e., an amount exceeding the aggregate

[4] Sec. 453(a).

[5] The purchaser can amortize over a 15-year period any amounts paid to the seller with respect to the agreement not to compete (Sec. 197).

[6] Sec. 1012.

[7] The liquidation may be taxable to any minority shareholders and to the subsidiary corporation upon distributions to the minority shareholders.

asset adjusted basis), this premium is lost upon liquidation because the parent's basis in the stock disappears. The stock basis "loss" cannot be deducted and provides no tax benefit. If the parent paid less than the aggregate asset adjusted basis, the "excess" asset basis is included in the asset carryover basis, which can provide additional tax benefits.

EXAMPLE C:7-3 ▶ Assume the same facts as in Example C:7-2 except that, following the stock acquisition, Alpha and Theta Corporations continue to file separate tax returns, and Theta liquidates into Alpha shortly after the acquisition. Theta's assets have the following adjusted bases and FMVs immediately before the sale:

Assets	*Adjusted Basis*	*FMV*
Cash	$ 50,000	$ 50,000
Marketable securities	49,000	55,000
Accounts receivable	60,000	60,000
Inventory	60,000	90,000
Building	27,000	44,000
Land	10,000	26,000
Machinery and equipment[a]	74,000	125,000
Total	$330,000	$450,000

[a]The machinery and equipment are Sec. 1245 property. Recapture potential of the machinery and equipment is $107,000.

Theta and Alpha recognize no gain or loss on the liquidation. Alpha assumes Theta's $100,000 in liabilities and takes a $330,000 total basis in Theta assets, the basis of each asset carrying over. In addition, Alpha inherits all of Theta's tax attributes, including any NOL carryovers, E&P, and the $107,000 depreciation recapture potential of the machinery and equipment. ◀

ADDITIONAL COMMENT

A Sec. 338 election triggers immediate taxation to the target corporation. Therefore, in most situations it makes little sense to pay an immediate tax to obtain a step-up in basis when such additional basis can be recovered only in future years. The election can be beneficial, however, if the target corporation has enough NOLs to offset most or all of the gain recognized on the deemed asset sale. The election also can be beneficial if Sec. 338(h)(10) applies (see footnote 9).

Section 338 Deemed Sale Election. The Sec. 338 **deemed sale election** operates as follows: First target corporation's shareholders sell their stock to the acquiring corporation. Then the acquiring corporation makes a Sec. 338 deemed sale election with respect to the purchased stock. This election results in a hypothetical sale of the "old" target corporation's assets to a "new" target corporation for their **aggregate deemed sale price (ADSP)** in a transaction that requires the seller ("old" target) to recognize gains and losses on its final tax return. The "old" target corporation goes out of existence for tax purposes only.[8] The "new" target corporation is treated as a new entity for tax purposes (i.e., it makes new accounting method and tax year elections). The bases of old target corporation assets are stepped-up or stepped-down to the price paid by the acquiring corporation for target corporation stock plus the amount of target corporation liabilities (including any federal income taxes owed on the hypothetical sale). Corporate purchasers generally do not find the Sec. 338[9] election appealing because, in the year of the election, the target corporation usually incurs a significant tax liability.

PRACTICAL APPLICATION

The purchasing corporation most likely would not make a Sec. 338 election if it resulted in the target corporation's asset tax bases being stepped-down.

Eligible Stock Acquisitions. Section 338 requires the acquiring corporation to purchase 80% or more of target corporation voting stock and 80% or more of the total value of all classes of target stock except certain nonvoting preferred stock during a continuous 12-month (or shorter) qualified stock acquisition period.[10] The acquisition period begins on the date the acquiring corporation first purchases target stock and ends on the date the qualified stock purchase is completed. If the acquiring corporation does not acquire the necessary 80% minimum within the 12-month acquisition period, it cannot make a Sec. 338 election.

---

[8] The target corporation's legal existence does not change under the applicable corporation laws. For federal income tax purposes only, the target corporation (commonly referred to as "old" target) goes out of existence. A "new" target corporation is created. For tax purposes, this new corporation acquires all the assets of the "old" corporation.

[9] An alternative Sec. 338 election is permitted under Sec. 338(h)(10) for members of an affiliated group. This election generally is used by affiliated groups that file consolidated tax returns. The Sec. 338(h)(10) election permits the target corporation (e.g., a subsidiary) to recognize gain or loss as if it had sold its assets in a single transaction. The corporation selling the stock (e.g., a parent corporation) does not recognize gain on the stock sale, thereby resulting in a single level of taxation. This special Sec. 338 election has become popular in recent years. In addition, the Treasury Department has issued Reg. Secs. 1.336-2–1.336-5, which would allow a parent corporation to elect under Sec. 336(e) to treat certain dispositions of a subsidiary corporation's stock as a taxable sale of the subsidiary's underlying assets. See page C:7-10.

[10] The basic Sec. 332 liquidation of a controlled subsidiary stock definition outlined in Chapter C:6 also is used for Sec. 338 purposes.

EXAMPLE C:7-4 ▶ Alpha Corporation purchases a 25% block of Theta Corporation's single class of stock on each of four dates: April 1, July 1, and December 1 of Year 1, and February 1 of Year 2. Because Alpha acquires at least 80% of Theta stock within a 12-month period (April 1 of Year 1 through February 1 of Year 2), it is eligible to make a Sec. 338 deemed sale election. ◀

EXAMPLE C:7-5 ▶ Assume the same facts as in Example C:7-4 except Alpha Corporation instead purchases the final 25% block on May 15 of Year 2. In this case, Alpha acquires only 75% of the Theta stock during a 12-month period. Two possible 12-month periods may occur—April 1 of Year 1 through March 31 of Year 2, and May 16 of Year 1 through May 15 of Year 2. The 80% stock ownership minimum is not achieved in either period. Thus, Alpha is not eligible to make a Sec. 338 election. ◀

For the purpose of the 80% requirement, the following stock acquisitions are not treated as purchases:

- Stock whose adjusted basis is determined in whole or part by its basis in the hands of the person from whom it was acquired (e.g., stock acquired as a capital contribution)
- Stock whose basis is determined under Sec. 1014(a) (i.e., FMV on the date of decedent's death or alternative valuation date)
- Stock acquired in a nontaxable transaction under Sec. 351, 354, 355, or 356 (e.g., corporate formations, divisions, or reorganizations)
- Stock acquired from a related party where stock ownership may be attributed to the purchaser under Secs. 318(a)(1) through (3)

The Election. A Sec. 338 election must be made no later than the fifteenth day of the ninth month beginning after the month in which the acquisition date falls. The acquisition date is the first date during the 12-month acquisition period on which the 80% stock ownership requirement is met.[11]

EXAMPLE C:7-6 ▶ On April 1 of Year 1, Alpha Corporation purchased 40% of Theta Corporation's single class of stock. On October 20 of Year 1, it purchases an additional 50% of Theta stock. The acquisition date is October 20 of Year 1. Alpha must make a Sec. 338 election on or before July 15 of Year 2. ◀

Deemed Sale Transaction. When the acquiring corporation makes a Sec. 338 election, the target corporation is treated as having sold all its assets at their aggregate deemed sale price (ADSP) in a single transaction at the close of the acquisition date. The asset sale is a taxable transaction, with gain or loss recognized by the target corporation. ADSP is calculated as follows:[12]

$$ADSP = \frac{G + L - (T_R \times B)}{(1 - T_R)}$$

Where: G = The acquiring corporation's grossed-up basis in recently purchased target corporation stock;
L = The target corporation's liabilities other than its tax liability for the deemed sale gain determined by reference to the ADSP;
T_R = the applicable federal income tax rate; and
B = the adjusted basis of the asset(s) deemed sold.

EXAMPLE C:7-7 ▶ Assume the same facts as in Examples C:7-2 and C:7-3 except Alpha makes a timely Sec. 338 election. Also assume that Theta's marginal tax rate is 34%. The aggregate deemed sale price is calculated as follows:

$$ADSP = \frac{G + L - (T_R \times B)}{(1 - T_R)}$$

---

[11] Secs. 338(g) and 338(h)(2).

[12] This equation is derived as follows:

$ADSP = G + L + [T_R \times (ADSP - B)]$

$ADSP = G + L + (T_R \times ADSP) - (T_R \times B)$

$ADSP - (T_R \times ADSP) = G + L - (T_R \times B)$

$ADSP \times (1 - T_R) = G + L - (T_R \times B)$

$$ADSP = \frac{G + L - (T_R \times B)}{(1 \times T_R)}$$

$$\text{ADSP} = \frac{\$350{,}000 + \$100{,}000 - (0.34 \times \$330{,}000)}{(1 - 0.34)}$$

$$0.66\ \text{ADSP} = \$337{,}800$$

$$\text{ADSP} = \$511{,}818$$

Thus, Theta recognizes a gain of $181,818 ($511,818 − $330,000) and pays a tax of $61,818 (0.34 × $181,818) on the gain. ◀

TAX STRATEGY TIP

Many taxpayers avoid Sec. 338 because it requires an advance payment of taxes to achieve a step-up in basis of target corporation's assets. A Sec. 338 election becomes more attractive, however, when the target corporation has NOLs that can offset its gain on the deemed sale of its assets, thereby reducing the cost of making the election.

The Sec. 338 election was intended for transactions in which the acquisition price of target stock exceeds the adjusted basis of target assets. In many of these transactions, the amount of gain recognized by the target corporation, as well as the associated tax liability, could be substantial. This potential tax cost might induce companies to forego the Sec. 338 election or lower the price they are willing to pay for target stock if they intend to make a Sec. 338 election.

Tax Basis of the Assets After the Deemed Sale. Similarly to the ADSP, the tax basis in the assets of the new target corporation is based on the amount paid by the acquiring corporation for target corporation stock. This amount is called the **adjusted grossed-up basis** in the target corporation stock. The adjusted grossed-up basis equals the sum of

- The purchasing corporation's grossed-up basis in recently purchased target corporation stock;
- The purchasing corporation's basis in nonrecently purchased target corporation stock;
- The liabilities of the new target corporation; and
- Other relevant items.[13]

The adjusted grossed-up basis is determined as of the beginning of the day following the acquisition date. Example C:7-10 illustrates the calculation of the adjusted grossed-up basis.

A target corporation's stock owned by the acquiring corporation falls into two categories: recently purchased stock and nonrecently purchased stock. This categorization is necessary because only the recently purchased stock is treated as consideration used in a deemed purchase of target corporation assets. Recently purchased stock includes any target corporation stock held on the acquisition date that the acquiring corporation purchased during the 12-month (or shorter) acquisition period. Nonrecently purchased stock includes all other target corporation stock acquired before the acquisition period and held by the acquiring corporation on the acquisition date.[14] The basis of the purchasing corporation's ownership interest equals the grossed-up basis of the recently purchased stock plus the basis of the nonrecently purchased stock.

EXAMPLE C:7-8 ▶ On July 23 of the current year, Alpha Corporation purchases all of Theta Corporation's single class of stock. All the Theta stock is considered to be recently purchased because it is purchased in a single transaction. The acquisition date is July 23 of the current year. ◀

EXAMPLE C:7-9 ▶ Assume the same facts as in Example C:7-8 except Alpha already owns 10% of Theta stock (purchased five years ago) and purchases the remaining 90% of Theta stock. The original block of Theta stock is not considered to be recently purchased because it was acquired more than 12 months before the acquisition date (July 23 of the current year). ◀

When the acquiring corporation does not own all of target corporation outstanding stock, the basis of the acquiring corporation's recently purchased stock must be increased or grossed-up to a hypothetical value that reflects ownership of all the stock.[15]

---

[13] Secs. 338(b)(1) and (2). The IRS has indicated that other relevant items include only items that arise from adjustment events that occur after the close of the new target's first tax year and items discovered as a result of an IRS examination of a tax return (e.g., the payment of contingent amounts for recently or nonrecently purchased stock).

[14] Sec. 338(b)(6). A special gain recognition election is available to adjust the basis of nonrecently purchased stock. This election, which is set forth in Sec. 338(b)(3), is beyond the scope of this text.

[15] Sec. 338(b)(4). The gross-up procedure involves taking the purchasing corporation's basis for the recently purchased target stock and dividing it by the percentage (by value) of recently purchased target stock owned (expressed as a decimal).

Specifically, the basis of the recently purchased stock must be increased by the face amount of any target liabilities outstanding on the day following the acquisition date, plus the tax liability incurred on any gain realized in the deemed sale.[16] This liability adjustment embodies the notion that, if the acquisition had been structured as an asset purchase, the assumption of liabilities would have been reflected in the total purchase price.

Allocation of Basis to Individual Assets. The adjusted grossed-up basis of the stock is allocated among seven classes of assets under the residual method.[17] The residual method requires that the adjusted grossed-up basis be allocated to the corporation's tangible and intangible property (other than goodwill and going concern value) on a sequential hierarchical basis. Any amount exceeding the aggregate FMVs of this property is assigned to target corporation goodwill and going concern value.

PRACTICAL APPLICATION

Because goodwill now can be amortized, the fact that the residual purchase price is allocated to goodwill may be a desirable tax result. Goodwill was not amortized under pre-Sec. 197 law because it had an indefinite life. On the negative side, however, the required 15-year amortization period under Sec. 197 is longer than the time period used by many taxpayers under pre-Sec. 197 law to amortize intangible assets that had a shorter determinable life.

The seven classes of assets to which the adjusted grossed-up basis is allocated are as follows:

- Class I: cash and general deposit accounts, including demand deposit and similar accounts in banks, savings and loan associations, and other financial institutions.
- Class II: actively traded personal property (as defined in Sec. 1092(d)(1)), such as U.S. government obligations and publicly traded securities.
- Class III: accounts receivable, mortgages, and credit card receivables that arise in the ordinary course of business.
- Class IV: inventory or other property held primarily for sale to customers in the ordinary course of business.
- Class V: all assets other than Class I, II, III, IV, VI, and VII assets. Included in this category are tangible and intangible property without regard to whether such property is depreciable, depletable, or amortizable.
- Class VI: all amortizable Sec. 197 intangible assets except goodwill and going concern value.
- Class VII: Sec. 197 intangible assets in the nature of goodwill and going concern value.[18]

ADDITIONAL COMMENT

The residual method ensures that any premium paid for the target stock is reflected in goodwill. Because the residual method is the only acceptable allocation method, the only uncertainty that remains is to determine the FMVs of the assets listed in Classes II through VI.

Class VI and VII intangible assets are amortizable over a 15-year period if they are used in the active conduct of a trade or business. Among such assets are goodwill, going concern value, and covenants not to compete.

The adjusted grossed-up basis is first allocated to individual Class I assets based on their actual dollar amounts.[19] Any excess is allocated to Class II assets based on, and to the extent of, their relative gross FMVs. Similar allocations are made to Class III through VI assets based on, and to the extent of, the relative gross FMVs of individual assets within each class. The intra-class allocation is based on the asset's total gross FMV, not its net FMV (gross FMV minus liabilities secured by the property). Any remaining adjusted grossed-up basis is assigned to Class VII (goodwill).

EXAMPLE C:7-10 ▶ Assume the same facts as in Example C:7-7, with assets classified as follows:

Asset Class	Assets	FMV
I	Cash	$ 50,000
II	Marketable securities	55,000
III	Accounts receivable	60,000
IV	Inventory	90,000
V	Building	44,000
V	Land	26,000
V	Machinery and equipment	125,000
	Total	$450,000

[16] Sec. 338(b)(2) and Reg. Secs. 1.338(b)-1(f)(1) and (2).
[17] Reg. Sec. 1.338-6(a).
[18] Reg. Sec. 1.338-6(b).
[19] Ibid.

The adjusted grossed-up basis of Alpha's interest in Theta stock is calculated as follows:

Recently purchased stock	$350,000
Plus: Theta's nontax liabilities	100,000
Theta's tax liability [($511,818 − $330,000) × 0.34]	61,818
Adjusted grossed-up basis	$511,818

ADDITIONAL COMMENT

The effects of a Sec. 338 election include termination of the "old" target corporation, creation of a "new" target corporation with the option of a new tax year and different accounting methods, new depreciation elections without regard to anti-churning rules, and elimination of the old target's tax attributes (i.e., NOL carryforwards). Because it is a separate legal entity, the "new" target corporation files a tax return separate from that of the acquiring corporation (unless the group files a consolidated return).[20]

The adjusted grossed-up basis is allocated to Theta's seven asset classes in the following steps:

Step 1: Allocate $50,000 to cash (Class I asset).

Step 2: Allocate $55,000 to marketable securities (Class II asset).

Step 3: Allocate $60,000 to accounts receivable (Class III asset).

Step 4: Allocate $90,000 to inventory (Class IV asset).

Step 5: Allocate $195,000 to the building, land, machinery, and equipment (Class V assets). Because the total basis that remains after the Step 4 allocation ($256,818) exceeds the aggregate FMV of the Class V assets ($195,000), each asset will take a basis exactly equal to its FMV.

Step 6: No allocation to Class VI assets.

Step 7: Allocate the residual $61,818 [$511,818 − ($50,000 + $55,000 + $60,000 + $90,000 + $195,000)] to goodwill (Class VII asset). The $61,818 is amortizable under Sec. 197. ◀

Topic Review C:7-1 summarizes the requirements for, and tax consequences of, a Sec. 338 deemed sale election.

TOPIC REVIEW C:7-1

Section 338 Deemed Sale Election

ELECTION REQUIREMENTS

1. The acquiring corporation must make a qualified stock purchase (i.e., within a 12-month period purchase 80% or more of target corporation voting stock and 80% or more of the total value of all target corporation stock).
2. Stock received in transactions that result in a substituted basis (e.g., nontaxable reorganizations, corporate formations, and gifts), transfers at death, and related party exchanges do not count toward the 80% minimum threshold.
3. The acquiring corporation must make the election not later than the fifteenth day of the ninth month beginning after the month in which the acquisition date falls. The acquisition date is the first date on which the 80% stock ownership requirement is met.

TAX CONSEQUENCES OF A SEC. 338 ELECTION

1. The old target corporation is treated as having sold all its assets to the new target corporation at their aggregate deemed sales price in a single transaction at the close of the acquisition date. The old target corporation recognizes gain or loss on the deemed sale.
2. The new target corporation takes an aggregate asset basis equal to the acquiring corporation's adjusted grossed-up basis in the target stock, that is, the sum of the acquiring corporation's basis in the target corporation stock on the day following the acquisition date, the target corporation's liabilities on the day after the acquisition date, and other relevant items (e.g., contingent liabilities that become fixed).
3. The total adjusted grossed-up basis is allocated to individual assets under the residual method. This method requires allocation of basis first to cash and near-cash items, then to other tangible and intangible assets, and finally to goodwill and going concern value.
4. After the Sec. 338 deemed asset sale, the tax attributes of the old target corporation disappear.
5. The new target corporation makes new tax year and accounting method elections.

[20] The "old" target also files a separate tax return that includes the gains from the Sec. 338 deemed sale. The "old" target may not file a consolidated tax return with the acquiring corporation.

Section 336(e) Deemed Sale Election. Another election similar in principle to the Sec. 338 election is available to shareholders who sell their target corporation stock. Under IRC Sec. 336(e) and associated Treasury Regulations, a domestic corporation (the seller) that sells, exchanges, or distributes stock in another domestic corporation (the target corporation) that it controls may, under certain circumstances, elect to have the transaction treated as if the target corporation disposed of its assets in a taxable transaction. As a result of the election, the seller recognizes no gain or loss on the sale, exchange, or distribution of the target corporation stock. On the other hand, the target corporation recognizes gain or loss, except in the case of certain distributions to shareholders.

To qualify for the election, the seller must dispose of at least 80% of the target stock by vote and value within a 12-month period. As a result of the election, the following events are deemed to occur:

- The old target corporation is deemed to sell all its assets in a single sale to an unrelated person at an aggregate deemed asset disposition price (ADADP), calculated and allocated to the assets in a manner similar to that of ADSP under Sec. 338. This deemed sale results in recognized taxable gain or loss to the target corporation.
- The new target is deemed to acquire the assets from an unrelated person for a value that is used to determine an aggregate grossed up basis (AGUB), allocated to the assets in a manner similar to the asset allocation under Sec. 338.
- The old target goes out of existence.

The Sec. 336(e) election is intended to provide relief to the parties in a stock sale where gain on the stock sale is subject to taxation, without a corresponding step up in the basis of the underlying assets. The election gives the parties an opportunity to adjust the bases of the target corporation's underlying assets via the AGUB allocation to a level that approximates the FMV of the assets. As a practical matter, the parties should negotiate the stock selling price to reflect the incidence of taxation on any recognized gain. Where a stock disposition under Sec. 336(e) also qualifies as a stock purchase under Sec. 338, the latter IRC provision controls. However, Sec. 336(e) can apply in situations where Sec. 338 cannot apply, for example, in stock sales to multiple parties, some of which can be entities other than a corporation.

Comparison of Taxable and Nontaxable Acquisitions

OBJECTIVE 2

Distinguish between taxable and nontaxable acquisitions

KEY POINT

Determining whether a transaction is taxable or nontaxable is doubly important to the target corporation because it is involved in two potentially taxable exchanges: the exchange between the target corporation and the acquiring corporation and the exchange between the acquiring corporation and its shareholders.

Taxable and Nontaxable Asset Acquisitions

One way to illustrate the difference between taxable and nontaxable asset acquisitions is to identify the type of consideration used to acquire the assets and to compare the tax consequences of the transactions. For this discussion, we assume that the acquiring corporation acquires all the target corporation's assets and liabilities and that the target corporation liquidates immediately after the acquisition. If the acquiring corporation uses cash and/or other property to purchase the assets, the target corporation is taxed on the sale, and its shareholders are taxed on the liquidation. On the other hand, if the acquiring corporation uses its own stock, the asset acquisition may qualify as a reorganization that is nontaxable to the target corporation and its shareholders. If the acquiring corporation supplements its stock with a limited amount of cash and/or other property, the transaction still may qualify as a reorganization but may be partially taxable.

Tax Consequences to the Target Corporation. Section 1001(c) requires that, with certain exceptions, the entire gain or loss realized on a sale or exchange of property be recognized. Thus, the target corporation recognizes all gains and losses realized on selling its assets.

A reorganization is one exception to the general rule. The target corporation generally recognizes no gain or loss when it exchanges its assets for acquiring corporation stock. It also recognizes no gain or loss when it distributes the acquiring corporation stock to its shareholders. The target corporation, however, could recognize gain if it receives boot and does not distribute the boot to its shareholders, or if it distributes boot or retained property whose FMV exceeds its adjusted basis. The term *retained property* refers to property not transferred to the acquiring corporation as part of the acquisition.

SELF-STUDY QUESTION

Why would an acquiring corporation want an acquisition to be nontaxable if it gets only a substituted basis rather than a FMV basis in the acquired assets?

ANSWER

Usually the motivation for an acquisition to be nontaxable comes from the target corporation and its shareholders. However, two reasons why the acquiring corporation may desire a nontaxable acquisition are (1) the acquiring corporation has no cash to acquire the assets, so it must use stock as the consideration for the purchase and (2) the target corporation may have favorable tax attributes (e.g., an NOL) that the acquiring corporation would like to use.

Tax Consequences to the Acquiring Corporation. The acquiring corporation recognizes no gain or loss when it issues its stock in exchange for property in either a taxable or nontaxable acquisition date. In a taxable acquisition, the acquiring corporation takes a cost (FMV) basis in the assets received, and the holding period for the acquired assets begins the day after the acquisition. In a reorganization, the acquiring corporation takes a carryover basis equal to target corporation's basis before the transfer. If the target corporation recognizes a gain because it does not distribute boot property to its shareholders, the carryover basis is adjusted upward to reflect this recognized gain. The acquiring corporation's holding period includes the target corporation's holding period.

In a taxable acquisition all the target corporation's tax attributes (e.g., an NOL carryover) disappear when it liquidates, while in a nontaxable reorganization, the acquiring corporation inherits the target corporation's tax attributes.

Tax Consequences to the Target Corporation Shareholders. If the target corporation liquidates as part of a taxable acquisition, its shareholders recognize gain or loss on the surrender of their stock. The target corporation assets they receive take a basis equal to their FMV. A reorganization requires the shareholders to recognize gain only to the extent they receive boot. The gain generally is capital in character. In some circumstances, however, target corporation shareholders could recognize dividend income. The stock and securities they receive take a substituted basis that references the basis of target corporation stock and securities surrendered. Their basis in any boot property received is its FMV.

Accounting for the Acquisition. For financial reporting purposes, only the purchase method is available to account for acquisitions. Thus, the acquired assets must be recorded at their fair market values. Any goodwill created in the acquisition cannot be amortized, but rather must be periodically tested for impairment. Also, any impairment of an indefinite-life intangible asset must be reported in the acquiring corporation's financial statements as a loss from continuing operations. For other accounting issues, see Financial Statement Implications at the end of this chapter.

Topic Review C:7-2 compares various aspects of taxable and nontaxable asset acquisitions.

TAX STRATEGY TIP

Taxes can be an important variable in determining the acquisition method used to acquire the target corporation's stock or assets. All parties also need to consider nontax variables associated with the transaction. For example, a stock-for-stock acquisition may minimize taxes but leave the target corporation's shareholders controlling the acquiring corporation. Facing loss of control, the acquiring corporation's owners may prefer financing the transaction with borrowed funds (and taxing the acquisition to the seller) while retaining control of the acquiring corporation.

COMPARISON OF TAXABLE AND NONTAXABLE STOCK ACQUISITIONS

For purposes of this discussion, we assume that the acquiring corporation acquires all the stock of target corporation instead of its assets and that the target corporation becomes a controlled subsidiary of the acquiring corporation. If the acquiring corporation uses cash and/or other property alone or along with its own stock to acquire the target stock, the acquisition is taxable. If the acquiring corporation uses solely its voting stock or voting stock of its parent corporation to acquire the target corporation stock, the acquisition may qualify as a nontaxable reorganization.

Tax Consequences to the Target Corporation. The target corporation's basis in its assets does not change as a result of either a taxable or nontaxable stock acquisition (unless the acquiring corporation makes a Sec. 338 election after a taxable

TOPIC REVIEW C:7-2

Comparison of Taxable and Nontaxable Asset Acquisitions

Tax Feature	Taxable Acquisition	Nontaxable Reorganization
1. Consideration used in acquisition	Primarily cash and debt instruments; may involve some stock of the acquiring corporation or its parent corporation.	Primarily stock and limited amount of cash or debt of the acquiring corporation or its parent corporation.
2. The target corporation		
a. Amount of gain or loss	All gains and losses are recognized. Installment method available if payments are deferred.	Generally, no gain or loss recognized. Gain recognized on an asset transfer when the target corporation receives boot property and does not distribute the boot property to its shareholders. Gain also recognized on the distribution of appreciated boot or retained property.
b. Character of gain or loss	Depends on nature of each asset transferred or distributed.	Depends on nature of each asset transferred or distributed.
c. Depreciation recapture	Sec. 1245 or 1250 depreciation is recaptured.	Sec. 1245 or 1250 depreciation is not recaptured unless boot triggers the recognition of gain.
3. The acquiring corporation		
a. Gain or loss when stock is exchanged for property	None recognized.	None recognized.
b. Gain or loss when boot is exchanged for property	Gain or loss recognized if noncash boot property is transferred to the target corporation.	Gain or loss recognized if noncash boot property is transferred to the target corporation.
c. Basis of acquired assets	Cost.	Same as the target corporation's basis, increased by gain recognized.
d. Holding period of acquired assets	Begins the day after the transaction date.	Includes holding period of the target corporation.
e. Acquisition of target corporation tax attributes	No.	Yes.
4. The target corporation shareholders		
a. Amount of gain or loss	Realized gain or loss is recognized. Installment method available if payments are deferred.	Realized gain is recognized to the extent of boot received; realized losses are not recognized.
b. Character of gain or loss	Capital gain or loss; may be Sec. 1244 loss.	Capital gain and/or dividend income if boot is received.
c. Basis of stock and securities received	Cost; generally FMV of stock, securities, or other property received.	Substituted basis referenced to the stock and securities surrendered; FMV for boot property.
d. Holding period of stock and securities received	Begins the day after the transaction date.	Includes holding period for the stock and securities surrendered; day after the transaction date for boot property.

stock purchase). Any depreciation recapture potential on the transaction date stays with target corporation assets and, therefore, is inherited by the purchaser. Also, the target corporation retains any loss or credit carryovers, which may be subject to special limitations in the post-acquisition tax years.

If the acquiring corporation is a member of an affiliated group that files a consolidated tax return, the target corporation must join in the consolidated return election if the acquiring corporation owns at least 80% of the target corporation stock, and the target corporation is an includible corporation. Otherwise, the acquiring corporation and the target corporation can make an initial consolidated tax return election (see Chapter C:8).

Tax Consequences to the Acquiring Corporation. In either a taxable or nontaxable stock acquisition, the acquiring corporation recognizes no gain or loss when it exchanges its own stock for target corporation stock. In a taxable acquisition, the acquiring corporation's basis in the target corporation stock is its acquisition cost. A taxable acquisition may qualify for the Sec. 338 deemed sale election. In a reorganization, the acquiring corporation's basis in the target corporation stock is the same as that in the hands of target corporation shareholders, and a Sec. 338 election is not available. The acquiring corporation recognizes any realized gain or loss when it exchanges noncash boot property for target corporation stock.

Tax Consequences to the Target Corporation Shareholders. The gain recognized in a taxable stock sale is capital in character if the target corporation stock is a capital asset in the seller's hands. The seller can account for the gain under the installment method if payment of part or all of the consideration is deferred to a later tax year and if the stock is not traded on an established securities exchange. Consideration received by the seller that represents compensation for an agreement not to compete with the purchaser for a specified time period is taxable as ordinary income.

Because only voting stock may be used in a nontaxable stock acquisition, the target corporation's shareholders recognize no gain or loss. The shareholders take a substituted basis in the acquiring corporation stock, which is the same as their basis in the target corporation stock.

Topic Review C:7-3 compares various aspects of taxable and nontaxable stock acquisitions.

TOPIC REVIEW C:7-3

Comparison of Taxable and Nontaxable Stock Acquisitions

Tax Feature	Taxable Acquisition	Nontaxable Reorganization
1. Consideration used in acquisition	Primarily cash and debt instruments; may include some stock of the acquiring corporation or its parent corporation.	Solely voting stock of the acquiring corporation or its parent corporation.
2. The target corporation		
a. Parent-subsidiary relationship established	Yes.	Yes.
b. Consolidated tax return election available	Yes.	Yes.
c. Basis in assets	Unchanged by stock acquisition unless a Sec. 338 election is made.	Unchanged by stock acquisition. No Sec. 338 election available.
d. Tax attributes	Retained by the target corporation.	Retained by the target corporation.
3. The acquiring corporation		
a. Basis in stock acquired	Cost basis.	Carryover basis from the target corporation shareholders.
4. The target corporation shareholders		
a. Amount of gain or loss recognized	Realized gain or loss is recognized.	No boot is received; therefore, no gain is recognized.
b. Character of gain or loss	Capital gain or loss; may be Sec. 1244 loss.	Not applicable.
c. Basis of stock, securities, or other property received	Cost; generally FMV of stock, securities, or other property received.	Substituted basis from stock surrendered.
d. Holding period of stock, securities, or other property received	Begins the day after the transaction date.	Includes holding period of the stock surrendered.

TYPES OF REORGANIZATIONS AND THEIR TAX CONSEQUENCES

OBJECTIVE 3

Recognize the types of nontaxable reorganizations and determine their tax consequences

Section 368(a)(1) authorizes seven types of nontaxable reorganizations that correspond to the principal forms of business acquisitions, divestitures, and restructurings. Generally, tax practitioners refer to the reorganization type by the subparagraph of Sec. 368(a)(1) that defines it. For example, a merger is referred to as a *Type A* reorganization because it is defined in Sec. 368(a)(1)(A). The seven types of reorganizations also can be classified according to the transactional form, with the most common forms being acquisitive and divisive. In an **acquisitive reorganization**, the acquiring corporation obtains part or all of a target (or transferor) corporation's assets or stock. Types A, B, and C reorganizations generally are acquisitive. In a **divisive reorganization**, some of a transferor corporation's assets are transferred to a second corporation that is controlled by either the transferor or its shareholders. As part of the reorganization, the controlled (or transferee) corporation's stock or securities exchanged for the transferor's assets are distributed to the transferor's shareholders. Subsequent to the transfer, the transferor corporation can either remain in existence or be liquidated. If the transferor corporation remains in existence, its assets usually are divided between at least two corporations. Types D and G reorganizations may be either acquisitive or divisive.

TYPICAL MISCONCEPTION

For an acquisition to be treated as nontaxable, the transaction must qualify as a reorganization. The term *reorganization* includes only transactions specified in Sec. 368. Other transactions that may constitute reorganizations in a more general context are not considered nontaxable reorganizations.

Two types of reorganizations are neither acquisitive or divisive. A Type E reorganization—a recapitalization—involves a change in a corporation's capital structure. A Type F reorganization—a change in identity, legal form, or state of incorporation—involves the transfer of an existing corporation's assets to a new corporation, in which the shareholders of the transferor corporation generally retain the same equity interest.

KEY POINT

A summary of the acquisitive reorganizations is presented below:

Type	*Description*
A	Merger or consolidation
B	Stock-for-stock
C	Asset-for-stock
D	Asset-for-stock
G	Bankruptcy

Not all reorganizations fit neatly into one of the seven categories. Some reorganizations satisfy the requirements of two or more reorganization provisions. In this situation, the IRC or the IRS generally determines which reorganization rules prevail. In other situations, a reorganization may satisfy the requirements of a reorganization provision, but for various reasons the IRS and courts prescribe an entirely different tax treatment (e.g., if the transaction lacks a business purpose, it may be treated as taxable). These issues are discussed further in the next section.

The remainder of this section examines the tax consequences of a reorganization to the target (or transferor) corporation, the acquiring (or transferee) corporation, and the shareholders and other security holders.[21]

THE TARGET OR TRANSFEROR CORPORATION

Recognition of Gain or Loss on Asset Transfer. Under Sec. 361(a), the target corporation recognizes no gain or loss on the exchange of property exclusively for stock in another corporation that is a party to the reorganization.[22] In addition, under Sec. 361(b), the target corporation recognizes no gain if it also receives cash or noncash boot property as part of the reorganization and distributes such property to its shareholders or

[21] The corporation that transfers its assets as part of a reorganization is referred to as either a **target** or **transferor corporation**. The term *target corporation* generally is used in the context of an acquisitive reorganization where substantially all of a corporation's assets are acquired by the acquiring corporation. The term *target corporation* also applies to a corporation whose stock is acquired from its shareholders. The term *transferor corporation* is used in the context of a divisive and other reorganizations where only part of a corporation's assets are transferred to a transferee corporation, and the transferor corporation may remain in existence. Tax law provisions generally are applied identically to target or transferor corporations and acquiring or transferee corporations, so usually only a single reference to the target or acquiring corporation is provided in the text.

[22] Section 361(a) permits securities (e.g., long-term debt obligations) to be received tax-free when the target corporation surrenders the same or a larger face amount of securities. Generally, a securities exchange does not occur in an acquisitive reorganization, so all debt obligations received by the target corporation are treated as boot property.

TYPICAL MISCONCEPTION

One perplexing aspect of the reorganization provisions is the overlap between the different statutory reorganizations. One transaction often can qualify as more than one type of reorganization.

creditors. On the other hand, the target corporation recognizes gain equal to the lesser of the realized gain or the amount of cash plus the FMV of any noncash boot property received unless it distributes the property to its shareholders. However, because most acquisitive and divisive reorganization provisions require the target corporation to be liquidated or distribute all its assets, the target corporation generally retains no boot and thus recognizes no gain on the exchange. (Note: the target corporation might recognize gain on the distribution of appreciated property to its shareholders, as discussed below.)

EXAMPLE C:7-11 ►

In a reorganization, Theta Corporation transfers assets having a $175,000 adjusted basis to Alpha Corporation in exchange for $400,000 of Alpha common stock. In the exchange, Theta realizes a $225,000 gain ($400,000 amount realized − $175,000 adjusted basis). Because Theta received no boot, however, it recognizes none of the gain. If Theta instead had received $350,000 of Alpha common stock plus $50,000 of cash or other property, Theta would have recognized no gain only if it had distributed the $50,000 of boot to its shareholders. ◄

TYPICAL MISCONCEPTION

Often, taxpayers do not realize that Sec. 361 applies to two exchanges. Section 361(a) applies to the exchange between the acquiring and target corporations (which already has been discussed). Section 361(c) deals with the exchange between the target corporation and its shareholders. Therefore, the target corporation is the only party to the reorganization that may recognize two separate gains.

Depreciation Recapture. The depreciation recapture rules of Secs. 1245 and 1250 do not override the gain or loss nonrecognition rules of Sec. 361.[23] The recapture potential that accumulates before the reorganization remains with the assets transferred to the acquiring corporation and is recognized when the acquiring corporation later sells or exchanges the assets in a taxable transaction.

Assumption of Liabilities. Neither the acquiring corporation's assuming the target corporation's liabilities nor its acquiring the target corporation's property subject to a liability triggers gain recognition on the asset transfer. Section 357(c), however, requires the target corporation to recognize gain if the sum of the liabilities assumed or acquired exceeds the total adjusted bases of the property transferred *and* the transaction is a divisive Type D reorganization.

SELF-STUDY QUESTION

How can the target corporation distribute appreciated boot property to its shareholders if it receives a FMV basis in all such property received from the acquiring corporation?

ANSWER

If the property appreciates in the hands of the target corporation before it is distributed, gain will result under Sec. 361(c). In addition, the target corporation may retain some of its own assets and distribute these assets to its shareholders, again causing the target corporation to recognize gain.

Recognition of Gain or Loss on Distribution of Stock and Securities. The target corporation recognizes no gain or loss when, pursuant to a plan of reorganization, it distributes to its shareholders or creditors either (1) its stock, stock rights, or obligations or (2) any stock, stock rights, or obligations of a party to a reorganization that it received in the reorganization (see page C:7-47 for an explanation of a plan of reorganization).[24] Distributions of noncash boot property (including property retained by the target corporation) pursuant to the reorganization plan result in the recognition of gain (but not loss) in the same manner as if the target corporation had sold such property at its FMV.[25] Normally the gain recognized upon the distribution of boot property is inconsequential because of the brief period of time between the receipt of the boot from the acquiring corporation (with a basis equal to its FMV) and its distribution to the shareholders.

EXAMPLE C:7-12 ►

In a statutory merger (Type A reorganization), Theta Corporation transfers all its assets and liabilities to Alpha Corporation, which exchanges $300,000 of its common stock and $100,000 of cash to Theta for Theta assets. Theta's basis in the assets is $250,000. In the exchange, Theta realizes a $150,000 [($300,000 + $100,000) − $250,000] gain. Theta recognizes none of this gain, even though it receives boot, because Theta must liquidate as a reorganization requirement. Upon distributing the Alpha stock to its shareholders, Theta recognizes no gain. However, depending on their Theta stock basis, Theta shareholders who receive cash may have to recognize gain. ◄

THE ACQUIRING OR TRANSFEREE CORPORATION

Amount of Gain or Loss Recognized. Under Sec. 1032, the acquiring corporation recognizes no gain or loss when it receives cash or other property in exchange for its stock. Similarly, a target corporation recognizes no gain or loss when in a reorganization it

[23] Secs. 1245(b)(3) and 1250(d)(3). Similar provisions are found in the other recapture rules.

[24] Secs. 361(c)(1)–(c)(3).

[25] Sec. 361(c).

SELF-STUDY QUESTION

Because the acquiring corporation is merely purchasing assets, can it ever recognize gain or loss on the transaction?

ANSWER

Yes. If the acquiring corporation uses noncash boot property, it recognizes gain or loss to the extent of the built-in gain or loss in the noncash boot property (Sec. 1001(a)).

receives cash or other property in exchange for its securities. Under Sec. 1001, however, the acquiring corporation recognizes gain or loss when it transfers appreciated or depreciated (in value) noncash boot property to the target corporation or its shareholders.[26]

Basis of Acquired Property. Under Sec. 362(b), property acquired from the target corporation in a reorganization takes a carryover basis, increased by the amount of gain recognized by the target corporation on the exchange. As a practical matter, however, because the target corporation generally recognizes no gain on the asset transfer, the carryover basis is not stepped up.

EXAMPLE C:7-13 ▶ Assume the same facts as in Example C:7-12. Alpha's basis in the acquired property is the same as Theta's basis, or $250,000. ◀

Holding Period of Acquired Property. The acquiring corporation's holding period for acquired property includes the target corporation's holding period.[27]

SHAREHOLDERS AND SECURITY HOLDERS

Amount of Gain or Loss Recognized. Under Sec. 354(a), shareholders recognize no gain or loss if, pursuant to a plan of reorganization, stock or securities in a corporate party to a reorganization are exchanged solely for stock or securities in the same corporation or another corporate party to the reorganization. The receipt of property other than stock or securities (nonqualifying property) does not necessarily disqualify the entire transaction from nontaxable treatment. Section 356(a) requires that a shareholder or security holder recognize gain to the extent of the lesser of the realized gain or the amount of cash received plus the FMV of any other property received. Thus, a shareholder recognizes gain to the extent he or she receives nonqualifying property that does not represent a continuation of the equity interest.

EXAMPLE C:7-14 ▶ Upon the liquidation of Theta Corporation in a reorganization, Brian surrenders 1,000 Theta shares having a $13,000 basis in exchange for Alpha Corporation stock having a $28,000 FMV. Brian's realized gain is $15,000 ($28,000 − $13,000), none of which is recognized. If instead Brian had received $25,000 of Alpha stock and $3,000 of cash, he would have recognized $3,000 of the $15,000 realized gain. ◀

ADDITIONAL COMMENT

The acquiring corporation may increase its basis in assets received only to the extent of gain recognized by the target corporation on its exchange with the acquiring corporation. Any gain recognized by the target corporation on distributing stock or other property to its shareholders does not increase the basis of any assets.

With some limitations, the general rule of Sec. 354(a) permits a nontaxable exchange of stock for securities. The receipt of securities is completely nontaxable only if the principal amount of the securities surrendered equals or exceeds the principal amount of the securities received. If the principal amount of securities received exceeds the principal amount of securities surrendered, the FMV of the "excess" constitutes boot.[28] If no securities are surrendered, the FMV of the entire principal amount received constitutes boot. Certain types of preferred stock (e.g., preferred stock that the issuer must redeem) also may constitute boot.

EXAMPLE C:7-15 ▶ Assume the same facts as in Example C:7-14 except Brian instead receives $25,000 of Alpha stock and Alpha debt securities having a $3,000 principal amount and a $2,850 FMV. Brian's realized gain is $14,850 [($25,000 + $2,850) − $13,000], of which $2,850 is recognized. If Brian had received $3,000 in Alpha securities and surrendered $2,000 of Theta securities, the FMV of the $1,000 "excess" principal amount, or $950 [$1,000 × ($2,850/$3,000)], would have been treated as boot. ◀

SELF-STUDY QUESTION

In addition to receiving stock in Alpha Corporation, shareholder Sue receives debt securities with a FMV of $120,000 and a principal amount of $100,000. In the exchange, Sue surrenders securities of Theta Corporation with a FMV and principal amount of $80,000. Is Sue treated as having received any boot?

Character of the Recognized Gain. Section 356(a)(2) requires that the recognized gain be taxed as a dividend if the receipt of the boot property has the same effect as the payment of a dividend. The amount of this dividend equals the lesser of the shareholder's recognized gain or the shareholder's ratable share of the transferor or target

[26] Rev. Rul. 72-327, 1972-2 C.B. 197.

[27] Sec. 1223(1).

[28] Secs. 354(a)(2) and 356(d)(2)(B). The FMV of the debt obligations surrendered is irrelevant when determining the amount of recognized gain.

ANSWER

Yes. $100,000 − $80,000 = $20,000 of excess principal amount received. The boot received is $24,000. This amount represents the FMV of the excess principal amount [($20,000/ $100,000) × $120,000].

corporation's current and accumulated earnings and profits (E&P). Any additional recognized gain generally is capital in character.

The Sec. 302(b) stock redemption rules determine whether the exchange has the effect of a dividend.[29] (See Chapter C:4 for a review of the Sec. 302(b) rules.) Reorganizations generally do not involve the actual redemption of target corporation stock. For purposes of Sec. 356, however, they involve the hypothetical redemption of a portion of acquiring corporation stock. When the distribution of boot meets the hypothetical Sec. 302 redemption requirements for sale treatment, the shareholder recognizes capital gain.

The following example applies the dividend equivalency test to the receipt of boot in a reorganization.

EXAMPLE C:7-16 ▶ Betty owns all 80 outstanding shares of Theta Corporation stock having a total FMV of $600,000. In a reorganization, Theta merges with Alpha Corporation, with Betty receiving $250,000 in cash and 35 shares of Alpha stock worth $350,000 in exchange for her Theta stock. Four other individuals own the remaining 100 shares of Alpha stock. Betty's Theta stock has a $200,000 basis. Theta and Alpha have E&P balances of $300,000 and $500,000, respectively. Betty's realized gain is $400,000 [($350,000 stock + $250,000 cash) − $200,000 adjusted basis], of which $250,000 must be recognized because the cash is treated as boot property.

Based on equivalent Alpha per share values, the Theta stock initially is treated as having been exchanged exclusively for Alpha stock (and not for a combination of cash and Alpha stock). Thus, because the Theta stock is worth $600,000 and the Alpha stock is worth $10,000 ($350,000 ÷ 35) per share, Betty initially is treated as having exchanged her 80 shares of Theta stock for 60 shares of Alpha stock, resulting in 160 (100 + 60) shares of Alpha stock deemed outstanding. Next, the $250,000 cash Betty actually received is treated as having been used to redeem 25 ($250,000 ÷ $10,000 per share) of the 60 shares of Alpha stock that Betty hypothetically received in the initial exchange. Because Betty is deemed to have owned 37.5% (60 shares ÷ 160 shares) of Alpha stock before the hypothetical redemption and 25.93% (35 shares ÷ 135 shares) after the hypothetical redemption, the $250,000 gain is capital in character under the Sec. 302(b)(2) substantially disproportionate redemption rules (i.e., 25.93% is less than 80% × 37.5% = 30%). ◀

TYPICAL MISCONCEPTION

Before the *Clark* decision, the IRS referenced the target corporation's E&P to measure the amount of dividend income. Since the *Clark* decision, the IRS has not ruled definitively and generally whether the parties look only to the target corporation's E&P or to the combined E&P of the acquiring and target corporations. However, in CCA 201032035, the IRS's Chief Counsel concluded that the parties must use the combined E&P based on the facts in that advice memorandum.

The Sec. 302(b) test would apply in the same manner where securities are received in the reorganization. In such a case, the boot portion of the transaction would equal the FMV of the "excess" principal amount received by the shareholder or security holder.

Whether capital gain treatment is available for boot received in a reorganization depends on the relative sizes of the target and acquiring corporations. If the acquiring corporation is larger in market value than the target corporation, the Sec. 302(b)(2) (substantially disproportionate redemption) or Sec. 302(b)(1) (not essentially equivalent to a dividend) rules generally will allow capital gain treatment. (See Chapter C:4 for an explanation of these rules.) If the acquiring corporation is smaller in market value than the target corporation, the target corporation's shareholder could be considered as having received dividend income or a combination of dividend income and capital gain (e.g., if the boot received exceeds the shareholder's ratable share of E&P).

Because dividends and capital gains are taxed at the same rate for noncorporate shareholders, the distinction between the two possible treatments in a reorganization may seem insignificant. Nevertheless, capital gains treatment can provide a benefit not available to dividend treatment in that the capital gains can be offset by (1) capital losses recognized in the current year or (2) capital loss carryovers from prior tax years. Dividend income, even though taxed at the capital gains rate, cannot be offset by capital losses.

Corporate shareholders may prefer dividend treatment because they can claim a 70%, 80%, or 100% dividends-received deduction to reduce their tax liability. On the other hand, capital gains recognized in the reorganization can be offset by capital losses

[29] *CIR v. Donald E. Clark*, 63 AFTR 2d 89-1437, 89-1 USTC ¶9230 (USSC, 1989). The IRS has agreed to follow the *Clark* decision in Rev. Rul. 93-61, 1993-2 C.B. 118.

recognized by corporate and noncorporate shareholders in other transactions. Finally, Sec. 453(f)(6)(C) permits a corporate or noncorporate shareholder who is a party to a reorganization to use the installment method to defer recognizing part of the gain realized, provided such gain is not characterized as a dividend.[30]

STOP & THINK

Question: The character of the shareholder's recognized gain is determined under the Sec. 302(b) stock redemption rules. Why are the relative sizes of the acquiring and target corporations in terms of market value important in determining the character of the gain recognized in a reorganization?

Solution: If the target corporation is smaller in market value than the acquiring corporation, the receipt of boot almost always will qualify for capital gains treatment under the redemption rules because generally no shareholder(s) will own more than 50% of the acquiring corporation's stock before and after the hypothetical redemption. If the boot is distributed proportionately to stock ownership, the pre-and post-redemption interests of the target corporation shareholder(s) are likely to be reduced. If the target corporation is larger in market value than the acquiring corporation, a shareholder could own more than 50% of the acquiring corporation stock before and after the hypothetical redemption, resulting in the characterization of boot as a dividend.

KEY POINT

In a nontaxable reorganization, shareholders defer recognition of their realized gain or loss. Consequently, they take a substituted basis in the new nonrecognition property received (i.e., any deferred gain or loss is reflected in the basis of the nonrecognition property received).

Basis of Stock and Securities Received. The basis of stock and securities (nonrecognition property) received by target corporation shareholders and security holders is determined according to the Sec. 358 rules, as discussed in Chapter C:2. Accordingly, the basis of nonrecognition property is calculated as follows:

Adjusted basis of stock and securities surrendered
Plus: Any gain recognized in the exchange
Minus: Cash received in the exchange
FMV of any noncash property received in the exchange
Basis of nonrecognition property received

If a shareholder or security holder receives no boot, the stock and securities take a substituted basis from the stock and securities surrendered. If the shareholder recognizes gain, the basis of stock and securities surrendered is increased by the amount of such gain and then reduced by the amount of cash plus the FMV of any other boot property received in the reorganization. The basis of any other boot property is its FMV.

EXAMPLE C:7-17 ▶ Keith owns Theta Corporation stock having a $10,000 adjusted basis. In a reorganization, Keith exchanges his Theta stock for $12,000 of Alpha stock and $4,000 of Alpha securities. Keith realizes a $6,000 gain [($12,000 + $4,000) − $10,000], of which he must recognize $4,000 because he received securities worth $4,000 but surrendered no securities. The basis of the Alpha securities that Keith received is $4,000. Keith's basis in the Alpha stock is $10,000 ($10,000 basis of Theta stock + $4,000 gain recognized − $4,000 FMV of Alpha securities). ◀

When the target corporation shareholders initially own a single class of stock (or a single class of securities) and exchange that stock for two or more classes of stock or securities in a reorganization, the total basis in the nonrecognition property as calculated under the above formula must be allocated among the stock and/or securities in proportion to the relative FMVs of each class.[31]

Holding Period. The holding period for the stock and securities that are nonrecognition property includes the holding period for the stock and securities surrendered. The holding period for boot property begins the day after the exchange date.[32]

[30] *King Enterprises, Inc. v. U.S.*, 24 AFTR 2d 69-5866, 69-2 USTC ¶9720 (Ct. Cls., 1969).

[31] Reg. Sec. 1.358-2(a)(2)-(4).

[32] Sec. 1223(1).

Topic Review C:7-4 summarizes the tax consequences of a reorganization to the target corporation, acquiring corporation, and target corporation shareholders and security holders.

TOPIC REVIEW C:7-4

Tax Consequences of a Reorganization

THE TARGET CORPORATION

1. The target corporation recognizes no gain or loss on the asset transfer except to the extent that it receives and retains cash or other boot property (Secs. 361(a)–(b)). Generally, boot is not retained because the reorganization provisions require the target corporation to liquidate or otherwise distribute all its assets.
2. The character of any recognized gain or loss depends on the nature of the assets transferred.
3. The acquiring corporation's assumption or acquisition of target corporation liabilities does not trigger recognition of gain on the asset transfer except where "excess" liabilities are assumed in divisive Type D reorganizations (Sec. 357(a)).
4. The target corporation recognizes no gain or loss when it distributes qualified stock and securities to its shareholders and security holders. The target corporation recognizes gain (but not loss) when it distributes to its shareholders or security holders noncash boot property or retained assets (Sec. 361(c)).

THE ACQUIRING CORPORATION

1. The acquiring corporation recognizes no gain or loss when it receives cash or other boot property in exchange for its stock or debt obligations (Sec. 1032).
2. On the other hand, the acquiring corporation recognizes gain or loss when it transfers appreciated or depreciated (in value) noncash boot property to the target corporation or its shareholders (Sec. 1001).
3. The basis of noncash property received by the acquiring corporation equals its basis in the transferor's hands increased by any gain recognized by the transferor (Sec. 362(b)).
4. The acquiring corporation's holding period for such property includes the transferor's holding period (Sec. 1223(1)).

SHAREHOLDERS AND SECURITY HOLDERS

1. Shareholders and security holders recognize no gain or loss if they receive only stock (Sec. 354(a)). They recognize gain (but not loss) when they receive cash, excess securities, or other boot property. The amount of recognized gain equals the lesser of the realized gain or the amount of cash plus the FMV of any other boot property received (Sec. 356(b)).
2. The character of recognized gain is based on Sec. 302(b) as applied hypothetically to receipt of acquiring corporation stock. Dividend income cannot exceed the shareholder's ratable share of the transferor or target corporation's E&P (Sec. 356(a)(2)).
3. The total basis of stock and securities received equals the adjusted basis of stock and securities surrendered plus any gain recognized by the shareholders and security holders on the exchange minus the sum of cash and FMV of other boot property received. This basis is allocated among the stock and securities received according to their relative FMVs. The basis of boot property is its FMV (Sec. 358(a)).
4. The holding period for stock and securities received includes the holding period for stock and securities surrendered. The holding period for boot property received begins the day after the exchange date (Sec. 1223(1)).

ACQUISITIVE REORGANIZATIONS

OBJECTIVE 4

Describe the structure and requirements of each type of acquisitive reorganization

This section is devoted to Types A, B, C, D, and G acquisitive reorganizations. Each of these types is explained below. Topic Review C:7-5 summarizes the tax aspects of acquisitive reorganizations.

TYPE A REORGANIZATION

Type A reorganizations encompass four transactional structures: mergers, consolidations, triangular mergers, and reverse triangular mergers. Each of these structures is summarized in Topic Review C:7-5.

TOPIC REVIEW C:7-5

Summary of Major Acquisitive Reorganizations

Type of Reorganization	The Target (T) Corporation Property Acquired	Consideration That Can Be Used	What Happens to the Target (T) Corporation?	Shareholders' Recognized Gain	Other Requirements
A—Merger or consolidation	Assets and liabilities of T Corporation.[a]	Voting and nonvoting stock, securities, and other property of A Corporation.[b]	T Corporation liquidates as part of the merger.	Lesser of realized gain or FMV of boot received.	Transaction must have a business purpose and meet continuity of interest and business enterprise requirements.
B—Stock for stock	At least 80% of voting and 80% of nonvoting T Corporation stock.	Voting stock of A Corporation.	Becomes a subsidiary of A Corporation.	None	Boot paid by the transferor may render the entire transaction taxable.
C—Assets for stock	Substantially all T Corporation assets (and possibly some or all of its liabilities).	A Corporation stock, securities, and other property, provided at least 80% of the assets are acquired for voting stock.	Stock, securities, and boot received in the reorganization and all of T Corporation's remaining properties must be distributed to its shareholders and creditors; as a practical matter, T Corporation liquidates.	Lesser of realized gain or FMV of boot received.	For advance ruling purposes, "substantially all" is 70% of the gross assets and 90% of the net assets of T Corporation.
D—Acquisitive	Substantially all T Corporation assets (and possibly some or all of its liabilities) are acquired by a " controlled" transferee corporation (A Corporation[b]).	A Corporation stock, securities, and other property.	Stocks, securities, and boot received in the reorganization and all of T Corporation's remaining property must be distributed to its shareholders and creditors; as a practical matter, T Corporation liquidates.	Lesser of realized gain or FMV of boot received.	"Substantially all" definition is same as in a Type C reorganization; continuity of interest requirement applies; control is defined as 50% of the voting power or 50% of the value of A Corporation stock.

[a]T Corporation is the target or transferor corporation.
[b]A Corporation is the acquiring or controlled transferee corporation. In a Type D reorganization, A Corporation is 50% or more controlled by T Corporation shareholders.

KEY POINT

The Type A reorganization is unique in comparison to other statutory reorganizations because corporation law is an important factor in determining whether a transaction qualifies as a nontaxable merger.

Merger or Consolidation. In its broadest sense, a Type A reorganization is a **merger** or a **consolidation** that satisfies the corporation laws of the United States, a state, the District of Columbia, or a foreign country.[33] State law authorizes several different merger forms. Two common forms are discussed below. Other permitted forms, such as triangular mergers and reverse triangular mergers, are discussed later in this chapter. The first form involves the acquiring corporation's transferring its stock, securities, and other consideration (boot) directly to the target corporation in exchange for its assets and liabilities. The acquiring corporation stock, securities, and other consideration received by the target corporation are then distributed to its shareholders and security holders in exchange for their target corporation stock and securities. The target corporation then goes out of existence (i.e., it is legally "dissolved"). Figure C:7-1 illustrates this type of merger. The second form involves the acquiring corporation's exchanging its stock, securities, and other consideration directly for target corporation stock and securities held by target corporation shareholders and security holders. The acquiring corporation then liquidates the target corporation and acquires its assets and liabilities.

In a consolidation, a new corporation uses stock, securities, and other consideration to acquire the assets of two or more existing target corporations. Each target corporation distributes the stock, securities, and other consideration to its shareholders and security holders in exchange for target corporation stock and securities. It then liquidates. Figure C:7-2 illustrates this type of consolidation. In another type, the new acquiring corporation transfers its stock, securities, and other consideration directly to target corporation shareholders and security holders in exchange for their target corporation stock and securities. Each target corporation transfers its assets and liabilities to the acquiring corporation and then liquidates.

KEY POINT

The Type A reorganization is the most flexible reorganization with respect to the type of consideration that may be used. The only requirement that must be satisfied concerns continuity of interest, which is discussed later in the chapter.

Requirements for Mergers and Consolidations. In terms of consideration, a Type A reorganization gives the acquiring corporation the greatest flexibility. Section 368 places no restrictions on the kind of consideration that can be used. Under the continuity of

ADDITIONAL COMMENT

The actual exchange of acquiring corporation stock for target corporation stock may be different from the illustrations provided in this chapter. These illustrations represent how the IRC construes the steps in each reorganization. As a practical matter, the exchange of stock between the parties usually is performed by an independent stock transfer agent rather than flowing from the acquiring corporation to the target corporation and finally to the target corporation shareholders.

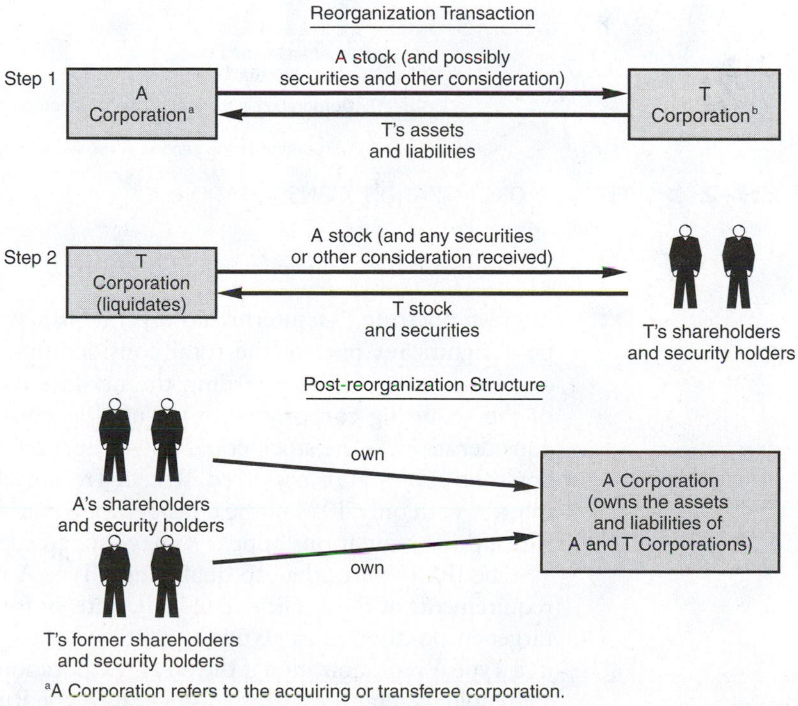

[a]A Corporation refers to the acquiring or transferee corporation.

[b]T Corporation refers to the target or transferor corporation.

FIGURE C:7-1 ▶ TYPE A REORGANIZATION—MERGER

[33] Sec. 368(a)(1)(A) and Reg. Sec. 1.368-2(b)(1).

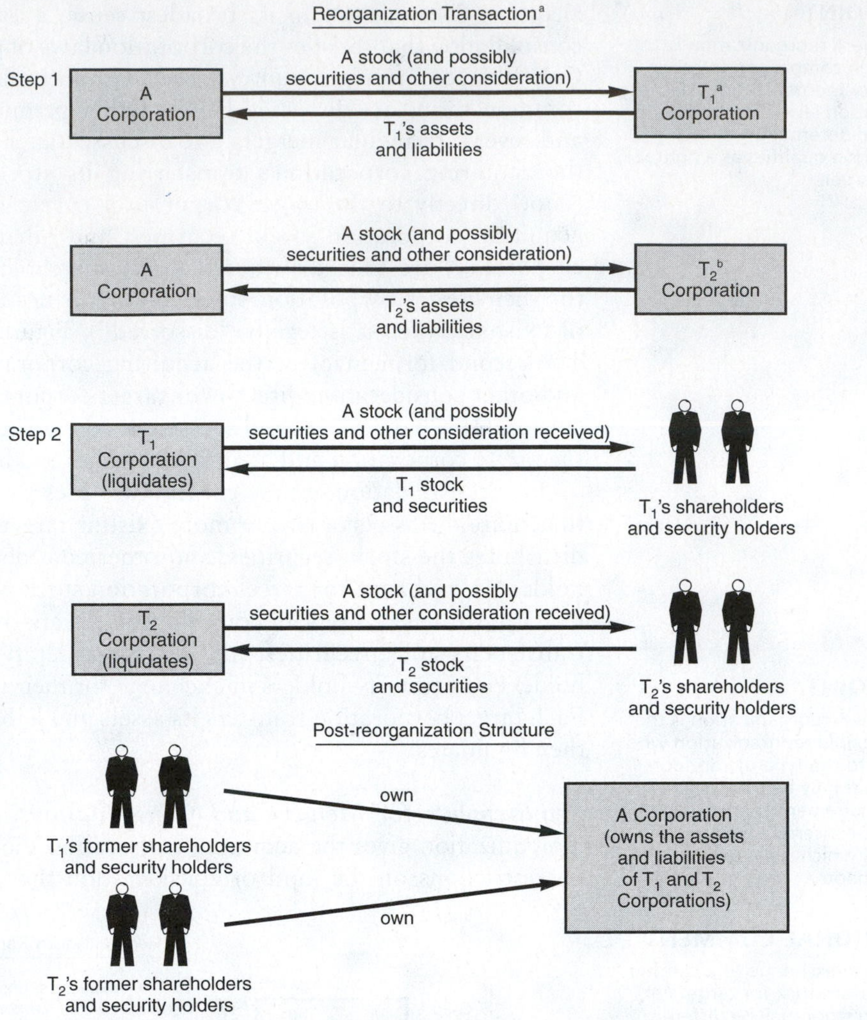

[a]T_1 Corporation is the first of two target corporations that are parties to the reorganization.

[b]T_2 Corporation is the second of two target corporations that are parties to the reorganization.

FIGURE C:7-2 ▶ TYPE A REORGANIZATION: CONSOLIDATION

interest doctrine, as interpreted by the IRS, stock of the acquiring corporation must be a significant part of the total consideration used. In the past, the IRS did not issue a private letter ruling regarding the tax-free nature of the transaction if the percentage of the acquiring corporation stock used as consideration was less than 50% of the total consideration.[34] The stock could be voting, nonvoting, or a combination of the two, and it could be common or preferred. Recent Treasury Regulations, however, allow continuity of interest with only 40% of the consideration consisting of the acquiring corporation stock.[35] Thus, these regulations appear to have superceded the IRS's previous ruling position.

The IRS requires that, to qualify as a Type A reorganization, the merger must satisfy the requirements of the applicable federal, state, or foreign corporate merger law. In addition, the target corporation must go out of existence or be dissolved.[36] An acquisition does not qualify as a Type A reorganization if the target corporation retains some assets and target corporation shareholders retain some target stock. Revenue Ruling 2000-5 holds that, if a target corporation merges under state law into two or more acquiring corporations and the target corporation does not go out of existence, the transaction does not qualify as a Type A reorganization.

[34] See Rev. Proc. 77-37, 1977-2 C.B. 568, Sec. 3.02. In recent years, tax opinions from tax counsel have largely replaced private letter rulings for most acquisitive reorganizations.

[35] Reg. Sec. 1.368-1(e)(2)(v), Example 1.

[36] Rev. Rul. 2000-5, 2000-1 C.B. 436.

ADDITIONAL COMMENT

Shareholder approval is time consuming, expensive, and not always possible to obtain, particularly in the case of large public corporations having shareholders that are widely dispersed.

Because a merger or consolidation must comply with state, federal, or foreign corporation laws, transactions that qualify as mergers or consolidations, and the procedures that must be followed to effect them, vary according to the laws of the jurisdictions in which the acquiring and target corporations are incorporated. Generally, these laws require approval by a majority of shareholders of the corporate parties to the merger. Where the stock in one or both of the companies is publicly traded, holding a shareholder's meeting, soliciting proxies, and obtaining the necessary corporate approvals may be costly and time consuming.

The rights of any dissenting shareholders are defined in merger law. Among these rights are the right to dissent and have shares independently valued and purchased for cash. Liquidating the interests of a substantial number of dissenting shareholders may require a large cash outlay and could, in some circumstances, violate the continuity-of-interest doctrine.

A transaction that does not satisfy the requirements of the applicable corporation law does not qualify as a Type A reorganization.[37] Generally, this shortcoming renders the entire transaction taxable.

Advantages and Disadvantages of a Type A Reorganization. A Type A reorganization offers a number of advantages and disadvantages.

Advantages:

- A Type A reorganization is more flexible than other types of reorganizations because the consideration need not be solely voting stock, as in the case of some other types. Cash, securities, other property, and the assumption of the target corporation's liabilities can constitute up to 60% of the total consideration used.[38]
- Substantially all the assets of the target corporation need not be acquired, as in the case of a Type C reorganization. Thus, dispositions of unwanted assets by the target corporation prior to, or as part of, the acquisition generally do not render the merger taxable.

Disadvantages:

- The parties to the merger must comply with applicable corporation laws. In most states, the shareholders of both the acquiring and target corporations must approve a plan of merger by a two-thirds majority. Such approvals can take time and be costly if stock in one or both of the corporations is publicly traded.
- Dissenting shareholders of both corporations generally have the right to have their shares independently appraised and purchased for cash, which may require a substantial cash outlay.
- All liabilities of the target corporation, including unknown and contingent liabilities, must be assumed.
- A merger requires the transfer of real estate titles, leases, and contracts. The target corporation may have licenses, rights, or other privileges that are nontransferable. This limitation may necessitate a reverse triangular merger or Type B reorganization discussed below.

Tax Consequences of a Merger. The following example illustrates the tax consequences of a merger.

EXAMPLE C:7-18 ▶ In a merger that qualifies as a Type A reorganization, Theta Corporation transfers to Alpha Corporation all its assets having a $2 million FMV and a $1.3 million adjusted basis, respectively, together with $400,000 in liabilities, in exchange for $1 million of Alpha common stock having a $16 per share market value and $600,000 of cash. At the time of the transfer, Alpha's E&P balance is $1 million, and Theta's is $750,000. Theta distributes the Acquiring stock and cash to its sole shareholder, Millie, in exchange for all her Theta stock, which has a $175,000 basis. If Millie had received only Alpha stock (instead of a combination of Alpha stock and cash), she would have held 6.25% of Alpha stock (100,000 out of 1.6 million shares deemed outstanding) immediately after the exchange.

---

[37] *Edward H. Russell v. CIR,* 15 AFTR 2d 1107, 65-2 USTC ¶9448 (5th Cir., 1965).

[38] Previous advance ruling requirements generally limited nonstock consideration to 50% of the total consideration. In certain circumstances, the courts have permitted the 50% ceiling to be exceeded. Treasury Regulations now allow up to 60% nonstock consideration. See footnote 37.

In the asset transfer, Theta realizes a $700,000 gain [($1,000,000 stock + $600,000 cash + $400,000 liabilities) − $1,300,000 adjusted basis] but recognizes none of this gain. Alpha takes a $1.3 million carryover basis in the assets it receives. Theta recognizes no gain when it distributes the stock and cash to Millie.

Upon Theta's liquidation, Millie realizes a $1,425,000 gain [($1,000,000 stock + $600,000 cash) − $175,000 adjusted basis], of which $600,000 must be recognized because of the cash (i.e., boot) received. The hypothetical redemption of Millie's Alpha stock required under the *Clark* case and Rev. Rul. 93-61 (see pages C:7-16 and C:7-17) qualifies for Sec. 302(b)(2) sale treatment because the deemed redemption of 37,500 ($600,000 cash ÷ $16) shares of Alpha stock reduces Millie's interest from 6.25% (100,000 shares ÷ 1,600,000 shares) to 4.00% (62,500 shares ÷ 1,562,500 shares). Millie's basis in her Alpha stock is $175,000 ($175,000 basis of Theta stock + $600,000 gain recognized − $600,000 cash received). Millie's holding period for the Alpha stock includes her holding period for the Theta stock. ◀

ADDITIONAL COMMENT

If the IRS applies Sec. 351 to the drop-down transaction, and if the total adjusted basis for all property transferred exceeds the total FMV of that property, the subsidiary's total basis will be limited to the total FMV (see Chapter C:2 for details).

Drop-Down Type a Reorganization. The reorganization rules permit the acquiring corporation to transfer (drop down) to a controlled subsidiary part or all the assets and liabilities acquired in the merger or consolidation.[39] The drop down does not affect the nontaxable nature of the transaction. Thus, neither the parent nor subsidiary recognize gain or loss. The subsidiary takes from its parent a carryover basis in the assets.

Triangular Mergers. Triangular mergers are authorized under Sec. 368(a)(2)(D). They are similar to straight mergers (previously discussed) except the parent corporation uses a controlled subsidiary to acquire target corporation stock or assets. The target corporation then merges into the subsidiary under one of the two merger structures described earlier (see Figure C:7-3).

Triangular mergers must satisfy the same legal requirements as straight mergers. In addition, the stock used as consideration in the transaction is restricted to that of the parent corporation. On the other hand, a limited amount of subsidiary cash and securities can be used, and the subsidiary can assume the target corporation's liabilities.

The "Substantially All" Requirement. To be nontaxable, the subsidiary must acquire substantially all of target corporation's assets pursuant to a plan of reorganization. For advance ruling purposes, the IRS has defined *substantially all* to be at least 70% of the FMV of the target corporation's gross assets and 90% of the FMV of its net assets.[40]

EXAMPLE C:7-19 ▶ In a triangular merger, Alpha Corporation's subsidiary, Alpha-Sub Corporation, plans to acquire $2.5 million (FMV) in assets and $1 million in liabilities of Theta Corporation. Under the IRS's advance ruling policy, Alpha must acquire at least 70% of Theta's gross assets ($1,750,000 = $2,500,000 FMV of assets × 0.70) and 90% of its net assets [$1,350,000 = ($2,500,000 FMV of assets − $1,000,000 liabilities) × 0.90], or $1.75 million in assets. Theta can sell or otherwise dispose of the remaining assets. ◀

Advantages of a Triangular Merger. The tax treatment of a triangular merger is the same as for a straight merger. A triangular merger, however, offers three advantages over a straight merger:

PRACTICAL APPLICATION

The triangular merger is a very popular type of acquisition because the consideration that may be used is still very flexible and yet the parent corporation does not have to assume the known or unknown liabilities of the target corporation. Rather, the controlled subsidiary assumes these liabilities.

- In a triangular merger, the target corporation's assets and liabilities become the responsibility of the subsidiary. Thus, the parent corporation generally cannot be held liable for any unknown or contingent liabilities. Potential claims against the parent corporation from the target corporation's creditors are thus minimized.
- Because the parent corporation is the principal shareholder in the acquiring subsidiary, obtaining shareholder approval for the transaction is relatively easy. Accordingly, the cost of obtaining shareholder approval may be less, especially if the parent corporation's stock is widely held.

---

[39] Sec. 368(a)(2)(C). As defined in Sec. 368(c), *control* requires the parent corporation to own at least 80% of the voting power and 80% of each class of nonvoting stock. The ability to "drop down" the assets acquired to a subsidiary corporation without recognizing any gain also applies to Type B, C, and G reorganizations.

[40] Rev. Proc. 77-37, 1977-2 C.B. 568, Sec. 3.01. Also see Rev. Rul. 2001-46, 2001-2 C.B. 321.

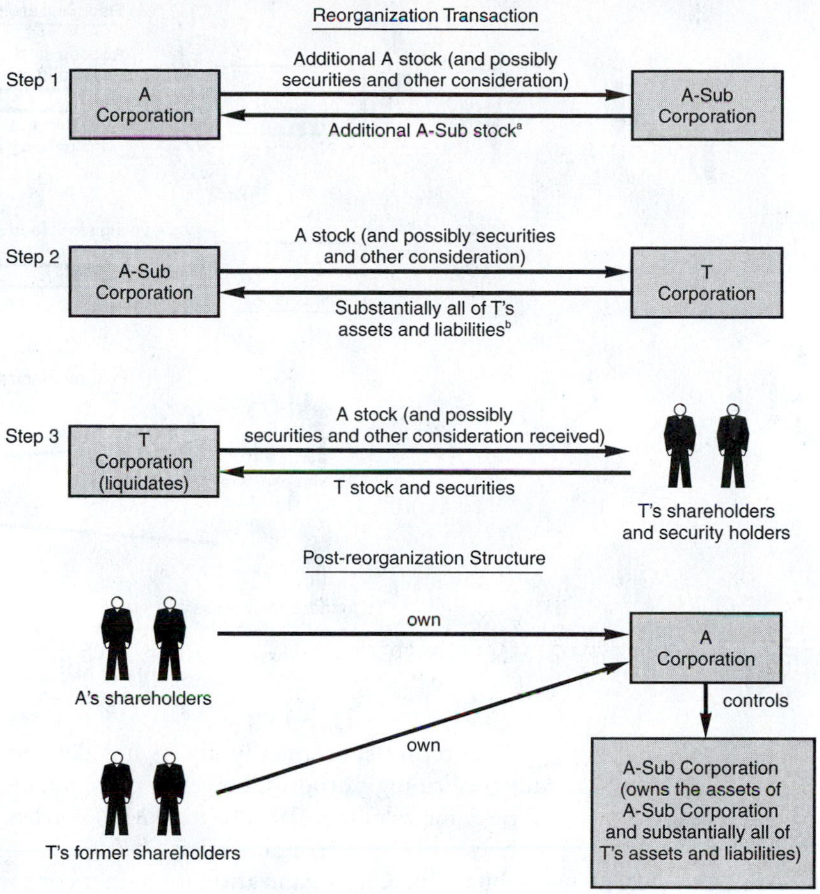

[a]A Corporation must control A-Sub Corporation. If A already owns 100% of A-Sub, the A stock may be treated as additional paid-in capital for the shares that are already owned.

[b]T's shareholders may receive any remaining T Corporation assets that A Corporation did not acquire and that T Corporation did not sell to third parties.

FIGURE C:7-3 ▶ TRIANGULAR TYPE A REORGANIZATION

- The target corporation shareholders may prefer to receive parent corporation stock, especially if such stock is publicly traded, because of its greater marketability. By selling shares of this stock over an extended period of time, target shareholders can recognize the gain as if they were using the installment method of accounting.

ADDITIONAL COMMENT

In addition to the Type B reorganization, which will be discussed later, the reverse triangular merger is an acquisitive reorganization that keeps the target corporation in existence. It is a popular reorganization form because, unlike the Type B reorganization, the acquiring corporation can use a limited amount of boot.

Reverse Triangular Mergers. A **reverse triangular merger** is similar to the triangular merger illustrated in Figure C:7-3 except the subsidiary (A-Sub Corporation) merges into the target corporation (T Corporation), the target corporation remains in existence as a subsidiary of the parent corporation (A Corporation), and A-Sub Corporation goes out of existence. Continuing the target corporation as a going concern may be desirable from a business standpoint where the corporation holds nontransferable rights, licenses, and contracts. Technical details of this type of acquisition are beyond the scope of this text.

TYPE C REORGANIZATION

A **Type C reorganization** is an asset-for-stock acquisition. This type of transaction, illustrated in Figure C:7-4, requires the acquiring corporation to obtain substantially all the target corporation's assets in exchange for acquiring corporation voting stock and possibly a limited amount of other consideration.[41]

[41] Sec. 368(a)(1)(C).

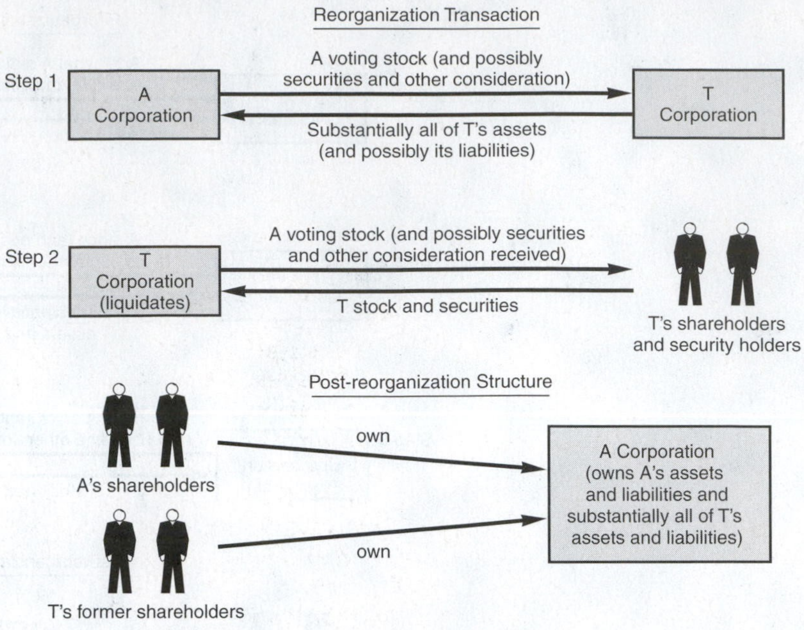

FIGURE C:7-4 ▶ TYPE C (ASSET-FOR-STOCK) REORGANIZATION

The term "substantially all" is not defined in the IRC or Treasury Regulations. For advance ruling purposes, however, the same minimum standard that applies to triangular Type A mergers (i.e., 70% of the FMV of gross assets and 90% of the FMV of net assets) applies to Type C reorganizations.[42]

ADDITIONAL COMMENT

The term "dissolution" means the corporation ceases to exist as a legal entity. The term "liquidation" means the corporation distributes all its assets without necessarily dissolving.

In a Type C reorganization the target corporation must distribute the stock, securities, and other property it receives, plus any other property it retains, to its shareholders as part of the reorganization. Although the corporation need not formally dissolve, as a practical matter it usually liquidates.[43] If it does dissolve, any liabilities not assumed by the acquiring corporation usually become the responsibility of the target corporation's directors by statute. Because the economic effect of a Type C reorganization is the same as that of a merger (i.e., the acquisition of target corporation assets) without dissolving the target corporation, many tax practitioners call it a practical merger.

In a Type C reorganization, the target corporation can retain its corporate charter to prevent others from using its corporate name or sell its corporate name to a third party. Assets other than the corporate charter can be retained to satisfy the minimum capital requirements of state law.[44]

ADDITIONAL COMMENT

Because of the solely-for-voting-stock requirement, a Type C reorganization is much less flexible than a Type A reorganization in terms of the consideration that can be used.

Consideration Used to Effect the Reorganization. Section 368(a)(1)(C) requires that the consideration used to effect the reorganization be solely voting stock of the acquiring corporation (or its parent corporation). Both the acquiring corporation's assumption of part or all of target corporation liabilities and its acquiring property subject to a liability are disregarded for purposes of the solely-for-voting-stock requirement.

Section 368(a)(2)(B) permits the acquiring corporation to use other consideration in the reorganization, provided it obtains at least 80% of target property solely for its voting stock. Effectively, this provision allows the acquiring corporation to use cash, securities, nonvoting stock, or other property to acquire up to 20% of target assets. Liabilities assumed or acquired reduce on a dollar-for-dollar basis the amount of cash or other property the acquiring corporation can use in the reorganization. If the liabilities assumed or acquired exceed 20% of the FMV of target assets, the transaction will qualify as a Type C reorganization only if the acquiring corporation uses no cash, securities, nonvoting stock, or other property as consideration.

---

42 Rev. Proc. 77-37, 1977-2 C.B. 568, Sec. 3.01.

43 Sec. 368(a)(2)(G).

44 Rev. Proc. 89-50, 1989-1 C.B. 631.

EXAMPLE C:7-20 ► Alpha Corporation wants to acquire all of Theta Corporation's assets and liabilities in a Type C reorganization. The following table illustrates how the solely-for-voting-stock test applies in four different situations:

	Situation 1	*Situation 2*	*Situation 3*	*Situation 4*
FMV of Theta assets	$200,000	$200,000	$200,000	$200,000
Theta liabilities assumed by Alpha	–0–	30,000	100,000	100,000
Consideration given by Alpha:				
FMV of Alpha voting stock	160,000	160,000	100,000	99,900
Cash	40,000	10,000	–0–	100

In Situation 1, because the FMV of the Alpha stock equals 80% of total assets, the transaction qualifies as a Type C reorganization. In Situation 2, although the liabilities assumed reduce the amount of cash Alpha can pay, the transaction is still a Type C reorganization because the amount of cash and liabilities, in total, do not exceed 20% of the FMV of Theta assets. In Situation 3, the high percentage of liabilities does not disqualify the transaction from Type C reorganization treatment because Alpha paid no cash.[45] In Situation 4, the transaction fails as a Type C reorganization because Alpha uses cash and stock, and the total amount of cash given plus liabilities assumed by Alpha exceed 20% of the total FMV of Theta assets. ◄

ADDITIONAL COMMENT

A target corporation's liabilities assumed by the acquiring corporation are not a problem unless the target corporation receives boot as part of the consideration. In this case, when applying the 20% boot relaxation rule, liabilities are treated as cash. Situation 4 in Example C:7-20 illustrates that, if the target corporation has liabilities exceeding 20% of the FMV of its assets, the boot relaxation rule is of no benefit.

Advantages and Disadvantages of a Type C Reorganization. Relative to a statutory merger, a Type C reorganization offers the following advantages and disadvantages.

SELF-STUDY QUESTION

Must the acquiring corporation assume all liabilities of the target corporation in a Type C reorganization?

ANSWER

No. The acquiring corporation may leave liabilities in the target corporation. These liabilities would then have to be satisfied with assets retained by the target corporation or with assets acquired by the target corporation in the reorganization.

Advantages:

- ► A Type C reorganization does not have to comply with the merger laws of a state or the federal government as does a Type A reorganization (merger). However, it might have to comply with other laws (e.g., corporate and securities laws).
- ► In a Type C reorganization, the acquiring corporation assumes only those target corporation liabilities specified in the acquisition agreement. Unknown and contingent liabilities are not assumed, as they are in a merger.
- ► In a Type C reorganization, shareholders of the acquiring corporation generally need not approve the acquisition, thereby reducing the total transaction cost. In a merger, however, acquiring and target corporation shareholders must approve the transaction.

Disadvantages:

- ► In a Type C reorganization, the acquiring corporation must use voting stock in contrast to a Type A reorganization, in which the acquiring corporation may use nonvoting stock.
- ► A Type C reorganization has much tighter boot restrictions than does a Type A reorganization in which up to 60% of consideration other than stock can be used (see footnote 37).
- ► In many cases, target liabilities assumed by the acquiring corporation may be so substantial (i.e., exceeding 20% of total consideration) as to preclude the use of any consideration other than voting stock.
- ► The target corporation might want to sell, dispose of, or retain assets the acquiring corporation does not want. However, doing so shortly before an asset-for-stock acquisition might cause the transaction to fail the substantially all test and thereby disqualify it as a Type C reorganization. By contrast, the substantially all test does not apply to a merger, and dispositions of unwanted assets generally will not disqualify a merger as a Type A reorganization.

ADDITIONAL COMMENT

In either a Type A or Type C reorganization, dissenting shareholders of the target corporation may have the right under state law to have their shares independently appraised and purchased for cash.

---

[45] The IRS, however, may attempt to treat a transaction as a purchase under the continuity of interest doctrine (see page C:7-41) when the amount of liabilities assumed or acquired is high relative to the total FMV of the assets acquired.

Tax Consequences of a Type C Reorganization. The following example illustrates the tax consequences of a Type C reorganization.

EXAMPLE C:7-21 ▶ Alpha Corporation acquires all Theta Corporation's assets and liabilities in exchange for \$1.2 million of Alpha voting stock. Theta distributes the Alpha stock to its sole shareholder, Andrew, in exchange for all his Theta stock. Theta's assets have a \$1.4 million FMV and a \$600,000 adjusted basis. Alpha assumes liabilities of \$200,000. Theta has a \$500,000 E&P balance. Andrew's basis in his Theta stock is \$400,000. Theta realizes an \$800,000 gain [(\$1,200,000 + \$200,000) − \$600,000], none of which is recognized. Alpha recognizes no gain when it exchanges its stock for the assets, in which it takes a \$600,000 carryover basis. Upon surrendering his Theta shares, Andrew realizes an \$800,000 (\$1,200,000 − \$400,000) gain, none of which is recognized. Andrew's substituted basis in the Alpha stock is \$400,000. Andrew's holding period for the Alpha stock includes his holding period for the Theta stock. Alpha inherits all of Theta's tax attributes, including the \$500,000 E&P balance. ◀

TYPICAL MISCONCEPTION

As with a Type A reorganization, a Type C reorganization can be structured as a triangular (but not reverse triangular) acquisition. Although this feature provides greater flexibility in tax planning, it makes the tax consequences more confusing because of the substantial overlap between the different types of reorganizations.

Drop-Down and Triangular Type C Reorganizations. In a Type C reorganization, the acquiring corporation can transfer (drop down) the acquired assets and liabilities to a controlled subsidiary without adversely affecting the nontaxable character of the Type C reorganization. Alternatively, an acquiring subsidiary can use parent corporation voting stock to acquire substantially all the target corporation's assets.[46] The triangular Type C reorganization requirements are the same as those for a basic Type C reorganization except the voting stock used by the acquiring subsidiary to acquire target corporation assets must consist solely of the parent's stock. The acquiring subsidiary, however, can provide additional consideration in the form of securities, cash, or other property.

TYPE D REORGANIZATION

KEY POINT

When a Type D reorganization is used as an acquisitive reorganization, it generally involves commonly controlled corporations. However, its most common usage is as part of a divisive reorganization under Sec. 355 (discussed later in this chapter).

Type D reorganizations can be either acquisitive or divisive. (Divisive Type D reorganizations are discussed on pages C:7-33 through C:7-38.) In an acquisitive Type D reorganization, a target (transferor) corporation transfers substantially all its assets to an acquiring (transferee) corporation in exchange for the transferee's stock and securities (and possibly other consideration) pursuant to a plan of reorganization. The exchange must be followed by a distribution of the stock, securities, and other consideration received in the reorganization, plus any other property retained by the transferor corporation, to the transferor's shareholders and security holders pursuant to a complete liquidation.[47] (See Figure C:7-5 for an illustration of an acquisitive Type D reorganization.)

What constitutes "substantially all" is based on the facts and circumstances. For advance ruling purposes, however, the 70% of the FMV of gross assets and 90% of the FMV of net assets tests used in the triangular Type A and Type C reorganizations also apply here.[48]

ADDITIONAL COMMENT

The 50% control requirement makes the Type D reorganization a useful tool for the IRS to recast certain tax avoidance transactions.

Control Requirements. The transferor (target) corporation or one or more of its shareholders must control the transferee (acquiring) corporation immediately after the asset transfer. Section 368(a)(2)(H) defines control as either 50% or more of the total combined voting power of all classes of voting stock, or 50% or more of the total value of all classes of stock.

In one version of an acquisitive Type D reorganization, an acquiring corporation acquires all the assets of a larger corporation (target corporation), and target corporation shareholders control the acquiring corporation after the reorganization. Type C reorganizations (in which the target corporation does not control the acquiring corporation) and Type A reorganizations (which must comply with state, federal, or foreign merger law) are more common than acquisitive Type D reorganizations.

Tax Consequences of a Type D Reorganization. Acquisitive Type D reorganization requirements are similar to those for a Type C reorganization. If the reorganization satisfies both the Type C and Type D reorganization requirements, Sec.

[46] Sec. 368(a)(2)(C) and Sec. 368(a)(1)(C).

[47] Secs. 368(a)(1)(D) and 354(b)(1).

[48] Rev. Proc. 77-37, 1977-2 C.B. 568, Sec. 3.01.

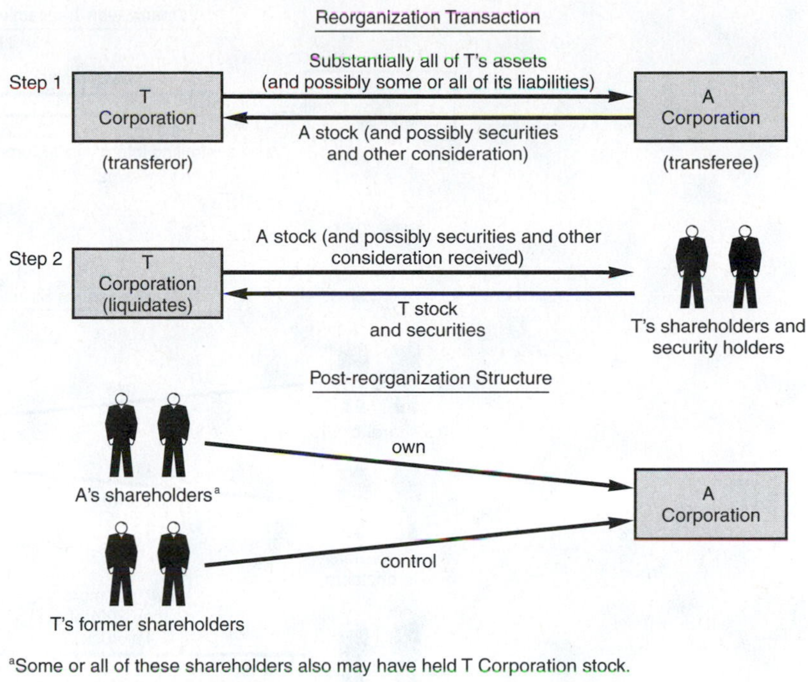

FIGURE C:7-5 ▶ ACQUISITIVE TYPE D REORGANIZATION

368(a)(2)(A) mandates that the reorganization be treated as Type D. The basic tax consequences of a Type D reorganization to the target corporation, the acquiring corporation, and target corporation shareholders are the same as those in a Type C reorganization.

ADDITIONAL COMMENT

If the acquiring corporation wants the target corporation to remain in existence, the two transactional alternatives in Sec. 368 that can accomplish this objective are a Type B reorganization or a reverse triangular merger.

TYPE B REORGANIZATION

A **Type B reorganization** is the simplest of acquisitive reorganizations. In this type of reorganization, target corporation shareholders (or parent company) exchange their stock for acquiring corporation voting stock, and the target corporation remains in existence as the acquiring corporation's subsidiary (see Figure C:7-6). No Sec. 338 election is available because, in any reorganization, the stock is not considered "purchased" for purposes of this election.

A Type B reorganization generally preserves the target corporation as a going concern. The basis of the target's assets (inside basis) and its tax attributes generally remain unchanged. After the reorganization, the target corporation and its parent may elect to file a consolidated tax return (see Chapter C:8). If the target corporation liquidates into its parent shortly after the stock-for-stock exchange, the IRS may attempt to collapse the two-step transaction into a single transaction and treat it as a Type C asset-for-stock reorganization.[49]

KEY POINT

The IRC allows no relaxation of the solely-for-voting-stock requirement for the Type B reorganization. Thus, the Type B reorganization has the least flexible consideration requirement of any of the reorganizations.

Solely-for-Voting-Stock Requirement. Under Sec. 368(a)(1)(B), the acquiring corporation must acquire target corporation stock solely in exchange for acquiring corporation voting stock. The acquiring corporation must own sufficient stock to be in control of the target corporation immediately after the exchange.

The solely-for-voting-stock requirement generally precludes the use of other property as consideration in the transaction. However, the voting stock used can be either common or preferred. If the acquiring corporation uses consideration other than voting stock (e.g., nonvoting preferred stock), the transaction will not qualify as a Type B reorganization and thus will be taxable to target corporation shareholders.

In a Type B reorganization, acquiring corporation debt obligations can be exchanged for target corporation debt obligations held by target shareholders, who will not recognize gain or loss if the face amounts of the two obligations are the same.[50]

[49] Rev. Rul. 67-274, 1967-2 C.B. 141. If the transaction is "collapsed" into a Type C reorganization, the Type C reorganization requirements (and not the Type B) must be satisfied.

[50] Rev. Rul. 98-10, 1998-1 C.B. 643.

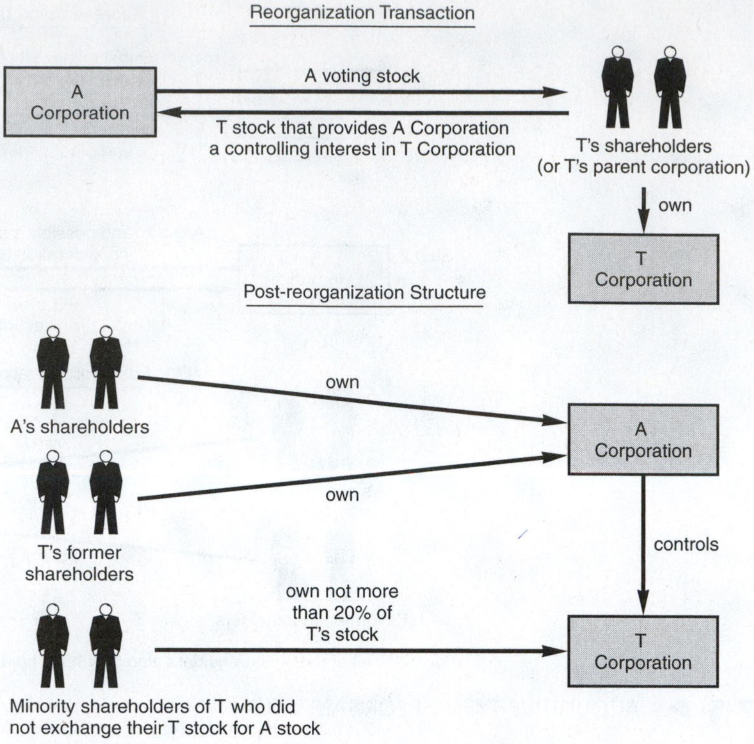

FIGURE C:7-6 ▶ TYPE B (STOCK-FOR-STOCK) REORGANIZATION

SELF-STUDY QUESTION

How can dissenters in a Type B reorganization be handled given the no-boot restriction?

ANSWER

The target corporation can redeem the dissenting shares before the reorganization. Also, the nondissenting shareholders could buy out the dissenters' stock.

ADDITIONAL COMMENT

"Creeping acquisitions" are allowed in a Type B reorganization because the requirement is merely that the acquiring corporation own 80% after the transaction. Transactions within 12 months generally are considered related transactions. This aggregation rule can be either an advantage or a disadvantage depending on what consideration the acquiring corporation used in the various acquisition steps.

Exceptions. The acquiring corporation can use cash in limited circumstances without violating the solely-for-voting-stock requirement. For example:

- The target corporation shareholders can receive cash in exchange for their right to receive a fractional share of acquiring corporation stock.[51]
- The acquiring corporation can pay reorganization expenses (such as legal expenses, accounting fees, and administrative costs) of the target corporation without violating the solely-for-voting-stock requirement.[52]

Control. For the purpose of a Type B reorganization, Section 368(c) defines control as 80% of the total combined voting power of all classes of voting stock and 80% of each class of nonvoting stock. Because the acquiring corporation need not acquire all the target corporation stock, a minority interest of up to 20% may remain. Under state law, minority shareholders can have their shares independently valued and acquired for cash without impairing the tax-free nature of the transaction. The target corporation can use its cash to redeem the minority shareholders' stock before or after the reorganization. The acquiring corporation, however, cannot use cash to purchase the dissenting minority shareholders' stock either before or as part of the reorganization. Doing so will render the entire transaction taxable.[53]

Timing of the Transaction. Some Type B reorganizations are conducted in a single transaction by exchanging stock of the acquiring corporation for 100% of target corporation shares. In other instances, the reorganization is accomplished through a series of transactions over an extended period of time. Regulation Sec. 1.368-2(c) provides that a cash purchase of stock may be disregarded for purposes of the solely-for-voting-stock requirement if it was independent of the stock-for-stock exchange. According to this regulation, stock acquisitions over a relatively short period of time—12 months or less—are to be aggregated for purposes of the solely-for-voting-stock requirement.

[51] Rev. Rul. 66-365, 1966-2 C.B. 116, as amplified by Rev. Rul. 81-81, 1981-1 C.B. 122.

[52] Rev. Rul. 73-54, 1973-1 C.B. 187.

[53] Rev. Rul. 68-285, 1968-1 C.B. 147.

EXAMPLE C:7-22 ► In July of last year, Alpha Corporation purchased for cash 12% of Theta Corporation's single class of stock. In January of the current year, Alpha acquires the remaining 88% in a stock-for-stock exchange. The IRS probably will aggregate the cash and stock-for-stock acquisitions because they occurred within a 12-month period. Even though Alpha achieves 80% control in a single stock-for-stock exchange, this transaction does not qualify as a Type B reorganization because, if the two stock purchases are aggregated, the solely-for-voting-stock requirement is not met. The transaction could qualify as a Type B reorganization if Alpha unconditionally sold its 12% interest in Theta and then acquired the requisite 80% interest in a single stock-for-stock exchange, or if Alpha postponed the stock-for-stock exchange until after July of the current year, when the exchange might be considered independent of the cash purchase.[54] ◄

EXAMPLE C:7-23 ► Seven years ago, Alpha Corporation acquired 85% of Theta Corporation's single class of stock in a transaction that qualified as a Type B reorganization. In December of the current year, Alpha acquires the remaining 15% of Theta stock in a stock-for-stock exchange. Even though Alpha already controls Theta, the second transaction qualifies for Type B reorganization treatment because Alpha owns at least 80% of Theta after the exchange. ◄

Tax Consequences of a Type B Reorganization. The tax consequences of a Type B reorganization are as follows:

- The target corporation shareholders (or parent company) recognize no gain or loss on the exchange unless their fractional shares are acquired for cash or the target corporation redeems some of their stock.
- The target corporation shareholders (or parent company) take a substituted basis in their acquiring corporation stock referenced to the basis of their target corporation stock surrendered. The holding period for the acquiring corporation stock includes the holding period for the target corporation stock.
- The acquiring corporation recognizes no gain or loss when it issues its voting stock for target corporation stock.
- The acquiring corporation's basis in the target corporation stock is the same as in the hands of target corporation shareholders (or parent company).

EXAMPLE C:7-24 ► Mark owns all of Theta Corporation's single class of stock, which has a $400,000 basis. Mark exchanges his Theta stock for $700,000 of Alpha Corporation voting stock. Mark realizes a $300,000 gain ($700,000 − $400,000), none of which is recognized. Mark's substituted basis in the Alpha stock is $400,000. Alpha recognizes no gain or loss when it issues its stock to Mark, and it takes a $400,000 carryover basis in the acquired Theta stock. ◄

? STOP & THINK

Question: Assume that stock in both Alpha and Theta Corporations is publicly traded and each corporation has several thousand shareholders. Alpha acquires Theta stock in a Type B reorganization. What problems might arise in determining Alpha's basis in the Theta stock?

Solution: Under Sec. 358(a), Alpha's basis in the Theta stock is the same as that in the hands of Theta's shareholders. Many shareholders may not know their basis in stock purchased several years ago. The basis for these shares may have changed as a result of stock dividends, stock splits, or nonliquidating distributions. This lack of information may make it difficult to accurately determine Alpha's basis in the Theta stock acquired. To address the issue, the IRS allows sampling to extrapolate Alpha's basis from the stock holdings of a small number of Theta shareholders' aggregate stock basis.

ADDITIONAL COMMENT

The IRS has concluded that compliance with the sampling standards in Rev. Proc. 81-70, 1981-2 C.B. 729, may be "unduly burdensome or impossible." Thus, the IRS has sought comments from those who perform basis studies and other interested parties in an effort to revise the revenue procedure (see Notice 2004-44, 2004-28 I.R.B. 32). So far, the IRS has not issued new guidance.

Advantages of a Type B Reorganization. A Type B reorganization has a number of advantages.

- The acquisition of target corporation stock usually can be accomplished in a single transaction without formal shareholder approval. Even if the target corporation's management does not approve the transaction, the acquiring corporation can acquire

[54] See, for example, *Eldon S. Chapman et al. v. CIR*, 45 AFTR 2d 80-1290, 80-1 USTC ¶9330 (1st Cir., 1980).

What Would You Do in This Situation?

You have just joined Professional CPA, LLP as a new associate. Professional CPA's principal audit client is Intergalactic Enterprises, a public company that accounts for roughly a quarter of Professional CPA's revenues. Intergalactic wants to acquire the stock of Nebula Industries in a tender offer that qualifies as a Type B reorganization. In the proposed transaction, Intergalactic would offer three shares of Intergalactic stock for every two shares of Nebula stock. Currently, in the open market, Intergalactic stock trades at $15 a share while Nebula stock trades at $25 a share. Intergalactic would terminate the offer upon the tender of 55% of Nebula's outstanding shares.

Because Intergalactic's principal shareholder, Herman Islander, wants to retain control of the Intergalactic board of directors, he proposes to restrict the voting rights of Intergalactic stock issued to Nebula's shareholders. Under the proposed restriction, holders of the newly issued Intergalactic shares would have the right to vote for only two out of seven Intergalactic board members while holders of currently issued Intergalactic shares have the right to vote for all seven board members. Moreover, the voting rights inherent in all Nebula shares issued and outstanding are unrestricted.

Islander has requested from Professional CPA a written opinion to the effect that the exchange of Nebula shares with unrestricted voting rights, for Intergalactic shares with restricted voting rights, meets the continuity of interest requirement. Although your supervisor questions whether the exchange in fact does meet the requirement, she recognizes that Intergalactic is a key audit client that contributes substantially to the firm's revenues.

Your supervisor approaches you with a request that you draft the opinion. What should be your response?

the requisite number of shares through a tender offer directly to target corporation shareholders including target's parent corporation, if applicable.

- The target corporation remains in existence, and its assets, liabilities, and tax attributes need not be transferred to the acquiring corporation. However, the use of its NOLs may be limited under Sec. 382 (see pages C:7-43 through C:7-45).[55]
- The corporate name, goodwill, licenses, and rights of the target corporation may be preserved after the acquisition.
- The acquiring corporation does not directly assume the target corporation's liabilities, as is the case in some other reorganizations.
- The acquiring and target corporations can report their post-acquisition results on a consolidated basis (see Chapter C:8).

Disadvantages of a Type B Reorganization. Offsetting those advantages are a number of disadvantages.

- The acquiring corporation can use only voting stock as consideration in the transaction.
- Issuing additional stock for the acquisition can dilute the voting power and control of acquiring corporation shareholders.
- The acquiring corporation must obtain at least 80% of target corporation stock even though effective control can be achieved through ownership of less than 80%.
- The acquisition of less than 100% of target corporation stock may give rise to dissenting minority shareholders. Under state law, these shareholders have the right to have their shares appraised and purchased for cash.
- The bases of target corporation stock (outside basis) and assets (inside basis) are not stepped-up (or stepped-down) to their FMVs upon the change in ownership, as would be the case in a taxable asset acquisition.

Drop-Down and Triangular Type B Reorganizations. As with Type A and C reorganizations, a triangular Type B reorganization, or a drop down of target corporation stock into a subsidiary before the stock-for-stock exchange, can be accomplished tax-free. In a triangular Type B reorganization, the acquiring subsidiary exchanges its parent stock for a controlling interest in the target corporation. As in a basic Type B reorganization,

[55] A Type B reorganization can result in an ownership change that, under Sec. 382, restricts the use of the target corporation's NOL carryovers but does not, in total, diminish the amount of its carryovers.

the target corporation remains in existence as a subsidiary of the acquiring subsidiary. In a triangular Type B reorganization, however, it becomes a second-tier subsidiary of the parent corporation.

TYPE G REORGANIZATION

Section 368(a)(1)(G) defines a **Type G reorganization** as "a transfer by a corporation of part or all of its assets to another corporation in a Title 11 [bankruptcy] or similar case, but only if, in pursuance of the plan, stock or securities of the corporation to which the assets are transferred are distributed in a transaction that qualifies under sections 354, 355, or 356." Type G reorganizations are infrequent because the reorganization must occur pursuant to a court-approved plan in a bankruptcy, receivership, or similar situation.

In an acquisitive Type G reorganization, an insolvent corporation might transfer substantially all its assets to an acquiring corporation under a court-approved plan (e.g., a bankruptcy reorganization plan). It then might distribute all the stock, securities, and other property received in the exchange, plus any property retained, to its shareholders and creditors in exchange for their stock and debt obligations.

DIVISIVE REORGANIZATIONS

OBJECTIVE 5

Describe the structure and requirements of divisive reorganizations

A divisive reorganization involves the transfer of some of a transferor corporation's assets to a controlled corporation in exchange for the controlled corporation's stock and securities (and possibly boot property).[56] The transferor then distributes the stock and securities (and possibly boot property) to its shareholders. A divisive reorganization generally is governed by the Type D reorganization rules, although a divisive reorganization involving an insolvent corporation could be governed by the Type G reorganization rules. Topic Review C:7-6 summarizes the requirements for divisive and other reorganizations.

ADDITIONAL COMMENT

In a divisive transaction governed by Sec. 355, the "transferor corporation" is referred to as the "distributing corporation." Accordingly, the discussion of divisive reorganizations in this text will use that terminology and thus refer to the transferor corporation as the distributing corporation.

TYPICAL MISCONCEPTION

The existence of a corporate business purpose is necessary before the stock of a controlled subsidiary can be distributed to the shareholders of the distributing corporation. This requirement is much more difficult to satisfy in a Sec. 355 distribution than it is in an acquisitive reorganization.

DIVISIVE TYPE D REORGANIZATION

A divisive Type D reorganization must satisfy the requirements of Secs. 368(a)(1)(D) and 355, which are explained below.[57] Divisive Type D reorganizations can assume three forms: spin-offs, split-offs, and split-ups (see Figure C:7-7).

In the reorganization, a distribution of a controlled corporation's stock may be nontaxable under Sec. 355 even if the distributing corporation transfers no assets to the controlled corporation, in which case the division is not classified as a reorganization. To be a nontaxable Type D reorganization, however, both the asset transfer and the Sec. 355 distribution must be part of a single transaction governed by a plan of reorganization.

A divisive Type D reorganization can accomplish various business objectives, including

- Dividing an enterprise into two or more corporations to separate a high-risk business from a low-risk business
- Splitting up a single business among two or more disputing shareholders
- Reorganizing an enterprise according to functions, profit centers, or geographical areas
- Divesting operations because of antitrust laws

Forms of Divisive Type D Reorganizations. Three types of divisive transactions are nontaxable under Sec. 368(a)(1)(D):

- **Split-off**—the distributing corporation transfers some of its assets to a controlled corporation in exchange for stock and possibly securities, cash, or other boot property. The distributing corporation then distributes stock in the controlled corporation to some or all of its shareholders in exchange for some of their stock. The context for such a transaction might be a management dispute between two distinct shareholder groups. To resolve the dispute, the parent corporation might redeem all the stock of one of the groups (see Figure C:7-7).

---

[56] In a divisive Type D reorganization, Sec. 368(c) defines the term control because Sec. 355 (not Sec. 354) governs the distribution. In such a reorganization, control requires ownership of at least 80% of the voting and nonvoting stock. In an acquisitive Type D reorganization, on the other hand, control requires ownership of only 50% of the voting and nonvoting stock.

[57] The requirements of a divisive Type D reorganization are contrasted with the acquisitive Type D reorganization (previously discussed), where substantially all the transferor's assets must be transferred to a controlled corporation.

TOPIC REVIEW C:7-6

Summary of Divisive and Other Reorganizations

Type of Reorganization	Distributing (D) or Transferor (T) Corporation Property Acquired	Consideration That Can Be Used	What Happens to the Distributing (D) or Transferor (T) Corporation?	Shareholders' Recognized Gain	Other Requirements
D—Divisive	D Corporation transfers part or all of its assets (and possibly some or all of its liabilities) to C Corporation.	Stock, securities, and other property of C Corporation.	D Corporation must distribute stock, securities, and boot received to its shareholders. D Corporation may liquidate or remain in existence.	Lesser of realized gain or FMV of boot received.	Transactions can assume three forms—spin-off, split-off, or split-up. Control is defined as 80% under Sec. 368(c).
E—Recapitalization	No increase or decrease in assets. The capital structure of T Corporation changes.	Stock, securities, and other property of T Corporation.	T Corporation remains in existence.	Lesser of realized gain or FMV of boot received.	May involve stock-for-stock, bond-for-bond, or bond-for-stock exchanges.
F—Change in form, identity, or place of organization	Old T Corporation transfers assets or stock to new T Corporation.	Stock, securities, and other property of new T Corporation.	Old T Corporation liquidates.	Lesser of realized gain or FMV of boot received.	Must involve only a single operating company.
G—Acquisitive or divisive	T Corporation transfers part or all of its assets (and possibly some or all of its liabilities) to A Corporation in bankruptcy.	Stock, securities, and other property of A Corporation.	T Corporation may liquidate, divide, or remain in existence.	Lesser of realized gain or FMV of boot received.	Stock and securities of A Corporation received by T Corporation must be distributed to its shareholders, security holders, or creditors.

Key:
D Corporation refers to the distributing corporation.
C Corporation refers to the controlled corporation.
T Corporation refers to the transferor corporation.
A Corporation refers to the transferee or acquiring corporation.

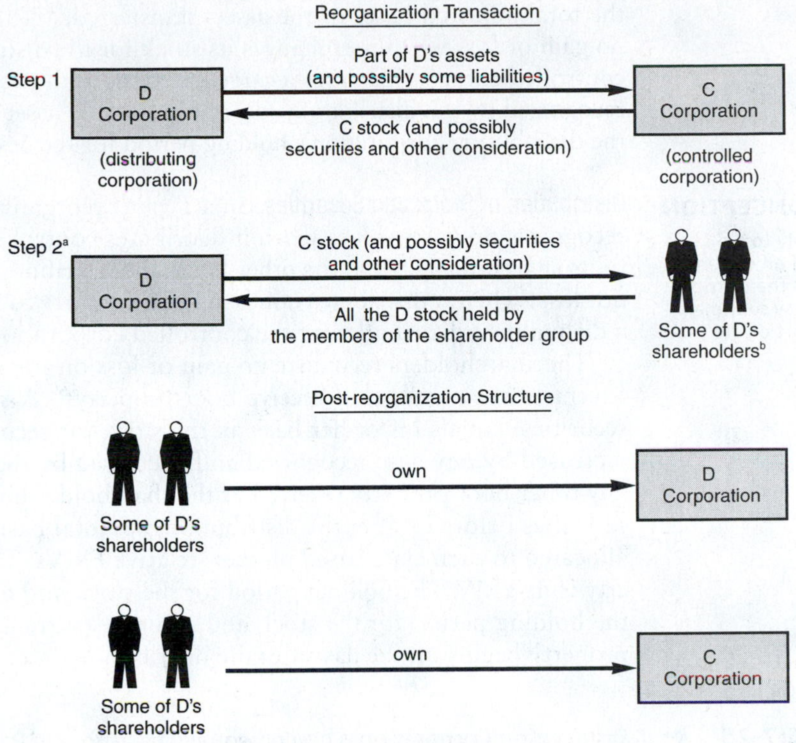

[a] Step 1 remains the same for a spin-off. In a spin-off, D's shareholders surrender no D stock. In a split-up, Step 1 involves the transfer of D Corporation's assets and liabilities to two controlled corporations. Step 2 involves the distribution of the stock of the two controlled corporations pursuant to the liquidation of D Corporation.

[b] This distribution also could be made on a pro rata basis to all of D's shareholders, in which case the shareholders surrender only a portion of their D shares.

FIGURE C:7-7 ► DIVISIVE TYPE D REORGANIZATION (SPLIT-OFF FORM)

- **Spin-off**—the distributing corporation transfers some of its assets to a controlled corporation in exchange for stock and possibly securities, cash, or other boot property. The distributing corporation then distributes the controlled corporation stock ratably to all its shareholders who do not surrender their distributing corporation stock. Such a transaction might be motivated by a desire to minimize the risk associated with distinct operations (e.g., automobile manufacturing and car financing) within a single corporation.
- **Split-up**—the distributing corporation transfers all its assets to two controlled corporations in exchange for controlled corporation stock and possibly securities, cash, or other boot property. The distributing corporation then distributes stock in the two controlled corporations to all its shareholders, in exchange for all its outstanding stock. Such a transaction might be motivated by a desire to separate and continue distinct operations of an old corporation having a weak brand or little goodwill.

If the Sec. 355 requirements discussed below are *not* met, a spin-off is taxed as a dividend to the shareholders; a split-off is taxed as a stock redemption to the shareholders; and a split-up is taxed to its shareholders as a liquidation of the distributing corporation.

ADDITIONAL COMMENT

If the IRS applies Sec. 351 to the asset transfer, and if the total adjusted basis for all property transferred exceeds the total FMV of that property, the subsidiary's total basis will be limited to the total FMV (see Chapter C:2 for details).

Asset Transfer. The distributing corporation recognizes no gain or loss on the asset transfer except where it receives and retains boot property or where the controlled corporation acquires or assumes distributing corporation liabilities, and total liabilities exceed the total adjusted bases of the assets transferred.[58] The controlled corporation recognizes no gain or loss when it exchanges its stock for the distributing corporation's property. The controlled corporation takes a carryover basis in the acquired assets, increased by any gain recognized by the distributing corporation on the asset transfer. Its holding period includes the distributing corporation's holding period for the assets.

TYPICAL MISCONCEPTION

Section 355 can apply to a distribution of stock of an existing subsidiary as well as the distribution of stock of a new subsidiary that is created as part of the transaction.

Distribution of Stock and Securities. In a Type D reorganization, the distributing corporation recognizes no gain or loss when it distributes controlled corporation stock (or securities) to its shareholders.[59] On the other hand, the distributing corporation recognizes gain (but not loss) when it distributes noncash boot property to its shareholders and when it makes a disqualified distribution of the controlled corporation's stock or securities.

The shareholders recognize no gain or loss on the receipt of the stock (and securities) except to the extent they receive boot property.[60] A shareholder's basis in the stock (or securities) equals his or her basis in the stock (or securities) held before the distribution, increased by any gain recognized and decreased by the sum of any cash and the FMV of any other boot property received. If the shareholder holds more than one class of stock or securities before or after the distribution, the total basis in the nonrecognition property is allocated to each class based on their relative FMVs. The basis in any noncash boot property is its FMV. The holding period for the stock and nonboot securities received includes the holding period for the stock and securities surrendered. The holding period for boot property begins on the day after the distribution date.

EXAMPLE C:7-25 ▶ Distributing Corporation is owned equally by Ruth and Pat, who cannot agree on how Distributing should be managed. Ruth and Pat agree to divide the business by organizing Controlled Corporation and by exchanging Pat's Distributing shares for Controlled shares while leaving Ruth's equity interest intact (i.e., a split-up). Pat's basis in her Distributing shares is $400,000. Pursuant to this plan, Distributing transfers assets having a $600,000 FMV and a $350,000 adjusted basis to Controlled in exchange for all of Controlled's single class of stock. In the asset transfer, Distributing realizes a $250,000 gain ($600,000 − $350,000), none of which is recognized. Distributing recognizes no gain on the distribution of the Controlled shares to Pat. Upon surrendering her Distributing shares, Pat realizes a $200,000 ($600,000 − $400,000) gain, none of which is recognized. Her basis in the Controlled stock is $400,000. The holding period for the Controlled shares includes Pat's holding period for the Distributing shares. Upon issuing its stock for Distributing assets, Controlled recognizes no gain and takes a $350,000 basis in the acquired assets. ◀

SELF-STUDY QUESTION

Does the receipt of boot make the entire Sec. 355 transaction taxable to the shareholders?

ANSWER

No. The shareholders may have a partial recognition of gain. The amount and type of gain recognized depends on whether the shareholders surrender stock of the distributing corporation in the transaction.

Under Sec. 355, boot consists of cash, short-term debt, property other than stock or securities of a controlled corporation, stock in the controlled corporation purchased within the previous five years in a taxable transaction, securities of the controlled corporation to the extent the principal amount of securities received exceeds the principal amount of securities surrendered, and stock or securities attributable to accrued interest.[61] When the shareholder receives boot, the amount and character of the recognized income or gain depend on whether he or she surrendered stock and securities in the distributing corporation (i.e., a split-off or split-up) or retained stock or securities (i.e., a spin-off).

When the shareholder receives boot in a spin-off, the FMV of the boot is treated as a dividend to the extent of the shareholder's ratable share of the distributing corporation's E&P. Any securities the shareholders receive in a spin-off are treated as boot because the

---

[58] Secs. 361(a) and 357(c)(1)(B).

[59] Sec. 361(c)(1). Two special rules may require the distributing corporation to recognize gain when it distributes stock and securities. A disqualifying distribution occurs if, immediately after the distribution, any person holds a 50% disqualified stock interest in either the distributing corporation or the controlled corporation. Disqualified stock generally is defined as any stock in the distributing or a controlled corporation purchased within the five-year period ending on the distribution date. The disqualifying distribution rules prevent a divisive transaction following a stock purchase to accomplish the disposition of a significant part of the historical shareholders' interests in one or more of the divided corporations. A second set of rules, the anti-Morris Trust rules, also requires the distributing corporation to recognize gain when a distribution of stock or securities is made and is preceded or followed by a disposition of the stock or securities.

[60] Sec. 355(a). As with an acquisitive reorganization, Sec. 361(a) permits securities (e.g., long-term debt obligations) to be received tax-free in a divisive transaction when the shareholders surrender the same face amount of securities, or a larger amount. The excess amount of securities received constitutes boot property.

[61] Secs. 355(a)(3) and 356(b).

shareholders do not surrender any securities in this type of transaction. Thus, the FMV of the securities constitutes a dividend to the extent of the shareholder's ratable share of the distributing corporation's E&P.

TYPICAL MISCONCEPTION

In a spin-off, the FMV of the boot received is treated as a Sec. 301 distribution to the shareholder. In a split-off or split-up, the shareholders recognize gain to the extent of the lesser of boot received or the gain realized. This gain may be a dividend or capital gain under Sec. 302.

In a split-off or split-up, in addition to the exchange of stock, a shareholder may receive boot property. If the shareholder realizes a loss on the exchange, the loss is not recognized, whether or not boot is received.[62] If the shareholder realizes a gain on the exchange, he or she recognizes the gain to the extent of the FMV of any boot received.

If the exchange is essentially equivalent to a dividend under the Sec. 302 stock redemption rules, the recognized gain is treated as a dividend to the extent of the shareholder's ratable share of the distributing corporation's E&P.[63] Otherwise it is treated as a capital gain. In either case, the income is taxed at the capital gains rate. Under the Sec. 302 rules, the shareholder is treated as though he or she continued to own stock in the distributing corporation and surrendered only the portion of his or her shares equal in value to the amount of boot received. This hypothetical redemption is then tested under the Sec. 302(b) rules to determine whether the shareholder is entitled to sale or dividend treatment.[64]

EXAMPLE C:7-26 ▶ Distributing Corporation owns assets with a $60,000 FMV plus all the outstanding shares of Controlled Corporation stock valued at $40,000. Distributing formed Controlled by transferring some of its assets to Controlled as part of the reorganization. Distributing's E&P balance is $35,000. Carl and Diane each own 100 shares of Distributing stock. In a split-off, Distributing distributes all the Controlled stock to Carl in exchange for his 100 shares. Carl also receives $10,000 in cash. Carl's basis in the surrendered Distributing shares is $22,000. Carl has a $28,000 realized gain, calculated as follows:

FMV of Controlled stock	$40,000
Plus: Cash received	10,000
Amount realized	$50,000
Minus: Basis of Distributing stock	(22,000)
Realized gain	$28,000

Carl recognizes $10,000 of this gain (i.e., the lesser of the $28,000 realized gain or the $10,000 FMV of boot received). If Carl surrenders Distributing stock solely for the $10,000 cash, he would effectively be exchanging 20 Distributing shares ($10,000 boot ÷ $500 FMV for each share of Distributing stock) worth $10,000. Before this hypothetical redemption, he owns 50% of the outstanding Distributing shares (100 ÷ 200). Afterward, he owns 44% (80 ÷ 180). Thus, the hypothetical redemption is not substantially disproportionate under Sec. 302(b)(2) because the 44% post-redemption stock ownership exceeds 80% of the pre-redemption stock ownership (50% × 0.80 = 40%). If the exchange can meet one of the other tests for sale treatment (e.g., not essentially equivalent to a dividend), the $10,000 will be taxed as a capital gain. Otherwise it will be taxed as a dividend. ◀

TYPICAL MISCONCEPTION

Unlike Sec. 351, securities (long-term debt) can be exchanged in a Sec. 355 transaction without the recognition of gain as long as the principal amount surrendered is equal to or greater than the principal amount received.

In a split-off or split-up, a shareholder will receive securities of the controlled corporation tax-free only if the shareholder surrenders securities in the distributing corporation with an equal or larger principal amount. To the extent the principal amount of securities received exceeds the principal amount of securities surrendered, the excess will be taxable.

The Sec. 355 Requirements. Under Sec. 355, a distributing corporation's distribution of a controlled corporation's stock is nontaxable to the shareholders if all six of the following conditions are met:[65]

- The property distributed consists solely of stock or securities of a corporation controlled by the distributing corporation immediately before the distribution. The distributing corporation owns and distributes stock possessing at least 80% of the total

[62] Sec. 356(c).
[63] Sec. 356(a)(2).
[64] Rev. Rul. 93-62, 1993-2 C.B. 118.
[65] Sec. 355(a) and Reg. Secs. 1.355-2(b) and (c). Also, Rev. Proc. 2013-30, 2013-36 I.R.B. 173, provides a checklist questionnaire of the information that must be included in a ruling request under Sec. 355. Appendix A of this revenue procedure contains guidelines regarding the business purpose of Sec. 355 transactions including information submission requirements for nine specific situations where rulings may or may not be granted.

ADDITIONAL COMMENT
The control requirement of Sec. 355 is the same control requirement relating to the formation of a corporation under Sec. 351 (see Chapter C:2).

TYPICAL MISCONCEPTION
The active trade or business requirement has two conditions: a pre-distribution five-year history must exist, and both the distributing and controlled corporations must be actively engaged in a trade or business immediately after the distribution.

combined voting power of all classes of stock entitled to vote and at least 80% of the total number of shares of all other classes of stock.[66]

- The distribution has not been used principally as a device to distribute the E&P of the distributing corporation, the controlled corporation, or both. Whether the distribution has been used as such a device will depend on the facts and circumstances of each case. A sale or exchange of distributing or controlled corporation stock after the distribution is evidence that the distribution was used as such a device, especially if the sale was prearranged.[67]
- Immediately after the distribution, the distributing and controlled corporations each engage in a trade or business that was actively conducted for at least five years before the distribution. This requirement prevents a corporation from spinning off a newly formed subsidiary whose only assets are unneeded cash and other liquid assets. The shareholders then could sell or liquidate the subsidiary and extract the liquid assets in a transaction characterized as a sale rather than a dividend.[68]
- The distributing corporation distributes either all controlled corporation stock and securities held by it immediately before the distribution or an amount of controlled corporation stock constituting control. The distributing corporation may retain some stock if it can establish to the IRS's satisfaction that the stock was not retained as part of a tax avoidance plan.
- The distribution has a substantial corporate business purpose. Qualifying distributions include those made to comply with antitrust laws and those made to separate businesses where the shareholders have major disagreements.[69]
- Shareholders who directly or indirectly owned the controlled corporation(s) and a substantial number of shareholders who owned the distributing corporation's stock before the distribution maintain a continuing equity interest in one or more of the corporations following the division.[70] The distribution of stock and securities need not be pro rata. Disproportionate distributions may be used to eliminate the stock ownership of dissenting shareholders. In a split-off, some shareholders may exchange all their distributing corporation stock for all the controlled corporation stock.

DIVISIVE TYPE G REORGANIZATION

A divisive Type G reorganization involves the transfer of some of a corporation's assets to a second corporation under a court-approved plan. The transferor corporation then distributes the transferee corporation's stock and securities to its shareholders, security holders, and creditors. The transferor corporation may continue as a separate enterprise after restructuring its operations. Alternatively, the transferor corporation may liquidate under a court approved bankruptcy plan.

OTHER REORGANIZATIONS

OBJECTIVE 6

Define other types of reorganizations

Two types of transactions do not fit into the acquisitive or divisive reorganization categories: Type E reorganizations, which are recapitalizations, and Type F reorganizations, which are changes in identity, form, or state of incorporation. Topic Review C:7-6 presented earlier summarizes the requirements for Type E and Type F reorganizations.

TYPE E REORGANIZATION

Section 368(a)(1)(E) refers to a **Type E reorganization** simply as a "recapitalization." A 1942 Supreme Court opinion defined **recapitalization** as "the reshuffling of the corporate

[66] Sec. 368(c).
[67] Reg. Sec. 1.355-2(d).
[68] Sec. 355(b)(2). A corporation is engaged in the active conduct of a trade or business if it actively conducts all activities necessary to generate a profit and these activities encompass all steps in the process of earning income. Specifically excluded are passive investment activities such as merely holding stock, securities, and land.
[69] Reg. Sec. 1.355-2(b)(5), Exs. (1) and (2).
[70] Reg. Sec. 1.355-2(c).

KEY POINT

A Type E reorganization is neither acquisitive nor divisive in nature. Instead, it simply allows a single corporation to restructure its capital without creating a taxable exchange between the corporation and its shareholders or creditors.

structure within the framework of an existing corporation."[71] To qualify as a nontaxable reorganization, a recapitalization must have a bona fide business purpose. One reason for a recapitalization is to reduce a corporation's interest payments and debt-to-equity ratio by exchanging additional common or preferred stock for outstanding bonds. Alternatively, a family corporation might exchange newly issued preferred stock for part or all of the common stock held by a retiring, controlling shareholder so the shareholder can transfer management control to his or her children. This type of recapitalization facilitates estate planning (see discussion after Example C:7-28).

Three types of corporate capital structure adjustments can qualify as a Type E reorganization: a stock-for-stock exchange, a bond-for-stock exchange, and a bond-for-bond exchange.[72] Normally, these exchanges do not result in an increase or decrease in the corporation's assets except to the extent shareholders or creditors receive a distribution of cash or other property.

Stock-for-Stock Exchange. An exchange of common stock for common stock, or preferred stock for preferred stock, in the same corporation can qualify as a recapitalization if it is pursuant to a plan of reorganization. Section 1036 permits similar types of exchanges in a non-reorganization context. In either context, shareholders recognize no gain or loss on the exchange and take a substituted basis in the shares received that references the basis in the shares surrendered.

EXAMPLE C:7-27 ▶ The shareholders of Epsilon Corporation exchange all their nonvoting Class B common stock for additional shares of Epsilon voting Class A common stock. The exchange is nontaxable under Sec. 1036 even if not pursuant to a plan of reorganization. An exchange of some of Epsilon Class A preferred stock for Class B preferred stock also would be nontaxable under Sec. 1036. ◀

Section 1036 does not apply to an exchange of common stock for preferred stock, or preferred stock for common stock, in the same corporation, or an exchange of stock of two corporations. On the other hand, the reorganization rules apply to an exchange of two different classes of stock (e.g., common for preferred) in the same corporation if the exchange is pursuant to a plan of reorganization. Under the Sec. 354(a) nonrecognition rules, the exchange is nontaxable to the shareholders except to the extent they receive boot property. If the FMV of stock received differs from that of stock surrendered, the difference may be recharacterized as a gift, a contribution to capital, compensation for services, a dividend, or a payment to satisfy a debt obligation, depending on the facts and circumstances.[73] The tax consequences of that portion of the exchange will not be governed by the reorganization rules.

EXAMPLE C:7-28 ▶ John owns 60% of Eta Corporation's common stock and all its preferred stock. The remainder of Eta common stock is held by 80 unrelated individuals. John's basis in his preferred stock is \$300,000. The preferred stock is valued at \$500,000. John exchanges his preferred stock for \$400,000 of additional common stock and \$100,000 in cash. In the exchange, John realizes a \$200,000 [(\$400,000 + \$100,000) − \$300,000] gain, of which he recognizes \$100,000 as dividend income (assuming Boise has sufficient E&P). None of the Sec. 302(b) exceptions that permit capital gain treatment applies. John's basis in the additional common stock is \$300,000 (\$300,000 + \$100,000 gain recognized − \$100,000 cash received). ◀

A recapitalization often is used as an estate planning device whereby a parent's controlling common stock interest is exchanged for both common and preferred stock. The common stock often is gifted to a child who, following the recapitalization, owns a controlling common stock interest in the corporation and manages its business. The parent derives a steady stream of income from preferred stock dividends. The preferred stock's

---

[71] *Helvering v. Southwest Consolidated Corp.*, 28 AFTR 573, 42-1 USTC ¶9248 (USSC, 1942).

[72] An exchange of stock for bonds has been held in *J. Robert Bazely v. CIR* (35 AFTR 1190, 47-2 USTC ¶9288 [USSC, 1947]) not to be a recapitalization. Even if it were a recapitalization, it generally would be taxable because receipt of the entire principal amount of the bonds represents boot under Sec. 356. Regulation Sec. 1.368-1(b) holds that continuity of interest and continuity of business enterprise are not necessary for a qualified Type E reorganization.

[73] Rev. Ruls. 74-269, 1974-2 C.B. 87, and 83-120, 1983-2 C.B. 170.

value is less likely to increase significantly over time, thereby limiting the value of that portion of the parent's estate and minimizing the estate tax liability. Relatively more capital appreciation could accrue to the child who owns the common stock.

Substantial income, estate, and gift tax planning opportunities previously existed in the recapitalization of a closely held corporation. To prevent abuses, Congress added Secs. 2701–2704, which, for transfer tax purposes, set forth procedures for more accurately valuing interests transferred to, and retained in, corporations and partnerships. Additional coverage of this topic is presented in Chapter C:12

Bond-for-Stock Exchange. A bond-for-stock exchange is nontaxable to the shareholder except to the extent the shareholder receives a portion of the stock in satisfaction of the corporation's liability to him or her for accrued interest.[74] The latter portion is taxed as ordinary income.

Bond-for-Bond Exchange. These exchanges are nontaxable only where the principal amount of the bonds received does not exceed the principal amount of the bonds surrendered. If the principal amount of the bonds received exceeds the principal amount of the bonds surrendered, the FMV of the "excess" is taxed to the bondholder as boot.

TYPE F REORGANIZATION

Section 368(a)(1)(F) defines a **Type F reorganization** as a "mere change in identity, form, or place of organization of one corporation, however effected." Typically, Type F reorganizations are used to change either the jurisdiction in which the business is incorporated or the name of a corporation, without requiring the old corporation or its shareholders to recognize gain or loss. In a Type F reorganization, the assets and liabilities of the old corporation are transferred to a new corporation in exchange for stock and possibly debt obligations. The shareholders and creditors of the old corporation then exchange their stock and debt interests for similar interests in the new corporation.

EXAMPLE C:7-29 ▶ Phi Corporation is incorporated in Illinois. Its management decides to change its state of incorporation to Delaware because of that state's favorable securities and corporation laws. To effect the change, Old Phi exchanges its assets for all the stock in New Phi, incorporated in Delaware. The shareholders of Old Phi then exchange their stock for New Phi stock. Old Phi goes out of existence. Neither the shareholders nor the "two" corporations recognize gain or loss. Each shareholder takes a substituted basis in the New Phi stock that references their basis in the Old Phi stock. Their holding period for the New Phi stock includes their holding period for the Old Phi stock. New Phi's asset bases are the same as Old Phi's asset bases, and New Phi acquires Old Phi's tax attributes. Although the two corporations are legally distinct, they represent the same enterprise that merely has changed its state of incorporation. ◀

The reorganization illustrated in Example C:7-29 also could be accomplished if Old Phi's shareholders exchanged their Old Phi stock for New Phi stock. Old Phi then would liquidate into New Phi. The tax consequences would be the same for both transactions.

JUDICIAL RESTRICTIONS ON THE USE OF CORPORATE REORGANIZATIONS

OBJECTIVE 7

Explain judicial doctrines pertaining to corporate reorganizations

The U.S. Supreme Court has held that compliance with the letter of the law of reorganization provisions does not necessarily make a transaction nontaxable.[75] Through four judicial doctrines, the courts have placed certain restrictions on reorganizations:

[74] Sec. 354(a)(2)(B).

[75] *Evelyn F. Gregory v. Helvering,* 14 AFTR 1191, 35-1 USTC ¶9043 (USSC, 1935).

- Continuity of proprietary interest
- Continuity of business enterprise
- A bona fide business purpose
- The step transaction doctrine

All four doctrines elevate economic substance over legal form.

CONTINUITY OF INTEREST

TYPICAL MISCONCEPTION

The continuity of interest requirement has nothing to do with the relative sizes of the acquiring and target corporations. The target shareholders may end up with a minimal amount of the total outstanding stock of the acquiring corporation, and yet the merger will be a valid reorganization as long as 40% of the consideration received by the target shareholders is an equity interest in the acquiring corporation.

The continuity of interest doctrine is based on the principle that the tax deferral associated with a reorganization is available because the shareholder merely has changed his or her investment from one form to another rather than liquidated that interest. According to Reg. Sec. 1.368-1(b), the requirements of this doctrine are met by a continuity of the business enterprise under a modified corporate form and a continuity of interest on the part of the shareholders who, directly or indirectly, own the enterprise before its reorganization. In a series of decisions, the courts have held that a continuing interest is ensured through ownership of common or preferred stock.[76] Thus, a transaction that involves the receipt of only cash or short-term debt obligations by the target corporation or its shareholders does not qualify as a nontaxable reorganization.

SELF-STUDY QUESTION

For which reorganizations is the continuity of interest requirement most important?

The IRC does not specify how much stock is necessary for continuity of interest. For advance ruling purposes, however, the IRS traditionally required that at least 50% of the total consideration received by target corporation shareholders consist of the acquiring corporation's stock. The courts, however, have accepted lower percentages, and Treasury Regulations now accept 40% as the continuity of interest threshold.[77]

EXAMPLE C:7-30 ▶ In a Type C reorganization, Theta Corporation transfers all its assets to Alpha Corporation in exchange for $200,000 of Alpha stock and the assumption of $800,000 of Theta liabilities. Theta distributes the Alpha stock to its sole shareholder, Nancy, in exchange for all her Theta stock. Even though the transaction meets the statutory requirements for a Type C reorganization, the IRS probably will claim that the transaction does not qualify for nontaxable treatment because it lacks continuity of proprietary interest. Only 20% of the total consideration paid consists of an equity interest in Alpha. ◀

ANSWER

The only limitation on consideration used for both regular and triangular mergers is the continuity of interest requirement. The other reorganizations, including reverse triangular mergers, have statutory requirements more restrictive than the continuity of interest doctrine.

Recently, the IRS amended Reg. Sec. 1.368-1(b) to clarify that neither the continuity of interest nor the continuity of business enterprise doctrine applies to Type E and Type F reorganizations.

CONTINUITY OF BUSINESS ENTERPRISE

SELF-STUDY QUESTION

Does the acquiring corporation have to continue its own historic business?

ANSWER

No. Treasury Regulations hold that continuity of business enterprise can be satisfied if the acquiring corporation uses a significant portion of the target's historic business assets in a business, not necessarily the target's old business (Reg. Sec. 1.368-1(d)(1)).

Continuity of business enterprise implies that the acquiring corporation either continue the target corporation's business or use a significant portion of the target corporation's operating assets in a new business.[78] This doctrine limits nontaxable reorganizations to transactions involving *continuing interests* in the target's business or target property under a modified corporate form. The **continuity of business enterprise doctrine**, however, does not require that the target corporation's historic business be continued.

Whether the continuity of business enterprise requirement is met depends on the facts and circumstances of each case. The historic business requirement can be satisfied if the acquiring corporation continues one or more of the target corporation's significant lines of business.

EXAMPLE C:7-31 ▶ Historically, Theta Corporation has manufactured resins and chemicals and has distributed chemicals for the production of plastics. All three lines of business generate the same level of revenues. Theta merges into Alpha Corporation. Two months after the merger, Alpha sells the resin manufacturing and chemicals distribution lines to an unrelated party for cash. The transaction satisfies the continuity of business enterprise requirement because Alpha continues at least one of Theta's three significant lines of business.[79] ◀

---

[76] See, for example, *V. L. LeTulle v. Scofield*, 23 AFTR 789, 40-1 USTC ¶9150 (USSC, 1940).

[77] Reg. Sec. 1.368-1(e)(2)(v), Example 1. See also *John A. Nelson Co. v. Helvering*, 16 AFTR 1262, 36-1 USTC ¶9019 (USSC, 1935), in which the Supreme Court permitted a nontaxable reorganization where the stock exchanged constituted only 38% of the total consideration.

[78] Reg. Sec. 1.368-1(d)(1).

[79] Reg. Secs. 1.368-1(d)(3) and −1(d)(5), Ex. (1).

The business (asset) continuity requirement is satisfied if the acquiring corporation uses in its business a significant portion of the assets used in the target corporation's business. Significance relates to the relative importance of the assets to target's historic business operations.

EXAMPLE C:7-32 ▶ Both Alpha and Theta Corporations manufacture computers. Theta merges into Alpha. Alpha terminates Theta's manufacturing activities and retains Theta's equipment as a source of supply for its components. Alpha satisfies the continuity of business enterprise requirement by continuing to use a significant portion of Theta's business assets. Thus, Alpha need not continue Theta's historic business to satisfy the continuity of business enterprise requirement.[80] If instead Alpha had sold Theta's assets for cash and placed the proceeds in an investment vehicle, the continuity of business enterprise requirement would not have been met. ◀

ADDITIONAL COMMENT

Because the target corporation and its shareholders have the most to lose, they should protect themselves by stipulating that the acquiring corporation retain the historic assets. If not, the acquiring corporation can unilaterally dispose of the historical assets and invalidate the nontaxable reorganization.

The acquiring corporation need not hold the target corporation's business assets for a prolonged period of time. The assets (business activities) may be held (conducted) by an 80%-or-more-owned subsidiary included in a chain of corporations that includes the acquiring corporation. In some cases, the acquired assets can be held by (or business conducted by) a partnership or LLC owned in full or in part by the acquiring corporation or one of its subsidiaries.

BUSINESS PURPOSE REQUIREMENT

To qualify for reorganization treatment, a transaction must serve a bona fide **business purpose.**[81] Regulation Sec. 1.368-1(c) states that a transactional scheme that uses "the form of a corporate reorganization as a disguise for concealing its real character, and the object and accomplishment of which is the consummation of a preconceived plan having no business or corporate purpose, is not a plan of reorganization."

EXAMPLE C:7-33 ▶ Distributing Corporation transfers appreciated stock from its investment portfolio to newly created Controlled Corporation in exchange for all its stock. It then distributes the Controlled stock to its sole shareholder, Kathy, in exchange for some of her Distributing stock. Shortly after the stock transfer, Controlled liquidates, and Kathy receives the appreciated stock held by Controlled. If the liquidation were treated as a separate event, Kathy would recognize a capital gain, which she could use to offset capital loss carryovers from other tax years. In addition, she could step up the basis in the appreciated stock to its FMV without incurring a tax liability. Even though the stock transfer to Controlled complies with the letter of Sec. 368(a)(1)(D) as a divisive Type D reorganization, the IRS probably will claim that the Sec. 355 trade or business requirement has not been met. It also will rely on the Supreme Court's decision in *Gregory v. Helvering* (see footnote 83) to rule that the series of transactions serves no business purpose. As a result, Kathy's receipt of the appreciated stock from Controlled most likely will be treated as a dividend. ◀

KEY POINT

Business purpose is much more difficult to establish in divisive (Sec. 355) transactions than it is in acquisitive (Sec. 354) transactions.

STEP TRANSACTION DOCTRINE

The IRS can invoke the **step transaction doctrine** to collapse a multistep reorganization into a single taxable transaction. Alternatively, the IRS can invoke the doctrine to collapse a series of steps, which the taxpayer claims as independent taxable events, into an integrated nontaxable reorganization. Both IRS actions prevent the taxpayer from elevating legal form over economic substance.

EXAMPLE C:7-34 ▶ Jody transfers business property from his sole proprietorship to wholly owned Theta Corporation. Three days after this transaction, purportedly in a Type C reorganization, Theta transfers all its assets to Alpha Corporation in exchange for Alpha stock. Subsequently, Theta liquidates and distributes the Alpha stock to Jody. After the liquidation, Jody owns 15% of the Alpha stock. The IRS might collapse the two steps (the Sec. 351 asset transfer to Theta and the Type C asset-for-stock reorganization) into a single transaction: an asset transfer by Jody to Alpha. It might claim that the Sec. 351 requirements have not been met because Jody does not own at least 80% of the Alpha stock immediately after the exchange. Furthermore, it might rule that, because Jody owns only 15% of Alpha stock, Jody must recognize gain or loss on the asset transfer.[82] ◀

---

[80] Reg. Secs. 1.368-1(d)(4) and −1(d)(5), Ex. (2).

[81] *Evelyn F. Gregory v. Helvering*, 14 AFTR 1191, 35-1 USTC ¶9043 (USSC, 1935). Other Sec. 355 requirements, such as not constituting a device for distributing of E&P, probably were not met in this case.

[82] Rev. Rul. 70-140, 1970-1 C.B. 73.

TAX ATTRIBUTES

OBJECTIVE 8

Assess what happens to NOL carryovers and other tax attributes in a reorganization

Under Sec. 381(a), the acquiring or transferee corporation inherits the target or transferor corporation's tax attributes (e.g., loss or tax credit carryovers) in certain types of reorganizations. Sections 269, 382, 383, and 384, however, restrict the taxpayer's ability to use certain corporate tax attributes (e.g., NOL carryovers) following the acquisition of a loss corporation's stock or assets.

ASSUMPTION OF TAX ATTRIBUTES

In Type A, C, acquisitive D, F, and acquisitive G reorganizations, the acquiring corporation obtains both the target corporation's tax attributes and assets. The tax attributes do not change hands in either a Type B or Type E reorganization because assets are not transferred from one corporation to another. Even though assets are transferred in divisive Type D and G reorganizations, the only tax attribute allocated to the transferee corporation is a pro rata portion of the transferor corporation's E&P.[83]

KEY POINT

An often-cited advantage of a nontaxable asset reorganization over a taxable acquisition is that the tax attributes (e.g., NOLs and net capital losses) carry over to the acquiring corporation.

In acquisitive reorganizations, tax attributes carried over under Sec. 381(c) include

- Net operating losses
- Capital losses
- Earnings and profits (E&P)
- General business credits
- Inventory methods

KEY POINT

The thrust of Sec. 381, as it relates to NOLs, is to allow a target corporation's NOL carryovers to offset only the post-acquisition income of the acquiring corporation.

The target corporation's NOL carryover is determined as of the acquisition date and carries over to tax years ending after such date. Generally, the acquisition date for a reorganization is that on which the transferor or target corporation transfers the assets. When losses carryover from more than one tax year, the loss from the earliest tax year is used first. NOLs from the period following the acquisition date cannot be carried back by the acquiring corporation to offset target corporation profits earned in tax years preceding the acquisition date.[84]

EXAMPLE C:7-35 ▶ Theta Corporation merges into Alpha Corporation at the close of business on June 30 of the current year. Both corporations use the calendar year as their tax year. At the beginning of the year, Theta reports a $200,000 NOL carryover from the preceding year. Theta must file a final tax return for the period January 1 through June 30 of the current year. Theta reports $60,000 of taxable income (before any NOL deductions) on its tax return for the short period. Theta's taxable income for the January 1 through June 30 period reduces its NOL carryover to $140,000 ($200,000 − $60,000). Alpha succeeds to this carryover. ◀

Section 381(c) restricts the acquiring corporation's use of the NOL carryover in its first tax year ending after the acquisition date. The NOL deduction is limited to the portion of the acquiring corporation's taxable income allocable on a daily basis to the post-acquisition period.

EXAMPLE C:7-36 ▶ Assume the same facts as in Example C:7-35 except Alpha's accountants determine that its taxable income is $146,000, earned evenly throughout the current year. Alpha can use Theta's NOL carryover to offset $73,600 [(184 ÷ 365) × $146,000] of its taxable income attributable to the 184 days in the July 1 through December 31 current year post-acquisition period. The remaining NOL of $66,400 ($140,000 − $73,600) carries over to offset Alpha's taxable income in the following year. Both the pre- and post-acquisition periods in the current year are treated as full tax years for loss carryover purposes. ◀

LIMITATION ON USE OF TAX ATTRIBUTES

Sections 382 and 269 are intended to discourage taxpayers from purchasing the assets or stock of a corporation having loss carryovers (known as the **loss corporation**) primarily to acquire the corporation's tax attributes. Similarly, Secs. 382 and 269 are intended to discourage

[83] Reg. Sec. 1.312-10.

[84] Special rules apply to Type F reorganizations. Because this type of reorganization involves only a change in form or identity of a single corporation, NOLs generated after the acquisition date can be carried back to offset profits earned in pre-acquisition tax years.

a loss corporation from acquiring assets or stock of a profitable corporation primarily to use its carryovers. Section 383 imposes similar restrictions on acquisitions intended to facilitate the use of capital loss and tax credit carryovers. Additionally, Sec. 384 restricts the use of pre-acquisition losses to offset built-in gains.

Section 382. The Sec. 382 NOL restrictions are triggered when a substantial change in the stock ownership of the loss corporation occurs.

TYPICAL MISCONCEPTION

To effect an ownership change, the 5% shareholders must increase their stock ownership by more than 50 *percentage points.* For example, if shareholder A increases her stock ownership from 10% to 20%, this increase is not an ownership change even though it doubles A's ownership.

Stock Ownership Change. A substantial change in stock ownership occurs where

- Stock ownership of any person(s) owning 5% or more of a corporation's stock has changed or a reorganization (other than a divisive Type D or G or a Type F reorganization) has occurred *and*
- The percentage of stock in the new loss corporation owned by one or more 5% shareholders has increased by more than 50% over the lowest percentage of stock in the old loss corporation owned by such shareholder(s) at any time during the preceding three-year (or shorter) "testing" period.[85]

The 5% shareholder test is based on the value of the loss corporation's stock. Nonvoting preferred stock is excluded from the calculation of ownership.

An **old loss corporation** is any corporation entitled to use an NOL carryover or that has an NOL for the tax year in which the ownership change occurs, and that undergoes the requisite stock ownership change. A **new loss corporation** is any corporation entitled to use an NOL carryover after the stock ownership change.[86] The old and new loss corporations are the same in most taxable acquisitions (e.g., the purchase of a loss corporation's stock by a new shareholder group). The identity of the old and new loss corporations differ, however, in many acquisitive reorganizations (e.g., a merger transaction where an unprofitable target [old loss] corporation merges into the acquiring [new loss] corporation).

KEY POINT

One of the burdensome aspects of Sec. 382 is that each time the stock ownership of a 5% shareholder changes, all 5% shareholders must be tested at that date to determine whether an ownership change has occurred.

Ownership changes are tested any time a transaction affects a person owning 5% or more of the stock either before or after the change. Such change may occur because a stock transaction involving a 5% shareholder or a person who does not own a 5% interest in the loss corporation affects the size of the stock interest owned by another 5% shareholder (i.e., a stock redemption). When applying the 5% test, all shareholders owning less than 5% of the loss corporation's stock are considered to be a single shareholder.

EXAMPLE C:7-37 ▶ Stock in Spencer Corporation is publicly traded with no single individual owning more than 5% of its outstanding shares. In recent years, Spencer has incurred a series of NOLs. On July 3, Barry acquires for cash 80% of Spencer's single class of stock. Barry owned none of the Spencer stock before the acquisition. A substantial stock ownership change has occurred because, as a result of a stock purchase, a 5% shareholder (Barry) now owns 80 percentage points more stock than the 0% he owned at any time during the three-year testing period. Because Spencer incurred the NOLs prior to the ownership change and can use the NOLs after the change, it is considered to be both the old and new loss corporation. Consequently, Spencer's NOLs are subject to the Sec. 382 limitations. ◀

In many acquisitive reorganizations, the Sec. 382 stock ownership test is applied first with respect to the old loss (or target) corporation and then with respect to the new loss (or acquiring) corporation.

EXAMPLE C:7-38 ▶ Theta Corporation has a single class of stock. None of its 300 shareholders owns more than 5% of the outstanding shares. Theta has incurred substantial NOLs in recent years. Pursuant to an agreement, Theta merges into Alpha Corporation. Alpha also has a single class of stock, and none of its 500 shareholders owns more than 5% of its outstanding shares, or any of the Theta shares before the merger. After the merger, Theta shareholders own 40% of the

[85] Sec. 382(g). For the purpose of determining the 50-percentage-point ownership change, special rules permit a testing period of less than three years. For example, where a recent previous change in stock ownership involving a 5% shareholder has occurred, the testing period begins on the date of the earlier ownership change.

[86] Secs. 382(k)(1)–(3).

Alpha stock. For purposes of applying the Sec. 382 stock ownership test, the stockholdings of all Alpha shareholders are aggregated. The Sec. 382 rules limit the use of Theta NOL carryovers because Alpha shareholders owned none of the old loss corporation (Theta) stock before the reorganization and own 60% of the new loss corporation (Alpha) stock immediately after the reorganization. ◀

Divisive Type D and G reorganizations or Type F reorganizations may be subject to the Sec. 382 limitations if the underlying transactions result in a more than 50% increase in the transferor corporation's stock ownership.

TYPICAL MISCONCEPTION

Section 382 does not necessarily disallow NOLs. It merely limits the amount of NOL carryovers the new loss corporation can use on an annual basis.

Loss Limitation. The Sec. 382 loss limitation for any tax year ending after the stock ownership change equals the value of the old loss corporation's stock (including nonvoting preferred) immediately before the ownership change multiplied by the long-term tax-exempt federal rate.[87] The IRS periodically publishes the long-term tax-exempt federal rate, which is the highest of the adjusted federal long-term tax-exempt rates applicable in any month during the three-calendar-month period ending with the month in which the stock ownership change occurs.[88]

ADDITIONAL COMMENT

The new loss corporation's use of the old loss corporation's NOLs is limited annually to the FMV of the old loss corporation multiplied by the long-term tax-exempt federal rate because this limitation approximates the rate at which the old loss corporation could have used the NOLs.

A new loss corporation first claims its current year deductions. It then deducts any NOLs from the old loss corporation (pre-change tax years) not limited by Sec. 382. If the NOL carryovers from the old loss corporation exceed the Sec. 382 loss limitation, the unused portion is deferred until the following year, provided the 20-year NOL carryforward period has not expired. If the Sec. 382 loss limitation exceeds the new loss corporation's taxable income for the current year, the unused loss portion carries forward and increases the Sec. 382 loss limitation in the following year.[89] Finally, any of its NOL and other carryovers from post-change taxable years are deducted. A new loss corporation that discontinues the business of the old loss corporation throughout the two-year period beginning on the stock ownership change date must use a zero Sec. 382 limitation for any post-change year. This zero limitation, in effect, disallows the use of the NOL carryovers.[90]

EXAMPLE C:7-39 ▶

Peter purchased all the stock in Taylor Corporation (the old and new loss corporation) from Karl at the close of business on December 31 of last year. Taylor manufactures brooms and has a $1 million NOL carryover from last year. Taylor continues to manufacture brooms after Peter's acquisition and in the current year earns $300,000 of taxable income. The value of the Taylor stock immediately before the acquisition is $3.5 million. The requisite stock ownership change has occurred because Peter has increased his stock ownership from zero during the three-year testing period to 100% immediately after the acquisition. Assume the applicable long-term tax-exempt federal rate is 5%. Thus, the Sec. 382 loss limitation for the current year is $175,000 ($3,500,000 × 0.05). Taylor can claim a $175,000 NOL deduction in the current year, thereby reducing its taxable income to $125,000. The remaining $825,000 ($1,000,000 − $175,000) NOL carries over to subsequent years, subject to the Sec. 382 limitation in those years. ◀

KEY POINT

If the old loss corporation is a very large corporation relative to its NOL carryovers, Sec. 382 will not be a real obstacle in the use of the NOLs by the new loss corporation. Only when the old loss corporation has a small FMV relative to its NOL carryovers does Sec. 382 become a major obstacle.

ADDITIONAL COMMENT

Although the legislative intent of Sec. 382 has not been seriously questioned, the complexity of the statute with its accompanying Treasury Regulations is of concern to many tax practitioners.

Special rules apply to the loss corporation for the year in which the stock ownership change occurs. Taxable income earned before the change is not subject to the Sec. 382 limitation. Taxable income earned after the change, however, is subject to the limitation. Allocation of income earned during the tax year to the time periods before and after the stock ownership change is based on the number of days in each of the two time periods under procedures similar to those for allocating tax attributes under Sec. 381.

Old loss corporation NOLs incurred before the date of the stock ownership change are limited by Sec. 382. These include NOLs incurred in tax years ending before the date of change plus the pre-change portion of the NOL for the tax year that includes the date of change. Allocation of an NOL for the tax year that includes the date of change is based on the number of days before and after the change.[91]

---

[87] Sec. 382(b)(1).

[88] Sec. 382(f).

[89] Sec. 382(b)(2).

[90] Sec. 382(c). In addition, failure to continue the old loss corporation's business enterprise may change the transaction's status from a nontaxable reorganization to a taxable acquisition.

[91] Sec. 382(b)(3).

Section 383. Section 383 restricts the use of tax credit and capital loss carryovers when a stock ownership change occurs, within the meaning of Sec. 382. The same restrictions that apply to NOLs apply to the general business credit, the minimum tax credit, and the foreign tax credit.

Section 384. Section 384 restricts the use of pre-acquisition losses of either the acquiring or target corporation (the loss corporation) to offset built-in gains recognized by another corporation (the gain corporation) during the five-year post-acquisition recognition period. Such gains may be offset only by pre-acquisition losses of the gain corporation. This limitation applies if a corporation acquires either a controlling stock interest or the assets of another corporation and either corporation is a gain corporation.

ADDITIONAL COMMENT

Section 269 represents the IRS's oldest and broadest weapon in dealing with trafficking in NOLs. However, because of the subjectivity of application, Secs. 382, 383, and 384 have turned out to be the IRS's main statutory weapons in this area.

Section 269. Section 269 applies where control of a corporation is obtained and the principal purpose of the transaction is "the evasion or avoidance of federal income tax by securing the benefit of a deduction" or credit that otherwise would not be available. The IRC defines control as 50% of the voting power or 50% of the value of the outstanding stock. The IRS can use this provision to disallow a loss or credit carryover in situations where Sec. 382 does not apply.

TAX PLANNING CONSIDERATIONS

OBJECTIVE 9

Identify tax planning opportunities in taxable acquisitions and reorganizations

WHY USE A REORGANIZATION INSTEAD OF A TAXABLE TRANSACTION?

Choosing between a taxable and nontaxable transaction can be difficult. The advantages and disadvantages of a nontaxable reorganization are important for both the buyer and the seller. Depending on their relative importance, they may serve as points of negotiation and compromise in the effort to structure the transaction.

From the target shareholders' perspective, several factors are relevant. First, a nontaxable reorganization affords shareholders a tax deferral except to the extent they receive boot. This tax deferral may permit a shareholder to preserve a higher percentage of his or her capital investment than otherwise would be possible in a taxable acquisition. Second, a taxable transaction permits target corporation shareholders to convert their former equity interests into liquid assets (e.g., when they receive cash or property other than stock or securities of the acquiring corporation). These liquid assets can be invested however the shareholder chooses.

ETHICAL POINT

The choice between structuring an acquisition as taxable or nontaxable involves a large number of considerations for both the buyer and the seller. All parties must examine the tax, financial, and legal considerations with the assistance of their own experts.

In a reorganization, the shareholder must obtain a proprietary interest in the acquiring corporation. The future success of the acquiring corporation is likely to enhance the value of this interest. Conversely, if the acquiring corporation encounters financial difficulties, the value of the shareholder's investment may diminish. Third, losses realized in a reorganization cannot be recognized. A taxable transaction permits the immediate recognition of realized losses. Fourth, gains recognized in a reorganization are taxed as dividends if the distribution of boot is substantially equivalent to a dividend. Taxable transactions generally result in the shareholder's recognizing capital gains. Finally, a taxable transaction permits the shareholder to step-up to FMV the basis of stock and securities received. A nontaxable transaction, however, results in a substituted basis.

SELF-STUDY QUESTION

Is a nontaxable reorganization always preferable to a taxable acquisition?

ANSWER

No. What form an acquisition should take involves a myriad of issues relating to the parties involved in the transaction. A number of these issues are discussed in this section.

From the transferor corporation's point of view, a reorganization permits the exchange of assets without gain recognition. In addition, depreciation is not recaptured in a reorganization. Instead, the recapture potential shifts to the acquiring corporation.

From the acquiring corporation's point of view, a reorganization permits an acquisition without the expenditure of substantial amounts of cash or securities. Because the target corporation shareholders do not recognize gain unless they receive boot, they may be

TYPICAL MISCONCEPTION

When an acquisition structure is developed, the tax consequences are only one of many factors the parties must consider. Often, the final acquisition structure will not be optimal from a tax perspective because other factors may be deemed more important.

willing to accept a lower sales price than would otherwise be the case in a taxable acquisition. In a reorganization, the transferee takes the same property basis as the transferor's. The inability to step up basis to cost or FMV reduces the attractiveness of a reorganization and could lower the price the acquirer is willing to pay.

In a reorganization, the acquirer obtains the benefits of NOL, tax credit, and other carryovers from the target corporation (subject to limitations). In a taxable transaction, such tax attributes are not inherited by the buyer although they can be used to reduce the seller's tax cost in the sale.

AVOIDING THE REORGANIZATION PROVISIONS

TYPICAL MISCONCEPTION

The reorganization provisions are not elective. If a transaction qualifies as a Sec. 368 reorganization, it must be treated as such. It usually is not difficult to disqualify a nontaxable reorganization if the parties desire a taxable acquisition.

An acquisition can be converted from a nontaxable reorganization into a taxable transaction if the restrictions on the use of consideration incidental to a particular type of reorganization are ignored. For example, the Type B reorganization rules can be skirted if the acquiring corporation obtains target corporation stock through a combination of acquiring corporation stock and cash. Because this structure does not meet the solely-for-voting-stock requirement, the transaction is taxable to the selling shareholders. It also is treated as a stock purchase, thereby permitting the acquiring corporation to make a Sec. 338 election and step-up the basis in target corporation assets.

EXAMPLE C:7-40 ►

Alpha Corporation offers to exchange one share of its common stock (valued at $40) plus $20 cash for each share of Theta Corporation's single class of common stock. All of Theta's shareholders accept the offer and exchange a total of 2,000 Theta shares for 2,000 Alpha shares and $40,000 cash. At the time of the exchange, Theta's assets have a $35,000 adjusted basis and a $110,000 FMV. Theta recognizes no gain or loss in the exchange. The basis of its assets remains $35,000 unless Alpha makes a Sec. 338 election. Theta's shareholders recognize gain or loss in the exchange, whether or not Alpha makes a Sec. 338 election. ◄

COMPLIANCE AND PROCEDURAL CONSIDERATIONS

OBJECTIVE 10

Comply with procedural rules for taxable acquisitions and reorganizations

SECTION 338 ELECTION

The acquiring corporation makes a Sec. 338 election by filing Form 8023 (Elections Under Section 338 for Corporations Making Qualified Stock Purchases) with the IRS. This election must be made by the fifteenth day of the ninth month beginning after the month of the acquisition date. The required information about the acquiring corporation, the target corporation, and the election is set forth in Reg. Sec. 1.338-1(d).

PLAN OF REORGANIZATION

Nonrecognition of gain by a transferor corporation in an asset acquisition (Sec. 361) or a shareholder in a stock acquisition (Sec. 354) requires that the acquisition be pursuant to a plan of reorganization. A **plan of reorganization** is a plan for restructuring an enterprise that complies with the reorganization provisions of the Internal Revenue Code and associated Treasury Regulations. Nonrecognition of gain or loss is limited to exchanges or distributions that are a direct part of a reorganization undertaken to continue the business of a corporation that is a party to a reorganization.[92] Although a written plan is not required, it would be prudent for all parties to the reorganization to reduce the plan to writing, either as a communication to the shareholders, a document in the corporate records, a memorandum of understanding, or a written agreement between the parties. The transaction generally is taxable if a plan of reorganization does not exist or if a transfer or distribution is not pursuant to a plan.[93]

[92] Reg. Sec. 1.368-2(g).

[93] *A. T. Evans*, 30 B.T.A. 746 (1934), *acq.* XIII-2 C.B. 7; and *William Hewitt*, 19 B.T.A. 771 (1930).

PARTY TO A REORGANIZATION

For an asset or stock transfer to be nontaxable under Secs. 354 and 361, a shareholder or a transferor must be a party to a reorganization. Section 368(b) includes as a **party to a reorganization** "any corporation resulting from a reorganization, and both corporations involved in a reorganization where one corporation acquires the stock or assets of a second corporation." In a triangular reorganization, the corporation controlling the acquiring corporation, and whose stock is used to effect the reorganization, also is a party to the reorganization.

RULING REQUESTS

Before proceeding with an acquisition or disposition, some taxpayers request an advance ruling from the IRS on the tax consequences of the transaction. They generally do so because of the complexity of tax reorganization law and the substantial dollar amounts involved in the transaction. An after-the-fact determination by the IRS or the courts that a completed transaction is taxable could be costly to all parties. The IRS will issue an advance ruling only for reorganizations that conform to the guidelines of Rev. Proc. 77-37 and other IRS pronouncements. It will not issue an advance ruling for a reorganization if the consequences are adequately addressed in the IRC, Treasury Regulations, Supreme Court decisions, tax treaties, revenue rulings, revenue procedures, notices, or other IRS pronouncements.[94] Because of IRS policy not to issue these so-called "comfort rulings," many taxpayers instead seek opinion letters from tax counsel.

FINANCIAL STATEMENT IMPLICATIONS

OBJECTIVE 11

Recognize the financial statement implications of corporate acquisitions

An acquiring corporation must use the acquisition method for financial statement purposes whether the business combination is a taxable purchase or a nontaxable reorganization.[95] However, differences occur in the recording of deferred tax accounts and the treatment of goodwill. Also, a stock acquisition has its own particularities because recording the transaction occurs in the process of consolidating the financial statements of the acquiring parent and the acquired subsidiary.

For subsequent illustrations, assume Theta Corporation (the target corporation) has the following balance sheet of identified assets and liabilities, where the tax basis and book basis are the same. Thus, prior to the acquisition, Theta has no temporary differences or deferred tax accounts.

	FMV	*Basis*	*Difference*
Accounts receivable	$ 12,000	$ 12,000	$ –0–
Inventory	30,000	25,000	5,000
Plant and equipment	100,000	75,000	25,000
Land	50,000	40,000	10,000
Total assets	$192,000	$152,000	$40,000
Liabilities	$ 20,000	$ 20,000	
Equity	172,000	132,000	
Total liabilities and equity	$192,000	$152,000	

TAXABLE ASSET ACQUISTION

In a taxable purchase, the acquiring corporation's tax basis in the purchased assets likely will be the same as the recorded book basis. If so, deferred tax liabilities and assets will not arise as a result of the business combination. Also, if tax goodwill and book goodwill

[94] Rev. Proc. 2014-1, 2014-1, I.R.B. 1, Rev. Proc. 2014-3, 2014-1 I.R.B. 111, and Rev. Proc. 2013-32, 2013-28 I.R.B. 55.

[95] Accounting Standards Codification (ASC) 805, Business Combinations, which codifies SFAS No. 141R.

are equal, future amortization of tax goodwill under Sec. 197 will create temporary differences because book goodwill can be expensed only if impaired.[96] (If tax and book goodwill differ in a taxable business combination, the financial statement treatment gets complicated, a topic beyond the scope of this textbook.)

EXAMPLE C:7-41 ▶ At the beginning of the current year, Alpha Corporation purchases all of Theta Corporation's assets for $207,000 cash and does not assume Theta's liabilities. For both book and tax purposes, each asset gets a FMV allocation of this purchase price with the remainder allocated to goodwill. Because the book and tax bases are equal, Alpha records no deferred tax accounts. Accordingly, Alpha makes the following book journal entry to record the purchase:

Accounts receivable	12,000	
Inventory	30,000	
Plant and equipment	100,000	
Land	50,000	
Goodwill	15,000	
Cash		207,000

In the acquisition year, Alpha deducts $1,000 of goodwill amortization for tax purposes but takes no impairment loss for book purposes. Assuming no other book-tax differences, $150,000 of pretax book income, and a 35% tax rate, Alpha realizes the following results for this year.

Net income before FIT expense	$150,000
Goodwill amortization (temporary difference)	(1,000)
Taxable income	$149,000

Thus, Alpha's federal income tax expense is $52,500 ($150,000 × 0.35), and its federal tax liability is $52,150 ($149,000 × 0.35). Also, Alpha records a deferred tax liability of $350 ($1,000 × 0.35). Accordingly, Alpha makes the following book journal entry:

Federal income tax expense	52,500	
Deferred tax liability		350
Federal income taxes payable		51,150

The deferred tax liability will increase by the same amount each year of the 15-year tax amortization period and will reverse if and when Alpha takes an impairment loss on the book goodwill. ◀

NONTAXABLE ASSET ACQUISTION

In a nontaxable business combination, such as a Type A or Type C reorganization, the bases recorded for financial statement purposes differ from the carryover tax bases of acquired assets. For business combinations, the acquiring corporation recognizes a deferred tax asset or liability for differences between the assigned financial statement values and the tax bases of the transferred assets and liabilities.[97] Goodwill for which the corporation is not allowed an amortization deduction for tax purposes, the usual situation in a nontaxable acquisition, does not give rise to a temporary difference.

EXAMPLE C:7-42 ▶ At the beginning of the current year, Alpha Corporation acquires all of Theta's assets and assumes Theta's liabilities in a Type A merger. In addition to assuming the liabilities, Alpha issues $187,000 worth of its preferred stock as consideration, for a total consideration of $207,000. For tax purposes, Alpha takes a carryover basis in each asset, but for financial statement purposes, Alpha records each asset at its FMV. Assuming a 35% corporate tax rate, the $40,000 difference between the total book value and total tax basis creates a $14,000 ($40,000 × 0.35) deferred tax liability. Thus, aside from $15,000 of goodwill from the excess of consideration paid ($207,000) over the FMV of identified assets ($192,000), Alpha records $14,000 of additional goodwill. Accordingly, Alpha makes the following book journal entry to record the acquisition:

Accounts receivable	12,000
Inventory	30,000
Plant and equipment	100,000

[96] Accounting Standards Codification (ASC) 350, Intangibles—Goodwill and Other, which codifies SFAS No. 142.

[97] Accounting Standards Codification (ASC) 740, Income Taxes, which codifies SFAS No. 109.

Land	50,000	
Goodwill	29,000	
Deferred tax liability		14,000
Liabilities		20,000
Preferred stock		187,000

In the acquisition year, Alpha's book net income before federal income tax (FIT) expense is $150,000, which includes $12,000 of book depreciation on the acquired plant and equipment and $2,800 of book goodwill impairment. For tax purposes, Alpha recognizes a $5,000 gain on the sale of the acquired inventory and takes $9,000 of depreciation on the acquired plant and equipment, but it amortizes no goodwill. The difference between the $2,800 book goodwill impairment and the zero tax goodwill amortization produces a permanent difference. The other book-tax differences are temporary, resulting in the following net income to taxable income reconciliation:

Net income before FIT expense	$150,000
Goodwill (permanent difference)	2,800
Net income after permanent differences	$152,800
Inventory sale (temporary difference)	5,000
Depreciation (temporary difference)	3,000
Taxable income	$160,800

Thus, assuming a 35% tax rate, Alpha's federal income tax expense is $53,480 ($152,800 × 0.35), and its federal tax liability is $56,280 ($160,800 × 0.35). Also, Alpha reduces its deferred tax liability by $2,800 ($8,000 × 0.35). Accordingly, Alpha makes the following book journal entry:

Federal income tax expense	53,480	
Deferred tax liability	2,800	
Federal income taxes payable		56,280

◀

STOCK ACQUISTION

In a stock acquisition, the target corporation remains intact as a subsidiary of the acquiring corporation. The adjustments necessary to implement acquisition accounting rules income tax accounting rules occur when the corporations prepare their consolidated financial statements.

EXAMPLE C:7-43 ▶ At the beginning of the current year, Alpha Corporation acquires 100% of Theta's stock for $187,000 cash. As a result, Theta's shareholders recognize gain or loss on their sale of the stock. Alpha makes the following book journal entry to record the purchase:

Investment in Theta Corporation	187,000	
Cash		187,000

If Alpha instead acquired the Theta stock in a Type B reorganization using $187,000 of common voting stock, Alpha would have made a similar journal entry with the credit being to common stock rather than cash. In the consolidating journal entry for either type acquisition, Alpha eliminates the investment account, adjusts Theta's tax bases to book value, and records the necessary deferred accounts as follows:

Inventory	5,000	
Plant and equipment	25,000	
Land	10,000	
Goodwill	29,000	
Theta's equity	132,000	
Deferred tax liability		14,000
Investment in Theta Corporation		187,000

◀

PRICING THE ACQUISITION

In the above examples, the numerical amount of consideration is the same for the taxable and nontaxable asset acquisitions ($207,000). Economically, however, they are not comparable because, in the taxable purchase, the seller bears the tax burden. In the nontaxable asset acquisition, however, the acquiring corporation assumes the tax burden because it pays the same amount of consideration for assets having a low tax basis and a built-in gain. Consequently, it incurs the tax liability when it sells or depreciates the low basis assets. To shift the tax burden back to the seller in a nontaxable acquisition, the acquiring corporation might want to negotiate a reduced price for the assets. Similarly, in either a taxable or nontaxable stock acquisition, the acquiring corporation obtains a subsidiary with low basis assets. Hence, it might want to negotiate a stock price that reflects that built-in tax liability.

NET OPERATING LOSSES

If the target corporation has net operation loss carryovers (NOLs), the acquiring corporation must establish a deferred tax asset along with a valuation allowance if necessary. See Chapter C:3 for a discussion of the valuation allowance as well as a general discussion of the financial implications of federal income taxes.

PROBLEM MATERIALS

DISCUSSION QUESTIONS

C:7-1 From the standpoint of the target corporation shareholders, what is the advantage of a taxable stock acquisition by a purchaser corporation compared to the purchaser's acquiring all the target's assets in a taxable transaction followed by a liquidating distribution from the target to its shareholders?

C:7-2 What tax advantages exist for a corporate buyer when it acquires the assets of another corporation in a taxable transaction? For a seller when he or she exchanges stock in a taxable transaction? In a nontaxable transaction?

C:7-3 What tax and nontax advantages and disadvantages accrue when an acquiring corporation purchases all of a target corporation's stock for cash and subsequently liquidates the target corporation?

C:7-4 Why might a parent corporation make a Sec. 338 election after acquiring a target corporation's stock? When would such an election not be advisable?

C:7-5 a. Holt Corporation acquires all the stock of Star Corporation and makes a timely Sec. 338 election. The adjusted grossed-up basis of the Star stock is $2.5 million. The FMV of tangible assets on Star's balance sheet is $1.8 million. How are the new bases in Star's individual assets determined?

b. How would your answer change if instead the adjusted grossed-up basis were $1.4 million?

C:7-6 Compare the tax consequences of a taxable asset acquisition and a Type C asset-for-stock reorganization, based on the following factors:

a. Consideration used to effect the transaction.

b. Recognition of gain or loss by the target corporation on the asset transfer.

c. Basis of property to the acquiring corporation.

d. Recognition of gain or loss when the target corporation liquidates.

e. Use and/or carryover of the target corporation's tax attributes.

C:7-7 Which of the following events as part of an acquisitive reorganization require the target corporation to recognize gain? Assume in all cases that the target corporation liquidates in the reorganization.

a. Transfer of appreciated target corporation assets in exchange for acquiring corporation stock and short-term notes.

b. Transfer of appreciated target corporation assets in exchange for acquiring corporation stock and the assumption of the target corporation's liabilities.

c. Assume the same facts as in Part b except the amount of liabilities assumed by the acquiring corporation exceeds the adjusted basis of the target corporation assets transferred.

d. Transfer of appreciated target corporation assets in exchange for stock and cash. The target corporation distributes the cash to its shareholders.

e. Transfer of appreciated target corporation assets in exchange for stock and cash. The target uses the cash to pay off its liabilities.

C:7-8 A shareholder receives stock and cash in an acquisitive reorganization. The shareholder recognizes a gain because of the boot (cash) received. What rules determine whether the character of the shareholder's recognized gain is dividend income or capital gain?

C:7-9 Evaluate the following statement: Individual shareholders who recognize gain as the result of receiving boot in a corporate reorganization generally prefer to report capital gain, whereas corporate shareholders generally prefer to report dividend income.

C:7-10 How is the basis in nonboot stock and securities received by a shareholder determined? How is the basis in boot property determined?

C:7-11 Compare the types of consideration that can be used in Type A, B, and C reorganizations.

C:7-12 How does the IRS interpret the continuity of interest doctrine for a Type A reorganization?

C:7-13 How does the IRS interpret the continuity of business enterprise requirement for a Type A reorganization?

C:7-14 What are the advantages of a Type C asset-for-stock reorganization as opposed to a Type A merger reorganization? The disadvantages?

C:7-15 How does the IRS interpret the "substantially all" asset requirement for a Type C reorganization?

C:7-16 Explain why an acquiring corporation might be prohibited from using cash as part of the consideration paid in a Type C reorganization.

C:7-17 Some acquisitive transactions may be characterized as either a Type C or a Type D reorganization. Which reorganization provision controls if the two types overlap?

C:7-18 What is the difference between an acquisitive Type C reorganization and an acquisitive Type D reorganization?

C:7-19 Explain the circumstances in which cash and other property can be used in a Type B reorganization.

C:7-20 Alpha Corporation purchased for cash a 5% interest in Theta Corporation stock. After buying the stock and examining Theta's books, Alpha's management wants to make a tender offer to acquire the remaining Theta stock in exchange for Alpha voting stock. Can this tender offer be accomplished as a Type B reorganization? What problems may be encountered in structuring the acquisition as a nontaxable reorganization?

C:7-21 In a tender offer, Alpha Corporation wants to exchange its voting common stock for all of Theta Corporation's single class of stock. Only 85% of Theta's shareholders agree to tender their shares. After the tender, what options exist for Alpha to acquire the remaining shares as part of the reorganization? At a later date? How will a subsequent cash acquisition of the remaining outstanding shares affect the tax treatment of the tender offer?

C:7-22 Explain the structure of a triangular reorganization? What advantages would a triangular reorganization provide the acquiring corporation?

C:7-23 Compare and contrast the requirements for, and the tax treatment of, the spinoff, split-off, and split-up forms of divisive Type D reorganizations.

C:7-24 Stock in a controlled subsidiary corporation can be distributed tax-free to the distributing corporation's shareholders under Sec. 355. Explain the difference between such a distribution and a divisive Type D reorganization.

C:7-25 Under what circumstances is the distribution of a controlled corporation's stock or securities nontaxable to the distributing corporation's shareholders? What events trigger the recognition of gain or loss by the shareholders?

C:7-26 When does the distributing corporation recognize gain or loss on the distribution of stock or securities of a controlled corporation to its shareholders?

C:7-27 What is a recapitalization? What types of recapitalizations are nontaxable?

C:7-28 In a family corporation, how can a recapitalization be used to transfer voting control tax-free from a retiring senior generation to an upcoming junior generation?

C:7-29 Explain why a transaction might satisfy the letter of Sec. 368 for a reorganization yet fail to be treated as a reorganization.

C:7-30 Which types of reorganizations (acquisitive, divisive, and other) permit the carryover of tax attributes from a target or transferor corporation to an acquiring or transferee corporation?

C:7-31 What restrictions are placed on the acquisition and use of a loss corporation's tax attributes?

C:7-32 Explain why Sec. 382 will not be an obstacle to the use of NOL carryovers following an acquistion if the value of the old loss corporation is large relative to its NOL carryovers.

C:7-33 What is a plan of reorganization? Does such a plan need to be reduced to writing?

C:7-34 Why do some taxpayers secure an advance ruling for a proposed reorganization transaction?

C:7-35 Does the receipt of a favorable advance ruling provide the taxpayer with a guarantee that the IRS will follow the ruling if it audits the completed transaction?

ISSUE IDENTIFICATION QUESTIONS

C:7-36 Rodger Powell owns all the stock in Fireside Bar and Grill Corporation in Pittsburgh. Now that he has turned 65, Rodger wants to sell his business and retire to sunny Florida. Karin Godfrey, a long-time bartender at Fireside, offers to purchase all the corporation's noncash assets in exchange for a 25% down payment, with the remaining 75% paid in five equal annual installments. Interest will accrue at a market rate on the unpaid installments. Rodger plans to liquidate the corporation that has operated the Bar and Grill. He also plans to have Fireside Bar and Grill distribute the installment notes and any remaining assets. What tax issues should Fireside Bar and Grill, Rodger, and Karin consider with respect to the proposed purchase?

C:7-37 Adolph Coors Co. transferred part of its assets to ACX Technologies Corporation in exchange for all of ACX's stock. The transferred assets included its aluminum unit, which makes aluminum sheet; its paper packaging unit, which makes consumer-products packaging; and its ceramic unit, which makes high-technology ceramics used in computer boards and automotive parts. The ACX Technologies stock received for the assets was distributed to the Coors shareholders. What tax issues should the parties to the divisive reorganization consider?

C:7-38 Johnson & Johnson announced that it had entered into a merger agreement with Alza Corporation, a research-based pharmaceutical company and a leader in drug delivery technologies. In a nontaxable reorganization, Alza shareholders were offered a fixed exchange ratio of 0.49 shares of Johnson & Johnson common stock for each share of Alza stock. Alza had approximately 295 million shares outstanding at the time of the announcement. The boards of directors of both companies approved the merger. What tax issues might have been important to the two companies and to the two shareholder groups?

PROBLEMS

C:7-39 ***Qualified Stock Purchase.*** Alpha Corporation purchased 20% of Theta Corporation's stock on each of the following dates in the current year: January 2, April 1, June 1, October 1, and December 31.

a. Has a qualified stock purchase occurred? If it so desires, when must Alpha make the deemed sale election under Sec. 338?

b. How would your answer to Part a change if instead the purchase dates were January 1, April 1, and September 2 of the current year, and January 3, and April 15 of the following year?

c. If either Part a or b fails to be a qualified stock purchase and Alpha made its initial purchase on April 1 of the current year, what is the latest date on which Alpha can make the final stock purchase needed to qualify for a Sec. 338 election?

C:7-40 ***Sec. 338 Election.*** Alpha Corporation purchases 20% of Theta Corporation stock from Milt on August 10 of the current year. Alpha purchases an additional 30% of the stock from Nick on November 15 of the current year. Alpha purchases the remaining 50% of the Theta stock from Phil on April 10 of the following year. The total price paid for the stock is $1.9 million. Theta's balance sheet on April 10 of the following year shows assets with a $2.5 million FMV, a $1.6 million adjusted basis, and $500,000 in liabilities.

a. What is the acquisition date for the Theta stock for Sec. 338 purposes? By what date must Alpha make the Sec. 338 election?

b. If Alpha makes a Sec. 338 election, what is the aggregate deemed sale price for the assets?

c. What is the total basis of the assets following the deemed sale, assuming a 34% corporate tax rate?

d. How does the tax liability attributable to the deemed sale affect the price Alpha should be willing to pay for the Theta stock?

e. What happens to Theta's tax attributes following the deemed sale?

C:7-41 ***Sec. 338 Election.*** Gator Corporation is considering the acquisition of Bulldog Corporation's stock in exchange for cash. Two options are under review: (1) Gator purchases the assets from Bulldog for $1.4 million or (2) Gator purchases the Bulldog stock for $1 million and makes a Sec. 338 election shortly after the stock purchase. Bulldog has no NOL or capital loss carryovers. Bulldog's balance sheet is presented below.

Assets	*Adjusted Basis*	*FMV*	*Liabilities and Equity*	*Amount*
Cash	$100,000	$ 100,000	Short-term debt	$ 200,000
Marketable securities	140,000	200,000	Long-term debt	200,000
Accounts receivable	100,000	100,000	Paid-in capital	300,000
Inventory (FIFO)	100,000	150,000	Retained earnings	700,000
Plant and equipment	200,000	500,000		
Intangibles	–0–	350,000		
Total	$640,000	$1,400,000	Total	$1,400,000

a. What advantages would accrue to Gator if it purchases the assets directly? What disadvantages would accrue to Bulldog if it sells the assets and then liquidates?

b. What advantages would accrue to Gator if it purchases the Bulldog stock for cash and subsequently makes a Sec. 338 election? What advantage would accrue to Bulldog if its shareholders sell the Bulldog stock?
c. How would your answers change if Bulldog had incurred $250,000 of NOLs in the current year that it cannot carry back in full due to insufficient taxable income in the preceding two years?

C:7-42 *Sec. 338 Election.* J.S. Bachman owns 100% of Legato Corporation's stock and has a $350,000 basis in his stock. On December 31 of the current year, Legato Corporation reported the following balance sheet:

Assets	*Adjusted Basis*	*FMV*	*Liabilities and Equity*	*Amount*
Inventory	$200,000	250,000	Liabilities	$100,000
Land	250,000	600,000	Equity	750,000
Total	$450,000	$850,000	Total	$850,000

Staccato Corporation wishes to purchase, for cash, 80% of Legato's stock from Mr. Bachman and then make a Sec. 338 election. Determine the following amounts resulting from the transaction and Sec. 338 election: Grossed-up basis (G), aggregated deemed sale price (ADSP), total gain (loss) recognized, tax liability, adjusted grossed-up basis (AGUB), basis of each asset after allocating the AGUB, and gain recognized by Mr. Bachman. Assume a 34% corporate tax rate, and determine the required amounts in each of the following independent situations.
a. Staccato pays $491,200 for the Legato stock.
b. Staccato pays $600,000 for the Legato stock.
c. Staccato pays $470,000 for the Legato stock.
d. Staccato pays $670,000 for the Legato stock.

C:7-43 *Sec. 338 Basis Allocation.* Alpha Corporation purchases all of Theta Corporation's stock for $300,000 cash. Alpha makes a timely Sec. 338 election. Theta's balance sheet at the close of business on the acquisition date is as follows:

Assets	*Adjusted Basis*	*FMV*	*Liabilities and Equity*	*Amount*
Cash	$ 50,000	$ 50,000	Accounts payable	$ 40,000
Marketable securities	18,000	38,000	Note payable	60,000
Accounts receivable	66,000	65,000	Owner's equity	300,000
Inventory (FIFO)	21,000	43,000		
Equipment[a]	95,000	144,000		
Land	6,000	12,000		
Building[b]	24,000	48,000		
Total	$280,000	$400,000	Total	$400,000

[a]The equipment cost $200,000.
[b]The building is MACRS property on which Theta has claimed $10,000 of depreciation.

a. What is the aggregate deemed sale price for the Theta assets (assume a 34% corporate tax rate)?
b. What amount and character of gain or loss must Theta recognize on the deemed sale?
c. What is the adjusted grossed-up basis for the Theta stock? What basis is allocated to each of the individual properties?
d. What happens to "old" Theta's tax attributes? Do they carry over to "new" Theta?
e. What amount (if any) of goodwill can Theta amortize following the acquisition? Over what period and under what method may Theta amortize the goodwill?

C:7-44 *Amount of Corporate Gain or Loss.* Thomas Corporation transfers to Andrews Corporation all its assets and $100,000 of its liabilities in exchange for Andrews voting common stock, having a $600,000 FMV, in a merger in which Thomas subsequently liquidates. Thomas's basis in its assets is $475,000.
a. What is the amount of Thomas's realized and recognized gain or loss on the asset transfer?
b. What is Andrews's basis in the assets received?
c. What is the amount of Thomas's realized and recognized gain or loss when it distributes the stock to its shareholders?
d. How would your answers to Parts a–c change if Thomas's basis in the assets instead had been $750,000?

e. How would your answers to Parts a–c change if Andrews instead had exchanged $600,000 cash for Thomas assets and Thomas subsequently liquidated. Assume a 34% corporate tax rate.

C:7-45 *Amount of Shareholder Gain or Loss.* Silvia exchanges all her Theta Corporation stock (acquired August 1, 2011) for $300,000 of Alpha Corporation voting common stock pursuant to Theta's merger into Alpha. Immediately after the stock-for-stock exchange Silvia owns 25% of Alpha's 2,000 outstanding shares of stock. Silvia's adjusted basis in the Theta stock is $200,000 before the merger.

a. What are the amount and character of Silvia's recognized gain or loss?
b. What is Silvia's basis in the Alpha stock? When does her holding period begin?
c. How would your answers to Parts a and b change if instead Silvia received $60,000 cash and Alpha common stock worth $240,000?

C:7-46 *Amount and Character of Shareholder Gain or Loss.* Yong owns 100% of Theta Corporation stock having a $600,000 adjusted basis. As part of the merger of Theta into Alpha Corporation, Yong exchanges his Theta stock for $750,000 cash and Alpha common stock having a $3 million FMV. Yong retains a 60% interest in Alpha's 100,000 shares of outstanding stock immediately after the merger.

a. What are the amount and character of Yong's recognized gain?
b. What is Yong's basis in the Alpha stock?
c. How would your answers to Parts a and b change if instead Yong's 60,000 Alpha shares were one-third of Alpha's outstanding shares?

C:7-47 *Amount and Character of Gain Recognized.* Springs Corporation has developed a nature park at the site of Blue Springs. Because Newberry Corporation wants to develop several other springs in the area, Newberry wants to merge with Springs under Florida law. Newberry offers $650,000 of nonvoting preferred shares plus 1,000 shares of voting common (FMV of $50,000) to Springs in exchange for all of Springs' assets. As part of the merger, Springs' sole shareholder, Mr. High, exchanges all his shares in Springs for the shares in Newberry. Immediately before this transaction, Mr. High had a $240,000 basis in his Springs shares and owned no shares in Newberry. After the transaction he owns 20% of the value of the Newberry stock.

a. Does this transaction qualify as a Type A reorganization?
b. Does Springs recognize any gain or loss on the asset sale or the exchange of shares with Mr. High?
c. Does Mr. High recognize any gain or loss? What is his basis and holding period in his Newberry shares?

C:7-48 *Characterization of the Shareholder's Gain or Loss.* Turbo Corporation has one million shares of common stock and 200,000 shares of nonvoting preferred stock outstanding. Pursuant to a merger under state law, Ace Corporation exchanges its common stock worth $15 million for the Turbo common stock and pays $10 million in cash for the Turbo preferred stock. Some shareholders of Turbo received only Ace common stock for their common stock. Some shareholders received only cash for their preferred stock. Some shareholders received both cash and Ace common stock for their Turbo preferred and common stock, respectively. Shareholders owning approximately 10% of the Turbo common stock also owned Turbo preferred stock. The total cash received by these shareholders amounted to $1.5 million. The Turbo common stockholders end up with 15% of the Ace stock. What is the tax treatment of the common stock and/or cash received by each of the three groups of Turbo shareholders? Assume that some Turbo shareholders realize a gain on the transaction while other shareholders realize a loss.

C:7-49 *Requirements for a Type A Reorganization.* In a merger under state law, Anchor Corporation acquires all the assets of Tower Corporation. Tower's assets have a $5 million FMV and a $2.2 million adjusted basis. Assuming Tower liquidates, which of the following transactions qualify as a Type A reorganization?

a. The assets are exchanged for $5 million of Anchor common stock.
b. The assets are exchanged for $5 million of Anchor nonvoting preferred stock.
c. The assets are exchanged for $5 million of Anchor securities.
d. The assets are exchanged for $3.5 million of Anchor nonvoting preferred stock and $1.5 million in cash.
e. The assets are exchanged for $3 million of Anchor common stock and Anchor's assumption of $2 million of Tower liabilities.
f. The assets are exchanged for $5 million in cash provided by Anchor. An "all cash" merger transaction is permitted under state law.

C:7-50 *Tax Consequences of a Merger.* Armor Corporation exchanges $1 million of its common stock and $300,000 of Armor bonds for all of Trail Corporation's outstanding stock. As part of the same transaction, Trail then merges into Armor, which receives assets having a $1.3 million FMV and an $875,000 adjusted basis. In the merger, Antonello, a Trail shareholder, exchanges his 20% interest in Trail's single class of stock for $200,000 in Armor stock and $60,000 in Armor bonds. Antonello's 20% interest in Trail is comprised of 4,000 shares having a $100,000 adjusted basis. Following the reorganization, Antonello owns 5% (1,000 shares) of Armor's stock. Armor's E&P balance is $375,000.

a. What is the amount of Trail's recognized gain or loss in the asset transfer?
b. What is Armor's basis in the assets received in the exchange?
c. What are the amount and character of Antonello's recognized gain or loss?
d. What is Antonello's basis in the Armor stock? In the Armor bonds?

C:7-51 *Requirements for a Type C Reorganization.* Arnold Corporation plans to acquire all the assets of Turner Corporation in an asset-for-stock exchange. Turner's assets have a $600,000 adjusted basis and a $1 million FMV. Which of the following transactions qualify as a Type C reorganization (assuming Turner liquidates as part of the reorganization)?

a. The assets are exchanged for $800,000 of Arnold voting common stock and $200,000 of cash.
b. The assets are exchanged for $800,000 of Arnold voting common stock and $200,000 of Arnold bonds.
c. The assets are exchanged for $1 million of Arnold nonvoting preferred stock.
d. The assets are exchanged for $700,000 of Arnold voting common stock and Arnold's assumption of $300,000 of Turner's liabilities.
e. The assets are exchanged for $700,000 of Arnold voting common stock, Arnold's assumption of $200,000 of Turner's liabilities, and $100,000 in cash.

C:7-52 *Tax Consequences of a Type C Reorganization.* As part of a Type C reorganization, Ash Corporation exchanges $250,000 of its voting common stock and $50,000 of its bonds for all of Texas Corporation's assets. Texas liquidates, with each of its two shareholders receiving equal amounts of the Ash stock and bonds. Barbara has a $50,000 basis in her stock, and George has a $200,000 basis in his stock. George and Barbara, who are unrelated, each own 8% of Ash's stock (5,000 shares) immediately after the reorganization. At the time of the reorganization, Texas's E&P balance is $75,000, and its assets have an adjusted basis of $225,000.

a. What is the amount of Texas's recognized gain or loss in the asset transfer? On the distribution of the stock and bonds?
b. What is Ash's basis in the assets it acquired?
c. What are the amount and character of each shareholder's recognized gain or loss?
d. What is the basis of each shareholder's Ash stock? Ash bonds?

C:7-53 *Tax Consequences of a Type C Reorganization.* As part of a Type C reorganization, Tulsa Corporation exchanges assets having a $300,000 FMV and a $175,000 adjusted basis for $250,000 of Akron Corporation voting common stock and Akron's assumption of $50,000 of Tulsa's liabilities. Tulsa liquidates, with its sole shareholder, Michelle, receiving the Akron stock in exchange for her Tulsa stock having an adjusted basis of $100,000. Michelle owns 12% (2,500 shares) of Akron's stock immediately after the reorganization.

a. What is the amount of Tulsa's recognized gain or loss in the asset transfer? On the distribution of the stock?
b. What is Akron's basis in the assets it receives?
c. What effect would the transfer of Tulsa's assets to Subsidiary Corporation (controlled by Akron) have on the reorganization?
d. What are the amount and character of Michelle's recognized gain or loss?
e. What is Michelle's basis and holding period for her Akron stock?
f. What are the tax consequences of the transaction if Akron first transfers its stock to Akron-Sub Corporation, which then acquires Tulsa's assets?

C:7-54 *Requirements for a Type B Reorganization.* Allen Corporation plans to acquire all the stock in Taylor Corporation in a stock-for-stock exchange. Which of the following transactions will qualify as a Type B reorganization?

a. All of Taylor's common stock is exchanged for $1 million of Allen voting preferred stock.
b. All of Taylor's common stock is exchanged for $1 million of Allen voting common stock, and $500,000 face amount of Taylor bonds are exchanged for $500,000 face amount of Allen bonds. Both bonds are trading at their par values.

c. All of Taylor's stock is exchanged for $750,000 of Allen voting common stock and $250,000 of Allen bonds.
d. All of Taylor's stock is exchanged for $1 million of Allen voting common stock, and Taylor shareholders end up with less than 1% of Allen stock.
e. Ninety percent of Taylor's stock is exchanged for $900,000 of Allen voting common stock. One shareholder who owns 10% of the Taylor stock exercises his right under state law to have his shares independently appraised and redeemed for cash by Taylor. He receives $100,000.
f. Assume the same facts as in Part d except the Allen stock is contributed to Allen-Sub Corporation. The Allen stock is exchanged by Allen-Sub for all the Taylor stock.

C:7-55 *Tax Consequences of a Type B Reorganization.* Trent Corporation's single class of stock is owned equally by Juan and Miguel, who are unrelated. Juan has a $125,000 basis in his 1,000 Trent shares, and Miguel has a $300,000 basis in his 1,000 Trent shares. In a single transaction, Adams Corporation exchanges 2,500 shares of its voting common stock for each shareholder's Trent stock. Immediately after the reorganization, each shareholder owns 15% of the Adams stock, which has a FMV of $100 per share.
a. What are the amount and character of each shareholder's recognized gain or loss?
b. What is each shareholder's basis in his Adams stock?
c. What is Adams's basis in the Trent stock?
d. How would your answers to Parts a–c change if Adams instead exchanged 2,000 shares of Adams common stock and $50,000 in cash for each shareholder's Trent stock?

C:7-56 *Tax Consequences of a Type B Reorganization.* Austin Corporation exchanges $1.5 million of its voting common stock for all of Travis Corporation's single class of stock. Ingrid, who owns all the Travis stock, has a $375,000 stock basis. Immediately after the reorganization, Ingrid owns 25% of the 15,000 outstanding shares of Austin stock.
a. What are the amount and character of Ingrid's recognized gain or loss?
b. What is Ingrid's basis in her Austin stock?
c. What is Austin's basis in the Travis stock?
d. What are the tax consequences for all parties if Austin subsequently liquidates Travis as part of the plan of reorganization?
e. As part of the reorganization, Austin exchanges $1 million of its 7% bonds for $1 million Travis 7% bonds held equally by ten private investors.

C:7-57 *Tax Consequences of a Type B Reorganization.* On January 30 of the current year, Ashton Corporation purchased from Cathy 10% of Todd Corporation stock for $250,000 in cash. On May 30 of the following year, Andrea and Bill each exchange one-half of the remaining 90% of the Todd stock for $1.2 million of Ashton voting common stock. Andrea and Bill each have a $150,000 basis in their Todd stock, and each owns 15% of the Ashton stock (12,000 shares) immediately after the reorganization.
a. What are the amount and character of each shareholder's recognized gain or loss?
b. What is each shareholder's basis in his or her Ashton stock?
c. What is Ashton's basis in the Todd stock?
d. How would your answers to Parts a–c change if instead Ashton had acquired the remaining Todd stock on May 30 of the current year?
e. What effect would the stock acquisition have on the adjusted bases of individual assets and the tax attributes of Todd?
f. Can the Ashton-Todd corporate group file a consolidated tax return?
g. Can a Sec. 338 election be made with respect to Todd's assets?

C:7-58 *Tax Consequences of a Divisive Type D Reorganization.* Road Corporation is owned equally by four shareholders. It conducts activities through two operating divisions: the road construction division and meat packing division. To segregate the two activities into distinct corporations, Road transfers the assets and liabilities of the meat packing division (60% of Road's total net assets) to Food Corporation in exchange for all of Food's single class of stock. The assets of the meat packing division have a $2.75 million FMV and a $1.1 million adjusted basis. Its liabilities total $500,000. Road distributes the $2.25 million of Food stock (90,000 shares) ratably to each of the four shareholders.
a. What is the amount of Road's recognized gain or loss on the asset transfer? On the distribution of the Food stock?
b. What are the amount and character of each shareholder's recognized gain or loss on the distribution? (Assume each shareholder's basis in Road stock is $200,000.)

c. What is the basis of each shareholder's Road and Food stock after the reorganization? (Assume the Road stock is worth $1.5 million immediately after the distribution.)

C:7-59 *Tax Consequences of a Divisive Type D Reorganization.* Light Corporation is owned equally by two individual shareholders, Bev and Tarek. The shareholders no longer agree on how to manage Light's operations. Tarek agrees to a plan whereby $500,000 of Light's assets (having an adjusted basis of $350,000) and $100,000 of Light's liabilities are transferred to Dark Corporation in exchange for all its single class of stock (5,000 shares). Tarek will exchange all his Light common stock, having a $150,000 adjusted basis, for the $400,000 of Dark stock. Bev will continue to operate Light.

a. What is the amount of Light's recognized gain or loss on the asset transfer? On the distribution of the Dark stock?
b. What are the amount and character of Tarek's recognized gain or loss?
c. What is Tarek's basis in his Dark stock?
d. What tax attributes of Light will be allocated to Dark?

C:7-60 *Distribution of Stock: Spin-Off.* Parent Corporation has been in the business of manufacturing and selling trucks for the past eight years. Its subsidiary, Diesel Corporation, has been in the business of manufacturing and selling diesel engines for the past seven years. Parent acquired control of Diesel six years ago when it purchased 100% of its single class of stock from Large Corporation. A federal court has ordered Parent to divest itself of Diesel pursuant to an antitrust ruling. Consequently, Parent distributes all its Diesel stock to its shareholders. Alan owns less than 1% of Parent's outstanding stock having a $40,000 basis. As a result of Parent's distribution, he receives 25 shares of Diesel stock having a $25,000 FMV. Parent distributes no cash or other assets. Parent's E&P at the end of the year in which the spinoff occurs is $2.5 million. The Parent stock held by Alan has a $75,000 FMV immediately after the distribution.

a. What are the amount and character of the gain, loss, or income Alan must recognize as a result of Parent's distributing the Diesel stock?
b. What basis does Alan take in the Diesel stock he receives?
c. When does Alan's holding period for the Diesel stock begin?
d. What amount and character of gain or loss does Parent recognize on the distribution?
e. How would your answer to Part a change if Parent had been in the truck business for only three years before the distribution, and it had acquired the Diesel stock in a taxable transaction only two years ago?

C:7-61 *Distribution of Stock: Split-Off.* Parent Corporation has owned all 100 shares of Subsidiary Corporation common stock since 2008. Parent has been in the business of manufacturing and selling light fixtures, and Subsidiary has been in the business of manufacturing and selling light bulbs. Amy and Bill are the two equal shareholders of the Parent stock and have owned their stock since 2008. Amy's basis in her 50 Parent shares is $80,000, and Bill's basis in his 50 Parent shares is $60,000. On April 10, 2015, Parent distributes all 100 Subsidiary shares to Bill in exchange for all his Parent shares (which are cancelled). The distribution has a bona fide business purpose. The Subsidiary stock had a $30,000 basis to Parent on the distribution date. At the end of 2015, Parent has $150,000 of E&P. Immediately after the distribution, the FMVs of the Parent and Subsidiary stocks are $3,000 and $1,000 per share, respectively.

a. What are the amount and character of the gain, loss, or income Bill must recognize as a result of Parent's distributing the Subsidiary stock?
b. What basis does Bill take in the Subsidiary stock?
c. When does Bill's holding period for the Subsidiary stock begin?
d. Assume instead that Andrew formed Subsidiary in 2011 to manufacture and sell lightbulbs. Andrew sold the Subsidiary stock to Parent for cash in 2013. How would your answers to Parts a–c change?

C:7-62 *Distribution of Stock and Securities: Split-Off.* Ruby Corporation has 100 shares of common stock outstanding. Fred, a shareholder of Ruby, exchanges his 25% interest in the Ruby stock for Garnet Corporation stock and securities. Ruby purchased 80% of the Garnet stock ten years ago for $25,000. At the time of the exchange, Fred has a $50,000 basis in his Ruby stock, and the stock has an $80,000 FMV. Fred receives Garnet stock that has a $60,000 FMV and Garnet securities that have a $20,000 FMV. Ruby has $50,000 of E&P. Assume that all the requirements of Sec. 355 are met except with respect to the receipt of boot.

a. What are the amount and character of Fred's recognized gain or loss in the exchange?
b. What is Fred's basis in the Garnet stock and the Garnet securities?
c. What are the amount and character of Ruby's recognized gain or loss on the distribution?

d. When does Fred's holding period begin for the Garnet stock and the Garnet securities?
e. How would your answers to Part a change if the exchange did not meet the requirements of Sec. 355 or Sec. 356?

C:7-63 *Distribution of Stock and Securities: Split-Up.* Jean Corporation has two divisions—home cookware and electric home appliances. Bill and Bob Jean own all of Jean Corporation's single class of stock. Bill, the older brother, owns 70% of the Jean stock, and Bob owns the remaining 30%. Bill and Bob's adjusted bases in their Jean stock are \$700,000 and \$300,000, respectively. They have owned the stock for eight years. The divisions have the following assets:

Division	*FMV Assets*	*Adjusted Basis*
Cookware	\$980,000	\$600,000
Home appliances	420,000	300,000

To divide the business, Jean transfers the cookware assets to Cookware Corporation in exchange for all of Cookware stock. Jean transfers the home appliance assets to Home Appliance Corporation in exchange for all of Home Appliance stock. Jean transfers the Cookware stock to Bill in exchange for all of his Jean stock. Jean transfers the Home Appliance stock to Bob in exchange for all of his Jean stock. Finally, Jean liquidates with its remaining cash used to pay off its liabilities.
a. What gain or loss is recognized on the transfer of the Jean assets to Cookware and Home Appliance? What basis do the two corporations take in the assets transferred?
b. What gain or loss do Bill and Bob recognize when they exchange their Jean stock for the Cookware and Home Appliance stock? What basis does each shareholder take in his or her new stock?

C:7-64 *Requirements for a Type E Reorganization.* Master Corporation plans a recapitalization. Explain the tax consequences of each of the following unrelated transactions:
a. Holders of Class A nonvoting preferred stock exchange their stock for newly issued common stock. Master paid \$300,000 of cash dividends on the preferred stock in the current year and each prior year.
b. Holders of Master bonds in the amount of \$3 million exchange their bonds for the same dollar amount of preferred stock. In addition, \$180,000 of unpaid interest will be paid by issuing additional Master preferred stock to the former bondholders.
c. Because of a decline in the prevailing rate of interest, Master 9% bonds in the amount of \$3 million are called and exchanged by their holders before their maturity date for the same dollar amount of Master 6% bonds. In addition, Master will pay with cash \$180,000 of unpaid interest.

C:7-65 *Tax Consequences of a Type E Reorganization.* Milan Corporation is owned by four shareholders. Andy and Bob each own 40% of the outstanding common and preferred stock. Chris and Doug each own 10% of the outstanding common and preferred stock. The shareholders want to retire the preferred stock that was issued five years ago when the corporation was in the midst of a major expansion. Retirement of the preferred stock will eliminate the need to pay annual preferred dividends. Explain the tax consequences of the following two alternatives to the shareholders:
- Milan redeems the \$100 par preferred stock for its \$120 call price. Each shareholder purchased his preferred stock at its par value five years ago.
- The shareholders exchange each share of the \$100 par value preferred stock for \$120 of additional common stock.

What nontax advantages might exist for selecting one alternative over the other?

C:7-66 *Types of Reorganizations.* Identify the type of each of the following reorganizations.
a. Briggs Corporation was originally incorporated in Georgia but now conducts most of its business in Florida. The firm transfers substantially all its Georgia assets to a new Florida corporation. The Georgia entity liquidates shortly after the transfer. All "Georgia" shareholders swap their "old" Briggs stock for "new" Briggs stock, thereby acquiring an ownership interest in the Florida entity.
b. Jones Corporation exchanges all \$1 million of its \$1,000 face amount, 6% bonds for the same amount of new convertible bonds bearing a lower interest rate.
c. Bill Smith owns 100% of Smith Corporation and James Jones owns 100% of Jones Corporation. The two corporations are combined into a single entity called Smith & Jones Corporation. Each shareholder in the two original corporations receives stock in the new combined entity in proportion to the value of his original stock holdings.

d. Dupree Corporation is in bankruptcy. The corporation works out an arrangement whereby bondholders and other creditors receive Dupree notes and stock in exchange for discharge of their original claims.

C:7-67 *Reorganization Requirements.* Discuss the tax consequences of the following corporate reorganizations to the parties to the reorganization:

a. Adobe Corporation and Tyler Corporation merge under Florida law. Tyler shareholders receive for their Tyler stock $300,000 of Adobe common stock and $700,000 of Adobe securities.
b. Alabama Corporation exchanges $1 million of its voting common stock for all the noncash assets of Texas Corporation. The transaction meets all requirements of a Type C reorganization. Alabama then splits the acquired business into two operating divisions: meat packing and meat distribution. Alabama retains the meat packing division's assets and continues its activities but sells for cash the assets of the meat distribution division. The meat distribution division's assets constitute 40% of Texas's noncash assets.
c. Parent Corporation transfers $500,000 of investment securities to Subsidiary Corporation in exchange for all its single class of stock. The Subsidiary stock is exchanged for one-third of the stock held by each of Parent's shareholders. Six months after the reorganization, Subsidiary distributes the investment securities to its shareholders pursuant to the liquidation of Subsidiary.

C:7-68 *Determining the Type of Reorganization Transaction.* For each of the following transactions, indicate the reorganization type (e.g., Type A, Type B, etc.). Assume all common stock is voting.

a. Anderson and Brown Corporations exchange their assets for all the single class of stock of newly created Computer Corporation. Following the exchange, Anderson and Brown liquidate. The transaction satisfies Michigan corporation law requirements.
b. Price Corporation (incorporated in Texas) exchanges all its assets for all the single class of stock in Price Corporation (incorporated in Delaware). Following the exchange, Price (Texas) liquidates.
c. All of Gates Corporation's noncumulative, 10% preferred stock is exchanged for Gates common stock.
d. Hobbs Corporation exchanges its common stock for 90% of the outstanding common stock and 80% of the outstanding nonvoting preferred stock in Calvin Corporation. The remaining Calvin stock is held by about 30 individual investors.
e. Scale Corporation transfers the assets of its two operating divisions to Major and Minor Corporations in exchange for all of each corporation's single class of stock. Scale then distributes the Major and Minor stock pursuant to the liquidation of Scale.
f. Tobias Corporation has $3 million of assets and $1 million of liabilities. Andrew Corporation exchanges $2 million of its voting common stock for all of Tobias' assets and liabilities. Tobias liquidates, and its shareholders end up with 11% of the Andrew stock.
g. How would your answer to Part f change (if at all) if Tobias' balance sheet indicates that liabilities constitute 90% of the corporation's capital structure and common stock, the remaining 10%?

C:7-69 *Tax Attribute Carryovers.* At the close of business on May 31, 2015, Alaska Corporation exchanges $2 million of its voting common stock for all the noncash assets of Tennessee Corporation. Tennessee uses its cash to pay off its liabilities and then liquidates. Tennessee and Alaska report the following taxable income (loss):

Tax Year Ending	*Alaska Corp.*	*Tennessee Corp.*
December 31, 2012	($100,000)	($95,000)
December 31, 2013	60,000	20,000
December 31, 2014	70,000	(90,000)
May 31, 2015	XXX	(40,000)
December 31, 2015	73,000	XXX

a. What tax returns must Alaska and Tennessee file for 2015?
b. What amount of the NOL carryover does Alaska acquire?
c. Ignoring any implications of Sec. 382, what amount of Tennessee's NOL can Alaska use in 2015?

C:7-70 *Sec. 382 Limitation: Purchase Transaction.* Murray Corporation's stock is owned by about 1,000 shareholders, none of whom own more than 1% of the outstanding shares. Pursuant to a tender offer, Said purchased all the Murray stock for $7.5 million cash at the close of business on December 31, 2014. Before the acquisition, Said owned no Murray stock. Murray had incurred substantial NOLs, which totaled $1 million at the end of 2014. Murray's taxable income is expected to be $200,000 and $600,000, respectively, for 2015 and 2016. Assuming the long-term tax-exempt federal rate is 5% and Murray continues in the same trade or business, what amount of NOLs can Murray use in 2015 and/or 2016? What amount of NOLs and Sec. 382 limitation carryover to 2017?

C:7-71 *Sec. 382 Limitation: Nontaxable Reorganization.* Albert Corporation is a profitable publicly traded corporation. None of its shareholders owns more than 1% of its outstanding shares. On December 31, 2014, Albert exchanged $8 million of its stock for all the stock of Turner Corporation as part of a merger. Turner is owned by Tara, who receives 15% of the Albert stock as part of the reorganization. Tara owned none of the Albert stock before the merger. Turner accumulated $2.5 million in NOL carryovers before merging into Albert. Albert expects to earn $1 million and $1.5 million in taxable income during 2015 and 2016, respectively. Assuming the long-term tax-exempt federal rate is 4.5%, what amount of NOLs can Albert use in 2015 and 2016?

C:7-72 *Sec. 338 Limitation: Value of NOLs.* At the beginning of the current year, Allegro Corporation acquires all of Tempo Corporation's stock in a Type B reorganization. At the time of the acquisition, Tempo's stock has a $900,000 FMV, and Tempo has a $115,000 net operating loss (NOL) carryover. Assuming a 3.25% long-term tax-exempt federal rate, a 34% corporate tax rate, and a 5% discount rate, determine the present value of the tax benefits that will result from the NOLs. Assume that any NOL benefit will occur at the end of each relevant tax year.

COMPREHENSIVE PROBLEM

C:7-73 Sid Kess, a long-time tax client of yours, has decided to acquire the snow blower manufacturing firm owned by Richard Smith, one of his closest friends. Richard has a $200,000 adjusted basis in his Richard Smith Snow Blowers (RSSB) stock. Sid Kess Enterprises (SKE), a C corporation 100%-owned by Sid Kess, will make the acquisition. RSSB operates as a C corporation and reports the following assets and liabilities as of November 1 of the current year.

Assets	*Adjusted Basis*	*FMV*
Cash	$ 200,000	$ 200,000
Inventory (LIFO)	470,000	600,000
Equipment	100,000	275,000
Building	200,000	295,000
Land	80,000	120,000
Goodwill	–0–	250,000
Total	$1,050,000	$1,740,000

Liabilities and Equity	*Amount*
Accounts payable	$ 60,000
Mortgage payable	120,000
Paid-in capital	220,000
Retained earnings	650,000
Total	$1,050,000

RSSB has claimed depreciation of $200,000 and $80,000 on the equipment and building, respectively, and has claimed no amortization on the goodwill. Retained earnings approximate RSSB's E&P. No NOL, capital loss, or credit carryovers exist at the time of the acquisition. What are the tax consequences of each alternative acquisition transaction to SKE and RSSB? Assume a 34% corporate tax rate.

a. SKE acquires all the single class of RSSB stock for $1.56 million in cash. RSSB is not liquidated.

b. SKE acquires all the noncash assets of RSSB for $1.54 million in cash. RSSB is liquidated.

c. SKE acquires all the RSSB stock for $1.56 million in cash. RSSB is liquidated into SKE shortly after the acquisition.
d. SKE acquires all the RSSB stock for $1.56 million in cash. SKE makes a timely Sec. 338 election. Assume that RSSB's corporate tax rate is 34%.
e. SKE exchanges $1.54 million of its common stock for all of RSSB's noncash assets ($1,540,000 = $1,740,000 total assets − $200,000 cash). SKE has 10,000 shares of stock outstanding with a $3 million FMV before the acquisition. RSSB liquidates as part of the transaction. RSSB uses part of the retained cash to pay off the corporation's liabilities. The remaining cash is distributed along with the SKE stock in the liquidation of RSSB.
f. SKE exchanges $1.56 million of its common stock for all of Richard Smith's RSSB stock. Assume that RSSB does not liquidate. Each share of SKE stock has a $300 FMV.
g. Assume the same facts as in Part d except SKE transfers $1.56 million of its common stock to SKE-Sub. In the transaction, SKE-Sub is the acquiring corporation and uses $1.56 million of the SKE stock to acquire RSSB's stock.
h. Assume the same facts as in Part e except SKE transfers $1.54 million of its common stock to SKE-Sub. In the transaction, SKE-Sub is the acquiring corporation and uses $1.54 million of the SKE stock to acquire RSSB's noncash assets.

TAX STRATEGY PROBLEMS

C:7-74 Angel Macias is considering selling his business (organized as Theta Corporation), which has the following assets and liabilities:

Assets	*Adjusted Basis*	*FMV*
Cash	$ 400,000	$ 400,000
Securities	400,000	300,000
Inventory (LIFO)	100,000	200,000
Equipment	200,000	400,000
Building	50,000	300,000
Goodwill	–0–	200,000
Total	$1,150,000	$1,800,000

Theta's balance sheet also shows $200,000 of accounts payable and $400,000 in bank loans. No NOL carryovers or carrybacks are available. Bill Jones and Sam Smith, each of whose net worth exceeds $1 million, are interested in acquiring the business by using S&J Corporation as the vehicle for making the acquisition. Theta's management and its owners are interested in selling the business. What advice would you give Bill and Sam about acquiring the assets directly from Theta, or by acquiring Theta stock from its shareholders and then liquidating Theta into S&J? Bill and Sam also have expressed concern about possible differences in the financial reporting of a nontaxable versus a taxable acquisition.

C:7-75 Pedernales, a cash-rich Texas company that produces petrochemicals, would like to expand its operations in the Southwest. It considers acquiring Dorado, a Nevada corporation that disposes chemical wastes. Dorado owns key licenses, facilities, and technological processes. Over the years, it has accumulated substantial business and foreign tax credits. Because waste disposal sites are scarce in the United States, the value of Dorado's assets has increased threefold, while the value of Dorado stock has increased fivefold. The Rodriguez family, which owns a 52% equity stake in Pedernales, wants to retain control of the Texas company. How might Pedernales structure an acquisition? What tax and other issues should it consider?

C:7-76 Tom Smith owns 100% of Alpha Corporation's single class of stock, and Alpha owns 100% of Beta Corporation's single class of stock. Alpha and Beta have filed separate tax returns for a number of years. Neither corporation has any NOL carryovers. Although in recent years Alpha and Beta have been profitable, Beta needs an infusion of additional capital from outside investors. The corporations have received a proposal from an investor, Karla Boroff, to invest $2 million in Beta to enable Beta to expand its operations and to eliminate a current working capital shortage. Karla has imposed one constraint on her capital contribution—that Alpha and Beta become two independent entities. Alpha would continue to be owned entirely by Tom, but Beta would be controlled by the two individuals, Tom and Karla, with each owning 50% of Beta's stock. What tax strategies can you offer for separating the two companies?

CASE STUDY PROBLEMS

TAX & FINANCIAL ACCOUNTING

C:7-77 *Comparative Acquisition Forms.* Bailey Corporation owns a number of automotive parts shops. Bill Smith owns an automotive parts shop that has been in existence for 40 years and has competed with one of Bailey's branches. Bill is considering retiring and would like to sell his business. He has his CPA prepare the following balance sheet, which he presents to John Bailey, president of Bailey Corporation and a long-time friend of Bill's.

Assets	*Adjusted Basis*	*FMV*
Cash	$ 250,000	$ 250,000
Accounts receivable	75,000	70,000
Inventories (LIFO)	600,000	1,750,000
Equipment	200,000	250,000
Building	30,000	285,000
Land	30,000	115,000
Total	$1,185,000	$2,720,000

If Bailey Corporation pursues the acquisition, it will operate the automotive parts shop under its own tradename in the location Bill has used for 40 years. Mr. Bailey has asked you to prepare a summary of the tax consequences of the following three transactions: (1) a cash purchase of the noncash assets, (2) a purchase of the stock of Bill's corporation with cash and Bailey notes, and (3) an asset-for-stock reorganization conducted exclusively with Bailey stock. Upon interviewing Bill, you obtain the following additional information: Bill's business is operated as a C corporation. Bill has a $160,000 adjusted basis in his stock. Accounts payable of $200,000 are outstanding. The corporation has depreciated the building under the straight-line method and to date has claimed $100,000 in depreciation. The equipment is Sec. 1245 property for which the corporation has claimed $150,000 in depreciation. The after-tax profits in each of the last three years have exceeded $300,000. Bill suspects that some goodwill value exists that is not shown on the balance sheet. No NOL carryovers are available from prior years.

Required: Prepare a memorandum that outlines the tax consequences of each of the three alternative acquisitions. Assume that the anticipated cash purchase price is $2.55 million for the noncash assets and $2.6 million for the stock. Furthermore, assume that the transaction takes place in the current year. How would the acquiring corporation report each of the three alternatives under GAAP?

C:7-78 The following advertisement appeared in a financial journal:

$17 MILLION CASH WITH
ADDITIONAL CASH AVAILABLE
$105 MM TAX LOSS GOOD THROUGH 2029
CAPITAL GROUP, INC.
NASDAQ listed w/300 shareholders
WANTS TO ACQUIRE COMPANY
with Net Before Tax Audited Earnings of $7MM to $10MM
Exceptional Opportunity and Participation for Sellers and
Existing Management. Contact: Albert M. Zlotnick or Ross P.
Lederer, Tel: (000)-000-0000 and Fax: (000)-000-0000.

Required: Prepare a memorandum explaining the tax advantages that would accrue to the Capital Group if it acquired the stock or assets of a profitable corporation in a non-taxable reorganization or a taxable transaction. Would the advantages be the same if a profitable corporation acquired Capital? In addition, explain any tax law provisions that might restrict the use of these loss carryovers.

TAX RESEARCH PROBLEMS

C:7-79 On January 10 of the current year, Austin Corporation acquires for cash 8% of Travis Corporation's single class of stock. On August 25 of the current year, Austin makes a tender offer to exchange Austin common stock for the remaining Travis shares. Travis shareholders tender an additional 75% of the outstanding Travis stock. The exchange is completed on September 25 of the current year. Austin ends up with slightly more than

83% of the Travis shares. The remaining 17% of the Travis stock is held by about 100 former shareholders of Travis who own small blocks of stock. Your tax manager has asked you to draft a memorandum explaining whether one or both of the two acquisition transactions qualify as a nontaxable reorganization. If part or all of either transaction is taxable to Travis' shareholders, suggest ways to restructure the acquisitions so as to maximize tax benefits of the transaction. Assume that Austin does not want to make a Sec. 338 election.

Matt Bonner, CEO of Travis, asked a question that might be relevant to reporting the transaction: To simplify the corporate structure, can Austin liquidate Travis into Austin without recognizing any gain or loss?

At a minimum you should consult:

- IRC Sec. 368(a)(1)(B)
- Reg. Sec. 1.368-2(c)
- *Eldon S. Chapman, et al. v. CIR*, 45 AFTR 2d 80-1290, 80-1 USTC ¶9330 (1st Cir., 1980)
- *Arden S. Heverly, et al. v. CIR*, 45 AFTR 2d 80-1122, 80-1 USTC ¶9322 (3rd Cir., 1980)

C:7-80 ABC Corporation is the object of a hostile takeover bid by XYZ Corporation. ABC incurs a total of $400,000 in attorneys' fees, accounting fees, and printing costs for information mailed to ABC shareholders in its effort to defeat the XYZ takeover bid. XYZ finally concedes, and ABC remains a separate corporation. What is the appropriate tax treatment of the $400,000 in fees? Would that treatment be different if XYZ succeeds in acquiring ABC? Tax authorities you should consult include the following:

- IRC Sec. 162
- IRC Sec. 165
- *INDOPCO, Inc. v. Comm.*, 69 AFTR 2d 92-694, 92-1 USTC ¶50,113 (USSC, 1992)
- *U.S. v. Federated Department Stores, Inc.*, 74 AFTR 2d 94-5519, 94-2 USTC ¶50,418 (S.D. Ohio, 1994)
- *A.E. Staley Manufacturing Co. v. Comm.*, 80 AFTR 2d 97-5060, 97-2 USTC ¶50,521 (7th Cir., 1997)
- Reg. Sec. 1.263(a)-5

C:7-81 Diversified Corporation operates a successful bank with ten branches. Al, Bob, and Cathy created Diversified six years ago and own all the Diversified stock in equal shares. Diversified has constructed in downtown Metropolis a new building that houses a banking facility on the first floor, offices for its employees on the second and third floors, and office space to be leased out to third party lessees on the fourth through twelfth floors. Since the building was completed six months ago, approximately 75% of the floor space on the upper floors has been occupied. Under a plan of reorganization, Diversified proposes to transfer the building to Metropolis Real Estate (MRE) Corporation in exchange for all the MRE common stock. A team of commercial real estate experts has been hired to manage MRE. Following the reorganization, the building will be the only property owned by MRE. Diversified owns no other real estate because it currently leases from third parties the facilities for its ten retail banking branches. Diversified will distribute the MRE common stock ratably to Al, Bob, and Cathy, who will end up with all the Diversified and MRE common stock. Your tax manager has asked you to draft a memorandum explaining whether or not the proposed transaction will satisfy the requirements of a nontaxable divisive reorganization. At a minimum you should consult:

- IRC Sec. 368(a)(1)(D)
- Reg. Sec. 1.355-3(b), (c)
- *Appleby v. Comm.*, 9 AFTR 2d 372, 62-1 USTC ¶9178 (3rd Cir., 1962)

CHAPTER 8

CONSOLIDATED TAX RETURNS

LEARNING OBJECTIVES

After studying this chapter, you should be able to

1. Determine whether a group of corporations is an affiliated group
2. Describe how an affiliated group makes a consolidated return election and how it discontinues the election
3. Calculate consolidated taxable income for a consolidated group
4. Apply the rules for reporting intercompany transactions
5. Compute on a consolidated basis deductions and credits subject to limitations
6. Determine a consolidated group's NOL, calculate the carryback or carryover of a consolidated NOL, and apply the SRLY restrictions on NOL usage
7. Adjust the parent's basis in stock of a consolidated subsidiary
8. Compare the advantages and disadvantages of filing a consolidated tax return
9. Comply with the procedures for making a consolidated return election
10. Explain the financial statement implications of various consolidated transactions

CHAPTER OUTLINE

Many corporations have complex entity structures. For example, a corporation may have one or more subsidiaries, and some of these subsidiaries may have their own subsidiaries. A group of corporations form into complex entity structures for many reasons. For example, a parent corporation may want to insulate itself from liabilities related to its subsidiaries, or it may want to make it easier to implement a plan that links the compensation of the subsidiary's managers to the subsidiary's performance.

An **affiliated group** of corporations generally is a parent corporation and all its subsidiaries that are at least 80%-owned by the parent and other subsidiaries in the group (this topic will be discussed later in the chapter). The affiliated group has two options for filing its federal income tax returns:

- Each member of the group can file a separate tax return that reports its own income, deductions, credits, and other items.[1]
- The affiliated group can file a single, consolidated tax return that reports a combined result for all its group members.

If the affiliated group elects to file a **consolidated tax return**, it does not merely add up the members' incomes, deductions, and other items. Instead, the group must make adjustments so that it generally is treated as if it were a single corporation, as discussed in more detail later in the chapter. For example, the capital gains and losses for all group members are netted to determine the deductibility of capital losses against capital gains rather than netting these items separately for each group member. The group also must make adjustments for transactions among themselves, called *intercompany transactions*, so the consolidated tax return reflects the correct amount of consolidated taxable income.

Some consolidated tax returns include as few as two corporations. Other consolidated tax returns include hundreds of corporations. Most of the nation's largest corporate groups file consolidated tax returns. In 2011, only 37,152 consolidated tax returns were filed, which was less than 3% of all Form 1120s filed. However, these tax returns reported more than 97% of total taxable income and paid more than 97% of total income taxes of all corporations filing Form 1120.[2]

This chapter discusses the requirements for a group of corporations to qualify as an affiliated group that can elect to file a consolidated tax return. It also explains several rules that pertain to computing consolidated taxable income and the consolidated tax liability. The discussion then turns to some issues that arise when corporations enter or leave an affiliated group that is filing a consolidated tax return, such as when subsidiaries are bought and sold. The chapter also considers the advantages and disadvantages of filing a consolidated tax return instead of separate tax returns and discusses some financial statement implications.

DEFINITION OF AN AFFILIATED GROUP

OBJECTIVE 1

Determine whether a group of corporations is an affiliated group

REQUIREMENTS

Stock Ownership Requirements. Only an affiliated group of corporations can elect to file a consolidated tax return. A group of corporations must satisfy the following stock ownership requirements to qualify as an affiliated group:

- The parent corporation must own directly at least 80% of the stock in one or more includible corporations (defined below).
- At least 80% of the stock of *each* corporation in the group (other than the parent corporation) must be owned directly by the parent corporation and other group members.

[1] If the affiliated group members file separate tax returns, some special tax rules apply because group members are related taxpayers under Sec. 267. These rules include, but are not limited to, matching of income and deductions (Sec. 267(a)(2)), deferral of loss on intragroup sales (Sec. 267(f)(2)), and ordinary income recognition on intragroup sales of depreciable property (Sec. 1239). The members also may constitute a controlled group subject to the restrictions of Sec. 1563. See Chapter C:3 for details.

[2] Internal Revenue Service, Statistics of Income Division (*www.irs.gov*).

- Both 80% stock ownership requirements must be satisfied in two ways for each includible corporation (other than the parent): the stock owned directly must be at least 80% of the total voting power of all the includible corporation's outstanding stock entitled to vote, and it must be at least 80% of the total value of all the includible corporation's outstanding stock.[3]

EXAMPLE C:8-1 ▶ P Corporation owns 95% of S1 Corporation's stock, and S1 owns 100% of S2 Corporation's stock. Unrelated individuals own the remainder of S1's stock. P, S1, and S2 comprise an affiliated group because P owns at least 80% of S1's stock, and S1 owns at least 80% of S2's stock. The P-S1-S2 affiliated group can elect to file a consolidated tax return with P as the common parent.[4] ◀

EXAMPLE C:8-2 ▶ P Corporation owns 90% of S1 Corporation's stock and 35% of S2 Corporation's stock. S1 owns 50% of S2's stock. Unrelated individuals own the remainder of S1's and S2's stock. P, S1, and S2 comprise an affiliated group because P owns at least 80% of S1's stock, and P and S1 together own 85% (50% + 35%) of S2's stock. ◀

EXAMPLE C:8-3 ▶ Ted (an individual) owns all the stock of Alpha and Beta Corporations. Alpha and Beta are not an affiliated group because a parent-subsidiary relationship is not present even though the same individual owns 100% of each corporation. Alpha and Beta cannot elect to file a consolidated tax return. The Tax Strategy Tip on page C:8-4 suggests ways to restructure the corporations so they qualify as an affiliated group. ◀

EXAMPLE C:8-4 ▶ S Corporation has 1,000 shares of common stock and 600 shares of preferred stock outstanding. Each share of common stock has two votes and is worth \$45. Each share of preferred stock has one vote and is worth \$75. P Corporation owns all 1,000 shares of S's common stock and 150 shares of S's preferred stock. Unrelated individuals own the remaining preferred stock.

The total voting power of S's stock is 2,600 [(1,000 × 2) + (600 × 1)] votes, and the total value of S's stock is \$90,000 [(1,000 × \$45) + (600 × \$75)]. P's ownership of S's stock possesses 2,150 [(1,000 × 2) + (150 × 1)] votes and is worth \$56,250 [(1,000 × \$45) + (150 × \$75)]. This ownership is 82.69% (2,150 ÷ 2,600) of S's total voting power and 62.50% (\$56,250 ÷ \$90,000) of the value of S's stock. Because both 80% stock ownership requirements are not met, P and S are not an affiliated group. ◀

BOOK-TO-TAX ACCOUNTING COMPARISON

The group of corporations included in a consolidated tax return may be quite different from the group of corporations included in a set of consolidated financial statements because of different stock ownership requirements and the different types of corporations that are included in or excluded from the groups. Page 1 of Schedule M-3 reconciles these differences (see Appendix B).

Includible Corporation Requirement. All corporations are includible except certain specified corporations having special tax statuses. Important types of corporations that are not includible are:

- Corporations exempt from tax under Sec. 501
- Life insurance companies subject to tax under Sec. 801[5]
- Foreign corporations[6]
- Regulated investment companies
- Real estate investment trusts
- S corporations

Most of the nation's largest corporations have a great number of subsidiaries, many of which are not part of an affiliated group because they are not includible corporations. Consequently, they cannot be included in a consolidated tax return, and they usually file their own separate corporate tax returns (if required to do so). Moreover, their stock ownership of other group members cannot be counted toward satisfying the 80% stock ownership requirement for an affiliated group.

---

[3] When determining whether these stock ownership requirements are met, nonvoting preferred stock is ignored if it is limited and preferred as to dividends (and does not participate in corporate growth to any significant extent), has redemption and liquidation rights limited to its issue price (plus a reasonable redemption or liquidation premium), and is not convertible into another class of stock (Sec. 1504(a)(4)).

[4] All corporations in this chapter are includible corporations and have a single class of stock unless otherwise indicated.

[5] Two or more Sec. 801 life insurance companies may elect to file a consolidated tax return. If an affiliated group contains one or more Sec. 801 domestic life insurance companies, Sec. 1504(c)(2)(A) permits the parent corporation to elect to treat as includible corporations all such companies that have met the affiliated group stock ownership tests for the five immediately preceding tax years.

[6] Section 1504(d) allows a domestic corporation to elect to treat a 100%-owned Canadian or Mexican corporation as a domestic corporation if such foreign corporation is maintained solely for the purpose of complying with local law regarding title and operation of property.

EXAMPLE C:8-5 ▶ P Corporation owns all the stock of S1 and S2 Corporations. S1 owns all of S3 Corporation's stock, and S2 (a foreign corporation) owns all of S4 Corporation's stock. S2 is not a member of the affiliated group because, as a foreign corporation, it is not an includible corporation. P, S1, S3, and S4 are includible corporations, but only P, S1, and S3 qualify as an affiliated group. Although S4 is an includible corporation, it is not a member of the affiliated group because the group's members (P, S1, and S3) do not own at least 80% of S4's stock. S2's ownership of S4's stock is disregarded because S2 is not an includible corporation even though S2 is wholly-owned by a group member. ◀

ADDITIONAL COMMENT

In Example C:8-5, P, S1, S3, and S4 (but not S2, generally) comprise a parent-subsidiary controlled group. P constructively owns all of S4's stock for controlled group purposes but not for affiliated group purposes. Thus, S4 is in the same controlled group as P, S1, and S3 even though it is not in their affiliated group.

Under the check-the-box regulations discussed in Chapter C:2, noncorporate entities can elect to be treated as a corporation. A partnership or LLC that makes this election (and that does not elect to be treated as an S corporation) is an affiliated group member and is eligible to participate in a consolidated tax return provided it is an includible corporation and satisfies the stock ownership requirements. If a partnership or LLC does not elect to be treated as a corporation, it cannot be a member of the affiliated group and cannot participate in a consolidated tax return. Instead, the partnership's or LLC's income and losses pass through to each affiliated group member having an ownership interest in it.

TYPICAL MISCONCEPTION

The terms *controlled group, affiliated group,* and *consolidated group* are easily confused. These terms have different definitions and applications.

TAX STRATEGY TIP

A brother-sister controlled group cannot file a consolidated tax return. One way to convert it into an affiliated group is for the owner(s) of one of the group's corporations to transfer 80% or more of the corporation's stock to one of its sibling corporations in a nontaxable transaction meeting the Sec. 351 requirements (see Chapter C:2). The two corporations, being in a parent-subsidiary relationship, then can make the consolidated return election and begin filing on a consolidated basis. Alternatively, the owner(s) could transfer the stock of all the sibling corporations to a new corporation, e.g., a holding company that would be the common parent.

COMPARISON WITH CONTROLLED GROUP DEFINITIONS

Chapter C:3 discusses the three types of controlled groups: parent-subsidiary, brother-sister, and combined controlled groups. Special tax rules apply to controlled groups of corporations to prevent them from avoiding taxes. For example, a controlled group's members are limited to a total of $50,000 of taxable income being taxed at 15%, $25,000 being taxed at 25%, and $9,925,000 being taxed at 34%. A brother-sister controlled group cannot elect to file a consolidated tax return because it does not qualify as an affiliated group, as illustrated in Example C:8-3. However, a parent-subsidiary controlled group and the parent-subsidiary portion of a combined controlled group often also qualify as an affiliated group and can elect to file a consolidated tax return if they so qualify.

The criteria for a parent-subsidiary controlled group and those for an affiliated group are similar but not identical. Differences in the criteria include:

- ▶ The stock ownership requirement for a parent-subsidiary controlled group is at least 80% of voting power *or* value. For an affiliated group, it is at least 80% of voting power *and* value.
- ▶ Through stock attribution rules, stock owned by certain related persons is taken into account in determining whether a controlled group exists. They are not used to determine whether an affiliated group exists.
- ▶ The types of corporations excluded from a controlled group differ from those excluded from an affiliated group.
- ▶ The controlled group definition is tested only on December 31, but the affiliated group definition is tested on each day of the year.

Because of these differences, a corporation could be a member of a controlled group but not be a member of an affiliated group.

CONSOLIDATED TAX RETURN ELECTION

OBJECTIVE 2

Describe how an affiliated group makes a consolidated return election and how it discontinues the election

CONSOLIDATED RETURN REGULATIONS

A consolidated group is an affiliated group of corporations that files a consolidated tax return. The IRC contains very few rules pertaining to consolidated tax returns, and these few rules primarily address the composition of affiliated groups. Instead of enacting voluminous IRC rules, Congress gave the Treasury Department the authority to issue regulations addressing the determination of the consolidated tax liability and the filing of consolidated tax returns. Thus, the IRC allows an affiliated group to elect to file a consolidated

TYPICAL MISCONCEPTION

A corporation's tax year can be both a consolidated return year and a separate return year. For example, P1 Corporation sells all of S Corporation's stock to P2 Corporation at the end of Year 1. If P1 and S file a consolidated tax return for Year 1, Year 1 is a consolidated return year for S with respect to the P1-S consolidated group, but it is a separate return year with respect to the P2-S consolidated group.

ADDITIONAL COMMENT

Filing a consolidated tax return does not affect the reporting of other taxes, such as payroll, sales, or property taxes. Also, some states do not allow the filing of consolidated tax returns for state income tax purposes.

tax return, but it does so on the condition that all the group's members abide by the consolidated return regulations.

Terminology. A **consolidated return year** is a corporation's tax year for which it files a consolidated tax return with the other members of its affiliated group. A **separate return year** is a corporation's tax year for which it files a separate tax return or files a consolidated tax return with another affiliated group. A corporation could have a separate return year because it was not a member of the affiliated group or because the group did not file a consolidated tax return.[7]

An affiliated group elects to file its tax return on a consolidated basis by filing a corporate tax return (Form 1120) that includes the income, expenses, etc. of all its members. The group must make the election no later than the due date for the common parent's tax return including any permitted extensions. Each corporation that is a member of the affiliated group during the initial consolidated return year must consent to the election. The Compliance and Procedural Considerations section later in this chapter provides further details about the election process.

TERMINATION OF CONSOLIDATED TAX RETURN FILING

Termination of the Affiliated Group. Once an affiliated group has elected to file a consolidated tax return, it must continue to file on a consolidated basis as long as the affiliated group exists unless the IRS permits it to file separate tax returns. An affiliated group "remains in existence for a tax year if the common parent remains as the common parent and at least one subsidiary that was affiliated with it at the end of the prior year remains affiliated with it at the beginning of the year."[8] The parent corporation need not own the *same* subsidiary throughout the entire tax year nor own any subsidiary throughout the entire tax year as long as the parent owns a subsidiary at the beginning of the current tax year that it owned at the end of the prior tax year.

EXAMPLE C:8-6 ▶ P and S1 Corporations have filed a consolidated tax return for several calendar years. At the close of business on August 31 of the current year, P purchases all of S2 Corporation's stock. At the close of business on September 30, P sells all its S1 stock. The affiliated group, P-S1-S2, must file a consolidated tax return for the current year because P remained the common parent and at least one subsidiary that was affiliated with it at the end of the prior year remained affiliated with it at the beginning of the current year (i.e., S1).

Alternatively, assume the order of the purchase and sale transactions are reversed, i.e., P sells the S1 stock on August 31 and purchases the S2 stock on September 30. In this case, the affiliated group still must file a consolidated tax return for the current year. Even though P did not have a subsidiary from September 1 through September 30, it nevertheless remained as the common parent, and S1 was affiliated with it at the end of the prior year and at the beginning of the current year. In both cases, the consolidated tax return will include S1's and S2's income only for the portion of the year S1 and S2 were in the group. ◀

EXAMPLE C:8-7 ▶ P and S Corporations have filed a consolidated tax return for several calendar years. At the close of business on December 31 of the current year, P sells all its S stock to an unrelated individual. On January 1 of the next year, P purchases all of T Corporation's stock. P and S must file a consolidated tax return for the current year. However, the P-S affiliated group terminates at the end of the current year and a new affiliated group, P-T, forms in the next year. P and T may elect to file a consolidated tax return in the next year but are not required to do so. ◀

ADDITIONAL COMMENT

The IRS seldom grants permission to discontinue the filing of consolidated tax returns when the request relates to a change in the tax situation of the affiliated group that is not related to a tax law change.

Good Cause Request to Discontinue Consolidation. The IRS may give an affiliated group permission to discontinue filing a consolidated tax return, even though the group remains in existence, if it makes a "good cause" request. The IRS ordinarily will grant the request if changes to the IRC or Treasury Regulations having effective dates in

[7] Reg. Sec. 1.1502-1.

[8] Reg. Sec. 1.1502-75(d)(1).

that tax year create a substantial adverse effect on the consolidated tax liability for the tax year (relative to what the aggregate tax liability would be if the group members filed separate tax returns).[9]

Effects on Former Members. The termination of a consolidated group affects its former members in several ways, two of which are examined later in this chapter.

- Any gains and losses that have been deferred on intercompany transactions (e.g., profits on inventory sales between group members) may have to be recognized under the acceleration rule.
- Consolidated tax attributes (e.g., NOLs, capital losses, tax credits, and charitable contribution carryovers) may have to be allocated among the former group members.

If a corporation departs an affiliated group and had been included in the group's consolidated tax return, it cannot be included again in the group's consolidated tax return (or that of another affiliated group with the same common parent corporation) until after the 60-month period beginning with the first tax year in which the corporation ceased to be a group member.[10] The IRS can waive this five-year rule.

CONSOLIDATED TAXABLE INCOME

OBJECTIVE 3

Calculate consolidated taxable income for a consolidated group

ACCOUNTING PERIODS AND METHODS

Accounting Periods. Beginning with the first year the affiliated group files a consolidated tax return, each subsidiary corporation in the group must adopt the parent corporation's tax year, and the group must file its return using the parent's tax year. The requirement for a common tax year also applies when a new member joins the affiliated group, such as when its stock is acquired.[11] Unless the IRS grants permission otherwise, a subsidiary that leaves a consolidated group must retain its former group's tax year (or adopt the tax year of the acquiring consolidated group, if applicable).

Accounting Methods. Each group member determines the accounting methods it uses by applying the same rules as if it were filing a separate tax return unless the IRS grants it permission to change its accounting method.[12] This requirement applies when the group makes a consolidated tax return election and when a new corporation joins an existing consolidated group. Thus, one group member may use the cash method and another group member may use the accrual method with respect to the same consolidated tax return. The possibility of finding a mixture of cash and accrual basis corporations in an affiliated group is limited because of the Sec. 448 restrictions on the use of the cash method by C corporations (see Chapter C:3).

KEY POINT

Even though members of a consolidated group must use the same tax year-end, members are not required to use the same tax accounting methods. For example, different inventory methods (e.g., LIFO and FIFO) can occur within the same consolidated group.

INCOME INCLUDED IN THE CONSOLIDATED TAX RETURN

An affiliated group includes in its consolidated tax return the parent corporation's income for its entire tax year except for any part of the year it was a member of another affiliated group that filed a consolidated tax return. The group includes a subsidiary corporation's income in the consolidated tax return only for the part of the year that it was a group member. The subsidiary's income for any part of the year it was not a group member is included in its own separate tax return or the consolidated tax return of another affiliated group.[13]

EXAMPLE C:8-8 ▶ P and S Corporations were unaffiliated prior to 2015 and filed separate tax returns. P uses a fiscal year ending May 31 as its tax year, and S uses a calendar year. At the close of business on February 12, 2015, P acquires all of S's stock, and the P-S affiliated group elects to file a

[9] Reg. Sec. 1.1502-75(c).
[10] Sec. 1504(a)(3).
[11] Reg. Sec. 1.1502-76(a).
[12] Reg. Sec. 1.1502-17(a).
[13] Reg. Sec. 1.1502-76(b)(1)(i).

consolidated tax return. S must change its tax year to a fiscal year ending May 31. The group's first consolidated tax return will include P's income for June 1, 2014, through May 31, 2015, and S's income for February 13, 2015, through May 31, 2015. S must file a separate, short-period tax return for January 1, 2015, through February 12, 2015. ◀

EXAMPLE C:8-9 ▶ P1 Corporation owns all of S Corporation's stock, and the two corporations have filed consolidated tax returns for several years on a calendar year basis. At the close of business on August 8 of the current year, P1 sells all of S's stock to P2 Corporation, which has a September 30 tax year. P2 has filed consolidated tax returns for several years with its other subsidiaries. S must change its tax year from a calendar year to a fiscal year ending September 30 when it leaves the P1 consolidated group and enters the P2 consolidated group. ◀

EXAMPLE C:8-10 ▶ P and S1 Corporations have filed consolidated tax returns for several calendar years. At the close of business on August 31 of the current year, P sells all its S1 stock to an unrelated individual. At the close of business on September 30 of the current year, P purchases all of S2 Corporation's stock from an unrelated individual. S2 had been using a fiscal year ending March 31 as its tax year. As discussed in Example C:8-6, the affiliated group, with P as the parent corporation, does not terminate. The current year's consolidated tax return includes P's income for the entire year, S1's income for January 1 through August 31 of the current year, and S2's income for October 1 through December 31 of the current year. S1 must file a short-period, separate tax return for September 1 through December 31 of the current year (unless the IRS grants it permission to change its tax year), and S2 must file a short-period, separate tax return for April 1 through September 30 of the current year. ◀

KEY POINT

Two basic rules determine what income must be included in a consolidated tax return: the common parent's income for the entire tax year and each subsidiary's income for the part of the tax year it is a member of the consolidated group.

A corporation that becomes or ceases to be a member of an affiliated group filing a consolidated tax return generally does so at the end of the day its status changes.[14] A corporation entering the consolidated group will have to file a separate tax return (or participate in the consolidated tax return of the affiliated group in which it previously was a member), and this tax return often will be a short-period return, which is a return for less than one year. However, the separate tax return does not require annualization of the corporation's taxable income.[15]

A corporation entering a consolidated group does not have to change its tax year if it already is using the same tax year as the group. In this case, the group can elect to ratably allocate the entering member's income, except for extraordinary items, between the separate return and consolidated return portions of the year. The group also can make this election for a departing group member that does not have to change its tax year.[16]

WHAT WOULD YOU DO IN THIS SITUATION?

The P-S-T affiliated group has filed consolidated tax returns for many years using the calendar year as its tax year. On October 1, P Corporation created a new subsidiary, X Corporation, with a $10,000 initial capital contribution, and X issued its stock to P. X opened a bank account and obtained a federal tax identification number. X did not conduct any business activities before year-end. Its only income was $125 in interest earned from the bank account. Due to a lack of communication or oversight, P's tax department did not include X's income in the current year's consolidated tax return.

Your CPA firm has provided tax advice to P for several years, but P's tax department has handled the federal tax return filings. Most of your work for P has been in the state and local tax area and on special federal tax assignments. You were aware of the affiliated group's future business plans for creating X. Will the oversight with respect to X disqualify the group from filing a consolidated tax return for the current year and future years? Can you avoid having to file a federal income tax return for X because of the small amount of its income? Does the failure to include X in this year's consolidated tax return prevent it from being included in future years? What advice can you give your client about needing to include X in the consolidated tax return?

---

[14] Reg. Sec. 1.1502-76(b)(1)(ii)(A).

[15] Reg. Sec. 1.1502-76(b)(2)(i).

[16] Reg. Sec. 1.1502-76(b)(2)(ii). The group can make this election only if the entering corporation does not have to change its accounting method (e.g., entering the group allows the corporation to retain the cash method because the group's gross receipts do not exceed the $5 million limit under Sec. 448(c)).

EXAMPLE C:8-11 ▶ P Corporation acquires all the stock of S Corporation on February 26 of the current year (the 57th day of the year, which is not a leap year). P has been filing consolidated tax returns on a calendar year basis for several years with its other subsidiaries. S previously was unaffiliated and had been filing separate tax returns using a calendar year. S's income for the current year is $730,000 and includes no extraordinary items. The consolidated group can elect to ratably allocate the $730,000 because S does not have to change its tax year when entering the group. If it so elects, $114,000 ($730,000 × (57 days ÷ 365 days)) will be allocated to S's separate tax return for January 1 through February 26, and the other $616,000 ($730,000 × (308 days ÷ 365 days)) will be allocated to the consolidated tax return for the current year. ◀

If the consolidated group does not elect to ratably allocate an entering or departing group member's income, the group must allocate the member's income according to its accounting method, i.e., a closing of its books. This treatment also applies to extraordinary items, even if a ratable allocation is elected, and to an entering or departing member that must change its tax year. Extraordinary items include capital gains and losses, Sec. 1231 gains and losses, NOL carrybacks and carryovers, and several other items that are beyond the scope of this textbook.

CALCULATION OF CONSOLIDATED TAXABLE INCOME AND TAX

To arrive at its consolidated federal income tax liability, the group first must calculate **consolidated taxable income**. The process is more complicated than merely adding the consolidated group members' taxable incomes and losses. Instead, the group must make adjustments so that it generally is treated as if it were a single corporation. The calculation of consolidated taxable income involves the five steps presented in Table C:8-1. Later in the chapter, after discussing the various components of consolidated taxable income, we will discuss the consolidated tax calculation.

INTERCOMPANY TRANSACTIONS

OBJECTIVE 4

Apply the rules for reporting intercompany transactions

Corporations in an affiliated group filing a consolidated tax return may engage in transactions with each other. The discussion here usually will designate the two consolidated group members involved in the intercompany transaction as S and B Corporations instead of the usual P and S Corporations. This designation makes it easier to remember which group member is the seller (S) or provider of services and which group member is the buyer (B) or recipient of services.

BASIC CONCEPTS

An **intercompany transaction** is a transaction between two corporations that are in the same consolidated group immediately after the transaction.[17] Intercompany transactions include:

- S's sale, exchange, contribution, or other transfer of property to B whether or not S recognizes gain or loss
- S's performance of services for B, and B's payment or accrual of its expense for the services
- S's licensing of technology, renting of property, or lending of money to B, and B's payment or accrual of its expense for these items
- A distribution by a subsidiary to its parent corporation in connection with the parent's investment in the subsidiary's stock, such as a dividend or a redemption

In general, S and B are treated as separate entities. S and B each report on their own books any income, gains, deductions, and losses related to intercompany transactions using the same basic rules that would apply if they were unaffiliated corporations. For

[17] Reg. Sec. 1.1502-13(b)(1)(i).

▼ TABLE C:8-1
Consolidated Taxable Income Calculation

Step 1: Compute each group member's taxable income (or loss) based on the member's own accounting methods as if it were filing its own separate tax return.

Step 2: Adjust each group member's taxable income as follows:
1. Income, gains, and losses on intercompany transactions occurring in the current year may be deferred until a later year.
2. Income, gains, and losses on intercompany transactions occurring in prior years may be taken into account in the current year.
3. Dividends received by one group member from another group member are excluded from the recipient's gross income.

Step 3: Remove certain items from each member's taxable income because they must be computed on a consolidated basis (see Step 5):
1. Section 1231 gains and losses
2. Capital gains and losses
3. Charitable contribution deduction
4. Dividends-received deduction
5. Net operating loss (NOL) deduction
6. U.S. production activities deduction

The result of making the adjustments to a member's taxable income in Steps 2 and 3 is the member's **separate taxable income (loss)**.

Step 4: Combine the members' separate taxable incomes and losses. This amount is called the group's **combined taxable income**.

Step 5: Adjust the group's combined taxable income for the following items computed on a consolidated basis (see Step 3):
1. Determine and deduct the consolidated Sec. 1231 net loss.
2. Determine the consolidated net capital gain or loss (taking into account any capital loss carrybacks and carryovers and net Sec. 1231 gains that are not treated as ordinary income). Add the consolidated net capital gain to combined taxable income.
3. Determine and deduct the consolidated charitable contribution deduction (taking into account any charitable contribution carryovers).
4. Determine and deduct the consolidated dividends-received deduction.
5. Determine and deduct the consolidated NOL deduction (taking into account any allowable NOL carryovers and carrybacks).
6. Determine and deduct the consolidated U.S. production activities deduction.

Consolidated taxable income (or consolidated NOL)[18]

ADDITIONAL COMMENT

These adjustments are listed in the same computational order as shown on page C:3-19, but they appear in a different order on Form 1120.

example, if B purchases some property from S for cash, B's adjusted basis in the property would be B's cost to acquire it, and B's holding period for it would begin the day after B purchases the property.

To determine consolidated taxable income, S and B give special treatment to income, gains, deductions, and losses related to intercompany transactions. Specifically, the consolidated return regulations usually require that S's income, gains, deductions, or losses be deferred, and therefore excluded, in determining consolidated taxable income until a subsequent event occurs for B. These subsequent events include the following situations:

- ▶ B sells property it acquired in an intercompany transaction to a party outside the consolidated group.
- ▶ S or B leaves the consolidated group while B still owns property it acquired from S in an intercompany transaction.
- ▶ B claims a depreciation, depletion, or amortization deduction on property it acquired in an intercompany transaction.

[18] Reg. Sec. 1.1502-11.

- The corporations in an affiliated group discontinue filing a consolidated tax return and begin filing separate tax returns.

The intercompany transaction rules, in effect, have the members calculate consolidated taxable income as though S and B were a single entity. That is, if S and B were two divisions of a single corporation, any transactions between them would be ignored in computing the single corporation's taxable income. Likewise, consolidated taxable income should reflect only the consolidated group's income, gains, deductions, and losses from transactions with parties outside the group. The intercompany transaction rules adjust the consolidated group members' income, gains, deductions, and losses related to intercompany transactions, which the members reported on their separate books. Thus, the intercompany adjustments transform separate entity treatment into single entity treatment for calculating consolidated taxable income. This coexistence of separate entity treatment and single entity treatment is a challenging aspect of consolidated tax returns.

EXAMPLE C:8-12 ▶ S and B Corporations are members of a consolidated group. S owns marketable securities having a $120,000 basis. S sells the securities to B in the current year for $200,000 cash. S's $80,000 ($200,000 − $120,000) gain is determined and reported on its books on a separate entity basis in the current year. However, the $80,000 gain is not included in the current year's consolidated taxable income. On a single entity basis, the consolidated group did not sell the securities to an outside party, so it makes an adjustment to remove the gain from consolidated taxable income in the current year. B's basis in the securities is its $200,000 cost, and B's holding period begins the day after it purchases the securities from S. The group will take the $80,000 gain into account for consolidated taxable income at a later time, in accordance with the matching and acceleration rules discussed below. ◀

MATCHING AND ACCELERATION RULES

Treasury Regulations have two principal rules regarding intercompany transactions: the matching rule and the acceleration rule. Unlike many tax rules, the matching and acceleration rules are not detailed and mechanical. Instead, they are broad and conceptual, thereby allowing enough flexibility to apply to the wide variety of intercompany transactions that arise in practice.[19] The purpose of the intercompany transaction rules is to clearly reflect a consolidated group's taxable income by preventing intercompany transactions from creating, accelerating, avoiding, or deferring consolidated taxable income.[20] The following three terms will be used in the discussion of the intercompany transaction rules:[21]

- **Intercompany item:** S's income, gain, deduction, and loss from an intercompany transaction
- **Corresponding item:** B's income, gain, deduction, and loss from an intercompany transaction or from property acquired in an intercompany transaction
- **Recomputed corresponding item:** The corresponding item B would take into account if S and B were divisions of a single corporation and the transaction occurred between those divisions

EXAMPLE C:8-13 ▶ S and B Corporations are members of a consolidated group. S owns property having a $70 basis. S sells this property to B for $100. A few years later, B sells the property to a third party for $110. The sale from S to B is an intercompany transaction. The intercompany item is S's $30 ($100 − $70) gain on its sale of the property to B. The corresponding item is B's $10 ($110 − $100) gain on its sale of the property to the third party. The recomputed corresponding item is the $40 ($110 − $70) gain that B would realize on the sale to the third party had S and B been divisions of a single corporation. ◀

ADDITIONAL COMMENT

The intercompany transaction rules are an excellent example of the additional recordkeeping necessary to file consolidated tax returns.

Matching Rule. To determine consolidated taxable income, the matching rule requires a consolidated group to take into account an intercompany item in a manner that produces the same result as if the transaction were between two divisions of a single

[19] Preamble to T.D. 8597.
[20] Reg. Sec. 1.1502-13(a)(1).
[21] Reg. Secs. 1.1502-13(b)(2), (3), and (4).

corporation.[22] That is, the amount of S's intercompany item taken into account for consolidated taxable income is such that, when combined (i.e., matched) with B's corresponding item, the result is the same as if the consolidated group were a single corporation. The amount of S's intercompany item taken into account for consolidated taxable income can be calculated as follows:

Amount of recomputed corresponding item
Minus: Amount of B's corresponding item
Amount of S's intercompany item taken into account for consolidated taxable income

Working backwards from the desired outcome for consolidated taxable income, the starting point of the calculation is the amount of the recomputed corresponding item. The portion of the desired outcome comprised of B's corresponding item is subtracted out, leaving the amount of S's intercompany item that needs to be taken into account.[23]

EXAMPLE C:8-14 ▶ S and B Corporations are members of a consolidated group. S owns property having a $150 basis. S sells this property to B for $200 in Year 1. In Year 3, B sells the property to an unrelated corporation, X, for $215.

S's intercompany item is the $50 ($200 − $150) gain on its sale of the property to B. B's corresponding item is the $15 ($215 − $200) gain in Year 3 on its sale of the property to X. The recomputed corresponding item is the $65 ($215 − $150) gain in Year 3 that B would realize on the sale to X had S and B been divisions of a single corporation.

Year 1: If S and B were two divisions of a single corporation, the single corporation would realize no gain or loss, so the recomputed corresponding item for Year 1 is zero. B has no gain or loss in Year 1, so its corresponding item is zero. Thus, none of S's gain is taken into account for consolidated taxable income.

Year 3: If S and B were two divisions of a single corporation, it would realize a $65 gain. Subtracting B's $15 corresponding item from this $65 recomputed corresponding item yields the $50 amount of S's intercompany item taken into account for Year 3. Thus, recognition of S's $50 gain in Year 1 is deferred for consolidated taxable income until Year 3. In Year 3, S's $50 gain is matched with B's $15 gain to produce the $65 gain that accrued while the group held the property. ◀

EXAMPLE C:8-15 ▶ Assume the same facts as in Example C:8-14 except B sold the property to X for $180. The intercompany item again is S's $50 gain. However, B's corresponding item now is a $20 ($180 − $200) loss, and the recomputed corresponding item is a $30 ($180 − $150) gain.

Year 1: The property has not yet been sold outside the group, and B has not yet sold the property, so the recomputed corresponding item and B's corresponding item are both zero. None of S's gain is taken into account for consolidated taxable income.

Year 3: The property now has been sold to a person outside the consolidated group. Subtracting B's corresponding item ($20 loss) from the recomputed corresponding item ($30 gain) results in all of S's $50 intercompany item being taken into account for consolidated taxable income ($30 − (− $20) = $50). Note that a negative number is being subtracted because B's corresponding item is a loss. In summary, S's $50 gain is matched with B's $20 loss to produce the net $30 gain that accrued while the group held the property. ◀

TAX STRATEGY TIP

A member of a consolidated group should consider selling property with a built-in loss to a party outside the group rather than to another group member. For example, S Corporation owns Sec. 1231 property with a $15,000 adjusted basis and a $9,000 FMV. If S sells the property to another group member, the $6,000 loss will not be deducted for consolidated taxable income until a later time. If S sells the property to an unrelated third party, the $6,000 loss will be deductible immediately for consolidated taxable income. Thus, the income tax savings from the $6,000 loss is accelerated.

Acceleration Rule. In some situations, it may not be possible to match S's intercompany item with B's corresponding item to produce the same outcome as if S and B were two divisions of a single corporation. For example, S may sell property to B while they are members of the same consolidated group, but B then departs the group before it has sold the property. In this situation, B's corresponding item will occur when B is outside the consolidated group, so it cannot be matched with S's intercompany item. The acceleration rule requires that the consolidated group take into account S's intercompany item immediately before the time it first becomes impossible to apply the matching rule.[24]

[22] Reg. Sec. 1.1502-13(c).

[23] In addition to the timing of income, gain, deduction, or loss, the matching rule requires that various other attributes be redetermined, such as the character and source of such amounts.

[24] Rec. Sec. 1.1502-13(d).

EXAMPLE C:8-16 ▶ Assume the same facts as in Example C:8-14 except P, the common parent of S and B, sells all of its B stock to an unrelated corporation, Y, on June 4 of Year 2, which is before B sells the property to X. On that date, B departs the consolidated group, so it becomes impossible to match B's subsequent corresponding item in Year 3 with S's intercompany item. This situation triggers the acceleration rule, and the portion of S's intercompany item that has not yet been taken into account, which is all $50, is taken into account in Year 2, immediately before the stock sale on June 4. ◀

APPLICATIONS OF MATCHING AND ACCELERATION RULES

The matching and acceleration rules are two principles used to implement the single entity approach to reporting intercompany transactions. The discussion below provides several examples to illustrate the two rules. Unless otherwise stated, S Corporation and B Corporation are in the same affiliated group, with P Corporation as their common parent. Also, the group has filed consolidated tax returns for several years on a calendar year basis.

EXAMPLE C:8-17 ▶ S purchased 1,000 shares of publicly traded stock as an investment several years ago for $175,000. In the current year (Year 1), S sells all the stock to B for $200,000. B sells 400 shares of the stock (40%) to a third party for $78,000 in Year 3, and B sells the other 600 shares (60%) to another third party for $134,000 in Year 5. S's intercompany item is its $25,000 ($200,000 − $175,000) gain on the sale to B. The timing of and extent to which S's intercompany item is taken into account for consolidated taxable income is as follows:

Year 1: No corresponding item or recomputed corresponding item occurs this year because B has not yet sold the stock. Therefore, none of S's $25,000 gain is taken into account.

Year 3: B's corresponding item is its $2,000 ($78,000 − (40% × $200,000)) loss on the sale of 400 shares to the third party. From the perspective of a single entity, the consolidated group acquired the 400 shares for $70,000 (40% × $175,000) and sold them for $78,000, producing an $8,000 gain (the recomputed corresponding item). To achieve this result in consolidated taxable income, $10,000 of S's intercompany item is taken into account. The $10,000 gain, when matched with B's $2,000 loss, results in the $8,000 gain.

Year 5: B's corresponding item is its $14,000 ($134,000 − (60% × $200,000)) gain on the sale of the 600 shares. The recomputed corresponding item, from a single-entity perspective, is a $29,000 gain ($134,000 − (60% × $175,000)). The remaining $15,000 ($25,000 − $10,000) of S's gain is taken into account. The matching of this $15,000 with B's $14,000 corresponding item produces a $29,000 gain in consolidated taxable income, which is the outcome that would occur if S and B were two divisions of a single corporation. ◀

The timing and extent to which S's $25,000 gain in Example C:8-17 is taken into account for consolidated taxable income can be determined by applying the formula for the matching rule.

ADDITIONAL COMMENT

Note that, for Year 3, a negative $2,000 is subtracted, which is equivalent to adding $2,000. Subsequent examples of this type use similar notation.

	Year 1	*Year 3*	*Year 5*
Recomputed corresponding item	$-0-	$ 8,000	$29,000
Minus: B's corresponding item	-0-	(−2,000)	(14,000)
S's intercompany item taken into account	$-0-	$10,000	$15,000

The consolidated group can report the three sales made by S and B in Example C:8-17 by using a worksheet format such as that illustrated in the consolidated tax return example in Appendix B (see partial worksheet below). Each transaction initially is reported in the selling corporation's separate tax return column. The adjustments for the deferred gain on S's sale of the stock to B appear as negative and positive entries in the adjustments and eliminations column of the worksheet. The Year 1 negative adjustment removes the $25,000 gain realized on the intercompany transaction from Year 1 consolidated taxable income. The Year 3 and Year 5 positive adjustments restore the deferred gain when B sells the stock outside the consolidated group.

Transaction	*Consolidated Taxable Income*	*Adjustments & Eliminations*	*S Corporation's Separate Reporting*	*B Corporation's Separate Reporting*
S's sale to B in Year 1	$ –0–	$(25,000)	$25,000	
B's sale to third party in Year 3	8,000	10,000		$(2,000)
B's sale to third party in Year 5	29,000	15,000		14,000
Total	$37,000	$ –0–	25,000	$12,000

EXAMPLE C:8-18 ▶ Assume the same facts as in Example C:8-17 except S's and B's common parent corporation, P, sells all its B stock to a third party in Year 4. B's departure from the consolidated group triggers the acceleration rule in Year 4 because it is not possible to match B's subsequent corresponding item with the $15,000 portion of S's intercompany item that has not yet been taken into account. Thus, the $15,000 is included in Year 4 consolidated taxable income rather than Year 5 consolidated taxable income. The results would be the same if the common parent sold all of S's stock in Year 4 rather than all of B's stock. B still has a $14,000 gain in Year 5, but B includes the gain in its separate tax return (or the consolidated tax return of the affiliated group to which B belongs at that time). ◀

Installment Sale of Property from Buyer to Third Party. Under the installment method, if some or all of the proceeds from the sale of property are to be received after the taxable year of sale, the seller spreads recognition of any gain on the sale over the years it collects the proceeds (see Chapter I:11). The installment method does not apply if the seller realizes a loss. Also, in a gain situation, the seller can elect to not use the installment method. Applying the matching rule to an installment sale requires an understanding of how the installment method operates on both a separate and single entity basis.

EXAMPLE C:8-19 ▶ S owns land having a $64,000 basis. In Year 1, S sells the land to B for $90,000. In Year 3, B sells the land to a third party for $100,000. The third party is to pay B $60,000 of the $100,000 in Year 4 and the remaining $40,000 in Year 5. B charges the third party an interest rate acceptable to the IRS on the unpaid balance.

Because S's sale of the land to B is an intercompany transaction, S's $26,000 ($90,000 − $64,000) gain on the sale will not be taken into account until a later time. When B sells the property in Year 3, it realizes a $10,000 ($100,000 − $90,000) gain. Under the installment method, B's gross profit percentage on the sale is 10% ($10,000 ÷ $100,000), so B has a $6,000 (10% × $60,000) corresponding item in Year 4 and a $4,000 (10% × $40,000) corresponding item in Year 5. From the perspective of a single entity, the consolidated group acquired the land for $64,000 and sold it for $100,000, which produces a $36,000 gain. The group's gross profit percentage is 36% ($36,000 ÷ $100,000), so the recomputed corresponding items are $21,600 (36% × $60,000) in Year 4 and $14,400 (36% × $40,000) in Year 5.

S's $26,000 gain on the intercompany transaction is taken into account for consolidated taxable income such that, when matched with B's corresponding items, they combine to be the same as the recomputed corresponding items as follows:

	Year 1	*Year 3*	*Year 4*	*Year 5*
Recomputed corresponding item	$–0–	$–0–	$21,600	$14,400
Minus: B's corresponding item	–0–	–0–	(6,000)	(4,000)
S's intercompany item taken into account	$–0–	$–0–	$15,600	$10,400 ◀

In Example C:8-19, all of S's $26,000 gain is removed in the calculation of Year 1 consolidated taxable income, $15,600 of it is restored in the calculation of Year 4 consolidated taxable income, and the other $10,400 of it is restored in Year 5.[25]

[25] Reg. Sec. 1.1502-13(c)(7) Example 5.

Transaction	*Consolidated Taxable Income*	*Adjustments & Eliminations*	*S Corporation's Separate Reporting*	*B Corporation's Separate Reporting*
S's sale to B in Year 1	$ -0-	$(26,000)	$26,000	
B's sale to third party in Year 3	-0-			
B's collection of first installment in Year 4	21,600	15,600		$ 6,000
B's collection of second installment in Year 5	14,400	10,400		4,000
Total	$36,000	$ -0-	$26,000	$10,000

EXAMPLE C:8-20 ▶ **Assume the same facts as in Example C:8-19 except B sells the land to a third party for $80,000 in Year 3. The third party is to pay B $48,000 of the $80,000 in Year 4 and the remaining $32,000 in Year 5. B's corresponding item is now its $10,000 ($80,000 − $90,000) loss in Year 3. The installment method does not apply to losses, so B reports the entire loss in the year of sale. From a single entity perspective, the consolidated group realizes a $16,000 ($80,000 − $64,000) gain, which produces a 20% ($16,000 ÷ $80,000) gross profit percentage. The group's recomputed corresponding items are $9,600 (20% × $48,000) in Year 4 and $6,400 (20% × $32,000) in Year 5. S's $26,000 gain on the intercompany transaction taken into account for consolidated taxable income is determined as follows:**

	Year 1	*Year 3*	*Year 4*	*Year 5*
Recomputed corresponding item	$-0-	$ -0-	$9,600	$6,400
Minus: B's corresponding item	-0-	(-10,000)	-0-	-0-
S's intercompany item taken into account	$-0-	$10,000	$9,600	$6,400 ◀

Example C:8-20 illustrates the process underlying the matching rule. It requires an understanding of how the transactions affect each of the group members on a separate entity basis and how the transactions would affect the corporations in the consolidated group if they were a single entity. Applying the same worksheet format used above, Example C:8-20 is presented as:

Transaction	*Consolidated Taxable Income*	*Adjustments & Eliminations*	*S Corporation's Separate Reporting*	*B Corporation's Separate Reporting*
S's sale to B in Year 1	$ -0-	$(26,000)	$26,000	
B's sale to third party in Year 3	-0-	10,000		$(10,000)
B's collection of first installment in Year 4	9,600	9,600		
B's collection of second installment in Year 5	6,400	6,400		
Total	$16,000	$ -0-	$26,000	$(10,000)

BOOK-TO-TAX ACCOUNTING COMPARISON
The intercompany rental income and expense in Example C:8-21 are eliminated in preparing the consolidated financial statements.

Performance of Services. Some intercompany transactions involve one consolidated group member performing services for another group member. For example, one group member may rent property or lend money to another group member. The matching rule generally applies in a manner similar to that for intercompany property transactions, matching S's intercompany item to B's corresponding item so their net effect results in the recomputed corresponding item.

EXAMPLE C:8-21 ▶ S rents land to B for $25,000 per year. S and B both use the accrual method of accounting. S's rental income is its intercompany item, and B's rental expense is its corresponding item. The recomputed corresponding item is zero because, from the perspective of a single corporation with divisions S and B, the single entity would have no rental income or expense. The group will take into account $25,000 ($0 − (−$25,000)) of S's annual rental income as B reports the $25,000 annual rental expense. Note that B's corresponding item is negative because it is an expense. S's rental income and B's rental expense are recognized simultaneously for consolidated taxable income and thus offset each other. ◀

EXAMPLE C:8-22 ▶ On March 1 of Year 1, S lends B $100,000 for one year. B pays the $100,000 debt, plus 12% annual interest, to S on March 1 of Year 2. S and B each use the accrual method of accounting. In determining their separate taxable incomes, S reports interest income of $10,000 ($100,000 × 12% × 10/12) in Year 1 and $2,000 ($100,000 × 12% × 2/12) in Year 2, and B reports interest expense of $10,000 in Year 1 and $2,000 in Year 2. The recomputed corresponding item is zero in Year 1 and in Year 2. Application of the matching rule results in S's intercompany items being reported in consolidated taxable income at the same time S reports them in its separate taxable income.

	Year 1	*Year 2*
Recomputed corresponding item	$ –0–	$ –0–
Minus: B's corresponding item	(–10,000)	(–2,000)
S's intercompany item taken into account	$ 10,000	$ 2,000

◀

Applying the worksheet format used for the earlier intercompany transactions, S and B report the interest income and expense as follows:

Year	*Consolidated Taxable Income*	*Adjustments & Eliminations*	*S Corporation's Separate Reporting*	*B Corporation's Separate Reporting*
Year 1	$–0–		$10,000	$(10,000)
Year 2	–0–		2,000	(2,000)
Total	$–0–		$12,000	$(12,000)

If S and B use different accounting methods, they might not report their respective sides of the intercompany transaction at the same time in determining their separate taxable incomes. The principle of the matching rule still applies, with S's intercompany item being matched with B's corresponding item.

EXAMPLE C:8-23 ▶ Assume the same facts as in Example C:8-22 except B uses the cash method of accounting. For separate taxable income, S reports interest income of $10,000 in Year 1 and $2,000 in Year 2, and B reports interest expense of $0 in Year 1 and $12,000 in Year 2. For consolidated taxable income, all $12,000 of S's interest income is reported in Year 2 under the matching rule.

	Year 1	*Year 2*
Recomputed corresponding item	$–0–	$ –0–
Minus: B's corresponding item	–0–	(–12,000)
S's intercompany item taken into account	$–0–	$ 12,000

◀

ADDITIONAL COMMENT

Corporations filing a consolidated tax return are related parties under Sec. 267 because they also are members of the same controlled group. One consequence of their related status is that B cannot deduct its expense from an intercompany transaction with S before S reports its income from the transaction. This rule also can apply to transactions with corporations that are in the same controlled group but not the same consolidated group, such as brother-sister corporations.

Applying the worksheet format used previously, S and B report the interest income and expense as follows:

Year	*Consolidated Taxable Income*	*Adjustments & Eliminations*	*S Corporation's Separate Reporting*	*B Corporation's Separate Reporting*
Year 1	$–0–	$(10,000)	$10,000	$ –0–
Year 2	–0–	10,000	2,000	(12,000)
Total	$–0–	$ –0–	$12,000	$(12,000)

In some circumstances, B might capitalize its expenditure for the services S provides. B's corresponding item still would be its income, gain, deduction, and loss from an intercompany transaction or from property in an intercompany transaction. However, the corresponding item might occur at a time later than S's intercompany item, requiring that some or all of S's intercompany item be deferred under the matching rule.

EXAMPLE C:8-24 ▶ S operates a drilling business, B operates a farming business. S and B both use the accrual method of accounting. In Year 1, S drills a water well and charges B $9,000 for the service. S incurs $8,000 of expenses in drilling the well, realizing a $1,000 profit. B capitalizes the $9,000 cost of its well and amortizes it over the four-year period Years 2 through 5.

From a single entity perspective, the group's cost of the well is $8,000, so its recomputed corresponding item is $2,000 ($8,000 ÷ 4 years) for each of Years 2 through 5. B's annual corresponding item is its $2,250 ($9,000 ÷ 4 years) amortization deduction. S's $1,000 intercompany item is reported for consolidated taxable income as follows:

	Year 1	*Year 2*	*Year 3*	*Year 4*	*Year 5*
Recomputed corresponding item	$–0–	$(2,000)	$(2,000)	$(2,000)	$(2,000)
Minus: B's corresponding item	–0–	(–2,250)	(–2,250)	(–2,250)	(–2,250)
S's intercompany item taken into account	$–0–	$ 250	$ 250	$ 250	$ 250

Transaction	*Consolidated Taxable Income*	*Adjustments & Eliminations*	*S Corporation's Separate Reporting*	*B Corporation's Separate Reporting*
Drilling of well in Year 1	$ –0–	$(1,000)	$1,000	
Amortization deductions:				
Year 2	(2,000)	250		$(2,250)
Year 3	(2,000)	250		(2,250)
Year 4	(2,000)	250		(2,250)
Year 5	(2,000)	250		(2,250)
Total	$(8,000)	$ –0–	$1,000	$(9,000)

◀

Intercompany Sale of Inventory. Many consolidated groups have sales of inventory within the group. For example, one group member (S) may manufacture goods and sell them to another group member (B). B subsequently resells the goods to third-party customers. The matching rule applies in this situation and allows the consolidated group to defer taxation of profit from the intercompany transaction until B sells the inventory to a third party.[26]

EXAMPLE C:8-25 ▶ P, S, and B Corporations comprise a consolidated group with P being the common parent of subsidiaries S and B. S begins selling inventory items to B in Year 1, and both subsidiaries use the first-in, first-out (FIFO) inventory method. Information and treatment regarding S's inventory sales to B during Years 1 and 2 follow:

[26] Reg. Sec. 1.1502-13(e)(1) provides simplifying rules for intercompany inventory sales when S or B uses a dollar-value LIFO method to account for intercompany transactions.

Year 1: S sells inventory to B for $400,000. The cost of this inventory to S was $300,000. Thus, S realizes a profit of $100,000 ($400,000 − $300,000) on the sale, which is S's intercompany item. During the year, B sells 88% of this inventory to third parties for $414,000. B's cost for this inventory is $352,000 ($400,000 × 0.88). Thus, B realizes a profit of $62,000 ($414,000 − $352,000) on the sale to third parties, which is B's corresponding item. S's cost for this same inventory had been $264,000 ($300,000 × 0.88). Thus, S realized a profit of $88,000 ($352,000 − $264,000) when it sold this portion of the inventory to B, which is S's intercompany item taken into account. From the perspective of a single entity, the consolidated group realizes a profit of $150,000 ($414,000 − $264,000) on the sale to third parties, which is the recomputed corresponding item. At year-end, B's inventory includes the remaining 12% of inventory it purchased from S in Year 1. B's cost in this remaining inventory is $48,000 ($400,000 × 0.12), and S's cost for this same inventory was $36,000 ($300,000 × 0.12). Thus, the remaining inventory contains a deferred profit of $12,000 ($48,000 − $36,000). Applying the matching rule, these transactions are summarized as follows:

Recomputed corresponding item	$150,000
Minus: B's corresponding item	(62,000)
S's intercompany item taken into account	$88,000

Year 2: B sells to third parties the remaining inventory it purchased from S in Year 1. The selling price is $55,000 and is deemed sold first in Year 2 under FIFO. Thus, B realizes a profit of $7,000 ($55,000 − $48,000) on this sale. From the perspective of a single entity, the consolidated group realizes a profit of $19,000 ($55,000 − $36,000) on this sale to third parties.

Also in Year 2, S sells additional inventory to B for $550,000. The cost of this inventory to S was $420,000. Thus, S realizes a profit of $130,000 ($550,000 − $420,000) on the sale. During the year, B sells 80% of this inventory to third parties for $515,000. B's cost for this inventory is $440,000 ($550,000 × 0.80). Thus, B realizes a profit of $75,000 ($515,000 − $440,000) on the sale to third parties. S's cost for this same inventory had been $336,000 ($420,000 × 0.80). Thus, S realized a profit of $104,000 ($440,000 − $336,000) when it sold this portion of the inventory to B. From the perspective of a single entity, the consolidated group realizes a profit of $179,000 ($515,000 − $336,000) on this sale to third parties. At year-end, B's inventory includes the remaining 20% of inventory it purchased from S in Year 2. B's cost in this remaining inventory is $110,000 ($550,000 × 0.20), and S's cost for this same inventory was $84,000 ($420,000 × 0.20). Thus, the remaining inventory contains a deferred profit of $26,000 ($110,000 − $84,000). Applying the matching rule, these transactions are summarized as follows:

Recomputed corresponding item ($19,000 + $179,000)	$198,000
Minus: B's corresponding item ($7,000 + $75,000)	(82,000)
S's intercompany item taken into account ($12,000 + $104,000)	$116,000

Applying the worksheet format for the intercompany transactions in Years 1 and 2, S and B report their inventory profits as follows:

Year	*Consolidated Taxable Income*	*Adjustments & Eliminations*	*S Corporation's Separate Reporting*	*B Corporation's Separate Reporting*
Year 1	$150,000	$(12,000)	$100,000	$ 62,000
Year 2	198,000	(14,000)*	130,000	82,000
Total	$348,000	$(26,000)	$230,000	$144,000

* Positive $12,000 adjustment for inventory S sold to B in Year 1 that B sells to third parties in Year 2, minus $26,000 adjustment for inventory S sells to B in Year 2 that B has not sold to third parties by the end of Year 2. ◀

EXAMPLE C:8-26 ▶ Assume the same facts as in Example C:8-25 except P sells all of B's stock on December 31 of Year 2. Because B no longer is a member of the consolidated group after that date, the remaining group cannot match S's intercompany items with B's corresponding items. Thus, the acceleration rule is triggered, and the $26,000 ($110,000 − $84,000) of S's intercompany inventory profits that otherwise would be included in Year 3 consolidated taxable income is now included in Year 2 consolidated taxable income. ◀

ADDITIONAL COMMENT

The matching and acceleration rules also apply to intercompany sales of depreciable property and involve complex depreciation adjustments that are beyond the scope of this textbook.

RELEVANCE OF MATCHING AND ACCELERATION RULES

The matching and acceleration rules are broad and conceptual, thereby allowing enough flexibility to apply to a wide variety of intercompany transactions that arise in practice. Applying the rules can seem tedious and irrelevant, possibly causing one to wonder why it is necessary to determine the intercompany items and corresponding items if the consolidated group's taxable income ultimately reflects the recomputed corresponding items. In response, we can cite the following reasons why the rules are important (some of which receive further discussion later in this chapter). The rules affect:

- The time for recognizing intercompany transactions, i.e., how much gain or loss to recognize currently or in the future.
- The amount by which a parent corporation adjusts the basis of stock it owns in its subsidiary corporations.
- The amount of consolidated net operating losses attributed to a particular consolidated group member.
- The amount of a member's separate return net operating losses that the group may use.
- The amount of each member's earning and profits (E&P).

Topic Review C:8-1 summarizes the intercompany transaction rules.

ITEMS COMPUTED ON A CONSOLIDATED BASIS

OBJECTIVE 5

Compute on a consolidated basis deductions and credits subject to limitations

An affiliated group filing a consolidated tax return generally is treated as if it were a single corporation. To accomplish this treatment, the group calculates on a consolidated basis its deductions and credits that are subject to limitations. The computation of these items for a consolidated tax return is similar to their computation for an unaffiliated corporation. The group also must calculate its regular tax and its alternative minimum tax on a consolidated basis.

TOPIC REVIEW C:8-1

Reporting Intercompany Transactions

INTERCOMPANY TRANSACTIONS

1. **Intercompany transaction:** A transaction between two corporations that are in the same consolidated group immediately after the transaction.
2. **Three concepts of reporting intercompany transactions:**
   a. **Intercompany item:** The selling corporation's income, gain, deduction, and loss from an intercompany transaction.
   b. **Corresponding item:** The buying corporation's income, gain, deduction, and loss from an intercompany transaction or from property acquired in an intercompany transaction.
   c. **Recomputed corresponding item:** The corresponding item the buying corporation would have if it and the selling corporation were two divisions of a single corporation and the transaction occurred between those divisions.
3. **Separate entity concept:** The selling and buying corporations involved in the intercompany transaction generally are treated as separate entities in determining the amount of income, gain, deduction, and loss that each one incurs.
4. **Matching rule:** The selling corporation's intercompany item is taken into account for consolidated taxable income so that, when it is combined with the buying corporation's corresponding item, the result is the same as if the consolidated group were a single corporation (i.e., the recomputed corresponding item).
5. **Acceleration rule:** If it is not possible to apply the matching rule to match the selling corporation's intercompany item with the buying corporation's corresponding item, the consolidated group takes into account the selling corporation's intercompany item immediately before the time it first becomes impossible to apply the matching rule.
6. **Examples of events that can trigger recognition of an intercompany item:**
   a. The buying corporation sells to a third party property acquired in an intercompany transaction (matching rule).
   b. The selling corporation or buying corporation leaves the consolidated group (acceleration rule).
   c. The buying corporation claims depreciation, amortization, or depletion deductions for property acquired in an intercompany transaction (matching rule).
   d. The corporations in the affiliated group discontinue filing a consolidated tax return and begin filing separate tax returns (acceleration rule).

KEY POINT

The consolidated charitable contribution deduction could be greater than or less than the total of the charitable contribution deductions if the group filed separate tax returns. The outcome depends on each individual situation.

CHARITABLE CONTRIBUTION DEDUCTION

Chapter C:3 discusses the charitable contribution deduction for an unaffiliated C corporation. Recall that the deduction is limited to 10% of adjusted taxable income. Adjusted taxable income is the corporation's taxable income computed without regard to its charitable contribution deduction, NOL carryback, capital loss carryback, dividends-received deduction, and U.S. production activities deduction. The corporation can carry forward to the five succeeding tax years its charitable contributions that exceed the 10% limitation. Any unused contributions remaining at the end of the five-year carryover period expire.

The consolidated charitable contribution deduction is calculated by first aggregating the consolidated group members' charitable contributions. The deductibility of the aggregate charitable contributions is limited to 10% of consolidated adjusted taxable income, and any aggregate contributions exceeding the 10% limitation carry forward for five years.[27] Adjusted consolidated taxable income is determined similarly to an unaffiliated corporation's adjusted taxable income except the group uses consolidated amounts.[28]

EXAMPLE C:8-27 ▶ P, S1, and S2 Corporations comprise a consolidated group. The group members have the following charitable contributions and adjusted taxable incomes for the current year:

Group Member	*Charitable Contributions*	*Adjusted Taxable Income*
P	$12,500	$150,000
S1	5,000	(40,000)
S2	2,000	10,000
Total	$19,500	$120,000

The consolidated group's charitable contribution deduction is limited to $12,000 (10% × $120,000). Because its aggregate charitable contributions exceed this limitation, it can deduct only $12,000 in the current year. The $7,500 ($19,500 − $12,000) excess charitable contribution carries over to the next five tax years in successive order until used. If not used, they expire at the end of the five-year carryover period. ◀

SELF-STUDY QUESTION

In Example C:8-27, what would be each corporation's current year charitable contribution deduction if the group filed separate tax returns?

ANSWER

$12,500 for P, $0 for S1, and $1,000 for S2. The total of these three deductions is $1,500 more than the $12,000 consolidated charitable contribution deduction. However, the total of the charitable contribution carryovers is $1,500 less than the consolidated charitable contribution carryover.

NET SEC. 1231 GAIN OR LOSS

An unaffiliated corporation determines its net Sec. 1231 gain or loss by netting its recognized gains and losses from the sale or exchange of Sec. 1231 property (see Chapter I:13). The corporation treats any net Sec. 1231 loss as an ordinary loss. A net Sec. 1231 gain generally is treated as a long-term capital gain, although some or all of it may be converted to ordinary income if the corporation has any unrecaptured Sec. 1231 losses from the prior five years (the lookback rule). A consolidated group determines its net Sec. 1231 gain or loss by netting the members' Sec. 1231 gains and losses on a consolidated basis rather than for each member separately.[29]

ADDITIONAL COMMENT

An affiliated group's ordinary gain or loss and capital gain or loss often will be different when it nets its various gains and losses on a consolidated basis rather than on a separate basis.

CAPITAL GAINS AND LOSSES

Chapter C:3 discusses the treatment of capital gains and losses for an unaffiliated corporation. The corporation's capital gain net income or net capital loss is determined by netting its capital gains, capital losses, and net Sec. 1231 gains (to the extent they are not recaptured as ordinary income under the five-year lookback rule). Unlike with individuals, a corporation's net capital gain receives no preferential tax treatment. Also, a corporation cannot deduct a net capital loss. Instead, it must carry back the net capital loss to the three previous tax years and five following tax years, using the net capital loss in the earliest year(s) possible.

In a similar manner, the consolidated group determines its capital gain net income or net capital loss by netting the group members' capital gains and capital losses, as well as

[27] If a member leaves the consolidated group before the group fully uses its charitable contribution carryovers, the departing member takes with it its allocable share of the unused carryover. The allocation is based on the relative amount of the member's charitable contributions (when compared to the group's total charitable contributions) for the consolidated return year in which they were made. The allocation is similar to that for unused NOL carryovers discussed later in the chapter.

[28] Reg. Sec. 1.1502-24.

[29] Reg. Sec. 1.1502-23.

any consolidated net Sec. 1231 gain not recaptured under the lookback rule. If the group has a net capital loss for a tax year, it cannot deduct it in that year but must carry it back to the three preceding and forward to the five succeeding tax years. The consolidated net capital loss can offset any consolidated net capital gain in those eight carryback and carryover years.[30]

EXAMPLE C:8-28 ▶ P and S Corporations comprise a consolidated group. The group has no capital loss carryovers, and it has recognized no net Sec. 1231 losses in the previous five years. During the current year, the group reports $200,000 of ordinary income before taking into account the following gains and losses:

	Capital Gains and Losses				
	Short-Term		*Long-Term*		
Group Member	*Gains*	*Losses*	*Gains*	*Losses*	*Net Sec. 1231 Gain (Loss)*
P	$ –0–	$ –0–	$ 500	$1,500	$(3,100)
S	2,000	7,500	6,000	–0–	8,000
	$2,000	$7,500	$6,500	$1,500	$ 4,900

The P-S group's $4,900 consolidated net Sec. 1231 gain is treated as a long-term capital gain and is combined with the group's $5,000 ($6,500 − $1,500) net long-term capital gain and its $5,500 ($2,000 − $7,500) net short-term capital loss. Thus, the current year consolidated capital gain net income is $4,400 ($4,900 + $5,000 − $5,500). This amount is taxed at the regular corporate tax rates. ◀

KEY POINT

One member of the consolidated group may have a gain or loss from the sale of Sec. 1231 property or a capital asset to another group member. This sale is an example of an *intercompany transaction*, discussed earlier in the chapter. The consolidated group defers recognition of the gain or loss until a later time, and it does not include the gain or loss in the consolidated Sec. 1231 netting process or in the consolidated capital gain and loss netting process until that time.

Departing Group Members' Capital Losses. A particular issue arises with consolidated groups of corporations that does not arise with unconsolidated corporations. This issue pertains to the carryback and carryover of unused capital losses when the composition of the consolidated group changes. For example, suppose a consolidated group has capital loss carryovers when the parent corporation sells the stock in one of its subsidiaries. To what extent are the unused capital losses available to the departed group member on its separate tax return versus the remaining group members on their consolidated tax return? The group must determine the portion of the net capital loss attributable to the departing group member, and this portion is available to the departing group member and is not available to the remaining consolidated group members. The apportionment procedure is similar to that for NOLs for departing group members, which will be discussed later in the chapter.

ADDITIONAL COMMENT

In Example C:8-28, if P and S had filed separate tax returns, P's $3,100 net Sec. 1231 loss would have been treated as an ordinary loss, and P would have had a $1,000 ($500 − $1,500) net capital loss that would not have been deductible in the current year. S's $8,000 net Sec. 1231 gain would have been treated as a long-term capital gain, making S's capital gain net income $8,500 ($8,000 + $6,000 + $2,000 − $7,500).

Srly Limitation. A consolidated group member may have net capital losses available from another tax year in which it was not member of the group. The consolidated group can use the net capital loss from this *separate return limitation year*, but the group's use of a member's SRLY net capital loss is limited to the member's cumulative contribution to consolidated capital gain net income. This restriction on the use of net capital losses is similar to the SRLY limitation on the use of NOLs, which will be discussed later in the chapter.

DIVIDENDS-RECEIVED DEDUCTION

ADDITIONAL COMMENT

The IRC does not allow corporations to forego the three-year carryback period for net capital losses. This restriction can complicate matters when some of the current year consolidated group members filed separate tax returns during any of the three prior years because they were not group members then.

Chapter C:3 discusses the dividends-received deduction for an unaffiliated corporation. Corporations that own less than 20% of the distributing corporation's stock may deduct 70% of the dividends received. If the shareholder (distributee) corporation owns 20% or more of the distributing corporation's stock but less than 80% of such stock, it may deduct 80% of the dividends received. The dividends-received deduction is limited to 70% of taxable income computed without regard to any NOL deduction, any capital loss carryback, the dividends-received deduction itself, or the U.S. production activities deduction. The limitation is 80% of such taxable income for dividends received qualifying

[30] Reg. Sec. 1.1502-22.

for the 80% deduction. The limitation does not apply if, after taking into account the full dividends-received deduction, the corporation has an NOL for the year.

Dividends Received from Non-Group Members. The calculation of the consolidated dividends-received deduction for dividends received from corporations that are not members of the consolidated group is similar to the calculation for an unaffiliated corporation. The group members' dividends-received deductions, calculated without regard to the limitation on them, are added. The sum of these dividends-received deductions is limited to 70% (or 80%) of consolidated taxable income computed without regard to any NOL deduction, any capital loss carryback, the dividends-received deduction itself, or the U.S. production activities deduction. Similar to an unaffiliated corporation, the limitation does not apply if the consolidated group would have an NOL for the year after taking the full dividends-received deduction.

EXAMPLE C:8-29 ▶ P and S Corporations comprise a consolidated group. Taxable income (without considering any dividends-received deductions, NOLs, capital loss carrybacks, or U.S. production activities deductions) is $16,000 for P and $18,000 for S. P received $20,000 of dividends from unaffiliated corporations that are less than 20%-owned; S received $15,000 of such dividends. The consolidated dividends-received deduction is $23,800, computed as follows:

Dividends-received deduction before limitation (($20,000 × 70%) + ($15,000 × 70%))	$24,500
Limitation (($16,000 + $18,000) × 70%)	$23,800
Dividends-received deduction (lesser of $24,500 or $23,800)	$23,800 ◀

ADDITIONAL COMMENT

In Example C:8-29, if P and S did not file a consolidated tax return, P would report an $11,200 dividends-received deduction on its separate tax return, which is the lesser of $14,000 (70% × $20,000) or $11,200 (70% × $16,000). S would report a $10,500 dividends-received deduction, which is the lesser of $10,500 (70% × $15,000) or $12,600 (70% × $18,000). The total dividends-received deductions of $21,700 ($11,200 + $10,500) would be less than the $23,800 dividends-received deduction allowed when P and S file a consolidated tax return.

Dividends Received From Group Members. The deduction for dividends received by one affiliated group member from another member is determined differently than the deduction for dividends received from a non-group member. If the corporations in the affiliated group do not file a consolidated tax return, the distributee corporation may claim a 100% dividends-received deduction on its separate tax return. Also qualifying for the 100% dividends-received deduction are dividends from a corporation that would be a member of the distributee's consolidated group but is not an includible corporation because it is a life insurance company. The 100% dividends-received deduction is not subject to the taxable income limitation and is taken before the 80% or 70% dividends received deduction.

If the affiliated group members file a consolidated tax return, the distribution of a dividend from one group member to another group member (e.g., from subsidiary to parent) qualifies as an intercompany transaction. An intercompany dividend distribution is not included in the distributee member's gross income if it produces a corresponding negative adjustment to that member's basis of its stock in the distributing member (this basis adjustment is discussed later in the chapter).[31] This exclusion eliminates the intercompany dividend from consolidated taxable income, but the consolidated group cannot also claim a 100% dividends-received deduction for the excluded dividend. If the intercompany distribution is in the form of property, the excess of the property's FMV over the distributing member's adjusted basis in it is reported by that member as a gain in its separate taxable income calculation under Sec. 311(b). However, the reporting of this gain for consolidated taxable income is deferred because it is an intercompany transaction. The consolidated group determines the timing of the gain's inclusion in consolidated taxable income by the matching and acceleration rules.[32]

SELF-STUDY QUESTION

Are dividends received from members of the same affiliated group entitled to a dividends-received deduction?

ANSWER

Not if the affiliated group files a consolidated tax return because intercompany dividends are excluded; hence, no dividends-received deduction is necessary.

EXAMPLE C:8-30 ▶ P, S1, and S2 Corporations comprise a consolidated group. Consolidated taxable income (without considering any dividends-received deduction, NOLs, capital loss carrybacks, or U.S. production activities deduction) is $200,000. The group members receive the following dividend income from unaffiliated corporations that are less than 20%-owned: P, $6,000; S1, $10,000; and S2, $34,000. In addition, P receives a $40,000 dividend from S1, and the distribution reduces P's basis in its S1 investment.

[31] Reg. Sec. 1.1502-13(f)(2)(ii).

[32] Reg. Sec. 1.1502-13(f)(2)(iii).

REAL-WORLD EXAMPLE

When each corporation in an affiliated group prepares (but does not file) its own separate tax return, intercompany dividends might be included in gross income. In such a situation, the group needs to make a worksheet adjustment during the consolidation process to remove the dividend amount from consolidated taxable income.

- P excludes from its gross income the $40,000 dividend received from S1 because the distribution reduces P's basis in its S1 investment.
- The 70% dividends-received deductions included in the separate taxable income calculations are P, $4,200 (70% × $6,000); S1, $7,000 (70% × $10,000); and S2, $23,800 (70% × $34,000). The total 70% dividends-received deduction of $35,000 ($4,200 + $7,000 + $23,800) is not restricted by the $140,000 dividends-received deduction limitation (70% × $200,000 consolidated taxable income given in the facts).

Thus, the consolidated dividends-received deduction is $35,000. ◀

STOP & THINK

Question: Alpha Corporation has owned the stock of a 100%-owned subsidiary for many years. The CPA who has prepared both corporations' tax returns since their creation has been trying to persuade Alpha's Director of Federal Taxes to begin filing a consolidated tax return based on the tax exemption for intragroup dividends. Is the CPA right or wrong in this approach?

Solution: The CPA is wrong. If Alpha and its subsidiary file separate tax returns, Alpha can claim a 100% deduction for dividends received from its subsidiary, which will offset the dividend received. If the corporations file a consolidated tax return, Alpha can exclude the dividends from its gross income. Typically, these two alternatives result in the same outcome. The outcomes for these two alternatives may differ, however, when preparing state tax returns. The CPA should focus on other factors, such as deferring profits on intercompany transactions and offsetting profits and losses between the two corporations.

SELF-STUDY QUESTION

What is the dividends-received deduction in Example C:8-30 if the group has consolidated taxable income before special deductions of (a) $35,000? (b) $34,999? Should a $1 difference in consolidated taxable income make a $10,500 difference in the dividends-received deduction?

ANSWER

(a) $24,500 (70% × $35,000) due to the consolidated taxable income limitation. (b) All $35,000 is allowed because the full dividends-received deduction creates an NOL. Maybe a $1 difference should not have such a radical effect, but it does. Therefore, as a tax strategy, the corporation should plan its taxable income level to avoid losing a portion of the dividends-received deduction.

U.S. PRODUCTION ACTIVITIES DEDUCTION

If an affiliated group files a consolidated tax return, the group calculates the U.S. production activities deduction on a consolidated basis (see Chapter C:3 for a discussion of this deduction). Accordingly, the deduction for the consolidated group is the least of (1) 9% of the group's consolidated qualified production activities income, (2) 9% of the group's consolidated taxable income before this deduction, or (3) 50% of the group's consolidated W-2 wages allocable to U.S. production activities.

EXAMPLE C:8-31 ▶ P and S Corporation file consolidated tax returns and compute their consolidated taxable income for the current year as follows:

	Consolidated Taxable Income	*Adjustments & Eliminations*	*P's Separate Reporting*	*S's Separate Reporting*
Gross profit on outside sales	$725,000		$500,000	$225,000
Operating expenses	(300,000)		(200,000)	(100,000)
Interest from corporate bonds	9,000		9,000	-0-
Charitable contributions	–0–	$23,000[b]	(7,000)[a]	(16,000)[a]
Consol. taxable income before the charitable contribution and U.S. production activities deductions	$434,000	$23,000	$ 302,000	$ 109,000
Consolidated charit. contrib. ded.	(23,000)			
Consol. taxable income before the U.S. production activities deduction	$411,000			
Consolidated U.S. prod. act. ded.	(36,990)			
Consolidated taxable income	$ 374,010			

[a]Amount of charitable contributions before applying the charitable contribution limitation.
[b]Removes amounts for later calculation on a consolidated basis.
[c]Consolidated taxable income before the deduction ($411,000) is less than consolidated qualified production activities income ($425,000 = $725,000 − $300,000). Therefore, the deduction equals $411,000 × 0.09. This example assumes that all gross profit and operating expenses are related to qualified production activities. It also assumes that the 50% of W-2 wages limitation is not limiting. ◀

For purposes of the U.S. production activities deduction, the tax law expands the definition of an affiliated group by reducing the stock ownership threshold from at least 80% to more than 50% and by including in the definition insurance companies and corporations that use the possessions tax credit. An **expanded affiliated group** includes corporations that are eligible to file a consolidated tax return because they are in the same affiliated group, but it also may include other corporations (e.g., 51%-owned subsidiaries).

For purposes of calculating the U.S. production activities deduction, the expanded affiliated group is treated as one combined corporation, and the deduction is the least of (1) 9% of the group's combined qualified production activities income, (2) 9% of the group's combined taxable income before this deduction, or (3) 50% of the group's combined W-2 wages allocable to U.S. production activities. Each of the three combined amounts is the aggregate across the separate members. The expanded affiliated group then allocates the resultant deduction to each separate member with positive qualified production activities income based on the relative amounts of such income. If the expanded affiliated group includes a consolidated group in addition to corporations filing separate tax returns, the consolidated group is treated as one separate member of the expanded affiliated group.[33]

EXAMPLE C:8-32 ▶ Assume the same facts as in the previous example except P and S file separate tax returns.

	P's Separate Tax Return	*S's Separate Tax Return*
Gross profit on outside sales	$500,000	$225,000
Operating expenses	(200,000)	(100,000)
Interest from corporate bonds	9,000	-0-
Taxable income before the charit. contrib. ded.	$309,000	$125,000
Charitable contribution deduction[a]	(7,000)	(12,500)
Taxable income before the U.S. prod. act. ded.	$302,000	$112,500
U.S. production activities deduction[b]	(26,333)	(10,972)
Taxable income	$275,667	$101,528

[a]P's deduction is limited to $30,900 ($309,000 × 0.10), and S's deduction is limited to $12,500 ($125,000 × 0.10).

[b]Combined qualified production activities income ($300,000 + $125,000)	$ 425,000
Combined taxable income before the U.S. prod. act. ded. ($302,000 + $112,500)	$ 414,500
Lesser of the two amounts	$ 414,500
Times: Percentage	0.09
Combined U.S. production activities deduction	$ 37,305

Combined deduction is allocated in proportion to each expanded affiliated group member's qualified production activities income as follows:

To P: 300/425 × $37,305 = $26,333
To S: 125/425 × $37,305 = $10,972

[33] Reg. Sec. 1.199-7.

REGULAR TAX LIABILITY

A consolidated group determines its consolidated regular income tax liability similarly to an unaffiliated corporation by applying the Sec. 11 corporate tax rates to its consolidated taxable income. These rates appear inside the back cover of this textbook.

The regular tax liability for a consolidated tax return resembles the total tax liability for a controlled group but is not exactly the same. As discussed in Chapter C:3, Sec. 1561 limits to an aggregate of $50,000 the taxable incomes of a controlled group's members to which the 15% tax rate applies, and it allows only an aggregate of $25,000 of the group's members' taxable incomes to be taxed at 25%. For a controlled group, however, each corporation computes its tax liability separately, with the benefits of the 15% and 25% tax brackets allocated among the group's members. In contrast, a consolidated group simply applies the normal corporate tax rate schedule to its consolidated taxable income.

CORPORATE ALTERNATIVE MINIMUM TAX

A consolidated group determines its corporate alternative minimum tax (AMT) on a consolidated basis.[34] In so doing the group calculates its AMT using an approach similar in many ways to the AMT calculation for an unaffiliated corporation except the amounts involved are determined on a consolidated basis (see Chapter C:5 for a detailed discussion of the corporate AMT for an unaffiliated corporation). The group increases or decreases its regular taxable income for each of its AMT preference and adjustment items (e.g., the difference between MACRS and AMT depreciation and the adjusted current earnings (ACE) adjustment) to arrive at alternative minimum taxable income (AMTI). The consolidated group reduces its AMTI by a $40,000 AMT exemption, but this amount phases out from $150,000 to $310,000 of AMTI.

EXAMPLE C:8-33 ▶ P and S Corporations comprise a consolidated group whose consolidated regular tax is $50,000. P's separate alternative minimum taxable income (AMTI) is $145,000, and S's separate AMTI is $140,000. The group's $40,000 exemption must be reduced by $33,750, calculated as follows: ($145,000 + $140,000) − $150,000 × 0.25 = $33,750. Thus, the reduced consolidated exemption is $6,250 ($40,000 − $33,750).

Even if P and S file separate returns instead of a consolidated tax return, the group is allowed only one $40,000 exemption under the controlled group rules discussed in Chapter C:3. In addition, the group members would have to limit that exemption in the same manner as does the consolidated group. The controlled group then apportions the reduced exemption between the two corporations. ◀

The group's tentative minimum tax (TMT) is 20% of its AMTI in excess of its AMT exemption, and this amount is reduced by the group's AMT foreign tax credit to arrive at its TMT. The AMT is the excess of the TMT over the regular tax liability for the tax year. The consolidated group must pay any consolidated AMT in addition to its regular tax liability, but this amount is available in future years as a consolidated minimum tax credit. The consolidated group is eligible for the small corporation exemption from the AMT, but the $5 million and $7.5 million tests are based on the entire group's gross receipts.

The consolidated group determines its preadjustment AMTI, ACE, and AMTI using an approach that generally parallels the determination of consolidated regular taxable income. For example, the group may defer recognition of income, gains, deductions, or losses from intercompany transactions, much like it would for consolidated regular taxable income. However, the intercompany items, corresponding items, and recomputed corresponding items may differ in amount for AMT and regular tax purposes, such as when the intercompany transaction involves depreciable property.

---

[34] Prop. Reg. Sec. 1.1502-55.

KEY POINT

Determining the AMT is complex for an unconsolidated corporation. Determining it on a consolidated basis adds greatly to the complexity of this computation.

Many complex issues arise for a consolidated group's AMT that do not arise for an unconsolidated corporation's AMT. For example, recall from Chapter C:5 that the negative ACE adjustment is limited to the cumulative net amount of positive and negative ACE adjustments. Applying this limitation on a consolidated basis requires the tracking of separate return and consolidated return positive and negative ACE adjustments in prior years if corporations enter or leave the consolidated group. Further discussion of these issues is beyond the scope of this textbook.

TAX CREDITS

A consolidated group can claim all tax credits available to corporate taxpayers. The group calculates these credits in much the same way as would an unaffiliated corporation. The discussion that follows examines the two major credits claimed by most consolidated groups—the general business credit and the foreign tax credit.

General Business Credit. A consolidated group determines its general business credit on a consolidated basis, combining its members' separate credit amounts into a single amount.[35] (See Chapter I:14 for more detailed coverage of the general business credit.) The extent to which this combined amount can be claimed as a credit is limited to the excess of the group's consolidated net income tax over the greater of (1) its consolidated tentative minimum tax or (2) 25% of its consolidated net regular tax liability exceeding $25,000. Any credit exceeding this limitation carries back one year and forward 20 years.[36]

The corporations in a consolidated group may find that the general business credit allowed in the current year is smaller on a consolidated basis than it would be on a separate return basis. For example, if the credit is attributable to a profitable group member and another group member has a loss, consolidation may result in that member's loss reducing the group's credit limitation. However, if the credit is attributable to an unprofitable group member, consolidation may allow the members to claim a greater amount of credit on a consolidated basis than on a separate return basis because the credit limitation is higher on a consolidated basis due to other group members' profits.

EXAMPLE C:8-34 ▶ P and S Corporations comprise a consolidated group. For the current year, P and S have separate taxable income and losses of $300,000 and ($100,000), respectively. P has a $40,000 research credit, and S has a $10,000 employer provided child care credit. P and S have $125,000 of AMT preference and adjustment items.

The group has a $50,000 ($40,000 + $10,000) tentative general business credit. The group's consolidated regular taxable income is $200,000 ($300,000 − $100,000), assuming no intercompany transactions or other items that would cause consolidated taxable income to differ from the sum of the separate taxable income and loss. The group's regular tax is $61,250 [$22,250 + (0.39 × ($200,000 − $100,000))]. The group's tentative minimum tax is $65,000 (20% × ($200,000 + $125,000)); the AMT exemption is fully phased-out), so the consolidated AMT is $3,750 ($65,000 − $61,250). The group's general business credit limitation is calculated as follows:

Regular tax		$61,250
Plus: Alternative minimum tax		3,750
Minus: Credits allowed under Secs. 21-30C		–0–
Net income tax		$65,000
Minus: Greater of:		
(1) 25% of group's net regular tax liability exceeding $25,000 [0.25 × ($61,250 − $25,000)]	$ 9,062	
(2) Group's tentative minimum tax for the year	65,000	(65,000)
General business credit limitation		$ –0–

The $50,000 ($50,000 tentative credit − $0 credit limitation) of unused general business credits carries back one year and forward 20 years. ◀

BOOK-TO-TAX ACCOUNTING COMPARISON

A general business credit carryover creates a deferred tax asset on the group's consolidated financial statements. The group also establishes a valuation allowance for any part of the deferred tax asset that does not have a more likely than not probability of being realized, and it should record a liability for unrecognized tax benefit for the portion of it that is not more likely than not to be realized upon effective settlement with the IRS (see Chapter C:3 regarding uncertain tax positions under ASC 740).

[35] Reg. Sec. 1.1502-3.

[36] Sec. 39(a).

Foreign Tax Credit. A consolidated group determines its foreign tax credit on a consolidated basis.[37] The parent corporation makes the election to claim either a deduction or a credit for the group's foreign income taxes. If the parent chooses to claim a credit, the consolidated group computes its foreign tax credit limitation by taking into account its consolidated foreign-source income, consolidated taxable income, and consolidated regular tax in the manner described in Chapter C:16.

ESTIMATED TAX PAYMENTS

For the first two years for which an affiliated group files consolidated tax returns, it may elect to make estimated tax payments on either a consolidated or separate basis. Once an affiliated group has filed consolidated tax returns for two consecutive years, it must pay estimated taxes on a consolidated basis and continue doing so until the group's members again file separate tax returns.[38] The group's estimated tax payments and any underpayment exceptions or penalties are based on its consolidated tax liability for the current and preceding tax years without regard to the number of corporations comprising the group. If new, profitable corporations join the group, this treatment can be advantageous due to the time value of money.

EXAMPLE C:8-35 ▶ The P-S1 affiliated group has filed consolidated tax returns for several years. In the preceding year, the group reported a $100,000 consolidated tax liability. The P-S1 group acquires all of S2 Corporation's stock during the current year. S2 is profitable and causes the P-S1-S2 group to report a $300,000 consolidated tax liability in the current year. Assuming the P-S1-S2 group does not fall under the large corporation rules discussed below, it can base its current year estimated tax payments on its $100,000 consolidated tax liability from the prior tax year. The group will not incur an underpayment penalty if it makes $25,000 ($100,000 ÷ 4) of estimated tax payments by the fifteenth day of the fourth, sixth, ninth, and twelfth months of its tax year. The group must pay the balance of its consolidated tax liability by the due date of its consolidated tax return (without regard to any extensions) to avoid a penalty. ◀

Large Corporation Rule. Chapter C:3 discusses the special underpayment rules for large corporations imposed by Sec. 6655(d)(2)(B). A large corporation's estimated tax payments cannot be based on its prior year's tax liability except for the first installment. A large corporation is one whose taxable income was $1 million or more in any of its three preceding tax years. A controlled group of corporations must allocate the $1 million amount among its group members. An affiliated group that files a consolidated tax return is treated as a single corporation for this purpose. An affiliated group that files separate tax returns generally must allocate this $1 million amount because it also qualifies as a parent-subsidiary controlled group.

Consolidated or Separate Basis. During the first two tax years of filing consolidated tax returns, a consolidated group sometimes can reduce its quarterly tax payments by making estimated tax payments on a separate basis in the first year and on a consolidated basis in the second year or vice versa. These reduced quarterly estimated tax payments will cause the group to pay a larger balance of tax by the due date of its tax return (without extensions). The group can apply different exceptions for the underpayment penalty (e.g., prior year's liability or annualization of current year's income) on a consolidated or separate basis the first two years. Determination of the actual required estimated tax payments on a consolidated or separate basis, however, is beyond the scope of this textbook.

Short-Period Return. If a corporation joins a consolidated group after the beginning of its tax year or leaves a consolidated group before its tax year ends, it generally must file a separate, short-period tax return covering the time period it was unaffiliated with the group (however, it would not file a separate tax return if it left one consolidated

---

[37] Reg. Sec. 1.1502-4.

[38] Reg. Sec. 1.1502-5.

group to enter another consolidated group). Treasury Regulations provide rules covering estimated tax payments for short tax years.[39] No estimated tax payment is required for a short tax year that is less than four months.

NET OPERATING LOSSES (NOLs)

OBJECTIVE 6

Determine a consolidated group's NOL, calculate the carryback or carryover of a consolidated NOL, and apply the SRLY restrictions on NOL usage

One advantage of filing a consolidated tax return is the ability of the consolidated group to offset one member's NOLs against the taxable income of other group members. However, the profitable group members' taxable income may not be sufficient to fully offset the other members' NOLs, resulting in a consolidated NOL. The consolidated NOL carries back two years and forward 20 years unless the parent elects out of the carryback. If corporations enter or depart the consolidated group between the year the NOL arose and the carryback or carryover year, the group must determine the portion of the NOL that carries to the entering or departing corporation's separate return year. In addition, if a corporation entering the consolidated group has unused NOLs from years prior to its entry into the group (or a departing corporation has unused NOLs from years after its departure), the group may be able to use the NOLs. Because of the potential for abuse, the tax law limits the group's ability to use a separate return NOL in a consolidated return year. In addition, NOL, capital loss, and tax credit carryovers can be subject to the consolidated limitations under Secs. 382-384. The rules that apply to carrybacks and carryovers are discussed below.

CURRENT YEAR NOL

KEY POINT

Generally, the most significant benefit of filing a consolidated tax return is the group's ability to offset one member's losses against the income of other members.

A consolidated group's NOL equals the excess of its deductions over its gross income (i.e., its negative taxable income).[40] The group combines each member's separate taxable income or loss to determine a combined taxable income before adjusting for NOL carryovers (see Table C:8-1). The combining process allows one group member's losses to offset the taxable income of other group members. The group determines its consolidated NOL after applying the intercompany transaction rules and after calculating on a consolidated basis the various items discussed earlier, such as Sec. 1231 and capital gains and losses. The group must use a member's current year loss to first offset other members' current-year profits. A group member cannot elect separately to carry back its own losses from a consolidated return year to one of its earlier or later profitable separate return years. Only the consolidated group's NOL (if any) may carry back or over.

EXAMPLE C:8-36 ▶ P and S Corporations comprise an affiliated group. During Year 1, their initial year of operation, P and S file calendar year separate tax returns. Beginning in Year 2, the group elects to file a consolidated tax return. P and S report the following results for Years 1 and 2:

	Taxable Income	
Group Member	*Year 1*	*Year 2*
P	($15,000)	$40,000
S	250,000	(27,000)
Consolidated taxable income	N/A	$13,000

N/A = Not applicable

P may not use its Year 1 NOL to offset S's Year 1 profits because they file separate returns. In its Year 2 consolidated tax return, the group must first offset S's $27,000 separate loss against P's separate taxable income. S cannot carry back the $27,000 to its Year 1 separate tax return. (Note that the tax savings from deducting the $27,000 would be greater if S could carry it back

[39] Reg. Sec. 1.6655-5.

[40] Reg. Sec. 1.1502-21(e).

to Year 1.) Because P did not exist before Year 1, P carries its Year 1 NOL forward to offset all $13,000 of Year 2 consolidated taxable income that the P-S group reports prior to deducting any of the NOL carryover. The group's Year 2 consolidated taxable income is zero. P carries over to Year 3 its remaining NOL of $2,000 ($15,000 NOL from Year 1 − $13,000 used in Year 2). ◀

CARRYBACKS AND CARRYOVERS OF CONSOLIDATED NOLS

A consolidated NOL carries back to the two preceding tax years and carries over to the 20 succeeding tax years. The parent corporation may elect for the consolidated group to relinquish the carryback period for a consolidated NOL and use the NOL only as a carryforward to succeeding years.[41] (Chapter C:3 discusses reasons for making this election.)

If the same corporations comprise the consolidated group during the carryback and carryover periods as during the year in which the NOL occurs, the treatment of the consolidated NOL is much like the treatment of an unaffiliated corporation's NOL. However, if the group's composition changes, the treatment of a consolidated NOL becomes complicated.

General Rule. The consolidated group apportions a fraction of its consolidated NOL to each member that incurred a separate loss during the year the NOL arose as follows:[42]

$$\frac{\text{Separate NOL of the particular group member}}{\text{Sum of the separate NOLs of all group members having such losses}} \times \text{Consolidated NOL} = \text{Portion of consolidated NOL attributable to the particular group member}$$

EXAMPLE C:8-37 ▶ P, S1, and S2 Corporations comprise an affiliated group. The group filed separate tax returns in Years 1 and 2 but elected to file a consolidated tax return in Year 3. The members report the following amounts of income and loss (before any NOL deduction):

	Year 1	*Year 2*	*Year 3*
P	$80,000	$90,000	$ 75,000
S1	11,000	7,000	(60,000)
S2	4,400	3,300	(40,000)
Consolidated taxable income	N/A	N/A	$(25,000)

N/A = Not applicable

Of the $25,000 Year 3 consolidated NOL, the group apportions $15,000 [$25,000 × ($60,000 ÷ ($60,000 + $40,000))] to S1 and $10,000 [$25,000 × ($40,000 ÷ ($60,000 + $40,000))] to S2. Assuming P does not elect to forego the NOL carryback period, S1 carries back $11,000 of its apportioned NOL to offset all its Year 1 separate return taxable income and the remaining $4,000 ($15,000 − $11,000) to offset part of its Year 2 separate return taxable income. S2 carries back $7,700 of its $10,000 apportioned NOL to offset its Years 1 and 2 separate return taxable incomes. The remaining $2,300 ($10,000 − $4,400 − $3,300) of consolidated NOL attributable to S2 carries forward to Year 4. ◀

KEY POINT

In Example C:8-37, because the P-S1-S2 affiliated group did not file a consolidated tax return prior to Year 3, P must either forgo the NOL carryback or allow $22,700 ($11,000 + $4,000 + $7,700) of the consolidated NOL to be carried back to S1's and S2's Years 1 and 2 separate tax returns.

If a corporation ceases to be a member of a consolidated group, any consolidated NOL carryover apportioned to it first must be used to offset consolidated taxable income in the year of departure. This requirement applies even when the entire NOL carryover is attributable to the departing member. Any NOL carryover apportioned to the departing member not absorbed by departure year consolidated taxable income becomes the member's separate carryover and may be used in its subsequent separate return years.[43]

---

[41] Reg. Sec. 1.1502-21(b)(3)(i).

[42] Reg. Sec. 1.1502-21(b)(2)(iv). The member's separate NOL is determined in a manner similar to the calculation of separate taxable income except for a series of adjustments to take into account the member's charitable contributions, dividends-received deductions, and Sec. 1231 and capital gains and losses. The consolidated NOL apportioned to a member might be reduced under the unified loss rules of Reg. Sec. 1.1502-36, which are beyond the scope of this text.

[43] Reg. Sec. 1.1502-21(b)(2)(ii)(A).

EXAMPLE C:8-38 ▶ P, S1, and S2 Corporations comprise an affiliated group that has filed consolidated tax returns on a calendar year basis for several years. At the close of business on September 30 of Year 2, P sells all its S1 stock. Therefore, S1 must file a separate tax return for the period October 1 through December 31 of Year 2. The members report the following amounts of income and loss (before any NOL deduction):

	Year 1	*Year 2*
P	$ 48,000	$20,000
S1	(50,000)	43,000*
S2	(100,000)	10,000
Total	$(102,000)	$73,000

*S1 earns $30,000 from January 1 through September 30 and $13,000 from October 1 through December 31.

Assuming P elects to forego the NOL carryback period, the consolidated NOL carryover of $102,000 from Year 1 offsets the $60,000 ($20,000 + $30,000 + $10,000) of taxable income reported by P, S1, and S2 in their Year 2 consolidated tax return. Of the remaining $42,000 ($102,000 − $60,000), the group apportions $14,000 [$42,000 × ($50,000 ÷ ($50,000 + $100,000))] to S1 and $28,000 [$42,000 × ($100,000 ÷ ($50,000 + $100,000))] to S2. Of S1's carryover, $13,000 can be used in its separate tax return for October 1 through December 31 of Year 2. The remaining $1,000 ($14,000 − $13,000) carries over to S1's Year 3 separate tax return. The consolidated group carries over S2's $28,000 apportioned share of the Year 1 NOL to Year 3 and subsequent years. ◀

TAX STRATEGY TIP

In Example C:8-38, the group is entitled to use the consolidated NOL before S1 determines its NOL carryover. This privilege can affect the negotiated purchase price for S1.

Offspring Rule. The offspring rule pertains to the consolidated NOL apportioned to a loss corporation that was newly formed by one or more of the affiliated group's members. The rule permits the NOL apportioned to the loss corporation to be carried back to a consolidated return year before it was a group member or to a separate return year of the parent corporation. Normally, the NOL apportioned to a loss member cannot be carried back in this way. The offspring rule applies if:[44]

- ▶ The loss corporation did not exist in the carryback year, and
- ▶ The loss corporation has been a member of the affiliated group continually since its organization.

If these two requirements are met, the part of the consolidated NOL apportioned to the loss member carries back to the two preceding consolidated return years (or separate return year of the common parent). The offspring rule does not apply if the common parent was a member of a different consolidated group or affiliated group filing separate returns for the year to which the loss carries.

EXAMPLE C:8-39 ▶ P and S1 Corporations were affiliated during Years 1 and 2 and filed consolidated tax returns in those years. On January 1 of Year 3, P creates S2 Corporation and acquires all its stock. S2 becomes a member of the affiliated group on that date. P, S1, and S2 report the following results for Years 1 through 3 (before any NOL deduction):

	Year 1	*Year 2*	*Year 3*
P	$ 9,000	$11,000	$ 16,000
S1	8,000	7,000	4,000
S2			(30,000)
Consolidated taxable income	$17,000	$18,000	$(10,000)

The entire Year 3 consolidated NOL is apportioned to S2. As discussed earlier, S2's $30,000 separate NOL is first used to offset the Year 3 taxable income of P and S1, leaving only a $10,000 consolidated NOL. If P does not elect to forego the NOL carryback period, the offspring rule allows the $10,000 NOL to carry back and offset $10,000 of the $17,000 Year 1 consolidated taxable income. The requirements for the offspring rule are met because S2 did not exist in Year 1 (the carryback year) and has been a group member continually since its organization in Year 3.

SELF-STUDY QUESTION

In Examples C:8-39 and C:8-40, what is the reason for allowing S2's portion of the consolidated NOL to carry back to Years 1 and 2?

ANSWER

The assets that make up S2 really were P's assets in Years 1 and 2, so it makes sense to allow the NOL to carry back to whatever tax return P filed in Years 1 and 2.

[44] Reg. Sec. 1.1502-21(b)(2)(ii)(B).

If P elects to forego the NOL carryback period, the $10,000 consolidated NOL offsets consolidated taxable income in Year 4 and up to 19 subsequent years assuming S2 does not depart the consolidated group before the $10,000 NOL is used. ◀

EXAMPLE C:8-40 ▶ Assume the same facts as in Example C:8-39 except P and S1 Corporations did not begin filing consolidated tax returns until Year 2. The offspring rule's requirements are still met, so the $10,000 consolidated NOL apportioned to S2 can carry back to P's Year 1 separate tax return, offsetting its $9,000 of taxable income (assuming P does not elect to forego the NOL carryback period). The remaining $1,000 offsets $1,000 of the $18,000 Year 2 consolidated taxable income. ◀

If the loss corporation is not a member of the affiliated group immediately after its organization, that member's portion of the consolidated NOL carries back only to its prior separate return years.

EXAMPLE C:8-41 ▶ Assume the same facts as in Example C:8-40 except a third party created S2 in Year 2, and P acquired all of S2's stock from the third party on January 1 of Year 3. P, S1, and S2 report the following results for Years 1 through 3 (before any NOL deduction):

Group Member		*Taxable Income*	
	Year 1	*Year 2*	*Year 3*
P	$ 9,000	$11,000	$16,000
S1	8,000	7,000	4,000
S2		8,000	(30,000)
Consolidated taxable income	N/A	$18,000[a]	($10,000)

N/A = Not applicable
[a] Includes only the results of P and S1.

The offspring rule does not apply because S2 was not affiliated with the P-S1 group in Year 2. Because the entire $10,000 consolidated NOL is attributable to S2, S2 can carry it back to Year 2 and offset all $8,000 of its taxable income on its Year 2 separate return. S2 cannot carry back the loss to Year 1 because S2 did not exist then. The remaining NOL of $2,000 ($10,000 − $8,000) carries over to offset the consolidated group's Year 4 and later taxable income. Alternatively, the P-S1-S2 affiliated group could elect to carry over the entire $10,000 loss to offset taxable income in Year 4 and later years. ◀

TAX STRATEGY TIP

In deciding whether to elect out of the NOL carryback, a parent corporation should consider whether its subsidiaries have minority shareholders who might benefit if the subsidiaries receive a refund.

SPECIAL LOSS LIMITATIONS

The term NOL trafficking refers to attempts by one tax entity to acquire NOL deductions from another entity. For example, a profitable corporation might consider acquiring an unprofitable corporation merely to obtain a tax benefit from the acquired corporation's unused NOLs. To inhibit NOL trafficking, the tax law imposes special limitations on the use of NOLs. The **Sec. 382 loss limitation rules**, which were discussed in Chapter C:7 on a separate return basis, also could apply to affiliated groups filing consolidated tax returns. The **separate return limitation year (SRLY) rules** apply only to consolidated groups and limit the use in a consolidated return year of a member's NOL that arose in a separate return year. Specifically, the SRLY rules limit use of the NOL to the loss member's subsequent contribution to consolidated taxable income. The SRLY rules are explained in detail below, as well as special aspects of the Sec. 382 rules with respect to consolidated tax returns.

BOOK-TO TAX ACCOUNTING COMPARISON

An NOL creates a deferred tax asset on an acquiring corporation's consolidated balance sheet, thereby highlighting the economic benefit the unprofitable corporation's NOLs provides for the acquiring corporation's consolidated group. However, a valuation allowance for this deferred tax asset may be needed because of the Sec. 382 and SRLY loss limitation rules.

Separate Return Limitation Year Rules. A SRLY generally is any separate return year (i.e., a year in which a corporation filed a separate tax return or joined in a consolidated tax return of another consolidated group). However, a SRLY does not include the following:[45]

- A separate return year of the group's parent corporation. The SRLY limitation thus does not apply to the parent corporation's NOLs, even if they arise in a separate return year.

[45] Reg. Sec. 1.1502-1(f).

KEY POINT

The SRLY rules limit a consolidated group's ability to acquire another corporation and use its already existing NOLs to offset the group's income.

ADDITIONAL COMMENT

These two exceptions to the SRLY rules exist because, in both cases, the group has not acquired already existing NOLs.

- A separate return year of a corporation that was a member of the affiliated group for every day of the loss year (e.g., the group did not elect to file a consolidated tax return in the loss year). The SRLY limitation does not apply in this circumstance because the loss year would not have been a SRLY had the group elected to file a consolidated tax return.

An NOL incurred in a SRLY carries back two years and forward 20 years unless the corporation elects to carry forward the NOL only for 20 years. If the year to which the NOL carries is a consolidated return year, the NOL's deductibility is limited to the SRLY limitation for that group member:[46]

Aggregate of consolidated taxable income for all consolidated return years of the group determined by taking into account only the loss member's items of income, gain, deduction, and loss
Minus: Any of the loss member's NOLs previously absorbed by the consolidated group
SRLY limitation (not less than zero)

The SRLY rules limit the consolidated group's use of the loss member's NOL to that member's aggregate contribution to consolidated taxable income in excess of zero. As a result, an NOL incurred in a SRLY that is deductible on a consolidated tax return equals the lesser of (1) the SRLY limitation, (2) consolidated taxable income, or (3) the amount of the NOL carryover or carryback. Any NOL carryover or carryback exceeding the lesser of these three amounts carries over to subsequent tax years.

EXAMPLE C:8-42 ▶ P and S Corporations are calendar year corporations that formed in Year 1. P acquires 100% of S's stock at the close of business on December 31 of Year 1.[47] P and S file separate tax returns for Year 1 and begin filing a consolidated tax return for Year 2. Assume the U.S. production activities deduction does not apply. The corporations report the following taxable incomes (losses), before any NOL deductions, for Years 1 through 5:

SELF-STUDY QUESTION

What is the consequence of having NOLs subject to the SRLY limitations?

ANSWER

The effect of having a member's NOLs tainted as SRLY NOLs is that they can be used only to offset taxable income of the loss member. This restriction could delay deduction of the NOLs and increases the likelihood that they will expire unused.

	Taxable Income				
Group Member	*Year 1*	*Year 2*	*Year 3*	*Year 4*	*Year 5*
P	$(9,000)	$17,000	$ 6,000	$(6,000)	$ 2,000
S	(20,000)	(2,000)	5,000	5,000	16,000
Consolidated taxable income	N/A	$15,000	$11,000	$(1,000)	$18,000

N/A = Not applicable

Under the SRLY rules, the P-S consolidated group uses the NOLs as follows:

- *Year 2:* P's Year 1 NOL offsets the group's consolidated taxable income (CTI). For P, Year 1 is not a SRLY because P is the group's parent corporation. S's only contribution to CTI by the end of Year 2 is its $2,000 loss in Year 2. Therefore, S's SRLY limitation for Year 2 is zero because S makes no positive aggregate contribution to CTI. The group's resulting CTI is $6,000 ($15,000 − $9,000).
- *Year 3:* S's SRLY limitation for Year 3 is $3,000 [($2,000) + $5,000]. S's $20,000 unused NOLs and the group's $11,000 CTI are both more than $3,000, so the group can deduct $3,000 of S's Year 1 NOL. The group's resulting CTI is $8,000 ($11,000 − $3,000), and $17,000 ($20,000 − $3,000) of S's NOL remains to carry forward.
- *Year 4:* S's SRLY limitation is $5,000 [($2,000) + $5,000 + $5,000 − $3,000]. However, none of S's Year 1 NOL can be used because the group has no positive CTI for the NOL to offset. Assuming the group carries back the Year 4 consolidated NOL to Year 2, CTI in Year 2 is reduced from $6,000 to $5,000 ($15,000 − $9,000 carryover from Year 1 − $1,000 carryback from Year 4).

[46] Reg. Sec. 1.1502-21(c). If multiple group members have unexpired NOLs or a loss member has unexpired NOLs from multiple SRLYs, the group uses the NOLs on a first-in, first-out (FIFO) basis. The group uses NOLs from tax years ending on the same date on a pro rata basis.

[47] P's acquisition of S stock might trigger both the SRLY rules and the Sec. 382 rules. To simplify the example, assume that the acquisition did not trigger the Sec. 382 rules. The SRLY-Sec. 382 overlap rules are discussed later in this chapter.

▶ *Year 5:* S's SRLY limitation is $21,000 [($2,000) + $5,000 + $5,000 − $3,000 + $16,000]. However, S has only $17,000 of NOLs remaining, so the group deducts this amount. The group's resulting CTI is $1,000 ($18,000 − $17,000), and no NOLs remain to carry forward to Year 6. ◀

The SRLY rules generally apply separately to each corporation that has a loss carryover from a SRLY.

EXAMPLE C:8-43 ▶ At the close of business on December 31 of Year 1, P Corporation purchases 100% of S Corporation's stock and 100% of T Corporation's stock. S and T were unaffiliated prior to these purchases. From Year 1, S has a $12,000 NOL carryover, and T has an $11,000 NOL carryover. Assume the Sec. 382 limitation does not apply to these stock purchases. The P-S-T affiliated group elects to file a consolidated tax return for Year 2, and the members report the following separate taxable income for that year:

P Corporation	$100,000
S Corporation	$ 14,000
T Corporation	$ 10,000

The Year 2 SRLY limitation for S's NOL is $14,000, and the limitation for T's NOL is $10,000. The P-S-T consolidated group can deduct all $12,000 of S's Year 1 NOL, but it can deduct only $10,000 of T's Year 1 NOL. As a result, the group's Year 2 consolidated taxable income is $102,000 ($100,000 + $14,000 + $10,000 − $12,000 − $10,000). The remaining $1,000 ($11,000 − $10,000) of T's Year 1 NOL carries forward to Year 3. ◀

The SRLY limitation applies to a SRLY subgroup on a joint basis rather than to each corporation separately. For NOL carryovers, a SRLY subgroup is the loss corporation and each other group member that (1) became a member of the current affiliated group at the same time as the loss corporation, (2) was affiliated with the loss corporation in another affiliated group before becoming a member of the current affiliated group, and (3) has been continuously affiliated with the loss corporation after ceasing to be a member of the former affiliated group.

EXAMPLE C:8-44 ▶ Assume the same facts as in Example C:8-43 except S owns 100% of T's stock, and P purchased 100% of S's stock at the close of business on December 31 of Year 1. S and T are a SRLY subgroup. The S-T subgroup SRLY limitation for Year 2 is $24,000 ($14,000 + $10,000), so the P-S-T consolidated group can deduct on its Year 2 tax return all $23,000 ($12,000 + $11,000) of S's and T's NOL carryovers from Year 1. ◀

KEY POINT

The SRLY rules apply to both carryovers and carrybacks. Remember that SRLYs stem from a year in which a member files a separate tax return or joins in the filing of a consolidated return with a different affiliated group.

In addition to NOL carryovers, the SRLY rules apply to NOL carrybacks. For example, suppose P Corporation owns 100% of S Corporation's stock, and they have filed consolidated tax returns for many years. P sells all its stock in S at the end of Year 2, and S incurs an NOL in Year 3. If S does not elect to forego the NOL carryback period, the Year 3 NOL first carries to the P-S Year 1 consolidated tax return, and any remaining NOL then carries to the P-S Year 2 consolidated tax return. In Years 1 and 2, the SRLY rules restrict the consolidated group's use of S's Year 3 NOL to S's contribution to consolidated taxable income for all consolidated return years.

The SRLY rules also limit the use of built-in losses. A built-in loss is a loss that accrues in a separate return year but is realized in a consolidated return year. For example, S Corporation purchases land in a separate return year for $100,000. The land's fair market value declines to $85,000 before P purchases all of S's stock, when they start filing tax returns on a consolidated basis. If S sells the land during the five-year period beginning on the date P purchases S's stock, the SRLY rules limit the extent to which the P-S consolidated group can use the realized loss. As with NOLs, the group must compute S's SRLY limitation in determining how much of the loss it can use.[48]

In a reverse acquisition, the acquired corporation's shareholders own more than 50% of the fair market value of the acquiring corporation's stock immediately after the

[48] Reg. Sec. 1.1502-15(a).

acquisition. In such an acquisition, the SRLY limitation applies to the acquiring corporation's NOLs and does not apply to the acquired corporation's NOLs.[49] For example, suppose P Corporation acquires all of S Corporation's stock in exchange for P stock. Because P is smaller than S, persons who were S shareholders immediately before the purchase own more than 50% of the fair market value of P's stock immediately after the purchase. The form of the transaction is that P acquires S, but its substance is that S acquires P. The transaction qualifies as a reverse acquisition, so the SRLY limitation applies to P's NOLs but not to S's NOLs. That is, S is treated as if it were the parent corporation for purposes of applying the SRLY limitation. The details of this rule and other aspects of the reverse acquisition rules are beyond the scope of this textbook.

A discussion of the financial statement implications of SRLY losses appears at the end of this chapter.

Consolidated Sec. 382 Rules. The Sec. 382 rules may apply when a consolidated group acquires a corporation with an unused NOL. Section 382 inhibits NOL trafficking by limiting the acquiring corporation's use of a loss corporation's NOL to the Sec. 382 limitation, which is the value of the old loss corporation's stock multiplied by the long-term tax-exempt federal interest rate.[50] The 50 percentage point stock ownership change needed to trigger the Sec. 382 rules can occur in acquisitive transactions involving a single corporation or a group of corporations that file separate or consolidated returns. (See Chapter C:7 for a discussion of Sec. 382.) The consolidated Sec. 382 rules generally provide that the ownership change and Sec. 382 limitation are determined with respect to the entire consolidated group (or a subgroup of a consolidated group) and not separately for each corporation.[51] The details of these rules are beyond the scope of this textbook.

Srly-Sec. 382 Overlap. A SRLY-Sec. 382 overlap occurs when an acquisition of a corporation falls under both the SRLY rules and the Sec. 382 rules (for example, a corporation in a consolidated group purchases 100% of the stock of a target corporation having an NOL carryover). Because both sets of rules inhibit NOL trafficking by restricting the use of NOLs, Treasury Regulations alleviate the burden of applying them by waiving the application of the SRLY rules in many SRLY-Sec. 382 overlap situations.[52]

To qualify for the overlap rule, a corporation must become a member of a consolidated group (the SRLY event) within six months of the date of an ownership change that triggers a Sec. 382 limitation (the Sec. 382 event). Often, the SRLY event and the Sec. 382 event are simultaneous.

EXAMPLE C:8-45 ▶ P Corporation purchases 60% of S Corporation's stock on February 28 of the current year. On June 30 of the current year, P purchases the other 40% of S's stock. P has filed consolidated tax returns with its other subsidiaries for several years. The Sec. 382 event occurs on February 28, when the 50 percentage-point ownership change takes place. The SRLY event occurs on June 30, when P's ownership of S reaches the 80% threshold needed to include S in the consolidated tax return. The overlap rule applies because the Sec. 382 event occurred within six months of the SRLY event, so the SRLY rules are waived beginning with the tax year that includes June 30. Instead, only the Sec. 382 rules apply. ◀

ADDITIONAL COMMENT

In some cases, the overlap rule will not apply. In Example C:8-45, if the 40% purchase had taken place on September 30, the SRLY event would have occurred more than six months after the Sec. 382 event. Consequently, the SRLY rules and the Sec. 382 rules both would apply.

If the SRLY event precedes the Sec. 382 event by six months or less, the overlap rule applies for the first tax year beginning after the Sec. 382 event (and the SRLY rules apply for the interim period). This situation could occur, for example, if the acquiring corporation had owned 45% of the target corporation's stock for many years, purchased 40% of the target's stock in the current year, and purchased the remaining 15% of the target's stock less than six months after the 40% purchase.

Topic Review C:8-2 summarizes the rules applying to carrybacks and carryovers of consolidated return and separate return NOLs.

---

[49] Reg. Sec. 1.1502-1(f)(3).

[50] The Sec. 382 limitation rules apply to the tax attributes limited by Secs. 382–384 (e.g., NOLs, capital losses, foreign tax credits, general business credits, minimum tax credit, built-in gains, and built-in losses).

[51] Reg. Sec. 1.1502-91(a)(1).

[52] Reg. Sec. 1.1502-21(g).

TOPIC REVIEW C:8-2

Rules Addressing NOL Carrybacks and Carryovers To or From Consolidated Tax Return Years

Loss Year	Carryover/ Carryback Year	Rule and Special Limitations
CRY[a]	CRY	1. Consolidated NOLs carry back two years and forward 20 years. The group's parent corporation can elect to forgo the carryback period. No special problems arise if the group members are the same in the loss year and the year to which the loss carries. 2. The Sec. 382 limitation applies to the loss carryover if a Sec. 382 ownership change occurs.
CRY	SRY[b]	1. Carryback to a member's prior separate return year is possible only if part or all of the NOL is apportioned to the member. Offspring rule permits carryback of an offspring member's allocable share of the consolidated NOL to a separate or consolidated return year of the group's parent corporation. 2. The departing member is allocated part of the consolidated NOL carryover. The consolidated NOL carryover is used first in the consolidated return year in which the member departs. The allocated share of the remaining consolidated NOL carryover is then available to be used in the departing member's first separate return year. The Sec. 382 loss limitation may apply to the loss carryover.
SRY	CRY	1. A separate return year NOL carries over to a consolidated return year, but the SRLY rules may limit the NOL's usage. The SRLY rules do not apply to the NOLs of the parent corporation or to a corporation that is a member of the affiliated group on each day of the loss year unless a reverse acquisition occurs. Section 382 loss limitation rules may apply to the loss carryover, but the SRLY rules may be waived under the overlap rule. 2. Carryback of a loss of a departed group member to a consolidated return year is a SRLY loss.

[a]Consolidated return year.
[b]Separate return year.

Stock Basis Adjustments

OBJECTIVE 7

Adjust the parent's basis in stock of a consolidated subsidiary

A consolidated group member must annually adjust the basis of stock it owns in a subsidiary for the subsidiary's profits and losses, for distributions from the subsidiary, and for other items. These rules are similar to those that apply to partners of partnerships and shareholders of S corporations (see Chapters C:9 and C:11) and are intended to prevent the duplication of income or loss in consolidated taxable income.[53]

EXAMPLE C:8-46 ▶ P Corporation purchases all of S Corporation's stock on January 1 of the current year for $100,000. The corporations elect to file a consolidated tax return. S recognizes a $25,000 profit during the current year and pays no dividends to P. P sells all its S stock on December 31 of the current year for $125,000. P increases the basis of its S stock by $25,000. As a result, P realizes no gain or loss on the sale of its S stock [$125,000 amount realized − $125,000 basis ($100,000 + $25,000)].

Had P not adjusted its basis for S's profit, it would have realized a $25,000 gain on the stock sale ($125,000 − $100,000), and this gain would have been taxed on the current year's consolidated tax return. However, the increase in the S stock's value that led to this $25,000 gain is attributable to the $25,000 profit that S earned. Without the basis adjustment to the S stock, the consolidated group would have been taxed twice on the $25,000 gain. ◀

KEY POINT

Positive stock basis adjustments reduce the amount of gain or increase the amount of loss reported when a sale of the stock of a consolidated group member (other than the parent) occurs.

A consolidated group may be comprised of many tiers of corporations. For example, a parent corporation may have a subsidiary corporation (a first-tier subsidiary), and the subsidiary, in turn, may have its own subsidiary (a second-tier subsidiary). The stock basis

[53] Losses realized on the sale by one consolidated group member of another member's stock involve complicated rules and calculations that are beyond the scope of this text.

adjustments itemized below are discussed with respect to a parent corporation that owns stock of a subsidiary, but they also apply to a higher-tier subsidiary that owns stock of a lower-tier subsidiary.

The starting point for the calculation is the parent corporation's original basis in its subsidiary stock, which depends on the method used to acquire it (e.g., purchase, nontaxable corporate formation, or nontaxable reorganization). The parent makes the following adjustments to the original basis:[54]

- Increase basis for the subsidiary's income and gain items and decrease it for the subsidiary's deduction and loss items taken into account in determining consolidated taxable income. Items whose recognition is deferred under the intercompany transaction rules do not increase or decrease basis until they are taken into account for consolidated taxable income.
- Increase basis for the subsidiary's income permanently excluded from taxation (e.g., tax-exempt bond interest and federal income tax refunds).
- Increase basis for the subsidiary's deductions that do not represent a recovery of basis or an expenditure of money as if they were tax-exempt income (for example, the dividends-received and U.S. production activities deductions). However, the parent also decreases basis for the deductions themselves, so these two adjustments usually net to zero and thus have no net effect on the parent's basis in the subsidiary.[55]
- Decrease basis for the subsidiary's expenses that are not deductible and are not capital expenditures (e.g., federal income taxes, the nondeductible 50% of meals and entertainment expenses, expenses related to tax-exempt income, and losses disallowed under Sec. 267).
- Decrease basis for distributions received from the subsidiary (without regard to the subsidiary's E&P or whether the E&P accumulated before or after the subsidiary became a member of the consolidated group).
- Decrease basis for the subsidiary's NOLs that arise and are used in the current year against other group members' taxable income. NOLs that carry forward reduce basis in the year used. NOLs that carry back reduce basis in the year they arise. Expiring NOLs reduce basis in the year they expire. However, basis is not decreased when the subsidiary's pre-acquisition NOLs expire unused if the group waives the use of part or all of such losses. Similar rules apply to capital losses.

EXAMPLE C:8-47 ▶ On January 1 of the current year, P Corporation purchases all of S Corporation's stock for $1 million. P and S elect to file a consolidated tax return. During the current year, S reports taxable income of $300,000 and tax-exempt bond interest of $25,000, and S pays P a $40,000 dividend. On January 1 of the next year, P sells the S stock for $1.2 million. Assume that the portion of the consolidated tax liability allocable to S is $102,000 ($300,000 × 0.34) and that S pays it. P's basis in its S stock on the sale date is $1,183,000 ($1,000,000 + $300,000 + $25,000 − $102,000 − $40,000). Thus, P realizes a $17,000 gain on the stock sale ($1,200,000 − $1,183,000).[56] ◀

ADDITIONAL COMMENT

Determining the federal income tax allocable to each group member often is more complex than in Example C:8-47 because members' losses, credits, and other items affect the consolidated tax liability. The regulations specify methods for allocating the tax liability among a group's members, but the details are beyond the scope of this textbook.

TIERING UP OF STOCK BASIS ADJUSTMENTS

In adjusting the basis of its first-tier subsidiary's stock, the parent corporation also takes into account the adjustments the first-tier subsidiary makes to its basis in second-tier subsidiary stock. The adjustments are applied in order of the tiers, from the lowest to the highest.

EXAMPLE C:8-48 ▶ P Corporation owns all of S Corporation's stock, and S owns all of T Corporation's stock. The three corporations have filed on a consolidated basis for several years. At the beginning of the current year, P's basis in its S stock was $800,000, and S's basis in its T stock was $500,000. During the current year, S reports $100,000 of taxable income, and T reports $50,000 of taxable

[54] Reg. Sec. 1.1502-32. If the parent owns less than 100% of the subsidiary's stock, it adjusts the stock basis by its ownership percentage multiplied by the various adjustment items.

[55] Reg. Sec. 1502-32(b)(3)(ii)(B).

[56] Separate basis calculations are required for regular tax and AMT purposes. The AMT basis calculations parallel those made for regular tax purposes but use the appropriate numbers from the AMT calculation. Because the stock basis adjustments for regular tax and AMT purposes may differ (e.g., different amounts of expenses), the sale of subsidiary stock may result in different gain or loss amounts for the two purposes.

income. Assume that the portions of the consolidated tax liability allocable to S and T are \$34,000 (\$100,000 × 0.34) and \$17,000 (\$50,000 × 0.34), respectively, and that each pays its allocable portion. S increases the basis in its T stock to \$533,000 (\$500,000 + \$50,000 − \$17,000). P increases the basis in its S stock to \$899,000 (\$800,000 + \$100,000 − \$34,000 + \$50,000 − \$17,000), reflecting adjustments for both tiers below P. ◀

EXCESS LOSS ACCOUNT

If the negative basis adjustments (e.g., for losses and distributions) are sufficiently large, the parent reduces its basis in the subsidiary stock to zero. Additional negative basis adjustments create or increase an excess loss account. Creation of or change in the balance of an excess loss account does not trigger recognition of income or gain. Instead, it is treated as negative basis. Subsequent profits or other positive basis adjustments first reduce or eliminate the excess loss account before producing a positive basis in the subsidiary stock. A corporation disposing of a subsidiary's stock recognizes its excess loss account in the disposed shares as income or gain from the disposition.[57]

EXAMPLE C:8-49 ▶ P Corporation owns all of S Corporation's stock, and the two corporations have filed on a consolidated basis for several years. P's basis in its S stock was \$900,000 at the beginning of the current year. During the current year, S incurs a \$950,000 NOL, which offsets part of P's \$2.5 million of taxable income. On January 1 of the next year, P sells its S stock for \$80,000. P first reduces its basis in the S stock to zero, and the remaining \$50,000 (\$950,000 − \$900,000) of the negative adjustment creates an excess loss account. When P sells the S stock, it recognizes a \$130,000 gain (\$80,000 amount realized − \$0 basis + \$50,000 excess loss account). ◀

TAX PLANNING CONSIDERATIONS

OBJECTIVE 8

Compare the advantages and disadvantages of filing a consolidated tax return

Filing a consolidated tax return has several advantages and disadvantages as discussed below. Thus, the decision whether or not to file a consolidated tax return is one of an affiliated group's tax planning considerations.

ADVANTAGES OF FILING A CONSOLIDATED TAX RETURN

- The consolidated group can offset one member's operating losses against another member's operating profits. This offset usually is beneficial because it allows the losses to immediately reduce taxes. If the group members filed separate returns, the losses carry back or forward as an NOL. However, discounting decreases the present value of the tax savings from an NOL that carries forward.
- The group can offset one member's net capital loss against another member's net capital gain. Again, this offset allows the net loss to immediately reduce taxes, and it reduces the chance that the losses will expire unused.
- The group computes various credit and deduction limitations on a consolidated basis (e.g., charitable contributions). If the group members filed separate tax returns, some members' credits or deductions might be only partially used due to the limitations, while other members' credits or deductions fall short of the limitations. By filing a consolidated tax return, group members with "excess" credits or deductions can take advantage of other members' "excess" limitations.
- In the consolidated tax return, the group eliminates dividends paid from one group member to another group member. However, the recipient member would be eligible for a 100% dividends-received deduction if they filed separate tax returns.
- The group defers gains and profits on intercompany transactions, which reduces the present value of the taxes on these items (assuming tax rates do not increase).

[57] Reg. Sec. 1.1502-19.

- The parent corporation (and upper tier corporations) increase their bases in subsidiary (and lower tier corporation) stock investments for the subsidiary's (and lower tier corporations') taxable income, much like pass-through entities, thereby eliminating multiple taxation at the higher tier levels.
- The group calculates its alternative minimum tax (AMT) on a consolidated basis. If the group members filed separate tax returns, some group members might incur an AMT because they have large amounts of AMT preference and adjustment items, while other group members have no AMT because they have relatively few preference and adjustment items. If the group files a consolidated tax return, members with "excess" tentative minimum taxes can use them to take advantage of other members' "excess" regular taxes.

DISADVANTAGES OF FILING A CONSOLIDATED TAX RETURN

- The group must continue to file consolidated tax returns for all subsequent tax years until the affiliated group terminates or the IRS grants permission for the group to discontinue filing on a consolidated basis. By filing a consolidated tax return, the group forfeits the flexibility to choose between filing on a separate or consolidated basis in future years.
- Offsetting one member's losses against other members' profits or gains reduces the limitations on various deductions and credits (e.g., charitable contributions), which may reduce the amounts of such items currrently allowed on a consolidated basis compared to those allowed on a separate return basis.
- All group members must use the same taxable year.
- The group defers losses and deductions on intercompany transactions, which reduces the present value of the tax savings on these items (assuming tax rates do not increase).
- The group may incur additional administrative costs to maintain the records necessary to account for intercompany transactions and the special loss limitations although it may realize some savings by filing a single tax return.

No general rule can be applied to determine whether an affiliated group should elect to file a consolidated tax return. Each group should examine the long- and short-term advantages and disadvantages of filing a consolidated tax return instead of separate tax returns before making this decision.

COMPLIANCE AND PROCEDURAL CONSIDERATIONS

OBJECTIVE 9

Comply with the procedures for making a consolidated return election

THE BASIC ELECTION AND RETURN

As discussed earlier in this chapter, an affiliated group elects to file its tax return on a consolidated basis by filing a corporate tax return (Form 1120) that includes the income, expenses, etc. of all its members. The group must make the election no later than the due date for the common parent's tax return including any permitted extensions.[58] Each corporation that is a member of the affiliated group during the initial consolidated return year must consent to the election. The parent corporation consents by joining in the consolidated tax return. Each subsidiary corporation consents to the election by filing Form 1122 (Authorization and Consent of Subsidiary Corporation To Be Included in a Consolidated Income Tax Return) as part of the initial consolidated tax return. Only newly acquired subsidiary corporations file Form 1122 with subsequent consolidated tax returns.

Each year's consolidated tax return also must include Form 851 (Affiliations Schedule). This form includes names, addresses, and identification numbers of the

[58] Reg. Sec. 1.1502-75(a)(1).

corporations in the consolidated group; the corporations' tax prepayments; the ownership of their stock at the beginning of the tax year; and all stock ownership changes occurring during the tax year. Treasury Regulations require the group to file supporting statements with its consolidated tax return. These statements show in columnar form a reconciliation of the members' taxable incomes with consolidated taxable income, and they also show the details of each member's gross income and deductions so the IRS can readily audit them.[59] An example of such a reconciliation appears in the consolidated tax return included in Appendix B.

Similar to unaffiliated corporations, the due date for the consolidated tax return is the fifteenth day of the third month after the end of the consolidated group's tax year. A six-month extension for filing the tax return is allowed if the parent corporation files Form 7004 (Application for Automatic Extension of Time To File Certain Business Income Tax, Information, and Other Returns) and pays the estimated balance of the consolidated tax liability. If a subsidiary corporation enters or departs the consolidated group, the due date for its separate tax return for the part of the year it was not affiliated with the group depends on the date the group files its consolidated tax return.[60]

Appendix B presents a sample Form 1120 for reporting the current year's results for the Alpha affiliated group described in Example C:8-50. The Form 1120 involves the three intercompany transactions mentioned in the example, and a worksheet that summarizes the income and expense items for the five companies illustrates the reporting of the intercompany transactions and presents the details of the consolidated taxable income calculation.

EXAMPLE C:8-50 ▶ Alpha Manufacturing Corporation owns 100% of Beta, Charlie, Delta, and Echo Corporations' stock. The affiliated group has filed consolidated tax returns for several years using the calendar year as its tax year. The five corporations' separate taxable income components are reported on the supporting schedule of the group's consolidated tax return contained in Appendix B. This return illustrates the following three common transactions involving members of a consolidated group:

- The sale of inventory from Alpha to Beta, the profit from which is deferred for consolidated taxable income. Beta sells additional inventory to outsiders.
- Intragroup dividends paid from Beta and Echo to Alpha
- Payment of interest from Delta to Alpha ◀

ADDITIONAL COMMENT

If an affiliated group is considering making a consolidated return election, a properly executed Form 1122 should be obtained before any corporation is sold during the election year. After the sale, the consent form may be difficult to obtain.

ADDITIONAL COMMENT

The treatment for state income tax purposes of corporations affiliated for federal income tax purposes varies. Many states allow such corporations to file on a separate or consolidated basis, but several other states require combined unitary reporting, which is somewhat similar to consolidated reporting. The corporations comprising a consolidated or unitary reporting group for state income tax purposes often differs from those comprising an affiliated group for federal income tax purposes (e.g., 50% rather than 80% minimum ownership).

Students should review this sample return to see how the group reports the transactions and how it transfers the numbers from the consolidated taxable income schedule to the consolidated group's Form 1120. Although not displayed in Appendix B, the consolidated return should include a Schedule M-3 if applicable (see Chapter C:3).

PARENT CORPORATION AS AGENT FOR THE CONSOLIDATED GROUP

A consolidated group's parent corporation generally acts as the sole agent for all matters relating to the group's consolidated tax liability.[61] This agency role means that a subsidiary corporation cannot act in its own behalf with respect to a consolidated return year except to the extent that Treasury Regulations prohibit the parent from acting in the subsidiary's behalf. For example, the parent, not the subsidiary, makes or changes any election used in computing the subsidiary's separate taxable income, corresponds with the IRS regarding a tax liability determination, files any requests for extensions of time in which to file a tax return, files a claim for a refund or credit relating to a consolidated return year, or elects to deduct or credit foreign tax payments.

---

59 Reg. Sec. 1.1502-75(j).

60 Reg. Sec. 1.1502-76(c). The details of these rules are beyond the scope of this text.

61 Reg. Sec. 1.1502-77(a).

SEPARATE ENTITY TREATMENT OF INTERCOMPANY TRANSACTIONS

The consolidated group's common parent can request consent from the IRS to treat the group's intercompany transactions on a separate entity basis, where the transactions are treated as if the group members involved were not members of the same consolidated group. When deciding whether to grant such consent, the IRS considers whether such treatment reduces the group's tax compliance burden and whether it has more than a 5% effect on the group's consolidated taxable income or consolidated tax liability. The group can make the request for all its intercompany transactions (other than those involving group members' stock or obligations) or only one or more classes of intercompany transactions. The group applies such separate entity treatment for the consolidated return year for which the IRS grants consent and subsequent tax years. The group's common parent can revoke such separate entity treatment if the IRS consents to it, and the IRS can revoke the group's use of such treatment.[62]

TAX STRATEGY TIP

Because of the several liability rule, the purchaser of a consolidated group's subsidiary should consider obtaining an agreement under which the purchaser will be reimbursed for any additional taxes, interest, and penalties the IRS assesses the subsidiary that are attributable to other group members.

LIABILITY FOR TAXES DUE

The parent corporation and every other corporation that was a group member for any part of the consolidated return year are liable for that year's consolidated tax liability.[63] Thus, the IRS may collect the entire consolidated tax liability from one group member if the other group members are unable to pay their allocable portion of the tax. The IRS can ignore any agreements among the group members to limit their share of the tax liability. A corporation that is a member of a consolidated group for even a few days during a tax year can be liable for the entire year's consolidated tax liability and related deficiencies.

An exception to this several liability rule occurs when a subsidiary corporation departs the consolidated group because its stock is sold or exchanged before the IRS assesses a deficiency against the group. The IRS can opt to assess a former subsidiary for only its allocable portion of the total deficiency if the IRS believes that the assessment and collection of the balance of the deficiency from the other group members will not be jeopardized.

FINANCIAL STATEMENT IMPLICATIONS

OBJECTIVE 10

Explain the financial statement implications of various consolidated transactions

INTERCOMPANY TRANSACTIONS

Intercompany transactions can raise deferred tax issues depending on the type of transaction and whether the affiliated group files consolidated tax returns or separate tax returns. The following discussion assumes a 100%-owned domestic subsidiary to avoid the complications of accounting for noncontrolling interests and for foreign subsidiaries. It also addresses just two types of intercompany transactions: (1) distributed and undistributed subsidiary profits and (2) intercompany sales of property.

For a parent with a 100%-owned domestic subsidiary, intercompany dividends and undistributed subsidiary earnings cause no temporary differences. If the group files a consolidated tax return, the intercompany dividend is eliminated for both tax and consolidated financial statement purposes. If the group files separate tax returns, the parent takes a 100% dividends-received deduction because it owns at least 80% of the subsidiary's stock. Therefore, in either case, no book-tax difference occurs that would create a temporary difference. Undistributed subsidiary earnings are included in consolidated financial statements, but a parent filing a separate tax return would not include these earnings in its income until the subsidiary distributes them as dividends. However, when ultimately distributed, the parent can take the 100% dividends-received deduction, thereby offsetting the dividend income. Consequently, undistributed subsidiary earnings also present no deferred tax issues (within the assumed parameters of this discussion).

---

[62] Reg. Sec. 1.1502-13(e)(3) and Rev. Proc. 2009-31, 2009-27 I.R.B. 107.

[63] Reg. Sec. 1.1502-6(a).

ADDITIONAL COMMENT

Although a consolidated group defers income or loss on intercompany sales for both tax and financial statement purposes, the amount of income or loss deferred may differ.

ADDITIONAL COMMENT

According to an internal memorandum, the FASB is considering a change to its accounting standards that would require the recognition of deferred tax consequences of intra-group asset transfers.

Intercompany sales, however, do raise deferred tax issues in certain cases. If the group files a consolidated tax return, the group defers income or loss on intercompany sales of inventory and other property for both tax and consolidated financial statement purposes. Thus, temporary differences and deferred tax issues do not arise. On the other hand, if the group members each file a separate tax return, the selling member recognizes income or loss for tax purposes but not for consolidated financial statement purposes, thereby creating a temporary difference. Accounting Standards Codification (ASC) 810, (formerly ARB No. 51) requires the group to defer recognizing income taxes on intercompany profits on assets remaining within the group,[64] but ASC 740 (formerly SFAS No. 109) prohibits "recognition of a deferred tax asset for the intra-entity difference between the tax basis of the assets in the buyer's tax jurisdiction and their cost as reported in the consolidated financial statements."[65] Thus, even though the buyer's tax basis (the intercompany purchase price) may exceed the financial statement basis (e.g., the original cost), the group does not recognize a deferred tax asset. Instead, the group recognizes a prepaid asset for the seller's tax on the intercompany profit.

EXAMPLE C:8-51 ▶ Parent forms Subsidiary on January 2 of the current year as a 100%-owned subsidiary. The corporations have no temporary or permanent differences aside from those that might arise on intercompany transactions. For the current year, Parent and Subsidiary report the following transactions:

	Parent	*Subsidiary*
Net income before intercompany transactions and income taxes	$300,000	$120,000
Profit on sale of inventory from Parent to Subsidiary	50,000	
Profit on partial sale of same inventory from Subsidiary to third parties		6,000
Dividend from Subsidiary to Parent	40,000	

The $50,000 profit to Parent is the difference between the inventory's $60,000 cost to Parent and its $110,000 selling price to Subsidiary. Subsidiary, in turn, sold 30% of this inventory to third parties for $39,000. This portion of the inventory had a $33,000 ($110,000 × 0.30) tax basis to Subsidiary, thereby generating the $6,000 profit.

If Parent and Subsidiary file a consolidated tax return for the current year, the $40,000 intercompany dividend and the $35,000 ($50,000 × 0.70) profit in the remaining inventory will be eliminated in both the consolidated financial statements and the consolidated tax return, leaving no temporary differences. Thus, consolidated taxable income (as well as net income before federal income taxes will equal $441,000 ($300,000 + $120,000 + $50,000 + $40,000 + $6,000 − $40,000 − $35,000)), and the federal income tax liability will be $149,940 ($441,000 × 0.34). Accordingly, the group makes the following book journal entry:

Federal income tax expense	149,940	
Federal income taxes payable		149,940

If instead Parent and Subsidiary file separate tax returns, Parent will claim a $40,000 dividends-received deduction. Parent, however, will eliminate the $35,000 inventory profit deferred for consolidated financial statement purposes but not for tax purposes. Thus, Parent's separate taxable income will be $350,000 ($300,000 + $50,000 + $40,000 − $40,000), and Subsidiary's taxable income will be $126,000 ($120,000 + $6,000). Even though Parent and Subsidiary do not file a consolidated tax return, they still comprise a parent-subsidiary controlled group. Consequently, Sec. 1563 limits the use of the 15% and 25% tax brackets. However, because the group's total taxable income ($350,000 + $126,000) exceeds $335,000, the benefit of the low brackets is completely phased out. Consequently, all taxable income for the group is taxed a flat 34% tax rate, giving Parent a $119,000 ($350,000 × 0.34) tax liability and Subsidiary a $42,840 ($126,000 × 0.34) tax liability, for a total of $161,840. At the same time, the group's consolidated net income before federal income taxes remains at $441,000, which is $35,000 ($350,000 + $126,000 − $441,000) less than the group's total taxable income. The group records as prepaid taxes the $11,900 ($35,000 × 0.34) tax that Parent pays on the eliminated intercompany inventory profit, so

[64] Accounting Standards Codification (ASC) 810-10-45-8.

[65] Accounting Standards Codification (ASC) 740-10-25-3.

the group's federal income tax expense is $149,940 ($161,840 − $11,900). This $149,940 also equals 34% of the group's $441,000 consolidated net income before federal income taxes. Accordingly, the group makes the following book journal entry:

Federal income tax expense	149,940	
Prepaid taxes	11,900	
Federal income taxes payable		161,840

Next year, Parent and Subsidiary earn the same income before intercompany transactions ($300,000 and $120,000, respectively) and file separate tax returns. However, they have no intercompany transactions next year, and Subsidiary sells the remaining inventory to third parties for a $14,000 profit. Thus, Parent's taxable income is $300,000, and Subsidiary's taxable income is $134,000 ($120,000 + $14,000). In addition, Parent's tax liability is $102,000 ($300,000 × 0.34), and Subsidiary's tax liability is $45,560 ($134,000 × 0.34), for a total of $147,560. At the same time, the group's consolidated net income after recognizing the $35,000 deferred profit but before federal income taxes is $469,000 ($300,000 + $134,000 + $35,000). The group now charges to federal income tax expense the $11,900 it previously recorded as prepaid taxes in the year the intercompany sale occurred, so the group's federal income tax expense is $159,460 ($147,560 + $11,900). This $159,460 also equals 34% of the group's $469,000 consolidated net income before federal income taxes. Accordingly, the group makes the following book journal entry:

Federal income tax expense	159,460	
Prepaid taxes		11,900
Federal income taxes payable		147,560

◀

SRLY LOSSES

A net operating loss (NOL) from a separate return limitation year (SRLY) will create a deferred tax asset, possibly subject to a valuation allowance.

EXAMPLE C:8-52 ▶ Parent Corporation acquires 100% of Subsidiary Corporation at the beginning of the current year, when Subsidiary has a $200,000 NOL. Parent and Subsidiary elect to file a consolidated tax return for the current year. Assuming Parent's acquisition of Subsidiary is not a Sec. 382 ownership change, the SRLY limitation restricts the Parent-Subsidiary group's use of Subsidiary's NOL. Accordingly, management estimates that the group will be able to use only $150,000 of the NOL before it expires. The group's tax rate is 34%. The deferred tax asset is $68,000 ($200,000 × 0.34), and the valuation allowance is $17,000 ($50,000 × 0.34).

If Parent's acquisition of Subsidiary qualifies as a Sec. 382 ownership change, the SRLY limitation does not apply because of the overlap rule. However, the Sec. 382 limitation applies to restrict the group's use of Subsidiary's NOL. Assuming management estimates that the group will be able to use only $140,000 of the NOL before it expires, the deferred tax asset is $68,000 ($200,000 × 0.34), and the valuation allowance is $20,400 ($60,000 × 0.34).

If Parent and Subsidiary file separate tax returns, Subsidiary's use of its own NOL is restricted. If Parent's acquisition of Subsidiary does not qualify as a Sec. 382 ownership change, Subsidiary can use the $200,000 NOL only to offset the taxable income on its separate tax return, which restricts Subsidiary's use of its own NOL in much the same was as the SRLY limitation restricts it on a consolidated tax return. If the acquisition qualifies as a Sec. 382 ownership change, Subsidiary's use of its own NOL is limited to the same Sec. 382 limitation that applies had the corporations file a consolidated tax return. ◀

See Chapter C:3 for a general discussion of financial implications of federal income taxes.

PROBLEM MATERIALS

DISCUSSION QUESTIONS

C:8-1 What minimum level of stock ownership does the IRC require for a corporation to be included in an affiliated group?

C:8-2 Which of the following entities are includible in an affiliated group (if the 80% stock ownership requirements are met)?
a. Domestic C corporation.
b. Foreign corporation.
c. Life insurance company taxed under Sec. 801.
d. Limited liability company.

C:8-3 Pamela (an individual) owns 100% of P Corporation's stock and 100% of R Corporation's stock. P owns 100% of S Corporation's stock and 49% of T Corporation's stock. S owns the remaining 51% of T's stock. All the corporations are includible corporations and have only one class of stock.
a. Which entities comprise an affiliated group?
b. Which entities comprise a controlled group?
c. How would your answer to Part a change if S were instead a foreign corporation?

C:8-4 P Corporation purchases all of S Corporation's stock in the current year. Both corporations are includible corporations. S is P's only subsidiary. Explain their federal income tax return filing alternatives.

C:8-5 How do the stock ownership requirements for an affiliated group of corporations differ from those for a controlled group?

C:8-6 P Corporation owns 100% of the stock of S1 and S2 Corporations. S1 owns 51% of S3 Corporation's stock, and unrelated persons own the remaining 49%. S2 is a foreign corporation. Explain why the corporations included in a consolidated tax return can differ from the corporations included in a set of consolidated financial statements.

C:8-7 Explain why the consolidated return Treasury Regulations are legislative regulations.

C:8-8 P Corporation has owned all the stock of S and T Corporations for several years. P sells all of T's stock to Z Corporation during the current year.
a. Does P's sale of T's stock cause the affiliated group to cease to exist?
b. Is T required to file a consolidated tax return with Z?
c. If P purchases all of T's stock from Z three years after it sells T's stock to Z, is T required to file a consolidated tax return with P and S?
d. How would your answers change if P did not own any of S's stock?

C:8-9 P Corporation owns all the stock of S and T Corporations, and the three corporations elected to file a consolidated tax return for the prior year. What circumstances would allow the corporations to file separate tax returns for the current year?

C:8-10 Define the following terms:
a. Intercompany transaction.
b. Intercompany item.
c. Corresponding item.
d. Recomputed corresponding item.
e. Matching rule.
f. Acceleration rule.

C:8-11 P and S1 Corporations have filed consolidated tax returns for several years. S1 acquires all of S2 Corporation's stock at the close of business on June 15 of the current year. Which of the following current year transactions are intercompany transactions?
a. S1 sells machinery (Sec. 1245 property) to S2 on September 1.
b. P sells inventory to S1 throughout the year.
c. S2 performs services for S1 throughout the year.
d. P sells inventory to the S1-S2 Partnership on July 23. S1 and S2 are equal partners in the partnership.

C:8-12 P, S1, and S2 Corporations comprise a consolidated group. The group members use the accrual method of accounting. For each of the following intercompany transactions that occur during the current year, determine the intercompany item and corresponding item.
a. P lends S1 money, and P charges interest at a 10% annual rate. The money and interest remain unpaid at the end of the tax year.
b. S1 sells inventory to P. At year end, P holds the entire inventory purchased from S1.
c. P sells land (Sec. 1231 property) to S2. S2 holds the land (Sec. 1231 property) at year-end.
d. S1 provides engineering services that are capitalized as part of the cost of S2's new factory building.

C:8-13 One consolidated group member lends money to another member of its group. Both corporations use the accrual method of accounting. Explain how the lending group member reports its interest income and how the borrowing group member reports its interest expense for consolidated tax return purposes. Discuss how this treatment compares to the consolidated financial accounting treatment of the transaction.

C:8-14 Brooklyn and Bronx Corporations become an affiliated group at the beginning of the current year. Will the corporations obtain a greater charitable contribution deduction for the current year by filing a consolidated tax return or separate tax returns?

C:8-15 An affiliated group elects to file a consolidated tax return. Explain why the group's consolidated capital gain net income or net capital loss is not merely the sum of the members' separate capital gain net incomes and net capital losses if they were to file separate tax returns.

C:8-16 Indicate the tax treatment for each of the following dividends received by a corporation that is a member of an affiliated group filing a consolidated tax return:

a. Dividend received from a corporation that is 5%-owned by the group member.
b. Dividend received from a corporation that is 100%-owned by the group member.
c. Dividend received from a foreign corporation that is 80%-owned by the group's parent corporation.
d. Dividend received from a life insurance company that is 100%-owned by the group's parent corporation.
e. Dividend received from a corporation that is 50%-owned by the group member and 50%-owned by the group's parent corporation.

C:8-17 P, S, and T Corporations comprise a consolidated group. In the current year, P has a profit, while S and T both incur a loss. The net of P's profit with S's and T's losses result in a consolidated NOL. In what years can P, S, and/or T deduct the consolidated NOL?

C:8-18 An affiliated group has a consolidated NOL for the current year. What factors could determine whether it would be advantageous or disadvantageous for the group to elect to forgo the carryback of the consolidated NOL?

C:8-19 Define the term SRLY and explain its significance and application to a consolidated tax return.

C:8-20 What is the SRLY-Sec. 382 overlap rule? Explain its significance and application to a consolidated tax return.

C:8-21 P Corporation owns 100% of S Corporation's stock, and the corporations file a consolidated tax return.

a. Explain why P must increase the basis in its S stock by S's taxable income and decrease the basis by the dividends S pays to P.
b. Suppose S owns 100% of T Corporation's stock. Explain the basis adjustments that P and S must make.

C:8-22 P Corporation owns 100% of the stock of S1 and S2 Corporations. The corporations currently are filing separate tax returns. P and S1 are profitable. S2 is a start-up company that has reported losses for its first two years of operations. S1 eventually will be purchasing cosmetics from S2 and reselling them to retailers. What are the advantages and disadvantages of the three corporations filing a consolidated tax return?

C:8-23 The president of your CPA firm's largest client, a medium-size manufacturing company, advises you that the firm is about to acquire its largest supplier. Both companies have been profitable for the past ten years. The president wants to know what tax return filing options are available for the two companies and the advantages and disadvantages of the options. What factors are likely to be most important for this decision? What additional information do you need to give the president an informed answer?

C:8-24 During what time period can an affiliated group elect to file a consolidated tax return? How does it make the election? During what time period can it request to terminate its consolidation?

C:8-25 For which of the following tax-related matters can an affiliated group's parent corporation act as the group's agent?

a. Making an initial consent for a subsidiary corporation to participate in a consolidated return election.
b. Changing an accounting method election for a subsidiary corporation.
c. Carrying on correspondence with the IRS during an audit regarding a transaction entered into by a subsidiary corporation that affects the group's determination of consolidated taxable income.
d. Requesting an extension of time within which to file a consolidated tax return.

ISSUE IDENTIFICATION QUESTIONS

C:8-26 Mark owns all the stock of Red and Green Corporations. Red has been reporting $125,000 in taxable income for each of the past five years. Green has been reporting $30,000 NOLs annually, which have accumulated to $150,000. Approximately one-third of Red's profits come from sales to Green. Intercompany sales between Red and Green have increased during each of the last five years. What tax issues should Mark consider with respect to his investments in Red and Green Corporations?

C:8-27 Alpha and Baker Corporations, two accrual method of accounting corporations that use the calendar year as their tax year, have filed consolidated tax returns for several years. Baker, a 100%-owned subsidiary of Alpha, is transferring a patent, equipment, and working capital to newly created Charter Corporation in exchange for 100% of its stock. In the current year, Charter will begin to produce parts for the automotive industry. Charter expects to incur organizational expenditures of $12,000 and start-up expenditures of $60,000. What tax issues should Charter consider with respect to the selection of its overall accounting method, inventory method, and tax year, the proper reporting of its organizational and start-up expenditures, and the type of income tax return to file?

C:8-28 Wildcat Corporation is the parent company of a three-member affiliated group. Wildcat and Badger Corporations have filed consolidated tax returns for several years. Early in the current year, Wildcat purchases Hawkeye Corporation, a start-up business that incurred net operating losses in each of its first three years prior to the purchase. Hawkeye's losses total $260,000. Can the Wildcat-Badger-Hawkeye group deduct the losses on its consolidated tax return? The group expects annual profits to be $300,000, with Hawkeye's contribution to the total being $50,000. What tax issues should the three corporations consider when determining how they can deduct the NOLs?

PROBLEMS

C:8-29 *Affiliated Group Definition.* In each of the following cases, determine the corporations that comprise an affiliated group. All corporations are includible corporations and have one class of stock.

a. B Corporation owns 100% of C Corporation's stock and 90% of D Corporation's stock. Unrelated persons own 10% of D's stock.
b. B Corporation owns 100% of C Corporation's stock and 90% of D Corporation's stock. C owns 80% of E Corporation's stock, and D owns 75% of F Corporation's stock. Unrelated persons own the remainder of D's, E's, and F's stock.
c. B Corporation owns 80% of C Corporation's stock and 40% of D Corporation's stock. C owns 41% of D's stock. Unrelated individuals own the remainder of C's and D's stock.
d. Luciano, an individual, owns all the stock of M and N Corporations.
e. Viviana, an individual, owns all the stock of W and X Corporations. W owns all of Y Corporation's stock, and X owns all of Z Corporation's stock.

C:8-30 *Affiliated Group Definition* In each of the following cases, determine the corporations that comprise an affiliated group. All corporations are includible corporations and have one class of stock unless otherwise indicated.

a. P Corporation owns all the stock of S and T Corporations. T owns all of U Corporation's stock. T and U are Belgian corporations.
b. Assume the same facts as in Part a except U is a domestic corporation.
c. Omar, an individual, owns 100% of P Corporation's stock and 30% of S Corporation's stock. P owns 70% of S's stock.
d. G is a German corporation. G owns all of P Corporation's stock. P owns all of S Corporation's stock.
e. P Corporation owns all of S Corporation's stock. P and S each own 50% of T, a domestic limited liability company.

C:8-31 *Stock Ownership Requirement.* Pierre Corporation's management is negotiating with Salem Corporation's management to purchase some of Salem's stock. Salem's outstanding shares are as follows:

Type of Stock	*Votes per Share*	*Shares Outstanding*	*FMV per Share*
Common stock	4	60,000	$40
Preferred stock	1	10,000	75

Pierre's management wants to acquire enough Salem stock to allow Pierre and Salem to file a consolidated tax return. Pierre and Salem are includible corporations.

a. If Pierre acquires all of Salem's common stock and none of Salem's preferred stock, will they be eligible to file a consolidated tax return?
b. What minimum amount of Salem's common stock and/or preferred stock must Pierre acquire for the two corporations to be eligible to file a consolidated tax return?
c. Suppose that Salem also has 10,000 shares of nonvoting preferred stock outstanding. Each share's FMV is $90. The stock is nonparticipating, has redemption and liquidation rights limited to its issue price, and is not convertible. If Pierre acquires all of Salem's common and voting preferred stock, what minimum amount of Salem nonvoting preferred stock must Pierre acquire for the two corporations to be eligible to file a consolidated tax return?

C:8-32 *Affiliated Group Termination.* P Corporation owns all of S Corporation's stock. P and S have filed consolidated tax returns for several years. Determine whether the affiliated group terminates in each of the following circumstances. Assume that all corporations use the calendar year as their tax year.

a. On February 1 of the current year, P purchases all of T Corporation's stock.
b. On March 1 of the current year, P purchases all of T Corporation's stock. On October 1 of the current year, P sells all of S's stock.
c. On April 1 of the current year, P sells all of S's stock. On September 1 of the current year, P purchases all of T Corporation's stock.
d. On May 1 of the current year, P sells all of S's stock. On January 1 of the next year, P purchases all of T Corporation's stock.
e. On June 1, R Corporation purchases all of P's stock. R had no subsidiaries prior to June 1.
f. On July 1, R Corporation purchases all of P's stock. On July 1, R has several wholly owned subsidiaries with which it has filed consolidated tax returns for several years.

C:8-33 *Consolidated Taxable Income.* Assume the same facts as in Problem C:8-32. What tax returns must the corporations file for the current year?

C:8-34 *Consolidated Taxable Income.* P Corporation owns all the stock of S1 and S2 Corporations. The corporations have filed calendar year, consolidated tax returns for several years. On September 15 of the current year, P sells all of S1's stock to Michelle, an unrelated individual. What effect does P's sale of S1's stock have on the P-S1-S2 group's current year consolidated taxable income?

C:8-35 *Consolidated Return Election.* P Corporation uses the calendar year as its tax year and the accrual method as its overall accounting method. S Corporation uses a fiscal year ending June 30 as its tax year and the cash method as its overall accounting method. On July 31, 2016, P acquires all of S's stock, and the P-S affiliated group elects to file a consolidated tax return for 2016.

a. What tax year must the group use in filing its consolidated tax return?
b. What overall accounting method(s) can P and S Corporations use?
c. What tax returns must the corporations file?

C:8-36 *Consolidated Taxable Income.* P Corporation acquires all the stock of S Corporation on October 15 of the current year, which is the 288th day of the year (and not a leap year). Neither corporation is affiliated with another corporation prior to the acquisition. P and S use the accrual method of accounting, and each uses the calendar year as its taxable year. P's and S's income for the current year, which includes no extraordinary items, are $876,000 and $292,000, respectively. For each of the following circumstances, what tax returns must the corporations file for the current year, and what amount of income must each of those returns include?

a. P and S elect to file a consolidated tax return and also elect to ratably allocate the entering subsidiary's income.
b. P and S do not elect to file a consolidated tax return.

C:8-37 *Intercompany Transactions.* P, S1, and S2 Corporations have filed consolidated tax returns for several years. In the current year (Year 1), S1 sells land to S2 for $275,000. S1 purchased the land for $120,000 several years ago and has held it for possible expansion. S2 constructs a new plant facility on the land. In Year 3, S2 sells the land and the plant facility to a third party for cash, with $400,000 of the sales price attributable to the land.

a. What are the intercompany item, the corresponding item, and the recomputed corresponding item for this intercompany transaction?
b. In what year(s) are S1's gain or loss and S2's gain or loss included in consolidated taxable income?

C:8-38 *Intercompany Transactions.* P Corporation owns all the stock of S and B Corporations. The three corporations have filed consolidated tax returns on a calendar year basis for several years. S owns property it had purchased for $40,000 several years ago. On August 1 of Year 1, S sells the property to B for $55,000. On February 1 of Year 3, B sells the property to an unrelated third party for $60,000.

a. What are the intercompany item, the corresponding item, and the recomputed corresponding item for this intercompany transaction?
b. In what year(s) are S's and B's gains or losses included in consolidated taxable income?

c. Suppose B sells the property to the third party for $53,000 instead of $60,000. How would your answers to Part b change?
d. Suppose P sells all of its B stock to an unrelated third party on October 1 of Year 2. How would your answers to Part b change?

C:8-39 *Intercompany Transactions.* P Corporation owns all the stock of S1 and S2 Corporations, and the three corporations have filed consolidated tax returns on a calendar year basis for several years. P owns 2,400 shares of publicly traded stock it purchased several years ago for $30 per share. P sells all the stock to S1 for $45 per share on January 25 of the current year (Year 1). S1 sells 1,400 shares of the stock to a third party for $48 per share on December 6 of Year 1, and S1 sells the other 1,000 shares to another third party for $52 per share on March 18 of Year 2.
a. What are the intercompany item, the corresponding items, and the recomputed corresponding items for this intercompany transaction?
b. In what year(s) are P's gain or loss and S1's gain or loss included in consolidated taxable income?
c. Suppose P sells all of S1's stock to a third party on December 30 of Year 1. How would your answer to Part b change?
d. Suppose S1 sells the 1,000 shares on March 18 of Year 2, for $44 per share instead of $52 per share. How would your answers to Parts a and b change?

C:8-40 *Intercompany Transactions.* P and S Corporations have filed consolidated tax returns for several years. In Year 1, P purchased land as an investment for $20,000. In Year 3, P sold the land to S for $60,000. S used the land for four years as additional parking space for its employees and made no improvements to the land. In Year 7, S sells the land to Z Corporation, an unrelated party, for $180,000. The sale's terms require Z to pay S $36,000 in each of Years 7 through 11. The terms also require Z to pay S interest at a rate acceptable to the IRS. Z pays all the required amounts.
a. What are the intercompany item, the corresponding items, and the recomputed corresponding items?
b. In what year(s) does the consolidated group include P's gain or loss and S's gain or loss in its taxable income?
c. How does the consolidated group report the interest income?

C:8-41 *Intercompany Transactions.* P owns all the stock of S1 and S2 Corporations. The corporations have filed consolidated tax returns for several years. In the current year (Year 1), S1 sells land to P for $100,000. S1 purchased the land several years earlier for $35,000. P sells the land to a unrelated third party in Year 3 for $115,000. The sale's terms require the third party to pay P $50,000 in Year 3, $40,000 in Year 4, and $25,000 in Year 5, plus interest at a rate acceptable to the IRS. The third party pays all the required amounts.
a. In what year(s) does the consolidated group include S1's gain or loss and P's gain or loss in its taxable income?
b. Suppose P sells all of S1's stock on December 31 of Year 4. How would this sale change your answer to Part a?
c. Suppose S1 sold the land to P in Year 1 for $120,000 instead of $100,000. How would this sale change your answer to Part a?

C:8-42 *Intercompany Transactions.* P Corporation owns all of S Corporation's stock. Both corporations use the accrual method of accounting, and they file a consolidated tax return. S provides cleaning services to P. In so doing, S charges P $6,000 for the services and incurs $5,000 of expenses to provide them. How does this transaction affect the group's consolidated taxable income?

C:8-43 *Intercompany Transactions.* P and S Corporations have filed consolidated tax returns on a calendar year basis for several years. Both corporations use the accrual method of accounting. On August 1 of the current year (Year 1), P loans S $250,000 on a one-year note. P charges interest at a 12% simple rate. S repays the loan plus interest on July 31 of Year 2. How does this intercompany transaction affect the group's consolidated taxable income?

C:8-44 *Intercompany Transactions.* P and S Corporations have filed consolidated tax returns on a calendar year basis for several years. Both corporations use the accrual method of accounting. On January 1 of the current year, S begins renting a warehouse to P for $10,000 per month. P pays S $10,000 on the first day of each month of the current year. How does this transaction affect the group's consolidated taxable income?

C:8-45 *Intercompany Transactions.* S and B corporations are members of an affiliated group that has filed consolidated tax returns for several years. S drills a water well for B in Year

1 and charges B $5,000 for the service. S incurs $4,400 of expenses when drilling the well. B capitalizes the $5,000 cost of its well and amortizes it over the five-year period Years 2 through 6. S and B both use the accrual method of accounting.

a. What are the intercompany item, the corresponding items, and the recomputed corresponding items for this intercompany transaction?

b. In what year(s) are S's profit or loss and B's deductions taken into account for consolidated taxable income?

C:8-46 *Intercompany Transactions.* P and S Corporations have filed consolidated tax returns for several years. In the current year (Year 1), P began selling inventory items to S. P and S use the first-in, first-out (FIFO) inventory method. P's profits on its Year 1 inventory sales to S are $75,000. S's sales to third parties during Year 1 include inventory items that P sells to S during Year 1 for a $40,000 profit; S sells these inventory items to third parties for a $25,000 profit. S's inventory at the end of Year 1 includes items that P sells to S for a $35,000 profit. S is deemed to sell these to third parties during Year 2 due to its use of the FIFO method and realizes a $22,000 profit on their sale. P's profits on its Year 2 inventory sales to S are $240,000. S's sales to third parties during Year 2 include items that P sells to S during Year 2 for a $160,000 profit. S sells these inventory items to third parties for a $105,000 profit. S's inventory at the end of Year 2 includes items that P sells to S for an $80,000 profit. The group's consolidated taxable income (before taking into account any adjustments for profits on intercompany inventory sales) is $100,000 in Year 1 and $367,000 in Year 2. For simplicity, assume P and S have no other transactions in these two years. Also, ignore the U.S. production activities deduction. What is the group's consolidated taxable income for Years 1 and 2?

C:8-47 *Intercompany Transactions.* P and S Corporations have filed consolidated tax returns for several years. The group had no intercompany inventory sales before the current year (Year 1). P and S use the first-in, first-out (FIFO) inventory method. During Year 1, S sells 50,000 widgets to P, earning $8 per unit profit on the sale. Also during Year 1, P sells 37,500 of these widgets to third parties for an additional $6 per unit profit. Thus, P's inventory at the end of Year 1 includes 12,500 of unsold widgets. During Year 2, S sells 80,000 widgets to P, earning $9 per unit profit on the sale. Also during Year 2, P sells to third parties 65,000 of these widgets and also sells the 12,500 widgets from beginning inventory, all for an additional $6 per unit profit. Thus, P's inventory at the end of Year 2 includes 15,000 widgets P purchased from S in Year 2. No intercompany inventory sales occur in Year 3. However, during Year 3, P sells all widgets in beginning inventory for an additional $7 per unit profit. In addition to these intercompany transactions, P incurs a $40,000 loss and S earns $500,000 of profit in each year from other business activities. What is the group's consolidated taxable income for each of Years 1, 2, and 3? Ignore the U.S. production activities deduction.

C:8-48 *Charitable Contribution Deduction.* Topeka and Wichita Corporations have filed consolidated tax returns for several years. Topeka and Wichita report current year taxable incomes (without regard to any dividend income received, charitable contribution deduction, or dividends-received deduction) of $200,000 and $150,000, respectively. The $200,000 includes $30,000 profit on inventory that Topeka sold to Wichita on December 29 of the current year. Wichita sold none of the inventory before the end of the year. Topeka and Wichita received dividends of $10,000 and $4,000, respectively, during the current year that qualify for the 70% dividends-received deduction. Wichita's and Topeka's cash contributions to public charities during the current year are $45,000 and $5,000, respectively. Ignore the U.S. production activities deduction.

a. What is the Topeka-Wichita group's consolidated taxable income?

b. What is the amount of the charitable contribution carryover? How long can it be carried back and/or forward?

c. What is the Topeka-Wichita group's regular tax liability?

C:8-49 *Sec. 1231 Gains and Losses and Capital Gains and Losses.* Mobile, Newark, and Omaha Corporations comprise an affiliated group that has filed separate tax returns prior to the current year. The corporations report the following amounts for the current year:

Transaction	*Mobile*	*Newark*	*Omaha*	*Total*
Sec. 1231 gains	$ 18,000	$ 9,000	$ –0–	$ 27,000
Sec. 1231 losses	12,000	14,000	–0–	26,000
Short-term capital gains	3,500	–0–	–0–	3,500
Short-term capital losses	(2,000)	–0–	(6,200)	(8,200)
Long-term capital gains	–0–	8,100	5,500	13,600
Long-term capital losses	(2,400)	(7,300)	–0–	(9,700)
Other separate taxable income	300,000	200,000	100,000	600,000

The corporations have no intercompany transactions, no capital loss carryovers, and no nonrecaptured net Sec. 1231 losses. Ignore the U.S. production activities deduction.

a. Determine each corporation's current year taxable income if they file separate tax returns for the current year.

b. Determine the group's current year taxable income if the corporations elect to file a consolidated tax return.

C:8-50 ***Capital Gains and Losses.*** Alpha and Beta Corporations comprise an affiliated group that has filed separate tax returns prior to the current year. The corporations report the following amounts for the current year:

Transaction	*Alpha*	*Beta*	*Total*
Long-term capital gains	$ 20,000	$ 15,000	$ 35,000
Long-term capital losses	(11,900)	(17,000)	(28,900)
Other separate taxable income	80,000	70,000	150,000

Alpha's long-term capital gains include a $4,400 gain on land it sold to Beta during the current year. Beta had not sold the land by the end of the current year. The corporations have no other intercompany transactions and no capital loss carryovers. Ignore the U.S. production activities deduction.

a. Determine each corporation's current year taxable income if they file separate tax returns for the current year.

b. Determine the group's current year taxable income if the corporations elect to file a consolidated tax return.

C:8-51 ***Dividends-Received Deduction.*** P, S, and T Corporations have filed consolidated tax returns for several years. P, S, and T report taxable incomes or losses (without regard to any dividends received and dividends-received deductions) of $200,000, $(70,000), and $175,000, respectively, for the current year. P and S received cash dividends this year as follows:

Shareholder	*Distributing Corporation*	*Amount*
P Corporation	T Corporation	$125,000
P Corporation	100%-owned nonconsolidated U.S.-based life insurance company	15,000
S Corporation	25%-owned domestic corporation	40,000
P Corporation	51%-owned foreign corporation	10,000

a. What amount of dividend income does the group include in its consolidated taxable income?

b. What is the amount of the consolidated dividends-received deduction?

c. What is the amount of consolidated taxable income and consolidated regular tax liability? Ignore the U.S. production activities deduction.

C:8-52 ***Regular Tax Liability.*** Miami and Tampa Corporations comprise a parent-subsidiary controlled group. The corporations also comprise an affiliated group that has filed separate tax returns prior to the current year. In each case for the current year, determine each corporation's regular tax liability if they file separate tax returns, and determine the group's consolidated regular tax liability if they elect to file a consolidated tax return. Ignore the U.S. production activities deduction. Assume that, if they file separate tax returns, Miami and Tampa do not elect a special apportionment plan for allocating the corporate tax rates. Assume also that, if the group elects to file a consolidated tax return, its consolidated taxable income equals the sum of Miami's and Tampa's separate taxable incomes.

a. Miami's separate taxable income is $50,000, and Tampa's separate taxable income is $30,000.

b. Miami's separate taxable income is $70,000, and Tampa's separate taxable income is $(15,000), i.e., a loss.

c. Miami's separate taxable income is $45,000, and Tampa's separate taxable income is $40,000.

C:8-53 ***Alternative Minimum Tax.*** Dallas and Houston Corporations comprise an affiliated group that formed at the beginning of the current year. The following items pertain to Dallas and Houston for the current year:

Transaction	*Dallas*	*Houston*	*Total*
Taxable income	$500,000	$400,000	$ 900,000
AMT preference & adjustment items	175,000	210,000	385,000
Adjusted current earnings	740,000	720,000	1,460,000

Determine each corporation's AMT liability if they file separate tax returns, and determine the group's consolidated AMT liability if they elect to file a consolidated tax return. Assume that, if the group elects to file a consolidated tax return, its consolidated taxable income, consolidated AMT preference and adjustment items, and consolidated adjusted current earnings equal the sum of the corporations' separate amounts. Assume also that the corporations do not qualify for the small corporation and first-year exemptions from the AMT. Ignore the U.S. production activities deduction.

C:8-54 ***General Business Credit.*** Peoria and Salem Corporations have filed consolidated tax returns for several years. For the current year, consolidated adjusted current earnings are $750,000. Consolidated preadjustment alternative minimum taxable income is $400,000. Consolidated taxable income is $300,000. The consolidated general business credit amount (computed without regard to the overall limitation) is $15,000. Assume the Peoria-Salem group is not eligible for the small corporation exemption from the AMT. Ignore the U.S. production activities deduction.

a. What is the group's federal tax liability?

b. Are any credit carryovers created in the current year? How are they used?

C:8-55 ***Consolidated NOL Carrybacks and Carryovers.*** P and S Corporations form in Year 1, with S as P's wholly-owned subsidiary. The corporations immediately elect to file consolidated tax returns. The group reports the following results:

	Taxable Income				
Group Member	*Year 1*	*Year 2*	*Year 3*	*Year 4*	*Year 5*
P	$9,000	$10,000	$(6,000)	$ 20,000	$15,000
S	(7,800)	2,000	2,000	(30,000)	10,000
Consolidated taxable income (before NOL deduction)	$1,200	$12,000	$(4,000)	$(10,000)	$25,000

The group does not elect to forego any NOL carrybacks. Ignore the U.S. production activities deduction. In what years can the group deduct the Years 3 and 4 consolidated NOLs?

C:8-56 ***Consolidated NOL Carryover.*** P Corporation owns all the stock of S1 and S2 Corporations. The corporations have filed consolidated tax returns since their creation in Year 1. At the close of business on July 10 of Year 3, P sells all of its S2 stock. The group reports the following results:

	Taxable Income		
Group Member	*Year 1*	*Year 2*	*Year 3*
P	$ 8,000	$(18,000)	$16,000
S1	9,000	(24,000)	(4,000)
S2	10,000	(28,000)	15,000[a]
Consolidated taxable income (before NOL deduction)	$27,000	$(70,000)	$19,000[b]

[a] $7,000 is attributable to January 1 through July 10 of Year 3, and $8,000 is attributable to July 11 through December 31 of Year 3.

[b] $16,000 − $4,000 + $7,000.

Ignore the U.S. production activities deduction.

a. In what year(s) can the corporations deduct the Year 2 consolidated NOL if the group does not elect to forego the carryback period?

b. In what year(s) can the corporations deduct the Year 2 consolidated NOL if the group elects to forego the carryback period?

C:8-57 *Consolidated NOL Carrybacks and Carryovers.* P Corporation owns all the stock of S Corporation, and P and S file a consolidated tax return. On January 1 of Year 2, P creates T Corporation and acquires all of its stock. P, S, and T report the following results for Years 1 through 3 (before any NOL deduction):

	Taxable Income		
Group Member	*Year 1*	*Year 2*	*Year 3*
P	$21,000	$22,000	$23,000
S	11,000	12,000	13,000
T		10,000	(50,000)
Consolidated taxable income	$32,000	$44,000	$(14,000)

The group does not elect to forego any NOL carrybacks. Ignore the U.S. production activities deduction.

a. In what year(s) can the group deduct the Year 3 NOL?

b. Assume the same facts as in Part a except a third party created T in Year 2 and P acquires all of T's stock from the third party on January 1 of Year 3. Thus, Year 2 consolidated taxable income is $34,000 ($22,000 + $12,000). In what year(s) can the group deduct the Year 3 NOL?

c. Assume the same facts as in Part a except the group does not begin filing consolidated tax returns until Year 3. In what year(s) can the group deduct the Year 3 NOL?

C:8-58 *Separate Return and Consolidated NOL Carryovers and Carrybacks.* P Corporation acquires all of S Corporation's stock on January 1 of Year 2. In Year 1, the corporations were unrelated entities that filed separate returns. P and S report the following results:

	Taxable Income		
Group Member	*Year 1*	*Year 2*	*Year 3*
P	$40,000	$(30,000)	$21,000
S	(29,000)	20,000	6,000
Consolidated taxable income (before NOL deduction)	N/A	$(10,000)	$ 27,000

N/A = Not applicable

Ignore the Sec. 382 loss limitation that might apply to P's acquisition of S, and ignore the U.S. production activities deduction.

a. What are the Year 2 tax consequences if P and S file a consolidated tax return? What are the Year 2 tax consequences if P and S instead file separate tax returns?

b. What are the Year 3 tax consequences if P and S file consolidated returns for Years 2 and 3?

C:8-59 *Consolidated NOL Carryovers and Intercompany Transactions.* P Corporation owns all the stock of S1 and S2 Corporations, and the group has filed consolidated tax returns on a calendar year basis for several years. In the current year (Year 1), S2 sells to S1 for $90,000 land S2 had purchased for $75,000. On December 31 of Year 2, S1 sells the land to a third party for $91,000. On January 18 of Year 3, P sells all of its S2 stock to a third party for a sales price equal to P's basis in the S2 stock. The consolidated group members report the following amounts of taxable income and loss (before deducting any NOLs or applying the matching and acceleration rules):

	Taxable Income (Loss)	
Group Member	*Year 2*	*Year 3*
P	$165,000	$(30,000)
S1	(120,000)	(20,000)
S2	(140,000)	7,000[a]
Consolidated taxable income or loss before deducting any NOLs or applying the matching and acceleration rules	$ (95,000)	$(43,000)

[a] Pertains to January 1 through January 18 of Year 3.

Assume that the group elects to forego the carryback period for the Year 2 consolidated NOL.

a. Determine the amount of NOL available for S2's Year 3 separate tax return.
b. Assume the same facts as in Part a except S1's land sale to a third party for $91,000 occurred on January 1 of Year 3. Determine the amount of NOL available for S2's Year 3 separate tax return.

C:8-60 *SRLY Limitation.* P Corporation acquires all of S Corporation's stock at the close of business on December 31 of Year 1. The corporations, which file on the calendar year, begin filing a consolidated tax return for Year 2. The corporations report the following taxable incomes (losses), before any NOL deduction, for Years 1 through 5:

	Taxable Income before NOL deduction				
Group Member	*Year 1*	*Year 2*	*Year 3*	*Year 4*	*Year 5*
P	$100,000	$125,000	$70,000	$(8,000)	$100,000
S	(63,000)	(15,000)	18,000	25,000	40,000
Consolidated taxable income (before NOL deduction)	N/A	$110,000	$ 88,000	$ 17,000	$140,000

N/A = Not applicable

P and S have no NOLs before Year 1, and S elects to forego the two-year carryback period for its Year 1 NOL. Ignore the Sec. 382 loss limitation that might apply to P's acquisition of S, assume that the acquisition does not qualify as a reverse acquisition, and ignore the U.S. production activities deduction. What is consolidated taxable income for each of Years 2 through 5?

C:8-61 *SRLY Limitation.* Bart, P's sole shareholder, creates P on January 1 of Year 1. P purchases all of S1's and S2's stock on September 1 of Year 1, after both corporations are in operation for about six months. P, S1, and S2 Corporations comprise the P-S1-S2 affiliated group and file separate tax returns for Year 1. The P-S1-S2 affiliated group then elects to file consolidated tax returns starting in Year 2. The group reports the following results:

	Taxable Income		
Group Member	*Year 1*	*Year 2*	*Year 3*
P	$(8,000)	$50,000	$10,000
S1	(24,000)	20,000	(18,000)
S2	(16,000)	(10,000)	15,000
Consolidated taxable income (before NOL deduction)	N/A	$60,000	$ 7,000

Ignore the Sec. 382 loss limitation that might apply to the acquisitions of S1 and S2, assume that P's purchase of S1 and S2 does not qualify as a reverse acquisition, and ignore the U.S. production activities deduction.

a. What is Year 2 consolidated taxable income?
b. What is Year 3 consolidated taxable income?
c. What NOL carryovers are available in Year 4?
d. How would your answer to Parts a through c change if Bart instead created P, S1, and S2 as an affiliated group on January 1 of Year 1?

C:8-62 *SRLY and Sec. 382 Loss Limitations.* P Corporation owns 100% of S Corporation's stock, and they have filed consolidated tax returns for several years. P also has owned 49% of T Corporation's stock for 10 years. On December 31 of the current year (Year 1), P purchases the other 51% of T's stock for $510,000 cash. T has $160,000 of NOLs it is carrying over on that date. In Year 2, the corporations report taxable profits as follows: P, $400,000; S, $250,000; and T, $90,000. Assume that the long-term tax-exempt federal interest rate is 5%.

a. Determine the amount of T's NOLs the group can deduct for its Year 2 consolidated taxable income.
b. Assume the same facts as in Part a except P purchases 45% of T's stock for $450,000 on December 31 of Year 1. Determine the amount of T's NOLs the group can deduct for its Year 2 consolidated taxable income.

C:8-63 *Stock Basis Adjustments.* P Corporation purchases 100% of S Corporation's stock for $2 million on January 1 of the current year. The corporations elect to file a consolidated tax return. During the current year, S reports $350,000 of taxable income and $30,000 of tax-exempt interest income, and it distributes a $100,000 dividend to P. Each corporation pays its portion of the consolidated tax liability. Assume a 34% corporate tax rate. What is P's basis for its S stock at the end of the current year?

C:8-64 *Stock Basis Adjustments.* P Corporation owns 100% of S Corporation's stock, and S owns 100% of T Corporation's stock. The three corporations have filed consolidated tax returns for several years. On January 1 of the current year, P's basis for its S stock is $5 million, and S's basis for its T stock is $3 million. The corporations' taxable incomes for the current year are $500,000 for P, $350,000 for S, and $250,000 for T. S and T pay no dividends during the year. Each corporation pays its portion of the consolidated tax liability. Assume a 34% corporate tax rate.

a. Determine P's basis for its S stock and S's basis for its T stock at the end of the current year.

b. Assume the same facts as in Part a except S pays an $80,000 dividend to P and T pays a $90,000 dividend to S. Determine P's basis for its S stock and S's basis for its T stock at the end of the current year.

C:8-65 *Financial Statement Implications.* P and S Corporations comprise an affiliated group that files separate tax returns. P and S had no intercompany inventory sales before the current year (Year 1). P and S use the first-in, first-out (FIFO) inventory method. During Year 1, S sells 40,000 widgets to P, earning $7 per unit profit on the sale. P's inventory at the end of Year 1 includes 10,000 of these widgets. During Year 2, S sells 75,000 widgets to P, earning $7.50 per unit profit on the sale. P's inventory at the end of Year 2 includes 12,000 of these widgets. During Year 3, no intercompany inventory sales occur, and P sells all widgets in beginning inventory. P's and S's taxable income each year (including any profits from intercompany inventory sales) is $380,000 and $300,000, respectively. Prepare the journal entries to record federal income tax expense for each of Years 1, 2, and 3. Assume a 34% corporate tax rate.

C:8-66 *Financial Statement Implications.* P Corporation acquires all of S Corporation's stock at the beginning of the current year in a transaction that qualifies as a Sec. 382 ownership change. P and S elect to file a consolidated tax return for the current year. At the time of the acquisition, S has $900,000 of NOLs it has not deducted. Management estimates that, because of the Sec. 382 limitation, the group will be able to use only $300,000 of the NOLs before they expire. The group's tax rate is 35%. Determine the amount of deferred tax asset and valuation allowance the group records for S's NOL.

COMPREHENSIVE PROBLEMS

C:8-67 P and S Corporations have filed consolidated tax returns for ten years. P and S use the accrual method of accounting, and they use the calendar year as their tax year. P and S report separate return taxable income (before any consolidation adjustments and eliminations, the NOL deduction, the charitable contributions deduction, and the dividends-received deduction) for the current year of $200,000 and $250,000, respectively. These amounts include the following current year transactions and events:

- P sells land to a third party for $80,000. P purchased the land from S two years ago for $70,000. S had purchased the land five years ago for $48,000.
- P's separate taxable income includes a $12,000 dividend S paid to P.
- P sold inventory to S in the previous year for which the deferred profit at the beginning of the current year is $5,000. S sells this inventory outside the consolidated group in the current year. P sells additional inventory to S in the current year, realizing a $100,000 profit. The intercompany profit on this unsold inventory is $8,000.
- The P-S group has a $20,000 consolidated NOL carryover available from the previous year. The NOL is wholly attributable to S.
- P receives $10,000 of dividends from corporations in which it owns less than 1% of the stock.
- P and S contribute cash to charities of $17,000 and $11,000, respectively.
- P lends S $150,000 early in the current year. S repays the loan later in the year. In addition, S pays P $6,000 interest at the time of repayment.

- S earns $1,600 of tax-exempt interest income, which is not included in S's $250,000 separate return taxable income.
- P and S have no qualified production activities income.

Determine the P-S group's consolidated taxable income and consolidated tax liability for the current year. What is P's basis for the S stock at the end of the current year? Assume that P's basis for the S stock was $1.4 million at the beginning of the current year.

C:8-68 Using the facts from Problem C:8-70 below, calculate the tax liabilities of Flying Gator and T Corporations for 2014. How much larger (or smaller) would be the total of the two separate return tax liabilities if they were to file separate tax returns than the affiliated group's consolidated return tax liability? What taxes are due (or refund available) if Flying Gator made $125,000 of estimated tax payments and T Corporation made $25,000 of estimated tax payments?

TAX STRATEGY PROBLEM

C:8-69 Sandra and John, who are unrelated, each own 50% of Alpha Corporation's stock and 50% of Beta Corporation's stock. For five years, Alpha has conducted manufacturing activities and sold machine parts primarily in the eastern United States. Alpha has reported $75,000 of operating profits in each of the last two years. Alpha's annual operating profits are expected to grow to $150,000 during the next five years. Alpha has $100,000 of NOLs it is carrying forward. Alpha sells 25% of its product to Beta. Beta has been working to establish a market niche for reselling Alpha products in the southwestern United States. In the start-up phase of establishing the market, Beta incurred $200,000 of NOLs. Under the sales arrangement with Alpha, probably the best that Beta can hope to achieve in the short-run is reach a break-even point.

Required: What suggestions can you offer Sandra and John about the short-term possibility of using Alpha's and Beta's NOLs against the profits that Alpha expects to earn and about minimizing their overall tax liabilities if both businesses become profitable? Sandra has specifically asked about merging the two companies into a single entity so the losses of one entity can offset the profits of the other and delay the need to pay income taxes to the federal government. Sandra indicates that the two companies were created for business reasons and not tax avoidance reasons. The operating situation has changed and, according to Sandra, now may be the time to combine the entities into one. However, John is not sure that bringing the two businesses together is a good idea.

TAX FORM/RETURN PREPARATION PROBLEM

C:8-70 The Flying Gator Corporation and its 100%-owned subsidiary, T Corporation, have filed consolidated tax returns for many years. Both corporations use the hybrid method of accounting and the calendar year as their tax year. During 2014 (which is the current year for this problem), they report the operating results as listed in Table C:8-2. Note the following additional information:

- Flying Gator and T Corporations are the only members of their controlled group.
- Flying Gator's address is 2101 W. University Ave., Gainesburg, FL 32611. Its employer identification number is 38-2345678. Flying Gator was incorporated on June 11, 2002. Its total assets are $430,000. Stephen Marks is Flying Gator's president.
- A $50,000 consolidated NOL carryover from the preceding year is available. The NOL is wholly attributable to Flying Gator.
- Flying Gator and T use the first-in, first-out (FIFO) inventory method. T began selling inventory to Flying Gator in the preceding year, which resulted in a $40,700 deferred intercompany profit at the end of the preceding year. Flying Gator is deemed to realize this profit in the current year because it uses the FIFO method. During the current year, T sells additional inventory to Flying Gator, realizing a $300,000 profit. At the end of the current year, Flying Gator holds inventory responsible for $45,100 of this profit.
- Flying Gator receives all its dividends from T. T receives all its dividends from a 60%-owned domestic corporation. All distributions are from E&P.
- Flying Gator receives all its interest income from T. T pays Flying Gator the interest on March 31 of the current year on a loan that was outstanding from October 1 of the

▼ TABLE C:8-2
Current Year Operating Results for Flying Gator and T Corporations (Problem C:8-67)

Income or Deductions	Flying Gator	T	Total
Gross receipts	$2,500,000	$1,250,000	$3,750,000
Cost of goods sold	(1,500,000)	(700,000)	(2,200,000)
Gross profit	$1,000,000	$ 550,000	$1,550,000
Dividends	100,000	50,000	150,000
Interest	15,000		15,000
Sec. 1231 gain		20,000	20,000
Sec. 1245 gain		25,000	25,000
Long-term capital gain (loss)	(5,000)	6,000	1,000
Short-term capital gain (loss)		(3,000)	(3,000)
Total income	$1,110,000	$ 648,000	$1,758,000
Salaries and wages	175,000	200,000	375,000
Repairs	25,000	40,000	65,000
Bad debts	10,000	5,000	15,000
Taxes	18,000	24,000	42,000
Interest	30,000	20,000	50,000
Charitable contributions	22,000	48,000	70,000
Depreciation (other than that included in cost of goods sold)	85,000	40,000	125,000
Other expenses	160,000	260,000	420,000
Total deductions	$ 525,000	$ 637,000	$1,162,000
Separate return taxable income (before the USPAD, NOL ded., and DRD)	$ 585,000	$ 11,000	$ 596,000

preceding year through March 31 of the current year. Flying Gator and T did not accrue any interest at the end of the preceding year because they use the hybrid method of accounting. T pays $5,000 of its interest expense to a third party.

- Officer's salaries are $80,000 for Flying Gator and $65,000 for T. These amounts are included in salaries and wages in Table C:8-2.
- Flying Gator's capital losses include a $9,000 long-term loss on a sale of land to T in the current year. T holds the land at year-end.
- The corporations have no nonrecaptured net Sec. 1231 losses from prior tax years.
- Qualified production activities income for Flying Gator is $340,000 and for T is $(35,000).
- Estimated tax payments for the current year are $150,000.

Determine the consolidated group's 2014 tax liability. Prepare the front page of the consolidated group's current year corporate income tax return (Form 1120). Hint: Prepare a spreadsheet similar to the one included in Appendix B to arrive at consolidated taxable income.

CASE STUDY PROBLEM

C:8-71 P Corporation operates six automotive service franchises in a metropolitan area. The service franchises have been a huge success in their first three years of operation, and P's annual taxable income exceeds $600,000. J Corporation owns the real estate associated with the six service franchises. P leases its automotive service franchise locations from J. J reports large interest and MACRS depreciation deductions because of a highly leveraged, capital intensive operation. As a result, J has reported NOLs in its first three years of operation. P and J file separate tax returns.

Carol owns 100% of both corporations. Carol sees the idea for the automotive service franchise chain starting to really develop and expects to add six more locations in each of the next two years. Because of the rapid expansion that is planned, she feels that she has outgrown her father's accountant and needs to have new ideas to help her save tax dollars so she can reinvest more money in the business.

Required: The tax partner that you are assigned to requests that you prepare a memorandum outlining your thoughts about Carol's tax problems and suggested solutions to those problems in preparation for his meeting next week with Carol.

TAX RESEARCH PROBLEMS

C:8-72 Angela owns all the stock of A, B, and P Corporations. P has owned all the stock of S1 Corporation for six years. The P-S1 affiliated group has filed a consolidated tax return in each of these six years using the calendar year as its tax year. On July 10 of the current year (a nonleap year). Angela sells her entire stock investment in A, which uses the calendar year as its tax year. No change takes place in Angela's ownership of B stock during the tax year. At the close of business on November 25 of this year, S1 purchases 90% of the common stock and 80% of the nonconvertible, nonvoting preferred stock (measured by value) of S2 Corporation. A, P, S1, and S2 are includible corporations. Which corporations are included in the affiliated group? In the controlled group? What income is included in the various tax returns? How is the allocation of the income between tax years made if the books are not closed on the sale or acquisition dates? If no special allocations are made, what portion of the reduced tax rate benefits of Sec. 11(b) can be claimed in the current year by the affiliated group? In future years?

A partial list of resources includes:

- IRC Sec. 1504
- IRC Sec. 1563
- Reg. Sec. 1.1502-76
- Reg. Sec. 1.1561-2

C:8-73 P, R, and T Corporations have filed a consolidated tax return for a number of years using the calendar year as its tax year. Current plans call for P to purchase all of X Corporation's stock at the close of business on June 30 of the current year from three individuals. X was created seven years ago and always has been an S corporation using the calendar year as its tax year. The chief financial officer of P comes to your office and makes a number of inquiries about the tax consequences of the acquisition including: Can X retain its S election? If so, does it file a federal income tax return separate from the consolidated group? Does X have to be included in the P-R-T group's consolidated tax return? Assuming the acquisition takes place as planned, what tax returns are required of the consolidated group and X? What income is included in the pre-affiliation tax return of X (if required) and the consolidated group's post-acquisition consolidated tax return? Prepare a brief memo for the chief financial officer outlining the answers to these questions and any other questions you feel are relevant.

A partial list of resources includes:

- IRC Sec. 1361(b)
- IRC Sec. 1362(d)(2)
- Reg. Sec. 1.1502-76

C:8-74 Mary owns all of Able Corporation's stock. Able owns all the shares of Baker and Cross Corporations. The three corporations have filed a consolidated calendar year tax return for several years. After consulting with her tax accountant, Mary decides that it will be more beneficial if the corporations are restructured as S corporations so their income is subject to a single layer of tax. The restructuring process is complex because Baker holds some valuable franchises that cannot be transferred. The restructuring occurred on October 23 of the current year. On October 23, Able transfers all of its assets and liabilities to Baker, and the two corporations merge with Baker as the survivor. As part of the restructuring, Mary receives all the stock of Baker. Six hours after the first transaction, Baker sells Mary all the stock in Cross for $2 million. Thus, the consolidated group survived for only six hours during the restructuring. Immediately after the restructuring, Baker incurs substantial losses. Can Baker file a consolidated return for the restructuring year and deduct the post-restructuring losses against prior year consolidated income?

A partial list of resources includes:

- Reg. Sec. 1.1502-75(a)(2)
- Reg. Sec. 1.1502-75(d)(2)
- Reg. Sec. 1.1502-76(b)(1)
- *The Falconwood Corporation v. U.S.* (96 AFTR 2d 2005-5977), 2005-2 USTC ¶50,597 (Fed. Cir., 2005)

[illegible]

TAX RESEARCH PROBLEMS

[illegible]

Research sources may include:

- IRC Sec. [illegible]
- [illegible]
- [illegible]
- [illegible]

[illegible]

A partial list of research sources includes:

- IRC Sec. [illegible]
- IRC Sec. [illegible]
- Reg. Sec. 1.[illegible]

[illegible]

- [illegible]
- [illegible]
- [illegible]

[illegible]

CHAPTER

9

PARTNERSHIP FORMATION AND OPERATION

LEARNING OBJECTIVES

After studying this chapter, you should be able to

1. Compare and contrast the various partnership forms
2. Describe the basic concepts of partnership taxation
3. Explain the tax results of a contribution of property or services in exchange for a partnership interest
4. Establish the permitted tax year for a partnership
5. Distinguish between items included in partnership ordinary income or loss and those that must be separately stated
6. Determine a partner's distributive share of partnership income, gain, loss, deduction, or credit items
7. Calculate a partner's basis in a partnership interest and its effect on losses allowed
8. Discuss the at-risk and passive activity loss limitations
9. Determine the tax consequences of property sales between a partner and the partnership and of guaranteed payments to a partner
10. Recognize the special tax issues associated with family partnerships
11. Identify planning techniques to get the best tax advantages from partnership losses
12. Comply with the requirements for filing a partnership tax return

CHAPTER OUTLINE

Partnerships have long been one of the major entities for conducting business activities. Partnerships vary in complexity from the corner gas station owned and operated by two brothers to syndicated tax partnerships with their partnership interests traded on major security markets. Two different sets of rules apply to partnerships depending on their size. The rules discussed in Chapter C:9 and most of Chapter C:10 apply to the majority of partnerships. A different set of rules, discussed at the end of Chapter C:10, apply to electing large partnerships. The partnership rules are found in Subchapter K of the IRC, which includes Secs. 701–777.

Chapters C:9 and C:10 discuss the income tax rules applying to partnership business operations. The first part of this chapter defines a partnership, describes the types of partnerships, and discusses the formation of a partnership. The remainder of the chapter deals with the ongoing operations of a partnership, such as the annual taxation of partnership earnings, transactions between partners and the partnership, and a partner's basis in a partnership interest. This chapter also considers procedural matters, such as reporting the annual partnership income and IRS audit procedures for partnerships and their partners. Chapter C:10 continues by discussing distributions to the partners and the tax implications of transactions used to terminate a partner's interest in a partnership. Chapter C:10 also discusses the unique problems of limited partnerships and the taxation of publicly traded partnerships and electing large partnerships.

Definition of a partnership

OBJECTIVE 1

Compare and contrast the various partnership forms

For tax purposes, the definition of a partnership includes "a syndicate, group, pool, joint venture, or other unincorporated organization" that carries on a business or financial operation or venture. However, a trust, estate, or corporation cannot be treated as a partnership. Unlike a corporation, which can exist only after incorporation documents are finalized, formation of a partnership requires no legal documentation. If two people (or business entities) work together to carry on any business or financial operation with the intention of making a profit and sharing that profit as co-owners, a partnership exists for federal income tax purposes.[1]

The IRC and Treasury Regulations define a **partner** simply as a member of a partnership. Years of case law and common business practice, however, have made clear that a partner can be an individual, trust, estate, or corporation. The only restriction on the number of partners is that a partnership must have at least two partners, but a large syndicated partnership may have hundreds or even thousands of partners.

ADDITIONAL COMMENT

Even though the formation of a partnership requires no legal documentation, the partners should draft a formal written partnership agreement to prevent subsequent disagreements and arguments.

GENERAL AND LIMITED PARTNERSHIPS

Each state has laws governing the rights and restrictions of partnerships. Almost all state statutes are modeled on the Uniform Partnership Act (UPA) or the Uniform Limited Partnership Act (ULPA) and thus have strong similarities to each other. A partnership can take two basic legal forms: a general partnership or a limited partnership. The differences between the two forms are substantial and extend to the partners' legal rights and liabilities as well as the tax consequences of operations to the partners. Because these differences are so important, we examine the two partnership forms before proceeding with further discussion of the partnership tax rules.

General Partnerships. A **general partnership** exists any time two or more partners join together and do not specifically provide that one or more of the partners is a limited partner (as defined below). In a general partnership, each partner has the right to

[1] Section 761(a) allows an election to avoid the Subchapter K rules for a very limited group of business owners.

participate in the management of the partnership. However, a general partnership is flexible enough to allow its business affairs to be managed by a single partner chosen by the general partners.

REAL-WORLD EXAMPLE

For 2012, 3.33 million domestic partnerships filed returns. Of these, 583,000 were general partnerships, 407,000 were limited partnerships, 129,000 were limited liability partnerships, and 2.21 million were limited liability companies. The average general partnership had 3.7 partners, the average limited partnership had 26.4 partners, the average limited liability partnership had 4.0 partners, and the average limited liability company had 4.0 members.

Although only one (or a few) of the general partners may exercise management duties, each **general partner** has the ability to make commitments for the partnership.[2] In a general partnership, each partner has unlimited liability for all partnership debts. If the partnership fails to pay its debts, each partner may have to pay far more than the amount he or she has invested in the venture. Thus, each partner faces the risk of losing personal assets if the partnership incurs business losses. This exposure is the single biggest drawback to the general partnership form of doing business.

Limited Partnerships. A **limited partnership** has two classes of partners. It must have at least one general partner, who essentially has the same rights and liabilities as any general partner in a general partnership,[3] and at least one **limited partner**. Even if a partnership becomes bankrupt, a limited partner can lose no more than his or her original investment plus any additional amount he or she has committed to contribute. However, a limited partner has no right to be active in the partnership's management.

The broad rights and obligations of general partners could make a general partnership an unwieldy form for operating a business with a large number of owners. On the other hand, a limited partnership having one (or a small number of) general partners can be useful for a business operation that needs to attract a large amount of capital. In fact, one common form for a tax shelter investment is a limited partnership having a corporation with a small amount of capital as its sole general partner. Such an arrangement allows the tax advantages of the partnership form while retaining the limited liability feature for virtually every investor.

Many of these limited partnerships are so large and widely held that in many ways they appear more like corporations than partnerships. As discussed in Chapter C:10, the tax laws provide that publicly traded partnerships may be reclassified for tax purposes as corporations.

Limited Liability Limited Partnerships (LLLPs). A recent variation on the limited partnership in some (but not all) states is the LLLP. As discussed above, a limited partnership, in addition to having limited partners, has one or more general partners whose personal liability exposure is unlimited. The LLLP is a partnership formed under a state's limited partnership laws but that can elect under the state's laws to provide the general partners with limited liability. Thus, the LLLP is similar to an LLC and becomes potentially useful in states that do not extend LLC status to personal service firms but allow such firms to operate as an LLLP.[4]

REAL-WORLD EXAMPLE

The number of limited liability companies has increased from 48,000 in 1994 to 2.21 million in 2012. Moreover, LLCs represented 66.4% of all domestic partnerships in 2012.

Limited Liability Companies (LLCs). With the advent of LLCs, businesses have the opportunity to be treated as a partnership for tax purposes while having limited liability protection for every owner. State law provides this limited liability. Unique tax rules for LLCs have not been developed. Instead, the check-the-box regulations (discussed in Chapter C:2) permit each LLC to choose whether to be treated as a partnership or taxed as a corporation. If an LLC is considered a partnership for tax purposes, the same tax rules apply to the LLC that apply to a traditional partnership. Chapter C:10 further discusses the tax treatment of LLCs.

TAX STRATEGY TIP

A business that expects losses in its early years may wish to form an LLC initially so that losses pass through to the owners. Later, if the business expects to grow, it can consider incorporating as a C corporation and retaining its earnings to fund this expansion.

Limited Liability Partnerships (LLPs). Initially, professional organizations in certain fields (e.g., public accounting and law) were not permitted to operate as LLCs and therefore remained general partnerships. Subsequently, many states have added LLPs to the list of permissible business forms. The primary difference between a general partnership and an LLP is that, in an LLP, a partner is not liable for damages resulting from failures in the

[2] Uniform Partnership Act.

[3] Uniform Limited Partnership Act.

[4] For a detailed discussion, see Shop Talk, "Service Firms Practicing as LLLPs: What Are the Tax Consequences?" *Journal of Taxation,* August 2005.

work of other partners or of people supervised by other partners. Under the check-the-box regulations, an LLP can be treated as a partnership or as a corporation. Like an LLC, the default tax classification of an LLP is a partnership. The same tax rules apply to an LLP that apply to a traditional partnership. Chapter C:10 further discusses the tax treatment of LLPs.

REAL-WORLD EXAMPLE

Only 100 or so partnerships file as electing large partnerships each year.

Electing Large Partnerships. Partnerships that qualify as "large partnerships" may elect to have a simplified set of reporting rules apply. To qualify as a large partnership, the partnership must not be a service partnership and must not be engaged in commodity trading. Further, to qualify to make this election, the partnership must have at least 100 partners throughout the tax year (excluding partners who provide substantial services in connection with the partnership's business activities). Once the partnership makes the election, it reports its income under a simplified reporting scheme, is subject to different rules about when the partnership terminates, and is subject to a different system of audits. The election is irrevocable without IRS permission. Chapter C:10 presents details about the tax treatment of electing large partnerships.

Overview of Taxation of Partnership Income

OBJECTIVE 2

Describe the basic concepts of partnership taxation

The following overview gives a broad perspective of the taxation of partnership income other than income earned by electing large partnerships. (Appendix F compares the tax characteristics of a partnership, a C corporation, and an S corporation.) More detailed descriptions follow this overview.

PARTNERSHIP PROFITS AND LOSSES

A partnership is not a taxpaying entity, and income earned by a partnership is not subject to two layers of federal income taxes. Instead, each partner reports a share of the partnership's income, gain, loss, deduction, and credit items in his or her income tax return. The partnership, however, must file Form 1065 (U.S. Partnership Return of Income), an information return that provides the IRS with information about partnership earnings as well as how the earnings are allocated among the partners. The partnership must elect a tax year and accounting methods to calculate its earnings. (Appendix B includes a completed partnership tax return that shows a Form 1065 and Schedule K-1 for a partner along with a set of supporting facts.)

ADDITIONAL COMMENT

Because most partnerships use the calendar year as their tax year, the K-1s are not due until April 15. Because a calendar year corporate partner's return is due on March 15 and an individual partner's return is due on April 15, partners often must request extensions for filing their returns. An electing large partnership must provide K-1s by March 15 following the close of the partnership tax year.

Each partner receives a Schedule K-1 from the partnership, which informs the partner of the amount and character of his or her share of partnership items. The partner then combines his or her partnership earnings and losses with all other items of income or loss for the tax year, computes the amount of taxable income, and calculates the tax liability. Partnership income is taxed at the applicable tax rate for its partners, which can range from 10% to 39.6% (in 2015) for partners who are individuals, trusts, or estates. Corporate partners pay tax on partnership income at rates ranging from 15% to 39%.

One of the major advantages of the partnership form of doing business is that partnership losses are allocated among the partners. If the loss limitation rules (explained later in this chapter) do not apply, these losses offset the partners' other income, resulting in immediate tax savings for the partners. The immediate tax saving available to the partner contrasts sharply with the net operating loss (NOL) carrybacks or carryforwards that may result from a C corporation's operations.

SELF-STUDY QUESTION

Why does a partner need to know his or her basis in his or her partnership interest?

ANSWER

Three important reasons are (1) to determine the gain or loss on a sale of the partnership interest, (2) to determine the amount of partnership losses a partner can deduct, and (3) to determine the amount of distributions that are nontaxable to the partner.

THE PARTNER'S BASIS

A partner's basis in his or her partnership interest is a crucial element in partnership taxation. When a partner makes a contribution to a partnership or purchases a partnership interest, he or she establishes a beginning basis. Because partners can be personally liable for partnership debts, a partner's basis in his or her partnership interest is increased by his or her share of any partnership liabilities. Accordingly, the partner's basis fluctuates as the partnership borrows and repays loans or increases and decreases its accounts payable. In addition, a partner's basis in his or her partnership interest increases by the partner's share of partnership income and decreases by his or her share of partnership losses. Because a partner's basis in his or her partnership interest can never be negative, the basis serves as one limit on the amount of deductible partnership losses. (See the discussion on pages C:9-26 and C:9-27 about the various loss limitations.)

EXAMPLE C:9-1 ► Tom purchases a 20% interest in the XY Partnership for $8,000 on January 1 of Year 1 and begins to materially participate in the partnership's business. The XY Partnership uses the calendar year as its tax year. At the time of the purchase, the XY Partnership has $2,000 in liabilities, of which Tom's share is 20%. Tom's basis in his partnership interest on January 1 is $8,400 [$8,000 + (0.20 × $2,000)]. ◄

EXAMPLE C:9-2 ► Assume the same facts as in Example C:9-1 except, during Year 1, the XY Partnership incurs $10,000 in losses, and its liabilities increase by $4,000. Tom's basis on December 31 of Year 1 is calculated as follows:

January 1, Year 1, basis	$8,400
Plus: Share of liability increase ($4,000 × 0.20)	800
Minus: Share of partnership losses ($10,000 × 0.20)	(2,000)
December 31, Year 1, basis	$7,200

◄

EXAMPLE C:9-3 ► Assume the same facts as in Example C:9-2, and further assume that, during Year 2, the XY Partnership incurs $60,000 in losses and its liabilities increase by $10,000. Tom's share of the losses is $12,000 ($60,000 × 0.20). The maximum amount Tom can deduct in Year 2 is calculated as follows:

January 1, Year 2, basis	$7,200
Plus: Share of liability increase	2,000
December 31, Year 2, basis before losses	$9,200
Minus: Maximum loss deduction allowed	(9,200)
December 31, Year 2, basis	$ -0-

Tom's remaining $2,800 in losses carry over to subsequent years, and he can deduct them when he regains sufficient basis in his partnership interest. ◄

PARTNERSHIP DISTRIBUTIONS

ADDITIONAL COMMENT
The increase in a partner's basis for earnings prevents double taxation of those earnings upon a subsequent distribution, sale of the partnership interest, or liquidation of the partnership.

When a partnership makes current (nonliquidating) distributions, the distributions generally are nontaxable to the partners because they represent the receipt of earnings that already have been taxed to the partners and that have increased the partners' bases in their partnership interests. Because they are a return of capital, these distributions reduce a partner's basis in his or her partnership interest. If a cash distribution is so large, however, that it exceeds a partner's basis in his or her partnership interest, the partner recognizes gain equal to the amount of the excess. When the partnership goes out of business or when a partner withdraws from the partnership, the partnership makes liquidating distributions to the partner. Like current distributions, these distributions cause the partner to recognize gain only if the cash received exceeds the partner's basis in his or her partnership interest. A partner may recognize a loss if he or she receives only cash, inventory, and unrealized receivables in complete liquidation of his or her partnership interest. Chapter C:10 presents detailed coverage of current and liquidating distributions.

TAX IMPLICATIONS OF FORMATION OF A PARTNERSHIP

OBJECTIVE 3

Explain the tax results of a contribution of property or services in exchange for a partnership interest

When two or more individuals or entities decide to operate an unincorporated business together, they form a partnership. The following sections examine the tax implications of property contributions, service contributions, and organization and syndication expenditures.

CONTRIBUTION OF PROPERTY

Nonrecognition of Gain or Loss. Section 721 governs the formation of a partnership. In most cases, a partner who contributes property in exchange for a partnership interest recognizes no gain or loss on the transaction. Likewise, the partnership recognizes no gain or loss on the contribution of property. The partner's basis for his or her partnership interest and the partnership's basis for the property are both the same as basis of the property transferred.[5]

Nonrecognition treatment is limited to transactions in which a partner receives a partnership interest in exchange for a contribution of property. As in the corporate formation area, the term *property* includes cash, tangible property (e.g., buildings and land), and intangible property (e.g., franchise rights, trademarks, and leases).[6] Services are specifically excluded from the definition of property, so a contribution of services for a partnership interest is a taxable transaction.

ADDITIONAL COMMENT

For contributions to a corporation to be nontaxable, the contributing shareholders must control (own at least 80%) the corporation immediately after the transaction. No such control requirement exists for contributions to a partnership to be nontaxable.

Recognition of Gain or Loss. The general rule of Sec. 721(a) provides that neither the partnership nor any partner recognizes gain or loss when partners contribute property in exchange for a partnership interest. Three exceptions to this general rule may require a partner to recognize a gain upon the contribution of property to a partnership in exchange for a partnership interest:

- Contribution of property to a partnership that would be treated as an investment company if it were incorporated
- Contribution of property followed by a distribution in an arrangement that may be considered a sale rather than a contribution
- Contribution of property to a partnership along with the partnership's assumption of the partner's liabilities if, as a result, the partner's share of partnership liabilities exceeds his or her basis in the partnership.

The investment company exception of Sec. 721(b) requires recognition of gain only if the exchange results in diversification of the transferor's property interest.[7] If the contribution of property is to an investment partnership, the contributing partner must recognize any gain (but not loss) realized on the property transfer as if he or she sold the stock or securities.

Sections 707(a)(2)(A) and (B) set out the second exception, which holds that a property contribution followed by a distribution (or an allocation of income or gain) may be treated as a property sale by the partner to the partnership rather than as a contribution by the partner to the partnership. For example, Treasury Regulations may require sale treatment (and the recognition of gain or loss) if the distribution would not have occurred except for the contribution.

EXAMPLE C:9-4 ▶ In return for a 40% interest in the CD Partnership, Cara contributed land with a $100,000 fair market value (FMV). The partners agreed that the partnership would distribute $100,000 in cash to Cara immediately after the contribution. Because the cash distribution would not have occurred had Cara not first contributed the land and become a partner, the transaction is likely to be treated as a sale of the land by Cara to the partnership. ◀

If the distribution does not occur simultaneously with the contribution, the transaction is treated as a sale if the later distribution is not dependent on the normal business risk of the enterprise.

EXAMPLE C:9-5 ▶ Elena received a 30% interest in the DEF Partnership in return for her contribution of land having a $60,000 FMV. The partnership waits six months and then distributes $60,000 in cash to Elena. If the $60,000 distribution is not contingent on the partnership's earnings or ability to borrow funds or other normal risks of doing business, the distribution and contribution will be treated as a sale of land by Elena to the partnership. ◀

[5] Secs. 722 and 723.

[6] For an excellent discussion of the definition of the term *property*, see footnote 6 of *D.N. Stafford v. U.S.*, 45 AFTR 2d 80-785, 80-1 USTC ¶9218 (5th Cir., 1980).

[7] Reg. Sec. 1.351-1(c)(1). This investment is taxed only when immediately after the exchange more than 80% of the value of the partnership's assets (excluding cash and nonconvertible debt obligations) is held for investment or is readily marketable stocks, securities, or interests in regulated investment companies or real estate investment trusts.

KEY POINT

A partner's relief of debt is treated as if the partner receives a cash distribution. A partner's assumption of debt is treated as if the partner makes a cash contribution. These two simple rules are critical to understanding transactions such as formations of partnerships, distributions from partnerships, and sales or liquidations of partnership interests.

Effects of Liabilities. The third condition that may cause a partner to recognize gain (but not loss) on the formation of a partnership is the contribution of property to a partnership along with the partnership's assumption of liabilities previously owed by the partner. Because each partner is liable for his or her share of partnership liabilities, increases and decreases in the partnership liabilities are reflected in each partner's basis. Specifically, Sec. 752 provides that two effects result from a partner's contribution of property to a partnership if the partnership also assumes the partner's liabilities.

- Each partner's basis is increased by his or her share of the partnership's liabilities as if he or she had contributed cash to the partnership in the amount of his or her share of partnership liabilities.
- The partner whose personal liabilities are assumed by the partnership has a reduction in the basis of his or her partnership interest as if the partnership distributed cash to him or her in the amount of the assumed liability. A cash distribution first reduces the partner's basis in the partnership interest. If the cash distribution exceeds the partner's predistribution basis in the partnership interest, the partner recognizes gain.

The net effect of these two basis adjustments, however, is seldom large enough to cause a transferor partner to recognize gain when he or she contributes property to the partnership. The transferor partner is deemed first to have made a contribution of property plus a contribution of cash equal to the partner's share of any partnership liabilities existing prior to his or her entrance into the partnership (or contributed by other partners concurrently with this transaction). The partner then is deemed to have received a cash distribution equal to the total amount of his or her own liability assumed by the *other* partners. Also, see the Additional Comment next to Example C:9-6 for an alternate way to view the transaction.

EXAMPLE C:9-6 ▶

In return for a 20% partnership interest, Mary contributes land having a $60,000 FMV and a $30,000 basis to the XY Partnership. The partnership assumes Mary's $15,000 liability arising from her purchase of the land, and Mary's share of partnership liabilities is 20%. The XY Partnership has $4,000 in liabilities immediately before her contribution. Mary's basis in her partnership interest is calculated as follows:

Basis of contributed property	$30,000
Plus: Mary's share of existing partnership liabilities ($4,000 × 0.20)	800
Minus: Mary's liabilities assumed by the other partners ($15,000 × 0.80)	(12,000)
Mary's basis in her partnership interest	$18,800

Mary recognizes no gain on the partnership's assumption of her liability because the deemed cash distribution from the assumption of her $12,000 in liabilities by the partnership does not exceed her $30,800 basis in the partnership interest immediately preceding the deemed distribution. ◀

ADDITIONAL COMMENT

In Example C:9-6, the $12,000 reduction in basis also can be viewed as the net of $3,000, which is Mary's 20% share of the $15,000 increase in partnership liabilities, and $15,000, which is Mary's liability assumed by the partnership.

EXAMPLE C:9-7 ▶

Assume the same facts as in Example C:9-6 except the amount of the liability assumed by the XY Partnership is $50,000. Mary's basis in her partnership interest is calculated as follows:

Basis of contributed property	$30,000
Plus: Mary's share of existing partnership liabilities ($4,000 × 0.20)	800
Predistribution basis	$30,800
Minus: Mary's liabilities assumed by the other partners ($50,000 × 0.80)	(40,000)
Basis in partnership interest (cannot be negative)	$ -0-

The cash deemed distributed in excess of Mary's predistribution basis causes her to recognize a $9,200 ($40,000 − $30,800) gain. Mary reduces her basis to zero by the distribution because a partner's basis in the partnership interest can never be less than zero. ◀

ADDITIONAL COMMENT

In contrast to partnership formations, had Example C:9-7 involved a formation of the XY Corporation, Mary would have recognized a $20,000 gain under Sec. 357(c) for the excess of the liability over basis ($50,000 − $30,000).

? STOP & THINK

Question: Assume the land Mary contributed in Example C:9-6 has a $60,000 FMV and an $85,000 adjusted basis. Should Mary contribute it to the partnership?

Solution: If Mary contributes the land, she cannot recognize her $25,000 ($60,000 FMV − $85,000 adjusted basis) loss until the partnership disposes of the property. Accordingly, Mary might prefer to sell the property and recognize her loss now. If the partnership

ADDITIONAL COMMENT

If Mary's interest in the partnership exceeded 50%, she could not deduct the loss on the sale of property to the partnership. See page C:9-27.

can afford the $60,000 price and needs this property, Mary could sell the land to the partnership, recognize her loss on the sale, and then contribute the cash she receives from the partnership in exchange for her partnership interest. If the partnership does not need the property, Mary could sell the land to a third party, recognize her loss, and contribute the sales proceeds to the partnership in exchange for her partnership interest. However, a problem arises if the partnership needs this property and cannot afford to buy it from Mary. In that case, contributing the property to the partnership may be the only alternative despite the less-than-optimal tax results.

TYPICAL MISCONCEPTION

Example C:9-7 illustrates another difference between partnership and corporate formations. In the example, XY Partnership does not increase its basis in the property for the gain recognized by Mary, but if XY were a corporation, XY would increase its basis in the property by Mary's recognized gain.

Because the partnership's assumption of a partner's liabilities is treated as a cash distribution, the character of any gain recognized by the partner is controlled by the partnership distribution rules. Cash distributions exceeding predistribution basis always result in gain recognition, and that gain is deemed to be gain from the sale of the partnership interest.[8] Because a partnership interest is usually a capital asset, any gain arising from assumption of a partner's liabilities normally is a capital gain.

Partner's Basis in the Partnership Interest (Commonly Called Outside Basis). In general, the transferor partner's beginning basis in the partnership interest equals the sum of money contributed plus his or her basis in contributed property. If the partner recognizes any gain on the contribution because the partnership is an investment company, the amount of recognized gain increases his or her basis in the partnership interest.[9] Beginning basis also includes the partner's share of partnership liabilities at the time of contribution. Any gain recognized because of the effects of liabilities on the partner's basis does not increase the basis for the partnership interest because, in this situation, the basis is zero.

In some instances, a partner may contribute valuable property having little or no basis. For example, accounts receivable or notes receivable of a partner using the cash method of accounting can be a valued contribution to a partnership, but if the receivables' bases are zero, the beginning basis of the partnership interest also is zero.

TYPICAL MISCONCEPTION

If a partner contributes both ordinary income property and capital gain property to a partnership, the partner apparently has two different holding periods for his or her partnership interest.

Holding Period for Partnership Interest. The holding period for the partnership interest includes the transferor's holding period for the contributed property if that property is a capital asset or Sec. 1231 property in the transferor's hands.[10] If the contributed property is an ordinary income asset (e.g., inventory) to the partner, the holding period for the partnership interest begins the day after the contribution date.[11]

EXAMPLE C:9-8 ▶ On April 1, Sue contributes a building (Sec. 1231 property) to the ST Partnership in exchange for a 20% interest. Sue purchased the building three years ago. Her holding period for her partnership interest includes the three years she held the contributed building. ◀

EXAMPLE C:9-9 ▶ On April 1, Ted contributes inventory to the ST Partnership in exchange for a 20% interest. No matter when Ted acquired the inventory, his holding period for his partnership interest begins on April 2, the day after his contribution. ◀

BOOK-TO-TAX ACCOUNTING COMPARISON

Although the partnership takes a carryover tax basis in property, the partnership also records the property at FMV for book purposes. Thus, the partnership essentially maintains two sets of books.

Partnership's Basis in Property. Under Sec. 723, the partnership's basis for contributed property is the same as the property's basis in the hands of the contributing partner. If, however, the contributing partner recognizes gain because the partnership is an investment company, such gain increases the partnership's basis in the contributed property. Gain recognized by the contributing partner because of the assumption of a partner's liability does not increase the partnership's basis in the property.[12]

Not only does the property's basis carry over to the partnership from the contributing partner, but for some property the character of gain or loss on a subsequent disposition of the property by the partnership also references the character of the property in the contributing

[8] Sec. 731(a).
[9] Sec. 722.
[10] Sec. 1223(1).
[11] Reg. Sec. 1.1223-1(a).
[12] Rev. Rul. 84-15, 1984-1 C.B. 158.

partner's hands. Section 724 prevents the transformation of ordinary income into capital gains (or capital losses into ordinary losses) when a partner contributes property to a partnership. Properties that were (1) unrealized receivables, inventory, or capital loss property in the hands of the contributing partner and (2) contributed to a partnership retain their character for some subsequent partnership dispositions.[13]

Unrealized Receivables. The concept of unrealized receivables plays a key role for tax purposes in many different partnership transactions. An **unrealized receivable** is any right to payment for goods or services the holder has not included in income because of the accounting method used.[14] The most common occurence of unrealized receivables is a cash basis taxpayer's accounts receivable.

If a partner contributes an unrealized receivable to his or her partnership, any gain or loss recognized on the partnership's later disposition or collection of the receivable is treated as ordinary income or loss. This rule mandates ordinary income or loss treatment regardless of how long the partnership holds the receivable or its character in the partnership's hands.

Inventory. If property was inventory to the contributing partner, its character remains ordinary for five years. Consequently, any gain or loss recognized by the partnership on the disposition of such property during the five-year period beginning on the date of contribution is ordinary gain or loss. Ordinary gain or loss treatment occurs even if the property is a capital asset or Sec. 1231 asset in the partnership's hands.

EXAMPLE C:9-10 ▶ On June 1, Jose, a real estate developer, contributes ten acres of land in an industrial park he developed to the Hi-Tech Partnership in exchange for a 30% interest in the partnership. Although Jose held the acreage in inventory, the land serves as the site for Hi-Tech's new research facility. Four years later Hi-Tech sells its research facility and the land. Although gain on the sale of the land usually would be taxed as Sec. 1231 gain, Hi-Tech must report it as ordinary income. ◀

ADDITIONAL COMMENT

Congress enacted Sec. 724 to eliminate the ability to transform the character of gain or loss on property by contributing the property to a partnership and having the partnership subsequently sell it.

Capital Loss Property. The final type of property whose character is fixed at the time of the contribution is property that would generate a capital loss if sold by the contributing partner rather than contributed to the partnership. A loss recognized by the partnership on the disposition of the property within five years of its contribution to the partnership is a capital loss. However, the amount of loss characterized as capital may not exceed the capital loss the contributing partner would have recognized had the partner sold the property on the contribution date. The character of any loss exceeding the difference between the property's FMV and its adjusted basis on the contribution date is determined by the property's character in the hands of the partnership.

EXAMPLE C:9-11 ▶ Pam holds investment land that she purchased six years ago for $50,000. The FMV of the land was only $40,000 two years ago when she contributed it to the PK Partnership, which is in the business of developing and selling lots. PK develops the contributed land and sells it in the current year for $28,000, or at a $22,000 loss. The $10,000 loss that accrued while Pam held the land as a capital asset retains its character as a capital loss. The remaining $12,000 of loss that accrues while the land is part of the partnership's inventory is an ordinary loss. ◀

Partnership's Holding Period. Under Sec. 1223(2), the partnership's holding period for its contributed assets includes the holding period of the contributing partner. This rule applies without regard to the character the property has in the contributing partner's hands or the partnership's hands.

Section 1245 and 1250 Property Rules. Although the Sec. 1245 and Sec. 1250 depreciation recapture rules override many gain nonrecognition provisions in the IRC, the partner incurs no depreciation recapture unless he or she recognizes gain upon contributing

---

[13] Sec. 724. The determination of whether property is an unrealized receivable, inventory, or a capital loss property in the contributing partner's hands occurs immediately before the contribution.

[14] Section 724(d)(1) references the unrealized receivables definition found in Sec. 751(c). For distributions and sale transactions, the unrealized receivables definition is broadened to include certain recapture items. This difference is discussed more fully in Chapter C:10.

property in exchange for a partnership interest.[15] Instead, both the adjusted basis and depreciation recapture potential carry over to the partnership. If the partnership later sells the property at a gain, the Sec. 1245 and 1250 provisions affect the character of the gain. In addition, any unrecaptured Sec. 1250 gain potential carries over to the partnership to affect gain characterization upon a future sale. Unrecaptured Sec. 1250 gain is taxed to individuals at a 25% capital gains rate (and possibly an additional 3.8% tax on net investment income).

Contribution of Property after Formation. Any time a partner contributes property in exchange for a partnership interest, the rules outlined above apply whether the contribution occurs during the formation of the partnership or at a later date. This treatment contrasts sharply with corporate contributions, where a nontaxable contribution after formation is rare because of the 80% control requirement. Most contributions of property in exchange for a partnership interest are nontaxable even if they occur years after forming the partnership.

CONTRIBUTION OF SERVICES

A partner who receives a partnership interest in exchange for services has been compensated as if he or she receives cash and thus must recognize ordinary income. The amount and timing of the income to be recognized are determined under Sec. 83. Consequently, receipt of an unrestricted interest in a partnership requires the service partner to immediately recognize income equal to the FMV of the partnership interest less any cash or property contributed by the partner. Generally, the service partner recognizes no income upon receiving a restricted interest in a partnership until the restriction lapses or the interest can be freely transferred.

ADDITIONAL COMMENT

The Treasury Department has issued proposed regulations, and the IRS will issue a new revenue procedure that will alter the landscape of taxing partnership interests transferred for services. The new rules also will make Rev. Proc. 93-27, discussed on the next page, obsolete. However, taxpayers may not rely on the proposed rules until they are finalized and may continue to rely on existing rules and procedures. See Notice 2005-43, 2005-24 I.R.B. 1221.

Although a partnership interest seems to be a unified interest, it really is made up of two components: a capital interest and a profits interest. A partner may receive both components or only a profits interest in exchange for his or her services. (A capital interest without a profits interest rarely occurs.) Treasury Regulations indicate that a **capital interest** can be valued by determining the amount the partner would receive if the partnership liquidated on the day the partner receives the partnership interest.[16] If the partner would receive proceeds from the sale of the partnership's assets or receive the assets themselves, he or she is considered to own a capital interest. Alternatively, if the partner's only interest is in the future earnings of the partnership (with no interest in the current partnership assets), the partner owns a **profits interest** (but not a capital interest).

Tax law has long been settled that receipt of a capital interest in a partnership in exchange for services is taxable under the rules outlined above. A profits interest, however, is no more than a right to future income taxable to the partners as the partnership earns it. To the extent the profits interest itself has a value, one might expect that value to be taxed when the partner receives the profits interest, as any other property received for services would be taxed.

EXAMPLE C:9-12 ▶ Carl arranges favorable financing for the purchase of an office building and receives a 30% profits interest in a partnership formed to own and operate the building. Less than three weeks later, Carl sells his profits interest to his partner for $40,000. Carl must recognize $40,000 as ordinary income from the receipt of a partnership profits interest in exchange for services. ◀

The facts in Example C:9-12 approximate those of *Sol Diamond,* a landmark partnership taxation case, which was the first case to tax the partner upon receipt of a profits interest.[17] The Tax Court pointed out that Sec. 61 included all compensation for services, and no other provision contained in the IRC or Treasury Regulations removed this transaction from taxation. The Seventh Circuit Court of Appeals seemed to limit the inclusion

---

[15] Secs. 1245(b)(3) and 1250(d)(3). Property acquired as a capital contribution where gain is not recognized under Sec. 721 is subject to the MACRS anti-churning rules of Sec. 168(i)(7)(A). In general, the anti-churning rules require the partnership to use the same depreciation method as the partner who contributed the property. See Chapter C:2 for a discussion of these rules in connection with a corporate formation transaction.

[16] Reg. Sec. 1.704-1(e)(1)(v). The capital interest definition in this regulation relates to family partnerships, but such definition should apply generally in the partnership area.

[17] 33 AFTR 2d 74-852, 74-1 USTC ¶9306 (7th Cir., 1974), *aff'g.* 56 T.C. 530 (1971).

of a profits interest to situations in which the market value of the profits interest could be determined. The IRS resolved much of the uncertainty in this area of tax law when it issued Rev. Proc. 93-27, which provides that the IRS generally will tax a profits interest received for services only in three specified instances in which a FMV is readily ascertainable.[18] In the general case, therefore, an income tax is not levied on the profits interest separately, but all partnership profits that pass through to the partner are taxed under the normal rules of partnership taxation.

Consequences to the Partnership. Payments by the partnership for services are either deductible as an expense or capitalized, including those paid for services with an interest in the partnership. If the payment constitutes a deductible expense, the partnership takes the deduction in the same year the partner includes the value of his or her partnership interest in income.[19] This rule matches the timing of the partnership's deduction to the partner's income recognition.

Allocating the Expense Deduction. The partnership allocates the expense deduction or the amortization of the capital expenditure among the partners other than the service partner. This allocation occurs because these partners make the outlay by relinquishing part of their interest in the partnership.

EXAMPLE C:9-13 ▶ In June of the current year Jay, a lawyer, receives a 1% capital and profits interest (valued at $4,000) in the JLK Partnership in return for providing legal services to JLK's employees during the first five months of the current year. The legal services were a fringe benefit for JLK's employees and were deductible by JLK. Jay must include $4,000 in his current year gross income, and JLK can deduct the expense in the current year. JLK allocates the $4,000 expense to all partners other than Jay. ◀

If the service performed is of a nature that should be capitalized, the partnership capitalizes the amount and amortizes it as appropriate. The related asset's basis is increased at the same time and in the same amount as the partner's gross income inclusion.[20]

EXAMPLE C:9-14 ▶ In June of the current year, Rob, an architect, receives a 10% capital and profits interest in the KLB Partnership for his services in designing a new building to house the partnership's operations. The June value of the partnership interest is $24,000. Rob must recognize $24,000 of ordinary income in the current year as a result of receiving the partnership interest. The KLB Partnership must capitalize the $24,000 as part of the building's cost and depreciate that amount (along with the building's other costs) over its recovery period. ◀

The timing of the partner's recognition of income is the same in the preceding two examples even though the partnership could deduct one payment but had to capitalize the other.

Partnership Gain or Loss. By exchanging an interest in the partnership for services, the partnership, in effect, pays for services by transferring an interest in the underlying partnership property. Generally, when a debtor uses property to pay a debt, the debtor must recognize gain or loss equal to the difference between the property's FMV and adjusted basis. Likewise, the partnership must recognize the gain or loss existing in the proportionate share of its assets deemed to be transferred to the service partner.[21] Furthermore, because the partnership recognizes gain or loss, it must adjust the bases of the assets.

EXAMPLE C:9-15 ▶ On January 1 of the current year, Maria is admitted as a 25% partner in the XYZ Partnership in exchange for services valued at $16,500. The partnership has no liabilities at the time but has assets with a basis of $50,000 and FMV of $66,000. The transaction is treated as if Maria received an undivided one-fourth interest in each asset. She is taxed on the $16,500 FMV of the

[18] 1993-2 C.B. 343. The three exceptions involve receipt of a profits interest having a substantially certain and predictable income stream, the partner disposes of the profits interest within two years of receipt, or the profits interest is a limited interest in a publicly traded partnership.

[19] Reg. Sec. 1.83-6(a)(1).

[20] Reg. Sec. 1.83-6(a)(4).

[21] Reg. Sec. 1.83-6(b).

assets and takes a $16,500 basis in her partnership interest. The partnership recognizes $4,000 of gain [0.25 × ($66,000 FMV − $50,000 adjusted basis)] on the assets deemed paid to Maria. The partnership calculates gain or loss for each asset XYZ holds, and the character of each asset determines the character of the gain or loss recognized. The recognized gain is allocated to the partners other than Maria. Also, the partnership's original basis in its assets ($50,000) is increased by the $4,000 recognized gain. ◀

SELF-STUDY QUESTION

What is the importance of the distinction between organizational expenditures and syndication expenditures?

ANSWER

Organizational expenditures can be deducted up to $5,000 and then amortized over a period of 180 months, but syndication expenditures are *not* deductible or amortizable.

ORGANIZATIONAL AND SYNDICATION EXPENDITURES

The costs of organizing a partnership are capital expenditures. However, under Sec. 709, the partnership can elect to deduct the first $5,000 of these expenditures in the tax year it begins business. As a limit, the partnership must reduce the $5,000 by the amount by which cumulative organizational expenditures exceed $50,000, although the $5,000 cannot be reduced below zero. The partnership can amortize the remaining organizational expenditures over an 180-month period beginning in the month it begins business.

For organizational expenditures paid or incurred after September 8, 2008, a partnership is deemed to have made the Sec. 709 election for the tax year the partnership begins business.[22] A partnership also can apply the amortization provisions for expenditures made after October 22, 2004, provided the statute of limitations is still open for the particular year. If the partnership chooses to forgo the deemed election, it can elect to capitalize the expenditures (without amortization) on a timely filed tax return for the tax year the partnership begins business. Either election, to amortize or capitalize, is irrevocable and applies to all organizational expenditures of the partnership.

Organizational expenditures that can be capitalized and amortized must meet the same requirements as the costs incurred by a corporation making the Sec. 248 election to amortize organizational expenditures (see Chapter C:3). The organizational expenditures must be incident to the creation of the partnership, chargeable to a capital account, and of a character that would be amortizable over the life of the partnership if the partnership had a limited life. Eligible expenditures include legal fees for negotiating and preparing partnership agreements, accounting fees for establishing the initial accounting system, and filing fees. Syndication expenditures for the issuing and marketing of interests in the partnership are not organizational expenditures and cannot be included in this election.[23] The partnership deducts unamortized organizational expenditures (but not capitalized syndication expenditures) when it terminates or liquidates.

Topic Review C:9-1 summarizes the tax consequences of forming a partnership.

PARTNERSHIP ELECTIONS

OBJECTIVE 4

Establish the permitted tax year for a partnership

Once formed, the partnership must make a number of elections. For example, a partnership must select a tax year and elect accounting methods for all but a few items affecting the computation of partnership taxable income or loss.

PARTNERSHIP TAX YEAR

The partnership's selection of a tax year is critical because it determines when each partner reports his or her share of partnership income or loss. Under Sec. 706(a), each partner's tax return includes his or her share of partnership income, gain, loss, deduction, or credit items for any taxable year of the partnership ending within or with the partner's tax year.

EXAMPLE C:9-16 ▶ Vicki is a member of a partnership having a November 30 year-end. In her tax return for calendar Year 1, she must include her share of partnership items from the partnership tax year that ends November 30 of Year 1. Results of partnership operations in December of Year 1 are reported in Vicki's Year 2 tax return along with her share of other partnership items from the partnership year that ends on November 30 of Year 2. She receives, in essence, a one-year deferral of the taxes due on December's partnership income. ◀

[22] Reg. Sec. 1.709-1.

[23] Reg. Sec. 1.709-2(b).

TOPIC REVIEW C:9-1

Formation of a Partnership

	Contribution to a Partnership: Property	Contribution to a Partnership: Services
Recognition of gain, loss, or income by partner	Nontaxable unless (1) liabilities assumed by the partnership exceed partner's predistribution basis in partnership interest (gain recognized is amount by which liabilities assumed by partnership exceed predistribution basis), (2) the partnership formed is an investment partnership (gain recognized is excess of FMV of partnership interest over basis of assets contributed), or (3) a contribution is followed by a distribution that is treated as a sale (gain or loss recognized on sale transaction).	Taxable to partner equal to FMV of partnership interest received in exchange for the services.
Basis of partnership interest	Substituted basis from property contributed plus share of partnership liabilities assumed minus the partner's liabilities assumed by the partnership. Gain recognized because of the investment company rules increases the basis of the partnership interest.	Amount of income recognized plus share of partnership liabilities assumed by the partner minus partner's liabilities assumed by the partnership.
Gain or loss recognized by the partnership	No gain or loss recognized by the partnership.	1. Deduction or capitalized expense is created depending on the type of service rendered. 2. Gain or loss recognized equals difference between FMV of portion of assets used to pay service partner and the basis of such portion of the assets.
Basis of assets to the partnership	Carryover basis is increased by a partner's gain recognized only if gain results from the formation of an investment partnership. No basis adjustment occurs when assumption of partner's liabilities results in a partner's gain recognition. In a sale transaction, assets take a cost basis.	Increased or decreased to reflect the FMV of the assets paid to the service partner.

Section 706 Restrictions. Because of a substantial opportunity for tax deferral, Congress enacted Sec. 706 to restrict the available choices for a partnership's tax year. The partnership must use the same tax year as the one or more **majority partners** who have an aggregate interest in partnership profits and capital exceeding 50%. This rule must be used only if these majority partners have a common tax year and have had this tax year for the shorter of the three preceding years or the partnership's period of existence. If the tax year of the partner(s) owning a majority interest cannot be used, the partnership must use the tax year of all its principal partners (or the tax year to which all of its principal partners are concurrently changing). A **principal partner** is defined as one who owns a 5% or more interest in capital or profits.[24] If the principal partners do not have a common tax year, the partnership must use the tax year that allows the least aggregate deferral. The least aggregate deferral test provided in Treasury Regulations[25] requires that, for each possible tax year-end, each partner's ownership percentage be multiplied by the number of months the partner would defer income (number of months from partnership year-end to partner year-end). The number arrived at for each partner is totaled across all partners. The same procedure is followed for each alternative tax year, and the partnership must use the tax year that produces the smallest total.

EXAMPLE C:9-17 ► Jane, Kerry Corporation, and Lanier Corporation form the JKL Partnership. The three partners use tax years ending on December 31, June 30, and September 30, respectively. Jane, Kerry

[24] Sec. 706(b)(3).

[25] Reg. Sec. 1.706-1.

WHAT WOULD YOU DO IN THIS SITUATION?

Bob Krause and his large family corporation have been longtime clients of your accounting firm. During the current year, Bob and his adult son, Tom, formed the BT Partnership to develop and sell vacation homes on the Suwanee River. Bob contributed a 1,000-acre tract of land in exchange for a 50% interest in BT Partnership's profits and losses. The land had a $300,000 FMV and a $30,000 adjusted basis. Tom contributed $150,000 in cash for the remaining 50% interest in the partnership. Two months after being formed, BT Partnership used the land as security for a $200,000 loan from a local bank. Of the $200,000 loan proceeds, the partnership used $50,000 to subdivide and plot the land. The partnership then distributed the other $150,000 of the loan proceeds to Bob. Bob plans not to report these transactions because property contributions in exchange for a partnership interest and distributions of money by a partnership that do not exceed the partner's basis are nontaxable transactions. What would you advise your client to do in this situation?

Corporation, and Lanier Corporation own 40%, 40%, and 20%, respectively, of the partnership. Neither the majority partner rule nor the principal partner rule can be applied to determine JKL's tax year because each partner has a different year-end. To determine the least aggregate deferral, all three possible year-ends must be analyzed as follows:

			Possible Tax Year-Ends					
			6/30		*9/30*		*12/31*	
Partner	*Partnership Interest*	*Partner Tax Year*	*Months Deferred*[a]	*Total*[b]	*Months Deferred*	*Total*	*Months Deferred*	*Total*
Jane	40%	12/31	6	2.4	3	1.2	0	0
Kerry	40%	6/30	0	0	9	3.6	6	2.4
Lanier	20%	9/30	3	0.6	0	0	9	1.8
				3.0		4.8		4.2

[a] Months from possible partnership tax year-end to partner tax year-end.
[b] Partnership interest × months deferred = Total.

The partnership must use a June 30 year-end because, with a total score of 3.0, that tax year-end produces the least aggregate deferral. ◀

If the partnership has a business purpose for using some tax year other than the year prescribed by these rules, the IRS may approve use of another tax year. Revenue Procedure 2002-39[26] states that an acceptable business purpose for using a different tax year is to end the partnership's tax year at the end of the partnership's natural business year. This revenue procedure explains that a business having a peak period and a nonpeak period completes its natural business year at the end of its peak season (or shortly thereafter). For example, a ski lodge has a natural business year that ends in early spring. Partnerships that do not have a peak period cannot use the natural business year exception.

EXAMPLE C:9-18 ▶ Amy, Brad, and Chris are equal partners in the ABC Partnership. Each partner uses a December 31 tax year-end. ABC earns 30% of its gross receipts in July and August each year and has experienced this pattern of earnings for more than three years. This two-month period is the peak season for their business each year. The IRS probably would grant approval for the partnership to use an August 31 tax year-end. ◀

KEY POINT

Because of the Sec. 706 requirements, most partnerships are required to adopt a calendar year. As a compromise, a Sec. 444 election permits a fiscal tax year as long as no more than a three-month deferral exists and as long as the deferral is not increased from any deferral already approved.

Section 444 provides an election that permits a partnership to use a year-end that results in a deferral of the lesser of the current deferral period or three months. The deferral period is the time from the beginning of the partnership's fiscal year to the close of the

[26] 2002-1 C.B. 1046. The IRS in Rev. Rul. 87-57, 1987-2 C.B. 117, has provided a series of situations illustrating the business purpose requirement. In addition, Rev. Proc. 2006-46, 2006-2 C.B. 859, provides expeditious IRS approval if the natural business year satisfies a 25% test. This test requires that 25% of the partnership's gross receipts be earned in the last two months of the requested year and in the last two months of the two preceding similar 12-month periods.

first required tax year ending within such year (i.e., usually December 31). The **Sec. 444 election** is available to both new partnerships making an initial tax year election or existing partnerships that are changing tax years. A partnership that satisfies the Sec. 706 requirements described above or has established a business purpose for its choice of a year-end (i.e., natural business year) does not need a Sec. 444 election.

STOP & THINK

Question: Suppose the ABC Partnership has had a December 31 year-end for many years. All its partners are individuals with calendar tax year-ends. Using Sec. 444, what tax year-ends are available for ABC?

Solution: Only December 31 can be used for a tax year-end for ABC even with Sec. 444. Section 444 allows a minimum deferral of the shorter of three months or the existing deferral. Because the existing deferral is zero months (the required tax year-end and the existing tax year-end are both December 31), no deferral is allowed under Sec. 444. The section allows a deferral only for new partnerships or for partnerships that already have a deferral.

HISTORICAL NOTE

Congress enacted Sec. 444, in part, as a concession to tax return preparers who already have the majority of their clients with calendar year-ends.

A partnership that makes a Sec. 444 election must make a required payment under Sec. 7519. (See the Compliance and Procedural Considerations section of this chapter for a discussion of the Sec. 444 election and Sec. 7519 required payment.) The required payment has the effect of assessing a tax on the partnership's deferred income at the highest individual marginal tax rate plus one percentage point.

Topic Review C:9-2 summarizes the allowable partnership tax year elections.

OTHER PARTNERSHIP ELECTIONS

With the exception of three specific elections reserved to the partners, Sec. 703(b) requires that the partnership make all elections that can affect the computation of taxable income derived from the partnership.[27] The three elections reserved to the individual partners relate to income from the discharge of indebtedness, deduction and recapture of certain mining exploration expenditures, and the choice between deducting or crediting foreign income taxes. Other than these elections, the partnership makes all elections at the entity level. Accordingly, the partnership elects its overall accounting method, which can differ from the methods used by its partners. The partnership also elects its inventory and depreciation methods.

TOPIC REVIEW C:9-2

Allowable Tax Year for a Partnership

Section 706 requires that a partnership select the highest ranked tax year-end from the ranking that follows:

1. The tax year-end used by the partners who own a majority interest in the partnership capital and profits.
2. The tax year-end used by all principal partners (i.e., partners who each owns an interest in at least 5% of the partnership capital or profits).
3. The tax year-end determined by the least aggregate deferral test.

The IRS may grant permission for the partnership to use a fiscal year-end if the partnership has a natural business year. If the partnership does not have a natural business year, it must either

- Use the tax year-end required by Sec. 706 or
- Elect a fiscal year-end under Sec. 444 and make a required payment that approximates the tax due on the deferred income.

[27] The partnership does not include depletion from oil or gas wells in its computation of income (Sec. 703(a)(2)(F)). Instead each partner elects cost or percentage depletion (Sec. 613A(c)(7)(D)).

PARTNERSHIP REPORTING OF INCOME

OBJECTIVE 5

Distinguish between items included in partnership ordinary income or loss and those that must be separately stated

PARTNERSHIP TAXABLE INCOME

Although the partnership is not a taxable entity, the IRC requires that the partnership calculate **partnership taxable income** for various computational reasons, such as adjusting the partners' basis in their partnership interests. Partnership taxable income for partnerships that are not electing large partnerships is calculated in much the same way as the taxable income of individuals, with a few differences mandated by the IRC. First, taxable income is divided into separately stated items and ordinary income or loss. Section 703(a) specifies a list of deductions available to individuals but that cannot be claimed by a partnership. The forbidden deductions include income taxes paid or accrued to a foreign country or U.S. possession, charitable contributions, oil and gas depletion, and net operating loss (NOL) carrybacks or carryovers. The first three items must be separately stated and may or may not be deductible by the partner. Because all losses are allocated to the partners for deduction on their tax returns, the partnership itself never has an NOL carryover or carryback. Instead, a partner may have an NOL if his or her deductible share of partnership losses exceeds his or her other business income. These NOLs are used at the partner level without any further regard for the partnership entity.

ADDITIONAL COMMENT

The applicable capital gains tax rate for net capital gains and qualified dividends of noncorporate taxpayers is 0% for taxpayers in tax brackets of 15% and below, 15% for taxpayers in the 25% through 35% tax brackets, and 20% for taxpayers in the 39.6% tax bracket. Also, 25% and 28% rates apply for gains on certain types of property. In addition, an incremental 3.8% rate applies to net investment income for taxpayers whose modified AGI exceeds $200,000 ($250,000 for married filing jointly). Net investment income includes, among other things, interest, dividends, annuities, royalties, rents, and net gains from the disposition of property not used in a trade or business, all reduced by deductions allocable to such income or gains.

SEPARATELY STATED ITEMS

Each partner must report his or her distributive share of partnership income. However, Sec. 702, related Treasury Regulations, and tax return instructions require that certain items be separately stated at the partnership level so their character can remain intact at the partner reporting level. For example, the following items must be separately stated:

- Net short-term capital gains and losses
- Net long-term capital gains and losses
- Sec. 1231 gains and losses
- Unrecaptured Sec. 1250 gains
- Sec. 179 expense
- Charitable contributions
- Dividends and interest income
- Taxes paid or accrued to a foreign country or to a U.S. possession
- Tax-exempt or partially tax-exempt interest
- Investment income and expenses
- Any items subject to special allocations (discussed below)
- Any other item provided by Treasury Regulations and tax form instructions

As a general rule, an item must be separately stated if the income tax liability of any partner that would result from treating the item separately is different from the liability that would result if that item were included in partnership ordinary income.[28] For a comprehensive list of separately stated items, see Form 1065, Schedule K included in Appendix B.

ADDITIONAL COMMENT

The pass-through aspect of partnerships reflects the aggregate theory of partnerships, which holds that the partnership is merely an aggregate of its partners. In other ways, however, partnerships conform to the entity theory, for example, they report income and make elections at the entity level.

Once the partnership separately states each item and allocates a distributive share to each partner, the partners report the separately stated items on their tax returns as if the partnership entity did not exist. A partner's share of partnership net long-term capital gains or losses is combined with the partner's personal long-term capital gains and losses to calculate the partner's net long-term capital gain or loss. Likewise, a partner's share of partnership charitable contributions is combined with the partner's own charitable contributions with the total subject to the partner's charitable contribution limitations. In summary, Sec. 702(b) requires that the character of each separately stated item be determined at the partnership level. The amount then passes through to the partners and is reported in each partner's return as if the partner directly realized the amount.

[28] Reg. Sec. 1.702-1(a)(8)(ii).

TYPICAL MISCONCEPTION

Partnership ordinary income or loss is the sum of all taxable income or loss items not separately stated. The partnership reports this amount as a residual number on line 22 of Form 1065. Partnership taxable income includes both the taxable separately stated items and the partnership ordinary income or loss. These two terms are not interchangeable.

PARTNERSHIP ORDINARY INCOME

All taxable items of income, gain, loss, or deduction that do not have to be separately stated are combined into a total called **partnership ordinary income** or **loss**. This ordinary income amount sometimes is incorrectly referred to as partnership taxable income. Partnership taxable income is the sum of all taxable items among the separately stated items plus the partnership ordinary income or loss. Therefore, partnership taxable income often is substantially greater than partnership ordinary income.

Included in the partnership's ordinary income are items such as gross profit on sales, administrative expenses, and employee salaries. Such items are always ordinary income or expenses not subject to special limitations. Partnership ordinary income also includes Sec. 1245 depreciation recapture because such ordinary income is not eligible for preferential treatment.

The partnership allocates a share of partnership ordinary income or loss to each partner. Such an allocation is reported on Schedules K and K-1 of the partnership's Form 1065 (see the completed partnership tax return in Appendix B). An individual partner reports his or her distributive share of ordinary income, or the deductible portion of his or her distributive share of ordinary loss, on Schedule E of Form 1040. Schedule E includes rental and royalty income and income or losses from estates, trusts, S corporations, and partnerships. A corporate partner reports partnership ordinary income or loss in the Other Income category of Form 1120.

EXAMPLE C:9-19 ▶ Harry and Rita have been operating the HR Partnership for several years. Each partner has a 50% interest in the partnership. In the current year, the partnership incurred the following items:

Sales	$450,000
Cost of goods sold	250,000
Dividend income	6,000
Gain on sale of stock held for three years	7,000
Loss on sale of stock held for seven months	1,000
Gain on sale of equipment ($10,000 total depreciation taken)	14,000
Salaries paid to employees	45,000
Depreciation	15,000

The partnership will report these items as follows:

Partnership ordinary income items:		
Sales		$450,000
Minus: Cost of goods sold		(250,000)
Gross profit		200,000
Plus: Sec. 1245 depreciation recapture		10,000
Minus: Ordinary expenses:		
Salaries	$45,000	
Depreciation	15,000	(60,000)
Partnership ordinary income		$ 150,000

Separately stated items:	
Dividends	6,000
Net short-term capital loss	(1,000)
Net long-term capital gain	7,000
Sec. 1231 gain ($14,000 - $10,000)	4,000

As discussed in the next section of this chapter, each partner will report a 50% distributive share of partnership ordinary income and each separately stated item. ◀

U.S. PRODUCTION ACTIVITIES DEDUCTION

Chapter C:3 describes the corporate version of the U.S. production activities deduction, whereby the deduction equals 9% times the lesser of (1) qualified production activities income for the year or (2) taxable income before the U.S. production activities deduction. Individuals use a modified form of AGI instead of taxable income for this computation. The deduction, however, cannot exceed 50% of the employer's W-2 wages allocable to production activities for the year. In the case of a partnership, the deduction applies at the partner level, so the partnership must report each partner's share of qualified production activities income on the partner's Schedule K-1. For the 50% salary limitation, each partner is allocated a share of the partnership's W-2 wages.

PARTNER REPORTING OF INCOME

OBJECTIVE 6

Determine a partner's distributive share of partnership income, gain, loss, deduction, or credit items

PARTNER'S DISTRIBUTIVE SHARE

Once the partnership determines separately stated income, gain, loss, deduction, or credit items, and partnership ordinary income or loss, the partnership must allocate the totals among the partners. Each partner must report and pay taxes on his or her distributive share. Under Sec. 704(b), the partner's distributive share normally is determined by the terms of the partnership agreement or, if the partnership agreement is silent, by the partner's overall interest in the partnership as determined by taking into account all facts and circumstances.

Note that the term **distributive share** is misleading because it has nothing to do with the amount actually distributed to a partner. A partner's distributive share is the portion of partnership taxable and nontaxable income that the partner has agreed to report for tax purposes. Actual distributions in a given year may be more or less than the partner's distributive share.

Partnership Agreement. The **partnership agreement** may describe a partner's distributive share by indicating the partner's profits and loss interest, or it may indicate separate profits and loss interests. For example, the partnership agreement may state that a partner has a 10% interest in both partnership profits and losses or a partner has only a 10% interest in partnership profits (i.e., profits interest) but has a 30% interest in partnership losses (i.e., loss interest).

If the partnership agreement states only one interest percentage, it is used to allocate both partnership profit and loss. If the partnership agreement states profit and loss percentages separately, the partnership's taxable income for the year is first totaled to determine whether a net profit or net loss has occurred. Then the appropriate percentage (either profit or loss) applies to each class of income for the year.[29]

EXAMPLE C:9-20 ▶ The ABC Partnership reports the following income and loss items for the current year:

Net long-term capital loss	$100,000
Net Sec. 1231 gain	90,000
Ordinary income	220,000

Carmelia has a 20% profits interest and a 30% loss interest in the ABC Partnership. Because the partnership earns a $210,000 ($90,000 + $220,000 − $100,000) net profit, Carmelia's distributive share is calculated using her 20% profits interest and is reported as follows:

Net long-term capital loss	$ 20,000
Net Sec. 1231 gain	18,000
Ordinary income	44,000

Her loss percentage is used only in years in which the partnership has a net loss. ◀

Varying Interest Rule. If a partner's ownership interest changes during the partnership tax year, the income or loss allocation takes into account the partner's varying interest.[30] This varying interest rule applies for changes occurring to a partner's interest as a result of buying an additional interest in the partnership, selling part (but not all) of a partnership interest, giving or being given a partnership interest, or admitting a new partner. The partner's ownership interest generally applies to the income earned on a pro rata basis.

EXAMPLE C:9-21 ▶ Maria owns 20% of the XYZ Partnership from January 1 through June 30 of the current year (not a leap year). On July 1 she buys an additional 10% interest in the partnership. During this

[29] This rule is derived from the House and Senate reports on the original Sec. 704(b) provisions. The two reports are identical and read, "The income ratio shall be applicable if the partnership has taxable income . . . and the loss ratio shall be applicable [if] the partnership has a loss." H. Rept. No. 1337, 83d Cong., 2d Sess., p. A223 (1954); S. Rept. No. 1622, 83d Cong., 2d Sess., p. 379 (1954).

[30] Sec. 706(d)(1).

year, XYZ Partnership has ordinary income of $120,000, which it earned evenly throughout the year. Maria's $30,049 ($11,901 + $18,148) distributive share of income is calculated as follows:

Pre-July 1: $$\$120{,}000 \times \frac{181 \text{ days}}{365 \text{ days}} \times 0.20 = \$11{,}901$$

Post-June 30: $$\$120{,}000 \times \frac{184 \text{ days}}{365 \text{ days}} \times 0.30 = \$18{,}148$$

Similar calculations would be made if the XYZ Partnership reported separately stated items such as capital gains and losses. ◀

SPECIAL ALLOCATIONS

Special allocations are unique to partnerships (and LLCs treated as partnerships). They allow tremendous flexibility in sharing specific items of income and loss among the partners. Special allocations can provide a specified partner with more or less of an item of income, gain, loss, or deduction than would be available using the partner's regular distributive share. Special allocations fall into two categories. First, Sec. 704 requires certain special allocations with respect to contributed property. Second, other special allocations are allowed as long as they meet the tests set forth in Treasury Regulations for having substantial economic effect. If the special allocation fails the substantial economic effect test, it is disregarded, and the income, gain, loss, or deduction is allocated according to the partner's interest in the partnership as expressed in the actual operations and activities.

BOOK-TO-TAX ACCOUNTING COMPARISON

For tax purposes, the partnership takes a carryover basis in contributed property. For book purposes, however, the partnership records the contributed property at its FMV.

Allocations Related to Contributed Property. As previously discussed, when a partner contributes property to a partnership, the property takes a carryover basis that references the contributing partner's basis. With no special allocations, this carryover basis rule would require the partnership (and each partner) to accept the tax burden of any gain or loss that accrued to the property before its contribution.

EXAMPLE C:9-22 ▶ In the current year, Elizabeth contributes land having a $4,000 basis and a $10,000 FMV to the DEF Partnership. Assuming the property continues to increase in value, or at least does not decline in value, DEF's gain on the ultimate sale of this property is $6,000 greater than the gain that accrues while the partnership owns the property. Without a special allocation, this $6,000 precontribution gain would be allocated among all partners. ◀

Section 704(c), however, requires precontribution gains or losses to be allocated to the contributing partner. Thus, the precontribution gain of $6,000 in Example C:9-22 would be allocated to Elizabeth. In addition, income and deductions reported with respect to contributed property must be allocated to take into account the difference between the property's basis and FMV at the time of contribution.

EXAMPLE C:9-23 ▶ Kay and Sam form an equal partnership when Sam contributes cash of $10,000 and Kay contributes land having a $6,000 basis and a $10,000 FMV. If the partnership sells the land two years later for $12,000, the $4,000 precontribution gain ($10,000 FMV − $6,000 basis) is allocated only to Kay. The $2,000 gain that accrued while the partnership held the land ($12,000 sales price − $10,000 FMV at contribution) is allocated to Kay and Sam equally. Kay reports a total gain of $5,000 ($4,000 + $1,000), and Sam reports a $1,000 gain on the sale of the land. ◀

BOOK-TO-TAX ACCOUNTING COMPARISON

The capital accounts for meeting the substantial economic effect requirements are maintained using book value accounting rather than tax accounting.

The allocation of depreciation is another common example of the special deduction allocation related to contributed property that is necessary under these rules. Tax Research Problem C:9-61 addresses the depreciation allocation issue.

Substantial Economic Effect. Special allocations not related to contributed property must meet several specific criteria established by Treasury Regulations. These criteria ensure that the allocations affect the partner's economic consequences and not just their tax consequences.

BOOK-TO-TAX ACCOUNTING COMPARISON

In Example C:9-23, the partnership records a $6,000 tax gain and a $2,000 book gain, which provides another example of the difference between partnership tax and book accounting.

To distinguish transactions affecting only taxes from those affecting the partner's economic position, Treasury Regulations look at whether the allocation has an economic effect and whether the economic effect is substantial. Under the Sec. 704 regulations, the allocation has economic effect if it meets all three of the following conditions:

- The allocation results in the appropriate increase or decrease in the partner's capital account.

- The proceeds of any liquidation occurring at any time in the partnership's life cycle are distributed in accordance with positive capital account balances.
- Partners must make up negative balances in their capital accounts upon the liquidation of the partnership, and these contributions are used to pay partnership debts or are allocated to partners having positive capital account balances.[31]

EXAMPLE C:9-24 ▶ Arnie and Bonnie each contribute $100,000 to form the AB Partnership on January 1 of Year 1. The partnership uses these contributions plus a $1.8 million mortgage to purchase a $2 million office building. To simplify the calculations, assume the partnership depreciates the building using the straight-line method over a 40-year life and that in each year income and expenses are equal before considering depreciation. AB makes a special allocation of depreciation to Arnie. The allocation reduces Arnie's capital account, and the partnership makes any liquidating distributions in accordance with the capital account balances. Allocations through Year 3 are as follows:

	Capital Account Balance	
	Arnie	*Bonnie*
January 1, Year 1, balance	$100,000	$100,000
Year 1 loss (from depreciation deduction)	(50,000)	–0–
Year 2 loss (from depreciation deduction)	(50,000)	–0–
Year 3 loss (from depreciation deduction)	(50,000)	–0–
December 31, Year 3, balance	$ (50,000)	$100,000

If we assume that the property has declined in value in an amount equal to the depreciation claimed and that the partnership now liquidates, the need for the requirement to restore negative capital account balances becomes apparent.

Sales price of property on December 31, Year 3	$1,850,000
Minus: Mortgage principal	(1,800,000)
Partnership cash to be distributed to partners	$ 50,000

If Arnie does not have to restore his negative capital account balance, Bonnie can receive only $50,000 in cash even though her capital account balance is $100,000. In effect, Bonnie has borne the economic burden of the Year 3 depreciation. Without a requirement to restore the negative capital account balance, the special allocation to Arnie would be ignored for Year 3, and Bonnie would receive the depreciation deduction. However, if Arnie must restore any negative capital account balance, he will contribute $50,000 when the partnership liquidates at the end of Year 3, and Bonnie will receive her full $100,000 capital account balance. The Year 3 special allocation to Arnie will then have economic effect. Note that Arnie's allocations for Years 1 and 2 are acceptable even without an agreement to restore negative capital account balances. This result occurs in each of these two years because Arnie has sufficient capital to absorb the economic loss if the property declines in value in an amount equal to the depreciation allocated to him.[32] ◀

ADDITIONAL COMMENT

The substantial economic effect rules ensure that cash flows ultimately conform to allocations and that allocations do not allow for abusive shifting of tax benefits among partners.

The second requirement for a special allocation to be accepted under Treasury Regulations is that the economic effect must be substantial, which requires that a reasonable possibility exists that the allocation will substantially affect the dollar amounts to be received by the partners independent of tax consequences.[33] Moreover, allocations that involve shifting will not pass the substantiality test. Shifting occurs when the following two conditions are present:

- The net change in the partner's capital accounts will be the same for a normal allocation and the special allocation.
- The total tax liability of the partners will be less with the special allocation than with a normal allocation.[34]

---

31 Reg. Sec. 1.704-1(b)(2)(ii). Treasury Regulations provide other alternatives for meeting this portion of the requirements.

32 Such allocations do not literally meet the three requirements outlined above for special allocations. However, allocations that meet the alternate standard—having sufficient capital to absorb the economic loss—are considered to have economic effect and will be allowed. See Reg. Sec. 1.704-1(b)(2)(ii)(d).

33 Reg. Sec. 1.704-1(b)(2)(iii)(a). It should be noted that the substantial economic effect regulations go far beyond the rules covered in this text.

34 Reg. Sec. 1.704-1(b)(2)(iii)(b). An allocation also can fail the substantiality test by being transitory, which is something like shifting except an allocation in one year is offset by another allocation in a future year (Reg. Sec. 1.704-1(b)(2)(iii)(c)).

EXAMPLE C:9-25 ▶ The AB Partnership earns $10,000 in tax-exempt interest income and $10,000 in taxable interest income each year. Andy and Becky each have 50% capital and profit interests in the partnership. An allocation of the tax-exempt interest income to Andy, a 33% tax bracket partner, and the taxable interest income to Becky, a 15% tax bracket partner, does not have substantial economic effect. In particular, the allocation lacks substantiality because of shifting. The allocation increases each partner's capital account by $10,000 as would an equal allocation, and it reduces the partner's overall tax liability (see Problem C:9-36 at the end of this chapter). ◀

STOP & THINK

Question: The special allocation rules require that a partner who receives a special allocation of loss or expense receive less cash or property when the partnership liquidates. As we will see later in this chapter, losses reduce the partner's basis in the partnership interest, so a sale or liquidation of the partnership interest will cause the partner to recognize a larger gain (or a smaller loss) than would have resulted without this loss allocation. Because the basis is reduced, the partner also is more likely to recognize taxable gain on a distribution from the partnership. With these negative consequences, why would anyone want to be given a special allocation of partnership loss or expense?

Solution: The answer is a matter of timing. The specially allocated loss reduces taxable income now and saves more taxes now for the partner than would a "normal" loss allocation. The negative consequences occur when the partner incurs a larger gain (or smaller loss) upon a future sale or liquidation of his or her partnership interest. The special allocation scenario may have a greater after-tax present value to the partner than would the after-tax present value of receiving a normal share of losses and an increased liquidating distribution.

BASIS FOR PARTNERSHIP INTEREST

OBJECTIVE 7

Calculate a partner's basis in a partnership interest and its effect on losses

The calculation of a partner's beginning basis in a partnership interest depends on the method used to acquire the interest, with different valuation techniques for a purchased interest, a gifted interest, and an inherited interest. The results of the partnership's operations and liabilities both cause adjustments to the beginning amount. Additional contributions to the partnership and distributions from the partnership further alter the partner's basis.

BEGINNING BASIS

ADDITIONAL COMMENT

A partner's basis in a partnership interest commonly is referred to as "outside basis" as opposed to "inside basis," which is the partnership's basis in its assets.

A partner's beginning basis for a partnership interest received for a contribution of property or services has been discussed. However, a partner also can acquire a partnership interest by methods other than contributing property or services to the partnership. If a person purchases the partnership interest from an existing partner, the new partner's basis is the price paid for the partnership interest, including assumption of partnership liabilities. If a person inherits the partnership interest, the heir's basis is the FMV of the partnership interest on the decedent's date of death or, if elected by the executor, the alternate valuation date but not less than liabilities assumed. If a person receives the partnership interest as a gift, the donee's basis generally equals the donor's basis (including the donor's ratable share of partnership liabilities) plus the portion of any gift tax paid by the donor that relates to appreciation attaching to the gift property. In summary, the usual rules for the method of acquisition dictate the beginning basis for a partnership interest.

SELF-STUDY QUESTION

What are some of the common methods of acquiring a partnership interest, and what is the beginning basis?

ANSWER

1. Contribution—substituted basis from contributed property
2. Purchase—cost basis
3. Inheritance—FMV
4. Gift—usually donor's basis with a possible gift tax adjustment

EFFECTS OF LIABILITIES

The early part of this chapter briefly discussed the effect of partnership liabilities on the basis of a partnership interest in connection with the contribution of property subject to a liability. However, further explanation is necessary to fully convey the pervasive impact of liabilities on partnership taxation.

Increases and Decreases in Liabilities. Two changes in a partner's liabilities are considered contributions of cash by the partner to the partnership.[35] The first is an

[35] Sec. 752.

increase in the partner's share of partnership liabilities. This increase can arise from either an increase in the partner's profit or loss interests or from an increase in total partnership liabilities. Accordingly, if a partnership incurs a large debt, the partners' bases in their partnership interests increase. The second way to increase a partner's basis is to have the partner assume partnership liabilities in his or her individual capacity.

Conversely, two liability changes are treated as distributions of cash from the partnership to the partner. These changes are a decrease in a partner's share of partnership liabilities and a decrease in the partner's individual liabilities resulting from the partnership's assumption of the partner's liability. Often, both an increase and a decrease in a partner's basis for his or her interest can result from a single transaction. The framework below illustrates the steps used to calculate the partner's basis in his or her partnership interest.

	Partner's basis before changes in liabilities
Plus:	Increases in share of partnership liabilities
Minus:	Decreases in share of partnership liabilities
Plus:	Partnership liabilities assumed by this partner
Minus:	This partner's liabilities assumed by the partnership
	Partner's basis in the partnership interest

EXAMPLE C:9-26 ▶ Juan, a 40% partner in the ABC Partnership, has a $30,000 basis in his partnership interest before receiving a partnership distribution of land. As part of the transaction, Juan agrees to assume a $10,000 mortgage on the land. First, Juan's basis in his partnership interest will decrease by $4,000 for the decline in Juan's share of partnership liabilities resulting from the partnership no longer owing the $10,000 mortgage. Second, his basis in the partnership interest will increase by $10,000, which is the partnership liability he assumes in his individual capacity. The net change in basis in his partnership resulting from the liabilities is $6,000 (−$4,000 + $10,000). His basis in his partnership interest also must be decreased for the land distribution he receives. Distributions will be discussed further in Chapter C:10. ◀

A Partner's Share of Liabilities. Having explained the general impact of liabilities on a partner's basis for his or her partnership interest, we now turn to how the specific amount of the partner's share of a partnership's liabilities is determined. All examples so far have considered only general partners who have the same interest in profits and losses. Partnerships, however, commonly have one or more limited partners, and thus partners can have differing profit and loss ratios. Moreover, the type of liability affects how it is allocated. Treasury Regulations provide guidelines for allocating partnership liabilities to the individual partners.

ADDITIONAL COMMENT

That a partner gets basis for his or her share of recourse debt is not controversial. That a partner gets basis for debt on which the partner is not personally liable seems questionable, yet other rules, such as the at-risk provisions, limit the benefit of the basis created by the nonrecourse debt.

Recourse and Nonrecourse Loans. A **recourse loan** is the usual kind of loan for which the borrower remains liable until the loan is paid. If the recourse loan is secured and the borrower fails to make payments as scheduled, the lender can sell the property used as security. If the sales proceeds are insufficient to repay a recourse loan, the borrower must make up the difference. Under Treasury Regulations, a recourse loan is one for which any partner or a related party will stand an economic loss if the partnership cannot pay the debt.[36] In contrast, a **nonrecourse loan** is one in which the lender may sell property used as security if the loan is not paid, but no partner is liable for any deficiency. In short, the lender has no recourse against the borrower for additional amounts. Nonrecourse debts most commonly occur in connection with the financing of real property that is expected to substantially increase in value over the life of the loan.

ADDITIONAL COMMENT

In January 2014, the Treasury Department issued proposed Treasury Regulations that would alter the way partnership liabilities are allocated to partners. These regulations would not be effective unless and until they are finalized. Also, in the interim, they could be modified before issuance. Therefore, the discussion in the text regarding liabilities does not reflect these proposed regulations.

General and Limited Partners. A limited partner normally is not liable to pay partnership debts beyond the original contribution (which already is reflected in his or her basis in the partnership interest) and any additional amount the partner has pledged to contribute.[37] Therefore, recourse debt increases a limited partner's basis only to the extent the

[36] Reg. Sec. 1.752-1(a).

[37] This rule may be modified by the limited partner agreeing to assume some of the risk of economic loss despite his or her limited partner status. For example, a limited partner may guarantee the debt or may agree to reimburse the general partner some amount if the general partner has to pay the debt. These arrangements mean that the limited partner shares the risk of loss.

partner has a risk of economic loss. Nonrecourse debts increase a limited partner's basis based primarily on the profit ratio.[38]

A general partner's share of nonrecourse liabilities also is determined primarily by his or her profit ratio. On the other hand, because limited partners seldom receive an allocated share of the recourse liabilities, the general partners share all recourse liabilities beyond any amounts the limited partners can claim according to their economic loss potential.

The Sec. 752 Treasury Regulations require that recourse liabilities be allocated to the partner who will bear the economic loss if the partnership cannot pay the debt. The regulations provide a complex procedure using a hypothetical liquidation to determine who would bear the loss. In this text, we assume that the hypothetical liquidation analysis has been completed and that the appropriate shares of economic loss as determined by the hypothetical liquidation procedure are stated as part of the problem or example information.

EXAMPLE C:9-27 ▶ The ABC Partnership has one general partner (Anna) and a limited partner (Clay) with the following partnership interests:

	Anna (General)	*Clay (Limited)*
Loss interest	75%	25%
Profits interest	60%	40%
Basis before liabilities	$100,000	$100,000

Clay has an obligation to make an additional $5,000 contribution. He has made no other agreements or guarantees. The partnership has two liabilities at year-end: a $300,000 nonrecourse liability and a $400,000 recourse liability. Clay has an economic risk of loss only to the extent he has agreed to make additional contributions. The partners' year-end bases are calculated as follows:

	Anna (General)	*Clay (Limited)*
Year-end basis (excluding liabilities)	$100,000	$100,000
Share of:		
Recourse liability	395,000	5,000
Nonrecourse liability	180,000[a]	120,000[b]
Year-end basis	$675,000	$225,000

[a] 60% × $300,000 = $180,000
[b] 40% × $300,000 = $120,000 ◀

If the partnership has more than one general partner, the economic risk of loss computation entails computing a hypothetical loss and allocating that loss to the general partners. The hypothetical loss computation assumes the partnership sells all its assets (including cash) for the amount of nonrecourse liabilities. If the partnership does not have nonrecourse liabilities, the assets are deemed sold for zero dollars. The hypothetical loss then is subtracted from the partners' capital accounts to determine the economic risk of loss.

EXAMPLE C:9-28 ▶ Assume the same facts as in Example C:9-27 except that Clay is a general partner. In addition, the partnership has $900,000 of assets, and each partner's capital account is $100,000. If the partnership sold its assets for the amount of the nonrecourse liability, it would realize a $600,000 loss ($300,000 − $900,000). The economic risk of loss is calculated as follows:

	Anna (General)	*Clay (General)*
Capital accounts	$100,000	$100,000
Minus: Hypothetical loss (allocated according to loss percentages)	(450,000)	(150,000)
Economic risk of loss	($350,000)	($ 50,000)

[38] Some nonrecourse debt allocations involve two steps before an allocation according to profits interests. These two steps of the allocation process are beyond the scope of this explanation.

The partners' year-end bases are calculated as follows:

	Anna (General)	Clay (General)
Year-end basis (excluding liabilities)	$100,000	$100,000
Share of:		
Recourse liability	350,000	50,000
Nonrecourse liability	180,000	120,000
Year-end basis	$630,000	$270,000 ◀

Determining the partners' share of recourse liabilities can be simplified if the partners have the same interest in losses as they do for profits and if their capital accounts are in accordance with those percentages. In this situation, the recourse liability allocation also will be in accordance with the profit/loss percentages.

EFFECTS OF OPERATIONS

A partner's basis is a summary of his or her contributions and the partner's share of partnership liabilities, earnings, losses, and distributions. Basis prevents a second tax levy on a distribution of income that was taxed previously as a partner's distributive share. Section 705 mandates a basis increase for additional contributions made by the partner to the partnership plus the partner's distributive share for the current and prior tax years of the following items:[39]

- Partnership taxable income (both separately stated items and partnership ordinary income)
- Tax-exempt income of the partnership

BOOK-TO-TAX ACCOUNTING COMPARISON

Although a partner's basis in the partnership cannot go below zero, a partner's book capital account (equity) may be negative.

Basis is decreased (but not below zero) by distributions from the partnership to the partner plus the partner's distributive share for the current and prior tax years of the following items:

- Partnership losses (both separately stated items and partnership ordinary loss)
- Expenditures that are not deductible for tax purposes and that are not capital expenditures

The positive basis adjustment for tax-exempt income and the negative basis adjustment for nondeductible expenses preserve that tax treatment for the partner. If these adjustments were not made, tax-exempt income would be taxable to the partner upon a subsequent distribution or upon the sale or other disposition of the partnership interest.

EXAMPLE C:9-29 ▶ LMN Partnership has only one asset—a $100,000 municipal bond. Marta has a $20,000 basis in her 20% partnership interest. In the current year, the partnership collects $4,000 tax-exempt interest from the bond. Marta's basis at year-end is calculated as follows:

Beginning basis	$20,000
Share of tax-exempt income	800
Basis at year end	$20,800

On the first day of the next year, the partnership sells the bond for $100,000 cash. At this point, the partnership has $104,000 in cash and no other assets. The partnership liquidates and distributes her 20% share of the cash ($20,800) to Marta. Marta has no gain or loss because her $20,800 basis exactly equals her distribution. If the tax-exempt income had not increased her basis, she would have recognized an $800 gain on the distribution ($20,800 cash distribution − $20,000 basis if no increase were made for the tax-exempt income). Thus, her basis must be increased by tax-exempt income to prevent a taxable gain upon its distribution. ◀

Loss Limitations. Each partner is allocated his or her distributive share of ordinary income or loss and separately stated income, gain, loss, or deduction items each year. The partner always reports income and gain items in his or her current tax year, and these items increase the partner's basis in the partnership interest. However, the partner may not be able to use his or her full distributive share of losses because Sec. 704(d) limits a partner's loss deduction to the amount of his or her basis in the partnership interest before the loss. All positive basis adjustments for the year and all reductions for actual or deemed distributions must be made before determining the amount of the deductible loss.[40]

[39] Section 705 also contains adjustments pertaining to depletion.

[40] Reg. Sec. 1.704-1(d)(2).

EXAMPLE C:9-30 ► On January 1 of the current year, Miguel has a $32,000 basis for his general interest in the MT Partnership. He materially participates in the partnership's business activities. On December 1, Miguel receives a $1,000 cash distribution. His distributive share of MT's current items are a $4,000 net long-term capital gain and a $43,000 ordinary loss. Miguel's deductible loss is calculated as follows:

January 1 basis	$32,000
Plus: Long-term capital gain	4,000
Minus: Distribution	(1,000)
Limit for loss deduction	$35,000

Miguel can deduct $35,000 of the ordinary loss in the current year, which reduces his basis to zero. He cannot deduct the remaining $8,000 of ordinary loss currently but can deduct it in the following year if he regains sufficient basis in his partnership interest. ◄

SELF-STUDY QUESTION

What happens to losses that are disallowed due to lack of basis in a partnership interest?

ANSWER

The losses are suspended until that partner obtains additional basis.

Any distributive share of loss that a partner cannot deduct because of the basis limit is simply noted in the partner's financial records. It is not reported on the partner's tax return, nor does it reduce the partner's basis. However, the losses carry forward until the partner again has positive basis from capital contributions, additional partnership borrowings, or partnership earnings.

EXAMPLE C:9-31 ► Assume the same facts as in Example C:9-30. Miguel makes no additional contributions in the following year, and the MT Partnership's liabilities remain unchanged. Miguel's distributive share of MT's partnership items in the following year is $2,500 of net short-term capital gain and $14,000 of ordinary income. These items restore his basis to $16,500 ($0 + $2,500 + $14,000), and he can deduct the $8,000 loss carryover. After taking these transactions into account, Miguel's basis is $8,500 ($16,500 − $8,000). ◄

Topic Review C:9-3 summarizes the rules for determining the initial basis for a partnership interest and the annual basis adjustments required to determine the adjusted basis of a partnership interest.

TOPIC REVIEW C:9-3

Basis of a Partnership Interest

Method of Acquisition	**Beginning Basis Is**
Property contributed	Substituted basis from property contributed plus gain recognized for contributions to an investment partnership
Services contributed	Amount of income recognized for services rendered (plus any additional amount contributed)
Purchase	Cost
Gift	Donor's basis plus gift tax on appreciation
Inheritance	Fair market value at date of death or alternative valuation date

Liability Impact on Basis

Increase basis for	Increases in the partner's share of partnership liabilities Liabilities of the partnership assumed by the partner in his or her individual capacity
Decrease basis for	Decreases in the partner's share of partnership liabilities Liabilities of the partner assumed by the partnership

Operations Impact on Basis

Increase basis for	Partner's share of ordinary income and separately stated income and gain items (including tax-exempt items) Additional contributions to the partnership Precontribution gain recognized
Decrease basis for	Distributions from the partnership to the partner Partner's share of ordinary loss and separately stated loss and deduction items (including items that are not deductible for tax purposes and are not capital expenditures) Precontribution loss recognized

Special Loss Limitations

OBJECTIVE 8

Discuss the at-risk and passive activity loss limitations

Three sets of rules limit the loss from a partnership interest that a partner may deduct. The Sec. 704(d) rules explained above limit losses to the partner's basis in the partnership interest. Two other rules establish more stringent limits. The at-risk rules limit losses to an amount called *at-risk basis*. The passive activity loss or credit limitation rules disallow most net passive activity losses.

AT-RISK LOSS LIMITATION

The Sec. 704(d) loss limitation rules were the only loss limits for many years. However, Congress became increasingly uncomfortable with allowing partners to increase their basis by a portion of the partnership's nonrecourse liabilities and then offset this basis with partnership losses. Accordingly, Congress established the **at-risk rules**, which limit loss deductions to the partner's at-risk basis. The **at-risk basis** is essentially the same amount as the regular partnership basis with the exception that liabilities increase the at-risk basis only if the partner is at risk for such an amount. The at-risk rules apply to individuals and closely held C corporations. Partners that are widely held C corporations are not subject to these rules.

REAL-WORLD EXAMPLE

In 2012, 44.5% of all domestic partnerships and LLCs reported net losses. These losses would have passed through to the partners and LLC members to offset income or gains from other sources.

Although much of the complexity of the *at-risk* term is beyond the scope of this text, a simplified working definition is possible. A partner is at risk for an amount if he or she would lose that amount should the partnership suddenly become worthless. Because a partner would not have to pay a partnership's nonrecourse liabilities even if the partnership became worthless, the usual nonrecourse liabilities cannot be included in any partner's at-risk basis. Under the at-risk rules, a partner's loss deduction may be substantially less than the amount deductible under the Sec. 704(d) rules.[41]

EXAMPLE C:9-32 ▶ Keesha is a limited partner in the KM Manufacturing Partnership. At the end of the partnership's tax year, her basis in the partnership interest is $30,000 ($10,000 investment plus a $20,000 share of nonrecourse financing). Keesha's distributive share of partnership losses for the tax year is $18,000. Although she has sufficient basis in the partnership interest, the at-risk rules limit her deduction to $10,000 because she is not at risk for the nonrecourse financing. ◀

The IRC allows one significant exception to the application of the at-risk rules. At-risk rules do not apply to nonrecourse debt if it is qualified real estate financing. The partner is considered at risk for his or her share of nonrecourse real estate financing if all of the following requirements are met:

TYPICAL MISCONCEPTION

The at-risk rules severely limit the use of nonrecourse debt to obtain loss deductions except for certain qualified real estate financing, yet this real estate exception is more apparent than real because of the final set of rules that must be satisfied: the passive activity limitations.

- The financing is secured by real estate used in the partnership's real estate activity.
- The debt is not convertible to any kind of equity interest in the partnership.
- The financing is from a qualified person or from any federal, state, or local government, or is guaranteed by any federal, state, or local government.[42] A qualified person is an unrelated party who is in the trade or business of lending money (e.g., bank, financial institution, or mortgage broker).

PASSIVE ACTIVITY LIMITATIONS

Subsequent to enacting the at-risk rules, Congress added still a third set of limitations to losses a partner may deduct: the passive activity loss and credit limitations of Sec. 469. Under these rules, income falls into one of three categories: (1) amounts derived from passive activities; (2) active income such as salary, bonuses, and income from businesses in which the taxpayer materially participates; and (3) portfolio income such as dividends, interest, and capital gains from investments other than passive activities. Generally, losses of an individual partner from a passive activity cannot be used to offset either active income or portfolio income. However, passive losses carry over to future years where they can offset passive income in those years. Moreover, passive losses are allowed in full when a taxpayer disposes of the entire interest in the passive activity. Passive losses generated by

[41] Sec. 465(a).

[42] Sec. 465(b)(6).

a passive rental activity in which an individual partner is an active participant can be deducted up to a maximum of $25,000 per year. This deduction phases out by 50% of the amount of the partner's adjusted gross income (AGI) that exceeds $100,000, so that no deduction is allowed if the partner has AGI of $150,000 or more. (The phase-out begins at $200,000 for low-income housing or rehabilitation credits.) Losses disallowed under the phase-out are deductible to the extent of passive income.

TAX STRATEGY TIP

If a partner is unable to use all of his or her share of partnership losses due to a lack of basis, contributions to capital or increasing partnership liabilities may provide the additional needed tax basis. If the passive activity limitation rules are the reason the partnership losses cannot be used, the possibility of investing in passive activities that generate passive income may be the best planning alternative. See Tax Planning Considerations for further discussion.

A passive activity is any trade or business in which the taxpayer does not materially participate. A taxpayer who owns a limited partnership interest in any activity generally fails the material participation test. Accordingly, losses from most limited partnership interests can be used only to offset income from passive activities even if the limited partner has sufficient Sec. 704(d) and at-risk basis.[43]

Although passive activity limitations may greatly affect the taxable income or loss reported by a partner, they have no unusual effect on basis. Basis is reduced (but not below zero) by the partner's distributive share of losses whether or not the losses are limited under the passive loss rules.[44] When the suspended passive losses later become deductible, the partner's basis in the partnership interest is not affected.

EXAMPLE C:9-33 ▶ Chris purchases a 20% capital and profits interest in the CJ Partnership in the current year, but he does not participate in CJ's business. Chris owns no other passive investments. His Sec. 704(d) basis in CJ is $80,000, and his at-risk basis is $70,000. Chris's distributive share of the CJ Partnership's loss for the current year is $60,000. After the results of this year's operations are taken into account, Chris's Sec. 704(d) basis is $20,000 ($80,000 − $60,000), and his at-risk basis is $10,000 ($70,000 − $60,000). However, Chris cannot deduct any of the CJ loss in the current year because it is a passive activity loss. The $60,000 loss, however, can be used in a subsequent year if the partner generates passive income. Because the $60,000 loss already has reduced basis for purposes of both Sec. 704(d) and the at-risk rules, the disallowed loss need not be tested against those rules a second time. ◀

TRANSACTIONS BETWEEN A PARTNER AND THE PARTNERSHIP

OBJECTIVE 9

Determine the tax consequences of property sales between a partner and the partnership and of guaranteed payments

The partner and the partnership are treated as separate entities for many transactions. Section 707(b) restricts sales of property between the partner and partnership by disallowing certain losses and converting certain capital gains into ordinary income. Section 707(c) permits a partnership to make guaranteed payments for capital and services to a partner that are separate from the partner's distributive share. Each of these rules is explored below.

SALES OF PROPERTY

Loss Sales. Without restrictions, a controlling partner could sell property to the partnership to recognize a loss for tax purposes while retaining a substantial interest in the property through ownership of a partnership interest. Congress closed the door to such loss recognition with the Sec. 707(b) rules.

KEY POINT

The IRC disallows losses on sales between persons and certain related partnerships, similar to the related party rules of Sec. 267. The concern is that tax losses can be artificially recognized without the property being disposed of outside the economic group.

The rules for partnership loss transactions are quite similar to the Sec. 267 related party rules discussed in Chapter C:3. Under Sec. 707(b)(1), no loss can be deducted on the sale or exchange of property between a partnership and a person who directly or indirectly owns more than 50% of the partnership's capital or profits interests. (Indirect ownership includes ownership by related parties such as members of the partner's family.[45]) Similarly, losses are disallowed on sales or exchanges of property between two partnerships in which the same persons own, directly or indirectly, more than 50% of the capital

---

[43] Sec. 469(h)(2).

[44] S. Rept. No. 99-313, 99th Cong., 2d Sess., p. 723, footnote 4 (1986).

[45] For purposes of Sec. 707, related parties include an individual and members of his or her family (spouse, brothers, sisters, lineal descendants, and ancestors), an individual and a more-than-50%-owned corporation, and two corporations that are members of the same controlled group.

or profits interests. If the seller is disallowed a loss under Sec. 707(b)(1), the purchaser can reduce any subsequent gain realized on a sale of the property by the previously disallowed loss.

EXAMPLE C:9-34 ▶ James, Karen, and Thelma own equal interests in the JKT Partnership. Karen and Thelma are siblings, but James is unrelated to the others. For purposes of Sec. 707, Karen owns two-thirds of the partnership (one-third directly and one-third indirectly from Thelma). Likewise, Thelma also owns two-thirds, but James has only a direct ownership interest of one-third. ◀

EXAMPLE C:9-35 ▶ Pat sold land having a $45,000 basis to the PTA Partnership for $35,000, its FMV. If Pat has a 60% capital and profits interest in the partnership, Pat realizes but cannot recognize a $10,000 loss on the sale. If Pat owns only a 49% interest, directly and indirectly, he can recognize the loss. ◀

EXAMPLE C:9-36 ▶ Assume the same facts as in Example C:9-35 except the partnership later sells the land for $47,000. The partnership's realized gain is $12,000 ($47,000 − $35,000 basis). If Pat has a 60% capital and profits interest, his previously disallowed loss of $10,000 reduces the partnership's recognized gain to $2,000. This $2,000 gain is then allocated to the partners according to the partnership agreement. ◀

Gain Sales. When gain is recognized on the sale of a capital asset between a partnership and a related partner, Sec. 707(b)(2) requires that the gain be ordinary (and not capital gain) if the property will not be a capital asset to its new owner. Sales or exchanges resulting in the application of Sec. 707(b)(2) include transfers between (1) a partnership and a person who owns, directly or indirectly, more than 50% of the partnership's capital or profits interests, or (2) two partnerships in which the same persons own, directly or indirectly, more than 50% of the capital or profits interests.[46] This provision prevents related parties from increasing the depreciable basis of assets (and thereby reducing future ordinary income) at the cost of recognizing only a current capital gain.

EXAMPLE C:9-37 ▶ Sharon and Tony have the following capital and profits interests in two partnerships:

Partner	*ST Partnership (%)*	*QRS Partnership (%)*
Sharon	42	58
Tony	42	30
Other unrelated partners	16	12
Total	100	100

The ST Partnership sells land having a $150,000 basis to the QRS Partnership for $180,000. The land was a capital asset for the ST Partnership, but QRS intends to subdivide and sell the land. Because the land is ordinary income property to the QRS Partnership and because Sharon and Tony control both partnerships, the ST Partnership must recognize $30,000 of ordinary income on the land sale. ◀

GUARANTEED PAYMENTS

A corporate shareholder can be an employee of the corporation. However, a partner generally is not an employee of the partnership, and most fringe benefits are disallowed for a partner who is "employed" by his or her partnership.[47]

A partner who provides services to the partnership in an ongoing relationship might be compensated like any other employee. Section 707(c) provides for this kind of payment and labels it a **guaranteed payment**. The term *guaranteed payment* also includes certain payments made to a partner for the use of invested capital. These payments are similar to interest. Both types of guaranteed payments must be determined without regard to the partnership's income.[48] Conceptually, this requirement separates guaranteed payments from distributive shares. As indicated below, however, such a distinction may not be so clear in practice.

46 Sec. 707(b)(2).

47 Rev. Rul. 91-26, 1991-1 C.B. 184, holds that accident and health insurance premiums paid for a partner by the partnership are guaranteed payments.

48 Sec. 707(c).

TYPICAL MISCONCEPTION

If a partner, acting in his or her capacity as a partner, receives payments from the partnership determined without regard to the partnership's income, the partner has received a guaranteed payment. If the partner is acting as a nonpartner, the partner is treated as any other outside contractor.

Determining the Guaranteed Payment. Sometimes the determination of the guaranteed payment is quite simple. For example, some guaranteed payments are expressed as specific amounts (e.g., $20,000 per year), with the partner also receiving his or her normal distributive share. Other times, the guaranteed payment is expressed as a **guaranteed minimum.** However, these guaranteed minimum arrangements make it difficult to distinguish the partner's distributive share and guaranteed payments because no guaranteed payment occurs under this arrangement unless the partner's distributive share is less than his or her guaranteed minimum. If the distributive share is less than the guaranteed minimum, the guaranteed payment is the difference between the distributive share and the guaranteed minimum.

EXAMPLE C:9-38 ▶ Tina manages the real estate owned by the TAV Partnership, in which she also is a partner. She receives 30% of all partnership income before guaranteed payments, but no less than $60,000 per year. In the current year, the TAV Partnership reports $300,000 in ordinary income. Tina's 30% distributive share is $90,000 (0.30 × $300,000), which exceeds her $60,000 guaranteed minimum. Therefore, she has no guaranteed payment. ◀

EXAMPLE C:9-39 ▶ Assume the same facts as in Example C:9-38 except the TAV Partnership reports $150,000 of ordinary income. Tina has a guaranteed payment of $15,000, which represents the difference between her $45,000 distributive share (0.30 × $150,000) and her $60,000 guaranteed minimum.[49] ◀

Tax Impact of Guaranteed Payments. Like salary or interest income, guaranteed payments are ordinary income to the recipient. The guaranteed payment must be included in income for the recipient partner's tax year during which the partnership year ends and the partnership deducts or capitalizes the payments.[50]

EXAMPLE C:9-40 ▶ In January of Year 2, a calendar year taxpayer, Will, receives a $10,000 guaranteed payment from the WRS Partnership, which uses the accrual method of accounting. WRS accrues and deducts the payment during its tax year ending December 31 of Year 1. Will must report the guaranteed payment in his Year 1 tax return because that return includes the Year 1 partnership income that reflects the partnership's deduction of the guaranteed payment. ◀

The partnership treats the guaranteed payment as if it is made to an outsider. If the payment is for a service that is a capital expenditure (e.g., architectural services for designing a building for the partnership), the guaranteed payment must be capitalized and, if allowable, amortized. If the payment is for services deductible under Sec. 162, the partnership deducts the payment from ordinary income. Thus, deductible guaranteed payments offset the partnership's ordinary income but never its capital gains. If the guaranteed payment exceeds the partnership's ordinary income, the payment creates an ordinary loss that is allocated among the partners.[51]

EXAMPLE C:9-41 ▶ Theresa is a partner in the STU Partnership. She is to receive a guaranteed payment for deductible services of $60,000 and 30% of partnership income computed after the partnership deducts the guaranteed payment. The partnership reports $40,000 of ordinary income and a $120,000 long-term capital gain before deducting the guaranteed payment. Theresa's income from the partnership is determined as follows:

		Theresa's Share	
	STU Partnership	*Ratable Share*	*Amount*
Ordinary income (before guaranteed payment)	$ 40,000		
Minus: Guaranteed payment	(60,000)	100%	$60,000
Ordinary loss	($ 20,000)	30%	(6,000)
Long-term capital gain	$120,000	30%	36,000 ◀

[49] Reg. Sec. 1.707-1(c), Exs. (1) and (2).
[50] Reg. Secs. 1.707-1(c) and 1.706-1(a).
[51] Reg. Sec. 1.707-1(c), Ex. (4).

Family Partnerships

OBJECTIVE 10

Recognize the special tax issues associated with family partnerships

CAPITAL OWNERSHIP

Because each partner reports and pays taxes on a distributive share of partnership income, a family partnership is an excellent way to spread income among family members and minimize the family's tax bill. However, to accomplish this tax minimization goal, the IRS must accept the family members as real partners. The question of whether someone is a partner in a family partnership is often litigated, but safe-harbor rules under Sec. 704(e) provide a clear answer if three tests are met: the partnership interest must be a capital interest, capital must be a material income-producing factor in the partnership's business activity, and the family member must be the true owner of the interest.

A capital interest gives the partner the right to receive assets if the partnership liquidates immediately upon the partner's acquisition of the interest. Capital is a material income-producing factor if the partnership derives substantial portions of gross income from the use of capital. For example, capital is a material income-producing factor if the business has substantial inventory or significant investment in plant or equipment. Capital is seldom considered a material income-producing factor in a service business.[52]

TAX STRATEGY TIP

In certain situations, family partnerships provide an excellent tax-planning tool, but the family members must be real partners. The rules that determine who is a real partner in a family partnership are guided by the assignment-of-income principle.

The remaining question is whether the family member is the true owner of the interest. Ownership is seldom questioned if one family member purchases the interest at a market price from another family member. However, when one family member gifts the interest to another, the major question is whether the donor retains so much control over the partnership interest that the donor is still the owner of the interest. If the donor still controls the interest, the donor is taxed on the distributive share.

Donor Retained Control. No mechanical test exists to determine whether the donor has retained too much control, but several factors may indicate a problem:[53]

- Retention of control over distributions of income can be a problem unless the retention occurs with the agreement of all partners or the retention is for the reasonable needs of the business.
- Retention of control over assets that are essential to the partnership's business can indicate too much control by the donor.
- Limitation of the donee partner's right to sell or liquidate his or her interest may indicate that the donor has not relinquished full control over the interest.
- Retention of management control that is inconsistent with normal partnership arrangements can be another sign that the donor retains control. This situation is not considered a fatal problem unless it occurs in conjunction with a significant limit on the donee's ability to sell or liquidate his or her interest.

If the donor has not directly or indirectly retained too much control, the donee is a full partner. As a partner, the donee must report his or her distributive share of income.

Minor Donees. When income splitting is the goal of a family, the appropriate donee for the partnership interest is often a minor. With the problem of donor-retained controls in mind, gifts to minors should be made with great attention to detail. Further, net unearned income of a child under age 18 is taxed to the child at the parents' marginal tax rate under the "kiddie tax" rules. This provision removes much of the incentive to transfer family partnership interests to young children, but gifting partnership interests to minors age 18 or older still can reap significant tax advantages, although in some situations the kiddie tax also applies to children ages 18 through 23.

DONOR-DONEE ALLOCATIONS OF INCOME

Partnership income must be properly allocated between a donor and a donee to be accepted by the IRS. Note that only the allocation between the donor and donee is questioned, with no impact on the distributive shares of any other partners.

---

[52] Reg. Sec. 1.704-1(e)(1)(iv).

[53] Reg. Sec. 1.704-1(e)(2)(ii).

Two requirements apply to donor-donee allocations. First, the donor must be allocated reasonable compensation for services rendered to the partnership. Then, after reasonable compensation is allocated to the donor, any remaining partnership income must be allocated based on relative capital interests.[54] This allocation scheme apparently overrides the partnership's ability to make special allocations of income.

EXAMPLE C:9-42 ▶ Andrew, a 40% partner in the ABC Partnership, gives one-half of his interest to his brother, John. During the current year, Andrew performs services for the partnership for which reasonable compensation is $65,000 but for which he accepts no pay. Andrew and John are each credited with a $100,000 distributive share, all of which is ordinary income. Reallocation between Andrew and John is necessary to reflect the value of Andrew's services.

Total distributive shares for the brothers	$200,000
Minus: Reasonable compensation for Andrew	(65,000)
Income to allocate	$135,000

John's distributive share: $\frac{20\%}{40\%} \times \$135{,}000 = \$67{,}500$

Andrew's distributive share: $\left(\frac{20\%}{40\%} \times \$135{,}000\right) + \$65{,}000 = \$132{,}500$ ◀

ETHICAL POINT

CPAs have a responsibility to review an entity's conduct of its activities to be sure it is operating as a partnership. If a donee receives a partnership interest as a gift and the donee is not the true owner of the interest (e.g., the donor retains too much control over the donee's interest), the partnership return must be filed without a distributive share of income or loss being allocated to the donee.

TAX PLANNING CONSIDERATIONS

OBJECTIVE 11

Identify planning techniques to get the best tax advantages from partnership losses

TIMING OF LOSS RECOGNITION

The loss limitation rules provide a unique opportunity for tax planning. For example, if a partner knows that his or her distributive share of active losses from a partnership for a tax year will exceed the Sec. 704 basis limitation for deducting losses, he or she should carefully examine the tax situation for the current and upcoming tax years. Substantial current personal income may make immediate use of the loss desirable. Current income may be taxed at a higher marginal tax rate than will future income because of, for example, an extraordinarily good current year, an expected retirement, or a decrease in future years' tax rates. If the partner chooses to use the loss in the current year, he or she can make additional contributions just before year-end (perhaps even from funds the partner borrows, as long as the additional benefit exceeds the cost of the funds). Alternatively, one partner may convince the other partners to have the partnership incur additional liabilities so that each partner's basis increases. This last strategy should be exercised with caution unless a business reason (rather than solely a tax reason) exists for the borrowing.

EXAMPLE C:9-43 ▶ Ted, a 60% general partner in the ST Partnership, expects to be allocated partnership losses of $120,000 for the current year from a partnership in which he materially participates but where his partnership basis is only $90,000. Because he has a marginal tax rate of 33% for the current year (and anticipates only a 25% marginal tax rate for next year), Ted wants to use the ST Partnership losses to offset his current year income. He could make a capital contribution to raise his basis by $30,000. Alternatively, he could get the partnership to incur $50,000 in additional liabilities, which would increase his basis by his $30,000 ($50,000 × 0.60) share of the liability. The partnership's $50,000 borrowing must serve a business purpose for the ST Partnership. ◀

Alternatively, if a partner has little current year income and expects substantial income in the following year, the partner may prefer to delay the deduction of partnership losses that exceed the current year's loss limitation. Similarly, if a partner has loss, deduction, or credit carryovers that expire in the current year, deferral of the distributive share of

[54] Sec. 704(e)(2).

partnership losses to the following year again may be desirable. Should the partner opt to deduct the loss in a later year, he or she needs only to leave things alone so that the distributive share of losses exceeds the loss limitation for the current year.

COMPLIANCE AND PROCEDURAL CONSIDERATIONS

OBJECTIVE 12

Comply with the requirements for filing a partnership tax return

REPORTING TO THE IRS AND THE PARTNERS

Forms. If the partnership is not an electing large partnership, the partnership must file a Form 1065 (U.S. Return of Partnership Income) with the IRS by the fifteenth day of the fourth month after the end of the partnership tax year. (See Appendix B for a completed Form 1065.) The IRS, however, allows an automatic five-month extension of time to file Form 1065. To obtain the extension, the partnership must file Form 7004 (Application for Automatic Extension of Time To File Certain Business Income Tax, Information, and Other Returns) on or before the partnership's normal filing date.[55] The IRS imposes penalties for failure to file a timely or complete partnership return. Because the partnership is only a conduit, Form 1065 is an information return and is not accompanied by any tax payment.[56] Included on the front page of Form 1065 are the ordinary items of income, gain, loss, and deduction that are not separately stated. Schedule K of Form 1065 reports both a summary of the ordinary income items and all the partnership's separately stated items. Schedule K-1, which the partnership must prepare for each partner, reflects a particular partner's distributive share of partnership ordinary income or loss, separately state items, and his or her special allocations. The partner's Schedule K-1 is notification of his or her share of partnership items for use in calculating income taxes and self-employment taxes.

ADDITIONAL COMMENT

The partnership Schedule K in Appendix B of this text makes apparent that the large number of items now having to be separately stated has substantially complicated the preparation of Form 1065.

Schedule M-3. A partnership must file Schedule M-3 in lieu of Schedule M-1 if any one of the following conditions holds:

- The amount of total assets reported in Schedule L of Form 1065 (Balance Sheet per Books) equals or exceeds $10 million.
- The amount of adjusted total assets equals or exceeds $10 million, where adjusted total assets equal the Schedule L amount plus the following items that appear in Schedule M-2 of Form 1065: (1) capital distributions made during the year, (2) net book loss for the year, and (3) other adjustments.
- Total receipts equal or exceed $35 million.
- A reportable entity partner owns at least a 50% interest in the partnership on any day of the tax year, where a reportable entity partner is one that had to file its own Schedule M-3.

Section 444 Election and Required Payments. A partnership can elect to use a tax year other than a required year by filing an election under Sec. 444. This election is made by filing Form 8716 (Election to Have a Tax Year Other Than a Required Tax Year) by the earlier of the fifteenth day of the fifth month following the month that includes the first day of the tax year for which the election is effective or the due date (without regard to extension) of the income tax return resulting from the Sec. 444 election. In addition, a copy of Form 8716 must be attached to the partnership's Form 1065 for the first tax year for which the Sec. 444 election is made.

A partnership making a Sec. 444 election must make a required payment annually under Sec. 7519. The required payment has the effect of remitting a deposit equal to the

[55] Reg. 1.6081-2.

[56] Reg. Sec. 301.6031-1(e)(2). Although the partnership pays no income tax, it still must pay the employer's share of social security taxes and any unemployment taxes as well as withhold income taxes from its employees' salaries. Remember, however, that the partners are not considered to be employees. In addition, some publicly traded partnerships may pay a tax as explained in Chapter C:10.

tax (at the highest individual tax rate plus one percentage point) on the partnership's deferred income.

A partnership can obtain a refund if past payments exceed the tentative payment due on the deferred income for the current year. Similar refunds are available if the partnership terminates a Sec. 444 election or liquidates. The required payments are not deductible by the partnership and are not passed through to a partner. The required payments are in the nature of a refundable deposit.

The Sec. 7519 required payment is due on or before May 15 of the calendar year following the calendar year in which the election year begins. The partnership remits the required payment with Form 8752 (Required Payment or Refund Under Section 7519) along with a computational worksheet, which is illustrated in the instructions to Form 1065. Refunds of excess required payments also are obtained by filing Form 8752.

Estimated Taxes. If the partnership is not an electing large partnership, it pays no income taxes and makes no estimated tax payments. However, the partners must make estimated tax payments based on their separate tax positions including their distributive shares of partnership income or loss for the current year. Thus, the partners are not making separate estimated tax payments for their partnership income but rather are including the effects of the partnership's results in the calculation of their normal estimated tax payments.

Self-Employment Income. Every partnership must report the net earnings (or loss) for the partnership that constitute self-employment income to the partners. The instructions to Form 1065 contain a worksheet to make such a calculation. The partnership's self-employment income includes both guaranteed payments, partnership ordinary income and loss, and some separately stated items, but generally excludes capital gains and losses, Sec. 1231 gains and losses, interest, dividends, and rentals. The distributive share of self-employment income for each partner is shown on a Schedule K-1 and is included with the partner's other self-employment income in determining his or her self-employment tax liability (Schedule SE, Form 1040). The distributive share of partnership income allocable to a limited partner is not self-employment income.

EXAMPLE C:9-44 ▶ Adam is a general partner in the AB Partnership. His distributive share of partnership income and his guaranteed payment for the year are as follows:

Ordinary income	$15,000
Short-term capital gain	9,000
Guaranteed payment	18,000

Adam's self-employment income is $33,000 ($15,000 + $18,000). ◀

EXAMPLE C:9-45 ▶ Assume the same facts as in Example C:9-44 except that Adam is a limited partner. His self-employment income includes only the $18,000 guaranteed payment. ◀

IRS AUDIT PROCEDURES

Any questions arising during an IRS audit about a partnership item must be determined at the partnership level (instead of at the partner level).[57] Section 6231(a)(3) defines **partnership items** as virtually all items reported by the partnership for the tax year including tax preference items, credit recapture items, guaranteed payments, and the at-risk amount. In fact, almost every item that can appear on the partnership return is treated as a partnership item. Each partner must either report partnership items in a manner consistent with the Schedule K-1 received from the partnership or notify the IRS of the inconsistent treatment.[58]

The IRS can bring a single proceeding at the partnership level to determine the characterization or tax impact of any partnership item. All partners have the right to participate in the administrative proceedings, and the IRS must offer a consistent settlement to all partners.

---

[57] Sec. 6221.

[58] Sec. 6222.

KEY POINT

To alleviate the administrative nightmare of having to audit each partner of a partnership, Congress has authorized the IRS to conduct audits of partnerships in a unified proceeding at the partnership level. This process is more efficient and should provide greater consistency in the treatment of the individual partners than did the previous system.

The partnership generally assigns a **tax matters partner** to facilitate communication between the IRS and the partners of a large partnership and to serve as the primary representative of the partnership.[59] If the partnership fails to assign the tax matters partner, the designation goes to the general partner having the largest profits interest at the close of the partnership's tax year.

These audit procedures, however, do not apply to small partnerships. For this purpose, a small partnership is defined as one having no more than ten partners who must be natural persons (but excluding nonresident aliens), C corporations, or estates. In counting partners, a husband and wife (or their estates) count as a single partner. Further, the IRS has announced that a partnership can be excluded from the audit procedures only if it can be established that all partners fully reported their shares of partnership items on timely filed tax returns.[60]

Problem Materials

DISCUSSION QUESTIONS

C:9-1 Yvonne and Larry plan to begin a business that will grow plants for sale to retail nurseries. They expect to have substantial losses for the first three years of operations while they develop their plants and their sales operations. Both Yvonne and Larry have substantial interest income, and both expect to work full-time in this new business. List three advantages for operating this business as a partnership instead of a C corporation.

C:9-2 Bob and Carol want to open a bed and breakfast inn as soon as they buy and renovate a turn-of-the-century home. What would be the major disadvantage of using a general partnership rather than a corporation for this business? Should they consider any other form for structuring their business?

C:9-3 Sam wants to help his brother, Lou, start a new business. Lou is a capable auto mechanic but has little business sense, so he needs Sam to help him make business decisions. Should this partnership be arranged as a general partnership or a limited partnership? Why? Should they consider any other form for structuring their business?

C:9-4 Doug contributes services but no property to the CD Partnership upon its formation. What are the tax implications of his receiving only a profits interest versus his receiving a capital and profits interest?

C:9-5 An existing partner wants to contribute property having a basis less than its FMV for an additional interest in a partnership.

a. Should he contribute the property to the partnership?
b. What are his other options?
c. Explain the tax implications for the partner of these other options.

C:9-6 Jane contributes valuable property to a partnership in exchange for a general partnership interest. The partnership also assumes the recourse mortgage Jane incurred when she purchased the property two years ago.

a. How will the liability affect the amount of gain that Jane must recognize?
b. How will it affect her basis in the partnership interest?

C:9-7 Which of the following items can be deducted (up to $5,000) and amortized as part of a partnership's organizational expenditures?

a. Legal fees for drawing up the partnership agreement
b. Accounting fees for establishing an accounting system
c. Fees for securing an initial working capital loan
d. Filing fees required under state law in initial year to conduct business in the state
e. Accounting fees for preparation of initial short-period tax return
f. Transportation costs for acquiring machinery essential to the partnership's business
g. Syndication expenses

C:9-8 The BW Partnership reported the following current year earnings: $30,000 interest from tax-exempt bonds, $50,000 long-term capital gain, and $100,000 net income from operations. Bob saw these numbers and told his partner, Wendy, that the partnership had $100,000 of taxable income. Is he correct? Explain your answer.

C:9-9 How will a partner's distributive share be determined if the partner sells one-half of his or her beginning-of-the-year partnership interest at the beginning of the tenth month of the partnership's tax year?

---

[59] Sec. 6231(a)(7).

[60] Rev. Proc. 84-35, 1984-1 C.B. 509.

C:9-10 Can a recourse debt of a partnership increase the basis of a limited partner's partnership interest? Explain.

C:9-11 The ABC Partnership has a nonrecourse liability that it incurred by borrowing from an unrelated bank. It is secured by an apartment building owned and managed by the partnership. The liability is not convertible into an equity interest. How does this liability affect the at-risk basis of general partner Anna and limited partner Bob?

C:9-12 Is the Sec. 704(d) loss limitation rule more or less restrictive than the at-risk rules? Explain.

C:9-13 Jeff, a 10% limited partner in the recently formed JRS Partnership, expects to have losses from the partnership for several more years. He is considering purchasing an interest in a profitable general partnership in which he will materially participate. Will the purchase allow him to use his losses from the JRS Partnership?

C:9-14 Helen, a 55% partner in the ABC Partnership, owns land (a capital asset) having a $20,000 basis and a $25,000 FMV. She plans to transfer the land to the ABC Partnership, which will subdivide the land and sell the lots. Discuss whether Helen should sell or contribute the land to the partnership.

C:9-15 The TUV Partnership is considering two compensation schemes for Tracy, the partner who runs the business on a daily basis. Tracy can be given a $10,000 guaranteed payment, or she can be given a comparably larger distributive share (and distribution) so that she receives about $10,000 more each year. From the standpoint of when the income must be reported in Tracy's tax return, are these two compensation alternatives the same?

C:9-16 Roy's father gives him a capital interest in the Family Partnership. Discuss whether the Sec. 704(e) family partnership rules apply to this interest.

C:9-17 Andrew gives his brother Steve a 20% interest in the AS Partnership, and he retains a 30% interest. Andrew works for the partnership but is not paid. How will this arrangement affect the income from the AS Partnership that Andrew and Steve report?

ISSUE IDENTIFICATION QUESTIONS

C:9-18 Bob and Kate form the BK Partnership, a general partnership, as equal partners. Bob contributes an office building with a $130,000 FMV and a $95,000 adjusted basis to the partnership along with a $60,000 mortgage, which the partnership assumes. Kate contributes the land on which the building sits with a $50,000 FMV and a $75,000 adjusted basis. Kate will manage the partnership for the first five years of operations but will not receive a guaranteed payment for her work in the first year of partnership operations. Starting with the second year of partnership operations, Kate will receive a $10,000 guaranteed payment for each year she manages the partnership. What tax issues should Bob, Kate, and the BK Partnership consider with respect to the formation and operation of the partnership?

C:9-19 Suzanne and Laura form a partnership to market local crafts. In April, the two women spent $1,600 searching for a retail outlet, $1,200 to have a partnership agreement drawn up, and $2,000 to have an accounting system established. During April, they signed contracts with a number of local crafters to feature their products in the retail outlet. The outlet was fitted and merchandise organized during May. In June, the store opened and sold its first crafts. The partnership paid $500 to an accountant to prepare an income statement for the month of June. What tax issues should the partnership consider with regard to beginning this business?

C:9-20 Cara, a CPA, established an accounting system for the ABC Partnership and, in return for her services, received a 10% profits interest (but no capital interest) in the partnership. Her usual fee for the services would be approximately $20,000. No sales of profits interests in the ABC Partnership occurred during the current year. What tax issues should Cara and the ABC Partnership consider with respect to the payment made for the services?

C:9-21 George, a limited partner in the EFG Partnership, has a 20% interest in partnership capital, profits, and losses. His basis in the partnership interest is $15,000 before accounting for events of the current year. In December of the current year, the EFG Partnership repaid a $100,000 nonrecourse liability. The partnership earned $20,000 of ordinary income this year. What tax issues should George consider with respect to reporting the results of this year's activities for the EFG Partnership on his personal return?

C:9-22 Katie works 40 hours a week as a clerk in the mall and earns $20,000. In addition, she works five hours each week in the JKL Partnership's office. Katie, a 10% limited partner in the JKL Partnership, has been allocated a $2,100 loss from the partnership for the current year. The basis for her interest in JKL before accounting for current operations is $5,000. What tax issues should Katie consider with respect to her interest in, and employment by, the JKL Partnership?

C:9-23 Daniel has no family to inherit his 80% capital and profits interest in the CD Partnership. To ensure the continuation of the business, he gives a 20% capital and profits interest in the partnership to David, his best friend's son, on the condition that David work in the partnership for at least five years. David receives guaranteed payments for his work. Daniel takes no salary from the partnership, but he devotes all his time to the business operations of the partnership. What tax issues should Daniel and David consider with respect to the gift of the partnership interest and Daniel's employment arrangement with the partnership?

PROBLEMS

C:9-24 ***Formation of a Partnership.*** Suzanne and Bob form the SB General Partnership as equal partners. They make the following contributions:

Individual	*Asset*	*Basis to Partner*	*FMV*
Suzanne	Cash	$45,000	$ 45,000
	Inventory (securities)	14,000	15,000
Bob	Land	45,000	40,000
	Building	50,000	100,000

The SB Partnership assumes the $80,000 recourse mortgage on the building that Bob contributes, and the partners share the economic risk of loss on the mortgage equally. Bob has claimed $40,000 in straight-line depreciation under the MACRS rules on the building. Suzanne is a stockbroker and contributed securities from her inventory. The partnership will hold them as an investment.

a. What amount and character of gain or loss must each partner recognize on the formation of the partnership?
b. What is each partner's basis in his or her partnership interest?
c. What is the partnership's basis in each asset?
d. What is the partnership's initial book value of each asset?
e. The partnership holds the securities for two years and then sells them for $20,000. What amount and character of gain must the partnership and each partner report?

C:9-25 ***Formation of a Partnership Compared to Formation of a Corporation.*** At the beginning of the current year, Able and Baker formed the AB Partnership by transferring cash and property to the partnership in exchange for a partnership interest, with each having a 50% interest. Specifically, Able transferred property having a $50,000 FMV, a $30,000 adjusted basis, and subject to a $10,000 liability, which the partnership assumed. Baker contributed $40,000 cash to the partnership. The partnership also borrowed $28,000 from the bank to use in its operations. All liabilities are recourse for which the partners have an equal economic risk of loss. During the current year, the partnership earned $24,000 of net ordinary income and reinvested this amount in new property.

a. What is the partnership's and each partner's gain or loss recognized on the formation of the partnership?
b. What is each partner's basis in his or her partnership interest at the end of the current year?
c. For the partnership, prepare a tax and book balance sheet at the end of the current year.
d. Assume instead that Able and Baker formed a corporation rather than a partnership. What is the corporation's and each shareholder's gain or loss recognized on the formation of the corporation? What is each shareholder's basis in his or her stock at the end of the current year?

C:9-26 ***Formation of a Partnership.*** On May 31, six brothers decided to form the Grimm Brothers Partnership to publish and print children's stories. The contributions of the brothers and their partnership interests are listed below. They share the economic risk of loss from liabilities according to their partnership interests.

Individual	*Asset*	*Basis to Partner*	*FMV*	*Partnership Interest*
Al	Cash	$15,000	$ 15,000	15%
Bob	Accounts receivable	–0–	20,000	20%
Clay	Office equipment	13,000	15,000	15%
Dave	Land	50,000	15,000	15%
Ed	Building	15,000	150,000	20%
Fred	Services	?	15,000	15%

The following other information about the contributions may be of interest:

- Bob contributes accounts receivable from his proprietorship, which uses the cash method of accounting.
- Clay uses the office equipment in a small business he owns. When he joins the partnership, he sells the remaining business assets to an outsider. He has claimed $8,000 of MACRS depreciation on the office equipment.
- The partnership assumes a $130,000 mortgage on the building Ed contributes. Ed claimed $100,000 of straight-line MACRS depreciation on the commercial property.
- Fred, an attorney, drew up all the partnership agreements and filed the necessary paperwork. He receives a full 15% capital and profits interest for his services.

a. How much gain, loss, or income must each partner recognize as a result of the formation?
b. How much gain, loss, or income must the partnership recognize as a result of the formation?
c. What is each partner's basis in his partnership interest?
d. What is the partnership's basis in its assets?
e. What is the partnership's initial book value of each asset?
f. What effects do the depreciation recapture provisions have on the property contributions?
g. How would your answer to Part a change if Fred received only a profits interest?
h. What are the tax consequences to the partners and the partnership when the partnership sells for $9,000 the land contributed by Dave? Prior to the sale, the partnership held the land as an investment for two years.

C:9-27 ***Formation of a Partnership.*** On January 1, Julie, Kay, and Susan form a partnership. The contributions of the three individuals are listed below. Julie received a 30% partnership interest, Kay received a 60% partnership interest, and Susan received a 10% partnership interest. They share the economic risk of loss from recourse liabilities according to their partnership interests.

Individual	*Asset*	*Basis to Partner*	*FMV*
Julie	Accounts receivable	$ –0–	$ 60,000
Kay	Land	30,000	58,000
	Building	45,000	116,000
Susan	Services	?	20,000

Kay has claimed $15,000 of straight-line MACRS depreciation on the building. The land and building are subject to a $54,000 mortgage, of which $18,000 is allocable to the land and $36,000 is allocable to the building. The partnership assumes the mortgage. Susan is an attorney, and the services she contributes are the drawing-up of all partnership agreements.

a. What amount and character of gain, loss, or income must each partner recognize on the formation of the partnership?
b. What is each partner's basis in her partnership interest?
c. What is the partnership's basis in each of its assets?
d. What is the partnership's initial book value of each asset?

e. To raise some immediate cash after the formation, the partnership decides to sell the land and building to a third party and lease it back. The buyer pays $40,000 cash for the land and $80,000 cash for the building in addition to assuming the $54,000 mortgage. Assume the partnership claim no additional depreciation on the building before the sale. What is each partner's distributive share of the gains, and what is the character of the gains?

C:9-28 *Contribution of Services.* Sean is admitted to the calender year XYZ Partnership on December 1 of the current year in return for his services managing the partnership's business during the year. The partnership reports ordinary income of $100,000 for the current year without considering this transaction. Assume a nonleap year.

a. What are the tax consequences to Sean and the calendar year XYZ Partnership if Sean receives a 20% capital and profits interest in the partnership with a $75,000 FMV?
b. What are the tax consequences to Sean and the XYZ Partnership if Sean receives only a 20% profits interest with no determinable FMV?

C:9-29 *Contribution of Services and Property.* Marjorie works for a large firm whose business is to find suitable real estate, establish a limited partnership to purchase the property, and then sell the limited partnership interests. In the current year, Marjorie received a 5% limited partnership interest in the Eldorado Limited Partnership. Marjorie received this interest partially in payment for her services in selling partnership interests to others, but she also was required to contribute $5,000 in cash to the partnership. Similar limited partnership interests sold for $20,000 at approximately the same time that Marjorie received her interest. What are the tax consequences for Marjorie and the Eldorado Limited Partnership of Marjorie's receipt of the partnership interest?

C:9-30 *Partnership Tax Year.* The BCD Partnership is being formed by three equal partners, Beta Corporation, Chi Corporation, and Delta Corporation. The partners' tax year-ends are June 30 for Beta, September 30 for Chi, and October 31 for Delta. The BCD Partnership's natural business year ends on January 31.

a. What tax year(s) can the partnership elect without IRS permission?
b. What tax year(s) can the partnership elect with IRS permission?
c. How would your answers to Parts a and b change if Beta, Chi, and Delta own 4%, 4%, and 92%, respectively, of the partnership?

C:9-31 *Partnership Tax Year.* The BCD Partnership is formed in April of the current year. The three equal partners, Boris, Carlton Corporation, and Damien have had tax years ending on December 31, August 30, and December 31, respectively, for the last three years. The BCD Partnership has no natural business year.

a. What tax year is required for the BCD Partnership under Sec. 706?
b. Can the BCD Partnership make a Sec. 444 election? If so, what are the alternative tax years BCD could select?

C:9-32 *Partnership Income and Basis Adjustments.* Mark and Pamela are equal partners in MP Partnership. The partnership, Mark, and Pamela are calendar year taxpayers. The partnership incurred the following items in the current year:

Sales	$450,000
Cost of goods sold	210,000
Dividends on corporate investments	15,000
Tax-exempt interest income	4,000
Sec. 1245 gain (recapture) on equipment sale	33,000
Sec. 1231 gain on equipment sale	18,000
Long-term capital gain on stock sale	12,000
Long-term capital loss on stock sale	10,000
Short-term capital loss on stock sale	9,000
Depreciation (no Sec. 179 or bonus depreciation components)	27,000
Guaranteed payment to Pamela	30,000
Meals and entertainment expenses	11,600
Interest expense on loans allocable to:	
Business debt	42,000
Stock investments	9,200
Tax-exempt bonds	2,800
Principal payment on business loan	14,000
Charitable contributions	5,000
Distributions to partners ($40,000 each)	80,000

a. Compute the partnership's ordinary income and separately stated items.
b. Show Mark's and Pamela's shares of the items in Part a.
c. Compute Mark's and Pamela's ending basis in their partnership interests assuming their beginning balances are $150,000 each.

C:9-33 *Financial Accounting and Partnership Income.* Jim, Liz, and Keith are equal partners in the JLK Partnership, which uses the accrual method of accounting. All three materially participate in the business. JLK reports financial accounting income of $186,000 for the current year. The partnership used the following information to determine financial accounting income.

Operating profit (excluding the items listed below)	$94,000
Rental income	30,000
Interest income:	
Municipal bonds (tax-exempt)	15,000
Corporate bonds	3,000
Dividend income (all from less-than-20%-owned domestic corporations)	20,000
Gains and losses on property sales:	
Gain on sale of land held as an investment (contributed by Jim six years ago when its basis was $9,000 and its FMV was $15,000)	60,000
Long-term capital gains	10,000
Short-term capital losses	7,000
Sec. 1231 gain	9,000
Unrecaptured Sec. 1250 gain	44,000
Depreciation:	
Rental real estate	12,000
Machinery and equipment	27,000
Interest expense related to:	
Mortgages on rental property	18,000
Loans to acquire municipal bonds	5,000
Guaranteed payments to Jim	30,000
Low-income housing expenditures qualifying for credit	21,000

The following additional information is available about the current year's activities.

- The partnership received a $1,000 prepayment of rent for next year but has not recorded it as income for financial accounting purposes.
- The partnership recorded the land for financial accounting purposes at $15,000.
- MACRS depreciation on the rental real estate and machinery and equipment were $12,000 and $29,000, respectively, in the current year.
- MACRS depreciation for the rental real estate includes depreciation on the low-income housing expenditures.

a. What is JLK's financial accounting income?
b. What is JLK's partnership taxable income? (See Appendix B for an example of a financial accounting-to-tax reconciliation.)
c. What is JLK's ordinary income (loss)?
d. What are JLK's separately stated items?

C:9-34 *Partner's Distributive Shares.* On January of the current year, Becky (20%), Chuck (30%), and Dawn (50%) are partners in the BCD Partnership. During the current year, BCD reports the following results. All items occur evenly throughout the year unless otherwise indicated. Assume the current year is not a leap year.

Ordinary income	$120,000
Long-term capital gain (recognized September 1)	18,000
Short-term capital loss (recognized March 2)	6,000
Charitable contribution (made October 1)	20,000

a. What are the distributive shares for each partner, assuming they all continue to hold their interests at the end of the year?
b. Assume that Becky purchases a 5% partnership interest from Chuck on July 1 so that Becky and Chuck each own 25% from that date through the end of the year. What are Becky and Chuck's distributive shares for the current year?

C:9-35 *Allocation of Precontribution Gain.* Last year, Patty contributed land with a $4,000 basis and a $10,000 FMV in exchange for a 40% profits, loss, and capital interest in the PD Partnership. Dave contributed land with an $8,000 basis and a $15,000 FMV for the remaining 60% interest in the partnership. During the current year, PD Partnership reported $8,000 of ordinary income and sold the land that Patty contributed for $14,000, thereby producing a taxable long-term capital gain of $10,000 ($14,000 – $4,000). What income or gain must Patty and Dave report from the PD Partnership in the current year?

C:9-36 *Special Allocations.* Refer to Example C:9-25 in the text. Provide computations showing that the partners' total tax liability under the special allocation is less than their total liability under an equal allocation of the two types of interest income.

C:9-37 *Special Allocations.* Clark sold securities for a $50,000 short-term capital loss during the current year, but he has no personal capital gains to recognize. The C&L General Partnership, in which Clark has a 50% capital, profits, and loss interest, reported a $60,000 short-term capital gain this year. In addition, the partnership earned $140,000 of ordinary income. Clark's only partner, Lois, agrees to divide the year's income as follows:

Type of Income	*Total*	*Clark*	*Lois*
Short-term capital gain	$ 60,000	$50,000	$10,000
Ordinary income	140,000	50,000	90,000

Both partners and the partnership use a calendar year-end, and both partners have a 33% marginal tax rate.

a. Have the partners made a special allocation of income that has substantial economic effect?
b. What amount and character of income must each partner report on his or her tax return?

C:9-38 *Special Allocations.* Diane and Ed have equal capital and profits interests in the DE Partnership, and they share the economic risk of loss from recourse liabilities according to their partnership interests. In addition, Diane has a special allocation of all depreciation on buildings owned by the partnership. The buildings are financed with recourse liabilities. The depreciation reduces Diane's capital account, and liquidation is in accordance with the capital account balances. Depreciation for the DE Partnership is $50,000 annually. Diane and Ed each have $50,000 capital account balances on January 1 of Year 1. Will the special allocation be acceptable for Year 1, Year 2, and Year 3 in the following independent situations?

a. The partners have no obligation to repay negative capital account balances, and the partnership's operations (other than depreciation) each year have no net effect on the capital accounts.
b. The partners have an obligation to repay negative capital account balances.
c. The partners have no obligation to repay negative capital account balances. The partnership operates at its break-even point (excluding any depreciation claimed) and borrows $200,000 on a full recourse basis on December 31 of Year 2.

C:9-39 *Basis in Partnership Interest.* What is Kelly's basis for her partnership interest in each of the following independent situations? The partners share the economic risk of loss from recourse liabilities according to their partnership interests.

a. Kelly receives her 20% partnership interest for a contribution of property having a $14,000 basis and a $17,000 FMV. The partnership assumes her $10,000 recourse liability but has no other debts.
b. Kelly receives her 20% partnership interest as a gift from a friend. The friend's basis (without considering partnership liabilities) is $34,000. The FMV of the interest at the time of the gift is $36,000. The partnership has liabilities of $100,000 when Kelly receives her interest. No gift tax was paid with respect to the transfer.
c. Kelly inherits her 20% interest from her mother. Her mother's basis was $140,000. The FMV of the interest is $120,000 on the date of death and $160,000 on the alternate valuation date. The executor chooses the date of death for valuing the estate. The partnership has no liabilities.

C:9-40 *Basis in Partnership Interest.* Yong received a 40% general partnership interest in the XYZ Partnership in each of the independent situations below. In each situation, assume the general partners share the economic risk of loss related to recourse liabilities according to their partnership interests. What is Yong's basis in his partnership interest?

a. Yong designs the building the partnership will use for its offices. Yong normally would charge a $20,000 fee for a similar building design. Based on the other partner's contributions, the 40% interest has a FMV of $25,000. The partnership has no liabilities.

b. Yong contributes land with a $6,000 basis and an $18,000 FMV, a car (which he has used in his business since he purchased it) with a $15,000 adjusted basis and a $6,000 FMV, and $2,000 cash. The partnership has recourse liabilities of $100,000.

C:9-41 ***Basis in Partnership Interest.*** Tina purchases an interest in the TP Partnership on January 1 of the current year for $50,000. The partnership uses the calendar year as its tax year and has $200,000 in recourse liabilities when Tina acquires her interest. The partners share economic risk of loss associated with recourse debt according to their loss percentage. Her distributive share of partnership items for the year is as follows:

Ordinary income (excluding items listed below)	$30,000
Long-term capital gains	10,000
Municipal bond interest income	8,000
Charitable contributions	1,000
Interest expense related to municipal bond investment	2,000

TP reports the following liabilities on December 31:

Recourse debt	$100,000
Nonrecourse debt (not qualified real estate financing)	80,000

a. What is Tina's basis on December 31 if she has a 40% interest in profits and losses? TP is a general partnership. Tina has not guaranteed partnership debt, nor has she made any other special agreements about partnership debt.
b. How would your answer to Part a change if Tina instead had a 40% interest in profits and a 30% interest in losses? Assume TP is a general partnership, and all other agreements continue in place. Also assume the partners share recourse liabilities in accordance with their loss interest percentages.
c. How would your answer to Part a change if Tina were instead a limited partner having a 40% interest in profits and 30% interest in losses? The partnership agreement contains no guarantees or other special arrangements.

C:9-42 ***At-Risk Loss Limitation.*** The KC Partnership is a general partnership that manufactures widgets. The partnership uses a calendar year as its tax year and has two equal partners, Kerry and City Corporation, a widely held corporation. On January 1 of the current year, Kerry and City Corporation each has a $200,000 basis in the partnership interest. Operations during the year produce the following results:

Ordinary loss	$900,000
Long-term capital loss	100,000
Short-term capital gain	300,000

The only change in KC's liabilities during the year is KC's borrowing $100,000 as a nonrecourse loan (not qualified real estate financing) that remains outstanding at year-end.
a. What is each partner's deductible loss from the partnership's activities before any passive loss limitation?
b. What is each partner's basis in the partnership interest after the year's operations?
c. How would your answers to Parts a and b change if the KC Partnership's business were totally in real estate but not a rental activity? Assume the loan is qualified real estate financing.

C:9-43 ***At-Risk Loss Limitation.*** Mary and Gary are partners in the MG Partnership. Mary owns a 40% capital, profits, and loss interest. Gary owns the remaining interest. Both materially participate in partnership activities. At the beginning of the current year, MG's only liabilities are $30,000 in accounts payable, which remain outstanding at year-end. In November, MG borrows $100,000 on a nonrecourse basis from First Bank. The loan is secured by property with a $200,000 FMV. These are MG's only liabilities at year-end. Bases for the partnership interests at the beginning of the year are $80,000 for Mary and $120,000 for Gary after considering the impact of liabilities but before considering operations. MG has a $200,000 ordinary loss during the current year. How much loss can Mary and Gary recognize?

C:9-44 ***Passive Loss Limitation.*** Eve and Tom own 40% and 60%, respectively, of the ET Partnership, which manufactures clocks. The partnership is a limited partnership, and Eve is the only general partner. She works full-time in the business. Tom essentially is an investor in the firm and works full-time at another job. Tom has no other income except his salary from his full-time employer. During the current year, the partnership reports the following gain and loss:

Ordinary loss	$140,000
Long-term capital gain	20,000

Before including the current year's gain and loss, Eve and Tom had $46,000 and $75,000 bases for their partnership interests, respectively. The partnership has no nonrecourse liabilities. Tom has no further obligation to make any additional investment in the partnership.

a. What gain or loss should each partner report on his or her individual tax return?

b. If the partnership borrowed an additional $100,000 of recourse liabilities, how would your answer to Part a change?

C:9-45 ***Passive Loss Limitation.*** Kate, Chad, and Stan are partners in the KCS Partnership, which operates a manufacturing business. The partners formed the partnership ten years ago with Kate and Chad each as general partners having a 40% capital and profits interest. Kate materially participates; Chad does not. Stan has a 20% interest as a limited partner. At the end of the current year, the following information was available:

	Kate	*Chad*	*Stan*
Basis in partnership (before gains and losses)	$100,000	$100,000	$50,000
Distributive share of:			
Nonrecourse liability (already included in basis and not qualified real estate financing)	50,000	50,000	25,000
Operating loss	(80,000)	(80,000)	(40,000)
Capital gain	20,000	20,000	10,000

a. How much operating loss can each partner deduct in the current year?

b. Assuming each partner's individual AGI is less than $100,000, how much loss could each partner deduct if the KCS Partnership were engaged in rental activities? Assume Kate and Chad both actively participate, but Stan does not.

C:9-46 ***At-Risk and Passive Loss Limitations.*** At the beginning of year 1, Ed and Fran each contributed $1,000 cash to EF Partnership as equal partners. The partnership immediately borrowed $98,000 on a nonrecourse basis and used the contributed cash and loan proceeds to purchase equipment costing $100,000. The partnership leases out the equipment on a five-year lease for $10,000 per year. Over the five-year period, the partnership makes the following principal and interest payments on the loan:

Year	*Principal*	*Interest*
1	$3,000	$7,000
2	3,500	6,500
3	3,500	6,500
4	4,000	6,000
5	4,000	6,000

Assume the partnership depreciates the equipment according to the following hypothetical schedule:

Year	*Depreciation*
1	$40,000
2	25,000
3	15,000
4	8,000
5	8,000
6	4,000

At the beginning of Year 6, the partnership sells the equipment for $82,000. The partnership claims the last $4,000 of depreciation at the beginning of Year 6 as an expense, so the equipment has a zero basis when sold. At the beginning of Year 6, the partnership also pays off the $80,000 loan balance and distributes any remaining cash to Ed and Fran. Assume that each partner has a 33% ordinary tax rate and an 18.8% capital gains tax rate (including the 3.8% tax on net investment income).

a. Determine the partnership's gain (loss) for each of the five years and the beginning of the sixth year.

b. Assume that depreciation recapture applies but that the at-risk and passive activity loss rules do not apply. Using the results from Part a and a 7% discount rate, determine the present value of tax savings for both partners combined over the five-year period including the beginning of the sixth year. Why do these tax savings occur?
c. Now assume the at-risk and passive activity loss rules do apply. Determine what the partners recognize over the five-year period including the beginning of the sixth year. Do the partners have any tax savings in this situation? Why or why not?
d. Provide a schedule analyzing each partner's outside basis over the five-year period including the sixth year.

C:9-47 *Related Party Transactions.* Susan, Steve, and Sandy own 15%, 35%, and 50%, respectively, in the SSS Partnership. Susan sells securities for their $40,000 FMV to the partnership. What are the tax implications of the following independent situations?
a. Susan's basis in the securities is $60,000. The three partners are siblings.
b. Susan's basis in the securities is $50,000. Susan is unrelated to the other partners.
c. Susan's basis in the securities is $30,000. Susan and Sandy are sisters. The partnership will hold the securities as an investment.
d. What are the tax consequences in Part a if the partnership subsequently sells the securities to an unrelated third party for $70,000? For $55,000? For $35,000?

C:9-48 *Related Party Transactions.* Kara owns 35% of the KLM Partnership and 45% of the KTV Partnership. Lynn owns 20% of KLM and 3% of KTV. Maura, Kara's daughter, owns 15% of KTV. No other partners own an interest in both partnerships or are related to other partners. The KTV Partnership sells to the KLM Partnership 1,000 shares of stock, which KTV has held for investment purposes, for its $50,000 FMV. What are the tax consequences of the sale in each of the following independent situations?
a. KTV's basis for the stock is $80,000.
b. KTV's basis for the stock is $23,000 and KLM holds the stock as an investment.
c. KTV's basis for the stock is $35,000 and KLM holds the stock as inventory.
d. What are the tax consequences in Part a if the KLM Partnership subsequently sells the stock to an unrelated third party for $130,000? For $70,000? For $40,000?

C:9-49 *Guaranteed Payments.* Scott and Dave each invested $100,000 cash when they formed the SD Partnership and became equal partners. They agreed that the partnership would pay each partner a 5% guaranteed payment on his $100,000 capital account. Before the two guaranteed payments, current year results were $23,000 of ordinary income and $14,000 of long-term capital gain. What amount and character of income will Scott and Dave report for the current year from their partnership?

C:9-50 *Guaranteed Payments.* Allen and Bob are equal partners in the AB Partnership. Bob manages the business and receives a guaranteed payment. What amount and character of income will Allen and Bob report in each of the following independent situations?
a. The AB Partnership earns $160,000 of ordinary income before considering Bob's guaranteed payment. Bob is guaranteed a $90,000 payment plus 50% of all income remaining after the guaranteed payment.
b. Assume the same facts as Part a except Bob's distributive share is 50% with a guaranteed minimum of $90,000.
c. The AB Partnership earns a $140,000 long-term capital gain and no ordinary income. Bob is guaranteed $80,000 plus 50% of all amounts remaining after the guaranteed payment.

C:9-51 *Guaranteed Payments.* Pam and Susan own the PS Partnership. Pam takes care of daily operations and receives a guaranteed payment for her efforts. What amount and character of income will each partner report in each of the following independent situations?
a. The PS Partnership reports a $10,000 long-term capital gain and no ordinary income. Pam receives a $40,000 guaranteed payment plus a 30% distributive share of all partnership income after deducting the guaranteed payment.
b. The PS Partnership reports $80,000 of ordinary income, before considering any guaranteed payment, and a $60,000 Sec. 1231 gain. Pam receives a $35,000 guaranteed payment plus a 20% distributive share of all partnership income after deducting the guaranteed payment.
c. The PS Partnership reports $120,000 of ordinary income before considering any guaranteed payment. Pam receives 40% of partnership income but no less than $60,000.

C:9-52 *Family Partnership.* Dad gives Son a 20% capital and profits interest in the Family Partnership. Dad holds a 70% interest, and Fred, an unrelated individual, holds a 10% interest. Dad and Fred work in the partnership, but Son does not. Dad and Fred receive reasonable compensation for their work. The partnership earns $100,000 ordinary income, and the partners agree to divide this amount based on their relative ownership interests. What income must Father, Son, and Fred report if Family Partnership is a manufacturing firm with substantial inventories?

C:9-53 *Family Partnership.* Steve wishes to pass his business on to his children, Tracy and Vicki, and gives each daughter a 20% partnership interest to begin getting them involved. Steve retains the remaining 60% interest. Neither daughter is employed by the partnership, which buys and manages real estate. Steve draws only a $40,000 guaranteed payment for his work for the partnership. Reasonable compensation for his services would be $70,000. The partnership reports ordinary income of $120,000 after deducting the guaranteed payment. Distributive shares for the three partners are tentatively reported as: Steve, $72,000; Tracy, $24,000; and Vicki, $24,000. What is the proper distributive share of income for each partner?

COMPREHENSIVE PROBLEMS

C:9-54 Rick has a $50,000 basis in the RKS General Partnership on January 1 of the current year, and he owns no other investments. He has a 20% capital interest, a 30% profits interest, and a 40% loss interest in the partnership. Rick does not work in the partnership. The partnership's only liability is a $100,000 nonrecourse debt borrowed several years ago, which remains outstanding at year-end. Rick's share of the liability is based on his profits interest and is included in his $50,000 partnership basis. Rick and the partnership each report on a calendar year basis. Income for the entire partnership during the current year is:

Ordinary loss	$440,000
Long-term capital gain	100,000
Sec. 1231 gain	150,000

a. What is Rick's distributive share of income, gain, and loss for the current year?
b. What partnership income, gain, and loss should Rick report on his tax return for the current year?
c. What is Rick's basis in his partnership interest on the first day of next year?

C:9-55 Charles and Mary formed CM Partnership on January 1 of the current year. Charles contributed Inventory A with a $100,000 FMV and a $70,000 adjusted basis for a 40% interest, and Mary contributed $150,000 cash for a 60% interest. The partnership operates on a calendar year. The partnership used the cash to purchase equipment for $50,000, Inventory B for $80,000, and stock in ST Corporation for $5,000. The partnership used the remaining $15,000 for operating expenses and borrowed another $5,000 for operating expenses. During the year, the partnership sold one-half of Inventory A for $60,000 (tax basis, $35,000), one-half of Inventory B for $58,000 (tax basis, $40,000), and the ST stock for $6,000. The partnership claimed $7,000 of depreciation on the equipment for both tax and book purposes. Thus, for the year, the partnership incurred the following items:

Sales—Inventory A	$60,000
Sales—Inventory B	58,000
COGS—Inventory A	35,000
COGS—Inventory B	40,000
Operating expenses	20,000
Depreciation	7,000
Short-term capital gain	1,000
Interest on business loan	500

On December 31 of the current year, the partnership made a $1,000 principal payment on the loan and distributed $2,000 cash to Charles and $3,000 cash to Mary.

a. Determine partnership ordinary income for the year and each partner's distributive share.
b. Determine the separately stated items and each partner's distributive share.
c. Determine each partner's basis in the partnership at the end of the current year.
d. Determine each partner's book capital account at the end of the current year.
e. Provide an analysis of the ending cash balance.
f. Provide beginning and ending balance sheets using tax numbers.
g. Provide beginning and ending balance sheets using book values.

TAX STRATEGY PROBLEM

C:9-56 Sarah and Rex formed SR Entity on December 28 of last year. The entity operates on a calendar tax year. Each individual contributed $800,000 cash in exchange for a 50% ownership interest in the entity (common stock if a corporation; partnership interest if a partnership). In addition, the entity borrowed $400,000 from the bank. The entity operates on a calendar year. On December 28 of last year, the entity used the $2 million cash (contributions and loan) to purchase assets as indicated in the following balance sheet as of December 28 of last year:

Cash	$ 100,000
Inventory	1,770,000
Investment in tax-exempt bonds	50,000
Investment in corporate stock (less than 20%-owned)	80,000
Total	$2,000,000
Liability	$ 400,000
Equity*	1,600,000
Total	$2,000,000

*If a partnership, each partner's beginning capital account is $800,000.

The balance sheet did not change between December 28 of last year and the beginning of the current year. Thus, the above balance sheet also represents the balance sheet at January 1 of the current year.

The following data apply to the entity for the current year:

Sales	$3,000,000
Purchase of additional inventory	2,100,000
Ending inventory at December 31 of the current year	1,650,000
Gain on sale of corporate stock on December 31 of the current year	20,000
Dividends received on stock prior to its sale	4,000
Tax-exempt interest received	2,200
Operating expenses	500,000
Interest paid on loan (no principal paid)*	30,000
Distribution on December 31 of the current year:	
Sarah	50,000
Rex	50,000

*For simplicity, assume all the $30,000 interest expense pertains to business (and not to investments).

Sarah and Rex actively manage the entity's business, and the business does not qualify for the U.S. production activities deduction. At the individual level, Sarah and Rex are each single with no dependents. Each individual claims a standard deduction and one personal exemption (if applicable). Neither individual has income from sources other than listed above.

a. First, assume the entity is a regular C corporation and the distributions are dividends to Sarah and Rex. For the current year, determine the following:
   (1) The corporation's taxable income and tax liability.
   (2) Sarah's and Rex's individual AGI, taxable income, and tax liability.
   (3) The total tax liability for the corporation and its owners.

b. Next, assume the entity is a partnership. For the current year, determine the following:
   (1) Partnership ordinary income and each partner's share of partnership ordinary income.
   (2) Partnership separately stated items and each partner's share of each item.
   (3) Sarah's and Rex's AGI, taxable income, and total tax liability. Assume each partner will incur a $17,660 self-employment tax.
   (4) Each partner's basis in the partnership (outside basis) at the end of the current year.

c. Based on your analysis for the current year, which entity is better from an overall tax perspective? What are the shortcomings of examining only one year?

d. Given the corporate form, explain how the corporation can restructure the $50,000 distribution to each individual to reduce the overall tax liability. Assume the corporation and each individual pay a 7.65% payroll tax.

TAX FORM/RETURN PREPARATION PROBLEMS

C:9-57 The Dapper-Dons Partnership was formed ten years ago as a general partnership to custom tailor men's clothing. Dapper-Dons is located at 123 Flamingo Drive in City, ST, 54321. Bob Dapper manages the business and has a 40% capital and profits interest. His address is 709 Brumby Way, City, ST, 54321. Jeremy Dons owns the remaining 60% interest but is not active in the business. His address is 807 Ninth Avenue, City, ST, 54321. The partnership values its inventory using the cost method and did not change the method used during the current year. The partnership uses the accrual method of accounting. Because of its simplicity, the partnership is not subject to the partnership audit procedures. The partnership has no foreign partners, no foreign transactions, no interests in foreign trusts, and no foreign financial accounts. This partnership is neither a tax shelter nor a publicly traded partnership. No changes in ownership of partnership interests occurred during the current year. The partnership made cash distributions of $155,050 and $232,576 to Dapper and Dons, respectively, on December 30 of the current year. It made no other property distributions. Financial statements for the current year are presented in Tables C:9-1 and C:9-2. Assume that Dapper-Dons' business qualifies as a U.S. production activity and that its qualified production activities income is $600,000. Dapper-Dons, being an eligible small pass-through partnership, uses the small business simplified overall method for reporting these activities (see discussion for Line 13d of Schedules K and K-1 in the Form 1065 instructions).

Prepare a current year (2014 for this problem) partnership tax return for Dapper-Dons Partnership.

C:9-58 Healthwise Medical Supplies Company is located at 2400 Second Street, City, ST 12345. The company is a general partnership that uses the calendar year and accrual basis for both book and tax purposes. It engages in the development and sale of specialized surgical tools to hospitals. The employer identification number (EIN) is XX-2016014. The company formed and began business on January 1, 2013. It has no foreign partners or other foreign dealings. The company is neither a tax shelter nor a publicly traded partnership. The company has made no distributions other than cash, and no changes in ownership have occurred during the current year. Dr. Bailey is the Tax Matters Partner. The partnership makes no special elections. Table C:9-3 contains book balance sheet information at the beginning and end of the current year, and Table C:9-4 presents a book income statement for the current year. Other information follows:

Information on Partnership Formation:
Two individuals formed the partnership on January 1, 2013: Dr. Leisa H. Bailey (1200 First Pike, City, ST 12345) and Dr. Thomas J. Firth (3600 Third Blvd., City, ST 54321). For a 30% interest, Dr. Bailey contributed $1.2 million cash. She is an active general partner who manages the company. For a 70% interest, Dr. Firth contributed $2.32 million cash and 1,000 shares of Fastgrowth, Inc. stock having, at the time of contribution, a $480,000 fair market value (FMV) and a $96,000 adjusted basis. Dr. Firth is an active general partner who designs and develops new products. For book purposes, the company recorded the contribution of stock at fair market value.

Inventory and Cost of Goods Sold (Form 1125-A):
The company uses the periodic inventory method and prices its inventory using the lower of FIFO cost or market. Only beginning inventory, ending inventory, and purchases should be reflected in Schedule A. No other costs or expenses are allocated to cost of goods sold. Note: the company is exempt from the uniform capitalization (UNICAP) rules because average gross income for the previous year was less than $10 million [Sec. 263A(b)(2)(B)].

Line 9	(a)	Check (ii)
	(b)–(d)	Not applicable
	(e) & (f)	No

Capital Gains and Losses (Schedule D):
The company sold all 1,000 shares of the Fastgrowth, Inc. common stock on July 2, 2014, for $1.44 million. Dr. Firth acquired the stock on January 2, 2011, for $96,000 and contributed the stock to the company on January 1, 2013, when its FMV was $480,000.

▼ TABLE C:9-1

Dapper-Dons Partnership Income Statement for the 12 Months Ending December 31 of the Current Year (Problem C:9-57)

Sales		$2,357,000
Returns and allowances		(20,000)
		$2,337,000
Beginning inventory (FIFO method)	$ 200,050	
Purchases	624,000	
Labor	600,000	
Supplies	42,000	
Other costs[a]	12,000	
Goods available for sale	$1,478,050	
Ending inventory[b]	(146,000)	(1,332,050)
Gross profit		$ 1,004,950
Salaries for employees other than partners (W-2 wages)	$51,000	
Guaranteed payment for Dapper	85,000	
Utilities expense	46,428	
Depreciation (MACRS depreciation is $74,311)[c]	49,782	
Automobile expense	12,085	
Office supplies expense	4,420	
Advertising expense	85,000	
Bad debt expense	2,100	
Interest expense (all trade- or business-related)	45,000	
Rent expense	7,400	
Travel expense (meals cost $4,050 of this amount)	11,020	
Repairs and maintenance expense	68,300	
Accounting and legal expense	3,600	
Charitable contributions[d]	16,400	
Payroll taxes	5,180	
Other taxes (all trade- or business-related)	1,400	
Total expenses		494,115
Operating profit		$ 510,835
Other income and losses:		
Gain on sale of AB stock[e]	$ 18,000	
Loss on sale of CD stock[f]	(26,075)	
Sec. 1231 gain on sale of land[g]	5,050	
Interest on U.S. Treasury bills for entire year ($80,000 face amount)	2,000	
Dividends from 15%-owned domestic corporation	11,000	9,975
Net income		$ 520,810

[a] Additional Sec. 263A costs of $7,000 for the current year are included in other costs.
[b] Ending inventory includes the appropriate Sec. 263A costs, and no further adjustment is needed to properly state cost of sales and inventories for tax purposes.
[c] The partnership reports a $10,000 positive AMT adjustment for property placed in service after 1986. Dapper-Dons acquired and placed in service $40,000 of rehabilitation expenditures for a certified historical property this year. The appropriate MACRS depreciation on the rehabilitation expenditures already is included in the MACRS depreciation total.
[d] The partnership made all contributions in cash to qualifying charities.
[e] The partnership purchased the AB stock as an investment two years ago on December 1 for $40,000 and sold it on June 14 of the current year for $58,000.
[f] The partnership purchased the CD stock as an investment on February 15 of the current year for $100,000 and sold it on August 1 for $73,925.
[g] The partnership used the land as a parking lot for the business. The partnership purchased the land four years ago on March 17 for $30,000 and sold it on August 15 of the current year for $35,050.

▼ TABLE C:9-2
Dapper-Dons Partnership Balance Sheet for January 1 and December 31 of the Current Year (Problem C:9-57)

	Balance January 1	Balance December 31
Assets:		
Cash	$ 10,000	$ 40,000
Accounts receivable	72,600	150,100
Inventories	200,050	146,000
Marketable securities[a]	220,000	260,000
Building and equipment	374,600	465,000
Minus: Accumulated depreciation	(160,484)	(173,100)
Land	185,000	240,000
Total assets	$901,766	$1,128,000
Liabilities and equities:		
Accounts payable	$ 35,000	$ 46,000
Accrued salaries payable	14,000	18,000
Payroll taxes payable	3,416	7,106
Sales taxes payable	5,200	6,560
Mortgage and notes payable (current maturities)	44,000	52,000
Long-term debt	210,000	275,000
Capital:		
Dapper	236,060	289,334
Dons	354,090	434,000
Total liabilities and equities	$901,766	$1,128,000

[a] Short-term investment.

▼ TABLE C:9-3
Healthwise Medical Supplies Company—Book Balance Sheet Information

Account	January 1, 2014 Debit	January 1, 2014 Credit	December 31, 2014 Debit	December 31, 2014 Credit
Cash	$ 978,900		$ 890,850	
Accounts receivable	756,000		840,000	
Inventory	1,400,000		1,680,000	
Investment in municipal bonds	30,000		30,000	
Investment in corporate stock	480,000		–0–	
Equipment	1,600,000		2,100,000	
Accumulated depreciation—Equipment		$ 228,640		$1,120,480
Accounts payable		140,000		182,000
Notes payable (short-term)		700,000		140,000
Accrued payroll expenses		4,900		7,350
Capital account balances:				
Dr. Leisa H. Bailey (30%)		1,251,408		1,227,306
Dr. Thomas J. Firth (70%)		2,919,952		2,863,714
Totals	$5,244,900	$5,244,900	$5,540,850	$5,540,850

▼ TABLE C:9-4
Healthwise Medical Supplies Company—Book Income Statement 2013

Sales		$7,000,000
Returns and allowances		(350,000)
Net sales		$6,650,000
Beginning inventory	$1,400,000	
Purchases	2,800,000	
Ending inventory	(1,680,000)	
Cost of goods sold		(2,520,000)
Gross profit		$4,130,000
Expenses:		
Depreciation (including Sec. 179)	$ 891,840	
Repairs	45,500	
General insurance	49,000	
Guaranteed payment (to Dr. Bailey)	180,000	
Other salaries	980,000	
Travel	28,000	
Utilities	84,000	
Rent expense	210,000	
Advertising expense	42,000	
Professional fees	70,000	
Employment taxes	98,000	
Business interest expense	33,600	
Investment expenses	4,800	
Investment interest expense	4,200	
Meals and entertainment	21,000	
Charitable contributions (cash)	56,000	
Total expenses		(2,797,940)
Other income:		
Interest on municipal bonds		1,200
Dividend income		26,400
Gain on stock sale:		
Selling price	$1,440,000	
Book value	(480,000)	
Book gain		960,000
Net income per books		$2,319,660

Fixed Assets and Depreciation (Form 4562):
The company acquired the equipment on January 2, 2013, and placed it in service on that date. The equipment, which originally cost $1.6 million, is MACRS seven-year property. The company did not elect Sec. 179 expensing in the acquisition year and elected out of bonus depreciation. The company claimed the following depreciation on this property:

Year	*Book and Regular Tax Depreciation*	*AMT Depreciation*
2013	$228,640	$171,360
2014	391,840	306,080

On March 1, 2014, the company acquired and placed in service additional equipment costing $500,000. The company made the Sec. 179 expensing election for the entire cost of this new equipment. No depreciation or expensing is reported on Schedule A.

Other Information

- The company paid Dr. Bailey a $180,000 guaranteed payment for her management services.
- The company made a $56,000 cash contribution to Fort Sanders Hospital System on December 1 of the current year.
- During the current year, the company made a $720,000 cash distribution to Dr. Bailey and a $1.68 million cash distribution to Dr. Firth.
- The municipal bonds, acquired in 2013, are general revenue bonds, not private-activity bonds. Assume that no expenses of the company are allocable to the tax-exempt interest generated from the municipal bonds.
- Assume qualified production activities income (QPAI) equals $2.24 million. Employer's W-2 wages allocable to U.S. production activities equal $980,000. The company, being an eligible small pass-through partnership, uses the small business simplification overall method for reporting these activities (see discussion for Line 13d of Schedule K and Line 13 of Schedule K-1 in the Form 1065 instructions).
- Use book numbers for Schedule L, Schedule M-2, and Line 1 of Schedule M-1. Also use book numbers for Item L of Schedule K-1, and check the box for Sec. 704(b) book.
- The partners share liabilities, which are recourse, in the same proportion as their ownership percentages.

Required: Prepare the 2014 partnership tax return (Form 1065), including the following additional schedules and forms: Schedule D, Form 4562, and Schedule K-1.

Optional: Prepare a schedule for each partner's basis in his or her partnership interest.

CASE STUDY PROBLEMS

C:9-59 Abe and Brenda formed the AB Partnership ten years ago as a general partnership and have been very successful with the business. However, in the current year, economic conditions caused them to lose significant amounts, but they expect the economy and their business to return to profitable operations by next year or the year after. Abe manages the partnership business and works in it full-time. Brenda has a full-time job as an accountant for a $39,000 annual salary, but she also works in the partnership occasionally. She estimates that she spent about 120 hours working in the partnership this year. Abe has a 40% profits interest, a 50% loss interest, and a basis in his partnership interest on December 31 (before considering this year's operations) of $81,000. Brenda has a 60% profits interest, a 50% loss interest, and a basis of $104,000 on December 31 (before considering this year's operations). The partnership has no liabilities at December 31. Neither Abe nor Brenda currently has other investments. The AB Partnership incurs the following amounts during the year.

Ordinary loss	$100,000
Sec. 1231 gain	10,000
Tax-exempt municipal bond income	14,000
Long-term capital loss	14,000
Short-term capital loss	136,000

Early next year, the AB Partnership is considering borrowing $100,000 from a local bank to be secured by a mortgage on a building owned by the partnership with $150,000 FMV.

Required: Prepare a presentation to be made to Abe and Brenda discussing this matter. Points that should be discussed include: What amounts should Abe and Brenda report on their income tax return for the current year from the AB Partnership? What are their bases in their partnership interests after taking all transactions into effect? What happens to any losses they cannot deduct in the current year? What planning opportunities are presented by the need to borrow money early next year? What planning ideas would you suggest for Brenda?

C:9-60 On the advice of his attorney, Dr. Andres, a local pediatrician, contributed several office buildings, which he had previously owned as sole proprietor, to a new Andres Partnership in which he became a one-third general partner. He gave the remaining limited partnership interests to his two sons, Miguel and Esteban. Last year, when the partnership was formed, the boys were 14 and 16. The real estate is well managed and extremely profitable. Dr. Andres regularly consults with a full-time hired manager about the business, but neither of his sons has any dealings with the partnership. Under the terms of the partnership agreement, the boys can sell their partnership interest to no one but their father. Distributions from the partnership have been large, and Dr. Andres has insisted that the boys put all their distributions into savings accounts to pay for their college education.

Last year's return (the partnership's first) was filed by Mr. Jones, a partner in the local CPA firm of Wise and Johnson. Mr. Jones, who was Dr. Andres's accountant for a decade, retired last summer. Dr. Andres's business is extremely profitable and is an important part of the client base of this small-town CPA firm. Ms. Watson, the young partner who has taken over Dr. Andres's account, asked John, a second-year staff accountant, to prepare the current year's partnership return.

John has done considerable research and is positive that the Andres Partnership does not qualify as a partnership at all because the father has retained too much control over the sons' interests. John has briefly talked to Mr. Jones about his concerns. Mr. Jones said he was really rushed in the prior year when he filed the partnership return and admitted he never looked into the question of whether the arrangement met the requirements for being taxed as a partnership. After hearing more of the details, Mr. Jones stated that John was probably correct in his conclusion. Dr. Andres's tax bill will be significantly larger if he has to pay tax on all the partnership's income. When John approached Ms. Watson with his conclusions, her response was, "Oh, no! Dr. Andres already is unhappy because Mr. Jones is no longer preparing his returns. He'll really be unhappy if we give him a big tax increase, too." She paused thoughtfully, and then went on. "My first thought is just to leave well enough alone and file the partnership return. Are you positive, John, that this won't qualify as a partnership? Think about it and let me know tomorrow."

Required: Prepare a list of points you want to go over with the tax partner that would support finding that the business activity is a partnership. Prepare a second list of points that would support finding that the business activity is not a partnership.

TAX RESEARCH PROBLEMS

C:9-61 Caitlin and Wally formed the C & W Partnership on September 20, 2015. Caitlin contributed cash of $195,000, and Wally contributed office furniture with a FMV of $66,000. He bought the furniture for $60,000 on January 5, 2015, and placed it in service on that date. Wally did not elect Sec. 179 expensing on the furniture. He also contributed an office building and land with a combined FMV of $129,000. The land's FMV is $9,000. Wally bought the land in 2008 for $8,000 and had the building constructed for $100,000. The building was placed in service in June 2011.

Required: Your tax manager has asked you to prepare a schedule for the file indicating the basis of property at the time of contribution that Wally contributed, the depreciation for each piece of property that the partnership can claim, and the allocation of the depreciation to the two partners. Also indicate the amount and type of any recapture to which the contributed property may be subject at the time of the contribution and at a later time when the partnership sells the property. Your tax manager knows that, under Reg. Sec. 1.704-3, several alternatives exist for allocating depreciation relating to contributed property. He remembers that the Treasury Regulations describe a traditional method and a couple of others, but he's not sure what method applies in this situation. He wants you to check the alternatives and indicate which method should be used. Be certain to clearly label your schedule so that anyone who looks at the file later can determine where your numbers came from and the authority for your calculations. The manager has suggested that, at a minimum, you consult the following authorities:

- IRC Secs. 1(h), 168, 704, 1231, 1245
- Prop. Reg. Sec. 1.168-5(b)
- Reg. Sec. 1.704-1(b)(2)(iv)(g)(3)
- Reg. Sec. 1.704-3

C:9-62 Your clients, Lisa and Matthew, plan to form Lima General Partnership. Lisa will contribute $50,000 cash to Lima for a 50% interest in capital and profits. Matthew will contribute land having a $35,000 adjusted basis and a $50,000 FMV to Lima for the remaining 50% interest in capital and profits. Lima will borrow additional funds of $100,000 from a bank on a recourse basis and then will subdivide and sell the land. Prepare a draft memorandum for your tax manager's signature outlining the tax treatment for the partnership formation transaction. As part of your memorandum, compare the reporting of this transaction on the tax and financial accounting books. References:

- IRC Sec. 721
- Accounting Standards Codification (ASC) 845 (Nonmonetary Transactions)

C:9-63 Almost two years ago, the DEF Partnership was formed when Demetrius, Ebony, and Farouk each contributed $100,000 in cash. They are equal general partners in the real estate partnership, which has a December 31 year-end. The partnership uses the accrual method of accounting for financial accounting purposes but uses the cash method of accounting for tax purposes. The first year of operations resulted in a $50,000 loss. Because the real estate market plummeted, the second year of operations will result in an even larger ordinary loss. On November 30, calculations reveal that the year's loss is likely to be $100,000 for financial accounting purposes. Financial accounting results for the year are as follows:

	Quarter			
	First	*Second*	*Third*	*Fourth**
Revenue	$40,000	$60,000	$80,000	$100,000
Maintenance expense	(30,000)	(58,000)	(70,000)	(85,000)
Interest expense	(10,000)	(30,000)	(35,000)	(50,000)
Utilities expense	(3,000)	(3,000)	(3,000)	(3,000)
Projected loss	($ 3,000)	($31,000)	($28,000)	($38,000)

* Fourth quarter results are the sum of actual October and November results along with estimates for December results. December estimates are revenue, $33,000; maintenance, $60,000; interest, $20,000; and utilities, $1,000.

Cash has been short throughout the second year of operations, so more than $65,000 of expenses for second year operations have resulted in bills that are currently due or overdue. The unpaid bills are for July 1 through November 30 interest on a loan from the bank. In addition, all but essential maintenance has been postponed during the fourth quarter so that most of the fourth quarter maintenance is scheduled to be completed during December.

The DEF partners wants to attract a new partner to obtain additional capital. Raj is interested in investing $100,000 as a limited partner in the DEF Partnership if a good deal can be arranged. Raj would have a 25% profits and loss interest in the partnership but would expect something extra for the current year. In the current tax year, Raj has passive income of more than $200,000 from other sources, so he would like to have large passive losses allocated to him from DEF.

Required: Your tax partner has asked you to prepare a memorandum suggesting a plan to maximize the amount of current year loss that can be allocated to Raj. Assume none of the partners performs more than one-half of his or her personal service time in connection with real estate trades or businesses in which he or she materially participates. She reminded you to consider the varying interest rules for allocating losses to new partners found in Sec. 706 and to look into the possibilities of somehow capitalizing on the cash method of accounting or of using a special allocation. She wants you to be sure to check all the relevant case law for the plan you suggest.

C:9-64 Alice, Beth, and Carl formed the ABC partnership early in Year 1. Alice and Beth each contributed $100,000 for their partnership interests, and Carl contributed land having a $100,000 FMV and $160,000 adjusted basis. The land remained a capital asset to the partnership. Late in Year 2, Carl sold his interest in the partnership to Dan for $100,000. Shortly after that transaction, the partnership sold the land to an outside party for $100,000. The partnership has no Sec. 754 election in effect (discussed in Chapter C:10). The partners have asked that you explain the consequences these transactions have to the partnership and the partners, especially Carl and Dan. At a minimum, you should consult the following resources:

- IRC Sec. 704
- Reg. Sec. 1.704-3(a)

CHAPTER

10

SPECIAL PARTNERSHIP ISSUES

LEARNING OBJECTIVES

After studying this chapter, you should be able to

1. Determine the gain, loss, and basis consequences of a nonliquidating partnership distribution
2. Identify a partnership's Sec. 751 assets and assess the tax consequences of a nonliquidating distribution when these assets are involved
3. Determine the gain, loss, and basis consequences of liquidating or selling a partnership interest
4. Recognize other means of terminating a partnership interest and related issues
5. Analyze the effects of optional and mandatory basis adjustments
6. Compare and contrast the various special forms a partnership might take
7. Identify tax planning opportunities in liquidating or selling a partnership interest

CHAPTER OUTLINE

Chapter C:10 continues the discussion of partnership taxation. The chapter first explains simple nonliquidating distributions and then discusses more complex nonliquidating and liquidating distributions. The chapter also explains methods of disposing of a partnership interest, including sales of the partnership interest and the retirement or death of a partner as well as transactions that terminate the entire partnership.

Finally, the chapter examines special partnership forms. These forms include publicly traded partnerships, limited liability companies, limited liability partnerships, and electing large partnerships.

NONLIQUIDATING DISTRIBUTIONS

OBJECTIVE 1

Determine the gain, loss, and basis consequences of a nonliquidating partnership distribution

Distributions from a partnership fall into two categories: liquidating distributions and nonliquidating (or current) distributions. A **liquidating distribution** is a single distribution, or one of a planned series of distributions, that terminates a partner's entire interest in the partnership. All other distributions, including those that substantially reduce a partner's interest in the partnership, are governed by the **nonliquidating (current) distribution** rules.

Although the tax consequences of the two types of distributions are similar in many respects, they are sufficiently different to require separate study. The chapter first discusses simple current distributions. It then covers complex current distributions involving Sec. 751 property and liquidating distributions.

RECOGNITION OF GAIN

A current distribution that does not bring Sec. 751 into play cannot result in the recognition of a loss by either the partnership or the partner who receives the distribution. Moreover, the partnership usually recognizes no gain on a current distribution (except for Sec. 751 property, defined later in this chapter). Under Sec. 731, partners who receive distributions recognize a gain if they receive money distributions that exceed their basis in the partnership. For distribution purposes, money includes cash, deemed cash from reductions in a partner's share of liabilities, and the fair market value (FMV) of marketable securities.

EXAMPLE C:10-1 ▶ Melissa is a 30% partner in the ABC Real Estate Partnership until Josh is admitted as a partner in exchange for a cash contribution. After Josh's admission, Melissa holds a 20% interest. Because of large loss deductions, Melissa's basis (before Josh's admission) is $20,000 including her 30% interest in the partnership liabilities of $250,000. She is deemed to receive a cash distribution equal to the $25,000 [(0.30 − 0.20) × $250,000] reduction in her share of partnership liabilities. Because the cash distribution exceeds her basis, Melissa recognizes a $5,000 ($25,000 distribution − $20,000 basis) gain. ◀

KEY POINT

Reductions in a partner's share of liabilities are treated as cash distributions.

SELF-STUDY QUESTION

Can gain or loss be recognized in a current distribution?

ANSWER

Current distributions with no Sec. 751 implications do not create losses to either the partner or partnership. Ignoring Sec. 751, the partnership recognizes no gains. However, a partner recognizes a gain if the partner receives a money distribution exceeding his or her basis in his or her partnership interest. A distribution also may trigger recognition of precontribution gain or loss for a partner.

Precontribution Gain Recognition. Although a current distribution usually causes gain recognition only if money distributions exceed a partner's basis, a distribution also may trigger recognition of previously unrecognized precontribution gain or loss. A precontribution gain or loss is the difference between the FMV and adjusted basis of property when contributed to the partnership. Two different distribution events may trigger recognition of precontribution gain or loss.

First, if a partner contributes property with a precontribution gain or loss, the contributing partner must recognize the precontribution gain or loss when the partnership distributes the property to any other partner within seven years of the contribution. The amount of precontribution gain or loss recognized by the contributing partner equals the amount of precontribution gain or loss remaining that would have been allocated to the contributing partner had the property instead been sold for its FMV on the distribution date. The partnership's basis in the property immediately before the distribution and the contributing partner's basis in his or her partnership interest are both increased by any gain recognized or decreased by any loss recognized.[1]

EXAMPLE C:10-2 ▶ Several years ago, Michael contributed land with a $3,000 basis and a $7,000 FMV to the AB Partnership. In the current year, the partnership distributed the land to Stephen, another partner in the partnership. At the time of the distribution, the land had a $9,000 FMV. Stephen recognizes no gain on the distribution. Michael, however, recognizes his $4,000 precontribution gain when the partnership distributes the property to Stephen. Michael increases the basis in his partnership interest by $4,000, and the partnership's basis in the land immediately before the distribution increases by $4,000. This increase in the partnership's basis for the land also increases the land's basis to the distributee partner (Stephen). ◀

KEY POINT

Note the differences in the two distributions that cause a contributing partner to recognize remaining precontribution gains. In the first distribution, the *contributed property* is distributed to *another partner.* In the second distribution, *property other than the contributed property* is distributed to the *contributing partner.*

Second, under Sec. 737, property distributions to a partner may cause the partner to recognize his or her remaining precontribution gain if the FMV of the distributed property exceeds the partner's basis in his or her partnership interest before the distribution. The gain recognized under Sec. 737 is the lesser of the remaining precontribution net gain or the excess of the FMV of the distributed property over the adjusted basis of the partnership interest immediately before the property distribution (but after reduction for any money distributed at the same time).[2] The remaining precontribution gain is the net of all precontribution gains and losses for property contributed to the partnership in the seven years immediately preceding the distribution to the extent that such precontribution gains and losses have not already been recognized. The character of the recognized gain is determined by referencing the type of property that had precontribution gains or losses. The gain recognized under Sec. 737 is in addition to any gain recognized on the same distribution because of distributed cash exceeding the partner's basis in his or her partnership interest.

EXAMPLE C:10-3 ▶ Several years ago, Sergio contributed land, a capital asset, with a $20,000 FMV and a $15,000 basis to the STU Partnership in exchange for a 30% general interest in the partnership. The partnership still holds the land on January 31 of the current year, and none of the $5,000 precontribution gain has been recognized. On January 31 of the current year, Sergio has a $40,000 basis in his partnership interest when he receives an $8,000 cash distribution plus property purchased by the partnership with a $45,000 FMV and a $30,000 basis. Under the Sec. 731 distribution rules Sergio recognizes no gain because the cash distribution ($8,000) does not exceed Sergio's predistribution basis in his partnership interest ($40,000). However, under Sec. 737 he recognizes gain equal to the lesser of the $5,000 remaining precontribution gain or the $13,000 difference between the FMV of the property distributed ($45,000) and the basis of the partnership interest after the cash distribution but before any property distributions ($32,000 = $40,000 adjusted basis − $8,000 cash distributed). Thus, Sergio recognizes a $5,000 capital gain. ◀

EXAMPLE C:10-4 ▶ Assume the same facts as in Example C:10-3 except the distribution was $20,000 in cash and $23,000 (FMV) in marketable securities, which are treated like money, plus the property. Sergio recognizes a $3,000 gain under Sec. 731 because he received a money distribution exceeding his basis in the partnership interest ($43,000 money distribution − $40,000 adjusted basis before distributions). Under Sec. 737 he also recognizes gain equal to the lesser of the remaining precontribution gain ($5,000) or the $45,000 excess of the FMV of the property distributed ($45,000) over the zero basis of the partnership interest after money distributions but before property distributions ($0 = $40,000 adjusted basis − $43,000 money distributed). Sergio, therefore, recognizes both a $5,000 capital gain under Sec. 737 and a $3,000 capital gain under Sec. 731. ◀

If a partner recognizes gain under Sec. 737, that gain increases the partner's basis in his or her partnership interest (illustrated in the next section). Further, the recognized gain also increases the partnership's basis in the property that was the source of the precontribution gain.

[1] Sec. 704(c). See Chapter C:9 for a discussion of precontribution gains and losses.

[2] Section 737 does not apply if the property distributed was contributed by this same partner. Only the provisions of Sec. 731 would be considered in such a situation.

EXAMPLE C:10-5 ▶ Assume the same facts as in Example C:10-3. At the time Sergio contributed the land, the partnership assumed Sergio's $15,000 basis in the land. Now, Sergio's $5,000 Sec. 737 gain increases the partnership's basis in the land to $20,000. ◀

BASIS EFFECTS OF DISTRIBUTIONS

In general, the partner's basis for property distributed by the partnership carries over from the partnership. The partner's basis in the partnership interest is reduced by the amount of money received and by the partner's basis in the distributed property.

EXAMPLE C:10-6 ▶ Jack has a $35,000 basis for his interest in the MLV Partnership before receiving a current distribution consisting of $7,000 in money, accounts receivable having a zero basis to the partnership, and land having an $18,000 basis to the partnership. Jack takes a carryover basis in the land and receivables. Following the distribution, his basis in the partnership interest is calculated as follows:

Predistribution basis in partnership interest		$35,000
Minus:	Money received	(7,000)
	Carryover basis in receivables	(–0–)
	Carryover basis in land	(18,000)
Postdistribution basis in partnership interest		$10,000

◀

The total bases of all distributed property in the partner's hands is limited to the partner's predistribution basis in his or her partnership interest plus any gain recognized on the distribution under Sec. 737.[3] If the partner's predistribution basis plus Sec. 737 gain is less than the sum of the money received plus the carryover basis of any noncash property received, the order in which the basis is allocated becomes crucial. First, cash and deemed cash distributions reduce the partner's basis in his or her partnership interest. Next, the remaining basis is allocated to provide a carryover of the partnership's basis for receivables and inventory. If the partner's predistribution basis is not large enough to allow a carryover of the partnership's basis for these two property categories, the partner's remaining basis is allocated among the receivables and inventory items based on both the partnership's basis in the assets and their FMV.[4] First, each asset is given its basis to the partnership. Then, the difference between the carryover basis from the partnership and the partner's basis in the partnership interest is

WHAT WOULD YOU DO IN THIS SITUATION?

You have done the personal and business tax work for Betty and Thelma for a number of years. Betty and Thelma are partners in a retail shop. In addition, the two have decided they want to exchange some property that is not associated with their partnership. Betty wants to exchange undeveloped land she personally holds as an investment, having a $40,000 FMV and a $10,000 adjusted basis, for machinery and office equipment that Thelma owns but no longer uses. Thelma's machinery and office equipment in total have a $40,000 FMV and a $28,000 adjusted basis. Recently, a friend told Betty that several years ago he and an associate did a similar swap tax-free by contributing both pieces of property to be exchanged to a partnership, having the partnership hold the property for a few months, and then having the partnership distribute the property to the partner who wanted to receive it. The friend said the arrangement was nontaxable because the initial transfer qualified as a nontaxable contribution of property to the partnership in exchange for a partnership interest, and the distribution was nontaxable because it was simply a pro rata property distribution made by the partnership. Thelma and Betty have come to you asking that you structure their exchange using their retail shop partnership so that the transfer will be tax-free also. How should you respond to their request?

---

3 Secs. 732(a)(2) and 737(c). Marketable securities have a basis equal to their Sec. 732 basis plus any gain recognized under Sec. 731(c).

4 Sec. 732(c).

calculated. A decrease must be allocated if the partner's basis in the partnership interest (after any money distribution) is less than the carryover basis from the partnership. The decrease is first allocated to any asset that has declined in value in an amount equal to the smaller of the decline in value for the asset or the asset's share of the decrease. If the decrease is not fully used at this point in the calculation, the remaining decrease is allocated to the assets based on their relative adjusted bases at this point in the calculation.

KEY POINT

If different types of property are distributed, the partnership distribution rules assume that the property is distributed in the following order: (1) cash, (2) receivables and inventory, and (3) other property. This ordering can affect both the recognition of gain to the partner and the basis the partner takes in the distributed property.

EXAMPLE C:10-7 ►

Tracy has a $15,000 basis in her interest in the TP Partnership and no remaining precontribution gain immediately before receiving a current distribution that consists of $6,000 in money, power tools held as inventory with a $4,000 basis to the partnership and FMV of $3,500, and steel rod held as inventory with an $8,000 basis to the partnership and FMV of $9,200. The basis of the distributed property in Tracy's hands is determined as follows:

Predistribution basis in partnership interest	$15,000
Minus: Money received	(6,000)
Plus: Sec. 737 gain	–0–
Basis to be allocated	$ 9,000

The calculation of bases for the steel rod and power tools is as follows:

		Steel Rods	*Power Tools*	*Total*
	FMV of asset	$9,200	$3,500	$12,700
	Minus: Partnership's basis for asset	(8,000)	(4,000)	(12,000)
	Difference	$1,200	($ 500)	$ 700
Step 1:	Give each asset the partnership's basis for the asset	$8,000	$4,000	$12,000
	Minus: Tracy's basis to be allocated			(9,000)
	Decrease to allocate			$ 3,000
Step 2:	Asset basis after Step 1	$8,000	$4,000	$12,000
	Allocate the decrease first to assets that have declined in value	–0–	(500)	(500)
	Adjusted bases at this point in the calculation	$8,000	$3,500	$11,500
Step 3:	Allocate $2,500 remaining decrease based on relative adjusted bases at this point in the calculation	(1,739)[a]	(761)[b]	(2,500)
	Tracy's bases in the assets	$6,261	$2,739	$ 9,000

[a][$8,000 ÷ ($8,000 + $3,500)] × $2,500 = $1,739
[b][$3,500 ÷ ($8,000 + $3,500)] × $2,500 = $ 761

This process results in Tracy's total basis in the two assets she receives being exactly equal to the $9,000 amount to be allocated. Moreover, Tracy's basis in her partnership interest is zero after the property distributions. ◄

EXAMPLE C:10-8 ►

Assume the same facts as in Example C:10-7 except Tracy recognizes $1,000 of remaining precontribution gain under Sec. 737 as a result of the distribution. The basis of the distributed property in Tracy's hands is determined as follows:

Predistribution basis in partnership interest	$15,000
Minus: Money received	(6,000)
Plus: Sec. 737 gain	1,000
Amount to be allocated	$10,000

The calculation of the basis for the steel rods and power tools are as follows:

	Steel Rods	*Power Tools*	*Total*
FMV of asset	$9,200	$3,500	$12,700
Minus: Partnership's basis for asset	(8,000)	(4,000)	(12,000)
Difference	$1,200	($ 500)	$ 700

Step 1: Give each asset the partnership's basis for the asset	$8,000	$4,000	$12,000
Minus: Tracy's basis to be allocated			(10,000)
Decrease to allocate			$ 2,000
Step 2: Adjusted basis after Step 1	$8,000	$4,000	$12,000
Allocate the decrease first to assets that have declined in value	–0–	(500)	(500)
Adjusted basis at this point in the calculation	$8,000	$3,500	$11,500
Step 3: Allocate $1,500 remaining decrease based on relative adjusted bases at this point in the calculation	(1,043)[a]	(457)[b]	(1,500)
Tracy's bases in the assets	$6,957	$3,043	$10,000

[a][$8,000 ÷ ($8,000 + $3,500)] × $1,500 = $1,043
[b][$3,500 ÷ ($8,000 + $3,500)] × $1,500 = $ 457

Again, Tracy's basis in her partnership interest is zero after the distributions. ◀

If a partner's predistribution basis plus Sec. 737 gain recognized exceeds the sum of his or her money distribution plus the carryover basis for any receivables and inventory, a carryover basis is allocated to the other property received. If the partner has an insufficient basis in the partnership interest to provide a carryover basis for all the distributed property, the remaining basis for the partnership interest is allocated to the other property first to any decrease in FMV below basis and then based on the relative bases of such property in the partnership's hands just as was calculated above.

SELF-STUDY QUESTION

Assume the same facts as in Example C:10-9 except the basis in the two parcels of land is only $4,000 in total. What are the tax consequences of the distribution?

ANSWER

If the basis in the two parcels of land were only $4,000 in total, the partner would take a $4,000 carryover basis in the land and retain a $2,000 basis in his partnership interest.

EXAMPLE C:10-9 ▶ John has a $15,000 basis in his partnership interest and no remaining precontribution gain before receiving the following property as a current distribution:

Property	*Basis to the Partnership*	*FMV*
Money	$ 5,000	$5,000
Inventory	4,000	4,500
Land parcel 1	4,500	6,000
Land parcel 2	3,000	4,000

John's basis in his distributed property is calculated as follows:

Predistribution basis	$15,000
Minus: Money received	(5,000)
Plus: Sec. 737 gain	–0–
Basis for noncash property	$10,000
Minus: Carryover basis for inventory	(4,000)
Remaining basis to be allocated	$ 6,000

The calculation of the basis for the two parcels of land is as follows:

	Parcel One	*Parcel Two*	*Total*
FMV of asset	$6,000	$4,000	$10,000
Minus: Partnership's basis for asset	(4,500)	(3,000)	(7,500)
Difference	$1,500	$1,000	$ 2,500
Step 1: Give each asset the partnership's basis for the asset	$4,500	$3,000	$ 7,500
Minus: John's basis to be allocated			(6,000)
Decrease to allocate			$ 1,500
Step 2: Adjusted basis after Step 1	$4,500	$3,000	$ 7,500
Allocate the decrease first to assets that have declined in value	–0–	–0–	–0–
Adjusted basis at this point in the calculation	$4,500	$3,000	$ 7,500

Step 3: Allocate $1,500 remaining decrease based on relative adjusted bases at this point in the calculation	(900)[a]	(600)[b]	(1,500)
John's bases in the assets	$3,600	$2,400	$ 6,000

[a][$4,500 ÷ ($4,500 + $3,000)] × $1,500 = $900
[b][$3,000 ÷ ($4,500 + $3,000)] × $1,500 = $600

TYPICAL MISCONCEPTION

The partner's basis in his or her partnership interest cannot be less than zero. However, a partner's capital account can be less than zero. One must distinguish between references to a partner's basis in his or her partnership interest (his outside basis) and the balance in a partner's capital account.

John's basis in his partnership interest is zero after the distribution because all its basis is allocated to the money and other property received. ◀

Two other points should be noted. First, even when a partner's basis in the partnership interest is reduced to zero by a current distribution, he or she retains an interest in the partnership. If the partner has no remaining interest in the partnership (as opposed to a zero basis), the distribution would have been a liquidating distribution. Second, the distributee's basis in property distributed as a current distribution is always equal to or less than the carryover basis. Basis for distributed property cannot be increased above the carryover basis amount when received as a nonliquidating distribution.

HOLDING PERIOD AND CHARACTER OF DISTRIBUTED PROPERTY

The partner's holding period for property distributed as a current distribution includes the partnership's holding period for such property.[5] The length of time the partner owns the partnership interest is irrelevant when determining the holding period for the distributed property. Thus, if a new partner receives a distribution of property the partnership held for two years before he or she became a partner, the new partner's holding period for the distributed property is deemed to begin when the partnership purchased the property (i.e., two years ago) rather than on the more recent date when the partner purchases the partnership interest.

KEY POINT

Consistent with the discussion in Chapter C:9, certain rules ensure that neither contributions to nor distributions from a partnership can be used to alter the character of certain gains and losses on property held by the partnership or by the individual partners.

Special rules determine the character of gain or loss recognized when a partner subsequently sells or exchanges unrealized receivables or inventory distributed to the partner. These properties are defined in the next section of this chapter.

If the partnership distributes property that is an unrealized receivable in its hands, the distributee partner recognizes ordinary income or loss on a subsequent sale of that property. This ordinary income or loss treatment occurs without regard to the character of the property in the distributee partner's hands or the length of time the partner holds the property before its disposition.[6]

If the partnership distributes property that is inventory in its hands, the distributee partner recognizes ordinary income or loss on a subsequent sale that occurs within five years of the distribution date.[7] The inventory rule mandates the ordinary income or loss result only for the five-year period beginning on the distribution date. After five years, the character of the gain or loss recognized on the sale of such property is determined by its character in the hands of the distributee partner.

NONLIQUIDATING DISTRIBUTIONS WITH SEC. 751

OBJECTIVE 2

Identify a partnership's Sec. 751 assets and assess the tax consequences of a nonliquidating distribution when these assets are involved

So far, the discussion of current distributions has ignored the existence of the Sec. 751 property rules. Now, we must expand our discussion to include them.

SECTION 751 ASSETS DEFINED

Section 751 assets include unrealized receivables and inventory. These two categories encompass all property likely to produce ordinary income when sold or collected. Each of these categories must be carefully defined before further discussion of Sec. 751.

---

[5] Sec. 735(b).
[6] Sec. 735(a)(1).
[7] Sec. 735(a)(2).

KEY POINT

Section 751 property represents property in a partnership that is likely to produce ordinary income or loss. The application of Sec. 751 in conjunction with partnership distributions or sales of a partnership interest is of concern to individual partners because the rules may trigger ordinary income recognition rather than capital gains.

Unrealized Receivables. **Unrealized receivables** includes a much broader spectrum of property than the name implies. Unrealized receivables are certain rights to payments to be received by a partnership to the extent they are not already included in income under the partnership's accounting methods. They include rights to payments for services performed or to be performed as well as rights to payment for goods delivered or to be delivered (other than capital assets). A common example of unrealized receivables is the accounts receivable of a cash method partnership.

In addition to rights to receive payments for goods and services, the term unrealized receivables includes most potential ordinary income recapture items. A primary example of this type of unrealized receivable is the potential Sec. 1245 or 1250 recapture on the partnership's depreciable property, which is the amount of depreciation that would be recaptured as ordinary income under Sec. 1245 or 1250 if the partnership sold property at its FMV.[8]

EXAMPLE C:10-10 ▶ The LK Partnership has two assets: $10,000 cash and a machine having a $14,000 basis and a $20,000 FMV. The partnership has claimed $8,000 of depreciation on the machine since its purchase. If the partnership sells the machine for its FMV, all $6,000 of the gain would be recaptured as ordinary income under Sec. 1245. Therefore, the LK Partnership has a $6,000 unrealized receivable. ◀

SELF-STUDY QUESTION

What is included in the definition of unrealized receivables?

ANSWER

Unrealized receivables include not only the obvious cash method accounts receivable that have yet to be recognized but also most of the potential ordinary income recapture provisions. Therefore, the term unrealized receivables is broader than it may appear.

The definition of unrealized receivables is not limited to Sec. 1245 and 1250 depreciation recapture. Among the other recapture provisions creating unrealized receivables are Sec. 617(d) (mining property), Sec. 1252 (farmland), and Sec. 1254 (oil, gas, and geothermal property). Assets covered by Sec. 1278 (market discount bonds) and Sec. 1283 (short-term obligations) generate unrealized receivables to the extent the partnership would recognize ordinary income if it sold the asset. This type of unrealized receivable is deemed to have a zero basis.

Inventory. Inventory is equally surprising in its breadth. Inventory for purposes of Sec. 751 includes three major types of property:

- Items held for sale in the normal course of partnership business
- Any other property that, if sold by the partnership, would not be considered a capital asset or Sec. 1231 property
- Any other property held by the partnership that, if held by the selling or distributee partner, would be property of the two types listed above[9]

TYPICAL MISCONCEPTION

The definition of inventory is broadly construed by Sec. 751. In fact, for purposes of determining whether inventory is substantially appreciated, even unrealized receivables are treated as inventory items.

In short, cash, capital assets, and Sec. 1231 assets are the only properties that are not inventory.

For purposes of calculating the impact of Sec. 751 on distributions, inventory is considered a Sec. 751 asset only if the inventory is **substantially appreciated**. (This substantially appreciated rule does not apply to sales of partnership interests, discussed later in this chapter.) The test to determine whether inventory is substantially appreciated (and therefore falling under Sec. 751) is purely mechanical. Inventory is substantially appreciated if its FMV exceeds 120% of its adjusted basis to the partnership. For purposes of testing whether the inventory is substantially appreciated (but *only* for that purpose), inventory also includes unrealized receivables. The inclusion of unrealized receivables in the definition of inventory increases the likelihood that the inventory will be substantially appreciated.

EXAMPLE C:10-11 ▶ The ABC Partnership owns the following assets on December 31:

Assets	*Basis*	*FMV*
Cash	$10,000	$ 10,000
Unrealized receivables	–0–	40,000
Inventory	30,000	34,000
Land (Sec. 1231 property)	40,000	70,000
Total	$80,000	$154,000

[8] Sec. 751(c). Unrealized receivables may have basis if costs or expenses have been incurred but not taken into account under the partnership's method of accounting (e.g., the basis of property sold in a nondealer installment sale).

[9] Sec. 751(d)(2).

For purposes of the substantially appreciated inventory test, both ABC's unrealized receivables and inventory are included. The inventory's $74,000 FMV exceeds 120% of its adjusted basis [($30,000 + $0) × 1.20 = $36,000]. Therefore, the ABC Partnership has substantially appreciated inventory. ◄

EXCHANGE OF SEC. 751 ASSETS AND OTHER PROPERTY

A current distribution receives treatment under Sec. 751 only if the partnership has Sec. 751 assets and an exchange of Sec. 751 property for non-Sec. 751 property occurs. Accordingly, if a partnership does not have *both* Sec. 751 property and other property, the rules discussed above for simple current distributions control the taxation of the distribution. Similarly, a distribution that is proportionate to all partners or (1) consists of only the partner's share of either Sec. 751 property or non-Sec. 751 property and (2) does not reduce the partner's interest in other property is not affected by the Sec. 751 rules.

TYPICAL MISCONCEPTION

Even if a partnership has Sec. 751 property, Sec. 751 is not applicable as long as a partner's interest in the ordinary income type assets is not altered. However, if a distribution of the partnership assets is disproportionate, Sec. 751 treats that portion of the distribution as a deemed sale between the partnership and the distributee partner, with the corresponding income or loss being recognized.

However, any portion of the distribution that represents an exchange of Sec. 751 property for non-Sec. 751 property must be isolated and is not treated as a distribution at all. Instead, it is treated as a sale between the partnership and the partner, and any gain or loss realized on the sale transaction is fully recognized.[10] The character of the recognized gain or loss depends on the character of the property deemed sold. For the party deemed the seller of the Sec. 751 assets, the gain or loss is ordinary income or loss.

Analyzing the transaction to determine what property was involved in the Sec. 751 transaction is best accomplished by using an orderly, step-by-step approach.

STEP 1: DIVIDE THE ASSETS INTO SEC. 751 ASSETS AND NON-SEC. 751 ASSETS. Inventory must be tested at this time to see whether it is substantially appreciated to know whether it is a Sec. 751 asset for distribution purposes.

STEP 2: DEVELOP A SCHEDULE, SUCH AS THE ONE IN TABLE C:10-1, TO DETERMINE WHETHER THE PARTNER EXCHANGED SEC. 751 ASSETS FOR NON-SEC. 751 ASSETS OR VICE VERSA. This schedule must be based on the FMV of all the partnership's assets. To make the determination, compare the partner's interest in the partnership's assets before the distribution with his or her interest in the assets after the distribution. This part of the analysis assumes a hypothetical nontaxable pro rata distribution equal to the partner's decreased interest in the assets. We can see whether the partner exchanged Sec. 751 assets for non-Sec. 751 assets by comparing the hypothetical distribution with the actual distribution. Thus, in Table C:10-1,

KEY POINT

Steps 2 and 3 try to identify whether a disproportionate distribution of Sec. 751 assets has taken place. In Table C:10-1, if the column 5 total for Sec. 751 assets is zero, Sec. 751 is not applicable. But as the table illustrates, Anne received $10,000 more than her share of the partnership cash without receiving any of her $10,000 share of Sec. 751 assets.

- Column 1 represents the partner's interest (valued at FMV) in each asset before the distribution.
- Column 2 represents the partner's interest (valued at FMV) in each asset after the distribution.
- Column 3 shows a hypothetical proportionate distribution that would have occurred had the partner's ownership interest been reduced by the partner taking a pro rata share of each asset. (As such, the proportionate distribution would be nontaxable.)
- Column 4 shows the amounts actually distributed.
- Column 5 shows the difference between the hypothetical and actual distributions. This column indicates whether a Sec. 751 exchange has occurred (see Step 3).

STEP 3: ANALYZE COLUMN 5 TO DETERMINE WHETHER SEC. 751 ASSETS WERE EXCHANGED FOR NON-SEC. 751 ASSETS. If the column 5 total for the Sec. 751 assets section of Table C:10-1 is zero, no Sec. 751 exchange has occurred. The partner simply received an additional amount of one type of Sec. 751 asset in exchange for relinquishing an interest in some other type of Sec. 751 asset. For example, no Sec. 751 exchange occurs if a partner exchanges an interest in substantially appreciated inventory for an interest in unrealized receivables. However, if the column 5 total for the Sec. 751

[10] Sec. 751(b).

▼ TABLE C:10-1
Analysis of Sec. 751 Nonliquidating Distribution (Example C:10-12)

	Beginning Partnership Amount[a]	(1) Anne's Interest Before Distribution[a] (1/3)	(2) Anne's Interest After Distribution[a] (1/5)	(3) Hypothetical Proportionate Distribution (3) = (1) − (2)[a]	(4) Actual Distribution[a]	(5) Difference[b] (5) = (4) − (3)
Sec. 751 assets:						
Unrealized receivables	$15,000	$ 5,000	$ 3,000	$ 2,000	$ –0–	$ (2,000)
Inventory	60,000	20,000	12,000	8,000	–0–	(8,000)
Total Sec. 751 assets	$75,000	$25,000	$15,000	$10,000	$ –0–	$ (10,000)
Non-Sec. 751 assets:						
Cash	$75,000	$25,000	$10,000[c]	$15,000	$25,000	$ 10,000
Total non-Sec. 751 assets	$75,000	$25,000	$10,000	$15,000	$25,000	$ 10,000

[a]Valued at fair market value.
[b]A negative amount means that Anne gave up her interest in a particular property. A positive amount means that she received more than her proportionate interest.
[c]One-fifth interest in remaining cash of $50,000.

assets is an amount other than zero, a Sec. 751 exchange has occurred. One (or more) Sec. 751 properties has been exchanged for one (or more) non-Sec. 751 properties.

EXAMPLE C:10-12 ▶ On January 1, the ABC Partnership holds the assets listed below before making a $25,000 cash distribution to Anne that reduces her interest in the partnership from one-third to one-fifth.

Assets	*Basis*	*FMV*
Cash	$ 75,000	$ 75,000
Unrealized receivables	–0–	15,000
Inventory	30,000	60,000
Total	$105,000	$150,000

ABC owes no liabilities on January 1. Before the distribution, Anne has a $35,000 basis in her partnership interest. The following three steps indicate that a Sec. 751 exchange has occurred:

STEP 1. Determine ABC's Sec. 751 and non-Sec. 751 assets. ABC's Sec. 751 assets include the unrealized receivables and the substantially appreciated inventory. The cash is ABC's only non-Sec. 751 property.

STEP 2. Complete the table used to analyze the Sec. 751 distribution (see Table C:10-1).

STEP 3. Analyze column 5 of Table C:10-1 to see whether a Sec. 751 exchange has occurred. Because Anne's Sec. 751 asset total declined by $10,000, we know she gave up $10,000 of her proportionate interest in ABC's Sec. 751 assets in exchange for cash. ◀

ADDITIONAL COMMENT

Step 4 is crucial if a student is to understand the deemed sale that Sec. 751 creates. In Example C:10-13, Anne is treated as if she had exchanged her $10,000 interest in the unrealized receivables and inventory for $10,000 of cash. Thus, Anne has a taxable gain or loss on the deemed sale. To determine Anne's gain or loss on the deemed sale, the adjusted basis of the unrealized receivables and inventory equals whatever her basis would have been had the partnership actually distributed those assets to her.

STEP 4: DETERMINE THE GAIN OR LOSS ON THE SEC. 751 DEEMED SALE. We must assume that the exchange occurring in Step 3 above was a sale of the exchanged property between the partnership and the partner. This step follows logically from the premise that the partner "bargained" to receive the amounts actually distributed rather than a proportionate distribution. She sold her interest in some assets to receive more than her proportionate interest in other assets. As with any sale, the gain (or loss) equals the difference between the FMV of the property received and the adjusted basis of the property given up. Note that, up to this point, we have been dealing only in terms of the FMV, so the adjusted basis of property given up must be determined as if the hypothetical distribution actually had occurred.

EXAMPLE C:10-13 ▶ Assume the same facts as in Example C:10-12. The Sec. 751 sale portion of the distribution is analyzed as Anne receiving $10,000 more cash than her proportionate share and giving up a $2,000 (FMV) interest in the unrealized receivables and an $8,000 (FMV) interest in the inventory. By examining the balance sheet, we can see that the partnership's bases for the unrealized receivables and inventory are $0 and $4,000 [$8,000 × ($30,000 ÷ $60,000)]. If Anne received these properties in a current distribution, her basis would be the same as the property's basis in the partnership's hands, or $0 and $4,000, respectively. Therefore, Anne's deemed sale of the Sec. 751 assets is analyzed as follows:

Amount realized (cash)	$10,000
Minus: Adjusted basis of property deemed sold	(4,000)
Realized and recognized gain	$ 6,000

The character of the recognized gain depends on the character of the property deemed sold (in this case, the unrealized receivables and inventory). Therefore, Anne's $6,000 gain is ordinary income. ◀

STEP 5: DETERMINE THE IMPACT OF THE CURRENT DISTRIBUTION. The last step in analyzing the distribution's effect on the partner is to determine the impact of the portion of the distribution that is not a Sec. 751 exchange. This distribution is treated exactly like any other nonliquidating distribution.

EXAMPLE C:10-14 ▶ Assume the same facts as in Examples C:10-12 and C:10-13. Examining the distribution, we see in column 4 of Table C:10-1 that, as part of the Sec. 751 exchange, Anne received only $10,000 of the $25,000 cash actually distributed. The remaining $15,000 represents a current distribution. As described earlier in this chapter, a partner recognizes gain on a current distribution only if the money distributed exceeds his or her basis in the partnership interest. Thus, Anne recognizes no gain because she has a $16,000 basis in the partnership interest immediately after the current distribution. This basis is calculated as follows:

Predistribution basis for partnership interest	$35,000
Minus: Basis of property deemed distributed in Sec. 751 exchange ($0 unrealized receivables + $4,000 inventory)	(4,000)
Basis before current distribution	$31,000
Minus: Money distributed	(15,000)
Postdistribution basis of partnership interest	$16,000

After the entire distribution is complete, Anne owns a one-fifth partnership interest with a basis of $16,000 and has $25,000 in cash. In addition, she has recognized $6,000 of ordinary income. ◀

? STOP & THINK

Question: Do most current distributions made by a partnership require a Sec. 751 calculation?

Solution: No. A partnership makes many current distributions pro rata to all partners, so Sec. 751 is not involved. Even if the distribution is not pro rata, the distribution often does not create an exchange of an interest in Sec. 751 assets for an interest in other assets. This exchange happens only when (1) the partner is reducing his or her overall interest in the partnership, (e.g., from a 15% to a 5% general partner) or (2) an explicit agreement provides that the distribution results in a partner giving up all or part of his or her interest in some asset(s) maintained by the partnership. Most current distributions do not involve Sec. 751.

LIQUIDATING OR SELLING A PARTNERSHIP INTEREST

A partner can terminate or dispose of an interest in a partnership in a number of ways. The two most common are receiving a liquidating distribution and selling the interest. Other possibilities include giving the interest away, exchanging the interest for corporate

OBJECTIVE 3

Determine the gain, loss, and basis consequences of liquidating or selling a partnership interest

stock, and transferring the interest at death. This part of the chapter considers each of these methods.

LIQUIDATING DISTRIBUTIONS

The IRC defines a liquidating distribution as a distribution, or one of a series of distributions, that terminates a partner's interest in the partnership.[11] If the partner's interest is drastically reduced but not terminated, the distribution is treated as a current distribution. A liquidating distribution can occur when only one member of a partnership terminates his or her interest, several partners terminate their interests but the partnership continues, or the entire partnership terminates and each partner receives a liquidating distribution. Rules for taxation of a liquidating distribution are the same whether one partner terminates his or her interest or the entire partnership liquidates.

Gain or Loss Recognition by the Partner. The rule for recognizing gain on a liquidating distribution is exactly the same rule used for a current distribution. A partner recognizes gain only if any money distributed exceeds the partner's predistribution basis in his or her partnership interest.[12] Distributed money includes money deemed distributed to the partner from a liability reduction or the FMV of marketable securities treated as money.

Although a partner can never recognize a loss from a current distribution, he or she can recognize a loss from a liquidating distribution. A partner recognizes a loss only if (1) the liquidating distribution consists of money (including money deemed distributed), unrealized receivables, and inventory, but no other property and (2) the partner's basis in the partnership interest exceeds the total basis of these distributed properties (including cash).[13] The amount of the loss is the difference between the partner's basis in the partnership interest before the distribution and the sum of money plus the bases of the receivables and inventory (to the partnership immediately before the distribution) that the partner receives.

EXAMPLE C:10-15 ▶ Maria terminates her interest in the ABC Partnership when her basis in the partnership is \$35,000. She receives a liquidating distribution of \$10,000 cash and inventory with a \$12,000 basis to the partnership. Her recognized loss is \$13,000 [\$35,000 − (\$10,000 + \$12,000)]. The inventory has a \$12,000 basis to Maria. ◀

Basis in Assets Received. A partner's basis of an asset received in a liquidating distribution is determined using rules similar to those used to determine the basis of an asset received in a current distribution. For both kinds of distributions, the basis in unrealized receivables and inventory is generally the same as the property's basis in the partnership's hands. Under no condition is the basis of these two types of assets increased. Occasionally, however, the partner's basis in his or her partnership interest is so small that after making the necessary reduction for money (and deemed money) distributions, the basis in the partnership interest is smaller than the partnership's bases for the unrealized receivables and inventory distributed. In such cases, the remaining basis in the partnership interest must be allocated among the unrealized receivables and inventory items based first on their decline in value and then on their relative bases as adjusted to reflect the decline in value.[14] As a result, the bases for the unrealized receivables and inventory are reduced, and the amount of ordinary income a partner recognizes on their ultimate sale, exchange, or collection increases.

TYPICAL MISCONCEPTION

The basis to a partner of distributed unrealized receivables or inventory can never be greater than the partnership's basis in those assets. Also, if the partner's basis in his or her partnership interest is not sufficient, the partner's basis in the distributed unrealized receivables and inventory is less than the partnership's basis in those assets.

Remember that a liquidating distribution of money, unrealized receivables, and inventory having a total basis to the partnership less than the partner's basis in his or her partnership interest results in the recognition of a loss. However, the partner recognizes no loss if the distribution includes any property other than money, unrealized receivables, and inventory. Instead, all the remaining basis in the partnership interest must be allocated

11 Sec. 761(d).
12 Sec. 731(a)(1).
13 Sec. 731(a)(2).
14 Sec. 732(c).

to the other property received regardless of that property's basis to the partnership or its FMV. Application of this rule can create strange results.

EXAMPLE C:10-16 ▶ Assume the same facts as in Example C:10-15 except Maria's distribution also includes an office typewriter having a $50 basis to the partnership and a $100 FMV. The allocation of basis proceeds as follows:

Predistribution basis for partnership interest	$35,000
Minus: Money received	(10,000)
Basis after money distribution	$25,000
Minus: Basis of inventory to partnership	(12,000)
Remaining basis of partnership interest	$13,000

The entire $13,000 remaining basis of the partnership interest is allocated to the typewriter. ◀

TAX STRATEGY TIP

The partnership in Example C:10-16 should avoid distributing low basis property along with cash, unrealized receivables, and inventory so that the partner can obtain an immediate loss deduction.

The basis allocation procedure illustrated in Example C:10-16 delays loss recognition until Maria either depreciates or sells the typewriter. The allocation procedure also may change the character of the loss because Maria would recognize a capital loss when she receives the liquidating distribution in Example C:10-15. In Example C:10-16, however, the character of Maria's loss is determined by the character of the typewriter in her hands (or in some cases by a series of specific rules that are discussed below). Worst of all, if she converts the typewriter into personal-use property, the loss on its sale or exchange is nondeductible.

If the partnership distributes two or more assets other than unrealized receivables or inventory in the same distribution, the remaining basis in the partnership interest is allocated among them based on both their relative FMVs and bases in the partnership's hands. Such an allocation process can lead to either a decrease or increase in the total basis of these assets. This potential for increasing the assets' bases is unique to liquidating distributions.

The allocation that results in a decrease in the basis of a distributed asset is identical to the allocation process described for current distributions. However, if the amount to be allocated is greater than the carryover bases of the distributed assets, the basis is first allocated among the distributed assets in an amount equal to their carryover basis from the partnership. Then, allocations are made based on relative appreciation of the assets up to the amount of appreciation, and further allocations are made to the assets based on their relative FMVs.

EXAMPLE C:10-17 ▶ Before receiving a liquidating distribution, Craig's basis in his interest in the BCD Partnership is $62,000. The distribution consists of $10,000 in cash, inventory having a $2,000 basis to the partnership and a $4,000 FMV, and two parcels of undeveloped land (not held as inventory) having bases of $6,000 and $18,000 to the partnership and having FMVs of $10,000 and $24,000, respectively. Assume that Sec. 751 does not apply. His bases in the assets received are calculated as follows:

Predistribution basis for partnership interest	$62,000
Minus: Money received	(10,000)
Basis of inventory to the partnership	(2,000)
Basis allocated to two parcels of land	$50,000

The calculation of the basis for the two parcels of land are as follows:

	Parcel One	*Parcel Two*	*Total*
FMV of asset	$10,000	$24,000	$34,000
Minus: Partnership's basis for asset	(6,000)	(18,000)	(24,000)
Difference	$ 4,000	$ 6,000	$10,000
Step 1: Give each asset the partnership's basis for the asset	$ 6,000	$18,000	$24,000
Minus: Craig's basis to be allocated			(50,000)
Increase to allocate			$26,000

Step 2:	Adjusted basis after Step 1	$ 6,000	$18,000	$24,000
	Allocate the increase first to assets that have increased in value	4,000	6,000	10,000
	Adjusted basis at this point in the calculation	$10,000	$24,000	$34,000
Step 3:	Allocate $16,000 remaining increase based on relative FMVs	4,706[a]	11,294[b]	16,000
	Craig's bases in the assets	$14,706	$35,294	$50,000

[a]$10,000 ÷ ($10,000 + $24,000) × $16,000 = $ 4,706
[b]$24,000 ÷ ($10,000 + $24,000) × $16,000 = $11,294 ◀

KEY POINT

If the partner recognizes neither gain nor loss in a liquidating distribution, the partner's total basis in the distributed assets always equals the partner's predistribution basis in his or her partnership interest.

In a liquidating distribution, the amount of money received plus the distributee partner's total basis of the noncash property received normally equals the partner's predistribution basis in the partnership interest. The only two exceptions to this rule apply when the money received exceeds the partner's basis in his or her partnership interest, causing the partner to recognize a gain, or when money, unrealized receivables, and inventory are the only assets distributed and the partner recognizes a loss. In all other liquidating distributions, the distributee partner recognizes no gain or loss. Instead, that partner's predistribution basis in his or her partnership interest is transferred to the cash and other property received.

Holding Period in Distributed Assets. The distributee partner's holding period for any assets received in a liquidating distribution includes the partnership's holding period for such property.[15] If the partnership received the property as a contribution from a partner, the partnership's holding period also may include the period of time the contributing partner held the property prior to making the contribution (see Chapter C:9). The distributee partner's holding period for his or her partnership interest is irrelevant in determining the holding period of the assets received.

EXAMPLE C:10-18 ▶ George purchased an interest in the DEF Partnership on June 1, 2013, but he cannot get along with the other partners. Therefore, on July 1, 2015, he receives a liquidating distribution that terminates his interest in the partnership. George's distribution includes land that the partnership has owned since August 1, 2007. George's holding period for the land begins on August 1, 2007, even though his holding period for the partnership interest begins much later. ◀

The character of the gain or loss recognized on a subsequent sale of distributed property is determined using the same rules as for a current distribution.

KEY POINT

The main difference in how the Sec. 751 rules apply to current versus liquidating distributions is that, after a liquidating distribution, the partner always has a zero interest in the partnership assets because he or she is no longer a partner in the partnership.

Effects of Sec. 751. Section 751 has essentially the same impact on both liquidating and current distributions. To the extent the partner exchanges an interest in Sec. 751 assets for an interest in other assets (or vice versa), that portion of the transaction bypasses the distribution rules. Instead, this portion of the transaction is treated as a sale occurring between the partnership and the partner. One notable difference occurs between liquidating distributions and current distributions having Sec. 751 implications: the postdistribution interest in partnership assets is zero for the liquidating distribution because it terminates the partner's interest in the partnership.

EXAMPLE C:10-19 ▶ The ABC Partnership holds the assets listed below on December 31 before making a $50,000 cash distribution that reduces Al's one-third interest in the partnership to zero.

Assets	*Basis*	*FMV*
Cash	$75,000	$ 75,000
Unrealized receivables	–0–	15,000
Inventory	15,000	60,000
Total	$90,000	$150,000

[15] Sec. 735(b).

The partnership has no liabilities, and Al's predistribution basis in his partnership interest is $30,000. The following steps lead to the tax effects of the liquidating distribution:

STEP 1. Determine ABC's Sec. 751 and non-Sec. 751 assets. The Sec. 751 assets include the unrealized receivables and the substantially appreciated inventory. The cash is ABC's only non-Sec. 751 asset.

STEP 2. Complete the table used to analyze the Sec. 751 distributions (see Table C:10-2).

STEP 3. Analyze column 5 of Table C:10-2 to see whether a Sec. 751 exchange has occurred. Table C:10-2 shows that Al exchanges $5,000 of unrealized receivables and $20,000 of inventory for $25,000 cash.

SELF-STUDY QUESTION

What is the deemed Sec. 751 exchange shown in Table C:10-2?

ANSWER

Column 5 shows that Al received $25,000 of excess cash in lieu of $25,000 of Sec. 751 assets. Thus, the Sec. 751 exchange is a deemed sale by Al of $25,000 of unrealized receivables and inventory to the partnership in exchange for $25,000 of cash. With a table similar to Table C:10-2, the Sec. 751 computations are much easier to understand.

STEP 4. Determine the gain or loss on the Sec. 751 deemed sale. Al is deemed to have sold unrealized receivables and inventory for cash. Assume Al first got the receivables and inventory in a current distribution. He obtains the partnership's bases for the assets of $0 and $5,000, respectively. The subsequent deemed sale results in Al recognizing a $20,000 gain.

Amount realized (cash)	$25,000
Minus: Adjusted basis of property deemed sold	(5,000)
Realized and recognized gain	$20,000

Al's gain is ordinary income because it results from his deemed sale of receivables and inventory to the partnership.

STEP 5. Determine the impact of the non-Sec. 751 portion of the distribution. The liquidating distribution is only the $25,000 cash he receives that was *not* a part of the Sec. 751 transaction. To determine its impact, we first must find Al's basis in his partnership interest after the Sec. 751 transaction but before the $25,000 liquidating distribution.

Predistribution basis in the partnership interest	$30,000
Minus: Basis of receivables and inventory deemed distributed in Sec. 751 exchange	(5,000)
Basis before money distribution	$25,000
Minus: Money distribution	(25,000)
Gain recognized on liquidating distribution	$ -0-

Al recognizes no further gain or loss from the liquidating distribution portion of the transaction. ◀

▼ TABLE C:10-2
Analysis of Sec. 751 Liquidating Distribution (Example C:10-19)

	Beginning Partnership Amount[a]	(1) Al's Interest Before Distribution[a] (1/3)	(2) Al's Interest After Distribution[a] (-0-)	(3) Hypothetical Proportionate Distribution[a] (3) = (1) − (2)	(4) Actual Distribution[a]	(5) Difference[b] (5) = (4) − (3)
Sec. 751 assets:						
Unrealized receivables	$15,000	$ 5,000	$ -0-	$ 5,000	$ -0-	$ (5,000)
Inventory	60,000	20,000	-0-	20,000	-0-	(20,000)
Total Sec. 751 assets	$75,000	$25,000	$ -0-	$25,000	$ -0-	$ (25,000)
Non-Sec. 751 assets:						
Cash	$75,000	$25,000	$ -0-	$25,000	$50,000	$ 25,000
Total non-Sec. 751 assets	$75,000	$25,000	$ -0-	$25,000	$50,000	$ 25,000

[a]Valued at fair market value.
[b]A negative amount means that Al gave up his interest in a particular property. A positive amount means that Al received more than his proportionate interest.

SELF-STUDY QUESTION

What is the character of gain or loss on the sale of a partnership interest?

ANSWER

Because a partnership interest is generally a capital asset, the sale of a partnership interest results in the partner recognizing a capital gain or loss. However, if a partnership has Sec. 751 assets, the partner is deemed to sell his or her share of the underlying Sec. 751 assets, thereby causing a corresponding ordinary gain or loss to be recognized.

Effects of Distribution on the Partnership. A partnership generally recognizes no gain or loss on liquidating distributions made to its partners.[16] If a Sec. 751 deemed sale occurs, however, the partnership may recognize gain or loss on assets deemed sold to its partner. Although a liquidating distribution normally does not itself terminate the partnership, the partnership terminates if none of the remaining partners continue to operate the business of the partnership in a partnership form. In this case, all partners will receive liquidating distributions. Finally, the partnership's assets may be subject to optional or mandatory basis adjustments (discussed later in this chapter).

Topic Review C:10-1 summarizes the tax consequences of current and liquidating distributions.

SALE OF A PARTNERSHIP INTEREST

Absence any contrary rules, a partner's sale or exchange of a partnership interest would generate a capital gain or loss under Sec. 741 because a partnership interest is usually a capital asset. Section 751, however, modifies this result by requiring the partner to recognize ordinary

TOPIC REVIEW C:10-1

Current and Liquidating Distributions

Tax Consequences	Current Distributions	Liquidating Distributions
Impact on Partner:		
Money (or deemed money from liability changes or marketable securities) distributed	Gain recognized only if money distributed exceeds basis in partnership interest before distribution.	Gain recognized only if money distributed exceeds basis in partnership interest before distribution.
Unrealized receivables and/or inventory distributed	Carryover basis (limited to basis in partnership interest before distribution reduced by money distributed).	Carryover basis (limited to basis in partnership interest before distribution reduced by money distributed).
	No gain or loss recognized.[a]	Loss recognized if partnership distributes money, inventory, and receivables with basis less than partner's basis in partnership interest before distribution and partnership distributes no other property.[a]
Other property distributed	Carryover basis (limited to basis in partnership interest before distribution reduced by money and carryover basis in inventory and receivables).	Basis equal to basis in partnership interest before distribution reduced by money and carryover basis in inventory and receivables.
	No gain or loss recognized.[a]	No gain or loss recognized.[a]
Impact on Partnership:		
General rule	No gain or loss recognized.	No gain or loss recognized.
Partnership assets	May be subject to optional basis adjustments.	May be subject to optional or mandatory basis adjustments.
Other Tax Consequences:	If a Sec. 751 deemed sale or exchange occurs, the partner and/or the partnership may recognize gain or loss on the deemed sale.	If a Sec. 751 deemed sale or exchange occurs, the partner and/or the partnership may recognize gain or loss on the deemed sale.

[a]A partner may recognize precontribution gain (but not loss) under Sec. 737 if a precontribution net gain remains and the FMV of the property distributed exceeds the adjusted basis of the partnership interest immediately before the property distribution (but after any money distribution). The contributing partner also may recognize precontribution gain or loss if the partnership distributes the contributed property to another partner within seven years of the contribution (Sec. 704(c)).

[16] Sec. 731(b).

income or loss (and possibly unrecaptured Sec. 1250 gain) on the sale or exchange of a partnership interest to the extent the consideration received is attributable to the partner's share of unrealized receivables and inventory items. The sale of a partnership interest also may have two other effects: the purchaser acquires the partner's share of the partnership's liabilities, and the partnership may be terminated. Each of these situations related to the sale of a partnership interest is examined below.

Section 751 Property. The definition of Sec. 751 property is slightly different for sales or exchanges than for distributions because inventory does not have to be substantially appreciated to be included as Sec. 751 property. Thus, all inventory and all unrealized receivables are Sec. 751 assets in a sale or exchange situation.[17]

Treasury Regulations under Sec. 751 take a hypothetical asset sale approach to determine the amount of ordinary income or loss the partner recognizes on the sale or exchange of a partnership interest.[18] Under the regulations, the partnership is deemed to sell all its assets for their FMV immediately before the partner sells his or her interest in the partnership. The partner then is allocated his or her share of ordinary gain or loss (and possibly unrecaptured Sec. 1250 gain) attributable to the Sec. 751 assets. With this approach, the results of the sale or exchange can be determined using the following three steps:

STEP 1. Determine the total gain or loss on the sale or exchange of the partnership interest.

STEP 2. Determine the ordinary gain or loss component and the unrecaptured Sec. 1250 gain component, if applicable, using the hypothetical asset sale approach.[19]

STEP 3. Determine the capital gain component by calculating the residual gain or loss after assigning the ordinary gain or loss and the unrecaptured Sec. 1250 gain components.

EXAMPLE C:10-20 ▶ Troy sells his one-fourth interest in the TV Partnership to Steve for $50,000 cash when the partnership's assets are as follows:

Assets	*Basis*	*FMV*
Cash	$ 20,000	$ 20,000
Unrealized receivables	–0–	24,000
Inventory	20,000	68,000
Building	40,000	56,000
Land	40,000	32,000
Total	$120,000	$200,000

The partnership has no liabilities on the sale date and has claimed $19,000 of straight-line depreciation on the building. Troy's basis in his partnership interest is $30,000 on such date. Both the receivables and inventory are Sec. 751 assets, and the building is Sec. 1250 property. Application of Step 1 yields the following gain on Troy's sale of his partnership interest:

Amount realized on sale	$50,000
Minus: Adjusted basis of partnership interest	(30,000)
Total gain realized	$20,000

Application of Step 2 yields the following allocation to Sec. 751 and Sec. 1250 property:

Deemed Sale of Assets	*Partnership Gain (Loss)*	*Troy's Share (25%)*
Unrealized receivables	$24,000	$ 6,000
Inventory	48,000	12,000
Building	16,000	4,000
Land	(8,000)	(2,000)

[17] Regulation Sec. 1.751-1(a)(1) is outdated to some extent and still speaks in terms of substantially appreciated inventory. However, Sec. 751(a) in the IRC, which deals with the sale or exchange of a partnership interest, includes all inventory items, not just those that are substantially appreciated.

[18] Reg. Sec. 1.751-1(a)(2). This hypothetical sale approach allows for easy incorporation of special allocations under Sec. 704 into the Sec. 751 calculation.

[19] The unrecaptured Sec. 1250 gain is the lesser of the hypothetical gain on Sec. 1250 property (e.g., buildings) or the amount of depreciation claimed on the Sec. 1250 property (assuming straight-line depreciation). This gain applies to non-corporate taxpayers and is subject to the 25% capital gains tax rate. A similar rule applies to a collectibles gain subject to the 28% capital gains tax rate. See Reg. Sec. 1.1(h)-1.

Thus, on the sale of his partnership interest, Troy recognizes ordinary income of $18,000 ($6,000 + $12,000). Because the $19,000 of depreciation exceeds the hypothetical gain on the building, the entire $16,000 gain is unrecaptured Sec. 1250 gain, $4,000 of which is Troy's share.

Application of Step 3 yields the following residual allocation to capital gain or loss:

Total gain realized	$ 20,000
Minus: Allocation to ordinary income and unrecaptured Sec. 1250 gain	(22,000)
Capital loss recognized	$ (2,000)

In summary, on the sale of his partnership interest, Troy recognizes $18,000 of ordinary income, $4,000 of unrecaptured Sec. 1250 gain, and a $2,000 capital loss. Without Sec. 751, these three components would have been netted together as a $20,000 capital gain. ◀

STOP & THINK

Question: Bill owns 20% of Kraco and plans to sell his ownership interest for a $40,000 gain. Kraco has both unrealized receivables and inventory. If Kraco is a corporation, Bill will report a $40,000 capital gain. If Kraco is a partnership, part of the $40,000 gain (the gain on his 20% share of the Sec. 751 assets) will be ordinary income, and the remainder will be capital gain. Why did Congress decide to tax the gain on the sale of corporate stock differently from the gain on the sale of a partnership interest?

Solution: The corporation itself will pay tax on the ordinary income realized when it collects unrealized receivables or sells inventory, and the corporation's tax is unaffected by the identity of the shareholder. Under no conditions will the shareholder have to report any of the corporation's ordinary income. Accordingly, the sale of the corporate stock does not provide an opportunity to avoid ordinary income for the owner, nor can the owner convert ordinary income into capital gain by selling the corporate stock.[20]

Because the partners report and pay taxes on the ordinary income earned by the partnership, a sale of a partnership interest that produces only capital gains would represent an opportunity for a partner to avoid recognizing ordinary income and recognize capital gains instead. Imagine, for example, that Kraco is a cash basis service business whose only asset is a large account receivable where all work has been completed. If Bill stays in the partnership, he will recognize ordinary income when the partnership collects the receivable. If he were allowed to sell his partnership interest in this setting for a capital gain, he could convert his ordinary income into capital gain. However, Sec. 751 prevents this conversion from happening by requiring him to recognize ordinary income on the sale of the partnership interest to the extent the sales proceeds are attributable to Sec. 751 assets.

ADDITIONAL COMMENT

Section 751 treatment is another application of the aggregate theory of partnership taxation as opposed to the entity theory.

Liabilities. When a partnership has liabilities, each partner's distributive share of any liabilities is always part of the basis for the partnership interest. When a partner sells his or her partnership interest, the partner is relieved of the liabilities. Accordingly, the amount realized on the sale of a partnership interest is made up of money plus the FMV of noncash property received plus the seller's share of partnership liabilities assumed or acquired by the purchaser.

EXAMPLE C:10-21 ▶ Andrew is a 30% partner in the ABC Partnership when he sells his entire interest to Miguel for $40,000 cash. At the time of the sale, Andrew's basis is $27,000 (which includes his $7,000 share of partnership liabilities). The partnership has no Sec. 751 assets. Andrew's $20,000 gain on the sale is calculated as follows:

Amount realized:		
Cash	$40,000	
Liabilities assumed by purchaser	7,000	$47,000
Minus: Adjusted basis		(27,000)
Gain recognized on sale		$20,000

◀

[20] An exception used to exist under Sec. 341 for a so-called collapsible corporation. However, Congress has permanently repealed this provision.

Impact on the Partnership. When one partner sells his or her partnership interest, the sale usually has no more impact on the partnership than the sale of corporate stock by one shareholder has on the corporation. Only the partner and the purchaser of the interest are affected. However, the partnership itself is affected if the partnership interest sold is sufficiently large that, under Sec. 708, its sale terminates the partnership for tax purposes. This effect is discussed later in this chapter. Also, the partnership may have to make optional or mandatory basis adjustments to its assets (discussed later in this chapter).

OTHER PARTNERSHIP TERMINATION ISSUES

OBJECTIVE 4

Recognize other means of terminating a partnership interest and related issues

RETIREMENT OR DEATH OF A PARTNER

If a partner dies or retires from a partnership, that partner's interest can be sold either to an outsider or to one or more existing partners.[21] The results of such a sale are outlined above. Often, however, a partner or a deceased partner's successor-in-interest departs from the partnership in return for payments made by the partnership itself. When the partnership buys out the partner's interest, the analysis of the tax results focuses on two types of payments: payments made in exchange for the partner's interest in partnership property and other payments.

Payments for Partnership Property. Generally, the IRS accepts the valuation placed on the retiring partner's interest in the partnership property by the partners in an arm's-length transaction. Payments made for the property interest are taxed under the liquidating distribution rules. Like any liquidating distribution made to a partner, payments made to a retiring partner or a deceased partner's successor-in-interest[22] in exchange for his or her property interest are not deductible by the partnership.[23]

If the retiring or deceased partner was a general partner and the partnership is a service partnership (i.e., capital is not a material income producing factor), payments made to a general partner for unrealized receivables and goodwill (when the partnership agreement does not provide for a goodwill payment on retirement or death) are not considered payments for property. Instead, any such payments are treated as other payments. The other payment treatment permits the partnership to deduct the amounts paid to the retiring or deceased partner or to reduce the distributive share allocable to the other partners.

TYPICAL MISCONCEPTION

The significance of the two different kinds of payments is not readily apparent to some taxpayers. The payments for partnership property are not deductible by the partnership and often are not income to the retiring partner. However, payments considered in the second category are deductible by the partnership (or they reduce the distributive shares that other partners must recognize) and usually are income to the retiring partner.

Other Payments. Payments made to a retiring partner or to a deceased partner's successor-in-interest that exceed the value of that partner's share of partnership property have a different tax result for both the retiring partner and for the partnership. A few payments that do represent payments for property (e.g., payments to a general partner retiring from a service partnership for his or her interest in unrealized receivables and for his or her interest in partnership goodwill) also are taxed under these rules.

Under these rules, a payment is treated as either a distributive share or a guaranteed payment. If the excess payment is a function of partnership income (e.g., 10% of the partnership's net income), the income is considered a distributive share of partnership income.[24] Accordingly, the character of the income flows through to the partner, and each of the remaining partners is taxed on a smaller amount of partnership income. The income must be reported in the partner's tax year that includes the partnership year-end from which the distributive share arises, regardless of when the partner actually receives the distribution.

If the amount of the excess payment is determined without regard to the partnership income, the payment is treated as a guaranteed payment.[25] If the payment is a guaranteed

TYPICAL MISCONCEPTION

The main difference between a payment being taxed as a distributive share or as a guaranteed payment is the character of the income recognized by the recipient partner. If the payment is taxed as a distributive share, the character of the income is determined by the type of income earned by the partnership. In contrast, the payment is always ordinary income if it is treated as a guaranteed payment.

[21] Retirement from the partnership in this context has nothing to do with reaching a specific age and leaving the employ of the partnership but instead refers to the partner's withdrawal at any age from a continuing partnership.

[22] A deceased partner's successor-in-interest is the party that succeeds to the rights of the deceased partner's partnership interest (e.g., the decedent's estate or an heir or legatee of the deceased partner). A deceased partner's successor-in-interest is treated as a partner by the tax laws until his or her interest in the partnership has been completely liquidated.

[23] Sec. 736(b).

[24] Sec. 736(a)(1).

[25] Sec. 736(a)(2).

payment, the retiring partner recognizes ordinary income, and the partnership generally has an ordinary deduction. Like all guaranteed payments, the income is includible in the recipient's income for his or her tax year within which ends the partnership tax year in which the partnership claims its deduction (see Chapter C:9).

EXAMPLE C:10-22 ▶ When Sam retires from the STU Partnership, he receives a cash payment of $30,000. At the time of his retirement, his basis for his one-fourth limited partnership interest is $25,000. The partnership has no liabilities and the following assets:

Assets	*Basis*	*FMV*	*Sam's 1/4 FMV*
Cash	$ 40,000	$ 40,000	$10,000
Marketable securities	25,000	32,000	8,000
Land	35,000	48,000	12,000
Total	$100,000	$120,000	$30,000

In the absence of a valuation agreement, the partnership presumably pays Sam a ratable share of the FMV of each asset (and he receives no payment for any partnership goodwill). The $30,000 amount paid to Sam equals the FMV of his one-fourth interest in the partnership assets. The $30,000 Sam receives in exchange for his interest in partnership property is analyzed as a liquidating distribution in the following manner:

Cash distribution received	$30,000
Minus: Basis in partnership interest	(25,000)
Gain recognized on liquidating distribution	$ 5,000

Because the partnership holds no Sec. 751 assets, the entire gain is a capital gain. The partnership gets no deduction for the distribution. ◀

EXAMPLE C:10-23 ▶ Assume the same facts as in Example C:10-22 except Sam receives $34,000 instead of $30,000. This amount represents payment for Sam's one-fourth interest in partnership assets plus an excess payment of $4,000. Accordingly, this excess payment must be either a distributive share or a guaranteed payment. Because the $4,000 payment is not contingent on partnership earnings, it is taxed as a guaranteed payment. The partnership deducts the $4,000 payment, and Sam recognizes $4,000 of ordinary income.

In summary, Sam receives $34,000 as a payment on his retirement from the STU Partnership, $4,000 of which is considered a guaranteed payment taxed as ordinary income to Sam and deductible by the partnership. The remaining $30,000 Sam receives is in exchange for his interest in partnership property. Because the $30,000 cash payment exceeds his $25,000 basis in his partnership interest, he recognizes a $5,000 gain on the liquidating distribution. The partnership gets no deduction for the $30,000, which is considered a distribution. ◀

If the partnership has Sec. 751 assets, the calculations for a retiring partner are slightly more difficult. First, payments for substantially appreciated inventory and unrealized receivables are payments for property and must be analyzed using the liquidating distribution rules along with Sec. 751. The remainder of the transaction is analyzed as indicated above. (For partnership retirements only, unrealized receivables do not include recapture items.)

A retiring partner who receives payments from the partnership is considered to be a partner in that partnership for tax purposes until he or she receives the last payment. Likewise, a deceased partner's successor-in-interest is a member of the partnership until receiving the last payment.[26]

EXCHANGE OF A PARTNERSHIP INTEREST

Exchange for Another Partnership Interest. A partner also may terminate a partnership interest by exchanging it for either an interest in another partnership or a different interest in the same partnership. Exchanges involving interests in different partnerships do not qualify for like-kind exchange treatment.[27] Nevertheless, the IRS allows exchanges of interests within a single partnership.[28]

[26] Reg. Sec. 1.736-1(a)(1)(ii).
[27] Sec. 1031(a)(2)(D).
[28] Rev. Rul. 84-52, 1984-1 C.B. 157, and Rev. Rul. 95-37, 1995-1 C.B. 130.

EXAMPLE C:10-24 ► Pam and Dean are equal partners in the PD General Partnership, which owns and operates a farm. The two partners agree to convert PD into a limited partnership, with Pam becoming a limited partner and Dean having both a general and a limited partnership interest in PD. Even though the partners exchange a general partnership interest for a limited partnership interest (plus an exchange of a general partnership interest for a general partnership interest for Dean), they recognize no gain or loss on the exchange. If, however, a partner's interest in the partnership's liabilities is changed, that partner's basis must be adjusted. If liabilities are reduced and a deemed distribution exceeding the basis for the partnership interest occurs, the partner must recognize gain on the excess. ◄

Exchange for Corporate Stock. A partnership interest may be exchanged for corporate stock in a transaction that qualifies under the Sec. 351 nonrecognition rules (see Chapter C:2). For Sec. 351 purposes, a partnership interest is property. If the other Sec. 351 requirements are met, a single partner's partnership interest can be transferred for stock in a new or an existing corporation in a nontaxable exchange. The partner treats this as if he or she had transferred any other property under the Sec. 351 rules. The basis in the corporate stock is determined by the partner's basis in the partnership interest. The holding period for the stock received in the exchange includes the holding period for the partnership interest. As a result of the exchange, one of the corporation's assets is an interest in a partnership, and the corporation (not the transferor) is now the partner of record. Thus, the corporation must report its distributive share of partnership income along with its other earnings.

Incorporation. When limited liability is important, the entire partnership may choose to incorporate. Normally such an incorporation can be structured to fall within the Sec. 351 provisions and can be partially or totally tax exempt. When a partnership chooses to incorporate, three possible alternatives are available:

- The partnership contributes its assets and liabilities to the corporation in exchange for the corporation's stock. The partnership then distributes the stock to the partners in a liquidating distribution of the partnership.
- The partnership liquidates by distributing its assets to the partners. The partners then contribute the property to the new corporation in exchange for its stock.
- The partners contribute their partnership interests directly to the new corporation in exchange for its stock. The partnership liquidates, with the corporation receiving all the partnership's assets and liabilities.

The tax implications of the incorporation and the impact of partnership liabilities, gain to be recognized, basis in the corporate assets, and the new shareholders' bases in their stock and securities may differ depending on the form chosen for the transaction.[29]

Formation of an LLC, LLP, or LLLP. A second option for obtaining limited liability protection for all owners is for the partnership to become an LLC. Under Rev. Rul. 95-37,[30] the conversion is viewed as a partnership-to-partnership transfer. The property transfer does not cause the partners to recognize gain or loss nor does the transfer terminate the tax year for the partnership or any partner. The basis for the partners' interest in the partnership will be changed only if the liability shares for the partners change. Under the check-the-box regulations, an LLC with more than one member is treated as a partnership unless it elects to be taxed as a corporation (see Chapter C:2). If the LLC elects to be taxed as a C or an S corporation, the transfer of the property to the LLC falls under the incorporation rules discussed above.

If a partnership chooses LLP status to reduce some of the liability risks facing the partners, the change from partnership to LLP status also falls under the partnership-to-partnership transfer rules described above. The transfer does not cause the partners to recognize

[29] Rev. Rul. 84-111, 1984-2 C.B. 88. In addition, Reg. Secs. 301.7701-1, 2, and 3 describe the tax consequences of a partnership electing to be taxed as a corporation under the check-the-box regulations.

[30] 1995-1 C.B. 130.

gain or loss nor does the property transfer terminate the tax year for the partnership or any partner. Basis for the partners' interest in the partnership will be changed only if the liability shares for the partners change.[31] Finally, in some states, partners can achieve limited liability through a limited liability limited partnership (LLLP) (see page C:10-31).

Topic Review C:10-2 summarizes the tax consequences of a number of alternative methods for terminating an investment in a partnership.

INCOME RECOGNITION AND TRANSFERS OF A PARTNERSHIP INTEREST

The partnership tax year closes with respect to any partner who sells or exchanges his or her entire interest in a partnership or any partner whose interest in the partnership is liquidated. The partnership tax year closes on the sale or exchange date or the date of final payment on a liquidation. As a result, that partner's share of all items earned by the partnership must be reported in the partner's tax year that includes the transaction date.[32]

A partner's tax year also closes on the date of death. The partner's final return will include all partnership income up to the date of death.

TERMINATION OF A PARTNERSHIP

Events Causing a Termination to Occur. Because of the complex relationships among partners and their liability for partnership debts, state partnership laws provide for the termination of a partnership under a wide variety of conditions. Section 708(b), however, avoids the tax complexity created by the wide variety of state laws and the numerous termination conditions. This IRC section provides that a partnership terminates for tax purposes only if

TOPIC REVIEW C:10-2

Terminating an Investment in a Partnership

Method	Tax Consequences to Partner
Death or retirement:	
Amounts paid for property[a]	Liquidating distribution tax consequences apply to the amount paid.
Amounts paid in excess of property values:	
Amounts not determined by reference to partnership income	Ordinary income.
Amounts determined by reference to partnership income	Distributive share of partnership income.
Sale of partnership interest to outsider	Capital gain (loss) except for ordinary income (loss) reported on Sec. 751 assets and unrecaptured Sec. 1250 gain on depreciable real property.
Exchange for partnership interest:	
In same partnership	No tax consequences
In different partnership	Capital gain (loss) except for ordinary income (loss) on Sec. 751 assets and unrecaptured Sec. 1250 gain on depreciable real property.
Exchange for corporate stock	No gain or loss generally recognized if it qualifies for Sec. 351 tax-free treatment. If the exchange does not qualify for Sec. 351 treatment, capital gain (loss) except for ordinary income (loss) on Sec. 751 assets and unrecaptured Sec. 1250 gain on depreciable real property.
Incorporation of partnership	Tax consequences depend on form of transaction used for incorporation.
Formation of LLC or LLP	No tax consequences except for distributions or contributions deemed to occur if liability shares change.

[a]Only for a general partner departing from a service partnership, property excludes unrealized receivables and goodwill if it is not mentioned in the partnership agreement.

[31] Ibid.

[32] Sec. 706(c)(2).

- ▶ No part of any business, financial operation, or venture of the partnership continues to be carried on by any of its partners in a partnership or
- ▶ Within a 12-month period a sale or exchange of at least 50% of the total interest in partnership capital and profits occurs.

TYPICAL MISCONCEPTION

Taxpayers often do not understand the difference between a partnership tax year closing for a specific partner versus a partnership tax year closing for all partners due to a termination of the partnership itself. The tax consequences of these two events are drastically different.

No Business Operated as a Partnership. If no partner continues to operate any business of the partnership through the same or another partnership, the original partnership terminates. To avoid termination, the partnership must maintain partners and business activity. For example, if one partner retires from a two-person partnership and the second partner continues the business alone, the partnership terminates. However, if one partner in a two-member partnership dies, the partnership does not terminate as long as the deceased's estate or successor-in-interest continues to share in the profits and losses of the partnership business.[33]

Likewise, a partnership terminates if it ceases to carry on any business or financial venture. The courts, however, have allowed a partnership to continue under this rule even though the partnership sold all its assets and retained only a few installment notes.[34] Despite the courts' flexibility in these circumstances, a partnership should maintain more than a nominal level of assets if continuation of the partnership is desired.

KEY POINT

For the 50% rule to terminate a partnership, a *sale* or *exchange* of 50% or more of the capital *and* profits interests must occur. Sales or exchanges occurring within a 12-month period are aggregated. However, if the same interest is sold twice within 12 months, it is only counted once.

Sale or Exchange of at Least a 50% Interest. The second condition that terminates a partnership is the sale or exchange of at least a 50% interest in both partnership capital and profits within a 12-month period.[35] The relevant 12-month period is determined without reference to the tax year of either the partnership or any partner but rather is any 12 consecutive months. To cause termination, the partner must transfer the partnership interest by sale or exchange. Transactions or occurrences that do not constitute a sale or exchange (e.g., the gifting of a partnership interest or the transferring of a partnership interest at death) do not cause a partnership to terminate as long as partners continue the partnership business. Likewise, as long as at least two partners remain, the removal of a partner who owns more than 50% of the total partnership capital and profits interests can be accomplished without terminating the partnership by making a liquidating distribution.[36]

Measuring the portion of the total partnership capital and profits interest transferred often presents difficulties. Multiple exchanges of the same partnership interest are counted only once for purposes of determining whether the 50% maximum is exceeded. When several different small interests are transferred within a 12-month period, the partnership's termination occurs on the date of the transfer that first crosses the 50% threshold.[37]

EXAMPLE C:10-25 ▶ On August 1 of Year 1, Miguel sells his 30% capital and profits interest in the LMN Partnership to Steve. On June 1 of Year 2, Steve sells the 30% interest acquired from Miguel to Andrew. For purposes of Sec. 708, the two sales are considered to be the transfer of a single partnership interest. Thus, the LMN Partnership does not terminate unless other sales of partnership interests occur totaling at least 20% of LMN's capital and profits interests during any 12-month period that includes either August 1 of Year 1, or June 1 of Year 2. ◀

EXAMPLE C:10-26 ▶ On July 15 of Year 1, Kelly sells Carlos a 37% capital and profits interest in the KRS Partnership. On November 14 of Year 1, Rick sells Diana a 10% capital and profits interest in the KRS Partnership. On January 18 of Year 2, Sherrie sells Evan a 5% capital and profits interest in the KRS Partnership. The KRS Partnership terminates on January 18 of Year 2 because the cumulative interest sold within the 12-month period that includes January 18 of Year 2, first exceeds 50% on that date. ◀

Effects of Termination.

Importance of Timing. When a partnership terminates, its tax year closes, requiring the partners to include their share of partnership earnings for the short-period partnership tax

---

33 Reg. Sec. 1.708-1(b)(1)(i)(A).

34 For example, see *Max R. Ginsburg v. U.S.*, 21 AFTR 2d 1489, 68-1 USTC ¶9429 (Ct. Cls., 1968).

35 Under Sec. 774(c), an electing large partnership does *not* terminate solely because 50% or more of its interests are sold within a 12-month period.

36 Reg. Sec. 1.708-1(b)(1)(ii).

37 Ibid.

year in their tax returns. If the termination is not properly timed, partnership income for a regular 12-month tax year already may be included in the same return that must include the short tax year, resulting in more than 12 months of partnership income or loss being reported in some partners' tax returns. As partners and partnerships are increasingly forced to adopt the same tax year, this problem will lessen.

EXAMPLE C:10-27 ▶ Joy is a calendar year taxpayer who owns a 40% capital and profits interest in the ATV Partnership. ATV has a natural business year-end of March 31 and with IRS permission uses that date as its tax year-end. For the partnership tax year ending March 31, 2015, Joy has an $80,000 distributive share of ordinary income. Pat, who owns the remaining 60% capital and profits interests, sells his interest to Collin on November 30, 2015. Because more than 50% of the capital and profits interests have changed hands, the ATV Partnership terminates on November 30, 2015, and the partnership's tax year ends on that date.

Joy's tax return for the tax year ending December 31, 2015, must include the $80,000 distributive share from the partnership tax year for the period April 1, 2014, through March 31, 2015, and the distributive share of partnership income for the short tax year including the period April 1, 2015, through November 30, 2015. ◀

Liquidating Distributions and Contributions. When a termination occurs for tax purposes, the partnership is deemed to have made a pro rata liquidating distribution to all partners. Accordingly, the partners must recognize gain or loss under the liquidating distribution rules. An actual liquidating distribution may occur if the termination occurs because of the cessation of business. However, if the termination occurs because of a 50% or greater change in ownership of the capital and profits interests, an actual distribution usually does not occur. In this case, the new group of partners continue the business, and Treasury Regulations provide for the termination of the old partnership and the formation of a new partnership. Specifically, the old partnership is deemed to contribute all its property and liabilities to a new partnership in exchange for the interests in the new partnership. The old partnership then is deemed to liquidate by distributing its only remaining asset (the interests in the new partnership) to its partners.[38]

EXAMPLE C:10-28 ▶ The AB Partnership terminates for tax purposes on July 15 when Anna sells her 60% capital and profits interest to Diane for $123,000. The partnership has no liabilities, and its assets at the time of termination are as follows:

Assets	*Basis*	*FMV*
Cash	$ 20,000	$ 20,000
Receivables	30,000	32,000
Inventory	22,000	28,000
Building	90,000	95,000
Land	40,000	30,000
Total	$202,000	$205,000

Beth, a 40% partner in the AB Partnership, has an $80,800 basis in her partnership interest at the time of the termination. She has held her AB Partnership interest for three years at the time of the termination.

The old AB Partnership is deemed to transfer all its assets to a new partnership (NewAB) on July 15 in exchange for all the interests in NewAB. The old partnership then is deemed to transfer all the NewAB interests to the partners of the old partnership (Diane and Beth). At this point, the old AB Partnership ceases to exist because it no longer has partners, nor does it carry on any business.

The basis and holding period of the assets held by NewAB are identical to the basis and holding period of the old AB Partnership assets.[39] The basis of Beth's interest in NewAB is identical to her basis in her interest in the AB Partnership ($80,800).[40] Her holding period for the NewAB partnership interest begins when she acquired the old AB Partnership interest. Diane's basis in her partnership interest is its $123,000 cost, and her holding period begins when she purchases the interest. ◀

[38] Reg. Sec. 1.708-1(b)(1)(iv).
[39] Secs. 723 and 1223(2).
[40] Sec. 722.

Changes in Accounting Methods. The termination ends all partnership elections. Thus, the new partnership must make all elections concerning its tax year and accounting methods in its first new tax year.

KEY POINT

The principal concern when two or more partnerships combine is which partnership's tax year, accounting methods, and elections will survive the merger. This determination is made by examining the capital and profits interests of the partners of the old partnerships.

MERGERS AND CONSOLIDATIONS

When two or more partnerships join together to form a new partnership, the parties to the transaction must determine which, if any, of the old partnerships are continued and which are terminated. An old partnership whose partner(s) own more than 50% of the profits and capital interests of the new partnership is considered to be continued as the new partnership.[41] Accordingly, the new partnership must continue with the tax year and accounting methods and elections of the old partnership that is considered to continue. All the other old partnerships are considered to have been terminated.

EXAMPLE C:10-29 ►

The AB and CD Partnerships merge to form the ABCD Partnership. April and Ben each own 30% of ABCD, and Carol and David each own 20% of ABCD. The ABCD Partnership is considered a continuation of the AB Partnership because April and Ben, the former partners of AB, own 60% of ABCD. ABCD is bound by the tax year, accounting method, and other elections made by AB. CD, formerly owned by Carol and David, is considered to terminate on the merger date. ◄

In some combinations, the partners of two or more of the old partnerships might hold the requisite profits and capital interest in the new partnership. When two or more old partnerships satisfy this requirement, the old partnership credited with contributing the greatest dollar value of assets to the new partnership is considered the continuing partnership, and all other partnerships terminate. Sometimes, none of the old partnerships account for more than 50% of the capital and profits of the new partnership. In that case, all the old partnerships terminate, and the merged partnership is a new entity that can make its own tax year and accounting method elections.

EXAMPLE C:10-30 ►

Three partnerships merge to form the ABCD Partnership. The AB Partnership (owned by Andy and Bill) contributes assets valued at $140,000 to ABCD. BC Partnership (owned by Bill and Cathy) and CD Partnership (owned by Cathy and Drew) contribute assets valued at $180,000 and $120,000, respectively. The capital and profits interests of the partners in the new partnership are Andy, 20%; Bill, 35%; Cathy, 19%; and Drew, 26%. Both the AB and BC Partnerships had partners who now own more than 50% of the new partnership (Andy and Bill own 55%, and Bill and Cathy own 54%). The BC Partnership contributed more assets ($180,000) to the new partnership than did the AB Partnership ($140,000). Therefore, the ABCD Partnership is a continuation of the BC Partnership. Both the AB and CD Partnerships terminate on the merger date. ◄

KEY POINT

The principal concern of a partnership division is to determine which of the new partnerships is the continuation of the prior partnership.

DIVISION OF A PARTNERSHIP

When a partnership divides into two or more new partnerships, all the new partnerships whose partners own collectively more than 50% of the profits and capital interests in the old partnerships are considered a continuation of the old partnership.[42] All partnerships that are continuations of the old partnership are bound by the old partnership's tax year and accounting method elections. Any other partnership created by the division is considered a new partnership eligible to make its own tax year and accounting method elections. If no new partnership meets the criteria for continuation of the divided partnership, the divided partnership terminates on the division date. The interest of any partner of the divided partnership who does not own an interest in a continuing partnership is considered to be liquidated on the division date.

EXAMPLE C:10-31 ►

The RSTV Partnership is in the real estate and insurance business. Randy owns a 40% interest and Sam, Thomas, and Vicki each own 20% of RSTV. The partners agree to split the partnership, with the RS Partnership receiving the real estate operations and the TV Partnership receiving the insurance business. Because Randy and Sam own more than 50% of the RSTV Partnership (40% + 20% = 60%), the RS Partnership is a continuation of the RSTV Partnership and must report its results using the same tax year and accounting method elections that RSTV

[41] Sec. 708(b)(2)(A).

[42] Sec. 708(b)(2)(B).

used. Thomas and Vicki are considered to have terminated their interests in RSTV and to have received a liquidating distribution of the insurance business property. The TV Partnership makes its tax year and accounting method elections following the rules for a new partnership. ◀

Optional and Mandatory Basis Adjustments

OBJECTIVE 5

Analyze the effects of optional and mandatory basis adjustments

In general, a partnership makes no adjustment to the basis of its property when a partner sells or exchanges his or her interest in the partnership, when a partner's interest transfers upon the partner's death, or when the partnership makes a property distribution to a partner. A partnership, however, may adjust basis of its assets if the partnership makes an **optional basis adjustment** election under Sec. 754. The following paragraphs compare the consequences of having no election to having such an election. The discussion focuses primarily on sale transactions but also briefly mentions distributions. Once made, the Sec. 754 election applies to all subsequent transfers of partnership interests (e.g., sales, exchanges, and transfers upon death) and all subsequent distributions. In addition, the partnership may have to make a **mandatory basis adjustment** in certain circumstances even if a Sec. 754 election is not in effect.

Adjustments on Transfers

Optional Adjustment. If a new incoming partner purchases his or her partnership interest from an existing partner, the new partner's basis in the partnership interest equals the purchase price plus the new partner's share of partnership liabilities. The new partner's basis in the partnership is likely to be different from his or her share of basis of the underlying assets in the partnership. This difference could lead to inequitable results as demonstrated by the following example.

EXAMPLE C:10-32 ▶ Amy, Bill, and Corey each own a one-third interest in ABC partnership, which has the following simple balance sheet:

	Basis	*FMV*
Assets:		
Cash	$30,000	$ 30,000
Inventory	60,000	90,000
Total	$90,000	$120,000
Liabilities and capital:		
Liabilities	$15,000	$ 15,000
Capital—Amy	25,000	35,000
—Bill	25,000	35,000
—Corey	25,000	35,000
Total	$90,000	$120,000

Eric purchases Amy's one-third interest for $35,000 cash and assumes her $5,000 share of partnerships liabilities. Eric pays this amount because one-third the FMV of the underlying partnership assets is $40,000 (1/3 × $120,000). In addition, the cash paid plus Eric's share of partnership liabilities gives him a $40,000 basis in his new partnership interest. Amy's basis at the time of sale is $30,000. Therefore, Amy recognizes a $10,000 gain ($40,000 amount realized − $30,000 basis). Amy's $10,000 gain also reflects her share of the difference between the inventory's FMV and basis at the partnership level. Thus, her gain will be ordinary income under Sec. 751.

Now suppose the partnership later sells the inventory for $90,000. The partnership recognizes $30,000 of ordinary income. Therefore, each partner, Bill, Corey, and Eric, recognizes a $10,000 distributive share of ordinary income from that sale, and each partner increases the basis of his partnership interest by the same amount. Accordingly, Eric increases his basis in the partnership from $40,000 to $50,000. In this situation, Eric appears to be taxed on the same gain as was Amy even though he paid a FMV price for his partnership interest (and the underlying partnership assets).

However, this result primarily is an issue of timing and possibly character of income and loss. For example, suppose further that, sometime after selling the inventory, the partnership distributes the $120,000 cash to the partners in liquidation. Eric would receive $40,000 and recognize a $10,000 ($40,000 distribution − $50,000 basis) capital loss.

In short, with no optional basis adjustment election in effect, Eric recognizes $10,000 of ordinary income when the partnership sells the inventory and a $10,000 capital loss when the partnership liquidates. This timing difference could be substantial if the partnership remains in existence for a long time. Also, the capital loss may offset only capital gains and up to $3,000 of ordinary income in the partner's personal tax return. ◀

ADDITIONAL COMMENT

The situation of a new partner purchasing an interest in a partnership is a good example of where a partner's outside basis can differ significantly from his or her share of the partnership's inside basis. The Sec. 754 election mitigates this difference.

Amount of the Adjustment. An incoming partner might view the situation in Example C:10-32 as unacceptable and wish the partnership to make a Sec. 754 election. If the partnership makes such an election or has a Sec. 754 election already in effect, Sec. 743 mandates a special basis adjustment equal to the difference between the transferee (purchasing) partner's basis in the partnership interest and the transferee partner's share of basis of partnership assets. This basis adjustment, arising from a transfer, belongs only to the transferee partner (and not to the other partners), and it eliminates the inequities noted in Example C:10-32.

EXAMPLE C:10-33 ▶ Assume the same facts as in Example C:10-32 except the partnership makes a Sec. 754 election. Eric's optional basis adjustment is calculated as follows:

Cash purchase price	$35,000
Share of partnership liabilities	5,000
Initial basis in partnership	$40,000
Minus: Eric's share of partnership's basis in assets (1/3 × $90,000)[43]	(30,000)
Optional basis adjustment	$10,000

Now when the partnership sells the inventory, Eric has an additional $10,000 basis in his share of the inventory that offsets the $10,000 income he otherwise would recognize. The other partners, however, still recognize their $10,000 distributive shares of income. Because Eric recognizes no income, he does not increase his partnership basis. Suppose the partnership liquidates sometime after selling the inventory. Again, Eric receives a $40,000 distribution, but he recognizes no capital gain or loss ($40,000 distribution − $40,000 basis). Thus, the optional basis adjustment eliminated both the timing and character differences that occurred in Example C:10-32. ◀

Mandatory Adjustment. The IRC imposes a mandatory basis adjustment for a sale or exchange of a partnership interest if the partnership has a substantial built-in loss and has no Sec. 754 optional basis adjustment election in effect. A substantial built-in loss exists if the partnership's adjusted basis in its property exceeds the FMV of the property by more than $250,000. This provision prevents the doubling of losses. Exceptions to the rule apply to certain specialized partnerships, discussion of which is beyond the scope of this textbook.

EXAMPLE C:10-34 ▶ David, Ellen, and Frank each own a one-third interest in DEF partnership, which has the following simple balance sheet:

	Basis	*FMV*
Assets:		
Cash	$ 100,000	$100,000
Land	1,100,000	800,000
Total	$1,200,000	$900,000

43 In some cases, the calculation of the transferee's share of the partnership's basis in assets can be more complicated than shown in this example. See Reg. Sec. 1.743-1(d).

Capital:		
David	$ 400,000	$300,000
Ellen	400,000	300,000
Frank	400,000	300,000
Total	$1,200,000	$900,000

Gwen purchases David's one-third interest for $300,000 cash, which gives Gwen a $300,000 initial basis in her new partnership interest. David's partnership interest basis at the time of sale is $400,000. Therefore, he recognizes a $100,000 loss. David's $100,000 loss also reflects his share of the difference between the land's FMV and basis at the partnership level.

Now suppose the partnership has no optional basis adjustment election in effect and later sells the land for $800,000. The partnership recognizes a $300,000 loss. As a result, each partner, Ellen, Frank, and Gwen, recognizes a $100,000 distributive share of that loss, and each partner decreases the basis of his or her partnership interest by the same amount. As a result, both David and Gwen recognize a $100,000 loss. To prevent this doubling of losses, the partnership must make a $100,000 mandatory downward basis adjustment with respect to Gwen's share of the land, thereby nullifying her distributive share of loss on the land sale. The adjustment is mandatory because the partnership has a substantial built-in loss (i.e., its $300,00 built-in loss exceeds $250,000). Note that, without this mandatory adjustment, Gwen's $100,000 loss would be temporary because her partnership basis would be reduced to $200,000, causing her to recognize a $100,000 gain should the partnership liquidate and distribute $300,000 to her. Nevertheless, Congress chose to eliminate the initial doubling of losses by requiring the mandatory basis adjustment. ◀

Other Issues. Examples C:10-32 through C:10-34 assume inventory or land is the only asset other than cash. If the assets instead had been depreciable property, the basis adjustments would give the transferee partner additional depreciation deductions in Examples C:10-32 and C:10-33 or reduced depreciation deductions in example C:10-34. Also, if a partnership has more than one asset other than cash, the optional or mandatory basis adjustment must be allocated to the assets under special rules found in Sec. 755 and related Treasury Regulations. These allocation rules are beyond the scope of this text.

ADJUSTMENTS ON DISTRIBUTIONS

Optional Adjustment. As mentioned earlier, if a partnership distributes property to a partner, the partnership makes no adjustment to the basis of its remaining property unless an optional basis adjustment election is in place or unless the mandatory basis adjustment rule discussed later applies. If the partnership has made a Sec. 754 election, the partnership makes the following adjustments upon the distribution to a partner:

- Increases the basis of *partnership* property by:
  1. Any gain recognized by the distributee partner on the distribution (e.g., cash distribution exceeding the partner's basis in his or her partnership interest)
  2. The amount by which the distributee partner decreases the basis of property received in a property distribution from the basis of the property in the partnership's hands
- Decreases the basis of *partnership* property by:
  1. Any loss recognized by the distributee partner on a liquidating distribution
  2. The amount by which the distributee partner increases the basis of property received in a property distribution from the basis of the property in the partnership's hands

Unlike the optional basis adjustments arising from a transfer of partnership interest, the basis adjustments arising from a distribution belong to the partnership as a whole. These adjustments eliminate many (but not all) basis and timing disparities resulting from distributions.

A partnership should take care in making a Sec. 754 election because, once made, the election affects many transactions in complicated ways. Moreover, the election can cause downward as well as upward adjustments. Finally, the election has long-range implications because it can be revoked only with IRS approval. The IRS will not grant such approval if the primary purpose of the revocation is to avoid reducing the basis of partnership assets.

Mandatory Adjustment. The discussion of the optional basis adjustment for distributions included increases and decreases to partnership property. The IRC makes the decreasing basis adjustment for distributions mandatory if it exceeds $250,000. As with exchange transactions, this provision prevents the doubling of losses. In effect, the mandatory adjustment rule applies only to liquidating distributions because such decreasing adjustments cannot occur in nonliquidating distribution situations.

SPECIAL FORMS OF PARTNERSHIPS

OBJECTIVE 6

Compare and contrast the various special forms a partnership might take

Here, we examine a series of special partnership forms, including tax shelters organized as limited partnerships, publicly traded partnerships, limited liability companies, limited liability partnerships, and electing large partnerships.

TAX SHELTERS AND LIMITED PARTNERSHIPS

Tax shelters at their best are good investments that reduce and/or defer the amount of an investor's tax bill. Traditionally, shelter benefits arise from leverage, income deferral, deduction acceleration, and tax credits.

ADDITIONAL COMMENT

The passive activity loss limitations eliminate the deferral benefit of tax shelters.

Many years ago, limited partnerships were the primary vehicle for tax shelter investments. However, subsequent tax law greatly reduced the benefits of limited partnerships as tax shelters by invoking the passive activity loss limitations for activity conducted in a limited partnership form. The limited partnership, however, still allows an investor to limit liability while receiving the benefits of the shelter's tax attributes to save taxes on other passive income. Moreover, limited partnerships that generate passive income rather than losses have become popular investments for investors who already hold loss-generating limited partnership interests. (See Problem C:9-46 in the previous chapter for an example of tax deferred benefits and their elimination by the at-risk and passive activity loss limitations.)

PUBLICLY TRADED PARTNERSHIPS

The IRC restricts still further the benefits of tax shelter ownership by imposing special rules on **publicly traded partnerships** (PTPs). A PTP is a partnership whose interests are traded either on an established securities exchange or in a secondary market or the equivalent thereof. A partnership that meets the requirements is taxed as a C corporation under Sec. 7704.

Two exceptions apply to partnerships that otherwise would be classified as PTPs:

- Partnerships that have 90% or more of their gross income being "qualifying income" continue to be taxed under the partnership rules.
- Partnerships that were in existence on December 17, 1987 and have not added a substantial new line of business since that date are grandfathered. In general, application of the PTP rules for these partnerships was delayed until tax years beginning after December 31, 1997.

REAL-WORLD EXAMPLE

Many PTPs are traded on major stock exchanges such as the New York Stock Exchange.

The Taxpayer Relief Act of 1997 added an election that allows the grandfathered partnerships to continue to be treated as partnerships after the original ten-year window and until the election is revoked. To elect to continue to be treated as a partnership, the publicly traded partnership (which must have been taxed as a partnership under the grandfather provision) must agree to pay a 3.5% annual tax on gross income from the active conduct of any trade or business.[44] The election may be revoked by the partnership, but once revoked, it cannot be reinstated.

[44] Sec. 7704(g)(3).

For the 90% of gross income test, Sec. 7704(d) defines qualifying income to include certain interest, dividends, real property rents (but not personal property rents), income and gains from the sale or disposition of a capital asset or Sec. 1231(b) trade or business property held for the production of passive income, and gain from the sale or disposition of real property. It also includes gains from certain commodity trading and natural resource activities. Any PTP not taxed as a corporation because of this 90% exception is subject to separate and more restrictive Sec. 469 passive loss rules than are partnerships that are not publicly traded.

If a partnership is first classified as a PTP taxed as a corporation during a tax year, the PTP incurs a deemed contribution of all partnership assets and all partnership liabilities to a corporation in exchange for all the corporation's stock. The stock is then deemed distributed to the partners in complete liquidation of the partnership. This transaction is taxed exactly as if it had physically occurred.

LIMITED LIABILITY COMPANIES

In recent years, the limited liability company (LLC) has emerged as a popular form of business entity in the United States. The LLC combines the legal and tax benefits of partnerships and S corporations. Currently, all 50 states have adopted LLC laws. The LLC business form combines the advantage of limited liability for all its owners with the ability of achieving the conduit treatment and the flexibility of being taxed as a partnership.

In the past, whether an LLC was characterized as a corporation or a partnership for federal tax purposes depended on the number of corporate characteristics the entity possessed, such as limited liability, free transferability of interests, centralized management, and continuity of life. The process of determining tax treatment was complex and time consuming. To alleviate this complexity, the Treasury Department issued regulations that allow entities (other than corporations and trusts) to choose whether to be taxed as a partnership or as an association. (An association is an unincorporated entity taxed as a corporation.) According to these check-the-box regulations, an LLC with two or more members can choose either partnership or association tax treatment. With a written and properly filed election, any LLC can choose to be taxed as an association. If the LLC makes no such election, an LLC with two or more members is treated as a partnership for tax purposes, while a single member LLC is treated as a sole proprietorship.

As already mentioned, an LLC with two or more members that does not elect association status is a partnership for tax purposes and is subject to all the rules applicable to other partnerships. Thus, the formation of the LLC; income, gain, loss, and deductions that flow through to the LLC members; current and liquidating distributions; and sale, gift, or exchange of an interest in the LLC all fall under the partnership rules. An LLC treated as a partnership is subject to the Sec. 704 rules for special allocations and allocations of precontribution gain or loss, to the Sec. 736 rules for retirement distributions, and to the Sec. 751 rules pertaining to unrealized receivables and inventory.

TAX STRATEGY TIP

The list of advantages of an LLC over an S corporation is substantial and suggests that an LLC should always be seriously considered as an option for a pass-through entity. However, one current, important advantage of an S corporation is that the shareholders are not subject to self-employment taxes on their share of the entity's earnings.

Using the LLC form for a business with publicly traded ownership interests is likely to result in taxation as a corporation. Even if the LLC does not elect association status, the public trading of the ownership interest brings the LLC under the publicly traded partnership rules. As discussed above, these rules result in the business being taxed as a corporation unless 90% or more of the income is qualifying income or unless the LLC is covered under the grandfather rules. However, given the recency of LLCs as a form for conducting business, the grandfather provisions are unlikely to apply.

If an LLC is treated as a partnership, it offers greater flexibility than does an S corporation because it is not subject to the restrictions that apply to S corporations as to the number of shareholders, the number of classes of stock, or the types of investments in related entities that the entity can make. Moreover, unlike S corporations, LLCs can use the special allocation rules of Sec. 704 to allocate income, gain, loss or deductions to their members. Finally, each member's basis in the LLC interest includes that member's share of the organization's debts (and not just shareholder debt as with an S corporation).

LIMITED LIABILITY PARTNERSHIPS

REAL-WORLD EXAMPLE

All the Big 4 accounting firms and a number of other national, regional, and local accounting firms operate as LLPs. Even though the non-responsible partners in an LLP are not liable for the responsible partner's negligence, all partners and employees can suffer if the partnership itself is deemed guilty, as demonstrated by the demise of a former national accounting firm several years ago.

Many states have added limited liability partnerships (LLPs) to the list of business forms that can be formed. Under the current state laws, the primary difference between a general partnership and an LLP is that in a limited liability partnership, a partner is not liable for damages resulting from failures in the work of other partners or of people supervised by other partners. For example, assume that a limited liability accounting partnership is assessed damages in a lawsuit that resulted from an audit partner in New York being negligent in an audit. The tax partner for the same firm, who is based in San Diego and who had no involvement with the audit or the auditor, should not be liable to pay damages resulting from the suit.

Like a general or limited partnership, this business form is a partnership for tax purposes. All the partnership tax rules and regulations apply to this business form just as they do to any other partnership.

STOP & THINK

Question: What issues do you expect the check-the-box regulations to raise for new businesses making their initial choice of entity decision? What effect do you expect these regulations to have on existing corporations?

Solution: Consider the options facing a new business. The business can be formed as a C corporation, which provides limited liability protection to owners but subjects the corporate income to double taxation. A business formed as a C corporation can make an S election for tax purposes, which keeps the limited liability protection for the owners and eliminates the double taxation by taxing all income directly to the owners. However, as you will see in Chapter C:11, a number of restrictions prevent many corporations from electing S status. In addition, all income and loss of an S corporation must be allocated among the shareholders on a pro rata basis. A partnership offers the most flexible tax treatment with no double taxation of income, but the traditional partnership must have at least one general partner whose liability for partnership debts is not limited. An LLC, which is treated as a partnership, provides limited liability protection to its owners while avoiding both the double taxation of income found in a regular C corporation as well as the restrictions placed on S corporations. Because an LLC is treated as a partnership, the income and loss shares reported by each partner is flexible, and the partner's basis for his partnership interest includes his or her share of the LLC's liabilities. Thus, in some ways, the LLC has the best attributes of both the corporation and the partnership.

These are strong reasons why a new entity would choose to form as an LLC and be treated as a partnership. However, because the LLC is a relatively new business form, statutes, case law, and regulations are still being developed, and thus many areas of uncertainty remain to be resolved over time.

The check-the-box regulations are not helpful to existing C corporations and S corporations because an existing corporation cannot elect to be treated as a partnership. Instead, it must liquidate (with all the tax consequences of a liquidation, as described in Chapter C:6) before it can form as a partnership or an LLC. Potentially, the change in entity form has a high tax cost for an existing corporation.

LIMITED LIABILITY LIMITED PARTNERSHIP

Another recent innovation in some states (but not all) is the limited liability limited partnership (LLLP). Remember that a limited partnership, in addition to having limited partners, has one or more general partners whose personal liability exposure is unlimited. The LLLP is a partnership formed under a state's limited partnership laws but that can elect under the state's laws to provide the general partners with limited liability. Thus, the LLLP is similar to an LLC and becomes potentially useful in states that do not extend LLC status to personal service firms but allow such firms to operate as an LLLP.[45]

[45] For a detailed discussion, see Shop Talk, "Service Firms Practicing as LLLPs: What Are the Tax Consequences?" *Journal of Taxation*, August 2005.

REAL-WORLD EXAMPLE
Only 100 or so partnerships file as electing large partnerships each year. Such partnerships file using Form 1065-B.

ELECTING LARGE PARTNERSHIPS

Partnerships that qualify as "large partnerships" may elect to be taxed under a simplified reporting arrangement.[46] The partnership must meet the following four qualifications to be treated as an electing large partnership:

- It must not be a service partnership.
- It must not be engaged in commodity trading.
- It must have at least 100 partners.
- It must file an election to be taxed as an electing large partnership.

Section 775 defines a service partnership as one in which substantially all the partners perform substantial services in connection with the partnership's activities or the partners are retired but in the past performed substantial services in connection with the partnership's activities. One example of a partnership that could not make this election is a partnership that provides accounting services. An electing large partnership also cannot be engaged in commodity trading. Further, to qualify to make this election, the partnership must have at least 100 partners (excluding those partners who do provide substantial services in connection with the partnership's business activities) throughout the tax year.

Once it makes the election, the partnership reports its income under a simplified reporting scheme, is subject to different rules about when the partnership terminates, and is subject to a different system of audits. The election is irrevocable without IRS permission.

Electing Large Partnership Taxable Income. Much like other partnerships, the calculation of electing large partnership taxable income includes separately stated income and other income. However, the items that must be separately stated are very different for the electing large partnership. Likewise, the items included in other income differ significantly. The main reason that Congress added electing large partnerships to the IRC was to provide a form of flow-through entity that does not require so much separate reporting to each partner of many different income, loss, and deduction items. Simpler reporting from the partnership to the partners was the goal, so fewer items are separately stated and many more items are combined at the partnership level.

Like a regular partnership, calculation of an electing large partnership's taxable income is similar to the calculation for an individual. For an electing large partnership (just like for other partnerships), the deductions for personal exemptions and net operating losses are disallowed as well as most additional itemized deductions, such as medical expenses and alimony. However, calculation of the items that would qualify as miscellaneous itemized deductions for an individual differs from the calculation for either individuals or other partnerships. For an electing large partnership, miscellaneous itemized deductions are combined at the partnership level and subject to a 70% deduction at the partnership level. After the 70% deduction, the remaining miscellaneous itemized deductions are combined with other income and passed through to the partners. Because they are combined with other income at the partnership level, they are not subject to the 2% nondeductible floor at the individual partner level.[47]

Instead of flowing through as a separately stated item as they do with a regular partnership, charitable contributions made by an electing large partnership are subject to the 10% of taxable income limit similar to the limit that normally applies to corporations. Once the limit is applied, the partnership deducts allowable charitable contribution from its ordinary income, and the partners do not report the charitable contributions as a separate item.[48]

For a regular partnership, the first-year expensing deduction allowed under Sec. 179 is both limited at the partnership level and is separately stated and limited at the partner level. For an electing large partnership, the only limit is at the partnership level. The

---

[46] Sec. 775.
[47] Sec. 773(b).
[48] Sec. 773(b)(2).

allowable deduction is calculated at the partnership level, and the deduction amount offsets the partnership's ordinary income. For an electing large partnership, the Sec. 179 deduction is not separately stated and the impact of the Sec. 179 deduction is buried in the ordinary income amount reported by the partnership to the partners.

Separately Stated Large Partnership Items. An electing large partnership nevertheless is a pass-through entity, so some items still must be separately stated at the partnership level, and these items maintain their character when reported in the partners' tax returns. Section 772 lists the following items the electing large partnership must report separately:

- Taxable income or loss from passive loss limitation activities
- Taxable income or loss from other partnership activities
- Net capital gain or loss from passive loss limitation activities
- Net capital gain or loss from other partnership activities
- Tax-exempt interest
- Applicable net alternative minimum tax adjustment separately computed for passive loss limitation activities and other activities
- General credits
- Low income housing credit
- Rehabilitation credit
- Foreign income taxes
- Credit for producing fuel from a nonconventional source
- Any other item the IRS determines should be separately stated

The differences between the treatment of other partnerships versus electing large partnerships is significant. The most interesting aspect of this list is what items are combined for reporting by an electing large partnership. For example, Sec. 1231 gains and losses are netted at the partnership level, net 1231 losses are included in ordinary income or loss, and net 1231 gains are reported with capital gains and losses. The capital gains and losses also are combined at the partnership level with only a single, net number reported to the partners. The capital gain or loss is treated as long-term at the partner level. However, if the net is a short-term capital gain, that gain is treated as ordinary income and combined at the partnership level with other ordinary income items. All the partnership's credits are combined at the partnership level with the exceptions of the low income housing credit and the rehabilitation credit.

Both ordinary income and capital gains attributed to passive loss activities are reported separately from the results of other partnership activities. In addition, the taxable income or loss from activities other than passive activities generally are treated as items of income or expense with respect to property held for investment rather than as active trade or business income. Dividend income, for example, would fall into this category.

For the electing large partnership, all limits, such as the charitable contributions limit and the Sec. 179 expensing deduction limit, are applied at the partnership level rather than at the individual partner level with three exceptions. The three limits applied at the partner level are the Sec. 68 limit on itemized deductions, the limit on at risk losses, and the limit on passive activity losses.[49] For the limitation to be applied at the partner level, these items must be separately stated.

For separately stated items, the character of amounts flowing through the partnership retain their character when reported on the partners' tax returns. However, because many more items are combined at the partnership level and not separately stated, the character of many fewer kinds of income is retained to flow through with the electing large partnership form.

[49] Sec. 773(a)

EXAMPLE C:10-35 ▶ The ABC Partnership is an electing large partnership that reports the following transactions for the current year. ABC has no passive activities.

Net long-term capital loss	$100,000
Sec. 1231 gain	120,000
Ordinary income	40,000
Dividend income	10,000
Charitable contributions	30,000
Tax-exempt income	4,000

ABC will report these earnings to its partners as follows:

Long-term capital gain	$20,000
Ordinary income	33,000
Dividend income	10,000
Tax-exempt income	4,000

Because the partnership has a net Sec. 1231 gain, it is treated as a long-term capital gain ($120,000) and combined at the partnership level with the long-term capital loss ($100,000) to result in a net long-term capital gain of $20,000. At the partnership level, the charitable contribution deduction is limited to 10% of taxable income, or $7,000 [0.10 × ($20,000 capital gain + $10,000 dividend income + $40,000 ordinary income)] and is subtracted from ordinary income of $40,000 before ordinary income is reported to the partners. The character of the long-term capital gain, dividend income, tax-exempt income, and ordinary income pass through to the partner. ◀

Reporting Requirement. An electing large partnership files Form 1065-B and must provide a Schedule K-1 to each of its partners on or before March 15 following the close of the partnership tax year without regard to when the partnership tax return is due.[50] Partnerships that are not electing large partnerships are only required to provide the information return by the due date of the partnership tax return—which, for a calendar year partnership, is April 15. The March 15 provision will help reduce the number of partners who must file an extension of their individual tax returns because they do not receive the Schedule K-1 from a regular partnership early enough to file a timely individual return.

Termination of the Partnership. Because electing large partnerships are quite large and often may be widely traded, Congress decided to change the conditions under which these partnership will be considered to terminate. An electing large partnership terminates only if its partners cease to conduct any business, financial operation, or venture in a partnership form. Unlike other partnerships, an electing large partnership will not terminate because of the sale or exchange of partnership interests involving at least a 50% interest in partnership capital or profits during a 12-month period.[51]

Electing Large Partnership Audits. An electing large partnership is not subject to the partnership audit rules but is subject to a much more restrictive set of partnership audit procedures.[52] First, all electing large partnership partners must report all items of partnership income, gain, loss, or deduction in the way the partnership reports the item. Deviations from that partnership reporting will be "corrected" by the IRS just as a math mistake is corrected.[53]

Because all partners are required to use identical reporting for partnership items, it becomes somewhat easier to audit partnership results only at the partnership level. Notice of audit proceedings, determination of errors, settlement offers, appeals proceedings, and court cases are all handled at the partnership level, and no individual partner can request separate treatment or refuse to participate in the partnership level result. In general, any adjustments determined at the partnership level by an audit agreement or court decision will be considered to be income or deduction that occurs in the year of the agreement or

[50] Sec. 6031.
[51] Sec. 774(c).
[52] Sec. 6240.
[53] Sec. 6241.

decision.[54] Accordingly, the effect of adjustments is borne by the partners who own interests in the year of the agreement or decision and not by the partners who originally reported the contested transaction results.

Tax planning considerations

OBJECTIVE 7

Identify tax planning opportunities in liquidating or selling a partnership interest

LIQUIDATING DISTRIBUTION OR SALE TO PARTNERS

An unusual tax planning opportunity exists when one partner withdraws from a partnership and the remaining partners proportionately increase their ownership of the partnership. The partners can structure the ownership change as either a liquidating distribution made by the partnership or as a sale of the partnership interest to the remaining partners. In fact, the substance of the two transactions is the same, only the form is different. However, this difference in form can make a substantial difference in the tax consequences in a number of areas.

- If the transferor partner receives payment for his or her interest in the partnership's Sec. 751 assets, he or she must recognize ordinary income no matter how the transaction is structured. The partnership's basis in Sec. 751 assets is increased in the case of a liquidating distribution. When a sale transaction takes place, the partnership's basis in Sec. 751 assets is increased only if the partnership has an optional basis adjustment election in effect.
- If the partnership has an optional basis adjustment election in effect, the allocation of the adjustment to the individual partnership assets can be different depending on whether the transaction is structured as a sale or as a liquidating distribution.
- If the interest being transferred equals or exceeds 50% of the profits and capital interests, a sale to the remaining partners terminates the partnership. A liquidating distribution does not cause a termination to occur.

Because the tax implications of the sale transaction and liquidating distribution alternatives are both numerous and complex, the partners should make their choice only after careful consideration. (See the Tax Strategy Problem later in the Problem Material.)

Problem materials

DISCUSSION QUESTIONS

C:10-1 Javier is retiring from the JKL Partnership. In January of the current year, he has a $100,000 basis in his partnership interest when he receives a $10,000 cash distribution. The partnership plans to distribute $10,000 each month this year, and Javier will cease to be a partner after the December payment. Is the January payment to Javier a current distribution or a liquidating distribution?

C:10-2 Mariel has a $60,000 basis in her partnership interest just before receiving a parcel of land as a liquidating distribution. She has no remaining precontribution gain and will receive no other distributions. Under what conditions will Mariel's basis in the land be $60,000?

C:10-3 Cindy has a $4,000 basis in her partnership interest before receiving a nonliquidating (current) distribution of property having a $4,500 basis and a $6,000 FMV from the CDE Partnership. Cindy has a choice of receiving either inventory or a capital asset. She will hold the distributed property as an investment for no more than two years before she sells it. What tax difference (if any) will occur as a result of Cindy's selection of one property or the other to be distributed by the partnership?

[54] Sec. 6242.

C:10-4 The AB Partnership purchases plastic components and assembles children's toys. The assembly operation requires a number of special machines that are housed in a building the partnership owns. The partnership has depreciated all its property under MACRS. The partnership sells the toys on account to a number of retail establishments and uses the accrual method of accounting. Identify any items you think might be classified as unrealized receivables.

C:10-5 Which of the following items are considered to be inventory for purposes of Sec. 751?
a. Supplies
b. Inventory
c. Notes receivable
d. Land held for investment purposes
e. Lots held for resale

C:10-6 Explain the conditions under which Sec. 751 has an impact on nonliquidating (current) distributions.

C:10-7 What conditions are required for a partner to recognize a loss upon receipt of a distribution from a partnership?

C:10-8 Can a partner recognize both a gain and a loss on the sale of a partnership interest? If so, under what conditions?

C:10-9 Tyra has a zero basis in her partnership interest and a share in partnership liabilities, which are quite large. Explain how these facts will affect the taxation of her departure from the partnership using the following methods of terminating her interest in the partnership.
a. A liquidating distribution of property
b. A sale of the partnership interest to a current partner for cash

C:10-10 Tom is a 55% general partner in the RST Partnership. Tom wants to retire, and the other two partners, Stacy and Rich, want to continue the partnership business. They agree that the partnership will liquidate Tom's interest in the partnership by paying him 20% of partnership profits for each of the next ten years. Explain why Sec. 736 does (or does not) apply to the partnership's payments to Tom.

C:10-11 Lucia has a $20,000 basis in her limited partnership interest before her retirement from the partnership. Her share of partnership assets have a $23,000 FMV, and the partnership has no Sec. 751 assets. In addition to being paid cash for her full share of partnership assets, Lucia will receive a share of partnership income for the next three years. Explain Lucia's tax treatment for the payments she receives.

C:10-12 What are the advantages and disadvantages to the partnership and its partners when a partnership termination is caused by a sale of at least a 50% capital and profits interest?

C:10-13 What is a publicly traded partnership? Are all publicly traded partnerships taxed as corporations?

C:10-14 What are the advantages of a firm being formed as a limited liability company (LLC) instead of as a limited partnership?

C:10-15 What is an electing large partnership? What are the advantages to the partnership of electing to be taxed under the electing large partnership rules?

ISSUE IDENTIFICATION QUESTIONS

C:10-16 When Kayla's basis in her interest in the JKL Partnership is $30,000, she receives a current distribution of office equipment. The equipment has an FMV of $40,000 and basis of $35,000. Kayla will not use the office equipment in a business activity. What tax issues should Kayla consider with respect to the distribution?

C:10-17 Joel receives a $40,000 cash distribution from the JM Partnership, which reduces his partnership interest from one-third to one-fourth. The JM Partnership is a general partnership that uses the cash method of accounting and has substantial liabilities. JM's inventory has appreciated substantially since it was purchased. What issues should Joel consider with regard to the distribution?

C:10-18 Scott sells his one-third partnership interest to Sally for $43,000 when his basis in the partnership interest is $33,000. On the date of sale, the partnership has no liabilities and the following assets:

Assets	*Basis*	*FMV*
Cash	$30,000	$30,000
Inventory	12,000	21,000
Building	45,000	60,000
Land	12,000	18,000

The partnership has claimed $5,400 of straight-line depreciation on the building. What tax issues should Scott and Sally consider with respect to the sale transaction?

C:10-19 David owns a 60% interest in the DDD Partnership, a general partnership, which he sells to the two remaining partners—Drew and Dana. The three partners have agreed that David will receive $150,000 in cash from the sale. David's basis in the partnership interest before the sale is $120,000, which includes his $30,000 share of partnership recourse liabilities. The partnership has assets with a $300,000 FMV and a $200,000 adjusted basis. What issues should David, Drew, and Dana consider before this sale takes place?

C:10-20 Andrew and Beth are equal partners in the AB Partnership. On December 30 of the current year, the AB Partnership agrees to liquidate Andrew's partnership interest for a cash payment on December 30 of each of the next five years. What tax issues should Andrew and Beth consider with respect to the liquidation of Andrew's partnership interest?

C:10-21 Alex owns 60% of the Hot Wheels LLC, which is treated as a partnership. He plans to give 15% of the LLC (one-fourth of his interest) to his daughter Haley for her high school graduation. He plans to put her interest in a trust, and he will serve as the trustee until Haley is 21. The trust will receive any distributions from the LLC, but Haley is unlikely to be given any of the cash until she is age 21. Alex's 60% interest has a $120,000 FMV and an $80,000 adjusted basis including his $48,000 share of the LLC's liabilities. Alex works full time for the LLC for a small salary and his share of LLC income. Alex also has a special allocation of income from rental property he manages for the LLC. What issues should Alex consider before he completes the gift?

C:10-22 Three individuals recently formed Krypton Company as a limited liability company (LLC). The three individuals—Jeff, Susan, and Richard—own equal interests in the company, and they all have substantial income from other sources. Krypton is a manufacturing firm and expects to earn approximately $130,000 of ordinary income and $30,000 of long term capital gain each year for the next several years. Jeff will be a full time manager and will receive a salary of $60,000 each year. What tax issues should the owners consider regarding the LLC's initial year of operations?

C:10-23 XYZ Limited Partnership has more than 300 partners and is publicly traded. XYZ was grandfathered under the 1987 Tax Act and has consistently been treated as a partnership. In the current year, XYZ will continue to be very profitable and will continue to pay out about 30% of its income to its owners each year. The managing partners of XYZ want to consider the firm's options for taxation in the current and later years.

PROBLEMS

C:10-24 *Current Distributions.* Lisa has a $25,000 basis in her partnership interest before receiving a current distribution of $4,000 cash and land with a $30,000 FMV and a $14,000 basis to the partnership. Assume that any distribution involving Sec. 751 property is pro rata, that any precontribution gains have been recognized before the distribution, and that no Sec. 754 election is in effect.

a. Determine Lisa's recognized gain or loss, Lisa's basis in distributed property, and Lisa's ending basis in her partnership interest.
b. How does your answer to Part a change if the partnership's basis in the land is $24,000 instead of $14,000?
c. How does your answer to Part a change if Lisa receives $28,000 cash instead of $4,000 (along with the land)?
d. How does your answer to Part a change if, in addition to the cash and land, Lisa receives inventory with a $25,000 FMV and a $10,000 basis and receivables with a $3,000 FMV and a zero basis?
e. Suppose instead that Lisa receives the distribution in Part a from a C corporation instead of a partnership. The corporation has $100,000 of E&P before the distribution, and Lisa's stock basis before the distribution is $25,000. What are the tax consequences to Lisa and the C corporation?
f. Note: This part can be answered only after the student studies Chapter C:11 but is placed here to allow comparison with Parts a and e. Suppose instead that Lisa receives the distribution in Part a from an S corporation instead of a partnership. Lisa is a 50% owner in the corporation, and her stock basis before the distribution is $25,000. What are the tax consequences to Lisa and the S corporation?

C:10-25 ***Current Distributions.*** Complete the chart for each of the following independent distributions. Assume that all distributions are nonliquidating and pro rata to the partners, that no contributed property was distributed, that all precontribution gain has been recognized before these distributions, and that no Sec. 754 election is in effect.

	Partner's Basis and Gain/Loss	*Property Distributed*	*Property's Basis to Partnership*	*Property's FMV*	*Property's Basis to Partner*
a. Basis:					
Predistribution	$20,000	Cash	$ 6,000	$ 6,000	
Postdistribution	$_____	Land	4,000	15,000	$_____
Gain or loss	$_____	Machinery	3,000	2,000	$_____
b. Basis:					
Predistribution	$20,000	Cash	$ 3,000	$ 3,000	
Postdistribution	$_____	Land	6,000	4,000	$_____
Gain or loss	$_____	Inventory	7,000	7,500	$_____
c. Basis					
Predistribution	$26,000	Cash	$35,000	$35,000	
Postdistribution	$_____	Land—Parcel 1	6,000	10,000	$_____
Gain or loss	$_____	Land—Parcel 2	18,000	18,000	$_____
d. Basis:					
Predistribution	$28,000	Land—Parcel 1	$ 4,000	$ 6,000	$_____
Postdistribution	$_____	Land—Parcel 2	6,000	10,000	$_____
Gain or loss	$_____	Land—Parcel 3	4,000	10,000	$_____

C:10-26 ***Current Distribution with Precontribution Gain.*** Three years ago, Mario joined the MN Partnership by contributing land with a $10,000 basis and an $18,000 FMV. On January 15 of the current year, Mario has a basis in his partnership interest of $20,000, and none of his precontribution gain has been recognized. On January 15, Mario receives a current distribution of a property other than the contributed land with a $15,000 basis and a $23,000 FMV.

a. Does Mario recognize any gain or loss on the distribution?
b. What is Mario's basis in his partnership interest after the distribution?
c. What is the partnership's basis in the land Mario contributed after Mario receives this distribution?

C:10-27 ***Current Distribution of Contributed Property.*** Andrew contributed investment land having an $18,000 basis and a $22,000 FMV along with $4,000 in money to the ABC Partnership when it was formed. Two years later, the partnership distributed the investment land Andrew had contributed to Bob, another partner. At the time of the distribution, the land had a $21,000 FMV, and Andrew and Bob's bases in their partnership interests were $21,000 and $30,000, respectively.

a. What gain or loss must be recognized on the distribution, and who must recognize it?
b. What are the bases for Andrew and Bob's interests in the partnership after the distribution?
c. What is Bob's basis in the distributed land?

C:10-28 ***Current Distribution of Contributed Property.*** The ABC Partnership made the following current distributions in the current year. The dollar amounts listed are the amounts before considering any implications of the distribution.

	Property Received			
Partner	*Type of Property*	*Basis*	*FMV*	*Partner's Basis in Partnership Interest*
Alonzo	Land	$ 4,000	$10,000	$19,000
Beth	Inventory	1,000	10,000	15,000
Cathy	Cash	10,000	10,000	18,000

The land Alonzo received had been contributed by Beth two years ago when its basis was $4,000 and its FMV was $8,000. The inventory Beth received had been contributed by Cathy two years ago when its basis was $1,000 and its FMV was $4,000. For each independent situation, what gain or loss must be recognized? What is the basis of the distributed property after the distribution? What are the bases of the partnership interests after the distribution? Assume the distribution has no Sec. 751 implications.

C:10-29 ***Current Distribution with Sec. 751.*** The KLM Partnership owns the following assets on March 1 of the current year:

Assets	*Partnership's Basis*	*FMV*
Cash	$ 30,000	$ 30,000
Receivables	–0–	16,000
Inventory	50,000	52,000
Supplies	6,000	6,500
Equipment[a]	9,000	10,500
Land (investment)	40,000	65,000
Total	$135,000	$180,000

[a]The partnership has claimed depreciation of $4,000 on the equipment.

a. Which partnership items are unrealized receivables?
b. Is the partnership's inventory substantially appreciated?
c. Assume the KLM Partnership has no liabilities and that Kay's basis for her partnership interest is $33,750. On March 1 of the current year, Kay receives a $20,000 current distribution in cash, which reduces her partnership interest from one-third to one-fourth. What are the tax results of the distribution (i.e., the amount and character of any gain, loss, or income recognized and Kay's basis in her partnership interest)?

C:10-30 ***Current Distribution with Sec. 751.*** The JKLM Partnership owns the following assets on October 1 of the current year:

Assets	*Partnership's Basis*	*FMV*
Cash	$ 48,000	$ 48,000
Receivables	12,000	12,000
Inventory	21,000	24,000
Machinery[a]	190,000	240,000
Land	36,500	76,000
Total	$307,500	$400,000

[a]Sale of the machinery for its FMV would result in $50,000 of Sec. 1245 depreciation recapture. Thus, the machinery's FMV and original cost are the same numerical value, $240,000.

a. Which partnership items are unrealized receivables?
b. Is the partnership's inventory substantially appreciated?
c. Assume the JKLM Partnership has no liabilities and Jack's basis in his partnership interest is $76,875. On October 1 of the current year, Jack receives a $25,000 current distribution in cash, which reduces his partnership interest from one-fourth to one-fifth. What are the tax results of the distribution (i.e., the amount and character of any gain, loss, or income recognized and Jack's basis in his partnership interest)?

C:10-31 ***Current Distribution with Sec. 751.*** The PQRS Partnership owns the following assets on December 30 of the current year:

Assets	*Partnership's Basis*	*FMV*
Cash	$ 20,000	$ 20,000
Receivables	–0–	40,000
Inventory	80,000	100,000
Total	$100,000	$160,000

The partnership has no liabilities, and each partner's basis in his or her partnership interest is $25,000. On December 30 of the current year, Paula receives a current distribution of inventory having a $10,000 FMV, which reduces her partnership interest from one-fourth to one-fifth. What are the tax consequences of the distribution to the partnership, Paula, and the other partners?

C:10-32 ***Current and Liquidating Distributions.*** The CL Partnership has two partners, Cleo and Leo. Each partner's basis in his or her partnership interest is $10,000 before any distribution. The partnership distributes $12,000 cash to Cleo and $8,000 cash to Leo.

a. Assuming a current distribution, determine for each partner (1) gain on loss recognized and (2) basis in the partnership interest after the distribution.

b. Assuming a liquidating distribution, determine each partner's gain or loss recognized.

C:10-33 ***Liquidating Distributions.*** Assume the same four independent distributions as in Problem C:10-25. Fill in the blanks in that problem assuming the only change in the facts is that the distributions are now liquidating distributions instead of nonliquidating distributions.

C:10-34 ***Liquidating Distribution.*** Marinda is a one-third partner in the MWH Partnership before she receives $100,000 cash as a liquidating distribution. Immediately before Marinda receives the distribution, the partnership has the following assets:

Assets	*Partnership's Basis*	*FMV*
Cash	$100,000	$100,000
Marketable securities	50,000	90,000
Investment land	90,000	140,000
Total	$240,000	$330,000

At the time of the distribution, the partnership has $30,000 of outstanding liabilities, which the three partners share equally. Marinda's basis in her partnership interest before the distribution was $80,000, which includes her share of liabilities. What are the amount and character of the gain or loss recognized by Marinda and the MWH Partnership on the liquidating distribution? Assume that no Sec. 754 election is in effect.

C:10-35 ***Liquidating Distributions.*** The AB Partnership pays its only liability (a $100,000 mortgage) on April 1 of the current year and terminates that same day. Alison and Bob were equal partners in the partnership but have partnership bases immediately preceding these transactions of $110,000 and $180,000, respectively, including his or her share of liabilities. The two partners receive identical distributions with each receiving the following assets:

Assets	*Partnership's Basis*	*FMV*
Cash	$ 20,000	$ 20,000
Inventory	33,000	35,000
Receivables	10,000	8,000
Building	40,000	60,000
Land	15,000	10,000
Total	$118,000	$133,000

The building has no depreciation recapture potential. What are the tax implications to Alison, Bob, and the AB Partnership of the April 1 transactions (i.e., basis of assets to Alison and Bob, amount and character of gain or loss recognized, etc.)? Assume that no Sec. 754 election is in effect.

C:10-36 ***Liquidating Distribution.*** The LQD Partnership distributes the following property to Larry in a distribution that liquidates Larry's interest in the partnership. Assume that no Sec. 754 election is in effect. Larry's basis in his partnership interest before the distribution is $40,000. The adjusted bases and FMVs of the distributed property to the partnership before the distribution are as follows:

Assets	*Partnership's Basis*	*FMV*
Cash	$ 2,500	$ 2,500
Inventory	8,000	9,000
Capital asset 1	10,000	15,000
Capital asset 2	15,000	17,500
Total	$35,500	$44,000

a. Determine Larry's basis in each distributed asset.
b. Same as Part a except Larry's partnership basis before the distribution is $46,500.
c. Same as Part b except the basis of capital asset 2 is $20,000 instead of $15,000.
d. Same as Part c except Larry's partnership basis before the distribution is $34,500.

C:10-37 ***Sale of a Partnership Interest.*** Pat, Kelly, and Yvette are equal partners in the PKY Partnership before Kelly sells her partnership interest. On January 1 of the current year, Kelly's basis in her partnership interest, including her share of liabilities, was $35,000. During January, the calendar year partnership earned $15,000 ordinary income and $6,000 of tax-exempt income. The partnership has a $60,000 recourse liability on January 1, and this amount remains constant throughout the tax year. Kelly's share of that liability is $20,000. The partnership has no other liabilities. Kelly sells her interest on February 1 to Margaret for a cash payment of $45,000. On the sale date the partnership had the following assets:

Assets	*Partnership's Basis*	*FMV*
Cash	$ 20,000	$ 20,000
Inventory	60,000	120,000
Building	36,000	40,000
Land	10,000	15,000
Total	$126,000	$195,000

The partnership has claimed $5,000 of depreciation on the building using the straight-line method.

a. What is Kelly's basis in her partnership interest on February 1 just before the sale?
b. What are the amount and character of Kelly's gain or loss on the sale?
c. What is Margaret's basis in her partnership interest?
d. What is the partnership's basis in its assets after the sale?

C:10-38 ***Sale of Partnership Interest and Termination.*** Clay owned 60% of the CAP Partnership and sold one-half of his interest (30%) to Steve for $75,000 cash. Before the sale, Clay's basis in his entire partnership interest was $168,000 including his $30,000 share of partnership liabilities and his share of income up to the sale date. Partnership assets on the sale date were

Assets	*Partnership's Basis*	*FMV*
Cash	$ 50,000	$ 50,000
Inventory	30,000	60,000
Land	200,000	190,000
Total	$280,000	$300,000

a. What are the amount and character of Clay's recognized gain or loss on the sale? What is his remaining basis in his partnership interest?
b. What is Steve's basis in his partnership interest?
c. How will the partnership's basis in its assets be affected?
d. How would your answers to Parts a and c change if Clay sold his entire interest to Steve for $150,000 cash?

C:10-39 ***Sale of a Partnership Interest.*** Alice, Bob, and Charles are one-third partners in the ABC Partnership. The partners originally formed the partnership with cash contributions, so no partner has precontribution gains or losses. Prior to Alice's sale of her partnership interest, the partnership has the following balance sheet:

	Partnership's Basis	*FMV*
Assets:		
Cash	$ 12,000	$ 12,000
Receivable	–0–	21,000
Inventory	57,000	72,000
Machinery[a]	90,000	132,000
Building[b]	120,000	165,000
Land	36,000	30,000
Investments[c]	15,000	48,000
Total	$330,000	$480,000

Liabilities and capital:		
Liabilities	$105,000	$105,000
Partners' capital:		
Alice	75,000	125,000
Bob	75,000	125,000
Charles	75,000	125,000
Total	$330,000	$480,000

[a]The machinery cost $126,000, and the partnership has claimed $36,000 of depreciation.
[b]The building cost $150,000, and the partnership has claimed $30,000 of straight-line depreciation.
[c]The partnership has held the investments for more than one year.

Alice has a $110,000 basis in her partnership interest including her share of partnership liabilities, and she sells her partnership interest to Darla for $125,000 cash.
a. What are the amount and character of Alice's recognized gain or loss on the sale?
b. What is Darla's basis in her partnership interest?

C:10-40 *Retirement of a Partner.* Suzanne retires from the BRS Partnership when the basis of her one-third interest is $105,000, which includes her share of liabilities. At the time of her retirement, the partnership had the following assets:

Assets	*Partnership's Basis*	*FMV*
Cash	$145,000	$145,000
Receivables	40,000	40,000
Land	130,000	220,000
Total	$315,000	$405,000

The partnership has $60,000 of liabilities when Suzanne retires. The partnership will pay Suzanne cash of $130,000 to retire her partnership interest.
a. What are the amount and character of the gain or loss Suzanne must recognize?
b. What is the impact of the retirement on the partnership and the remaining partners?

C:10-41 *Retirement of a Partner.* Brian owns 40% of the ABC Partnership before his retirement on April 15 of the current year. On that date, his basis in the partnership interest is $40,000 including his share of liabilities. The partnership's balance sheet on that date is as follows:

	Partnership's Basis	*FMV*
Assets:		
Cash	$ 60,000	$ 60,000
Receivables	24,000	24,000
Land	16,000	40,000
Total	$100,000	$124,000
Liabilities and capital:		
Liabilities	$ 20,000	$ 20,000
Capital—Abner	16,000	20,800
—Brian	32,000	41,600
—Charles	32,000	41,600
Total	$100,000	$124,000

What are the amount and character of gain or loss that Brian and the ABC Partnership recognize for the following independent retirement payments?
a. Brian receives $41,600 cash on April 15.
b. Brian receives $50,000 cash on April 15.

C:10-42 *Retirement of a Partner.* Kim retires from the KLM Partnership on January 1 of the current year. At that time, her basis in the partnership is $75,000, which includes her share of liabilities. The partnership reports the following balance sheet:

	Partnership's Basis	FMV
Assets:		
Cash	$100,000	$100,000
Receivables	30,000	30,000
Inventory	40,000	40,000
Land	55,000	100,000
Total	$225,000	$270,000
Liabilities and capital:		
Liabilities	$ 75,000	$ 75,000
Capital—Kim	50,000	65,000
—Larry	50,000	65,000
—Michael	50,000	65,000
Total	$225,000	$270,000

Explain the tax consequences (i.e., amount and character of gain or loss recognized and Kim's basis for any assets received) of the partnership making the retirement payments described in the following independent situations. Kim's share of liabilities is $25,000.

a. Kim receives $65,000 cash on January 1.

b. Kim receives $75,000 cash on January 1.

C:10-43 *Death of a Partner.* When Jerry died on April 16 of the current year, he owned a 40% interest in the JM Partnership, and Michael owns the remaining 60% interest. All his assets are held in his estate for a two-year period while the estate is being settled. Jerry's estate is his successor-in-interest for the partnership interest. Under a formula contained in the partnership agreement, the partnership must pay Jerry's successor-in-interest $40,000 cash shortly after his death plus $90,000 for each of the two years immediately following a partner's death. The partnership agreement provides that all payments to a retiring partner will first be payments for the partner's share of assets, and then any additional payments will be Sec. 736(a) payments. When Jerry died, the partnership had the following balance sheet:

	Partnership's Basis	FMV
Assets:		
Cash	$100,000	$100,000
Land	200,000	300,000
Total	$300,000	$400,000
Liabilities and capital:		
Liabilities	$ 75,000	$ 75,000
Capital—Jerry	90,000	130,000
—Michael	135,000	195,000
Total	$300,000	$400,000

Jerry's basis for the partnership interest on the date of his death was $120,000 including his $30,000 share of partnership liabilities.

a. How will the payments be taxed to Jerry's successor-in-interest?

b. What are the tax implications of the payments for the partnership?

C:10-44 *Death of a Partner.* Bruce died on June 1 of the current year. On the date of his death, he held a one-third interest in the ABC Partnership, which had a $100,000 basis including his share of liabilities. Under the partnership agreement, Bruce's successor-in-interest, his wife, is to receive the following amounts from the partnership: $130,000 cash, the partnership's assumption of Bruce's $20,000 share of partnership liabilities, plus 10% of partnership net income for the next three years. The partnership's balance sheet immediately before Bruce's death is as follows:

	Partnership's Basis	FMV
Assets:		
Cash	$100,000	$100,000
Receivables	90,000	90,000
Inventory	40,000	40,000
Land	70,000	220,000
Total	$300,000	$450,000
Liabilities and capital:		
Liabilities	$ 60,000	$ 60,000
Capital—Bruce	80,000	130,000
—Others	160,000	260,000
Total	$300,000	$450,000

a. What are the amount and character of the gain or loss that Bruce's wife must recognize when she receives the first year's payment?
b. What is the character of the gain recognized from the partnership interest when she receives the payments in each of the following three years?
c. When does Bruce's successor-in-interest cease to be a member of the partnership?

C:10-45 ***Liquidation or Sale of a Partnership Interest.*** John has a 60% capital and profits interest in the JAS Partnership with a basis of $333,600, which includes his share of liabilities, when he decides to retire. Andrew and Stephen want to continue the partnership's business. On the date John retires, the partnership's balance sheet is as follows:

	Partnership's Basis	FMV
Assets:		
Cash	$160,000	$160,000
Receivables	100,000	100,000
Building[a]	200,000	300,000
Land	96,000	180,000
Total	$556,000	$740,000
Liabilities and capital:		
Liabilities	$120,000	$120,000
Capital—John	261,600	372,000
—Andrew	87,200	124,000
—Stephen	87,200	124,000
Total	$556,000	$740,000

[a]The partnership has claimed $60,000 of straight-line depreciation on the building.

a. What are the tax implications for John, Andrew, Stephen, and the JAS Partnership if Andrew and Stephen each purchase one-half of John's partnership interest for a cash price of $186,000 each? Include in your answer the amount and character of the recognized gain or loss, basis of the partnership assets, and any other relevant tax implications.
b. What are the tax implications for John, Andrew, Stephen, and the JAS Partnership if the partnership pays John a liquidating distribution equal to 60% of each partnership asset other than cash plus $24,000 of cash? Assume the assets are easily divisible.

C:10-46 ***Liquidation or Sale of a Partnership Interest.*** Amy, a one-third partner, retires from the AJS Partnership on January 1 of the current year. Her basis in her partnership interest is $120,000 including her share of liabilities. Amy receives $160,000 in cash from the partnership for her interest. On that date, the partnership balance sheet is as follows:

	Partnership's Basis	FMV
Assets:		
Cash	$180,000	$180,000
Receivables	60,000	60,000
Land	120,000	300,000
Total	$360,000	$540,000

Liabilities and capital:		
Liabilities	$ 60,000	$ 60,000
Capital—Amy	100,000	160,000
—Joan	100,000	160,000
—Stephanie	100,000	160,000
Total	$360,000	$540,000

a. What are the amount and character of Amy's recognized gain or loss?
b. How would your answers to Part a change if Joan and Stephanie each purchased one-half of Amy's partnership interest for $80,000 cash instead of having the partnership distribute the $160,000 in cash to Amy?

C:10-47 *Exchange of Partnership Interests.* Josh holds a general partnership interest in the JLK Partnership having a $40,000 basis and a $60,000 FMV. The JLK Partnership is a limited partnership that engages in real estate activities. Diana has an interest in the CDE Partnership having a $20,000 basis and a $60,000 FMV. The CDE Partnership is a general partnership that also engages in real estate activities. Neither partnership has any Sec. 751 assets or any liabilities.
a. What are the tax implications if Josh and Diana simply exchange their partnership interests?
b. What are the tax implications if instead Diana exchanges her general partnership interest in the CDE Partnership for a limited partnership interest in the same partnership (and Josh retains his general partnership interest in the JLK Partnership)?

C:10-48 *Termination of a Partnership.* Wendy, Xenia, and Yancy own 40%, 8%, and 52%, respectively, of the WXY Partnership. For each of the following independent situations occurring in the current year, determine whether the WXY Partnership terminates and, if so, the date on which the termination occurs.
a. Wendy sells her entire interest to Alan on June 1. Alan sells one-half of the interest to Beth on November 15.
b. Yancy receives a series of liquidating distributions totaling $100,000. He receives four equal annual payments on January 1 of the current year and the three subsequent years.
c. Wendy and Xenia each receive a liquidating distribution on September 14.
d. Yancy sells his interest to Karen on June 1 for $10,000 cash and a $90,000 installment note. The note will be paid in monthly installments of $10,000 principal plus interest (at a rate acceptable to the IRS) beginning on July 1.
e. The WXY and ABC Partnerships combine their businesses on December 30. Ownership of the new, combined partnership is as follows: Wendy, 20%; Xenia, 4%; Yancy, 26.5%; Albert, 20%; Beth, 19.5%; and Carl, 10%.
f. On January 1, the WXY Partnership divides its business into two new businesses. The WX Partnership is owned equally by Wendy and Xenia. Yancy continues his share of the business as a sole proprietorship.

C:10-49 *Termination of a Partnership.* For each of the following independent situations, determine which partnership(s) (if any) terminate and which partnership(s) (if any) continue.
a. The KLMN Partnership is created when the KL Partnership merges with the MN Partnership. The ownership of the new partnership is held 25% by Katie, 30% by Laura, 25% by Michael, and 20% by Neal.
b. The ABC Partnership, with $150,000 in assets, is owned equally by Amy, Beth, and Chuck. The CD Partnership, with $100,000 in assets, is owned equally by Chuck and Drew. The two partnerships merge, and the resulting ABCD Partnership is owned as follows: Amy, 20%; Beth, 20%; Chuck, 40%; and Drew, 20%.
c. The WXYZ Partnership results when the WX and YZ Partnerships merge. Ownership of WXYZ is held equally by the four partners. WX contributes $140,000 in assets, and YZ contributes $160,000 in assets to the new partnership.
d. The DEFG Partnership is owned 20% by Dawn, 40% by Eve, 30% by Frank, and 10% by Greg. Two new partnerships are formed by the division of DEFG. The two new partnerships, the DE and FG Partnerships, are owned in proportion to their relative interests in the DEFG Partnership by the individuals for whom they are named.
e. The HIJK Partnership is owned equally by its four partners, Hal, Isaac, Juan, and Katherine, before its division. Two new partnerships, the HI and JK Partnerships, are formed out of the division with the new partnerships owned equally by the partners for whom they are named.

C:10-50 *Disposal of a Tax Shelter.* Maria purchased an interest in a real estate tax shelter many years ago and deducted losses from its operation for several years. The real property owned by the tax shelter when Maria made her investment has been fully depreciated on a straight-line basis. Her basis in her limited partnership interest is zero, but her share of partnership liabilities is $100,000. Explain the tax results if Maria sells her partnership interest for $5 cash.

C:10-51 *Optional Basis Adjustment.* Patty pays $100,000 cash for Stan's one-third interest in the STU Partnership. The partnership has a Sec. 754 election in effect. Just before the sale of Stan's interest, STU's balance sheet appears as follows:

	Partnership's Basis	*FMV*
Assets:		
Cash	$ 80,000	$ 80,000
Land	160,000	220,000
Total	$240,000	$300,000
Partners' capital:		
Stan	$ 80,000	$100,000
Traffic Corporation	80,000	100,000
Union Corporation	80,000	100,000
Total	$240,000	$300,000

a. What is Patty's total optional basis adjustment?
b. If STU Partnership sells the land for its $220,000 FMV immediately after Patty purchases her interest, how much gain or loss will the partnership recognize?
c. How much gain will Patty report as a result of the sale?

C:10-52 *Mandatory Basis Adjustment.* The JKL Partnership has three equal partners, Jingjing, Kevin, and Latisha. Latisha sells her interest to Larry for $690,000. The partnership does not have a Sec. 754 election in effect. Just before the sale of Latisha's interest, the partnership's balance sheet appears as follows:

	Partnership's Basis	*FMV*
Assets:		
Inventory	$ 800,000	$1,070,000
Land	1,600,000	1,000,000
Total	$2,400,000	$2,070,000
Partners' capital:		
Jingjing	$ 800,000	$ 690,000
Kevin	800,000	690,000
Latisha	800,000	690,000
Total	$2,400,000	$2,070,000

a. What is Latisha's recognized net loss on the sale, and what is the character of its components?
b. What is Larry's mandatory basis adjustment?

C:10-53 *Taxation of LLC Income.* ABC Company, a limited liability company (LLC) organized in the state of Florida, reports using a calendar tax year-end. The LLC chooses to be taxed as a partnership. Alex, Bob, and Carrie (all calendar year taxpayers) own ABC equally, and each has a basis of $40,000 in his or her ABC interest on the first day of the current tax year. ABC has the following results for the current year's operation:

Operating income	$30,000
Short-term capital gain	12,000
Long-term capital loss	6,000

Each owner received a $12,000 cash distribution during the current year.
a. What are the amount and character of the income, gain, and loss Alex must report on his tax return as a result of ABC's operations?
b. What is Alex's basis in his ownership interest in ABC after the current year's operations?

C:10-54 *Electing Large Partnership.* Austin & Becker is an electing large partnership. During the current year, the partnership has the following income, loss, and deduction items:

Ordinary income	$5,200,000
Rental loss	(2,000,000)
Long-term capital loss from investments	(437,100)
Short-term capital gain from investments	827,400
Charitable contributions	164,000

a. What ordinary income will Austin & Becker report?
b. What are the separately stated items for Austin & Becker?

C:10-55 *Electing Large Partnership.* Happy Times Film Distributions is an electing large partnership. During the current year, the partnership has the following income, loss, and deduction items:

Ordinary income	$ 700,000
Passive income	3,000,000
Sec. 1231 gains	27,000
Sec. 1231 losses	(134,800)
Long-term capital gains from investments	437,600
General business tax credits	43,000

a. What ordinary income will Happy Times report?
b. What are the separately stated items reported by Happy Times?

COMPREHENSIVE PROBLEMS

C:10-56 Refer to the facts in Comprehensive Problem C:6-54. Now assume the entity is a partnership named Lifecycle Partnership. Additional facts are as follows:

- Except for precontribution gains and losses, the partners agree to share profits and losses in a 60% (Able)—40% (Baker) ratio.
- The partners actively and materially participate in the partnership's business. Thus, the partnership is not a passive activity.
- Partnership debt is recourse debt.
- The salary to Able is a guaranteed payment.
- The refund for the NOL is not relevant to the partnership, nor are the E&P numbers.
- In addition to the numbers provided for the assets on January 2, 2018, the following partnership book values apply:

Equipment	$ 215,000
Building	926,000
Land A	30,000
Land B	20,000
Total	$1,191,000

- On January 2, 2018, the partnership sells its assets and pays off the $1.87 million debt. The partnership then makes liquidating distributions of the $490,000 remaining cash to Able and Baker in accordance with their book capital account balances.

Required:

a. Determine the tax consequences of the partnership formation to Able, Baker, and Lifecycle Partnership.
b. For 2015 through 2017, prepare a schedule showing:
(1) Partnership ordinary income and other separately stated items
(2) Able's and Baker's book capital accounts at the end of 2015, 2016, and 2017
(3) Able's and Baker's bases in their partnership interests at the end of 2015, 2016, and 2017

c. For 2018, determine:
   (1) The results of the asset sales
   (2) Able's and Baker's book capital accounts after the asset sales but before the final liquidating distribution
   (3) Able's and Baker's bases in their partnership interests after the asset sales but before the final liquidating distribution
   (4) The results of the liquidating distributions, assuming a 23.8% tax rate (the 20% maximum capital gain rate plus the 3.8% rate on net investment income)

C:10-57 Anne decides to leave the ABC Partnership after owning the interest for many years. She owns a 52% capital, profits, and loss interest in the general partnership (which is not a service partnership). Anne's basis in her partnership interest is $120,000 just before she leaves the partnership. The partnership agreement does not mention payments to partners who leave the partnership. The partnership has not made an optional basis adjustment election (Sec. 754). All partnership liabilities are recourse liabilities, and Anne's share is equal to her loss interest. When Anne leaves the partnership, the assets and liabilities for the partnership are as follows:

	Partnership's Basis	*FMV*
Assets:		
Cash	$240,000	$240,000
Receivables	–0–	64,000
Inventory	24,000	24,000
Land	60,000	100,000
Total	$324,000	$428,000
Liabilities	$ 60,000	$ 60,000

Analyze the following two alternatives, and answer the associated questions for each alternative.

a. Anne could receive a cash payment of $220,000 from the partnership to terminate her interest in the partnership. Does Anne or the partnership have any income, deduction, gain, or loss? Determine both the amount and character of any items.

b. Carrie already owns a 30% general interest in the ABC partnership prior to Anne's departure. Carrie is willing to buy Anne's partnership interest for a cash payment of $220,000. What income, gain, loss, or deduction will Anne recognize on the sale? What are the tax implications for the partnership if Carrie buys Anne's interest?

TAX STRATEGY PROBLEM

C:10-58 Consider the following balance sheet for DEF Partnership:

	Partnership's Basis	*FMV*
Assets:		
Cash	$60,000	$ 60,000
Receivables	–0–	60,000
Land A	10,000	20,000
Land B	10,000	20,000
Land C	10,000	20,000
Total	$90,000	$180,000
Partners' capital:		
Daniel	$30,000	$ 60,000
Edward	30,000	60,000
Frances	30,000	60,000
Total	$90,000	$180,000

Note: Land A, B, and C are Sec. 1231 property, and each partner's outside basis is $30,000.

Suppose Daniel wishes to exit the partnership completely. After discussions with Edward and Frances, the partners agree to let Daniel choose one of three options:

1. Daniel takes a liquidating distribution of $60,000 cash.
2. Daniel takes a pro rata liquidating distribution of $20,000 cash, $20,000 receivables, and Land A (FMV $20,000).

3. Daniel sells his entire partnership interest to Doris for $60,000 cash.
   Required:
a. Determine the tax consequences to Daniel of each option including gains (losses) realized, recognized, and deferred; character of gains (losses); and bases of assets.
b. Discuss the relative merits of each option to Daniel, that is, what are the advantages and disadvantages of each option? What factors could sway your recommendation one way or the other?

Note: See Case Study Problem C:10-59 for another situation involving various exit strategies.

CASE STUDY PROBLEM

C:10-59 Mark Green and his brother Michael purchased land in Orlando, Florida many years ago. At that time, they began their investing as Green Brothers Partnership with capital they obtained from placing second mortgages on their homes. Their investments have flourished both because of the prosperity and growth of the area and because they have shown an ability to select prime real estate for others to develop. Over the years, they have acquired a great amount of land and have sold some to developers.

Their current tax year has just closed, and the partnership has the following balance sheet:

	Partnership's Basis	*FMV*
Assets:		
Cash	$200,000	$ 200,000
Accounts receivable	90,000	90,000
Land held for investment	310,000	1,010,000
Total	$600,000	$1,300,000
Liabilities and capital:		
Mortgages	$400,000	$ 400,000
Capital—Mark	100,000	450,000
—Michael	100,000	450,000
Total	$600,000	$1,300,000

Mark and Michael each have a basis in their partnership interest of $300,000 including their share of liabilities. They share the economic risk of loss from the liabilities equally. Last spring, Mark had a serious heart attack. On his doctor's advice, Mark wants to retire from all business activity and terminate his interest in the partnership. He is interested in receiving some cash now but is not averse to receiving part of his payment over time.

You have been asked to provide the brothers with information on how to terminate Mark's interest in the partnership. Several possibilities have occurred to Mark and Michael, and they want your advice as to which is best for Mark from a tax standpoint. Michael understands that the resulting choice may not be the best option for him. The possibilities they have considered include the following:

- Michael has substantial amounts of personal cash and could purchase Mark's interest directly. However, the brothers think that option probably would take almost all the cash Michael could raise, and they are concerned about any future cash needs Michael might have. They would prefer to have Mark receive $120,000 now plus $110,000 per year for each of the next three years. Mark also would receive interest at a market rate on the outstanding debt. This alternative would qualify for installment reporting. However, the installment sale rules for related parties would apply.
- The partnership could retire Mark's interest. They have considered the option of paying Mark $150,000 now plus 50% of partnership profits for the next three years. Alternatively, they could arrange for Mark to have a $150,000 payment now and a guaranteed payment of $100,000 per year for the next three years. They expect that the dollar amounts to be received by Mark would be approximately the same for the next three years under these two options. Mark also would receive interest at a market rate on any deferred payments.
- John Watson, a long-time friend of the family, has expressed an interest in buying Mark's interest for $450,000 cash immediately. Michael and John are comfortable that they could work well together.

Mark has substantial amounts of money in savings accounts and in stocks and bonds that have a ready market. He has invested in no other business directly. Assume that, for each year, Mark's ordinary tax rate is 33% and his capital gains tax rate is 18.8% (the 15% capital gain rate for his tax bracket plus the 3.8% rate on net investment income).

TAX & FINANCIAL ACCOUNTING

Required: Prepare a memorandum summarizing the advice you would give the two brothers on the options that they have considered.

TAX RESEARCH PROBLEMS

C:10-60 Arnie, Becky, and Clay are equal partners in the ABC General Partnership. The three individuals each have a $120,000 tax basis in their partnership interest. For business reasons, the partnership needs to be changed into the ABC Corporation, and all three owners agree to the change. The partnership is expected to have the following assets on the date that the change is to occur:

Assets	*Partnership's Tax Basis & Book Value*	*FMV*
Cash	$ 50,000	$ 50,000
Accounts receivable	60,000	55,000
Inventory	150,000	200,000
Land	100,000	295,000
Total	$360,000	$600,000

Liabilities of $75,000 are currently outstanding. The liabilities are shared equally and are already included in the $120,000 bases of the partnership interests. The structure being considered for making the change is as follows:

- ABC Partnership transfers all its assets and liabilities to the new ABC Corporation in exchange for all the corporation's stock.
- ABC Partnership then liquidates by distributing the ABC stock to Arnie, Becky, and Clay.

Required: The tax manager you work for has asked you to determine the tax and financial accounting consequences. Describe the financial and tax treatments in a short memorandum to the partnership. Be sure to mention any relevant IRC sections, Treasury Regulations, revenue rulings, and accounting standards. Assume a 35% corporate tax rate.

C:10-61 Della retires from the BCD General Partnership when her basis in her partnership interest is $70,000 including her $10,000 share of liabilities. The partnership is in the business of providing house cleaning services for local residences. At the date of Della's retirement, the partnership's balance sheet is as follows:

	Partnership's Basis	*FMV*
Assets:		
Cash	$ 50,000	$ 50,000
Receivables	–0–	30,000
Equipment[a]	40,000	50,000
Building[b]	90,000	100,000
Land	30,000	40,000
Total	$210,000	$270,000
Liabilities and capital:		
Liabilities	$ 30,000	$ 30,000
Capital—Bruce	60,000	80,000
—Celia	60,000	80,000
—Della	60,000	80,000
Total	$210,000	$270,000

[a]If the equipment were sold for $50,000, the entire gain would be recaptured as Sec. 1245 ordinary income.
[b]The building has been depreciated using the straight-line method.

Della will receive payments of $20,000 cash plus 5% of partnership ordinary income for each of the next five years. The partnership agreement specifies that goodwill will be paid for when a partner retires. Bruce, Celia, and Della agree that the partnership has $21,000 in goodwill when Della retires and that she will be paid for her one-third share.

Required: A tax manager in your firm has asked you to determine the amount and character of the income Della must report for each of the next five years. In addition, he wants you to research the tax consequences of the retirement on the partnership for the next five years. (Assume the partnership earns $100,000 of ordinary income each year for the next five years.) Prepare an oral presentation to be made to Della explaining the tax consequences of the payments she will receive.

C:10-62 Pedro owns a 60% interest in the PD General Partnership having a $40,000 basis and $200,000 FMV. His share of partnership liabilities is $100,000. Because he is nearing retirement age, he has decided to give away his partnership interest on June 15 of the current year. The partnership's tax year ends on December 31. Pedro's tax year ends on June 30. He intends to give a 30% interest to his son, Juan, and the remaining 30% interest to the American Red Cross.

Required: A tax manager in your firm has asked you to prepare a letter to Pedro explaining fully the tax consequences of this gift to him, the partnership, and the donees. She reminds you to be sure to include information about the allocation of the current year's partnership income.

C:10-63 Frank, Greta, and Helen each have a one-third interest in the FGH Partnership. On December 31, 2014, the partnership reported the following balance sheet:

	Partnership's Basis	*FMV*
Assets:		
Cash	$120,000	$120,000
Asset 1	262,380	360,000
Asset 2	115,200	90,000
Total	$497,580	$570,000
Partners' Capital:		
Frank	$165,860	$190,000
Greta	165,860	190,000
Helen	165,860	190,000
Total	$497,580	$570,000

The partnership placed Asset 1 (seven-year property) in service in 2012 and Asset 2 (five-year property) in service in 2013. The partnership did not elect Sec. 179 expensing and elected out of bonus depreciation in both years. Accordingly, it computed the assets' adjusted bases at December 31, 2014 as follows:

		Asset 1		*Asset 2*
Cost		$600,000		$240,000
Depreciation:				
2012	$85,740			
2013	146,940		$48,000	
2014	104,940	(337,620)	76,800	(124,800)
Adjusted basis		$262,380		$115,200

On January 2, 2015, Helen sold her partnership interest to Hank for $190,000. At the time of sale, the partnership had a Sec. 754 optional basis election in effect but has not elected to use the remedial method for allocating partnership items.

Required: The partners have asked you to determine (1) the amount and character of Helen's gain or loss; (2) Hank's optional basis adjustment and its allocation to Asset 1 and Asset 2; and (3) the amount of depreciation allocated to Hank in 2015, including the effects of the optional basis adjustment. At a minimum, you should consult the following resources:

- IRC Secs. 743 and 751
- Reg. Sec. 1.743-1(j)
- Reg. Sec. 1.755-1

CHAPTER

11

S CORPORATIONS

LEARNING OBJECTIVES

After studying this chapter, you should be able to

1 Discuss the advantages and disadvantages of making the S election

2 List the requirements for being eligible to elect S corporation status

3 Explain how a corporation elects, revokes, or terminates S corporation status

4 Classify an S corporation's ordinary and separately stated items, and calculate special S corporation taxes

5 Allocate an S corporation's ordinary and separately stated items to its shareholders and apply loss limitation rules

6 Calculate a shareholder's basis in his or her S corporation stock and debt

7 Determine the taxability of an S corporation's distributions to its shareholders

8 Explain other rules that pertain to S corporations

9 Identify tax planning opportunities for an S corporation and its shareholders

10 Comply with S corporation procedural and filing requirements

CHAPTER OUTLINE

This chapter discusses a special type of corporate entity known as an S corporation. The S corporation rules, located in Subchapter S of the Internal Revenue Code, permit small corporations to enjoy the nontax advantages of the corporate form of organization without being subject to the possible tax disadvantages of the corporate form (e.g., double taxation when the corporation pays a dividend to its shareholders). When enacting these rules, Congress stated three purposes:

- To permit businesses to select a particular form of business organization without being influenced by tax considerations
- To provide aid for small businesses by allowing the income of the business to be taxed to shareholders rather than being taxed at the corporate level
- To permit corporations realizing losses to obtain a tax benefit of offsetting the losses against income at the shareholder level[1]

As discussed in Chapter C:2, S corporations are treated as corporations for legal and business purposes. For federal income tax purposes, however, they are treated much like partnerships.[2] As in a partnership, the profits and losses of the S corporation pass through to the owners, and the S corporation can make nontaxable distributions of earnings previously taxed to its shareholders. Although generally taxed like a partnership, the S corporation still follows many of the basic Subchapter C tax provisions (e.g., S corporations use the corporate tax rules regarding formations, liquidations, and nontaxable reorganizations instead of the partnership rules). A tabular comparison of the S corporation, partnership, and C corporation rules appears in Appendix F.

ADDITIONAL COMMENT

An LLC (or partnership) that wishes to be treated as an S corporation can file the S election (Form 2553) and automatically be classified as an association (corporation) under the check-the-box regulations without having to file the entity classification election (Form 8832).

Changes over the past several years have caused many businesses to reexamine the implications of an S election. First, the restrictive nature of the S corporation requirements has caused many new businesses that were potential S corporations to look at alternative business forms. All 50 states have adopted limited liability company (LLC) legislation. LLCs offer many of the same tax advantages of S corporations because they are treated as partnerships. LLCs, however, are not subject to the same requirements that an S corporation and its shareholders must satisfy to make and retain an S election. Partially because of the S corporation restrictions, some new businesses have organized as LLCs to take advantage of the greater operational flexibility the LLC form provides the entity and its owners, as well as its liability protection. A number of small businesses, however, elected to be S corporations because of the greater certainty available within the legal system for corporate entities.

Over the last several years, tax legislation has relaxed restrictions and increased the S corporation's popularity. For example, the shareholder limit was increased to 100, and the prohibitions against certain entities and trusts becoming S corporation shareholders were lessened. Moreover, current law now treats family members as one shareholder for the 100-shareholder limit. In effect, these changes have reduced some of the differences between S corporations and LLCs and have renewed interest in the S corporation form of doing business.

For many existing C corporations, the tax cost of liquidating the corporate entity and creating an LLC may be a prohibitively expensive way to avoid the corporate level income tax (see Chapter C:6). However, many of these C corporations have taken the next best alternative, that is, making an S election.

This chapter examines the requirements for making an S election and the tax rules that apply to S corporations and their shareholders.

---

[1] S. Rept. No. 1983, 85th Cong., 2d Sess., p. 87 (1958).

[2] Some states do not recognize an S corporation as a conduit for state income tax purposes. Instead, they are taxed under the state income tax laws in the same manner as a C corporation.

Should an S Election Be Made?

OBJECTIVE 1

Discuss the advantages and disadvantages of making the S election

Advantages of S Corporation Treatment

A number of advantages are available to a corporation that makes an S election.

- The corporation's income is exempt from the corporate income tax. An S corporation's income is taxed only to its shareholders, whose tax bracket may be lower than a C corporation's tax bracket.
- The corporation's losses pass through to its shareholders and can be used to reduce the taxes owed on other types of income. This feature can be especially important for new businesses. The corporation can make an S election, pass through the start-up losses to the owners, and terminate the election once a C corporation becomes advantageous.
- Undistributed income taxed to the shareholder is not taxed again when subsequently distributed unless the distribution exceeds the shareholder's basis for his or her stock.
- Capital gains, dividends, and tax-exempt income are separately stated and retain their character when passed through to the shareholders. Such amounts become commingled with other corporate earnings and are taxed as dividends when distributed by a C corporation. However, the applicable capital gains tax rate on qualified dividends may alleviate the detrimental tax effect of C corporation dividends.
- Deductions, losses, and tax credits are separately stated and retain their character when passed through to the shareholders. These amounts may be subject to the various limitations at the shareholder level. This treatment can permit the shareholder to claim a tax benefit when it otherwise would be denied to the corporation (e.g., a shareholder can claim the general business credit benefit even though the S corporation reports a substantial loss for the year).
- Splitting the S corporation's income among family members is possible. However, income splitting is restricted by the requirement that reasonable compensation be provided to family members who provide capital and services to the S corporation.
- An S corporation's earnings that pass through to the individual shareholders are not subject to the self-employment tax. In contrast, a partnership must determine what portion of each general partner's net earnings constitutes self-employment income.
- An S corporation is not subject to the personal holding company tax or the accumulated earnings tax (although, as discussed later, passive income can trigger a corporate-level tax in special circumstances).

ADDITIONAL COMMENT

The applicable capital gains tax rate for net capital gains and qualified dividends of noncorporate taxpayers is 0% for taxpayers in tax brackets of 15% and below, 15% for taxpayers in the 25% through 35% tax brackets, and 20% for taxpayers in the 39.6% tax bracket. Also, 25% and 28% rates apply for gains on certain types of property. In addition, an incremental 3.8% rate applies to net investment income for taxpayers whose modified AGI exceeds $200,000 ($250,000 for married filing jointly). Net investment income includes, among other things, interest, dividends, annuities, royalties, rents, and net gains from the disposition of property not used in a trade or business, all reduced by deductions allocable to such income or gains.

REAL-WORLD EXAMPLE

The number of S corporations has grown from 725,000 in 1985 to 4.6 million in 2013.

Disadvantages of S Corporation Treatment

A number of tax disadvantages also exist for a corporation that makes an S election.

- A C corporation is treated as a separate tax entity from its shareholders, thereby permitting its first $50,000 of income to be taxed at a 15% marginal rate instead of the shareholder's marginal rate.
- The S corporation's earnings are taxed to the shareholders even though they are not distributed. This treatment may require the corporation to make distributions or salary payments so the shareholder can pay taxes owed on the S corporation's earnings.
- S corporations are subject to an excess net passive income tax and a built-in gains tax. Partnerships are not subject to either of these taxes.
- Dividends received by the S corporation are not eligible for the dividends-received deduction, as is the case for a C corporation.
- Allocation of ordinary income or loss and the separately stated items is based on the stock owned on each day of the tax year. Special allocations of particular items are not permitted, as they are in a partnership.

KEY POINT

The structure of an S corporation can create a real hardship for a shareholder if large amounts of income pass through without any compensation payments or distributions of cash to help pay the tax on the income.

- The loss limitation for an S corporation shareholder is smaller than for a partner in a partnership because of the treatment of liabilities. Shareholders can increase their loss limitations by the basis of any debt they loan to the S corporation. Partners, on the other hand, can increase their loss limitation by their ratable share of all partnership liabilities.
- S corporations and their shareholders are subject to the at-risk, passive activity limitation, and hobby loss rules. C corporations generally are not subject to these rules.
- An S corporation is somewhat restricted in the type and number of shareholders it can have and the capital structure it can use. Partnerships and C corporations are not so restricted.
- S corporations must use a calendar year as their tax year unless they can establish a business purpose for a fiscal year or unless they make a special election to use an otherwise nonpermitted tax year. Similar restrictions also apply to partnerships.

TAX STRATEGY TIP

With the top 39.6 % individual marginal tax rate now above the top 35% corporate marginal tax rate (ignoring the 39% and 38% bubble ranges), S corporations with positive income may be less attractive to high-bracket individuals than would C corporations, but S corporations with losses may be more attractive than would C corporations. Assuming an S corporation shareholder has sufficient offsetting income (and loss limitations do not apply), he or she could use the loss pass-through immediately at a high tax savings whereas a C corporation might have to carry over the loss to offset income in later years at perhaps a low tax savings.

Once the owners decide to incorporate, no general rule determines whether the corporation should make an S election. Before making a decision, management and the shareholders should examine the long- and short-run tax and nontax advantages and disadvantages of filing as a C corporation versus filing as an S corporation. Unlike a consolidated return election, the S election can be revoked or terminated at any time with minimal effort.

S CORPORATION REQUIREMENTS

OBJECTIVE 2

List the requirements for being eligible to elect S corporation status

The S corporation requirements are divided into two categories: shareholder-related and corporation-related requirements. A corporation that satisfies all the requirements is known as a small business corporation. Only small business corporations can make an S election. Each set of requirements is outlined below.

SHAREHOLDER-RELATED REQUIREMENTS

Three shareholder-related requirements must be satisfied on each day of the tax year.[3]

- The corporation must not have more than 100 shareholders.
- All shareholders must be individuals, estates, certain tax-exempt organizations, or certain kinds of trusts.
- None of the individual shareholders can be classified as a nonresident **alien**.

ADDITIONAL COMMENT

The Sec. 1244 stock rules (Chapter C:2) and the S corporation rules both use the term *small business corporations.* The definitions have different requirements, although most S corporation stock can qualify as Sec. 1244 stock.

100-Shareholder Rule. For purposes of applying the 100-shareholder limit, members of a family (and their estates) count as one shareholder. Members of a family include the common ancestor, lineal descendants of the common ancestor, spouses (or former spouses) of the common ancestor or lineal descendents, and estates of family members. An individual will not be considered a common ancestor if he or she is more than six generations removed from the youngest generation of family member shareholders. When two unmarried or nonfamily individuals own stock jointly (e.g., as tenants in common or as joint tenants), each owner is considered a separate shareholder.

REAL-WORLD EXAMPLE

In 2011, 62.1% of all S corporations had one owner. Only 0.12% of the 4.2 million S corporations that filed in 2011 had more than 30 owners.

Eligible Shareholders. C corporations and partnerships cannot own S corporation stock. This restriction prevents a corporation or a partnership having a large number of owners from avoiding the 100-shareholder limitation by purchasing S corporation stock and being treated as a single shareholder. Organizations exempt from the federal

[3] Sec. 1361.

income tax under Sec. 501(a) (e.g., a tax-exempt public charity or private foundation) can hold S corporation stock, and each such organization counts as one shareholder when calculating the 100-shareholder limit.

Seven types of trusts can own S corporation stock: grantor trusts, voting trusts,[4] testamentary trusts, **qualified Subchapter S trusts (QSSTs)**,[5] qualified retirement plan trusts, small business trusts, and beneficiary-controlled trusts (i.e., trusts that distribute all their income to a single income beneficiary who is treated as the owner of the trust). Grantor trusts, QSSTs, and beneficiary-controlled trusts can own S corporation stock only if the grantor or the beneficiary is a qualified shareholder. Each beneficiary of a voting trust also must be an eligible shareholder. A qualified retirement plan trust is one formed as part of a qualified stock bonus, pension, or profit sharing plan or employee stock ownership plan (ESOP) that is exempt from the federal income tax under Sec. 501(a).

Small business trusts can own S corporation stock. These trusts can be complex trusts and primarily are used as estate planning devices. No interest in a small business trust can be acquired in a purchase transaction, that is, a transaction where the holder's interest takes a cost basis under Sec. 1012. Interests in small business trusts generally are acquired as a result of a gift or bequest. All current beneficiaries of a small business trust must be individuals, estates, or charitable organizations. Current beneficiaries are parties that can receive an income distribution for the period in question. Each beneficiary counts separately for purposes of the 100-shareholder limit. QSSTs and tax-exempt trusts are ineligible to elect to be a small business trust. The trustee must make an election to obtain small business trust status.

ETHICAL POINT

Tax professionals must assist their clients in monitoring that the S corporation requirements are met on each day of the tax year. Failing to meet one of the requirements for even one day terminates the election. Ignoring a terminating event until the IRS discovers it upon an audit probably will cause the corporation to be taxed as a C corporation and prevent it from having the termination treated as being inadvertent.

A testamentary trust (i.e., a trust created under the terms of a will) that receives S corporation stock can hold the stock and continue to be an eligible shareholder for a two-year period, beginning on the date the stock transfers to the trust. A grantor trust that held S corporation stock immediately before the death of the deemed owner, and which continues in existence after the death of the deemed owner, can continue to hold the stock and be an eligible shareholder for the two-year period beginning on the date of the deemed owner's death. Charitable remainder unitrusts and charitable remainder annuity trusts do not qualify as small business trusts.

EXAMPLE C:11-1 ▶ Joan, a U.S. citizen, owns 25% of Walden Corporation's stock. Walden is an S corporation. At the time of Joan's death in the current year, the Walden stock passes to her estate. The estate is a qualifying shareholder, and the transfer does not affect the S election. If the stock subsequently transfers to a trust provided for in Joan's will, the testamentary trust can hold the Walden stock for a two-year period before the S election terminates. ◀

The trust in Example C:11-1 can hold the S corporation stock for an indefinite period only if the trust's income beneficiary makes an election to have it treated as a QSST or small business trust. Otherwise, the S election terminates at the end of the two-year period.

Alien Individuals. Individuals who are not U.S. citizens (i.e., alien individuals) can own S corporation stock only if they are U.S. residents or are married to a U.S. citizen or resident alien and make an election to be taxed as a resident alien. The S election terminates if an alien individual purchases S corporation stock and does not reside in the United States or has not made the appropriate election.

CORPORATION-RELATED REQUIREMENTS

The corporation must satisfy the following three requirements on each day of the tax year:

---

[4] A **voting trust** is an arrangement whereby the stock owned by a number of shareholders is placed under the control of a trustee, who exercises the voting rights possessed by the stock. One reason for creating a voting trust is to increase the voting power of a group of minority shareholders in the selection of corporate directors or the establishment of corporate policies.

[5] A QSST is a domestic trust that owns stock in one or more S corporations and distributes (or is required to distribute) all its income to its sole income beneficiary. The income beneficiary must make an irrevocable election to have the QSST rules of Sec. 1361(d) apply. The beneficiary is treated as the owner (and, therefore, the shareholder) of the portion of the trust consisting of the S corporation stock. A separate election is made for each S corporation's stock owned by the trust.

ADDITIONAL COMMENT

An unincorporated eligible entity that makes a valid S election is automatically treated as making an election to be treated as a corporation under the check-the-box regulations. Thus, the entity does not have to make two separate elections.

- The corporation must be a domestic corporation or an unincorporated entity that elects to be treated as a corporation under the check-the-box regulations.
- The corporation must not be an "ineligible" corporation.
- The corporation must have only one class of stock.[6]

The first requirement precludes a foreign corporation from making an S election.

A corporation may be an ineligible corporation and thereby violate the second requirement in one of two ways:

- Corporations that maintain a special federal income tax status are not eligible to make an S election. For example, financial institutions (e.g., banks) that use the reserve method to account for bad debts and insurance companies are not eligible.
- Corporations that have elected the special Puerto Rico and U.S. possessions tax credit (Sec. 936) or that had elected the special Domestic International Sales Corporation tax exemption are ineligible to make the S election.

ADDITIONAL COMMENT

Current S corporation stock ownership rules and the approval of the check-the-box regulations permit great flexibility in creating groups of entities that fit the business needs of their owners.

S corporations can own the stock of a C corporation without any limitation on the percentage of voting power or value held. However, as mentioned earlier, a C corporation cannot own the stock of an S corporation. An S corporation that owns the stock of a C corporation cannot participate in the filing of a consolidated tax return. An S corporation also can own the stock of a **Qualified Subchapter S Subsidiary (QSub)**. A QSub is a domestic corporation that qualifies as an S corporation, is 100% owned by an S corporation, and for which the parent S corporation elects to treat the subsidiary as a QSub. The assets, liabilities, income, deductions, losses, etc. of the QSub are treated as those of its S corporation parent and reported on the parent's tax return.[7]

A corporation that has two classes of stock issued and outstanding has violated the third requirement and cannot be an S corporation. The single class of stock determination is more difficult than it appears at first glance because of the many different financial arrangements that are possible between an S corporation and its shareholders. A corporation is treated as having only one class of stock if all of its outstanding shares of stock possess identical rights to distribution and liquidation proceeds and the corporation has not issued any instrument or obligation, or entered into any arrangement, that is treated as a second class of stock.[8] A second class of stock is not created if the only difference between the two classes of stock pertains to voting rights.[9]

EXAMPLE C:11-2 ▶ Kelly Corporation has two classes of common stock outstanding. The Class A and Class B common stock give the shareholders identical rights and interests in the profits and assets of the corporation. Class A stock has one vote per share. Class B stock is nonvoting. Kelly Corporation is treated as having only one class of stock outstanding and can make an S election. ◀

General Rules. The determination of whether all outstanding shares of stock confer identical rights to distribution and liquidation proceeds is based on the corporate charter, articles of incorporation, bylaws, applicable state law, and binding agreements relating to distribution and liquidation proceeds (i.e., the governing agreements).[10] Treasury Regulations permit certain types of state laws, agreements, distributions, etc., to be disregarded in determining whether all of a corporation's outstanding shares confer identical rights to distribution and liquidation proceeds. These include

- Agreements to purchase stock at the time of death, divorce, disability, or termination of employment
- Distributions made on the basis of the shareholder's varying stock interests during the year
- Distributions that differ in timing (e.g., one shareholder receives a distribution in the current year and a second shareholder receives a similar dollar amount distribution shortly after the beginning of the next tax year)

---

[6] Sec. 1361(b)(1).
[7] Sec. 1361(b)(3).
[8] Reg. Sec. 1.1361-1(l).
[9] Sec. 1361(c)(4).
[10] Reg. Sec. 1.1361-1(l)(2).

Agreements to increase cash or property distributions to shareholders who bear heavier state income tax burdens so as to provide equal after-tax distributions provide unequal distribution and liquidation rights. The unequal distributions probably will cause a second class of stock to be created. However, state laws that require a corporation to pay or withhold state income taxes on behalf of some or all of a corporation's shareholders are disregarded.

Debt Instruments. Debt instruments, corporate obligations, and deferred compensation arrangements, in general, are not treated as a second class of stock. A number of safe harbors exist for characterizing corporate obligations as debt (and not as a second class of stock):[11]

- Unwritten advances from a shareholder that do not exceed $10,000 during the tax year, are treated as debt by the two parties, and are expected to be repaid within a reasonable time
- Obligations that are considered equity under the general tax laws but are owned solely by the shareholders in the same proportion as the corporations's outstanding stock

KEY POINT

If debt instruments satisfy the safe harbor rules, such instruments cannot be construed as equity. However, such debt must have been issued in an S corporation tax year.

In addition, Sec. 1361(c)(5) provides a safe harbor for straight debt instruments so that the debt is not treated as a second class of stock. For debt to qualify under the safe harbor, it must meet the following requirements if issued while an S election is in effect:

- The debt must represent an unconditional promise to pay a certain sum of money on a specified date or on demand.
- The interest rate and interest payment dates must not be contingent on profits, the borrower's discretion, or similar factors.[12]
- The debt must not be convertible directly or indirectly into stock.
- The creditor must be an individual, estate, or trust eligible to be an S corporation shareholder, or a nonindividual creditor actively and regularly engaged in the business of lending money.[13]

The safe harbor rules can apply to debt even if the debt otherwise would be considered a second class of stock under case law or other IRC provisions. An obligation that originally qualifies as straight debt may no longer qualify if it is materially modified so that it no longer satisfies the safe harbor or is transferred to a third party who is not an eligible shareholder.[14]

Election of S Corporation Status

OBJECTIVE 3

Explain how a corporation elects, revokes, or terminates S corporation status

The S election exempts a corporation from all taxes imposed by Chapter 1 of the Internal Revenue Code (Secs. 1-1399) except for the following:

- Sec. 1374 built-in gains tax
- Sec. 1375 excess net passive income tax
- Sec. 1363(d) LIFO recapture tax

This rule exempts the S corporation from the regular income tax, accumulated earnings tax, the personal holding company tax, and the corporate alternative minimum tax for all tax years the election remains in effect.

[11] Reg. Sec. 1.1361-1(l)(4). An exception applies to debt instruments, corporate obligations, and deferred compensation arrangements that are treated as stock under the general principles of the federal tax law where the principal purpose for the debt instrument, etc., is to circumvent the distribution or liquidation proceeds rights provided for by the outstanding stock or to circumvent the 100-shareholder limit.

[12] That the interest rate depends on the prime rate or a similar factor not related to the debtor corporation will not disqualify the instrument from coming under the safe harbor rules. If the interest being paid is unreasonably high, an appropriate portion may be treated as a payment of something other than interest.

[13] Sec. 1361(c)(5).

[14] Reg. Sec. 1.1361-1(l)(5)(ii) and (iii).

The S election affects the shareholders in three ways:

- Shareholders report their pro rata share of the S corporation's ordinary income or loss as well as any separately stated items.
- Shareholders treat most distributions as a nontaxable recovery of their stock investments.
- Shareholders' stock bases are adjusted for the shareholders' ratable share of ordinary income or loss and any separately stated items.

MAKING THE ELECTION

Only small business corporations can make the S election.[15] For a small business corporation to make a valid S election, the corporation must file a timely election (Form 2553), and all the corporation's shareholders must consent to the election. Existing corporations can make a timely S election at any time during the tax year preceding the year for which the election is to be effective or on or before the fifteenth day of the third month of the year for which the election is to be effective.

For a new corporation, the S election can be made at any time on or before the fifteenth day of the third month of its initial tax year. A new corporation's initial tax year begins with the first day the corporation has shareholders, acquires assets, or begins business.

If the corporation makes the S election during the first 2½ months of the tax year for which the election is first to be effective, the corporation also must meet all the small business corporation requirements on each day of the tax year preceding and including the election date. If the corporation fails to satisfy this requirement, the election becomes effective in the corporation's next tax year.

The tax law, however, provides some relief for improper elections. First, if the corporation misses the deadline for making the S corporation election, the IRS can treat the election as timely made if the IRS determines that the corporation had reasonable cause for making the late election. Second, if the election was ineffective because the corporation inadvertently failed to qualify as a small business corporation or because it inadvertently failed to obtain shareholder consents (see below), the IRS nevertheless can honor the election if the corporation and shareholders take steps to correct the deficiency within a reasonable period of time.[16]

EXAMPLE C:11-3 ▶ Wilco Corporation, a calendar year taxpayer, has been in existence for several years. Wilco wants to be treated as an S corporation for 2016 and subsequent years. The corporation can make the election any time during 2015 or from January 1 through March 15, 2016. If the corporation makes the election after March 15, 2016, it becomes effective in 2017. However, if Wilco can show reasonable cause for making the late election, the IRS may allow the election to be effective for 2016. ◀

SELF-STUDY QUESTION

Would the answer to Example C:11-3 change if Wilco is a member of an affiliated group through January 15, 2016?

ANSWER

Yes. Because Wilco is an ineligible corporation for a portion of the 2½-month period of 2016, an S election would not be effective until January 1, 2017.

Consent of Shareholders. Each person who is a shareholder on the election date must consent to the election. The consent is binding on the current tax year and all future tax years. No additional consents are required of shareholders who acquire the stock between the election date and its effective date or at any subsequent date.

Section 1362(b)(2) imposes a special rule on the shareholders when the corporation makes an election after the beginning of the tax year for which it is to be effective. Each shareholder who owned stock during any portion of the year preceding the election date, and who is not a shareholder on the election date, also must consent to the election.

EXAMPLE C:11-4 ▶ Sara and Harry own all of Kraft Corporation's stock. Sara sells all her Kraft stock to Lisa on February 10. The next day Kraft makes an S election. For the election to apply in the current year, Sara, Harry, and Lisa must consent to the election. If Sara refuses to consent, the election will not be effective until next year. ◀

[15] Election rules are in Sec. 1362.

[16] IRS spells out detailed procedures for relief in Rev. Proc. 97-48, 1997-2 C.B. 521, Rev. Proc. 2003-43, 2003-23 C.B. 998, Rev. Proc. 2004-48, 2004-2 C.B. 172, Rev. Proc. 2007-62, 2007-41, C.B. 786, and Rev. Proc. 2013-30, 2013-36 I.R.B. 173.

Each tenant (whether or not husband and wife) must consent to the S election if the shareholders own the stock as tenants in common, joint tenants, or tenants in the entirety. If the shareholders own the S corporation stock as community property, each person having a community property interest must consent to the election. If the shareholder is a minor, either the minor or the minor's legal representative (e.g., a natural parent or legal guardian) can make the consent.

Topic Review C:11-1 summarizes the S corporation requirements and procedures for making the S election.

TERMINATION OF THE ELECTION

Once made, the S election remains in effect until the corporation either revokes the election or terminates the election because it ceases to meet the small business corporation requirements. The following discussion examines each action and outlines the requirements for making a new S election following a termination.[17]

Revocation of the Election. A corporation can revoke its S election in any tax year as long as it meets the requirements regarding shareholder consent and timeliness. Shareholders owning more than one-half the corporation's stock (including nonvoting stock) on the day the corporation makes the revocation must consent to the revocation. A revocation made on or before the fifteenth day of the third month of the tax year is effective on the first day of that tax year. A revocation made after the first 2½ months of the tax year takes effect on the first day of the next tax year. An exception permits the S corporation to select a prospective date for the revocation to be effective. The prospective date can be the date the corporation makes the revocation or any subsequent date.

TOPIC REVIEW C:11-1

S Corporation Requirements and Election Procedures

REQUIREMENTS

Shareholder-related:

1. The corporation may have no more than 100 shareholders. Family members and their estates count as one shareholder.
2. All shareholders must be individuals, estates, certain kinds of trusts, or certain kinds of tax-exempt organizations. Eligible trusts include grantor trusts, voting trusts, testamentary trusts, beneficiary-controlled trusts, qualified Subchapter S trusts, qualified retirement plan trusts, and small business trusts.
3. All the individual shareholders must be U.S. citizens or resident aliens.

Corporation-related:

1. The corporation must be a domestic corporation or an unincorporated entity. An unincorporated entity that makes an S election is automatically treated as having elected to be taxed as a domestic corporation under the check-the-box regulations.
2. The corporation must not be an ineligible corporation (e.g., an ineligible bank or other financial institution, an insurance company, or a foreign corporation).
3. The corporation must have only one class of stock issued and outstanding. Differences in voting rights are ignored.

MAKING THE ELECTION

1. The corporation can make the S election any time during the tax year preceding the year for which the election is effective or on or before the fifteenth day of the third month of the tax year for which the election is effective. Late elections are effective with the next tax year unless the corporation obtains IRS relief for reasonable cause.
2. Each shareholder who owns stock on the date the corporation makes the election must consent to the election. If the corporation makes the election after the beginning of the tax year, each person who was a shareholder during the portion of the tax year preceding the election also must consent to the election.

[17] Termination and revocation rules are in Sec. 1362.

EXAMPLE C:11-5 ▶ Adobe Corporation, a calendar year taxpayer, has been an S corporation for several years. However, the corporation has become quite profitable, and management feels that it would be advantageous to make a public stock offering to obtain additional capital during 2016. Adobe can revoke its S election any time on or before March 15, 2016, making the revocation effective on January 1, 2016. If the corporation revokes the election after March 15, 2016, it takes effect January 1, 2017. In either case, the corporation may specify a prospective 2016 effective date as long as the date occurs on or after the date it makes the revocation. ◀

TAX STRATEGY TIP

When it is difficult to obtain the majority shareholder vote necessary for revocation, consideration should be given to purposely triggering a termination event.

Termination of the Election. The S election terminates if the corporation fails one or more of the small business corporation requirements any time after the election's effective date. The termination generally occurs on the day of the terminating event. Events that can terminate the election include

- Exceeding the 100-shareholder limit
- Having an ineligible shareholder own some of the stock
- Creating a second class of stock
- Attaining a prohibited tax status
- Selecting an improper tax year
- Failing the passive investment income test for three consecutive years

The passive investment income test applies annually. It terminates the S election if more than 25% of the corporation's gross receipts are passive investment income for each of three consecutive tax years *and* the corporation has Subchapter C earnings and profits (E&P) at the end of each of the three consecutive tax years. If the corporation meets these conditions for three consecutive tax years, the election terminates on the first day of the next (fourth) tax year.

Passive investment income includes royalties, rents,[18] dividends, interest, annuities, and gains from the sale or exchange of stocks and securities. Treasury Regulations hold that passive investment income excludes income derived from the active conduct of a trade or business. Subchapter C E&P includes only earnings that accrued in tax years in which an S election was not in effect (i.e., the corporation was taxed under the C corporation rules).

EXAMPLE C:11-6 ▶ Shareholders formed Silver Corporation in the current year, and the corporation promptly made an S election. Silver can earn an unlimited amount of passive income during a tax year without any fear of losing its S corporation status or being subject to the Sec. 1375 tax on excess net passive income because it has never been a C corporation and thus has no Subchapter C E&P. However, if a C corporation containing E&P merged into Silver, Silver would then have potential exposure to the passive income rules. (See page C:11-16 for a discussion of the Sec. 1375 tax.) ◀

HISTORICAL NOTE

Previously, a termination was deemed effective on the first day of the tax year in which the terminating event occurred. To stop potential abuse, Congress changed the rule so that an S election terminates on the day of the terminating event.

Allocation of Income. A terminating event occurring at some time other than the first day of the tax year creates an S termination year. The **S termination year** is divided into an S short year and C short year. The **S short year** begins on the first day of the tax year and ends on the day preceding the termination date. The **C short year** begins on the termination date and continues through the last day of the corporation's tax year.

EXAMPLE C:11-7 ▶ Dixon Corporation has been an S corporation for several years. Paula and Frank each own one-half of Dixon's stock. Paula sells one-half of her Dixon stock to Eagle Corporation on July 1. The sale terminates the S election on July 1 because Eagle is an ineligible shareholder. Assuming Dixon is a calendar year taxpayer, the S short year runs from January 1 through June 30. The C short year runs from July 1 through December 31. ◀

[18] Regulation Sec. 1.1362-2(c)(5)(ii)(B)(2) excludes from rents payments received for the use or occupancy of property if the corporation provides significant services or incurs substantial costs in the rental business. See page C:11-37 for additional explanations of the significant services and substantial costs definitions.

TAX STRATEGY TIP

Income or loss can be allocated in the termination year under either of two methods. Careful consideration should be given to the possible tax advantages of a daily allocation versus an actual closing of the books. See Tax Planning Considerations for further details.

ADDITIONAL COMMENT

To use an actual closing of the books to allocate Dixon's income or loss in Example C:11-7, Eagle must consent. Due to the consequences of such an election, the method of allocation should be considered in negotiating the Dixon stock sale.

The S corporation's shareholders report the S short year income according to the normal reporting rules described below. The C corporation reports the income earned during the C short year and calculates its C short year income tax liability on an annualized basis (see Chapter C:3). The S short year and C short year returns are due on the due date for the corporation's tax return for the tax year had the termination not occurred (including any extensions).

An S corporation can use either of two rules to allocate the termination year's income between the S short year and the C short year. The general rule of Sec. 1362(e)(2) allocates the ordinary income or loss and the separately stated items between the S short year and C short year based on the number of days in each year. A special election under Sec. 1362(e)(3) permits an allocation that accords with the corporation's normal tax accounting rules if all persons who were shareholders at any time during the S short year and all persons who are shareholders on the first day of the C short year consent to the election. The corporation cannot use a daily allocation when an S termination year occurs and, during such year, sales or exchanges of 50% or more of the corporation's outstanding stock occur. In such a case, the corporation must use its normal accounting rules to make the allocation.

Inadvertent Termination. Special rules permit the corporation to continue its S election if an inadvertent termination occurs by its ceasing to be a small business corporation or by its failing the passive investment income test for three consecutive years. If such a termination occurs, the S corporation or its shareholders must take the necessary steps, within a reasonable time period after discovering the event creating the termination, to restore the corporation's small business status. If the IRS determines that the termination was inadvertent, the corporation and all persons owning stock during the termination period must agree to make the adjustments necessary to report the income for this period as if the S election had been in effect continuously.[19]

EXAMPLE C:11-8 ► Shareholders formed Frye Corporation in 2012 and operated it as a C corporation during that year. Frye made an S election in 2013. During 2012, the corporation incorrectly computed its E&P and believed that no Subchapter C E&P existed for its only pre–S corporation tax year. From 2013 through 2015, Frye earned large amounts of passive income but did not pay the Sec. 1375 excess net passive income tax or worry about terminating its election because it thought it had no accumulated E&P from 2012. Upon auditing Frye's tax returns, the IRS finds that Subchapter C E&P, in fact, did exist from 2012 and terminates the S election effective on January 1, 2016. If the corporation distributes the E&P and the shareholders report the dividend income, the IRS probably will treat the occurrence as an inadvertent termination and not revoke the election. ◄

The IRS also can grant relief for inadvertent terminations of the election to treat a subsidiary as a Qualified Subchapter S Subsidiary (QSub). For example, a parent S corporation might inadvertently transfer shares of a QSub to another person, thereby violating the 100% ownership requirement. If the S corporation takes the necessary steps to correct the inadvertent transfer, the IRS can grant relief, thereby allowing the election to remain in effect.

Other IRS Waivers. The IRS not only can waive a termination it deems to be inadvertent, it also can validate certain invalid elections. Validation of an invalid election can occur when the election failed to meet the basic S corporation requirements of Sec. 1361 or failed to provide the necessary shareholder consents. The IRS also can exercise this authority in situations where a corporation never filed an election. In addition, the IRS can treat a late S election as being timely filed if the IRS determines that reasonable cause

[19] Regulation Sec. 1.1362-4(b) holds that a termination will be inadvertent if the terminating event was not reasonably within the control of the corporation and was not part of a plan to terminate the election or if it took place without the corporation's knowledge and reasonable safeguards were in place to prevent the event from occurring.

existed for failing to make a timely election and the corporation meets certain other requirements.[20]

New Election Following a Termination. A corporation that revokes or terminates its S election must wait five tax years before making a new election.[21] This delay applies unless the IRS consents to an earlier reelection. Regulation Sec. 1.1362-5(a) indicates that permission for an early reelection can occur (1) when more than 50% of the corporation's stock is owned by persons who did not own stock on the termination date or (2) when the event causing the termination was not reasonably within the control of the corporation or the shareholders having a substantial interest in the corporation *and* was not part of a plan to terminate the election involving the corporation or such shareholders.

EXAMPLE C:11-9 ▶ Terri owned Vector Corporation, a calendar year taxpayer that has been an S corporation for ten years. In January of last year, Terri sold all the Vector stock to Michelle with payments to be made over a five-year period. Two years after the sale, Michelle fails to make the necessary payments, and Terri repossesses the stock. During the time Michelle held the stock, Vector revoked its S election. Vector should immediately apply for reelection of S status because a more than 50% ownership change occurred since the revocation date. ◀

Avoiding Termination of an S Election. Termination of an S election potentially can increase corporate or shareholder taxes. The S corporation's owners, management, and tax advisor need to understand the various events that can cause the termination of the S election. Some steps shareholders can take to prevent an untimely termination include the following:

- Monitor all transfers of S corporation stock. Make certain the purchaser or transferee of the stock is not an ineligible shareholder (e.g., corporation, partnership, or nonresident alien) or that the total number of shareholders does not exceed 100 (e.g., an excess shareholder resulting from creation of a joint interest).
- Establish procedures for the S corporation to purchase the stock of deceased shareholders to avoid the stock being acquired by a trust that is ineligible to be a shareholder.
- Establish restrictions on the transferability of the S corporation stock by having shareholders enter into a stock purchase agreement. Such an agreement could provide that the stock cannot be transferred without the prior consent of all other shareholders

WHAT WOULD YOU DO IN THIS SITUATION?

Harry Baker formed Xeno Corporation on January 4, 2013. The corporation filed a valid S corporation election on January 19, 2013, to be in effect for 2013. Harry, the corporation's sole shareholder, consented to the election. The corporation had business ties to Mexico, and to strengthen these ties, Harry sold 25% of his Xeno shares to Pedro Gonzales on February 10, 2014. Pedro is one of Harry's business associates and is a citizen and resident of Mexico. Harry continued to operate Xeno as an S corporation throughout 2014. Early in March 2015, Harry became aware that, by selling stock to an ineligible shareholder, he may have jeopardized the corporation's S election. Thus, Harry immediately contacted Pedro and persuaded Pedro to sell his Xeno shares back to him (Harry). Harry hires you as his tax advisor on December 17, 2015, at which time you learn about the sale and repurchase of the Xeno shares. However, Harry tells you not to worry because, by buying back the shares, he already has rectified the situation, and thus the IRS need not be told about the transfers. How do you advise Harry on this matter?

[20] See footnote 16.

[21] *Termination* includes both revocation of the S election and loss of the election because one or more of the small business corporation requirements were not met.

and, if the necessary consent cannot be obtained, the corporation will repurchase the stock at a specified price (e.g., at book value).

- Monitor the passive income earned by an S corporation that previously had been a C corporation for one or more years. Make certain the passive income requirement is not failed for three consecutive years by reducing the level of passive income or by distributing the Subchapter C E&P.

S CORPORATION OPERATIONS

OBJECTIVE 4

Classify an S corporation's ordinary and separately stated items, and calculate special S corporation taxes

S corporations make the same accounting period and accounting method elections that a C corporation makes. Each year, the S corporation must compute and report to the IRS and to its shareholders its ordinary income or loss and its separately stated items. The special S corporation rules are explained below.

TAXABLE YEAR

Section 1378(a) requires that the S corporation's taxable year be a permitted year, defined as

- A tax year ending on December 31 (including a 52–53 week year)
- Any fiscal year for which the corporation establishes a business purpose[22]

Section 1378(b) specifically notes that income deferral for the shareholders is not a necessary business purpose. An S corporation that adopts a fiscal year coinciding with its natural business year has satisfied the business purpose requirement. The natural business year for an S corporation depends on the type of business conducted. When a trade or business has nonpeak and peak periods of business, the natural business year is considered to end at, or soon after, the close of the peak business period. A business whose income is steady throughout the year, does not have a natural business year.[23]

EXAMPLE C:11-10 ▶ Sable Corporation, an S corporation, operates a ski resort and reports $1 million of gross receipts for each of its last three tax years. If at least $250,000 (25% of gross receipts) of the receipts occurred in February and March for each of the three consecutive years, Sable can adopt, or change to, or continue to use a natural business year ending March 31.[24] ◀

An S corporation's adoption of, or a change to, a fiscal year that is an ownership tax year also is permitted. An ownership tax year is the same tax year used by shareholders owning more than 50% of the corporation's outstanding stock. The 50% requirement must be met on the first day of the tax year to which the change relates. Failure to meet the 50% ownership requirement on the first day of any later tax year requires a change to a calendar year or other approved fiscal year. S corporations also can adopt or change to a fiscal year for which it obtains IRS approval, based on the facts and circumstances of the situation.[25]

ADDITIONAL COMMENT

The requirement that all S corporations adopt calendar years (with March 15 return due dates) caused a hardship for tax return preparers. Section 444 is a compromise provision that allows a fiscal year for filing purposes, but it mandates a special payment of the deferred taxes.

Section 444 permits an S corporation to elect a fiscal year other than a permitted year. The fiscal year elected under Sec. 444 must have a deferral period of three months or less (e.g., a September 30 or later fiscal year-end for an S corporation otherwise required to use a calendar year). An S corporation that changes its tax year can elect to use a new fiscal year under Sec. 444 only if the deferral period is no longer than the shorter of three months or the deferral period of the tax year being changed.[26] A Sec. 444 election is not required of an S corporation that satisfies the business purpose exception.

---

22 Some S corporations use a "grandfathered" fiscal year, which is a fiscal year for which IRS approval was obtained after June 30, 1974. Excluded are fiscal years that result in an income deferral of three months or less.

23 Rev. Procs. 2002-39, 2002-1 C.B. 1046, and 2006-46, 2006-2 C.B. 859.

24 See Rev. Proc. 2006-46, 2006-2 C.B. 859, for an explanation of the 25% test.

25 Regulation Sec. 1.1378-1 and Rev. Proc. 2006-46, 2006-2 C.B. 859, explain the procedures for an S corporation adopting a fiscal year or changing the tax year of a new or existing S corporation. Rev. Rul. 87-57, 1987-2 C.B. 117, examines eight situations concerning whether the tax year is a permitted year.

26 Special Sec. 444 transitional rules for 1986 permitted many S corporations to retain a previously adopted fiscal year (e.g., January 31) even though the deferral period is longer than three months.

S corporations that elect a fiscal year under Sec. 444 must make required payments under Sec. 7519, which approximate the deferral benefit of the fiscal year. Revocation or termination of the S election also terminates the Sec. 444 election unless the corporation becomes a personal service corporation. Termination of the Sec. 444 election permits the S corporation to obtain a refund of prior Sec. 7519 payments.

Topic Review C:11-2 summarizes the alternative tax years available to an S corporation.

ACCOUNTING METHOD ELECTIONS

As with a partnership, an S corporation makes accounting method elections independent of accounting method elections made by its shareholders. Three elections generally reserved for the S corporation's shareholders are as follows:

- Section 617 election relating to deduction and recapture of mining exploration expenditures
- Section 901 election to take a credit for foreign income taxes[27]

ORDINARY INCOME OR LOSS AND SEPARATELY STATED ITEMS

S corporations are treated much like partnerships and thus report both an ordinary income or loss amount and a series of separately stated items. Ordinary income or loss is the net of income and deductions other than the separately stated items described in the next paragraph.

KEY POINT

S corporations are much like partnerships in their method of reporting income and losses. Both are pass-through entities that provide K-1s to their owners with their respective shares of income and loss items.

The S corporation's separately stated items are the same ones that apply in partnership taxation under Sec. 702(a), related Treasury Regulations, and tax return instructions.[28] For example, the following items must be separately stated:

- Net short-term capital gains and losses
- Net long-term capital gains and losses
- Sec. 1231 gains and losses
- Unrecaptured Sec. 1250 gains
- Sec. 179 expense
- Charitable contributions

TOPIC REVIEW C:11-2

Alternative S Corporation Tax Years

Tax Year	Requirements
Calendar year (including certain 52–53 week years)	The permitted tax year unless an exception applies.
Permitted fiscal year:	IRS will grant approval if:
a. Ownership year	The tax year requested is the same as that used by shareholders owing more than 50% of the corporation's outstanding stock. This test must be met on the first day of the year for which approval is requested as well as for each succeeding year.
b. Natural business year	25% or more of the gross receipts for each of the three most recent 12-month periods are in the last two months of the requested tax year.
c. Facts and circumstances year	The corporation establishes a business purpose (other than an ownership year or natural business year) using the facts and circumstances of the situation.
Nonpermitted fiscal year	A Sec. 444 election permits the S corporation to use an otherwise nonpermitted tax year if the deferral period is three months or less and the corporation makes the necessary required payments.

[27] Secs. 1363(c).

[28] Sec. 1366(a).

- Dividends and interest income[29]
- Taxes paid or accrued to a foreign country or to a U.S. possession
- Tax-exempt or partially tax-exempt interest
- Investment income and expenses
- Any other item provided by Treasury Regulations and tax form instructions

For a comprehensive list of separately stated items, see Form 1120S, Schedule K included in Appendix B.

Section 1366(b) requires that the character of any separately stated item be determined as if the item were (1) realized directly by the shareholder from the same source from which it was realized by the corporation or (2) incurred by the shareholder in the same manner as it was incurred by the corporation. Thus, the character of an income, gain, deduction, loss, or credit item does not change merely because the item passes through to the shareholders.

Deductions that cannot be Claimed. S corporations also have several deductions that it cannot claim, including

- The 70%, 80%, or 100% dividends-received deduction (because dividends pass through to the S corporation's shareholders)
- The U.S. production activities deduction (because that deduction passes through to the S corporation's shareholders)
- The same deductions disallowed to a partnership under Sec. 703(a)(2) (e.g., personal and dependency exemptions, additional itemized deductions for individuals, taxes paid or accrued to a foreign country or to a U.S. possession, charitable contributions, oil and gas depletion, and NOL carrybacks and carryforwards).[30]

Similarity to C Corporation Treatment. S corporations are treated as corporations for certain tax matters. For example, an S corporation can elect to amortize its organizational expenditures under Sec. 248 (after deducting up to $5,000). Also, the 20% reduction in certain tax preference benefits under Sec. 291 applies to an S corporation if the corporation was a C corporation in any of its three preceding tax years.[31]

ADDITIONAL COMMENT

The 20-year carryover period continues to run on C corporation NOLS even during subsequent S corporation years.

Carryovers and Carrybacks When Status Changes. Some S corporations may operate as C corporations during a period of years that either precede the making of an S election or follow the termination of an S election. No carryovers or carrybacks that originate in a C corporation tax year can carry to an S corporation tax year other than carryovers that can be used to offset the built-in gains tax (see pages C:11-16 through C:11-18). Similarly, no carryovers or carrybacks created in an S corporation tax year can carry to a C corporation tax year.[32] Losses from an S corporation tax year pass through to the shareholder and, if greater than the shareholder's income for the year, can create an NOL carryover or carryback for the shareholder.

---

[29] Partnerships are permitted to have C corporations as owners of partnership interests. Thus, dividends eligible for the dividends-received deduction also are separately stated. Such is not the case with an S corporation, which cannot have a corporate shareholder.

[30] Sec. 1363(b)(2).

[31] Secs. 1363(b)(3) and (4).

[32] Sec. 1371(b).

U.S. PRODUCTION ACTIVITIES DEDUCTION

Chapter C:3 describes the C corporation version of the U.S. production activities deduction, whereby the deduction equals 9% times the lesser of (1) qualified production activities income for the year or (2) taxable income before the U.S. production activities deduction. Individuals use a modified form of AGI instead of taxable income for this computation. The deduction, however, cannot exceed 50% of the employer's W-2 wages allocable to U.S. production activities for the year. In the case of an S corporation, the deduction applies at the shareholder level, so the S corporation must report each shareholder's share of qualified production activities income on the shareholder's Schedule K-1. For the 50% salary limitation, each shareholder is allocated his or her share of the S corporation's W-2 wages.

SPECIAL S CORPORATION TAXES

The S corporation is subject to three special taxes: the excess net passive income tax, the built-in gains tax, and the LIFO recapture tax. Each of these taxes is explained below.

Excess Net Passive Income Tax. The **excess net passive income (or Sec. 1375) tax** applies when an S corporation has passive investment income for the tax year that exceeds 25% of its gross receipts and, at the close of the tax year, the S corporation has Subchapter C E&P. The excess net passive income tax equals the S corporation's excess net passive income times the highest corporate tax rate (35% in 2014).[33]

The **excess net passive income** is determined as follows:

$$\text{Excess net passive income} = \text{Net passive income} \times \frac{\text{Passive investment income} - 25\% \text{ of gross receipts}}{\text{Passive investment income}}$$

KEY POINT

The excess net passive income tax is of concern to a former C corporation that has accumulated E&P. A corporation that always has been an S corporation will not have a passive income problem.

The excess net passive income is limited to the corporation's taxable income, which is defined as a C corporation's taxable income except with no reduction for the NOL deduction or the dividends-received deduction. Net passive income equals passive investment income minus any deductions directly related to its production. Passive investment income excludes income derived from the active conduct of a trade or business.[34]

EXAMPLE C:11-11 ▶ Paoli Corporation, an S corporation, reports the following results for the current year:

Service (nonpassive) income	$35,000
Dividend income	37,000
Interest income	28,000
Passive income-related expenses	10,000
Other expenses	25,000

At the end of this year, Paoli's E&P from its prior C corporation tax years amounts to $60,000. Paoli's excess net passive income is determined as follows:

$$\$33{,}846 = (\$65{,}000 - \$10{,}000) \times \frac{\$65{,}000 - (0.25 \times \$100{,}000)}{\$65{,}000}$$

The excess net passive income tax is $11,846 ($33,846 × 0.35). The special tax reduces (on a pro rata basis) the dividend income and interest income items that pass through to the shareholders. The S election is not terminated at the end of the current year unless Paoli also was subject to the tax in the prior two tax years. ◀

TAX STRATEGY TIP

A former C corporation can avoid the Sec. 1375 tax (and the possibility of having its S election terminated) by electing to distribute its Subchapter C E&P. See Tax Planning Considerations for further details.

Built-in Gains Tax. A second corporate level tax may apply to gains recognized by an S corporation that formerly was a C corporation. This tax, called the **built-in gains (or Sec. 1374) tax**, applies to any income or gain the corporation would have included in

[33] Passive investment income and Subchapter C E&P for this purpose have the same definition here as given on page C:11-10.

[34] Reg. Sec. 1.1362-2(c)(5). Also, Reg. Sec. 1.1375-1(f), Ex. (2) indicates that passive income subject to the Sec. 1375 tax includes municipal bond interest that otherwise is exempt from the federal income tax.

ADDITIONAL COMMENT

A special rule provides reduced recognition periods for tax years beginning in 2009 through 2014. As an example, for 2011 through 2014, a calendar year S corporation recognizes no built-in gains tax if the fifth year of the recognition period precedes the applicable year.

gross income while a C corporation had the corporation used the accrual method of accounting (known as a **built-in gain**) and that the corporation reports during the ten-year period beginning on the date the S election took effect (known as the recognition period). **Built-in losses** are any deductions or losses the corporation would have deducted while a C corporation had the corporation used the accrual method of accounting and that the corporation reports during the ten-year period beginning on the date the S election took effect. Built-in gains and losses also include the differences between the FMVs and adjusted bases of assets held at the time the S election takes effect. Built-in losses reduce the amount of recognized built-in gains in determining the built-in gains tax liability.

Congress enacted this tax to prevent taxpayers from avoiding the corporate level tax by making an S election before distributing or selling its assets. The built-in gains tax applies to S corporation tax years beginning after December 31, 1986, where the S corporation was formerly a C corporation and made the current S election after December 31, 1986.

EXAMPLE C:11-12 ▶ Theta Corporation, a calendar year taxpayer, incorporated 12 years ago and operated as a C corporation through the end of last year. On February 4 of the current year, Theta filed an S election that was effective for the current year and later tax years. Theta is subject to the built-in gains tax for ten years starting with January 1 of the current year. ◀

The Sec. 1374 tax is determined by using the following four-step calculation:

STEP 1: Determine the corporation's net recognized built-in gain for the tax year.

STEP 2: Reduce the net recognized built-in gain from Step 1 (but not below zero) by any NOL or capital loss carryovers from prior C corporation tax years.

STEP 3: Compute a tentative tax by multiplying the amount determined in Step 2 by the highest corporate tax rate (35% in 2015).

STEP 4: Reduce the tax determined in Step 3 (but not below zero) by the general business credit and minimum tax credit carryovers from any prior C corporation tax years and by the nonhighway use of gasoline and other fuels credit.

TAX STRATEGY TIP

An S corporation with NOL, capital loss, general business credit, and minimum tax credit carryovers from C corporation years can use these carryovers to reduce the effect of the built-in gains tax. Both NOL and capital loss carryforwards reduce the amount of recognized built-in gain taxed under Sec. 1374. The general business and minimum tax credit carryforwards reduce the actual built-in gains tax.

A recognized built-in gain or loss is any gain or loss recognized on an asset disposition during the ten-year recognition period unless the S corporation can establish that it did not hold the asset on the first day of the first tax year to which the S election applies. A recognized built-in gain cannot exceed the excess of a property's FMV over its adjusted basis on the first day of the ten-year recognition period. Dispositions include sales or exchanges and other events, including the collection of accounts receivable by a cash basis taxpayer, collection of an installment sale obligation, and the completion of a long-term contract by a taxpayer using the completed contract method.[35]

PRACTICAL APPLICATION

The application of the Sec. 1374 tax requires detailed records, which enable the taxpayer to track the built-in gain assets and determine when the corporation recognizes these gains.

Built-in losses include not only losses originating from a disposition of property, but also any deductions claimed during the ten-year recognition period that are attributable to periods before the first S corporation tax year. A recognized built-in loss cannot exceed the excess of a property's adjusted basis over its FMV on the first day of the ten-year recognition period. Built-in losses, however, do not include any loss, deduction, or carryover originating from the disposition of an asset acquired before or during the recognition period where the principal purpose of such acquisition was avoiding the Sec. 1374 tax.

The net recognized built-in gain for a tax year is limited to the smaller of:

- The excess of (1) the net unrealized built-in gain (i.e., excess of the FMV of the S corporation's assets at the beginning of its first tax year for which the S election is in effect over their total adjusted basis on such date) over (2) the total net recognized built-in gain for prior tax years beginning in the ten-year recognition period.[36]

---

[35] Income and gains potentially can be taxed under both the excess net passive income (Sec. 1375) and built-in gains (Sec. 1374) taxes. Any such income or gain is fully taxed under the Sec. 1374 rules. The portion of the income or gain taxed under the Sec. 1374 tax is exempt from the Sec. 1375 tax.

[36] The recognition period can be extended beyond ten years if property having a carryover basis is acquired in a tax-free transaction (e.g., a tax-free reorganization) from a C corporation. For such property, the ten-year recognition period begins on the date the S corporation acquired the property.

- The S corporation's taxable income as if it were a C corporation but with no dividends-received deduction or NOL deduction allowed.

If the net of the recognized built-in gains and losses exceeds the corporation's taxable income and the corporation made the S election after March 30, 1988, the excess built-in gain carries over to the next tax year, where it may be subject to the Sec. 1374 built-in gains tax in the carryover year. The built-in gain carryover consists of a ratable share of each of the income categories (e.g., ordinary income or capital gains) making up the net recognized built-in gain for the tax year.

The built-in gains tax passes through to the shareholders as if it were a loss. The loss must be allocated proportionately among the net recognized built-in gains that resulted in the tax being imposed.

EXAMPLE C:11-13 ▶ Assume the same facts as in Example C:11-12 and that Theta Corporation uses the accrual method of accounting. Theta owns the following assets on January 1 of the current year:

Assets	*Adjusted Basis*	*FMV*
Cash	$ 10,000	$ 10,000
Marketable securities	39,000	45,000
Accounts receivable	60,000	60,000
Inventory (FIFO)	60,000	75,000
Building	27,000	44,000
Land	10,000	26,000
Machinery and equipment[a]	74,000	140,000
Total	$280,000	$400,000

[a] $50,000 of the gain is subject to recapture under Sec. 1245.

ETHICAL POINT

A C corporation that has substantially appreciated assets and wants to make an S election should obtain an appraisal of its assets on or about the first day of the S election period. The S corporation's tax accountant must make sure the appraiser does not assign an artificially low value to these assets to minimize the potential built-in gains tax burden.

During the current year, Theta collects $58,000 of accounts receivable and declares $2,000 uncollectible. It sells the FIFO inventory at a $25,000 profit in the first quarter, replacing the sold inventory with new inventory. It also sells two machines during the current year. One machine, having an $18,000 FMV and an $11,000 adjusted basis on January 1, produced a $7,000 gain (Sec. 1245 recapture income) on September 2. A second machine, having a $15,000 FMV and a $19,000 adjusted basis on January 1, produced a $4,000 loss on March 16.

- Theta recognizes no built-in gain or loss on collecting the receivables because it is an accrual method taxpayer. The $2,000 uncollectible debt is not a built-in loss because the loss arose after January 1. It is deductible as part of the ordinary income or loss calculation.
- Of the $25,000 inventory profit, $15,000 ($75,000 − $60,000) is a built-in gain taxed under Sec. 1374. Theta includes the entire $25,000 profit in ordinary income or loss.
- Theta recognizes a $7,000 built-in gain ($18,000 − $11,000) and a $4,000 ($15,000 − $19,000) built-in loss on the sale of the two machines. The $7,000 gain is ordinary income due to Sec. 1245 recapture and becomes part of Theta's S corporation ordinary income or loss. The $4,000 Sec. 1231 loss passes through separately to the shareholders.

In total, an $18,000 ($15,000 + $7,000 − $4,000) net recognized built-in gain is taxed under Sec. 1374, subject to the taxable income ceiling. Assuming C corporation taxable income (with no NOL deduction or dividends-received deduction) is at least $18,000, the built-in gains tax is $6,300 ($18,000 × 0.35). The entire tax amount reduces the shareholder's ordinary income from the inventory and machinery sales. ◀

REAL-WORLD EXAMPLE

The special S corporation taxes account for only a small amount of federal revenues. For example, collections on the built-in gains and excess net passive income taxes are less than 0.5% of total C corporation tax revenues.

LIFO Recapture Tax. If a C corporation using the LIFO inventory method makes an S election, Sec. 1363(d)(3) requires the corporation to include its LIFO recapture amount in gross income for its last C corporation tax year. The LIFO recapture amount is the excess of the inventory's basis for tax purposes under the FIFO method over its basis under the LIFO method at the close of the final C corporation tax year. Any tax increase incurred in the final C corporation tax year is payable in four annual installments, on or before the due date for the final C corporation tax return and on or before the due date for the first three S corporation tax returns. The S corporation's inventory basis is increased by the LIFO recapture amount included in gross income.

EXAMPLE C:11-14 ► Taylor Corporation, a calendar year C corporation since its inception in 2003, made an S election on December 21, 2015, effective for its 2016 tax year. Taylor has used the LIFO inventory method for a number of years. Its LIFO inventory has a $400,000 adjusted basis, a $650,000 FIFO inventory value, and an $800,000 FMV. Taylor's LIFO recapture amount is $250,000 ($650,000 − $400,000). Taylor includes this amount in gross income reported on its 2015 corporate tax return. Assuming a 34% corporate tax, Taylor's increased tax liability is $85,000 (0.34 × $250,000), of which $21,250 (0.25 × $85,000) is due with Taylor's 2015 C corporation tax return. An additional $21,250 is due with the 2016 through 2018 S corporation tax returns. Taylor increases the basis of its inventory by the $250,000 LIFO recapture amount. ◄

STOP & THINK

Question: Former C corporations that are now treated as S corporations are subject to three corporate level taxes—the **LIFO recapture tax**, the built-in gains tax, and the excess net passive income tax. Why did Congress enact these three taxes?

Solution: Prior to enacting the LIFO recapture tax, Congress debated making the conversion of a C corporation into an S corporation a taxable event subject to the corporate liquidation rules. The corporation would have recognized all gains and losses at the time of conversion. As a compromise, only LIFO users are subject to an "automatic" tax when conversion occurs, and this tax applies only to the LIFO recapture amount and not all inventory appreciation. The built-in gains tax applies only when the corporation sells or exchanges assets during its first ten years after the S election. Assets not sold or exchanged during this time period escape the tax. The excess net passive income tax encourages S corporations to distribute their accumulated E&P. No tax is imposed, however, if the corporation keeps its passive income below the 25% of gross receipts threshold. Thus, former C corporations and their shareholders generally are better off under the current system than had Congress mandated corporate liquidation treatment.

TAXATION OF THE SHAREHOLDER

OBJECTIVE 5

Allocate an S corporation's ordinary and separately stated items to its shareholders and apply loss limitation rules

INCOME ALLOCATION PROCEDURES

An S corporation's shareholders must report their pro rata share of the ordinary income or loss and separately stated items for the S corporation's tax year that ends with or within the shareholder's tax year.[37] Each shareholder's pro rata share of these items is determined by

1. Allocating an equal portion to each day in the tax year (by dividing the amount of the item by the number of days in the S corporation's tax year)
2. Allocating an equal portion of the daily amount to each share of stock outstanding on each day (by dividing the daily amount for the item by the number of shares of stock outstanding on a particular day)
3. Totaling the daily allocations for each share of stock
4. Totaling the amounts allocated for each share of stock held by the shareholder

TYPICAL MISCONCEPTION

An S corporation's income or loss is allocated basically the same as a partnership's except that a partnership may have the added flexibility of making certain special allocations under Sec. 704(b).

These allocation rules are known as the "per day/per share" method. Special allocations (such as those possible under the partnership tax rules) of the ordinary income or loss and separately stated items are not permitted.

If a sale of the S corporation stock occurs during the year, the transferor reports the earnings allocated to the transferred shares through the day of the transfer.[38] The transferee reports his or her share of the earnings from the day after the transfer date through the end of the tax year.

[37] Sec. 1366(a). If the shareholder dies during the S corporation's tax year, the income earned during the portion of the tax year preceding death is reported on the shareholder's tax return. Income for the period the estate holds the S corporation stock is reported on the estate's fiduciary tax return.

[38] Reg. Sec. 1.1377-1(a)(2)(ii). Also see examples under Reg. Sec. 1.1377-1(c).

EXAMPLE C:11-15 ▶ Fox Corporation is an S corporation owned equally by Arnie and Bonnie during all of the current year (assume not a leap year). During this year, Fox reports ordinary income of $146,000 and a long-term capital gain of $36,500. Arnie and Bonnie each report $73,000 (0.50 × $146,000) of ordinary income and $18,250 (0.50 × $36,500) of long-term capital gain. ◀

EXAMPLE C:11-16 ▶ Assume the same facts as in Example C:11-15, except Bonnie sells one-half of her shares to Clay on March 31 of the current year (the 90th day of Fox's tax year). Arnie reports the same ordinary income and long-term capital gain from his investment. Bonnie and Clay report ordinary income and long-term capital gain as follows:

Ordinary Income

$$\text{Bonnie: } \left(\$146{,}000 \times \frac{1}{2} \times \frac{90}{365}\right) + \left(\$146{,}000 \times \frac{1}{4} \times \frac{275}{365}\right) = \$45{,}500$$

$$\text{Clay: } \$146{,}000 \times \frac{1}{4} \times \frac{275}{365} = \underline{27{,}500}$$

$$\text{Total} \quad \underline{\underline{\$73{,}000}}$$

Long-Term Capital Gain

$$\text{Bonnie: } \left(\$36{,}500 \times \frac{1}{2} \times \frac{90}{365}\right) + \left(\$36{,}500 \times \frac{1}{4} \times \frac{275}{365}\right) = \$11{,}375$$

$$\text{Clay: } \$36{,}500 \times \frac{1}{4} \times \frac{275}{365} = \underline{6{,}875}$$

$$\text{Total} \quad \underline{\underline{\$18{,}250}}$$ ◀

KEY POINT

Shareholders of an S corporation need to be aware that when they dispose of their stock, they have the option of having income or loss determined by an actual closing of the books rather than an allocation on a daily basis.

A special election is available for allocating the ordinary income or loss and separately stated items when the shareholder's interest in the S corporation terminates or is substantially reduced during the tax year. Under this election, the income is allocated according to the accounting methods used by the S corporation (instead of on a daily basis). The election divides the S corporation's tax year into two parts ending on

- The day the shareholder's interest in the corporation terminates
- The last day of the S corporation's tax year

The corporation can make this election only if all affected shareholders agree to the election.[39] Affected shareholders include the shareholder whose interest terminated and all shareholders who received S corporation shares during the year. The Tax Planning Considerations section of this chapter explores this election in greater detail.

LOSS AND DEDUCTION PASS-THROUGH TO SHAREHOLDERS

The S corporation's ordinary loss and separately stated loss and deduction items pass through to the shareholders at the end of the corporation's tax year. The shareholders report these items in their tax year in which the S corporation's tax year ends.

Allocation of the Loss. Under the rules outlined above, allocation of the loss also occurs on a daily basis. Thus, shareholders receive an allocation of ordinary loss and separately stated items even if they own the stock for only a portion of the year. If ordinary loss and other separately stated loss and deduction pass-through items exceed the shareholder's income, the excess may create an NOL for the shareholder and result in a carryback or carryover at the shareholder level.

EXAMPLE C:11-17 ▶ Kauai Corporation, an S corporation, reports a $73,000 ordinary loss during the current year (not a leap year). At the beginning of the currrent year, Edward and Frank own equally all of Kauai's stock. On June 30 of the current year (the 181st day of Kauai's tax year), Frank gives

39 Sec. 1377(a)(2).

one-fourth of his stock to his son George. Edward is allocated \$36,500 (\$73,000 × 0.50) of ordinary loss. Frank and George are allocated ordinary losses as follows:

Frank:	$\left(\$73{,}000 \times \frac{1}{2} \times \frac{181}{365}\right)$	+ $\left(\$73{,}000 \times \frac{3}{8} \times \frac{184}{365}\right)$	=	\$31,900
George:	$\$73{,}000 \times \frac{1}{8} \times \frac{184}{365}$		=	4,600
	Total			\$36,500

All three shareholders can deduct these losses on their individual tax returns subject to the loss limitations described below. ◀

REAL-WORLD EXAMPLE

A U.S. Supreme Court case held that discharge of indebtedness income excluded from gross income under Sec. 108 nevertheless is a pass-through item that increases the shareholders' stock bases, thereby allowing loss pass-through items to be deducted by the shareholders. *Gitlitz et al. v. Comm.* 87 AFTR 2d 2001-417, 2001-1 USTC ¶50,147 (USSC, 2001). A subsequent tax act, however, disallowed the pass-through and stock basis increase for debt cancellations. This situation is a good example of Congress "overruling" the Supreme Court with its legislative power.

Shareholder Loss Limitations. Each shareholder's deduction for his or her share of the ordinary loss and the separately stated loss and deduction items is limited to the sum of the adjusted basis for his or her S corporation stock plus the adjusted basis of any indebtedness owed *directly* by the S corporation to the shareholder. Thus, a shareholder must account for stock basis and debt basis. Unlike the partnership taxation rules, however, a shareholder cannot increase his or her stock basis by a ratable share of the general S corporation liabilities.[40]

In determining the stock basis limitation for losses, the shareholder makes the following positive and negative adjustments:[41]

- Increase stock basis for any capital contributions during the year
- Increase stock basis for ordinary income and separately stated income or gain items
- Decrease stock basis for distributions not included in the shareholder's income
- Decrease stock basis for nondeductible, noncapital expenditures (unless the shareholder elects to determine the loss limitation without this decrease)

Sequencing the basis reduction for distributions ahead of losses means that distributions reduce the deductibility of S corporation loss and deduction pass-throughs, but losses do not affect the treatment of S corporation distributions.

TAX STRATEGY TIP

Rather than having the corporation borrow money, an S corporation shareholder might consider borrowing money directly from the bank and then lending the loan proceeds to the corporation with the corporation guaranteeing the bank loan. In this way, the shareholder obtains debt basis.

Many S corporations are nothing more than incorporated forms of sole proprietorships or partnerships. As a result, banks and other lending institutions often require one or more shareholders to personally guarantee loans the institutions make to the S corporation. The IRS and courts, however, have held that these guaranteed loans do not create corporate indebtedness to the shareholder. As a result, the shareholder's loss limitation does not increase until the shareholder pays part or all of the corporation's liability or the shareholder executes a note at the bank in full satisfaction of the corporation's liability. Such action by the shareholder converts the guarantee into an indebtedness of the corporation to the shareholder, which increases the shareholder's debt basis and loss limitation.[42]

The adjusted basis of S corporation stock and debt generally is determined as of the last day of the S corporation's tax year. If the shareholder disposes of the S corporation stock before that date, the stock and debt bases are instead determined immediately prior to the disposition.

Loss and deduction pass-through items are allocated to each share of stock and reduce each share's basis. Once the losses and deductions have reduced stock basis to zero, they then reduce the basis of any debt owed by the S corporation to the shareholder.

EXAMPLE C:11-18 ▶ Pat and Bill equally own Tillis Corporation, an S corporation. During the current year, Tillis reports an ordinary loss of \$104,000. Tillis's liabilities at the end of the current year include \$110,000 of accounts payable, \$150,000 of mortgage payable, and a \$20,000 note owed to Bill.

---

40 Sec. 1366(d)(1). Amounts owed by an S corporation to a conduit entity that has the shareholder as an owner or beneficiary will not increase the shareholder's loss limitation.

41 Sec. 1366(d) and Reg. Sec. 1.1366-2(a)(3). Special basis adjustment rules apply to oil and gas depletion.

42 Rev. Ruls. 70-50, 1970-1 C.B. 178; 71-288, 1971-2 C.B. 319; and 75-144, 1975-1 C.B. 277. See also *Estate of Daniel Leavitt v. CIR*, 63 AFTR 2d 89-1437, 89-1 USTC ¶9332 (4th Cir., 1989) among a series of decisions that uphold the IRS's position. However, see *Edward M. Selfe v. U.S.*, 57 AFTR 2d 86-464, 86-1 USTC ¶9115 (11th Cir., 1986) for a transaction where a guarantee was held to increase the shareholder's loss limitation because the transaction was structured so the bank looked primarily to the shareholder instead of the corporation for repayment.

Thus, Bill has a $20,000 debt basis for the amount he loaned to the corporation. Pat and Bill each had a $40,000 adjusted basis in their Tillis stock on January 1. The ordinary loss is allocated equally to Pat and Bill. Pat's $52,000 loss allocation is only partially deductible this year (i.e., up to $40,000) because the loss exceeds his $40,000 stock basis. Bill's $52,000 loss allocation is fully deductible this year because his loss limitation is $60,000 ($40,000 stock basis + $20,000 debt basis). After the loss pass-through, Pat and Bill each have a zero stock basis and Bill has an $8,000 debt basis.[43] ◀

Any loss or deduction pass-through not currently deductible is suspended until the shareholder regains basis in his stock or debt. The carryover period for the loss or deduction item is unlimited.[44] The additional adjusted basis amount can originate from a number of sources, including subsequent profits earned by the S corporation, additional capital contributions or loans made by the shareholder to the corporation, or purchases of additional stock from other shareholders.

EXAMPLE C:11-19 ▶ Assume the same facts as in Example C:11-18 and that Tillis Corporation reports ordinary income of $24,000 next year. Pat and Bill each are allocated $12,000 of ordinary income. This income provides Pat with the necessary $12,000 stock basis to deduct the $12,000 loss carryover. The $12,000 income allocated to Bill restores his debt basis to $20,000 (see footnote 43). ◀

If a limited loss is made up of more than one type of income, the loss limitation is prorated between the different types of losses. For example, if a shareholder has a $6,000 stock basis, a $9,000 ordinary loss pass-through, and a $3,000 long-term capital loss pass-through, $4,500 ($6,000 × $9,000/$12,000) of the allowed loss is ordinary, and $1,500 ($6,000 × $3,000/$12,000) of the allowed loss is a long-term capital loss.

If a shareholder sells his or her S corporation stock still having unused losses due to lack of stock or debt basis, these losses do not transfer to the new shareholder. Instead, the unused losses lapse when the shareholder sells the stock. If the shareholder transfers the S corporation stock to a spouse or former spouse incident to a divorce, however, the suspended losses transfer to the spouse or former spouse. Thus, the spouse or former spouse can deduct the losses when he or she obtains sufficient basis.

Special Shareholder Loss and Deduction Limitations. S corporation shareholders are subject to three special loss and deduction limitations. These limitations may prevent an S corporation's shareholder from using losses or deductions even though the general loss limitation described above does not otherwise apply. Application of the special loss limitations occurs as follows:

KEY POINT

An advantage of an S election is that losses pass through to the shareholders. This advantage, however, is significantly limited by the at-risk and passive activity rules.

- *At-Risk Rules:* The Sec. 465 at-risk rules apply at the shareholder level. Thus, a shareholder can deduct a loss from a particular S corporation activity only to the extent the shareholder is at risk in the S corporation's activity at year-end.
- *Passive Activity Limitation Rules:* Losses and credits from a passive activity offset income earned from that passive activity or other passive activities in the same or subsequent tax year. An S corporation shareholder personally must meet the material participation standard for an activity to avoid the passive activity limitation. The S corporation's material participation in an activity does not allow a passive investor to deduct S corporation losses against his or her salary and other "active" income.
- *Hobby Loss Rules:* S corporation losses are subject to the Sec. 183 hobby loss rules, which limit deductions to the activity's gross income unless the S corporation can establish that it is engaged in the activity for profit.

In addition, various separately stated loss and deduction items are subject to shareholder limitations (e.g., charitable contributions, capital losses, and investment interest expenses), but they are not subject to corporate limitations. Conversely, some separately stated items are subject to corporate limitations but not shareholder limitations (e.g., the 50% nondeductible portion of meal and entertainment expenses).

Post-Termination Loss Carryovers. Loss and deduction carryovers incurred in S corporation tax years can carry over at the shareholder level even though the

[43] See pages C:11-24 through C:11-27 for a detailed discussion of basis adjustments.

[44] Sec. 1366(d)(2). If more than one type of loss or deduction item passes through to the shareholder, the carryover amount is allocated to each of the pass-through items based on their relative amounts.

SELF-STUDY QUESTION

If losses are suspended due to the lack of basis in S corporation stock, do the losses expire when the S election terminates?

ANSWER

No. These loss carryovers may be deducted in the post-termination transition period (usually one year) if the shareholder creates additional stock basis in that period of time.

S election has terminated. Shareholders can deduct these carryovers only in the **post-termination transition period.**[45] The length of the post-termination transition period depends on the event causing the termination. In general, the period begins on the day after the last day of the corporation's final S corporation tax year and ends on the later of one year after the last day or the due date for the final S corporation tax return (including any extensions).

If the S election terminates for a prior tax year as a result of a determination, the period runs for 120 days beginning on the determination date. Section 1377(b)(2) defines a determination as a court decision that becomes final, a closing agreement entered into, a final disposition of a refund claim by the IRS, or an agreement between the corporation and the IRS that the corporation failed to qualify as an S corporation.

The shareholder can deduct the loss carryovers only up to his or her adjusted basis of the stock at the end of the post-termination transition period.[46] Losses that cannot be deducted because of the basis limitation are lost forever. Deducted losses reduce the shareholder's stock basis.

EXAMPLE C:11-20 ▶ Sigma Corporation has been a calendar year S corporation for several years. Helen's stock basis is $45,000. On July 1, 2015, its S election terminates when an ineligible shareholder acquires part of its stock. For the period ended June 30, 2015, Helen is allocated $60,000 of Sigma's ordinary loss. Helen can deduct only $45,000 of this loss because of her Sigma stock basis, which the loss reduces to zero. The $15,000 unused loss carries over to the post-termination transition period, which ends on June 30, 2016, assuming Sigma does not extend the March 15, 2016, due date for the S short -year tax return. Helen must have an adjusted basis for the Sigma stock of at least $15,000 at the close of business on June 30, 2016, to use the loss. Helen should consider making additional capital contributions of at least $15,000 between July 1, 2015, and June 30, 2016, to use the loss. ◀

Topic Review C:11-3 summarizes the rules governing deductibility of S corporation losses and deductions that pass through to the shareholders.

TOPIC REVIEW C:11-3

Deductibility of S Corporation Losses and Deductions

Allocation Process

1. Losses and deductions are allocated based on the number of shares of stock owned by each shareholder on each day of the tax year. Special allocations of losses and deductions are not permitted.
2. Termination of the S election requires the tax year to be divided into two parts. The corporation can elect (with the shareholders' consent) to allocate the loss or deduction according to the corporation's accounting methods. This election also is available when a shareholder's interest in the S corporation terminates.

Loss Limitations

1. Losses and deductions pass through on a per-share basis and are limited to the shareholder's basis in stock and debt. Once the basis for all the shareholder's stock is reduced to zero, the losses reduce the basis of any S corporation indebtedness to the shareholder.
2. Losses and deductions that are not deducted carry over to a tax year in which the shareholder regains stock or debt basis. The time period for the carryover is unlimited. The unused losses lapse if the shareholder transfers the stock to anyone other than a spouse or former spouse incident to a divorce.
3. S corporation shareholders are subject to three special loss limitations:
   - At-risk rules
   - Passive activity limitations
   - Hobby loss rules

   Some separately stated loss and deduction items also are subject to shareholder limitations (e.g., investment interest expense). Other separately stated items are subject to corporate limitations but not shareholder limitations (e.g., the 50% nondeductible portion of meal and entertainment expenses).

[45] Sec. 1366(d)(3). The loss carryovers that carry over include those disallowed by the at-risk rules.

[46] Sec. 1366(d)(3)(B).

FAMILY S CORPORATIONS

Family S corporations have been an important tax planning device. This type of tax planning often involves a high-tax-bracket taxpayer gifting stock to a minor child who generally has little other income. The transfer results in income splitting among family members. The IRS has enjoyed success in litigating cases dealing with intrafamily transfers of S corporation stock when the transferor (usually a parent) retains the economic benefits and control over the stock transferred to the transferee (usually a child).[47] The IRS has attained less success when one family member purchases the stock from another family member at its market value.

ADDITIONAL COMMENT

The advantages of family S corporations have been somewhat curtailed. For example, income from stock of an S corporation gifted to a child under age 18 (and, in some cases, age 18 through 23) is subject to the "kiddie tax," where unearned income exceeding $2,100 (in 2015) is taxed at the parents' marginal tax rate.

The IRS also has the statutory authority to adjust the income, loss, deduction, or credit items allocated to a family member to reflect the value of services rendered or capital provided to the corporation. Section 1366(e) defines family as including spouse, ancestors, lineal descendants, and trusts created for such individuals. This provision permits the reallocation of income to provide for full compensation of a shareholder or nonshareholder for services and capital provided to the corporation. It also reduces the residual income reported by the S corporation and allocated to the shareholders according to their stock ownership. Such a reallocation prevents not only the shifting of income from the family member providing the services or capital to other family members, but also the avoidance of employment taxes. Alternatively, the IRS can determine that the corporation paid too much compensation to a shareholder and reduce that shareholder's salary and increase the residual income allocated based on stock ownership.

EXAMPLE C:11-21 ▶ Harvest Corporation, an S corporation, reports ordinary income of $200,000 after it claims a $20,000 deduction for Sid's salary. Sid and his three children own the Harvest stock equally. Harvest employs none of Sid's three children. The IRS subsequently determines that reasonable compensation for Sid is $80,000. This adjustment increases Sid's salary income and Harvest's compensation deduction by $60,000 ($80,000 − $20,000) and reduces Harvest's ordinary income to $140,000 ($200,000 − $60,000). Each shareholder's ratable share of ordinary income is reduced from $50,000 ($200,000 ÷ 4) to $35,000 ($140,000 ÷ 4). These adjustments have a twofold effect. First, they increase the amount of income allocable to Sid ($80,000 + $35,000 vs. $20,000 + $50,000), where Sid may be in a higher tax bracket than his children. Second, the increased salary increases Sid's employment taxes. Alternatively, if the IRS can prove that the stock transfer to the three children is not a bona fide transfer, all $220,000 of Harvest's income is taxed to Sid—$80,000 as salary and $140,000 as an allocation of ordinary income. ◀

BASIS ADJUSTMENTS

OBJECTIVE 6

Calculate a shareholder's basis in his or her S corporation stock and debt

Shareholder's must adjust their S corporation stock basis annually. In addition, if the S corporation is indebted to the shareholder, he or she may have to adjust the debt basis downward for loss or deduction pass-throughs and upward to reflect restoration of the debt basis when the corporation earns subsequent profits. Each of these adjustments is described below.

BASIS ADJUSTMENTS TO S CORPORATION STOCK

Basis adjustments to the shareholder's stock are made in the following order:[48]

Initial investment (or basis at beginning of tax year)
Plus: Additional capital contributions made during the year
Allocable share of ordinary income
Allocable share of separately stated income and gain items

[47] See, for example, *Gino A. Speca v. CIR*, 47 AFTR 2d 81-468, 80-2 USTC ¶9692 (7th Cir., 1980) and *Henry D. Duarte*, 44 T.C. 193 (1965), where the IRS's position prevailed. See also *Gavin S. Millar*, 1975 PH T.C. Memo ¶75,113, 34 TCM 554, and *Donald O. Kirkpatrick*, 1977 PH T.C. Memo ¶77,281, 36 TCM 1122, where the taxpayers prevailed.

[48] Sec. 1367(a) and Reg. Sec. 1.1367-1(f).

SELF-STUDY QUESTION

Why is the determination of stock basis in an S corporation important?

ANSWER

To determine gain or loss on the sale of the stock, to determine the amount of losses that can be deducted, and to determine the amount of distributions to shareholders that are nontaxable.

Minus: Distributions excluded from the shareholder's gross income
Allocable share of any expense not deductible in determining ordinary income (loss) and not chargeable to the capital account (A shareholder, however, can elect to make this adjustment *after* the two following adjustments.)
Allocable share of ordinary loss
Allocable share of separately stated loss and deduction items

Adjusted basis for stock (but not less than zero)

A shareholder's initial basis for S corporation stock depends on how he or she acquires it. Stock purchased from the corporation or another shareholder takes a cost basis. Stock received as part of a corporate formation takes a substituted basis from the assets transferred. Stock acquired by gift takes the donor's basis (adjusted for gift taxes paid) or FMV (if lower). Stock acquired at death takes its FMV on the decedent's date of death or the alternate valuation date (if elected). The basis of S corporation stock inherited from a deceased shareholder is its FMV minus any corporate income that would have been income in respect of a decedent (see Chapter C:14) if the income had been acquired from the decedent. No basis adjustment occurs when the corporation makes the initial S election.

The basis adjustments to the S corporation stock parallel those made to a partnership interest. The ordinary income and separately stated income and gain items increase the shareholder's basis whether they are taxable, tax-exempt, or receive preferential tax treatment.

EXAMPLE C:11-22 ► Cathy owns Marlo Corporation, an S corporation. At the beginning of the current year, Cathy's adjusted basis in her Marlo stock is $105,000. Marlo reports the following operating results this year:

Ordinary income	$70,000
Municipal bond interest income	15,000
Dividends from domestic corporations	6,000
Long-term capital gain	8,000
Short-term capital loss	17,000

Cathy's adjusted basis in her Marlo stock at year-end is $187,000 ($105,000 + $70,000 + $15,000 + $6,000 + $8,000 − $17,000). ◄

Cathy makes the basis adjustment at the end of the S corporation's tax year, when the results for the entire period are known. Because profits and losses are allocated ratably on a daily basis to all shares held on each day of the tax year, a shareholder's gain or loss realized on the sale of S corporation stock during the tax year is not determinable until the ordinary income or loss and separately stated items allocable to the shares sold are known. Similarly, when S corporation stock becomes worthless during a tax year, the shareholder must make the necessary positive and negative basis adjustments before determining the amount of the worthless security loss.

EXAMPLE C:11-23 ► Mike, Carlos, and Juan equally own Diaz Corporation, an S corporation. Mike's 100 shares of Diaz stock have a $25,000 adjusted basis at the beginning of the current year (not a leap year). Diaz reports ordinary income of $36,500 and municipal bond interest income of $14,600 in the current year. On February 14 of the current year (the 45th day of Diaz's tax year), Mike sells all his Diaz stock for $30,000. Assuming the corporation uses the daily method to allocate the income items, Mike's basis for the Diaz stock is $27,100, determined as follows:

$$\$27{,}100 = \$25{,}000 + \left(\$36{,}500 \times \frac{45}{365} \times \frac{1}{3}\right) + \left(\$14{,}600 \times \frac{45}{365} \times \frac{1}{3}\right)$$

Mike reports a $2,900 ($30,000 − $27,100) gain on the sale. ◄

KEY POINT

Losses first reduce basis in stock and then any amount of debt owed to the shareholder by the S corporation. Subsequent *net* increases in basis are added first to debt and then to stock.

BASIS ADJUSTMENTS TO SHAREHOLDER DEBT

After the shareholder's basis in S corporation stock is reduced to zero, basis in any S corporation indebtedness to the shareholder is reduced (but not below zero) by the remainder of the available loss and deduction items.[49] If a shareholder has more than one loan outstanding at year-end, the basis reduction applies to all the indebtednesses based on the relative adjusted basis of each loan. Ordinary income and separately stated gain or income items allocated to the shareholder in subsequent tax years (net of distributions and losses to the shareholders) first restore debt basis. Once all previous decreases to debt basis are restored, any additional positive basis adjustments increase the shareholder's stock basis.[50]

Repayment of a shareholder indebtedness results in gain recognition to the shareholder if the payment amount exceeds the debt's adjusted basis. If the indebtedness is secured by a note, the difference is a capital gain. If the indebtedness is not secured by a note or other evidence of the indebtedness, the repayment is ordinary income.[51]

EXAMPLE C:11-24 ▶ At the beginning of Year 1, Betty owns one-half the stock of Trailer Corporation, an S corporation. Betty's basis in the Trailer stock is $40,000. Trailer owes Betty $20,000 on January 1, Year 1, evidenced by a note. Thus, Betty has a $20,000 debt basis. During Year 1, Trailer reports an ordinary loss of $100,000 and during Year 2 reports ordinary income of $10,000. Betty's $50,000 loss pass-through from Year 1 first reduces her stock basis from $40,000 to zero. Next, the $10,000 remainder of the loss pass-through reduces Betty's debt basis from $20,000 to $10,000. Betty's $5,000 allocation of Year 2's ordinary income increases her debt basis from $10,000 to $15,000. If the corporation repays the note before the end of Year 2, Betty reports a $5,000 ($20,000 − $15,000) long-term capital gain resulting from the repayment plus $5,000 of ordinary income from Trailer's Year 2 operations. If the debt instead were unsecured (i.e., an advance from the shareholder not secured by a note), the gain would be ordinary income. ◀

? STOP & THINK

Question: The text preceding Example C:11-24 says that ordinary income and separately stated gain or income items (net of losses and distributions) restore debt basis before increasing stock basis; that is, debt is restored first by any net increase. The following rule also applies: total basis for the loss limitation equals (1) stock basis *after* all current year adjustments other than for losses plus (2) debt basis *before* any current year adjustments.

Consider the following situation: Omega Corporation is an S corporation with one shareholder. At the beginning of last year, the shareholder's stock basis was $15,000, and her debt basis was $20,000. Last year, Omega incurred a $45,000 ordinary loss, $35,000 of which the shareholder could deduct and $10,000 of which carries over. The loss affected basis as follows:

	Stock Basis	*Debt Basis*
Basis at beginning of last year	$15,000	$20,000
Ordinary loss last year ($45,000)	(15,000)	(20,000)
Basis at beginning of current year	$ –0–	$ –0–

In the current year, Omega earns $18,000 of ordinary income. What does the shareholder recognize in the current year, and what is the effect on her stock and debt bases? Why is the net increase rule for debt basis restoration beneficial to the shareholder?

Solution: The shareholder recognizes $18,000 of ordinary income and deducts the entire $10,000 loss carryover. Current year basis adjustments are as follows:

	Stock Basis	*Debt Basis*
Balance at beginning of current year	$ –0–	$ –0–
Ordinary income	10,000	8,000
Loss carryover allowed	(10,000)	–0–
Basis at end of current year	$ –0–	$8,000

The net increase approach benefits the shareholder because it allows her to deduct the $10,000 loss carryover in the current year rather than next year. The net increase for debt

---

[49] The shareholder makes no basis reductions to debt repaid before the end of the tax year. Regulation Sec. 1.1367-2(d)(1) holds that restoration occurs immediately before a shareholder repays or disposes of indebtedness during the tax year.

[50] Sec. 1367(b)(2)(B).

[51] Rev. Ruls. 64-162, 1964-1 (Part I) C.B. 304 and 68-537, 1968-2 C.B. 372.

restoration is $8,000 ($18,000 − $10,000), which leaves $10,000 of the $18,000 ordinary income to increase stock basis. This net increase approach to debt restoration allows a stock basis increase sufficient to use the loss carryover. Alternatively, if debt were restored by ordinary income without netting, the debt basis would increase by the entire $18,000, leaving no positive adjustment to the stock basis. This increase to debt basis would not help the shareholder in the current year because debt basis for the loss limitation is the balance before any current year adjustments. Under this hypothetical alternative approach, the shareholder could deduct the loss next year because next year's beginning debt basis would be $18,000. However, the net increase approach is better than the alternative because it allows the shareholder to deduct the loss in the current year.

S CORPORATION DISTRIBUTIONS

OBJECTIVE 7

Determine the taxability of an S corporation's distributions to its shareholders

Two sets of rules apply to S corporation distributions. One applies to S corporations having accumulated E&P. Accumulated E&P may exist if an S corporation was a C corporation in a pre–S election tax year. Another set of distribution rules applies to S corporations that do not have E&P (e.g., a corporation formed after 1982 that makes a timely S election in its initial tax year). These rules are explained below.

CORPORATIONS HAVING NO EARNINGS AND PROFITS

For S corporations with no accumulated E&P, a two-tier rule applies. Distributions are initially nontaxable and reduce the shareholder's stock basis (but not below zero). If the distribution exceeds the shareholder's stock basis, the shareholder treats the excess as a gain from the sale or exchange of the stock. Stock basis for determining excess distributions is that after positive adjustments for ordinary income and separately stated income and gain items but before negative adjustments.[52]

EXAMPLE C:11-25 ▶ Sandy owns 100% of Liberty Corporation, an S corporation. At the beginning of the current year, Sandy's adjusted basis in her Liberty stock (a capital asset) is $20,000, and she has no debt basis. In the current year, Liberty reports ordinary income of $30,000 and a long-term capital loss of $7,000. Liberty makes a $35,000 cash distribution to Sandy on June 15. Sandy's basis for the stock must be adjusted for the ordinary income before determining the taxability of the distribution. Because Sandy's $50,000 ($20,000 + $30,000) adjusted stock basis exceeds the $35,000 distribution, she excludes the entire distribution from her gross income. The distribution reduces her stock basis to $15,000 ($50,000 − $35,000). Because Sandy still has sufficient stock basis, she can deduct the $7,000 capital loss, which further reduces her stock basis to $8,000.

If Liberty instead reports only $5,000 of ordinary income and a $7,000 capital loss, $10,000 of the distribution is taxable. The ordinary income increases the stock's basis to $25,000 ($20,000 + $5,000). Because the distribution exceeds the stock's adjusted basis by $10,000 ($35,000 − $25,000), Sandy recognizes a capital gain on the excess distribution. The distribution not included in Sandy's income ($25,000) reduces her stock basis to zero at year-end. Because the stock basis after the distribution is zero, Sandy cannot deduct the $7,000 capital loss in the current year. She must wait until she regains a positive stock basis (or obtains debt basis by lending money to the corporation). ◀

SELF-STUDY QUESTION

Can distributions that exceed stock basis be nontaxable to the extent of shareholder loans?

ANSWER

No. Although the amount of deductible losses can be increased by the amount of shareholder loans, nontaxable distributions are strictly limited to stock basis. Also, distributions never reduce debt basis.

If an S corporation distributes appreciated property to its shareholders, the S corporation recognizes gain as if it sold the property.[53] The corporation recognizes no loss, however, when it distributes property that has declined in value. The gain recognized on the distribution may be taxed at the corporate level as part of the S corporation's built-in gains or excess net passive income. The gain also becomes part of the S corporation's ordinary income or loss, or is passed through as a separately stated item, depending on the type of

[52] Secs. 1368(b)and (d).

[53] Sec. 311(b).

property distributed and the character of the gain recognized. After this recognition occurs, the distributed property causes no further taxation provided the sum of the money plus the FMV of the noncash property distributed does not exceed the shareholder's stock basis. The shareholder's stock basis is reduced by the FMV of the distribution, and the shareholder takes a FMV basis in the distributed property.

EXAMPLE C:11-26 ▶ Tad owns 100% of Echo Corporation, which always has been an S corporation. Tad's stock basis at the beginning of the current year is $50,000. Echo reports $30,000 of ordinary income for this year (exclusive of the effects of a property distribution to Tad). On December 1, Echo distributes some Cable Corporation stock to Tad. The stock cost $40,000 and has a $100,000 FMV, and Echo has held it as an investment for three years. Echo reports $60,000 ($100,000 − $40,000) of capital gain from distributing the stock. Tad reports $30,000 of ordinary income and $60,000 of long-term capital gain from Echo's current year activities. Tad's stock basis increases to $140,000 ($50,000 + $30,000 + $60,000). The distribution is free of further taxation because the $140,000 stock basis exceeds the $100,000 distribution. The stock basis is $40,000 ($140,000 − $100,000) at year-end. Tad takes a $100,000 FMV basis in the Cable stock. ◀

ADDITIONAL COMMENT

The distribution of appreciated stock in Example C:11-26 produced income to Echo, which passed through to Tad. A similar distribution by a C corporation would result in a double tax by causing income recognition to both Echo and Tad.

CORPORATIONS HAVING ACCUMULATED EARNINGS AND PROFITS

Prior Rules. Under pre-1983 rules, a corporation's undistributed taxable income was taxed to its shareholders as a deemed distribution at year-end. This income accumulated in a **previously taxed income (PTI)** account, which can be a source of S corporation distributions. For simplicity in this text, however, the following discussion assumes that S corporation status occurs after 1982 and thus ignores the implications of PTI.

KEY POINT

The AAA represents the cumulative income and loss recognized in post-1982 S corporation years. To the extent the AAA is positive and sufficient basis exists in the stock, distributions from an S corporation are nontaxable and reduce stock basis.

Current Rules. Under current (post-1982) rules, some S corporations have a post-1982 accumulated E&P balance earned while a C corporation. Part or all of a distribution may be treated as made from this balance. The current rules, however, also require S corporations that have accumulated E&P balances to maintain an **accumulated adjustments account (AAA)** from which they make most of their distributions. The existence of accumulated E&P and AAA balances makes the tax treatment of cash and property distributions somewhat more complicated than do the rules explained in the preceding section.

Money Distributions. For corporations making a post-1982 S election and having an accumulated E&P balance, money distributions come from the two tiers of earnings illustrated in Table C:11-1. The corporation makes distributions from the first tier until it is exhausted. The corporation then makes distributions from the second tier until that tier is used up. Amounts distributed after the two tiers of earnings are exhausted reduce the shareholder's remaining basis in his or her S corporation stock. Any additional amounts distributed once stock basis has been reduced to zero are taxed to the shareholder as a capital gain. The corporation usually maintains these tiers as working paper accounts and not as general ledger accounts.

The AAA is the cumulative total of the ordinary income or loss and separately stated items accumulated for the S period but excluding tax-exempt income and expenses related to its production. The S period is the most recent continuous period during which the corporation has been an S corporation. No tax years beginning before 1983 are included in this period.[54]

The year-end AAA balance is determined as follows:

AAA balance at the beginning of the year
Plus: Ordinary income
Separately stated income and gain items (except for tax-exempt income)

[54] Sec. 1368(e). An S corporation without accumulated E&P need not maintain the AAA to determine the tax effect of its distributions. If an S corporation having no E&P subsequently acquires E&P in a transaction where it assumes tax attributes under Sec. 381(a) (e.g., a merger), the corporation must calculate its AAA at the merger date to determine the tax effects of post-merger distributions. To accomplish this calculation, a firm may need to make calculations back to the original S election date. To reduce this hardship, the IRS, in the Form 1120S instructions, recommends that all S corporations maintain AAA information.

▼ TABLE C:11-1
Source of Money or Property Distributions Made by S Corporations Having Accumulated Earnings and Profits

Tier	Classification	Treatment of Distributions
1	Accumulated adjustments account	Nontaxable[a]
2	Accumulated E&P	Taxable (dividend)
3	Basis of S corporation stock	Nontaxable[a]
4	Excess over stock basis	Taxable (capital gain)

[a] These distributions reduce the basis of the S corporation stock. Although generally nontaxable, gain can be recognized if the amount of money plus the FMV of the noncash property distributed exceeds the shareholder's adjusted basis in the S corporation stock as indicated in Tier 4.

Minus: Distributions made from AAA (see first bullet item below)
Ordinary loss
Separately stated loss and deduction items (except for expenses or losses related to the production of tax-exempt income)
Expenses not deductible in determining ordinary income (loss) and not chargeable to the capital account

AAA balance at the end of the year

Four differences exist between the positive and negative adjustments required for the AAA and the basis calculation for S corporation stock:

- Distributions not included in gross income reduce *stock* basis *before* other negative adjustments. Distributions reduce the AAA *after* other negative adjustments unless the other negative adjustments, when netted against positive adjustments, produce a "net negative adjustment." In this case, positive adjustments increase the AAA and negative adjustments other than distributions reduce the AAA to the extent of the positive adjustments. Then, distributions reduce the AAA before the net negative adjustment, and the net negative adjustment reduces the AAA after the distribution.[55]
- Tax-exempt income does not increase the AAA but increases the basis of S corporation stock.
- Nondeductible expenses that reduce stock basis also reduce the AAA except for expenses related to the production of tax-exempt income and federal income taxes related to a C corporation tax year.
- The AAA balance can be negative (e.g., when the cumulative losses exceed the cumulative profits), but a shareholder's stock basis cannot be less than zero.

TYPICAL MISCONCEPTION
Even though stock basis cannot be less than zero, the AAA can be negative if cumulative losses exceed cumulative profits.

Allocation of the AAA balance to individual distributions occurs at year-end after taking into account current year income and loss items. In general, the AAA balance is allocated ratably to individual distributions within a tax year (other than distributions coming from E&P) based on the amount of money or FMV of noncash property distributed.

[55] Reg. Secs. 1.1367-1(f) and 1.1368-2(a)(5). This ordering for AAA preserves nontaxable treatment for S corporation earnings from prior years distributed in the loss year.

Corporations also maintain an Other Adjustments Account (OAA) if they have accumulated E&P at year-end. The corporation increases this account for tax-exempt income earned and decreases it by expenses incurred in earning the tax-exempt income, distributions out of the OAA, and federal taxes paid by the S corporation that are attributable to C corporation tax years. The effect of creating a separate account for tax-exempt income earned by companies having accumulated E&P is that the AAA is determined by taking into account only the taxable portion of the S corporation's income and any expenses and losses other than those related to the production of the tax-exempt income. Although the corporation reports the OAA balance on page 4 of the Form 1120S, it is not an accumulated earnings account. Municipal bond interest and other forms of tax-exempt income (net of related deductions) become part of the stock basis and thus appear after accumulated E&P in the distribution order. A corporation having an accumulated E&P balance might consider having the tax-exempt income-producing property owned at the shareholder level rather than at the corporate level.

EXAMPLE C:11-27 ▶ Omega Corporation is an S corporation with one shareholder, George. George's stock basis at the beginning of the current year is $22,000. Omega reports the following results for the current year:

Ordinary loss	$10,000
Dividend income	2,000

In addition, at the beginning of the current year, the corporation has a $12,000 AAA balance and a $4,000 accumulated E&P balance. In December of the current year, Omega distributes $7,500 cash to George. Because the ordinary loss and dividend income produce an $8,000 ($2,000 − $10,000) net negative adjustment, the predistribution AAA remains at $12,000 while the $2,000 dividend increases predistribution stock basis. Accordingly, the predistribution balances are as follows:

	Stock Basis	*AAA*	*E&P*
Beginning balances	$22,000	$12,000	$4,000
Dividend income	2,000	2,000	
Partial ordinary loss		(2,000)	
Predistribution balance	$24,000	$12,000	$4,000

Given these predistribution balances, the distribution has the following effects:

	Stock Basis	*AAA*	*E&P*
Predistribution balance	$24,000	$12,000	$4,000
AAA distribution	(7,500)	(7,500)	
Ordinary loss	(10,000)		
Net negative adjustment		(8,000)	
Ending balance	$ 6,500	($3,500)	$4,000

Because the net negative adjustment to the AAA occurs after the distribution, the entire distribution comes out of the AAA, and none comes out of accumulated E&P. Also, the distribution does not exceed the predistribution stock basis. Thus, the entire distribution is nontaxable. ◀

EXAMPLE C:11-28 ▶ Sigma Corporation, an S corporation, reports the following results during the current year:

Ordinary income	$30,000
Long-term capital gain	15,000
Municipal bond interest income	5,000
Dividend from domestic corporation	3,000
Charitable contribution	8,000

Sigma's sole shareholder, Silvia, has a $60,000 stock basis on January 1. On January 1, Sigma has a $40,000 AAA balance, a $27,000 accumulated E&P balance, and a zero OAA balance. Sigma makes $50,000 cash distributions to Silvia, its sole shareholder, on June 1 and December 1. The stock basis, AAA, OAA, and accumulated E&P activity for the year (before any distributions) is summarized as follows:

TYPICAL MISCONCEPTION

If shareholders sell their S corporation stock, the AAA account remains with the S corporation. But if an S election terminates, other than for the post-termination transition period, the AAA disappears.

	Stock Basis	*AAA*	*E&P*	*OAA*
Beginning balance	$ 60,000	$40,000	$27,000	$ -0-
Ordinary income	30,000	30,000		
Long-term capital gain	15,000	15,000		
Municipal bond interest	5,000			5,000
Dividend income	3,000	3,000		
Charitable contribution		(8,000)		
Predistribution balance	$113,000	$80,000	$27,000	$5,000

The $80,000 AAA balance is allocated ratably to each of the distributions as follows:

$$\$40{,}000 = \$50{,}000 \times \frac{\$80{,}000}{\$50{,}000 + \$50{,}000}$$

The charitable contribution does not reduce the predistribution stock basis but does reduce the predistribution AAA because the reduction does not produce a net negative adjustment. Accordingly, $40,000 of each distribution comes out of AAA. This portion of the distribution is nontaxable because the AAA distributions in total are less than the stock's $113,000 predistribution basis. The remaining $10,000 ($50,000 − $40,000) of each distribution comes out of accumulated E&P and is taxable as dividend income. Accumulated E&P is reduced to $7,000 ($27,000 − $20,000) at year-end. The OAA balance reported on Form 1120S is not affected by the distribution because the accumulated E&P has not been exhausted. The stock's basis is $25,000 ($113,000 − $80,000 − $8,000) at year-end because a dividend distribution from accumulated E&P does not reduce its basis, but the charitable contribution does. After adjustment for the distribution, the AAA is zero. The effects of the distribution are summarized below:

	Stock Basis	*AAA*	*E&P*	*OAA*
Predistribution balance	$113,000	$80,000	$27,000	$5,000
AAA distribution	(80,000)	(80,000)		
E&P distribution			(20,000)	
Charitable contribution	(8,000)			
Ending balance	$ 25,000	$ -0-	$ 7,000	$5,000

◀

Property Distributions. Property distributions (other than money) made by an S corporation having accumulated E&P trigger gain recognition according to the general rules described on pages C:11-27 and C:11-28. The FMV of the noncash property distributed reduces AAA.

TAX STRATEGY TIP

If a shareholder has NOL carryforwards that are about to expire, the election to treat distributions as dividend income to the extent of E&P (as opposed to AAA distributions) may make sense.

Distribution Ordering Elections. An S corporation can elect to change the distribution order of E&P and the AAA. Specifically, the S corporation can elect to skip over the AAA in determining the source of a cash or property distribution, in which case distributions will come from accumulated E&P and then AAA. This election permits the S corporation to distribute Subchapter C E&P so as to avoid the excess net passive income tax and termination of the S election. The Tax Planning Considerations section of this chapter contains further discussion of this election.

Post-Termination Transition Period. Nontaxable distributions of money made during the S corporation's post-termination transition period can be made to those shareholders who owned S corporation stock on the termination date. These distributions come first from the former S corporation's AAA balance and then from current and accumulated E&P. The amounts from the AAA are nontaxable and reduce the shareholder's stock basis.[56] The AAA balance disappears when the post-termination period ends. Even though the profits earned during the S election period no longer can be distributed tax-free from the AAA after the post-termination period ends, they still can be distributed tax-free to the extent of the shareholder's stock basis once the corporation

[56] Sec. 1371(e).

TOPIC REVIEW C:11-4

Taxation of S Corporation Income and Distributions

Taxation of Income to the Corporation

1. Unlike with a partnership, special entity level taxes apply to an S corporation.
   a. Built-in gains tax: applicable to the net recognized built-in gain of an S corporation that formerly was a C corporation and that made its S election after December 31, 1986.
   b. Excess net passive income tax: applicable to S corporations that have Subchapter C E&P at year-end and that earn passive investment income exceeding 25% of gross receipts during the tax year.
   c. LIFO recapture tax: imposed when a C corporation that uses the LIFO inventory method in its final C corporation tax year makes an S election.

Allocation of Income to the Shareholders

1. Income and gains are allocated based on the number of shares of stock owned by each shareholder on each day of the tax year.
2. Termination of the S election or termination of the shareholder's interest in the S corporation during the tax year requires the tax year to be divided into two parts. The S corporation can elect to allocate the income or gain according to the general rule in (1) or the accounting methods used by the corporation.

Shareholder Distributions

1. Income and gain allocated to the shareholder increase the basis of the S corporation stock. For any S corporation that does not have an E&P balance, the amount of money plus the FMV of any noncash property distributed is nontaxable provided it does not exceed the shareholder's stock basis, determined before negative adjustments. The corporation recognizes gain (but not loss) when it distributes noncash property. The gain passes through to the shareholders.
2. If the S corporation made the S election after 1982 and has accumulated E&P, two earnings tiers must be maintained: the AAA and accumulated E&P. Distributions come from each tier in succeeding order until the tier is exhausted. Distributions out of accumulated E&P are taxable to the shareholder as dividends. Other distributions are nontaxable unless stock basis is reduced to zero, in which case the shareholder recognizes capital gain on the excess distribution.

distributes its current and accumulated E&P. Any distributions made from current or accumulated E&P and noncash distributions made during the post-termination transition period are taxable.

Topic Review C:11-4 summarizes the taxation of S corporation income and gains that pass through to the shareholders and the treatment of S corporation distributions.

STOP & THINK

Question: Special earnings tracking rules apply to S corporations that formerly were C corporations. Why do we need to have these special rules, which add complexity to the distribution topic?

Solution: Former C corporations that were profitable usually have an accumulated E&P balance when they become an S corporation. These earnings have never been taxed as a dividend to the corporation's shareholders. If separate tracking of the S corporation earnings (AAA) and C corporation earnings (accumulated E&P) did not occur, it would be impossible to determine which cash and property distributions came from S corporation earnings and which ones came from C corporation earnings, thereby frustrating the government's ability to collect taxes on distributed E&P.

Other rules

OBJECTIVE 8

Explain other rules that pertain to S corporations

In addition to the differences discussed above, S corporations differ from C corporations in a number of other ways. As discussed below, these differences include tax preference items and other alternative minimum tax (AMT) adjustments, expenses owed by the S corporation to a shareholder, related party sales and exchanges, and fringe benefits paid by the S corporation to a shareholder-employee.

TAX PREFERENCE ITEMS AND OTHER AMT ADJUSTMENTS

The S corporation is not subject to the corporate AMT. Instead, the S corporation computes and passes through tax preference items contained in Sec. 57(a) to its shareholders. The shareholders then include these tax preference items in their individual AMT calculations. Allocation of the tax preference items occurs on a daily basis unless the corporation makes one of the two special elections to allocate the items based on the corporation's tax accounting methods.

Section 56(a) prescribes a number of adjustments to the tax reporting of certain transactions and occurrences for AMT purposes from that used for income tax purposes. As with tax preference items, these special AMT adjustments pass through to the S corporation's shareholders to be included in their individual AMT calculations.

S corporations do not have to make an adjustment for the difference between adjusted current earnings and preadjustment alternative minimum taxable income that a C corporation makes in calculating its AMT liability. For certain corporations, this difference may make an S election attractive.[57]

TRANSACTIONS INVOLVING SHAREHOLDERS AND OTHER RELATED PARTIES

The Sec. 267(a)(2) related party transaction rules deny a payor a deduction for an expense paid to a related payee when a mismatching of the expense and income items occurs because of differences in accounting methods. A number of related party situations directly involve S corporations. Some of these transactions involve two S corporations or an S corporation and a C corporation where the same shareholders directly or indirectly own more than 50% of the value of each corporation's stock. Section 267(a)(2), for example, prevents an S corporation using the accrual method from currently deducting a year-end expense accrued for an item owed to a second S corporation that uses the cash method when the same shareholders own both corporations. The first S corporation can deduct the expense on the day the second S corporation includes the income in its gross income.

The S corporation, being a pass-through entity, is subject to Sec. 267(e), which extends the Sec. 267(a)(2) related party transaction rules described above to any payment made by the S corporation to *any* person who directly or indirectly owns S corporation stock. This rule prevents the S corporation from deducting a payment to be made to one of its shareholders or to someone who indirectly owns such stock until the payee reports the income. Payments made to the S corporation by a person who directly or indirectly owns S corporation stock are similarly restricted.

EXAMPLE C:11-29 ▶ Vassar Corporation, an S corporation, uses the accrual method of accounting and a calendar tax year. On September 1, Year 1, Vassar borrows $50,000 from Joan, a cash basis taxpayer who owns 10% of the Vassar stock. Joan charges interest at an 8% annual rate. At year-end, Vassar accrues $1,000 of interest expense on the loan. The corporation pays six months of interest (including the $1,000 of accrued interest) to Joan on April 1, Year 2. Vassar cannot deduct the Year 1 accrued interest until it pays the interest in Year 2. ◀

Section 267(a)(1) denies a deduction for losses incurred on the sale or exchange of property directly or indirectly between related parties. The same definition of a related party applies for this purpose as in applying Sec. 267(a)(2) to expense transactions involving an S corporation. Any loss disallowed to the seller on the related party sale or exchange can offset gains realized by the purchaser on a subsequent sale or exchange.

FRINGE BENEFITS PAID TO A SHAREHOLDER-EMPLOYEE

The S corporation is not treated as a corporate taxpayer with respect to many fringe benefits paid to 2% shareholders.[58] Instead, the S corporation is treated the same as a partnership,

---

[57] Sec. 56(g)(6).

[58] Section 1372(b) defines a 2% shareholder as any person who directly or indirectly owns on any day of the S corporation's tax year more than 2% of its outstanding stock or stock possessing more than 2% of its voting power. The Sec. 318 stock attribution rules apply to determine whether the 2% threshold has been exceeded.

TYPICAL MISCONCEPTION

Most fringe benefits provided by a C corporation are deductible to the corporation and nontaxable to the employee. However, fringe benefits paid to a more-than-2% shareholder-employee of an S corporation are in many cases nondeductible unless taxable to the shareholder-employee as compensation.

and a 2% shareholder is treated as a partner of such partnership.[59] Because of this restriction, many fringe benefits paid to a 2% shareholder-employee of an S corporation are deductible by the corporation and taxable to the shareholder unless the benefit is specifically excludible from the shareholder's gross income under the particular fringe benefit provision. Shareholders owning 2% or less of the S corporation stock are treated as ordinary employees.

The special fringe benefit rules apply only to statutory fringe benefits. They do not apply to stock options, qualified retirement plans, and nonqualified deferred compensation. The fringe benefits limited by the more-than-2%-shareholder rule include group term life insurance premiums (Sec. 79), accident and health benefit plan insurance premiums and payments (Secs. 105 and 106), meals and lodging furnished by the employer (Sec. 119), and cafeteria plan benefits (Sec. 125). Fringe benefits that may be excluded by more-than-2%-shareholders include compensation for injuries and sickness (Sec. 104), educational assistance program benefits (Sec. 127), dependent care assistance program benefits (Sec. 129), and certain other fringe benefits (Sec. 132). For purposes of the Sec. 162(l) above-the-line deduction for self-employed taxpayer's health insurance premiums, a more-than-2%-shareholder is deemed to be self-employed.

EXAMPLE C:11-30 ▶ Bill and his wife Cathy each own 50% of Edison Corporation, an S corporation. Edison employs Bill and ten other individuals. All employees receive group term life insurance benefits based on their annual salaries. All employees except Bill can qualify for the Sec. 79 group term life insurance premium exclusion. Bill is treated as a partner and, therefore, does not qualify as an employee. Bill's premiums are taxable to Bill. Nevertheless, Edison can deduct the premiums paid to all its employees, including Bill. Because Bill is treated as self-employed under the 2% shareholder rules, he can deduct a portion of the premiums paid on the health insurance as a "for" AGI deduction under the Sec.162(l) rules applicable to health insurance payments made by all self-employed individuals. ◀

TAX PLANNING CONSIDERATIONS

OBJECTIVE 9

Identify tax planning opportunities for an S corporation and its shareholders

ELECTION TO ALLOCATE INCOME BASED ON THE S CORPORATION'S ACCOUNTING METHODS

As a general rule, the S corporation's ordinary income or loss and separately stated items are allocated based on the amount of stock owned by each shareholder on each day of the S corporation's tax year. A special "closing of books" election allows the income to be allocated based on the S corporation's accounting methods when the S election terminates or when a shareholder terminates or substantially reduces his or her entire interest in the S corporation.[60] The use of the S corporation's tax accounting method to allocate the year's profit or loss can permit income shifting among shareholders.

EXAMPLE C:11-31 ▶ At the beginning of the current year (assume not a leap year), Rod and Dana equally own Apex Corporation, an S corporation. During the current year, Apex reports ordinary income of \$146,000. On March 31 of the current year (the 90th day of Apex's tax year), Dana sells all his Apex stock to Randy. Apex earns \$125,000 of its ordinary income after March 31 of the current year. Rod is allocated \$73,000 (\$146,000 × 0.50) of ordinary income. His income allocation is the same whether the corporation uses the daily allocation method or the special allocation election. In total, Dana and Randy are allocated \$73,000 of ordinary income. Dana and Randy can allocate the ordinary income amount in the following ways:

[59] Sec. 1372(a).

[60] The shareholder, however, still can be a creditor, director, or employee of the corporation. Sections 1362(e) and 1377(a) prevent the daily allocation method from applying to any items resulting from a sale or exchange of 50% or more of the S corporation's stock during an S termination year.

	Daily Allocation	*Closing of Books Election*
Dana:	$\$146{,}000 \times \frac{1}{2} \times \frac{90}{365} = \$18{,}000$	$(\$146{,}000 - \$125{,}000) \times \frac{1}{2} = \$10{,}500$
Randy:	$\$146{,}000 \times \frac{1}{2} \times \frac{275}{365} = \$55{,}000$	$\$125{,}000 \times \frac{1}{2} = \$62{,}500$

The shifting of the $7,500 in income from Dana ($18,000 − $10,500) to Randy ($62,500 − $55,000) under the special election also reduces Dana's adjusted basis for his Apex stock when determining his gain or loss on the sale. The $7,500 difference between the income allocations under the two methods may be a point for negotiation between Dana and Randy, particularly if their marginal tax rates differ. ◀

By electing to use the S corporation's tax accounting method to allocate profits or losses between the C short year and S short year in the termination year, the corporation can shift losses into an S short year where the shareholders obtain an immediate benefit at a marginal tax rate of up to 39.6%, or it can shift profits into a C short year to take advantage of the 15% and 25% marginal corporate tax rates. The C corporation, however, must annualize its short-year income in determining its tax liability.

EXAMPLE C:11-32 ▶ Delta Corporation has been an S corporation for several years using a calendar year as its tax year. The corporation has one shareholder whose marginal tax rate is 33%. Delta's S election terminates on July 1. The S short year includes January 1 through June 30, and the C short year includes July 1 through December 31. Total ordinary income this year is $10,000. If the corporation closes its books on June 30, $40,000 of ordinary loss is allocable to the S short year, and $50,000 of ordinary income is allocable to the C short year. Assuming each month has 30 days, the following income allocations are possible:

Period	*Daily Allocation*	*Closing of Books Election*
S short year	$ 5,000	($40,000)
C short year	5,000	50,000
Total	$10,000	$10,000

With the daily allocation, one-half the income is taxed to the shareholder, and the other half is taxed to the C corporation.[61] The daily allocation method causes the shareholder's tax to be $1,650 ($5,000 × 0.33) on the pass-through income and the C corporation's tax to be $750 ($5,000 × 2 × 0.15 × 0.5) on its annualized income, for a total tax of $2,500. By closing the books, the corporation passes the $40,000 S short year loss through to its shareholder and is taxed on the $50,000 C short year income as a C corporation. This method provides the shareholder with a $13,200 ($40,000 pass-through loss × 0.33) tax savings and causes the C corporation's tax to be $11,125 ($22,250 tax on $100,000 of annualized income × 0.5), for a net tax savings of $2,075 ($13,200 − $11,125). Thus, in this situation, the closing of books method provides the greater overall tax advantage ($2,075 vs. $2,500). ◀

INCREASING THE BENEFITS FROM S CORPORATION LOSSES

At the shareholder level, the deduction for S corporation pass-through losses is limited to the S corporation stock basis plus the basis of debt owed by the S corporation to the shareholder. Pass-through losses exceeding this limitation carry over to a subsequent tax year when the shareholder regains stock or debt basis. If the shareholder expects his or her marginal tax rate to be the same or lower in a carryover tax year, the shareholder should consider either increasing his or her stock basis or loaning additional funds to the corporation before the end of the current tax year. Conversely, if the shareholder never expects the loans to be repaid, he or she should not lend the S corporation additional amounts just to secure an additional tax deduction, which is worth at most 39.6 cents (at 2015 rates) for

61 Section 1362(e)(5)(A) requires calculation of the tax liability for the C short year to be based on the annualized income of the former S corporation (see Chapter C:3 for a discussion of annualization).

each dollar loaned. If the shareholder expects his or her marginal tax rate to be higher in future tax years, the shareholder should consider deferring additional capital contributions or loans until after the end of the current tax year.

EXAMPLE C:11-33 ▶ Nancy owns 100% of Bailey Corporation, an S corporation. Bailey expects a $100,000 ordinary loss in the current year. Nancy's stock basis (before adjustment for the current loss) is $35,000. Bailey also owes Nancy $25,000. Nancy's current marginal tax rate is 33%, but she expects her marginal tax rate to decline to 15% next year. Nancy should consider making $40,000 [$100,000 loss − ($35,000 stock basis + $25,000 debt basis)] of additional capital contributions or loans before the end of the current year to obtain an additional $7,200 [(0.33 − 0.15) × $40,000] of tax benefits from deducting the loss in the current year rather than next year. If Nancy instead expects her marginal tax rates to be 15% in the current year and 33% next year, she can defer $7,200 [(0.33 − 0.15) × $40,000] of tax benefits (less the time value of money for one year) by postponing her capital contributions or loans until next year. Alternatively, Nancy could use the loss carryover to offset profits reported next year. These profits would restore part or all of her debt basis (and possibly increase her stock basis). The stock basis then would be partially or fully offset by the $40,000 loss carryover. ◀

KEY POINT

If an S corporation shareholder has losses that have been suspended due to lack of basis, either contributions to capital or bona fide loans to the corporation will create the necessary basis to use the losses.

The S corporation loss carryover is available only to the shareholder who held the stock when the loss occurred. A shareholder should consider increasing the stock basis to take advantage of the carryover before selling the stock. The purchasing shareholder does not acquire the carryover.

PASSIVE INCOME REQUIREMENTS

The S corporation can earn an unlimited amount of passive income each year without incurring any penalty provided it has no E&P accumulated in a C corporation tax year (known as Subchapter C E&P) at the end of its tax year. Thus, a corporation can make an S election to avoid the personal holding company tax that otherwise might apply to a C corporation's passive income.

S corporations that have operated as C corporations and have accumulated Subchapter C E&P are potentially liable for the excess net passive income tax. In addition, their S election may terminate if the passive investment income exceeds 25% of gross receipts for three consecutive tax years. The S corporation can avoid both of these possible problems by making a special election under Sec. 1368(e)(3) to distribute its entire Subchapter C E&P balance to its shareholders. A corporation that elects to distribute Subchapter C E&P before distributing from its accumulated adjustments account (AAA) can make a second special election to treat part or all of this "distribution" as a deemed dividend, which is deemed distributed to the shareholders and immediately contributed by the shareholders to the corporation on the last day of the corporation's tax year.[62] Such an election requires no cash outlay. The distribution, however, results in a tax cost for the shareholders who pay tax on the resulting deemed dividend income. To the shareholders, the cost of the election can be small if the accumulated E&P balance is insignificant or if the shareholder has a current year NOL (excluding the distribution) or an NOL carryover. The tax cost also could be low given the shareholder's applicable tax rate on dividends. The ultimate long-run benefit, however, may be great because it permits the S corporation to earn an unlimited amount of passive investment income free from corporate taxes in subsequent tax years.

EXAMPLE C:11-34 ▶ Hawaii Corporation incorporated 12 years ago and operated for a number of years as a C corporation, during which time it accumulated $30,000 of E&P. Most of Hawaii's gross income now comes from rentals and interest, constituting passive investment income. Hawaii makes an S election starting in the current year. The excess net passive income tax will apply in the current year if Hawaii's rentals and interest exceed 25% of its gross receipts for the year unless the corporation elects to distribute the accumulated E&P and then distributes the earnings by the end of the currrent year. ◀

[62] Reg. Sec. 1.1368-1(f)(3).

S corporations that earn rental income also can avoid the passive income tax and the possibility of having its election terminated if the corporation renders significant services to the occupant of the space or if the corporation incurs significant costs in the rental business.[63] Whether the corporation performs significant services or incurs substantial costs in the rental business depends on the facts and circumstances including, but not limited to, the number of persons employed to provide the services and the types and amounts of costs and expenses incurred (other than depreciation).

EXAMPLE C:11-35 ▶ Assume the same facts as in Example C:11-34 except Hawaii Corporation provides significant services to its tenants in connection with its rental activities. Because the services are significant, Hawaii has a passive income problem only if its interest income exceeds 25% of its gross receipts. If the 25% threshold is not exceeded, Hawaii can avoid having to distribute its Subchapter C E&P in the current year. ◀

S corporations that experience a passive income problem in two consecutive tax years should carefully monitor their passive income in the next year. If they see that their passive income for the third year will exceed the 25% threshold, they should elect to distribute their accumulated Subchapter C E&P before year-end. This strategy not only will prevent loss of the S election but also will avoid having to pay the Sec. 1375 tax.

COMPLIANCE AND PROCEDURAL CONSIDERATIONS

OBJECTIVE 10

Comply with S corporation procedural and filing requirements

MAKING THE ELECTION

A corporation makes the S election by filing Form 2553 (Election by a Small Business Corporation). Any person authorized to sign the S corporation's tax return under Sec. 6037 can sign the election form. The corporation files Form 2553 with the IRS Service Center designated in the instructions. The IRS can treat a late election as timely made if the corporation can show reasonable cause.[64]

A shareholder can consent to the S election either on Form 2553 or on a separate consent statement signed by the shareholder and attached to the corporation's election form. Regulation Sec. 1.1362-6(b) outlines other information that must be provided with a separate consent. The IRS can grant extensions of time for filing shareholder consents to the S election.[65]

A corporation makes a Sec. 444 election to use a fiscal year on Form 8716, which the corporation must file by the earlier of (1) the fifteenth day of the fifth month following the month that includes the first day of the tax year for which the election will first be effective or (2) the due date for the income tax return resulting from the election.[66] The corporation must attach a copy of Form 8716 to Form 1120S for the first tax year for which the Sec. 444 election is effective. A corporation desiring to make a Sec. 444 election also must state its intention in a statement attached to its S election form (Form 2553).[67]

FILING THE CORPORATE TAX RETURN

All S corporations, whether or not they owe taxes under Secs. 1374 or 1375, must file a tax return if they exist for part or all of the tax year. An S corporation must file its corporate tax return not later than the fifteenth day of the third month following the end of the tax year.[68] The S corporation reports its results on Form 1120S (U.S. Income Tax Return for an S Corporation). A completed S corporation tax return and the facts supporting the return appear in Appendix B. An S corporation is allowed an automatic six-month extension of

---

63 According to Reg. Sec. 1.1362-2(c)(5)(ii)(B)(2), however, significant services are not rendered and substantial costs are not incurred in connection with net leases.

64 Sec. 1362(b)(5). Also see footnote 16.

65 Reg. Sec. 1.1362-6(b)(3)(iii).

66 Temp. Reg. Sec. 1.444-3T(b)(1).

67 Temp. Reg. Sec. 1.444-3T(b)(3).

68 Sec. 6072(b).

time for filing its tax return by filing Form 7004 (Application for Automatic Extension of Time to File Certain Business Income Tax, Information, and Other Returns), also illustrated in Appendix B.[69]

EXAMPLE C:11-36 ▶ Simpson Corporation, an S corporation, uses the calendar year as its tax year. Its tax return generally is due on March 15. Simpson can file Form 7004 and obtain an automatic six-month extension for the return, thereby extending its due date until September 15. ◀

All S corporations that file a tax return must furnish each person who is a shareholder at any time during the tax year with pertinent information from the tax return, usually via Form 1120S, Schedule K-1. The corporation must make the Schedule K-1 available to the shareholder not later than the day on which it files its tax return.[70] An individual shareholder reports the S corporation's pass-through ordinary income or loss and certain passive income or loss items on his or her Form 1040, Schedule E. The shareholder reports most separately stated items on other supporting schedules to Form 1040, as illustrated on the Form 1120S, Schedule K-1 presented in Appendix B.

An S corporation is subject to the same basic three-year statute of limitations that applies to other taxpayers. This three-year limitations period applies for purposes of determining the time period during which

- The corporation remains liable for assessments of the excess net passive income and built-in gains taxes
- The IRS can question the correctness of an S election made for a particular tax year

The limitation period for assessing the income tax liability of an S corporation shareholder (e.g., for an erroneous S corporation loss deduction claimed), however, runs from the date on which the shareholder files his or her return and not from the date the S corporation files its tax return.[71]

If the corporation elects a fiscal year under Sec. 444, it determines the Sec. 7519 required payment on a computation worksheet provided in the instructions for the Form 1120S. The corporation need not make a required payment if the total of such payments for the current year and all preceding years is $500 or less. Amounts equal to or less than the $500 threshold carry over to succeeding years. The required payment is due on or before May 15 regardless of the fiscal year used. The required payment and the computation worksheet must accompany a Form 8752, which also is used to secure a refund of prior Sec. 7519 payments.[72]

ESTIMATED TAX PAYMENTS

S corporations must make estimated tax payments if their estimated tax liability is reasonably expected to be $500 or more.[73] Estimated tax payments are required for the corporate liability attributable to the built-in gains tax (Sec. 1374) and the excess net passive income tax (Sec. 1375). In addition, the S corporation's shareholders must include their income, gain, loss, deduction, and credit pass-through items in their own estimated tax calculations.

The corporate estimated tax payment requirements described for a C corporation in Chapter C:3 also apply to an S corporation's tax liabilities. The required quarterly installment is 25% of the lesser of (1) 100% of the tax shown on the return for the tax year or (2) the sum of 100% of the built-in gains tax shown on the return for the tax year plus 100% of the excess net passive income tax shown on the return for the preceding tax year.

An S corporation cannot use the prior year tax liability exception when determining the required payment to be made with respect to the built-in gains tax. This exception, however, is available with respect to the excess net passive income tax portion of the

---

69 Reg. Sec. 1.6081-3.

70 Sec. 6037(b).

71 *Sheldon B. Bufferd v. CIR*, 71 AFTR 2d 93-573, 93-1 USTC ¶50,038 (USSC, 1993).

72 Temp. Reg. Sec. 1.7519-2T.

73 Estimate tax rules appear in Sec. 6655.

SELF-STUDY QUESTION

Is an S corporation required to make estimated tax payments?

ANSWER

Yes. An S corporation is required to pay estimated taxes if the corporation is subject to built-in gains or excess net passive income taxes. Also, shareholders are required to include their S corporation income, loss, and credit pass-through items in determining their estimated tax payments.

required payment without regard to whether the corporation owed any tax in the prior year. All corporations can use the prior year tax liability exception for the excess net passive income tax whether or not they are "large" corporations under Sec. 6655(d)(2). The annualization election of Sec. 6655(e) also is available when determining the quarterly estimated tax payment amounts. An S corporation's failure to make timely estimated tax payments, or a timely final payment when it files the tax return, will trigger interest and penalties.

The S corporation's shareholders must include their ratable share of ordinary income or loss and separately stated items in determining their estimated tax liability. Such amounts are treated as having been received concurrently by the shareholders throughout the S corporation's tax year. Thus, ordinary income or loss and separately stated items for an S corporation tax year that ends with or within the shareholder's tax year are included in the estimated tax calculation to the extent they are attributable to months in the S corporation tax year that precede the month in which the installment is due.[74]

CONSISTENCY RULES

ADDITIONAL COMMENT

When examining an S corporation, the IRS conducts the audit in a unified proceeding at the corporate level rather than in separate audits of each S corporation shareholder.

Section 6037(c) requires an S corporation shareholder to report on his or her return a Subchapter S item in a manner consistent with the treatment accorded the item on the S corporation's return. A Subchapter S item is any item (e.g., income, gain, deduction, loss, credit, accounting method, or tax year) of an S corporation where the reporting of the item is more appropriately determined at the corporation level than at the shareholder level. A shareholder must notify the IRS of any inconsistency when the corporation has filed a return but the shareholder's treatment on his return is (or may be) inconsistent with the treatment of the item on the corporation return. Failure to do so may result in the imposition of a negligence penalty under Sec. 6662. Any adjustment required to produce consistency with the corporate return is treated as a mathematical or clerical error for penalty calculation purposes. A similar notification also is required when the corporation has not filed a return. If a shareholder receives incorrect information from the S corporation regarding a Subchapter S item, the shareholder's consistent reporting of the item consistently with the information provided by the corporation generally will eliminate the imposition of any penalty.

SAMPLE S CORPORATION TAX RETURN

REAL-WORLD EXAMPLE

In 2013, of the 6.81 million corporate tax returns filed, 67% were S corporations.

A sample S corporation Form 1120S and supporting Schedule K-1 appear in Appendix B, along with the facts supporting the return. Two differences should be noted between the S corporation tax return and a partnership tax return. First, the S corporation tax return provides for the determination of a corporate tax liability and the payment of the special taxes that can be levied on the S corporation. No such items appear in the partnership return. Second, the S corporation return does not require a reconciliation of the shareholders' basis adjustments as occurs on a partnership tax return. Schedule M-1, M-2, and M-3 reconciliations similar to those required of a C corporation are required of an S corporation. Schedule M-1 requires a reconciliation of book income with the income or loss reported on line 23 of Schedule K, which includes not only the ordinary income (loss) amount but also separately stated income and deduction items. For tax years ending on or after December 31, 2006, an S corporation must file Schedule M-3 in lieu of Schedule M-1 if the amount of total assets reported in Schedule L of Form 1120S (Balance Sheet per Books) equals or exceeds $10 million. The S corporation also may file Schedule M-3 voluntarily even if not required to do so. If the corporation files Schedule M-3, in either case, it checks the appropriate box on page 1 of Form 1120S and does not file Schedule M-1. (The sample tax return in Appendix B does not include Schedule M-3.) Schedule M-2 requires a reconciliation of the AAA, OAA, and PTI accounts. (The PTI account pertains to pre-1983 S corporations.) Only S corporations that have an accumulated E&P balance must provide the AAA reconciliation and OAA balance although the IRS recommends that all S corporations maintain AAA and OAA balances.

[74] For example, see Ltr. Rul. 8639008 (June 23, 1986).

Problem Materials

DISCUSSION QUESTIONS

C:11-1 List five advantages and five disadvantages of making an S election. Briefly explain each item.

C:11-2 Julio, age 50, is a U.S. citizen who has a 28% marginal tax rate. He has operated the A&B Automotive Parts Company for a number of years as a C corporation. Last year, A&B reported $200,000 of pre-tax profits, from which it paid $50,000 in salary and $25,000 in dividends to Julio. The corporation expects this year's pre-tax profits to be $300,000. To date, the corporation has created no fringe benefits or pension plans for Julio. Julio asks you to explain whether an S corporation election would reduce his taxes. How do you respond to Julio's inquiry?

C:11-3 Celia, age 30, is leaving a major systems development firm to establish her own firm. She will design computer-based systems for small- and medium-sized businesses. Celia will invest $100,000 in the business. She hopes to operate near her breakeven point during her first year, although a small loss is possible. Profits will build up slowly over the next four years until she is earning $150,000 a year in her fifth year. Celia has heard about S corporations and asks you whether the S corporation form would be advisable for her new business. How do you respond to Celia's inquiry?

C:11-4 Lance and Rodney are contemplating starting a new business to manufacture computer software games. They expect to encounter losses in the initial years. Lance's CPA has talked to them about using an S corporation. Rodney, while reading a business publication, encounters a discussion on limited liability companies (LLCs). The article talks about the advantages of using an LLC instead of an S corporation. How would you respond to their inquiry?

C:11-5 Which of the following classifications make a shareholder ineligible to own stock in an S corporation?
- a. U.S. citizen
- b. Domestic corporation
- c. Partnership where all the partners are U.S. citizens
- d. Estate of a deceased U.S. citizen
- e. Grantor trust created by a U.S. citizen
- f. Nonresident alien individual

C:11-6 Will the following events cause an S election to terminate?
- a. The S corporation earning 100% of its gross receipts in its first tax year from passive sources
- b. The S corporation issuing nonvoting stock that has a dividend preference
- c. The S corporation purchasing 100% of the single class of stock of a second domestic corporation that has conducted business activities for four years
- d. An individual shareholder donating 100 shares of S corporation stock to a charity that is exempt from tax under Sec. 501(c)(3)
- e. The S corporation earning tax-exempt interest income

C:11-7 What is an inadvertent termination? What actions must the S corporation and its shareholders take to correct an inadvertent termination?

C:11-8 After an S corporation revokes or terminates its S election, how long must the corporation wait to make a new election? What circumstances permit an early reelection?

C:11-9 What tax years can a newly created corporation that makes an S election adopt for its first tax year? If a fiscal year is permitted, does it require IRS approval?

C:11-10 At the time Cable Corporation makes its S election, it elects to use a fiscal year based on a Sec. 444 election. What other requirements must Cable satisfy to continue to use its fiscal year election for future tax years?

C:11-11 What are Subchapter C earnings and profits (E&P)? How does the existence of such E&P affect the S corporation's ability to earn passive income?

C:11-12 Explain the procedures for allocating an S corporation's ordinary income or loss to each of the shareholders. What special allocation elections are available?

C:11-13 What limitations apply to the amount of loss pass-through an S corporation shareholder can deduct? What happens to any losses exceeding this limitation? What happens to losses if the shareholder transfers his or her stock?

C:11-14 What actions can an S corporation shareholder take before year-end to increase the amount of the S corporation's losses he or she can deduct in the year they are incurred?

C:11-15 What is a post-termination transition period? What loss carryovers can an S corporation shareholder deduct during this period?

C:11-16 Explain the positive and negative adjustments to the basis of an S corporation shareholder's stock investment and the basis of an S corporation debt owed to the shareholder.

C:11-17 Explain the differences between the tax treatment accorded nonliquidating property distributions made by S corporations and partnerships.

C:11-18 What nonliquidating distributions made by an S corporation are taxable to its shareholders? Tax-free to its shareholders?

C:11-19 What is an accumulated adjustments account (AAA)? What income, gain, loss, and deduction items *do not* affect this account assuming the S corporation has an accumulated E&P balance?

C:11-20 Explain the differences between the way the following items are reported by a C corporation and an S corporation:

a. Ordinary income or loss
b. Dividend income
c. Capital gains and losses
d. Tax-exempt interest income
e. Charitable contributions
f. Nonliquidating property distributions
g. Fringe benefits paid to a shareholder-employee

C:11-21 When is the S corporation's tax return due? What extensions are available for filing the return?

C:11-22 What taxes must an S corporation prepay by making quarterly estimated tax payments? Can a shareholder owning S corporation stock use the corporation's estimated tax payments to reduce the amount of his or her individual estimated tax payments? Explain.

C:11-23 Review the completed C corporation, partnership, and S corporation tax returns presented in Appendix B. List three major tax reporting similarities and three major tax reporting differences in either content or format among the three tax returns.

ISSUE IDENTIFICATION QUESTIONS

C:11-24 Jennelle and Paula are equal partners in the J&P Manufacturing Partnership. The partnership will form J&P Corporation by exchanging the assets and liabilities of the J&P Manufacturing Partnership for all the corporation's stock on September 1 of the current year. The partnership then will liquidate by distributing the J&P Corporation stock equally to Jennelle and Paula. Both shareholders use the calendar year as their tax year and desire that the corporation make an S election. What tax issues should Jennelle and Paula consider with respect to the incorporation?

C:11-25 Williams Corporation has operated as a C corporation for the last seven years. The corporation has assets with a $450,000 adjusted basis and an $800,000 FMV. Liabilities amount to $100,000. Dan Williams, who uses a calendar year as his tax year, owns all the Williams Corporation stock. The corporation uses the accrual method of accounting and a June 30 year-end. Dan's CPA has suggested that he convert the corporation to S corporation status to reduce his total corporate/personal federal income tax liability. Dan would like to complete the conversion on the last day of the corporation's tax year. What tax issues should Dan and his CPA consider with respect to the S election?

C:11-26 Peter owns 50% of Air South Corporation, an air charter service. His S corporation stock basis at beginning of the year is $100,000. Air South has not done well this year and will report an ordinary loss of $375,000. What tax issues should Peter consider with respect to the loss?

C:11-27 Glacier Smokeries has been an S corporation since its inception six years ago. On January 1 of the current year, the corporation's two equal shareholders, Adam and Rodney, had adjusted bases of $175,000 and $225,000, respectively, for their S corporation's stock. The shareholders plan to have the corporation distribute land with a $75,000 adjusted basis and a $300,000 FMV in the current year. The shareholders also expect ordinary income to be $125,000 in the current year. What tax issues should Adam and Rodney consider with respect to the distribution?

PROBLEMS

C:11-28 *Comparison of Entity Forms.* Carl Carson, a single taxpayer, owns 100% of Delta Corporation. During 2015, Delta reports $150,000 of taxable income. Carl reports no income other than that earned from Delta, and Carl claims the standard deduction.

a. What is Delta's income tax liability assuming Carl withdraws none of the earnings from the C corporation? What is Carl's income tax liability? What is the total tax liability for the corporation and its shareholder?

b. Assume that Delta instead distributes $80,000 of its after-tax earnings to Carl as a dividend in the current year. What is the total income tax liability for the C corporation and its shareholder?

c. How would your answer to Part a change if Carl withdrew $80,000 from the business in salary? Assume the corporation pays $6,120 of Social Security taxes on the salary, which it can deduct from the $150,000 taxable income amount in Part a. Carl also pays $6,120 of Social Security taxes on the salary, which he cannot deduct.

d. How would your answers to Parts a–c change if Delta were instead an S corporation?

C:11-29 *Making the Election.* Voyles Corporation, a calendar year taxpayer formed five years ago, desires to make an S election beginning in 2015. Sue and Andrea each own one-half of the Voyles stock.

a. How does Voyles make the S election?

b. When can Voyles file its election form?

c. If in Part b the corporation does not file the election in a timely manner, when will the election take effect?

C:11-30 *Termination of the Election.* Orlando Corporation, a calendar year taxpayer, has been an S corporation for several years. On July 9, 2015, Orlando authorizes a second class of nonvoting preferred stock that pays a 10% annual dividend. The corporation issues the stock to Sid on September 11, 2015, to raise additional equity capital. Sid owns no other Orlando stock.

a. Does Orlando's S election terminate? If so, when is the termination effective?

b. What tax returns must Orlando file for 2015? When are they due?

c. How would your answer to Parts a and b change if instead the second class of stock were nonvoting Class B common stock?

C:11-31 *Revocation of the Election.* Tango Corporation, a calendar year taxpayer, has been an S corporation for several years. Tango's business activities have become very profitable in recent years. On June 16, 2015, its sole shareholder desires to revoke the S election.

a. How does Tango revoke its S election? When does the revocation take effect?

b. Assume Tango files a prospective revocation effective July 1, 2015. What tax returns are required of Tango for 2015? For 2016? When are these returns due?

c. If the corporation makes a new S election after the revocation, when does it take effect?

C:11-32 *Sale of S Corporation Interest.* Peter and his wife, Alice, own all the stock of Galleon Corporation. Galleon made its S election 12 years ago. Peter and Alice sold one-half their Galleon stock to a partnership owned by Rob and Susan (not husband and wife) at the close of business on December 31 of the current year for a $75,000 profit. What are the tax consequences of the sale transaction for Peter and Alice? For the corporation? As Peter and Alice's CPA, do you have any advice for them if all parties would like the S election to continue?

C:11-33 *Selecting a Tax Year.* Indicate in each of the following independent situations whether the taxpayer can accomplish what is proposed. Provide adequate authority for your answer including any special elections that are needed or requirements that must be satisfied. Assume all individuals use the calendar year as their tax year unless otherwise indicated.

a. Will and Carol form Classic Corporation. They want the corporation to adopt a fiscal year ending January 31 as its tax year to provide a maximum deferral for their income. The corporation makes an S election for its initial tax year ending January 31, 2016.

b. Mark and Dennis have owned and operated the Plastic Corporation for several years. Plastic has used a fiscal year ending June 30 since its organization as a C corporation because it conforms to the corporation's natural business year. The corporation makes an S election for its tax year beginning July 1, 2015.

C:11-34 *Passive Income Tax.* Oliver organized North Corporation 15 years ago. The corporation made an S election last year after it accumulated $60,000 of E&P as a C corporation. As of December 31 of the current year, the corporation has distributed none of its accumulated E&P. In the current year, North reports the following results:

Dividends from domestic corporations	$ 60,000
Rental income	100,000
Services income	50,000
Expenses related to rental income	30,000
Expenses related to services income	15,000
Other expenses	5,000

The corporation has not provided significant services nor incurred substantial costs in connection with earning the rental income. The services income is derived from the active conduct of a trade or business.

a. Is North subject to the excess net passive income tax? If so, what is its tax liability?

b. What is the effect of the excess net passive income tax liability on North's pass-throughs of ordinary income and separately stated items?

c. What advice would you give North regarding its activities?

C:11-35 *Built-in Gains Tax.* Theta Corporation formed 15 years ago. In its first year, it elected to use the cash method of accounting and adopted a calendar year as its tax year. It made an S election on August 15 of last year, effective for Theta's current tax year. At the beginning of the current year, Theta had assets with a $600,000 FMV and a $180,000 adjusted basis. During the current year, Theta reports taxable income of $400,000.

- In the current year, Theta collects all $200,000 of accounts receivables outstanding on January 1 of the current year. The receivables had a zero adjusted basis.
- On February 1, Theta sells an automobile for $3,500. The automobile had a $2,000 adjusted basis and a $3,000 FMV on January 1 of the current year. Theta claimed $800 of MACRS depreciation on the automobile in the current year.
- On March 1, Theta sells land (a Sec. 1231 asset) that it held three years in anticipation of building its own office building for a $35,000 gain. The land had a $45,000 FMV and a $25,000 adjusted basis on January 1 of the current year.
- In the current year, Theta paid $125,000 of accounts payable outstanding on January 1 of the current year. All the payables are deductible expenses.

What is the amount of Theta's built-in gains tax liability?

C:11-36 *Determination of Pass-Throughs and Stock Basis Adjustments.* Mike and Nancy are equal shareholders in MN Corporation, an S corporation. The corporation, Mike, and Nancy are calendar year taxpayers. The corporation has been an S corporation during its entire existence and thus has no accumulated E&P. The shareholders have no loans to the corporation. The corporation incurred the following items in the current year:

Sales	$300,000
Cost of goods sold	140,000
Dividends on corporate investments	10,000
Tax-exempt interest income	3,000
Sec. 1245 gain (recapture) on equipment sale	22,000
Sec. 1231 gain on equipment sale	12,000
Long-term capital gain on stock sale	8,000
Long-term capital loss on stock sale	7,000
Short-term capital loss on stock sale	6,000
Depreciation	18,000
Salary to Nancy	20,000
Meals and entertainment expenses	7,800
Interest expense on loans allocable to:	
Business debt	32,000
Stock investments	6,400
Tax-exempt bonds	1,800
Principal payment on business loan	9,000
Charitable contributions	2,000
Distributions to shareholders ($15,000 each)	30,000

a. Compute the S corporation's ordinary income and separately stated items.
b. Show Mike's and Nancy's shares of the items in Part a.
c. Compute Mike's and Nancy's ending stock bases assuming their beginning balances are $100,000 each. When making basis adjustments, apply the adjustments in the order outlined on pages C:11-24 and C:11-25 of the text.

C:11-37 *Allocation of Income to Shareholders.* John owns all the stock of Lucas Corporation, an S corporation. John's basis for the 1,000 shares is $130,000. On June 11 of the current year (assume a non-leap year), John gifts 100 shares of stock to his younger brother Michael, who has been working in the business for one year. Lucas Corporation reports $125,000 of ordinary income for the current year. What amount of income is allocated to John? To Michael?

C:11-38 *Sale of S Corporation Interest.* Al and Ruth each own one-half the stock of Chemical Corporation, an S corporation. During the current year (assume a non-leap year), Chemical earns $15,000 per month of ordinary income. On April 5, Ruth sells her entire stock interest to Patty. The corporation sells a business asset on August 18 and realizes a $75,000 Sec. 1231 gain. What alternatives (if any) exist for allocating Chemical's current year income?

C:11-39 *Allocation of Income to Shareholders.* Toyland Corporation, an S corporation, uses the calendar year as its tax year. Bob, Alice, and Carter own 60, 30, and 10 shares, respectively, of the Toyland stock. Carter's basis for his stock is $26,000 on January 1 of the current year (assume a non-leap year). On June 30, Alice gifted one-half of her stock to Mike. On November 30, Carter sold his stock to Mike for $45,000. Toyland reports the following results for the current year:

Ordinary income	$120,000
Long-term capital loss	10,000
Charitable contributions	6,000

a. What amount of income, loss, or deduction do the four shareholders report (assuming the corporation makes no special allocation election)?
b. What gain or loss does Carter recognize when he sells the Toyland stock?

C:11-40 *Allocation of Income to Shareholders.* Redfern Corporation, a calendar year taxpayer, has been an S corporation for several years. Rod and Kurt each own 50% of Redfern's stock. On July 1 of the current year (assume a non-leap year), Redfern issues additional common stock to Blackfoot Corporation for cash. Rod, Kurt, and Blackfoot each end up owning one-third of Redfern's stock. Redfern reports ordinary income of $125,000 and a short-term capital loss of $15,000 in the current year. Eighty percent of the ordinary income and all the capital loss accrue after Blackfoot purchases its stock. Redfern makes no distributions to its shareholders in the current year. What income and losses do Redfern, Blackfoot, Rod, and Kurt report as a result of the current year's activities?

C:11-41 *Allocation of Income Between Family Members.* Bright Corporation, an S corporation, has been 100% owned by Betty since its creation 12 years ago. The corporation has been profitable in recent years and, in the current year (assume a non-leap year), reports ordinary income of $240,000 after paying Betty a $60,000 salary. On January 1, Betty gifts 15% of her Bright stock to each of her three sons, John, Andrew, and Stephen, hoping they will work in the family business. Betty pays gift taxes on the transfers. The sons are ages 24, 17, and 15 at present and are not currently active in the business. Bright distributes $7,500 in cash to each son and $27,500 in cash to Betty in the current year.
a. What income does Betty, John, Andrew, and Stephen report for the current year as a result of Bright's activities assuming the sons are considered bona fide owners of the stock? How will the income be taxed to the children?
b. Assuming the IRS determines a reasonable salary for Betty to be $120,000, how would your answer to Part a change?
c. How would your answer to Part a change if the sons were not considered bona fide owners of the stock?

C:11-42 *Use of Losses by Shareholders.* Monte and Allie each own 50% of Raider Corporation, an S corporation. Both individuals actively participate in Raider's business. On January 1, Monte and Allie have adjusted bases for their Raider stock of $80,000 and $90,000, respectively. During the current year, Raider reports the following results:

Ordinary loss	$175,000
Tax-exempt interest income	20,000
Long-term capital loss	32,000

Raider's balance sheet at year-end shows the following liabilities: accounts payable, $90,000; mortgage payable, $30,000; and note payable to Allie, $10,000.
a. What income and deductions will Monte and Allie report from Raider's current year activities?
b. What is Monte's stock basis on December 31?
c. What are Allie's stock basis and debt basis on December 31?
d. What loss carryovers are available for Monte and Allie?
e. Explain how the use of the losses in Part a would change if instead Raider were a partnership and Monte and Allie were partners who shared profits, losses, and liabilities equally.

C:11-43 *Use of Loss Carryovers.* Assume the same facts as in Problem C:11-42. Assume further that Raider Corporation reports $75,000 of ordinary income, $20,000 of tax-exempt income, and a $25,000 long-term capital gain in the next year.
a. What income and deductions will Monte and Allie report from next year's activities?
b. What is Monte's stock basis on December 31 of next year?
c. What are Allie's stock basis and note basis on December 31 of next year?
d. What loss carryovers (if any) are available to Monte and Allie?

C:11-44 *Use of Losses by Shareholders.* Tom owns 100% of Hammer Corporation, an S corporation. Tom has a $100,000 stock basis on January 1. Tom actively participates in Hammer's business. Hammer operating results were not good in the current year, with the corporation reporting an ordinary loss of $175,000. The size of the loss required Tom to lend Hammer $50,000 on August 10 of the current year to provide funds needed for operations. The loan is secured by a Hammer Corporation note. Hammer rebounds during the next year and reports ordinary income of $60,000. Hammer repays the $50,000 note on December 15.

a. What amount of Hammer's current year loss can Tom deduct on his income tax return?
b. What is Tom's basis for the Hammer stock and note at the end of the loss year?
c. What income and deductions will Tom report next year from Hammer's activities and the loan repayment?

C:11-45 *S Corporation and Partnership Losses.* In the current year, Harold and Faye form Entity Company by each contributing $50,000 to the company in exchange for a 50% ownership interest. In addition, the company borrows $40,000 from First Bank. In the current year, the company incurs a $110,000 loss from operations.

a. How much of the loss can each shareholder deduct in the current year if Entity is an S Corporation, and what is each shareholder's basis in his or her stock at the end of the year?
b. How much of the loss can each partner deduct in the current year if Entity is a partnership, and what is each partner's basis in his or her partnership interest at the end of the year?

C:11-46 *Allocation of Losses to Shareholders.* Harry and Rita formed Alpha Corporation as an S corporation, with each shareholder contributing $10,000 in exchange for stock. In addition, Rita loaned the corporation $7,000, and the corporation borrowed another $8,000 from the bank. In the current year, the corporation incurred a $26,000 operating loss. In the next year, the corporation will earn $16,000 of operating income.

a. For the current year and next year, determine the pass-through items for each shareholder and each shareholder's stock basis at the end of each year. Also, determine Rita's debt basis at the end of each year.
b. Same as Part a except the corporation also distributes $6,000 cash to each shareholder at the end of next year.
c. Assume the same facts as in Part b and that Alpha is a partnership instead of an S corporation. For the current year and next year, determine the pass-through items for each partner and each partner's basis in his or her partnership interest at the end of each year.

C:11-47 *Post-Termination Loss Use.* Stein Corporation, an S corporation, has 400 shares of stock outstanding. Chuck and Linda own an equal number of these shares, and both actively participate in Stein's business. Chuck and Linda each contributed $60,000 when they organized Stein on September 9 of Year 1. Start-up losses during Year 1 resulted in Stein reporting a $210,000 ordinary loss. Stein's activities have since become profitable, and the corporation voluntarily revokes the S election on March 1 of Year 2, with no prospective revocation date being specified. In Year 2, Stein reports $360,000 of taxable income ($30,000 per month). Stein makes no distributions to its shareholders in either year.

a. What amount of loss can Chuck and Linda deduct in Year 1?
b. What amount of loss do Chuck and Linda carry over to Year 2?
c. If Chuck reported only $5,000 of other business income in Year 1, what happens to the "excess" deductible S corporation losses?
d. What portion of the loss carryover from Part b can Chuck and Linda deduct in Year 2? What happens to any unused portion of the loss?
e. What advice can you offer to Chuck and Linda to enhance their use of the Stein loss?

C:11-48 *Use of Losses by Shareholders.* Tina, a single taxpayer, owns 100% of Rocket Corporation, an S corporation. She has an $80,000 stock basis for her investment on January 1 of the current year (Year 1). During the first 11 months of Year 1, Rocket reports an ordinary loss of $100,000. The corporation expects an additional $20,000 loss for December. Tina earns $295,000 of ordinary income from her other activities in Year 1. She expects her other income to decline to $125,000 in Year 2 and continue at that level in future years. The corporation expects Year 2 losses to be only $20,000. Rocket projects a $35,000 profit for Year 3 and each of the subsequent four years. What advice can you offer Tina about using her Rocket losses and retaining S corporation status in future years? How would your answer change if Tina expected her income from other activities to be $75,000 in Year 1 and $295,000 in Year 2?

C:11-49 *Stock Basis Adjustment.* For each of the following items, indicate whether the item will increase, decrease, or cause no change in the S corporation's ordinary income (loss), AAA, and in the shareholder's stock basis. The corporation was formed four years ago and made its S election two years ago. During the time it was a C corporation, it accumulated $30,000 of E&P. The corporation has not distributed any of this accumulated E&P.

a. Operating profit
b. Dividend income received from domestic corporation
c. Interest income earned on corporate bond held as an investment
d. Life insurance proceeds paid on death of corporate officer
e. Long-term capital gain
f. Sec. 1231 loss
g. Sec. 1245 gain (depreciation recapture)
h. Charitable contributions
i. Fines paid for having overweight trucks
j. Depreciation
k. Pension plan contributions for employees
l. Salary paid to owner
m. Premiums paid on life insurance policy in Part d
n. Distribution of money (but not exceeding current year's earnings)

C:11-50 *Taxability of Distributions.* Tammy organized Sweets Corporation in January of the current year, and the corporation immediately elected to be an S corporation. Tammy, who contributed $40,000 in cash to start the business, owns 100% of the corporation's stock. Sweets' current year results are reported below:

Ordinary income	$36,000
Short-term capital loss	5,000

On July 10, Sweets makes a $10,000 cash distribution to Tammy.

a. What income (if any) do Sweets and Tammy recognize as a result of the distribution?
b. What is Tammy's basis for the Sweets stock on December 31?
c. How would your answers to Parts a and b change if Sweets' distribution were instead $80,000?

C:11-51 *Property Distributions.* George and Martha formed Washington Corporation as an S corporation several years ago. George and Martha each have a 50% interest in the corporation. At the beginning of the current year, their stock bases are $45,000 each. In the current year, the corporation earns $40,000 of ordinary income. In addition, the corporation distributes property to George having a $26,000 FMV and a $40,000 adjusted basis and distributes property to Martha having a $26,000 FMV and a $16,000 adjusted basis.

a. Determine what George and Martha recognize in the current year, and determine their ending stock bases. What bases do George and Martha have in the distributed property?
b. What tax planning disadvantages do you see with these property distributions?
c. How would you answer to Part a change if George and Martha form the Washington Partnership instead of an S corporation?

C:11-52 *Taxability of Distributions.* Curt incorporates Vogel Corporation on January 15 of the current year. Curt makes a $70,000 capital contribution including land having a $12,000 FMV, and Vogel makes a timely S election for this year. Vogel reports $60,000 of ordinary income, $40,000 of Sec. 1231 gain, $5,000 of tax-exempt interest income, and $3,000 of charitable contributions this year. On December 1, Vogel distributes $5,000 cash plus the land contributed by Curt because the corporation no longer needs it in the business. The land, which had a $10,000 basis and a $12,000 FMV when contributed to the corporation in January, has an $18,000 FMV when distributed.

a. What income do Vogel Corporation and Curt report as a result of the distribution?
b. What is Curt's basis in the Vogel stock on December 31?
c. What is Vogel's accumulated adjustments account (AAA) balance on December 31?

C:11-53 *Taxability of Distributions.* Hal organized Stable Corporation five years ago and has continued to own all its stock. The corporation made an S election one year after its incorporation. At the beginning of the current year, Stable reports the following earnings accumulations:

Accumulated adjustments account (AAA)	$85,000
Accumulated E&P	22,000

Hal's basis in his Stable stock on January 1 of the current year is $120,000. During the current year, Stable reports the following results from its operations:

Ordinary income	$30,000
Tax-exempt interest income	15,000
Long-term capital loss	20,000

Stable makes a $65,000 cash distribution to Hal on August 8.

a. What income, gain, or loss (if any) do Stable and Hal recognize as a result of the distribution?

b. What is Hal's basis in the Stable stock on December 31?

c. What are Stable's AAA, E&P, and OAA balances on December 31?

d. How would your answers to Parts a-c change if Stable instead distributed $120,000?

C:11-54 *Taxability of Distributions.* Sigma Corporation, an S corporation with one shareholder, incurred the following items Year 1 and Year 2:

Year 1	
Tax-exempt income	$ 5,000
Ordinary income	30,000
Year 2	
Ordinary loss	($40,000)
Cash distribution	15,000

At the beginning of Year 1, the corporation had AAA and OAA balances of zero and accumulated E&P of $6,000. At the beginning of Year 1, the shareholder had a $10,000 basis in stock and a $12,000 basis in debt he loaned to the corporation.

a. Determine items reported by the shareholder in Year 1 and Year 2.

b. Determine the balances in each corporate account and the shareholder's stock and debt bases at the end of each year.

c. Determine the results if the distribution in Year 2 is $35,000 instead of $15,000.

d. How does the answer to Part c change if, in Year 2, the corporation has an $18,000 long-term capital gain in addition to the $40,000 ordinary loss?

C:11-55 *Taxability of Distributions.* Beta Corporation, an S corporation with one shareholder, incurred the following items:

Year 1	
Ordinary loss	($40,000)
Year 2	
Ordinary income	$27,000
Cash distribution	10,000
Year 3	
Ordinary income	$22,000
Cash distribution	17,000

At the beginning of Year 1, the shareholder's stock basis was $20,000, and her debt basis was $16,000.

a. Assuming the corporation has no accumulated E&P, show items reported by the shareholder in each year, show all basis adjustments to stock and debt, and show the stock and debt bases at the end of each year.

b. Redo Part a for Year 2 and Year 3 assuming ordinary income in Year 2 is $8,000 instead of $27,000.

c. Go back to the original facts and again redo Part a for all years assuming that, at the beginning of Year 1, the corporation had a AAA balance of zero and accumulated E&P of $12,000.

COMPREHENSIVE PROBLEMS

C:11-56 *Comparison of Entity Formations.* Cara, Bob, and Steve want to begin a business on January 1, 2016. The individuals are considering three business forms—C corporation, partnership, and S corporation.

- Cara has investment land with a $36,000 adjusted basis and a $50,000 FMV that she is willing to contribute. The land has a rundown building on it having a $27,000 basis and a $15,000 FMV. Cara has never used the building nor rented it. She would like to get rid of the building. Because she needs cash, Cara will take out a $25,000 mortgage on the property before the formation of the new business and have the new business assume the debt. Cara obtains a 40% interest in the entity.

- Bob will contribute machinery and equipment, which he purchased for his sole proprietorship in January 2010. He paid $100,000 for the equipment and has used the MACRS rules with a half-year convention on this seven-year recovery period property. He did not make a Sec. 179 expensing election for this property, and he elected out of bonus depreciation. The FMV of the machinery and equipment is $39,000. Bob obtains a 39% interest in the entity.
- Steve will contribute cash of $600 and services worth $20,400 for his interest in the business. The services he will contribute include drawing up the necessary legal documentation for the new business and setting up the initial books. Steve obtains a 21% interest in the entity.

To begin operations, the new business plans to borrow $50,000 on a recourse basis from a local bank. Each owner will guarantee his or her ownership share of the debt.

What are the tax and nontax consequences for the new business and its owners under each alternative? Assume that any corporation will have 200 shares of common stock authorized and issued. For the partnership alternative, each partner receives a capital, profits, and loss interest. How would your answer to the basic facts change if instead Steve contributes $2,600 in cash and $18,400 in services?

C:11-57 ***Comparison of Operating Activities.*** RST business entity reported the following items during the current year:

Dividends from 25%-owned domestic corporation	$ 19,000
Municipal bond interest received	18,000
Corporate bond interest received	29,000
Gain on land contributed by Karen[a]	40,000
Operating profit (excluding depreciation)[b]	120,000
MACRS depreciation	36,000
Sec. 1245 gain (depreciation recapture)	5,000
Sec. 1231 loss	28,000
Long-term capital losses	4,000
Short-term capital losses	5,000
Charitable contributions	23,000
Investment interest expense (related to General Electric bonds)	16,000
Salary (guaranteed payment)	37,000

[a] Karen held the land as an investment prior to contributing it to RST business entity three years ago in exchange for her ownership interest. When Karen contributed the land, it had a basis of $15,000 and a FMV of $40,000. RST sold the land in the current year for $55,000. RST business entity held the land as an investment. Assume that Sec. 351 applied to any corporate formation transaction.

[b] Assume that qualified production activities income is $47,000 and that operating profit includes sufficient W-2 wages so as not to be a limiting factor.

a. What is the corporate taxable income and income tax liability for the current year if RST is taxed as a C corporation?

b. What is the ordinary income and separately stated items for the current year if RST elects to be an S corporation? Assume that RST has never operated as a C corporation.

c. What are the ordinary income and separately stated items if RST is treated as a general partnership?

C:11-58 ***Comparison of Nonliquidating Distributions.*** Jeff and John organized Tampa Corporation 18 years ago and have each owned 50% of the corporation since its inception. In the current year, Tampa reports ordinary income/taxable income of $40,000. Assume the business does not qualify for the U.S. production activities deduction. On April 5, Tampa distributes $100,000 cash to Jeff and distributes land with a $100,000 FMV and a $70,000 adjusted basis to John. Tampa had purchased the land as an investment two years ago. What are the tax implications to Tampa, Jeff, and John of the land distribution in each of the four situations that follow?

a. Tampa has been a C corporation since its formation. On January 1 of the current year, Jeff's basis in his stock is $50,000, and John's stock basis is $45,000. Tampa has accumulated E&P of $155,000 on January 1 of the current year.

b. Tampa was formed as a C corporation but made an S election three years after its formation. On January 1 of the current year, Jeff's basis in his stock is $100,000, and John's stock basis is $80,000. Tampa had the following earnings balances on January 1 of the current year:

Accumulated Adjustments Account	$125,000
Accumulated E&P	30,000

c. Tampa was formed as a partnership and continues to operate in that form. On January 1 of the current year, Jeff's basis in his partnership interest is $100,000, and John's partnership basis is $80,000. The partnership has no liabilities and no unrecognized precontribution gains.

d. How would your answers to Parts a–c change if the land held as an investment and then distributed to John had been contributed to Tampa by Jeff two years ago? At the time of Jeff's contribution, the land had a FMV of $95,000 and a $70,000 basis.

TAX STRATEGY PROBLEMS

C:11-59 Alice, a single taxpayer, will form Morning Corporation in the current year. Alice plans to acquire all of Morning's common stock for a $100,000 contribution to the corporation. Morning will obtain additional capital by borrowing $75,000 from a local bank. Morning will conduct a variety of service activities with little need to retain its capital in the business. Alice expects start-up losses of $90,000 during Morning's first year of operation. She expects the corporation to earn pre-tax operating profits of $250,000 (before reduction for Alice's salary) starting next year. Alice plans to withdraw $100,000 of Morning's profits as salary. Her other income consists primarily of ordinary income (no dividends) from other sources, and she expects these amounts to total $120,000 annually. What advice can you provide Alice about the advisability of making an S election in the initial tax year? In the next tax year? In answering these questions, compare the following alternatives: (1) S corporation in both the current year and the next year, (2) S corporation in the current year and C corporation in the next year (i.e., by revoking the S election next year), (3) C corporation in both the current year and the next year, and (4) C corporation in the current year and S corporation in the next year. When analyzing these alternatives, consider the total taxes associated with each alternative, specifically, at the corporate and shareholder levels and across both years. Ignore payroll taxes, however. Also, assume the following facts: (1) for both years, Alice's combined standard deduction and exemption is $10,300; (2) 2015 tax rate schedules remain the same for both years; and (3) a 7% discount rate applies for present value calculations. Although this problem asks for only a two-year analysis, discuss some shortcomings of such a short time frame. Ignore the U.S. production activities deduction for this problem.

C:11-60 One way to compare the accumulation of income by alterative business entity forms is to use mathematical models. The following models express the investment after-tax accumulation calculation for a particular entity form:

Flow-through entities (S corporations, partnerships, and LLCs): $ATA = [1 + R(1 - t_p)]^n$

C corporation: $ATA = [1 + R(1 - t_c)]^n(1 - t_g) + t_g$

where: ATA = after-tax accumulation in n years

R = before-tax rate of return;

t_p = owner's marginal tax rate on ordinary income

t_c = corporation's marginal tax rate

t_g = owner's tax rate on capital gains

n = number of periods

For each alternative business form, the owner makes an initial investment of $1. The following operating assumptions apply:

Before-tax rate of return (R) = 0.18

Marginal tax rate for owner (t_p) = 0.396

Corporate tax rate (t_c) = 0.35

Capital gains rate (t_g) = 0.238 for regular capital gains, including the 3.8% tax on net investment income (assume the Sec. 1202 50% exclusion for small business corporations does not apply)

Investment horizon (n) = 2, 4, 20, 50, or 101 years

A flow-through entity distributes only enough cash each year for the owners to pay their taxes. The corporation pays no dividends. The shareholders sell their stock at the end of the investment horizon, and their gains are taxed at capital gains rates. (See Chapter I:18 of the *Individuals* volume for a detailed explanation of these models.)

Required: What is the after-tax accumulation if each business form is operated for the investment horizon and then sold for the amount of the accumulation? Which entity form is best for each investment horizon? How would your calculations and conclusions change if the C corporation's tax rate is 25%?

C:11-61 Problem C:6-56 considered two alternative forms for doing business. Now consider a third alternative. The C corporation could make an S election effective at the beginning of the current year (the 13th year), operate as an S corporation for the next 20 years, and liquidate the S corporation at that time (32 years in total). Compare this alternative to the other two alternatives in Problem C:6-56.

C:11-62 Assume the corporation in Problem C:11-61 (and C:6-56) had been an S corporation for its first 12 years, during which it distributed just enough cash for the shareholder to pay taxes on the pass-through income. Thus, the S corporation reinvested after-tax income. Now the corporation is considering revoking its S election and operating as a C corporation for the remaining 20 years with no dividend distributions. Show the results of remaining an S corporation versus revoking the election. Also show supporting models and calculations. Which alternative should the corporation adopt? Ignore the accumulated earnings tax for C corporations. How does your answer change if the C corporation's tax rate is 15% instead of 35%?

TAX FORM/RETURN PREPARATION PROBLEMS

C:11-63 Bottle-Up, Inc., was organized on January 8, 2005, and made its S election on January 24, 2005. The necessary consents to the election were filed in a timely manner. Its address is 1234 Hill Street, City, ST 33333. Bottle-Up uses the calendar year as its tax year, the accrual method of accounting, and the first-in, first-out (FIFO) inventory method. Bottle-Up manufactures ornamental glass bottles. It made no changes to its inventory costing methods this year. It uses the specific identification method for bad debts for book and tax purposes. Herman Hiebert and Melvin Jones own 500 shares each. Both individuals materially participate in Bottle-Up's single activity. Herman Hiebert is the tax matters person. Financial statements for Bottle-Up for the current year are shown in Tables C:11-2 through C:11-4. Assume that Bottle-Up's business qualifies as a U.S. production activity and that its qualified production activities income is $90,000. The S corporation uses the small business simplified overall method for reporting these activities (see discussion for Line 12d of Schedules K and K-1 in the Form 1120S instructions). Prepare a 2014 S corporation tax return for Bottle-Up, showing yourself as the paid preparer.

C:11-64 Refer to the facts in Tax Form/Return Preparation Problem C:9-58. Now assume the company is an S corporation rather than a partnership. Additional facts are as follows:

- Drs. Bailey and Firth formed the corporation on January 1, 2013, and the corporation immediately elected S corporation status effective at the beginning of 2013.
- Upon formation of the corporation, Dr. Bailey received common stock worth $1.2 million, and Dr. Firth received common stock worth $2.8 million.
- The balance sheet information is the same as in Table C:9-3 except the equity section is as follows:

	January 1, 2014	*December 31, 2014*
Common stock	$4,000,000	$4,000,000
Retained earnings	171,360	91,020

- The $180,000 paid to Dr. Bailey is salary constituting W-2 wages (instead of a guaranteed payment). Ignore employment taxes (Social Security, etc.) on Dr. Bailey's salary.
- Qualified production activities income (QPAI) still equals $2.24 million, but employer's W-2 wages allocable to U.S. production activities equal $1.16 million (because of Dr. Bailey's salary). The company, being an eligible small pass-through S corporation, uses the small business simplification overall method for reporting these activities (see discussion for Line 12d of Schedule K and Line 12 of Schedule K-1 in the Form 1120S instructions).
- Use book numbers for Schedule L and Schedule M-1 in Form 1120S.

▼ **TABLE C:11-2**

Bottle-Up, Inc. Income Statement for the Year Ended December 31 of the Current Year (Problem C:11-63)

Sales		$2,500,000
Returns and allowances		(15,000)
Net sales		$2,485,000
Beginning inventory	$ 102,000	
Purchases	900,000	
Labor	200,000	
Supplies	80,000	
Utilities	100,000	
Other manufacturing costs	188,000[a]	
Goods available for sale	$1,570,000	
Ending inventory	(96,000)	1,474,000[b]
Gross profit		$1,011,000
Salaries[c]	$ 451,020	
Utilities expense	54,000	
Depreciation (MACRS depreciation is $36,311)	11,782	
Automobile and truck expense	26,000	
Office supplies expense	9,602	
Advertising expense	105,000	
Bad debts expense	620	
Rent expense	30,000	
Interest expense[d]	1,500	
Meals and entertainment expense	21,000	
Selling expenses	100,000	
Repairs and maintenance expense	38,000	
Accounting and legal expense	4,500	
Charitable contributions[e]	9,000	
Insurance expense[f]	24,500	
Hourly employees' fringe benefits	11,000	
Payroll taxes	36,980	
Other taxes	2,500	
Penalties (fines for overweight trucks)	1,000	(938,004)
Operating profit		$ 72,996
Other income and losses:		
Long-term gain on sale of capital assets	$ 48,666[g]	
Sec. 1231 loss	(1,100)[h]	
Interest on U.S. Treasury bills	1,200	
Interest on State of Florida bonds	600	
Dividends from domestic corporations	11,600	
Investment expenses	(600)	60,366
Net income		$ 133,362

[a] Total MACRS depreciation is $74,311. Assume that $38,000 of depreciation has been allocated to cost of sales for both book and tax purposes so that the book and tax inventory and cost of sales amounts are the same. The AMT depreciation adjustment on personal property is $9,000.

[b] The cost of goods sold amount reflects the Uniform Capitalization Rules of Sec. 263A. The appropriate restatements have been made in prior years.

[c] Officer salaries of $120,000 are included in the total. All are employer's W-2 wages.

[d] Investment interest expense is $500. All other interest expense is trade- or business-related. None of the interest expense relates to the production of tax-exempt income.

[e] The corporation made all contributions in cash to qualifying charities.

[f] Includes $3,000 of premiums paid for policies on lives of corporate officers. Bottle-Up is the beneficiary for both policies.

[g] The corporation acquired the capital assets on March 3, 2012 for $100,000 and sold them on September 15, 2014, for $148,666.

[h] The corporation acquired the Sec. 1231 property on June 5, 2013 for $10,000 and sold it on December 21, 2014, for $8,900.

▼ TABLE C:11-3
Bottle-Up, Inc. Balance Sheet for January 1 and December 31 of the Current Year (Problem C:11-63)

	January 1	December 31
Assets:		
Cash	$ 15,000	$116,948
Accounts receivable	41,500	45,180
Inventories	102,000	96,000
Stocks	103,000	74,000
Treasury bills	15,000	16,000
State of Florida bonds	10,000	10,000
Building and equipment	374,600	375,000
Minus: Accumulated depreciation	(160,484)	(173,100)
Land	160,000	190,000
Total	$660,616	$750,028
Liabilities and equities:		
Accounts payable	$ 36,000	$ 10,000
Accrued salaries payable	12,000	6,000
Payroll taxes payable	3,416	7,106
Sales taxes payable	5,200	6,560
Due to Mr. Hiebert	10,000	5,000
Mortgage and notes payable (current maturities)	44,000	52,000
Long-term debt	210,000	260,000
Capital stock	10,000	10,000
Retained earnings	330,000	393,362
Total	$660,616	$750,028

▼ TABLE C:11-4
Bottle-Up, Inc. Statement of Change in Retained Earnings, for the Current Year Ended December 31 (Problem C:11-63)

Balance, January 1		$330,000[a]
Plus: Net income	$133,362	
Minus: Dividends	(70,000)	63,362
Balance, December 31		$393,362

[a] The January 1 accumulated adjustments account balance is $274,300.

Required: Prepare the 2014 S corporation tax return (Form 1120S), including the following additional schedules and forms: Schedule D, Form 4562, and Schedule K-1.

Optional: (1) Complete Schedule M-2 in Form 1120S even though the company has never been a C corporation. For this purpose, the accumulated adjustments account at the beginning of 2014 is $171,360. (2) Prepare a schedule for each shareholder's basis in his or her S corporation stock. For this purpose, Bailey's stock basis at the beginning of 2014 is $1,251,408 and Firth's is $2,535,952.

CASE STUDY PROBLEM

C:11-65 Debra has operated a family counseling practice for a number of years as a sole proprietor. She owns the condominium office space that she occupies in addition to her professional library and office furniture. She has a limited amount of working capital and little need to accumulate additional business assets. Her total business assets are about $150,000, with an $80,000 mortgage on the office space being her only liability. Typically, she has withdrawn any unneeded assets at the end of the year. Debra has used her personal car for business travel and charged the business for the mileage at the appropriate mileage rate provided by the IRS. Over the last three years, Debra's practice has grown so that she now forecasts $80,000 of income being earned this year. Debra has contributed small amounts to an Individual Retirement Account (IRA) each year, but her contributions have never reached the annual limits. Although she has never been sued, Debra recently has become concerned about legal liability. An attorney friend of hers has suggested that she incorporate her business to protect herself against being sued and to save taxes.

Required: You are a good friend of Debra's and a CPA; she asks your opinion on incorporating her business. You are to meet with Debra tomorrow for lunch. Prepare a draft of the points you feel should be discussed over lunch about incorporating the family counseling practice.

TAX RESEARCH PROBLEMS

C:11-66 Cato Corporation incorporated six years ago in California, with Tim and Elesa, husband and wife, owning all the Cato stock. Immediately thereafter, Cato made an S election effective for that year. Tim and Elesa filed the necessary consents to the election. On March 10 of last year, Tim and Elesa transferred 15% of the Cato stock to the Reid and Susan Trust, an irrevocable trust created three years earlier for the benefit of their two minor children. Early in the current year, Tim and Elesa's tax accountant learns about the transfer and advises the couple that the transfer of the stock to the trust may have terminated Cato's S election. Prepare a memorandum for your tax manager indicating any action Tim and Elesa can take that will permit Cato to retain its S election. Research sources suggested by the tax manager include Secs. 1361(c)(2), 1362(d)(2), and 1362(f).

C:11-67 One of your wealthy clients, Cecile, invests $100,000 for sole ownership of an electing S corporation's stock. The corporation is in the process of developing a new food product. Cecile anticipates that the new business will need approximately $200,000 in capital (other than trade payables) during the first two years of its operations before it starts to earn sufficient profits to pay a return on the shareholder's investment. The first $100,000 of this total is to come from Cecile's contributed capital. The remaining $100,000 of funds will come from one of the following three sources:

- Have the corporation borrow the $100,000 from a local bank. Cecile is required to act as a guarantor for the loan.
- Have the corporation borrow $100,000 from the estate of Cecile's late husband. Cecile is the sole beneficiary of the estate.
- Have Cecile lend $100,000 to the corporation from her personal funds.

The S corporation will pay interest at a rate acceptable to the IRS. During the first two years of operations, the corporation anticipates losing $125,000 before it begins to earn a profit. Your tax manager has asked you to evaluate the tax ramifications of each of the three financing alternatives. Prepare a memorandum to the tax manager outlining the information you found in your research.

C:11-68 Joe Stephens formed Sigma Corporation on January 4 of Year 1, and the corporation immediately made an S election effective for that year. In forming the corporation, Joe contributed $50,000 cash in exchange for 100% of Sigma's stock. Shortly thereafter, the corporation obtained a $75,000 bank loan to assist with operations. Sigma's first two years did not go as well as expected, with Sigma incurring a $60,000 ordinary loss in Year 1 and a $12,000 ordinary loss in Year 2. Moreover, in Year 2, Joe and his wife Marsha divorced. As part of the divorce settlement, on March 31 of Year 2, Joe gave Marsha 50% of the Sigma stock. In Year 3, Sigma's performance improved, with the corporation earning $40,000 of ordinary income. Joe asks your help in determining the tax consequences of these events, particularly the usage of the S corporation losses. At a minimum, you should consider the following resources:

- IRC Sec. 1366
- Reg. Sec. 1.1366-2

CHAPTER

12

THE GIFT TAX

LEARNING OBJECTIVES

After studying this chapter, you should be able to

1. Explain the basic concepts of the unified transfer tax system
2. Apply the gift tax formula
3. Recognize a number of transactions subject to the gift tax
4. Determine whether an annual gift tax exclusion is available
5. Identify the deductions available for gift tax purposes
6. Apply the gift-splitting rules
7. Calculate the gift tax liability
8. Recognize how basis affects the overall tax consequences
9. Determine the tax consequences of below-market loans
10. Identify tax planning opportunities in gift situations
11. Comply with the filing requirements for gift tax returns

The **gift tax** is a **wealth transfer tax** that applies if a person transfers property while alive. It is similar to the estate tax, which applies to transfers associated with death. Both the gift tax and the estate tax (discussed in Chapter C:13) are part of the unified transfer tax system that subjects gratuitous transfers of property between persons to taxation. Most property transfers are exempt from these transfer taxes because of the annual exclusion and the various deductions and credits.[1] However, planning for reducing these transfer taxes is a significant matter for wealthy individuals.

Various tax acts over the years have modified the unified transfer tax system in terms of (1) the threshold (called the exemption equivalent or applicable exclusion amount) above which the tax becomes effective, (2) the tax rates applicable to estates and gifts, and (3) a number of other aspects of the unified transfer tax system. For 2014, the amount that could be transferred tax free was $5 million indexed to $5.34 million. For 2015, the threshold is indexed to $5.43 million. For both years, the top tax rate is 40%. The unified credit amounts (and exemption equivalents), and the unified transfer tax rates for all years, appear inside the back cover of this textbook. These amounts also are discussed within this chapter and Chapter C:13 where appropriate.

This chapter discusses both the structure of the gift tax (including the exclusion, deduction, and credit provisions) and exactly which property transfers fall within its purview. It reviews the income tax basis rules in the context of their implications for selecting properties to transfer by gift instead of at death.

The Unified Transfer Tax System

OBJECTIVE 1

Explain the basic concepts of the unified transfer tax system

The recipient of a gift incurs no income tax liability because Sec. 102 explicitly excludes gifts and inheritances from the recipient's gross income.[2] The gift tax, a type of excise tax, is levied on the donor, the person who transferred the property. The gift tax applies to the act of transferring property to a recipient who pays either no consideration or consideration smaller than the value of the property received.

History and Purpose of Transfer Taxes

ADDITIONAL COMMENT

The continuity of the estate tax was interrupted for 2010 for estates whose executors elected to have a modified carryover basis rule apply instead of the estate tax applying.

The United States has had an estate tax since 1916 and a gift tax continuously since 1932. The structure of the gift and estate taxes has remained fairly constant, but details such as the amount of the exclusion and the rate schedules have changed numerous times. The Tax Reform Act of 1976 (the 1976 Act) made a very significant change by enacting a unified rate schedule for gift and estate tax purposes.

The gift tax has had several purposes, one of the most important of which was to raise revenue. However, because of the fairly generous annual exclusion and unified credit legislated by Congress, the gift tax yields only a small fraction of the federal government's total revenues. Only donors making relatively large gifts owe any gift taxes. Another purpose of the gift tax is to serve as a backstop to the estate tax and to prevent individuals from avoiding a significant amount of—or all—estate taxes by disposing of property before death. For example, without the gift tax, persons who know they are terminally ill could dispose of property "on their deathbed" and escape the transfer tax. In addition, the gift tax provides revenue to offset some of the reduction in income tax revenue resulting from the fact that income from gifted property sometimes is shifted to persons in lower income tax brackets. Another purpose for levying gift and estate taxes is to redistribute wealth.

No one knows what the distribution of wealth would have been had Congress not enacted transfer taxes. However, one study estimated that the top 1% of the population held 22.5% of this nation's personal wealth in 1995, about the same percentage as in 1992.[3]

---

[1] For example, in 2012, of 9,412 estate tax returns filed, 3,738 paid an estate tax. Of these 3,738 returns, all but 311 reported a gross estate over $5 million.

[2] The income earned from property received as a gift or an inheritance, however, is not exempt from the income tax.

[3] "Tax Report," *The Wall Street Journal* (April 19, 2000), p. A1.

In 1976, Congress greatly revamped the transfer tax system by combining the separate estate and gift tax systems into one unified transfer tax system. Although Chapters C:12 and C:13 use the terms *gift tax* and *estate tax,* these taxes actually are components of the same unified transfer tax system. The system also includes the generation-skipping transfer tax, a topic discussed in Chapter C:13. The unification of the transfer tax system removed the previous law's bias favoring the tax treatment of lifetime gifts in comparison with transfers at death. The three most significant elements of the unified system—the unified rate schedule, the inclusion of taxable gifts in the death tax base, and the unified credit—are discussed below.

SELF-STUDY QUESTION

Use the rate schedule inside the back cover of this text to determine the amount of gift tax (before credits) on 2015 taxable gifts of $6 million.

ANSWER

The tax is $2,345,800 [$345,800 + 0.40 × ($6,000,000 − $1,000,000)].

UNIFIED RATE SCHEDULE

Before the 1976 Act mandated a **unified rate schedule,** effective for gifts made after 1976 and deaths occurring after 1976 and applicable to both lifetime transfers and transfers at death, the gift tax rates were only 75% of the estate tax rates on a transfer of the same size. The rates are progressive and have varied over the years. The 2001 Act reduced the unified transfer tax rates beginning in 2002 by replacing the former top two brackets (on amounts exceeding $2.5 million) with a 50% maximum tax rate in 2002. The top rate declined to 49% in 2003, 48% in 2004, 47% in 2005, and 46% in 2006. In those years, the top rate applied to tax bases above $2 million. In 2007 through 2009, for both estate and gift tax purposes, a maximum tax rate of 45% applied to tax bases exceeding $1.5 million.

For 2010 through 2012, the top estate and gift tax rate was 35%, applicable to tax bases exceeding $500,000. For 2013 and after, a top rate of 40% applies to tax bases above $1 million. The estate and gift tax unified transfer tax rates appear inside the back cover of this textbook.

IMPACT OF TAXABLE GIFTS ON DEATH TAX BASE

Before 1977, a separate system applied to lifetime gifts compared with dispositions at death. By making gifts, an individual could shift the taxation of property from the top of the estate tax rate schedule to the bottom of the gift tax rate schedule. Few taxpayers could take advantage of this shifting, however, because only people with a relatively large amount of property could afford to part with sizable amounts of their assets while alive.

ADDITIONAL COMMENT

At the taxpayer's death, the unified tax is computed on the sum of the taxable estate plus the adjusted taxable gifts. The tax on this sum is reduced by the tax that would have been payable (at current rates) on the taxable gifts made after December 31, 1976.

Under today's unified system, taxable gifts affect the size of the tax base at death. Any post-1976 taxable gifts (other than gifts included in the gross estate) are called **adjusted taxable gifts,** and such gifts are included in the donor's death tax base. Although they are valued at their fair market value (FMV) on the date of the gift, the addition of such taxable gifts to the tax base at death can cause the donor-decedent's estate to be taxed at a higher marginal tax rate. However, such gifts are not taxed for a second time upon the donor's death because gift taxes (computed at current rates) on these gifts are subtracted in determining the estate tax liability.

EXAMPLE C:12-1 ▶ In 1994, Dan made taxable gifts totaling $500,000. When Dan died the value of the gifted property had tripled. Dan's death tax base includes the $500,000 of post-1976 taxable gifts. They are valued for estate tax purposes at their FMV on the date of the gift; the post-gift appreciation escapes the transfer tax system. Thus, the transfer tax value is fixed or frozen at the date-of-gift value. ◀

Note that unification (including taxable gifts that become part of the tax base at death) extends only to gifts made after 1976. Congress exempted gifts made before 1977 from unification because it did not want to retroactively change the two separate transfer tax systems of the prior tax regime.

UNIFIED CREDIT

The **unified credit** reduces dollar for dollar a certain amount of the tax computed on the taxable gifts or the taxable estate. The amount of the credit has varied depending on the year of the transfer (see discussion on page C:12-6). In the gift and estate tax formulas, the full credit is available for lifetime transfers and again in determining the tax payable at death. In concept, however, an individual's estate does not receive the benefit of this unified credit amount at death to the extent the decedent had used the credit against lifetime transfers (as explained in Chapter C:13). The gift tax formula, including the unified credit, is discussed below.

Gift tax formula

OBJECTIVE 2

Apply the gift tax formula

The formula described in this section is used to calculate a donor's gift tax liability for the year of the transfer. Gift tax reporting is done on an annual basis, always on a calendar year. Figure C:12-1 illustrates the formula for determining the donor's annual gift tax liability. This formula is discussed in detail later in the chapter.

ADDITIONAL COMMENT

The gift tax applies to cumulative lifetime gifts made since the enactment of the gift tax in 1932. The unified gift and estate tax, enacted in 1976, applies only to cumulative lifetime taxable gifts made after 1976. Thus, a taxable gift of $75,000 made in 1970 would not be included in a decedent's unified tax base for calculating the estate tax but would affect the gift tax payable by that person.

DETERMINATION OF GIFTS

The starting point in the process is to determine which, if any, of the taxpayer's transfers constitute gifts. The next section discusses the various types of transfers that the statute views as gifts. All gifts are valued at their FMVs on the date of the gift. Next, the aggregate amount of gifts for the period is determined. The aggregate gifts are then reduced by any exclusions and deductions. Finally, the tax is computed according to the formula illustrated in Figure C:12-1.

EXCLUSIONS AND DEDUCTIONS

For many years the maximum amount excludible annually was $10,000 per donee, but Congress amended the IRC to allow indexation beginning with gifts made after 1998. Inflation adjustments are rounded to the next *lowest* multiple of $1,000.[4] Accordingly, the annual exclusion rose to $11,000 for 2002 through 2005, to $12,000 for 2006 through 2008, to $13,000 for 2009 through 2012, and to $14,000 beginning in 2013. If the gifts made to a donee are less than the annual exclusion amount, the amount excludible is limited to the amount of the gift made to that donee. A donor may claim exclusions for transfers to an unlimited number of donees.

Two types of deductions (marital and charitable) reduce the amount of the taxable gifts. Most transfers to one's spouse generate a marital deduction; there is no ceiling on the amount of this deduction. Similarly, most transfers to charitable organizations are cancelled out by the charitable contribution deduction, which also is unlimited.

KEY POINT

The annual exclusion applies to each *donee* per year; therefore, the total amount of tax-free gifts in a given year can be much greater than the annual exclusion amount. Also, gift-splitting can double the tax-free amount per donee.

GIFT-SPLITTING ELECTION

Congress authorized gift-splitting provisions to achieve more comparable tax consequences between taxpayers of community property and noncommunity property (common law) states.[5] Under **community property law**, assets acquired after marriage are community property unless they are acquired by gift or inheritance. Typically, in a **community property state**, a large portion of the spouses' assets is community property, property in which each spouse has a one-half interest. One-half of a community property gift is automatically considered to be given by each spouse. By contrast, in a **common law state**, all assets acquired during the marriage are the property of the acquiring spouse. The other spouse does not automatically acquire an interest in the property. Thus, sometimes only one spouse owns enough assets to consider making large gifts.

Section 2513 authorizes spouses to elect gift splitting, which treats gifts made by each spouse to third parties as if each spouse made one-half of the gift. As a result, spouses in common law states can achieve the same benefits that apply automatically for gifts of community property. Thus, both spouses can claim a $14,000 per donee exclusion although only one spouse actually makes the gift, and the spouses can give each donee a total of $28,000 before either spouse's gift becomes taxable.

[4] Sec. 2503(b).

[5] The eight traditional community property states are Louisiana, Texas, New Mexico, Arizona, California, Washington, Idaho, and Nevada. Wisconsin's marital property law, though not providing for community property, is basically the same as community property.

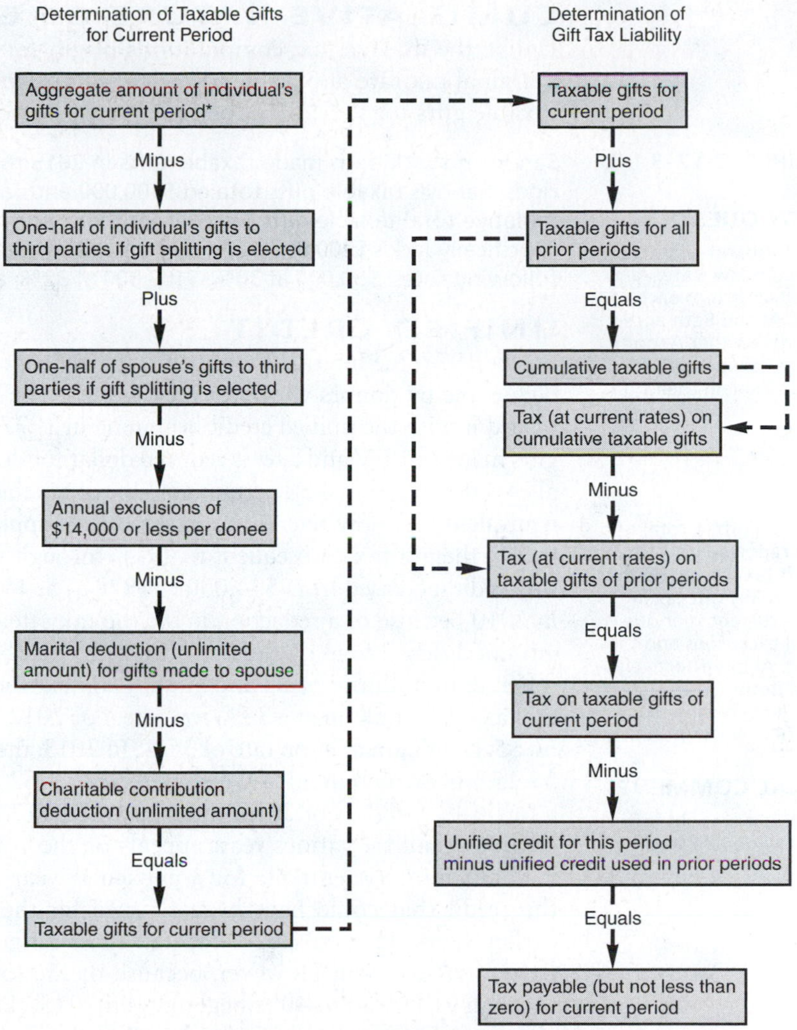

* Valued at FMV on date of gift.

FIGURE C:12-1 ▶ THE GIFT TAX FORMULA

As a result of the Supreme Court's 2013 decision in *U.S. v. Windsor*,[6] same-sex spouses are eligible for the gift-splitting election. The Court ruled unconstitutional the section of the Defense of Marriage Act (DOMA) that recognized only marriages between a man and a woman as a marriage for purposes of federal law. The IRS announced that it will honor the *Windsor* decision for same-sex spouses whose domicile is in states that do not recognize such marriages if the spouses were married in jurisdictions permitting such marriages.[7] The ruling does not apply, however, to civil unions or domestic partnerships.

EXAMPLE C:12-2 ▶

ADDITIONAL COMMENT

Because the gift tax is a tax on *cumulative* lifetime gifts, taxpayers must keep track of all taxable gifts. All previous taxable gifts are part of the calculation for current gift tax due, and post-1976 taxable gifts affect the estate tax liability.

Andy and Bonnie, residents of a common law state, are married throughout 2015. In that year, Andy gives his brother $100,000 cash. Andy and Bonnie may elect gift splitting and thereby treat the $100,000 gift as if each spouse gave $50,000. As a result, the excludible portion of the gift totals $28,000 ($14,000 per donee for each of the two deemed donors). If they elect gift splitting, each donor's $36,000 taxable gift may be taxed at a lower marginal tax rate. In addition, Bonnie can use a unified credit amount that she might not otherwise be able to use. As a result of gift splitting, the tax consequences are the same as if Andy and Bonnie were residents of a community property state and each gave $50,000 of community property to Andy's brother. ◀

[6] 111 AFTR2d 2013-2385, 2013-2 USTC ¶50,400 (USSC, 2013).

[7] Rev. Rul. 2013-17, 2013-38 I.R.B. 201.

CUMULATIVE NATURE OF GIFT TAX

Unlike the income tax, computations of gift tax liabilities are cumulative in nature. The marginal tax rate applicable to the current period's taxable gifts is a function of both the taxable gifts for the current period and the aggregate taxable gifts for all earlier periods.

EXAMPLE C:12-3 ▶ Sandy and Jack each made taxable gifts in 2015 totaling $200,000. However, for previous periods, Sandy's taxable gifts totaled $100,000 and Jack's totaled $1.5 million. Because Jack's cumulative total taxable gifts were larger than Sandy's, Jack's marginal tax rate exceeds Sandy's. Specifically Jack's $200,000 gift is taxed at a 40% rate, while Sandy's $200,000 gift is taxed at the following rates: $50,000 at 30%, $100,000 at 32%, and $50,000 at 34%. ◀

SELF-STUDY QUESTION

Al and Beth, husband and wife, live in a common law state. Al gives a $3 million gift to each of two children. Al and Beth agree to split the gift. Neither Al nor Beth has made taxable gifts in any prior year. Explain their gift tax liability.

ANSWER

One-half of each gift, a total of $6 million, is reported on each taxpayer's gift tax return. Neither Al nor Beth has any gift tax liability for the current year due to the annual exclusions and the unified credit. Al has effectively used some of Beth's unified credit without Beth ever having ownership or control over Al's property.

ADDITIONAL COMMENT

The unified credit amounts after 2011 are $5 million adjusted for inflation.

UNIFIED CREDIT

Before 1977, the Internal Revenue Code (IRC) allowed donors a $30,000 specific exemption deductible by donors whenever they desired. The 1976 Act repealed this exemption and replaced it with the unified credit beginning in 1977.[8] Consequently, the gift tax computed for gifts made in 1977 and later is reduced dollar for dollar by the unified credit. The unified credit allows donors to make a certain amount of taxable gifts (known originally as the **exemption equivalent** and now referred to in the IRC as **applicable exclusion amount**) without needing to pay the gift tax. Subsequent to 1977, through various tax acts, the maximum amount of the credit increased from $34,000 in 1978 to $345,800 in 2009, but it decreased to $330,800 in 2010 because of a reduction in the top tax rate. For 2004 through 2010, the credit for the gift tax differed from the credit for the estate tax because the gift and estate exempt amounts differed. In both the estate and gift tax context for 2011, the unified credit was $1,730,800, the tax on $5 million at a 35% top rate. For 2012, the unified credit was $1,772,800, the tax on $5.12 million at a top rate of 35%. In 2013, the unified credit was $2,045,800, the tax on $5.25 million, and in 2014 the unified credit is $2,081,800, the tax on $5.34 million, both at a top rate of 40%. For 2015, the credit is $2,117,800, the tax on $5.43 million. The unified credit amount for various years appears on the inside back cover of this textbook.

The amount creditable for a particular year is the credit amount for that year minus the credit that could have been claimed for the taxable gifts made by the individual in earlier years. Prior to 2010, top tax rates ranged from 45% to 55% depending on the particular tax year. However, because of the lowering of the top rate to 35% in 2010 through 2012 and to 40% beginning in 2013, the credit is reduced not by the credit actually claimed in earlier years but by what the unified credit would have been, if lower, had the credit been calculated using the rates for the current year. Recall that no credit was allowed for gifts made before 1977.[9]

EXAMPLE C:12-4 ▶ Zheng made her first taxable gift ($325,000) in 1984. She used the $96,300 unified credit available for 1984 (as shown on the inside back cover) to reduce her $96,300 gift tax liability to zero. Zheng made her next taxable gift ($100,000) in 1985. Zheng's 1985 gift tax is computed as follows:

Tax on cumulative gifts [$70,800 + 0.34 × ($425,000 − $250,000)]	$130,300
Minus: Tax on 1984 taxable gift	(96,300)
Tax on 1985 gift	$ 34,000
Minus: Unified credit available in 1985 ($121,800 − $96,300)	(25,500)
Tax in 1985	$ 8,500

Thus, by 1985, Zheng has claimed credits totaling $121,800. If she makes taxable gifts in 2015, the maximum credit she can claim against her 2015 tax is $1,996,000 ($2,117,800 – $121,800 already used). In this situation, the credit actually claimed and the amount of the credit calculated using the 2015 rate are the same because the earlier gifts were not taxed at rates above 40%. ◀

ADDITIONAL COMMENT

Taxpayers must keep a record of how much of the specific exemption they used between September 9 and December 31, 1976, to determine how much of the unified credit is available to them.

After passage of the 1976 Act, prospective donors quickly realized they could make gifts before the end of 1976 and avoid the unification provisions, but Congress adopted a special rule that affects donors who used any portion of their specific exemption between September 9, 1976, and December 31, 1976.[10] The rule reduced the amount of unified

[8] Sec. 2505.

[9] Also, no credit is used for a gift that is completely nontaxable.

[10] Sec. 2505(b). Congress repealed this exemption for post-1976 years.

credit otherwise available to such donors by 20% of the amount of the specific exemption they claimed against gifts made between September 9 and December 31, 1976. The maximum reduction in the unified credit as a result of this provision is $6,000 (0.20 × $30,000 maximum specific exemption).

EXAMPLE C:12-5 ▶ In November 1976, Maria made a large taxable gift, her first gift, and used her $30,000 specific exemption. As a result, the unified credit that Maria could otherwise claim after 1976 is reduced by $6,000 (0.20 × $30,000). Her 1976 taxable gifts are not includible in her death tax base. ◀

TRANSFERS SUBJECT TO THE GIFT TAX

OBJECTIVE 3

Recognize a number of transactions subject to the gift tax

In general, property transferred for less than adequate consideration in money or money's worth is deemed to be a gift in the gift tax context. The gift occurs when the donor gives up control over the transferred property. Congress has legislated several provisions that exempt various property transfers that otherwise might be viewed as gifts from the scope of the gift tax. These exemptions include direct payments of medical expenses and tuition, transfers to political organizations, property settlements in conjunction with a divorce, and qualified disclaimers.

TRANSFERS FOR INADEQUATE CONSIDERATION

As mentioned earlier, the initial step in determining the donor's gift tax liability is deciding which transactions constitute gifts for gift tax purposes. Section 2501(a) states that a gift tax is imposed on "the transfer of property by gift." Thus, if *property* is transferred *by gift,* the transferor potentially incurs a gift tax liability. Perhaps surprisingly, the IRC does not define the term *gift*. Section 2511(a), however, elaborates on the gift concept by indicating that the tax is applicable "whether the transfer is in trust or otherwise, whether the gift is direct or indirect, and whether the property is real or personal, tangible or intangible."

A transaction is subject to the gift tax even though not entirely gratuitous if "the value of the property transferred by the donor exceeds the value in money or money's worth of the consideration given therefor."[11] In such circumstances, the amount of the gift is the difference between the value of the property the donor gave up and the value of the consideration in money or money's worth received. The following discussion examines in more depth the scope of the rule regarding transfers for less than adequate consideration.

ADDITIONAL COMMENT
At times, a transferor can inadvertently make a gift by selling property to a family member for an amount determined in an IRS audit to be less than its fair market value.

Bargain Sales. Often, an individual wants to sell an asset to a family member, but the prospective buyer cannot afford to pay the full FMV of the property. If the buyer pays consideration of less than the FMV of the transferred property, the seller makes a gift to the buyer equal to the bargain element of the transaction, which is the excess of the property's FMV over its sales price.

EXAMPLE C:12-6 ▶ Martha sells her ranch, having a $1 million FMV, to her son Stan, who can afford to pay only $300,000 of consideration. In the year of the sale, Martha makes a gift to Stan of $700,000, the excess of the ranch's FMV over the consideration received. ◀

Transfers in Normal Course of Business. Treasury Regulations provide an exception to the general rule that a transfer for inadequate consideration triggers a gift. Specifically, a transaction arising "in the ordinary course of business (a transaction which is bona fide, at arm's length, and free from any donative intent)" is considered to have been made for adequate consideration.[12] Thus, no gift arises when a buyer acquires property for less than its FMV *if* the acquisition is in the ordinary course of business.

EXAMPLE C:12-7 ▶ John, a merchant, has a clearance sale and sells a diamond bracelet valued at $30,000 to Bess who pays $14,000, the clearance sale price. Because the clearance sale arose in the ordinary course of John's business, the bargain element ($16,000) does not constitute a gift to Bess. ◀

[11] Reg. Sec. 25.2512-8.

[12] Ibid.

STATUTORY EXEMPTIONS FROM THE GIFT TAX

For various reasons, including simplifying the administration of the gift tax, Congress enacted several provisions that exempt certain transactions from the purview of the gift tax. In the absence of these statutory rules, some of these transactions could constitute gifts.

Payment of Medical Expenses or Tuition. Section 2503(e) states that a qualified transfer is not treated as a transfer of property by gift. The IRC defines *qualified transfer* as an amount paid on behalf of an individual to an educational organization for tuition or to any person who provides medical care as payment for such medical care. Such payments are exempt from gift treatment only if made *directly* to the educational organization or to the person or entity providing the medical care. *Educational organization* has the same definition as for charitable contribution purposes,[13] and *medical care* has the same definition as for medical expense deduction purposes.[14] Note that the rule addresses only tuition, not room, board, and books. Moreover, the identity of the person whose expenses are paid is not important. The special exemption applies even if an individual makes payments on behalf of a non-relative.

SELF-STUDY QUESTION

Ben's adult son Clarence, who is not Ben's dependent, needs a liver transplant. Because Clarence cannot afford the surgical procedure, Ben pays the medical fee directly to the hospital. Is Ben's payment for Clarence's benefit a taxable gift?

ANSWER

The payment is not a taxable gift because of Sec. 2503(e).

If a taxpayer pays amounts benefitting someone else and the expenditures constitute support that the payor must furnish under state law, such payments are support, not gifts. State law determines the definition of support. Generally, payments of medical expenses for one's minor child would be categorized as support and not a gift, even in the absence of Sec. 2503(e). On the other hand, state law generally does not require parents to pay medical expenses or tuition for an adult child. Thus, the enactment of Sec. 2503(e) removed such payments from the gift tax.

According to the Staff of the Joint Committee on Taxation, special rules concerning tuition and medical expense payments were enacted because

> Congress was concerned that certain payments of tuition made on behalf of children who have attained their majority, and of special medical expenses on behalf of elderly relatives, technically could be considered gifts under prior law. The Congress believed such payments should be exempt from gift taxes.[15]

EXAMPLE C:12-8 ▶ Sergio (a widower) pays $20,000 for his adult grandson's tuition at medical school and $15,000 for the grandson's room and board in the medical school's dormitory. Sergio makes all payments directly to the educational organization. Section 2503(e) exempts the direct payment of the tuition to the medical school (but not the room and board) from being treated as a gift. Because Sergio is not required under state law to pay room and board for a grandson, such payments are not support. Sergio has made a $15,000 gift to the grandson. ◀

EXAMPLE C:12-9 ▶ Assume the same facts as in Example C:12-8 except that Sergio writes a $35,000 check to his grandson, who in turn pays the medical school. Sergio has made a $35,000 gift. Because Sergio does not pay the tuition directly to the school, Sergio does not meet all the conditions for exempting the tuition payments from gift tax treatment. Here, and in Example C:12-8, Sergio receives a $14,000 annual exclusion. ◀

Transfers to Political Organizations. Congress adopted a provision specifically exempting transfers to political organizations from being deemed to be a transfer of property by gift.[16] Without this special rule, these transfers generally would be subjected to gift tax treatment.

EXAMPLE C:12-10 ▶ Ann transfers $2,000 to a political organization founded to promote Thomas's campaign for governor. Ann's $2,000 transfer does not fall within the statutory definition of a gift. ◀

Property Settlements in Conjunction with Divorce. To reduce litigation, Congress enacted special rules addressing property transfers in the context of a divorce. Section 2516 and underlying Treasury Regulations specify the circumstances in which it automatically exempts property settlements in connection with a divorce from being treated as gifts.

For Sec. 2516 to be applicable, the spouses must adopt a written agreement concerning their marital and property rights and the divorce must occur during a three-year

[13] Section 170(b)(1)(A)(ii) defines *educational organization* in the context of the charitable contribution deduction.

[14] Section 213(d) defines *medical care* in the context of the medical expense deduction.

[15] U.S. Congress, Staff of the Joint Committee on Taxation, *General Explanation of the Economic Recovery Tax Act of 1981* (Washington, DC: U.S. Government Printing Office, 1981), p. 273.

[16] Sec. 2501(a)(4).

WHAT WOULD YOU DO IN THIS SITUATION?

You are a CPA with a very wealthy client, Ms. Atsushi Trong, who is a model of the U.S. success story. She immigrated to the United States as a teenager and studied clothing trends in both high school and college. She started her own clothing company, which has been very sucessful. She has a net worth of over $100 million and no immediate family.

She decided to plow some of her good fortune back into the educational system, which provided the intellectual foundation for her success. She selected the current class of her old high school, and in 2015 gave each of 100 graduating students $100,000 to be used to pay tuition costs for four years at her college alma mater. Each of the 100 student donees used the $100,000 to prepay the four-year tuition costs in 2015.

You have been asked to determine the tax consequences of these transactions. What position would you take after considering the requirements of the IRC and *Statements on Standards for Tax Services* (reproduced in Appendix E)?

period beginning one year before they make the agreement. No gift arises from any transfer made in accordance with such agreement if a spouse transfers property to settle the other spouse's marital or property rights or to provide reasonable support for the children while they are minors. In addition, Sec. 1041 provides for no gain or loss recognition, with the transferred property having a carryover basis.

EXAMPLE C:12-11 ▶ In June 2014, Hal and Wanda signed a property agreement whereby Hal is to transfer $750,000 to Wanda in settlement of her property rights. Hal makes the transfer in May 2015. Hal and Wanda receive a divorce decree in July 2015. Hal is not deemed to have made a gift to Wanda when he transferred property to her. ◀

Qualified Disclaimers. Sometimes a person named to receive property under a decedent's will prefers not to receive such property and would like to disclaim (not accept) it. Typically, the person is quite ill and/or elderly or very wealthy. State disclaimer statutes allow individuals to say "no thank you" to the property willed to them. State law or another provision in the will addresses how to determine who will receive the property after the original beneficiary (the disclaimant) declines to accept it.

ADDITIONAL COMMENT

Individuals who execute disclaimers, in a sense, participate in shifting wealth to another.

Section 2518(a) states that individuals making a qualified disclaimer are treated as if the disclaimed property were never transferred to them. Thus, the person making the disclaimer is not deemed to have made a gift to the person who receives the property because of the disclaimer.

A **qualified disclaimer** must meet the following four tests:

- It must be an irrevocable, unqualified, written refusal to accept property.
- The transferor or his or her legal representative must receive the refusal no later than nine months after the later of the day the transfer is made or the day the person named to receive the property becomes age 21.
- The disclaiming person must not have accepted the property interest or any of its benefits.
- As a result of the disclaimer, the property must pass to the decedent's spouse or a person other than the one disclaiming it. In addition, the person disclaiming the property cannot direct who is to receive the property.[17]

EXAMPLE C:12-12 ▶ Doug dies on February 1, 2015, and wills 500 acres of land to Joan. If Joan disclaims the property in a manner that meets all four of the tests for a qualified disclaimer, Joan will not be treated as making a gift to the person who receives the property as a result of her disclaimer. ◀

[17] Sec. 2518(b).

EXAMPLE C:12-13 ▶ Assume the same facts as in Example C:12-12 except Joan instead disclaims the property on January 2, 2016. Joan's action arose too late to meet the second qualified disclaimer test above. Thus, Joan makes a gift to the person who receives the property she disclaims. ◀

CESSATION OF DONOR'S DOMINION AND CONTROL

A gift occurs when a transfer becomes complete and is valued as of the date the transfer becomes complete. Thus, the concept of a completed transfer is important in two contexts: determination of whether a gift has arisen and, if so, the value of the gift. According to Treasury Regulations, a gift becomes complete—and is thus deemed made and valued—when the donor "has so parted with dominion and control as to leave in him no power to change its disposition, whether for his own benefit or for the benefit of another."[18] A gift is not necessarily complete just because the transferor cannot receive any further personal benefits, such as income, from the property. If the transferor still can influence the benefits others may receive from the transferred property, the transfer is incomplete with respect to the portion of the property over which the transferor retained control.

Revocable Trusts. A transferor who conveys property to a revocable trust makes an incomplete transfer because the creator of a revocable trust can change the trust provisions, including the identity of the beneficiaries. Moreover, the creator may demand the return of the trust property. Because the transferor does not give up any control over property conveyed to a revocable trust, the individual does not make a gift upon funding the trust. Once the trustee distributes trust income to a beneficiary, however, the creator of the trust loses control over the distributed funds and then makes a completed gift of the income the trustee pays out.

EXAMPLE C:12-14 ▶ On May 1, Ted transfers $500,000 to a revocable trust with First National Bank as trustee. The trustee must pay out all the income to Ed during Ed's lifetime and at Ed's death distribute the property to Ed, Jr. On December 31, the trustee distributes $35,000 of income to Ed. The May 1 transfer is incomplete because Ted may revoke the trust; thus, no gift arises upon the funding of the trust. A $35,000 gift to Ed occurs on December 31 because Ted no longer has control over the income distributed to Ed. The gift is eligible for the annual exclusion. ◀

EXAMPLE C:12-15 ▶ Assume the same facts as in Example C:12-14 and that Ted amends the trust instrument on July 7 of the next year to make the trust irrevocable. By this date, the trust property has appreciated to $612,000. Ted makes a completed gift of $612,000 on July 7 of the next year because he gives up his powers over the trust. The gift is eligible for the annual exclusion. ◀

KEY POINT

If the donor retains control over any portion of the property, no gift is considered to have been made with respect to the portion of the property the donor still controls.

Other Retained Powers. Transfers to an irrevocable trust can be deemed incomplete for the portion of the trust over which the creator kept control. Treasury Regulations state that if "the donor reserves any power over its [the property's] disposition, the gift may be wholly incomplete, or may be partially complete and partially incomplete, depending upon all the facts in the particular case."[19] One must examine the trust agreement language to determine the scope of the donor's retention of control. The regulations elaborate by indicating that "[a] gift is . . . incomplete if and to the extent that a reserved power gives the donor the power to name new beneficiaries or to change the interests of the beneficiaries."[20]

EXAMPLE C:12-16 ▶ On May 3, Art transfers $300,000 of property in trust with a bank as trustee. Art names his friends Bob and/or Sue to receive the trust income for 15 years and Karl to receive the trust property at the end of 15 years. Art reserves the power to determine how that income is to be divided between Bob and Sue each year, but the trustee must distribute all of the income each year. Because Art reserves the power over payment of the income for the 15-year period, this portion of the transfer is incomplete on May 3. Actuarial tables discussed in the next section of the chapter address the valuation of the completed gift to Karl. As discussed in Chapter C:14, under the grantor trust rules, Art is taxed on the trust income. ◀

[18] Reg. Sec. 25.2511-2(b).
[19] Ibid.
[20] Reg. Sec. 25.2511-2(c).

EXAMPLE C:12-17 ► Assume the same facts as in Example C:12-16 and that on December 31 Art instructs the trustee to distribute the trust's $34,000 of income as follows: $18,000 to Bob and $16,000 to Sue. Once the trustee pays out income, Art loses control over it. Thus, Art makes an $18,000 gift to Bob and a $16,000 gift to Sue on December 31. Each gift qualifies for the annual exclusion. ◄

EXAMPLE C:12-18 ► Assume the same facts as in Example C:12-16 and that on May 3 of the next year, when the trust assets are valued at $360,000, Art relinquishes his powers over payment of income and gives this power to the trustee. Art's transfer of the income interest (with a remaining term of 14 years) becomes complete on May 3 of the next year. The valuation of the gift of a 14-year income interest is determined from actuarial tables in Appendix H. ◄

Topic Review C:12-1 provides examples of various complete, incomplete, and partially complete transfers.

VALUATION OF GIFTS

ADDITIONAL COMMENT

Because the determination of value is such a subjective issue, a large number of gift tax controversies involve valuation disagreements.

General Rules. All gifts are valued at their FMV as of the date of the gift (i.e., the date the transfer becomes complete). Treasury Regulations state that a property's value is "the price at which such property would change hands between a willing buyer and a willing seller, neither being under any compulsion to buy or to sell, and both having reasonable knowledge of relevant facts."[21] According to the regulations, stocks and bonds traded on a stock exchange or over the counter are valued at the mean of the highest and lowest selling price on the date of the gift.[22] In general, the guidelines for valuing properties are the same, regardless of whether the property is conveyed during life or at death. An exception is life insurance policies, which are less valuable while the insured is alive. Valuation of life insurance policies is discussed in a later section of this chapter, as well as in Chapter C:13's coverage of the estate tax.

KEY POINT

The value of the life estate plus the value of the remainder interest equals the total FMV of the property.

Life Estates and Remainder Interests. Often a donor transfers less than his or her entire interest in an asset. For example, an individual may transfer property in trust and reserve the right to the trust's income for life and name another individual to receive the property upon the transferor's death. In such a situation, the transferor retains a **life estate** and gives a **remainder interest.** In general, only the remainder interest is subject to the gift tax. An exception applies if the gift is to a family member, as discussed in the estate freeze section below. If the transferor keeps an annuity (a fixed amount) for life and names another person to receive the remainder at the transferor's death, in all situations the gift is of just the remainder interest.

A grantor also may transfer property in trust with the promise that another person will receive the income for a certain number of years and at the end of that time period the

TOPIC REVIEW C:12-1

Examples of Complete and Incomplete Transfers

1. Complete Transfers, Subject to Gift Tax:
   a. Property transferred outright to donee
   b. Property transferred to an irrevocable trust over which the donor retains no powers
2. Incomplete Transfers, Not Subject to Gift Tax:
   a. Property transferred to a revocable trust
   b. Property transferred to an irrevocable trust for which the donor retains discretionary powers over both income and the remainder interest
3. Partially Complete Transfers, Only a Portion Subject to Gift Tax:
   a. Property transferred to an irrevocable trust for which the donor retains discretionary powers over who receives the income but not the remainder interest[a]

[a]The gift of the remainder interest constitutes a completed transfer.

[21] Reg. Sec. 25.2512-1.

[22] Reg. Sec. 25.2512-2.

TAX STRATEGY TIP

When gifting a remainder interest, the donor should consider giving property with an anticipated appreciation rate greater than the Sec. 7520 interest rate.

property will revert to the grantor. In this case, the donor retains a reversionary interest, whereas the other party receives a **term certain interest.**[23] As explained later in the discussion of estate freezes, unless the donee is a family member, only the term certain interest is subject to the gift tax. Trusts in which the grantor retains a reversionary interest have disadvantageous income tax consequences to the grantor if they were created after March 1, 1986. Chapter C:14 discusses the income tax treatment of such trusts.

Life estates, annuity interests, remainders, and term certain interests are valued from actuarial tables that incorporate the Sec. 7520 interest rate. In general, these tables must be used regardless of the actual earnings rate of the transferred assets. Excerpts from the tables appear in Appendix H. Table S is used for valuing life estates and remainders and Table B for term certain interests. The factor for a life estate or term certain interest is 1.0 minus the remainder factor. The remainder factor simply represents the present value of the right to receive a property at the end of someone's life (in the case of Table S) or at the end of a specified time (in the case of Table B). The value of the income interest plus the remainder interest is 1.0, the entire value of the property. The factor for an annuity is the life estate or the term factor divided by the Sec. 7520 interest rate. Section 7520 calls for the interest rate to be revised every month to the rate, rounded to the nearest 0.2%, that is 120% of the federal midterm rate applicable for the month of the transfer.[24] Congress mandated that at least once every ten years the tables be revised to reflect mortality experience. The most recent revised life tables are effective for transfers beginning on May 1, 2009.

EXAMPLE C:12-19 ▶ Refer to Example C:12-16, in which on May 3 Art transfers $300,000 of property in trust with a bank as trustee. Art names his friends Bob and Sue to receive the trust income for 15 years but reserves the power to determine how the income is to be divided between them each year. However, the trustee must distribute all the income. Art specifies that Karl is to receive the trust property at the end of the fifteenth year. Because Art keeps power over the income, only the gift of the remainder interest is a completed transfer on May 3. The gift is valued from Table B. If the interest rate is 4%, the amount of the gift is $166,580 (0.555265 × $300,000), the present value of the property to be received by Karl at the end of 15 years. ◀

EXAMPLE C:12-20 ▶ Assume the same facts as in Example C:12-19 and that three years later, when the trust assets are valued at $360,000, Art relinquishes to the trustee his power over the payment of trust income. The income interest has a remaining term of 12 years. The gift is the present value of the 12-year income interest, which is valued from Table B by subtracting the factor for a remainder interest (0.624597 if the interest rate is 4%) from 1.0. Thus, the amount of the gift is $135,145 [(1.0 − 0.624597) × $360,000]. ◀

EXAMPLE C:12-21 ▶ On July 5 of the current year, Don transfers $100,000 of property in trust with a bank trustee and names his friends Larry (age 60) to receive all of the income for the rest of Larry's life and Ruth (age 25) to receive the assets upon Larry's death. The amount of each donee's gift is reported on the gift tax return and is determined from Table S. If the interest rate is 4% and Larry is age 60, the value of the remainder interest gift to Ruth, as calculated from the single life remainder factors column of Table S, is $46,310 (0.46310 × $100,000). This amount represents the present value of the property Ruth will receive after the death of Larry, age 60. The remaining portion of the $100,000 of property, $53,690 ($100,000 − $46,310), is the value of Larry's life estate. The total value of the income plus remainder interests is 1.0. ◀

EXAMPLE C:12-22 ▶ In July of the current year, Amy (age 62) transferred $1 million of stock to a trust from which she retained the right to receive $120,000 per year for five years. She provided that the remainder will pass to her son, Arthur, at the end of the fifth year. Assume that 4% was the Sec. 7520 rate at the time of her transfer. She anticipated that the stock would continue to appreciate at its recent appreciation rate of 6% a year. The factor for a five-year annuity, assuming a 4%

---

[23] *Term certain interest* means that a particular person has an interest in the property held in trust for a specified time period. The person having such interest does not own or hold title to the property but has a right to receive the income from such property for a specified time period. At the end of the time period, the property reverts to the grantor (or passes to another person, the remainderman).

[24] The IRS regularly issues revenue rulings with applicable rate information.

rate, is 4.451825 [(1.0 − 0.821927, the factor for a remainder interest)/(0.04, the Sec. 7520 rate)]. Thus, Amy is deemed to have retained $534,219 (4.451825 × $120,000) and is deemed to have gifted the difference of $465,781 ($1,000,000 − $534,219) to Arthur. ◄

STOP & THINK

Question: In which scenario would the amount of the gift be larger: (1) a gift of a remainder interest to a friend if a 68-year-old donor retained the income for life or (2) a gift of a remainder interest to a friend if an 86-year-old donor retained the income for life? Assume that each donor makes the gift on the same day so that the applicable interest rates are the same for each scenario.

Solution: The gift of the remainder interest would be larger if the donor is 86, instead of 68, because the actuarial value of the income interest the donor retains would be smaller if the donor is older. Under actuarial assumptions, older donors have shorter life expectancies.

ADDITIONAL COMMENT

In estate freeze transfers, Congress provided rules that generally increase the amount classified as a gift at the time of the actual transfer.

Special Valuation Rules: Estate Freezes. A number of years ago, Congress became concerned that individuals were able to shift wealth to other individuals, usually in a younger generation, without paying their "fair share" of the transfer taxes. An approach donors commonly used was to recapitalize a corporation (by exchanging common stock for both common and preferred shares) and then give the common stock to individuals in the younger generation. This technique was one of a variety of transactions known as estate freezes.

In 1990, Congress decided to address the perceived problem of estate freezes by writing new valuation rules that apply for certain gifts. The thrust of these rules—current IRC Chapter 14 (Secs. 2701 through 2704)—is to ensure that gifts are not undervalued. A couple of the more common situations governed by the new rules are described below, but the rules are too complicated to warrant a complete discussion. If a parent owns 100% of a corporation's stock and then gives the common stock to his or her children and retains the preferred stock, the value of the right to the preferred dividends is treated as zero unless the stock is cumulative preferred. Consequently, unless the donor retains *cumulative* preferred stock, the value assigned to the common stock given away is relatively high. If the donor creates a trust in which he or she retains an interest and in which he or she gives an interest to a family member, the value of the transferor's retained interest is treated as zero unless the interest is an annuity interest (fixed payments) or a unitrust interest (calling for distributions equal to a specified percentage of the current FMV of the trust). Thus, the donor who retains an income interest is treated as having kept nothing. The effect of these rules increases the amount classified as a gift, compared with the result under prior law, unless the transferor structures the transaction to avoid having a zero value assigned to his or her retained interest.[25]

GIFT TAX CONSEQUENCES OF CERTAIN TRANSFERS

Some transactions that cause the transferor to make a gift are straightforward. It is easy to see that the disposition is within the scope of the gift tax if, for example, an individual places the title to stock or real estate solely in another person's name and receives less than adequate consideration in return. Treasury Regulations include the following examples of transactions that may be subject to the gift tax: forgiving of a debt; assignment of the benefits of a life insurance policy; transfer of cash; and transfer of federal, state, or municipal bonds.[26] The gratuitous transfer of state and local bonds falls within the scope of the gift tax, even though interest on such bonds is exempt from federal income taxation. The following discussion concerns the gift tax rules for several transfers that are more complicated than, for example, transferring the title to real property or stock to another person.

[25] See Reg. Secs. 25.2701-1 through -6 and 25.2702-1 through -6 for guidance concerning the estate freeze provisions.

[26] Reg. Sec. 25.2511-1(a).

Creation of Joint Bank Accounts. Parties depositing money to a jointly owned bank account potentially face gift tax consequences. Funding a joint bank account is an incomplete transfer because the depositor is free to withdraw the amount deposited into the account. A gift occurs when one party withdraws an amount exceeding the amount he or she deposited.[27] The transfer is complete at that time because only the person who withdrew funds can control those funds.

EXAMPLE C:12-23 ▶ On May 1, Connie deposits $100,000 into a joint bank account in the names of Connie and Ben. Her friend Ben makes no deposits. On December 1, Ben withdraws $30,000 from the joint account. No gift arises upon the creation of the bank account. However, on December 1, Connie makes a gift to Ben of $30,000, the excess of Ben's withdrawal over Ben's deposit. ◀

Creation of Other Joint Tenancies. **Joint tenancy** is a popular form of property ownership from a convenience standpoint because, when one joint owner dies, the property is automatically owned by the survivor(s). Each joint tenant is deemed to have an equal interest in the property. A completed gift arises when the transferor titles real estate or other property in the names of himself or herself and another (e.g., a spouse, a sibling, or a child) as joint tenants. The person furnishing the consideration to acquire the property is deemed to have made a gift to the other joint tenant in an amount equal to the value of the donee's pro rata interest in the property.[28]

EXAMPLE C:12-24 ▶ Kwame purchases land for $250,000 and immediately has it titled in the names of Kwame and Kesha, as joint tenants with right of survivorship. Kwame and Kesha are not husband and wife. Kwame makes a gift to Kesha of $125,000, which is one-half the value of the property. ◀

TAX STRATEGY TIP

An owner of a life insurance policy who wishes to gift the ownership to someone else, such as the beneficiary, can use the following strategies to avoid the gift tax:
(1) Before making the gift, borrow enough against the policy to reduce its net value to the amount of the annual exclusion ($14,000 in 2015). The former owner (borrower) then can pay premiums and make loan repayments, not to exceed the annual exclusion in any given year.
(2) Have the insurance company rewrite the policy into separate policies, each having a value that does not exceed the annual exclusion. Then, gift one policy each year for several years.

Transfer of Life Insurance Policies. The mere naming of another as the beneficiary of a life insurance policy is an incomplete transfer because the owner of the policy can change the beneficiary designation at any time. However, if an individual irrevocably assigns all ownership rights in an insurance policy to another party, this event constitutes a gift of the policy to the new owner.[29] Ownership rights include the ability to change the beneficiary, borrow against the policy, and cash the policy in for its cash surrender value.

The payment of a premium on an insurance policy owned by another person is considered a gift to the policy's owner. The amount of the gift is the amount of the premium paid. The tax result is the same as if the donor transferred cash to the policy owner and the owner used the cash to pay the premium.

According to Reg. Sec. 25.2512-6, the value of the gift of a life insurance policy is the amount it would cost to purchase a comparable policy on the date of the gift. The regulations point out, however, that if the policy is several years old, the cost of a comparable policy is not readily ascertainable. In such a situation, the policy is valued at its interpolated terminal reserve (i.e., an amount similar to the policy's cash surrender value) plus the amount of any unexpired premiums. The insurance company will furnish information concerning the interpolated terminal reserve.

EXAMPLE C:12-25 ▶ On September 1, Bill transfers his entire ownership rights in a $300,000 life insurance policy on his own life to his sister Susan. The policy's interpolated terminal reserve is $24,000 as of September 1. On July 1, Bill had paid the policy's $4,800 annual premium. Bill makes a gift to Susan on September 1 of $28,000 [$24,000 + ($\frac{10}{12}$ × $4,800)] because he transferred ownership to Susan. If, however, the policy had been a term insurance policy, which has no interpolated terminal reserve, the gift would have been $4,000 ($\frac{10}{12}$ × $4,800), the amount of the unexpired premium.

On July 1 of the next year, Bill pays the $4,800 annual premium on the policy now owned by Susan. As a result of the premium payment, Bill makes a $4,800 gift to Susan that year, the same result as if he had given her $4,800 of cash to pay the premium. ◀

---

27 Reg. Sec. 25.2511-1(h)(4).

28 Reg. Sec. 25.2511-1(h)(5). If the two joint tenants are husband and wife, no taxable gift will arise because of the unlimited marital deduction.

29 Reg. Sec. 25.2511-1(h)(8).

EXAMPLE C:12-26 ▶ Assume the same facts as in Example C:12-25 and that later Susan, who now owns the policy, changes the beneficiary of the policy from Frank to John. Susan does not make a gift because she has not given up control; she can change the beneficiary again in the future. ◀

Exercise of a General Power of Appointment. Section 2514 provides the rules concerning powers of appointment. A **power of appointment** exists when a person transfers property (perhaps in trust) and grants someone else the power to specify who eventually will receive the property. Thus, possession of a power of appointment over property has some of the same benefits as ownership of the property. Powers can be general or special. *Potential* gift tax consequences are associated with the powerholder's exercise of a **general power of appointment**. A person possesses a general power of appointment if he or she has the power to appoint the property (have the property distributed) to him- or herself, his or her creditors or estate, or the creditors of his or her estate. The words *his or her estate* mean that there are no restrictions concerning to whom the individual may bequeath the property. By default, a power that is not general is a special power.

A gift occurs when a powerholder exercises a general power of appointment and names some other person to receive the property.[30] The donee is the person named to receive the property. A person who exercises a general power of appointment in favor of himself or herself does not make a gift (i.e., one cannot make a gift to him- or herself).

EXAMPLE C:12-27 ▶ In 2015, Tina funds an irrevocable trust with $600,000 and names Van to receive the income for life. In addition, Tina grants Van a general power of appointment exercisable during his life as well as at his death. Tina made a gift to Van of $600,000 at the time she transferred the property to the trust in 2015. In 2016, Van instructs the bank trustee to distribute $50,000 of trust property to Kay. Through the exercise of his general power of appointment in favor of Kay, Van makes a $50,000 gift to Kay in 2016 because he diverted property to her. ◀

Net Gifts. A **net gift** occurs when an individual makes a gift to a donee who agrees to pay the gift tax as a condition of receiving the gift. The donee's payment of the gift tax is treated as consideration paid to the donor. The amount of the gift is the excess of the FMV of the transferred property over the amount of the gift tax paid by the donee. Because the amount of the gift depends on the amount of gift tax payable, which in turn depends on the amount of the gift, the calculations require the use of simultaneous equations.[31]

The net gift strategy is especially attractive for people who would like to remove a rapidly appreciating asset from their estate but are unable to pay the gift tax because of liquidity problems. However, a net gift has one potential disadvantage: the Supreme Court has ruled that the donor must recognize as a gain the excess of the gift tax payable over his or her adjusted basis in the property.[32] The Court's rationale is that the donee's payment of the donor's gift tax liability constitutes an "amount realized" for purposes of determining the gain or loss realized on a sale, exchange, or other disposition. From a practical standpoint, this decision affects only donors who transfer property so highly appreciated that the property's adjusted basis is less than the gift tax liability.

EXAMPLE C:12-28 ▶ Mary, who previously had made sizable taxable gifts, transferred land with a $3 million FMV to her son, Sam, who agreed to pay the gift tax liability. Mary's adjusted basis in the land was $15,000. Earlier in 2015, she gave him $14,000, which was covered by the annual exclusion. The taxable gift was $3 million, less the gift tax paid by Sam. Simultaneous equations are necessary to calculate the amount of the gift and the gift tax liability. Mary must recognize gain equal to the excess of the gift tax liability paid by Sam minus Mary's $15,000 basis in the property.

---

30 In general, the exercise of a special power of appointment is free of gift tax consequences. In the case of special powers of appointment, the holder of the power does not have an unrestricted ability to name the persons to receive the property. For example, he or she may be able to appoint to only his or her descendants.

31 In Rev. Rul. 75-72 (1975-1 C.B. 310), the IRS explained how to calculate the amount of the net gift and the gift tax. In Ltr. Rul. 7842068 (July 20, 1978), the IRS stated that the donor's available unified credit, not the donee's, is used to calculate the gift tax payable.

32 *Victor P. Diedrich v. CIR*, 50 AFTR 2d 82-5054, 82-1 USTC ¶9419 (USSC, 1982).

TAX STRATEGY TIP

As a general rule, substantially appreciated property should not be transferred by gift. It should be transferred at death to take advantage of the step-up in basis to the estate tax value (usually FMV at date of death). If Mary in Example C:12-28 were elderly, it might be better to transfer an asset other than the land to preserve a step-up in basis for the land.

Assume that, because of sizable previous taxable gifts, any additional gifts Mary made were subject to the 40% maximum gift tax rate for 2015. Assume Mary had used all of her unified credit. If G represents the amount of the gift and T is the amount of the tax, then

$$G = \$3,000,000 - T$$
$$T = 0.40G$$

Substituting 0.40G for T in the first equation and solving for G yields G = $3,000,000 ÷ 1.40 = $2,142,857, the amount of the gift. The tax is 40% of this amount, or $857,143. Mary's gain equals the $857,143 gift tax paid by Sam minus her $15,000 basis in the property, or $842,143. ◀

Exclusions

OBJECTIVE 4

Determine whether an annual gift tax exclusion is available

In many instances, a portion or all of a transfer by gift is tax-free because of the annual exclusion authorized by Sec. 2503(b). In 1932, the Senate Finance Committee explained the purpose of the **annual exclusion** as follows:

> Such exemption . . . is to obviate the necessity of keeping an account of and reporting numerous small gifts, and . . . to fix the amount sufficiently large to cover in most cases wedding and Christmas gifts and occasional gifts of relatively small amount.[33]

In most gift transactions, the donor makes no taxable gift because of the annual exclusion. Consequently, administration of the gift tax provisions is a much simpler task than it otherwise would be.

AMOUNT OF THE EXCLUSION

The amount of this exclusion, which is analogous to an exclusion from gross income for income tax purposes, is $14,000.[34] It is available each year for an unlimited number of donees. For transfers made in trust, each beneficiary is deemed to be a separate donee. Any number of donors may make a gift to the same donee, and each is eligible to claim the exclusion. The only limitations on the annual exclusion are the donor's wealth, generosity, and imagination in identifying donees.

EXAMPLE C:12-29 ▶ In 2015, Ann and Bob each give $14,000 cash to each of Tad and Liz. Ann and Bob again make $14,000 cash gifts to Tad and Liz in 2016. For both 2015 and 2016, Ann receives $28,000 of exclusions ($14,000 for the gift to Tad and $14,000 for the gift to Liz). The same result applies to Bob. ◀

TAX STRATEGY TIP

Gifts up to the amount of the annual exclusion not only remove the gifted amounts from the donor's estate with no gift tax cost but also remove the property's future income from the donor's estate. In addition, the property's income can be shifted to someone whose tax bracket might be lower than the donor's, thereby reducing income taxes.

The annual exclusion is a significant tax planning device that has no estate tax counterpart. So long as a donor's gifts to a particular donee do not exceed the excludable amount, the donor will never make any taxable gifts or incur any gift tax liability. Because taxable gifts will be zero, the donor's estate tax base will not include any adjusted taxable gifts. A donor, who each year for ten years prior to 2002 gave $10,000 per donee to each of ten donees, removed $1 million (10 × $10,000 × 10) from being taxed in his or her estate. The donor accomplished these transfers without making any taxable gifts or paying any gift tax. If retained, the $1 million would have been taxed in the donor's estate unless the property was willed to the donor's surviving spouse.

PRESENT INTEREST REQUIREMENT

Although we generally speak of the annual exclusion as if it were available automatically for all gifts, in actuality it is not. A donor receives an exclusion only for gifts that constitute a present interest.

---

33 S. Rept. No. 665, 72nd Cong., 1st Sess. (1932), reprinted in 1939-1 C.B. (Part 2), pp. 525–526.

34 On January 1, 1982, Congress increased the annual exclusion from $3,000 to $10,000. Later, Congress provided that the exclusion would be indexed after 1998, with inflation adjustments rounded to the next lowest multiple of $1,000. In 2002, the exclusion rose to $11,000 and remained there through 2005. It rose to $12,000 in 2006, to $13,000 in 2009, and to $14,000 in 2013.

Definition of Present Interest. A **present interest** is "an unrestricted right to the immediate use, possession, or enjoyment of property or the income from property (such as a life estate or term certain)."[35] Only present interests qualify for the annual exclusion. If only a portion of a transfer constitutes a present interest, the excluded portion of the gift may not exceed the value of the present interest.

Definition of Future Interest. A future interest is the opposite of a present interest. A **future interest** "is a legal term, and includes reversions, remainders, and other interests . . . which are limited to commence in use, possession, or enjoyment at some future date or time."[36] Gifts of future interests are ineligible for the annual exclusion. The following examples help demonstrate the attributes of present and future interests.

EXAMPLE C:12-30 ► Nancy transfers $500,000 of property to an irrevocable trust with a bank serving as trustee. Nancy names Norm (age 55) to receive all the trust income quarterly for the rest of Norm's life. At Norm's death, the property is to pass to Ellen (age 25) or Ellen's estate. Norm receives an unrestricted right to immediate enjoyment of the income. Thus, Norm has a present interest. Ellen, however, has a future interest because Ellen cannot enjoy the property or any of the income until Norm dies. The taxable gift is $486,000 ($500,000 − $14,000). ◄

EXAMPLE C:12-31 ► Greg transfers $800,000 of property to an irrevocable trust with a bank serving as trustee and instructs the trustee to distribute all the trust income semiannually to Greg's three adult children, Jill, Katy, and/or Laura. The trustee is to use its discretion in deciding how much to distribute to each beneficiary. Moreover, the trustee is authorized to distribute nothing to a particular beneficiary if it deems such action to be in the beneficiary's best interest. Although all the income must be paid out, the trustee has complete discretion to determine how much to pay to each particular beneficiary. No beneficiary has the assurance that he or she will receive a trust distribution. Thus, Greg created no present interests, and the annual exclusion does not apply. The taxable gift, therefore, is $800,000. ◄

Special Rule for Trusts for Minors. Congress realized that many donors would not want to require trusts for minor children to distribute all their income to the young children. Accordingly, Congress enacted Sec. 2503(c), which authorizes special trusts for minors, to address donors' concerns about the distribution of trust income to minors. Section 2503(c) authorizes an annual exclusion for gifts to trusts for beneficiaries under age 21 even though the trusts need not distribute all their income annually. Such trusts, known as **Sec. 2503(c) trusts**, allow donors to claim the annual exclusion if the following two conditions are met:

- Until the beneficiary becomes age 21, the trustee may pay the income and/or the underlying assets to the beneficiary.
- Any income and underlying assets not paid to the beneficiary will pass to that beneficiary when he or she reaches age 21. If the beneficiary should die before becoming age 21, the income and underlying assets are payable to either the beneficiary's estate or to any person the minor may appoint if the minor possesses a general power of appointment over the property.

ADDITIONAL COMMENT

The donor may serve as trustee of a Sec. 2503(c) trust, but this approach generally is not advisable. If the donor's powers are not sufficiently limited, the trust property will be included in the donor's estate if the donor's death occurs before the trust terminates.

If the trust instrument contains both the provisions listed above, no part of the trust is considered to be a gift of a future interest. Therefore, the entire transfer is treated as a present interest and is eligible for the annual exclusion.

As a result of Sec. 2503(c), donors creating trusts for donees under age 21 receive an exclusion even though the trustee has discretion over paying out the trust income. However, the IRC requires the trustee to distribute the assets and accumulated income at age 21.

ADDITIONAL COMMENT

The holder of a *Crummey* power must be given notice of a contribution to the trust to which the power relates and must be given a reasonable time period within which to exercise the power. The donor receives the annual exclusion regardless of whether the donee exercises the power.

Crummey Trust. The **Crummey trust** is yet another technique that allows the donor to obtain an annual exclusion upon funding a discretionary trust. The trust can terminate at whatever age the donor specifies and can be created for a beneficiary of any age. Thus, the *Crummey* trust is a much more flexible arrangement than the Sec. 2503(c) trust.

[35] Reg. Sec. 25.2503-3(b).

[36] Reg. Sec. 25.2503-3(a).

The *Crummey* trust is named for a Ninth Circuit Court of Appeals decision holding that the trust beneficiaries received a present interest as a result of certain language in the trust instrument.[37] That language, which is referred to interchangeably as a *Crummey* power, *Crummey* demand power, or *Crummey* withdrawal power, entitled each beneficiary to demand a distribution of the lesser of $4,000 (the amount in the case) or the amount transferred to the trust that year. If the beneficiary did not exercise the power by a specified date, it expired. The trust instrument included the "lesser of" language for the demand power because the donor did not want to create a present interest larger than the annual exclusion amount. In years in which the gift is smaller than the annual exclusion amount, the donor simply wants to be able to exclude the amount of that year's gift. In addition, the donor wants to restrict the amount to which the beneficiary can have access. Because of potential changes in the annual exclusion amount, the trust instrument often states that the maximum amount the beneficiary can withdraw is "an amount equal to the annual exclusion for federal gift tax purposes" or twice that amount if gift splitting is anticipated.

The court held that the demand power provided each beneficiary with a present interest equal to the maximum amount the beneficiary could require the trustee to pay over to him or her that year. Use of the *Crummey* trust technique entitles the donor to receive the annual exclusion while creating a discretionary trust that terminates at whatever age the donor deems appropriate. The donor thereby avoids the restrictive rules of Sec. 2503(c). Generally, the donor hopes the beneficiary will not exercise the demand right.

EXAMPLE C:12-32 ▶ Al funds two $100,000 irrevocable trusts and names First Bank the trustee. The first trust is for the benefit of Kay, his 15-year-old daughter. The trustee has discretion to distribute income and/or principal to Kay until she reaches age 21. If she dies before age 21, the trust assets are payable to whomever she appoints in her will or to her estate if she dies without a will. The second trust is for the benefit of Bob, Al's 25-year-old son. Income and/or principal are payable to Bob in the trustee's discretion until Bob reaches age 35, whereupon Bob will receive the trust assets. Bob may demand by December 31 of each year that the trustee pay him the lesser of the amount of the gift tax annual exclusion or the amount transferred to the trust that calendar year. The trust for Kay is a Sec. 2503(c) trust, and the one for Bob is a *Crummey* trust. An annual exclusion is available for each trust. ◀

STOP & THINK

Question: For which of the following gifts would the donor receive an annual exclusion:

- A gift of a remainder interest in land if the donor retains the income interest for life
- A gift outright of a life insurance policy that has a cash surrender value
- A gift to a discretionary trust that is classified as a Sec. 2503(c) trust
- A gift to a Crummey trust?

Solution: All the transfers except the gift of the remainder interest in land (a future interest) are eligible for the annual exclusion. Even though the gift to the Sec. 2503(c) trust does not literally involve a gift of a present interest (the right to current income or enjoyment), the IRC explicitly allows this kind of transfer to qualify for the annual exclusion.

GIFT TAX DEDUCTIONS

OBJECTIVE 5

Identify the deductions available for gift tax purposes

The formula for determining taxable gifts allows both an unlimited marital deduction and an unlimited charitable contribution deduction. The **marital deduction** is for transfers to one's spouse. The **charitable contribution deduction** is for gifts to charitable organizations. Section 2524 states that the deductible amount in either case may not exceed the amount of the "includible gift"—that is, the amount of the gift exceeding the annual exclusion. Thus, the lowest possible taxable gift is zero, not a negative number, as could be the case if the deduction equaled the total amount of the gift.

[37] *D. Clifford Crummey v. CIR*, 22 AFTR 2d 6023, 68-2 USTC ¶12,541 (9th Cir., 1968).

MARITAL DEDUCTION

ADDITIONAL COMMENT

Congress allowed a marital deduction because a taxpayer who transfers property to his or her spouse has not made a transfer outside the economic (husband/wife) unit. For similar reasons, the interspousal gift has no *income* tax consequences. The donor spouse recognizes no gain or loss, and the donee spouse takes a carryover basis.

Generally, the marital deduction results in tax-free interspousal transfers, but an exception discussed below applies to gifts of certain terminable interests. Congress enacted the marital deduction in 1948 to provide more uniform treatment of community property and noncommunity property donors. To recap, in community property states, most property acquired after marriage is owned equally by each spouse. In noncommunity property states, however, the spouses' wealth often is divided unequally, and such spouses can equalize each individual's share of the wealth only by engaging in a gift-giving program. As a result of the marital deduction, spouses, including those in same sex marriages, can shift wealth between themselves completely free of any gift tax consequences.

Unlimited Amount. Over the years, the maximum marital deduction has varied, but since 1981 a spouse has been able to deduct up to 100% of the amount of gifts made to the other spouse. The amount of the marital deduction, however, is limited to the portion of the gift that exceeds the annual exclusion.[38] After 1981, transfers of community property became eligible for the marital deduction.

EXAMPLE C:12-33 ► Jane gives her husband stock valued at $450,000. She excludes $14,000 because of the annual exclusion and claims a $436,000 marital deduction. Thus, no taxable gift arises. ◄

Gifts of Terminable Interests: General Rule.

Nondeductible Terminable Interests. A **terminable interest** is an interest that ends or is terminated when some event occurs (or fails to occur) or a specified amount of time passes. Some, but not all, terminable interests are ineligible for the marital deduction.[39] A marital deduction is denied only when the transfer is of a *nondeductible* terminable interest. A nondeductible terminable interest has one of the following characteristics:

- The donee-spouse's interest ceases at a set time (such as at death) and the property then either passes back to the donor or passes to a third party who does not pay adequate consideration.
- Immediately after making the gift, the donor has the power to name someone else to receive an interest in the property, and the person named may possess the property upon the termination of the donee-spouse's interest.[40]

The next three examples illustrate some of the subtleties of the definition of nondeductible terminable interests. In Example C:12-34, a marital deduction is available because the transfer involves neither characteristic of a nondeductible terminable interest.

EXAMPLE C:12-34 ► A donor gives a patent to a spouse. A patent is a terminable interest because the property interest terminates at the end of the patent's legal life. Nevertheless, the patent does not constitute a nondeductible terminable interest. When the patent's legal life expires, a third party will not possess an interest in the patent. Thus, a donor will receive a marital deduction. ◄

In Example C:12-35, a marital deduction is denied because the first of the two alternative characteristics of a nondeductible terminable interest exists.

EXAMPLE C:12-35 ► A donor transfers property in trust and (1) names his wife to receive trust income, at the trustee's discretion, annually for the next 15 years and (2) states that at the end of the 15-year period the trust's assets are to be distributed to their child. The donor gave his wife a nondeductible terminable interest. When the spouse's interest ceases, the property passes to their child, who did not pay adequate consideration. Thus, the donor receives no marital deduction. ◄

In Example C:12-36, a marital deduction is available. In addition to having a lifetime income interest, the donee-spouse has a general power of appointment over the trust's assets and can specify who eventually receives the property.

---

[38] Sec. 2524.
[39] Sec. 2523(b).
[40] Ibid.

EXAMPLE C:12-36 ▶ The donor gives his wife the right to all the income from a trust annually for life plus a general power of appointment over the trust's assets. He has transferred an interest eligible for the marital deduction. The general power of appointment may be exercisable during life, at death, or at both times. In addition, the donee-spouse is entitled to receive the income annually. ◀

TAX STRATEGY TIP

Granting the spouse a general power of appointment can qualify a transfer for the marital deduction. For example, Brad transferred property to a trust, income to be distributed annually to his wife Sonia until her death, with a general power of appointment in Sonia over the remainder. Sonia's general power of appointment qualified the transfer for the marital deduction.

The rationale behind the nondeductible terminable interest rule is that a donor should obtain a marital deduction only if he or she conveys an interest that will have transfer tax significance to the donee-spouse. In other words, when a donee spouse later gives away property received as a result of an interspousal transfer, a transfer subject to the gift tax occurs. If the donee-spouse retains such property until death, the asset is included in the donee-spouse's gross estate.

TAX STRATEGY TIP

By using a QTIP, a donor can achieve a marital deduction while exercising some control over the property. For example, assume the same facts as in the previous annotation except that Brad has been married twice. He had two children by his first wife and three children with Sonia. Brad could not be sure his first two children would receive any assets from the trust because Sonia could exercise her general power of appointment in favor of just their three children (or someone else). If Brad funded a QTIP, the trust instrument could specify that the remainder, on Sonia's death, would go equally to all five children. Brad could thus control the ultimate disposition of the remainder and still receive a marital deduction.

QTIP Provisions. Beginning in 1982, Congress made a major change to the nondeductible terminable interest rule and allowed transfers of qualified terminable interest property to be eligible for the marital deduction.[41] Such transfers are commonly referred to as *QTIP transfers*. **Qualified terminable interest property** is property

- That is transferred by the donor-spouse,
- In which the donee has a "qualifying income interest for life," and
- For which a special election has been made.

A spouse has the necessary "qualifying income interest for life" if

- The spouse is entitled to all the income from the property annually or more often, and
- No person has a power to appoint any part of the property to any person other than the donee-spouse unless the power cannot be exercised until after the spouse dies.

The QTIP rule enhances the attractiveness of making transfers to one's spouse because a donor can receive a marital deduction—and thereby make a nontaxable transfer—without having to grant the spouse full control over the gifted property. The QTIP rule is especially attractive for a donor who wants to ensure that the children by a previous marriage will receive the property upon the donee-spouse's death.

The donor does not have to claim a marital deduction even though the transfer otherwise qualifies as a QTIP transfer. Claiming the deduction on such transfers is elective.[42] If the donor elects to claim a marital deduction, the donee-spouse must include the QTIP trust property in his or her estate at its value as of the donee-spouse's date of death. Thus, as with other transfers qualifying for the marital deduction, the interspousal transfer is tax-free, and the taxable event is postponed until the donee-spouse transfers the property.

EXAMPLE C:12-37 ▶ Jo transfers $1 million of property in trust with a bank acting as trustee. All the trust income is payable to Jo's husband, Ed (age 64), quarterly for the rest of his life. Upon Ed's death, the property will pass to Jo's nieces. This gift is eligible for a marital deduction. If Jo elects to claim the marital deduction, she will receive a $986,000 ($1,000,000 − $14,000) marital deduction. The deduction is limited to the amount of the includible gift, i.e., the gift exceeding the annual exclusion. Jo's taxable gift will be zero. ◀

Note that Jo's marital deduction in the preceding example is for $986,000 and not for the value of Ed's life estate. If Jo elects to claim the marital deduction, Ed's gross estate will include the value of the entire trust, valued as of the date of Ed's death. The QTIP provision permits Jo to receive a marital deduction while still being able to specify who will receive the property upon her husband's death.

Topic Review C:12-2 summarizes the eligibility of a transfer for the marital deduction and the amount of the marital deduction that can be claimed.

---

41 Sec. 2523(f).

42 The donor might decide not to claim the marital deduction if the donee-spouse has substantial assets already or a short life expectancy, especially if the gifted property's value is expected to appreciate at a high annual rate.

TOPIC REVIEW C:12-2

Eligibility for and Amount of the Marital Deduction

Examples of Transfers Eligible for the Marital Deduction

Property transferred to spouse as sole owner

Property transferred in trust with all the income payable to the spouse for life and over which the donee-spouse receives a general power of appointment

Property transferred in trust with all the income payable annually or more often to the spouse for life and for which the donor-spouse designated the remainderman—marital deduction available if elected under QTIP rule

Examples of Transfers Ineligible for the Marital Deduction

Property transferred in trust with the income payable in the trustee's discretion to the spouse for life, and for which the donor-spouse designated the remainderman

Property transferred in trust with all the income payable to the spouse for a specified number of years and for which the donor-spouse designated the remainderman

Amount of the Marital Deduction, if Available

The amount of the transfer minus the portion eligible for the annual exclusion

CHARITABLE CONTRIBUTION DEDUCTION

A donor who makes no noncharitable gifts in excess of the excludible amount does not have to report gifts to charitable organizations on a gift tax return, provided a charitable contribution deduction is available and the charitable organization receives the donor's entire interest in the property. Claiming an income tax deduction for a charitable contribution does not preclude the donor from also obtaining a gift tax deduction. In contrast with the income tax provisions, the gift tax charitable contribution deduction has no percentage limitation. The only ceiling is imposed by Sec. 2524, which limits the deduction to the amount of the gift that exceeds the excluded portion.

EXAMPLE C:12-38 ► Julio gives stock valued at $76,000 to State University. Julio receives a $14,000 annual exclusion and a $62,000 charitable contribution deduction for *gift* tax purposes. However, he need not report the gift on a gift tax return if he does not have to file a return to report gifts to noncharitable donees. On his *income* tax return, he receives a $76,000 charitable contribution deduction, subject to AGI limitations. ◄

TAX STRATEGY TIP

A charitably minded taxpayer could avoid the gift (and the estate) tax entirely by giving all his or her property to a qualified charitable organization. Actually, in 2015 the taxpayer could give $5.43 million plus the amount shielded by the annual exclusion to noncharitable donees and still pay no gift tax, assuming the taxpayer had not earlier made any taxable gifts.

Transfers Eligible for the Deduction. To be deductible, the gift must be made to a charitable organization. The rules defining charitable organizations are quite similar for income, gift, and estate tax purposes.[43] According to Sec. 2522, a gift tax deduction is available for contributions to the following:

- The United States or any subordinate level of government within the United States as long as the transfer is solely for public purposes
- A corporation, trust fund, etc., organized exclusively for religious, charitable, scientific, literary, or educational purposes, or to foster amateur sports competition, including the encouragement of art and the prevention of cruelty to children or animals
- A fraternal society or similar organization operating under the lodge system if the gifts are to be used in the United States only for religious, charitable, scientific, literary, or educational purposes
- A war veterans' post or organization organized in the United States or one of its possessions if no part of its net earnings accrues to the benefit of private shareholders or individuals

[43] In contrast to the income tax rules, a charitable contribution deduction is available under the gift tax rules for transfers made to foreign charitable organizations. No deduction is available, however, for gifts made to foreign governments.

Split-Interest Transfers. Specialized rules apply when a donor makes a transfer for both private (i.e., an individual) and public (i.e., a charitable organization) purposes. Such arrangements are known as **split-interest transfers**. An example of a split-interest transfer is the gift of a residence to one's sister for life with the remainder interest to a university. If a donor gives a charitable organization a remainder interest, the donor forfeits the charitable contribution deduction unless the remainder interest is in either a personal residence (not necessarily the donor's principal residence), a farm, a charitable remainder annuity trust or unitrust, or a pooled income fund.[44] A split-interest gift of a present interest to a charity qualifies for a charitable contribution deduction only if the charity receives a guaranteed annuity interest or a unitrust interest. Actuarial tables are used to value split-interest transfers (see Appendix H).

EXAMPLE C:12-39 ▶ Al transfers $800,000 of property to a charitable remainder annuity trust. He reserves an annuity of $52,000 per year for his remaining life and specifies that upon his death the trust property will pass to the American Red Cross. Al must report this transaction on a gift tax return because the Red Cross did not receive his entire interest in the property. In the same year, Al gives a museum a remainder interest in his antique furniture collection and reserves a life estate for himself.

Each of these is a split-interest transfer. Unfortunately for the donor, only the remainder interest in the charitable remainder annuity trust is eligible for a charitable contribution deduction. Consequently, Al makes a taxable gift equal to the value of the remainder interest in the antique furniture. (If Al had given a remainder interest in a personal residence or farm, he would have received a charitable contribution deduction for this gift.) Even though the furniture is not an income-producing property, the value of the remainder interest is determined from the actuarial tables found in Appendix H.

Assume that Al was age 60 at the time of the gifts and that the Sec. 7520 interest rate was 4%. What is the amount of Al's charitable contribution deduction?

Answer: The portion of the annuity trust retained by Al is $697,970 {[(1.0 − 0.46310)/0.04] × $52,000}. The charitable deduction on the gift tax return is $102,030 ($800,000 − $697,970), the value of the remainder interest, a future interest. The same amount also is allowable—subject to the ceiling rules—as a charitable contribution deduction on Al's income tax return for that year. ◀

SELF-STUDY QUESTION

In Example C:12-39, does Al receive an annual exclusion for the gift of the furniture?

ANSWER

No. The remainder interest is a future interest, as is the remainder in the trust.

THE GIFT-SPLITTING ELECTION

OBJECTIVE 6

Apply the gift-splitting rules

The gift-splitting provisions of Sec. 2513 allow spouses to treat a gift actually made by just one of them as if each spouse made one-half of the gift. This election offers several advantages, as follows:

- ▶ If only one spouse makes a gift to a particular donee, the election enables a spouse to give $28,000 (instead of $14,000) to the donee before a taxable gift arises.
- ▶ If per-donee annual transfers exceed $28,000 and taxable gifts occur, the election may reduce the applicable marginal gift tax rate.
- ▶ Each spouse may use a unified credit to reduce the gift tax payable.

TAX STRATEGY TIP

Donors can magnify the benefits of the annual exclusion by using gift splitting techniques.

To take advantage of the gift-splitting election, the spouses must meet the following requirements at the time of the transfer:

- ▶ They must be U.S. citizens or residents.
- ▶ At the time of the gift(s) for which the spouses make an election, the donor-spouse must be married to the person who consents to gift splitting. In addition, the donor-spouse must not remarry before the end of the year.

[44] In a **charitable remainder annuity trust**, an individual receives trust distributions for a certain time period or for life. The annual distributions are a uniform percentage (5% or higher) of the value of the trust property, valued on the date of the transfer. For a **charitable remainder unitrust**, the distributions are similar, except that they are a uniform percentage (5% or higher) of the value of the trust property, revalued at least annually. Thus, the annual distributions from a unitrust, but not an annuity trust, vary from one year to the next. Both unitrusts and annuity trusts must meet the requirements that the payout rate does not exceed 50% of the value of the property and the value of the remainder interest is at least 10% of the initial FMV. A **pooled income fund** is similar in concept to a mutual fund. The various individual beneficiaries receive annual distributions of their proportionate shares of the pooled income fund's total income.

ADDITIONAL COMMENT

A wife makes a gift of $40,000 to a child in March and a gift of $60,000 to another child in November of the same year. The gift-splitting election, if made, will apply to both gifts because the election to gift split applies to all gifts made during the year. With gift splitting, her husband will be treated as making one-half of each gift.

The gift-splitting election is effective for all transfers to third parties made during the portion of the year that the spouses were married to each other.

A spouse living in a community property state who makes a gift of separate property (e.g., an asset received by inheritance) may desire to use gift splitting. In this case, the election automatically extends to gifts of community property even though splitting each spouse's gifts of community property has no impact on the "bottom-line" amount of taxable gifts.

Note that gift splitting is an all-or-nothing proposition. Spouses wanting to elect it for one gift must elect it for all gifts to third parties for that year. Each year's election stands alone, however, and is not binding on future years.[45] The procedural aspects of the gift-splitting election are discussed in the Compliance and Procedural Considerations section of this chapter.

EXAMPLE C:12-40 ►

Eli married Joy on April 1 of the current year. They are still married to each other at the end of the year. In March, Eli gave Amy $60,000. In July, Eli gave Barb $52,000, and Joy gave Claire $28,000. If the couple elects gift splitting, the election is effective only for the July gifts. Each spouse is treated as giving $26,000 and $14,000 to Barb and Claire, respectively. Because they may not elect gift splitting for the gift Eli made before their marriage, Eli is treated as giving $60,000—the amount he actually transfers—to Amy. Under gift splitting, Eli and Joy each exclude $14,000 of gifts to both Barb and Claire, or a total of $56,000. Eli also excludes $14,000 of his gift to Amy. ◄

ADDITIONAL COMMENT

The gift-splitting election is a year-by-year election. For example, a husband and wife could elect to gift split in 2010, 2012, and 2014, but not elect to gift split in 2011, 2013, and 2015.

Upon the death of the actual donor or the spouse who consented to gift splitting, such decedent's estate tax base includes that decedent's post-1976 taxable gifts, known as adjusted taxable gifts. By electing gift splitting, a couple can reduce the amount of the taxable gifts the donor-decedent is deemed to have made. Under gift splitting, the adjusted taxable gifts include only the portions of the gifts that are taxable on the gift tax returns filed by the donor-decedent. Of course, the nondonor-spouse's estate reports his or her post-1976 taxable gifts.

? STOP & THINK

Question: Bob made taxable gifts of $5.5 million in 2014, and Betty, his spouse, has not made any taxable gifts. Betty inherited a large fortune and is contemplating gifting $500,000 in 2015 to each of her two children. Bob does not anticipate making any taxable gifts in 2015. Should they elect gift splitting for Betty's gifts?

Solution: They should not necessarily elect gift splitting because the main advantage of the election will be that the aggregate annual exclusions will be $56,000 instead of $28,000. An adverse effect will be that Bob, who has exhausted his unified credit (except for the small increase to the current year amount) and whose rate is 40%, will be the deemed donor of $472,000 [(0.50 × $1,000,000) − $28,000] of taxable gifts.

COMPUTATION OF THE GIFT TAX LIABILITY

OBJECTIVE 7

Calculate the gift tax liability

EFFECT OF PREVIOUS TAXABLE GIFTS

The gift tax computation involves a cumulative process. All the donor's previous taxable gifts (i.e., those made in 1932 or later years) plus the donor's taxable gifts for the current year affect the marginal tax rate for current taxable gifts. Thus, two donors who make the same taxable gifts in the current period may incur different gift tax liabilities because one donor may have made substantially larger taxable gifts in earlier periods than did the other donor. The process outlined below must be used to compute the gross tax levied on the current period's taxable gifts.

1. Determine the gift tax liability (at current rates) on the donor's cumulative taxable gifts (taxable gifts of current period plus aggregate taxable gifts of previous periods).

[45] If the nondonor-spouse has made substantial taxable gifts relative to those made by the donor-spouse, the gift tax liability for the period in question may be lower if the spouses do not elect gift splitting because the nondonor-spouse may have little or no unified credit left and may have reached the highest marginal transfer tax rate.

2. Determine the gift tax liability (at current rates) on the donor's cumulative taxable gifts made through the end of the preceding period.
3. Subtract the gift tax determined in Step 2 from that in Step 1. The difference equals the gross gift tax on the current period's taxable gifts.

This calculation process results in taxing the gifts on a progressive basis over the donor's lifetime.

Note that, although the gift tax rates have varied over the years, the current rate schedule is used in the calculation even when the donor made some or all the earlier gifts when different rates were in effect. This process ensures that current taxable gifts are taxed at the appropriate rate, given the donor's earlier gift history.

EXAMPLE C:12-41 ▶ In 1975, Tony made $2 million in taxable gifts. These gifts were the first Tony ever made. The tax imposed under the 1975 rate schedule was $564,900. Tony made his next taxable gifts in 2015. The taxable amount of these gifts was $400,000. The tax on Tony's 2015 taxable gifts before applying the unified credit is calculated as follows:

Tax at current rates on $2.4 million of cumulative taxable gifts	$905,800
Minus: Tax at current rates on $2 million of prior period taxable gifts	(745,800)
Tax on $400,000 of taxable gifts made in the current period	$160,000 ◀

This cumulative process results in the $400,000 gift in Example C:12-41 being taxed at the maximum 40% gift tax rate for 2015, which applied to taxable transfers exceeding $1 million. If the gift tax computations were not cumulative, the tax on the $400,000 of gifts would be determined by using the lowest marginal rates and would have been only $121,800. Because the tax on taxable transfers made in previous periods is determined by reference to the current rate schedule, Tony's actual 1975 gift tax liability, incurred when the gift tax rates were lower, is not relevant to the determination of his current gift tax. As discussed below, the unified credit will reduce the tax liability.

UNIFIED CREDIT AVAILABLE

Congress enacted a unified credit for both gift and estate tax purposes beginning in 1977. The unified credit reduces the amount of the gross gift tax owed on current period gifts. The size of the tax base for which the unified credit exactly offsets the tax liability is referred to as the exemption equivalent (or applicable exclusion amount). The amount of the credit has increased over the years (see inside back cover). The credit for gift tax purposes rose to $345,800 in 2002 and remained at that amount through 2009 even though the credit against estate taxes increased further through 2009. In 2010, the unified credit for gift taxes was $330,800. In 2011, it rose to $1,730,800, the tax at a maximum 35% tax rate on the $5 million exemption equivalent for 2011. For 2012, the $5 million became indexed. Beginning in 2013, the top tax rate rose to 40%. The exemption equivalent for 2015 is $5 million indexed to $5.43 million. Thus, for 2015 the credit is $2,117,800. Donors who made taxable gifts in the post-1976 period have used some of their credit. Thus, the credit available for the current year is reduced by the aggregate amount allowable as a credit in all preceding years. Because of the reduction of the top rate beginning in 2010 the credit for the current year is reduced by what the credit would have been, if lower than the credit actually claimed, calculated using the rates for the current year.

EXAMPLE C:12-42 ▶ Hu made her first taxable gift in 1985. The taxable amount of the 1985 gift was $100,000, which resulted in a gross gift tax of $23,800. Hu claimed $23,800 (of the $121,800 credit then available) on her 1985 return to reduce her net gift tax liability to zero. Hu made her next taxable gift in 1994. The taxable amount of the gift was $400,000. The tax on the $400,000 gift equaled (1) the tax on $500,000 of total gifts (at 1994 gift tax rates) of $155,800 minus (2) the tax on $100,000 of previous gifts (at 1994 gift tax rates) of $23,800, or $132,000. The credit amount for 1994 was $192,800. Hu's gift tax was reduced to zero by a credit of $132,000 because for 1994 she had a credit of $169,000 ($192,800 − $23,800) left. If in 2015 Hu makes additional taxable gifts, $1,926,000 [$2,117,800 − ($23,800 + $132,000)] of unified credit is available to reduce Hu's gift tax liability in 2015. Note that none of Hu's earlier gifts were taxed at rates above 40%. Thus, the credit available for the current year is reduced by the total amount of the credits actually claimed earlier. ◀

STOP & THINK

Question: In the process of preparing a current year gift tax return, you reviewed a 2011 gift tax return a different CPA prepared for your new client, George Winston. The tax return reported 2011 taxable gifts of $5 million and $500,000 of taxable gifts made in 1999. You note that the return showed tax of $1,730,800, claimed a unified credit of $1,730,800, and thus reported zero gift tax payable. What should you discuss with your new client?

Solution: You should explain that the 2011 unified credit of $1,730,800 (which equaled the tax on the first $5 million of taxable gifts) was not an annual credit maximum but rather the credit available during a donor's lifetime. Because in 1999 the client made $500,000 of taxable gifts, he used $155,800 of his $211,300 unified credit then available. In addition, you should explain the cumulative nature of the gift tax calculations. The tax calculated on the first $5 million of taxable gifts was $1,730,800. If the other CPA claimed a $1,730,800 unified credit and showed zero tax payable, he or she did not calculate the tax on the $5 million 2011 taxable gift by performing the cumulative calculations that take into effect the $500,000 of earlier taxable gifts. The tax *before* the credit was calculated incorrectly. The credit actually available was $1,575,000 ($1,730,800 − $155,800), the 2011 credit less the credit already used. In this situation you subtract the credit actually used in 1999 because that credit was calculated at a top rate of 34%. Therefore, you should advise the client to file an amended return and pay the correct gift tax.

COMPREHENSIVE ILLUSTRATION

The following comprehensive illustration demonstrates the computation of one donor's gift tax liability for the situation where the spouses elect gift splitting. It demonstrates the computation of the wife's gift tax liability.

ADDITIONAL COMMENT

This illustration pertains to 2014 because tax forms for that year are the latest available at the time this textbook was published.

Background Data. Hugh and Wilma Brown are married to each other throughout 2014. Hugh made no taxable gifts in earlier periods. Wilma's previous taxable gifts were $300,000 in 1975 and $200,000 in 1988. In August 2014, Wilma makes the following gratuitous transfers:

- $80,000 in cash to son Billy
- $30,000 in jewelry to daughter Betsy
- $34,000 in medical expense payments to Downtown Infirmary for medical care of grandson Tim
- Remainder interest in vacation cabin to friend Ruth Cain. Wilma (age 60) retains a life estate. The vacation cabin is valued at $100,000.
- $600,000 of stocks to a bank in trust with all of the income payable semiannually to husband Hugh (age 72) for life and remainder payable at Hugh's death to Jeff Bass, Wilma's younger brother, or Jeff's estate. Wilma wants to elect the marital deduction.

In 2014, Hugh's only gifts were

- $100,000 of stock to State University
- $600,000 of land to daughter Betsy

Assume the applicable interest rate for valuing life estates and remainders is 4%.

Calculation of Tax Liability. Section 2503(e) exempts the medical expense payments from the gift tax. The Browns need to report the gift made to State University even though the university received Hugh's entire interest in the property, and even though the transfer is nontaxable, because they must file a gift tax return to report gifts to noncharitable donees. The vacation cabin is valued at $100,000, and the remainder interest therein at $46,310 (0.46310 × $100,000) (see Table S, age 60, 4%, in Appendix H). The stock is transferred to a QTIP trust, and the marital deduction election treats the entire interest (not just the life estate) as having been given to Hugh Brown.

Table C:12-1 shows the computation of Wilma's gift tax liability for 2014. These same facts are used for the sample United States Gift Tax Return, Form 709, in Appendix B. The form's format for reporting the gift-splitting aspects differs slightly from the format in the table. On the form, Part 1 of Schedule A splits the gifts earlier than Table C:12-1 does. Wilma does not have a predeceased spouse.

▼ TABLE C:12-1
Comprehensive Gift Tax Illustration

Wilma's actual 2014 gifts:			
	Billy, cash		$ 80,000
	Betsy, jewelry		30,000
	Ruth, remainder interest in vacation cabin (future interest)		46,310
	Husband Hugh and son Jeff, transfer to QTIP trust		600,000
	Total gifts made by Wilma		$756,310
Minus:	One-half of Wilma's gifts made to third parties that are deemed made by Hugh [0.50 × ($80,000 + $30,000 + $46,310)]		(78,155)
Plus:	One-half of Hugh's gifts made to third parties (Betsy and State University) that are deemed made by Wilma [0.50 × ($100,000 + $600,000)]		350,000
Minus:	Annual exclusions for gifts of present interests ($14,000 each for gifts made to Billy, Betsy, Hugh, and State University)		(56,000)
Minus:	Marital deduction ($600,000 − $14,000 exclusion)		(586,000)
Minus:	Charitable contribution deduction ($50,000 deemed gift by Wilma − $14,000 exclusion)		(36,000)
Taxable gifts for current period			$350,155
Tax on cumulative taxable gifts of $850,155[a]			$287,360
Minus:	Tax on previous taxable gifts of $500,000 (current rate schedule)		(155,800)
Tax on taxable gifts of $350,155 for the current period			$131,560
Minus:	Unified credit:		
	Credit for 2014	$2,081,800	
	Minus: Credit allowable for prior periods	(68,000)[b]	
	Remaining credit; credit actually used	$2,013,800	$131,560
Tax payable for 2014			$ -0-

[a]$300,000 (in 1975) + $200,000 (in 1988) + $350,155 (in 2014).
[b]$0 (for 1975) + $68,000 (for 1988). The $68,000, which is smaller than the maximum credit of $192,800 for 1988, is the excess of the $155,800 tax on cumulative taxable gifts less the $87,800 tax on the $300,000 previous taxable gifts. Taxpayer subtracts the same amount as the credit actually used because the credit was calculated at rates below 37%.

BASIS CONSIDERATIONS FOR A LIFETIME GIVING PLAN

OBJECTIVE 8

Recognize how basis affects the overall tax consequences

Prospective donors should consider the tax-saving features of making a series of lifetime gifts (discussed in the Tax Planning Considerations section of this chapter). Lifetime giving plans can remove income from the donor's income tax return and transfer it to the donee's income tax return, where it may be taxed at a lower marginal tax rate. A series of gifts may permit property to be transferred to a donee without incurring a gift tax liability and thus enable the donor to eliminate part or all of his or her estate tax liability. These two advantages must be weighed against the unattractive basis rules (discussed below) applicable for such transfers.

PROPERTY RECEIVED BY GIFT

The carryover basis rules apply to property received by gift. Provided the property's FMV on the date of the gift exceeds its adjusted basis, the donor's basis in the property carries over as the donee's basis. In addition, the donee's basis may be increased by some or all of the gift tax paid by the donor. For pre-1977 gifts, all the gift taxes paid by the donor may be added to the donor's adjusted basis. For post-1976 transfers, however, the donee may add only the portion of the gift taxes represented by the following fraction:

SELF-STUDY QUESTION

Barkley purchased land in 1965 for $90,000. In 1974, when the FMV of the land was $300,000, he gave the land to his son Tracy, claimed a $3,000 annual exclusion, and paid gift taxes of $23,000. What is Tracy's basis in the land? What if the gift had been made in 2015? For simplicity, assume the 2015 tax was $23,000.

ANSWER

If the gift were made in 1974, Tracy's basis is $90,000 plus the $23,000 gift tax, or $113,000. Had Barkley made the gift in 2015, Tracy's basis would be $90,000 plus [($210,000/$286,000) × $23,000], or $106,888.

$$\frac{\text{Amount of property's appreciation from acquisition date through date of gift}}{\text{FMV of property on the date of the gift minus exclusions and deductions}}$$

In no event, however, can the gift tax adjustment increase the donee's basis above the property's FMV on the date of the gift.[46]

If the gifted property's FMV on the date of the gift is less than the donor's adjusted basis, the basis rules are more complicated. For purposes of determining gain, the donee's basis is the same as the donor's adjusted basis. In determining loss, the donee's basis is the property's FMV on the date of the gift. If the donee sells the property for an amount between its FMV as of the date of the gift and the donor's adjusted basis, the donee recognizes no gain or loss. The property's basis cannot be increased by any gift taxes paid if the donor's adjusted basis exceeds the property's FMV as of the date of the gift. In general, prospective donors should dispose of property that has declined in value by selling it instead of gifting it.

PROPERTY RECEIVED AT DEATH

ADDITIONAL COMMENT

Phil owns investment property worth $350,000 in which his adjusted basis is $500,000. Unless there are reasons why the property should be kept in the family, Phil should sell the property and recognize an income tax loss. If he gifts the property to his child, the loss basis in the child's hands is $350,000 (and the gain basis is $500,000). Thus, if the value does not increase, a loss deduction for the $150,000 decline in market value can never be taken. If Phil dies holding the loss property, his heirs will take the estate tax return value (FMV) as their basis, and the potential income tax loss will not be recognized.

In general, the basis rules that apply to property received as a result of another's death call for a step up or step down to the property's FMV as of the decedent's date of death. The recipient's basis is the same as the amount at which the property is valued on the estate tax return, which is its FMV on either the decedent's date of death or the alternate valuation date. Generally, the alternate valuation date is six months after the date of death. Although these rules are usually thought of as providing for a step-up in basis, if the property has declined in value as of the transferor's death, the basis is stepped-down to its FMV at the date of death or alternate valuation date.

In certain circumstances, no step up in basis occurs for appreciated property transferred at death.[47] This exception applies if both of the following conditions are present:

- ▶ The decedent receives the appreciated property as a gift during the one-year period preceding his or her death, and
- ▶ The property passes to the donor or to the donor's spouse as a result of the donee-decedent's death.

Before the enactment of this rule, a widely publicized planning technique involved transferring appreciated property to one's ill spouse who, in turn, could will the property back to the donor-spouse, who would receive the property at a stepped-up basis. Interspousal transfers by gift and at death are tax-free because of the unlimited marital deduction for both gift tax and estate tax purposes. Consequently, before the rule change, the property received a step-up in basis at no transfer tax cost.

EXAMPLE C:12-43 ▶ In June 2014, Sarah gave property valued at $700,000 to Tom, her husband. Sarah's adjusted basis in the property was $120,000. Tom died in March 2015. At this time, the property was worth $740,000. If the property passed back to Sarah under Tom's will upon Tom's death, Sarah's basis would be $120,000. However, if the property passed to someone other than Sarah at Tom's death, its basis would be stepped-up to $740,000. If Tom lived for more than one year after receiving the gift, the basis would be stepped-up to its FMV as of Tom's date of death regardless of whether the property passed at Tom's death to Sarah or someone else. If Tom (the donee) sold the property a few months before his death in March 2015, Tom's basis would be the same as Sarah's was, or $120,000. ◀

For estates of decedents dying in 2010, the executor could elect to exempt the estate from the estate tax and forego the basis step-up and use instead a modified carryover basis rule. Under this rule, a person receiving property from a decedent obtained a basis equal to the lesser of (1) the decedent's adjusted basis in the property or (2) the property's fair market value at the date of the decedent's death. A special rule, however, allowed a total basis increase of

[46] See Reg. Sec. 1.1015-5(c) for examples of how to calculate the gift tax that can increase the property's basis.

[47] Sec. 1014(e).

$1.3 million to all assets (and an additional $3 million basis increase for property transferred to a surviving spouse) not to exceed the property's fair market value. Assume a decedent's estate consisted of $10 million cash and land the decedent purchased for $2 million. He died in 2010, when the land was worth $12 million and willed the land to his spouse and the cash to his children. The executor elected to be exempt from the estate tax. The spouse's basis in the land is $6.3 million ($2,000,000 + $1,300,000 + $3,000,000), compared with $12 million under the fair market value basis rule. Some additional special rules apply to the basis of property received from a decedent but are not detailed in this text.

Below-market loans: gift and income tax consequences

OBJECTIVE 9

Determine the tax consequences of below-market loans

GENERAL RULES

Section 7872 addresses the gift and income tax consequences of below-market loans. In general, it treats the lender as both making a gift to the borrower and receiving interest income. The borrower is treated as receiving a gift and paying interest expense.

In the case of a demand loan, the lender is treated as having made a gift in each year in which the loan is outstanding. The amount of the gift equals the forgone interest income for the portion of the year the loan is outstanding. The forgone interest income is calculated by referring to the excess of the federal short-term rate of Sec. 1274(d), for the period in question, over the interest rate the lender charged.

For income tax purposes, the forgone interest is treated as being retransferred from the borrower to the lender on the last day of each calendar year in which the loan is outstanding. The amount of the forgone interest is the same as for gift tax purposes and is reported by the lender as income for the year in question. The borrower gets an interest expense deduction for the same amount unless one of the rules limiting the interest deduction applies (e.g., personal interest or investment interest limitations).

EXAMPLE C:12-44 ▶ On July 1, Frank lends $500,000 to Susan, who signs an interest-free demand note. The loan is still outstanding on December 31. Assume that 10% is the applicable annual interest rate. Frank is deemed to have made a gift to Susan on December 31 of $25,000 (0.10 × $500,000 × 6/12). Frank must report $25,000 of interest income. Susan deducts $25,000 of interest expense provided the interest expense deduction rules do not otherwise limit or disallow her deduction. ◀

DE MINIMIS RULES

Under one of the *de minimis* rules, neither the income nor the gift tax rules apply to any gift loan made directly between individuals for any day on which the aggregate loans outstanding between the borrower and the lender are $10,000 or less. The *de minimis* exception does not apply to any loan directly attributable to the purchase or carrying of income-producing assets.

A second *de minimis* exception potentially permits loans of $100,000 or less to receive more favorable income tax (but not gift tax) treatment by limiting the lender's imputed income to the borrower's net investment income (as defined in Sec. 163(d)(3)) for the year. Moreover, if the borrower's net investment income for the year is $1,000 or less, such amount is treated as being zero.

The *de minimis* provisions do not apply to transactions having tax avoidance as a principal purpose and do not apply to any day on which the total outstanding loans between the borrower and the lender exceed $100,000. For purposes of the $100,000 or $10,000 loan limitations, a husband and wife are treated as one person.

EXAMPLE C:12-45 ▶ On August 1, Mike lends $100,000 to Don. No other loans are outstanding between the parties. Avoidance of federal taxes is not a principal purpose of the loan. Don signs an interest-free demand note when 10% is the applicable interest rate. The loan is still outstanding on December 31. Mike is treated as having made a present interest gift to Don on December 31 of $4,167 [$100,000 × 0.10 × 5/12]. Mike need not report this gift on a gift tax return unless his aggregate gifts to Don exceed the $14,000 gift tax annual exclusion.

The income tax consequences depend on Don's (the borrower's) net investment income. If Don's net investment income for the year exceeds $4,167, Mike reports $4,167 of imputed interest income under Sec. 7872. Subject to rules that may disallow some or all of the interest expense deduction, Don deducts the $4,167 interest expense imputed under Sec. 7872 . If Don's net investment income is between $1,001 and $4,167, each party reports imputed interest income or expense equal to Don's net investment income. Mike and Don report no interest income or expense under Sec. 7872 if Don's net investment income is $1,000 or less. ◄

TAX PLANNING CONSIDERATIONS

OBJECTIVE 10

Identify tax planning opportunities in gift situations

The 1976 Act, which introduced the unification concept, reduced the tax law's bias in favor of lifetime transfers. The 2001 Act, on the other hand, was more favorable toward transfers at death because the unified credit for gift tax purposes peaked at $345,800 beginning in 2004 whereas the credit against the estate tax continued to increase. Beginning in 2011, the unified credit again became the same amount for gift and estate tax purposes. Nevertheless, lifetime gifts provide more advantages than disadvantages. Many factors, including the expected appreciation rate, should affect the decision of whether to make gifts. Thus, the optimal result is not always clear. The pros and cons of lifetime gifts from an estate planning perspective are discussed below.

ADDITIONAL COMMENT

For 2015, the credit for gift tax is $2,117,800.

TAX-SAVING FEATURES OF INTER VIVOS GIFTS

Use of Annual Exclusion. The annual exclusion offers donors the opportunity to start making gifts to several donees per year relatively early in their lifetime and keep substantial amounts of property off the transfer tax rolls. The tax-free amount doubles if a husband and wife use the gift-splitting election.

The law provides no estate tax counterpart to the annual gift tax exclusion. Consequently, a terminally ill person whose will includes bequests of approximately $14,000 to numerous individuals would realize substantial transfer tax savings if gifts—instead of bequests—were made to these individuals.

Removal of Post-Gift Appreciation from Tax Base. Another important advantage of lifetime gifts is that their value is frozen at their date-of-gift value. That is, any post-gift appreciation escapes the transfer tax rolls. Consequently, transfer tax savings are maximized if the donor gives away the assets that appreciate the most.

Removal of Gift Tax Amount from Transfer Tax Base. With one exception, gift taxes paid by the donor are removed from the transfer tax base. The lone exception applies to gift taxes paid on gifts the donor makes within three years of dying. Under the gross-up rule (discussed in Chapter C:13), the donor's gross estate includes only gift taxes paid on gifts made within three years of the donor's death.

ADDITIONAL COMMENT

If a terminally ill spouse, Sam, has no property, an election to gift split can effectively use up Sam's unified credit. Another method of using Sam's unified credit is for Sam's spouse to give Sam property in trust with the income payable to Sam for life, and the remainder subject to a general power of appointment in Sam. If the general power of appointment is not exercised during Sam's lifetime (or by will on Sam's death), the remainder must pass to specified beneficiaries other than the donor. If Sam exercises the general power while alive, he will be subject to gift tax. Otherwise, the trust will be in Sam's gross estate.

Income Shifting. Originally, one of the most favorable consequences of lifetime gifts was income shifting, but the compression of the income tax rate schedules beginning in 1987 has lessened these benefits. The 2003 Act, which lowered the tax rate on dividends, further reduced income shifting benefits from giving stock. The income produced by the gifted property is taxed to the donee, whose marginal income tax rate may be lower than the donor's. In addition, a high-income donor may be subject to the incremental 3.8% rate on net investment income, but the donee may not be subject to this rate if his or her income is sufficiently low. If income tax savings do arise, they accrue each year during the post-gift period. Thus, the income tax savings can be quite sizable over a span of several years. This tax saving aspect of gifts is a major reason Congress retained the gift tax in the 2001 Act.

Gift in Contemplation of Donee-Spouse's Death. At times, a terminally ill spouse may have very few assets. If such a spouse died, a sizable portion of his or her unified credit would be wasted in general because the decedent's estate would be well below the amount of the exemption equivalent provided by the unified credit. If the healthier spouse is relatively wealthy, he or she could give the ill spouse a gift in an amount equal to the estate tax exemption equivalent. Because of the unlimited marital deduction, the gift would be tax-free. Upon the death of the donee-spouse, no estate tax would be payable because the estate tax liability would not exceed the unified credit. The donee-spouse should not transfer his or her property back to the donor-spouse at death. Otherwise, the donee-spouse's unified credit would be wasted, and the original tax planning would be negated. Moreover, the retransferred property would be included in the surviving spouse's estate.

TAX STRATEGY TIP

Trying to be sure that the first spouse to die makes use of the exemption equivalent is no longer as important an issue because the unused exemption equivalent of the first spouse to die is portable to the surviving spouse. The "portability" rule is discussed in Chapter C:13.

A gift of appreciated property in contemplation of the donee-spouse's death provides an additional advantage. If the property does not pass back to the donor-spouse, its basis is increased to its value on the donee's date of death. In the event the property is willed to the donor-spouse, a step-up in basis still occurs if the date of the gift precedes the donee-spouse's date of death by more than one year.

Lessening State Transfer Tax Costs. Currently about 22 states levy an estate or inheritance tax, but only one state imposes a gift tax.[48] State death taxes are deductible in calculating the taxable estate, but they still add to death-associated costs. Therefore, in some states, the tax cost of lifetime transfers is lower than that for transfers at death.

Income Tax Savings from Charitable Gifts. Some individuals desire to donate a portion of their property to charitable organizations. Assuming the donation is eligible for a charitable contribution deduction, the transfer tax implications are the same—no taxable transfer—irrespective of whether the transfer occurs *inter vivos* or at death. From an income tax standpoint, however, a lifetime transfer is preferable because only lifetime transfers produce an income tax deduction for charitable contributions.

NEGATIVE ASPECTS OF GIFTS

Loss of Step-Up in Basis. Taxpayers deliberating about whether to make gifts or which property to give should keep in mind that the donee receives no step-up in basis for property acquired by gift. From a practical standpoint, sacrifice of the step-up in basis is insignificant if the donee does not plan to sell the property or if the property is not subject to an allowance for depreciation. Also, keep in mind that gain on the sale is likely to be taxed at the applicable long-term capital gain rate, and property in the estate may be taxed at 40%.

Prepayment of Estate Tax. A donor who makes taxable gifts that exceed the exemption equivalent (applicable exclusion amount) must pay a gift tax. Upon the donor's death, the taxable gift is included in his or her estate tax base as an adjusted taxable gift. Because the gift tax paid during the donor's lifetime reduces the donor's estate tax liability, in a sense, the donor's payment of the gift tax results in prepayment of a portion of the estate tax.

COMPLIANCE AND PROCEDURAL CONSIDERATIONS

OBJECTIVE 11

Comply with the filing requirements for gift tax returns

FILING REQUIREMENTS

Section 6019 specifies the circumstances in which a donor should file a gift tax return. In general, the donor will file Form 709 (United States Gift Tax Return). A completed Form 709 appears in Appendix B. The facts used in the preparation of the completed Form 709 are the same as the facts in the comprehensive illustration, which uses a format for the gift-splitting aspects that differs slightly from that used in the form.

---

48 Only one state imposes a gift tax—Connecticut. Beginning with 2011, the Connecticut gift tax applies only if cumulative gifts exceed $2 million. Minnesota enacted a tax applicable to gifts made after June 30, 2013, but subsequently repealed the tax. Louisiana repealed its gift tax effective July 1, 2008, and North Carolina its gift tax effective January 2009. Tennessee repealed its gift tax in May 2012 retroactive to the beginning of 2012.

As is the case for income tax returns, a return can be necessary even though the taxable amount and the tax payable are both zero. A donor must file a gift tax return for any calendar year in which the donor makes gifts other than

- Gifts to the spouse that qualify for the marital deduction
- Gifts that are fully shielded from taxation because they fall within the annual exclusion amount or are exempted from classification as a gift under the exception for educational or medical expenses
- Gifts to charitable organizations if the gift is deductible and the organization receives the donor's entire interest in the property

In addition, if the gift to the spouse is of qualified terminable interest property (QTIP), the donor must report the gift on the gift tax return. The marital deduction is not available for these transfers unless the donor makes the election, which is done by claiming a marital deduction on the gift tax return.

United States persons who receive aggregate gifts from foreign corporations or foreign partnerships exceeding $15,601 (in 2015) or aggregate gifts or bequests from nonresident aliens or foreign estates exceeding $100,000 (in 2015) must report such amounts as prescribed in Treasury Regulations.[49]

DUE DATE

All gift tax returns must be filed on a calendar-year basis. Under the general rule, gift tax returns are due no later than April 15 following the close of the year of the gift.[50] An extension of time granted for filing an individual income tax return is deemed to automatically extend the filing date for the individual's gift tax return for that year. The automatic extension period is until October 15.

If the donor dies early in the year in which a gift is made, the due date for the donor's final gift tax return may be earlier than April 15. Because information concerning the decedent's taxable gifts is necessary to complete the estate tax return, the gift tax return for the year of death is due no later than the due date (including extensions) for the donor's estate tax return.[51] Estate tax returns are due nine months after the date of death.

Receipt of an extension for filing a gift tax return does not postpone the due date for payment of the tax. Interest is imposed on any gift tax not paid by April 15. Donors should submit Form 8892 if they anticipate owing gift tax and/or if they need an extension for only their gift tax return. Unlike with the income tax, a donor does not have to make estimated payments of gift taxes.

GIFT-SPLITTING ELECTION

For taxable gifts to be computed under the gift-splitting technique, both spouses must indicate their consent to gift splitting in one of the following ways:[52]

- Each spouse signifies his or her consent on the other spouse's gift tax return.
- Each spouse signifies his or her consent on his or her own gift tax return.
- Both spouses signify their consent on one of the gift tax returns.

Treasury Regulations state that the first approach listed above is the preferred manner for designating consent.

KEY POINT

Similarly to a husband and wife filing a joint income tax return, if gift splitting is elected, the husband and wife have joint and several liability for the entire gift tax liability regardless of who actually made the gifts.

LIABILITY FOR TAX

The donor is responsible for paying the gift tax,[53] and if the spouses consent to gift splitting, the entire gift tax liability is a joint and several liability of the spouses.[54] Thus, if spouses do not pay the tax voluntarily, the IRS may attempt to collect whatever amount it deems appropriate from either spouse, irrespective of the size of the gift that spouse actually made.

In the rare event that the donor does not pay the gift tax, the donee becomes personally liable for the gift tax.[55] However, a donee's liability is limited to the value of the gift.

---

49 Sec. 6039F.

50 Sec. 6075(b).

51 The decedent's post-1976 taxable gifts affect the size of his or her estate tax base, as discussed in the next chapter.

52 Reg. Sec. 25.2513-2(a)(1).

53 Sec. 2502(c).

54 Sec. 2513(d).

55 Reg. Sec. 301.6324-1.

DETERMINATION OF VALUE

One of the most difficult problems encountered by donors and their tax advisors is determining the gifted property's FMV. This task is especially difficult if the gifted property is stock in a closely held business, an oil and gas property, or land in an area where few sales occur.

If a transaction involves a sale, the IRS can argue that the asset's value exceeds its sales price and, thus, there is a gift to the extent of the bargain element. This problem is especially common with sales to family members. If the donor gives or sells to a family member property whose value is not readily determinable, the donor should obtain an appraisal of the property before filing the gift tax return.

ETHICAL POINT

A CPA who advises a client about the tax consequences of making a gift also has a responsibility to make sure the property is correctly valued. Otherwise, if the valuation claimed is too low, the IRS can levy a penalty on the donor. For example, a gift of noncash property (e.g., land) may require that an appraisal be obtained. Failure to obtain an appraisal, or failure to investigate an appraisal that seems too low, may result in an undervaluation of the gift property, which may lead to the IRS imposing additional gift taxes, interest, and penalties.

Penalty for Undervaluation. Section 6662 imposes a penalty, at one of two rates, on underpayments of gift or estate taxes resulting from too low a valuation of property. The amount on which the penalty is imposed is the underpayment of the transfer tax attributable to the valuation understatement.

No penalty applies if the valuation shown on the return exceeds 65% of the amount determined during an audit or court trial to be the correct value. If the value reported on the return is 65% or less of the correct value, the penalty rate is as shown below.

Ratio of Value per Return to Correct Value	*Penalty Rate*
More than 40% but 65% or less	20%
40% or less	40%

Section 6662(g)(2) exempts a taxpayer from the penalty if the underpayment is less than $5,000.

EXAMPLE C:12-46 ▶ Assume Donna already had used her available unified credit when she gave land to her son and reported its value at $400,000 on her 2014 gift tax return. The IRS audited Donna's return in 2015, and she agreed that $900,000 was the correct value of the property. Because the value stated on the return was 44.44% [($400,000 ÷ $900,000) × 100] of the correct value, the IRS levied a 20% penalty on the underpayment attributable to the valuation understatement. If Donna was in the 40% marginal gift tax bracket, the gift tax underpayment was $200,000 [0.40 × ($900,000 − $400,000)]. Thus, the penalty is $40,000 (0.20 × $200,000) unless Donna can demonstrate reasonable cause and good faith for the valuation. ◀

STATUTE OF LIMITATIONS

ADDITIONAL COMMENT

If a taxpayer is unsure whether a taxable gift has been made, it is a good idea to file a gift tax return and at least disclose the transaction. The filing of the return with adequate disclosure of the transaction causes the statute of limitations to begin and limits the time during which the IRS may question the valuation and the amount of the gift, if any.

In general, the statute of limitations for gift tax purposes is three years after the later of the date the return was filed or the return's due date.[56] The statute of limitations increases from three to six years if the donor omits from the gift tax return gifts whose total value exceeds 25% of the gifts reported on the return. If the donor files no return because, for example, he or she is unaware that he or she made any gifts, the IRS may assess the tax at any time.

The cumulative nature of the gift tax causes the taxable gifts of earlier years to affect the gift tax owed in subsequent periods. After the statute of limitations has expired for pre-1997 gifts, the IRS cannot argue that taxable gifts of prior periods were undervalued (and thus that the current period's gifts should be taxed at a higher rate than that used by the donor) as long as the donor paid gift tax on the earlier gifts. However, for gifts reported after August 5, 1997, this rule applies even if the donor has paid no gift tax.[57]

For gifts made in 1997 and later, it is important to adequately disclose potential gift transactions for which the gift status is unclear. The statute of limitations will not expire on a transaction unless the donor makes adequate disclosure.[58]

EXAMPLE C:12-47 ▶ Andy filed a gift tax return for 2015, reporting taxable gifts of $5.85 million made in October 2015. Andy paid gift tax. If Andy adequately disclosed all potential gifts, once the statute of limitations expires for 2015, the IRS cannot contend that, for purposes of calculating the tax on later taxable gifts, the 2015 taxable gifts exceeded $5.85 million. ◀

[56] Sec. 6501.
[57] Sec. 2504(c).
[58] Sec. 6501(c)(9).

Problem Materials

Discussion Questions

C:12-1 Describe two ways in which the transfer tax (estate and gift tax) system is a unified system.

C:12-2 What was the Congressional purpose for enacting the gift-splitting provisions?

C:12-3 Determine whether the following statement is true or false: Every donor who makes a taxable gift incurs a gift tax liability. Explain your answer.

C:12-4 Under what circumstances must the amount of the unified credit usually available be reduced (by a maximum amount of $6,000) even though the donor has never claimed any unified credit?

C:12-5 Does the exemption from the gift tax for direct payment of tuition encompass payments of nonrelatives' tuition? Explain.

C:12-6 Steve is considering the following transactions. Explain to him which actions will constitute gifts for gift tax purposes.

a. Transferring all his ownership rights in a life insurance policy to another person

b. Depositing funds into a joint bank account in the names of himself and another party (who deposits nothing)

c. Paying half the consideration for land and having it titled in the names of Steve and his son as joint tenants with right of survivorship if the son furnishes the other half of the consideration

d. Paying a hospital for the medical expenses of a neighbor

e. Making a $1 million demand loan to an adult child and charging no interest

C:12-7 Dick wants to transfer property with a $600,000 FMV to an irrevocable trust with a bank as the trustee. Dick will name his distant cousin Earl to receive all of the trust income annually for the next eight years. Then the property will revert to Dick. In the last few years, the income return (yield) on the property has been 6%. Assume this yield is not likely to decline and that the applicable rate from the actuarial tables is 4%.

a. What will be the amount of Dick's gift to Earl?

b. Would you recommend that Dick transfer the property yielding 6% to this type of a trust? Explain. If not, what type of property would you recommend that Dick transfer to the trust?

C:12-8 Antonio would like to make a gift of a life insurance policy. Explain to him what action he must take to make a completed gift.

C:12-9 In what circumstances might a potential donor be interested in making a net gift? Explain the potential income tax problem with making a net gift.

C:12-10 What is the purpose of the gift tax annual exclusion?

C:12-11 In what circumstances do gifts fail to qualify for the annual exclusion?

C:12-12 Compare and contrast a Sec. 2503(c) trust and a *Crummey* trust.

C:12-13 From a nontax standpoint, would a parent probably prefer to make a transfer to a minor child by using a Sec. 2503(c) trust or a *Crummey* trust?

C:12-14 Explain the requirements for classifying a transaction as a transfer of a qualified terminable interest property (QTIP).

C:12-15 Why do some donors consider the qualified terminable interest property (QTIP) transfer an especially attractive arrangement for making gifts to their spouses?

C:12-16 A client is under the impression that a donor cannot incur a gift tax liability if he or she makes gifts to only U.S. charitable organizations. What should you say to the client?

C:12-17 Describe to a married couple three advantages of making the gift-splitting election.

C:12-18 Both Damien and Latoya make taxable gifts of $250,000 in the current year. Will their current year gift tax liabilities necessarily be identical? Explain.

C:12-19 A donor made large taxable gifts beginning in 1999 and a taxable gift in the current year. In the intervening years, the highest gift tax rates declined. In calculating the tax on taxable gifts of previous periods, which rate schedule is applicable: the one for the year in which the donor made the earlier gifts or the one for the current period?

C:12-20 A mother is trying to decide which of the two assets listed below to give to her adult daughter.

Asset	*FMV*	*Adjusted Basis*	*Annual Net Income from the Asset*
Apartment	$600,000	$400,000	$(10,000)
Bonds	600,000	530,000	80,000

The mother's marginal income tax rate exceeds her daughter's. Describe the pros and cons of giving each of the two properties. Which option would be preferable?

C:12-21 Phil and Marcy have been married for a number of years. Marcy is very wealthy, but Phil is not. In fact, Phil, who has only $10,000 of property, is very ill, and his doctor believes that he probably will die within the next few months. Make one (or more) tax planning suggestions for the couple. Assume the year is 2015 and that Phil may die in 2015.

C:12-22 Assume the same facts as in Problem C:12-21 and that Marcy has decided to give Phil property valued at $5.42 million. Phil probably will leave the gifted property to their children under his will.

a. What are the gift tax consequences to Marcy and the estate tax consequences to Phil of the transfer (assuming the property does not appreciate before his death)?

b. Assume Marcy is trying to decide whether to give Phil stock with an adjusted basis of $1,285,000 or land with an adjusted basis of $2.8 million. Each asset is valued at $5.42 million. Which asset would you recommend she give and why?

C:12-23 Carlos has heard about the unified transfer tax system and does not understand how making gifts can be beneficial. Explain to Carlos how a lifetime gift fixes (freezes) the gifted property's value for transfer tax purposes.

C:12-24 Describe for a client five advantages and two disadvantages of disposing of property by gift instead of at death.

C:12-25 In general, what is the due date for the gift tax return? What are two exceptions?

C:12-26 In 2006, Frank made an installment sale of real property to Stu, his son, for $1 million. Payments are due over a 10-year period. Frank did not file a gift tax return. For 2013, Frank reported taxable gifts so large that he used all of his unified credit then available. In 2015, the IRS audits Frank's 2013 income tax return and discovers the sale. The IRS then contends that the property Frank sold was worth $2.5 million in 2006 and that Frank made a $1.5 million gift to Stu in 2006.

a. Can the IRS collect the gift tax on the 2006 gift? If not, will the 2006 gift affect the tax due on gifts that Frank makes in the future?

b. Will Frank potentially incur any penalty? Explain.

ISSUE IDENTIFICATION QUESTIONS

C:12-27 Kwambe is thinking of making a substantial gift of stock to his fiancée, Maya. The wedding is scheduled for October 1 of the current year. Kwambe already has exhausted his unified credit. He also is considering giving $28,000 cash this year to each of his three children by a previous marriage. What tax issues should Kwambe consider with respect to the gifts he plans to make to Maya and his three children?

C:12-28 Janet (who has made no taxable gifts) is considering transferring assets valued at $9 million to an irrevocable trust (yet to be created) for the benefit of her son, Gordon, age 15, with Farmers Bank as trustee. Her attorney has drafted a trust agreement that provides that Gordon is to receive income in the trustee's discretion for the next 20 years and that at age 35 the trust assets will be distributed equally between Gordon and his sister Joanna. Janet anticipates that her husband will consent to gift splitting. What tax issues should Janet and her husband consider with respect to the trust?

C:12-29 Melvin funds an irrevocable trust with Holcomb Bank as trustee and reserves the right to receive the income for seven years. He provides that at the end of the seventh year the trust assets will pass outright to his adult daughter, Pamela, or to Pamela's estate should Pamela not be alive. Melvin transfers assets valued at $1 million to the trust; the assets at present are producing income of about 4.5% per year. Assume that the Sec. 7520 rate per the actuarial tables for the month of the transfer is 6%. What tax issues should Melvin consider regarding the trust?

PROBLEMS

C:12-30 *Calculation of Gift Tax.* In 2015, Sondra makes taxable gifts aggregating $300,000. Her only other taxable gifts amount to $200,000, all of which she made in 1997.

a. What is Sondra's 2015 gift tax liability?

b. What is her 2015 gift tax liability under the assumption that she made the $200,000 of taxable gifts in 1974 instead of 1997?

C:12-31 *Calculation of Gift Tax.* Amir made taxable gifts as follows: $800,000 in 1975, $1.2 million in 1999, and $600,000 in 2015. What is Amir's gift tax liability for 2015?

C:12-32 *Determination of Taxable Gifts.* In the current year, Beth, who is single, sells stock valued at $40,000 to Linda for $18,000. Later that year, Beth gives Linda $12,000 in cash.

a. What is the amount of Beth's taxable gifts?

b. How would your answer to Part a change if Beth instead gave the cash to Patrick?

C:12-33 *Determination of Taxable Gifts.* In the current year, Kent gives $42,000 cash to each of his eight grandchildren. His wife makes no gifts during the current year.

a. What are Kent's taxable gifts, assuming Kent and his wife do *not* elect gift splitting?

b. How would your answer to Part a change if the couple elects gift splitting?

C:12-34 *Determination of Taxable Gifts.* In the current year, David gives $180,000 of land to David, Jr. In the current year, David's wife gives $200,000 of land to George and $44,000 cash to David, Jr. Assume the couple elects gift splitting for the current year.

a. What are the couple's taxable gifts?

b. How would your answer to Part a change if David's wife gave the $44,000 of cash to Ollie (instead of to David, Jr.)?

C:12-35 *Determination of Taxable Gifts.* Yolanda and Xavier, spouses, have four adult children, Andy, Betty, Cathy, and Danny. In 2015, they made a number of gifts. Yolanda gave Andy cash of $40,000 and Betty stock valued at $60,000. Xavier gave Cathy stock valued at $38,000 and deposited $80,000 in a bank account in the names of Xavier and Danny, joint tenants with right of survivorship. Later in the year, Xavier withdrew $10,000 from the account, and Danny withdrew $8,000. Xavier gave stock valued at $70,000 to his alma mater, State Technological Institute. Calculate the amount of taxable gifts for each spouse if they elect gift splitting.

C:12-36 *Recognition of Transactions Treated as Gifts.* In the current year, Emily, a widow, engages in the following transactions. Determine the amount of the completed gift, if any, arising from each of the following occurrences.

a. Emily names Lauren the beneficiary of a $100,000 life insurance policy on Emily's life. The beneficiary designation is not irrevocable.

b. Emily deposits $50,000 cash into a checking account in the joint names of herself and Matt, who deposits nothing to the account. Later that year, Matt withdraws $15,000 from the account.

c. Emily pays $22,000 of nephew Noah's medical expenses directly to County Hospital.

d. Emily transfers the title to land valued at $60,000 to Olive.

C:12-37 *Calculation of Gift Tax.* Refer to the facts of Problem C:12-36 and assume the current year is 2015. Emily's prior gifts are as follows:

Year	*Amount of Taxable Gifts*
1974	$ 500,000
1998	1,000,000

What is Emily's 2015 gift tax liability?

C:12-38 *Recognition of Transactions Treated as Gifts.* In the current year, Marge (age 67) engages in the following transactions. Determine the amount of the completed gift, if any, arising from each of the following events. Assume 4% is the applicable interest rate.

a. Marge transfers $100,000 of property in trust and irrevocably names herself to receive $8,000 per year for life and daughter Joy (age 37) to receive the remainder.

b. Marge pays her grandson's $15,000 tuition to State University.

c. Marge gives the same grandson stock valued at $72,000.

d. Marge deposits $150,000 into a revocable trust. Later in the year, the bank trustee distributes $18,000 of income to the named beneficiary, Gail.

C:12-39 *Recognition of Transactions Treated as Gifts.* Determine the amount of the completed gift, if any, arising from each of the following occurrences.

a. A parent sells real estate valued at $1.8 million to an adult child, who pays $1 million in consideration.

b. A furniture store holds a clearance sale and sells a customer a $5,000 living room suite for $1,500.

c. During the year, a father purchases food and clothing costing $8,500 for his minor child.

d. A citizen contributes $1,500 cash to a political organization.

e. Zeke lends $600,000 interest free to Henry, who signs a demand note on August 1. Assume 6% is the applicable interest rate and the note remains unpaid at year-end.

C:12-40 *Determination of Unified Credit.* In March 1976, Sue made a taxable gift of $200,000. In arriving at the amount of her taxable gift, Sue elected to deduct the $30,000 specific exemption formerly available. In 2015, Sue makes her next gift; the taxable amount is $6.5 million.

a. What unified credit can Sue claim on her 2015 return?

b. What unified credit can Sue claim on her 2015 return if she made the 1976 gift in December instead of March?

C:12-41 *Valuation of Gifts.* On September 1 of the current year, Mario irrevocably transfers a $100,000 whole life insurance policy on his life to Mario, Jr. as owner. On September 1, the policy's interpolated terminal reserve is $30,000. Mario paid the most recent annual premium ($1,800) on June 1. What is the amount of the gift Mario made in the current year?

C:12-42 *Determination of Gift Tax Deductions.* In June, Tina makes cash gifts of $700,000 to her husband and $100,000 to the City Art Museum. What are the amounts of the deductions available for these gifts when calculating Tina's income tax and gift tax liabilities if she does not elect gift splitting?

C:12-43 *Determination of Annual Exclusion.* For each of the following transactions that occur in the current year, indicate the amount of the annual exclusion available. Explain your answer.

a. Tracy creates a trust in the amount of $300,000 for the benefit of her eight-year-old daughter, May. She names a bank as trustee. Before May reaches age 21, the trustee in its discretion is to pay income or corpus (trust assets) to May or for her benefit. When May reaches age 21, she will receive the unexpended portion of the trust income and corpus. If May dies before reaching age 21, the unexpended income and corpus will be paid to her estate or a person (or persons) she appoints under a general power of appointment.

b. Assume the same facts as in Part a except May is age 28 when Tracy creates the trust and the trust agreement contains age 41 wherever age 21 appears in Part a.

c. Assume the same facts as in Part b except the trust instrument allows May to demand a distribution by December 31 of each year equal to the lesser of the amount of the annual exclusion for federal gift tax purposes or the amount transferred to the trust that year.

C:12-44 *Determination of Annual Exclusion.* During 2015, Will gives $40,000 cash to Will, Jr. and a remainder interest in a few acres of land to his friend Suzy. The remainder interest is valued at $32,000. Will and his wife, Helen, elect gift splitting, and during the current year Helen gives Joyce $8,000 of stock. What is the total amount of the annual gift tax exclusions available to Will and Helen?

C:12-45 *Availability of Annual Exclusion.* Bonnie, a widow, irrevocably transfers $1 million of property to a trust and names a bank as trustee. For as long as Bonnie's daughter Carol is alive, Carol is to receive all the trust income annually. Upon Carol's death, the property is to be distributed to Carol's children. Carol is age 32 and currently has three children. How many gift tax exclusions does Bonnie receive for the transfer?

C:12-46 *Calculation of Gift Tax.* In earlier years, neither Hugo nor Wanda, his wife, made any taxable gifts. In 2014, Hugo gave $14,000 cash to each of his 30 nieces, nephews, and grandchildren. In 2015, Wanda gives $34,000 of stock to each of the same people. What is the *minimum* legal gift tax liability *before* reduction for the unified credit for each spouse for each year?

C:12-47 *Calculation of Marital Deduction.* Hugh makes the gifts listed below to Winnie, his wife, age 37. What is the amount of the marital deduction, if any, attributable to each?

a. Hugh transfers $500,000 to a trust with a bank named as trustee. All the income must be paid to Winnie monthly for life. At Winnie's death, the property passes to Hugh's sisters or their estates.

b. Hugh transfers $300,000 to a trust with a bank named as trustee. Income is payable at the trustee's discretion to Winnie annually until the earlier of her death or her remarriage. When payments to Winnie cease, the trustee must distribute the property to Hugh's children by a previous marriage or to their estates.

C:12-48 *Calculation of the Marital Deduction.* In the current year, Louise makes the transfers described below to Lance, her husband, age 47. Assume 4% is the applicable interest rate. What is the amount of her marital deduction, if any, attributable to each transfer?

a. In June, she gives him land valued at $45,000.

b. In October, she gives him a 12-year income interest in a trust with a bank named as trustee. She names their daughter to receive the remainder interest. She funds the irrevocable trust with $400,000 in assets.

C:12-49 *Charitable Contribution Deduction.* Tien (age 70) transfers a remainder interest in a vacation cabin (with a total value of $100,000) to a charitable organization and retains a life estate in the cabin for herself.

a. What is the amount of the gift tax charitable contribution deduction, if any, attributable to this transfer? Assume that 4% is the applicable interest rate.

b. How will your answer to Part a change if Tien instead gives a remainder interest in a valuable oil painting (worth $100,000) to the organization?

C:12-50 ***Calculation of Gift Tax.*** In 2015, Homer and his wife, Wilma (residents of a non– community property state) make the gifts listed below. Homer's previous taxable gifts consist of $100,000 made in 1975 and $1.4 million made in 1996. Wilma has made no previous taxable gifts.

Wilma's current year gifts were	
to Art	$400,000
to Bart	6,000
Homer's current year gifts were	
to Linda	$600,000
to a charitable organization	100,000
to Norma (future interest)	200,000

a. What are the gift tax liabilities of Homer and Wilma for 2015 if they elect gift splitting and everyone except Norma receives a present interest?
b. How would the gift tax liabilities for each spouse in Part a change if they do not elect gift splitting?

C:12-51 ***Calculation of Gift Tax.*** In 2015, Henry and his wife, Wendy, made the gifts shown below. All gifts are of present interests. What is Wendy's gift tax payable for 2015 if the couple elects gift splitting and Wendy's previous taxable gifts (made in 1995) total $1 million?

Wendy's current gifts were	
to Janet	$80,000
to Cindy	70,000
to Henry	50,000
Henry's current gifts were	
to Janet	30,000

C:12-52 ***Basis Rules.*** In June 2014, Karen transferred property with a $75,000 FMV and a $20,000 adjusted basis to Hal, her husband. Hal dies in March 2015; the property has appreciated to $85,000 in value by then. His gross estate is $1 million.
a. What is the amount of Karen's taxable gift for 2014?
b. What gain would Hal have recognized if he sold the property for $95,000 in July 2014?
c. If Hal wills the property to Dot, his daughter, what basis would Dot have?
d. How would your answer to Part c change if Hal instead willed the property to Karen?
e. How would your answer to Part d change if Hal did not die until August 2015?

C:12-53 ***Basis Rules.*** Siu is considering giving her son stock in Ace Corporation or Gold Corporation. Each has a current FMV of $500,000, and each has the same estimated future appreciation rate. Siu's basis in the Ace stock is $100,000, and her basis in the Gold stock is $450,000. Assume Siu has total assets of $7 million. Which stock would you suggest that she give away and why, or does it make any difference?

C:12-54 ***Below-Market Loans.*** On October 1, Sam lends Tom $10 million. Tom signs an interest-free demand note. The loan is still outstanding on December 31. Explain the income tax and gift tax consequences of the loan to both Sam and Tom. Assume that the federal short-term rate is 5%.

COMPREHENSIVE PROBLEM

C:12-55 In 2015, Ginger Graham, age 46 and wife of Greg Graham, engaged in the transactions described below. Determine Ginger's gift tax liability for 2015 if she and Greg elect gift splitting and Greg gave their son Stevie stock valued at $80,000 during 2015. Ginger's grandmother Mamie died November 12, 2014, and Mamie's will bequeathed $250,000 to Ginger. On March 4, 2015, Ginger irrevocably disclaimed the $250,000 in writing, and, as a result, the property passed instead to Ginger's sister Gertie. In 2015, Ginger gave $100,000 cash to her alma mater, State University. In 1996, Ginger gave ownership of a life insurance policy on her own life to her daughter, Denise, and in 2015 Ginger paid the $22,000 annual premium on the policy. In 2014, Ginger deposited $45,000 into a bank account in the name of herself and son Stevie, joint tenants with rights of survivorship.

Stevie deposited nothing. Neither party made a withdrawal until 2015, when Stevie withdrew $30,000. In 2015, Ginger created a trust with County Bank as trustee and transferred $300,000 of stock to the irrevocable trust. She named her husband Greg (age 47) to receive all the trust income semi-annually for life and daughter Drucilla to receive the remainder. In 2015, she gave a remainder interest in her beach cottage to the American Red Cross and kept the right to use the cottage rent free for the rest of her life. The fair market value of the cottage was $70,000.

Other information: Ginger's earlier *taxable* gifts are $175,000, all made in 1996. Ginger will make whatever elections are necessary to minimize her current gift tax liability. Assume the Sec. 7520 interest rate is 4%.

TAX STRATEGY PROBLEMS

C:12-56 *Determination of Taxable Gifts.* George and Martha, spouses, made a number of gifts during 2015. Their accountant is trying to help them decide whether to elect gift splitting. If they elect gift splitting, each spouse will have $4 million of taxable gifts. If they do not elect gift splitting, George's taxable gifts will be $2 million, and Martha's will be $6 million. George has not made any earlier taxable gifts, but Martha made $250,000 of taxable gifts in 2009. Calculate the amount of gift tax each spouse will owe if they elect gift splitting and if they do not elect gift splitting for 2015. What do you recommend they do concerning the election to split gifts?

C:12-57 Ilene Ishi is planning to fund an irrevocable charitable remainder annuity trust with $100,000 of cash. She will designate her sister, age 60, to receive an annuity of $5,000 per year for 15 years and State University to receive the remainder at the end of the fifteenth year. The valuation of the charitable portion of the transfer, according to Reg. Sec. 25.2522(c)-3(d)(2)(i), is to be determined under Reg. Sec. 1.664-2(c), an income tax regulation. Regulation Sec. 1.664-2(c) provides that, in valuing the remainder interest, the donor may elect to use the Sec. 7520 interest rate for either of the two months preceding the month of the transfer as an alternative to using the rate for the actual month of transfer. Otherwise, the value will be determined by using the Sec. 7520 rate for the month of the transfer. Assume that in the month of the transfer the interest rate was 4% but that in the two preceding months the rate was 4.2%. Should the donor elect to calculate the value of the remainder interest by using the interest rate for one of the two preceding months? Explain your answer. Note: The 4.2% rate does not appear in the excerpts from the actuarial tables, but the absence of such rate from the tables will not preclude you from answering this question.

TAX FORM/RETURN PREPARATION PROBLEMS

C:12-58 Use the information shown below to prepare a 2014 gift tax return (Form 709) for Joel Bruton. Pages 4 and 5 of the form are not applicable. Joel and his wife Janis, both U.S. citizens, want to elect gift splitting. They reside at 117 Panther Place, South City, NC 28000. Joel had not been married prior to his marriage to Janis in 1966. For simplicity, assume that the Sec. 7520 rate is 4%. Joel's transactions, all in July, are as shown below. Assume whatever amount you like for the adjusted basis of gifted property.

	Value on Date of Gift
1. Stock given to daughter Belinda	$ 78,000
2. Apartment building and land given to daughter Belinda	2,476,000
3. Tuition to university, paid for grandson Jacob	24,000
4. Pottery collection given to Atlanta Art Museum	120,000
5. Trust for benefit of wife Janis (age 67) for life with remainder to Belinda. All of the income is to be distributed quarterly to Janis	3,000,000

During the year Janis gave $40,000 cash to Belinda and $200,000 of stock to her sister Jeanette Johnson. Joel made a $1 million taxable gift in 2000. It was the first and only gift he ever made.

C:12-59 Alice Arnold, Social Security number, a widow, engages in the transactions listed below in 2014. Use this information to prepare a gift tax return (Form 709) for Alice.

	Amount
1. Stock given to daughter, Brenda Bell.	$700,000
2. Cash transferred to son, Al Arnold.	600,000
3. $500,000 interest-free demand loan made to Brenda Bell on July 1. The loan is still outstanding on December 31.	
4. Land given to niece, Lou Lane	100,000

Assume 6% is the applicable interest rate. Alice has made only one previous taxable gift: $300,000 (taxable amount) in 2000. Alice, a U.S. citizen, resides at 105 Peak Rd., Western City, CO 80000. Page 4 of the form does not apply to Alice.

CASE STUDY PROBLEMS

C:12-60 Your client, Karen Kross, recently married Larry Kross. Karen is age 72, quite wealthy, and in reasonably good health. To date, she has not made any taxable gifts, but Larry made taxable gifts totaling $900,000 in 1998. Karen is considering giving each of her five college-age grandchildren approximately $34,000 of cash for them to use to pay their college expenses of tuition and room and board for the year. In addition, she is considering giving her three younger grandchildren $3,000 each to use for orthodontic bills. Karen wants to give her daughter property valued at $400,000. She is trying to choose between giving her daughter cash or stock with a basis of $125,000. She would like to give her son $400,000 of property also, but prefers to tie the property up in a discretionary trust with a bank as trustee for the son for at least 15 years. An agricultural museum approached Karen about making a contribution to it and, as a result, she is contemplating deeding her family farm to the museum but retaining a life estate in the farm.

Required: Prepare a memorandum to the tax partner of your firm that discusses the transfer tax and income tax consequences of the proposed transactions described above. Also, make any recommendations that you deem appropriate.

C:12-61 Morris Jory, a long-time tax client of the firm you work for, has made substantial gifts during his lifetime. Mr. Jory transferred Jory Corporation stock to 14 donees in December 2014. Each donee received shares valued at $14,000. Two of the donees were Mr. Jory's adult children, Amanda and Peter. The remaining 12 donees were employees of Jory Corporation who are not related to Mr. Jory. Mr. Jory, a widower, advised the employees that within two weeks of receiving the stock certificates they must endorse such certificates over to Amanda and Peter. Six of the donees were instructed to endorse their certificates to Amanda and six to Peter. During 2014, Mr. Jory also gave $35,000 cash to his favorite grandchild, Robin. Your firm has been engaged to prepare Mr. Jory's 2014 gift tax return. In early 2015, you meet with Mr. Jory, who insists that his 2014 taxable gifts are only $21,000 ($35,000 to Robin − $14,000 annual exclusion). After your meeting with Mr. Jory, you are uncertain about his position regarding the amount of his 2014 taxable gifts and have scheduled a meeting with your firm's senior tax partner, who has advised Mr. Jory for more than 20 years. In preparation for the meeting, prepare a summary of the tax and ethical considerations (with supporting authority where possible) regarding whether you should prepare a gift tax return that reports the taxable gifts in accordance with Mr. Jory's wishes.

TAX RESEARCH PROBLEMS

C:12-62 Your manager advises you that clients Mike and Winona Marsh, residents of Bath, Maine, acquired beachfront property in Maine in 2002 and titled the property in their names as joint tenants with right of survivorship. Under Maine law, either joint tenant can sever the joint tenancy unilaterally. Mike died in July 2015, survived by Winona and their two adult children. His will provided that all his property passes to Winona if she survives him. Otherwise it passes to the children equally. In September 2015, Winona executed a written disclaimer of the one-half interest in the beachfront property that otherwise would pass to her by survivorship. As a result, this interest passed to the two children equally. Winona and the children represent that Winona has not accepted the interest in the property or any of its benefits. Your manager requests that you research the issue of whether Winona made a gift to the children and that you address your conclusions in a memo. She recommends that you search only in private letter rulings.

C:12-63 In July of the current year, Horace Hiatt, a widower, transferred $14,000 worth of publicly traded stock to an irrevocable trust with Benton National Bank as trustee. He named his granddaughter, Heather, then age 15, the beneficiary. The trust instrument provides that, until Heather reaches age 21, the trustee is to distribute amounts of income and/or principal to her as it "shall deem to be in the best interest of Heather." In addition, the trust instrument states that, if Heather dies before reaching age 21, the trust assets are to be distributed in accordance with Heather's appointment under a general power of appointment. The trust instrument provides further that the trust assets, including undistributed income, will be paid over to Heather upon her attaining age 21. However, if Heather does not ask for such property within 60 days of being notified of her right to ask for it, the trust is to continue until Heather reaches age 45, and the trustee is to continue to have the distribution powers it received at inception. Your manager asks you to research the effect, if any, on the eligibility for the gift tax annual exclusion resulting from the language stating that the trust will continue until age 45 if Heather does not ask for the trust assets within a certain time frame. Your manager suggests that she seems to recall reading a 2006 letter ruling on this issue and asks that you try to locate it and that you also try to locate applicable higher authority, if any. Draft a memo to your manager addressing the availability of the annual exclusion.

C:12-64 Janet Mason filed a 2012 gift tax return to report the gift on June 3, 2012, of closely held stock in Mason Meat Co., Inc. The tax return, which your firm prepared, reflected a value of $1,500 per share (determined by an appraiser) and a taxable gift of $6.3 million. This was Janet's first taxable gift, and she exhausted her unified credit then available of $1,772,800. On October 22, 2013, Janet's father, Mason Meat's CEO and founder, died unexpectedly at age 59. In addition, two months prior to her father's death the firm had recalled much of its meat from distributors and supermarkets because of contamination in the meat plant. The meat plant closed for six weeks while the problem was corrected. An appraiser valued the stock for her father's estate at $1,000 per share. Janet, a new client, would like for your firm to prepare an amended gift tax return and value her gift at $1,000 per share because of the decline in value resulting from the two events described. She would like a refund of the gift tax she paid and have some of her unified credit restored. Prepare a memo that addresses whether Janet should be entitled to a refund of the gift tax paid and restoration of some of her unified credit.

C:12-65 *Internet Research Problem.* Go to the IRS Web site, www.irs.gov and under "Learn About IRS," select "Tax Stats, Facts, & Figures." Then consult statistics regarding estate and gift taxes. Finally, select "Gift Tax—Gift Tax One Sheet." Compare the number of nontaxable gift tax returns filed for 2008 with those for 2013. Also compare the number of taxable returns filed for 2008 with those for 2013. In addition, for 2013 indicate the total amount of nontaxable and taxable gifts reported.

C:12-66 *Internet Research Problem.* Your manager wants you to participate in delivering a staff training course on the basics of gift taxation. Your assignment is to discuss *Crummey* trusts. You want to increase your knowledge of some of the advantages and disadvantages of such trusts. Conduct research on the Internet and summarize the advantages and disadvantages. Also indicate which site(s) is (are) the source(s) of your information.

C:12-67 *Internet Research Problem.* What was the Sec. 7520 rate for May, June, and July 2014?

CHAPTER

13

THE ESTATE TAX

LEARNING OBJECTIVES

After studying this chapter, you should be able to

1. Explain the formula for the estate tax
2. Describe the methods for valuing interests in the gross estate
3. Recognize which interests are includible in the gross estate
4. Identify the deductions available for estate tax purposes
5. Calculate the estate tax liability
6. Explain tax provisions that alleviate liquidity problems
7. Summarize the basic concepts of the generation-skipping transfer tax
8. Recognize tax planning opportunities for estates
9. Comply with the filing requirements for estate tax returns

CHAPTER OUTLINE

Gift taxes and estate taxes are part of a unified system that taxes the transfer of wealth. Thus, they are fundamentally different than income or property taxes. Chapter C:12 discussed their history and purposes.

As previously noted, the term *gift taxes* applies to lifetime transfers and the term *estate taxes* applies to dispositions of property resulting from the transferor's death. This chapter discusses the structure of the federal estate tax and examines the types of interests and transactions that cause inclusions in the decedent's gross estate. It also discusses the various deductions and credits affecting the federal estate tax liability and the rules concerning the taxable gifts that affect the estate tax base, an important issue because of the unified nature of the tax levied at death.

The Economic Growth and Tax Relief Reconciliation Act of 2001 (the 2001 Act) was an important landmark in the history of the estate and gift tax. It provided phased-in increases to the unified credit and phased-in reductions to the unified tax rate schedule beginning with 2002. In addition, it provided that the estate and generation skipping transfer taxes would not apply, effective January 1, 2010. However, the 2001 Act further provided that, in the absence of additional legistation, the rules for gift, estate, and generation skipping taxes would revert on January 1, 2011, to what they were before the 2001 Act.

REAL-WORLD EXAMPLE

In 2007, the top 2.29 million U.S. wealth holders held total assets worth $13.2 trillion in the following proportions:

Personal residences	9.4%
Other real property	12.6
Closely held stock	11.9
Publicly traded stock	19.3
Tax-exempt bonds	6.0
Various taxable bonds	2.6
Cash accounts	7.9
Retirement assets	9.1
Various other assets	21.2

Thus, as of January 1, 2010, the estate tax was automatically repealed and was scheduled to return in 2011 at pre-2001 Act levels. With the repeal of the estate tax, a decedent's assets, except for a limited amount, were not permitted to be stepped-up to fair market value. Rather, the basis of the assets transferred to beneficiaries was determined using a modified carryover basis system discussed at C:12-27 and 12-28. In December 2010, Congress enacted the Tax Relief, Unemployment Insurance Reauthorization, and Job Creation Act of 2010 (hereinafter referred to as the Tax Relief Act), which reinstated the estate tax retroactive to January 1, 2010 along with the basis of assets being set to fair market value at the date of death. However, for decedents who died in 2010, it allowed the executor to choose between (1) no estate tax with a modified carryover basis or (2) the estate tax with a $5 million applicable exclusion amount, a top rate of 35%, and FMV bases for the estate's assets. Thus, estates below the $5 million threshold could step up the assets' bases to FMV without incurring any estate tax liability. A step-up occurs when the estate's assets have a FMV exceeding their bases. A step-down will occur for assets whose bases exceed their FMV.

The Tax Relief Act set the maximum estate and gift tax rates at 35% for 2011 and 2012 and the amount that could be transferred tax free in either context at $5 million for 2011 and $5 million indexed to $5.12 million for 2012. The American Taxpayer Relief Act of 2012 (ATRA 2012) increased the top estate and gift tax rate from 35% to 40% beginning in 2013 and retained a nontaxable amount of $5 million, indexed to $5.25, $5.34, and $5.43 million for 2013, 2014, and 2015, respectively.

ESTATE TAX FORMULA

OBJECTIVE 1

Explain the formula for the estate tax

The tax base for the federal estate tax is the *total* of the decedent's taxable estate (i.e., the gross estate less the deductions discussed below) and adjusted taxable gifts (post-1976 taxable gifts). After the gross tax liability on the tax base is determined, various credits—including the unified credit—are subtracted to arrive at the net estate tax payable. The estate tax formula appears in Figure C:13-1.

GROSS ESTATE

As illustrated in Figure C:13-1, calculation of the decedent's estate tax liability begins with determining which items are included in the gross estate. Such items are valued at either the decedent's date of death or the alternate valuation date.[1] As a transfer tax, the estate tax is levied on dispositions that are essentially testamentary in nature. Transactions are viewed as being essentially **testamentary transfers** if the transferor's control or enjoyment of the property in question ceases at death, not before death.[2]

[1] Under Sec. 2032, the alternate valuation date is the earlier of six months after the date of death or the date the property is disposed of. See pages C:13-7 and C:13-8 for details.

[2] An example of a transaction that is essentially **testamentary** in nature is a situation where the donor transfers property in trust but reserves a lifetime right to receive the trust income and, thus, continues to enjoy the economic benefits.

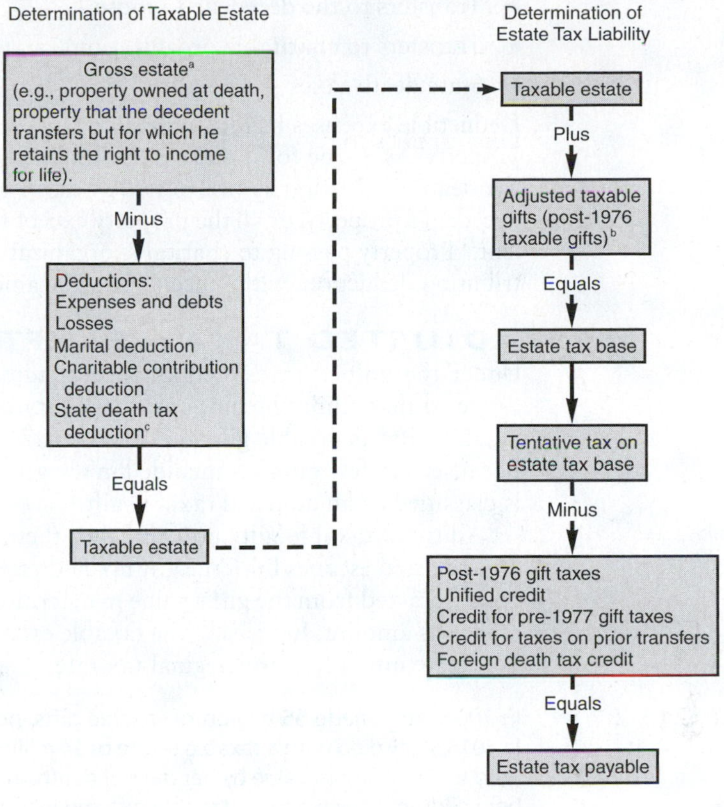

[a]Valued at decedent's date of death or alternate valuation date.
[b]Valued at date of gift.
[c]For decedents dying after 2004.

FIGURE C:13-1 ▶ ESTATE TAX FORMULA

Inclusions in the gross estate extend to a much broader set of properties than merely assets to which the decedent holds title at the time of death. Making a lifetime transfer that generates a taxable gift does not guarantee that the donor removes the transferred property from his or her gross estate. Although an individual usually removes property from his or her gross estate by giving it to another before death, the donor's gross estate must include the gifted property if the donor retains either the right to receive the income generated by the transferred property or control over the property for the donor's lifetime.

EXAMPLE C:13-1 ▶ In the current year, Ted transfers stocks to an irrevocable trust with a bank named as trustee. Under the terms of the trust agreement, Ted is to receive the trust income annually for the rest of his life and Ted's cousin Ed (or Ed's estate) is to receive the remainder. In the current year, Ted made a taxable gift of the remainder interest (but not the income interest) in the trust. If, for example, Ted already has used his entire unified credit, he incurs a gift tax liability. When Ted dies, the entire value of the trust is included in Ted's gross estate, even though Ted has made a taxable gift and does not have legal title to the property. Because the shift in the right to the income does not occur until Ted's death, the transfer is testamentary in nature. ◀

SELF-STUDY QUESTION

Six years ago Barb transferred $500,000 in trust, income for life to herself, remainder to her cousin. What part, if any, of the value of the trust's assets will be included in Barb's estate?

ANSWER

The value of the entire trust will be included in Barb's estate, because she retained the income from the trust until her death.

The categories of items included in the gross estate and their valuation are examined in detail later in this chapter. Once the components of the gross estate have been determined and valued, the deductions from the gross estate are calculated.

DEDUCTIONS

The IRC authorizes five categories of items that may be deducted in arriving at the amount of the taxable estate:

- ▶ Expenses and debts
- ▶ Casualty and theft losses

- Transfers to the decedent's spouse
- Transfers to charitable organizations
- State death taxes

Deductible expenses include funeral expenses and expenses of administering the decedent's property. As is true for gift tax purposes, there is no ceiling on the marital deduction. Thus, the death of the first spouse is free of estate taxes if the decedent's spouse receives all the decedent's property, or all the property except for an amount equal to the exemption equivalent.[3] Property passing to charitable organizations qualifies, in general, for a charitable contribution deduction, with no ceiling on the amount of such deductions.

ADJUSTED TAXABLE GIFTS AND TAX BASE

Under the unified transfer tax concept, adjusted taxable gifts are added to the taxable estate to determine the amount of the estate tax base. Section 2001(b) defines adjusted taxable gifts as taxable gifts made after 1976 *other than* gifts included in the gross estate. Because very few gifts are included in the gross estate, almost every post-1976 taxable gift is classified as an adjusted taxable gift.

Adjusted taxable gifts are valued at their date-of-gift values. Therefore, any post-gift appreciation escapes both the gift tax and estate tax. Allowable deductions and exclusions are subtracted from the gift's value in determining taxable gifts and, thus, the adjusted taxable gifts amount. Increasing the taxable estate by adjusted taxable gifts potentially forces the estate into a higher marginal tax rate.

EXAMPLE C:13-2 ▶ In 2004, Amy made $5 million of taxable gifts, none of which were included in her gross estate. In 2015, Amy died with a taxable estate of $4 million. The property Amy gave away in 2004 appreciated to $7 million in value by her date of death. In 2005, Amy gave stock valued at $8,000 to one of her children. Amy made no taxable gift and incurred no transfer tax on the 2005 transaction. The stock had appreciated to $70,000 when Amy died. Amy's estate tax base is calculated as follows:

Taxable estate	$4,000,000
Plus: Adjusted taxable gifts (valued at date-of-gift values)	5,000,000
Estate tax base	$9,000,000

The $2 million of post-gift appreciation on the property gifted in 2004 escapes transfer taxation. Amy's $9 million tax base includes the property gifted in 2004, whose value was "frozen" at its date-of-gift value. The 2005 gift did not affect Amy's estate tax base because the 2005 *taxable* gift was zero. ◀

ADDITIONAL COMMENT

Income earned on gifted property is the donee's and is not included in the donor's estate.

TENTATIVE TAX ON ESTATE TAX BASE

Once the amount of the tax base has been determined, the next step is to calculate the tax on this base using the unified tax rates, which are reproduced on the inside back cover of this textbook. In 2007 through 2009, a maximum tax rate of 45% applied to tax bases exceeding $1.5 million for both estate and gift tax purposes. For 2010 through 2012, the top estate and gift tax rate was 35%, applicable to tax bases exceeding $500,000. If, however, an estate's executor so elected for 2010, the estate tax did not apply that year, but the 35% top tax rate nevertheless applied to 2010 gifts. Beginning in 2013 the maximum rate rose to 40%, and it applies to transfers above $1 million.

EXAMPLE C:13-3 ▶ Assume the same facts as in Example C:13-2. The gross tax on Amy's $9 million tax base is $3,545,800. The estate was taxed at a 40% marginal tax rate, the highest rate applicable in the year Amy died. ◀

REDUCTION FOR POST-1976 GIFT TAXES

Adjusted taxable gifts, in effect, are not taxed twice because Sec. 2001(b)(2) allows a reduction to the estate tax for gift taxes imposed on post-1976 taxable gifts. If the rate schedule for the year of death differs from the schedule applicable for the year of the gift, the tax on post-1976 taxable gifts is determined by using the rate schedule in effect for the year of

[3] The estate tax exemption equivalent ($5 million for 2011, $5.12 million for 2012, $5.25 million for 2013, $5.34 million for 2014, and $5.43 million for 2015), as explained in Chapter C:12, is the size of the tax base for which the estate tax liability is exactly cancelled by the unified credit, $1,730,800 in 2011, $1,772,800 in 2012, $2,045,800 in 2013, $2,081,800 in 2014, and $2,117,800 in 2015.

death. The unified credit subtracted from the gift tax is recalculated to arrive at what the credit *would have been* if the tax rates in effect at the date of death had been in effect at the time of the gift. The rule regarding rates works to the disadvantage of decedents who made taxable gifts and paid taxes at a higher rate than the rate in effect on the date of death. This recalculation approach ensures that the estate pays tax at the current marginal tax rate applicable for the decedent's amount of taxable estate and adjusted taxable gifts.

EXAMPLE C:13-4 ▶ Assume the same facts as in Examples C:13-2 and C:13-3. Recall that in 2004 Amy made $5 million of taxable gifts. The tax on $5 million of 2004 taxable gifts was $2,220,800. Amy was entitled to a $345,800 unified credit on the $1 million exemption equivalent amount and paid $1,875,000 of gift taxes. Amy's 2004 gifts were taxed at a 48% marginal rate. For the year of Amy's death (2015), the marginal rate for $5 million of transfers is 40%. Consequently, the reduction for gift taxes on post-1976 taxable gifts is limited to the amount of gift taxes that would be payable if the 2015 rate schedule were in effect in the year of the gift. This amount is calculated as follows:

Tax on $5 million at 2015 rates	$1,945,800
Minus: Unified credit for 2004 (the year of the gift)	(345,800)
Tax that would have been payable on $5 million if 2015 rates were in effect	$1,600,000

Note that the only changes to the gift tax computation are that the 2015 transfer tax rates are used. The credit applicable for the year of the gift (and not the credit for the year of death) is subtracted. This amount is recalculated (when necessary) to take into consideration the tax rates in effect for the year of the donor's death. Because the tax on the first $1 million was the same in 2004 as it is in 2015, the unified credit subtracted is the same amount as the credit used on the 2004 tax return. ◀

EXAMPLE C:13-5 ▶ From Examples C:13-3 and C:13-4, Amy's estate tax, before reduction for any credits, is calculated as follows:

Tax on $9 million tax base (Example C:13-3)	$3,545,800
Minus: Tax that would have been payable on $5 million of post-1976 taxable gifts, at 2015 rates (Example C:13-4)	(1,600,000)
Estate tax, before reduction for credits (discussed below)	$1,945,800 ◀

SELF-STUDY QUESTION

Taxpayer made $3 million of taxable gifts in 1992 and paid gift taxes of $1,098,000 (gross tax of $1,290,800 minus the unified credit of $192,800). Taxpayer died in 2015 with a taxable estate of $100,000. At 2015 rates and a credit recalculated at 2015 rates, the gift taxes payable on $3 million would be $953,000 ($1,145,800 − $192,800). Determine the amount of her estate tax liability.

ANSWER

The unified transfer tax base was $3.1 million, the sum of the $3 million of 1992 taxable gifts and the $100,000 estate. The 2015 tax on $3.1 million is $1,185,800. The unified credit of $2,117,800 and the subtraction for gift taxes of $953,000 reduce the tax liability to zero.

UNIFIED CREDIT

As shown in the inside back cover, the unified credit has varied over the years since its inception in 1977. The credit enables a certain size tax base, referred to as the exemption equivalent or applicable exclusion amount, to be completely free of transfer taxes. For 2009, the unified credit was the equivalent of the tax on $3.5 million for estates and $1 million for gifts. The Tax Relief Act did not revise the amount in effect for 2010 for gift tax purposes. It, however, increased the exempt amount to $5 million for estate tax purposes for the years 2010 and 2011, and for gift tax purposes for 2011. As a result, the unified credit rose to $1,730,800. In addition, this amount was indexed in 2012 to a $5.12 million exempt amount and a $1,772,800 credit. For 2013 and later, the exempt amount remains at $5 million, indexed annually for inflation. In 2015, the inflation-adjusted exempt amount is $5.43 million, resulting in a $2,117,800 unified credit for 2015. This exempt amount often is referred to as the exemption equivalent and/or the applicable exclusion amount.

The estate tax computation permits an estate to subtract the entire unified credit applicable for the year of death (reduced by any phaseout for certain pre-1977 gifts) regardless of how much unified credit the decedent claimed for gift tax purposes. As a conceptual matter, however, only one unified credit is available. Under the unification concept, the estate tax is computed on a tax base consisting of the taxable estate plus the adjusted taxable gifts. The tentative tax on the tax base is reduced not by the amount of the "gross" tax on the adjusted taxable gifts, but by the "gross" tax on such gifts reduced by the unified credit. Ignoring changes in the amount of the unified credit, this computation achieves the same result as allowing the unified credit amount to be subtracted only once against all of a person's transfers but allowing a reduction to the estate tax for the gift tax liability *before* reduction for the unified credit.

ADDITIONAL COMMENT

Three additional credits are available for estates. See Figure C:13-1 and pages C:13-24 and C:13-25.

The Gross Estate: Valuation

OBJECTIVE 2

Describe the methods for valuing interests in the gross estate

DATE-OF-DEATH VALUATION

All property included in the gross estate is valued at either its fair market value (FMV) on the date of death or the alternate valuation date. The valuation date election is an all-or-nothing proposition. Each item included in the gross estate must be valued as of the same date. In other words, the executor (called the personal representative in some states) cannot value some items as of the date of death and others as of the alternate valuation date.

TYPICAL MISCONCEPTION

The basis of inherited property is the FMV of the property on the decedent's date of death, which could be higher or lower than the decedent's basis. This change is referred to as a step-up or a step-down in basis. Many taxpayers hear so much about step-up that they forget that a step-down can occur. However, see pages C:12-27 and C:12-28 for carryover basis rules applicable to deaths in 2010.

Fair market value is defined as "the price at which the property would change hands between a willing buyer and a willing seller, neither being under any compulsion to buy or to sell and both having reasonable knowledge of relevant facts."[4] In general, the FMV of a particular asset on a certain date is the same regardless of whether the property is being valued for gift or estate tax purposes. Life insurance on the life of the transferor is an exception to this rule. Upon the death of the insured, the policy is valued at its face value, whereas it is valued at a lesser amount while the insured is alive. Generally, this lesser amount is either the cost of a comparable contract or the policy's interpolated terminal reserve plus the unexpired portion of the premium.

For certain types of property, Treasury Regulations contain detailed descriptions of the valuation approach. However, the valuation of interests in closely held businesses is described in only very general terms. Judicial decisions and revenue rulings provide additional guidance for valuation of assets. Valuation rules for several interests are discussed below. For purposes of this discussion, it is assumed that date-of-death valuation is elected.

ETHICAL POINT

The executor may need to engage a qualified appraiser to value interests in closely held corporations and real estate. Because appraisals are subjective, two appraisers may arrive at different values. Using the highest appraisal may mean additional estate taxes, but it will provide a greater step-up in basis. Using too low an appraisal may subject the estate to undervaluation penalties (see page C:13-35).

Listed Stocks. Stocks traded on a stock exchange are valued at the average of their highest and lowest selling prices on the date of death.[5] If no sales occur on the date of death, but sales do take place within a few days of such date, the estate tax value is a weighted average of the high and low sales prices on the nearest trade dates before and after the date of death. The average is weighted inversely in relation to the number of days separating the sales dates and the date of death.

EXAMPLE C:13-6 ▶ Juan, who died on November 12, 2015, owned 100 shares of Jet Corporation stock. Jet stock, traded on the New York Stock Exchange, traded at a high of $120 and a low of $114 on November 12. On Juan's estate tax return, the stock was valued at $117 per share, the average of $120 and $114. The total value of the block of Jet stock was $11,700 (100 × $117). ◀

EXAMPLE C:13-7 ▶ Susan, who died on May 7, 2015 owned 100 shares of Top Corporation stock, traded on the New York Stock Exchange. No sales of Top stock occurred on May 7. The sales occurring closest to May 7 took place two business days before May 7 and three business days after May 7. On the earlier date, the stock traded at a high of $500 and a low of $490, with an average of $495. On the later date, the high was $492 and the low was $490, for an average of $491. The date-of-death per-share valuation of the stock is computed under the inverse weighted average approach, as follows:

$$\frac{[3 \times \$495] + [2 \times \$491]}{5} = \$493.40$$

The total value of the block of Top stock is $49,340 (100 × $493.40). ◀

In certain circumstances, the decedent may own such a large block of stock that the price at which the stock trades in the market may not represent the FMV per share for the decedent's number of shares. In such circumstances, Treasury Regulations allow a departure from the traditional valuation rule for stocks. These regulations, referred to as the blockage regulations, state that

[4] Reg. Sec. 20.2031-1(b).

[5] Reg. Sec. 20.2031-2(b).

> In certain exceptional cases, the size of the block of stock to be valued in relation to the number of shares changing hands in sales may be relevant in determining whether selling prices reflect the fair market value of the block of stock to be valued. If the executor can show that the block of stock to be valued is so large in relation to the actual sales on the existing market that it could not be liquidated in a reasonable time without depressing the market, the price at which the block could be sold as such outside the usual market, as through an underwriter, may be a more accurate indication of value than market quotations.[6]

Interests in Firms Whose Stock is not Publicly Traded. Often, the decedent owns stock in a firm whose shares are not publicly traded. Treasury Regulations do not specifically address the valuation rules for this type of an interest. However, detailed guidelines about relevant factors, including book value and earning capacity, are found in Rev. Rul. 59-60.[7] If the stock is a minority interest in a closely held firm, the courts often grant a discount for the minority interest.

SELF-STUDY QUESTION

Compare a situation where capitalization of earnings might be used instead of or in addition to comparable sales when valuing real estate.

ANSWER

Capitalization of earnings might be used instead of or in addition to comparable sales in the valuation of an apartment or office building. Comparable sales would be used for valuing a personal residence.

Real Estate. Perhaps surprisingly, Treasury Regulations do not specifically address the valuation approach for real estate. Thus, the general valuation principles concerning a price that would be acceptable to a willing buyer and a willing seller must be implemented without the benefit of more specific guidance. Appraisal literature discusses three techniques for valuing real property: comparable sales, reproduction cost, and capitalization of earnings.[8] Unfortunately, for some properties, it may be difficult to locate a comparable real estate sale. The reproduction cost, of course, is not applicable to valuing land. Capitalization of earnings often is used in valuing commercial real property. At times, an appraiser may use all three approaches.

Annuities, Interests for Life or a Term of Years, Reversions, Remainders. Actuarial tables are used to value annuities, interests for life or a term of years, reversions, and remainders included in the gross estate.[9] The same tables apply for both estate and gift tax purposes. (See Chapter C:12 for a discussion of the use of these tables.) The following example illustrates a situation when the actuarial tables must be used to value an inclusion in the decedent's estate.

EXAMPLE C:13-8 ► Tony gives property to a trust with a bank named as trustee and his cousin named to receive all of the trust income for the next 15 years (i.e., a term certain interest). At the end of the fifteenth year, the property reverts to Tony or his estate. Tony dies exactly four years after creating the trust, and the trust property is valued at $100,000 at Tony's death. At Tony's death, the trust has 11 years to continue until the property reverts to Tony's estate. The inclusion in Tony's estate is the value of a reversionary interest following a term certain interest with 11 remaining years. If 4% is the applicable rate, the reversionary interest is valued at $64,958 (0.649581 × $100,000) from Table B of the actuarial tables included in Appendix H. ◄

ALTERNATE VALUATION DATE

Section 2032 authorizes the executor to elect to value all property included in the gross estate at its FMV on the alternate valuation date. Congress enacted this provision in response to the stock market crash of 1929 to make sure that an entire estate could not be confiscated for taxes because of a sudden, substantial drop in values.

In general, the **alternate valuation date** is six months after the date of death. However, if the property is distributed, sold, exchanged, or otherwise disposed of within six months of the date of death, the alternate valuation date is the date of sale or other disposition.

EXAMPLE C:13-9 ► Ron died on March 3, 2015. Ron's estate included two items: stock and land. The estate still owned the stock on September 3, but the executor sold the land on August 20. If Ron's executor elected the alternate valuation date, the stock was valued as of September 3. The land, however, was valued as of August 20 because it was disposed of before the end of the six-month period. Of course, the value of land generally would change very little, if any, between August 20 and September 3. ◄

---

[6] Reg. Sec. 20.2031-2(e). As examples of cases dealing with the blockage discount, see *Horace Havemeyer v. U.S.*, 33 AFTR 1069, 45-1 USTC ¶10,194 (Ct. Cls., 1945); *Estate of Charles M. Prell*, 48 T.C. 67 (1967); and *Estate of David Smith*, 57 T.C. 650 (1972). The *Smith* case extended the blockage concept to large holdings of works of art.

[7] 1959-1 C.B. 237.

[8] For a discussion of techniques for appraising real estate, see The Appraisal Institute, *The Appraisal of Real Estate*, 11th ed. (Arlington Heights, IL: The Appraisal Institute, 1996).

[9] Section 7520 provides that the interest rate potentially changes every month. Regulation Sec. 20.7520-1(a)(2) provides these tables. An excerpt from these tables is included in Appendix H.

REAL-WORLD EXAMPLE

Proposed Treasury Regulations, if adopted, would allow the alternative valuation only for reductions due to "market conditions."

If the executor elects the alternate valuation date, generally any changes in value that occur *solely* because of a "mere lapse of time" must be ignored in determining the property's value.[10] In a limited number of situations, one must concentrate on the meaning of the phrase "the mere passage of time." For example, if the executor elects the alternate valuation date to value a patent, he or she must ignore any change in value attributable to the fact that the patent's remaining life is six months shorter on the alternate valuation date than it was on the date of death. Changes in value resulting from the invention of a competing patented product are relevant.

ADDITIONAL COMMENT

The limitation on the use of alternate valuation is especially important now that the exemption equivalent is $5 million, adjusted annually for inflation.

The alternate valuation date election can be made only if it decreases the value of the gross estate *and* the estate tax liability (after reduction for credits).[11] As a result of this provision, electing the alternate valuation date cannot produce a higher step-up in basis. Congress enacted this strict rule because the alternate valuation date formerly offered a substantial tax planning advantage in situations where, because of the unlimited marital deduction, no estate tax was owed. If the property appreciated between the date of death and the alternate valuation date, the recipient could receive an increased basis if the executor elected the alternate valuation date.[12] Because of the unlimited marital deduction, the estate formerly could achieve an additional step-up in basis without increasing the estate tax liability.

STOP & THINK

Question: Joan died on December 1, 2015. Her estate consisted of three assets: an apartment building valued at $3.2 million on December 1, 2015, stock valued at $3.7 million on December 1, and $400,000 of cash. On June 1 of the next year, 1, the values were as follows: apartment building—$3.5 million, stock—$3.1 million, and cash of $400,000. Joan willed all her property to her son, who anticipates owning the property for a long time. The deductions for Joan's estate were negligible. Is there an estate tax benefit in electing the alternate valuation date? Is there an income tax benefit in electing the alternate valuation date?

Solution: An estate tax benefit results from using the alternate valuation date. The estate tax liability would be lower because the taxable estate would be $300,000 smaller if the alternate valuation date value ($7 million minus deductions) were used instead of the date of death value ($7.3 million minus deductions). Some income tax benefit also results from using the alternate valuation date. By using the alternate valuation date value, the tax basis for calculating cost recovery on the apartment building is $300,000 higher, ignoring any allocation of value to the land. However, a related detriment occurs because the basis of the stock is $600,000 lower with the alternate valuation date. If the son sells the stock soon after June 1, the $600,000 capital loss that would arise by using the date of death value might permit Joan's son to sell a number of highly-appreciated assets and offset a very large capital gain with the $600,000 capital loss.

THE GROSS ESTATE: INCLUSIONS

OBJECTIVE 3

Recognize which interests are includible in the gross estate

As Figure C:13-1 illustrates, the process of calculating the decedent's estate tax liability begins with determining the components of the gross estate. The **gross estate** is analogous to gross income. Once the components of the gross estate have been identified, they must be valued. As previously mentioned, the gross estate encompasses a much wider array of items than merely those to which the decedent held legal title at death. For example, under certain statutory provisions, referred to as the *transferor sections,* the gross estate includes items previously transferred by the decedent. For decedents other than nonresident aliens, the fact that property is located in a foreign country does not preclude it from being included in the gross estate. Table C:13-1 provides an overview of the inclusions in the gross estate.

---

[10] Reg. Sec. 20.2032-1(f).
[11] Sec. 2032(c).
[12] Sec. 1014(a).

▼ **TABLE C:13-1**
Inclusions in the Gross Estate

IRC Section	Type of Property or Transaction Included
2033	Property in which the decedent had an interest
2035	Gift taxes on property given away within three years of death plus certain property (primarily life insurance) given away within three years of death
2036	Property that the decedent transferred during life but in which the decedent retained economic benefits or the power to control enjoyment
2037	Property that the decedent transferred during life but for which the decedent has too large a reversionary interest
2038	Property that the decedent transferred during life but over which the decedent held the power to alter, amend, revoke, or terminate an interest
2039	Annuities
2040	Jointly owned property
2041	Property over which the decedent possessed a general power of appointment
2042	Life insurance on the decedent's life
2044	QTIP trust for which a marital deduction was claimed by the decedent's spouse

COMPARISON OF GROSS ESTATE WITH PROBATE ESTATE

The gross estate is a federal tax law concept, and the probate estate is a state law concept. To oversimplify, the **probate estate** can be defined as encompassing property that passes subject to the will (or under an intestacy statute) and is subject to court administration. Often, a decedent's gross estate is substantially larger than his or her probate estate. For example, suppose that at the time of death, a decedent owned a life insurance policy on his own life with his daughter as the beneficiary. The policy is not a part of the decedent's probate estate because the policy proceeds are payable directly to the named beneficiary (the daughter), but it is included in the gross estate.

STOP & THINK

Question: Karl died in 2015, and Karl's executor included the following properties in Karl's gross estate: life insurance payable to the beneficiary, Karl's wife; savings account solely in Karl's name; land titled in the names of Karl and his son as joint tenants with right of survivorship; and a trust created under the will of Karl's mother. Karl had an income interest in the trust for his lifetime and complete power to designate the owners of the property on his death. With the exception of the trust assets (willed to his children), Karl's will left all his property to his beloved cousin, Karla. Which assets passed under the terms of Karl's will? Which assets did Karla receive?

Solution: This scenario illustrates the difference between the property included in a decedent's gross estate and in the probate estate. Karl's gross estate was larger than his probate estate. Only two assets included in his gross estate—the savings account and the trust property—passed under the terms of Karl's will. Karla received only the savings account because Karl willed the trust property to his children. The life insurance passed outside the will to the named beneficiary, the spouse, and the land passed outside the will to the surviving joint tenant, the son.

SELF-STUDY QUESTION

Which of the following properties will be included in (1) the probate estate, (2) the gross estate, (3) both the probate and gross estate, or (4) neither estate?

1. Real property held in joint tenancy with the decedent's spouse. (The answer is 2.)
2. Real property held as a tenant in common with the decedent's spouse. (The answer is 3.)
3. A life insurance policy owned by the decedent in which the decedent's spouse is named the beneficiary. (The answer is 2.)
4. A life insurance policy always owned by the decedent's spouse in which the decedent's children are named the beneficiaries. (The answer is 4.)

PROPERTY IN WHICH THE DECEDENT HAD AN INTEREST

Section 2033, sometimes called the *generic section,* provides that the gross estate includes the value of all property the decedent beneficially owned at the time of death. Its broad language taxes such items as a personal residence, an automobile, stocks, and any other asset titled in the decedent's name. Because the rule refers to beneficial ownership, however, its scope extends beyond assets to which the decedent held legal title. For example, such items as remainder interests also are included in the gross estate.

EXAMPLE C:13-10 ▶ At the time of his death, Raj held the following assets in his name: personal residence, mountain cabin, Zero Corporation stock, checking account, and savings account. Raj beneficially owned each of these items when he died. Under Sec. 2033, each item was included in Raj's gross estate. ◀

EXAMPLE C:13-11 ▶ Ken's will named Ann to receive trust income for life and Raj or Raj's estate to receive the trust remainder upon Ann's death. Raj's gross estate, therefore, included the value of the remainder interest if Raj predeceased Ann because Raj's will controlled the passage of the remainder interest Raj beneficially owned. The transfer was associated with Raj's death, and, hence, was subject to the estate tax. ◀

DOWER OR CURTESY RIGHTS

Certain state laws provide wealth protection to surviving spouses through **dower** or **curtesy** rights.

ADDITIONAL COMMENT

Any property that passes outright to the decedent's spouse, due to dower or curtesy rights under state law, is eligible for the marital deduction and will not increase the unified tax base.

- Dower is a widow's interest in her deceased husband's property.
- Curtesy is a widower's interest in his deceased wife's property.

Dower or curtesy rights entitle the surviving spouse to a certain portion of the decedent spouse's estate, even though the decedent may have willed a smaller portion to the spouse. Because the decedent spouse does not have complete control over the portion of his or her estate that is subject to dower or curtesy rights, some might think that the gross estate excludes the portion of the estate that the surviving spouse is entitled to receive. Thus, Congress made it crystal clear that the decedent's gross estate is not reduced for the value of the property in which the surviving spouse has a dower or curtesy interest or some other statutory interest.[13]

EXAMPLE C:13-12 ▶ The laws of a certain state provide that widows are entitled to receive one-third of their deceased husband's property. The husband's gross estate does not exclude his widow's dower rights (one-third interest) in his property. ◀

SELF-STUDY QUESTION

When Dorothy died on April 10, 2015, she owned Z Corporation bonds, which paid interest on April 1 and October 1, and stock in X and Y Corporations. X Corporation had declared a dividend on March 15 payable to stockholders of record on April 1. Y Corporation had declared a dividend on March 31 payable to stockholders of record on April 15. Dorothy's estate received the interest and dividends on the payment dates. Are any of the interest or dividends includible in Dorothy's gross estate?

ANSWER

The X Corporation dividend is included because the date of record preceded Dorothy's death. The Y Corporation dividend is not included because the date of record was after her death. The Z Corporation bond interest included is the interest that accrued between the April 1 payment date and the April 10 date of death.

TRANSFEROR PROVISIONS

Sections 2035 through 2038 are called the *transferor provisions*. They apply if the decedent made a transfer while alive of a type specified in the IRC section in question, *and* the decedent did not receive adequate consideration in money or money's worth for the transferred interest. If one of the transferor provisions applies, the gross estate includes the transferred property at its date-of-death or alternate valuation date value.

Gifts Made Within Three Years of Death. Section 2035(a) specifies the circumstances in which a gift that a decedent makes within three years of death triggers an inclusion in the gross estate. The scope of this provision, which is relatively narrow, encompasses the following two types of transfers made by the donor-decedent within three years before death:

- A life insurance policy on the decedent's life that would have been taxed under Sec. 2042 (life insurance proceeds received by the executor or for the benefit of the estate) had the policy not been given away, or
- An interest in property that would have been taxed under Sec. 2036 (transfers with a retained life estate), Sec. 2037 (transfers taking effect at death), or Sec. 2038 (revocable transfers) had it not been transferred.

Of these situations, the most common involves the insured's gifting a life insurance policy on his or her own life and dying within three years of the transfer. With new insurance policies, the potential for an inclusion can be avoided if the decedent never owns the new policy. In other words, instead of the insured purchasing a new policy and then giving it to a transferee as owner, the other party should buy the new policy. A common planning

[13] Sec. 2034.

technique involves a transfer of cash by an individual to a trust, and the trust (a life insurance trust) using the cash to purchase an insurance policy on the transferor's life.

EXAMPLE C:13-13 ▶ On April 1, 2012, Roy transferred to Sally ownership of a $400,000 life insurance policy on his own life purchased in 1997. Sally is the policy's beneficiary. Roy died on February 3, 2015. Because Roy died within three years of giving away the policy, the policy was included in Roy's gross estate. The estate tax value of the policy is its $400,000 face value. If Roy had died on April 2, 2015, the policy transfer would have fallen outside the three-year rule by one day, and the policy would not have been included in Roy's gross estate. ◀

EXAMPLE C:13-14 ▶ Roy gave stock to Troy on May 1, 2014. Roy died on February 3, 2015. The stock was worth $80,000 on the gift date and $125,000 at the time of Roy's death. The gifted property was not included in Roy's gross estate because it is not life insurance on Roy's life, nor is it property that would have been taxed in Roy's estate under Secs. 2036 through 2038 had he kept such property. ◀

Gross-Up Rule. The donor-decedent's gross estate is increased by any gift tax that he or she, or his or her estate pays on any gift the decedent or his or her spouse makes during the three-year period ending with the decedent's death.[14] This provision, known as the gross-up rule, applies to the gift tax triggered by a gift of any type of property during the three-year look-back period.

The purpose of the gross-up rule is to foreclose the opportunity that existed under pre-1977 law to reduce one's gross estate (and thereby one's taxable estate) by removing the gift tax on "deathbed" gifts from the gross estate. Because the donor's estate received a credit for some or all of the gift tax paid, under the pre-1977 rules, a person on his or her deathbed in effect could prepay a portion of his or her estate tax and at the same time reduce his or her gross estate by the amount of the gift tax.

The gross-up rule, as illustrated in the two examples below, reinstates the estate to the position it would have been in had no gift tax liability been incurred.

EXAMPLE C:13-15 ▶ In late 2013, Cheron made her first gift, a $6 million taxable gift of stock, and paid a gift tax of $300,000 ($2,345,800 gross tax − $2,045,800 unified credit). Cheron died in early 2015. Cheron's gross estate did not include the stock, but it did include the $300,000 gift tax paid because she made the gift within three years of her death. ◀

EXAMPLE C:13-16 ▶ In late 2013, Hal gave Jody stock having a $12,028,000 FMV, and he and Wanda, his wife, elected gift splitting. Each was deemed to have made a $6 million [($12,028,000 ÷ 2) − $14,000 annual exclusion] taxable gift, and each paid $300,000 ($2,345,800 gross tax − $2,045,800 unified credit) of gift tax. Wanda died in early 2015. Wanda's gross estate included the $300,000 in gift tax she paid on the portion of her husband's gift that she was deemed to have made within three years of her death. Her cash balance declined because of paying the gift tax, and the gross-up for the tax reinstated her estate to the position it would have been in had she paid no gift tax. ◀

SELF-STUDY QUESTION

Refer to Example C:13-16. Assume that Hal, the spouse who actually made the gift, paid Wanda's $300,000 gift tax as well as his own $300,000 gift tax. Would Wanda's $300,000 gift tax be included in her gross estate?

ANSWER

No. It would not be included because payment of the tax from Hal's account did not reduce Wanda's cash balance.

Transfers with Retained Life Estate. Section 2036, although titled "Transfers with Retained Life Estate," extends beyond taxing solely lifetime transfers made by the decedent in which he or she retained a life estate (the right to income or use for life). The two primary types of transfers taxed under Sec. 2036 are those for which the decedent

- Kept possession or enjoyment of the property or the right to its income
- Retained the power to designate the person who is to possess or enjoy the property or to receive its income

Thus, Sec. 2036 applies when the transferor kept the income or enjoyment *or* the right to control other individuals' income or enjoyment.

The direct or indirect retention of voting rights in stock of a controlled corporation that the decedent transferred also can cause the gifted stock to be included in the

[14] Sec. 2035(b).

transferor's gross estate.[15] A controlled corporation is one in which the decedent owned (directly, indirectly, or constructively), or had the right to vote, stock that possessed at least 20% of the voting power.[16]

The retention of income, control, or voting rights for one of the three retention periods listed below causes the transferred property to be included in the transferor's gross estate. The three periods are

- The transferor's lifetime
- A period that cannot be determined without referring to the transferor's death (e.g., the transferor retained the right to quarterly payments of income, but payments ceased with the last quarterly payment before the transferor's death)
- A period that does not end, in fact, before the transferor's death

An implied agreement or understanding is sufficient to trigger inclusion. For example, if a mother gives a residence to her daughter and continues to occupy the residence alone and rent-free, the residence probably will be included in the mother's gross estate under the argument that the parties had an implied understanding allowing the mother to reside in the residence for life without paying rent.

If Sec. 2036 applies to a transfer and if the decedent's retention of enjoyment or control extends to all the transferred property, 100% of the transferred property's value is included in the transferor's gross estate.[17] However, if the transferor keeps the right to only one-third of the income for life and retains no control over the remaining two-thirds, his estate includes just one-third of the property's date-of-death value. The following three examples illustrate some of the transactions that cause Sec. 2036 to apply.

EXAMPLE C:13-17 ▶ In 2008, David (age 30) transferred an office building to Ellen but retained the right to collect all the income from the building for life. David died in 2015. Because David retained the income right for life, the Sec. 2036 inclusion applied. The amount included was 100% of the building's date-of-death value. ◀

EXAMPLE C:13-18 ▶ Assume the same facts as in Example C:13-17 except that David retained the right to income for only 16 years. David died seven years after the transfer; therefore, David had the right to receive the income for the remaining nine-year period. Because the retention period did not *in fact* end before David's death, his gross estate included 100% of the property's date-of-death value. ◀

EXAMPLE C:13-19 ▶ Tracy created a trust with a bank as trustee and named Alice, Brad, and Carol to receive the trust income for their joint lives and Dick to receive the remainder upon the death of the first among Alice, Brad, or Carol to die. Tracy retained some control by reserving the right to designate the portion of the income to be paid to each income beneficiary each year. Only the transfer to Dick was a completed transfer and subject to gift taxes. Tracy predeceased the other parties. Because her control over the flow of income did not end before her death, the date-of-death value of the trust assets was included in Tracy's gross estate even though a portion of the transfer was subject to gift taxes. If Tracy had instead "cut the string" and not kept control over the income flow, she could have removed the trust property from her estate. ◀

SELF-STUDY QUESTION

Refer to Example C:13-19. Assume the same facts except that the trustee was directed to distribute its annual income equally to Alice, Brad, and Carol for their joint lives. Also assume that Tracy named Dick the remainderman. Was the value of the trust included in Tracy's gross estate?

ANSWER

No, because Tracy retained no power to control the enjoyment of the property.

Reversionary Interests. If, under the terms of the transfer, the chance exists that the property will pass back to the transferor the transferor has a **reversionary interest**. Under Sec. 2037, the transferor's gross estate includes earlier transferred property if the transferor stipulates that another person must survive him or her to own the property and the value of the decedent's reversionary interest exceeds 5% of the value of the transferred property. Actuarial techniques are used to value the reversionary interest.[18] Section 2037 does not apply if the value of the reversionary interest does not exceed the 5% *de minimis* amount.

EXAMPLE C:13-20 ▶ Beth transferred an asset to Tammy for life and then to Doug for life. The asset is to revert to Beth, if Beth is still alive, upon the death of either Tammy or Doug, whoever dies second. If Beth is not alive upon the death of the survivor of Tammy and Doug, the asset is to pass to Don or to

---

[15] Sec. 2036(b)(1).

[16] Sec. 2036(b)(2).

[17] Reg. Sec. 20.2036-1(a).

[18] The **reversionary interest** is the interest that will return to the transferor. Often, it will return only if certain contingencies occur. The value of Beth's reversionary interest in Example C:13-20 is a function of the present value of the interest Beth would receive after the deaths of Tammy and Doug, valued as from actuarial tables (see Appendix H), and coupled with the probability that Tammy and Doug would die before Beth.

a charitable organization if Don is not alive. Thus, Don must survive Beth to receive the property. Beth predeceases Tammy and Doug, and there is an inclusion in her estate if the value of Beth's reversionary interest exceeds 5% of the property's value. The amount included is not the value of Beth's reversionary interest, but rather the date-of-death value of the asset less the value of Tammy's and Doug's intervening life estates. ◀

ADDITIONAL COMMENT

Sections 2036 through 2038 draw back into the gross estate certain previously transferred property and include it at its FMV on the date of the decedent's death. For income tax purposes, if the property has appreciated in value, donees will obtain a stepped-up basis rather than a carryover gift tax basis for property included in the gross estate.

Revocable Transfers. Section 2038 covers the rules for revocable transfers (i.e., revocable trusts). However, this provision also taxes all transfers over which the decedent has, at the time of his or her death, the power to change the enjoyment of property by altering, amending, revoking, or terminating an interest. Revocable trusts, sometimes called living trusts, are popular arrangements from a non-tax standpoint because assets held by a revocable trust pass outside of probate. Advantages of avoiding probate include lower probate costs and easier administration for real property located in a state that is not the decedent's state of domicile. In addition, unlike a will, a revocable trust is not a matter of public record.

Section 2038 can apply even though the decedent does not originally retain powers over the property. The crucial factor is that the transferor possesses the powers at the time of death regardless of whether the transferor retained such powers originally. The estate includes only the value of the interest that is subject to the decedent's power to change. Sections 2038 and 2036 overlap greatly, and if one amount is taxable under one section and a different amount is taxable under the other section, the gross estate includes the larger amount. Two types of transfers taxed by Sec. 2038 are illustrated in the following examples.

EXAMPLE C:13-21 ▶ Joe funded a revocable trust and named his son to receive the income for life and his grandson to receive the property upon the son's death. Because the trust was revocable, Joe could change the terms of the trust or take back the trust property during his lifetime. Joe's power to revoke the transfer extended to the entire trust. Thus, Joe's gross estate included the date-of-death value of the entire trust. ◀

EXAMPLE C:13-22 ▶ Vicki created a trust and irrevocably named Gina to receive the income for life and Matt to receive the remainder. Vicki, however, retained the right to substitute Liz (for Matt) as remainderman. When Vicki died, she had the authority to change the enjoyment of the remainder. Thus, the value of the trust's remainder interest was includible in Vicki's estate. ◀

SELF-STUDY QUESTION

Reggie purchased an annuity and elected to collect benefits for 15 years. If Reggie dies before the end of the 15-year term of the annuity, his estate will be entitled to the remaining payments. Assume Reggie died after receiving nine payments. Will the value of the remaining six payments be included in Reggie's estate?

ANSWER

Yes. Section 2039 requires that the cost of a comparable contract of six payments be included in his gross estate.

ANNUITIES AND OTHER RETIREMENT BENEFITS

Section 2039 explicitly addresses the estate tax treatment of annuities. Even if this section had not been enacted, some annuities probably would have been taxable under the general language of Sec. 2033 because the decedent would have been viewed as having an interest in the property. For an annuity to be included in the gross estate, it must involve payments made under a contract or an agreement. In addition, the decedent must be receiving such payments at the time of his or her death or must have the right to collect such payments alone or with another person. If the annuity simply ceases with the death of the decedent in question, nothing is to be received by another party and nothing is included in the gross estate. For the payments to be included in the decedent's estate, they must be payable for the decedent's life, a period that may not be determined without referring to the decedent's date of death or for a period that does not actually end before the decedent's death.

Annuities not Related to Employment. The purchase of an annuity designed to pay benefits to the purchaser and then to a named survivor upon the purchaser's death, or to both parties simultaneously and then to the survivor, is a form of wealth shifting. The survivor receives wealth that originates with the purchaser. This type of transfer is different from most other wealth transfers because it involves a series of annuity payments instead of a transfer of a tangible property.

The amount included in the gross estate with respect to annuities or other retirement benefits is a fraction (described below) of the value of the annuity or lump-sum payment to be received by the surviving beneficiary. Annuities are valued at the cost of a comparable contract.[19] To determine the inclusion in the gross estate, this cost is multiplied by a fraction that represents the portion of the purchase price the decedent contributed.

EXAMPLE C:13-23 ▶ Twelve years ago, Jim purchased a joint and survivor annuity and selected the payment option of benefits to be paid to himself and his son concurrently and then to the survivor for life. Jim and his son started collecting payments four years before Jim died, survived by his son. At the time of Jim's death, the cost of a comparable contract providing the same benefits was $180,000. Because Jim provided all the consideration to purchase the annuity, his gross estate included 100% of the $180,000 cost of a comparable contract. This annuity arrangement represents a shifting of wealth from Jim to his son upon Jim's death. ◀

SELF-STUDY QUESTION

On his retirement at age 65, Winslow elected to take a joint and survivor annuity from his qualified pension plan. The plan provided Winslow and his wife with a monthly pension of $7,500 until the death of the survivor. Winslow died seven years later. What amount (if any) was included in Winslow's gross estate if his wife survived?

ANSWER

The gross estate included the cost of a comparable contract providing $7,500 a month for the rest of the spouse's life. The younger the spouse, the higher the cost.

Employment-Related Retirement Benefits. Recall that, to determine the amount of an annuity includible in the decedent's gross estate, the cost of a comparable contract is multiplied by a fraction representing the portion of the purchase price contributed by the decedent. Section 2039(b) states that contributions from the decedent's employer (or former employer) are treated as contributions made by the decedent, provided such payments are made as a result of the employment relationship. Thus, 100% of the benefits from an employment-related annuity are included in the gross estate.

EXAMPLE C:13-24 ▶ Pat was employed by Wheel Corporation at the time of his death. Wheel Corporation maintains a qualified retirement plan to which it makes 60% of the contributions and its employees contribute 40%. Pat's spouse is to receive an annuity valued at $350,000 from the retirement plan. Because the employer's contributions are considered to have been made by the employee, Pat is deemed to have provided all the consideration for the retirement benefits. Consequently, Pat's gross estate includes 100% of the annuity's $350,000 date-of-death value. ◀

JOINTLY OWNED PROPERTY

Section 2040 addresses the estate tax treatment of jointly owned property (i.e., property owned in a joint tenancy with right of survivorship or tenancy by the entirety arrangement).[20] An important characteristic of this form of ownership is that, upon the death of one joint owner, the decedent's interest passes automatically (by right of survivorship) to the surviving joint owner(s). Thus, the property is not part of the probate estate and does not pass under the will. Section 2040 contains two sets of rules, one for property jointly owned by spouses and one for all other jointly owned properties.

Ownership Involving Persons Other than Spouses. When persons other than spouses or persons in addition to spouses own property as joint owners, the amount includible is determined by the consideration-furnished test.[21] Under this test, property is included in a joint owner's gross estate in accordance with the portion of the consideration he or she furnished to acquire the property. Obviously, this portion can range between 0% and 100%.

---

[19] Reg. Sec. 20.2031-8(a).

[20] Both joint tenancies with right of survivorship and tenancies by the entirety have the feature of survivorship. When one joint owner dies, his or her interest passes by right of survivorship to the remaining joint owner(s). Only spouses may use the tenancy by the entirety arrangement, whereas any persons may own as joint tenants with right of survivorship. A joint tenancy with right of survivorship may be severed by the action of any joint owner, whereas a tenancy by the entirety arrangement continues unless severed by the joint action of both joint owners.

The following definitions are from Henry Campbell Black, *Black's Law Dictionary*, Rev. 6th ed., Ed. by Joseph R. Nolan and Jacqueline M. Nolan-Haley (St. Paul, MN: West Publishing Co., 1990), p. 1465.

Joint tenancy with right of survivorship: The primary incident of joint tenancy is survivorship, by which the entire tenancy on the decease of any joint tenant remains to the survivors, and at length to the last survivor.

Tenancy by the entirety: A tenancy which is created between husband and wife and by which together they hold title to the whole with right of survivorship so that upon death of either, other takes whole to exclusion of deceased heirs. It is essentially a "joint tenancy" modified by the common-law theory that husband and wife are one person, and survivorship is the predominant and distinguishing feature of each. Neither party can alienate or encumber the property without the consent of the other.

[21] Sec. 2040(a).

EXAMPLE C:13-25 ►

Seven years ago, Fred and Jack provided $10,000 and $30,000 of consideration, respectively, to purchase real property titled in the names of Fred and Jack as joint tenants with right of survivorship. Fred died and was survived by Jack. The real property was valued at $60,000. Fred's gross estate included $15,000 ($0.25 \times \$60,000$) because Fred furnished 25% of the consideration to acquire the property. If Jack instead predeceased Fred when the property was worth $60,000, his estate would have included $45,000 ($0.75 \times \$60,000$). ◄

ADDITIONAL COMMENT

The tracing rule is easy to understand but difficult to implement. Suppose a joint tenancy between a parent and a child was created in a parcel of real estate 30 years ago when the parent paid for the property. The child died of a heart attack, and the parent is senile. Nothing should be included in the child's gross estate. However, the burden of proof to keep a portion of the property out of the estate is on the estate, not the IRS.

If part of the consideration furnished by one joint tenant is originally received gratuitously from another joint tenant, the consideration is attributable to the joint tenant who made the gift. If all joint owners acquire their interests by gift, devise, bequest, or inheritance, the decedent joint owner's estate includes his or her proportionate share of the date-of-death value of the jointly owned property.

EXAMPLE C:13-26 ►

Ray gave stock valued at $50,000 to Sam. Three years later Sam transferred this stock (now valued at $60,000) as partial consideration to acquire real property costing $120,000. Ray furnished the remaining $60,000 of consideration. The real property was titled in the names of Ray and Sam as joint tenants with right of survivorship. Because Sam received the asset that he used for consideration as a gift from Ray (the other joint tenant), Sam is treated as having furnished no consideration. If Sam dies before Ray, Sam's estate will include none of the real property's value. If Ray predeceases Sam, however, Ray's estate will include the entire date-of-death value. ◄

SELF-STUDY QUESTION

Fred and Myrtle, husband and wife, held title to their home in joint tenancy with right of survivorship. Fred died in an airplane crash. What part of the value of the residence was included in Fred's gross estate? Who will own the residence if Fred willed all his property to their children?

Ownership Involving Only Spouses. If spouses are the only joint owners, the property is classified as a **qualified joint interest**. Section 2040(b)(1) provides that, in the case of qualified joint interests, the decedent's gross estate includes one-half the value of the qualified joint interest. The 50% inclusion rule applies automatically regardless of the relative amount of consideration provided by either spouse.

EXAMPLE C:13-27 ►

Wilma provided all the consideration to purchase stock costing $80,000. She registered the stock in her name and her husband's name as joint tenants with right of survivorship. The estate of the first spouse to die, regardless of which spouse it is, will include 50% of the value of the jointly owned stock. Upon the second spouse's death, all the property will be included in that spouse's gross estate because the property no longer is jointly owned property. ◄

ANSWER

One-half the value of the residence was included in Fred's gross estate. Myrtle will own the residence after Fred's death because it passed to her by right of survivorship.

GENERAL POWERS OF APPOINTMENT

Section 2041 requires inclusion in the gross estate of certain property interests that the decedent never owned in a legal sense. Inclusion occurs because the decedent had the power to designate who eventually would own the property. The authority to designate the owner—a significant power—is called a power of appointment. Powers of appointment can be general or special (i.e., more restricted). By default, a power that is not general is classified as special.

Only a general power of appointment results in an addition to the gross estate. If a general power was created before October 22, 1942, however, no inclusion occurs unless the decedent exercised the power. For a post-1942 general power of appointment, inclusion occurs regardless of whether the power is exercised. A general power of appointment exists if the holder can exercise the power in favor of him- or herself, his or her estate or creditors, *or* the creditors of his or her estate. Being exercisable in favor of the decedent's estate means there is no restriction on the powerholder's ability to specify the person(s) to receive the property. The power may be exercisable during the decedent's life, by his or her will, or both.

EXAMPLE C:13-28 ►

Kathy died in 2007, and her will created a trust from which Doris is to receive the income for life. In addition, Doris was granted the power to designate by will the person or persons to receive the trust's assets. Doris has a testamentary general power of appointment. The trust's assets are included in Doris's gross estate regardless of whether Doris exercises the power. If Kathy had instead died in 1940, Doris would have had a pre-1942 power of appointment. Such powers are taxed only if exercised. ◄

If a powerholder can exercise a power for only specified purposes and/or in favor of only certain persons such as children, the power is a special power. Appointment powers that can be exercised solely for purposes of the decedent's health, support, maintenance, or education are governed by a so-called "ascertainable standard" and also are free of estate tax consequences.

EXAMPLE C:13-29 ▶ Assume the same facts as in Example C:13-28 except that Kathy's will merely empowered Doris to name which of her descendants shall receive the trust assets. Doris now has only a special power of appointment because she does not have the power to leave the property to whomever she desires (e.g., the power to appoint the property to her estate). Because Doris's power of appointment is only a special power, the value of the trust is not included in Doris's gross estate. ◀

LIFE INSURANCE

TYPICAL MISCONCEPTION

Many taxpayers who own life insurance policies on their own lives mistakenly believe that their estates will not owe estate taxes on the life insurance proceeds if they name someone other than their estate as the beneficiary. Life insurance will be included in the gross estate of the decedent if, at the time of death, the decedent held *any* (one) of the incidents of ownership in the policy.

Section 2042 addresses the estate tax treatment of life insurance policies on the decedent's life. Life insurance policies owned by the decedent on the lives of others are taxed under the general language of Sec. 2033. According to Sec. 2042, a decedent's gross estate includes the value of policies on his or her own life if the proceeds are receivable by the executor or for the benefit of the estate, or if the decedent had any "incidents of ownership" in the policy at the time of death. Treasury Regulations list the following powers as a partial inventory of the incidents of ownership:

- To change the beneficiary
- To surrender or cancel the policy
- To borrow against the policy
- To pledge the policy for a loan
- To revoke an assignment of the policy[22]

Examples in the regulations pertaining to incidents of ownership involve economic rights over the insurance policies. Judicial decisions also have been important in defining what constitutes incidents of ownership. In some jurisdictions, the phrase has been interpreted to be broader than simply relating to economic powers.[23]

If the decedent could have exercised the incidents of ownership only in conjunction with another party, the policy nevertheless is included in the gross estate. Moreover, it is the legal power to exercise ownership rights, not the practical ability to do so, that leads to an inclusion. The Supreme Court in the *Estate of Marshal L. Noel* emphasized the importance of the decedent-insured's legal versus practical powers in a situation where the insured was killed in a plane crash and the policies he owned on his life were on the ground in the possession of his spouse. The Court held that the decedent possessed incidents of ownership and thus the policies were includible in his gross estate.[24]

EXAMPLE C:13-30 ▶ Tracy purchased an insurance policy on her life, and several years later she transferred all her incidents of ownership in the policy to her daughter. Seven years after the transfer, Tracy died. Tracy's niece has always been the policy's beneficiary. The policy was not included in Tracy's gross estate because Tracy did not have any incidents of ownership in the policy at the time of her death, nor was her estate the beneficiary. (Also, she did not give the policy away within three years of death.) ◀

EXAMPLE C:13-31 ▶ Assume the same facts as in Example C:13-30 except that Tracy's estate instead was the policy's beneficiary. Because Tracy's estate was designated as the beneficiary, the policy was included in her gross estate and valued at its face value. ◀

It is not sufficient to consider only Sec. 2042 in determining whether a life insurance policy on the decedent's life is includible in the gross estate. Recall from the discussion earlier in this chapter that a life insurance policy is includible in a decedent's gross estate if the individual makes a gift of the life insurance policy on his or her own life within three years of dying.[25]

EXAMPLE C:13-32 ▶ Two years prior to his death, Peng gave all his incidents of ownership in a life insurance policy on his own life to his son, Phong. The face value of the policy is $400,000. Phong was

---

[22] Reg. Sec. 20.2042-1(c)(2).

[23] See, for example, *Estate of James H. Lumpkin, Jr. v. CIR*, 31 AFTR 2d 73-1381, 73-1 USTC ¶12,909 (5th Cir., 1973), wherein the court held that the right to choose how the proceeds were to be paid—in a lump sum or in installments—was an incident of ownership.

[24] *CIR v. Estate of Marshal L. Noel*, 15 AFTR 2d 1397, 65-1 USTC ¶12,311 (USSC, 1965).

[25] The gifted insurance policy is included under Sec. 2035(a)(2).

always the beneficiary. Because Peng died within three years of giving Phong the policy, Peng's gross estate included the policy, valued at its $400,000 date-of-death value. The potential problem of making a transfer of a life insurance policy within three years of death could have been avoided had Phong been the original owner of the policy. In that case, Peng would not have made a transfer and need not have been concerned with the three-year rule. ◀

TAX STRATEGY TIP

A very wealthy individual may be concerned that his or her estate will not have sufficient cash to pay its estate taxes. The individual could buy life insurance so his or her estate will have sufficient cash. However, if the individual owns the policy or names his or her estate the beneficiary, the proceeds of the policy will be taxed in the gross estate. In this case, the individual should have his or her children (or an irrevocable life insurance trust) buy the life insurance and name themselves the beneficiaries, even if the individual has to provide the funds for the premiums (by making gifts). If the children are the beneficiaries, they can use the policy proceeds to buy an asset from the estate so the estate can raise cash needed to pay the estate taxes.

CONSIDERATION OFFSET

Property is included in the gross estate at its FMV on the date of death or alternate valuation date. Section 2043 allows an offset against the amount included in the gross estate for consideration received in certain transactions.[26] This offset is allowed only if the decedent received some, but less than adequate, consideration in connection with an earlier transaction. The gross estate is reduced by an offset for the partial consideration received. The offset is for the actual dollars received, not for the pro rata portion of the cost paid by the decedent. This offset, called the consideration offset, serves the same function as a deduction in that it reduces the taxable estate. If the decedent receives consideration equal to the value of the property transferred, the property in question is not included in the gross estate. No offset is permitted if the property is excluded from the decedent's gross estate.

The consideration offset prevents a double counting of property in the decedent's estate. For example, if an individual makes a transfer that is includible in the gross estate and receives partial consideration in return, the consideration received is part of the gross estate unless it has been consumed. Sections 2035 through 2038 also require the transferred property to be included in the gross estate, even though the transferor does not own it at the date of death.

EXAMPLE C:13-33 ▶ Two years ago, Steve transferred a $300,000 life insurance policy on his life to Earl. The policy was worth $75,000 at the time of transfer, but Earl paid Steve only $48,000 consideration for the policy. Steve dies in the current year with the $48,000 still in his savings account. Steve's gross estate includes both the amount in the savings account and the $300,000 face value of the insurance policy. Under Sec. 2043, Steve's gross estate is reduced by the $48,000 consideration received on the transfer of the insurance policy. The insurance policy on Steve's life would be excluded from Steve's estate if Steve survived the transfer by more than three years, and no consideration offset would be permitted because the insurance is not included in the gross estate. ◀

RECIPIENT SPOUSE'S INTEREST IN QTIP TRUST

Recall from Chapter C:12 that a gift tax marital deduction is available for transferring qualified terminable interest property (QTIP) to one's spouse. A QTIP interest involves a transfer entitling the recipient spouse to all the income for life. The estate tax rules for QTIP interests are explained on page C:13-22. Claiming a marital deduction with respect to QTIP interests is voluntary. If the donor or the executor elects to claim a marital deduction for QTIP interests transferred to the spouse during life or at death, the transferred property generally is included in the recipient spouse's gross estate.[27] A QTIP interest included in the gross estate, like other property included in the gross estate, is valued at its date-of-death or alternate valuation date value.

The gross estate of the surviving spouse excludes the QTIP interest if the transferor spouse does not elect to claim a marital deduction. If the recipient spouse has a life estate, has no general power of appointment, and was not the transferor, no IRC sections other than Sec. 2044 (dealing with QTIPs) include the property in the gross estate.

No inclusion in the gross estate is required for QTIP interests for which a marital deduction was elected if the recipient spouse disposes of all or a portion of his or her income interest during his or her lifetime. However, Sec. 2519 treats dispositions of all or a portion of a spouse's income interest in a QTIP as a transfer of all interests in the QTIP other than the qualifying income interest. Thus, such dispositions are subject to the gift tax.

[26] Section 2043 provides a consideration offset for items included in the gross estate under Secs. 2035 through 2038 and Sec. 2041.

[27] Sec. 2044.

EXAMPLE C:13-34 ▶ Henry died, and his will created a $3 million QTIP trust for his widow, Wendy, age 75. Henry's executor elected to claim a marital deduction for the QTIP trust. Wendy died five years later. By then, the assets in the QTIP trust had appreciated to $3.8 million. Wendy's gross estate included the QTIP trust, valued at $3.8 million. If Henry's executor had not claimed a marital deduction for the QTIP trust, the value of the trust would have been excluded from Wendy's estate. If Henry's executor had made a partial QTIP election for 70% of the trust, only 70% of the $3.8 million value would have been in Wendy's gross estate. ◀

Deductions

OBJECTIVE 4

Identify the deductions available for estate tax purposes

As mentioned earlier in this chapter, deductions from the gross estate currently fall into five categories. Three of these categories (debts and funeral and administration expenses, casualty and theft losses, and state death taxes) allow the tax base to reflect the net wealth passed to the decedent's heirs, legatees, or devisees. Two other deduction categories reduce the estate tax base for transfers to the surviving spouse (the marital deduction) or to charitable organizations (the charitable contribution deduction). No deduction is available, however, for the amount of wealth diverted to the federal government in the form of estate taxes. The aggregate amount of the deductions is subtracted from the gross estate amount to determine the taxable estate. Each deduction category is examined below. Table C:13-2 provides an overview of the estate tax deductions.

SELF-STUDY QUESTION

Compare the estate tax treatment for a mortgage compared with the accrued interest on a mortgage on a principal residence.

ANSWER

A mortgage and the accrued interest are deductible on the estate tax return as debts, and the accrued interest is deductible on the estate's income tax return when paid.

DEBTS AND FUNERAL AND ADMINISTRATION EXPENSES

Section 2053 authorizes deductions for mortgages and other debts owed by the decedent, as well as for the decedent's funeral and administration expenses. Mortgages and all other debts of the decedent are deductible provided they represent bona fide contracts for an adequate and full consideration in money or money's worth. Even personal debts relating to an expenditure for which no income tax deduction would be allowable are deductible. Interest, state and local taxes, and trade or business expenses accrued at the date of death are deductible on both the estate tax return (as a debt of the decedent) and on the estate's income tax return (as an expense known as a deduction in respect of a decedent) when they are paid. (See Chapter C:14 for a discussion of the income tax implications.)

Examples of administration expenses include executor's commissions, attorneys' fees, court costs, accountants' fees, appraisers' fees, and expenses of preserving and distributing the estate. The executor must decide whether to deduct administration expenses on the estate tax return (Form 706) or the estate's income tax return (Form 1041). Such expenses cannot be deducted twice, although some may be deducted on the estate tax return and others on the estate's income tax return.

▼ TABLE C:13-2
Estate Tax Deductions

IRC Section	Type of Deduction
2053	Funeral and administration expenses[a] and debts
2054	Casualty and theft losses[a]
2055	Charitable contributions[b]
2056	Marital deduction[b]
2058	State death taxes[c]

[a]Administration expenses and losses are deductible on the estate tax return or on the estate's income tax return.
[b]No limit on deductible amount.
[c]Available (instead of a credit) after 2004.

ADDITIONAL COMMENT

In addition to the 39.6% top income tax rate, an estate or trust can incur an incremental 3.8% on net investment income. The 3.8% rate applies to the lesser of undistributed net investment income or the excess (if any) of the entity's AGI over the dollar amount at which the highest tax bracket begins ($12,300 in 2015). Net investment income includes, among other things, interest, dividends, annuities, royalties, rents, and net gains from the disposition of certain property, all reduced by allocable deductions.

An estate that owes no estate tax (e.g., because of the unlimited marital deduction or the unified credit) should deduct administration expenses on its income tax return because no tax savings will result from a deduction on the estate tax return. If an estate owes estate taxes, its marginal estate tax rate will be 40% because this rate applies to tax bases exceeding $1 million. The highest income tax rate for an estate is 39.6% plus potentially 3.8% on net investment income. Thus, at times, the tax savings will be greater if the administration expenses are deducted on the income tax returns.

Funeral expenses are deductible only on the estate tax return. The estate may deduct any funeral expenses allowable under local law including "[a] reasonable expenditure for a tombstone, monument, or mausoleum, or for a burial lot, either for the decedent or his family, including a reasonable expenditure for its future care." The transportation costs of the person bringing the body to the burial place also are deductible as funeral expenses.[28]

EXAMPLE C:13-35 ►

At Ed's date of death in 2015, Ed owed a $75,000 mortgage on his residence, plus $280 of interest accrued thereon, and $320 of personal expenditures charged to a credit card. The estate's administration expenses were $32,000. His funeral expenses totaled $12,000. Under Sec. 2053, Ed's estate could deduct $75,600 ($75,000 + $280 + $320) for debts and $12,000 for funeral expenses. The $32,000 of administration expenses were deductible on the estate tax return, on the estate's income tax return for the year in which they were paid, or some on each return. As Chapter C:14 points out, Ed's estate receives an income tax deduction for the accrued mortgage interest whenever it is paid. ◄

TAX STRATEGY TIP

The executor should elect to deduct any casualty or theft loss, when such loss is allowable, from the estate tax return if the marginal estate tax rate exceeds the marginal income tax rate.

LOSSES

Section 2054 authorizes a deduction for losses incurred from theft or casualty while the estate is being settled. Just as in the context of the income tax, examples of casualties include fires, storms, and earthquakes. Any insurance compensation received affects the amount of the loss. If the alternate valuation date is elected, the loss may not be used to reduce the alternate value and then used again as a loss deduction. As with administration expenses, the executor must decide whether to deduct the loss on the estate tax return or the estate's income tax return. No double deduction is allowed for these losses, and the nondeductible floor applicable for income tax purposes does not exist for estate tax purposes.

EXAMPLE C:13-36 ►

Sam dies on May 3, 2015. One of the items included in Sam's gross estate is a mountain cabin valued at $125,000. The uninsured cabin is totally destroyed in a landslide on August 18. If the date-of-death valuation is chosen, the cabin is included in the gross estate at $125,000. The executor must choose between claiming a Sec. 2054 loss deduction on the estate tax return or a Sec. 165 casualty loss deduction on the estate's income tax return. ◄

EXAMPLE C:13-37 ►

Assume the same facts as in Example C:13-36 except that Sam's executor elects the alternate valuation date. The cabin is valued at zero when determining the value of the gross estate. No loss deduction is available for the casualty on the estate tax return. Likewise, the estate cannot claim an income tax deduction for the casualty loss because the property's adjusted basis in its hands is zero. ◄

CHARITABLE CONTRIBUTION DEDUCTION

Section 2055 authorizes a deduction for transfers to charitable organizations. The rules concerning eligible donee organizations are the same as for gift tax purposes.

Because the estate tax charitable contribution deduction is unlimited, a decedent could eliminate his or her estate tax liability by willing all his or her property (or all property except for an amount equal to the exemption equivalent) to a charitable organization. Similarly, a decedent could eliminate an estate tax liability by willing an amount equal to the exemption equivalent to the children and the rest of the estate to the surviving spouse and a charitable organization (e.g., in equal shares).[29] People who desire to leave some property to a charity at their death should be encouraged to consider giving the property before death, so they can obtain an income tax deduction for the gift and also reduce their gross estate by the amount of the gift.

---

[28] Reg. Sec. 20.2053-2.

[29] Another way the estate could owe no taxes is if all of the property, or all of the property except for the exemption equivalent, is shielded from taxation by the marital deduction.

Computing the Deduction. In certain circumstances, computation of the estate tax charitable contribution deduction can be somewhat complicated. Suppose the decedent (a widow) has an $11 million gross estate and no Sec. 2053 or 2054 deductions. The decedent's will specifies that her son is to receive $8 million and a charitable organization is to receive the residue (the rest not explicitly disposed of). Assume that state law specifies that death taxes are payable from the residue. Because $8 million of property passes to the decedent's child, the estate will definitely owe some estate taxes. The charitable organization will receive $3 million, less the estate taxes payable from the residue. The estate tax liability depends on the amount of the charitable contribution deduction, which in turn depends on the amount of the estate tax liability. Simultaneous equations are required to calculate the charitable contribution deduction.[30]

EXAMPLE C:13-38 ▶ Ahmed, a widower, died with a gross estate of $9 million. Ahmed willed State University $1 million and the residue of his estate to his children. Under state law, death taxes are payable from the residue. In this scenario, Ahmed's estate receives a charitable contribution deduction for $1 million because the estate taxes were charged against the children's share (the residue). ◀

Split-Interest Transfers. If the decedent's will provides for a split-interest transfer (i.e., a transfer of interests to both an individual and a charitable organization), the rules concerning whether a charitable contribution deduction is available are very technical. Basically, the rules are the same as for gift tax purposes (discussed in Chapter C:12).

EXAMPLE C:13-39 ▶ Jane dies with a gross estate of $8 million. In 2005, she gave City Art Museum a remainder interest in her personal residence but retained the right to live there rent-free for the rest of her life. Upon Jane's death, no other individuals have an interest in the residence. Jane received an income tax deduction in 2005 for the value of the remainder interest and incurred no gift tax liability. Under Sec. 2036, Jane's gross estate includes her residence, valued at $350,000. Her estate receives a $350,000 charitable contribution deduction.

Her lifetime transfer triggers no added estate tax cost. The residence is included in her gross estate, but the inclusion is a wash because of the estate tax charitable contribution deduction allowed for the value of the residence. ◀

MARITAL DEDUCTION

The fourth category of deductions is the marital deduction for certain property passing to the decedent's surviving spouse.[31] Because the marital deduction is unlimited, the decedent's estate does not owe any federal estate taxes if all the items includible in the gross estate (or all items except an amount equal to the exemption equivalent) pass to the surviving spouse.[32] If the surviving spouse is not a U.S. citizen, however, a marital deduction is not available unless the decedent's property passes to a special trust called a qualified domestic trust.

TAX STRATEGY TIP

The marital deduction defers the estate tax until the death of the surviving spouse and protects against liquidity problems when the first spouse dies. Moreover, the surviving spouse can reduce the overall estate tax through personal consumption and a lifetime gifting program.

The marital deduction helps provide equal treatment for decedents of common law and community property states because marital property is treated differently under each type of state law. In community property states, for example, a large portion of the assets acquired after marriage constitute community property (i.e., property owned equally by each spouse). On the other hand, in common law states, one spouse may own the majority of the assets acquired after marriage. Thus, with no marital deduction and no portability election (discussed on Page C:13-24), the progressive estate tax rates could cause the combined estate tax liability to be higher for a couple living in a noncommunity property state. Nevertheless, a marital deduction is available to decedents who own nothing but community property.

Under the Supreme Court's 2013 decision in *U.S. v. Windsor*[33] and according to IRS policy,[34] same-sex spouses qualify for the marital deduction.

---

[30] The simultaneous equation problem generally does not occur if a charity receives a bequest of a specific dollar amount. See Reg. Sec. 20.2055-3 for a discussion of death taxes payable from charitable transfers.

[31] Sec. 2056.

[32] Some states have not adopted an unlimited marital deduction; therefore, some estates may owe state death taxes even though no federal liability would otherwise exist. Payment of a substantial amount of state taxes will reduce the amount passing to the spouse as a marital deduction and can cause federal taxes to be owed.

[33] 111 AFTR2d 2013-2385, 2013-2 USTC 50,400 (USSC, 2013). Also see page C:12-5.

[34] Rev. Rul. 2013-17, 2013-38 I.R.B. 201.

Only certain transfers to the surviving spouse are eligible for the marital deduction. The estate does not receive a marital deduction unless the interest conveyed to the surviving spouse will be included in the recipient spouse's gross estate or will be subject to the gift tax if transferred while the surviving spouse is alive.

The following three tests must be met before an interest qualifies for the marital deduction:

- The property must be included in the decedent's gross estate.
- The property must pass to the recipient spouse in a qualifying manner.
- The interest conveyed must not be a nondeductible terminable interest.

Test 1: Inclusion in the Gross Estate. No property passing to the surviving spouse is eligible for the marital deduction unless the property is included in the decedent's gross estate. The reason for this rule is obvious: Assets excluded from the gross estate cannot generate a deduction.

EXAMPLE C:13-40 Gail is insured under a life insurance policy for which her husband, Al, is the beneficiary. Gail's sister always had the incidents of ownership in the policy. Even though the insurance proceeds are payable to Al, Gail's estate receives no marital deduction for the insurance. The policy is excluded from Gail's gross estate because she had no incidents of ownership, her estate was not the beneficiary, and the policy was not transferred within three years of her death. Gail held the title to the personal residence in which she and Al lived. She willed the residence to Al, and the residence qualifies for the marital deduction.

TEST 2: The Passing Requirement. Property is not eligible for the marital deduction unless it passes to the decedent's spouse in a qualifying manner. According to Sec. 2056(c), property is deemed to pass from one spouse to the other if the surviving spouse receives the property because of

- A bequest or devise under the decedent's will
- An inheritance resulting from the decedent dying intestate
- Dower or curtesy rights
- An earlier transfer from the decedent
- Right of survivorship
- An appointment by the decedent under a general power of appointment or in default of appointment
- A designation as the beneficiary of a life insurance policy on the decedent's life

In addition, a surviving spouse's interest in a retirement benefit plan is considered to have passed from the decedent to the survivor to the extent the retirement benefits are included in the gross estate.[35]

Test 3: The Terminable Interest Rule. The last statutory test (also applicable for gift tax purposes) requires that the recipient-spouse's interest *not* be classified as a nondeductible terminable interest.[36] A terminable interest is one that ceases with the passage of time or the occurrence of some event. Some terminable interests qualify for the marital deduction, however, because only *nondeductible* terminable interests fail to generate a marital deduction. Nondeductible terminable interests have the following features:

- An interest in the property must pass or have passed from the decedent to a person other than the surviving spouse, and such person must have paid less than adequate consideration in money or money's worth.
- The other person may possess or enjoy any part of the property after the termination of the surviving spouse's interest.

---

[35] Reg. Sec. 20.2056(e)-1(a)(6).

[36] Nondeductible terminable interests also are precluded from eligibility for the marital deduction for gift tax purposes.

Thus, if the decedent makes a transfer granting the surviving spouse the right to receive all the income annually for life and a general power of appointment over the property, the property is eligible for the marital deduction. As discussed below, the QTIP provisions allow a marital deduction for certain transfers that otherwise would be disqualified under the nondeductible terminable interest rule.

EXAMPLE C:13-41 ▶ Louis wills a copyright with a ten-year remaining legal life to his wife, Tina, age 42. His will also sets up a trust for the benefit of Tina, whom he entitles to receive all of the income semiannually until the earlier of her remarriage or her death. Upon Tina's remarriage or death, the trust property is to be distributed to the couple's children or their estates. Both the copyright and the trust are terminable interests. The copyright is eligible for the marital deduction because it is not a nondeductible terminable interest; the copyright simply ends at the expiration of its legal life. No person other than Tina receives an interest in the copyright. No marital deduction is available for the trust because it is a nondeductible terminable interest. Upon the termination of Tina's interest, which will occur if she remarries, the children will possess the property, and they will receive their interests from Louis without paying adequate consideration. ◀

SELF-STUDY QUESTION

A decedent, by will, creates a trust with income to the surviving spouse for 25 years, the remainder to their children. The surviving spouse's life expectancy is 16 years. Does the property qualify for the marital deduction?

ANSWER

The property does not qualify because the surviving spouse's interest terminates at the end of a specified number of years. The spouse's shorter life expectancy is irrelevant.

QTIP Transfers. Section 2056(b)(7) authorizes a marital deduction for transfers of qualified terminable interest property (called QTIP transfers). The QTIP provisions are somewhat revolutionary compared with earlier law because they allow a marital deduction in situations where the recipient spouse holds no power to designate which parties eventually receive the property.

Qualified terminable interest property is defined as property that passes from the decedent, in which the surviving spouse has a qualifying income interest for life, and to which an election applies. A spouse has a qualifying income interest for life if the following are true:

- ▶ He or she is entitled to all the income from the property, payable at least annually.
- ▶ No person has a power to appoint any portion of the property to anyone other than the surviving spouse unless the power cannot be exercised during the spouse's lifetime (e.g., it is exercisable only at or after the death of the surviving spouse).

SELF-STUDY QUESTION

How does the donor spouse or decedent spouse who establishes a QTIP trust control the disposition of the trust corpus?

ANSWER

The donor or decedent spouse states in the trust instrument or in his or her will who will receive the remainder interest on the death of the recipient spouse.

Claiming the marital deduction with respect to QTIP transfers is not mandatory, and partial elections also are allowed. In the event the executor elects to claim a marital deduction for 100% of the QTIP transfer, the marital deduction is for the entire amount of the QTIP transfer. In other words, the deduction is not limited to the value of the surviving spouse's life estate.

If the marital deduction is elected in the first spouse's estate, the property is taxed in the surviving spouse's estate under Sec. 2044 or is subject to the gift tax in such spouse's hands if disposed of during the spouse's lifetime.[37] Thus, as with other interspousal transfers, the QTIP provisions allow a postponement of the taxable event until the second spouse dies or disposes of the interest by gift. If the taxable event is postponed, the property is valued at its FMV as of the date the second spouse transfers the property by gift or at death.

EXAMPLE C:13-42 ▶ Tom died in 2005, survived by his wife, Mary. Tom's will called for setting up a $1 million trust from which Mary receives all the income quarterly for the rest of her life. Upon Mary's death, the property is to be distributed to Tom's children by a previous marriage. If Tom's executor elected to claim a marital deduction, Tom's estate received a $1 million marital deduction. At Mary's death, the trust assets are valued at $2.2 million. Section 2044 includes $2.2 million in Mary's gross estate. If Tom's executor forgoes electing the marital deduction, Mary's gross estate excludes the value of the trust. In either event, the trust assets will be taxed in the estate of one of the spouses, but not both. ◀

ADDITIONAL COMMENT

Refer to Example C:13-42. The executor may elect QTIP status for less than the entire property in the trust. For example, the executor might elect QTIP treatment for only 60% of the $1 million placed in the trust. On Mary's death, 60% of $2.2 million, or $1.32 million, is included in Mary's gross estate.

State Death Taxes. For estates of decedents dying after 2004, Sec. 2058 allows a deduction for state death taxes. Eligible taxes include estate, inheritance, legacy, and succession taxes paid to a state or the District of Columbia. The taxes must be paid no later than four years after the filing of the estate tax return. The amount of the deduction is the amount paid and, unlike the state death tax credit formerly available, is not restricted to a maximum amount.

---

[37] Section 2519 states that, if a recipient spouse disposes of a qualifying income interest for life for which the donor or the executor elected a marital deduction under the QTIP rules, the recipient spouse is treated as having made a gift of everything except the qualifying income interest. Under the generic gift rules of Sec. 2511, the gift of the income interest is treated as a gift.

COMPUTATION OF TAX LIABILITY

OBJECTIVE 5

Calculate the estate tax liability

As mentioned earlier, the estate tax base is the aggregate of the decedent's taxable estate and his or her adjusted taxable gifts. Figure C:13-1 earlier in this chapter illustrates how the estate tax formula combines these two concepts.

TAXABLE ESTATE AND TAX BASE

The gross estate's value is reduced by the deductions to arrive at the amount of the taxable estate. Under the unification provisions effective after 1976, the estate tax base consists of the taxable estate plus the adjusted taxable gifts, defined as *all* taxable gifts made *after 1976 other than* gifts included in the gross estate. The addition of the adjusted taxable gifts to the estate tax base may cause an estate to be taxed at a higher marginal tax rate. If the decedent elects gift splitting (discussed in Chapter 12), the decedent's adjusted taxable gifts equal the amount of the taxable gifts the individual is deemed to have made after applying the gift-splitting provisions. Adjusted taxable gifts can arise from consenting to gift splitting, even though the decedent never actually gives away any property.

Adjusted taxable gifts are valued at date-of-gift values; therefore, any post-gift appreciation is exempt from the transfer taxes. The estate tax computations for decedents who never made gifts exceeding the excludable amount reflect no adjusted taxable gifts.

SELF-STUDY QUESTION

Verda died penniless in 2015. Because of consenting to gift splitting, her taxable gifts for 1999 were $1.75 million. She paid $457,000 of gift taxes on these gifts. What was her unified tax base?

ANSWER

Her unified tax base was $1.75 million, the amount of her lifetime taxable gifts. Note that the gifts are valued at what they were worth on the date of the gift.

SELF-STUDY QUESTION

Refer to the previous self-study question. What was the amount of the unified tax before credits? After credits?

ANSWER

The unified tax before credits was $645,800. This tax was reduced by the unified credit of $2,117,800 and by post-1976 gift taxes, which leaves zero tax due. Verda's unified tax base of $1.75 million was below the $5.43 million exemption equivalent for 2015.

TENTATIVE TAX AND REDUCTION FOR POST-1976 GIFT TAXES

The tentative tax is computed on the estate tax base, which is the sum of the taxable estate and the adjusted taxable gifts, if any.[38] The unified transfer tax rates are found in Sec. 2001(c) and are reproduced on the inside back cover. The tentative tax is reduced by the decedent's post-1976 gift taxes. In determining the tax on post-1976 taxable gifts, the effect of gift splitting is taken into consideration. That is, the amount of the post-1976 gift taxes is usually the levy imposed on the taxable gifts the decedent is deemed to have made after applying any gift-splitting election.

If the tax rates change between the time of the gift and the time of death, the subtraction for gift taxes equals the amount of gift taxes that *would have been payable* on post-1976 gifts had the rate schedule applicable in the year of death been in effect in the year of the gift. In addition to the "as if" computation for the gross tax amount, the unified credit subtracted to determine the amount of gift tax that would have been payable is based on current rates.

UNIFIED CREDIT

The excess of the tentative tax over the post-1976 gift taxes is reduced by the unified credit. The amount of this credit has changed over the years (see inside back cover). If a decedent died in 2010 and the executor opted to incur the estate tax and obtain a FMV basis, the unified credit was $1,730,800, the tax on $5 million at a 35% top rate. In both the estate and gift tax context for 2011, the unified credit was $1,730,800, which again is the tax on $5 million at a 35% top rate. In 2012, the $5 million amount became indexed for inflation, and the credit that year was $1,772,800, the tax on $5.12 million at the top rate of 35%. Beginning in 2013, the top rate rose to 40%, and the credit for 2013 was $2,045,800, the tax on $5.25 million. For 2014, the credit was $2,081,800, the tax on $5.34 million. For 2015, the credit is $2,117,800, the tax on $5.43 million. The unified credit never generates a refund; the most relief it can provide is to eliminate an estate's federal estate tax liability.

Section 2010(c) provides that the unified credit otherwise available for estate tax purposes must be reduced because of certain pre-1977 gifts. Before 1977, a $30,000 lifetime exemption was available for the gift tax. Donors could claim some or all of this exemption whenever they so desired. For post-1976 years, Congress repealed the exemption and replaced it with the unified credit. If the decedent claimed any portion of the $30,000 exemption against gifts made after September 8, 1976, and before January 1, 1977, the unified credit was reduced by 20% of the exemption claimed.

[38] Sec. 2001(b).

EXAMPLE C:13-43 ▶ Carl died in 2015 with a tax base of $6 million. In October 1976, Carl made his first taxable gift and claimed the $30,000 exemption to reduce the amount of his taxable gifts. Thus, Carl's $2,117,800 unified credit is reduced by $6,000 (0.20 × $30,000). If Carl claimed the exemption by making a gift on or before September 8, 1976, his estate would have been entitled to the full $2,117,800 credit. ◀

PORTABILITY BETWEEN SPOUSES OF EXEMPTION AMOUNT

Prior to 2011, both a husband and wife had estate tax exemption amounts that could be used only by that individual. For example, in 2009, when the exempt amount was $3.5 million, the husband could use $3.5 million at his death, and the wife could use $3.5 million at her death. This situation was the case even if one spouse's estate tax base was much smaller than $3.5 million and the other spouse's estate was considerably larger than $3.5 million. For many years, a number of estates used a technique called "credit shelter trusts" or "bypass trusts" to make sure the $3.5 million (the 2009 amount) or the relevant amount for the year of death passed in such a way as to take advantage of the unified credit. The Tax Relief Act made the exemption equivalent portable between spouses for 2011 and 2012, and ATRA 2012 made the provision permanent. As a result, any nontaxable amount that remains unused at the first spouse's death can be used by the second spouse. However this concept, called portability, applies only if the executor elects it. If a surviving spouse was predeceased by more than one spouse who died after 2010, the surviving spouse can use the unused exemption amount of only the last deceased spouse. The portable amount is called the "deceased spousal unused exclusion amount." As a result of the Supreme Court's decision in *Windsor*, same-sex spouses qualify for the benefits of portability.

EXAMPLE C:13-44 ▶ Joe died early in 2012 with a taxable estate of $2.12 million. He is survived by his spouse, Joanne. Joe's executor elected portability. Thus, Joe's remaining $3 million ($5,120,000 − $2,120,000) exemption equivalent is added to Joanne's $5 million (ignoring indexing), so she now would have an exempt amount of $8 million (again ignoring indexing). The amount portable from Joe is not indexed. ◀

EXAMPLE C:13-45 ▶ Joanne from the previous example married Karl late in 2012. Karl died in July 2013 with a taxable estate of $11 million. Thus, Karl has no unused exemption. If Joanne dies in December 2015, her exempt amount will be $5.43 million as she cannot use Joe's remaining exemption equivalent because Joe is not Joanne's last deceased spouse. ◀

OTHER CREDITS

The IRC authorizes three additional credits: a gift tax credit on pre-1977 gifts, a credit for another decedent's estate taxes paid on prior transfers, and a credit for foreign death taxes. (Prior to 2005, the IRC also allowed a state death tax credit.) These credits apply less often than the unified credit. Like the unified credit, these credits cannot exceed the amount of the estate tax actually owed.

Pre-2005 State Death Tax Credit. For many years, all states levied some form of death tax: an inheritance tax, an estate tax, or both. Many states enacted a simple system whereby the state death tax liability equaled the credit for state death taxes allowed on the federal estate tax return.

Prior to 2005, Sec. 2011 allowed a credit calculated in accordance with the table contained in Sec. 2011(b). As mentioned earlier, beginning in 2005, a deduction replaced the credit. Consequently, if a jurisdiction had earlier imposed a state death tax that was equal to the credit allowed on the federal return for state death taxes, no state death tax will be owed after 2004 *unless* that jurisdiction changes its tax rules.

EXAMPLE C:13-46 ▶ John died in 2015 with a taxable estate of $6 million. If he resided in a state whose statute imposes an estate tax equal to the credit available on the federal return for state death taxes, his estate owed nothing to the state. In effect, his state no longer has an estate tax. On the other hand, if he resided in a state that levies an inheritance tax based on the value of the property the various heirs receive, his estate received a deduction (not a credit) for the inheritance tax paid. ◀

Credit for Pre-1977 Gift Taxes. Section 2012(a) authorizes a credit for gift taxes paid by the decedent on pre-1977 gifts that must be included in the gross estate.

Remember that Sec. 2001(b)(2) allows a reduction for gift taxes paid on post-1976 gifts, but the IRC does not refer to this item as a credit.

In general, the credit for pre-1977 gift taxes equals the amount of gift taxes paid with respect to transfers included in the gross estate. Because of a ceiling rule, however, the amount of the credit sometimes is lower than the amount of gift taxes paid. A discussion of the ceiling computation is beyond the scope of this text.

Credit for Tax on Prior Transfers. The credit available under Sec. 2013 for the estate taxes paid on prior transfers reduces the cost of having property taxed in more than one estate in quick succession. Without this credit, the overall tax cost could be quite severe if the legatee dies soon after the original decedent. The credit applies if the person who transfers the property (i.e., the transferor-decedent) to the decedent in question (i.e., the transferee-decedent) dies no more than ten years before, or within two years after, the date of the transferee-decedent's death. The potential credit is the smaller of the federal estate tax of the transferor-decedent attributable to the transferred interest or the federal estate tax of the transferee-decedent attributable to the transferred interest.

To determine the final credit, the potential credit is multiplied by a percentage that varies inversely with the period of time separating the two dates of death. If the transferor dies no more than two years before or after the transferee, the credit percentage is 100%. As specified in Sec. 2013(a), the other percentages are as follows:

Number of Years by Which Transferor's Death Precedes the Transferee's Death	*Credit Percentage*
More than 2, but not more than 4	80
More than 4, but not more than 6	60
More than 6, but not more than 8	40
More than 8, but not more than 10	20

EXAMPLE C:13-47 ► Mary died on March 1, 2010. All of Mary's property passed to Debra, her daughter. Debra died on June 1, 2015. All of Debra's property passed to her son. Both Mary's and Debra's estates paid federal estate taxes. Debra's estate was entitled to a credit for a percentage of some, or all, of the taxes paid by Mary's estate. Because Mary's death preceded Debra's death by five years and three months, the credit for the tax paid on prior transfers was 60% of the potential credit. ◄

EXAMPLE C:13-48 ► Ed died on August 7, 2013. One of the items included in Ed's estate was a life insurance policy on Sam's life. Sam gave Ed all his incidents of ownership in this policy on December 13, 2012. Sam died on June 15, 2015, within three years of making a gift of the insurance policy on his own life. The policy was included in Sam's gross estate under Sec. 2035. Because Sam died within two years of Ed's death, Ed's estate was entitled to a credit for 100% of the potential credit and an amended return had to be filed to claim this credit. ◄

SELF-STUDY QUESTION

What is the effect of the maximum credit provision for the foreign death tax credit?

ANSWER

The effect is to tax the property located in the foreign country at the higher of the U.S. estate tax rate or the foreign death tax rate.

Foreign Death Tax Credit. Under Sec. 2014, the estate is entitled to a credit for some or all of the death taxes paid to a foreign country for property located in that foreign country and included in the gross estate. The maximum credit is the smaller of the foreign death tax attributable to the property located in the foreign country that imposed the tax or the federal estate tax attributable to the property located in the foreign country and taxed by such country.

COMPREHENSIVE ILLUSTRATION

The following comprehensive illustration demonstrates the computation of the estate tax liability.

ADDITIONAL COMMENT

This illustration pertains to 2014 because tax forms for that year are the latest available at the time this textbook was published.

Background Data. Herman Estes died on October 13, 2014. Herman, a Florida resident, was survived by his widow, Ann, and three adult children. During his lifetime, Herman made two gifts, as follows:

- In 1978, he gave his daughter, Dotty, $203,000 cash. He claimed a $3,000 annual exclusion available then and thus made a $200,000 taxable gift on which he paid a $20,800 gift tax, after claiming the $34,000 unified credit.
- In April 2013, he gave his son, Johnny, stock then worth $6,514,000. Herman claimed a $14,000 annual exclusion and thus made a $6.5 million taxable gift. He claimed the available unified credit of $2,011,800 ($2,045,800 − $34,000) and paid $559,200 ($2,571,000 − $2,011,800) gift tax. On October 13, 2014, the stock was worth $6.75 million.

Property discovered after Herman's death appears below. All amounts represent date-of-death values.

- Checking account containing $19,250.
- Savings account containing $75,000.
- Land worth $440,000 held in the names of Herman and Ann, joint tenants with right of survivorship (JTWROS). Herman provided all the consideration to buy the land in January 1993.
- Life insurance policy 123-A with a face value of $200,000. Herman had incidents of ownership; Johnny is the beneficiary.
- A personal residence titled in Herman's name worth $325,000.
- Stock in Ajax Corporation worth $4.4 million.
- Qualified pension plan to which Herman's employer made 60% of the contributions and Herman made 40%. Ann is to receive a lump-sum distribution of $240,000.
- A trust created under the will of Herman's mother, Amelia, who died in 1999. Herman was entitled to receive all the income quarterly for life. In his will, Herman could appoint the trust assets to such of his descendants as he desired. The trust assets are valued at $375,000.

At his death, Herman owes a $25,200 bank loan, including $200 accrued interest. Balances due on his various charge cards total $6,500. Herman's funeral expenses are $15,000, and his administration expenses are $70,000. Assume the maximum tax savings will occur by deducting the administration expenses on the estate tax return instead of on the income tax return.

Herman's will contains the following provisions:

- "To my wife, Ann, I leave my residence, my savings account, and $10,000 from my checking account."
- "I leave $200,000 of property in trust with First Bank as trustee. My wife, Ann, is to receive all the income from this trust fund quarterly for the rest of her life. Upon Ann's death, the trust property is to be divided equally among our three children."
- "To the American Cancer Society I leave $10,000."
- "I appoint the property in the trust created by my mother, Amelia Estes, to my daughter, Dotty."
- "The residue of my estate is to be divided equally between my sons, Johnny and Billy."

Calculation of Tax Liability. Table C:13-3 illustrates the computation of Herman's estate tax liability. These same facts are used for the sample Estate Tax Return (Form 706) included in Appendix B. For illustration purposes, it is assumed that the executor elects to claim the marital deduction on the QTIP trust and that the laws for Florida levy death taxes equal to the maximum federal credit for state death taxes. As mentioned earlier, after 2004 an estate receives a deduction instead of a credit for state death taxes. Thus, because the federal government allows no credit for state death taxes, Herman's estate owes nothing to the state.

▼ **TABLE C:13-3**
Comprehensive Estate Tax Illustration

Gross estate:	
Checking account (Sec. 2033)	$ 19,250
Savings account (Sec. 2033)	75,000
Land held in joint tenancy with wife (0.50 × $400,000) (Sec. 2040)	220,000
Life insurance (Sec. 2042)	200,000
Personal residence (Sec. 2033)	325,000
Ajax stock (Sec. 2033)	4,400,000
Qualified pension plan (Sec. 2039)	240,000
Gross-up for gift tax paid on 2013 gift (Sec. 2035)	559,200
Total gross estate	$6,038,450
Minus:	
Debts (Sec. 2053):	
Bank loan, including $200 accrued interest	(25,200)
Charge cards	(6,500)
Funeral expenses (Sec. 2053)	(15,000)
Administration expenses (Sec. 2053)	(70,000)
Marital deduction (Sec. 2056):	
Residence (under will)	(325,000)
Cash from checking account (under will)	(10,000)
Savings account (under will)	(75,000)
QTIP trust (under will)	(200,000)
Land (JTWROS)	(220,000)
Qualified pension plan (beneficiary)	(240,000)
Charitable contribution deduction (Sec. 2055)	(10,000)
Total reductions to gross estate	($1,196,700)
Taxable estate	$4,841,750
Plus adjusted taxable gifts (Sec. 2001(b)):	
1978 taxable gifts	200,000[a]
2013 taxable gifts	6,500,000[a]
Estate tax base	$11,541,750
Tentative tax on tax base (2014 tax rates) (Sec. 2001)	$4,562,500
Minus:	
Reduction for post-1976 gift taxes (Sec. 2001(b))	(580,000)[b]
Unified credit (Sec. 2010)	(2,081,800)
Estate tax payable	$ 1,900,700

[a]Valued at date-of-gift fair market values.
[b]If rates differ at the time of death from the time of the gift, the reduction for gift taxes is recalculated using the rates for the year of death, and the unified credit applied in determining the gift taxes also is recalculated using the rates for the year of death. In this illustration, the rates are the same for each year. Thus, in this scenario, the $580,000 subtraction is the total of the gift taxes paid, $20,800 plus $559,200.

Note that several factors affect the computation set out in Table C:13-3:

ADDITIONAL COMMENT

In 2013, the top *income* tax rate is 39.6% plus, potentially, 3.8% on net investment income, and the top *estate* tax rate is 40%. Ann, the surviving spouse, will not benefit from portability from Herman's estate because Herman's tax base exceeded $5.25 million.

- Herman had only a special power of appointment over the assets in the trust created by his mother because he could will the property only to his descendants. Therefore, the trust property is not included in his estate.
- Assets that pass to the surviving spouse outside the will, such as by survivorship and by beneficiary designation, can qualify for the marital deduction.
- Adjusted taxable gifts (added to the taxable estate) include only post-1976 taxable gifts.
- Because the highest marginal income tax rate for the estate is assumed to be lower than its 40% marginal estate tax rate and because the estate owes a tax liability (even with the available credits), administration expenses should be deducted on the estate tax return.

Liquidity concerns

OBJECTIVE 6

Explain tax provisions that alleviate liquidity problems

Liquidity is one of the major problems facing individuals planning their estates and executors eventually managing the estates. Individuals often use life insurance to help address this problem. In general, the entire amount of the estate tax liability is due nine months after the decedent's death. Certain provisions, however, allow the executor to pay some or all of the estate tax liability at a later date. Deferral of part or all of the estate tax payments and two other provisions aimed at alleviating a liquidity problem are discussed below.

DEFERRAL OF PAYMENT OF ESTATE TAXES

Reasonable Cause. Section 6161(a)(1) authorizes the Secretary of the Treasury to extend the payment date for the estate taxes for a *reasonable period,* defined as a period of not longer than 12 months. Moreover, the Secretary of the Treasury may extend the payment date for a maximum period of ten years if the executor shows reasonable cause for not being able to pay some, or all, of the estate tax liability on the regular date.[39]

Whenever the executor pays a portion of the estate tax after the regular due date, the estate owes interest on the portion of the tax for which it postpones payment. In general, the interest rate, which is governed by Sec. 6621, is the same as that applicable to underpayments. The interest rate on underpayments potentially fluctuates quarterly with changes in the rate paid on short-term U.S. Treasury obligations.[40]

Remainder or Reversionary Interests. If the gross estate includes a relatively large remainder or reversionary interest, liquidity problems could result if the estate had to pay the entire estate tax liability soon after the decedent's death. For example, the estate might include a remainder interest in an asset in which a healthy, 30-year-old person has a life estate. The estate might not gain possession of the assets until many years after the decedent's death. Section 6163 permits the executor to elect to postpone payment of the tax attributable to a remainder or reversionary interest until six months after the other interests terminate, which in the example would be after the person currently age 30 died. In addition, upon being convinced of reasonable cause, the Secretary of the Treasury may grant an additional extension of up to three years.

TAX STRATEGY TIP

A person who owns a substantial interest in a small business might choose to gift property other than the business interest. He or she may want to retain the business interest so that his or her estate will qualify for the five-year deferral, ten-installment option of Sec. 6166. See Tax Planning Considerations for further details.

Interests in Closely Held Businesses. Section 6166 authorizes the executor to pay a portion of the estate tax in as many as ten annual installments in certain situations. Executors may elect to apply Sec. 6166 if

- The gross estate includes an interest in a closely held business, and
- The value of the closely held business exceeds 35% of the value of the adjusted gross estate.

Closely held businesses are defined as proprietorships and partnerships or corporations having no more than 45 owners.[41] If a corporation or partnership has more than 45 owners, it nevertheless can be classified as closely held if the decedent's gross estate includes 20% or more of the capital interest (in the partnership) or 20% or more of the value of the voting stock (in the corporation).[42]

The adjusted gross estate is defined as the gross estate less *allowable* Sec. 2053 and 2054 deductions. Consequently, in determining whether the estate meets the 35% requirement, all administration expenses and casualty and theft losses are subtracted, regardless of whether the executor elects to deduct them on the estate tax return or the estate's income tax return.

Once the election is chosen, the following provisions apply:

- The portion of the estate tax that can be paid in installments is the ratio of the value of the closely held business interest to the value of the adjusted gross estate.

[39] Sec. 6161(a)(2).

[40] Sec. 6621. The interest rate is discussed in Chapter C:15.

[41] Sec. 6166(b)(1).

[42] Ibid.

- The first of the ten allowable installments generally is not due until five years after the due date for the return. (This provision defers the last payment for as many as 15 years.)
- Interest on the tax due is payable annually, even during the first five years.

Some or all of the installment payments may accrue interest at a rate of only 2%. The maximum amount of deferred tax to which the 2% rate applies is (1) the tax on the total of $1 million of value (as indexed) and the exemption equivalent amount less (2) the unified credit. In no event, however, may the amount exceed the tax postponed under Sec. 6166.[43] The $1 million amount is indexed for inflation with inflation adjustments rounded to the next lowest $10,000; for 2015, this amount is $1.47 million. The interest rate on any additional deferred tax is 45% of the rate applicable to underpayments. The downside is the interest paid is not deductible as interest expense on the estate's income tax return or as an administrative expense on the estate tax return.

STOCK REDEMPTIONS TO PAY DEATH TAXES

Sometimes an estate's major asset is stock in a closely held corporation. In this situation, the corporation may have to redeem some of the corporate stock to provide the estate sufficient liquidity to pay death taxes. As discussed in Chapter C:4, stock redemptions generally receive sale or exchange treatment only if they meet certain requirements under Sec. 302, such as being substantially disproportionate or involving a complete termination of the shareholder's interest. Without exchange treatment and assuming sufficient earnings and profits, the redeemed shareholder (e.g., the estate) would recognize a dividend equal to the redemption proceeds rather than a capital gain equal to the difference between the redemption proceeds and the stock's adjusted basis. Because of the applicable capital gain tax rate on dividends, the primary benefit of sale or exchange treatment is being able to apply basis against proceeds. To reduce the income tax cost upon a shareholder's death, Sec. 303 allows exchange treatment to an estate on a redemption that otherwise does not meet the requirements of Sec. 302 for such treatment. This treatment minimizes any gain recognized because the stock's adjusted basis, which is subtracted from the redemption proceeds, was stepped up to its FMV upon the decedent's death.

To qualify for Sec. 303 treatment, the stock in the corporation redeeming the shares must make up more than 35% of the value of the decedent's gross estate, less any *allowable* Sec. 2053 and 2054 deductions. The maximum amount of redemption proceeds eligible for exchange treatment is the total of the estate's death taxes and funeral and administration expenses, regardless of whether they are deducted on the estate tax return or the estate's income tax return.

SELF-STUDY QUESTION

Why might an heir to farmland want an estate to forego the special valuation method of Sec. 2032A?

ANSWER

The heir may contemplate selling the land and prefer the higher basis he or she would get if FMV is used rather than the special farmland value, especially if the estate taxes are payable out of the residual estate and the heir does not share in that residual.

SPECIAL USE VALUATION OF FARM REAL PROPERTY

In 1976, Congress became concerned that farms sometimes had to be sold to generate funds to pay estate taxes. This situation was attributable, in part, to the FMV of farm land in many areas being relatively high, perhaps because of suburban housing being built nearby. Congress enacted Sec. 2032A, which allows real property used for farming or in a trade or business other than farming to be valued using a formula approach that attempts to value the property at what it is worth for farming purposes. The lowest valuation permitted is $750,000 below the property's FMV, but the $750,000 became indexed after 1998 with adjustments rounded to the next lowest $10,000. For 2015 the indexed amount is $1.10 million.

The estate must meet a number of requirements before the executor can elect the special valuation rules.[44] Moreover, if during the ten-year period after the decedent's death the new owner of the property disposes of it or no longer uses it as a farm, in general, an additional tax equal to the estate tax savings that arose from the lower Sec. 2032A valuation is levied.

[43] Sec. 6601(j).

[44] For example, the farm real and personal property must make up at least 50% of the adjusted value of the gross estate, and the farm real property must make up 25% or more of the adjusted value of the gross estate.

GENERATION-SKIPPING TRANSFER TAX

OBJECTIVE 7

Summarize the basic concepts of the generation-skipping transfer tax

The Tax Reform Act of 1976 enacted a third transfer tax—the generation-skipping transfer tax (GSTT)—to fill a void in the gift and estate tax structure. In 1986, Congress repealed the original GSTT retroactive to its original effective date and replaced it with a revised GSTT. The revised GSTT generally applies to *inter vivos* transfers made after September 25, 1985, and transfers at death made after October 22, 1986.

For years, a popular estate planning technique, especially among the very wealthy, involved giving individuals in several generations an interest in the same property. For example, a decedent might set up a testamentary trust creating successive life estates for a child and a grandchild and a remainder interest for a great grandchild. Under this arrangement, an estate tax would be imposed at the death of the person establishing the trust but not again until the great grandchild's death. The GSTT's purpose is to ensure that some form of transfer taxation is imposed one time a generation. It accomplishes its purpose by subjecting transfers that escape gift or estate taxation for one or more generations to the GSTT.

Originally, every grantor was entitled to a $1 million exemption from the GSTT, but the exemption became indexed for inflation (with adjustments rounded to the next lowest $10,000) for estates of decedents dying after 1998.[45] Beginning in 2004, Congress changed the exemption to the same amount as the "applicable exclusion amount" for estate tax purposes, which was $3.5 million in 2009. With the increase in the unified credit beginning in 2011, the exemption rose to $5 million in 2011 and now is $5.43 million in 2015. The grantor elects when, and against which transfers, to apply this exemption. Appreciation on the property for which the exemption is elected is also exempt from the GSTT.

The GSTT is levied at a flat rate, the highest estate tax rate.[46] The tax applies to direct skip gifts and bequests and to taxable terminations of and taxable distributions from generation-skipping transfers. A **generation-skipping transfer** involves a disposition that

- ▶ Provides interests for more than one generation of beneficiaries who are in a younger generation than the transferor, or
- ▶ Provides an interest solely for a person two or more generations younger than the transferor.[47]

The recipient must be a skip person, a person two or more generations younger than the decedent (or the donor). For family members, generation assignments are made according to the family tree. Transfers to skip persons outside of a trust are known as direct skips because they skip one or more generations.

EXAMPLE C:13-49 ▶ Tom transfers an asset directly to his grandson, Tom, III. This is a direct skip type of generation-skipping transfer because the transferee (Tom, III) is two generations younger than the transferor (Tom). ◀

The termination of an interest in a generation-skipping arrangement is known as a taxable termination.[48] This event triggers imposition of the GSTT. The tax is levied on the before-tax amount transferred, and the trustee pays the tax.

EXAMPLE C:13-50 ▶ Tom created a trust with income payable to his son, Tom, Jr., for life and a remainder interest distributable to Tom, III upon the death of Tom, Jr. (his father). This is a generation-skipping transfer because Tom, Jr., and Tom, III are one and two generations younger, respectively, than the transferor (Tom). A taxable termination occurs when Tom, Jr., dies. ◀

---

[45] Sec. 2631(a).
[46] Sec. 2641.
[47] Sec. 2611.
[48] Sec. 2612(a).

EXAMPLE C:13-51 ▶ The trust in Example C:13-50 was worth $2 million when Tom, Jr., died in 2015. Assume Tom, Jr., had used his GSTT exemption against other transfers. The amount of the taxable termination was $2 million. The tax was $800,000 (0.40 × $2,000,000). The trustee paid the tax and distributed the $1.2 million of remaining assets to the beneficiary. ◀

In the case of a direct skip, the amount subject to the GSTT is the value of the property received by the transferee.[49] The transferor is liable for the tax. If the direct skip occurs *inter vivos*, the GSTT paid by the transferor is treated as an additional transfer subject to the gift tax.[50] As a result, the total transfer tax liability (GSTT plus gift tax) can exceed the value of the property the donee received.

EXAMPLE C:13-52 ▶ In 2015, Susan gave $1 million to her granddaughter. Assume Susan had used her entire unified credit and was in the 40% marginal gift tax bracket; ignore the annual exclusion and the exemption. The GSTT was $400,000 (0.40 × $1,000,000). The amount subject to the gift tax was the value of the property transferred ($1 million) plus the GSTT paid ($400,000). Thus, the gift tax is $560,000 (0.40 × $1,400,000). It cost $960,000 ($400,000 + $560,000) to shift $1 million of property to the granddaughter. ◀

TAX PLANNING CONSIDERATIONS

OBJECTIVE 8

Recognize tax planning opportunities for estates

The effectiveness of many of the pre-1977 transfer tax-saving strategies was diluted by the unification of the transfer tax system in general and by the adoption of a unified rate schedule and the concept of adjusted taxable gifts in particular. To some extent, provisions that allow a larger tax base to be free of estate taxes and permit most interspousal transfers to be devoid of transfer tax consequences counterbalance unification. This section discusses various tax planning considerations that tax advisors should explore to reduce the transfer taxes applicable to a family unit.

WHAT WOULD YOU DO IN THIS SITUATION?

You are a CPA specializing in wealth transfer taxation. One of your clients is an unmarried resident of Aspen, Colorado and his health has recently taken a downhill turn. His doctor told him to consider putting his affairs in order.

This client is a merchant who owns a number of assets with FMVs totaling approximately $5.7 million. His largest asset is his Victorian era store building. Based on comparable sales in the area, your client's building appears to be worth approximately $760,000. Because your client is in poor health, he does not use all the store space and occasionally rents out some space to other vendors. During the ski season, the full price fair market rental value of the space would be over $1,000 per week.

Your client's only son has indicated that he is not interested in moving to Aspen but plans to continue the rental practices initiated by his father.

The estate probably will have no deductions. Would you propose to the client that this asset be listed in the estate as Special Use Value property pursuant to Sec. 2032A? Would it be ethical to propose a valuation method based on the historical income generated by this property for the client's estate tax return? Using the historical income stream, the capitalized value would be $460,000. With this value, his estate would be lower by $300,000 and no tax would be owed because of an overall valuation of $5.4 million for the entire estate.

---

[49] Sec. 2623.

[50] Sec. 2515.

TAX STRATEGY TIP

Prospective donors should weigh the opportunities for reducing transfer taxes through the use of lifetime gifts against the income tax disadvantage of foregoing the step up in basis that occurs if the donor retains the property until death. On the other hand, unless the donee is the donor's spouse, income taxes on the income produced by the gifted property often can be reduced if shifted to a donee in a lower tax bracket.

USE OF *INTER VIVOS* GIFTS

One of the most significant strategies for reducing transfer taxes is a well-designed, long-term gift program. As long as the gifts to each donee do not exceed the annual exclusion, there will be no additions to the gross estate and no adjusted taxable gifts. A donor may pass thousands of dollars of property to others free of any transfer tax consequences if he or she selects enough donees and makes gifts over a substantial number of years. If taxable gifts do occur, the donor removes the post-gift appreciation from the estate tax base. Moreover, if the donor lives more than three years after the date of the gift, the gift tax paid is removed from the gross estate.

USE OF EXEMPTION EQUIVALENT

ADDITIONAL COMMENT

As mentioned earlier, the so-called exemption equivalent amount ($5.43 million in 2015) is portable between spouses. Thus, any amount that remains unused at the first spouse's death can be used by the second spouse. However, this benefit applies only if the executor elects portability.

The exemption equivalent allows a certain amount of property—$5.43 million in 2015—to pass to people other than the decedent's spouse without any estate taxes being extracted therefrom. The exemption equivalent also is called the applicable exclusion amount. Recall that a donor can transfer property to a spouse tax-free without limit. Because the spouse presumably will die before any children or grandchildren (i.e., individuals to whom people often will property), a very wealthy person should contemplate leaving at least an amount equal to the exemption equivalent to people other than his or her spouse. (If one leaves this amount of property in trust, the trust is often called a credit shelter or bypass trust.) This technique precludes the decedent from wasting some or all of the exemption equivalent and thereby prevents the property from being taxed when the surviving spouse dies. Taking advantage of the portability provision is another opportunity for making use of the decedent's exemption equivalent.

Making full use of the exemption equivalent enables a husband and wife to transfer to third parties an aggregate of $10.86 million (using 2015 amounts) without incurring any estate taxes. The strategy of making gifts to an ill spouse, who is not wealthy, to keep the donee-spouse's exemption equivalent from being wasted was discussed earlier (see Chapter C:12). Under this technique, the wealthier spouse makes gifts to the other spouse free of gift taxes because of the marital deduction. The recipient spouse then has an estate that can be passed tax-free to children, grandchildren, or other individuals because of the exemption equivalent. This strategy no longer is the only planning technique because the portability rule allows the decreased spouse's unused exemption equivalent to shift to the surviving spouse.

STOP & THINK

Question: Sol made $600,000 in taxable gifts in 2006 but did not have to pay any gift tax. Sol died in 2015, when the gifted property was worth $825,000. Sol's taxable estate (gross estate minus estate tax deductions) was $5.43 million. Did the exemption equivalent enable Sol's estate to owe zero tax?

Solution: No. In concept, the unified credit of $2,117,800, which cancels out the tax on the $5.43 million taxable estate because of the exemption equivalent of equal amount (in 2015), is available only once. Sol's total tranfers—by gift and at death—exceeded $5.43 million. Calculation of Sol's estate tax payable would be as follows:

Taxable estate	$5,430,000
Plus: Adjusted taxable gifts	600,000
Estate tax base	$6,030,000
Tentative tax on estate tax base	$2,357,800
Minus:	
Post-1976 gift tax (on $600,000 gift)	–0–
Unified credit	(2,117,800)
Estate tax payable	$ 240,000

The $240,000 represents the tax on the incremental $600,000, the amount over and above the $5.43 million *aggregate* taxable amount that could be passed free of transfer taxes (both gift and estate).

WHAT SIZE MARITAL DEDUCTION IS BEST?

To reiterate, the tax law imposes no ceiling on the amount of property eligible for the marital deduction. Even so, the availability of an unlimited marital deduction does not necessarily mean that a person should use it. From a tax perspective, wealthier people should consider leaving an amount equal to the exemption equivalent to someone other than the spouse. Alternatively, they could leave the spouse an income interest in property equal to the exemption equivalent along with the power to invade such property for reasons of health, support, maintenance, or education. These powers do not cause an inclusion in the gross estate. Making use of the exemption equivalent has become less important because the portability election allows the surviving spouse to use the decedent's exemption equivalent.

In certain circumstances, it may be preferable for an amount exceeding the exemption equivalent to pass directly to third parties. It might be beneficial for the first spouse's estate to pay some estate taxes if the surviving spouse already has substantial property and has a relatively short life expectancy, especially if the decedent spouse's assets are expected to rapidly increase in value.

? STOP & THINK

Question: Tarik died in 2015 at age 78. He was survived by his wife, Saliah, and several children and grandchildren. Saliah is 54 and in excellent health. Tarik's adjusted gross estate was \$8 million, and his will left \$5.43 million outright to his children and the rest to a trust for Saliah. The trust is eligible for the QTIP election. An investment advisor believes that the trust assets will likely appreciate annually at the rate of at least 10%. Name two advantages and one disadvantage of electing the marital deduction on the entire trust.

Solution: One advantage is that the tax on the trust property will be deferred, perhaps for a long time, given the wife's age and health. Another advantage is that, because no tax is owed at Tarik's death, the trust assets remain intact to appreciate and produce more income for Saliah. That is, there is no current capital drain to pay transfer taxes. A disadvantage is that, because of the anticipated appreciation and the long time before Saliah's estimated death, the amount taxed in Saliah's estate will likely be much greater than the residue (here, \$2.57 million) Tarik willed to Saliah. Note that Tarik took full advantage of his unified credit.

USE OF DISCLAIMERS

Because the IRC does not treat a **qualified disclaimer** as a gift, disclaimers can be valuable estate planning tools (see Chapter C:12). For example, if a decedent wills all his or her property to the surviving spouse, such spouse could disclaim an amount at least equal in size to the exemption equivalent and thereby enable the decedent's estate to take full advantage of the unified credit. However, in the absence of the spouse's disclaiming, the portability election keeps the exemption equivalent from being wasted. In a different scenario, a decedent's children might disclaim some bequests if, as a result of their disclaimer, the property would pass to the surviving spouse. This approach might be desirable if a large estate otherwise would receive a relatively small marital deduction. A disclaimer also could be appropriate if the disclaimant is elderly and in poor health and wishes to preclude the property from being taxed again relatively soon. (Of course, the credit for tax on prior transfers would provide some relief from double taxation.) Bear in mind, however, that the person making the qualified disclaimer has no input concerning which individuals receive the disclaimed property.

ROLE OF LIFE INSURANCE

Life insurance is an important asset with respect to estate planning for the following reasons:

- It can help provide the liquidity for paying estate taxes and other costs associated with death.
- It has the potential for a large increase in value. If the insured gives away his or her incidents of ownership in the policy and survives the gift by more than three years, the estate benefits by keeping the policy's increased value out of the estate.

Assume an individual is contemplating purchasing a new insurance policy on his or her life and transferring it to another individual as a gift. The insured must live for more than three years after making the gift to exclude the face amount of the policy from his or her gross estate. Should the insured die within three years of gifting the policy, the donor's gross estate includes the policy's face amount. If the donee instead purchases the policy, the insured will not make a gift of the policy, and the three-year rule will not be of concern.

QUALIFYING THE ESTATE FOR INSTALLMENT PAYMENTS

TAX STRATEGY TIP

The payment of estate taxes can be deferred as much as 14 years if the estate's executor makes a timely Sec. 6166 election. The interest charged on the deferred taxes is at a favorable rate.

It can be quite beneficial for an estate owning an interest in a closely held business to qualify for installment payment of estate taxes under Sec. 6166. In a sense, the estate can borrow a certain amount of dollars from the government at 2% and the rest at a higher, but still favorable, rate. The closely held business interest must comprise more than 35% of the adjusted gross estate, defined as the gross estate less Sec. 2053 and Sec. 2054 deductions.

Retaining closely held business interests and gifting other assets will increase the likelihood of the estate's being able to elect the installment payments. However, closely held business interests often have a potential for great appreciation. Consequently, from the standpoint of reducing the size of the estate by freezing values, they are good candidates for gifts.

People cannot make gifts to restructure their estates and thereby qualify for Sec. 6166 if they postpone restructuring until soon before their death. If the decedent makes gifts within three years of dying, the closely held business interest must make up more than 35% of the adjusted gross estate in both of the following calculations:

1. Calculate the ratio of the closely held business to the actual adjusted gross estate.
2. Redo the calculations after revising the ratio to include (at date-of-death values) any property given away within three years of death.

EXAMPLE C:13-53 ▶ Joe died in 2015. Joe's gross estate included a closely held business interest valued at $2 million and other property valued at $3.6 million. Joe's allowable Sec. 2053 and 2054 deductions totaled $100,000. In 2013, partly in hopes of qualifying his estate for Sec. 6166 treatment, Joe made gifts of listed securities of $300,000 (at 2015 valuations) and paid no gift tax on the gifts. The two tests for determining whether Joe's estate qualified for Sec. 6166 are as follows:

Excluding gifts:	$2,000,000 ÷ $5,500,000 = 36.36%
Including gifts:	$2,000,000 ÷ $5,800,000 = 34.48%

Joe's estate could not elect Sec. 6166 treatment because it met the greater than 35% test in only one of the two computations. ◀

WHERE TO DEDUCT ADMINISTRATION EXPENSES

Another tax planning opportunity concerns the choice of where to deduct administration expenses: on the estate tax return, on the estate's income tax return, or some in each place. The executor should claim the deduction where it will yield the greatest tax savings. For 2015 the top tax rate is 40% for estate tax purposes and 39.6% for income tax purposes. In addition, an estate could owe an incremental 3.8% tax on its undistributed net investment income. Thus, for some estates, the tax savings will be slightly higher if the expenses are deducted on the income tax return. However, some decedents may have made bequests to certain persons or charitable organizations based on the size of the adjusted gross or taxable estate. In such circumstances, the tax return on which the administration expenses are deducted will affect the amount of the adjusted gross and taxable estates and the amount that some beneficiaries of the estate receive. If no estate taxes are owed because of the exemption equivalent or the marital and/or charitable contribution deduction, administration expenses should be deducted on the estate's income tax return.

Compliance and Procedural Considerations

OBJECTIVE 9

Comply with the filing requirements for estate tax returns

FILING REQUIREMENTS

Section 6018 indicates the circumstances in which estate tax returns are necessary. In general, no return is necessary unless the value of the gross estate plus adjusted taxable gifts exceeds the exemption equivalent (also known as the applicable exclusion amount). An exception applies, however, if the decedent made any post-1976 taxable gifts or claimed any portion of the $30,000 specific exemption after September 8, 1976, and before January 1, 1977. In such circumstances, a return must be filed if the value of the gross estate exceeds the amount of the exemption equivalent reduced by the total of the decedent's adjusted taxable gifts and the amount of the specific exemption claimed against gifts made after September 8, 1976, and before January 1, 1977.

REAL-WORLD EXAMPLE

The IRS expects 119,400 estate tax returns to be filed in 2015.

To elect the portability of the deceased spouse's unused exemption equivalent, the executor must file an estate tax return even though a return would not otherwise be required. In such situations the executor must calculate the unused amount but is allowed to make a good faith estimate of the value of the gross estate. If a return is filed, but for some reason the executor does not want to take advantage of portability, the executor must check a box on the estate tax return to denote the decision to opt out of the portability election.

A completed sample Estate Tax Return (Form 706) appears in Appendix B. The facts on which the return is based are the same as for the comprehensive illustration appearing on pages C:13-25 through C:13-27.

DUE DATE

Estate tax returns generally must be filed within nine months after the decedent's death.[51] The Secretary of the Treasury is authorized to grant a reasonable extension of time for filing.[52] The maximum extension period is six months. Obtaining an extension does not extend the time for paying the estate tax. Section 6601 imposes interest on any portion of the tax not paid by the due date of the return, determined without regard to the extension period. Thus, to avoid interest, the estate must pay the tax by the original due date.

VALUATION

One of the most difficult tasks of preparing estate tax returns is valuing the items included in the gross estate. Some items (e.g., one-of-a-kind art objects) may truly be unique. For many properties the executor should arrange for appraisals by experts.

If the value of any property reported on the return is 65% or less of the amount determined to be the proper value during an audit or court case, a 20% undervaluation penalty is imposed.[53] The penalty is higher if a gross valuation misstatement occurs; that is, the estate tax valuation is 40% or less than the amount determined to be the proper value.[54] Chapter C:12 discusses these penalties in more detail.

ELECTION OF ALTERNATE VALUATION DATE

The executor may value the gross estate on the alternate valuation date instead of on the date of death by making an irrevocable election on the estate tax return. The election does not necessarily have to be made on a timely return, but no election is possible if the return is filed more than a year after the due date (including extensions).

Problem Materials

DISCUSSION QUESTIONS

C:13-1 In general, at what amount are items includible in the gross estate valued? (Answer in words.) Indicate one exception to the general valuation rules and the reason for this exception.

C:13-2 A client requests that you explain the valuation rules used for gift tax and estate tax purposes. Explain the similarities and differences of the two sets of rules.

51 Sec. 6075(a).

52 Sec. 6081(a).

53 Sec. 6662(g).

54 Sec. 6662(h).

C:13-3 Compare the valuation for gift and estate tax purposes of a $150,000 group term life insurance policy on the transferor's life.

C:13-4 Explain how shares of stock traded on a stock exchange are valued. What is the blockage rule?

C:13-5 Assume that the properties included in Alex's gross estate have appreciated during the six-month period immediately after his death. May Alex's executor elect the alternate valuation date and thereby achieve a larger step-up in basis? Explain.

C:13-6 Explain to an executor an advantage and a disadvantage of electing the alternate valuation date.

C:13-7 A decedent transferred land to an adult child by gift two years before death. Is the land included in the decedent's gross estate? In the estate tax base?

C:13-8 From a tax standpoint, which of the following alternatives is more favorable for a client's estate?

a. Buying a new insurance policy on his life and soon thereafter giving it to another person

b. Encouraging the other person to buy the policy with funds previously received from the client

Explain your answer.

C:13-9 Explain the difference between the estate tax treatment for gift taxes paid on gifts made two years before death and on gifts made ten years before death.

C:13-10 A client is considering making a very large gift. She wants to know whether the gross-up rule will apply to the entire amount of gift taxes paid by both her and her spouse if the spouses elect gift splitting and she dies within three years of the gift. Explain.

C:13-11 A widow owns a valuable eighteenth-century residence that she would like the state historical society to own someday. Explain to her the estate tax consequences of the following two alternatives:

a. Deeding the state historical society a remainder interest in the residence and reserving the right to live there rent free for the rest of her life.

b. Giving her entire interest in the house to the society and moving to another home for the rest of her life.

C:13-12 When does the consideration furnished test apply to property that the decedent held as a joint tenant with right of survivorship?

C:13-13 Describe two circumstances in which life insurance on a decedent's life is includible in the gross estate under Sec. 2042. If insurance policies on the decedent's life escape being included under Sec. 2042, are they definitely excluded from the gross estate? Explain.

C:13-14 Indicate two situations in which property that has previously been subject, at least in part, to gift taxation is nevertheless included in the donor-decedent's gross estate.

C:13-15 Joe's will required property to be put in trust with a bank as trustee. His will named his sister Tess to receive the trust income annually for life and empowered Tess to will the property to whomever she so desires. In addition, Tess may require that the trustee make distributions of principal to her for her health or support needs. Tess plans to leave the property by will to two of her three children in equal shares. Tess seeks your advice about whether the trust will be included in her gross estate. Respond to Tess.

C:13-16 Determine the accuracy of the following statement: The gross estate includes a general power of appointment possessed by the decedent only if the decedent exercised the power.

C:13-17 Carlos died six years before his wife. His will called for the creation of a trust to be funded with $1 million of property. The bank trustee was required to distribute all the trust income semiannually to Carlos's widow for the rest of her life. Upon her death, the trust assets were to be distributed to the couple's children. When the widow died, the trust assets had appreciated to $1.7 million. Are the trust assets included in the widow's gross estate? Explain.

C:13-18 List the various categories of estate tax deductions, and compare them with the categories of gift tax deductions. What differences exist?

C:13-19 Compare the tax treatment of administration expenses with that of the decedent's debts.

C:13-20 Judy died and was survived by her husband, Jason, who received the following interests as a result of his wife's death. Does Judy's estate receive a marital deduction for them? Explain.

a. $400,000 of life insurance proceeds; Jason is the beneficiary; Judy held the incidents of ownership.

b. Outright ownership of $700,000 of land held by Judy and Jason as joint tenants. Jason provided all the consideration to purchase the land.

C:13-21 Compare the credits available for estate tax purposes with the credits available for gift tax purposes. What differences exist?

C:13-22 Explain to a client the tax policy reason Congress allowed estates to make installment payments of the portion of the estate taxes attributable to closely held business interests.

C:13-23 Assume that Larry is wealthier than Jane, his wife, and that he is likely to die before her. From an overall tax standpoint (considering transfer taxes and income taxes), is it preferable for Larry to transfer property to Jane *inter vivos* or at death, or does it matter? Explain.

C:13-24 Bala desires to freeze the value of his estate. Explain which of the following assets you would recommend that Bala transfer during his lifetime (more than one asset may be suggested):
a. Life insurance on his life
b. Cash
c. Corporate bonds (assume interest rates are expected to rise)
d. Stock in a firm with a bright future
e. Land in a boom town

C:13-25 Refer to Problem C:13-24. Explain the negative tax considerations (if any) with respect to Bala's making gifts of the assets that you recommended.

C:13-26 From a tax standpoint, describe an advantage a very wealthy married person would achieve by disposing of an amount equal to the exemption equivalent (applicable exclusion amount) to individuals other than his or her spouse?

C:13-27 In general, when is the estate tax due? What are some exceptions?

ISSUE IDENTIFICATION QUESTIONS

C:13-28 Henry Arkin (a widower) is quite elderly and is beginning to engage in some estate planning. His goal is to reduce his transfer taxes. He is considering purchasing land with a high potential for appreciation and having it titled in the names of himself and his grandson as joint tenants with rights of survivorship. Henry would provide all of the consideration, estimated to be about $14 million. What tax issues should Henry Arkin consider with respect to the purchase of the land?

C:13-29 Annie James died early in 2015. All her property passed subject to her will, which provides that her surviving husband, Dave James, is to receive all the property outright. Her will further states that any property Dave disclaims will pass instead to their children in equal shares. Annie's gross estate is $6.3 million, and her Sec. 2053 deductions are $300,000. Dave, who is in poor health, already owns about $5 million of property. What tax issues should Dave James consider with respect to the property bequeathed to him by his wife?

C:13-30 Assume the same facts as in Problem C:13-29 except that Annie's will leaves all her property to a QTIP trust for Dave for life with the remainder to their children. What tax issues should Dave James and the estate's executor consider with respect to the property that passes to the QTIP trust?

C:13-31 Jeung Hong, a widower, died in March 2015. His gross estate was $6.5 million and, at the time of his death, he owed debts of $60,000. His will made a bequest of $200,000 to his undergraduate alma mater and left the rest of his property to his children. His administrative expenses were $75,000. What tax issues should the estate's CPA consider when preparing Jeung's estate tax return and his estate's income tax return?

PROBLEMS

C:13-32 *Valuation.* Beth died on May 8, 2015. Her executor elected date-of-death valuation. Beth's gross estate included, among other properties, the items listed below. What is the estate tax value of each item?
a. 4,000 shares of Highline Corporation stock, traded on a stock exchange on May 8, 2015 at a high of 30, a low of 25, and a close of 26.
b. Life insurance policy on the life of Beth having a face value of $600,000. The cost of a comparable policy immediately before Beth's death was $187,430.
c. Life insurance policy on the life of Beth's son having a face value of $100,000. The interpolated terminal reserve immediately before Beth's death was $14,000. Unexpired premiums were $920.
d. Beach cottage appraised at a FMV of $175,000 and valued for property tax purposes at $152,000.

C:13-33 *Valuation.* Mary died on April 3, 2015. As of this date, Mary's gross estate was valued at $6.5 million. On October 3, Mary's gross estate was valued at $5.8 million. The estate neither distributed nor sold any assets before October 3, 2015. Mary's estate had no deductions or adjusted taxable gifts. What was Mary's *lowest* possible estate tax liability?

C:13-34 *Estate Tax Formula.* Sue died on May 3, 2015. On October 1, 2012, Sue gave Tom land valued at $7,013,000. Sue applied a unified credit of $1,772,800 against the gift tax due on this transfer. On Sue's date of death the land was valued at $9.4 million.

a. With respect to this transaction, what amount was included in Sue's gross estate?
b. What is the amount of Sue's adjusted taxable gifts attributable to the 2012 gift?

C:13-35 *Transferor Provisions.* Val died on May 13, 2015. On July 3, 2012, she gave a $400,000 life insurance policy on her own life to son Ray. Because the value of the policy was relatively low, the transfer did not cause any gift tax to be payable.

a. What amount was included in Val's gross estate as a result of the 2012 gift?
b. What amount was included in Val's gross estate if the property given was land instead of a life insurance policy?
c. Refer to Part a. What amount would have been included in Val's gross estate if she instead gave Ray the policy on April 30, 2011?

C:13-36 *Transferor Provisions.* In December 2012, Jody transferred stock having an $8,113,000 FMV to her daughter Joan. Jody paid $1,043,000 ($2,815,800 − $1,772,800) of gift taxes on this transfer. When Jody died in January 2015, the stock was valued at $9 million. Jody made no other gifts during her lifetime. With respect to this gift transaction, what amount was includible in Jody's gross estate, and what amount was reportable as adjusted taxable gifts?

C:13-37 *Transferor Provisions.* In December 2012, Curt and Kate elected gift splitting to report $16,226,000 of gifts of stocks Curt made. Each paid gift taxes of $1,043,000 by spending his or her own funds. Kate died in January 2015 and was survived by Curt. Her only taxable gift was the one reported for 2012. When Kate died in 2015, the stock had appreciated to $18.8 million. With respect to the 2012 gift, what amount was included in Kate's gross estate, and what amount was reportable as adjusted taxable gifts?

C:13-38 *Transferor Provisions.* John died in 2015. What amount, if any, was included in his gross estate in each of the following situations:

a. In 1997, John created a revocable trust, funded it with $400,000 of assets, and named a bank as trustee. The trust instrument provided that the income is payable to John annually for life. Upon John's death, the assets were to be divided equally among John's descendants. When John died at the age of 72, the trust was still revocable. The trust assets were then worth $480,000.
b. In 1997, John transferred title to his personal residence to a charitable organization but retained the right to live there rent free for 20 years. The residence was worth $150,000 on the transfer date. At John's death, the residence was worth $230,000.
c. In 1997, John created an irrevocable trust, funded it with $200,000 of assets, and named a bank as trustee. According to the trust agreement, all the trust income was to be paid out annually for 25 years. The trustee, however, is to decide how much income to pay each year to each of the three beneficiaries (John's children). Upon termination of the trust, the assets are to be distributed equally among John's three children (now adults) or their estates. The trust's assets were worth $500,000 when John died.
d. In 1997, John created an irrevocable trust with a bank named as trustee. He designated his grandson Al as the beneficiary of all the income for life. Upon Al's death, the property is to be distributed equally among Al's descendants. The trust assets were worth $400,000 when John died.

C:13-39 *Transferor Provisions.* Twelve years ago, Latoya transferred property to an irrevocable trust with a bank trustee. Latoya named Al to receive the trust income annually for life and Pat or Pat's estate to receive the remainder upon Al's death. Latoya reserved the power to designate Mike or Mike's estate (instead of Pat or Pat's estate) to receive the remainder. Upon Latoya's death in August 2015, the trust assets were valued at $200,000; Al was age 50; Mike, age 27; and Pat, age 32. Assume a 4% rate for the actuarial tables.

a. How much, if any, is included in Latoya's gross estate?
b. How much would have been included in Latoya's gross estate if she had *not* retained any powers over the trust?

C:13-40 *Annuities.* Maria died two years after her retirement. At the time of her death at age 67, she was covered by the two annuities listed below.

- An annuity purchased by Maria's father providing benefits to Maria upon her attaining age 65. Upon Maria's death, survivor benefits are payable to her sister. The sister's total benefits are valued at $45,000.

- An annuity purchased by Maria's former employer under a qualified plan to which only the employer contributed. Benefits became payable to Maria upon her retirement. Upon Maria's death a survivor annuity valued at $110,000 is payable to her son.

a. What is the amount of the inclusion in Maria's gross estate with respect to each annuity?
b. How would your answer for the first annuity change if Maria had instead purchased the annuity?
c. How would your answer for the second annuity change if the employer had instead made 70% of the contributions to the qualified plan and Maria had made the remaining 30%?

C:13-41 ***Jointly Owned Property.*** Ten years ago, Art purchased land for $60,000 and immediately titled it in the names of Art and Bart, joint tenants with right of survivorship. Bart paid no consideration. In 2015, Art died and was survived by Bart, his brother. The land's value had appreciated to $300,000.

a. What was the amount of the inclusion in Art's gross estate?
b. Assume Bart died (instead of Art). What amount would have been included in Bart's gross estate?
c. Assume that Art died in January 2015 and Bart died in November 2015, when the land was worth $320,000. What amount was included in Bart's gross estate?

C:13-42 ***Jointly Owned Property.*** Five years ago, Andy and Sandy, siblings, pooled their resources and purchased a warehouse. Andy provided $50,000 of consideration, and Sandy furnished $100,000. Andy died and was survived by Sandy. The property, which they had titled in the names of Andy and Sandy, joint tenants with right of survivorship, was valued at $450,000 when Andy died. What amount was includible in Andy's gross estate?

C:13-43 ***Jointly Owned Property.*** Fifteen years ago, Mrs. Cobb purchased land costing $80,000. She had the land titled in the names of Mr. and Mrs. Cobb, joint tenants with right of survivorship. Mrs. Cobb died and was survived by Mr. Cobb. At Mrs. Cobb's death, the land's value was $200,000.

a. What amount was included in Mrs. Cobb's gross estate?
b. What amount, if any, of the marital deduction could Mrs. Cobb's estate claim for the land?
c. Assume Mr. Cobb died after Mrs. Cobb and the land was worth $240,000 at his death. What amount was included in his gross estate?

C:13-44 ***Powers of Appointment.*** Tai was the sole income beneficiary for life of each of the trusts described below. For each trust, indicate whether and why it was includible in Tai's gross estate.

a. A trust created under the will of Tai's mother, who died in 1996. Upon Tai's death, the trust assets are to pass to those of Tai's descendants whom Tai directs by his will. Should Tai fail to appoint the trust property, the trust assets are to be distributed to the Smithsonian Institution. Tai willed the property to his twin daughters in equal shares.
b. An irrevocable *inter vivos* trust created in 2001 by Tai's father. The trust agreement authorizes Tai to appoint the property to whomever he so desires. The appointment could be made only by his will. In his will, Tai appointed the property to an elderly neighbor.
c. An irrevocable trust created by Tai's uncle in 2005. The trust instrument authorized Tai to demand that the trustee distribute trust assets to Tai for his health and/or maintenance needs. Any property remaining in the trust at Tai's death will pass in accordance with the trust instrument to Tai's descendants in equal shares.
d. A trust created under the will of Tai's great-grandmother, who died in 1941. Her will authorizes Tai to appoint the property by his will to whomever he so desires. In default of appointment, the property is to pass to Tai's descendants in equal shares. Tai's will did not mention this trust.
e. Assume the same facts as in Part b except Tai's will did not mention the trust property.

C:13-45 ***Life Insurance.*** Joy died on November 5, 2015. Soon after Joy's death, the executor discovered the following insurance policies on Joy's life.

Policy Number	*Owner*	*Beneficiary*	*Face Value*
123	Joy	Joy's husband	$400,000
757	Joy's son	Joy's estate	225,000
848	Joy's son	Joy's son	300,000
414	Joy's daughter	Joy's husband	175,000

Joy transferred ownership of policies 757 and 848 to her son in 2009. She gave ownership of policy 414 to her daughter in 2013. Indicate the amount includible in Joy's gross estate for each policy.

C:13-46 *Life Insurance.* Refer to Problem C:13-45. What is the net addition to Joy's *taxable estate* with respect to the insurance policies listed above if all the property passing under Joy's will was left to Joy's son?

C:13-47 *Deductions.* When Yuji died in March 2015, his gross estate was valued at $8 million. He owed debts totaling $300,000. Funeral and administration expenses were $12,000 and $120,000, respectively. The marginal estate tax rate exceeded his estate's marginal income tax rate. Yuji willed his church $300,000 and his spouse $1.1 million. Calculate Yuji's taxable estate.

C:13-48 *Marital Deduction.* Assume the same facts as in Problem C:13-47 except that Yuji's will also provided for setting up a trust to be funded with $400,000 of property with a bank named as trustee. His wife is to receive all the trust income semiannually for life, and upon her death the trust assets are to be distributed equally among Yuji's children and grandchildren.

a. What was the amount of Yuji's taxable estate? Provide two possible answers.
b. Assume Yuji's widow died in December 2015. With respect to Yuji's former assets, which items will be included in the widow's gross estate? Provide two possible answers, but you need not indicate amounts.

C:13-49 *Marital Deduction.* Assume the same facts as in Problem C:13-48 and that before Yuji's death in 2015 his wife already owned property valued at $300,000. Assume that each asset owned by each spouse increased 8% in value by the surviving spouse's date of death later in 2015 and that Yuji's executor elected to claim the maximum marital deduction possible. Assume there were no state death taxes. From a tax standpoint, was the executor's strategy of electing the marital deduction on the QTIP trust a wise decision? Support your answer with computations.

C:13-50 *Portability of Exemption.* Sam Snider died February 14, 2014, survived by his spouse Janet and several children. Sam had not made any taxable gifts. Sam's gross estate was $7 million. In each of the following independent situations, indicate the amount of Sam's exemption equivalent that is portable to Janet and that can be used by Janet's estate if Sam's executor makes the appropriate election.

a. Sam's deductions, including the marital deduction, total $3.7 million; Janet dies in 2015.
b. Sam's deductions, including the marital deduction, total $1.1 million; Janet dies in 2015.
c. Sam's deductions, including the marital deduction, total $6 million; Janet dies in 2019.
d. Sam's deductions, including the marital deduction, total $5.5 million. Janet remarries late in 2014. Her new spouse dies early in 2015 with a $9 million taxable estate, and Janet dies late in 2015.

C:13-51 *Adjusted Taxable Gifts.* Will, a bachelor, died in 2015. At that time, his sole asset was cash of $6 million. Assume no debts or funeral and administration expenses and no charitable bequests. His gift history was as follows:

Date	*Amount of Taxable Gifts*	*FMV of Gift Property at Date of Death*
October 1987	$270,000	$290,000
October 1991	90,000	45,000

a. What was Will's estate tax base?
b. How would your answer to Part a change if Will made the first gift in 1974 (instead of 1987)?

C:13-52 *Estate Tax Base.* Bess, a widow, died in October 2015. Her gross estate, which totaled $7 million, included a $100,000 life insurance policy on her life that she gave away in 2013. The taxable gift that arose from giving away the policy was $15,000. In December 2012, Bess made a $740,000 taxable gift of stock whose value increased to $790,000 by the time Bess died. She owed debts of $80,000 at the time of her death.

a. What was her estate tax base?
b. What unified credit could her estate claim?

C:13-53 *Estate Tax Base.* Maria Martinez died in 2015, survived by her spouse, Sergio, and two adult children. Her gross estate, all of which passed under her will, was valued at $7.2 million. She had Sec. 2053 deductions of $100,000. Her will left $200,000 to her church, 20% of her gross estate to her spouse, and the rest to her children in equal shares. She made taxable gifts of $20,000 in 1975 and $500,000 in 1999. The gifted assets have increased in value to $120,000 and $715,000, respectively. Calculate her taxable estate, her adjusted taxable gifts, and her estate tax base.

C:13-54 *Estate Tax Calculation.* Joseph Jernigan died in 2015 with a taxable estate of $4.1 million. He was survived by his spouse Josephine and several children. He made taxable gifts of $100,000 in 1974 and $650,000 in 2000. The property given in 1974 was valued at $425,000 when he died, and the property given in 2000 was valued at $400,000 when he died. Determine his estate tax base, his estate tax before subtraction of the unified credit, the amount of unified credit available to his estate, the reduction for post-1976 gift taxes, and his estate tax payable. Also, indicate the amount, if any, of his exemption equivalent that is portable to Josephine.

C:13-55 *Installment Payments.* Elaine died on May 1, 2015. Her gross estate consisted of the following items:

Cash	$ 40,000
Stocks traded on a stock exchange	4,200,000
Personal residence	550,000
25% capital interest in a 60-person partnership	3,100,000

Elaine's Sec. 2053 deductions totaled $200,000. She had no other deductions.

a. What percentage of Elaine's federal estate taxes can be paid in installments under Sec. 6166? When was the first installment payment due?

b. Could Elaine's estate elect Sec. 6166 treatment if the stocks were valued at $6.2 million instead of $4.2 million?

C:13-56 *State Death Taxes.* Giovanni died in 2015 with a gross estate of $6.9 million and debts of $30,000. He made post-1976 taxable gifts of $100,000, valued at $80,000 when Giovanni died. His estate paid state death taxes of $110,200. Calculate his estate tax base.

COMPREHENSIVE PROBLEMS

C:13-57 Bonnie died on June 1, 2015, survived by her husband, Abner, and two sons, Carl and Doug. Bonnie's only lifetime taxable gift was made in October 2013 in the taxable amount of $6.25 million. She did not elect gift splitting. By the time of her death, the value of the gifted property (stock) had declined to $5.1 million.

Bonnie's executor discovered the items shown below. Amounts shown are the FMVs of the items as of June 1, 2015.

Cash in checking account in her name	$ 127,750
Cash in savings account in her name	430,000
Stock in names of Bonnie and Doug, joint tenants with right of survivorship. Bonnie provided all the consideration ($3,000) to purchase the stock.	25,000
Land in names of Bonnie and Abner, joint tenants with right of survivorship. Abner provided all the consideration to purchase the land.	360,000
Personal residence in only Bonnie's name	450,000
Life insurance on Bonnie's life. Bonnie was owner, and Bonnie's estate was beneficiary (face value)	5,000,000
Trust created under the will of Bonnie's mother (who died in 2000). Bonnie was entitled to all the trust income for life, and she could will the trust property to whomever she desired. She willed it to her sons in equal amounts.	700,000

Bonnie's debts, as of her date of death, were $60,000. Her funeral and administration expenses were $9,000 and $71,000, respectively. Her estate paid state death taxes of $65,000. The executor elected to deduct the administration expenses on the estate tax return.

Bonnie's will included the following:

> I leave my residence to my husband Abner.
>
> $250,000 of property is to be transferred to a trust with First Bank named as trustee. All of the income is to be paid to my husband, Abner, semiannually for the rest of his life. Upon his death the property is to be divided equally between my two sons or their estates.
>
> I leave $47,000 to the American Cancer Society.

Assume the executor elected to claim the maximum marital deduction possible. Compute the following with respect to Bonnie's estate:

a. Gross estate
b. Taxable estate
c. Adjusted taxable gifts
d. Estate tax base and basic exclusion amount portable to Abner
e. Tentative tax on estate tax base
f. Federal estate tax payable

C:13-58 Assume the same facts as in Problem C:13-57 except the joint tenancy land was held in the names of Bonnie and her son Doug, joint tenants with right of survivorship. Also assume that Bonnie provided 55% of the consideration to buy the land and that Bonnie's executor did not elect to claim the marital deduction on the QTIP trust. Assume further that, because of the annual exclusion, no taxable gift arose on the purchase of the joint tenancy land.

TAX STRATEGY PROBLEMS

C:13-59 Gaylord Gunnison (GG) died January 13, 2015, and his gross estate consisted of three properties—cash, land, and stock in a public company. The amount of cash on the date of his death was $2.9 million, which went into the estate. On January 13, 2015, the land had a fair market value of $1 million, and the stock had a fair market value of $2 million. On July 13, 2015, the fair market values of the land and stock were $1.1 million and $1.6 million, respectively, and the cash remained at $2.9 million. Assume, for simplicity, that the estate has no deductions and GG made no taxable gifts. GG willed all of his property to his daughter, Gilda, who anticipated that, beginning in July 2015, the stock would appreciate at the rate of 9% per year before taxes. She anticipates selling the stock on or about July 13, 2021. Assume that the land's fair market value will remain at $1.1 million through 2021 and that she anticipates retaining the land for the rest of her life.

Considering both income tax and estate tax effects, compare after-tax wealth using the alternate valuation date or the date of death to value the estate. Which date should the executor have elected? For simplicity, assume that the cash is not invested. (Incidentally, the factor for the future value, six years hence, at 9% is 1.677.) Prepare a worksheet on which you calculate the amount of after-tax wealth using the two possible valuation dates. Assume that the gain will be taxed at a 20% capital gains rate and will be subject to the 3.8% tax on net investment income (i.e., at a 23.8% rate).

C:13-60 Steve Silver, a new client, owns stock in HyTeche, Inc., which recently had an initial public offering. In early 2015, his stock is valued at $8 million. His only other asset is $9 million of cash. Unfortunately, he has a terminal illness and has a life expectancy of less than a year. He believes that the stock's value will escalate to about $10 million by the time of his death. Steve is a widower and wants his daughter Sylvia to end up with the stock. He wants you to do a projection of his total transfer tax cost (gift and estate) if he gives the stock to Sylvia immediately compared with his total transfer tax cost if he leaves the stock to Sylvia under his will. He explains that Sylvia is not likely to sell the stock. Thus, the stock's basis is a moot issue. Prepare projections for the total transfer tax cost of the gift now versus pass on at death scenarios under the assumption that he will die in late 2015 when the stock will be worth $10 million.

C:13-61 Matt Patterson died in early 2015 with a $4.5 million gross estate and no deductions other than a potential marital deduction. He bequeathed all his property to his spouse, Nancy, with the provision that, if Nancy predeceases him, the couple's two adult children will receive the entire property in equal amounts. Nancy survived Matt, but she has a recently diagnosed terminal illness. Nancy's own assets have an estimated $6.1 million fair market value as of Matt's date of death. Her estate will likely have only a minimal amount of deductions. Her current will leaves her property 50% each to the two children. Your manager will soon meet with Nancy, who wants to discuss the implications of disclaiming Matt's bequest to her. Your manager requests that you prepare projections of the combined estate tax liability of Matt and Nancy if Nancy disclaims and does not disclaim. Assume the assets do not appreciate by Nancy's date of death. Nancy requested the projections be based on the assumption that her death will occur near the end of 2015, at the latest.

TAX FORM/RETURN PREPARATION PROBLEMS

C:13-62 Prepare an estate tax return (Form 706) for Marcia Miller, who died July 23, 2014. Marcia (born April 2, 1930) resided at 117 Brandywine Way, Eastern City, PA 19000 and was a lifelong Pennsylvania resident. Her first husband, Arthur Adams, died in 1995. In June 1999, she married Matt Miller, a U.S. citizen, who survived her. Marcia has three children (Andy, Annie, and Archie Adams) from her first marriage.

Date of death values of the properties discovered at Marcia's death are listed below.

- Principal residence with a value of $420,000. Purchased by Marcia in 2001 and titled in the names of Matt and Marcia Miller, joint tenants with right of survivorship.
- Household furnishings acquired by Marcia during her first marriage and valued at $62,000 when she died.
- $1 million cash in a money market account in Marcia's name. On her date of death, there also was $2,200 of accrued interest in the account.
- $17,000 checking account at Keystone State Bank in the names of Marcia and Matt as tenants in common.
- Stock portfolio in Marcia's name with fair market value at her death of $5.6 million.
- $1 million life insurance policy. Marcia purchased the policy in 1990 and held incidents of ownership. Beneficiary is Marcia's estate, and Marcia held incidents of ownership.
- QTIP trust established at Franklin State Bank by Arthur Adams. His executor claimed a 60% marital deduction on the trust, valued then at $750,000. Marcia received all the income monthly for life, and the remainder is to go to the three Adams children in equal shares. The trust was valued at $1.8 million at Marcia's death.
- Trust at Quaker State Bank with value of $500,000. The trust was created under the will of Marcia's uncle, Josh Judson, who died in 1992. Marcia was entitled to receive all the income annually for life and was granted the power to will the property to such of her descendants as she so desired with the specification that, if she did not exercise the power, the property would pass to Josh's former housekeeper, Yvonne Jones.

Marcia's will included the following provisions:

- I bequeath to Matt all of my tangible, personal property.
- To First Lutheran Church I leave $50,000.
- To a trust with PHL Bank I leave $200,000. Matt is to receive all the trust income quarterly for life, and the remainder is to be divided equally at his death among my three children or their estates.
- I leave my sister Annette $100,000, but if she disclaims this amount, it will go instead to my beloved Matthew.
- I appoint the property in the trust at Quaker State Bank to Annie Adams.
- The rest of my property I leave to Andy (my first born).

Other pertinent information follows:

- As of her date of death, Marcia owed her country club $800.
- The cost of Marcia's funeral and tombstone totaled $15,000.
- Her accountant's, attorney's, and executor's fees are estimated to be $120,000.
- Annette made a qualified disclaimer of the $100,000 bequest.
- Marcia's executor, Hy Phee, will make whatever elections will result in the lowest estate tax payable. During her life, Marcia never made any taxable gifts and never consented to gift splitting.
- Assume that, under state law, taxes and any other costs associated with death are payable from the estate's residue and that the state death tax owed is equal to the state death tax credit available on the federal estate tax return.

C:13-63 Prepare an estate tax return (Form 706) for Adam Zugg of 45 Cornfield Place, Midwest City, IL 60000. Adam died October 31, 2014. He was survived by his wife,

Callie, and their son, Zebulon. At the time of his death, Adam was employed by a farm equipment distributor as its office manager. The executor reports that he has discovered the property listed below.

Checking account, Adam and Callie, joint tenants with right of survivorship	$ 10,200
Stocks in public companies in the name of Adam	1,300,000
Undeveloped land (not leased or farmed) in the name of Adam	4,400,000
Qualified retirement plan funded by Adam's employer	800,000
Face value of term life insurance policy on Adam's life	2,000,000
Automobile in Adam's name	22,000

Other information includes the following:

1. Adam owned the life insurance policy, and his estate is the beneficiary.
2. Callie is the beneficiary of the retirement plan.
3. Adam willed his stocks to Callie and the rest of his property to Zebulon.
4. Adam owed $13,200 on a car loan.
5. The estate's administrative expenses were $32,000, and his funeral expenses were $8,000.
6. Assume that the estate paid state estate taxes of $45,000.
7. Adam made his only taxable gift, $6 million in amount, in December 2013 and paid all the gift taxes from an account solely in his name.
8. Assume the estate's marginal income tax rate will be 33%.

CASE STUDY PROBLEMS

C:13-64 Your long-time client, Harold (Hal) Holland will meet with your supervising partner next week for an estate planning appointment. Hal has been married to Winona Holland for 25 years. Hal is age 68 and retired. Winona, age 60, retired early to spend more time with Hal. They are residents of Topeka, Kansas. Hal is a U.S. citizen, and Winona is a citizen of Australia. Winona has indicated she plans to return to Australia if Hal predeceases her. Your supervising partner has requested that you identify any potential pitfalls in Hal's current estate plan so she can bring them to his attention.

Hal has stated that, in addition to providing some wealth transfers to his wife Winona, he wants to treat his three children by his prior marriage (Gina, Halbert, and Julianna) approximately equally in terms of total wealth received from him by gift plus as a result of his death.

Hal and Winona prepared and submitted via e-mail the list of assets shown below.

- Principal residence in Topeka titled in the names of Hal and Winona, joint tenants with right of survivorship; purchased with $280,000 of consideration furnished solely by Winona; fair market value of $400,000.
- Household furnishings in the Topeka house; fair market value of $34,000. Winona owned almost all of these furnishings before she married Hal.
- Portfolio of publicly traded stocks in Hal's name; fair market value of $7.12 million.
- Mountain cabin and land in Vail, Colorado. Hal purchased the property in 1998 for $60,000; fair market value is $460,000. Hal never visits the cabin, but Halbert spends every summer and several weeks during the winter at the cabin.
- Stock (12 shares) in Harold's Hammocks, Inc. (a closely held C corporation) transferred to the Oz State Bank Revocable Trust in 1992; fair market value of $226,000, and basis of $15,000. Hal acquired the 12 shares in 1988 in a Sec. 351 transaction. Julianna and Gina own the remaining stock, 44 shares each, which Hal gifted to them in 2010.
- Individual retirement account at ToKan State Bank. The account consists of the funds rolled directly into the IRA from the non-contributory qualified retirement plan of Hal's former employer when Hal retired. Fair market value of the IRA is $540,000. Hal has not yet received any distributions. He is the IRA beneficiary, and Winona is the contingent beneficiary if Hal predeceases her.
- Cash of $825,000 in checking and savings accounts in Hal's name.
- Mutual fund shares in the names of Hal and Julianna, joint tenants with right of survivorship. Hal provided all the consideration ($9,000); fair market value of $64,000. He intended to use the money to help finance Julianna's education, but she received a full scholarship.

- Stock in Dolrah, Inc. (a firm that elected S corporation status in 1990 upon its formation). The stock is in Hal's name, and he is one of six stockholders; fair market value of his shares was $79,000.

Hal's current will reads as follows:

> To my wife, Winona, I leave outright any household furnishings that I own, $500,000 of stock from my portfolio of publicly traded stocks, and all of my stock in Dolrah, Inc.
>
> To my grandchild, Halbert, Jr., I leave $5,750,000 of publicly traded stock from my portfolio.
>
> I leave the rest of my estate outright in equal shares to my children, Gina, Halbert, and Julianna.

Required:
Prepare a memo to your supervising partner to help her prepare for the appointment with Hal. In the memo, advise the partner of any pitfalls (problems) you have identified that she should discuss with Hal. You need not make any calculations of estate tax liabilities.

C:13-65 Your client is Jon Jake, the executor of the Estate of Beth Adams, a widow. Mrs. Adams died 11 years after the death of her husband, Sam. Mr. Jake seeks assistance in the preparation of the estate tax return for Mrs. Adams, whose estate consists primarily of real estate. Mrs. Adams's estate will be divided among her three adult children except for $50,000 willed to charity. The real estate has been appraised at $6.8 million by her son-in-law (who is married to one of Mrs. Adams's three children), a real estate appraiser. You have a number of real estate clients and have considerable familiarity with property values for real estate located in the same general area as the estate's property. Your "gut feeling" is that the appraised values may be somewhat understated. As a tax advisor, what responsibilities do you have to make additional inquiries? What information should you provide Mr. Jake concerning possible penalties?

TAX RESEARCH PROBLEMS

C:13-66 Arthur Zolnick died at age 84 on June 7, 2014. In March 2008, he transferred $4 million of stock to a charitable remainder annuity trust (CRAT) from which he named himself to receive $200,000 per year for life. He designated a charitable organization to receive the remainder interest after his death and appointed his nephew Luther as trustee. Luther never distributed cash to Arthur because Arthur indicated he had no need for additional funds that "would just add to my gross estate." At Arthur's date of death, the value of the assets in the CRAT had risen to $4.3 million. Another firm prepared the estate tax return, on which it claimed a charitable contribution deduction for the CRAT. The IRS proposed disallowing the deduction. Arthur's executor has asked your firm to address whether a charitable contribution deduction should be available.

C:13-67 In May 2008, Jasper Mason died, survived by his spouse Amber Mason and four adult children. His gross estate was valued at $3 million, and he had Sec. 2053 deductions of $120,000. His will left the personal residence on which the mortgage had been paid off to Amber. Its value was $450,000. The will stated that the rest of Jasper's property was to pass to a trust at Seaman's Bank with Amber to receive all the trust income semi-annually for life and the four children to receive the remainder in equal shares. Amber was the beneficiary of a $1 million life insurance policy included in Jasper's gross estate. The insurance policy was the only non-probate asset. Jasper made no post-1976 taxable gifts. A CPA with a small firm that does not specialize in taxation prepared the estate tax return for Jasper's estate and elected to claim the marital deduction for the trust. The firm with whom you are employed has been engaged to prepare the estate tax return for Amber, who died in May 2015. The Seaman's Bank trust has increased in value to $3 million as of Amber's date of death. Amber owned assets valued at $4 million in her own name. Your manager asks you to research whether the Seaman's Bank trust has to be included in Amber's gross estate. He is hoping that it does not because, even if the marital deduction had not been claimed for the trust, Jasper's estate still would not have owed any tax. Draft a memo to your manager reporting the results of your research. Confine your research to IRS pronouncements.

C:13-68 Gordon Hall and Thomas Settles, a same-sex couple, were legally married in Lenox, MA in June 2012. However, they are residents of a state that does not recognize same-sex marriages. In August 2012, Gordon transferred stock valued at $7 million to Thomas. He filed a gift tax return, under extension, in October 2013. Because of the Defense of Marriage Act (DOMA), he could not claim a marital deduction on the gift and consequently paid a large amount of gift tax in October 2013. This was his first taxable gift. For 2012 and 2013, Gordon and Thomas each filed a federal income tax return in March using the status of "single" taxpayer. Each is in the highest marginal income tax bracket because of large taxable income. Gordon contacted your firm after returning from an extended vacation and inquired whether he is entitled to a refund of the gift tax he paid on the 2012 gift and, if so, the approximate amount of the refund. Write a letter to Gordon in which you address his inquiry.

C:13-69 George Tanner died October 2, 2014, survived by his son Thomas and his daughter Gigi Tanner Stewart and her children, Sam and Cindy. George was the sole stockholder of Tanner, Inc., a C corporation. Gigi served as president of Tanner from its inception until early January 2015. However, she never had an employment agreement or a noncompete agreement with Tanner. George was not involved with the business; he simply provided the funding. Gigi executed all of Tanner's contracts with its customers and was very involved with the business. George's will left half of the Tanner stock to Gigi and the other half to Thomas. In late December 2014, Gigi and Thomas had major disagreements, and soon thereafter Gigi formed a C corporation (GTS, Inc.) to compete with Tanner. Because of the personal relationships Gigi had with Tanner's customers, almost all of them broke their contracts with Tanner and began doing business with GTS. Preparation of George's estate tax return is underway, and one of the estate's major assets is the Tanner stock. A question has arisen whether the valuation of the Tanner stock should take into account the value of Gigi's personal goodwill due to the absence of an employment agreement or a noncompete agreement. If so, the value of her personal goodwill would adversely affect the value otherwise determined for the stock. Your supervisor requested that you research this issue and present your results in a memo so she can discuss the valuation issue with the person who is preparing an appraisal of the Tanner stock.

C:13-70 *Internet Research Problem.* Philip Seymour Hoffman died in February 2014, survived by three children (Cooper, Tallulah, and Willa) and their mother Marianne O'Donnell. His estate is estimated to have a net value of $35 million. Perform a Google search using the words "Philip Seymour Hoffman will" and read the February 20, 2014 article by Deborah L. Jacobs from *Forbes*. Answer the following questions:

a. When did he execute the will?
b. Whom does his will name to receive his property?
c. What marital deduction will his estate receive?
d. If his will provides for a disclaimer, summarize its terms.
e. If Hoffman owned a $10 million life insurance policy on his own life, who will receive the insurance proceeds?

C:13-71 *Internet Research Problem.* Soon you will be meeting with a client who is considering moving to one of several other states and who currently does not have a will. You want to do some research regarding how property often passes if the decedent dies intestate (without a will). The client is married, has no children, has one living parent, and has an estate of approximately $3 million. Go to http://www.uniformlaws.org and consult Section 2-102 of the probate provisions on the site. They describe the "model" rules for property dispositions if this client dies intestate. Prepare a brief memo about what you learn regarding the client's situation.

CHAPTER

14

INCOME TAXATION OF TRUSTS AND ESTATES

LEARNING OBJECTIVES

After studying this chapter, you should be able to

1. Describe the basic concepts concerning trusts and estates
2. Distinguish between the accounting concepts of principal and income
3. Calculate the income tax liability of a trust or an estate
4. Explain the significance of distributable net income
5. Calculate the taxable income of a simple trust
6. Calculate the taxable income of a complex trust and an estate
7. Recognize the significance of income in respect of a decedent
8. Explain the effect of the grantor trust provisions
9. Identify tax planning opportunities in trust and estate income taxation
10. Comply with procedural rules for trust and estate income taxation

CHAPTER OUTLINE

Chapters C:12 and C:13 examined two components of the transfer tax system: the gift tax and the estate tax. This chapter returns to income taxation by exploring the basic rules for taxing trusts and estates, two special tax entities often called **fiduciaries**. Income generated by property owned by an estate or a **trust** is reported on an income tax return for that entity. In general, the tax rules governing estates and trusts are identical. Unless the text states that a rule applies to only one of these entities, the discussion concerns both estates and trusts. Subchapter J (Secs. 641-692) of the IRC contains the special tax rules applicable to estates and trusts, and this chapter describes its basic provisions.

This chapter also discusses principles of fiduciary accounting, a concept that influences the tax consequences. The chapter focuses on determining the fiduciary's taxable income and the amount taxable to the beneficiaries. It includes comprehensive examples concerning the computations of taxable income, and Appendix B displays completed tax returns (Form 1041) for both a simple and a complex trust. The chapter also explores the circumstances that cause the grantor (transferor) to be taxed on the trust's income.

BASIC CONCEPTS

OBJECTIVE 1

Describe the basic concepts concerning trusts and estates

INCEPTION OF TRUSTS

Often a very wealthy person (one concerned with gift and/or estate taxes) will create trusts for tax and/or other reasons (e.g., conserving assets). A person may create a trust at any point in time by transferring property to the trust. A **trustee** (named by the transferor) administers the trust property for the benefit of the beneficiary. The trustee may be either an individual or an institution, such as a bank, and there can be more than one trustee.

If the transfer occurs during the transferor's lifetime, the trust is called an **inter vivos trust**, meaning among the living. The transferor is known as the **grantor** or the **trustor**. A trust created under the direction of a decedent's will is called a **testamentary trust** and contains assets formerly held by the decedent's estate. A trust may continue to exist for whatever time the trust instrument or the will specifies, subject to the constraints of the **Rule Against Perpetuities.**[1]

INCEPTION OF ESTATES

REAL-WORLD EXAMPLE

The IRS projects that 3.2 million fiduciary income tax returns will be filed in 2015.

Estates originate only upon the death of the person whose assets are being administered. The estate continues in existence until the executor[2] (i.e., the person(s) named in the will to manage the property and distribute the assets) or administrator (where the decedent died without a will) completes his or her duties. An executor's or administrator's duties include collecting the assets, paying the debts and taxes, and distributing the property. The time needed to perform the duties may vary from a year or two to over a decade, depending on many factors (e.g., whether anyone contests the will).

Because the estate is a separate tax entity, continuing the estate's existence results in an additional personal exemption and achieves having some income taxed to yet another taxpayer, but the estate's income tax rates are very compressed. Nevertheless, the decedent's survivors sometimes can reduce their personal income taxes by preserving the estate's existence as a separate taxpayer. Treasury Regulations provide, however, that if the IRS considers that the administration of an estate has been unreasonably prolonged, it will view the estate as having been terminated for federal tax purposes after a reasonable period for performance of the administrative duties has expired.[3] In such a situation, the income is taxed directly to the individuals entitled to receive the estate's assets, and sometimes these individuals have a higher marginal tax rate than does the estate.

---

[1] The Rule Against Perpetuities addresses how long property may be tied up in trust and is the "principle that no interest in property is good unless it must vest, if at all, not later than 21 years, plus period of gestation, after some life or lives in being at time of creation of interest." Henry Campbell Black, *Black's Law Dictionary,* Rev. 6th ed., Ed. by Joseph R. Nolan and Jacqueline M. Nolan-Haley (St. Paul, MN: West Publishing Co., 1990), p. 1331. Some states have abolished the Rule Against Perpetuities.

[2] In some states, this individual is called a personal representative.

[3] Reg. Sec. 1.641(b)-3(a).

REASONS FOR CREATING TRUSTS

A myriad of reasons—both tax and nontax—exist for creating trusts. A discussion of some of these reasons follows.

KEY POINT

A trust is a contract between two parties: the grantor and the trustee. The grantor gives the trustee legal title to property, which the trustee holds for the benefit of a third party(ies), the beneficiary(ies). The trustee, acting in a fiduciary capacity, manages the property for the duration of the trust. Beneficiaries may have an income interest, which means that they receive part or all of the trust's income, or they may have a remainder interest, which means that they will receive the trust property on some specified future date. A beneficiary may hold both an income interest and a remainder interest. The grantor may also be a beneficiary and/or the trustee.

Tax Saving Aspects of Trusts. If the trust is irrevocable, meaning the grantor cannot require the trustee to return the assets, one of the primary tax purposes for establishing the trust traditionally was to achieve income splitting, whereby the income from the trust assets was taxed to at least one taxpayer (i.e., the trust or the beneficiary) at a lower marginal tax rate than that of the grantor. Today's compressed fiduciary tax rate schedules, under which the top rate of 39.6% (in 2015) occurs at an income level above $12,300, often make achieving income tax reduction difficult. Sometimes the trust instrument grants the trustee discretion in "sprinkling" the income among several beneficiaries or accumulating it within the trust. In such circumstances, the trustee may consider the tax effects of making a distribution of income to one beneficiary rather than to another or retaining income in the trust.

Individuals also have created trusts to minimize their estate taxes. As discussed in Chapter C:13, for the transferor to exclude the property conveyed to the trust from the gross estate, the transferor must not retain the right to receive the trust income or the power to control which other people receive the income or have, at the time of death, the power to alter the identity of anyone named earlier to receive such assets.[4]

Nontax Aspects of Trusts. Reduction of taxes is not always the foremost reason for establishing trusts. Individuals, some of whom are very wealthy, often use trusts, including Sec. 2503(c) trusts and *Crummey* trusts, when minors are the donees so that a trustee can manage the assets. (See Chapter C:12 for a discussion of such trusts.) Even when the donee is an adult, donors sometimes may prefer that the assets be managed by a trustee deemed to have better management skills than the donee. Other donors may want to avoid conveying property directly to a donee if they fear the donee would soon consume most of the assets. In addition, donors sometimes use trusts to protect assets from creditors.

The creation of a **revocable trust** (i.e., one in which the grantor may demand that the assets be returned) does not yield any income or estate tax savings for the grantor. Nevertheless, donors often establish revocable trusts, including ones in which the grantor is also the beneficiary, for nontax purposes such as having the property managed by another person or an institution with superior management skills. Use of a revocable trust reduces probate costs because assets in a revocable trust avoid probate. Such a strategy is especially important in states where probate costs are high. In this text, a trust is deemed to be an **irrevocable trust** unless explicitly denoted as being revocable.

ADDITIONAL COMMENT

Estates and trusts potentially owe the 3.8% incremental tax on net investment income, but the inception point for this tax is at a much lower amount than it is for individuals. The tax is levied on the lesser of (1) the entity's undistributed net investment income or (2) its modified adjusted gross income (MAGI) in excess of the amount at which the top tax rate of 39.6% begins ($12,300 in 2015). MAGI is AGI reduced by the personal exemption, expenses that would not have been incurred if the property were not held by an estate or trust, and the distribution deduction. Net investment income includes, among other things, interest, dividends, annuities, royalties, rents, and net gains from certain property dispositions, all reduced by allocable deductions.

BASIC PRINCIPLES OF FIDUCIARY TAXATION

Throughout the rest of this chapter, you should keep several basic principles of **fiduciary taxation** in mind. These features (discussed below) apply to all trusts other than grantor trusts, a type of trust where generally the grantor instead of the trust or the beneficiary pays tax on the income. (See pages C:14-30 through C:14-33 for a description of the tax treatment of grantor trusts.)

Trusts and Estates as Separate Taxpayers. An estate or a trust is a separate taxpaying entity that files a Form 1041, and if it has any taxable income, it pays an income tax. The 2015 tax rates applicable to estates and trusts appear on the inside back cover. These rates, which are indexed annually for inflation, are very compressed in comparison with the rates for individuals. As is true for individuals, an estate's or trust's long-term capital gains and qualified dividends are taxed at a maximum rate of 15% or 20% depending on the entity's tax bracket. Also, see the adjoining Additional Comment.

[4] Sec. 2036, relating to retention of income or control, and Sec. 2038, relating to the power to alter the identity of beneficiaries.

EXAMPLE C:14-1 ▶ For calendar year 2015, a trust reports taxable income of $15,000, all from interest on corporate bonds. Its tax liability is $4,249, ignoring the 3.8% tax on net investment income. In contrast, an unmarried individual not qualifying as a head of household would owe taxes of $1,789 on $15,000 of taxable income. Assuming that MAGI also is $15,000, the additional tax on the trust net investment income is $103 [($15,000 − $12,300) × 0.038]. ◀

No Double Taxation. Unlike the situation for corporations, no double taxation of income earned by an estate or trust (a fiduciary taxpayer) occurs because an estate or trust receives a deduction for the income it distributes to its beneficiaries. The beneficiaries, in turn, report the taxable portion of their receipts as income on their individual returns. Thus, the current income is taxed once, to the fiduciary or to the beneficiary or some to each, depending on how much is distributed. In total, all the estate or trust's current income is taxed, sometimes some to the fiduciary and the remaining amount to the beneficiary. One of the primary purposes of the Subchapter J rules is to address exactly where the estate or trust's current income is taxed.

EXAMPLE C:14-2 ▶ In the current year, the Lopez Trust receives corporate bond interest of $25,000, $15,000 of which the trustee in its discretion distributes to Lupe. Lupe is taxed on $15,000, the amount of the distribution. The trust is taxed on the income it retains or accumulates, $10,000 in this case, less a $100 personal exemption (discussed on pages C:14-9 and C:14-10). ◀

Conduit Approach. A conduit approach governs fiduciary income taxation. Under this approach, the distributed income has the same character in the hands of the beneficiary as it has to the trust. Thus, if the trust distributes nontaxable interest income on state and local bonds, such income retains its tax-free character at the beneficiary level.

EXAMPLE C:14-3 ▶ In the current year, the Lopez Trust receives $15,000 of dividends and $10,000 of nontaxable interest. It distributes all of its receipts to its beneficiary, who is deemed to receive $15,000 of dividend income and $10,000 of nontaxable interest. The 15% tax rate applies to the dividends if the beneficiary's tax bracket exceeds 15%. However, if the beneficiary has low AGI and taxable income, and is in the 15% or lower tax bracket, the 0% tax rate will apply to the dividends. ◀

SELF-STUDY QUESTION

King Trust receives interest on a savings account and distributes it to Anne. Because the trust is treated as a conduit, the interest is reported by Anne as taxable interest. Why might this be important?

ANSWER

For purposes of the 3.8% tax on net investment income and the limitation on the investment interest deduction, the interest from the trust is part of Anne's investment income.For purposes of the passive loss limitations, it is classified as portfolio income.

Similarity to Rules for Individuals. Section 641(b) states "[T]he taxable income of an estate or trust shall be computed in the same manner as in the case of an individual, except as otherwise provided in this part." Sections 641-683 appear in this part (Part I) of Subchapter J. Thus, the tax effect for fiduciaries is the same as for individuals if the provisions of Secs. 641-683 do not specify rules that differ from those applicable for individual taxpayers. Sections 641-683 do not provide any special treatment for interest income from state and local bonds or for state and local tax payments. Consequently, an estate or trust receives an exclusion for state and local bond interest and the same deductions as individuals for state and local taxes. On the other hand, Sec. 642(b) specifies the amount of the personal exemption for fiduciaries. Thus, this subsection preempts the Sec. 151 rule concerning the amount of the personal exemption for individuals.

PRINCIPLES OF FIDUCIARY ACCOUNTING

OBJECTIVE 2

Distinguish between the accounting concepts of principal and income

To better understand the special tax treatment of fiduciary income, especially the determination of to whom the estate or trust's current income is taxed, one needs a general knowledge of the principles of fiduciary accounting. Receipts and disbursements are classified in either the income or principal (corpus) account.

THE IMPORTANCE OF IDENTIFYING INCOME AND PRINCIPAL

When computing taxable income, we generally are concerned with whether a particular item is included in or deducted from gross income. When answering fiduciary tax questions, however, we also need to consider whether an item is classified as principal (corpus) or income for fiduciary accounting purposes. For example, certain items (e.g., interest on state bonds) may constitute fiduciary accounting gross income but are not included in calculating gross income for tax purposes. Other items (e.g., capital gains) are included in gross income but generally classified as principal for fiduciary accounting purposes. If the trust instrument stipulates that the trustee can distribute only income prior to the termination of the trust, the amount of fiduciary accounting income sets the ceiling on the current distribution that the trustee can make to a beneficiary.

One of the most difficult aspects of feeling comfortable with the fiduciary taxation rules is appreciating the difference between fiduciary accounting income and income in the general tax sense. To understand and apply the IRC, one has to know in which context the word *income* is used. Section 643(b) provides guidance for this matter by providing that the word *income* refers to income in the fiduciary accounting context unless other words, such as "distributable net," "undistributable net," "taxable," or "gross," modify the word *income*. In this text, the term **net accounting income** is used to refer to the excess of accounting gross income over expenses charged to accounting income.

Under state law, the definitions in the trust instrument that classify items as principal or income preempt any definitions contained in state statutes. In the absence of definitions in the trust instrument, the applicable state statute controls. For purposes of defining principal and income, many states follow the Uniform Principal and Income Act of 2000 (hereafter referred to as the Uniform Act) in its entirety or with minor modifications.[5]

SELF-STUDY QUESTION

A trust agreement provides that all trust income is to be distributed to Janet until her thirty-fifth birthday, at which time the trust is to terminate and distribute all of its corpus to Joe. Stock is the only property owned by the trust. If the trust sells the stock, is Janet entitled to a distribution equal to the gain?

ANSWER

This question stresses the importance of differentiating between income and principal. The trustee must follow the definitions of income and corpus stated in the trust agreement, or if not there, under state law. Janet receives no distribution if the proceeds are classified as corpus unless the trustee under the Uniform Act makes an adjustment and moves money from corpus to income.

The Uniform Act allows the trustee to make adjustments between the principal and income accounts to the extent the trustee deems them necessary (such as to increase the amount distributable), provided certain additional requirements are met. A trustee, however, will not always deem adjustments necessary. The rationale behind allowing adjustments is grounded in modern portfolio theory. By allowing trustees to transfer cash from the principal to the income account, the Uniform Act enables a trustee to apply prudent investor standards when making investment decisions. If dividends are low because of growth stock investments, the Uniform Act allows the trustee to adjust and transfer some cash to the income account, thereby increasing the amount distributable to a beneficiary entitled to receive nothing but income.

The categorization of a receipt or disbursement as principal or income generally affects the amount that can be distributed and the amount taxed to the fiduciary or the beneficiary. A trustee cannot distribute a receipt that constitutes gross income for tax purposes if it constitutes principal under the fiduciary accounting rules unless the trust instrument authorizes the trustee to distribute principal or unless, under the Uniform Act, the trustee makes adjustments by transferring some cash from principal to income. For example, if a gain is classified as principal and the trustee can distribute only income, the trust is taxed on the gain.

EXAMPLE C:14-4 ▶ In the current year, the Bell Trust collects $18,000 of dividends, classified as accounting income. In addition, it sells stock for a $40,000 capital gain. The trust instrument states that the gain is allocated to principal and does not allow the trustee to make adjustments. The trust instrument requires the trustee to distribute all the trust's income to Beth annually until she reaches age 45. The trust assets are to be held and paid to Beth on her forty-fifth birthday (five years from now). The trustee must distribute $18,000 to Beth in the current year. The capital gain cannot be distributed currently because it is allocated to principal, and the trustee is not empowered to make distributions of principal this year. The trust will pay tax on the gain. ◀

PRINCIPAL AND INCOME: THE UNIFORM ACT

Income Receipts. The Uniform Act defines *income* as amounts received "as current return from a principal asset." It lists income as including rent, interest, and dividends.

[5] The *Uniform Principal and Income Act* (2000) is a model set of rules proposed by the National Conference of Commissioners on Uniform State Laws. States can voluntarily adopt such provisions verbatim or in amended form.

The rules provide details for receipts from the disposition of minerals and other natural resources. A portion (90%) of the receipts from royalties is added to principal so the trustee can use funds to buy other assets to replace income from the depleting assets. The remainder of the royalties constitutes income.

Principal Receipts. ***Principal*** is defined in the Uniform Act as "property held in trust for distribution to a remainder beneficiary when the trust terminates." Among the categories of receipts included in principal are the following: consideration received on the sale or other transfer of principal property, capital gain dividends (from mutual funds), life insurance proceeds, and 90% of royalties received from natural resources.

Expenditures. The Uniform Act provides guidance for expenditures also. Among the important charges that reduce income are the following:

- Ordinary expenses, including regularly recurring property taxes, insurance premiums on property, interest, and ordinary repairs
- One-half the regular compensation of the trustee
- Income tax payable by the trustee levied on receipts classified as income

Some of the significant expenditures chargeable to principal are

- Principal payments on debts
- One-half the regular compensation of the trustee
- Tax based on receipts allocated to principal even if the tax is described as an income tax

As with income, provisions in the trust instrument regarding allocation of principal payments take precedence over state law or the Uniform Act.

EXAMPLE C:14-5 ▶ The governing instrument for the Wang Trust does not define income and principal. The state in question has adopted the Uniform Act. In the current year, the trust reports the following receipts and disbursements:

Dividends	$12,000
Proceeds from sale of stock, including $20,000 of gain	70,000
Trustee's fee	1,000
CPA's fee for preparation of tax return	300

The trust's net accounting income is $11,200 ($12,000 − $500 − $300). The gain on the sale of stock and the remaining sales proceeds constitute corpus. One-half the trustee's fee is charged to income. If the trustee can distribute nothing but income, the maximum distribution is $11,200. ◀

SELF-STUDY QUESTION

Wilson Trust, which owns a commercial building, is required to distribute all of its income each year. The building is leased to a tenant on a net lease, so the trust's only expense is depreciation. The rental income is $25,000, and the depreciation is $11,000. If depreciation is charged to income, the distribution to the income beneficiary will be $14,000, and the trustee will set aside $11,000 of the income for the remainderman. What is the impact if depreciation is chargeable to principal?

ANSWER

The income distribution will be $25,000. If the trust holds the building to the end of its useful life, the building will theoretically "turn to dust" overnight, and the remainderman would receive nothing (as far as the building is concerned) because the trust had no depreciation reserve.

CATEGORIZATION OF DEPRECIATION

The Uniform Act does not provide specific mandates regarding depreciation. Rather, it states that a "trustee may transfer to principal a reasonable amount of the net cash receipts from a principal asset that is subject to depreciation." Thus, the trustee has freedom to decide whether to charge depreciation against income. The Drafting Committee for the Uniform Act indicated that it believed the trustee should have discretion about how to handle depreciation. It added that a "purpose served by transferring cash from income to principal for depreciation is to provide funds to pay the principal of an indebtedness secured by the depreciable property." If depreciation is charged against income, it reduces accounting income and thereby the maximum amount the trustee can distribute to the beneficiary if it can distribute only income. If depreciation is charged against principal, the maximum amount that can be distributed to the income beneficiaries is not reduced by the depreciation deduction. This result is advantageous to the income beneficiary. (See page C:14-9 for a discussion of the tax treatment of depreciation.)

A statement in the trust instrument concerning the accounting treatment for depreciation overrides the discretion granted to the trustee by the Uniform Act.

EXAMPLE C:14-6 ▶ Park Trust, whose trust instrument is silent with respect to depreciation, collects rental income of $17,000 and pays property taxes of $1,000. Its depreciation expense is $4,000. If the trustee does not transfer an amount for depreciation to principal, the trust's net accounting income is $16,000 ($17,000 − $1,000). If the trust instrument mandates current distribution of all the income, the beneficiary receives $16,000. If the trustee transfers $4,000 to principal, the income distribution is limited to $12,000. ◀

Topic Review C:14-1 summarizes the treatment under the Uniform Act of the major receipts and expenditures of fiduciaries. The discussion in the rest of the chapter assumes the Uniform Act governs the trust and that the trustee makes no adjustments from principal to income.

Formula for Taxable Income and Tax Liability

OBJECTIVE 3

Calculate the income tax liability of a trust or an estate

With three major exceptions, the formula for determining a fiduciary's taxable income and income tax liability is very similar to the formula applicable to individuals. A fiduciary's deductions are not divided between deductions *for* and *from* adjusted gross income (AGI). Instead, a fiduciary's deductions are simply deductible in arriving at taxable income. A fiduciary receives no standard deduction. A type of deduction unique to fiduciaries—the distribution deduction—is available in computing a fiduciary's taxable income. Figure C:14-1 illustrates the formula for computing a fiduciary's taxable income and tax liability.

Gross Income

The items included in a trust or estate's gross income are the same as those included in an individual's gross income. However, the categorization of a fiduciary's income is not identical for tax and accounting purposes. For example, a gain usually constitutes principal for accounting purposes, but it is part of gross income for tax purposes.

EXAMPLE C:14-7 ▶ In the current year, Duke Trust receives $8,000 interest on corporate bonds, $20,000 interest on state bonds, and a $50,000 capital gain. The trust reports gross income of $58,000 ($8,000 + $50,000). Its accounting income is $28,000 ($8,000 + $20,000) because tax-exempt interest is accounting income, and the gain is generally part of principal. ◀

Deductions for Expenses

Fiduciaries incur numerous deductible expenses that parallel those of individuals and include interest, taxes (e.g., state and local income taxes and property taxes), fees for tax return preparation, expenses associated with producing rental income, and trade or business expenses. In addition, fiduciaries may deduct some or all of the trustee's fee under Sec. 212 as an expense incurred for the management of property held for the production of income.

TOPIC REVIEW C:14-1

Classification of Receipts and Expenditures as Principal or Income Under the Uniform Act of 2000

Income Account	Principal Account
Income:	Receipts:
Rent	Consideration (including gains) received upon disposition of property
Interest	Capital gain dividends from mutual funds
Dividends	90% of royalties
10% of royalties	Life insurance proceeds
Expenses:	Expenditures:
Ordinary expenses (e.g., property taxes, insurance, interest, and ordinary repairs)	Principal payments on debt
Taxes levied on accounting income	Taxes levied on gains and other items of principal

Note that the Uniform Act gives the trustee discretion whether to charge depreciation to income.

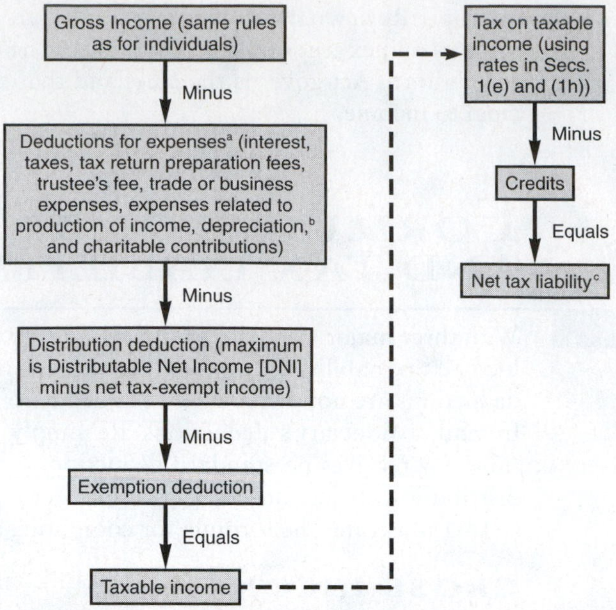

[a] No deduction is available for expenses allocable to tax-exempt income.

[b] When the trust instrument is silent, depreciation is allocated for tax purposes between the fiduciary and the beneficiary according to the portion of income attributable to each.

[c] Trusts and estates are subject to the alternative minimum tax (AMT). The AMT may be owed by a trust or estate in addition to the income tax levy described in this figure. The AMT is calculated in the same way as for individual taxpayers. Trusts and estates, however, are allowed only a $23,800 statutory exemption in 2015. The phase-out for the exemption begins at $79,450.

FIGURE C:14-1 ▶ FORMULA FOR DETERMINING THE TAXABLE INCOME AND TAX LIABILITY OF A FIDUCIARY

For individuals, miscellaneous itemized deductions are deductible only to the extent they exceed 2% of AGI. Section 67(e) provides that a hypothetical AGI amount for an estate or trust is determined in the same fashion as for an individual *except* that (1) expenses paid or incurred in connection with the administration of the estate or trust *that would not have been incurred if the property were not held in such trust or estate,* (2) the personal exemption, and (3) the distribution deduction are treated as deductible for hypothetical AGI. Thus, these deductions, such as the cost of preparing a fiduciary return, are not subject to the 2% floor. Controversy arose about whether investment counsel fees paid by trusts were subject to the 2% floor. The Supreme Court in *Knight*[6] concluded that, to escape the 2% rule, the costs must be "uncommon, unusual, or unlikely" for an individual to incur. It emphasized that individuals commonly engage investment advisers and concluded that the fees in question were subject to the 2% floor. The IRS stated that it would allow bundled trustee's fees (where there are no details of the amount billed for each service) to be fully deductable even if some of the fee was for services normally subject to the 2% floor if paid to an investment advisory firm.[7] This treatment applied to any tax year beginning before final Treasury Regulations were published.[8] For tax years beginning after 2014, Reg. Sec. 1.67-4 provides that, in general, investment advisory fees are subject to the 2% floor but that "certain incremental costs of investment advice beyond the amount that would be charged to an individual investor are not subject to the 2% floor." This regulation states that, if bundled fees for various services are not computed on an hourly basis, "only the portion of that fee that is attributable to investment advice is subject to the 2% floor." For simplicity, this chapter assumes that all trustee fees are exempt from classification as a miscellaneous itemized deduction.

---

[6] *Knight vs. Comm.*, 101 AFTR 2d 2008-544, 2008-1 USTC ¶50,332 (USSC, 2008). Prior to the Supreme Court's decision, the Treasury Department issued Prop. Reg. 1.67-4, which adopted a harsher position than that of the Supreme Court. It provided that miscellaneous expenses incurred by estates and trusts need to be expenses *unique* to estates and trusts to avoid the 2% floor rule. The Treasury Department issued final Treasury Regulations in 2014.

[7] Notice 2010-32, 2010-16 I.R.B. 594.

[8] Notice 2011-37, 2011-20 I.R.B. 652.

An executor can deduct administration expenses on the estate's income tax return if he or she does not deduct such items on the estate tax return. Unlike the situation for individuals, a fiduciary's charitable contribution deduction is not limited. The IRC does not allow a deduction, however, unless the trust instrument authorizes a charitable contribution.[9]

A depreciation or depletion deduction is available to an estate or trust only to the extent it is not allowable to beneficiaries under Secs. 167(d) or 611(b).[10] According to Sec. 167(d), the depreciation deduction for trusts is apportioned between the income beneficiaries and the trust pursuant to the terms of the trust instrument. If the instrument is silent, the depreciation is divided between the parties on the basis of the trust income allocable to each. For estates, however, the depreciation always must be apportioned according to the share of the income allocable to each party. The Sec. 611(b) rules for depletion parallel those described above for the allocation of depreciation.

EXAMPLE C:14-8 ▶ In the current year, Nunn Trust distributes 20% of its income to Bob and 50% to Clay. It accumulates the remaining 30%. The trust's current year depreciation is $10,000. The trust instrument is silent concerning the depreciation deduction, and the trustee exercised discretion to charge depreciation to principal. Even though net accounting income and the maximum distributable amount are not reduced by the depreciation deduction, Bob receives a $2,000 (0.20 × $10,000) depreciation deduction, and Clay receives a $5,000 (0.50 × $10,000) depreciation deduction. The remaining $3,000 (0.30 × $10,000) of depreciation is deducted in calculating the trust's taxable income. ◀

DISTRIBUTION DEDUCTION

Simple Trusts. Some trusts must distribute all their income currently and are not empowered to make charitable contributions. Treasury Regulations refer to such trusts as **simple trusts.**[11] According to Sec. 651(a), these trusts receive a distribution deduction for the income required to be distributed currently, that is, 100% of the trust income. No words modify the word *income;* therefore, *income* means accounting income. If the accounting income that must be distributed exceeds the trust's distributable net income, the distribution deduction may not exceed the distributable net income (see discussion beginning on page C:14-10). As used in this context, distributable net income does not include any tax-free income (net of related deductions) that the trust earned.[12] Whatever amount is deductible at the trust level is taxed to the beneficiaries, and they are taxed on all the income, irrespective of the amount they receive.

KEY POINT

If a trust *must* distribute all of its income currently, has no charitable beneficiary, *and* does *not* distribute corpus during the year, it is a simple trust for that year. *Income* as used here, is accounting net income.

Complex Trusts. Trusts that are not required to distribute all their income currently are referred to as **complex trusts.**[13] The distribution deduction for complex trusts and all estates is the sum of the income required to be distributed currently and any other amounts (such as discretionary payments) properly paid, credited, or required to be distributed for the year. As is the case for simple trusts, the distribution deduction may not exceed the trust or estate's distributable net income (reduced by its tax-exempt income net of any related deductions).[14] The complex trust or estate's beneficiaries report, in the aggregate, gross income equal to the amount of the distribution deduction.[15]

EXAMPLE C:14-9 ▶ Green Trust must distribute 25% of its income annually to Amy. In addition, the trustee in its discretion may distribute additional income to Amy or Brad. In the current year, the trust has net accounting income and distributable net income of $100,000, none from tax-exempt sources. The trust makes a $25,000 mandatory distribution to Amy and discretionary distributions of $10,000 each to Amy and Brad. The trust's distribution deduction is $45,000 ($25,000 + $10,000 + $10,000). Amy and Brad report trust income of $35,000 and $10,000, respectively, on their individual returns. ◀

PERSONAL EXEMPTION

One of the differences between the rules for individuals and for fiduciaries is the amount of the personal exemption. Under Sec. 151, individuals are allowed personal exemptions. Section 642(b) authorizes an exemption for fiduciaries that applies in lieu of the amount for individuals. A trust or estate, however, receives no exemption in the year of its termination.

---

9 Sec. 642(c)(1).
10 Sec. 642(e).
11 Reg. Sec. 1.651(a)-1.
12 Sec. 651(b).
13 Reg. Sec. 1.661(a)-1.
14 Secs. 661(a) and (c).
15 Sec. 662(a).

Estates are entitled to a $600 exemption. The exemption amount for trusts differs, depending on the terms of the trust. If the trust instrument requires that the trustee distribute all the income annually, the trust receives a $300 exemption. Otherwise, $100 is the exemption amount. Some trusts may be required to make current distributions of all their income in certain years, whereas in other years they may be directed to accumulate the income or to make distributions at the trustee's discretion. For such trusts the exemption amount is $300 in some years and $100 in other years.

EXAMPLE C:14-10 ▶ Marion Gold establishes a trust in 2012 with Jack Silver as the beneficiary. The trust instrument instructs the trustee to make discretionary distributions of income to Jack during the years 2012 through 2016. Beginning in 2017, the trustee is to pay all the trust income to Jack currently. For 2012 through 2016, the trust's exemption is $100. Beginning in 2017, it rises to $300. ◀

Recall that a trust receives a distribution deduction for income currently distributed to its beneficiaries. At first blush, it appears that the distribution deduction balances out the income of trusts that must distribute all their income currently, and such trusts receive no tax benefits from their exemption deduction. True, the exemption produces no tax savings for such trusts if they have no gains credited to principal. Tax savings do result from the personal exemption, however, if the trust has undistributed gains. The exemption reduces the amount of gain otherwise taxed at the trust level.

EXAMPLE C:14-11 ▶ Rizzo Trust must distribute all of its income currently. Capital gains are characterized as principal. In the current year, Rizzo Trust has $25,000 of interest income from corporate bonds and a $10,000 capital gain. It has no expenses. It receives a distribution deduction of $25,000 and a $300 personal exemption. Its taxable income is $9,700 ($25,000 + $10,000 − $25,000 − $300), which represents the capital gain less the personal exemption. ◀

SELF-STUDY QUESTION

A trust, although not required to do so, distributes all of its income in the current year. In the same year, it has a long-term capital gain. The trust agreement allocates the gain to principal. The trust does not distribute corpus, and none of its beneficiaries are charities. Is the trust a simple trust? What is its personal exemption?

ANSWER

It is a complex trust because it is not required to distribute all of its income. The exemption is $100 because distributions are discretionary.

The personal exemption amount for individuals is adjusted annually for changes in the consumer price index, but no comparable provision exists for the personal exemption for fiduciaries. On the other hand, the tax rate schedules for both fiduciaries and individuals are indexed for inflation.

CREDITS

In general, the rules for tax credits for fiduciaries are the same as those for individuals, but a fiduciary generally does not incur expenditures of the type that trigger some of the personal credits, such as the credit for household and dependent care expenses. Trusts and estates are allowed a foreign tax credit determined in the same manner as for individual taxpayers except that the credit is limited to the amount of foreign taxes not allocable to the beneficiaries.[16]

U.S. PRODUCTION ACTIVITIES DEDUCTION

The 2004 Jobs Act added a new deduction for businesses engaged in U.S. production activities for tax years beginning after 2004. Chapter C:3 describes the corporate version of this deduction, but the deduction also applies to individuals. In the fiduciary context, the deduction can arise when a sole proprietor dies, and his or her business passes to an estate or trust. To the extent income is distributed from the estate or trust, the U.S. production activities deduction applies at the beneficiary level. Thus, the estate or trust will need to determine each beneficiary's share of the business's qualified production activities income and report these amounts to the beneficiaries. Further discussion of this topic with respect to estates and trusts is beyond the scope of this text.

DISTRIBUTABLE NET INCOME

OBJECTIVE 4

Explain the significance of distributable net income

As stated earlier in this chapter, the primary function of Subchapter J is to determine to whom—the fiduciary, the beneficiary, or some to each—the estate or the trust's current income is to be taxed. **Distributable net income** (DNI) plays a key role in determining the amount taxed to each party. In fact, DNI has been called the pie to be cut for tax purposes.[17]

[16] Sec. 642(a)(1).

[17] M. Carr Ferguson, James L. Freeland, and Richard B. Stephens, *Federal Income Taxation of Estates and Beneficiaries* (Boston, MA: Little, Brown, 1970), p. 1x.

SIGNIFICANCE OF DNI

DNI sets the ceiling on the amount of distributions taxed to the beneficiaries. As mentioned earlier, beneficiaries are taxed on the lesser of the amount of the distributions they receive or their share of DNI (reduced by net tax-exempt income).

Just as the total amount taxed to the beneficiaries equals the fiduciary's distribution deduction, DNI represents not only the maximum that can be taxed to the beneficiaries but also the maximum that can be deducted at the fiduciary level. Recall from the preceding section that the distribution deduction is the smaller of the amount distributed or the fiduciary's DNI. The distribution deduction, however, may not include any portion of tax-exempt income (net of any related deductions) deemed to have been distributed.

DNI also determines the character of the beneficiaries' income. Under the conduit approach, each beneficiary's distribution is deemed to consist of various categories of income (net of deductions) in the same proportion as the total of each class of income bears to the total DNI. For example, if 40% of the trust's income consists of dividends, 40% of each beneficiary's distribution is deemed to consist of dividends.

EXAMPLE C:14-12 ▶ Southern Trust has $30,000 of DNI for the current year. Its DNI includes $10,000 of rental income and $20,000 of corporate bond interest. The trust instrument requires that each year the trustee distribute 30% of the trust's income to Jose and 70% to Petra. Because the trust has no tax-exempt income and must distribute all of its income, it receives a $30,000 distribution deduction.

Jose reports $9,000 (0.30 × $30,000) of trust income, and Petra reports $21,000 (0.70 × $30,000) of trust income. Because rents make up one-third ($10,000 ÷ $30,000) of DNI, the composition of the income reported by Jose and Petra is one-third rental income and two-thirds corporate bond interest. ◀

SELF-STUDY QUESTION

What functions does distributable net income (DNI) serve?

ANSWER

1. It establishes the maximum amount on which the beneficiaries may be taxed.
2. It establishes the maximum amount the trust or estate may deduct as a distribution deduction.
3. It establishes the character of the income or expense in DNI that flows to the beneficiaries (income or expense flows to the beneficiaries in proportion to the part each different type of income or expense bears to DNI).

DEFINITION OF DNI

Section 643(a) defines *DNI* as the fiduciary's taxable income, adjusted as follows:

- No distribution deduction is subtracted.
- No personal exemption is subtracted.
- Capital gains are not included and capital losses are not subtracted unless such gains and losses are allocated to accounting income instead of to principal.
- Extraordinary dividends and taxable stock dividends are not included if they are allocable to principal.
- An addition is made for tax-exempt interest (minus the expenses allocable thereto).

Because one purpose of DNI is to set a ceiling on the distribution deduction, the distribution deduction is not subtracted from taxable income in determining DNI. If capital gains and extraordinary dividends are allocated to corpus, they are excluded from DNI because they cannot be distributed. Tax-exempt interest is part of accounting income and can be distributed even though it is excluded from gross income. Consequently, DNI includes tax-exempt income (net of the nondeductible expenses allocable to such income). Even though net tax-exempt income is included in DNI, no distribution deduction is available for the portion of the distribution deemed to consist of tax-exempt income.

KEY POINT

A significant difference between net accounting income and DNI is that DNI is reduced by certain expenses charged to principal. These expenses do not decrease net accounting income, nor do they decrease the amount of money that can be distributed.

Aside from complicated scenarios, net accounting income and DNI are the same, with one other exception. Any expenses (e.g., trustee's fees) charged to principal reduce DNI even though they do not lessen net accounting income. The trustee's fees (whether charged to income or to principal) are deductible in arriving at taxable income, and no adjustment is made to taxable income for such expenses when calculating DNI. Reducing DNI by the expenses charged to principal provides a tax advantage for the income beneficiary because these fees lessen the amount taxable to the beneficiary. However, such fees do not decrease the money that can be distributed to the beneficiary.

MANNER OF COMPUTING DNI

The amount of taxable income is in large measure a function of the distribution deduction, and the distribution deduction depends on the amount of DNI. The distribution deduction cannot exceed DNI. Thus, the Sec. 643(a) definition of DNI, which involves starting with a fiduciary's taxable income and then making adjustments, is not a workable definition from a practical standpoint because the computation is circular. The distribution deduction must be computed to arrive at the amount of income taxable to the fiduciary, and the distribution deduction depends, in part, on the amount of DNI.

However, there are two practical means of determining DNI. The first approach, as illustrated below, begins with taxable income exclusive of the distribution deduction and makes the adjustments (other than the distribution deduction) to taxable income that the IRC specifies.

EXAMPLE C:14-13 ▶ **In the current year, Darby Trust reports the following results. The trust must distribute all of its income annually and cannot distribute capital gains. The trust instrument requires charging all trustee's fees to principal.**

	Amounts Allocable to	
	Income	*Principal*
Corporate bond interest	$20,000	
Rental income	30,000	
Gain on sale of investment land		$40,000
Property taxes	5,000	
Trustee's fee charged to corpus		2,000
Distribution to beneficiary	45,000	

The trust's taxable income exclusive of the distribution deduction is computed as follows:

Corporate bond interest	$20,000
Rental income	30,000
Capital gain	40,000
Minus: Property taxes	(5,000)
Trustee's fee	(2,000)
Personal exemption	(300)
Taxable income exclusive of distribution deduction	$82,700

Now that taxable income exclusive of the distribution deduction has been determined, DNI can be computed in the following manner:

Taxable income exclusive of distribution deduction	$82,700
Plus: Personal exemption	300
Minus: Capital gain	(40,000)
DNI	$43,000 ◀

A second method that often can be used to determine DNI is to calculate net accounting income and reduce such amount by expenses charged to corpus (e.g., the trustee's fee). In some complicated situations, however, DNI would not be correctly arrived at under this approach, but the discussion of such situations is beyond the scope of this book.

EXAMPLE C:14-14 ▶ **Assume the same facts as in Example C:14-13. The following steps illustrate the second approach to calculating the DNI amount.**

Corporate bond interest	$20,000
Rental income	30,000
Minus: Property taxes	(5,000)
Net accounting income	$45,000
Minus: Trustee's fee charged to corpus	(2,000)
DNI	$43,000 ◀

Although the beneficiary receives a cash distribution of $45,000 (net accounting income), he or she reports only $43,000 (DNI) as income. The beneficiary receives $2,000 tax-free. Thus, an income beneficiary benefits from trustee's fees charged to principal by getting to report a smaller amount of gross income than the amount of cash he or she receives. The trust's distribution deduction cannot exceed $43,000 (DNI) even though the amount paid to the beneficiary exceeds this amount.

Topic Review C:14-2 summarizes the DNI concept.

STOP & THINK

Question: Wei is the beneficiary of a two unrelated simple trusts. From which trust would Wei receive the larger amount of after-tax cash?

- Trust A collects corporate bond interest of $40,000 and pays a trustee's fee of $1,000. The trustee's fee is charged to corpus.
- Trust B collects corporate bond interest of $40,000 and pays a trustee's fee of $800. The trustee's fee is charged to income.

Solution: Wei would receive $40,000 in cash from Trust A but pay federal income taxes on only $39,000, which is the trust's DNI. The trust's distribution is based on net accounting income, which is not reduced by the trustee's fee charged to corpus. Wei's gross income is based on the trust's DNI, which is reduced by the trustee's fee. Wei would receive $39,200 in cash from Trust B. He would pay federal income taxes on the same $39,200 amount, which is the trust's DNI. The trustee's fee paid by Trust B reduces both net accounting income and DNI. Even though the trust's economic income is larger with Trust B, Wei would have a larger amount of after-tax cash flow from Trust A.

DETERMINING A SIMPLE TRUST'S TAXABLE INCOME

OBJECTIVE 5

Calculate the taxable income of a simple trust

The term *simple trust* does not appear in the IRC. Treasury Regulations interpreting Secs. 651 and 652—the statutory rules for trusts that distribute current income only—introduce the term *simple trust*. The provisions of Secs. 651 and 652 govern only trusts whose trust agreements require that all income be distributed currently and do not authorize charitable contributions. Moreover, such provisions are inapplicable if the trust makes distributions of principal.

Some trust instuments may require trusts to pay out all their income currently in certain years but permit them to retain a portion of their income in other years. In some of the years in which the instument mandates distribution of all the income, it also permits distributions of principal. These trusts are simple trusts in some years and complex trusts in others. The amount of the personal exemption, however, turns not on whether the trust is simple or complex but on whether it must pay out all its income currently. Suppose, for

TOPIC REVIEW C:14-2

The Distributable Net Income (DNI) Concept

Significance of DNI

DNI, exclusive of net tax-exempt interest included therein, sets the ceiling on:

1. The distribution deduction, and
2. The aggregate amount of gross income reportable by the beneficiaries.

Calculation of DNI

Taxable income, exclusive of distribution deduction[a]	
Plus:	Personal exemption
Minus:	Capital gains (or plus deductible capital losses)[b]
Plus:	Tax-exempt interest (net of allocable expenses)
Distributable net income (DNI)[c]	

[a]Gross income (dividends, taxable interest, rents, and capital gains) minus deductible expenses and the personal exemption.
[b]In certain situations beyond the scope of this textbook, the trustee's exercise of the power to adjust can result in the inclusion of capital gains in DNI.
[c]Frequently, DNI is the same amount as net accounting income minus trustee's fees charged to corpus.

▼ TABLE C:14-1
Trust Classification Rules and the Size of the Exemption

Situation	Classification	Exemption Amount
Required to pay out all of its income, makes no charitable contributions, distributes no principal	Simple	$300
Required to pay out all of its income, makes no charitable contributions, distributes principal	Complex	$300
Required to pay out all of its income, authorized to make charitable contributions, distributes no principal	Complex	$300
Authorized to make discretionary distributions of income, but not principal, makes no charitable contributions	Complex	$100
Authorized to make discretionary distributions of both income and principal, makes no charitable contributions	Complex	$100

example, a trust must pay out all of its current income and one-fourth of its principal. Because the trust distributes principal, it is a complex trust. It claims a $300 personal exemption because of the mandate to distribute all of its income. Table C:14-1 highlights the trust classification rules and the $300 or $100 exemption dichotomy.

ALLOCATION OF EXPENSES TO TAX-EXEMPT INCOME

Recall that expenses related to producing tax-exempt income are not deductible.[18] Thus, if a trust with income from both taxable and tax-exempt sources incurs expenses that are not directly attributable to the production of taxable income, a portion of such expenses may not be deducted. Regulation Secs. 1.652(b)-3 and 1.652(c)-4(e) address the issue of the allocation of deductions. An expense directly attributable to one type of income, such as a repair expense for rental property, is allocated thereto. Expenses not directly related to a particular item of income, such as a trustee's fee for administering the trust's assets, may be allocated to any type of income included in computing DNI, provided a portion of the expense is allocated to nontaxable income. Regulation Sec. 1.652(b)-3 sets forth the following formula for determining the amount of indirect expenses allocable to nontaxable income:

$$\frac{\text{Tax-exempt income (net of expenses directly attributable thereto)}}{\text{Accounting income (net of all direct expenses)}^{19}} \times \text{Expenses not directly attributable to any item of income} = \text{Indirect expenses allocable to nontaxable income}$$

EXAMPLE C:14-15 ▶ In the current year, the Mason Trust reports the following results:

Dividends	$16,000
Interest from corporate bonds	6,000
Tax-exempt interest from state bonds	18,000
Capital gain (allocated to corpus)	20,000
Trustee's fee, all allocated to corpus	4,000

[18] Sec. 265(a)(1).

[19] A discrepancy exists in the Treasury Regulations with respect to how to allocate expenses to tax-exempt income. According to Reg. Sec. 1.652(b)-3(b), the denominator is accounting income net of direct expenses. Regulation Sec. 1.652(c)-4(e), however, shows computations where the denominator is accounting income unreduced by direct expenses. The text uses the latter approach.

SELF-STUDY QUESTION

A trust can allocate indirect expenses arbitrarily (after the appropriate allocation is made to tax-exempt income). Hill Trust has rental income, taxable interest income, and dividend income. Its sole beneficiary has unused passive rental losses of her own. To which income would you suggest allocating the trustee's fee?

ANSWER

If possible, the trust should take into consideration the tax status of its beneficiaries. The trust should maximize passive rental income and not allocate the fee to its rental income. Moreover, because of the low tax rate on dividends, the trust should allocate the fee against interest income.

Accounting gross income is \$40,000 (\$16,000 + \$6,000 + \$18,000). The trustee's fee is an indirect expense that must be allocated to the tax-exempt income as follows:

$$\frac{\$18,000}{\$40,000} \times \$4,000 = \$1,800$$

Thus, the Mason Trust cannot deduct \$1,800 of its \$4,000 trustee's fee. The remaining \$2,200 may be allocated to dividends or corporate bond interest in whatever amounts the return preparer selects. Because of the low tax rate on dividends, allocating the fee to the higher taxed interest income would reduce taxes. The 3.8% tax on net investment income also is a factor for consideration in making the allocation. ◄

DETERMINATION OF DNI AND THE DISTRIBUTION DEDUCTION

As mentioned above, DNI is defined as taxable income with several adjustments, including a subtraction for capital gains credited to principal. As described earlier, a practical technique for determining DNI involves beginning with taxable income exclusive of the distribution deduction. Once DNI has been determined, both the distribution deduction and the trust's taxable income can be calculated.

A simple trust must distribute all of its net accounting income currently. Thus, a simple trust generally receives a distribution deduction equal to the amount of its net accounting income.[20] The following two exceptions modify this general rule:

- The distribution deduction may not exceed DNI. Therefore, if a trust has expenses that are charged to corpus (as in Example C:14-13), the distribution deduction is limited to the DNI amount because DNI is smaller than net accounting income.
- Because tax-exempt income is not included in the trust's gross income, no distribution deduction is available for tax-exempt income (net of the expenses allocable thereto) included in DNI.[21]

TAX TREATMENT FOR BENEFICIARY

The aggregate gross income reported by the beneficiaries equals the trust's net accounting income, subject to the constraint that the aggregate of their gross income amount does not exceed the trust's DNI. If DNI is lower than net accounting income and the trust has more than one beneficiary, each beneficiary's share of gross income is the following fraction of total DNI:[22]

$$\frac{\text{Income required to be distributed to such beneficiary}}{\text{Income required to be distributed to all beneficiaries}}$$

The income received by the beneficiaries retains the character it had at the trust level. Thus, if the trust receives tax-exempt interest, the beneficiaries are deemed to have received tax-exempt interest. Unless the trust instrument specifically allocates particular types of income to certain beneficiaries, each beneficiary is viewed as receiving income consisting of the same fraction of each category of income as the total of such category bears to total DNI.

EXAMPLE C:14-16 ►

In the current year, Crane Trust collects \$22,000 of tax-exempt interest and \$66,000 of dividends and pays \$8,000 of trustee's fees from corpus. Its net accounting income is \$88,000, and its DNI is \$80,000: \$20,000 of net tax-exempt interest and \$60,000 of net dividends. The trust instrument requires distribution of one-eighth of the income annually to Matt and the remaining seven-eighths of the income to Pat. The cash distributions to Matt and Pat are \$11,000 and \$77,000, respectively. The distribution deduction and the aggregate gross income of the beneficiaries are limited to \$60,000 (\$80,000 DNI − \$20,000 net tax-exempt interest). Matt and Pat will report gross income of \$7,500 (0.125 × \$60,000) and \$52,500 (0.875 × \$60,000), respectively. Dividends make up 75% (\$60,000 ÷ \$80,000) of DNI and 100% (\$60,000 ÷ \$60,000) of taxable DNI. Therefore, all of Matt's and Pat's *gross* income is deemed to consist of dividends. Matt and Pat also are deemed to receive \$2,500 (0.125 × \$20,000) and \$17,500 (0.875 × \$20,000), respectively, of tax-exempt interest. ◄

---

[20] Sec. 651(a).

[21] Sec. 651(b).

[22] Sec. 652(a).

Because a simple trust must distribute all of its income currently, trustees cannot defer the taxation of trust income to the beneficiaries by postponing distributions until the next year. Beneficiaries of simple trusts are taxed currently on their pro rata share of taxable DNI regardless of the amount distributed to them during the year.[23]

SHORTCUT APPROACH TO PROVING CORRECTNESS OF TAXABLE INCOME

A shortcut approach may be used to verify the correctness of the amount calculated as a simple trust's taxable income. Because a simple trust must distribute all of its income currently, the only item taxable at the trust level should be the amount of gains (net of losses) credited to principal, reduced by the personal exemption. The taxable income calculated under the shortcut approach should equal the taxable income determined under the formula illustrated in Figure C:14-1. The steps of the shortcut approach are as follows:

1. Start with the excess of gains over losses credited to principal.
2. Subtract the $300 personal exemption.

EXAMPLE C:14-17 ▶ In the current year, West Trust, which must distribute all of its income currently, reports $25,000 of corporate bond interest, a $44,000 long-term capital gain, and a $4,000 long-term capital loss. Under the shortcut approach, the test-check calculation of its taxable income is $39,700 [($44,000 − $4,000) − $300 personal exemption]. On its tax return, the trust reports $25,000 of gross income from interest, $40,000 from net long-term capital gains, a $25,000 distribution deduction, a $300 exemption, and $39,700 of taxable income. ◀

EFFECT OF A NET OPERATING LOSS

If a trust incurs a net operating loss (NOL), the loss does not pass through currently to the beneficiaries unless the loss arises in the year the trust terminates, but the trust can carry the NOL back and forward. In determining the amount of the NOL, deductions are not allowed for charitable contributions or the distribution deduction.[24] In the year a trust terminates, any loss that would otherwise qualify for a loss carryover at the trust level passes through to the individual return(s) of the beneficiary(ies) succeeding to the trust's property.[25]

EXAMPLE C:14-18 ▶ In 2015, the year it terminates, New Trust incurs a $10,000 NOL. It also has a $40,000 NOL carryover from 2013 and 2014. At termination, New Trust distributes 30% of its assets to Kay and 70% to Liz. Because 2015 is the termination year, Kay may report a $15,000 (0.30 × $50,000) NOL on her 2015 return, and Liz may report a $35,000 (0.70 × $50,000) NOL on her 2015 return. Before 2015, the beneficiaries cannot report any of the trust's NOLs on their returns. ◀

EFFECT OF A NET CAPITAL LOSS

The maximum capital loss that a trust can deduct is the lesser of $3,000 or the excess of its capital losses over capital gains.[26] Because simple trusts must distribute all of their accounting income currently and the distribution deduction reduces their taxable income to zero, they receive no current tax benefit from capital losses that exceed capital gains. Nevertheless, the trust's taxable income for the year of the loss is reduced by its net capital loss, up to $3,000. In determining the capital loss carryover, capital losses that produced no tax benefit are available as a carryover to offset capital gains realized by the trust in subsequent years. In addition, if all of the capital loss carryovers have not been absorbed by capital gains before the trust's termination date, the remaining capital loss is passed through in the termination year to the beneficiaries succeeding to the trust's property.[27]

---

23 Reg. Sec. 1.652(a)-1.

24 Reg. Sec. 1.642(d)-1(b).

25 Reg. Sec. 1.642(h)-1. A trust is never categorized as a simple trust in the year it terminates because in its final year it always makes distributions of principal.

26 Sec. 1211(b).

27 Reg. Sec. 1.642(h)-1.

EXAMPLE C:14-19 ► Lev Trust, which must distribute all of its income currently, sold two capital assets before it terminates. In Year 1, it sold an asset at a $20,000 loss. In Year 2, it sold an asset for a $6,000 gain. In Year 3, it terminates and distributes its assets equally between its two beneficiaries, Joy and Tim. The trust is not a simple trust in Year 3 because it distributes principal that year. Because the $20,000 loss provided no benefit on the Year 1 return, the carryover to Year 2 was $20,000, and $6,000 of it offset Year 2's $6,000 capital gain. The remaining $14,000 carries over to Year 3. Because Year 3 is the termination year, a $7,000 (0.50 x $14,000) capital loss passes through to both Joy's and Tim's individual returns for Year 3. Joy realizes a $12,000 capital gain by selling assets in Year 3. Joy offsets the $7,000 trust loss against her own gain. Tim sells no assets in Year 3. Therefore, Tim deducts $3,000 of the loss from the trust against his other income. His remaining $4,000 loss carries over to Year 4. ◄

SELF-STUDY QUESTION

Why do Treasury Regulations (see footnotes 26 and 27) allow unused NOLs and capital losses to be used by the remainderman on the termination of a trust?

ANSWER

Losses have depleted the corpus of the trust. Because the remainderman's interest has been depleted by these losses, it is reasonable to allow the trust to pass these losses through to the remainderman at the end of its life.

Topic Review C:14-3 describes how to calculate a trust's taxable income.

ADDITIONAL COMMENT

This illustration pertains to 2014 because tax forms for that year are the latest available at the time this textbook was published.

COMPREHENSIVE ILLUSTRATION: DETERMINING A SIMPLE TRUST'S TAXABLE INCOME

The following comprehensive illustration reviews a number of the points discussed previously. The facts for this illustration are used to complete the 2014 Form 1041 for a simple trust that appears in Appendix B.

Background Data. Zeb Brown established the Bob Adams Trust by a gift in 2003. The trust instrument requires that the trustee (First Bank) distribute all of the trust income at least annually to Bob Adams for life and that trustee's fees be paid from principal. Capital gains are credited to principal and cannot be distributed. The 2014 results of the trust are as follows:

	Amounts Allocable to	
	Income	*Principal*
Dividends	$30,000	
Rental income from land	5,000	
Tax-exempt interest	15,000	
Rental expenses (realtor's commission on rental income)	1,000	
Trustee's fee		$ 1,200
Fee for preparation of tax return	500	
Capital gain on sale of stock[a]		12,000
Distribution of net accounting income to Bob	48,500	
Payments of estimated tax		2,600

[a]The trust sold the stock in October for $15,000, having acquired it four years earlier.

TOPIC REVIEW C:14-3

Calculation of Trust Taxable Income

Gross income[a]
Minus: Deductions for expenses[a]
Distribution deduction[b]
Personal exemption ($300 or $100)

Taxable income

[a]Rules for calculating these amounts are generally the same as for individual taxpayers.
[b]Deduction cannot exceed the amount of DNI from taxable sources.

Trustee's Fee. As mentioned earlier, a portion of the trustee's fee is nondeductible because it must be allocated to tax-exempt income. The trust receives $50,000 ($30,000 + $5,000 + $15,000) of gross accounting income, of which $15,000 is tax-exempt. Therefore, $360 [($15,000 ÷ $50,000) × $1,200] of the trustee's fee is allocated to tax-exempt income and is nondeductible. The entire return preparation fee is deductible because no such fee would have been incurred had the trust's income been entirely from tax-exempt sources.

Distribution Deduction and DNI. One of the key amounts affecting taxable income is the distribution deduction. Taxable income exclusive of the distribution deduction is the starting point for determining the amount of DNI, a number crucial in quantifying the distribution deduction. The trust's taxable income, exclusive of the distribution deduction, is calculated as follows:

Dividends		$30,000
Rental income		5,000
Capital gain on sale of stock		12,000
Minus:	Rental expenses	(1,000)
	Deductible portion of trustee's fee	(840)
	Fee for tax return preparation	(500)
	Personal exemption	(300)
Taxable income, exclusive of distribution deduction		$44,360

DNI now can be calculated by making the adjustments shown below to taxable income, exclusive of the distribution deduction.[28]

Taxable income, exclusive of distribution deduction		$44,360
Plus:	Personal exemption	300
Minus:	Capital gain on sale of stock	(12,000)
Plus:	Tax-exempt interest ($15,000), net of $360 of allocable expenses	14,640
DNI		$47,300

Recall that the distribution deduction cannot exceed the DNI, as reduced by tax-exempt income (net of any allocable expenses). Nor can it exceed net accounting income of $48,500 ($30,000 + $5,000 + $15,000 – $1,000 – $500). The distribution deduction may be computed as follows:

Smaller of:	Net accounting income ($48,500) or DNI ($47,300)		$47,300
Minus:	Tax-exempt interest	$15,000	
	Minus: Allocable expenses	(360)	(14,640)
Distribution deduction			$32,660

Trust's Taxable Income and Tax. Once the amount of the distribution deduction is determined, the trust's taxable income and tax can be calculated as illustrated in Table C:14-2.

Categorizing a Beneficiary's Income. Because income reported by the beneficiary retains the character it had at the trust level, the amount of each category of income received by the beneficiary must be determined. Bob is deemed to have received dividends, rents, and tax-exempt interest. Rental expenses are charged entirely against rental income. The deductible portion of the trustee's fee and the tax return preparation fee can be allocated in full to rents or dividends, or some to each. However, because of the low tax rate

28 Another way of determining the amount of DNI in this scenario is to reduce the net accounting income of $48,500 by the $1,200 of expenses charged to principal. The resulting amount is $47,300.

on dividends, the fees should be allocated against the higher taxed rents. Consequently, the character of Bob's income is determined as follows:

	Dividends	*Rents*	*Tax-Exempt Interest*	*Total*
Accounting income	$30,000	$5,000	$15,000	$50,000
Minus: Expenses:				
Rental expenses		(1,000)		(1,000)
Trustee's fee		(840)	(360)	(1,200)
Tax return preparation fee		(500)		(500)
DNI	$30,000	$2,660	$14,640	$47,300

Bob reports $30,000 of dividend income and $2,660 of rental income on his individual return. His dividend income is taxed at the low rate applicable to dividends.

Determining Taxable Income for Complex Trusts and Estates

OBJECTIVE 6

Calculate the taxable income of a complex trust and an estate

The caption to Subpart C of Part I of Subchapter J (Secs. 661-664) reads "Distribution for Estates and Trusts Accumulating or Distributing Corpus." In general, the rules applicable to estates and these trusts (complex trusts) are the same. The IRC does not contain the term *complex trust*, but according to Treasury Regulations, "A trust to which subpart C is applicable is referred to as a 'complex' trust."[29] Recall from the discussion about simple trusts that a trust that must distribute all of its income currently can be classified as a

ADDITIONAL COMMENT

The short-cut approach to computing taxable income used in Table C:14-2 consists of reducing the income allocated to corpus by the personal exemption.

▼ TABLE C:14-2
Comprehensive Illustration: Determining a Simple Trust's Taxable Income and Tax Liability

Gross income:	
Dividends	$30,000
Rental income	5,000
Capital gain on sale of stock	12,000[a]
Minus: Expense deductions:	
Rental expenses	(1,000)
Deductible portion of trustee's fee	(840)
Tax return preparation fee	(500)
Minus: Distribution deduction	(32,660)
Minus: Personal exemption	(300)
Taxable income	$ 11,700[b]
Tax liability on taxable income (2014 rates)	$ 1,380[c]
Minus: Estimated tax payments	(2,600)
Tax owed (refunded)	$ (1,220)

[a]The stock sale took place in October and involved stock purchased four years earlier.
[b]The short-cut approach to verifying taxable income is as follows:

Long-term capital gain	$12,000
Minus: Personal exemption	(300)
Taxable income	$11,700

[c]The taxable income consists of a long-term capital gain, which, in 2014, is taxed at a maximum rate of 0% on the first $2,500 and 15% on the rest. The trust in this situation is not subject to the 3.8% tax on net investment income.

[29] Reg. Sec. 1.661(a)-1.

complex trust for a particular year if it also pays out some principal during the year. Trusts that can accumulate income are categorized as complex trusts, even in years in which they make discretionary distributions of all their income. A trust is a complex trust also if the trust instrument provides for amounts to be paid to, or set aside for, charitable organizations (see Table C:14-1).

Many of the rules are the same for simple and complex trusts, but some differences exist. Different rules apply to determine the distribution deduction for the two types of trusts. The rules for determining an estate's distribution deduction are the same as those applicable to complex trusts. The personal exemption, however, is $600 for an estate and $300 or $100 for a complex trust. The $300 amount applies for years in which a trust must pay out all of its income; otherwise, the exemption is $100.

TAX STRATEGY TIP

Trust managers can reduce overall taxes by carefully planning the amount and timing of distributions. See Tax Planning Considerations later in text for details.

DETERMINATION OF DNI AND THE DISTRIBUTION DEDUCTION

Section 661(a) defines the distribution deduction for complex trusts and estates as the sum of the total current income *required* to be paid out currently plus any other amounts "properly paid or credited or required to be distributed" (i.e., discretionary distributions) to the beneficiary during the year. If the fiduciary can make mandatory distributions from either the income or the principal account, distributions are treated as "current income required to be paid" if paid out of the trust's income account; thus, some of the income is taxed to the beneficiary. Like simple trusts, the amount of the trust's DNI limits the amount of the distribution deduction.

EXAMPLE C:14-20 ▶ In the current year, Able Trust has net accounting income and DNI of $30,000, all from taxable sources. It makes a $15,000 mandatory distribution of income to Kwame and a $4,000 discretionary distribution to Kesha. Its distribution deduction is computed as follows:

Income required to be distributed currently	$15,000
Plus: Other amounts properly paid, etc.	4,000
Tentative distribution deduction	$19,000
DNI	$30,000
Distribution deduction (lesser of tentative distribution deduction or DNI)	$19,000 ◀

As is the case for simple trusts, an additional constraint applies to the amount of the distribution deduction. No distribution deduction is allowed with respect to tax-exempt income (net of allocable expenses).

EXAMPLE C:14-21 ▶ Assume the same facts as in Example C:14-20 except that net accounting income and DNI consist of $20,000 of corporate bond interest and $10,000 of tax-exempt interest. Because one-third ($10,000 ÷ $30,000) of the DNI is from tax-exempt sources, tax-exempt income is deemed to make up one-third of the distributions. Thus, the distribution deduction is only $12,667 (0.667 × $19,000). ◀

If a trust makes charitable contributions, DNI is not reduced by the charitable contribution deduction when determining the maximum distribution deduction available for mandatory distributions. However, DNI is reduced by the charitable contribution deduction when calculating the deduction for discretionary distributions.

EXAMPLE C:14-22 ▶ Assume instead that Kwamsha Trust has net accounting income (all from taxable sources) and DNI (exclusive of the charitable contribution deduction) of $16,000. The trust makes a $15,000 mandatory distribution to Kwame and a $4,000 mandatory distribution to Kesha. In accordance with its trust instrument, the trust pays $3,000 to a charitable organization.

Tentative distribution deduction (required distributions)	$19,000
DNI (excluding charitable contribution deduction)	16,000
Distribution deduction (lesser of tentative distribution deduction or DNI)	16,000

If the distributions to both Kwame and Kesha were discretionary, the $3,000 charitable contribution would be deductible by the trust and, in determining the maximum distribution deduction, would reduce DNI to $13,000, thereby limiting the distribution deduction to $13,000. Thus, in total, the beneficiaries would report $3,000 ($16,000 − $13,000) less gross income than if the distributions were mandatory. ◀

TAX TREATMENT FOR BENEFICIARY

KEY POINT

Distributions to beneficiaries retain the character that the income has at the fiduciary level; for example, the character of rents, interest, dividends, or tax-exempt income flows through to the beneficiary.

General Rules. In general, the amount of distributions from estates or complex trusts includible in a beneficiary's gross income equals the sum of income required to be distributed currently to the beneficiary plus any other amounts properly paid or credited, or required to be distributed (i.e., discretionary distributions) to the beneficiary during the year.[30] This general rule has three exceptions, all discussed later in this section.

Because income retains the character it has at the fiduciary level, beneficiaries do not include distributions of tax-exempt income in their gross income. Each beneficiary's distribution is deemed to consist of tax-exempt income in the proportion that total tax-exempt income bears to total DNI.[31] Thus, if 30% of DNI is from tax-exempt income, 30% of each beneficiary's distribution is deemed to consist of tax-free income.

Even in the absence of distributions of principal, mandatory payments to beneficiaries sometimes exceed DNI because at times accounting income exceeds DNI. When the total income required to be distributed currently exceeds DNI (before reduction for the charitable contribution deduction), each beneficiary reports as gross income the following ratio of DNI attributable to taxable sources:

$$\frac{\text{Income required to be distributed currently to this beneficiary}}{\text{Aggregate income required to be distributed to all beneficiaries currently}}$$ [32]

In calculating the portion of DNI includible in the gross income of each beneficiary who receives mandatory distributions, DNI is not reduced for the charitable contribution deduction.

EXAMPLE C:14-23 ▶ In the current year, Yui Trust reports net accounting income of $125,000 but DNI of only $95,000 because of certain expenses charged to principal. The trust must distribute $100,000 of income to Tai and $10,000 to Tien. It makes no discretionary distributions or charitable contributions but is a complex trust because it is not required to distribute all of its income. Because the trust's mandatory distributions of $110,000 exceed its DNI of $95,000, the amount each beneficiary reports as gross income is as follows:

Beneficiary	*Gross Income*
Tai	$86,364 = ($100,000 ÷ $110,000) × $95,000
Tien	$8,636 = ($10,000 ÷ $110,000) × $95,000

◀

Exception—The Tier System. Some trust instruments require mandatory distributions to some beneficiaries and allow discretionary distributions to the same or other beneficiarries. If the sum of current income required to be distributed currently and all other amounts distributed (e.g., discretionary payments of income or any payments of corpus) exceed DNI, the amount taxable to each beneficiary is calculated under a tier system. Beneficiaries to whom income distributions must be made are commonly called **tier-1 beneficiaries.**[33] All other beneficiaries are known as **tier-2 beneficiaries.** An individual who receives both mandatory and discretionary payments in the same year can be both a tier-1 and a tier-2 beneficiary.

Under the tier system, tier-1 beneficiaries are the first to absorb income. The total income taxed to this group is the lesser of the aggregate mandatory distributions or DNI, which is determined without reduction for charitable contributions. If required income distributions plus all other payments exceed DNI, each tier-2 beneficiary includes in income a fraction of the remaining DNI, the DNI minus the income required to be distributed currently. Section 662(a)(2) states that the fraction for each beneficiary is as follows:

$$\frac{\text{Other amounts properly paid or required to be distributed to the beneficiary}}{\text{Aggregate of amounts properly paid or required to be distributed to \textit{all} beneficiaries}}$$

30 Sec. 662(a).
31 Sec. 662(b).
32 Sec. 662(a)(1).
33 The terms *tier-1* and *tier-2* do not appear in the IRC or Treasury Regulations.

EXAMPLE C:14-24 ▶ In the current year, Eagle Trust reports net accounting income and DNI of $80,000, all from taxable sources. The trust instrument requires the trustee to distribute $30,000 of income to Holly currently. In addition, the trustee makes $60,000 of discretionary distributions, $15,000 to Holly and $45,000 to Irene. The trust distributes $90,000 total and pays $10,000 of the $60,000 discretionary distributions from corpus. The gross income reported by each beneficiary is determined as follows:

1. Gross income from mandatory distributions:	
Lesser of:	
a. Amount required to be distributed, or	$30,000
b. DNI	80,000
Amount reportable by Holly	30,000
2. Gross income from other amounts paid:	
Lesser of:	
a. All other amounts paid, or	60,000
b. DNI minus amount required to be distributed ($80,000 − $30,000)	50,000
Amount reportable by Holly and Irene	50,000
3. Total amount reportable (1) + (2b) = (3)	80,000

The portions of the $50,000 remaining DNI from Step 2 to be reported by each beneficiary are calculated under a pro rata approach as follows:

Holly: $50,000 × ($15,000 ÷ $60,000) = $12,500
Irene: $50,000 × ($45,000 ÷ $60,000) = $37,500

A recapitulation of the beneficiaries' gross income is as follows:

	Amount Reported by	
Type of Distribution	*Holly*	*Irene*
Mandatory distributions	$30,000	$ -0-
Discretionary distributions	12,500	37,500
Total	$42,500	$37,500 ◀

Tier-1 beneficiaries generally have gross income equal to their total distributions if they receive no tax-exempt interest, whereas tier-2 beneficiaries are more likely to receive a portion of their distributions tax-free. Thus, tier-2 beneficiaries potentially receive more favorable tax treatment than tier-1 beneficiaries.

SELF-STUDY QUESTION

What is the ultimate effect of the separate share rule?

ANSWER

It has the effect of treating a trust or estate as two or more separate entities, each with its own DNI. This "separate" DNI is allocated to the specific beneficiary of each share of the trust or estate.

Exception—Separate Share Rule. Some trusts and estates with more than one beneficiary can be treated as consisting of more than one entity in determining the amount of the distribution deduction and the beneficiaries' gross income.[34] In calculating the fiduciary's income tax liability, however, these trusts or estates are treated as one entity with the result that taxable income is taxed under one rate schedule. Entities eligible for this treatment, known as the **separate share rule**, have governing instruments requiring that distributions be made in substantially the same manner as if separate entities had been created.[35] If the separate share rule applies, the amount of the income taxable to a beneficiary can differ from the amount taxable under the general rules. Because of this rule, beneficiaries often report gross income that is less than the distributions they receive.

EXAMPLE C:14-25 ▶ Bart Berry created the Berry Trust for the benefit of Dale and John. According to the trust instrument, no income is to be distributed until a beneficiary reaches age 21. Moreover, income is to be divided into two equal shares. Once a beneficiary reaches age 21, the trustee may make discretionary distributions of income and principal to such beneficiary, but distributions may not exceed a beneficiary's share of the trust. Each beneficiary is to receive his remaining share of the trust assets on his thirtieth birthday. Earlier distributions of income and principal must be taken into account in determining each beneficiary's final distribution.

On January 1 of the current year, Dale reaches age 21; John is age 16. In the current year, the trust has DNI and net accounting income of $50,000, all from taxable sources.

[34] Sec. 663(c).

[35] Reg. Sec. 1.663(c)-3(a).

The trustee distributes $25,000 of income (Dale's 50% share) and $80,000 of principal to Dale. The trustee makes no distribution of income or corpus to John. Under the separate share rule, the trust's distribution deduction and Dale's gross income inclusion cannot exceed his share of DNI, or $25,000. Dale receives the remaining $80,000 distribution tax-free. Berry Trust pays tax on John's separate share of the income (all accumulated), or $25,000, less the personal exemption. In the absence of the separate share rule, Dale would be taxed on $50,000 (the lesser of DNI or his total distributions). ◀

Exception—Specific Bequests. Recall that a beneficiary is taxed on other amounts properly paid, credited, or required to be distributed,[36] subject to the constraint that the maximum amount taxed to all beneficiaries is the fiduciary's DNI. Thus, a beneficiary can be required to report gross income even though he or she receives a distribution paid from the principal account.

EXAMPLE C:14-26 ▶ Doug died last year, leaving a will that stated, "I bequeath all my property to my sister Tina." During the current year, Doug's estate reports $50,000 of DNI, all from taxable sources. Also during the current year, the executor distributes Doug's coin collection, valued at $22,000, to Tina. The adjusted basis of the coin collection also is $22,000, its value at the date of death. The distribution of the coin collection is classified as an "other amount properly paid" and, even though the executor distributes nothing from the income account, Tina must report $22,000 of gross income. If the coin collection's adjusted basis and FMV exceed $50,000 (DNI), Tina's gross income would be only $50,000, the DNI amount. ◀

ADDITIONAL COMMENT

The executor of an estate should carefully consider the timing of property distributions if the property being distributed is not the subject of a specific bequest. If possible, property (other than specific bequests) should be distributed in a year when the trust has little or no DNI to minimize the beneficiary's gross income.

On the other hand, a distribution of property does not trigger a distribution deduction at the estate level or the recognition of gross income at the beneficiary level if such property constitutes a bequest of a specific sum of money or of specific property to be paid at one time or in not more than three installments.[37] If Doug's will in Example C:14-26 instead includes specific bequest language (e.g., "I bequeath my coin collection to Tina"), Tina would not report any gross income upon receiving the coin collection.

More income is generally taxed at the estate level (and less at the beneficiary level) if the decedent's will includes numerous specific bequests. If the estate has a lower marginal income tax rate than its beneficiaries' marginal tax rates, the optimal tax result is to have the income taxed to the estate because the tax liability is lower.

EXAMPLE C:14-27 ▶ Dick died last year and bequeathed $100,000 cash to Fred and devised his residence, valued at $300,000, to Gary. The executor distributes the cash and the residence in the current year, when the estate has $80,000 of DNI, all from taxable sources. Because the cash and residence constitute specific bequests, the estate receives no distribution deduction and the beneficiaries report no gross income. Most of the income will be taxed to the estate at the top tax rate. ◀

? STOP & THINK

Question: Sally is the sole beneficiary of her uncle Harry's estate. Uncle Harry's will made a specific bequest of the rare book collection to Sally. Another part of his will left Sally the rest of his estate. In the current year, the estate had DNI of $36,000, all from dividends and corporate interest. During the current year, the estate's executor distributed to Sally $12,200 of cash and her uncle Harry's rare book collection, valued at $5,400 on both date of death and date of distribution. How much gross income should Sally report from the estate during the current year? What is the amount of the estate's distribution deduction?

Solution: Sally does not have to report gross income as a result of receiving the specific bequest of the book collection. Because Sally's $12,200 cash distribution does not exceed the estate's $36,000 DNI, Sally should report gross income equal to the cash distributed to her ($12,200). The estate's distribution deduction equals the amount included in Sally's gross income ($12,200). If Harry had not specifically willed the books to Sally, the distribution of the books would be taxable to Sally because the $17,600 ($12,200 + $5,400) distributed by the estate is less than the estate's DNI.

---

[36] Sec. 662(a)(2).

[37] Sec. 663(a)(1).

KEY POINT

Generally, the tax consequences of both NOLs and net capital losses are the same for estates, complex trusts, and simple trusts.

EFFECT OF A NET OPERATING LOSS

As with simple trusts, an NOL of an estate or complex trust can be carried back and carried forward. In the year the trust or estate terminates, any remaining NOL passes through to the beneficiaries who succeed to the assets. In addition, in its year of termination the estate passes through to its beneficiaries any excess of current nonoperating expenses (e.g., executor's fees) over current income. If the estate incurs NOLs over a series of years, a tax incentive exists for terminating the estate as early as possible so the loss can pass through to the beneficiaries.

EFFECT OF A NET CAPITAL LOSS

The tax effect of having capital losses that exceed capital gains generally is the same for estates and complex trusts as for simple trusts. As for an individual taxpayer, the maximum capital loss deduction is the lesser of $3,000 or the excess of its capital losses over capital gains.[38] Simple trusts, however, receive no immediate tax benefit when capital losses exceed capital gains because no income is retained against which to offset the capital loss. Estates and complex trusts often do not distribute all their income and, thus, have taxable income against which they can offset a capital loss.

EXAMPLE C:14-28 ▶ Last year, Green Trust reported $30,000 of net accounting income and DNI, all from taxable sources. It made discretionary distributions totaling $7,000 to Amy. It sold one capital asset at an $8,000 long-term capital loss. The trust deducted $3,000 of capital losses in arriving at last year's taxable income. The trust carries over the remaining $5,000 of capital loss to the current year. If in the current year, Green Trust sells a capital asset for a $7,000 long-term capital gain, it will offset the $5,000 loss carryover against the $7,000 capital gain. ◀

ADDITIONAL COMMENT

This illustration pertains to 2014 because tax forms for that year are the latest available at the time this textbook was published.

COMPREHENSIVE ILLUSTRATION: DETERMINING A COMPLEX TRUST'S TAXABLE INCOME

The comprehensive illustration below reviews a number of points discussed earlier. A sample Form 1041 for a complex trust appears in Appendix B; it is prepared for 2014 on the basis of the facts in this illustration.

Background Data. Ted Tims established the Cathy and Karen Stephens Trust in 2003. Its trust instrument empowers the trustee (Merchants Bank) to distribute income in its discretion to Cathy and Karen for the next 20 years. The trust will then be terminated, and the trust assets will be divided equally between Cathy and Karen, irrespective of the amount of distributions each has previously received. In other words, no separate shares are to be maintained. The trust instrument states that capital gains are part of principal and that trustee's fees are to be paid from principal.

The 2014 income and expenses of the trust appear below. With the exception of the information concerning distributions and payments of estimated tax, the amounts are the same as in the comprehensive illustration for a simple trust discussed previously in the chapter. As before, the holding period for the stock sold in October was four years.

	Amounts Allocable to	
	Income	*Principal*
Dividends	$30,000	
Rental income from land	5,000	
Tax-exempt interest	15,000	
Rental expenses (realtor's commissions on rental income)	1,000	
Trustee's fee		$ 1,200
Fee for preparation of tax return	500	
Capital gain on sale of stock		12,000
Distribution of net accounting income to:		
Cathy	14,000	
Karen	7,000	
Payments of estimated tax		5,360

Trustee's Fee. Recall that some of the trustee's fee must be allocated to tax-exempt income, with the result that this portion is nondeductible. Of the trust's gross accounting income of $50,000 ($30,000 + $5,000 + $15,000), $15,000 is from tax-exempt sources.

[38] Sec. 1211(b).

Consequently, the nondeductible trustee's fee is \$360 [(\$15,000 ÷ \$50,000) × \$1,200]. The remaining \$840 of the fee is deductible, as is the \$500 tax return preparation fee.

Distribution Deduction and DNI. Recall that the primary function of the Subchapter J rules is to provide guidance for calculating the amounts taxable to the beneficiaries and to the fiduciary. One of the crucial numbers in the process is the distribution deduction, which requires knowledge of the DNI amount. Taxable income, exclusive of the distribution deduction, is the starting point for calculating DNI and is computed as follows:

Dividends		\$30,000
Rental income		5,000
Capital gain on sale of stock		12,000
Minus:	Rental expenses	(1,000)
	Deductible portion of trustee's fee	(840)
	Fee for tax return preparation	(500)
	Personal exemption	(100)
Taxable income, exclusive of distribution deduction		\$44,560

DNI is calculated by adjusting taxable income, exclusive of the distribution deduction, as follows:

Taxable income, exclusive of distribution deduction		\$44,560
Plus:	Personal exemption	100
Minus:	Capital gain on sale of stock	(12,000)
Plus:	Tax-exempt interest (net of \$360 of allocable expenses)	14,640
DNI		\$47,300

The distribution deduction is the lesser of (1) amounts required to be distributed, plus all other amounts properly paid or credited, or required to be distributed, or (2) DNI. This lesser-of amount must be reduced by tax-exempt income (net of allocable expenses). DNI, exclusive of net tax-exempt income, is calculated as follows:

DNI		\$47,300
Minus:	Tax-exempt income (net of \$360 of allocable expenses)	(14,640)
DNI, exclusive of net tax-exempt income		\$32,660

In no event may the distribution deduction exceed \$32,660, the DNI, exclusive of net tax-exempt income. The DNI ceiling is of no practical significance in this example, however, because the trust distributed only \$21,000.

ADDITIONAL COMMENT

This example dealing with a complex trust clearly illustrates the computational complexity that exists in situations with multiple categories of income and multiple beneficiaries.

Because a portion of the payments to each beneficiary is deemed to consist of tax-exempt income, the distribution deduction is less than the \$21,000 distributed. Each beneficiary's share of tax-exempt income is determined by dividing DNI into categories of income. In this categorization process, the rental expenses are direct expenses that must be charged against rental income, and \$360 of the trustee's fees must be charged against tax-exempt income. In this example, the deductible trustee's fee and the tax return preparation fee are charged against rental income. Alternatively, they could be charged against dividend income or pro rata against each income category, but an allocation to dividend income would be disadvantageous because dividends are taxed at a preferential rate. As with the simple trust illustrated earlier, total DNI of \$47,300 consists of the following categories:

	Dividends	*Rents*	*Tax-Exempt Interest*	*Total*
Accounting income	\$30,000	\$5,000	\$15,000	\$50,000
Minus: Expenses:				
Trustee's fee		(840)	(360)	(1,200)
Rental expenses		(1,000)		(1,000)
Tax return preparation fee		(500)		(500)
DNI	\$30,000	\$2,660	\$14,640	\$47,300

Because there are two beneficiaries and three categories of income, we must calculate the amount of each beneficiary's distribution attributable to each income category. These steps were not needed in the simple trust illustration because the simple trust had only one beneficiary.

Category of Income	*Proportion of DNI*
Dividends	63.4249% = $30,000 ÷ $47,300
Rental income	5.6237% = $ 2,660 ÷ $47,300
Tax-exempt income	30.9514% = $14,640 ÷ $47,300
Total	100.0000%

As shown above, 30.9514% of each beneficiary's distribution represents tax-exempt interest and is ineligible for a distribution deduction. The amount of the distribution deduction (which cannot exceed the $32,660 DNI, exclusive of net tax-exempt income) is determined as follows:

Total amount distributed	$21,000
Minus: Net tax-exempt income deemed distributed (0.309514 × $21,000)	(6,500)
Distribution deduction	$14,500

The distributions received by the beneficiaries are deemed to consist of three categories of income in the amounts shown below.

Components of Distributions	*Cathy*	*Karen*	*Total*
Dividends (63.4249%)	$ 8,879	$4,440	$13,319
Plus: Rental income (5.6237%)	788	393	1,181
Gross income (69.0486%)	$ 9,667	$4,833	$14,500
Plus: Tax-exempt interest (30.9514%)	4,333	2,167	6,500
Total income (100%)	$14,000	$7,000	$21,000

Trust's Taxable Income. Once the taxable and tax-exempt distributions have been quantified, the trust's taxable income can be calculated. Table C:14-3 illustrates this calculation. Unlike the simple trust situation, no short-cut approach exists for verifying taxable income for complex trusts and estates except in the years when they distribute all their income.

Trust's Tax On Net Investment Income. The trust has investment income of $47,000 ($30,000 dividends + $5,000 rents + $12,000 capital gain) and net investment income of $44,660 ($47,000 − $2,340). Of this amount, $14,500 is distributed, resulting in an undistributed amount of $30,160 ($44,660 − $14,500). For purposes of the tax on net investment income, the trust's adjusted gross income (AGI) is deemed to consist of investment income less deductions for expenses, the distribution deduction, and the personal exemption. This AGI amount is $30,060 ($47,000 − $2,340 − $14,500 − $100). Thus, AGI exceeds the amount at which the 39.6% tax bracket begins by $17,910 ($30,060 − $12,150). Because the AGI in excess of the point at which the 39.6% rate begins is the smaller amount, the tax on net investment income is $681 ($17,910 × 0.038).

Additional Observations. A few additional observations are in order concerning the Stephens Trust:

- ▶ If the entity is an estate instead of a trust, all amounts except the personal exemption are the same. The estate's personal exemption would be $600 instead of $100.
- ▶ Assume that (1) the trust owns a building instead of land and incurs $2,000 of depreciation expense, charged in the trustee's discretion against principal. Because approximately 56% of the trust's income is accumulated (i.e., $26,300 of its $47,300 DNI), $1,120 (0.56 × $2,000) of the depreciation is deductible by the trust and its taxable income is $1,120 lower. The remaining $880 (0.44 × $2,000) is deductible on the

▼ **TABLE C:14-3**

Comprehensive Illustration: Determining a Complex Trust's Taxable Income and Tax Liability

Gross income:	
Dividends	$30,000
Rental income	5,000
Capital gain on sale of stock	12,000
Minus: Expense deductions:	
Rental expenses	(1,000)
Deductible portion of trustee's fee	(840)
Tax return preparation fee	(500)
Minus: Distribution deduction	(14,500)
Minus: Personal exemption	(100)
Taxable income	$30,060
Tax on taxable income (2014 rates)[a]	$ 5,237
Plus: 3.8% tax on net investment income (see Page C:14-26)	681
Total tax liability	$ 5,918
Minus: Estimated taxes	(5,360)
Tax owed	$ 558

[a]The $12,000 long-term capital gain and the $16,681 of dividends retained by the trust ($28,681 in total) are taxed at the lower rates. The $16,681 amount is $30,000 minus the $13,319 dividends distributed, as calculated on p. C:14-26. The tax liability is calculated as follows:

Tax on ordinary, non-dividend income [0.15 × $1,379 (where $1,379 = $30,060 − $12,000 − $16,681)]	$ 207
Plus: Tax on capital gains and dividends at 0% [0.0 × $1,121 (where $1,121 = $2,500 − $1,379)]	−0−
Tax on capital gains and dividends at 15% [0.15 × $9,650 (where $9,650 = $12,150 income taxed at rates below 39.6% − $2,500 income already taxed)]	1,448
Tax on remaining capital gains and dividends at 20% [0.20 × $17,910 ($28,681 − $1,121 – $9,650)]	3,582
Tax on taxable income	$5,237

beneficiaries' returns and is divided between them according to their pro rata share of the total distributions. Cathy deducts $587 [$880 × ($14,000 ÷ $21,000)], and Karen deducts $293 [$880 × ($7,000 ÷ $21,000)]. In summary, the depreciation is deductible as follows $1,120 to the trust, $587 to Cathy, and $293 to Karen.

▶ If the trustee had charged against income an amount equal to the depreciation expense for tax purposes, accounting income would have been reduced by the depreciation. In addition, the entire $2,000 of depreciation would have been deducted on the trust return, and DNI would have been $45,300 instead of $47,300.

INCOME IN RESPECT OF A DECEDENT

OBJECTIVE 7

Recognize the significance of income in respect of a decedent

DEFINITION AND COMMON EXAMPLES

Section 691 specifies the tax treatment for specific types of income known as income in respect of a decedent. **Income in respect of a decedent (IRD)** is gross income that the decedent earned before death but was not includible on the decedent's income tax return for the tax year ending with the date of death or for an earlier tax year because the decedent (a cash basis taxpayer) had not collected the income. Because most individuals use the cash method of accounting, IRD generally consists of income earned, but not actually or constructively received, prior to death. Common examples of IRD include the following:

- Interest earned, but not received, before death
- Salary, commission, or bonus earned, but not received, before death
- Dividends collected after the date of death, for which the record date precedes the date of death
- The gain portion of principal collected on a pre-death installment sale

SELF-STUDY QUESTION

Roger, a cash basis taxpayer, is a medical doctor. At the time of Roger's death, patients owe him $150,000. These accounts receivable are "property" in which Roger has an interest at the time of his death and are included in his gross estate. Why are the accounts receivable income in respect of a decedent?

ANSWER

Because they are income Roger earned while alive, but did not report as income under his accounting method, they constitute income to his estate (or his heirs) when they are collected. Thus, they are income in respect of a decedent (IRD).

SIGNIFICANCE OF IRD

Double Taxation. Recall from Chapter C:13 that a decedent's gross estate includes property to the extent of his or her interest therein. The decedent has an interest in any income earned but not actually or constructively received before death. Thus, the decedent's gross estate includes income accrued as of the date of death. If the decedent used the cash method of accounting, the decedent did not include this accrued income in gross income because he or she had not yet collected it. The income is taxed to the party (i.e., the estate or a named individual) entitled to receive it. Thus, IRD is taxed under both the transfer tax system and the income tax system. Income also is taxed under two systems if the decedent collects a dividend check, deposits it into his or her bank account, and dies before consuming the cash. In the latter case, the dividend is included in the decedent's individual income tax return, and the cash (from the dividend check) is included in the decedent's gross estate. The individual income taxes owed on the dividend income are deductible as a debt on the estate tax return.

EXAMPLE C:14-29 ▶

Doug dies on July 1. Included in Doug's gross estate is an 8%, $1,000 corporate bond that pays interest each September 1 and March 1. Doug's gross estate also includes accrued interest for the period March 2 through July 1 of $27 ($\$1,000 \times 0.08 \times 4/12$). On September 1, Doug's estate collects $40 of interest, of which $27 constitutes IRD. The calendar year income tax return for Doug's estate includes $40 of interest income, consisting of $27 of IRD and $13 earned after death. ◀

SELF-STUDY QUESTION

Karl receives his April monthly paycheck on May 1 and deposits the paycheck in his savings account. He dies on May 10. He made no withdrawals from the account before his death. On June 1, Karl's employer pays Karl's estate one-third of Karl's May salary (the amount Karl had earned prior to his death on May 10). What are the tax consequences?

ANSWER

Karl's gross estate will include his savings account, which includes a deposit of his April paycheck. Karl's final income tax return will include his salary through April 30. His May 1 check is subject to both the individual income and the estate tax. The income taxes owed on the April salary are deductible as a debt on his estate tax return.

Karl's gross estate will include the one-third of his May salary. His estate's income tax return also will report this amount as income. The salary is income in respect of a decedent, so the estate will receive some relief under Sec. 691(c) from the double tax on the May salary.

Deductions in Respect of a Decedent. Section 691(b) authorizes **deductions in respect of a decedent** (DRD). Such deductions include trade or business expenses, expenses for the production of income, interest, taxes, depletion, etc. that are accrued before death but are not deductible on the decedent's final income tax return because the decedent used the cash method of accounting. Because these accrued expenses have not been paid before death, they also may be deductible as debts on the estate tax return. In addition, the accrued expenses are deductible on the estate's income tax return when paid by the estate (if they are for deductible expenses). Thus, a double benefit can be obtained for DRD.

EXAMPLE C:14-30 ▶

Dan dies on September 20. At the time of his death, Dan owes $18,000 of salaries to the employees of his proprietorship. The executor pays the total September payroll of $29,000 on September 30. The $18,000 of accrued salaries is deductible as a debt on the estate tax return. As a trade or business (Sec. 162) expense, the salaries also constitute DRD. The $18,000 of DRD and any other salaries paid are deductible on the estate's income tax return for the period in which paid. ◀

Section 691(c) Deduction. The Sec. 691(c) deduction provides some relief for the double taxation of IRD. This deduction equals the federal estate taxes attributable to the net IRD included in the gross estate. The total Sec. 691(c) deduction is the excess of the decedent's actual federal estate tax over the federal estate tax that would be payable if the net IRD were excluded from the decedent's gross estate. Net IRD means IRD minus deductions in respect of a decedent (DRD). If the IRD is collected in more than one tax year, the Sec. 691(c) deduction for a particular tax year is determined by the following formula:[39]

$$\begin{array}{c}\text{Sec. 691(c)}\\\text{deduction}\\\text{for the year}\end{array} = \begin{array}{c}\text{Total}\\\text{Sec. 691(c)}\\\text{deduction}\end{array} \times \frac{\text{Net IRD included in gross income for the year}}{\text{Total Net IRD}}$$

[39] Sec. 691(c)(1).

EXAMPLE C:14-31 ▶ Latoya (a widow) died in 2014, and her estate tax base was $6 million. Latoya's gross estate included $300,000 of IRD, primarily from gains on installment sales. Her estate had no DRD. The estate collects $250,000 of the IRD during its 2015 tax year. The Sec. 691(c) deduction for Latoya's estate for 2015 is calculated as shown below.

Actual 2014 federal estate tax on base of $6 million	$264,000[a]
Minus: 2014 federal estate tax on base of $5.7 million determined by excluding net IRD from gross estate	(144,000)[b]
Total Sec. 691(c) deduction	$120,000
Sec. 691(c) deduction available in 2015 [($250,000 ÷ $300,000) × $120,000]	$100,000 ◀

[a] [$345,800 + ($6,000,000 − $1,000,000) × 0.40] − $2,081,800
[b] [$345,800 + ($5,700,000 − $1,000,000) × 0.40] − $2,081,800

ADDITIONAL COMMENT

For decedents dying in 2010, Congress retroactively reinstated the estate tax along with the FMV basis rule. However, for 2010, estate executors could elect out of the estate tax and use the modified carryover basis rules that were in effect for 2010 before the reinstatement.

No Step-Up in Basis. Most property received as the result of a decedent's death acquires a basis equal to its FMV on the date of death or the alternate valuation date. Property classified as IRD retains the basis it had in the decedent's hands.[40]

This carryover basis rule for IRD items is especially unfavorable when the decedent sells a highly appreciated asset soon before death, collects a relatively small portion of the sales price before death, and reports the sale under the installment method of accounting. For example, if the gain is 80% of the sales price, 80% of each principal payment in the post-death period will continue to be characterized as gain. If the sale instead had been postponed until after the date of death, the gain would be restricted to the post-death appreciation (if any) because the step-up in basis rules apply to the asset.

EXAMPLE C:14-32 ▶ On June 3 of last year, Joel sold a parcel of investment land for $40,000. The land had a $10,000 adjusted basis in Joel's hands. The buyer paid $8,000 down and signed a $32,000 note at an interest rate acceptable to the IRS. The note is payable June 3 of the current year. Joel, a cash basis taxpayer, uses the installment method for reporting the $30,000 ($40,000 − $10,000) gain. The gross profit ratio is 75% ($30,000 gain ÷ $40,000 contract price). Joel died accidentally on June 13 of last year with a gross estate of $1 million. Joel's final individual income tax return reported a gain of $6,000 (0.75 × $8,000). The estate reports a gain of $24,000 (0.75 × $32,000) on its current year income tax return because it collects the $32,000 balance on June 3 of the current year. Had the sale contract been entered into immediately after Joel's death, the gain would have been zero because the land's basis would have been its $40,000 FMV at the date of death. ◀

SELF-STUDY QUESTION

Roger (a cash basis taxpayer) died leaving $150,000 of accounts receivable. What basis does his estate have in these accounts receivable?

ANSWER

Zero. The accounts receivable constitute IRD. If they were stepped-up in basis, they would never be subject to an income tax.

STOP & THINK

Question: Isaac, a cash basis, calendar year taxpayer, died on May 12 of the current year. On which income tax return—Isaac's or his estate's—should the following income and expenses be reported? Assume the estate's tax year is the calendar year.

- Dividends declared in January and paid in February
- Interest income on a corporate bond that pays interest each June 30 and December 31
- Rent collected in June for a vacation home rented to tenants for the month of March, but the tenants were allowed to pay after occupying the property
- Balance due on Isaac's state income taxes for the previous year, paid in July because the return was extended
- Federal estimated income tax for the previous year that Isaac paid in January

Solution: Income received before death and deductible expenses paid before death (in this case the dividends and nothing more) should be reported on Isaac's individual return. Income received after his death, even though earned before his death, is to be reported on the estate's income tax return. The same is true for deductible expenses paid by the estate. Items to be reported on the estate's income tax return include the interest income, the rental income, and the state income taxes. The federal income taxes paid are not deductible on the federal income tax return of either taxpayer. The federal tax payment, however, reduced the cash Isaac owned at his date of death and thereby his gross estate.

40 Sec. 1014(c).

Grantor Trust Provisions

OBJECTIVE 8

Explain the effect of the grantor trust provisions

This portion of the chapter examines the provisions affecting a special type of trust known as a **grantor trust**, which is governed by Secs. 671-679. As discussed previously, income of a regular (or nongrantor) trust or an estate is taxed to the beneficiary to the extent distributed and to the fiduciary to the extent accumulated. In the case of a grantor trust, however, the trust's grantor (creator) is taxed on some or all of the trust's income even if such income is distributed to a third-party beneficiary. In certain circumstances, a person other than the grantor or the beneficiary (e.g., a person with powers over the trust) must pay taxes on the trust's income.

PURPOSE AND EFFECT

The grantor trust rules require grantors who do not give up enough control or economic benefits when they create a trust to pay a price by being taxed on part or all of the trust's income. A grantor must report some or all of a trust's income on his or her individual tax return if he or she does not part with enough control over the trust assets or give up the right to income produced by the assets for a sufficiently long time period. For transfers after March 1, 1986, the grantor generally is taxed on the trust's income if the trust property will eventually return to the grantor or the grantor's spouse.[41] According to the Tax Court, the grantor trust rules have the following purpose and result:

> This subpart [Secs. 671–679] enunciates the rules to be applied where, in described circumstances, a grantor has transferred property to a trust but has not parted with complete dominion and control over the property or the income which it produces. . . .[42]

Sections 671–679 use the term *treated as owner* instead of taxed. Section 671 specifies that when a grantor is treated as owner, the income, deductions, and credits attributable to the portion of the trust with respect to which the grantor is treated as owner are reported directly on the grantor's tax return and not on the trust's return. The fiduciary tax return contains only the items attributable to the portion of the trust for which the grantor is not treated as the owner.

ADDITIONAL COMMENT

Many trust provisions can cause the grantor trust rules to apply. A trust need *not* be a revocable trust to be a grantor trust.

Unfortunately, the rules governing when the grantor has given up enough to avoid being taxed on the trust's income do not agree completely with the rules concerning whether the transfer is complete for gift tax purposes or the transferred property is removed from the donor's gross estate. In certain circumstances, a donor can make a taxable gift and still be taxed on the income from the transferred property. For example, if a donor transfers property to a trust with the income payable annually to the donor's cousin for six years and a reversion of the property to the donor at the end of the sixth year, the donor makes a gift, subject to the gift tax, of the value of a six-year income interest. Under the grantor trust rules, however, the donor is taxed on the trust's income because the property reverts to the donor within too short a time period.

Retention of certain powers over property conveyed in trust can cause the trust assets to be included in the donor's gross estate even though these powers do not result in the donor being taxed on the trust income. Assume a donor to a trust reserves the discretionary power to pay out or accumulate trust income until the beneficiary (a grandchild) reaches age 21. The trust assets, including any accumulated income, are to be distributed to the beneficiary on his or her twenty-first birthday. The donor is not taxed on the trust income because he can exercise his powers only until the beneficiary reaches age 21. If the donor dies before the beneficiary attains age 21, however, the donor's gross estate will include the trust property because the donor retained control over the beneficiary's economic benefits (see discussion of Sec. 2036 in Chapter C:13).

---

[41] For trusts created before March 2, 1986, the grantor was treated as the owner with respect to the trust's capital gains but not its ordinary income if the property returned to the grantor after a period of more than ten years. In such a situation, the grantor is taxed on the capital gains and the trust and/or the beneficiary on the ordinary income. The trusts usually terminated slightly more than ten years after their funding. Thus, few (if any) of these trusts exist today.

[42] *William Scheft*, 59 T.C. 428, at 430-431 (1972).

REVOCABLE TRUSTS

The grantor of a revocable trust can control assets conveyed to the trust by altering the terms of the trust (including changing the identity of the beneficiaries) and/or withdrawing assets from the trust. Often the grantor also is a beneficiary. Sec. 676 provides that the grantor is treated as the owner of the trust and therefore is taxed on the income generated by the trust. As Chapter C:12 points out, a transfer of assets to a revocable trust is an incomplete transfer and not subject to the gift tax.

EXAMPLE C:14-33 ► In the current year, Tom transfers property to a revocable trust and names Ann to receive the income for life and Beth to receive the remainder. The trust's income for the current year consists of $15,000 of dividends and an $8,000 long-term capital gain. The trustee distributes the dividends to Ann but retains the gain and credits it to principal. Because the trust is revocable, the dividend and capital gain income are taxed directly to Tom on his current year individual tax return. Nothing is taxed to the trust or its beneficiaries. ◄

ADDITIONAL COMMENT

A common use of the revocable trust is to avoid probate for the property held by the trust. On the death of the grantor, who also is the beneficiary, the trustee of the revocable trust distributes the trust property in accordance with the trust agreement. Because the trustee holds legal title to the property, he or she can distribute the property without the trust assets going through the probate process. The trust assets are included in the gross estate because the trust is revocable.

POST-1986 REVERSIONARY INTEREST TRUSTS

The 1986 Tax Reform Act amended Sec. 673(a) for transfers made after March 1, 1986, to provide that, generally, the grantor is treated as the owner of the trust and is taxed on the accounting income of the trust if he or she has a reversionary interest in either income or principal. Under Sec. 672(e), a grantor is treated as holding any interest held by his or her spouse. These rules have two exceptions.

The first exception makes the grantor trust rules inapplicable if, as of the inception of the trust, the value of the reversionary interest, as valued under the actuarial tables, does not exceed 5% of the value of the trust. The second exception applies if the reversion will occur only if the beneficiary dies before reaching age 21 and the beneficiary is a lineal descendant of the grantor.

EXAMPLE C:14-34 ► In the current year, Paul establishes a trust with income payable to his elderly parents for 15 years. The assets of the trust will then revert to Paul. The value of Paul's reversionary interest exceeds 5%. Because Paul has a reversionary interest valued at above 5% and the transfer arose after March 1, 1986, Paul is taxed currently on the trust's accounting income and capital gains. ◄

EXAMPLE C:14-35 ► In the current year, Paul transfers property to a trust with income payable to his daughter Ruth until Ruth reaches age 21. On Ruth's twenty-first birthday, she is to receive the trust property outright. In the event Ruth dies before reaching age 21, the trust assets will revert to Paul. Paul is not taxed on the accounting income because his reversion is contingent on the death of the beneficiary (a lineal descendant) before age 21. ◄

RETENTION OF ADMINISTRATIVE POWERS

Under Sec. 675, the grantor is taxed on the accounting income and gains if he or she or his or her spouse holds certain administrative powers. Such powers include, but are not limited to, the following:

- The power to purchase or exchange trust property for less than adequate consideration in money or money's worth
- The power to borrow from the trust without adequate interest or security except where the trustee (who is someone other than the grantor) has a general lending power to make loans irrespective of interest or security
- The power exercisable in a role other than as trustee to (1) vote stock of a corporation in which the holdings of the grantor and the trust are significant from the standpoint of voting control and (2) reacquire the trust property by substituting other property of equal value.

RETENTION OF ECONOMIC BENEFITS

Section 677 taxes the grantor on the portion of the trust with respect to which the income may be

- Distributed to the grantor or his or her spouse,
- Held or accumulated for future distribution to the grantor or his or her spouse, or
- Used to pay premiums on life insurance policies on the life of the grantor or his or her spouse

Using trust income to provide support for a child whom the grantor is legally obligated to support yields obvious economic benefits to the grantor. A grantor is taxed on any trust income distributed by the trustee to support individuals whom the grantor is legally obligated to support (e.g., children). However, the mere existence of the discretionary power to use trust income for support purposes does not cause the grantor to be taxed on the trust income. Taxation turns on whether the trust income is actually used to meet the support obligation.

The next example concerns use of trust income to support the grantor's minor child.

EXAMPLE C:14-36 ▶ Hal creates a trust and empowers the bank trustee to distribute income to his minor son, Louis, until the son reaches age 21. When Louis reaches age 21, the trust assets including accumulated income are to be paid over to the child. In the current year, when Louis is age 15, the trustee distributes $5,000 that is used to support Louis and $8,000 that is deposited into Louis's savings account. The remaining $12,000 of income is accumulated. Hal (the grantor) is taxed on the $5,000 used to support his son. Louis includes $8,000 in his gross income, and the trust pays tax on $12,000 less its $100 exemption. Note, however, that the kiddie tax rules apply to Louis's income of $8,000. ◀

The following example deals with the payment of premiums on an insurance policy on the grantor's life.

EXAMPLE C:14-37 ▶ Maria is the grantor of the Martinez Trust, one of whose assets is a life insurance policy on Maria's life. The trust instrument requires that $1,000 of trust income be used to pay the annual insurance premiums and that the rest be distributed to Maria's adult son Juan. Section 677 requires Maria (the grantor and insured) to be taxed on $1,000 of accounting income. The remaining income is taxed to Juan under the general trust rules. ◀

ADDITIONAL COMMENT

If the grantor were a parent of the insured, the income required to be used for paying life insurance premiums would not be taxed to the grantor because the insured is not the grantor or the grantor's spouse.

CONTROL OF OTHERS' ENJOYMENT

Section 674 taxes the grantor on trust income if he or she, his or her spouse, or someone without an interest in the trust (e.g., a trustee) has the power to control others' beneficial enjoyment such as by deciding how much income to distribute. Many exceptions, including one for independent trustees, exist for the general rule.

EXAMPLE C:14-38 ▶ Otto is grantor and trustee of a trust over which the trustee has complete discretion to pay out the income or corpus in any amount he deems appropriate to some or all of the three adult beneficiaries, Kay, Fay, and May (none related to Otto). In the current year, the trustee distributes all the income to Kay. Otto, the grantor, is taxed on the income. If instead the trustee were independent, Kay would be taxed on the income she received. ◀

Under Sec. 678, an individual other than the trust's grantor or beneficiary can be required to report the trust income. This individual is taxed on the trust income if he or she has the power under the trust instrument to vest the trust principal or the income in him- or herself, provided such power is exercisable solely by such individual.

Topic Review C:14-4 summarizes the grantor trust rules.

WHAT WOULD YOU DO IN THIS SITUATION?

You, a CPA, have prepared the income tax returns for the Candy Cain Trust, an irrevocable trust, since the inception of the trust five years ago. The grantor is Able Cain, another client and the father of Candy Cain, the income beneficiary. First Bank, the trustee, is authorized to distribute income at its descretion to Candy, who reached age 18 August of last year. Last year, the trust's DNI of $4,000, all from interest on corporate bonds, was distributed to Candy in June to pay her medical bills incurred in an accident. You advised Mr. Cain that he must include the $4,000 trust distribution on his individual tax return because he used the distribution to satisfy his obligation to support Candy until age 18. Candy began working after her high school graduation and, last year, used her earned income to provide over half of her own support. Mr. Cain reminds you of how many clients he has referred to you and demands that you instead show the distribution as taxable to Candy so the income will be taxed at her low rates instead of at his rate, the highest marginal rate. How will you react to Mr. Cain's request?

TOPIC REVIEW C:14-4

Grantor Trust Rules

Factual Situation	Tax Treatment
1. Trust is revocable.	Ordinary income (including dividends) and capital gains are taxed to grantor.
2. Irrevocable trust is funded on or after March 2, 1986, with income payable to third-party beneficiary for 25 years after which property reverts to grantor; the value of the reversionary interest exceeds 5% of the value of the trust.	Ordinary income (including dividends) and capital gains are taxed to grantor.
3. The grantor of an irrevocable trust retains administrative powers described in the IRC.	Ordinary income (including dividends) and capital gains are taxed to grantor.
4. The income of an irrevocable trust is disbursed to meet the grantor's obligation to support his or her children.	Ordinary income (including dividends) used for support are taxed to grantor.
5. The income of an irrevocable trust is disbursed to pay the premium on a life insurance policy on the life of the grantor or the grantor's spouse.	Ordinary income (including dividends) and capital gains are taxed to grantor to the extent they may be used to pay the premiums.

Tax planning considerations

OBJECTIVE 9

Identify tax planning opportunities in trust and estate income taxation

Many tax planning opportunities exist with respect to estates and trusts, including the ability to shift income to the fiduciary and/or the beneficiaries and the opportunity for executors or trustees of discretionary trusts to consider the tax consequences of the timing of distributions. These and other tax planning considerations are discussed below.

ABILITY TO SHIFT INCOME

Before 1987, one of the primary tax advantages of using trusts was the ability to shift income from the grantor to the trust or the beneficiary. Four changes have made the tax advantages of shifting income difficult to achieve. First, the tax rate schedules for fiduciaries are very compressed. In fact, an estate or trust has only $2,500 (in 2015) of income subject to the 15% tax rate, and the 39.6% rate begins at $12,300. Second, unearned income exceeding $2,100 (in 2015) of children under age 18 (and in some cases age 18 through 23) is taxed at the higher of the parents' or the child's tax rate, even if distributed from a trust or estate. Third, dividend income is eligible for a low or zero tax rate regardless of whether it is taxed to the grantor, the beneficiary, or the trust. Fourth, the taxpayer may owe the 3.8% tax on net investment income. Depending on whether the trust income is distributed or retained, it is taxed to the trust or the beneficiary or a portion to each. Because the trust is a separate taxpayer, income taxed to the trust is taxed under the trust's rate schedule. If the beneficiary has income from other sources, the income shifted from the trust to the beneficiary is not necessarily taxed in the lowest tax bracket. An income tax savings nevertheless can occur whenever a portion of the shifted income is taxed at a rate lower than the rate the grantor would pay on such income.

ADDITIONAL COMMENT

In 2015, the first $2,500 of trust income is taxed at 15%. A complex trust pays no tax on $100 of income (because of its personal exemption) and only 15% on the next $2,500 of income. If the trust distributes income to a child subject to the kiddie tax rules who is a dependent and has no other unearned income, the child pays no tax on the first $1,050 of that income and pays taxes at his or her own rate on the next $1,050. The rest is taxed at the parents' rates. If the parents are always in the top income tax bracket, nontrivial income tax savings still can be achieved by using a trust to spread non-dividend income over different taxpayers. In such scenarios, a Sec. 2503(c) trust (trust for minors) is commonly used.

TIMING OF DISTRIBUTIONS

Individuals managing estates and discretionary trusts can reduce taxes by carefully planning the timing of distributions. From a tax standpoint, the executor or trustee should consider the beneficiary's income from other sources and make distributions in amounts that equalize the marginal tax rates of the beneficiary and the fiduciary. If the trust is a **sprinkling trust** (a discretionary trust with several beneficiaries), the trustee can accomplish tax savings for the beneficiaries by making distributions to the beneficiaries who have the lowest marginal tax rate that year. Of course, nontax reasons might require a trustee to distribute income to other beneficiaries as well. A special 65-day

KEY POINT

Given that one often cannot determine the exact amount of income a trust (or any other entity) has earned until after the end of the tax year, the importance of the 65-day rule for distribution planning becomes readily apparent.

rule allows trustees of complex trusts and estates to treat distributions made during the first 65 days of the new tax year as if they had been made on the last day of the preceding tax year. If the trustee or executor does not make the election, the distributed income is deducted by the fiduciary and taxed to the beneficiary in the year of the actual distribution.

PROPERTY DISTRIBUTIONS

Under the general rule affecting property distributions, the trust receives a distribution deduction equal to the lesser of the fiduciary's adjusted basis in the property or the property's FMV.[43] If the trust distributes appreciated property, however, the trustee can elect to recognize a gain on the distribution equal to the excess of the property's FMV over its adjusted basis on the distribution date. If the trustee does not make the election, the trust recognizes no gain when it distributes the property.

If the trustee elects to recognize the gain, the distribution deduction equals the property's FMV. The beneficiary, in turn, takes a basis equal to the property's adjusted basis to the trust plus the gain the trust recognized on the distribution. If the beneficiary likely will sell the property soon after distribution, the election provision allows the trustee to choose where the appreciation will be taxed, at the trust level or the beneficiary level. If the distribution involves appreciated capital gain property, the capital gain the trust recognizes can offset the trust's current capital loss and carryovers from prior tax years.

EXAMPLE C:14-39 ▶ Todd Trust owns a number of assets, including an asset with a FMV of $35,000 and an adjusted basis of $12,000. In the current year, the trust distributes the asset to its sole beneficiary, Susan. The trust does not make any other distributions to Susan. If the trustee elects to recognize gain of $23,000, the trust receives a distribution deduction of $35,000, the FMV of the asset. If the trust has a $23,000 capital loss, it can offset the loss against the gain. Susan includes $35,000 of income in her tax return and obtains a $35,000 basis in the asset. Thus, if she sells the asset for $35,000, she will report no gain. If the trustee had not elected to recognize gain on the in-kind distribution, the distribution deduction would have been $12,000, the asset's adjusted basis to the trust. Susan's basis in the asset also would have been $12,000, and she would have reported $12,000 income from the trust. ◀

CHOICE OF YEAR-END FOR ESTATES

Distributions from an estate or trust are taxed to the beneficiaries in the beneficiaries' tax year in which the fiduciary's year ends.[44] Congress in 1986 required all trusts (even existing fiscal-year trusts) other than tax-exempt and wholly charitable trusts to use a calendar year as their tax year to eliminate their ability to defer the taxation of trust distributions to beneficiaries by choosing a noncalendar year.[45] Estates, however, are completely free to choose a year-end as long as the tax year does not exceed 12 months.

EXAMPLE C:14-40 ▶ Molly Madison died on February 7, 2014. Madison Estate adopted a fiscal year ending January 31. During the period February 7, 2014, through January 31, 2015, Madison Estate distributes $30,000 to Bob, a calendar year beneficiary. The estate's DNI exceeds $30,000. Bob reports $30,000 of estate income on his individual return for 2015, Bob's tax year during which the estate's tax year ended. By choosing the January 31 year-end (instead of a calendar year-end), the executor postpones the taxation of income to Bob from 2014 to 2015. ◀

ADDITIONAL COMMENT

For 2015, 39.6% is the top tax rate for income tax purposes, and 40% is the highest estate tax rate. Also, both the estate and individuals can owe an additional 3.8% tax on net investment income.

DEDUCTION OF ADMINISTRATION EXPENSES

Chapter C:13 points out that the executor elects where to deduct administration expenses, i.e., on the estate tax return, the estate's income tax return, or some on each return. Unlike the situation for deductions in respect of a decedent, Sec. 642(g) denies a double deduction for administration expenses. Such expenses should be deducted where they will yield the greatest tax savings. Of course, if the surviving spouse receives all the

[43] Sec. 643(e)(2).
[44] Secs. 652(c) and 662(c).
[45] Sec. 644.

decedent's property or all except for an amount equal to the exemption equivalent, deducting administration expenses on the estate tax return will produce no tax savings because the estate will owe no estate taxes.

COMPLIANCE AND PROCEDURAL CONSIDERATIONS

OBJECTIVE 10

Comply with procedural rules for trust and estate income taxation

FILING REQUIREMENTS

General Rule. Every estate that has gross income of at least $600 for the tax year must file an income tax return (Form 1041-U.S. Income Tax Return for Estates and Trusts). A trust income tax return (generally Form 1041) is required for every trust that has taxable income or has gross income of $600 or more.[46] In addition, every estate or trust that has a nonresident alien as a beneficiary must file a return.[47]

ETHICAL POINT

Individual beneficiaries report their share of income from trusts and estates on their Form 1040. CPAs have a responsibility to monitor clients' beneficial interests in trusts and estates to prevent underreporting. Some clients may unintentionally forget to disclose income from a simple trust if they received no cash distributions from the fiduciary during the year.

DUE DATE FOR RETURN AND TAX

The due date for fiduciary returns (Form 1041) is the same as for individuals, the fifteenth day of the fourth month following the end of the tax year.[48] If an extension is desired, Form 7004 must be filed. The automatic extension period is five months.

Both trusts and estates generally must make estimated tax payments using the general rules applicable to individual taxpayers.[49] The IRC, however, exempts estates from making estimated tax payments for their first two tax years. If the fiduciary's tax liability exceeds the estimated tax payments, the balance of the tax is due on or before the due date for the return.[50] Estimated tax payments for a trust or an estate should be accompanied by Form 1041-ES (Estimated Income Tax for Fiduciaries).

DOCUMENTS TO BE FURNISHED TO IRS

Although the executor or the trustee need not file a copy of the will or the trust instrument with the return, at times the IRS may request a copy of such documents. If the IRS makes such a request, the executor or the trustee also should transmit the following:

- A statement signed under penalty of perjury that the copy is true and complete
- A statement naming the provisions of the will or trust agreement that the executor or the trustee believes control how the income is to be divided among the fiduciary, the beneficiaries, and the grantor (if applicable)

SAMPLE SIMPLE AND COMPLEX TRUST RETURNS

Appendix B contains samples of simple and complex trust returns (Form 1041). The Appendix also illustrates completed Schedules K-1 for the reporting of distributed income, etc. to the beneficiaries. One copy of Schedule K-1 for each beneficiary is filed with Form 1041. In addition, each beneficiary receives a copy of his or her Schedule K-1, so that he or she knows the amount and type of gross income to report for the distributions received as well as other pertinent information.

In the two sets of facts illustrated in the sample returns, the trusts do not owe the alternative minimum tax (AMT). Trusts that owe the AMT report it on Schedule I of Form 1041.

---

46 Secs. 6012(a)(3) and (4). A special grantor trust rule, however, permits a revocable trust's income to be reported on the grantor's tax return. See Reg. Sec. 1.671-4(b).

47 Sec. 6012(a)(5).

48 Sec. 6072(a).

49 Sec. 6654(l).

50 Sec. 6151(a).

Problem Materials

Discussion Questions

C:14-1 Explain to a client in laymen's language what portion of the income of an estate or trust is subject to taxation at the fiduciary level.

C:14-2 Given the tax rate schedule for trusts, what reasons (tax and/or nontax) exist today for creating a trust?

C:14-3 List some major differences between the taxation of individuals and trusts.

C:14-4 Explain to a client the significance of the income and principal categorization scheme used for fiduciary accounting purposes.

C:14-5 List some common examples of principal and income items under the Uniform Act.

C:14-6 A client asks about the relevance of state law in classifying items as principal or income. Explain the relevance.

C:14-7 A trust instrument provides that, for life, Irene is entitled to receive distributions of income only and Beth is to receive the remainder interest. The trust sells property at a gain. Income and corpus are classified in accordance with the Uniform Act. Is the gain classified as income? Explain.

C:14-8 Refer to Question C:14-7. Which taxpayer (the trust, Irene, or Beth) pays the tax on the gain?

C:14-9 A trust owns an asset on which depreciation is claimed. The trust distributes all of its income to its sole income beneficiary. Whose taxable income is reduced by the depreciation?

C:14-10 What is the amount of the personal exemption for trusts and estates?

C:14-11 A client inquires about the significance of distributable net income (DNI). Explain.

C:14-12 a. Are net accounting income and DNI always the same amount?
b. If not, explain a common reason for a difference.
c. Are capital gains usually included in DNI?

C:14-13 Assume that a trust collects rental income and interest income on tax-exempt bonds. Will a portion of the rental expenses, such as repairs, have to be allocated to tax-exempt income and thereby become nondeductible? Explain.

C:14-14 a. Describe the shortcut approach for verifying that the amount calculated as a simple trust's taxable income is correct.
b. Can a shortcut verification process be applied for trusts and estates that accumulate some of their income? Explain.

C:14-15 When does the NOL of a trust or estate produce tax deductions for the beneficiaries?

C:14-16 The Mary Morgan Trust, a simple trust governed by the Uniform Act, sells one capital asset in the current year. The sale results in a loss.
a. When will the capital loss produce a tax benefit for the trust or its beneficiary? Explain.
b. Would the result necessarily be the same for a complex trust? Explain.

C:14-17 Describe the tier system for taxing trust beneficiaries.

C:14-18 Determine the accuracy of the following statement: Under the tier system, beneficiaries who receive mandatory distributions of income are more likely to be taxed on the entire distributions they receive than are beneficiaries who receive discretionary distributions.

C:14-19 a. Describe to a client what income in respect of a decedent (IRD) is.
b. Describe to the client one tax disadvantage and one tax advantage that occur because of the classification of a receipt as IRD.

C:14-20 Describe three situations that cause trusts to be subject to the grantor trust rules.

C:14-21 Can a client escape the grantor trust rules by providing in a trust instrument that income is payable to a nephew for 20 years and that the trust assets pass at the end of 20 years to the client's spouse?

C:14-22 Amelia, a widow, is in the top marginal income tax bracket and has considerably more income than she can spend. She is considering creating a trust for the benefit of her son Jason but is reluctant to make it irrevocable, at least presently. If she funds a revocable trust that must distribute all of its income to Jason, will Jason be taxed on the income? How may this trust help reduce the size of Amelia's gross estate?

C:14-23 What is the benefit of the 65-day rule?

C:14-24 a. When are fiduciary income tax returns due?
b. Must estates and trusts pay estimated income taxes?

ISSUE IDENTIFICATION QUESTIONS

C:14-25 Art Rutter sold an apartment building in May 2015 for a small amount of cash and a note payable with payments beginning in 2016. Principal and interest payments are due annually on the note in April of 2016 through 2020. Art died in August 2015. He willed all his assets to his daughter Amelia. Art's gross estate is about $6 million, and his estate tax deductions are very small. What tax issues should the executor of his estate consider with respect to reporting the sale of the building and the collection of the installments?

C:14-26 For the first five months of its existence (August through December 2015), the Estate of Amy Ennis had gross income (net of expenses) of $7,000 per month. For January through July 2016, the executor estimates that the estate will have gross income (net of expenses) totaling $5,000. The estate's sole beneficiary is Amy's uncle, Joe, an unmarried, calendar year taxpayer. Joe incurred a large NOL from his sole proprietorship years ago, and $34,000 of the NOL carryover remains but expires at the end of 2015. During 2015, Joe's only income was $10,000 from part-time employment. What tax issues should the executor of Amy's estate consider with respect to distributions of the estate's income?

C:14-27 Raj Kothare funded an irrevocable simple trust in May of last year. The trust benefits Raj's son for life and grandson upon the son's death. One of the assets he transferred to the trust was Webbco stock, which had a $35,000 FMV on the transfer date. Raj's basis in the stock was $39,000, and he paid no gift tax on the transfer. The stock's value has dropped to $27,000, and the trustee thinks that now (October of the current year) might be the time to sell the stock and recognize the loss. For the current year, the trust will have $20,000 of income exclusive of any gain or loss. What tax and non-tax issues should the trustee consider concerning the possible sale of the stock?

PROBLEMS

C:14-28 *Calculation of the Tax Liability.* A complex trust has taxable income of $29,900 in 2015. The $29,900 includes $5,000 of rental income and $25,000 of taxable interest income, reduced by the $100 personal exemption. The trust makes no distributions during the year. What is the trust's total tax liability? Compare this tax to the amount of tax an unmarried individual filing single would pay on the same amount of rental and interest income (with no other income). Assume the individual claims the standard deduction.

C:14-29 *Determination of Taxable Income and Tax Liability.* Suellen Symmes died on January 15, 2015. Her estate elected a November 30 year end. The executor projects that the estate will receive interest income of $50,000 by November 30, 2015, and will have no other gross income. In addition, it will have no deductions other than the personal exemption. The beneficiary of the estate is Thomas Symmes, a calendar year taxpayer who is projected to have $195,000 of taxable income in 2015, not including any distributions from the estate. Compare the overall tax costs for the estate and Thomas if (1) the executor distributes $37,250 to Thomas prior to November 30, 2015, and (2) the estate makes no distributions before November 30, 2015. Thomas is unmarried and files as a single taxpayer.

C:14-30 *Determination of Taxable Income.* A simple trust has the following receipts and expenditures for the current year. The trust instrument classifies gains, losses, and trustee's fees as part of principal.

Dividends	$20,000
Long-term capital gain	15,000
Trustee's fees	1,500
Distribution to beneficiary	20,000

a. What is the trust's taxable income under the formula approach of Figure C:14-1?
b. What is the trust's taxable income under the short-cut approach?

C:14-31 *Determination of Taxable Income.* Refer to Problem C:14-30. How would your answer to Part a change if the trust in addition received $8,000 interest from tax-exempt bonds, and it distributed $28,000 instead of $20,000?

C:14-32 ***Determination of Taxable Income and Tax Liability.*** A simple trust has the following receipts and expenditures for 2015. The trust instrument is silent with respect to capital gains, and state law concerning trust accounting income follows the Uniform Act. Assume the trustee's fee is charged equally to income and to principal.

Corporate bond interest	$40,000
Tax-exempt interest	9,000
Long-term capital gain	5,000
Trustee's fee	2,000
Distribution to beneficiary	48,000

a. What is the trust's taxable income under the formula approach of Figure C:14-1?
b. What is the trust's tax liability?

C:14-33 ***Determination of Taxable Income.*** During the current year, a simple trust has the following receipts and expenditures. The Uniform Act governs the accounting classification.

Corporate bond interest	$60,000
Long-term capital gain	20,000
Trustee's fees	3,000

a. What amount must be distributed to the beneficiary?
b. What is the trust's taxable income under the shortcut approach?

C:14-34 ***Determination of Distribution Deduction.*** A trust has net accounting income of $24,000 and incurs a trustee's fee of $1,000 in its principal account. What is its distribution deduction under the following situations:
a. It distributes $24,000, and all of its income is from taxable sources.
b. It distributes $24,000, and it has tax-exempt income (net of allocable expenses) of $2,000.
c. It distributes $10,000, and all of its income is from taxable sources.

C:14-35 ***Determination of Beneficiary's Income.*** A complex trust is authorized to make discretionary distributions of income and principal to its two beneficiaries, Roy and Sandy. Separate shares are not required. For the current year, it has DNI and net accounting income of $80,000, all from taxable sources. It distributes $60,000 to Roy and $40,000 to Sandy. How much gross income should each beneficiary report?

C:14-36 ***Determination of Beneficiary's Income.*** Refer to Problem C:14-35. How would your answer change if the trust instrument required that $10,000 per year be distributed to Sandy, and the trustee also made discretionary distributions of $60,000 to Roy and $30,000 to Sandy with separate shares not required?

C:14-37 ***Determination of Beneficiary's Income.*** A complex trust is required to distribute $20,000 and $30,000 annually to its beneficiaries, Bart and Thelma, respectively. In addition, it can distribute other amounts at its discretion. In Year 1, it had DNI of $62,000 and distributed $20,000 to Bart and $47,000 to Thelma. All of its income is from dividends. In Year 2, it had DNI of $66,000 and distributed $25,000 to Bart and $36,000 to Thelma. Again, all of its income is from dividends. Determine the amount of income each beneficiary should report with respect to the distributions for each year.

C:14-38 ***Determination of Accounting Income and Distribution.*** The Trotter Trust has the receipts and expenditures listed below for the current year. Assume the Uniform Act governs an item's classification as principal or income. The trustee's fee is charged one-half to principal and one-half to income. What is the trust's net accounting income and the maximum amount it can distribute? Assume the trust instrument precludes distributing principal currently.

Dividends	$15,000
Interest on tax-exempt bonds	7,000
Loss on sale of capital asset	(9,000)
Rental income from land	6,000
Property taxes on rental property	1,000
Trustee's fee	1,800

C:14-39 ***Determination of Taxable Income.*** Refer to Problem C:14-38. Assume the trustee must pay out all of its income currently to its beneficiary, Julio.
a. What is the deductible portion of the trustee's fee?
b. What is the trust's taxable income exclusive of the distribution deduction?
c. What is the trust's DNI?
d. What is the trust's taxable income using the formula approach of Figure C:14-1?

C:14-40 ***Determination of Taxable Income.*** Refer to Problem C:14-39. How would your answers change if the trust were a discretionary trust that distributes $12,000 to its beneficiary, Julio?

C:14-41 ***Calculation of Deductible Expenses.*** The George Grant Trust reports the receipts and expenditures listed below. What are the trust's *deductible* expenses?

U.S. Treasury interest	$25,000
Rental income	9,000
Interest from tax-exempt bonds	6,000
Property taxes on rental property	2,000
CPA's fee for tax return preparation	800
Trustee's fee	1,900

C:14-42 ***Tax Treatment of Capital Losses.*** A simple trust had a long-term capital loss of $10,000 for 2014 and a long-term capital gain of $15,000 for 2015. Its net accounting income and DNI are equal. Explain the tax treatment for the 2014 capital loss assuming the trust is in existence at the end of 2016.

C:14-43 ***Tax Treatment of Capital Losses.*** Refer to Problem C:14-42. How would your answer change if instead the trust were a complex trust that makes no distributions in 2014 and 2015? Assume the trust earns $8,000 of corporate bond interest income each year.

C:14-44 ***Revocable Trusts.*** A revocable trust created by Amir realizes $30,000 of rental income and a $5,000 capital loss. It distributes $22,000 to Ali, its beneficiary. How much income is taxed to the trust, the grantor, and the beneficiary?

C:14-45 ***Reversionary Interest Trusts.*** Holly funded the Holly Marx Trust in January 2015. The entire trust income is payable to her adult son, Jack for 20 years. At the end of the twentieth year, the trust assets are to pass to Holly's husband. In the current year, the trust realizes $30,000 of dividend income and a $15,000 long-term capital gain. How much income is taxed to the trust, the grantor, and the beneficiary in the current year?

C:14-46 ***Reversionary Interest Trusts.*** Refer to Problem C:14-45. Explain how your answers would change for each independent situation indicated below:
a. At the end of the trust term, the property passes instead to Holly's nephew Nathan.
b. Holly creates the trust in October 2015 for a term of 25 years, after which the property will revert to her.

C:14-47 ***Income in Respect of Decedent.*** The following items are relevant for the first income tax return for the Ken Kimble Estate. Mr. Kimble, a cash method of accounting taxpayer, died on July 1, 2015.

Dividends	$10,000
Interest on corporate bonds	18,000
Collection on installment note from sale of investment land	24,000

The record date was June 14 for $6,000 of the dividends and October 31 for the remaining $4,000 of dividends. The bond interest is payable annually on October 1. Mr. Kimble's basis in the land was $8,000. He sold it in May of 2014 for a total sales and contract price of $48,000 and reported his gain under the installment method. Ignore interest on the installment note. What amount of IRD should be reported on the estate's calendar year income tax return?

C:14-48 ***Income in Respect of Decedent.*** Julie Brown died on May 27 of the current year. She was employed before her death at a gross salary of $4,000 per month. Her pay day was the last day of each month, and her employer did not pro rate her last monthly salary payment. She owned preferred stock that paid quarterly dividends of $800 per quarter each March 31, June 30, September 30, and December 31. The record date for the June dividend was June 10. Assume her estate chooses a calendar year as its tax year. What amount of gross income should be reported on the estate's first income tax return? Identify the items of IRD included in gross income.

C:14-49 *Property Distributions.* In the current year, Maddox Trust, a complex trust, distributed an asset with a $42,000 adjusted basis and a $75,000 FMV to its sole beneficiary, Marilyn Maddox-Mason. The trustee elected to recognize gain on the distribution. Marilyn received no other distributions from the trust during the year. The distributable net income for the year was $87,000, and none of it was from tax-exempt sources.

a. What is the trust's distribution deduction?
b. On her individual income tax return, how much gross income should Marilyn report from the trust?
c. What is Marilyn's basis in the asset distributed in kind from the trust?

C:14-50 *Income Recognition by Beneficiary.* Joan died April 17, 2014. Joan's executor chose March 31 as the tax year end for the estate. The estate's only beneficiary, Kathy, reports on a calendar year. The executor of Joan's estate makes the following distributions to Kathy:

June 2014	$ 5,000
August 2014	10,000
March 2015	12,000
August 2015	14,000

The 2014 and 2015 distributions do not exceed DNI. How much income should Kathy report on her 2014 return as a result of the distributions from the estate? On her 2015, return?

COMPREHENSIVE PROBLEM

C:14-51 Dana Dodson died October 31, 2014, with a gross estate of $6.7 million, debts of $200,000, and a taxable estate of $6.5 million. Dana made no taxable gifts. All of her property passed under her will to her son, Daniel Dodson. The estate chose a June 30 year-end. Its receipts, disbursements, and gains for the period ended June 30, 2015, were as follows:

Dividend income	$27,000
Interest income from corporate bonds	18,000
Interest income from tax-exempt bonds	9,000
Gain on sale of land	10,000
Executor's fee (charged to principal)	4,000
Distribution to Daniel Dodson	–0–

Of the $27,000 dividends received in the estate's first tax year, $7,000 were declared October 4, 2014, with a record date of October 25 and a payment date of November 4, 2014. The corporate bonds pay interest each August 31 and February 28. The estate collected $18,000 corporate bond interest in February 2015 and August 2015. The tax-exempt bonds pay interest each June 30 and December 31. The estate collected $4,500 in December 2014 and December 2015 and $4,500 in June 2015 and June 2016 from the tax-exempt bonds. Dana, a cash basis taxpayer, sold land in 2011 for a total gain of $60,000 and used installment reporting. She collected principal in 2012 and 2013 and reported gain of $30,000 on her 2012 return and $10,000 on her 2013 return. The estate collected additional principal in March 2015 and the remaining principal payment in March 2016. The gain attributable to the March 2015 and March 2016 principal collections is $10,000 per tax year. Ignore interest on the sale.

Calculate the following:

a. Deductible executor's fee.
b. Total IRD and the IRD reported on the return for the period ended June 30, 2015.
c. Total Sec. 691(c) deduction if none of the debts are DRD.
d. Section 691(c) deduction deductible on the estate's income tax return for the period ended June 30, 2015.
e. Taxable income of the estate for its tax year ended June 30, 2015.
f. Marginal income tax rate for the estate for its tax year ended June 30, 2015.

TAX STRATEGY PROBLEMS

C:14-52 Glorietta Trust is an irrevocable discretionary trust that Grant Glorietta funded in 2005. The discretionary income beneficiary for life is Grant's son, Gordon Glorietta (single). Gordon is a partner in a partnership in which he materially participates, and he has a large basis in his partnership interest. For 2015, the trust had $50,000 of corporate bond interest, net of expenses, and no other income. It made no distributions to Gordon in 2015. Assume that it is now February 22, 2016, and Gordon has just learned that his share of loss from the partnership will be $72,000. Gordon has other income for 2015 of approximately $52,000. The trustee anticipates distributing $40,000 cash to Gordon before the end of February. For the last few years, Gordon's marginal tax rate was 15%. He claims the standard deduction, has only one exemption, and files as a single individual. Discuss a tax-saving opportunity presented by this scenario. Also show a comparative analysis of the alternatives.

C:14-53 Carla plans to create a trust and transfer to it oil and gas properties producing royalty income. She will transfer no other properties. The sole income beneficiary of the trust will be Carla's son, Marshall, who is in the top marginal income tax bracket and is expected to remain there. Carla estimates that the trust, a simple trust, will receive about $30,000 of royalty income each year and have $2,000 of cash expenses each year. The situs of the trust will be a state that has enacted the latest version of the Uniform Principal and Income Act. Carla seeks your advice about the total combined income tax cost to the trust and Marshall if the Uniform Principal and Income Act governs, compared with the combined tax cost to the two taxpayers if the trust instrument states that 27.5% of the royalty income is to be allocated to principal (corpus) and the rest to income. For simplicity, use 2015 tax rates and ignore the depletion deduction that would actually be available with respect to the royalty income. In addition, ignore the 3.8% tax on net investment income. You will need to follow the instructions for Problem C:14-63 to find the rules under the Uniform Principal and Income Act.

C:14-54 Cate Cole died in 2013, and her will left her entire estate in equal shares to her two adult children, Calvin and Corrine. Both children anticipate being in the top income tax bracket for at least ten years. The Cate Cole Estate is a calendar year taxpayer. The year 2015 is almost over, and to date the estate has received $18,000 of interest income from a certificate of deposit (CD). The executor does not expect to collect any more income before the end of the year. However, in January 2016, the estate will collect $1,500 of interest income from the CD. The executor has distributed all the estate's assets except for the CD, which matures in early January 2016. The executor anticipates distributing the funds from the CD when it matures, after which he will close the estate. Because the taxable estate did not exceed the "exemption equivalent," the executor did *not* deduct administration expenses on the estate tax return. The estate owes administration expenses totaling $25,000. Propose an income tax minimization strategy for timing, between 2015 and 2016, the payment of the administration expenses, and prepare a schedule to support your recommendation.

TAX FORM/RETURN PREPARATION PROBLEMS

C:14-55 Marion Mosley created the Jenny Justice Trust in 2005 with First Bank named as trustee. For 20 years, the trust is to pay out all its income semiannually to the beneficiary, Jenny Justice. At the end of the twentieth year, the trust assets are to be distributed to Jenny's descendants. According to the trust instrument, capital gains are credited to principal, and depreciation is charged to principal. For the current year, the irrevocable trust reports the following results:

	Amounts Allocable to	
	Income	*Principal*
Rental income	$15,000	
Corporate bond interest	27,000	
Interest on tax-exempt (non-private activity) bonds	8,000	
Long-term capital gain on sale of land		11,000[a]
Maintenance and repairs of rental property	1,500	
Property taxes on rental property	700	
CPA's fee for tax return preparation	500	
Trustee's fee		2,000
Depreciation		2,400
Estimated federal income taxes paid from principal		2,000

[a]The sales price and adjusted basis are $91,000 and $80,000, respectively. The trustee acquired the land in 2006 and the trustee sold it in November of the current year.

Prepare a Form 1041, including any needed Schedule K-1s, for the Jenny Justice Trust. Ignore the alternative minimum tax (AMT). The trustee's address is P.O. Box 100, Southwest City, TX 75000. The identification number of the trust is 74-1234567. Jenny, resides at 2 Mountain View, South City, AL 35000.

C:14-56 In 2005, Belinda Barclay established the Barclay Trust, an irrevocable trust, and named as trustee Local Bank, 1234 Tide Freeway, South City, AL 35000. She funded the trust with corporate and municipal bonds. The trustee is directed to distribute income in its discretion to Belinda's adult sons, Anthony and Patrick Barclay, for 15 years and then to pay out the remaining trust assets, including any accumulated income, equally between the two sons. The tax ID number for the trust is 74-7654321. Half of the trustee's fee is charged to principal and half to income. Gains and losses are classified as principal. During the current year, the trustee distributed $12,400 to Anthony, who resides at 37 Crimson Cove, South City, AL 35000, and nothing to Patrick. Other current year information for the trust is as follows:

Corporate bond interest	$17,000
Municipal bond interest	19,000
Long-term capital gain on sale of corporate bonds	2,200
CPA's fee for prior year's tax return	800
Trustee's fee	1,500
Estimated federal income taxes paid from principal	3,700

The trust has a $700 short-term capital loss carryover from the prior year.

Prepare a Form 1041, and any needed Schedule K-1s, for the Barclay Trust. Ignore the alternative minimum tax (AMT). The bonds are not private activity bonds.

C:14-57 Mark Meadows funded a trust in 2004 with Merchants Bank named as trustee. He paid no gift tax on the transfer. The trustee in its discretion is to pay out income, but not principal, to Mark's children, Angela and Barry, for 15 years. Then the trust will terminate, and its assets, including accumulated income, will be paid to Angela and Barry in equal amounts. (Separate shares are *not* to be maintained.) In the current year, the trustee distributes $3,000 to Angela and $9,000 to Barry. The trust paid estimated federal income taxes of $6,000 from the principal account and reported the following additional results for the current year. The trust instrument requires trustee's fees to be paid from principal.

	Amounts Allocable to	
	Income	*Principal*
Dividends	$50,000	
Interest on corporate bonds	4,000	
Interest on City of Cleveland (non-private activity) bonds	9,000	
Long-term capital loss on sale of stock		$12,000[a]
Trustee's fee		2,400
CPA's fee for tax return preparation	400	

[a]Mr. Meadows purchased the stock for $30,000 in 2000. It was valued at $44,000 when he transferred it to the trust in 2004. The price declined and the trust sold the stock for $18,000 in December of the current year.

Prepare a Form 1041, including any needed Schedule K-1s, for the trust established by Mr. Meadows. Ignore the alternative minimum tax (AMT). The trustee's address is 201 Fifth Ave., Northeast City, NY 10000. The trust's identification number is 74-1212121. Angela and Barry reside at 3 East 46th St., North City, NY 11000.

CASE STUDY PROBLEMS

C:14-58 Arthur Rich, a widower, is considering setting up an irrevocable trust (or trusts) with a bank as trustee for his three minor children. He will fund the trust at $900,000 (or $300,000 each in the case of three trusts). A friend suggested that he might want to consider a January 31 year-end for the trusts. The friend also suggested that Arthur might want to make each trust a complex discretionary trust. Arthur is a little apprehensive about the idea of a trust that would be complex. The friend warned that trust income should not be spent on support of the children.

Required: Prepare a memorandum to the tax partner of your firm concerning the above client matter. As part of your analysis, consider the following:

a. What tax reasons, if any, can you think of for having three trusts instead of one?
b. Why do you think the friend suggested a January 31 year-end?
c. What is your reaction to the friend's suggestion about the year-end?
d. Which taxpayer, the beneficiary, the grantor, or the trust, is taxed on the income from a discretionary trust?
e. To what extent do trusts serve as income-shifting arrangements?
f. What can you advise Arthur concerning his apprehension about a complex trust?
g. Why did the friend warn against spending trust income for the children's support?

C:14-59 You are preparing a current year (Year 2) individual tax return for Robert Lucca, a real estate developer and long-time client. While preparing Robert's individual tax return you learn that he has interest income from a trust his 75-year-old father created last year (Year 1). Robert's Year 2 income from the trust is properly reflected on a Schedule K-1 prepared by the accounting firm that prepared the trust's Year 2 return. Robert prepared the trust's return for Year 1, and decided that he should not be taxed on any of the trust's income because the trust distributed nothing to him. Upon reviewing Robert's copy of the trust instrument, you learn that the instrument calls for mandatory distributions of all the income to Robert every year. Assume that the trust reported $8,000 of taxable income for Year 1 and claimed no distribution deduction and that Robert was in the highest marginal tax bracket for Year 1.

a. What responsibility do you have to correct the error made for the tax Year 1? Refer to the *Statements on Standards for Tax Services* in Appendix E.
b. Assume instead that an IRS agent has just begun to audit Robert's Year 1 individual tax return. What is your responsibility if you have discovered the error on the Year 1 trust return, and you are representing Robert in the audit?

TAX RESEARCH PROBLEMS

C:14-60 You are in the process of doing income tax projections for the Estate of Esther Simmons, who died January 3, 2015. The Estate has paid appraisal fees for having her real estate holdings appraised for estate tax valuation purposes, probate court fees, and newspaper costs for having notices regarding debts published in the local newspaper. Draft a memo in which you address whether these costs will be classified as miscellaneous itemized deductions subject to the 2% nondeductible floor.

C:14-61 Roy Ritter died two years ago. Among the assets he owned were Ritter Ranch, a cattle ranch consisting of 12,220 acres in Texas. In accordance with Roy's will, the ranch passed to a testamentary trust (the Ritter Trust) with grandson Gene Ritter as trustee. The sole asset of the trust is the ranch, and unfortunately the ranch is operating at a loss. Gene is an accountant and devotes some hours to day-to-day ranching issues but does not meet the material participation test in the context of the passive activity loss (PAL) rules. Gene employs a well-trained, full-time ranch manager and 20 "ranch hands." Ritter Trust is a new client of your firm. Write a memo in which you discuss the applicability of the PAL rules to the Ritter Trust. In particular, you should discuss whether "material participation" is measured by just the trustee's hours and activities or whether the hours and efforts of the trustee, the ranch manager, and all of the other employees should be considered. Recall that Sec. 469 is the primary IRC section for the PAL rules.

C:14-62 Joyce Ingalls is the daughter of the late Fred Ingalls, who died August 15, 2014. One of the items included in his gross estate was a traditional (non-Roth) IRA valued at several million dollars. Mr. Ingalls's estate will owe estate taxes, but none had been paid by March 1, 2015, the date Joyce filed her 2014 individual income tax return, which she prepared herself. Included in her gross income for 2014 was a $50,000 distribution from her father's IRA. After talking with a friend, she wonders whether a Sec. 691(c) deduction was available on her 2014 return, and she has contacted you to resolve this issue. Write a memo in which you address whether Joyce is entitled to claim a Sec. 691(c) deduction for income in respect of a decedent (IRD) she collected, given that no estate tax has yet been paid on the IRD or any other inclusion in her father's gross estate. Also address in a conceptual manner how the deduction, assuming it is available, is calculated. At a minimum you should consult the following sources:

- IRC Sec. 691(c)
- FSA 200011023

C:14-63 *Internet Research Problem.* A client, Sam Curren, established the Curren Trust earlier this year. In addition to stocks and cash, the trust's assets include a life insurance policy on the life of Mr. Curren. The trust is both the owner and beneficiary of the policy. The insurance premiums are $8,250 per year. Are the premium payments classified as payments from the principal account or from the income account if the state that is the situs of the trust has adopted the latest version of the Uniform Principal and Income Act? Go to the Web site for the National Conference of Commissioners of Uniform State Laws, www.uniformlaws.org, and find the Uniform Principal and Income Act. Consult Section 502 of the Act and prepare a memo that addresses the classification of the payment of the insurance premium.

C:14-64 *Internet Research Problem.* You are preparing for a client meeting at which the client has indicated he wants to discuss revocable trusts. Use the search engine Google and locate a discussion about revocable trusts (also known as living trusts). Summarize the points from a site's discussion about revocable (living) trusts, and indicate which Web site you visited.

CHAPTER

15

ADMINISTRATIVE PROCEDURES

LEARNING OBJECTIVES

After studying this chapter, you should be able to

1. Describe the role of the IRS in our tax system
2. Discuss how returns are selected for audit and the alternatives available to taxpayers whose returns are audited
3. Explain the IRS's ruling process
4. Identify the due dates for filing tax returns and paying taxes
5. Distinguish the various types of penalties imposed by the IRS
6. Calculate the penalty for not paying estimated taxes
7. Describe the more severe penalties, including the fraud penalty
8. Recognize when the statute of limitations applies
9. Explain from whom the government may collect unpaid taxes
10. Apply the professional and governmental standards for tax practitioners

CHAPTER OUTLINE

This chapter provides an overview of the administrative and procedural aspects of tax practice, an area with which all tax advisors should be familiar. The specific matters discussed include the role of the Internal Revenue Service (IRS) in tax enforcement and collection, the manner in which the IRS chooses tax returns for audit, taxpayers' alternatives to immediately agreeing to pay a proposed deficiency, due dates for returns, taxpayer penalties, and the statute of limitations. Chapter C:1 briefly discussed the AICPA's *Statements on Standards for Tax Services* and Treasury Department *Circular 230* guidelines for tax practioners. Chapter C:15 expands the discussion on professional standards and examines additional tax practice topics, including Internal Revenue Code (IRC) penalty provisions that affect tax advisors and tax return preparers.

ROLE OF THE INTERNAL REVENUE SERVICE

OBJECTIVE 1

Describe the role of the IRS in our tax system

The IRS is part of the Treasury Department. Its chief administrative officer is the IRS Commissioner. Overseeing the activities of the IRS is a nine-member board consisting of the Secretary of the Treasury, the IRS Commissioner, a public sector representative, and six private sector representatives. All board members are appointed by the President of the United States.

ENFORCEMENT AND COLLECTION

KEY POINT

The U.S. tax structure is based on a self-assessment system. The level of voluntary compliance actually is quite high, but one of the principal purposes of the IRS is to enforce the federal tax laws and identify taxpayers who willfully or inadvertently fail to pay their fair share of the tax burden.

One of the IRS's most significant functions is enforcing tax laws.[1] The IRS is responsible for ensuring that taxpayers file returns, correctly report their tax liabilities, and pay any tax due.

Voluntary compliance with U.S. tax laws is relatively high. However, because some persons do not voluntarily comply, the IRS must audit selected taxpayers' returns and investigate the activities of nonfilers. In addition, because numerous ambiguities (gray areas) in the tax law exist, taxpayers and the IRS do not always agree on the proper tax treatment of transactions and events. As part of its enforcement duties, the IRS attempts to discover whether the reporting of these transactions and events differs from the way the IRS thinks they should be reported. As we point out later, taxpayers who disagree with the IRS in an audit may litigate.

The IRS must ensure that taxpayers not only report the correct tax liability, but also pay their taxes on time. For various reasons, some taxpayers file returns without paying any or all of the tax owed. The IRS's collection agents are responsible for collecting as much of the tax as possible from such persons.

INTERPRETATION OF THE STATUTE

As noted in Chapter C:1, the statutory language of the Internal Revenue Code (IRC) often is so vague that the courts and IRS must interpret it so that it can be readily applied. The IRS publishes its interpretations in revenue rulings, revenue procedures, notices, and information releases, which are available to the general public. In addition, the IRS offers guidance to specific taxpayers in the form of letter rulings, which have no precedential value for third-party taxpayers. Each of these authorities is discussed in detail in Chapter C:1.

[1] The IRS, however, does not have enforcement duties with respect to the taxes on guns and alcohol.

AUDITS OF TAX RETURNS

OBJECTIVE 2

Discuss how returns are selected for audit and the alternatives available to taxpayers whose returns are audited

The IRS operates service centers across the country, which receive and process tax returns.[2] One of the IRS's principal enforcement functions is auditing these returns. All returns are subject to some verification. One task the IRS service centers perform is checking whether amounts are properly calculated and faithfully carried from one line of a return to another. Another task is determining whether any items, such as signatures and Social Security numbers, are missing. Computers compare (or "match") by Social Security number the amounts reported on a taxpayer's return with employer- or payer-prepared documents (e.g., Forms W-2 and 1099) filed with the IRS service center.[3] To date, however, a 100% matching of these documents with tax return information has been difficult to achieve.

If the service center detects a calculation error in the tax reported on the return, it will send to the taxpayer a notice proposing an additional tax or granting a refund. If the information reported on a return is inconsistent with the information on Forms W-2 or 1099 reported by an employer or payer, the IRS asks the taxpayer to account for the discrepancy in writing or pay some additional tax.

PERCENTAGE OF RETURNS EXAMINED

REAL-WORLD EXAMPLE

Percentage examined of all returns filed in 2013:

Individuals	1.0%
C corporations	1.4%
S corporations	0.4%
Partnerships	0.4%

The IRS exams only a small fraction of all returns filed. For example, see the Real World Example in the margin. However in fiscal year 2013, for individuals with total positive income (i.e., gross income before losses and other deductions) of $1 million or more, the audit rate was 10.8%, and corporations with assets of at least $250 million faced a 33.9% audit rate. As a result of its audit activities, the IRS recommended additional taxes totaling $37.1 billion and civil penalies of $25.9 billion in that year.[4]

The examination percentages described above may be misleading because over half the returns filed are subject to a computerized matching in which the IRS compares the tax return information with documents (Forms 1099 and W-2) submitted by taxpayers and employers. Because wages, interest, alimony, pensions, unemployment compensation, Social Security benefits, and other items of income are reported to the IRS by the payers, and because state income taxes, local real estate taxes, home mortgage interest, and other items of deduction are reported to the IRS by the payees, taxpayers who report only these items on their returns effectively face a 100% audit rate. According to a former IRS commissioner, "[M]ore than half of the individual returns filed are simple enough so that a matching with forms filed by employers and interest payors is sufficient to insure compliance."[5] In fact, 60% of individual assessments were by correspondence.

SELECTION OF RETURNS FOR AUDIT

Returns are chosen for audit in various ways, with many being selected under the *discriminant function (DIF)* process described below. The IRS's objective in using the DIF process is to make the audit process as productive as possible by maximizing the number of audits that result in the collection of additional taxes.[6] The DIF process has improved the IRS's ability to select returns for audit. In recent years, the IRS failed to collect additional taxes on only 10% to 15% of the individual returns audited by its revenue agents and examiners. By comparison, in the late 1960s, before the advent of the DIF program, the IRS failed to collect additional taxes in 45% to 50% of its audits.[7] The IRS conducts an audit initiative known as the Market Segment Specialization Program (MSSP). Examples of market segments include manufacturing, wholesale trade, retail trade (auto

[2] For returns filed during calendar year 2014, the IRS maintains nine centers to process returns.

[3] Form W-2 reports employees' salaries and withholding tax, and Form 1099 reports income such as interest and dividends.

[4] "Examination Coverage: Recommended and Average Recommended Additional Tax Examination, by Type and Size of Return, Fiscal Year 2013," *Internal Revenue Service 2013 Data Book*, available for download at *www.irs.gov/pub/irs-soi/13databk.pdf*. Examinations are performed by revenue agents, tax auditors, and service center personnel.

[5] Bureau of National Affairs, *BNA Daily Tax Reports*, June 20, 1984, p. G-1.

[6] J. L. Wedick, Jr., "Looking for a Needle in a Haystack—How the IRS Selects Returns for Audit," *The Tax Adviser*, November 1983, pp. 673–674.

[7] Letter from Sheldon S. Cohen, former IRS Commissioner, to Representative Nancy L. Johnson, Chairman of House Ways and Means Subcommittee on Oversight Regarding the TCMP, dated July 20, 1995, reprinted in *Tax Notes Today*, August 10, 1995, Document 95 TNT 156-63.

and boat dealers and service stations), and services (medical and health).[8] Under the MSSP, IRS personnel develop industry expertise, and the IRS prepares MSSP audit guidelines. As IRS personnel become more familiar with specific industries, their ability to spot industry-specific items that taxpayers incorrectly report likely will improve.

HISTORICAL NOTE

Taxpayers have made several attempts to make the DIF variables public information. However, so far the courts have refused to require the IRS to provide such information. The basic thrust of the DIF program is that a return will be flagged if enough items on the return are out of the norm for a taxpayer in that particular income bracket.

Discriminant Function (DIF) Program. Of the individual returns audited in 1982, the IRS selected two-thirds under the **DIF** program. In fiscal year 2006, the IRS selected only 27% under the DIF program, with the rest being selected under 12 different audit initiatives, some of which involve nonfilers, tax-shelter related write-offs, computer matching of third-party information, claims for refund, return preparers, and unallowable items.[9]

Returns with a relatively high DIF score have characteristics in common with returns for which the IRS earlier assessed a deficiency upon audit (e.g., the return may have reported a relatively high casualty loss or charitable contribution deduction). Because the IRS does not have the resources to audit all returns with a relatively high DIF score, IRS agents choose which of the higher scored returns should receive top priority for an audit.[10]

The IRS developed its DIF formulas based on data gathered in its **Taxpayer Compliance Measurement Program (TCMP)**. Under the TCMP, the IRS conducted special audits of taxpayers selected at random. In these audits, the IRS examined every line item of taxpayers' returns to develop a statistical norm for the taxpayers' industry or profession as a whole. The IRS "indefinitely postponed" the TCMP in 1995, but in 2002, the IRS launched the **National Research Program (NRP)**. The NRP updates data compiled in TCMP audits and develops new statistical models for identifying returns most likely to contain errors. The NRP differs from the TCMP in two significant respects. First, it relies on pre-existing audit data as well as data compiled in ordinary, as opposed to special, audits. Second, it focuses on specific portions of a tax return, not all line-by-line items, some of which can be verified without face-to-face meetings. Like the TCMP, the NRP is based on data gathered primarily in audits of randomly selected individual tax returns.[11] Starting in 2007, the IRS began selecting 13,000 returns per year and will combine the audit results over rolling three year periods.

The IRS also conducts what are called "financial status" or "lifestyle" audits. These audits seek to identify inconsistencies between the income that a taxpayer reports and income suggested by his or her lifestyle. In the course of the audit, IRS agents review the taxpayer's overall economic situation. They may ask questions concerning where the taxpayer vacations, where his or her children go to school, and the cost and model of his or her vehicles. Although the courts generally have sanctioned the use of financial status audits, Congress has limited their use to situations in which the IRS has a reasonable indication of unreported income.

Other Methods. The IRS widely uses other methods for selecting returns for audit. Some returns are chosen because the taxpayer filed a claim for a refund of taxes paid previously, and the IRS decides to audit the tax return before refunding the requested amount. A few returns are audited because the IRS receives a tip from one taxpayer (perhaps a disgruntled former employee or ex-spouse) that another taxpayer did not file a correct return. If the IRS does collect additional taxes as a result of the audit, it will pay a reward to the individual who provided the tip. The amount of the award must be at least 15% of the additional taxes, penalties, and interest collected, but it cannot exceed 30%. The award can be reduced if the whistleblower's contribution was less than substantial. Whistleblowers can appeal to the Tax Court if the award is reduced below 15%.[12] If the tax, penalties, and interest exceed $2 million, the reward ranges from 15% to 30% of the amount collected. Sometimes, examining the return of an entity (e.g., a corporation) leads to an audit of a related party's return (e.g., a major stockholder).

Occasionally, the IRS investigates particular types of transactions or entities to ascertain taxpayer compliance with the tax law. As a result of these investigations, the IRS may

---

[8] K. D. Bakhai and G. E. Bowers, "A New Era in IRS Auditing," *Florida CPA Today*, November 1994, pp. 26–30.

[9] J. L. Wedick, Jr., "Looking for a Needle in a Haystack—How the IRS Selects Returns for Audit," *The Tax Adviser*, November 1983, pp. 673–674.

[10] Ibid.

[11] The NRP also targets taxes other than individual taxes. For example, the IRS is in the final stages of a project involving S corporations. It also announced a multi-year employment tax project beginning in 2010.

[12] Sec. 7623 and Reg. Sec. 301.7623-1(c).

select a number of returns for audit. For example, in 1989 the IRS examined 3,000 to 4,000 individual returns to determine whether taxpayers avoided classifying expenses as miscellaneous itemized deductions to escape the 2% floor. In 1997, the IRS investigated the returns of about 200,000 trusts (representing approximately 7% of total trust returns) to determine whether taxpayers had established them to avoid taxes.[13] In 2003, through a combination of audits, summons, and targeted litigation, the IRS launched an initiative to identify and deter promoters of abusive tax shelters.[14] In November 2009, the IRS announced its first major employment tax research study in 25 years.

DISCLOSURE OF UNCERTAIN TAX POSITIONS

In 2010, the IRS introduced a new reporting requirement for Form 1120, specifically, Schedule UTP (Uncertain Tax Position Statement). An uncertain tax position is a tax position taken on a tax return that would result in an adjustment to a line on the tax return if the position is not sustained. Schedule UTP requires a description of each uncertain tax position for which the taxpayer recorded a reserve in its audited financial statements or for which no reserve has been recorded because of expected litigation. Taxpayers also must rank the uncertain positions and disclose whether any tax position exceeds 10% of the aggregate amount of the reserves for all tax positions. For 2010 and 2011 tax years, corporations with assets exceeding $100 million that issued audited financial statements had to report uncertain tax positions on Schedule UTP. For 2012 and 2013, the threshold was $50 million and was decreased to $10 million in 2014.

The schedule will help the IRS identify and prioritize issues for audit. The IRS hopes that Schedule UTP will make their auditors more efficient and increase taxpayer compliance. Taxpayers' primary objection is that the schedule provides a detailed roadmap of vulnerable tax positions, which would affect who was audited and what issues should be addressed. In response to this concern (in Announcement 2010-76), the IRS expanded its policy of restraint and will refrain from requesting particular documents related to uncertain tax positions and the workpapers used to complete Schedule UTP. As part of the restraint policy, the IRS will not assert that the attorney-client privilege, tax advice privilege under Sec. 7525, or the work product doctrine has been waived by providing otherwise privileged documents to financial auditors for their use in preparing financial statements. However, privilege is not created for any other document of the taxpayer or third party. Refer to "Accountant-Client Privilege" on page C:15-36.

ALTERNATIVES FOR A TAXPAYER WHOSE RETURN IS AUDITED

When the IRS notifies a taxpayer of an impending audit, the notice indicates whether the audit is a correspondence, office, or field audit. In a correspondence audit, communication, such as documenting a deduction or explaining why the taxpayer did not report certain income, is handled through the mail. In an office audit, the taxpayer and/or his or her tax advisor meet with an IRS employee at a nearby IRS office. The audit notice indicates which items the IRS will examine and what information the taxpayer should bring to the audit. Field audits are common for business returns and complex individual returns. IRS officials conduct these audits either at the taxpayer's place of business or residence or at his or her tax advisor's office.

ADDITIONAL COMMENT

This special relief rule was designed to reduce the likelihood that the IRS could harass a taxpayer by repeatedly auditing a taxpayer on the same issue.

Special Relief Rule. A special relief rule exists for repetitive audit examinations of the same item. A taxpayer who receives an audit notice can request that the IRS suspend the examination and review whether the audit should proceed if (1) the IRS audited the taxpayer's return for the same item in at least one of the two previous years and (2) the earlier audit did

[13] Jacob M. Schlesinger, "IRS Cracks Down on Trusts It Believes Were Set up as Tax-Avoidance Schemes," *The Wall Street Journal*, April 4, 1997, p. A2.

[14] I.R. 2003-51, April 15, 2003.

not result in a change to his or her tax liability. To request the suspension, the taxpayer should call the IRS official whose name and telephone number appear on the audit notice.

EXAMPLE C:15-1 ▶ In October 2015, the IRS notifies Tony that it will audit his 2013 medical expense deduction. Two years ago, the IRS audited Tony's 2011 medical expense deduction but did not assess an additional tax. Consequently, Tony may request that the IRS suspend the audit of his 2013 return regarding this issue. ◀

EXAMPLE C:15-2 ▶ Assume the same facts as in Example C:15-1 except the IRS audited Tony's 2011 employee business expenses. Because that audit dealt with a different item, Tony may not request a suspension. ◀

ADDITIONAL COMMENT

Taxpayers should encourage the tax practitioner to handle an IRS audit. Because taxpayers usually have a limited understanding of the complexities of the tax law and its administration, having the taxpayer present at the audit generally is not a good idea.

TYPICAL MISCONCEPTION

Taxpayers should be cautious in signing a Form 870. Once this form is executed, the taxpayer no longer is permitted to administratively pursue the items under audit.

Meeting with a Revenue Agent. Generally, the first step in the audit process is a meeting between the IRS agent and the taxpayer or the taxpayer's advisor. If the taxpayer is fortunate, the agent will agree that the return was correct as filed or, even better, that the taxpayer is entitled to a refund. In most instances, however, the agent will contend that the taxpayer owes additional taxes. Taxpayers who do not agree with the outcome of their meeting may ask to confer with the agent's supervisor. A meeting with the supervisor could lead to an agreement concerning the additional tax due.

Should the taxpayer agree and the agent's supervisor concur in the amount owed, the taxpayer must sign Form 870 (Waiver of Restrictions on Assessment and Collection of Deficiency in Tax). This form indicates that the taxpayer waives any restrictions on the IRS's authority to assess the tax and consents to the IRS's collecting it. However, signing Form 870 does not preclude the taxpayer from filing a refund claim later.

If the taxpayer agrees that he or she owes additional tax and pays the tax upon signing the Form 870 waiver, interest accrues on the tax deficiency from the due date of the return through the payment date. Interest also ceases to accrue 30 days after the taxpayer signs the Form 870 waiver but begins to accrue again when the IRS issues a notice and demand for payment. However, the IRS charges no additional interest if the taxpayer pays the tax due within 21 days of the notice and demand (ten days for $100,000 or more).

Technical Advice Memoranda. Occasionally, a highly technical issue with which an IRS agent or appeals officer has had little or no experience arises in the course of the audit. Regardless of the type of audit, the official may request advice from the IRS's national office. Sometimes, the taxpayer urges the official to seek such advice. The advice is given in a Technical Advice Memorandum, which the IRS makes public in the form of a letter ruling. If the advice is favorable to the taxpayer, the agent or appeals officer must follow it. Even if the advice is pro-IRS, the official may consider the hazards of litigation in deciding whether to compromise.

Appeal to Appeals Division. If the taxpayer does not sign the Form 870 waiver, the IRS will send the taxpayer a **30-day letter**, detailing the proposed changes in the taxpayer's liability and advising the taxpayer of his or her right to pursue the matter with the IRS appeals office. The taxpayer has 30 days from the date of the letter to request a conference with an IRS appeals officer.

If the additional tax and penalty is less than $25,000 (a small case request), taxpayers may initiate an appeal indicating the unagreed adjustments and briefly stating the reasons for the appeal. If the amount of additional tax plus penalties and interest in question exceeds $25,000, the taxpayer must submit a formal **protest letter** within the 30-day period. If the taxpayer does not respond to the 30-day letter, the IRS will follow up with a 90-day letter, discussed below.

Protest letters are submitted to an official in the appropriate IRS functional division and should include the following information:

- The taxpayer's name, address, and telephone number
- A statement that the taxpayer wishes to appeal the IRS findings to the appeals office
- A copy of the letter showing the proposed adjustments
- The tax years involved

- A list of the proposed changes with which the taxpayer disagrees and the reasons for disagreement
- A statement of facts supporting the taxpayer's position on any issue with which he or she disagrees
- The law or other authority on which the taxpayer relied[15]

The taxpayer must declare, under penalties of perjury, that the statement of facts is true. If the taxpayer's representative prepares the protest letter, the representative must indicate whether he or she knows personally that the statement of facts is true.

KEY POINT

The appeals officer currently has the authority to settle or compromise issues with the taxpayer. To alleviate some of the workload and to make the audit process more efficient, the IRS currently is considering giving more of this settlement authority to revenue agents.

Unlike IRS agents, appeals officers generally have the authority to settle (compromise) cases after considering the hazards of litigation. For example, if the appeals officer believes that the IRS has approximately a 40% chance of winning in court, the appeals officer may agree to close the case if the taxpayer will pay an amount equal to 40% of the originally proposed deficiency. The settlement authority of appeals officers extends to questions of fact and law.

In some matters, however, an appeals officer has no settlement authority. For example, if the matter involves an appeals coordinated issue, the appeals officer must obtain concurrence or guidance from a director of appeals to reach a settlement. An **appeals coordinated issue** usually has wide impact or importance, frequently involving an entire industry or occupation group, for which the IRS desires consistent treatment. An example of an appeals coordinated issue is the income tax treatment of a sale in/lease out (SILO) transaction.[16]

If, after the appeals conference, the taxpayer completely agrees with the IRS's position, he or she signs a Form 870 waiver. However, if the appeals officer makes some concessions and the parties agree that the additional tax is less than that originally proposed, the taxpayer signs Form 870-AD (Waiver of Restrictions on Assessment and Collection). Unlike the case of a Form 870 waiver, a Form 870-AD waiver generally does not permit the taxpayer later to file a refund claim for the tax year in question. A Form 870-AD waiver is effective only if accepted by the IRS.

90-DAY LETTER

If the taxpayer and appeals officer fail to reach an agreement, or if the taxpayer does not file a written protest within 30 days of the date of the initial letter, the IRS issues a **90-day letter** (officially, a "Statutory Notice of Deficiency").[17] The 90-day letter specifies the amount of the deficiency; explains how the amount was calculated; and states that the IRS will assess it unless, within 90 days of the date of mailing, the taxpayer files a petition with the Tax Court.[18] During the 90-day period (and whether or not the taxpayer files the petition), the IRS may not assess the deficiency or attempt to collect it. After the 90-day period (and only if the taxpayer timely files the petition), the IRS still may not assess or collect the deficiency until the Court's decision becomes final.

LITIGATION

As mentioned earlier, taxpayer litigation can begin in one of three courts of first instance: the Tax Court, a U.S. district court, and the U.S. Court of Federal Claims. Before deciding where to litigate, a taxpayer should consider the precedents, if any, of the various courts. Chapter C:1 discusses the issues of precedent and "forum shopping" and provides an overview of the organization and key attributes of the federal courts. After considering the time and expense of litigation, some taxpayers decide to pay the deficiency even though they believe their position is correct.

U.S. Tax Court. Taxpayers seeking to litigate in the Tax Court must file their petition with the Tax Court within 90 days of the date on which the IRS mails the Statutory Notice of Deficiency. The Tax Court strictly enforces this time limit. Before the scheduled hearing date, taxpayers still may reach an agreement with the IRS. Going the Tax Court route has some advantages, including not having to pay the deficiency as a precondition to filing suit.

---

[15] IRS, *Publication No. 5* [Your Appeal Rights and How to Prepare a Protest If You Don't Agree], January 1999, p. 1. A sample protest letter is published in Robert E. Meldman and Richard J. Sideman, *Federal Taxation Practice and Procedure,* Ninth Edition (Chicago: CCH Incorporated, 2006).

[16] IRS Appeals Coordinated Issue Program Settlement Guidelines, UIL No. 9300.38-00.

[17] Upon request, the IRS may grant an extension of time for filing a protest letter.

[18] Sec. 6213(a). If the notice is addressed to a person outside the United States, the time period is 150 days instead of 90.

If the amount in question does not exceed $50,000 for a given year, the taxpayer may use the informal small cases procedure, an alternative not available in other courts. A potential disadvantage of this procedure is that the taxpayer may not appeal the Court's decision.

Taxpayers must pay the additional tax, plus any interest and penalties, if they lose in Tax Court and choose not to appeal their case. In some situations, the Tax Court leaves the computation of the additional tax up to the litigating parties. When this happens, the phrase "Entered under Rule 155" appears at the end of the Tax Court's opinion.

U.S. District Court or U.S. Court of Federal Claims. To litigate in either a U.S. district court or the U.S. Court of Federal Claims, the taxpayer must first pay the deficiency and then file a claim for a refund with the IRS. In all likelihood, the IRS will deny this claim on the ground that the IRS correctly calculated the deficiency amount and properly assessed it. Upon notice of denial or six months after filing the claim, whichever is earlier, the taxpayer may sue the IRS for a refund. In no event, however, may the taxpayer file this lawsuit two years after the IRS denies the claim.

Appeal of a Lower Court's Decision. Whichever party loses—the taxpayer or the IRS—may appeal the lower court's decision to an appellate court. If the lawsuit was filed in the Tax Court or a federal district court, the case is appealable to the circuit court of appeals with jurisdiction over the taxpayer. For individuals, the taxpayer's place of residence generally determines which court of appeals has jurisdiction. In the case of corporations, the firm's principal place of business or state of incorporation generally controls. Cases originating in the U.S. Court of Federal Claims are appealable to the Circuit Court of Appeals for the Federal Circuit; that is, all the latter cases are heard by the same circuit, irrespective of the taxpayer's residence, principal place of business, or state of incorporation.

Either the taxpayer or the government can request that the U.S. Supreme Court review an appellate court's decision by preparing a writ of certiorari. If the Supreme Court decides to hear a case, it grants **certiorari**. If the Court decides not to hear a case, it denies certiorari. In any given year, the Supreme Court hears only a few cases dealing with tax matters.

? STOP & THINK

Question: Two years ago, Pete deducted an expenditure in the year he paid it. Recently, the IRS audited Pete's return for that year and contended that the expenditure is not deductible. Pete is a resident of California, which is in the Ninth Circuit. In a similar case a few years ago, the Tax Court held that the expenditure is deductible, and the IRS did not appeal the decision. In yet another similar case litigated in a U.S. district court in California, the government lost at the trial level but won on appeal to the Ninth Circuit. If Pete decides to litigate, in which forum (lower court) should he file suit, and why?

Solution: If he litigates in the Tax Court, he need not pay the proposed deficiency tax in advance. However, under the *Golsen* Rule (see Chapter C:1), the Tax Court would depart from its earlier pro-taxpayer decision and rule for the IRS. (Pete's case would be appealable to the Ninth Circuit, and the Ninth Circuit has adopted a pro-government position.) Because the court for his California district would be bound by Ninth Circuit precedent, he should not litigate in that court. This likely outcome would disappoint Pete if he believed that a jury would rule in his favor because only U.S. district courts allow for jury trials. The only forum in which he could win is the U.S. Court of Federal Claims. No precedent that this court must follow exists because neither the U.S. Supreme Court, the Court of Appeals for the Federal Circuit, nor the U.S. Court of Federal Claims has previously adjudicated the issue. (For a discussion of "forum-shopping," see Chapter C:1.)

Burden of Proof. In civil cases, the IRS has the burden of proving any factual issue relevant to a determination of the taxpayer's liability, provided the taxpayer meets four conditions.[19] First, the taxpayer introduces "credible evidence" regarding the issue. Credible evidence means evidence of a quality sufficient to serve as the basis of a court decision.[20]

---

[19] See Sec. 7491.

[20] See S. Rept. No. 105-174, (PL. 105-206), pp. 45-46.

Second, the taxpayer complies with the recordkeeping and substantiation requirements of the IRC. These requirements include the proper documentation of meal and entertainment expenses (Sec. 274), charitable contributions (Sec. 170), and foreign controlled businesses (Sec. 6038). Third, the taxpayer "cooperates" with the reasonable requests of the IRS for witnesses, information, documents, meetings, and interviews. Cooperation includes providing access to, and inspection of, persons and items within the taxpayer's control. It also includes exhausting all administrative remedies available to the taxpayer.[21] Fourth, the taxpayer is either a legal person with net worth not exceeding $7 million, or a natural person.

Requests for rulings

OBJECTIVE 3

Explain the IRS's ruling process

As discussed in Chapter C:1, a taxpayer can seek to clarify the tax treatment of a transaction by requesting that the IRS rule on the transaction. The IRS will respond to certain requests by issuing a letter ruling (sometimes referred to as a private letter ruling) directly to the taxpayer. A letter ruling is a written determination that interprets and applies the tax laws to the taxpayer's specific set of facts.[22] The IRS releases letter rulings to the public but eliminates all confidential information before doing so. The IRS charges a user fee for issuing a ruling, with the 2014 fees ranging from $180 for identical accounting method changes to $50,000 for pre-filing agreements. The fee for ruling on a proposed transaction is $28,300.[23]

ADDITIONAL COMMENT

The information requirements for requesting a letter ruling are very precise (see Rev. Proc. 2015-1). In general, a tax professional experienced in dealing with the national office of the IRS should be consulted. Also, a good blueprint of what should be included in a ruling request often can be found by locating an already-published letter ruling and examining its format.

INFORMATION TO BE INCLUDED IN TAXPAYER'S REQUEST

Early each calendar year, the IRS issues a revenue procedure that details how to request a letter ruling and the information that the request must contain. Taxpayers or tax advisors should consult this procedure before requesting a ruling. Appendix B of the procedure contains a checklist the taxpayer may use to ensure that the request is in order. The IRS has issued additional guidelines concerning the data to be included in the ruling request. For example, the IRS has specified what information the taxpayer must provide in a request for a ruling on the tax effects of transfers to a controlled corporation under Sec. 351. All ruling requests must contain a statement of all the relevant facts, including the following:

- Names, addresses, telephone numbers, and taxpayer identification numbers of all interested parties
- The taxpayer's annual accounting period and method
- A description of the taxpayer's business operations
- A complete statement of the business reasons for the transaction
- A detailed description of the transaction[24]

The taxpayer also should submit copies of the contracts, agreements, deeds, wills, instruments, and other documents that pertain to the transaction. The taxpayer must provide an explicit statement of all the relevant facts and not merely incorporate by reference language from the documents. The taxpayer also should indicate what confidential data should be deleted from the ruling before its release to the public.

If the taxpayer takes a position, he or she must disclose the basis for this position and the authorities relied on. Even if the taxpayer does not argue for a particular position, he or she must furnish an opinion of the expected tax effects, along with a statement of authorities supporting this opinion. In addition, the taxpayer should disclose and discuss any authorities to the contrary. The IRS suggests that, if no authorities to the contrary exist, the taxpayer should state so.

---

21 Ibid.

22 Rev. Proc. 2015-1, 2015-1 I.R.B. 1, Sec. 2.01.

23 Rev. Proc. 2015-1, 2015-1 I.R.B. 1, Appendix A.

24 Rev. Proc. 2015-1, 2015-1 I.R.B. 1, Sec. 7.01. Certain revenue procedures provide a checklist of information to be included for frequently occurring transactions. See, for example, Rev. Proc. 83-59, 1983-2 C.B. 575, which includes guidelines for requesting rulings regarding a corporate formation under Sec. 351.

The person on whose behalf a ruling is requested should sign the following declaration: "Under penalties of perjury, I declare that I have examined this request, including accompanying documents, and, to the best of my knowledge and belief, the request contains all the relevant facts relating to the request, and such facts are true, correct, and complete."[25]

WILL THE IRS RULE?

In income and gift tax matters, the IRS will rule only on proposed transactions and on completed transactions for which the taxpayer has not yet filed a return.[26] In estate tax matters, the IRS generally will not rule if the estate has filed a tax return. On the other hand, the IRS will rule on the estate tax consequences of a living person.[27] If no temporary or final Treasury Regulations relating to a particular statutory provision have been issued, the following policies govern a ruling unless another IRS pronouncement holds otherwise:

- If the answer seems clear by applying the statute to the facts, the IRS will rule under the usual procedures.
- If the answer seems reasonably certain by applying the statute to the facts, but not entirely free from doubt, the IRS will likewise rule.
- If the answer does not seem reasonably certain, the IRS will rule if so doing is in the best interests of tax administration.[28]

TYPICAL MISCONCEPTION

It is easy to be confused about the difference between letter rulings, which pertain to either prospective transactions or completed transactions for which a return has not yet been filed, and Technical Advice Memoranda, which pertain to completed transactions for which the return has been filed and is under audit.

The IRS will not rule on a set of alternative ways of structuring a proposed transaction or on the tax consequences of hypothetical transactions. Generally, the IRS will not rule on certain issues because of the factual nature of the problem involved or for other reasons.[29]

From time to time, the IRS discloses, by means of a revenue procedure, the topics with respect to which it will not rule. The list of topics, however, is not all-inclusive. The IRS may refuse to rule on other topics whenever, in its opinion, the facts and circumstances so warrant.

According to Rev. Proc. 2015-3, the matters on which the IRS will not rule include the following:

- Whether property qualifies as the taxpayer's principal residence
- Whether compensation is reasonable in amount
- Whether a capital expenditure for an item ordinarily used for personal purposes (e.g., a swimming pool) has medical care as its primary purpose
- The determination of the amount of a corporation's earnings and profits.[30]

In addition, the IRS will not rule privately on issues that it proposes to address in revenue rulings, revenue procedures, or otherwise, or that the Treasury Department proposes to address in Treasury Regulations.

SELF-STUDY QUESTION

How are letter rulings different from other IRS administrative pronouncements (i.e., revenue rulings, revenue procedures, notices, and information releases)?

ANSWER

Letter rulings are written for specific taxpayers (not the general public) and have no precedential value.

WHEN RULINGS ARE DESIRABLE

Private letter rulings serve to "insure" the taxpayer against adverse, after-the-fact tax consequences. They are desirable where (1) the transaction is proposed, (2) the potential tax liability is high, and (3) the law is unsettled or unclear. They also are desirable where the IRS has issued to another taxpayer a favorable ruling regarding similar facts and issues. Because only the other taxpayer may rely on the latter ruling, *this* taxpayer may seek a ruling on which he or she may confidently rely. On the other hand, private letter rulings are undesirable where the IRS has issued to another taxpayer an unfavorable ruling regarding similar facts and issues. They also are undesirable where the IRS might publicly rule on a related matter, and the taxpayer has an interest in this matter. Private letter rulings offer insight into the IRS's thinking on the tax treatment of proposed transactions. Although third parties may not cite them as authority for the tax consequences of their transactions, they may cite them as authority for avoiding a substantial understatement penalty (discussed later in this chapter).

ADDITIONAL COMMENT

Requesting a letter ruling makes most sense for transactions that the taxpayer would not undertake without being assured of certain tax consequences. For example, certain divisive reorganizations are tax-free under Sec. 355. Taxpayers often request a ruling that a proposed transaction satisfies the intricate requirements of Sec. 355.

[25] Rev. Proc. 2015-1, 2015-1 I.R.B. 1, Sec. 7.01.
[26] Ibid., Sec. 5.01.
[27] Ibid., Sec. 5.06.
[28] Ibid., Sec. 5.16.
[29] Ibid., Sec. 6.02.
[30] Rev. Proc. 2015-3, 2015-1 I.R.B. 111, Sec. 3.

Due Dates

OBJECTIVE 4

Identify the due dates for filing tax returns and paying taxes

DUE DATES FOR RETURNS

Returns for individuals, fiduciaries, and partnerships are due on or before the fifteenth day of the fourth month following the year-end of the individual or entity.[31] C corporation and S corporation tax returns are due no later than the fifteenth day of the third month after the corporation's year-end. To be subject to reporting requirements, individuals and fiduciaries, but not corporations and partnerships, must have earned a minimum level of gross income during the year.[32]

EXTENSIONS

Congress realized that, in some instances, gathering the requisite information and completing the return by the designated due date is difficult. Consequently, it authorized extensions of time for filing returns. Unless the taxpayer is abroad, the extension period cannot exceed six months.[33]

Individuals. By filing Form 4868 (Application for Automatic Extension of Time to File U.S. Individual Income Tax Return), an individual taxpayer may request an automatic six-month extension of time to file the tax return.[34] The extension is automatic in the sense that the taxpayer need not convince the IRS that an extension is necessary.

EXAMPLE C:15-3 ► Bob and Alice, his wife, are calendar year taxpayers. By filing Form 4868, they may get an automatic extension until October 15 of the following year for filing their current year's return. However, if the fifteenth falls on Saturday, Sunday, or a holiday, the due date is the next business day. ◄

Corporations. Corporations request an automatic extension by filing Form 7004 (Application for Automatic Extension of Time to File Corporation Income Tax Return) by the original due date for the return. Although the IRC specifies an automatic extension period of three months, Treasury Regulations and the Form 7004 instructions specify six months.[35] No additional extensions are available.

EXAMPLE C:15-4 ► Lopez Corporation reports on a fiscal year ending March 31. The regular due date for its return is June 15. It may file Form 7004 and request an automatic six-month extension that postpones the due date until December 15. ◄

DUE DATES FOR PAYMENT OF THE TAX

TYPICAL MISCONCEPTION

Obtaining an extension defers the date by which the return must be filed, but it does *not* defer the payment date of the tax liability. Therefore, an extension for filing must be accompanied by a payment of an estimate of the taxpayer's tax liability. Computing this estimated tax liability can be difficult because much of the information necessary to complete the return may be incomplete or not yet available.

The granting of an extension merely postpones the due date for filing the return. It does not extend the due date for paying the tax. In general, the due date for the tax payment is the same as the unextended due date for filing the return.[36] In addition, the first estimated tax installment for extinguishing an individual's annual income tax liability must be paid by the due date for the preceding year's return, and the remaining payments must be made, respectively, two, five, and nine months later. Taxpayers who elect to let the IRS compute their tax must pay it within 30 days of the date the IRS mails a notice of the amount payable.[37]

When individuals request an automatic extension, they should project the amount of their tax liability to the extent possible. Any tax owed, net of tax withholding and estimated tax payments, should be remitted with the extension request. In addition, if an extension for filing a gift tax return is requested (on the same form), the estimated amount of gift tax liability should be remitted. Similarly, corporations should remit with their automatic extension request the amount of tax they estimate to be due, reduced by any estimated tax already paid.

---

[31] Sec. 6072(a). Section 6072(c) extends the due date for returns of nonresident alien individuals and foreign corporations to the fifteenth day of the sixth month after the end of their tax year.

[32] Secs. 6012(a) and 6031(a).

[33] Sec. 6081(a).

[34] Reg. Sec. 1.6081-4.

[35] Sec. 6081(b) and Reg. Sec. 1.6081-3(a).

[36] Sec. 6151(a).

[37] Sec. 6151(b)(1). The estimated tax payment rules for C corporations, S corporations, and trusts and estates are described in Chapters C:3, C:11, and C:14, respectively, of this volume.

INTEREST ON TAX NOT TIMELY PAID

Interest accrues on any tax not paid by the original due date for the return even if the taxpayer extends the filing date.[38] Taxpayers incur interest charges in four situations.

- They file late, without having requested an extension, and pay late.
- They request an extension for filing but underestimate their tax liability and, thus, must pay additional tax when they file their return.
- They file in a timely manner but are not financially able to pay some, or all, of the tax.
- The IRS audits their return and determines that they owe additional taxes.

EXAMPLE C:15-5 ▶ Ann filed her Year 1 individual return in a timely manner on April 15 of Year 2, and the IRS audits it in March of Year 4. Ann is a calendar year taxpayer. The IRS contends that Ann owes $2,700 of additional taxes. Ann pays the additional taxes on March 30 of Year 4. Ann also must pay interest on the $2,700 deficiency for the period April 16 of Year 2 through March 30 of Year 4. The applicable interest rates for various segments of time appear in the schedule below. ◀

Rate Determination. The IRS fixes the interest rate that it charges taxpayers under rules provided in Sec. 6621 and announces changes in Revenue Rulings. The rate varies with fluctuations in the quarterly federal short-term rate. Thus, the interest rate could change at the beginning of each calendar quarter. For noncorporate taxpayers, the interest rate on both underpayments and overpayments is three percentage points higher than the federal rate. For corporate tax overpayments exceeding $10,000, the interest rate is reduced to the federal short-term rate plus one-half percentage point. For corporate underpayments exceeding $100,000, the rate is five percentage points above the federal short-term rate if the deficiency is not paid before a certain date. Rates are rounded to the nearest full percent. Recent applicable interest rates are as follows:

Period	*General Rate for Underpayments and Overpayments*
October 1, 2011, through December 31, 2014	3%
April 1, 2011, through September 30, 2011	4%
October 1, 2011, through March 31, 2012	3%
January 1, 2011, through March 31, 2011	3%
April 1, 2009, through December 31, 2010	4%
January 1, 2009, through March 31, 2009	5%
October 1, 2008, through December 31, 2008	6%

HISTORICAL NOTE

Probably two of the most significant changes in tax administration have been the daily compounding of interest and tying the interest rate charged to the federal short-term rate, which has resulted in a higher rate used to calculate the interest charge than in years past. Before these two changes, taxpayers who played the "audit lottery" and took aggressive positions incurred little risk.

Daily Compounding. Daily compounding applies to both the interest taxpayers owe to the government and the interest the government owes to taxpayers who have overpaid their taxes. The IRS has issued Rev. Proc. 95-17 containing tables to be used for calculating interest.[39] The major tax services have published these tables. In addition, software packages are available for interest calculations.

Accrual Period. Interest usually accrues from the original due date for the return until the payment date. However, two important exceptions apply. First, if the IRS fails to send an individual taxpayer a notice within 36 months after the original due date or the date on which a return is timely filed (including extensions), whichever is later, the accrual of interest (and penalties) is suspended.[40] The suspension period begins on the

[38] Secs. 6601(a) and (b)(1).
[39] Rev. Proc. 95-17, 1995-1 C.B. 556.
[40] Sec. 6404(g).

day after the 36-month period and ends 21 days after the IRS sends the requisite notice. Second, if the IRS does not issue a notice and demand for payment within 30 days after the taxpayer signs a Form 870 waiver, no interest is charged for the period between the end of the 30-day period and the date the IRS issues its notice and demand.[41] Taxpayers litigating in the Tax Court may make a deposit to reduce interest potentially owed. If the court decides that the taxpayer owes a deficiency, interest will not accrue on the deposit.

EXAMPLE C:15-6 ▶ Cindy receives an automatic extension for filing this year's return. On June 24 of the following year, she submits her return, along with the $700 balance she owes on this year's tax liability. She owes interest on $700 for the period April 16 of this year through June 24 of the following year. Interest is compounded daily based on the interest rate for underpayments determined under Sec. 6621. ◀

EXAMPLE C:15-7 ▶ After filing for an automatic extension, Hans filed his Year 1 return on August 15 of Year 2. On August 29 of Year 5, the IRS sends Hans a notice of deficiency in which it assesses interest. Because the IRS failed to send Hans the notice by August 15 of Year 5 (36 months after the date on which the return was timely filed), the accrual of interest is suspended. The suspension period begins on August 16 of Year 5 (the day after the 36-month period) and ends on September 19 of Year 5 (21 days after the IRS sends the requisite notice). ◀

EXAMPLE C:15-8 ▶ Raj filed his Year 1 individual return on March 15 of Year 2. The IRS audits the return early in Year 4, and on January 27 of Year 4, Raj signs a Form 870 waiver, in which he agrees that he owes a $780 deficiency. The IRS does not issue a notice and demand for payment until March 21 of Year 4. Raj pays the deficiency two days later. Raj owes interest, compounded daily at the Sec. 6621 underpayment rate, for the period April 16 of Year 2 (the day after the original due date) through February 26 of Year 4 (30 days after Raj signed Form 870). No interest can be assessed for the period February 27 through March 21 of Year 4 because the IRS did not issue its notice and demand for payment until more than 30 days after Raj signed the Form 870 waiver. ◀

Abatement. The IRS does not abate interest except for unreasonable errors or delays resulting from its managerial or ministerial acts.[42] A "managerial act" involves the temporary or permanent loss of records or the exercise of judgment or discretion relating to the management of personnel.[43] A "ministerial act" involves routine procedure without the exercise of judgment or discretion.[44] A decision concerning the proper application of federal law is neither a managerial nor a ministerial act.

EXAMPLE C:15-9 ▶ Omar provides documentation to an audit agent, who assures him that he will receive a copy of an audit report shortly. Before the agent has had an opportunity to act, however, the divisional manager transfers him to another office. An extended period of time elapses before the manager assigns another audit agent to Omar's case. The decision to reassign is a managerial act. The IRS may abate interest attributable to any unreasonable delay in payment resulting from this act. ◀

EXAMPLE C:15-10 ▶ Chanelle requests information from an IRS employee concerning the balance due on her current year tax liability. The employee fails to access the most current computerized database and provides Chanelle with incorrect information. Based on this information, Chanelle pays less than the full balance due. The employee's failing to access the most current database is a ministerial act. The IRS may abate interest attributable to any unreasonable delay in payment resulting from this act. ◀

FAILURE-TO-FILE AND FAILURE-TO-PAY PENALTIES

Objective 5

Distinguish the various types of penalties imposed by the IRS

Penalties add teeth to the accounting and reporting provisions of the Internal Revenue Code. Without them, these provisions would be mere letters on the books of the legislature—words without effect. Tax-related penalties fall into two broad categories: taxpayer and preparer. As the name suggests, taxpayer penalties apply only to taxpayers, be they individuals, corporations, estates, or trusts. Preparer penalties apply only to tax return

[41] Sec. 6601(c).
[42] Sec. 6404(e).
[43] Reg. Sec. 301.6404-2(b)(1).
[44] Reg. Sec. 301.6404-2(b)(2).

REAL-WORLD EXAMPLE

In fiscal 2013, as a result of the audit process, the IRS assessed a total of $25.9 billion in civil penalties and abated about $11.5 billion for reasonable cause.

preparers, be they firms that employ tax professionals or the professionals themselves. Within these broad categories are two distinct subcategories: civil and criminal. Civil penalties are imposed on taxpayers for negligently, recklessly, or intentionally failing to fulfill their accounting or reporting obligations. Criminal penalties are imposed for maliciously or willfully failing to do so. Taxpayers may raise as a defense to some penalties "reasonable cause" and a good faith belief in the correctness of their position. Sometimes, for the defense to be valid, they also must disclose this position on their tax return. This section of the text discusses two commonly encountered penalties in income, estate, and gift taxation: failure to file and failure to pay. The IRS may assess these penalties, in addition to interest, on overdue tax liabilities. Subsequent sections of the text discuss other taxpayer and preparer penalties. Topic Review C:15-1 presents a summary of IRC penalty provisions. The Topic Review is provided here rather than later in the chapter to give readers a framework for following the discussion of the various penalties.

TOPIC REVIEW C:15-1

Overview of Penalties

Penalty	IRC Section	Applicability	Rules/Calculation	Defenses/Waiver
A. TAXPAYER—CIVIL				
Failure to file	6651(a)	All persons	*General rule:* 5% per month or fraction thereof; 25% maximum *Minimum penalty if late more than 60 days:* lesser of $135 or 100% of tax due	Reasonable cause, not willful neglect
	6651(f)	All persons	*Fraudulent reason for not filing: 15% per month or fraction thereof;* 75% maximum	
Failure to pay tax	6651(a)	All persons	*General rule:* 0.5% per month or fraction thereof; 25% maximum*	Reasonable cause, not willful neglect
Failure by individual to pay estimated tax	6654	Individuals, certain estates, trusts	*General rule:* penalty at same rate as interest rate for deficiency; imposed for period between due date for estimated tax payments and earlier of payment date or due date for return	Waiver in unusual circumstances
Failure by corporation to pay estimated tax	6655	Corporations	*General rule:* penalty at same rate as interest rate for deficiency; imposed for period between due date for estimated tax payments and earlier of payment date or due date for return	—
Negligence	6662(c)	All persons	*General rule:* 20% of underpayment attributable to negligence	Reasonable cause, good faith
Substantial understatement	6662(d)	All persons	*General rule:* 20% of underpayment attributable to substantial understatement (portion for which no substantial authority and no disclosure exists)	Reasonable cause, good faith; also, substantial authority, disclosure
Civil fraud	6663	All persons	*General rule:* 75% of portion of understatement attributable to fraud.	Reasonable cause, good faith
B. TAXPAYER—CRIMINAL				
Willful attempt to evade tax	7201	All persons	*General rule:* Up to $100,000 ($500,000 for corporations) and/or up to five years in prison	—
Willful failure to collect or pay over tax	7202	All persons	*General rule:* Up to $10,000 and/or up to five years in prison	—
Willful failure to pay or file	7203	All persons	*General rule:* Up to $25,000 ($100,000 for corporations) and/or up to one year in prison	—
Willfully making false or fraudulent statements	7206	All persons	*General rule:* Up to $100,000 ($500,000 for corporations) and/or up to three years in prison	—

TOPIC REVIEW C:15-1 (CONT.)

C. PREPARER—CIVIL				
Understatement of tax by preparer	6694(a)	Tax return preparers	*General rule:* greater of $1,000 or half of preparer's income from return	Reasonable cause, good faith; also, disclosure
Willful attempt to understate taxes	6694(b)	Tax return preparers	*General rule:* greater of $5,000 or half of preparer's income from return	—
Failure to furnish copy to taxpayer	6695(a)	Tax return preparers	*General rule:* $50; $25,000 maximum	Reasonable cause, not willful neglect
Failure to sign return	6695(b)	Tax return preparers	*General rule:* $50; $25,000 maximum	Reasonable cause, not willful neglect
Failure to furnish identifying number	6695(c)	Tax return preparers	*General rule:* $50; $25,000 maximum	Reasonable cause, not willful neglect
Failure to retain copy or list	6695(d)	Tax return preparers	*General rule:* $50; $25,000 maximum	Reasonable cause, not willful neglect
Failure to file correct information returns	6695(e)	Tax return preparers	*General rule:* $50 for each failure to file a return or each failure to set forth an item in a return; $25,000 maximum	Reasonable cause, not willful neglect
Improper negotiation of checks	6695(f)	Tax return preparers	*General rule:* $500 per check	—
Aiding and abetting in understatement	6701(b)	All persons	*General rule:* $1,000 ($10,000 for corporations)	—

* If the taxpayer owes both the failure-to-file and the failure-to-pay penalties for a given month, the total penalty for such month is limited to 5% of the net tax due.

FAILURE TO FILE

Taxpayers who do not file a return by the due date generally are liable for a penalty of 5% per month (or fraction thereof) of the net tax due.[45] A fraction of a month, even just a day, counts as a full month. The maximum penalty for failing to file is 25%. If the taxpayer receives an extension, the extended due date is treated as the original due date. In determining the net tax due (i.e., the amount subject to the penalty), the IRS reduces the taxpayer's gross tax by any taxes paid by the return's due date (e.g., withholding and estimated tax payments) and tax credits claimed on the return. If any failure to file is fraudulent, the penalty rate is 15% per month up to a maximum penalty of 75%. For purposes of this provision, "fraud" is actual, intentional wrongdoing or the commission of an act for the specific purpose of evading a tax known or believed to be due.[46]

ADDITIONAL COMMENT

The most common reason given by taxpayers to support reasonable cause for failing to file a timely tax return is reliance on one's tax advisor. Other reasons include severe illness or serious accident. Reliance on a tax advisor is not always sufficient cause to obtain a waiver of the penalties.

Penalties are not levied if a taxpayer can prove that he or she failed to file a timely return because of reasonable cause (as opposed to willful neglect). According to Treasury Regulations, reasonable cause exists if "the taxpayer exercised ordinary business care and prudence and was nevertheless unable to file the return within the prescribed time."[47] Not surprisingly, much litigation deals with the issue of reasonable cause.

Note that the penalty imposed for not filing on time generally is a function of the net tax due. However, a minimum penalty applies in some cases. Congress enacted the minimum penalty provision because of the cost to the IRS of identifying nonfilers. If a taxpayer does not file an income tax return within 60 days of the due date (including any extensions), the penalty will be no less than the smaller of $135 or 100% of the tax due on the return. Taxpayers who owe no tax are not subject to the **failure-to-file penalty**. Also, the IRS may waive the penalty if the taxpayer shows reasonable cause for not filing.

[45] Rules for failure to file penalties are in Sec. 6651.

[46] *Robert W. Bradford v. CIR*, 58 AFTR 2d 86-5532, 86-2 USTC ¶9602 (9th Cir., 1996) *Chris D. Stoltzfus v. U.S.*, 22 AFTR 2d 5251, 68-2 USTC ¶9499 (3rd Cir., 1968): and *William E. Mitchell v. CIR*, 26 AFTR 684, 41-1 USTC ¶9317 (5th Cir., 1941).

[47] Reg. Sec. 301.6651-1(c)(1).

EXAMPLE C:15-11 ▶ Earl files his current year individual income tax return on July 5 of the following year. Earl requested no extension and did not have reasonable cause for his late filing, but he committed no fraud. Earl's current year return shows a balance due of $400. Under the regular rules, the late filing penalty would be $60 (0.05 × 3 months × $400). Earl's penalty is $135 because of the minimum penalty provision applicable to his failure to file the return within 60 days of the due date. ◀

In general under Sec. 6601(e)(2), interest does not accrue on any penalty paid within 21 days of the date that the IRS notifies the taxpayer of the penalty (ten days if the amount exceeds $100,000). However, interest accrues on the failure-to-file penalty, from the due date of the return (including any extensions) until the payment date.

FAILURE TO PAY

The **failure-to-pay penalty** is imposed at 0.5% per month (or fraction thereof).[48] The maximum penalty is 25%. The penalty is based on the gross tax shown on the return less any tax payments made and credits earned before the beginning of the month for which the penalty is calculated. As with the failure-to-file penalty, the IRS may waive the failure-to-pay penalty if the taxpayer shows reasonable cause.

Because the tax is due on the original due date for the return, taxpayers who request an extension without paying 100% of their tax liability potentially owe a failure-to-pay penalty. Treasury Regulations provide some relief by exempting a taxpayer from the penalty if the additional tax due with the filing of the extended return does not exceed 10% of the tax owed for the year.[49]

EXAMPLE C:15-12 ▶ Gary requests an extension for filing his current year individual income tax return. His current year tax payments include withholding of $4,500, estimated tax payments of $2,000, and $1,000 submitted with his request for an automatic extension. He files his return on June 6 of the following year, showing a total tax of $8,000 and a balance due of $500. Gary is exempt from the failure-to-pay penalty because the $500 balance due does not exceed 10% of his current year liability (0.10 × $8,000 = $800). Had Gary's current year tax instead been $9,000, he would have owed an additional tax of $1,500 and a failure-to-pay penalty of $15 (0.005 × 2 months × $1,500). ◀

The 0.5% penalty increases to 1% a month, or fraction thereof, in certain circumstances. The rate is 1% for any month beginning after the earlier of

- Ten days after the date the IRS notifies the taxpayer that it plans to levy on his or her salary or property and
- The day the IRS notifies and demands immediate payment from the taxpayer because it believes that collection is in jeopardy

EXAMPLE C:15-13 ▶ Ginny filed her Year 1 individual income tax return on April 13 of Year 2. However, Ginny did not pay her tax liability at that time. On October 7 of Year 4, the IRS notifies Ginny of its plans to levy on her property. The failure-to-pay penalty is 0.5% per month for the period April 16 of Year 2 through October 16 of Year 4. Beginning on October 17 of Year 4, ten days following the notice of levy, the penalty rises to 1% per month, or a fraction thereof. ◀

SELF-STUDY QUESTION

If a taxpayer does not have sufficient funds to pay his or her tax liability by the due date, should the taxpayer wait until the funds are available before filing the tax return?

ANSWER

No. He or she should file the return on a timely basis. This filing avoids the 5% per month failure-to-file penalty. The taxpayer still will owe the failure-to-pay penalty, but at least this penalty is only 0.5% per month.

Some taxpayers file on time to avoid the failure-to-file penalty even though they cannot pay the balance of the tax due. Barring a showing of reasonable cause, these taxpayers still will incur the failure-to-pay penalty. Because taxpayers who do not timely file a return are likely to owe additional taxes, they often owe both the failure-to-file and the failure-to-pay penalties.

The IRC provides a special rule for calculating the 5% per month failure-to-file penalty for periods in which the taxpayer owes both penalties. The 5% per month failure-to-file penalty is reduced by the failure-to-pay penalty. Thus, the total penalties for a given month will not exceed 5%. For months when the taxpayer incurs both penalties, the failure-to-file penalty is effectively 4.5% (5% − 0.5%). Note, however, that no reduction occurs if the minimum penalty for failure to file applies.

[48] Rules for failure to pay penalties are in Sec. 6651.

[49] Reg. Sec. 301.6651-1(c)(3) and (4).

EXAMPLE C:15-14 ▶ Tien files her current year individual income tax return on August 5 of the following year, without having requested an extension. Her total tax is $20,000. Tien pays $15,000 in a timely manner and the $5,000 balance when she files the return. Although Tien committed no fraud, she can show no reasonable cause for the late filing and late payment. Tien's penalties are as follows:

Failure-to-pay penalty:		
$5,000 × 0.005 × 4 months		$ 100
Failure-to-file penalty:		
$5,000 × 0.05 × 4 months	$1,000	
Minus: Reduction for failure-to-pay penalty imposed for same period	(100)	900
Total penalties		$1,000 ◀

EXAMPLE C:15-15 ▶ Assume the same facts as in Example C:15-14 except that Tien instead pays the $5,000 balance on November 17 of the following year. The penalties are as follows:

Failure-to-pay penalty:		
$5,000 × 0.005 × 8 months (April 16 through November 17)		$ 200
Failure-to-file penalty:		
$5,000 × 0.05 × 4 months (April 16 through August 5)	$1,000	
Minus: Reduction for failure-to-pay penalty levied for April 16 through August 5 ($5,000 × 0.005 × 4 months)	(100)	900
Total penalties		$1,100 ◀

Estimated taxes

OBJECTIVE 6

Calculate the penalty for not paying estimated taxes

Individuals earning only salaries and wages generally pay their annual income tax liability through payroll withholding. The employer is responsible for remitting these withheld amounts, along with Social Security taxes, to a designated federal depository. By contrast, individuals earning other types of income, as well as C corporations, S corporations, and trusts, must estimate their annual income tax liability and prepay their taxes on a quarterly basis.[50] Estates must do the same with respect to income earned during any tax year ending two years after the decedent's death.[51] Although partnerships do not pay estimated income taxes, their separate partners do if they are individuals or taxable entities. Chapters C:3, C:11, and C:14 discuss the estimated income tax requirements for C corporations, S corporations, and fiduciaries, respectively.

PAYMENT REQUIREMENTS

Individuals should pay quarterly estimated income taxes if they have a significant amount of income from sources other than salaries and wages.[52] The amount of each payment should be the same if this outside income accrues uniformly throughout the year. To avoid an estimated income tax penalty for the current year, individuals with AGI of $150,000 or less in the previous year should calculate each payment as follows:

Step 1: Determine the lesser of
- a. 90% of the taxpayer's regular tax, alternative minimum tax (if any), and self-employment tax for the current year, or
- b. 100% of the taxpayer's prior year regular tax, alternative minimum tax (if any), and self-employment tax if the taxpayer filed a return for the prior year and the year was not a short tax year.

Step 2: Calculate the total of
- a. Tax credits for the current year
- b. Taxes withheld on the current year's wages
- c. Overpayments of the prior year's tax liability the taxpayer requests be credited against the current year's tax

50 S corporations must pay quarterly estimated taxes on their net recognized built-in gains, passive investment income, and credit recapture amounts.

51 For example, if the decedent's death were June 15 of the current year, and the assets of the decedent's estate are not distributed by June 14 of the following year, the estate must pay estimated taxes on income earned on estate assets for the following tax year.

52 Rules pertaining to individuals' estimated taxes are in Sec 6654.

Step 3: Multiply the excess of the amount from Step 1 over the amount from Step 2 by 25%.

Calendar year individual taxpayers should pay their quarterly installments on April 15, June 15, September 15, and January 15.

Individuals with AGI exceeding $150,000 ($75,000 for married filing separately) in the prior year can avoid the estimated tax penalty for the current year if they pay at least 90% of the current year's tax, or at least 110% of the prior year's tax.[53]

EXAMPLE C:15-16 ▶ Mike's regular tax on his current year taxable income is $35,000. Mike also owes $2,000 of self-employment tax but no alternative minimum tax. Mike's total liability last year for both income and self-employment taxes was $24,000. His AGI last year did not exceed $150,000. Taxes withheld from Mike's current year wages were $8,000. Mike did not overpay his tax last year or earn any credits this year. For the current year, Mike should have made quarterly estimated tax payments of $4,000, as calculated below.

Lesser of:	90% of current year's tax (0.90 × $37,000 = $33,300) or 100% of prior year's $24,000 tax liability	$24,000
Minus:	Taxes withheld from current year's wages	(8,000)
Minimum estimated tax payment to avoid penalty under general rule		$16,000
Quarterly estimated tax payments (0.25 × $16,000)		$ 4,000

◀

ADDITIONAL COMMENT

Although it is simpler to use the amount of tax paid (or, if necessary, the applicable percentage of the amount of tax paid) in the preceding year as a safe harbor, the estimate of the current year's tax liability is preferable if the current year's tax liability is expected to be significantly less than the preceding year's tax liability.

The authority to make estimated tax payments based on the preceding year's income is especially significant for taxpayers with rising levels of income. To avoid an estimated income tax penalty, these taxpayers need to pay only an amount equal to the prior year's tax liability. Using this safe harbor eliminates the need for estimating the current year's tax liability with a high degree of accuracy.

EXAMPLE C:15-17 ▶ Peter, a single calendar year taxpayer, incurs a regular tax liability of $76,000 in the current year. Peter owes no alternative minimum tax liability nor can he claim any tax credits. No overpayments of last year's taxes are available to offset this year's tax liability. Taxes withheld evenly from Peter's wages throughout the current year are $68,000. Peter's AGI last year exceeded $150,000, and his regular tax liability was $60,000. Because Peter's $17,000 of withholding for each quarter exceeds the $15,000 minimum required quarterly payments, as calculated below, he incurs no underpayment penalty.

Lesser of:	90% of current year's (0.90 × $76,000 = $68,400) or 110% of prior year's $60,000 tax liability	$66,000
Minus:	Taxes withheld from current year's wages	(68,000)
Minimum estimated tax payment to avoid penalty under general rule		$ –0–

The $8,000 ($76,000 − $68,000) balance of the current's year taxes is due on or before April 15 of next year with the filing of the return or the request for extension of time to file. ◀

ADDITIONAL COMMENT

If a taxpayer is having taxes withheld and making estimated tax payments, a certain amount of tax planning is possible. Withholdings are deemed to have occurred equally throughout the year. Thus, disproportionately large amounts could be withheld in the last quarter to allow the taxpayer to avoid the underpayment penalty.

PENALTY FOR UNDERPAYING ESTIMATED TAXES

With the exceptions discussed in the next section, taxpayers who do not remit the requisite amount of estimated tax by the appropriate date are subject to a penalty for underpayment of estimated taxes. The penalty is calculated at the same rate as the interest rate applicable under Sec. 6621 to late payments of tax.[54] The penalty for each quarter is calculated on Form 2210.

The amount subject to the penalty is the excess of the total tax that should have been paid during the quarter (e.g., $6,000 [$24,000 prior year's tax liability ÷ 4] in Example C:15-16) over the sum of the estimated tax actually paid during that quarter on or before

[53] Included in the definition of *individuals* are estates and trusts. Section 67(e) defines AGI for estates and trusts. (See Chapter C:14.)

[54] Daily compounding is not applicable in calculating the penalty.

the installment date plus the withholding attributable to that quarter. Unless the taxpayer proves otherwise, the withholding is deemed to take place equally during each quarter. This rule creates a planning opportunity. Taxpayers who have not paid sufficient amounts of estimated tax in the first three quarters can avoid a penalty by having large amounts of tax withheld during the last quarter.

The penalty is assessed for the time period beginning on the due date for the quarterly installment and ending on the earlier of the date the underpayment actually is paid or the due date for the return (April 15 assuming a calendar year taxpayer). The next example illustrates the computation of the underpayment penalty.

EXAMPLE C:15-18 ▶ Assume the same facts as in Example C:15-16 except Mike pays only $3,000 of estimated tax payments on April 15, June 15, and September 15 of the current year and January 15 of next year and, for simplicity, that 6% is the Sec. 6621 underpayment rate for the entire time period. Mike files his current year return on March 30 of next year and pays the $17,000 ($37,000 − $8,000 withholding − $12,000 estimated taxes) balance due at that time. Mike's underpayment penalty is determined as follows:

TYPICAL MISCONCEPTION

Many self-employed taxpayers assume they are not liable for estimated taxes if they have sufficient itemized deductions and exemptions to create zero taxable income or a taxable loss. However, a self-employment tax liability may exist even if the individual has no taxable income. Thus, taxpayers in this situation can end up with an overall tax liability and an accompanying estimated tax penalty.

	Installment			
	First	*Second*	*Third*	*Fourth*
Amount that should have been paid ($24,000 ÷ 4)	$6,000	$6,000	$6,000	$6,000
Minus: Wage withholding	(2,000)	(2,000)	(2,000)	(2,000)
Estimated tax payment	(3,000)	(3,000)	(3,000)	(3,000)
Underpayment	$1,000	$1,000	$1,000	$1,000
Number of days of underpayment (ends March 30 of next year because earlier than April 15 of next year);	349	288	196	74
Penalty at 6% assumed annual rate for number of days of underpayment*	$ 57	$ 47	$ 32	$ 12

*Calculated as follows: Underpayment × 0.06 × (No. of days/365)

The total penalty equals $148 ($57 + $47 + $32 + $12). The $148 penalty is not deductible. ◀

Interest does not accrue on underpayments of estimated tax.[55] However, if the entire tax is not paid by the due date for the return, interest and perhaps also a failure-to-pay penalty will be levied on the unpaid amount.

EXCEPTIONS TO THE PENALTY

In certain circumstances, individuals who have not remitted the required estimated tax payments nevertheless will be exempt from the underpayment penalty. The IRS imposes no penalty if the taxpayer's tax liability exceeds by less than $1,000 taxes actually withheld from wages during the year. Similarly, the taxpayer will not owe a penalty, regardless of the underpayment amount, if the taxpayer owed no taxes for the prior tax year, the prior tax year consisted of the full 12 months, and the taxpayer was a U.S. citizen or resident alien throughout that year. The Secretary of the Treasury can waive the penalty otherwise due in the case of "casualty, disaster, or other unusual circumstances" or for newly retired or disabled individuals.[56]

EXAMPLE C:15-19 ▶ Paul's current year tax liability is $2,200, the same as last year's. His wage withholding amounts to $1,730, and Paul does not pay any estimated taxes. Paul pays the $470 balance due on March 15 of next year. Under the general rules, Paul is subject to the underpayment penalty because he does not reach either the 90% of the current year tax threshold or 100% of the prior year

[55] Sec. 6601(h).

[56] Sec. 6654(e).

tax threshold. However, because Paul's tax exceeds wage withholding by less than $1,000, he owes no penalty for underpaying his estimated tax liability. ◀

Taxpayers are exempt from the underpayment penalty in certain other circumstances, a discussion of which is beyond the scope of this text. Chapter I:14 of *Prentice Hall's Federal Taxation: Principles* and *Comprehensive* texts, however, discusses one such circumstance where the taxpayer annualizes his or her income and bases the estimated tax payment on the annualized amount.[57] Annualizing income often is beneficial for taxpayers who realize a high percentage of their income later in the year (e.g., large year-end bonus).

Other more severe penalties

OBJECTIVE 7

Describe the more severe penalties, including the fraud penalty

In addition to the penalties for failure to file, failure to pay, and underpayment of estimated tax, taxpayers may be subject to other more severe penalties. These include the accuracy-related penalty (applicable in several contexts) and the fraud penalty, each of which is discussed below. A 20% accuracy-related penalty applies to any underpayment attributable to negligence, any substantial understatement of income tax, transactions without economic substance, and various types of errors, a discussion of which is beyond the scope of this text.[58] An accuracy-related penalty is not levied, however, if the government imposed the fraud penalty or if the taxpayer filed no return.

NEGLIGENCE

ADDITIONAL COMMENT

To shift the burden of proof to the IRS, the taxpayer must introduce credible evidence regarding a factual issue relating to his or her tax liability.

The accuracy-related **negligence penalty** applies whenever the IRS determines that a taxpayer has underpaid any part of his or her taxes as a result of negligence or disregard of the rules or regulations (but without intending to defraud). The penalty is 20% of the underpayment attributable to negligence. Interest accrues on the negligence penalty at the rate applicable to underpayments.[59]

EXAMPLE C:15-20 ▶ The IRS audits Ted's individual return and assesses a $7,500 deficiency, of which $2,500 is attributable to negligence. Ted agrees to the assessment and pays the additional tax of $7,500 the following year. Ted incurs a negligence penalty of $500 (0.20 × $2,500). ◀

The IRC defines ***negligence*** as "any failure to make a reasonable attempt to comply with the provisions" of the IRC. It defines disregard of the rules or regulations as "any careless, reckless, or intentional disregard."[60] According to Treasury Regulations, a presumption of negligence exists if the taxpayer does not include in gross income an amount of income reported on an information return or does not reasonably attempt to ascertain the correctness of a deduction, credit, or exclusion that a reasonable and prudent person would think was "too good to be true."[61]

A taxpayer is careless if he or she does not diligently try to determine the correctness of his or her position. A taxpayer is reckless if he or she exerts little or no effort to determine whether a rule or regulation exists. A taxpayer's disregard is intentional if he or she knows about the rule or regulation he or she disregards.[62]

The penalty will not be imposed for any portion of an underpayment if the taxpayer had reasonable cause for his or her position and acted in good faith.[63] Failure to follow a regulation must be disclosed on Form 8275-R (Regulation Disclosure Statement), but disclosure alone is not sufficient as a defense against negligence.

---

[57] Section 6654(d)(2) allows for computation of the underpayments, if any, by annualizing income. Relief from the underpayment penalty may result from applying the annualization rules. Corporations, but not individuals, are permitted a seasonal adjustment to the annualization rules.

[58] Rules pertaining to accuracy-related penalties are in Sec. 6662.

[59] Sec. 6601(e)(2)(B).

[60] Sec. 6662(c).

[61] Reg. Sec. 1.6662-3(b)(1).

[62] Reg. Sec. 1.6662-3(b)(2).

[63] Sec. 6664(c)(1).

EXAMPLE C:15-21 ▶ The IRS audits Mario's current year individual return, and Mario agrees to a $4,000 deficiency. Mario had reasonable cause for adopting his tax return positions (which were not contrary to the applicable rules or regulations) and acted in good faith. Mario will not be liable for a negligence penalty. ◀

SUBSTANTIAL UNDERSTATEMENT

ADDITIONAL COMMENT

Theoretically, penalties are designed to deter taxpayers from willfully disregarding federal tax laws. Some taxpayers have been concerned that the IRS has used the multitude of tax penalties primarily as a source of revenue. The IRS achieved this result by "stacking" penalties (i.e., applying several penalties to a single underpayment). Recent legislation has alleviated some of this concern.

SELF-STUDY QUESTION

How is an understatement different from an underpayment?

ANSWER

An underpayment can be larger than an understatement. Understatements do not include underpayments for which there was either substantial authority or adequate disclosure.

Taxpayers who substantially understate their income tax are liable for an accuracy-related penalty for their substantial understatements. The IRC defines a substantial understatement as an understatement of tax exceeding the greater of 10% of the tax required to be shown on the return or $5,000 (or $10,000 in the case of a C corporation). For a C corporation, an additional rule applies. Specifically, if 10% of the required tax exceeds $10 million, a substantial understatement exists if the understatement exceeds $10 million. The penalty equals 20% of the underpayment of tax attributable to the substantial understatement. It does not apply to understatements for which the taxpayer shows reasonable cause and good faith for his or her position.

Understatement Versus Underpayment. The amount of tax attributable to the substantial understatement may be less than the amount of the underpayment. In general, the amount of the understatement is calculated as the amount by which the tax required to be shown (i.e., the correct tax) exceeds the tax shown on the return. Because the amount of tax attributable to certain items is not treated as an understatement, the additional tax attributed to such items is not subject to the penalty. An underpayment for an item other than a tax shelter is *not* an understatement if either of the following is true:

- The taxpayer has substantial authority (discussed below) for the tax treatment of the item.
- The taxpayer discloses, either on the return or in a statement attached to the return, the relevant facts affecting the tax treatment of the item, and the taxpayer has a reasonable basis for such treatment.

Although neither the IRC nor Treasury Regulations define "reasonable basis," Reg. Sec. 1.6662-3(b)(3) states that a "reasonable basis" standard is significantly higher than the "not frivolous" standard that usually applies to tax preparers. The latter standard involves a tax position that is not patently improper. The taxpayer meets the adequate disclosure requirement if he or she properly completes either Form 8275 or Form 8275-R and attaches it to the return, or discloses information on the return in a manner prescribed by an annual revenue procedure.[64] Large corporations required to disclose uncertain tax positions will meet the disclosure requirement by filing Schedule UTP.

EXAMPLE C:15-22 ▶ The IRS examines Val's current year individual income tax return, and Val agrees to a $9,000 deficiency, which increases her tax liability from $25,000 to $34,000. Val neither made adequate disclosure concerning the items for which the IRS assessed the deficiency nor had substantial authority for her tax treatment. Thus, Val's understatement also is $9,000. This understatement is substantial because it exceeds both 10% of her correct tax liability ($3,400 = 0.10 × $34,000) and the $5,000 minimum. Val incurs a substantial understatement penalty of $1,800 (0.20 × $9,000). ◀

EXAMPLE C:15-23 ▶ Assume the same facts as in Example C:15-22 except Val has substantial authority for the tax treatment of an item that results in a $1,000 additional assessment. In addition, she makes adequate disclosure for a second item with respect to which the IRS assesses additional taxes of $1,500. Although Val's underpayment is $9,000, her understatement is only $6,500 [$9,000 − ($1,000 + $1,500)]. The $6,500 understatement is substantial because it is more than the greater of 10% of Val's tax or $5,000. Thus, the penalty in this case is $1,300 (0.20 × $6,500). ◀

Like the negligence penalty, the substantial understatement penalty bears interest at the rate applicable for underpayments. The interest accrues from the due date of the return.

---

[64] Reg. Secs. 1.6662-4(f)(1) and (2). See Rev. Proc. 99-41, 1999-2 C.B. 566, Rev. Proc. 2001-11, 2001-1 C.B. 275, and Rev. Proc. 2002-66, 2002-2 C.B. 724, where the Treasury Department identifies circumstances where disclosure of a position on a taxpayer's return is adequate to reduce the understatement penalty of Sec. 6662(d) and tax preparer penalties of Sec. 6694(a).

ADDITIONAL COMMENT

Even though the substantial understatement penalty is a taxpayer penalty, tax preparers have a duty to make their clients aware of the potential risk of substantial understatement. In some situations, failure to do so has resulted in the client's attempting to collect the amount of the substantial understatement penalty from the preparer.

Concept of Substantial Authority. Treasury Regulations indicate that substantial authority

- Exists only if the weight of authorities supporting the tax treatment of an item is substantial relative to the weight of those supporting the contrary treatment, and
- Is based on an objective standard involving an analysis of law and its application to the relevant facts. This standard is more stringent than the "reasonable basis" standard that the taxpayer must meet to avoid the negligence penalty but less stringent than the "more likely than not" standard that applies to tax shelters.[65] (See discussion below.)

According to these regulations, the following are considered to be "authority": statutory provisions; proposed, temporary, and final regulations; court cases; revenue rulings; revenue procedures; tax treaties; Congressional intent as reflected in committee reports and joint statements of a bill's managers; private letter rulings; technical advice memoranda; information or press releases; notices; and any other similar documents published by the IRS in the *Internal Revenue Bulletin* and the *General Explanation of the Joint Committee on Taxation* (also known as the "Blue Book"). Conclusions reached in treatises, periodicals, and the opinions of tax professionals are not considered to be authority. The applicability of court cases in the taxpayer's district is not taken into account in determining the existence of substantial authority. On the other hand, the applicability of Court of Appeals cases in the taxpayer's circuit *is* taken into account in determining the existence of substantial authority.

EXAMPLE C:15-24 ▶ Authorities addressing a particular issue are as follows:

- For the government: Tax Court and Fourth Circuit Court of Appeals
- For taxpayers: U.S. District Court for Rhode Island and First Circuit Court of Appeals

The taxpayer (Tina) is a resident of Rhode Island, which is in the First Circuit. Tina would have substantial authority for a pro-taxpayer position because such a position is supported by the circuit court of appeals for Tina's geographical jurisdiction. ◀

Taxpayers should be aware that, while sparing them a substantial understatement penalty, disclosure (even with a reasonable basis for the tax treatment of the item) might raise a "red flag" that could prompt an IRS audit.

Tax Shelters and Reportable Transactions. A different set of rules applies to a tax shelter, which is any arrangement for which a significant purpose is the avoidance or evasion of federal income tax.[66] See page C:15-30 and C:15-31 for a discussion of this topic.

TRANSACTIONS WITHOUT ECONOMIC SUBSTANCE

As part of its 2010 health care legislation, Congress added a 20% accuracy-related penalty for underpayments that result from transactions lacking economic substance.[67] Further, if the understatement results from a nondisclosed noneconomic substance transaction, the penalty is increased to 40%.

Prior to 2010, the law existed in the form of a judicial doctrine (i.e., the economic substance doctrine), but the courts did not agree on what constituted economic substance. Section 7701(o)(1) states that a transaction will have economic substance if (1) the transaction changes in a meaningful way the taxpayer's economic position (apart from federal income tax effects) and (2) the taxpayer has a substantial business purpose (apart from federal income tax effects) for entering into the transaction.

CIVIL FRAUD

Fraud differs from simple, honest mistakes and negligence in that it involves a deliberate attempt to deceive. Because the IRS cannot establish intent per se, it attempts to prove

[65] Reg. Sec. 1.6662-4(d). Substantial authority usually is considered to require a 40% chance that the position would be sustained if challenged.

[66] Sec. 6662(d)(2)(C).

[67] Sec. 6662(b)(6)

intent indirectly by emphasizing the taxpayer's actions and the circumstances surrounding these actions. One leading authority referred to fraud cases in this manner:

> Fraud cases ordinarily involve systematic or substantial omissions from gross income or fictitious deductions or dependency claims, accompanied by the falsification or destruction of records or false or inconsistent statements to the investigating agents, especially where records are not kept by the taxpayer. The taxpayer's education and business experience are relevant.[68]

The penalty equals 75% of the portion of the underpayment attributable to fraud.[69] If the IRS establishes that any portion of an underpayment is due to fraud, the entire underpayment is treated as having resulted from fraud unless the taxpayer establishes otherwise by a preponderance of the evidence. Like the negligence penalty, the fraud penalty bears interest.

EXAMPLE C:15-25 ▶ The IRS audits Ned's individual return and claims that Ned's underpayment is due to fraud. Ned agrees to the $40,000 deficiency but establishes that only $32,000 of the deficiency is attributable to fraud. The remainder results from mistakes that the IRS did not believe were due to fraud. Ned's civil fraud penalty is $24,000 (0.75 × $32,000). ◀

The fraud penalty can be imposed on taxpayers filing income, gift, or estate tax returns. If it is imposed, the negligence and substantial understatement penalties are not assessed on the portion of the underpayment attributable to fraud.[70] With respect to a joint return, no fraud penalty can be imposed on a spouse who has not committed fraud. In other words, one spouse is not liable for the other spouse's fraudulent acts.

? STOP & THINK

Question: A few years ago, Joyce filed her individual income tax return in which she reported $250,000 of taxable income. She paid all the tax shown on the return on the day she filed. She, however, fraudulently omitted an additional $100,000 of gross income and, of course, does not have substantial authority for this omission. If the IRS proves that Joyce committed fraud, will she be liable for both the civil fraud penalty and the substantial understatement penalty? What are the rates for the two penalties?

Solution: Because the penalties cannot be stacked, Joyce will not owe both penalties. If the IRS successfully proves fraud, she will owe a penalty of 75% of the tax due on the omitted income. She will not owe the 20% penalty for substantial understatements.

CRIMINAL FRAUD

REAL-WORLD EXAMPLE

In fiscal 2013, the IRS initiated 5,314 criminal investigations (up from 5,125 in 2012), and it referred 4,364 for prosecution. During fiscal 2013, the IRS filed 3,865 indictments and handed down sentences in 2,812 of those cases. Of those sentenced, 80.1% were incarcerated. (Source: IRS *2013 Data Book;* see footnote 4.)

Civil and criminal fraud are similar in that both involve a taxpayer's intent to misrepresent facts. They differ primarily in terms of the weight of evidence required for conviction. Civil fraud requires proof by a preponderance of the evidence. Criminal fraud requires proof beyond a reasonable doubt. Because the latter standard is more stringent than the former, the government charges relatively few taxpayers with criminal fraud. To do so, the IRS and Justice Department must agree on the charges.

Criminal Fraud Investigations. The Criminal Investigation Division of the IRS conducts criminal fraud investigations. The agents responsible for the investigation are called **special agents**. Under IRS policy, at the first meeting of the special agent and the taxpayer, the special agent must

- Identify himself or herself as such
- Advise the taxpayer that he or she is the subject of a criminal investigation
- Advise the taxpayer of his or her rights to remain silent and consult legal counsel

[68] Boris I. Bittker and Lawrence Lokken, *Federal Taxation of Income, Estates, and Gifts* (Boston, MA: Warren, Gorham & Lamont, 1999), vol. 4, ¶ 114–6.

[69] Rules pertaining to fraud penalties are in Sec. 6663.

[70] Sec. 6662(b).

ADDITIONAL COMMENT

Any time a tax professional learns a client has engaged in activities that may constitute criminal fraud, he or she immediately should refer the client to qualified legal counsel. Counsel should then hire the accountant as a consultant. Taxpayer's communications will be confidential under the attorney–client relationship. This relationship encompasses agents of the attorney.

Penalty Provisions. Sections 7201-7216 provide for criminal penalties. Three of these penalties are discussed below.

Section 7201. Section 7201 provides for an assessment of a penalty against any person who "willfully attempts . . . to evade or defeat any tax." The maximum penalty is $100,000 ($500,000 for corporations), a prison sentence of up to five years, or both.

Section 7203. Section 7203 imposes a penalty on any person who willfully fails to pay any tax or file a return. The maximum penalty is $25,000 ($100,000 for corporations), a prison sentence of no more than one year, or both. If the government charges the taxpayer with willfully failing to prepare a return, it need not prove that the taxpayer owes additional tax.

Section 7206. Persons other than the taxpayer can be charged under Sec. 7206. This section applies to any person who

> [W]illfully aids or assists in, or procures, counsels, or advises the preparation or presentation under, or in connection with any matter arising under the internal revenue laws, of a return, affidavit, claim, or other document, which is fraudulent or is false as to any material matter, whether or not such falsity or fraud is with the knowledge or consent of the person authorized or required to present such return, affidavit, claim, or document.[71]

What constitutes a material matter has been litigated extensively.[72] The maximum penalty under Sec. 7206 is $100,000 ($500,000 for corporations), a prison sentence of up to three years, or both. The government need not prove that the taxpayer owes additional tax.

STATUTE OF LIMITATIONS

OBJECTIVE 8

Recognize when the statute of limitations applies

The **statute of limitations** has the same practical implications in a tax context as in other contexts. It specifies a timeframe (called the "limitations period") during which the government must assess the tax or initiate a court proceeding to collect the tax.[73] The statute of limitations also defines the limitations period during which a taxpayer may file a lawsuit against the government or a claim for a refund.

GENERAL THREE-YEAR RULE

Under the general rule of Sec. 6501(a), the limitations period is three years after the date on which the return is filed, regardless of whether the return is timely filed. A return filed before its due date is treated as filed on the due date.

EXAMPLE C:15-26 ▶ Ali files his Year 1 individual return on March 5 of Year 2. The government may not assess additional taxes for Year 1 after April 15 of Year 5, three years after the due date. If instead Ali files his Year 1 individual return on October 7 of Year 2, the limitations period for his return expires on midnight of October 7 of Year 5, three years after Ali files his tax return. ◀

SIX-YEAR RULE FOR SUBSTANTIAL OMISSIONS

Income Tax Returns. In the case of substantial omissions, the limitations period is six years after the later of the date the return is filed or the return's due date. For income tax purposes, the six-year period is applicable if the taxpayer omits from gross income an amount exceeding 25% of the gross income shown on the return. If an item is disclosed either on the return or in a statement attached to the return, it is not treated as an omission if the disclosure adequately apprises the IRS of the nature and amount of the item. In the case of taxpayers conducting a trade or business, gross income for purposes of the 25% omission test means the taxpayer's sales revenues (not the taxpayer's gross profit).[74] Taxpayers benefit from this special definition because it renders the 25% test applicable to a gross amount (implying a higher threshold).

---

[71] Sec. 7206(2).

[72] See, for example, *U.S. v. Joseph DiVarco*, 32 AFTR 2d 73-5605, 73-2 USTC ¶9607 (7th Cir., 1973), wherein the court held that the source of the taxpayer's income as stated on the tax return is a material matter.

[73] Rules pertaining to the statute of limitations are Sec. 6501.

[74] Regulation Sec. 1.61-3(a) defines *gross income* as sales less cost of goods sold.

WHAT WOULD YOU DO IN THIS SITUATION?

After working eight years for a large CPA firm, you begin your practice as a sole practitioner CPA. Your practice is not as profitable as you had expected, and you consider how you might attract additional clients. One idea is to obtain for your clients larger refunds than they anticipate. Your reputation for knowing tax-saving tips might grow, and your profits might increase. You think further and decide that maybe you could claim itemized deductions for charitable contributions that actually were not made and for business expenses that actually were not paid. You are aware of Sec. 7206, regarding false and fraudulent statements but think that you can avoid the "as to any material matter" stipulation by keeping the deduction overstatements relatively insubstantial. Would you try this scheme for increasing your profits? If so, would you escape the scope of Sec. 7206? What ramifications might these deeds have on your standing as a CPA under the AICPA's *Statements on Standards for Tax Services* and *Code of Professional Conduct*?

EXAMPLE C:15-27 ► Peg files her Year 1 return on March 28 of Year 2. Her return shows $6,000 of interest from corporate bonds and $30,000 of salary. Peg attaches a statement to her return that indicates why she thinks an additional $2,000 receipt of income is nontaxable. However, because of an oversight, she does not report an $8,000 capital gain. Peg is deemed to have omitted only $8,000 rather than $10,000 (the $8,000 capital gain plus the $2,000 receipt) because she disclosed the $2,000 receipt. The $8,000 amount is 22.22% ($8,000/$36,000) of her reported gross income. Because the omission does not exceed 25% of Peg's reported gross income, the limitations period expires on April 15 of Year 5. ◄

EXAMPLE C:15-28 ► Assume the same facts as in Example C:15-27 except Peg does not make adequate disclosure of the $2,000 receipt. Thus, she is considered to have omitted $10,000 from gross income. The $10,000 amount is 27.77% ($10,000/$36,000) of her reported gross income. Therefore, the limitations period expires on April 15 of Year 8. ◄

EXAMPLE C:15-29 ► Rita conducts a business as a sole proprietorship. Rita's Year 1 return, filed on March 18 of Year 2, indicates sales of $100,000 and cost of goods sold of $70,000. Rita inadvertently fails to report $9,000 of interest earned on a loan to a relative. For purposes of the 25% omission test, her gross income is $100,000, not $30,000. The omitted interest is 9% ($9,000/$100,000) of her reported gross income. Because the $9,000 does not exceed 25% of the gross amount, the limitations period expires on April 15 of Year 5. ◄

KEY POINT

A 25% omission of gross income extends the basic limitations period to six years, whereas a 25% overstatement of deductions is still subject to the basic three-year limitations period. However, if fraud can be shown, there is no limitations period.

Note that the six-year rule applies only to omitted income. Thus, claiming excessive deductions will not result in a six-year limitations period. In *U.S. v. Home Concrete and Supply LLC*,[75] the Supreme Court confirmed that overstating the basis of an asset sold was not an omission from income for purposes of extending the statute of limitations to six years. However, if the omission involves fraud, no limitations period applies.

Gift and Estate Tax Returns. A similar six-year limitations period applies for gift and estate tax purposes. If the taxpayer omits items that exceed 25% of the gross estate value or the total amount of gifts reported on the return, the limitations period expires six years after the later of the date the return is filed or the due date. Items disclosed on the return or in a statement attached to the return that adequately apprises the IRS of the nature and amount of the item do not constitute omissions. Understatements of the value of assets disclosed on the return also are not considered omissions.

EXAMPLE C:15-30 ► John files his Year 1 gift tax return on April 3 of Year 2. The return reports a cash gift to his son of $600,000. In Year 1, John also sold land to his son for $700,000. At the time of the sale, John thought the land's FMV was $700,000. Upon audit, the IRS determines that the FMV of the land on the sale date was $900,000. Thus, John effectively gifted an additional $200,000 to his son as a result of the less than FMV, or bargain element, of the original sale. The $200,000 amount is 33⅓% ($200,000/$600,000) of all gifts reported. The limitations period expires on April 15 of Year 8. ◄

[75] 109 AFTR 2d 2012-1692 (USSC, 2012).

WHEN NO RETURN IS FILED

No limitations period exists if the taxpayer does not file a return. Thus, the government may assess the tax or initiate a court proceeding for collection at any time.

EXAMPLE C:15-31 ▶ Jill does not file a tax return for Year 1. No limitations period applies. Consequently, if the government discovers 20 years later that Jill did not file a return, it may assess the Year 1 tax, along with penalties and interest. ◀

OTHER EXCEPTIONS TO THREE-YEAR RULE

SELF-STUDY QUESTION

Should a taxpayer ever agree to extend the limitations period?

ANSWER

Yes. When an audit is in progress, if a taxpayer refuses to extend the limitations period, the agent may assert a deficiency for each item in question. Had the taxpayer granted an extension, perhaps many of the items in question never would have been included in the examining agent's report.

Extension of the Three-Year Limitations Period. The IRC provides other exceptions to the three-year statute of limitations rule, some of which are discussed here. The taxpayer and the IRS can mutually agree in writing to extend the limitations period for taxes other than the estate tax. In such situations, the limitations period is extended until the date agreed on by the two parties. Such agreements usually are concluded when the IRS is auditing a return near the end of the statutory period. Taxpayers often agree to extending the limitations period because they think that, if they do not do so, the IRS will assess a higher deficiency than otherwise would have been the case. Before concluding such an agreement, the IRS must notify the taxpayer that he or she may refuse to extend the limitations period or may limit the extension to particular issues.

NOL Carrybacks. For a year to which a net operating loss (NOL) carries back, the applicable limitations period is for the year in which the NOL arose.

When Fraud is Proven.

Deficiency and Civil Fraud Penalty. If the government successfully proves that a taxpayer filed a false or fraudulent return "with the intent to evade tax" or engaged in a "willful attempt . . . to defeat or evade tax," there is no limitations period. In other words, the government may at any time assess the tax or begin a court proceeding to collect the tax and the interest thereon. In addition, if the government proves fraud, it may impose a civil penalty. If it fails to prove fraud and the normal three-year limitations period and special six-year period for 25% omissions have expired, it may not assess additional taxes. The fraud issue is significant in tax litigation because the burden of proving fraud is unconditionally on the government.

EXAMPLE C:15-32 ▶ The IRS audits Trey's 2015 return late in 2018. It also examines Trey's prior years' returns and contends that Trey had willfully attempted to evade tax on his timely filed 2012 return. Trey litigates in the Tax Court, and the Court decides the fraud issue in his favor. Because the IRS did not prove fraud, it may not assess additional taxes for 2012. Had the IRS proven fraud, the limitations period for the 2012 return would have remained open, and the IRS could have assessed the additional taxes. ◀

ADDITIONAL COMMENT

Even though a taxpayer is home free from criminal prosecution after six years of an act or omission, he or she still is subject to civil fraud penalties if fraud is proven at any time after the six-year period.

Criminal Provisions. If taxpayers are not indicted for criminal violations of the tax law within a certain period of time, they are home free. For most criminal offenses, the maximum period is six years after the commission of the offense.[76] Taxpayers cannot be prosecuted, tried, or punished unless an indictment is made within that timeframe. The six-year period begins on the date the taxpayer committed the offense, not the date he or she files the return. Taxpayers who file fraudulent returns might commit offenses related to the returns at a subsequent date. An example of an offense that some taxpayers commit after filing a return is depositing money into a new bank account under a fictitious name.

EXAMPLE C:15-33 ▶ In March of Year 2, Tony files a fraudulent Year 1 return through which he attempts to evade tax. Before filing, Tony keeps a double set of books. In Year 1, Tony deposits some funds into a bank account under a fictitious name. In Year 3, he moves to another state, and on May 5 of Year 3, he transfers these funds to a new bank account under a different fictitious name. Depositing money into the new account is an offense relating to the fraudulent return. Provided Tony commits no

---

[76] Sec. 6531.

SELF-STUDY QUESTION

Suppose a taxpayer incorrectly includes a receipt in a tax return and then, after the limitations period has expired for that year, correctly includes the receipt in a subsequent return. Is it equitable for the taxpayer to have to pay tax on the same income twice?

ANSWER

No. A complicated set of provisions (Secs. 1311-1314) allows, in specific situations, otherwise closed years to be opened if a position taken in an open year is inconsistent with a position taken in a closed year.

additional offenses, the limitations period for indictment expires on May 5 of Year 9, six years after committing the latest fraudulent offense. ◀

REFUND CLAIMS

Taxpayers generally are not entitled to a refund for overpayments of tax unless they file a claim for refund by the later of three years from the date they file the return or two years from the date they pay the tax.[77] The limitations period for individuals is suspended when the individual is financially disabled. A return filed before the due date is deemed to have been filed on the due date. The due date is determined without regard to extensions. In most cases, taxpayers pay the tax concurrently with filing the return. Typically, the taxpayer files a claim for a refund in the following circumstance: the IRS has audited the taxpayer's return, has proposed a deficiency, and has assessed additional taxes. The taxpayer may have paid the additional taxes two years after the due date for the return. In such a situation, the taxpayer may file a claim for a refund at any time within two years after making the additional payment (or a total of four years after the filing date). If the taxpayer does not file a claim until more than three years after the date of filing the return, the maximum refund is the amount of tax paid during the two-year period immediately preceding the date on which he or she files the claim.[78]

EXAMPLE C:15-34 ▶ Pat files his Year 1 return on March 12 of Year 2. The return reports a tax liability of $5,000, and Pat pays this entire amount when he files his return. He pays no additional tax. Pat must file a claim for refund by April 15 of Year 5, three years from the later of the date filed or the original due date without extensions. The maximum refundable amount is $5,000. ◀

EXAMPLE C:15-35 ▶ Assume the same facts as in Example C: 15-34 except the IRS audits Pat's Year 1 return, and Pat pays a $1,200 deficiency on October 2 of Year 4. Pat may file a claim for refund as late as October 2 of Year 6. However, if Pat files the claim later than April 15 of Year 5, the refund may not exceed $1,200 (the amount of tax paid during the two-year period immediately preceding the filing of the claim). ◀

LIABILITY FOR TAX

OBJECTIVE 9

Explain from whom the government may collect unpaid taxes

Taxpayers are primarily liable for paying their tax. Spouses and transferees may be secondarily liable, as discussed below.

JOINT RETURNS

Ordinarily, if spouses file a joint return, their liability to pay the tax is joint and several.[79] **Joint and several liability** means that each spouse is potentially liable for the full amount due. If one spouse fails to pay any or all of the tax, the other spouse is responsible for paying the deficiency. Joint and several liability has facilitated IRS collection efforts where one spouse absconds from the country, and the other spouse remains behind.

Validity of Joint Return. To be valid, a joint return generally must include the signatures of both spouses. However, if one spouse cannot sign because of a disability, the return still is valid if that spouse orally consents to the other spouse's signing for him or her.[80] A joint return is invalid if one spouse forces the other to file jointly.

Innocent Spouse Provision. Congress has provided for **innocent spouse relief** where holding one spouse liable for the taxes due from both spouses would be inequitable.[81] Relief is available if all five of the following conditions are met:

- ▶ The spouses file a joint return.
- ▶ The return contains an understatement of tax attributable to the erroneous item(s) of an individual filing it.

---

[77] Sec. 6511(a).

[78] Under Sec. 6512, special rules apply if the IRS has mailed a notice of deficiency and if the taxpayer files a petition with the Tax Court.

[79] Sec. 6013(d)(3).

[80] Reg. Sec. 1.6012-1(a)(5).

[81] The innocent spouse provisions are in Sec. 6015.

- The other individual establishes that he or she neither knew nor had reason to know of any or all of the understatement.
- Based on all the facts and circumstances, holding the other individual liable for the deficiency would be inequitable.
- The other individual elects innocent spouse relief no later than two years after the IRS begins its collection efforts.

The degree of relief available depends on the extent of the electing spouse's knowledge. If the spouse neither knew nor had reason to know of *an understatement,* full relief will be granted. Full relief encompasses liability for taxes, interest, and penalties attributable to the full amount of the understatement. On the other hand, if the spouse either knew or had reason to know of an understatement, but not *the extent of the understatement,* only partial relief will be granted. Partial relief encompasses liability for taxes, interest, and penalties attributable to that portion of the understatement of which the spouse was unaware.

EXAMPLE C:15-36 ▶ Jim and Joy jointly filed a tax return for Year 1. Joy fraudulently reported on Schedule C two expenses: one amounting to $4,000 and the other amounting to $3,000. The IRS audits the return, assesses a $2,170 deficiency, and begins its collection efforts on June 3 of Year 3. If (1) Jim elects innocent spouse relief no later than June 3 of Year 5, (2) Jim establishes that he neither knew nor had reason to know of the understatement, and (3) holding Jim liable for the deficiency would be inequitable under the circumstances, Jim will be relieved of liability for the full $2,170. ◀

EXAMPLE C:15-37 ▶ Assume the same facts as in Example C:15-36 except Jim had reason to know the $3,000 expense was fraudulent. If (1) Jim elects innocent spouse relief no later than June 3 of Year 5, (2) Jim establishes that he neither knew nor had reason to know the *extent* of the understatement (i.e., $7,000 as opposed to $3,000), and (3) holding Jim liable for the full amount of the deficiency would be inequitable under the circumstances, Jim will be relieved of liability for that portion of the deficiency attributable to the $4,000 expense. ◀

Proportional liability is liability for only that portion of a deficiency attributable to the taxpayer's separate taxable items. A joint filer incurs proportional liability if all the following conditions are met:

- The joint filer elects proportional liability within two years after the IRS begins its collection efforts.
- The electing filer is either divorced or separated at the time of the election.
- The electing filer did not reside in the same household as the other filer at any time during the 12-month period preceding the election.
- The electing filer does not have actual knowledge of any item giving rise to the deficiency.

The electing filer bears the burden of proving the amount of his or her proportional liability. The fraudulent transfer of property between joint filers immediately before the election will invalidate it.

EXAMPLE C:15-38 ▶ Sam and Sue jointly filed a Year 1 tax return. Sam intentionally omitted to report $8,000 in gambling winnings. Sue fraudulently deducted $1,600 in business expenses. The IRS audits the return, assesses a $3,600 deficiency, and begins its collection efforts on August 19 of Year 4. Sam and Sue are subsequently divorced. If Sue (1) elects innocent spouse relief no later than August 19 of Year 6, (2) did not reside in the same household as Sam at any time during the 12-month period preceding the election, and (3) did not actually know of Sam's omission, she will be liable for only that portion of the deficiency attributable to her fraudulent deduction. ◀

Equitable Relief. Spouses unable to obtain relief under the standard innocent spouse provisions still may petition the IRS for equitable relief. The IRS uses a facts and circumstances test and, beginning in 2013, relaxed the requirements for obtaining relief, particularly in cases where one spouse was abusive or where the spouse seeking relief missed a statutory deadline.

The Effect of Community Property Laws. Community property laws are ignored in determining to whom income (other than income from property) is attributable. For example, if one spouse living in a community property state wins money by gambling, the gambling income is not treated as community property for purposes of the innocent spouse provisions. If the gambling winnings are omitted from a joint return, they are deemed to be solely the income of the spouse who gambled.

TYPICAL MISCONCEPTION

A taxpayer cannot escape paying taxes by transferring assets to a transferee (donee, heir, legatee, etc.) or a fiduciary (executor, trustee, etc.).

TRANSFEREE LIABILITY

The Internal Revenue Code authorizes the IRS to collect taxes from persons other than the taxpayer.[82] The two categories of persons from whom the IRS may collect taxes are transferees and fiduciaries. Transferees include donees, heirs, legatees, devisees, shareholders of dissolved corporations, parties to a reorganization, and other distributees.[83] Fiduciaries include executors and administrators of estates. In general, the limitations period for transferees expires one year after the limitations period for transferors. The transferors may be income earners in the case of income taxes, executors in the case of estate taxes, and donors in the case of gift taxes.

EXAMPLE C:15-39 ▶ Lake Corporation is liquidated in the current year, and it distributes all its assets to its sole shareholder, Leo. If the IRS audits Lake's return and assesses a deficiency, Leo (the distributee) is responsible for paying the deficiency. ◀

TAX PRACTICE ISSUES

OBJECTIVE 10

Apply the professional and governmental standards for tax practitioners

A number of statutes and guidelines address what constitutes proper behavior of CPAs and others engaged in tax practice, including the AICPA's *Statements on Standards for Tax Services* (see Appendix E).

STATUTORY PROVISIONS CONCERNING TAX RETURN PREPARERS

KEY POINT

As evidenced by the formidable list of possible penalties, an individual considering becoming a tax return preparer needs to be aware of certain procedures set forth in the IRC.

Sections 6694–6696 impose penalties on tax return preparers for misconduct. Section 7701(a)(36) defines a tax return preparer as a "person who prepares for compensation, or who employs one or more persons to prepare for compensation, any return of tax imposed by this title or any claim for refund of tax imposed by this title."[84] Tax return preparers are divided into two categories: signing preparers and non-signing preparers. A signing preparer has primary responsibility for the overall substantive accuracy of the preparation of the return or refund claim. A non-signing preparer gives advice to a taxpayer or another preparer, and the advice leads to a position or entry that is a substantial portion of the return or refund claim. As a result, more than one preparer can be subject to the preparer penalties. The preparer responsible for the position giving rise to the understatement is subject to preparer penalties related to that position.[85]

Section 6695 imposes penalties for

- Failure to furnish the taxpayer with a copy of the return or claim ($50 per failure)
- Failure to sign a return or claim ($50 per failure)
- Failure to furnish one's identification number ($50 per failure)
- Failure to keep a copy of a return or claim or, in lieu thereof, to maintain a list of taxpayers for whom returns or claims were prepared ($50 per failure)
- Failure to file a correct information return ($50 per failure)
- Endorsement or other negotiation of an income tax refund check made payable to anyone other than the preparer ($500 per check)
- Failure to be diligent in determining eligibility for the earned income credit ($500 per case)

The first five penalties are not assessable if the preparer shows that the failure is due to reasonable cause and not willful neglect, and the maximum penalty cannot exceed $25,000 for a return period.[86]

A preparer will owe a maximum penalty equal to $1,000 or 50% of the income derived from the return if he or she lacked substantial authority for a non-disclosed position. Substantial authority is an objective standard that involves the analysis of the law

[82] Sec. 6901.

[83] Reg. Sec. 301.6901-1(b).

[84] The 2007 Small Business Act broadened the definition of tax return preparer to include a person preparing non-income tax returns, such as estate, gift, excise, or employment tax returns. This Act also expanded the definition of a preparer from "one preparer per firm" to "one preparer per position per firm."

[85] Reg. Sec. 1.6694-1(b).

[86] Regulation Sec. 1.6695-1(b)(3) states that, for the purpose of avoiding the failure-to-sign penalty, reasonable cause is "a cause which arises despite ordinary care and prudence exercised by the individual preparer."

REAL-WORLD EXAMPLE

In addition to these penalties, the IRS may suspend or bar a tax practitioner from practicing before the IRS. Each week the IRS publishes a list of suspended practitioners.

and application of the law to the relevant facts.[87] The standard is less stringent than the "more likely than not" (greater than 50%) test but more stringent than the reasonable basis standard. Reasonable basis refers to a position that is arguable and reasonably based on an acceptible authority such as the Internal Revenue Code, Treasury Regulations, court cases, and other pronouncements listed in Treasury Regulations.[88] Consequently, a tax position meets the substantial authority test if the authorities supporting the position are more substantial than authorities that take a contrary position. The preparer may avoid the penalty if the preparer has reasonable basis for the position and the position is properly disclosed. The IRS will impose no penalty if the preparer shows that he or she has reasonable cause for the understatement, and he or she acted in good faith.

If any portion of the understatement results from the preparer's willful attempt to understate taxes or from reckless or intentional disregard of rules or regulations, the penalty will be the greater of $5,000 or 50% of the income derived from the return. Treasury Regulations state that preparers are considered to have willfully understated taxes if they have attempted to wrongfully reduce taxes by disregarding pertinent information.[89] A preparer generally is deemed to have recklessly or intentionally disregarded a rule or regulation if he or she adopts a position contrary to a rule or regulation about which he or she knows, or is reckless in not knowing about such rule or regulation. A preparer may adopt a position contrary to a revenue ruling if the position has reasonable basis. In addition, a preparer may depart from following a Treasury Regulation without penalty if he or she has a good faith basis for challenging its validity and adequately discloses his or her position on Form 8275-R (Regulation Disclosure Statement).

? STOP & THINK

Question: While preparing a client's tax return two days before the due date, Tevin reviews an item that arguably is deductible. He weighs the cost of researching whether he has substantial authority for the position. In so doing, he calculates that researching the issue will cost him $300 in forgone revenues and that not researching the issue will cost him $250 in preparer penalties. What should Tevin do?

Solution: Undoubtedly, Tevin should research the issue and determine whether the deduction either has substantial authority or has a reasonable basis. If he has a reasonable basis, he should disclose his position on the tax return. At stake here is not merely $300 in foregone revenues but also Tevin's professional reputation. His taking a position that does not meet the applicable standards subjects not only him as tax preparer, but also his client as taxpayer, to penalties. If the IRS imposes a penalty on the client, the client might terminate the professional relationship with Tevin or sue Tevin for negligence. Besides, Tevin may have miscalculated his own professional liability. If the IRS determines that Tevin recklessly or intentionally disregarded tax rules and regulations, it may impose a penalty of $5,000, not $250.

Tax preparers who offer advice relating to the preparation of a document, knowing that such advice will result in a tax understatement, will be liable for aiding and abetting in the understatement.[90] The penalty for aiding and abetting is $1,000 for advice given to noncorporate taxpayers and $10,000 for advice given to corporate taxpayers. If a preparer is assessed an aiding-and-abetting penalty, the preparer will not be assessed a Sec. 6694 preparer penalty for the same infraction.

REPORTABLE TRANSACTION DISCLOSURES

The IRS has continued its focus on tax shelters, including reportable and listed transactions, and has issued extensive and detailed reporting requirements on individuals who advise clients on certain aggressive tax schemes. Section 6111 sets forth the required disclosures by material advisors for reportable transactions, and Section 6112 requires material advisors to maintain a list of tax shelter clients and file information returns with the IRS.

[87] Reg. Sec. 1.6662-4(d).
[88] Reg. Sec. 1.6662-3(b)(3) and Reg. Sec. 1.6662-4(d)(3).
[89] Reg. Sec. 1.6694-3.
[90] Sec. 6701.

A reportable transaction is any transaction required to be disclosed because the IRS has determined it to have the potential for tax evasion or avoidance.[91] Reportable transactions include the following: (1) listed transactions as defined by the IRS, (2) confidential transactions, (3) transactions with contractual protection, (4) loss transactions where the losses claimed exceed certain thresholds ranging from $50,000 in a single year for individuals to $20 million for corporations over a number of years, (5) transactions of interest as designated by the IRS, and (6) patented transactions.[92]

A material advisor is any person who provides material aid, assistance, or advice with respect to any reportable transaction, and who receives gross income from the activity in excess of $50,000 if the tax benefits flow primarily to individuals or $250,000 for corporations and other entities.[93] The income thresholds are sharply reduced for listed transactions and transactions of interest ($10,000 for individuals and $25,000 for corporations).[94]

In general, a material advisor complies with the disclosure requirements by filing Form 8918 which details the transaction, the expected tax treatment, and the potential tax benefits in sufficient detail for the IRS to fully understand the transaction. Failure to make the required disclosures subjects taxpayers and material advisors to severe penalties as follows:

- *Imposed on the taxpayer:* Failure to disclose a reportable or listed transaction (ranging from $10,000 to $200,000, depending on the nature of the transaction and the status of the taxpayer)[95]
- *Imposed on the taxpayer:* Accuracy-related penalty for listed and reportable transactions (20% of the understatement for disclosed transactions; 30% for undisclosed transactions)[96]
- *Imposed on the organizer or advisor:* Failure to furnish information on reportable transactions ($50,000 in the case of tax benefits provided to individuals; $250,000 in any other case)[97]
- *Imposed on the organizer or advisor:* Failure to maintain an investor list ($10,000 per day after the twentieth business day following notice)[98]
- *Imposed on the organizer or advisor:* Tax shelter fraud (lesser of $1,000 or 100% of gross income derivable from the tax shelter)[99]

In addition, if a taxpayer fails to report information regarding a listed transaction on a required return or statement, the limitations period is extended to one year after the earlier of the date on which the information is furnished to the IRS or the date on which a material advisor meets the list maintenance requirements.[100]

ETHICAL POINT

In deciding whether to adopt a pro-taxpayer position on a tax return or in rendering tax advice, a tax advisor should keep in mind his or her responsibilities under the tax return preparer rules of the IRC, *Treasury Department Circular 230,* and the *Statements on Standards for Tax Services,* especially Statement No. 1. Statement No. 1 (reproduced in Appendix E) requires that a CPA have a good faith belief that the position adopted on the tax return is supported by existing law or by a good faith argument for extending, modifying, or reversing existing law.

RULES OF *CIRCULAR 230*

Treasury Department *Circular 230* regulates the practice of attorneys, CPAs, enrolled agents, and enrolled actuaries before the IRS. Practice before the IRS includes representing taxpayers in meetings with IRS audit agents and appeals officers. Tax professionals who do not comply with the rules and regulations of *Circular 230* can be barred from practicing before the IRS and may be subject to censure and/or monetary penalties. Such professionals are entitled to an administrative hearing before being penalized.

Circular 230 rules apply to all paid preparers (signing and non-signing), including "registered tax return preparers" (RTRP). All paid preparers must register with the IRS, pay an annual fee, and obtain a preparer tax identification number. An RTRP is limited to preparing and signing tax returns, claims for refund, and other documents to be filed with the IRS and

[91] Sec. 6707A(c).
[92] Reg. Sec. 1.6011-4 and Prop. Reg. Sec. 1.6011-4.
[93] Sec 6111(b).
[94] Reg. Sec. 301.6111-3(b)(3).
[95] Sec. 6707A.
[96] Sec. 6662A.
[97] Sec. 6111.
[98] Sec. 6708.
[99] Sec. 6700(a).
[100] Sec. 6501(c)(10).

ADDITIONAL COMMENT

The IRS amended Circular 230 in 2011 to include additional requirements on tax return preparers who only prepare returns and do not otherwise appear before the IRS. In *Loving v. IRS*, 111 AFTR 2d 2013-589 (DC Washington D.C., 2013), the court concluded that this authority exceeded the IRS's statutory authority.

may represent a taxpayer before revenue agents, Taxpayer Advocate Service representatives, or similar employees of the IRS. However, RTRPs may not provide tax advice beyond the advice necessary to prepare the tax return and may not represent taxpayers before appeals officers, counsel, or similar IRS employees.

Among the rules governing the conduct of practitioners before the IRS are the following:[101]

- If the practitioner knows that a client has not complied with federal tax laws or has made an error in or an omission from any return, the practitioner should promptly advise the client of the error or omission. The practitioner also must advise the client of possible corrective action and the consequences of not taking such action.
- Each person practicing before the IRS must exercise due diligence in preparing returns, determining the correctness of representations made to the Treasury Department, and determining the correctness of representations made to clients about tax matters.

Circular 230 provides that a practitioner may not sign a return or advise a client to take a position that lacks a reasonable basis, is an unreasonable position as described in Sec. 6694(a)(2), is a willful attempt to understate tax, or is a reckless or intentional disregard of rules or regulations as described in Sec. 6694(b)(2).[102]

Circular 230 also lists best practices standards for tax advisors.[103] Such standards include the following:

- Communicate clearly with the client regarding the terms of the engagement.
- Establish the relevant facts, evaluate the reasonableness of assumptions or representations, relate the applicable law to the relevant facts, and arrive at a conclusion supported by the law and relevant facts.
- Advise the client of the implications of conclusions reached, including the applicability of accuracy-related penalties.
- Act fairly and with integrity in practice before the IRS.

Circular 230 also provides detailed substantive and format requirements for practitioners who provide written advice.[104] Accordingly, a practitioner must meet all of the following standards:

- Base the written advice on reasonable factual and legal assumptions
- Reasonably consider all relevant facts and circumstances that the practitioner knows or reasonably should know
- Use reasonable efforts to identify the facts relevant to the written advice
- Not rely on representations, statements, findings, or agreements of the taxpayer or any other person if reliance on them would be unreasonable
- Relate applicable law and authorities to the facts
- Not take into account whether or not the return will be audited or the matter will be raised in audit

Circular 230 also provides that the IRS will apply a "reasonable practitioner standard" to determine whether the requirements listed above have been met. In written advice related to tax shelters, the IRS is specifically directed to consider the additional risk caused by the practitioner's lack of knowledge of the taxpayer's particular circumstances when determining whether a practitioner has failed to comply with this section of *Circular* 230.

STATEMENTS ON STANDARDS FOR TAX SERVICES

Tax advisors confronted with ethical issues frequently turn to a professional organization for guidance. Although the guidelines set forth by such organizations are not *legally* enforceable, they carry significant moral weight, and may be cited in a negligence lawsuit as the proper "standard of care" for tax practitioners. They also may provide grounds for the termination or suspension of one's professional license. One such set of guidelines is

---

[101] *Treasury Department Circular 230* (2014), Secs. 10.21 and 10.22.
[102] Ibid., Sec. 10.34.
[103] Ibid., Sec. 10.33.
[104] Written advice is discussed in Sec. 10.37.

the *Statements on Standards for Tax Services* (SSTSs), issued by the American Institute of Certified Public Accountants (AICPA) and reproduced in Appendix E.[105] Inspired by the principles of honesty and integrity, these guidelines define standards of ethical conduct for CPAs engaged in tax practice. In the words of the AICPA:

> In our view, practice standards are the hallmark of calling one's self a professional. Members should fulfill their responsibilities as professionals by instituting and maintaining standards against which their professional performance can be measured. The promulgation of practice standards also reinforces one of the core values of the AICPA Vision—that CPAs conduct themselves with honesty and integrity.[106]

The SSTSs are professionally enforceable; that is, they may be enforced through a disciplinary proceeding conducted by the AICPA, which may terminate or suspend a practitioner from AICPA membership.

Statement No. 1 defines the circumstances under which a CPA should (or should not) recommend a tax return position to a taxpayer. It also prescribes a course of conduct that the CPA should follow when making such a recommendation. Specifically,

- A member should not recommend that a tax return position be taken with respect to any item unless the member has a good-faith belief that the position has a realistic possibility of being sustained administratively or judicially on its merits if challenged.
- [A] member may recommend a tax return position that the member concludes that the position has a reasonable basis and the member recommends that the taxpayer appropriately disclose the position.
- When recommending tax return positions and when preparing or signing a return on which a tax return position is taken, a member should, when relevant, advise the taxpayer regarding potential penalty consequences of such tax return position and the opportunity, if any, to avoid such penalties through disclosure.

The *realistic possibility standard* set forth in Statement No. 1 parallels that of Sec. 6694. Regulation Sec. 1.6694-2(b)(2) states that the relevant authorities for the realistic- possibility-of-being-sustained test are the same as those that apply in the substantial authority context. The IRS will treat a position as having met the realistic possibility of being sustained on "its merits" if a reasonable and well informed analysis by a person knowledgeable in the tax law would lead such a person to conclude that the position has approximately a one in three, or greater, likelihood of being sustained on its merits.

However, the *realistic possibility standard* set forth in Statement No. 1 differs from the IRC standard in that it allows as support for a tax return position well reasoned articles or treatises, in addition to primary tax authorities. The IRC standard allows as support for a tax return position only primary tax authorities.

Statement No. 2 sets forth the standards when signing the preparer's declaration that the return is true, correct, and complete. Specifically,

- A member should make a reasonable effort to obtain all necessary information from the taxpayer to provide answers to all questions on the tax return.
- A request for information may necessitate a disclosure for the return to be considered complete or to avoid penalties.

Statement No. 3 addresses (1) whether tax practitioners can reasonably rely on information supplied to them by the taxpayer, (2) when they have a duty to examine or verify such information, (3) when they have a duty to make inquiries of the taxpayer, and (4) what information they should consider in preparing a tax return. Specifically,

[105] The AICPA's Tax Executive Committee issued revised standards in November 2009, which were effective January 1, 2010.

[106] Letter to AICPA members by David A. Lifson, Chair, AICPA Tax Executive Committee, and Gerald W. Padwe, Vice President, AICPA Taxation Section (April 18, 2000).

- In preparing or signing a return, a member may in good faith rely, without verification, on information furnished by the taxpayer or by third parties. However, a member should make reasonable inquiries if the information furnished appears to be incorrect, incomplete, or inconsistent either on its face or on the basis of other facts known to a member.
- If the tax law or regulations impose a condition with respect to the deductibility or other tax treatment of an item . . . a member should make appropriate inquiries to determine to the member's satisfaction whether such condition has been met.
- When preparing a tax return, a member should consider information actually known to that member from the tax return of another taxpayer if the information is relevant to that tax return and its consideration is necessary to properly prepare that tax return.

Note that the duty to verify arises only when taxpayer provided information appears "strange" on its face. Otherwise, the tax practitioner has no duty to investigate taxpayer facts and circumstances. The taxpayer has the ultimate responsibility for the contents of the return.

Statement No. 4 defines the circumstances in which a tax practitioner may use estimates in preparing a tax return. In addition, it cautions practitioners as to the manner in which they may use estimates. Specifically,

- A member may advise on estimates used in the preparation of a tax return, but the taxpayer has the responsibility to provide the estimated data. Appraisals or valuations are not considered estimates.
- [A] member may use the taxpayer's estimates in the preparation of a tax return if it is not practical to obtain exact data and if the member determines that the estimates are reasonable. If the taxpayer's estimates are used, they should be presented in a manner that does not imply greater accuracy than exists.

Notwithstanding this statement, the tax practitioner may not use estimates when such use is implicitly prohibited by the IRC. For example, Sec. 274(d) disallows deductions for certain expenses (e.g., meals and entertainment) unless the taxpayer can substantiate the expenses with adequate records or sufficient corroborating information. The documentation requirement effectively precludes the taxpayer from estimating such expenses and the practitioner from using such estimates.

Statement No. 5 sets forth the standards for members in recommending a tax return position that departs from the position determined in an administrative proceeding or in a court decision with respect to the taxpayer's prior return.

Statement No. 6 defines a tax practitioner's duty when he or she becomes aware of an error in the taxpayer's return or a return that is the subject of an administrative proceeding. Specifically,

- A member should inform the taxpayer promptly upon becoming aware of (1) an error in a previously filed return, (2) an error in a return that is the subject of an administrative proceeding (e.g., an IRS audit or appeals conference), or (3) a taxpayer's failure to file a required return. A member should advise the taxpayer of the potential consequences of the error and recommend the corrective measures to be taken. The member is not obligated to inform the taxing authority, and a member may not do so without the taxpayer's permission, except when required by law.
- If a member is requested to prepare the current year's return and the taxpayer has not taken appropriate action to correct an error in a prior year's return, the member should consider whether to withdraw from preparing the return and whether to continue a professional or employment relationship with the taxpayer.
- If a member is representing a taxpayer in an administrative proceeding with respect to a return that contains an error of which the member is aware, the member should request the taxpayer's agreement to disclose the error to the taxing authority.

This statement implies that the tax practitioner's primary duty is to the taxpayer, not the taxing authority. Furthermore, upon the taxpayer's failure to correct a tax related error, the practitioner may exercise discretion in deciding whether or not to terminate the professional relationship. The standard also permits the member to provide oral recommendations, but the member should document any oral advice.

Finally, Statement No. 7 addresses the quality of advice provided by the tax practitioner, what consequences presumably ensue from such advice, and whether the practitioner has a duty to update advice to reflect subsequent developments. Specifically,

- A member should use professional judgment to ensure that tax advice provided to a taxpayer reflect competence and appropriately serves the taxpayer's needs. When communicating tax advice to a taxpayer in writing, a member should comply with relevant taxing authorities' standards applicable to written tax advice. A member should use professional judgment about any need to document oral advice.
- A member should assume that tax advice provided to a taxpayer will affect the manner in which the matters or transactions considered would be reported on the taxpayer's tax returns.
- A member has no obligation to communicate with a taxpayer when subsequent developments affect advice previously provided with respect to significant matters except while assisting a taxpayer in implementing procedures or plans associated with the advice provided or when a member undertakes an obligation by specific agreement.

The statement implies that practitioner-taxpayer dealings should not be casual, nonconsensual, open ended. Rather, they should be professional, contractual, and definite. Oral advice may be appropriate in routine matters, but written communications are recommended in important, complicated, or significant dollar value transactions. When giving tax advice, a member should consider the standards in SSTS No. 1.

TAX ACCOUNTING AND TAX LAW

Accountants and lawyers frequently deal with the same issues. These issues pertain to incorporation and merger, bankruptcy and liquidation, purchases and sales, gains and losses, compensation and benefits, and estate planning. Both types of professionals are competent to practice in many of the same areas. In some areas, however, accountants are more competent than lawyers, and in other areas, lawyers are more competent than accountants. What are these areas, and where does one draw the line?

In the realm of federal taxation, achieving a clear delineation always has been difficult. When an accountant prepares a tax return, he or she invariably delves into the intricacies of tax law. When a lawyer gives tax advice, he or she frequently applies principles of accounting. Toward clarifying the responsibilities of each, the AICPA and American Bar Association have issued the *Statement on Practice in the Field of Federal Income Taxation.*[107] This statement indicates five areas in which CPAs and attorneys are equally competent to practice and several areas in which each is exclusively competent to practice. The areas of mutual competence are as follows:

- Preparing federal income tax returns
- Determining the tax effects of proposed transactions
- Representing taxpayers before the Treasury Department
- Practicing before the U.S. Tax Court
- Preparing claims for refunds

Areas in which an accountant is exclusively competent to practice include:

- Resolving accounting issues
- Preparing financial statements included in financial reports or submitted with tax returns
- Advising clients as to accounting methods and procedures
- Classifying transactions and summarizing them in monetary terms
- Interpreting financial results

[107] National Conference of Lawyers and Certified Public Accountants, *Statement on Practice in the Field of Federal Income Taxation*, November 1981.

Areas in which an attorney is exclusively competent to practice include:

- Resolving issues of law
- Preparing legal documents such as agreements, conveyances, trust instruments, and wills
- Advising clients as to the sufficiency or effect of legal documents
- Taking the necessary steps to create, amend, or dissolve a partnership, corporation, or trust
- Representing clients in criminal investigations

State bar and CPA associations have issued similar guidelines for their constituencies, and the courts generally have followed these and the national guidelines.[108]

What happens if an accountant oversteps his or her professional bounds? The transgression may constitute the **unauthorized practice of law**. The unauthorized practice of law involves the engagement, by nonlawyers, in professional activities traditionally reserved for the bar. In most states, it is actionable by injunction, damages, or both. Allegations of the unauthorized practice of law typically arise in the context of a billing dispute.[109] The CPA bills a client for professional services, and the client disputes the bill on the ground that the accountant engaged in the unauthorized practice of law. Occasionally, the court sustains the client's allegation and thus denies the accountant the amount in dispute. With this and the public interest in mind, accountants should always confine their practice to areas in which they are most competent.

ACCOUNTANT-CLIENT PRIVILEGE

ADDITIONAL COMMENT

The protected status of client prepared tax accrual workpapers is still being litigated. In 2009, the U.S. Court of Appeals for the First Circuit in *United States v. Textron Inc.*, 104 AFTR 2d 2009-5719, held that the IRS can obtain tax accrual workpapers. Given the complex issues involved and conflicts among the circuits, additional litigation is likely.

According to judicial doctrine, certain communications between an attorney and a client are "privileged," i.e., nondiscoverable in the course of litigation. In 1998, Congress extended this privilege to similar communications between a federally authorized tax advisor and a client. A federally authorized tax advisor includes a certified public accountant.

The accountant-client privilege is similar to the attorney-client privilege in two respects. First, it encompasses communications for the purpose of obtaining or giving professional advice. Second, it excludes communications for the sole purpose of preparing a tax return. The accountant-client privilege is dissimilar in three respects. First, it is limited only to *tax* advice. Second, it may be asserted only in a noncriminal tax proceeding before a federal court or the IRS. Third, it excludes written communications between an accountant and a corporation regarding a tax shelter. A tax shelter is any plan or arrangement, a significant purpose of which is tax avoidance or evasion.

EXAMPLE C:15-40 ▶ Alec, Chief Financial Officer of MultiCorp, has solicited the advice of his tax accountant, Louise, concerning a civil dispute with the IRS. Louise has advised Alec in a series of letters spanning the course of five months. An IRS appeals officer asks Louise if he can review the letters. Louise may refuse the officer's request because her professional advice was offered in anticipation of civil litigation and therefore is "privileged." ◀

EXAMPLE C:15-41 ▶ Assume the same facts as in Example C:15-40 except Louise sends Alec a letter concerning a foreign sales scheme. Because Louise communicates tax advice to a corporation concerning a "tax shelter" and because this communication is written, it is *not* privileged. ◀

The creation of an accountant-client privilege reflects Congress' belief that the selection of a tax advisor should not hinge on the question of privilege. It ensures that all tax advice is accorded the same protection regardless of the tax advisor's professional status.

---

108 See for example *Lathrop v. Donahue*, 367 U.S. 820, 81 S. Ct. 1826 (1961), *U.S. v. Gordon Buttorff*, 56 AFTR 2d 85-5247, 85-1 USTC ¶9435 (5th Cir., 1985), *Morton L. Simons v. Edgar T. Bellinger*, 643 F.2d 774, 207 U.S. App. D.C. 24 (1980), *Emilio L. Ippolito v. The State of Florida*, 824 F. Supp. 1562, 1993 U.S. Dist. LEXIS 13091 (M.D. Fla., 1993), *In re Application of New Jersey Society of Certified Public Accountants*, 102 N.J. 231, 507 A.2d 711 (1986).

109 See for example, *In re Bercu*, 299 N.Y. 728, 87 N.E.2d 451 (1949), and *Agran v. Shapiro*, 46 AFTR 896, 127 Cal. App.2d 807 (App. Dept. Super. Ct., 1954).

Problem Materials

Discussion Questions

C:15-1 Describe how the IRS verifies tax returns at its service centers.

C:15-2 Name some of the IRS administrative pronouncements.

C:15-3 a. Through what programs has the IRS gathered data to develop its DIF statistical models?
b. How do these programs differ?
c. How has the IRS used these programs to select returns for audit?

C:15-4 On his individual return, Al reports salary and exemptions for himself and seven dependents. His itemized deductions consist of mortgage interest, real estate taxes, and a large loss from breeding dogs. On his individual return, Ben reports self-employment income, a substantial loss from partnership operations, a casualty loss deduction equal to 25% of his AGI, charitable contribution deductions equal to 30% of his AGI, and an exemption for himself. Al's return reports higher taxable income than does Ben's. Which return is more likely to be selected for audit under the DIF program? Explain.

C:15-5 The IRS notifies Tom that it will audit his current year return for an interest deduction. The IRS audited Tom's return two years ago for a charitable contribution deduction. The IRS, however, did not assess a deficiency for the prior year return. Is any potential relief available to Tom with respect to the audit of his current year return?

C:15-6 The IRS informs Brad that it will audit his current year employee business expenses. Brad just met with a revenue agent who contends that Brad owes $775 of additional taxes. Discuss briefly the procedural alternatives available to Brad.

C:15-7 What course(s) of action is (are) available to a taxpayer upon receipt of the following notices:
a. The 30-day letter?
b. The 90-day letter?
c. IRS rejection of a claim for a refund?

C:15-8 List the courts in which a taxpayer can begin tax-related litigation.

C:15-9 Why do taxpayers frequently litigate in the Tax Court?

C:15-10 In what situations is a protest letter necessary?

C:15-11 What information should be included in a request for a private letter ruling?

C:15-12 What conditions must the taxpayer meet to shift the burden of proof to the IRS?

C:15-13 In what circumstances will the IRS rule on estate tax issues?

C:15-14 On which of the following issues will the IRS likely issue a private letter ruling and why? In your answer, assume that no other IRS pronouncement addresses the issue and that pertinent Treasury Regulations are not forthcoming.
a. Whether the taxpayer correctly calculated a capital gain reported on last year's tax return.
b. The tax consequences of using stock derivatives in a corporate reorganization.
c. Whether a mathematical formula correctly calculates the fair market value of a stock derivative.
d. Whether the cost of an Internet course that purports to improve existing employment skills may be deducted this year as a business expense.

C:15-15 Tracy wants to take advantage of a "terrific business opportunity" by engaging in a transaction with Homer. Homer, domineering and impatient, wants Tracy to conclude the transaction within two weeks and under the terms proposed by Homer. Otherwise, Homer will offer the opportunity to another party. Tracy is unsure about the tax consequences of the proposed transaction. Would you advise Tracy to request a ruling? Explain.

C:15-16 Provide the following information relating to both individual and corporate taxpayers:
a. Due date for an income tax return assuming the taxpayer requests no extension.
b. Due date for the return assuming the taxpayer files an automatic extension request.

C:15-17 Your client wants to know whether she must file any documents for an automatic extension to file her tax return. What do you tell her?

C:15-18 A client believes that obtaining an extension for filing an income tax return would give him additional time to pay the tax at no additional cost. Is the client correct?

C:15-19 Briefly explain the rules for determining the interest rate charged on tax underpayments. Is this rate the same as that for overpayments? In which months might the rate(s) change?

C:15-20 In April of the current year, Stan does not have sufficient assets to pay his tax liability for the previous year. However, he expects to pay the tax by August of the current year. He wonders if he should request an extension for filing his return instead of simply filing his return and paying the tax in August. What is your advice?

C:15-21 At what rate is the penalty for underpaying estimated taxes imposed? How is the penalty amount calculated?

C:15-22 The IRS audited Tony's return, and Tony agreed to pay additional taxes plus the negligence penalty. Is this penalty necessarily imposed on the total additional taxes that Tony owes? Explain.

C:15-23 Assume that a taxpayer owes additional taxes as a result of an audit. Give two reasons why the IRS might not impose a substantial understatement penalty on the additional amount owed.

C:15-24 Upon audit, the IRS determines Maria's tax liability to be $40,000. Maria agrees to pay a $7,000 deficiency. Will she necessarily have to pay a substantial understatement penalty? Explain.

C:15-25 Distinguish between the circumstances that give rise to the civil fraud penalty and those that give rise to the negligence penalty.

C:15-26 Distinguish between the burdens of proof the government must meet to prove civil and criminal fraud.

C:15-27 Explain why the government might bring criminal fraud charges against a taxpayer under Sec. 7206 instead of Sec. 7201. Compare the maximum penalties imposed under Secs. 7201, 7203, and 7206.

C:15-28 In general, when does the limitations period for tax returns expire? List four exceptions to the general rule.

C:15-29 What is the principal purpose of the innocent spouse provisions?

C:15-30 Is the tax return preparer limited to the person who signs the return? Explain.

C:15-31 List five IRC penalties that can be imposed on tax return preparers. Does the IRC require a CPA to verify the information a client furnishes?

C:15-32 According to *Treasury Department Circular 230,* what standard should a CPA meet to properly take a position on a tax return?

C:15-33 Under the AICPA's *Statements on Standards for Tax Services*, what is the tax practitioner's professional duty in each of the following situations?

a. Client erroneously deducts $5,000 (instead of $500) on a previous year's tax return.
b. Client refuses to file an amended return to correct the deduction error.
c. Client informs tax practitioner that client incurred $200 in out-of-pocket office supplies expenses.
d. Client informs tax practitioner that client incurred $700 in business related entertainment expenses.
e. Tax practitioner learns that the exemption amount for single taxpayers has been increased by $1,000. Client is a single taxpayer.

ISSUE IDENTIFICATION QUESTIONS

C:15-34 You are preparing the tax return of Bold Corporation, which had sales of $60 million. Bold made a $1 million expenditure for which the appropriate tax treatment—deductible or capitalizable—is a gray area. Bold's director of federal taxes and chief financial officer urgently wants to deduct the expenditure. What tax compliance issues should you consider in advising her?

C:15-35 Your client, Hank Goedert, earned $100,000 of salary and received $40,000 of dividends in the current year. His itemized deductions total $37,000. In addition, Hank received $47,000 from a relative who was his former employer. You have researched whether the $47,000 should be classified as a gift or compensation and are confident that substantial authority exists for classifying the receipt as a gift. What tax compliance issues should you consider in deciding whether to include or exclude the amount in Hank's gross income?

C:15-36 The IRS audited the tax returns of Darryl Strawberry, a former major league outfielder. It contended that, between 1986 and 1990, Strawberry earned $422,250 for autograph signings, appearances, and product endorsements, but he reported only $59,685 of income. Strawberry attributed the shortfall to his receipt of cash for autograph sessions and promotional events. He allegedly concealed the cash payments in separate bank accounts of which his CPA was unaware. What tax compliance issues regarding the alleged underreporting are pertinent?

PROBLEMS

C:15-37 *Calculation of Penalties.* Amy files her current year tax return on August 13 of the following year. She pays the amount due without requesting an extension. The tax shown on her return is $24,000. Her current year wage withholding amounts to $15,000. Amy pays no estimated taxes and claims no tax credits on her current year return.

a. What penalties will the IRS likely impose on Amy (ignoring the penalty for underpayment of estimated taxes)? Assume Amy committed no fraud.
b. On what dollar amount, and for how many days, will Amy owe interest?

C:15-38 *Calculation of Penalties.* In the preceding problem, how would your answers change if Amy instead files her return on June 18 and, on September 8 pays the amount due? Assume her wage withholding tax amounts to

a. $19,000
b. $24,500
c. How would your answer to Part a change if Amy requests an automatic extension?

C:15-39 *Calculation of Penalties.* The taxes shown on Hu's tax returns for Year 1 and Year 2 are \$5,000 and \$8,000, respectively. Hu's wage withholding for Year 2 was \$5,200, and she paid no estimated taxes. Hu filed her Year 2 return on March 18 of Year 3, but she did not have sufficient funds to pay any taxes on that date. She paid the \$2,800 balance due on June 24 of Year 4. Hu's AGI for Year 1 did not exceed \$150,000. Calculate the penalties Hu owes with respect to her Year 2 tax return.

C:15-40 *Calculation of Penalties.* Ted's current year return reported a tax liability of \$1,800. Ted's wage withholding for the current year was \$2,200. Because of his poor memory, Ted did not file his current year return until May 28 of the following year. What penalties (if any) does Ted owe?

C:15-41 *Calculation of Penalties.* Bob, a calendar year taxpayer, files his current year individual return on July 17 of the following year without having requested an extension. His return indicates an amount due of \$5,100. Bob pays this amount on November 3 of the following year. What are Bob's penalties for failing to file and failing to pay his tax on time? Assume Bob committed no fraud.

C:15-42 *Calculation of Penalties.* Carl's tax liability for last year was \$19,000, and his AGI did not exceed \$150,000. Carl requests an automatic extension for filing his current year individual return but does not pay any additional tax with his extension request. By April 15 of the following year, Carl has paid \$20,000 of taxes in the form of wage withholding and estimated taxes. Carl files his current year return and pays the balance of the taxes due on June 18 of the following year. What penalties will Carl owe if his current year tax is \$23,000? \$20,800?

C:15-43 *Determination of Interest.* Refer to the preceding problem.

a. Will Carl owe interest? If so, on what amount and for how many days?

b. Assume the applicable interest rate is 6%. Compute Carl's interest payable if his current year tax is \$23,000. (See a major tax service for the compounding tables.)

C:15-44 *Penalty for Underpayment of Estimated Taxes.* Ed's tax liability for last year was \$24,000. Ed projects that his tax for this year will be \$34,000. Ed is self-employed and, thus, will have no withholding. His AGI for last year did not exceed \$150,000. How much estimated tax should Ed pay for this year to avoid the penalty for underpaying estimated taxes?

C:15-45 *Penalty for Underpayment of Estimated Taxes.* Refer to the preceding problem. Assume that Ed expects his income for this year to decline and his tax liability for this year to be only \$15,000. What minimum amount of estimated taxes should Ed pay this year? What problem will Ed encounter if he pays this minimum amount and his current year income exceeds last year's because of a large capital gain realized in December of this year?

C:15-46 *Penalty for Underpayment of Estimated Taxes.* Pam's prior year (Year 1) income tax liability was \$23,000. Her current year (Year 2) AGI did not exceed \$150,000. On April 2 of next year (Year 3), Pam, a calendar year taxpayer, timely files her current year individual return, which indicates a \$30,000 income tax liability (before reduction for withholding). In addition, the return indicates self-employment taxes of \$2,600. Taxes withheld from Pam's current year (Year 2) salary total \$20,000; she has paid no estimated taxes.

a. Will Pam owe a penalty for not paying sufficient estimated taxes? Explain.

b. What amount (if any) per quarter is subject to the penalty, and for what period will the penalty be imposed for each quarter's underpayment?

c. How would your answers to parts a and b change if Pam's current year (Year 2) tax liability (including self-employment taxes) instead were \$17,000?

C:15-47 *Penalty for Underpayment of Estimated Taxes.* Amir's projected tax liability for the current year is \$23,000. Although Amir has substantial dividend and interest income, he does not pay any estimated taxes. Amir's withholding for January through November of the current year is \$1,300 per month. He wants to increase his withholding for December to avoid the penalty for underpaying estimated taxes. Amir's previous year's liability (excluding withholding) is \$21,000. His previous year's AGI did not exceed \$150,000. What amount should Amir have withheld from his December paycheck? Explain.

C:15-48 *Negligence Penalty.* The IRS audits Tan's individual return for the current year and assesses a \$9,000 deficiency, \$2,800 of which results from Tan's negligence. What is the amount of Tan's negligence penalty? Does the penalty bear interest?

C:15-49 *Negligence Penalty.* The IRS audits Pearl's current year individual return and determines that, among other errors, she negligently failed to report dividend income of \$8,000. The deficiency relating to the dividends is \$2,240. The IRS proposes an additional \$12,000 deficiency for the other errors that do not involve negligence. What is the amount of Pearl's negligence penalty for the \$14,240 in deficiencies?

C:15-50 *Substantial Understatement Penalty.* Carmen's current year individual return reports a $6,000 deduction for a questionable item not relating to a tax-shelter. Carmen does not make a disclosure regarding this item. The IRS audits Carmen's return, and she consents to a deficiency. As a result, her tax liability increases from $20,000 to $21,860. Assume Carmen lacks substantial authority for the deduction.

a. What substantial understatement penalty (if any) will be imposed?
b. Will the penalty bear interest?
c. How would your answer to Parts a and b change if Carmen reported a $20,000 deduction instead of $6,000, and her tax liability increased by $6,200 to $26,200?

C:15-51 *Substantial Understatement Penalty.* Refer to Part c of the previous problem. Assume that Carmen discloses her position, which is not frivolous. How would your original answer change assuming the item does not involve a tax shelter?

C:15-52 *Fraud Penalty.* Luis, a bachelor, owes $56,000 of additional taxes, all due to fraud.

a. What is the amount of Luis' civil fraud penalty?
b. What criminal fraud penalty might the government impose on Luis under Sec. 7201?

C:15-53 *Fraud Penalty.* Hal and Wanda, his wife, are in the 35% marginal tax bracket in the current year. Wanda fraudulently omits from their joint return $50,000 of gross income. Hal does not participate in or know of her fraudulent act. Hal, however, overstates his deductions by $10,000 because of an oversight.

a. If the government successfully proves fraud in a civil suit against Wanda, what fines and/or penalties might she owe? If Hal and Wanda establish that the overstatement is not attributable to fraud, can the government impose a civil fraud penalty on Hal?
b. If the government successfully proves fraud in a criminal suit against Wanda, what fines or penalties might she owe? Could she or Hal be sentenced to prison?

C:15-54 *Statute of Limitations.* Frank, a calendar year taxpayer, reports $100,000 of gross income and $60,000 of taxable income on his Year 1 return, which he files on March 12 of Year 2. He fails to report on the return a $52,000 long-term capital gain and a $10,000 short-term capital loss. When does the limitations period for the government's collecting the tax deficiency expire if

a. Frank's omission results from an oversight?
b. His omission results from a willful attempt to evade the tax?

C:15-55 *Statute of Limitations.* Refer to the previous problem. Assume Frank subsequently commits fraud with respect to his Year 1 return as late as October 8, of Year 3. When does the limitations period for charging Frank with criminal tax fraud expire?

C:15-56 *Claim for Refund.* Maria, a calendar year taxpayer, files her Year 1 individual return on March 12 of Year 2 and pays the amount of tax due. She later discovers that she overlooked some deductions that she should have reported on the return. By what date must she file a claim for refund?

C:15-57 *Innocent Spouse Provisions.* Wilma earns no income in the current year but files a joint return with her husband, Hank. The return reports $40,000 of gross income and AGI, and $24,000 of taxable income. Hank realized $12,000 of gambling winnings (no losses) in the current year but failed to report the winnings on the return. Wilma does not know about Hank's gambling activities, much less his winnings. The IRS audits the return and assesses additional taxes. Is Wilma entitled to innocent spouse relief? Explain.

C:15-58 *Innocent Spouse Provisions.* Joe and Joan file a joint return for the current year. They are in the 35% marginal tax bracket. Unbeknownst to Joe, Joan fails to report on the return the $8,000 value of a prize she won. She, however, used the prize to buy Joe a new boat. Is Joe entitled to innocent spouse relief? Explain.

C:15-59 *Unauthorized Practice of Law.* Your client, Meade Technical Solutions, proposes to merge with Dealy Cyberlabs. In advance of the merger, you (a) issue an opinion concerning the FMV of Dealy, (b) prepare pro forma financials for the merged entity to be, (c) draft Meade shareholder resolutions approving the proposed merger, (d) file a shareholder proxy statement with the U.S. Securities and Exchange Commission, and (e) advise Meade's board of directors concerning the advantages of a Type A versus a Type B reorganization. Which of these activities, if any, constitutes the unauthorized practice of law?

C:15-60 *Unauthorized Practice of Law.* Your client, Envirocosmetics, recently has filed for bankruptcy. In the course of bankruptcy proceedings, you (a) prepare a plan of reorganization that alters the rights of preferred stockholders, (b) notify the Envirocosmetics' creditors of an impending bulk transfer of the company's assets, (c) review IRS secured claims against these assets, (d) restructure the company's debt by reducing its principal amount and extending its maturity, (e) advise the bankruptcy court as to how this restructuring will impact the company's NOLs. Which of these activities, if any, constitutes the unauthorized practice of law?

C:15-61 *Accountant-Client Privilege* Which of the following communications between an accountant and client are privileged?

a. For tax preparation purposes only, client informs the accountant that she contributed $10,000 to a homeless shelter.
b. Client informs the accountant that he forgot to report on his tax return the $5,000 value of a prize and asks how he should correct the error.
c. Client informs the accountant that she no longer will pay alimony to her ex-husband.

C:15-62 *Accountant-Client Privilege.* Which of the following communications between an accountant and client are *not* privileged?

a. In a closed-door meeting, the accountant orally advises the client to set up a foreign subsidiary to shift taxable income to a low-tax jurisdiction.
b. In a closed-door meeting, the accountant submits to the client a plan for shifting taxable income to a low-tax jurisdiction.
c. In soliciting professional advice relating to criminal fraud, the client informs the accountant that he (the client) lied to the IRS.

COMPREHENSIVE PROBLEM

C:15-63 This year, Ark Corporation acquired substantially all the voting stock of BioTech Consultants, Inc. for cash. Subsequent to the acquisition, Ark's chief financial officer, Jonathan Cohen, approached Edith Murphy, Ark's tax advisor, with a question: Could Ark amortize the "general educational skills" of BioTech's employees? Edith researched the issue but found no primary authorities on point. She did, however, find a tax journal article, co-authored by two prominent academics, that endorsed amortizing "general educational skills" for tax purposes. The article referred to numerous primary authorities that support the amortization of "technical skills," but not "general educational skills." Edith consulted these authorities directly. Based on her research, Edith in good faith advised Jonathan that Ark could amortize the "general educational skills" over a 15-year period. In so doing, has Edith met the "realistic possibility standard" of

a. The IRC?
b. The AICPAs *Statements on Standards for Tax Services* (see Appendix E)?

TAX STRATEGY PROBLEM

C:15-64 The IRS is disputing a deduction reported on your Year 1 tax return, which you filed on April 12 of Year 2. On April 4 of Year 5, the IRS audit agent asks you to waive the statute of limitations for the entire return so as to give her additional time to obtain a Technical Advice Memorandum. The agent proposes in return for the waiver a "carrot"—the prospect of an offer in compromise—and a "stick"—the possibility of a higher penalty. Although you have substantial authority for the deduction, you consider the following alternatives: (1) waive the statute of limitations for the entire return, (2) waive the statute of limitations for the deduction only, or (3) do not waive the statute of limitations in any way, shape, or form. Which alternative should you choose, and why?

CASE STUDY PROBLEM

C:15-65 A long-time client, Horace Haney, wishes to avoid currently recognizing revenue in a particular transaction. A recently finalized Treasury Regulation provides that, in such a transaction, revenue should be currently recognized. Horace insists that you report no revenue from the transaction and, furthermore, that you make no disclosure about contravening the regulation. The IRC is unclear about whether the income should be recognized currently. No relevant cases, revenue rulings, or letter rulings deal specifically with the transaction in question.

Required: Discuss whether you, a CPA, should prepare Horace's tax return and comply with his wishes. Assume that recognizing the income in question would increase Horace's tax liability by about 25%.

TAX RESEARCH PROBLEMS

C:15-66 Art is named executor of the Estate of Stu Stone, his father, who died on February 3 of the current year. Art hires Larry to be the estate's attorney. Larry advises Art that the estate must file an estate tax return but does not mention the due date. Art, a pharmacist, has no experience in tax matters other than preparing his own tax returns. Art provides Larry with all the necessary information by June 15 of the current year. On six occasions, Art contacts Larry to check on the progress of the estate tax return. Each time, Larry assures

Art that "everything is under control." On November 15, Art contacts Larry for the seventh time. He learns that because of a clerical oversight, the return—due on November 2 of the current year—has not been filed. Larry apologizes and says he will make sure that an associate promptly files the return. The return, which reports an estate tax liability of $75,200, is filed on December 7 of the current year. Your manager requests that you prepare a memorandum addressing whether the estate will owe a failure-to-file penalty. Your manager suggests that, at a minimum, you consult

- IRC Sec. 6151(a)
- *U.S. v. Robert W. Boyle,* 55 AFTR 2d 85-1535, 85-1 USTC ¶13,602 (USSC, 1985)

C:15-67 Harold and Betty, factory workers who until this year prepared their own individual tax returns, purchased an investment from a broker last year. Although they reviewed the prospectus for the investment, the broker explained the more complicated features of the investment. Early this year, they struggled to prepare their individual return for last year but, because of the investment, found it too complicated to complete. Consequently, they hired a CPA to prepare the return. The CPA deducted losses generated from the investment against income that Harold and Betty generated from other sources. The IRS audited the return for last year and contended that the loss is not deductible. After consulting their CPA, who further considered the tax consequences of the investment, Harold and Betty agreed that the loss is not deductible and consented to paying the deficiency. The IRS also contended that the couple owes the substantial understatement penalty because they did not disclose the value of the investment on their return and did not have substantial authority for their position. Assume you are representing the taxpayers before the IRS and intend to argue that they should be exempted from the substantial understatement penalty. Your tax manager reminds you to consult Secs. 6662 and 6664 when conducting your research.

C:15-68 Gene employed his attorney to draft identical trust instruments for each of his three minor children: Judy (age 5), Terry (age 7), and Grady (age 11). Each trust instrument names the Fourth City Bank as trustee and states that the trust is irrevocable. It provides that, until the beneficiary reaches age 21, the trustee at its discretion is to pay income and/or principal (corpus) to the beneficiary. Upon reaching age 21, the beneficiary will have 60 days in which to request that the trust assets be paid over to him or her. Otherwise, the assets will stay in the trust until the beneficiary reaches age 35. The beneficiary also is granted a general testamentary power of appointment over the trust assets. If the beneficiary dies before the trust terminates and does not exercise his or her power of appointment (because, for example, he or she dies without a will), trust assets will be distributed to family members in accordance with state intestacy laws. Each trust will be funded with property valued at $100,000. Before he signs the instruments, Gene wants to obtain a ruling from the IRS concerning whether the trusts qualify for the annual gift tax exclusion. Your task is to prepare a request for a letter ruling.

A partial list of research sources is

- IRC Secs. 2503(b) and (c)
- Reg. Sec. 25.2503-4
- Rev. Rul. 67-270, 1967-2 C.B. 349
- Rev. Rul. 74-43, 1974-1 C.B. 285
- Rev. Rul. 81-7, 1981-1 C.B. 474

C:15-69 On April 15 of Year 2, Adam and Renee Tyler jointly filed a Year 1 return that reported AGI of $68,240 ($20,500 attributable to Renee) and a tax liability of $3,050. They paid this amount in a timely fashion. On their return, the Tylers claimed a $18,405 deduction for Adam's distributive share of a partnership loss. If not for the loss, the Tylers' tax liability would have been $8,358. In the previous year, Adam had withdrawn $20,000 cash from the partnership, which he used to buy Renee a new car. Although Renee, a marketing consultant, is not active in the partnership business, she has worked for the partnership as a part-time receptionist. Adam and his partner (who incidentally is Renee's brother) failed to file a partnership return for Year 1. Upon audit, the IRS discovered that the Year 1 partnership records were missing. In Year 3, Adam had a heart attack. He remains in serious condition. Unable to reach Adam, the IRS sends Renee a 30-day letter proposing a $5,308 deficiency. She intends to protest. Your supervisor has asked you to write a memorandum discussing Renee's potential liabilities and defenses. In your memorandum, you should consult the following authorities:

- IRC Secs. 6013 and 6662
- *Rebecca Jo Reser v. CIR,* 79 AFTR 2d 97-2743, 97-1 USTC ¶50,416 (5th Cir., 1997)

C:15-70 A colleague comes to you with the following investment proposal that he would like to market for Client:

- Client obtains cash of $60,000 from Bank.
- Bank loan agreement specifies that $40,000 of this amount represents principal; the remaining $20,000 represents interest.
- Client contributes the $60,000 cash to Partnership, which agrees to assume Client's $40,000 debt.
- Under Sec. 752, Partnership's debt assumption is treated as a distribution of money that reduces Client's basis in partnership interest from $60,000 to $20,000.
- Partnership invests the $60,000 in a resort hotel project.
- Before the project comes onstream, Client sells partnership interest for $15,000.

Net result: Partnership, not Client, is responsible for repayment of Bank loan. Client realizes a $5,000 capital loss without having spent any of its own funds.

Prepare a memorandum that sets forth the tax and reporting implications of this investment proposal. At a minimum, consult the following authorities:

- IRC Secs. 6707A and 6111
- Reg. Secs. 1.6111-4 and 301.6112-1
- Notice 2000-44, 2000-2 C.B. 255

C:15-71 Five years ago, Spyros Dietrich wanted to sell IMPEXT, Inc., his wholly owned import-export business. He also wanted to avoid recognizing the substantial gain that would result from his selling his IMPEXT shares on the open market. Spyros' basis in the shares ($100,000) was well below their market value ($600,000).

To avoid gain recognition, Spyros formed the SH Partnership with his brother Hussein. To capitalize the partnership, Spyros transferred all his IMPEXT shares to SH in exchange for 99 SH Partnership units. Hussein transferred $100 cash in exchange for one SH Partnership unit. Subsequently, Spyros formed Fu Yung, Inc., an S corporation, and transferred his 99 SH Partnership units to Fu Yung in exchange for 99 Fu Yung shares.

Under Sec. 708, the transfer to Fu Yung technically caused a dissolution of SH. However, Spyros and Hussein agreed to continue the SH "business" in reconstituted form as the FYH Partnership. Thereupon, FYH elected under Sec. 754 to step up its basis in the IMPEXT shares from $100,000 to $600,000. Then FYH sold the IMPEXT shares to disinterested investor Gonzalez for $615,000, thereby realizing only a $15,000 gain. Ninety-nine percent of this gain passed through to Spyros' separate return via Fu Yung and FYH.

The series of transactions went unnoticed by the IRS until the current year, when it audited Spyros' return. On that return, Spyros reported $525,000 of ordinary income and $14,850 (i.e., 99% of $15,000) of capital gain. When the IRS alleged that Spyros had substantially understated his income, Spyros raised the "statute of limitations" as a defense. Is the IRS correct in its allegation? If so, is it precluded by the statute of limitations from collecting additional taxes from Spyro?

Before answering these questions, please consult the following sources:

- IRC Secs. 708, 704, 6501
- *Brandon Ridge Partners v. U.S.*, 100 AFTR 2d 2007-5347, 2007-2 USTC ¶50,573 (DC FL, July 30, 2007)

2014 TAX TABLES AND RATE SCHEDULES

2015 WITHHOLDING TABLES (PARTIAL)

2014 Tax Table

CAUTION

See the instructions for line 44 to see if you must use the Tax Table below to figure your tax.

Example. Mr. and Mrs. Brown are filing a joint return. Their taxable income on Form 1040, line 43, is $25,300. First, they find the $25,300-25,350 taxable income line. Next, they find the column for married filing jointly and read down the column. The amount shown where the taxable income line and filing status column meet is $2,891. This is the tax amount they should enter on Form 1040, line 44.

Sample Table

At Least	But Less Than	Single	Married filing jointly*	Married filing sepa-rately	Head of a house-hold
		Your tax is—			
25,200	**25,250**	3,330	2,876	3,330	3,136
25,250	**25,300**	3,338	2,884	3,338	3,144
25,300	**25,350**	3,345	(2,891)	3,345	3,151
25,350	**25,400**	3,353	2,899	3,353	3,159

If line 43 (taxable income) is— At least	But less than	And you are— Single	Married filing jointly *	Married filing sepa-rately	Head of a house-hold
		Your tax is—			
0	**5**	0	0	0	0
5	**15**	1	1	1	1
15	**25**	2	2	2	2
25	**50**	4	4	4	4
50	**75**	6	6	6	6
75	**100**	9	9	9	9
100	**125**	11	11	11	11
125	**150**	14	14	14	14
150	**175**	16	16	16	16
175	**200**	19	19	19	19
200	**225**	21	21	21	21
225	**250**	24	24	24	24
250	**275**	26	26	26	26
275	**300**	29	29	29	29
300	**325**	31	31	31	31
325	**350**	34	34	34	34
350	**375**	36	36	36	36
375	**400**	39	39	39	39
400	**425**	41	41	41	41
425	**450**	44	44	44	44
450	**475**	46	46	46	46
475	**500**	49	49	49	49
500	**525**	51	51	51	51
525	**550**	54	54	54	54
550	**575**	56	56	56	56
575	**600**	59	59	59	59
600	**625**	61	61	61	61
625	**650**	64	64	64	64
650	**675**	66	66	66	66
675	**700**	69	69	69	69
700	**725**	71	71	71	71
725	**750**	74	74	74	74
750	**775**	76	76	76	76
775	**800**	79	79	79	79
800	**825**	81	81	81	81
825	**850**	84	84	84	84
850	**875**	86	86	86	86
875	**900**	89	89	89	89
900	**925**	91	91	91	91
925	**950**	94	94	94	94
950	**975**	96	96	96	96
975	**1,000**	99	99	99	99

If line 43 (taxable income) is— At least	But less than	And you are— Single	Married filing jointly *	Married filing sepa-rately	Head of a house-hold
		Your tax is—			
1,000					
1,000	**1,025**	101	101	101	101
1,025	**1,050**	104	104	104	104
1,050	**1,075**	106	106	106	106
1,075	**1,100**	109	109	109	109
1,100	**1,125**	111	111	111	111
1,125	**1,150**	114	114	114	114
1,150	**1,175**	116	116	116	116
1,175	**1,200**	119	119	119	119
1,200	**1,225**	121	121	121	121
1,225	**1,250**	124	124	124	124
1,250	**1,275**	126	126	126	126
1,275	**1,300**	129	129	129	129
1,300	**1,325**	131	131	131	131
1,325	**1,350**	134	134	134	134
1,350	**1,375**	136	136	136	136
1,375	**1,400**	139	139	139	139
1,400	**1,425**	141	141	141	141
1,425	**1,450**	144	144	144	144
1,450	**1,475**	146	146	146	146
1,475	**1,500**	149	149	149	149
1,500	**1,525**	151	151	151	151
1,525	**1,550**	154	154	154	154
1,550	**1,575**	156	156	156	156
1,575	**1,600**	159	159	159	159
1,600	**1,625**	161	161	161	161
1,625	**1,650**	164	164	164	164
1,650	**1,675**	166	166	166	166
1,675	**1,700**	169	169	169	169
1,700	**1,725**	171	171	171	171
1,725	**1,750**	174	174	174	174
1,750	**1,775**	176	176	176	176
1,775	**1,800**	179	179	179	179
1,800	**1,825**	181	181	181	181
1,825	**1,850**	184	184	184	184
1,850	**1,875**	186	186	186	186
1,875	**1,900**	189	189	189	189
1,900	**1,925**	191	191	191	191
1,925	**1,950**	194	194	194	194
1,950	**1,975**	196	196	196	196
1,975	**2,000**	199	199	199	199

If line 43 (taxable income) is— At least	But less than	And you are— Single	Married filing jointly *	Married filing sepa-rately	Head of a house-hold
		Your tax is—			
2,000					
2,000	**2,025**	201	201	201	201
2,025	**2,050**	204	204	204	204
2,050	**2,075**	206	206	206	206
2,075	**2,100**	209	209	209	209
2,100	**2,125**	211	211	211	211
2,125	**2,150**	214	214	214	214
2,150	**2,175**	216	216	216	216
2,175	**2,200**	219	219	219	219
2,200	**2,225**	221	221	221	221
2,225	**2,250**	224	224	224	224
2,250	**2,275**	226	226	226	226
2,275	**2,300**	229	229	229	229
2,300	**2,325**	231	231	231	231
2,325	**2,350**	234	234	234	234
2,350	**2,375**	236	236	236	236
2,375	**2,400**	239	239	239	239
2,400	**2,425**	241	241	241	241
2,425	**2,450**	244	244	244	244
2,450	**2,475**	246	246	246	246
2,475	**2,500**	249	249	249	249
2,500	**2,525**	251	251	251	251
2,525	**2,550**	254	254	254	254
2,550	**2,575**	256	256	256	256
2,575	**2,600**	259	259	259	259
2,600	**2,625**	261	261	261	261
2,625	**2,650**	264	264	264	264
2,650	**2,675**	266	266	266	266
2,675	**2,700**	269	269	269	269
2,700	**2,725**	271	271	271	271
2,725	**2,750**	274	274	274	274
2,750	**2,775**	276	276	276	276
2,775	**2,800**	279	279	279	279
2,800	**2,825**	281	281	281	281
2,825	**2,850**	284	284	284	284
2,850	**2,875**	286	286	286	286
2,875	**2,900**	289	289	289	289
2,900	**2,925**	291	291	291	291
2,925	**2,950**	294	294	294	294
2,950	**2,975**	296	296	296	296
2,975	**3,000**	299	299	299	299

(Continued)

* This column must also be used by a qualifying widow(er).

(Continued on page T-3)

2014 Tax Table — *Continued*

If line 43 (taxable income) is— At least	But less than	And you are— Single	Married filing jointly *	Married filing separately	Head of a household
		Your tax is—			
3,000					
3,000	3,050	303	303	303	303
3,050	3,100	308	308	308	308
3,100	3,150	313	313	313	313
3,150	3,200	318	318	318	318
3,200	3,250	323	323	323	323
3,250	3,300	328	328	328	328
3,300	3,350	333	333	333	333
3,350	3,400	338	338	338	338
3,400	3,450	343	343	343	343
3,450	3,500	348	348	348	348
3,500	3,550	353	353	353	353
3,550	3,600	358	358	358	358
3,600	3,650	363	363	363	363
3,650	3,700	368	368	368	368
3,700	3,750	373	373	373	373
3,750	3,800	378	378	378	378
3,800	3,850	383	383	383	383
3,850	3,900	388	388	388	388
3,900	3,950	393	393	393	393
3,950	4,000	398	398	398	398
4,000					
4,000	4,050	403	403	403	403
4,050	4,100	408	408	408	408
4,100	4,150	413	413	413	413
4,150	4,200	418	418	418	418
4,200	4,250	423	423	423	423
4,250	4,300	428	428	428	428
4,300	4,350	433	433	433	433
4,350	4,400	438	438	438	438
4,400	4,450	443	443	443	443
4,450	4,500	448	448	448	448
4,500	4,550	453	453	453	453
4,550	4,600	458	458	458	458
4,600	4,650	463	463	463	463
4,650	4,700	468	468	468	468
4,700	4,750	473	473	473	473
4,750	4,800	478	478	478	478
4,800	4,850	483	483	483	483
4,850	4,900	488	488	488	488
4,900	4,950	493	493	493	493
4,950	5,000	498	498	498	498
5,000					
5,000	5,050	503	503	503	503
5,050	5,100	508	508	508	508
5,100	5,150	513	513	513	513
5,150	5,200	518	518	518	518
5,200	5,250	523	523	523	523
5,250	5,300	528	528	528	528
5,300	5,350	533	533	533	533
5,350	5,400	538	538	538	538
5,400	5,450	543	543	543	543
5,450	5,500	548	548	548	548
5,500	5,550	553	553	553	553
5,550	5,600	558	558	558	558
5,600	5,650	563	563	563	563
5,650	5,700	568	568	568	568
5,700	5,750	573	573	573	573
5,750	5,800	578	578	578	578
5,800	5,850	583	583	583	583
5,850	5,900	588	588	588	588
5,900	5,950	593	593	593	593
5,950	6,000	598	598	598	598
6,000					
6,000	6,050	603	603	603	603
6,050	6,100	608	608	608	608
6,100	6,150	613	613	613	613
6,150	6,200	618	618	618	618
6,200	6,250	623	623	623	623
6,250	6,300	628	628	628	628
6,300	6,350	633	633	633	633
6,350	6,400	638	638	638	638
6,400	6,450	643	643	643	643
6,450	6,500	648	648	648	648
6,500	6,550	653	653	653	653
6,550	6,600	658	658	658	658
6,600	6,650	663	663	663	663
6,650	6,700	668	668	668	668
6,700	6,750	673	673	673	673
6,750	6,800	678	678	678	678
6,800	6,850	683	683	683	683
6,850	6,900	688	688	688	688
6,900	6,950	693	693	693	693
6,950	7,000	698	698	698	698
7,000					
7,000	7,050	703	703	703	703
7,050	7,100	708	708	708	708
7,100	7,150	713	713	713	713
7,150	7,200	718	718	718	718
7,200	7,250	723	723	723	723
7,250	7,300	728	728	728	728
7,300	7,350	733	733	733	733
7,350	7,400	738	738	738	738
7,400	7,450	743	743	743	743
7,450	7,500	748	748	748	748
7,500	7,550	753	753	753	753
7,550	7,600	758	758	758	758
7,600	7,650	763	763	763	763
7,650	7,700	768	768	768	768
7,700	7,750	773	773	773	773
7,750	7,800	778	778	778	778
7,800	7,850	783	783	783	783
7,850	7,900	788	788	788	788
7,900	7,950	793	793	793	793
7,950	8,000	798	798	798	798
8,000					
8,000	8,050	803	803	803	803
8,050	8,100	808	808	808	808
8,100	8,150	813	813	813	813
8,150	8,200	818	818	818	818
8,200	8,250	823	823	823	823
8,250	8,300	828	828	828	828
8,300	8,350	833	833	833	833
8,350	8,400	838	838	838	838
8,400	8,450	843	843	843	843
8,450	8,500	848	848	848	848
8,500	8,550	853	853	853	853
8,550	8,600	858	858	858	858
8,600	8,650	863	863	863	863
8,650	8,700	868	868	868	868
8,700	8,750	873	873	873	873
8,750	8,800	878	878	878	878
8,800	8,850	883	883	883	883
8,850	8,900	888	888	888	888
8,900	8,950	893	893	893	893
8,950	9,000	898	898	898	898
9,000					
9,000	9,050	903	903	903	903
9,050	9,100	908	908	908	908
9,100	9,150	915	913	915	913
9,150	9,200	923	918	923	918
9,200	9,250	930	923	930	923
9,250	9,300	938	928	938	928
9,300	9,350	945	933	945	933
9,350	9,400	953	938	953	938
9,400	9,450	960	943	960	943
9,450	9,500	968	948	968	948
9,500	9,550	975	953	975	953
9,550	9,600	983	958	983	958
9,600	9,650	990	963	990	963
9,650	9,700	998	968	998	968
9,700	9,750	1,005	973	1,005	973
9,750	9,800	1,013	978	1,013	978
9,800	9,850	1,020	983	1,020	983
9,850	9,900	1,028	988	1,028	988
9,900	9,950	1,035	993	1,035	993
9,950	10,000	1,043	998	1,043	998
10,000					
10,000	10,050	1,050	1,003	1,050	1,003
10,050	10,100	1,058	1,008	1,058	1,008
10,100	10,150	1,065	1,013	1,065	1,013
10,150	10,200	1,073	1,018	1,073	1,018
10,200	10,250	1,080	1,023	1,080	1,023
10,250	10,300	1,088	1,028	1,088	1,028
10,300	10,350	1,095	1,033	1,095	1,033
10,350	10,400	1,103	1,038	1,103	1,038
10,400	10,450	1,110	1,043	1,110	1,043
10,450	10,500	1,118	1,048	1,118	1,048
10,500	10,550	1,125	1,053	1,125	1,053
10,550	10,600	1,133	1,058	1,133	1,058
10,600	10,650	1,140	1,063	1,140	1,063
10,650	10,700	1,148	1,068	1,148	1,068
10,700	10,750	1,155	1,073	1,155	1,073
10,750	10,800	1,163	1,078	1,163	1,078
10,800	10,850	1,170	1,083	1,170	1,083
10,850	10,900	1,178	1,088	1,178	1,088
10,900	10,950	1,185	1,093	1,185	1,093
10,950	11,000	1,193	1,098	1,193	1,098
11,000					
11,000	11,050	1,200	1,103	1,200	1,103
11,050	11,100	1,208	1,108	1,208	1,108
11,100	11,150	1,215	1,113	1,215	1,113
11,150	11,200	1,223	1,118	1,223	1,118
11,200	11,250	1,230	1,123	1,230	1,123
11,250	11,300	1,238	1,128	1,238	1,128
11,300	11,350	1,245	1,133	1,245	1,133
11,350	11,400	1,253	1,138	1,253	1,138
11,400	11,450	1,260	1,143	1,260	1,143
11,450	11,500	1,268	1,148	1,268	1,148
11,500	11,550	1,275	1,153	1,275	1,153
11,550	11,600	1,283	1,158	1,283	1,158
11,600	11,650	1,290	1,163	1,290	1,163
11,650	11,700	1,298	1,168	1,298	1,168
11,700	11,750	1,305	1,173	1,305	1,173
11,750	11,800	1,313	1,178	1,313	1,178
11,800	11,850	1,320	1,183	1,320	1,183
11,850	11,900	1,328	1,188	1,328	1,188
11,900	11,950	1,335	1,193	1,335	1,193
11,950	12,000	1,343	1,198	1,343	1,198

(Continued)

* This column must also be used by a qualifying widow(er).

(Continued on page T-4)

2014 Tax Table — *Continued*

If line 43 (taxable income) is—		And you are—			
At least	But less than	Single	Married filing jointly *	Married filing sepa-rately	Head of a house-hold
		Your tax is—			
12,000					
12,000	12,050	1,350	1,203	1,350	1,203
12,050	12,100	1,358	1,208	1,358	1,208
12,100	12,150	1,365	1,213	1,365	1,213
12,150	12,200	1,373	1,218	1,373	1,218
12,200	12,250	1,380	1,223	1,380	1,223
12,250	12,300	1,388	1,228	1,388	1,228
12,300	12,350	1,395	1,233	1,395	1,233
12,350	12,400	1,403	1,238	1,403	1,238
12,400	12,450	1,410	1,243	1,410	1,243
12,450	12,500	1,418	1,248	1,418	1,248
12,500	12,550	1,425	1,253	1,425	1,253
12,550	12,600	1,433	1,258	1,433	1,258
12,600	12,650	1,440	1,263	1,440	1,263
12,650	12,700	1,448	1,268	1,448	1,268
12,700	12,750	1,455	1,273	1,455	1,273
12,750	12,800	1,463	1,278	1,463	1,278
12,800	12,850	1,470	1,283	1,470	1,283
12,850	12,900	1,478	1,288	1,478	1,288
12,900	12,950	1,485	1,293	1,485	1,293
12,950	13,000	1,493	1,298	1,493	1,299
13,000					
13,000	13,050	1,500	1,303	1,500	1,306
13,050	13,100	1,508	1,308	1,508	1,314
13,100	13,150	1,515	1,313	1,515	1,321
13,150	13,200	1,523	1,318	1,523	1,329
13,200	13,250	1,530	1,323	1,530	1,336
13,250	13,300	1,538	1,328	1,538	1,344
13,300	13,350	1,545	1,333	1,545	1,351
13,350	13,400	1,553	1,338	1,553	1,359
13,400	13,450	1,560	1,343	1,560	1,366
13,450	13,500	1,568	1,348	1,568	1,374
13,500	13,550	1,575	1,353	1,575	1,381
13,550	13,600	1,583	1,358	1,583	1,389
13,600	13,650	1,590	1,363	1,590	1,396
13,650	13,700	1,598	1,368	1,598	1,404
13,700	13,750	1,605	1,373	1,605	1,411
13,750	13,800	1,613	1,378	1,613	1,419
13,800	13,850	1,620	1,383	1,620	1,426
13,850	13,900	1,628	1,388	1,628	1,434
13,900	13,950	1,635	1,393	1,635	1,441
13,950	14,000	1,643	1,398	1,643	1,449
14,000					
14,000	14,050	1,650	1,403	1,650	1,456
14,050	14,100	1,658	1,408	1,658	1,464
14,100	14,150	1,665	1,413	1,665	1,471
14,150	14,200	1,673	1,418	1,673	1,479
14,200	14,250	1,680	1,423	1,680	1,486
14,250	14,300	1,688	1,428	1,688	1,494
14,300	14,350	1,695	1,433	1,695	1,501
14,350	14,400	1,703	1,438	1,703	1,509
14,400	14,450	1,710	1,443	1,710	1,516
14,450	14,500	1,718	1,448	1,718	1,524
14,500	14,550	1,725	1,453	1,725	1,531
14,550	14,600	1,733	1,458	1,733	1,539
14,600	14,650	1,740	1,463	1,740	1,546
14,650	14,700	1,748	1,468	1,748	1,554
14,700	14,750	1,755	1,473	1,755	1,561
14,750	14,800	1,763	1,478	1,763	1,569
14,800	14,850	1,770	1,483	1,770	1,576
14,850	14,900	1,778	1,488	1,778	1,584
14,900	14,950	1,785	1,493	1,785	1,591
14,950	15,000	1,793	1,498	1,793	1,599
15,000					
15,000	15,050	1,800	1,503	1,800	1,606
15,050	15,100	1,808	1,508	1,808	1,614
15,100	15,150	1,815	1,513	1,815	1,621
15,150	15,200	1,823	1,518	1,823	1,629
15,200	15,250	1,830	1,523	1,830	1,636
15,250	15,300	1,838	1,528	1,838	1,644
15,300	15,350	1,845	1,533	1,845	1,651
15,350	15,400	1,853	1,538	1,853	1,659
15,400	15,450	1,860	1,543	1,860	1,666
15,450	15,500	1,868	1,548	1,868	1,674
15,500	15,550	1,875	1,553	1,875	1,681
15,550	15,600	1,883	1,558	1,883	1,689
15,600	15,650	1,890	1,563	1,890	1,696
15,650	15,700	1,898	1,568	1,898	1,704
15,700	15,750	1,905	1,573	1,905	1,711
15,750	15,800	1,913	1,578	1,913	1,719
15,800	15,850	1,920	1,583	1,920	1,726
15,850	15,900	1,928	1,588	1,928	1,734
15,900	15,950	1,935	1,593	1,935	1,741
15,950	16,000	1,943	1,598	1,943	1,749
16,000					
16,000	16,050	1,950	1,603	1,950	1,756
16,050	16,100	1,958	1,608	1,958	1,764
16,100	16,150	1,965	1,613	1,965	1,771
16,150	16,200	1,973	1,618	1,973	1,779
16,200	16,250	1,980	1,623	1,980	1,786
16,250	16,300	1,988	1,628	1,988	1,794
16,300	16,350	1,995	1,633	1,995	1,801
16,350	16,400	2,003	1,638	2,003	1,809
16,400	16,450	2,010	1,643	2,010	1,816
16,450	16,500	2,018	1,648	2,018	1,824
16,500	16,550	2,025	1,653	2,025	1,831
16,550	16,600	2,033	1,658	2,033	1,839
16,600	16,650	2,040	1,663	2,040	1,846
16,650	16,700	2,048	1,668	2,048	1,854
16,700	16,750	2,055	1,673	2,055	1,861
16,750	16,800	2,063	1,678	2,063	1,869
16,800	16,850	2,070	1,683	2,070	1,876
16,850	16,900	2,078	1,688	2,078	1,884
16,900	16,950	2,085	1,693	2,085	1,891
16,950	17,000	2,093	1,698	2,093	1,899
17,000					
17,000	17,050	2,100	1,703	2,100	1,906
17,050	17,100	2,108	1,708	2,108	1,914
17,100	17,150	2,115	1,713	2,115	1,921
17,150	17,200	2,123	1,718	2,123	1,929
17,200	17,250	2,130	1,723	2,130	1,936
17,250	17,300	2,138	1,728	2,138	1,944
17,300	17,350	2,145	1,733	2,145	1,951
17,350	17,400	2,153	1,738	2,153	1,959
17,400	17,450	2,160	1,743	2,160	1,966
17,450	17,500	2,168	1,748	2,168	1,974
17,500	17,550	2,175	1,753	2,175	1,981
17,550	17,600	2,183	1,758	2,183	1,989
17,600	17,650	2,190	1,763	2,190	1,996
17,650	17,700	2,198	1,768	2,198	2,004
17,700	17,750	2,205	1,773	2,205	2,011
17,750	17,800	2,213	1,778	2,213	2,019
17,800	17,850	2,220	1,783	2,220	2,026
17,850	17,900	2,228	1,788	2,228	2,034
17,900	17,950	2,235	1,793	2,235	2,041
17,950	18,000	2,243	1,798	2,243	2,049
18,000					
18,000	18,050	2,250	1,803	2,250	2,056
18,050	18,100	2,258	1,808	2,258	2,064
18,100	18,150	2,265	1,813	2,265	2,071
18,150	18,200	2,273	1,819	2,273	2,079
18,200	18,250	2,280	1,826	2,280	2,086
18,250	18,300	2,288	1,834	2,288	2,094
18,300	18,350	2,295	1,841	2,295	2,101
18,350	18,400	2,303	1,849	2,303	2,109
18,400	18,450	2,310	1,856	2,310	2,116
18,450	18,500	2,318	1,864	2,318	2,124
18,500	18,550	2,325	1,871	2,325	2,131
18,550	18,600	2,333	1,879	2,333	2,139
18,600	18,650	2,340	1,886	2,340	2,146
18,650	18,700	2,348	1,894	2,348	2,154
18,700	18,750	2,355	1,901	2,355	2,161
18,750	18,800	2,363	1,909	2,363	2,169
18,800	18,850	2,370	1,916	2,370	2,176
18,850	18,900	2,378	1,924	2,378	2,184
18,900	18,950	2,385	1,931	2,385	2,191
18,950	19,000	2,393	1,939	2,393	2,199
19,000					
19,000	19,050	2,400	1,946	2,400	2,206
19,050	19,100	2,408	1,954	2,408	2,214
19,100	19,150	2,415	1,961	2,415	2,221
19,150	19,200	2,423	1,969	2,423	2,229
19,200	19,250	2,430	1,976	2,430	2,236
19,250	19,300	2,438	1,984	2,438	2,244
19,300	19,350	2,445	1,991	2,445	2,251
19,350	19,400	2,453	1,999	2,453	2,259
19,400	19,450	2,460	2,006	2,460	2,266
19,450	19,500	2,468	2,014	2,468	2,274
19,500	19,550	2,475	2,021	2,475	2,281
19,550	19,600	2,483	2,029	2,483	2,289
19,600	19,650	2,490	2,036	2,490	2,296
19,650	19,700	2,498	2,044	2,498	2,304
19,700	19,750	2,505	2,051	2,505	2,311
19,750	19,800	2,513	2,059	2,513	2,319
19,800	19,850	2,520	2,066	2,520	2,326
19,850	19,900	2,528	2,074	2,528	2,334
19,900	19,950	2,535	2,081	2,535	2,341
19,950	20,000	2,543	2,089	2,543	2,349
20,000					
20,000	20,050	2,550	2,096	2,550	2,356
20,050	20,100	2,558	2,104	2,558	2,364
20,100	20,150	2,565	2,111	2,565	2,371
20,150	20,200	2,573	2,119	2,573	2,379
20,200	20,250	2,580	2,126	2,580	2,386
20,250	20,300	2,588	2,134	2,588	2,394
20,300	20,350	2,595	2,141	2,595	2,401
20,350	20,400	2,603	2,149	2,603	2,409
20,400	20,450	2,610	2,156	2,610	2,416
20,450	20,500	2,618	2,164	2,618	2,424
20,500	20,550	2,625	2,171	2,625	2,431
20,550	20,600	2,633	2,179	2,633	2,439
20,600	20,650	2,640	2,186	2,640	2,446
20,650	20,700	2,648	2,194	2,648	2,454
20,700	20,750	2,655	2,201	2,655	2,461
20,750	20,800	2,663	2,209	2,663	2,469
20,800	20,850	2,670	2,216	2,670	2,476
20,850	20,900	2,678	2,224	2,678	2,484
20,900	20,950	2,685	2,231	2,685	2,491
20,950	21,000	2,693	2,239	2,693	2,499

(Continued)

* This column must also be used by a qualifying widow(er).

(Continued on page T-5)

2014 Tax Table — *Continued*

If line 43 (taxable income) is—		And you are—			
At least	But less than	Single	Married filing jointly *	Married filing sepa-rately	Head of a house-hold
		Your tax is—			
21,000					
21,000	21,050	2,700	2,246	2,700	2,506
21,050	21,100	2,708	2,254	2,708	2,514
21,100	21,150	2,715	2,261	2,715	2,521
21,150	21,200	2,723	2,269	2,723	2,529
21,200	21,250	2,730	2,276	2,730	2,536
21,250	21,300	2,738	2,284	2,738	2,544
21,300	21,350	2,745	2,291	2,745	2,551
21,350	21,400	2,753	2,299	2,753	2,559
21,400	21,450	2,760	2,306	2,760	2,566
21,450	21,500	2,768	2,314	2,768	2,574
21,500	21,550	2,775	2,321	2,775	2,581
21,550	21,600	2,783	2,329	2,783	2,589
21,600	21,650	2,790	2,336	2,790	2,596
21,650	21,700	2,798	2,344	2,798	2,604
21,700	21,750	2,805	2,351	2,805	2,611
21,750	21,800	2,813	2,359	2,813	2,619
21,800	21,850	2,820	2,366	2,820	2,626
21,850	21,900	2,828	2,374	2,828	2,634
21,900	21,950	2,835	2,381	2,835	2,641
21,950	22,000	2,843	2,389	2,843	2,649
22,000					
22,000	22,050	2,850	2,396	2,850	2,656
22,050	22,100	2,858	2,404	2,858	2,664
22,100	22,150	2,865	2,411	2,865	2,671
22,150	22,200	2,873	2,419	2,873	2,679
22,200	22,250	2,880	2,426	2,880	2,686
22,250	22,300	2,888	2,434	2,888	2,694
22,300	22,350	2,895	2,441	2,895	2,701
22,350	22,400	2,903	2,449	2,903	2,709
22,400	22,450	2,910	2,456	2,910	2,716
22,450	22,500	2,918	2,464	2,918	2,724
22,500	22,550	2,925	2,471	2,925	2,731
22,550	22,600	2,933	2,479	2,933	2,739
22,600	22,650	2,940	2,486	2,940	2,746
22,650	22,700	2,948	2,494	2,948	2,754
22,700	22,750	2,955	2,501	2,955	2,761
22,750	22,800	2,963	2,509	2,963	2,769
22,800	22,850	2,970	2,516	2,970	2,776
22,850	22,900	2,978	2,524	2,978	2,784
22,900	22,950	2,985	2,531	2,985	2,791
22,950	23,000	2,993	2,539	2,993	2,799
23,000					
23,000	23,050	3,000	2,546	3,000	2,806
23,050	23,100	3,008	2,554	3,008	2,814
23,100	23,150	3,015	2,561	3,015	2,821
23,150	23,200	3,023	2,569	3,023	2,829
23,200	23,250	3,030	2,576	3,030	2,836
23,250	23,300	3,038	2,584	3,038	2,844
23,300	23,350	3,045	2,591	3,045	2,851
23,350	23,400	3,053	2,599	3,053	2,859
23,400	23,450	3,060	2,606	3,060	2,866
23,450	23,500	3,068	2,614	3,068	2,874
23,500	23,550	3,075	2,621	3,075	2,881
23,550	23,600	3,083	2,629	3,083	2,889
23,600	23,650	3,090	2,636	3,090	2,896
23,650	23,700	3,098	2,644	3,098	2,904
23,700	23,750	3,105	2,651	3,105	2,911
23,750	23,800	3,113	2,659	3,113	2,919
23,800	23,850	3,120	2,666	3,120	2,926
23,850	23,900	3,128	2,674	3,128	2,934
23,900	23,950	3,135	2,681	3,135	2,941
23,950	24,000	3,143	2,689	3,143	2,949

If line 43 (taxable income) is—		And you are—			
At least	But less than	Single	Married filing jointly *	Married filing sepa-rately	Head of a house-hold
		Your tax is—			
24,000					
24,000	24,050	3,150	2,696	3,150	2,956
24,050	24,100	3,158	2,704	3,158	2,964
24,100	24,150	3,165	2,711	3,165	2,971
24,150	24,200	3,173	2,719	3,173	2,979
24,200	24,250	3,180	2,726	3,180	2,986
24,250	24,300	3,188	2,734	3,188	2,994
24,300	24,350	3,195	2,741	3,195	3,001
24,350	24,400	3,203	2,749	3,203	3,009
24,400	24,450	3,210	2,756	3,210	3,016
24,450	24,500	3,218	2,764	3,218	3,024
24,500	24,550	3,225	2,771	3,225	3,031
24,550	24,600	3,233	2,779	3,233	3,039
24,600	24,650	3,240	2,786	3,240	3,046
24,650	24,700	3,248	2,794	3,248	3,054
24,700	24,750	3,255	2,801	3,255	3,061
24,750	24,800	3,263	2,809	3,263	3,069
24,800	24,850	3,270	2,816	3,270	3,076
24,850	24,900	3,278	2,824	3,278	3,084
24,900	24,950	3,285	2,831	3,285	3,091
24,950	25,000	3,293	2,839	3,293	3,099
25,000					
25,000	25,050	3,300	2,846	3,300	3,106
25,050	25,100	3,308	2,854	3,308	3,114
25,100	25,150	3,315	2,861	3,315	3,121
25,150	25,200	3,323	2,869	3,323	3,129
25,200	25,250	3,330	2,876	3,330	3,136
25,250	25,300	3,338	2,884	3,338	3,144
25,300	25,350	3,345	2,891	3,345	3,151
25,350	25,400	3,353	2,899	3,353	3,159
25,400	25,450	3,360	2,906	3,360	3,166
25,450	25,500	3,368	2,914	3,368	3,174
25,500	25,550	3,375	2,921	3,375	3,181
25,550	25,600	3,383	2,929	3,383	3,189
25,600	25,650	3,390	2,936	3,390	3,196
25,650	25,700	3,398	2,944	3,398	3,204
25,700	25,750	3,405	2,951	3,405	3,211
25,750	25,800	3,413	2,959	3,413	3,219
25,800	25,850	3,420	2,966	3,420	3,226
25,850	25,900	3,428	2,974	3,428	3,234
25,900	25,950	3,435	2,981	3,435	3,241
25,950	26,000	3,443	2,989	3,443	3,249
26,000					
26,000	26,050	3,450	2,996	3,450	3,256
26,050	26,100	3,458	3,004	3,458	3,264
26,100	26,150	3,465	3,011	3,465	3,271
26,150	26,200	3,473	3,019	3,473	3,279
26,200	26,250	3,480	3,026	3,480	3,286
26,250	26,300	3,488	3,034	3,488	3,294
26,300	26,350	3,495	3,041	3,495	3,301
26,350	26,400	3,503	3,049	3,503	3,309
26,400	26,450	3,510	3,056	3,510	3,316
26,450	26,500	3,518	3,064	3,518	3,324
26,500	26,550	3,525	3,071	3,525	3,331
26,550	26,600	3,533	3,079	3,533	3,339
26,600	26,650	3,540	3,086	3,540	3,346
26,650	26,700	3,548	3,094	3,548	3,354
26,700	26,750	3,555	3,101	3,555	3,361
26,750	26,800	3,563	3,109	3,563	3,369
26,800	26,850	3,570	3,116	3,570	3,376
26,850	26,900	3,578	3,124	3,578	3,384
26,900	26,950	3,585	3,131	3,585	3,391
26,950	27,000	3,593	3,139	3,593	3,399

If line 43 (taxable income) is—		And you are—			
At least	But less than	Single	Married filing jointly *	Married filing sepa-rately	Head of a house-hold
		Your tax is—			
27,000					
27,000	27,050	3,600	3,146	3,600	3,406
27,050	27,100	3,608	3,154	3,608	3,414
27,100	27,150	3,615	3,161	3,615	3,421
27,150	27,200	3,623	3,169	3,623	3,429
27,200	27,250	3,630	3,176	3,630	3,436
27,250	27,300	3,638	3,184	3,638	3,444
27,300	27,350	3,645	3,191	3,645	3,451
27,350	27,400	3,653	3,199	3,653	3,459
27,400	27,450	3,660	3,206	3,660	3,466
27,450	27,500	3,668	3,214	3,668	3,474
27,500	27,550	3,675	3,221	3,675	3,481
27,550	27,600	3,683	3,229	3,683	3,489
27,600	27,650	3,690	3,236	3,690	3,496
27,650	27,700	3,698	3,244	3,698	3,504
27,700	27,750	3,705	3,251	3,705	3,511
27,750	27,800	3,713	3,259	3,713	3,519
27,800	27,850	3,720	3,266	3,720	3,526
27,850	27,900	3,728	3,274	3,728	3,534
27,900	27,950	3,735	3,281	3,735	3,541
27,950	28,000	3,743	3,289	3,743	3,549
28,000					
28,000	28,050	3,750	3,296	3,750	3,556
28,050	28,100	3,758	3,304	3,758	3,564
28,100	28,150	3,765	3,311	3,765	3,571
28,150	28,200	3,773	3,319	3,773	3,579
28,200	28,250	3,780	3,326	3,780	3,586
28,250	28,300	3,788	3,334	3,788	3,594
28,300	28,350	3,795	3,341	3,795	3,601
28,350	28,400	3,803	3,349	3,803	3,609
28,400	28,450	3,810	3,356	3,810	3,616
28,450	28,500	3,818	3,364	3,818	3,624
28,500	28,550	3,825	3,371	3,825	3,631
28,550	28,600	3,833	3,379	3,833	3,639
28,600	28,650	3,840	3,386	3,840	3,646
28,650	28,700	3,848	3,394	3,848	3,654
28,700	28,750	3,855	3,401	3,855	3,661
28,750	28,800	3,863	3,409	3,863	3,669
28,800	28,850	3,870	3,416	3,870	3,676
28,850	28,900	3,878	3,424	3,878	3,684
28,900	28,950	3,885	3,431	3,885	3,691
28,950	29,000	3,893	3,439	3,893	3,699
29,000					
29,000	29,050	3,900	3,446	3,900	3,706
29,050	29,100	3,908	3,454	3,908	3,714
29,100	29,150	3,915	3,461	3,915	3,721
29,150	29,200	3,923	3,469	3,923	3,729
29,200	29,250	3,930	3,476	3,930	3,736
29,250	29,300	3,938	3,484	3,938	3,744
29,300	29,350	3,945	3,491	3,945	3,751
29,350	29,400	3,953	3,499	3,953	3,759
29,400	29,450	3,960	3,506	3,960	3,766
29,450	29,500	3,968	3,514	3,968	3,774
29,500	29,550	3,975	3,521	3,975	3,781
29,550	29,600	3,983	3,529	3,983	3,789
29,600	29,650	3,990	3,536	3,990	3,796
29,650	29,700	3,998	3,544	3,998	3,804
29,700	29,750	4,005	3,551	4,005	3,811
29,750	29,800	4,013	3,559	4,013	3,819
29,800	29,850	4,020	3,566	4,020	3,826
29,850	29,900	4,028	3,574	4,028	3,834
29,900	29,950	4,035	3,581	4,035	3,841
29,950	30,000	4,043	3,589	4,043	3,849

(Continued)

* This column must also be used by a qualifying widow(er).

(Continued on page T-6)

2014 Tax Table — *Continued*

If line 43 (taxable income) is—		And you are—			
At least	But less than	Single	Married filing jointly *	Married filing separately	Head of a household
		Your tax is—			
30,000					
30,000	30,050	4,050	3,596	4,050	3,856
30,050	30,100	4,058	3,604	4,058	3,864
30,100	30,150	4,065	3,611	4,065	3,871
30,150	30,200	4,073	3,619	4,073	3,879
30,200	30,250	4,080	3,626	4,080	3,886
30,250	30,300	4,088	3,634	4,088	3,894
30,300	30,350	4,095	3,641	4,095	3,901
30,350	30,400	4,103	3,649	4,103	3,909
30,400	30,450	4,110	3,656	4,110	3,916
30,450	30,500	4,118	3,664	4,118	3,924
30,500	30,550	4,125	3,671	4,125	3,931
30,550	30,600	4,133	3,679	4,133	3,939
30,600	30,650	4,140	3,686	4,140	3,946
30,650	30,700	4,148	3,694	4,148	3,954
30,700	30,750	4,155	3,701	4,155	3,961
30,750	30,800	4,163	3,709	4,163	3,969
30,800	30,850	4,170	3,716	4,170	3,976
30,850	30,900	4,178	3,724	4,178	3,984
30,900	30,950	4,185	3,731	4,185	3,991
30,950	31,000	4,193	3,739	4,193	3,999
31,000					
31,000	31,050	4,200	3,746	4,200	4,006
31,050	31,100	4,208	3,754	4,208	4,014
31,100	31,150	4,215	3,761	4,215	4,021
31,150	31,200	4,223	3,769	4,223	4,029
31,200	31,250	4,230	3,776	4,230	4,036
31,250	31,300	4,238	3,784	4,238	4,044
31,300	31,350	4,245	3,791	4,245	4,051
31,350	31,400	4,253	3,799	4,253	4,059
31,400	31,450	4,260	3,806	4,260	4,066
31,450	31,500	4,268	3,814	4,268	4,074
31,500	31,550	4,275	3,821	4,275	4,081
31,550	31,600	4,283	3,829	4,283	4,089
31,600	31,650	4,290	3,836	4,290	4,096
31,650	31,700	4,298	3,844	4,298	4,104
31,700	31,750	4,305	3,851	4,305	4,111
31,750	31,800	4,313	3,859	4,313	4,119
31,800	31,850	4,320	3,866	4,320	4,126
31,850	31,900	4,328	3,874	4,328	4,134
31,900	31,950	4,335	3,881	4,335	4,141
31,950	32,000	4,343	3,889	4,343	4,149
32,000					
32,000	32,050	4,350	3,896	4,350	4,156
32,050	32,100	4,358	3,904	4,358	4,164
32,100	32,150	4,365	3,911	4,365	4,171
32,150	32,200	4,373	3,919	4,373	4,179
32,200	32,250	4,380	3,926	4,380	4,186
32,250	32,300	4,388	3,934	4,388	4,194
32,300	32,350	4,395	3,941	4,395	4,201
32,350	32,400	4,403	3,949	4,403	4,209
32,400	32,450	4,410	3,956	4,410	4,216
32,450	32,500	4,418	3,964	4,418	4,224
32,500	32,550	4,425	3,971	4,425	4,231
32,550	32,600	4,433	3,979	4,433	4,239
32,600	32,650	4,440	3,986	4,440	4,246
32,650	32,700	4,448	3,994	4,448	4,254
32,700	32,750	4,455	4,001	4,455	4,261
32,750	32,800	4,463	4,009	4,463	4,269
32,800	32,850	4,470	4,016	4,470	4,276
32,850	32,900	4,478	4,024	4,478	4,284
32,900	32,950	4,485	4,031	4,485	4,291
32,950	33,000	4,493	4,039	4,493	4,299

If line 43 (taxable income) is—		And you are—			
At least	But less than	Single	Married filing jointly *	Married filing separately	Head of a household
		Your tax is—			
33,000					
33,000	33,050	4,500	4,046	4,500	4,306
33,050	33,100	4,508	4,054	4,508	4,314
33,100	33,150	4,515	4,061	4,515	4,321
33,150	33,200	4,523	4,069	4,523	4,329
33,200	33,250	4,530	4,076	4,530	4,336
33,250	33,300	4,538	4,084	4,538	4,344
33,300	33,350	4,545	4,091	4,545	4,351
33,350	33,400	4,553	4,099	4,553	4,359
33,400	33,450	4,560	4,106	4,560	4,366
33,450	33,500	4,568	4,114	4,568	4,374
33,500	33,550	4,575	4,121	4,575	4,381
33,550	33,600	4,583	4,129	4,583	4,389
33,600	33,650	4,590	4,136	4,590	4,396
33,650	33,700	4,598	4,144	4,598	4,404
33,700	33,750	4,605	4,151	4,605	4,411
33,750	33,800	4,613	4,159	4,613	4,419
33,800	33,850	4,620	4,166	4,620	4,426
33,850	33,900	4,628	4,174	4,628	4,434
33,900	33,950	4,635	4,181	4,635	4,441
33,950	34,000	4,643	4,189	4,643	4,449
34,000					
34,000	34,050	4,650	4,196	4,650	4,456
34,050	34,100	4,658	4,204	4,658	4,464
34,100	34,150	4,665	4,211	4,665	4,471
34,150	34,200	4,673	4,219	4,673	4,479
34,200	34,250	4,680	4,226	4,680	4,486
34,250	34,300	4,688	4,234	4,688	4,494
34,300	34,350	4,695	4,241	4,695	4,501
34,350	34,400	4,703	4,249	4,703	4,509
34,400	34,450	4,710	4,256	4,710	4,516
34,450	34,500	4,718	4,264	4,718	4,524
34,500	34,550	4,725	4,271	4,725	4,531
34,550	34,600	4,733	4,279	4,733	4,539
34,600	34,650	4,740	4,286	4,740	4,546
34,650	34,700	4,748	4,294	4,748	4,554
34,700	34,750	4,755	4,301	4,755	4,561
34,750	34,800	4,763	4,309	4,763	4,569
34,800	34,850	4,770	4,316	4,770	4,576
34,850	34,900	4,778	4,324	4,778	4,584
34,900	34,950	4,785	4,331	4,785	4,591
34,950	35,000	4,793	4,339	4,793	4,599
35,000					
35,000	35,050	4,800	4,346	4,800	4,606
35,050	35,100	4,808	4,354	4,808	4,614
35,100	35,150	4,815	4,361	4,815	4,621
35,150	35,200	4,823	4,369	4,823	4,629
35,200	35,250	4,830	4,376	4,830	4,636
35,250	35,300	4,838	4,384	4,838	4,644
35,300	35,350	4,845	4,391	4,845	4,651
35,350	35,400	4,853	4,399	4,853	4,659
35,400	35,450	4,860	4,406	4,860	4,666
35,450	35,500	4,868	4,414	4,868	4,674
35,500	35,550	4,875	4,421	4,875	4,681
35,550	35,600	4,883	4,429	4,883	4,689
35,600	35,650	4,890	4,436	4,890	4,696
35,650	35,700	4,898	4,444	4,898	4,704
35,700	35,750	4,905	4,451	4,905	4,711
35,750	35,800	4,913	4,459	4,913	4,719
35,800	35,850	4,920	4,466	4,920	4,726
35,850	35,900	4,928	4,474	4,928	4,734
35,900	35,950	4,935	4,481	4,935	4,741
35,950	36,000	4,943	4,489	4,943	4,749

If line 43 (taxable income) is—		And you are—			
At least	But less than	Single	Married filing jointly *	Married filing separately	Head of a household
		Your tax is—			
36,000					
36,000	36,050	4,950	4,496	4,950	4,756
36,050	36,100	4,958	4,504	4,958	4,764
36,100	36,150	4,965	4,511	4,965	4,771
36,150	36,200	4,973	4,519	4,973	4,779
36,200	36,250	4,980	4,526	4,980	4,786
36,250	36,300	4,988	4,534	4,988	4,794
36,300	36,350	4,995	4,541	4,995	4,801
36,350	36,400	5,003	4,549	5,003	4,809
36,400	36,450	5,010	4,556	5,010	4,816
36,450	36,500	5,018	4,564	5,018	4,824
36,500	36,550	5,025	4,571	5,025	4,831
36,550	36,600	5,033	4,579	5,033	4,839
36,600	36,650	5,040	4,586	5,040	4,846
36,650	36,700	5,048	4,594	5,048	4,854
36,700	36,750	5,055	4,601	5,055	4,861
36,750	36,800	5,063	4,609	5,063	4,869
36,800	36,850	5,070	4,616	5,070	4,876
36,850	36,900	5,078	4,624	5,078	4,884
36,900	36,950	5,088	4,631	5,088	4,891
36,950	37,000	5,100	4,639	5,100	4,899
37,000					
37,000	37,050	5,113	4,646	5,113	4,906
37,050	37,100	5,125	4,654	5,125	4,914
37,100	37,150	5,138	4,661	5,138	4,921
37,150	37,200	5,150	4,669	5,150	4,929
37,200	37,250	5,163	4,676	5,163	4,936
37,250	37,300	5,175	4,684	5,175	4,944
37,300	37,350	5,188	4,691	5,188	4,951
37,350	37,400	5,200	4,699	5,200	4,959
37,400	37,450	5,213	4,706	5,213	4,966
37,450	37,500	5,225	4,714	5,225	4,974
37,500	37,550	5,238	4,721	5,238	4,981
37,550	37,600	5,250	4,729	5,250	4,989
37,600	37,650	5,263	4,736	5,263	4,996
37,650	37,700	5,275	4,744	5,275	5,004
37,700	37,750	5,288	4,751	5,288	5,011
37,750	37,800	5,300	4,759	5,300	5,019
37,800	37,850	5,313	4,766	5,313	5,026
37,850	37,900	5,325	4,774	5,325	5,034
37,900	37,950	5,338	4,781	5,338	5,041
37,950	38,000	5,350	4,789	5,350	5,049
38,000					
38,000	38,050	5,363	4,796	5,363	5,056
38,050	38,100	5,375	4,804	5,375	5,064
38,100	38,150	5,388	4,811	5,388	5,071
38,150	38,200	5,400	4,819	5,400	5,079
38,200	38,250	5,413	4,826	5,413	5,086
38,250	38,300	5,425	4,834	5,425	5,094
38,300	38,350	5,438	4,841	5,438	5,101
38,350	38,400	5,450	4,849	5,450	5,109
38,400	38,450	5,463	4,856	5,463	5,116
38,450	38,500	5,475	4,864	5,475	5,124
38,500	38,550	5,488	4,871	5,488	5,131
38,550	38,600	5,500	4,879	5,500	5,139
38,600	38,650	5,513	4,886	5,513	5,146
38,650	38,700	5,525	4,894	5,525	5,154
38,700	38,750	5,538	4,901	5,538	5,161
38,750	38,800	5,550	4,909	5,550	5,169
38,800	38,850	5,563	4,916	5,563	5,176
38,850	38,900	5,575	4,924	5,575	5,184
38,900	38,950	5,588	4,931	5,588	5,191
38,950	39,000	5,600	4,939	5,600	5,199

(Continued)

* This column must also be used by a qualifying widow(er).

(Continued on page T-7)

2014 Tax Table — *Continued*

If line 43 (taxable income) is—		And you are—			
At least	But less than	Single	Married filing jointly *	Married filing separately	Head of a household
		Your tax is—			
39,000					
39,000	39,050	5,613	4,946	5,613	5,206
39,050	39,100	5,625	4,954	5,625	5,214
39,100	39,150	5,638	4,961	5,638	5,221
39,150	39,200	5,650	4,969	5,650	5,229
39,200	39,250	5,663	4,976	5,663	5,236
39,250	39,300	5,675	4,984	5,675	5,244
39,300	39,350	5,688	4,991	5,688	5,251
39,350	39,400	5,700	4,999	5,700	5,259
39,400	39,450	5,713	5,006	5,713	5,266
39,450	39,500	5,725	5,014	5,725	5,274
39,500	39,550	5,738	5,021	5,738	5,281
39,550	39,600	5,750	5,029	5,750	5,289
39,600	39,650	5,763	5,036	5,763	5,296
39,650	39,700	5,775	5,044	5,775	5,304
39,700	39,750	5,788	5,051	5,788	5,311
39,750	39,800	5,800	5,059	5,800	5,319
39,800	39,850	5,813	5,066	5,813	5,326
39,850	39,900	5,825	5,074	5,825	5,334
39,900	39,950	5,838	5,081	5,838	5,341
39,950	40,000	5,850	5,089	5,850	5,349
40,000					
40,000	40,050	5,863	5,096	5,863	5,356
40,050	40,100	5,875	5,104	5,875	5,364
40,100	40,150	5,888	5,111	5,888	5,371
40,150	40,200	5,900	5,119	5,900	5,379
40,200	40,250	5,913	5,126	5,913	5,386
40,250	40,300	5,925	5,134	5,925	5,394
40,300	40,350	5,938	5,141	5,938	5,401
40,350	40,400	5,950	5,149	5,950	5,409
40,400	40,450	5,963	5,156	5,963	5,416
40,450	40,500	5,975	5,164	5,975	5,424
40,500	40,550	5,988	5,171	5,988	5,431
40,550	40,600	6,000	5,179	6,000	5,439
40,600	40,650	6,013	5,186	6,013	5,446
40,650	40,700	6,025	5,194	6,025	5,454
40,700	40,750	6,038	5,201	6,038	5,461
40,750	40,800	6,050	5,209	6,050	5,469
40,800	40,850	6,063	5,216	6,063	5,476
40,850	40,900	6,075	5,224	6,075	5,484
40,900	40,950	6,088	5,231	6,088	5,491
40,950	41,000	6,100	5,239	6,100	5,499
41,000					
41,000	41,050	6,113	5,246	6,113	5,506
41,050	41,100	6,125	5,254	6,125	5,514
41,100	41,150	6,138	5,261	6,138	5,521
41,150	41,200	6,150	5,269	6,150	5,529
41,200	41,250	6,163	5,276	6,163	5,536
41,250	41,300	6,175	5,284	6,175	5,544
41,300	41,350	6,188	5,291	6,188	5,551
41,350	41,400	6,200	5,299	6,200	5,559
41,400	41,450	6,213	5,306	6,213	5,566
41,450	41,500	6,225	5,314	6,225	5,574
41,500	41,550	6,238	5,321	6,238	5,581
41,550	41,600	6,250	5,329	6,250	5,589
41,600	41,650	6,263	5,336	6,263	5,596
41,650	41,700	6,275	5,344	6,275	5,604
41,700	41,750	6,288	5,351	6,288	5,611
41,750	41,800	6,300	5,359	6,300	5,619
41,800	41,850	6,313	5,366	6,313	5,626
41,850	41,900	6,325	5,374	6,325	5,634
41,900	41,950	6,338	5,381	6,338	5,641
41,950	42,000	6,350	5,389	6,350	5,649

If line 43 (taxable income) is—		And you are—			
At least	But less than	Single	Married filing jointly *	Married filing separately	Head of a household
		Your tax is—			
42,000					
42,000	42,050	6,363	5,396	6,363	5,656
42,050	42,100	6,375	5,404	6,375	5,664
42,100	42,150	6,388	5,411	6,388	5,671
42,150	42,200	6,400	5,419	6,400	5,679
42,200	42,250	6,413	5,426	6,413	5,686
42,250	42,300	6,425	5,434	6,425	5,694
42,300	42,350	6,438	5,441	6,438	5,701
42,350	42,400	6,450	5,449	6,450	5,709
42,400	42,450	6,463	5,456	6,463	5,716
42,450	42,500	6,475	5,464	6,475	5,724
42,500	42,550	6,488	5,471	6,488	5,731
42,550	42,600	6,500	5,479	6,500	5,739
42,600	42,650	6,513	5,486	6,513	5,746
42,650	42,700	6,525	5,494	6,525	5,754
42,700	42,750	6,538	5,501	6,538	5,761
42,750	42,800	6,550	5,509	6,550	5,769
42,800	42,850	6,563	5,516	6,563	5,776
42,850	42,900	6,575	5,524	6,575	5,784
42,900	42,950	6,588	5,531	6,588	5,791
42,950	43,000	6,600	5,539	6,600	5,799
43,000					
43,000	43,050	6,613	5,546	6,613	5,806
43,050	43,100	6,625	5,554	6,625	5,814
43,100	43,150	6,638	5,561	6,638	5,821
43,150	43,200	6,650	5,569	6,650	5,829
43,200	43,250	6,663	5,576	6,663	5,836
43,250	43,300	6,675	5,584	6,675	5,844
43,300	43,350	6,688	5,591	6,688	5,851
43,350	43,400	6,700	5,599	6,700	5,859
43,400	43,450	6,713	5,606	6,713	5,866
43,450	43,500	6,725	5,614	6,725	5,874
43,500	43,550	6,738	5,621	6,738	5,881
43,550	43,600	6,750	5,629	6,750	5,889
43,600	43,650	6,763	5,636	6,763	5,896
43,650	43,700	6,775	5,644	6,775	5,904
43,700	43,750	6,788	5,651	6,788	5,911
43,750	43,800	6,800	5,659	6,800	5,919
43,800	43,850	6,813	5,666	6,813	5,926
43,850	43,900	6,825	5,674	6,825	5,934
43,900	43,950	6,838	5,681	6,838	5,941
43,950	44,000	6,850	5,689	6,850	5,949
44,000					
44,000	44,050	6,863	5,696	6,863	5,956
44,050	44,100	6,875	5,704	6,875	5,964
44,100	44,150	6,888	5,711	6,888	5,971
44,150	44,200	6,900	5,719	6,900	5,979
44,200	44,250	6,913	5,726	6,913	5,986
44,250	44,300	6,925	5,734	6,925	5,994
44,300	44,350	6,938	5,741	6,938	6,001
44,350	44,400	6,950	5,749	6,950	6,009
44,400	44,450	6,963	5,756	6,963	6,016
44,450	44,500	6,975	5,764	6,975	6,024
44,500	44,550	6,988	5,771	6,988	6,031
44,550	44,600	7,000	5,779	7,000	6,039
44,600	44,650	7,013	5,786	7,013	6,046
44,650	44,700	7,025	5,794	7,025	6,054
44,700	44,750	7,038	5,801	7,038	6,061
44,750	44,800	7,050	5,809	7,050	6,069
44,800	44,850	7,063	5,816	7,063	6,076
44,850	44,900	7,075	5,824	7,075	6,084
44,900	44,950	7,088	5,831	7,088	6,091
44,950	45,000	7,100	5,839	7,100	6,099

If line 43 (taxable income) is—		And you are—			
At least	But less than	Single	Married filing jointly *	Married filing separately	Head of a household
		Your tax is—			
45,000					
45,000	45,050	7,113	5,846	7,113	6,106
45,050	45,100	7,125	5,854	7,125	6,114
45,100	45,150	7,138	5,861	7,138	6,121
45,150	45,200	7,150	5,869	7,150	6,129
45,200	45,250	7,163	5,876	7,163	6,136
45,250	45,300	7,175	5,884	7,175	6,144
45,300	45,350	7,188	5,891	7,188	6,151
45,350	45,400	7,200	5,899	7,200	6,159
45,400	45,450	7,213	5,906	7,213	6,166
45,450	45,500	7,225	5,914	7,225	6,174
45,500	45,550	7,238	5,921	7,238	6,181
45,550	45,600	7,250	5,929	7,250	6,189
45,600	45,650	7,263	5,936	7,263	6,196
45,650	45,700	7,275	5,944	7,275	6,204
45,700	45,750	7,288	5,951	7,288	6,211
45,750	45,800	7,300	5,959	7,300	6,219
45,800	45,850	7,313	5,966	7,313	6,226
45,850	45,900	7,325	5,974	7,325	6,234
45,900	45,950	7,338	5,981	7,338	6,241
45,950	46,000	7,350	5,989	7,350	6,249
46,000					
46,000	46,050	7,363	5,996	7,363	6,256
46,050	46,100	7,375	6,004	7,375	6,264
46,100	46,150	7,388	6,011	7,388	6,271
46,150	46,200	7,400	6,019	7,400	6,279
46,200	46,250	7,413	6,026	7,413	6,286
46,250	46,300	7,425	6,034	7,425	6,294
46,300	46,350	7,438	6,041	7,438	6,301
46,350	46,400	7,450	6,049	7,450	6,309
46,400	46,450	7,463	6,056	7,463	6,316
46,450	46,500	7,475	6,064	7,475	6,324
46,500	46,550	7,488	6,071	7,488	6,331
46,550	46,600	7,500	6,079	7,500	6,339
46,600	46,650	7,513	6,086	7,513	6,346
46,650	46,700	7,525	6,094	7,525	6,354
46,700	46,750	7,538	6,101	7,538	6,361
46,750	46,800	7,550	6,109	7,550	6,369
46,800	46,850	7,563	6,116	7,563	6,376
46,850	46,900	7,575	6,124	7,575	6,384
46,900	46,950	7,588	6,131	7,588	6,391
46,950	47,000	7,600	6,139	7,600	6,399
47,000					
47,000	47,050	7,613	6,146	7,613	6,406
47,050	47,100	7,625	6,154	7,625	6,414
47,100	47,150	7,638	6,161	7,638	6,421
47,150	47,200	7,650	6,169	7,650	6,429
47,200	47,250	7,663	6,176	7,663	6,436
47,250	47,300	7,675	6,184	7,675	6,444
47,300	47,350	7,688	6,191	7,688	6,451
47,350	47,400	7,700	6,199	7,700	6,459
47,400	47,450	7,713	6,206	7,713	6,466
47,450	47,500	7,725	6,214	7,725	6,474
47,500	47,550	7,738	6,221	7,738	6,481
47,550	47,600	7,750	6,229	7,750	6,489
47,600	47,650	7,763	6,236	7,763	6,496
47,650	47,700	7,775	6,244	7,775	6,504
47,700	47,750	7,788	6,251	7,788	6,511
47,750	47,800	7,800	6,259	7,800	6,519
47,800	47,850	7,813	6,266	7,813	6,526
47,850	47,900	7,825	6,274	7,825	6,534
47,900	47,950	7,838	6,281	7,838	6,541
47,950	48,000	7,850	6,289	7,850	6,549

(Continued)

* This column must also be used by a qualifying widow(er).

(Continued on page T-8)

2014 Tax Table — *Continued*

If line 43 (taxable income) is—		And you are—			
At least	But less than	Single	Married filing jointly *	Married filing separately	Head of a household
		Your tax is—			
48,000					
48,000	48,050	7,863	6,296	7,863	6,556
48,050	48,100	7,875	6,304	7,875	6,564
48,100	48,150	7,888	6,311	7,888	6,571
48,150	48,200	7,900	6,319	7,900	6,579
48,200	48,250	7,913	6,326	7,913	6,586
48,250	48,300	7,925	6,334	7,925	6,594
48,300	48,350	7,938	6,341	7,938	6,601
48,350	48,400	7,950	6,349	7,950	6,609
48,400	48,450	7,963	6,356	7,963	6,616
48,450	48,500	7,975	6,364	7,975	6,624
48,500	48,550	7,988	6,371	7,988	6,631
48,550	48,600	8,000	6,379	8,000	6,639
48,600	48,650	8,013	6,386	8,013	6,646
48,650	48,700	8,025	6,394	8,025	6,654
48,700	48,750	8,038	6,401	8,038	6,661
48,750	48,800	8,050	6,409	8,050	6,669
48,800	48,850	8,063	6,416	8,063	6,676
48,850	48,900	8,075	6,424	8,075	6,684
48,900	48,950	8,088	6,431	8,088	6,691
48,950	49,000	8,100	6,439	8,100	6,699
49,000					
49,000	49,050	8,113	6,446	8,113	6,706
49,050	49,100	8,125	6,454	8,125	6,714
49,100	49,150	8,138	6,461	8,138	6,721
49,150	49,200	8,150	6,469	8,150	6,729
49,200	49,250	8,163	6,476	8,163	6,736
49,250	49,300	8,175	6,484	8,175	6,744
49,300	49,350	8,188	6,491	8,188	6,751
49,350	49,400	8,200	6,499	8,200	6,759
49,400	49,450	8,213	6,506	8,213	6,769
49,450	49,500	8,225	6,514	8,225	6,781
49,500	49,550	8,238	6,521	8,238	6,794
49,550	49,600	8,250	6,529	8,250	6,806
49,600	49,650	8,263	6,536	8,263	6,819
49,650	49,700	8,275	6,544	8,275	6,831
49,700	49,750	8,288	6,551	8,288	6,844
49,750	49,800	8,300	6,559	8,300	6,856
49,800	49,850	8,313	6,566	8,313	6,869
49,850	49,900	8,325	6,574	8,325	6,881
49,900	49,950	8,338	6,581	8,338	6,894
49,950	50,000	8,350	6,589	8,350	6,906
50,000					
50,000	50,050	8,363	6,596	8,363	6,919
50,050	50,100	8,375	6,604	8,375	6,931
50,100	50,150	8,388	6,611	8,388	6,944
50,150	50,200	8,400	6,619	8,400	6,956
50,200	50,250	8,413	6,626	8,413	6,969
50,250	50,300	8,425	6,634	8,425	6,981
50,300	50,350	8,438	6,641	8,438	6,994
50,350	50,400	8,450	6,649	8,450	7,006
50,400	50,450	8,463	6,656	8,463	7,019
50,450	50,500	8,475	6,664	8,475	7,031
50,500	50,550	8,488	6,671	8,488	7,044
50,550	50,600	8,500	6,679	8,500	7,056
50,600	50,650	8,513	6,686	8,513	7,069
50,650	50,700	8,525	6,694	8,525	7,081
50,700	50,750	8,538	6,701	8,538	7,094
50,750	50,800	8,550	6,709	8,550	7,106
50,800	50,850	8,563	6,716	8,563	7,119
50,850	50,900	8,575	6,724	8,575	7,131
50,900	50,950	8,588	6,731	8,588	7,144
50,950	51,000	8,600	6,739	8,600	7,156
51,000					
51,000	51,050	8,613	6,746	8,613	7,169
51,050	51,100	8,625	6,754	8,625	7,181
51,100	51,150	8,638	6,761	8,638	7,194
51,150	51,200	8,650	6,769	8,650	7,206
51,200	51,250	8,663	6,776	8,663	7,219
51,250	51,300	8,675	6,784	8,675	7,231
51,300	51,350	8,688	6,791	8,688	7,244
51,350	51,400	8,700	6,799	8,700	7,256
51,400	51,450	8,713	6,806	8,713	7,269
51,450	51,500	8,725	6,814	8,725	7,281
51,500	51,550	8,738	6,821	8,738	7,294
51,550	51,600	8,750	6,829	8,750	7,306
51,600	51,650	8,763	6,836	8,763	7,319
51,650	51,700	8,775	6,844	8,775	7,331
51,700	51,750	8,788	6,851	8,788	7,344
51,750	51,800	8,800	6,859	8,800	7,356
51,800	51,850	8,813	6,866	8,813	7,369
51,850	51,900	8,825	6,874	8,825	7,381
51,900	51,950	8,838	6,881	8,838	7,394
51,950	52,000	8,850	6,889	8,850	7,406
52,000					
52,000	52,050	8,863	6,896	8,863	7,419
52,050	52,100	8,875	6,904	8,875	7,431
52,100	52,150	8,888	6,911	8,888	7,444
52,150	52,200	8,900	6,919	8,900	7,456
52,200	52,250	8,913	6,926	8,913	7,469
52,250	52,300	8,925	6,934	8,925	7,481
52,300	52,350	8,938	6,941	8,938	7,494
52,350	52,400	8,950	6,949	8,950	7,506
52,400	52,450	8,963	6,956	8,963	7,519
52,450	52,500	8,975	6,964	8,975	7,531
52,500	52,550	8,988	6,971	8,988	7,544
52,550	52,600	9,000	6,979	9,000	7,556
52,600	52,650	9,013	6,986	9,013	7,569
52,650	52,700	9,025	6,994	9,025	7,581
52,700	52,750	9,038	7,001	9,038	7,594
52,750	52,800	9,050	7,009	9,050	7,606
52,800	52,850	9,063	7,016	9,063	7,619
52,850	52,900	9,075	7,024	9,075	7,631
52,900	52,950	9,088	7,031	9,088	7,644
52,950	53,000	9,100	7,039	9,100	7,656
53,000					
53,000	53,050	9,113	7,046	9,113	7,669
53,050	53,100	9,125	7,054	9,125	7,681
53,100	53,150	9,138	7,061	9,138	7,694
53,150	53,200	9,150	7,069	9,150	7,706
53,200	53,250	9,163	7,076	9,163	7,719
53,250	53,300	9,175	7,084	9,175	7,731
53,300	53,350	9,188	7,091	9,188	7,744
53,350	53,400	9,200	7,099	9,200	7,756
53,400	53,450	9,213	7,106	9,213	7,769
53,450	53,500	9,225	7,114	9,225	7,781
53,500	53,550	9,238	7,121	9,238	7,794
53,550	53,600	9,250	7,129	9,250	7,806
53,600	53,650	9,263	7,136	9,263	7,819
53,650	53,700	9,275	7,144	9,275	7,831
53,700	53,750	9,288	7,151	9,288	7,844
53,750	53,800	9,300	7,159	9,300	7,856
53,800	53,850	9,313	7,166	9,313	7,869
53,850	53,900	9,325	7,174	9,325	7,881
53,900	53,950	9,338	7,181	9,338	7,894
53,950	54,000	9,350	7,189	9,350	7,906
54,000					
54,000	54,050	9,363	7,196	9,363	7,919
54,050	54,100	9,375	7,204	9,375	7,931
54,100	54,150	9,388	7,211	9,388	7,944
54,150	54,200	9,400	7,219	9,400	7,956
54,200	54,250	9,413	7,226	9,413	7,969
54,250	54,300	9,425	7,234	9,425	7,981
54,300	54,350	9,438	7,241	9,438	7,994
54,350	54,400	9,450	7,249	9,450	8,006
54,400	54,450	9,463	7,256	9,463	8,019
54,450	54,500	9,475	7,264	9,475	8,031
54,500	54,550	9,488	7,271	9,488	8,044
54,550	54,600	9,500	7,279	9,500	8,056
54,600	54,650	9,513	7,286	9,513	8,069
54,650	54,700	9,525	7,294	9,525	8,081
54,700	54,750	9,538	7,301	9,538	8,094
54,750	54,800	9,550	7,309	9,550	8,106
54,800	54,850	9,563	7,316	9,563	8,119
54,850	54,900	9,575	7,324	9,575	8,131
54,900	54,950	9,588	7,331	9,588	8,144
54,950	55,000	9,600	7,339	9,600	8,156
55,000					
55,000	55,050	9,613	7,346	9,613	8,169
55,050	55,100	9,625	7,354	9,625	8,181
55,100	55,150	9,638	7,361	9,638	8,194
55,150	55,200	9,650	7,369	9,650	8,206
55,200	55,250	9,663	7,376	9,663	8,219
55,250	55,300	9,675	7,384	9,675	8,231
55,300	55,350	9,688	7,391	9,688	8,244
55,350	55,400	9,700	7,399	9,700	8,256
55,400	55,450	9,713	7,406	9,713	8,269
55,450	55,500	9,725	7,414	9,725	8,281
55,500	55,550	9,738	7,421	9,738	8,294
55,550	55,600	9,750	7,429	9,750	8,306
55,600	55,650	9,763	7,436	9,763	8,319
55,650	55,700	9,775	7,444	9,775	8,331
55,700	55,750	9,788	7,451	9,788	8,344
55,750	55,800	9,800	7,459	9,800	8,356
55,800	55,850	9,813	7,466	9,813	8,369
55,850	55,900	9,825	7,474	9,825	8,381
55,900	55,950	9,838	7,481	9,838	8,394
55,950	56,000	9,850	7,489	9,850	8,406
56,000					
56,000	56,050	9,863	7,496	9,863	8,419
56,050	56,100	9,875	7,504	9,875	8,431
56,100	56,150	9,888	7,511	9,888	8,444
56,150	56,200	9,900	7,519	9,900	8,456
56,200	56,250	9,913	7,526	9,913	8,469
56,250	56,300	9,925	7,534	9,925	8,481
56,300	56,350	9,938	7,541	9,938	8,494
56,350	56,400	9,950	7,549	9,950	8,506
56,400	56,450	9,963	7,556	9,963	8,519
56,450	56,500	9,975	7,564	9,975	8,531
56,500	56,550	9,988	7,571	9,988	8,544
56,550	56,600	10,000	7,579	10,000	8,556
56,600	56,650	10,013	7,586	10,013	8,569
56,650	56,700	10,025	7,594	10,025	8,581
56,700	56,750	10,038	7,601	10,038	8,594
56,750	56,800	10,050	7,609	10,050	8,606
56,800	56,850	10,063	7,616	10,063	8,619
56,850	56,900	10,075	7,624	10,075	8,631
56,900	56,950	10,088	7,631	10,088	8,644
56,950	57,000	10,100	7,639	10,100	8,656

(Continued)

* This column must also be used by a qualifying widow(er).

(Continued on page T-9)

2014 Tax Table — *Continued*

If line 43 (taxable income) is— At least	But less than	And you are— Single	Married filing jointly *	Married filing sepa-rately	Head of a house-hold
		Your tax is—			
57,000					
57,000	57,050	10,113	7,646	10,113	8,669
57,050	57,100	10,125	7,654	10,125	8,681
57,100	57,150	10,138	7,661	10,138	8,694
57,150	57,200	10,150	7,669	10,150	8,706
57,200	57,250	10,163	7,676	10,163	8,719
57,250	57,300	10,175	7,684	10,175	8,731
57,300	57,350	10,188	7,691	10,188	8,744
57,350	57,400	10,200	7,699	10,200	8,756
57,400	57,450	10,213	7,706	10,213	8,769
57,450	57,500	10,225	7,714	10,225	8,781
57,500	57,550	10,238	7,721	10,238	8,794
57,550	57,600	10,250	7,729	10,250	8,806
57,600	57,650	10,263	7,736	10,263	8,819
57,650	57,700	10,275	7,744	10,275	8,831
57,700	57,750	10,288	7,751	10,288	8,844
57,750	57,800	10,300	7,759	10,300	8,856
57,800	57,850	10,313	7,766	10,313	8,869
57,850	57,900	10,325	7,774	10,325	8,881
57,900	57,950	10,338	7,781	10,338	8,894
57,950	58,000	10,350	7,789	10,350	8,906
58,000					
58,000	58,050	10,363	7,796	10,363	8,919
58,050	58,100	10,375	7,804	10,375	8,931
58,100	58,150	10,388	7,811	10,388	8,944
58,150	58,200	10,400	7,819	10,400	8,956
58,200	58,250	10,413	7,826	10,413	8,969
58,250	58,300	10,425	7,834	10,425	8,981
58,300	58,350	10,438	7,841	10,438	8,994
58,350	58,400	10,450	7,849	10,450	9,006
58,400	58,450	10,463	7,856	10,463	9,019
58,450	58,500	10,475	7,864	10,475	9,031
58,500	58,550	10,488	7,871	10,488	9,044
58,550	58,600	10,500	7,879	10,500	9,056
58,600	58,650	10,513	7,886	10,513	9,069
58,650	58,700	10,525	7,894	10,525	9,081
58,700	58,750	10,538	7,901	10,538	9,094
58,750	58,800	10,550	7,909	10,550	9,106
58,800	58,850	10,563	7,916	10,563	9,119
58,850	58,900	10,575	7,924	10,575	9,131
58,900	58,950	10,588	7,931	10,588	9,144
58,950	59,000	10,600	7,939	10,600	9,156
59,000					
59,000	59,050	10,613	7,946	10,613	9,169
59,050	59,100	10,625	7,954	10,625	9,181
59,100	59,150	10,638	7,961	10,638	9,194
59,150	59,200	10,650	7,969	10,650	9,206
59,200	59,250	10,663	7,976	10,663	9,219
59,250	59,300	10,675	7,984	10,675	9,231
59,300	59,350	10,688	7,991	10,688	9,244
59,350	59,400	10,700	7,999	10,700	9,256
59,400	59,450	10,713	8,006	10,713	9,269
59,450	59,500	10,725	8,014	10,725	9,281
59,500	59,550	10,738	8,021	10,738	9,294
59,550	59,600	10,750	8,029	10,750	9,306
59,600	59,650	10,763	8,036	10,763	9,319
59,650	59,700	10,775	8,044	10,775	9,331
59,700	59,750	10,788	8,051	10,788	9,344
59,750	59,800	10,800	8,059	10,800	9,356
59,800	59,850	10,813	8,066	10,813	9,369
59,850	59,900	10,825	8,074	10,825	9,381
59,900	59,950	10,838	8,081	10,838	9,394
59,950	60,000	10,850	8,089	10,850	9,406
60,000					
60,000	60,050	10,863	8,096	10,863	9,419
60,050	60,100	10,875	8,104	10,875	9,431
60,100	60,150	10,888	8,111	10,888	9,444
60,150	60,200	10,900	8,119	10,900	9,456
60,200	60,250	10,913	8,126	10,913	9,469
60,250	60,300	10,925	8,134	10,925	9,481
60,300	60,350	10,938	8,141	10,938	9,494
60,350	60,400	10,950	8,149	10,950	9,506
60,400	60,450	10,963	8,156	10,963	9,519
60,450	60,500	10,975	8,164	10,975	9,531
60,500	60,550	10,988	8,171	10,988	9,544
60,550	60,600	11,000	8,179	11,000	9,556
60,600	60,650	11,013	8,186	11,013	9,569
60,650	60,700	11,025	8,194	11,025	9,581
60,700	60,750	11,038	8,201	11,038	9,594
60,750	60,800	11,050	8,209	11,050	9,606
60,800	60,850	11,063	8,216	11,063	9,619
60,850	60,900	11,075	8,224	11,075	9,631
60,900	60,950	11,088	8,231	11,088	9,644
60,950	61,000	11,100	8,239	11,100	9,656
61,000					
61,000	61,050	11,113	8,246	11,113	9,669
61,050	61,100	11,125	8,254	11,125	9,681
61,100	61,150	11,138	8,261	11,138	9,694
61,150	61,200	11,150	8,269	11,150	9,706
61,200	61,250	11,163	8,276	11,163	9,719
61,250	61,300	11,175	8,284	11,175	9,731
61,300	61,350	11,188	8,291	11,188	9,744
61,350	61,400	11,200	8,299	11,200	9,756
61,400	61,450	11,213	8,306	11,213	9,769
61,450	61,500	11,225	8,314	11,225	9,781
61,500	61,550	11,238	8,321	11,238	9,794
61,550	61,600	11,250	8,329	11,250	9,806
61,600	61,650	11,263	8,336	11,263	9,819
61,650	61,700	11,275	8,344	11,275	9,831
61,700	61,750	11,288	8,351	11,288	9,844
61,750	61,800	11,300	8,359	11,300	9,856
61,800	61,850	11,313	8,366	11,313	9,869
61,850	61,900	11,325	8,374	11,325	9,881
61,900	61,950	11,338	8,381	11,338	9,894
61,950	62,000	11,350	8,389	11,350	9,906
62,000					
62,000	62,050	11,363	8,396	11,363	9,919
62,050	62,100	11,375	8,404	11,375	9,931
62,100	62,150	11,388	8,411	11,388	9,944
62,150	62,200	11,400	8,419	11,400	9,956
62,200	62,250	11,413	8,426	11,413	9,969
62,250	62,300	11,425	8,434	11,425	9,981
62,300	62,350	11,438	8,441	11,438	9,994
62,350	62,400	11,450	8,449	11,450	10,006
62,400	62,450	11,463	8,456	11,463	10,019
62,450	62,500	11,475	8,464	11,475	10,031
62,500	62,550	11,488	8,471	11,488	10,044
62,550	62,600	11,500	8,479	11,500	10,056
62,600	62,650	11,513	8,486	11,513	10,069
62,650	62,700	11,525	8,494	11,525	10,081
62,700	62,750	11,538	8,501	11,538	10,094
62,750	62,800	11,550	8,509	11,550	10,106
62,800	62,850	11,563	8,516	11,563	10,119
62,850	62,900	11,575	8,524	11,575	10,131
62,900	62,950	11,588	8,531	11,588	10,144
62,950	63,000	11,600	8,539	11,600	10,156
63,000					
63,000	63,050	11,613	8,546	11,613	10,169
63,050	63,100	11,625	8,554	11,625	10,181
63,100	63,150	11,638	8,561	11,638	10,194
63,150	63,200	11,650	8,569	11,650	10,206
63,200	63,250	11,663	8,576	11,663	10,219
63,250	63,300	11,675	8,584	11,675	10,231
63,300	63,350	11,688	8,591	11,688	10,244
63,350	63,400	11,700	8,599	11,700	10,256
63,400	63,450	11,713	8,606	11,713	10,269
63,450	63,500	11,725	8,614	11,725	10,281
63,500	63,550	11,738	8,621	11,738	10,294
63,550	63,600	11,750	8,629	11,750	10,306
63,600	63,650	11,763	8,636	11,763	10,319
63,650	63,700	11,775	8,644	11,775	10,331
63,700	63,750	11,788	8,651	11,788	10,344
63,750	63,800	11,800	8,659	11,800	10,356
63,800	63,850	11,813	8,666	11,813	10,369
63,850	63,900	11,825	8,674	11,825	10,381
63,900	63,950	11,838	8,681	11,838	10,394
63,950	64,000	11,850	8,689	11,850	10,406
64,000					
64,000	64,050	11,863	8,696	11,863	10,419
64,050	64,100	11,875	8,704	11,875	10,431
64,100	64,150	11,888	8,711	11,888	10,444
64,150	64,200	11,900	8,719	11,900	10,456
64,200	64,250	11,913	8,726	11,913	10,469
64,250	64,300	11,925	8,734	11,925	10,481
64,300	64,350	11,938	8,741	11,938	10,494
64,350	64,400	11,950	8,749	11,950	10,506
64,400	64,450	11,963	8,756	11,963	10,519
64,450	64,500	11,975	8,764	11,975	10,531
64,500	64,550	11,988	8,771	11,988	10,544
64,550	64,600	12,000	8,779	12,000	10,556
64,600	64,650	12,013	8,786	12,013	10,569
64,650	64,700	12,025	8,794	12,025	10,581
64,700	64,750	12,038	8,801	12,038	10,594
64,750	64,800	12,050	8,809	12,050	10,606
64,800	64,850	12,063	8,816	12,063	10,619
64,850	64,900	12,075	8,824	12,075	10,631
64,900	64,950	12,088	8,831	12,088	10,644
64,950	65,000	12,100	8,839	12,100	10,656
65,000					
65,000	65,050	12,113	8,846	12,113	10,669
65,050	65,100	12,125	8,854	12,125	10,681
65,100	65,150	12,138	8,861	12,138	10,694
65,150	65,200	12,150	8,869	12,150	10,706
65,200	65,250	12,163	8,876	12,163	10,719
65,250	65,300	12,175	8,884	12,175	10,731
65,300	65,350	12,188	8,891	12,188	10,744
65,350	65,400	12,200	8,899	12,200	10,756
65,400	65,450	12,213	8,906	12,213	10,769
65,450	65,500	12,225	8,914	12,225	10,781
65,500	65,550	12,238	8,921	12,238	10,794
65,550	65,600	12,250	8,929	12,250	10,806
65,600	65,650	12,263	8,936	12,263	10,819
65,650	65,700	12,275	8,944	12,275	10,831
65,700	65,750	12,288	8,951	12,288	10,844
65,750	65,800	12,300	8,959	12,300	10,856
65,800	65,850	12,313	8,966	12,313	10,869
65,850	65,900	12,325	8,974	12,325	10,881
65,900	65,950	12,338	8,981	12,338	10,894
65,950	66,000	12,350	8,989	12,350	10,906

(Continued)

* This column must also be used by a qualifying widow(er).

(Continued on page T-10)

2014 Tax Table — *Continued*

If line 43 (taxable income) is—		And you are—			
At least	But less than	Single	Married filing jointly *	Married filing separately	Head of a household
		Your tax is—			
66,000					
66,000	66,050	12,363	8,996	12,363	10,919
66,050	66,100	12,375	9,004	12,375	10,931
66,100	66,150	12,388	9,011	12,388	10,944
66,150	66,200	12,400	9,019	12,400	10,956
66,200	66,250	12,413	9,026	12,413	10,969
66,250	66,300	12,425	9,034	12,425	10,981
66,300	66,350	12,438	9,041	12,438	10,994
66,350	66,400	12,450	9,049	12,450	11,006
66,400	66,450	12,463	9,056	12,463	11,019
66,450	66,500	12,475	9,064	12,475	11,031
66,500	66,550	12,488	9,071	12,488	11,044
66,550	66,600	12,500	9,079	12,500	11,056
66,600	66,650	12,513	9,086	12,513	11,069
66,650	66,700	12,525	9,094	12,525	11,081
66,700	66,750	12,538	9,101	12,538	11,094
66,750	66,800	12,550	9,109	12,550	11,106
66,800	66,850	12,563	9,116	12,563	11,119
66,850	66,900	12,575	9,124	12,575	11,131
66,900	66,950	12,588	9,131	12,588	11,144
66,950	67,000	12,600	9,139	12,600	11,156
67,000					
67,000	67,050	12,613	9,146	12,613	11,169
67,050	67,100	12,625	9,154	12,625	11,181
67,100	67,150	12,638	9,161	12,638	11,194
67,150	67,200	12,650	9,169	12,650	11,206
67,200	67,250	12,663	9,176	12,663	11,219
67,250	67,300	12,675	9,184	12,675	11,231
67,300	67,350	12,688	9,191	12,688	11,244
67,350	67,400	12,700	9,199	12,700	11,256
67,400	67,450	12,713	9,206	12,713	11,269
67,450	67,500	12,725	9,214	12,725	11,281
67,500	67,550	12,738	9,221	12,738	11,294
67,550	67,600	12,750	9,229	12,750	11,306
67,600	67,650	12,763	9,236	12,763	11,319
67,650	67,700	12,775	9,244	12,775	11,331
67,700	67,750	12,788	9,251	12,788	11,344
67,750	67,800	12,800	9,259	12,800	11,356
67,800	67,850	12,813	9,266	12,813	11,369
67,850	67,900	12,825	9,274	12,825	11,381
67,900	67,950	12,838	9,281	12,838	11,394
67,950	68,000	12,850	9,289	12,850	11,406
68,000					
68,000	68,050	12,863	9,296	12,863	11,419
68,050	68,100	12,875	9,304	12,875	11,431
68,100	68,150	12,888	9,311	12,888	11,444
68,150	68,200	12,900	9,319	12,900	11,456
68,200	68,250	12,913	9,326	12,913	11,469
68,250	68,300	12,925	9,334	12,925	11,481
68,300	68,350	12,938	9,341	12,938	11,494
68,350	68,400	12,950	9,349	12,950	11,506
68,400	68,450	12,963	9,356	12,963	11,519
68,450	68,500	12,975	9,364	12,975	11,531
68,500	68,550	12,988	9,371	12,988	11,544
68,550	68,600	13,000	9,379	13,000	11,556
68,600	68,650	13,013	9,386	13,013	11,569
68,650	68,700	13,025	9,394	13,025	11,581
68,700	68,750	13,038	9,401	13,038	11,594
68,750	68,800	13,050	9,409	13,050	11,606
68,800	68,850	13,063	9,416	13,063	11,619
68,850	68,900	13,075	9,424	13,075	11,631
68,900	68,950	13,088	9,431	13,088	11,644
68,950	69,000	13,100	9,439	13,100	11,656
69,000					
69,000	69,050	13,113	9,446	13,113	11,669
69,050	69,100	13,125	9,454	13,125	11,681
69,100	69,150	13,138	9,461	13,138	11,694
69,150	69,200	13,150	9,469	13,150	11,706
69,200	69,250	13,163	9,476	13,163	11,719
69,250	69,300	13,175	9,484	13,175	11,731
69,300	69,350	13,188	9,491	13,188	11,744
69,350	69,400	13,200	9,499	13,200	11,756
69,400	69,450	13,213	9,506	13,213	11,769
69,450	69,500	13,225	9,514	13,225	11,781
69,500	69,550	13,238	9,521	13,238	11,794
69,550	69,600	13,250	9,529	13,250	11,806
69,600	69,650	13,263	9,536	13,263	11,819
69,650	69,700	13,275	9,544	13,275	11,831
69,700	69,750	13,288	9,551	13,288	11,844
69,750	69,800	13,300	9,559	13,300	11,856
69,800	69,850	13,313	9,566	13,313	11,869
69,850	69,900	13,325	9,574	13,325	11,881
69,900	69,950	13,338	9,581	13,338	11,894
69,950	70,000	13,350	9,589	13,350	11,906
70,000					
70,000	70,050	13,363	9,596	13,363	11,919
70,050	70,100	13,375	9,604	13,375	11,931
70,100	70,150	13,388	9,611	13,388	11,944
70,150	70,200	13,400	9,619	13,400	11,956
70,200	70,250	13,413	9,626	13,413	11,969
70,250	70,300	13,425	9,634	13,425	11,981
70,300	70,350	13,438	9,641	13,438	11,994
70,350	70,400	13,450	9,649	13,450	12,006
70,400	70,450	13,463	9,656	13,463	12,019
70,450	70,500	13,475	9,664	13,475	12,031
70,500	70,550	13,488	9,671	13,488	12,044
70,550	70,600	13,500	9,679	13,500	12,056
70,600	70,650	13,513	9,686	13,513	12,069
70,650	70,700	13,525	9,694	13,525	12,081
70,700	70,750	13,538	9,701	13,538	12,094
70,750	70,800	13,550	9,709	13,550	12,106
70,800	70,850	13,563	9,716	13,563	12,119
70,850	70,900	13,575	9,724	13,575	12,131
70,900	70,950	13,588	9,731	13,588	12,144
70,950	71,000	13,600	9,739	13,600	12,156
71,000					
71,000	71,050	13,613	9,746	13,613	12,169
71,050	71,100	13,625	9,754	13,625	12,181
71,100	71,150	13,638	9,761	13,638	12,194
71,150	71,200	13,650	9,769	13,650	12,206
71,200	71,250	13,663	9,776	13,663	12,219
71,250	71,300	13,675	9,784	13,675	12,231
71,300	71,350	13,688	9,791	13,688	12,244
71,350	71,400	13,700	9,799	13,700	12,256
71,400	71,450	13,713	9,806	13,713	12,269
71,450	71,500	13,725	9,814	13,725	12,281
71,500	71,550	13,738	9,821	13,738	12,294
71,550	71,600	13,750	9,829	13,750	12,306
71,600	71,650	13,763	9,836	13,763	12,319
71,650	71,700	13,775	9,844	13,775	12,331
71,700	71,750	13,788	9,851	13,788	12,344
71,750	71,800	13,800	9,859	13,800	12,356
71,800	71,850	13,813	9,866	13,813	12,369
71,850	71,900	13,825	9,874	13,825	12,381
71,900	71,950	13,838	9,881	13,838	12,394
71,950	72,000	13,850	9,889	13,850	12,406
72,000					
72,000	72,050	13,863	9,896	13,863	12,419
72,050	72,100	13,875	9,904	13,875	12,431
72,100	72,150	13,888	9,911	13,888	12,444
72,150	72,200	13,900	9,919	13,900	12,456
72,200	72,250	13,913	9,926	13,913	12,469
72,250	72,300	13,925	9,934	13,925	12,481
72,300	72,350	13,938	9,941	13,938	12,494
72,350	72,400	13,950	9,949	13,950	12,506
72,400	72,450	13,963	9,956	13,963	12,519
72,450	72,500	13,975	9,964	13,975	12,531
72,500	72,550	13,988	9,971	13,988	12,544
72,550	72,600	14,000	9,979	14,000	12,556
72,600	72,650	14,013	9,986	14,013	12,569
72,650	72,700	14,025	9,994	14,025	12,581
72,700	72,750	14,038	10,001	14,038	12,594
72,750	72,800	14,050	10,009	14,050	12,606
72,800	72,850	14,063	10,016	14,063	12,619
72,850	72,900	14,075	10,024	14,075	12,631
72,900	72,950	14,088	10,031	14,088	12,644
72,950	73,000	14,100	10,039	14,100	12,656
73,000					
73,000	73,050	14,113	10,046	14,113	12,669
73,050	73,100	14,125	10,054	14,125	12,681
73,100	73,150	14,138	10,061	14,138	12,694
73,150	73,200	14,150	10,069	14,150	12,706
73,200	73,250	14,163	10,076	14,163	12,719
73,250	73,300	14,175	10,084	14,175	12,731
73,300	73,350	14,188	10,091	14,188	12,744
73,350	73,400	14,200	10,099	14,200	12,756
73,400	73,450	14,213	10,106	14,213	12,769
73,450	73,500	14,225	10,114	14,225	12,781
73,500	73,550	14,238	10,121	14,238	12,794
73,550	73,600	14,250	10,129	14,250	12,806
73,600	73,650	14,263	10,136	14,263	12,819
73,650	73,700	14,275	10,144	14,275	12,831
73,700	73,750	14,288	10,151	14,288	12,844
73,750	73,800	14,300	10,159	14,300	12,856
73,800	73,850	14,313	10,169	14,313	12,869
73,850	73,900	14,325	10,181	14,325	12,881
73,900	73,950	14,338	10,194	14,338	12,894
73,950	74,000	14,350	10,206	14,350	12,906
74,000					
74,000	74,050	14,363	10,219	14,363	12,919
74,050	74,100	14,375	10,231	14,375	12,931
74,100	74,150	14,388	10,244	14,388	12,944
74,150	74,200	14,400	10,256	14,400	12,956
74,200	74,250	14,413	10,269	14,413	12,969
74,250	74,300	14,425	10,281	14,425	12,981
74,300	74,350	14,438	10,294	14,438	12,994
74,350	74,400	14,450	10,306	14,450	13,006
74,400	74,450	14,463	10,319	14,463	13,019
74,450	74,500	14,475	10,331	14,477	13,031
74,500	74,550	14,488	10,344	14,491	13,044
74,550	74,600	14,500	10,356	14,505	13,056
74,600	74,650	14,513	10,369	14,519	13,069
74,650	74,700	14,525	10,381	14,533	13,081
74,700	74,750	14,538	10,394	14,547	13,094
74,750	74,800	14,550	10,406	14,561	13,106
74,800	74,850	14,563	10,419	14,575	13,119
74,850	74,900	14,575	10,431	14,589	13,131
74,900	74,950	14,588	10,444	14,603	13,144
74,950	75,000	14,600	10,456	14,617	13,156

(Continued)

* This column must also be used by a qualifying widow(er).

(Continued on page T-11)

2014 Tax Table — *Continued*

If line 43 (taxable income) is— At least	But less than	And you are— Single	Married filing jointly *	Married filing separately	Head of a household
		Your tax is—			
75,000					
75,000	75,050	14,613	10,469	14,631	13,169
75,050	75,100	14,625	10,481	14,645	13,181
75,100	75,150	14,638	10,494	14,659	13,194
75,150	75,200	14,650	10,506	14,673	13,206
75,200	75,250	14,663	10,519	14,687	13,219
75,250	75,300	14,675	10,531	14,701	13,231
75,300	75,350	14,688	10,544	14,715	13,244
75,350	75,400	14,700	10,556	14,729	13,256
75,400	75,450	14,713	10,569	14,743	13,269
75,450	75,500	14,725	10,581	14,757	13,281
75,500	75,550	14,738	10,594	14,771	13,294
75,550	75,600	14,750	10,606	14,785	13,306
75,600	75,650	14,763	10,619	14,799	13,319
75,650	75,700	14,775	10,631	14,813	13,331
75,700	75,750	14,788	10,644	14,827	13,344
75,750	75,800	14,800	10,656	14,841	13,356
75,800	75,850	14,813	10,669	14,855	13,369
75,850	75,900	14,825	10,681	14,869	13,381
75,900	75,950	14,838	10,694	14,883	13,394
75,950	76,000	14,850	10,706	14,897	13,406
76,000					
76,000	76,050	14,863	10,719	14,911	13,419
76,050	76,100	14,875	10,731	14,925	13,431
76,100	76,150	14,888	10,744	14,939	13,444
76,150	76,200	14,900	10,756	14,953	13,456
76,200	76,250	14,913	10,769	14,967	13,469
76,250	76,300	14,925	10,781	14,981	13,481
76,300	76,350	14,938	10,794	14,995	13,494
76,350	76,400	14,950	10,806	15,009	13,506
76,400	76,450	14,963	10,819	15,023	13,519
76,450	76,500	14,975	10,831	15,037	13,531
76,500	76,550	14,988	10,844	15,051	13,544
76,550	76,600	15,000	10,856	15,065	13,556
76,600	76,650	15,013	10,869	15,079	13,569
76,650	76,700	15,025	10,881	15,093	13,581
76,700	76,750	15,038	10,894	15,107	13,594
76,750	76,800	15,050	10,906	15,121	13,606
76,800	76,850	15,063	10,919	15,135	13,619
76,850	76,900	15,075	10,931	15,149	13,631
76,900	76,950	15,088	10,944	15,163	13,644
76,950	77,000	15,100	10,956	15,177	13,656
77,000					
77,000	77,050	15,113	10,969	15,191	13,669
77,050	77,100	15,125	10,981	15,205	13,681
77,100	77,150	15,138	10,994	15,219	13,694
77,150	77,200	15,150	11,006	15,233	13,706
77,200	77,250	15,163	11,019	15,247	13,719
77,250	77,300	15,175	11,031	15,261	13,731
77,300	77,350	15,188	11,044	15,275	13,744
77,350	77,400	15,200	11,056	15,289	13,756
77,400	77,450	15,213	11,069	15,303	13,769
77,450	77,500	15,225	11,081	15,317	13,781
77,500	77,550	15,238	11,094	15,331	13,794
77,550	77,600	15,250	11,106	15,345	13,806
77,600	77,650	15,263	11,119	15,359	13,819
77,650	77,700	15,275	11,131	15,373	13,831
77,700	77,750	15,288	11,144	15,387	13,844
77,750	77,800	15,300	11,156	15,401	13,856
77,800	77,850	15,313	11,169	15,415	13,869
77,850	77,900	15,325	11,181	15,429	13,881
77,900	77,950	15,338	11,194	15,443	13,894
77,950	78,000	15,350	11,206	15,457	13,906
78,000					
78,000	78,050	15,363	11,219	15,471	13,919
78,050	78,100	15,375	11,231	15,485	13,931
78,100	78,150	15,388	11,244	15,499	13,944
78,150	78,200	15,400	11,256	15,513	13,956
78,200	78,250	15,413	11,269	15,527	13,969
78,250	78,300	15,425	11,281	15,541	13,981
78,300	78,350	15,438	11,294	15,555	13,994
78,350	78,400	15,450	11,306	15,569	14,006
78,400	78,450	15,463	11,319	15,583	14,019
78,450	78,500	15,475	11,331	15,597	14,031
78,500	78,550	15,488	11,344	15,611	14,044
78,550	78,600	15,500	11,356	15,625	14,056
78,600	78,650	15,513	11,369	15,639	14,069
78,650	78,700	15,525	11,381	15,653	14,081
78,700	78,750	15,538	11,394	15,667	14,094
78,750	78,800	15,550	11,406	15,681	14,106
78,800	78,850	15,563	11,419	15,695	14,119
78,850	78,900	15,575	11,431	15,709	14,131
78,900	78,950	15,588	11,444	15,723	14,144
78,950	79,000	15,600	11,456	15,737	14,156
79,000					
79,000	79,050	15,613	11,469	15,751	14,169
79,050	79,100	15,625	11,481	15,765	14,181
79,100	79,150	15,638	11,494	15,779	14,194
79,150	79,200	15,650	11,506	15,793	14,206
79,200	79,250	15,663	11,519	15,807	14,219
79,250	79,300	15,675	11,531	15,821	14,231
79,300	79,350	15,688	11,544	15,835	14,244
79,350	79,400	15,700	11,556	15,849	14,256
79,400	79,450	15,713	11,569	15,863	14,269
79,450	79,500	15,725	11,581	15,877	14,281
79,500	79,550	15,738	11,594	15,891	14,294
79,550	79,600	15,750	11,606	15,905	14,306
79,600	79,650	15,763	11,619	15,919	14,319
79,650	79,700	15,775	11,631	15,933	14,331
79,700	79,750	15,788	11,644	15,947	14,344
79,750	79,800	15,800	11,656	15,961	14,356
79,800	79,850	15,813	11,669	15,975	14,369
79,850	79,900	15,825	11,681	15,989	14,381
79,900	79,950	15,838	11,694	16,003	14,394
79,950	80,000	15,850	11,706	16,017	14,406
80,000					
80,000	80,050	15,863	11,719	16,031	14,419
80,050	80,100	15,875	11,731	16,045	14,431
80,100	80,150	15,888	11,744	16,059	14,444
80,150	80,200	15,900	11,756	16,073	14,456
80,200	80,250	15,913	11,769	16,087	14,469
80,250	80,300	15,925	11,781	16,101	14,481
80,300	80,350	15,938	11,794	16,115	14,494
80,350	80,400	15,950	11,806	16,129	14,506
80,400	80,450	15,963	11,819	16,143	14,519
80,450	80,500	15,975	11,831	16,157	14,531
80,500	80,550	15,988	11,844	16,171	14,544
80,550	80,600	16,000	11,856	16,185	14,556
80,600	80,650	16,013	11,869	16,199	14,569
80,650	80,700	16,025	11,881	16,213	14,581
80,700	80,750	16,038	11,894	16,227	14,594
80,750	80,800	16,050	11,906	16,241	14,606
80,800	80,850	16,063	11,919	16,255	14,619
80,850	80,900	16,075	11,931	16,269	14,631
80,900	80,950	16,088	11,944	16,283	14,644
80,950	81,000	16,100	11,956	16,297	14,656
81,000					
81,000	81,050	16,113	11,969	16,311	14,669
81,050	81,100	16,125	11,981	16,325	14,681
81,100	81,150	16,138	11,994	16,339	14,694
81,150	81,200	16,150	12,006	16,353	14,706
81,200	81,250	16,163	12,019	16,367	14,719
81,250	81,300	16,175	12,031	16,381	14,731
81,300	81,350	16,188	12,044	16,395	14,744
81,350	81,400	16,200	12,056	16,409	14,756
81,400	81,450	16,213	12,069	16,423	14,769
81,450	81,500	16,225	12,081	16,437	14,781
81,500	81,550	16,238	12,094	16,451	14,794
81,550	81,600	16,250	12,106	16,465	14,806
81,600	81,650	16,263	12,119	16,479	14,819
81,650	81,700	16,275	12,131	16,493	14,831
81,700	81,750	16,288	12,144	16,507	14,844
81,750	81,800	16,300	12,156	16,521	14,856
81,800	81,850	16,313	12,169	16,535	14,869
81,850	81,900	16,325	12,181	16,549	14,881
81,900	81,950	16,338	12,194	16,563	14,894
81,950	82,000	16,350	12,206	16,577	14,906
82,000					
82,000	82,050	16,363	12,219	16,591	14,919
82,050	82,100	16,375	12,231	16,605	14,931
82,100	82,150	16,388	12,244	16,619	14,944
82,150	82,200	16,400	12,256	16,633	14,956
82,200	82,250	16,413	12,269	16,647	14,969
82,250	82,300	16,425	12,281	16,661	14,981
82,300	82,350	16,438	12,294	16,675	14,994
82,350	82,400	16,450	12,306	16,689	15,006
82,400	82,450	16,463	12,319	16,703	15,019
82,450	82,500	16,475	12,331	16,717	15,031
82,500	82,550	16,488	12,344	16,731	15,044
82,550	82,600	16,500	12,356	16,745	15,056
82,600	82,650	16,513	12,369	16,759	15,069
82,650	82,700	16,525	12,381	16,773	15,081
82,700	82,750	16,538	12,394	16,787	15,094
82,750	82,800	16,550	12,406	16,801	15,106
82,800	82,850	16,563	12,419	16,815	15,119
82,850	82,900	16,575	12,431	16,829	15,131
82,900	82,950	16,588	12,444	16,843	15,144
82,950	83,000	16,600	12,456	16,857	15,156
83,000					
83,000	83,050	16,613	12,469	16,871	15,169
83,050	83,100	16,625	12,481	16,885	15,181
83,100	83,150	16,638	12,494	16,899	15,194
83,150	83,200	16,650	12,506	16,913	15,206
83,200	83,250	16,663	12,519	16,927	15,219
83,250	83,300	16,675	12,531	16,941	15,231
83,300	83,350	16,688	12,544	16,955	15,244
83,350	83,400	16,700	12,556	16,969	15,256
83,400	83,450	16,713	12,569	16,983	15,269
83,450	83,500	16,725	12,581	16,997	15,281
83,500	83,550	16,738	12,594	17,011	15,294
83,550	83,600	16,750	12,606	17,025	15,306
83,600	83,650	16,763	12,619	17,039	15,319
83,650	83,700	16,775	12,631	17,053	15,331
83,700	83,750	16,788	12,644	17,067	15,344
83,750	83,800	16,800	12,656	17,081	15,356
83,800	83,850	16,813	12,669	17,095	15,369
83,850	83,900	16,825	12,681	17,109	15,381
83,900	83,950	16,838	12,694	17,123	15,394
83,950	84,000	16,850	12,706	17,137	15,406

(Continued)

* This column must also be used by a qualifying widow(er).

(Continued on page T-12)

2014 Tax Table — *Continued*

If line 43 (taxable income) is— At least	But less than	And you are— Single	Married filing jointly *	Married filing sepa-rately	Head of a house-hold
		Your tax is—			
84,000					
84,000	84,050	16,863	12,719	17,151	15,419
84,050	84,100	16,875	12,731	17,165	15,431
84,100	84,150	16,888	12,744	17,179	15,444
84,150	84,200	16,900	12,756	17,193	15,456
84,200	84,250	16,913	12,769	17,207	15,469
84,250	84,300	16,925	12,781	17,221	15,481
84,300	84,350	16,938	12,794	17,235	15,494
84,350	84,400	16,950	12,806	17,249	15,506
84,400	84,450	16,963	12,819	17,263	15,519
84,450	84,500	16,975	12,831	17,277	15,531
84,500	84,550	16,988	12,844	17,291	15,544
84,550	84,600	17,000	12,856	17,305	15,556
84,600	84,650	17,013	12,869	17,319	15,569
84,650	84,700	17,025	12,881	17,333	15,581
84,700	84,750	17,038	12,894	17,347	15,594
84,750	84,800	17,050	12,906	17,361	15,606
84,800	84,850	17,063	12,919	17,375	15,619
84,850	84,900	17,075	12,931	17,389	15,631
84,900	84,950	17,088	12,944	17,403	15,644
84,950	85,000	17,100	12,956	17,417	15,656
85,000					
85,000	85,050	17,113	12,969	17,431	15,669
85,050	85,100	17,125	12,981	17,445	15,681
85,100	85,150	17,138	12,994	17,459	15,694
85,150	85,200	17,150	13,006	17,473	15,706
85,200	85,250	17,163	13,019	17,487	15,719
85,250	85,300	17,175	13,031	17,501	15,731
85,300	85,350	17,188	13,044	17,515	15,744
85,350	85,400	17,200	13,056	17,529	15,756
85,400	85,450	17,213	13,069	17,543	15,769
85,450	85,500	17,225	13,081	17,557	15,781
85,500	85,550	17,238	13,094	17,571	15,794
85,550	85,600	17,250	13,106	17,585	15,806
85,600	85,650	17,263	13,119	17,599	15,819
85,650	85,700	17,275	13,131	17,613	15,831
85,700	85,750	17,288	13,144	17,627	15,844
85,750	85,800	17,300	13,156	17,641	15,856
85,800	85,850	17,313	13,169	17,655	15,869
85,850	85,900	17,325	13,181	17,669	15,881
85,900	85,950	17,338	13,194	17,683	15,894
85,950	86,000	17,350	13,206	17,697	15,906
86,000					
86,000	86,050	17,363	13,219	17,711	15,919
86,050	86,100	17,375	13,231	17,725	15,931
86,100	86,150	17,388	13,244	17,739	15,944
86,150	86,200	17,400	13,256	17,753	15,956
86,200	86,250	17,413	13,269	17,767	15,969
86,250	86,300	17,425	13,281	17,781	15,981
86,300	86,350	17,438	13,294	17,795	15,994
86,350	86,400	17,450	13,306	17,809	16,006
86,400	86,450	17,463	13,319	17,823	16,019
86,450	86,500	17,475	13,331	17,837	16,031
86,500	86,550	17,488	13,344	17,851	16,044
86,550	86,600	17,500	13,356	17,865	16,056
86,600	86,650	17,513	13,369	17,879	16,069
86,650	86,700	17,525	13,381	17,893	16,081
86,700	86,750	17,538	13,394	17,907	16,094
86,750	86,800	17,550	13,406	17,921	16,106
86,800	86,850	17,563	13,419	17,935	16,119
86,850	86,900	17,575	13,431	17,949	16,131
86,900	86,950	17,588	13,444	17,963	16,144
86,950	87,000	17,600	13,456	17,977	16,156
87,000					
87,000	87,050	17,613	13,469	17,991	16,169
87,050	87,100	17,625	13,481	18,005	16,181
87,100	87,150	17,638	13,494	18,019	16,194
87,150	87,200	17,650	13,506	18,033	16,206
87,200	87,250	17,663	13,519	18,047	16,219
87,250	87,300	17,675	13,531	18,061	16,231
87,300	87,350	17,688	13,544	18,075	16,244
87,350	87,400	17,700	13,556	18,089	16,256
87,400	87,450	17,713	13,569	18,103	16,269
87,450	87,500	17,725	13,581	18,117	16,281
87,500	87,550	17,738	13,594	18,131	16,294
87,550	87,600	17,750	13,606	18,145	16,306
87,600	87,650	17,763	13,619	18,159	16,319
87,650	87,700	17,775	13,631	18,173	16,331
87,700	87,750	17,788	13,644	18,187	16,344
87,750	87,800	17,800	13,656	18,201	16,356
87,800	87,850	17,813	13,669	18,215	16,369
87,850	87,900	17,825	13,681	18,229	16,381
87,900	87,950	17,838	13,694	18,243	16,394
87,950	88,000	17,850	13,706	18,257	16,406
88,000					
88,000	88,050	17,863	13,719	18,271	16,419
88,050	88,100	17,875	13,731	18,285	16,431
88,100	88,150	17,888	13,744	18,299	16,444
88,150	88,200	17,900	13,756	18,313	16,456
88,200	88,250	17,913	13,769	18,327	16,469
88,250	88,300	17,925	13,781	18,341	16,481
88,300	88,350	17,938	13,794	18,355	16,494
88,350	88,400	17,950	13,806	18,369	16,506
88,400	88,450	17,963	13,819	18,383	16,519
88,450	88,500	17,975	13,831	18,397	16,531
88,500	88,550	17,988	13,844	18,411	16,544
88,550	88,600	18,000	13,856	18,425	16,556
88,600	88,650	18,013	13,869	18,439	16,569
88,650	88,700	18,025	13,881	18,453	16,581
88,700	88,750	18,038	13,894	18,467	16,594
88,750	88,800	18,050	13,906	18,481	16,606
88,800	88,850	18,063	13,919	18,495	16,619
88,850	88,900	18,075	13,931	18,509	16,631
88,900	88,950	18,088	13,944	18,523	16,644
88,950	89,000	18,100	13,956	18,537	16,656
89,000					
89,000	89,050	18,113	13,969	18,551	16,669
89,050	89,100	18,125	13,981	18,565	16,681
89,100	89,150	18,138	13,994	18,579	16,694
89,150	89,200	18,150	14,006	18,593	16,706
89,200	89,250	18,163	14,019	18,607	16,719
89,250	89,300	18,175	14,031	18,621	16,731
89,300	89,350	18,188	14,044	18,635	16,744
89,350	89,400	18,201	14,056	18,649	16,756
89,400	89,450	18,215	14,069	18,663	16,769
89,450	89,500	18,229	14,081	18,677	16,781
89,500	89,550	18,243	14,094	18,691	16,794
89,550	89,600	18,257	14,106	18,705	16,806
89,600	89,650	18,271	14,119	18,719	16,819
89,650	89,700	18,285	14,131	18,733	16,831
89,700	89,750	18,299	14,144	18,747	16,844
89,750	89,800	18,313	14,156	18,761	16,856
89,800	89,850	18,327	14,169	18,775	16,869
89,850	89,900	18,341	14,181	18,789	16,881
89,900	89,950	18,355	14,194	18,803	16,894
89,950	90,000	18,369	14,206	18,817	16,906
90,000					
90,000	90,050	18,383	14,219	18,831	16,919
90,050	90,100	18,397	14,231	18,845	16,931
90,100	90,150	18,411	14,244	18,859	16,944
90,150	90,200	18,425	14,256	18,873	16,956
90,200	90,250	18,439	14,269	18,887	16,969
90,250	90,300	18,453	14,281	18,901	16,981
90,300	90,350	18,467	14,294	18,915	16,994
90,350	90,400	18,481	14,306	18,929	17,006
90,400	90,450	18,495	14,319	18,943	17,019
90,450	90,500	18,509	14,331	18,957	17,031
90,500	90,550	18,523	14,344	18,971	17,044
90,550	90,600	18,537	14,356	18,985	17,056
90,600	90,650	18,551	14,369	18,999	17,069
90,650	90,700	18,565	14,381	19,013	17,081
90,700	90,750	18,579	14,394	19,027	17,094
90,750	90,800	18,593	14,406	19,041	17,106
90,800	90,850	18,607	14,419	19,055	17,119
90,850	90,900	18,621	14,431	19,069	17,131
90,900	90,950	18,635	14,444	19,083	17,144
90,950	91,000	18,649	14,456	19,097	17,156
91,000					
91,000	91,050	18,663	14,469	19,111	17,169
91,050	91,100	18,677	14,481	19,125	17,181
91,100	91,150	18,691	14,494	19,139	17,194
91,150	91,200	18,705	14,506	19,153	17,206
91,200	91,250	18,719	14,519	19,167	17,219
91,250	91,300	18,733	14,531	19,181	17,231
91,300	91,350	18,747	14,544	19,195	17,244
91,350	91,400	18,761	14,556	19,209	17,256
91,400	91,450	18,775	14,569	19,223	17,269
91,450	91,500	18,789	14,581	19,237	17,281
91,500	91,550	18,803	14,594	19,251	17,294
91,550	91,600	18,817	14,606	19,265	17,306
91,600	91,650	18,831	14,619	19,279	17,319
91,650	91,700	18,845	14,631	19,293	17,331
91,700	91,750	18,859	14,644	19,307	17,344
91,750	91,800	18,873	14,656	19,321	17,356
91,800	91,850	18,887	14,669	19,335	17,369
91,850	91,900	18,901	14,681	19,349	17,381
91,900	91,950	18,915	14,694	19,363	17,394
91,950	92,000	18,929	14,706	19,377	17,406
92,000					
92,000	92,050	18,943	14,719	19,391	17,419
92,050	92,100	18,957	14,731	19,405	17,431
92,100	92,150	18,971	14,744	19,419	17,444
92,150	92,200	18,985	14,756	19,433	17,456
92,200	92,250	18,999	14,769	19,447	17,469
92,250	92,300	19,013	14,781	19,461	17,481
92,300	92,350	19,027	14,794	19,475	17,494
92,350	92,400	19,041	14,806	19,489	17,506
92,400	92,450	19,055	14,819	19,503	17,519
92,450	92,500	19,069	14,831	19,517	17,531
92,500	92,550	19,083	14,844	19,531	17,544
92,550	92,600	19,097	14,856	19,545	17,556
92,600	92,650	19,111	14,869	19,559	17,569
92,650	92,700	19,125	14,881	19,573	17,581
92,700	92,750	19,139	14,894	19,587	17,594
92,750	92,800	19,153	14,906	19,601	17,606
92,800	92,850	19,167	14,919	19,615	17,619
92,850	92,900	19,181	14,931	19,629	17,631
92,900	92,950	19,195	14,944	19,643	17,644
92,950	93,000	19,209	14,956	19,657	17,656

(Continued)

* This column must also be used by a qualifying widow(er).

(Continued on page T-13)

2014 Tax Table — *Continued*

If line 43 (taxable income) is—		And you are—			
At least	But less than	Single	Married filing jointly *	Married filing separately	Head of a household
		Your tax is—			
93,000					
93,000	93,050	19,223	14,969	19,671	17,669
93,050	93,100	19,237	14,981	19,685	17,681
93,100	93,150	19,251	14,994	19,699	17,694
93,150	93,200	19,265	15,006	19,713	17,706
93,200	93,250	19,279	15,019	19,727	17,719
93,250	93,300	19,293	15,031	19,741	17,731
93,300	93,350	19,307	15,044	19,755	17,744
93,350	93,400	19,321	15,056	19,769	17,756
93,400	93,450	19,335	15,069	19,783	17,769
93,450	93,500	19,349	15,081	19,797	17,781
93,500	93,550	19,363	15,094	19,811	17,794
93,550	93,600	19,377	15,106	19,825	17,806
93,600	93,650	19,391	15,119	19,839	17,819
93,650	93,700	19,405	15,131	19,853	17,831
93,700	93,750	19,419	15,144	19,867	17,844
93,750	93,800	19,433	15,156	19,881	17,856
93,800	93,850	19,447	15,169	19,895	17,869
93,850	93,900	19,461	15,181	19,909	17,881
93,900	93,950	19,475	15,194	19,923	17,894
93,950	94,000	19,489	15,206	19,937	17,906
94,000					
94,000	94,050	19,503	15,219	19,951	17,919
94,050	94,100	19,517	15,231	19,965	17,931
94,100	94,150	19,531	15,244	19,979	17,944
94,150	94,200	19,545	15,256	19,993	17,956
94,200	94,250	19,559	15,269	20,007	17,969
94,250	94,300	19,573	15,281	20,021	17,981
94,300	94,350	19,587	15,294	20,035	17,994
94,350	94,400	19,601	15,306	20,049	18,006
94,400	94,450	19,615	15,319	20,063	18,019
94,450	94,500	19,629	15,331	20,077	18,031
94,500	94,550	19,643	15,344	20,091	18,044
94,550	94,600	19,657	15,356	20,105	18,056
94,600	94,650	19,671	15,369	20,119	18,069
94,650	94,700	19,685	15,381	20,133	18,081
94,700	94,750	19,699	15,394	20,147	18,094
94,750	94,800	19,713	15,406	20,161	18,106
94,800	94,850	19,727	15,419	20,175	18,119
94,850	94,900	19,741	15,431	20,189	18,131
94,900	94,950	19,755	15,444	20,203	18,144
94,950	95,000	19,769	15,456	20,217	18,156
95,000					
95,000	95,050	19,783	15,469	20,231	18,169
95,050	95,100	19,797	15,481	20,245	18,181
95,100	95,150	19,811	15,494	20,259	18,194
95,150	95,200	19,825	15,506	20,273	18,206
95,200	95,250	19,839	15,519	20,287	18,219
95,250	95,300	19,853	15,531	20,301	18,231
95,300	95,350	19,867	15,544	20,315	18,244
95,350	95,400	19,881	15,556	20,329	18,256
95,400	95,450	19,895	15,569	20,343	18,269
95,450	95,500	19,909	15,581	20,357	18,281
95,500	95,550	19,923	15,594	20,371	18,294
95,550	95,600	19,937	15,606	20,385	18,306
95,600	95,650	19,951	15,619	20,399	18,319
95,650	95,700	19,965	15,631	20,413	18,331
95,700	95,750	19,979	15,644	20,427	18,344
95,750	95,800	19,993	15,656	20,441	18,356
95,800	95,850	20,007	15,669	20,455	18,369
95,850	95,900	20,021	15,681	20,469	18,381
95,900	95,950	20,035	15,694	20,483	18,394
95,950	96,000	20,049	15,706	20,497	18,406
96,000					
96,000	96,050	20,063	15,719	20,511	18,419
96,050	96,100	20,077	15,731	20,525	18,431
96,100	96,150	20,091	15,744	20,539	18,444
96,150	96,200	20,105	15,756	20,553	18,456
96,200	96,250	20,119	15,769	20,567	18,469
96,250	96,300	20,133	15,781	20,581	18,481
96,300	96,350	20,147	15,794	20,595	18,494
96,350	96,400	20,161	15,806	20,609	18,506
96,400	96,450	20,175	15,819	20,623	18,519
96,450	96,500	20,189	15,831	20,637	18,531
96,500	96,550	20,203	15,844	20,651	18,544
96,550	96,600	20,217	15,856	20,665	18,556
96,600	96,650	20,231	15,869	20,679	18,569
96,650	96,700	20,245	15,881	20,693	18,581
96,700	96,750	20,259	15,894	20,707	18,594
96,750	96,800	20,273	15,906	20,721	18,606
96,800	96,850	20,287	15,919	20,735	18,619
96,850	96,900	20,301	15,931	20,749	18,631
96,900	96,950	20,315	15,944	20,763	18,644
96,950	97,000	20,329	15,956	20,777	18,656
97,000					
97,000	97,050	20,343	15,969	20,791	18,669
97,050	97,100	20,357	15,981	20,805	18,681
97,100	97,150	20,371	15,994	20,819	18,694
97,150	97,200	20,385	16,006	20,833	18,706
97,200	97,250	20,399	16,019	20,847	18,719
97,250	97,300	20,413	16,031	20,861	18,731
97,300	97,350	20,427	16,044	20,875	18,744
97,350	97,400	20,441	16,056	20,889	18,756
97,400	97,450	20,455	16,069	20,903	18,769
97,450	97,500	20,469	16,081	20,917	18,781
97,500	97,550	20,483	16,094	20,931	18,794
97,550	97,600	20,497	16,106	20,945	18,806
97,600	97,650	20,511	16,119	20,959	18,819
97,650	97,700	20,525	16,131	20,973	18,831
97,700	97,750	20,539	16,144	20,987	18,844
97,750	97,800	20,553	16,156	21,001	18,856
97,800	97,850	20,567	16,169	21,015	18,869
97,850	97,900	20,581	16,181	21,029	18,881
97,900	97,950	20,595	16,194	21,043	18,894
97,950	98,000	20,609	16,206	21,057	18,906
98,000					
98,000	98,050	20,623	16,219	21,071	18,919
98,050	98,100	20,637	16,231	21,085	18,931
98,100	98,150	20,651	16,244	21,099	18,944
98,150	98,200	20,665	16,256	21,113	18,956
98,200	98,250	20,679	16,269	21,127	18,969
98,250	98,300	20,693	16,281	21,141	18,981
98,300	98,350	20,707	16,294	21,155	18,994
98,350	98,400	20,721	16,306	21,169	19,006
98,400	98,450	20,735	16,319	21,183	19,019
98,450	98,500	20,749	16,331	21,197	19,031
98,500	98,550	20,763	16,344	21,211	19,044
98,550	98,600	20,777	16,356	21,225	19,056
98,600	98,650	20,791	16,369	21,239	19,069
98,650	98,700	20,805	16,381	21,253	19,081
98,700	98,750	20,819	16,394	21,267	19,094
98,750	98,800	20,833	16,406	21,281	19,106
98,800	98,850	20,847	16,419	21,295	19,119
98,850	98,900	20,861	16,431	21,309	19,131
98,900	98,950	20,875	16,444	21,323	19,144
98,950	99,000	20,889	16,456	21,337	19,156
99,000					
99,000	99,050	20,903	16,469	21,351	19,169
99,050	99,100	20,917	16,481	21,365	19,181
99,100	99,150	20,931	16,494	21,379	19,194
99,150	99,200	20,945	16,506	21,393	19,206
99,200	99,250	20,959	16,519	21,407	19,219
99,250	99,300	20,973	16,531	21,421	19,231
99,300	99,350	20,987	16,544	21,435	19,244
99,350	99,400	21,001	16,556	21,449	19,256
99,400	99,450	21,015	16,569	21,463	19,269
99,450	99,500	21,029	16,581	21,477	19,281
99,500	99,550	21,043	16,594	21,491	19,294
99,550	99,600	21,057	16,606	21,505	19,306
99,600	99,650	21,071	16,619	21,519	19,319
99,650	99,700	21,085	16,631	21,533	19,331
99,700	99,750	21,099	16,644	21,547	19,344
99,750	99,800	21,113	16,656	21,561	19,356
99,800	99,850	21,127	16,669	21,575	19,369
99,850	99,900	21,141	16,681	21,589	19,381
99,900	99,950	21,155	16,694	21,603	19,394
99,950	100,000	21,169	16,706	21,617	19,406

$100,000 or over use the Tax Computation Worksheet

* This column must also be used by a qualifying widow(er).

2014 Tax Rate Schedules

CAUTION

The Tax Rate Schedules are shown so you can see the tax rate that applies to all levels of taxable income. Do not use them to figure your tax. Instead, see chapter 30.

Schedule X—If your filing status is **Single**

If your taxable income is: *Over—*	*But not over—*	The tax is:	*of the amount over—*
$0	$9,075	.... **10%**	**$0**
9,075	36,900	**$907.50 + 15%**	**9,075**
36,900	89,350	**5,081.25 + 25%**	**36,900**
89,350	186,350	**18,193.75 + 28%**	**89,350**
186,350	405,100	**45,353.75 + 33%**	**186,350**
405,100	406,750	**117,541.25 + 35%**	**405,100**
406,750	....	**118,118.75 + 39.6%**	**406,750**

Schedule Y-1—If your filing status is **Married filing jointly** or **Qualifying widow(er)**

If your taxable income is: *Over—*	*But not over—*	The tax is:	*of the amount over—*
$0	$18,150	.... **10%**	**$0**
18,150	73,800	**$1,815.00 + 15%**	**18,150**
73,800	148,850	**10,162.50 + 25%**	**73,800**
148,850	226,850	**28,925.00 + 28%**	**148,850**
226,850	405,100	**50,765.00 + 33%**	**226,850**
405,100	457,600	**109,587.50 + 35%**	**405,100**
457,600	....	**127,962.50 + 39.6%**	**457,600**

Schedule Y-2—If your filing status is **Married filing separately**

If your taxable income is: *Over—*	*But not over—*	The tax is:	*of the amount over—*
$0	$9,075	.... **10%**	**$0**
9,075	36,900	**$907.50 + 15%**	**9,075**
36,900	74,425	**5,081.25 + 25%**	**36,900**
74,425	113,425	**14,462.50 + 28%**	**74,425**
113,425	202,550	**25,382.50 + 33%**	**113,425**
202,550	228,800	**54,793.75 + 35%**	**202,550**
228,800	....	**63,981.25 + 39.6%**	**228,800**

Schedule Z—If your filing status is **Head of household**

If your taxable income is: *Over—*	*But not over—*	The tax is:	*of the amount over—*
$0	$12,950	.... **10%**	**$0**
12,950	49,400	**$1,295.00 + 15%**	**12,950**
49,400	127,550	**6,762.50 + 25%**	**49,400**
127,550	206,600	**26,300.00 + 28%**	**127,550**
206,600	405,100	**48,434.00 + 33%**	**206,600**
405,100	432,200	**113,939.00 + 35%**	**405,100**
432,200	....	**123,424.00 + 39.6%**	**432,200**

Combined Federal Income Tax, Employee Social Security Tax, and Employee Medicare Tax Withholding Tables

SINGLE Persons—**MONTHLY** Payroll Period

(For Wages Paid through December 2015)

And the wages are–		And the number of withholding allowances claimed is—										
At least	But less than	0	1	2	3	4	5	6	7	8	9	10
		The amount of income, social security, and Medicare taxes to be withheld is—										
$ 0	$220	7.65%	7.65%	7.65%	7.65%	7.65%	7.65%	7.65%	7.65%	7.65%	7.65%	7.65%
220	230	$20.21	$17.21	$17.21	$17.21	$17.21	$17.21	$17.21	$17.21	$17.21	$17.21	$17.21
230	240	21.98	17.98	17.98	17.98	17.98	17.98	17.98	17.98	17.98	17.98	17.98
240	250	23.74	18.74	18.74	18.74	18.74	18.74	18.74	18.74	18.74	18.74	18.74
250	260	25.51	19.51	19.51	19.51	19.51	19.51	19.51	19.51	19.51	19.51	19.51
260	270	27.27	20.27	20.27	20.27	20.27	20.27	20.27	20.27	20.27	20.27	20.27
270	280	29.04	21.04	21.04	21.04	21.04	21.04	21.04	21.04	21.04	21.04	21.04
280	290	30.80	21.80	21.80	21.80	21.80	21.80	21.80	21.80	21.80	21.80	21.80
290	300	32.57	22.57	22.57	22.57	22.57	22.57	22.57	22.57	22.57	22.57	22.57
300	320	35.72	23.72	23.72	23.72	23.72	23.72	23.72	23.72	23.72	23.72	23.72
320	340	39.25	25.25	25.25	25.25	25.25	25.25	25.25	25.25	25.25	25.25	25.25
340	360	42.78	26.78	26.78	26.78	26.78	26.78	26.78	26.78	26.78	26.78	26.78
360	380	46.31	28.31	28.31	28.31	28.31	28.31	28.31	28.31	28.31	28.31	28.31
380	400	49.84	29.84	29.84	29.84	29.84	29.84	29.84	29.84	29.84	29.84	29.84
400	420	53.37	31.37	31.37	31.37	31.37	31.37	31.37	31.37	31.37	31.37	31.37
420	440	56.90	32.90	32.90	32.90	32.90	32.90	32.90	32.90	32.90	32.90	32.90
440	460	60.43	34.43	34.43	34.43	34.43	34.43	34.43	34.43	34.43	34.43	34.43
460	480	63.96	35.96	35.96	35.96	35.96	35.96	35.96	35.96	35.96	35.96	35.96
480	500	67.49	37.49	37.49	37.49	37.49	37.49	37.49	37.49	37.49	37.49	37.49
500	520	71.02	39.02	39.02	39.02	39.02	39.02	39.02	39.02	39.02	39.02	39.02
520	540	74.55	41.55	40.55	40.55	40.55	40.55	40.55	40.55	40.55	40.55	40.55
540	560	78.08	45.08	42.08	42.08	42.08	42.08	42.08	42.08	42.08	42.08	42.08
560	580	81.61	48.61	43.61	43.61	43.61	43.61	43.61	43.61	43.61	43.61	43.61
580	600	85.14	52.14	45.14	45.14	45.14	45.14	45.14	45.14	45.14	45.14	45.14
600	640	90.43	57.43	47.43	47.43	47.43	47.43	47.43	47.43	47.43	47.43	47.43
640	680	97.49	64.49	50.49	50.49	50.49	50.49	50.49	50.49	50.49	50.49	50.49
680	720	104.55	71.55	53.55	53.55	53.55	53.55	53.55	53.55	53.55	53.55	53.55
720	760	111.61	78.61	56.61	56.61	56.61	56.61	56.61	56.61	56.61	56.61	56.61
760	800	118.67	85.67	59.67	59.67	59.67	59.67	59.67	59.67	59.67	59.67	59.67
800	840	125.73	92.73	62.73	62.73	62.73	62.73	62.73	62.73	62.73	62.73	62.73
840	880	132.79	99.79	65.79	65.79	65.79	65.79	65.79	65.79	65.79	65.79	65.79
880	920	139.85	106.85	72.85	68.85	68.85	68.85	68.85	68.85	68.85	68.85	68.85
920	960	146.91	113.91	79.91	71.91	71.91	71.91	71.91	71.91	71.91	71.91	71.91
960	1,000	154.97	120.97	86.97	74.97	74.97	74.97	74.97	74.97	74.97	74.97	74.97
1,000	1,040	164.03	128.03	94.03	78.03	78.03	78.03	78.03	78.03	78.03	78.03	78.03
1,040	1,080	173.09	135.09	101.09	81.09	81.09	81.09	81.09	81.09	81.09	81.09	81.09
1,080	1,120	182.15	142.15	108.15	84.15	84.15	84.15	84.15	84.15	84.15	84.15	84.15
1,120	1,160	191.21	149.21	115.21	87.21	87.21	87.21	87.21	87.21	87.21	87.21	87.21
1,160	1,200	200.27	156.27	122.27	90.27	90.27	90.27	90.27	90.27	90.27	90.27	90.27
1,200	1,240	209.33	163.33	129.33	96.33	93.33	93.33	93.33	93.33	93.33	93.33	93.33
1,240	1,280	218.39	170.39	136.39	103.39	96.39	96.39	96.39	96.39	96.39	96.39	96.39
1,280	1,320	227.45	177.45	143.45	110.45	99.45	99.45	99.45	99.45	99.45	99.45	99.45
1,320	1,360	236.51	186.51	150.51	117.51	102.51	102.51	102.51	102.51	102.51	102.51	102.51
1,360	1,400	245.57	195.57	157.57	124.57	105.57	105.57	105.57	105.57	105.57	105.57	105.57
1,400	1,440	254.63	204.63	164.63	131.63	108.63	108.63	108.63	108.63	108.63	108.63	108.63
1,440	1,480	263.69	213.69	171.69	138.69	111.69	111.69	111.69	111.69	111.69	111.69	111.69
1,480	1,520	272.75	222.75	178.75	145.75	114.75	114.75	114.75	114.75	114.75	114.75	114.75
1,520	1,560	281.81	231.81	185.81	152.81	119.81	117.81	117.81	117.81	117.81	117.81	117.81
1,560	1,600	290.87	240.87	192.87	159.87	126.87	120.87	120.87	120.87	120.87	120.87	120.87
1,600	1,640	299.93	249.93	199.93	166.93	133.93	123.93	123.93	123.93	123.93	123.93	123.93
1,640	1,680	308.99	258.99	208.99	173.99	140.99	126.99	126.99	126.99	126.99	126.99	126.99
1,680	1,720	318.05	268.05	218.05	181.05	148.05	130.05	130.05	130.05	130.05	130.05	130.05
1,720	1,760	327.11	277.11	227.11	188.11	155.11	133.11	133.11	133.11	133.11	133.11	133.11
1,760	1,800	336.17	286.17	236.17	195.17	162.17	136.17	136.17	136.17	136.17	136.17	136.17
1,800	1,840	345.23	295.23	245.23	202.23	169.23	139.23	139.23	139.23	139.23	139.23	139.23
1,840	1,880	354.29	304.29	254.29	209.29	176.29	142.29	142.29	142.29	142.29	142.29	142.29
1,880	1,920	363.35	313.35	263.35	216.35	183.35	149.35	145.35	145.35	145.35	145.35	145.35
1,920	1,960	372.41	322.41	272.41	223.41	190.41	156.41	148.41	148.41	148.41	148.41	148.41
1,960	2,000	381.47	331.47	281.47	231.47	197.47	163.47	151.47	151.47	151.47	151.47	151.47
2,000	2,040	390.53	340.53	290.53	240.53	204.53	170.53	154.53	154.53	154.53	154.53	154.53
2,040	2,080	399.59	349.59	299.59	249.59	211.59	177.59	157.59	157.59	157.59	157.59	157.59
2,080	2,120	408.65	358.65	308.65	258.65	218.65	184.65	160.65	160.65	160.65	160.65	160.65
2,120	2,160	417.71	367.71	317.71	267.71	225.71	191.71	163.71	163.71	163.71	163.71	163.71
2,160	2,200	426.77	376.77	326.77	276.77	232.77	198.77	166.77	166.77	166.77	166.77	166.77
2,200	2,240	435.83	385.83	335.83	285.83	239.83	205.83	172.83	169.83	169.83	169.83	169.83
2,240	2,280	444.89	394.89	344.89	294.89	246.89	212.89	179.89	172.89	172.89	172.89	172.89
2,280	2,320	453.95	403.95	353.95	303.95	253.95	219.95	186.95	175.95	175.95	175.95	175.95
2,320	2,360	463.01	413.01	363.01	313.01	263.01	227.01	194.01	179.01	179.01	179.01	179.01
2,360	2,400	472.07	422.07	372.07	322.07	272.07	234.07	201.07	182.07	182.07	182.07	182.07

Combined Federal Income Tax, Employee Social Security Tax, and Employee Medicare Tax Withholding Tables

SINGLE Persons—**MONTHLY** Payroll Period

(For Wages Paid through December 2015)

And the wages are–		And the number of withholding allowances claimed is—										
At least	But less than	0	1	2	3	4	5	6	7	8	9	10
		The amount of income, social security, and Medicare taxes to be withheld is—										
$2,400	$2,440	$481.13	$431.13	$381.13	$331.13	$281.13	$241.13	$208.13	$185.13	$185.13	$185.13	$185.13
2,440	2,480	490.19	440.19	390.19	340.19	290.19	248.19	215.19	188.19	188.19	188.19	188.19
2,480	2,520	499.25	449.25	399.25	349.25	299.25	255.25	222.25	191.25	191.25	191.25	191.25
2,520	2,560	508.31	458.31	408.31	358.31	308.31	262.31	229.31	196.31	194.31	194.31	194.31
2,560	2,600	517.37	467.37	417.37	367.37	317.37	269.37	236.37	203.37	197.37	197.37	197.37
2,600	2,640	526.43	476.43	426.43	376.43	326.43	276.43	243.43	210.43	200.43	200.43	200.43
2,640	2,680	535.49	485.49	435.49	385.49	335.49	285.49	250.49	217.49	203.49	203.49	203.49
2,680	2,720	544.55	494.55	444.55	394.55	344.55	294.55	257.55	224.55	206.55	206.55	206.55
2,720	2,760	553.61	503.61	453.61	403.61	353.61	303.61	264.61	231.61	209.61	209.61	209.61
2,760	2,800	562.67	512.67	462.67	412.67	362.67	312.67	271.67	238.67	212.67	212.67	212.67
2,800	2,840	571.73	521.73	471.73	421.73	371.73	321.73	278.73	245.73	215.73	215.73	215.73
2,840	2,880	580.79	530.79	480.79	430.79	380.79	330.79	285.79	252.79	218.79	218.79	218.79
2,880	2,920	589.85	539.85	489.85	439.85	389.85	339.85	292.85	259.85	225.85	221.85	221.85
2,920	2,960	598.91	548.91	498.91	448.91	398.91	348.91	299.91	266.91	232.91	224.91	224.91
2,960	3,000	607.97	557.97	507.97	457.97	407.97	357.97	307.97	273.97	239.97	227.97	227.97
3,000	3,040	617.03	567.03	517.03	467.03	417.03	367.03	317.03	281.03	247.03	231.03	231.03
3,040	3,080	626.09	576.09	526.09	476.09	426.09	376.09	326.09	288.09	254.09	234.09	234.09
3,080	3,120	635.15	585.15	535.15	485.15	435.15	385.15	335.15	295.15	261.15	237.15	237.15
3,120	3,160	644.21	594.21	544.21	494.21	444.21	394.21	344.21	302.21	268.21	240.21	240.21
3,160	3,200	653.27	603.27	553.27	503.27	453.27	403.27	353.27	309.27	275.27	243.27	243.27
3,200	3,240	662.33	612.33	562.33	512.33	462.33	412.33	362.33	316.33	282.33	249.33	246.33
3,240	3,280	671.39	621.39	571.39	521.39	471.39	421.39	371.39	323.39	289.39	256.39	249.39
3,280	3,320	680.45	630.45	580.45	530.45	480.45	430.45	380.45	330.45	296.45	263.45	252.45
3,320	3,360	692.51	639.51	589.51	539.51	489.51	439.51	389.51	339.51	303.51	270.51	255.51
3,360	3,400	705.57	648.57	598.57	548.57	498.57	448.57	398.57	348.57	310.57	277.57	258.57
3,400	3,440	718.63	657.63	607.63	557.63	507.63	457.63	407.63	357.63	317.63	284.63	261.63
3,440	3,480	731.69	666.69	616.69	566.69	516.69	466.69	416.69	366.69	324.69	291.69	264.69
3,480	3,520	744.75	675.75	625.75	575.75	525.75	475.75	425.75	375.75	331.75	298.75	267.75
3,520	3,560	757.81	684.81	634.81	584.81	534.81	484.81	434.81	384.81	338.81	305.81	272.81
3,560	3,600	770.87	693.87	643.87	593.87	543.87	493.87	443.87	393.87	345.87	312.87	279.87
3,600	3,640	783.93	702.93	652.93	602.93	552.93	502.93	452.93	402.93	352.93	319.93	286.93
3,640	3,680	796.99	712.99	661.99	611.99	561.99	511.99	461.99	411.99	361.99	326.99	293.99
3,680	3,720	810.05	726.05	671.05	621.05	571.05	521.05	471.05	421.05	371.05	334.05	301.05
3,720	3,760	823.11	739.11	680.11	630.11	580.11	530.11	480.11	430.11	380.11	341.11	308.11
3,760	3,800	836.17	752.17	689.17	639.17	589.17	539.17	489.17	439.17	389.17	348.17	315.17
3,800	3,840	849.23	765.23	698.23	648.23	598.23	548.23	498.23	448.23	398.23	355.23	322.23
3,840	3,880	862.29	778.29	707.29	657.29	607.29	557.29	507.29	457.29	407.29	362.29	329.29
3,880	3,920	875.35	791.35	716.35	666.35	616.35	566.35	516.35	466.35	416.35	369.35	336.35
3,920	3,960	888.41	804.41	725.41	675.41	625.41	575.41	525.41	475.41	425.41	376.41	343.41
3,960	4,000	901.47	817.47	734.47	684.47	634.47	584.47	534.47	484.47	434.47	384.47	350.47
4,000	4,040	914.53	830.53	747.53	693.53	643.53	593.53	543.53	493.53	443.53	393.53	357.53
4,040	4,080	927.59	843.59	760.59	702.59	652.59	602.59	552.59	502.59	452.59	402.59	364.59
4,080	4,120	940.65	856.65	773.65	711.65	661.65	611.65	561.65	511.65	461.65	411.65	371.65
4,120	4,160	953.71	869.71	786.71	720.71	670.71	620.71	570.71	520.71	470.71	420.71	378.71
4,160	4,200	966.77	882.77	799.77	729.77	679.77	629.77	579.77	529.77	479.77	429.77	385.77
4,200	4,240	979.83	895.83	812.83	738.83	688.83	638.83	588.83	538.83	488.83	438.83	392.83
4,240	4,280	992.89	908.89	825.89	747.89	697.89	647.89	597.89	547.89	497.89	447.89	399.89
4,280	4,320	1,005.95	921.95	838.95	756.95	706.95	656.95	606.95	556.95	506.95	456.95	406.95
4,320	4,360	1,019.01	935.01	852.01	769.01	716.01	666.01	616.01	566.01	516.01	466.01	416.01
4,360	4,400	1,032.07	948.07	865.07	782.07	725.07	675.07	625.07	575.07	525.07	475.07	425.07
4,400	4,440	1,045.13	961.13	878.13	795.13	734.13	684.13	634.13	584.13	534.13	484.13	434.13
4,440	4,480	1,058.19	974.19	891.19	808.19	743.19	693.19	643.19	593.19	543.19	493.19	443.19
4,480	4,520	1,071.25	987.25	904.25	821.25	752.25	702.25	652.25	602.25	552.25	502.25	452.25
4,520	4,560	1,084.31	1,000.31	917.31	834.31	761.31	711.31	661.31	611.31	561.31	511.31	461.31
4,560	4,600	1,097.37	1,013.37	930.37	847.37	770.37	720.37	670.37	620.37	570.37	520.37	470.37
4,600	4,640	1,110.43	1,026.43	943.43	860.43	779.43	729.43	679.43	629.43	579.43	529.43	479.43
4,640	4,680	1,123.49	1,039.49	956.49	873.49	789.49	738.49	688.49	638.49	588.49	538.49	488.49
4,680	4,720	1,136.55	1,052.55	969.55	886.55	802.55	747.55	697.55	647.55	597.55	547.55	497.55
4,720	4,760	1,149.61	1,065.61	982.61	899.61	815.61	756.61	706.61	656.61	606.61	556.61	506.61
4,760	4,800	1,162.67	1,078.67	995.67	912.67	828.67	765.67	715.67	665.67	615.67	565.67	515.67
4,800	4,840	1,175.73	1,091.73	1,008.73	925.73	841.73	774.73	724.73	674.73	624.73	574.73	524.73
4,840	4,880	1,188.79	1,104.79	1,021.79	938.79	854.79	783.79	733.79	683.79	633.79	583.79	533.79
4,880	4,920	1,201.85	1,117.85	1,034.85	951.85	867.85	792.85	742.85	692.85	642.85	592.85	542.85
4,920	4,960	1,214.91	1,130.91	1,047.91	964.91	880.91	801.91	751.91	701.91	651.91	601.91	551.91
4,960	5,000	1,227.97	1,143.97	1,060.97	977.97	893.97	810.97	760.97	710.97	660.97	610.97	560.97
5,000	5,040	1,241.03	1,157.03	1,074.03	991.03	907.03	824.03	770.03	720.03	670.03	620.03	570.03
$5,040 and over		Do not use this table. See page 48 for instructions.										

Combined Federal Income Tax, Employee Social Security Tax, and Employee Medicare Tax Withholding Tables

MARRIED Persons—**MONTHLY** Payroll Period

(For Wages Paid through December 2015)

And the wages are–		And the number of withholding allowances claimed is—										
At least	But less than	0	1	2	3	4	5	6	7	8	9	10
		The amount of income, social security, and Medicare taxes to be withheld is—										
$ 0	**$720**	7.65%	7.65%	7.65%	7.65%	7.65%	7.65%	7.65%	7.65%	7.65%	7.65%	7.65%
720	**760**	$58.61	$56.61	$56.61	$56.61	$56.61	$56.61	$56.61	$56.61	$56.61	$56.61	$56.61
760	**800**	65.67	59.67	59.67	59.67	59.67	59.67	59.67	59.67	59.67	59.67	59.67
800	**840**	72.73	62.73	62.73	62.73	62.73	62.73	62.73	62.73	62.73	62.73	62.73
840	**880**	79.79	65.79	65.79	65.79	65.79	65.79	65.79	65.79	65.79	65.79	65.79
880	**920**	86.85	68.85	68.85	68.85	68.85	68.85	68.85	68.85	68.85	68.85	68.85
920	**960**	93.91	71.91	71.91	71.91	71.91	71.91	71.91	71.91	71.91	71.91	71.91
960	**1,000**	100.97	74.97	74.97	74.97	74.97	74.97	74.97	74.97	74.97	74.97	74.97
1,000	**1,040**	108.03	78.03	78.03	78.03	78.03	78.03	78.03	78.03	78.03	78.03	78.03
1,040	**1,080**	115.09	82.09	81.09	81.09	81.09	81.09	81.09	81.09	81.09	81.09	81.09
1,080	**1,120**	122.15	89.15	84.15	84.15	84.15	84.15	84.15	84.15	84.15	84.15	84.15
1,120	**1,160**	129.21	96.21	87.21	87.21	87.21	87.21	87.21	87.21	87.21	87.21	87.21
1,160	**1,200**	136.27	103.27	90.27	90.27	90.27	90.27	90.27	90.27	90.27	90.27	90.27
1,200	**1,240**	143.33	110.33	93.33	93.33	93.33	93.33	93.33	93.33	93.33	93.33	93.33
1,240	**1,280**	150.39	117.39	96.39	96.39	96.39	96.39	96.39	96.39	96.39	96.39	96.39
1,280	**1,320**	157.45	124.45	99.45	99.45	99.45	99.45	99.45	99.45	99.45	99.45	99.45
1,320	**1,360**	164.51	131.51	102.51	102.51	102.51	102.51	102.51	102.51	102.51	102.51	102.51
1,360	**1,400**	171.57	138.57	105.57	105.57	105.57	105.57	105.57	105.57	105.57	105.57	105.57
1,400	**1,440**	178.63	145.63	112.63	108.63	108.63	108.63	108.63	108.63	108.63	108.63	108.63
1,440	**1,480**	185.69	152.69	119.69	111.69	111.69	111.69	111.69	111.69	111.69	111.69	111.69
1,480	**1,520**	192.75	159.75	126.75	114.75	114.75	114.75	114.75	114.75	114.75	114.75	114.75
1,520	**1,560**	199.81	166.81	133.81	117.81	117.81	117.81	117.81	117.81	117.81	117.81	117.81
1,560	**1,600**	206.87	173.87	140.87	120.87	120.87	120.87	120.87	120.87	120.87	120.87	120.87
1,600	**1,640**	213.93	180.93	147.93	123.93	123.93	123.93	123.93	123.93	123.93	123.93	123.93
1,640	**1,680**	220.99	187.99	154.99	126.99	126.99	126.99	126.99	126.99	126.99	126.99	126.99
1,680	**1,720**	228.05	195.05	162.05	130.05	130.05	130.05	130.05	130.05	130.05	130.05	130.05
1,720	**1,760**	235.11	202.11	169.11	135.11	133.11	133.11	133.11	133.11	133.11	133.11	133.11
1,760	**1,800**	242.17	209.17	176.17	142.17	136.17	136.17	136.17	136.17	136.17	136.17	136.17
1,800	**1,840**	249.23	216.23	183.23	149.23	139.23	139.23	139.23	139.23	139.23	139.23	139.23
1,840	**1,880**	256.29	223.29	190.29	156.29	142.29	142.29	142.29	142.29	142.29	142.29	142.29
1,880	**1,920**	263.35	230.35	197.35	163.35	145.35	145.35	145.35	145.35	145.35	145.35	145.35
1,920	**1,960**	270.41	237.41	204.41	170.41	148.41	148.41	148.41	148.41	148.41	148.41	148.41
1,960	**2,000**	277.47	244.47	211.47	177.47	151.47	151.47	151.47	151.47	151.47	151.47	151.47
2,000	**2,040**	284.53	251.53	218.53	184.53	154.53	154.53	154.53	154.53	154.53	154.53	154.53
2,040	**2,080**	291.59	258.59	225.59	191.59	158.59	157.59	157.59	157.59	157.59	157.59	157.59
2,080	**2,120**	298.65	265.65	232.65	198.65	165.65	160.65	160.65	160.65	160.65	160.65	160.65
2,120	**2,160**	305.71	272.71	239.71	205.71	172.71	163.71	163.71	163.71	163.71	163.71	163.71
2,160	**2,200**	312.77	279.77	246.77	212.77	179.77	166.77	166.77	166.77	166.77	166.77	166.77
2,200	**2,240**	319.83	286.83	253.83	219.83	186.83	169.83	169.83	169.83	169.83	169.83	169.83
2,240	**2,280**	327.89	293.89	260.89	226.89	193.89	172.89	172.89	172.89	172.89	172.89	172.89
2,280	**2,320**	336.95	300.95	267.95	233.95	200.95	175.95	175.95	175.95	175.95	175.95	175.95
2,320	**2,360**	346.01	308.01	275.01	241.01	208.01	179.01	179.01	179.01	179.01	179.01	179.01
2,360	**2,400**	355.07	315.07	282.07	248.07	215.07	182.07	182.07	182.07	182.07	182.07	182.07
2,400	**2,440**	364.13	322.13	289.13	255.13	222.13	189.13	185.13	185.13	185.13	185.13	185.13
2,440	**2,480**	373.19	329.19	296.19	262.19	229.19	196.19	188.19	188.19	188.19	188.19	188.19
2,480	**2,520**	382.25	336.25	303.25	269.25	236.25	203.25	191.25	191.25	191.25	191.25	191.25
2,520	**2,560**	391.31	343.31	310.31	276.31	243.31	210.31	194.31	194.31	194.31	194.31	194.31
2,560	**2,600**	400.37	350.37	317.37	283.37	250.37	217.37	197.37	197.37	197.37	197.37	197.37
2,600	**2,640**	409.43	359.43	324.43	290.43	257.43	224.43	200.43	200.43	200.43	200.43	200.43
2,640	**2,680**	418.49	368.49	331.49	297.49	264.49	231.49	203.49	203.49	203.49	203.49	203.49
2,680	**2,720**	427.55	377.55	338.55	304.55	271.55	238.55	206.55	206.55	206.55	206.55	206.55
2,720	**2,760**	436.61	386.61	345.61	311.61	278.61	245.61	211.61	209.61	209.61	209.61	209.61
2,760	**2,800**	445.67	395.67	352.67	318.67	285.67	252.67	218.67	212.67	212.67	212.67	212.67
2,800	**2,840**	454.73	404.73	359.73	325.73	292.73	259.73	225.73	215.73	215.73	215.73	215.73
2,840	**2,880**	463.79	413.79	366.79	332.79	299.79	266.79	232.79	218.79	218.79	218.79	218.79
2,880	**2,920**	472.85	422.85	373.85	339.85	306.85	273.85	239.85	221.85	221.85	221.85	221.85
2,920	**2,960**	481.91	431.91	381.91	346.91	313.91	280.91	246.91	224.91	224.91	224.91	224.91
2,960	**3,000**	490.97	440.97	390.97	353.97	320.97	287.97	253.97	227.97	227.97	227.97	227.97
3,000	**3,040**	500.03	450.03	400.03	361.03	328.03	295.03	261.03	231.03	231.03	231.03	231.03
3,040	**3,080**	509.09	459.09	409.09	368.09	335.09	302.09	268.09	235.09	234.09	234.09	234.09
3,080	**3,120**	518.15	468.15	418.15	375.15	342.15	309.15	275.15	242.15	237.15	237.15	237.15
3,120	**3,160**	527.21	477.21	427.21	382.21	349.21	316.21	282.21	249.21	240.21	240.21	240.21
3,160	**3,200**	536.27	486.27	436.27	389.27	356.27	323.27	289.27	256.27	243.27	243.27	243.27
3,200	**3,240**	545.33	495.33	445.33	396.33	363.33	330.33	296.33	263.33	246.33	246.33	246.33
3,240	**3,280**	554.39	504.39	454.39	404.39	370.39	337.39	303.39	270.39	249.39	249.39	249.39
3,280	**3,320**	563.45	513.45	463.45	413.45	377.45	344.45	310.45	277.45	252.45	252.45	252.45
3,320	**3,360**	572.51	522.51	472.51	422.51	384.51	351.51	317.51	284.51	255.51	255.51	255.51
3,360	**3,400**	581.57	531.57	481.57	431.57	391.57	358.57	324.57	291.57	258.57	258.57	258.57

Combined Federal Income Tax, Employee Social Security Tax, and Employee Medicare Tax Withholding Tables

MARRIED Persons—**MONTHLY** Payroll Period

(For Wages Paid through December 2015)

And the wages are–		And the number of withholding allowances claimed is—										
At least	But less than	0	1	2	3	4	5	6	7	8	9	10
		The amount of income, social security, and Medicare taxes to be withheld is—										
$3,400	**$3,440**	$590.63	$540.63	$490.63	$440.63	$398.63	$365.63	$331.63	$298.63	$265.63	$261.63	$261.63
3,440	**3,480**	599.69	549.69	499.69	449.69	405.69	372.69	338.69	305.69	272.69	264.69	264.69
3,480	**3,520**	608.75	558.75	508.75	458.75	412.75	379.75	345.75	312.75	279.75	267.75	267.75
3,520	**3,560**	617.81	567.81	517.81	467.81	419.81	386.81	352.81	319.81	286.81	270.81	270.81
3,560	**3,600**	626.87	576.87	526.87	476.87	426.87	393.87	359.87	326.87	293.87	273.87	273.87
3,600	**3,640**	635.93	585.93	535.93	485.93	435.93	400.93	366.93	333.93	300.93	276.93	276.93
3,640	**3,680**	644.99	594.99	544.99	494.99	444.99	407.99	373.99	340.99	307.99	279.99	279.99
3,680	**3,720**	654.05	604.05	554.05	504.05	454.05	415.05	381.05	348.05	315.05	283.05	283.05
3,720	**3,760**	663.11	613.11	563.11	513.11	463.11	422.11	388.11	355.11	322.11	288.11	286.11
3,760	**3,800**	672.17	622.17	572.17	522.17	472.17	429.17	395.17	362.17	329.17	295.17	289.17
3,800	**3,840**	681.23	631.23	581.23	531.23	481.23	436.23	402.23	369.23	336.23	302.23	292.23
3,840	**3,880**	690.29	640.29	590.29	540.29	490.29	443.29	409.29	376.29	343.29	309.29	295.29
3,880	**3,920**	699.35	649.35	599.35	549.35	499.35	450.35	416.35	383.35	350.35	316.35	298.35
3,920	**3,960**	708.41	658.41	608.41	558.41	508.41	458.41	423.41	390.41	357.41	323.41	301.41
3,960	**4,000**	717.47	667.47	617.47	567.47	517.47	467.47	430.47	397.47	364.47	330.47	304.47
4,000	**4,040**	726.53	676.53	626.53	576.53	526.53	476.53	437.53	404.53	371.53	337.53	307.53
4,040	**4,080**	735.59	685.59	635.59	585.59	535.59	485.59	444.59	411.59	378.59	344.59	311.59
4,080	**4,120**	744.65	694.65	644.65	594.65	544.65	494.65	451.65	418.65	385.65	351.65	318.65
4,120	**4,160**	753.71	703.71	653.71	603.71	553.71	503.71	458.71	425.71	392.71	358.71	325.71
4,160	**4,200**	762.77	712.77	662.77	612.77	562.77	512.77	465.77	432.77	399.77	365.77	332.77
4,200	**4,240**	771.83	721.83	671.83	621.83	571.83	521.83	472.83	439.83	406.83	372.83	339.83
4,240	**4,280**	780.89	730.89	680.89	630.89	580.89	530.89	480.89	446.89	413.89	379.89	346.89
4,280	**4,320**	789.95	739.95	689.95	639.95	589.95	539.95	489.95	453.95	420.95	386.95	353.95
4,320	**4,360**	799.01	749.01	699.01	649.01	599.01	549.01	499.01	461.01	428.01	394.01	361.01
4,360	**4,400**	808.07	758.07	708.07	658.07	608.07	558.07	508.07	468.07	435.07	401.07	368.07
4,400	**4,440**	817.13	767.13	717.13	667.13	617.13	567.13	517.13	475.13	442.13	408.13	375.13
4,440	**4,480**	826.19	776.19	726.19	676.19	626.19	576.19	526.19	482.19	449.19	415.19	382.19
4,480	**4,520**	835.25	785.25	735.25	685.25	635.25	585.25	535.25	489.25	456.25	422.25	389.25
4,520	**4,560**	844.31	794.31	744.31	694.31	644.31	594.31	544.31	496.31	463.31	429.31	396.31
4,560	**4,600**	853.37	803.37	753.37	703.37	653.37	603.37	553.37	503.37	470.37	436.37	403.37
4,600	**4,640**	862.43	812.43	762.43	712.43	662.43	612.43	562.43	512.43	477.43	443.43	410.43
4,640	**4,680**	871.49	821.49	771.49	721.49	671.49	621.49	571.49	521.49	484.49	450.49	417.49
4,680	**4,720**	880.55	830.55	780.55	730.55	680.55	630.55	580.55	530.55	491.55	457.55	424.55
4,720	**4,760**	889.61	839.61	789.61	739.61	689.61	639.61	589.61	539.61	498.61	464.61	431.61
4,760	**4,800**	898.67	848.67	798.67	748.67	698.67	648.67	598.67	548.67	505.67	471.67	438.67
4,800	**4,840**	907.73	857.73	807.73	757.73	707.73	657.73	607.73	557.73	512.73	478.73	445.73
4,840	**4,880**	916.79	866.79	816.79	766.79	716.79	666.79	616.79	566.79	519.79	485.79	452.79
4,880	**4,920**	925.85	875.85	825.85	775.85	725.85	675.85	625.85	575.85	526.85	492.85	459.85
4,920	**4,960**	934.91	884.91	834.91	784.91	734.91	684.91	634.91	584.91	534.91	499.91	466.91
4,960	**5,000**	943.97	893.97	843.97	793.97	743.97	693.97	643.97	593.97	543.97	506.97	473.97
5,000	**5,040**	953.03	903.03	853.03	803.03	753.03	703.03	653.03	603.03	553.03	514.03	481.03
5,040	**5,080**	962.09	912.09	862.09	812.09	762.09	712.09	662.09	612.09	562.09	521.09	488.09
5,080	**5,120**	971.15	921.15	871.15	821.15	771.15	721.15	671.15	621.15	571.15	528.15	495.15
5,120	**5,160**	980.21	930.21	880.21	830.21	780.21	730.21	680.21	630.21	580.21	535.21	502.21
5,160	**5,200**	989.27	939.27	889.27	839.27	789.27	739.27	689.27	639.27	589.27	542.27	509.27
5,200	**5,240**	998.33	948.33	898.33	848.33	798.33	748.33	698.33	648.33	598.33	549.33	516.33
5,240	**5,280**	1,007.39	957.39	907.39	857.39	807.39	757.39	707.39	657.39	607.39	557.39	523.39
5,280	**5,320**	1,016.45	966.45	916.45	866.45	816.45	766.45	716.45	666.45	616.45	566.45	530.45
5,320	**5,360**	1,025.51	975.51	925.51	875.51	825.51	775.51	725.51	675.51	625.51	575.51	537.51
5,360	**5,400**	1,034.57	984.57	934.57	884.57	834.57	784.57	734.57	684.57	634.57	584.57	544.57
5,400	**5,440**	1,043.63	993.63	943.63	893.63	843.63	793.63	743.63	693.63	643.63	593.63	551.63
5,440	**5,480**	1,052.69	1,002.69	952.69	902.69	852.69	802.69	752.69	702.69	652.69	602.69	558.69
5,480	**5,520**	1,061.75	1,011.75	961.75	911.75	861.75	811.75	761.75	711.75	661.75	611.75	565.75
5,520	**5,560**	1,070.81	1,020.81	970.81	920.81	870.81	820.81	770.81	720.81	670.81	620.81	572.81
5,560	**5,600**	1,079.87	1,029.87	979.87	929.87	879.87	829.87	779.87	729.87	679.87	629.87	579.87
5,600	**5,640**	1,088.93	1,038.93	988.93	938.93	888.93	838.93	788.93	738.93	688.93	638.93	588.93
5,640	**5,680**	1,097.99	1,047.99	997.99	947.99	897.99	847.99	797.99	747.99	697.99	647.99	597.99
5,680	**5,720**	1,107.05	1,057.05	1,007.05	957.05	907.05	857.05	807.05	757.05	707.05	657.05	607.05
5,720	**5,760**	1,116.11	1,066.11	1,016.11	966.11	916.11	866.11	816.11	766.11	716.11	666.11	616.11
5,760	**5,800**	1,125.17	1,075.17	1,025.17	975.17	925.17	875.17	825.17	775.17	725.17	675.17	625.17
5,800	**5,840**	1,134.23	1,084.23	1,034.23	984.23	934.23	884.23	834.23	784.23	734.23	684.23	634.23
5,840	**5,880**	1,143.29	1,093.29	1,043.29	993.29	943.29	893.29	843.29	793.29	743.29	693.29	643.29
5,880	**5,920**	1,152.35	1,102.35	1,052.35	1,002.35	952.35	902.35	852.35	802.35	752.35	702.35	652.35
5,920	**5,960**	1,161.41	1,111.41	1,061.41	1,011.41	961.41	911.41	861.41	811.41	761.41	711.41	661.41
5,960	**6,000**	1,170.47	1,120.47	1,070.47	1,020.47	970.47	920.47	870.47	820.47	770.47	720.47	670.47
6,000	**6,040**	1,179.53	1,129.53	1,079.53	1,029.53	979.53	929.53	879.53	829.53	779.53	729.53	679.53
6,040	**6,080**	1,188.59	1,138.59	1,088.59	1,038.59	988.59	938.59	888.59	838.59	788.59	738.59	688.59
$6,080 and over		Do not use this table. See page 48 for instructions.										

APPENDIX A

TAX RESEARCH WORKING PAPER FILE

INDEX TO TAX RESEARCH FILE*

*Most accounting firms maintain a **client file** for each of their clients. Typically, this file contains copies of client letters, memoranda-to-the-file, relevant primary and secondary authorities, and billing information. In our case, the client file for Mercy Hospital would include copies of the following: (1) the December 12 letter to Elizabeth Feghali, (2) the December 9 memorandum-to-the-file, (3) Sec. 119, (4) Reg. Sec. 1.119-1, (5) the *Kowalski* opinion, (6) the *Standard Federal Tax Reporter* annotation, and (7) pertinent billing information.

Tax Research File

As mentioned in Chapter C:1 the tax research process entails six steps.

1. Determine the facts
2. Identify the issues
3. Locate applicable authorities
4. Evaluate these authorities
5. Analyze the facts in terms of applicable authorities
6. Communicate conclusions and recommendations to others.

Let us walk through each of these steps.

Determine the Facts Assume that we have determined the facts to be as follows:

> *Mercy Hospital maintains a cafeteria on its premises. In addition, it rents space to MacDougal's, a privately owned sandwich shop. The cafeteria closes at 8:00 p.m. MacDougal's is open 24 hours. Mercy provides meal vouchers to each of its 240 medical employees to enable them to remain on call in case of emergency. The vouchers are redeemable either at the cafeteria or at MacDougal's. Although the employees are not required to remain on or near the premises during meal hours, they generally do. Elizabeth Fegali, Mercy's Chief Administrator, has approached you with the following question: Is the value of a meal voucher includible in the employees' gross income?*

At this juncture, be sure you understand the facts before proceeding further. Remember, researching the wrong facts could produce the wrong results.

Identify the Issues Identifying the issues presupposes a minimum level of proficiency in tax accounting. This proficiency will come with time, effort, and perseverance. The central issue raised by the facts is the taxability of the meal vouchers. A resolution of this issue will hinge on the resolution of other issues raised in the course of the research.

Locate Applicable Authorities For some students, this step is the most difficult in the research process. It raises the perplexing question, "Where do I begin to look?" The answer depends on the tax resources at one's disposal, as well as one's research preferences. Four rules of thumb apply:

1. *Adopt an approach with which you are comfortable, and that you are confident will produce reliable results.*
2. *Always consult the IRC and other primary authorities.*
3. *Be as thorough as possible, taking into consideration time and billing constraints.*
4. *Make sure that the authorities you consult are current.*

One approach is to conduct a topical search. Begin by consulting the index to the Internal Revenue Code (IRC). Then read the relevant IRC section(s). If the language of the IRC is vague or ambiguous, turn to the Treasury Regulations. Read the relevant regulation section that elaborates or expounds on the IRC provision. If the language of the regulation is confusing or unclear, go to a commercial tax service. Read the relevant tax service paragraphs that explain or analyze the statutory and regulatory provisions. For references to other authorities, browse through the footnotes and annotations of the service. Then, consult these authorities directly. Finally, check the currency of the authorities consulted, with the aid of a citator or status (finding) list.

If a pertinent court decision or IRS ruling has been called to your attention, consult this authority directly. Alternatively, browse through the status (finding) list of a tax service for references to tax service paragraphs that discuss this authority. Better still, consult a citator or status list for references to court opinions or rulings that cite the authority. If you subscribe to a computerized tax service, conduct a keyword, citation, contents, or topical search. (For a discussion of these types of searches, see the computerized research supplement available for download at *www.prenhall.com/phtax*.) Then, hyperlink to the authorities cited within the text of the documents retrieved. So numerous are the approaches to tax research that one is virtually free to pick and choose. All that is required of the researcher is a basic level of skill and some imagination.

Let us adopt a topical approach to the issue of the meal vouchers. If we consult an index to the IRC, we are likely to find the heading "Meals and Lodging." Below this heading are likely to be several subheadings, some pertaining to deductions, others to exclusions. Because the voucher issue pertains to an exclusion, let us browse through these subheadings. In so doing, we will notice that most of these subheadings refer to Sec. 119. If we look up this IRC section, we will see the following passage:

Sec. 119. Meals or lodging furnished for the convenience of the employer.

(a) **Meals and lodging furnished to employee, his spouse, and his dependents, pursuant to employment.**
There shall be excluded from gross income of an employee the value of any meals or lodging furnished to him . . . by, or on behalf of his employer for the convenience of the employer, but only if—

(1) in the case of meals, the meals are furnished on the business premises of the employer . . .

(b) **Special rules. For purposes of subsection (a)—**
(4) **Meals furnished to employees on business premises where meals of most employees are otherwise excludable.** All meals furnished on the business premises of an employer to such employer's employees shall be treated as furnished for the convenience of the employer if . . . more than half of the employees to whom such meals are furnished on such premises are furnished such meals for the convenience of the employer.

Section 119 appears to be applicable. It deals with meals furnished to an employee on the business premises of the employer. Our case deals with meal vouchers furnished to employees for redemption at employer-maintained and employer-rented-out facilities. But here, additional issues arise. For purposes of Sec. 119, are meal vouchers the same as "meals"? (Do not assume they are.) Are employer-maintained and employer-rented-out facilities the same as "the business premises of the employer"? (Again, do not assume they are.) And what does the IRC mean by "for the convenience of the employer"? Because the IRC offers no guidance in this respect, let us turn to the Treasury Regulations.

The applicable regulation is Reg. Sec. 1.119-1. How do we know this? Because Treasury Regulation section numbers track the IRC section numbers. Regulation Sec. 1.119-1 is the only regulation under Sec. 119. If we browse through this regulation, we will find the following provision:

(a) **Meals . . .**
(2) **Meals furnished without a charge**
(i) Meals furnished by an employer without charge to the employee will be regarded as furnished for the convenience of the employer if such meals are furnished for a substantial noncompensatory business reason of the employer . . .
(ii) (a) Meals will be regarded as furnished for a substantial noncompensatory business reason of the employer when the meals are furnished to the employee during his working hours to have the employee available for emergency call during his meal period . . .

(c) **Business premises of the employer.**
(1) **In general.** For purposes of this section, the term "business premises of the employer" generally means the place of employment of the employee . . .

Based on a reading of this provision, we might conclude that the hospital meals are furnished "for the convenience of the employer." Why? Because they are furnished for a "substantial noncompensatory business reason of the employer," namely, to have the employees available for emergency call during their meal periods. They also are furnished during the employees' working hours. Moreover, under Sec. 119(b)(4), if more than half the employees satisfy the "for the convenience of the employer" test, all employees will be regarded as satisfying the test. But are the meals furnished on "the business premises of the employer"? Under the regulation, the answer would depend. If the meals are furnished in the hospital cafeteria, they probably are furnished on "the business premises of the employer." The hospital is the place of employment of the medical employees. The cafeteria is part of the hospital. On the other hand, if the meals are furnished at MacDougal's, they probably are not furnished on "the business premises of the employer." MacDougal's is not the place of employment of the medical employees. Nor is it a part of the hospital. Thus, Reg. Sec. 1.119-1 is enlightening with respect to two statutory terms: "for the convenience of the employer" and "the business premises of the employer." However, it is obscure with respect to the third term, "meals." Because of this obscurity, let us turn to a tax service.

Although the index to CCH's *Standard Federal Tax Reporter* does not list "meal vouchers," it does list "cash allowances in lieu of meals" as a subtopic under Meals and Lodging. Are meal vouchers the same as cash meal allowances?—perhaps so; let us see. Next to the heading "cash allowances in lieu of meals" is a reference to CCH ¶7222.59. If we look up this reference, we will find the following annotation:

¶7222.59 Meal allowances.—Cash meal allowances received by an employee (state trooper) from his employer were not excludible from income. *R.J. Kowalski*, SCt, 77-2 USTC ¶9748, 434 US 77.[1]

Here we discover that, in the *Kowalski* case, the U.S. Supreme Court decided that cash meal allowances received by an employee were not excludible from the employee's income. Is the *Kowalski* case similar to our case? It might be. Let us find out. If we turn to paragraph 9748 of the second 1977 volume of *United States Tax Cases,* we will find the text of the *Kowalski* opinion. A synopsis of this opinion is present below.

In the mid-1970s, the State of New Jersey provided cash meal allowances to its state troopers. The state did not require the troopers to use the allowances exclusively for meals. Nor did it require them to consume their meals on its business premises. One trooper, Robert J. Kowalski, failed to report a portion of his allowance on his tax return. The IRS assessed a deficiency, and Kowalski took the IRS to court. In court, Kowalski argued that the meal allowances were excludible, because they were furnished "for the convenience of the employer." The IRS contended that the allowances were taxable because they amounted to compensation. The Supreme Court took up the case and sided with the IRS. The Court held that the Sec. 119 income exclusion does not apply to cash payments; it applies only to meals in kind.[2]

For the sake of illustration, let us assume that Sec. 119, Reg. Sec. 1.119-1, and the *Kowalski* case are the *only* authorities "on point." How should we evaluate them?

Evaluate Authorities Section 119 is the key authority applicable to our case. It supplies the operative rule for resolving the issue of the meal vouchers. It is vague, however, with respect to three terms: "meals," "business premises of the employer," and "for the convenience of the employer." The principal judicial authority is the *Kowalski* case. It provides an official interpretation of the term "meals." Because the U.S. Supreme Court decided *Kowalski*, the case should be assigned considerable weight. The relevant administrative authority is Reg. Sec. 1.119-1. It expounds on the terms "business premises of the employer" and "for the convenience of the employer." Because neither the IRC nor *Kowalski* explain these terms, Reg. Sec. 1.119-1 should be accorded great weight. But what if *Kowalski* had conflicted with Reg. Sec. 1.119-1? Which should be considered more authoritative? As a general rule, high court decisions "trump" the Treasury Regulations (and all IRS pronouncements for that matter). The more recent the decision, the greater its precedential weight. Had there been no Supreme Court decision and a division of appellate authority, equal weight should have been assigned to each of the appellate court decisions.

Analyze the Facts in Terms of Applicable Authorities Analyzing the facts in terms of applicable authorities involves applying the abstraction of the law to the concreteness of the facts. It entails expressing the generalities of the law in terms of the specifics of the facts. In this process, every legal condition must be satisfied for the result implied by the

[1] The researcher also might read the main *Standard Federal Tax Reporter* paragraph that discusses meals and lodging furnished by the employer (CCH ¶7222.01). Within this paragraph are likely to be references to other primary authorities.

[2] At this juncture, the researcher should consult a citator to determine whether *Kowalski* is still "good law," and to locate other authorities that cite *Kowalski.*

general rule to ensue. Thus, in our case, the conditions of furnishing "meals," "on the business premises of the employer," and "for the convenience of the employer" must be satisfied for the value of the "meals" to be excluded from the employee's income.

When analyzing the facts in terms of case law, the researcher should always draw an *analogy* between case facts and client facts. Likewise, he or she should always draw a *distinction* between case facts and client facts. Remember, under the rule of precedent, a court deciding the client's case will be bound by the precedent of cases involving *similar* facts and issues. By the same token, it will *not* be bound by the precedent of cases involving *dissimilar* facts and issues.

The most useful vehicle for analyzing client facts is the memorandum-to-the-file (see page A-6). The purpose of this document is threefold: first, it assists the researcher in recollecting transactions long transpired; second, it apprises colleagues and supervisors of the nature of one's research; third, it provides "substantial authority" for the tax treatment of a particular item. Let us analyze the facts of our case by way of a memorandum-to-the-file. Notice the format of this document; it generally tracks the steps in the research process itself.

Communicate Conclusions and Recommendations to Others For three practical reasons, research results always should be communicated to the client *in writing*. First, a written communication can be made after extensive revisions. An oral communication cannot. Second, in a written communication, the researcher can delve into the intricacies of tax law. Often, in an oral communication, he or she cannot. Third, a written communication reinforces an oral understanding. Alternatively, it brings to light an oral misunderstanding.

The written communication usually takes the form of a client letter (see page A-7). The purpose of this letter is two-fold: first, it apprises the client of the results of one's research and, second, it recommends to the client a course of action based on these results. A sample client letter is presented below. Notice the organization of this document; it is similar to that of the memorandum-to-the-file.

Memorandum-to-the-File

Date: December 9, 20X1
From: Rosina Havacek
Re: The taxability of meal vouchers furnished by Mercy Hospital to its medical staff.

Facts

[*State only the facts that are relevant to the Issue(s) and necessary for the Analysis.*] Our client, Mercy Hospital ("Mercy"), provides meal vouchers to its medical employees to enable them to remain on emergency call. The vouchers are redeemable at Mercy's onsite cafeteria and at MacDougal's, a privately owned sandwich shop. MacDougal's rents business space from the hospital. Although Mercy does not require its employees to remain on or near its premises during their meal hours, the employees generally do. Elizabeth Fegali, Mercy's Chief Administrator, has asked us to research whether the value of the meal vouchers is taxable to the employees.

Issues

[*Identify the issue(s) raised by the facts. Be specific.*] The taxability of the meal vouchers depends on three issues: first, whether the meals are furnished "for the convenience of the employer"; second, whether they are furnished "on the business premises of the employer"; and third, whether the vouchers are equivalent to cash.

Applicable Law

[*Discuss those legal principles that both strengthen and weaken the client's case. Because the primary authority for tax law is the IRC, begin with the IRC.*] Section 119 provides that the value of meals is excludible from an employee's income if the meals are furnished for the convenience of, and on the business premises of the employer. [*Discuss how administrative and/or judicial authorities expound on statutory terms.*] Under Reg. Sec. 1.119-1, a meal is furnished "for the convenience of the employer" if it is furnished for a "substantial noncompensatory business reason." A "substantial noncompensatory business reason" includes the need to have the employee available for emergency calls during his or her meal period. Under Sec. 119(b)(4), if more than half the employees satisfy the "for the convenience of the employer" test, all employees will be regarded as satisfying the test. Regulation Sec. 1.119-1 defines "business premises of the employer" as the place of employment of the employee.

[*When discussing court cases, present case facts in such a way as to enable the reader to draw an analogy with client facts.*] A Supreme Court case, *Kowalski v. CIR*, 434 U.S. 77, 77-2 USTC ¶9748, discusses what constitutes "meals" for purposes of Sec. 119. In *Kowalski*, the State of New Jersey furnished cash meal allowances to its state troopers to enable them to eat while on duty. It did not require the troopers to use the allowances exclusively for meals. Nor did it require them to consume their meals on its business premises. One trooper, R.J. Kowalski, excluded the value of his allowances from his income. The IRS disputed this treatment, and Kowalski took the IRS to Court. In Court, Kowalski argued that the allowances were excludible because they were furnished "for the convenience of the employer." The IRS contended that the allowances were taxable because they amounted to compensation. The U.S. Supreme Court took up the case and decided for the IRS. The Court held that the Sec. 119 income exlusion does not apply to payments in cash.

Analysis

[*The analysis should (a) apply applicable law to the facts and (b) address the issue(s). In this section, every proposition should be supported by either authority, logic, or plausible assumptions.*]

Issue 1: The meals provided by Mercy seem to be furnished "for the convenience of the employer." They are furnished to have employees available for emergency call during their meal breaks. This is a "substantial noncompensatory reason" within the meaning of Reg. Sec. 1.119-1.

Issue 2: Although the hospital cafeteria appears to be the "business premises of the employer," MacDougal's does not appear to be. The hospital is the place of employment of the medical employees. MacDougal's is not.

Issue 3: [*In applying case law to the facts, indicate how case facts are similar to/dissimilar from client facts. If the analysis does not support a "yes-no" answer, do not give one.*] Based on the foregoing authorities, it is unclear whether the vouchers are equivalent to cash. On the one hand, they are redeemable only in meals. Thus, they resemble meals-in-kind. On the other hand, they are redeemable at more than one institution. Thus, they resemble cash. Nor is it clear whether a court deciding this case would reach the same conclusion as the Supreme Court did in *Kowalski*. In the latter case, the State of New Jersey provided its meal allowances in the form of cash. It did not require its employees to use the allowances exclusively for meals. Nor did it require them to consume their meals on its business premises. In our case, Mercy provides its meal allowances in the form of vouchers. Thus, it indirectly requires its employees to use the allowances exclusively for meals. On the other hand, it does not require them to consume their meals on its business premises.

Conclusion

[*The conclusion should (a) logically flow from the analysis, and (b) address the issue(s).*] Although it appears that the meals acquired by voucher in the hospital cafeteria are furnished "for the convenience of the employer" and "on the business premises of the employer," it is unclear whether the vouchers are equivalent to cash. If they *are* equivalent to cash, *or* if they are redeemed at MacDougal's, their value is likely to be taxable to the employees. On the other hand, if they are not equivalent to cash, *and* they are redeemed only in the hospital cafeteria, their value is likely to be excludible.

Professional Accounting Associates
2701 First City Plaza
Suite 905
Dallas, Texas 75019

December 12, 20X1

Elizabeth Feghali, Chief Administrator
Mercy Hospital
22650 West Haven Drive
Arlington, Texas 75527

Dear Ms. Feghali:

[*Introduction. Set a cordial tone.*] It was great to see you at last Thursday's football game. If not for that last minute fumble, the Longhorns might have taken the Big 12 Conference championship!

[*Issue/Purpose.*] In our meeting of December 6, you asked us to research whether the value of the meal vouchers that Mercy provides to its medical employees is taxable to the employees. [*Short Answer.*] I regret to inform you that if the vouchers are redeemed at MacDougal's, their value is likely to be taxable to the employees. On the other hand, if the vouchers are redeemed in the hospital cafeteria, their value is likely to be excludible from the employee's income. [*The remainder of the letter should elaborate, support, and qualify this answer.*]

[*Steps taken in deriving conclusion.*] In reaching this conclusion, we consulted relevant provisions of the Internal Revenue Code ("IRC"), applicable Treasury Regulations under the IRC, and a pertinent Supreme Court case. In addition, we reviewed the documents on employee benefits that you submitted to us at our earlier meeting.

[*Facts. State only the facts that are relevant to the issue and necessary for the analysis.*] The facts as we understand them are as follows: Mercy provides meal vouchers to its medical employees to enable them to eat while on emergency call. The vouchers are redeemable either in the hospital cafeteria or at MacDougal's. MacDougal's is a privately owned institution that rents business space from the hospital. Although Mercy's employees are not required to remain on or near the premises during their meal hours, they generally do.

[*Applicable law. State, do not interpret.*] Under the IRC, the value of meals is excludible from an employee's income if two conditions are met: first, the meals are furnished "for the convenience of the employer" and second, they are provided "on the business premises of the employer." Although the IRC does not explain what is meant by "for the convenience of the employer," "business premises of the employer," and "meals," other authorities do. Specifically, the Treasury Regulations define "business premises of the employer" to be the place of employment of the employees. The regulations state that providing meals during work hours to have an employee available for emergency calls is "for the convenience of the employer." Moreover, under the IRC, if more than half the employees satisfy the "for the convenience of the employer" test, all the employees will be regarded as satisfying the test. The Supreme Court has interpreted "meals" to mean food-in-kind. The Court has held that cash allowances do not qualify as "meals."

[*Analysis. Express the generalities of applicable law in terms of the specifics of the facts.*] Clearly, the meals furnished by Mercy are "for the convenience of the employer." They are furnished during the employees' work hours to have the employees available for emergency call. Although the meals provided in the hospital cafeteria appear to be furnished "on the business premises of the employer," the meals provided at MacDougal's do not appear to be. The hospital is the place of employment of the medical employees. MacDougal's is not. What is unclear is whether the meal vouchers are equivalent to food-in-kind. On the one hand, they are redeemable at more than one institution and thus resemble cash allowances. On the other hand, they are redeemable only in meals and thus resemble food-in-kind.

[*Conclusion/Recommendation.*] Because of this lack of clarity, we suggest that you modify your employee benefits plan to allow for the provision of meals-in-kind exclusively in the hospital cafeteria. In this way, you will dispel any doubt that Mercy is furnishing "meals," "for the convenience of the employer," "on the premises of the employer."

[*Closing/Follow Up.*] Please call me at 475-2020 if you have any questions concerning this conclusion. May I suggest that we meet next week to discuss the possibility of revising your employee benefits plan.

Very truly yours,
Professional Accounting Associates

By: Rosina Havacek, Junior Associate

APPENDIX

B TAX FORMS

Note: Because of the availability of tax forms from many sources, only a limited number of forms are reprinted in this textbook. All federal forms are available from the Internal Revenue Service, either in paper form or from the IRS Web site, http://www.irs.gov

Form **706** (Rev. August 2013) Department of the Treasury Internal Revenue Service

United States Estate (and Generation-Skipping Transfer) Tax Return

▶ Estate of a citizen or resident of the United States (see instructions). To be filed for decedents dying after December 31, 2012.
▶ Information about Form 706 and its separate instructions is at *www.irs.gov/form706.*

OMB No. 1545-0015

Part 1—Decedent and Executor

1a Decedent's first name and middle initial (and maiden name, if any)	Herman
1b Decedent's last name	Estes
2 Decedent's social security no.	XXX XX XXXX
3a City, town, or post office; county; state or province; country; and ZIP or foreign postal code.	County, FL 22222
3b Year domicile established	1941
4 Date of birth	1935
5 Date of death	10-13-2014
6a Name of executor (see instructions)	John Johnson
6b Executor's address (number and street including apartment or suite no.; city, town, or post office; state or province; country; and ZIP or foreign postal code) and phone no.	10 Main Place City, FL 22222 Phone no.
6c Executor's social security number (see instructions)	123 45 6789
6d If there are multiple executors, check here ☐ and attach a list showing the names, addresses, telephone numbers, and SSNs of the additional executors.	
7a Name and location of court where will was probated or estate administered	
7b Case number	
8 If decedent died testate, check here ▶ ☒ and attach a certified copy of the will.	
9 If you extended the time to file this Form 706, check here ▶ ☐	
10 If Schedule R-1 is attached, check here ▶ ☐	
11 If you are estimating the value of assets included in the gross estate on line 1 pursuant to the special rule of Reg. section 20.2010-2T(a) (7)(ii), check here ▶ ☐	

Part 2—Tax Computation

Line	Description		Amount		Amount
1	Total gross estate less exclusion (from Part 5—Recapitulation, item 13)			1	6,038,450
2	Tentative total allowable deductions (from Part 5—Recapitulation, item 24)			2	1,196,700
3a	Tentative taxable estate (subtract line 2 from line 1)			3a	4,841,750
b	State death tax deduction			3b	
c	Taxable estate (subtract line 3b from line 3a)			3c	4,841,750
4	Adjusted taxable gifts (see instructions)			4	6,700,000
5	Add lines 3c and 4			5	11,541,750
6	Tentative tax on the amount on line 5 from Table A in the instructions			6	4,562,500
7	Total gift tax paid or payable (see instructions)			7	580,000
8	Gross estate tax (subtract line 7 from line 6)			8	3,982,500
9a	Basic exclusion amount	9a	5,340,000		
9b	Deceased spousal unused exclusion (DSUE) amount from predeceased spouse(s), if any (from Section D, Part 6—Portability of Deceased Spousal Unused Exclusion).	9b			
9c	Applicable exclusion amount (add lines 9a and 9b)	9c	5,340,000		
9d	Applicable credit amount (tentative tax on the amount in 9c from Table A in the instructions)	9d	2,081,800		
10	Adjustment to applicable credit amount (May not exceed $6,000. See instructions.)	10			
11	Allowable applicable credit amount (subtract line 10 from line 9d)			11	2,081,800
12	Subtract line 11 from line 8 (but do not enter less than zero)			12	1,900,700
13	Credit for foreign death taxes (from Schedule P). (Attach Form(s) 706-CE.)	13			
14	Credit for tax on prior transfers (from Schedule Q)	14			
15	Total credits (add lines 13 and 14)			15	
16	Net estate tax (subtract line 15 from line 12)			16	1,900,700
17	Generation-skipping transfer (GST) taxes payable (from Schedule R, Part 2, line 10)			17	
18	Total transfer taxes (add lines 16 and 17)			18	1,900,700
19	Prior payments (explain in an attached statement)			19	
20	Balance due (or overpayment) (subtract line 19 from line 18)			20	1,900,700

Under penalties of perjury, I declare that I have examined this return, including accompanying schedules and statements, and to the best of my knowledge and belief, it is true, correct, and complete. Declaration of preparer other than the executor is based on all information of which preparer has any knowledge.

Sign Here

▶ *John Johnson* Signature of executor ▶ 5-14-15 Date

▶ Signature of executor ▶ Date

Paid Preparer Use Only

Print/Type preparer's name: Mary Wilson, CPA	Preparer's signature: *Mary Wilson, CPA*	Date: 5-12-15	Check ☒ if self-employed	PTIN
Firm's name ▶ Mary Wilson, CPA			Firm's EIN ▶	
Firm's address ▶ 15 Main Place, City, ST 22222			Phone no.	

For Privacy Act and Paperwork Reduction Act Notice, see instructions. Cat. No. 20548R Form **706** (Rev. 8-2013)

Note: Pages not pertinent to the tax consequences are omitted.

See the Comprehensive Illustration on text page C:13-25 for tax form facts.

Form 706 (Rev. 8-2013)

Estate of: Herman Estes | **Decedent's social security number** XXX XX XXXX

Part 3—Elections by the Executor

Note. For information on electing portability of the decedent's DSUE amount, including how to opt out of the election, see Part 6—Portability of Deceased Spousal Unused Exclusion.

Note. Some of the following elections may require the posting of bonds or liens.

Please check "Yes" or "No" box for each question (see instructions).		Yes	No
1 Do you elect alternate valuation?	1		X
2 Do you elect special-use valuation? If "Yes," you must complete and attach Schedule A-1	2		X
3 Do you elect to pay the taxes in installments as described in section 6166? If "Yes," you must attach the additional information described in the instructions. **Note. By electing section 6166 installment payments, you may be required to provide security for estate tax deferred under section 6166 and interest in the form of a surety bond or a section 6324A lien.**	3		X
4 Do you elect to postpone the part of the taxes due to a reversionary or remainder interest as described in section 6163?	4		X

Part 4—General Information

Note. Please attach the necessary supplemental documents. **You must attach the death certificate.** (See instructions)

Authorization to receive confidential tax information under Reg. section 601.504(b)(2)(i); to act as the estate's representative before the IRS; and to make written or oral presentations on behalf of the estate:

Name of representative (print or type)	State	Address (number, street, and room or suite no., city, state, and ZIP code)
Mary Wilson	ST	15 Main Place, City, ST 22222

I declare that I am the ☐ attorney/ ☒ certified public accountant/ ☐ enrolled agent (check the applicable box) for the executor. I am not under suspension or disbarment from practice before the Internal Revenue Service and am qualified to practice in the state shown above.

Signature	CAF number	Date	Telephone number
Mary Wilson, CPA		5-12-15	

1 Death certificate number and issuing authority (attach a copy of the death certificate to this return).
1246, County Coroner

2 Decedent's business or occupation. If retired, check here ► ☒ and state decedent's former business or occupation.
Executive

3a Marital status of the decedent at time of death:
☒ Married ☐ Widow/widower ☐ Single ☐ Legally separated ☐ Divorced

3b For all prior marriages, list the name and SSN of the former spouse, the date the marriage ended, and whether the marriage ended by annulment, divorce, or death. Attach additional statements of the same size if necessary.

4a Surviving spouse's name	4b Social security number	4c Amount received (see instructions)
Ann Estes	XXX XX XXXX	1,070,000

5 Individuals (other than the surviving spouse), trusts, or other estates who receive benefits from the estate (do not include charitable beneficiaries shown in Schedule O) (see instructions).

Name of individual, trust, or estate receiving $5,000 or more	Identifying number	Relationship to decedent	Amount (see instructions)
Johnny Estes	XXX-XX-XXXX	Son	1,290,925
Billy Estes	XXX-XX-XXXX	Son	1,090,925
Daughter, Dorothy Estes, received the corpus in the special power of appointment trust created by Amelia Estes			
All unascertainable beneficiaries and those who receive less than $5,000 ►			
Total			2,381,850*

If you answer "Yes" to any of the following questions, you must attach additional information as described.	Yes	No
6 Is the estate filing a protective claim for refund? If "Yes," complete and attach two copies of Schedule PC for each claim.		X
7 Does the gross estate contain any section 2044 property (qualified terminable interest property (QTIP) from a prior gift or estate)? (see instructions)		X
8a Have federal gift tax returns ever been filed? If "Yes," attach copies of the returns, if available, and furnish the following information:	X	
b Period(s) covered: 1978, 2013 — c Internal Revenue office(s) where filed: Cincinnati, OH		
9a Was there any insurance on the decedent's life that is not included on the return as part of the gross estate?		X
b Did the decedent own any insurance on the life of another that is not included in the gross estate?		X

* $4,841,750 – $559,200 – $1,900,700

Form 706 (Rev. 8-2013)

Estate of: Herman Estes

Decedent's social security number: XXX XX XXXX

Part 4—General Information *(continued)*

If you answer "Yes" to any of the following questions, you must attach additional information as described.		Yes	No
10	Did the decedent at the time of death own any property as a joint tenant with right of survivorship in which **(a)** one or more of the other joint tenants was someone other than the decedent's spouse, and **(b)** less than the full value of the property is included on the return as part of the gross estate? If "Yes," you must complete and attach Schedule E		X
11a	Did the decedent, at the time of death, own any interest in a partnership (for example, a family limited partnership), an unincorporated business, or a limited liability company; or own any stock in an inactive or closely held corporation?		X
b	If "Yes," was the value of **any** interest owned (from above) discounted on this estate tax return? If "Yes," see the instructions on reporting the total accumulated or effective discounts taken on Schedule F or G		
12	Did the decedent make any transfer described in sections 2035, 2036, 2037, or 2038? (see instructions) If "Yes," you must complete and attach Schedule G	X	
13a	Were there in existence at the time of the decedent's death any trusts created by the decedent during his or her lifetime?		X
b	Were there in existence at the time of the decedent's death any trusts not created by the decedent under which the decedent possessed any power, beneficial interest, or trusteeship?	X	
c	Was the decedent receiving income from a trust created after October 22, 1986, by a parent or grandparent?	X	
	If "Yes," was there a GST taxable termination (under section 2612) on the death of the decedent?		X
d	If there was a GST taxable termination (under section 2612), attach a statement to explain. Provide a copy of the trust or will creating the trust, and give the name, address, and phone number of the current trustee(s).		
e	Did the decedent at any time during his or her lifetime transfer or sell an interest in a partnership, limited liability company, or closely held corporation to a trust described in lines 13a or 13b?		X
	If "Yes," provide the EIN for this transferred/sold item. ▶		
14	Did the decedent ever possess, exercise, or release any general power of appointment? If "Yes," you must complete and attach Schedule H		X
15	Did the decedent have an interest in or a signature or other authority over a financial account in a foreign country, such as a bank account, securities account, or other financial account?		X
16	Was the decedent, immediately before death, receiving an annuity described in the "General" paragraph of the instructions for Schedule I or a private annuity? If "Yes," you must complete and attach Schedule I	X	
17	Was the decedent ever the beneficiary of a trust for which a deduction was claimed by the estate of a predeceased spouse under section 2056(b)(7) and which is not reported on this return? If "Yes," attach an explanation		X

Part 5—Recapitulation.

Note. If estimating the value of one or more assets pursuant to the special rule of Reg. section 20.2010-2T(a)(7)(ii), enter on both lines 10 and 23 the amount noted in the instructions for the corresponding range of values. (See instructions for details.)

Item no.	Gross estate		Alternate value	Value at date of death
1	Schedule A—Real Estate	1		325,000
2	Schedule B—Stocks and Bonds	2		4,400,000
3	Schedule C—Mortgages, Notes, and Cash	3		94,250
4	Schedule D—Insurance on the Decedent's Life (attach Form(s) 712)	4		200,000
5	Schedule E—Jointly Owned Property (attach Form(s) 712 for life insurance)	5		220,000
6	Schedule F—Other Miscellaneous Property (attach Form(s) 712 for life insurance)	6		
7	Schedule G—Transfers During Decedent's Life (att. Form(s) 712 for life insurance)	7		559,200
8	Schedule H—Powers of Appointment	8		
9	Schedule I—Annuities	9		240,000
10	Estimated value of assets subject to the special rule of Reg. section 20.2010-2T(a)(7)(ii)	10		
11	Total gross estate (add items 1 through 10)	11		6,038,450
12	Schedule U—Qualified Conservation Easement Exclusion	12		
13	Total gross estate less exclusion (subtract item 12 from item 11). Enter here and on line 1 of Part 2—Tax Computation	13		6,038,450

Item no.	Deductions		Amount
14	Schedule J—Funeral Expenses and Expenses Incurred in Administering Property Subject to Claims	14	85,000
15	Schedule K—Debts of the Decedent	15	31,700
16	Schedule K—Mortgages and Liens	16	
17	Total of items 14 through 16	17	116,700
18	Allowable amount of deductions from item 17 (see the instructions for item 18 of the Recapitulation)	18	116,700
19	Schedule L—Net Losses During Administration	19	
20	Schedule L—Expenses Incurred in Administering Property Not Subject to Claims	20	
21	Schedule M—Bequests, etc., to Surviving Spouse	21	1,070,000
22	Schedule O—Charitable, Public, and Similar Gifts and Bequests	22	10,000
23	Estimated value of deductible assets subject to the special rule of Reg. section 20.2010-2T(a)(7)(ii)	23	
24	Tentative total allowable deductions (add items 18 through 23). Enter here and on line 2 of the Tax Computation	24	1,196,700

Form 706 (Rev. 8-2013)

Estate of: Herman Estes

Decedent's social security number XXX XX XXXX

Part 6—Portability of Deceased Spousal Unused Exclusion (DSUE)

Portability Election

A decedent with a surviving spouse elects portability of the deceased spousal unused exclusion (DSUE) amount, if any, by completing and timely-filing this return. No further action is required to elect portability of the DSUE amount to allow the surviving spouse to use the decedent's DSUE amount.

Section A. Opting Out of Portability

The estate of a decedent with a surviving spouse may opt out of electing portability of the DSUE amount. Check here and do not complete Sections B and C of Part 6 only if the estate opts **NOT** to elect portability of the DSUE amount. ☐

Section B. QDOT

	Yes	No
Are any assets of the estate being transferred to a qualified domestic trust (QDOT)?		X

If "Yes," the DSUE amount portable to a surviving spouse (calculated in Section C, below) is preliminary and shall be redetermined at the time of the final distribution or other taxable event imposing estate tax under section 2056A. See instructions for more details.

Section C. DSUE Amount Portable to the Surviving Spouse (To be completed by the estate of a decedent making a portability election.)

Complete the following calculation to determine the DSUE amount that can be transferred to the surviving spouse.

1	Enter the amount from line 9c, Part 2—Tax Computation	1	
2	Reserved	2	
3	Enter the value of the cumulative lifetime gifts on which tax was paid or payable (see instructions)	3	
4	Add lines 1 and 3	4	
5	Enter amount from line 10, Part 2—Tax Computation	5	
6	Divide amount on line 5 by 40% (0.40) (do not enter less than zero)	6	
7	Subtract line 6 from line 4	7	
8	Enter the amount from line 5, Part 2– Tax Computation	8	
9	Subtract line 8 from line 7 (do not enter less than zero)	9	
10	DSUE amount portable to surviving spouse (Enter lesser of line 9 or line 9a, Part 2 – Tax Computation)	10	

Section D. DSUE Amount Received from Predeceased Spouse(s) (To be completed by the estate of a deceased surviving spouse with DSUE amount from predeceased spouse(s))

Provide the following information to determine the DSUE amount received from deceased spouses.

A Name of Deceased Spouse (dates of death after December 31, 2010, only)	B Date of Death (enter as mm/dd/yy)	C Portability Election Made? Yes	C No	D If "Yes," DSUE Amount Received from Spouse	E DSUE Amount Applied by Decedent to Lifetime Gifts	F Year of Form 709 Reporting Use of DSUE Amount Listed in col E	G Remaining DSUE Amount, if any (subtract col. E from col. D)
Part 1 — DSUE RECEIVED FROM LAST DECEASED SPOUSE							
Part 2 — DSUE RECEIVED FROM OTHER PREDECEASED SPOUSE(S) AND USED BY DECEDENT							
Total (for all DSUE amounts from predeceased spouse(s) applied)							

Add the amount from Part 1, column D and the total from Part 2, column E. Enter the result on line 9b, Part 2—Tax Computation ▶

Note: The DSUE is not available.

Form 706 (Rev. 8-2013)

Estate of: Herman Estes

Decedent's social security number XXX XX XXXX

SCHEDULE A—Real Estate

- For jointly owned property that must be disclosed on Schedule E, see instructions.
- Real estate that is part of a sole proprietorship should be shown on Schedule F.
- Real estate that is included in the gross estate under sections 2035, 2036, 2037, or 2038 should be shown on Schedule G.
- Real estate that is included in the gross estate under section 2041 should be shown on Schedule H.
- If you elect section 2032A valuation, you must complete Schedule A and Schedule A-1.

Note. If the value of the gross estate, together with the amount of adjusted taxable gifts, is less than the basic exclusion amount and the Form 706 is being filed solely to elect portability of the DSUE amount, consideration should be given as to whether you are required to report the value of assets eligible for the marital or charitable deduction on this schedule. See the instructions and Reg. section 20.2010-2T (a)(7)(ii) for more information. If you are not required to report the value of an asset, identify the property but make no entries in the last three columns.

Item number	Description	Alternate valuation date	Alternate value	Value at date of death
1	Personal residence, house and lot, located at 105 Elm Court, City, ST			325,000
	Total from continuation schedules or additional statements attached to this schedule . . .			
	TOTAL. (Also enter on Part 5—Recapitulation, page 3, at item 1.)			325,000

(If more space is needed, attach the continuation schedule from the end of this package or additional statements of the same size.)

Form 706 (Rev. 8-2013)

Estate of: Herman Estes

Decedent's social security number XXX XX XXXX

SCHEDULE B—Stocks and Bonds

(For jointly owned property that must be disclosed on Schedule E, see instructions.)

Note. If the value of the gross estate, together with the amount of adjusted taxable gifts, is less than the basic exclusion amount and the Form 706 is being filed solely to elect portability of the DSUE amount, consideration should be given as to whether you are required to report the value of assets eligible for the marital or charitable deduction on this schedule. See the instructions and Reg. section 20.2010-2T (a)(7)(ii) for more information. If you are not required to report the value of an asset, identify the property but make no entries in the last four columns.

Item number	Description, including face amount of bonds or number of shares and par value for identification. Give CUSIP number. If trust, partnership, or closely held entity, give EIN.	CUSIP number or EIN, where applicable	Unit value	Alternate valuation date	Alternate value	Value at date of death
1	Stock in Ajax Corporation 1,000 shares, $10 per share		4,400			4,400,000
	Total from continuation schedules (or additional statements) attached to this schedule					
	TOTAL. (Also enter on Part 5—Recapitulation, page 3, at item 2.)					4,400,000

(If more space is needed, attach the continuation schedule from the end of this package or additional statements of the same size.)

Form 706 (Rev. 8-2013)

Estate of: Herman Estes

Decedent's social security number XXX XX XXXX

SCHEDULE C—Mortgages, Notes, and Cash

(For jointly owned property that must be disclosed on Schedule E, see instructions.)

Note. If the value of the gross estate, together with the amount of adjusted taxable gifts, is less than the basic exclusion amount and the Form 706 is being filed solely to elect portability of the DSUE amount, consideration should be given as to whether you are required to report the value of assets eligible for the marital or charitable deduction on this schedule. See the instructions and Reg. section 20.2010-2T (a)(7)(ii) for more information. If you are not required to report the value of an asset, identify the property but make no entries in the last three columns.

Item number	Description	Alternate valuation date	Alternate value	Value at date of death
1	Checking account			19,250
2	Savings account (includes accrued interest through date of death)			75,000
	Total from continuation schedules (or additional statements) attached to this schedule . .			
	TOTAL. (Also enter on Part 5—Recapitulation, page 3, at item 3.)			94,250

(If more space is needed, attach the continuation schedule from the end of this package or additional statements of the same size.)

Form 706 (Rev. 8-2013)

Estate of: Herman Estes

Decedent's social security number XXX XX XXXX

SCHEDULE D—Insurance on the Decedent's Life

You must list all policies on the life of the decedent and attach a Form 712 for each policy.

Note. If the value of the gross estate, together with the amount of adjusted taxable gifts, is less than the basic exclusion amount and the Form 706 is being filed solely to elect portability of the DSUE amount, consideration should be given as to whether you are required to report the value of assets eligible for the marital or charitable deduction on this schedule. See the instructions and Reg. section 20.2010-2T (a)(7)(ii) for more information. If you are not required to report the value of an asset, identify the property but make no entries in the last three columns.

Item number	Description	Alternate valuation date	Alternate value	Value at date of death
1	Life insurance policy No. 123-A issued by the Life Insurance Company of Ohio. Beneficiary — Johnny Estes			200,000
	Total from continuation schedules (or additional statements) attached to this schedule . .			
	TOTAL. (Also enter on Part 5—Recapitulation, page 3, at item 4.)			200,000

(If more space is needed, attach the continuation schedule from the end of this package or additional statements of the same size.)

Form 706 (Rev. 8-2013)

Estate of: Herman Estes | **Decedent's social security number** XXX XX XXXX

SCHEDULE E—Jointly Owned Property

(If you elect section 2032A valuation, you must complete Schedule E and Schedule A-1.)

PART 1. Qualified Joint Interests—Interests Held by the Decedent and His or Her Spouse as the Only Joint Tenants (Section 2040(b)(2))

Note. If the value of the gross estate, together with the amount of adjusted taxable gifts, is less than the basic exclusion amount and the Form 706 is being filed solely to elect portability of the DSUE amount, consideration should be given as to whether you are required to report the value of assets eligible for the marital or charitable deduction on this schedule. See the instructions and Reg. section 20.2010-2T (a)(7)(ii) for more information. If you are not required to report the value of an asset, identify the property but make no entries in the last three columns.

Item number	Description. For securities, give CUSIP number. If trust, partnership, or closely held entity, give EIN.	CUSIP number or EIN, where applicable	Alternate valuation date	Alternate value	Value at date of death
1	Land				440,000
	Total from continuation schedules (or additional statements) attached to this schedule				
1a	Totals		1a		440,000
1b	Amounts included in gross estate (one-half of line **1a**)		1b		220,000

PART 2. All Other Joint Interests

2a State the name and address of each surviving co-tenant. If there are more than three surviving co-tenants, list the additional co-tenants on an attached statement.

	Name	Address (number and street, city, state, and ZIP code)
A.		
B.		
C.		

Item number	Enter letter for co-tenant	Description (including alternate valuation date if any). For securities, give CUSIP number. If trust, partnership, or closely held entity, give EIN	CUSIP number or EIN, where applicable	Percentage includible	Includible alternate value	Includible value at date of death
1						
		Total from continuation schedules (or additional statements) attached to this schedule				
2b		Total other joint interests		2b		
3		**Total includible joint interests** (add lines 1b and 2b). Also enter on Part 5—Recapitulation, page 3, at item 5		3		220,000

(If more space is needed, attach the continuation schedule from the end of this package or additional statements of the same size.)

Form 706 (Rev. 8-2013)

Estate of: Herman Estes	Decedent's social security number XXX XX XXXX

SCHEDULE G—Transfers During Decedent's Life

(If you elect section 2032A valuation, you must complete Schedule G and Schedule A-1.)

Note. If the value of the gross estate, together with the amount of adjusted taxable gifts, is less than the basic exclusion amount and the Form 706 is being filed solely to elect portability of the DSUE amount, consideration should be given as to whether you are required to report the value of assets eligible for the marital or charitable deduction on this schedule. See the instructions and Reg. section 20.2010-2T (a)(7)(ii) for more information. If you are not required to report the value of an asset, identify the property but make no entries in the last three columns.

Item number	Description. For securities, give CUSIP number. If trust, partnership, or closely held entity, give EIN	Alternate valuation date	Alternate value	Value at date of death
A.	Gift tax paid or payable by the decedent or the estate for all gifts made by the decedent or his or her spouse within 3 years before the decedent's death (section 2035(b))	X X X X X		559,200
B.	Transfers includible under sections 2035(a), 2036, 2037, or 2038:			
	Total from continuation schedules (or additional statements) attached to this schedule . .			
	TOTAL. (Also enter on Part 5—Recapitulation, page 3, at item 7.)			559,200

SCHEDULE H—Powers of Appointment

(Include "5 and 5 lapsing" powers (section 2041(b)(2)) held by the decedent.)
(If you elect section 2032A valuation, you must complete Schedule H and Schedule A-1.)

Note. If the value of the gross estate, together with the amount of adjusted taxable gifts, is less than the basic exclusion amount and the Form 706 is being filed solely to elect portability of the DSUE amount, consideration should be given as to whether you are required to report the value of assets eligible for the marital or charitable deduction on this schedule. See the instructions and Reg. section 20.2010-2T (a)(7)(ii) for more information. If you are not required to report the value of an asset, identify the property but make no entries in the last three columns.

Item number	Description	Alternate valuation date	Alternate value	Value at date of death
1				
	Total from continuation schedules (or additional statements) attached to this schedule . . .			
	TOTAL. (Also enter on Part 5—Recapitulation, page 3, at item 8.)			

(If more space is needed, attach the continuation schedule from the end of this package or additional statements of the same size.)

Form 706 (Rev. 8-2013)

Estate of: Herman Estes

Decedent's social security number XXX XX XXXX

SCHEDULE I—Annuities

Note. Generally, no exclusion is allowed for the estates of decedents dying after December 31, 1984 (see instructions).

Note. If the value of the gross estate, together with the amount of adjusted taxable gifts, is less than the basic exclusion amount and the Form 706 is being filed solely to elect portability of the DSUE amount, consideration should be given as to whether you are required to report the value of assets eligible for the marital or charitable deduction on this schedule. See the instructions and Reg. section 20.2010-2T (a)(7)(ii) for more information. If you are not required to report the value of an asset, identify the property but make no entries in the last three columns.

		Yes	No
A	Are you excluding from the decedent's gross estate the value of a lump-sum distribution described in section 2039(f)(2) (as in effect before its repeal by the Deficit Reduction Act of 1984)? . . . . If "Yes," you must attach the information required by the instructions.		X

Item number	Description. Show the entire value of the annuity before any exclusions	Alternate valuation date	Includible alternate value	Includible value at date of death
1	Qualified pension plan issued by Buckeye Corporation. Beneficiary — Ann Estes, spouse			240,000
	Total from continuation schedules (or additional statements) attached to this schedule . .			
	TOTAL. (Also enter on Part 5—Recapitulation, page 3, at item 9.)			240,000

(If more space is needed, attach the continuation schedule from the end of this package or additional statements of the same size.)

Form 706 (Rev. 8-2013)

Estate of: Herman Estes

Decedent's social security number XXX XX XXXX

SCHEDULE J—Funeral Expenses and Expenses Incurred in Administering Property Subject to Claims

► Use Schedule PC to make a protective claim for refund due to an expense not currently deductible.
For such a claim, report the expense on Schedule J but without a value in the last column.

Note. Do not list expenses of administering property not subject to claims on this schedule. To report those expenses, see instructions.

If executors' commissions, attorney fees, etc., are claimed and allowed as a deduction for estate tax purposes, they are not allowable as a deduction in computing the taxable income of the estate for federal income tax purposes. They are allowable as an income tax deduction on Form 1041, U.S. Income Tax Return for Estates and Trusts, if a waiver is filed to forgo the deduction on Form 706 (see Instructions for Form 1041).

Are you aware of any actual or potential reimbursement to the estate for any expense claimed as a deduction on this schedule? . . . . Yes / No

If "Yes," attach a statement describing the expense(s) subject to potential reimbursement. (see instructions)

Item number	Description	Expense amount	Total amount
	A. Funeral expenses:	15,000	
	Total funeral expenses . . . . ►		15,000

B. Administration expenses:

1 Executors' commissions—amount estimated/agreed upon/paid. (Strike out the words that do not apply.)	
2 Attorney fees—amount estimated/agreed upon/paid. (Strike out the words that do not apply.) . .	70,000
3 Accountant fees—amount estimated/agreed upon/paid. (Strike out the words that do not apply.) .	

Item number	Description	Expense amount	Total amount
	4 Miscellaneous expenses:		
	Total miscellaneous expenses from continuation schedules (or additional statements) attached to this schedule		
	Total miscellaneous expenses . . . . ►		
	TOTAL. (Also enter on Part 5—Recapitulation, page 3, at item 14.) . . . . ►		85,000

(If more space is needed, attach the continuation schedule from the end of this package or additional statements of the same size.)

Form 706 (Rev. 8-2013)

Estate of: Herman Estes

Decedent's social security number XXX XX XXXX

SCHEDULE K—Debts of the Decedent, and Mortgages and Liens

▶ **Use Schedule PC to make a protective claim for refund due to a claim not currently deductible. For such a claim, report the expense on Schedule K but without a value in the last column.**

	Yes	No
Are you aware of any actual or potential reimbursement to the estate for any debt of the decedent, mortgage, or lien claimed as a deduction on this schedule?		X
If "Yes," attach a statement describing the items subject to potential reimbursement. (see instructions)		
Are any of the items on this schedule deductible under Reg. section 20.2053-4(b) and Reg. section 20.2053-4(c)?		X
If "Yes," attach a statement indicating the applicable provision and documenting the value of the claim.		

Item number	Debts of the Decedent—Creditor and nature of debt, and allowable death taxes	Amount
1	Bank loan (including $200 interest accrued through date of death)	25,200
2	American Express, Visa, and Master Card credit card debts	6,500
	Total from continuation schedules (or additional statements) attached to this schedule	
	TOTAL. (Also enter on Part 5—Recapitulation, page 3, at item 15.)	31,700

Item number	Mortgages and Liens—Description	Amount
	Total from continuation schedules (or additional statements) attached to this schedule	
	TOTAL. (Also enter on Part 5—Recapitulation, page 3, at item 16.)	

(If more space is needed, attach the continuation schedule from the end of this package or additional statements of the same size.)

Form 706 (Rev. 8-2013)

Estate of: Herman Estes	Decedent's social security number XXX XX XXXX

SCHEDULE M—Bequests, etc., to Surviving Spouse

Note. If the value of the gross estate, together with the amount of adjusted taxable gifts, is less than the basic exclusion amount and the Form 706 is being filed solely to elect portability of the DSUE amount, consideration should be given as to whether you are required to report the value of assets eligible for the marital or charitable deduction on this schedule. See the instructions and Reg. section 20.2010-2T (a)(7)(ii) for more information. If you are not required to report the value of an asset, identify the property but make no entry in the last column.

			Yes	No
1	Did any property pass to the surviving spouse as a result of a qualified disclaimer? If "Yes," attach a copy of the written disclaimer required by section 2518(b).	1		X
2a	In what country was the surviving spouse born? United States			
b	What is the surviving spouse's date of birth? 3-12-1948			
c	Is the surviving spouse a U.S. citizen?	2c	X	
d	If the surviving spouse is a naturalized citizen, when did the surviving spouse acquire citizenship? N/A			
e	If the surviving spouse is not a U.S. citizen, of what country is the surviving spouse a citizen? N/A			
3	**Election Out of QTIP Treatment of Annuities.** Do you elect under section 2056(b)(7)(C)(ii) not to treat as qualified terminable interest property any joint and survivor annuities that are included in the gross estate and would otherwise be treated as qualified terminable interest property under section 2056(b)(7)(C)? (see instructions)	3		X

Item number	Description of property interests passing to surviving spouse. For securities, give CUSIP number. If trust, partnership, or closely held entity, give EIN	Amount
	QTIP property:	
A1	Trust with First Bank as trustee	200,000
	All other property:	
B1	Residence	325,000
	Savings account	75,000
	Checking account	10,000
	Land held in joint tenancy	220,000
	Qualified pension plan	240,000
	Total from continuation schedules (or additional statements) attached to this schedule	

4	**Total** amount of property interests listed on Schedule M			4	1,070,000
5a	Federal estate taxes payable out of property interests listed on Schedule M	5a			
b	Other death taxes payable out of property interests listed on Schedule M	5b			
c	Federal and state GST taxes payable out of property interests listed on Schedule M	5c			
d	Add items 5a, 5b, and 5c			5d	
6	Net amount of property interests listed on Schedule M (subtract 5d from 4). Also enter on Part 5—Recapitulation, page 3, at item 21			6	1,070,000

(If more space is needed, attach the continuation schedule from the end of this package or additional statements of the same size.)

Form 706 (Rev. 8-2013)

Estate of: Herman Estes

Decedent's social security number XXX XX XXXX

SCHEDULE O—Charitable, Public, and Similar Gifts and Bequests

Note. If the value of the gross estate, together with the amount of adjusted taxable gifts, is less than the basic exclusion amount and the Form 706 is being filed solely to elect portability of the DSUE amount, consideration should be given as to whether you are required to report the value of assets eligible for the marital or charitable deduction on this schedule. See the instructions and Reg. section 20.2010-2T (a)(7)(ii) for more information. If you are not required to report the value of an asset, identify the property but make no entry in the last column.

		Yes	No
1a	If the transfer was made by will, has any action been instituted to contest or have interpreted any of its provisions affecting the charitable deductions claimed in this schedule? . . . . If "Yes," full details must be submitted with this schedule.		X
b	According to the information and belief of the person or persons filing this return, is any such action planned? . If "Yes," full details must be submitted with this schedule.		X
2	Did any property pass to charity as the result of a qualified disclaimer? . . . . If "Yes," attach a copy of the written disclaimer required by section 2518(b).		X

Item number	Name and address of beneficiary	Character of institution	Amount
1	American Cancer Society	Charity	10,000
	Total from continuation schedules (or additional statements) attached to this schedule		

3	Total			3	10,000
4a	Federal estate tax payable out of property interests listed above	4a			
b	Other death taxes payable out of property interests listed above	4b			
c	Federal and state GST taxes payable out of property interests listed above .	4c			
d	Add items 4a, 4b, and 4c			4d	
5	Net value of property interests listed above (subtract 4d from 3). Also enter on Part 5—Recapitulation, page 3, at item 22			5	10,000

(If more space is needed, attach the continuation schedule from the end of this package or additional statements of the same size.)

Form **709** | **United States Gift (and Generation-Skipping Transfer) Tax Return** | OMB No. 1545-0020

▶ Information about Form 709 and its separate instructions is at *www.irs.gov/form709*.

(For gifts made during calendar year 2013)

▶ **See instructions.**

Department of the Treasury
Internal Revenue Service

2014

1 Donor's first name and middle initial	2 Donor's last name	3 Donor's social security number
Wilma	Brown	XXX-XX-XXXX
4 Address (number, street, and apartment number)		5 Legal residence (domicile)
2 Main Street		State
6 City or town, state or province, country, and ZIP or foreign postal code		7 Citizenship (see instructions)
City, ST 22222		U.S.A.

Part 1—General Information

Line		Yes	No
8	If the donor died during the year, check here ▶ ☐ and enter date of death ______, ______.		
9	If you extended the time to file this Form 709, check here ▶ ☐		
10	Enter the total number of donees listed on Schedule A. Count each person only once. ▶ 6		
11a	Have you (the donor) previously filed a Form 709 (or 709-A) for any other year? If "No," skip line 11b	X	
b	Has your address changed since you last filed Form 709 (or 709-A)?		X
12	**Gifts by husband or wife to third parties.** Do you consent to have the gifts (including generation-skipping transfers) made by you and by your spouse to third parties during the calendar year considered as made one-half by each of you? (see instructions.) (If the answer is "Yes," the following information must be furnished and your spouse must sign the consent shown below. **If the answer is "No," skip lines 13–18.**)	X	
13	Name of consenting spouse Hugh Brown — 14 SSN XXX-XX-XXXX		
15	Were you married to one another during the entire calendar year? (see instructions)	X	
16	If 15 is "No," check whether ☐ married ☐ divorced or ☐ widowed/deceased, and give date (see instructions) ▶		
17	Will a gift tax return for this year be filed by your spouse? (If "Yes," mail both returns in the same envelope.)	X	
18	**Consent of Spouse.** I consent to have the gifts (and generation-skipping transfers) made by me and by my spouse to third parties during the calendar year considered as made one-half by each of us. We are both aware of the joint and several liability for tax created by the execution of this consent.		
	Consenting spouse's signature ▶ *Hugh Brown* — **Date** ▶ 3-2-2015		
19	Have you applied a DSUE amount received from a predeceased spouse to a gift or gifts reported on this or a previous Form 709? If "Yes," complete Schedule C		

Part 2—Tax Computation

Line			Amount
1	Enter the amount from Schedule A, Part 4, line 11	1	350,155
2	Enter the amount from Schedule B, line 3	2	500,000
3	Total taxable gifts. Add lines 1 and 2	3	850,155
4	Tax computed on amount on line 3 (see *Table for Computing Gift Tax* in instructions)	4	287,360
5	Tax computed on amount on line 2 (see *Table for Computing Gift Tax* in instructions)	5	155,800
6	Balance. Subtract line 5 from line 4	6	131,560
7	Applicable credit amount. If donor has DSUE amount from predeceased spouse(s), enter amount from Schedule C, line 4; otherwise, see instructions	7	2,081,800
8	Enter the applicable credit against tax allowable for all prior periods (from Sch. B, line 1, col. C)	8	68,000
9	Balance. Subtract line 8 from line 7. Do not enter less than zero	9	2,013,800
10	Enter 20% (.20) of the amount allowed as a specific exemption for gifts made after September 8, 1976, and before January 1, 1977 (see instructions)	10	
11	Balance. Subtract line 10 from line 9. Do not enter less than zero	11	2,013,800
12	Applicable credit. Enter the smaller of line 6 or line 11	12	131,560
13	Credit for foreign gift taxes (see instructions)	13	-0-
14	Total credits. Add lines 12 and 13	14	131,560
15	Balance. Subtract line 14 from line 6. Do not enter less than zero	15	-0-
16	Generation-skipping transfer taxes (from Schedule D, Part 3, col. H, Total)	16	-0-
17	Total tax. Add lines 15 and 16	17	-0-
18	Gift and generation-skipping transfer taxes prepaid with extension of time to file	18	
19	If line 18 is less than line 17, enter **balance due** (see instructions)	19	-0-
20	If line 18 is greater than line 17, enter **amount to be refunded**	20	

Attach check or money order here.

Sign Here

Under penalties of perjury, I declare that I have examined this return, including any accompanying schedules and statements, and to the best of my knowledge and belief, it is true, correct, and complete. Declaration of preparer (other than donor) is based on all information of which preparer has any knowledge.

May the IRS discuss this return with the preparer shown below (see instructions)? ☒ Yes ☐ No

▶ *Wilma Brown* — Signature of donor — Date 3-2-2015

Paid Preparer Use Only

Print/Type preparer's name	Preparer's signature	Date	Check ☒ if self-employed	PTIN
Sally Preparer	*Sally Preparer*	3-1-2015		
Firm's name ▶ Sally Preparer			Firm's EIN ▶	
Firm's address ▶ 110 Last Bank Tower, City, ST 22222			Phone no.	

For Disclosure, Privacy Act, and Paperwork Reduction Act Notice, see the instructions for this form. Cat. No. 16783M Form **709** (2014)

Note: Page 4 and 5, which are not pertinent to the tax consequences, are omitted because the donor made no generation–skipping transfers and had no deceased spousal unused exclusion amount. See the Comprehensive Illustration on text page C:12-25 for tax form facts.

Form 709 (2014) Page 2

SCHEDULE A **Computation of Taxable Gifts** (Including transfers in trust) (see instructions)

A Does the value of any item listed on Schedule A reflect any valuation discount? If "Yes," attach explanation . . . . . . Yes ☐ No ☒

B ☐ ◄ Check here if you elect under section 529(c)(2)(B) to treat any transfers made this year to a qualified tuition program as made ratably over a 5-year period beginning this year. See instructions. Attach explanation.

Part 1—Gifts Subject Only to Gift Tax. Gifts less political organization, medical, and educational exclusions. (see instructions)

A Item number	B • Donee's name and address • Relationship to donor (if any) • Description of gift • If the gift was of securities, give CUSIP no. • If closely held entity, give EIN	C	D Donor's adjusted basis of gift	E Date of gift	F Value at date of gift	G For split gifts, enter 1/2 of column F	H Net transfer (subtract col. G from col. F)
1-4	} Schedule attached		593,000	2014	756,310	78,155	678,155
*Gifts made by spouse —complete **only** if you are splitting gifts with your spouse and he/she also made gifts.*							
5	State University, stock		32,000*	2014	100,000	50,000	50,000
6	Betsy Brown, land		112,000*	2014	600,000	300,000	300,000
Total of Part 1. Add amounts from Part 1, column H . . . ►							1,028,155

Part 2—Direct Skips. Gifts that are direct skips and are subject to both gift tax and generation-skipping transfer tax. You must list the gifts in chronological order.

A Item number	B • Donee's name and address • Relationship to donor (if any) • Description of gift • If the gift was of securities, give CUSIP no. • If closely held entity, give EIN	C 2632(b) election out	D Donor's adjusted basis of gift	E Date of gift	F Value at date of gift	G For split gifts, enter 1/2 of column F	H Net transfer (subtract col. G from col. F)
*Gifts made by spouse —complete **only** if you are splitting gifts with your spouse and he/she also made gifts.*							
Total of Part 2. Add amounts from Part 2, column H . . . ►							

Part 3—Indirect Skips. Gifts to trusts that are currently subject to gift tax and may later be subject to generation-skipping transfer tax. You must list these gifts in chronological order.

A Item number	B • Donee's name and address • Relationship to donor (if any) • Description of gift • If the gift was of securities, give CUSIP no. • If closely held entity, give EIN	C 2632(c) election	D Donor's adjusted basis of gift	E Date of gift	F Value at date of gift	G For split gifts, enter 1/2 of column F	H Net transfer (subtract col. G from col. F)
*Gifts made by spouse —complete **only** if you are splitting gifts with your spouse and he/she also made gifts.*							
Total of Part 3. Add amounts from Part 3, column H . . . ►							

(If more space is needed, attach additional statements.) Form **709** (2014)

*Assumed amounts not listed in the facts.

Form 709 (2014) Page 3

Part 4—Taxable Gift Reconciliation

1	Total value of gifts of donor. Add totals from column H of Parts 1, 2, and 3	1	1,028,155
2	Total annual exclusions for gifts listed on line 1 (see instructions)	2	56,000 *
3	Total included amount of gifts. Subtract line 2 from line 1	3	972,155

Deductions (see instructions)

4	Gifts of interests to spouse for which a marital deduction will be claimed, based on item numbers 4 of Schedule A	4	600,000		
5	Exclusions attributable to gifts on line 4	5	14,000		
6	Marital deduction. Subtract line 5 from line 4	6	586,000		
7	Charitable deduction, based on item nos. 5 less exclusions	7	36,000		
8	Total deductions. Add lines 6 and 7			8	622,000
9	Subtract line 8 from line 3			9	350,155
10	Generation-skipping transfer taxes payable with this Form 709 (from Schedule D, Part 3, col. H, Total)			10	
11	**Taxable gifts.** Add lines 9 and 10. Enter here and on page 1, Part 2—Tax Computation, line 1			11	350,155

Terminable Interest (QTIP) Marital Deduction. (see instructions for Schedule A, Part 4, line 4)

If a trust (or other property) meets the requirements of qualified terminable interest property under section 2523(f), and:

a. The trust (or other property) is listed on Schedule A, and

b. The value of the trust (or other property) is entered in whole or in part as a deduction on Schedule A, Part 4, line 4,

then the donor shall be deemed to have made an election to have such trust (or other property) treated as qualified terminable interest property under section 2523(f).

If less than the entire value of the trust (or other property) that the donor has included in Parts 1 and 3 of Schedule A is entered as a deduction on line 4, the donor shall be considered to have made an election only as to a fraction of the trust (or other property). The numerator of this fraction is equal to the amount of the trust (or other property) deducted on Schedule A, Part 4, line 6. The denominator is equal to the total value of the trust (or other property) listed in Parts 1 and 3 of Schedule A.

If you make the QTIP election, the terminable interest property involved will be included in your spouse's gross estate upon his or her death (section 2044). See instructions for line 4 of Schedule A. If your spouse disposes (by gift or otherwise) of all or part of the qualifying life income interest, he or she will be considered to have made a transfer of the entire property that is subject to the gift tax. See *Transfer of Certain Life Estates Received From Spouse* in the instructions.

12 Election Out of QTIP Treatment of Annuities

☐ ◀ Check here if you elect under section 2523(f)(6) **not** to treat as qualified terminable interest property any joint and survivor annuities that are reported on Schedule A and would otherwise be treated as qualified terminable interest property under section 2523(f). See instructions. Enter the item numbers from Schedule A for the annuities for which you are making this election ▶ ____________

SCHEDULE B **Gifts From Prior Periods**

If you answered "Yes," on line 11a of page 1, Part 1, see the instructions for completing Schedule B. If you answered "No," skip to the Tax Computation on page 1 (or Schedules C or D, if applicable). Complete Schedule A before beginning Schedule B. See instructions for recalculation of the column C amounts. Attach calculations.

A Calendar year or calendar quarter (see instructions)	B Internal Revenue office where prior return was filed	C Amount of applicable credit (unified credit) against gift tax for periods after December 31, 1976	D Amount of specific exemption for prior periods ending before January 1, 1977	E Amount of taxable gifts
1975	Atlanta, GA	-0-		300,000
1988	Atlanta, GA	68,000		200,000
1 Totals for prior periods	1	68,000		500,000

2	Amount, if any, by which total specific exemption, line 1, column D is more than $30,000	2	
3	Total amount of taxable gifts for prior periods. Add amount on line 1, column E and amount, if any, on line 2. Enter here and on page 1, Part 2—Tax Computation, line 2	3	500,000

(If more space is needed, attach additional statements.) Form **709** (2014)

*$14,000 each for Billy, Betsy, State University, and Hugh.

Form 709 (2014), Schedule A, Part 1

A	B	C	D	E	F	G	H
1	Billy Brown, son, cash		$ 80,000	2014	$ 80,000	$40,000	$ 40,000
2	Betsy Brown, daughter, jewelry		18,000*	2014	30,000	15,000	15,000
3	Ruth Cain, remainder interest in vacation cabin (0.46310 + 100,000)		15,000*	2014	46,310	23,155	23,155
4	Trust at First Bank, income to Hugh Brown, spouse, for life. Remainder to Jeff Bass, brother, (QTIP trust)		480,000*	2014	600,000	-0-	600,000
			$593,000		$756,310	$78,155	$678,155

*Assumed amounts not listed in the facts.

Note: To save space, addresses are not shown here.

Facts for Sole Proprietorship (Schedule C)

Andrew Lawrence is the sole proprietor of a business that operates under the name Andrew Lawrence Furniture (Business Code 337000). The proprietorship is located at 1234 First Avenue, City, ST 55555. Andrew started the business with a $200,000 capital investment on June 1, 2008. The proprietorship uses the calendar year as its tax year (the same as its proprietor) and the accrual method of accounting. The following information pertains to its 2014 activities:

A trial balance is included as part of the accompanying worksheet. Notes accompanying the account balances are presented below.

1. Cost of goods sold is determined as follows:

Inventory at beginning of year	$ 64,000
Plus: Purchases	340,800
Cost of labor	143,204
Additional Sec. 263A adjustment	7,000
Other costs	90,000
Goods available for sale	$645,004
Minus: Inventory at end of year	(104,800)
Cost of goods sold	$540,204

The proprietorship values its inventory using the first-in, first-out method and historical costs. The Sec. 263A rules apply to the proprietorship. No change in valuing inventories occurred between the beginning and end of the tax year.

2. The proprietorship uses MACRS depreciation for tax purposes. The current year tax depreciation is $27,476. Of this amount, $15,000 is included in cost of goods sold and inventory. The AMT depreciation adjustment on post-1986 personal property is $1,514. This amount is reported on Andrew Lawrence's Form 6251 (Alternative Minimum Tax—Individuals), which is not reproduced here.

3. Using its excess funds, the proprietorship has purchased various temporary investments, including a 2% investment in Plaza Corporation stock, 50 shares of Service Corporation stock, and some tax-exempt municipal bonds. The proprietorship has held the Plaza stock for two years and sold it in July for $4,500 more than its $7,000 adjusted basis. Prior to the sale, Plaza paid a $1,000 dividend. The 50 shares of Service stock, which had been purchased during the year, was declared worthless during the year. The proprietorship recovered none of its $2,100 adjusted basis.

4. Employees other than Andrew Lawrence receive limited fringe benefits. One employee also receives a $2,000 contribution to an Individual Retirement Account paid by the proprietorship.

5. Miscellaneous expenses include $150 of expenses related to the production of the dividend income.

6. The proprietorship paid no estimated taxes.

7. Balance sheet information is not provided for the sole proprietorship because it is not reported on the Schedule C. Balance sheet information, however, can be found on page 4 of the C corporation tax return.

8. For additional information, see Schedule C and the worksheet on page B-6.

SCHEDULE C (Form 1040)
Department of the Treasury Internal Revenue Service (99)

Profit or Loss From Business
(Sole Proprietorship)

► For information on Schedule C and its instructions, go to *www.irs.gov/schedulec.*
► Attach to Form 1040, 1040NR, or 1041; partnerships generally must file Form 1065.

OMB No. 1545-0074
2014
Attachment Sequence No. 09

Name of proprietor: Andrew Lawrence
Social security number (SSN): XXX-XX-XXXX

A Principal business or profession, including product or service (see instructions): Manufacturing Furniture
B Enter code from instructions ► 3 3 7 0 0 0

C Business name. If no separate business name, leave blank.
D Employer ID number (EIN), (see instr.) X X X X X X X X X

E Business address (including suite or room no.) ► 1234 Avenue
City, town or post office, state, and ZIP code: City, ST 55555

F Accounting method: (1) ☐ Cash (2) ☒ Accrual (3) ☐ Other (specify) ►

G Did you "materially participate" in the operation of this business during 2013? If "No," see instructions for limit on losses . ☒ Yes ☐ No

H If you started or acquired this business during 2013, check here . . . ► ☐

I Did you make any payments in 2013 that would require you to file Form(s) 1099? (see instructions) . . . ☐ Yes ☒ No

J If "Yes," did you or will you file required Forms 1099? . . . ☐ Yes ☐ No

Part I Income

1	Gross receipts or sales. See instructions for line 1 and check the box if this income was reported to you on Form W-2 and the "Statutory employee" box on that form was checked . . . ► ☐	1	869,658
2	Returns and allowances	2	29,242
3	Subtract line 2 from line 1	3	840,416
4	Cost of goods sold (from line 42)	4	540,204
5	**Gross profit.** Subtract line 4 from line 3	5	300,212
6	Other income, including federal and state gasoline or fuel tax credit or refund (see instructions)	6	
7	**Gross income.** Add lines 5 and 6 ►	7	300,212

Part II Expenses

Enter expenses for business use of your home only on line 30.

8	Advertising	8	13,000	18	Office expense (see instructions)	18	16,000
9	Car and truck expenses (see instructions)	9	4,000	19	Pension and profit-sharing plans	19	2,000
				20	Rent or lease (see instructions):		
10	Commissions and fees	10	10,400	a	Vehicles, machinery, and equipment	20a	36,000
11	Contract labor (see instructions)	11		b	Other business property	20b	
12	Depletion	12		21	Repairs and maintenance	21	
13	Depreciation and section 179 expense deduction (not included in Part III) (see instructions)	13	12,476	22	Supplies (not included in Part III)	22	
				23	Taxes and licenses	23	9,840
				24	Travel, meals, and entertainment:		
14	Employee benefit programs (other than on line 19)	14	4,000	a	Travel	24a	4,000
15	Insurance (other than health)	15		b	Deductible meals and entertainment (see instructions)	24b	4,000
16	Interest:			25	Utilities	25	
a	Mortgage (paid to banks, etc.)	16a		26	Wages (less employment credits)	26	52,000
b	Other	16b	8,000	27a	Other expenses (from line 48)	27a	8,650
17	Legal and professional services	17		b	**Reserved for future use**	27b	

28	**Total expenses** before expenses for business use of home. Add lines 8 through 27a ►	28	184,366
29	Tentative profit or (loss). Subtract line 28 from line 7	29	
30	Expenses for business use of your home. Do not report these expenses elsewhere. Attach Form 8829 unless using the simplified method (see instructions). **Simplified method filers only:** enter the total square footage of: (a) your home: ______ and (b) the part of your home used for business: ______. Use the Simplified Method Worksheet in the instructions to figure the amount to enter on line 30	30	115,846
31	**Net profit or (loss).** Subtract line 30 from line 29. • If a profit, enter on both **Form 1040, line 12** (or **Form 1040NR, line 13**) and on **Schedule SE, line 2.** (If you checked the box on line 1, see instructions). Estates and trusts, enter on **Form 1041, line 3.** • If a loss, you **must** go to line 32.	31	115,846

32 If you have a loss, check the box that describes your investment in this activity (see instructions).
• If you checked 32a, enter the loss on both **Form 1040, line 12,** (or **Form 1040NR, line 13**) and on **Schedule SE, line 2.** (If you checked the box on line 1, see the line 31 instructions). Estates and trusts, enter on **Form 1041, line 3.**
• If you checked 32b, you **must** attach **Form 6198.** Your loss may be limited.

32a ☐ All investment is at risk.
32b ☐ Some investment is not at risk.

Schedule C (Form 1040) 2014 Page 2

Part III **Cost of Goods Sold** (see instructions)

33 Method(s) used to value closing inventory: a [X] Cost b [ ] Lower of cost or market c [ ] Other (attach explanation)

34 Was there any change in determining quantities, costs, or valuations between opening and closing inventory? If "Yes," attach explanation . . . [ ] Yes [X] No

35 Inventory at beginning of year. If different from last year's closing inventory, attach explanation	35	64,000
36 Purchases less cost of items withdrawn for personal use	36	340,800
37 Cost of labor. Do not include any amounts paid to yourself	37	143,204
38 Materials and supplies	38	
39 Other costs	39	97,000
40 Add lines 35 through 39	40	645,004
41 Inventory at end of year	41	104,800
42 **Cost of goods sold.** Subtract line 41 from line 40. Enter the result here and on line 4	42	540,204

Part IV **Information on Your Vehicle.** Complete this part **only** if you are claiming car or truck expenses on line 9 and are not required to file Form 4562 for this business. See the instructions for line 13 to find out if you must file Form 4562.

43 When did you place your vehicle in service for business purposes? (month, day, year) ▶ 3 / 12 / 13

44 Of the total number of miles you drove your vehicle during 2013, enter the number of miles you used your vehicle for:

a Business 17,000 b Commuting (see instructions) 4,500 c Other 12,000

45 Was your vehicle available for personal use during off-duty hours? . . . [X] Yes [ ] No

46 Do you (or your spouse) have another vehicle available for personal use?. . . [X] Yes [ ] No

47a Do you have evidence to support your deduction? . . . [X] Yes [ ] No

b If "Yes," is the evidence written? . . . [X] Yes [ ] No

Part V **Other Expenses.** List below business expenses not included on lines 8–26 or line 30.

Repairs	4,800
General and administrative	3,000
Miscellaneous	850
48 **Total other expenses.** Enter here and on line 27a . . . 48	8,650

Schedule C (Form 1040) 2014

Andrew Lawrence, Sole Proprietorship Reconciliation of Book and Taxable Income For Year Ending December 31, 2014

	Book Income		Adjustments		Taxable Income		Schedule	Other Tax	
Account Name	Debit	Credit	Debit	Credit	Debit	Credit	C	Forms	
Sales		$869,658				$869,658	$869,658		
Sales returns & allowances	$ 29,242				$ 29,242		(29,242)		
Cost of sales	540,204				540,204		(540,204)		
Dividends		1,000			1,000	1,000		$ 1,000	(Sch. B)
Tax-exempt interest		18,000	$18,000			0			
Gain on July stock sale		4,500				4,500		4,500	(Sch. D)
Worthless stock loss	2,100				2,100			(2,100)	(Sch. D)
Proprietor's salary[a]	36,000			$36,000	0		0	0	
Other salaries	52,000				52,000		(52,000)		
Rentals	36,000				36,000		(36,000)		
Bad debts	4,000				4,000		(4,000)		
Interest:									
Working capital loans	8,000				8,000		(8,000)		
Purchase tax-exempt bonds	2,000			2,000	0				
Employment taxes	8,320				8,320		(8,320)		
Taxes	1,520				1,520		(1,520)		
Repairs	4,800				4,800		(4,800)		
Depreciation[b]	12,000		476		12,476		(12,476)		
Charitable contributions	12,000				12,000			(12,000)	(Sch. A)
Travel	4,000				4,000		(4,000)		
Meals and entertainment[c]	8,000			4,000	4,000		(4,000)		
Office expenses	16,000				16,000		(16,000)		
Advertising	13,000				13,000		(13,000)		
Transportation expense	10,400				10,400		(10,400)		
General and administrative	3,000				3,000		(3,000)		
Pension plans[d]	2,000				2,000		(2,000)		
Employee benefit programs[e]	4,000				4,000		(4,000)		
Miscellaneous	1,000				1,000		(850)	(150)	(Form 4952)
Net profit/Taxable income	83,572		23,524		107,096				
Total	$893,158	$893,158	$42,000	$42,000	$875,158	$875,158	$115,846		

[a] The $3,000 monthly salary for Andrew Lawrence is treated as a withdrawal from the proprietorship and is not deducted on Schedule C. The salary does not reduce Schedule C income and therefore is taxed as self-employment income.

[b] MACRS depreciation is $27,476 − $15,000 = $12,476

[c] 50% of the meals and entertainment expense is not deductible for tax purposes.

[d] The pension plan expense is the same for book and tax purposes for this business. No pension expenses relate to pensions for the proprietor.

[e] The employee benefit expense is the same for book and tax purposes for this business. None relates to proprietor benefits.

SCHEDULE SE (Form 1040) Department of the Treasury Internal Revenue Service (99)	**Self-Employment Tax** ▶ Information about Schedule SE and its separate instructions is at *www.irs.gov/schedulese.* ▶ Attach to Form 1040 or Form 1040NR.	OMB No. 1545-0074 2014 Attachment Sequence No. 17
Name of person with **self-employment** income (as shown on Form 1040 or Form 1040NR)	Social security number of person with **self-employment** income ▶	

Before you begin: To determine if you must file Schedule SE, see the instructions.

May I Use Short Schedule SE or Must I Use Long Schedule SE?

Note. Use this flowchart **only if** you must file Schedule SE. If unsure, see *Who Must File Schedule SE* in the instructions.

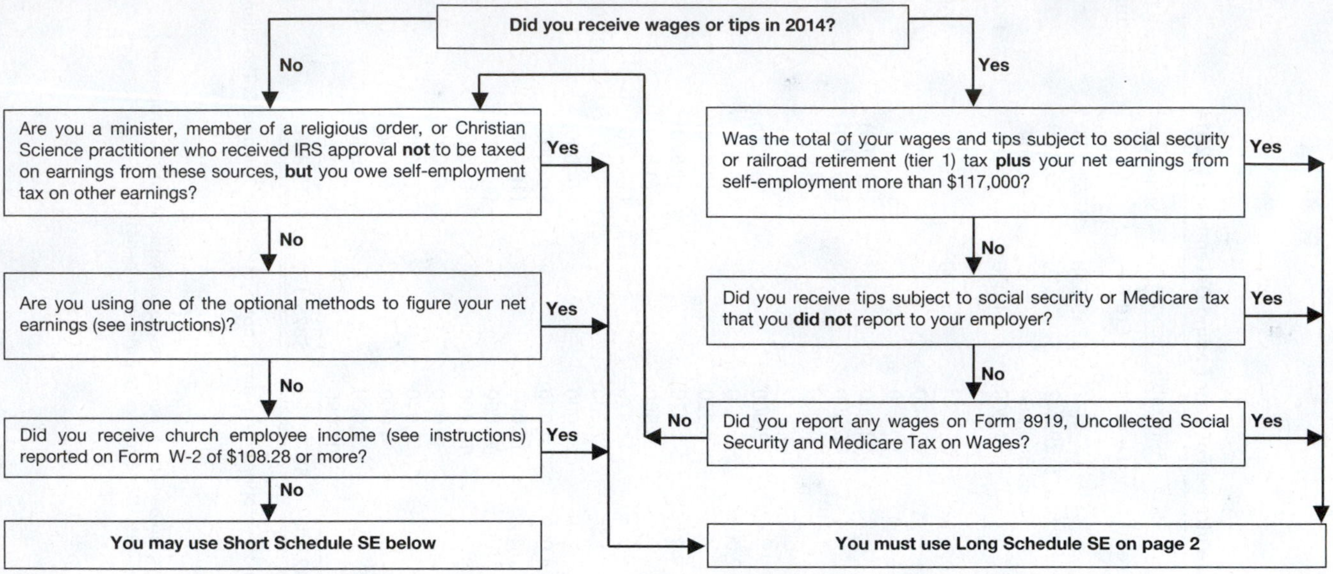

Section A—Short Schedule SE. Caution. Read above to see if you can use Short Schedule SE.

1a	Net farm profit or (loss) from Schedule F, line 34, and farm partnerships, Schedule K-1 (Form 1065), box 14, code A	**1a**	
b	If you received social security retirement or disability benefits, enter the amount of Conservation Reserve Program payments included on Schedule F, line 4b, or listed on Schedule K-1 (Form 1065), box 20, code Z	**1b**	( )
2	Net profit or (loss) from Schedule C, line 31; Schedule C-EZ, line 3; Schedule K-1 (Form 1065), box 14, code A (other than farming); and Schedule K-1 (Form 1065-B), box 9, code J1. Ministers and members of religious orders, see instructions for types of income to report on this line. See instructions for other income to report	**2**	
3	Combine lines 1a, 1b, and 2	**3**	
4	Multiply line 3 by 92.35% (.9235). If less than $400, you do not owe self-employment tax; **do not** file this schedule unless you have an amount on line 1b . . . . ▶	**4**	
	Note. If line 4 is less than $400 due to Conservation Reserve Program payments on line 1b, see instructions.		
5	**Self-employment tax.** If the amount on line 4 is: • $117,000 or less, multiply line 4 by 15.3% (.153). Enter the result here and on **Form 1040, line 57,** or **Form 1040NR, line 55** • More than $117,000, multiply line 4 by 2.9% (.029). Then, add $14,508 to the result. Enter the total here and on **Form 1040, line 57,** or **Form 1040NR, line 55**	**5**	
6	**Deduction for one-half of self-employment tax.** Multiply line 5 by 50% (.50). Enter the result here and on **Form 1040, line 27,** or **Form 1040NR, line 27** **6**		

Schedule SE (Form 1040) 2014 | Attachment Sequence No. 17 | Page 2

Name of person with **self-employment** income (as shown on Form 1040)	Social security number of person with **self-employment** income ▶	

Section B—Long Schedule SE

Part I Self-Employment Tax

Note. If your only income subject to self-employment tax is **church employee income,** see instructions. Also see instructions for the definition of church employee income.

A If you are a minister, member of a religious order, or Christian Science practitioner **and** you filed Form 4361, but you had $400 or more of **other** net earnings from self-employment, check here and continue with Part I . . . . ▶ ☐

Line	Description		Line	Amount	Cents
1a	Net farm profit or (loss) from Schedule F, line 34, and farm partnerships, Schedule K-1 (Form 1065), box 14, code A. **Note.** Skip lines 1a and 1b if you use the farm optional method (see instructions)		1a		
b	If you received social security retirement or disability benefits, enter the amount of Conservation Reserve Program payments included on Schedule F, line 4b, or listed on Schedule K-1 (Form 1065), box 20, code Z		1b	(	)
2	Net profit or (loss) from Schedule C, line 31; Schedule C-EZ, line 3; Schedule K-1 (Form 1065), box 14, code A (other than farming); and Schedule K-1 (Form 1065-B), box 9, code J1. Ministers and members of religious orders, see instructions for types of income to report on this line. See instructions for other income to report. **Note.** Skip this line if you use the nonfarm optional method (see instructions) . . .		2		
3	Combine lines 1a, 1b, and 2 . . .		3		
4a	If line 3 is more than zero, multiply line 3 by 92.35% (.9235). Otherwise, enter amount from line 3		4a		
	Note. If line 4a is less than $400 due to Conservation Reserve Program payments on line 1b, see instructions.				
b	If you elect one or both of the optional methods, enter the total of lines 15 and 17 here . .		4b		
c	Combine lines 4a and 4b. If less than $400, **stop**; you do not owe self-employment tax. **Exception.** If less than $400 and you had **church employee income,** enter -0- and continue ▶		4c		
5a	Enter your **church employee income** from Form W-2. See instructions for definition of church employee income . . .	5a			
b	Multiply line 5a by 92.35% (.9235). If less than $100, enter -0- . . .		5b		
6	Add lines 4c and 5b . . .		6		
7	Maximum amount of combined wages and self-employment earnings subject to social security tax or the 6.2% portion of the 7.65% railroad retirement (tier 1) tax for 2013 . . .		7	113,700	00
8a	Total social security wages and tips (total of boxes 3 and 7 on Form(s) W-2) and railroad retirement (tier 1) compensation. If $113,700 or more, skip lines 8b through 10, and go to line 11	8a			
b	Unreported tips subject to social security tax (from Form 4137, line 10)	8b			
c	Wages subject to social security tax (from Form 8919, line 10)	8c			
d	Add lines 8a, 8b, and 8c . . .		8d		
9	Subtract line 8d from line 7. If zero or less, enter -0- here and on line 10 and go to line 11 . ▶		9		
10	Multiply the **smaller** of line 6 or line 9 by 12.4% (.124) . . .		10		
11	Multiply line 6 by 2.9% (.029) . . .		11		
12	**Self-employment tax.** Add lines 10 and 11. Enter here and on **Form 1040, line 56,** or **Form 1040NR, line 54**		12		
13	**Deduction for one-half of self-employment tax.** Multiply line 12 by 50% (.50). Enter the result here and on **Form 1040, line 27,** or **Form 1040NR, line 27** . . .	13			

Part II Optional Methods To Figure Net Earnings (see instructions)

Farm Optional Method. You may use this method **only** if **(a)** your gross farm income[1] was not more than $6,960, **or (b)** your net farm profits[2] were less than $5,024.

Line	Description	Line	Amount	Cents
14	Maximum income for optional methods . . .	14	4,640	00
15	Enter the **smaller** of: two-thirds (2/3) of gross farm income[1] (not less than zero) **or** $4,640. Also include this amount on line 4b above . . .	15		

Nonfarm Optional Method. You may use this method **only** if **(a)** your net nonfarm profits[3] were less than $5,024 and also less than 72.189% of your gross nonfarm income,[4] **and (b)** you had net earnings from self-employment of at least $400 in 2 of the prior 3 years. **Caution.** You may use this method no more than five times.

Line	Description	Line	Amount	Cents
16	Subtract line 15 from line 14 . . .	16		
17	Enter the **smaller** of: two-thirds (2/3) of gross nonfarm income[4] (not less than zero) **or** the amount on line 16. Also include this amount on line 4b above . . .	17		

[1] From Sch. F, line 9, and Sch. K-1 (Form 1065), box 14, code B.

[2] From Sch. F, line 34, and Sch. K-1 (Form 1065), box 14, code A—minus the amount you would have entered on line 1b had you not used the optional method.

[3] From Sch. C, line 31; Sch. C-EZ, line 3; Sch. K-1 (Form 1065), box 14, code A; and Sch. K-1 (Form 1065-B), box 9, code J1.

[4] From Sch. C, line 7; Sch. C-EZ, line 1; Sch. K-1 (Form 1065), box 14, code C; and Sch. K-1 (Form 1065-B), box 9, code J2.

Form 1041 U.S. Income Tax Return for Estates and Trusts 2014

Department of the Treasury—Internal Revenue Service

OMB No. 1545-0092

▶ Information about Form 1041 and its separate instructions is at *www.irs.gov/form1041.*

A Check all that apply:
- ☐ Decedent's estate
- ☒ Simple trust
- ☐ Complex trust
- ☐ Qualified disability trust
- ☐ ESBT (S portion only)
- ☐ Grantor type trust
- ☐ Bankruptcy estate-Ch. 7
- ☐ Bankruptcy estate-Ch. 11
- ☐ Pooled income fund

For calendar year 2013 or fiscal year beginning , 2013, and ending , 20

Name of estate or trust (If a grantor type trust, see the instructions.): Bob Adams Trust (Simple Trust)

Name and title of fiduciary: First Bank

Number, street, and room or suite no. (If a P.O. box, see the instructions.): Post Office Box 100

City or town, state or province, country, and ZIP or foreign postal code: City, ST 44444

C Employer identification number: XX-XXXXXXX

D Date entity created: 2003

E Nonexempt charitable and split-interest trusts, check applicable box(es), see instructions.
- ☐ Described in sec. 4947(a)(1). Check here if not a private foundation . . . ▶ ☐
- ☐ Described in sec. 4947(a)(2)

B Number of Schedules K-1 attached (see instructions) ▶ 1

F Check applicable boxes: ☐ Initial return ☐ Final return ☐ Amended return ☐ Net operating loss carryback ☐ Change in trust's name ☐ Change in fiduciary ☐ Change in fiduciary's name ☐ Change in fiduciary's address

G Check here if the estate or filing trust made a section 645 election . . . . . . ▶ ☐ Trust EIN ▶

Income	1	Interest income	1	
	2a	Total ordinary dividends	2a	30,000
	b	Qualified dividends allocable to: (1) Beneficiaries 30,000 (2) Estate or trust -0-		
	3	Business income or (loss). Attach Schedule C or C-EZ (Form 1040)	3	
	4	Capital gain or (loss). Attach Schedule D (Form 1041)	4	12,000
	5	Rents, royalties, partnerships, other estates and trusts, etc. Attach Schedule E (Form 1040)	5	4,000 *
	6	Farm income or (loss). Attach Schedule F (Form 1040)	6	
	7	Ordinary gain or (loss). Attach Form 4797	7	
	8	Other income. List type and amount	8	
	9	**Total income.** Combine lines 1, 2a, and 3 through 8 ▶	9	46,000
Deductions	10	Interest. Check if Form 4952 is attached ▶ ☐	10	
	11	Taxes	11	
	12	Fiduciary fees ($1,200 – $360)	12	840
	13	Charitable deduction (from Schedule A, line 7)	13	
	14	Attorney, accountant, and return preparer fees	14	500
	15a	Other deductions **not** subject to the 2% floor (attach schedule)	15a	
	b	Net operating loss deduction (see instructions)	15b	
	c	Allowable miscellaneous itemized deductions subject to the 2% floor	15c	
	16	Add lines 10 through 15c ▶	16	1,340
	17	Adjusted total income or (loss). Subtract line 16 from line 9 — 17: 44,660		
	18	Income distribution deduction (from Schedule B, line 15). Attach Schedules K-1 (Form 1041)	18	32,660
	19	Estate tax deduction including certain generation-skipping taxes (attach computation)	19	
	20	Exemption	20	300
	21	Add lines 18 through 20 ▶	21	32,960
Tax and Payments	22	Taxable income. Subtract line 21 from line 17. If a loss, see instructions	22	11,700
	23	**Total tax** (from Schedule G, line 7)	23	1,380
	24	**Payments: a** 2013 estimated tax payments and amount applied from 2012 return	24a	2,600
	b	Estimated tax payments allocated to beneficiaries (from Form 1041-T)	24b	
	c	Subtract line 24b from line 24a	24c	2,600
	d	Tax paid with Form 7004 (see instructions)	24d	
	e	Federal income tax withheld. If any is from Form(s) 1099, check ▶ ☐	24e	
		Other payments: **f** Form 2439 ; **g** Form 4136 ; Total ▶	24h	
	25	**Total payments.** Add lines 24c through 24e, and 24h ▶	25	2,600
	26	Estimated tax penalty (see instructions)	26	
	27	**Tax due.** If line 25 is smaller than the total of lines 23 and 26, enter amount owed	27	
	28	**Overpayment.** If line 25 is larger than the total of lines 23 and 26, enter amount overpaid	28	1,220
	29	Amount of line 28 to be: **a Credited to 2014 estimated tax** ▶ 1,220 ; **b Refunded** ▶	29	

Sign Here — Under penalties of perjury, I declare that I have examined this return, including accompanying schedules and statements, and to the best of my knowledge and belief, it is true, correct, and complete. Declaration of preparer (other than taxpayer) is based on all information of which preparer has any knowledge.

Signature of fiduciary or officer representing fiduciary: Tom Trusty — Date: 3-14-15 — EIN of fiduciary if a financial institution: XX-XXXXXXX

May the IRS discuss this return with the preparer shown below (see instr.)? ☒ Yes ☐ No

Paid Preparer Use Only

Print/Type preparer's name	Preparer's signature	Date	Check ☒ if self-employed	PTIN
Karen Certified	Karen Certified	3-14-15		

Firm's name ▶ Karen Certified — Firm's EIN ▶

Firm's address ▶ One Some Place, City, ST 44444 — Phone no.

For Paperwork Reduction Act Notice, see the separate instructions. Cat. No. 11370H Form **1041** (2014)

*Line 5: Net rental income = Rental income $5,000 – Realtor's commissions $1,000 = $4,000

Note: Pages concerning the AMT are omitted because the trust does not owe the AMT.

See the Comprehensive Illustration on text page C:14-17 for tax form facts.

Form 1041 (2014) Page 2

Schedule A **Charitable Deduction.** Do not complete for a simple trust or a pooled income fund.

1	Amounts paid or permanently set aside for charitable purposes from gross income (see instructions)	1	
2	Tax-exempt income allocable to charitable contributions (see instructions)	2	
3	Subtract line 2 from line 1	3	
4	Capital gains for the tax year allocated to corpus and paid or permanently set aside for charitable purposes	4	
5	Add lines 3 and 4	5	
6	Section 1202 exclusion allocable to capital gains paid or permanently set aside for charitable purposes (see instructions)	6	
7	**Charitable deduction.** Subtract line 6 from line 5. Enter here and on page 1, line 13	7	

Schedule B **Income Distribution Deduction**

1	Adjusted total income (see instructions)	1	44,660	
2	Adjusted tax-exempt interest ($15,000 – $360)	2	14,640	*
3	Total net gain from Schedule D (Form 1041), line 19, column (1) (see instructions)	3		
4	Enter amount from Schedule A, line 4 (minus any allocable section 1202 exclusion)	4		
5	Capital gains for the tax year included on Schedule A, line 1 (see instructions)	5		
6	Enter any gain from page 1, line 4, as a negative number. If page 1, line 4, is a loss, enter the loss as a positive number	6	(12,000)	
7	**Distributable net income.** Combine lines 1 through 6. If zero or less, enter -0-	7	47,300	
8	If a complex trust, enter accounting income for the tax year as determined under the governing instrument and applicable local law — 8			
9	Income required to be distributed currently	9	48,500	
10	Other amounts paid, credited, or otherwise required to be distributed	10	-0-	
11	Total distributions. Add lines 9 and 10. If greater than line 8, see instructions	11	48,500	
12	Enter the amount of tax-exempt income included on line 11	12	14,640	
13	Tentative income distribution deduction. Subtract line 12 from line 11	13	33,860	
14	Tentative income distribution deduction. Subtract line 2 from line 7. If zero or less, enter -0-	14	32,660	
15	**Income distribution deduction.** Enter the smaller of line 13 or line 14 here and on page 1, line 18	15	32,660	

Schedule G **Tax Computation** (see instructions)

1	**Tax: a** Tax on taxable income (see instructions)	1a	1,380			
	b Tax on lump-sum distributions. Attach Form 4972	1b				
	c Alternative minimum tax (from Schedule I (Form 1041), line 56)	1c				
	d **Total.** Add lines 1a through 1c ▶			1d	1,380	
2a	Foreign tax credit. Attach Form 1116	2a				
b	General business credit. Attach Form 3800	2b				
c	Credit for prior year minimum tax. Attach Form 8801	2c				
d	Bond credits. Attach Form 8912	2d				
e	**Total credits.** Add lines 2a through 2d ▶			2e		
3	Subtract line 2e from line 1d. If zero or less, enter -0-			3	1,380	
4	Net investment income tax from Form 8960, line 21			4	-0-	**
5	Recapture taxes. Check if from: ☐ Form 4255 ☐ Form 8611			5		
6	Household employment taxes. Attach Schedule H (Form 1040)			6		
7	**Total tax.** Add lines 3 through 6. Enter here and on page 1, line 23 ▶			7	1,380	

	Other Information	Yes	No
1	Did the estate or trust receive tax-exempt income? If "Yes," attach a computation of the allocation of expenses. Enter the amount of tax-exempt interest income and exempt-interest dividends ▶ $ 15,000	X	
2	Did the estate or trust receive all or any part of the earnings (salary, wages, and other compensation) of any individual by reason of a contract assignment or similar arrangement?		X
3	At any time during calendar year 2014, did the estate or trust have an interest in or a signature or other authority over a bank, securities, or other financial account in a foreign country?		X
	See the instructions for exceptions and filing requirements for FinCEN Form 114. If "Yes," enter the name of the foreign country ▶		
4	During the tax year, did the estate or trust receive a distribution from, or was it the grantor of, or transferor to, a foreign trust? If "Yes," the estate or trust may have to file Form 3520. See instructions		X
5	Did the estate or trust receive, or pay, any qualified residence interest on seller-provided financing? If "Yes," see the instructions for required attachment		X
6	If this is an estate or a complex trust making the section 663(b) election, check here (see instructions) ▶ ☐		
7	To make a section 643(e)(3) election, attach Schedule D (Form 1041), and check here (see instructions) ▶ ☐		
8	If the decedent's estate has been open for more than 2 years, attach an explanation for the delay in closing the estate, and check here ▶ ☐		
9	Are any present or future trust beneficiaries skip persons? See instructions		X

Form **1041** (2014)

* Line 2: Allocation of expenses: $\frac{\$15,000}{\$50,000}$ x $1,200 = $360 of trustee's fee allocated to tax-exempt income

** Zero because AGI of $11,700 ($44,660 – $32,660 – $300) does not exceed the beginning of the 39.6% tax bracket.

SCHEDULE D (Form 1041)
Department of the Treasury
Internal Revenue Service

Capital Gains and Losses

▶ Attach to Form 1041, Form 5227, or Form 990-T.
▶ Use Form 8949 to list your transactions for lines 1b, 2, 3, 8b, 9 and 10.
▶ Information about Schedule D and its separate instructions is at *www.irs.gov/form1041*.

OMB No. 1545-0092
2014

Name of estate or trust	Employer identification number
Bob Adams Trust	XX-XXXXXXX

Note: *Form 5227 filers need to complete **only** Parts I and II.*

Part I Short-Term Capital Gains and Losses—Assets Held One Year or Less

See instructions for how to figure the amounts to enter on the lines below. This form may be easier to complete if you round off cents to whole dollars.	(d) Proceeds (sales price)	(e) Cost (or other basis)	(g) Adjustments to gain or loss from Form(s) 8949, Part I, line 2, column (g)	(h) Gain or (loss) Subtract column (e) from column (d) and combine the result with column (g)
1a Totals for all short-term transactions reported on Form 1099-B for which basis was reported to the IRS and for which you have no adjustments (see instructions). However, if you choose to report all these transactions on Form 8949, leave this line blank and go to line 1b .				
1b Totals for all transactions reported on Form(s) 8949 with **Box A** checked				
2 Totals for all transactions reported on Form(s) 8949 with **Box B** checked				
3 Totals for all transactions reported on Form(s) 8949 with **Box C** checked				

4 Short-term capital gain or (loss) from Forms 4684, 6252, 6781, and 8824	4	
5 Net short-term gain or (loss) from partnerships, S corporations, and other estates or trusts . .	5	
6 Short-term capital loss carryover. Enter the amount, if any, from line 9 of the 2012 Capital Loss Carryover Worksheet	6	( )
7 **Net short-term capital gain or (loss).** Combine lines 1a through 6 in column (h). Enter here and on line 17, column (3) on the back . . . . ▶	7	

Part II Long-Term Capital Gains and Losses—Assets Held More Than One Year

See instructions for how to figure the amounts to enter on the lines below. This form may be easier to complete if you round off cents to whole dollars.	(d) Proceeds (sales price)	(e) Cost (or other basis)	(g) Adjustments to gain or loss from Form(s) 8949, Part II, line 2, column (g)	(h) Gain or (loss) Subtract column (e) from column (d) and combine the result with column (g)
8a Totals for all long-term transactions reported on Form 1099-B for which basis was reported to the IRS and for which you have no adjustments (see instructions). However, if you choose to report all these transactions on Form 8949, leave this line blank and go to line 8b .	15,000	3,000		12,000
8b Totals for all transactions reported on Form(s) 8949 with **Box D** checked				
9 Totals for all transactions reported on Form(s) 8949 with **Box E** checked				
10 Totals for all transactions reported on Form(s) 8949 with **Box F** checked.				

11 Long-term capital gain or (loss) from Forms 2439, 4684, 6252, 6781, and 8824	11	
12 Net long-term gain or (loss) from partnerships, S corporations, and other estates or trusts . .	12	
13 Capital gain distributions	13	
14 Gain from Form 4797, Part I	14	
15 Long-term capital loss carryover. Enter the amount, if any, from line 14 of the 2012 Capital Loss Carryover Worksheet	15	( )
16 **Net long-term capital gain or (loss).** Combine lines 8a through 15 in column (h). Enter here and on line 18a, column (3) on the back . . . . ▶	16	12,000

Part III Summary of Parts I and II

Caution: *Read the instructions **before** completing this part.*

			(1) Beneficiaries' (see instr.)	(2) Estate's or trust's	(3) Total
17	**Net short-term gain or (loss)**	17			
18	**Net long-term gain or (loss):**				
a	Total for year	18a		12,000	12,000
b	Unrecaptured section 1250 gain (see line 18 of the wrksht.)	18b			
c	28% rate gain	18c			
19	**Total net gain or (loss).** Combine lines 17 and 18a ▶	19		12,000	12,000

Note: *If line 19, column (3), is a net gain, enter the gain on Form 1041, line 4 (or Form 990-T, Part I, line 4a). If lines 18a and 19, column (2), are net gains, go to Part V, and **do not** complete Part IV. If line 19, column (3), is a net loss, complete Part IV and the **Capital Loss Carryover Worksheet,** as necessary.*

Part IV Capital Loss Limitation

20	Enter here and enter as a (loss) on Form 1041, line 4 (or Form 990-T, Part I, line 4c, if a trust), the **smaller** of:		
a	The loss on line 19, column (3) **or b** $3,000	20	( )

Note: *If the loss on line 19, column (3), is more than $3,000, **or** if Form 1041, page 1, line 22 (or Form 990-T, line 34), is a loss, complete the **Capital Loss Carryover Worksheet** in the instructions to figure your capital loss carryover.*

Part V Tax Computation Using Maximum Capital Gains Rates

Form 1041 filers. Complete this part **only** if both lines 18a and 19 in column (2) are gains, or an amount is entered in Part I or Part II and there is an entry on Form 1041, line 2b(2), **and** Form 1041, line 22, is more than zero.

Caution: *Skip this part and complete the **Schedule D Tax Worksheet** in the instructions if:*

- *Either line 18b, col. (2) or line 18c, col. (2) is more than zero, or*
- *Both Form 1041, line 2b(1), and Form 4952, line 4g are more than zero.*

Form 990-T trusts. Complete this part **only** if both lines 18a and 19 are gains, or qualified dividends are included in income in Part I of Form 990-T, **and** Form 990-T, line 34, is more than zero. Skip this part and complete the **Schedule D Tax Worksheet** in the instructions if either line 18b, col. (2) or line 18c, col. (2) is more than zero.

21	Enter taxable income from Form 1041, line 22 (or Form 990-T, line 34)			21	11,700		
22	Enter the **smaller** of line 18a or 19 in column (2) but not less than zero	22	12,000				
23	Enter the estate's or trust's qualified dividends from Form 1041, line 2b(2) (or enter the qualified dividends included in income in Part I of Form 990-T)	23					
24	Add lines 22 and 23	24	12,000				
25	If the estate or trust is filing Form 4952, enter the amount from line 4g; otherwise, enter -0- ▶	25					
26	Subtract line 25 from line 24. If zero or less, enter -0-			26	12,000		
27	Subtract line 26 from line 21. If zero or less, enter -0-			27	-0-		
28	Enter the **smaller** of the amount on line 21 or $2,500			28	2,500		
29	Enter the **smaller** of the amount on line 27 or line 28			29	-0-		
30	Subtract line 29 from line 28. If zero or less, enter -0-. This amount is taxed at 0% ▶					30	2,500
31	Enter the smaller of line 21 or line 26			31	11,700		
32	Subtract line 30 from line 26			32	9,500		
33	Enter the **smaller** of line 21 or $12,150			33	11,700		
34	Add lines 27 and 30			34	2,500		
35	Subtract line 34 from line 33. If zero or less, enter -0-			35	9,200		
36	Enter the **smaller** of line 32 or line 35			36	9,200		
37	Multiply line 36 by 15% ▶					37	1,380
38	Enter the amount from line 31			38	11,700		
39	Add lines 30 and 36			39	11,700		
40	Subtract line 39 from line 38. If zero or less, enter -0-			40	-0-		
41	Multiply line 40 by 20% ▶					41	-0-
42	Figure the tax on the amount on line 27. Use the 2014 Tax Rate Schedule for Estates and Trusts (see the Schedule G instructions in the instructions for Form 1041)			42	-0-		
43	Add lines 37, 41, and 42			43	1,380		
44	Figure the tax on the amount on line 21. Use the 2014 Tax Rate Schedule for Estates and Trusts (see the Schedule G instructions in the instructions for Form 1041)			44	2,992		
45	**Tax on all taxable income.** Enter the **smaller** of line 43 or line 44 here and on Form 1041, Schedule G, line 1a (or Form 990-T, line 36) ▶					45	1,380

661113

☐ Final K-1 ☐ Amended K-1 OMB No. 1545-0092

Schedule K-1 (Form 1041) **2014**
Department of the Treasury
Internal Revenue Service

For calendar year 2014, or tax year beginning ________, 2014, and ending ________, 20 ____

Beneficiary's Share of Income, Deductions, Credits, etc.

▶ See back of form and instructions.

Part I Information About the Estate or Trust

A Estate's or trust's employer identification number
XX-XXXXXXX

B Estate's or trust's name
Bob Adams Trust

C Fiduciary's name, address, city, state, and ZIP code
First Bank
Post OfficeBox 100
City, ST 44444

D ☐ Check if Form 1041-T was filed and enter the date it was filed ________

E ☐ Check if this is the final Form 1041 for the estate or trust

Part II Information About the Beneficiary

F Beneficiary's identifying number
XXX-XX-XXXX

G Beneficiary's name, address, city, state, and ZIP code
Bob Adams
3 Jackson Highway
City, ST 44444

H ☒ Domestic beneficiary ☐ Foreign beneficiary

Part III Beneficiary's Share of Current Year Income, Deductions, Credits, and Other Items

1	Interest income	11	Final year deductions
2a	Ordinary dividends 30,000		
2b	Qualified dividends 30,000		
3	Net short-term capital gain		
4a	Net long-term capital gain		
4b	28% rate gain	12	Alternative minimum tax adjustment
4c	Unrecaptured section 1250 gain		
5	Other portfolio and nonbusiness income		
6	Ordinary business income		
7	Net rental real estate income 2,660*	13	Credits and credit recapture
8	Other rental income		
9	Directly apportioned deductions		
		14	Other information
10	Estate tax deduction		A 14,640

*See attached statement for additional information.

Note. A statement must be attached showing the beneficiary's share of income and directly apportioned deductions from each business, rental real estate, and other rental activity.

For IRS Use Only

For Paperwork Reduction Act Notice, see the Instructions for Form 1041. IRS.gov/form1041 Cat. No. 11380D **Schedule K-1 (Form 1041) 2014**

*5,000 − ($1,000 + $840 + $500) = $2,660

This list identifies the codes used on Schedule K-1 for beneficiaries and provides summarized reporting information for beneficiaries who file Form 1040. For detailed reporting and filing information, see the Instructions for Schedule K-1 (Form 1041) for a Beneficiary Filing Form 1040 and the instructions for your income tax return.

	Report on
1. Interest income	Form 1040, line 8a
2a. Ordinary dividends	Form 1040, line 9a
2b. Qualified dividends	Form 1040, line 9b
3. Net short-term capital gain	Schedule D, line 5
4a. Net long-term capital gain	Schedule D, line 12
4b. 28% rate gain	28% Rate Gain Worksheet, line 4 (Schedule D Instructions)
4c. Unrecaptured section 1250 gain	Unrecaptured Section 1250 Gain Worksheet, line 11 (Schedule D Instructions)
5. Other portfolio and nonbusiness income	Schedule E, line 33, column (f)
6. Ordinary business income	Schedule E, line 33, column (d) or (f)
7. Net rental real estate income	Schedule E, line 33, column (d) or (f)
8. Other rental income	Schedule E, line 33, column (d) or (f)
9. Directly apportioned deductions	
Code	
A Depreciation	Form 8582 or Schedule E, line 33, column (c) or (e)
B Depletion	Form 8582 or Schedule E, line 33, column (c) or (e)
C Amortization	Form 8582 or Schedule E, line 33, column (c) or (e)
10. Estate tax deduction	Schedule A, line 28
11. Final year deductions	
A Excess deductions	Schedule A, line 23
B Short-term capital loss carryover	Schedule D, line 5
C Long-term capital loss carryover	Schedule D, line 12; line 5 of the wksht. for Sch. D, line 18; and line 16 of the wksht. for Sch. D, line 19
D Net operating loss carryover — regular tax	Form 1040, line 21
E Net operating loss carryover — minimum tax	Form 6251, line 11
12. Alternative minimum tax (AMT) items	
A Adjustment for minimum tax purposes	Form 6251, line 15
B AMT adjustment attributable to qualified dividends	See the beneficiary's instructions and the Instructions for Form 6251
C AMT adjustment attributable to net short-term capital gain	See the beneficiary's instructions and the Instructions for Form 6251
D AMT adjustment attributable to net long-term capital gain	See the beneficiary's instructions and the Instructions for Form 6251
E AMT adjustment attributable to unrecaptured section 1250 gain	See the beneficiary's instructions and the Instructions for Form 6251
F AMT adjustment attributable to 28% rate gain	See the beneficiary's instructions and the Instructions for Form 6251
G Accelerated depreciation	See the beneficiary's instructions and the Instructions for Form 6251
H Depletion	See the beneficiary's instructions and the Instructions for Form 6251
I Amortization	See the beneficiary's instructions and the Instructions for Form 6251
J Exclusion items	2014 Form 8801

13. Credits and credit recapture	
Code	*Report on*
A Credit for estimated taxes	Form 1040, line 63
B Credit for backup withholding	Form 1040, line 62
C Low-income housing credit	See the beneficiary's instructions
D Rehabilitation credit and energy credit	See the beneficiary's instructions
E Other qualifying investment credit	See the beneficiary's instructions
F Work opportunity credit	See the beneficiary's instructions
G Credit for small employer health insurance premiums	See the beneficiary's instructions
H Biofuel producer credit	See the beneficiary's instructions
I Credit for increasing research activities	See the beneficiary's instructions
J Renewable electricity, refined coal, and Indian coal production credit	See the beneficiary's instructions
K Empowerment zone and renewal community employment credit	See the beneficiary's instructions
L Indian employment credit	See the beneficiary's instructions
M Orphan drug credit	See the beneficiary's instructions
N Credit for employer-provided child care and facilities	See the beneficiary's instructions
O Biodiesel and renewable diesel fuels credit	See the beneficiary's instructions
P Nonconventional source fuel credit	See the beneficiary's instructions
Q Credit to holders of tax credit bonds	See the beneficiary's instructions
R Agricultural chemicals security credit	See the beneficiary's instructions
S Energy efficient appliance credit	See the beneficiary's instructions
T Credit for employer differential wage payments	See the beneficiary's instructions
U Recapture of credits	See the beneficiary's instructions
14. Other information	
A Tax-exempt interest	Form 1040, line 8b
B Foreign taxes	Form 1040, line 47 or Sch. A, line 8
C Qualified production activities income	Form 8903, line 7, col. (b) (also see the beneficiary's instructions)
D Form W-2 wages	Form 8903, line 17
E Net investment income	Form 4952, line 4a
F Gross farm and fishing income	Schedule E, line 42
G Foreign trading gross receipts (IRC 942(a))	See the Instructions for Form 8873
H Adjustment for section 1411 net investment income or deductions	Form 8960, line 7 (also see the beneficiary's instructions)
I Other information	See the beneficiary's instructions

Note. If you are a beneficiary who does not file a Form 1040, see instructions for the type of income tax return you are filing.

Form **1041** Department of the Treasury—Internal Revenue Service
U.S. Income Tax Return for Estates and Trusts **2014** OMB No. 1545-0092

▶ **Information about Form 1041 and its separate instructions is at *www.irs.gov/form1041.***

A Check all that apply:
- ☐ Decedent's estate
- ☐ Simple trust
- ☒ Complex trust
- ☐ Qualified disability trust
- ☐ ESBT (S portion only)
- ☐ Grantor type trust
- ☐ Bankruptcy estate-Ch. 7
- ☐ Bankruptcy estate-Ch. 11
- ☐ Pooled income fund

For calendar year 2013 or fiscal year beginning , 2013, and ending , 20

Name of estate or trust (If a grantor type trust, see the instructions.): Cathy and Karen Stephens Trust (Complex Trust)

C Employer identification number: XX-XXXXXXX

Name and title of fiduciary: Merchants Bank

D Date entity created: 2003

Number, street, and room or suite no. (If a P.O. box, see the instructions.): 3000 Sun Plaza

E Nonexempt charitable and split-interest trusts, check applicable box(es), see instructions.
- ☐ Described in sec. 4947(a)(1). Check here if not a private foundation . . ▶ ☐
- ☐ Described in sec. 4947(a)(2)

City or town, state or province, country, and ZIP or foreign postal code: City, ST 88888

B Number of Schedules K-1 attached (see instructions) ▶ 2

F Check applicable boxes: ☐ Initial return ☐ Final return ☐ Amended return ☐ Net operating loss carryback ☐ Change in trust's name ☐ Change in fiduciary ☐ Change in fiduciary's name ☐ Change in fiduciary's address

G Check here if the estate or filing trust made a section 645 election . . . . . . ▶ ☐ Trust EIN ▶

Income	1	Interest income	1	
	2a	Total ordinary dividends	2a	30,000
	b	Qualified dividends allocable to: (1) Beneficiaries 13,319 (2) Estate or trust 16,681		
	3	Business income or (loss). Attach Schedule C or C-EZ (Form 1040)	3	
	4	Capital gain or (loss). Attach Schedule D (Form 1041)	4	12,000
	5	Rents, royalties, partnerships, other estates and trusts, etc. Attach Schedule E (Form 1040)	5	4,000
	6	Farm income or (loss). Attach Schedule F (Form 1040)	6	
	7	Ordinary gain or (loss). Attach Form 4797	7	
	8	Other income. List type and amount	8	
	9	**Total income.** Combine lines 1, 2a, and 3 through 8 ▶	9	46,000
Deductions	10	Interest. Check if Form 4952 is attached ▶ ☐	10	
	11	Taxes	11	
	12	Fiduciary fees ($1,200 – $360)	12	840
	13	Charitable deduction (from Schedule A, line 7)	13	
	14	Attorney, accountant, and return preparer fees	14	500
	15a	Other deductions **not** subject to the 2% floor (attach schedule)	15a	
	b	Net operating loss deduction (see instructions)	15b	
	c	Allowable miscellaneous itemized deductions subject to the 2% floor	15c	
	16	Add lines 10 through 15c ▶	16	1,340
	17	Adjusted total income or (loss). Subtract line 16 from line 9 — 17: 44,660		
	18	Income distribution deduction (from Schedule B, line 15). Attach Schedules K-1 (Form 1041)	18	14,500
	19	Estate tax deduction including certain generation-skipping taxes (attach computation)	19	
	20	Exemption	20	100
	21	Add lines 18 through 20 ▶	21	14,600
Tax and Payments	22	Taxable income. Subtract line 21 from line 17. If a loss, see instructions	22	30,060
	23	**Total tax** (from Schedule G, line 7)	23	5,918
	24	**Payments: a** 2013 estimated tax payments and amount applied from 2012 return	24a	5,360
	b	Estimated tax payments allocated to beneficiaries (from Form 1041-T)	24b	
	c	Subtract line 24b from line 24a	24c	5,360
	d	Tax paid with Form 7004 (see instructions)	24d	
	e	Federal income tax withheld. If any is from Form(s) 1099, check ▶ ☐	24e	
		Other payments: f Form 2439 ; g Form 4136 ; Total ▶	24h	
	25	**Total payments.** Add lines 24c through 24e, and 24h ▶	25	5,360
	26	Estimated tax penalty (see instructions)	26	
	27	**Tax due.** If line 25 is smaller than the total of lines 23 and 26, enter amount owed	27	558
	28	**Overpayment.** If line 25 is larger than the total of lines 23 and 26, enter amount overpaid	28	
	29	Amount of line 28 to be: **a Credited to 2014 estimated tax** ▶ ; **b Refunded** ▶	29	

Sign Here

Under penalties of perjury, I declare that I have examined this return, including accompanying schedules and statements, and to the best of my knowledge and belief, it is true, correct, and complete. Declaration of preparer (other than taxpayer) is based on all information of which preparer has any knowledge.

Fred Fidus — Signature of fiduciary or officer representing fiduciary | 3-14-15 — Date | ▶ XX-XXXXXXX — EIN of fiduciary if a financial institution

May the IRS discuss this return with the preparer shown below (see instr.)? ☒ Yes ☐ No

Paid Preparer Use Only

Print/Type preparer's name	Preparer's signature	Date	Check ☒ if self-employed	PTIN
Sarah Public	Sarah Public	3-13-15		

Firm's name ▶ Sarah Public — Firm's EIN ▶

Firm's address ▶ 200 Sun Plaza City, ST 88888 — Phone no.

For Paperwork Reduction Act Notice, see the separate instructions. Cat. No. 11370H Form **1041** (2014)

*Line 5: Net Rental income = Rental income $5,000 – Rental expenses $1,000 = $4,000

Note: Pages concerning the AMT are omitted because the trust does not owe the AMT.

See the Comprehensive Illustration on text page C:14-24 for tax form facts.

Form 1041 (2014) Page 2

Schedule A — Charitable Deduction. Do not complete for a simple trust or a pooled income fund.

1	Amounts paid or permanently set aside for charitable purposes from gross income (see instructions)	1	
2	Tax-exempt income allocable to charitable contributions (see instructions)	2	
3	Subtract line 2 from line 1	3	
4	Capital gains for the tax year allocated to corpus and paid or permanently set aside for charitable purposes	4	
5	Add lines 3 and 4	5	
6	Section 1202 exclusion allocable to capital gains paid or permanently set aside for charitable purposes (see instructions)	6	
7	**Charitable deduction.** Subtract line 6 from line 5. Enter here and on page 1, line 13	7	

Schedule B — Income Distribution Deduction

1	Adjusted total income (see instructions)	1	44,660
2	Adjusted tax-exempt interest ($15,000 – $360)	2	14,640
3	Total net gain from Schedule D (Form 1041), line 19, column (1) (see instructions)	3	
4	Enter amount from Schedule A, line 4 (minus any allocable section 1202 exclusion)	4	
5	Capital gains for the tax year included on Schedule A, line 1 (see instructions)	5	
6	Enter any gain from page 1, line 4, as a negative number. If page 1, line 4, is a loss, enter the loss as a positive number	6	(12,000)
7	**Distributable net income.** Combine lines 1 through 6. If zero or less, enter -0-	7	47,300
8	If a complex trust, enter accounting income for the tax year as determined under the governing instrument and applicable local law — 8: 48,500		
9	Income required to be distributed currently	9	-0-
10	Other amounts paid, credited, or otherwise required to be distributed	10	21,000
11	Total distributions. Add lines 9 and 10. If greater than line 8, see instructions	11	21,000
12	Enter the amount of tax-exempt income included on line 11	12	6,500
13	Tentative income distribution deduction. Subtract line 12 from line 11	13	14,500
14	Tentative income distribution deduction. Subtract line 2 from line 7. If zero or less, enter -0-	14	32,660
15	**Income distribution deduction.** Enter the smaller of line 13 or line 14 here and on page 1, line 18	15	14,500

Schedule G — Tax Computation (see instructions)

1	**Tax:** a Tax on taxable income (see instructions)	1a	5,237		
	b Tax on lump-sum distributions. Attach Form 4972	1b			
	c Alternative minimum tax (from Schedule I (Form 1041), line 56)	1c			
	d **Total.** Add lines 1a through 1c ▶			1d	5,237
2a	Foreign tax credit. Attach Form 1116	2a			
b	General business credit. Attach Form 3800	2b			
c	Credit for prior year minimum tax. Attach Form 8801	2c			
d	Bond credits. Attach Form 8912	2d			
e	**Total credits.** Add lines 2a through 2d ▶			2e	
3	Subtract line 2e from line 1d. If zero or less, enter -0-			3	5,237
4	Net investment income tax from Form 8960, line 21			4	681
5	Recapture taxes. Check if from: ☐ Form 4255 ☐ Form 8611			5	
6	Household employment taxes. Attach Schedule H (Form 1040)			6	
7	**Total tax.** Add lines 3 through 6. Enter here and on page 1, line 23 ▶			7	5,918

Other Information

		Yes	No
1	Did the estate or trust receive tax-exempt income? If "Yes," attach a computation of the allocation of expenses. Enter the amount of tax-exempt interest income and exempt-interest dividends ▶ $ 15,000; (see below)	X	
2	Did the estate or trust receive all or any part of the earnings (salary, wages, and other compensation) of any individual by reason of a contract assignment or similar arrangement?		X
3	At any time during calendar year 2013, did the estate or trust have an interest in or a signature or other authority over a bank, securities, or other financial account in a foreign country? See the instructions for exceptions and filing requirements for FinCEN Form 114. If "Yes," enter the name of the foreign country ▶		X
4	During the tax year, did the estate or trust receive a distribution from, or was it the grantor of, or transferor to, a foreign trust? If "Yes," the estate or trust may have to file Form 3520. See instructions		X
5	Did the estate or trust receive, or pay, any qualified residence interest on seller-provided financing? If "Yes," see the instructions for required attachment		X
6	If this is an estate or a complex trust making the section 663(b) election, check here (see instructions) ▶ ☐		
7	To make a section 643(e)(3) election, attach Schedule D (Form 1041), and check here (see instructions) ▶ ☐		
8	If the decedent's estate has been open for more than 2 years, attach an explanation for the delay in closing the estate, and check here ▶ ☐		
9	Are any present or future trust beneficiaries skip persons? See instructions		X

Form **1041** (2014)

Line 2: Allocation of expenses: $\frac{\$15,000}{\$50,000} \times \$1,200 = \$360$ of trustee's fee allocated to tax-exempt income

SCHEDULE D (Form 1041)

Department of the Treasury Internal Revenue Service

Capital Gains and Losses

▶ Attach to Form 1041, Form 5227, or Form 990-T.

▶ Use Form 8949 to list your transactions for lines 1b, 2, 3, 8b, 9 and 10.

▶ Information about Schedule D and its separate instructions is at *www.irs.gov/form1041*.

OMB No. 1545-0092

2014

Name of estate or trust	Employer identification number
Cathy and Karen Stephens Trust	XX-XXXXXXX

Note: *Form 5227 filers need to complete* ***only*** *Parts I and II.*

Part I Short-Term Capital Gains and Losses—Assets Held One Year or Less

See instructions for how to figure the amounts to enter on the lines below. This form may be easier to complete if you round off cents to whole dollars.	(d) Proceeds (sales price)	(e) Cost (or other basis)	(g) Adjustments to gain or loss from Form(s) 8949, Part I, line 2, column (g)	(h) Gain or (loss) Subtract column (e) from column (d) and combine the result with column (g)
1a Totals for all short-term transactions reported on Form 1099-B for which basis was reported to the IRS and for which you have no adjustments (see instructions). However, if you choose to report all these transactions on Form 8949, leave this line blank and go to line 1b				
1b Totals for all transactions reported on Form(s) 8949 with **Box A** checked				
2 Totals for all transactions reported on Form(s) 8949 with **Box B** checked				
3 Totals for all transactions reported on Form(s) 8949 with **Box C** checked				

4 Short-term capital gain or (loss) from Forms 4684, 6252, 6781, and 8824	4	
5 Net short-term gain or (loss) from partnerships, S corporations, and other estates or trusts	5	
6 Short-term capital loss carryover. Enter the amount, if any, from line 9 of the 2012 Capital Loss Carryover Worksheet	6	( )
7 **Net short-term capital gain or (loss).** Combine lines 1a through 6 in column (h). Enter here and on line 17, column (3) on the back ▶	7	

Part II Long-Term Capital Gains and Losses—Assets Held More Than One Year

See instructions for how to figure the amounts to enter on the lines below. This form may be easier to complete if you round off cents to whole dollars.	(d) Proceeds (sales price)	(e) Cost (or other basis)	(g) Adjustments to gain or loss from Form(s) 8949, Part II, line 2, column (g)	(h) Gain or (loss) Subtract column (e) from column (d) and combine the result with column (g)
8a Totals for all long-term transactions reported on Form 1099-B for which basis was reported to the IRS and for which you have no adjustments (see instructions). However, if you choose to report all these transactions on Form 8949, leave this line blank and go to line 8b	15,000	3,000		12,000
8b Totals for all transactions reported on Form(s) 8949 with **Box D** checked				
9 Totals for all transactions reported on Form(s) 8949 with **Box E** checked				
10 Totals for all transactions reported on Form(s) 8949 with **Box F** checked				

11 Long-term capital gain or (loss) from Forms 2439, 4684, 6252, 6781, and 8824	11	
12 Net long-term gain or (loss) from partnerships, S corporations, and other estates or trusts	12	
13 Capital gain distributions	13	
14 Gain from Form 4797, Part I	14	
15 Long-term capital loss carryover. Enter the amount, if any, from line 14 of the 2012 Capital Loss Carryover Worksheet	15	( )
16 **Net long-term capital gain or (loss).** Combine lines 8a through 15 in column (h). Enter here and on line 18a, column (3) on the back ▶	16	12,000

Schedule D (Form 1041) 2014 Page 2

Part III Summary of Parts I and II
Caution: *Read the instructions* ***before*** *completing this part.*

		Line	(1) Beneficiaries' (see instr.)	(2) Estate's or trust's	(3) Total
17	**Net short-term gain or (loss)**	17			
18	**Net long-term gain or (loss):**				
a	Total for year	18a		12,000	12,000
b	Unrecaptured section 1250 gain (see line 18 of the wrksht.)	18b			
c	28% rate gain	18c			
19	**Total net gain or (loss).** Combine lines 17 and 18a ►	19		12,000	12,000

Note: *If line 19, column (3), is a net gain, enter the gain on Form 1041, line 4 (or Form 990-T, Part I, line 4a). If lines 18a and 19, column (2), are net gains, go to Part V, and* ***do not*** *complete Part IV. If line 19, column (3), is a net loss, complete Part IV and the* ***Capital Loss Carryover Worksheet,*** *as necessary.*

Part IV Capital Loss Limitation

20 Enter here and enter as a (loss) on Form 1041, line 4 (or Form 990-T, Part I, line 4c, if a trust), the **smaller** of:
a The loss on line 19, column (3) **or b** $3,000 . . . 20 ( )

Note: *If the loss on line 19, column (3), is more than $3,000,* ***or*** *if Form 1041, page 1, line 22 (or Form 990-T, line 34), is a loss, complete the* ***Capital Loss Carryover Worksheet*** *in the instructions to figure your capital loss carryover.*

Part V Tax Computation Using Maximum Capital Gains Rates

Form 1041 filers. Complete this part **only** if both lines 18a and 19 in column (2) are gains, or an amount is entered in Part I or Part II and there is an entry on Form 1041, line 2b(2), **and** Form 1041, line 22, is more than zero.

Caution: *Skip this part and complete the* ***Schedule D Tax Worksheet*** *in the instructions if:*

- *Either line 18b, col. (2) or line 18c, col. (2) is more than zero, or*
- *Both Form 1041, line 2b(1), and Form 4952, line 4g are more than zero.*

Form 990-T trusts. Complete this part **only** if both lines 18a and 19 are gains, or qualified dividends are included in income in Part I of Form 990-T, **and** Form 990-T, line 34, is more than zero. Skip this part and complete the **Schedule D Tax Worksheet** in the instructions if either line 18b, col. (2) or line 18c, col. (2) is more than zero.

		Line	Amount	Line	Amount	Line	Amount
21	Enter taxable income from Form 1041, line 22 (or Form 990-T, line 34)			21	30,060		
22	Enter the **smaller** of line 18a or 19 in column (2) but not less than zero	22	12,000				
23	Enter the estate's or trust's qualified dividends from Form 1041, line 2b(2) (or enter the qualified dividends included in income in Part I of Form 990-T)	23	16,681				
24	Add lines 22 and 23	24	28,681				
25	If the estate or trust is filing Form 4952, enter the amount from line 4g; otherwise, enter -0- ►	25	-0-				
26	Subtract line 25 from line 24. If zero or less, enter -0-			26	28,681		
27	Subtract line 26 from line 21. If zero or less, enter -0-			27	1,379		
28	Enter the **smaller** of the amount on line 21 or $2,500			28	2,500		
29	Enter the **smaller** of the amount on line 27 or line 28			29	1,379		
30	Subtract line 29 from line 28. If zero or less, enter -0-. This amount is taxed at 0% ►					30	1,121
31	Enter the smaller of line 21 or line 26			31	28,681		
32	Subtract line 30 from line 26			32	27,560		
33	Enter the **smaller** of line 21 or $12,150			33	12,150		
34	Add lines 27 and 30			34	2,500		
35	Subtract line 34 from line 33. If zero or less, enter -0-			35	9,650		
36	Enter the **smaller** of line 32 or line 35			36	9,650		
37	Multiply line 36 by 15% ►					37	1,448
38	Enter the amount from line 31			38	28,681		
39	Add lines 30 and 36			39	10,771		
40	Subtract line 39 from line 38. If zero or less, enter -0-			40	17,910		
41	Multiply line 40 by 20% ►					41	3,582
42	Figure the tax on the amount on line 27. Use the 2014 Tax Rate Schedule for Estates and Trusts (see the Schedule G instructions in the instructions for Form 1041)			42	207		
43	Add lines 37, 41, and 42			43	5,237		
44	Figure the tax on the amount on line 21. Use the 2014 Tax Rate Schedule for Estates and Trusts (see the Schedule G instructions in the instructions for Form 1041)			44	10,233		
45	**Tax on all taxable income.** Enter the **smaller** of line 43 or line 44 here and on Form 1041, Schedule G, line 1a (or Form 990-T, line 36) ►					45	5,237

Form **8960** Department of the Treasury Internal Revenue Service (99)

Net Investment Income Tax—Individuals, Estates, and Trusts

▶ Attach to Form 1040 or Form 1041.

▶ Information about Form 8960 and its separate instructions is at *www.irs.gov/form8960.*

OMB No. 1545-2227 | 2014 | Attachment Sequence No. 72

Name(s) shown on Form 1040 or Form 1041: Cathy and Karen Stephens Trust

Your social security number or EIN: XX-XXXXXXX

Part I Investment Income ☐ Section 6013(g) election (see instructions) ☐ Regulations section 1.1411-10(g) election (see instructions)

1	Taxable interest (Form 1040, line 8a; or Form 1041, line 1)			1	
2	Ordinary dividends (Form 1040, line 9a; or Form 1041, line 2a)			2	30,000
3	Annuities from nonqualified plans (see instructions)			3	
4a	Rental real estate, royalties, partnerships, S corporations, trusts, etc. (Form 1040, line 17; or Form 1041, line 5)	4a	4,000		
b	Adjustment for net income or loss derived in the ordinary course of a non-section 1411 trade or business (see instructions)	4b			
c	Combine lines 4a and 4b			4c	4,000
5a	Net gain or loss from disposition of property from Form 1040, combine lines 13 and 14; or from Form 1041, combine lines 4 and 7	5a	12,000		
b	Net gain or loss from disposition of property that is not subject to net investment income tax (see instructions)	5b			
c	Adjustment from disposition of partnership interest or S corporation stock (see instructions)	5c			
d	Combine lines 5a through 5c			5d	12,000
6	Changes to investment income for certain CFCs and PFICs (see instructions)			6	
7	Other modifications to investment income (see instructions)			7	
8	Total investment income. Combine lines 1, 2, 3, 4c, 5d, 6, and 7			8	46,000

Part II Investment Expenses Allocable to Investment Income and Modifications

9a	Investment interest expenses (see instructions)	9a			
b	State income tax (see instructions)	9b			
c	Miscellaneous investment expenses (see instructions)	9c	1,340		
d	Add lines 9a, 9b, and 9c			9d	1,340
10	Additional modifications (see instructions)			10	
11	Total deductions and modifications. Add lines 9d and 10			11	1,340

Part III Tax Computation

12	Net investment income. Subtract Part II, line 11 from Part I, line 8. Individuals complete lines 13–17. Estates and trusts complete lines 18a–21. If zero or less, enter -0-			12	44,660
	Individuals:				
13	Modified adjusted gross income (see instructions)	13			
14	Threshold based on filing status (see instructions)	14			
15	Subtract line 14 from line 13. If zero or less, enter -0-	15			
16	Enter the smaller of line 12 or line 15			16	
17	Net investment income tax for individuals. Multiply line 16 by 3.8% (.038). Enter here and on Form 1040, line 60			17	
	Estates and Trusts:				
18a	Net investment income (line 12 above)	18a	44,660		
b	Deductions for distributions of net investment income and deductions under section 642(c) (see instructions)	18b	14,500		
c	Undistributed net investment income. Subtract line 18b from 18a (see instructions)	18c	30,160		
19a	Adjusted gross income (see instructions) *	19a	30,060*		
b	Highest tax bracket for estates and trusts for the year (see instructions)	19b	12,150		
c	Subtract line 19b from line 19a. If zero or less, enter -0-	19c	17,910		
20	Enter the smaller of line 18c or line 19c			20	17,910
21	Net investment income tax for estates and trusts. Multiply line 20 by 3.8% (.038). Enter here and on Form 1041, Schedule G, line 4			21	681

For Paperwork Reduction Act Notice, see your tax return instructions. Cat. No. 59474M Form **8960** (2014)

*$44,660–$14,500–$100=$30,060

661113

☐ Final K-1 ☐ Amended K-1 OMB No. 1545-0092

Schedule K-1 (Form 1041) **2014**
Department of the Treasury
Internal Revenue Service

For calendar year 2013,
or tax year beginning ____________, 2013,
and ending ____________, 20 ____

Beneficiary's Share of Income, Deductions, Credits, etc.

► See back of form and instructions.

Part I Information About the Estate or Trust

A Estate's or trust's employer identification number
XX-XXXXXXX

B Estate's or trust's name
Cathy and Karen Stephens Trust

C Fiduciary's name, address, city, state, and ZIP code
Merchants Bank
3000 Sun Plaza
City, ST 88888

D ☐ Check if Form 1041-T was filed and enter the date it was filed ____________

E ☐ Check if this is the final Form 1041 for the estate or trust

Part II Information About the Beneficiary

F Beneficiary's identifying number
XXX-XX-XXXX

G Beneficiary's name, address, city, state, and ZIP code
Cathy Stephens
13 Sunny Shores
City, ST 77777

H ☒ Domestic beneficiary ☐ Foreign beneficiary

Part III Beneficiary's Share of Current Year Income, Deductions, Credits, and Other Items

1	Interest income	
2a	Ordinary dividends	8,879
2b	Qualified dividends	8,879
3	Net short-term capital gain	
4a	Net long-term capital gain	
4b	28% rate gain	
4c	Unrecaptured section 1250 gain	
5	Other portfolio and nonbusiness income	
6	Ordinary business income	
7	Net rental real estate income	788
8	Other rental income	
9	Directly apportioned deductions	
10	Estate tax deduction	
11	Final year deductions	
12	Alternative minimum tax adjustment	
13	Credits and credit recapture	
14	Other information	A 4,333

*See attached statement for additional information.

Note. A statement must be attached showing the beneficiary's share of income and directly apportioned deductions from each business, rental real estate, and other rental activity.

For IRS Use Only

661113

☐ Final K-1 ☐ Amended K-1

OMB No. 1545-0092

Schedule K-1 (Form 1041)
Department of the Treasury
Internal Revenue Service

2014

For calendar year 2013, or tax year beginning ______, 2013, and ending ______, 20 ____

Beneficiary's Share of Income, Deductions, Credits, etc.

▶ See back of form and instructions.

Part I Information About the Estate or Trust

A Estate's or trust's employer identification number
XX-XXXXXXX

B Estate's or trust's name
Cathy and Karen Stephens Trust

C Fiduciary's name, address, city, state, and ZIP code
Merchants Bank
3000 Sun Plaza
City, ST 88888

D ☐ Check if Form 1041-T was filed and enter the date it was filed ______

E ☐ Check if this is the final Form 1041 for the estate or trust

Part II Information About the Beneficiary

F Beneficiary's identifying number
XXX-XX-XXXX

G Beneficiary's name, address, city, state, and ZIP code
Karen Stephens
1472 Ski Run
City, ST 11111

H ☒ Domestic beneficiary ☐ Foreign beneficiary

Part III Beneficiary's Share of Current Year Income, Deductions, Credits, and Other Items

1	Interest income	
2a	Ordinary dividends	4,440
2b	Qualified dividends	4,440
3	Net short-term capital gain	
4a	Net long-term capital gain	
4b	28% rate gain	
4c	Unrecaptured section 1250 gain	
5	Other portfolio and nonbusiness income	
6	Ordinary business income	
7	Net rental real estate income	393
8	Other rental income	
9	Directly apportioned deductions	
10	Estate tax deduction	
11	Final year deductions	
12	Alternative minimum tax adjustment	
13	Credits and credit recapture	
14	Other information	A 2,167

*See attached statement for additional information.

Note. A statement must be attached showing the beneficiary's share of income and directly apportioned deductions from each business, rental real estate, and other rental activity.

For IRS Use Only

Facts for General Partnership (Form 1065)

The same basic facts presented for the Andrew Lawrence proprietorship are used for the partnership except for the following:

1. Johns and Lawrence is instead a general partnership. Andrew Lawrence and Stephen Johns are both general partners and have equal capital and profits interests. The partners formed the partnership on June 1, 2008. Johns and Lawrence each exchanged their $100,000 of property for a 50% interest in capital and profits.

2. The book income for Johns and Lawrence is presented in the attached worksheet, which reconciles book income and partnership taxable income.

3. The $18,000 salaries paid to each partner are stipulated in the partnership agreement and are treated as guaranteed payments.

4. The partnership pays federal and state employment taxes on the wages paid to employees other than the partners Johns and Lawrence. The employment tax expense is $52,000 × 0.16 = $8,320. The guaranteed payments made to Johns and Lawrence are treated as self-employment income by the two partners.

5. The partnership paid no estimated federal income taxes.

6. The partnership distributed $14,106 to each of the two partners.

7. Other deductions include:

Travel	$ 4,000
Meals and entertainment	8,000
Minus: 50% disallowance	(4,000)
Office expenses	16,000
Transportation	10,400
General and administrative	3,000
Advertising	13,000
Miscellaneous*	850
Total	$51,250

*$150 of the miscellaneous expenses are related to the production of the dividend income and are separately stated.

8. The following schedule reconciles net income for the C corporation and the partnership:

Net income per books for C corporation	$63,412
Plus: Federal income taxes	14,000
Employment tax adjustment ($14,480 − $8,320)	6,160
Net income per books for partnership	$83,572

9. Total paid-in capital and accumulated profits were divided equally between the two partners in accordance with the actual contributions and allocation of partnership profits in the partnership agreement. Actual business operations may provide for an unequal allocation.

10. Qualified production activities income (QPAI) equals $80,000. Employer's W-2 wages allocable to U.S. production activities equal $52,000.

11. The balance sheet for Johns and Lawrence appears on page 4 of Form 1065.

12. For additional information, see the worksheet on page B-36.

Form **1065** Department of the Treasury Internal Revenue Service

U.S. Return of Partnership Income

For calendar year 2013, or tax year beginning ________, 2013, ending ________, 20 ____.

▶ Information about Form 1065 and its separate instructions is at *www.irs.gov/form1065.*

OMB No. 1545-0099

2014

A Principal business activity: Manufacturing	Name of partnership: Johns and Lawrence	D Employer identification number: XX-XXXXXXX
B Principal product or service: Furniture	Type or Print — Number, street, and room or suite no. If a P.O. box, see the instructions.: 1234 First Avenue	E Date business started: 6-1-2008
C Business code number: 337000	City or town, state or province, country, and ZIP or foreign postal code: City, ST 55555	F Total assets (see the instructions): $ 499,484

G Check applicable boxes: (1) ☐ Initial return (2) ☐ Final return (3) ☐ Name change (4) ☐ Address change (5) ☐ Amended return (6) ☐ Technical termination - also check (1) or (2)

H Check accounting method: (1) ☐ Cash (2) ☒ Accrual (3) ☐ Other (specify) ▶

I Number of Schedules K-1. Attach one for each person who was a partner at any time during the tax year ▶

J Check if Schedules C and M-3 are attached ☐

Caution. *Include **only** trade or business income and expenses on lines 1a through 22 below. See the instructions for more information.*

Income	1a	Gross receipts or sales	1a	869,658		
	b	Returns and allowances	1b	29,242		
	c	Balance. Subtract line 1b from line 1a			1c	840,416
	2	Cost of goods sold (attach Form 1125-A)			2	540,204
	3	Gross profit. Subtract line 2 from line 1c			3	300,212
	4	Ordinary income (loss) from other partnerships, estates, and trusts (attach statement)			4	
	5	Net farm profit (loss) (attach Schedule F (Form 1040))			5	
	6	Net gain (loss) from Form 4797, Part II, line 17 (attach Form 4797)			6	
	7	Other income (loss) (attach statement)			7	
	8	**Total income (loss).** Combine lines 3 through 7			8	300,212
Deductions (see the instructions for limitations)	9	Salaries and wages (other than to partners) (less employment credits)			9	52,000
	10	Guaranteed payments to partners			10	36,000
	11	Repairs and maintenance			11	4,800
	12	Bad debts			12	4,000
	13	Rent			13	36,000
	14	Taxes and licenses (8,320 + 1,520)			14	9,840
	15	Interest			15	8,000
	16a	Depreciation (if required, attach Form 4562)	16a	27,476		
	b	Less depreciation reported on Form 1125-A and elsewhere on return	16b	15,000	16c	12,476
	17	Depletion **(Do not deduct oil and gas depletion.)**			17	
	18	Retirement plans, etc.			18	2,000
	19	Employee benefit programs			19	4,000
	20	Other deductions (attach statement)			20	51,250
	21	**Total deductions.** Add the amounts shown in the far right column for lines 9 through 20			21	220,366
	22	**Ordinary business income (loss).** Subtract line 21 from line 8			22	79,846

Sign Here

Under penalties of perjury, I declare that I have examined this return, including accompanying schedules and statements, and to the best of my knowledge and belief, it is true, correct, and complete. Declaration of preparer (other than general partner or limited liability company member manager) is based on all information of which preparer has any knowledge.

▶ *Andrew Lawrence* ▶ 4-14-15

Signature of general partner or limited liability company member manager — Date

May the IRS discuss this return with the preparer shown below (see instructions)? ☐ Yes ☐ No

Paid Preparer Use Only

Print/Type preparer's name	Preparer's signature	Date	Check ☒ if self-employed	PTIN
Michael S. Prepper	*Michael S. Prepper*	4-14-15		

Firm's name ▶ Michael S. Prepper — Firm's EIN ▶

Firm's address ▶ 1111 Second Street, City, ST 55555 — Phone no.

Schedule B Other Information

		Yes	No
1	What type of entity is filing this return? Check the applicable box: a ☒ Domestic general partnership b ☐ Domestic limited partnership c ☐ Domestic limited liability company d ☐ Domestic limited liability partnership e ☐ Foreign partnership f ☐ Other ▶		
2	At any time during the tax year, was any partner in the partnership a disregarded entity, a partnership (including an entity treated as a partnership), a trust, an S corporation, an estate (other than an estate of a deceased partner), or a nominee or similar person?		X
3	At the end of the tax year:		
a	Did any foreign or domestic corporation, partnership (including any entity treated as a partnership), trust, or tax-exempt organization, or any foreign government own, directly or indirectly, an interest of 50% or more in the profit, loss, or capital of the partnership? For rules of constructive ownership, see instructions. If "Yes," attach Schedule B-1, Information on Partners Owning 50% or More of the Partnership		X
b	Did any individual or estate own, directly or indirectly, an interest of 50% or more in the profit, loss, or capital of the partnership? For rules of constructive ownership, see instructions. If "Yes," attach Schedule B-1, Information on Partners Owning 50% or More of the Partnership *	X	
4	At the end of the tax year, did the partnership:		
a	Own directly 20% or more, or own, directly or indirectly, 50% or more of the total voting power of all classes of stock entitled to vote of any foreign or domestic corporation? For rules of constructive ownership, see instructions. If "Yes," complete (i) through (iv) below		X

(i) Name of Corporation	(ii) Employer Identification Number (if any)	(iii) Country of Incorporation	(iv) Percentage Owned in Voting Stock

		Yes	No
b	Own directly an interest of 20% or more, or own, directly or indirectly, an interest of 50% or more in the profit, loss, or capital in any foreign or domestic partnership (including an entity treated as a partnership) or in the beneficial interest of a trust? For rules of constructive ownership, see instructions. If "Yes," complete (i) through (v) below		X

(i) Name of Entity	(ii) Employer Identification Number (if any)	(iii) Type of Entity	(iv) Country of Organization	(v) Maximum Percentage Owned in Profit, Loss, or Capital

		Yes	No
5	Did the partnership file Form 8893, Election of Partnership Level Tax Treatment, or an election statement under section 6231(a)(1)(B)(ii) for partnership-level tax treatment, that is in effect for this tax year? See Form 8893 for more details		X
6	Does the partnership satisfy **all four** of the following conditions?		
a	The partnership's total receipts for the tax year were less than $250,000.		
b	The partnership's total assets at the end of the tax year were less than $1 million.		
c	Schedules K-1 are filed with the return and furnished to the partners on or before the due date (including extensions) for the partnership return.		
d	The partnership is not filing and is not required to file Schedule M-3		X
	If "Yes," the partnership is not required to complete Schedules L, M-1, and M-2; Item F on page 1 of Form 1065; or Item L on Schedule K-1.		
7	Is this partnership a publicly traded partnership as defined in section 469(k)(2)?		X
8	During the tax year, did the partnership have any debt that was cancelled, was forgiven, or had the terms modified so as to reduce the principal amount of the debt?		X
9	Has this partnership filed, or is it required to file, Form 8918, Material Advisor Disclosure Statement, to provide information on any reportable transaction?		X
10	At any time during calendar year 2014, did the partnership have an interest in or a signature or other authority over a financial account in a foreign country (such as a bank account, securities account, or other financial account)? See the instructions for exceptions and filing requirements for FinCEN Form 114, Report of Foreign Bank and Financial Accounts (FBAR) (formerly TD F 90-22.1). If "Yes," enter the name of the foreign country. ▶		X

*Schedule B-1 is not attached. If attached, it would list Stephen Johns and Andrew Lawrence, each of whom own a 50% interest in the partnership.

Form 1065 (2014) Page 3

Schedule B Other Information *(continued)*

		Yes	No
11	At any time during the tax year, did the partnership receive a distribution from, or was it the grantor of, or transferor to, a foreign trust? If "Yes," the partnership may have to file Form 3520, Annual Return To Report Transactions With Foreign Trusts and Receipt of Certain Foreign Gifts. See instructions		X
12a	Is the partnership making, or had it previously made (and not revoked), a section 754 election? . . . . . . See instructions for details regarding a section 754 election.		X
b	Did the partnership make for this tax year an optional basis adjustment under section 743(b) or 734(b)? If "Yes," attach a statement showing the computation and allocation of the basis adjustment. See instructions		X
c	Is the partnership required to adjust the basis of partnership assets under section 743(b) or 734(b) because of a substantial built-in loss (as defined under section 743(d)) or substantial basis reduction (as defined under section 734(d))? If "Yes," attach a statement showing the computation and allocation of the basis adjustment. See instructions		X
13	Check this box if, during the current or prior tax year, the partnership distributed any property received in a like-kind exchange or contributed such property to another entity (other than disregarded entities wholly-owned by the partnership throughout the tax year) . . . . ▶ ☐		
14	At any time during the tax year, did the partnership distribute to any partner a tenancy-in-common or other undivided interest in partnership property?		X
15	If the partnership is required to file Form 8858, Information Return of U.S. Persons With Respect To Foreign Disregarded Entities, enter the number of Forms 8858 attached. See instructions ▶		
16	Does the partnership have any foreign partners? If "Yes," enter the number of Forms 8805, Foreign Partner's Information Statement of Section 1446 Withholding Tax, filed for this partnership. ▶		X
17	Enter the number of Forms 8865, Return of U.S. Persons With Respect to Certain Foreign Partnerships, attached to this return. ▶		
18a	Did you make any payments in 2013 that would require you to file Form(s) 1099? See instructions		X
b	If "Yes," did you or will you file required Form(s) 1099?		
19	Enter the number of Form(s) 5471, Information Return of U.S. Persons With Respect To Certain Foreign Corporations, attached to this return. ▶ -0-		
20	Enter the number of partners that are foreign governments under section 892. ▶ -0-		

Designation of Tax Matters Partner (see instructions)

Enter below the general partner or member-manager designated as the tax matters partner (TMP) for the tax year of this return:

Name of designated TMP ▶	Andrew Lawrence	Identifying number of TMP ▶	XXX-XX-XXXX
If the TMP is an entity, name of TMP representative ▶		Phone number of TMP ▶	
Address of designated TMP ▶	333 Third Street City, ST 55555		

Form **1065** (2014)

Form 1065 (2014) Page 4

Schedule K		Partners' Distributive Share Items	Line	Total amount
Income (Loss)	1	Ordinary business income (loss) (page 1, line 22)	1	79,846
	2	Net rental real estate income (loss) (attach Form 8825)	2	
	3a	Other gross rental income (loss) 3a		
	b	Expenses from other rental activities (attach statement) 3b		
	c	Other net rental income (loss). Subtract line 3b from line 3a	3c	
	4	Guaranteed payments	4	36,000
	5	Interest income	5	
	6	Dividends: a Ordinary dividends	6a	1,000
		b Qualified dividends 6b 1,000		
	7	Royalties	7	
	8	Net short-term capital gain (loss) (attach Schedule D (Form 1065))	8	(2,100)
	9a	Net long-term capital gain (loss) (attach Schedule D (Form 1065))	9a	4,500
	b	Collectibles (28%) gain (loss) 9b		
	c	Unrecaptured section 1250 gain (attach statement) 9c		
	10	Net section 1231 gain (loss) (attach Form 4797)	10	
	11	Other income (loss) (see instructions) Type ▶	11	
Deductions	12	Section 179 deduction (attach Form 4562)	12	
	13a	Contributions	13a	12,000
	b	Investment interest expense	13b	150
	c	Section 59(e)(2) expenditures: (1) Type ▶ (2) Amount ▶	13c(2)	
	d	Other deductions (see instructions) Type ▶	13d	
Self-Employment	14a	Net earnings (loss) from self-employment	14a	115,846
	b	Gross farming or fishing income	14b	
	c	Gross nonfarm income	14c	300,212
Credits	15a	Low-income housing credit (section 42(j)(5))	15a	
	b	Low-income housing credit (other)	15b	
	c	Qualified rehabilitation expenditures (rental real estate) (attach Form 3468)	15c	
	d	Other rental real estate credits (see instructions) Type ▶	15d	
	e	Other rental credits (see instructions) Type ▶	15e	
	f	Other credits (see instructions) Type ▶	15f	
Foreign Transactions	16a	Name of country or U.S. possession ▶		
	b	Gross income from all sources	16b	
	c	Gross income sourced at partner level	16c	
		Foreign gross income sourced at partnership level		
	d	Passive category ▶ e General category ▶ f Other ▶	16f	
		Deductions allocated and apportioned at partner level		
	g	Interest expense ▶ h Other ▶	16h	
		Deductions allocated and apportioned at partnership level to foreign source income		
	i	Passive category ▶ j General category ▶ k Other ▶	16k	
	l	Total foreign taxes (check one): ▶ Paid ☐ Accrued ☐	16l	
	m	Reduction in taxes available for credit (attach statement)	16m	
	n	Other foreign tax information (attach statement)		
Alternative Minimum Tax (AMT) Items	17a	Post-1986 depreciation adjustment	17a	1,514
	b	Adjusted gain or loss	17b	
	c	Depletion (other than oil and gas)	17c	
	d	Oil, gas, and geothermal properties—gross income	17d	
	e	Oil, gas, and geothermal properties—deductions	17e	
	f	Other AMT items (attach statement)	17f	
Other Information	18a	Tax-exempt interest income	18a	18,000
	b	Other tax-exempt income	18b	
	c	Nondeductible expenses	18c	6,000 *
	19a	Distributions of cash and marketable securities	19a	28,212
	b	Distributions of other property	19b	
	20a	Investment income	20a	1,000 **
	b	Investment expenses	20b	
	c	Other items and amounts (attach statement)		

Form **1065** (2014)

*Disallowed meals and entertainment expenses ($4,000) plus interest on loan used to purchase tax-exempt bonds ($2,000).

**Investment income only if partners elect to tax dividends at ordinary rates under Sec. 163(d)(4)(B).

Analysis of Net Income (Loss)

1	Net income (loss). Combine Schedule K, lines 1 through 11. From the result, subtract the sum of Schedule K, lines 12 through 13d, and 16l . . . 1	107,096

2 Analysis by partner type:	(i) Corporate	(ii) Individual (active)	(iii) Individual (passive)	(iv) Partnership	(v) Exempt Organization	(vi) Nominee/Other
a General partners		107,096				
b Limited partners						

Schedule L Balance Sheets per Books

	Beginning of tax year (a)	Beginning of tax year (b)	End of tax year (c)	End of tax year (d)
Assets				
1 Cash		60,000		92,760
2a Trade notes and accounts receivable	25,100		24,000	
b Less allowance for bad debts	1,000	24,000	1,000	23,000
3 Inventories		64,000		104,800
4 U.S. government obligations				
5 Tax-exempt securities		200,000		200,000
6 Other current assets (attach statement)		7,000		-0-
7a Loans to partners (or persons related to partners)				
b Mortgage and real estate loans				
8 Other investments (attach statement)				
9a Buildings and other depreciable assets	151,600		151,600	
b Less accumulated depreciation	45,200	106,400	72,760	78,924
10a Depletable assets				
b Less accumulated depletion				
11 Land (net of any amortization)				
12a Intangible assets (amortizable only)				
b Less accumulated amortization				
13 Other assets (attach statement)				
14 Total assets		461,400		499,484
Liabilities and Capital				
15 Accounts payable		26,000		19,000
16 Mortgages, notes, bonds payable in less than 1 year		4,000		4,000
17 Other current liabilities (attach statement)		3,600		3,600
18 All nonrecourse loans				
19a Loans from partners (or persons related to partners)				
b Mortgages, notes, bonds payable in 1 year or more		130,000		119,724
20 Other liabilities (attach statement)				
21 Partners' capital accounts		297,800		353,160
22 Total liabilities and capital		461,400		499,484

Schedule M-1 Reconciliation of Income (Loss) per Books With Income (Loss) per Return

Note. Schedule M-3 may be required instead of Schedule M-1 (see instructions).

1 Net income (loss) per books	83,572	6 Income recorded on books this year not included on Schedule K, lines 1 through 11 (itemize):	
2 Income included on Schedule K, lines 1, 2, 3c, 5, 6a, 7, 8, 9a, 10, and 11, not recorded on books this year (itemize):		a Tax-exempt interest $ 18,000	18,000
3 Guaranteed payments (other than health insurance)	36,000	7 Deductions included on Schedule K, lines 1 through 13d, and 16l, not charged against book income this year (itemize):	
4 Expenses recorded on books this year not included on Schedule K, lines 1 through 13d, and 16l (itemize):		a Depreciation $ 476	476
a Depreciation $		8 Add lines 6 and 7	18,476
b Travel and entertainment $	6,000*	9 Income (loss) (Analysis of Net Income (Loss), line 1). Subtract line 8 from line 5	107,096
5 Add lines 1 through 4	125,572		

Schedule M-2 Analysis of Partners' Capital Accounts

1 Balance at beginning of year	297,800	6 Distributions: a Cash	28,212
2 Capital contributed: a Cash		b Property	
b Property	83,572	7 Other decreases (itemize):	
3 Net income (loss) per books			
4 Other increases (itemize):		8 Add lines 6 and 7	28,212
5 Add lines 1 through 4	381,372	9 Balance at end of year. Subtract line 8 from line 5	353,160

*$4,000 travel and entertaiment plus $6,000 on loan to buy tax-exempt bonds.

651113

☐ Final K-1 ☐ Amended K-1 OMB No. 1545-0099

Schedule K-1 (Form 1065) **2014**

Department of the Treasury
Internal Revenue Service

For calendar year 2013, or tax year beginning ________, 2013 ending ________, 20____

Partner's Share of Income, Deductions, Credits, etc.

► See back of form and separate instructions.

Part I Information About the Partnership

A Partnership's employer identification number
XX-XXXXXXX

B Partnership's name, address, city, state, and ZIP code
Johns and Lawrence
1234 Avenue
City, ST 55555

C IRS Center where partnership filed return
Ogden, UT

D ☐ Check if this is a publicly traded partnership (PTP)

Part II Information About the Partner

E Partner's identifying number
XXX-XX-XXXX

F Partner's name, address, city, state, and ZIP code
Andrew Lawrence*
333 Third Street
City, ST 55555

G ☒ General partner or LLC member-manager ☐ Limited partner or other LLC member

H ☐ Domestic partner ☐ Foreign partner

I1 What type of entity is this partner? Individual

I2 If this partner is a retirement plan (IRA/SEP/Keogh/etc.), check here (see instructions) ☐

J Partner's share of profit, loss, and capital (see instructions):

	Beginning	Ending
Profit	50 %	50 %
Loss	50 %	50 %
Capital	50 %	50 %

K Partner's share of liabilities at year end:

Nonrecourse	$
Qualified nonrecourse financing	$
Recourse	$ 73,162

L Partner's capital account analysis:

Beginning capital account	$ 148,900
Capital contributed during the year	$ -0-
Current year increase (decrease)	$ 41,786
Withdrawals & distributions	$ (14,106)
Ending capital account	$ 176,580

☐ Tax basis ☐ GAAP ☒ Section 704(b) book
☐ Other (explain)

M Did the partner contribute property with a built-in gain or loss?
☐ Yes ☒ No
If "Yes," attach statement (see instructions)

Part III Partner's Share of Current Year Income, Deductions, Credits, and Other Items

Line	Item	Amount
1	Ordinary business income (loss)	39,923
2	Net rental real estate income (loss)	
3	Other net rental income (loss)	
4	Guaranteed payments	18,000
5	Interest income	
6a	Ordinary dividends	500
6b	Qualified dividends	500
7	Royalties	
8	Net short-term capital gain (loss)	(1,050)
9a	Net long-term capital gain (loss)	2,250
9b	Collectibles (28%) gain (loss)	
9c	Unrecaptured section 1250 gain	
10	Net section 1231 gain (loss)	
11	Other income (loss)	
12	Section 179 deduction	
13	Other deductions	A 6,000
		G 75
		U 40,000
		V 26,000
14	Self-employment earnings (loss)	A 57,923
		A 150,106
15	Credits	
16	Foreign transactions	
17	Alternative minimum tax (AMT) items	A 757
18	Tax-exempt income and nondeductible expenses	A 9,000
		C 3,000
19	Distributions	A 14,106
20	Other information	A 500**

*See attached statement for additional information.

For IRS Use Only

For Paperwork Reduction Act Notice, see Instructions for Form 1065. IRS.gov/form1065 Cat. No. 11394R **Schedule K-1 (Form 1065) 2014**

*Schedule K-1 for Stephen Johns is similar to this one and is not reproduced here.

**Investment income only if partner elects to tax dividends at ordinary rates under Sec. 163(d)(4)(B).

Schedule K-1 (Form 1065) 2014 Page **2**

This list identifies the codes used on Schedule K-1 for all partners and provides summarized reporting information for partners who file Form 1040. For detailed reporting and filing information, see the separate Partner's Instructions for Schedule K-1 and the instructions for your income tax return.

1. Ordinary business income (loss). Determine whether the income (loss) is passive or nonpassive and enter on your return as follows.

	Report on
Passive loss	See the Partner's Instructions
Passive income	Schedule E, line 28, column (g)
Nonpassive loss	Schedule E, line 28, column (h)
Nonpassive income	Schedule E, line 28, column (j)
2. Net rental real estate income (loss)	See the Partner's Instructions
3. Other net rental income (loss)	
Net income	Schedule E, line 28, column (g)
Net loss	See the Partner's Instructions
4. Guaranteed payments	Schedule E, line 28, column (j)
5. Interest income	Form 1040, line 8a
6a. Ordinary dividends	Form 1040, line 9a
6b. Qualified dividends	Form 1040, line 9b
7. Royalties	Schedule E, line 4
8. Net short-term capital gain (loss)	Schedule D, line 5
9a. Net long-term capital gain (loss)	Schedule D, line 12
9b. Collectibles (28%) gain (loss)	28% Rate Gain Worksheet, line 4 (Schedule D instructions)
9c. Unrecaptured section 1250 gain	See the Partner's Instructions
10. Net section 1231 gain (loss)	See the Partner's Instructions
11. Other income (loss)	
Code	
A Other portfolio income (loss)	See the Partner's Instructions
B Involuntary conversions	See the Partner's Instructions
C Sec. 1256 contracts & straddles	Form 6781, line 1
D Mining exploration costs recapture	See Pub. 535
E Cancellation of debt	Form 1040, line 21 or Form 982
F Other income (loss)	See the Partner's Instructions
12. Section 179 deduction	See the Partner's Instructions
13. Other deductions	
A Cash contributions (50%)	See the Partner's Instructions (A–G)
B Cash contributions (30%)	
C Noncash contributions (50%)	
D Noncash contributions (30%)	
E Capital gain property to a 50% organization (30%)	
F Capital gain property (20%)	
G Contributions (100%)	
H Investment interest expense	Form 4952, line 1
I Deductions—royalty income	Schedule E, line 19
J Section 59(e)(2) expenditures	See the Partner's Instructions
K Deductions—portfolio (2% floor)	Schedule A, line 23
L Deductions—portfolio (other)	Schedule A, line 28
M Amounts paid for medical insurance	Schedule A, line 1 or Form 1040, line 29
N Educational assistance benefits	See the Partner's Instructions
O Dependent care benefits	Form 2441, line 12
P Preproductive period expenses	See the Partner's Instructions
Q Commercial revitalization deduction from rental real estate activities	See Form 8582 instructions
R Pensions and IRAs	See the Partner's Instructions
S Reforestation expense deduction	See the Partner's Instructions
T Domestic production activities information	See Form 8903 instructions
U Qualified production activities income	Form 8903, line 7b
V Employer's Form W-2 wages	Form 8903, line 17
W Other deductions	See the Partner's Instructions
14. Self-employment earnings (loss)	

Note. *If you have a section 179 deduction or any partner-level deductions, see the Partner's Instructions before completing Schedule SE.*

A Net earnings (loss) from self-employment	Schedule SE, Section A or B
B Gross farming or fishing income	See the Partner's Instructions
C Gross non-farm income	See the Partner's Instructions
15. Credits	
A Low-income housing credit (section 42(j)(5)) from pre-2008 buildings	See the Partner's Instructions (A–G)
B Low-income housing credit (other) from pre-2008 buildings	
C Low-income housing credit (section 42(j)(5)) from post-2007 buildings	
D Low-income housing credit (other) from post-2007 buildings	
E Qualified rehabilitation expenditures (rental real estate)	
F Other rental real estate credits	
G Other rental credits	
H Undistributed capital gains credit	Form 1040, line 71; check box a
I Biofuel producer credit	See the Partner's Instructions (I–K)
J Work opportunity credit	
K Disabled access credit	

Code	*Report on*
L Empowerment zone employment credit	See the Partner's Instructions (L–P)
M Credit for increasing research activities	
N Credit for employer social security and Medicare taxes	
O Backup withholding	
P Other credits	
16. Foreign transactions	
A Name of country or U.S. possession	Form 1116, Part I (A–C)
B Gross income from all sources	
C Gross income sourced at partner level	
Foreign gross income sourced at partnership level	
D Passive category	Form 1116, Part I (D–F)
E General category	
F Other	
Deductions allocated and apportioned at partner level	
G Interest expense	Form 1116, Part I
H Other	Form 1116, Part I
Deductions allocated and apportioned at partnership level to foreign source income	
I Passive category	Form 1116, Part I (I–K)
J General category	
K Other	
Other information	
L Total foreign taxes paid	Form 1116, Part II
M Total foreign taxes accrued	Form 1116, Part II
N Reduction in taxes available for credit	Form 1116, line 12
O Foreign trading gross receipts	Form 8873
P Extraterritorial income exclusion	Form 8873
Q Other foreign transactions	See the Partner's Instructions
17. Alternative minimum tax (AMT) items	
A Post-1986 depreciation adjustment	See the Partner's Instructions and the Instructions for Form 6251 (A–F)
B Adjusted gain or loss	
C Depletion (other than oil & gas)	
D Oil, gas, & geothermal—gross income	
E Oil, gas, & geothermal—deductions	
F Other AMT items	
18. Tax-exempt income and nondeductible expenses	
A Tax-exempt interest income	Form 1040, line 8b
B Other tax-exempt income	See the Partner's Instructions
C Nondeductible expenses	See the Partner's Instructions
19. Distributions	
A Cash and marketable securities	See the Partner's Instructions (A–C)
B Distribution subject to section 737	
C Other property	
20. Other information	
A Investment income	Form 4952, line 4a
B Investment expenses	Form 4952, line 5
C Fuel tax credit information	Form 4136
D Qualified rehabilitation expenditures (other than rental real estate)	See the Partner's Instructions
E Basis of energy property	See the Partner's Instructions
F Recapture of low-income housing credit (section 42(j)(5))	Form 8611, line 8
G Recapture of low-income housing credit (other)	Form 8611, line 8
H Recapture of investment credit	See Form 4255
I Recapture of other credits	See the Partner's Instructions
J Look-back interest—completed long-term contracts	See Form 8697
K Look-back interest—income forecast method	See Form 8866
L Dispositions of property with section 179 deductions	See the Partner's Instructions (L–Z)
M Recapture of section 179 deduction	
N Interest expense for corporate partners	
O Section 453(l)(3) information	
P Section 453A(c) information	
Q Section 1260(b) information	
R Interest allocable to production expenditures	
S CCF nonqualified withdrawals	
T Depletion information—oil and gas	
U Amortization of reforestation costs	
V Unrelated business taxable income	
W Precontribution gain (loss)	
X Section 108(i) information	
Y Net investment income	
Z Other information	

Form **1125-A**
(Rev. December 2012)
Department of the Treasury
Internal Revenue Service

Cost of Goods Sold

▶ Attach to Form 1120, 1120-C, 1120-F, 1120S, 1065, or 1065-B.
▶ Information about Form 1125-A and its instructions is at *www.irs.gov/form1125a*.

OMB No. 1545-2225

Name: Johns and Lawrence

Employer identification number: XX-XXXXXXX

1	Inventory at beginning of year	1	64,000
2	Purchases	2	340,800
3	Cost of labor	3	143,204
4	Additional section 263A costs (attach schedule)	4	7,000
5	Other costs (attach schedule)	5	90,000
6	**Total.** Add lines 1 through 5	6	645,004
7	Inventory at end of year	7	104,800
8	**Cost of goods sold.** Subtract line 7 from line 6. Enter here and on Form 1120, page 1, line 2 or the appropriate line of your tax return (see instructions)	8	540,204

9a Check all methods used for valuing closing inventory:
(i) ☒ Cost
(ii) ☐ Lower of cost or market
(iii) ☐ Other (Specify method used and attach explanation.) ▶

b Check if there was a writedown of subnormal goods ▶ ☐

c Check if the LIFO inventory method was adopted this tax year for any goods (if checked, attach Form 970) ▶ ☐

d If the LIFO inventory method was used for this tax year, enter amount of closing inventory computed under LIFO | 9d |

e If property is produced or acquired for resale, do the rules of section 263A apply to the entity (see instructions)? ☐ Yes ☒ No

f Was there any change in determining quantities, cost, or valuations between opening and closing inventory? If "Yes," attach explanation ☐ Yes ☒ No

Section references are to the Internal Revenue Code unless otherwise noted.

General Instructions

Purpose of Form

Use Form 1125-A to calculate and deduct cost of goods sold for certain entities.

Who Must File

Filers of Form 1120, 1120-C, 1120-F, 1120S, 1065, or 1065-B, must complete and attach Form 1125-A if the applicable entity reports a deduction for cost of goods sold.

Inventories

Generally, inventories are required at the beginning and end of each tax year if the production, purchase, or sale of merchandise is an income-producing factor. See Regulations section 1.471-1. If inventories are required, you generally must use an accrual method of accounting for sales and purchases of inventory items.

Exception for certain taxpayers. If you are a qualifying taxpayer or a qualifying small business taxpayer (defined below), you can adopt or change your accounting method to account for inventoriable items in the same manner as materials and supplies that are not incidental.

Under this accounting method, inventory costs for raw materials purchased for use in producing finished goods and merchandise purchased for resale are deductible in the year the finished goods or merchandise are sold (but not before the year you paid for the raw materials or merchandise, if you are also using the cash method).

If you account for inventoriable items in the same manner as materials and supplies that are not incidental, you can currently deduct expenditures for direct labor and all indirect costs that would otherwise be included in inventory costs. See the instructions for lines 2 and 7.

For additional guidance on this method of accounting, see Pub. 538, Accounting Periods and Methods. For guidance on adopting or changing to this method of accounting, see Form 3115, Application for Change in Accounting Method, and its instructions.

Qualifying taxpayer. A qualifying taxpayer is a taxpayer that, (a) for each prior tax year ending after December 16, 1998, has average annual gross receipts of $1 million or less for the 3 prior tax years and (b) its business is not a tax shelter (as defined in section 448(d)(3)). See Rev. Proc. 2001-10, 2001-2 I.R.B. 272.

Qualifying small business taxpayer. A qualifying small business taxpayer is a taxpayer that, (a) for each prior tax year ending on or after December 31, 2000, has average annual gross receipts of $10 million or less for the 3 prior tax years, (b) whose principal business activity is not an ineligible activity, and (c) whose business is not a tax shelter (as defined in section 448 (d)(3)). See Rev. Proc. 2002-28, 2002-18 I.R.B. 815.

Uniform capitalization rules. The uniform capitalization rules of section 263A generally require you to capitalize, or include in inventory, certain costs incurred in connection with the following.

- The production of real property and tangible personal property held in inventory or held for sale in the ordinary course of business.
- Real property or personal property (tangible and intangible) acquired for resale.
- The production of real property and tangible personal property by a corporation for use in its trade or business or in an activity engaged in for profit.

See the discussion on section 263A uniform capitalization rules in the instructions for your tax return before completing Form 1125-A. Also see Regulations sections 1.263A-1 through 1.263A-3. See Regulations section 1.263A-4 for rules for property produced in a farming business.

Johns and Lawrence General Partnership Reconciliation of Book and Taxable Income For Year Ending December 31, 2014

	Book Income		Adjustments		Taxable Income		Form 1065 Schedule K	
Account Name	Debit	Credit	Debit	Credit	Debit	Credit	Ordinary Income	Separately Stated Items
Sales		$869,658				$869,658	$869,658	
Sales returns & allowances	$ 29,242				$ 29,242		(29,242)	
Cost of sales	540,204				540,204		(540,204)	
Dividends		1,000				1,000		$ 1,000
Tax-exempt interest		18,000	$18,000			0		18,000
Gain on stock sale		4,500				4,500		4,500
Worthless stock loss	2,100				2,100			(2,100)
Guaranteed payments[(a)]	36,000			$36,000	0		(36,000)	
Other salaries	52,000				52,000		(52,000)	
Rentals	36,000				36,000		(36,000)	
Bad debts	4,000				4,000		(4,000)	
Interest:								
Working capital loans	8,000				8,000		(8,000)	
Purchase tax-exempt bonds	2,000			2,000	0			(2,000)
Employment taxes	8,320				8,320		(8,320)	
Taxes	1,520				1,520		(1,520)	
Repairs	4,800				4,800		(4,800)	
Depreciation[(b)]	12,000		476		12,476		(12,476)	
Charitable contributions	12,000				12,000			(12,000)
Travel	4,000				4,000		(4,000)	
Meals and entertainment[(c)]	8,000			4,000	4,000		(4,000)	
Meals and ent. nondeductible								(4,000)
Office expenses	16,000				16,000		(16,000)	
Advertising	13,000				13,000		(13,000)	
Transportation expense	10,400				10,400		(10,400)	
General and administrative	3,000				3,000		(3,000)	
Pension plans[(d)]	2,000				2,000		(2,000)	
Employee benefit programs[(e)]	4,000				4,000		(4,000)	
Miscellaneous	1,000				1,000		(850)	(150)
Net profit/Taxable income	83,572		$23,524		107,096			
Total	$893,158	$893,158	$42,000	$42,000	$875,158	$875,158	$ 79,846	

[(a)] Guaranteed payments have no net effect on taxable income. The guaranteed payments both reduce ordinary income and increase separately stated income items that are taxable.

[(b)] MACRS depreciation = $27,476 total − $15,000 allocated to COGS = $12,476

[(c)] 50% of the meals and entertainment expense is not deductible for tax purposes but must be separately stated on Schedules K and K-1.

[(d)] The pension plan expense is the same for book and tax purposes for this partnership. No pension expenses relate to pensions for the partners.

[(e)] The employee benefit expense is the same for book and tax purposes for this partnership. None relates to partner benefits.

Facts for C Corporation (Form 1120)

The same basic facts presented for the Andrew Lawrence proprietorship are used for the C corporation except for the following:

1. Andrew Lawrence and Stephen Johns are the two 50% shareholders of Johns and Lawrence, Inc., a furniture manufacturer (Business Code 337000). Johns and Lawrence is located at 1234 First Avenue, City, ST 55555. The following information pertains to the 2014 corporate tax return:

Compensation of Officers

Name	Share	Title	Compensation
Stephen Johns	1,000	President	$18,000
Andrew Lawrence	1,000	V.P.	18,000
Total	2,000		$36,000

The corporation paid all salaries owed to the shareholders in 2014. The corporation paid none of the interest or rentals to the shareholders.

2. The book income for the corporation appears in the attached worksheet, which reconciles the corporation's book income and its taxable income before special deductions.

3. The company was incorporated on June 1, 2008. Each of the two officers hold one-half the stock, which they acquired on that date for a total cash and property contribution of $200,000. No change in the stockholdings has occurred since incorporation. Johns and Lawrence each devote 100% of their time to the business. The corporation provides no expense allowances. The corporation, however, reimburses properly substantiated expenses. Both officers are U.S. citizens. Johns and Lawrence is not a member of a controlled group.

4. Addresses for the officers are: Andrew Lawrence, 333 Third Street, City, ST 55555; Stephen Johns, 777 Seventh Street, City, ST 55555.

5. The corporation paid estimated taxes of $14,000 for tax year 2014.

6. Other deductions include:

Travel	$ 4,000
Meals and entertainment	8,000
Minus: 50% disallowance	(4,000)
Office expenses	16,000
Transportation	10,400
General and administrative	3,000
Miscellaneous	1,000
Total	$38,400

7. The charitable contributions deduction limitation is $7,694 (see footnote b in Reconciliation worksheet on page B-16). The remaining $4,306 ($12,000 − $7,694) carries over to 2015 and the four succeeding tax years.

8. Qualified production activities income (QPAI) equals $80,000. Employer's W-2 wages allocable to U.S. production activities equal $88,000.

9. The $28,212 of withdrawals made by the two owners are dividends out of the corporation's earnings and profits. They are reported as gross income on the shareholders' individual tax returns.

10. The beginning-of-the-year balance sheets for all entity forms are the same, which permits a direct comparison of the 2014 tax differences. Actually, the corporation would have reported tax differences in all prior years (2008 through 2013), which would have been included in the January 1, 2014 balance sheet. If these differences were so included, the direct comparisons would be much more difficult.

11. For additional information, see the worksheet on page B-16.

Form **1120** Department of the Treasury Internal Revenue Service

U.S. Corporation Income Tax Return

For calendar year 2013 or tax year beginning ________, 2013, ending ________, 20 ___

► **Information about Form 1120 and its separate instructions is at *www.irs.gov/form1120*.**

OMB No. 1545-0123

2014

A Check if: 1a Consolidated return (attach Form 851) ☐ b Life/nonlife consolidated return ☐ 2 Personal holding co. (attach Sch. PH) ☐ 3 Personal service corp. (see instructions) ☐ 4 Schedule M-3 attached ☐	**TYPE OR PRINT** Name: Johns and Lawrence, Inc. Number, street, and room or suite no. If a P.O. box, see instructions.: 1234 First Avenue City or town, state, or province, country and ZIP or foreign postal code: City, ST 55555	**B Employer identification number** XX-XXXXXXX C Date incorporated 6/1/2008 D Total assets (see instructions) $ 479,324

E Check if: (1) ☐ Initial return (2) ☐ Final return (3) ☐ Name change (4) ☐ Address change

Income	1a	Gross receipts or sales	1a 869,658	
	b	Returns and allowances	1b 29,242	
	c	Balance. Subtract line 1b from line 1a		1c 840,416
	2	Cost of goods sold (attach Form 1125-A)		2 540,204
	3	Gross profit. Subtract line 2 from line 1c		3 300,212
	4	Dividends (Schedule C, line 19)		4 1,000
	5	Interest		5
	6	Gross rents		6
	7	Gross royalties		7
	8	Capital gain net income (attach Schedule D (Form 1120))		8
	9	Net gain or (loss) from Form 4797, Part II, line 17 (attach Form 4797)		9 2,400
	10	Other income (see instructions—attach statement)		10
	11	**Total income.** Add lines 3 through 10 ►		11 303,612
Deductions (See instructions for limitations on deductions.)	12	Compensation of officers (see instructions—attach Form 1125-E) ►		12 36,000
	13	Salaries and wages (less employment credits)		13 52,000
	14	Repairs and maintenance		14 4,800
	15	Bad debts		15 4,000
	16	Rents		16 36,000
	17	Taxes and licenses		17 16,000
	18	Interest		18 8,000
	19	Charitable contributions		19 7,694
	20	Depreciation from Form 4562 not claimed on Form 1125-A or elsewhere on return (attach Form 4562)		20 12,476
	21	Depletion		21
	22	Advertising		22 13,000
	23	Pension, profit-sharing, etc., plans		23 2,000
	24	Employee benefit programs		24 4,000
	25	Domestic production activities deduction (attach Form 8903) Not Reproduced		25 6,169
	26	Other deductions (attach statement)		26 38,400
	27	**Total deductions.** Add lines 12 through 26 ►		27 240,539
	28	Taxable income before net operating loss deduction and special deductions. Subtract line 27 from line 11.		28 63,073
	29a	Net operating loss deduction (see instructions)	29a	
	b	Special deductions (Schedule C, line 20)	29b 700	
	c	Add lines 29a and 29b		29c 700
Tax, Refundable Credits, and Payments	30	**Taxable income.** Subtract line 29c from line 28 (see instructions)		30 62,373
	31	Total tax (Schedule J, Part I, line 11)		31 10,593
	32	Total payments and refundable credits (Schedule J, Part II, line 21)		32 14,000
	33	Estimated tax penalty (see instructions). Check if Form 2220 is attached ► ☐		33
	34	**Amount owed.** If line 32 is smaller than the total of lines 31 and 33, enter amount owed		34
	35	**Overpayment.** If line 32 is larger than the total of lines 31 and 33, enter amount overpaid		35 3,407
	36	Enter amount from line 35 you want: **Credited to 2015 estimated tax** ► 3,407 **Refunded** ►		36

Sign Here

Under penalties of perjury, I declare that I have examined this return, including accompanying schedules and statements, and to the best of my knowledge and belief, it is true, correct, and complete. Declaration of preparer (other than taxpayer) is based on all information of which preparer has any knowledge.

► Andrew Lawrence | 3-14-15 | ► Vice-President

Signature of officer | Date | Title

May the IRS discuss this return with the preparer shown below (see instructions)? ☒ Yes ☐ No

Paid Preparer Use Only

Print/Type preparer's name	Preparer's signature	Date	Check ☒ if self-employed	PTIN
Michael Prepper	Michael Prepper	3-14-15		
Firm's name ► Michael S. Prepper			Firm's EIN ►	
Firm's address ► 1111 Second Street, City, ST 55555			Phone no.	

Form 1120 (2014) Page 2

Schedule C **Dividends and Special Deductions** (see instructions)	**(a)** Dividends received	**(b)** %	**(c)** Special deductions (a) × (b)
1 Dividends from less-than-20%-owned domestic corporations (other than debt-financed stock)	1,000	70	700
2 Dividends from 20%-or-more-owned domestic corporations (other than debt-financed stock)		80	
3 Dividends on debt-financed stock of domestic and foreign corporations		see instructions	
4 Dividends on certain preferred stock of less-than-20%-owned public utilities		42	
5 Dividends on certain preferred stock of 20%-or-more-owned public utilities		48	
6 Dividends from less-than-20%-owned foreign corporations and certain FSCs		70	
7 Dividends from 20%-or-more-owned foreign corporations and certain FSCs		80	
8 Dividends from wholly owned foreign subsidiaries		100	
9 **Total.** Add lines 1 through 8. See instructions for limitation			700
10 Dividends from domestic corporations received by a small business investment company operating under the Small Business Investment Act of 1958		100	
11 Dividends from affiliated group members		100	
12 Dividends from certain FSCs		100	
13 Dividends from foreign corporations not included on lines 3, 6, 7, 8, 11, or 12			
14 Income from controlled foreign corporations under subpart F (attach Form(s) 5471)			
15 Foreign dividend gross-up			
16 IC-DISC and former DISC dividends not included on lines 1, 2, or 3			
17 Other dividends			
18 Deduction for dividends paid on certain preferred stock of public utilities			
19 **Total dividends.** Add lines 1 through 17. Enter here and on page 1, line 4 ►	1,000		
20 **Total special deductions.** Add lines 9, 10, 11, 12, and 18. Enter here and on page 1, line 29b ►			700

Form **1120** (2014)

Form 1120 (2014) Page 3

Schedule J Tax Computation and Payment (see instructions)

Part I–Tax Computation

1	Check if the corporation is a member of a controlled group (attach Schedule O (Form 1120)) ► ☐				
2	Income tax. Check if a qualified personal service corporation (see instructions) ► ☐			2	10,593
3	Alternative minimum tax (attach Form 4626)			3	
4	Add lines 2 and 3			4	10,593
5a	Foreign tax credit (attach Form 1118)	5a			
b	Credit from Form 8834 (see instructions)	5b			
c	General business credit (attach Form 3800)	5c			
d	Credit for prior year minimum tax (attach Form 8827)	5d			
e	Bond credits from Form 8912	5e			
6	**Total credits.** Add lines 5a through 5e			6	-0-
7	Subtract line 6 from line 4			7	10,593
8	Personal holding company tax (attach Schedule PH (Form 1120))			8	
9a	Recapture of investment credit (attach Form 4255)	9a			
b	Recapture of low-income housing credit (attach Form 8611)	9b			
c	Interest due under the look-back method—completed long-term contracts (attach Form 8697)	9c			
d	Interest due under the look-back method—income forecast method (attach Form 8866)	9d			
e	Alternative tax on qualifying shipping activities (attach Form 8902)	9e			
f	Other (see instructions—attach statement)	9f			
10	**Total.** Add lines 9a through 9f			10	-0-
11	**Total tax.** Add lines 7, 8, and 10. Enter here and on page 1, line 31			11	10,593

Part II–Payments and Refundable Credits

12	2012 overpayment credited to 2013			12	
13	2013 estimated tax payments			13	14,000
14	2013 refund applied for on Form 4466			14	( )
15	Combine lines 12, 13, and 14			15	14,000
16	Tax deposited with Form 7004			16	
17	Withholding (see instructions)			17	
18	**Total payments.** Add lines 15, 16, and 17			18	14,000
19	Refundable credits from:				
a	Form 2439	19a			
b	Form 4136	19b			
c	Form 8827, line 8c	19c			
d	Other (attach statement—see instructions)	19d			
20	**Total credits.** Add lines 19a through 19d			20	-0-
21	**Total payments and credits.** Add lines 18 and 20. Enter here and on page 1, line 32			21	14,000

Schedule K Other Information (see instructions)

		Yes	No
1	Check accounting method: a ☐ Cash b ☒ Accrual c ☐ Other (specify) ►		
2	See the instructions and enter the:		
a	Business activity code no. ► 337,000		
b	Business activity ► Manufacturing		
c	Product or service ► Furniture		
3	Is the corporation a subsidiary in an affiliated group or a parent-subsidiary controlled group? If "Yes," enter name and EIN of the parent corporation ►		X
4	At the end of the tax year:		
a	Did any foreign or domestic corporation, partnership (including any entity treated as a partnership), trust, or tax-exempt organization own directly 20% or more, or own, directly or indirectly, 50% or more of the total voting power of all classes of the corporation's stock entitled to vote? If "Yes," complete Part I of Schedule G (Form 1120) (attach Schedule G)		X
b	Did any individual or estate own directly 20% or more, or own, directly or indirectly, 50% or more of the total voting power of all classes of the corporation's stock entitled to vote? If "Yes," complete Part II of Schedule G (Form 1120) (attach Schedule G)*	X	

Form 1120 (2014)

*Schedule G is not attached. If attached, it would list the same individuals listed on Form 1125-E.

Form 1120 (2014) Page 4

Schedule K **Other Information** *continued* (see instructions)

		Yes	No
5	At the end of the tax year, did the corporation:		
a	Own directly 20% or more, or own, directly or indirectly, 50% or more of the total voting power of all classes of stock entitled to vote of any foreign or domestic corporation not included on **Form 851,** Affiliations Schedule? For rules of constructive ownership, see instructions. If "Yes," complete (i) through (iv) below.		X

(i) Name of Corporation	**(ii)** Employer Identification Number (if any)	**(iii)** Country of Incorporation	**(iv)** Percentage Owned in Voting Stock

		Yes	No
b	Own directly an interest of 20% or more, or own, directly or indirectly, an interest of 50% or more in any foreign or domestic partnership (including an entity treated as a partnership) or in the beneficial interest of a trust? For rules of constructive ownership, see instructions. If "Yes," complete (i) through (iv) below.		X

(i) Name of Entity	**(ii)** Employer Identification Number (if any)	**(iii)** Country of Organization	**(iv)** Maximum Percentage Owned in Profit, Loss, or Capital

		Yes	No
6	During this tax year, did the corporation pay dividends (other than stock dividends and distributions in exchange for stock) in excess of the corporation's current and accumulated earnings and profits? (See sections 301 and 316.)		X
	If "Yes," file **Form 5452,** Corporate Report of Nondividend Distributions. If this is a consolidated return, answer here for the parent corporation and on Form 851 for each subsidiary.		
7	At any time during the tax year, did one foreign person own, directly or indirectly, at least 25% of **(a)** the total voting power of all classes of the corporation's stock entitled to vote or **(b)** the total value of all classes of the corporation's stock? . . .		X
	For rules of attribution, see section 318. If "Yes," enter: **(i)** Percentage owned ▶ ________ and **(ii)** Owner's country ▶ ________		
	(c) The corporation may have to file **Form 5472,** Information Return of a 25% Foreign-Owned U.S. Corporation or a Foreign Corporation Engaged in a U.S. Trade or Business. Enter the number of Forms 5472 attached ▶ ________		
8	Check this box if the corporation issued publicly offered debt instruments with original issue discount . . . . . . ▶ ☐ If checked, the corporation may have to file **Form 8281,** Information Return for Publicly Offered Original Issue Discount Instruments.		
9	Enter the amount of tax-exempt interest received or accrued during the tax year ▶ $ 18,000		
10	Enter the number of shareholders at the end of the tax year (if 100 or fewer) ▶ 2		
11	If the corporation has an NOL for the tax year and is electing to forego the carryback period, check here . . . . . ▶ ☐ If the corporation is filing a consolidated return, the statement required by Regulations section 1.1502-21(b)(3) must be attached or the election will not be valid.		
12	Enter the available NOL carryover from prior tax years (do not reduce it by any deduction on line 29a.) ▶ $ -0-		
13	Are the corporation's total receipts (page 1, line 1a, plus lines 4 through 10) for the tax year **and** its total assets at the end of the tax year less than $250,000?		X
	If "Yes," the corporation is not required to complete Schedules L, M-1, and M-2. Instead, enter the total amount of cash distributions and the book value of property distributions (other than cash) made during the tax year ▶ $ ________		
14	Is the corporation required to file Schedule UTP (Form 1120), Uncertain Tax Position Statement (see instructions)? . . . . If "Yes," complete and attach Schedule UTP.		X
15a	Did the corporation make any payments in 2013 that would require it to file Form(s) 1099?		X
b	If "Yes," did or will the corporation file required Forms 1099?		
16	During this tax year, did the corporation have an 80% or more change in ownership, including a change due to redemption of its own stock?		X
17	During or subsequent to this tax year, but before the filing of this return, did the corporation dispose of more than 65% (by value) of its assets in a taxable, non-taxable, or tax deferred transaction?		X
18	Did the corporation receive assets in a section 351 transfer in which any of the transferred assets had a fair market basis or fair market value of more than $1 million?		X

Form 1120 (2014) Page 5

Schedule L Balance Sheets per Books

Assets		Beginning of tax year (a)	(b)	End of tax year (c)	(d)
1	Cash		60,000		72,600
2a	Trade notes and accounts receivable	25,000		24,000	
b	Less allowance for bad debts	(1,000)	24,000	(1,000)	23,000
3	Inventories		64,000		104,800
4	U.S. government obligations				
5	Tax-exempt securities (see instructions)		200,000		200,000
6	Other current assets (attach statement)		7,000		
7	Loans to shareholders				
8	Mortgage and real estate loans				
9	Other investments (attach statement)				
10a	Buildings and other depreciable assets	151,600		151,600	
b	Less accumulated depreciation	(45,200)	106,400	(72,676)	78,924
11a	Depletable assets				
b	Less accumulated depletion	( )		( )	
12	Land (net of any amortization)				
13a	Intangible assets (amortizable only)				
b	Less accumulated amortization	( )		( )	
14	Other assets (attach statement)				
15	Total assets		461,400		479,324
	Liabilities and Shareholders' Equity				
16	Accounts payable		26,000		19,000
17	Mortgages, notes, bonds payable in less than 1 year		4,000		4,000
18	Other current liabilities (attach statement)		3,600		3,600
19	Loans from shareholders				
20	Mortgages, notes, bonds payable in 1 year or more		130,000		119,724
21	Other liabilities (attach statement)				
22	Capital stock: a Preferred stock				
	b Common stock	200,000	200,000	200,000	200,000
23	Additional paid-in capital				
24	Retained earnings—Appropriated (attach statement)				
25	Retained earnings—Unappropriated		97,800		133,000
26	Adjustments to shareholders' equity (attach statement)				
27	Less cost of treasury stock		( )		( )
28	Total liabilities and shareholders' equity		461,400		479,324

Schedule M-1 Reconciliation of Income (Loss) per Books With Income per Return

Note: Schedule M-3 required instead of Schedule M-1 if total assets are $10 million or more—see instructions

1	Net income (loss) per books	63,412	7	Income recorded on books this year not included on this return (itemize): Tax-exempt interest $ 18,000	18,000
2	Federal income tax per books	14,000			
3	Excess of capital losses over capital gains				
4	Income subject to tax not recorded on books this year (itemize):				
5	Expenses recorded on books this year not deducted on this return (itemize): a Depreciation $ 4,306; b Charitable contributions $ 4,000; c Travel and entertainment $; Nondeductable interest* $2,000	10,306	8	Deductions on this return not charged against book income this year (itemize): a Depreciation $ 476; b Charitable contributions $; U.S. prod. act. ded. $6,169	6,645
			9	Add lines 7 and 8	24,645
6	Add lines 1 through 5	87,718	10	Income (page 1, line 28)—line 6 less line 9	63,073

Schedule M-2 Analysis of Unappropriated Retained Earnings per Books (Line 25, Schedule L)

1	Balance at beginning of year	97,800	5	Distributions: a Cash	28,212
2	Net income (loss) per books	63,412		b Stock	
3	Other increases (itemize):			c Property	
			6	Other decreases (itemize):	
			7	Add lines 5 and 6	28,212
4	Add lines 1, 2, and 3	161,212	8	Balance at end of year (line 4 less line 7)	133,000

*On loans to acquire municipal bonds.

Form **1125-A** (Rev. December 2012) Department of the Treasury Internal Revenue Service

Cost of Goods Sold

▶ Attach to Form 1120, 1120-C, 1120-F, 1120S, 1065, or 1065-B.
▶ Information about Form 1125-A and its instructions is at *www.irs.gov/form1125a.*

OMB No. 1545-2225

Name	Employer identification number
Johns and Lawrence, Inc.	XX-XXXXXXX

1	Inventory at beginning of year	1	64,000
2	Purchases	2	340,800
3	Cost of labor	3	143,204
4	Additional section 263A costs (attach schedule)	4	7,000
5	Other costs (attach schedule)	5	90,000
6	**Total.** Add lines 1 through 5	6	645,004
7	Inventory at end of year	7	104,800
8	**Cost of goods sold.** Subtract line 7 from line 6. Enter here and on Form 1120, page 1, line 2 or the appropriate line of your tax return (see instructions)	8	540,204

9a Check all methods used for valuing closing inventory:

(i) [X] Cost

(ii) [ ] Lower of cost or market

(iii) [ ] Other (Specify method used and attach explanation.) ▶

b Check if there was a writedown of subnormal goods ▶ [ ]

c Check if the LIFO inventory method was adopted this tax year for any goods (if checked, attach Form 970) ▶ [ ]

d If the LIFO inventory method was used for this tax year, enter amount of closing inventory computed under LIFO | 9d |

e If property is produced or acquired for resale, do the rules of section 263A apply to the entity (see instructions)? [ ] Yes [X] No

f Was there any change in determining quantities, cost, or valuations between opening and closing inventory? If "Yes," attach explanation [ ] Yes [X] No

Section references are to the Internal Revenue Code unless otherwise noted.

General Instructions

Purpose of Form

Use Form 1125-A to calculate and deduct cost of goods sold for certain entities.

Who Must File

Filers of Form 1120, 1120-C, 1120-F, 1120S, 1065, or 1065-B, must complete and attach Form 1125-A if the applicable entity reports a deduction for cost of goods sold.

Inventories

Generally, inventories are required at the beginning and end of each tax year if the production, purchase, or sale of merchandise is an income-producing factor. See Regulations section 1.471-1. If inventories are required, you generally must use an accrual method of accounting for sales and purchases of inventory items.

Exception for certain taxpayers. If you are a qualifying taxpayer or a qualifying small business taxpayer (defined below), you can adopt or change your accounting method to account for inventoriable items in the same manner as materials and supplies that are not incidental.

Under this accounting method, inventory costs for raw materials purchased for use in producing finished goods and merchandise purchased for resale are deductible in the year the finished goods or merchandise are sold (but not before the year you paid for the raw materials or merchandise, if you are also using the cash method).

If you account for inventoriable items in the same manner as materials and supplies that are not incidental, you can currently deduct expenditures for direct labor and all indirect costs that would otherwise be included in inventory costs. See the instructions for lines 2 and 7.

For additional guidance on this method of accounting, see Pub. 538, Accounting Periods and Methods. For guidance on adopting or changing to this method of accounting, see Form 3115, Application for Change in Accounting Method, and its instructions.

Qualifying taxpayer. A qualifying taxpayer is a taxpayer that, (a) for each prior tax year ending after December 16, 1998, has average annual gross receipts of $1 million or less for the 3 prior tax years and (b) its business is not a tax shelter (as defined in section 448(d)(3)). See Rev. Proc. 2001-10, 2001-2 I.R.B. 272.

Qualifying small business taxpayer. A qualifying small business taxpayer is a taxpayer that, (a) for each prior tax year ending on or after December 31, 2000, has average annual gross receipts of $10 million or less for the 3 prior tax years, (b) whose principal business activity is not an ineligible activity, and (c) whose business is not a tax shelter (as defined in section 448 (d)(3)). See Rev. Proc. 2002-28, 2002-18 I.R.B. 815.

Uniform capitalization rules. The uniform capitalization rules of section 263A generally require you to capitalize, or include in inventory, certain costs incurred in connection with the following.

- The production of real property and tangible personal property held in inventory or held for sale in the ordinary course of business.
- Real property or personal property (tangible and intangible) acquired for resale.
- The production of real property and tangible personal property by a corporation for use in its trade or business or in an activity engaged in for profit.

See the discussion on section 263A uniform capitalization rules in the instructions for your tax return before completing Form 1125-A. Also see Regulations sections 1.263A-1 through 1.263A-3. See Regulations section 1.263A-4 for rules for property produced in a farming business.

Form **1125-E**
(Rev. December 2013)
Department of the Treasury
Internal Revenue Service

Compensation of Officers

► Attach to Form 1120, 1120-C, 1120-F, 1120-REIT, 1120-RIC, or 1120S.
► Information about Form 1125-E and its separate instructions is at *www.irs.gov/form1125e*.

OMB No. 1545-2225

Name: Johns and Lawrence, Inc.

Employer identification number: XX-XXXXXXX

Note. Complete Form 1125-E only if total receipts are $500,000 or more. See instructions for definition of total receipts.

	(a) Name of officer	(b) Social security number (see instructions)	(c) Percent of time devoted to business	Percent of stock owned (d) Common	(e) Preferred	(f) Amount of compensation
1	Stephen Johns	XXX-XX-XXXX	100 %	50 %	%	18,000
	Andrew Lawrence	XXX-XX-XXXX	100 %	50 %	%	18,000
			%	%	%	
			%	%	%	
			%	%	%	
			%	%	%	
			%	%	%	
			%	%	%	
			%	%	%	
			%	%	%	
			%	%	%	
			%	%	%	
			%	%	%	
			%	%	%	
			%	%	%	
			%	%	%	
			%	%	%	
			%	%	%	
			%	%	%	
			%	%	%	

2	Total compensation of officers	2	36,000
3	Compensation of officers claimed on Form 1125-A or elsewhere on return	3	
4	Subtract line 3 from line 2. Enter the result here and on Form 1120, page 1, line 12 or the appropriate line of your tax return	4	36,000

Johns and Lawrence, Inc. (C Corporation) Reconciliation of Book Income to Taxable Income before Special Deductions for Year Ending December 31, 2014

	Book Income		Adjustments		Taxable Income	
Account Name	Debit	Credit	Debit	Credit	Debit	Credit
Sales		$869,658				$869,658
Sales returns & allowances	$ 29,242				$ 29,242	
Cost of sales	540,204				540,204	
Dividends		1,000				1,000
Tax-exempt interest		18,000	$18,000			0
Gain on stock sale		4,500				4,500
Worthless stock loss	2,100				2,100	
Officers' salaries	36,000				36,000	
Other salaries	52,000				52,000	
Rentals	36,000				36,000	
Bad debts	4,000				4,000	
Interest:						
Working capital loans	8,000				8,000	
Purchase tax-exempt bonds	2,000			$ 2,000	0	
Employment taxes	14,480				14,480	
Taxes	1,520				1,520	
Repairs	4,800				4,800	
Depreciation[(a)]	12,000		476		12,476	
Charitable contributions[(b)]	12,000			4,306	7,694	
Travel	4,000				4,000	
Meals and entertainment[(c)]	8,000			4,000	4,000	
Office expenses	16,000				16,000	
Advertising	13,000				13,000	
Transportation expense	10,400				10,400	
General and administrative	3,000				3,000	
Pension plans	2,000				2,000	
Employee benefit programs	4,000				4,000	
Miscellaneous	1,000				1,000	
U.S. prod. act. ded.	0		6,169		6,169	
Federal income taxes	14,000			14,000	0	
Net income/Taxable income before spec. deds.	63,412			339	63,073[(e)]	
Total	$893,158	$893,158	$24,645	$24,645	$875,158	$875,158

[(a)] MACRS depreciation = $27,476 total − $15,000 included in COGS = $12,476

[(b)] Charitable contribution deduction limitation:

Total income (Form 1120, page 1, line 11)	$303,612
Minus: Deductions other than char. cont., DRD, & U.S. prod. act. ded.	(226,676)
Charitable contribution base	$ 76,936
Times: 10%	0.10
Charitable contribution deduction	$ 7,694

[(c)] $8,000 × 0.50 disallowance rate = $4,000 disallowed expenses

[(d)]

Total income (Form 1120, page 1, line 11)	$303,612
Minus: Deductions other than the U.S. prod. act. ded.	(235,070)
Taxable income before the U.S. prod. act. ded.	$ 68,542
Times: 9%	0.09
U.S. prod. act. ded.	$ 6,169

[(e)] Taxable income:

Taxable income before spec. deds.	$ 63,073
Minus: Div. rec. ded. ($1,000 × 0.70)	(700)
Taxable income	$ 62,373

SCHEDULE M-3 (Form 1120)

Department of the Treasury
Internal Revenue Service

Net Income (Loss) Reconciliation for Corporations With Total Assets of $10 Million or More

► Attach to Form 1120 or 1120-C. ► Information about Schedule M-3 (Form 1120) and its separate instructions is available at *www.irs.gov/form1120*.

OMB No. 1545-0123

2014

Name of corporation (common parent, if consolidated return): Valley Corporation

Employer identification number: XX-XXXXXXX

Check applicable box(es): (1) [X] Non-consolidated return (2) [ ] Consolidated return (Form 1120 only)

(3) [ ] Mixed 1120/L/PC group (4) [ ] Dormant subsidiaries schedule attached

Part I Financial Information and Net Income (Loss) Reconciliation (see instructions)

1a Did the corporation file SEC Form 10-K for its income statement period ending with or within this tax year?
[ ] **Yes.** Skip lines 1b and 1c and complete lines 2a through 11 with respect to that SEC Form 10-K.
[X] **No.** Go to line 1b. See instructions if multiple non-tax-basis income statements are prepared.

b Did the corporation prepare a certified audited non-tax-basis income statement for that period?
[ ] **Yes.** Skip line 1c and complete lines 2a through 11 with respect to that income statement.
[X] **No.** Go to line 1c.

c Did the corporation prepare a non-tax-basis income statement for that period?
[X] **Yes.** Complete lines 2a through 11 with respect to that income statement.
[ ] **No.** Skip lines 2a through 3c and enter the corporation's net income (loss) per its books and records on line 4a.

2a Enter the income statement period: Beginning 1/1/14 Ending 12/31/14

b Has the corporation's income statement been restated for the income statement period on line 2a?
[ ] **Yes.** (If "Yes," attach an explanation and the amount of each item restated.)
[X] **No.**

c Has the corporation's income statement been restated for any of the five income statement periods preceding the period on line 2a?
[ ] **Yes.** (If "Yes," attach an explanation and the amount of each item restated.)
[X] **No.**

3a Is any of the corporation's voting common stock publicly traded?
[ ] **Yes.**
[X] **No.** If "No," go to line 4a.

b Enter the symbol of the corporation's primary U.S. publicly traded voting common stock . . . . . ______

c Enter the nine-digit CUSIP number of the corporation's primary publicly traded voting common stock . . . . . ______

4a	Worldwide consolidated net income (loss) from income statement source identified in Part I, line 1	4a	372,000
b	Indicate accounting standard used for line 4a (see instructions): (1) [X] GAAP (2) [ ] IFRS (3) [ ] Statutory (4) [ ] Tax-basis (5) [ ] Other (specify) ______		
5a	Net income from nonincludible foreign entities (attach statement)	5a	( )
b	Net loss from nonincludible foreign entities (attach statement and enter as a positive amount)	5b	
6a	Net income from nonincludible U.S. entities (attach statement)	6a	( )
b	Net loss from nonincludible U.S. entities (attach statement and enter as a positive amount)	6b	
7a	Net income (loss) of other includible foreign disregarded entities (attach statement)	7a	
b	Net income (loss) of other includible U.S. disregarded entities (attach statement)	7b	
c	Net income (loss) of other includible entities (attach statement)	7c	
8	Adjustment to eliminations of transactions between includible entities and nonincludible entities (attach statement)	8	
9	Adjustment to reconcile income statement period to tax year (attach statement)	9	
10a	Intercompany dividend adjustments to reconcile to line 11 (attach statement)	10a	
b	Other statutory accounting adjustments to reconcile to line 11 (attach statement)	10b	
c	Other adjustments to reconcile to amount on line 11 (attach statement)	10c	
11	**Net income (loss) per income statement of includible corporations.** Combine lines 4 through 10	11	372,000

Note. Part I, line 11, must equal the amount on Part II, line 30, column (a), and Schedule M-2, line 2.

12 Enter the total amount (not just the corporation's share) of the assets and liabilities of all entities included or removed on the following lines.

	Total Assets	Total Liabilities
a Included on Part I, line 4 ►	2,306,980*	1,320,420
b Removed on Part I, line 5 ►		
c Removed on Part I, line 6 ►		
d Included on Part I, line 7 ►		

For Paperwork Reduction Act Notice, see the Instructions for Form 1120. Cat. No. 37961C **Schedule M-3 (Form 1120) 2014**

*For this information, see Comprehensive Example, Year 1, Step 11 on text Page C:3-50.

See text Example C:3-51 for tax form facts.

Schedule M-3 (Form 1120) 2014 Page 2

Name of corporation (common parent, if consolidated return): Valley Corporation

Employer identification number: XX-XXXXXXX

Check applicable box(es): (1) ☐ Consolidated group (2) ☐ Parent corp (3) ☐ Consolidated eliminations (4) ☐ Subsidiary corp (5) ☐ Mixed 1120/L/PC group

Check if a sub-consolidated: (6) ☐ 1120 group (7) ☐ 1120 eliminations

Name of subsidiary (if consolidated return)

Employer identification number

Part II Reconciliation of Net Income (Loss) per Income Statement of Includible Corporations With Taxable Income per Return (see instructions)

Income (Loss) Items (Attach statements for lines 1 through 11)	(a) Income (Loss) per Income Statement	(b) Temporary Difference	(c) Permanent Difference	(d) Income (Loss) per Tax Return
1 Income (loss) from equity method foreign corporations				
2 Gross foreign dividends not previously taxed				
3 Subpart F, QEF, and similar income inclusions				
4 Section 78 gross-up				
5 Gross foreign distributions previously taxed				
6 Income (loss) from equity method U.S. corporations				
7 U.S. dividends not eliminated in tax consolidation	10,000			10,000
8 Minority interest for includible corporations				
9 Income (loss) from U.S. partnerships				
10 Income (loss) from foreign partnerships				
11 Income (loss) from other pass-through entities				
12 Items relating to reportable transactions (attach statement)				
13 Interest income (attach Form 8916-A) *	3,000		(3,000)	-0-
14 Total accrual to cash adjustment				
15 Hedging transactions				
16 Mark-to-market income (loss)				
17 Cost of goods sold (attach Form 8916-A)	(550,000)			(550,000)
18 Sale versus lease (for sellers and/or lessors)				
19 Section 481(a) adjustments				
20 Unearned/deferred revenue Prepaid rent	-0-	8,000		8,000
21 Income recognition from long-term contracts				
22 Original issue discount and other imputed interest				
23a Income statement gain/loss on sale, exchange, abandonment, worthlessness, or other disposition of assets other than inventory and pass-through entities	(12,000)	12,000		
b Gross capital gains from Schedule D, excluding amounts from pass-through entities				
c Gross capital losses from Schedule D, excluding amounts from pass-through entities, abandonment losses, and worthless stock losses				
d Net gain/loss reported on Form 4797, line 17, excluding amounts from pass-through entities, abandonment losses, and worthless stock losses				
e Abandonment losses				
f Worthless stock losses (attach statement)				
g Other gain/loss on disposition of assets other than inventory				
24 Capital loss limitation and carryforward used				
25 Other income (loss) items with differences (attach statement)				
26 **Total income (loss) items.** Combine lines 1 through 25	(549,000)	20,000	(3,000)	(532,000)
27 **Total expense/deduction items** (from Part III, line 38)	(314,440)	(110,000)	128,440	(296,000)
28 Other items with no differences **	1,200,000			1,200,000
29a Mixed groups, see instructions. All others, combine lines 26 through 28	336,560	(90,000)	125,440	372,000
b PC insurance subgroup reconciliation totals				
c Life insurance subgroup reconciliation totals				
30 **Reconciliation totals.** Combine lines 29a through 29c	336,560	(90,000)	125,440	372,000

Note. Line 30, column (a), must equal the amount on Part I, line 11, and column (d) must equal Form 1120, page 1, line 28.

Schedule M-3 (Form 1120) 2014

*Tax-exempt interest $3,000

**Sales $1,500,000 minus operating expenses $300,000

Schedule M-3 (Form 1120) 2014 Page 3

Name of corporation (common parent, if consolidated return): Valley Corporation

Employer identification number: XX-XXXXXXX

Check applicable box(es): (1) ☐ Consolidated group (2) ☐ Parent corp (3) ☐ Consolidated eliminations (4) ☐ Subsidiary corp (5) ☐ Mixed 1120/L/PC group

Check if a sub-consolidated: (6) ☐ 1120 group (7) ☐ 1120 eliminations

Name of subsidiary (if consolidated return)

Employer identification number

Part III **Reconciliation of Net Income (Loss) per Income Statement of Includible Corporations With Taxable Income per Return—Expense/Deduction Items** (see instructions)

Expense/Deduction Items	(a) Expense per Income Statement	(b) Temporary Difference	(c) Permanent Difference	(d) Deduction per Tax Return
1 U.S. current income tax expense *	124,100		(124,100)	
2 U.S. deferred income tax expense *	27,540		(27,540)	
3 State and local current income tax expense				
4 State and local deferred income tax expense				
5 Foreign current income tax expense (other than foreign withholding taxes)				
6 Foreign deferred income tax expense				
7 Foreign withholding taxes				
8 Interest expense (attach Form 8916-A) **	75,000			75,000
9 Stock option expense				
10 Other equity-based compensation				
11 Meals and entertainment				
12 Fines and penalties				
13 Judgments, damages, awards, and similar costs				
14 Parachute payments				
15 Compensation with section 162(m) limitation				
16 Pension and profit-sharing				
17 Other post-retirement benefits				
18 Deferred compensation				
19 Charitable contribution of cash and tangible property				
20 Charitable contribution of intangible property				
21 Charitable contribution limitation/carryforward				
22 Domestic production activities deduction			35,000	35,000
23 Current year acquisition or reorganization investment banking fees				
24 Current year acquisition or reorganization legal and accounting fees				
25 Current year acquisition/reorganization other costs				
26 Amortization/impairment of goodwill				
27 Amortization of acquisition, reorganization, and start-up costs				
28 Other amortization or impairment write-offs				
29 Reserved				
30 Depletion				
31 Depreciation	60,000	110,000		170,000
32 Bad debt expense	25,000		(9,000)	16,000
33 Corporate owned life insurance premiums	2,800		(2,800)	-0-
34 Purchase versus lease (for purchasers and/or lessees)				
35 Research and development costs				
36 Section 118 exclusion (attach statement)				
37 Other expense/deduction items with differences (attach statement)				
38 **Total expense/deduction items.** Combine lines 1 through 37. Enter here and on Part II, line 27, reporting positive amounts as negative and negative amounts as positive	314,440	110,000	(128,440)	296,000

Schedule M-3 (Form 1120) 2014

*$151,640 FIT per books – $124,100 FIT liability (current income tax expense) = $27,540 deferred income tax expense. Also see Comprehensive Problem, Year 1, Step 7 on text Page C:3-49.

**Business interest

Form **1120** Department of the Treasury Internal Revenue Service

U.S. Corporation Income Tax Return

For calendar year 2013 or tax year beginning ________, 2013, ending ________, 20 ____

► Information about Form 1120 and its separate instructions is at *www.irs.gov/form1120.*

OMB No. 1545-0123 **2014**

A Check if: 1a Consolidated return (attach Form 851) [X]; b Life/nonlife consolidated return [ ]; 2 Personal holding co. (attach Sch. PH) [ ]; 3 Personal service corp. (see instructions) [ ]; 4 Schedule M-3 attached [ ]	TYPE OR PRINT — Name: Alpha Manufacturing Corp. and Subsidaries	**B** Employer identification number: XX-XXXXXXX
	Number, street, and room or suite no. If a P.O. box, see instructions. 800 Tenth Place	**C** Date incorporated: 9/15/2004
	City or town, state, or province, country and ZIP or foreign postal code: City, ST 55555	**D** Total assets (see instructions): $ 3,976,492

E Check if: (1) [ ] Initial return (2) [ ] Final return (3) [ ] Name change (4) [ ] Address change

Income	1a	Gross receipts or sales	1a	6,121,000		
	b	Returns and allowances	1b	-0-		
	c	Balance. Subtract line 1b from line 1a			1c	6,121,000
	2	Cost of goods sold (attach Form 1125-A)			2	2,275,000
	3	Gross profit. Subtract line 2 from line 1c			3	3,846,000
	4	Dividends (Schedule C, line 19)			4	40,000
	5	Interest			5	156,000
	6	Gross rents			6	195,000
	7	Gross royalties			7	
	8	Capital gain net income (attach Schedule D (Form 1120))			8	67,939
	9	Net gain or (loss) from Form 4797, Part II, line 17 (attach Form 4797)			9	48,760
	10	Other income (see instructions—attach statement)			10	10,000
	11	**Total income.** Add lines 3 through 10 ►			11	4,363,699
Deductions (See instructions for limitations on deductions.)	12	Compensation of officers (see instructions—attach Form 1125-E) ►			12	165,000
	13	Salaries and wages (less employment credits)			13	1,356,000
	14	Repairs and maintenance			14	83,000
	15	Bad debts			15	48,500
	16	Rents			16	179,000
	17	Taxes and licenses			17	138,000
	18	Interest			18	58,000
	19	Charitable contributions			19	15,000
	20	Depreciation from Form 4562 not claimed on Form 1125-A or elsewhere on return (attach Form 4562)			20	168,693
	21	Depletion			21	
	22	Advertising			22	269,140
	23	Pension, profit-sharing, etc., plans			23	140,000
	24	Employee benefit programs			24	105,000
	25	Domestic production activities deduction (attach Form 8903)			25	29,013
	26	Other deductions (attach statement)			26	1,284,000
	27	**Total deductions.** Add lines 12 through 26 ►			27	4,038,346
	28	Taxable income before net operating loss deduction and special deductions. Subtract line 27 from line 11.			28	325,353
	29a	Net operating loss deduction (see instructions)	29a			
	b	Special deductions (Schedule C, line 20)	29b	32,000		
	c	Add lines 29a and 29b			29c	32,000
Tax, Refundable Credits, and Payments	30	**Taxable income.** Subtract line 29c from line 28 (see instructions)			30	293,353
	31	Total tax (Schedule J, Part I, line 11)			31	97,658
	32	Total payments and refundable credits (Schedule J, Part II, line 21)			32	100,000
	33	Estimated tax penalty (see instructions). Check if Form 2220 is attached ► [ ]			33	
	34	**Amount owed.** If line 32 is smaller than the total of lines 31 and 33, enter amount owed			34	
	35	**Overpayment.** If line 32 is larger than the total of lines 31 and 33, enter amount overpaid			35	2,342
	36	Enter amount from line 35 you want: **Credited to 2015 estimated tax** ► 2,342	Refunded ►		36	

Sign Here

Under penalties of perjury, I declare that I have examined this return, including accompanying schedules and statements, and to the best of my knowledge and belief, it is true, correct, and complete. Declaration of preparer (other than taxpayer) is based on all information of which preparer has any knowledge.

► *U. R. Stuck* — Signature of officer | 3-14-15 — Date | ► President — Title

May the IRS discuss this return with the preparer shown below (see instructions)? [ ] Yes [ ] No

Paid Preparer Use Only

Print/Type preparer's name	Preparer's signature	Date	Check [X] if self-employed	PTIN
John A. Prepper	*John A. Prepper*	3-14-15		
Firm's name ► Prepper and Associates			Firm's EIN ►	
Firm's address ► 2222 Fifth Street, City, ST 55555			Phone no.	

For Paperwork Reduction Act Notice, see separate instructions. Cat. No. 11450Q Form **1120** (2014)

See text Example C:8-50 and the worksheet on appendix page B-25 for tax form facts.

Form 1120—Consolidated Taxable Income Computation

Line	Title	Consolidated	Adjustments and Eliminations	1 Alpha Mfg. Corp.	2 Beta Corp.	3 Charlie Corp.	4 Delta Corp.	5 Echo Corp.
1	Net gross receipts	$6,121,000	($50,000)	$1,566,000	$2,680,000	$676,000		$1,249,000
2	Cost of goods sold	(2,275,000)	26,000	(783,000)	(1,390,000)	(128,000)		–0–
3	Gross profit	$3,846,000	($24,000)[1]	$ 783,000	$1,290,000	$548,000	$ –0–	$1,249,000
4	Dividends (Sch. C)	40,000	(170,000)[2]	210,000				
5	Interest	156,000[3]		46,000	89,000			21,000
6	Gross rents	195,000					$195,000	
7	Gross royalties							
8	Capital gain net income (Sch. D)	67,939		67,939				
9	Net gain or loss from Form 4797	48,760		52,760	(4,000)			
10	Other income	10,000[4]		10,000				
11	Total income	$4,363,699	($194,000)	$1,169,699	$1,375,000	$548,000	$195,000	$1,270,000
12	Compensation of officers	$ 165,000		$ 165,000				
13	Salaries and wages	1,356,000		138,000	$ 240,000	$ 377,000	$ 36,000	$ 565,000
14	Repairs and maintenace	83,000		19,000	18,000	7,000	18,000	21,000
15	Bad debts	48,500			36,500	4,000		8,000
16	Rents	179,000		93,000	39,000	11,000		36,000
17	Taxes	138,000		36,000	27,000	10,000	16,000	49,000
18	Interest	58,000[3]		27,000			29,000	2,000
19	Charitable contributions	15,000		9,000	4,000			2,000
20	Depreciation	168,693		24,500	62,930	24,370	24,043	32,850
21	Depletion	–0–						
22	Advertising	269,140			223,140	27,000		19,000
23	Pension, profit-sharing, etc. plans	140,000		39,000	21,000	35,000		45,000
24	Employee benefit programs	105,000		26,000	16,000	29,000		34,000
25	Domestic prod. act. ded.	29,013	29,013[5]					
26	Other deductions	1,284,000[4]		409,000	401,000	72,000	49,000	353,000
27	Total deductions	$4,038,346	$ 29,013	$ 985,500	$1,088,570	$596,370	$172,043	$1,166,850

Line	Title	Consolidated	Adjustments and Eliminations	1 Alpha Mfg. Corp.	2 Beta Corp.	3 Charlie Corp.	4 Delta Corp.	5 Echo Corp.
28	Taxable income before NOL ded. and special deductions	$325,353	($223,013)	$184,199	$286,430	($48,370)	$22,957	$103,150
29a	NOL deduction							
29b	Special deductions	(32,000)	(32,000)[3]					
30	Taxable income	$293,353	($255,013)					

Explanatory Notes

1 Beta's inventory at the beginning of the current year includes items Alpha acquired for a $90,000 cost and sold to Beta for $175,000 during the preceding year. Beta sells the items to third parties during the current year. Beta's inventory at the end of the current year includes items Alpha acquired for a $116,000 cost and sold to Beta for $225,000 during the current year. Beta sells the items to third parties during the next year.

Under the matching rule, the consolidated group defers inclusion of the $85,000 ($175,000 − $90,000) intercompany profit from the preceding year to the current year and defers inclusion of the $109,000 ($225,000 − $116,000) intercompany profit from the current year to the next year. The net adjustment for net gross receipts on Line 1 for the current year is negative $50,000 ($175,000 − $225,000), and the net adjustment for cost of goods sold on Line 2 for the current year is positive $26,000 ($116,000 − $90,000). The net adjustment for gross profit on Line 3 for the current year is negative $24,000 [($50,000) + $26,000].

2 Dividends of $100,000 and $70,000 paid by Beta and Echo, respectively, to Alpha are an adjustment to consolidated taxable income because they were included in Alpha's separate reporting. The remaining $40,000 of dividends are from unaffiliated domestic corporations that are more than 20%-owned and eligible for an 80% dividends-received deduction (see Line 29b). The group claims a $32,000 dividends-received deduction.

3 Alpha Manufacturing loaned money to Delta Corporation. Delta accrued and paid $12,000 in interest during the year. Under the matching rule, Delta's $12,000 of interest expense (the corresponding item) is matched with Alpha's $12,000 of interest income (the intercompany item). The two amounts offset, resulting in a zero net effect on consolidated taxable income (the recomputed corresponding item). The individual firms reported these amounts in their separate expense and income items, so no adjustment or elimination is needed.

4 The supporting schedule of component items is not reproduced here.

5 The consolidated U.S. production activities deduction is computed as $322,366 × 0.09, where $322,366 is consolidated taxable income before that deduction and is less than consolidated qualified production activities income.

Facts for S Corporation (Form 1120S)

The same basic facts presented for the Andrew Lawrence proprietorship are used for the S corporation except for the following:

1. Johns and Lawrence, Inc. made an S corporation election on June 13, 2008. The election was effective for its initial tax year.

2. The book income for Johns and Lawrence is presented in the attached worksheet, which reconciles book income and S corporation taxable income.

3. The $18,000 salaries paid to each employee are subject to the same employment tax requirements as when paid by the C corporation. The total employment taxes ($14,480) are the same as for the C corporation.

4. The S corporation paid no estimated federal income taxes.

5. The corporation distributed $14,106 to each of the two shareholders.

6. Other deductions include:

Travel	$ 4,000
Meals and entertainment	8,000
Minus: 50% disallowance	(4,000)
Office expenses	16,000
Transportation	10,400
General and administrative	3,000
Miscellaneous*	850
Total	$38,250

*$150 of the miscellaneous expenses are related to the production of the dividend income and are separately stated.

7. The following schedule reconciles net income for the C corporation and the S corporation:

Net income per books for C corporation	$63,412
Plus: Federal income taxes	14,000
Net income per books for S corporation	$77,412

The S corporation return can be tied back to the partnership return. The only difference between the two returns is that the S corporation pays an additional $6,160 in employment taxes with respect to the shareholder-employee salaries, as compared to the partnership's guaranteed payments. This dollar difference is reflected in the net income numbers, the ordinary income numbers, capital account balances, and total asset amounts.

8. Qualifed production activities income (QPAI) equals $80,000. Employer's W-2 wages allocable to U.S. production activities equal $88,000.

9. The balance sheet for Johns and Lawrence appears on page 4 of Form 1120S.

10. For additional information, see worksheet on page B-46.

Form **1120S**

Department of the Treasury
Internal Revenue Service

U.S. Income Tax Return for an S Corporation

▶ Do not file this form unless the corporation has filed or is attaching Form 2553 to elect to be an S corporation.
▶ Information about Form 1120S and its separate instructions is at *www.irs.gov/form1120s.*

OMB No. 1545-0130

2014

For calendar year 2013 or tax year beginning , 2013, ending , 20

A S election effective date: 6-13-2008
B Business activity code number (see instructions): 337000
C Check if Sch. M-3 attached ☐

TYPE OR PRINT
Name: Johns and Lawrence, Inc.
Number, street, and room or suite no. If a P.O. box, see instructions.: 1234 First Avenue
City or town, state or province, country, and ZIP or foreign postal code: City, ST 55555

D Employer identification number: XX-XXXXXXX
E Date incorporated: 6-1-2008
F Total assets (see instructions): $ 498,324

G Is the corporation electing to be an S corporation beginning with this tax year? ☐ Yes ☐ No If "Yes," attach Form 2553 if not already filed
H Check if: (1) ☐ Final return (2) ☐ Name change (3) ☐ Address change (4) ☐ Amended return (5) ☐ S election termination or revocation
I Enter the number of shareholders who were shareholders during any part of the tax year . . . . ▶ 2

Caution. Include **only** trade or business income and expenses on lines 1a through 21. See the instructions for more information.

Income	1a	Gross receipts or sales	1a	869,658		
	b	Returns and allowances	1b	29,242		
	c	Balance. Subtract line 1b from line 1a			1c	840,416
	2	Cost of goods sold (attach Form 1125-A)			2	540,204
	3	Gross profit. Subtract line 2 from line 1c			3	300,212
	4	Net gain (loss) from Form 4797, line 17 (attach Form 4797)			4	
	5	Other income (loss) (see instructions—attach statement)			5	
	6	**Total income (loss).** Add lines 3 through 5 ▶			6	300,212
Deductions (see instructions for limitations)	7	Compensation of officers (see instructions—attach Form 1125-E)			7	36,000
	8	Salaries and wages (less employment credits)			8	52,000
	9	Repairs and maintenance			9	4,800
	10	Bad debts			10	4,000
	11	Rents			11	36,000
	12	Taxes and licenses			12	16,000
	13	Interest			13	8,000
	14	Depreciation not claimed on Form 1125-A or elsewhere on return (attach Form 4562)			14	12,476
	15	Depletion **(Do not deduct oil and gas depletion.)**			15	
	16	Advertising			16	13,000
	17	Pension, profit-sharing, etc., plans			17	2,000
	18	Employee benefit programs			18	4,000
	19	Other deductions (attach statement)			19	38,250
	20	**Total deductions.** Add lines 7 through 19 ▶			20	226,526
	21	**Ordinary business income (loss).** Subtract line 20 from line 6			21	73,686
Tax and Payments	22a	Excess net passive income or LIFO recapture tax (see instructions)	22a			
	b	Tax from Schedule D (Form 1120S)	22b			
	c	Add lines 22a and 22b (see instructions for additional taxes)			22c	NONE
	23a	2013 estimated tax payments and 2012 overpayment credited to 2013	23a			
	b	Tax deposited with Form 7004	23b			
	c	Credit for federal tax paid on fuels (attach Form 4136)	23c			
	d	Add lines 23a through 23c			23d	NONE
	24	Estimated tax penalty (see instructions). Check if Form 2220 is attached ▶ ☐			24	
	25	**Amount owed.** If line 23d is smaller than the total of lines 22c and 24, enter amount owed			25	NONE
	26	**Overpayment.** If line 23d is larger than the total of lines 22c and 24, enter amount overpaid			26	
	27	Enter amount from line 26 **Credited to 2014 estimated tax** ▶		**Refunded** ▶	27	

Sign Here

Under penalties of perjury, I declare that I have examined this return, including accompanying schedules and statements, and to the best of my knowledge and belief, it is true, correct, and complete. Declaration of preparer (other than taxpayer) is based on all information of which preparer has any knowledge.

▶ Andrew Lawrence (Signature of officer) | 3-14-15 (Date) | ▶ Vice-President (Title)

May the IRS discuss this return with the preparer shown below (see instructions)? ☒ Yes ☐ No

Paid Preparer Use Only

Print/Type preparer's name	Preparer's signature	Date	Check ☒ if self-employed	PTIN
Michael Prepper	Michael Prepper	3-14-15		

Firm's name ▶ Michael S. Prepper — Firm's EIN ▶
Firm's address ▶ 1111 Second Street, City, ST 55555 — Phone no.

Form 1120S (2014) Page 2

Schedule B **Other Information** (see instructions)

		Yes	No
1	Check accounting method: a ☐ Cash b ☒ Accrual c ☐ Other (specify) ▶		
2	See the instructions and enter the: a Business activity ▶ Manufacturing b Product or service ▶ Furniture		
3	At any time during the tax year, was any shareholder of the corporation a disregarded entity, a trust, an estate, or a nominee or similar person? If "Yes," attach Schedule B-1, Information on Certain Shareholders of an S Corporation		X
4	At the end of the tax year, did the corporation:		
a	Own directly 20% or more, or own, directly or indirectly, 50% or more of the total stock issued and outstanding of any foreign or domestic corporation? For rules of constructive ownership, see instructions. If "Yes," complete (i) through (v) below		X

(i) Name of Corporation	(ii) Employer Identification Number (if any)	(iii) Country of Incorporation	(iv) Percentage of Stock Owned	(v) If Percentage in (iv) is 100%, Enter the Date (if any) a Qualified Subchapter S Subsidiary Election Was Made

		Yes	No
b	Own directly an interest of 20% or more, or own, directly or indirectly, an interest of 50% or more in the profit, loss, or capital in any foreign or domestic partnership (including an entity treated as a partnership) or in the beneficial interest of a trust? For rules of constructive ownership, see instructions. If "Yes," complete (i) through (v) below		X

(i) Name of Entity	(ii) Employer Identification Number (if any)	(iii) Type of Entity	(iv) Country of Organization	(v) Maximum Percentage Owned in Profit, Loss, or Capital

		Yes	No
5 a	At the end of the tax year, did the corporation have any outstanding shares of restricted stock? If "Yes," complete lines (i) and (ii) below. (i) Total shares of restricted stock ▶ (ii) Total shares of non-restricted stock ▶		X
b	At the end of the tax year, did the corporation have any outstanding stock options, warrants, or similar instruments? If "Yes," complete lines (i) and (ii) below. (i) Total shares of stock outstanding at the end of the tax year ▶ (ii) Total shares of stock outstanding if all instruments were executed ▶		X
6	Has this corporation filed, or is it required to file, **Form 8918,** Material Advisor Disclosure Statement, to provide information on any reportable transaction?		X
7	Check this box if the corporation issued publicly offered debt instruments with original issue discount ▶ ☐ If checked, the corporation may have to file **Form 8281,** Information Return for Publicly Offered Original Issue Discount Instruments.		
8	If the corporation: **(a)** was a C corporation before it elected to be an S corporation **or** the corporation acquired an asset with a basis determined by reference to the basis of the asset (or the basis of any other property) in the hands of a C corporation **and (b)** has net unrealized built-in gain in excess of the net recognized built-in gain from prior years, enter the net unrealized built-in gain reduced by net recognized built-in gain from prior years (see instructions) ▶ $ N/A		
9	Enter the accumulated earnings and profits of the corporation at the end of the tax year. $ -0-		
10	Does the corporation satisfy **both** of the following conditions?		
a	The corporation's total receipts (see instructions) for the tax year were less than $250,000		
b	The corporation's total assets at the end of the tax year were less than $250,000 If "Yes," the corporation is not required to complete Schedules L and M-1.		X
11	During the tax year, did the corporation have any non-shareholder debt that was canceled, was forgiven, or had the terms modified so as to reduce the principal amount of the debt? If "Yes," enter the amount of principal reduction $		X
12	During the tax year, was a qualified subchapter S subsidiary election terminated or revoked? If "Yes," see instructions		X
13a	Did the corporation make any payments in 2013 that would require it to file Form(s) 1099?		X
b	If "Yes," did the corporation file or will it file required Forms 1099?		

Form **1120S** (2014)

Form 1120S (2014) Page 3

Schedule K Shareholders' Pro Rata Share Items

Section	Line	Description			Line	Total amount
Income (Loss)	1	Ordinary business income (loss) (page 1, line 21)			1	73,686
	2	Net rental real estate income (loss) (attach Form 8825)			2	
	3a	Other gross rental income (loss)	3a			
	b	Expenses from other rental activities (attach statement)	3b			
	c	Other net rental income (loss). Subtract line 3b from line 3a			3c	
	4	Interest income			4	
	5	Dividends: a Ordinary dividends			5a	1,000
		b Qualified dividends	5b	1,000		
	6	Royalties			6	
	7	Net short-term capital gain (loss) (attach Schedule D (Form 1120S))			7	(2100)
	8a	Net long-term capital gain (loss) (attach Schedule D (Form 1120S))			8a	4,500
	b	Collectibles (28%) gain (loss)	8b			
	c	Unrecaptured section 1250 gain (attach statement)	8c			
	9	Net section 1231 gain (loss) (attach Form 4797)			9	
	10	Other income (loss) (see instructions) Type ▶			10	
Deductions	11	Section 179 deduction (attach Form 4562)			11	
	12a	Charitable contributions			12a	12,000
	b	Investment interest expense			12b	150
	c	Section 59(e)(2) expenditures (1) Type ▶ (2) Amount ▶			12c(2)	
	d	Other deductions (see instructions) Type ▶			12d	
Credits	13a	Low-income housing credit (section 42(j)(5))			13a	
	b	Low-income housing credit (other)			13b	
	c	Qualified rehabilitation expenditures (rental real estate) (attach Form 3468)			13c	
	d	Other rental real estate credits (see instructions) Type ▶			13d	
	e	Other rental credits (see instructions) Type ▶			13e	
	f	Biofuel producer credit (attach Form 6478)			13f	
	g	Other credits (see instructions) Type ▶			13g	
Foreign Transactions	14a	Name of country or U.S. possession ▶				
	b	Gross income from all sources			14b	
	c	Gross income sourced at shareholder level			14c	
		Foreign gross income sourced at corporate level				
	d	Passive category			14d	
	e	General category			14e	
	f	Other (attach statement)			14f	
		Deductions allocated and apportioned at shareholder level				
	g	Interest expense			14g	
	h	Other			14h	
		Deductions allocated and apportioned at corporate level to foreign source income				
	i	Passive category			14i	
	j	General category			14j	
	k	Other (attach statement)			14k	
		Other information				
	l	Total foreign taxes (check one): ▶ ☐ Paid ☐ Accrued			14l	
	m	Reduction in taxes available for credit (attach statement)			14m	
	n	Other foreign tax information (attach statement)				
Alternative Minimum Tax (AMT) Items	15a	Post-1986 depreciation adjustment			15a	1,514
	b	Adjusted gain or loss			15b	
	c	Depletion (other than oil and gas)			15c	
	d	Oil, gas, and geothermal properties—gross income			15d	
	e	Oil, gas, and geothermal properties—deductions			15e	
	f	Other AMT items (attach statement)			15f	
Items Affecting Shareholder Basis	16a	Tax-exempt interest income			16a	18,000
	b	Other tax-exempt income			16b	
	c	Nondeductible expenses			16c	6,000 *
	d	Distributions (attach statement if required) (see instructions)			16d	28,212
	e	Repayment of loans from shareholders			16e	

Form **1120S** (2014)

*Disallowed meals and entertainment expenses ($4,000) plus interest on loan to purchase tax-exempt bonds ($2,000).

Form 1120S (2014) Page 4

Schedule K **Shareholders' Pro Rata Share Items** (continued)

				Total amount	
Other Information	17a	Investment income	17a	1,000	*
	b	Investment expenses	17b		
	c	Dividend distributions paid from accumulated earnings and profits	17c		
	d	Other items and amounts (attach statement)			
Recon-ciliation	18	**Income/loss reconciliation.** Combine the amounts on lines 1 through 10 in the far right column. From the result, subtract the sum of the amounts on lines 11 through 12d and 14l	18		

Schedule L **Balance Sheets per Books**

	Assets	Beginning of tax year (a)	Beginning of tax year (b)	End of tax year (c)	End of tax year (d)
1	Cash		60,000		86,600
2a	Trade notes and accounts receivable	25,000		24,000	
b	Less allowance for bad debts	(1,000)	24,000	(1,000)	23,000
3	Inventories		64,000		104,800
4	U.S. government obligations				
5	Tax-exempt securities (see instructions)		200,000		200,000
6	Other current assets (attach statement)		7,000		
7	Loans to shareholders				
8	Mortgage and real estate loans				
9	Other investments (attach statement)				
10a	Buildings and other depreciable assets	151,600		151,600	
b	Less accumulated depreciation	(45,200)	106,400	(72,676)	78,924
11a	Depletable assets				
b	Less accumulated depletion	( )		( )	
12	Land (net of any amortization)				
13a	Intangible assets (amortizable only)				
b	Less accumulated amortization	( )		( )	
14	Other assets (attach statement)				
15	Total assets		461,400		493,324
	Liabilities and Shareholders' Equity				
16	Accounts payable		26,000		19,000
17	Mortgages, notes, bonds payable in less than 1 year		4,000		4,000
18	Other current liabilities (attach statement)		3,600		3,600
19	Loans from shareholders				
20	Mortgages, notes, bonds payable in 1 year or more		130,000		119,724
21	Other liabilities (attach statement)				
22	Capital stock		200,000		200,000
23	Additional paid-in capital				
24	Retained earnings		97,800		147,000
25	Adjustments to shareholders' equity (attach statement)				
26	Less cost of treasury stock		( )		( )
27	Total liabilities and shareholders' equity		461,400		493,324

Form **1120S** (2014)

* Investment income only if shareholders elect to tax dividends at ordinary rates under Sec. 163(d)(4)(B).

Form 1120S (2014) Page 5

Schedule M-1 **Reconciliation of Income (Loss) per Books With Income (Loss) per Return**

Note. Schedule M-3 required instead of Schedule M-1 if total assets are $10 million or more—see instructions

1	Net income (loss) per books	77,412	5	Income recorded on books this year not included on Schedule K, lines 1 through 10 (itemize): a Tax-exempt interest $ 18,000	18,000
2	Income included on Schedule K, lines 1, 2, 3c, 4, 5a, 6, 7, 8a, 9, and 10, not recorded on books this year (itemize)				
3	Expenses recorded on books this year not included on Schedule K, lines 1 through 12 and 14l (itemize): a Depreciation $ b Travel and entertainment $ 4,000 Interest on loans* $2,000	6,000	6	Deductions included on Schedule K, lines 1 through 12 and 14l, not charged against book income this year (itemize): a Depreciation $ 476	476
			7	Add lines 5 and 6	18,476
4	Add lines 1 through 3	83,412	8	Income (loss) (Schedule K, line 18). Line 4 less line 7	64,936

Schedule M-2 **Analysis of Accumulated Adjustments Account, Other Adjustments Account, and Shareholders' Undistributed Taxable Income Previously Taxed** (see instructions)

		(a) Accumulated adjustments account	(b) Other adjustments account	(c) Shareholders' undistributed taxable income previously taxed
1	Balance at beginning of tax year	86,100	11,700	
2	Ordinary income from page 1, line 21	73,686		
3	Other additions	5,500**	18,000	
4	Loss from page 1, line 21	( )		
5	Other reductions	(18,250***)	(2,000)	
6	Combine lines 1 through 5	147,036	27,700	
7	Distributions other than dividend distributions	28,212		
8	Balance at end of tax year. Subtract line 7 from line 6	118,824	27,700	

Form **1120S** (2014)

*For municipal bonds

**$1,000 + $4,500 = $5,500

***$12,000 + $4,000 + $150 +$2,100 = $18,250

671113

☐ Final K-1 ☐ Amended K-1 OMB No. 1545-0130

Schedule K-1 (Form 1120S) **2014**
Department of the Treasury
Internal Revenue Service

For calendar year 2013, or tax year beginning ________, 2013 ending ________, 20____

Shareholder's Share of Income, Deductions, Credits, etc.

► See back of form and separate instructions.

Part I Information About the Corporation

A Corporation's employer identification number
XX-XXXXXXX

B Corporation's name, address, city, state, and ZIP code
Johns and Lawrence, Inc.
1234 First Avenue
City, ST 55555

C IRS Center where corporation filed return
Ogden, UT

Part II Information About the Shareholder

D Shareholder's identifying number
XXX-XX-XXXX

E Shareholder's name, address, city, state, and ZIP code
Andrew Lawrence
333 Third Street
City, ST 55555

F Shareholder's percentage of stock ownership for tax year . . . . 50 %

For IRS Use Only

Part III Shareholder's Share of Current Year Income, Deductions, Credits, and Other Items

Line	Item	Amount
1	Ordinary business income (loss)	36,843
2	Net rental real estate income (loss)	
3	Other net rental income (loss)	
4	Interest income	
5a	Ordinary dividends	500
5b	Qualified dividends	500
6	Royalties	
7	Net short-term capital gain (loss)	(1,050)
8a	Net long-term capital gain (loss)	2,250
8b	Collectibles (28%) gain (loss)	
8c	Unrecaptured section 1250 gain	
9	Net section 1231 gain (loss)	
10	Other income (loss)	
11	Section 179 deduction	
12	Other deductions	
	A	6,000
	G	75
	Q	40,000
	R	44,000
13	Credits	
14	Foreign transactions	
15	Alternative minimum tax (AMT) items	
	A	757
16	Items affecting shareholder basis	
	A	9,000
	C	3,000
	D	14,106
17	Other information	
	A	500 **

* See attached statement for additional information.

*Schedule K-1 for Stephen Johns is similar to this one and is not reproduced here.

**Investment income only if shareholder elects to tax dividends at ordinary rates under Sec. 163(d)(4)(B).

Schedule K-1 (Form 1120S) 2014 Page **2**

This list identifies the codes used on Schedule K-1 for all shareholders and provides summarized reporting information for shareholders who file Form 1040. For detailed reporting and filing information, see the separate Shareholder's Instructions for Schedule K-1 and the instructions for your income tax return.

1. Ordinary business income (loss). Determine whether the income (loss) is passive or nonpassive and enter on your return as follows:

	Report on
Passive loss	See the Shareholder's Instructions
Passive income	Schedule E, line 28, column (g)
Nonpassive loss	Schedule E, line 28, column (h)
Nonpassive income	Schedule E, line 28, column (j)
2. Net rental real estate income (loss)	See the Shareholder's Instructions
3. Other net rental income (loss)	
Net income	Schedule E, line 28, column (g)
Net loss	See the Shareholder's Instructions
4. Interest income	Form 1040, line 8a
5a. Ordinary dividends	Form 1040, line 9a
5b. Qualified dividends	Form 1040, line 9b
6. Royalties	Schedule E, line 4
7. Net short-term capital gain (loss)	Schedule D, line 5
8a. Net long-term capital gain (loss)	Schedule D, line 12
8b. Collectibles (28%) gain (loss)	28% Rate Gain Worksheet, line 4 (Schedule D instructions)
8c. Unrecaptured section 1250 gain	See the Shareholder's Instructions
9. Net section 1231 gain (loss)	See the Shareholder's Instructions

10. Other income (loss)

Code		
A	Other portfolio income (loss)	See the Shareholder's Instructions
B	Involuntary conversions	See the Shareholder's Instructions
C	Sec. 1256 contracts & straddles	Form 6781, line 1
D	Mining exploration costs recapture	See Pub. 535
E	Other income (loss)	See the Shareholder's Instructions

11. Section 179 deduction — See the Shareholder's Instructions

12. Other deductions

A	Cash contributions (50%)	See the Shareholder's Instructions
B	Cash contributions (30%)	See the Shareholder's Instructions
C	Noncash contributions (50%)	See the Shareholder's Instructions
D	Noncash contributions (30%)	See the Shareholder's Instructions
E	Capital gain property to a 50% organization (30%)	See the Shareholder's Instructions
F	Capital gain property (20%)	See the Shareholder's Instructions
G	Contributions (100%)	See the Shareholder's Instructions
H	Investment interest expense	Form 4952, line 1
I	Deductions—royalty income	Schedule E, line 19
J	Section 59(e)(2) expenditures	See the Shareholder's Instructions
K	Deductions—portfolio (2% floor)	Schedule A, line 23
L	Deductions—portfolio (other)	Schedule A, line 28
M	Preproductive period expenses	See the Shareholder's Instructions
N	Commercial revitalization deduction from rental real estate activities	See Form 8582 instructions
O	Reforestation expense deduction	See the Shareholder's Instructions
P	Domestic production activities information	See Form 8903 instructions
Q	Qualified production activities income	Form 8903, line 7b
R	Employer's Form W-2 wages	Form 8903, line 17
S	Other deductions	See the Shareholder's Instructions

13. Credits

A	Low-income housing credit (section 42(j)(5)) from pre-2008 buildings	See the Shareholder's Instructions
B	Low-income housing credit (other) from pre-2008 buildings	See the Shareholder's Instructions
C	Low-income housing credit (section 42(j)(5)) from post-2007 buildings	See the Shareholder's Instructions
D	Low-income housing credit (other) from post-2007 buildings	See the Shareholder's Instructions
E	Qualified rehabilitation expenditures (rental real estate)	See the Shareholder's Instructions
F	Other rental real estate credits	See the Shareholder's Instructions
G	Other rental credits	See the Shareholder's Instructions
H	Undistributed capital gains credit	Form 1040, line 71, box a
I	Biofuel producer credit	See the Shareholder's Instructions
J	Work opportunity credit	See the Shareholder's Instructions
K	Disabled access credit	See the Shareholder's Instructions
L	Empowerment zone employment credit	See the Shareholder's Instructions
M	Credit for increasing research activities	See the Shareholder's Instructions

Code		*Report on*
N	Credit for employer social security and Medicare taxes	See the Shareholder's Instructions
O	Backup withholding	See the Shareholder's Instructions
P	Other credits	See the Shareholder's Instructions

14. Foreign transactions

A	Name of country or U.S. possession	Form 1116, Part I
B	Gross income from all sources	Form 1116, Part I
C	Gross income sourced at shareholder level	Form 1116, Part I
	Foreign gross income sourced at corporate level	
D	Passive category	Form 1116, Part I
E	General category	Form 1116, Part I
F	Other	Form 1116, Part I
	Deductions allocated and apportioned at shareholder level	
G	Interest expense	Form 1116, Part I
H	Other	Form 1116, Part I
	Deductions allocated and apportioned at corporate level to foreign source income	
I	Passive category	Form 1116, Part I
J	General category	Form 1116, Part I
K	Other	Form 1116, Part I
	Other information	
L	Total foreign taxes paid	Form 1116, Part II
M	Total foreign taxes accrued	Form 1116, Part II
N	Reduction in taxes available for credit	Form 1116, line 12
O	Foreign trading gross receipts	Form 8873
P	Extraterritorial income exclusion	Form 8873
Q	Other foreign transactions	See the Shareholder's Instructions

15. Alternative minimum tax (AMT) items

A	Post-1986 depreciation adjustment	See the Shareholder's Instructions and the Instructions for Form 6251
B	Adjusted gain or loss	See the Shareholder's Instructions and the Instructions for Form 6251
C	Depletion (other than oil & gas)	See the Shareholder's Instructions and the Instructions for Form 6251
D	Oil, gas, & geothermal—gross income	See the Shareholder's Instructions and the Instructions for Form 6251
E	Oil, gas, & geothermal—deductions	See the Shareholder's Instructions and the Instructions for Form 6251
F	Other AMT items	See the Shareholder's Instructions and the Instructions for Form 6251

16. Items affecting shareholder basis

A	Tax-exempt interest income	Form 1040, line 8b
B	Other tax-exempt income	See the Shareholder's Instructions
C	Nondeductible expenses	See the Shareholder's Instructions
D	Distributions	See the Shareholder's Instructions
E	Repayment of loans from shareholders	See the Shareholder's Instructions

17. Other information

A	Investment income	Form 4952, line 4a
B	Investment expenses	Form 4952, line 5
C	Qualified rehabilitation expenditures (other than rental real estate)	See the Shareholder's Instructions
D	Basis of energy property	See the Shareholder's Instructions
E	Recapture of low-income housing credit (section 42(j)(5))	Form 8611, line 8
F	Recapture of low-income housing credit (other)	Form 8611, line 8
G	Recapture of investment credit	See Form 4255
H	Recapture of other credits	See the Shareholder's Instructions
I	Look-back interest—completed long-term contracts	See Form 8697
J	Look-back interest—income forecast method	See Form 8866
K	Dispositions of property with section 179 deductions	See the Shareholder's Instructions
L	Recapture of section 179 deduction	See the Shareholder's Instructions
M	Section 453(l)(3) information	See the Shareholder's Instructions
N	Section 453A(c) information	See the Shareholder's Instructions
O	Section 1260(b) information	See the Shareholder's Instructions
P	Interest allocable to production expenditures	See the Shareholder's Instructions
Q	CCF nonqualified withdrawals	See the Shareholder's Instructions
R	Depletion information—oil and gas	See the Shareholder's Instructions
S	Amortization of reforestation costs	See the Shareholder's Instructions
T	Section 108(i) information	See the Shareholder's Instructions
U	Net investment income	See the Shareholder's Instructions
V	Other information	See the Shareholder's Instructions

Form **1125-A**
(Rev. December 2012)
Department of the Treasury
Internal Revenue Service

Cost of Goods Sold

► Attach to Form 1120, 1120-C, 1120-F, 1120S, 1065, or 1065-B.
► Information about Form 1125-A and its instructions is at *www.irs.gov/form1125a.*

OMB No. 1545-2225

Name: Johns and Lawrence, Inc.

Employer identification number: XX-XXXXXXX

1	Inventory at beginning of year	1	64,000
2	Purchases	2	340,800
3	Cost of labor	3	143,204
4	Additional section 263A costs (attach schedule)	4	7,000
5	Other costs (attach schedule)	5	90,000
6	**Total.** Add lines 1 through 5	6	645,004
7	Inventory at end of year	7	104,800
8	**Cost of goods sold.** Subtract line 7 from line 6. Enter here and on Form 1120, page 1, line 2 or the appropriate line of your tax return (see instructions)	8	540,204

9a Check all methods used for valuing closing inventory:
- *(i)* ☒ Cost
- *(ii)* ☐ Lower of cost or market
- *(iii)* ☐ Other (Specify method used and attach explanation.) ►

b Check if there was a writedown of subnormal goods ► ☐

c Check if the LIFO inventory method was adopted this tax year for any goods (if checked, attach Form 970) ► ☐

d If the LIFO inventory method was used for this tax year, enter amount of closing inventory computed under LIFO **9d**

e If property is produced or acquired for resale, do the rules of section 263A apply to the entity (see instructions)? ☐ Yes ☒ No

f Was there any change in determining quantities, cost, or valuations between opening and closing inventory? If "Yes," attach explanation ☐ Yes ☒ No

Section references are to the Internal Revenue Code unless otherwise noted.

General Instructions

Purpose of Form

Use Form 1125-A to calculate and deduct cost of goods sold for certain entities.

Who Must File

Filers of Form 1120, 1120-C, 1120-F, 1120S, 1065, or 1065-B, must complete and attach Form 1125-A if the applicable entity reports a deduction for cost of goods sold.

Inventories

Generally, inventories are required at the beginning and end of each tax year if the production, purchase, or sale of merchandise is an income-producing factor. See Regulations section 1.471-1. If inventories are required, you generally must use an accrual method of accounting for sales and purchases of inventory items.

Exception for certain taxpayers. If you are a qualifying taxpayer or a qualifying small business taxpayer (defined below), you can adopt or change your accounting method to account for inventoriable items in the same manner as materials and supplies that are not incidental.

Under this accounting method, inventory costs for raw materials purchased for use in producing finished goods and merchandise purchased for resale are deductible in the year the finished goods or merchandise are sold (but not before the year you paid for the raw materials or merchandise, if you are also using the cash method).

If you account for inventoriable items in the same manner as materials and supplies that are not incidental, you can currently deduct expenditures for direct labor and all indirect costs that would otherwise be included in inventory costs. See the instructions for lines 2 and 7.

For additional guidance on this method of accounting, see Pub. 538, Accounting Periods and Methods. For guidance on adopting or changing to this method of accounting, see Form 3115, Application for Change in Accounting Method, and its instructions.

Qualifying taxpayer. A qualifying taxpayer is a taxpayer that, (a) for each prior tax year ending after December 16, 1998, has average annual gross receipts of $1 million or less for the 3 prior tax years and (b) its business is not a tax shelter (as defined in section 448(d)(3)). See Rev. Proc. 2001-10, 2001-2 I.R.B. 272.

Qualifying small business taxpayer. A qualifying small business taxpayer is a taxpayer that, (a) for each prior tax year ending on or after December 31, 2000, has average annual gross receipts of $10 million or less for the 3 prior tax years, (b) whose principal business activity is not an ineligible activity, and (c) whose business is not a tax shelter (as defined in section 448 (d)(3)). See Rev. Proc. 2002-28, 2002-18 I.R.B. 815.

Uniform capitalization rules. The uniform capitalization rules of section 263A generally require you to capitalize, or include in inventory, certain costs incurred in connection with the following.

- The production of real property and tangible personal property held in inventory or held for sale in the ordinary course of business.
- Real property or personal property (tangible and intangible) acquired for resale.
- The production of real property and tangible personal property by a corporation for use in its trade or business or in an activity engaged in for profit.

See the discussion on section 263A uniform capitalization rules in the instructions for your tax return before completing Form 1125-A. Also see Regulations sections 1.263A-1 through 1.263A-3. See Regulations section 1.263A-4 for rules for property produced in a farming business.

Johns and Lawrence, Inc. (S Corporation) Reconciliation of Book and Taxable Income For Year Ending December 31, 2014

	Book Income		Adjustments		Taxable Income		Form 1120S Schedule K	
Account Name	Debit	Credit	Debit	Credit	Debit	Credit	Ordinary Income	Separately Stated Items
Sales		$869,658				$869,658	$869,658	
Sales returns & allowances	$ 29,242				$ 29,242		(29,242)	
Cost of sales	540,204				540,204		(540,204)	
Dividends		1,000				1,000		1,000
Tax-exempt interest		18,000	$18,000			0		$18,000
Gain on stock sale		4,500				4,500		4,500
Worthless stock loss	2,100				2,100			(2,100)
Officers salaries[a]	36,000				36,000		(36,000)	
Other salaries	52,000				52,000		(52,000)	
Rentals	36,000				36,000		(36,000)	
Bad debts	4,000				4,000		(4,000)	
Interest:								
Working capital loans	8,000				8,000		(8,000)	
Purchase tax-exempt bonds	2,000			$ 2,000	0			(2,000)
Employment taxes	14,480				14,480		(14,480)	
Taxes	1,520				1,520		(1,520)	
Repairs	4,800				4,800		(4,800)	
Depreciation[b]	12,000		476		12,476		(12,476)	
Charitable contributions	12,000				12,000			(12,000)
Travel	4,000				4,000		(4,000)	
Meals and entertainment[c]	8,000			4,000	4,000		(4,000)	
Meals and ent. nondeductible								(4,000)
Office expenses	16,000				16,000		(16,000)	
Advertising	13,000				13,000		(13,000)	
Transportation expense	10,400				10,400		(10,400)	
General and administrative	3,000				3,000		(3,000)	
Pension plans[d]	2,000				2,000		(2,000)	
Employee benefit programs[e]	4,000				4,000		(4,000)	
Miscellaneous	1,000				1,000		(850)	(150)
Net profit/Taxable income	77,412			12,476	64,936			
Total	$893,158	$893,158	$18,476	$18,476	$875,158	$875,158	$ 73,686	

[a] Salaries for the S corporation's shareholder-employees are deductible by the S corporation and are subject to the same employee taxes imposed on nonshareholder-employees.

[b] MACRS depreciation = $27,476 total − $15,000 allocated to COGS = $12,476

[c] 50% of the meals and entertainment expense is not deductible for tax purposes but must be separately stated on the Schedules K and K-1.

[d] The pension plan expense is the same for book and tax purposes for this corporation. No pension expenses relate to pensions for the shareholder-employees.

[e] The employee benefit expense is the same for book and tax purposes for this corporation. None relates to shareholder-employee benefits.

Form **2210**

Department of the Treasury
Internal Revenue Service

Underpayment of Estimated Tax by Individuals, Estates, and Trusts

▶ Information about Form 2210 and its separate instructions is at *www.irs.gov/form2210*.
▶ Attach to Form 1040, 1040A, 1040NR, 1040NR-EZ, or 1041.

OMB No. 1545-0074
2014
Attachment Sequence No. **06**

Name(s) shown on tax return | **Identifying number**

Do You Have To File Form 2210?

- Complete lines 1 through 7 below. Is line 7 less than $1,000?
  - **Yes** → **Do not file Form 2210.** You do not owe a penalty.
  - **No** ↓
- Complete lines 8 and 9 below. Is line 6 equal to or more than line 9?
  - **Yes** → You do not owe a penalty. **Do not file Form 2210** (but if box **E** in Part II applies, you must file page 1 of Form 2210).
  - **No** ↓
- You may owe a penalty. Does any box in Part II below apply?
  - **No** → **Do not file Form 2210.** You are not required to figure your penalty because the IRS will figure it and send you a bill for any unpaid amount. If you want to figure it, you may use Part III or Part IV as a worksheet and enter your penalty amount on your tax return, but **do not file Form 2210.**
  - **Yes** → You **must** file Form 2210. Does box **B, C,** or **D** in Part II apply?
    - **Yes** → You must figure your penalty.
    - **No** → You are **not** required to figure your penalty because the IRS will figure it and send you a bill for any unpaid amount. If you want to figure it, you may use Part III or Part IV as a worksheet and enter your penalty amount on your tax return, but **file only page 1 of Form 2210.**

Part I Required Annual Payment

1	Enter your 2014 tax after credits from Form 1040, line 56 (see instructions if not filing Form 1040)	1	
2	Other taxes, including self-employment tax and, if applicable, Additional Medicare Tax and/or Net Investment Income Tax (see instructions)	2	
3	Refundable credits, including the premium tax credit (see instructions)	3	( )
4	Current year tax. Combine lines 1, 2, and 3. If less than $1,000, **stop;** you do not owe a penalty. **Do not** file Form 2210	4	
5	Multiply line 4 by 90% (.90) 5		
6	Withholding taxes. **Do not** include estimated tax payments (see instructions)	6	
7	Subtract line 6 from line 4. If less than $1,000, **stop**; you do not owe a penalty. **Do not** file Form 2210	7	
8	Maximum required annual payment based on prior year's tax (see instructions)	8	
9	**Required annual payment.** Enter the **smaller** of line 5 or line 8	9	

Next: Is line 9 more than line 6?

☐ **No.** You **do not** owe a penalty. **Do not** file Form 2210 unless box **E** below applies.

☐ **Yes.** You may owe a penalty, but **do not** file Form 2210 unless one or more boxes in Part II below applies.

- If box **B, C,** or **D** applies, you must figure your penalty and file Form 2210.
- If box **A** or **E** applies (but not **B, C,** or **D**) file only page 1 of Form 2210. You are **not** required to figure your penalty; the IRS will figure it and send you a bill for any unpaid amount. If you want to figure your penalty, you may use Part III or IV as a worksheet and enter your penalty on your tax return, but **file only page 1 of Form 2210.**

Part II Reasons for Filing. Check applicable boxes. If none apply, **do not** file Form 2210.

A ☐ You request a **waiver** (see instructions) of your entire penalty. You must check this box and file page 1 of Form 2210, but you are not required to figure your penalty.

B ☐ You request a **waiver** (see instructions) of part of your penalty. You must figure your penalty and waiver amount and file Form 2210.

C ☐ Your income varied during the year and your penalty is reduced or eliminated when figured using the **annualized income installment method.** You must figure the penalty using Schedule AI and file Form 2210.

D ☐ Your penalty is lower when figured by treating the federal income tax withheld from your income as paid on the dates it was actually withheld, instead of in equal amounts on the payment due dates. You must figure your penalty and file Form 2210.

E ☐ You filed or are filing a joint return for either 2013 or 2014, but not for both years, and line 8 above is smaller than line 5 above. You must file page 1 of Form 2210, but you are **not** required to figure your penalty (unless box **B, C,** or **D** applies).

Form 2210 (2014) Page **2**

Part III Short Method

Can You Use the Short Method?

You may use the short method if:

- You made no estimated tax payments (or your only payments were withheld federal income tax), **or**
- You paid the same amount of estimated tax on each of the four payment due dates.

Must You Use the Regular Method?

You must use the regular method (Part IV) instead of the short method if:

- You made any estimated tax payments late,
- You checked box **C** or **D** in Part II, **or**
- You are filing Form 1040NR or 1040NR-EZ and you did not receive wages as an employee subject to U.S. income tax withholding.

Note: *If any payment was made earlier than the due date, you may use the short method, but using it may cause you to pay a larger penalty than the regular method. If the payment was only a few days early, the difference is likely to be small.*

10	Enter the amount from Form 2210, line 9		**10**	
11	Enter the amount, if any, from Form 2210, line 6	**11**		
12	Enter the total amount, if any, of estimated tax payments you made .	**12**		
13	Add lines 11 and 12		**13**	
14	**Total underpayment for year.** Subtract line 13 from line 10. If zero or less, **stop**; you do not owe a penalty. **Do not file Form 2210 unless you checked box E in Part II**		**14**	
15	Multiply line 14 by .01995		**15**	
16	• If the amount on line 14 was paid **on or after** 4/15/15, enter -0-. • If the amount on line 14 was paid **before** 4/15/15, make the following computation to find the amount to enter on line 16. Amount on line 14 × Number of days paid before 4/15/15 × .00008		**16**	
17	**Penalty.** Subtract line 16 from line 15. Enter the result here and on Form 1040, line 79; Form 1040A, line 51; Form 1040NR, line 76; Form 1040NR-EZ, line 26; or Form 1041, line 26. **Do not file Form 2210 unless you checked a box in Part II** . . . . ►		**17**	

Form **2210** (2014)

Form 2210 (2014) Page 3

Part IV Regular Method (See the instructions if you are filing Form 1040NR or 1040NR-EZ.)

Section A—Figure Your Underpayment		Payment Due Dates (a) 4/15/14	(b) 6/15/14	(c) 9/15/14	(d) 1/15/15
18 **Required installments.** If box C in Part II applies, enter the amounts from Schedule AI, line 25. Otherwise, enter 25% (.25) of line 9, Form 2210, in each column	18				
19 Estimated tax paid and tax withheld (see the instructions). For column (a) only, also enter the amount from line 19 on line 23. If line 19 is equal to or more than line 18 for all payment periods, stop here; you do not owe a penalty. **Do not file Form 2210 unless you checked a box in Part II**	19				
Complete lines 20 through 26 of one column before going to line 20 of the next column.					
20 Enter the amount, if any, from line 26 in the previous column	20				
21 Add lines 19 and 20	21				
22 Add the amounts on lines 24 and 25 in the previous column	22				
23 Subtract line 22 from line 21. If zero or less, enter -0-. For column (a) only, enter the amount from line 19	23				
24 If line 23 is zero, subtract line 21 from line 22. Otherwise, enter -0-	24				
25 **Underpayment.** If line 18 is equal to or more than line 23, subtract line 23 from line 18. Then go to line 20 of the next column. Otherwise, go to line 26 ▶	25				
26 Overpayment. If line 23 is more than line 18, subtract line 18 from line 23. Then go to line 20 of the next column	26				

Section B—Figure the Penalty (Use the Worksheet for Form 2210, Part IV, Section B—Figure the Penalty in the instructions.)

27 **Penalty.** Enter the total penalty from line 14 of the Worksheet for Form 2210, Part IV, Section B—Figure the Penalty. Also include this amount on Form 1040, line 79; Form 1040A, line 51; Form 1040NR, line 76; Form 1040NR-EZ, line 26; or Form 1041, line 26. **Do not file Form 2210 unless you checked a box in Part II** ▶	27	

Form **2210** (2014)

Form 2210 (2014) Page 4

Schedule AI—Annualized Income Installment Method (See the instructions.)

Estates and trusts, **do not** use the period ending dates shown to the right. Instead, use the following: 2/28/14, 4/30/14, 7/31/14, and 11/30/14.

Part I Annualized Income Installments

		(a) 1/1/14–3/31/14	(b) 1/1/14–5/31/14	(c) 1/1/14–8/31/14	(d) 1/1/14–12/31/14
1 Enter your adjusted gross income for each period (see instructions). (Estates and trusts, enter your taxable income without your exemption for each period.)	1				
2 Annualization amounts. (Estates and trusts, see instructions)	2	4	2.4	1.5	1
3 Annualized income. Multiply line 1 by line 2	3				
4 If you itemize, enter itemized deductions for the period shown in each column. All others enter -0-, and skip to line 7. **Exception:** Estates and trusts, skip to line 9 and enter amount from line 3	4				
5 Annualization amounts	5	4	2.4	1.5	1
6 Multiply line 4 by line 5 (see instructions if line 3 is more than $152,525)	6				
7 In each column, enter the full amount of your standard deduction from Form 1040, line 40, or Form 1040A, line 24. (Form 1040NR or 1040NR-EZ filers, enter -0-. **Exception:** Indian students and business apprentices, see instructions.)	7				
8 Enter the **larger** of line 6 or line 7	8				
9 Subtract line 8 from line 3	9				
10 In each column, multiply $3,950 by the total number of exemptions claimed. (see instructions if line 3 is more than $152,525) (Estates, trusts, and Form 1040NR or 1040NR-EZ filers, see instructions.)	10				
11 Subtract line 10 from line 9. If zero or less, enter -0-	11				
12 Figure your tax on the amount on line 11 (see instructions)	12				
13 Self-employment tax from line 34 (complete Part II below)	13				
14 Enter other taxes for each payment period including, if applicable, Additional Medicare Tax and/or Net Investment Income Tax (see instructions)	14				
15 Total tax. Add lines 12, 13, and 14	15				
16 For each period, enter the same type of credits as allowed on Form 2210, Part I, lines 1 and 3 (see instructions)	16				
17 Subtract line 16 from line 15. If zero or less, enter -0-	17				
18 Applicable percentage	18	22.5%	45%	67.5%	90%
19 Multiply line 17 by line 18	19				
Complete lines 20–25 of one column before going to line 20 of the next column.					
20 Enter the total of the amounts in all previous columns of line 25	20				
21 Subtract line 20 from line 19. If zero or less, enter -0-	21				
22 Enter 25% (.25) of line 9 on page 1 of Form 2210 in each column	22				
23 Subtract line 25 of the previous column from line 24 of that column	23				
24 Add lines 22 and 23	24				
25 Enter the **smaller** of line 21 or line 24 here and on Form 2210, Part IV, line 18 ►	25				

Part II Annualized Self-Employment Tax (Form 1040 and Form 1040NR filers only)

		(a)	(b)	(c)	(d)
26 Net earnings from self-employment for the period (see instructions)	26				
27 Prorated social security tax limit	27	$29,250	$48,750	$78,000	$117,000
28 Enter actual wages for the period subject to social security tax or the 6.2% portion of the 7.65% railroad retirement (tier 1) tax. **Exception:** If you filed Form 4137 or Form 8919, see instructions	28				
29 Subtract line 28 from line 27. If zero or less, enter -0-	29				
30 Annualization amounts	30	0.496	0.2976	0.186	0.124
31 Multiply line 30 by the **smaller** of line 26 or line 29	31				
32 Annualization amounts	32	0.116	0.0696	0.0435	0.029
33 Multiply line 26 by line 32	33				
34 Add lines 31 and 33. Enter here and on line 13 above ►	34				

Form **2220**

Department of the Treasury
Internal Revenue Service

Underpayment of Estimated Tax by Corporations

► Attach to the corporation's tax return.
► Information about Form 2220 and its separate instructions is at *www.irs.gov/form2220*.

OMB No. 1545-0142

2014

Name: Globe Corporation

Employer identification number: XX-XXXXXXX

Note: *Generally, the corporation is not required to file Form 2220 (see Part II below for exceptions) because the IRS will figure any penalty owed and bill the corporation. However, the corporation may still use Form 2220 to figure the penalty. If so, enter the amount from page 2, line 38 on the estimated tax penalty line of the corporation's income tax return, but* **do not** *attach Form 2220.*

Part I Required Annual Payment

1	Total tax (see instructions)			1	100,000
2a	Personal holding company tax (Schedule PH (Form 1120), line 26) included on line 1	2a			
b	Look-back interest included on line 1 under section 460(b)(2) for completed long-term contracts or section 167(g) for depreciation under the income forecast method	2b			
c	Credit for federal tax paid on fuels (see instructions)	2c			
d	**Total.** Add lines 2a through 2c			2d	
3	Subtract line 2d from line 1. If the result is less than $500, **do not** complete or file this form. The corporation does not owe the penalty			3	100,000
4	Enter the tax shown on the corporation's 2012 income tax return (see instructions). **Caution:** ***If the tax is zero or the tax year was for less than 12 months, skip this line and enter the amount from line 3 on line 5***			4	125,000
5	**Required annual payment.** Enter the **smaller** of line 3 or line 4. If the corporation is required to skip line 4, enter the amount from line 3			5	100,000

Part II Reasons for Filing—Check the boxes below that apply. If any boxes are checked, the corporation **must** file Form 2220 even if it does not owe a penalty (see instructions).

6 ☐ The corporation is using the adjusted seasonal installment method.
7 ☐ The corporation is using the annualized income installment method.
8 ☐ The corporation is a "large corporation" figuring its first required installment based on the prior year's tax.

Part III Figuring the Underpayment

			(a)	(b)	(c)	(d)
9	**Installment due dates.** Enter in columns (a) through (d) the 15th day of the 4th (***Form 990-PF filers:*** Use 5th month), 6th, 9th, and 12th months of the corporation's tax year	9	4-15-14	6-15-14	9-15-14	12-15-14
10	**Required installments.** If the box on line 6 and/or line 7 above is checked, enter the amounts from Schedule A, line 38. If the box on line 8 (but not 6 or 7) is checked, see instructions for the amounts to enter. If none of these boxes are checked, enter 25% of line 5 above in each column	10	25,000	25,000	25,000	25,000
11	Estimated tax paid or credited for each period (see instructions). For column (a) only, enter the amount from line 11 on line 15	11	16,000	16,000	21,000	35,000
	Complete lines 12 through 18 of one column before going to the next column.					
12	Enter amount, if any, from line 18 of the preceding column	12		-0-	-0-	-0-
13	Add lines 11 and 12	13		16,000	21,000	35,000
14	Add amounts on lines 16 and 17 of the preceding column	14		9,000	18,000	22,000
15	Subtract line 14 from line 13. If zero or less, enter -0-	15	16,000	7,000	3,000	13,000
16	If the amount on line 15 is zero, subtract line 13 from line 14. Otherwise, enter -0-	16		-0-	-0-	
17	**Underpayment.** If line 15 is less than or equal to line 10, subtract line 15 from line 10. Then go to line 12 of the next column. Otherwise, go to line 18	17	9,000	18,000	22,000	12,000
18	**Overpayment.** If line 10 is less than line 15, subtract line 10 from line 15. Then go to line 12 of the next column	18				

Go to Part IV on page 2 to figure the penalty. Do not go to Part IV if there are no entries on line 17—no penalty is owed.

See text Example C:3-48 for tax form facts.

Form 2220 (2014) Page **2**

Part IV Figuring the Penalty

			(a)	(b)	(c)	(d)
19	Enter the date of payment or the 15th day of the 3rd month after the close of the tax year, whichever is earlier (see instructions). ***(Form 990-PF and Form 990-T filers:*** Use 5th month instead of 3rd month.)	19	6-15-14	9-15-14	12-15-14	3-15-15
20	Number of days from due date of installment on line 9 to the date shown on line 19	20	61	92	91	90
21	Number of days on line 20 after 4/15/2014 and before 7/1/2014	21	61	15		
22	Underpayment on line 17 × (Number of days on line 21 / 365) × 3%	22	$ 45	$ 22	$	$
23	Number of days on line 20 after 6/30/2014 and before 10/1/2014	23		77	15	
24	Underpayment on line 17 × (Number of days on line 23 / 365) × 3%	24	$	$ 114	$ 27	$
25	Number of days on line 20 after 9/30/2014 and before 1/1/2015	25			76	16
26	Underpayment on line 17 × (Number of days on line 25 / 365) × 3%	26	$	$	$ 137	$ 16
27	Number of days on line 20 after 12/31/2014 and before 4/1/2015	27				74
28	Underpayment on line 17 × (Number of days on line 27 / 365) × 3%	28	$	$	$	$ 73
29	Number of days on line 20 after 3/31/2015 and before 7/1/2015	29				
30	Underpayment on line 17 × (Number of days on line 29 / 365) × *%	30	$	$	$	$
31	Number of days on line 20 after 6/30/2015 and before 10/1/2015	31				
32	Underpayment on line 17 × (Number of days on line 31 / 365) × *%	32	$	$	$	$
33	Number of days on line 20 after 9/30/2015 and before 1/1/2016	33				
34	Underpayment on line 17 × (Number of days on line 33 / 365) × *%	34	$	$	$	$
35	Number of days on line 20 after 12/31/2015 and before 2/16/2016	35				
36	Underpayment on line 17 × (Number of days on line 35 / 365) × *%	36	$	$	$	$
37	Add lines 22, 24, 26, 28, 30, 32, 34, and 36	37	$ 45	$ 136	$ 164	$ 89
38	**Penalty.** Add columns (a) through (d) of line 37. Enter the total here and on Form 1120, line 33; or the comparable line for other income tax returns				38	$ 434

*Use the penalty interest rate for each calendar quarter, which the IRS will determine during the first month in the preceding quarter. These rates are published quarterly in an IRS News Release and in a revenue ruling in the Internal Revenue Bulletin. To obtain this information on the Internet, access the IRS website at ***www.irs.gov***. You can also call 1-800-829-4933 to get interest rate information.

Form **2220** (2014)

Form **2441**

Department of the Treasury
Internal Revenue Service (99)

Child and Dependent Care Expenses

► Attach to Form 1040, Form 1040A, or Form 1040NR.

► Information about Form 2441 and its separate instructions is at *www.irs.gov/form2441*.

1040
1040A
1040NR
2441

OMB No. 1545-0074

2014

Attachment Sequence No. **21**

Name(s) shown on return | **Your social security number**

Part I **Persons or Organizations Who Provided the Care**—You **must** complete this part.
(If you have more than two care providers, see the instructions.)

1 **(a)** Care provider's name	**(b)** Address (number, street, apt. no., city, state, and ZIP code)	**(c)** Identifying number (SSN or EIN)	**(d)** Amount paid (see instructions)

Did you receive **dependent care benefits?**
No → Complete only Part II below.
Yes → Complete Part III on the back next.

Caution. If the care was provided in your home, you may owe employment taxes. If you do, you cannot file Form 1040A. For details, see the instructions for Form 1040, line 60a, or Form 1040NR, line 59a.

Part II **Credit for Child and Dependent Care Expenses**

2 Information about your **qualifying person(s).** If you have more than two qualifying persons, see the instructions.

(a) Qualifying person's name — First	Last	**(b)** Qualifying person's social security number	**(c) Qualified expenses** you incurred and paid in 2014 for the person listed in column (a)

3 Add the amounts in column (c) of line 2. **Do not** enter more than $3,000 for one qualifying person or $6,000 for two or more persons. If you completed Part III, enter the amount from line 31 . . . . **3**

4 Enter your **earned income.** See instructions **4**

5 If married filing jointly, enter your spouse's earned income (if you or your spouse was a student or was disabled, see the instructions); **all others**, enter the amount from line 4 . **5**

6 Enter the **smallest** of line 3, 4, or 5 . . . . **6**

7 Enter the amount from Form 1040, line 38; Form 1040A, line 22; or Form 1040NR, line 37. . . . . **7**

8 Enter on line 8 the decimal amount shown below that applies to the amount on line 7

If line 7 is: Over	But not over	Decimal amount is	If line 7 is: Over	But not over	Decimal amount is
$0	15,000	.35	$29,000	31,000	.27
15,000	17,000	.34	31,000	33,000	.26
17,000	19,000	.33	33,000	35,000	.25
19,000	21,000	.32	35,000	37,000	.24
21,000	23,000	.31	37,000	39,000	.23
23,000	25,000	.30	39,000	41,000	.22
25,000	27,000	.29	41,000	43,000	.21
27,000	29,000	.28	43,000	No limit	.20

8 X .

9 Multiply line 6 by the decimal amount on line 8. If you paid 2013 expenses in 2014, see the instructions **9**

10 Tax liability limit. Enter the amount from the Credit Limit Worksheet in the instructions. **10**

11 **Credit for child and dependent care expenses.** Enter the **smaller** of line 9 or line 10 here and on Form 1040, line 49; Form 1040A, line 31; or Form 1040NR, line 47 . . . . **11**

Form 2441 (2014) Page 2

Part III Dependent Care Benefits

12 Enter the total amount of **dependent care benefits** you received in 2014. Amounts you received as an employee should be shown in box 10 of your Form(s) W-2. **Do not** include amounts reported as wages in box 1 of Form(s) W-2. If you were self-employed or a partner, include amounts you received under a dependent care assistance program from your sole proprietorship or partnership **12**

13 Enter the amount, if any, you carried over from 2013 and used in 2014 during the grace period. See instructions **13**

14 Enter the amount, if any, you forfeited or carried forward to 2015. See instructions . . . **14** ( )

15 Combine lines 12 through 14. See instructions **15**

16 Enter the total amount of **qualified expenses** incurred in 2014 for the care of the **qualifying person(s)** . . . **16**

17 Enter the **smaller** of line 15 or 16 . . . . **17**

18 Enter your **earned income.** See instructions **18**

19 Enter the amount shown below that applies to you.
- If married filing jointly, enter your spouse's earned income (if you or your spouse was a student or was disabled, see the instructions for line 5).
- If married filing separately, see instructions.
- All others, enter the amount from line 18.

. . . **19**

20 Enter the **smallest** of line 17, 18, or 19 . . . . **20**

21 Enter $5,000 ($2,500 if married filing separately **and** you were required to enter your spouse's earned income on line 19) **21**

22 Is any amount on line 12 from your sole proprietorship or partnership? (Form 1040A filers go to line 25.)

☐ **No.** Enter -0-.

☐ **Yes.** Enter the amount here **22**

23 Subtract line 22 from line 15 . . . . . **23**

24 **Deductible benefits.** Enter the **smallest** of line 20, 21, or 22. Also, include this amount on the appropriate line(s) of your return. See instructions **24**

25 **Excluded benefits. Form 1040 and 1040NR filers:** If you checked "No" on line 22, enter the smaller of line 20 or 21. Otherwise, subtract line 24 from the smaller of line 20 or line 21. If zero or less, enter -0-. **Form 1040A filers:** Enter the **smaller** of line 20 or line 21 . . **25**

26 **Taxable benefits. Form 1040 and 1040NR filers:** Subtract line 25 from line 23. If zero or less, enter -0-. Also, include this amount on Form 1040, line 7, or Form 1040NR, line 8. On the dotted line next to Form 1040, line 7, or Form 1040NR, line 8, enter "DCB." **Form 1040A filers:** Subtract line 25 from line 15. Also, include this amount on Form 1040A, line 7. In the space to the left of line 7, enter "DCB" **26**

To claim the child and dependent care credit, complete lines 27 through 31 below.

27 Enter $3,000 ($6,000 if two or more qualifying persons) **27**

28 **Form 1040 and 1040NR filers:** Add lines 24 and 25. **Form 1040A filers:** Enter the amount from line 25 . . . . **28**

29 Subtract line 28 from line 27. If zero or less, **stop.** You cannot take the credit. **Exception.** If you paid 2013 expenses in 2014, see the instructions for line 9 . . . . . **29**

30 Complete line 2 on the front of this form. **Do not** include in column (c) any benefits shown on line 28 above. Then, add the amounts in column (c) and enter the total here **30**

31 Enter the **smaller** of line 29 or 30. Also, enter this amount on line 3 on the front of this form and complete lines 4 through 11 . . . . **31**

Form **2441** (2014)

Form **4626** Department of the Treasury Internal Revenue Service

Alternative Minimum Tax—Corporations

► Attach to the corporation's tax return.
► Information about Form 4626 and its separate instructions is at *www.irs.gov/form4626*.

OMB No. 1545-0175

2014

Name	Employer identification number
Glidden Corporation	XX-XXXXXXX

Note: *See the instructions to find out if the corporation is a small corporation exempt from the alternative minimum tax (AMT) under section 55(e).*

1	Taxable income or (loss) before net operating loss deduction			1	130,278
2	**Adjustments and preferences:**				
a	Depreciation of post-1986 property			2a	7,500
b	Amortization of certified pollution control facilities			2b	
c	Amortization of mining exploration and development costs			2c	
d	Amortization of circulation expenditures (personal holding companies only)			2d	
e	Adjusted gain or loss			2e	(6,918)
f	Long-term contracts			2f	
g	Merchant marine capital construction funds			2g	
h	Section 833(b) deduction (Blue Cross, Blue Shield, and similar type organizations only)			2h	
i	Tax shelter farm activities (personal service corporations only)			2i	
j	Passive activities (closely held corporations and personal service corporations only)			2j	
k	Loss limitations			2k	
l	Depletion			2l	
m	Tax-exempt interest income from specified private activity bonds			2m	
n	Intangible drilling costs			2n	
o	Other adjustments and preferences			2o	
3	Pre-adjustment alternative minimum taxable income (AMTI). Combine lines 1 through 2o			3	130,860
4	**Adjusted current earnings (ACE) adjustment:**				
a	ACE from line 10 of the ACE worksheet in the instructions	4a	312,360		
b	Subtract line 3 from line 4a. If line 3 exceeds line 4a, enter the difference as a negative amount (see instructions)	4b	181,500		
c	Multiply line 4b by 75% (.75). Enter the result as a positive amount	4c	136,125		
d	Enter the excess, if any, of the corporation's total increases in AMTI from prior year ACE adjustments over its total reductions in AMTI from prior year ACE adjustments (see instructions). **Note:** *You **must** enter an amount on line 4d (even if line 4b is positive).*	4d	311,296		
e	ACE adjustment. • If line 4b is zero or more, enter the amount from line 4c • If line 4b is less than zero, enter the **smaller** of line 4c or line 4d as a negative amount			4e	136,125
5	Combine lines 3 and 4e. If zero or less, stop here; the corporation does not owe any AMT			5	266,985
6	Alternative tax net operating loss deduction (see instructions)			6	-0-
7	**Alternative minimum taxable income.** Subtract line 6 from line 5. If the corporation held a residual interest in a REMIC, see instructions			7	266,985
8	**Exemption phase-out** (if line 7 is $310,000 or more, skip lines 8a and 8b and enter -0- on line 8c):				
a	Subtract $150,000 from line 7 (if completing this line for a member of a controlled group, see instructions). If zero or less, enter -0-	8a	116,985		
b	Multiply line 8a by 25% (.25)	8b	29,246		
c	Exemption. Subtract line 8b from $40,000 (if completing this line for a member of a controlled group, see instructions). If zero or less, enter -0-			8c	10,754
9	Subtract line 8c from line 7. If zero or less, enter -0-			9	256,231
10	Multiply line 9 by 20% (.20)			10	51,246
11	Alternative minimum tax foreign tax credit (AMTFTC) (see instructions)			11	-0-
12	Tentative minimum tax. Subtract line 11 from line 10			12	51,246
13	Regular tax liability before applying all credits except the foreign tax credit			13	34,058
14	**Alternative minimum tax.** Subtract line 13 from line 12. If zero or less, enter -0-. Enter here and on Form 1120, Schedule J, line 3, or the appropriate line of the corporation's income tax return			14	17,188

See the Comprehensive Example on text page C:5-10 for tax form facts.

Form **4684**

Department of the Treasury
Internal Revenue Service

Casualties and Thefts

► Information about Form 4684 and its separate instructions is at *www.irs.gov/form4684.*
► Attach to your tax return.
► Use a separate Form 4684 for each casualty or theft.

OMB No. 1545-0177
2014
Attachment Sequence No. 26

Name(s) shown on tax return | Identifying number

SECTION A—Personal Use Property (Use this section to report casualties and thefts of property **not** used in a trade or business or for income-producing purposes.)

1 Description of properties (show type, location, and date acquired for each property). Use a separate line for each property lost or damaged from the same casualty or theft.

Property **A** ______
Property **B** ______
Property **C** ______
Property **D** ______

		Properties A	Properties B	Properties C	Properties D
2 Cost or other basis of each property	2				
3 Insurance or other reimbursement (whether or not you filed a claim) (see instructions)	3				
Note: *If line 2 is **more** than line 3, skip line 4.*					
4 Gain from casualty or theft. If line 3 is **more** than line 2, enter the difference here and skip lines 5 through 9 for that column. See instructions if line 3 includes insurance or other reimbursement you did not claim, or you received payment for your loss in a later tax year	4				
5 Fair market value **before** casualty or theft	5				
6 Fair market value **after** casualty or theft	6				
7 Subtract line 6 from line 5	7				
8 Enter the **smaller** of line 2 or line 7	8				
9 Subtract line 3 from line 8. If zero or less, enter -0-	9				

10 Casualty or theft loss. Add the amounts on line 9 in columns A through D	10	
11 Enter the **smaller** of line 10 or $100	11	
12 Subtract line 11 from line 10	12	
Caution: *Use only one Form 4684 for lines 13 through 18.*		
13 Add the amounts on line 12 of all Forms 4684	13	
14 Add the amounts on line 4 of all Forms 4684	14	
15 • If line 14 is **more** than line 13, enter the difference here and on Schedule D. **Do not** complete the rest of this section (see instructions). • If line 14 is **less** than line 13, enter -0- here and go to line 16. • If line 14 is **equal** to line 13, enter -0- here. **Do not** complete the rest of this section.	15	
16 If line 14 is **less** than line 13, enter the difference	16	
17 Enter 10% of your adjusted gross income from Form 1040, line 38, or Form 1040NR, line 37. Estates and trusts, see instructions	17	
18 Subtract line 17 from line 16. If zero or less, enter -0-. Also enter the result on Schedule A (Form 1040), line 20, or Form 1040NR, Schedule A, line 6. Estates and trusts, enter the result on the "Other deductions" line of your tax return	18	

Form 4684 (2014) Attachment Sequence No. 26 Page 2

Name(s) shown on tax return. Do not enter name and identifying number if shown on other side. | **Identifying number**

SECTION B—Business and Income-Producing Property

Part I **Casualty or Theft Gain or Loss** (Use a separate Part I for each casualty or theft.)

19 Description of properties (show type, location, and date acquired for each property). Use a separate line for each property lost or damaged from the same casualty or theft. **See instructions if claiming a loss due to a Ponzi-type investment scheme and Section C is not completed.**

Property **A** ____________________

Property **B** ____________________

Property **C** ____________________

Property **D** ____________________

	Line	Properties A		B		C		D	
20 Cost or adjusted basis of each property	20								
21 Insurance or other reimbursement (whether or not you filed a claim). See the instructions for line 3	21								
Note: *If line 20 is* ***more*** *than line 21, skip line 22.* 22 Gain from casualty or theft. If line 21 is **more** than line 20, enter the difference here and on line 29 or line 34, column (c), except as provided in the instructions for line 33. Also, skip lines 23 through 27 for that column. See the instructions for line 4 if line 21 includes insurance or other reimbursement you did not claim, or you received payment for your loss in a later tax year	22								
23 Fair market value **before** casualty or theft	23								
24 Fair market value **after** casualty or theft	24								
25 Subtract line 24 from line 23	25								
26 Enter the **smaller** of line 20 or line 25	26								
Note: *If the property was totally destroyed by casualty or lost from theft, enter on line 26 the amount from line 20.* 27 Subtract line 21 from line 26. If zero or less, enter -0-	27								
28 Casualty or theft loss. Add the amounts on line 27. Enter the total here and on line 29 **or** line 34 (see instructions)							28		

Part II **Summary of Gains and Losses** (from separate Parts I)

	(a) Identify casualty or theft		(b) Losses from casualties or thefts (i) Trade, business, rental or royalty property	(b) (ii) Income-producing and employee property		(c) Gains from casualties or thefts includible in income
	Casualty or Theft of Property Held One Year or Less					
29			( )	( )		
			( )	( )		
30	Totals. Add the amounts on line 29	30	( )	( )		
31	Combine line 30, columns (b)(i) and (c). Enter the net gain or (loss) here and on Form 4797, line 14. If Form 4797 is not otherwise required, see instructions				31	
32	Enter the amount from line 30, column (b)(ii) here. Individuals, enter the amount from income-producing property on Schedule A (Form 1040), line 28, or Form 1040NR, Schedule A, line 14, and enter the amount from property used as an employee on Schedule A (Form 1040), line 23, or Form 1040NR, Schedule A, line 9. Estates and trusts, partnerships, and S corporations, see instructions				32	
	Casualty or Theft of Property Held More Than One Year					
33	Casualty or theft gains from Form 4797, line 32				33	
34			( )	( )		
			( )	( )		
35	Total losses. Add amounts on line 34, columns (b)(i) and (b)(ii)	35	( )	( )		
36	Total gains. Add lines 33 and 34, column (c)				36	
37	Add amounts on line 35, columns (b)(i) and (b)(ii)				37	
38	If the loss on line 37 is **more** than the gain on line 36:					
a	Combine line 35, column (b)(i) and line 36, and enter the net gain or (loss) here. Partnerships (except electing large partnerships) and S corporations, see the note below. All others, enter this amount on Form 4797, line 14. If Form 4797 is not otherwise required, see instructions				38a	
b	Enter the amount from line 35, column (b)(ii) here. Individuals, enter the amount from income-producing property on Schedule A (Form 1040), line 28, or Form 1040NR, Schedule A, line 14, and enter the amount from property used as an employee on Schedule A (Form 1040), line 23, or Form 1040NR, Schedule A, line 9. Estates and trusts, enter on the "Other deductions" line of your tax return. Partnerships (except electing large partnerships) and S corporations, see the note below. Electing large partnerships, enter on Form 1065-B, Part II, line 11				38b	
39	If the loss on line 37 is **less** than or **equal** to the gain on line 36, combine lines 36 and 37 and enter here. Partnerships (except electing large partnerships), see the note below. All others, enter this amount on Form 4797, line 3				39	

Note: *Partnerships, enter the amount from line 38a, 38b, or line 39 on Form 1065, Schedule K, line 11. S corporations, enter the amount from line 38a or 38b on Form 1120S, Schedule K, line 10.*

Form **6251**

Department of the Treasury
Internal Revenue Service (99)

Alternative Minimum Tax—Individuals

▶ Information about Form 6251 and its separate instructions is at *www.irs.gov/form6251*.
▶ Attach to Form 1040 or Form 1040NR.

OMB No. 1545-0074
2014
Attachment Sequence No. **32**

Name(s) shown on Form 1040 or Form 1040NR | **Your social security number**

Part I Alternative Minimum Taxable Income (See instructions for how to complete each line.)

Line	Description	Line	Amount
1	If filing Schedule A (Form 1040), enter the amount from Form 1040, line 41, and go to line 2. Otherwise, enter the amount from Form 1040, line 38, and go to line 7. (If less than zero, enter as a negative amount.)	1	
2	Medical and dental. If you or your spouse was 65 or older, enter the **smaller** of Schedule A (Form 1040), line 4, **or** 2.5% (.025) of Form 1040, line 38. If zero or less, enter -0-	2	
3	Taxes from Schedule A (Form 1040), line 9	3	
4	Enter the home mortgage interest adjustment, if any, from line 6 of the worksheet in the instructions for this line	4	
5	Miscellaneous deductions from Schedule A (Form 1040), line 27	5	
6	If Form 1040, line 38, is $152,525 or less, enter -0-. Otherwise, see instructions	6	( )
7	Tax refund from Form 1040, line 10 or line 21	7	( )
8	Investment interest expense (difference between regular tax and AMT)	8	
9	Depletion (difference between regular tax and AMT)	9	
10	Net operating loss deduction from Form 1040, line 21. Enter as a positive amount	10	
11	Alternative tax net operating loss deduction	11	( )
12	Interest from specified private activity bonds exempt from the regular tax	12	
13	Qualified small business stock (7% of gain excluded under section 1202)	13	
14	Exercise of incentive stock options (excess of AMT income over regular tax income)	14	
15	Estates and trusts (amount from Schedule K-1 (Form 1041), box 12, code A)	15	
16	Electing large partnerships (amount from Schedule K-1 (Form 1065-B), box 6)	16	
17	Disposition of property (difference between AMT and regular tax gain or loss)	17	
18	Depreciation on assets placed in service after 1986 (difference between regular tax and AMT)	18	
19	Passive activities (difference between AMT and regular tax income or loss)	19	
20	Loss limitations (difference between AMT and regular tax income or loss)	20	
21	Circulation costs (difference between regular tax and AMT)	21	
22	Long-term contracts (difference between AMT and regular tax income)	22	
23	Mining costs (difference between regular tax and AMT)	23	
24	Research and experimental costs (difference between regular tax and AMT)	24	
25	Income from certain installment sales before January 1, 1987	25	( )
26	Intangible drilling costs preference	26	
27	Other adjustments, including income-based related adjustments	27	
28	**Alternative minimum taxable income.** Combine lines 1 through 27. (If married filing separately and line 28 is more than $242,450, see instructions.)	28	

Part II Alternative Minimum Tax (AMT)

29 Exemption. (If you were under age 24 at the end of 2014, see instructions.)

IF your filing status is . . .	**AND line 28 is not over . . .**	**THEN enter on line 29 . . .**
Single or head of household	$117,300	$52,800
Married filing jointly or qualifying widow(er)	156,500	82,100
Married filing separately	78,250	41,050

If line 28 is **over** the amount shown above for your filing status, see instructions. . . . **29**

30 Subtract line 29 from line 28. If more than zero, go to line 31. If zero or less, enter -0- here and on lines 31, 33, and 35, and go to line 34 . . . **30**

31
- If you are filing Form 2555 or 2555-EZ, see instructions for the amount to enter.
- If you reported capital gain distributions directly on Form 1040, line 13; you reported qualified dividends on Form 1040, line 9b; **or** you had a gain on both lines 15 and 16 of Schedule D (Form 1040) (as refigured for the AMT, if necessary), complete Part III on the back and enter the amount from line 64 here.
- **All others:** If line 30 is $182,500 or less ($91,250 or less if married filing separately), multiply line 30 by 26% (.26). Otherwise, multiply line 30 by 28% (.28) and subtract $3,650 ($1,825 if married filing separately) from the result.

. . . **31**

32 Alternative minimum tax foreign tax credit (see instructions) . . . **32**

33 Tentative minimum tax. Subtract line 32 from line 31 . . . **33**

34 Add Form 1040, line 44 (minus any tax from Form 4972), and Form 1040, line 46. Subtract from the result any foreign tax credit from Form 1040, line 48. If you used Schedule J to figure your tax on Form 1040, line 44, refigure that tax without using Schedule J before completing this line (see instructions) . . . **34**

35 **AMT.** Subtract line 34 from line 33. If zero or less, enter -0-. Enter here and on Form 1040, line 45 . . . **35**

Form 6251 (2014) Page 2

Part III Tax Computation Using Maximum Capital Gains Rates

Complete Part III only if you are required to do so by line 31 or by the Foreign Earned Income Tax Worksheet in the instructions.

36	Enter the amount from Form 6251, line 30. If you are filing Form 2555 or 2555-EZ, enter the amount from line 3 of the worksheet in the instructions for line 31	36	
37	Enter the amount from line 6 of the Qualified Dividends and Capital Gain Tax Worksheet in the instructions for Form 1040, line 44, or the amount from line 13 of the Schedule D Tax Worksheet in the instructions for Schedule D (Form 1040), whichever applies (as refigured for the AMT, if necessary) (see instructions). If you are filing Form 2555 or 2555-EZ, see instructions for the amount to enter	37	
38	Enter the amount from Schedule D (Form 1040), line 19 (as refigured for the AMT, if necessary) (see instructions). If you are filing Form 2555 or 2555-EZ, see instructions for the amount to enter	38	
39	If you did not complete a Schedule D Tax Worksheet for the regular tax or the AMT, enter the amount from line 37. Otherwise, add lines 37 and 38, and enter the **smaller** of that result or the amount from line 10 of the Schedule D Tax Worksheet (as refigured for the AMT, if necessary). If you are filing Form 2555 or 2555-EZ, see instructions for the amount to enter	39	
40	Enter the **smaller** of line 36 or line 39	40	
41	Subtract line 40 from line 36	41	
42	If line 41 is $182,500 or less ($91,250 or less if married filing separately), multiply line 41 by 26% (.26). Otherwise, multiply line 41 by 28% (.28) and subtract $3,650 ($1,825 if married filing separately) from the result ▶	42	
43	Enter: • $73,800 if married filing jointly or qualifying widow(er), • $36,900 if single or married filing separately, or • $49,400 if head of household.	43	
44	Enter the amount from line 7 of the Qualified Dividends and Capital Gain Tax Worksheet in the instructions for Form 1040, line 44, or the amount from line 14 of the Schedule D Tax Worksheet in the instructions for Schedule D (Form 1040), whichever applies (as figured for the regular tax). If you did not complete either worksheet for the regular tax, enter the amount from Form 1040, line 43; if zero or less, enter -0-. If you are filing Form 2555 or 2555-EZ, see instructions for the amount to enter	44	
45	Subtract line 44 from line 43. If zero or less, enter -0-	45	
46	Enter the **smaller** of line 36 or line 37	46	
47	Enter the **smaller** of line 45 or line 46. This amount is taxed at 0%	47	
48	Subtract line 47 from line 46	48	
49	Enter: • $406,750 if single • $228,800 if married filing separately • $457,600 if married filing jointly or qualifying widow(er) • $432,200 if head of household	49	
50	Enter the amount from line 45	50	
51	Enter the amount from line 7 of the Qualified Dividends and Capital Gain Tax Worksheet in the instructions for Form 1040, line 44, or the amount from line 19 of the Schedule D Tax Worksheet, whichever applies (as figured for the regular tax). If you did not complete either worksheet for the regular tax, enter the amount from Form 1040, line 43; if zero or less, enter -0-. If you are filing Form 2555 or Form 2555-EZ, see instructions for the amount to enter	51	
52	Add line 50 and line 51	52	
53	Subtract line 52 from line 49. If zero or less, enter -0-	53	
54	Enter the smaller of line 48 or line 53	54	
55	Multiply line 54 by 15% (.15) ▶	55	
56	Add lines 47 and 54	56	
	If lines 56 and 36 are the same, skip lines 57 through 61 and go to line 62. Otherwise, go to line 57.		
57	Subtract line 56 from line 46	57	
58	Multiply line 57 by 20% (.20) ▶	58	
	If line 38 is zero or blank, skip lines 59 through 61 and go to line 62. Otherwise, go to line 59.		
59	Add lines 41, 56, and 57	59	
60	Subtract line 59 from line 36	60	
61	Multiply line 60 by 25% (.25) ▶	61	
62	Add lines 42, 55, 58, and 61	62	
63	If line 36 is $182,500 or less ($91,250 or less if married filing separately), multiply line 36 by 26% (.26). Otherwise, multiply line 36 by 28% (.28) and subtract $3,650 ($1,825 if married filing separately) from the result	63	
64	Enter the **smaller** of line 62 or line 63 here and on line 31. If you are filing Form 2555 or 2555-EZ, do not enter this amount on line 31. Instead, enter it on line 4 of the worksheet in the instructions for line 31	64	

Form **7004**
(Rev. December 2012)
Department of the Treasury
Internal Revenue Service

Application for Automatic Extension of Time To File Certain Business Income Tax, Information, and Other Returns

▶ File a separate application for each return.
▶ Information about Form 7004 and its separate instructions is at *www.irs.gov/form7004.*

OMB No. 1545-0233

Print or Type

Name	Identifying number
Palmer Corporation	XX-XXXXXXX
Number, street, and room or suite no. (If P.O. box, see instructions.) 222 Sixth Avenue	
City, town, state, and ZIP code (If a foreign address, enter city, province or state, and country (follow the country's practice for entering postal code)). City, ST 55555	

Note. ***File request for extension by the due date of the return for which the extension is granted. See instructions before completing this form.***

Part I Automatic 5-Month Extension

1a Enter the form code for the return that this application is for (see below) . . . . ☐

Application Is For:	Form Code	Application Is For:	Form Code
Form 1065	09	Form 1041 (estate other than a bankruptcy estate)	04
Form 8804	31	Form 1041 (trust)	05

Part II Automatic 6-Month Extension

b Enter the form code for the return that this application is for (see below) . . . . ☐

Application Is For:	Form Code	Application Is For:	Form Code
Form 706-GS(D)	01	Form 1120-ND (section 4951 taxes)	20
Form 706-GS(T)	02	Form 1120-PC	21
Form 1041 (bankruptcy estate only)	03	Form 1120-POL	22
Form 1041-N	06	Form 1120-REIT	23
Form 1041-QFT	07	Form 1120-RIC	24
Form 1042	08	Form 1120S	25
Form 1065-B	10	Form 1120-SF	26
Form 1066	11	Form 3520-A	27
Form 1120	12	Form 8612	28
Form 1120-C	34	Form 8613	29
Form 1120-F	15	Form 8725	30
Form 1120-FSC	16	Form 8831	32
Form 1120-H	17	Form 8876	33
Form 1120-L	18	Form 8924	35
Form 1120-ND	19	Form 8928	36

2 If the organization is a foreign corporation that does not have an office or place of business in the United States, check here . . . . ▶ ☐

3 If the organization is a corporation and is the common parent of a group that intends to file a consolidated return, check here . . . . ▶ ☐
If checked, attach a statement, listing the name, address, and Employer Identification Number (EIN) for each member covered by this application.

Part III All Filers Must Complete This Part

4 If the organization is a corporation or partnership that qualifies under Regulations section 1.6081-5, check here . ▶ ☐

5a The application is for calendar year 20 ____ , or tax year beginning Oct. 1 , 2014, and ending Sept. 30 , 2015

b **Short tax year.** If this tax year is less than 12 months, check the reason: ☐ Initial return ☐ Final return
☐ Change in accounting period ☐ Consolidated return to be filed ☐ Other (see instructions-attach explanation)

6	Tentative total tax	6	72,000
7	**Total** payments and credits (see instructions)	7	68,000
8	**Balance due.** Subtract line 7 from line 6 (see instructions)	8	4,000

For Privacy Act and Paperwork Reduction Act Notice, see separate Instructions. Cat. No. 13804A Form **7004** (Rev. 12-2012)

See text Example C:3-50 for the tax form facts.

Form **8615**

Department of the Treasury
Internal Revenue Service (99)

Tax for Certain Children Who Have Unearned Income

► Attach only to the child's Form 1040, Form 1040A, or Form 1040NR.
► Information about Form 8615 and its separate instructions is at *www.irs.gov/form8615*.

OMB No. 1545-0074
2014
Attachment Sequence No. **33**

Child's name shown on return | **Child's social security number**

Before you begin: If the child, the parent, or any of the parent's other children for whom Form 8615 must be filed must use the Schedule D Tax Worksheet or has income from farming or fishing, see **Pub. 929,** Tax Rules for Children and Dependents. It explains how to figure the child's tax using the **Schedule D Tax Worksheet** or **Schedule J** (Form 1040).

A Parent's name (first, initial, and last). **Caution:** *See instructions before completing.* | **B** **Parent's social security number**

C Parent's filing status (check one):
☐ Single ☐ Married filing jointly ☐ Married filing separately ☐ Head of household ☐ Qualifying widow(er)

Part I Child's Net Unearned Income

1	Enter the child's unearned income (see instructions)	1	
2	If the child **did not** itemize deductions on **Schedule A** (Form 1040 or Form 1040NR), enter $2,000. Otherwise, see instructions	2	
3	Subtract line 2 from line 1. If zero or less, **stop;** do not complete the rest of this form but **do** attach it to the child's return	3	
4	Enter the child's **taxable income** from Form 1040, line 43; Form 1040A, line 27; or Form 1040NR, line 41. If the child files Form 2555 or 2555-EZ, see the instructions	4	
5	Enter the **smaller** of line 3 or line 4. If zero, **stop;** do not complete the rest of this form but **do** attach it to the child's return	5	

Part II Tentative Tax Based on the Tax Rate of the Parent

6	Enter the parent's **taxable income** from Form 1040, line 43; Form 1040A, line 27; Form 1040EZ, line 6; Form 1040NR, line 41; or Form 1040NR-EZ, line 14. If zero or less, enter -0-. If the parent files Form 2555 or 2555-EZ, see the instructions	6	
7	Enter the total, if any, from Forms 8615, line 5, of **all other** children of the parent named above. **Do not** include the amount from line 5 above	7	
8	Add lines 5, 6, and 7 (see instructions)	8	
9	Enter the tax on the amount on line 8 based on the **parent's** filing status above (see instructions). If the Qualified Dividends and Capital Gain Tax Worksheet, Schedule D Tax Worksheet, or Schedule J (Form 1040) is used to figure the tax, check here ► ☐	9	
10	Enter the parent's tax from Form 1040, line 44; Form 1040A, line 28, minus any alternative minimum tax; Form 1040EZ, line 10; Form 1040NR, line 42; or Form 1040NR-EZ, line 15. **Do not** include any tax from **Form 4972** or **8814** or any tax from recapture of an education credit. If the parent files Form 2555 or 2555-EZ, see the instructions. If the Qualified Dividends and Capital Gain Tax Worksheet, Schedule D Tax Worksheet, or Schedule J (Form 1040) was used to figure the tax, check here ► ☐	10	
11	Subtract line 10 from line 9 and enter the result. If line 7 is blank, also enter this amount on line 13 and go to **Part III**	11	
12a	Add lines 5 and 7 — 12a		
b	Divide line 5 by line 12a. Enter the result as a decimal (rounded to at least three places)	12b	× .
13	Multiply line 11 by line 12b	13	

Part III Child's Tax—If lines 4 and 5 above are the same, enter -0- on line 15 and go to line 16.

14	Subtract line 5 from line 4 — 14		
15	Enter the tax on the amount on line 14 based on the **child's** filing status (see instructions). If the Qualified Dividends and Capital Gain Tax Worksheet, Schedule D Tax Worksheet, or Schedule J (Form 1040) is used to figure the tax, check here ► ☐	15	
16	Add lines 13 and 15	16	
17	Enter the tax on the amount on line 4 based on the **child's** filing status (see instructions). If the Qualified Dividends and Capital Gain Tax Worksheet, Schedule D Tax Worksheet, or Schedule J (Form 1040) is used to figure the tax, check here ► ☐	17	
18	Enter the **larger** of line 16 or line 17 here and on the **child's** Form 1040, line 44; Form 1040A, line 28; or Form 1040NR, line 42. If the child files Form 2555 or 2555-EZ, see the instructions	18	

Form **8283**
(Rev. December 2014)
Department of the Treasury
Internal Revenue Service

Noncash Charitable Contributions

▶ Attach to your tax return if you claimed a total deduction of over $500 for all contributed property.
▶ Information about Form 8283 and its separate instructions is at *www.irs.gov/form8283*.

OMB No. 1545-0908
Attachment Sequence No. **155**

Name(s) shown on your income tax return | **Identifying number**

Note. Figure the amount of your contribution deduction before completing this form. See your tax return instructions.

Section A. Donated Property of $5,000 or Less and Publicly Traded Securities—List in this section **only** items (or groups of similar items) for which you claimed a deduction of $5,000 or less. Also list publicly traded securities even if the deduction is more than $5,000 (see instructions).

Part I **Information on Donated Property—**If you need more space, attach a statement.

1	**(a)** Name and address of the donee organization	**(b)** If donated property is a vehicle (see instructions), check the box. Also enter the vehicle identification number (unless Form 1098-C is attached).	**(c)** Description of donated property (For a vehicle, enter the year, make, model, and mileage. For securities, enter the company name and the number of shares.)
A		☐	
B		☐	
C		☐	
D		☐	
E		☐	

Note. If the amount you claimed as a deduction for an item is $500 or less, you do not have to complete columns (e), (f), and (g).

	(d) Date of the contribution	**(e)** Date acquired by donor (mo., yr.)	**(f)** How acquired by donor	**(g)** Donor's cost or adjusted basis	**(h)** Fair market value (see instructions)	**(i)** Method used to determine the fair market value
A						
B						
C						
D						
E						

Part II **Partial Interests and Restricted Use Property—**Complete lines 2a through 2e if you gave less than an entire interest in a property listed in Part I. Complete lines 3a through 3c if conditions were placed on a contribution listed in Part I; also attach the required statement (see instructions).

2a Enter the letter from Part I that identifies the property for which you gave less than an entire interest ▶
If Part II applies to more than one property, attach a separate statement.

b Total amount claimed as a deduction for the property listed in Part I: **(1)** For this tax year ▶
(2) For any prior tax years ▶

c Name and address of each organization to which any such contribution was made in a prior year (complete only if different from the donee organization above):

Name of charitable organization (donee)

Address (number, street, and room or suite no.)

City or town, state, and ZIP code

d For tangible property, enter the place where the property is located or kept ▶

e Name of any person, other than the donee organization, having actual possession of the property ▶

		Yes	**No**
3a	Is there a restriction, either temporary or permanent, on the donee's right to use or dispose of the donated property?		
b	Did you give to anyone (other than the donee organization or another organization participating with the donee organization in cooperative fundraising) the right to the income from the donated property or to the possession of the property, including the right to vote donated securities, to acquire the property by purchase or otherwise, or to designate the person having such income, possession, or right to acquire?		
c	Is there a restriction limiting the donated property for a particular use?		

Form 8283 (Rev. 12-2014) Page 2

Name(s) shown on your income tax return	Identifying number

Section B. Donated Property Over $5,000 (Except Publicly Traded Securities)— Complete this section for one item (or one group of similar items) for which you claimed a deduction of more than $5,000 per item or group (except contributions of publicly traded securities reported in Section A). Provide a separate form for each property donated unless it is part of a group of similar items. An appraisal is generally required for property listed in Section B. See instructions.

Part I Information on Donated Property—To be completed by the taxpayer and/or the appraiser.

4 Check the box that describes the type of property donated:

- **a** ☐ Art* (contribution of $20,000 or more)
- **b** ☐ Qualified Conservation Contribution
- **c** ☐ Equipment
- **d** ☐ Art* (contribution of less than $20,000)
- **e** ☐ Other Real Estate
- **f** ☐ Securities
- **g** ☐ Collectibles**
- **h** ☐ Intellectual Property
- **i** ☐ Vehicles
- **j** ☐ Other

*Art includes paintings, sculptures, watercolors, prints, drawings, ceramics, antiques, decorative arts, textiles, carpets, silver, rare manuscripts, historical memorabilia, and other similar objects.

**Collectibles include coins, stamps, books, gems, jewelry, sports memorabilia, dolls, etc., but not art as defined above.

Note. In certain cases, you must attach a qualified appraisal of the property. See instructions.

5	(a) Description of donated property (if you need more space, attach a separate statement)	(b) If tangible property was donated, give a brief summary of the overall physical condition of the property at the time of the gift	(c) Appraised fair market value
A			
B			
C			
D			

	(d) Date acquired by donor (mo., yr.)	(e) How acquired by donor	(f) Donor's cost or adjusted basis	(g) For bargain sales, enter amount received	See instructions: (h) Amount claimed as a deduction	See instructions: (i) Date of contribution
A						
B						
C						
D						

Part II Taxpayer (Donor) Statement—List each item included in Part I above that the appraisal identifies as having a value of $500 or less. See instructions.

I declare that the following item(s) included in Part I above has to the best of my knowledge and belief an appraised value of not more than $500 (per item). Enter identifying letter from Part I and describe the specific item. See instructions. ▶ ____________

Signature of taxpayer (donor) ▶ Date ▶

Part III Declaration of Appraiser

I declare that I am not the donor, the donee, a party to the transaction in which the donor acquired the property, employed by, or related to any of the foregoing persons, or married to any person who is related to any of the foregoing persons. And, if regularly used by the donor, donee, or party to the transaction, I performed the majority of my appraisals during my tax year for other persons.

Also, I declare that I perform appraisals on a regular basis; and that because of my qualifications as described in the appraisal, I am qualified to make appraisals of the type of property being valued. I certify that the appraisal fees were not based on a percentage of the appraised property value. Furthermore, I understand that a false or fraudulent overstatement of the property value as described in the qualified appraisal or this Form 8283 may subject me to the penalty under section 6701(a) (aiding and abetting the understatement of tax liability). In addition, I understand that I may be subject to a penalty under section 6695A if I know, or reasonably should know, that my appraisal is to be used in connection with a return or claim for refund and a substantial or gross valuation misstatement results from my appraisal. I affirm that I have not been barred from presenting evidence or testimony by the Office of Professional Responsibility.

Sign Here Signature ▶ Title ▶ Date ▶

Business address (including room or suite no.)	Identifying number
City or town, state, and ZIP code	

Part IV Donee Acknowledgment—To be completed by the charitable organization.

This charitable organization acknowledges that it is a qualified organization under section 170(c) and that it received the donated property as described in Section B, Part I, above on the following date ▶ ____________

Furthermore, this organization affirms that in the event it sells, exchanges, or otherwise disposes of the property described in Section B, Part I (or any portion thereof) within 3 years after the date of receipt, it will file **Form 8282,** Donee Information Return, with the IRS and give the donor a copy of that form. This acknowledgment does not represent agreement with the claimed fair market value.

Does the organization intend to use the property for an unrelated use? . . . . ▶ ☐ Yes ☐ No

Name of charitable organization (donee)	Employer identification number	
Address (number, street, and room or suite no.)	City or town, state, and ZIP code	
Authorized signature	Title	Date

Form **8582**

Department of the Treasury
Internal Revenue Service (99)

Passive Activity Loss Limitations

▶ See separate instructions.
▶ Attach to Form 1040 or Form 1041.
▶ Information about Form 8582 and its instructions is available at *www.irs.gov/form8582*.

OMB No. 1545-1008
2014
Attachment Sequence No. **88**

Name(s) shown on return	**Identifying number**

Part I **2014 Passive Activity Loss**

Caution: *Complete Worksheets 1, 2, and 3 before completing Part I.*

	Rental Real Estate Activities With Active Participation (For the definition of active participation, see **Special Allowance for Rental Real Estate Activities** in the instructions.)				
1a	Activities with net income (enter the amount from Worksheet 1, column (a))	1a			
b	Activities with net loss (enter the amount from Worksheet 1, column (b))	1b	( )		
c	Prior years unallowed losses (enter the amount from Worksheet 1, column (c))	1c	( )		
d	Combine lines 1a, 1b, and 1c			1d	
	Commercial Revitalization Deductions From Rental Real Estate Activities				
2a	Commercial revitalization deductions from Worksheet 2, column (a)	2a	( )		
b	Prior year unallowed commercial revitalization deductions from Worksheet 2, column (b)	2b	( )		
c	Add lines 2a and 2b			2c	( )
	All Other Passive Activities				
3a	Activities with net income (enter the amount from Worksheet 3, column (a))	3a			
b	Activities with net loss (enter the amount from Worksheet 3, column (b))	3b	( )		
c	Prior years unallowed losses (enter the amount from Worksheet 3, column (c))	3c	( )		
d	Combine lines 3a, 3b, and 3c			3d	
4	Combine lines 1d, 2c, and 3d. If this line is zero or more, stop here and include this form with your return; all losses are allowed, including any prior year unallowed losses entered on line 1c, 2b, or 3c. Report the losses on the forms and schedules normally used			4	

If line 4 is a loss and:
- Line 1d is a loss, go to Part II.
- Line 2c is a loss (and line 1d is zero or more), skip Part II and go to Part III.
- Line 3d is a loss (and lines 1d and 2c are zero or more), skip Parts II and III and go to line 15.

Caution: *If your filing status is married filing separately and you lived with your spouse at any time during the year,* **do not** *complete Part II or Part III. Instead, go to line 15.*

Part II **Special Allowance for Rental Real Estate Activities With Active Participation**

Note: *Enter all numbers in Part II as positive amounts. See instructions for an example.*

5	Enter the **smaller** of the loss on line 1d or the loss on line 4			5	
6	Enter $150,000. If married filing separately, see instructions	6			
7	Enter modified adjusted gross income, but not less than zero (see instructions)	7			
	Note: *If line 7 is greater than or equal to line 6, skip lines 8 and 9, enter -0- on line 10. Otherwise, go to line 8.*				
8	Subtract line 7 from line 6	8			
9	Multiply line 8 by 50% (.5). **Do not** enter more than $25,000. If married filing separately, see instructions			9	
10	Enter the **smaller** of line 5 or line 9			10	

If line 2c is a loss, go to Part III. Otherwise, go to line 15.

Part III **Special Allowance for Commercial Revitalization Deductions From Rental Real Estate Activities**

Note: *Enter all numbers in Part III as positive amounts. See the example for Part II in the instructions.*

11	Enter $25,000 reduced by the amount, if any, on line 10. If married filing separately, see instructions	11	
12	Enter the loss from line 4	12	
13	Reduce line 12 by the amount on line 10	13	
14	Enter the **smallest** of line 2c (treated as a positive amount), line 11, or line 13	14	

Part IV **Total Losses Allowed**

15	Add the income, if any, on lines 1a and 3a and enter the total	15	
16	**Total losses allowed from all passive activities for 2014.** Add lines 10, 14, and 15. See instructions to find out how to report the losses on your tax return	16	

Caution: *The worksheets must be filed with your tax return. Keep a copy for your records.*

Worksheet 1—For Form 8582, Lines 1a, 1b, and 1c (See instructions.)

Name of activity	Current year		Prior years	Overall gain or loss	
	(a) Net income (line 1a)	(b) Net loss (line 1b)	(c) Unallowed loss (line 1c)	(d) Gain	(e) Loss
Total. Enter on Form 8582, lines 1a, 1b, and 1c . . . . ▶					

Worksheet 2—For Form 8582, Lines 2a and 2b (See instructions.)

Name of activity	(a) Current year deductions (line 2a)	(b) Prior year unallowed deductions (line 2b)	(c) Overall loss
Total. Enter on Form 8582, lines 2a and 2b . . . . ▶			

Worksheet 3—For Form 8582, Lines 3a, 3b, and 3c (See instructions.)

Name of activity	Current year		Prior years	Overall gain or loss	
	(a) Net income (line 3a)	(b) Net loss (line 3b)	(c) Unallowed loss (line 3c)	(d) Gain	(e) Loss
Total. Enter on Form 8582, lines 3a, 3b, and 3c . . . . ▶					

Worksheet 4—Use this worksheet if an amount is shown on Form 8582, line 10 or 14 (See instructions.)

Name of activity	Form or schedule and line number to be reported on (see instructions)	(a) Loss	(b) Ratio	(c) Special allowance	(d) Subtract column (c) from column (a)
Total . . . . ▶			1.00		

Worksheet 5—Allocation of Unallowed Losses (See instructions.)

Name of activity	Form or schedule and line number to be reported on (see instructions)	(a) Loss	(b) Ratio	(c) Unallowed loss
Total . . . . ▶			1.00	

Worksheet 6—Allowed Losses (See instructions.)

Name of activity	Form or schedule and line number to be reported on (see instructions)	(a) Loss	(b) Unallowed loss	(c) Allowed loss
Total . . . . ▶				

Worksheet 7—Activities With Losses Reported on Two or More Forms or Schedules (See instructions.)

Name of activity:	(a)	(b)	(c) Ratio	(d) Unallowed loss	(e) Allowed loss
Form or schedule and line number to be reported on (see instructions):					
1a Net loss plus prior year unallowed loss from form or schedule . ▶					
b Net income from form or schedule . . . . ▶					
c Subtract line 1b from line 1a. If zero or less, enter -0- ▶					
Form or schedule and line number to be reported on (see instructions):					
1a Net loss plus prior year unallowed loss from form or schedule . ▶					
b Net income from form or schedule . . . . ▶					
c Subtract line 1b from line 1a. If zero or less, enter -0- ▶					
Form or schedule and line number to be reported on (see instructions):					
1a Net loss plus prior year unallowed loss from form or schedule . ▶					
b Net income from form or schedule . . . . ▶					
c Subtract line 1b from line 1a. If zero or less, enter -0- ▶					
Total . . . . ▶			1.00		

APPENDIX

C MACRS TABLES

MACRS, ADS and ACRS Depreciation Methods Summary

		Depreciation Method		Table No.[a]	
System	Characteristics	MACRS	ADS	MACRS	ADS
MACRS & ADS	Personal Property:				
	1. Accounting convention	Half-year or mid-quarter	Half-year or mid-quarter[b]		
	2. Life and method				
	a. 3-year, 5-year, 7-year, 10-year	200% DB or elect straight-line	150% DB or elect straight-line	1, 2, 3, 4, 5	10, 11[c]
	b. 15-year, 20-year	150% DB or elect straight-line	150% DB or elect straight-lined	1, 2, 3, 4, 5	
				6	
	3. Luxury Automobile Limitations				
	Real property:				
	1. Accounting convention	Mid-month	Mid-month		
	2. Life and method				
	a. Residential rental property	27.5 years, straight-line	40 years straight-line	7	12
	b. Nonresidential real property	39 years, straight-line[e]	40 years straight-line	9	12

	Characteristics	ACRS
ACRS[f]	Personal Property	
	1. Accounting convention	Half-year
	2. Life and method	
	a. 3-year, 5-year, 10-year, 15-year	150% DB or elect straight-line
	Real Property	
	1. Accounting convention	First of month or mid-month
	2. Life	
	a. 15-year property	Placed in service after 12/31/80 and before 3/16/84
	b. 18-year property	Placed in service after 3/15/84 and before 5/9/85
	c. 19-year property	Placed in service after 5/8/85 and before 1/1/87
	3. Method	
	a. All but low-income housing	175% DB or elect straight-line
	b. Low-income housing property	200% DB or elect straight-line

[a] All depreciation tables in this appendix are based upon tables contained in Rev. Proc. 87-57, as amended.
[b] General and ADS tables are available for property lives from 2.5–50.0 years using the straight-line method. These tables are contained in Rev. Proc. 87-57 and are only partially reproduced here.
[c] The mid-quarter tables are available in Rev. Proc. 87-57, but are not reproduced here.
[d] Special recovery periods are assigned certain MACRS properties under the alternative depreciation system.
[e] A 31.5-year recovery period applied to nonresidential real property placed in service under the MACRS rules prior to May 13, 1993 (see Table 8).
[f] ACRS was effective for years 1981–1986. ACRS tables are no longer reproduced here.

▼ **TABLE 1**

General Depreciation System—MACRS
Personal Property Placed in Service after 12/31/86
Applicable Convention: Half-year
Applicable Depreciation Method: 200 or 150 Percent Declining Balance Switching to Straight Line

If the Recovery Year Is:	And the Recovery Period Is: 3-Year	5-Year	7-Year	10-Year	15-Year	20-Year
	The Depreciation Rate Is:					
1	33.33	20.00	14.29	10.00	5.00	3.750
2	44.45	32.00	24.49	18.00	9.50	7.219
3	14.81	19.20	17.49	14.40	8.55	6.677
4	7.41	11.52	12.49	11.52	7.70	6.177
5		11.52	8.93	9.22	6.93	5.713
6		5.76	8.92	7.37	6.23	5.285
7			8.93	6.55	5.90	4.888
8			4.46	6.55	5.90	4.522
9				6.56	5.91	4.462
10				6.55	5.90	4.461
11				3.28	5.91	4.462
12					5.90	4.461
13					5.91	4.462
14					5.90	4.461
15					5.91	4.462
16					2.95	4.461
17						4.462
18						4.461
19						4.462
20						4.461
21						2.231

▼ **TABLE 2**

General Depreciation System—MACRS
Personal Property Placed in Service after 12/31/86
Applicable Convention: Mid-quarter (Property Placed in Service in First Quarter)
Applicable Depreciation Method: 200 or 150 Percent Declining Balance Switching to Straight Line

If the Recovery Year Is:	And the Recovery Period Is: 3-Year	5-Year	7-Year	10-Year	15-Year	20-Year
	The Depreciation Rate Is:					
1	58.33	35.00	25.00	17.50	8.75	6.563
2	27.78	26.00	21.43	16.50	9.13	7.000
3	12.35	15.60	15.31	13.20	8.21	6.482
4	1.54	11.01	10.93	10.56	7.39	5.996
5		11.01	8.75	8.45	6.65	5.546
6		1.38	8.74	6.76	5.99	5.130
7			8.75	6.55	5.90	4.746
8			1.09	6.55	5.91	4.459
9				6.56	5.90	4.459
10				6.55	5.91	4.459
11				0.82	5.90	4.459
12					5.91	4.460
13					5.90	4.459
14					5.91	4.460
15					5.90	4.459
16					0.74	4.460
17						4.459
18						4.460
19						4.459
20						4.460
21						0.557

▼ **TABLE 3**

General Depreciation System—MACRS
Personal Property Placed in Service after 12/31/86
Applicable Convention: Mid-quarter (Property Placed in Service in Second Quarter)
Applicable Depreciation Method: 200 or 150 Percent Declining Balance Switching to Straight Line

If the Recovery Year Is:	And the Recovery Period Is: 3-Year	5-Year	7-Year	10-Year	15-Year	20-Year
	The Depreciation Rate Is:					
1	41.67	25.00	17.85	12.50	6.25	4.688
2	38.89	30.00	23.47	17.50	9.38	7.148
3	14.14	18.00	16.76	14.00	8.44	6.612
4	5.30	11.37	11.97	11.20	7.59	6.116
5		11.37	8.87	8.96	6.83	5.658
6		4.26	8.87	7.17	6.15	5.233
7			8.87	6.55	5.91	4.841
8			3.33	6.55	5.90	4.478
9				6.56	5.91	4.463
10				6.55	5.90	4.463
11				2.46	5.91	4.463
12					5.90	4.463
13					5.91	4.463
14					5.90	4.463
15					5.91	4.462
16					2.21	4.463
17						4.462
18						4.463
19						4.462
20						4.463
21						1.673

▼ **TABLE 4**

General Depreciation System—MACRS
Personal Property Placed in Service after 12/31/86
Applicable Convention: Mid-quarter (Property Placed in Service in Third Quarter)
Applicable Depreciation Method: 200 or 150 Percent Declining Balance Switching to Straight Line

If the Recovery Year Is:	And the Recovery Period Is: 3-Year	5-Year	7-Year	10-Year	15-Year	20-Year
	The Depreciation Rate Is:					
1	25.00	15.00	10.71	7.50	3.75	2.813
2	50.00	34.00	25.51	18.50	9.63	7.289
3	16.67	20.40	18.22	14.80	8.66	6.742
4	8.33	12.24	13.02	11.84	7.80	6.237
5		11.30	9.30	9.47	7.02	5.769
6		7.06	8.85	7.58	6.31	5.336
7			8.86	6.55	5.90	4.936
8			5.53	6.55	5.90	4.566
9				6.56	5.91	4.460
10				6.55	5.90	4.460
11				4.10	5.91	4.460
12					5.90	4.460
13					5.91	4.461
14					5.90	4.460
15					5.91	4.461
16					3.69	4.460
17						4.461
18						4.460
19						4.461
20						4.460
21						2.788

▼ TABLE 5

General Depreciation System—MACRS
Personal Property Placed in Service after 12/31/86
Applicable Convention: Mid-quarter (Property Placed in Service in Fourth Quarter)
Applicable Depreciation Method: 200 or 150 Percent Declining Balance Switching to Straight Line

If the Recovery Year Is:	And the Recovery Period Is: 3-Year	5-Year	7-Year	10-Year	15-Year	20-Year
	The Depreciation Rate Is:					
1	8.33	5.00	3.57	2.50	1.25	0.938
2	61.11	38.00	27.55	19.50	9.88	7.430
3	20.37	22.80	19.68	15.60	8.89	6.872
4	10.19	13.68	14.06	12.48	8.00	6.357
5		10.94	10.04	9.98	7.20	5.880
6		9.58	8.73	7.99	6.48	5.439
7			8.73	6.55	5.90	5.031
8			7.64	6.55	5.90	4.654
9				6.56	5.90	4.458
10				6.55	5.91	4.458
11				5.74	5.90	4.458
12					5.91	4.458
13					5.90	4.458
14					5.91	4.458
15					5.90	4.458
16					5.17	4.458
17						4.458
18						4.459
19						4.458
20						4.459
21						3.901

▼ TABLE 6

Luxury Automobile Depreciation Limits

	Year Automobile is Placed in Service[a] 2015	2012–2014	2010–2011	2009	2008
Maximum Allowable Depreciation (100% Business Use):					
Year 1	$3,160	$3,160[b]	$3,060[c]	$2,960[d]	$2,960[e]
Year 2	5,100	5,100	4,900	4,800	4,800
Year 3	3,050	3,050	2,950	2,850	2,850
Year 4 and Each Succeeding Year	1,875	1,875	1,775	1,775	1,775

[a]For years prior to 2008, see the Revenue Procedure for the appropriate year.
[b]$11,160 in Year 1 (2014, 2013, or 2012) if taxpayer claims bonus depreciation.
[c]$11,060 in Year 1 (2011 or 2010) if taxpayer claims bonus depreciation.
[d]$10,960 in Year 1 (2009) if taxpayer claims bonus depreciation.
[e]$10,960 in Year 1 (2008) if taxpayer claimed bonus depreciation.

▼ **TABLE 6 (continued)**

Truck and Van Depreciation Limits

	Year Truck or Van is Placed in Service[a]							
	2015	2014	2013	2012	2011	2010	2009	2008
Maximum Allowable Depreciation (100% Business Use):								
Year 1	$3,460	$3,460[b]	$3,360[c]	$3,360[c]	$3,260[d]	$3,160[f]	$3,060[e]	$3,160[f]
Year 2	5,600	5,550	5,400	5,300	5,200	5,100	4,900	5,100
Year 3	3,350	3,350	3,250	3,150	3,150	3,050	2,950	3,050
Year 4 and Each Succeeding Year	1,975	1,975	1,975	1,875	1,875	1,875	1,775	1,875

[a]For years prior to 2008, see the Revenue Procedure for the appropriate year.
[b]$11,460 in Year 1 (2014) if taxpayer claims bonus depreciation.
[c]$11,360 in Year 1 (2012 and 2013) if taxpayer claims bonus depreciation.
[d]$11,260 in Year 1 (2011) if taxpayer claims bonus depreciation.
[e]$11,060 in Year 1 (2009) if taxpayer claims bonus depreciation.
[f]$11,160 in Year 1 (2010 and 2008) if taxpayer claimed bonus depreciation.

▼ **TABLE 7**

General Depreciation System—MACRS
Residential Rental Real Property Placed in Service after 12/31/86
Applicable Recovery Period: 27.5 Years
Applicable Convention: Mid-month
Applicable Depreciation Method: Straight Line

If the Recovery Year Is:	And the Month in the First Recovery Year the Property Is Placed in Service Is: 1	2	3	4	5	6	7	8	9	10	11	12
	The Depreciation Rate Is:											
1	3.485	3.182	2.879	2.576	2.273	1.970	1.667	1.364	1.061	0.758	0.455	0.152
2	3.636	3.636	3.636	3.636	3.636	3.636	3.636	3.636	3.636	3.636	3.636	3.636
3	3.636	3.636	3.636	3.636	3.636	3.636	3.636	3.636	3.636	3.636	3.636	3.636
4	3.636	3.636	3.636	3.636	3.636	3.636	3.636	3.636	3.636	3.636	3.636	3.636
5	3.636	3.636	3.636	3.636	3.636	3.636	3.636	3.636	3.636	3.636	3.636	3.636
6	3.636	3.636	3.636	3.636	3.636	3.636	3.636	3.636	3.636	3.636	3.636	3.636
7	3.636	3.636	3.636	3.636	3.636	3.636	3.636	3.636	3.636	3.636	3.636	3.636
8	3.636	3.636	3.636	3.636	3.636	3.636	3.636	3.636	3.636	3.636	3.636	3.636
9	3.636	3.636	3.636	3.636	3.636	3.636	3.636	3.636	3.636	3.636	3.636	3.636
10	3.637	3.637	3.637	3.637	3.637	3.637	3.636	3.636	3.636	3.636	3.636	3.636
11	3.636	3.636	3.636	3.636	3.636	3.636	3.637	3.637	3.637	3.637	3.637	3.637
12	3.637	3.637	3.637	3.637	3.637	3.637	3.636	3.636	3.636	3.636	3.636	3.636
13	3.636	3.636	3.636	3.636	3.636	3.636	3.637	3.637	3.637	3.637	3.637	3.637
14	3.637	3.637	3.637	3.637	3.637	3.637	3.636	3.636	3.636	3.636	3.636	3.636
15	3.636	3.636	3.636	3.636	3.636	3.636	3.637	3.637	3.637	3.637	3.637	3.637
16	3.637	3.637	3.637	3.637	3.637	3.637	3.636	3.636	3.636	3.636	3.636	3.636
17	3.636	3.636	3.636	3.636	3.636	3.636	3.637	3.637	3.637	3.637	3.637	3.637
18	3.637	3.637	3.637	3.637	3.637	3.637	3.636	3.636	3.636	3.636	3.636	3.636
19	3.636	3.636	3.636	3.636	3.636	3.636	3.637	3.637	3.637	3.637	3.637	3.637
20	3.637	3.637	3.637	3.637	3.637	3.637	3.636	3.636	3.636	3.636	3.636	3.636
21	3.636	3.636	3.636	3.636	3.636	3.636	3.637	3.637	3.637	3.637	3.637	3.637
22	3.637	3.637	3.637	3.637	3.637	3.637	3.636	3.636	3.636	3.636	3.636	3.636
23	3.636	3.636	3.636	3.636	3.636	3.636	3.637	3.637	3.637	3.637	3.637	3.637
24	3.637	3.637	3.637	3.637	3.637	3.637	3.636	3.636	3.636	3.636	3.636	3.636
25	3.636	3.636	3.636	3.636	3.636	3.636	3.637	3.637	3.637	3.637	3.637	3.637
26	3.637	3.637	3.637	3.637	3.637	3.637	3.636	3.636	3.636	3.636	3.636	3.636
27	3.636	3.636	3.636	3.636	3.636	3.636	3.637	3.637	3.637	3.637	3.637	3.637
28	1.970	2.273	2.576	2.879	3.182	3.485	3.636	3.636	3.636	3.636	3.636	3.636
29	0.000	0.000	0.000	0.000	0.000	0.000	0.152	0.455	0.758	1.061	1.364	1.667

▼ TABLE 8

General Depreciation System—MACRS
Nonresidential Real Property Placed in Service after 12/31/86 and before 5/13/93
Applicable Recovery Period: 31.5 Years
Applicable Convention: Mid-month
Applicable Depreciation Method: Straight Line

If the Recovery Year Is:	And the Month in the First Recovery Year the Property Is Placed in Service Is: 1	2	3	4	5	6	7	8	9	10	11	12
	The Depreciation Rate Is:											
1	3.042	2.778	2.513	2.249	1.984	1.720	1.455	1.190	0.926	0.661	0.397	0.132
2	3.175	3.175	3.175	3.175	3.175	3.175	3.175	3.175	3.175	3.175	3.175	3.175
3	3.175	3.175	3.175	3.175	3.175	3.175	3.175	3.175	3.175	3.175	3.175	3.175
4	3.175	3.175	3.175	3.175	3.175	3.175	3.175	3.175	3.175	3.175	3.175	3.175
5	3.175	3.175	3.175	3.175	3.175	3.175	3.175	3.175	3.175	3.175	3.175	3.175
6	3.175	3.175	3.175	3.175	3.175	3.175	3.175	3.175	3.175	3.175	3.175	3.175
7	3.175	3.175	3.175	3.175	3.175	3.175	3.175	3.175	3.175	3.175	3.175	3.175
8	3.175	3.174	3.175	3.174	3.175	3.174	3.175	3.175	3.175	3.175	3.175	3.175
9	3.174	3.175	3.174	3.175	3.174	3.175	3.174	3.175	3.174	3.175	3.174	3.175
10	3.175	3.174	3.175	3.174	3.175	3.174	3.175	3.174	3.175	3.174	3.175	3.174
11	3.174	3.175	3.174	3.175	3.174	3.175	3.174	3.175	3.174	3.175	3.174	3.175
12	3.175	3.174	3.175	3.174	3.175	3.174	3.175	3.174	3.175	3.174	3.175	3.174
13	3.174	3.175	3.174	3.175	3.174	3.175	3.174	3.175	3.174	3.175	3.174	3.175
14	3.175	3.174	3.175	3.174	3.175	3.174	3.175	3.174	3.175	3.174	3.175	3.174
15	3.174	3.175	3.174	3.175	3.174	3.175	3.174	3.175	3.174	3.175	3.174	3.175
16	3.175	3.174	3.175	3.174	3.175	3.174	3.175	3.174	3.175	3.174	3.175	3.174
17	3.174	3.175	3.174	3.175	3.174	3.175	3.174	3.175	3.174	3.175	3.174	3.175
18	3.175	3.174	3.175	3.174	3.175	3.174	3.175	3.174	3.175	3.174	3.175	3.174
19	3.174	3.175	3.174	3.175	3.174	3.175	3.174	3.175	3.174	3.175	3.174	3.175
20	3.175	3.174	3.175	3.174	3.175	3.174	3.175	3.174	3.175	3.174	3.175	3.174
21	3.174	3.175	3.174	3.175	3.174	3.175	3.174	3.175	3.174	3.175	3.174	3.175
22	3.175	3.174	3.175	3.174	3.175	3.174	3.175	3.174	3.175	3.174	3.175	3.174
23	3.174	3.175	3.174	3.175	3.174	3.175	3.174	3.175	3.174	3.175	3.174	3.175
24	3.175	3.174	3.175	3.174	3.175	3.174	3.175	3.174	3.175	3.174	3.175	3.174
25	3.174	3.175	3.174	3.175	3.174	3.175	3.174	3.175	3.174	3.175	3.174	3.175
26	3.175	3.174	3.175	3.174	3.175	3.174	3.175	3.174	3.175	3.174	3.175	3.174
27	3.174	3.175	3.174	3.175	3.174	3.175	3.174	3.175	3.174	3.175	3.174	3.175
28	3.175	3.174	3.175	3.174	3.175	3.174	3.175	3.174	3.175	3.174	3.175	3.174
29	3.174	3.175	3.174	3.175	3.174	3.175	3.174	3.175	3.174	3.175	3.174	3.175
30	3.175	3.174	3.175	3.174	3.175	3.174	3.175	3.174	3.175	3.174	3.175	3.174
31	3.174	3.175	3.174	3.175	3.174	3.175	3.174	3.175	3.174	3.175	3.174	3.175
32	1.720	1.984	2.249	2.513	2.778	3.042	3.175	3.174	3.175	3.174	3.175	3.174
33	0.000	0.000	0.000	0.000	0.000	0.000	0.132	0.397	0.661	0.926	1.190	1.455

▼ TABLE 9

General Depreciation System—MACRS
Nonresidential Real Property Placed in Service after 5/12/93
Applicable Recovery Period: 39 years
Applicable Depreciation Method: Straight Line

If the Recovery Year Is:	And the Month in the First Recovery Year the Property Is Placed in Service Is: 1	2	3	4	5	6	7	8	9	10	11	12
	The Depreciation Rate Is:											
1	2.461	2.247	2.033	1.819	1.605	1.391	1.177	0.963	0.749	0.535	0.321	0.107
2-39	2.564	2.564	2.564	2.564	2.564	2.564	2.564	2.564	2.564	2.564	2.564	2.564
40	0.107	0.321	0.535	0.749	0.963	1.177	1.391	1.605	1.819	2.033	2.247	2.461

▼ TABLE 10

Alternative Depreciation System—MACRS (Partial Table)
Property Placed in Service after 12/31/86
Applicable Convention: Half-year
Applicable Depreciation Method: 150 Percent Declining Balance Switching to Straight Line

If the Recovery Year Is:	And the Recovery Period Is: 3	4	5	7	10	12
	The Depreciation Rate Is:					
1	25.00	18.75	15.00	10.71	7.50	6.25
2	37.50	30.47	25.50	19.13	13.88	11.72
3	25.00	20.31	17.85	15.03	11.79	10.25
4	12.50	20.31	16.66	12.25	10.02	8.97
5		10.16	16.66	12.25	8.74	7.85
6			8.33	12.25	8.74	7.33
7				12.25	8.74	7.33
8				6.13	8.74	7.33
9					8.74	7.33
10					8.74	7.33
11					4.37	7.32
12						7.33
13						3.66

▼ TABLE 11

Alternative Depreciation System—MACRS (Partial Table)
Property Placed in Service after 12/31/86
Applicable Convention: Half-year
Applicable Depreciation Method: Straight Line

If the Recovery Year Is:	And the Recovery Period Is: 3	4	5	7	10	12
	The Depreciation Rate Is:					
1	16.67	12.50	10.00	7.14	5.00	4.17
2	33.33	25.00	20.00	14.29	10.00	8.33
3	33.33	25.00	20.00	14.29	10.00	8.33
4	16.67	25.00	20.00	14.28	10.00	8.33
5		12.50	20.00	14.29	10.00	8.33
6			10.00	14.28	10.00	8.33
7				14.29	10.00	8.34
8				7.14	10.00	8.33
9					10.00	8.34
10					10.00	8.33
11					5.00	8.34
12						8.33
13						4.17

▼ TABLE 12

Alternative Depreciation System—MACRS
Real Property Placed into Service after 12/31/86
Applicable Recovery Period: 40 years
Applicable Convention: Mid-month
Applicable Depreciation Method: Straight Line

If the Recovery Year Is:	And the Month in the First Recovery Year the Property Is Placed in Service Is: 1	2	3	4	5	6	7	8	9	10	11	12
	The Depreciation Rate Is:											
1	2.396	2.188	1.979	1.771	1.563	1.354	1.146	0.938	0.729	0.521	0.313	0.104
2 to 40	2.500	2.500	2.500	2.500	2.500	2.500	2.500	2.500	2.500	2.500	2.500	2.500
41	0.104	0.312	0.521	0.729	0.937	1.146	1.354	1.562	1.771	1.979	2.187	2.396

▼ **TABLE 13**

Lease Inclusion Dollar Amounts for Automobiles (Other Than for Trucks, Vans, or Electronic Automobiles) With a Lease Term Beginning in Calendar Year 2015

REV. PROC. 2015-19 TABLE 3 *DOLLAR AMOUNTS FOR PASSENGER AUTOMOBILES (THAT ARE NOT TRUCKS OR VANS) WITH A LEASE TERM BEGINNING IN CALENDAR YEAR 2015*

Fair Market Value of Passenger Automobile		Tax Year During Lease				
Over	Not Over	1st	2nd	3rd	4th	5 and Later
$17,500	$18,000	3	6	9	10	11
18,000	18,500	4	7	11	13	15
18,500	19,000	4	9	14	15	18
19,000	19,500	5	11	15	19	21
19,500	20,000	6	12	18	22	24
20,000	20,500	6	14	20	25	27
20,500	21,000	7	15	23	27	31
21,000	21,500	8	17	25	30	34
21,500	22,000	9	18	28	32	38
22,000	23,000	10	21	31	37	42
23,000	24,000	11	24	36	42	49
24,000	25,000	12	27	41	48	55
25,000	26,000	14	30	45	54	62
26,000	27,000	15	34	49	60	68
27,000	28,000	17	37	54	65	75
28,000	29,000	18	40	59	71	81
29,000	30,000	20	43	64	76	87
30,000	31,000	21	46	69	81	95
31,000	32,000	23	49	73	88	100
32,000	33,000	24	52	78	93	107
33,000	34,000	25	56	82	99	114
34,000	35,000	27	59	87	104	120
35,000	36,000	28	62	92	110	126
36,000	37,000	30	65	96	116	133
37,000	38,000	31	68	102	121	139
38,000	39,000	33	71	106	127	146
39,000	40,000	34	75	110	132	153
40,000	41,000	35	78	115	138	159
41,000	42,000	37	81	120	143	166
42,000	43,000	38	84	125	149	172
43,000	44,000	40	87	129	155	179
44,000	45,000	41	90	134	161	185
45,000	46,000	43	93	139	166	191
46,000	47,000	44	97	143	172	198
47,000	48,000	45	100	148	177	205
48,000	49,000	47	103	153	183	210
49,000	50,000	48	106	158	188	218
50,000	51,000	50	109	162	194	224
51,000	52,000	51	112	167	200	230
52,000	53,000	53	115	172	205	237
53,000	54,000	54	119	176	211	243
54,000	55,000	56	122	180	217	250
55,000	56,000	57	125	186	222	256

▼ TABLE 13 (continued)

REV. PROC. 2015-19 TABLE 3 *DOLLAR AMOUNTS FOR PASSENGER AUTOMOBILES (THAT ARE NOT TRUCKS OR VANS) WITH A LEASE TERM BEGINNING IN CALENDAR YEAR 2015*

Fair Market Value of Passenger Automobile		Tax Year During Lease				
Over	**Not Over**	**1st**	**2nd**	**3rd**	**4th**	**5 and Later**
$ 56,000	$ 57,000	58	128	191	227	263
57,000	58,000	60	131	195	234	269
58,000	59,000	61	135	199	239	276
59,000	60,000	63	137	205	244	283
60,000	62,000	65	142	212	253	292
62,000	64,000	68	149	220	265	304
64,000	66,000	71	155	230	275	318
66,000	68,000	73	162	239	287	331
68,000	70,000	76	168	249	298	343
70,000	72,000	79	174	258	309	357
72,000	74,000	82	180	268	320	370
74,000	76,000	85	186	277	332	383
76,000	78,000	88	193	286	343	396
78,000	80,000	91	199	296	354	408
80,000	85,000	96	210	312	374	431
85,000	90,000	103	226	335	402	464
90,000	95,000	110	242	359	430	496
95,000	100,000	117	258	382	458	529
100,000	110,000	128	281	418	500	577
110,000	120,000	142	313	464	556	643
120,000	130,000	157	344	511	613	707
130,000	140,000	171	376	558	668	772
140,000	150,000	185	408	604	725	837
150,000	160,000	200	439	651	781	902
160,000	170,000	214	470	699	837	966
170,000	180,000	228	502	745	894	1,031
180,000	190,000	243	533	792	950	1,096
190,000	200,000	257	565	839	1,006	1,161
200,000	210,000	271	597	886	1,061	1,226
210,000	220,000	286	628	933	1,118	1,290
220,000	230,000	300	660	979	1,174	1,356
230,000	240,000	315	691	1,026	1,231	1,420
240,000	and over	329	723	1,073	1,286	1,485

▼ **TABLE 14**

Lease Inclusion Dollar Amounts for Trucks and Vans With a Lease Term Beginning in Calendar Year 2015

REV. PROC. 2015-19 TABLE 4 *DOLLAR AMOUNTS FOR TRUCKS AND VANS WITH A LEASE TERM BEGINNING IN CALENDAR YEAR 2015*

Fair Market Value of Truck or Van		Tax Year During Lease				
Over	Not Over	1st	2nd	3rd	4th	5 and Later
$18,500	$19,000	2	4	6	8	9
19,000	19,500	3	6	8	11	12
19,500	20,000	4	7	11	13	16
20,000	20,500	4	9	13	16	19
20,500	21,000	5	11	15	19	22
21,000	21,500	6	12	18	22	25
21,500	22,000	6	14	20	25	28
22,000	23,000	7	16	24	29	33
23,000	24,000	9	19	29	34	40
24,000	25,000	10	23	33	40	46
25,000	26,000	12	25	38	46	53
26,000	27,000	13	29	42	51	60
27,000	28,000	15	32	47	57	65
28,000	29,000	16	35	52	62	73
29,000	30,000	18	38	56	68	79
30,000	31,000	19	41	61	74	85
31,000	32,000	20	45	66	79	91
32,000	33,000	22	48	70	85	98
33,000	34,000	23	51	75	91	104
34,000	35,000	25	54	80	96	111
35,000	36,000	26	57	85	101	118
36,000	37,000	28	60	89	108	124
37,000	38,000	29	63	94	113	131
38,000	39,000	30	67	98	119	137
39,000	40,000	32	70	103	124	144
40,000	41,000	33	73	108	130	150
41,000	42,000	35	76	113	135	157
42,000	43,000	36	79	118	141	163
43,000	44,000	38	82	122	147	169
44,000	45,000	39	85	127	153	176
45,000	46,000	40	89	131	158	183
46,000	47,000	42	92	136	163	189
47,000	48,000	43	95	141	169	195
48,000	49,000	45	98	145	175	202
49,000	50,000	46	101	151	180	208
50,000	51,000	48	104	155	186	215
51,000	52,000	49	108	159	192	221
52,000	53,000	51	110	165	197	228
53,000	54,000	52	114	169	203	234
54,000	55,000	53	117	174	208	241
55,000	56,000	55	120	178	214	248
56,000	57,000	56	123	183	220	254
57,000	58,000	58	126	188	225	261
58,000	59,000	59	130	192	231	267
59,000	60,000	61	133	197	236	273
60,000	62,000	63	137	204	245	283
62,000	64,000	66	144	213	256	296
64,000	66,000	68	150	223	268	308

▼ TABLE 14 (continued)

REV. PROC. 2015-19 TABLE 4 *DOLLAR AMOUNTS FOR TRUCKS AND VANS WITH A LEASE TERM BEGINNING IN CALENDAR YEAR 2015*

Fair Market Value of Truck or Van		Tax Year During Lease				
Over	Not Over	1st	2nd	3rd	4th	5 and Later
$ 66,000	$ 68,000	71	157	232	278	322
68,000	70,000	74	163	241	290	335
70,000	72,000	77	169	251	301	348
72,000	74,000	80	175	261	312	361
74,000	76,000	83	182	269	324	374
76,000	78,000	86	188	279	335	386
78,000	80,000	89	194	288	346	400
80,000	85,000	94	205	305	366	422
85,000	90,000	101	221	328	394	455
90,000	95,000	108	237	351	422	488
95,000	100,000	115	253	375	450	519
100,000	110,000	126	276	410	492	569
110,000	120,000	140	308	457	548	633
120,000	130,000	155	339	504	604	698
130,000	140,000	169	371	551	660	763
140,000	150,000	183	403	597	717	827
150,000	160,000	198	434	644	773	893
160,000	170,000	212	466	691	829	957
170,000	180,000	226	497	738	885	1,023
180,000	190,000	241	528	785	942	1,087
190,000	200,000	255	560	832	997	1,152
200,000	210,000	269	592	878	1,054	1,217
210,000	220,000	284	623	925	1,110	1,282
220,000	230,000	298	655	972	1,166	1,346
230,000	240,000	312	687	1,019	1,222	1,411
240,000	and over	327	718	1,066	1,278	1,476

APPENDIX

D GLOSSARY

Ability to pay A concept in taxation that holds that taxpayers be taxed according to their ability to pay such taxes, that is, taxpayers who have sufficient financial resources should pay the tax. This concept is an integral part of vertical equity.

Accountable plan A type of employee reimbursement plan that meets two tests, (1) substantiation, and (2) return of excess reimbursement. Under an accountable plan, reimbursements are excluded from the employee's gross income and the expenses are not deductible by the employee.

Accounting method The rules used to determine the tax year in which income and expenses are reported for tax purposes. Generally, the same accounting method must be used for tax purposes as is used for keeping books and records. The accounting treatment used for any item of income or expense and for specific items (e.g., installment sales and contracts) is included in this term.

Accounting period The period of time, usually 12 months, used by taxpayers to compute their taxable income. Taxpayers who do not keep records must use a calendar year. Taxpayers who do keep books and records may choose between a calendar year or a fiscal year. The accounting period election is made on the taxpayer's first filed return and cannot be changed without IRS consent. The accounting period may be less than 12 months if it is the taxpayer's first or final return or if the taxpayer is changing accounting periods. Certain restrictions upon the use of a fiscal year apply to partnerships, S corporations, and personal service corporations.

Accrual method of accounting Accounting method under which income is reported and expenses are deducted when (1) all events have occurred that fix the taxpayer's right to receive the income and (2) the amount of the item can be determined with reasonable accuracy. Taxpayers with inventories to report must use this method to report sales and purchases.

Accumulated Adjustments Account (AAA) Account that must be kept by S corporations. The cumulative total of the ordinary income or loss and separately stated items for the most recent S corporation election period.

Accumulated earnings and profits The sum of the undistributed current earnings and profits balances (and deficits) from previous years reduced by any distributions that have been made out of accumulated earnings and profits.

Accumulated earnings credit Deduction that reduces the accumulated taxable income amount. It does not offset the accumulated earnings tax on a dollar-for-dollar basis. Different rules apply for operating companies, service companies, and holding or investment companies.

Accumulated earnings tax Penalty tax on corporations other than those subject to the personal holding company tax among others. It is levied on a corporation's current year addition to its accumulated earnings balance in excess of the amount needed for reasonable business purposes and not distributed to the shareholders. This tax is intended to discourage companies from retaining excessive amounts of earnings if the funds are invested in activities that are unrelated to business needs. The tax is 20% of accumulated taxable income.

Accumulated taxable income The tax base for the accumulated earnings tax which is determined by taking the corporation's taxable income and increasing (decreasing) it by positive (negative) adjustments and decreasing it by the accumulated earnings credit and available dividends-paid deductions.

Accumulation distribution rules (throwback rules) Exception to the general rule that distributable net income (DNI) serves as a ceiling on the amount taxable to a beneficiary. Under the general rule, the beneficiary excludes the portion of any distribution in excess of DNI from his gross income. Accumulation distributions made by a trust are taxable to the beneficiaries in the year received.

ACE See adjusted current earnings.

Acquiescence policy IRS policy of announcing whether it agrees or disagrees with a court decision decided in favor of the taxpayer. Such statements are not issued for every case.

Acquisitive reorganization A transaction in which the acquiring corporation obtains all or part of the stock or assets of a target corporation.

Additional depreciation The excess of the actual amount of accelerated depreciation (or cost-recovery deductions under ACRS) over the amount of depreciation that would be deductible under the straight-line method. Such depreciation applies to Sec. 1250 depreciable real property acquired prior to 1987.

Adjusted current earnings (ACE) Alternative minimum taxable income for the tax year plus or minus a series of special adjusted current earnings adjustments specified in Sec. 56(g)(4).

Adjusted gross income (AGI) A measure of taxable income that falls between gross income and taxable income. It is the income amount that is used as the basis for calculating the floor or the ceiling for numerous other tax computations.

Adjusted grossed-up basis For Sec. 338 purposes, the sum of (1) the basis of a purchasing corporation's stock interest in a target corporation plus (2) an adjustment for the target corporation's liabilities on the day following the acquisition date plus or minus (3) other relevant items.

Adjusted income from rents (AIR) This amount is equal to the corporation's gross income from rents reduced by the deductions claimed for amortization or depreciation, property taxes, interest, and rent.

Adjusted ordinary gross income (AOGI) A corporation's adjusted ordinary gross income is its ordinary gross income reduced by (1) certain expenses incurred in connection with gross income from rents, mineral, oil and gas royalties, and working interests in oil or gas wells, (2) interest received by dealers on certain U.S. obligations, (3) interest received from condemnation awards, judgments, or tax refunds, and (4) rents from certain tangible personal property manufactured or produced by the corporation.

Adjusted sales price The amount realized from the sale of a residence less any fixing-up expenses.

Adjusted taxable gift Taxable gifts made after 1976 that are valued at their date-of-gift value. These gifts affect the size of the transfer tax base at death.

Administrative pronouncement Treasury Department or IRS statement that interprets provisions of the IRC. Such pronouncements may be in the form of Treasury Regulations, revenue rulings, or revenue procedures.

Ad valorem tax A tax based on the value of real property or personal property. Typically, these taxes are levied at the time of a transaction, as is the case with a sales tax or a value-added tax (VAT). However, the taxes also can be levied annually, as with a real estate tax that a local government levies annually on the value of property.

Affiliated group A group consisting of a parent corporation and at least one subsidiary corporation.

Alien Individuals who are not U.S. citizens.

Alimony Payments made pursuant to divorce or separation or written agreement between spouses subject to conditions specified in the tax law. Alimony payments (as contrasted to property settlements) are deductible for AGI by the payor and are included in the gross income of the recipient.

All events test Rule holding that an accrual basis taxpayer must report an item of income (1) when all events have occurred that fix the taxpayer's right to receive the item of income and (2) when the amount of the item can be determined with reasonable accuracy. This test is not satisfied until economic performance has taken place.

Alternate valuation date The alternate valuation date is the earlier of six months after the date of death or the date the property is sold, exchanged, distributed, etc. by the estate. Unless this option is elected, the gross estate is valued at its FMV on the date of the decedent's death.

Alternative minimum tax (AMT) Tax which applies to individuals, corporations, and estates and trusts if it exceeds the taxpayer's regular tax. Most taxpayers are not subject to this tax. This tax equals the amount by which the tentative minimum tax exceeds the regular tax.

Alternative minimum taxable income (AMTI) The taxpayer's taxable income (1) increased by tax preference items and (2) adjusted for income, gain, deduction, and loss items that have to be recomputed under the AMT system.

Amount realized The amount realized equals the sum of money plus the fair market value of all other property received from the sale or other disposition of the property less any selling expenses (e.g., commissions, advertising, deed preparation costs, and legal expenses) incurred in connection with the sale.

Announcement Information release issued by the IRS to provide a technical explanation of a current tax issue. Announcements are aimed at tax practitioners rather than the general public.

Annual exclusion An exemption that is intended to relieve a donor from keeping an account of and reporting the numerous small gifts (e.g., wedding and Christmas gifts) made throughout the year. This exclusion currently is $14,000 per donee (in 2014 and 2015).

Annuity A series of regular payments that will continue for either a fixed period of time or until the death of the recipient. Pensions are usually paid in this way.

Appeals coordinated issue Issue over which the appeals officer must obtain a concurrence of guidance from the regional director of appeals in order to render a decision.

Applicable federal rate The rate determined monthly by the federal government which is based on the rate paid by the government on borrowed funds. The rate varies with the term of the loan. Thus, short-term loans are for a period of under three years, mid-term loans are for over three years and under nine years, and long-term loans are for over nine years.

Asset depreciation range (ADR) system of depreciation Depreciation method allowed for property placed in service before January 1, 1981. This method prescribed useful lives for various classes of assets.

Assignment of income doctrine A judicial requirement that income be taxed to the person that earns it.

At-risk basis Essentially the same amount as the regular partnership basis with the exception that liabilities increase the at-risk basis only if the partner is at-risk for such an amount.

At-risk rules These rules limit the partner's loss deductions to his at-risk basis.

Average tax rate The taxpayer's total tax liability divided by the amount of his taxable income.

Bad debt Bona fide debt that is uncollectible because it is worthless. Such debts are further characterized as "business bad debts," which give rise to an ordinary deduction, and "nonbusiness bad debts," which are treated as a short-term capital loss. A determination of whether a debt is worthless is made by reference to all the pertinent evidence (e.g., the debtor's general financial condition and whether the debt is secured by collateral). Such debts are deductible subject to certain requirements.

Bardahl formula Mathematical formula for determining the amount of working capital that a business reasonably needs for accumulated earnings tax purposes. For a manufacturing company, the formula is based on the business's operating cycle.

Bona fide debt A debt that (1) arises from a valid and enforceable obligation to pay a fixed or determinable sum of money and (2) results in a debtor-creditor relationship.

Bonus Depreciation Special first year depreciation on qualified property (non-real estate) placed in service at various times over the past ten years. Most recently, 50% bonus depreciation was allowable in 2008, 2009, and through September 8, 2010. After September 8, 2010 to December 31, 2011, the rate was increased to 100%. For 2012 through 2014, the rate returned to 50%. Congress had not yet extended bonus depreciation for 2015.

Boot Property that may not be received tax-free in certain nontaxable transactions (i.e., any money, debt obligations, and so on).

Bootstrap acquisition An acquisition where an investor purchases part of a corporation's stock and then has the corporation redeem the remainder of the seller's stock.

Brother-sister controlled group Under the narrow 50%–80% definition, this type of controlled group exists if (1) five or fewer individuals, estates, or trusts own at least 80% of the voting stock or 80% of the value of each corporation and (2) the shareholders have common ownership of more than 50% of the voting power or 50% of the value of all classes of stock. Under the broad 50%-only definition, the five or fewer shareholders need only to meet the 50% test.

Built-in gain A gain that accrued prior to the conversion of a C corporation to an S corporation.

Built-in gains (Sec. 1374) tax Tax on built-in gains that are recognized by the S corporation during the ten-year period beginning on the date that the S corporation election took effect.

C corporation Form of business entity that is taxed as a separate taxpaying entity. Its income is subject to an initial tax at the corporate level. Its shareholders are subject to a second tax if dividends are paid from the corporation's earnings and profits. This type of corporation is sometimes referred to as a regular corporation.

C short year That portion of an S termination year that begins on the day on which the termination is effective and continues through to the last day of the corporation's tax year.

Capital asset This category of assets includes all assets except inventory, notes and accounts receivable, and depreciable property or land used in a trade or business (e.g., property, plant, and machinery).

Capital expenditure An expenditure that adds to the value of, substantially prolongs the useful life of, or adapts the property to a new or different use qualifies as a capital expenditure.

Capital gain Gain realized on the sale or exchange of a capital asset.

Capital gain dividend A distribution by a regulated investment company (i.e., a mutual fund) of capital gains realized from the sale of investments in the fund. Such dividends also include undistributed capital gains allocated to the shareholders.

Capital gain property For charitable contribution deduction purposes, property upon which a long-term capital gain would be recognized if that property was sold at its FMV.

Capital interest An interest in the assets owned by a partnership.

Capital recovery A capital recovery amount is a deduction for depreciation or cost recovery. It is a factor in the determination of a property's adjusted basis.

Cash method of accounting Accounting method that requires the taxpayer to report income for the taxable year in which payments are actually or constructively received. Expenses are reported in the year they are paid. Most individuals and service businesses (i.e., businesses without inventories) use this method.

Cash receipts and disbursements method of accounting See Cash method of accounting.

Casualty loss Loss that arises from an identifiable event that was sudden, unexpected, or unusual (e.g., fire, storm, shipwreck, other casualty, or theft). Within certain limitations, individuals may deduct such losses from AGI. Business casualty losses are deductible for AGI.

Certiorari An appeal from a lower court (i.e., a federal court of appeals) which the U.S. Supreme Court agrees to hear. Such appeals, which are made as a writ of certiorari, are generally not granted unless (1) a constitutional issue needs to be decided or (2) a conflict among the lower court decisions that must be clarified.

Charitable remainder annuity trust This type of trust makes distributions to individuals for a certain time period or for life. The annual distributions are a uniform percentage (5% or higher) of the value of the trust property as valued on the date of transfer.

Charitable remainder unitrust This type of trust makes annual distributions for either a specified time period or for life. The distributions are a uniform percentage (5% or higher) of the value of the property as revalued annually.

Circular 230 Rules and standards issued by the Treasury Department regarding practice before the IRS.

Clifford trust A trust that is normally held for a ten-year period after which the principal reverts to the grantor. The trust accounting income is not generally taxed to the grantor.

Closed transaction Situation where the property in question (e.g., property distributed in a corporate liquidation) can be valued with reasonable certainty. The gain or loss reported on the transaction is determinable at the time the transaction occurs. See open transaction doctrine.

Closed-fact situation or tax compliance situation Situation or transaction that has already occurred. In such situations, the tax advisor's task is to analyze the facts to determine the appropriate tax treatment.

Closely held C corporation For purposes of the at-risk rules, a C corporation in which more than 50% of the stock is owned by five or fewer individuals at any time during the last half of the corporation's tax year.

Closely held corporation A corporation that is owned by either a single individual or a small group of individuals who may or may not be family members.

Combined controlled group A group of three or more corporations which are members of a parent-subsidiary or brother-sister controlled group. In addition, at least one of the corporations must be the parent corporation of the parent-subsidiary controlled group and a member of a brother-sister controlled group.

Common law state All states other than the community property states are common law states. In such states, all assets acquired during the marriage are the property of the acquiring spouse.

Community income In any of the eight community property states, such income consists of the income from the personal efforts, investments, etc. of either spouse. Community income belongs equally to both spouses.

Community property law Law in community property states mandating that all property acquired after marriage is generally community property unless acquired by gift or inheritance. Each spouse owns a one-half interest in community property.

Community property state The eight traditional community property states (Louisiana, Texas, New Mexico, Arizona, California, Washington, Idaho, and Nevada) and Wisconsin (which adopted a similar law). These states do not follow the common law concept of property ownership.

Compensation Payment for personal services. Salaries, wages, fees, commissions, tips, bonuses, and specialized forms of compensation such as director's fees and jury's fees fall into this category. However, certain fringe benefits and some foreign-earned income are not taxed.

Completed contract method of accounting Accounting method for long-term contracts undertaken by smaller companies. Income from the contract is reported in the taxable year in which the contract is completed. The completed contract method is limited to construction contracts undertaken by smaller companies.

Consolidated tax return A single tax return filed by an affiliated group of includible corporations.

Consolidation A form of nontaxable reorganization involving two or more corporations whose assets are acquired by a new corporation. The stock, securities, and other consideration transferred by the acquiring corporation is then distributed by each target corporation to its shareholders and security holders in exchange for their stock and securities.

Constant interest rate method Used to amortize the original issue discount ratably over the life of the bond, this method determines the amount of interest income by multiplying the interest yield to maturity by the adjusted issue price.

Constructive dividend The manner in which the IRS or the courts might recharacterize an excessive corporate payment to a shareholder to reflect the true economic benefit conferred upon the shareholder. As a result of the recharacterization, the IRS or the courts usually recast a corporate-shareholder transaction as an E&P distribution, deny the corporation an offsetting deduction, and treat all or a portion of the income recognized by the shareholder as a dividend.

Contributory pension plan A qualified pension plan to which employees make voluntary contributions.

Controlled group A controlled group is two or more separately incorporated businesses owned by a related group of individuals or entities. Such groups include parent-subsidiary groups, brother-sister groups, or combined groups.

Corporation A separate taxpaying entity (such as an association, joint stock company, or insurance company) that must file a tax return every year, even when it had no income or loss for the year.

Corresponding item The buyer's income, gain, deduction, or loss from an intercompany transaction, or from property acquired in an intercompany transaction.

Cost depletion method Calculation of the depletion of an asset (e.g., oil and gas properties) under which the asset's adjusted basis is divided by the estimated recoverable units to arrive at a per-unit depletion. This amount is then multiplied by the number of units sold to determine the cost depletion. This method may be alternated with the percentage depletion method as long as the calculation takes that into account.

Cost The amount paid for property in cash or the fair market value of the property given in exchange. The costs of acquiring the property and preparing it for use are included in the cost of the property.

Crummey trust Technique that allows a donor to set up a discretionary trust and obtain an annual exclusion. Such a trust arrangement allows the beneficiary to demand an annual distribution of the lesser of the annual exclusion ($14,000 in 2014 and 2015) or the amount transferred to the trust that year.

Current year's exclusion The amount of the annuity payment that is excluded from gross income. This amount is determined by multiplying the exclusion ratio by the amount received during the year.

Customs duties A federal excise tax on imported goods.

DIF See Discriminant Function Program.

Deductions for AGI Expenses one would see on an income statement prepared for financial accounting purposes, for example, compensation paid to employees, repairs to business property, and depreciation expenses. Certain nonbusiness deductions (e.g., alimony payments, moving expenses, and deductible payments to an individual retirement account (IRA)) are also deductible for AGI.

Deductions from AGI Generally, deductions are allowed for certain personal expenses such as medical deductions and charitable contributions which are referred to as itemized deductions. Alternatively, individuals may deduct the standard deduction. Personal and dependency deductions are also deductions from AGI.

Deferred tax asset A book balance sheet item that results from temporary differences that produce tax deductions in the future when the differences reverse. The amount is the applicable tax rate times the temporary difference.

Deferred tax liability A book balance sheet item that results from temporary differences that produce taxable income in the future when the differences reverse. The amount is the applicable tax rate times the temporary difference.

Deficiency dividend This type of dividend substitutes an income tax levy on the dividend payment at the shareholder level for the payment of the personal holding company tax.

Defined contribution pension plan Qualified pension plan under which a separate account is maintained for each participant and fixed amounts are contributed based upon a specific percentage-of-compensation formula. The retirement benefits are based on the value of the participant's account at the time of retirement. Defined contribution plans for self-employed individuals are referred to as *H.R. 10 plans*.

Discriminant Function Program Program used by the IRS to select individual returns for audit. This system is intended to identify those tax returns that are most likely to contain errors.

Dissolution A legal term implying that a corporation has surrendered the charter that it originally received from the state.

Distributable net income (DNI) Maximum amount of distributions taxed to the beneficiaries and deducted by a trust or estate.

Distributive share The portion of partnership taxable and nontaxable income, losses, credits, and so on that the partner must report for tax purposes.

Dividend A distribution of property made by a corporation out of its earnings and profits.

Dividends-paid deduction Distributions made out of a corporation's earnings and profits are eligible for this deduction for personal holding company tax and accumulated earnings tax purposes. The deduction is equal to the amount of money plus the adjusted basis of the nonmoney property distributed.

Dividends-received deduction This deduction attempts to mitigate the triple taxation that would occur if one corporation paid dividends to a corporate shareholder who, in turn, distributed such amounts to its individual shareholders. Certain restrictions and limitations apply to this deduction.

Divisive reorganization Transaction in which part of a transferor corporation's assets are transferred to a second, newly created corporation that is controlled by either the transferee or its shareholders.

E&P See Earnings and profits.

Earnings and profits A measure of the corporation's ability to pay a dividend from its current and accumulated earnings without an impairment of capital.

Economic performance test Economic performance occurs when the property or services to be provided are actually delivered.

Effective tax rate The taxpayer's total tax liability divided by his total economic income. In financial statements, the term means total book income tax expense divided by pretax book income. In footnotes to the financial statements, firms reconcile the effective tax rate to the statutory tax rate.

Employee achievement award Award given under circumstances that does not create a likelihood that it is really disguised compensation. It must be in the form of tangible personal property (other than cash) and be valued at no more than $400.

Employee stock ownership plan (ESOP) A qualified stock bonus plan or combined stock bonus plan and money purchase pension plan. ESOP's are funded by contributions of the employer's stock which are held for the employees' benefit.

Employment taxes Social security (FICA) and federal and state unemployment compensation taxes.

Entertainment expense Entertainment expenses (e.g., business meals) that are either directly related to or associated with the active conduct of a trade or business are deductible within certain limitations and restrictions. Directly related expenses are those that (1) derive a business benefit other than goodwill and (2) are incurred in a clear business setting. Expenses that are associated with the business are those that show a clear business purpose (e.g., obtaining new business) and occur on the same day the business is discussed.

Estate A legal entity which comes into being only upon the death of the person whose assets are being administered. The estate continues in existence until the duties of the executor have been completed.

Estate tax Part of the federal unified transfer tax system, this tax is based upon the total property transfers an individual makes during his lifetime and at death.

Excess depreciation See Additional depreciation.

Excess net passive income An amount equal to the S corporation's net passive income multiplied by the fraction consisting of its passive investment income less 25% of its gross receipts divided by its passive investment income. It is limited to the corporation's taxable income.

Excess net passive income (Sec. 1375) tax Tax levied when (1) an S corporation has passive investment income for the taxable year that exceeds 25% of its gross receipts and (2) at the close of the tax year the S corporation has earnings and profits from C corporation tax years.

Exclusion Any item of income that the tax law says is not taxable.

Exclusion ratio The portion of the annuity payment that is excluded from taxation. This amount equals the investment in the contract (its cost) divided by the expected return from the annuity.

Exemption equivalent That portion of the tax base that is completely free of transfer taxes as a result of the unified credit. (Also called the applicable exclusion amount.)

Expanded affiliated group A group of corporations treated as one corporation for purposes of determining the U.S. production activities deduction allowed to the group. A 50% ownership test applies for identifying members of the group.

Expected return The amount which a taxpayer can expect to receive from an annuity. It is determined by multiplying the amount of the annuity's annual payment by the expected return multiple.

Expected return multiple The number of years that the annuity is expected to continue. This amount may be a stated term or for the remainder of the taxpayer's life.

FICA Tax withheld through the payment of payroll taxes, FICA is intended to finance social security benefits for individuals who are not self-employed. Employees and employers contribute matching amounts until a federally-set annual earnings ceiling is reached. At that time, no further contributions need be made for that year. No ceiling exists for the hospital insurance (HI) portion of the tax. Self-employed individuals are subject to self-employment tax and currently receive a *for* AGI income tax deduction equal to 50% of their self-employment tax payments.

FIFO method of inventory valuation This flow of cost method assumes that the first goods purchased will be the first goods sold. Thus, the ending inventory consists of the last goods purchased.

Failure-to-file penalty Penalty imposed for the failure to file a timely return. The penalty is assessed at 5% per month (or fraction thereof) on the amount of the net tax due. The maximum penalty for failing to file is 25%. The minimum penalty is the lesser of $135 or 100% of the tax due.

Failure-to-pay penalty Penalty imposed at the rate of 0.5% per month (or fraction thereof) on the amount of tax shown on the return less any tax payments made before the beginning of the month for which the penalty is being calculated. The maximum penalty is 25%.

Fair market value (FMV) The amount that would be realized from the sale of a property at a price that is agreeable to both the buyer and the seller when neither party is obligated to participate in the transaction.

Federal estate tax See estate tax.

Fiduciary A person or other entity (e.g., a guardian, executor, trustee, or administrator) who holds and manages property for someone else.

Fiduciary accounting income The excess of accounting income over expenses for a fiduciary (i.e., an estate or trust). Excluded are any items credited to or charged against capital.

Fiduciary taxation The special tax rules that apply to fiduciaries (e.g., trusts and estates).

Field audit procedure Audit procedure generally used by the IRS for corporations or individuals engaged in a trade or business and conducted at either the taxpayer's place of business or his tax advisor's office. Generally, several items on the tax return are examined.

Fiscal year An annual accounting period that ends on the last day of any month other than December. A fiscal year may be elected by taxpayers that keep books and records, such as businesses.

Fixing-up expenses Expenses incurred to assist in the sale of a residence (e.g., normal repairs and painting costs). Capital expenditures do not qualify as fixing-up expenses.

Flat tax See Proportional tax.

Foreign corporation A corporation that is incorporated under the laws of a country other than the United States.

Foreign tax credit Tax credit given to mitigate the possibility of double taxation faced by U.S. citizens, residents, and corporations earning foreign income.

Foreign-earned income An individual's earnings from personal services rendered in a foreign country.

Former passive activity An activity that was formerly considered passive, but which is not considered to be passive with respect to the taxpayer for the current year.

Forum shopping The ability to consider differing precedents in choosing the forum for litigation.

Franchise tax State tax levy sometimes based upon a weighted average formula consisting of net worth, income, and sales.

Functional-use test A test used to determine whether property is considered similar or related in service or use for purposes of involuntary conversions of property under Sec. 1033. The functional-use test requires that the replacement property be functionally the same as the converted property.

Future interest Such interests include reversions, remainders, and other interests that may not be used, owned, or enjoyed until some future date.

General business credit Special credit category consisting of tax credits commonly available to businesses. The more significant credit items are (1) the investment tax credit, (2) the targeted jobs credit, (3) the research credit, (4) the low-income housing credit, (5) the empowerment zone employment credit, (6) the disabled access credit.

General partnership A partnership with two or more partners where no partner is a limited partner.

General power of appointment Power of appointment under which the holder can appoint the property to himself, his estate, his creditors, or the creditors of his estate. Such power may be exercisable during the decedent's life, by his will, or both.

Generally accepted accounting principles (GAAP) The accounting principles that govern the preparation of financial reports to shareholders. GAAP does not apply to the tax treatment unless the method clearly reflects income. It is used only when the regulations do not specify the treatment of an item or when the regulations provide more than one alternative accounting method.

Generation-skipping transfer A disposition that (1) provides interests for more than one generation of beneficiaries who are in a younger generation than the transferor or (2) provides an interest solely for a person two or more generations younger than the transferor.

Gift tax A wealth transfer tax that applies if the property transfer occurs during a person's lifetime. A $14,000 (2014 and 2015) per donee annual exclusion is allowed.

Grantor trust Trust governed by Secs. 671 through 679. The income from such trusts is taxed to the grantor even if some or all of the income has been distributed.

Grantor The transferor who creates a trust.

Gross estate The gross estate includes items to which the decedent held title at death as well as certain incomplete transfers made by the decedent prior to death.

Gross income All income received in cash, property, or services, from whatever source derived and from which the taxpayer derives a direct economic benefit.

Gross tax For income tax purposes, the amount determined by multiplying taxable income by the appropriate tax rate(s). The gross tax may also be found in the appropriate tax table for the taxpayer's filing status.

Guaranteed minimum Minimum amount of payment guaranteed to a partner. This amount is important if the partner's distributive share is less than his guaranteed minimum. See also Guaranteed payment.

Guaranteed payment Minimum amount of payment guaranteed to a partner in the form of a salary-like payment made for services provided to the partnership and interest-like payments for the use of invested capital. Guaranteed payments, which may be in the form of a guaranteed minimum amount or a set amount, are taxed as ordinary income. See also Guaranteed minimum.

H.R. 10 Plan Special retirement plan rules applicable to self-employed individuals. Such plans are often referred to as "Keogh plans."

Hedge agreement This is an obligation on the part of a shareholder-employee to repay to the corporation any portion of salary that is disallowed by the IRS as a deduction. It is also used in connection with other corporate payments to shareholder-employees (e.g., travel and entertainment expenses).

Horizontal equity A concept in taxation that refers to the notion that similarly-situated taxpayers should be treated equally under the tax law.

Hybrid method of accounting Accounting method that combines the cash and accrual methods. Under this method, taxpayers can report sales and purchases under the accrual method and other income and expense items under the cash method. See also the cash method of accounting and the accrual method of accounting.

IRS See Internal Revenue Service.

Income The economic concept of income measures the amount an individual can consume during a period and remain as well off at the end of the period as at the beginning. The accounting concept of income is a measure of the income that is realized in a transaction. The tax concept of income is close to the accounting concept. It includes both taxable and nontaxable income from any source. However, it does not include a return of capital.

Income beneficiary Entity or individual that receives the income from a trust.

Income in respect of a decedent (IRD) Amount to which the decedent was entitled as gross income but which was not properly includible in computing his or her taxable income for the tax year ending with his or her date of death or for a previous tax year under the method of accounting employed by the decedent.

Income tax expense A subtraction item in the book income statement that represents a firm's current and deferred tax expense for the year. It is the total tax expense and sometimes is called the total tax provision.

Incremental A concept in taxation that described how the tax law has been changed or modified over the years. Under incrementalism, the tax law is changed on an incremental basis rather than a complete revision basis.

Indeterminate market value If the market value of the property in question cannot be determined by the usual methods, the "open transaction" doctrine may be applied and the tax consequences may be deferred until the transaction is closed. Alternatively, the property may be valued by using the fair market value of the property that is given in the exchange (e.g., the value of the services rendered).

Information release An administrative pronouncement concerning an issue the IRS thinks the general public will be interested in. Such releases are issued in lay terms.

Innocent spouse provision This provision exempts a spouse from penalty and liability for tax if such spouse had no knowledge of nor reason to know about an item of taxable income that is in dispute.

Innocent spouse rule Rule that exempts a spouse from penalty or from liability for the tax if such spouse had no knowledge of nor reason to know about an item of community income.

Installment sale Any disposition of property which involves receiving at least one payment after the close of the taxable year in which the sale occurs.

Installment sale method of accounting Taxpayers may use this method of accounting to reduce the tax burden from gains on the sale of property paid for in installments. Under this method, payment of the tax is deferred until the sale proceeds are collected. This method is not applicable to sales of publicly traded property or to losses.

Intangible drilling and development costs (IDCs) Expenditures made by an operator for wages, fuel, repairs, hauling supplies, and so forth, incident to and necessary for the preparation and drilling of oil and gas wells.

Inter vivos trust Transfer to a trust that is made during the grantor's lifetime.

Interest The cost charged by a lender for the use of money. For example, finance charges, loan discounts, premiums, loan origination fees, and points paid by a buyer to obtain a mortgage loan are all interest expenses. The deductibility of the expense depends upon the purpose for which the indebtedness was incurred.

Interpretative regulations Treasury Regulations that serve to interpret the provisions of the Internal Revenue Code.

Investment expenses All deductions other than interest that are directly connected with the production of investment income.

Investment interest Interest expense on indebtedness incurred to purchase or carry property held for investment (e.g., income from interest, dividends, annuities, and royalties). Interest expenses incurred from passive activities are not subject to the investment interest limitations and interest incurred to purchase or carry tax-exempt securities is not deductible. Interest incurred from passive activities is subject to the passive activity loss limitation rules.

Involuntary conversion Such a conversion occurs when property is compulsorily converted into money or other property due to theft, seizure, requisition, condemnation, or partial or complete destruction. For example, an involuntary conversion occurs when the government exercises its right of eminent domain.

Irrevocable trust Trust under which the grantor cannot require the trustee to return the trust's assets.

Itemized deductions Also known as "deductions from AGI," these personal expenditures are allowable for such items as medical expenses, state and local taxes, charitable contributions, unreimbursed employee business expenses, interest on a personal residence, and casualty and theft losses. Specific requirements and limitations apply to the deductibility of each of these items. In addition, only taxpayers whose total itemized deductions exceed the standard deduction amount can itemize their deductions. Total itemized deductions are subject to reduction based on AGI.

Joint income Income from jointly-held property.

Joint tenancy A popular form of property ownership that serves as a substitute for a will. Each joint tenant is deemed to have an equal interest in the property.

Judicial decisions Decision rendered by a court deciding the case that is presented to it by a plaintiff and defendant. These decisions are important sources of the tax law and can come from trial courts and appellate courts.

Keogh plan Retirement plan for self-employed individuals. This type of plan is also known as an "H.R. 10 plan."

LIFO method of inventory valuation This method assumes a last-in, first out flow of cost. It results in the lowest taxable income during periods of inflation because it shows the lowest inventory value. Price indexes are used for the valuation. The information in these indexes is grouped into groups (pools) of similar items. See also Simplified LIFO method.

LIFO recapture tax A tax imposed on a C corporation that uses the LIFO inventory method and which elects S corporation treatment. The tax is imposed in the final C corporation tax year and paid over a four-year period.

Legislative reenactment doctrine Rule holding that Congress's failure to change the wording in the Code over an extended period signifies that Congress has approved the treatment provided in the regulations.

Letter ruling Letter rulings originate from the IRS at the taxpayer's request. They describe how the IRS will treat a proposed transaction. It is only binding on the person requesting the ruling providing the taxpayer completes the transaction as proposed in the ruling. Those of general interest are published as Revenue Rulings.

Life estate A property transfer in trust that results in the transferor reserving the right to income for life. Another individual is named to receive the property upon the transferor's death.

Like class Classes of assets defined by the Regulations that are considered to be property of a like kind for purposes of Sec. 1031. Like class property is tangible personal property that is in the same General Asset Class or the Same Product Class as other property.

Like-kind exchange A direct exchange of like-kind property. The transferred property and the received property must be held for productive use either (1) in a trade or business or (2) as an investment. Nonrecognition of gain or loss is mandatory. Certain like-kind exchanges between related parties are restricted if either party disposes of the property within two years of the exchange.

Limited liability company (LLC) A business entity that combines the legal and tax benefits of partnerships and S corporations. These entities are treated as partnerships for federal tax purposes unless they elect to be taxed as a corporation under the check-the-box regulations.

Limited liability partnership (LLP) Similar to a limited liability company, but formed under a separate state statute that generally applies to service companies.

Limited partnership A partnership where one or more of the partners is designated as a limited partner.

Liquidating distribution A distribution that (1) liquidates a partner's entire partnership interest due to retirement, death, or other business reason or (2) partially or totally liquidates a shareholder's stock interest in a corporation following the adoption of a plan at liquidation.

Long-term capital gain (LTCG) Gain realized on the sale or exchange of a capital asset held longer than one year.

Long-term contracts Building, manufacturing, installation, and construction contracts that are not completed in the same taxable year in which they are entered into. Service contracts do not qualify as long-term contracts. See also Completed contract method of accounting.

Look-back interest Interest that is assessed on any additional tax that would have been paid if the actual total cost of the contract was used to calculate the tax rather than the estimated cost. Thus, it is applicable to any contract or portion of a contract that is accounted for under either the hybrid or percentage of completion method of accounting.

Loss corporation A corporation entitled to use a net operating loss carryover or having a net operating loss for the taxable year in which an ownership change occurs.

Majority partners The one or more partners in a partnership who have an aggregate interest in partnership profits and capital exceeding 50%.

Mandatory basis adjustment Required basis adjustment if the partnership has a substantial built-in loss at the time a partner sells his or her partnership interest or if the partnership has a decreasing basis adjustment at the time of a liquidating distribution.

Marginal tax rate The tax that is applied to an incremental amount of taxable income that is added to the tax base. This rate can be used to measure the tax effect of a proposed transaction. Currently, the highest marginal tax rate for individuals is 39.6%. An additional 3.8% may apply to net investment income for individuals having modified AGI exceeding \$200,000 (\$250,000 for married filing jointly). For corporations, the highest statutory marginal tax rate also is 35%. However, in certain taxable income ranges (called "bubbles"), the marginal tax is 39% (\$100,000 to \$335,000 range) or 38% (\$15 million to \$18,333,333 range).

Marital deduction Deduction allowed for nontaxable inter-spousal transfers other than those for gifts of certain terminable interests.

Market value This term refers to replacement cost under the lower of cost or market inventory method. That is, it is the price at which the taxpayer can replace the goods in question. See also Fair market value.

Material participation The level of participation by a taxpayer in an activity that determines whether the activity is either passive or active. If a taxpayer does not meet the material participation requirements, the activity is treated as a passive activity.

Medical expense deduction Unreimbursed medical expenses incurred for medical procedures or treatments that are (1) legal in the locality in which they are performed and (2) incurred for the purpose of alleviating a physical or mental defect or illness that affects the body's structure or function, are deductible from AGI. Out-of-pocket travel costs incurred while en route to a medical facility, certain capital expenditures affecting the sick person, premiums for medical insurance, and in-patient hospital care are also deductible. Certain restrictions and limitations apply to this deduction.

Memorandum decision Decision issued by the Tax Court. They deal with factual variations on matters which were decided in earlier cases.

Merger A nontaxable reorganization one form of which has the acquiring corporation transfer its stock, securities, and other consideration to the target corporation in exchange for its assets and liabilities. The target corporation then distributes the consideration that it receives to its shareholders and security holders in exchange for their stock and securities.

Minimum tax credit (MTC) A tax credit allowed for the amount of alternative minimum tax that arose because of deferral and permanent adjustments and preference items. This credit may be carried over and used to offset regular tax liabilities in subsequent years, subject to limitations.

Miscellaneous itemized deductions Certain unreimbursed employee expenses (e.g., required uniforms, travel, entertainment, and so on) fall into this category. Miscellaneous itemized deductions also include certain investment expenses, appraisal fees for charitable contributions and fees for tax return preparation. The nature of the deduction depends on whether the taxpayer is an employee or a self-employed individual.

Modified percentage of completion method A variation of the regular percentage of completion method where an election may be made to defer reporting profit from a long-term contract until at least 10% of the estimated total cost has been incurred.

Necessary expense Expense that is deductible because it is appropriate and helpful in the taxpayer's business. Such expenses must also qualify as ordinary.

Negligence The IRC defines negligence as (1) any failure to reasonably attempt to comply with the IRC and (2) "careless, reckless, or intentional disregard" of the rules and regulations.

Negligence penalty Penalty assessed if the IRS finds that the taxpayer has filed an incorrect return because of negligence. Generally this penalty is 20% of the underpayment attributable to negligence.

Net gift A gift upon which the donee pays the gift tax as a condition to receiving the gift.

Net investment income The excess of the taxpayer's investment income over his investment expenses. See also Investment income.

Net operating loss (NOL) A net operating loss occurs when business expenses exceed business income for any taxable year. Such losses generally may be carried back two years or carried forward 20 years to a year in which the taxpayer has taxable income. The loss is carried back first and must be deducted from years in chronological order unless the taxpayer makes a special election to forgo the carryback.

New loss corporation Any corporation permitted to use a net operating loss carryover after an ownership change occurs.

Ninety (90)-day letter Officially called a Statutory Notice of Deficiency, this letter is sent when (1) the taxpayer does not file a protest letter within 30 days of receipt of the 30-day letter or (2) the taxpayer has met with an appeals officer but no agreement was reached. The letter notifies the taxpayer of the amount of the deficiency, how that amount was determined, and that a deficiency will be assessed if a petition is not filed with the Tax Court within 90 days. The taxpayer is also advised of the alternatives available to him.

Nonaccountable plan A type of employee reimbursement plan that does not meet either of the two tests for an accountable plan (see accountable plan). Under a nonaccountable plan, reimbursements are included in the employee's gross income and the expenses are deductible by the employee, subject to the 2% of AGI floor.

Nonqualified deferred compensation plan Type of plan used by employer to provide incentives or supplementary retirement benefits for executives. Such plans are not subject to the nondiscrimination and vesting rules.

Nonqualified stock option Stock option that does not meet the requirements for an incentive stock option.

Nonrecourse loan Loan for which the borrower has no liability.

Notice An interpretation by the IRS that provides guidance concerning how to interpret a statute, perhaps one recently enacted.

Office audit procedure IRS audit of a specific item on an individual's tax return. An office audit takes place at the IRS branch office.

Old loss corporation Any corporation that is allowed to use a net operating loss carryover, or which has a net operating loss for the tax year in which an ownership change occurs, and which undergoes the requisite stock ownership change.

Open transaction doctrine Valuation technique for property that can only be valued on the basis of uncertain future payments. This doctrine determines the shareholder's gain or loss when the asset is sold, collected, or able to be valued. Assets that cannot be valued are assigned a value of zero.

Open-fact or tax-planning situation Situation or transaction in which the facts have not yet occurred. In such situations, the tax advisor's task is to plan for the facts or shape them so as to produce a favorable tax result.

Optional basis adjustment An elective technique that adjusts the basis for the underlying partnership assets up or down as a result of (1) distributions from the partnership to its partners, (2) sales of partnership interests by existing partners, or (3) transfers of the interest following the death of a partner.

Ordinary expense An expense that is deductible because it is reasonable in amount and bears a reasonable and proximate relationship to the income-producing activity or property.

Ordinary gross income (OGI) A corporation's ordinary gross income is its gross income reduced by (1) capital gains and (2) Sec. 1231 gains.

Ordinary income property For charitable contribution deduction purposes, any property that would result in the recognition of ordinary income if it was sold. Such property includes inventory, works of art or manuscripts created by the taxpayer, capital assets that have been held for one year or less, and Sec. 1231 property that results in ordinary income due to depreciation recapture.

Parent-subsidiary controlled group To qualify as such, a common parent must own at least 80% of the voting stock or at least 80% of the value of at least one subsidiary corporation and at least 80% of each other component member of the controlled group must be owned by other members of the controlled group.

Partial liquidation This occurs when a corporation discontinues one line of business, distributes the assets related to that business to its shareholders, and continues in at least one other line of business.

Partner A member of a partnership. The member may be an individual, trust, estate, or corporation. See also general partner and limited partner.

Partnership Syndicate, group, pool, joint venture, or other unincorporated organization which carries on a business or financial operation or venture and which has at least two partners.

Partnership agreement Agreement that governs the relationship between the partners and the partnership.

Partnership interest The capital and/or profits interest in a partnership received in exchange for a contribution of properties or services (e.g., money or business equipment). The nature of a partnership interest is similar to that of corporate stock.

Partnership item Virtually all items reported by the partnership for the taxable year, including tax preference items, credit recapture items, guaranteed payments, and at-risk amounts.

Partnership ordinary income The positive sum of all partnership items of income, gain, loss, or deduction that do not have to be separately stated.

Partnership ordinary loss The negative sum of all partnership items of income, gain, loss, or deduction that do not have to be separately stated.

Partnership taxable income The sum of all taxable items among the separately stated items plus the partnership ordinary income or ordinary loss.

Party to a reorganization Such parties include (1) corporations that result from a reorganization and (2) the corporations involved in a reorganization where one corporation acquires the stock or assets of the other corporation.

Passive activity limitation Separate limitation on the amount of losses and credits that can be claimed with respect to a passive activity.

Passive income Income from an activity that does not require the taxpayer's material involvement or participation. Thus, income from tax shelters and rental activities generally fall into this category.

Passive loss Loss generated from a passive activity. Such losses are computed separately. They may be used to offset income from other passive activities, but may not be used to offset either active income or portfolio income.

Percentage depletion method Depletion method for assets such as oil and gas that is equal to a specified percentage times the gross income from the property but which may not exceed 100% of the taxable income before depletion is deducted. Lease bonuses, advance royalties, and other amounts payable without regard to production may not be included in the calculation. This method is only available to small oil and gas producers and royalty owners and for certain mineral properties.

Percentage of completion method of accounting Accounting method generally used for long-term contracts under which income is reported in proportion to the amount of work that has been completed in a given year.

Permanent difference Items reported in taxable income but not book income or vice versa. Such differences include book income items that are nontaxable in the current year and will never be taxable and book expense items that are nondeductible in computing taxable income for the current year and will never be deductible.

Personal exemption A deduction in an amount mandated by Congress. The amount for 2015 is $4,000 ($3,950 in 2014). The amount is adjusted each year for increases in the cost of living. An additional exemption is allowed for each individual who is a dependent.

Personal holding company (PHC) A closely held corporation (1) that is owned by five or fewer shareholders who own more than 50% of the corporation's outstanding stock at any time during the last half of its tax year and (2) whose PHC income equals at least 60% of the corporation's adjusted ordinary gross income for the tax year. Certain corporations (e.g., S corporations) are exempt from this definition.

Personal holding company income (PHCI) Categories of income including the following: dividends; interest; annuities; royalties (other than minerals, oil and gas, computer software, and copyright royalties); adjusted income from rents; adjusted income from mineral, oil and gas royalties or working interests in oil and gas wells; computer software royalties; copyright royalties; produced film rents; income from personal service contracts involving a 25% or more shareholder; rental income from corporate property used by a 25% or more shareholder; and distributions from estates and trusts.

Personal holding company (PHC) tax This tax equals 20% of undistributed personal holding company income and, if applicable, is assessed in addition to the regular corporate income tax and the AMT.

Personal interest All interest other than active business interest, investment interest, interest incurred in a passive activity, qualified residence interest, and interest incurred when paying the estate tax on an installment basis. Personal interest is currently treated as a nondeductible personal expenditure. See also Interest.

Personal service corporation (PSC) A regular C corporation whose principal activity is the performance of personal services that are substantially performed by owner-employees who own more than 10% of the value of the corporation's stock.

Plan of liquidation A written document detailing the steps to be undertaken while carrying out the complete liquidation of a corporation.

Plan of reorganization A consummated transaction that is specifically defined as a reorganization.

Pooled income fund A fund in which individuals receive an income interest for life and a charitable contribution deduction equal to the remainder interest for amounts contributed to the fund. The various individual beneficiaries receive annual distributions of income based upon their proportionate share of the fund's earnings.

Portfolio income Dividends, interest, annuities, and royalties not derived in the ordinary course of business. Gains and losses on property that produces portfolio income are included in such income.

Post-termination transition period The period of time following the termination of the S corporation election during which (1) loss and deduction carryovers can be deducted or (2) distributions of S corporation previously taxed earnings can be made tax-free.

Power of appointment The power to designate the eventual owner of a property. Such appointments may be general or specific. See also General power of appointment.

Preadjustment AMTI Alternative minimum taxable income determined without the adjusted current earnings adjustment and the alternative tax NOL deduction.

Preadjustment year For purposes of the innocent spouse provisions, the most recent tax year of the spouse ending before the date the deficiency is mailed.

Preferential dividend Dividends are preferential if (1) the amount distributed to a shareholder exceeds his ratable share of the distribution as determined by the number of shares that are owned or (2) the distribution amount for a class of stock is more or less than its rightful amount.

Preferred stock bailout A tax treatment mandated by Sec. 306 which prevents shareholders who receive nontaxable preferred stock dividends from receiving capital gain treatment upon the sale or redemption of the preferred stock.

Premium Tax Credit A personal tax credit for a portion of the cost of a taxpayer's health insurance premiums. To be eligible for the credit, a taxpayer must have household income between 100% and 400% of the federal poverty line. The credit is based on the excess of the qualifying premiums over what is deemed to be affordable based on the taxpayer's household income.

Present interest An unrestricted right to the immediate use, possession, or enjoyment of property or the income from property (e.g., a life estate or term certain).

Previously taxed income (PTI) Income earned in a pre-1983 S corporation tax year and which was taxed to the shareholder. A money distribution of PTI can be distributed tax-free once all of a corporation's AAA balance has been distributed. See Accumulated Adjustments Account.

Primary cite The highest level official reporter which reports a particular case is called the primary cite.

Principal partner Partner who owns at least a 5% interest in the partnership's capital or profits.

Probate estate Those properties that (1) pass subject to the will or under an intestacy statute and (2) are subject to court administration are part of the probate estate.

Profit-sharing plan A qualified defined benefit plan which may be established in lieu of or in addition to a qualified pension plan. Contributions to a profit-sharing plan are usually based upon profits. Incidental benefits may or may not be included. In addition, the plan must meet certain requirements concerning determination of the amount and timing of the employer's contribution, how the employee wants to receive the employer's contribution, vesting, and forfeitures.

Profits interest Interest in the partnership's future earnings.

Progressive rate Tax that increases as the taxpayer's taxable income increases. The U.S. income tax is an example of a progressive tax.

Property Cash, tangible property (e.g., buildings and land) and intangible property (e.g., franchise rights, trademarks, and leases).

Property settlement The division of property between spouses upon their separation or divorce.

Property tax Federal, state, or local tax levied on real and/or personal property (e.g., securities, a personal automobile).

Proportional tax A method of taxation under which the tax rate is the same for all taxpayers regardless of their income. State and local sales taxes are examples of this form of tax.

Protest letter If the additional tax in question is more than $25,000 and the IRS audit was a field audit, the taxpayer must file a protest letter within 30 days. If no such letter is sent, then the IRS will follow-up with a 90-day letter. See also Ninety (90) day letter.

Qualified disclaimer Disclaimer made by a person named to receive property under a decedent's will who wishes to renounce the property and any of its benefits. Such a disclaimer must be in written form and be irrevocable. In addition, it must be made no later than nine months after the later of the day the transfer is made or the day the recipient becomes 21 years old. The property must pass to either the decedent's spouse or another person not named by the person making the disclaimer.

Qualified joint interest If spouses are the only joint owners of a property, that property is classified as a qualified joint interest.

Qualified pension plan Pension plan that includes (1) systematic and definite payments made to a pension trust based upon actuarial methods and (2) usually provides for incidental benefits such as disability, or medical insurance benefits.

Qualified plan award Employee achievement awards given under a written plan or program that does not discriminate in favor of highly compensated employees. Such awards must be in the form of tangible personal property other than cash and be worth no more than $1,600.

Qualified residence interest Interest on an indebtedness which is secured by the taxpayer's qualified residence when it is paid or accrued. A taxpayer may have two qualified residences: a principal residence and a residence that he has personally used more than the greater of 14 days or 10% of the rental days during the year.

Qualified Subchapter S trusts (QSSTs) A domestic trust that owns stock in one or more S corporations and distributes (or is required to distribute) all of its income to its sole income beneficiary. The beneficiary must make an irrevocable election to be treated as the owner of the trust consisting of the S corporation stock. A separate QSST election must be made for each corporation's stock that is owned by the trust.

Qualified terminable interest property (QTIP) QTIP property is property for which a special election has been made that makes it eligible for the marital deduction. Such property must be transferred by the donor-spouse to a donee-spouse who has a qualifying interest for life. In other words, the donor does not have to grant full control over the property to his spouse.

Readily ascertainable fair market value The fair market value of nonqualified stock options can be readily ascertained where the option is traded on an established options exchange.

Realized gain or loss The gain or loss computed by taking the amount realized from a sale of property and subtracting the property's adjusted basis.

Reasonable business needs For accumulated earnings tax purposes, the amount that a prudent businessman would consider appropriate for the business's bona fide present and future needs, Sec. 303 (death tax) redemption needs, and excess business holding redemption needs.

Recapitalization A nontaxable change in the capital structure of an existing corporation for a bona fide business purpose.

Recapture provision A provision requiring recapture of earlier alimony payments as ordinary income by the payor if the payments decline sharply in either the second or third year.

Recomputed corresponding item The corresponding item that would occur if the selling and buying group members were divisions of a single corporation.

Recourse loan Loan for which the borrower remains liable until repayment is complete. If the loan is secured, the lender can be repaid by selling the security. Any difference in the sale amount and the loan amount must be paid by the borrower.

Recovery of basis doctrine Rule that allows taxpayers to recover the basis of an asset without being taxed. Such amounts are considered a return of capital.

Refundable credit See Tax credit.

Regressive tax A form of taxation under which the tax rate decreases as the tax base (e.g., income) increases.

Regular corporation See C corporation.

Regular decision Tax Court decision that is issued on a particular issue for the first time.

Regular tax A corporation's tax liability for income tax purposes reduced by foreign tax credits allowable for income tax purposes.

Remainder interest The portion of an interest in the property retained by a transferor who is not transferring his entire interest in a property.

Remainderman The person entitled to the remainder interest.

Reorganization A corporate acquisition or division that meets specific requirements to qualify as a nontaxable transaction. Reorganizations are classified as Type A, B, C, D, E, F, or G.

Replacement property Property that is acquired to replace converted property to retain nonrecognition of gain status. Such property must generally be functionally the same as the converted property. For example, a business machine must be replaced with a similar business machine. There are exceptions to this rule: The taxpayer-use test applies to the involuntary conversion of rental property owned by an investor; condemnations of real property held for business or investment use may be replaced by like-kind property.

Residential rental property Property from which at least 80% of the gross rental income is rental from dwelling units. Residential units include manufactured homes that are used for rental purposes, but not hotels, motels, or other establishments for transient use.

Restricted property plan Such plans are used to attract and retain key executives by giving them an ownership interest in the corporation. The income recognition rules contained in Sec. 83 govern this type of plan.

Revenue Amounts received by the taxpayer from any source. It includes both taxable and nontaxable amounts and items that are a return of capital. Although closely related to income or gross income, differences between these items do exist.

Revenue procedure Issued by the national office of the IRS and reflects the IRS's position on procedural aspects of tax practice issues. Revenue procedures are published in the Cumulative Bulletin.

Revenue ruling Issued by the national office of the IRS and reflects the IRS's interpretation of a narrow tax issue. Revenue rulings, which are published in the Cumulative Bulletin, have less weight than the Treasury Regulations.

Reverse triangular merger Type of nontaxable transaction in which a subsidiary corporation is merged into a target corporation and the target corporation stays alive as a subsidiary of the parent corporation.

Reversionary interest The interest in a property that might revert back to the transferor under the terms of the transfer. If the amount of reversionary interest is 5% or less, it is not included in the gross estate.

Revocable trust Trust under which the grantor may demand that the assets be returned.

Royalties Ordinary income arising from amounts paid for the right to use property that belongs to another and is transferred for valuable consideration (e.g., a patent right where substantially all rights are transferred).

Rule against perpetuities The requirement that no property interest vest more than 21 years, plus the gestation period, after some life or lives in being at the time the interest is created.

S corporation Election that can be made by small business corporations that allows them to be taxed like partnerships rather than like C corporations. Small business corporations are those that meet the 100-shareholder limitation, the type of shareholder restrictions, and the one class of stock restriction.

S short year That portion of an S termination year that commences on the first day of the tax year and ends on the day preceding the day on which the termination is effective.

S termination year A tax year in which a termination event occurs on any day other than the first day of the tax year. It is divided into an S short year and a C short year.

Sale A transaction where one receives cash and/or the equivalent of cash, including the assumption of debt, in exchange for an asset.

Sales tax State or local tax on purchases. Generally, food items and medicines are exempt from such tax.

Section 444 election Personal service corporations, partnerships, and S corporations that are unable to otherwise elect a fiscal year, instead of their required tax year, can under Sec. 444 elect a fiscal year as their taxable year.

Secondary cite Citation to a secondary source (i.e., an unofficial reporter) for a particular case.

Section 1231 property Real or depreciable property that is (1) held for more than one year and (2) used in a trade or business. Certain property, such as inventory, U.S. government publications, copyrights, literary, musical, or artistic compositions, and letters, are excluded from this definition.

Section 1245 property Certain property subject to depreciation and, in some cases, amortization. Depreciable personal property such as equipment is Section 1245 property. However, most real property is not.

Section 1250 property Any real property that (1) is not Section 1245 property and (2) is subject to a depreciation allowance.

Section 306 stock Preferred stock that is received as a stock dividend or a part of a nontaxable reorganization. Section 306 stock is subject to the special preferred stock bailout rules when sold or redeemed. See Preferred stock bailouts.

Security A security includes (1) shares of stock in a corporation; (2) a right to subscribe for, or the right to receive, a share of stock in a corporation; and (3) a bond, debenture, note, or other evidence of indebtedness issued by a corporation with interest coupons or in registered form.

Self employment tax A tax imposed on self-employed (SE) individuals. The SE tax is comprised of two parts, (1) 12.4% for Social Security taxes (limited to a maximum amount of SE income) and (2) 2.9% for Medicare taxes (no limit on SE income). For 2015, the maximum SE income subject to the tax is $118,500 ($117,000 in 2014). An additional 0.9% Medicare tax applies for individuals whose earned income exceeds certain thresholds.

Separate property All property that is owned before marriage and any gifts or inheritances acquired after marriage are separate property. This distinction depends on the state of residence. However, it is possible even in community property states.

Separate share rule Rule permitting a trust with several beneficiaries to treat each beneficiary as having a separate trust interest for purposes of determining (1) the amount of the distribution deduction and (2) the beneficiary's gross income.

Severance damages Compensation for a decline in the value of the property remaining after part of the taxpayer's property is condemned. The IRS considers such damages analogous to the proceeds from property insurance.

Shared Responsibility Payment An excise tax assessed on taxpayers not having the required minimum essential health insurance coverage. The penalty tax is collected with the federal income tax return.

Shifting income The process of transferring income from one family member to another. Methods for shifting income include gifts of stock or bonds to family members who are in lower tax brackets.

Short-period tax return A tax return covering a period of less than 12 months. Short period returns are commonly filed in the first or final tax year or when a change in tax year is made.

Short-term capital gain (STCG) Gain realized on the sale or exchange of a capital asset held for one year or less.

Short-term trust Trust whose period is long enough for the grantor to escape being taxed on the trust's accounting income. A *Clifford* trust is a short-term trust.

Simple trust Trust that must distribute all of its income currently and is not empowered to make a charitable contribution.

Simplified LIFO method This method of inventory valuation allows taxpayers to use a single LIFO pool rather than multiple pools. See also LIFO method.

Small cases procedure When $50,000 or less is in question for a particular year, a taxpayer may opt to have the case heard by a special commissioner rather than a Tax Court judge. The commissioner's opinion cannot be appealed and has no precedential value.

Sole proprietorship Form of business entity owned by an individual who reports all items of income and expense on Schedule C (or Schedule C-EZ) of his individual return.

Special agents The IRS agents responsible for criminal fraud investigations.

Specific write-off method of accounting Method of accounting used for bad debts. Under this method, the taxpayer deducts each bad debt individually as it becomes worthless. This is the only allowable accounting method for bad debts arising after 1986.

Spin-off A nontaxable distribution in which a parent corporation distributes the stock and securities of a subsidiary to its shareholders without receiving anything in exchange.

Split-interest transfer A transfer made for both private (i.e., an individual) and public (i.e., a charitable organization) purposes.

Split-off A nontaxable distribution in which a parent corporation distributes a subsidiary's stock and securities to some or all of its shareholders in exchange for part or all of their stock and securities in the parent corporation.

Split-up A nontaxable distribution in which a parent corporation distributes the stock or securities of two or more subsidiaries to its shareholders in exchange for all of their stock and securities in the parent corporation. The parent corporation then goes out of existence.

Splitting income The process of creating additional taxable entities, especially corporations, in order to reduce an individual's effective tax rate.

Sprinkling trust A discretionary trust with several beneficiaries.

Standard deduction A floor amount set by Congress to simplify the tax computation. It is used by taxpayers who do not have enough deductions to itemize. The amount of the deduction varies according to the taxpayer's filing status, age, and vision. Taxpayers who use this standard deduction are not required to keep records.

Standards for Tax Services (SSTS) Ethical standards of practice and compliance set by the Tax Division of the American Institute of Certified Public Accountants. The AICPA enforces these standards, and thus they have a great deal of influence over ethics in tax practice.

Statute of limitations A period of time as provided by law in which a taxpayer's return may not be changed either by the IRS or the taxpayer. The limitations period is generally three years from the later of the date the tax return is filed or its due date. A fraudulent return has no statute of limitations.

Step transaction doctrine A judicial doctrine which the IRS can use to collapse a multistep transaction into a single transaction (either taxable or nontaxable) to prevent the taxpayers from arranging a series of business transactions to obtain a tax result that is not available if only a single transaction is used.

Stock bonus plan A special type of defined benefit plan under which the employer's stock is contributed to a trust. The stock is then allocated and distributed to the participants. See also Employee stock ownership plan.

Stock dividend A dividend paid in the form of stock in the corporation issuing the dividend.

Stock option plan This category includes incentive stock options and nonqualified stock option arrangements. Such plans are used to attrack and retain key employees.

Stock redemption The acquisition by a corporation of its own stock in exchange for property. Such stock may be cancelled, retired, or held as treasury stock.

Stock rights Rights issued by a corporation to its shareholders or creditors which permit the purchase of an additional share(s) of stock at a designated exercise price with the surrender of one or more of the stock rights.

Substantially appreciated inventory This type of inventory includes (1) items held for sale in the normal course of partnership business, (2) other property which would not be considered a capital asset or Sec. 1231 property if it was sold by the partnership, and (3) any other property held by the partnership which would fall into the above classification if it was held by the selling or distributee partner.

Surviving spouse A special filing status available to widows and widowers who file a joint return for the year his or her spouse dies and for the following two years. The surviving spouse may not have remarried, must be a U.S. citizen or resident, have qualified to file a joint return for the year, and must have at least one dependent child living at home during the year.

Target corporation The corporation that transfers its assets as part of a taxable or nontaxable acquisition. Also may be known as the acquired or transferor company.

Tax A mandatory assessment levied under the authority of a political entity for the purpose of raising revenue to be used for public or governmental purposes. Such taxes may be levied by the federal, state, or local government.

Tax attributes Corporations have various tax items, such as earnings and profits, deduction and credit carryovers, and depreciation recapture potential, that are called tax attributes. The tax attributes of a target or liquidating corporation are assumed by the acquiring or parent corporation, respectively, in acquisitive reorganizations and tax-free liquidations.

Tax base The amount to which the tax rate is applied to determine the tax due. For income tax purposes, the tax base is taxable income.

Tax benefit rule Recovery of an amount in a subsequent year that produced a tax benefit in a prior year and is thus taxable to the recipient.

Tax credit Amount that can be deducted from the gross tax to arrive at the net tax due or refund due. Prepaid amounts, that is, amounts paid to the government during the year, are tax credits. Such prepaid amounts are often referred to as "refundable credits."

Tax deferred bonds Bonds on which the interest is not subject to current taxation but is deferred to a future period of time, such as Series EE U.S. Savings Bonds.

Tax exempt bonds Bonds on which the interest is completely exempt from federal income taxation, such as state and municipal bonds.

Tax law The tax law is comprised of the Internal Revenue Code, administrative and judicial interpretations, and the committee reports issued by the Congressional committees involved in the legislative process.

Tax matters partner (1) Partner who is designated by the partnership or (2) the general partner having the largest profits interests at the close of the partnership's tax year.

Tax preference items Designated items that increase taxable income to arrive at AMTI. Unlike AMT adjustments, tax preference items do not reverse in later years and reduce AMTI.

Tax research The process of solving a specific tax related question on the basis of both tax law sources and the specific circumstances surrounding the particular situation.

Tax services Multivolume commentaries on the tax law. Generally these commentaries contain copies of the Internal Revenue Code and the Treasury Regulations. Also included are editorial comments prepared by the publisher of the tax service, current matters, and a cross-reference to various government promulgations and judicial decisions. Most tax services now are available on the Internet.

Tax shelter Passive activity which may lack economic substance other than creating tax deductions and credits that enable taxpayers to reduce or eliminate the income tax liability from their regular business activities. Section 469 restricts the current use of deductions and credits arising from passive activities.

Tax treaties Bilateral agreements entered into between two nations which address tax and other matters. Treaties provide for modifications to the basic tax laws involving residents of the two countries (e.g., reductions in the withholding rates).

Tax year The period of time (usually 12 months) selected by a taxpayer to compute their taxable income. The tax year may be a calendar year or a fiscal year. The election is made on the taxpayer's first return and cannot be changed without IRS approval. The tax year may be less than 12 months if it is the taxpayer's first or final return or if the taxpayer is changing accounting periods.

Taxable income For individuals, taxable income is adjusted gross income reduced by deductions from adjusted gross income.

Taxpayer Compliance Measurement Program (TCMP) A stratified random sample used to select tax returns for audit. The program is intended to test the extent to which taxpayers are in compliance with the law.

Taxpayer-use test A test used to determine whether property is considered similar or related in service or use for purposes of involuntary conversions of property. This test is used by owner-investors (as opposed to owner-users) of property.

Technical advice memorandum Such memoranda are administrative interpretations issued in the form of letter ruling. Taxpayers may request them if they need guidance about the tax treatment of complicated technical matters which are being audited.

Temporary differences Items which are included in book income in the current year but which were included in taxable income in the past or will be included in the future. Book income items that are nontaxable in the current year even though they were taxed in the past or will be taxed in the future and book expenses that are not currently deductible even though that status was different in the past or will be different in the future are categorized as temporary differences.

Tentative minimum tax (TMT) Tax calculated by (1) multiplying 20% times a corporation's alternative minimum taxable income less a statutory exemption amount and (2) deducting allowable foreign tax credits.

Term certain interest A person holding such an interest has a right to receive income from property for a specified term, but does not own or hold title to such property. The property reverts to the grantor at the end of the term.

Terminable interest A property interest that ends when (1) some event occurs (or fails to occur) or (2) a specified amount of time passes.

Testamentary Of, pertaining to, or of the nature of a testament or will.

Testamentary gift Transfer of property made at the death of the donor (i.e., bequests, devises, and inheritances).

Testamentary transfers A transferor's control or enjoyment of a property ceases at death.

Testamentary trust Trust created under the direction of a decedent's will and funded by the decedent's estate.

Thirty (30)-day letter A report sent to the taxpayer if the taxpayer does not sign Form 870 (Waiver of Statutory Notice) concerning any additional taxes assessed. The letter details the proposed changes and advises the taxpayer of his right to pursue the matter with the Appeals Office. The taxpayer then has 30 days in which to request a conference.

Throwback dividends For accumulated earnings tax and personal holding company tax purposes, these are distributions made out of current or accumulated earnings and profits in the first two and one-half months after the close of the tax year.

Tier-1 beneficiary Beneficiary to whom a distribution must be made.

Tier-2 beneficiary Beneficiary who receives a discretionary distribution.

Total economic income The amount of the taxpayer's income, including exclusions and deductions from the tax base (e.g., tax-exempt bonds), is categorized as total economic income.

Transferor corporation The corporation that transfers its assets as part of a reorganization. May also be known as acquired or target corporation.

Transportation expense The deductibility of this type of expense depends upon whether it is trade- or business-related, whether it is related to the production of income, whether the expense is employment related and therefore subject to the 2% nondeductible floor for miscellaneous itemized deductions. Commuting expenses are nondeductible. See also Travel expense.

Travel expense Such expenses include transportation, meals, and lodging incurred in the pursuit of a trade, business, or employment-related activity. There are limitations and restrictions on the deductibility of these expenses. See also Transportation expense.

Triangular reorganization A type of reorganization (i.e., Type A, B, or C) where the parent corporation uses a subsidiary corporation to serve as the acquiring corporation. See triangular merger.

Trustee An individual or institution which administers a trust for the benefit of a beneficiary.

Trustor The grantor or transferor of a trust.

Type A reorganization Type of corporate reorganization that meets the requirements of state or federal law, may take the form of a consolidation, a merger, a triangular merger, or a reverse triangular merger.

Type B reorganization Reorganization characterized by a stock-for-stock exchange. The target corporation remains in existence as a subsidiary of the acquiring corporation.

Type C reorganization A transaction that requires the acquiring corporation to obtain substantially all of the target corporation's assets in exchange for its voting stock and a limited amount of other consideration. The target corporation is generally liquidated.

Type D reorganization This type of reorganization may be either acquisitive or divisive. In the former, substantially all of the transferor corporation's assets (and possibly some or all of its liabilities) are acquired by a controlled corporation. The target corporation is liquidated. The latter involves the acquisition of the part or all of the transferor corporation's assets (and liabilities) by a controlled subsidiary corporation(s). The transferor corporation may either remain in existence or be liquidated.

Type E reorganization This type of reorganization changes the capital structure of a corporation. The corporation remains in existence.

Type F reorganization The old corporation's assets or stock are transferred to a single newly formed corporation in this type of transaction. The "old" corporation is liquidated.

Type G reorganization This type of reorganization may be either acquisitive or divisive. In either case, part or all of the target or transferor corporation's assets (and possibly some or all of its liabilities) are transferred to another corporation as part of a bankruptcy proceeding. The target or transferor corporation may either remain in existence or be liquidated.

Unfunded deferred compensation plan This type of plan is used for highly-compensated employees who wish to defer the recognition of income until future periods. Funding is generally accomplished through an escrow account for the employee's benefit.

Unified credit The unified credit enables a tax base of a certain size (i.e., the exemption equivalent or applicable exclusion amount) to be completely free of transfer taxes. It may be subtracted only once against all of a person's transfers—throughout one's lifetime and at death. See exemption equivalent and applicable exclusion amount.

Unified rate schedule Progressive rate schedule for estate and gift taxes. These rates are effective for gifts made after 1976 and deaths occurring after 1976.

Unrealized receivable Right to payment for goods and services that has not been included in the owner's income because of its method of accounting.

Unreported decisions District court decisions that are not reported in official reporters. Such decisions may be reported in secondary reporters that report only tax-related cases.

U.S. production activities deduction A deduction equal to 9% times the lesser of (1) qualified production activities income for the year or (2) taxable income before the U.S. production activities deduction. The deduction, however, cannot exceed 50% of the corporation's W-2 wages allocable to U.S. production activities for the year.

Valuation allowance A contra-type account that represents the portion of a deferred tax asset that likely will not be realized.

Vertical equity A concept in taxation that provides that the incidence of taxation should be borne by taxpayers who have the ability to pay the tax. Taxpayers who are not similarly situated should be treated differently under the tax law.

Voting trust An arrangement whereby the stock owned by a number of shareholders is placed under the control of a trustee for purposes of exercising the voting rights possessed by the stock. This practice increases the voting power of the minority shareholders.

Wash sale A wash sale results when the taxpayer (1) sells stock or securities and (2) purchases substantially identical stock or securities within the 61-day period extending from 30 days before the date of sale to 30 days after the date of sale.

Wealth transfer taxes Estate taxes (i.e., the tax on dispositions of property that occur as a result of the transferor's death) and gift taxes (i.e., the tax on lifetime transfers) are wealth transfer taxes.

Writ of certiorari A petition to the U.S. Supreme court to request that the Court agree to hear a case. A writ of certiorari is requested by the party (IRS or taxpayer) that lost at the Court of Appeals level.

APPENDIX E

AICPA STATEMENTS ON STANDARDS FOR TAX SERVICES NOS. 1–7

Note: The AICPA released revised Statements on Standards for Tax Services (SSTS) effective on January 1, 2010. These statements are enforceable standards of tax practice for AICPA members. Changes to Statements No. 1 and 7 (formerly No. 8) were substantive in nature. As a result, Interpretations No. 1-1 and 1-2 relating to former Statement No. 1 are currently being updated. The new statements as well as the old statements can be found on the AICPA website at www.aicpa.org.

PREFACE

1. Standards are the foundation of a profession. The AICPA aids its members in fulfilling their ethical responsibilities by instituting and maintaining standards against which their professional performance can be measured. Compliance with professional standards of tax practice also reaffirms the public's awareness of the professionalism that is associated with CPAs as well as the AICPA.

2. This publication sets forth enforceable tax practice standards for members of the AICPA, Statements on Standards for Tax Services (SSTSs or statements). These statements apply to all members providing tax services regardless of the jurisdictions in which they practice. Interpretations of these statements may be issued as guidance to assist in understanding and applying the statements. The SSTSs and their interpretations are intended to complement other standards of tax practice, such as Treasury Department Circular No. 230, *Regulations Governing the Practice of Attorneys, Certified Public Accountants, Enrolled Agents, Enrolled Actuaries, Enrolled Retirement Plan Agents, and Appraisers before the Internal Revenue Service*; penalty provisions of the Internal Revenue Code; and state boards of accountancy rules.

3. The SSTSs are written in as simple and objective a manner as possible. However, by their nature, practice standards provide for an appropriate range of behavior and need to be interpreted to address a broad range of personal and professional situations. The SSTSs recognize this need by, in some sections, providing relatively subjective rules and by leaving certain terms undefined. These terms are generally rooted in tax concepts and, therefore, should be readily understood by tax practitioners. Accordingly, enforcement of these rules, as part of the AICPA's Code of Professional Conduct Rule 201, *General Standards*, and Rule 202, *Compliance With Standards* (AICPA, *Professional Standards*, vol. 2, ET sec. 201 par. .01 and ET sec. 202 par. .01), will be undertaken on a case-by-case basis. Members are expected to comply with them.

History

4. The SSTSs have their origin in the Statements on Responsibilities in Tax Practice (SRTPs), which provided a body of advisory opinions on good tax practice. The guidelines as originally set forth in the SRTPs became more important than many members had anticipated when the guidelines were issued. The courts, the IRS, state accountancy boards, and other professional organizations recognized and relied on the SRTPs as the appropriate articulation of professional conduct in a CPA's tax practice. The SRTPs became *de facto* enforceable standards of professional practice, because state disciplinary organizations and courts regularly held CPAs accountable for failure to follow the guidelines set forth in the SRTPs.

5. The AICPA's Tax Executive Committee concluded it was appropriate to issue tax practice standards that would become a part of the AICPA's *Professional Standards*. At its July 1999 meeting, the AICPA Board of Directors approved support of the executive committee's initiative and placed the matter on the agenda of the October 1999 meeting of the AICPA's governing Council. On October 19, 1999, Council approved designating the Tax Executive Committee as a standardsetting body, thus authorizing that committee to promulgate standards of tax practice. As a result, the original SSTSs, largely mirroring the SRTPs, were issued in August 2000.

6. The SRTPs were originally issued between 1964 and 1977. The first nine SRTPs and the introduction were promulgated in 1976; the tenth SRTP was issued in 1977. The original SRTPs concerning the CPA's responsibility to sign the tax return (SRTP No. 1, *Signature of Preparers*, and No. 2, *Signature of Reviewer: Assumption of Preparer's Responsibility*) were withdrawn in 1982 after Treasury Department regulations were issued adopting

substantially the same standards for all tax return preparers. The sixth and seventh SRTPs, concerning the responsibility of a CPA who becomes aware of an error, were revised in 1991. The first interpretation of the SRTPs, Interpretation No. 1-1, "Realistic Possibility Standard," was approved in December 1990. The SSTSs and Interpretation No. 1-1, "Realistic Possibility Standard," of SSTS No. 1, *Tax Return Positions*, superseded and replaced the SRTPs and their Interpretation No. 1-1, effective October 31, 2000. Although the number and names of the SSTSs, and the substance of the rules contained in each of them, remained the same as in the SRTPs, the language was revised to both clarify and reflect the enforceable nature of the SSTSs. In addition, because the applicability of these standards is not limited to federal income tax practice (as was the case with the SRTPs), the language was changed to indicate the broader scope. In 2003, in connection with the tax shelter debate, SSTS Interpretation No. 1-2, "Tax Planning," of SSTS No. 1 was issued to clarify a member's responsibilities in connection with tax planning; that interpretation became effective December 31, 2003.

7. When the original SSTSs were issued, an effort was made to keep to a minimum any changes in the language of the SSTSs from that of the predecessor SRTPs. This was done to alleviate concerns regarding the enforceability of standards that differed from the SRTPs under which members had been practicing. Since the issuance of the original SSTSs, members have asked for clarification on certain matters, such as the duplication of the language in SSTS No. 6, *Knowledge of Error: Return Preparation*, and No. 7, *Knowledge of Error: Administrative Proceedings*. Also, certain changes in federal and state tax laws have raised concerns regarding the need to revise SSTS No. 1. As a result, in 2008, the original SSTS Nos. 1–8 were updated, effective January 1, 2010. The original SSTS Nos. 6–7 were combined into the revised SSTS No. 6, *Knowledge of Error: Return Preparation and Administrative Proceedings*. The original SSTS No. 8, *Form and Content of Advice to Taxpayers*, was renumbered SSTS No. 7. In addition, various revisions were made to the language of the original SSTSs.

Ongoing Process

8. The following SSTSs and any interpretations issued thereunder reflect the AICPA's standards of tax practice and delineate members' responsibilities to taxpayers, the public, the government, and the profession. The statements are intended to be part of an ongoing process of articulating standards of tax practice for members. These standards are subject to change as necessary or appropriate to address changes in the tax law or other developments in the tax practice environment.

9. Members are encouraged to assess the adequacy of their practices and procedures for providing tax services in conformity with these standards. This process will vary according to the size of the practice and the nature of tax services performed.

10. The Tax Executive Committee promulgates the SSTSs and their interpretations. Acknowledgment is also due to the many members who have devoted their time and efforts over the years to developing and revising the AICPA's standards.

STATEMENT ON STANDARDS FOR TAX SERVICES NO. 1, *TAX RETURN POSITIONS*

Introduction

1. This statement sets forth the applicable standards for members when recommending tax return positions, or preparing or signing tax returns (including amended returns, claims for refund, and information returns) filed with any taxing authority. For purposes of these standards

a. a *tax return position* is (i) a position reflected on a tax return on which a member has specifically advised a taxpayer or (ii) a position about which a member has knowledge of all material facts and, on the basis of those facts, has concluded whether the position is appropriate.

b. a *taxpayer* is a client, a member's employer, or any other third-party recipient of tax services.

2. This statement also addresses a member's obligation to advise a taxpayer of relevant tax return disclosure responsibilities and potential penalties.

3. In addition to the AICPA, various taxing authorities, at the federal, state, and local levels, may impose specific reporting and disclosure standards with regard to recommending tax return positions or preparing or signing tax returns.[1] These standards can vary between taxing authorities and by type of tax.

Statement

4. A member should determine and comply with the standards, if any, that are imposed by the applicable taxing authority with respect to recommending a tax return position, or preparing or signing a tax return.

5. If the applicable taxing authority has no written standards with respect to recommending a tax return position or preparing or signing a tax return, or if its standards are lower than the standards set forth in this paragraph, the following standards will apply:

a. A member should not recommend a tax return position or prepare or sign a tax return taking a position unless the member has a good-faith belief that the position has at least a realistic possibility of being sustained administratively or judicially on its merits if challenged.

b. Notwithstanding paragraph 5(a), a member may *recommend a tax return position* if the member (i) concludes that there is a reasonable basis for the position and (ii) advises the taxpayer to appropriately disclose that position. Notwithstanding paragraph 5(a), a member may *prepare or sign a tax return* that reflects a position if (i) the member concludes there is a reasonable basis for the position and (ii) the position is appropriately disclosed.

[1]A member should refer to the current version of Internal Revenue Code Section 6694, Understatement of taxpayer's liability by tax return preparer, and other relevant federal, state, and jurisdictional authorities to determine the reporting and disclosure standards that are applicable to preparers of tax returns.

6. When recommending a tax return position or when preparing or signing a tax return on which a position is taken, a member should, when relevant, advise the taxpayer regarding potential penalty consequences of such tax return position and the opportunity, if any, to avoid such penalties through disclosure.

7. A member should not recommend a tax return position or prepare or sign a tax return reflecting a position that the member knows

a. exploits the audit selection process of a taxing authority, or
b. serves as a mere arguing position advanced solely to obtain leverage in a negotiation with a taxing authority.

8. When recommending a tax return position, a member has both the right and the responsibility to be an advocate for the taxpayer with respect to any position satisfying the aforementioned standards.

Explanation

9. The AICPA and various taxing authorities impose specific reporting and disclosure standards with respect to tax return positions and preparing or signing tax returns. In a given situation, the standards, if any, imposed by the applicable taxing authority may be higher or lower than the standards set forth in paragraph 5. A member is to comply with the standards, if any, of the applicable taxing authority; if the applicable taxing authority has no standards or if its standards are lower than the standards set forth in paragraph 5, the standards set forth in paragraph 5 will apply.

10. Our self-assessment tax system can function effectively only if taxpayers file tax returns that are true, correct, and complete. A tax return is prepared based on a taxpayer's representation of facts, and the taxpayer has the final responsibility for positions taken on the return. The standards that apply to a taxpayer may differ from those that apply to a member.

11. In addition to a duty to the taxpayer, a member has a duty to the tax system. However, it is well established that the taxpayer has no obligation to pay more taxes than are legally owed, and a member has a duty to the taxpayer to assist in achieving that result. The standards contained in paragraphs 4–8 recognize a member's responsibilities to both the taxpayer and the tax system.

12. In reaching a conclusion concerning whether a given standard in paragraph 4 or 5 has been satisfied, a member may consider a well-reasoned construction of the applicable statute, well-reasoned articles or treatises, or pronouncements issued by the applicable taxing authority, regardless of whether such sources would be treated as *authority* under Internal Revenue Code Section 6662, *Imposition of accuracy-related penalty on underpayments*, and the regulations thereunder. A position would not fail to meet these standards merely because it is later abandoned for practical or procedural considerations during an administrative hearing or in the litigation process.

13. If a member has a good-faith belief that more than one tax return position meets the standards set forth in paragraphs 4–5, a member's advice concerning alternative acceptable positions may include a discussion of the likelihood that each such position might or might not cause the taxpayer's tax return to be examined and whether the position would be challenged in an examination. In such circumstances, such advice is not a violation of paragraph 7.

14. A member's determination of whether information is appropriately disclosed by the taxpayer should be based on the facts and circumstances of the particular case and the disclosure requirements of the applicable taxing authority. If a member recommending a position, but not engaged to prepare or sign the related tax return, advises the taxpayer concerning appropriate disclosure of the position, then the member shall be deemed to meet the disclosure requirements of these standards.

15. If particular facts and circumstances lead a member to believe that a taxpayer penalty might be asserted, the member should so advise the taxpayer and should discuss with the taxpayer the opportunity, if any, to avoid such penalty by disclosing the position on the tax return. Although a member should advise the taxpayer with respect to disclosure, it is the taxpayer's responsibility to decide whether and how to disclose.

16. For purposes of this statement, preparation of a tax return includes giving advice on events that have occurred at the time the advice is given if the advice is directly relevant to determining the existence, character, or amount of a schedule, entry, or other portion of a tax return.

STATEMENT ON STANDARDS FOR TAX SERVICES NO. 2, *ANSWERS TO QUESTIONS ON RETURNS*

Introduction

1. This statement sets forth the applicable standards for members when signing the preparer's declaration on a tax return if one or more questions on the return have not been answered. The term *questions* includes requests for information on the return, in the instructions, or in the regulations, whether or not stated in the form of a question.

Statement

2. A member should make a reasonable effort to obtain from the taxpayer the information necessary to provide appropriate answers to all questions on a tax return before signing as preparer.

Explanation

3. It is recognized that the questions on tax returns are not of uniform importance, and often they are not applicable to the particular taxpayer. Nevertheless, there are at least three reasons why a member should be satisfied that a reasonable effort has been made to obtain information to provide appropriate answers to the questions on the return that are applicable to a taxpayer:

a. A question may be of importance in determining taxable income or loss, or the tax liability shown on the return, in which circumstance an omission may detract from the quality of the return.
b. A request for information may require a disclosure necessary for a complete return or to avoid penalties.
c. A member often must sign a preparer's declaration stating that the return is true, correct, and complete.

4. Reasonable grounds may exist for omitting an answer to a question applicable to a taxpayer. For example, reasonable grounds may include the following:

a. The information is not readily available and the answer is not significant in terms of taxable income or loss, or the tax liability shown on the return.
b. Genuine uncertainty exists regarding the meaning of the question in relation to the particular return.
c. The answer to the question is voluminous; in such cases, a statement should be made on the return that the data will be supplied upon examination.

5. A member should not omit an answer merely because it might prove disadvantageous to a taxpayer.

6. A member should consider whether the omission of an answer to a question may cause the return to be deemed incomplete or result in penalties.

7. If reasonable grounds exist for omission of an answer to an applicable question, a taxpayer is not required to provide on the return an explanation of the reason for the omission.

STATEMENT ON STANDARDS FOR TAX SERVICES NO. 3, *CERTAIN PROCEDURAL ASPECTS OF PREPARING RETURNS*

Introduction

1. This statement sets forth the applicable standards for members concerning the obligation to examine or verify certain supporting data or to consider information related to another taxpayer when preparing a taxpayer's tax return.

Statement

2. In preparing or signing a return, a member may in good faith rely, without verification, on information furnished by the taxpayer or by third parties. However, a member should not ignore the implications of information furnished and should make reasonable inquiries if the information furnished appears to be incorrect, incomplete, or inconsistent either on its face or on the basis of other facts known to the member. Further, a member should refer to the taxpayer's returns for one or more prior years whenever feasible.

3. If the tax law or regulations impose a condition with respect to deductibility or other tax treatment of an item, such as taxpayer maintenance of books and records or substantiating documentation to support the reported deduction or tax treatment, a member should make appropriate inquiries to determine to the member's satisfaction whether such condition has been met.

4. When preparing a tax return, a member should consider information actually known to that member from the tax return of another taxpayer if the information is relevant to that tax return and its consideration is necessary to properly prepare that tax return. In using such information, a member should consider any limitations imposed by any law or rule relating to confidentiality.

Explanation

5. The preparer's declaration on a tax return often states that the information contained therein is true, correct, and complete to the best of the preparer's knowledge and belief based on all information known by the preparer. This type of reference should be understood to include information furnished by the taxpayer or by third parties to a member in connection with the preparation of the return.

6. The preparer's declaration does not require a member to examine or verify supporting data; a member may rely on information furnished by the taxpayer unless it appears to be incorrect, incomplete, or inconsistent. However, there is a need to determine by inquiry that a specifically required condition, such as maintaining books and records or substantiating documentation, has been satisfied and to obtain information when the material furnished appears to be incorrect, incomplete, or inconsistent. Although a member has certain responsibilities in exercising due diligence in preparing a return, the taxpayer has the ultimate responsibility for the contents of the return. Thus, if the taxpayer presents unsupported data in the form of lists of tax information, such as dividends and interest received, charitable contributions, and medical expenses, such information may be used in the preparation of a tax return without verification unless it appears to be incorrect, incomplete, or inconsistent either on its face or on the basis of other facts known to a member.

7. Even though there is no requirement to examine underlying documentation, a member should encourage the taxpayer to provide supporting data where appropriate. For example, a member should encourage the taxpayer to submit underlying documents for use in tax return preparation to permit full consideration of income and deductions arising from security transactions and from pass-through entities, such as estates, trusts, partnerships, and S corporations.

8. The source of information provided to a member by a taxpayer for use in preparing the return is often a pass-through entity, such as a limited partnership, in which the taxpayer has an interest but is not involved in management. A member may accept the information provided by the pass-through entity without further inquiry, unless there is reason to believe it is incorrect, incomplete, or inconsistent, either on its face or on the basis of other facts known to the member. In some instances, it may be appropriate for a member to advise the taxpayer to ascertain the nature and amount of possible exposure to tax deficiencies, interest, and penalties by taxpayer contact with management of the pass-through entity.

9. A member should make use of a taxpayer's returns for one or more prior years in preparing the current return whenever feasible. Reference to prior returns and discussion of prior-year tax determinations with the taxpayer should provide information to determine the taxpayer's general tax status, avoid the omission or duplication of items, and afford a basis for the treatment of similar or related transactions. As with the examination of information supplied for the current year's return, the extent of comparison of the details of income and deduction between years depends on the particular circumstances.

STATEMENT ON STANDARDS FOR TAX SERVICES NO. 4, *USE OF ESTIMATES*

Introduction

1. This statement sets forth the applicable standards for members when using the taxpayer's estimates in the preparation of a tax return. A member may advise on estimates used in the preparation of a tax return, but the taxpayer has the responsibility to provide the estimated data. Appraisals or valuations are not considered estimates for purposes of this statement.

Statement

2. Unless prohibited by statute or by rule, a member may use the taxpayer's estimates in the preparation of a tax return if it is not practical to obtain exact data and if the member determines that the estimates are reasonable based on the facts and circumstances known to the member. The taxpayer's estimates should be presented in a manner that does not imply greater accuracy than exists.

Explanation

3. Accounting requires the exercise of professional judgment and, in many instances, the use of approximations based on judgment. The application of such accounting judgments, as long as not in conflict with methods set forth by a taxing authority, is acceptable. These judgments are not estimates within the purview of this statement. For example, a federal income tax regulation provides that if all other conditions for accrual are met, the exact amount of income or expense need not be known or ascertained at year end if the amount can be determined with reasonable accuracy.

4. When the taxpayer's records do not accurately reflect information related to small expenditures, accuracy in recording some data may be difficult to achieve. Therefore, the use of estimates by a taxpayer in determining the amount to be deducted for such items may be appropriate.

5. When records are missing or precise information about a transaction is not available at the time the return must be filed, a member may prepare a tax return using a taxpayer's estimates of the missing data.

6. Estimated amounts should not be presented in a manner that provides a misleading impression about the degree of factual accuracy.

7. Specific disclosure that an estimate is used for an item in the return is not generally required; however, such disclosure should be made in unusual circumstances where nondisclosure might mislead the taxing authority regarding the degree of accuracy of the return as a whole. Some examples of unusual circumstances include the following:

a. A taxpayer has died or is ill at the time the return must be filed.
b. A taxpayer has not received a Schedule K-1 for a pass-through entity at the time the tax return is to be filed.
c. There is litigation pending (for example, a bankruptcy proceeding) that bears on the return.
d. Fire, computer failure, or natural disaster has destroyed the relevant records.

STATEMENT ON STANDARDS FOR TAX SERVICES NO. 5, *DEPARTURE FROM A POSITION PREVIOUSLY CONCLUDED IN AN ADMINISTRATIVE PROCEEDING OR COURT DECISION*

Introduction

1. This statement sets forth the applicable standards for members in recommending a tax return position that departs from the position determined in an administrative proceeding or in a court decision with respect to the taxpayer's prior return.

2. For purposes of this statement, *administrative proceeding* includes an examination by a taxing authority or an appeals conference relating to a return or a claim for refund.

3. For purposes of this statement, *court decision* means a decision by any court having jurisdiction over tax matters.

Statement

4. The tax return position with respect to an item as determined in an administrative proceeding or court decision does not restrict a member from recommending a different tax position in a later year's return, unless the taxpayer is bound to a specified treatment in the later year, such as by a formal closing agreement. Therefore, the member may recommend a tax return position or prepare or sign a tax return that departs from the treatment of an item as concluded in an administrative proceeding or court decision with respect to a prior return of the taxpayer provided the requirements of Statement on Standards for Tax Services (SSTS) No. 1, *Tax Return Positions*, are satisfied.

Explanation

5. If an administrative proceeding or court decision has resulted in a determination concerning a specific tax treatment of an item in a prior year's return, a member will usually recommend this same tax treatment in subsequent years. However, departures from consistent treatment may be justified under such circumstances as the following:

a. Taxing authorities tend to act consistently in the disposition of an item that was the subject of a prior administrative proceeding but generally are not bound to do so. Similarly, a taxpayer is not bound to follow the tax treatment of an item as consented to in an earlier administrative proceeding.
b. The determination in the administrative proceeding or the court's decision may have been caused by a lack of documentation. Supporting data for the later year may be appropriate.

c. A taxpayer may have yielded in the administrative proceeding for settlement purposes or not appealed the court decision, even though the position met the standards in SSTS No. 1.

d. Court decisions, rulings, or other authorities that are more favorable to a taxpayer's current position may have developed since the prior administrative proceeding was concluded or the prior court decision was rendered.

6. The consent in an earlier administrative proceeding and the existence of an unfavorable court decision are factors that the member should consider in evaluating whether the standards in SSTS No. 1 are met.

STATEMENT ON STANDARDS FOR TAX SERVICES NO. 6, *KNOWLEDGE OF ERROR: RETURN PREPARATION AND ADMINISTRATIVE PROCEEDINGS*

Introduction

1. This statement sets forth the applicable standards for a member who becomes aware of (a) an error in a taxpayer's previously filed tax return; (b) an error in a return that is the subject of an administrative proceeding, such as an examination by a taxing authority or an appeals conference; or (c) a taxpayer's failure to file a required tax return. As used herein, the term *error* includes any position, omission, or method of accounting that, at the time the return is filed, fails to meet the standards set out in Statement on Standards for Tax Services (SSTS) No. 1, *Tax Return Positions*. The term *error* also includes a position taken on a prior year's return that no longer meets these standards due to legislation, judicial decisions, or administrative pronouncements having retroactive effect. However, an error does not include an item that has an insignificant effect on the taxpayer's tax liability. The term *administrative proceeding* does not include a criminal proceeding.

2. This statement applies whether or not the member prepared or signed the return that contains the error.

3. Special considerations may apply when a member has been engaged by legal counsel to provide assistance in a matter relating to the counsel's client.

Statement

4. A member should inform the taxpayer promptly upon becoming aware of an error in a previously filed return, an error in a return that is the subject of an administrative proceeding, or a taxpayer's failure to file a required return. A member also should advise the taxpayer of the potential consequences of the error and recommend the corrective measures to be taken. Such advice and recommendation may be given orally. The member is not allowed to inform the taxing authority without the taxpayer's permission, except when required by law.

5. If a member is requested to prepare the current year's return and the taxpayer has not taken appropriate action to correct an error in a prior year's return, the member should consider whether to withdraw from preparing the return and whether to continue a professional or employment relationship with the taxpayer. If the member does prepare such current year's return, the member should take reasonable steps to ensure that the error is not repeated.

6. If a member is representing a taxpayer in an administrative proceeding with respect to a return that contains an error of which the member is aware, the member should request the taxpayer's agreement to disclose the error to the taxing authority. Lacking such agreement, the member should consider whether to withdraw from representing the taxpayer in the administrative proceeding and whether to continue a professional or employment relationship with the taxpayer.

Explanation

7. While performing services for a taxpayer, a member may become aware of an error in a previously filed return or may become aware that the taxpayer failed to file a required return. The member should advise the taxpayer of the error and the potential consequences, and recommend the measures to be taken. Similarly, when representing the taxpayer before a taxing authority in an administrative proceeding with respect to a return containing an error of which the member is aware, the member should advise the taxpayer to disclose the error to the taxing authority and of the potential consequences of not disclosing the error. Such advice and recommendation may be given orally.

8. It is the taxpayer's responsibility to decide whether to correct the error. If the taxpayer does not correct an error, a member should consider whether to withdraw from the engagement and whether to continue a professional or employment relationship with the taxpayer. Although recognizing that the taxpayer may not be required by statute to correct an error by filing an amended return, a member should consider whether a taxpayer's decision not to file an amended return or otherwise correct an error may predict future behavior that might require termination of the relationship.

9. Once the member has obtained the taxpayer's consent to disclose an error in an administrative proceeding, the disclosure should not be delayed to such a degree that the taxpayer or member might be considered to have failed to act in good faith or to have, in effect, provided misleading information. In any event, disclosure should be made before the conclusion of the administrative proceeding.

10. A conflict between the member's interests and those of the taxpayer may be created by, for example, the potential for violating Code of Professional Conduct Rule 301, *Confidential Client Information* (AICPA, *Professional Standards*, vol. 2, ET sec. 301 par. .01) (relating to the member's confidential client relationship); the tax law and regulations; or laws on privileged communications, as well as by the potential adverse impact on a taxpayer of a member's withdrawal. Therefore, a member should consider consulting with his or her own legal counsel before deciding upon recommendations to the taxpayer and whether to continue a professional or employment relationship with the taxpayer.

11. If a member believes that a taxpayer may face possible exposure to allegations of fraud or other criminal misconduct, the member should advise the taxpayer to consult with an attorney before the taxpayer takes any action.

12. If a member decides to continue a professional or employment relationship with the taxpayer and is requested to prepare a tax return for a year subsequent to that in which the error occurred, the member should take reasonable steps to ensure that the error is not repeated. If the subsequent year's tax return cannot be prepared without perpetuating the error, the member should consider withdrawal from the return preparation. If a member learns that the taxpayer is using an erroneous method of accounting and it is past the due date to request permission to change to a method meeting the standards of SSTS No. 1, the member may sign a tax return for the current year, providing the tax return includes appropriate disclosure of the use of the erroneous method.

13. Whether an error has no more than an insignificant effect on the taxpayer's tax liability is left to the professional judgment of the member based on all the facts and circumstances known to the member. In judging whether an erroneous method of accounting has more than an insignificant effect, a member should consider the method's cumulative effect, as well as its effect on the current year's tax return or the tax return that is the subject of the administrative proceeding.

14. If a member becomes aware of the error while performing services for a taxpayer that do not involve tax return preparation or representation in an administrative proceeding, the member's responsibility is to advise the taxpayer of the existence of the error and to recommend that the error be discussed with the taxpayer's tax return preparer. Such recommendation may be given orally.

STATEMENT ON STANDARDS FOR TAX SERVICES NO. 7, *FORM AND CONTENT OF ADVICE TO TAXPAYERS*

Introduction

1. This statement sets forth the applicable standards for members concerning certain aspects of providing advice to a taxpayer and considers the circumstances in which a member has a responsibility to communicate with a taxpayer when subsequent developments affect advice previously provided. The statement does not, however, cover a member's responsibilities when the expectation is that the advice rendered is likely to be relied on by parties other than the taxpayer.

Statement

2. A member should use professional judgment to ensure that tax advice provided to a taxpayer reflects competence and appropriately serves the taxpayer's needs. When communicating tax advice to a taxpayer in writing, a member should comply with relevant taxing authorities' standards, if any, applicable to written tax advice. A member should use professional judgment about any need to document oral advice. A member is not required to follow a standard format when communicating or documenting oral advice.

3. A member should assume that tax advice provided to a taxpayer will affect the manner in which the matters or transactions considered would be reported or disclosed on the taxpayer's tax returns. Therefore, for tax advice given to a taxpayer, a member should consider, when relevant (*a*) return reporting and disclosure standards applicable to the related tax return position and (*b*) the potential penalty consequences of the return position. In ascertaining applicable return reporting and disclosure standards, a member should follow the standards in Statement on Standards for Tax Services No. 1, *Tax Return Positions*.

4. A member has no obligation to communicate with a taxpayer when subsequent developments affect advice previously provided with respect to significant matters, except while assisting a taxpayer in implementing procedures or plans associated with the advice provided or when a member undertakes this obligation by specific agreement.

Explanation

5. Tax advice is recognized as a valuable service provided by members. The form of advice may be oral or written and the subject matter may range from routine to complex. Because the range of advice is so extensive and because advice should meet the specific needs of a taxpayer, neither a standard format nor guidelines for communicating or documenting advice to the taxpayer can be established to cover all situations.

6. Although oral advice may serve a taxpayer's needs appropriately in routine matters or in welldefined areas, written communications are recommended in important, unusual, substantial dollar value, or complicated transactions. The member may use professional judgment about whether, subsequently, to document oral advice.

7. In deciding on the form of advice provided to a taxpayer, a member should exercise professional judgment and should consider such factors as the following:

a. The importance of the transaction and amounts involved
b. The specific or general nature of the taxpayer's inquiry
c. The time available for development and submission of the advice
d. The technical complexity involved
e. The existence of authorities and precedents
f. The tax sophistication of the taxpayer
g. The need to seek other professional advice
h. The type of transaction and whether it is subject to heightened reporting or disclosure requirements
i. The potential penalty consequences of the tax return position for which the advice is rendered
j. Whether any potential applicable penalties can be avoided through disclosure
k. Whether the member intends for the taxpayer to rely upon the advice to avoid potential penalties

8. A member may assist a taxpayer in implementing procedures or plans associated with the advice offered. When providing such assistance, the member should review and revise such advice as warranted by new developments and factors affecting the transaction.

9. Sometimes a member is requested to provide tax advice but does not assist in implementing the plans adopted. Although such developments as legislative or administrative changes or future judicial interpretations may affect the advice previously provided, a member cannot be expected to communicate subsequent developments that affect such advice unless the member undertakes this obligation by specific agreement with the taxpayer.

10. Taxpayers should be informed that (*a*) the advice reflects professional judgment based upon the member's understanding of the facts, and the law existing as of the date the advice is rendered and (*b*) subsequent developments could affect previously rendered professional advice. Members may use precautionary language to the effect that their advice is based on facts as stated and authorities that are subject to change.

11. In providing tax advice, a member should be cognizant of applicable confidentiality privileges.

These Statements on Standards for Tax Services were unanimously adopted by the assenting votes of the 17 members of the 18-member Tax Executive Committee who participated in the August 6, 2009, Tax Executive Committee meeting.

Note: *Statements on Standards for Tax Services are issued by the Tax Executive Committee, the senior technical body of the AICPA designated to promulgate standards of tax practice. Rule 201, General Standards, and Rule 202, Compliance With Standards, of the Code of Professional Conduct (AICPA, Professional Standards, vol. 2, ET sec. 201 par. .01 and ET sec. 202 par. .01), require compliance with these standards.*

APPENDIX F

COMPARISON OF TAX ATTRIBUTES FOR C CORPORATIONS, PARTNERSHIPS, AND S CORPORATIONS

APPENDIX F: COMPARISON OF TAX ATTRIBUTES FOR C CORPORATIONS, PARTNERSHIPS, AND S CORPORATIONS

Tax Attribute	C Corporation	Partnership	S Corporation
I. General Characteristics			
1. Application of the separate entity versus conduit (flow through) concept.	*Entity:* The corporation is treated as a separate taxpaying entity. If the corporation distributes income to shareholders in the form of dividends, the shareholders are subject to a second tax on such amounts. Shareholders also are subject to a second tax if they sell their stock.	*Conduit:* The partners report their distributive share of partnership ordinary income and separately stated items on their tax returns. Most elections, such as depreciation methods, accounting period and methods, are made at the partnership level. Special tax rules apply to electing large partnerships.	*Conduit:* Similar to the partnership form of organization. However, the S corporation may be subject to tax at the corporate level on excess net passive income, or built-in gains under special circumstances.
2. Period of existence.	Continues until dissolution; not affected by stock sales by shareholders.	Termination can occur by agreement, or by death, retirement, or disaffiliation of a partner.	Same as for C corporation.
3. Transferability of interest.	Stock can be transferred easily; corporation may retain right to buy back shares.	Addition of new partner or transfer of partner's interest generally requires approval of other partners.	Same as for C corporation.
4. Liability exposure.	Shareholders generally liable only for capital contributions.	General partners are personally, jointly, and severally liable for partnership obligations. Limited partners usually are liable only for capital contributions.	Same as for C corporation.
5. Management responsibility.	Shareholders may be part of management or may hire outside management.	All general partners participate in management. Limited partners generally do not participate.	Because of limited number of shareholders, shareholders usually are part of management.
II. Election and Restrictions			
1. Restrictions on: a. Type of owners.	No restriction.	No restriction.	Limited to individuals, estates, charitable organizations, and certain kinds of trusts.
b. Number of owners.	No restriction.	No restriction.	Limited to 100 shareholders, where a family counts as one shareholder.
c. Type of entity.	Includes domestic or foreign corporations, unincorporated entities known as associations, and certain kinds of trusts. A publicly traded partnership is taxed as a corporation unless more than 90% of its income is qualifying passive income. Grandfathered publicly traded partnerships can avoid corporate taxation by paying an excise tax. Partnerships, LLCs, and proprietorships can elect to be taxed as a corporation under the check-the-box regulations.	Includes a variety of unincorporated entities including limited liability company and limited liability partnership forms. Certain joint undertakings are excluded from partnership status.	Domestic corporations and unincorporated entities (e.g., associations) are eligible. A partnership, LLC, or proprietorship that elects to be treated as an S corporation automatically is considered to have elected to be treated as a corporation under the check-the-box regulations.

APPENDIX F: COMPARISON OF TAX ATTRIBUTES FOR C CORPORATIONS, PARTNERSHIPS, AND S CORPORATIONS

Tax Attribute	C Corporation	Partnership	S Corporation
d. Special tax classifications.	No restriction.	No restriction.	S corporation cannot be a former Domestic International Sales Corporation, or have elected the special Puerto Rico and U.S. Possessions tax credit. Certain financial institutions and insurance companies also are ineligible.
e. Investments made by entity.	No restriction.	No restriction.	S corporation can own 80% or more of a C corporation but cannot file a consolidated tax return with the C corporation.
f. Capital structure.	No restriction.	No restriction.	Limited to a single class of stock that is outstanding. Differences in voting rights are disregarded. Special "safe harbor" rules are available for debt issues.
g. Passive interest income.	No restriction.	No restriction.	Passive investment income cannot exceed 25% of gross receipts for three consecutive tax years when the corporation also has Subchapter C E&P at the end of the year.
2. Election and shareholder consent.	No election required.	No election required.	Election can be made during the preceding tax year or first 2 1/2 months of the tax year. Shareholders must consent to the election.
3. Termination of election.	Not applicable.	The partnership can terminate if it does not carry on any business, financial operation, or venture or if a sale or exchange of at least 50% of the profits and capital interests occurs within a 12-month period.	Occurs if one of the requirements is failed after the election is first effective or if the passive investment income test is failed for three consecutive tax years. IRS can waive invalid elections and permit inadvertent terminations not to break the S election.
4. Revocation of election.	Not applicable.	Not applicable.	Election may be revoked only by shareholders owning more than one-half of the stock. Must be made in first 2 1/2 months of tax year or on a prospective basis.
5. New election.	Not applicable.	Not applicable.	Not permitted for five-year period without IRS consent to early reelection.

APPENDIX F: COMPARISON OF TAX ATTRIBUTES FOR C CORPORATIONS, PARTNERSHIPS, AND S CORPORATIONS

Tax Attribute	C Corporation	Partnership	S Corporation
III. Accounting Periods and Elections			
1. Taxable year.	Calendar year or fiscal year is permitted. Personal service corporations are restricted to using a calendar year unless IRS grants approval to use a fiscal year. A special election is available to use a fiscal year resulting in a three-month or less income deferral if the corporation meets a series of minimum distribution requirements.	Generally use tax year of majority or principal partners. Otherwise use of the least aggregate deferral year is required. Can use a fiscal year that has a business purpose for which IRS approval is obtained. An electing partnership may use a fiscal year resulting in a three-month or less income deferral if an additional required payment is made.	Can use a fiscal year that has a business purpose for which IRS approval is obtained. An S corporation may use a fiscal year resulting in a three-month or less income deferral if an additional required payment is made. If neither of the above applies, a calendar year must be used.
2. Accounting methods.	Elected by the corporation. Use of cash method of accounting is restricted for certain personal service corporations and C corporations having $5 million or more annual gross receipts.	Elected by the partnership. Restrictions on the use of the cash method of accounting apply to partnerships having a C corporation as a partner or that are tax shelters.	Elected by the S corporation. Restrictions on the use of the cash method of accounting apply to S corporations that are tax shelters.
IV. Taxability of Profits			
1. Taxability of profits.	Ordinary income and capital gains are taxed to the corporation. Profits are taxed a second time when distributed.	Ordinary income and separately stated income and gain items pass through to the partners at the end of the partnership's tax year whether or not distributed.	Same as partnership.
2. Allocation of profits.	Not applicable.	Based on partnership agreement. Special allocations are permitted.	Based on stock ownership on each day of the tax year. Special allocations are not permitted.
3. Character of income.	Distributed profits (including tax-exempt income) are dividends to extent of earnings and profits (E&P).	Items receiving special treatment (e.g., capital gains or tax-exempt income) pass through separately to the partner and retain same character as when earned by the partnership.	Same as partnership.
4. Maximum tax rate for earnings.	15% on the first $50,000; 25% from $50,000 to $75,000; 34% from $75,000 to $10 million. The rate is 35% for taxable income above $10 million. A 5% surcharge applies to taxable income between $100,000 and $335,000, and a 3% surcharge applies to taxable income between $15 million and $18,333,333. Special rules apply to controlled groups. Personal service corporations are taxed at a flat 35% rate.	Rates of tax applicable to noncorporate partners from 10% through 39.6% are levied on pass-through income from the partnership. An additional 3.8% tax may apply to net investment income. C corporation rates apply to corporate partners.	Same as partnership except for certain special situations where a special corporate tax applies to the S corporation.

Tax Attribute	C Corporation	Partnership	S Corporation
5. Special tax levies.	Can be subject to accumulated earnings tax, personal holding company tax, and corporate alternative minimum tax.	Not applicable.	Can be subject to built-in gains tax, excess net passive income tax, and LIFO recapture tax.
6. Income splitting between family members.	Only possible when earnings are distributed to shareholder. Dividends received by shareholder under age 18 (or, in some cases, ages 18 through 23) are taxed at parents' marginal tax rate.	Transfer of partnership interest by gift will permit income splitting. Subject to special rules for transactions involving family members requiring payment of reasonable compensation for capital and services. Income received by partner under age 18 is taxed at parents' marginal tax rate.	Transfer of S corporation interest by gift will permit income splitting. Special rules apply to transactions involving family members requiring payment of reasonable compensation for capital and services. Income received by shareholder under age 18 is taxed at parents' marginal tax rate.
7. Sale of ownership interest.	Gain is taxed as capital gain; from 50% to 100% of gain may be excluded under Sec. 1202 qualified small business stock rules. Loss is eligible for Sec. 1244 treatment.	Gain may be either ordinary income or capital gain depending on the nature of underlying partnership assets. Losses usually are capital.	Gain is capital in nature but is not eligible for special Sec. 1202 small business stock rules. Loss is eligible for Sec. 1244 treatment.
V. Treatment of Special Income, Gain, Loss, Deduction and Credit Items			
1. Capital gains and losses.	Long-term capital gains are taxed at regular tax rates. Capital losses offset capital gains; excess losses carried back three years and forward five years.	Passed through to partners (according to partnership agreement).	Passed through to shareholders (on a daily basis according to stock ownership).
2. Section 1231 gains and losses.	Eligible for long-term capital gain or ordinary loss treatment. Loss recapture occurs at the corporate level.	Passed through to partners. Loss recapture occurs at the partner level.	Same as partnership.
3. Dividends received from domestic corporation.	Eligible for 70%, 80%, or 100% dividends-received deduction.	Passed through to noncorporate partners, subject to the applicable capital gains tax rate if qualified, possibly including an additional 3.8% on net investment income. Corporate partners may be eligible for the dividends-received deduction.	Same as partnership except S corporation cannot have corporate shareholders.
4. U.S. production activities deduction.	Deduction equals a 9% times the lesser of (1) qualified production activities income for the year or (2) taxable income before the U.S. production activities deduction. The deduction, however, cannot exceed 50% of the corporation's W-2 wages allocable to U.S. production activities for the year.	Passed through to partners. Limitations apply at partner level.	Same as partnership.
5. Organizational expenditures.	Deduct up to $5,000 and amortize balance over 180 months.	Same as C corporation.	Same as partnership.
6. Charitable contributions.	Limited to 10% of taxable income.	Passed through to partners. Limitations apply at partner level.	Same as partnership.
7. Expensing of asset acquisition costs.	Limited to the Sec. 179 limits in effect for the year property is placed in service.	Limited to the Sec. 179 limits in effect for the year property is placed in service for the partnership and for each partner.	Same as partnership.

APPENDIX F: COMPARISON OF TAX ATTRIBUTES FOR C CORPORATIONS, PARTNERSHIPS, AND S CORPORATIONS

Tax Attribute	C Corporation	Partnership	S Corporation
8. Expenses owed to related parties.	Regular Sec. 267 rules apply to payments and sales or exchanges made to or by the corporation and certain other related parties (e.g., controlling shareholder and corporation or members of a controlled group).	Regular Sec. 267 rules can apply. Special Sec. 267 rules for passthrough entities apply to payments made by the partnership to a partner.	Same as partnership.
9. Employment-related tax considerations.	An owner-employee may be treated as an employee for Social Security tax and corporate fringe benefit purposes. The corporate qualified pension and profit-sharing benefits available to owner-employees are comparable to the plan benefits for self-employed individuals (partners and sole proprietors).	A partner is not considered an employee of the business. Therefore, the partner must pay self-employment tax on the net self-employment income from the business. Corporate fringe benefit exclusions such as group term life insurance are not available (i.e., the premiums are not deductible by the business and are not excludable from the partner's income). Fringe benefits may be provided as nontaxable distribution or as taxable compensation.	Corporate fringe benefit exclusions generally are not available to S corporation shareholders. Fringe benefits usually are provided as nontaxable distribution or taxable compensation. S corporation shareholders may be treated as employees, however, for Social Security tax payments and qualified pension and profit sharing plan rules.
10. Tax preference items and AMT adjustments.	Subject to the corporate alternative minimum tax at the corporate level.	Passed through to partners and taxed under the alternative minimum tax rules applicable to the partner.	Same as partnership.
VI. Deductibility of Losses and Special Items			
1. Deductibility of losses.	Losses create net operating loss (NOL) that carry back two years (unless an extended carryback period applies) or forward 20 years or capital loss that carry back three years or forward five years.	Ordinary losses and separately stated loss and deduction items pass through to the partners at the end of the partnership tax year. May create a personal NOL.	Same as partnership.
2. Allocation of losses.	Not applicable.	Based on partnership agreement. Special allocations are permitted.	Based on stock ownership on each day of the tax year. Special allocations are not permitted.
3. Shareholder and entity loss limitations.	Passive losses may be restricted under the passive activity limitation if the C corporation is closely held.	Limited to partner's basis for the partnership interest. Ratable share of all partnership liabilities is included in basis of partnership interest. Excess losses carry over indefinitely until partnership interest again has a basis. Subject to at-risk, passive activity, and hobby loss restrictions.	Limited to shareholder's basis for the stock interest plus basis of S corporation debts to the shareholder. Excess losses carry over indefinitely until shareholder again has basis for stock or debt. Subject to the at-risk, passive activity, and hobby loss restrictions.
4. Basis adjustments for debt and equity interests.	Not applicable.	Basis in partnership interest reduced by loss and deduction passthrough. Subsequent profits increase basis of partnership interest.	Basis in S corporation stock reduced by loss and deduction passthrough. Once basis of stock has been reduced to zero, any other losses and deductions reduce basis of debt (but not below zero). Subsequent net increases restore basis reductions to debt before increasing basis of stock.

APPENDIX F: COMPARISON OF TAX ATTRIBUTES FOR C CORPORATIONS, PARTNERSHIPS, AND S CORPORATIONS

Tax Attribute	C Corporation	Partnership	S Corporation
5. Investment interest deduction limitation.	Not applicable.	Investment interest expenses and income pass through to the partners. Limitation applies at partner level.	Same as partnership.
VII. Distributions			
1. Taxability of nonliquidating distributions to shareholder.	Taxable as dividends if made from current or accumulated E&P. Additional distributions first reduce shareholder's basis for stock, and distributions exceeding stock basis trigger capital gain recognition.	Nontaxable unless money, money equivalents, or marketable securities received by the partner exceeds his or her basis for the partnership interest.	Nontaxable if made from the accumulated adjustment account or shareholder's basis for his or her stock. Taxable if made out of accumulated E&P or after stock basis has been reduced to zero.
2. Taxability of nonliquidating distributions to distributing entity.	Gain (but not loss) recognized as if the corporation had sold the property for its FMV immediately before the distribution.	No gain or loss recognized by the partnership except when a disproportionate distribution of Sec. 751 property occurs.	Gain (but not loss) recognized and passed through to the shareholders as if the corporation had sold the property for its FMV immediately before the distribution. Gain may be taxed to the S corporation under one of the special tax levies.
3. Basis adjustment to owner's investment for distribution.	None unless the distribution exceeds E&P.	Amount of money or adjusted basis of distributed property reduces basis in partnership interest.	Amount of money or FMV of distributed property reduces basis of stock except when distribution is made out of accumulated E&P.
VIII. Other Items			
1. Tax return.	Form 1120. Schedule M-3 may be required.	Form 1065 (Information Return). Schedule M-3 may be required.	Form 1120S (Information Return). Schedule M-3 may be required.
2. Due date.	March 15 for calendar year C corporations.	April 15 for calendar year partnerships.	March 15 for calendar year S corporations.
3. Extensions of time permitted.	Six months.	Five months.	Six months.
4. Estimated tax payments required.	Yes—April 15, June 15, September 15, and December 15 for calendar year C corporations.	No—Estimated taxes are required of the partners for passed through income, etc.	Yes—Applies to built-in gains tax and excess net passive income tax.
5. Audit rules.	IRS audits corporation independently of its shareholders.	Special audit rules apply requiring audit of partnership and requiring partners to take a position consistent with the partnership tax return.	Special rules require consistent tax treatment for Subchapter S items on the corporation and shareholder returns.

APPENDIX

G RESERVED

APPENDIX

H ACTUARIAL TABLES

TRANSFERS MADE AFTER APRIL 30, 2009
EXCERPT FROM TABLE S
SINGLE LIFE REMAINDER FACTORS

	INTEREST RATE								
AGE	**2%**	**4%**	**6%**	**8%**	**AGE**	**2%**	**4%**	**6%**	**8%**
25	.36464	.14924	.06960	.03724	58	.64573	.43790	.31103	.23053
26	.37134	.15440	.07288	.03929	59	.65553	.45041	.32348	.24197
27	.37819	.15980	.07639	.04153	60	.66534	.46310	.33625	.25380
28	.38520	.16542	.08012	.04396	61	.67515	.47595	.34933	.26603
29	.39233	.17126	.08406	.04656	62	.68494	.48892	.36267	.27862
30	.39959	.17730	.08820	.04933	63	.69470	.50200	.37625	.29155
31	.40698	.18355	.09255	.05229	64	.70443	.51519	.39010	.30484
32	.41449	.19002	.09712	.05543	65	.71411	.52849	.40420	.31850
33	.42213	.19671	.10192	.05878	66	.72385	.54203	.41872	.33273
34	.42988	.20360	.10693	.06231	67	.73359	.55575	.43363	.34749
35	.43774	.21070	.11217	.06605	68	.74331	.56963	.44887	.36272
36	.44572	.21803	.11764	.06999	69	.75299	.58360	.46438	.37837
37	.45381	.22557	.12335	.07416	70	.76260	.59764	.48013	.39443
38	.46201	.23334	.12932	.07856	71	.77215	.61176	.49614	.41090
39	.47032	.24133	.13554	.08320	72	.78162	.62593	.51237	.42776
40	.47873	.24954	.14201	.08807	73	.79098	.64009	.52876	.44494
41	.48724	.25797	.14873	.09319	74	.80019	.65417	.54523	.46235
42	.49585	.26662	.15572	.09856	75	.80923	.66813	.56169	.47991
43	.50457	.27552	.16301	.10422	76	.81807	.68192	.57810	.49754
44	.51338	.28465	.17057	.11016	77	.82671	.69553	.59444	.51525
45	.52228	.29400	.17843	.11640	78	.83515	.70894	.61068	.53298
46	.53129	.30360	.18659	.12294	79	.84337	.72213	.62680	.55071
47	.54037	.31343	.19505	.12980	80	.85135	.73507	.64272	.56836
48	.54955	.32351	.20383	.13699	81	.85910	.74773	.65844	.58590
49	.55882	.33383	.21294	.14453	82	.86660	.76009	.67391	.60330
50	.56819	.34442	.22242	.15247	83	.87385	.77214	.68909	.62050
51	.57766	.35528	.23226	.16080	84	.88084	.78385	.70396	.63745
52	.58722	.36641	.24249	.16957	85	.88757	.79521	.71849	.65412
53	.59687	.37781	.25309	.17876	86	.89402	.80619	.73264	.67046
54	.60658	.38945	.26406	.18837	87	.90021	.81679	.74638	.68642
55	.61635	.40131	.27537	.19838	88	.90612	.82700	.75971	.70200
56	.62613	.41335	.28697	.20875	89	.91176	.83681	.77259	.71714
57	.63593	.42555	.29887	.21947	90	.91713	.84620	.78500	.73181

Source: Reg. Sec. 20.2031-7(d)(7), as supplemented by IRS Pub. 1457: Actuarial Values, Table S.

EXCERPT FROM TABLE B
TERM CERTAIN REMAINDER FACTORS

	INTEREST RATE			
YEARS	**2%**	**4%**	**6%**	**8%**
1	.980392	.961538	.943396	.925926
2	.961169	.924556	.889996	.857339
3	.942322	.888996	.839619	.793832
4	.923845	.854804	.792094	.735030
5	.905731	.821927	.747258	.680583
6	.887971	.790315	.704961	.630170
7	.870560	.759918	.665057	.583490
8	.853490	.730690	.627412	.540269
9	.836755	.702587	.591898	.500249
10	.820348	.675564	.558395	.463193
11	.804263	.649581	.526788	.428883
12	.788493	.624597	.496969	.397114
13	.773033	.600574	.468839	.367698
14	.757875	.577475	.442301	.340461
15	.743015	.555265	.417265	.315242
16	.728446	.533908	.393646	.291890
17	.714163	.513373	.371364	.270269
18	.700159	.493628	.350344	.250249
19	.686431	.474642	.330513	.231712
20	.672971	.456387	.311805	.214548
21	.659776	.438834	.294155	.198656
22	.646839	.421955	.277505	.183941
23	.634156	.405726	.261797	.170315
24	.621721	.390121	.246979	.157699
25	.609531	.375117	.232999	.146018

Source: Reg. Sec. 20.2031-7(d)(6), Table B, as supplemented by IRS Pub. 1457: Actuarial Values, Table B.

APPENDIX

I INDEX OF CODE SECTIONS

Entries in **BOLD** denote references to **Corporations.**
Entries in *ITALICS* denote references to *Individuals.*

BOLD = Corporations
ITALICS = Individuals

BOLD = Corporations
ITALICS = Individuals

BOLD = Corporations
ITALICS = Individuals

APPENDIX

J INDEX OF TREASURY REGULATIONS

Final Regulations

Entries in **BOLD** denote references to **Corporations.**
Entries in *ITALICS* denote references to *Individuals.*

BOLD = Corporations
ITALICS = Individuals

APPENDIX

K INDEX OF GOVERNMENT PROMULGATIONS

Entries in **BOLD** denote references to **Corporations.**
Entries in *ITALICS* denote references to *Individuals.*

BOLD = Corporations
ITALICS = Individuals

APPENDIX

L INDEX OF COURT CASES

Entries in **BOLD** denote references to **Corporations.**
Entries in *ITALICS* denote references to *Individuals.*

BOLD = Corporations
ITALICS = Individuals

APPENDIX

M SUBJECT INDEX

Entries in BOLD denote references to **Corporations**
Entries in *ITALICS* denote references to *Individuals*

BOLD = Corporations
ITALICS = Individuals

BOLD = Corporations
ITALICS = Individuals

BOLD = Corporations
ITALICS = Individuals

BOLD = Corporations
ITALICS = Individuals

BOLD = Corporations
ITALICS = Individuals

BOLD = Corporations
ITALICS = Individuals

BOLD = Corporations
ITALICS = Individuals

BOLD = Corporations
ITALICS = Individuals

BOLD = Corporations
ITALICS = Individuals

BOLD = Corporations
ITALICS = Individuals

BOLD = Corporations
ITALICS = Individuals